Sociology

IAN ROBERTSON

Sociology

THIRD EDITION

WORTH PUBLISHERS, INC.

Sociology, THIRD EDITION

Editors: Peter Deane, Linda Baron Davis

Make-up and Production: George Touloumes, Sarah J. Segal

Picture Editor: June Lundborg Whitworth

Design: Malcolm Grear Designers

Typography: York Graphic Services, Inc.

Printing and Binding: R. R. Donnelley & Sons Company

Cover photograph: © Geoffrey Gove

Text and illustration credits appear on pages 628–631,

which constitute an extension of the copyright page.

Worth Publishers, Inc.

33 Irving Place

New York, New York 10003

PREFACE

Like its predecessors, this edition of *Sociology* rests on two basic premises. The first is that sociology is both a humanistic art and a rigorous science; in fact, much of its excitement arises from the insights offered by this unique blend of two intellectual traditions. The second premise is that sociology can be, and should be, a profoundly liberating discipline. By challenging conventional wisdoms and by dissolving the myths about social reality, the discipline provides an acute awareness of the human authorship of, and responsibility for, both the social world and much of our personal experience and identity. Sociology thus offers that crucial sense of options and choice that is essential to human freedom.

The original impetus to write this book grew out of several years' experience as a teacher and professional writer in radically different societies in North America, Europe, and Africa. Sociology fascinates me and informs my daily observations of the social world. I count the book successful to the extent that it conveys to the reader the sheer pleasure that I draw from sociology myself.

Changes in This Edition

The changes in the present edition are extensive: I have written three new chapters, combined or reorganized several others, rewritten much of the rest of the book, and replaced most of the illustrations and artwork.

The first of the new chapters deals with the important social institution of medicine, a subject that I have found has high student interest. The second of these chapters covers technology and environment and concentrates on a crucial feature of the modern world, the interaction between technological innovation and our social and natural surroundings. The third new chapter deals with

war and peace, with a particular focus on warfare in the nuclear age. I am particularly eager to include this novel chapter in a sociology text. It has long been a matter of regret to me that certain journals in our field contain so much material of so little real import, while crucial issues such as warfare—which, after all, has claimed nearly 100 million lives over the course of this century and now threatens the very future of society—go almost completely neglected.

To accommodate these new chapters and to improve the narrative flow, I have (1) combined the two original chapters on social stratification and on social inequality in the United States, (2) combined the original chapters on urbanization and population, and (3) eliminated the science chapter while transferring its core features to the new chapter on technology and environment.

I have also added a new theme to the book: the emergence of postindustrial society. The United States is now such a society, in the sense that most workers are engaged in providing services and information rather than in industrial manufacturing. At appropriate points the book explores the meaning and implications of this development. The change from preindustrial to industrial and now to postindustrial society has been accompanied by a shift in loyalties away from the community and tradition, and I examine the implications of this trend toward self-fulfillment and individualism in such areas as deviance, sexuality, gender roles, family life, religion, and the economy.

The additional new material in this edition is too extensive to list in full, but some of the new topics discussed are the sociology of art; the sociology of emotions; the sociology of time and space; mental disorder; the Japanese corporation; the medicalization of deviance; the death penalty; AIDS and new styles in sexual behavior; new immigration patterns; women and work; the changing economic status of children and the aged; problems of the black family; the abortion dilemma; academic standards in the schools; changes in the Islamic world; the American fundamentalist revival; socioeconomic changes in China; trends in the American political system; world-system theory; terrorism; and "urban legends." As before, I have tried throughout the book to convey a sense of the "cutting edge" of the discipline by including much material that is not traditionally covered in sociology texts.

Organization

In general, the coverage of the field continues to reflect the same goal that I had for the first edition, when I decided at the outset not to write a slender "core" text covering a few selected topics. The problem with such an approach, of course, is that one person's core may be another's apple—or vice versa—with the result that some instructors are left without text discussion of material they consider essential. Instead, I have tried to give a broad coverage of the main areas of the discipline, while keeping the text sufficiently flexible to be adapted to the needs of individual instructors.

I have again divided the book into five units. Unit I provides an introduction to sociology and to the methods of sociological research. Unit II deals with the individual, culture, and society, and focuses on the influence of social and cultural forces on personal experience and social behavior. The chapters in this unit cover culture, society, socialization, social interaction, social groups, deviance, and sexual behavior. Unit III discusses various forms of social inequality, and emphasizes the role of ideology as well as coercion and tradition in the maintenance of inequalities. The first chapter in the unit deals with the general problem of social stratification, and then discusses the United States in detail; the second deals with inequalities of race and ethnicity; and the third, with inequalities of gender and of age. Unit IV discusses several important social institutions: the family, education, religion, medicine, the economic order, and the political order. Finally, Unit V focuses on some issues of social change; it contains chapters on social change, collective behavior and social movements, population and urbanization, technology and environment, and war and peace.

I have taken great care, however, to structure the book in such a way that instructors can, if they wish, omit some chapters and present others in a different order. Nearly all instructors will want to cover the first five chapters, in which the most important terms and concepts of the discipline are introduced. (Chapter 2, on methods, could be omitted, but devoting some lecture time to research methods would then be advisable.) The sequence of the remaining chapters can then be freely rearranged to suit the convenience of the individual instructor, and there are ample cross-references to the five basic chapters and to relevant topics in other chapters to facilitate the use of any alternative sequence.

Features

The book includes a number of distinctive features that are intended to enhance its effectiveness as a teaching and learning tool.

Cross-cultural material. While this book is not intended as an exercise in comparative sociology, I have started from the assumption that sociology is something more than the study of American society. Throughout the text there are frequent references to other cultures and to the historical past. This material is intended to serve two purposes. The first is to enliven the text, for the ways of life of other peoples—particularly in preindustrial societies—are inherently fascinating. The second purpose, more serious, is to undermine ethnocentric attitudes by highlighting, through comparison, distinctive aspects of American society that might otherwise pass unnoticed or be taken for granted.

Art. The sociology of art has long been a personal interest of mine, and I have always regarded the artwork and other illustrations as integral to the book—nearly as important, in fact, as the writing. Users have responded very positively to the inclusion of fine art in previous editions, and I have expanded this feature in the present revision, paying particular attention to pieces that convey points of historical or cross-cultural interest. I have also taken particular care in selecting photographs, cartoons, and other graphic materials that best complement the narrative. Additionally, I have tried to provide full and informative captions that reinforce and amplify the text discussion. Numerous tables and charts, up-to-date and easy to read, are also used to aid the students' understanding of concepts and sociological data.

Theory. I have always believed that a sound introduction to sociological theory should be an essential feature of the introductory course, and that we fail both the discipline and our students if we do not provide it. The treatment of theory in this book is shaped by two convictions. The first is that theory can be presented in a clear, concise, interesting, and understandable manner, and that its practical value can be readily appreciated by the student. The second conviction is that theory must not, as happens all too often, be briefly introduced in the first chapter and then hastily buried: this tactic can only confirm the student's worst suspicions that theory is an irrelevant luxury.

I have again taken a fairly eclectic approach to sociological theory and have utilized all three of the main perspectives in the contemporary discipline: functionalist theory (primarily for issues of social order and stability), conflict theory (primarily for issues of social tension and change), and interactionist theories (primarily for "micro" issues). Above all, I have made use of these perspectives throughout the book—not by applying them mechanically to everything, but by introducing particular theoretical perspectives where they will genuinely enhance the understanding of a specific issue. Where the perspectives complement one another, as they often do, this is made clear; where they seem contradictory, the problem is discussed, and, if possible, resolved. I have drawn extensively, of course, on the ideas of contemporary sociologists; but in keeping with the continuing resurgence of interest in classical thinkers, I have given due emphasis to such writers as Marx, Durkheim, and Weber.

Readings. I have included a number of readings from original sources at appropriate places in the text. These readings have been chosen for their interest and relevance, and are designed to give the student a deeper, more first-hand experience of sociological writing and research.

Pedagogical aids. Several features of the book are designed to aid the learning process. Each chapter begins with a brief overview of its major topics and closes with a numbered, point-by-point summary of the contents. All important terms are printed in bold-face italics and immediately defined—and the definitions are consistent throughout. These important terms are also listed (with the number of the page on which they are defined) for end-of-chapter review. Throughout the book, there are also occasional boxes containing short and relevant items of interest.

Glossary. The book contains an extensive glossary—virtually a mini-dictionary—of over three hundred important sociological terms. The glossary can be used both for ready reference and for reviewing purposes.

Library research techniques. I have included a brief appendix on techniques of library research. This appendix is intended as a handy guide to library facilities, including data-base computer files; it offers many suggestions for tracking down sources and information and should prove useful to students working on term papers or research projects.

Supplementary Materials

A new *Study Guide* is available to help students both in understanding and in reviewing the course. The guide, prepared by Carla B. Howery of the American Sociological Association, includes learning objectives, chapter summaries, multiple-choice questions, application exercises, and case studies.

The text is further complemented by a comprehensive *Instructor's Resource Manual,* extensively revised by Donald P. Irish (Hamline University) and Carla B. Howery. The revised manual includes essay and application questions, discussions and demonstrations, projects, sample lectures, additional lecture topics, a film guide, a new software guide, sample syllabi, and other teaching resources.

A *Test Bank* of multiple-choice questions has been prepared by Jeffrey P. Rosenfeld (Nassau Community College) and John N. Short (University of Arkansas, Monticello). The test bank is accompanied by *Computest,* a computerized test-generation system.

A new supplement to the text is a set of *Computer Simulations.* The simulations contain eight personal-computer games that allow students to practice and apply sociological concepts in an interesting and stimulating way. The simulations have been prepared by John Stimson (William Paterson College), Ardyth Stimson (Kean College), Stephen Shalom (William Paterson College), and Robert C. Rosen (William Paterson College). They are designed for use with an Apple II+/IIe/IIc.

The text has also served as the basis for a series of video programs, *Focus on Society,* prepared for open-circuit broadcast and cable television by the Dallas County Community College District. This series is supplemented by a separate study guide by Paul McGee (North Lake College).

Finally, I have prepared a new edition of my

anthology of readings in sociology, *The Social World.* Organized in the same sequence of topics as the text, the reader should provide a useful accompaniment to it.

Thanks

I have been greatly helped in the preparation of this book by a number of people, including the many instructors and students who have offered their comments and suggestions either in writing or in person. I particularly want to thank those of my colleagues who evaluated various parts of the published second edition and of the manuscript for the third edition for accuracy, coverage, readability, currency, and teachability. The book owes a great deal to the many constructive criticisms and suggestions they offered. Of course, I have not always agreed with the reviewers (nor have they always agreed with one another), and the responsibility for the final manuscript is entirely my own. The reviewers were

Mark Abrahamson, University of Connecticut
H. Paul Chalfant, Texas Tech University
Rodney Coe, St. Louis University School of Medicine
Carolie Coffey, Cabrillo College
Randall Collins, University of California, Riverside
Glen Elder, Cornell University
Frederick Elkin, York University
Richard Fantasia, Smith College
Joe R. Feagin, University of Texas, Austin
Paul Gebhard, Kinsey Institute
Tom Gervasi, Center for Military Research and Analysis
Barbara Hargrove, Iliff School of Theology
Barbara Heyns, New York University
Carla B. Howery, American Sociological Association
Donald P. Irish, Hamline University
Barclay D. Johnson, Carleton University
Judith Lorber, City College of New York
Robert F. Meier, Washington State University
Linda Nilson, University of California, Los Angeles

Anthony Orum, University of Texas, Austin
Vincent N. Parrillo, William Paterson College
James T. Richardson, University of Nevada
Jeffrey P. Rosenfeld, Nassau Community College
Daniel Rossides, Bowdoin College
Edward Sagarin, City College of New York
Steven R. Severin, Kellogg Community College
Randall Stokes, University of Massachusetts
Shirley Strom, Henry Ford Community College
Larry Stern, College of the Holy Cross
Ralph Tomlinson, California State University, Los Angeles
Kenrick S. Thompson, Northern Michigan University
Andrew C. Twaddle, University of Missouri-Columbia
Victoria Swigert, College of the Holy Cross
Robin M. Williams, Cornell University
John Wilson, Duke University

I am especially grateful to Donald Irish, who read the entire manuscript for all three editions; the book has benefited greatly from his cogent criticisms and humane wisdom. I have gained a great deal since the previous edition from my teaching of introductory sociology at the University of California, Los Angeles, and at William Paterson College, New Jersey, and I am indebted to my students and colleagues at both institutions.

I am grateful also to June Lundborg Whitworth, who is once again responsible for the photo and art research for the text. My thanks also go to two graduate students at Columbia University who helped with the research for the book, Tracey Dewart and Rosa Haritos.

Finally, I am fortunate to continue my association with Worth Publishers, a company with a deserved reputation for its commitment to excellence at every stage of the publishing process. For the effort they put into this book and the extraordinary support they have given me, my thanks go to Bob Worth and all his staff, notably George Touloumes, Sarah J. Segal, and Demetrios Zangos of the production department, and particularly my good friends and superb editors, Peter Deane and Linda Baron Davis.

February 1987   IAN ROBERTSON

CONTENTS

The Author

Ian Robertson spent most of his early years in South Africa, where he obtained a B.A. degree in Political Science at the University of Natal. As president of the multiracial National Union of South African Students he organized several campaigns against that country's apartheid laws, until he was arbitrarily placed under restriction by Prime Minister Vorster. Among other prohibitions, he was forbidden to teach, write, belong to organizations, enter college premises, or be with more than one other person at any time. He was eventually allowed to leave South Africa, and thereafter he studied at Oxford, Cambridge, and Harvard universities, supporting himself through scholarships and writing. During this period his articles on various social topics appeared in such publications as the *Times* and *Guardian* in England and the *New Republic* and *Nation* in the United States.

Ian Robertson trained as a teacher at Oxford, where he was awarded a Diploma in Education in English and Latin. At Cambridge he took a First-Class Honors degree and M.A. in sociology and was elected Senior Scholar in Sociology at King's College. At Harvard he was awarded both a master's degree and a doctorate in the sociology of education. Dr. Robertson has a wide teaching experience: he has taught basic curriculum to retarded children in England, high school social studies in Massachusetts, sociology of education to Harvard graduates, and social sciences to Cambridge undergraduates. Most recently, he has taught introductory sociology at the University of California, Los Angeles (1983) and the William Paterson College of New Jersey (1985). He is currently devoting himself to his writing.

In addition to various articles, Dr. Robertson has published *Readings in Sociology: Contemporary Perspectives* (Harper & Row, 1976), *Race and Politics in South Africa* (Transaction Books, 1978), *Social Problems* (Random House, 1980), and *The Social World* (Worth, 1987).

Sociology

Introduction to Sociology

Like any subject that deals with people, sociology can be truly fascinating. This introductory unit explains what sociology is, as well as what sociologists do and how they go about their work. In reading it you will discover sociology's distinctive perspective on human society and social behavior.

The first chapter offers you a general overview of the discipline, presenting sociologists as "strangers" in the familiar landscape of their own society: in other words, as people who look afresh at the world others take for granted. The chapter explains the "sociological imagination"—the vivid awareness you will gain of the close link between personal experience and wider social forces. It also discusses the scientific nature of sociology, the relationship of sociology to other social sciences, the history of the discipline, and the major theoretical approaches that sociologists use to make sense of their subject matter.

The second chapter discusses the methods sociologists use to investigate the social world. Sociological research is essentially a form of detective work, in which the sociologist tries to find out what is happening in society and why. The value of sociologists' conclusions is obviously influenced by the accuracy and reliability of the methods they use to collect and analyze the evidence. The chapter therefore examines the problems of tracing cause and effect in social behavior, the unique difficulties sociologists face in their research, and the methods they use to uncover the facts about social life.

The illustration opposite is a detail from Sunday Afternoon on the Island of La Grande Jatte, *by the French artist Georges Seurat. The work was painted in Europe a century ago and shows one aspect of the diverse and changing milieu in which the discipline of sociology developed.*

CHAPTER 1

Sociology: A New Look at a Familiar World

Alone among living creatures, human beings are fully self-aware—capable of inquiring and reflecting about themselves. Throughout history, our ancestors pondered human nature as it seemed to reveal itself in the social life of our species. Why do human beings form families, and why do they worship gods? Why is the way of life of one group so different from that of another? What makes some people break social rules while others obey them? Why are some people rich when others are poor? What makes one group go to war with another? What might a human being who had not been raised in the company of other people be like? What holds societies together, and why do all societies continually change over time?

Until quite recently the answers to these and similar questions came from intuition, from speculation, and from the dead weight of myth, superstition, and "folk wisdom" handed down from the past. Only in the course of the past century or so has a new method been applied to the study of human society and social behavior—the method of science, which provides answers drawn from facts collected by systematic research.

This new mode of inquiry has produced the lively discipline of sociology. *Sociology* is the scientific study of human society and social behavior. Its subject matter is huge, complex, and varied, and the knowledge produced by sociological research remains imperfect in many ways. Yet, in the brief time that the discipline has been in existence, it has taught us a great deal about ourselves that we could never have learned by relying on speculation alone. We have learned to conceive of human beings and social life in an entirely new way—a way you will find sometimes disconcerting, yet often fascinating.

3

Figure 1.1 *To an outsider, the appearance of this woman from the South Pacific island of New Guinea may seem bizarre, but in the context of her own society, it is perfectly understandable. She is a widow, attending the funeral ceremonies of her late husband. She is covered in gray clay, for gray is the color of mourning in her society, and she wears voluminous strings of beads, the beads being symbolic of tears. In enacting the funeral rituals of her society, this widow does more than express her bereavement and honor her dead husband. Although she may be unaware of it, she is also affirming her loyalty to the group, its way of life, its traditions, its beliefs. Sociology invites us to look with the same inquiring eye at behavior we have always taken for granted in our own society—for example, at the rituals of Thanksgiving, Christmas, the Fourth of July, or even the dress and behavior of our own people at funerals.*

Sociology as a Perspective

The world does not consist of a reality that everyone sees in exactly the same way. A house may seem to be simply a house, but different people will look at it and interpret it quite differently. An architect, a real estate broker, a burglar, an artist, and a demolition expert, for instance, would each view the house from a distinctive perspective and would see quite different things as a result. In the same way, sociology offers a particular perspective on society and social behavior, a viewpoint quite unlike that of, say, the poet, the philosopher, the theologian, the lawyer, or the police officer.

The sociological perspective invites us to look at our familiar surroundings as if for the first time. It allows us to get a fresh view of a world we have always taken for granted, to examine our own social landscape with the same curiosity and fascination that we might bring to an exotic, alien culture. As Peter Berger (1963) has observed, sociology is nothing less than a special form of consciousness. It encourages us to focus on features of our social environment we have never noticed before and to interpret them in a new and richer light.

Sociology also gives us a window on the wider world that lies beyond our immediate experience, leading us into areas of society we might otherwise have ignored or misunderstood. Ordinarily, our own view of the world is shaped by our personal experience of it. However, sociology can take us into the worlds of the rich and the powerful, the poor and the weak, the worlds of politicians, doctors, professional athletes, and of slum dwellers, addicts, cult members, and criminals. Because these people have different social experiences, they have quite different definitions of social reality. Sociology enables us to appreciate viewpoints other than our own, to understand how these viewpoints came into being, and in the process, to better understand our attitudes, ourselves, and our own lives.

The Basic Insight

Sociology starts from the premise that we are basically social animals—not just from force of habit but because otherwise we could not survive. We live out our brief lives, for better or worse, in a society that existed long before we were born and presumably will exist long after we are gone. We are all born into human groups and derive our identities, hopes, fears, troubles, and satisfactions from them. *The basic insight of sociology is this: human behavior is largely shaped by the groups to which people belong and by the social interaction that takes place within those groups.* We are what we are and we behave the way we do because we happen to live in particular societies at particular points in space and time. If you had been born, say, a modern Chinese peasant, or an African Pygmy, or an ancient Greek, or a feudal aristocrat, your personality, your options in life, and your social experience would be utterly different. This fact seems obvious enough, but it is easily overlooked. People everywhere tend to take their social world for granted, accepting their society and its customs as unquestioningly as they do the physical world that also surrounds them. But the sociological perspective enables us to see society not as something to be taken for granted as "natural" but as a temporary social product, created by human beings and therefore capable of being changed by them as well.

The main focus of sociology is the group rather than the individual. Studies of particular individuals are useful to sociologists, but the sociologist is mainly interested in *social interaction—the ways in which people act toward, respond to, and influence one another.* All social behavior, from shaking hands to murder, and all social institutions, from the economy to the family, are ultimately the product of social interaction. The group, then, provides the sociologist's main frame of reference—whether the group being studied is as small as a gang or a rock band, as large as an ethnic community or a city, or as vast as a modern industrial society with a population of millions.

The Sociological Imagination

This emphasis on the group always leads back to the individual, however, for by understanding society, we more fully understand ourselves. C. Wright Mills (1959) described the perspective of the discipline as "the sociological imagination"—a vivid awareness of the relationship between private experience and the wider society. People usually see the world through their limited experience in a small orbit of family, relatives, friends, and fellow workers. This viewpoint places blinders on their view of the wider society. But it does more than that. Paradoxically, it also narrows their view of their own personal worlds, for those worlds are shaped by broader social forces that can easily pass unrecognized.

Figure 1.2 *The "sociological imagination" enables us to trace the links between individual experience and social forces. The options and lifestyles of these people—from the upper class in urban Europe, from a Pygmy tribe in an African rain forest, and from a lakeside village in South America—are very different. People's lives are shaped by historical and social forces over which they have little personal control.*

The sociological imagination allows us to escape from this cramped personal vision—to stand apart mentally from our own place in society and to see with a new clarity the link between private and social events. When a society becomes industrialized, rural peasants become urban workers, whether they like it or not. When a nation goes to war, spouses are widowed and children grow up as orphans, for reasons that are beyond their personal power to control. When an economy sags, workers are thrown out of their jobs, no matter how efficiently they have performed them. The sociological imagination permits us to trace the intricate connection between the patterns and events of our own lives and the patterns and events of our society. As Mills expressed it,

> the sociological imagination enables us to grasp history and biography and the relationship between the two within society. That is its task and its promise. . . . It is by means of the sociological imagination that men now hope to grasp what is happening to themselves as minute points of the intersection of biography and history within society.

What Is Science?

Science refers to the logical, systematic methods by which knowledge is obtained and to the actual body of knowledge produced by these methods. The sciences are usually divided into two main branches: the *natural sciences,* disciplines that study physical and biological phenomena, and the *social sciences,* disciplines that study various aspects of human behavior. There are important differences between the two branches, but both have the same commitment to the scientific method.

All science, natural and social, assumes that there is some underlying order in the universe. Events, whether they involve molecules or human beings, are not haphazard. They follow a pattern that is sufficiently regular for us to be able to make *generalizations*—statements that apply not just to a specific case but to most cases of the same type. It is possible to generalize, for example, that hydrogen and oxygen will always form water if they are combined at an appropriate temperature. Similarly, it is possible to generalize that all human societies will create some system of marriage and family. Generalizations are crucial to science because they place isolated, seemingly meaningless events in patterns we can understand. It then becomes possible to analyze relation-

ships of cause and effect and thus to *explain* why something happens and to *predict* that it will happen again under the same conditions in the future.

Science relies for its generalizations, explanations, and predictions on careful, systematic analysis of verifiable evidence—that is, evidence that can be checked by others and will always yield the same results. Nonscientific, "common-sense" explanations, on the other hand, are based on belief. The ancient Romans, for example, believed that the sun is drawn across the skies each day by a god in a chariot, although none of them had actually seen this happen. Scientists have since observed, of course, that the apparent movement of the sun is caused by the daily rotations of the earth, an observation any competent scientist can verify by using the same methods. In short, the scientific approach leads to a more reliable interpretation of reality than can be arrived at by common-sense assumptions.

This does not mean that common sense cannot provide accurate explanations and predictions; it can, and often does. However, the problem is that without using the methods of science, there is no way to tell whether common sense is correct. For centuries common sense told people that the world is the center of the universe and that the earth is flat. Using scientific methods, Copernicus found that the world is simply one planet among others; and the investigations of Columbus and other geographers proved that the earth is round. In making their factual investigations, these people and others like them risked their reputations and sometimes even their lives, for their findings contradicted important social beliefs of the time. But their challenge to ideas held dear by their societies tells us something else about science: there are no areas so sacred that science cannot explore them. Any question that can be answered by the scientific method is, in principle, an appropriate subject for scientific inquiry—even if the investigation and the findings outrage powerful interests or undermine cherished values. Yet science is not arrogant: it recognizes no ultimate, final truths. The body of scientific knowledge at any particular moment represents nothing more than the most logical interpretations of the existing data. It is always possible that new facts will come to light or that the available data will be reinterpreted in a new way, shattering the existing assumptions. Science therefore takes nothing for granted: everything is always open for further testing, reinterpretation, correction, and even refutation. That is why

Figure 1.3 *In their work, scientists sometimes run afoul of the popular assumptions and the established authorities of their time. Galileo, who invented the telescope early in the seventeenth century, proved that the earth moves around the sun, and not vice versa. His finding contradicted Church teachings, and in 1633 he was placed on trial by the Inquisition. Galileo was forced to recant his view on pain of death—but legend has it that he muttered under his breath, "It moves nevertheless."*

scientists, and especially sociologists, are so often "the destroyers of myths" (Elias, 1978). And sometimes the myths they destroy are their own.

Sociology as a Science

On the whole, social life does not consist of a series of random events: under most conditions, society and its processes are ordered and patterned. Most Americans or most Russians, for example, will continue to think and act in much the same way tomorrow as they did yesterday. Consequently, sociology is able to employ the same general methods of investigation that all sciences do, and to use its findings to make reasonably reliable generalizations. Like natural scientists, sociologists construct theories, collect and analyze data, conduct experiments and make observations, keep careful records, and try to arrive at precise and accurate conclusions.

The Scientific Status of Sociology

Like the other social sciences, however, sociology is relatively less advanced as a discipline than most of the natural sciences. There are two reasons for this. First, the scientific method has been used to study social behavior only in recent times, whereas the scientific method has been applied to the natural world for centuries. Second, and more important, the study of human behavior presents many problems that natural scientists do not have to confront. Sociologists are dealing with people—in other words, with subjects who are self-aware and capable of changing their behavior when they choose to. Unlike rocks or molecules, people may be deliberately uncooperative. They may behave in unforeseen ways for private reasons of their own. They may radically change their behavior when they know they are being studied. They cannot in good conscience be made the subject of experiments that affront their dignity or infringe on their basic human rights. And their behavior usually has extremely complex causes that may be difficult to pinpoint. (We shall explore these problems more fully in Chapter 2 when we discuss how sociologists go about their research.)

Although both natural and social scientists recognize that it may be impossible to prove the existence of "universal laws" that apply to anything or event in all circumstances, the natural sciences can generally offer more precise explanations and predictions than can sociologists. But the accumulated results of sociological research are already extensive, solid, and important. Sociological research methods are constantly being improved, and we can expect that they will achieve still greater precision in the future.

Strangers in a Familiar World

In the following selection, sociologist Peter Berger explains some of the intellectual fascination of the discipline.

Anthropologists use the term "culture shock" to describe the impact of a totally new culture upon a newcomer. In an extreme instance such shock will be experienced by the Western explorer who is told, halfway through dinner, that he is eating the nice old lady he had been chatting with the previous day. Most explorers no longer encounter cannibalism in their travels today. However, the first encounters with polygamy or with puberty rites or even with the way some nations drive their automobiles can be quite a shock to an American visitor. With the shock may go not only disapproval or disgust but a sense of excitement that things can *really* be that different from what they are at home. To some extent, at least, this is the excitement of any first travel abroad. The experience of sociological discovery could be described as "culture shock" minus geographical displacement. In other words, the sociologist travels at home—with shocking results. He is unlikely to find that he is eating a nice old lady for dinner. But the discovery, for instance, that his own church has considerable money invested in the missile industry or that a few blocks from his home there are people who engage in cultic orgies may not be drastically different in emotional impact. Yet we would not want to imply that sociological discoveries are always or even usually outrageous to moral sentiment. Not at all. What they have in common with exploration in distant lands, however, is the sudden illumination of new and unsuspected facets of human existence in society.

People who like to avoid shocking discoveries, who prefer to believe that society is just what they were taught in Sunday School, who like the safety of the rules and the maxims of what Alfred Schutz has called the "world-taken-for-granted," should stay away from sociology. People who feel no temptation before closed doors, who have no curiosity about human beings, who are content to admire scenery without wondering about the people who live in those houses on the other side of that river, should probably also stay away from sociology. They will find it unpleasant or, at any rate, unrewarding. People who are interested in human beings only if they can change, convert or reform them should also be warned, for they will find sociology much less useful than they hoped. And people whose interest is mainly in their own conceptual constructions will do just as well to turn to the study of little white mice. Sociology will be satisfying, in the long run, only to those who can think of nothing more entrancing than to watch and to understand things human.

SOURCE: Peter L. Berger, *Invitation to Sociology* (Garden City, N.Y.: Doubleday & Company, Inc., Anchor Books, 1963).

Sociology, then, is not less "scientific" than biochemistry or astronomy: it simply faces greater problems of generalization, explanation, and prediction. Yet the suspicion persists in some quarters that sociology is not "really" a science. In part this is because the popular image of the scientist is often that of someone working in a laboratory in a white coat, something sociologists rarely do. But the origin of the suspicion probably lies deeper. Few people are experts in molecular biology or planetary motions, but all of us can consider ourselves experts on society, because we have had years of experience in social living. Sociologists, it is sometimes suggested, merely state the obvious in complicated language, telling us virtually nothing that our common sense has not told us already.

It is true that the language of sociology is sometimes a little strange to the beginner. The sociologist uses a specialized vocabulary and often employs everyday words, such as "status," "role," and "culture," in precise but unfamiliar ways. Sociologists use this vocabulary for the same reason that all scientists must: unless terms have an agreed-upon, definite meaning, communication will be ambiguous and confusing, and findings will be difficult to verify. We do not expect a chemist to say, "I took some white crystals, mixed in a bit of black powder, chucked in some yellow stuff, threw in a match, and blew the place up." Unless the chemist tells us he or she was using potassium chlorate, carbon, and sulfur in specific quantities under particular conditions, the information is useless.

Similarly, it is not enough for a sociologist to say, "I showed this violent movie to some kids, and afterward they started acting much rougher than before." We need to know what is meant by "violent": what sort of violence, in what context, involving what kind of people? We need to know about the "kids": how old, which sex, what background? We need to know what is meant by "rougher than before": what is "roughness," how is it measured, how rough were they, in what ways, under what circumstances, for how long afterward, and toward whom? Only when the experiment is described with precision does it have any value as science, for it can then be repeated by other scientists to check the original findings. The need for precision means that, as a general rule, sociological writing will not have you chewing your fingernails in suspense or guffawing out of your armchair at an author's wit and humor. Some sociological writing, in fact, is quite deadly. But you will find many sociological articles and books that are absorbing to read because they expand our understanding of the human animal.

Sociology and Common Sense

But does sociology merely state the obvious by reporting what common sense tells us anyway? Here are some widely held common-sense views about society and social behavior. As you read through them, you might like to check them off as true or false.

1. Human beings have a natural instinct to mate with the opposite sex. (T/F)

2. Lower-class people are more likely to commit crimes than upper-class people. (T/F)

3. Ronald Reagan was elected president by a large majority of American adults. (T/F)

4. Revolutions are more likely to occur when conditions remain very bad than when bad conditions are rapidly improving. (T/F)

5. It makes sense to choose a college major in the same field as one's intended career, because most graduates are employed in the general field of their college major. (T/F)

6. The amount of money spent on a school's facilities has a strong effect on the academic success of its pupils. (T/F)

7. A substantial proportion of the people on welfare could work if they really wanted to. (T/F)

8. One thing found in every society is romantic love. (T/F)

9. Regular churchgoers are less likely to be prejudiced against people of other races than those who do not attend church. (T/F)

10. The best way to get an accurate assessment of public opinion is to poll as many people as possible. (T/F)

11. The income gap between American blacks and whites has narrowed significantly in recent years. (T/F)

12. The income gap between American male and female workers has narrowed significantly in recent years. (T/F)

13. Husbands are more likely to kill their wives in family fights than wives are to kill their husbands. (T/F)

14. Every society forbids sexual relations between parent and child and between brother and sister. (T/F)

15. Experts foresee a big expansion in well-paid "high technology" jobs in the American economy. (T/F)

16. For religious reasons, most American Catholics oppose birth control and are less likely than Protestants to get divorces. (T/F)

17. The population explosion in the less developed countries of the world is caused by high birth rates in those regions. (T/F)

18. The better you do in college, the more successful you are likely to be in your career. (T/F)

19. Physicians can correctly diagnose the medical problems of most patients who bring complaints to them. (T/F)

20. Natural disasters such as earthquakes cause panic and a breakdown in the organization and cohesion of the communities involved. (T/F)

All the above assumptions may seem to be in accord with common sense, but sociological-research has shown that every single one of them is false.

1. Human beings do not have a specific instinct to mate with the opposite sex. Our sexual preferences are learned (Chapter 9); in fact, if instinct is defined as an inherited complex behavior pattern, human beings do not have any instincts at all (Chapters 3 and 5).

2. There is no evidence whatever that poor people are more likely to commit crimes than rich ones. However, poor people commit different kinds of crime (for example, petty theft rather than expense-account fraud) and are more likely to be arrested and convicted (Chapter 8).

3. Fewer than one in every three eligible voters actually voted for Ronald Reagan in 1984. He won 59 percent of the votes cast, but 47 percent of the potential electorate did not vote (Chapter 18).

4. Revolutions are actually more likely to occur when conditions have been bad but are

rapidly improving. When conditions are bad and stay bad, people take their misfortune for granted, but when conditions suddenly improve, people develop higher aspirations and become easily frustrated (Chapter 19).

5. Most college graduates are not employed in the field of their college major. The percentage who are is likely to decrease even further in the years ahead, since people are increasingly likely to change jobs several times in their careers (Chapter 14).

6. The amount of money spent on a school's facilities seems to have little influence on pupils' achievement. Performance is related primarily to pupils' family and social-class backgrounds (Chapter 14).

7. Less than 2 percent of the people on welfare are adult males who have been out of work for several months. Nearly all are children, old people, handicapped people, or mothers who stay home to look after young children and have no other source of income (Chapter 10).

8. Romantic love may seem part of "human nature" to us, but in many societies it is unknown, and in many others it is regarded as ridiculous or tragic (Chapter 13).

9. Regular churchgoers are generally not less prejudiced than nonchurchgoers; in fact, they tend to be more prejudiced (Chapter 15).

10. The number of people involved in an opinion poll is largely irrelevant. What matters is that the sample be representative of the population whose opinion is wanted. A properly chosen sample of a few thousand people can give a highly accurate test of national opinion; a poorly chosen sample of 3 million, or even 30 million, could be hopelessly off target (Chapter 2).

11. Despite civil rights and other legislation, the income gap between blacks and whites has widened in recent years; black workers hold lower-paying jobs than whites and have a much higher unemployment rate (Chapter 11).

12. The income gap between male and female workers has narrowed very little: few women hold high-level positions; most are in low-paying occupations (Chapter 12).

13. Husbands and wives are equally likely to kill one another in marital disputes. Although husbands are usually stronger, wives are more likely to resort to lethal weapons, such as kitchen knives (Chapter 13).

14. Different societies define incest in very dif-ferent ways, and a few have permitted parent-child or brother-sister incest in certain circumstances (Chapters 9 and 13).

15. No big expansion in well-paid "high tech" jobs is foreseen. Although more people will use "high tech" equipment, such as word processors, they will be doing much the same jobs as before, for much the same pay (Chapter 17).

16. More than 80 percent of American Catholics favor birth control, and Catholics have a higher divorce rate than Protestants (Chapter 15).

17. The population explosion in the less developed countries is caused not by high birth rates but by a decrease in death rates. Birth rates have actually declined, but people are living much longer, causing overall population size to swell (Chapter 21).

18. There is no consistent relationship between people's performance in college and their later career achievements. The talents required for academic success in college and practical success in the world beyond are not the same (Chapter 14).

19. Physicians are unable to find anything wrong with more than half the patients who come to them—although the physicians may not tell that to the patients (Chapter 16).

20. Natural disasters such as earthquakes rarely cause panic, and in fact, generally produce greater social organization and cohesion in the community affected (Chapter 22).

Of course, common-sense views are not always so relentlessly contradicted by sociological research. Indeed, intuition and common sense in sociology are a rich source of insights. But they can provide only hunches. The hunch must be tested by the methods of science.

The Social Sciences

We have already referred to the social sciences, a related group of disciplines that study various aspects of human behavior. The social sciences are sociology, economics, psychology, political science, and anthropology. Of course, human behavior does not fit neatly into compartments, and in practice the boundaries between the social sciences are vague and constantly shifting. Each of the disciplines has different historical origins, and the distinctions among them have been preserved

Figure 1.4

"*I'm a social scientist, Michael. That means I can't explain electricity or anything like that, but if you want to know about people I'm your man.*"

Drawing by Handelsman; © 1986
The New Yorker Magazine, Inc.

largely as a matter of convenience. Nobody could possibly be an expert in all of them, and the fragmentation of the social sciences permits specialization. But social scientists realize how much the concerns of the various disciplines overlap, and they freely invade each other's territory whenever it seems useful.

Economics

Economics studies the production, distribution, and consumption of goods and services. Economists examine, for example, how prices are determined or what effects taxes will have. Economics is in many ways the most advanced of the social sciences. Its subject matter is often more easily measured than that of the other disciplines, and economists have developed sophisticated mathematical tools for their explanations and predictions. But the economy is also a part of society: goods and services do not produce, distribute, and consume themselves. These social aspects of economic life are the subject of the sociology of economics.

Psychology

Psychology studies human mental processes, such as emotion, memory, perception, and intelligence. This discipline, more than any other social science, focuses on the individual. Partly because it has its roots in natural sciences such as biology, it also relies more heavily on laboratory and clinical experiments. Psychology shares one major field of interest with sociology: *social psychology,* the study of how personality and behavior are influenced by the social context. Social psychology is a genuine hybrid discipline. In many colleges and universities, in fact, social psychology is as likely to be taught in sociology as in psychology departments.

Political Science

Political science has traditionally focused on two main areas: political philosophy and actual forms of government, with special emphasis on how the two are related. In recent years, however, the discipline has been strongly influenced by political sociology, which analyzes political behavior and studies the social interaction involved in the process of government. Political scientists are now asking more "sociological" questions, such as why people vote the way they do, or what happens "behind the scenes" in the informal manipulation of power. Sociological research, too, is increasingly used in shaping government policies. The interests of political scientists and political sociologists have been gradually converging and now often overlap.

Anthropology

Anthropology is sociology's sister discipline. It differs from sociology mainly in that it has usually focused on entire, small-scale, "primitive" societies, whereas sociology concentrates more on group processes within large modern industrial societies. Anthropology has several branches: archaeology, which deals with the remains of extinct civilizations; linguistics, which deals with certain aspects of language; physical anthropology, which uses fossil and other evidence to trace human evolution; and *cultural anthropology,* the study of the ways of life of other peoples. An *ethnography* is an anthropological report about some aspects of a people's way of life, and sociologists often find ethnographic evidence useful when they want to compare modern societies with other societies that are very different. In fact, now that

Figure 1.5 *Anthropology differs from sociology mainly in that it focuses on small-scale, traditional societies, such as these nomadic Lapps in northern Scandinavia. Anthropological reports from these fast-vanishing communities provide valuable information about the diversity of human social life.*

small-scale, traditional societies are rapidly becoming extinct, many cultural anthropologists are studying groups in modern industrial societies. Sociologists and cultural anthropologists draw freely on one another's work.

In this book we shall make use of findings from the other social sciences whenever this is helpful for the understanding of social behavior. We shall place particular emphasis on information from social psychology and cultural anthropology. The research of social psychologists often throws light on the ways in which the social environment influences behavior, and the ethnographies of cultural anthropologists enable us to highlight aspects of our own society by comparing our practices with those of other peoples.

The Development of Sociology

Before the mid-1800s the study of society was the domain of social philosophers, thinkers who were often less concerned about what society actually *is* like than what they thought it *ought* to be like. Yet in a relatively short period this entire emphasis was reversed.

The Origins

The new discipline of sociology began to emerge in the middle of the nineteenth century, in the context of the sweeping changes the Industrial Revolution brought to Europe. No social changes in history had been as widespread or as far-reaching, and this transformation—which is still taking place in the less developed nations of the world—cried out for analysis and explanation.

Industrialization threw into turmoil societies that had been relatively stable for centuries. New industries and technologies changed the face of the social and physical environment. Peasants left rural areas and flocked to the towns, where they worked as industrial laborers under appalling conditions. Cities grew at an unprecedented rate, providing an anonymous environment in which the customs and values of the small, tight-knit traditional community could scarcely survive. Social problems became rampant in the teeming cities. The ancient view that the social order was preordained by God began to collapse. A rising middle class, spurred by the examples of the French and American revolutions, clamored for democracy, and aristocracies and monarchies crumbled and fell. Religion began to lose its force as an unquestioned source of moral authority. Rapid social change became the norm rather than an abnormal state of affairs, and people could no longer expect that their children's lives would be much the same as their own. The direction of change was unclear, and the stability of the social order seemed threatened. An understanding of what was happening was urgently needed.

Two other factors besides industrialization encouraged the development of sociology. One was the example of the natural sciences—if their methods could make so much sense of the physical world, could they not be applied successfully to the social world as well? The second factor was the exposure of Europeans to the radically different societies in Africa, Asia, and the Americas that

Figure 1.6 *Sociology emerged as a separate discipline during the early stages of the Industrial Revolution, when traditional societies were suddenly thrust into an era of rapid social change and* *unprecedented social problems. Sociology was born out of the attempt to understand the transformations that seemed to threaten the stability of European society.*

their new colonial empires had engulfed. Information about the widely contrasting social practices of these peoples raised fresh questions about society in general. Why, for instance, were some societies apparently more advanced than others, and what lessons could the European countries learn from comparisons of various societies?

Early Sociologists

Given the social conditions that provoked their inquiry, the early sociologists focused their attention on the forces that hold society together and on the forces that fragment it.

Auguste Comte

The title "founder of sociology" usually goes to the French philosopher Auguste Comte (1798–1857). Comte was a somewhat eccentric person (he claimed to practice "mental hygiene," meaning that he refused to read anyone else's books), but was one of the most original thinkers of his time. It was he who coined the term "sociology" and who argued, in 1838, that the methods of science should be applied to the study of society. Comte established two specific problems for sociological investigation, "social statics" and "social dynamics." Social statics refers to the problem of order and stability—how and why do societies hold together and endure? Social dynamics refers to the problem of social change—what makes societies change and what shapes the nature and direction of the changes? Comte was so confident that the scientific method would unlock the secrets of society that he came to regard sociologists as a "priesthood of humanity," experts who would not only explain social events but would also guide society in the direction of greater progress. Although later sociologists have generally had more modest ambitions, they have continued to wrestle with the problems of social order and social change.

Figure 1.7 *Auguste Comte*   Figure 1.8 *Herbert Spencer*   Figure 1.9 *Karl Marx*

Herbert Spencer

Another important nineteenth-century figure was Herbert Spencer (1820–1903), who devised a theory to explain the problems of social order and change. Spencer compared human societies to living organisms. The parts of an animal, such as the lungs and the heart, are interdependent and contribute to the survival of the total organism. Similarly, Spencer argued, the various parts of society, such as the state and the economy, are also interdependent and work to ensure the stability and survival of the entire system. This theory took care of the problem of order. To explain change, Spencer pushed his analogy even further. Applying Darwin's theory of evolution to human societies, he argued that they gradually evolve from the forms found in the "primitive" societies of the world to the more complex forms found in the industrializing societies of his own time. Spencer believed that evolution means progress, and he strongly opposed attempts at social reform on the grounds that they might interfere with a natural evolutionary process. Spencer's ideas seem rather strange today, but they remain influential in a very modified form. Many sociologists still see society as a more or less harmonious system whose various parts contribute to overall stability. Many also believe there has been a general tendency for societies to move from the simple to the complex, although they do not necessarily equate this evolution with "progress" toward something better.

Karl Marx

The third and most important of the nineteenth-century social thinkers was Karl Marx (1818–

1883). Marx was born in Germany, but after being expelled from various countries for his revolutionary activities, he eventually settled in England. An erratic genius, he wrote brilliantly on subjects as broad and diverse as philosophy, economics, political science, and history. He did not think of himself as a sociologist, but his work is so rich in sociological insights that he is now regarded as one of the most profound and original sociological thinkers. His influence has been immense. Millions of people accept his theories with almost religious fervor, and modern socialist and communist movements owe their inspiration directly to him. It is important to realize, however, that Marxism is not the same as communism. Marx would probably be dismayed at many of the practices of communist movements, and he cannot be held responsible for policies pursued in his name a century after his death. Even in his own lifetime, he was so appalled at the various interpretations of his ideas by competing factions that he declared, "I am not a Marxist."

To Marx, the task of the social scientist was not merely to describe the world: it was to change it. Whereas Spencer saw social harmony and the inevitability of progress, Marx saw social conflict and the inevitability of revolution. The key to history, he believed, is class conflict—the bitter struggle between those who own the means of producing wealth and those who do not. This contest, Marx claimed, would end only with the overthrow of the ruling exploiters and the establishment of a free, humane, classless society. Marx placed special emphasis on the economic base of society. He argued that the character of virtually all other social arrangements is shaped by the way

Figure 1.10 *Emile Durkheim*   Figure 1.11 *Max Weber*   Figure 1.12 *George Herbert Mead*

goods are produced and by the relationships that exist between those who work to produce them and those who live off the production of others. Modern sociologists, including many who reject other aspects of Marx's theories, generally recognize the fundamental influence of the economy on other areas of society.

Emile Durkheim

The French sociologist Emile Durkheim (1858–1917) has strongly influenced the discipline. Durkheim dealt with the problem of social order; he argued that societies are held together by the shared beliefs and values of their members, especially as these are expressed in religious doctrine and ritual. Like Spencer, he wanted to establish how the various parts of society contribute to the maintenance of the whole. His method was to ask what function, or positive consequence for the social system, a given element has—an approach that has been highly influential in modern American sociology. Durkheim also made the first real breakthrough in sociological research with his painstaking statistical study of suicide in various population groups. He was able to show that suicide rates vary consistently from one group to another, proving that the act of suicide is influenced by social forces and is not simply the individual matter that it might appear to be.

Max Weber

The German sociologist Max Weber (1864–1920), a contemporary of Durkheim, has perhaps had a stronger influence on Western sociology than any other single individual. He was a man of prodi-

gious learning whose sociological investigations covered such diverse fields as politics, law, economics, music, cities, and the major world religions. Throughout his adult life Weber felt a great tension between his role as a scholar, dispassionately observing society, and his desire to influence events through political leadership. This tension may have contributed to a severe mental breakdown that incapacitated him for several years of his academic career. Weber remains an enigmatic and somewhat melancholy figure in sociological history. He viewed the direction of social change in industrial societies with distaste, feeling that the world was being "disenchanted" by bureaucracy, by the cold rationality of petty experts who knew no value other than efficiency. Humanity, he believed, was becoming trapped in an "iron cage."

Much of Weber's work can be seen as "a debate with the ghost of Karl Marx." Although he deeply admired much of Marx's writing, Weber took issue with him on several points. He regarded trends toward greater social equality as inevitable, but he did not particularly welcome them, because he foresaw that such moves would involve an increase in the power of the state over the individual. Weber did not believe that social change could always be directly traced to changes in the economy, as Marx had implied. He suggested that other factors, such as religious ideas, could also play an independent role. Perhaps most important, Weber believed that sociologists should aim at the goal of *value-freedom*—the absence of personal values or biases—in their professional work. His stance in this respect was quite unlike that of Marx, who had no qualms about using a ***value judgment***—an opinion based on personal values or biases—whenever he felt so inclined.

Figure 1.13 *Talcott Parsons*   Figure 1.14 *C. Wright Mills*   Figure 1.15 *Robert Merton*

Modern Developments

The major development of sociology in this century has taken place in the United States, where the discipline has sunk roots far deeper than in any other country. Lester Ward (1841–1913) repeated Comte's call for social progress guided by sociological knowledge, and under his influence the discipline rapidly became committed to social reform. William Graham Sumner (1840–1910) studied the minute aspects of daily life found in the ordinary customs of the people. Under the influence of these men, American sociologists lost most of their interest in the larger problems of social order and social change and began to concentrate instead on the study of smaller and more specific social problems.

Until about 1940 the University of Chicago's sociology department dominated the discipline in the United States. Sociologists such as George Herbert Mead developed the new discipline of social psychology, and others such as Robert E. Park and Ernest Burgess turned their attention to social problems and the lives of criminals, drug addicts, prostitutes, and juvenile delinquents. Many of the "Chicago School" sociologists were Protestant ministers or the sons of Protestant ministers, and under their leadership sociology became strongly identified with the concerns of social reform.

From the 1940s to the early 1960s, the center of attention shifted from Chicago to such universities as Harvard, Columbia, Michigan, and Wisconsin, and from reform to the much more neutral field of developing theories. Talcott Parsons (1902–1979) influenced a generation of American sociologists, such as Kingsley Davis and Robert Merton, with his abstract models of society as a fairly stable, harmonious system of parts with interrelated functions. Other sociologists concentrated on perfecting research methods and statistical techniques, and the earlier activist strain in the discipline was almost lost. C. Wright Mills, a vociferous critic of this trend, seemed to be crying in the wilderness. During the 1960s, however, the social turmoil caused by the Vietnam war and the civil rights movement encouraged a revival of the activist tradition in American sociology. During that decade, a survey found that over 70 percent of sociologists felt that part of their role was to be a critic of society and acknowledged that their work was not always value-free (Gouldner and Sprehe, 1965). For the first time, too, female and minority-group sociologists began to play a significant part in a discipline that had previously been almost wholly dominated by white males.

The sociology of the 1970s and 1980s has not been dominated by any one viewpoint or concern; its interests are more diverse than ever, and range from such old problems as inequality to such new ones as the impact of modern industrial society on the natural environment. Sociologists, too, are playing ever more diverse professional roles. Twenty years ago, nearly all sociologists were engaged in teaching and research. Today, many sociologists are employed in such fields as criminology, epidemiology, city planning, personnel management, social work, demography, or policy-making at every level of government. Others, although not employed specifically as sociologists, put their training to use in politics, journalism, business, and other professions.

Still, the question of whether the sociologist should be detached and value-free or activist and committed remains controversial. Some sociologists take the view that the science should be "ethically neutral," that it should attempt only to understand social processes and add to the sum of scientific knowledge. Others argue that sociological knowledge should be used to criticize and reform existing social arrangements.

Theoretical Perspectives

A crucial element in sociology, as in all science, is theory. A *theory* is a statement that organizes a set of concepts in a meaningful way by explaining the relationship among them. If the theory is valid, it will correctly predict that identical relationships will occur in the future if the conditions are identical. Although it is sometimes thought that "the facts speak for themselves," they do nothing of the kind. Facts are silent. They have no meaning until we give meaning to them, and that meaning is given by theory.

We are often prone to poke fun at "theorists" and to regard more highly the "practical" person. But theory and practice cannot be separated; virtually every practical decision you make and every practical opinion you hold has some theory behind it. A person may reject the views of prison reformers as being "theory" and prefer the "practical" approach that criminals should be severely punished in order to discourage crime. But in actuality this practical approach implies several theories—the theory that people always rationally choose whether or not to commit crimes, the theory that people try to avoid punishment, the theory that the most severe punishments make the best deterrents to crime. Even the most practical gadgets of everyday life, from can openers to automobiles, could not be constructed or used without some theory of how they operate. Theory is not an intellectual luxury practiced only by academics in their ivory towers.

Theory makes the facts of social life comprehensible. It places seemingly meaningless events in a general framework that enables us to determine cause and effect, to explain, and to predict. Sociological theories vary greatly in their scope and sophistication. Some attempt to explain only a small aspect of reality (such as why some people become heroin addicts). Others are more sweeping and confront large-scale societal problems (such as those of social order and social change). The leading figures in the early development of sociology, including Spencer, Marx, Durkheim, and Weber, offered grand theories of the latter type. Later sociologists, with the notable exception of Talcott Parsons, have generally felt that such attempts involve biting off more than one can chew and have concentrated instead on narrower theories aimed at explaining specific, limited social issues.

Despite this preference for more limited theories, most sociologists are guided in their work by a major *theoretical perspective*—a broad assumption about society and social behavior that provides a point of view for the study of specific problems. There are three of these general perspectives in modern sociology, and you will meet them repeatedly throughout this book. They are the functionalist, the conflict, and the interactionist perspectives. We shall look at each in turn.

The Functionalist Perspective

The *functionalist perspective* in sociology is a view of society that focuses on the way various parts of society have functions, or positive effects, that maintain the stability of the whole. The perspective draws its original inspiration from the work of Herbert Spencer and Emile Durkheim. As we have seen, Spencer compared societies to living organisms. Any organism has a *structure*—that is, a set of interrelated components, such as a head, limbs, a heart, and so on. Each of these parts has a *function*—that is, a positive consequence for the whole system, in this case a living organism. In the same way, Spencer argued, a society has a structure. Its interrelated parts are the family, religion, the military, and so on. Ideally, each of these components also has a function that contributes to the overall stability of the social system. Modern structural-functionalism (usually called functionalism) does not press the analogy between a society and an organism. But it does retain the same general idea of society as a system of interrelated parts. Functionalism in modern American sociology is associated particularly with the work of Talcott Parsons (1951) and has subsequently been much refined and modified by his student Robert Merton (1968).

The Social System

Functionalist theory implies that society tends to be an organized, stable, well-integrated system, in which most members agree on basic values. Under normal conditions, all the elements in the social system—such as the schools, the family, and the state—tend to "fit together," with each element helping to maintain overall stability. The family, for example, functions to regulate sexual behavior, to transmit social values to children, and to take care of young and aged people who could not otherwise survive.

In the functionalist view, a society has an underlying tendency to be in equilibrium, or balance. Social change is therefore likely to be disruptive unless it takes place relatively slowly, because changes in one part of the system usually provoke changes elsewhere in the system. If the economy, for example, requires an increasing number of highly trained workers, the government will pour more money into education, and the schools and colleges will produce more graduates. But if the economy expands (or contracts) so rapidly that the other elements in the social system cannot "catch up," disequilibrium will result. In times of very rapid economic growth, the educational system may be unable to provide qualified personnel quickly enough to fill the new jobs; during a recession, on the other hand, the system may continue to produce graduates even though there are not enough jobs for them.

Functions and Dysfunctions

How does one determine what the functions of a given element in the social system are? Essentially, sociologists ask what its *consequences* are—not what its *purposes* are believed to be. They do this because a component can have functions other than those that were intended. Robert Merton (1968) distinguishes between a ***manifest function***—a consequence that is obvious and intended—and a ***latent function***—a consequence that is unrecognized and unintended. The schools, for example, have the manifest function of teaching literacy and other skills that are essential in a modern industrial society. But they also have latent functions that are not intended or generally recognized. For example, they keep children in an industrial society off the streets and occupied until they are old enough to work. In the same way, the welfare system has the manifest function of preventing the poor from starving, but it also has the latent function of averting the civil disorder that might result if millions of people had no source of income.

Merton also points out that not all features of the social system are functional at all times: on occasion some element can have a ***dysfunction,*** a negative consequence that may disrupt the social system. Population growth in the less developed countries of the world, for example, is dysfunctional for societies whose economies cannot support ever increasing numbers of people. Some-

Figure 1.16 *The functionalist perspective focuses on the functions, or consequences, that a given element has in society. Economic activity, for example, functions to provide the goods and services on which society depends for its existence. It also gives people roles in life, enabling them to earn a living and to draw a sense of identity from the work they do. These functions contribute to the stability of the social system as a whole.*

times a component of the social system can be functional in one respect and dysfunctional in another. American industry, for example, is functional in that it provides the goods on which the society's way of life depends, but it is also dysfunctional in that it seriously pollutes the environment. The full implications of any element in the social system therefore have to be carefully explored.

The functionalist perspective, then, is obviously useful in explaining why some elements in a society exist and persist, but it also has some disadvantages. An important criticism of the functionalist view is that it tends in practice to be inherently conservative. Because their main emphasis is on social order and stability, functionalists risk the temptation of dismissing disruptive changes as dysfunctional, even if those changes are necessary, inevitable, and beneficial in the long run.

The Conflict Perspective

The **conflict perspective** in sociology is a view of society that focuses on social processes of tension, competition, and change. The perspective derives its inspiration from the work of Karl Marx, who saw the struggle between social classes as the "engine" of history and the main source of change. Although the conflict perspective has dominated sociology in Western Europe ever since, it was largely neglected in American sociology until the 1960s. The social and political turmoil of that decade was more readily analyzed through the conflict perspective than through the functionalist perspective. Conflict theory has been popular among American sociologists since that time.

Modern conflict theory, which is associated with such sociologists as C. Wright Mills (1956), Ralf Dahrendorf (1959), and Randall Collins (1975), does not simply focus, as Marx did, on class conflict; it sees conflict among many groups and interests as a fact of life in any society. These conflicts may involve, for example, the old versus the young, producers versus consumers, urbanites versus suburbanites, or one racial or ethnic group versus another.

Conflict and Change

Conflict theorists assume that societies are in a constant state of change, in which conflict is a permanent feature. "Conflict" does not necessarily mean outright violence; it includes tension, hostility, competition, and disagreement over goals and

Figure 1.17 *The conflict perspective focuses on tensions, disagreements, and competition in society. Conflict is assumed to be a permanent and inevitable aspect of social life and an important source of change. Conflict over nuclear energy, for example, may lead to significant changes in American energy policies in the future.*

values. This conflict is not an occasional event that disrupts the generally smooth workings of society: it is a continuing and inevitable part of social life. The things that people desire—such as power, wealth, and prestige—are always scarce, and the demand for them exceeds the supply. Those who gain control of these resources are able to protect their own interests at other people's expense. Conflict theorists regard the functionalists' vision of a general consensus on values as pure fiction: what actually happens, they argue, is that the powerful coerce the rest of the population into compliance and conformity. In other words, social order is maintained not by popular agreement but rather by force or the implied threat of force.

Conflict theorists do not see social conflict as necessarily destructive, although they admit that it may sometimes have that effect. They argue that conflict can often have positive results. It binds groups together as they pursue their own interests, and the conflict among competing groups focuses attention on social problems and leads to beneficial changes that might otherwise not have occurred. In this way, social movements—such as those for women's rights or against nuclear power—become an important source of change. The changes caused by social conflict prevent society from stagnating.

Who Benefits?

The conflict perspective, then, leads the sociologist to inquire into whose interests are involved in, and who benefits or suffers from, existing arrangements. In analyzing social inequality, for example, conflict theorists argue that it exists not because it is functional for society as a whole but because some people have been able to achieve political and economic power and have managed to pass on these advantages to their descendants. In the same way, conflict theorists would not see environmental pollution as a "dysfunction" of industrialism. Instead, they would point to the fact that powerful corporate interests make their profits from manufacturing processes that they fully realize pollute the environment. To take another case, tobacco, an addictive drug that has been conclusively linked to lung cancer, is freely marketed in the United States, but the use of marijuana, which on present evidence does not seem to be as physically harmful, is generally illegal. Why? A conflict analysis would point out that wealthy and influential interests benefit by manufacturing, advertising, and selling tobacco. Marijuana, on the other hand, is used chiefly by the young and the powerless. However, if marijuana spreads to more influential groups in society, or if large corporations become interested in marketing the drug themselves, pressures to decriminalize its use would be likely to increase. Social change, in this area as in others, is influenced by the shifting relationships and interests of groups competing for their own advantage.

A modern society contains a wide spectrum of opinions, occupations, lifestyles, and social groups.

On any social issue there are some people who stand to gain and some who stand to lose. Social processes cannot be fully understood without referring to this conflict of interest, a conflict whose outcome always favors the stronger party. To understand many features of American society, then, we must pay particular attention to the values and interests of those who exercise power—primarily people who are white, middle-aged, Protestant, wealthy, male, and of Anglo-Saxon background.

The conflict perspective has the advantage of highlighting aspects of society that the functionalist perspective, with its emphasis on consensus and stability, tends to ignore. But this fact also suggests an important criticism of the conflict perspective. By focusing so narrowly on issues of competition and change, it fails to come to grips with the more orderly, stable, and less controversial dimensions of social reality.

The Interactionist Perspective

The *interactionist perspective* in sociology is a view of society that focuses on the way in which people act toward, respond to, and influence one another. The perspective draws much of its original inspiration from Max Weber, who emphasized the importance of understanding the social world from the viewpoint of the individuals who act within it. Later developments in interactionist theory have been strongly influenced by social psychology and by the work of early leaders in the Chicago School, particularly George Herbert Mead. The important difference between this perspective and the two we have considered is that it does not focus on such large structures as the state, the economy, or social classes. Instead, it is concerned primarily with the everyday social interaction that takes place as people go about their lives.

Interaction: The Basis of Social Life

The main reason interactionist theorists are wary of the emphasis other sociologists place on the major components of society is that concepts such as "the economy" or "the state" are, after all, abstractions; they cannot exist or act by themselves. It is people that exist and act, and it is only through their social behavior that society can come into being at all. Society is ultimately created, maintained, and changed by the social interaction of its members.

Figure 1.18 *The interactionist perspective focuses on social behavior in everyday life. It tries to understand how people create and interpret the situations they experience, and it emphasizes how countless instances of social interaction produce the larger structures of society—government, the economy, and other institutions.*

The interactionist perspective is a broad one, containing a number of loosely linked approaches. Erving Goffman (1959), for example, took a "dramaturgical" approach to social interaction. In other words, he saw social life as a form of theater, in which people play different roles and "stage-manage" their lives and the impressions they create on others. George Homans (1974) takes an "exchange" approach. He focuses on the way people influence one another's behavior by exchanging various forms of rewards and punishments for approved or disapproved behavior. Harold Garfinkel (1967) adopts what he calls an "ethnomethodological" approach. This formidable term simply implies an attempt to scrape below the surface of social behavior to find out how people create and share their understandings of social life, and how they base their actions on those understandings. The most widely used approach is that of "symbolic interaction" (Mead, 1934; Blumer, 1969), and this is the one we shall emphasize here and elsewhere in this book.

Symbolic Interaction

A *symbol* is anything that can meaningfully represent something else. Signs, gestures, shared rules, and, most important, written and spoken language are examples of symbols. *Symbolic interaction* is the interaction that takes place between people through symbols. Much of this interaction takes place on a face-to-face basis, but it can also occur in other forms: symbolic interaction is taking place between you and the author as you read this sentence, and it occurs whenever you obey (or disobey) a traffic signal or a no-trespassing notice. The essential point is that people do not respond to the world directly: they place a social meaning on it and respond to that meaning. The words of this book, the red light of a traffic signal, a wolf whistle in the street, have no meaning in themselves. Rather, people learn to attach symbolic meaning to these things, and they order their lives on the basis of these meanings. We live in a symbolic as well as in a physical world, and our social life involves a constant process of interpreting the meanings of our own acts and those of others.

The interactionist perspective, then, leads the sociologist to inquire into people's interpretations of, and responses to, their interaction with others. Sociologists using this perspective usually focus on the specific, detailed aspects of personal everyday life. By what process, for example, does someone become a prostitute? Why is it that strangers in elevators so scrupulously avoid eye contact with each other, staring anywhere—at their shoes, at the ceiling, at the nearest wall—rather than directly into another passenger's face? How does someone learn to experience marijuana smoking as pleasurable? What unspoken tactics are used by a male doctor and a female patient to minimize embarrassment during a vaginal examination? What processes are involved in group decision making? What happens if you stand "too" close to someone during a conversation, and why?

The interactionist perspective provides a fascinating insight into the mechanics of everyday life, and it has the advantage of revealing fundamental social processes that other perspectives easily overlook. But the perspective is open to the important criticism that it neglects larger social institutions and societal processes of stability and change—institutions and processes which, after all, have powerful effects on social interaction and on our personal experience.

An Evaluation

Since each of these perspectives starts from different assumptions, and each leads the investigator to ask different questions, each viewpoint is likely to produce different types of conclusions. In many respects the theories seem quite contradictory. But this does not mean that one of them is "better" than the others, or even that they are always incompatible. The reason is that each perspective focuses on a different aspect of reality: functionalism, primarily on social order and stability; conflict theory, primarily on social tension and change; and interactionism, primarily on the ordinary experiences of everyday life. Each perspective has a part to play in the analysis of society. In fact, there is nothing unusual in a scientist's using apparently incompatible theories to study the same subject. Physicists find it useful to regard

Figure 1.19 *People's views of the world are largely shaped by their own experience of it. Their age, race, sex, nationality, social class, and personal histories all affect their values, attitudes, and inter-*

pretations of the reality that surrounds them. These two groups of Americans, each from different walks of life, probably interpret many social issues in different ways.

light sometimes as a continuous wave and sometimes as streams of particles, depending on the situation, and they gain a better understanding of the nature of light as a result.

Thus all three perspectives could be applied, for example, to the study of education. A functionalist approach would emphasize the functions that the schools play in maintaining the social system as a whole. It would point out how education provides the young with skills they need in later life, how it sorts and selects people for different kinds of jobs, how it transmits cultural values from one generation to the next, and even how it keeps millions of adolescents off the streets. A conflict approach would emphasize that while education is believed to be an important avenue to social and financial success in life, this avenue is obstructed for certain groups. It would point out, for example, how social-class background affects a pupil's academic achievement, how school districts tend to be segregated along class and racial lines, and how educational credentials are used by different individuals and groups jockeying for competitive advantage. An interactionist approach would emphasize the daily activities within the school. It would point to the forms of interaction between teachers and pupils, the influence of the student peer group over its individual members, or the ways in which the school rules are broken or followed. None of these approaches gives answers that are any more "true" than the others, and taken together they provide a broader and deeper understanding of the entire institution of education.

Some sociologists, of course, do argue that one or another of the perspectives gives an understanding generally superior to the others, and they systematically try to apply their chosen perspective to all or most problems. No such approach is adopted here—not just because the author does not accept that any one perspective is always the most useful, but because it would be a disservice to the introductory student to offer only one viewpoint.

In this book, then, you will regularly encounter all three perspectives. The interactionist perspective will be used particularly in the discussion of "micro" (small-scale) processes; the functionalist and conflict perspectives, in the discussion of "macro" (large-scale) processes. Sometimes the perspectives will contradict each other. When this happens, we shall evaluate their respective merits. At other times they will complement each other, giving a fuller and richer understanding of the subject.

The Problem of Objectivity

We have seen that people in different walks of life may interpret the same phenomenon—whether it is a house, a riot, a president's policies, a religious doctrine, or a military budget—in very different ways. In other words, people tend to see the world from a viewpoint of *subjectivity*—an interpretation based on personal values and experiences. We have also seen that sociologists themselves can adopt varying perspectives on the same problem and can come to different and even contradictory conclusions as a result. This fact raises a very important issue. Is it possible to understand society from a viewpoint of *objectivity*—an interpretation that eliminates the influence of personal values and experiences?

If the world consisted simply of some self-evident reality that everyone perceived in exactly the same way, there might be no disagreement among observers. But the truth of the matter is that what we see in the world is not determined by what exists "out there." It is shaped by what our past experience has prepared us to see and by what we consciously or unconsciously want to see. Knowledge and belief about the world do not exist in a vacuum; they are social products whose content depends on the context in which they are produced. A fundamentalist preacher will tend to view pornography in one way; the owner of a striptease establishment, in another way. Each is inclined to perceive facts selectively and to interpret them accordingly.

The same is inevitably true of social scientists, whose outlook on the world is also influenced by their background, training, and prior experiences. Most American social scientists are well educated, urban, white, middle-class, and male, and they naturally tend to interpret reality differently from people who do not share these characteristics. Their background and interests, for example, make them significantly more liberal than scholars in other disciplines (Lipset and Ladd, 1972). Inevitably, then, sociologists, like anyone else, will be guilty of some measure of *bias*—the tendency, often unconscious, to interpret facts according to one's own values. This problem occurs in all sciences, but it becomes particularly acute in the social sciences, whose subject matter often involves issues of deep human and moral concern. How can the problem be resolved?

The first step is to recognize that subjectivity and objectivity are not two neat and separate categories; they are really matters of degree. By exer-

FIRST-YEAR STUDENTS' ATTITUDES ON POLITICAL AND SOCIAL ISSUES
Percentage of those who agree somewhat or strongly with the statements below

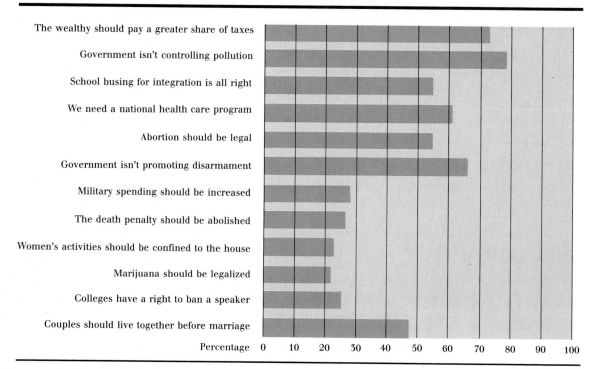

SOURCE: Alexander Astin, *The American Freshman: National Norms for Fall*
(American Council of Education and University of California at Los Angeles, 1986).

Figure 1.20 *This graph shows some attitudes of a recent national sample of first-year college students. Essentially, the findings reveal biases on one side or another of public issues. Do any of the findings surprise you? How do your own attitudes compare?*

If your attitudes differ in some respects, what social factors—such as religion, age, sex, class, place of residence, race, or peer-group influences—might explain these differences? How "biased" or "unbiased" do you think you are?

cising scrupulous caution the sociologist can attempt to be as objective as possible. This caution involves a deliberate effort to be conscious of one's own biases so that they can be kept out of the process of research and interpretation. The ethical code of the discipline requires that sociologists be intellectually honest—that they attempt to be aware of their own values and not allow these values to distort their work; that they relentlessly hunt down the relevant facts and not ignore those that are inconvenient for their pet theories; that they not manipulate data to prove a point; and that they not use research to suppress or misuse knowledge. Moreover, the sociological community does not have to rely entirely on the integrity of the individual to ensure that objectivity is strived for. When research is published, other sociologists can assess the findings and attempt to verify them by repeating the research to see if it yields the same results. This procedure provides an extremely ef-

fective check against bias and other distortions.

Total objectivity is probably impossible to achieve in any science, since some bias is always unconscious. But a self-conscious effort to be as objective as possible will produce vastly less biased results than not making this attempt. And if objectivity is defined as thought sufficiently disciplined to minimize the distortions caused by personal bias, then it is certainly possible. The pursuit of objectivity does not necessarily mean that sociologists should not express personal opinions, or value judgments. It means that these judgments should be clearly labeled as such and that they should not intrude into the actual process of research and interpretation. It would be perfectly legitimate, therefore, for a sociologist to give as objective an account as possible of a social problem, and then to add a subjective judgment—provided that the judgment was presented as a matter of personal opinion.

Summary

1. Sociology is the scientific study of human society; it differs from other modes of understanding the social world in that it relies on systematic observation of verifiable facts.

2. Sociology provides a unique perspective on society, enabling us to see the intimate relationships between social forces and individual experience.

3. Science refers to the logical, systematic methods by which reliable knowledge of the universe is obtained and also to the actual knowledge produced by these methods. Science assumes order in the universe, and it attempts to establish generalizations that can be used for the purposes of explanation and prediction.

4. The subject matter of sociology poses many problems the natural sciences do not face, but sociology nonetheless has the same commitment to the scientific method. Sociological explanations are therefore more reliable than those based only on common sense.

5. The social sciences are a related group of disciplines that study various aspects of human behavior. The main social sciences are sociology, economics, psychology, political science, and anthropology.

6. Sociology emerged in the middle of the nineteenth century, in the context of the changes caused by the Industrial Revolution.

7. Early sociologists, such as Comte, Spencer, Marx, Weber, and Durkheim, concentrated on problems of social order and social change. The subsequent development of sociology, which has taken place largely in the United States, has focused primarily on more restricted theories and studies and on the refinement of research techniques. There has been controversy over whether sociologists should be value-free or socially committed.

8. There are three major theoretical perspectives in modern sociology. The functionalist perspective focuses primarily on processes of order and stability; the conflict perspective, on processes of competition and change; the interactionist perspective, on processes of everyday social behavior. These three perspectives are not necessarily incompatible.

9. Complete objectivity is particularly difficult to achieve in the social sciences. By rigorously excluding personal biases and by submitting research findings to the criticism of the sociological community, however, sociologists can guard against subjective distortions and can reach a high degree of objectivity.

Important Terms

sociology (3)

social interaction (5)

science (6)

natural sciences (6)

social sciences (6)

generalization (6)

social psychology (11)

cultural anthropology (11)

ethnography (11)

value-freedom (15)

value judgment (15)

theory (17)

theoretical perspective (17)   conflict perspective (19)

functionalist perspective (17)   interactionist perspective (20)

structure (17)   symbol (21)

function (17)   symbolic interaction (21)

manifest function (18)   subjectivity (23)

latent function (18)   objectivity (23)

dysfunction (18)   bias (23)

Suggested Readings

ABRAHAMSON, MARK. *Functionalism*. Englewood Cliffs, N.J.: Prentice-Hall, 1978.

A succinct introduction to functionalist theory, with a consideration of some criticisms of the perspective.

AMERICAN SOCIOLOGICAL ASSOCIATION. *Careers in Sociology*. Washington, D.C.: American Sociological Association, 1984.

A short guide to career opportunities for sociology majors.

BART, PAULINE, and LINDA FRANKEL. *The Student Sociologist's Handbook*. 4th ed. New York: Random House, 1986.

A useful and comprehensive guide to sociological literature and sources of information.

BERGER, PETER L. *Invitation to Sociology: A Humanistic Perspective*. Garden City, N.Y.: Doubleday, Anchor Books, 1963.

A brief and elegantly written introduction to the field. Berger provides an absorbing account of the distinctive "sociological perspective."

COLLINS, RANDALL, and MICHAEL MAKOWSKY. *The Discovery of Society*. 3rd ed. New York: Random House, 1983.

A short and readable account of the history of sociology.

MILLS, C. WRIGHT. *The Sociological Imagination*. New York: Oxford University Press, 1959.

Written from a conflict perspective, this book has become a classic introduction to sociology. Mills elaborates on the intimate connection between private experience and social context.

ROBBOY, HOWARD, and CANDACE CLARK (eds.). *Social Interaction: Introductory Readings in Sociology*. 2nd ed. New York: St. Martin's Press, 1983.

A collection of interesting articles on a wide range of social topics. The book provides an excellent sampling of research conducted from an interactionist perspective.

SHOSTAK, ARTHUR B. (ed.). *Our Sociological Eye: Personal Essays on Society and Culture*. Port Washington, N.Y.: Alfred Publishing, 1977.

An anthology of first-person essays, in which sociologists apply the insights of their discipline to a variety of personal experiences.

Invitation to Sociology

PETER L. BERGER

In this reading, Berger describes the inherent fascination of sociology and invites the newcomer to this "very special kind of passion." It should be noted that Berger was writing at a time when an unconscious sexism was reflected in the general usage of the language—hence, the sociologist was assumed to be "he," and "his" subject matter, "men." Berger's "invitation" nevertheless deservedly has remained a classic portrait of the discipline's appeal.

The sociologist . . . is a person intensively, endlessly, shamelessly interested in the doings of men. His natural habitat is all the human gathering places of the world, wherever men come together. The sociologist may be interested in many other things. But his consuming interest remains in the world of men, their institutions, their history, their passions. And since he is interested in men, nothing that men do can be altogether tedious for him. He will naturally be interested in the events that engage men's ultimate beliefs, their moments of tragedy and grandeur and ecstasy. But he will also be fascinated by the commonplace, the everyday. He will know reverence, but this reverence will not prevent him from wanting to see and to understand. He may sometimes feel revulsion or contempt. But this also will not deter him from wanting to have his questions answered. The sociologist, in his quest for understanding, moves through the world of men without respect for the usual lines of demarcation. Nobility and degradation, power and obscurity, intelligence and folly—these are equally *interesting* to him, however unequal they may be in his personal values or tastes. Thus his questions may lead him to all possible levels of society,

the best and the least known places, the most respected and the most despised. And, if he is a good sociologist, he will find himself in all these places because his own questions have so taken possession of him that he has little choice but to seek for answers.

It would be possible to say the same things in a lower key. We could say that the sociologist, but for the grace of his academic title, is the man who must listen to gossip despite himself, who is tempted to look through keyholes, to read other people's mail, to open closed cabinets. Before some otherwise unoccupied psychologist sets out now to construct an aptitude test for sociologists on the basis of sublimated voyeurism, let us quickly say that we are speaking merely by way of analogy. . . . What interests us is the curiosity that grips any sociologist in front of a closed door behind which there are human voices. If he is a good sociologist, he will want to open that door, to understand these voices. Behind each closed door he will anticipate some new facet of human life not yet perceived and understood.

The sociologist will occupy himself with matters that others regard as too sacred or as too distasteful for dispassionate investigation. He will find rewarding the company of priests or of prostitutes, depending not on his personal preferences but on the questions he happens to be asking at the moment. He will also concern himself with matters that others may find much too boring. He will be interested in the human interaction that goes with warfare or with great intellectual discoveries, but also in the relations between people employed in a restaurant or between a group of little girls playing with their dolls. His main focus of attention is not the ultimate significance of what men do, but the action in itself, as another example of the infinite richness of human conduct. . . .

The sociologist moves in the common world of men, close to what most of them would call real. The categories he employs in his analyses are only refinements of the categories by which other men live—power, class, status, race, ethnicity. As a result, there is a deceptive simplicity and obviousness about some sociological investigations. One reads them, nods at the familiar scene, remarks that one has heard all this before and don't people have better things to do than to waste their time on truisms—until one is suddenly brought up against an insight that radically questions everything one had previously assumed about this familiar scene. This is the point at which one begins to sense the excitement of sociology. . . . It can be said that the first wisdom of sociology is this—things are not what they seem. This too is a deceptively simple statement. It ceases to be simple after a while. Social reality turns out to have many layers of meaning. The discovery of each new layer changes the perception of the whole. . . . To be sure, sociology is an individual pastime in the sense that it interests some men and bores others. Some like to observe human beings, others to experiment with mice. The world is big enough to hold all kinds and there is no logical priority for one interest as against another. But the word "pastime" is weak in describing what we mean. Sociology is more like a passion. The sociological perspective is more like a demon that possesses one, that drives one compellingly, again and again, to the questions that are its own. An introduction to sociology is, therefore, an invitation to a very special kind of passion.

SOURCE: Peter L. Berger, *Invitation to Sociology* (Garden City, N.Y.: Doubleday & Company, Inc., Anchor Books, 1963).

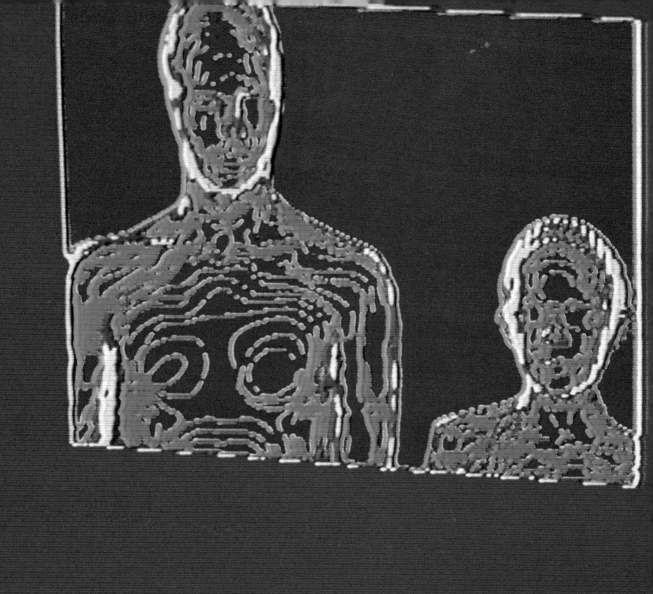

CHAPTER 2

Doing Sociology: The Methods of Research

Sociological research offers the challenge of going as a "stranger" into the familiar world, often to find one's assumptions shattered by the facts that one discovers. Research in sociology is really a form of detective work—it poses the same early puzzles and suspicions, the same moments of routine sifting through the evidence and inspired guessing, the same disappointments over false leads and facts that do not fit, and, perhaps, the same triumph when the pieces finally fall into place and an answer emerges. Research in sociology is where the real action takes place. It is in the field, far more than in the lecture room, that the sociologist comes to grips with the subject.

There are two sides to the sociological enterprise: theory and research. Both are essential, and each thrives on the other. Facts without theory are utterly meaningless, for they lack a framework in which they can be understood. Theories without facts are unproved speculations of little practical use, because there is no way to tell whether they are correct. Theory and research are thus parts of a constant cycle. A theory inspires research that can be used to verify or disprove it, and the findings of research are used to confirm, reject, or modify the theory, or even to provide the basis of new theories. The process recurs endlessly, and the accumulation of sociological knowledge is the result.

Guesswork, intuition, and common sense all have an important part to play in sociological research, but on their own they cannot produce reliable evidence: that requires a reliable research methodology. A *methodology* is a system of rules, principles, and procedures that guides scientific investigation. The sociologist is interested in discovering what happens in the social world and why it happens. Research methodology provides guidelines for collecting evidence about what takes place, for explaining why it takes place, and for doing so in such a way that the findings can be checked by other researchers. It is vital that the sociologist use appropriate methodology, for an invalid method can produce only flawed results.

The methods of sociology can be applied only to questions that can be answered by reference to observable, verifiable facts. The sociologist cannot tell us if God exists, because there is no scientific way to test theories on the subject. But the sociologist can tell us what percentage of a population claims to believe in God, or what reasons they have for believing in God, because these facts can be established by using appropriate methods.

The Logic of Cause and Effect

To explain any aspect of society or social behavior, the sociologist must understand relationships of cause and effect. One basic assumption of science is that all events have causes—whether the event is a ball rolling down a hill, a nuclear bomb exploding, an economy improving, a political party losing support, or a student passing an examination. A second basic assumption is that under the identical circumstances, the same cause will repeatedly produce the same effect. If we did not make these assumptions, the world would be utterly unpredictable and therefore unintelligible to us. The problem facing the sociologist is to sort out cause from effect in the complexities of social life, and to determine which of several possible causes, or which combination of causes, is producing a particular effect.

Variables

Like all scientists, the sociologist analyzes cause and effect in terms of the influence of variables on one another. A *variable* is any characteristic that can change or differ—for example, from time to time, from place to place, or from one individual or group to another. Differences in age, sex, race, and social class are variables. So are the rates of homicide, divorce, and narcotics addiction. So are differences in intelligence, nationality, income, and sense of humor. Causation occurs when one variable, such as the quantity of alcohol a driver consumes, influences another variable, such as the likelihood of the driver being involved in a traffic accident. A theory simply attempts to generalize

about the influence of one variable on another: "Drunken driving contributes to traffic accidents." "Malnutrition causes children to perform poorly in schoolwork." Such statements serve to link variables in a cause-and-effect relationship.

An *independent variable* is one that influences another variable—in other words, it acts as a cause. A *dependent variable* is one that is influenced by another variable—in other words, it is affected. Thus, degree of drunkenness is one independent variable (though not necessarily the only one) that can produce the dependent variable of a traffic accident. Similarly, childhood nutrition is an independent variable (though, again, not necessarily the only one) that can affect the dependent variable of school performance.

Recurrent relationships among particular variables allow us to make generalizations about the links between them. Such a statement applies to the general category of variables that is being considered, not to any specific case within it. Thus, medical scientists can tell us the characteristics of the people most likely to suffer a heart attack at some time in their lives, but they cannot tell us precisely which individuals will be affected. In the same way, a sociologist can tell us about the general characteristics of the marriages most likely to end in divorce, but cannot predict the fate of specific marriages. All generalizations in science are statements of *probability*—not certainty—for the entire category of variables under consideration.

Correlations

Determining cause and effect, then, involves tracing the effect of variables upon one another. But how does the sociologist do this?

The basic method is to establish whether there is a *correlation*—that is, a relationship between variables that occurs regularly. By analyzing the statistics, the sociologist can easily establish whether there is a correlation between drunk driving and traffic accidents and between malnutrition and poor school performance. In both cases, the evidence shows that the correlation is very high. In fact, not only are drunk driving and traffic accidents closely associated, but the more alcohol drivers consume, the more likely they are to have traffic accidents. Similarly, malnutrition is associated with poor school performance, and the more malnourished children are, the worse their school performance is likely to be. This seems to prove the case. But does it?

Figure 2.1 *There are many similarities between courtroom and scientific procedures. In fact, both emerged in the seventeenth century, when people realized that more rigorous methods of establishing facts were necessary. Both the courts and science are concerned with objectivity: scientists must try to exclude biases from their work; judges and jurors must disqualify themselves from cases in which they are biased. Both the courts and science have strict rules about what evidence is admissible (in each case, for example, hearsay is not acceptable). Both keep careful records—in the case of the courts, for possible use in the event of an appeal; in the case of science, for possible use by other scientists who wish to check the results. Both assume that valid findings can be replicated: the courts assume that the same evidence would normally yield the same verdict with different juries; science assumes that an identical study will yield identical results with different researchers.*

Logically, no. The fact that two variables are highly correlated does not prove that one caused the other, or even that they are related in any way at all. Consider another example: in North America there is a high correlation between the sale of ice cream and the incidence of rape. The more ice cream that is sold, the more likely it is that rapes will occur. If a high correlation between two variables were sufficient to prove a causal connection, we would have to conclude that eating ice cream causes rape or, alternatively, that rape causes people to eat huge amounts of ice cream. Clearly, neither of these theories is acceptable: they fail to link the facts in a meaningful way. But what explains the correlation? A moment's thought suggests the answer, in the form of a third variable that influences the other two: the heat of summer. People eat more ice cream when it is hot than when it is cold. Rapes are far more likely to occur in the summer than in the winter, partly because people are more likely to venture out of their homes at night and partly because the nature of rape is such that the act is not easily performed outdoors in freezing weather. The rape–ice cream association exists, but it is a ***spurious correlation***—one that is merely coincidental and does not imply any causal relationship whatever. Spurious correlations present a constant trap for the careless researcher.

Controls

How, then, can we determine whether a correlation is a causal one? To find out, sociologists must apply **controls**—ways of excluding the possibility that some other factors might be influencing the relationship between two variables. It might be, for example, that most people who drive when they are drunk do their drunken driving after dark and that poor visibility, not alcohol consumption, is the prime cause of the accidents. The sociologist has to control for this variable by comparing the accident rates of both drunken and sober drivers during daylight and at night. If the drunken drivers are still proportionately more likely to become involved in traffic accidents under both driving conditions, the possibility that visibility is the independent variable is eliminated. Similarly, it might be that children who are malnourished typically do not have a father in the home and therefore lack paternal encouragement in their academic work. Again, the sociologist has to control for this possibility by comparing the school performance of both well-nourished and malnourished children with and without a father in the home.

Only when the sociologist has controlled for the other possibilities—often a difficult task, because some possibilities are not immediately obvious and may be overlooked—can it be said with confidence that a causal connection exists between the variables. In the cases of our drunken drivers and malnourished children, a high correlation still exists when other possible independent variables have been eliminated. Have we now proved conclusively that drunken driving causes traffic accidents and that malnutrition causes poor school performance?

Not necessarily. The fact that variable A has a causal connection with variable B does not necessarily mean that A causes B. Until we probe deeper, we can conclude with equal justification that B causes A. In other words, the fact that a causal relationship exists between two variables does not tell us which is the independent and which is the dependent variable. That remains to be established, by one or both of two methods.

The first method is to make a logical, realistic assessment about which of the two possibilities is more likely. Either drunken driving causes traffic accidents, or traffic accidents cause some drivers to immediately become drunk. Either malnutrition causes poor school performance, or poor school performance causes malnutrition in children. In each case the latter relationship is logically impossible—ridiculous, in fact   and we can dismiss it, leaving the former as the only remaining possibility. In most instances, simple logic will tell us which variable influences which.

Figure 2.2 *There is some evidence that overweight people watch more TV than people of normal weight. But does this mean that extensive TV viewing is a cause of obesity? It may be true that people who watch a lot of TV get little exercise, and so become overweight. But it may also be true that overweight people avoid physical activity, and so spend more time watching TV. Or the apparent link between the two characteristics may be a mere coincidence. The point is that any correlation between variables must be very carefully analyzed before conclusions can be drawn about cause and effect.*

Basic Statistical Terms

Although some sociological research uses sophisticated mathematics, introductory students will be able to find their way through most sociological writing by relying on a few basic statistical concepts. The concepts you will encounter most frequently are those of averages and correlations.

Averages. The word "average" is often used loosely in ordinary conversation. There are actually three ways of calculating averages, or *central tendencies,* and each method can produce a different figure from the same data.

Suppose a researcher has studied nine individuals and finds that their annual incomes are

$3000	$3800	$9000
$3000	$6500	$9000
$3500	$9000	$150,000

For some purposes it may be sufficient to present all this information in the form given above, but it is often more useful to provide a single figure that reveals the central tendency of all the numbers involved.

The *mode* is the number that appears most often in the data. In our example the mode is $9000. The mode is useful for the researcher to show which figure recurs most frequently. It has the disadvantage, however, of not giving any idea of the range of the data as a whole.

The *mean* is the figure obtained by dividing the total of all the figures by the number of individual cases involved. In this case the total is $196,800; divided by nine, it gives a mean figure of $21,866.66. The mean has the advantage of taking account of all the data, but it can give misleading results. In our example, the central tendency is distorted by the presence of one extreme figure, $150,000, which hides the fact that all the other individuals earn $9000 a year or less. (The mean is the measure of central tendency that we usually call the "average" in ordinary speech.)

The *median* is the number that falls midway in a range of numbers; in our example, it would be $6500. If the number of cases were an even rather than an odd number—say, ten instead of nine—the median would be the mean ("average") of the two numbers in the middle, namely the fifth and sixth items. The median is sometimes useful because it does not allow extreme cases, such as the income of $150,000, to distort the central tendency. Sociologists often present an average in more than one form, particularly when a single measure might give a misleading impression.

Correlations. A correlation is a regular relationship between two variables. The strength of that relationship is usually expressed as a number called a *correlation coefficient.* When two variables have absolutely no consistent relationship to one another (as in the case of volcanic eruptions in Japan and the birth rate in Dallas), the correlation coefficient is zero. When one variable is always associated with the other (as in the case of the moon's gravitational pull and the oceans' tides), there is a perfect *positive* correlation, expressed as a correlation coefficient of 1.0. Weak positive correlations of around 0.2 or 0.3 are not very significant (the variables in these cases being related only two or three times out of ten), but stronger correlations of around 0.6 and above indicate an increasingly significant relationship between the variables. When the presence of one variable is always associated with the absence of the other (as in the case of snowstorms and sunbathers), there is a perfect *negative* correlation, and the correlation coefficient is −1.0.

A high correlation coefficient may suggest a causal relationship between the variables involved, but it is always possible that the correlation is coincidental or is produced by a third variable that influences the other two. Correlations therefore have to be interpreted with great care.

Sometimes, however, this kind of analysis does not yield such an obvious answer. We may find, for example, that there is a high correlation between cocaine abuse and dropping out of college. We may be able to eliminate the possibility that some third variable, such as low grades, has produced the other two and that the relationship between cocaine abuse and dropping out of college is causal, not spurious. But which causes which? One person's hunch might be that dropping out makes people more likely to abuse cocaine; another person's hunch might be that cocaine abuse makes people more likely to drop out. Both conclusions seem reasonable. To determine which is the independent (causal) variable and which is the dependent (resulting) variable, a second logical approach is needed—one that considers the variable of *time.* An event that causes another event must always precede it. If students drop out first and use cocaine afterward, then dropping out is the independent variable; if they use the drug first and then drop out, cocaine abuse is the independent variable. We can also use this method to validate further our conclusions about drunken drivers and malnourished children, by asking which came first—the drunkenness or the accidents, the malnutrition or poor school performance?

In summary, then, there are three criteria for a causal relationship: a correlation, or a regular association, between variables; the elimination, through controls, of other possible causes; and an analysis of the logic of the relationship in question, particularly of the time order involved. These criteria do not apply just to science; they apply to our everyday experience, where misinterpretation of cause-and-effect relationships is a major source of sloppy thinking. You will continually hear, in public statements and in private conversations, unproved assertions based on mere statistical association—for example, that an increase in sex education has caused an increase in teenage pregnancy; that an increase in executions has slowed an increase in homicides; that an increase in divorce has led to an increase in juvenile delinquency; and so on. Any of these statements might be true, reflecting a cause-and-effect relationship, but they might just as easily be false, reflecting a spurious correlation. A hallmark of an educated mind is the realization that such statements are merely hunches, requiring more evidence and analysis before final conclusions can be drawn.

Difficulties in Sociological Research

As we noted in Chapter 1, the sociologist's subject matter presents research problems of a kind that natural scientists rarely have to deal with. The sociologist's subjects are not inanimate objects or unreflecting animals. They are people who are self-aware, who have complex individual personalities, and who are capable of choosing their own courses of action for both rational and irrational reasons. The fact that the sociologist is studying human beings poses five major challenges to research methodology.

1. *The mere act of investigating social behavior may alter the very behavior that is being investigated.* When people know that they are being studied, they may not behave as they normally would. Suppose, for example, that a sociologist who was studying family interaction patterns visited your home. Would your family behave in exactly the same way as usual? The presence, personality, and actions of the observer can affect the behavior under investigation. Sometimes the problem is compounded when the subjects know or guess (correctly or incorrectly) what the sociologist is trying to find out: they may try to "help" by consciously or unconsciously behaving in ways they feel will conform to the researcher's expectations.

2. *People—unlike bacteria or hydrogen atoms—have emotions, motives, and other highly individual personality characteristics.* People may give false information deliberately, to put themselves in a better light, or unintentionally, because they misinterpret a question or do not understand the reasons for their own behavior or attitudes. They may also behave in unpredictable ways for a variety of peculiar reasons of their own, something inanimate objects do not do. As a result, sociological explanations and predictions are often less precise than those of the natural sciences.

3. *The origins of social behavior are almost always extremely complex, involving many social, psychological, historical, and other factors.* It is usually much more difficult for the sociologist than for the natural scientist to sort out cause and effect because so many more variables tend to be involved. It is relatively easy to establish why water boils or what effect pressure has on the volume of a gas. It is much more difficult to establish why fashions change, why civilizations decay, why new religions emerge, or why people fall in love with the people that they do.

4. *It is not permissible, for ethical reasons, to perform certain kinds of experiments on human beings.* The natural scientist has no moral qualms about experimenting with rays of light and often few qualms about experimenting with animals. But the dignity and privacy of human beings must be respected. We cannot deliberately raise boys as girls to see what effect the experience would have on their later sex-role adjustment, however interesting and valuable the findings might be. Nor can we arrange to have parents abuse their children so that we can see how such mistreatment affects personality, no matter how useful the results might be to social workers or psychiatrists. Ethical considerations place severe limitations on the methods the sociologist can use.

Figure 2.3 *"Streaking"—running stark naked through a public place—was an international fad of the early 1970s. During the brief period that the fad lasted, naked people charged down streets, through shopping malls, across college campuses, and even onto playing fields during major sport events. Sociological study of this behavior reveals some of the difficulties faced by social scientists in their research: (1) By observing, photographing, or interviewing a streaker, the researcher might alter the very behavior that is being studied. (2) The streaker's behavior, unlike that of a virus or molecule, is highly personal and unpredictable; it is difficult to know when or where streaking might occur. (3) The reasons for the emergence and then the disappearance of the fad are very complex and hard to untangle. (4) Streaking is essentially spontaneous and is therefore difficult to study under controlled conditions. (5) The researcher might have a personal attitude toward streaking—perhaps amusement, perhaps disgust—and this bias may hamper objective analysis. Natural scientists rarely face problems like these.*

5. *The sociologist, unlike the natural scientist, is part of the very subject he or she is studying.* The geologist may be interested in establishing the composition of a particular rock sample but is unlikely to be emotionally involved in the findings. The sociologist, who may be studying such issues as race relations or poverty, may find it much more difficult to maintain a detached attitude, and can even become passionately involved in the outcome of a study. The researcher may identify strongly with the problems and experiences of the subjects, and there is a risk that the process of investigation and interpretation will be distorted as a result.

All sociologists recognize these problems, but not all are agreed on how to deal with them. Some favor "quantitative" methods: they focus on refining statistical and other mathematical techniques, modeling their research as closely as possible after the example of the natural sciences. They aim to make sociology as rigorous and exact a science as possible. Others protest that excessive dependence on these methods produces mounds of figures, often about trivial issues, but very little understanding. Instead, these sociologists favor "quali-

tative" methods: they rely on their own subjective descriptions and interpretations of behavior, even when these may be difficult for others to verify. They concede that some precision is lost by their method, but claim that it provides more insights, a better "feel" for the texture of social life. Debate between the more zealous advocates of each approach has at times become heated. Advocates of a strongly interpretative approach have referred to sociologists relying on statistical techniques as "number crunchers" or "the IBM mafia," while advocates of the latter approach have dismissed the descriptive writings of the other camp as "pop sociology" or "soft sociology." Most sociologists, however, probably accept that there is a valid place for both approaches—a viewpoint expressed by Max Weber many decades ago. Weber asserted that sociology must model itself as far as possible on the natural sciences but that its subject matter, being so different, sometimes also calls for an interpretative, subjective approach.

Subjective interpretation—which Weber called **Verstehen,** the German word for empathetic understanding—is in no sense a substitute for the scientific method. Wherever possible, the conclu-

Figure 2.4 *In attempting to show a link between the "Protestant ethic" and the development of capitalism, Max Weber tried to gain a subjective understanding of the psychology of the early European Puritan merchants and entrepreneurs. Their fear of damnation, Weber claimed, had led them to work and invest for the glory of God—thereby creating modern capitalism. Weber's insights enriched his work, but (as he himself emphasized) subjective interpretation alone is no substitute for scientific analysis. Such interpretations do have a place in sociology, but they must be tested where possible against verifiable facts.*

sions drawn from subjective interpretation must be verified scientifically. Weber himself used *Verstehen* when he was trying to prove a causal link between two variables, the religious beliefs of early Puritans and the development of capitalism in Europe. The Puritans, he argued, believed that they were predestined to either heaven or damnation. According to their doctrine, they could not know what their actual fate would be, but they all had the duty of working for the greater glory of God. In their anxiety to find out if they were to be saved, they took signs of success in work as an indication of God's favor, and so worked all the harder. But their Puritan ethic forbade them to spend the resulting income on luxurious living, so they simply reinvested it. By accumulating and reinvesting wealth—instead of immediately spending it, as others were prone to do—they unwittingly created modern capitalism. This argument seems plausible, but there is no way to prove it scientifically because we cannot know whether the Puritans really did experience this "salvation panic." Weber's method was to place himself in the Puritans' shoes in order to understand their feelings and motives. By combining his subjective interpretations of Puritan psychology with a rigorous comparison of other religious doctrines and a historical analysis of the development of capitalism, he enhanced the richness (but not necessarily the validity) of his study.

Basic Research Methods

At the heart of the research process are the actual procedures sociologists use to collect their facts. One or more of four basic methods can be used: the experiment, the survey, the observational study, and the use of existing sources of information. Each of these has its advantages and its drawbacks, and the success of a research project depends largely on the researcher's choice of an appropriate method.

Experiments

An *experiment* is a method for studying the relationship between two variables under carefully controlled conditions. Experiments can be conducted either in the laboratory or in the field. In a laboratory experiment the subjects and any necessary materials are brought into an artificial environment that can be carefully regulated by the researcher. A field experiment takes place outside the laboratory under less artificial conditions, perhaps in a prison, hospital, or even a street. The laboratory experiment is more appropriate when the researcher wants to control the situation in minute detail, whereas the field experiment is more suitable when the researcher wants to study people in their more normal settings.

The Experimental Method

In the typical experiment, an independent variable is introduced into a carefully designed situation and its influence on a dependent variable is recorded. Let's say that the researcher decides to run an experiment on the effect that social interaction with Russian students has on American students' attitudes toward the Soviet Union. The researcher must first measure the American students' attitudes toward the Soviet Union, then arrange for social interaction to take place between visiting Russian students and American students, and then, after a suitable period, measure the American students' attitudes again to find out if any change has taken place. But this procedure is not enough to establish a causal link between the independent variable (interaction with the Russians) and the dependent variable (American students' attitudes). Any changes in the students' attitudes might have been caused by coincidental factors, such as favorable or unfavorable news about the Soviet Union that happened to appear while the experiment was in progress.

The researcher therefore has to control the situation in such a way that other possible influences can be discounted. The standard method of doing this would be to divide the American students into two groups whose members are similar in all relevant respects. One group would then become the *experimental group*—the subjects in an experiment who are exposed to the independent variable. The other group would become the *control group*—the subjects in an experiment who are exposed to all the experimental conditions except the independent variable. Thus, both groups would be tested on their attitudes toward the Soviet Union, but only the experimental group would interact with Russian students. Finally, both groups would again be tested on their attitudes. Any difference between the two groups is then assumed to be the result of the independent variable.

The "Hawthorne Effect"

One of the best-known experiments in sociology was conducted before World War II at the Hawthorne plant of Western Electric (Roethlisberger and Dickson, 1939). The management wanted to know what would encourage the workers to increase output. The researcher who investigated the problem, Elton Mayo, separated a group of women from the other workers and systematically varied lighting, coffee breaks, lunch hours, methods of payment, and so on. At first, Mayo and his associates were delighted: each new change increased levels of productivity. But when the researchers found that productivity rose no matter which variables were changed, they became suspicious. When the workers were finally returned to their original conditions, their productivity rose yet again! Something was seriously wrong with the researchers' theoretical assumptions. Whatever had caused the changes in the dependent variable—productivity—it was not the independent variables the experimenters had introduced, and from this point of view the experiment was a failure. But the reasons for the experiment's failure have taught sociologists a great deal. Production rose, it seems, because the women enjoyed all the attention they were getting: they became a tight-knit, cooperative group, they knew what effects the sociologists were trying to produce, and they did their best to please. This phenomenon is still known as the *Hawthorne effect*—the contamination of an experiment by the subjects' assumptions about what the experimenter is trying to discover. Sometimes, in fact, the effect takes a more negative form. There is now extensive evidence that some subjects—particularly college students required to participate in psychology experiments—become so suspicious or resentful that they alter their behavior, even to the extent of sabotaging the experiment (Diener and Crandall, 1978).

Figure 2.5 *Survey research can be an interesting but demanding task, particularly in open-ended interviews where the questioner has the chance to follow up on unexpected opinions or information. The researcher usually tries to remain as neutral as possible to avoid influencing the subjects' responses.*

The experimental method is useful because it allows the researcher to investigate specific topics that often cannot be systematically examined under everyday conditions, where so many other influences might conceal or distort the processes involved. The method has some disadvantages, however. It can be used only for narrowly defined issues. People may behave very differently in the artificial experimental situation than they would in the world beyond. And experimenters may sometimes unwittingly produce the effect they are looking for, or even its opposite.

Surveys

A *survey* is a method for systematically obtaining standardized information about the attitudes, behavior, or other characteristics of a population. Surveys are frequently used in sociological research, either simply to get facts (such as the political views of college students) or to find the relationships between facts (such as how social class or parental opinions influence students' political views). Surveys are perhaps the form of sociological research best known to the general public, for opinion polls have become a regular news feature and an important influence on political life.

The "population" in any survey is simply the total group of people the sociologist is interested in. It may consist of all college seniors, all mothers with children under the age of five, all twins in Ontario, or even the entire nation. In some cases it is possible to survey an entire population, but time and expense make this procedure impractical unless the population is a small one. In most cases it is necessary to survey a *sample,* a small number of individuals drawn from a larger population. This sample must accurately represent the population in question. If it does not, then any conclusions are valid only for the *respondents*—the actual subjects of a survey—and cannot be applied to the entire population from which the sample was drawn. (The same is true, incidentally, of experiments: the findings of an experiment cannot be generalized to a larger population unless the subjects are representative of the population concerned.)

In 1936, the popular magazine *Literary Digest* conducted an opinion poll to predict the outcome of that year's presidential election. The subjects were selected from telephone directories and automobile registration lists, and 2 million responses were obtained. The results pointed to a landslide victory for the Republican candidate, Alfred E. Landon, who had a lead of nearly 15 percentage points over his Democratic opponent. If you have never heard of Alfred E. Landon, you need not be unduly concerned over your ignorance. He was beaten by Franklin D. Roosevelt in every state except Maine and Vermont and swiftly disappeared into the footnotes of political history. The correct outcome of the election was predicted, however,

Figure 2.6 *Harry S Truman holds aloft a copy of the* Chicago Daily Tribune *on the night of his victory over Thomas E. Dewey in the 1948 presidential elections. The paper had gone to press before the results were announced, relying for its unfortunate headline on earlier opinion polls. In this case, the polls were inaccurate primarily because polling stopped too soon before the election. In the closing stages of the campaign, the great majority of the "undecideds" swung to Truman, but this trend went undetected. Modern opinion polls continue until the final days of a presidential campaign.*

by a young man named George Gallup, who used a much smaller sample for his purposes. The *Literary Digest* became a national laughingstock and soon went out of business, while the Gallup poll has become a regular feature of the American scene.

Why was Gallup's poll so much more reliable than the *Literary Digest*'s, even though it used a much smaller sample? The answer, of course, is that his sample was more representative than the *Literary Digest*'s. During the Depression years only middle- and upper-class people could afford telephones and automobiles, and these people were mostly Republicans. As a result, lower- and working-class people, who were overwhelmingly Democratic, were largely excluded from the *Digest*'s sample. In effect, the poll was a survey of how a predominantly Republican sample intended to vote, and so it produced a wildly inaccurate prediction for the nation as a whole. Gallup was able to predict the result more accurately because his sample faithfully represented the proportions of Democrats and Republicans in the electorate.

Random Samples

Whether a sample is representative has very little to do with its size. A representative sample of two or three thousand Americans can be used to predict the outcome of a presidential election to within a few percentage points of the actual result; as we have seen, an unrepresentative sample of several million can be hopelessly off target. Representativeness can be ensured by using a ***random sample***—one chosen in such a way that every member of the population in question has the same chance of being selected. Perhaps the simplest way to select a random sample is to pull names out of a hat, but sociologists can use more sophisticated techniques for drawing random samples from large populations.

One method is to systematically take, say, every tenth or thirty-ninth person from the population. This must be done with care: if you were surveying your college's student population, for example, you could not obtain a random sample by asking every fifth person who entered your sociology lecture room. All you would get would be a random sample of students who study sociology and don't cut class. To make your sample representative you would have to draw it from a complete listing of all students. A second method of obtaining a random sample is to assign a number to each member of the population and then to se-

lect the sample by using random numbers generated by a computer. This method is the most reliable because it eliminates most sources of human error.

Questionnaires and Interviews

A survey may use questionnaires, interviews, or a combination of the two. If the questionnaire is self-administered without an interview, the respondents are asked to complete it and often to return it by themselves. If the interview technique is used, the researcher asks the questions directly. The interview itself may be structured or unstructured. In a structured interview the researcher has a checklist of questions and asks them in exactly the same form and exactly the same order with each respondent. The respondent is asked to choose among several predetermined answers, such as "yes/no/don't know" or "very likely/likely/unlikely/very unlikely." The structured interview is inflexible, but it enables the researcher to make careful tabulations and comparisons of the answers. If other information about the respondents is included, such as income, geographical location, or age, all these variables can be fed into a computer, and correlations between them can be extracted in a few seconds. By using statistical controls on the data, the researcher can often explore causal links between the different variables in the survey. The unstructured interview is much more flexible and "open-ended." The researcher puts more general questions to the respondents, allows them to answer freely, and follows up on their comments. This approach allows the researcher to get insights that a structured interview may overlook, but it has some disadvantages. The answers are often extremely difficult to compare. If people are asked, for example, "Do you intend to vote in the next election?" they will give such answers as "Maybe," "I might if I feel like it," "Depends on who's running," "I suppose so," "I haven't decided yet," and so on. The interviewer also has to be on guard against influencing the respondents' answers by such subtle signals as choice of words, tone of voice, and facial expressions.

To be useful, survey questions must be put in straightforward, unemotional language and must be phrased so that all respondents will understand them in the same way. The question "Are you religious?" is almost useless because it will be interpreted in various ways by different people; it is necessary to ask more specific questions about church attendance, belief in God, and so on. Ques-

AMERICAN ATTITUDES TOWARD ABORTION

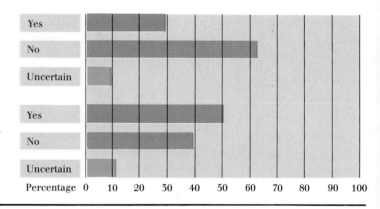

Do you think there should be an amendment to the Constitution prohibiting abortions?

Yes
No
Uncertain

Do you believe there should be an amendment to the Constitution protecting the life of the unborn child?

Yes
No
Uncertain

Percentage 0   10   20   30   40   50   60   70   80   90   100

SOURCE: CBS–New York Times Poll, 1980.

Figure 2.7 *Does the American public think abortion should be legal? The answer depends on how the question is phrased. When pollsters asked the question in two different ways, they got rather different results, as this chart shows. It is important that survey questions be neutrally phrased.*

tions should be stated in a neutral manner: one that begins "Do you agree that . . . ?" will draw more "yes" responses than one that begins "Do you think that . . . ?" Double-barreled questions, such as "Do you think that marijuana and heroin should be legalized?" inevitably produce confusion because people may have different opinions about the two issues. The word "not" should be avoided if possible: if the researcher asks "Do you think the United States should not get militarily involved in Central America?" many people will skip over the word "not" and misunderstand the question.

The survey is an indispensable source of information about social characteristics and the relationships among them. It is particularly useful for tracing changes in these characteristics over time, for questionnaires or interviews can be repeated at suitable intervals. The method has its disadvantages, however. People will sometimes express opinions on subjects they know nothing whatever about. (Even if people are asked to express opinions on a nonexistent law—say, the "Hodge Act"— a large minority will declare themselves for or against it!) In addition, many people—often more than half—fail to return self-administered questionnaires. An unsatisfactory response rate introduces bias into the sample because those who do return questionnaires may be different in important respects from those who do not—in particular,

they are more likely to have strong views on the subject being surveyed. To complicate matters, at least 10 percent of American adults are not sufficiently literate to complete a questionnaire, and in some countries the proportion may be much higher. Respondents may also give false information, particularly in face-to-face interviews. People may deny their racist views, for example, because they know these views are not "respectable." Finally, surveys rarely permit in-depth study of social behavior, and they can be expensive (Sudman and Bradburn, 1982).

Observational Studies

An observational study is an intensive examination of a particular group, event, or social process. The researcher does not attempt to influence what happens in any way, but aims instead at an accurate description and analysis of what takes place. The analysis usually traces cause-and-effect relationships, but some sociologists are content merely to give a precise account of their observations. This information often provides rich insights into social behavior and for that reason alone adds to the sum of sociological knowledge. Moreover, one researcher's description can be used by other researchers for other purposes.

How to Read a Table

Sociologists make considerable use of statistical tables, both as a source of data and as a way of presenting the results of their own research. You will be able to grasp the information in a table quickly if you follow a systematic procedure. Here are the main steps you should follow (using the accompanying table as a model).

1. *Read the title.* The title should tell you exactly what information the table contains. Our table tells about the willingness of Americans to vote for a female president.

2. *Look for headnotes.* Immediately below the title you will sometimes find a headnote. The headnote may give information about how the data were collected, how they are presented, or why they are presented in a particular way. In this case, the headnote tells us the exact form of the question that was asked.

3. *Examine the source.* At the bottom of a table you will find a statement of the source of the data. The source helps you to judge the reliability of the information and tells you where to find the original data if you want to check the statistics further. In the example the source is a reliable one, the Gallup poll.

4. *Read the labels.* There are two kinds of labels in a table, the column headings at the top and the headings along the left-hand side. You must make sure that you understand the labels, and you will have to keep both column and side headings in mind as you read the table. In our table the column headings represent national, female, and male opinions, while the side headings indicate the years in which the surveys were made.

5. *Find out what units are used.* The statistics in a table may be presented in hundreds, thousands, percentages, rates per 1000, rates per 100,000, and so on. Sometimes this information is not contained in the headnote but appears instead in the column or side headings. In our table, the overall column head indicates that figures are presented as percentages.

6. *Make comparisons.* Compare the data in the table, both horizontally and vertically, and notice any differences, similarities, or trends in the statistics. If you read our table horizontally, you will be able to compare the percentage of the nation willing to vote for a female president with the percentages of women and men willing to do so. If you read the table vertically, you will be able to compare opinions in any category from one year to another.

7. *Draw conclusions.* Finally, draw conclusions about the data and consider any questions that the statistics raise. You will notice, for example, that willingness to vote for a woman president has increased dramatically between 1937, when a minority of both men and women were favorable, and 1984, when an overwhelming majority of both sexes would vote for a woman. You will also note that in earlier years the idea of a woman president drew comparatively more support from women, but that in later years both sexes favored it equally, and you may want to investigate this further.

WILLINGNESS OF AMERICANS TO VOTE
FOR A WOMAN PRESIDENT

Question: If your party nominated a woman for president, would you vote for her if she were qualified for the job?

	Would Vote for Woman President (in percent)		
	National	Women	Men
1937	34	41	27
1949	50	53	47
1955	54	59	49
1963	57	55	61
1978	80	81	80
1984	78	78	78

SOURCE: Gallup poll.

Like the experiment, an observational study can be conducted in the laboratory or in the field. In a laboratory observation, for example, the sociologist might present a group of subjects with a problem in order to observe how leaders emerge and decisions are made. The researcher may choose to tape-record the interaction and to watch and film it through a two-way mirror rather than risk influencing the course of events by joining the group and taking notes on the spot. In field observation the sociologist studies something that is happening or has happened without attempting to structure the conditions of observation. Most observational studies take place in the field.

Case Studies

The most common form of field observation is the *case study*—a complete and detailed record of an event, group, or social process. Some case studies deal with events that have already taken place. The sociologist reconstructs these events through extensive interviews with the participants and by referring to other sources of data, ranging from police records to newspaper files. This method is often used for the analysis of infrequent, temporary events such as riots. Other case studies are conducted at the time the action is taking place. These "eyewitness" studies are a rich source of sociological information and insights.

The sociologist in a case study may choose to be either a detached or a participant observer. *Detached observation* is a method in which the researcher remains as aloof as possible, and the subjects may not even know they are being studied. Observing from a distance may obscure the view, however. Many sociologists therefore prefer *participant observation,* a method in which the researcher becomes directly involved in the social behavior under study. Sometimes the participant observer makes it clear to the subjects at the outset that he or she is a sociologist; at other times the sociologist pretends to be an ordinary member of the group. The latter approach has the advantage that people will behave in more typical ways if they

do not know they are being observed, and it also enables the sociologist to gain access to groups—such as some religious sects—that would not normally allow themselves to be studied. Concealing one's identity can raise serious ethical problems, however, because the sociologist is using deceit to observe the details of people's lives.

The case-study tradition in American sociology is full and varied. An influential early study was that of William Whyte (1943, 1984), who became a participant observer in a Boston slum neighborhood, and showed that, contrary to the assumptions of the time, it was a highly organized and cohesive community. He said of his research role, "As I sat and listened, I learned the answers to questions I would not even have had the sense to ask." Leon Festinger and his associates (1956) penetrated a cult whose members believed that the earth was doomed to imminent destruction but that a select few would be saved by aliens in a flying saucer. He eventually found himself on a hilltop awaiting the event with members of the cult, and he detailed their reactions when the prophecy failed. Erving Goffman (1961) spent many months as an observer in a mental hospital, where he worked as an aide. His account of how an asylum can systematically depersonalize patients and even aggravate their problems has been influ-

Figure 2.8 *Infrequent, spontaneous events, such as riots, usually have to be studied after they have occurred. It would be almost impossible to make an objective analysis on the spot, even if a trained observer happened to be there at the time. Such events can often be reconstructed and analyzed through a retrospective case study.*

Figure 2.9 *Sociology deals with people, and therefore with human hopes and passions, fears and frailties. Under these circumstances it is often difficult for researchers to be objective, especially when they are working closely with their subjects. In recent years, for example, many American farmers have gone bankrupt, and have had to watch their lands repossessed by banks and their equipment sold at auction. A sociologist who made a participant observer's study of this process might become deeply involved with the people and issues concerned.*

ential. Ned Polsky (1964) spent long periods as a participant observer with poolroom hustlers, noting how they "set up" their victims and analyzing their code of ethics. John Lofland (1966) participated in a religious sect—the "Moonies"—at a time when it had only a handful of converts, and he was later (1977) able to use the knowledge from his case study to analyze the reasons for the sect's rapid subsequent growth.

Observational studies of this kind place a heavy obligation on the sociologist. The identities of informants must be protected, especially when their behavior is disreputable. Systematic notes must be kept each day while memory is fresh. The observer must be careful not to influence the behavior he or she is studying. Gaining access to the group and winning the trust of its members can be difficult, especially if the backgrounds of the sociologist and the subjects are dissimilar. The assumption behind participant observation is that some things can be fully understood only by intimate experience of them, but the method relies heavily on the skills and subjective interpretations of the observer.

Observational studies have the advantage that they come to grips with real-life situations, thereby offering insights that years of experimenting and surveying might overlook. They have the disadvantage, however, of sacrificing scientific precision to some extent. The observer may misinter-

pret events, may unwittingly ignore things that are relevant and focus on things that are trivial, and may become so emotionally involved with the lives of the subjects that objectivity suffers. Another disadvantage is that the case studied may have been exceptional in unknown but important ways, so the findings of a single observational study cannot be generalized to all apparently similar cases.

Existing Sources

Sometimes the sociologist does not have to generate new information through experiments, surveys, or observational studies. The relevant data may already exist and may merely have to be collected and analyzed. A great deal of useful information is available in published or unpublished form, whether it consists of the statistics issued by government agencies, newsreels, diaries, letters, court records, song lyrics, works of art and literature, historical records, or the research findings of other social scientists.

One of the most important sources of information for the American sociologist is the census report published every ten years by the U.S. Bureau of the Census and supplemented annually with a wealth of information on subjects ranging from birth and death rates to details of income, sex ratios, and urbanization trends. Other government departments issue statistical data every year on subjects as diverse as education, trade, health, transport, and military spending. Similar material for Canadian society is issued by Statistics Canada, a government agency that collects important social, economic, and other data.

Another important source of existing information is the accumulated body of sociological research. Information from this source can be collected and reinterpreted; findings of previously isolated reports can be related to one another in new and revealing ways; the data that one sociologist collected to answer one question can sometimes be used by another sociologist to answer a different question.

Durkheim's Study of Suicide

Emile Durkheim's classic study of suicide, first published in 1897, remains an outstanding example of the use of existing sources. Durkheim wanted to find out why people commit suicide, and he suspected that explanations focusing on the psychology of the individual were inadequate. Experiments on suicide were obviously out of the question. Case studies of past suicides would be of little use, because they could not provide reliable generalizations about all suicides. Survey methods were hardly appropriate, because one cannot survey dead people. But statistics on suicide were readily available, and Durkheim chose to analyze them.

Durkheim was able to dismiss some theories of suicide—such as the possibility that suicidal tendencies are inherited—by applying statistical controls to the data and eliminating those variables. He was left with an interesting and suggestive pattern: suicide rates varied from one social group to another and did so in a consistent manner over the years. Protestants were more likely to commit suicide than Catholics; people in large cities were more likely to commit suicide than people in small communities; people living alone were more likely to commit suicide than people living in families. Durkheim isolated one independent variable that lay behind these differences: the extent to which the individual was integrated into a social bond with others. People with fragile ties to their community are more likely to take their own lives than people who have stronger ties.

Durkheim then compared suicide in such circumstances with a form of suicide that is more typical of traditional societies: the suicide that takes place because it is expected by the community. In ancient Rome or traditional Japan, for example, a suicide was regarded as a highly honorable act under some circumstances. In traditional Indian society, a widow was sometimes expected to burn

Figure 2.10 *Suicide seems a highly individual act, yet the motives for a suicide can be fully understood only by reference to the social context in which it occurs. The drawing here shows an Indian woman throwing herself on her husband's funeral pyre—an act that was once considered a moral duty in parts of India. Her behavior is approved and encouraged by her community, and she kills herself in response to social pressure. In the photo opposite, the young American leaping to his death probably has very different reasons, stemming from loneliness, despair, and a lack of meaningful bonds with other people. His behavior is disapproved by the community—in fact, police officers try unsuccessfully to prevent it—but social pressure is inadequate to keep him from killing himself.*

herself to death on her husband's funeral pyre and considered a dutiful wife if she did so. In these cases it is not the weakness but the strength of the individual's ties to the community that accounts for the suicide. People in these societies may actually take their own lives in response to social expectations they themselves share, whereas in our society people may take their lives because they do not share social expectations with anybody.

Durkheim was thus able to show that suicide—surely the most individual act anyone is capable of—can be fully understood only in its social context, particularly in terms of the presence or absence of shared social expectations that influence individual behavior. To understand why a specific person commits suicide, of course, we must look at that person's personality and the pressures to which he or she has been subjected. To understand why suicide rates are higher for some groups than for others, however, we have to look at the larger social forces that predispose individuals to suicide. Durkheim's insight—that individual behavior can be fully understood only in its social environment—has become the basis of the modern sociological perspective. And his careful, systematic use of the evidence he gleaned from existing sources helped to establish sociology as something more than inspired speculation: it proved that the young discipline was a science.

A Research Model

Suppose you wanted to conduct some sociological research. Exactly how might you go about it? Most research in sociology—and indeed in all science—follows the same basic, step-by-step procedure. The one outlined here is merely an ideal model, and not all sociologists stick to it in every detail, but it does provide the guidelines for most research projects.

1. *Define the problem.* The first step is to choose a suitable topic for a research project. The general area selected will usually be one in which the sociologist takes a personal interest. The specific topic can be chosen for a variety of reasons: perhaps because it raises issues of fundamental sociological importance; perhaps because it has suddenly become a focus of controversy; perhaps because research funds have become available to investigate it.

2. *Review the literature.* The existing sociological research bearing on the problem must be tracked down and reviewed. Knowledge of the relevant literature is essential. It provides background information, suggests theoretical approaches, indicates which areas of the topic have already been covered and which have not, and saves the sociologist the labor and embarrassment of unwittingly duplicating research that has already been done.

3. *Formulate a hypothesis.* The research problem must be stated in such a way that it can actually be tested. This is achieved by formulating a *hypothesis,* a tentative statement that predicts a relationship between variables. The hypothesis might be "Exposure to antiracist material reduces racial prejudice." However, ideas like "exposure," "antiracist material," and "racial prejudice" are too vague to operate with effectively, for their meanings are open to different interpretations. For each idea in the hypothesis, therefore, the researcher must create an *operational definition*—one that states a concept, for the purposes of research, in terms that can be measured. Thus, "exposure" might be an intense one-hour session repeated once a week for three weeks; "antiracist material" might be a specific series of films; "racial prejudice" might be measured by a particular questionnaire. Different researchers may produce different operational definitions of the same terms, which is one reason why investigations of what seems to be the same subject may produce varying conclusions.

A RESEARCH MODEL

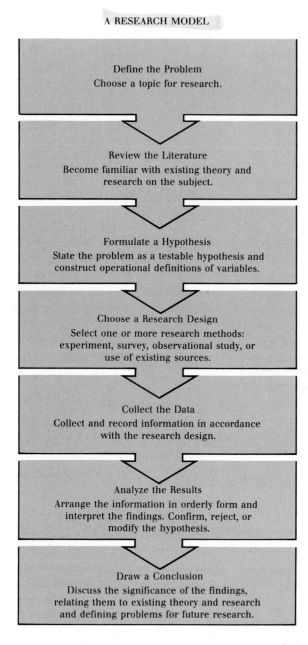

Define the Problem
Choose a topic for research.

Review the Literature
Become familiar with existing theory and research on the subject.

Formulate a Hypothesis
State the problem as a testable hypothesis and construct operational definitions of variables.

Choose a Research Design
Select one or more research methods: experiment, survey, observational study, or use of existing sources.

Collect the Data
Collect and record information in accordance with the research design.

Analyze the Results
Arrange the information in orderly form and interpret the findings. Confirm, reject, or modify the hypothesis.

Draw a Conclusion
Discuss the significance of the findings, relating them to existing theory and research and defining problems for future research.

Figure 2.11 *This chart shows the seven basic steps that a researcher might follow in any sociological research project.*

4. *Choose a research design.* The sociologist must now select one or more means of gathering data—a survey, an experiment, an observational study, the use of existing sources, or a combination of these. The advantages and disadvantages of each method must be carefully weighed because the ***research design***—the actual plan for the collection and analysis of the data—is the crux of the research process.

5. *Collect the data.* The conclusions will be no better than the data on which they are based, so the researcher must take great care in collecting and recording information. As we have seen, each research method has its limitations, and the researcher must scrupulously take them into account at all times.

6. *Analyze the results.* When all the data are in, the sociologist can begin to classify the facts, clarifying trends and relationships and tabulating the information in such a way that it can be accurately analyzed and interpreted. This task also requires scrupulous attention, for a given set of facts can often be interpreted in several different ways, and the researcher has to evaluate each of these possibilities with as much objectivity as possible. The theory, as expressed in the hypothesis, can now be confirmed, rejected, or modified.

7. *Draw a conclusion.* Assuming that all has gone as planned, the sociologist can now draw up a succinct report of the project, tracing the steps already mentioned and concluding with a discussion of the findings. The report will relate the conclusions to the existing body of theory and research, suggesting where current assumptions should be modified to take account of the new evidence. The report may also identify unanswered questions, and the sociologist may suggest new hypotheses that others can explore. If the research makes a significant contribution to sociological knowledge, it may be published, probably in the form of an article in a scholarly journal. It then becomes the common property of the scientific community, whose members can attempt to "replicate" the study—that is, repeat it to verify the findings—if they wish to do so.

Being an ideal, this model does not reveal the messiness that often accompanies the actual process of research. It tells us nothing, for instance, about the sheer frustrations, the inspired guesses, or the pure luck involved in research. Then, too, some researchers hardly use the model at all; they are more interested in describing social behavior and leaving it at that. Some researchers start with a vaguely defined hypothesis but continually modify it and their operational definitions as they go along. Sometimes the data disprove the hypothesis the researcher had in mind at the beginning but seem to prove some other hypothesis he or she had not thought of. The researcher may then try to fit the facts to the new hypothesis. The final report, however, should make clear what happened and why it happened.

Research Ethics

Until World War II, it was widely taken for granted that scientists would pursue their work in an ethical manner and that scientific innovation would advance human welfare. Two aspects of the war challenged those assumptions. The first was the activities of Nazi scientists, who gave advice on the design of facilities for mass murder and who engaged in horrifyingly unethical experiments, such as freezing people and carefully noting how long it took them to die. The second aspect was the American use of atomic bombs on the civilian populations of the Japanese cities of Hiroshima and Nagasaki. In applying the abstract theories of nuclear physics to the technology of war, scientists helped create a weapon of such awesome power that all humanity now lives under the threat of nuclear devastation and even extinction.

Over the past four decades, both scientists and the general public have become more sensitive to the potential ethical problems that scientific research can raise. The American Sociological Association, for example, has a code of ethics for researchers, which specifies that they should maintain objectivity and integrity, respect the privacy and dignity of subjects, protect subjects from harm, preserve confidentiality of personal data collected during research, and acknowledge sources of assistance, collaboration, and funding. This code helps to ensure that research, for the most part, is conducted in responsible ways. In some ambiguous situations, however, researchers may find these principles difficult to apply, for dilemmas can sometimes arise that are not easily resolved simply by referring to abstract standards (Diener and Crandall, 1976; Reynolds, 1982; Bulmer, 1982; Beauchamp et al., 1982).

What kind of ethical dilemmas are sociologists likely to encounter in their work? There are five basic types of dilemma, although they often overlap in practice.

1. *Harm to participants.* It would seem self-evident that research should not risk physical, psychological, or moral harm to the participants, but in practice this principle is occasionally violated. The U.S. military has been much criticized in the past for some of its experiments: for example, military researchers gave the psychedelic drug LSD to unsuspecting subjects to test their reactions, and even faked an impending air crash to see how the passengers, all young military personnel, would react to the belief that they were about to die (Berkun et al., 1962).

Studies that might cause harm to participants are rare in social science, but they do occur. In one case, for example, social psychologists wanted to find out if fictional crimes on television encourage viewers to commit actual crimes in real life. Subjects in the experiment watched a drama in which a character broke into a charity donation box and stole the contents. Later, all the subjects were given a chance to steal a small sum from a charity. Some did steal—and they were allowed to keep the money and were never told they had been subjects in this research. As it happened, members of the experimental group, who watched the drama, were no more likely to steal than members of the control group, who were not exposed to it—an important finding (Milgram and Shotland, 1973). But suppose the results had been different—that some suggestible subjects had been tempted into crimes, perhaps even against other charities or persons outside the study? Does the information gained from such research justify the potential risks to the individual and society?

2. *Invasion of privacy.* Any research into people's lives risks invading their privacy. The problem arises particularly when the sociologist uses unobtrusive measures—that is, ways of studying people without their knowledge. This issue frequently arises when sociologists, acting as participant observers, disguise their professional identity in order to win entry to some group, such as a religious cult or a criminal network, that would not normally permit themselves to be studied. It occurs, too, whenever the sociologist gains information about people who are not aware that their privacy might be intruded upon.

A study of consumer behavior in Tucson, Arizona, for example, relied on an examination of household garbage collected from outside people's homes. The researchers announced in the media that they would be using this technique but did not obtain consent from individual households. Of course, one bag of garbage looks much like another, but anonymity could not be guaranteed, as it would have been possible to identify individual households through discarded mail. Several interesting findings emerged from the study; in particular, there was a remarkable discrepancy between people's self-reports about their alcohol use and the actual evidence from their garbage, which indicated much higher consumption (Rathje and Hughes, 1976). In this specific study, the invasion of privacy was not a particularly serious one. But much sociological research focuses on attitudes and behaviors people would rather keep to them-

themselves, and the boundary between legitimate investigation and invasion of privacy may be difficult to define.

3. *Informed consent.* A basic respect for one's subjects suggests that the researcher should not only make them aware that they are being studied but should also obtain their permission. Yet, as we have seen, many studies could not be done at all under those circumstances, particularly when the subjects are acting in disreputable or even illegal ways. An additional problem is that the Hawthorne effect may come into play, especially if people know what the purpose of the research is.

A sociological study by Albert Reiss (1968, 1970) illustrates these problems. In an investigation of police brutality, Reiss and his team worked closely with police officers on duty, but pretended they were studying citizens' behavior toward the police. The researchers recorded an astonishing amount of violence and other mistreatment of civilians by the police. Although police chiefs were told the purpose of the study, the individual officers did not realize what the real purpose of the study was, nor that they themselves were the research subjects. Clearly, this study could not have been done with the informed consent of the subjects—so should it not have been done at all, or did its value outweigh that failing? Such studies pose an additional problem: they give sociologists a bad reputation among certain groups, making them reluctant to cooperate in future research.

4. *Applications of research.* Social science research does not occur in a vacuum; its findings can be put to a variety of uses. Sociological research on propaganda techniques, for example, might be used by advertisers to sell worthless goods, or research on political movements might be used by people who are interested in suppressing those movements. These possibilities raise questions about the relationship between the researcher and those who fund the research, particularly when the funders specify the precise topic and are hoping for a particular finding.

A classic example of this kind of dilemma occurred in 1964, when the Pentagon attempted to recruit social scientists for its "Project Camelot." The goal of this research was to find out what conditions might cause revolutions in Latin American countries, and what steps governments might take to prevent them. The results of the research, then, could be used to influence and even interfere in the domestic affairs of other nations. Several million dollars were made available for the project, and many social scientists agreed to participate in it. As it happened, news of the project leaked be-

fore it could begin, provoking such a furor in Latin America that the Pentagon canceled it (Horowitz, 1967). The affair contributed to a persistent wariness in other nations about the motives of American social scientists. American sociologists conducting research abroad sometimes encounter the suspicion that they are spies working for the CIA or some other branch of the U.S. government.

Why did the social scientists allow themselves to become involved in the project? Irving Louis Horowitz (1967) found that they did not regard themselves as "spies," nor were they interested in maintaining antidemocratic regimes in Latin America. They described themselves as "reformers" whose insights into the real causes of revolutions—poverty and oppression—might "educate" the army. None of them actually believed, however, that the military would take their recommendations seriously. They had been presented with an opportunity to do major research with almost unlimited funds, and they simply overlooked some of the ethical issues involved.

5. *Deception.* A final sensitive issue is the use of deception in order to gain information in the course of research. For example, in 1970 Laud Humphreys published *Tearoom Trade,* a controversial observational study of homosexual acts that took place between strangers in certain men's rest rooms ("tearooms"). Very few homosexually inclined people participate in this highly impersonal form of sexual activity, and Humphreys was interested in finding out more about their social characteristics. Because the participants wanted to avoid any involvement with juveniles or the police, one person always served as a lookout. By taking this role, Humphreys was able to observe hundreds of sexual encounters without his identity as an outsider becoming known. He also noted the automobile registration numbers of the participants and traced their addresses. After waiting a year to ensure that he would not be recognized, he visited their homes in the guise of a researcher conducting a survey on a quite different topic. He was thus able to obtain a great deal more information about them—including, for example, the surprising fact that the majority of them were married, were living with their wives, and led seemingly conventional lives—which was presumably the reason that their sexual adventures took such a fleeting and impersonal form.

Humphreys's ingenious study won the C. Wright Mills award of the Society for the Study of Social Problems for outstanding research, but it was strongly criticized by some sociologists and by editorial writers in the press. One charge was that

Figure 2.12 *The horrors of military repression and revolutionary war in Latin America may seem far removed from the world of the sociologist in the United States, but some American social scientists have become involved in Pentagon attempts to learn more about revolutions in order that they might be prevented. Any research on such issues is likely to have ethical implications, no matter whether one supports or opposes specific revolutions in particular countries. The picture,* The Revolution, *by the Mexican artist Manuel Rodriguez Lozano was painted in 1946 and (unlike a photograph) makes a universal statement without identifying sides.*

Humphreys had endangered his subjects: if his data on their identities and illegal acts had fallen into the wrong hands, blackmail, extortion, or arrest could have followed. Humphreys replied that he had kept his list of names secure in a bank deposit box and that he once allowed himself to be arrested rather than disclose his identity to the police. His attitude seems to have been a responsible one, but the fact remains that other researchers would not necessarily have been as careful. A second and more serious criticism was that Humphreys had used systematic deception both to observe the sexual encounters and later to gain entry to the subjects' homes. In the second edition of his book (1975), Hymphreys agreed that he should have identified himself as a researcher, even at the cost of sacrificing some sources of information. His dilemma highlights a problem that keeps recurring in sociological research: the distinction between legitimate investigation and unjustified intrusion is often difficult to make. In many marginal cases there are no clear guidelines for ethical conduct, and the sociologist may have to make a personal decision on the issue.

Summary

1.   Research methodology refers to the system of rules, principles, and procedures that regulates scientific investigation. Reliable research findings can be produced only by the use of a reliable research method.

2.   All events have causes, and the task of science is to trace these causes in the form of the influence of variables upon one another. Generalizations are statements of probability about relationships between particular variables.

3.   Cause and effect can be traced by establishing correlations between independent and dependent variables. It is necessary, however, to apply controls to exclude the possibility that some variable other than the one being studied is influencing the relationship under investigation. Logical analysis is also necessary to establish that a relationship is causal, not spurious.

4.   Sociological research presents several difficulties that derive from the nature of the subject matter: the act of investigating behavior may change the behavior; people may behave in unpredictable ways; the origins of social behavior are extremely complex; certain kinds of experiments cannot be performed on human beings; and the sociologist's personal involvement with the subjects can introduce bias into research.

5.   Some of these problems can be resolved by combining a rigorous scientific methodology with subjective interpretation, which Weber called *Verstehen*. Subjective interpretation on its own, however, is no substitute for the scientific method. It must be checked where possible by the methods of science.

6.   There are five basic methods of sociological research. The experiment permits careful study of the effect of independent upon dependent variables, but requires the use of experimental and control groups for valid conclusions to be drawn. The survey is useful for obtaining information about a population, but must be based on a random sample if it is to be representative. Observational studies, particularly case studies using detached or participant observation, are useful for in-depth analyses of social processes but rely heavily on the skills of the researcher. Existing sources of various kinds can often be used to generate new information, as in the case of Durkheim's pioneering study of suicide.

7.   An ideal research model consists of the following basic steps: defining the problem, reviewing the literature, formulating a hypothesis, choosing a research design, collecting the necessary data, analyzing the results, and drawing a conclusion.

8.   Sociological research can pose important ethical problems, notably those involving possible harm to participants, invasion of privacy, lack of informed consent, improper applications of research, and deception. A code of ethics helps guide sociologists through many of these pitfalls, but in some ambiguous cases the researcher may have to rely on personal judgments.

Important Terms

methodology (29)
variable (30)
independent variable (30)
dependent variable (30)
correlation (30)
spurious correlation (31)
controls (32)
Verstehen (35)
experiment (36)
experimental group (37)
control group (37)

Hawthorne effect (37)
survey (38)
sample (38)
respondents (38)
random sample (39)
case study (42)
detached observation (42)
participant observation (42)
hypothesis (45)
operational definition (45)
research design (46)

Suggested Readings

BABBIE, EARL R. *The Practice of Social Research*. 3rd ed. Belmont, Calif.: Wadsworth, 1983.

An excellent text, providing a clear and comprehensive coverage of social science research methods.

GLAZER, MYRON. *The Research Adventure*. New York: Random House, 1972.

An interesting account of several sociological research projects. Each example is chosen to illustrate the challenges and problems the researchers had to overcome.

GOLDEN, PATRICIA M. (ed.). *The Research Experience*. Itasca, Ill.: Peacock, 1976.

A good collection of firsthand accounts by researchers, who explain why they chose specific strategies and what problems they encountered.

HUFF, DARRELL, and IRVING GEIS. *How to Lie with Statistics*. New York: Norton, 1954.

A short and readable volume on the use and abuse of statistics. The writers alert the reader to the many ways statistics can be misleadingly presented or interpreted.

LIEBOW, ELLIOT. *Tally's Corner*. Boston: Little, Brown, 1967.

A classic participant-observation study, recording a period that the author spent "hanging out" with lower-class men on a street corner in Washington, D.C. The book is an excellent introduction to this research method.

REYNOLDS, PAUL D. *Ethics and Social Science Research*. Englewood Cliffs, N.J.: Prentice-Hall, 1982.

A good general introduction to some of the ethical dilemmas—and potential solutions—faced by researchers of human behavior.

SANDERS, WILLIAM B. (ed.). *The Sociologist as Detective: An Introduction to Research Methods*. New York: Praeger, 1974.

A useful anthology of articles about sociological research. In his introduction and overviews, the editor draws interesting parallels between the work of social researchers and detectives.

The Individual, Culture, and Society

The theme of this unit is the dynamic interrelationship among individuals, their society, and its culture. The personality and social behavior of individuals are deeply influenced by the culture and society in which they happen to live, while culture and society are themselves produced and maintained by the interaction of countless individuals.

The first chapter in the unit discusses culture—that is, the total way of life of a society. The second focuses on society itself, showing how every society has a social structure that helps it to "work" in a fairly smooth and predictable way. We then explore socialization, the process through which the human animal becomes a fully social being by learning the culture of his or her society. Then we take a close-up view of social interaction, showing how sociological analysis can throw fascinating light on the taken-for-granted reality of our everyday lives. The following chapter discusses social groups, both small and large, and the ways in which groups can influence the behavior of their members. The next chapter turns to the problem of deviance—that is, behavior that violates significant social expectations. Finally, we discuss human sexuality as a specific example of the complex process by which individual, culture, and society interact in the shaping of human behavior and social life.

The illustration opposite locates a single individual squarely within a cultural context—a context that the artist skillfully implies through hints of architecture and lifestyle. The painting, Portrait of Nick Wilder, *is by David Hockney, a contemporary British artist who has lived in southern California.*

CHAPTER 3

Culture

Human beings, unlike other animals, are not born with rigid, complex, behavior patterns that enable them to survive in specific habitats. Instead, we must learn and invent cultural means of adapting to different environments, ranging from arctic snows to desert wastelands and teeming cities. These learned ways of life, which are modified and passed on from one generation to the next, are basic to the understanding of human society.

In ordinary speech, the word "culture" is often used to refer to sophisticated tastes in art, literature, or music. The sociological use of the term is much wider, for it includes the entire way of life of a society. In this sense, everyone who participates in society is "cultured." To the sociologist, *culture* consists of all the shared products of human society. These products are of two basic kinds, material and nonmaterial. *Material culture* consists of all the artifacts, or physical objects, human beings create and give meaning to—wheels, clothing, schools, factories, cities, books, spacecraft, totem poles. *Nonmaterial culture* consists of abstract human creations—languages, ideas, beliefs, rules, customs, myths, skills, family patterns, political systems.

It is possible, at least conceptually, to distinguish "culture" from "society." Culture consists of the shared *products* of society; society consists of the interacting *people* who share a culture. But the two are closely interrelated. A society could not exist without culture. A culture cannot exist without a society to maintain it (although traces may remain in the form of archaeological ruins and historical records). Society and culture are closely linked, and because the English language does not have a word meaning "culture-and-society," sociologists often use either word interchangeably to refer to the complex whole. In this chapter, however, we shall try as far as possible to keep the two concepts distinct and shall use the term "culture" in its more specific sense.

Figure 3.1 *Culture and society are interwoven, and neither can exist without the other—although cultural artifacts, such as the ruined pyramids of ancient Egypt, may outlast the society that created them. Similarly, we may know about an extinct society through its surviving literature.*

The anthropologist Clifford Geertz (1968) observes that noncultured human beings "do not in fact exist, never have existed, and most important, could not in the nature of the case exist." Without culture, neither individual human beings nor human society could survive. To understand why this is so, we must examine the unique characteristics of our own species.

The Human Species: What Kind of Animal?

"What a piece of work is man!" exclaims Hamlet in Shakespeare's play. "How noble in reason! How infinite in faculty! In form, and moving, how express and admirable! In action, how like an angel! In apprehension, how like a god! The beauty of the world! The paragon of animals! And yet . . . what is this quintessence of dust?"

What are we? Hamlet's question is probably as old as the unique human capacity for self-aware-ness, a capacity that extends perhaps hundreds of thousands of years back into prehistory. Modern science can give no simple answer to the question, for we are an extraordinarily complex species—the most intelligent, resourceful, and adaptable that has ever existed on the planet. Yet today we do know infinitely more about the human species than we did even a few years ago, and we have learned that many traditional ideas about "human nature" are hopelessly naive and misguided. This book is about a particular animal, *Homo sapiens,* about the societies this animal forms, and about social behavior within those societies. Before we proceed to the study of culture and society, then, we must try to establish exactly what kind of creature we are talking about.

The Evolutionary Background

The universe we live in is about 10 billion years old. Its main visible components are over 100 billion galaxies, containing, on average, around 200 billion to 400 billion stars each. We inhabit one of the nine planets that circle a small, obscure star near the edge of a minor galaxy of about 100 billion stars. Astronomers have found strong evidence that other stars also have planets, and it may be that they are quite common in the universe. Even if only a tiny fraction of these planets could support life, the statistical probability would be that hundreds of millions of other inhabited worlds exist. If that is the case, the universe teems with life. Or it may be that in all these unimaginably vast reaches of space and time, we are utterly alone. Perhaps we will never know.

Our earth, at least, abounds with life, but how did we get here, in the form that we did? Over the centuries, thousands of cultures around the world have explained human origins in unique, moving, and poetic ways, sometimes through religious doctrines, sometimes through nonreligious myths. These diverse beliefs, handed down in oral or written form through the generations, were based on faith: they could not be checked against scientific evidence, for such evidence was not forthcoming until the middle of the last century. By that time, however, a mass of data was available from three major disciplines—geology, the science of the earth; biology, the science of life; and paleontology, the science of fossilized organisms. In 1859, after years of studying this evidence, Charles Darwin, an ordained minister of the Church of England, published *On the Origin of Species*, a book that has dramatically altered the human self-concept. With detailed evidence and careful reasoning, Darwin argued that all life forms are shaped by physical evolution, a slow and endless process in which new species emerge and diverge from older ones. Darwin did not mention the human species in his book, but his implication was inescapable: we, too, are a product of the evolutionary process, linked by ancient common ancestry to the very beginnings of life on earth.

As Darwin had foreseen, his book aroused immediate controversy. The Western religious tradition had long reserved a special place for humanity—a little lower than the angels, but far removed from the rest of the animal world. However, Darwin's ideas made sense of a growing body of evidence that could not be scientifically explained in any other way, and even in his own lifetime his theory won wide acceptance. Today, virtually the entire scientific community regards evolution as fact, and—despite opposition from fundamentalist groups—the Catholic Church and the mainstream Protestant and Jewish denominations of the world

have accepted it also, seeing the hand of God in the evolutionary process.

When scientists speak of the "theory" of evolution, they are referring not to *whether* evolution takes place, but rather to *how* the process can be explained. How do the bodily forms and potential behaviors of living organisms change over many generations? Darwin's theory was perhaps best summarized by the sociologist Herbert Spencer in his phrase "the survival of the fittest." All species tend to produce far more offspring than their environment can support, and a high proportion fall victim to starvation, predators, disease, and other perils. But there is great physical variation among the individuals in any species: some are swifter, some more resistant to disease, some equipped with better eyesight, some better camouflaged. Those that have any advantage in the struggle for survival are more likely to live longer and to breed, and they therefore tend to pass on their characteristics to the next generation. Nature thus "selects" the fittest members of each species to survive and reproduce. Darwin called this process "natural selection," to distinguish it from the much quicker "artificial selection" that occurs when people deliberately breed, say, a bulldog or poodle from its wolflike ancestor. In time, the characteristics that nature "selects" tend to spread throughout the entire population, and the old species evolves into a new one.

Like all scientific knowledge, evolutionary theory is being continually evaluated and refined as new evidence comes to light. Some modern theorists, for example, argue that new species sometimes form when a natural barrier, like a river or mountain range, permanently splits off part of an animal or plant population from the rest of its species. Over countless generations, minor variations in the genetic composition of the two groups may become magnified, particularly if each is subject to different environmental pressures or opportunities. Over time, the two groups may become so genetically distinct that they can no longer interbreed—meaning that they have become different species. Some modern paleontologists, too, claim that evolution sometimes happens much faster than Darwin envisioned. The fossil evidence often shows new species evolving quite rapidly— perhaps in as few as tens or hundreds of thousands of years—and then persisting over a much longer time with only minor changes. These evolutionary "spurts" are probably caused by relatively sudden changes in the species' environments—for example, by the spread of deserts, the shrinking of ice

Figure 3.2 *Pictured here are our three closest relatives: the chimpanzee, the gorilla, and the orangutan. Our own ancestral line has evolved separately from that of the great apes for several million years, and we have become unlike them in several important ways. Apart from the obvious physical* *differences (such as our comparative hairlessness, habitual upright posture, and vocal apparatus), we have very much larger brains. As a result, we are capable of highly complex and abstract thought, and our behavior is shaped by learning rather than by "instinct."*

caps, the rise and fall of sea levels, the extinctions of old predators or food resources and the appearance of new ones, the effects of volcanos, and perhaps even catastrophic impacts of large comets or meteors on the earth's surface (Stanley, 1982; Schneider and Londer, 1984; Eldredge, 1985).

What of our own origins? Tracing the actual evolution of the human species is no easy task. At one time, anthropologists were looking for a "missing link," an intermediate creature between ourselves and our distant ancestors. In recent years the fossils of many such hominid (human-like, rather than apelike) creatures have been found and dated, and the problem is to sort them into the various species and subspecies that evidently existed at different times. The fossil evidence is still scanty, however—partly because fossils form only under unusual conditions, partly because hominids were never numerous, and partly because most fossils are never discovered. As a result, there are still long gaps in our knowledge of our own origins. Peering into our ancestral past is like peering into a landscape shrouded in mist. The mist parts periodically to reveal the dim outlines of creatures like us yet not like us, but growing more recognizably human with the passage of time.

We do know that we are a member of the primate order, a group of related species that emerged relatively late in evolutionary time. The

planet earth is about 4.7 billion years old. The first living organisms emerged in the oceans approximately 3 billion years ago. The earliest land animals, amphibian creatures, appeared about 400 million years ago and eventually evolved into reptiles. Mammals, which evolved from reptiles about 180 million years ago, are a recent but very successful evolutionary development, primarily because they are more intelligent and adaptable than other life forms. They have an exceptional capacity to learn from experience, and in the higher mammals learning becomes progressively more important in shaping behavior. This development reaches its climax in human beings. Our almost total reliance on learned behavior is the single most important characteristic distinguishing us from other creatures.

The first primates emerged about 70 million years ago, and our own line diverged from our closest relatives, the great apes, between 5 and 8 million years ago. We are so closely related to chimpanzees and gorillas, in fact, that over 90 percent of our DNA, or genetic material, is identical with theirs (Gribbin, 1982). The first distinctively human species appears in the fossil record well over 3 million years ago. What was the physical and behavioral heritage of our ancestor?

The higher primates share a number of common characteristics, all of which give us clues to our own evolutionary background.

1. *Sociability.* Primates tend to be very sociable; they live in groups with a high degree of affection and interaction among their members. Humans, too, live almost exclusively in groups.

2. *Intelligence.* Primates have high intelligence, with brains that are exceptionally heavy in relation to body weight. In humans, the brain has evolved to an unparalleled complexity.

3. *Sensitive hands.* The higher primates have a very unusual physical characteristic: hands in which the thumb can be placed opposite the forefinger to give a firm, precise grip. The importance of this single feature cannot be overestimated: try writing, sewing, or using any tool efficiently without opposing the thumb to the forefinger!

4. *Vocality.* Primates are extremely vocal; they are among the noisiest of all land species and constantly call and chatter to one another. In humans, this characteristic has developed into the capacity for language.

5. *Acute eyesight.* Primates need stereoscopic, color vision to judge distance in leaping or swinging through trees and to spot their main food source, ripe fruit. Humans rely overwhelmingly on their acute eyesight, and compared to most other mammals, our other senses (especially smell) are very poorly developed.

6. *Upright posture.* As tree climbers, primates have a potential to stand upright. Many primate species are able to walk on their hind legs, although they do so rarely and only for short distances. In humans, however, bipedal (two-footed) standing and walking have become normal.

In the course of their evolution, our hominid ancestors developed two additional characteristics. The first, found in few other animals, is the potential for *year-round mating.* Human beings do not have a breeding season, a fact that encourages mates to form stable, long-lasting bonds. The second, found to a much greater extent in human beings than in any other animal, is the infant's *long period of dependence* on adults. This lengthy dependence provides the young human being with the opportunity to learn the cultural knowledge necessary for survival as an adult.

The fossil record shows that the modern human form of *Homo sapiens* was achieved about 50,000 years ago. The long evolutionary process made us what we are: an almost hairless, bipedal, tool-using, talking, family-forming, self-aware, highly intelligent social animal.

The Significance of Culture

Our physical adaptations and the behavioral flexibility offered by our huge and complex brains have made us the most creative species in the planet's history. *Homo sapiens* has spread to every continent, frequently driving other animal species to extinction in the process. It has become the most widely dispersed species on the planet, occupying mountains and valleys, deserts and jungles, shorelines and tundra, yet always finding some specialized means of living in these widely differing environments. The total weight of all living members of the species far exceeds that of any other animal,

Figure 3.3 *The significance of culture is that it enables us to invent and learn ways of adapting to our environments and to changing conditions. All other animals must rely on the slow and accidental process of biological evolution to adapt them to their environments, but we can use cultural knowledge and artifacts to adapt quickly to radically different conditions.*

and the human population is now growing so rapidly that, if current rates persist, it will double from 5 billion to 10 billion people in about forty years.

What accounts for the unprecedented success that our species has enjoyed thus far? The answer, in a word, is culture. We create culture, but culture in turn creates us. We make our own social environment, inventing and sharing the rules and patterns of behavior that shape our lives, and we use our learned knowledge to modify the natural environment. Our shared culture is what makes social life possible. Without a culture transmitted from the past, each new generation would have to solve the most elementary problems of human existence over again. It would be obliged to devise a family system, to invent a language, to discover fire, to create the wheel, and so on.

Clearly, the contents of culture cannot be genetically transmitted. There is no gene that tells us to believe in a particular god, to get married, to drive on the right, to build houses, or to write computer programs. Everything in culture is learned. Culture is thus a substitute for "instinct" as a means of responding to the environment, and it provides a vastly superior way of doing so. Culture frees us from reliance on the slow, random, accidental process of physical evolution by offering us a purposive and efficient means of adapting to changing conditions. If we waited for natural selection to enable us to live at the North Pole, to fly, or to live under the sea, we would wait forever. But cultural inventions enable us to be insulated from the cold of the arctic, to travel through air, and to live in submarines—all without any recourse to physical evolution. The emergence of a species that depends for its survival on a learned culture is perhaps the greatest breakthrough in evolutionary history.

"Human Nature"

Popular but utterly misguided views about our species abound and persist. For example, a substantial majority of Americans agree with the statement "Human nature being what it is, there will always be wars and conflict." The problem with such ideas about "human nature" is that they are deeply colored by the cultural beliefs of the societies in which they are found. In the industrialized countries of the world, particularly in the West, we tend to think of people as being "naturally" self-seeking, selfish, competitive, and even aggressive. But this kind of behavior is virtually unknown among

many of the "primitive" peoples of the world, such as the Arapesh of New Guinea, the Pygmies of the Ituri forest in central Africa, the Shoshone of the western United States, or the Lepcha of the Himalayas. These and many other societies never fight wars at all, and their inhabitants obviously have a very different conception of "human nature" (Montagu, 1978).

In fact, "human nature," if there is such a thing at all, is highly flexible. Our behavior is a product of an interaction between our basic biological heritage and the learning experiences of the particular culture in which we happen to live. For example, we have the biological capacity to speak, but which language we use and how we use it depend on our environment. We have the biological capacity to laugh, to cry, to blush, to become angry, but the circumstances under which we might do any of these things are learned. Nature provides us with legs, but we are not obliged to use them only for walking. We can use them to kick a ball, or to kick other people, or to ride a bicycle, or to do a war dance, or to cover with pants, or to sit cross-legged while contemplating.

Most modern psychologists agree that human beings do not have any "instincts." An *instinct* is a behavior pattern with three essential features: it is complex, it is unlearned, and it appears in all normal members of the species under identical conditions. For example, all members of some bird or insect species will build complex nests of exactly the same type, even if they have never seen such nests built before, as soon as the nesting season begins. Any instincts we once had, however, have been lost in the course of our evolution. The idea that we do not have instincts is difficult for some people to accept, because it seems to run counter to "common sense." One reason for the difficulty is that the word "instinct" is often used very loosely in ordinary speech. People talk about "instinctively" stepping on the brake or "instinctively" mistrusting someone, when these actions and attitudes are, in fact, culturally learned. Another reason is that much of our learned behavior is so taken for granted that it becomes "second nature" to us. The behavior seems so "natural" that we lose the awareness that it is learned, not inherited. But if you think about it, you will see that there is no human behavior that fits the definition of instinct above.

We do have some genetically determined types of behavior, of course, but these are *simple reflexes*—involuntary muscular responses, such as starting at an unexpected loud noise, throwing out

Sociobiology: A New Science?

The question of exactly what human nature is has recently been stimulated by the appearance of sociobiology, a new discipline that applies biological principles to explain the behavior of all social animals, including human beings. In the past, biologists and others who study animal behavior usually restricted their observations to species other than *Homo sapiens,* but in his groundbreaking survey of sociobiology, the insect specialist Edward O. Wilson (1975) laid claim to human behavior as well. Social sciences such as sociology, psychology, and anthropology, he announced, would eventually be absorbed by the new discipline, because our behavior could be better explained in terms of inborn, genetic programming. The essence of his argument is that social behavior, whether in ants, geese, or people, is bred into the species' genes through the same evolutionary pressures that shape its physical characteristics. According to Wilson, human cultural expressions as varied as religion, genocide, cooperation, competition, slavery, envy, territoriality, and altruism are grounded in our genes.

This argument received a sharp response from many social scientists, and in the ensuing debate each camp has approached human behavior from a very different perspective.

Sociobiologists, used to seeing genetically programmed behavior (such as mating rituals) in other species, are quick to assume that apparently similar behavior in human beings (such as courtship rituals) has the same origins; social scientists, whose training and experience make them sensitive to the flexibility of human behavior, see cultural diversity as proof that social behavior is learned. Social scientists (and many biologists) argue that analogies between human beings and other animal species are fundamentally faulty: one can no more explain human behavior in terms of the genetic principles that govern the behavior of, say, a sheep, than one can explain a sheep's behavior in terms of the social and psychological principles that govern human behavior. Human beings differ from other animals in their capacity for cultural learning—which, in fact, has a biological basis in their huge cerebral cortex, the part of the brain that is responsible for higher mental functions such as abstract thought. The cerebral cortex is entirely absent in most animals, and even in the species that have it, such as the other primates, it is relatively undeveloped. All sheep, all swans, all lobsters behave in much the same way because their behavior closely follows a genetic blueprint. Human individuals and human cultures display such a bewildering variety of behavior precisely because they are *not* prisoners of their genes.

Some sociobiologists claim that very specific human behaviors are genetically determined. Others merely suggest that genetic influences provide the limits and possibilities for our behavior—a position that social scientists already accept. The work of the sociobiologists is provocative, but they have yet to show that a single example of human social behavior is under the control of a specific gene or genes. So far, their work on the subject consists almost exclusively of speculation, and the future direction of the fledgling discipline is unclear.

SOURCES: Edward O. Wilson, *Sociobiology: The New Synthesis* (Cambridge, Mass.: Harvard University Press, 1975) and *On Human Nature* (Cambridge, Mass.: Harvard University Press, 1978); David P. Barash, *Sociobiology and Behavior* (New York: Elsevier, 1977); Kenneth Bock, *Human Nature and History: A Response to Sociobiology* (New York: Columbia University Press, 1981); R. C. Lewontin, Steven Rose, and Leon J. Kamin, *Not in Our Genes: Biology, Ideology, and Human Nature* (New York: Pantheon, 1984).

our arms when we lose our balance, pulling back our hand when it touches a hot surface. We also have a few inborn, basic *drives*—organic urges that need satisfaction, such as our desires for self-preservation, for food and drink, for sex, and perhaps for the company of other people. But the way we actually satisfy these drives is learned through cultural experience. Most people, of course, learn to fulfill their drives in the way their culture tells them to. But we are not programmed to satisfy them in any particular way. If we were, we would all fulfill our drives in a rigid, identical manner. In fact, unlike all other species, we can even override our drives completely. We can ignore the drive for self-preservation by committing suicide or by risking our lives for others. Protesters can ignore the drive for food and go on hunger strikes, even if it means starvation. Priests and others can suppress the sex drive and live out their lives in celibacy. Hermits can override the drive for human company, and live in isolation.

Within very broad limits, "human nature" is what we make of it, and what we make of it depends largely on the culture in which we happen to live. One of the most liberating aspects of the sociological perspective is that it strips away myths about our social behavior, showing that what seems "natural" or "instinctive" is usually nothing more than a cultural product of a specific human society at a particular moment in history.

Norms

When the explorer Captain Cook asked the chiefs in Tahiti why they always ate apart and alone, they replied, "Because it is right" (Linton, 1945). If we ask Americans why they eat with knives and forks, or why their men wear pants instead of skirts, or why they may be married to only one person at a time, we are likely to get similar and very uninformative answers: "Because it's right." "Because that's the way it's done." "Because it's the custom." Or even "I don't know."

The reason for these and countless other patterns of social behavior is that they are controlled by social *norms*—shared rules or guidelines that prescribe the behavior appropriate in a given situation. Norms define how people "ought" to behave under particular circumstances in a particular society. We conform to norms so readily that we are hardly aware they exist. In fact, we are much more likely to notice departures from norms than conformity to them. You would not be surprised if a stranger tried to shake hands when you were introduced, but you might be a little startled if he or she bowed, curtsied, started to stroke you, or kissed you on both cheeks. Yet each of these other forms of greeting is appropriate in other parts of the world. When we visit another society whose norms are different, we quickly become aware that we do things *this* way, they do them *that* way.

Some norms apply to every member of society. In the United States, for example, nobody is permitted to marry more than one person at the same time. Other norms apply to some people but not to others. There is a very strong norm in American society against the taking of human life, but this norm generally does not apply to police officers in shootouts, soldiers in combat, or people acting in self-defense against armed attackers. Other norms are even more specific and prescribe the appropriate behavior for people in particular situations, such as college students in lecture rooms, waiters in restaurants, or presidential candidates on the campaign trail.

Folkways and Mores

Norms ensure that social life proceeds smoothly, for they give us guidelines for our own behavior and reliable expectations for the behavior of others. This function of norms is so important that there is always strong social pressure on people to conform. But although most of us conform to most norms most of the time, all of us tend to violate some norms occasionally. In the case of certain norms, the folkways, a fair amount of nonconformity may be tolerated, but in the case of certain other norms, the mores, very little leeway is permitted (Sumner, 1906).

Folkways are the ordinary usages and conventions of everyday life. Conformity to folkways is expected but not absolutely insisted upon. We expect people to keep their lawns mowed, to refrain from picking their noses in public, to show up on time for appointments, and to wear a matching pair of shoes. Those who do not conform to these and similar folkways are considered peculiar and eccentric, particularly if they consistently violate a number of folkways. But they are not considered immoral or depraved, nor are they treated as criminals.

Mores (pronounced "mor-ays") are strong norms that are regarded as morally significant, and violations of them are considered a serious matter. (The word "mores" was the ancient Romans' term for their most respected and even sacred customs.) A man who walks down a street wearing nothing on the upper half of his body is violating a folkway; a man who walks down the street wearing nothing on the lower half of his body is violating one of our most important mores, the requirement that people cover their genitals and buttocks in public. Theft, drug abuse, murder, rape, desecration of the national flag, and contemptuous use of religious symbols all bring a strong social reaction. People believe that their mores are crucial for the maintenance of a decent and orderly society, and the offender may be strongly criticized, punched, restrained, imprisoned, committed to a mental asylum, or even executed. Some violations of mores are made almost unthinkable by a *taboo*—a powerful social belief that some specific act is utterly loathsome. In the United States, for example, there is a strong taboo against eating human flesh, a taboo so effective that most of the states do not even have laws prohibiting the practice.

Not all norms can be neatly categorized as either folkways or mores. In practice, norms fall at various points on a continuum, depending on how seriously they are taken by society. There is also a constant shift in the importance attached to some norms. Throughout most of the history of the Western world, for example, it has been the norm for men to wear their hair long. This was true in the early United States: national heroes such as Washington, Jefferson, and Franklin wore very long

Figure 3.4 *In American society, the norms concerning men's hair styles change from time to time. However, people tend to lose the awareness that these norms merely reflect passing fashions, and may become dismayed or angered at any violation* *of them. The long hair of the nation's second president, John Adams, and the "Mohawk" style of this contemporary youth would be acceptable in some places and times, but not in others.*

hair, even if it was in the form of wigs. But during World War I (1914–1918) troops kept their hair closely cropped to prevent infestations of lice in the unsanitary conditions of the trenches. Thereafter, it became fashionable for men to wear their hair short. At first a folkway, this fashion gradually developed into one of American society's mores. In the 1960s, when youths once more began to grow their hair long, they found that much of adult society considered the practice morally offensive. Family fights erupted, high schools suspended boys with long hair, employers fired workers who defied rules about hair length, and bumper stickers and highway billboards proclaimed: "Keep America beautiful—get a haircut!" In public, long-haired youths were frequently insulted, occasionally attacked, and in a few cases shot at. By the early 1970s, however, long hair on males had become almost a folkway, and today the society's norms allow males a much wider personal choice in the matter—although shorter hair is presently more fashionable. But in time, no doubt, the norms will change again, and people will be outraged at

long hair, short hair, dyed hair, hats, helmets, wigs, ribbons, or even bald heads on the young men, or young women, or both, of the future. (How will you react in the years ahead if *your* children shave their heads or wear long green hair or sport powdered wigs?)

Some norms, particularly mores, are encoded in law. A *law* is a rule that has been formally enacted by a political authority and is backed by the power of the state. The law usually codifies important norms that already exist, but sometimes political authorities attempt to introduce new norms by enacting appropriate laws. Civil rights legislation in the United States, for example, was aimed at destroying some traditional segregationist norms of race relations and replacing them with new ones. Attempts to introduce new norms in this way are not always successful. As the American attempt to legislate the prohibition of liquor in the 1920s clearly demonstrated, laws that run counter to cultural norms, particularly in the area of personal morality, are often ineffectual and eventually tend to fall into disuse.

Social Control

Every society must have some system of *social control,* a set of means of ensuring that people generally behave in expected and approved ways. Some of this social control over the individual can be exercised by others—either formally through such agencies as the police and government inspectors, or informally through the reactions of other people in the course of everyday life. All norms, whether they are codified in law or not, are supported by *sanctions,* rewards for conformity and punishments for nonconformity. The positive sanctions may range from an approving nod to a ceremony of public acclaim; the negative sanctions may range from mild disapproval to imprisonment or even execution. Only a tiny fraction of social behavior can be policed by formal agencies of control, and most sanctions are applied informally. If you help your neighbors and are polite to them, you will be rewarded with smiles and popularity. If you use "bad" language in the wrong company or offer your left hand rather than your right when someone wants to shake hands with you, you will receive raised eyebrows, glares, stares, or comments designed to make you uncomfortable—and therefore more likely to conform to social expectations in the future.

Most social control, however, does not have to be exercised through the direct influence of other people. We exercise it ourselves, internally. Growing up in society involves the *internalization of norms*—the unconscious process of making conformity to the norms of one's culture a part of one's personality, so that one usually follows social expectations automatically, without question. Like the chiefs on Tahiti and like people all over the world, we think and act in ways that are to a great extent shaped by the society we live in, though we are seldom aware of this fact. For the most part, we behave the way we do because "That's the way it's done."

Values

The norms of a society are ultimately an expression of its *values*—socially shared ideas about what is good, right, and desirable. The difference between values and norms is that values are abstract, general concepts, whereas norms are specific guidelines for people in particular kinds of situations.

The Importance of Values

The values of a society are important because they influence the content of its norms. If a society values education highly, its norms will make provision for mass schooling. If it values a large population, its norms will encourage big families. In principle at least, all norms can be traced to a basic social value. For example, the norms that require a student to be more polite and formal to a professor than to other students express the value society places on respect for authority and learning. The mid-century norms that insisted on short hair for men reflected the high value placed on men's "masculinity" in American culture—a value that was threatened by long hair because it was regarded as "effeminate."

Although all norms express social values, many norms persist long after the conditions that gave rise to them have been forgotten. The folkway that requires us to shake hands, especially when greeting a stranger, seems to have originated long ago in the desire to show that no weapon was concealed in the right hand. The folkway of throwing rice or confetti over a bride and groom may seem rather meaningless, but it actually stems from an ancient practice of showering newlyweds with nuts, fruits, and seeds as symbols of fertility.

American Values

Unlike norms, whose existence can easily be observed in everyday behavior, values are often more difficult to identify. The values of a society have to be inferred from its norms, so any analysis of social values relies heavily on the interpretations of the observer. The United States presents a particular problem, for it has a heterogeneous culture drawn from many different racial, ethnic, religious, and regional traditions, and so lacks the unquestioned consensus on values that smaller, traditional communities tend to display. Sociologists have therefore concentrated on detecting "core" values that appear to be shared by the majority of Americans. The most influential of these attempts is that of Robin Williams (1970), who found fifteen basic value orientations in the United States.

1. *Achievement and success.* The society is highly competitive, and great value is placed on the achievement of power, wealth, and prestige.

2. *Activity and work.* Regular, disciplined work is highly valued for its own sake; those who

do not work are considered lazy and even immoral.

3. *Moral orientation.* Americans tend to be moralists, seeing the world in terms of right and wrong and constantly evaluating the moral behavior of others.

4. *Humanitarianism.* Americans regard themselves as a kindly, charitable people, always ready to come to the aid of the less fortunate or the underdog.

5. *Efficiency and practicality.* Americans believe that problems have solutions, and they are an intensely practical people; the ability to "get things done" is widely admired.

6. *Progress.* Americans look to the future rather than the past, sharing a conviction that things can and should get better; their outlook is fundamentally optimistic.

7. *Material comfort.* Americans value the "good life," which they define in terms of a high standard of living and the possession of material goods.

8. *Equality.* Americans claim to believe in human equality, particularly in equality of opportunity; they generally relate to one another in an informal, egalitarian way.

9. *Freedom.* The freedom of the individual is regarded as one of the most important values in American life; Americans believe devoutly that they are and should remain "free."

10. *External conformity.* Despite their expressed belief in "rugged individualism," Americans tend to be conformist and are suspicious of those who are not.

11. *Science and rationality.* Americans believe in a scientific, rational approach to the world and in the use of applied science to gain mastery over the environment.

12. *Nationalism-patriotism.* Americans are proud of their country and its achievements; the "American way of life" is highly valued and assumed to be the best in the world.

13. *Democracy.* Americans regard their form of government as highly democratic, and believe that every citizen should have the right of political participation.

14. *Individual personality.* To be a responsible, self-respecting individual is very important, and Americans are reluctant to give the group priority over the individual.

15. *Group-superiority themes.* A strong countervalue to that of individual personality is the one

Printed by permission of the Estate of Norman Rockwell.
Copyright © 1943 Estate of Norman Rockwell.

Figure 3.5 *Freedom is one of the most strongly held of all American values. This 1943 painting,* Freedom of Speech, *by the American artist Norman Rockwell, captures an important aspect of this ideal.*

that places a higher value on some racial, ethnic, class, or religious groups than on others.

It is obvious that some of these values are not entirely consistent with one another. Many of them, too, are accepted by some Americans but rejected by others. Also, Williams's list does not exhaust all the possibilities, and other writers have identified rather different values. James Henslin (1975), for example, includes several items on Williams's list but adds others such as education, religiosity, male supremacy, romantic love, monogamy, and heterosexuality. Moreover, values change over time, and some of those listed by Williams may be eroding. Questions have been raised, for example, about the meaning of "progress," and about new problems posed by science and technology, such as pollution of the environment. There is perhaps less insistence now on the value of conformity, and certainly less emphasis on group superiority, than there was a few decades ago (Spates, 1983). But are any new values emerging?

A New Value?

Several observers have suggested that, at least among relatively young, middle-class people, an important new value has been gaining ground in the United States over the past decade or so—*self-fulfillment,* the commitment to achieving the development of one's individual personality, talents, and potential. This preoccupation with the self as "number one" is distinctive and unusual: it would be quite foreign to many cultures, where individualism is less valued—even discouraged—and where obligations to kin, work, and community are assigned more priority.

The evidence for the spread of the new value is still fragmentary. One strong indication is the growth of a diffuse but huge "human potential" movement, containing thousands of groups focused on raising consciousness, improving character, developing interpersonal skills, and "relating" generally. A similar phenomenon is the profusion of "self-help" or "personal development" books that fill whole sections in bookstores and are perennially on the best-seller lists—books with titles like *Power and How to Use It, How to Be Your Own Best Friend, Looking Out for Number 1, Living Alone and Liking It, How to Get What You Really Want, The Art of Selfishness, Self-Hypnosis in Two Days, Eat to Win, Having It All, Rich Is Better, How to Find Another Husband, Psychocybernetics and Self-Fulfillment,* and so on. The number of such titles on the best-seller lists has sharply increased over the past three decades (Mullins and Kopelman, 1984).

Other evidence for the new value comes from public opinion research conducted by Daniel Yankelovich (1981), who found that about 17 percent of Americans are deeply committed to a philosophy of self-fulfillment, even at the expense of the needs of their spouses and children. Yankelovich reports that another 63 percent embrace the value in varying degrees, while only 20 percent adhere to more traditional values. It seems the new value is so pervasive that even the U.S. military has been forced to acknowledge it. Earlier in the century, the army sought recruits with its famous "Uncle Sam wants YOU" poster, which gave the nation's need as sufficient reason for the individual to want to enlist. Even as recently as the mid-1970s, recruitment advertisements asserted that "everybody has an obligation to serve their country in some way." By the 1980s, however, the military was using a quite different tactic, stressing the opportunity for personal growth, not service to the nation, as the principal reason for joining up.

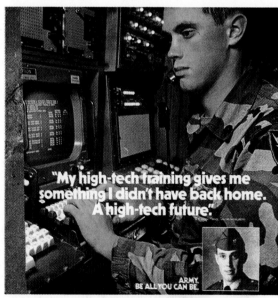

Figure 3.6 *Military recruitment posters reveal a long-term shift from an older value that emphasized duty to country to a newer value that emphasizes self-fulfillment. The famous "Uncle Sam" poster of World War I appealed to the individual's sense of obligation; recent posters appeal to the individual's wish for adventure, job training, or personal development.*

The potential recruit was offered "a whole world of choices," and a TV and radio jingle urged, "Be all that you can be/In the army." The navy, too, declared in its advertisements: "It's not just a job, it's an adventure."

Most social critics have reacted unfavorably to the new value, primarily because it seems to undermine other values, particularly those relating to work and social responsibility. Edwin Schur (1976) regards the human potential movement as substituting self-absorption for commitment to others. Daniel Bell (1976) points out that the capitalist system of the United States demands self-denial and discipline from the individual as a worker, but self-gratification and indulgence from the same person as a consumer. The result is a "cultural contradiction" that will threaten the entire system if self-fulfillment becomes the dominant value. Amitai Etzioni (1982) argues that an "ego-centered mentality" is crippling the family, the economy, and the schools. He claims, for example, that marriage is often less a permanent bonding than a potentially breakable alliance between two self-seeking individuals; that an emphasis on interesting experiences has led to a retreat from hard work; that misguided notions of the child as self-educator have led to unstructured classrooms filled with ill-disciplined pupils who learn very little. And Robert Bellah and his colleagues (1985) see rampant individualism destroying Americans' commitment to community. This new value has already affected several aspects of American social and cultural life, and in later chapters we will trace its impact on such areas as the family, religion, gender roles, and the economy.

Variation Among Cultures

The culture of every society is unique, containing combinations of norms and values that are found nowhere else. Americans eat oysters but not snails. The French eat snails but not locusts. The Zulus eat locusts but not fish. The Jews eat fish but not pork. The Hindus eat pork but not beef. The Russians eat beef but not snakes. The Chinese eat snakes but not people. The Jalé of New Guinea find people delicious. We spend our lives accumulating possessions for our private use; the BaMbuti of the Congo forests spend their lives sharing their goods; the Kwakiutl of the Pacific Northwest periodically gave their possessions away or even destroyed them at great ceremonies. Women in traditional Arab societies must cover the entire body

and even the face; American women may expose their faces but must keep their breasts and the entire pelvic region concealed; women in many parts of Africa may expose their breasts and buttocks but not the genital region; women in Tierra del Fuego may not expose their backs; and the Mundurcú of Brazil proceed about their daily lives stark naked. The range of cultural variation is so immense that probably no specific norm appears in every human society. How can we account for this variation?

The Ecological Context

People create culture as a means of adapting to the environment, and so their cultural practices are necessarily affected by the particular pressures and opportunities of the surroundings in which they live. Many anthropologists study cultural variations through an *ecological approach*—one that analyzes cultural elements in the context of the total environment in which a society exists (for example, Harris, 1977, 1979, 1986; Bennett, 1976; Hardesty, 1977).

The culture of the desert Bedouin Arabs offers an obvious illustration for this approach, because their harsh desert environment sets severe limits on their cultural options. They live in a region so arid that farming is impossible: accordingly, they cannot form permanent settlements or live in houses. Instead, they are nomads, spending a large part of the year wandering from one oasis to another, always moving on when the water dries up. Their shelter necessarily consists of tents, the only form of housing that can be easily transported. They have herds of camels, not pigs or moose, because camels are the only animals living in the region that can withstand long periods without water. Their material possessions are neither many, large, nor heavy, for they must be regularly packed, moved for tens or hundreds of miles, and then unpacked again. The Bedouins have evolved norms about the conservation of water, and unlike North Americans, they are not offended if people do not wash for days or weeks on end. They place a high value on the ability to navigate the almost featureless desert. Their religion does not include gods of the sea or spirits of the jungle; instead, like many pastoral peoples, they conceive of a god who is like a shepherd to his human flock. When they think of paradise, they imagine a place of cool shade, pleasing fountains, and an abundance of fresh fruits—the things that they lack in this world.

Figure 3.7 *Many of the variations among cultures can be explained in ecological terms. The way of life of the Eskimos of the Arctic Circle differs radically from that of these New Guinea villagers, for each people faces very different environmental pressures. The clothing of the Eskimo, for example, reflects the need for protection against the intense cold. In the tropical climate of New Guinea, where elaborate clothing would be a hindrance, more emphasis is given to body ornaments.*

In short, many important elements of their culture can be traced to the influence of the environment in which they live (Vidal, 1976).

The relationship of other cultural practices to the total environment is not always as obvious, but the ecological approach has been applied to several otherwise puzzling practices. Marvin Harris (1974, 1986), for example, uses it to explain a striking cultural feature of India: the apparently irrational veneration Indians have for cows. Although only one Indian in fifty has an adequate diet, the Hindu religion has a taboo against the slaughter of cows. As a result, over 100 million cows roam freely through the countryside and cities of India, snarling traffic and defecating in public places. Western observers (and some Indians in the more industrialized parts of the country) are apt to regard most of these cows as "useless." They are scrawny animals, yielding little milk and apparently contributing nothing of value to Indian social or economic life.

Harris points out, however, that the cows are vital to the Indian economy. A large part of the population lives on small farms that require at least one pair of oxen for plowing. These farm families live on the brink of starvation and cannot afford tractors. They must use oxen, and their oxen can be produced only by cows. Widespread cow slaughter would worsen the already critical shortage of draft animals, making the existing farms too unproductive and driving tens of millions of people into the severely crowded cities. Moreover, the cows provide India annually with some 700 million tons of manure. About half is used as fertilizer by farmers who could not possibly afford chemical substitutes. The remainder serves as cooking fuel, a vital resource in a country that has little oil or coal and an acute shortage of wood. And when the cows finally die, they are eaten, not by Hindus, but by outcastes who are not bound by the Hindu religion and who are generally even poorer and hungrier than the rest of the population. The hides of the animals are then used in India's huge leatherworking industry. The cows themselves do not compete with human beings for food. Unlike American cattle, which are often fed grain, they scavenge what they can from roadsides and other unproductive land. In short, the sacred cow is an important element in the entire Indian ecology. Harris observes that the Indians might rather eat their cows than starve, but they would surely starve if they did eat them.

Different societies, of course, may adopt different solutions to similar ecological problems. Many societies, for instance, face the problem that their

Figure 3.8 *Cows are highly valued in India—so much so that they roam the streets unmolested, even though many Indians are poorly nourished. This veneration of the cow seems inexplicable—yet it is a fundamental assumption of sociology that all human behavior, no matter how puzzling it may seem at first, can be rationally explained.*

environment does not offer enough resources to maintain a growing population. The Eskimos solved the problem by deliberately leaving many aged, unproductive people out in the snow to die. The Yanamamö of Brazil control their population by killing or deliberately starving female infants and by practicing incessant and bloody fighting among males. The Keraki of New Guinea limit population increase by requiring males to engage in exclusively homosexual relations for several years after puberty. The Chinese restrict population growth by penalizing parents of large families, by encouraging abortion, and by using such cultural artifacts as contraceptives. But whatever their specific solutions to problems posed by the ecological context, all cultures must ultimately adapt to the constraints of their environment—a fact that we are often inclined to overlook in the more industrialized nations of the world. As we shall see later in this book, however, we may have to adapt some of our own cultural practices in the future in order to deal with problems of overpopulation, resource depletion, and the poisoning of the environment.

Culture: A Functionalist View

The environment provides the general context in which culture develops. One way of analyzing specific components of culture more closely is to look for the *functions* they perform, or effects they have, in maintaining the social order as a whole. Functionalist theorists regard society and culture as a system of interdependent parts. To explain a par-

ticular cultural trait, therefore, one has to establish its functions in making the entire system "work." The functionalist approach has long been popular in studies of other cultures (for example, Radcliffe-Brown, 1935, 1952; Malinowski, 1926) and has been influential in American sociology during much of this century (for example, Parsons, 1951; Merton, 1968).

An important value in traditional Eskimo society was that of hospitality to travelers, including complete strangers. A host was obliged to do everything possible to make travelers comfortable, even if he found them personally offensive. (There was even a norm requiring a host to offer his wife to a male guest for the night.) As strange as this culture trait of obligatory hospitality might seem to us, it was highly functional in Eskimo culture. Travel through snows and arctic blizzards would be utterly impossible unless the traveler could rely on the certainty of food, warmth, and rest at the next settlement, and the host in turn could expect the same hospitality when he traveled. Without this norm, communication and trade among various groups might have been too hazardous to undertake. A similar norm does not exist in modern societies, where it would make no sense. These societies have created other cultural arrangements, such as restaurants and motels, to serve the same function.

The Cheyenne Indians periodically gathered for a sun-dance ceremony. Why? The activity brought no obvious rewards and seemed only to distract the various bands from the more mundane activities of making a living in their own areas. A functionalist analysis again suggests the reason.

Figure 3.9 *Every four years, a significant public ritual occurs in the United States, the presidential inauguration. It would be much easier for the newly elected president to get straight to work without all the fuss and expense that this event involves—so why bother with the ceremony? A functionalist analysis suggests an answer. Each inauguration celebrates the people's right to choose their leader every four years and shows that leader swearing loyalty to the Constitution. The ritual thus functions to provide a regular, public affirmation of the democratic way of life, a vital element in American culture. Functionalists frequently analyze rituals and other cultural phenomena in terms of their (recognized or unrecognized) social effects.*

The sun dance gave the entire tribe an opportunity to gather together for a common purpose, to reestablish social bonds, and to confirm their sense that they were not simply a scattering of isolated bands but rather a tribe united by similar cultural practices. In the same way, an American ritual such as Thanksgiving can be explained in terms of its function in drawing families together to reaffirm faith in the American way of life.

By showing that certain cultural elements serve to meet specific needs, functionalist theory can help us to understand why a particular trait may be present in one society but not in others. The approach sometimes has the disadvantage, however, of focusing on how things "fit together" at a particular moment in cultural history and thus neglecting cultural change. It must be remembered that changes—the introduction of snowmobiles to the Eskimo or Christianity to the Cheyenne, for example—may throw other parts of the cultural system into some disorder, creating new problems that require fresh cultural solutions.

Culture: A Conflict View

Another way to analyze some components of culture is to see them as the product of social tension. Conflict theorists regard society and culture as being in a constant state of change, much of it caused by tension and competition among different groups. In any society, they argue, various groups will create cultural arrangements that serve their own interests, and the strongest groups may be able to impose their own cultural preferences on the society as a whole. Cultural change occurs as different groups, each with its own values and norms, gain or lose power. To explain aspects of culture—or to explain the direction of cultural change—it may therefore be useful to ask, Who benefits? This approach has long been the dominant one in European sociology, and has been popular in American sociology over the past three decades (for example, Mills, 1956; Collins, 1974).

A good illustration for the conflict approach is the political culture of the Republic of South Africa, where a small white minority enforces racial segregation and inequality on a large nonwhite majority. The country has a total population of almost 33 million, classified at birth into one of four groups: whites (15 percent); Asians (3 percent); "coloreds," or people of mixed race (9 percent); and blacks (73 percent). There are over 300 racial laws that require members of each group to live in their own areas and to use separate facilities such as hospitals, schools, and colleges. Asians and coloreds have limited political rights, but the blacks have no vote or direct representation in the government, even though they constitute nearly three-quarters of the population.

Instead of giving blacks democratic political

rights, South Africa has created ten black reservations, or "homelands." These territories, which consist of a mostly barren 13 percent of the country's area, are gradually being granted "independence." In theory, blacks are expected to become citizens of the "homelands" and to exercise political rights there—even though they mostly live and work in South Africa itself. Already, four "homelands" have been granted independence, enabling the government to deprive 5 million blacks of some citizenship rights on the grounds that they are now foreigners. None of these independent states has been recognized by the rest of the world, and it is fairly easy to see why. Consider KwaNdebele, which will be the next "homeland" to achieve independence. This "country" consists of 380 square miles of prairie, with a capital of tin huts and enough jobs for 2 percent of its population. It has no resident doctor and only one paved road, which is used primarily to transport its citizens back to their jobs in South Africa.

How can we make sense of the cultural phenomenon of South Africa's political system? Conflict theorists suggest that it arises from competition among racially defined groups for control of South Africa's wealth and other resources. Most of those resources are presently enjoyed by the whites (see Figure 3.10). If we ask who benefits from this disparity, the answer, obviously, is the ruling minority. To conflict theorists, the elaborate but meaningless political "rights" granted to the other groups are simply a way to divide the majority, deflect their power, and make it easier to control them. Moreover, a conflict analysis also predicts that tension will produce social and cultural change in South Africa in the future. Since 1985, in fact, riots, shootings, and interracial disturbances have become so commonplace that a revolution may already be under way.

Conflict theory cannot explain all aspects of culture: it does not help us understand, for example, why the Eskimo sometimes built igloos or why

Figure 3.10 *As this chart shows, South Africa's resources are unequally distributed among the ruling white minority and the large black majority. A conflict analysis suggests that many aspects of South African culture, such as racial segregation and lack of democratic rights, are the outcome of a competition for control of these resources. Conflict theorists argue that many other cultural phenomena reflect underlying social tensions.*

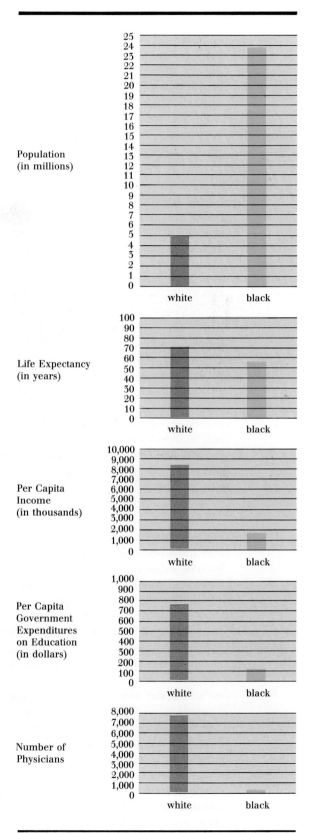

SOUTH AFRICA: RACIAL CONTRASTS

SOURCE: *Time*, August 25, 1985, p. 29.

Americans are so fond of hamburgers. But wherever different groups are in competition—whether they are white settlers and Indians on the American frontier in the nineteenth century, or different industries lobbying Congress for preferential treatment today—the cultural outcomes can be analyzed in terms of the shifting power relationships of the contenders.

Cultural Universals

In the midst of this variety, are there any **cultural universals**—that is, practices found in every culture? The answer is that there are a fairly large number of general cultural universals, but there do not seem to be any specific ones. Every culture, for example, has norms prohibiting murder, but different cultures have different ideas about which homicides constitute murder and which do not. We would consider human sacrifice murder, but the Aztecs did not. Vietnamese peasants no doubt considered the bombing of their communities by American forces as murder, but many Americans did not. We would consider the slaughter of an inoffensive stranger as murder, but there are still some small, isolated societies in which the norms permit any outsider to be killed on the spot, as a potential threat to the group.

Cultural universals derive from the common problems the natural and social environments pose for our species. The weather is often too hot or too cold for comfort, so clothing and housing must be made to adapt us to the climate. Children need care and attention, and some cultural provision must be made for this requirement. People become sick, and attempts must be made to cure them. Individuals must be distinguished from one another, and so they are given names. Life is often hard and death awaits us all, and people everywhere maintain religious beliefs to explain the human predicament.

The anthropologist George Murdock (1945) compiled a lengthy list of cultural universals, including the following: athletic sports, bodily adornment, cooking, cooperative labor, courtship, dancing, dream interpretation, family, feasting, folklore, food taboos, funeral ceremonies, games, gift-giving, incest taboos, laws, medicine, music, myths, numerals, personal names, property rights, religion, sexual restrictions, toilet training, toolmaking, and weather-making efforts. But these are only general traits; their specific content varies from one culture to another.

Ethnocentrism

Cultures may vary, but most human beings spend their entire lives within the culture in which they were born. Knowing little about other ways of life, they see their own norms and values as inevitable rather than optional. As Ralph Linton (1936) observed:

> It has been said that the last thing which a dweller in the deep sea would discover would be water. He would become conscious of its existence only if some accident brought him to the surface and introduced him to air. . . . The ability to see the culture of one's own society as a whole . . . calls for a degree of objectivity which is rarely if ever achieved.

For this reason, people in every society have some measure of **ethnocentrism**—the tendency to judge other cultures by the standards of one's own. People everywhere are apt to take it for granted that their morality, their marriage forms, their clothing styles, or their conceptions of beauty are right, proper, and the best of all possible choices. Here are some examples of ethnocentric thinking. Our women put rings through their ears and cosmetics on their faces because it enhances their beauty; their women put bones through their noses and scars on their faces because, in their pitiful ignorance, they don't realize how ugly it makes them. We won't eat cats or worms because that would be cruel or disgusting; they won't eat beef or drink milk because of some silly food taboo. We cover our private parts because we are decorous and civilized; they walk around naked because they are ignorant and shameless. Our brave troops achieve glorious victories over them; their fanatical hordes perpetrate bloody massacres on us. Our religion is divinely inspired truth; theirs is heathen superstition.

Ethnocentrism is particularly strong in isolated, traditional societies that have had little contact with other cultures. But even in the modern world, where citizens have such advantages as formal education, mass communication, and international travel, such attitudes still prevail. As Linton observes, one reason for the persistence of ethnocentrism is that it is almost impossible to view one's own culture objectively; but another reason is that ethnocentrism can be functional to a society. It provides faith and confidence in one's own tradition, discourages penetration by outsiders, and thus ensures the solidarity and unity of the group. But under some conditions ethnocentrism can have many undesirable effects. It can encourage racism, it can cause hostility and conflict be-

Figure 3.11 *The norms and values of a culture cannot be arbitrarily judged by those of another culture. From the perspective of American culture, the traditional Middle Eastern practice of hiding the entire female body from view seems silly; from the perspective of these Arab women, the American practice of exposing so much of the female body would be shameful and obscene. Neither viewpoint* *is objectively "right," for each practice can be fully understood only in its own cultural context. In fact, before we smile too quickly at how easily other people are shocked by matters of public attire, we might consider the reaction that would be likely to be provoked if the American women wore their bikinis to a church, a corporate office, or a college lecture hall.*

tween groups, and it can make a people unwilling to see the need for changes in their own culture.

Ethnocentrism also poses a severe problem for social scientists analyzing other cultures, because they may bring to the task unconscious and often unfounded assumptions about other people and their practices. Even trained observers experience "culture shock" when confronted with cultures radically unlike their own. Napoleon Chagnon, an anthropologist who studied the Yanamamö of Brazil, was aghast when he first met his subjects. They stank to him (though not, of course, to themselves), the heads of the men were covered with scars from their incessant fighting, and they were under the influence of a local psychedelic drug—one of

whose effects was to produce thick strings of green mucus that seemed to hang constantly from their noses. Chagnon (1967) recalls:

> I am not ashamed to admit . . . that had there been a diplomatic way out, I would have ended my field-work there and then. I did not look forward to the next day when I would be left alone with the Indians: I did not speak a word of their language, and they were decidedly different from what I had imagined them to be. The whole situation was depressing, and I wondered why I had ever decided to switch from civil engineering to anthropology in the first place.

Yet Chagnon was eventually able, after living among the Yanamamö for many months, to adjust to their culture and to develop a sympathetic understanding of their way of life.

Cultural Relativism

The ability to fully understand another culture depends largely on one's willingness to adopt the position of *cultural relativism,* the recognition that one culture cannot be arbitrarily judged by the standards of another. We are quick to complain when foreign critics—the Russians, for example—judge us in terms of their own values, for we feel that such a judgment distorts the reality of our culture and society. We have to be equally on guard against arbitrarily using our own standards to judge other cultures.

It is probably never possible to be entirely free of bias in favor of the cultural world we know. Opinion polls consistently show, for example, that Americans in every state of the Union are overwhelmingly convinced that their state is the very best place in the world to live—even though most of them have visited only a few other states, let alone other countries! Thus, no matter how hard we try, the sneaking feeling is likely to persist that our standards *are* better. Yet we must recognize that judgments about good and bad, moral and immoral, depend very much on who is doing the judging; there is no universally accepted standard to appeal to. An inability to adopt the position of cultural relativism is simply another example of ethnocentrism, and the problem with ethnocentrism is that it works both ways. We are shocked at the traditional Eskimo practice of leaving the aged to perish in the snow, or the Yanamamö practice of killing unwanted female children; but the Japanese are appalled at our practice of leaving aged parents to die in nursing homes, and the San ("Bushmen") of the Kalahari could not begin to comprehend how we can permit poverty to exist in our country in the midst of so much wealth.

Cultural relativism does *not* mean moral relativism—the position that one morality is as good as another. That view could quickly lead us to an "anything goes" position, in which wife-beating, scalping, cannibalism, and gas chambers are all equally acceptable. No responsible social scientist, for example, could fail to condemn the mass murders perpetrated by the Nazis. What cultural relativism does mean is that the practices of another society can be fully understood only in terms of its own norms and values. Thus, if we inquire why the Eskimo sometimes left old people to die in the cold, we find that they did so only in times when dwindling food supplies threatened the group with starvation. Under such conditions, those most likely to die were the weakest—the very young and the very old. The Eskimo chose to sacrifice the old, who represented a growing burden, in favor of the young, who represented the group's future. The aged went to their deaths willingly, for they had been taught since childhood that this was a sacrifice they might one day have to make—just as, years before, others might have made the same sacrifice for them. Once we have learned all this, we can better *understand* the Eskimo practice, even though we still may not *approve* of it. For the practical purposes of studying human behavior it is vital that we try, as far as possible, to remove the blinders of our own culture when we are looking at another. In the process, we may lose a certain self-righteousness about our own assumptions, and may even learn something more about our own culture, too.

Variation Within Cultures

There is variation not only among different cultures but also within any specific culture. This variation can take many forms, but usually reflects differences in the norms and values of different groups in the population. As a general rule, there is less variation in traditional, preindustrial societies than in modern, industrialized ones. In traditional societies, which tend to be smaller, people live similar lives and share similar values, and cultural change takes place relatively slowly. Modern societies tend to be larger, to contain more diverse populations, and to experience more rapid and uneven cultural change.

No matter how much diversity there is within a culture, however, no culture is simply a random collection of elements. There has to be some degree of *cultural integration*—the tendency for norms, values, beliefs, practices, and other characteristics to complement one another. The reason is that a culture must "fit together" to a considerable extent if it is to survive at all. Thus, rapid and massive cultural change—occurring, for example, when one society invades and subjugates another—can jeopardize a culture's very existence. This was the fate of the culture of the Plains Indians, which was threatened with disintegration by white settlers' slaughter of the buffalo (see Figure 3.12).

Real Culture and Ideal Culture

One common source of variation within a culture is the discrepancy that sometimes exists between *ideal culture*—the norms and values a society

Figure 3.12 *The culture of some of the Plains Indian tribes centered on the buffalo. Their religion emphasized the buffalo hunt, and the prestige of individual men was linked to their skills and courage as hunters. The carcass of the buffalo provided most of the items in the Indians' material culture—hides, tendons, bones, and membranes were all put to use for various purposes, including clothing and shelter. The Indians' nomadic way of life was based on the need to follow the migrations of the animals on which they depended for a living. When white settlers used their superior technology to systematically slaughter the buffalo, the traditional culture of the Plains Indians disintegrated, and their existing societies collapsed. When the Indians were settled on reservations and given cattle to raise, they sometimes turned the animals loose and hunted them like buffalo: there was nothing in their culture that prepared them to tend and milk cows.*

adheres to in principle—and **real culture**—the norms and values a society adheres to in practice. Americans, for example, claim to believe in the value of human equality, yet the United States contains people who are millionaires and people who are impoverished. Similarly, Americans are especially proud of their democratic rights, yet almost half the adults cannot be bothered to go to the polls in presidential elections. Americans also have a traditional norm that sex should take place only in the context of marriage, but the statistics on premarital and extramarital intercourse show that this norm is violated by the great majority of Americans at one time or another.

A society is often able to overlook the contradictions between its real and ideal culture. As devout Buddhists, fishermen in Burma are forbidden to kill anything, including fish. Yet they must fish to live. How do they overcome the contradiction? What happens is that the fish are first caught and then "are merely put on the bank to dry after their long soaking in the river, and if they are foolish or ill-judged enough to die while undergoing the process, it is their own fault" (Lowie, 1940). Sometimes, however, the discrepancy between real culture and ideal culture creates serious social problems. For example, strain in the United States between the value of equality and the reality of

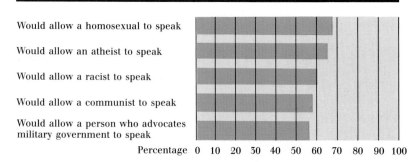

AMERICAN ATTITUDES TOWARD FREEDOM OF SPEECH

Would allow a homosexual to speak

Would allow an atheist to speak

Would allow a racist to speak

Would allow a communist to speak

Would allow a person who advocates military government to speak

Percentage   0 10 20 30 40 50 60 70 80 90 100

Figure 3.13 *Although freedom of speech is an important American ideal, opinion polls show that, in reality, Americans are sometimes reluctant to allow those who disagree with them to speak in the community. Such gaps between ideal and real culture are common, particularly in large, hetero-geneous societies.*

SOURCE: *Public Opinion,* October/November 1982, p. 35; October/November 1984, p. 28.

slavery and then continuing racial discrimination led to a civil war and decades of tension before the society was brought into a condition of greater, but by no means complete, cultural integration. Other practices that contradict the norms and values in ideal culture, such as crime and drug abuse, also pose severe problems—a topic we will discuss in detail in Chapter 8 ("Deviance").

High Culture and Popular Culture

Cultural variation and even strain also arise from the differing cultural tastes of a society's elite and its masses. Some aspects of a society's way of life are considered **high culture**—creations of a relatively profound and serious nature that primarily appeal to, and are supported by, a fairly small and elite group. Examples of high culture are classical music, fine art, poetry, formal banquets, and live theater. In contrast, other aspects of a society's way of life comprise the general category of **popular culture**—creations of a relatively less serious and less intellectually demanding nature that appeal primarily to, and are supported by, a large audience of typical members of the society. Examples of popular culture are "top forty" recordings, tabloid newspapers, TV soap operas, family outings at McDonald's, and ball games.

Many people participate to some extent in both high and popular culture, but high culture draws most of its support from the wealthier and better-educated levels of society. Because this elite has so much wealth and influence, its tastes, rather than those of the majority, become the standard for esthetic judgments. Thus, an artist who wins the favor of the elite can command high prices and museum showings, even if his or her work is ridi-

culed as utter rubbish in the popular culture ("My five-year-old could draw better than that"). The differing tastes represented by high and popular culture often lead to strain, particularly in the media, which are among the most important means of disseminating culture in modern society. Television programmers, for example, are constantly subject to contrary pressures—from the supporters of high culture, anxious that the public be exposed to what it supposedly *ought* to like (drama, classical music, current affairs), and from the supporters of popular culture, anxious to increase viewer ratings by giving the larger public what it actually *does* like ("Dynasty," rock video, game shows).

Subcultures and Countercultures

Another source of variation and often strain within a culture arises from the existence of groups that do not participate fully in the dominant culture of the society. These groups are especially common in large, heterogeneous industrialized societies, in which there are many cultural differences among members of different regional, religious, occupational, and other communities.

Subcultures

A **subculture** is a group that shares in the overall culture of the society but also has its own distinctive values, norms, and lifestyle. In North America, for example, there are subcultures of the young, of the rich and the poor, of different racial and ethnic groups, and of different regions. Smaller subcultures exist in the military, in prisons, on college campuses, among drug addicts, or among streetcorner gangs. People in each of these subcultures tend to be ethnocentric in relation to other subcultures, for membership in a subculture colors one's view of reality. A member of a wealthy subculture of Wall Street stockbrokers doubtless has a different perspective on American social reality than someone from, say, a subculture of Hell's Angels. If the differences between subcultures are sufficiently great, the results may be social tension and conflict.

It is important that sociologists—and sociology students, also—adopt a position of cultural relativism toward subcultures as well as toward other cultures. It is all too easy for sociologists—most of whom are white and middle class—to adopt ethnocentric attitudes toward different subcultures, arbitrarily judging other groups by the standards of the dominant culture. The practices of any subculture can be fully understood only by reference to its own norms and values.

Countercultures

A *counterculture* is a subculture whose values, norms, and lifestyle are fundamentally at odds with the dominant culture. Such a group consciously rejects some of the most important norms of the wider society, and is usually proud of it. In North America, the Hare Krishna movement is one such counterculture: in religion, dress, values, behavior, and general lifestyle, its members challenge basic assumptions of the surrounding society. The movement has few adherents, however,

and so has little cultural impact. In contrast, the youth movement of the 1960s attracted millions of participants and supporters. It challenged a whole range of treasured American norms and values, including those centered on conformity, drug use, dress, hard work, materialism, wartime patriotism, white superiority, and sexual restrictiveness (Roszak, 1969; Wuthnow, 1976; Yinger, 1982). A large counterculture inevitably generates strain in society, and indeed the 1960s were a time of great social turmoil. In this particular case, a measure of cultural integration was eventually achieved—partly because some countercultural norms and values came to be incorporated into the mainstream culture, partly because others were gradually abandoned by the young people of the period.

Language

One of the most important of all human characteristics is our capacity to communicate with one another through language. Although apes can be taught to construct "sentences" by using hand signs or by manipulating physical objects (Mounin, 1976; Hill, 1978; Premack and Premack, 1983), only human beings have spoken language. Language is a form of communication that differs radically from the kinds used by other species. Other animals can communicate with sounds, gestures, touch, and smell, but the meanings of these signals are fixed, and their use is limited to the immediate

Figure 3.14 *The youthful counterculture of the 1960s was a significant, though relatively short-lived, phenomenon. With an ethic of "Tune in, turn on, drop out," its members challenged many of the basic attitudes and values of the mainstream culture of the time.*

situation. With the exception of the artificial "languages" that gorillas and chimpanzees have been taught to use, the signals in animal communication are genetically predetermined responses to given conditions. These signals can be used to warn of danger, to indicate the presence of food, to claim territory, or to express fear, contentment, aggression, and sexual arousal—but little else. They cannot be combined in new ways to produce different or more complex information. A monkey can signal "food!" but not "bananas, tomorrow!"

Language, on the other hand, does not consist of fixed signals: it consists of learned symbols. A *symbol* is anything that can meaningfully represent something else. Gestures, facial expressions, drawings, and numbers are all symbols, but the most useful and flexible symbols are spoken or written words. Words are symbols for objects and concepts, and every human language consists of hundreds of thousands of words whose meaning is socially agreed upon. These words can be combined according to grammatical rules to express any idea of which the human mind is capable.

The Importance of Language

Language is the keystone of culture. Without it, culture could not exist. Culture, by definition, is shared, and without the medium of the spoken word, complex patterns of thought, emotion, knowledge, and belief could not be passed from individual to individual or generation to generation. When an animal dies, everything it has learned from experience perishes with it. But language gives human beings a history—access to the social experience and accumulated knowledge of the generations that have gone before.

Equally important, language enables us to give meaning to the world. Events in themselves have no meaning; we impose meaning on them by interpreting the evidence of our senses. Without language, all but the most rudimentary forms of thought are impossible. With language, we can apply reason to the world. We can think logically from premises to conclusions: we can categorize; we can order our experience; we can contemplate the past and the future, the abstract and the hypothetical; we can formulate and utter ideas that are entirely new. Nearly all that we learn in human culture is learned through language in social interaction with others. It is through language that we become cultured and thus fully human.

Linguistic Relativity

Shortly after World War II, George Orwell published his futuristic novel *1984,* which depicted a totalitarian dictatorship where every aspect of social behavior was strictly controlled. The rulers of the state had even deliberately constructed a new language, Newspeak, whose vocabulary and grammar made it impossible for people to think certain thoughts:

> The word *free* still existed in Newspeak, but it could only be used in such statements as "This dog is free from lice" or "This field is free from weeds." It could not be used in the old sense of "politically free," or "intellectually free," since political and intellectual freedom no longer existed as concepts, and were therefore of necessity nameless.... Countless other words such as *honor, justice, morality, internationalism, democracy, science,* and *religion* had simply ceased to exist. A few blanket words covered them, and, in covering them, abolished them. All words grouping themselves around the concepts of liberty and equality, for instance, were contained in the single word *crimethink,* while all words grouping themselves around the concepts of objectivity and rationalism were contained in the single word *oldthink.* [Orwell, 1949]

Is it possible for the language we speak to structure our reality in this way? For centuries people assumed that all languages reflect reality in the same basic way and that words and concepts can be freely and accurately translated from one language to another. But in the course of this century some social scientists have raised the intriguing possibility that this assumption is unfounded. Studies of many of the thousands of languages in the world have revealed that they often interpret the same phenomenon quite differently, and several writers have suggested that languages do not so much mirror reality as structure it.

The Linguistic-Relativity Hypothesis

The *linguistic-relativity hypothesis* holds that speakers of a particular language must necessarily interpret the world through the unique vocabulary and grammar their language supplies. This hypothesis was strongly propounded by two American linguists, Edward Sapir and his student Benjamin Whorf, and is sometimes known as the Sapir-Whorf hypothesis. Sapir (1929) argued forcefully that "the worlds in which different societies live are distinct worlds, not merely the same world with different labels attached."

In what ways do languages "slice up" and organize the world differently? The most common differences are in vocabulary: some languages have words for objects and concepts for which other languages have no words at all. The Aztecs, for example, had only one word for snow, frost, ice, and cold, and presumably tended to see these as essentially the same phenomenon. We have only one word for snow; the Eskimo have no general word for snow at all, but have over twenty words for different kinds of snow—snow on the ground, snow falling, snow drifting, and so on. Their language forces them to perceive these distinctions, while our language predisposes us to ignore them. The Koya of South India do not distinguish among snow, fog, and dew, but their language forces them to make distinctions among seven types of bamboo—distinctions that are important to them but that we would be unlikely to notice.

Even the color spectrum is dissected in different ways by different languages. The human eye can make between 7 million and 10 million different color discriminations, but all languages recognize only a handful of different colors. Most European languages recognize black, white, and at least six basic colors—red, orange, yellow, green, blue, and purple. Many languages, however, recognize only two colors: the Jalé of New Guinea, for example, divide the spectrum into the colors *hui* and *ziza*, representing the warm and cold colors of the spectrum, respectively. Other cultures, such as the Arawak of Surinam, the Toda of India, and the Baganda of Uganda, recognize only three colors (Berlin and Kay, 1969). All these peoples see the same color spectrum, but they divide it up in their own ways.

Other distinctions exist in the grammatical usages of different languages. The language of the Navajo Indians contains no real equivalent of our active verbs; in Navajo thought, people do not so much act on the world as participate passively in actions that are taking place. This linguistic feature is perhaps related to the extremely passive nature of the Navajo people. Even more startling to us is the language of the Hopi Indians, which does not recognize the categories of time and space that we do. The Hopi language lacks the equivalent of past, present, and future tenses, and organizes the universe instead into categories of "manifest" (everything that is or has been accessible to the physical senses) and "manifesting" (everything that is not physically accessible to the senses). If this concept is difficult to understand, it is because our language is poorly equipped to express it, just

as the Hopi language has difficulty expressing our concepts of time and space.

Evaluation

The linguistic-relativity hypothesis does not imply that speakers of different languages are *incapable* of expressing the same ideas or seeing the world in the same way. What the hypothesis does suggest is that the language we speak *predisposes* us to make particular interpretations of reality. We need only consider the likely attitudes of a white child who is taught to call blacks "niggers" or of a black child who is taught to call whites "honkies" to see the truth of this statement. A different kind of example is the widespread use of euphemism and jargon to conceal rather than to reveal meaning. Advertisements tell of a car that is "affordable" and "previously owned," meaning expensive and used. Politicians speak of the need for "revenue enhancement," meaning a tax increase. Hospitals record a "negative patient-care outcome," meaning that the patient died. Corporations report a "negative contribution to profits," which means a loss. Military statements tell of "air support," which is bombing, and "pacification," which is making war. We have learned of an "energetic disassembly and rapid oxidation" at a nuclear power plant, which turned out to be an explosion and a fire. And the event in which hundreds of millions of living human beings might be annihilated is called a "nuclear exchange"—as if it involved no more than some sort of technological swap. All these linguistic usages are calculated to, and do, predispose us to see things in a less concerned way. Language and culture, then, are in constant interaction: culture influences the structure and use of language, and language can influence cultural interpretations of reality.

The Arts

Among the most striking of human endeavors are the *arts*—unique, skilled, and creative cultural products intended to inspire or entertain. Depending on the culture or subculture in which they are produced, the arts can take innumerable forms, ranging from jazz and tribal dance to vampire movies or disco light shows. Some art is high culture—classical music, ballet, sculpture, "masterpiece" paintings, and so on. Other art is part of

Figure 3.15 *The arts take a variety of forms, sometimes as popular culture and sometimes as high culture. All artistic production, however, is influenced by its social context, for that context makes certain art forms possible and influences the public reaction to them.*

popular culture—country music, breakdancing, romance paperbacks, TV "sitcoms," and the like.

The fundamental insight of the sociology of art is this: artistic expression tends to reflect the social and cultural concerns of the society in which it is produced. Religious societies produce predominantly religious art; traditionalist societies produce mainly traditional art; conformist societies produce mostly conformist art; diverse societies produce diverse art. Over the centuries, art has flourished best in places that offered the favorable conditions of peace, prosperity, and above all, intellectual freedom: Athens, Rome, Florence, Venice, Amsterdam, London, Paris, and New York. In contrast, societies that try to repress or control the artist—like Nazi Germany or the Soviet Union—produce work that is generally uncreative and therefore dreary and banal. Even so, there are always some artists in every society who work in reaction to, rather than in conformity with, the prevailing norms. Novels by Soviet dissidents (such as *Dr. Zhivago* or *The Gulag Archipelago*) have been virtually the only Soviet art to win international approval in recent decades.

The creation of art thus requires much more than a talented individual. Artistic production is a social process, for the form that art takes, and the amount of acceptance it wins, are deeply influenced by the surrounding cultural environment. What artists can actually *do,* for example, depends on the technology available to them: someone using clay pigment, a chisel, or a flute has different options from someone working with computer graphics, a laser, or a synthesizer. Additionally, artistic success depends not only on what the artist produces, but also on what the audience of the time and place in question is willing to accept. For example, Hollywood westerns once depicted sturdy white settlers being inexplicably attacked by cruel and savage Indians; but Americans are now more sensitive to the Indians' viewpoint, and such westerns are no longer made. Instead, movie makers have transposed the basic themes of the western—frontier exploration, gun-toting heroism, rescues of innocent victims, battles with alien hordes—to a realm of greater contemporary interest, outer space. Captain Kirk and Luke Skywalker have replaced Roy Rogers and the Lone Ranger—a transformation aided by a new cinematographic technology of "special effects" that lends realism to extraterrestrial locales and characters, but which would be useless for traditional westerns.

The social process of artistic production can be illustrated by two examples: rock music and the abstract painting known as "modern art."

Rock Music

Rock music provides a good illustration of the interplay of social, cultural, and technological factors in the creation and acceptance of art. This form of popular culture emerged in a particular context— the United States and Britain in the prosperous years of the late 1950s. This was the era when the word "teenager" came into common usage for the first time, reflecting the emergence of a vast and unprecedented market of young people with money to spend on their own cultural interests. The new art form arose in the United States, where it drew heavily on the existing tradition of popular music (especially rhythm and blues) and then spread quickly to Britain, a culturally akin society. (Even today, rock remains primarily an American and a British art form, and rock artists of other nationalities still tend to write lyrics in English, the only language that now seems "right" for rock.) The growth and spread of rock music, too, was greatly influenced by available technologies: the amplified guitar, FM radio, techniques for creating and recording synthetic and layered sounds, and, more recently, cable TV and rock video. The success of rock, too, has always been a social process involving not just musicians but also talent scouts, producers, engineers, promoters, publicists, disk jockeys, agents, journalists, corporate personnel, retailers, managers, roadies, and, of course, the mass audience.

The cultural appeal of rock depends not only on its intrinsic musical qualities but also on an energy that derives from rock's aura of rebellion. Yet rock always risks becoming stale—partly because its audience and their tastes constantly change, partly because big business attempts to package and market the music (and even the musicians) as widely as possible, even if vitality is lost in the process. To maintain excitement, therefore, rock artists have always replenished the music by using it to challenge social conventions. Sometimes they have done this through their lyrics, which spread messages (often inaudible or incomprehensible to an older generation) about sex, drugs, politics, materialism, or whatever issues are of current concern to the young. Sometimes the artists create excitement through behavior that is deliberately calculated to outrage the establishment. The short history of rock is thus filled with such phenomena as Elvis Presley's pelvis; the Rolling Stones' surly arrogance; the Beatles' long hair; Jimi Hendrix's drug lyrics; Janis Joplin's raucous lifestyle; Alice Cooper's live python; Kiss's elaborate makeup; the Sex Pistols' profanities; Donna

Figure 3.16 *Rock music has always been most successful when it has an aura of innovation and even rebellion. The Rolling Stones's unusually long career has depended in large measure on their continuing ability to appear provocative.*

Summer's erotic innuendos; Boy George's ambiguous gender; Madonna's brash public persona. In time, of course, all their art may eventually seem tame, to be relegated to the status of "golden oldies." But the irreverent, iconoclastic nature of rock tells us why this music, despite its huge international popularity, is created and performed primarily in the Western democracies. Rock flourishes only in an atmosphere that can tolerate diversity of opinions and lifestyles. Authoritarian governments, ranging from communist regimes to right-wing dictatorships, loathe rock, which they uniformly brand as immoral and depraved—for they fear that it will introduce their young to subversive cultural influences. Thus, like any art form, rock's emergence, development, and spread can be fully understood only in its social context.

Figure 3.17 *The subject matter of art always reflects the characteristics and concerns of the society in which it is produced, and the most highly prized art is always that which the affluent are willing to support. It is hardly surprising that Raphael, working in the early sixteenth century, produced this* Madonna and Child with the Infant Baptist, *for religion provided the basic theme of the art of his day. Conversely, the untitled work by the modern American artist Cy Twombly reflects the high value currently placed on innovative abstract works in a society that emphasizes change, individualism, and diversity. At present, religious art is generally out of favor, while some of Twombly's works have sold for over a quarter million dollars. In time, of course, cultural tastes may change again, and the relative evaluation of these and other paintings may change as well.*

Modern Art

If, five centuries ago, Michelangelo had completely covered his surfaces with black paint and declared them art, his contemporaries would surely have considered him a lunatic; but when the American artist Frank Stella painted all-black pictures a few decades ago, he was hailed as a genius. The most striking aspect of contemporary high-culture painting—or "modern art," as it is usually known—is its heavy reliance on abstract forms. Contemporary paintings by abstract artists often command huge prices, even though most people in most cultures might not recognize them as works of art at all. How can this possibly be the case?

Throughout the history of Western culture, a primary goal of painting was to achieve as realistic a depiction of life as possible—to use techniques of color and perspective to reproduce three-dimensional reality on a flat surface. But in the nineteenth century this entire effort was made to appear futile by a new technology: photography, which can reproduce the world more accurately than any artist ever could. Gradually, many Western artists began to redefine their purpose: it was now to express, rather than merely depict, reality. By the early twentieth century, artists such as Picasso were using "unrealistic" colors and distorted forms to reveal mood and other aspects of reality that might escape the camera lens. Eventually, some artists abandoned the attempt to paint reality altogether, and instead explored geometric and other abstractions. This trend reached a climax in the United States in the 1950s, when artists, primarily in New York, created the genre of "abstract expressionism," which is characterized by huge canvases bearing mostly amorphous forms.

But why is abstraction the most prized form of art in the United States? By definition, the most prized art is the art people will pay the most for, and those who can pay the most are the elite. The tastes of the elite determine the contents of high culture. In earlier centuries, artists were commissioned by the elite—members of the royal courts, the aristocracy, and ranking clergy—to paint specific subjects that celebrated, and decorated, their way of life. Modern art, by contrast, is much more democratic and capitalistic: painters paint whatever they wish to and the elite do or do not buy it. In large measure, what art does get bought today is determined by the judgments of art dealers and critics, who are instrumental in promoting careers, endorsing trends, and setting prices. Currently, what these people and the elite value most in painting is innovation, a situation that reflects the culture's emphasis on diversity and novelty (Wolfe, 1975; Hughes, 1981; Wolff, 1981; Becker, 1982).

Therefore, the most prized art is that which seems to achieve something new. The first artist to drip paint rather than apply it with a brush, or to adorn a canvas with household objects, or to slash it, or to paint it all one color, or to make it trapezoid rather than rectangular, or to scribble on it, or to paint on fur instead of canvas, is hailed as a major talent; the second artist to do so is ignored. (That is why a black canvas by Stella is worth tens of thousands of dollars; the identical canvas by you is worth nothing.)

In this book there are a number of reproductions of paintings, which can sometimes illustrate a sociological point as well as, or even better than, a photograph. When you come across them, you might try to practice the sociology of art for yourself, by asking what these paintings tell you about the assumptions of the artist and the cultural environment in which they were produced.

Cultural Change

All cultures change, but they do so in different ways and at different rates. Under most conditions, cultural change is fairly slow: culture tends to be

Figure 3.18 *A great deal of cultural change takes place through diffusion, the spread of cultural traits from one society to another. This Nigerian Santa is enacting a ritual that has diffused to his country in a long route through several societies and over many centuries. Christianity arose in the Middle East and spread to western Europe. There, the celebration of the birth of Christ was combined with an ancient pagan tradition of a midwinter feast presided over by a figure much like the modern Santa. Eventually, the British colonized Nigeria, taking their western European version of Christmas with them—including reindeer, sleighbells, holly, and other items never found in the Middle East. Today, Santas are to be plentifully found in Nigerian stores over the Christmas period, complete with the traditional red snowwear that is hardly suited to the hot West African climate.*

inherently conservative, especially in its nonmaterial aspects, for people are reluctant to give up old values, customs, and beliefs in favor of new ones. When changes do occur in one area of a culture, they are usually accompanied, sooner or later, by changes elsewhere. If this were not the case, cultures would inevitably become poorly integrated over time. Some of the most important changes involve the ways in which a society earns its living and exploits the environment. Economic activity is so basic to human life that all other cultural elements have to adapt to it.

Three different social processes can lead to cultural change: discovery, invention, and diffusion. *Discovery* is a new perception of an aspect of reality that already exists—the hallucinogenic properties of peyote, the social structure of a termite colony, the functions of the heart, the cultural practices of another society. *Invention* is the combination or new use of existing knowledge to produce something that did not exist before—the compass, the United Nations, the atomic bomb, rock music. All inventions are based on previous discoveries and inventions. *Diffusion* is the spread of cultural elements from one culture to another—American technology to China, Italian opera to America, Christianity from Europe to Africa. One reason that different cultures change at different rates is that they may encourage or discourage these processes. A society that favors research and exploration will be likely to make discoveries; a society that wants to change its environment will devote resources to invention; a society that practices censorship or international isolation will experience little diffusion. Of the three processes, diffusion is probably the source of most cultural change. As implied by "The One Hundred Percent American," the reading at the end of this chapter, countless cultural elements that we consider to be distinctively our own are in fact derived from other, often distant cultures and frequently have histories that span many hundreds or even thousands of years.

Prisoners of Culture?

Through its profound effects on our behavior, values, attitudes, and personalities, the culture into which we are born influences our sense of who we are and what our goals in life should be. As Karl Marx declared:

> Men make their own history, but they do not make it just as they please; they do not make it under circumstances chosen by themselves, but under circumstances directly encountered, given, and transmitted from the past. [1969, originally published 1852]

But where does this leave human freedom? Are we simply the prisoners of our cultures?

The answer is no. Culture makes us, but we also make culture. Culture sets certain limitations on our options and behavior, but it cannot control us completely. If it did, there would be no cultural change, for we would all conform rigidly to existing norms and values. Culture provides general guidelines for behavior, but there are times when human beings must be creative, imaginative, and ready to improvise. The broad limits within which we do these things are determined by culture, but our specific acts often break with tradition and generate change. As individuals, few of us have the opportunity to modify culture; collectively, we do it all the time. Culture is created, sustained, and changed by the acts of human beings, and that is the measure of our freedom.

Summary

1.   Culture consists of all the shared products of human society, both material and nonmaterial. Culture and society are closely related and cannot exist independent of one another.

2.   According to evolutionary theory, human beings have evolved as the most advanced of the primates. Our species has exceptional capacity for learning. Culture provides a superior mode of adaptation to the environment. It enables us to adapt quickly to changed conditions, or even to change the environment to meet our needs.

3.   Social scientists generally accept that human nature is extremely flexible, and is the product of an interaction between biological potentials and cultural learning.

4.   Norms are shared rules or guidelines that prescribe appropriate behavior. Violations of folkways are more readily tolerated than violations of mores. Some acts are prohibited by taboos and some by laws. Norms are an important element in the system of social control through which a society ensures that its members behave in approved

ways. Norms are formally or informally enforced through positive or negative sanctions.

5.   Values are shared ideas about what is good or desirable. Norms express social values, although the origin of the norms may be forgotten. The United States has a unique set of important values, some of them contradictory or changing. Self-fulfillment may be emerging as an important new value.

6.   Cultures vary widely and each is unique. Ecological factors provide environmental influences on every culture. Some cultural variation can be explained in terms of the functions that particular elements (such as Eskimo hospitality) serve in maintaining the social system. Some cultural variation (such as the South African political system) can be explained as the product of conflict over scarce resources.

7.   There are a number of general cultural universals, but no specific practices are found in every society. We tend to be ethnocentric toward other cultures, judging them in terms of our own standards. It is important that a social scientist adopt a position of cultural relativism and attempt to understand other cultures and subcultures in their own terms.

8.   The norms, values, beliefs, and practices of a culture tend to be integrated, so changes in one area of culture often provoke changes in other areas. One source of cultural strain is the gap between real and ideal culture. Another source of strain is between high and popular culture. Strain can also arise from differences between the dominant culture and subcultures or countercultures.

9.   Language is fundamental to society and culture; it permits the transmission of culture and the interpretation of reality. The linguistic-relativity hypothesis holds that different languages predispose speakers to interpret reality in different ways.

10.   The creation and acceptance of art is a social process that reflects features of the surrounding society, as the cases of rock music and modern art illustrate.

11.   Cultural change is inevitable, and stems mainly from discovery, invention, and diffusion. Changes tend to be accepted into a culture only if they are compatible with existing norms and values. Changes in material culture are usually more readily accepted than changes in nonmaterial culture.

12.   We are not the prisoners of culture. Culture shapes us, but collectively we, in turn, shape and change the culture we pass on from generation to generation.

Important Terms

culture (55)	law (63)
material culture (55)	social control (64)
nonmaterial culture (55)	sanctions (64)
norms (62)	internalization of norms (64)
folkways (62)	values (64)
mores (62)	self-fulfillment (66)
taboo (62)	ecological approach (67)

cultural universals (72)   subculture (76)
ethnocentrism (72)   counterculture (77)
cultural relativism (74)   symbol (78)
cultural integration (74)   linguistic-relativity hypothesis (78)
ideal culture (74)   arts (79)
real culture (75)   discovery (84)
high culture (76)   invention (84)
popular culture (76)   diffusion (84)

Suggested Readings

AHRENS, W., and SUSAN P. MONTAGUE (eds.). *The American Dimension: Cultural Myths and Social Realities.* Port Washington, N.Y.: Alfred, 1976.

A fascinating collection of articles about various aspects of American culture, ranging from soap operas to bagels.

CAPLAN, ARTHUR L. (ed.). *The Sociobiology Debate.* New York: Harper and Row, 1979.

A useful collection of articles about sociobiology. The book provides a good introduction to this controversial and important topic.

FRITH, SIMON. *Sound Effects: Youth, Leisure, and the Politics of Rock 'n' Roll.* New York: Pantheon, 1982.

A good sociological analysis of rock music, tracing its development as an important part of contemporary popular culture.

HARRIS, MARVIN. *Cannibals and Kings: The Origins of Cultures.* New York: Random House, 1977.

An entertaining and provocative application of the ecological perspective to a variety of peculiar and apparently inexplicable cultural practices.

KEPHART, WILLIAM M. *Extraordinary Groups: The Sociology of Unconventional Life-Styles.* 2nd ed. New York: St. Martin's Press, 1982.

An interesting examination of various subcultures in the United States, revealing an extraordinary range of cultural diversity.

SPRADLEY, JAMES P., and DAVID W. MCCURDY. *Conformity and Conflict: Readings in Cultural Anthropology.* 5th ed. Boston: Little, Brown, 1984.

An interesting collection of articles that view aspects of various cultures from an anthropological perspective.

YANKELOVICH, DANIEL. *New Rules.* New York: Random House, 1981.

A discussion of recent changes in American values, based on extensive survey research.

YINGER, MILTON J. *Countercultures: The Promise and Peril of a World Turned Upside Down.* New York: Free Press, 1982.

A sociological analysis of groups whose values and norms directly contradict those of the surrounding culture.

READING

The One Hundred Percent American

RALPH LINTON

This classic essay pointedly demonstrates that many cultural traits we consider distinctively American have in fact diffused from other cultures and often have histories of thousands of years.

There can be no question about the average American's Americanism or his desire to preserve this precious heritage at all costs. Nevertheless, some insidious foreign ideas have already wormed their way into his civilization without his realizing what was going on. Thus dawn finds the unsuspecting patriot garbed in pajamas, a garment of East Indian origin; and lying in a bed built on a pattern which originated in either Persia or Asia Minor. He is muffled to the ears in un-American materials; cotton, first domesticated in India; linen, domesticated in the Near East; wool from an animal native to Asia Minor; or silk whose uses were first discovered by the Chinese. All these substances have been transformed into cloth by a method invented in Southwestern Asia. If the weather is cold enough he may even be sleeping under an eiderdown quilt invented in Scandinavia.

On awakening he glances at the clock, a medieval European invention, uses one potent Latin word in abbreviated form, rises in haste, and goes to the bathroom. Here, if he stops to think about it, he must feel himself in the presence of a great American institution; he will have heard stories of both the quality and frequency of foreign plumbing and will know that in no other country does the average man perform his ablutions in the midst of such splendor. But the invidious foreign influence pursues him even here. Glass was invented by the ancient Egyptians, the use of glazed tiles for floors and walls in the Near East, porcelain in China, and the art of enameling on metal by Mediterranean artisans of the Bronze Age. Even his bathtub and toilet are but slightly modified copies of Roman originals. The only purely American contribution to the ensemble is the steam radiator.

In this bathroom the American washes with soap invented by the ancient Gauls. Next he cleans his teeth, a subversive European practice which did not invade America until the latter part of the eighteenth century. He then shaves, a masochistic rite first developed by the heathen priests of ancient Egypt and Sumer. The process is made less of a penance by the fact that his razor is of steel, an iron-carbon alloy discovered in either India or Turkestan. Lastly, he dries himself on a Turkish towel.

Returning to the bedroom, the unconscious victim of un-American practices removes his clothes from a chair, invented in the Near East, and proceeds to dress. He puts on close-fitting tailored garments whose form derives from the skin clothing of the ancient nomads of the Asiatic steppes and fastens them with buttons whose prototypes appeared in Europe at the close of the Stone Age. This costume is appropriate enough for outdoor exercise in a cold climate, but is quite unsuited to American summers, steam-heated houses, and Pullmans. Nevertheless, foreign ideas and habits hold the unfortunate man in thrall even when common sense tells him that the authentically American costume of gee string and moccasins would be far more comfortable. He puts on his feet stiff coverings made from hide prepared by a process invented in ancient Egypt and cut to a pattern which can be traced back to ancient Greece, and makes sure they are properly polished, also a Greek idea. Lastly, he ties about his neck a strip of bright-colored cloth which is a vestigial survival of the shoulder shawls worn by seventeenth-century Croats. He gives himself a final appraisal in the mirror, an old Mediterranean invention, and goes downstairs to breakfast.

Here a whole new series of foreign things confronts him. His food and drink are placed before him in pottery vessels, the popular name of which—china—is sufficient evidence of their origin. His fork is a medieval Italian invention and his spoon a copy of a Roman original. He will usually begin the meal with coffee, an Abyssinian plant first discovered by the Arabs. . . . He will follow this with a bowl of cereal made from grain domesticated in the Near East and prepared by methods also invented there. From this he will go on to waffles, a Scandinavian invention, with plenty of butter, originally a Near-Eastern cosmetic. . . .

Breakfast over, he places upon his head a molded piece of felt, invented by the nomads of Eastern Asia, and if it looks like rain, puts on outer shoes of rubber, discovered by the ancient Mexicans, and takes an umbrella, invented in India. He then sprints for his train—the train, not the sprinting, being an English invention. At the station he pauses for a moment to buy a newspaper, paying for it with coins invented in ancient Lydia. Once on board he settles back to inhale the fumes of a cigarette invented in Mexico, or a cigar invented in Brazil. Meanwhile, he reads the news of the day, imprinted in characters invented by the ancient Semites by a process invented in Germany upon a material invented in China. As he scans the latest editorial pointing out the dire results to our institutions of accepting foreign ideas, he will not fail to thank a Hebrew God in an Indo-European language that he is a one hundred percent (decimal system invented by the Greeks) American (from Americus Vespucci, Italian geographer).

SOURCE: Ralph Linton, *The American Mercury*, 40 (April 1937), pp. 427–429.

CHAPTER 4

Society

Human beings are social animals. The quality we call "humanity" can be achieved only through social living, for there is no such thing as a person whose personality and behavior have not developed within some human society. We take social living so much for granted that we sometimes overlook the immense influence society has on us. But in the complex interaction between the individual and society, the latter is usually dominant. Society exists long before we are born into it, and it exists long after we are gone. Society gives content, direction, and meaning to our lives, and we, in turn, in countless ways, reshape the society that we leave to the next generation.

We are not social animals just because we happen to find social living convenient. Without society we could not survive. No infant could reach maturity without the care and protection of other people, and no adult could remain alive without using the vast store of information about the world that has been learned and passed on through society. Almost everything that we do is social in some sense—learned from others, done with others, directed toward others. Some very rare individuals try to escape from society, yet even they carry with them into their isolation the techniques, the ideas, and the identities they have learned from others. Hermits in their caves live with society in their memories.

What exactly is a society? Several conditions must be met before people can be said to be living in one. First, they must occupy a common territory. Second, they must share the same government or other political authority. Third, they must to some extent have a common culture and a sense of membership in, and commitment to, the same group. We may say, then, that a *society* is a population that occupies the same territory, is subject to the same political authority, and participates in a common culture. In the modern world, most societies are nation-states—that is, countries like Canada or China. Societies and nation-states are not necessarily identical, however, as many nation-states include smaller societies within their borders. Most of the countries of South America, for example, contain tribal societies of indigenous Indian peoples who have not been integrated into the larger society.

Many other animals are also social—such as ants, herrings, geese, and elephants. But these species depend for their survival primarily on unlearned ("instinctive") patterns of behavior. As a result, different societies of any one species, be they termites or zebras, are virtually identical, with little difference in the social behavior of the members from one society to another. When you have seen one nest of a particular termite species, you have for most purposes seen all the nests of that species. Human societies, on the other hand, are astonishingly diverse, because they are created by human beings themselves and are learned and modified by each new generation. Consequently, every human society is different—so different that a person suddenly transplanted from, say, the United States to a jungle tribe of Brazil (or vice versa) would be mystified by the new social environment and unable to behave appropriately. Each society thus presents a unique and exciting challenge to the sociologist's understanding.

In this chapter we shall look at two main topics. First, we shall examine the social structure that underlies all human societies. Second, we shall consider some basic types of societies, showing how and why they differ from one another. In particular, we shall examine the radical differences between modern industrialized societies and the traditional, preindustrial societies that they are rapidly replacing all over the world.

Social Structure

All complex things, from bacteria to planets, have a structure—that is, they consist of a set of interrelated parts. The structure of a building, for example, consists of a floor, walls, a roof, an entrance, and probably such fittings as windows and utility lines. All buildings have much the same basic structure, although the character of any particular building—such as a cottage, a warehouse, a shack, or a high-rise office tower—depends on the precise nature of its parts and their relationship to one another.

Sociologists sometimes find it helpful to use the metaphor of "structure" when they analyze human societies. A society is not just a chaotic collection of randomly interacting people: there is an underlying regularity, or pattern, to social behavior in any society. To sociologists, therefore, *social structure* is the pattern of relationships among the basic components in a social system. These components provide the framework for all human societies, although the precise character of the components and the relationships among them vary from one society to another. The most important components of social structure are statuses, roles, groups, and institutions. These concepts are of fundamental importance in sociology, and you will encounter them throughout this book.

Statuses

In ordinary speech, "status" usually refers to prestige, but the sociological use of the word is different. To the sociologist, a *status* is a position in society. Everybody occupies a number of statuses—positions such as student, carpenter, son, old person, senator, and so on. A person's status determines where that individual "fits" in society and how he or she should relate to other people. The status of daughter, for example, determines the occupant's basic relationships with other family members; the status of corporation president determines the occupant's basic relationships with employees, shareholders, or presidents of other corporations.

Naturally, a person can have several statuses simultaneously, but one of them, usually an occupational status, tends to be the most significant. This becomes a *master status,* the position most important in establishing an individual's social identity. Generally, a person's various statuses fit together fairly smoothly, but some people experience *status inconsistency,* a situation in which aspects of an individual's status or statuses appear contradictory. For example, black professionals find that they sometimes receive honor for their occupational status but at other times suffer prejudice because of their racial status. Successful blacks who move to affluent suburbs sometimes find that visiting white salespeople assume they are household servants (Williams, 1985).

In fact, there is a crucial distinction between statuses that society arbitrarily attaches to us and those that we can earn (or lose) by our own actions. An *ascribed status* is one that is attached to people on grounds over which they have no control. Whether you are young or old, male or female, or black or white, for example, there is not much you can do about it. On the other hand, an *achieved status* is one that depends to some extent on characteristics over which the individual has some control. At least partly through your own efforts you can become a spouse, a college graduate, a convict, or a member of a different religion. Sometimes an ascribed status can make it difficult for the individual to earn an achieved status. For example, if you are Hispanic and female (ascribed statuses), you will find it more difficult to become president of the United States (an achieved status) than if you were an "Anglo" male.

In most societies there is considerable inequality among different statuses. The person who has the status of Supreme Court justice, for example, enjoys more wealth, power, and prestige than the person who has the status of janitor. A *social class* is a category of people of roughly equivalent status in an unequal society. The members of any particular social class enjoy greater access to the society's wealth and other resources than do people with lower statuses, but have less access than people with higher statuses. The fact that statuses may be ranked unequally has profound consequences for both the individual and society, as we shall see in later chapters.

Roles

An actor plays many different parts, or roles, whose content depends on the demands of the particular character being portrayed. The sociological concept of "role" is derived directly from the theater, and refers to the part or parts a person plays in society. Specifically, a *role* is a set of expected behavior patterns, obligations, and privileges attached to a particular social status. The distinction between status and role is a simple one: you *occupy* a status, but you *play* a role (Linton, 1936). Status and role are thus two sides of the same coin.

College professor, for example, is a social status. Attached to this status is a professorial role, defined by social norms prescribing how the occupier of the status should behave. The status of professor is a fixed position in society, but the role is more flexible, for different occupants of the status actually play their roles in somewhat different ways. One reason is that, in practice, a single status may involve a number of roles. The status of col-

Figure 4.1 *There are two kinds of social status—those that are* ascribed *to people on grounds over which they have no control, and those that are* achieved *by individuals through personal effort. The status of the queen of Great Britain is an ascribed one: Elizabeth II has the status because she was next in line of succession to her father, the late king. The status of prime minister of Great Britain is an achieved one: Margaret Thatcher has the status because she won the leadership of her party and a national election. Of course, both the queen and the prime minister have other statuses as well—for example, each has the ascribed status of middle-aged woman, and each has the achieved status of wife.*

STATUS AND ROLES

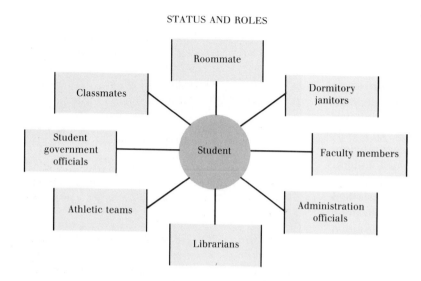

Figure 4.2 *Any status carries with it a number of different roles. Your status of student, for example, requires that you adopt somewhat different roles in your interaction with people who have other statuses and roles. Although student is only one of your statuses, it is probably your most important status, or master status, at present.*

lege professor includes one role as teacher, one role as colleague to other professors, one role as researcher, and perhaps other roles, such as student adviser or writer of scholarly articles.

The roles we play in life thus depend on the statuses we happen to occupy at a given time. If you are talking to your professor as a student, you will behave differently than you might if, years later, you return to visit the campus as a wealthy benefactor. Similarly, we respond to people according to the roles they play for us. If someone playing the role of physician asks you to undress, you will comply, but if the same person asks you to undress when playing the role of host at dinner, you will probably respond quite differently.

The actual content of our role behavior is determined primarily by **role expectations,** the generally accepted social norms that prescribe how a role ought to be played. These expectations may be at odds with our **role performance,** the actual behavior of a person playing a role. The fact that a person may have several different statuses, each with a number of roles attached, can often cause difficulty and confusion in social relationships. One such problem is **role strain,** a situation in which contradictory expectations are built into a single role. An office supervisor, for example, is expected to maintain good relations with the workers but is also expected to enforce regulations that the workers may resent. The more the supervisor's role performance satisfies one of these expectations, the more it may violate the other. Another problem is **role conflict,** a situation in which two or more of a person's roles have contradictory requirements. For example, police officers some-

times find themselves in a position where they ought to arrest their own children; in such circumstances, the role expectations of parent and police officer can be at odds with one another. But although role expectations may sometimes cause strains and conflicts in role performances, they do for the most part ensure the smooth and predictable course of social interaction. Roles enable us to structure our own behavior along socially expected lines. We can anticipate the behavior of others in most situations, and we can fashion our own actions accordingly.

Groups

Most social behavior takes place within and among groups that are constantly being formed and reformed. A **group** is a collection of people interacting together in an orderly way on the basis of shared expectations about each other's behavior. Put another way, a group is a number of persons whose statuses and roles are interrelated. A group therefore differs from a mere aggregate of people who just happen to be in the same place at the same time, such as pedestrians in a busy street. Because human beings are essentially cooperative social animals, groups are a vital part of social structure.

The distinctive characteristics of any society depend largely on the nature and activities of the groups that it contains. Groups can be classified into two main types, primary and secondary. A **primary group** consists of a small number of people who interact over a relatively long period on a direct, intimate basis. The members know one another personally and interact in a manner that is informal and has at least some emotional depth. Examples of this kind of group are families, cliques of friends and peers, and close neighbors. These groups are important building blocks of social structure; in fact, some small-scale, traditional societies are organized almost entirely around family or kinship groups.

In contrast, a *secondary group* consists of a number of people who interact on a relatively temporary, anonymous, and impersonal basis. The members either do not know one another personally, or, at best, know one another only in terms of particular formal roles (such as mail carrier or math teacher) rather than as whole people. Secondary groups are usually established to serve specific purposes, and people are generally less emotionally committed to them than they are to their primary groups. Examples of secondary groups are formal organizations such as corporations, political parties, or government bureaucracies. These large organizations are not found in the simplest of human societies, but they are increasingly important in large modern societies. (Both primary and secondary groups are discussed in more detail in Chapter 7, "Social Groups.")

Institutions

Every society must meet certain basic social needs if it is to survive and provide a satisfying life for its members. For example, children must be raised and cared for; the cultural knowledge of one generation must be passed on to the next; important social values must be shared and upheld; social order must be maintained; goods and services must be produced. Over time, the members of each society create patterns of thought and action that provide an appropriate solution for these recurrent challenges. These patterns of behavior are what sociologists call institutions.

An *institution* is a stable cluster of values, norms, statuses, roles, and groups that develops around a basic social need. (Figure 4.3 on page 94 lists major institutions of modern societies, with examples of each of these elements.) Thus, the family institution provides for the care of children. The educational institution transmits cultural knowledge to the young. The religious institution provides a set of shared values and the rituals that reaffirm them. The political institution allocates power and maintains order. The economic institu-

tion provides goods and services. These major institutions, too, contain smaller units within themselves: for example, baseball is an activity within the overarching institution of sport; the hospital is part of the overall medical institution; the prison is an aspect of the legal institution; and so on.

Characteristics of Institutions

Institutions such as the family, science, religion, and medicine may seem very different, but in fact the institutions of any society tend to share certain common features.

1. *Institutions tend to be resistant to change.* Patterns of social behavior become "institutionalized," or securely established, only when they have been reinforced by custom and tradition to the point where they are accepted almost without question. People tend to resent and resist any attack on the institutions they know. (Imagine, for example, the likely response in North America to a serious attempt to abolish the family, to end compulsory schooling, to replace existing churches with new cults, or to apply communist principles to the economy.) This resistance to change is often functional, for it can ensure social stability; but in times of social conflict or rapid change, resistance may be dysfunctional if the old forms of institutions have become outmoded, ineffectual, or even oppressive.

2. *Institutions tend to be interdependent.* A society's major institutions tend to uphold similar values and norms, to reflect compatible goals and priorities, and to benefit or penalize the same groups or interests. Thus a society with a capitalist economy is likely to have a political system that supports capitalism, a major religion or other belief system that endorses free enterprise, an educational system that encourages competition and teaches the superiority of capitalism, and so on. Conversely, a society with a socialist economy will tend to have institutions that mesh with and uphold norms and values appropriate to that particular system. Because all a society's institutions share common features, any one of them can yield insights into the others and can serve to some extent as a microcosm of the larger society.

3. *Institutions tend to change together.* When institutions do change, they rarely do so in isolation. Because institutions are so interdependent, significant modifications in one must usually be accompanied by changes in others if cultural integration is to be maintained. This is especially true

MAJOR SOCIAL INSTITUTIONS

Institution	Some Social Needs	Some Values	Some Norms	Some Statuses/ Roles	Some Groups
Family	Regulate sexual behavior; provide care for children.	Marital fidelity.	Have only one spouse.	Husband; grandmother.	Kinship group.
Education	Transmit cultural knowledge to the young.	Intellectual curiosity.	Attend school.	Teacher; student.	High school clique; college seminar.
Religion	Share and reaffirm community values and solidarity.	Belief in God.	Attend regular worship.	Rabbi; cardinal.	Synod; congregation.
Medical system	Take care of the sick.	Good health.	Save life if possible.	Physician; patient.	Hospital staff; ward of patients.
Economic system	Produce and distribute goods and services.	Free enterprise.	Maximize profits.	Accountant; vendor.	Corporate board; labor union.
Political system	Distribute power; maintain order.	Freedom.	Vote by secret ballot.	Senator; lobbyist.	Legislature; political party.
Science	Investigate social and natural world.	Unbiased search for truth.	Conduct research.	Physicist; anthropologist.	Research team; science society.
Military	Aggress or defend against enemies of the state.	Discipline.	Follow orders.	General; marine.	Platoon; army division.
Legal system	Maintain social control.	Fair trial.	Inform suspects of their rights.	Judge; lawyer.	Jury; cell mates.
Sport	Provide for recreation and exercise.	Winning.	Play by the rules.	Umpire; coach.	Baseball team; fan club.

Figure 4.3 *Institutions arise over time as people develop social responses to the particular needs of their society. Each institution is a stable cluster of values, norms, statuses, roles, and groups; and each provides an established pattern of thought and action that offers a solution to recurrent demands of social living. This table lists the major institutions that have been created to serve the needs of modern society, with examples of each of the elements involved.*

of changes in the economy, for the way in which a society makes its living has multiple effects on almost everything else. The Industrial Revolution of the eighteenth and nineteenth centuries, which we mentioned in Chapter 1, provides a classic example of how economic change can provoke multiple institutional adjustments. In that case, the transformation from a predominantly rural, agricultural society to an urban, industrial one resulted in sweeping changes in every other institution—families became smaller, government expanded, people stayed in school longer, traditional religion lost some of its influence, science developed rapidly, and so on.

4. *Institutions tend to be the site of major social problems.* Because institutions are centered on basic social needs, any significant institutional failure is likely to be regarded as a serious social problem. For example, unemployment is a social problem of the economy; marital breakdown is a problem of the family; high crime rates are a problem of the legal institution. Social problems have many sources, but one recurs constantly: being so stable, institutions continue to reflect the status quo, and so are slow to respond to changing social needs. Social problems that are located in social institutions are not easily solved: there are some groups that benefit and some that suffer under any

institutional arrangement, so there is always controversy over the need for change, as well as over its rate and direction.

Functionalist and Conflict Approaches

We have seen in earlier chapters that functionalist and conflict theories provide two rather different ways of examining large-scale aspects of society. This is especially true when it comes to their approaches to institutions.

Functionalist theorists are apt to ask what functions, or effects, a given institution has in maintaining the social system. They recognize that stability is essential if a society is to survive, and see institutions as regulating and channeling human behavior into predictable patterns that help the social system work smoothly. Functionalists are inclined to regard any failings of institutional arrangements as dysfunctions—negative effects that must be corrected to bring the system into balance once more. Conflict theorists, on the other hand, are inclined to ask who benefits from existing institutional arrangements. They are generally more critical of institutions, arguing that if they maintain order, they thereby support the status quo and the "haves" against the "have nots"; if they channel behavior, they thereby inhibit freedom. Conflict theorists are likely to see failings in institutions as the result of power struggles among various interests—struggles that may bring about needed changes in the long run.

As we shall see in later chapters when we examine specific institutions in detail, there is often validity to both the functionalist and conflict approaches, for each addresses a different aspect of society. Institutions do, indeed, make life stable and predictable by providing for central human needs; but they also tend to favor one group over another and to restrict choice—and thereby individual liberty. This dual nature of society—as something that makes human life possible, stable, and worthwhile, but that at the same time channels human behavior and imposes limits on our freedom—is an enduring paradox that sociology must confront.

An Illustration: Sport

Many of the principles of social structure that we have discussed can be illustrated by the institution of **sport**—competitive physical activity guided by established rules. Like other institutions, sport is in some respects a microcosm of the entire society. By understanding crucial aspects of sport—the kinds of games that are popular, the social groups that participate, the statuses and roles of those involved, the distribution of power and wealth within the institution, the linkages of sport with other institutions, and the values sport represents—we can learn much about a society as a whole. We can also, incidentally, see what is distinctive about the sociological approach to a familiar aspect of life.

Figure 4.4 *In all societies, sport is used to uphold social norms and values. This is especially evident when a team represents a community, region, or especially a nation. As the surrounding nationalistic pageantry of flags and anthems suggests, international competitions are far more than a test of athletic skills. Citizens are apt to feel that their nation's prestige depends on the performance of its athletes, almost as it would if they were gladiators representing the country in battle. Political considerations sometimes affect the Olympic Games: the United States boycotted the 1980 games in Moscow, and the Soviet Union boycotted the 1984 games in Los Angeles.*

Sport in American Society

In American society, sport is an important institution directly affecting the lives of the majority of the population who are either participants in, or spectators of, various sports. Three out of four Americans report that they discuss sports frequently, and an event like the Superbowl may attract well over 100 million viewers. The sports section of newspapers is by far the most popular part of the paper; in fact, it is the only section that millions of Americans ever read. Clearly, sport is not a trivial aspect of American life. Indeed, in recent years it has been the subject of extensive sociological study (Loy et al., 1978; Leonard, 1980; Snyder and Spreitzer, 1983; Eitzen, 1984; Coakley, 1986).

Like any other institution, sport serves various functions for the social system as a whole. Among the functions that have been identified are the following:

1. *Leisure activities.* Sport provides organized leisure activities for the population—a useful function in a society where people have a good deal of free time.

2. *Physical exercise.* Sport encourages people to engage in vigorous physical activity, which is important in a society where people get little exercise.

3. *Role models.* Sport provides, through famous athletes, role models whose skills and determination are held up for public emulation.

4. *Outlet for energies.* Sport may act as a "safety valve" for spectators and participants, allowing them to express aggressive or competitive energies in a generally harmless way.

5. *Reinforcement of values.* Sport serves to reinforce many of the basic values of society, such as teamwork, competition, discipline, and obedience to rules.

Changes in sport, like those in any other institution, parallel changes in the wider society. Until about a hundred years ago, Americans' favorite sports were such activities as foot racing, boat racing, cockfighting, hunting, and fishing; the large-scale spectator sports of football, baseball, hockey, and basketball were virtually unknown, and became popular only as the nation was transformed from a predominantly rural, agricultural society into an urban, industrial one. The development of these mass sports was spurred by several social factors: economic development, which led to a shorter work week and more leisure time; the growth of cities, which provided the concentrated populations necessary to support huge stadiums; the spread of radio and television, which brought spectator sport into homes across the nation; and innovations in land and air transport, which facilitated competition among regions and even among nations. Other changes in sport have likewise reflected trends in the wider society. As workers in general have become more and more specialized, a new role has emerged, that of the full-time professional athlete who specializes not only in a single sport but also in a single status, such as pitcher or quarterback. Similarly, as large organizations have proliferated in society, control of sport has passed from small, primary groups of players to large, secondary groups like unions, associations, and even corporations.

The American economic institution emphasizes free enterprise and the pursuit of profit, and its capitalist spirit inevitably affects sport. The teams of the major professional sports are corporate organizations, similar in most respects to other businesses; they even buy, sell, and trade players, as though athletes were economic commodities. Sport, in fact, is a big business that generates huge revenues, running into billions of dollars each year. But who benefits from the immense wealth generated by the industry? Conflict theorists argue that here, as elsewhere in the society, the wealth is unequally shared, with most of it going to high-status people such as sports "stars" and the owners of the various businesses that directly or indirectly profit from sport. Few people who participate in sport get rich, a fact that is perhaps obscured by the enormous earnings of the tiny minority of athletes who do. The full-time players in the four major team sports are, in fact, well paid, but their total number is less than 2,500; and only a handful of athletes in other sports are able to make a good living from the profession. Nevertheless, millions of Little Leaguers and other juvenile athletes are encouraged to aspire to become professionals in their sport, a status more than 99 percent of them will fail to achieve (Rosenberg, 1979; Eitzen and Sage, 1978). The idea that sport is an avenue to social and economic success is part of the general "rags to riches" dream that pervades American life. It is widely believed in America that if you work hard, you will grow rich—even though, in fact, most people do not get especially rich, no matter how hard they work (about 95 percent of American taxpayers earn less than $50,000 a year).

Sport and American Values

Sport in America embodies some highly regarded social values: perseverance, discipline, hard work, competition, success. These same values are called for in other American institutions—in the political system, for example, which relies on the competition of ideas, interests, and candidates, or in the educational system, which prizes diligence, conformity to rules, and competition among students for high grades. Perhaps most important, the principles of free enterprise that underlie the economy assume that the way to success is to work one's way up by competing with others.

Winning is so highly valued in American sports that the result of a contest seems to have become more important than the playing of it. A century ago it might have been said, "It matters not who won or lost, but how you played the game"; today, a much more appropriate slogan would appear to be, "Winning isn't everything; it's the only thing." This exclusive emphasis on victory extends throughout the institution, and is a familiar feature of that uniquely American system, intercollegiate sports. Students and alumni tend to regard a winning team as a superb advertisement for a college, serving to attract students, alumni contributions, and grants from state legislatures. For this reason the schools compete vigorously for promising athletes, often offering athletic scholarships to people who are not really "scholars" in the

traditional sense of the word (and frequently causing role conflict for those who try to meet the rival demands of their academic and their sporting roles). So intense does the competition for new recruits become that there is a good deal of cheating, usually in the form of attracting athletes by offering them disguised bribes.

The idea that victory is the only possible purpose of competition is so deeply embedded in American culture—and, indeed, in that of most modern industrialized societies—that it is difficult for us to imagine any alternative. Yet there are many societies where sports have a quite different objective. The Tangu people of New Guinea play a game in which each of two teams throws a spinning top at a cluster of stakes that have been driven into the ground. The object of the game is not to have one team win by hitting the most stakes; instead, it is to have each team hit exactly the same number of stakes, at which point the game ends. The Tangu, who place great emphasis on equality in their sharing of food and in other interpersonal relationships, have created a game that reflects their cultural values (Burridge, 1957). The Gahuku people of New Guinea use sport as a harmless substitute for combat between hostile groups. When one group has a grievance against another, a team from the offending group enters a contest with one score in its favor. The object of the game is for the team from the aggrieved group to even the score. Once a tie has been achieved, the game is over and the grievance has been satisfactorily redressed (Read, 1965). The Zuñi of northern New Mexico viewed rivalry as socially destructive. A person who constantly won footraces would be disqualified from future competition: the Zuñi preferred a game that gave the participants fairly equal chances, and felt that an outstanding athlete spoiled the fun for everybody else (Benedict, 1961). In short, societies that are interested in sharing and cooperation tend to prefer to play sports in a noncompetitive way; those that are interested in individual achievement and success tend to prefer more competitive sports (Stipes, 1973).

Class and Sport

Class, race, and sex statuses influence a person's chances to play a role in a variety of American institutions. In the political institution, for example, the wealthy are heavily overrepresented in the Senate (millionaires comprise less than 0.3 percent of the population but almost a third of the sen-

Figure 4.5

"And, in a sports first, the New York Rangers lost last night, three to two, but claimed victory anyway."

Drawing by Dana Fradon; © 1985
The New Yorker Magazine, Inc.

ators), whereas blacks and women are strikingly underrepresented (blacks comprise nearly 12 percent of the population, but there are no black senators; women comprise 53 percent of the population, but only 2 percent of the senators are female). A similar situation exists in other institutions, including sport.

Social class strongly affects the individual's access to, and preference for, particular sports, whether as a participant or as a spectator. Only the upper classes, for example, can take part in such expensive sports as yachting and polo. Both the upper and the middle classes may be able to afford tennis, golf, skiing, or scuba diving. The working class, however, may be able to participate only in such sports as bowling, pool, baseball, basketball, or boxing. These class biases toward particular sports tend to be passed on from one generation to the next. A child whose parents belong to a country club is likely to develop an interest in golf, tennis, or swimming, and to develop the necessary skills. A child who grows up in an inner city slum is more likely to turn to basketball, a game that needs little more in the way of facilities than a strip of asphalt and a backboard and hoop. Members of different social classes also tend to have different tastes as spectators: people of higher social status are more likely to view college sports or such genteel games as golf and tennis; people of lower status gravitate toward games that offer more daring, strength, and even violence, such as boxing and demolition derbies (Loy, 1969; Axthelm, 1970; Luschen, 1969; Gruneau, 1975).

Race and Sport

Blacks have always experienced prejudice and discrimination in American society, but it is widely believed that sport is exempt from racism—that it is a color-blind institution offering unique opportunities for talented ghetto youths to reach the heights of celebrity and fortune. The main evidence for this view is the high proportion of blacks in the major professional sports of baseball, football, and basketball. Unhappily, however, a sociological analysis contradicts the popular belief.

Actually, blacks are virtually absent from most forms of sport except football, baseball, basketball, and boxing: there are virtually no black figure skaters, race-car drivers, polo players, or skiers. Even in the few sports where blacks are well represented, their participation is a relatively new phenomenon, dating mainly from the late 1950s— a period when the civil rights movement was be-

ginning to achieve parallel changes in other institutions like the schools. Moreover, several studies have shown that blacks actually have to be better players than whites if they are to get into and remain in professional baseball, basketball, and football. And even within these teams, blacks are largely excluded from the central positions that offer most opportunity for leadership: there are hardly any black catchers and shortstops in baseball, or centers and quarterbacks in football, a situation that parallels the allocation of statuses in the society beyond (see Figure 4.6). Additionally, sport offers virtually no career opportunities for blacks in any role other than that of athlete: coaches, managers, umpires, administrators, sportscasters, and owners are almost all white. Indeed, the total number of blacks in the entire country who are involved in professional sports in some full-time capacity is probably fewer than 3,000. If young blacks were urged to aspire to a career in any other national industry that could offer fewer than 3,000 mostly temporary jobs, the idea would seem absurd; but the myth of sport as an avenue for black opportunity is so powerful that it persists in the face of the facts (Luschen and Sage, 1981; H. Edwards, 1982; Coakley, 1986).

It remains true, however, that blacks are disproportionately represented in professional baseball (over 20 percent of the players), football (over 40 percent), and basketball (over 60 percent). Why is this so? A frequent explanation is that blacks have inborn, genetic traits that make them especially talented at these sports. This argument is unconsciously racist—partly because it denies black athletes the same credit for individual work and perseverance that would be accorded to white players, and partly because no similar argument is made to explain the special skills that other groups have in particular sports. Nobody proposes genetic factors, for example, to explain why East Germany has produced so many excellent swimmers, why Canadians do well at hockey, why Japanese-Americans are disproportionately represented in judo—or, for that matter, why the British are hopeless at baseball while white Americans are equally inept at cricket. In each case, it is easy to see that cultural factors, not genetic ones, are at work.

What cultural factors, then, explain the black predominance in some American sports? Sport is one of the few fields in which blacks have achieved publicly recognized success, and one of the few that offers successful, highly visible role models for the ambitious young black. White children correctly perceive that they have a wide array of ca-

CONCENTRATION BY RACE IN PROFESSIONAL FOOTBALL AND BASEBALL

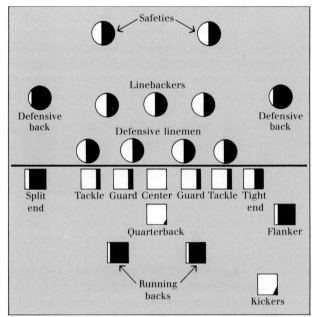

Proportion of black players in offensive and defensive
positions at the opening of the 1984 season

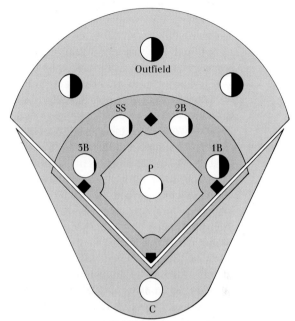

Proportion of black players in regular starting
positions in the 1985 season

SOURCE: Jay J. Coakley, *Sport in Society: Issues and Controversies* (St. Louis: Mosby, 1986), pp. 151, 152.

Figure 4.6 *The shaded areas in these illustrations show the proportion of black players in each position in NFL football in 1984 and in major league baseball in 1985. Despite rapid increases in the overall number of black players in professional football and baseball over the past thirty years, blacks are still underrepresented in the central positions in both sports.*

reer opportunities other than sport, so they are less apt to give sport the same single-minded dedication that many black children do. It is likely, then, that a much higher proportion of blacks than of whites see sport as a potential career, and that they work harder to achieve entry. As to why they choose baseball, football, and basketball, the answer is obvious enough: the facilities for these games are freely available in the school or neighborhood. Naturally, then, black athletes will excel at these sports and not at skiing, skating, or golfing, where facilities and coaching are not available to them (H. Edwards, 1982; Yetman and Eitzen, 1984; Coakley, 1986).

Sex and Sport

Like blacks, women have been, and to a great extent still are, denied entry to many athletic roles:

sport has long been an almost exclusively male preserve. In this respect, sport once again parallels such other American institutions as religion, the economy, politics, law, the military, and science, in which women were also refused access to high statuses. As we shall see in Chapter 12 ("Inequalities of Gender and Age"), there are many non-Western societies in which heavy physical labor is considered a woman's job, not a man's. But for centuries in Western culture, there has been a basic assumption that women are biologically incapable of vigorous, competitive activity. In North America it is widely felt that the more active and dominant a man is, the more "masculine" he is; the more passive and delicate a women, the more "feminine" she is. As a result, the combined role expectations of a feminine woman and a competitive athlete have raised the prospect of severe role conflicts, and a woman who wanted an athletic pastime, let alone a career, put her femininity at some risk. The institution of sport thus served to reinforce the role expectations of the larger society. The men were the active doers on the field; the women, the cutely dressed cheerleaders giving emotional support to their menfolk—a suitable preparation for the later roles of each (Hoepner, 1974; Gerber et al., 1974; Eitzen and Sage, 1982).

In recent years gender roles have changed significantly, primarily because unprecedented numbers of women have entered the economic institution and have demanded equality with men, at first in the workplace and then in other areas of life. Thanks to the efforts of the women's movement, court decisions, and legislation, female athletes are now enjoying adequate coaching and other facilities, instead of being treated as athletic afterthoughts. Women are becoming increasingly evident as joggers, soccer players, race-car drivers, javelin throwers, high-jumpers, golfers, tennis players, gymnasts, basketball players, and long-distance runners and swimmers. In fact, no matter what the sport, there is no physical reason why women cannot participate; they can avoid injury to vulnerable parts of the body the same way men do, through the use of protective clothing and rules of fair play. Why, then, do women not take part, even today, in *every* sport?

The key factor is a cultural one: men, who still control sport, want female athletes to appear "ladylike." On the playing field as elsewhere in life, women are often still valued for their decorative aspects rather than their individual talent. It is acceptable, it seems, for women to take part in sports involving the display of grace and beauty, such as figure skating, tennis, swimming, or skiing, and in noncontact sports such as basketball, baseball, and track. It is much less acceptable, however, for women to take part in any sport in which they have physical confrontation with an opponent, or in which they become too unkempt, exhausted, and sweaty. Football, ice hockey, and boxing therefore remain among the male preserves, for it is not so much talent as the individual's ascribed status (male or female) that determines access to an achieved status in sport (Metheny, 1977).

Our analysis of a single American institution and the statuses, roles, and groups within it has illuminated many other aspects of the society—its social changes, its other institutions, its values and myths, its gender roles, its typical patterns of intergroup relations and inequalities. We shall explore many such aspects of this specific society in more detail later, but we must first turn to a consideration of human societies in general.

Figure 4.7 *On average, men are stronger, faster, and heavier than women, so there are some sports, like football, in which most women will be unable to compete on equal terms with most men. In other events that require long-term physical endurance, trained women may prove superior, for they are able to convert body fat to energy for longer periods than most men. This is especially true of long-distance swimming, which is becoming a predominantly female sport, and marathons of fifty miles or more. Women are closing the gap on men in a number of other sports as well. In the 1984 Olympics, for instance, the difference between the women's and men's winning times in the 4 × 100 relays was half what it was in 1928, the first year women were allowed to enter the event.*

Types of Societies

If we compressed the entire history of life on the planet into a single year, the first modern human being would not appear until December 31 at about 11:53 P.M., and the first civilizations would have emerged only about a minute before the end of the year. Yet our cultural achievements in the brief time that we have occupied the planet have been remarkable. Some 15,000 years ago our ancestors were practicing religious rituals and painting superb pictures on the walls of their caves. Around 11,000 years ago, some human groups began to domesticate animals and plants, thereby freeing themselves from total dependence on the food that they could hunt and gather. About 6,000 years ago people began to live in cities, to specialize in different forms of labor, to divide into social classes, and to create distinct political and economic institutions. Within a few thousand years empires were created, linking previously isolated groups and bringing millions of people under centralized rule. Advanced agricultural technologies improved the productivity of the land, resulting in growing populations and the emergence of large nation-states. A mere 250 years ago the Industrial Revolution began, thrusting us into the modern world of factories and computers, jet aircraft and nuclear reactors, instant global communications and terrifying military technologies.

These historical developments are part of a general trend of *sociocultural evolution,* the tendency for societies' social structures and cultures to grow more complex over time. This process has some similarities with biological evolution. Like an organism, a society has to subsist by adapting to its environment in order to exploit food and other resources. Various societies have used different subsistence strategies, and those societies that have found more productive strategies have tended to grow larger and more complex, often enjoying their success at the expense of societies using more primitive technologies. This process of sociocultural evolution is not in any sense a "law" applicable to all societies. Some societies have evolved further and faster than others; some have become "stuck" at a particular level; some have disintegrated and disappeared; and all have changed in ways that are unique to themselves. Sociocultural evolution represents only a widespread pattern that has been observed in the historical and archaeological evidence (Steward, 1955; L. White, 1959; Sahlins and Service, 1960; Parsons, 1966; Fried, 1967; Lenski and Lenski, 1982).

As we indicated in the previous chapter, the *ecological approach* analyzes social and cultural elements in the context of the total environment in which a society exists. By applying this approach to different societies that have existed in the course of sociocultural evolution, we can account for much of the variation in their social structure and culture. In fact, although thousands of often dissimilar societies have existed since the beginning of human history, they can be broadly classified into five basic types according to the technologies they have used to exploit the environment—hunting and gathering, pastoralism, horticulture, agriculture, or industrialism. Additionally, a new, sixth type of society is beginning to emerge in the most technologically advanced parts of the world: the postindustrial society.

At each stage in this evolutionary process, social structure and culture grow more complex. The reason is that a more efficient subsistence strategy allows a society to create a greater amount of *surplus wealth,* that is, more food and other goods than is necessary to meet their producers' basic needs. As a result, an increasing proportion of the population is freed from the job of food production and can play a whole range of other social roles instead. The result is a significant increase in the *division of labor,* the specialization by individuals or groups in particular economic activities. In the most technologically simple societies, virtually the entire able-bodied population is engaged in food production. But in the most technologically advanced societies, less than 5 percent of the work force can feed the rest, enabling them to pursue a variety of occupational, social, and cultural opportunities (Lenski, 1966; Vayda, 1969; Y. Cohen, 1974; D. Bell, 1973; Bennet, 1976; Hardesty, 1977; M. Harris, 1979, 1980).

Hunting and Gathering Societies

As the name implies, a *hunting and gathering society* is one relying for its subsistence on such wild animals and vegetation as its members can hunt or gather. All societies used this subsistence strategy from the dawn of human existence until only a few thousand years ago, and even today there are still a handful of isolated peoples, such as the Aranda of the central Australian desert, who retain this way of life.

An immediate consequence of this strategy is that hunting and gathering societies usually consist of very small, scattered groups. The reason is simple: the environment cannot support a large concentration of people who rely on whatever food they can find or catch from one day to the next. Hunting and gathering peoples therefore live in small primary groups that rarely exceed forty members. Even so, each group may require several hundred square miles of territory to support itself, so contact between groups is brief and infrequent. The groups are based on kinship, with most members being related by ancestry or marriage. In fact, the family is almost the only distinct institution in these societies. It fulfills many of the functions that are met by more specialized institutions in other societies, such as economic production, the education of the young, and the defense of the group. Political institutions are absent: statuses in these societies are essentially equal, and although there is sometimes a part-time headman with very limited authority, most decisions are arrived at through group discussion.

Actually, there are very few statuses in these societies except for those based on sex, age, or kinship. The roles performed by men and women, by the young and the old, and by various kin are somewhat different, but there are no other specialized roles. Most members of the group do much the same things most of the time, and as a result of their common life experiences, they share almost identical values. Their religion almost never includes a belief in a powerful god or gods who are active in human affairs; instead, they tend to see the world as populated by unseen spirits that must be taken account of, but not necessarily worshiped.

Hunting and gathering peoples are constantly on the move because they must leave an area as soon as they have exhausted its food resources. As a result, possessions would be a hindrance to them, so they own very few goods. No one can acquire wealth, because there is no wealth to be acquired. Individuals who find food, the only significant resource in these societies, are expected to share it with the whole community. Intergroup fighting is extremely uncommon among hunters and gatherers, partly because they have so little in the way of material goods to fight about. Yet, contrary to popular belief, the life of these groups is not usually one of constant hardship on the brink of starvation. Their needs are simple and easily satisfied, and they spend less time working for their living than the average inhabitants of any other type of society. They are among the most leisured people on earth (Lee, 1968, 1979; Sahlins, 1972).

The use of hunting and gathering as a subsistence strategy thus has a very strong influence on social structure and culture. The social structure of these societies is necessarily very simple, and their cultures cannot become elaborate and diversified.

Figure 4.8 *The San people of the Namibian desert are one of the few hunting and gathering peoples that have survived into the modern world. They live in small nomadic groups based mainly on kinship. Accustomed to our own affluent lifestyle, we are inclined to regard their life as a hard one. But the San feel very few "needs," and are able to satisfy them with only a few hours' work each day. Their way of life is doomed, however, for their society is being influenced and absorbed by the industrializing societies of southern Africa.*

Figure 4.9 *Pastoralists in Afghanistan rest their camel herds at a temporary camp. The camel is well suited to the nomadic life of these pastoralists, for the animal can go without food or water for long periods and is an excellent beast of burden. The pastoralists take their herds from one place to another in search of grazing and water, using some of their camels for meat and milk. Surplus camels are sold or traded for other needed items. Not all pastoralists, however, are nomadic; those that live in areas that can support continuous grazing are able to form small, settled communities.*

Pastoral Societies

A ***pastoral society*** is one relying for its subsistence primarily on domesticated herd animals. The first pastoral societies emerged between 10,000 and 12,000 years ago, when some hunting and gathering groups began to capture, breed, and tend species of wild animals they had previously hunted. This strategy has since been adopted by many peoples living in deserts or other regions that are not suited to the cultivation of plants, but which contain animals—such as goats or sheep— that can be readily tamed and used as a food source. Many pastoral societies still exist in the modern world, particularly in Africa and in the Middle East.

Pastoralism is a much more reliable and productive strategy than hunting and gathering. It assures a steady food supply, and the size of the herds can be increased over time through careful animal husbandry. An important result is that societies can grow much larger, perhaps to include hundreds or even thousands of people. Equally significant, the greater productivity of this strategy allows pastoralists to accumulate a surplus of livestock and food. Through such means as trade, this surplus can be converted into other forms of wealth, such as wine, weapons, or gold—which can be used, in turn, to acquire power. For the first time, some individuals can become more powerful than others and can even pass on their status to

their descendants. Patterns of hereditary chieftainship begin to appear, as powerful and wealthy families are able to secure their positions.

Pastoralists are usually nomadic because they must constantly take their herds to new grazing grounds. As a result, their material possessions are few in number, but are more elaborate than those of hunting and gathering peoples because they can be carried by animals. Cultural artifacts in these societies therefore consist of items that are easily transportable—tents, woven carpets, simple utensils, jewelry, and so on. Their nomadic way of life often brings pastoralists into contact with other groups. One consequence is the development of systematic trading; a second is that disputes over grazing rights frequently lead to intergroup fighting. Slavery, unknown in hunting and gathering societies, makes its appearance as captives in battle are put to work for their conquerors.

Pastoral peoples tend to develop a belief that is found in very few religions: they commonly believe in a god or gods who take an active interest in human affairs and look after the people who worship them. This belief seems to have been suggested by the pastoralists' experience of the relationship between themselves and their flocks. The few modern religions based on this view of the relationship between human beings and a god— Judaism and its offshoots, Christianity and Islam— originated among pastoral peoples. (In fact, the word "pastor" originally meant shepherd.)

The subsistence strategy of pastoral societies thus provides distinctive social and cultural opportunities and limitations. Populations become larger, political and economic institutions begin to develop, and both social structure and culture become more complex.

Horticultural Societies

A *horticultural society* is one relying for its subsistence primarily on the hoe cultivation of domesticated plants. These societies also first appeared between 10,000 and 12,000 years ago, when some hunters and gatherers began to deliberately sow, tend, and harvest edible vegetation. Horticulturalists are essentially gardeners, working small plots by hand with hoes or digging sticks. Unlike pastoralists, they live a relatively settled life, although they must periodically move their gardens or villages short distances. Their subsistence strategy is typically based on a "slash and burn" technology, in which they clear areas of land, burn the vegetation they have cut down for use as fertilizer, raise crops for two or three years until the soil is exhausted, and then repeat the process elsewhere. Horticulture is really an alternative to pastoralism, and the choice of one strategy or the other depends primarily on environmental factors. Horticulture is much more likely to be adopted if the soil and climate favor crop cultivation. Many horticultural societies still exist in Africa, Asia, South America, and Australasia.

Like pastoralism, horticulture is much more efficient than hunting and gathering because it provides an assured, expandable food supply and the possibility of a surplus. Again, this surplus allows some wealthy individuals and families to become more powerful than others, and in advanced horticultural societies political institutions emerge in the form of hereditary chieftainships. The existence of a food surplus also means that some people can do work other than cultivation, so specialized new statuses and roles appear, such as those of shaman, trader, or craft worker. Because they live in relatively permanent settlements, horticulturalists can create more elaborate cultural artifacts than can hunters and gatherers or pastoralists. They can produce, for example, houses, thrones, or large stone sculptures. In the more advanced horticultural societies, political and economic institutions become well developed as conquest and trade link various villages together, and populations can run to several thousand people.

The emergence of some of humanity's grim-

Figure 4.10 *Lacking draft animals, horticulturalists have to tend their gardens by hand, a laborious process that limits the productivity of the land. Because the soil may quickly become exhausted, many horticultural peoples must either leave some of their gardens fallow every two or three years or find new areas for cultivation. These horticulturalists in the Amazon jungle are using a "slash and burn" technology: they cut down the vegetation, burn it, grow crops until the land is exhausted, and then repeat the process elsewhere. Horticulture permits relatively settled communities, and it can also provide enough food to support fairly large populations in the same area.*

mer endeavors is also closely associated with horticulture. Intertribal fighting and blood feuds, for example, are fairly common in horticultural societies, and the rare practices of cannibalism, headhunting, and human sacrifice are found almost exclusively in a few of the more aggressive societies of this type. The emergence of human sacrifice coincides with the tendency of advanced horticultural peoples to believe in capricious gods who must be worshiped and appeased, a development that is probably associated with their own experience of chieftainship and social inequality (Swanson, 1960).

The use of the horticultural strategy thus produces another set of distinctive consequences. It permits a settled way of life with relatively large populations, a situation that in turn encourages more complex social structures and cultures that are richer in material artifacts.

Agricultural Societies

An **agricultural society** is one relying for its subsistence primarily on the cultivation of crops through the use of plows and draft animals. The invention of the plow, about 6,000 years ago, was an event so significant that we still speak of the "agricultural revolution." The use of this tool greatly improves the productivity of the land; it brings to the surface nutrients that have sunk out of reach of the roots of plants, and it returns weeds to the soil to act as fertilizers. The same land can be cultivated almost continuously, and fully permanent settlements become possible. The use of animal power to pull the plow makes one agriculturalist far more productive than several horticulturalists. As a result, large fields replace small gardens, food output is greatly increased, and a substantial surplus can be produced.

The potential size of agricultural societies is much greater than that of horticultural or pastoral communities; it can run to several million people. A substantial minority of this population does not have to work the land and can engage instead in highly specialized, full-time roles (such as that of blacksmith or barber), most of which are conveniently performed among concentrations of other people. Agricultural subsistence thus allows for the establishment of cities, consisting essentially of people who directly or indirectly trade their spe-cialized skills for the agricultural products of those who still work the land. The society itself often consists of several such cities and their hinterlands, loosely welded together through periodic shows of force by those in central authority.

As political institutions grow much more elaborate, power becomes concentrated in the hands of a single individual, and a hereditary monarchy tends to emerge. The power of the monarch is usually absolute, literally involving the power of life and death over his or her subjects. In the more advanced agricultural societies the state emerges for the first time as a separate social institution with an elaborate court and government bureaucracy. Distinct social classes also make their appearance in virtually all agricultural societies. The wealth of these societies is almost always very unequally shared, with a small landowning minority of nobles enjoying the surplus produced by a working majority of peasants; one example of this pattern was the old feudal system of Europe. Religion also becomes a separate social institution, with full-time officials, temples, and considerable political influence. The religions of agricultural societies often include a belief in a "family" of gods, one of whom, the "high god," is regarded as more powerful than other, lesser gods. This belief probably stems from people's experience of different levels of political authority, ranging from local rulers to the absolute monarch. A distinct economic institu-

Figure 4.11 *Agriculture can be a highly productive strategy. Agriculturalists, like these Asian peasants, cultivate the soil with plows instead of hoes and digging sticks. Nutrients are thus returned to the soil, and the land can be continuously cultivated year after year. The high productivity of agriculture frees a large part of the population from the need to toil on the land, permitting them to engage in other specialized roles.*

tion also develops; trade becomes more elaborate, and money comes into use as a medium of exchange. The need for accurate records of crop harvests, taxation, and government transactions provides a powerful incentive for the development of some system of writing, which appears in virtually all advanced agricultural societies.

Agricultural societies tend to be almost constantly at war and sometimes engage in systematic empire-building. These conditions demand an effective military organization, and permanent armies appear for the first time. The need for efficient transport and communications in these large societies leads to the development of roads and navies, and previously isolated communities are brought into contact with one another. The relative wealth of agricultural societies and their settled way of life permit surplus resources to be invested in new cultural artifacts—paintings and statues, public buildings and monuments, palaces and stadiums.

A society relying on agriculture as a subsistence strategy thus has a far more complex social structure and culture than any of the less evolved types of societies. The number of statuses and roles multiplies, population size increases, cities appear, new institutions emerge, social classes arise, political and economic inequality becomes built into the social structure, and culture becomes much more diversified.

Industrial Societies

An *industrial society* is one relying for its subsistence primarily on mechanized production. Originating in England in the Industrial Revolution about 250 years ago, this mode of production proved so immensely successful that it has since spread all over the world, absorbing, transforming, or destroying other types of society in the process.

Industrialism is based on the application of scientific knowledge to the technology of production, enabling new energy sources to be harnessed and permitting machines to do the work that was previously done by people or animals. Because inventions and discoveries build upon one another, the rate of technological innovation in industrial societies is swift. New technologies—such as the steam engine, the internal combustion engine, electrical power, or atomic energy—tend to stimulate changes in the economy and other institutions. Unlike preindustrial societies, therefore, industrial societies are in a continual state of rapid social change.

Industrialism is a highly efficient subsistence strategy, for it allows a small minority to feed the rest of the people. Industrial societies can thus become very large, with populations running into tens or even hundreds of millions. In fact, populations grow very rapidly in the early stages of industrialization because people live longer as a result of better health and living standards. (In more advanced industrial societies population size tends to stabilize as birth control becomes popular.) Industrial societies are also highly urbanized, with the bulk of the population living in or around cities, where most jobs are located and where new ones are continually created. In this mass environment, more and more social life takes place in secondary groups rather than primary groups: organizations such as corporations and government bureaucracies flourish, and a good deal of social interaction becomes anonymous and impersonal.

Industrialism has a dramatic effect on institutions. The economy, of course, becomes vast, complex, and pervasive in its effects on the whole society. The family loses many of its earlier functions; it is no longer a unit of economic production, nor does it have the main responsibility for the education of the young. The influence of religion as an unquestioned source of moral authority also shrinks, for people no longer share similar life experiences and consequently hold many different and competing values and beliefs. Science, however, emerges as a new and important social institution, because technological innovation depends on the growth and refinement of scientific knowledge. Similarly, education becomes a distinct institution: an industrial society requires mass literacy, and for the first time formal education becomes compulsory for the many rather than a luxury for the few. Other institutions, such as law, sport, medicine, and the military, grow more elaborate.

Another effect of industrialism is, on the whole, to reduce social inequality. In a preindustrial society, most statuses are ascribed: a person is born into the circumstances of, say, a lord or a peasant and can do little to change this fate. But a person can actively achieve many of the new statuses, such as bus driver or politician, that appear in industrial societies. In the early stages of industrialism there is usually a yawning gap between the incomes of the rich and the poor as the rural peasantry is transformed into an urban work force, often under the most wretched conditions; but thereafter there is usually a steady reduction in inequalities of social class. Government becomes more representative as hereditary monarchies pass away, generally to be replaced by more representative political institutions.

Figure 4.12 *Industrial societies rely on advanced technology and mechanized production for their subsistence. This strategy is so efficient and produces so much wealth that industrialism is rapidly becoming the dominant mode of production all over the world. Despite its many advantages, however, industrialism poses a host of new problems to human society, ranging from pollution to overpopulation.*

The historical record shows that industrial societies have frequently used their superior military technology to invade and even colonize preindustrial societies. But industrial societies are not as inclined to fight one another: although preparedness for war may reach new heights of intensity, actual outbreaks of warfare are relatively infrequent. One study of preindustrial European societies found that, over a period of several centuries, they were at war, on average, almost every second year (Sorokin, 1937). In contrast, most of the industrial societies of modern Europe have been at war with each other only twice in the course of this century, and some have not been at war at all. The reason may lie more in self-interest than in pacifism: warfare can be ruinous for an advanced industrial society, largely because it involves such devastating weaponry and such severe economic dislocation. Indeed, were there to be a nuclear war, it is doubtful if the major industrial societies would survive at all.

Industrial society is rapidly becoming the dominant form in the modern world. Its huge surplus wealth makes possible extraordinary material conveniences and a far more heterogeneous culture than any found in preindustrial societies. The triumph of industrialism is due to its unprecedented effectiveness in exploiting the natural environment, but this success has caused a variety of new problems. Industrial societies have to contend with the ravaging of the environment through pollution, resource depletion, and species extinction; the destruction of traditional values and communi-

ties; the disruption of kinship systems; mass anonymity in mushrooming cities; the threat of nuclear war; and a breakneck rate of social change that constantly threatens to disorganize the existing social structure.

Postindustrial Societies

There is no reason to suppose that sociocultural evolution has come to a dead end with the development of industrial societies. But what lies beyond? Predicting the future is always a risky exercise, but many sociologists are convinced that the most advanced industrial nations, such as the United States, Canada, Japan, Sweden, Switzerland, and West Germany, are in transition to a new societal type. This is the ***postindustrial society,*** one relying for its subsistence primarily on the production of services and information. The United States is regarded as the pioneer in this trend because, in the latter half of the twentieth century, it has become the first society in history whose population does not work mostly at food production or industrial manufacturing. Instead, a majority of the workers provide services, ranging from auto repairs to teaching to investment banking. Many of these service jobs involve the production or manipulation of information by people in such roles as scientist, news reporter, government clerk, computer programmer, travel agent, consultant, lawyer, and the like (Touraine, 1971; D. Bell, 1973; Lipset, 1979; Toffler, 1980).

Figure 4.13 *An unprecedented feature of the emerging postindustrial societies is that the bulk of their workers do not produce food or other goods. Instead, most people make their living by providing services or information. Postindustrial societies rely heavily on scientific innovation and international communications and trade. These exceptionally affluent societies are highly complex and diversified, with an extraordinary number of statuses, roles, and subcultural lifestyles.*

Postindustrial society produces knowledge—particularly technological knowledge—that can be leased, sold, or used to produce goods, services, or still more knowledge. Agriculture and manufacturing do not disappear in a postindustrial society; they are simply made more efficient through automation and other technological innovations that allow fewer workers to produce an ever greater surplus. However, certain industries that still rely heavily on manual labor, like clothes making or shipbuilding, go into decline: they can operate more cheaply in less technologically advanced societies where wages are far lower. Indeed, a postindustrial society can exist only in an environment of global interdependence, where labor, capital, raw materials, and technological expertise can be combined and utilized with little regard for national boundaries. In turn, the postindustrial society thrives by supplying itself and other societies with advanced theoretical knowledge and with products based on this knowledge, such as computers, telecommunications, defense systems, genetic engineering, medical equipment, or aerospace vehicles.

In an environment that values theoretical knowledge and technical efficiency, two institutions become crucial: education and science. Education becomes a key to knowledge and thus to high statuses, for the most successful people are typically those who can control information and decision making—and not necessarily, as in other societal types, just those who own property. The average educational level in a postindustrial society is far higher than in any industrial or preindustrial society. Science grows in importance because technological innovation depends on continued scientific research, which is supported by massive infusions of public and corporate funds. Indeed, a feature of the emerging postindustrial society is its supreme faith in technology—including a conviction that technology can be used to solve the problems, such as the threats of pollution or modern weapons, that earlier technologies have created.

The postindustrial subsistence strategy has profound effects on the economy, for its huge surplus wealth permits an unprecedented standard of living and more diverse statuses and roles than ever. In fact, the postindustrial society offers so many different jobs that workers can anticipate changing their occupational statuses several times during their careers. Most people are "white collar" workers, doing jobs that require mental rather than physical effort (and new technologies like the computer eliminate even some of that effort, by taking over such menial tasks as billing and bookkeeping). As a result of the size, mobility, educational level, and widely differing life experiences of their populations, postindustrial societies have relatively varied, tolerant, and heterogeneous cultures. Subcultures and "lifestyles" proliferate, and people become deeply concerned with individual self-fulfillment. The emerging postindustrial societies show an unprecedented concern for the equality of the sexes and for the rights of individuals and minorities, and it is no accident that they are all highly democratic societies in which governments can be periodically chosen or dismissed by the voters. (This raises the interesting question of whether a still-industrial society like the Soviet Union, which attempts to control information and thus stifles creativity, can become a postindustrial society without making major changes in its political institution.)

Figure 4.14

"There're a billion people in China. At some point, some of them are going to need agents."

Drawing by D. Reilly; © 1985
The New Yorker Magazine, Inc.

Inhabitants of the emerging postindustrial societies face many problems, some of them a legacy from industrialism: the search for self-fulfillment in a mass society; economic imbalances caused by rapid change; unprecedented shortages of water, energy, land, and living space; and dilemmas of global interdependence in an overpopulated world where, despite the affluence of a handful of technologically advanced societies, billions of people are desperately poor. And lurking in the background is another problem, potentially devastating but easy to overlook. Despite their appearance of supreme mastery of the environment, postindustrial societies are ultimately dependent on two delicate systems: the biological life-supports of the planetary ecosystem, and the network of international political and economic cooperation. In any serious global disruption—caused, say, by natural disasters, nuclear war, or economic collapse—the hunters and gatherers of the world might continue to feed themselves, and be unaffected. But what would become of societies where most people are trained to produce neither food nor goods, nor little else besides that ultimate inedible, knowledge? This inherent danger does not imply that all postindustrial societies are necessarily doomed; it does mean that they are more fragile than they might appear.

Because the United States is a society in transition from one societal type to another, it displays shared characteristics of both industrial and post-industrial societies. On the one hand, the country remains the most powerful and productive industrial society in the world; on the other, most workers are now employed outside manufacturing in service and information jobs. But if the American present is still ambiguous, the future is surely postindustrial. We cannot know what form the society will take in the decades ahead, for there are no precedents to guide us, and the future will be influenced in any case by technological and other developments we cannot yet foresee. But therein lies part of the challenge and fascination of American life. In many other parts of the world, people wait for the future to arrive, as it were, second hand—for the latest fads and fashions, trends and techniques, goods and gadgets, to arrive from the distant lands where they have already been tried out. But we inhabit a society that is (among other things) a veritable sociological laboratory, a place where experiments are being made—here, now, and by ourselves—that may shape the human future.

Preindustrial and Industrialized Societies: A Comparison

The story of sociocultural evolution gives us a powerful reminder that, no matter what we make of our lives, we do it in the context provided by our society and the subsistence strategy it offers. Most readers of this book will spend their working lives sitting at a desk. Yet, in an earlier societal type, you might have spent your days on an assembly line; plowing fields for your feudal lord; hoeing your turnip patch or tending your yaks; or poking under a likely rock for some chewy bug.

In the course of sociocultural evolution thus far, however, the sharpest break occurs between the various traditional preindustrial societies on the one hand and modern industrial (and postindustrial) societies on the other. The changes involved are profound, and a major task of sociology has been to identify their nature.

In 1887, for example, the German sociologist Ferdinand Tönnies distinguished between the *Gemeinschaft,* a "community" in which most people know one another, and the *Gesellschaft,* an "association" in which most people are strangers to one another. The former type of society, he argued, is characterized by intimate, face-to-face contact, strong feelings of social solidarity, and a

Figure 4.15 *The most significant change in the history of sociocultural evolution is that between traditional, preindustrial societies and modern, industrialized ones. This table lists some of the typical differences between each type of society.*

THE GREAT TRANSFORMATION

	Preindustrial Society	Industrialized Society
Subsistence strategy	Hunting and gathering, pastoralism, horticulture, agricultural.	Industrialism, postindustrialism.
Social structure	Relatively simple: few statuses and roles; few developed institutions other than the family.	Complex: many statuses and roles; many highly developed institutions, such as education, science, etc.
Statuses	Mostly ascribed.	Some ascribed, but many achieved.
Social groups	Mostly primary (personal, intimate).	Mostly secondary (impersonal, anonymous).
Community size	Typically small (villages).	Typically large (cities).
Division of labor	Relatively little, except on grounds of age and sex.	A great deal: occupations are highly specialized.
Social control	Mostly informal, relying on spontaneous community reaction.	Often formal, relying on laws, police, and courts.
Values	Tradition-oriented, religious.	Future-oriented, secular.
Culture	Homogeneous: most people share similar norms and values; few subcultures.	Heterogeneous: many subcultures holding different norms and values.
Technology	Primitive, based mainly on human and animal muscle power.	Advanced, based mainly on machines and energy in the form of electricity, etc.
Social change	Slow.	Rapid.

commitment to tradition. The latter is marked by impersonal contacts, individualism rather than group loyalty, and a slackening of traditional ties and values. In 1893 the French sociologist Emile Durkheim also distinguished between a society that is held together by **mechanical solidarity,** a form of social cohesion based on the similarity of the members, and one held together by ***organic solidarity,*** a form of social cohesion based on the differences among members, which make them interdependent. In the former type, people perform much the same roles and share the same values; in the latter, they rely on each other's specialized roles but are more socially diverse. These and other writers were trying to describe essentially the same phenomenon: the differences between what in this book we shall call "traditional,"

or "preindustrial," societies, and "modern," or "industrialized," ones.

Some of the basic differences between preindustrial and industrialized societies are summarized in Figure 4.15. The changes wrought by this great transformation are entirely new in the history of the human species, and modern societies are still in the difficult process of adjusting to them. In this book we shall be dealing primarily with the most technologically advanced society in the world, the United States. But from time to time we shall refer to preindustrial and other industrialized societies—both to give some sense of the immense and often fascinating variety of human social behavior and to offer, through comparison, a greater awareness of the distinctive features of our own society.

Summary

1.   Human beings are social animals, by habit and by necessity. A society is a population occupying the same territory, subject to the same political authority, and sharing a common culture.

2.   Social processes are generally patterned and predictable. The basic components of a social system tend to be linked in an organized relationship, called social structure. Important components of social structure are statuses, roles, groups, and institutions.

3.   A status is a socially defined position in society. Ascribed statuses are arbitrarily assigned by society; achieved statuses are earned. Some statuses rank higher or lower than others; people of roughly equivalent status form a class.

4.   A role is the set of behavior patterns, obligations, and privileges attached to a particular status. Social norms prescribe how particular roles should be played. Role performance, however, may differ from role expectations. Role strains occurs when a person has difficulty in meeting role expectations; role conflict occurs when two or more of a person's roles impose conflicting demands.

5.   A group consists of a number of people interacting on the basis of shared expectations. A primary group is small and intimate; a secondary group is more anonymous. Groups are important building blocks of social structure.

6.   Institutions are stable clusters of norms, values, statuses, roles, and groups that develop around basic needs of society. They tend to be conservative, to be closely interrelated within social structure, to adjust to significant changes in other institutions, and to be the site of major social problems. Functionalist and conflict analyses emphasize different aspects of institutions.

7.   Sport is a significant American institution with important social functions. In some respects it provides a microcosm of the society, reflecting basic social values and patterns of class, race, and sex participation similar to those of other major social institutions.

8.   There has been a general trend of sociocultural evolution from small and simple societies to large and complex ones. This involves a progressively greater division of labor (resulting in more statuses and roles) within the population. Societies can be classified according to their basic subsistence strategies. The main types of societies are hunting and gathering societies, pastoral societies, horticultural societies, agricultural societies, and industrial societies. A new type, the postindustrial society, is emerging. Culture and social structure grow more complex at each stage, for more productive strategies produce greater surplus wealth, which can support larger and more diverse populations.

9.   Modern industrial (and postindustrial) societies are radically unlike traditional, preindustrial societies. They experience a rapid rate of social change, and virtually all aspects of culture and social structure are transformed by the modernization process that accompanies industrialization. Sociologists are still attempting to grasp the full significance of these changes.

Important Terms

society (89)

social structure (90)

status (90)

master status (90)

status inconsistency (90)

ascribed status (90)

achieved status (91)

social class (91)

role (91)

role expectations (92)

role performance (92)

role strain (92)

role conflict (92)

group (92)

primary group (92)

secondary group (93)

institution (93)

sport (95)

sociocultural evolution (101)

ecological approach (101)

surplus wealth (101)

division of labor (101)

hunting and gathering society (101)

pastoral society (103)

horticultural society (104)

agricultural society (105)

industrial society (106)

postindustrial society (107)

Gemeinschaft/Gesellschaft (109)

mechanical solidarity/organic solidarity (110)

Suggested Readings

AHRENS, W., and SUSAN P. MONTAGUE (eds.). *The American Dimension.* Port Washington, N.Y.: Alfred, 1976.

A collection of interesting articles on various aspects of American culture and society. Many of the contributions are both insightful and amusing.

COAKLEY, JAY J. *Sport in Society: Issues and Controversies.* 3rd ed. St. Louis: Mosby, 1986.

A good general introduction to the sociology of sport.

EITZEN, D. STANLEY (ed.). *Sport in Contemporary Society: An Anthology.* 2nd ed. New York: St. Martin's, 1984.

An excellent selection of articles on various aspects of the sociology of sport.

LENSKI, GERHARD, and JEAN LENSKI. *Human Societies.* 4th ed. New York: McGraw-Hill, 1982.

This book examines societies from the perspective of sociocultural evolution and traces the changes that take place in social structure in the course of the process.

PLOG, FRED, and DANIEL G. BATES. *Cultural Anthropology.* 3rd ed. New York: Knopf, 1986.

A concise account of human societies from an anthropological perspective. The book includes sections on hunting and gathering, pastoral, horticultural, agricultural, and industrial societies.

SKOLNICK, JEROME H., and ELLIOTT CURIE. *Crisis in American Institutions.* 6th ed. Boston: Little, Brown, 1985.

A collection of readings on modern American social problems. The book systematically relates these problems to strains and failures in American institutions and stresses the conflicts of interest involved in many of the problems.

TOFFLER, ALVIN. *The Third Wave.* New York: Morrow, 1980.

An account for the general reader of the transition to postindustrial society—the "third wave" after the agricultural and industrial revolutions.

READING

Status and Role in a Mock Prison

PHILIP ZIMBARDO

Philip Zimbardo, a social psychologist, set up a mock "prison" in which students played the roles of prisoners and guards. The results were frightening. Zimbardo's report shows how the roles that we play deeply influence our social behavior.

In an attempt to understand just what it means psychologically to be a prisoner or a prison guard, Craig Haney, Curt Banks, Dave Jaffe and I created our own prison. We carefully screened over 70 volunteers who answered an ad in a Palo Alto city newspaper and ended up with about two dozen young men who were selected to be part of this study. They were mature, emotionally stable, normal, intelligent college students from middle-class homes throughout the United States and Canada. They appeared to represent the cream of this generation. None had any criminal record and all were relatively homogeneous on many dimensions initially.

Half were arbitrarily designated as prisoners by a flip of a coin, the others as guards. These were the roles they were to play in our simulated prison. The guards were made aware of the potential seriousness and danger of the situation and their own vulnerability. They made up their own formal rules for maintaining law, order and respect, and were generally free to improvise new ones during their eight-hour, three-man shifts. The prisoners were unexpectedly picked up at their homes by a city policeman in a squad car, searched, handcuffed, fingerprinted, booked at the Palo Alto station house and taken blindfolded to our jail. There they were stripped, deloused, put into a uniform, given a number and put into a cell with two other prisoners where they expected to live for the next two weeks. The pay was good ($15 a day) and their motivation was to make money. We observed and recorded on videotape the events that occurred in the prison, and we interviewed and tested the prisoners and guards at various points throughout the study. . . .

At the end of only six days we had to close down our mock prison because what we saw was frightening. It was no longer apparent to most of the subjects (or to us) where reality ended and their roles began. The majority had indeed become prisoners or guards, no longer able to clearly differentiate between role playing and self. There were dramatic changes in virtually every aspect of their behavior, thinking and feeling. In less than a week the experience of imprisonment undid (temporarily) a lifetime of learning; human values were suspended, self-concepts were challenged and the ugliest, most base, pathological side of human nature surfaced. We were horrified because we saw some boys (guards) treat others as if they were despicable animals, taking pleasure in cruelty, while other boys (prisoners) became servile, dehumanized robots who thought only of escape, of their own individual survival and of their mounting hatred for the guards.

We had to release three prisoners in the first four days because they had such acute situational traumatic reactions as hysterical crying, confusion in thinking and severe depression. Others begged to be paroled, and all but three were willing to forfeit all the money they had earned if they could be paroled. By then (the fifth day) they had been so programmed to think of themselves as prisoners that when their request for parole was denied, they returned docilely to their cells. Now, had they been thinking as college students acting in an oppressive experiment, they would have quit once they no longer wanted the $15 a day we used as our only incentive. However, the reality was not quitting an experiment but "being paroled by the parole board from the Stanford County Jail." By the last days, the earlier solidarity among the prisoners (systematically broken by the guards) dissolved into "each man for himself." Finally, when one of their fellows was put in solitary confinement (a small closet) for refusing to eat, the prisoners were given a choice by one of the guards: give up their blankets and the incorrigible prisoner would be let out, or keep their blankets and he would be kept in all night. They voted to keep their blankets and to abandon their brother.

About a third of the guards became tyrannical in their arbitrary use of power, in enjoying their control over other people. They were corrupted by the power of their roles and became quite inventive in their techniques of breaking the spirit of the prisoners and making them feel they were worthless. Some of the guards merely did their jobs as tough but fair correctional officers, and several were good guards from the prisoners' point of view since they did them small favors and were friendly. However, no good guard ever interfered with a command by any of the bad guards; they never intervened on the side of the prisoners, they never told the others to ease off because it was only an experiment, and they never even came to me as prison superintendent or experimenter in charge to complain. . . .

By the end of the week the experiment had become a reality. . . . A Catholic priest who was a former prison chaplain in Washington, D.C. talked to our prisoners after four days and said they were just like the other first-timers he had seen.

SOURCE: Philip G. Zimbardo, "Pathology of Imprisonment," *Society*, 9 (April 1972), pp. 4–8.

CHAPTER 5

Socialization

At birth the human infant is a helpless organism. The newborn knows nothing, and cannot survive for more than a few hours without the help of other people. Unlike other animals, the infant will have to learn virtually all its later patterns of behavior. Somehow this biological being must be transformed into a fully human being, a person able to participate effectively in society. That transformation is achieved through the complex process of socialization.

Socialization is the process of social interaction through which people acquire personality and learn the way of life of their society. It is the essential link between the individual and society—a link so vital that neither individual nor society could survive without it. Socialization enables the individual to learn the norms, values, languages, skills, beliefs, and other patterns of thought and action that are essential for social living. And socialization enables the society to reproduce itself socially as well as biologically, thus ensuring its continuity from generation to generation.

One of the most important outcomes of socialization is individual *personality*, the fairly stable patterns of thought, feeling, and action that are typical of an individual. Personality thus includes three main elements: the *cognitive* component of thought, belief, perception, memory, and other intellectual capacities; the *emotional* component of love, hate, envy, sympathy, anger, pride, and other feelings; and the *behavioral* component of skills, aptitudes, competence, and other abilities. Nobody is born a great mathematician, the life of the party, or a skillful carpenter. People may be born with the potential to become any of these, but what they actually become is primarily the product of their unique experiences.

Social interaction takes place according to the norms and values of the culture in question. The content of socialization and the personality types

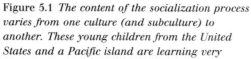

Figure 5.1 *The content of the socialization process varies from one culture (and subculture) to another. These young children from the United States and a Pacific island are learning very* *different ways of life. Within each society, there are typical personality patterns and types of social behavior that differ from those in other societies— yet each person grows up to be unique.*

that are most admired therefore vary from one society to another. However, attempts to pinpoint "national character" have met with only limited success. One difficulty is that personality is hard to measure scientifically, especially in a way that would allow valid cross-cultural comparisons. Another difficulty is that ideas of what other people are like are often influenced by ethnocentrism or even by the prevailing climate of international relations. During World War II, for example, Americans viewed the Japanese as cruel and treacherous, but now that they are our allies, they are regarded as ingenious and industrious.

Nonetheless, it is clear that there are characteristic personality traits in every society—patterns that result from a common experience of socialization in a unique culture. Within every society, however, each person is different, and these differences are also largely the product of socialization. We are born and live not only in a society but also in a specific part of it, and we are therefore influenced by particular subcultures of class, race, religion, and region, as well as by specific groups such as family and friends. Distinctive new experiences in these contexts are continually blended with old ones, so every person's biography and personality are unique. The socialization process thus helps to explain both the general *similarities* in personality and social behavior within a society and the many *differences* that exist between one person and another.

Socialization continues throughout the *life course*—the biological and social sequence of birth, childhood, maturity, old age, and death. At each stage in this lifelong process, we continually encounter new or changing conditions, both personal and social, and must learn to adjust to them. The most important socialization, however, occurs during infancy and childhood, when the foundations of later personality are laid. For this reason we shall concentrate in this chapter primarily on early socialization.

"Nature" and "Nurture"

From the middle of the last century until relatively recently, social scientists debated whether our personalities and social behavior are the product of heredity ("nature") or of learning ("nurture"). The debate led absolutely nowhere and is now recognized, in its "either/or" form, to have been one of the most futile controversies in the history of social science.

The "nature" viewpoint was dominant during the late nineteenth and early twentieth centuries, when various psychologists began to compile endless lists of supposed human "instincts." Warfare was attributed to an "aggressive" instinct, society to a "herding" instinct, capitalism to an "acquisitive" instinct, and so on. The problem with this enterprise was that it soon got out of hand. One researcher reviewed the existing literature and found that over 10,000 supposed instincts had already been "discovered" by various authors (Bernard, 1924). To make matters worse, evidence mounted to show that behavior which social scientists in Western cultures had declared "instinctive" in the human species often did not appear at all in other cultures—or was reversed in them. The situation became ludicrous, and the old concept of "instinct" quickly went out of fashion. Most contemporary psychologists do not regard the word as meaningful and refuse to use it in discussing human behavior.

Throughout most of this century, the "nurture" viewpoint held sway. At the turn of the century Ivan Pavlov, a Russian physiologist, noticed that dogs salivate not only at the presence of food but also at exposure to anything they have associated with feeding, such as their dish or even the ringing of a bell. If dogs could learn by association, would not human beings have an even greater capacity to do so? Pavlov's theories were taken up by the American psychologist John B. Watson, who argued that human behavior and personality are completely flexible and can be molded in any direction. Watson triumphantly taught an infant to call his milk bottle "mama" by offering him a bottle whenever he uttered the word. He capped his performance by teaching a little boy named Albert to fear white rats by frightening the boy with a loud noise whenever he was shown a white rat. In a widely quoted statement Watson (1924) declared without hesitation:

> Give me a dozen healthy infants, well-formed, and my own specified world to bring them up in, and I'll guarantee to take any one at random and train him to become any type of specialist I might select— doctor, lawyer, artist, merchant-chief and, yes, even beggar, and thief, regardless of his talents, penchants, tendencies, abilities, vocations, and race of his ancestors.

Today, most social scientists regard this view as hopelessly naive. The current consensus is that the "nature versus nurture" debate was a pointless one, for it opposed two factors that are closely interrelated and cannot be separated. We are the product not of either heredity or learning but rather of a complex interaction between the two.

We can readily see that this is the case with some of our physical features. Height and weight are partly determined by heredity. But people born with genes for tallness or fatness may not actually become tall or fat. If they are underfed, they will be shorter and thinner than they might otherwise have been. The same appears to be true of many aspects of personality. So far, scientists have not found any specific genes that can be shown to influence personality, but many suspect that some traits, such as intelligence, shyness, and artistic abilities, are partly influenced by hereditary factors. The methodological difficulties of sorting out heredity from environment are formidable, however. For example, even from the moment of birth, infants seem different: some are active, some passive, some irritable, some easily pleased. But this does not necessarily mean that these characteristics are inherited. They may have been influenced by the newborn's environment, which began in the womb nine months before and included such prenatal factors as the mother's emotional condition, nutrition, drug usage, hormonal balance, and general state of health. Moreover, socialization is already under way in the first few hours and days of life. Extensive studies have shown that mother-infant interaction is an extraordinarily rich and complex process in which each participant influences the other in ways that are unique to their relationship. Our personalities, therefore, are subject to social influence virtually as soon as we are born (Pines, 1982; Kaye, 1983; Kagan, 1984; K. Berger, 1986.)

The best evidence for some genetic influence on personality comes from studies of identical twins, who share exactly the same genetic heritage. If genes alone determined personality traits, then identical twins would have identical personalities. Of course, they never do, and some are very unlike each other in temperament and skills. On the whole, however, identical twins are much more likely to share personality traits than fraternal (nonidentical) twins or nontwin siblings. Even when identical twins are raised apart in different families, they tend to have more similar personalities than fraternal twins raised together, although they are significantly less similar than identical twins raised together. But these findings, too, are blurred by methodological problems. First, identical twins are subject to the same prenatal environment. Second, family, friends, and teachers tend to treat identical twins alike, especially when they have trouble telling them apart. In addition, people react to others partly according to their appearance, and to that extent even identical twins reared apart share similar social experiences. But these environmental factors do not seem sufficient to explain entirely the similarities in identical twins' personalities (Holden, 1980; Farber, 1981).

At most, however, hereditary factors provide a basic potential. People learn to develop and satisfy their potentials in a social setting, and it is primarily their social experience that will determine whether they realize or fall short of these potentials. A placid baby, if systematically ill-treated, can become a psychologically disturbed adult; a person born with a capacity for high intelligence, if raised in a stultifying environment, can grow up to be a dullard. Biology may set the broad outlines and limits of our potential, but how or whether we use that potential depends on the environment in which we live. The key to understanding the interaction of "nature" and "nurture" is the process of socialization, where biology and culture meet and blend.

Effects of Childhood Isolation

For many centuries people have wondered what human beings would be like if they were raised in isolation from human society. Some speculated that such children would be mere brutes, revealing the essence of our real "human nature." Others felt that they would be perfect beings, perhaps speaking the language of Adam and Eve in the Garden of Eden. Today there are obvious ethical considerations that make any experiment involving the deliberate isolation of children impossible, but earlier ages were not always under such moral inhibitions. In the thirteenth century the emperor Frederick II conducted just such an experiment, recorded by a medieval historian in the following terms:

> His . . . folly was that he wanted to find out what kind of speech and what manner of speech children would have when they grew up, if they spoke to no one beforehand. So he bade foster mothers and nurses to suckle the children, to bathe and wash them, but in no way to prattle with them or to speak to them, for he wanted to learn whether they would speak the Hebrew language, which was the oldest, or Greek, or Latin, or Arabic, or perhaps the language of their parents, of whom they had been born. But he laboured in vain, because the children all died. For they could not live without the petting and joyful faces and loving words of their foster mothers. [Quoted in Ross and McLaughlin, 1949]

The unhappy fate of the children comes as no surprise to modern social scientists, for it has been proved beyond doubt that children need more than mere physical care if they are to prosper. They need close emotional attachments with at least one other person; without this bond, socialization is impaired, and irreversible damage may be done to the personality. Evidence for this view comes from four main sources: reports of so-called feral (untamed) children who were allegedly raised by wild animals; studies of children who were deliberately reared in isolation by their own families; studies of children in institutions; and laboratory experiments that study the effects of isolation on other primates.

"Feral" Children

The evidence relating to "feral" children is highly dramatic but also highly unreliable. Many societies have myths about children being raised by animals. In the late nineteenth and early twentieth

Figure 5.2 *The myths of several societies tell of children who were raised by wild animals. This illustration shows the discovery of the legendary founders of ancient Rome, the twin brothers Romulus and Remus, who were supposedly raised by a wolf.*

centuries, however, a few cases of the discovery of children whose behavior seemed more like that of animals than human beings were reported from India, France, and elsewhere (Singh and Zingg, 1942; Malson, 1972; H. Lane, 1976; MacLean, 1978; Shattuck, 1980). In every case the children appeared to live alone in the wild, could not speak, reacted with fear or hostility toward other human beings, slouched or walked on all fours, and tore ravenously at their food. Attempts to socialize these children are said to have met with little success, and all died at a young age.

There are two difficulties with these reports. The first is that the children were never systematically examined by trained investigators, and the second is that we know nothing about their history before they were discovered. It seems highly improbable that they had been raised by wild animals. It is far more likely that they had been deserted by their own parents shortly before they were discovered by other people, and that they were already mentally disturbed, autistic, or had been raised in some form of isolation before being abandoned.

Children Raised in Isolation

Much more convincing evidence comes from studies of children who were deliberately raised in isolation by their own families. The sociological implications of these situations were first discussed by Kingsley Davis (1940, 1947, 1948), who reported on two such cases in the United States.

The first child, Anna, was discovered at the age of six. She had been born illegitimate, and her grandfather had insisted that she be kept hidden in an attic room. Anna received a bare minimum of physical care and attention and had virtually no opportunities for social interaction. When she was found, she could not talk, walk, keep herself clean, or feed herself; she was totally apathetic, expressionless, and indifferent to human beings. Davis (1948) comments: "Here, then, was a human organism which had missed nearly six years of socialization. Her condition shows how little her purely biological resources, when acting alone, could contribute to making her a complete person."

Attempts to socialize Anna had only limited success. The girl died of jaundice about four years later, but in that time she was able to learn some words and phrases, although she could never speak sentences. She also learned to use building blocks, to string beads, to wash her hands and brush her teeth, to follow directions, and to treat a doll with affection. She learned to walk but could run only clumsily. By the time of her death at almost eleven she had reached the level of socialization of a child of two or three.

The second child, Isabelle, was discovered around the same time as Anna and was approximately the same age, about six. She too was an illegitimate child, and her grandfather had kept her and her mother—a deaf-mute—in a dark room most of the time. Isabelle had the advantage, compared to Anna, of social interaction with her mother; but she had no chance to develop speech, for the two communicated with gestures. When Isabelle was discovered, her behavior toward other people, especially men, was "almost that of a wild animal." At first it was thought that she was deaf, for she did not appear to hear the sounds around her, and her only speech was a strange croaking sound. The specialists who worked with her pronounced her feebleminded and did not expect that she could ever be taught to speak.

Unlike Anna, however, Isabelle had the training of a skilled team of doctors and psychologists. After a slow start, she suddenly spurted through the stages of learning that are usually characteristic of the first six years of childhood, taking every stage in the usual order but at much greater speed than normal. By the time she was about eight years old she had reached an apparently normal level of intellectual development and was able to attend school with other children. Her greater success seems to have been related to the skills of her trainers, the fact that her mother was present during her isolation, and the fact that she was eventually able to gain the use of language.

Since these early cases, there have been several subsequent reports of children raised in isolation. The effects on all these children are similar: without socialization, they lack normal social, psychological, and even physical development. (One recent case is discussed in the reading "Genie" at the end of this chapter.)

Institutionalized Children

The socialization of children who are raised in orphanages and similar institutions differs in one important respect from that of children who are raised in families. Institutionalized children rarely have the chance to develop close emotional ties with specific adults, for although the children may interact with a large number of staff members, the attendants simply do not have the time to devote much personal attention to any one child. The standard of nutrition and other physical care in institutions is sometimes good and comparable to that in private homes, but relationships between child and adult are usually minimal.

In 1945, the psychologist René Spitz published an influential article on the effects that these conditions have on children's personalities. Spitz compared some infants who were being raised by their own mothers with infants of the same age who had been placed in the care of an orphanage. The infants living with their mothers had plenty of opportunity for close social interaction, but those in the institution received only routine care at mealtimes and when their clothing or bedding was changed. Spitz found that the infants in the orphanage were physically, socially, and emotionally retarded compared with the other infants—a difference, moreover, that increased steadily as the children grew older.

Spitz's report was followed by a large number of studies on the effects of institutionalization on infants and children, most of which have arrived at similar conclusions (Bowlby, 1969; Rutter, 1974). William Goldfarb (1945), for example, compared forty children who had been placed in foster homes soon after birth with forty children who had spent the first two years of life in institutions before being transferred to foster homes. He found that the institutionalized children suffered a number of personality defects that persisted even after they had left the institutions. They had lower IQ scores, seemed more aggressive and distractible, showed less initiative, and were more emotionally cold. Many other studies have reported similar depressing effects on physical, cognitive, emotional, and social development, and have confirmed that such disabilities suffered in early childhood tend to persist or even to grow worse in later years (for example, Provence and Lipton, 1962; Yarrow, 1963; Dennis, 1960, 1973).

Monkeys Raised in Isolation

Harry Harlow and his associates have conducted a series of important experiments on the effects of isolation on rhesus monkeys (Harlow, 1958, 1965; Harlow and Harlow, 1962; Novak, 1979). Harlow's work has shown that even in monkeys, social behavior is learned, not inherited. The monkeys

Figure 5.3 *In his experiments with monkeys raised in isolation, Harry Harlow has found that the animals prefer a soft, cuddly "mother" substitute to a "mother" that feeds them but is made of wire. The young monkeys clung to this cuddly "mother" for much of the time, especially if they were frightened. The wire "mother" was used only as a source of food. Harlow's study shows that the young monkeys placed great priority on intimate contact.*

raised in isolation in his labs behave in some ways like human psychotics. They are fearful of, or hostile to, other monkeys, make no attempt to interact with them, and are generally withdrawn and apathetic. Monkeys reared in isolation do not know how to mate with other monkeys and usually cannot be taught how to do so. If female monkeys who have been isolated since birth are artificially impregnated, they become unloving and abusive mothers, making little or no attempt to take care of their offspring. In one experiment Harlow provided isolated monkey infants with two substitute mothers—one made of wire and containing a feeding bottle and one covered with soft cloth but without a bottle. The infant monkeys preferred the soft, cuddly "mother" to the one that fed them. This wretched substitute for affection became the most important focus in their lives.

Like all animal studies, Harlow's experiments must be treated with caution when inferences are made for human behavior. After all, we are not monkeys. His studies show, however, that without socialization, monkeys cannot develop normal social, sexual, emotional, or maternal behavior. Since we know that human beings rely much more heavily on learning than monkeys do, it seems fair to conclude that the same would be true of us.

The evidence from these varied sources, then, points overwhelmingly in the same direction: without socialization, we are almost devoid of personality and are utterly unable to face even the simplest challenges of life. Lacking the "instincts" that guide the behavior of other animals, we can become social and thus fully human only by learning through interaction with other people.

The Emergence of the Self

At the core of personality lies the *self*—the individual's conscious experience of a distinct, personal identity that is separate from all other people and things. Unlike other animals, we are fully self-conscious, capable of thinking as subjects about ourselves as objects. You can be "proud of yourself" or "ashamed of yourself"; you can "love yourself," "change yourself," or "lose control of yourself"; and you can even "talk to yourself."

The concept of "self" is perhaps a rather vague one. But we certainly experience it as real; all of us have some fairly definite notion of who and what we are. A standard sociological method of investigating this sense of self is the "twenty questions" test, in which subjects (usually college students) are asked to complete twenty statements that begin "I am . . . ." The answers show that the self seems to consist primarily of the various social roles we play and the various personality traits we believe we possess. Over the past three decades, however, there has been a shift in the way respondents conceive of the self. In the 1950s, college students seemed to think of themselves mainly in terms of roles (student, female, Catholic, sorority member, and so on); but by the 1970s, most seemed to think of themselves in terms of traits (generous, friendly, honest, hardworking, and the like). The reasons for the shift are not clear, but it seems that today's students place more value on who rather than what they are, on development and self-fulfillment rather than on established statuses and settled roles (Kuhn and McPartland, 1954; Zurcher, 1977; Snow and Phillips, 1982).

But whatever our sense of self consists of, where does it come from? The answer is that it is a social product, created and modified throughout life by interaction with other people. At the time of birth we have no sense of self, no awareness of having a separate identity. The infant shows no recognition of other people as distinct beings until around six months of age and does not begin to use words such as "I," "me," and "mine" until at least the age of two. Only in the years that follow do young children gradually come to realize that other people also have distinct selves, with needs and outlooks that are different from their own. And only then can the child begin to appreciate that his or her own self is an identity separate from all others. Two related theories explain how social interaction leads to the emergence of the self.

Cooley: The Looking-Glass Self

Charles Horton Cooley (1864–1929) was an American economist turned social psychologist. He held that self-concepts are formed early in childhood and are then reevaluated throughout life whenever a person enters a new social situation.

The central concept in Cooley's theory is the **looking-glass self**—a self-concept derived from a social "mirror" in which we can observe how others react to us. Our concept of ourselves is derived from this reflection, for we learn from other people's responses to us whether we are attractive or ugly, popular or unpopular, respectable or disreputable. According to Cooley (1902), the process of developing the self involves three steps.

1. *Imagining our own appearance.* First, we imagine what appearance we present to others—particularly to "significant others" whose opinions are important to us, like family members, close friends, or teachers. Do we imagine ourselves as witty, intelligent, slim, helpful?

2. *Interpreting others' reactions.* Second, we imagine how others judge the appearance that we think we present. Do they really see us the way we imagine we appear, or are they receiving a different impression?

3. *Developing self-concept.* Third, we use our interpretation of others' judgments to develop feelings about ourselves. If the image we find in the social mirror is favorable, our self-concept is enhanced and our behavior is likely to be repeated; if the image is unfavorable, our self-concept is diminished and the behavior is more likely to change.

Figure 5.4 *According to Charles Horton Cooley, we learn our concept of self through the "looking glass" provided by society. Just as we learn what we look like by examining our reflection, so we learn our sense of self through the reflection provided by the "mirror" of other people's reactions to us.*

Of course, people may misjudge the way others see them. All of us make misinterpretations at times, and some people habitually misjudge the opinion of others and have unrealistically high or low self-concepts as a result. But whether our reading of the image in the "looking glass" is accurate or not, it is through this interpretation that we learn our identity. There can be no self without society, no "I" without a corresponding "they" to provide our self-image.

Mead: Role-Taking

George Herbert Mead (1863–1931) is one of the most important figures in American social science. A philosopher and social psychologist, Mead was by all accounts a fascinating lecturer, yet he never wrote a book—his attempts to commit his ideas to paper led him to agonies of frustration. His students and colleagues, however, compiled and published his work from lecture notes and other sources.

Mead (1934) elaborated on Cooley's ideas by introducing the concept of **symbolic interaction,** the interaction between people that takes place through symbols such as signs, gestures, and language. Mead placed particular importance on language, for this system of symbols is essential for all but the most simple forms of thought. Without language, he argued, there can hardly be a mind, and because language is socially learned, the mind itself is, in a sense, a social product.

Mead pointed out that a vital outcome of socialization is the ability to anticipate what others expect of us and to shape our own behavior accordingly. This capacity, he argued, is achieved by **role-taking**—pretending to take or actually taking the roles of other people, so that one can see the world and one's self from their viewpoints. In childhood we are able to internalize the expectations only of the **particular other**—specific other people such as parents. But as we grow older, we gradually learn to internalize the expectations of the **generalized other,** the attitudes and viewpoint of society as a whole. This internalized general concept of social expectations provides the basis for self-evaluation and hence for self-concept.

Mead showed how, as children progress through three stages of increasingly sophisticated role-taking, they gain a better understanding of themselves and of social life.

1. *Imitation.* Children under the age of about three lack a developed sense of self and so have difficulty distinguishing their roles from those of others. They merely mimic or imitate people in the immediate environment, such as family members, and they do so only occasionally and spontaneously—a gesture here, a word there. This is not really role-taking, but serves as preparation for it.

2. *Play.* After the age of about three, children begin to play at taking the roles of specific other people: they walk around in their parent's shoes; pretend to be an adult and scold a doll; or play "house," "doctors and nurses," and so on. By pretending to take the roles of specific other people in this kind of play, children are for the first time learning to see the world from a perspective that is not their own.

3. *Games.* By the early school years, children are ready to take part in organized games—preludes to the "game" of life—in which their

Figure 5.5 *George Herbert Mead pointed out that the development of the self requires that we learn to take the role of other people, if only in our imagination. Once we can do this, we realize that others also have selves, and can see our own self from their viewpoint. Children's games of pretending to be someone else are one of the first steps in this direction.*

roles are real and in which they must simultaneously take account of the roles and expectations of all the participants. A baseball pitcher, for example, must be aware not only of his or her own role requirements but also of the roles and likely responses of every other player—and of the symbolic system of rules that guides the game. Very young children cannot play organized games, for they do not understand the rules, cannot take the role of other players, and thus cannot anticipate how others will respond to their actions.

Mead pointed out that socialization is never perfect or complete. He distinguished between what he called the "I" (the spontaneous, self-interested, impulsive, unsocialized self) and the "me" (the socialized self that is conscious of social norms, values, and expectations). The "I," he insisted, is never completely under the control of the "me." The socialized self is usually dominant, but we all have the capacity to break social rules and violate the expectations of others.

Learning to Think

Mead emphasized that the mind is a social product; and, indeed, one of the most important achievements of socialization is the development of cognitive abilities—intellectual capacities such as perceiving, remembering, reasoning, calculating, believing. Our knowledge of this process is based largely on the work of Jean Piaget (1896–1980), who emphasized that "social life is necessary for the individual to become conscious of his own mind."

Piaget's many experiments with children suggest that human beings gradually pass through stages of cognitive development, with the attainment of new skills at each stage requiring successful completion of the previous stage. Each stage is characterized by the particular kinds of "operations," or intellectual processes, that a person at that stage can perform (1950, 1954).

The Sensorimotor Stage

In the sensorimotor stage, which lasts from birth until about the age of two, the intelligence of children is expressed only through sensory and physical contact with the environment. Lacking language, infants cannot "think" about the world. In fact, until the age of four months or so, infants cannot even differentiate themselves from their environment. They are thus unaware of the results of their acts; they do not realize, for example, that their own movements cause a rattle to make a sound. Similarly, children under the age of eight months do not understand that objects have a permanent existence: if a toy is removed from their sight, or if a parent leaves the room, they react as though the toy or parent has ceased to exist. By the end of the sensorimotor stage, however, children will look for a missing object with persistence—meaning that they realize the object still exists even though they cannot see it. At this point, the child begins to experience the world as a stable environment, not simply a shifting chaos.

The Preoperational Stage

This stage, on which Piaget focused most of his attention, lasts from around the age of two to seven. Piaget called the stage "preoperational" because during this period children are unable to do many simple mental operations, largely because they have no real understanding of such concepts as

Figure 5.6 *Children at the preoperational stage have great difficulty in realizing that the quantity of water does not change in volume when it is poured from one container to another of a different shape. If water is poured before the children's eyes from a tall, thin bottle into a short, wide flask, they insist that there is now less water than before. Children at this stage judge the volume of the water only by the height of the water level, and cannot understand that its volume remains constant no matter what the shape of the container is.*

speed, weight, number, quantity, or causality. Particularly during the early years of this stage, for example, children invariably assume that the larger of two objects must be the heavier. (They will typically state that a pound of feathers weighs more than a pound of lead.) Although they may be able to count, they do not really understand the concept of number. They assert that a long row of beads contains more beads than a shorter row, even if the short row is more densely packed with a greater number of beads. They have a limited understanding of cause and effect—often believing, for example, that trees waving in the wind are actually making the wind. They attribute life to inanimate objects, such as the sun and moon, and may believe that a table is "hurt" when it is bumped.

One of Piaget's discoveries ties in with Mead's earlier work on the importance of role-taking in socialization. Piaget found that children in the early part of the preoperational stage are highly egocentric: they see the world almost entirely from their own perspective and therefore have difficulty taking the social roles of others into account. If a young boy is asked "How many brothers do you have?" he may correctly answer "One." But if he is asked "How many brothers does your brother have?" he is likely to answer "None," because he cannot see himself from his brother's point of view. Similarly, if such children are asked to draw an object as it appears to them from their own location in the room, they can do so. But if they are asked to draw the same object from the point of view of someone situated elsewhere in the room, they will draw it exactly as before, being unable to fully take another person's perspective.

The Concrete Operational Stage

In this stage, which lasts from about seven to twelve, children can reason about concrete situations, but not about abstract or purely hypothetical ones. If children of this age are asked to talk about abstract concepts, such as death or justice, they have great difficulty in doing so without referring to actual events or images, such as the death of a pet or the physical appearance of police officers.

Children at this stage, however, are able to handle the concrete world with much the same cognitive skill as an adult. They can perform the various mental operations related to weight, speed, number, quantity, or causality that were not possible in the previous stage. They can also take the roles of others and appreciate their perspectives, and therefore can participate effectively in games and other organized social relationships.

The Formal Operational Stage

In this stage, which usually begins at the onset of adolescence, people are able to achieve formal, abstract thought. They can think in terms of theories and hypotheses and can manipulate complex mathematical, moral, and other concepts that are not tied to the immediate environment. They are able to use general rules to solve whole classes of problems, and they can reason logically from premises to conclusions with a sophistication that would not be possible in earlier stages. They can think about abstract personal goals and even utopian social conditions. Philosophic brooding may appear, on perennially favored topics of youth. (If sex is pleasant, why is it wrong? If God is good and all-powerful, why is there evil in the world and suffering among the innocent? If parents know best, why do they make mistakes?)

It seems that the *process* of cognitive socialization is universal: in all societies, people advance through the same sequence of development. But the *content* is culturally variable: what and how much we learn depend on our social environment. If our culture believes the earth is flat, or that cause and effect are related to magic, then it is through these concepts that we will interpret the world. Moreover, not everyone reaches the final stage of formal operations; many adults have great difficulty in understanding abstract concepts, particularly if they have little exposure to formal thinking in their own socialization. In fact, more than half the people in the world today cannot read or write, for they live in societies that lacked the resources to make formal education available to them. They are thus denied intellectual access to the vast storehouse of facts, ideas, and literature that the rest of us, socialized differently, can take for granted. Even within a given society, too, social and cultural factors encourage different categories of the population to think in different ways about different subjects: American men, for example, are socialized to be more likely than women to think in mathematical or engineering terms. Also, people who have an enriched educational environment may develop intellectually at a more rapid pace than others who lack those advantages.

As we move into a postindustrial society, we face the interesting question of what effect computers may have on the socialization of children. Computers introduce children to a purely logical universe defined by rigid rules, a world quite unlike the rest of their environment. Sherry Turkle (1984), who has pioneered studies of the influence

Figure 5.7 *There has been little research so far on how computers are affecting childhood socialization. It is already clear, though, that children often learn how to use the machines in a manner different from adults—they tend to be more intuitive, more inclined to trial-and-error experimentation, and less intimidated than adults approaching computers for the first time. Children also seem to develop a certain "intimacy" with computers, almost as though the machines had personality. Children can be heard discussing among themselves such issues as whether a computer can think or cheat, or even whether it is alive; and they sometimes compare themselves to computers.*

of computers on children's thought, claims that the machines can alter the way people think about themselves and social relationships—even to the extent of becoming "the basis for new esthetic values, new rituals, new philosophy, new cultural forms." These are bold but vague claims and further research will be needed to trace the impact of computers on the cognitive socialization of the first young generation to be exposed to them.

Learning to Feel

Another vital achievement of socialization is the development of emotional capacities—feelings such as love, hate, empathy, confidence, envy. One of the founders of modern psychology, Sigmund Freud (1856–1939), emphasized the importance of

emotions in human personality, and showed that a good deal of emotional life is unconscious—that is, we are often unaware of the real reasons for our feelings and the actions that spring from them. Although Freud developed an elaborate theory of emotions, later psychologists found his ideas increasingly unsatisfactory because of their highly speculative nature. In fact, emotions seemed so vague and inaccessible that social scientists were generally reluctant to study the subject systematically until fairly recently.

Within the past decade, however, psychologists and sociologists have begun to study emotions in detail. They have learned, perhaps not too surprisingly, that emotional socialization parallels cognitive socialization in important respects. First, the *process* of learning emotions seems to be the same in all normal human beings: the various feelings develop in an orderly sequence, with each new emotion being built on those already attained. Second, the *content* of emotions is culturally variable: social factors strongly influence what, when, and how emotions are expressed (Hochschild, 1975; Kemper, 1978; Shott, 1979; Kagan, 1984; Goleman, 1984).

Preliminary studies by Jerome Kagan and his colleagues indicate that emotional development takes the following course. Initially, during the first few days and weeks of life, the emotions of the child consist of little more than reflexive reactions to the environment: pleasure, surprise, disgust, distress, and curiosity. Then, in the first few months, new emotions begin to appear as a result of accumulating experience: joy, anger, sadness, and fear. By the middle of the second year, the child shows signs of tenderness and affection toward others, but without any recognition that these others have separate selves and identities of their own. But by the time they are five or six years old, children are developing a clear sense of self, an ability to compare themselves to others, and a sense of how others judge them. The "looking glass" provided by this new social awareness then makes possible, for the first time, emotions that require a consideration of other people's judgments: confidence, insecurity, pride, humility, jealousy, envy. Being able to take the role of others, children can now understand other people's emotions too, and so develop feelings of sympathy and empathy. By the teenage years, the growing cognitive capacity for abstract thought allows the young person to extend empathy to whole categories of people, such as the poor or the oppressed. Around this time, too, the deepening awareness of self and others opens the possibility of romantic passion.

Although the various emotions seem always to emerge in the same order, the process—as with the development of cognitive abilities—can be speeded up or slowed down by social factors. For example, infants do not normally show signs of fear and sadness until about seven or eight months, but infants who have been abused show these emotions as early on as three months (Greensbauer and Hiatt, 1984).

Social life is clearly pervaded by emotions. Love, hate, pride, jealousy, and the like provide the motives for a great deal of social behavior. What is perhaps not so obvious is that emotions, in turn, are pervaded by social life. In other words, social conditions influence how we interpret our emotions and whether, and in what form, we express them. Even the physical sensations that accompany some emotions have to be interpreted: What does this tightening of the chest, that quickening of the pulse, actually mean? Fear, lust, hope, anxiety, or something else? In one experiment, Stanley Schachter and Jerome Singer (1962) injected subjects with a stimulant, adrenaline, and found that the resulting state of physical arousal was interpreted differently according to the social setting. If the subjects were not told about the drug's physical effects, they attributed their arousal to emotional feelings—and if they were exposed to an angry person, they interpreted the feelings as anger, while if they were exposed to a euphoric person, they interpreted the feelings as euphoria. On the other hand, subjects who were told about the drug's physical effects did not interpret their subsequent arousal as emotional at all and simply reported a bodily reaction.

Even when we have learned to interpret our emotions, we must learn also under what social conditions, if any, they may be expressed. It may be appropriate to vent feelings of romantic passion toward one's date in private, but not toward one's employer's spouse in public, even if the feeling is as strong and sincere in both cases. Indeed, each culture has its own "feeling rules," norms that encourage or discourage certain emotions like anger or envy and specify how we shall express them, if we do so at all (Hochschild, 1979).

Figure 5.8 *Different cultures permit or discourage the display of particular emotions. In many parts of the Middle East, women are permitted and sometimes expected to display grief at funerals by uttering loud lamentations, beating their breast, tearing their hair, and collapsing to the ground and rocking their entire body. In North America, in contrast, the norms call for more reserve. A female mourner is permitted to sob and perhaps to feel so* *faint that she requires the physical support of relatives, but any more extreme display of grief is likely to be viewed as an embarrassing loss of emotional control. In both the Middle East and North America, moreover, men are socialized to repress their grief in public because they are, in general, expected to be less overtly emotional than women—however strong their private feelings may happen to be.*

Emotions do more than enrich social life; they help make it possible, too. As we noted in Chapter 3 ("Culture"), every society, if it is to survive, must have some form of social control—a set of means of ensuring that people generally behave in socially approved ways. Some of this control, we saw, is exercised externally, through such agencies as the police; but most of it is applied internally, through our self-control over our own behavior. Emotions play an important part in this process, for the experience of such learned feelings as pride, shame, guilt, and embarrassment enables us, consciously or unconsciously, to guide our own thoughts and actions along paths that are generally socially acceptable (Shott, 1979).

Agents of Socialization

The socialization process involves many different influences that affect the individual throughout life. The most important of these influences are *agents of socialization*—significant individuals, groups, or institutions that provide structured situations in which socialization takes place. Four of these agents—the family, the school, the peer group, and the mass media—are especially important in modern societies, for they affect almost everyone in a powerful and lasting way.

The Family

The family is without doubt the most significant single agent of socialization in all societies. One reason for the importance of the family is that it has the main responsibility for socializing children in the crucial early years of life. The family is where children establish their first close emotional ties, learn language, and begin to internalize cultural norms and values. To young children the family is all-encompassing. They have little social experience beyond its boundaries and therefore lack any basis for comparing and evaluating what is learned from family members. Each family therefore offers a unique experience to the children within it. In fact, different children within the same family have differing experiences, for they have a different set of older or younger brothers and sisters. There is considerable evidence that first-born children get more attention and discipline than children born subsequently, and that this may affect their later personalities: first-borns tend to do better in school and to be higher achiev-

ers later in life, while younger brothers and sisters tend to be more sociable and relaxed (Forer, 1976; Dunn and Kendrick, 1983).

A great deal of the socialization that takes place in the family is deliberate, but much of it is quite unconscious. The patterns of social interaction within the family may provide unintended models for the later behavior and personality traits of the children when they grow to adulthood. For example, parents who abuse their children were often abused by their own parents—and their own children, in turn, are more likely to become aggressive and abusive adults themselves (Huesmann and Eron, 1984). In this way, personality traits may be passed down over one or more generations.

Another reason for the importance of the family is that it has a specific location in the social structure. From the moment of birth, therefore, children have an ascribed status in a subculture of race, class, ethnicity, religion, and region—all of which may strongly influence the nature of later social interaction and socialization. For example, the values and expectations that children learn depend very much on the social class of their parents. Studies by Melvin Kohn (1963, 1976, 1977) show that working-class and middle-class parents raise their children in different ways. Working-class parents place greater value on conformity to traditional standards of behavior: they teach their children to obey the rules and stay out of trouble. These parents also tend to punish their children for the consequences of their misbehavior, and are more likely to use physical discipline. Middle-class parents, on the other hand, place greater value on curiosity and initiative: they teach their children to rely more on self-control in deciding how to behave. These parents punish their children for the motives rather than the consequences of their misbehavior, and are more likely to reason with them and to use the temporary withdrawal of privileges or love as a means of discipline. As Kohn points out, these styles of parenting are related to the occupational experiences of the parents. Blue-collar jobs generally require that the worker follow exactly the instructions of the supervisor; white-collar jobs require more independence and initiative. Parents thus socialize their children for that part of the social world that they know best—and in doing so, they help to reproduce the class system in the next generation. In part because of such influences, the social-class background of a child's family is an excellent predictor of that child's later IQ, educational achievement, and ultimate social-class status.

The School

The school is an agent formally charged by society with the task of socializing the young in particular skills and values. Unlike preindustrial societies, modern industrial and especially postindustrial societies require a skilled and literate work force, and so the facilities and professional staff for schooling are provided at public expense. In this setting, the young come for the first time under the direct supervision of people who are not relatives. The individual child is no longer considered somebody special; he or she is now one of a crowd, subject to the same regulations and expectations that everyone else is subject to. Personal behavior and academic achievements or failures become part of a permanent official record, and the children learn to evaluate themselves by the same standards that others apply to them. Participation in the life of the school also lessens the children's dependence on the family and creates new links to the wider society beyond.

The immediate task of the schools is to socialize the young in cognitive skills such as reading or mathematics and to provide knowledge about a variety of subjects, such as history or chemistry, that may not be available in the home. But the schools in every society also engage in outright indoctrination in values. We may find this fact more apparent in societies other than our own—until we consider the content of civics classes or the daily ritual of the Pledge of Allegiance. A schoolteacher who attended church and espoused capitalism would pass unnoticed in an American school; one who professed atheism and praised communism would soon be out of a job, for these views are inconsistent with American values. At a more subtle level, the school socializes through the "hidden curriculum" implicit in the content of school activities, ranging from regimented classroom schedules to organized sports. Children learn that they must be neat and punctual. They learn to sit still, keep quiet, wait their turn, and not be distracted from their work. They learn that individuals who can outdo their classmates are rewarded, while those who cannot compete successfully are regarded as failures. They learn that they should respect and obey without question the commands of those who have social authority over them. In teaching these attitudes and behaviors, the school is subtly socializing children for their later roles in the work force, where punctuality and obedience are highly valued.

The Peer Group

As children grow older, they spend more and more time in the company of their *peers*—people of roughly equivalent age and other social characteristics. As the influence of the peer group increases, that of the parents diminishes—especially in modern industrialized societies, where most parents work away from the home and where there has been a long-term erosion of the authority of elders. Young Americans of school-going age spend, on

Figure 5.9 *The peer group is an important agency of socialization from childhood on, but it is particularly influential during late childhood and adolescence. Young people at this stage are exploring their identities, a process that may involve a reaction against earlier behavior patterns learned in the family and school. The peer group provides new norms and values for its members and the opportunity to interact with others as equals.*

average, twice as much time with peers as with parents, and most of them prefer it that way. The influence of the peer group climaxes in adolescence, when young people are apt to form a distinctive subculture with its own tastes, leisure activities, dress, jargon, symbols, values, and heroes.

Membership in a peer group places children for the first time in a context where most socialization occurs without any deliberate design. Unlike the family or the school, the peer group is entirely centered on its own concerns and interests, and indeed its members can explore topics (like sex, drugs, and rock-and-roll) that other agents of socialization may wish to avoid. Within the peer group, the young are able for the first time to choose their own companions and to interact with others on a basis of equality. However, they cannot expect the automatic acceptance from peers that they can from family members, and so have to learn to present the self in ways that win the approval of the group. By rewarding members for conformity to group norms and criticizing or ostracizing them for nonconformity, the peer group helps shape their social behavior and personality. But although young people often seem to give their primary loyalty to their peers, appearances can be deceptive. Peers do have greater influence over matters of immediate lifestyle, such as musical tastes or leisure activities, but values learned in the family regarding religion, politics, education, and career goals tend to have greater long-term impact (Troll and Bengston, 1982; Davies and Kandell, 1981).

The Mass Media

The **mass media** are the various forms of communication that reach a large audience without any personal contact between the senders and the receivers of the messages: newspapers, magazines, books, television, radio, movies, videos, and records. This agent of socialization introduces the individual to an extraordinarily diverse array of people who are "known" only indirectly: sports figures, historic personages, politicians, authors, columnists, announcers, disk jockeys, talk-show hosts, newscasters, musicians, and even ordinary people interviewed in eyewitness news reports. Some of these people become "celebrities," who may be "known" in an emotional sense: members of the mass audience may follow the events of their lives, mimic their styles of dress and behavior, and even (especially in the case of "teen idols") imag-

ine they are in love with them (Caughey, 1984). Indeed, when national samples of teenagers are asked to name their "ten most admired people," about half their selections turn out to be movie stars and entertainers. We take this barrage of media socialization so much for granted that it is easy to forget that, until a few generations ago, most people's social exposure was limited to face-to-face contact with a handful of neighbors who were, in most respects, very similar to one another.

The media provide instant coverage of social events and social changes, ranging from news and opinions to fads and fashions. They offer role models, viewpoints, and glimpses of lifestyles that people might otherwise never have access to. Through the media, children can learn about courtroom lawyers, cowboys, police detectives, or even such improbable characters as Batman, E.T., and Rambo. (The fact that many of these images are not very realistic does not necessarily lessen their influence.) Through media advertising, too, the young learn about their future roles as consumers in the marketplace, and about the high value the society places on youth, success, beauty, and materialism. Changing social norms and values are quickly reflected in the media and may be readily adopted by people who might not otherwise be exposed to them. The rapid spread of new trends in youth culture, for example, depends heavily on such media as popular records, television, FM radio, youth-oriented magazines, and movies.

The most influential medium is probably television. There is a TV set in 98 percent of American homes, and the average American between the ages of three and sixteen spends more time in front of the TV set than in school. Yet the influence of television, like that of the other media, is difficult to trace with any certainty, because it is inevitably entangled in a multitude of influences on personality. One major point of controversy has been the impact of television violence: by the time the average American reaches the age of sixteen, he or she has witnessed over 18,000 fictional murders, not to mention innumerable other acts of violence—but what effects does this have? After surveying over 2,500 studies on the relationship of television violence to actual behavior, the National Institute of Mental Health (1982) found overwhelming evidence that these portrayals do, in fact, encourage aggressive conduct among children and teenagers.

Television is often acclaimed as a marvelous educational instrument. Some critics charge, however, that the medium actually impedes learning by hindering the acquisition of reading skills and encouraging intellectual passivity, but these claims are difficult to prove or disprove. Also, although television does bring a flood of information into the home, much of it is highly selective or distorted. News programs, for example, tend to feature the visually exciting or emotionally moving stories that draw large viewing audiences—even if this means omitting issues that are more sober but perhaps more significant also. Fictional portrayals, too, often overrepresent some categories of the population, such as the wealthy or physicians, and underrepresent others, such as the aged or minorities (Gerbner, 1981; Wright, 1986).

Other Agents

The individual may be influenced by many other agents of socialization—religious groups, youth organizations, and later in life, such agents as corporations or other employers and voluntary associations like clubs, political movements, and retirement homes.

In extreme cases, the individual may experience *resocialization,* learning that involves a sharp break with the past and socialization into radically different norms and values. This frequently takes place in a context where people have been partly or wholly isolated from their previous background. Resocialization occurs, for example, in conversion to a religious cult, in the experience of an anthropologist who lives among an alien people, or in "brainwashing" situations in which the individual's personality is systematically stripped away and rebuilt. It also occurs within a *total institution*—a place of residence where the inmates are confined for a set period of their lives, where they are cut off from the rest of society, and where they are under the almost absolute control of a hierarchy of officials (Goffman, 1961). Examples of a total institution are an army boot camp, a naval vessel, a prison, a mental asylum, and a traditional boarding school. In each case the inmates experience an abrupt break from their former existence; they surrender control over much of their lives to an administrative staff; they are to some extent depersonalized by having to wear uniforms and obey rigid rules; and they are under great pressure to conform to the values and regulations of their new environment.

It is obvious that the influences of the various agencies are not always complementary and can often be in outright conflict. The church, for example, may hold quite different values from the military; the peer group, quite different values from the school. It is also obvious that people do not always learn what they are supposed to learn. The socialization process may fail in certain respects, and people may come to behave in ways that were never anticipated or intended. Personality and behavior are never entirely stable; they change under the influence of socialization experiences throughout the life course.

Figure 5.10 *Military trainees are subjected to systematic resocialization, a form of socialization that involves an abrupt break with earlier experiences. Resocialization takes place in the context of "total institutions," such as boot camps, mental hospitals, and prisons, where the inmates are segregated from the rest of society, placed in uniforms and treated alike, and made subject to rigid rules and the authority of officials.*

The Life Course

The human life course seems at first sight to be purely a matter of biology. But the sequence of birth, childhood, maturity, old age, and death is also a social one, for its length, stages, challenges, and opportunities depend very much on the society in which one lives. How long we live, for example, is strongly influenced by social as well as biological factors. In North America, people are not considered old until they are in their sixties or seventies; among the malnourished Ik of Uganda, old age sets in by the late twenties. In modern industrialized societies, we associate the idea of death with the aged, but in traditional, preindustrial societies more people died in childhood than in old age. Thanks to such social factors as modern medicine, improved nutrition, and higher standards of sanitation, infectious diseases such as smallpox, diphtheria, and cholera no longer kill more than half of all children before the age of ten. For the first time in history, most people can now expect to grow old.

Every society imposes its own conception of a life course upon the physical process of growing up and growing old. Consequently, the period from birth to death is arbitrarily sliced up into a series of stages, each offering distinctive rights and responsibilities to the relevant age group. The number, length, and content of these stages vary from one society to another. But each society must socialize its members into accepting and effectively performing their changing roles at each stage in the sequence from early childhood until death.

Childhood

Childhood seems a "natural" part of the life course to us, yet the very concept of childhood is a comparatively recent one: preindustrial societies typically did not recognize it as a separate stage of life. Instead, the young passed directly from a prolonged infancy into their adult roles. There was no separate way of life reserved for childhood, with the distinctive songs, toys, privileges, and activities that we take for granted today (Ariès, 1962; Gilles, 1974; de Mause, 1974). People began to play adult economic and social roles as soon as they were physically able to do so, and children of five or six would work in the fields as long as any adult. Child labor was not considered a scandal; there can be no concept of children's rights without a concept of childhood. Even in early industrial societies, children continued to perform adult economic roles: in the United States in 1900, a quarter of the boys aged ten to fourteen were in the labor force. Some countries that are now in the early stages of industrialization still have only a limited concept of childhood and continue to make use of child labor. In such countries as Morocco, India, and Colombia, for example, tens of millions of children between the ages of five and thirteen work full time, even in factories and coal mines.

Advanced industrialized societies, on the other hand, tend to be very child-centered. Children are socialized quite differently from adults: they have distinctive forms of dress and their own separate spheres of activity, ranging from children's TV and games to kindergartens and elementary schools. They are exempted from playing full economic roles—in fact, the law forbids it—and have minimal social responsibilities. Adults tend to romanticize childhood as a period of carefree innocence, and they take pains to protect children from premature knowledge of such taboo subjects as death and sex. The "ideal" parents are those who derive great gratification from their children, and indulgently devote their resources to ensuring the optimum development of their offspring during the crucial formative years of primary socialization.

Figure 5.11 *The stages of the life course are influenced by social as well as biological factors. Preindustrial societies generally did not recognize separate stages of infancy, childhood, and adolescence. Childhood was not recognized in Europe until after the Middle Ages, and adolescence has been recognized in industrial societies only in this century. More recently, an additional, optional stage, that of youth, has appeared in the life course in the emerging postindustrial societies.*

THE LIFE COURSE

Preindustrial Societies	infancy-childhood		mature adulthood	old age
Industrialized Societies	infancy childhood	adolescence youth	mature adulthood	old age

The Nightmare of Childhood in Ages Past

In the modern world we tend to think of childhood as a period of special innocence in which the developing person needs and deserves care, kindness, and comfort. But as this account reveals, childhood in earlier ages was often a nightmare of neglect, misery, and pain.

For most people in our society, infants and children are small people to whom we should try to offer aid and comfort whenever possible. This attitude is new. A search of historical sources shows that until the last century children were instead offered beatings and whippings, with instruments usually associated with torture chambers. In fact, the history of childhood is a nightmare from which we have only recently begun to awaken.

. . .

Virtually every child-rearing tract from antiquity to the 18th century recommended the beating of children. We found no examples from this period in which a child wasn't beaten, and hundreds of instances of not only beating, but battering, beginning in infancy.

. . .

One 19th-century German schoolmaster who kept score reported administering 911,527 strokes with a stick, 124,000 lashes with a whip, 136,715 slaps with his hand and 1,115,800 boxes on the ear. The beatings described in most historical sources began at an early age, continued regularly throughout childhood, and were severe enough to cause bruising and bloodying.

. . .

The baby was tied up tightly in swaddling bands for its first year, supposedly to prevent it from tearing off its ears, breaking its legs, touching its genitals or crawling around like an animal. Traditional swaddling, as one American doctor described it, "consists in entirely depriving the child of the use of its limbs by enveloping them in an endless bandage, so as to not unaptly resemble billets of wood, and by which the skin is sometimes excoriated, the flesh compressed, almost to gangrene . . ."

Swaddled infants were not only more convenient to care for, since they withdrew into themselves in sleep most of the day, but they were also more easily laid for hours behind hot ovens, hung on pegs on the wall, and, wrote one doctor, "left, like a parcel, in every convenient corner." In addition, they were often thrown around like a ball for amusement. In 16th-century France, a brother of Henri IV, while being tossed from one window to another, was dropped and killed.

. . .

Although there were many exceptions to the general pattern, the average child of parents with some wealth spent his earliest years in the home of a wet nurse, returned home at age three or four to the care of other servants, and was sent out to service, apprenticeship, or school by age seven, so that the amount of time parents of means actually spent raising their children was minimal. . . . Of 21,000 children born in Paris in 1780, 17,000 were sent into the country to be wet-nursed, 3,000 were placed in nursery homes, 700 were wet-nursed at home and only 700 were nursed by their own mothers. Even those mothers who kept their infants at home often did not breastfeed them, giving them pap (water and grain) instead.

. . .

Children were always felt to be on the verge of turning into actual demons, or at least to be easily susceptible to "the power of the Devil." To keep their small devils cowed, adults regularly terrorized them with a vast army of ghostlike figures, from the Lamia and Striga of the ancients, who ate children raw, to the witches of Medieval times, who would steal bad children away and suck their blood. One 19th-century tract described in simplified language the tortures God had in store for children in Hell: "The little child is in this red-hot oven. Hear how it screams to come out . . ."

. . .

Another method that parents used to terrorize their children employed corpses. A common moral lesson involved taking children to visit the gibbet, where they were forced to inspect rotting corpses hanging there as an example of what happens to bad children when they grow up. Whole classes were taken out of school to witness hangings, and parents would often whip their children afterwards to make them remember what they had seen.

. . .

In antiquity infanticide was so common that every river, dung-heap and cesspool used to be littered with dead infants. Polybius blamed the depopulation of Greece on the killing of legitimate children, even by wealthy parents. Ratios of boys to girls in census figures ran four to one, since it was rare for more than one girl in a family to be spared. Christians were considered odd for their opposition to infanticide, although even that opposition was mild, with few penalties. Large-scale infanticide of legitimate babies continued well into Medieval times, with boy-girl ratios in rich as well as poor families often still running two to one. As late as 1527, one priest admitted that "the latrines resound with the cries of children who have been plunged into them."

SOURCE: Lloyd DeMause, "Our Forebears Made Childhood a Nightmare," *Psychology Today,* April 1975.

Figure 5.12 *Most traditional, preindustrial societies lacked a clear concept of childhood as a separate stage of life, and there was no distinct sphere of childhood games and other activities. Preindustrial Western art reflects this attitude: even as late as the middle of the eighteenth century, when this family portrait was painted by an unknown Dutch artist, children were portrayed as "little adults" with serious, mature faces and none of the innocence or "cuteness" that we might look for in children today.*

Interestingly, some observers now suggest that children in sophisticated postindustrial societies like the United States are growing up "too fast" and that the period of childhood is in danger of shrinking, or even "vanishing" from the life course again (Postman, 1981; Suransky, 1982; Winn, 1984; Elkind, 1984).

Adolescence

In simple, preindustrial societies there were, in effect, only two main stages of life, immaturity and adulthood. In such societies the change from one status to another was usually a clear and abrupt one, often marked, in the case of males, by initiation ceremonies involving great pain or feats of endurance. As soon as these rituals were completed, the young person became an adult, with the same rights and responsibilities as other mature members of the community.

In the course of their development, modern industrial societies have added a new stage to the life course: instead of passing directly from prolonged infancy or childhood to adulthood, we go through adolescence, a period roughly coinciding with the teenage years. Like childhood, adolescence is a social invention; in fact, the word came into use only at the beginning of this century. This new stage was introduced into the life course as a consequence of extended education.

In preindustrial and early industrial societies, most teenagers were full-time workers, and many were married, often in their early teens. But industrial societies required a work force whose members could at least read and write, and they needed a substantial number of professionals with highly sophisticated skills. Prolonged education therefore became necessary, but this inevitably entailed changes in the statuses and roles of those who remained in school. The result was a large and unprecedented category of people who were physically and sexually mature, yet denied such adult responsibilities as full-time employment and marriage. At the turn of the century less than 7 percent of Americans completed high school, compared with over 80 percent today—a significant and rapid change which, not surprisingly, has disrupted the traditional life course.

Because it is a relatively new stage of the life course in a rapidly changing society, adolescence is an ambiguous and often confusing period, marked by vaguely defined rights and responsibilities. The American socialization process equips people poorly for the challenges of adolescence, for teenagers are constantly confronted with contradictory demands and pressures. The media, for example, extol the virtues of sexual satisfaction and the value of material goods, but adolescents are usually forbidden full access to both, even though they have the physical maturity to achieve them. Having more freedom than children but less than adults, adolescents are constantly tempted to question or test the authority of parents and teachers. Segregated from other age groups in high schools, they tend to form their own subculture, with norms, values, and attitudes that may differ significantly from those of the society that surrounds them.

In emerging postindustrial societies, a large proportion of high school graduates continue on to college and even graduate school, further delaying their acceptance of full adult responsibilities. Kenneth Keniston (1970) suggests that yet another stage is now being introduced into the life course, that of "youth." This stage is an optional one that

Figure 5.13 *In many preindustrial societies the transition from childhood to adulthood is very abrupt. This transition usually takes place at puberty and is often marked by a social ceremony of initiation. These aboriginal boys in Australia are being held down by their elders while they undergo a painful circumcision ceremony, after which they will be able to take their place as adult members of the society. Traces of initiation ceremonies that mark changes in a young person's status are still found in modern societies—for example, the Jewish bar mitzvah, the "sweet sixteen" birthday party, the high school graduation ceremony, and the "hazing" that college freshmen sometimes face.*

Most people marry in their twenties or early thirties, establishing a home and a family. Their task becomes that of developing a fulfilling lifestyle and maintaining a warm relationship with their spouse and their offspring. In a rapidly changing modern society these tasks are harder, perhaps, than they would have been in a traditional society, for the future is more uncertain. The only real certainty, in fact, is that social change will render a good deal of prior socialization irrelevant. Only a few decades ago, for example, the roles of husband and wife were fairly rigid: the husband worked and was the economic mainstay of the family; the wife stayed home and raised the children. This pattern is now the exception rather than the rule, yet many adults have not been socialized for this change in traditional roles.

The forties and fifties are a period of consolidation. There is no more time now for illusion: root changes in personal, social, and economic life grow more unlikely, and what people have become is what, more or less, they will continue to be. Men and women both face the inevitable physical and psychological signs of aging: physical prowess and beauty fade, and an awareness grows that one's life is more than half over. It is now recognized that this period can sometimes include a "mid-life crisis," marked by increased rates of depression, alcoholism, divorce, and suicide. Men in particular must face the fact that if they have not "made it" in their chosen field by now, they probably never will. At the same time, women socialized to regard their beauty and their children as their main sources of

runs from about eighteen to thirty and contains students and other young people who for one reason or another do not immediately "settle down" into the usual defining characteristics of mature adulthood—a steady job, a permanent home, marriage, and a family.

Mature Adulthood

Sometime around the mid-twenties the individual enters mature adulthood. At this stage primary socialization is virtually completed, and the individual has developed a core identity that is henceforth unlikely to be radically modified (except under such extreme conditions as resocialization in a prison, mental hospital, or religious cult). For the most part, socialization is now of the developmental kind, building on the fairly stable foundations of prior experience.

Figure 5.14

"Are you sure this doesn't have mid-life crisis written all over it?"

Drawing by Richter; © 1985
The New Yorker Magazine, Inc.

identity are often dismayed as they increasingly lose both. Now without maternal responsibilities, and perhaps feeling that she has in some sense wasted a part of her life, a wife may strike out for a fresh career, a new independence, only to find this causes more problems with a husband whose self-confidence is faltering. Yet the "crisis" is by no means inevitable, and, even if it occurs, it can usually be overcome. For the many people who have successfully negotiated the life course up to this point, these years are among the most comfortable and satisfying of their lives (Levinson, 1978; Gould, 1978; Haan and Day, 1974; Rubin, 1979; Perlin, 1980).

Old Age

Perhaps the greatest failure of the American socialization process is its inability to equip people adequately to face old age (and later, death). Preindustrial societies were generally oriented toward the old rather than the young: the aged were respected for their wisdom and held an honored

Figure 5.15 *The elderly had an honored and respected role in traditional societies, and typically spent their last years living with their children and grandchildren. In the modern United States, however, the old are relatively segregated from the rest of society, sometimes being placed in old-age homes or nursing homes. More than two-thirds of all deaths now take place in hospitals and geriatric institutions.*

place in the family and the community. They had many roles to fill—familial, social, religious, and even economic, for they typically worked until advanced old age. In modern industrialized societies the situation is quite different. The knowledge of the elderly may seem obsolete, their authority may be negligible, and they may even be unwanted by their children: often, the best they can do is attempt not to be a "burden." There are few useful roles for the aged: they generally retire around age sixty-five, and are left with little or no part to play in economic life. On the whole, however, the situation of the elderly in the United States is much brighter than it was a decade or two ago. The average age of Americans is now higher than at any time in the nation's history, and the aged have used their numbers and influence to gain many benefits that have improved the quality of their lives.

In time, too, the burden of the years affects everyone: signs such as baldness, wrinkling, and stiffness in the limbs all announce the gradual degeneration of the body that comes with advanced age. Of course, different people age physically at very different rates; but ill-health becomes steadily more common until more than three-quarters of those aged sixty-five or over suffer from some chronic health condition. Yet the infirmity of some of the aged can have social as well as physical causes: if we offer the very old the role of an infirm person who has outlived any real usefulness to society, we must not be surprised that some of the elderly live up to these social expectations. Most of the aged, of course, are able to enjoy their retirement and to review a life with its share of satisfaction and fulfillment. But in a society that worships youth and gives power, wealth, and prestige to the middle-aged, old age can easily become an ambiguous period (Foner, 1986). (The problems of the aged are discussed in more detail in Chapter 12, "Inequalities of Gender and Age.")

Death

Socialization for death is almost nonexistent in the United States. In preindustrial societies, deaths usually took place at home in the context of the family, and young people grew up with a close understanding of the experience. In modern America, however, death is very much a taboo subject; we speak of it in hushed tones and use such euphemisms as "passed away." As children we fear the subject; as adults we avoid it—even, and sometimes especially, when we are in the presence of someone who is dying.

The reason for this distinctively modern taboo seems to be that death, almost alone of natural processes, remains beyond the control of our advanced technology. Modern medicine, nutrition, and sanitation have all helped to extend our *life expectancy*—the length of life the average newborn will enjoy. But they have had little, if any, effect on our *life span*—the maximum length of life possible in the species. The final point of the life course—the annihilation of the self, the ultimate confrontation with the unknown—mocks our claim to human mastery of the world, and we therefore try to deny the mystery and power of death by excluding it from our discussions and thoughts.

We also effectively exclude the dying from the ongoing life of the community. We have sanitized death and removed it as far as possible from everyday experience by ensuring that most people die in nursing homes, hospitals, and similar formal organizations that care for the sick and aged. Typically, therefore, the dying face their end in a bureaucratic environment, surrounded by other sick people and a professional staff, rather than in the intimacy of their homes with their loved ones. Often, in fact, there is a conspiracy of professionals and relatives to hide the fact of death from the dying person. Research into the sociology of death and dying, however, has produced an impressive body of evidence to suggest that people die far more happily—even contentedly—if death is openly discussed with them beforehand (Glaser and Strauss, 1965, 1968; Charmaz, 1980; DeSpelder and Strickland, 1983).

Our understanding of death and dying has been greatly increased by the pioneering work of Elisabeth Kübler-Ross (1969, 1975), who conducted extensive interviews with dying people. She suggested that there are five stages through which a terminally ill person often proceeds after learning the truth. The first is *denial,* usually expressed in disbelief—"It can't be happening to me." The second stage is *anger*—"Why me?" The third stage is *bargaining*—an implicit agreement to go willingly if God or fate will just allow the dying person to live a little longer, perhaps until some significant event such as a family birthday or wedding. The fourth stage is *depression,* a state of deep anxiety over the loss of self and the loss to one's family. The final stage is *acceptance,* in which the dying person approaches death with true peace of mind. Some of the most healthy and accepting attitudes toward death, in fact, are found in old-age homes and other places where the elderly live together and have been able to frankly discuss their dying

with others (Rosenfeld, 1978). As the findings of sociological research into death and dying become more widely known, socialization for death is likely to become more effective: in recent years, for example, courses on the subject have appeared at high schools and colleges and have attracted large enrollments.

Socialization and Free Will

If our behavior and personalities depend so much on the content of our individual socialization, what becomes of human free will? Do we have any choice over our personal behavior, or is it all shaped for us by our past experiences?

Dennis Wrong (1961) has drawn attention to what he calls the "oversocialized conception" of human beings—the view that we are little more than the predictable products of a harmonious socialization into the social order. Wrong points out that people often feel coerced by society into doing things they do not want to do, a clear indication that socialization is less than perfect. Socialization, he argues, can never completely wipe out any basic personality traits with which we are born. Our innate drives for food, sex, and security are not as easily channeled as some people might like to think, nor are our socially acquired desires for power, wealth, or prestige.

The experiences of past socialization are blended in unique ways by each person. Everyone faces the problem that different socializing influences contradict one another. Parents may tell us one thing, friends something else, the media something else again. And the different roles that a person plays may also be in conflict. As a student, you should stay home and work on your term paper; as a member of your peer group, you should go to a party. The individual is pushed this way and that and constantly has to make personal judgments and decisions in unanticipated situations. Our personal histories may strongly influence our choices of action, of course. That is why courts are often willing to take an offender's past background into account before passing sentence, particularly when dealing with juveniles. But in practice the courts, like the rest of society, always insist at some point that people (unless they are mentally disordered) are capable of choosing courses of action and of "reforming" their personalities. We hold people responsible for their behavior precisely because they *can* exercise choice—particularly moral choice—over what they do.

For whatever reasons, everyone violates social norms at some time or another, often in novel and sometimes socially disapproved ways. Hearing a "different drummer," we do not keep pace with our companions—or, in George Herbert Mead's more sociological terms, the unsocialized "I" is never completely subservient to the socialized "me." Within the very broad limits provided by our place in history and society, we are free to fabricate our selves and our behavior as we wish—particularly if we understand the social process through which we became what we are.

Summary

1.   Socialization is the lifelong process of social interaction through which people acquire personality and learn the way of life of their society. The process is essential for the survival of both the individual and society. People in the same culture tend to be similar in some general respects, but their unique experiences make them different.

2.   The "nature versus nurture" debate is now recognized as a pointless one. Human personality and social behavior are the outcome of an interaction between biological potentials and cultural learning.

3.   Evidence concerning children reared in isolation, children reared in institutions, and monkeys reared in isolation indicates that intimate social interaction is essential if later personal development is not to be severely impaired.

4.   The emergence of the self is crucial for the development of personality. Cooley argued that the self emerges through experience of the "looking glass" supplied by the reactions of other people. Mead emphasized symbolic interaction, particularly through language, and the development of the ability to take the role of others.

5.   Cognitive or intellectual abilities develop through four basic stages: the sensorimotor stage, the preoperational stage, the concrete operational stage, and the formal operational stage. The content of thought, however, depends on the cultural environment. For example, computers may have some effect on cognitive socialization.

6.   Emotional development also seems to proceed in a definite sequence, although social factors affect how and whether emotions are expressed.

7.   In the United States and most industrialized societies, there are four main agents of socialization: the family, the school, the peer group, and the mass media. Other agents also socialize the individual throughout life.

8.   In "total institutions," such as the military, resocialization may occur. The content and stages of the life course are influenced by social as well as biological factors. American socialization often fails to equip people adequately for certain stages of the life course, particularly adolescence, old age, and dying. In modern industrialized societies, the life course now includes infancy and childhood, adolescence, youth (optionally), mature adulthood, old age, and death.

9.   There is a danger of accepting an "oversocialized conception" of human beings. Socialization is never fully successful. We still retain a measure of free will and are responsible for our acts.

Important Terms

socialization (115)	generalized other (123)
personality (115)	agents of socialization (128)
life course (117)	peers (129)
self (121)	mass media (130)
looking-glass self (122)	resocialization (131)
symbolic interaction (123)	total institution (131)
role-taking (123)	life expectancy (137)
particular other (123)	life span (137)

Suggested Readings

BERGER, KATHLEEN. *The Developing Person Through Childhood and Adolescence.* 2nd ed. New York: Worth, 1986.

An excellent introduction to the study of human development, especially in the early years of life.

CLAUSEN, JOHN A. *The Life Course: A Sociological Perspective.* Englewood Cliffs, N.J.: Prentice-Hall, 1986.

A good introduction to the sociological perspective on the life course from birth to death.

DESPELDER, LYNNE ANN, and ALBERT LEE STRICKLAND. *The Last Dance: Encountering Death and Dying.* Palo Alto, Calif.: Mayfield, 1983.

A broad survey of the sociological literature on death and dying.

ELKIN, FREDERICK, and GERALD HANDEL. *The Child and Society.* 4th ed. New York: Random House, 1984.

A brief but thorough overview of the process of socialization. The book incorporates both sociological and social psychological material.

ERIKSON, ERIK H. *Childhood and Society.* New York: W. W. Norton, 1964.

A classic work that deals with the interaction between the social environment and personality during the socialization process. The book includes a discussion of the life course and of the "identity crises."

PIAGET, JEAN, and BARBEL INHELDER. *The Psychology of the Child.* New York: Basic Books, 1969.

A concise account of Piaget's theory of cognitive development, with descriptions of many of his experiments with children and their thought processes.

ROSE, PETER I. (ed.). *Socialization and the Life Cycle.* New York: St. Martin's Press, 1979.

An excellent collection of articles covering various aspects of socialization.

SHATTUCK, ROGER. *The Forbidden Experiment.* New York: Farrar, Straus, and Giroux, 1980.

A fascinating account of the discovery and subsequent life of a "wild boy" who was found in France in the nineteenth century. The book includes some information on other "feral" children.

SPIRO, MELFORD. *Children of the Kibbutz.* Rev. ed. Cambridge, Mass.: Harvard University Press, 1975.

An interesting study of socialization in an Israeli kibbutz, where the community rather than the parents has the responsibility for raising children.

Genie: A Case of Childhood Isolation

SUSAN CURTISS

Cases of childhood isolation reveal a great deal about "human nature," for they give us a harrowing glimpse of what a virtually unsocialized person can be like. The following case concerns Genie, a California girl who was kept locked in a room by her father from the time she was twenty months old until the age of thirteen and a half. The descriptions that follow were written by Susan Curtiss, a psycholinguist who worked with Genie for several years after she was discovered in 1970. They describe the circumstances of Genie's isolation and her typical behavior during her first year of treatment. (After six years of being cared for, first in a hospital and then in a foster home, Genie could speak in sentences, attend a special school, and form emotional attachments.)

. . . Genie was confined to a small bedroom, harnessed to an infant's potty seat. Genie's father sewed the harness, himself; unclad except for the harness, Genie was left to sit on that chair. Unable to move anything except her fingers and hands, feet and toes, Genie was left to sit, tied-up, hour after hour, often into the night, day after day, month after month, year after year. At night, when Genie was not forgotten, she was removed from her harness only to be placed into another restraining garment—a sleeping bag which her father had fashioned to hold Genie's arms stationary (allegedly to prevent her from taking it off). In effect, it was a straight jacket. Therein constrained, Genie was put into an infant's crib with wire mesh sides and a wire mesh cover overhead. Caged by night, harnessed by day, Genie was left to somehow endure the hours and years of her life.

There was little for her to listen to; there was no TV or radio in the house. Genie's bedroom was in the back of the house next to . . . a bathroom. . . . The father had an intolerance for noise, so what little conversation there was between family members in the rest of the house was kept at a low volume. Except for moments of anger, when her father swore, Genie did not hear any language outside her door, and thus received practically no auditory stimulation of any kind, aside from bathroom noises. There were two windows in her room, and one of them was kept open several inches. She may, therefore, have occasionally heard an airplane overhead or some other traffic or environmental noises; but set in the back of the house, Genie would not have heard much noise from the street.

Hungry and forgotten, Genie would sometimes attempt to attract attention by making noise. Angered, her father would often beat her for doing so. In fact, there was a large piece of wood left in the corner of Genie's room which her father used solely to beat her whenever she made any sound. Genie learned to keep silent and to suppress all vocalization; but sometimes, desperate for attention or food, Genie would use her body or some object to make noise. Her father would not tolerate this either, and he often beat her with his wooden stick on these occasions as well. During these times, and on all other occasions that her father dealt with Genie, he never spoke to her. Instead, he acted like a wild dog. He made barking sounds, he growled at her . . . he bared his teeth at her; and if he wished to merely threaten her with his presence, he stood outside the door and made his dog-like noises—to warn her that he was there and if she persisted in whatever she was doing, he would come in and beat her. That terrible noise, the sound of her father standing outside her door growling or barking or both, was almost the only sound Genie heard during those years she was imprisoned in her room. . . .

Just as there was little to listen to, there was not much for Genie to touch or look at. The only pieces of furniture in her room were the crib and the potty seat. There was no carpet on the floor, no pictures on the walls. There were two windows, but they were covered up except for a few inches at the top out of which Genie could see the sky from one and the side of a neighboring house from the other. There was one dim, bare ceiling light bulb, a wall of closets, and another wall with the bedroom door. . . . Occasionally, two plastic raincoats, one clear and one yellow, hung outside the closet in the room, and once in a while Genie was allowed to "play" with them. In addition, Genie was sometimes given "partly edited" copies of the TV log, with pictures that her father considered too suggestive removed (like women advertising swimming pools, etc.). She was also given an occasional empty cottage cheese container, empty thread spools, and the like. These were Genie's toys; and together with the floor, her harness, and her body, they were her primary sources of visual and tactile stimulation. . . .

. . .

Genie was pitiful. Hardly ever having worn clothing, she did not react to temperature, heat or cold. Never having eaten solid food, Genie did not know how to chew, and had great difficulty in swallowing. Having been strapped down and left sitting on a potty chair, she could not stand erect, could not straighten her arms or legs, could not run, hop, jump, or climb; in fact, she could only walk with difficulty, shuffling her feet, swaying from side to side. Hardly ever having seen more than a space of 10 feet in front of her (the distance from her potty chair to the door), she had become nearsighted exactly to that distance. Having been beaten for making noise, she had learned to suppress almost all vocalization save a whimper. Suffering from malnutrition, she weighed only 59 pounds and stood only 54 inches tall. She was incontinent of feces and urine. Her hair was sparse and stringy. She salivated copiously, spitting onto anything at hand. Genie was unsocialized, primitive, hardly human.

Surprisingly, however, Genie was alert and curious. She maintained good eye contact and avidly explored her new surroundings. She was intensely eager for human contact and attention. In the face of her hunger for contact with her new world, her almost total silence had an eerie quality. Except for a high-pitched whimpering and a few words she is reported to have imitated when she was first admitted to the hospital, she was a silent child who did not vocalize in any way, who did not even sob when she cried. Her silence was complete even in the face of frenzied emotion. Sometimes, frightened and frustrated by both her former life and her new surroundings, Genie would erupt and have a raging tantrum, flailing about, scratching, spitting, blowing her nose, and frantically rubbing her face and hair with her own mucus, all the time trying to gouge or otherwise inflict pain on herself—all in silence. Unable to vocalize, Genie would use objects and parts of her body to make noise and help express her frenzy: a chair scratching against the floor, her fingers scratching against a balloon, furniture falling, objects thrown or slammed against other objects, her feet shuffling. These were Genie's noises during her sobless silent tantrum. At long last, physically exhausted, her rage would subside, and Genie would silently return to her undemonstrative self.

There was no real language during her placid times either. Except for a few words, Genie never spoke. . . . The hospital staff had the general impression that Genie could understand a fair amount based on the fact that she maintained good eye contact and seemed to pay special attention to faces when people spoke to her. Yet all the staff interviewed admitted on questioning that they tended to point and demonstrate when relating to Genie, and thus a fair amount of gesturing most probably accompanied their speech to her. They also stated that often Genie did not respond to very common, simple commands or questions.

Genie had a habit of walking around during mealtime, stopping at other children's places at the table, sometimes attempting to take their portions of foods she especially liked (applesauce, milk, ice cream, etc.). She often walked around with her mouth stuffed with food, and during her journey around the dining room she would sometimes spit it out onto the nearest plate. Perhaps, in her bizarre unsocialized way, she was giving the other children an "offering" of food, to make up for the (unwilling and unoffered) offering of what she was about to take from them. In any case, her "offering" was never welcome, and mealtime with Genie was usually not a pleasant event.

Genie had other personal habits that were not socially acceptable. She blew her nose onto anything or nothing, often making a mess of her clothing. At times, when excited or agitated, she would urinate in inappropriate places—leaving her companion to deal with the results. But it was her lack of socialization that was most difficult to deal with, especially in public. Genie had a special fondness for certain things—anything made of plastic, certain foods, certain articles of clothing or accessories. If anyone she encountered in the street or in a store or other public place had something she liked, she was uncontrollably drawn to him or her, and without obeying any rules of psychological distance or social mores, she would go right up to the person and put her hands on the desired item. It was bad enough when she went up to someone else's shopping cart to reach in to take something out; but when the object of attention was an article of clothing, and Genie would simply attach herself to the person wearing that clothing and refuse to let go, the situations were extremely trying.

Even when Genie did not attach herself in quite such an embarrassing manner, she still went right up to strangers, stood directly in front of them, without any accepted distance between them, and peered into their faces with her face directly in front of theirs, pointing (without looking) at whatever possession of theirs held her interest. Other times, she very simply walked up to them and linked her arm through theirs or put her arm around them and was ready to walk on. All of this behavior, though charming and even endearing in the abstract, was quite embarrassing.

Genie masturbated excessively, which proved to be the most serious antisocial behavior problem of all. Despite admonishments, she continued to masturbate as often as possible, anywhere and everywhere. . . . Many of the items she coveted were objects with which to masturbate, and she would attempt to do so, regardless of where she was. She was drawn to chair backs, chair arms, counter edges, door knobs, door edges, table corners, car handles, car mirrors, and so forth; in essence, indoors and outdoors she was continually attempting to masturbate. . . . The first month, when I saw Genie almost daily, I spent the time trying to get to know her and to establish a relationship with her that would help her develop trust in me and enable me to work with her effectively. At that time she was still not testable, and was so bizarre in her behavior that had I attempted to gain information formally from her, I would not have known how to interpret her performance.

SOURCE: Susan Curtiss, *Genie* (New York: Academic Press, 1977).

CHAPTER 6

Social Interaction in Everyday Life

The most basic unit of human behavior is an act. Anything you can do is an act—waking in the morning, getting dressed, going to class, reading this sentence. Some of our acts have implications for nobody but ourselves, but most of them involve some relationship to other people, and thus constitute interaction with them.

Social interaction is the process by which people act toward or respond to other people. It includes any and all social behavior—smiling at a friend, asking a professor a question, moving aside to avoid an oncoming pedestrian, having an argument, buying a cup of coffee, or leaving personal "markers" at your seat in the library so that nobody will take it while you are away. Human social interaction is extraordinarily flexible and varied. In this respect it is quite unlike that of other social animals, which interact with one another in rather rigid, genetically programmed ways.

Our social interaction is utterly different for the reason that we live in a *meaningful* world, one that we can consciously reflect on and interpret. We respond to the natural and social environment according to the learned meanings that objects and events have for us. To us, a piece of wood is not simply an object: the same item can be a hockey stick, a potential weapon, or firewood, and we will act toward it in terms of the meaning we place on it. The same is true of other people: we have to *interpret* their behavior in order to interact with them. A person's act in jumping up and down is meaningless in itself; we cannot respond unless we know whether the person is doing a rain dance, is training for an athletic event, or has just stubbed a toe. Similarly, we cannot respond to an outstretched hand until we decide whether it is extended in friendship or is about to deliver a karate chop. Social interaction can take place in an orderly manner only if we and other people are able to interpret the endless variety of situations in which we find ourselves.

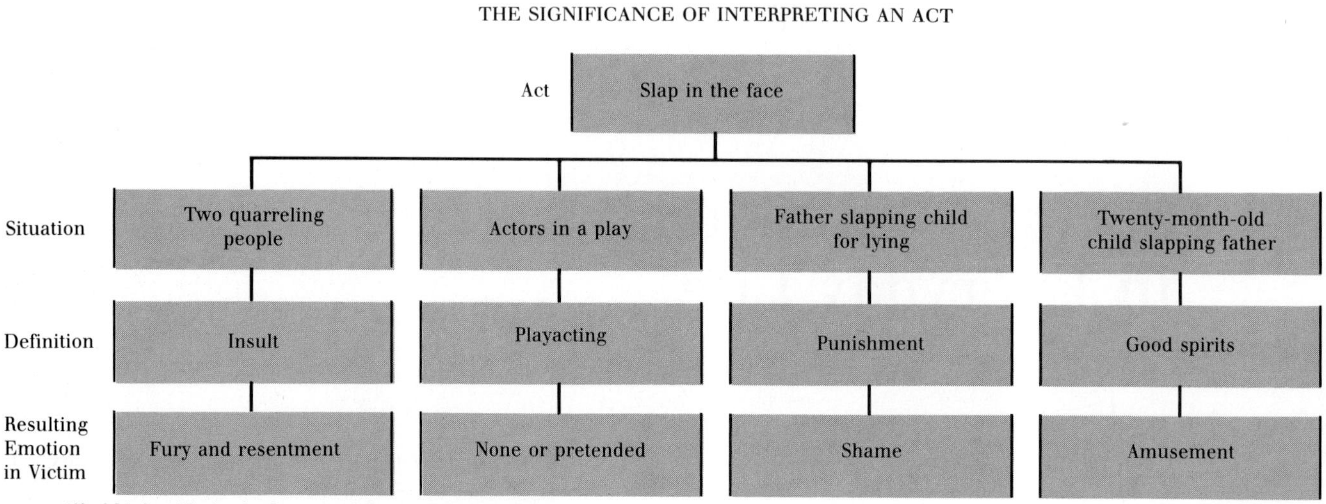

THE SIGNIFICANCE OF INTERPRETING AN ACT

	Act	Slap in the face		
Situation	Two quarreling people	Actors in a play	Father slapping child for lying	Twenty-month-old child slapping father
Definition	Insult	Playacting	Punishment	Good spirits
Resulting Emotion in Victim	Fury and resentment	None or pretended	Shame	Amusement

SOURCE: Alfred Lindesmith, Anselm Strauss, and Norman Denzin, *Social Psychology,* 4th ed. (New York: Holt, Rinehart and Winston, 1975), p. 213.

Figure 6.1 *As this chart suggests, a person's reaction to an event may depend, not on the event itself, but rather on the interpretation that he or she places on the situation.*

Most studies of social interaction rely, of course, on the interactionist perspective. As we saw in Chapter 1, this theoretical approach focuses primarily on "micro," or small-scale, processes, on the intricate web of minute, day-to-day activities that make up the ongoing life of society. Many of these events pass unnoticed because they are so much taken for granted, yet cumulatively they produce and make possible what we call society. Societies and cultures have no independent existence: they exist only through the people who inhabit and act upon them. Although social institutions—such as religion, education, the economy, the family—reach back into and influence social interaction, they are themselves the product of that interaction. The study of everyday life, then, provides a useful complement to the more common sociological emphasis on the "macro," or large-scale, processes and structures.

The interactionist perspective is a broad one. It includes contributions from several schools of thought that differ somewhat in their interests, assumptions, and methods, but which all emphasize the importance of meaning and interpretation in social life. In this chapter we will examine some of these approaches and illustrate their applications. We will find that when we subject the taken-for-granted reality of micro processes to sociological analysis, the supposedly familiar and obvious social world suddenly takes on a new and unexpected appearance.

Symbolic Interaction

We inhabit a meaningful world because our environment is not merely physical; it is also symbolic. A *symbol* is something that can meaningfully represent something else. Anything can be a symbol—a laugh, a gesture, a style of clothing, a crucifix, a piece of colored cloth marked with stars and stripes. A symbol has meaning only because people arbitrarily give meaning to it and agree on that meaning. Your college insignia, for example, represents your college simply because people share the same interpretation of an otherwise meaningless design. Words, too, are symbols, arbitrarily attached to agreed-upon meanings, and language is the richest and most flexible system of symbols there is. Through language and other symbols people define and interpret the world around them, piece together the buzz and confusion of life into meaningful patterns, and negotiate their interactions with others.

The most influential of all approaches to the micro processes of society emphasizes *symbolic interaction,* the interaction between people that takes place through symbols such as signs, gestures, and language. The symbolic interactionist approach thus focuses on the distinctive feature of human relationships already mentioned: we do not respond to other people directly, but rather to the meaning that we place on their actions (Mead, 1934; Blumer, 1969; Stryker, 1984).

How is it possible for us to interpret the actions and even the intentions of others? As we saw in Chapter 5 ("Socialization"), the key is our development of a concept of self—of an "inner person" that we can think about and reflect upon, almost as though our "self" were someone else. Our sense of self enables us to appreciate that other people also have selves and allows us to take the role of other people in our imaginations: that is, we can try to see things from their point of view, understand how they feel, predict how they are likely to behave, and anticipate their responses to our actions. This ability to interpret the behavior of others, combined with shared understandings of symbols, makes meaningful social interaction possible.

Punks and Nurses

A study by Andrew Travers (1982) illustrates how people may use symbols to establish their identities and convey meanings to others. Like much symbolic interactionist research, his study is based on participant observation—in this case, of two social groups, punks and nurses. Although these two groups are very different, they have this much in common: both are obsessed with their symbolic appearance. The punks are anxious to create an unconventional identity by symbolically polluting themselves; the nurses, who work in contact with disease, are anxious to symbolically rid themselves of pollution.

Punk is a youth fashion that started in England in the mid-1970s and spread to other countries in Western Europe and North America, where traces of it are still to be found in the mid-1980s among disaffected young people. Punk appearance violates social norms. Hair is sometimes wholly or partly shaved off, sometimes tousled into starched spikes, and often dyed in such arresting colors as pink or lime green. Safety pins and chains are sometimes hung from the ears or the nose. Boys are always clean-shaven (to distinguish them from their archenemies, the hippies), and girls wear dark makeup, perhaps with a swastika as a beauty spot. Clothes are torn and frequently hand-lettered with slogans like "I'm a dog," and the punk wardrobe often includes such unconventional items as kilts for boys and military boots for girls. The most favored neckwear is a leather collar with metal studs, and other accessories include padlocks and razor blades.

Punk behavior is also unconventional. Much time is spent hanging around on the street, since employment opportunities for people of this ap-

Figure 6.2 *Punks and nurses maintain a very different appearance—but each uses such symbols as clothing to communicate messages to other people.*

pearance are rather limited. Curiosity or criticism from passers-by is completely ignored, but the punks seem pleased by media descriptions of themselves as morons or hooligans. Dancing at concerts sometimes consists of jumping up and down on the same spot and punching a fist into the air, and enthusiasm for a singer may be indicated by a generous spit in his or her direction.

What is all this about? As Travers points out, punk symbols and behavior are carefully calculated to offend: punks actually want to appear vile in the eyes of "straight" society. They are deliberately trying to violate social expectations by symbolically polluting themselves. They make no attempt to apologize for their condition, and by this attitude, they gain a certain symbolic power. For the punks are mostly ordinary young working-class people, with little education or social status and few prospects. Their appearance is simply that, an appearance—one that disguises their basic ordinariness. By showing that they could not care less about the criticisms of others, they gain a sense of specialness: conventional society has no power over the punks, but the punks have the power to outrage conventional society.

Nurses, like punks, undergo a far-reaching socialization, but in the opposite direction. Despite their claims to professional status, nurses work in an environment that constantly threatens them with pollution, both symbolic and real. They are in daily contact with the diseased and dying. They serve them meals, make their beds, lift and wash them. They have to insert suppositories, clean wounds, help people urinate. They handle dirty laundry, clean up blood, vomit, and excrement, and attend to dead bodies. They are exposed to pain, grief, and every imaginable infection. And they do all this for long hours at low pay.

Travers suggests that there is only one way the nurse can transcend all this contamination, and that is to look and act as much as possible like a nurse—a clean, competent professional, with a vocation to help the sick. All over the world, nurses—the vast majority of whom are women— have a standard and immediately recognizable appearance: uniformed, well-laundered, stainless, demure. A nurse wears her hair tucked under a little white hat that has no possible use other than as a symbol, to make her look like a nurse. On the hospital ward the nurse's manner, under all circumstances, is supposed to be cheerful and efficient, unruffled and in control. Indeed, a nurse who does not look and act the part of a nurse is unlikely to be permitted to remain on the ward for very long.

The appearance and social behavior of the nurse give her a certain symbolic power, too, for they show that she is a truly remarkable individual who can rise above conditions that would daunt ordinary people. Clean and wholesome amid sickness and dirt, she reveals her identity as a person with a noble calling, a being superior to a "mere" secretary who works with nothing less sterile than a keyboard or telephone. Like the punk, the nurse uses symbols to create her social identity—but in her case it is to ensure social approval.

The Door Ceremony

The social relations of men and women are characterized by a variety of apparently trivial rituals and ceremonies that are freighted with symbolic meaning. Despite all the changes that have taken place in gender roles over the past two decades, it is still widely expected that a man will help a woman on with her coat, rather than the other way around; that a man rather than a woman will drive a car in which both are traveling, even if it is jointly owned; that a man rather than a woman will pick up the check on a date. Of all such rituals, the most common is undoubtedly the door ceremony. Even if they are complete strangers, a man and a woman arriving simultaneously at a door generally enact the same behavior: the woman waits expectantly while the man opens the door and allows her to enter first.

As Laurel Richardson Walum (1974) has pointed out, this apparently trivial form of social interaction has a much deeper symbolic meaning. It affirms the "appropriate" relationship of the sexes—the independence of the male and the dependence of the female. In our culture, to be "masculine" is to be active; to be "feminine" is to be passive. In the door ceremony the male actively opens the door, the female waits passively for it to be opened; the male communicates an ability to manage the tasks of daily life, the female communicates the need to have someone help her in these tasks. In performing the door ceremony, he *feels* masculine, she *feels* feminine. (We can better understand the symbolic meanings of such rituals if we imagine the roles of the sexes reversed, with men waiting for women to light their cigarettes, open doors, and drive them around.)

Until the 1960s, these social rituals were taken for granted, but since that time the changing status of women has made them problematic. Some people now see the door ceremony not as symbolic of chivalry, but rather as behavior that is demeaning.

In her research on college students, Walum found that the door ceremony, once a matter of flawless, unreflecting routine, had become a source of uncertainty and confusion. Should a man open a door for a woman or not? Do women want doors opened for them?

Some students, Walum found, were unsure of the appropriate behavior. One woman, for example, reported:

> I approached a door ahead of a fellow and then with common courtesy, I held it open for him to go through. He bumped right into me even though he could see me. He looked awfully puzzled and it took him forever to get through.

Others felt there is no place for the door ceremony in modern life, as both sexes should be treated equally:

> A male shouldn't circle the car to open the door for a woman. I believe each sex should treat the other with mutual courtesy. If a woman reaches the car first, there is nothing wrong with her opening it.

There were traditionalists of both sexes who felt strongly that the door ceremony should still be performed. One woman declared:

> I opened a door to enter a building and a boy walked in ahead of me. It was just like he expected me to open the door for him. My first reaction was frowning and thinking some people have a lot of nerve. I believe in manners that did not enter the mind of the boy. I wondered if most boys now take it for granted that girls . . . will want to hold the door open for boys.

Other students flatly refused to participate in the ceremony at all. A male student saw it as silly and pointless:

> I don't open doors for women. I'm glad not to. I don't want to serve them just because they're women. If they had their heads screwed on right they wouldn't trade doing laundry for me lighting their cigarettes.

How do these reactions compare with your own and your classmates' views and experience? Actually, people's responses to these issues tend to be influenced by such variables as age, education, region, religion, race, social class, and social trends. For example, the uncertainty Walum found in her college subjects in the early 1970s is not found in the general population today; in fact, a 1983 survey indicated that 94 percent of Americans approve of traditional customs like men opening

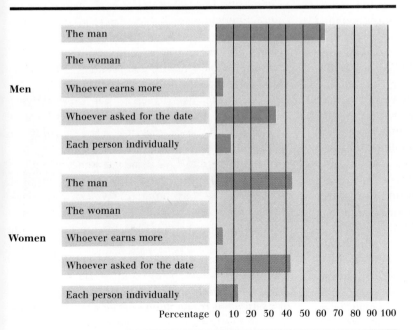

WHO SHOULD PAY FOR A DATE?

Question: Who do you believe should pay for an evening's entertainment in a dating relationship? Would you say the man, the woman, whoever earns more, whoever asked for the date, or each person individually?

Figure 6.3 *Are the "chivalrous" ceremonies that ritualize female dependence a thing of the past? As the results of one poll reveal, Americans no longer take it for granted that a man should pay the costs of a date with a woman. Other polls, however, show continued strong support for many similar "courtesy" rituals between the sexes.*

SOURCE: Survey by Audits and Surveys for the Merit Report, September 24, 1982.

doors for women. In any event, Walum's analysis does illustrate two important points about social interaction. First, the identical act, the door ceremony, is interpreted quite differently by different people according to the particular symbolic meaning that it has for them. Second, social interaction at the micro level is intimately related to the macro structure of society. As long as women are treated as delicate and helpless, they will continue to be largely excluded from positions of power and independence. When women are regarded as symbolically incapable of opening doors, the fact that there are hardly any female senators, governors, or major corporation presidents should not surprise us.

Dramaturgy

Our social interaction consists, essentially, of our playing various roles in relation to one another. As a student, for example, you play different roles in relation to your professor, your dormitory janitor, or your seminar group. Each of these audiences consequently sees a different aspect of your self.

As we noted in Chapter 4 ("Society"), the sociological concept of role is taken directly from the theater. One approach used in the interactionist perspective takes the idea of acting a role seriously. This approach is *dramaturgy,* a method of analyzing social interaction as though the participants were actors on a stage. Using this metaphor, the dramaturgical approach focuses on the way we play out various social parts and scenes, following the script where we can, and improvising when the script is unclear or incomplete.

The dramaturgical approach was founded and developed by Erving Goffman (1922–1982). Goffman's work often seems to lie beyond the mainstream of sociological research. His eye for the minute and subtle details of social behavior is more like a novelist's than a scientist's, yet his writing seems so aloof and impersonal that he might almost be describing the behavior of another species. Goffman's methods of gathering data are obscure, but his insights into the "little salutations, compliments, and apologies that punctuate social life" are often brilliant and convincing. He maintains that orderly social life is made possible by the unwritten scripts, or unspoken rules, of social interaction. A fully accurate picture of society must therefore take account of these rules, as well as the more explicit ones that people consciously recognize (1959, 1963a, 1966, 1969, 1971).

An example of these unspoken rules is what

Goffman (1963a) calls "civil inattention" toward strangers in public: we behave in a way that shows we are aware of their presence, but we avoid eye contact with them at close quarters. In effect, we politely ignore them. Goffman points out how the role of pedestrian often involves civil inattention:

> In performing this courtesy the eyes of the looker may pass over the eyes of the other, but no "recognition" is typically allowed. Where the courtesy is performed between two persons passing on the street, civil inattention may take the form of eyeing the other up to eight feet . . . and then casting the eyes down as the other passes—a kind of dimming of the lights. In any case, we have here what is perhaps the slightest of interpersonal rituals, yet one that constantly regulates the social intercourse of persons in our society.

These little rules and rituals, according to Goffman, form the backdrop to the stage on which we present our performances.

Presenting the Self

A major focus of dramaturgy is on how we present our selves to the world, for the disconcerting fact is that whatever you think your "true" self may be, the actual self you present to others varies from one situation to another. From early childhood we are taught to "behave" in the presence of others, or not to do such-and-such "in front of the neighbors." The self you present to your parents is dif-

Figure 6.4

"I believe that's Roger Hillard.
He's never mastered the art of entering a crowded room."

ferent from the one you present to your friends or to the police officer who stops you for a traffic violation. This does not necessarily mean that we are habitually insincere; insincerity arises only when we present a self that we do not ourselves believe in. In fact, social life requires that we present different aspects of ourselves in different situations. If everyone behaved in exactly the same way to everyone else, social chaos would result. We would be unable to fulfill our various roles as teachers, students, sons, daughters, employers, workers, and so on.

We are so used to presenting ourselves in particular ways in particular situations that we are usually not even aware we are doing it, for much of this behavior becomes an everyday routine. It is only when we realize that we are being scrutinized by others—when we are introduced to a stranger, perhaps, or, most excruciatingly of all, when we go through a job interview—that we become conscious of what we are doing. How, then, do we go about creating the impressions we offer to others?

People, Goffman argues, are deeply concerned with "impression management": they attempt to control the impressions they make on others by presenting themselves in the most favorable light. In acting their parts, people are careful to construct their "scenery," perhaps with posters on the wall or a lavishly illustrated book on the coffee table, and they make use of personal "props," such as a pipe or an expensive briefcase. People are careful to wear appropriate clothing for particular social occasions, presenting a different self by dressing casually for a friend, fashionably for a party, formally for a job interview.

Goffman suggests that we may have both a "back stage" and a "front stage" for our performances. Waiters in restaurants, for example, play one role while attending to their customers, switch to a more relaxed role in the private back stage of the kitchen, and then revert to their original role when they return to the customers. Similarly, a husband and wife who are entertaining another couple at dinner may seize a private moment to exchange thoughts on their performance as hosts and how it might be improved. A good deal of impression management, in fact, involves "teamwork" of this kind. Parents collaborate to prevent their children from knowing about their marital quarrels. Professors who loathe each other take care to hide this animosity when students are present. Political opponents and their staffs radiate a common air of confidence about forthcoming election results, regardless of what the opinion polls may show.

The attempt to present the self in a favorable light is not always successful. Frequently the audience knows perfectly well what the actor is trying to do and carefully evaluates the performance, noting both the impressions the actor "gives" deliberately and the impressions he or she "gives off" without intending to. The actor may sweat, stutter, blush, laugh too heartily, tremble, stand too close, cower, or drop things. If gestures seem carefully rehearsed or do not match the verbal part of the presentation, the audience may suspect insincerity. Sometimes, of course, people are able to claim a response—such as respect, trust, or a favor—to which they are not entitled. In this case, a "con" has been achieved. Sometimes, in fact, all parties to an encounter may manage to convince the others that the selves they are portraying are authentic, even when they are not.

Figure 6.5 *By using various "props," people create particular impressions about themselves. This Englishman offers various clues in his dress and appearance (such as his bowler hat and three-piece suit) that enable others to make some assessment of his personality and social status. Would you say that he is upper class or middle class? Conservative or liberal?*

Although we can use various clues to assess a performance, we rarely challenge the credentials of an actor even when we suspect that a false impression is being created. The reason is that all participants in a social encounter shoulder a common responsibility to maintain one another's "face." An encounter is a perilous exercise, liable to be disrupted at any time if an actor "loses face" by being successfully challenged. The discredited performer's acute embarrassment is highly discomforting to everyone else as well. We therefore participate in what Goffman calls a "studied nonobservance" of potentially embarrassing particulars—the stomach rumble of a dinner guest, the secretive nose picking of a new dating partner, the slightly slipped hairpiece of an employer, the obviously fictitious excuse of a student who has handed in a late term paper. Much of what we call "polite behavior" consists of an implicit bargain among actors to help one another "keep face" by not questioning the performances they offer.

Male Doctor and Female Patient

A pelvic examination, especially when it is performed by a male physician, involves an extremely delicate social encounter. Women in our society are socialized from early childhood to regard the vagina as a singularly private part of the body, and access to it is normally granted only to the husband or other highly specific individuals in an intimate and sexually charged context. As a result, women often find the experience of a pelvic examination threatening—so much so that many put off such examinations even when they know there is a pressing medical reason for having one. When the doctor is male, therefore, the examination requires an elaborate ritual on the part of the doctor, nurse, and patient to desexualize the interaction and to maintain the fiction that nothing out of the ordinary is happening.

James Henslin and Mae Briggs (1971) analyzed this ritual, drawing their information from several thousand pelvic examinations observed by Briggs, a trained nurse. Using the dramaturgical approach, they analyzed the interaction as though it consisted of a series of scenes in a play, in which the participants shift roles in order to maintain their definitions of reality. In the "prologue" to the play, the woman enters the doctor's reception room, casting off her previous role and preparing to assume the role of patient. When she is summoned into the consulting room, she fully takes on

this new role, and the first "scene" opens. In this part of the performance, the doctor presents himself as a competent physician, responding to the patient role that the other is acting. The doctor treats the patient as a full person, maintaining eye contact with her and discussing her medical problems in a courteous and professional manner. If he decides a pelvic examination is necessary, he announces his decision and leaves the room.

The second "scene" then opens with the nurse's appearance. Her arrival and the disappearance of the doctor both serve important purposes. The nurse is essentially "a stagehand for the scene that is to follow." Her role is to help transform the patient from a "person" to a "nonperson," a "pelvic" to be clinically examined. The nurse soothes any anxieties that the patient might express: many women, for example, make such comments as "The things we women have to put up with!" and the nurse sympathetically agrees. The nurse supervises the patient's undressing and prepares the clinical "props" for the examination. Nearly all women are anxious to conceal their discarded underclothing before the doctor returns, and the nurse facilitates these wishes. The doctor's absence is highly significant, for it ensures that the patient does not undress in his presence and thus eliminates any suggestion that she is performing a striptease. By the time the nurse summons him back into the room, the patient is lying on an examination table with a sheet over most of her body.

In this next crucial "scene" all three actors are present. The presence of the nurse has two purposes. It serves to desexualize the interaction, and it protects the doctor's interests by providing a legal witness if the patient should interpret his performance as unprofessional. The patient is now "dramaturgically transformed for the duration of this scene into a nonperson." The drape sheet separates her pubic area from the rest of her body. From her position on the table, she can see only the drape sheet and can maintain the sense that she is almost fully covered. More important, she cannot see the doctor's face. He sits out of view on a low stool, and there is no eye contact between them. The doctor may address occasional questions or instructions of a medical nature to the patient, but he can otherwise ignore her completely. The patient "plays the role of object," engaging in a studied nonobservance of the entire scene. She typically initiates no conversation, avoids eye contact even with the nurse by staring at the wall or ceiling, and tries to present an image of immobility and self-control.

The next "scene" begins as soon as the examination is over. The doctor departs, allowing the patient to dress in his absence. The nurse helps the patient make the transition back to the role of "person" once more. The two engage in conversation, with the patient often making such comments as "I'm glad that's over with." The nurse again provides sympathetic reassurance. Once the patient is recostumed and regroomed, the last "scene" takes place. The doctor reenters for a final interview, interacting with the patient in terms of the more normal role she is now playing. His manner, courteous and professional as before, affirms that nothing out of the ordinary has occurred and that his view of her self is essentially unaffected by the interaction that has just taken place. In the "epilogue" to the whole performance, the patient departs, resuming her everyday roles in the world beyond.

Ethnomethodology

We share with others in our culture the same basic understandings about commonplace social reality. We assume, for example, that people will shake our hand if we extend it in greeting, that relatives will wish us well on our birthday, that dentists will attend to our teeth and not give us a haircut. These taken-for-granted assumptions serve as the basis for the most routine, down-to-earth social intercourse. Even when dealing with people we have never met before, we can smoothly negotiate interactions with them because we all share understandings of how social life is conducted.

Yet these understandings are problematic. What are they, and where do they come from? If we ask people about the background rules of social interaction, they are often perplexed. The question is one they "hadn't thought about," and they may be unable to identify the assumptions by which they live their social lives. In fact, background understandings are so easily overlooked that they have been generally ignored even by sociologists. During the past twenty years or so, however, some sociologists have developed a new approach to this aspect of social interaction—one that has links to symbolic interactionism and to dramaturgical analysis, but which differs from them in its methods and focus. This approach is ***ethnomethodology,*** the study of how people construct and share their definitions of reality in their everyday interactions (Garfinkel, 1967; Dreitzel, 1970; Sudnow, 1972; Cicourel, 1974; Psathas, 1979). "Ethnos" is a Greek word meaning "people" or "folk," so the somewhat indigestible title of this approach simply refers to a method for studying folk understandings of the social world.

It must be said that ethnomethodology has the reputation, thus far, of being a "fringe" element in the interactionist perspective. Some of its advocates believe that it is one of the most important enterprises in sociology, while some of its critics regard it as little more than an off-beat peculiarity. The issue is far from settled, but we can give a brief idea here of why the approach is controversial.

Exposing the Rules

In a sense, rules are known by the exceptions that are made to them. If a rule were always followed, people might be unaware of it, for there would be nothing to indicate its existence. Many "background" social rules, the ethnomethodologists claim, are obeyed so widely that we are not conscious of them. The principal technique of ethnomethodology, as developed by its founder Harold Garfinkel, is therefore to expose the rules by breaking them, to lay bare the shared understandings by violating them. In experiments designed to do this, Garfinkel (1967) had his students act as though they did not understand certain unspoken assumptions that regulate social interaction: for example, they might try to bargain for items in a supermarket, break the rules in a game of tic-tac-toe, or move closer and closer to someone in a con-

Figure 6.6

"Obviously, some people here do not appreciate the gravity of our situation."

Drawing by Modell; © 1985
The New Yorker Magazine, Inc.

versation until they were standing nose-to-nose. In each case, the reactions of the subjects—surprise, anger, or embarrassment—showed that their understandings of social reality had been breached.

In one experiment, Garfinkel asked his students to behave at home as though they were boarders, not sons or daughters. The students addressed their parents as "Mr." and "Mrs.," displayed gracious table manners, politely asked for permission to open the refrigerator, and so on. Garfinkel reports that in most cases

> family members were stupefied. They vigorously sought to make the strange actions intelligible and to restore the situation to normal appearances. Reports were filled with accounts of astonishment, bewilderment, shock, anxiety, embarrassment, and anger, and with charges by various family members that the student was mean, inconsiderate, selfish, nasty, or impolite. Family members demanded explanations: What's the matter? What's gotten into you? Did you get fired? Are you sick? What are you being so superior about? Why are you mad? Are you out of your mind or are you just stupid?

Although the students were supposed to keep up the performance for only about fifteen minutes to an hour, their violation of taken-for-granted rules of household behavior was so disruptive that few could maintain the role that long.

Ethnomethodologists are particularly interested in communication through language, for words can carry more or less meaning than they seem to, depending on the understandings that the partners in a conversation share. Consider, for example, the following fictitious dialogue between a father and his rebellious teenage son:

> FATHER: Where are you going?
> SON: Out.
> FATHER: What are you going to do?
> SON: Nothing.
> FATHER: When will you be back?
> SON: Later.

The real meaning of this conversation, as implicitly understood by both participants, might run something like this:

> FATHER: You're not going out again tonight, are you? Where to this time?
> SON: Yes I am going out, I don't want to tell you where, and please don't bug me about it.
> FATHER: I'm worried you might get into trouble. Who are you going out with, and what do you plan to do?
> SON: I'm old enough to take care of myself, and I shouldn't have to tell you about every move I make.
> FATHER: Well, don't come home too late.
> SON: I'll probably be quite late, and I don't want to be tied down to a specific time.

In another of his experiments, Garfinkel asked

his students to engage in ordinary conversation with a friend or acquaintance, but to insist that the other person clarify the meaning of commonplace remarks and phrases. These are three of the student experimenters' reports on what happened:

> SUBJECT: I had a flat tire.
> EXPERIMENTER: What do you mean, you had a flat tire?
> SUBJECT: What do you mean, "What do you mean?" A flat tire is a flat tire. That is what I meant. Nothing special. What a crazy question!

> SUBJECT: All these old movies have the same kind of old iron bedstead in them.
> EXPERIMENTER: What do you mean? Do you mean all old movies, or some of them, or just the ones you have seen?
> SUBJECT: What's the matter with you? You know what I mean.
> EXPERIMENTER: I wish you would be more specific.
> SUBJECT: You know what I mean! Drop dead!

> SUBJECT: How are you?
> EXPERIMENTER: How am I in regard to what? My health, my finances, my school work, my peace of mind, my . . .
> SUBJECT: Look! I was just trying to be polite. Frankly, I don't give a damn how you are. [Adapted from Garfinkel, 1967]

As these examples show, breaking the rules always produces anger, anxiety, or confusion—thus exposing the shared understandings that we scarcely realize we live our lives by. The experiments are extremely simple, too. You could easily perform one the next time you are in an elevator, for example, by staring directly into the face of someone you don't know. If you are brazen enough to keep up the performance—and you probably won't be—the subject's reaction will soon show that you have violated an apparently trivial but very important social understanding about close-range eye contact between strangers.

Social Psychology

A well-developed academic discipline in its own right, *social psychology* is the study of how personality and behavior are influenced by the social context. The discipline is a true hybrid. From sociology, it draws upon the symbolic interactionist focus on meaning and interpretation in social life; from psychology, it derives a strong emphasis on experiments as a method of research. Social psychology covers a huge field, but we can give some idea here of its flavor and interests.

Helping Others

In 1964 a woman named Kitty Genovese was murdered outside her home in New York in the early morning. Her assailant took half an hour to kill her, and her screams were heard by at least thirty-eight of her neighbors. These people watched the entire scene from their windows, but not one of them came to her aid or even bothered to call the police. Their behavior was an extreme example of a fairly common phenomenon, **bystander apathy**—the reluctance of people to "get involved" in an apparent emergency affecting a stranger in public. Even people who will readily help friends or acquaintances in private often become mere onlookers in a public crisis. Why? The case of Kitty Genovese stimulated hundreds of research studies on bystander apathy, and this apparently callous behavior is now well understood.

Two factors appear to be operating. The first is that many emergencies are somewhat ambiguous. A person lying in a city street might be ill or dying, or might merely be asleep or drunk. What appears to be smoke pouring from a window might actually be steam from a radiator. People will not act in these situations until they have interpreted them, and this is where the second factor comes into play. In order to interpret the situation, people look for cues from other bystanders. If other people appear unconcerned, the individual is unlikely to define the situation as an emergency. Each person is hesitant about "overreacting," because he or she

will "lose face" and appear foolish if the wrong interpretation is made. In many situations, of course, the bystanders collectively mislead one another. Just as an entire crowd can panic when some of its members define a situation as dangerous, so it can maintain a collective unconcern when none of its members makes such a definition. Only when someone takes the responsibility to act do others tend to follow suit. But the larger the crowd, the less likely it is that anyone will assume this responsibility. If you encounter an emergency on your own, there is no way of escaping the moral responsibility to do something about it. But if a number of people are present, the moral responsibility to act is much more diffused; everyone tends to wait for "someone else" to take the initiative (Darley and Latané, 1968).

A number of studies have demonstrated this process quite clearly. In one experiment, Bibb Latané and Jean Rodin (1969) had subjects enter a room, one at a time, and fill out a form on the instructions of a female receptionist. The receptionist then left the room. A few moments later the subjects clearly heard an apparent emergency in the next room. A loud crashing noise was followed by cries of "Oh my God, my foot . . . I . . . I . . . can't move . . . it. Oh . . . my ankle . . . I can't get this thing . . . off me." The cries continued for about a minute longer and finally grew more subdued. Some 70 percent of the subjects intervened and came to the receptionist's assistance. Latané and Rodin then varied the experiment by having two

Figure 6.7 *Bystander apathy, or the unwillingness of bystanders to "get involved" in the problems of others, is especially common in cities and other crowded environments. People are reluctant to interpret a situation as an emergency unless "someone else" does so first, with the result that they all tend to ignore the problem.*

people present. In this case, only 40 percent came to the aid of the lady in distress. They then varied the experiment further by pairing individual subjects with another who, unknown to the subject, was actually an accomplice of the experimenters. The accomplice was instructed to ignore the screams. Under these conditions, only 7 percent of the subjects went to the receptionist's aid—a mere tenth of those who did so when there was nobody else in the room. Interpretations of the situation, derived from cues transmitted by other participants, were the decisive factors in determining whether one person would help another who was in apparent distress.

If bystanders are reluctant to come to the aid of people, they are even more apathetic about property. Harold Takooshian and Herzel Bodinger (1979) arranged for volunteers disguised as derelicts and street toughs to stage mock break-ins of automobiles in several busy New York streets. In each case, the "suspect" used a wire coat hanger to pry open a car door, and then removed a valuable object such as a TV set, camera, or fur coat. The experimenters watched from a hidden location and noted what happened.

The results showed a remarkably low rate of bystander intervention. In only 6 out of a total of 214 separate "break-ins" did passers-by challenge the "suspects," usually with such mild questions as "Does this car belong to you?" More than 3,000 people walked past the cars during the incidents, but most of them completely ignored the apparent crime. About a third would stop, stare, appear to deliberate for a moment, and then casually walk away. Not one person reported the incidents to the police. As one of the "suspects" later commented, "It was getting boring. Nothing was happening, and I felt I was wasting time. Nobody was reacting, no matter how furtive or outrageous I acted." In fact, a few of the passers-by actually assisted the "suspects." One of them, for example, warned that a police officer was approaching. Another declared, "Hey, baby, this is my schtick," took the hanger, forced open the door, watched while a TV set was removed, and then demanded a tip.

Takooshian and Bodinger repeated the experiments in fourteen North American cities. They found that the intervention rate varied greatly—from zero in Baltimore, Buffalo, Toledo, Miami, and Ottawa to 20 percent in Chicago, Los Angeles, San Francisco, and Fort Lauderdale to 25 percent in Phoenix. Overall, however, the intervention rate

Figure 6.8 *In these consecutive photographs from one of Takooshian and Bodinger's experiments, a "suspect" breaks into a car and walks away with a fur coat, while bystanders either ignore or merely watch the event. This was the typical reaction in several cities.*

was 10.8 percent, meaning that passers-by did nothing about nearly nine out of ten apparent property crimes.

Hurting Others

Would you deliberately apply severe electric shocks to an inoffensive stranger, even if that person were screaming in agony, begging you to stop, and had a heart condition? Under the appropriate circumstances, you probably would. That is the disturbing conclusion to be drawn from research by Stanley Milgram (1973), who conducted a series of studies of people's willingness to obey authority. Milgram showed that a substantial majority of subjects in his experiments were quite willing to hurt others, provided they defined their behavior as an appropriate response to an order by a legitimate authority.

Milgram secured volunteers by advertising in a newspaper for subjects to take part in a psychological experiment. The experiment took place in a Yale University laboratory, where each subject was introduced to the experimenter and to another volunteer. The experimenter explained that the research was to test the effects of punishment—in this case, electric shock—on learning. By drawing pieces of paper from a hat, the experimenter assigned one volunteer to the role of "teacher" and the other to the role of "learner." In fact, however, the draw, and the experiment, were rigged: the "learner," unknown to the subject, was an accomplice of the experimenter; and the "shock" was fake.

The experimenter then explained that the teacher was to read word pairs to the learner, and to give him an electric shock of increasing voltage every time he failed to recall a word pair correctly. The learner protested at this point that he had a heart condition, but the experimenter replied that the test would be painful but not dangerous. The learner was then strapped into a chair in an adjoining room, and the teacher was given an "electric shock generator." The control board of the generator was scaled from 15 volts at one end to 450 volts at the other, and there were verbal descriptions above the shock levels, ranging from "slight shock" at one end to "intense shock" in the middle and "danger—severe shock" at the other end. Milgram wanted to find the shock level at which volunteer teachers would refuse to cooperate further in the experiment.

First, Milgram did a preliminary test of the experiment on Yale University students. To his complete astonishment, they all applied "shocks" right up to the maximum level. It seemed that a more daunting situation was required. Milgram therefore varied the experiment for his nonstudent volunteers by introducing tape-recorded protests from the learner. At 125 volts, the learner shouted, "I can't stand the pain." At 195 volts, he complained of heart trouble. At 270 volts, he gave an agonized scream. Thereafter he did not respond at all, and further shocks were greeted by an ominous silence. Under these conditions, 65 percent of the subjects obediently pulled the levers all the way to 450 volts. Milgram, who was incredulous at this point, varied the experiment again. He put the learner in the same room as the teacher and required the teacher to physically force the learner's hand down onto a "shock plate" in order to receive the punishment. Under these rather gruesome conditions—with the learner struggling violently and hollering about his heart—30 percent of the subjects still applied shocks all the way to 450 volts.

How can this apparent cruelty in ordinary American citizens be explained? Milgram rejects any suggestion that his subjects were brutal or sadistic. They did not enjoy what they were doing. They often sweated, trembled, and protested to the experimenter, who met their complaints with a firm "The experiment requires that you continue." The behavior can be explained, Milgram contends, only in terms of the meaning that subjects placed on the situation. A substantial part of the population will simply do what they are told to do, irrespective of the content of the act and without any limitations of conscience, as long as they believe that the commands come from a legitimate authority. In this case, they regarded the experimenter as such an authority and accepted his interpretation of the situation—that the shocks were not dangerous, despite their painfulness, and that the research was justified in the interest of science.

These findings may have implications far beyond the laboratory—including helping us understand the atrocities that ordinary people sometimes commit during warfare. In 1968, for example, the public was shocked to learn that a platoon of American soldiers had entered the Vietnamese hamlet of My Lai and systematically murdered several hundred of its inhabitants—almost all of them infants, children, women, and old men. At the subsequent inquiry, the soldiers seemed as bewildered as anyone else by what had happened. They repeatedly offered two explanations for their behavior: that they were just doing what those around them were doing, and that they thought they were "following orders" (Hirsch, 1970).

Complying with Authority

This is a partial transcript from one of Stanley Milgram's experiments, in which the subject (the "teacher") is told by a person of authority to give electric shocks to a "learner" whom the subject believes is in great pain and is suffering from a heart condition.

LEARNER *(who, from the teacher's point of view, is heard but not seen, an offstage voice):* Ow, I can't stand the pain. Don't do that. . . .

TEACHER *(pivoting around in his chair and shaking his head):* I can't stand it. I'm not going to kill the man in there. You hear him hollering?

EXPERIMENTER: As I told you before, the shocks may be painful, but—

TEACHER: But he's hollering. He can't stand it. What's going to happen to him?

EXPERIMENTER *(his voice is patient, matter-of-fact):* The experiment requires that you continue, Teacher.

TEACHER: Aaah, but, unh, I'm not going to get that man sick in there . . . know what I mean?

EXPERIMENTER: Whether the learner likes it or not, we must go on, through all the word pairs.

TEACHER: I refuse to take the responsibility. He's in there hollering!

EXPERIMENTER: It's absolutely essential that you continue, Teacher.

TEACHER *(indicating the unused questions):* There's too many left here, I mean, Geez, if he gets them wrong, there's too many of them left. I mean who's going to take the responsibility if anything happens to that gentleman?

EXPERIMENTER: I'm responsible for anything that happens to him. Continue please.

TEACHER: All right. *(Consults list of words.)* The next one's "Slow—walk, truck, dance, music." Answer, please. *(A buzzing sound indicates the learner has signaled his answer.)* Wrong. A hundred and ninety-five volts. "Dance." *(Zzumph!)*

LEARNER: Let me out of here. My heart's bothering me! *(Teacher looks at experimenter.)*

EXPERIMENTER: Continue, please.

LEARNER *(screaming):* Let me out of here, you have no right to keep me here. Let me out of here, let me out, my heart's bothering me, let me out! *(Teacher shakes head, pats the table nervously.)*

TEACHER: You see, he's hollering. Hear that? Gee, I don't know.

EXPERIMENTER: The experiment requires . . .

TEACHER *(interrupting):* I know it does, sir, but I mean—hunh! He don't know what he's getting in for. He's up to 195 volts! *(Experiment continues, through 210 volts, 225 volts, 240 volts, 255 volts, 270 volts, delivered to the man in the electric chair, at which point the teacher, with evident relief, runs out of word-pair questions.)*

EXPERIMENTER: You'll have to go back to the beginning of that page and go through them again until he's learned them all correctly.

TEACHER: Aw, no. I'm not going to kill that man. You mean I've got to keep going up with the scale? No sir. He's hollering in there. I'm not going to give him 450 volts.

EXPERIMENTER: The experiment requires that you go on.

TEACHER: I know it does, but that man is hollering in there, sir.

LEARNER: Ohhh. I absolutely refuse to answer any more. *(Shouting urgently, now.)* Let me out of here. You can't hold me here. Get—me—out—of—here.

EXPERIMENTER: Continue. The next word is "Green," please.

TEACHER: "Green—grass, hat, ink, apple." *(Nothing happens. No answering buzz. Just gloomy silence.)*

TEACHER: I don't think he is going to answer.

EXPERIMENTER: If the learner doesn't answer in a reasonable time, about four or five seconds, consider the answer wrong. And follow the same procedures you have for wrong answers. Say "Wrong," tell him the number of volts, give him the punishment, read him the correct answer. Continue, please.

TEACHER: "Green—grass, hat, ink, apple." Answer, please. *(More silence. Teacher just sits there.)*

EXPERIMENTER: Go on with the procedure, please . . .

TEACHER: Three hundred and fifteen volts. The answer is "ink." *(Zzumph!)*

LEARNER: Ohh. Ooohh.

TEACHER *(relieved to hear response):* Next one. . . .

LEARNER: I absolutely refuse to answer.

TEACHER: You got to. You get a shock if you don't answer. *(Experiment continues with learner refusing to answer, and, finally, failing even to grunt or groan. . . .*

EXPERIMENTER: Please continue, Teacher. Continue, please. *(Teacher pushes lever. Zzumph!)*

TEACHER *(swiveling around in his chair):* Something's happened to that man in there. *(Swiveling back.)* Next one. "Low—dollar, necklace, moon, paint." *(Turning around again.)* Something's happened to that man in there. You better check in on him, sir. He won't answer or nothing.

EXPERIMENTER: Continue. Go on, please.

TEACHER: You accept all responsibility.

EXPERIMENTER: The responsibility is mine. Correct. Please go on. *(Teacher returns to his list, starts running through words as rapidly as he can read them, works through to 450 volts.)*

SOURCE: From the film *Obedience*, distributed by the New York University Film Library. Copyright 1965 by Stanley Milgram.

Nonverbal Communication

Despite the importance of language in human relationships, a great deal of social interaction involves **nonverbal communication**—the exchange of information through nonlinguistic symbols such as signs, gestures, and facial expressions. Nonverbal communication has attracted the attention of sociologists, psychologists, and anthropologists, and there is now a considerable body of research on the subject. Most of this research relies on nonparticipant observation: typically, social interaction is filmed and then minutely analyzed in slow motion to detect nonverbal cues that normally escape conscious attention. Two important forms of nonverbal communication are "body language" and the manipulation of the physical space between people (Argyle, 1975; Morris, 1977, 1979).

Body Language

It is estimated that the human face is capable of about 250,000 different expressions, many of them extremely subtle. Additionally, the head, fingers, hands, arms, shoulders, trunk, hips, and legs can also be used to signify meaning. Taken together, these potential sources of communication make possible the transmission of literally millions of messages through the "language" of body movement. If two people were enclosed in a box and every aspect of their behavior recorded down to microscopic levels, it would be possible to isolate as many as 5,000 separate bits of information every second (Birdwhistell, 1970). Although nearly all this behavior passes unnoticed in ordinary social interaction, some of it "gives off" information that others are consciously or unconsciously aware of.

Incidentally, the polygraph, or "lie detector," records some of this information. The assumption is that the stress of lying will cause heightened physical reactions in the liar, who is usually unaware of, or unable to control, such signals. The polygraph's sensors therefore measure such responses as pulse rate, blood pressure, breathing, and perspiration as the subject answers a series of yes-or-no questions. However, the machines are not always reliable. Pathological liars are not disturbed by lying and show little physiological response; and some people become so nervous when attached to the polygraph that they show signs of stress even when telling the truth. Actually, there are some simple guidelines for spotting liars, although these, too, are not always reliable. A smile or look of amazement that lingers too long is probably false; authentic facial expressions fade after four or five seconds. Asymmetrical facial expressions, such as a crooked smile, are usually deceitful unless they are normal for that person. And poor synchronization between facial expressions and body gestures (such as banging on a table a split second before looking angry) are signs of faking (Ekman, 1985).

Indeed, facial expressions and hand gestures are the most obvious forms of body language. The facial expressions that convey such basic emotions as anger, fear, sadness, amusement, puzzlement, and disgust are culturally universal; they appear to

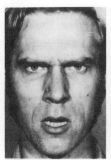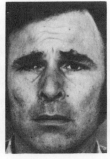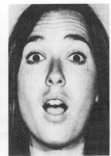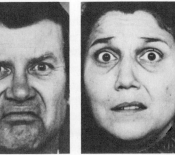

Figure 6.9 *Although the meaning of gestures varies greatly from one culture to another, the facial expressions that convey basic emotions of happiness, anger, sadness, surprise, disgust, and fear are innate in our species, and can be understood by people in any culture. (Another universal facial expression is a slight raising of the eyebrows whenever one person recognizes or meets another. You have probably never noticed this particular form of body language before—but watch for it when next you meet someone, in both that person and yourself.)*

be reflexes in our species and can be understood by people socialized in any culture (Ekman et al., 1972). Gestures, however, are culturally relative, and there does not seem to be any gesture that has the same meaning in all societies. Not all peoples point with the hand the way we do; some use the eyes, the chin, or the angle of the head for that purpose. Nor are "yes" or "no" universally indicated by nodding or shaking the head. In the Admiralty Islands, for example, a decisive "no" is indicated by a quick stroke of the nose with a finger of the right hand, and a less decisive "no" by a slower stroking. We beckon someone by moving our hands toward our own bodies, but the Islanders beckon by moving the hand in the direction of the person being beckoned (Hillier, 1933). In North America, tugging the ear usually means nothing more than that it itches. But in Yugoslavia the gesture signifies disdain for effeminacy; in Turkey, it provides protection against the evil eye; in Greece, it warns children that they are about to be punished; in Scotland, it is a sign of skepticism; in Malta, it refers to an informer (Morris et al., 1979).

Gestures, then, can be understood only by people of similar cultural background who attribute the same symbolic meaning to them. As Birdwhistell (1970) points out, a gesture cannot stand alone; it has meaning only in a particular context. The American gesture of "giving the finger" is meaningless in Britain, where the same message is conveyed by holding up the middle finger and forefinger with the palm facing inward. An American who was urinated upon by another person would not take the gesture kindly, but in parts of Africa the act symbolizes a welcome transfer of healing powers. Staring at a stranger does not have the same meaning in many other parts of the world that it does for Americans. American travelers to Latin America, for example, often have great difficulty in adapting to the experience of being openly scrutinized at close quarters by complete strangers.

Other forms of body language, such as posture, positioning of legs, or inclination of the body toward or away from another person, are not as readily noticed as facial expressions and overt gestures, nor do we have the same degree of control over them. Yet these signals can convey powerful messages even when neither participant in an encounter is consciously aware of them. Sexual interest on the part of one person, for example, causes the pupils of his or her eyes to dilate. The other person may well sense the nature of the message without being able to pinpoint its source. You will find it revealing to focus on the subtle messages that people "give off" by the way they move their

Figure 6.10 *The proximity of these girls, their facial expressions, and the inclination of their bodies all convey a definite impression: they are sharing some secret or gossip.*

bodies. You might try observing the different ways of walking that are apparent on any street, or you can look around your lecture hall and notice how students communicate their degree of interest in what the professor is saying by the inclination of their heads, the positioning of their limbs, the focus of their gaze, and how much they fidget.

Physical Proximity

Another way that people can communicate with one another is by manipulating the space between them. People have a very strong sense of some personal space that surrounds them and are greatly discomforted when it is invaded. Crowded subway cars, for example, are experienced as psychologically stressful even if they are not actually physically uncomfortable, and outbreaks of aggression are more likely in crowded situations than in less crowded situations that are otherwise similar. Edward T. Hall (1959, 1966) studied attitudes toward physical proximity in several cultures. He found that different peoples vary in the degree of closeness they will tolerate from strangers or acquaintances, with Americans seeming to require more personal space than any other people—a distance of at least 30 to 36 inches, unless the relationship is a very intimate one. American travelers to other countries, particularly in the Middle East, find that the inhabitants stand almost offensively close. But people in these cultures are apt to consider Americans—who are always backing away when one tries to talk to them—disdainful and rude.

Hall suggests that there are four distinct zones of private space:

1. *Intimate distance.* This zone extends up to 18 inches from the body. It is reserved for people with whom one may have such intimate physical contact as lying together with bodies touching.

2. *Personal distance.* This zone extends from 18 inches to 4 feet. It is reserved for friends and acquaintances. Some physical intimacy is permitted within this zone, such as putting one's arm around another's shoulder or greeting someone with a hug, but there are limits.

3. *Social distance.* This zone extends from 4 to 12 feet. It is maintained in relatively formal situations, such as job interviews. There is no actual physical contact within this zone.

4. *Public distance.* This zone extends for 12 feet and beyond, and is maintained by people wishing to distinguish themselves from the general public. Speakers addressing an audience, for example, maintain this distance.

Invasion of intimate or personal space always excites some reaction on the part of the person whose space is being invaded. People in this situation will, for example, pull their elbows in, lean away from the invader, construct physical barricades (of library books or other convenient objects), avoid eye contact with, or else glare at, the invader, make "distress" gestures such as scratching the head or fidgeting, or, if all else fails, actively increase the distance by outright retreat (Garfinkel, 1964; Felipe and Sommer, 1966; Patterson et al., 1971; Argyle, 1975).

Research has shown that the physical environment has some influence over standing and seating arrangements. The larger the area in which an interaction takes place, the closer the participants will approach one another. Living-room seating is generally arranged within an arc of 8 feet, since this is the maximum distance for comfortable conversation. Within such physical constraints, people's proximity is influenced by their precise relationship to one another. People generally approach closer to a friend than to an acquaintance or stranger, and maintain greater distance between themselves and others who are of a different age, race,

Figure 6.11 *People have a strong sense of personal space, and in the absence of other constraints will tend to arrange themselves more or less evenly over the available territory.*

or other social status (Burgoon and Jones, 1976). Pairs of females sit closer than pairs of males: the average distance between male pairs is as much as a foot greater than between female pairs (Pederson, 1973; Rosengrant, 1973). The distance between opposite-sexed pairs is more variable, for it depends on how intimate the partners are. Seating arrangements are affected by the kind of interaction that is taking place. When the relationship is a friendly or cooperative one, the partners usually choose adjacent or corner seating; when it is competitive or formal, they tend to sit opposite one

Figure 6.12

"Are Mommy and Patty and Kenny mad at Daddy?"

Drawing by Ziegler; © 1986
The New Yorker Magazine, Inc.

another (Cook, 1970; Norum et al., 1967; Sommer, 1979). All these manipulations of physical space convey subtle symbolic messages, for they reflect and maintain the social intimacy or distance that exists among people.

The Social Construction of Reality

Up to this point, we have focused on how people interpret the immediate situation in which they find themselves. But the interactionist perspective on society has far wider implications, extending to our interpretation of reality itself.

People generally take the world "out there" for granted. Its components appear to be prearranged long before we arrive on the scene, merely awaiting our discovery. "Reality" just seems to be there, presenting the same face to everyone: in short, it seems self-evident. Yet this is not the case. The "reality" that we encounter is merely the interpretation we place on the evidence of our senses, and people in different cultures may interpret that reality very differently (Schutz, 1962).

All knowledge and belief, including our own, is influenced by the historical and social location of those who produce it. Each society constructs its own understandings of reality according to the conceptual frameworks available to its members. Depending on the circumstances, therefore, reality may include witches, x-rays, ancestral spirits, viruses, demons, the will of Allah, or gravity. As these items suggest, what is real in one society is not

necessarily real in another. Much of the reality of medieval Europe, for example, seems naive and ignorant to us, and no doubt much of our reality will look rather quaint (to put it mildly) to people hundreds or thousands of years from now. But whether a society's understanding of reality is accurate has little consequence for social behavior. Half a century ago, the American sociologist W. I. Thomas made a simple but profound observation that has come to be known as the **Thomas theorem:** "If people define situations as real, they are real in their consequences." If members of a society believe that the earth is flat, that Jupiter rules the heavens, that illness is caused by witches, or that there are such things as x-rays, then the supposed flatness of the earth, the rule of Jupiter, the presence of witches, or the existence of x-rays will become as much a part of reality to people in that society as any other feature of their social or physical world. They will act in terms of that reality—by not sailing toward the edge of the earth, by making sacrifices to Jupiter, by burning witches at the stake, by avoiding or making use of radiation.

In an influential analysis, Peter Berger and Thomas Luckmann (1963) have described the **social construction of reality**—the process by which people create their understanding of the nature of their environment. According to Berger and Luckmann, the process involves three stages:

1. *People create material and nonmaterial products.* In the course of their social interaction, people create cultural products. Some are material products, such as cities, computers, baseballs, and arrows; some are nonmaterial, such as gods, Saturdays, democracy, and theories of physics.

2. *Cultural creations become part of overall reality.* In time, cultural products seem to take on a reality of their own. Cities and computers, gods and Saturdays, become just another part of the real world, like the wind and the moon. Often, in fact, people forget that these things are cultural creations and take them for granted as part of the overall reality that surrounds them.

3. *People learn about, and accept, their culture's reality.* Through the socialization process, people learn their society's explicit and implicit assumptions about what reality is. As a result, people socialized in a particular culture share the same perceptions of reality, rarely questioning the origins or validity of these understandings. It just seems to them that "that's the way it is."

We can illustrate this social process by examining what we consider the most basic aspects of reality, space and time.

Figure 6.13 *Throughout history, various cultures have created different understandings of reality. This picture, from the early sixteenth century, offers one speculation about the universe. The image seems quaint to us today—but how might our own understandings appear to our descendants a few hundred years from now?*

Space

Perhaps no part of reality seems more fundamental than space and the matter it contains, from the vastness of the universe to the tiniest particle within it. Yet the nature of the space that surrounds us has always been highly problematic, and different societies have understood it quite differently according to their own cultural assumptions. The ancient Egyptians, for example, saw the universe as a box, with the earth as its floor and the sky as a cow whose feet rested on the four corners of the earth. The ancient Greeks assumed that the earth is the center of the universe (what could be more obvious?) with the sun, moon, and planets revolving around it. The Greeks were much intrigued with musical and mathematical relationships, and concluded that the heavenly bodies must make a slight hum as they moved in perfect circles around the earth—"the music of the spheres."

The effort to maintain the earth in the center of the universe kept Western mathematicians and astronomers busy for the next fifteen hundred years, primarily because the Church insisted that reality had to be that way. A literal reading of the Bible seemed to indicate that the earth should be rectangular (like the holy tabernacle), that it should be surrounded by water, that Jerusalem should be at its center, and that the stars should be carried across the roof of the universe by angels—and that is the reality millions of people over the centuries learned and presumably accepted. By the seventeenth century, however, this view of reality was beginning to collapse—partly because no amount of tortuous mathematics could make it work, and partly because the invention of the telescope in 1608 revolutionized understandings of the universe. Galileo showed that space is not a cozy little system surrounding the earth, and that it might even be infinite—a concept his contemporaries found deeply shocking. The new reality was consequently constructed only as rapidly as social conditions would allow. The Church forced Galileo to recant his opinions, and it took decades of controversy before his modern view became accepted (Koestler, 1959).

From Galileo's time until the middle of this century, any intelligent, educated person "knew" that the universe consisted of what optical telescopes revealed: galaxies, stars, planets, asteroids, moons, comets, meteors. Recently, advances in theoretical physics and in means of detecting invisible radiation have again changed our understanding of the universe. Space is littered, it now seems, with exotic objects such as quasars, pulsars, black holes, and dense bodies spewing matter at speeds approaching that of light—and new discoveries are constantly forthcoming. Simultaneously, our understanding of the reality of the minutest objects is changing. To you, the reality of this book is that it is a solid object; to an atomic physicist, the reality is that it is mostly empty, electrically charged space. Only a generation ago, physics would have told us that the basic particles

of the book are atoms containing electrons, pro-
tons, and neutrons. But today we "know" better:
the fundamental particles that now constitute reality are leptons (electrons, neutrinos, muons, and
tauons) and quarks (known whimsically by what
physicists, at a loss for words, call their "flavors"—
up, down, top, bottom, strange, charm, truth, and
beauty). We also know that most of the matter that
should be in the universe, mathematically speaking, is actually missing. Physicists have therefore
constructed a theory of antimatter, which contains
such candidates for reality as a series of sleptons
and squarks. Although they are as "real" as anything can get, the particles in subatomic physics
have behavior and qualities that defy everyday
comprehension. For example, they have no size,
but have such qualities as mass, spin, and electric
charge, and may exist in ten or so dimensions.
Some physicists, in fact, suspect that we will never
achieve a "true" understanding of reality, because
there may be as many realities as there are possibilities. This brings us a long way from the ancient
Egyptians and their cow astride a box; but in all
this time the nature of space and matter has presumably remained constant. It is human understanding of the reality, constructed through social
interaction under changing cultural conditions,
that has altered, and will doubtless alter again
(Davies, 1984; Pickering, 1984).

Figure 6.14 *Like all past understandings of reality,
our contemporary views are shaped by the particular theories and methods that our society makes
available to us—in this case, a theory of electromagnetic radiation and a laser technology.*

Time

Like space, time is part of everyone's experience,
and understanding it is just as problematic. We in
the modern world know from Einstein's theory of
relativity that time is not constant. The faster you
travel, the slower time passes, so that astronauts
who traveled near the speed of light for a few
months by spaceship time might return to earth to
find their contemporaries decades older. Indeed,
some modern physicists suspect that time is
merely an illusion. If time is just another dimension, they claim, then the entire history of the universe is spread along this timeline, so that past,
present, and future all exist; we happen to be able
to experience only that part of the line on which we
are located. Illusion or not, the nature of time is
clearly not self-evident. We have to construct a social understanding of it (Zerubavel, 1981; E. Hall,
1983; Herbert, 1985).

As individuals, we experience time differently.
On some occasions, time may drag; on others, it
seems to fly. Collectively, however, we have to
create some agreed-upon sense of what time is. In
simple, preindustrial societies, time was often conceived as a cycle that repeats endlessly in much
the same way as natural rhythms—the rising and
setting of the sun, the repetition of the seasons, the
growth and decay of living organisms. Peasants
who spent their lives working the land had little
need to "know the time," and so agricultural societies attempted to track time only, perhaps, for astronomical and religious purposes. They measured
time largely in the terms that are still familiar to
us: the year (the time needed for the cycle of the
seasons), the month (the time for the cycle of the
phases of the moon), and the day (the time from
one dawn to the next). (An incident from sixteenth-
century Europe shows how people can lose the
awareness that their measures of time are social
constructs, and mistake them for immutable reality. Because the concept of the leap year had not
been invented, the solar and calendar years had
been slipping out of phase for several centuries. In
1582, Pope Gregory XIII decided to readjust them
by cutting ten days from the calendar. The public
response was furious rioting. Convinced that they
were losing ten days of income, and, indeed, ten
days of life itself, outraged mobs demanded their
time back!)

The mechanical clock was invented in Europe
around the fourteenth century and was in wide use
by the eighteenth century. This cultural innovation
changed conceptions of time, which could now be
measured off in brief, regular intervals (Landes,

Figure 6.15 *As this fifteenth-century European calendar suggests, precise measures of time were not important to the average person in traditional societies. The calendar merely serves as a rough, twelve-month reminder of how duties and possibilities change with the seasons.*

1983). Societies in which the clock is common-place tend to think of time not in a cyclical but in a linear way—as a straight line from the past to the future on which we travel, at a constant speed, in the present. It is impossible to imagine modern industrialized society without the clock and the socially constructed time that it implies. When people are working from 9 to 5 or are being paid by the hour, it becomes vital to know the time with precision. In our society, "time is money," and we often speak of time and money in the same terms; you can spend time, save time, waste time, use time, invest time, borrow time. Correspondingly, punctuality is regarded as a civic virtue, to be taught in the schools and practiced throughout life. Whereas people in less industrialized societies might agree to meet "in the afternoon," Americans would want to meet "at 2:15, sharp." This difference in attitude is, incidentally, a source of misunderstanding when Americans travel abroad. Anxious not to waste time, Americans expect instant service in restaurants and elsewhere, and take anything less to be a sign of indifference; the locals, on the other hand, assume that people will not mind waiting and in fact may wish to while away the time.

The creation of standard time zones in the United States provides a good example of how an aspect of reality is constructed through social

Figure 6.16 *In a modern industrialized society, where "time is money," the lives of most people are regulated, in one way or another, by precise, socially constructed measures of time.*

interaction, for these zones emerged only after decades of political negotiation and debate (Zerubavel, 1982, 1985). Until early in the nineteenth century, most cities and towns across the country had their own time, figuring noon when the sun was directly overhead. Consequently, local times varied by about four minutes for every degree of longitude. But the discrepancy was not a particular problem: punctuality was not especially important, and travelers were not bothered about the gain or loss of a few odd minutes. Once railroads were in use, however, the situation became chaotic— for how could timetables be maintained when trains and locations were all on different times? Apart from the irritation of arriving on time for your connection only to find that it had already left, there was a real danger of collisions. After much confusion and local resistance, the railroads and then Congress divided the continental United States into four main time zones. (In contrast, the Soviet Union, a society with a strongly centralized government, opted for a different, but characteris-

tic, solution. Although this huge country has eleven time zones, all airports and railroads run on Moscow time.) Negotiated agreements also led to the creation of the International Date Line at the 180th meridian, which runs through an unpopulated part of the globe. If you stand over that line you can have one foot in Monday and one in Tuesday, or, if you are there on December 31 or January 1, you can walk back and forth between one year and the next—a vivid indication that time is socially constructed.

The Hopi Indian language has no tenses to express time; the ancient Chinese developed water clocks, but only for astronomical purposes; we have instruments to measure picoseconds, or trillionths of a second. Each society constructs its own reality through a complex process of social interaction, in which people collectively act on the world and are influenced in turn by the results of their own actions. Seen in this light, the routines and "realities" of everyday life take on new and enhanced significance.

Summary

1.   Social interaction is the process by which people act toward or respond to other people. Because we live in a meaningful world, we have to interpret human behavior in order to interact with others. Sociologists emphasize the interactionist perspective in their studies of the micro processes of daily life. This perspective includes several related approaches.

2.   Symbolic interaction is the interaction that takes place through symbols such as gestures and language. We interact largely through shared understandings of such symbols. Examples are the symbolic appearance of punks and nurses, and the symbolic meaning of the door ceremony.

3.   Dramaturgy is a method of analyzing social interaction as though the participants were stage actors. It emphasizes the way people manage the impressions they create, within the context of unspoken rules of social interaction. Examples are the way people present aspects of their selves to others, and more specifically, the ritualized behaviors involved in such interactions as a pelvic examination.

4.   Ethnomethodology is the study of how people construct and share their definitions of reality in their everyday interactions. People interact on the basis of shared definitions and rules concerning social reality that they are hardly aware of. Ethnomethodology exposes these background social understandings by violating the rules.

5.   Social psychology, a hybrid of sociology and psychology, studies how personality and behavior are influenced by the social context. It uses primarily experimental methods to reveal these processes, as illustrated by studies of the conditions under which people may help or hurt each other.

6. Nonverbal communication is the exchange of information through nonlinguistic symbols. Some of this communication takes the form of body language, including facial expressions and physical gestures. Some of it occurs through the manipulation of personal space, which reflects the social intimacy or distance between people.

7. The social construction of reality is the process by which people create their understanding of the nature of their environment. People create cultural products, are confronted by these products as part of "reality," and are socialized to accept the total reality their society offers. This process can be seen in changing cultural understandings of space and time.

Important Terms

social interaction (143)

symbol (144)

symbolic interaction (144)

dramaturgy (148)

ethnomethodology (151)

social psychology (152)

bystander apathy (153)

nonverbal communication (157)

Thomas theorem (160)

social construction of reality (160)

Suggested Readings

BERGER, PETER L., and THOMAS LUCKMANN. *The Social Construction of Reality.* New York: Doubleday, 1963.

An influential analysis of the way in which interpretations of reality are created and sustained through social interaction.

GOFFMAN, ERVING. *Behavior in Public Places.* New York: Free Press, 1963.

A shrewd and acute description and analysis of social behavior in public settings. Goffman illuminates many aspects of interactive behavior that we normally take for granted or do not even notice.

GOFFMAN, ERVING. *The Presentation of Self in Everyday Life.* New York: Doubleday, 1959.
The classic statement of Goffman's dramaturgical perspective.

HEWITT, JOHN P. *Self and Society: A Symbolic Interactionist Social Psychology.* 3rd ed. Boston: Allyn and Bacon, 1983.

A good introduction to social psychology for the student who wants to explore the discipline from a sociological perspective.

MORRIS, DESMOND. *Manwatching: A Field Guide to Human Behavior.* New York: Abrams, 1979.

An interesting and well-illustrated introduction to "body language," written in an entertaining style.

ROBBOY, HOWARD L., and CANDACE CLARK (eds.). *Social Interaction: Introductory Readings in Sociology.* 2nd ed. New York: St. Martin's Press, 1983.

An excellent collection of articles written from the interactionist perspective.

ZERUBAVEL, EVIATAR. *The Seven Day Circle: The History and Meaning of the Week.* New York: Free Press, 1985.

An interesting sociological study of the social creation and meanings of the week.

Social Groups

"No man is an island," wrote the poet John Donne several centuries ago. He was acknowledging one of our most distinctive characteristics: the fact that we are social animals whose behavior and personalities are shaped by the groups to which we belong. Throughout life, most of our daily activities are performed in the company of others. Whether our purpose is working, playing, raising a family, learning, worshiping, or simply relaxing, we usually pursue it in groups, even if the group is as small as two or three people. Our need for human contacts is not merely a practical one; it is a deep psychological need as well. If people are deprived of the company of others for prolonged periods, mental breakdown is the usual result. Even the Geneva Convention, an international agreement that regulates the treatment of prisoners of war, recognizes this need. It regards solitary confinement for more than thirty days as a cruel and barbarous form of torture.

In its strictest sense, a *group* is a collection of people interacting together in an orderly way on the basis of shared expectations about one another's behavior. As a result of this interaction, members feel a common sense of "belonging." They distinguish members from nonmembers and expect certain kinds of behavior from one another that they would not necessarily expect from outsiders. A group differs from an *aggregate,* a collection of people who happen to be in the same place at the same time, such as the passengers in a bus or a crowd in a street. People in an aggregate do not interact to any significant extent and do not feel any shared sense of belonging. A group also differs from a *category,* a number of people who may never have met one another but who share similar characteristics, such as age, race, or sex. Although sociologists sometimes do use the word "group" loosely to refer to aggregates and categories, in this chapter we shall use the term only in its stricter sense.

As a result of the interaction that takes place among its members, a group develops an internal structure. Every group has its own boundaries, norms, values, and interrelated statuses and roles, such as those of leader, follower, joker, or scapegoat. In some groups this structure is rigid and explicit: members may hold official positions, and values and norms may be embodied in written objectives and rules. In other groups the structure may be much more flexible: values and norms may be vague and shifting, and statuses and roles may be subject to negotiation and change.

People form groups for a purpose, generally one that the members cannot achieve satisfactorily through individual effort. The purpose of a group may be an explicit one, such as raising money for charity or waging war against an enemy, or it may be less clearly defined, such as having a good time. The fact that the members of a group share common goals means that they tend to be generally similar to one another in ways that are relevant to the group's purpose. If the goals of the group are political, the members tend to share similar political opinions. If the goals are leisure activities, the members tend to be of similar age and social class and to have common leisure interests. The more the members interact within the group, the more they are influenced by its norms and values and the more similar they are likely to become.

Primary and Secondary Groups

There are two basic types of social groups: primary and secondary.

A ***primary group*** consists of a small number of people who interact over a relatively long period on a direct, intimate basis. The relationships among the members have emotional depth, and the group tends to endure over time. Primary groups are always small because large numbers of people cannot interact in a highly personal, face-to-face manner. Large groups therefore tend to break down into smaller, more intimate cliques. Typical primary groups include the family, the gang, or a college peer group.

A ***secondary group*** consists of a number of people who interact on a relatively temporary, anonymous, and impersonal basis. The members come together for some specific, practical purpose, such as making a committee decision or attending a convention. There is limited face-to-face contact, and members relate to one another only in terms of specific roles, such as division manager, supervisor, and employee. Secondary groups can be either small or large. Any newly formed small group is a secondary group at first, although it may become a primary group if its members eventually come to know one another well and begin to inter-

Figure 7.1 *A primary group consists of a small number of people who interact in direct and intimate ways, usually over a long period of time. In traditional societies virtually all social life took place in the context of primary groups. These women, members of a small community on the edge of the Sahara desert, form a primary group. They know one another well and interact together as full persons, not in terms of specific roles. Although in modern societies we still spend a good deal of time in primary groups, much of our social life takes place in less intimate settings.*

Figure 7.2 *A secondary group contains a number of people who have few emotional ties to one another. The members usually meet together for some practical purpose, and they interact with one another in terms of specific roles rather than as full persons. Secondary groups, such as these employees of a large organization, are characteristic of modern societies.*

act on a more intimate basis. A college seminar group, for example, may start out as a secondary group, but after a while it may become a primary group, or smaller primary groups may develop within it. All large groups, however, are secondary groups. These groups, which are often called "associations," include organizations such as business corporations, large factories, government departments, political parties, and religious movements. Large secondary groups always contain smaller primary groups within them. Colleges and army camps, for example, are secondary groups, but they may contain hundreds of primary groups.

In traditional, preindustrial societies almost all social life took place in the context of primary groups, such as the kinship network or the small village. In modern industrialized societies, dense urban populations and the spread of large associations have made social life much more anonymous. Many of our daily interactions involve secondary relationships with people we encounter in limited and specific roles and may never meet again. As we saw in Chapter 4 ("Society"), the growth of secondary groups and the multiplication of secondary relationships is one of the outstanding features of modern societies.

Small Groups

A *small group* is one that contains few enough members for the participants to relate to one another as individuals. Whether a small group is primary or secondary depends on the nature of the relationships among its members. A gathering of old friends is a primary group; a number of previously unacquainted people trapped in an elevator for half an hour is a small secondary group.

Over half a century ago the German sociologist Georg Simmel suggested that the interaction within small groups would prove to be an important subject for sociological research. His suggestion was largely neglected until after World War II, when Robert Bales and his associates began an influential series of studies of small-group processes (Bales, 1950, 1970; Homans, 1950; Hare et al., 1965; Hollander, 1964; T. Mills, 1967). Most of these studies took place in a laboratory setting, in which groups of volunteers were given some task to work on while researchers observed the interaction that took place. Although there is some question whether it is valid to apply the findings of these studies to "real life" situations, this research has illuminated many aspects of small-group interaction (Hare, 1976; McGrath 1978; Shaw, 1981).

The Effects of Size

The single most important feature of small groups is probably their size, for this characteristic determines the kinds of interaction that can take place among the members. The smaller the group is, the more personal and intense the interaction can become.

The smallest possible group is a *dyad,* a group containing two people. A dyad differs from all other groups in that its members have to take account of each other. If one member ignores the conversation of the other or begins daydreaming, the interaction is disrupted, and if one member withdraws from the group, it simply ceases to exist. If another member is added, forming a *triad,* a group containing three people, the situation alters significantly. Any one member can ignore the conversation of the others without destroying the interaction in the group. Two members can form a coalition against one, so any individual can become subject to group pressure. As more members are added, the nature of the interaction continues to change. People can take sides in discussions, and more than one coalition can be formed. In a group of up to about seven people, all the members can take part in the same conversation, but beyond that point it becomes progressively more likely that smaller groups will form, with several conversations taking place at the same time.

If the group becomes larger than about ten or twelve people, it is virtually impossible for them to take part in the same conversation unless one member takes the role of leader and regulates the interaction so that everyone has a chance to contribute. In groups of this size, the style of conversation changes because people can no longer tailor their speech to meet the expectations of specific people. As a result, their language becomes more formal: members no longer "talk" to the group; they "address" it, with a grammar and vocabulary unlike that used in ordinary conversation. The interaction is now markedly different from that in our original dyad.

Sudden changes in group size tend to be disruptive, particularly if there is a rapid increase in the number of new members. This disruption is partly caused by the fact that interaction grows more difficult as the group becomes larger, but another factor is that members often resist the assimilation of newcomers. The presence of new members threatens the norms of interaction that the group has already developed, and old members are uncomfortable until new norms have evolved.

Leadership

One element is always present in groups: leadership. A *leader* is someone who, largely by virtue of certain personality characteristics, is consistently able to influence the behavior of others. Groups have leaders even if the leaders do not hold formal positions of authority (and even if the group is determined *not* to have a leader).

Research has indicated that there are two distinct types of leadership in small groups (Bales, 1953; Slater, 1955). *Instrumental leadership* is the kind necessary to organize a group in pursuit of its goals. An instrumental leader proposes courses of action and influences the members to follow them. *Expressive leadership* is the kind necessary to create harmony and solidarity among group members. An expressive leader is concerned about keeping morale high and minimizing conflicts. The expressive leader is well liked by the group. When a newly formed group is asked to choose a leader, it usually gives both roles to the same person, because individuals who are well liked also tend to dominate group activities. Leaders generally do not fill both roles for long, however, because people who direct group activities tend to lose popularity. In one experiment on small groups, Philip Slater (1955) found that most members gave top rating to the same person for both expressive and instrumental leadership at the first meeting, but by the end of the fourth meeting, only 8 percent of the members still considered the leader likable. In such cases, the original leader may retain the instrumental role, but another group member emerges to assume the expressive role.

Do leaders have distinctive characteristics that are not shared by their followers? While there are certainly no hard and fast rules, it seems that leaders are likely to be taller than the average group member, to be judged better-looking than other members, to have a higher IQ, and to be more sociable, talkative, determined, and self-confident. In addition, leaders also tend to be more liberal in outlook, even in conservative groups (Stouffer, 1955; Stogdill, 1974; Crosbie, 1975). But personality characteristics alone cannot tell us who is likely to be a good leader, because different conditions require different leadership qualities. The kind of leadership required in a military battle or the aftermath of an earthquake may call for different qualities, and different people, than the kind of leadership required at a corporation board meeting or a political convention.

Style of leadership may be one of three basic kinds: *authoritarian,* in which the leader simply gives orders; *democratic,* in which the leader attempts to win a consensus on a course of action; and *laissez-faire,* in which the leader is easygoing and makes little attempt to direct or organize the group. In the United States, at least, the leaders

Figure 7.3 *In situations where quick, life-and-death decisions may have to be made—such as in hospitals or the military—leadership is usually authoritarian. In other contexts, however, authoritarian leadership may be counterproductive because of the resentment it may cause.*

who seem to be most effective in holding small groups together and seeing that they accomplish their tasks tend to be democratic. Authoritarian leaders are much less effective, because the work of the group becomes bogged down in internal conflicts. Laissez-faire leaders are usually ineffectual, for the group lacks directives and tackles problems in a haphazard way (White and Lippitt, 1960). This does not mean, however, that democratic leadership is the most effective in all situations. An authoritarian leader, for example, is more effective in emergency situations, where speed and efficiency outweigh other considerations. For this reason, leadership in armies, police forces, and hospital emergency rooms is typically authoritarian. Democratic leaders are more effective in situations where group members are concerned about individual rights or where there is disagreement over goals. However, research on American subjects, who have been socialized to react negatively to authoritarian leaders, cannot be automatically generalized to cultures in which authoritarian leadership is expected and in which there is virtually no experience of democratic decision making.

Group Decision Making

People often assume that when it comes to making decisions, two heads, or preferably several heads, are better than one. Americans have great faith in democratic decision making, believing that group decisions are likely to be wiser than decisions made by individuals acting alone. How valid is this belief?

The answer depends to some extent on the problem that has to be solved. In "determinate tasks"—problems that have only one correct solution, such as a crossword puzzle—group effort increases the chances of finding the answer. As a matter of simple probability, a group is more likely to come up with the correct solution than a single person is. If the problem is a complex one, involving specialized knowledge, the efficiency of the group is far superior to that of the individual, because group members can contribute a broader range of expertise and skills. The situation is rather different for "indeterminate tasks"— problems that have no necessarily correct solution, such as selecting one of several applicants for a job or deciding on how to handle an aircraft hijacking. In such cases different groups may arrive at very different decisions, probably because each group is influenced by the opinions of particular dominant members. Sometimes group decisions for solving indeterminate problems seem better than those of individuals, but sometimes they seem worse.

When groups do make decisions, they usually do so through consensus and only rarely by the majority imposing its view on a reluctant minority. No matter what the views of the members are at the outset, the general tendency is for discussion to bring about greater agreement. This is typically the case, for example, in jury deliberations. Although jury members often begin their discussions in disagreement or uncertainty, they tend to move toward a common opinion and usually render a unanimous verdict. The only consistent exceptions occur in groups whose participants are representing the fixed opinions of others outside the group, and thus cannot easily budge—for example, in groups involving party politics or labor-management disputes.

It was long assumed that in arriving at a consensus, groups are likely to make less risky decisions than individuals. But when J. A. Stoner (1961) investigated the matter, he found that people often made much more risky decisions in groups than they made alone on the same issues. Stoner called this change to a more daring course of action the "risky shift." The reasons for this tendency remain unclear, but two possibilities have been suggested. One is that in group decisions, responsibility is diffused among the members: nobody need feel personally accountable if the decision turns out to be the wrong one. A second possibility is that firm and even daring decisions win cultural approval: bold is cool. Research has also shown that some groups are capable of a "tame shift" toward much safer action than the members prefer as individuals. It seems that the very process of group discussion tends not merely to produce a consensus but also to intensify opinions in one direction or another. Accordingly, groups whose members start out tentatively approving or disapproving a proposal often end up strongly favoring or rejecting it (Kogan and Wallach, 1964; Myers and Lamm, 1976; Johnson, Stemler, and Hunter, 1977).

However, unanimous but bold decisions can cause a great deal of trouble if they also happen to be wrong. Irving Janis (1972; Janis and Mann, 1977) suggests one source of such poor judgment in groups: loyalty to the group may prevent individual members from raising controversial and uncomfortable questions. The members become so concerned with maintaining group harmony and consensus, particularly when a difficult moral problem is involved, that they withhold their reservations and criticisms. This "don't rock the boat" attitude results in what Janis calls "groupthink," a decision-making process in which members ignore information and alternatives that do not fit with the group's original assumptions. As an example of groupthink Janis cites the 1961 decision of President Kennedy and his top advisers to sponsor the Bay of Pigs invasion of Cuba by Cuban exiles dedicated to overthrowing Castro. This decision, which produced a military and diplomatic fiasco, was based on strategic assumptions that were almost ludicrous. Several members of the decision-making group had strong private objections to the plan, yet the decision to launch the invasion was unanimous. Janis quotes one of the participants as commenting afterward: "Our meeting was taking place in an atmosphere of assumed consensus. Had one senior adviser opposed the venture, I believe Kennedy would have canceled it. Not one spoke up." (The ancient Persians seem to have been aware of the groupthink phenomenon. The historian Herodotus tells us that whenever their leaders made an important decision in a sober, rational frame of mind, they always reconsidered the matter later while thoroughly drunk.)

Most group decision making, however, does involve debate among the participants. The process of decision making in small groups generally proceeds through a sequence of stages. The first stage is that of collecting information; the members orient themselves to the problem by analyzing the facts. The second stage is that of evaluating the information; at this point members express opinions and react to the opinions of others. The third stage is that of reaching a decision. Emotional tensions may rise at this stage, particularly if coalitions form and disagreements persist. The fourth stage occurs once the decision is made; it involves a general effort to restore harmony in the group. The members react more positively to one another, and there may be a certain amount of joking and frivolity. In this way the continuing solidarity of the group is assured (Bales and Strodtbeck, 1951).

Group Conformity

The pressure to conform to social expectations is strong in every aspect of life, but it seems to be particularly powerful in the intense atmosphere of a small group (Festinger et al., 1956). One of the most dramatic examples of this tendency comes from some experiments by Solomon Asch (1955), who found that people seem willing to disavow the evidence of their own senses if it is contradicted by the judgment of the rest of the group.

Asch assembled groups consisting of between seven and nine college students in what was described as a test of visual discrimination. However, in each group only one of the students was actually a subject in the experiment: the others were secret accomplices of the experimenter. In a series of eighteen trials Asch displayed pairs of cards like those shown in Figure 7.4. One card contained a single line, which was to serve as a standard. The other card contained three lines, one the same length as the standard, and the other two of significantly different lengths from the standard and from each other. The members of the group were asked one by one to state aloud which of the lines matched the standard.

When the first pair of cards was presented, the group unanimously picked the correct line. The same thing happened on the second trial. In twelve of the remaining sixteen trials, however, all Asch's secret accomplices agreed on what was clearly an incorrect answer. How did the real subject of the experiment react to this uncomfortable situation?

STANDARD AND COMPARISON LINES IN THE ASCH EXPERIMENT

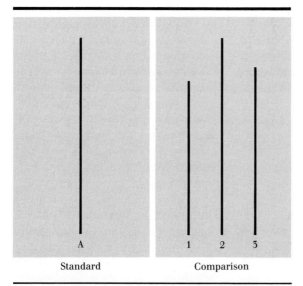

Standard   Comparison

SOURCE: Adapted from Solomon Asch, "Effects of Group Pressure upon the Modification and Distortion of Judgments," in H. Proshansky and B. Seidenberg (eds.), *Basic Studies in Social Psychology* (New York: Holt, Rinehart and Winston, 1965), pp. 393–401.

Figure 7.4 *These are the lines presented to subjects in one trial in Asch's experiments. Asch asked the subjects to state which of the comparison lines appeared to be the same length as the standard line. Control subjects (who made the judgment without any group pressure) chose the correct line over 99 percent of the time; but experimental subjects who were under group pressure to choose the wrong line did so in nearly a third of the cases.*

In about a third of the cases, the subject yielded to the majority and conformed to its decision. Subsequent interviews with these yielders revealed that only a few of them had, in fact, perceived the majority choice as correct. Although these few subjects actually disbelieved the evidence of their own senses, most of the yielders admitted that they thought they had judged the length of the lines correctly but did not want to be the "odd one out" by giving the right answer. The experiment vividly shows a group's power to induce conformity, although, like all laboratory experiments, it leaves open the question of whether people would react exactly the same way in "real life."

Ingroups and Outgroups

Every group must have some boundaries, for there would otherwise be no way of distinguishing between members and nonmembers. Sometimes these boundaries are formal and clearly defined, with access to the group available to "members only" on the basis of specific criteria. In such cases the boundary may be maintained by symbols, such as badges, membership cards, or even secret signs. A police department, a family, or a labor union has no difficulty in maintaining boundaries, because the criteria for membership are formally defined. In other cases the boundaries are not nearly as clear. A high school or college peer group, for example, has no specific criteria for membership, and the boundary between actual members and hangers-on may be very blurred.

All groups, however, tend to maintain their boundaries by developing a strong sense of the distinction between the "we" of the group and the "they" who are outside it. People tend to regard the *ingroup*—any group one belongs to and identifies with—as being somehow special. Correspondingly, they tend to regard the *outgroup*—any alternative group that one does not belong to or identify with—as less worthy, and may even view it with hostility. A common way of maintaining boundaries between groups, in fact, is through some form of conflict between them. The presence of a common enemy (real or imaginary) draws members together and increases the solidarity and cohesion of the group (Coser, 1956).

An experiment by Muzafer Sherif (1956) illustrates how ingroup loyalties can help to maintain group boundaries and solidarity. Sherif's subjects were eleven-year-old boys who did not know each other before the experiment began. Sherif took the boys for an extended stay at a summer camp, where they soon began to form friendship cliques. Once these groups had been formed, Sherif randomly divided the boys into two main groups and lodged them in separate cabins some distance apart. In doing so, he disrupted the cliques that had already formed, but the boys soon began to develop strong loyalties to their new groups. Next, Sherif pitted the two groups against each other in various competitive activities. The result was increasingly intense antagonism and hostility between the groups, including between those members on either side who had earlier been in the same friendship cliques. Finally, Sherif created some emergency situations, such as an interruption of the water supply, that required both groups to cooperate as a team. Within a short period, members of the two groups began to interact as a single group, their old hostilities forgotten. Sherif's experiment shows clearly how loyalty contributes to the maintenance of group boundaries, how conflict between groups heightens these loyalties, and how ingroup feelings lessen and disappear once the members of different groups unite in pursuit of common goals.

Networks

People and groups continually interact with other people and groups. These multiple contacts are organized into *social networks*—webs of relationships that link the individual directly to other people, and through these others, indirectly to even more people. Your own network, for example, consists of all your primary ties (like relatives and close friends) and all your secondary ties (like your classmates or your dentist); additionally, it potentially includes all the ties of the members of your own network. A person's network is not exactly a group, because its members do not all interact together, but networks do contain groups and do provide indirect access to still other groups.

In principle, your social network can be depicted diagrammatically on a piece of paper, with a point to represent each acquaintance and a line between the points to represent a relationship. In practice, such a diagram would soon blunt your pencil in an illegible chaos of dots and crossing lines. The average person in a modern society has a pool of between 500 and 2,500 acquaintances, many of whom are in turn acquainted with one another (Milgram, 1967). If we tried adding the full networks of these other individuals to our diagram, it would soon include millions of people. That is why we sometimes find, on meeting a stranger, that we share a mutual acquaintance—a "coincidence" that leaves us musing, "It's a small world."

Actually, you are only a few removes from knowing just about anybody else living in the society. You may, for example, be only a few people away from knowing the president of the United States: you may know a professor, who may know the college president, who may know a member of Congress—who knows the president. The same linkages apply throughout the society, as the social psychologist Stanley Milgram (1967) showed through a simple experiment. He gave a number of "starting persons" in the American Midwest a

booklet containing the name, address, and occupation of a "target person" on the East Coast, whom the starters did not know personally. They were to send the booklet on, by mail, toward the target person, but could actually address it only to an acquaintance they knew on a first-name basis. Each of these acquaintances was asked, in turn, to advance the booklet further toward its target in the same manner. Although some chains were never completed (perhaps because some intermediaries could not be bothered to participate), many were successful. Some took as few as two moves, most took between five and eight, and none required more than ten.

Networks form a vital part of social life. People's sense of "community," for example, depends to a great extent on the density of their local network—on the presence of many familiar faces. Similarly, people use their networks to get advice when they face unexpected problems or events: friends and acquaintances are asked to recommend a lawyer, a psychiatrist, a building contractor. Research has also shown that networks are important for getting jobs and for career advancement. In fact, some people engage in what they actually call "networking"'—going to parties, joining clubs, and attending specific functions in order

Figure 7.5

*"It's not what you know, it's who you know,
And who do I know? You!"*

Drawing by Dana Fradon; © 1974
The New Yorker Magazine, Inc.

to meet people who might prove influential or helpful later, on the general principle of "It isn't what you know, it's who you know." Part of the difficulty women have had in achieving high-status jobs is that their networks generally contain smaller, fewer, and lower-status groups than those of men, who are better able to utilize what is, literally, an "old-boy network." In general, people who join many groups, or who join large groups, greatly increase the size of their social networks—a fact that has long been appreciated by insurance agents, political candidates, and others who want ready access to many "contacts" (Granovetter, 1973; Lin, Ensler, and Vaughn, 1981; McPherson and Smith-Lovin, 1981).

Reference Groups

There is one kind of group to which people may feel they "belong" even if they are not actually members. This is the *reference group,* a group to which people refer when making evaluations of themselves and their behavior.

We constantly evaluate ourselves—our behavior, our appearance, our values, our ambitions, our lifestyles, and so on. In making these evaluations, we always refer to the standards of some group. The group may be one of which we are a member, such as the family or the peer group. But it may also be one we do not actually belong to. People may judge themselves, for example, by the standards of a community they previously lived in or of a community they hope to join in the future. A sociology student who plans eventually to take a graduate degree may evaluate his or her progress in terms of the standards of graduate students rather than those of an undergraduate peer group. A medical student may refer to the standards of physicians rather than those of fellow students.

Our evaluations of ourselves are strongly influenced by the reference groups we choose: if you get a B in an examination and compare yourself with A students, your self-evaluation will be very different than it would be if you were to compare yourself with C students. Reference groups are therefore an important element in the socialization process, for they can shape individual behavior and personality just as powerfully as any other group to which a person feels loyalty.

The concept of reference groups, incidentally, underlies a great deal of modern advertising. Advertisers commonly "pitch" certain products by implying that the products are popular among groups the target audience imagine themselves to be part of. Beer commercials, for example, typically show the advertised brew being quaffed by cheerful, hardworking, manly sports lovers. Other products, however, are "pitched" by implying that they are enjoyed among groups that the target audience would like to belong to. Because most Americans aspire to higher social status, advertisers try to give the impression that some products—like perfumes or liquors—are typically used by people whose social status appears higher than that of the actual target audience.

Formal Organizations

Until a century or so ago, nearly all social life took place within the context of small primary groups—the family, the church congregation, the school-house, the farm or shop, and the village community. Today the social landscape is dominated by large, impersonal organizations that influence our lives from the moment of birth. Some of these organizations are *voluntary,* in the sense that people may freely join them or withdraw from them. Examples include religious movements, political parties, and professional associations. Some are *coercive,* in the sense that people are forced to join them—for example, prisons or elementary schools. Other organizations are *utilitarian,* in the sense that people enter them for practical reasons: they join business enterprises, for example, in order to earn a living (Etzioni, 1975). But whichever organizations we belong to and whatever our reasons for joining them, we spend a good part of our lives within these large, impersonal groups.

Associations of this type are generally *formal organizations,* large secondary groups that are deliberately and rationally designed to achieve specific objectives. Unlike primary groups, which are informal, these organizations have a carefully designed structure that coordinates the activities of the members in the interests of the organization's goals. For example, formal organizations typically include a number of official statuses, such as those of president, secretary, and treasurer. Rights and responsibilities within the organization are attached primarily to the office a person occupies, not to the person as an individual. It is possible to draw a chart of any formal organization, showing the relationship of the various official positions to one another, without any reference to the actual individuals involved (see Figure 7.6 on the next page).

ORGANIZATIONAL CHART OF A PUBLISHING COMPANY

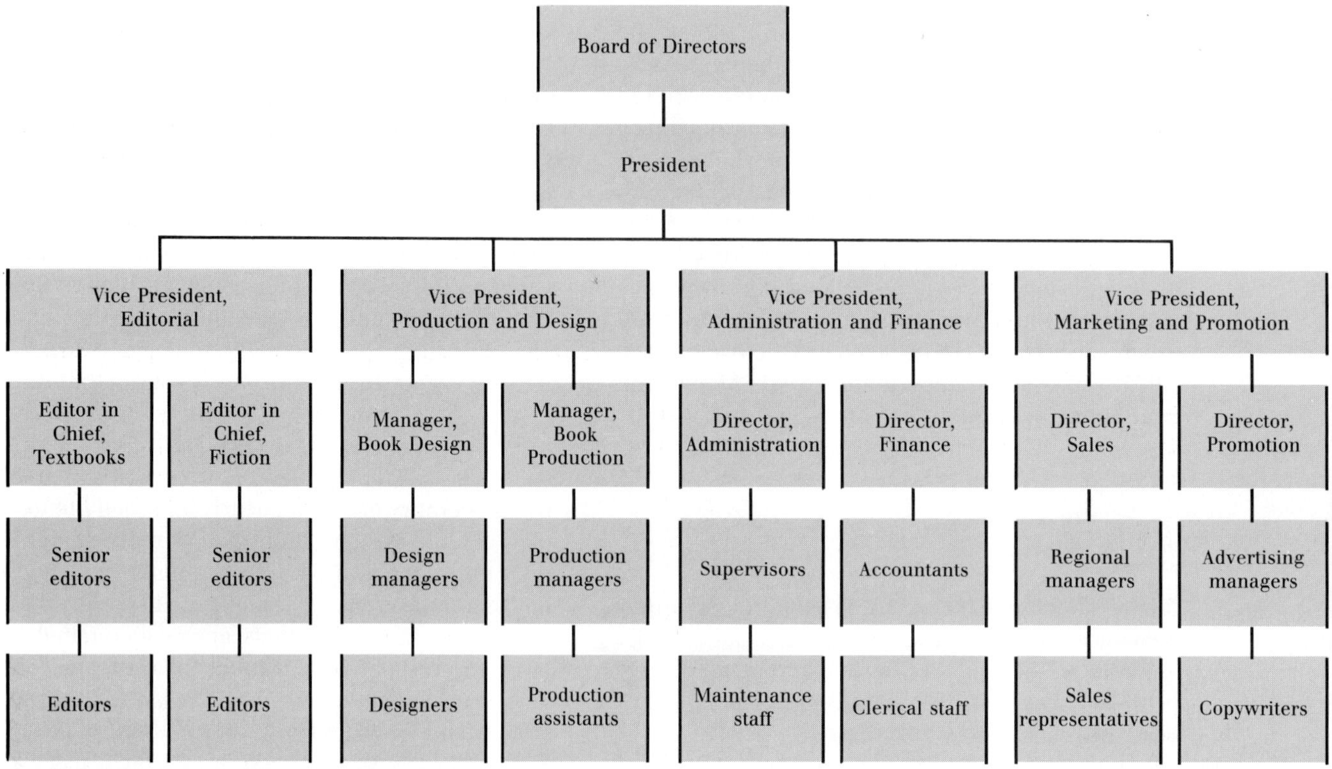

| Board of Directors |
| President |

Vice President, Editorial	Vice President, Production and Design	Vice President, Administration and Finance	Vice President, Marketing and Promotion
Editor in Chief, Textbooks	Editor in Chief, Fiction	Manager, Book Design	Manager, Book Production	Director, Administration	Director, Finance	Director, Sales	Director, Promotion
Senior editors	Senior editors	Design managers	Production managers	Supervisors	Accountants	Regional managers	Advertising managers
Editors	Editors	Designers	Production assistants	Maintenance staff	Clerical staff	Sales representatives	Copywriters

Figure 7.6 *This diagram is a typical organizational chart, setting out the formal chains of command and communication within a formal organization, a hypothetical publishing company. Similar charts, some of them extremely complex, can be drawn for any formal organization.*

Most people seem to have an ambiguous attitude toward formal organizations. On the one hand, our affluence and our very way of life are clearly dependent on the existence of organizations such as corporations, colleges, government departments, and large factories. On the other hand, the size, impersonality, and power of formal organizations are often seen as dehumanizing and threatening, and they have been held responsible for much of the feeling of alienation that is said to characterize modern industrialized societies. The significance of formal organizations in the modern world is so great, in fact, that they have become one of the most important areas of study in the discipline of sociology.

Bureaucracy

The larger and more complex a formal organization becomes, the greater is the need for a chain of command to coordinate the activities of its mem-

bers. This need is fulfilled by a **bureaucracy,** a hierarchical authority structure that operates under explicit rules and procedures. Understanding bureaucracy is the key to the analysis of formal organizations.

The word "bureaucracy" usually carries negative connotations in everyday speech. It brings to mind images of "red tape," forms in triplicate, lost files, incorrect bills, unanswered letters, counter clerks blinded by petty regulations, "runarounds," and "buck-passing." Yet although "bureaucracy" often seems synonymous with "inefficiency" from the point of view of the individual, the bureaucratic form has thrived for the simple reason that it is, for most purposes, highly efficient. It is the most effective means ever devised of making a large organization work. Sociologists therefore use the word in a neutral sense, without the overtones it generally has in ordinary usage.

This does not mean, however, that sociologists are uncritical of the bureaucratic form. In fact, there is a deep current of distaste for bureaucracy running through Western sociology, right back to such early thinkers as Karl Marx and Max Weber. Marx (1967, orig. 1843) loathed bureaucracy, which he saw as an "excrescence" on society. Weber, whose writings have provided the foundation for almost all later research on bureaucracy, declared in 1909:

> The passion for bureaucracy is enough to drive one to despair. . . . The great question is . . . not how we can promote and hasten it, but what we can oppose to this machinery in order to keep a portion of mankind free from this parcelling out of the soul, from this supreme mastery of the bureaucratic way of life.

Despite these misgivings, however, it was Weber who first systematically analyzed bureaucracy and demonstrated its efficiency.

Weber's Analysis

To Max Weber (1922), the master trend in the modern world was the process he referred to as **rationalization**—the way in which traditional, spontaneous, rule-of-thumb methods of social organization are replaced by abstract, explicit, carefully calculated rules and procedures. This gradual rationalization process can be seen in nearly every aspect of modern social life. In education, the tutor with a small circle of students is replaced by the vast modern college campus, with lectures supplied on videotape and multiple-choice examinations graded by computer. The traditional market of small stalls is succeeded by the modern supermarket. The "justice" meted out by a village headman evolves into an intricate system of laws and

Figure 7.7 *A characteristic feature of bureaucracies is the anonymous, impersonal nature of the relationships between officials and outsiders. This painting,* Government Bureau, *by the modern American artist George Tooker, captures that impersonality.*

courtroom procedures. Individual craft workers are replaced by laborers on the assembly line. Varied forms of architecture give way, in country after country, to the familiar slablike office building. In each case, the result of the rationalization process is a marked increase in efficiency, but this efficiency is achieved at a cost. The world, Weber felt, was becoming dull, drab, and "disenchanted," its mystery and beauty subverted by the new value of technical rationality. Weber believed bureaucracy is an especially threatening form of rationalization. Unlike other forms, which involve the manipulation of physical objects (such as machinery) or of procedures (such as the legal system), bureaucracy involves the calculated organization and subordination of *human beings* in the interests of impersonal, technical goals. As a result, Weber felt, people were becoming imprisoned in an "iron cage" of their own making.

Weber analyzed bureaucracy in terms of what he called an ideal type. An ***ideal type*** is an abstract description, constructed from a number of real cases in order to reveal their essential features. (For example, an ideal type of an American college might refer to such features as the roles of college administrators, professors, and students; to such activities as teaching, learning, and research; and to other characteristics such as fraternities, sororities, honor societies, and so on. The result would be an abstract description of a "typical" American college. For some purposes—explaining American education to a foreigner, for instance—this ideal type might be more useful than a description of a particular college.) Weber's ideal type of bureaucracy therefore shows us the essential characteristics of the bureaucratic form, although any individual bureaucracy will not necessarily conform to this description in every way.

According to Weber, a bureaucracy has the following typical features:

1. *Division of labor.* There is a clear-cut division of labor among the various officials. Each member of the organization has a specialized job to do and concentrates on this specific task.

2. *Hierarchy.* There is a hierarchy of authority within the organization. This hierarchy takes the shape of a pyramid, with greater authority for the few at the top and less for the many at the bottom. The scope of an individual's authority is clearly defined; each official takes orders from the officials immediately above and takes responsibility for those immediately below.

3. *Regulations.* An elaborate system of rules and regulations (mostly in written form) governs the day-to-day functioning of the bureaucracy. Decisions are based on these rules and on established precedents.

4. *Impersonality.* The members of the organization remain impersonal in their contacts with

Figure 7.8 *The bureaucratic form is generally efficient because it relies on highly rationalized procedures. For example, officials do not attempt to keep track of information in their heads or in the form of jottings on odd scraps of paper. All information is carefully coded and filed in a uniform manner.*

the public. Officials treat people as "cases," not as individuals. They also adopt a detached attitude to other members of the organization, interacting with them in terms of their official roles. Personal feelings are thus excluded from official business and do not enter into or distort the decision-making process.

5. *Record-keeping.* Complete written records—"the files"—are kept of all the organization's activities, and where possible, information is kept in a standardized format.

6. *Administrative staff.* There is a specialized administrative staff of managers, secretaries, record-keepers, and others. Their sole function is to keep the organization as a whole running smoothly.

7. *Career structure.* Employees are assumed to anticipate a career with the organization. Candidates for positions in the hierarchy are appointed on the basis of seniority or merit, or some combination of the two—not on the grounds of favoritism, family connections, or other criteria that are irrelevant to organizational efficiency.

Weber argued that such an organization would be highly efficient at coordinating the activities of its members and achieving specific objectives. As an ideal type, his analysis has stood the test of time. Later researchers have found it necessary to make one major modification, however, to take account of the informal, primary relationships that exist in all bureaucracies.

The Informal Structure of Bureaucracy

The formal structure of a bureaucracy is easily determined by a glance at its organizational chart, which will show the lines of authority along which communications flow from one official to another, usually in writing. In practice, however, no bureaucracy ever works strictly by the book. People get to know one another as individuals, not simply as officials. They establish primary relationships with one another, they bend and break the rules, they develop informal procedures for handling problems, and they take shortcuts through the hierarchy whenever they can (Blau and Meyer, 1971; Lehman and Etzioni, 1980; R. Hall, 1982; Perrow, 1986).

The existence of these informal networks was established in the course of research carried out between 1927 and 1932 at the Hawthorne plant of the Western Electric Company. Industrial sociologists were trying to discover incentives that would encourage the employees to work harder. In a classic study of fourteen men who wired telephone switchboards, the researchers found that output was determined, not by the official rules or even by bonuses, but rather by informal norms within the group itself. The men worked rapidly in the mornings, but eased off in the afternoons. To make their work more interesting they often traded tasks, although this practice was against the regulations. The workers had strong informal norms against working too hard; anyone who attempted to do so was called a "rate buster." They also had norms against working too slowly; anyone who appeared to slack off was called a "chiseler." They had an informal norm, too, against telling a superior about the failings of any individual; anyone who did so was considered a "squealer." The output of the workers was determined by an informal, unspoken agreement on what they felt was reasonable—not by what the management, for all its rational and careful calculations, believed they could or should do (Roethlisberger and Dickson, 1939).

More recent research has confirmed that the formal structure of a bureaucracy always breeds informal relationships and practices. Employees establish their own norms about how long a "lunch hour" should be. They swap tasks to make their work more varied and take over one another's duties when someone wants unofficial time off. They develop norms about the type and amount of company property that they can "take home" for private use. Because information travels slowly through official channels and because some decisions at the executive level are deliberately concealed from subordinates, an informal social network—"the grapevine"—develops to disseminate rumors. People who, in terms of the organizational chart, ought not to be in possession of important information often gain access to it.

Lower-status members of the hierarchy (such as secretaries in corporations or nurses in hospitals) often have a good deal of influence over higher-status officials. The underlings cannot exercise this influence too blatantly, however, so they develop subtle means of ensuring that their superiors still consider themselves fully in charge. In the following late-night telephone conversation between a ward nurse and a doctor on hospital call, for example, both parties try to preserve the illusion that it is the doctor, not the nurse, who is making a medical diagnosis and issuing a professional recommendation:

DOCTOR: This is Dr. Jones.
[An open and direct communication.]

NURSE: Dr. Jones, this is Miss Smith on 2W—Mrs. Brown, who learned today of her father's death, is unable to fall asleep.
[This message has two levels. Openly, it describes a set of circumstances, a woman who is unable to sleep and who that morning received word of her father's death. Less openly, but just as directly, it is a diagnostic and recommendation statement; i.e., Mrs. Brown is unable to sleep because of her grief, and she should be given a sedative. Dr. Jones, accepting the diagnostic statement and replying to the recommendation statement, answers.]

DOCTOR: What sleeping medication has been helpful to Mrs. Brown in the past?
[Dr. Jones, not knowing the patient, is asking for a recommendation from the nurse, who does know the patient, about what sleeping medication should be prescribed. Note, however, his question does not appear to be asking her for a recommendation. Miss Smith replies.]

NURSE: Pentobarbital mg 100 was quite effective night before last.
[A disguised recommendation statement. Dr. Jones replies with a note of authority in his voice.]

DOCTOR: Pentobarbital mg 100 before bedtime as needed for sleep; got it?
[Miss Smith ends the conversation with the tone of a grateful supplicant.]

NURSE: Yes, I have, and thank you very much doctor.
[Quoted in L. Stein, 1977]

In fact, the formal structure of the organization provides only a general framework in which people play out, often in highly personal ways, their bureaucratic roles. The organization has no real existence: without its participants it is merely an abstraction. It is people who create, operate, change, and *are* the organization. For this reason, some sociologists have stressed that a bureaucracy is a ***negotiated reality***—an organization that derives its existence and character from the social interaction through which the members continuously create and re-create it (Day and Day, 1977; Blankenship, 1977; Fine, 1984). Within the broad confines of bureaucracy, people "negotiate" relationships and establish social networks that may bear little relationship to the formal hierarchy.

Members of a bureaucracy are never treated entirely in terms of the offices they hold. One person, despite his or her high office, may be known as an incompetent whose advice should never be taken; another as an "old-timer," with valuable knowledge of rules and precedents and how to bend them; another as a "rising star" marked out for future promotion and worth cultivating in the meanwhile. Following the tortuous route of the official channels is no less irritating to members of a bureaucracy than it is to outsiders, and they quickly learn shortcuts through the system by way of informal networks of friendly officials. Government bureaucrats may bend the rules to help someone who has gained their sympathy, or they may subtly obstruct a case involving a member of the public who has been rude or offensive.

Figure 7.9 *Formal organizations are never quite as formal in practice as they are in theory, for informal networks and relationships always develop within the organizational structure. By helping to cut bureaucratic "red tape," these networks probably facilitate rather than hinder the work of the organization.*

Dysfunctions of Bureaucracy

Although Weber did not make it explicit, his view of bureaucracy was essentially a functionalist one. He analyzed bureaucracy as a response to a problem in social organization, showing how the various elements in a bureaucratic structure function to promote the survival, efficiency, and goals of the organization as a whole. Weber did not elaborate on the dysfunctions, or negative effects, of bureaucracy, although he was certainly aware of them. Other sociologists have subsequently identified a number of dysfunctions that are built into the bureaucratic form and that may well hinder its workings.

1. *Inefficiency in unusual cases.* Perhaps the most obvious dysfunction of bureaucracy is occasional inefficiency—a failing which, paradoxically, is an inevitable by-product of the overall efficiency of the system. Bureaucracies are efficient because their rules are designed for *typical* cases and problems. Officials can handle these cases quickly and effectively by applying uniform rules and procedures. Yet this means that the bureaucracy is ill equipped to handle *unusual* cases—the taxpayer whose file has been lost; the illiterate who cannot complete the necessary forms; the American citizen who was born in Romania eighty years ago, wants a passport, but cannot produce or trace the necessary birth certificate. When an unprecedented case arises that does not fit the rules, the bureaucracy is stumped. The problem may then circulate from desk to desk for weeks, months, or even years, before it finally reaches someone who is authorized and willing to make a decision on the problem.

2. *"Trained incapacity."* Blind adherence to existing rules and procedures may result in what Thorstein Veblen caustically termed "trained incapacity"— the inability to make any new, imaginative response because of previous bureaucratic training. A good illustration of this failing comes from the Soviet Union, where government bureaucrats are accustomed to controlling the news by suppressing, delaying, or altering it at will. For example, air crashes or other disasters occurring within the country are generally not reported in the Soviet media. So, when a serious nuclear accident occurred in the Soviet Union in 1986, officials at first made no public announcement of it. Only two days later, after neighboring countries detected very high levels of radiation coming from the direction of the Soviet Union, did Soviet officials issue a grudging, four-sentence statement. The result was a diplomatic disaster for the Soviet Union, for it undermined the country's efforts to convince Western European nations of its responsibility and reliability. In their trained incapacity, the Soviet officials relied on the only methods they knew—which happened to be entirely inappropriate in the unfamiliar conditions of the world beyond. Bureaucracies, then, face a perennial problem: that of balancing their own need for stability and predictability with the requirement that they respond effectively to—or even anticipate—change in the social environment outside.

3. *Goal displacement.* There is always a risk that, over time, officials will tend to forget the supposed goals of their organization and focus their energies elsewhere. Frequently, the task of running a large organization generates its own budgetary, personnel, and other administrative problems, and day-to-day bureaucratic behavior may concentrate on the "office politics" of these internal issues, displacing attention from the original goals. Even charitable organizations sometimes spend a disproportionate amount of their funds on "administration," leaving only a quarter or less to be spent on the stated purpose of their existence. Another form of goal displacement occurs when an organization's objective has been achieved. The bureaucrats do not simply resign and look for other jobs: on the contrary, they tend either to claim that there is still work to do, or to look for other goals to keep the organization going. Government bureaucracies are particularly notorious for finding a new reason for existence once their original purpose has been achieved, stalled, or abandoned (Selznick, 1943; Sills, 1957).

4. *Bureaucratic enlargement.* A related problem is the general tendency of all bureaucracies to grow. C. Northcote Parkinson (1957) has suggested, only half satirically, that "work expands to fill the time available for its completion" (see box on page 183). It is almost unknown for a bureaucracy to voluntarily spend less than its budget, or to hire fewer officials than it is authorized to employ. Officials tend to believe that their organization's work is so important that more resources should be devoted to it, and that more resources would lead to greater effectiveness. United States government agencies, for example, invariably seek annual budget increases—and sometimes go on a spending spree at the end of the fiscal year, fearing that if they underspend, Congress will cut their budgets the following year.

ILLINOIS DEPARTMENT OF LABOR
BUREAU OF EMPLOYMENT SECURITY

MEMORANDUM

To: David Gassman, Statistician

From: Benjamin Greenstein, Chief
              Research and Statistics

Subject: Hazardous Use of Coffee Pot

The afternoon of April 29, while Mr. Arthur Haverly was on vacation, an electric coffee pot was plugged in his office and left unattended. It spread noxious fumes through the office and scorched a table belonging to the State.

You admitted that you plugged in that coffee pot and that you did it, although Mr. Haverly had told you that I had requested that it should not be done due to previous adverse experience. When I asked you why you plugged in that coffee pot, although I had requested that it should not be done, you stated that you did not take it seriously.

I may note also that Mr. Haverly informed me the previous day that he had not authorized you to connect the coffee pot in his office.

The following facts, therefore, emerge:

1. You had used your supervisor's office for cooking coffee without his authorization.

2. You did so, although you knew that I had requested that it should not be done.

3. You had left the coffee pot unattended. For that matter, there may have been a conflict between performing agency work and attending to the coffee pot.

4. You created a fire hazard for your fellow workers and subjected them to noxious fumes.

5. When I asked you why you plugged in the coffee pot in spite of my request to the contrary, you stated that you did not take it seriously. This is a rejection of supervision.

6. Your disregard of my authority has resulted in discomfort to your fellow workers and damage to State property.

7. On April 30, the day following the above actions and conversation, at 8:25 in the morning, I noted that you had again plugged in the coffee pot. When I pointed out that you were aware that I had asked you not to plug it in, you replied that it is not 8:30 yet. I then told you that I am in charge of the section, even though it is not 8:30 yet.

What should be done with respect to your actions, as specified above, is under consideration. In the meantime, you are emphatically requested not to repeat the hazard you created by plugging in the coffee pot.

SOURCE: *The Washington Monthly*, 1974, reprinted in Rafael Steinberg, *Man and the Organization* (New York: Time-Life Books, 1975), p. 115.

Figure 7.10 *This memo reveals several features that distinguish formal organizations from more informal groups. (1) The communication is in writing. Composing, dictating, typing, and transmitting it may have taken hours of official time. (2) The people involved are relating to each other in their official roles, as "Chief, Research and Statistics," and "Statistician." (3) The superior officer is deeply concerned that appropriate hierarchical relationships should be observed. (4) An excessive amount of effort has been put into resolving an issue that would be regarded as trivial in a less formal group, where it would be handled with a few spoken words. (5) Officials are devoting energy to an internal organizational problem rather than to the goals of the group.*

"Parkinson's Law" and the "Peter Principle"

Bureaucracies have been the subject of many satirical criticisms. The two best-known onslaughts are expressed in "Parkinson's Law" and the "Peter Principle." Parkinson's Law is named after the writer who proposed it, C. Northcote Parkinson. The law is a simple one: In any bureaucracy, "work expands to fill the time available for its completion." The natural tendency of any formal organization, Parkinson points out, is to grow. Officials have to appear busy, and therefore they create tasks for themselves. In due course they have so much work to do that they need assistants. When an official has an assistant, however, the burden of work on the official actually increases, because he or she now has to supervise the subordinate. Much of the subordinate's time is taken up in turn with submitting reports to the superior official. As work continues to expand, more assistants and officials are added, some of whom are responsible solely for supervising others or handling the flow of communications between the multiplying personnel. An immense amount of time and effort is then spent on form filling, memo writing, and file keeping and on checking the form filling,

memo writing, and file keeping of others. Parkinson argues that virtually all of this activity is unnecessary.

The Peter Principle is named after its discoverer, Lawrence J. Peter. This principle, too, is a simple one: "In any hierarchy every employee tends to rise to his level of incompetence." Peter points out that officials who are competent at their jobs tend to be promoted. If they are competent at their new jobs, they are promoted again. This process continues until they finally reach a job that is beyond their abilities—and there they stay. The result is expressed in "Peter's corollary": "In time, every post tends to be occupied by an employee who is incompetent to carry out its duties." Bureaucracies are able to function, Peter suggests, only because at any given time there are enough officials who have not yet reached their level of incompetence and are capable of performing their jobs efficiently.

SOURCE: C. Northcote Parkinson, *Parkinson's Law* (Boston: Houghton Mifflin, 1957); Lawrence J. Peter and Raymond Hull, *The Peter Principle* (New York: William Morrow, 1969).

---

5. *Authoritarian structure.* The very nature of bureaucracy as a hierarchy generates problems. Because the structure of a bureaucracy is essentially authoritarian, officials at lower levels may conceal defects, mistakes, and inefficiencies from superiors. In theory, communications flow upward and downward through appropriate channels. In practice, communications flow almost entirely downward and are often distorted at the middle levels during the process. Those at the top of the hierarchy are unlikely to be aware of the problems or feelings of those at the bottom. The authoritarian structure can also generate internal friction. A bureaucracy is by nature a hierarchy of unequals. The level of an official's status may be indicated by such things as a convenient parking space, the presence of a secretary, the type of carpeting in the office, and the size of the desk and the amount of paper on it (the less paper and the bigger the desk, the higher the official). There is consequently always a tendency for an "us against them" attitude to develop at different levels in the hierarchy,

causing all the problems that the presence of ingroup-versus-outgroup conflicts can create.

6. *Bureaucratic personality.* Robert Merton (1968) has suggested another dysfunction of bureaucracy—its effects on the personalities of the bureaucrats. Merton argues that rigid routines and pressures for conformity may stifle individual creativity and imagination. In extreme cases, he claims, the bureaucrat focuses obsessively on means rather than ends, ritually following rules and procedures without any concern for the goals they were designed to serve. The title of William Whyte's book *The Organization Man* (1956), which presented a roughly similar picture, has entered popular speech to describe people so involved in an organization that other areas of their personal experience are distorted and impoverished. Merton's argument is controversial, however, as more recent research shows that workers in bureaucracies tend to be fairly open-minded, self-directed, and willing to accept change (Kohn, 1971, 1978).

Figure 7.11 *For nearly two decades, the space agency NASA was regarded as a model of bureaucratic efficiency. However, the 1986 explosion of the space shuttle Challenger has been attributed to a booster-rocket fault in combination with problems that are commonly associated with bureaucracy. Before the launch, lower-level engineers argued strongly that the space vehicle was unsafe to fly. They were overruled, disastrously, in an apparent "risky shift" by middle-level administrators. And upper-level officials, who made the actual decision to launch, were apparently unaware of the objections and fears of those lower down in the hierarchy.*

The current stereotype of the bureaucrat may yet prove to be based on myth. Perhaps the real danger that large-scale bureaucratization poses to the human spirit is a different one: an insidious and alienating loss of freedom.

The Problem of Oligarchy

The relationship between human freedom and bureaucracy is a complex one, for it involves much more than the subordination of individuals to the needs of organizations. Bureaucracy tends to result in *oligarchy,* or rule by the few—in this case, by officials at the top of the hierarchy. In a society dominated by large formal organizations, therefore, there is a danger that social, political, and economic power will become concentrated in the hands of those who hold high positions in the most influential formal organizations, such as large corporations, government departments, or the military services.

This issue was first raised in 1911 by Robert Michels, a sociologist and friend of Max Weber. Michels was a dedicated socialist at the time and was dismayed to find that the new socialist parties of Europe seemed to be dominated by their leaders just as much as the traditional, authoritarian, conservative parties were. Yet this should have been impossible: the socialists had deliberately designed their new parties with a democratic struc-

ture, so as to ensure mass participation in decision making. What had gone wrong? Michels pondered the issue, and came to the conclusion that the problem lay in the very nature of large organizations. "Whoever says organization," he wrote, "says oligarchy." According to his "iron law of oligarchy," democracy and large-scale organizations are incompatible.

Any large organization, Michels pointed out, is faced with administrative problems that can be solved only by creating a bureaucracy. A bureaucracy, in turn, must be a hierarchy, because the many decisions that have to be made every day cannot be made by large numbers of people. If an organization is to be run effectively, power must be in the hands of a few people at the top.

This situation is aggravated by certain characteristics of both leaders and members. People become leaders of political parties and similar organizations because they are adept at persuading others and getting their own way. Once they hold high positions, their power and prestige are further increased. They have access to knowledge and facilities that are not available to others, and they can control much of the information that flows down to the rank-and-file members of the organization. For their part, the members tend to admire the leaders and to look to them for direction. Unlike the leaders, the members usually have only a part-time commitment to the organization, and are willing to defer to their leaders' judgment on most matters. Moreover, the leaders are strongly motivated to maintain their own position, and they use all their skills and opportunities to do so. In particular, they tend to promote junior officials who support them and share their opinions, with the result that the oligarchy becomes self-perpetuating. Organization thus breeds oligarchy, which, in turn, prevents real democracy. This "iron law" so disillusioned Michels that he abandoned his hopes of achieving human equality through socialism: in fact, while teaching in Italy later in his life, he became for a while an ardent supporter of Mussolini's Fascist party.

Michels's argument seems persuasive, but it should not be accepted uncritically. Although he was correct in his view that power in organizations tends to be concentrated among the top officeholders, he neglected certain checks on the power of the leadership. In many organizations, from corporations to political parties, there are usually two or more groups competing for control. If the dominant group gets too far out of line with rank-and-file opinion, it risks being displaced by another group. Successful challenges to the power of the oligarchy have been recorded in a variety of bureaucratic organizations, ranging from labor unions to political parties to the military (Lipset et al., 1956; Zald and Berger, 1978). Michels also overlooked another vital aspect of organizations: whether they are oligarchic or not, they are often the best means of achieving a given goal. Many of the democratic advances of the past century have resulted, directly or indirectly, from the efforts of large-scale organizations.

The relationship between bureaucracy and freedom is a paradoxical one: human freedom in a modern industrialized society is dependent on bureaucracy, yet bureaucracy tends to undermine human freedom. Max Weber pointed out that the preservation of liberty requires impartial rules and procedures and formal organizations to apply them. For example, we cannot have impartial justice if judges rule on the basis of whim or favoritism: there must be a rational system of laws and a judicial bureaucracy to ensure that everyone is treated in the same way. We cannot have free elections without a representative list of voters, but then we need a formal bureaucracy to register voters and keep the lists up to date. We cannot prevent some people from infringing on the liberties of others unless there are formal organizations, ranging from police forces to federal regulatory agencies, to protect those liberties.

Yet bureaucracy may undermine as well as protect human freedom. The reason is that large, complex bureaucracies separate individuals from control over the decisions that affect their lives. Government departments, for example, are theoretically responsible to the electorate, but this responsibility is almost entirely fictional. It often happens, in fact, that the electorate—and even Congress—do not know what these bureaucracies are doing. In the mid-1970s, congressional investigations following the Watergate scandal revealed that government agencies such as the CIA and the FBI had been guilty of thousands of crimes, ranging from burglarizing legitimate opposition groups to giving the drug LSD to unsuspecting subjects. It also emerged that for a period of at least fifteen years, the United States had been involved in attempts to assassinate the heads of state of several foreign countries through plots that included the use of Mafia "hit men." Very few of the elected representatives of the American people had any idea that these policies were being pursued.

Our democratic theories have their roots in the small-scale world of the eighteenth century. The thinkers and revolutionaries who created those theories could not anticipate the growth and spread of vast, formal organizations that separate us from control over major social, political, and economic decisions. In this respect, as in many others, the radical changes that have taken place in the group basis of social life present a range of new problems.

Figure 7.12

"I was just going to say 'Well, I don't make the rules.' But, of course, I _do_ make the rules."

Drawing by Leo Cullum; © 1986
The New Yorker Magazine, Inc.

Other Forms of Organization

Most formal organizations today may conform closely to Weber's ideal type, but this is not the only conceivable type. Like any other aspect of culture, organizations are shaped by their social environment, and so vary from one time and place to another. There are significant differences, for example, among the Japanese corporation of the post–World War II years, the collectivist organization that has emerged in Western industrialized nations in recent years, and the modified formal organizations that may be emerging today.

Figure 7.13 *In many large Japanese corporations, the workers are expected to wear company uniforms, sing company songs, and perform calisthenics before starting the day's duties. Americans, who value individualism, would probably resent these rules as an intrusion into their privacy, but the Japanese, who are more community-oriented, seem to appreciate them as a means of cementing the bonds between worker and organization.*

The Japanese Corporation

Japan emerged from the ruins of defeat in World War II to become one of the leading industrial powers of the world. This extraordinary achievement is often attributed to unique features of the Japanese industrial corporation, a social invention that combines aspects of traditional Japanese culture with modern Western organizational techniques (Vogel, 1979; Rohlen, 1979; Pascale and Athos, 1981; Reischauer, 1981; Ouchi, 1981).

The model followed by the largest Japanese corporations draws on a long cultural tradition that emphasizes the importance of the group over the individual. When people join a major Japanese corporation, they are making a lifetime commitment, which the corporation reciprocates. Unless the employee commits a crime, he or she will not be fired or laid off. All promotions are made from inside the organization; outsiders are not even considered. Most promotions are based on seniority, so people of the same age move more or less together through the organizational hierarchy, with little competition among them. Workers are organized into small teams, and it is the teams—not the individual workers—whose performance is evaluated. Over the years, each individual may belong to many such teams, thereby gaining experience throughout the corporation. Decision making is collective: rather than issue new policies, the top officials merely ratify them after they have been discussed and approved at every level of the organization (the Japanese word for this process literally means "bottom-up" decision making).

Unlike Western corporations, which usually limit the relationship between organization and employee to matters that are "strictly business," Japanese corporations take considerable responsibility for their workers' welfare. They provide a whole range of services, sometimes including housing, recreation, health care, and continuing education. The workers, in turn, show great loyalty to the company—perhaps by wearing company uniforms, singing the company song, working exceptionally long hours, or taking part in company-organized sporting and other activities. In short, the activities of the corporation and the lives of its members are closely intertwined. This relationship between organization and worker reflects a deep difference between Japanese and Western cultures: to the Japanese, it indicates a bond of commitment that ensures security and solidarity; to Americans, it would seem like suffocating paternalism that prevents individual achievement and overlooks "whiz kid" potential.

The Collective

The period since the late 1960s has seen the spread in Western industrialized societies of a nonbureaucratic kind of organization, the collective. Typically, collectivist groups consist largely of volunteers or part-time workers who administer community projects such as free schools, alternative newspapers, medical or legal-aid clinics, or art centers. Those who choose this work often view the "establishment," as represented by large, formal organizations, with distaste.

As Joyce Rothschild-Whitt (1979) points out, the collectivist form differs sharply from the bureaucratic one in several respects. First, there is little division of labor, and individual members are encouraged to contribute a variety of talents to different jobs. Second, authority arises from the consensus of the collective as a whole, not from a hierarchy of officials. Third, individual initiative is more highly valued than rigid adherence to a set of rules. Fourth, members of the collective treat the public as individual people, not as a set of "cases." Fifth, the status of group members depends more on their personal qualities than on any official titles they might have.

Essentially, then, members of collectives are deliberately trying to create a setting that is the polar opposite of bureaucracy. But this effort is not without its own costs. Democracy is time-consuming, for long periods must be spent on staff discussions and consensus-seeking. The unconventional nature of collectives can cause them problems in dealing with more conventional organizations—for example, in trying to get bank loans. Most important, perhaps, collectives are suited only for small-scale enterprises in which virtually all relationships are primary; if collectives grew large, their informality would breed inefficiency. Although many thousands of collectives now exist in Western industrialized societies, there is little prospect of them replacing or even seriously competing with bureaucracies.

Organizational Reform

There is increasing pressure for reform of formal organizations. One source of this pressure is the new value of "self-fulfillment" discussed in Chapter 3 ("Culture"). The rigid requirements of bureaucracy are inconsistent with a value that emphasizes the personal growth of the individual. Rosabeth Kanter (1977) suggests various changes that might make formal organizations a more sat-

isfying work environment. These include job rotation, periodic sabbaticals, the elimination of some levels of management so as to spread authority more evenly, and rewards for length of service as well as for position in the hierarchy.

Pressure for reform also comes from the professional advisers who are increasingly employed in formal organizations, such as economists, physicists, computer scientists, sociologists, and other highly trained experts. These professionals do not readily fit into the hierarchical structure of the bureaucracy. Their knowledge and expertise are individual properties, attaching to them as people rather than to their offices. Professionals require the freedom to innovate, experiment, and take risks, and they expect their work to be judged by others in their own reference group—not by a bureaucrat who has no knowledge of their field of expertise. As formal organizations come to rely more and more on advanced technologies and expert advice, there is likely to be some change in traditional hierarchical relationships (Benson, 1973; Blankenship, 1977).

The changing environment outside organizations may also lead to reforms. Some writers have suggested that bureaucracies will tend to become less centralized, perhaps through being reorganized into self-contained, more temporary units. For example, Alvin Toffler (1970, 1980) argues that traditional, impersonal organizations are not capable of meeting the challenges of modern postindustrial societies. Rapidly changing conditions, he argues, demand a more fluid organization, containing special-purpose units that are dissolved when their tasks are done. Other critics claim that organizations will have to become more flexible and less hierarchical—partly to meet their members' growing demands for self-fulfillment, partly to give their professional advisers the autonomy that they require in their work. In time, then, organizational charts might consist of a series of project groups, often making decisions through consensus, instead of the traditional hierarchies (Weiss and Barton, 1979; Kochen and Deutch, 1980). But this prospect is perhaps more tempting than persuasive. Although organizations may have to modify their structures to deal with new problems, many of their traditional concerns will remain, and their traditional structures are likely to remain as well. The real challenge of reform will be to develop better means of social control over bureaucracy and thus to ensure that we shall not be dominated by the organizations that were first established, after all, for our own efficiency and convenience.

Summary

1.   Human beings are social animals who spend much of their time in groups. Groups are distinguished from aggregates and categories by the fact that their members interact.

2.   Primary groups consist of a small number of people who interact on an intimate basis. Secondary groups may be large or small, but their members interact without any emotional commitment to one another.

3.   Extensive research has been devoted to small-group interaction. The size of groups influences the kind of interaction that can take place. Leadership in groups may be instrumental or expressive. Democratic leaders are more effective than authoritarian or laissez-faire leaders, at least in American laboratory experiments. Groups are more effective than individuals at solving determinate problems, but group performance on indeterminate problems varies. Groups tend to arrive at decisions by consensus. There is sometimes a tendency toward a "risky shift" or other polarized opinion, and sometimes toward "groupthink." Most group decisions proceed through a regular sequence of stages. As Asch's experiments suggest, there is strong pressure for conformity in groups.

4.   Members of groups tend to regard their group as an "ingroup" and other groups as "outgroups." Conflict and tension between groups heighten feelings of group solidarity and loyalty, as Sherif's experiment shows.

5.   Networks are webs of direct and indirect relationships. Networks are a vital part of social life.

6.   Reference groups are those to which an individual refers when making self-evaluations. One need not be a member of a reference group in order to identify with it.

7.   Large secondary groups, or associations, generally take the form of formal organizations. These social groups dominate modern life.

8.   Formal organizations are coordinated through bureaucracies. Weber saw bureaucracy as a form of rationalization, and by constructing an ideal type, analyzed the way bureaucracies operate. His analysis has since been modified to take account of the informal structure that exists in all bureaucracies. Although bureaucracies are highly efficient, they have many dysfunctions as well, particularly when faced with unprecedented or unfamiliar situations.

9.   Bureaucracies tend to be oligarchic, a feature that Michels argued was incompatible with democracy. Although bureaucracies are necessary for a mass democracy, they also undermine liberty by separating people from the decision-making processes that affect their lives.

10. Some alternative forms of organization are the Japanese corporation, the collective, and emerging types of reformed organization.

Important Terms

group (167)   ingroup (173)
aggregate (167)   outgroup (173)
category (167)   social network (174)
primary group (168)   reference group (175)
secondary group (168)   formal organization (175)
small group (169)   bureaucracy (176)
dyad (169)   rationalization (177)
triad (170)   ideal type (178)
leader (170)   negotiated reality (180)
instrumental leadership (170)   oligarchy (184)
expressive leadership (170)

Suggested Readings

HALL, RICHARD H. *Organizations*. 3rd ed. Englewood Cliffs, N.J.: Prentice-Hall, 1982.

A good and comprehensive overview of sociological research on formal organizations and bureaucracy.

JANIS, IRVING L., and LEON MANN. *Decision Making*. New York: Free Press, 1977.

An excellent overview of theory and research on the question of how groups arrive at their decisions.

KANTER, ROSABETH MOSS, and BARRY STEIN (eds.). *Life in Organizations: Workplaces as People Experience Them*. New York: Basic Books, 1979.

An interesting collection of accounts of life in modern corporate and governmental bureaucracies.

MICHELS, ROBERT. *Political Parties*. New York: Free Press, 1967.

Although this book was first published more than half a century ago, it remains a readable and relevant analysis of the relationship between democracy and oligarchic organizations.

PARKINSON, C. NORTHCOTE. *Parkinson's Law*. Boston: Houghton Mifflin, 1957.

A satirical account of the inefficiencies of large organizations. The book includes a presentation of "Parkinson's Law," which states that in any organization, work expands to fill the amount of time available for its completion.

PERROW, CHARLES. *Complex Organizations*. 3rd ed. New York: Random House, 1986.

An important critical discussion of formal organizations and their implications for modern society.

SHAW, MARVIN E. *Group Dynamics*. 3rd ed. New York: McGraw-Hill, 1981.

A brief and readable summary of the main findings of social science research on small groups.

CHAPTER 8

Deviance

In the preceding chapters we have emphasized the basically orderly nature of society. Most people conform to most norms most of the time, and social life therefore takes on a fairly regular and predictable pattern. Yet this picture is incomplete. We need only look at the world around us to see that social norms are often violated as well as adhered to. People rob, rape, and defraud others. They wear peculiar clothing, smoke crack, and take part in riots. They embrace alien religions, become mentally disordered, and commit bigamy. A full picture of society, therefore, must include deviance from social norms as well as conformity to them.

What exactly is deviance? Strictly speaking, the concept would include any behavior that does not conform to social norms. In practice, though, many norms are not regarded as particularly important, and nonconformity to them may be tolerated or even ignored. The social reaction you get if you turn up late for appointments, don't eat three meals a day, or occasionally wear mismatched socks is very different from the reaction you get if you mug an old lady in the street, participate in orgies, or announce that you are Napoleon.

Minor deviations from norms, or deviations from norms that nobody bothers much about, have few if any social consequences and are not of particular sociological interest. The sociology of deviance is primarily concerned with violations that are considered offensive by a large number of people. The one characteristic shared by those who are widely regarded as deviant is *stigma*—the mark of social disgrace that sets the deviant apart from those who consider themselves "normal." Erving Goffman (1963b) perceptively remarked that the stigmatized person has a "spoiled identity" as a result of negative evaluations by others. For our purposes, then, *deviance* is behavior that violates significant social norms and is disapproved by large numbers of people as a result. This defini-

Figure 8.1 *Behavior that one culture admires may be regarded as deviant in another. The first of these pictures shows a member of the Maori of New Zealand, a people who used tattoos and incisions to create elaborate—and highly valued—facial patterns. The second shows a modern American, whose extensive tattoos would be regarded as deviant by most people in the culture.*

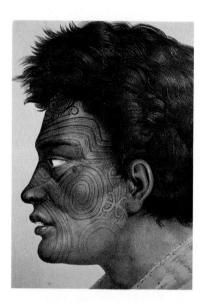 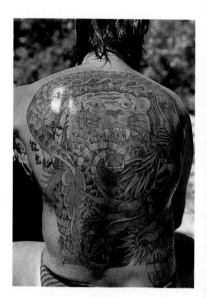

tion brings us closer to an understanding of deviance, and two additional points will clarify the concept further.

The first point is that society cannot be divided neatly into the sheep and the goats, the "normals" who conform and the "deviants" who do not. Although a majority of people usually conform to any specific norm that is important to society, most people have violated one or more important norms at some time in their lives. If we were to subtract from "normal" society all the people who have engaged in prohibited sexual acts, all the people who have ever stolen something, all the people who have suffered a mental disorder, and all the people who have used illegal drugs—to mention just a few out of hundreds of possibilities—we would have very few "normal" people left. Most people, however, escape discovery of their deviant behavior, are not stigmatized, and generally do not regard themselves as deviant at all.

The second point is that deviance is relative. No act is inherently deviant. It becomes deviant only when it is socially defined as such, and definitions vary greatly from time to time, place to place, and group to group. The heretic of one age may be the saint of the next; the "freedom fighter" of one group may be a "terrorist" to another; conservative views in one society may seem dangerously radical in a different society. Who and what are defined as deviant depend on who is doing the defining and who has the power to make the definition stick.

It is even possible for the same act to be differently interpreted depending on the precise context in which it takes place. If you talk to God in a synagogue or church, your behavior is regarded as perfectly normal; if you talk to God in a bus or a restaurant, or if God talks back to you, you are considered mentally disordered. It is quite acceptable for you to "do nothing" at home, but our society demands that you be "doing something" in public. If you stand around a street corner long enough, you will probably be arrested for loitering. The police are entitled to ask you what you are doing, and "nothing" is usually not an acceptable answer. An act may also draw different reactions depending on the social status of the person concerned. If a lower-class male exposes himself in a park, he will probably be charged with public indecency. If a corporation president does the same, he has an excellent chance of being referred to a psychiatrist for treatment.

Deviance and Social Control

Under most conditions, social behavior is remarkably orderly and predictable. You can generally rely on your sociology professor to show up for class, and you can expect that he or she will talk mostly about sociology and not something else. You can take it on faith that banks will be open during working hours, not closed because the tellers became bored and decided to throw a private party. And you can be almost certain that your neighbors will dress in much the same way tomorrow as they did yesterday, and will not appear on the streets half naked or painted with blue dye. In short, people generally fulfill their roles in accordance with social expectations. In doing so they make social order, and therefore society, possible.

As we noted in Chapter 3 ("Culture"), social order can exist only if there is an effective system of *social control*—a set of means of ensuring that people generally behave in expected and approved ways. Social control starts with the socialization process, which ideally ensures that everyone internalizes and follows the norms of the society. On the whole, socialization is highly successful: people conform to social norms most of the time through sheer habit, and rarely question why they act as they do. In general, human beings abide by the rules—not just when the rules seem sound and useful, but even when they are petty, arrogant, outdated, contradictory, or oppressive. Nevertheless, socialization is always to some extent imperfect and incomplete. People may be born with different potentials; they are exposed to different socializing influences; they interpret these influences in different ways; and they are often faced with novel situations in which they must improvise new behavior on their own.

When socialization cannot guarantee sufficient conformity, further means of social control are necessary. Society has to enforce its norms through *sanctions*—rewards for conformity and punishments for nonconformity. Both types of sanction can be applied either formally, in a patterned and organized way, or informally, through the spontaneous reactions of other people. A formal positive sanction, for example, might be the presentation of a medal or graduation certificate; a formal negative sanction might be imprisonment or execution. An informal positive sanction might be a pat on the back or a congratulatory handshake; an informal negative sanction might be a shouted insult or simply avoidance of the offender. The award of positive sanctions indicates that social control is working effectively and that people are fulfilling the expectations others have of them. But the use of negative sanctions implies that social control has failed and that deviance has occurred.

Paradoxically, however, the presence of deviance can actually make social control more effective. Emile Durkheim (1964a, orig. 1893) strongly argued that some deviance is necessary to define what the boundaries of permissible behavior are. When society stigmatizes thieves or prostitutes, it does more than punish them. It also reaffirms the existing norms and implicitly warns other people what their fate will be if they stray from the rules.

Figure 8.2 *Deviance can indirectly strengthen social control, for when a society punishes deviants, the rules—and the penalties for breaking them— are made clear to everyone. Throughout history, in fact, many societies have applied formal negative sanctions in public, so that the entire community can express its solidarity against the offender. In early New England, deviants were often placed in the stocks, where they had to endure the taunts and censure of the populace. In modern China, convicted criminals are often displayed in public before their execution.*

The public example of the stigmatized deviant provides evidence that social control has failed, but it also tends to restrain others from deviating and thus strengthens the norms. In applying sanctions to deviants, moreover, other people are made conscious of their own conformity, and so feel solidarity as the normal "us" against the deviant "them."

Explaining Deviance

The extent and the content of deviant behavior vary a great deal from one society to another and among different groups within a society, a fact that requires explanation. Psychologists may be interested in the reasons why specific people adopt the deviant practices that they do. But the sociological problem is not to explain why a particular person becomes deviant: it is to understand why deviance arises at all, why it follows specific patterns, and why some acts rather than others are defined as deviant in the first place. Four main sociological theories of deviance have been offered. Although none of them provides a comprehensive explanation of all deviance, the theories do tend to overlap and complement one another, and bring us much closer to an understanding of the phenomenon.

Cultural-Transmission Theory

One approach to an understanding of deviance is *cultural-transmission theory,* which explains deviance as behavior that is learned in the same way as conformity—through interaction with other people. In effect, this approach draws on the insights of symbolic interactionism, and applies them to the process of socialization into deviance.

Early in this century, sociologists noticed that high crime rates persisted in the same neighborhoods over many years. This fact suggested that deviance might have become rooted in the local cultures and then transmitted over time from one person or even one generation to another. Edwin Sutherland (1939) produced an influential theory to explain exactly how this process of cultural transmission takes place. According to Sutherland, deviant behavior is learned through *differential association,* or social relationships oriented toward particular types of people, such as criminals. This concept is really a sophisticated version of the old "bad companions" formula ("He was such a good kid until he started hanging out with *that*

bunch"). Just as people will tend to be conformists if their socialization emphasizes a respect for the prevailing norms, so they will tend to become deviant if their socialization encourages a contempt for these norms.

Since nobody is exposed exclusively to conformists or to deviants, several factors determine which influences will be the stronger. One is the *intensity* of contacts with others; a person is more likely to be influenced by deviant friends or family members than by more distant acquaintances who are deviant. Another is the *age* at which the contacts take place; influences in childhood and adolescence are more powerful than those occurring later in life. Another is the *ratio* of contacts with deviants to contacts with conformists; the more one associates with deviants rather than conformists, the more likely one is to become deviant.

In short, nobody is born with the knowledge, the techniques, or the justifications that are available to the deviant. Like any other elements of culture, these things must be transmitted from one person or group to another.

Evaluation

Cultural-transmission theory has an interesting implication: behavior that the dominant culture views as deviant may actually be conformist from the point of view of a subculture. For example, a Jehovah's Witness who refuses to salute the flag or swear allegiance, or who denies permission for a blood transfusion, is regarded as deviant by the wider society—yet that person is merely conforming to the group's norms, which are based on specific passages in the Bible. Several sociologists have applied this insight to gang delinquency, arguing that mere acceptance of certain lower-class norms and values—such as those related to "toughness," "street smarts," and the search for "kicks"—can put juveniles in trouble with the law. Simply by accepting the values of their own subculture, lower-class juveniles may come to be regarded as delinquent by the society beyond. Cultural-transmission theory also helps to explain why so many criminals, drug addicts, and other deviants relapse into their former behavior after release or treatment: they rejoin their social networks of deviant associates, and renew the activities.

Yet the theory has some problems. Many people, despite their deviant associations, fail to become deviant themselves: most children raised in high-crime neighborhoods, for example, do not

Figure 8.3 *Cultural-transmission theory implies that people socialized in a particular environment may become deviant simply through learning the norms of their own subculture. Raised in an area where gang activities are commonplace, a boy may learn patterns of behavior that the mainstream culture defines as deviant.*

become criminals. Additionally, some people become deviant without any actual contact with deviants: a check forger or rapist need not have had personal instruction in how to perform the acts. And some forms of deviant behavior are actually learned in contact with conforming citizens. One can learn the techniques of embezzlement, for example, by taking a course in bookkeeping. Some sociologists have extended Sutherland's theory by arguing that deviance can be learned partly by imitation of others or through incidental contact with ideas (Akers, 1985). Even with this modification, however, an important criticism still remains: cultural-transmission theory explains only how deviance is learned, not how it arose in the culture or why it was defined as deviance in the first place.

Structural-Strain Theory

Another approach is **structural-strain theory,** which explains deviance as the outcome of social strains that put pressure on some people to deviate. A very simplistic version of structural-strain theory is the ancient adage that "poverty breeds crime": it supposes that the very existence of a category of poor people within the social structure creates pressures for certain deviance.

Modern structural-strain theory uses an important concept that Emile Durkheim (1964a, orig. 1893) introduced to modern sociology—**anomie,** a condition of confusion that exists in both individ-

ual and society when social norms are weak, absent, or conflicting. Modern societies, Durkheim warned, are especially prone to anomie, for their cultural diversity creates confusion over norms and values and leaves people without clear moral guidelines. Individuals who are in a condition of anomie lack rules for behavior, for they feel little sense of social discipline over their personal desires and acts. (Anomie is discussed in more detail in Chapter 17, "The Economic Order.")

Robert Merton (1938, 1968) has developed the concept of anomie and applied it to deviant behavior. Like Durkheim, Merton writes from a functionalist perspective, and he regards deviance as the outcome of an imbalance in the social system. Anomie may arise, he claims, when there is an imbalance between socially approved *goals* and the availability of socially approved *means* of achieving them. In the United States, for example, the population is socialized into the belief that one has to "make it" in the world, by achieving financial success, or be a "failure." But not everybody can be wealthy, and some categories of the population—such as people with little education or few job skills—may find wealth difficult to achieve. Someone who accepts the goal of success but finds the approved means blocked may then fall into a state of anomie and seek success by disapproved methods such as theft or fraud, or may become deviant in other ways, such as turning to drugs. Strains within society itself thus exert pressure on some people to deviate rather than conform.

MERTON'S TYPOLOGY OF DEVIANCE

Modes of Adapting	Accepts Culturally Approved Goals	Accepts Culturally Approved Means
Conformist	yes	yes
Innovator	yes	no
Ritualist	no	yes
Retreatist	no	no
Rebel	no (creates new goals)	no (creates new means)

SOURCE: Adapted from Robert K. Merton, *Social Theory and Social Structure* (New York: Free Press, 1968), p. 194.

Figure 8.4 *According to Merton's theory, people will conform or deviate depending on their acceptance or rejection of culturally approved means and/or culturally approved goals. This table illustrates the various outcomes that are possible.*

Merton suggests that people may respond to a discrepancy between approved goals and approved methods of reaching them in one of five different ways, depending on their acceptance or rejection of the goals or the means (see Figure 8.4).

1. *Conformity* occurs when people accept both the approved goals and the approved means. Conformists want to achieve such goals as success, and generally use approved means—even if they are unsuccessful.

2. *Innovation* occurs when people accept the approved goals but resort to disapproved means. This is the most common form of deviance: it occurs, for example, when a student wants to pass a test but resorts to cheating; or when a woman wants to earn money but becomes a prostitute.

3. *Ritualism* occurs when people abandon the goals as irrelevant to their lives but still accept and compulsively enact the means. The classic example is the bureaucrat who becomes obsessed with petty rules and procedures, losing sight of the objectives that the rules were designed to achieve.

4. *Retreatism* occurs when people abandon both the approved goals and the approved means of achieving them. The retreatist is the "double failure" in the eyes of society—the vagrant, the chronic narcotics addict, the "skid-row bum."

5. *Rebellion* occurs when people reject both the approved goals and means and then substitute new, disapproved ones instead. The rebel, for example, may reject the goal of personal wealth and a business career as the way to achieve it, turning instead to a goal of social equality to be achieved through revolution.

Evaluation

Merton's theory of deviance is an elegant, thoughtful, and influential one. It not only locates the source of deviance squarely in social structure and culture rather than in the deviants themselves, but it also provides a plausible explanation of why people commit certain deviant acts, particularly crimes involving property. Albert Cohen (1955) pointed out, for example, that gangs are generally composed of lower-class boys who, lacking the social and educational background that would enable them to achieve success via approved channels, try to gain the respect of their peers through "hell-raising" and other forms of behavior that conform to gang norms. The gang provides people who cannot achieve a "respectable" status with the opportunity for other forms of achievement, even if these are disapproved by the wider society.

Unfortunately, structural-strain theory is less useful for explaining other forms of deviance, such as exhibitionism or mental disorder. Nor does it explain why very wealthy people, who have access to means of earning money legitimately, may resort to fraud and embezzlement to gain even more wealth. And because Merton shares the implicit functionalist assumption that there is a general consensus of values in society, he largely ignores the process by which some people and certain acts are defined as deviant by others—a process that often involves a conflict of values between those who have the power to apply these definitions and those who do not.

Control Theory

A third approach to the problem of deviance is *control theory,* which explains deviance as the outcome of a failure of social control. Unlike other theories of deviance, which begin with the question of why people deviate, control theory begins by asking why they conform in the first place. Control theorists suggest that deviance, not conformity, should be taken for granted: after all, life is full of temptations, and some deviant acts may be quite rewarding. People conform only because society is able to control their behavior, and if there were no such control, there might be little conformity (Nye, 1958; Hirschi, 1969; Gibbs, 1981; Meier, 1982).

This theory, too, is influenced by Durkheim's work. As we noted in Chapter 2 ("Doing Sociology: The Methods of Research"), Durkheim found that the rate of a certain form of deviance—suicide—is related to the strength of the bonds that tie the individual to the community: the stronger the bonds, the less the likelihood of suicide. On the basis of this discovery, Durkheim advanced a more general theory of deviance: in a society with strong social solidarity, the members are likely to conform to shared norms and values, but in a society with weak bonds among the members, people are more likely to deviate. Modern control theory relies on this insight, for it holds that people who are integrated into their community tend to follow its rules, whereas people who are isolated from their community may be inclined to break them.

Travis Hirschi (1969) suggests that a strong bond to society has four main elements. The first of these is *attachment,* or significant links to specific other people. Those who have affection and respect for others take the welfare and feelings of these people into account, and so are inclined to act in a responsible way. Conversely, people who are unattached need not worry about putting their social relationships at risk, and are more likely to steal or to abuse drugs. The second element is *commitment,* or the "stake" that people have in society. The greater people's investment in their education, their careers, or their homes and other possessions, the more reason they have to conform so as to protect what they have achieved. Conversely, those who have little investment in society may see little risk in deviating—and perhaps a chance to benefit from doing so. The third element in the bond with society is *involvement,* or continued participation in nondeviant activities. Time and energy are limited, so a person who is generally busy—perhaps with a job, hobbies, or family life—has little opportunity to take part in deviant acts. Conversely, "idle hands do the devil's work": people who are unemployed or otherwise uninvolved in conventional activities have greater chances for deviance. The final element is *belief,* the individual's allegiance to the values and moral code of the group. If people firmly believe that certain deviant acts are wrong, participation in those acts becomes almost unthinkable to them. Conversely, those who have weak allegiance to the beliefs of the community may be more inclined to

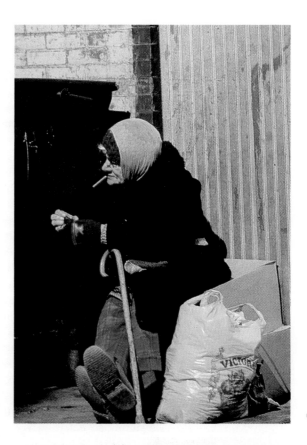

Figure 8.5 *According to control theory, people may become deviant if they have loose bonds with society and therefore experience weak social control. Urban "bag ladies," who live an isolated existence on city streets, may have originally fallen into this deviant way of life because they lacked strong bonds with others. In turn, their solitary lifestyle may make further deviance more likely.*

ignore its values and deviate from its norms. Hirschi concludes that a group whose members have strong mutual ties is better able to exert social control over their behavior than one whose members are not closely bonded together.

Evaluation

Control theory, like structural-strain theory, focuses on the social sources of deviance. It offers a plausible reason why some kinds of deviance are more likely to be present among certain types of people who lack close social bonds: consider, for example, the homeless "bag ladies" who live on big-city streets, carrying their possessions with them, or the hobos and drifters who ride freight cars on endless journeys around the country.

Those who join certain religious cults, too, are often young, unattached people who have recently left home and are in a new environment in which they have no strong bonds with others (which is why the cults often look for potential converts in airports and bus stations). Control theory seems particularly applicable to juvenile delinquency, since delinquency tends to occur at precisely the time when young people are loosening their bonds to their parents, and tapers off later as they begin to take steady jobs and to develop stable new relationships, particularly through marriage.

However, the theory runs into some problems. It cannot easily explain the extensive criminal, sexual, drug-related, and other deviance that occurs among respectable, high-status people who appear well integrated into society. Also, the theory does not help explain why people's deviance takes the various forms that it does—why, for example, one corporate executive might turn to cocaine, another to embezzlement. And control theory does not really come to grips with the possibility that some people have weak bonds with society because of their deviance, and not the other way around—that their behavior is so offensive that most people simply do not want very much to do with them.

Labeling Theory

Another theory confronts several of the problems that other explanations are unable to resolve. This is *labeling theory,* which explains deviance as a process by which some people successfully define others as deviant. This theory emphasizes the relativity of deviance, claiming that a person or act becomes deviant only when the "label" of deviance has been applied by other people. Accordingly, labeling theorists assert that the way in which people are labeled as deviant, not their acts, should be the focus of sociological attention. The theory draws heavily on the insights of the interactionist perspective for its understanding of the labeling process, and in recent years has also used aspects of conflict theory to explain why some people and behaviors rather than others are called deviant.

Early labeling theorists, notably Edwin Lemert (1951, 1967) and Howard Becker (1963b), point out that virtually everyone behaves in a deviant manner at some time or other. Most of this behavior falls into the category of *primary deviance*—nonconformity that is temporary, exploratory, triv-

ial, or easily concealed. The primary deviant may be a wealthy person who hides income from the tax collector, an overburdened parent who sometimes becomes hysterical, an adolescent who has a passing homosexual relationship with a friend, or a youth who tries an illicit drug "to see what it's like." This behavior may go unnoticed, and the individuals concerned do not regard themselves as deviants and are not regarded as such by others.

The situation changes markedly, however, if deviant acts are discovered and made public by significant other people—friends, parents, employers, school principals, or even the police and the courts. The offender is confronted by the evidence, often in a situation that Harold Garfinkel (1956) calls a "degradation ceremony." In this "ceremony" the person is accused of the deviant act, lectured to and perhaps punished, and forced to acknowledge the moral superiority of the accusers. Most important, the person is now labeled by others as a deviant—as a "nut," "whore," "queer," "weirdo," "crook," "dope addict." Other people begin to respond to the offender in terms of this label. As a result, the person consciously or unconsciously accepts the label, develops a new self-concept, and begins to behave accordingly. The label proves prophetic, and the deviance becomes habitual. The behavior now takes the form of *secondary deviance*—persistent nonconformity by a person who accepts the label of deviant. Often, in fact, the stigma that is applied to those now identified as deviants forces them into the company of other deviants, restricting their options, reinforcing their deviance, and thrusting them into a "deviant career," in which much of their behavior is interpreted by other people in the light of this single characteristic.

Evaluation

Labeling theory addresses the important question of why certain people and acts—rather than other people and different acts—are considered deviant. Many types of behavior, labeling theorists argue, become "deviant" because they offend *some* people's moral codes. Certain "moral entrepreneurs," such as religious groups or citizens' committees, try to arouse public opinion against behaviors they disapprove of, such as pornography, marijuana use, abortion, vagrancy, and the like. As Edwin Schur (1965, 1980) points out, the ensuing argument becomes a "stigma contest," a clash of competing moralities in which the winners declare themselves to be normal and moral and the losers

Figure 8.6

"Someone once labelled me a reactionary, and it stuck."

Drawing by Weber; © 1985
The New Yorker Magazine, Inc.

to be deviant and immoral. In general, the decision to stigmatize or even criminalize particular acts will depend on which of the contending groups has the most wealth, power, prestige, and other resources. For example, begging in the streets is considered deviant, but living in idleness off inherited wealth is not (Liazos, 1972; Lemert, 1974; Chambliss and Seidman, 1982).

Labeling theory can be used to explain the different social attitudes toward various forms of drug use. Consider that in the United States the two most dangerous and socially costly drugs are alcohol and tobacco, both of them potentially habit-forming and lethal. Alcohol is a factor in about 25,000 traffic deaths and about 10,000 homicides each year, and is implicated in thousands more deaths arising from such causes as liver damage and job accidents. Between 9 million and 12 million Americans are compulsive alcoholics, and the destructive effects of their addiction on family life, human relationships, and the economy are incalculable. Tobacco, a drug to which about 50 million Americans are addicted, kills around 340,000 people in the United States each year, mainly through such diseases as lung cancer and emphysema. In spite of these widely known facts, both alcohol and tobacco are publicly used in the most respectable circles; they are manufactured, marketed, and advertised by some of the largest and most powerful corporations in the land. On the

other hand, the use of marijuana, which is not physically addictive and has not been shown to directly cause any fatalities, is generally illegal, and around 365,000 Americans are arrested each year for possessing the drug. Although further research may yet disclose some adverse effects of marijuana, the scientific consensus is that it is far less dangerous to health than alcohol or tobacco.

How can the different social reactions toward drugs be explained? One reason is that alcohol and tobacco are "traditional" drugs, well entrenched in the culture. Another is that powerful economic interests benefit from their continued consumption. But Jock Young (1971) has suggested an additional reason: the social attitude toward a drug depends more on who uses it than on what its effects are. If the users of a drug are socially disapproved and negatively labeled, so is the drug. In the past, marijuana use was associated with such "disreputable" groups as jazz musicians, "hippies," and the rebellious young. The drug was made illegal, in fact, through the efforts of "moral entrepreneurs" in the federal drug-control bureaucracy, who were looking for a new cause after the repeal of Prohibition in 1933. Similar social processes can be seen in the reaction to other drugs and their users: barbiturates or amphetamines, for example, are approved if prescribed to respectable people who "need" them, but not if used by juveniles for "kicks."

Despite its broad usefulness, there are several objections to labeling theory. One is that empirical research has shown that in many cases, labeling is not an important influence on deviant behavior (Gove, 1980). For example, some habitual shoplifters or users of pornography might never have been discovered and labeled, yet many still behave in a consistently deviant way. However, this objection overlooks the possibility that some people may become secondary deviants by labeling *themselves* in terms of how they think others would see them. Another objection to the theory is that it ignores the fact that labeling may actually jolt the offender out of deviance altogether. Another problem with labeling theory is that it tends to encourage an indiscriminate sympathy for the "underdog" as the helpless victim of definitions arbitrarily imposed by the powerful. But not all inmates of a prison or an asylum are there simply because somebody chose to label them, although labeling was certainly part of the process that put them there. Some deviant acts are so socially disruptive that society must impose severe sanctions if social order is to be maintained, and the extreme relativism of labeling theory sometimes obscures this fact.

It is doubtful whether any single theory could account for behavior as diverse as drug addiction, compulsive gambling, child molestation, religious heresy, juvenile delinquency, or insurance fraud. Taken together, however, the four theories do show how deviant behavior occurs as a result of social processes, though each focuses on a different aspect of the phenomenon. We turn now to an examination of crime, one of the most widespread forms of deviance in American society today.

Crime

A *crime* is an act that contravenes a law. Political authorities are likely to make behavior illegal if it meets two conditions: first, it must be considered too socially disruptive to be permitted, and second, it must be difficult to control through informal sanctions alone. By formally declaring certain acts to be crimes, political authorities can ensure that the social reaction to them takes place in an orderly and predictable way. Thus, the law defines the exact nature of the offense, indicates who is prohibited from performing it, and specifies the formal, negative sanctions that may be applied to the offender.

Like all forms of deviance, crime is a relative matter. In medieval Iceland it was illegal to write verses of more than a certain length about another person; in the Soviet Union it has long been illegal to form a new political party; in South Africa it is illegal for a black student to attend a "white" college without a government permit. Although certain acts, such as murder, are regarded as criminal in all societies, each society defines these crimes in different ways. What may be murder in one society is regarded as a justifiable and even praiseworthy act in another. People in every society tend to regard the difference between criminal and non-criminal behavior as absolute, but these distinctions merely reflect the cultural assumptions of the time and place in question.

Types of Crime

The main types of crime in the United States can be conveniently classified into four principal categories: crimes of violence; crimes against property; crimes without victims; and white-collar and corporate crime. Our information about crime comes primarily from the annual reports of the Federal Bureau of Investigation (FBI), which compiles data provided by local police forces. The FBI regards crimes of violence and crimes against property as the most serious offenses. These acts—homicide, robbery, rape, aggravated assault, burglary, larceny, auto theft, and arson—are known as the eight "crime index" offenses, and the FBI reports concentrate on them.

Crimes of Violence

Crimes of violence are the ones that Americans fear the most. FBI statistics for 1986 show that, on average, a violent crime reportedly occurred in the United States every 24 seconds: a murder every 28 minutes, a forcible rape every 6 minutes, a robbery every 63 seconds, and an aggravated assault every 44 seconds. The rate of violent crime almost doubled during the 1970s, declined somewhat in the early 1980s, and rose slightly in the mid-1980s. Violent crime represents only a minuscule proportion of crimes as a whole, but this is small consolation to its victims.

The fear of violent crime is heightened by anxiety about being attacked—and particularly, murdered—by a complete stranger. Actually, most people who are murdered are already acquainted with the attacker. Some 57 percent of murders, in fact, are committed by a relative or acquaintance of the victim, usually in the context of a heated argument or a sexual triangle. Only 18 percent of murders occur in the course of "street" crimes—robbery, burglary, and other crimes directed against persons and property. A striking feature of American homicide is that a person's prospects of becoming a murder victim vary a great deal according to race and sex. Although blacks constitute about 12 percent of the population, they represent 45 percent of murder victims—and 94 percent of these are slain by other blacks. Whites, in contrast, are killed by whites in nearly 90 percent of the cases.

The high involvement of American blacks in homicide results primarily from the profound social disaster—involving broken families, drug abuse, poor education, and unemployment—that has afflicted a small segment of black youth in the ghetto "underclass." Much of this black-on-black homicide appears random, mindless, wantonly malign, psychopathic: the reasons offered by the perpetrators often run along the lines of "He stepped on my foot," or "He took my coat." Murder of this kind is committed by people who feel that, even if they lose their own lives, they are not losing

Street Criminals—Born or Bred?

The notion that, one way or another, "criminals are born" has a certain appeal, for it offers a simple answer to a complex problem. Not too surprisingly, many attempts have been made over the years to explain crime in terms of biological factors.

In the early twentieth century, it was widely assumed that criminals suffered from "moral insanity" or some other form of inherited degeneracy. In 1911, for example, the Italian criminologist Cesare Lombroso declared that criminals typically had such features as shifty eyes, receding hairlines, strong jaws, and red hair—apparently the results of an "evolutionary throwback" that produced "ferocious instincts" and "an irresistible craving for evil." Research soon showed, however, that these physical features did not appear any more frequently in criminals than in the general population.

Biological theories of crime have reappeared periodically since Lombroso's time. In the 1940s and 1950s William Sheldon and his associates reported that juvenile delinquents in Boston seemed disproportionately likely to have a muscular, agile build—which presumably facilitated their involvement in such activities as gang fights, burglaries, or muggings. This finding caused some interest—until further research showed that there was nothing particularly distinctive about the delinquents' typical body types. Then, in the 1960s, attention switched to genetic abnormalities that were found in a few violent criminals: unlike normal males, who have an X and a Y chromosome, these criminals had an extra Y chromosome, giving them the combination XYY. Researchers investigated this possible genetic factor, only to find that the apparent link was a coincidence: there is no consistent association between the extra chromosome and criminality.

The question of biological influences on crime receded for a while, but emerged again in 1985 when James Q. Wilson and Richard Herrnstein argued in *Crime and Human Nature* that inborn factors may predispose some people toward "street" crime—acts of violence and theft directed against people and property. On the basis of their review of the literature on crime, Wilson and Herrnstein claim that these offenders often have two traits that are known to be partly inherited: low intelligence and a squarish, muscular body. How could these traits be linked to crime? Low intelligence, Wilson and Herrnstein suggest, might cause failure and frustration in school, while making it difficult for the individual to conceptualize the sanctions against crime. And muscular build might encourage the person to envisage criminal acts, such as beating up and robbing people. If social circumstances were also unfavorable, the strongly built dullard might turn to street crime.

This analysis seemed plausible, and it caused a mild stir when it was published. But critics like Leon Kamin and Steven Rose soon argued that Wilson and Herrnstein had repeatedly made the elementary mistake of assuming that correlations between physique and crime implied cause-and-effect, and that they had ignored data that did not fit their theory. For example, research has shown that the squarish, muscular body type supposedly typical of young street criminals was even more typical in samples of bus drivers, California children, army recruits, and Princeton students! Actually, the evidence is that body type and intelligence (or any other partially inherited traits) usually do *not* lead to crime: the vast majority of people of muscular build and low intelligence are as law-abiding as anyone else. Conversely, many people who have other body types and high intelligence commit a variety of crimes, including street crime. And of course biological explanations tell us nothing about other crimes—like fraud or embezzlement—that may be committed by people of average or above-average intelligence, or of a different body type. Crime is a social phenomenon, not a biological one, and it has to be explained accordingly.

SOURCES: Cesare Lombroso, *Crime: Its Causes and Remedies* (Boston: Little, Brown, 1911); William H. Sheldon et al., *Varieties of Delinquent Youth* (New York: Harper and Row, 1949); Sheldon Glueck and Eleanor Glueck, *Physique and Delinquency* (New York: Harper and Row, 1956); Ian Taylor et al., *The New Criminology* (London: Routledge and Kegan Paul, 1973); James Q. Wilson and Richard Herrnstein, *Crime and Human Nature* (New York: Simon and Schuster, 1985); Leon J. Kamin, "Is Crime in the Genes? The Answer May Depend on Who Chooses What Evidence," *Scientific American*, February 1986, pp. 22–27; Steven Rose, "Stalking the Criminal Chromosome," *The Nation*, 242:50, 732–736, 1986.

much; who see no reason to adopt society's values, for society offers them nothing; who get no nearer to affluence or success than what they see on their TV set; whose repressed rage and even self-hate erupts against those around them (Silberman, 1978; Meredith, 1984).

In international terms, the United States is an extremely violent society, with a homicide rate far exceeding that of any other industrialized nation. A single American city like Chicago, Houston, or Los Angeles records more murders in a typical year than does the whole of England, where even the

Figure 8.7 *An American's chances of being murdered are strongly influenced by social characteristics. According to FBI calculations, a white female has a 1-in-606 lifetime chance of becoming a murder victim; a white male has a 1-in-186 chance; a black female has a 1-in-124 chance; and a black male has a 1-in-29 chance.*

police do not normally carry guns. Most other countries severely restrict private handgun ownership, but there are at least 60 million handguns in the United States—and weapons of this type are used in 44 percent of the 19,000 or so murders that occur each year. In 1980, the American handgun homicide rate was 77 times the average rate for England, Japan, Sweden, Switzerland, Australia, Israel, and Canada combined (Shields, 1981; Anderson, 1985). Why, then, does the United States permit such widespread access to handguns? One reason is the persistent belief that, since criminals have guns, law-abiding people need them for self-protection. Actually, gun-owning households are much more likely to suffer fatalities from their own weapons than from those of outsiders. One study found that only 2 percent of all slayings in gun-owning households were for self-protection; the remainder were suicides, homicides, or accidental deaths, almost all involving family members, friends, or acquaintances (Kellerman, 1986). A second reason for the proliferation of handguns is the belief, deeply held by many Americans, that gun ownership is an individual right. For granting this liberty to the individual, American society pays the price in the deviance of those who abuse it.

Crimes Against Property

Crimes against property are those offenses in which the criminal steals or damages something that belongs to someone else. These crimes are far more common than those involving violence: on average, one occurs every 3 seconds. The main forms of this offense are burglary, which involves an unlawful entry to commit a theft or other serious crime (one every 10 seconds); larceny, or theft (one every 5 seconds); motor-vehicle theft (one every 29 seconds); and arson, or maliciously setting fire to property. The FBI began to keep detailed statistics on arson only in 1979. Over 100,000 cases were reported in 1986, but since arson is a difficult crime to prove, the total number of cases is undoubtedly much higher. Although vandalism and revenge are frequently the motives behind this crime, insurance fraud is probably its most common cause.

Like the rate for violent crime, the property-crime rate rose sharply in the 1970s (by over one-third) but declined in the early 1980s before rising slightly in the mid-1980s. The main reason for the rapid earlier rise and subsequent leveling in the violent- and property-crime rate lies in changes in the average age of the population. More than half of those arrested for violent crimes, and two-thirds of those arrested for property crimes, are between the ages of sixteen and twenty-five. Any increase or decrease in the proportion of this age group in the total population, therefore, affects the crime rate—which is what has happened over the past couple of decades. As the large "baby boom" generation—born in the period from about 1946 to 1964—passed through its youthful years, crime rates rose sharply. When this huge generation entered adulthood, the proportion of youth in the general population shrank and the crime rate dropped—a trend that sociologists predicted years ago.

The slight upturn in crime rates since the mid-1980s was not expected, however. The causes of this trend are not yet clear, but another form of deviance, drug addiction, is certainly a significant factor. One reason is that hundreds of thousands of addicts have to find large sums of money to support their habits, and they frequently turn to crime to do so. A study of 354 Baltimore heroin addicts found that they had committed more than 775,000 crimes during a nine-year period (Ball et al., 1981). A second reason for the involvement of drugs in crime is that social control tends to fail over people who are under the influence of mind-altering chemicals. The National Institute of Justice (1986)

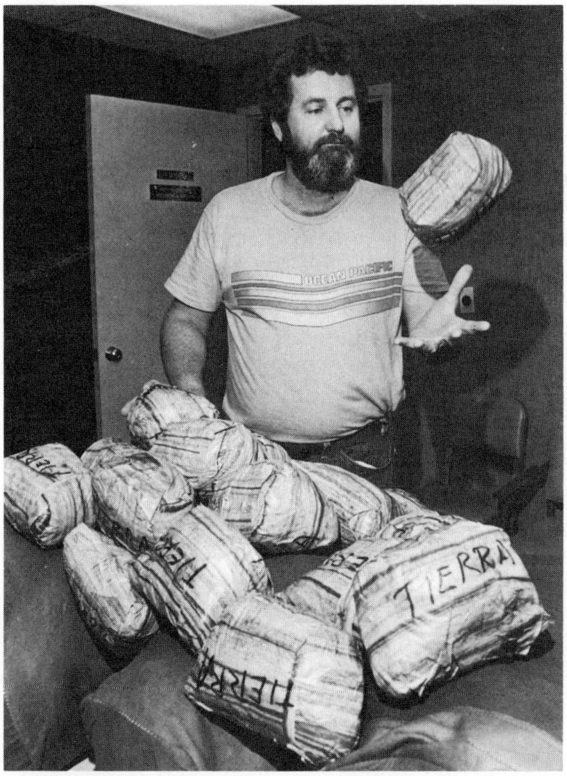

Figure 8.8 *Drugs are deeply involved in crime in several ways: users sometimes commit crimes while under the influence of drugs; addicts often commit crimes in order to pay for their drug habits; and suppliers commit crimes in the course of smuggling and distributing the drugs. This photo shows a 400-pound cocaine bust in Florida.*

reported that 56 percent of suspects arrested for serious crimes in New York City and Washington, D.C., over a two-year period had been using at least one of five drugs within the previous two days. (The drugs were cocaine, PCP, heroin, methadone, and amphetamines; no test was made for alcohol or marijuana.)

Crimes Without Victims

There is an entire category of offenses from which nobody usually suffers *directly*, except perhaps the offenders themselves. These are the victimless crimes, such as gambling, prostitution, vagrancy, illicit drug use, prohibited sexual acts between consenting adults, and the like. Well over a third of all arrests each year involve offenses of this kind. The 1986 FBI report shows that there were over 960,000 arrests for public drunkenness and about

33,000 for vagrancy, 32,000 for illegal gambling, 113,000 for prostitution, 81,000 for curfew violations and loitering, and 811,000 for various drug offenses.

Victimless crime is notoriously difficult to control. One reason, of course, is that there is no aggrieved victim to bring a charge, or to give evidence, against the offender. Another reason is that the offenders often regard the laws, not themselves, as immoral: although they may be lawabiding in other respects, they feel no guilt at committing an offense such as gambling or a prohibited sexual act. The fact that such behavior is illegal presents two additional problems. First, the prosecution of these petty offenders consumes an enormous amount of police effort and clogs the jails and the courts, at a time when the system can scarcely cope with more serious offenders. Second, the illegal nature of these pursuits stimulates the activities of organized crime, which, ever since Prohibition, has depended for its existence on supplying illegal goods and services, such as narcotics and gambling, to others who are willing to pay for them. Indeed, the President's Commission on Organized Crime (1986) reported that organized crime is now a $100-billion-a-year enterprise—comparable in size to the American steel or textile industry.

The most notorious group in organized crime, of course, is the Mafia—also known as Cosa Nostra, the Syndicate, or the Mob—which has Sicilian origins and which has long been involved in such activities as gambling, drug smuggling, and prostitution. More recently, Chinese organized crime, based on ancient secret groups known as Triads, has penetrated the United States; it is now responsible for much of the heroin trade from Southeast Asia. Colombian organized crime, too, has begun to play an important part in drug smuggling and distribution, particularly in the lucrative cocaine trade.

White-Collar and Corporate Crime

The phrase "white-collar crime" refers to all the crimes typically committed by high-status people, such as tax evasion, toxic pollution, copyright infringement, stock manipulation, price fixing, corruption of public officials, embezzlement, and fraud. Much of this crime takes place in the context of corporate activities. Even though individual corporate officers are involved in these offenses, fines and other sanctions are often directed instead at the corporation itself, for a corporation is, for most legal purposes, a "person." Additionally, many white-collar offenses escape prosecution because they are dealt with through regulatory agencies (such as the Securities and Exchange Commission, which scrutinizes the stock market) rather than through the criminal courts.

White-collar and corporate crime is generally regarded with more tolerance than other forms of crime, yet its economic impact is much greater. The U.S. Department of Justice estimates that this type of crime costs about $200 billion a year—about eighteen times the cost of street crime. These costs involve inflated prices, poisoned air and water, lost tax revenue, hazardous products, and the like. And this crime is by no means rare: studies have shown that about half of the leading 500 corporations have been convicted in recent years of at least one major crime or other serious misbehavior (Clinard and Yeager, 1980; Ermann and Lundman, 1982; Simon and Eitzen, 1986; Coleman, 1985). In 1985 alone, some 27 major oil companies agreed to repay over $630 million in illegal customer overcharges; several leading banks were charged with illegal money-laundering; a major brokerage house was convicted of defrauding hundreds of banks; and some 45 of the largest 100 military contractors were under criminal investigation for fraud. (Corporations are discussed in more detail in Chapter 17, "The Economic Order.")

The fact that this form of crime is so prevalent, even at the highest levels of society, raises serious doubts about traditional notions of criminals and

Figure 8.9

"In examining our books, Mr. Mathews promises to use generally accepted accounting principles, if you know what I mean."

Drawing by Wm. Hamilton; © 1972
The New Yorker Magazine, Inc.

crime. It may well be that "poverty breeds crime" by giving low-status people an incentive to steal and rob, but it seems that greed can just as easily breed crime in high-status people as well. In fact, there is not the slightest evidence that criminal behavior is any more common at the lower level of society than at any other. It seems, rather, that people of different statuses have different opportunities to commit various crimes. The criminal poor are hardly in a position to embezzle trust funds or manipulate the price of stocks, so they resort to high-risk, low-yield crimes such as larceny and burglary. The criminal nonpoor have no need to hold up gas stations or snatch purses, so they resort to low-risk, high-yield crimes such as tax evasion and computer fraud.

Who Are the Criminals?

At first sight it seems easy enough to establish who the criminals are: we need only look at the statistics published each year by the FBI in its *Uniform Crime Reports.* The 1986 report tells us that 50 percent of all persons arrested were under twenty-five, that males were four times more likely than females to be arrested, that persons arrested were much more likely to live in large cities than in small towns or rural areas, and that they were disproportionately likely to be black—in fact, blacks constituted 12 percent of the total population, but 29 percent of all arrestees.

Unfortunately, the official statistics may not give an accurate picture of society's "criminal element." One problem is that a great deal of crime is not reported at all, even if it is detected: Justice Department surveys indicate that the actual crime rate is about three times as high as the reported rate. A second problem is that the FBI presents data on only twenty-nine categories of crime and concentrates on the eight "crime index" offenses. White-collar crimes are hardly mentioned in the reports—although the inclusion of statistics on these crimes would substantially alter our picture of the "typical" criminal, who would become significantly whiter, older, more suburban, and more "respectable."

Most significant, the crime statistics exclude the largest group of criminals—those who escape detection. And the disconcerting fact is that this category includes virtually all of us. This does not mean, of course, that there are not important differences between people who are habitually law-abiding and people who are habitually criminal, or between people who commit minor crimes and people who commit serious ones. But a large number of self-report studies, in which people were asked to give anonymous details of any crimes they had committed, indicate that close to 100 percent of Americans have committed some kind of illegal offense (Doleschal and Klapmuts, 1973). These studies have a disturbing implication for our traditional distinctions between criminal and law-abiding citizens. The "typical" criminal is not the typical criminal at all but rather the one who typically gets arrested, prosecuted, and convicted. The tiny proportion of offenders who actually experience formal negative sanctions are the product of a long process of social selection.

Selecting the Criminal

There are several stages in the process of selecting the criminal. Only a proportion of crimes are detected, only a proportion of those detected are reported to the police, only a proportion of those reported lead to an arrest, only a proportion of arrests lead to prosecution, only a proportion of prosecutions lead to conviction, and only a proportion of convictions lead to imprisonment. The chances of going from one stage to the next depend largely on two factors: the seriousness of the offense, and the social status of the offender (Hazel et al., 1980; Reiman, 1984).

The crimes that go either undetected or unreported are predominantly petty crimes against property and "white-collar" offenses such as inflated insurance claims or tax evasion. When a crime is actually detected, the social status of the offender, all other things being equal, appears to be the determinant of whether an arrest and prosecution will follow. This tendency is especially apparent in the treatment of juvenile offenders. The great majority of juveniles in the arrest statistics are lower-class males, but this does not necessarily mean they commit most delinquent acts—only that they are more likely to be arrested. Self-report studies of juveniles, in which the subjects anonymously admit any illegal offenses they may have committed, have found little or no relationship between delinquent behavior and social class (Doleschal and Klapmuts, 1973; Tittle et al., 1978).

Why, then, are lower-class youths more likely to be selected for arrest? Two classic studies suggest an answer. Irvin Piliavan and Scott Briar (1964) spent nine months riding in police cars of the juvenile bureau of a West Coast police department. They found that more than 90 percent of the incidents that came to police attention were very

CRIMES CLEARED BY ARREST

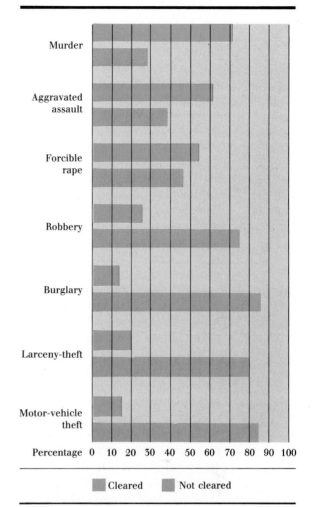

SOURCE: *Crime in the United States: Uniform Crime Reports* (Washington, D.C.: U.S. Government Printing Office, 1986), p. 155.

Figure 8.10 *On the whole, the police are not very successful at solving crimes: of all the serious offenses shown in this chart, only homicide, aggravated assault, and forcible rape result in an arrest in the majority of cases. The arrest rate for other crimes, such as white-collar offenses, is very much lower. Moreover, not all those arrested are actually prosecuted. The process of selecting the criminal continues in the courts, where some defendants are found guilty of lesser crimes or are acquitted. Of those convicted, only a minority are eventually imprisoned.*

minor. In these cases the police were reluctant to take official action unless they felt that the offender had a basically "bad character." In making this assessment the police were guided by such cues as race, dress, and demeanor. Of those who were polite, contrite, and cooperative, less than 5 percent were arrested; but of those who were defiant, nonchalant, and uncooperative, fully two-thirds were arrested. William Chambliss (1973) studied two teenage gangs in the same town, a lower-class gang he called the "Roughnecks" and a middle-class gang he called the "Saints." The Saints committed far more delinquent acts than the Roughnecks, but it was the Roughnecks, who were perceived and labeled by the community as delinquents, who were constantly in trouble. (Chambliss's analysis, "The Saints and the Roughnecks," appears as the reading at the end of this chapter.)

The process of selecting the adult criminal is especially apparent once the offender appears in court. Although every accused person has the right to counsel, to a jury trial, and to appeal to higher courts, the system does not work quite this way in practice. Many people cannot afford bail and may spend weeks or months in jail awaiting trial. Actual courtroom procedure rarely follows the stylized confrontations seen in TV dramas. Over 90 percent of the people who appear in lower courts plead guilty and are sentenced on the spot—usually after an unofficial "plea-bargaining" in which the accused agrees to plead guilty in return for a reduced sentence. Poor people, who cannot afford their own lawyers, are frequently urged to plead guilty by overworked public defenders. People who demand a jury trial and are eventually convicted tend to receive a more severe sentence than those who plead guilty: in effect, they are punished for wasting the court's time.

In comparison with their counterparts in other countries, American judges have exceptional discretion in determining the severity of the sentence, and there is strong evidence that the race and social class of the offender influence judicial decisions. In one experiment, three dozen judges were given fact sheets on hypothetical cases and asked to determine an appropriate sentence. The sheets contained the following basic information:

> "Joe Cut," 27, pleads guilty to battery. He slashed his common-law wife on the arms with a switchblade. His record showed convictions for disturbing the peace, drunkenness, and hit-and-run driving. He told a probation officer that he acted in self-defense after his wife attacked him with a broom handle. The prosecutor recommended not more than five days in jail or a $100 fine.

On half of the fact sheets, however, "Joe Cut" was described as white and on the other half as black. The judges who thought he was white gave him sentences of three to ten days, while those who thought he was black gave him sentences of five to thirty days (D. Jackson, 1974).

Judges also tend to take the social status of a convicted criminal into account before passing sentence, frequently reasoning that a higher-status offender has "already suffered" through damage to reputation and perhaps loss of employment. Although around 70 percent of people convicted of crime-index offenses go to prison, about 60 percent of white-collar criminals receive no jail terms, and of those who are jailed, the great majority serve one year or less. In part this discrepancy reflects the greater public fear of, and outrage at, crimes that are physically directed toward individuals or their property. But in part it also reflects the greater ability of high-status people to evade the full impact of the law.

Corrections

Corrections are the sanctions and other measures that society applies to convicted criminals—in the United States, primarily imprisonment, probation, and parole. Ideally, corrections serve several distinct purposes:

1. *Retribution.* Corrections serve to punish the offender, applying revenge on behalf of both the victim and society as a whole.

2. *Deterrence.* Through punishment, corrections serve both to deter the offender from deviating again, and to scare others who might be tempted into crime.

3. *Incapacitation.* By imposing restrictions on the freedom of the offender, corrections help prevent that person from committing further crimes, at least for the duration of the restrictions.

4. *Rehabilitation.* Corrections may serve to reform the offender by providing the skills and attitudes that make return to a law-abiding life possible and more attractive.

For most adults convicted of the serious crime-index offenses, corrections are likely to include imprisonment. This was not always the case, for prisons are a relatively recent innovation. Until two centuries ago, convicts were more likely to be executed, tortured, deported, or exposed to public ridicule in the stocks. Originally, imprisonment was intended to provide the convict with the opportunity for solitary reflection and thus for peni-

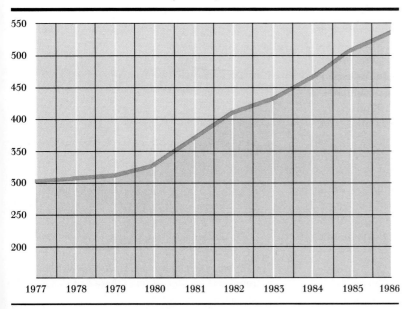

U.S. PRISON POPULATION
Number of inmates, in thousands

SOURCE: U.S. Department of Justice, 1986.

Figure 8.11 *The United States prison population has increased rapidly in recent years, and has grown much faster than the population as a whole. In 1977, 132 of every 100,000 Americans were in prison, but the rate rose to 210 of every 100,000 in 1986.*

tence and rehabilitation, but this goal has certainly not been achieved in practice. In fact, the rate of ***recidivism,*** or repeated crime by those who have been convicted before, seems alarmingly high. Nearly three-quarters of all offenders released after serving prison time are rearrested within four years—sometimes for the same crimes. Since other released prisoners presumably also return to crime but are not arrested, the actual crime rate among released convicts is even greater.

Clearly, prisons fail to rehabilitate. One reason, no doubt, is that relatively few resources are devoted to rehabilitation in the first place. A major reason, however, lies in the very nature of a prison, in which the authorities' custodial duties take priority over all other goals. As we noted in Chapter 5 ("Socialization"), a prison is organized as what Erving Goffman (1961) called a ***total institution***—a place of residence where the inmates are confined for a set period of their lives, where they are cut off from the rest of society, and where they surrender personal control of their lives, submitting instead to the almost absolute rule of a hierarchy of officials. Goffman argued that the very nature of a total institution aggravates the existing problems of the inmates, and in the long run can leave them incapable of assuming normal social responsibilities. Additionally, the prison environment guarantees differential associ-

ation with other criminals—so the inmates can scarcely fail to learn about new techniques and possibilities for crime. Imprisonment may thus lead to further crime, not rehabilitation.

Imprisonment rates have been increasing sharply in the United States in recent years: nearly 529,000 Americans were in prison in 1986, a record rate of about 210 per 10,000 people. More than 95 percent of inmates are male, and most have been in prison before. In international terms, the United States has an exceptionally high imprisonment rate, exceeded by only two other countries in the world—South Africa (which imprisons huge numbers of blacks as part of its apartheid policy) and the Soviet Union (which routinely imprisons people for minor offenses that might be overlooked or treated more leniently elsewhere).

The vast majority of the 2.4 million convicted offenders undergoing corrections in the United States are not imprisoned: they are on probation or parole. Probation is a supervised period in which offenders are required to hold a job and commit no further offense, after which their case is closed; parole is a partial reduction of a prison sentence, given conditionally to convicts who have behaved well in prison. (As of 1988, federal prisoners—a small minority of all prisoners—cannot receive parole, and federal judges will thereafter have less discretion in sentencing.) Few people believe that imprisonment does the offender any good; rather, it is used as a last-resort means of punishing criminals and protecting society from them (Currie, 1986). Several observers argue that society should waste little energy on imprisoning petty offenders, for whom other forms of correction—like probation or community service—might be more appropriate, and should concentrate instead on incapacitating dangerous and persistent offenders by locking them up—if necessary, for very long periods indeed (Moore et al., 1985). The great bulk of the street crimes that the public most fears are committed by a very small minority of repeat offenders, who can sometimes be identified quite early in their careers. About 7 percent of youngsters, for example, are responsible for about 70 percent of juvenile offenses (Tracey, Wolfgang, and Figlio, 1985).

Incidentally, the fact that so many criminals are repeatedly rearrested does not necessarily mean that prison fails to deter people from crime: it certainly fails to deter *these* individuals, but the example of their fate no doubt provides a strong enough warning to deter most other people. As Jack Gibbs (1975) points out, the best deterrence is not necessarily the most severe punishment; rather, it is punishment that is *swift* and *certain*. If punishment follows soon after the crime, and if there is little doubt that it will follow, the crime rate will be low; but if people think they may escape punishment indefinitely, then the sanctions will have much less deterrent effect. (See the box on the death penalty on the next page.)

Crime: A Conflict View

The conflict perspective draws attention to the competing interests of the deviants and their accusers. Like labeling theory, which it influenced, the conflict perspective asks, Exactly whose "law and order" do legal sanctions uphold? Extending Karl Marx's contention that the state supports the powerful against the weak, the rich against the poor, and the rulers against the ruled, some conflict theorists argue that a great deal of "crime" is merely behavior that powerful groups consider a threat to their position or interests (Quinney, 1979, 1980; Chambliss and Seidman, 1982).

Conflict theorists advance a good deal of evidence to support this general view. In the early United States, for example, the law was used to deprive the Indians of their rights and lands. The legal system also upheld slavery, and later enforced racial segregation. During the 1920s and

Figure 8.12

"There's no justice in the world, Kirkby, but I'm not convinced that this is an entirely bad thing."

Drawing by Handelsman; ©1986
The New Yorker Magazine, Inc.

1930s, labor unions were treated as criminal conspiracies, and employers could call on the police and courts to break workers' strikes. In the 1960s, during the Vietnam war, antiwar groups were systematically infiltrated and harassed by law-enforcement agencies. Conflict theorists see such outcomes as inevitable, for the laws tend to reflect the interests of the powerful and affluent rather than the powerless and poor. For that reason, the legal penalties for theft may be more severe than the penalties for, say, the failure of slum landlords to provide heat for their tenants in winter: those in power have more to lose from theft than the poor, and are less likely to live in unheated rental dwellings.

Conflict theorists also focus on how crimes against people and property, which are mostly committed by low-status people, are often punished with prison sentences, while crimes by people of higher status, such as embezzlement or fraud, tend to be treated more leniently (Reiman, 1984). Consider the case of tax evasion, which is primarily a crime of high-income people. According to Internal Revenue Service estimates, about $200 billion of taxable income went unreported in 1984. This is a great deal of money—the equivalent of the much deplored federal deficit of that year.

The Death Penalty

A handful of murderers in the United States receive society's ultimate negative sanction: execution. The Supreme Court struck down the death penalty in 1972, but reinstated it in 1976 on condition that judges and juries consider aggravating and mitigating circumstances. Executions began again the following year, and today some thirty-nine states have laws providing for the death penalty. Eighteen of these states permit execution by electrocution, thirteen by lethal injection, eight by gas, four by hanging, and four by firing squad.

By 1986 there were over 1,700 inmates under sentence of death. Their number is increasing steadily; the courts sentence about 150 people to die each year, while overturning about 50 existing death sentences. The total number of executions has thus far been relatively low—about two dozen a year—but may increase rapidly over the next decade as a large backlog of appeals is finally dealt with. More than thirty people on death row in 1986 were juveniles at the time of their crime; three of them were fifteen when the offense was committed. Sixteen states permit executions of juveniles, with age limits ranging from seventeen to ten years of age (in Indiana), and eleven states have no age limit at all.

The usefulness and morality of the death sentence are controversial, particularly because the United States is virtually the only Western democracy that allows executions. A principal argument for the death penalty is that it will deter murder—but what is the evidence for this view? Although people on both sides of the debate have wrenched the statistics this way and that in support of their claims, there does not appear to be any consistent difference in homicide rates between states with the death penalty and otherwise similar states without it. And if the death penalty alone deterred murder, there would be hardly any homicide in the United States, which has the death penalty, and a great deal of homicide among other industrialized nations, which do not. Yet the reverse is true: the American homicide rate is by far the highest in the industrialized world.

It seems, then, that the fear of death frequently fails to act as a powerful deterrent—but why? There appear to be two main reasons. The first is that homicide, unlike most other crimes, is rarely premeditated: it usually occurs in the heat of the moment—in such situations as family arguments or bungled robberies—when the perpetrator is least likely to think about the possible consequences. In the few cases where murder is premeditated, on the other hand, the offender obviously does not expect to get caught or punished anyway. (In many cases this expectation is borne out: about a quarter of murders do not lead to any arrest, and many arrests do not lead to conviction.)

The second reason the death penalty often fails to deter is that, as presently applied, no punishment is less swift or less certain. A death sentence is never carried out immediately: to minimize the chance of an innocent person being executed, courts permit an elaborate review process that sometimes lasts a decade or more. And far from being a certain punishment for murder, the death sentence is almost certain *not* to be given or applied. Only about 5 percent of convicted murderers arrive on death row, and many of them will never be executed. Most convicted murderers are sentenced to "life" imprisonment—but a 1986 Bureau of Justice Statistics survey found that more than half of them serve less than seven years behind bars.

Who are the unlucky few who do get sentenced to death or even executed? Several factors affect the selection process. One is the specific state: 90 percent of all executions since 1976 have taken place in the South, and 75 percent have occurred in just four states—Florida, Texas, Georgia, and Lousiana. Another factor is the ability to afford a skilled lawyer: more than 90 percent of death-row inmates were so poor that they had to rely on court-appointed defenders. Another factor is the race of the homicide victim: people are four times more likely to die for murdering a white as for murdering a black—in fact, 96 percent of those on death row killed whites—and about 70 percent of the blacks awaiting execution murdered a white person.

All in all, risking the death penalty is a gamble in which the odds strongly favor the killer. In theory, of course, it would be possible to make death the swift and certain punishment for homicide—but that could involve the specter of about fifty executions in the United States every day of the year, something without parallel or precedent in a civilized society.

Decisions about capital punishment, then, are not really about deterrence. They are about retribution—about society's revenge on a person who takes another's life. Whether such retribution is justified is not a matter of measurable *facts;* it is a moral *judgment* for each individual to make. Some people feel that those who kill another human being should pay the supreme penalty and forfeit their own lives; others feel that human life is so sacred that society is demeaned when the state kills its citizens, however grave their offense. In any event, a large and increasing majority of Americans—some 75 percent in a 1985 Gallup poll—favor the death penalty.

SOURCES: Ernest van den Haag and John P. Conrad (eds.), *The Death Penalty: A Debate* (New York: Plenum, 1985); James A. Yunker, "The Relevance of the Identification Problem to Statistical Research on Capital Punishment," *Crime and Delinquency,* 28, 96–124, 1982; Isaac Ehrlich, "The Deterrent Effect of Capital Punishment: A Question of Life and Death," *American Economic Review,* 65, 397–417, 1975; Richard M. McGahey, "Dr. Ehrlich's Magic Bullet: Econometric Theory, Econometrics, and the Death Penalty," *Crime and Delinquency,* 26, 485–502, 1980; Thorstein Sellin, *The Penalty of Death* (Beverly Hills, Calif.: Sage, 1980).

Figure 8.13 *During the Vietnam war, several Buddhist monks burned themselves to death in public as a dramatic form of political protest. This behavior is an example of principled deviance— acts done for a moral cause rather than for personal gratification.*

We might expect, therefore, that hundreds of thousands of tax dodgers would be hauled before the courts to receive severe sanctions. Yet the total number of people sentenced for tax fraud in 1984 was 1,854, of whom 1,149 were sentenced to prison, for an average term of two years. This works out, incidentally, to about one prison sentence for every $174 million of tax evasion in that year. In the same year, in contrast, some 1,291,700 people were arrested for larceny—the kinds of nonviolent stealing typically committed by lower-status people, such as shoplifting. Similarly, there is great concern about food-stamp fraud by poor people; New York State alone prosecutes about as many people for this offense as the federal government prosecutes tax evaders. But there is virtually no concern about pervasive mealtime fraud by executives who routinely dine with friends at expensive restaurants and deduct most of the costs from personal or corporate taxes as a business expense—a crime of fraud that is almost never prosecuted, even though it is probably one of the commonest in America.

Conflict theory also draws attention to "principled deviance"—socially disapproved acts that people commit out of moral conviction rather than in pursuit of personal goals. The outstanding examples of such deviance are political crimes, ranging from illegal demonstrations and draft evasion to sedition, sabotage, treason, and revolution. The people who do these things are not "typical" criminals; they include activists as different as George Washington and Fidel Castro. In many countries around the world, ranging from totalitarian communist societies to right-wing dictatorships, such people are often imprisoned or even tortured for their opposition to the status quo (Turk, 1982). This principled deviance and the conflict it creates can play an important part in social change—for what is deviant today can be conformist tomorrow. Anyone who sets out to change the existing norms risks being branded as a deviant, but the changes may be necessary and may not come about unless people are prepared to take this risk.

Not all deviance, of course, is simply a matter of the interests of the powerful taking precedence over those of the weak. Laws against crimes of violence, such as homicide and armed robbery, are intended to protect rich and poor alike—indeed, the poor are the primary victims of such offenses. The conflict approach is helpful because it shows how controversial questions of conformity or deviance may be influenced by the relative resources of the contending groups, and how deviance can sometimes provide the thrust for social change (Schur, 1980).

Mental Disorder

Another important form of deviance is *mental disorder,* the psychological inability to cope realistically and effectively with the ordinary challenges of life. Mentally disordered people violate social norms concerning reality, for their behavior can range from irrational depression to delusions, hallucinations, and fractured forms of thought and speech. The behavior of such people may be unpredictable, incomprehensible, or even frightening to others, making mutual social interaction difficult or even impossible. Consequently, mental disorder attracts the stigma of deviance—a stigma that may linger even if the deviant should return to normality.

How common is mental disorder in the United States? According to a 1985 report by the National Institutes of Mental Health, some 29 million Americans, or about one adult in five, suffer from such mental problems as severe anxiety and depression, although few of these people try to get professional help. These statistics are open to some question, however, for there is wide disagreement on exactly what constitutes mental disorder. Behavior that might seem disturbed in one context (like talking to oneself, or losing one's temper) might appear acceptable or understandable in another. To complicate matters, most mental disorders have no known physical cause or definitive symptoms. This means that there is rarely a simple, clinical test to determine if and how someone is mentally disordered. Instead, the decision depends on the opinion of trained observers—who frequently disagree among themselves (Eaton, 1980; Cockerham, 1981).

The Medical Model

In the past, most societies attributed mental disorder to supernatural influences: the victims were believed to be "possessed" by an evil spirit that had entered the body. Over 4,000 years ago, for example, the Egyptians chipped holes in the skulls of mentally disordered people to allow these spirits to escape; and, centuries later, the medieval Church tried to exorcise the demons, often by flogging, drowning, burning, or hanging the people they supposedly inhabited. By the eighteenth century, however, physicians began to claim that mental disorder was a medical problem—an "illness" best dealt with by doctors. A medical model was applied to the behavior: in other words, physicians came to "diagnose" and "treat" the "patient" for a specific "disease," just as they might in the case of a physical ailment. This trend accelerated in the late nineteenth century when psychiatry emerged as a specialized branch of medicine. Even so, medical science had little impact on mental disorders until the middle of the twentieth century, when newly available sedatives and tranquilizers made it possible to suppress some symptoms of disordered behavior. To this day, however, psychiatrists are

unable to cure most mental disorders through any conventional medical methods, and many critics question whether the medical model is always appropriate.

A few mental disorders do result from physical damage to the brain; these are universally regarded as physical diseases and are treated by neurologists rather than psychiatrists. However, no consistent physical causes are known for the remaining disorders. The most serious of this type of disorder is **psychosis,** a profound mental disturbance involving such a severe break with reality that the affected person cannot function in society. The psychoses include extreme paranoia (delusions of persecution or grandeur); manic-depression (severe and irrational mood changes); and schizophrenia (intellectual and emotional derangement). Understandably, most people consider the psychotic to be "mad," "crazy," or

Figure 8.14 *By the middle of the nineteenth century, physicians began to view mental disorder as a "disease" that they could "treat" by "medical" methods, such as suspending patients in the air and spinning them around. Treatment methods have changed a great deal since that time, but physicians are still unable to cure most mental disorders by standard medical means.*

"insane." The psychoses are the core of the problem of mental disorder: psychotics may be highly disruptive to others and represent four out of five of all first admissions to mental hospitals.

If there is no physical basis for these mental disorders, what causes them? Currently, the origins are believed to lie primarily in people's earlier social and psychological experiences, although there is good evidence that hormonal and other biological factors may make at least some people more vulnerable to certain disorders. One problem in applying a medical model to these disorders is that their symptoms, unlike those of such physical diseases as lung cancer or acne, are culturally variable. Different cultures have different ideas of how "mad" people should act—in one culture, perhaps, they might hear voices, while in another they might run amok in public—and these ideas actually influence how deranged people behave (Kleinman, 1979). A judgment about someone's sanity therefore depends to an extent on the assumptions of the culture, of the subculture, and of the individual making the judgment: for example, someone who talks to spirits may be normal to one observer, eccentric to another, and a raving lunatic to a third. Indeed, studies show that psychiatrists disagree about 20 percent of the time on the question of whether someone is psychotic or not, and about 50 percent of the time on the question of which particular psychosis a diagnosed psychotic is suffering from. Sometimes, eminent psychiatrists testify at trials as "expert" witnesses—only to give conflicting opinions on the sanity of the accused (Sandifer et al., 1964; Church, 1978; Conover, 1972; Lipkowitz and Idupaganti, 1983; Clinard and Meier, 1985).

This ambiguity about the medical model has led one critic, Thomas Szasz (1970, 1986), to declare that "mental illness is a myth." The *behavior* called mental illness exists, of course, but it is not an *illness*—it is a learned but defective means of dealing with the world. Unable to handle their environment in any other way, some people resort to paranoid, depressive, manic, or otherwise deranged approaches to reality. Psychiatry, Szasz argues, is not really a medical science at all, but rather a pseudoscience like astrology and alchemy; its various diagnostic labels are just mumbo-jumbo that lends it a veneer of scientific respectability. This does not mean that psychiatrists cannot help people through their problems—they very often can, but probably because of their personal qualities of insight and compassion rather than their medical training. All in all, argues

Szasz, the psychiatrist is just an agent of social control, much like the priest or judge—someone who interprets the social norms of the time, decides who is deviating from them, and tries to return the deviants to normality.

The potential for the psychiatrist to act as an agent of social control is perhaps clearer in the case of other cultures where different psychiatric assumptions prevail. In the Soviet Union, for example, psychiatry is sometimes used in much the same way as Americans might use the law—as a sanction against deviance. Since about 1960, Soviet authorities have committed thousands of political dissidents to mental hospitals—thus avoiding the inconvenience of political trials and eliminating critics on the grounds that there is something wrong with them, not their society. One man, for example, was diagnosed as schizophrenic for preferring the Bible to communism as a source of morality; another, who urged more freedom of speech for scientists, was committed because of his "paranoid delusion of reforming society"; and another, who had criticized Marx, was said to be suffering from "intoxication with philosophy." These practices have aroused so much international criticism that the Soviet Union resigned from the World Psychiatric Union in 1983. Yet Soviet psychiatrists continue to label as insane people who might be regarded as normal, or even admired, elsewhere. And it is possible that the Soviet psychiatrists are not being cynical: to them, the very expression of dissidence is so unusual that it may well seem to violate their society's norms of reality (Gershman, 1984).

Becoming Mentally Disordered

How, at least in conventional American terms, do people become mentally disordered? Most sociological explanations concur with Szasz's view that mental disorder is a learned form of behavior, unconsciously adopted by some people as a means of dealing with—or avoiding—personal pressures that threaten to overwhelm them. These pressures are assumed to arise from the social and particularly the family environment. Pathological family interaction patterns, in which the victim is subject to subtle, contradictory, and manipulative demands in an emotionally charged atmosphere, may lead certain people—particularly those who are biologically so predisposed—to "crack" under stress. In an influential statement, Thomas Scheff (1966, 1984) offers what is essentially a labeling theory of mental disorder. Everyone, he says, violates norms of reality on occasion—by talking to themselves, making irrelevant responses to questions, suffering memory lapses, irrationally fearing persecution, laughing inappropriately, and so on. Under pressure, some people violate these norms too often or too noticeably, and other people, suspecting that the offenders have taken leave of their senses, label them as "mentally ill." The offenders may find that this label has some advantages, for it lessens the pressures on them—it frees them, for example, from many normal social obligations, such as the duty to work, to show love to other family members, and so on. But, although the label was first applied because of a temporary inability to cope with reality, it is not as easily cast off as it was taken on, and the deviance may become habitual. Those who have been labeled as mentally ill may unconsciously adopt the behaviors that their culture teaches are appropriate for such people.

Who, then, becomes mentally disordered? Extensive sociological research has shown that mental disorder, like criminality, is not randomly distributed in the population: it, too, varies according to social status. By far the highest rates of severe disorders are found in the lowest social classes. The exact reason is a matter of debate. It could be that the pressures of lower-class life make people more susceptible to mental problems; or it could be that mental problems make people more likely to end up in lower social statuses; or it could be that lower-class people are simply more likely to be labeled as mentally disordered. Treatment, too, varies according to social class: higher-status people are more likely to be seen by private psychiatrists and given psychotherapy; lower-status people are more likely to be seen by hospital psychiatrists and to be given drugs or committed to the hospital. There are also marked differences along the lines of race and sex: blacks have higher hospitalization rates for mental disorders than whites, and women have higher rates than men (Srole et al., 1977; Dohrenwend et al., 1980; Eaton, 1985).

The number of people hospitalized for mental disorder has actually been declining—from 550,000 asylum patients in 1955 to around 130,000 in 1985. The emptying of mental hospitals began after the discovery of the drugs that make it unnecessary to closely control or even restrain many mentally disordered people. The process was hastened by civil libertarians, who urged the release of people who had been confined against their own will, and by politicians, who called for the discharge of patients in order to cut public spending. The results have often been tragic. Tens of thousands of seriously disordered people have been "returned to the community"—where, isolated and abandoned, they live in dilapidated urban rooming houses, eke out an existence on permanent welfare, or are even to be seen mumbling, raging, and scavenging their way about the streets of the great American cities (Skull, 1977; Mechanic, 1980; Bell, 1980).

Figure 8.15 *Many mentally disordered people have been "returned to the community" as part of a policy of reducing the number of mental-hospital patients. Hundreds of thousands of these people have become hopeless derelicts in the large cities.*

The Medicalization of Deviance

The application of a medical model to mental disorder is only one aspect of **medicalization,** the process by which the influence of medicine is extended over areas of life that were previously considered nonmedical. During this century, medicine has rapidly developed into one of modern society's major institutions. One effect of this trend is that physicians have extended their expertise to new areas. Consequently, many human experiences—such as pregnancy, child development, anxiety, insomnia, attempted suicide, alcoholism, addictions, voyeurism, or compulsive stealing—have gradually come to be regarded largely as medical matters, rather than as moral, religious, biological, or legal ones (Freidson, 1970; Zola, 1972; Conrad and Schneider, 1980; Starr, 1982).

Obesity provides a case in point. Until a few decades ago, people who deviated from the ideal physical form by being overweight were held to have a personal problem of eating too much or exercising too little. Gradually, however, physicians have succeeded in defining obesity as a disease, to be cured by such means as scientific diets, psychotherapy, or even surgery. Another example is gender confusion, a deviant identity in which someone feels like, or wishes to be, a member of the opposite sex. This personal dilemma is now subject to medical intervention in the form of a "sex-change" operation. Similarly, repeated shoplifting—which the church might regard as immoral, or the courts as illegal—is defined by psychiatry as the "disease" of "kleptomania." One form of deviance, in fact, became a "disease" only after a drug was accidentally found to "cure" it. Hyperactive children have long been disruptive in classrooms, where their behavior was considered a discipline problem. Then researchers discovered that a stimulant drug, ritalin, had the unexpected effect of pacifying these children. Having found the "medicine," physicians soon discovered the "disease" of "hyperkinesis"—which, despite its scientific sound, is merely the Greek word for "overenergetic." An important implication of this medicalization of deviance, however, is that offenders are *treated* as "sick" people rather than *punished* as "bad" people (Conrad and Schneider, 1980).

In this manner medicine has greatly extended its influence as an agent of social control, with psychiatrists defining the approved norms, labeling those who deviate from them, and trying to ensure that the deviants conform once more. This process can be clearly seen in the example of homosexuality—a form of deviance that has been both medicalized and then demedicalized as social attitudes have evolved. For centuries, the Western world generally viewed homosexuality as a moral matter, as a sin that might evoke divine retribution. Then, around the end of the nineteenth century, many Western countries redefined homosexuality as a crime, punishable by imprisonment. But by the middle of the twentieth century, public opinion—encouraged by psychiatry—once again shifted, and homosexuality was viewed primarily in medical terms. Homosexuals were considered "sick," and psychiatrists tried (and failed) to change their sexual orientation in order to "cure" them. By the 1960s, however, an emerging gay liberation movement insisted that homosexuality is simply a different lifestyle. In 1974 the American Psychiatric Association accepted this view, and gave millions of homosexuals an instant cure by simply voting the "disease" out of existence (Bayer, 1981). The obvious fact that physi-

Figure 8.16

"Yes, yes—angst, indefinable cravings, sleeplessness, weltschmerz, and occasional outbursts of rage. Just something that's going around."

Drawing by Ed Fisher; © 1985
The New Yorker Magazine, Inc.

cians cannot similarly vote away cancer or diabetes points up the difference between deviant behaviors and physical ailments.

It is doubtful, then, whether deviant behaviors are medical problems in any scientific sense. Yet our taken-for-granted social reality now includes the notion that certain forms of deviance are "diseases." In practice, therefore, the medical profession's definitions and redefinitions of deviance both shape and reflect the changing norms and values of society (Szasz, 1970, 1974; Kittrie, 1974; Shrag, 1978; Gross, 1978). (The medical profession is discussed in detail in Chapter 16, "Medicine.")

The Social Implications of Deviance

Deviance has a number of social consequences, some of which are functional and some of which are dysfunctional to society.

Functions of Deviance

Strange as it may seem, deviance may actually be useful to society, for—provided that it is kept within reasonable limits—it can help maintain social control and social stability in several different ways.

1. *Clarification of norms.* As we have noted previously, deviance is necessary to define the limits of permissible behavior. The existence of rule-breakers reminds us what the rules are, and the punishment of rule-breakers demonstrates to everyone how far society's tolerance extends on any specific issue at any particular time.

2. *Enhancement of solidarity.* By collectively reacting against deviants, conforming members of society reaffirm their shared norms and values, and are thus made more aware of their group solidarity. Emile Durkheim maintained that this function of deviance is so important that if there were no deviants, they would have to be invented. There is evidence, in fact, that some communities do attempt to create deviants in order to shore up their sense of "us" against "them."

3. *Diversion of discontent.* Deviance may sometimes serve as a "safety valve" for individual or social discontent, allowing people to violate the rules rather than attack the institutions that the rules uphold. For example, minor forms of delinquency, such as writing graffiti on public walls, may provide a more tolerable outlet for frustrated people than outright challenges to political authority. Deviance can thus function to take the strain off the social system by preventing an excessive accumulation of discontent.

4. *Identification of problems.* Deviance can help to identify social problems by signaling some defect in the social system. Sometimes norms are violated through "institutionalized evasion"—large-scale, patterned deviance involving many or most people in society. The institutionalized evasion that accompanied the prohibition of alcohol is a useful example: it showed that existing legislation was simply unenforceable. Other forms of deviance—such as high rates of mental disorder in a particular social group, or of truancy in a specific school—also provide a signal that something is amiss.

Dysfunctions of Deviance

Of course, deviance also has negative effects on society, which is why every society attempts to restrain deviant behavior within tolerable limits. There are several such dysfunctions.

1. *Disruption of social order.* Widespread violation of social norms can disrupt social order by making social life difficult and unpredictable. This is true for small groups as well as for the larger society. The idle worker can clog the flow of the assembly line, the psychotic can disrupt the family, the embezzler can become a threat to the commercial enterprise.

2. *Confusion of norms and values.* Extensive deviance leads to confusion over norms and values, making it difficult for people to know what behavior is expected, or even what is considered right or wrong. This is particularly true if deviants are seen to "get away with it," or if there is a growing perception that "everyone does it." Moreover, when a variety of different moralities compete in society, social tension may arise between conventional and deviant groups.

3. *Diversion of resources.* The need to control widespread deviance often diverts resources that could be more usefully directed elsewhere. For example, in the United States vast resources are devoted to the attempt to control crime and drug abuse—resources that could be channeled instead to other social needs and more productive uses, such as education or health care.

Figure 8.17 *The seventeenth-century Puritans of Salem, Massachusetts, created deviants where they did not exist, in the form of witches. By the time the Puritan witchhunt was over, several women had been executed. In persecuting "witches," the Puritans reaffirmed their own solidarity as a community and enhanced their sense of righteousness. A witchhunt of a different sort occurred in the United States during the 1950s, when the late Senator Joseph McCarthy made indiscriminate charges that "Reds" were infesting various areas of American life, including the State Department.*

Congress set up a committee on un-American activities, which tried to track down alleged communist sympathizers. These were the early days of the "cold war" with the Soviet Union, and the search for political deviants closer to home provided a focus for national solidarity against communism. Although he recklessly smeared the reputations of hundreds of people, McCarthy could never substantiate his claims. When he finally began to attack the U.S. Army, public revulsion led his colleagues in the Senate to formally censure him, and his search for un-American deviants came to an end.

4. *Violation of trust.* An important dysfunction of deviance is that it undermines trust. Social relationships are based on the assumption that people will behave according to the accepted norms of conduct: that they will not break contracts, not exploit friendships, not molest children left in their care, not rob strangers they meet in the street, not hijack airliners on which they are passengers. Widespread deviance undermines this trust for everyone, conformists and deviants alike. It also imposes many inconveniences on society: for example, because a handful of people hijack airliners, millions of air passengers must be searched for weapons.

Freedom, Diversity, and Deviance

Deviance is not intrinsically good or bad. It can be socially useful or socially destructive, depending on the circumstances. Deviance arises from the very nature of society and the necessity for establishing and maintaining social order. Without rules there can be no rule-breakers; but where there

are rules, there will always be people who are tempted—or pressured—to break them. The individual deviant may be abnormal, but deviance itself is intrinsic to social living.

Some societies, however, seem to have more deviance than others. The United States, a nation embarked on the historical experiment of giving its citizens an unprecedented degree of freedom, is confronted with the fact that some people abuse that freedom. For example, if people are free to own guns, some will use them to rob and kill each other; if people have freedom of religion, some will join obscure cults and sects; if people have freedom of expression, some will produce hard-core pornography; if people have freedom to travel, some will smuggle drugs. Conversely, a society that places greater emphasis on conformity to the rules—like China, for example—tends to have less deviance, though at the cost of personal freedom. After all, freedom implies choice; the exercise of choice leads to differences; and one group's differences soon become another group's deviance. In this sense, deviance may be part of the price that a free society pays for the liberty its members enjoy.

Summary

1.   Deviance refers to socially disapproved violations of important norms and expectations; deviants share the characteristic of stigma. Deviance is a relative matter, because the determination of who is deviant varies from one social context to another.

2.   Deviance signals a failure of social control. Social control is applied through the socialization process and through sanctions, which may be formal or informal, positive or negative. Some measure of deviance, however, reinforces social control by demonstrating the consequences of deviance to the rest of society.

3.   Several explanations of deviance (particularly crime) have been offered. Cultural-transmission theory regards deviant behavior as learned through differential association with other deviants. Structural-strain theory sees deviance as arising from a discrepancy between socially approved goals and the availability of socially approved means of achieving them; those who lack the approved means may fall into a state of anomie and use disapproved means instead. Control theory sees deviance as the result of inadequate social control over the behavior of people who have weak bonds to the community. Labeling theory explains deviance as a process by which some people are able to label others as deviant.

4.   The main types of crime in the United States may be classified as crimes of violence, crimes against property, crimes without victims, and white-collar and corporate crimes. Most crime data focus on the crimes of violence and crimes against property.

5.   The selection of criminals is a process in which higher-status offenders are disproportionately more likely to escape sanctions, which usually take the form of corrections such as imprisonment, probation, or parole. Only a small minority of offenders is ultimately imprisoned. The prison incapacitates these offenders, but its nature as a total institution makes it ineffective at rehabilitation. Conflict theorists emphasize that much crime is actually behavior that acts against the interests of the most powerful groups in society.

6.   Mental disorder represents deviance from norms of reality. Most psychotic disorders have no known physical cause, but are treated by psychiatrists according to a medical model. Definitions of mental disorder are culturally relative and depend in part on the assumptions of the observer. Critics charge that mental disorder is a form of learned but socially defective behavior and that psychiatrists may serve as agents of social control over this deviance.

7.   Many forms of deviance are becoming medicalized, or treated as sickness rather than as moral failings or criminal acts. This trend reflects the growing power of the medical profession, and the fact that society finds medicalization a convenient way of controlling some deviance.

8.   Deviance has several functions: it clarifies norms, enhances solidarity, diverts discontent, and identifies problems. It also has dysfunctions: it disrupts social order, confuses norms and values, diverts resources, and violates trust. Its effects, therefore, can be both positive and negative. Freedom and diversity may encourage deviance.

Important Terms

stigma (191)

deviance (191)

social control (193)

sanctions (193)

cultural-transmission
theory (194)

differential association (194)

structural-strain theory (195)

anomie (195)

control theory (196)

labeling theory (198)

primary deviance (198)

secondary deviance (198)

crime (200)

corrections (206)

recidivism (207)

total institution (207)

mental disorder (210)

psychosis (211)

medicalization (214)

Suggested Readings

BECKER, HOWARD S. *Outsiders.* Enlarged ed. New York: Free Press, 1973.

A highly influential book in which Becker outlines the labeling theory of deviance and applies the theory to various "outsiders," such as marijuana smokers.

CLINARD, MARSHALL B., and ROBERT F. MEIER. *Sociology of Deviant Behavior.* 6th ed. New York: Holt, Rinehart and Winston, 1985.

A short but comprehensive text on the sociology of deviance. The book is recommended for the student who wants a good overview of the subject.

CONRAD, PETER, and JOSEPH W. SCHNEIDER. *Deviance and Medicalization: From Badness to Sickness.* St. Louis, Mo.: Mosby, 1980.

An analysis of the tendency to treat certain forms of deviance as medical problems.

ERIKSON, KAI T. *Wayward Puritans.* New York: Wiley, 1966.

A study of the early Puritans in Massachusetts. Erikson shows that the Puritans created deviants where none really existed and thus affirmed their own normality and solidarity.

NETTLER, GWYNN. *Explaining Crime.* 3rd ed. New York: McGraw-Hill, 1983.

An excellent analysis of criminal behavior and theories of crime.

OAKLEY, RAY. *Drugs, Society, and Human Behavior.* 3rd ed. St. Louis, Mo.: Mosby, 1983.

A good overview of the sociology of drug use and abuse.

SIMON, DAVID K., and STANLEY EITZEN. *Elite Deviance.* 2nd ed. Boston: Allyn and Bacon, 1986.

A good up-to-date study of the nature, impact, and implications of white-collar and corporate crime.

SZASZ, THOMAS. *The Myth of Mental Illness.* Rev. ed. New York: Harper and Row, 1986.

A controversial but influential book, in which Szasz argues that the label "mental illness" is often used by society as a means of social control over certain types of deviants.

The Saints and the Roughnecks

WILLIAM J. CHAMBLISS

Two youth gangs in a small community were equally delinquent. Yet one gang was perceived by the community as nothing more than a group of high-spirited youths having a good time, while the other was perceived as delinquent. Chambliss uses labeling theory to explain why.

Eight promising young men— children of good, stable, white upper-middle-class families, active in school affairs, good pre-college students—were some of the most delinquent boys at Hanibal High School. The Saints were constantly occupied with truancy, drinking, wild driving, petty theft and vandalism. Yet not one was officially arrested for any misdeed during the two years I observed them.

This record was particularly surprising in light of my observations during the same two years of another gang of Hanibal High School students, six lower-class white boys known as the Roughnecks. The Roughnecks were constantly in trouble with police and community even though their rate of delinquency was about equal with that of the Saints. What was the cause of this disparity?

By midnight on Fridays and Saturdays the Saints were usually thoroughly high, and one or two of them were often so drunk they had to be carried to the cars. Then the boys drove around town, calling obscenities to women and girls; occasionally trying (unsuccessfully so far as I could tell) to pick girls up; and driving recklessly through red lights and at high speeds with their lights out. Occasionally they played "chicken." One boy would climb out the back window of the car and across the roof to the driver's side of the car while the car was moving at high speed (between 40 and 50 miles an hour); then the driver would move over and the boy who had just crawled across the car roof would take the driver's seat.

Searching for "fair game" for a prank was the boys' principal activity after they left the tavern. The boys would drive alongside a foot patrolman and ask directions to some street. If the policeman leaned on the car in the course of answering the question, the driver would speed away, causing him to lose his balance. The Saints were careful to play this prank only in an area where they were not going to spend much time and where they could quickly disappear around a corner to avoid having their license plate number taken.

Construction sites and road repair areas were the special province of the Saints' mischief. A soon-to-be-repaired hole in the road inevitably invited the Saints to remove lanterns and wooden barricades and put them in the car, leaving the hole unprotected. The boys would find a safe vantage point and wait for an unsuspecting motorist to drive into the hole. Often, though not always, the boys would go up to the motorist and commiserate with him about the dreadful way the city protected its citizenry.

Leaving the scene of the open hole and the motorist, the boys would then go searching for an appropriate place to erect the stolen barricade. An "appropriate place" was often a spot on a highway near a curve in the road where the barricade would not be seen by an oncoming motorist. The boys would wait to watch an unsuspecting motorist attempt to stop and (usually) crash into the wooden barricade. With saintly bearing the boys might offer help.

Abandoned houses, especially if they were located in out-of-the-way places, were fair game for destruction and spontaneous vandalism. The boys would break windows, remove furniture to the yard and tear it apart, urinate on the walls and scrawl obscenities inside.

The Saints were highly successful in school. The average grade for the group was "B," with two of the boys having close to a straight "A" average. Almost all of the boys were popular and many of them held offices in the school. One of the boys was vice-president of the student body one year. Six of the boys played on athletic teams.

At the end of their senior year, the student body selected ten seniors for special recognition as the "school wheels"; four of the ten were Saints. Teachers and school officials saw no problem with any of these boys and anticipated that they would all "make something of themselves."

How the boys managed to maintain this impression is surprising in view of their actual behavior while in school. Their technique for covering truancy was so successful that teachers did not even realize that the boys were absent from school much of the time. Occasionally, of course, the system would backfire and then the boy was on his own. A boy who was caught would be most contrite, would plead guilty and ask for mercy. He inevitably got the mercy he sought.

Cheating on examinations was rampant, even to the point of orally communicating answers to exams as well as looking at one another's papers. Since none of the group studied, and since they were primarily dependent on one another for help, it is surprising that grades were so high. Teachers contributed to the deception in their admitted inclination to give these boys (and presumably others like them) the benefit of the doubt. When asked how the boys did in school, and when pressed on specific examinations, teachers might admit that they were disappointed in John's performance, but would quickly add that they "knew that he was capable of doing better," so John was given a higher grade than he had actually earned. How often this happened is impossible to know. During the time that I observed the group, I never saw any of the boys take homework home. Teachers may have been "understanding" very regularly.

The local police saw the Saints as good boys who were among the leaders of the youth in the community. Rarely, the boys might be stopped in town for speeding or for running a stop sign. When this happened the boys were always polite, contrite and pled for mercy. As in school, they received the mercy they asked for. None ever received a ticket or was taken into the precinct by the local police.

Hanibal townspeople never perceived the Saints' high level of delinquency. The Saints were good boys who just went in for an occasional prank. After all, they were well dressed, well mannered and had nice cars. The Roughnecks were a different story. Although the two gangs of boys were the same age, and both groups engaged in an equal amount of wild-oat sowing, everyone agreed that the not-so-well-dressed, not-so-well-mannered, not-so-rich boys were heading for trouble.

The fighting activities of the group were fairly readily and accurately perceived by almost everyone. At least once a month, the boys would get into some sort of fight, although most fights were scraps between members of the group or involved only one member of the group and some peripheral hanger-on.

More serious than fighting, had the community been aware of it, was theft. Although almost everyone was aware that the boys occasionally stole things, they did not realize the extent of the activity. Petty stealing was a frequent event for the Roughnecks. Sometimes they stole as a group and coordinated their efforts; other times they stole in pairs. Rarely did they steal alone.

The thefts ranged from very small things like paperback books, comics and ballpoint pens to expensive items like watches. The nature of the thefts varied from time to time. The gang would go through a period of systematically shoplifting items from automobiles or school lockers. Types of thievery varied with the whim of the gang. Some forms of thievery were more profitable than others, but all thefts were for profit, not just thrills.

Roughnecks siphoned gasoline from cars as often as they had access to an automobile, which was not very often. Unlike the Saints, who owned their own cars, the Roughnecks would have to borrow their parents' cars, an event which occurred only eight or nine times a year. The boys claimed to have stolen cars for joy rides from time to time.

There was a high level of mutual distrust and dislike between the Roughnecks and the police. The boys felt very strongly that the police were unfair and corrupt. Some evidence existed that the boys were correct in their perception.

The main source of the boys' dislike for the police undoubtedly stemmed from the fact that the police would sporadically harass the group. From the standpoint of the boys, these acts of occasional enforcement of the law were whimsical and uncalled for. It made no sense to them, for example, that the police would come to the corner occasionally and threaten them with arrest for loitering when the night before the boys had been out siphoning gasoline from cars and the police had been nowhere in sight. To the boys, the police were stupid on the one hand, for not being where they should have been and catching the boys in a serious offense, and unfair on the other hand, for trumping up "loitering" charges against them.

Over the period that the group was under observation, each member was arrested at least once. Several of the boys were arrested a number of times and spent at least one night in jail. While most were never taken to court, two of the boys were sentenced to six months' incarceration in boys' schools.

The Roughnecks' behavior in school was not particularly disruptive. During school hours they did not all hang around together, but tended instead to spend most of their time with one or two other members of the gang who were their special buddies. Although every member of the gang attempted to avoid school as much as possible, they were not particularly successful and most of them attended school with surprising regularity. They considered school a burden—something to be gotten through with a minimum of conflict.

Teachers saw the boys the way the general community did, as heading for trouble, as being uninterested in making something of themselves. Some were also seen as being incapable of meeting the academic standards of the school. Most of the teachers expressed concern for this group of boys and were willing to pass them despite poor performance, in the belief that failing them would only aggravate the problem.

Why did the community, the school and the police react to the Saints as though they were good, upstanding, nondelinquent youths with bright futures but to the Roughnecks as though they were tough, young criminals who were headed for trouble? Why did the Roughnecks and the Saints in fact have quite different careers after high school—careers which, by and large, lived up to the expectations of the community?

Differential treatment of the two gangs resulted in part because one gang was infinitely more visible than the other. This differential visibility was a direct function of the economic standing of the families. The Saints had access to automobiles and were able to remove themselves from the sight of the community. In as routine a decision as to where to go to have a milkshake after school, the Saints stayed away from the mainstream of community life. Lacking transportation, the Roughnecks could not make it to the edge of town. The center of town was the only practical place for them to meet since their homes were scattered throughout the town and any non-central meeting place put an undue hardship on some members. Through necessity the Roughnecks congregated in a crowded area where everyone in the community passed frequently, including teachers and law enforcement officers. They could easily see the Roughnecks hanging around the drugstore.

On their escapades the Saints were also relatively invisible, since they left Hanibal and travelled to Big City. Here, too, they were mobile, roaming the city, rarely going to the same area twice.

To the notion of visibility must be added the difference in the responses of group members to outside intervention with their activities. If one of the Saints was confronted with an accusing policeman, even if he felt he was truly innocent of a wrongdoing, his demeanor was apologetic and penitent. A Roughneck's attitude was almost the polar opposite. When confronted with a threatening adult authority, even one who tried to be pleasant, the Roughneck's hostility and disdain were clearly observable. Sometimes he might attempt to put up a veneer of respect, but it was thin and was not accepted as sincere by the authority.

[Furthermore,] even if the Saints had been less discreet, their favorite delinquencies would have been perceived as less serious than those of the Roughnecks.

In the eyes of the police and school officials, a boy who drinks in an alley and stands intoxicated on the street corner is committing a more serious offense than is a boy who drinks to inebriation in a nightclub or a tavern and drives around afterwards in a car. Similarly, a boy who steals a wallet from a store will be viewed as having committed a more serious offense than a boy who steals a lantern from a construction site.

Perceptual bias also operates with respect to the demeanor of the boys in the two groups when they are confronted by adults. It is not simply that adults dislike the posture affected by boys of the Roughneck ilk; more important is the conviction that the posture adopted by the Roughnecks is an indication of their devotion and commitment to deviance as a way of life. The posture becomes a cue, just as the type of the offense is a cue, to the degree to which the known transgressions are indicators of the youths' potential for other problems.

Visibility, demeanor and bias are surface variables which explain the day-to-day operations of the police. Why do these surface variables operate as they do? Why did the police choose to disregard the Saints' delinquencies while breathing down the backs of the Roughnecks?

The answer lies in the class structure of American society and the control of legal institutions by those at the top of the class structure. Obviously, no representative of the upper class drew up the operational chart for the police which led them to look in the ghettoes and on street corners—which led them to see the demeanor of lower-class youth as troublesome and that of upper-middle-class youth as tolerable. Rather, the procedures simply developed from experience—experience with irate and influential upper-middle-class parents insisting that their son's vandalism was simply a prank and his drunkenness only a momentary "sowing of wild oats"— experience with cooperative or indifferent, powerless, lower-class parents who acquiesced to the law's definition of their son's behavior.

The community responded to the Roughnecks as boys in trouble, and the boys agreed with that perception. Their pattern of deviancy was reinforced, and breaking away from it became increasingly unlikely. Once the boys acquired an image of themselves as deviants, they selected new friends who affirmed that self-image. As that self-conception became more firmly entrenched, they also became willing to try new and more extreme deviances. With their growing alienation came freer expression of disrespect and hostility for representatives of the legitimate society. This disrespect increased the community's negativism, perpetuating the entire process of commitment to deviance. Lack of a commitment to deviance works the same way.

Selective perception and labeling—finding, processing and punishing some kinds of criminality and not others—means that visible, poor, nonmobile, outspoken, undiplomatic "tough" kids will be noticed, whether their actions are seriously delinquent or not. Other kids, who have established a reputation for being bright (even though underachieving), disciplined and involved in respectable activities, who are mobile and monied, will be invisible when they deviate from sanctioned activities. They'll sow their wild oats —perhaps even wider and thicker than their lower-class cohorts—but they won't be noticed. When it's time to leave adolescence most will follow the expected path, settling into the ways of the middle class, remembering fondly the delinquent but unnoticed fling of their youth. The Roughnecks and others like them may turn around, too. It is more likely that their noticeable deviance will have been so reinforced by police and community that their lives will be effectively channelled into careers consistent with their adolescent background.

SOURCE: William J. Chambliss, "The Saints and the Roughnecks," Society (November 1973), pp. 24–31.

CHAPTER 9

Sexuality and Society

For centuries, the societies of the Western world have shrouded sexuality in myth, taboo, and ignorance. Even sociologists, supposedly dedicated to studying social behavior regardless of the prejudices and obstacles in the way, did not accept human sexuality as a legitimate field of research until after World War II. Yet the fact remains that every society contains two sexes, a feature that obviously has important and far-reaching implications for personal behavior and social life.

Sexuality is a significant ingredient of individual personality. Much of our leisure time is occupied with sexual acts, thoughts, feelings, and sometimes fears. Even in situations that are not defined as sexual—the street, the workplace, the college cafeteria—undertones and overtones of sexuality are frequently present. Social interaction is often rich in various forms of sexual expression, ranging from overt acts to the most subtle glances, gestures, and other signals.

Sexual relationships have an even greater importance in the broader societal context, especially when they are institutionalized in the form of marriage. The sexual bond between husband and wife is the basis of marriage, which, in turn, is the basis of the family. The family is the most basic institution in all societies. It has the responsibility for, among other things, legitimate birth, primary socialization, the allocation of various statuses and roles to its members, and the transmission of property and other rights from generation to generation. It is small wonder, then, that every society carefully regulates the sexual behavior of its members, channeling their biological potentials into outlets that are socially regarded as natural and moral.

Some aspects of human sexuality are still imperfectly researched, partly because continuing social inhibitions have hindered the accumulation of the necessary information. Nevertheless, there

Figure 9.1 *Sexuality is an important element in both personal and social life. As this picture suggests, sexual implications are present in everyday situations that are not usually defined as sexual, including public places.*

The Nature of Human Sexuality

Researchers in several disciplines now recognize that human sexual behavior is highly flexible, so much so that we can learn to attach our erotic desires to almost anything—human beings, animals, inanimate objects such as shoes or underwear, or even the experience of pain and humiliation. Kingsley Davis (1971), one of the first sociologists to study sexual behavior, states flatly that "like other forms of behavior, sexual activity must be learned. Without socialization, human beings would not even know how to copulate." Alfred Kinsey (1953), a zoologist, wrote, "It is not so difficult to explain why a human animal does a particular thing sexually. It is more difficult to explain why each and every individual is not involved in every type of activity." Similar views have been expressed by psychologists, anthropologists, and medical scientists (for example, J. C. Coleman, 1976; Gregersen, 1982; Money and Tucker, 1975). The same principle seems to apply to some higher primates as well. Harry Harlow's experiments with rhesus monkeys (discussed in Chapter 5, "Socialization") have shown that if monkeys are raised in isolation, they do not know how to mate in later life, and it is extremely difficult, especially in the case of the males, to teach them how to do so. Even monkeys must learn their sexual conduct.

The human sex drive can usefully be compared to the hunger drive. We all have an innate tendency to feel hungry periodically, but we have to learn through the socialization process what we may eat and what we may not eat, although different societies teach rather different lessons in this regard. Unlike the inhabitants of some societies, the well-socialized American who encounters a dog, rat, or spider does not for one moment consider the creature as "food": we have what seems to be an "instinctive," but what is in fact a learned, aversion to the idea. The way we come to follow our society's norms of sexual conduct is similar. We start with a basic, undirected drive and learn through the socialization process to recognize some stimuli as nonsexual, some as sexual and appropriate, and some as potentially sexual but inappropriate or even taboo. The fact that our sex drive is so flexible is, of course, the reason every society goes to such lengths to regulate it. If we all behaved "instinctively" in a rigid and predictable manner, there would be no need for the guidelines supplied by powerful norms and taboos, and they would not exist.

is now sufficient scientific knowledge about sexual attitudes and behavior, in our own society and in many others, to provide an intelligent understanding of the subject. Even so, the sociological perspective on human sexuality may at first seem to run counter to common sense and everyday experience. To most people nothing seems more natural, or even more "instinctive," than their particular sexual preferences. But this popular view is simply wrong, for unlike the sexual behavior of most other animals, our sexual responses are not dictated by genes. Human sexual behavior and feelings are primarily learned through the socialization process and generally conform to the prevailing norms of the society concerned. Ideas about what is sexually appropriate or inappropriate, moral or immoral, erotic or offensive, are purely social in origin. In fact, even people who deviate from the prevailing norms of their culture tend to do so in predictable, patterned ways that are typical of each society.

Certain features of human sexuality, particularly those relating to love, courtship, and marriage, will be discussed in greater detail in Chapter 13 ("The Family"). In this chapter we will concentrate more on other aspects of sexuality that seem to require some explanation, such as cross-cultural variations in sexual practices, the incest taboo, and rape, showing how sociological analysis aids our understanding.

Sexual Behavior in Other Cultures

We can get an idea of how flexible human sexuality is by looking at sexual expression in other societies. There are two comprehensive surveys of cross-cultural variations in sexual behavior. The first is by Clellan Ford and Frank Beach (1951), who analyzed information on 190 traditional, pre-industrial societies from all over the world; the second is by Edgar Gregersen, whose preliminary report (1982) draws on data from 294 such societies. Both surveys are based primarily on the ethnographic reports of anthropologists who lived among and studied the people concerned. The information that follows is from these surveys unless otherwise indicated.

Cultural Universals

There is a great deal of variation in the sexual practices of different societies, and much variety, too, within each society. There are, however, three *cultural universals*—practices that are found in every society.

1. *The incest taboo.* Every society that we know of, past and present, has an *incest taboo,* a powerful moral prohibition against sexual contact between certain categories of relatives. The taboo almost always applies to relations between parent and child and between brother and sister. Additionally, all societies apply an incest taboo to sex between certain other categories of relatives—but each society has its own rules in this regard, so sexual relationships that are quite acceptable to one people might be utterly outrageous to another. As we shall see later in the chapter, the incest taboo is necessary to prevent the disintegration of the family.

2. *Marriage.* Every society expects at least some sexual behavior to be expressed within the context of *marriage,* a socially approved mating arrangement between two or more people. The practice of marriage helps to regulate sexual behavior by narrowing its context and encouraging a bonding of the partners. Marriage also ensures that children will be born legitimate: the identity of a child's mother is usually known, but if a child is born outside marriage, there may be nobody to play the social role of father—a situation every society tries to avoid. In practice, the great majority of people in every society get married. Most societies frown on extramarital sex: about two-thirds of the societies in the cross-cultural samples forbid *adultery,* or sexual relations involving partners at least one of whom is married to someone else. In these societies, the sanctions against adultery range from ridicule to execution. Most societies are more lax about premarital intercourse, which may be tolerated, approved, or in some cases even required. Societies that permit extensive premarital intercourse have to make provision for children born outside marriage—for example, by assigning the social role of father to an uncle, by creating rules for adoption, or by requiring welfare agencies to help support the children.

3. *Heterosexuality.* Every society insists on some conformity to a norm of *heterosexuality,* or sexual orientation toward the opposite sex. The reason is obvious enough: without genital, heterosexual intercourse, a society could not reproduce and would be extinct within a generation. In practice, of course, the great majority of people learn to become heterosexual. About a third of the societies included in the cross-cultural samples totally forbid *homosexuality,* or sexual orientation toward the same sex. In these societies, the sanctions against homosexuality range from ridicule to execution. In the remaining societies, homosexual behavior is tolerated, approved, and occasionally required. All societies that permit very extensive homosexual practices, however, require those involved to also practice heterosexuality or *bisexuality*—sexual orientation toward both sexes—at some point in their life course. Exclusive homosexuality is never tolerated for more than a small minority, because it might otherwise significantly affect reproduction. Two predominantly homosexual societies have been recorded: the Marindanim, a New Guinea tribe, and their neighbors, the Etoro, who actually place a taboo on sex between men and women for 295 days a year. However, even these societies expect everyone to marry and practice heterosexuality some of the time (Van Baal, 1966; Kelly, 1977; Herdt, 1981).

Conceptions of Beauty

Ideas about beauty and sexual attractiveness vary a great deal from one society to another. But although much is known about conceptions of female beauty in other cultures, there is little information on how other peoples judge the attractiveness of men. The main reason, it seems, is that most societies have more specific ideas about

Figure 9.2 *Conceptions of beauty and sexual attractiveness are culturally learned; in fact, what may be attractive in one culture may seem strange or unattractive in another. The pictures here show* *women from India, Panama, and Japan, and men from Kenya, Brazil, and New Guinea. Concepts of beauty also vary by time, and these cultures' concepts of beauty may well vary in the future.*

female than about male beauty, for men are much more likely to be valued for characteristics other than appearance, such as wealth and power.

There are few if any universal standards of female attractiveness. Some peoples regard the shape and color of the eyes as the main determinant of beauty; others are more concerned about the formation of the mouth, nose, or ears. Cultural preferences in these respects vary widely: the Mayans, for example, admired cross-eyes, while

the Yapese of the South Pacific consider black teeth attractive. In some societies small, slim women are admired, but there is a strong cross-cultural tendency for men to prefer fat women; in some West African societies the sexy woman is one who is positively obese. The Thonga of eastern Africa admire a woman who is tall and powerful; the Tongans of Polynesia are more concerned that a woman's ankles be small. The Masai of eastern Africa prefer women with small breasts, whereas the Apache prefer women with very large breasts. In many tropical societies women do not cover their breasts, but this does not mean that the men are in a constant state of erotic frenzy. The breasts are simply not considered a sexual stimulus at all, and attention may focus instead on the legs, buttocks, back, or elsewhere.

Restrictiveness and Permissiveness

Societies vary a great deal in their degree of sexual *restrictiveness,* or insistence on adherence to narrowly defined sexual norms—and in their degree of sexual *permissiveness,* or acceptance of some latitude in sexual norms and conduct.

Most societies in the cross-cultural samples are more permissive than restrictive in their attitudes toward sexual behavior. Only a handful of societies, in fact, wholly disapprove of both premarital and extramarital intercourse. People in these restrictive societies practice a public conspiracy to keep sexual knowledge from young children, but some of them carry their prohibitions even further. Among the Arapaho Indians, for example, the sexes were strictly segregated from childhood and could not play together; in later adolescence they could meet only in the presence of chaperones. Among the Gilbertese Islanders of the Pacific, a girl who was seduced could be put to death with her seducer, and among the Vedda of Ceylon, a man seen merely talking to an unmarried woman could be killed by her relatives. In restrictive societies, punishment for adultery can also be severe, although a husband's infidelity is likely to be treated more leniently than a wife's. Many societies permit a husband to beat, mutilate, or kill an adulterous wife. The Muslim tradition, for example, calls for stoning an unfaithful wife to death.

These attitudes contrast sharply with those of more permissive societies. Among some peoples, such as the Lesu of the Pacific, sexual knowledge is fully available to young children, and the parents openly copulate in front of them. The Trukese of the Carolines encourage sexual experimentation by children, and little huts are constructed outside the main compound for this purpose. The Lepcha of the Himalayas believe that young girls will not mature without the benefit of sexual experience, and Trobriand Island parents gave their children sexual instruction at a very early age, enabling them to begin practicing at the age of six to eight for girls and ten to twelve for boys. In addition,

Ford and Beach noted that over a third of the societies in their sample allow some form of what we would call adultery. The Siriono of Bolivia permit a man to have sexual relations with his wife's sisters and with his brothers' wives and their sisters. Among the Toda of southern India, married men and women are free to form sexual liaisons with others; their language contains no word for adultery. And sex hospitality, in which a husband offers his wife to guests, has been common in a number of societies—including, as we saw in Chapter 3 ("Culture"), the Eskimo.

Sexual Conduct

There is wide cross-cultural variation in the norms governing the particulars of sexual conduct. Even the position that the partners adopt in the sexual act differs from one society to another. The usual position in most Western societies is for the couple to lie face to face with the male on top; in his groundbreaking study of sexual behavior, Alfred Kinsey (1948) found that 70 percent of American couples had never tried any other position. In the South Sea Islands incredulous women laughingly called this approach the "missionary position," for it had been quite unknown to them until they had sex with visiting missionaries. In a survey of the evidence from 131 other societies, the anthropologist Clyde Kluckhohn (1948) found that the "missionary position" was customary or preferred in only 17 cases. Other peoples conduct intercourse from the side, from the rear, with the female on top, with the male kneeling over the female, and in other positions.

The context and content of sexual intercourse is also highly variable. Some peoples regard full nakedness as desirable or obligatory; others, as quite improper or even dangerous. The Hopi Indians insist that sex take place indoors; the Witoto of South America insist that it take place outside. The Masai of eastern Africa believe that sex in the daytime can be fatal; the Chenchu of India believe that intercourse at night can lead to the birth of a blind child. Some people insist on privacy; others are indifferent to the presence of observers. Some, such as the Trobriand Islanders, believe that women are sexually insatiable and expect them to take the initiative; others, such as the Chiricahua Indians, expect that a woman will remain completely passive. Kissing is unknown in some societies; the Siriono consider it a particularly disgusting act. Foreplay before intercourse is unknown

Figure 9.3 *This picture shows a child wedding in a remote part of India. In many traditional societies, weddings are arranged by the parents as a means of creating an alliance between the two kinship* *groups involved. The wedding serves to pledge the children to each other until they can assume normal marital responsibilities at around the age of puberty.*

among the Lepcha but may occupy several hours among the Ponapeans of the Pacific. Kinsey (1948) found that in the 1940s, the great majority of American males reached orgasm within two minutes of starting intercourse, but the Marquesan men of the Pacific habitually perform for several hours. Even the frequency of intercourse is related to cultural norms. The Keraki of New Guinea are reported to average once a week; Americans, two or three times a week; the Aranda of Australia, three to five times a day; and the Chagga of eastern Africa are alleged to manage ten episodes in a single night. Some peoples have learned to experience violence during sex as erotically exciting. The Siriono find pleasure in poking their fingers into each other's eyes; Choroti women in South America spit in their partner's face; Ponapean men tug out tufts of their mate's hair; and Apinaye women in the Brazilian jungle are reported to bite off pieces of their lover's eyebrows, noisily spitting them aside to enhance the erotic effect.

Evaluation

This cross-cultural evidence can be misleading in an important respect, for it deals only with the sexual practices of small, preindustrial societies, many of which have changed their cultural practices or have even become extinct since anthropologists first reported on them. No comparable study of modern industrial societies has been made, but it seems likely that sexual behavior in these societies, like most other aspects of their cultures, is much less variable. Since the majority of the world's population lives in industrialized or industrializing societies, it is probably safe to conclude that the sexual practices of most people in the world no longer differ radically from those of Western nations. The value of the evidence from these preindustrial societies is that it shows how the interplay between biological potentials and cultural norms can produce extraordinarily diverse kinds of sexual conduct.

The conclusion from the cross-cultural data may be disconcerting to some, but it is inescapable. If you were raised in one of these other societies, you would probably follow its rules of sexual conduct. You would do these things with the full knowledge and approval of your community, and if your personal tastes ran counter to the prevailing norms, you might be considered distinctly odd—even wicked. Being no less ethnocentric than peoples in other societies, you would also regard American sexual attitudes and practices as most peculiar, to say the least.

Sexual Behavior in America

The most striking feature of sexuality in America is the tension between a tradition of highly restrictive standards, on the one hand, and a climate that values individuality and personal freedom, on the other. Restrictive patterns of sexual behavior have long been regarded as the cornerstone of public and private morality, yet the pleasures of sexual gratification are constantly extolled, implicitly and explicitly, especially through the mass media. Not surprisingly, the attempt to maintain the standards of earlier generations is largely unsuccessful. As a result, there is a discrepancy between the sexuality that is portrayed in the **ideal culture**—the norms and values a society adheres to in principle—and the sexuality that is actually expressed in the **real culture**—the norms and values a society adheres to in practice.

Traditional Values

The traditional sexual values of American society, and of Western society in general, have their roots in a particular interpretation of ancient Judeo-Christian morality. Sexual activity can have two basic purposes: reproduction and pleasure. The Western tradition has strongly emphasized the former and has generally disapproved of the latter: sex was morally acceptable if the partners were married and if their primary purpose was reproduction; sex for pleasure alone, especially by unmarried partners, was considered immoral (Boswell, 1980).

The tradition that the main purpose of sex is to produce children comes from the Old Testament, which urges the faithful to "be fruitful and multiply," censures those who "waste" their seed, and imposes severe penalties for nonreproductive

Figure 9.4

"You should be ashamed of yourself, sitting there so sexy and everything, while people all over the world are starving and living in slums and things like that."

Drawing by Joseph Farris; © 1973
The New Yorker Magazine, Inc.

sexual acts. Sexuality itself, however, was not regarded as sinful, and the Old Testament permitted a married man with an infertile wife to have sex with unmarried women, particularly household servants, if the intent was to produce children. The negative emphasis on sexuality, with its blanket prohibition on sex outside marriage, comes from the New Testament—not from the teachings of Jesus, who had little to say about sex, but from those of Saint Paul, who recommended total abstention from sex and tolerated marriage only on the grounds that it was "better to marry than to burn." By the early Middle Ages sex was virtually equated with sin; the doctrines of the medieval Church "were based, quite simply, upon the conviction that the sexual act was to be avoided like the plague, except for the bare minimum necessary to keep the race in existence" (G. Taylor, 1970). The Church not only insisted that priests be celibate, but even tried to limit marital sex, forbidding it on Sundays, Wednesdays, and eventually Fridays, with the result that sexual activity was prohibited for the equivalent of about five months of the year.

Figure 9.5 *Traditional Western attitudes toward sexuality derive from a particular interpretation of Judeo-Christian morality. The Genesis account of the sin of Adam and Eve and their subsequent expulsion from the Garden of Eden, depicted in this painting by the Italian artist Masaccio, has strong sexual overtones: the human species is sinful, nakedness is shameful, and sex for pleasure's sake is immoral.*

Subsequent centuries were marked by alternating periods of restrictiveness and relative permissiveness, with particularly restrictive attitudes occurring among the early Puritans and among the Victorians of the past century. Prudery reached a climax with the middle-class Victorians, who were unable to refer to anything remotely sexual except in the most discreet terms. Sweat became "perspiration" and then "glow"; legs became "limbs"; underwear became "unmentionables"; chicken breast became "white meat"; prostitutes became "fallen women"; pregnancy became "an interesting condition." Women were careful to cover even their ankles from the gaze of men, and some zealots actually covered the legs of their furniture from the public view. Masturbation was regarded as a dreadful vice that caused such maladies as deafness, blindness, heart disease, epilepsy, hair on the palms, and insanity. Some lunatic asylums even had separate wards for inmates who were believed to be victims of this "self-abuse."

For centuries, the sense of the erotic as sinful has been compounded by the ***double standard,*** an unspoken expectation that restrictive rules of sexual conduct should be strictly applied to women, but leniently to men. Women were considered pure and chaste, a notion which ultimately led to a widely accepted myth that (with the possible exception of prostitutes) they were essentially sexless. William Acton, a nineteenth-century expert on marriage, wrote that "the belief that women have a sexual appetite is a vile aspersion," and a surgeon-general of the United States stated that "nine-tenths of the time decent women feel not the slightest pleasure in intercourse" (Hunt, 1959). The double standard has persisted until the present, particularly in the working class of the Western world. Nonmarital sex is frequently seen as a matter of surrender by the female and conquest by the male, with the woman's reputation being cheapened in the process and the man's being elevated in the eyes of his peers.

These traditional values remain powerful in America today, although attitudes vary greatly according to age, sex, religion, place of residence, and level of education. Sex is still sometimes regarded as somehow dirty and unmentionable, and practices that do not potentially lead to reproduction are widely considered perverted. Despite the introduction of sex-education programs into many schools, a conspiracy of silence may still prevent the young from obtaining accurate and objective information about sex. The mass media generally refuse to carry advertisements for birth-control

Figure 9.6 *Edouard Manet's painting* Luncheon on the Grass *caused a sensation when it was first exhibited in Paris in 1863. Guards had to restrain crowds of outraged visitors who wanted to destroy the picture, and every night attendants had to wipe gobs of spit from the canvas. Manet's image was deeply shocking to people at the time, for it portrayed a nude woman in an everyday environment, rather than in a remote, artificial pose. Social concepts of what is acceptable have changed a good deal since then.*

products. Parents, if they discuss sex with their offspring at all, often do so with embarrassment, and most information is acquired from the peer group.

Over the years state legislatures have made countless attempts to control the private sexual behavior of consenting adults by law. Until the 1940s, for example, half the states of the Union prohibited interracial sex. Until the 1960s, all the states prohibited homosexual acts, half had laws against premarital or extramarital sex, some banned the use or sale of contraceptives, and a few regarded any coital position except the "missionary position" as a crime. Many of these laws have since been repealed or amended, but in 1986 twenty-four states still had "sodomy" laws prohibiting oral-genital or anal-genital contacts, even by consenting adults in private. (In five states the laws cover only homosexual acts, but in nineteen they also cover heterosexual acts—even within marriage.) Although these laws are difficult to enforce and have tended to fall into disuse, prosecutions of consenting adults for private sexual acts (particularly prostitution) are by no means unknown.

Such laws have few parallels in the modern world; Canada and the Western European nations have generally abandoned similar legislation, in some cases as long as a century ago, and many other countries have never had such laws to begin with. Indeed, the few other societies that still

actively attempt to police private sexual behavior fall almost exclusively into two categories—communist-ruled states like the Soviet Union and Cuba, and fundamentalist Muslim nations like Iran and Saudi Arabia. The American laws seem particularly paradoxical, for Americans—perhaps more than any other people on earth—are suspicious of government regulation, protective of their privacy, and zealous in their defense of individual rights. Yet in 1986 the U.S. Supreme Court ruled, by a one-vote majority, to uphold a state law that provides up to twenty years imprisonment for "any sexual act involving the sex organs of one person and the mouth or anus of another."

Contemporary Practices

Research into the sexual practices of Americans is very limited and often unreliable. The greatest obstacle is the difficulty of surveying a representative, random sample of the population. It is easy enough to discover how Americans will vote or which brand of soap they use, but it is much more difficult for researchers to inquire in depth into the sex lives of complete strangers. Understandably, many of those sampled will refuse to respond. Since these people differ in unknown but perhaps significant ways from those who are willing to answer, the results of the survey may be biased. In addition, many who do answer may not always tell the truth. No sex researchers have yet been able to fully overcome these problems.

The first major research into the sexual behavior of Americans was that of Alfred Kinsey in the 1940s and 1950s. Despite considerable harassment, including denunciation in churches, the media, and Congress by those who found his research immoral because of its subject matter, Kinsey was able to obtain full histories of the sex lives of more than 18,000 people who were a fairly representative cross-section of the white American population. His study was not statistically perfect by any means, but it remains the most ambitious and reliable sex survey ever undertaken. Other attempts at a "national" survey have been made periodically by such magazines as *Playboy, Psychology Today, Cosmopolitan,* and *Ladies' Home Journal,* but since these publications appeal to specific audiences, their surveys are not based on random samples of the population and so have little scientific value. The same is true of most of the various "studies," "surveys," and "exposés" that appear in the bestseller lists from time to time. However, we do have a good deal of data from public opinion polls, even if the questions are brief and superficial in comparison with Kinsey's in-depth interviews; and there are numerous sociological studies of specific groups—prostitutes, unwed mothers, teenagers, and so on.

Despite the methodological difficulties, all the evidence points overwhelmingly in the same direction. There is a gap between the traditional moral norms specifying how Americans ought to behave and the statistical data revealing how they actually do behave. Nowhere is this more evident than in Kinsey's volumes *Sexual Behavior in the Human Male* (1948) and *Sexual Behavior in the Human Female* (1953), which stunned American society with revelations of widespread deviation from moral norms.

Kinsey found, for example, that 85 percent of all men had experienced premarital sex. Nearly 70 percent of the men had visited a prostitute. Some 37 percent of men had experienced at least one homosexual act to the point of orgasm, and 18 percent of men had as much homosexual as heterosexual experience. Over 90 percent of the men had masturbated, and nearly 60 percent had engaged in heterosexual oral-genital contacts. Half the married men had committed adultery, and a further 25 percent favored the idea of doing so. About 8 percent of the men admitted to sexual contacts with animals, and among some rural populations

the proportion rose as high as 50 percent. In accordance with the double standard, 40 percent of the men wanted their wives to be virgins at the time of marriage. Nearly half the women had experienced premarital sex, although in the great majority of cases their only partner had been their prospective husband. Some 13 percent of the women had experienced homosexual contacts, and a further 15 percent had experienced homosexual desires but had not acted on them. A quarter of the married women had committed adultery, nearly 60 percent had masturbated, nearly 60 percent had engaged in heterosexual oral-genital contacts, and nearly 4 percent had taken part in sexual activities with animals. On this evidence, Kinsey concluded that "a call for a cleanup of sex offenders in the community is in effect a proposal that 5 percent of the population should support the other 95 percent in penal institutions."

Kinsey's findings caused such a furor because few people at the time realized how much the sexuality of the real culture diverged from that of the ideal culture. Actually, a sexual revolution had taken place much earlier, during the "roaring twenties," when many young people began discreet experimentation in forbidden areas. But, in an atmosphere where sexuality was rarely discussed, the full extent of the changes had gone unrecognized: people kept their disapproved behavior secret, unaware that it was shared by millions of others. After the Kinsey reports, the atmosphere changed radically, and public discussion of sex—in such media as newspapers, print, film, television, and the lyrics of popular music—became a distinctive and continuing feature of American popular culture. It was in this environment that a second major sexual revolution of the century took place.

This more recent revolution lasted from about the mid-1960s until the mid-1970s, and was part of much broader social and cultural changes that occurred as the United States embarked on the transition from an industrial to a postindustrial society. A new, affluent generation of young people challenged traditional norms and values in many areas of society, sexuality included. The women's movement arose, demanding changes in the established relationships of the sexes. And, crucially, a new technology became widely available: the birth-control pill, which permitted a separation of the pleasurable from the reproductive aspects of sexual behavior. The changes that resulted have had significant implications for several areas of contemporary sexual and social life. What are these changes?

Figure 9.7 *A star of the 1920s, Lina Basquette, dances the Charleston. The first sexual revolution of this century began in this era, but because people professed values they no longer practiced, it passed largely unnoticed. In the second revolution of the 1960s and 1970s, people openly advocated new sexual values and mores.*

Permissive Attitudes

In general, sexual attitudes have become more permissive. Phenomena that were once considered scandalous, such as open cohabitation by unmarried couples, X-rated movies, or nudity on the stage, now arouse far less concern. The most significant change has been in attitudes toward premarital sex: according to a 1985 Gallup poll, 58 percent of the public consider premarital sex acceptable—compared with 47 percent in 1973 and only 24 percent in 1969. This permissiveness is not indiscriminate, however. A 1982 National Opinion Research Center poll found that some 72 percent of the public believe adultery is "always wrong," and only 3 percent felt it is "not wrong at all." Similarly, the public believes by 58 to 32 percent that homosexuality should not be considered an "acceptable alternative lifestyle," although a majority favor laws to prevent discrimination against homosexuals. In general, permissive attitudes correlate strongly with youth and education; older or less educated people tend to take a more conservative stand.

Premarital Sex

Although a minority chooses not to have premarital sex, most young people are willing to enter a sexual relationship with a steady partner, and some are quite promiscuous. Surveys consistently show that over 80 percent of unmarried women and over 90 percent of unmarried men have experienced sexual intercourse. The increase in premarital sexual behavior is primarily the result of greater sexual participation by women; rates of premarital sex by men have remained constant for forty years. The rates of premarital sex are somewhat lower for college students than for the rest of the population, involving about 77 percent of male students and 64 percent of female students (Zelnick et al., 1979; Robinson and Jedlicka, 1982; Horn and Bachrach, 1985).

The Double Standard

The double standard of sexual conduct for men and women is eroding rapidly, partly because of the greater equality of the sexes and partly because contraception frees many women from the fear of pregnancy. In sharp contrast to the situation a few decades ago, only a small minority of young people of both sexes feel it is desirable that a woman be a virgin at the time of marriage. Nonetheless, promiscuous behavior in a woman is still more likely to attract stigma than similar behavior in a man—although a strong sexual appetite in a woman is no longer likely to be seen as a sign of psychological maladjustment or "nymphomania" (Haas, 1979; Zelnick and Kanter, 1980).

One interesting effect of the changing relationships of the sexes is that the responsibility for a successful sexual encounter has been largely shifted from the female to the male partner. A common sexual "problem" until the 1960s was female "frigidity"—the inability of a woman to achieve orgasm or even to enjoy sex. Today, "frigidity" has all but disappeared; instead, the same problem is more likely to be labeled as one of poor "performance" by the male.

Teenage Pregnancy

The new sexual freedom has not always been accompanied by responsibility: more than one-third of mothers under twenty-four are unmarried. A comparative international study by the Allan Guttmacher Institute (1985) found that the United States has a much higher rate of teenage pregnancy and illegitimacy than other Western industrialized nations. Moreover, the United States is the only such society where teenage pregnancy—which now involves over a million adolescents a year—is increasing. Why should this be? Permissiveness alone cannot account for the phenomenon, for rates of teenage sexual activity are similar in the other nations. Nor does the reason lie in welfare benefits for unmarried mothers, for these are more generous in the other societies. Nor are the lower pregnancy rates elsewhere the result of easier abortions, for the other societies have lower abortion rates than the United States. The reason seems to lie in birth control, which is easily and cheaply available to adolescents elsewhere but is

TEENAGE PREGNANCY
IN CULTURALLY SIMILAR COUNTRIES
Pregnancy rate per 1,000 women

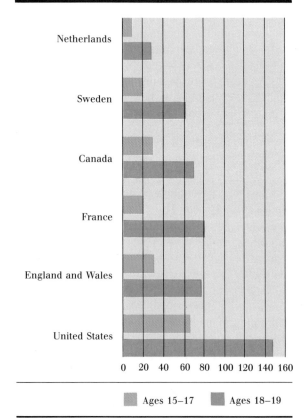

Ages 15–17   Ages 18–19

SOURCE: The Alan Guttmacher Institute, 1985.

Figure 9.8 *American teenagers become pregnant and give birth at significantly higher rates than adolescents in other countries. The main reason seems to be that American teenagers are less likely to use contraception.*

more difficult for American teens to get. The other nations are concerned that teenagers not get pregnant, and so encourage sexually active adolescents to use contraception. The United States is concerned that teenagers not have sex, and so discourages their use of contraception on the grounds that it might facilitate sexual activity. Thus, a combination of old values and new permissiveness leads to pregnancy—and thence to abortion or illegitimacy. (These issues are discussed in more detail in Chapter 13, "The Family.")

Pornography

Another obvious change is in the amount and availability of ***pornography,*** or pictorial and written material intended to arouse sexual excitement. Most users of pornography are men; about a quarter of the male population uses it frequently, either for entertainment or as an aid to masturbation. Pornography is now a $7-billion-a-year industry, whose products can be seen at corner newsstands in cities throughout North America. This material ranges from the "soft-core" type, consisting essentially of nude women in various poses, to the "hard-core" variety, which shows women in various sexual acts and often depicts them being stripped, bound, assaulted, tortured, and otherwise humiliated and degraded (Lederer, 1980; Faust, 1980; Dworkin, 1981).

Pornography has become deeply controversial, largely because many people believe that it directly or indirectly causes sex crimes. Studies of the issue have generally produced inconclusive findings, for it is difficult in practice to prove or disprove a general causal link between the use of pornography and acts such as rape or incest. The President's Commission on Obscenity and Pornography (1970) concluded that pornographic material "does not cause sexual misconduct," and recommended that restrictions on the distribution of pornography be lifted. But more recently, the Attorney-General's Commission on Pornography (1986) found that violent pornography "bears a causal relationship to sexual violence," and urged a legal crackdown on the material. Why the different conclusions? One reason, no doubt, is that each report tended to reflect the prevailing social climate: at the end of the 1960s, a commission stacked with liberals and civil libertarians took a permissive view; in the mid-1980s, a commission stacked with conservatives and law-enforcement officials drew a more restrictive conclusion. A second reason, however, is that the nature of por-

Figure 9.9 *Pornography and other public features of the sex industry have become highly controversial, for many people feel that these displays are distasteful and dehumanizing.*

nography had changed in the intervening years. The flood of newer, "hard-core" and sadomasochistic material—much of it now available in the form of video recordings—has reopened the whole question of the impact pornography may have on behavior.

Although the link between pornography and behavior is still undetermined, the link between pornography and attitudes is not. There is now ample evidence that men who are exposed to pornography tend, at least temporarily, to have more callous attitudes toward women afterward (Malamuth and Donnerstein, 1984). There can be little question that, whether or not pornography causes violence, it creates a climate in which women come to be seen as mere sex objects, existing solely to satisfy men's desires. Because of this, some feminist groups have formed an unusual alliance with conservative religious organizations to demand that pornography be restricted or banned. Other people, ranging from pornography consumers to civil-liberties groups, resist the suggestion. One objection is to the difficulty of agreeing on what is pornographic. A second objection derives from the First Amendment to the Constitution, which protects freedom of expression on the grounds that censorship itself is a greater danger to a free society than any censored material could

ever be (Lapham et al., 1984). The public remains divided on the issue. A 1985 Gallup poll found that a bare majority oppose further restrictions on pornography in general, but nearly three-quarters favor a ban on portrayals of sexual violence. Public opinion is also divided along sex lines: a 1986 Yankelovich poll found that half of all women, but only a quarter of men, are "very concerned" about pornography.

Sexually Transmitted Diseases

A direct effect of the more permissive environment has been an explosion in the incidence of sexually transmitted diseases, which are contracted by about 33,000 Americans every day. These include syphilis (about 70,000 cases a year), gonorrhea (about 2 million cases), venereal warts (1 million cases a year), chlamydia (3 million cases), trichomoniasis (1 million cases), and genital herpes (500,000 cases). Most of these diseases can be cured with antibiotics, although several can cause dangerous complications—not only in the immediate victims, but also in babies born to infected mothers. Herpes, however, is currently incurable, and this lifelong and often painful disease now afflicts an estimated 20 million Americans; additionally, tens of millions more are believed to be permanent carriers of herpes, although they have no symptoms. The disease is now so common in the sexually active population that a promiscuous person is almost certain to be exposed to it.

Most ominously of all, a new and lethal sexually transmitted disease has appeared in the United States in the 1980s: acquired immune deficiency syndrome (AIDS). In global terms, the great majority of the victims of this viral disease are heterosexual men and women—most of them in central Africa, where AIDS seems to have originated. In the United States, however, about 70 percent of the early AIDS victims are male homosexuals, perhaps because the disease was first introduced to, and then quickly amplified within, the promiscuous section of the homosexual population. AIDS is steadily spreading to the heterosexual population, however, and it is quite possible that the infection will soon become fairly common. By mid-1986, at the end of the first five-year period after the disease was recognized, over 20,000 Americans had been diagnosed with the severe, life-threatening form of AIDS; and tens of thousands more had been diagnosed with the milder AIDS-related complex, which in some cases leads to AIDS. In addition, between 1 and 3 million people had been infected with the AIDS virus. It is not known how many of these will develop AIDS; but the incubation period for the disease may run to five or more years—and infected people remain infected, and perhaps capable of infecting others, for life (Fettner and Check, 1985; Liebmann-Smith, 1985; Nichols, 1986). Estimates are that the number of cases of AIDS could increase tenfold during the second five-year period ending in 1991, by which time several million more Americans may be infected. (AIDS is discussed in more detail in Chapter 16, "Medicine.")

The 1980s have been a period of stability rather than flux in sexual norms, values, and practices, and there is general agreement among researchers that the sexual revolution which characterized the 1960s and 1970s is over. Opinion polls show substantial tolerance for diversity in sexual behavior, but they also show a continued commitment to marital fidelity and a declining interest in promiscuity. The epidemic of sexually transmitted diseases may have played a part in this trend, but it also seems that the sexual climate now calls for caring and commitment rather than rebellion and experimentation (Blumstein and Schwartz, 1983; Leo, 1984). The most important result of the preceding years of change, perhaps, has been widespread acceptance of newer concepts of sexual morality. Many people still adhere to the stern rules of earlier generations, and some seem not to believe in sexual morality at all. But increasingly, judgments about right and wrong in sexual matters are based on the attitude that moral behavior is that which involves mutual affection and respect and does no physical or psychological harm to those involved.

The real question mark hanging over contemporary sexual attitudes and practices is AIDS. If a permanent cure or effective vaccination can be found for this complex disease, its social consequences over the longer term will be more limited. But if AIDS continues to spread in the United States and the world as it has thus far—which could mean many millions of cases before the end of the century—the implications may be incalculable. We are socialized to associate sex with the most loving, life-giving human impulses. The equation of sex with death is something our culture is utterly unprepared for, and wrenching changes would be needed to deal with it.

We will turn now from the unique sexual practices of a specific society to consider four general topics in human sexual behavior: the incest taboo, rape, homosexuality, and prostitution.

The Incest Taboo

The question of why the incest taboo exists—and of why it is a cultural universal—offers a useful example of how sociological analysis can explain an otherwise puzzling practice. Why does every known society prohibit sexual relations between certain categories of relatives?

We have already noted that the taboo almost always applies to sex between parent and child and brother and sister. The exceptions are few and far between. Brother and sister were expected to marry in the royal families of ancient Egypt, Hawaii, and Peru, probably to prevent the royal lineage from being tainted by commoners. The Thonga of West Africa permit a father to have ritual sex with his daughter before he goes on a lion hunt; the Azande of central Africa expect their highest chiefs to marry their daughters; and the mothers of Burundi are expected to cure impotence in their adult sons by having intercourse with them. There is also evidence that brother-sister and parent-child marriages were occasionally practiced among the general population at certain periods in ancient Egypt and Iran, perhaps as a means of keeping property within the family

(Ford and Beach, 1951; Murdock, 1949; La Barre, 1954; Albert, 1963; Middleton, 1962). The general cross-cultural rule, however, is that people regard sex with certain close relatives as utterly immoral and even unthinkable. Why?

A ready response might be that the taboo is instinctive, because we certainly experience our aversion to incest as though it were an "instinct." But this view is clearly wrong, for several reasons. First, no other animal observes an incest taboo, and it is highly unlikely that we, who rely less than any other species on inherited behavior, would have evolved an instinct that all other animals lack. Second, if the attitude to incest were instinctive, there would be no need for the taboo—yet every society finds it necessary to have the taboo and laws to prevent the behavior. In fact, incest—most often between father and daughter or step-father and step-daughter—is a fairly common crime, although it is rarely reported. The American Psychological Association estimates that 12 to 15 million American women have been involved in incest, usually through sexual abuse in childhood or adolescence. A third reason why the taboo cannot be instinctive is that definitions of incest vary from one society to another. In some societies it is incestuous to marry any cousin; in other societies all cousins may intermarry. In some societies it is incestuous to marry the child of one's father's brother or one's mother's sister, but it is obligatory to marry the child of one's father's sister or one's mother's brother, even though all these cousins are equally closely related. The Mundugumor of New Guinea recognize blood relationships in such a complex way that three-quarters of all women in the society are ineligible as sex partners for any given man, and seven women out of eight are ineligible as wives. It would be a very strange instinct indeed that turned up in such different guises in different societies, scrupulously observing local and national boundaries in the process!

If the taboo is not instinctive, then might it exist to prevent the physical and mental degeneration that comes from inbreeding? This explanation sounds plausible, but for several reasons it is also incorrect. First, inbreeding does not necessarily produce degeneration: it merely intensifies certain traits, good or bad, that are already present in the related partners. Brother-sister marriages in Egypt and among the Inca resulted in no degeneration over as many as fourteen generations; indeed, the beautiful and intelligent Cleopatra was the product of such a union. Agricultural scientists use selective inbreeding, in fact, to produce healthier stock. Second, any ill effects of inbreeding usually take place too slowly and too haphazardly to be noticeable over a few generations. People living in simple, traditional societies would not be likely to link cause and effect, especially when other explanations, such as illness or witchcraft, are more readily available. Third, some peoples were apparently unaware that pregnancy is the result of sexual intercourse: the Trobriand Islanders, for example, denied that sex leads to conception, and other peoples attribute pregnancy to the work of their dead ancestors. Yet these societies have some of the most complex incest taboos ever recorded.

Then why the taboo? There are three main reasons, and they are social, not biological. The first is that early human beings—living primarily in small kinship groups of hunters and gatherers—needed to protect themselves by forming alliances with other groups. By forcing their children to marry into families outside their own, each group widened its social links and provided itself with allies in time of conflict and help in time of famine or other hazards. These groups, it has been said, faced the alternatives of marrying out or dying out. Marriage in most traditional societies is a practical alliance between groups, not a love match between individuals. That is why marriages are arranged by the parents, often when their offspring are still children and sometimes even before they are born (White, 1969).

The second reason for the incest taboo is that the family itself could not function without it, for the statuses of family members would be utterly and hopelessly confused. As Kingsley Davis (1948) points out:

> The incestuous child of a father-daughter union would be a brother of his own mother, i.e. the son of his own sister; a stepson of his own grandmother; possibly a brother of his own uncle; and certainly a grandson of his own father.

The third reason is that without an incest taboo, sexual rivalry among family members would disrupt the normal roles and attitudes of the various relatives. The father, for example, might experience role conflict as both the disciplinarian and the lover of his daughter; the mother might be jealous of both; and the child, of course, would be caught in the middle. Faced with constant conflict and tension, the family institution might simply disintegrate.

The incest taboo has developed over time because it is vital to the survival of the family and thus of society itself. Of course, neither traditional nor modern societies consciously appreciate the reasons for the taboo. They and we simply accept it as natural and moral.

Rape

The tender, romantic, and passionate intimacies of men and women are among the supreme human emotional experiences. Perhaps no other subject is so universally celebrated and even idealized in literature, art, and daily life. But the relationships of the sexes can have a darker side, one that may involve extremes of exploitation and violence.

Rape is forcible sexual intercourse against the will of the victim. It is a terrifying, brutal, and sometimes life-threatening crime, one that often leaves deep, long-term psychological scars. In the United States about 87,000 rapes are reported to the police every year, but these cases probably represent only about a tenth of the real total. One reason that rape is so underreported is that many victims are unwilling to relive the experience by submitting to police interrogation, medical examination, and court proceedings.

The fear of the crime touches virtually all women, instilling in them a wariness of male strangers and an apprehension about walking alone at night or being in deserted places. Yet, contrary to popular belief, most rapes are actually committed by an acquaintance of the victim—a family friend, a neighbor, a teacher, an employer, an ex-lover, a new dating partner. Victims of "date rape" are particularly reluctant to report the crime, for they are afraid that other people—including family, friends, and jurors—will suspect they did something to "ask for it" (Russell, 1984; Seligman et al., 1984).

"Date rape" is a threat even among American college students. One study found that 35 percent of male students said they might commit rape if they could be assured they would not be caught. Such attitudes seem to develop quite early: another study found that over 50 percent of male high school students believed that it is acceptable "for a guy to hold a girl down and force her to have sexual intercourse" in various situations, such as when "she gets him sexually excited" or "she says she's going to have sex with him and then changes her mind." Obviously, such attitudes are not always translated into action—but a female student is more likely to be forced into sex by a fellow student than by a stranger. Studies of college males have found that 10 percent admit to having had sex with a woman against her will—although most of them do not regard the act as rape. These students tend to regard sexual aggression as normal, and to believe that women "don't really mean it" when they say "no" to sexual advances. They are likely to answer "true" to such statements as "Most women

Figure 9.10 *When a man and a woman pass close together, they almost always turn as they do in this picture—the man toward the woman, the woman away from the man. This subtle form of body language reflects the different roles that men and women commonly play in their interaction with one another: the man as aggressor and pursuer, the woman as nonaggressive and pursued.*

are sly and manipulating when they want to attract a man," "A woman will only respect a man who will lay down the law to her," and "A man's got to show the woman who's boss right from the start or he'll end up henpecked." Additionally, many female students who have been forced into sex against their will (the legal definition of rape) likewise do not perceive the act as rape—just because a dating partner was the perpetrator (Malmuth, 1981; Sweet, 1985).

Although many people still regard rape as an expression of unrestrained, impulsive sexual desire, the sociological and psychological research of recent years has proven this view to be a myth.

Rape is a crime of violence, not of passion; it is a ritual of power and humiliation which, although socially regarded as intolerable, has its origins in approved patterns of interaction between the sexes (Chappell et al., 1977; Scully and Marolla, 1983).

The Social Context

In some cultures rape is virtually unknown, while in others it is relatively common. In a survey of 95 societies, Peggy Sanday (1982a) found that 47 percent were rape-free or almost rape-free, 17 percent were rape-prone, and 36 percent had a limited but undetermined amount of rape. The extent of rape seems to depend on cultural factors: rape-prone societies often have male gods, accord women low status, and encourage aggressiveness in boys, whereas rape-free societies believe in gods who are female or of both sexes, accord women more equality with men, and discourage male aggression. Thus the Ashanti of West Africa, who have a rape-free society, emphasize an earth goddess, treat women with great respect, and admire nurturant rather than aggressive traits. On the other hand, the Gusei of Kenya, who have a rape-prone society, emphasize male gods, treat women as inferiors, and conceive of normal heterosexual intercourse as an assault on women. In rape as in other aspects of human behavior, the conduct of the individual is influenced by the norms of the surrounding society.

In the United States, as in most other societies, the social relations of the sexes are marked by two cultural features relevant to rape: inequality between women and men, and a tendency for men to view women as actual or potential sexual property—that is, as sex objects. A classic example of this tendency is the barrage of whistles, catcalls, and obscene suggestions that often assails a young woman walking past a group of male construction workers. Since the likelihood that the woman will respond favorably to this kind of attention is approximately zero, the behavior clearly serves some other purposes. What it actually does is to allow the men to bolster their own egos, to demonstrate their "masculinity" to their peers, and to reassert the view that the role of women is to gratify men. The woman's feelings are not at issue.

In fact, this view of women is quite prevalent in the workplace, where the sexual harassment of women is a common and serious problem. In the office or factory, as elsewhere in society, men have a virtual monopoly of power and influence. Frequently, they take advantage of this superior status to indulge in uninvited and unwanted sexual advances, ranging from ogling, leering, squeezing, pinching, bottom-patting, and the like to outright propositions accompanied by the implied or explicit threat of dismissal (MacKinnon, 1979).

The norms of this kind of interaction require comparatively little self-control by the men; instead, it is the women who are expected to manage the situation. Many men, it seems, are convinced that any normal woman will be flattered by sexual attention in any form; women, for their part, have been socialized to receive these advances as gracefully as possible, regardless of their private response. The myth has it that they enjoy the attention, that they find it easy to deal with, and that the behavior is trivial in any case. But surveys show the reverse to be true: almost unanimously, women declare that sexual advances in the workplace make them feel powerless, trapped, defeated, intimidated, or demeaned. This reaction is understandable, for these norms of sexual harassment have a wider social significance. In all cases, the male's message is the same: Your responsibility is to satisfy me, you are not my equal, don't compete, your real value is your body. Sexual harassment in the workplace is now illegal, and—since corporate and other employers may be held responsible for their employees' conduct—may well be curtailed in the future. The incidence of rape, however, is increasing.

Figure 9.11

"I know you expect something in return for the movie, the flowers, and the dinner. Wait here and I'll get you a receipt."

The Nature of Rape

Rape is an extreme outcome of culturally approved activities in which one segment of society dominates another, socially and sexually. It is usually not an act of sudden impulse, for the majority of these crimes are planned in advance, with the rapist—whether a stranger or an acquaintance—carefully selecting a time, place, and victim for the attack. Nor is rape the result of any lack of alternative sexual outlets: many rapists are married, many have other sexual partners, and most could easily afford a prostitute. In fact, lust seems to have remarkably little to do with rape: a high proportion of rapists are completely impotent, and many more become sexually aroused only when they have sufficiently terrified and debased their victim through verbal and physical abuse. This victim's report is fairly typical:

> He hit me in the face and knocked me on the floor. He pulled off my robe and nightgown and I screamed and he threatened to kill me. He stuffed the nightgown in my mouth and tied the rest around my throat and the gown strangled me. He tied my hands behind my back and he pressed my neck so hard I passed out. Then he asked me if I needed air and I nodded and he let it loose a bit but still kept it in my mouth. He tied my legs up to the tie on my hands . . . then he got my butcher knife from the kitchen and ran the point all over my body. [Quoted in Shram, 1978]

All the evidence indicates that the sexual aspect of rape is of secondary importance. The primary object is to humiliate and subjugate the woman, and thus to bolster the aggressor's feelings of power, superiority, and masculinity (Amir, 1971; Brownmiller, 1975; Walker and Brodsky, 1976; Scully and Marolla, 1983; Russell, 1984).

The effects of rape can be devastating for the victim, involving physical and emotional damage and the disruption of personal, social, familial, and sexual life. If the victim reports the attack to the police, the emotional trauma may be reexperienced months or years later in a courtroom, where the intimate details of the rape are dissected before an audience of strangers. Typically, defense lawyers try to shift the burden of guilt from the accused to the victim. They may try to show that the woman is "loose," implying that if she has consented to any man before, she must have been willing on this occasion also. Or, utilizing the myth that women somehow enjoy being raped, they may claim that the victim consciously or subconsciously encouraged the assault. They may even argue that she was provocatively dressed and was

therefore at fault—another example of the way in which responsibility for the control of male advances is shifted to the female. Such a line of defense is unique to the crime of rape—a well-dressed man stepping from an expensive limousine would never be accused of thereby tempting someone to mug him. Even this aspect of the act and its aftermath can be fully understood only in terms of the overall patterns of sexual interaction in the society (Hilberman, 1976; Holmstrom and Burgess, 1976).

Homosexuality

As the principal variation on the norm of heterosexuality, homosexuality presents a recurring issue for both society and sociology. The behavior occurs all over the world and throughout history, although its form, acceptability, and apparent extent vary greatly from one society to another. There is a good deal of cross-cultural evidence about male homosexuality, but much less information about female homosexuality, or lesbianism. In many societies, as we have seen, homosexuality is taboo and therefore practiced in secret, while in others the behavior is more acceptable and thus more public. It seems that in any given society where male homosexuality is tolerated or encouraged, it takes *one* of three quite different types: pederasty, involving a relationship between a man and a boy; or transvestism, in which certain men take on the social and sexual role of women; or homophilia, in which both partners are adult men who play otherwise conventional masculine roles. The other two types tend to be rare and highly disapproved—not just by society at large, but also by most of those who practice the tolerated type of homosexuality (Gregersen, 1983).

Cross-culturally, pederasty is by far the most widespread form of socially accepted homosexual behavior, although it usually occurs in a bisexual context. Several societies, such as the Aranda of Australia, the Siwans of North Africa, and the Keraki of New Guinea, require every male to have exclusively homosexual relations with adults during adolescence but to be bisexual or heterosexual thereafter. Among the Keraki, for example, the initiation of adolescent males into adulthood requires them to take the passive role in anal intercourse for a year; when they become older, but before they get married, they initiate younger boys in like manner. The outstanding historical exam-

Figure 9.12 *The nature and extent of homosexual behavior depend very much on the social context in which they arise. Large, publicly visible gay subcultures based on relationships between otherwise conventional adults are found and tolerated almost exclusively in the democratic nations of the industrialized Western world. Other societies have tolerated quite different forms of homosexual behavior.*

ple of socially approved pederasty occurred in ancient Greece, where an elaborate system of sexual and spiritual relationships between adults and youths was apparently more highly valued than heterosexuality. But, like other societies that accept pederasty, the ancient Greeks regarded sex between adult men, or effeminate behavior by any males, as contemptible (Herdt, 1985; Dover, 1980).

Transvestism is cross-culturally much more rarely approved. This behavior has been accepted primarily among Asian people and North American Indian tribes, where there was often a clearly defined transvestite role with specific social duties, frequently those of tribal shaman. Clyde Kluck-

hohn (1948) found male homosexual behavior, generally of this type, accepted by 120 American Indian peoples and rejected by 54. A few societies that recognize the transvestite role, such as the Chukchi of Siberia, allow marriage between men. In such cases, the transvestite plays the social role of wife, while the husband is regarded as a normal heterosexual. Societies that accept transvestism generally regard pederasty as intolerable and consider homophilia almost incomprehensible.

Homophilia, involving adult males without any gender-role changes, is historically and cross-culturally very unusual. The behavior is found almost exclusively in the industrialized world—particularly in the emerging postindustrial societies of North America and Western Europe, where a distinct "gay" subculture is tolerated, but not encouraged, in larger cities. Homophilia is virtually unknown in simple, preindustrial societies, and there is very little evidence for it anywhere before the nineteenth century: most languages do not even have a name for this role, and our word "homosexual" was first coined in 1869. Societies that tolerate this type of homosexual behavior take a dim view of transvestism and particularly of pederasty, as do most homosexuals within these cultures.

The cross-cultural evidence on lesbianism is fragmentary, but the behavior seems to be generally less common than male homosexuality. The reason may lie in the fact that women in most societies have less freedom to experiment and deviate sexually than men, but it may also be the case that lesbian behavior is typically so discreet that visiting anthropologists may have interpreted it as mere "affection" and overlooked its real meaning. In any event, Gregersen (1983) found only five traditional societies that specifically approve of lesbianism, although the behavior is reported to be especially common in societies where men have many wives, particularly if the wives live together in harems. Lesbianism generally appears to take the homophilic form; relations between adult women and girls and relations involving gender-role reversals appear to be cross-culturally rare and are never socially approved. In general, lesbianism does not appear to arouse the strong reactions that male homosexuality sometimes does, and in practice most cultures appear to tolerate or not notice it. (The classic example of this phenomenon was a nineteenth-century British law that forbade male homosexuality but ignored lesbianism—because Queen Victoria refused to believe that women did such things!)

Western attitudes toward homosexuality have generally been negative. The reason lies yet again in the Western moral tradition that tolerates sexual acts only if they occur within marriage and can lead to reproduction. Homosexual acts are pursued for nonmarital love or pleasure and are necessarily nonreproductive. Until the global population explosion of the present century, widespread exclusive homosexuality would have been highly dysfunctional, for a society that did not encourage high birth rates might risk extinction. In a world faced with a crisis of overpopulation, however, homosexuality (and contraception, masturbation, oral-genital sex, and other nonreproductive forms of heterosexual activity) are no longer dysfunctional in this respect, and so receive more acceptance than in the past.

The Gay and Lesbian Community

How common is homosexuality in the United States? The answer to this question depends in part on the definition of homosexuality. Americans, unlike many other peoples, tend to see homosexuality and heterosexuality as "either/or" categories. Yet any attempt to divide the population into two distinct categories must fail because of the countless ambiguous cases that arise—people whose desires are heterosexual but whose behavior is homosexual; people who have homosexual histories but whose current behavior is heterosexual; people who alternate between the two forms of behavior; and so on. On the basis of his research,

Kinsey recognized that sexual orientation is a continuum, and he accordingly constructed a seven-point rating scale, with exclusive homosexuality at one end and exclusive heterosexuality at the other (see Figure 9.13). Subsequent studies of the topic have been tentative and fragmentary, but they have generally indicated that 10 percent or so of the population can be considered exclusively or predominantly homosexual. Such an estimate would include somewhere in the region of 25 million Americans. There is no evidence, however, that the percentage of homosexuals in the population has increased over time, although homosexuality has certainly become more visible.

Over the past decade and a half, the gay liberation movement has substantially changed attitudes toward homosexuality, and gay men and lesbian women (the names they prefer) are able to pursue their lifestyles with relative freedom in larger cities, many of which now have local laws to guarantee their civil rights. Of course, some homosexuals attempt throughout their lives to "pass" as heterosexuals, even to the extent of marrying. On the whole, they seem successful in this attempt: according to one national poll, less than a third of Americans are sure they know a homosexual, and more than half believe they do not know any homosexuals at all (Schneider and Lewis, 1984). This is a remarkable finding, given that there are about as many substantially homosexual people in the United States as there are blacks or people aged sixty-five or over—and they, obviously, all have to be *somebody's* child, parent, cousin, co-worker, teacher, neighbor, friend, or fellow student.

KINSEY HETEROSEXUAL–HOMOSEXUAL RATING SCALE

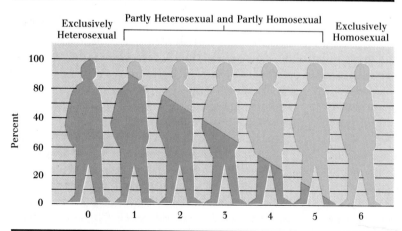

Figure 9.13 *Alfred Kinsey's research established that homosexuality and heterosexuality are not mutually exclusive categories, for elements of both are found in most people in varying degrees. Kinsey's seven-point scale provides a way of measuring the balance in particular individuals. The scale runs from one extreme of exclusively heterosexual acts or feelings through to the other extreme of exclusively homosexual acts or feelings.*

SOURCE: Adapted from Alfred C. Kinsey et al., *Sexual Behavior in the Human Male* (Philadelphia: W. B. Saunders, 1948), p. 638.

Most large cities contain definable areas that are occupied primarily by gays and lesbians and in which shops, restaurants, bars, hotels, churches, beaches, and other amenities cater primarily to them. Homosexuals are drawn together not only by a shared sexual orientation but also by a common social experience of stigma as deviants. As gay and lesbian people grow up they, like anyone else, experience sexual emotions, desires, and acts that feel natural and right. Yet at some point, each maturing gay or lesbian person experiences the shock of realizing that these deep personal feelings are often despised in the society beyond, and that to express them, even in acts of love, may sometimes be a crime. Some homosexuals react to this wound to their self-concept by accepting society's attitude toward homosexuality and falling into self-hatred. Some spend a lifetime denying their homosexual tendencies, to others and perhaps even to themselves. Most, however, find ways to resolve the conflict, and many are able to do so in the gay and lesbian communities, subcultures in which they can be resocialized by learning new roles, norms, and values. The new climate helps to neutralize earlier conceptions of homosexuality as perverted or sinful, and enables gays and lesbians to build positive self-concepts (Warren, 1974; Altman, 1972, 1982; Wolf, 1979).

The great majority of gay men tend to form long-lasting, affectionate relationships, and lesbians seem to maintain even more stable and enduring relationships than heterosexuals do (Hooker, 1965; Masters and Johnson, 1979; Blumstein and Schwartz, 1983; Ettmore, 1980). It is true, however, that male homosexuals are more promiscuous as a group than heterosexuals. This is not surprising. Men in general are expected to be more promiscuous than women. We would therefore expect to find, and do find, that sexual relationships involving only men are more promiscuous than those involving men and women, while those involving only women are the least promiscuous of all. In the first decade or so of gay liberation, in fact, some gay men seemed to initiate their own sexual revolution, reacting to their new freedom by almost celebrating promiscuity. The appearance of AIDS has abruptly chastened that attitude, and encouraged many gay men to revert to more traditional practices of dating and settling down with a single partner. The gay community's collective response to AIDS—especially through the support services it has provided to gays, drug addicts, children, and others stricken by the disease—has cemented its bonds in a way that promiscuous sex never could.

Learning Sexual Orientation

Many people, including some homosexuals, believe that gays and lesbians are simply "born that way." But since we know that even heterosexuals are not "born that way," this explanation seems unlikely. Despite extensive research, no consistent evidence has been found for genetic or hormonal factors that might predispose individuals toward homosexuality—or, for that matter, toward any of the other acts or preferences that occur in the vast spectrum of human sexual experience. Those who offer a biological explanation for homosexuality seem to do so, in fact, only because they can think of no other (for example, Bell, Weinberg, and Hammersmith, 1981). But biological factors cannot explain the different extent of homosexuality in different societies at different times, or the changes of sexual orientation that may take place during the lifetime of an individual. Homosexuality, like any other sexual behavior ranging from oral sex to sadomasochism to a pursuit of brunettes, is learned (Marmor, 1980).

How do people learn their eventual sexual orientation—and, more specifically, why do some become homosexual in the face of so much discouragement in the socialization process? The question has been widely discussed and several theories have been offered.

1. *Early experiences.* A common popular view is that homosexuality is caused by early childhood experiences, particularly seduction. But while this may be true in some specific instances, it cannot provide a comprehensive explanation. Most American preadolescents and a substantial proportion of adolescents have had some homosexual experience, but only a small minority of them become exclusive homosexuals. Other people who have never had any homosexual experience in their entire lives may still privately define themselves as homosexual (Dank, 1971). Conversely, most gays and lesbians have had some youthful heterosexual experience—but it obviously did not make them heterosexual.

2. *Family environment.* Psychoanalysts have focused on the family background of homosexuals, usually in the belief that homosexuality is a form of mental disorder or "sickness" resulting from pathological family interactions. The leading proponent of this theory is Irving Bieber (1962), who claimed that homosexual males typically had domineering, possessive mothers and ineffectual or hostile fathers. Bieber's study, which was based entirely on psychiatric patients, has not been sup-

Figure 9.14 *A significant category of the population does not conform to heterosexual norms. This fact, which is often perplexing to the rest of society, presents an important question for socialization theory: How do people learn their sexual orientation?*

ported by subsequent studies, which have found no significant relationship between family background and sexual orientation. Other studies have found no consistent personality differences between homosexuals and heterosexuals (Hooker, 1965, 1969). Correspondingly, in 1973, the American Psychiatric Association removed homosexuality from its list of mental disorders.

3. *Social learning.* Another view comes from some psychologists, who argue that sexual orientation is learned through rewards and punishments. A person who finds a homosexual experience pleasurable may continue to repeat the experience, and a homosexual identity may result. This approach is helpful, but it still has two major defects. First, the balance of rewards and punishments in society heavily favors a heterosexual orientation, and it is difficult to see how specific rewards in a limited context would counter this powerful social experience. Second, some homosexuals clearly do not find their orientation rewarding. They may wish to abandon their homosexual lifestyle but seem unable to do so. It is difficult to see how their sexual preference can be fully explained in terms of the punishments and rewards it offers them.

4. *Self-labeling.* A more recent approach to the problem avoids many of these difficulties. It recognizes the flexibility of the human sex drive and sees homosexual identity—or indeed any other sexual identity, including a heterosexual one—as the result of a self-definition, or label that people apply to themselves. This self-labeling usually occurs in late childhood or adolescence. At this age, young people may not even be fully aware that

they are labeling themselves, and in some cases they may apply the label reluctantly—but their self-definition shapes their later sexual orientation.

How does this self-labeling work? Consider the quite common case of an adolescent boy who experiences a mild sexual interest in another male. It is possible for him to interpret this interest in various ways. If he thinks, "This means nothing, it's just a phase many straight people go through," then he is defining himself as heterosexual and is likely to continue on that path. If he thinks, "Hmm. This means that I'm attracted to boys as well as girls," then he is considering himself bisexual and may develop a bisexual identity in later years. And if he thinks, "I'm attracted to another male—I must be gay," then his self-labeling may propel him further in the direction of homosexuality. In short, people become trapped within their own self-definition of their sexual orientation and, particularly if they are labeled as homosexuals (or heterosexuals) by others, they usually cannot escape from it. Regardless of social rewards or punishments, they can find no road back from their orientation, for they believe there is none (Sagarin, 1973, 1975; Blumstein and Schwartz, 1974).

Cultural beliefs strongly influence the self-definition that the individual makes. It is quite possible to engage in homosexual acts without defining oneself as, or becoming, homosexual, provided one's culture or subculture offer this option. Among American male prison communities, in which homosexuality is very common, the dominant partner in a sexual encounter is defined as heterosexual (even though he achieves sexual gratification from his homosexual acts) and the submissive partner is defined as homosexual (even if he is unwilling and even if he is raped). The participants in the acts learn to accept these definitions, regardless of their prior orientation (Kirkham, 1971; A. Davis, 1968; Lockwood, 1979). Similarly, many homosexual prostitutes think of themselves as fully heterosexual, because their subculture permits them to believe that they are "just doing it for the money" (Reiss, 1961; Humphreys, 1971). In general, exclusive homosexuality is found only in societies that define heterosexuality and homosexuality as mutually exclusive. In societies that offer bisexuality as a cultural option, people with homosexual tendencies are more likely to define themselves and to be defined by others as bisexual and to behave accordingly. The precise content of the homosexual, heterosexual, bisexual, or any other sexual role, and the process through which people come to learn it, can be understood only in terms of the prevailing cultural definitions.

Prostitution

Prostitution is the relatively indiscriminate exchange of sexual favors for economic gain. Not all exchanges of sex for gain are prostitution: the person who "marries for money," the "kept" lover, the actor or actress who sleeps with film directors en route to stardom, are not generally considered prostitutes. What distinguishes the prostitute is a willingness to perform sexual services for virtually anyone in return for some gain. In theory, four forms of prostitution are possible: women for men, men for men, women for women, and men for women. In practice the last two types are very rare indeed. Male homosexual prostitution is common in large cities, but by far the greatest number of prostitutes are women offering their services to men.

In some preindustrial societies the prostitute enjoyed high social status. In ancient Greece high-class prostitutes, the *hetairae*, were welcomed in literary and political circles. They appeared in public with leading statesmen, and their portraits and statues adorned public buildings. In many ancient societies of the Middle and Far East, prostitution was practiced in the temples as a religious ritual. Sacred prostitution even occurred among the early Hebrews, although the Old Testament later forbade the practice. But since early Christian times the occupation of prostitute in the West has

been anything but a respected one. Although she may consort on the most intimate terms with politicians and judges, bishops and bankers, the prostitute's status is very low.

The reason can again be traced to the Judeo-Christian moral tradition. Men use prostitution for pleasure alone, and neither they nor the prostitute have any intention that the relationship should lead to reproduction. By definition, prostitution can take place only outside the context of marriage. In further violation of social norms, the prostitute in Western cultures offers her services for money in a society that regards love as a prerequisite for legitimate sex. And to make matters worse still, she flouts the double standard with her promiscuity.

Figure 9.15 *Prostitution has often been called "the world's oldest profession." These prostitutes and their rather elegant surroundings were painted by the Italian artist Carpaccio in the sixteenth century. Despite repeated attempts to stamp it out, prostitution continues to thrive.*

Prostitution as an Occupation

The occupation of prostitute takes several basic forms. Most female prostitutes work as street-walkers, soliciting clients in public places such as streets and hotel lobbies. These women are generally poorly educated and include a high proportion of minority-group members, teenage runaways, and older prostitutes who are nearing the end of their careers. Other women work in brothels, which are today disguised as "massage parlors" or "clubs"; these prostitutes have higher status and better earnings than the streetwalker and they face less danger from their clients or the police. Still others work as call girls, operating out of hotel rooms or apartments, either on their own or through an "escort agency." These are usually the better-educated prostitutes, who may regard the occupation as a potential avenue to higher social status as the mistress or even the wife of a wealthy man. Male prostitutes catering to homosexuals solicit clients on certain streets, in some gay bars, and occasionally through "escort agencies." Male prostitutes catering to women generally work through private introductions and try to establish regular relationships with a small number of clients rather than transient relationships with many women (Winick and Kinsie, 1971; Laner, 1974; Bullough and Bullough, 1979; Cohen, 1980; Symanski, 1981).

Recruitment into prostitution is rarely the result of an abrupt decision. People tend to drift into the role and to serve a period of apprenticeship before finally defining themselves as prostitutes and relying on the occupation as a major or sole source of income. Drift into prostitution may begin when a woman accepts a casual offer from a man, or when she meets another prostitute or a pimp—a man who organizes female prostitution and lives off the proceeds. The pimp introduces women to their new role and thereafter serves as lover, business manager, protector, and exploiter. He arranges contacts, pays court fines and bail, and safeguards the prostitute's territory against competitors. Housegirls, call girls, and male prostitutes have little need of pimps, but a high proportion of streetwalkers have arrangements with them. They generally take pride in the lifestyle they provide for the pimp, since his affluence provides evidence of their occupational success. The relationship between prostitute and pimp is a curious one. It involves a reversal of the usual gender-role expectations, for the female partner or partners are more promiscuous than the male and serve as breadwinners for him.

Perspectives on Prostitution

Prostitution is actually a well-established, though minor, social institution. As such, it has been carefully researched by sociologists and has been analyzed from the functionalist, conflict, and interactionist perspectives. The functionalist theorist Kingsley Davis (1932, 1976) argues that, like other institutions, prostitution exists because it must have some effect, or function, that contributes to the maintenance of society as a whole. Both men and women, he claims, have sound reasons for entering into the relationship. From the point of view of the prostitute, the occupation offers some advantages: it can be less tedious and better paid than many alternative unskilled jobs, such as office cleaner or assembly-line worker, and there is often the possibility of forming relationships with high-status men. From the point of view of the clients, prostitution provides a convenient opportunity for sexual contacts. Men who are away from home may find the prostitute a convenient substitute for their usual partners; men with unusual sexual preferences may find that prostitutes will cater to tastes that other women will not; and old or unattractive men may use prostitution as the only way to enjoy sex with a young and attractive woman. Most important, these services involve no complications, obligations, or emotional entanglements. Prostitution, therefore, is functional, for it meets men's needs for a variety of sexual outlets without undermining the family system in the way that more affectionate and involved extramarital relationships would.

Conflict theorists have been critical of this approach, which they see as an example of functionalist bias in favor of the status quo. If prostitution exists to cater to sexual needs, why are there not hordes of males waiting to prostitute themselves to women? Like any other institution, conflict theorists argue, prostitution reflects the power relationships in the society beyond. Prostitution therefore benefits primarily the men involved—the pimps and especially the clients—at the expense of the women, who are exploited. Prostitution may be "convenient" for men—but what is the long-term effect on the women of servicing the lonely, the kinky, and the ugly? Most prostitutes, conflict theorists point out, have little education and come from lower- and working-class backgrounds, and many of them have suffered emotional, physical, and even sexual abuse as children. They enter prostitution because their only economic resource is their sexual availability. Not only are they trapped in a dead-end job—for youth

Figure 9.16 *Conflict theorists argue that the institution of prostitution reflects, in microcosm, the power relations of the sexes. Arrests of female prostitutes are commonplace—but how often are their male clients led off in handcuffs?*

and beauty are assets that fade quickly—but the work is dangerous, stigmatized, and criminal. And when the police crack down on this crime, it is the prostitutes who get arrested, not their respectable clients. Prostitution thus institutionalizes the tendency to regard women as sex objects, and represents, in microcosm, the economic and political inequality of the sexes (Chapman and Gates, 1978; James, 1978; Dworkin, 1981).

Interactionist researchers have looked less at the broader societal context than at the ordinary human relationships involved in prostitution—at how the participants interact and how they understand their own behavior. One focus of research, for example, is on the resocialization that takes place as a new recruit enters the occupation. From pimps and other prostitutes, she learns various techniques: how to solicit in public, how to recognize undercover police officers, how to handle difficult customers, how to perform minimum services in the least possible time for a maximum fee. She also acquires a new set of values that help to maintain her own relative self-concept: she learns to despise her clients, to hold "respectable" women in contempt as prostitutes in disguise, to regard society as hypocritical, and to justify her own activities as socially valuable (Bryant, 1965; N. Davis, 1971; Heyl, 1977).

The three perspectives may seem contradic-

tory, but, as is often the case, they complement each other to some extent, for each focuses on a rather different aspect of reality. The functionalist approach shows how prostitution may fulfill a certain social need; the conflict approach shows how the institution favors some groups at the expense of others; and the interactionist approach reveals the dynamics of the everyday social relationships involved. Taken together, they may provide a more comprehensive view of the topic than could be offered by any one perspective alone.

A sociological analysis also suggests why, for centuries, prostitution has resisted every effort to eradicate it. Many countries have legalized prostitution, justifying their action on the grounds that it is a victimless crime involving a private act by consenting adults. The idea that prostitution should be legalized is strongly resisted in the United States, however, mainly on the grounds that this would legitimate the practice, encourage more use of prostitutes' services, and so undermine public morality.

As Kingsley Davis (1932, 1976a) points out, however, prostitution cannot be completely eliminated in a sexually restrictive society, for it arises in response to those very restrictions. In the more permissive societies in the Ford and Beach cross-cultural sample, prostitution is extremely rare, for the reason that people have considerable opportunity for legitimate outlets beyond marriage. As Davis points out, prostitution could be completely eliminated only in a society that was totally permissive and in which sexual relations were freely available to all. Such a society could never exist, for total sexual freedom would imply a breakdown of the family system. The more restrictive a society is, the greater the pressure for prostitution to provide outlets for those who are not married or who find that exclusive sexual relationships with their spouses are unsatisfactory.

There is also an economic reason why prostitution cannot be eliminated. Police crackdowns might temporarily reduce the number of prostitutes, but the demand for their services would remain constant. The result would be an immediate increase in the fees for prostitution, which in turn would attract more women into the profession—including some who would not otherwise have considered it.

The sociological perspective on prostitution, as on all other forms of human sexual expression, offers a more acute insight into this aspect of social behavior—and with that insight, perhaps, comes a better understanding of the varied ways of men and women in our own society and elsewhere.

Summary

1.   Sexuality is an important element in social life. Human sexual behavior is not innate, but is learned through the socialization process. The subject has been poorly researched until recently.

2.   Human sexuality is extremely flexible; for this reason, every society makes strong efforts to regulate it in culturally approved ways.

3.   There are three cultural universals in human sexuality: the incest taboo, marriage, and heterosexuality. Other than that, there are considerable variations in sexual practices in other societies, particularly preindustrial societies. Societies vary in their conception of beauty, their permissiveness or restrictiveness, and their norms of sexual conduct. This variation reveals the interplay of biological potentials and cultural learning.

4.   Sexual behavior in the United States is marked by a contrast between real and ideal norms and values. Traditional values emphasize sex as legitimate only in the context of marriage and only if its primary purpose is reproduction, but they tolerate a double standard of behavior for males and females. The work of Kinsey and others indicates that these norms and values are extensively violated. A sexual revolution from the mid-1960s to the mid-1970s brought changes in attitudes, premarital sex, the double standard, teenage pregnancy, pornography, and sexually transmitted disease, notably herpes and AIDS. Sexual norms and values have now become more stable.

5.   Some form of incest taboo is universal. The taboo is not instinctive, nor does it exist to prevent any ill effects of inbreeding. It exists to encourage alliances between groups through marriage, to prevent confusion of statuses in the family, and to prevent sexual jealousies between family members.

6.   Rape is a crime of violence, not of passion, rooted in cultural norms. Many men tend to view women as sex objects, often subjecting them to sexual harassment in the workplace and elsewhere. Rape is an extreme manifestation of such established patterns of behavior, in which the aggressor bolsters his feelings of power and masculinity by abusing and humiliating the victim.

7.   Where societies approve or tolerate homosexuality, it takes one of three main forms: pederasty, transvestism, or homophilia. Homosexuality has long been stigmatized in Western societies. Homosexual life, particularly in urban centers, focuses on a defined homosexual community. Several theories of causation have been offered: early experiences, family environment, social learning, and self-labeling in terms of cultural beliefs.

8.   The practice of prostitution violates several traditional values and is stigmatized in the United States. Functionalist theory sees prostitution as meeting sound needs without placing too much strain on the family system; conflict theory sees it as a reflection of wider sexual inequalities; interactionist theory concentrates on the social behavior involved, such as the socialization of prostitutes.

Important Terms

cultural universals (225)
incest taboo (225)
marriage (225)
adultery (225)
heterosexuality (225)
homosexuality (225)
bisexuality (225)
restrictiveness (227)

permissiveness (227)
ideal culture (229)
real culture (229)
double standard (230)
pornography (234)
rape (238)
prostitution (245)

Suggested Readings

BLUMSTEIN, PHILLIP, and PEPPER SCHWARTZ. *American Couples.* New York: Morrow, 1983.

A sociological study of relationships of couples in the United States. Based on surveys and interviews, the book gives an interesting and readable view of contemporary intimate relationships.

BULLOUGH, VERN L. *Sexual Variance in Society and History.* Chicago: University of Chicago Press, 1980.

An interesting historical and cross-cultural survey of human sexual practices.

FORD, CLELLAN S., and FRANK A. BEACH. *Patterns of Sexual Behavior.* New York: Harper & Row, 1951.

An important study of sexual behavior in other cultures and in other species. The authors use this material to draw basic conclusions about human sexuality.

HENSLIN, JAMES M., and EDWARD SAGARIN (eds.). *The Sociology of Sex: An Introductory Reader.* 2nd ed. New York: Schocken, 1978.

A collection of articles on various aspects of the sociology of sex. The book provides a useful overview of research in this field.

HYDE, JANET SHIBLEY. *Understanding Human Sexuality.* 3rd ed. New York: McGraw-Hill, 1986.

A readable and up-to-date college text that provides a good overview of human sexuality. The book integrates material from several disciplines.

MARMOR, JUDD (ed.). *Homosexuality: A Modern Reappraisal.* New York: Basic Books, 1980.

A useful collection of articles covering various social and psychological aspects of homosexuality.

RUSSELL, DIANA E. H. *Sexual Exploitation: Rape, Child Sexual Abuse, and Workplace Harassment.* Beverly Hills, Calif.: Sage, 1984.

A thorough and up-to-date survey of social-science research on forms of sexual abuse.

SYMANSKI, RICHARD. *The Immoral Landscape: Female Prostitution in Western Societies.* Toronto: Butterworth, 1981.

A good descriptive and analytic study of prostitution in Europe and North America.

UNIT 3

Social Inequality

Social inequality exists when some people have a greater share of power, wealth, or prestige than others. Such inequality is as old as society itself, and throughout history it has been a constant source of tension, conflict, violence, injustice, and oppression. In most societies, social inequality is built into the social structure in such a way that it is passed down from generation to generation. When this happens, whole categories of a population are denied a fair share of their society's resources virtually from the moment of birth.

The first chapter in this unit deals with the general problem of social stratification, or the ranking of a population into unequal "strata." The chapter takes up the issue of social class, focusing on the United States, a country that is formally committed to human equality but in which there are severe inequalities among different segments of the population. The second chapter discusses race and ethnicity, and examines the hostility and inequality that are often present between peoples who are physically or culturally different from one another. The last chapter discusses inequalities of gender and of age, showing how traditional roles have ensured the dominance of men over women, and how changing social conditions have affected the status of the elderly in relation to that of other age categories.

Throughout the unit, we will find that these social inequalities are rarely maintained primarily through force. They are sustained largely by social custom and the power of ideas. Members of both the dominant and the subordinate group are inclined to accept unquestioningly the ideologies, or sets of ideas, that justify the inequalities and make them seem "natural" and even moral.

The illustration opposite, with its disturbing image of people trapped as potential victims of circumstances that seem beyond their control, is Target with Four Faces, by the contemporary American artist Jasper Johns.

CHAPTER 10

Social Stratification

All societies treat people who have certain characteristics differently from those who do not. Every society, for example, distinguishes between the old and the young and also between males and females. In addition, a society may treat its members differently on such grounds as skin color, physical strength, religious belief, educational achievement, or whatever other feature it considers important. The usual result of these distinctions is *social inequality*—the unequal sharing of such social rewards as wealth, power, and prestige.

For perhaps 99 percent of the time our ancestors inhabited the planet, they lived in small groups of hunters and gatherers, sharing whatever food, shelter, or other resources they had. In these societies, social inequality (other than that based on age or sex) meant only minor differences in the status of particular *individuals*. One person might have higher status than others, for example, because of some personal quality such as wisdom, beauty, or hunting skill. But as societies have become more complex over the past few thousand years, a quite different kind of inequality has appeared—inequality among entire *categories* of people. Like the layers of rock that can be seen in cliffs such as those of the Grand Canyon, the inhabitants of these societies are grouped into "strata." They generally regard people in their own stratum as equals, those in any higher stratum as in some way superior, and those in any lower stratum as somehow inferior. This kind of inequality is actually built into the social structure, in the sense that it tends to be passed down from one generation to the next. Wealth and poverty, for example, existed in your own society before you entered it, and will probably confront your children, too. And because children are born to families in different economic circumstances, they begin to experience the effects of wealth, poverty, or something in between from the earliest years of their lives.

To the sociologist, then, *social stratification* is the structured inequality of entire categories of people, who have different access to social rewards as a result of their status in a social hierarchy. Although there are still a few simple societies whose members are more or less equal, almost the entire human population now lives in stratified societies. A fundamental task of sociology is to find out why this is so, whether it is inevitable, and what effects this inequality has on human lives.

Stratification is perhaps the most profoundly important subject in the entire discipline. Sociologists have found that almost every aspect of our lives is linked to our status in the social hierarchy: our scores on IQ tests, our educational achievements, the size of our families, our standards of nutrition, the chances that we will be arrested or imprisoned or divorced or committed to a mental hospital, our tastes in literature and art, our political opinions, the diseases we suffer, our life expectancy, even the probability of our keeping the lights on during sexual intercourse.

What this means is that people within a particular stratum share similar *life chances,* or probabilities of benefiting or suffering from the opportunities or disadvantages their society offers. By its very nature, therefore, stratification raises issues of deep moral and emotional significance—wealth and poverty, greed and misery, ambition and failure, brutality and compassion, oppression and rebellion. Throughout history it has generated bloody conflict between slave and master, peasant and noble, worker and employer, poor and rich. Today, the nuclear superpowers are divided primarily over their views on how a society's wealth should be distributed. If these nations ever came into open conflict, much of the human life on earth could be wiped out.

In this chapter we will first examine the general principles of stratification, and will then apply them in detail to the world's leading postindustrial society, the United States. In the following chapters we will find that these principles are also relevant to other forms of structured inequality—of race and ethnicity, of gender, and of age. Issues of stratification will recur, too, throughout this book.

Stratification Systems

Forms of stratification vary widely from one society to another according to how "closed" or "open" they are. In a closed, or "caste," system, the boundaries between the strata are very clearly drawn, and there is no way for people to change their statuses. In an open, or "class," system, the boundaries between the strata are more flexible, and there are opportunities for people to change their statuses. Additionally, some societies, such as the Soviet Union, claim to have no stratification, and thus to be "classless." Examples of each type of system will make these distinctions clear.

Caste

A *caste system* is a closed form of social stratification in which status is determined by birth and is lifelong. Caste membership is therefore an *ascribed status,* one that is attached to people on grounds over which they have no control, such as skin color or parental religion. A person's status is, obviously, the same as that of his or her parents, and there is virtually no way to change it.

What would happen, though, if someone were born to parents from two different castes? The result would be confusion—a blurring of the boundaries of caste by individuals who did not fit into the system. All caste societies therefore insist on *endogamy,* or marriage within the same social category. Endogamy is usually reinforced by a taboo against sexual relations across caste lines. Additionally, caste societies recognize and guard against *ritual pollution*—types of contact or proximity between members of different castes that are considered unclean for the superior caste. The risk of such pollution helps keep the strata physically as well as socially separate.

Caste systems were historically quite common, but they are rare today. Traces of caste are still to be found in isolated areas of North Africa, the Middle East, and Asia, where, according to a 1981 United Nations report, at least a million people live in slavery. Apart from these remnants, only two rigid caste systems still exist. South Africa is a caste society, with four distinct racial strata. As we saw in Chapter 3 ("Culture"), this system is crumbling; laws against interracial sex were repealed in 1985, and revolutionary violence is under way. The other system is in India.

India

Caste has been a fundamental feature of Indian life for over 2,500 years. Although the caste system was officially abolished in 1949, it still persists in rural areas, where it dominates the lives of tens of millions of people. In theory India has four main castes, or *varnas.* The highest varna is that of the

Figure 10.1 *These people are members of the outcaste category that is still recognized in many parts of India. Their inherited social status is so low that they are not even included in the caste system. Members of higher strata may consider it a form of "ritual pollution" to be touched by the shadow on an outcaste—and, in some cases, even to be looked at by such a person.*

Brahmans, or priests and scholars; next are the Kshatriyas, or nobles and warriors; below them are the Vaishyas, or merchants and skilled artisans; and finally there are the Shudras, or common laborers. Beyond the actual castes are the lowest of the low—the Harijans, or outcastes. In practice, the caste system actually consists of thousands of subcastes, or *jati*. These *jati* are usually linked to a particular occupation—scavenging, silkworm-raising, or even snake-charming—and everyone born into one is expected to do the same work. Intermarriage between castes is taboo, and intermarriage between *jati* is strongly disapproved.

The rules concerning ritual pollution are highly elaborate. Shudras and Harijans are often considered "untouchable": a member of a higher caste can be polluted by the slightest physical contact with them, an outrage that must be remedied by washing or other ritual cleansing. In some regions an untouchable's mere glance at a cooking pot is sufficient to defile the food, and a low-caste person's passage over a bridge can pollute the entire stream beneath. In some areas untouchables are not allowed in the villages during early morning or late afternoon because their long shadows are a ritual danger to others. Some low-caste groups are not only untouchable but also unseeable: there is one group of washerwomen who for this reason may work only at night.

Not surprisingly, the whole system breaks down in the urban areas where an increasing number of Indians live. A crowded and anonymous environment makes it difficult to ascertain other people's caste or to avoid constant ritual pollution, and industrialism shatters the old order, producing such anomalies as poor Brahmans and even wealthy outcastes. Gradually, therefore, India is moving from a caste to a class system of social inequality (Hutton, 1963; Berreman, 1973; Robertson, 1976; Srinivas et al., 1978; Leonard, 1978).

Class

A *class system* is an open form of stratification based primarily on economic statuses, which may be subject to change. The boundaries between the strata are more flexible than in a caste system, with no clear division between one class and the next. An individual's status usually depends on the occupation and income of the family breadwinner, so people sometimes move up or down the class system as their economic circumstances improve or decline. In addition, there are no formal restrictions against marriages between people from different classes. Class membership, then, is an *achieved status,* one that depends to some extent on characteristics over which the individual has some control.

Almost all societies now have class systems, although their actual shape differs from one society to another. In predominantly agricultural societies there are usually two main classes: a small and wealthy class of landowners, and a large and poor class of peasants. In industrialized societies, on the other hand, there are usually three main classes: a small and wealthy upper class, a fairly large middle class of professionals and other white-collar workers, and a large working class of less skilled blue-collar workers.

Figure 10.2 *Modern British society is marked by significant class divisions. These inequalities are made more noticeable by some remaining traces of the country's feudal past, such as the monarchy and the House of Lords—a legislative assembly consisting mostly of men who inherited their titles. The roles of the queen and the lords are now mainly symbolic, but the persistence of an aristocracy is a reminder of how the society's wealth is distributed along traditional class lines.*

Great Britain

Great Britain provides a good illustration of a class system. The country has a small upper class, a large middle class, and a working class containing somewhat more than half of the total population. Wealth is very unequally shared: a 1976 royal commission found that the richest 1 percent of the population owned a quarter of the nation's wealth, while the richest 5 percent owned nearly half of it. An important means of maintaining the system is education. About 5 percent of the nation's children go to exclusive private boarding schools whose graduates enjoy great advantages later in life. (To give one illustration of the influence of these schools, no fewer than eighteen former pupils of the most exclusive of them, Eton, have become prime ministers. Imagine the chances of a single American high school producing eighteen presidents!) The pattern is repeated at the college level. Two universities, Oxford and Cambridge, enjoy the greatest prestige, and about half their entrants come from that 5 percent of children at the private schools. Graduates of Oxford and Cambridge are disproportionately represented at the upper levels of British society and dominate politics, law, religion, the media, corporations, and government service (Gathorne-Hardy, 1978; Halsey et al., 1980; Sampson, 1983).

Class differences in lifestyles are far more evident in Britain than in North America, and people are much more aware of class relationships. One reason is that the British monarchy has survived into the twentieth century, along with its ritual pomp and an intricate system of prestige awards—earldoms, knighthoods, dameships. Another reason, interestingly enough, is that voice accent is the most important indicator of social class, overriding such other symbols as style of dress.

There are distinct differences among and within the accents of the upper, middle, and lower classes, and any inhabitant of the country is unavoidably aware of the social status of another the moment that person utters a sentence. The observant American tourist will notice that the British tend to respond to one another quite differently on the basis of accent: a salesperson may address someone with an upper-class accent as "sir" or "madam," but may call someone with a lower-class accent "mate" or "dear." Despite these peculiarities, the British system shares basic features with all class systems: unequal distribution of wealth, differences in lifestyle from one stratum to another, and reproduction of the system from one generation to the next through such means as education and inheritance (Goldthorpe, 1980; Halsey, 1986).

A Classless Society?

A *classless society* is one with no economically based strata. Can a modern society be classless? This is an important question, for such a society is the stated goal of one of the major political forces of our time: communism. Although countries such as the Soviet Union are often described as "communist" in the West, none of these societies actually regards itself as communist. The communist-ruled nations claim only to have reached the intermediate stage of socialism, in which classes have been formally abolished but some inequality among individuals remains, pending the transition to a completely equal communist society. (Socialism and communism are discussed in more detail in Chapter 17, "The Economic Order.")

Figure 10.3 *Although the Soviet Union claims to have abolished classes, there are marked inequalities of power, wealth, and prestige between the ordinary citizens and the select group within the Communist party who form the country's bureaucratic elite. These huge portraits of Marx, Engels, and Lenin on a Moscow public building suggest the role of state officialdom in Soviet life.*

The Soviet Union

How valid is the claim that Soviet classes no longer exist? Actually, there is great social and economic inequality in the Soviet Union. About 9 percent of the people belong to the Communist party, which dominates national life. However, the real elite—consisting of about 1 percent of the population—is concentrated in what the Russians call the *nomenklatura,* a listing of high officials in the government, economy, military, media, education, and science. This elite and their families have incomes several times that of ordinary citizens, and enjoy a variety of privileges, such as better housing and medical facilities, free automobiles and vacations, and even coupons for use in special shops that stock luxury consumer goods that other people cannot buy. The *nomenklatura* is also overwhelmingly old, male, and Russian, in a country where Russians constitute only half the population (there are 128 other nationalities in the Soviet Union, speaking 125 different languages). Moreover, the political leadership does not face free elections, and its policies are not subject to public criticism. In the 1985 national elections, over 99.99 percent of citizens are said to have voted—but there was only one candidate for each position. Once elected, the representatives meet only a few days a year to unanimously acclaim the decisions of the unelected leaders, the Politburo (Matthews, 1979; Voslensky, 1984).

The Soviet Union admits that it has social inequality among individuals, but denies that it has social stratification among classes. The country certainly does not have a dominant class living partly off profits and inherited wealth, as all capitalist industrial societies do. Private ownership of the means of production has been abolished and the amassing of huge fortunes is illegal. On the other hand, there are at least three economic strata that surely *look* like classes: a large class of poor peasants and urban laborers, a smaller middle class of white-collar workers, and the tiny, affluent, privileged elite. Perhaps more to the point, members of the *nomenklatura* use their influence to get their children into elite schools and high-paying jobs, with the result that existing inequalities are becoming more structured into the system, not less. Also, the Soviet Union (like China, Hungary, and most other communist-ruled nations) increasingly uses financial rewards to encourage productivity, even though these incentives lead to greater income inequality. A totally classless society might be possible—but the Soviet Union is far from this goal, is getting no nearer to it, and seems to have no specific plans to achieve it (Dobson, 1977; Lane, 1978; Hollander, 1981; Shipler, 1982).

Social Mobility

A key question about any stratification system is what chance it offers people for *social mobility*—movement from one social status to another. Such movement can be either upward or downward, depending on whether people rise to higher statuses or fall to lower ones. Sociologists are especially interested in *intergenerational mobility,* or movement up or down the hierarchy by family members from one generation to the next. The amount of this movement—which occurs, for example, when a janitor's child becomes a doctor, or a doctor's child becomes a janitor—tells how rigidly inequality is structured into the society. But what factors determine how much mobility a society has?

Figure 10.4 *Most social mobility in industrialized societies is caused by structural changes in the economy. During the Great Depression, for example, millions of workers—like this man photographed in a makeshift home in 1932—lost their jobs when the economy collapsed. When the economy revived once more, most workers experienced upward social mobility as new jobs were created and incomes rose. Your own chances for social mobility will depend in large measure on whether the economy as a whole prospers or suffers during your lifetime.*

Actually, there are two quite different kinds of social mobility, and each has its own source. The first kind is *exchange mobility,* changes in people's social statuses as they exchange places with one another at different levels of the hierarchy. For example, high-level incompetents may lose their jobs and fall to lower statuses, while more competent people at lower levels are promoted to higher statuses. The amount of this mobility depends on how closed or open the society is: in a closed system there can be little exchange mobility, but in an open system there is potential for much more.

The second kind of mobility is *structural mobility,* changes in people's social statuses as a result of changes in the structure of the economy. For example, in times of economic recession there is a general downward trend in mobility as incomes shrink and workers are laid off. College graduates, no matter how keen they are to get good jobs, may find themselves driving cabs or collecting unemployment benefits. In times of economic growth, on the other hand, there is an upward trend in mobility as incomes rise and new jobs are created. College graduates, even the less promising ones, may find many excellent jobs available for the asking. The amount of this mobility depends on economic conditions: in a static economy there is little structural mobility, but in times of economic change there may be a good deal.

Which kind of mobility is more common? The answer is that most mobility in all modern societies is structural mobility. Over the past century or so, the mechanization of agriculture and the automation of industry have steadily eliminated millions of low-status blue-collar jobs, no matter how hard those who occupied them worked. Simultaneously, the growth of service industries and of government and corporate bureaucracies has created millions of new, higher-status white-collar jobs, which had to be filled. Under such structural conditions, social mobility is *guaranteed* for a large part of the population: huge numbers of people are forced out of a lower status and pulled into a higher one by factors that have little to do with them as individuals. But despite this trend, mobility from one stratum to another is the exception rather than the rule in *all* stratified societies. Even in the most open systems, like those of the United States, Canada, and other advanced industrialized nations, most people remain throughout their lives in the social class of their parents (Lipset and Bendix, 1959; Fox and Miller, 1965, 1966; Lipset, 1982; Grusky and Hauser, 1984).

Analysis of Class

In a caste system, people know their place because the boundaries between the strata are very sharp and rigidly maintained. In a class society, the matter is not so simple. What, for example, is your own social class? Middle class? Upper class? Lower-middle class? Working class? You may hesitate over the answer, and you may find that other people disagree about your exact social position, or that you disagree about theirs. Given that class lines are so blurred and uncertain, how do we determine the outlines of classes and who their members are?

Marx's Analysis

Karl Marx spent most of his life writing about social class. His pioneering work on the subject—voluminous, passionate, sometimes contradictory—has had such immense influence that almost all subsequent discussion of class systems has had to confront his ideas.

To Marx (1967, orig. 1876), a class consists of all those people who share a common relationship to the means of production. Those who own and therefore control the means of production—people such as slaveholders, feudal landowners, or the owners of property such as factories and capital—make up the dominant class. Those who work for them—such as slaves, peasants, or industrial laborers—are the subordinate class. The relationship between the classes involves not only inequality but also exploitation, because the dominant class takes unfair advantage of the subordinate one. The workers produce **surplus wealth**—more goods and services than are necessary to meet their producers' basic needs. But the workers do not enjoy the use of the surplus they have created. Instead, those who own the means of production are able to seize it as "profit" for their own use. Often the owners have merely inherited what they own, and often they do less work than their workers—yet they enjoy much higher incomes. This, in Marx's view, is the essence of exploitation, and the main source of conflict between the classes throughout history.

Marx wrote in an era when industry was owned and controlled by individual capitalists, and the bulk of the population comprised a poorly paid labor force living in wretched conditions. But changes in industrial societies since that time have thrown doubt on Marx's concept of class. One significant change is in the occupational structure: the middle class has expanded rapidly, and a variety of new jobs have emerged that do not seem to fit Marx's concept. Many middle-class people, for example, work not for capitalists but rather for their fellow citizens, perhaps as teachers, nurses, or civil servants. Others do not work for anybody: they are self-employed. Some blue-collar workers, too, are paid more than some white-collar professionals. An American truck driver, for example, may sometimes earn more than a high school principal—so what is their relative class status?

Another important change since Marx's time is that most industry is now run by large corporations, which are owned by thousands or even hundreds of thousands of stockholders but are con-

Figure 10.5 *Karl Marx's views, like those of anyone else, were deeply influenced by the social environment. Marx wrote in England at a time when a large and impoverished working class labored for a handful of wealthy capitalists who owned the factories and other means of production. Marx assumed that this situation would inevitably lead to revolution. But Marx did not foresee many of the changes that later occurred in industrial societies, such as the growth of a large middle class. No revolution has ever occurred in an advanced industrialized society.*

trolled by salaried managers. As a result, the *ownership* and the *control* of the means of production are no longer identical. True, corporate managers and directors typically own stock in the companies that employ them, but—especially in the case of large companies—they rarely own a controlling interest. Indeed, it may be that a "new class" is appearing, consisting of well-educated experts whose high social status is based on knowledge, not ownership. It is not clear where these salaried executives, bureaucrats, scientists, and others fit in Marx's concept of class (Gouldner, 1979; Bruce-Biggs, 1979; Herman, 1981).

Sociologists differ on the merits of Marx's analysis. Some insist that it is still relevant, although they often modify it by regarding the richest stratum as a general, property-owning class that directly or indirectly controls the economy and enjoys an unfair share of the wealth that other classes produce (Wright, 1979; Walker, 1979; Wright et al., 1982). Other sociologists, however, are troubled by the difficulties of Marx's concept as it applies to the contemporary scene.

Weber's Analysis

The German sociologist Max Weber (1946) offered an influential analysis of class that confronts the limitations of Marx's view. Weber's approach is a multidimensional one. He breaks the single concept of class into three distinct but related elements, which we may translate as economic status, or *wealth;* political status, or *power;* and social status, or *prestige.* So, instead of trying to decide whether a truck driver is of higher or lower class than a high school principal, we can rank them on all three dimensions. In this case the truck driver might have greater wealth, whereas the principal might have superior power and prestige.

Wealth, power, and prestige can thus be independent of each other. In practice, though, they are usually closely related. The reason is that any one of them can often be "converted" into any of the others. This is particularly true of wealth, which can readily be used to acquire power or prestige. Over the years, sociologists have used opinion polls to find out how the public in the United States, Canada, and several other industrialized societies ranks the prestige of various occupations. The results show that, as a general rule, prestige is closely linked to positions of political power and to occupations with high income (Inkeles and Rossi, 1956; Hodge, Siegel, and Rossi, 1964; Treiman, 1977; Davis and Smith, 1983). Prestige ratings for a number of different occupations are shown in Figure 10.6.

PRESTIGE RATINGS OF OCCUPATIONS IN THE UNITED STATES

Occupation	Score	Occupation	Score	Occupation	Score	Occupation	Score
Physician	82	Registered nurse	62	Foreman	45	Baker	34
College professor	78	Pharmacist	61	Real estate agent	44	Shoe repairman	33
Judge	76	Veterinarian	60	Fireman	44	Bulldozer operator	33
Lawyer	76	Elementary school		Postal clerk	43	Bus driver	32
Physicist	74	teacher	60	Advertising agent	42	Truck driver	32
Dentist	74	Accountant	57	Mail carrier	42	Cashier	31
Banker	72	Librarian	55	Railroad conductor	41	Sales clerk	29
Aeronautical		Statistician	55	Typist	41	Meat cutter	28
engineer	71	Social worker	52	Plumber	41	Housekeeper	25
Architect	71	Funeral director	52	Farmer	41	Longshoreman	24
Psychologist	71	Computer specialist	51	Telephone operator	40	Gas station	
Airline pilot	70	Stock broker	51	Carpenter	40	attendant	22
Chemist	69	Reporter	51	Welder	40	Cab driver	22
Minister	69	Office manager	50	Dancer	38	Elevator operator	21
Civil engineer	68	Bank teller	50	Barber	38	Bartender	20
Biologist	68	Electrician	49	Jeweler	37	Waiter	20
Geologist	67	Machinist	48	Watchmaker	37	Farm laborer	18
Sociologist	66	Police officer	48	Bricklayer	36	Maid/servant	18
Political scientist	66	Insurance agent	47	Airline stewardess	36	Garbage collector	17
Mathematician	65	Musician	46	Meter reader	36	Janitor	17
High school teacher	63	Secretary	46	Mechanic	35	Shoe shiner	9

SOURCE: James A. Davis and Tom W. Smith, *General Social Survey Cumulative File, 1972–1982.* Ann Arbor, Mich.: Inter-University Consortium for Political and Social Research.

Figure 10.6 *This table shows the average prestige ratings, on a scale of 1 to 100, that Americans give to various occupations. The most prestigious jobs in this ranking appear to be those that yield high income or that require extensive educational credentials.*

Influenced by Weber, many sociologists now assess people's social positions in terms of their overall *socioeconomic status,* or *SES,* a complex of factors such as income, type of occupation, years of education, and sometimes place of residence. Because an SES rating includes the dimensions of power and prestige as well as that of wealth, it takes account of inconsistencies that the Marxist approach is blind to. Using an SES rating, we can rank truck drivers and school principals relative to each other. Also, we can recognize differences in wealth, power, or prestige between people in the same line of work: for example, between a rich plumber and a poor one, or between a U.S. senator and a state legislator.

Maintaining Stratification

How can stratification systems possibly survive? At first sight, it seems unlikely that any of them would last very long, because the great majority of the people are denied an equal share of what the society produces. Yet revolutions are rare events, and some of the most apparently unfair and rigid systems—like the Indian caste system—persist for centuries. Two factors, it seems, are vital in maintaining stratification: the ruling stratum's control of the resources necessary to preserve the system; and a general belief throughout the society that the inequality is actually "natural" or "right."

Control of Resources

Marx emphasized that the economic base of society influences the general character of all other aspects of culture and social structure, such as law, religion, education, and government. For this reason, he claimed, social institutions tend to reflect the interests of those who control the economy rather than the interests of those who do not. In any society, therefore, the laws tend to protect the rich, not the poor. The established religion supports the social order, rather than preaching its overthrow. Education teaches the virtues of the present system, not its vices. Government upholds the status quo, rather than undermining it. In fact, any attempt to dislodge the ruling class is likely to be regarded as a revolutionary assault on the state as a whole, because the interests of the two are so closely identified.

This does not necessarily mean that the domi-

nant class actually plots to ensure that government and other institutions protect its advantages. Its members achieve this effect merely by acting in their common interests. Like anyone else, high-status people form *social networks*—webs of relationships that link the individual directly to other people, and through these others, indirectly to even more people. They enter these networks through socialization in their families, schools, clubs, corporate boards, and other elite circles where they associate with people of similar background and advantages. Because the social networks of the dominant stratum have much greater resources of wealth, power, and prestige than those of other strata, their members have far more "leverage" in society, despite their fewer numbers. In effect, they have not only economic but also "cultural" capital—easier access to the best education, the highest-paying jobs, the most useful contacts, the most powerful positions, the most crucial information. They influence, control, or occupy the commanding heights of the economic and political order, and their actions tend to preserve the advantages of their class as a whole (Collins, 1974, 1979; Bordieu, 1977).

A stratification system therefore survives for as long as the resources of those who benefit from it outweigh the resources of those who are disadvantaged by it. Change may come about if members of the lower stratum successfully mobilize

Figure 10.7

"Tom Willoughby, meet Howard Sylvester—one of us."

Drawing by Bernard Schoenbaum; © 1977
The New Yorker Magazine, Inc.

their own resources. Typically, they do this by forming a social movement—such as the labor movement or the civil rights movement—that organizes such resources as their votes, funds, access to the media, ability to cause demonstrations and strikes, and so on (Oberschall, 1973; Tilly, 1978; Zald and McCarthy, 1979). In extreme cases social movements aim at revolution, using violence as a resource. World history, particularly of the past two hundred years, has seen the revolutionary overthrow of several ruling classes—from the French Revolution of the eighteenth century to the Russian, Chinese, Cuban, Iranian, and Nicaraguan revolutions of the twentieth century. (There is a more detailed discussion of revolutions in Chapter 19, "Social Change," and of social movements in Chapter 20, "Collective Behavior and Social Movements.")

Revolutions are exceptional, however, and even violent class conflict is unusual. Although the ruling elite can use its ultimate resource—force—to maintain its advantage, this is rarely necessary. Instead, over time, the existing inequality becomes a tradition, to be taken for granted as "the way things are." In short, it gains *legitimacy,* the generally held belief that a given political system is valid and justified. Stratification thus tends to be widely accepted and even defended—not just by members of the privileged higher strata, but often by members of the lower strata as well.

Ideology

An *ideology* is a set of beliefs that explains and justifies some actual or potential social arrangements. Karl Marx explored the role of ideologies in legitimating social stratification, and his views are now widely accepted, even by sociologists who reject some of his other ideas. Marx's argument was simple. The dominant ideology in any society is always the ideology of the ruling class, and it always justifies that class's economic interests. Of course, other ideologies may exist in a society, but none can ever become dominant unless the class that holds it, and whose own interests it justifies, becomes the dominant class. In a society controlled by capitalists, therefore, the dominant ideology will be capitalism, not communism. In a society controlled by communists, the dominant ideology will be communism, not capitalism. In a society controlled by slaveholders, the dominant ideology will justify slavery, not freedom for all.

It is obvious why members of the upper stratum might regard the dominant ideology as "natural," but what about members of the lower stratum? Their acceptance of the ideology is what Marx called *false consciousness,* a subjective understanding that does not accord with the objective facts of one's situation. Members of the lower stratum fail to realize that their individual life chances are linked to their common circumstances as an

Figure 10.8 *A common feature of all stratified societies is that members of the lower stratum tend to accept the ideology that justifies the system—a phenomenon sociologists call "false consciousness." This working-class English woman, for example, proudly displays a picture of the queen in her window—thus giving implicit support to a system in which she herself is at a disadvantage.*

Figure 10.9 *In the feudal system of late medieval Europe, stratification was based on the ownership of land. The peasants spent their lives working for a landowning aristocracy, who in turn made financial contributions to a hereditary monarch. The entire system was legitimated by the ideology of the "divine right of kings"—the notion that feudalism had divine approval because the king ruled through the will of God.*

oppressed group. Instead of blaming the system, they attribute their low status as slaves, peasants, outcastes, or laborers to luck, fate, nature, the will of God, or other factors beyond their control. Only if they gain *class consciousness*—an objective awareness of the lower stratum's common plight and interests as an oppressed group—do they begin to question the legitimacy of the system. They then develop a new ideology, one that justifies their own class interests and consequently seems revolutionary to the dominant stratum. At that point, according to Marx, class conflict will begin.

An ideology is a complex belief system, often containing religious, political, economic, and other ideas. The Indian caste system provides a good example of an ideology in operation, for it is legitimated by the Hindu religion. According to Hindu doctrine, everyone is reincarnated through a series of lifetimes, and one's status in the next lifetime depends on how well one observes the required behavior in the present one. Failure to

live up to the duties of one's caste may result in reincarnation as a member of a lower caste, or even as an animal. This ideology thus serves the interests of the upper stratum—while giving the lower strata powerful reason to accept their own status.

Another example comes from the feudal system of medieval Europe, in which, generation after generation, a great mass of peasants worked for a tiny aristocracy of hereditary landowners. Feudalism was legitimated by the political and religious doctrine of the divine right of kings, which held that the monarch derives authority directly from God. When the king delegated some of this authority to the feudal lords, it followed logically that the peasants were under a divine imperative to obey the lords also. The Church lent full support to this system. The whole social order thus seemed unchallengeable because it had been ordained by God—a view that the peasants appear, on the whole, to have accepted as unquestioningly as their masters did.

In later centuries, Europeans used the ideology of colonialism to justify their invasion of faraway continents and their exploitation of the labor and wealth of the native populations. Under this colonial ideology, the ruling class of colonists were not considered invaders and exploiters: instead, they were pictured as the unselfish bearers of the "white man's burden," the noble but demanding task of bringing "civilization" to "inferior" peoples. The subject peoples seem for a while to have accepted the legitimacy of colonialism, and vast populations submitted to rule by tiny settler minorities. Eventually, however, they developed a consciousness of their common plight and created an ideology that expressed their own interests, nationalism. The entire colonial system collapsed in the resulting conflict between the strata.

Stratification in modern industrial societies is also legitimated by ideologies that tend to be accepted without question by members of all classes. In America, for example, inequality is justified as a means of providing incentives and rewarding achievement. It is believed that people have equal opportunity to improve their status: everyone is supposed to have the same chance to get rich by working hard. Actually, most Americans do work very hard, but most stay in the same class all their lives. Yet those who do not get rich (that is, most of us, and especially those who started out from low-status families) tend to blame only themselves or their bad luck: the well-socialized American who becomes a failure in the class system does not blame the system itself. Such "failure," however, is *inevitable* for a large part of the population, because the American system—like a caste system, feudalism, colonialism, or any other form of stratification—presupposes the existence of a large lower stratum that has to be filled by somebody (Robertson, 1976; Huber and Form, 1973; Dalphin, 1981).

Control of resources and the power of ideology thus help maintain stratification. But why are most societies stratified at all? Both functionalist and conflict theorists have offered answers to this question.

Stratification: A Functionalist View

In keeping with their assumption that features of society have functions, or effects, that contribute to the stability and survival of society as a whole, functionalists argue that stratification must have some useful social function, particularly since it is so widespread. In a classic statement, Kingsley Davis and Wilbert Moore (1945) contend that some form of stratification is a social necessity.

Davis and Moore point out that some vital social roles require scarce talents or prolonged training. If a society is to function effectively, it must fill these roles with talented, skilled people. Because the roles often involve stress and sacrifice, people must be attracted to them by rewards—such as wealth, power, or prestige. Thus, a society that values surgeons more than priests will give higher status and rewards to the surgeons, and one that values senators above garbage collectors will give higher status to the senators. This unequal distribution of social rewards is functional for the society as a whole because the ablest individuals are drawn to the most demanding roles. Social stratification, however, is the inevitable result.

This explanation was initially popular with American social scientists, perhaps because it fits so well with cultural values about individual success. Over the years, however, it has led to some skepticism (e.g., Tumin, 1953, 1955, 1963; Buckley, 1958; Wrong, 1959). The main criticism is that stratification systems do not work so neatly in practice. Some people who have no apparent value to society, such as the jet-setting inheritors of family fortunes, are highly rewarded. Some people whose roles are of limited value, such as movie or football stars, are more highly rewarded than people who play vital roles, such as prime ministers and presidents. Yoko Ono, for example, is worth over $150 million, but it is not immediately clear that her social value is *that* much greater than that of, say, your sociology professor. Above all, every society contains many people who have low rewards wholly or partly because their status is ascribed (outcastes in India, blacks in the United States) and many who have high rewards for the same reason (wealthy aristocrats in Britain, whites in South Africa). In all societies, as we have seen, the rate of intergenerational mobility from one stratum to another is actually rather low. Thus, stratification does not ensure that the ablest people fill the most demanding roles. It ensures that most people stay more or less where they are.

Actually, the theory of Davis and Moore shows how inequality among *individuals*—not stratification among whole *categories* of people—might be functional as a way of matching skilled people with demanding roles. But even when people do gain high status through their own efforts, they, like the poor, tend to pass this status on to their descendants. Inequality thus spreads with the passage of time, until the ultimate stratification system bears little resemblance to its origin, whether it was functional or not. At that point, in fact, stratification may have dysfunctions, or negative social effects. One dysfunction is that stratification, by denying people equal access to social roles, prevents a society from making the best use of its members' talents. A second dysfunction lies in the strain that stratification can cause—leading, perhaps, to disruption rather than stability in the social order.

Stratification: A Conflict View

Conflict theorists reject the functionalist view of society as a balanced system whose various features contribute to overall social stability. Instead, they regard tension and competition as a powerful factor in shaping culture and social structure. The conflict approach to stratification has always found favor with European sociologists, perhaps because their societies have a long history of class conflict. The approach derives from Marx's work, but has been much modified by later conflict theorists.

Marx held that stratification exists only because some groups become rich and powerful, and then preserve and enhance their own interests at the expense of other classes. Marx saw class conflict as the key to historical change: every ruling class is eventually overthrown by the subordinate class, which then becomes the new ruling class. This process repeats itself until a final confrontation between workers and capitalists in industrial society: the capitalists would grow fewer as a result of their endless competition, the middle class would disappear into an ever larger and more impoverished working class, and a successful revolution would inevitably result. The triumphant workers would then create a new socialist society in which the means of producing and distributing wealth would be owned by the public, for the good of all. Socialism would lead ultimately to a communist society, in which inequality, alienation, conflict, oppression, and human misery would be things of the past. This is a powerful vision—so powerful that, long after Marx's death, it continues to provoke revolutionary zeal against class systems in many parts of the world.

American sociologists tended to neglect Marx's theories until the 1960s. One reason is that Marx has been associated, perhaps unfairly, with the corruption of his ideas in the Soviet Union. But the main reason is that his predictions about the future of industrial capitalism and its class system

were, as we have seen, hopelessly inaccurate. He was even wrong in predicting that successful socialist revolutions would take place in highly industrialized societies: without exception, these uprisings have occurred in such countries as Russia, China, and Cuba when they were advanced agricultural societies. Very few Western sociologists accept Marx's view that historical forces will lead us inevitably, through revolution, to a classless society.

Recognizing these limitations, many modern conflict theorists have tried to modify some of Marx's insights and apply them to the changed conditions of the contemporary world. For example, Ralf Dahrendorf (1959) downplays competition between classes, and focuses instead on struggles among other groups in society, such as unions and employers. He argues that much inequality today is shaped not by who owns or does not own property, but rather by who gives orders and who takes them. Others, like Randall Collins (1974, 1979), emphasize how different groups jockey for position by acquiring such resources as educational credentials, which they can then use to secure jobs and other advantages for themselves. Some writers, such as Immanuel Wallerstein (1979), have even applied the conflict model to the international scene, suggesting a parallel between the relationship of rich and poor classes on the one hand and that of developed and less developed nations on the other. In any case, Marx's failure as a prophet does not necessarily invalidate his basic insight: that conflict over scarce resources leads to

Figure 10.10

"Sir, we've come to the conclusion that it's absolutely impossible to assemble a tax plan that doesn't benefit the rich."

Drawing by Dana Fradon; © 1985
The New Yorker Magazine, Inc.

the creation of caste and class systems, and that in every case the interests of the dominant class are served by the ideology and power of the state. The implication is that stratification is not a functional necessity at all—although it is certainly convenient for those who benefit from it.

But does this view provide a complete explanation for stratification? People, after all, grow up to be unequal in talents, skills, determination, perseverance, thrift, and so on. Surely, then, they will tend to achieve unequal rewards. And if there is no validity to the functionalist argument, then why do all societies—even communist-ruled ones—offer greater social rewards to people with rare and valued talents?

A Synthesis?

The conflict and functionalist views of stratification are not necessarily incompatible. Gerhard Lenski (1966) combines aspects of both in an influential theory that shows why some types of societies are more stratified than others. He claims that the basic resources a society needs for survival are allocated much the way the functionalists claim—that is, to meet basic social needs by matching roles with resources. This seems an efficient procedure, so it happens to some extent in every society. But Lenski maintains that a society's surplus resources are mostly allocated the way the conflict theorists claim—through struggle among different groups. The resulting inequalities may sometimes be functional, but most societies become much more stratified than they need to be.

As we noted in Chapter 4 ("Society"), there has been a general historical trend of *sociocultural evolution,* the tendency for societies' social structures and cultures to grow more complex over time. Lenski uses this idea to show that societies are stratified largely according to how much surplus wealth they have. *Hunting and gathering* societies generally lack a surplus, and so have no stratification: there is no way for people to become wealthier than others, let alone to pass their status on to their descendants. In the more productive *horticultural* societies and *pastoral* societies there is a limited surplus, which permits some inequality of wealth among specific families. These societies are usually not stratified, however, because there is insufficient surplus to support entire castes or classes. In *agricultural* societies, on the other hand, a considerable surplus is possible, and the

picture changes radically. Rigid strata invariably emerge, with wealth, power, and prestige concentrated in the hands of a hereditary, landowning aristocracy, usually headed by a monarch.

Industrial societies produce unprecedented wealth, and in the early stages of industrialism there is often a vast gap between the rich and the poor, as a rural peasantry is transformed into an urban work force living in slums and shantytowns. In the more advanced industrial societies, however, there is usually less inequality—even though there is more surplus wealth than ever. Why should this be? The reason is that industrialism creates a multitude of jobs that require a skilled, educated, and mobile labor force. As a result, structural social mobility causes the lower class to shrink and the middle class to expand. In response to demands from this large, rising class, governments become more democratic, and new social inventions, such as social-security programs and progressive income taxes, limit extremes of poverty and wealth. Lenski therefore expects that the long-term trend in most industrialized societies may be toward greater equality. This trend may well continue in the emerging *postindustrial* societies, where the middle class is expanding even further as technological innovations steadily create more new white-collar jobs. For the present, however, postindustrial societies still contain noticeable class divisions.

Social Stratification in the United States

The founders of the United States declared in ringing tones that "all men are created equal," and this value has been a central one in American culture ever since. Yet, from the moment of its birth, the United States has been a stratified society. For nearly a century after the Declaration of Independence, the nation had a caste system in the form of racial slavery. Like caste in India, the American version insisted on endogamy (through laws against intermarriage and taboos on sex across caste lines) and had strict rules about ritual pollution. These rules persisted until the middle of the twentieth century, in the form of segregation laws designed to prevent blacks from ritually polluting whites in such public facilities as restrooms, restaurants, and buses. Moreover, for decades after the founding of the new republic, the vote was restricted to adult white males who owned property.

Figure 10.11 *Racial segregation in the United States was a form of caste stratification. As in all caste systems, there was a taboo on sex between the strata, and the upper stratum was anxious to prevent "ritual pollution" through certain forms of contact with the lower stratum.*

Women were not permitted to vote until early in this century, and until recently were generally paid much less than men for doing the identical job. And despite its professed commitment to human equality, the United States today contains over 600,000 millionaires—while roughly 33 million people, including one child in every five, live below the official poverty line. Thus, the world's leading postindustrial society remains a visibly stratified one, marked by a very unequal distribution of wealth, power, and prestige.

Wealth

The most obvious sign of stratification in the United States is its unequal distribution of wealth. Wealth actually contains two components—*assets* (property such as real estate and stock) and *income* (earnings such as salaries and wages). Although both kinds of wealth usually become more equally shared in the most economically advanced societies, the United States seems to be an exception to this trend. For at least the past quarter century there has been little equalization of wealth in the form of assets, and none in the form of income. Moreover, the economic inequalities between the rich and the poor are enormous.

Assets

The bulk of the nation's wealth in the form of assets is owned by a tiny minority of the population. It is difficult to get precise data on the subject, but, using various sources, the Office of Management and the Budget (1973) reported that the poorest fifth of Americans owned only 0.2 percent of the national wealth, while the richest fifth owned 76 percent (see Figure 10.12). More recently, the Bureau of the Census (1986b) calculated that the top 12 percent of American families own 38 percent of the nation's assets. There is an important difference, too, in the assets of the poor and those of the rich. The wealth of the poor consists mostly of items that depreciate in value and produce no income, such as household goods. The wealth of the rich consists largely of assets that may appreciate in value and produce income, such as real estate and stocks. In fact, the Bureau of the Census (1984) reported that 46 percent of all corporate stock is owned by 1 percent of the population.

Who are the highly wealthy? Their numbers are small: less than 0.3 percent of Americans are millionaires, and many of these owe this status to huge but unexpected increases in the value of their

THE DISTRIBUTION OF WEALTH IN THE
UNITED STATES BY HOUSEHOLDS

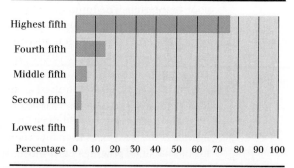

SOURCE: Executive Office of the President, Office of Management and the Budget, *Social Indicators, 1973* (Washington, D.C.: U.S. Government Printing Office, 1973), Chart 5/15.

Figure 10.12 *Wealth—that is, assets such as property and other capital—is very unequally distributed in the United States. As this chart shows, the richest fifth of American households own more than three-quarters of the society's wealth.*

own homes. But if the gap between the poor and those with assets of a million dollars yawns wide, it is nothing compared to the gulf between the "just millionaires" and those who form the real elite of the wealthy. Our best peek at the super-rich comes from *Forbes* magazine's regular survey of the 400 wealthiest Americans, which draws on a variety of public and private sources of information. Its 1986 survey included 400 people worth over $180 million, 50 of whom were worth at least $500 million, and 26 of whom were worth at least $1 billion. In addition, there were 90 family groups with assets of more than $500 million. In the recipe for all this success, one ingredient stands out: rich parents. All of the 90 families and 168 of the 400 individuals inherited all or part of their wealth. Relative to its size, the resources this super-rich elite can control are staggering. In an analysis of recent *Forbes*-400 data, the economist Lester Thurow (1985) calculates that these few hundred individuals and families are able to control about 40 percent of the fixed nonresidential capital of the United States— mainly with money inherited from someone else.

Income

The income received annually by Americans is also very unequally distributed. As Figure 10.13 shows, there is a huge gap between the incomes of the very rich and the very poor. The bottom fifth of American families receives only 4.7 percent of total income, while the highest fifth receives 42.9 percent. These shares are similar to those at the end of World War II, over four decades ago. After 1980, moreover, the Reagan administration's budgetary policies tended to shift income shares from the poor to the rich. The immediate effect of these policies, according to a 1984 analysis by the Congressional Office of the Budget, was that households with incomes of less than $10,000 suffered an average annual loss of $390, while households with incomes of over $80,000 showed an average gain of $8,270 (Sawhill and Palmer, 1984).

Who receives the highest incomes? Their numbers are few. Less than 5 percent of American individuals and families earn more than $50,000 a year, and less than 1 percent earn more than $100,000. Only about 12,000 people—less than .005 percent of the population—receive more than $1 million a year. These high-income people consist primarily of two overlapping groups. The first includes those living off earnings from businesses, stocks, and other capital investments. These assets of the wealthy produce income in such forms as

PERCENTAGE SHARE OF TOTAL INCOME
RECEIVED BY EACH FIFTH AND TOP 5 PERCENT
OF FAMILIES, 1958 TO 1984

Year	Percent Distribution of Aggregate Income					
	Lowest Fifth	Second Fifth	Middle Fifth	Fourth Fifth	Highest Fifth	Top 5 Percent
1984	4.7	11.0	17.0	24.4	42.9	15.7
1982	4.7	11.2	17.1	24.3	42.7	16.0
1980	5.1	11.6	17.5	24.1	41.5	15.6
1978	5.2	11.6	17.5	24.1	41.5	15.6
1976	5.4	11.8	17.6	24.1	41.1	15.6
1974	5.4	12.0	17.6	24.1	41.0	15.3
1972	5.4	11.9	17.5	23.9	41.4	15.9
1970	5.4	12.2	17.6	23.8	40.9	15.6
1968	5.6	12.4	17.7	23.7	40.5	15.6
1966	5.6	12.4	17.8	23.8	40.5	15.6
1964	5.1	12.0	17.7	24.0	41.2	15.9
1962	5.0	12.1	17.6	24.0	41.3	15.7
1960	4.8	12.2	17.8	24.0	41.3	15.9
1958	5.0	12.5	18.0	23.9	40.6	15.4

SOURCE: U.S. Bureau of the Census.

Figure 10.13 *The distribution of income—salaries, wages, and other earnings—has remained virtually unchanged for many years. The highest-earning fifth of American families has consistently earned over 40 percent of the national income, while the poorest fifth has consistently received around 5 percent.*

rents, interest, dividends, and capital gains— income that is often disproportionate to the amount of work the receivers actually do. For example, during a stock market surge in 1982–1983, some fifty wealthy stockholders watched their investments increase in value by at least $100 million each, and one stockholder became richer by over $1 billion (Main, 1983).

The second major group of high-income earners are executives of major corporations. In a 1985 survey of corporate incomes, *U.S. News and World Report* found that the highest officials of 202 of the largest corporations were paid over half a million dollars each. In fact, 51 officers were paid over $1 million a year, and 6 received more than $2 million. And these salaries are not the full story, since the highest executives may receive bonuses and other "perks" worth far more than their salaries. In 1984, for example, the chairman of Ford, with a salary of nearly $1.4 million, received an extra $5.9 million as well; the chairman of NCR, with a salary of just over $1 million, got an additional $12 million—more than sixty times the salary of the president of the United States. In contrast, the median family income of all Americans is just over $27,000, a figure that often includes the earnings of two or more family members. More than 70 percent of American individuals and households earn less than this amount.

Despite these marked disparities in assets and income, however, overall living standards have generally been improving. The real median income of Americans has more than doubled over the past quarter century, and the proportion of the population that lives in poverty has declined, with some sharp fluctuations, from about 27 percent in the late 1940s to under 15 percent in the mid-1980s.

Power

Like wealth, power is very unequally shared in the United States. The historical extension of voting rights to the poor, to blacks, and to women represents progress in one direction, but this has been offset by the growth of huge federal bureaucracies and influential private interest groups, leading to a concentration of power at the upper levels of government and the corporate economy. American voters can periodically elect or dismiss their political leaders, but the electorate is only one of several sources of influence over day-to-day government decisions. Americans generally suspect that they are excluded from much of the important decision making in the society: opinion polls regularly show large majorities agreeing that government is run for the benefit of a few private interests looking after themselves.

Indeed, if everyone had equal access to power, we might expect high officeholders to represent a cross-section of the American people. In fact, these officials are overwhelmingly white, middle-aged, male, Protestant, and, perhaps most significant, wealthy—for in the United States, as elsewhere, wealth is readily convertible to power. Of the 100 top officials appointed by President Reagan when he took office, 98 were white and 95 were male; almost half were earning over $100,000 a year

before their appointment, and a fifth were earning over $200,000 (Brownstein and Easton, 1983). Money is no disadvantage to those seeking public office in the United States: in 1986, almost a third of the senators were millionaires. Indeed, it is doubtful that the Rockefeller family would have produced three state governors (and a vice-president) or the Kennedy family three senators (and a president) without the backing of vast family fortunes.

Sociologists have debated not *whether* power is unequally shared but, rather, *how* unequally it is shared. Some, such as C. Wright Mills (1956) and Michael Useem (1986), argue that the United States is dominated by an elite of high officials in government and corporations. They claim that this elite operates informally and behind the scenes, making most of the important decisions that affect economic and political life. Other sociologists, such as David Riesman (1961) and Robert Dahl (1982), take a more pluralistic view. They claim that a variety of powerful interest groups struggle for advantage, sometimes privately and sometimes publicly, but tend to counterbalance each other in the long run. It is difficult to prove or disprove either of these views, but it is significant that the ordinary voter does not figure in the elite model and is a marginal element in the pluralistic model. Several studies have also shown that there is a tight-knit "establishment" or "governing class" of high-income individuals in government and corporate life that has a strong informal influence, especially in economic and foreign affairs (for example, Dye, 1976; G. Moore, 1979; Useem, 1978, 1979; Domhoff, 1983).

The successful use of behind-the-scenes influence is revealed in the history of the tax laws, which have long contained loopholes that were inserted under pressure from powerful interests. In theory, the tax system is progressive—the more you earn, the more you should be taxed. In practice, the income of the wealthy has always received favorable treatment. Until recent tax reforms, many super-rich Americans paid little—or even nothing—in income taxes, quite legally. In 1983, for example, twenty taxpayers with annual incomes of over $1 million avoided federal tax completely. And year after year, some of the largest and most profitable corporations in America—like General Dynamics, Boeing, and General Electric—paid no federal income taxes at all. By common consent, this tax system had become an unwieldy and inequitable absurdity, and it was greatly simplified in 1986. High-income taxpayers are no longer allowed innumerable deductions, but in return their maximum tax is now reduced from 50 percent to 28 percent, one of the lowest rates in the world. Additionally, a number of loopholes still remain for both individuals and businesses. (Power in the United States is discussed in more detail in Chapter 18, "The Political Order.")

Prestige

Differences in prestige seem less significant in the United States than differences in wealth and power. Some people have high prestige—the wealthy, the powerful, and a variety of other "celebrities," such as stars from the worlds of sport and entertainment. Others have low prestige—essentially the poor, the deviant, and other social rejects. On the whole, however, Americans treat one another in a way which, by international standards, is remarkably equal and informal. A beggar in the street may be viewed with distaste, or the occupant of a chauffeured limousine with envy, but there is much less of the deference toward "superiors" and arrogance toward "inferi-

Figure 10.14 *In the United States, prestige often depends on "conspicuous consumption"—the socially noticeable display of desired material goods.*

ors" that is typical of most other stratified societies. In many stratified societies in the past, such displays were actually institutionalized, with members of the lower strata being required to kneel, bow, curtsey, doff their hats, or offer other submissive gestures to their superiors. Many societies used such outward signs as the type or color of clothing to ensure that everyone knew who their superiors or inferiors were. In ancient Rome, for example, only members of the imperial family were allowed to wear purple, while in sixteenth-century England, no woman below the rank of countess could wear cloth of gold or silver.

Such inequalities in prestige can be sustained only if the relevant symbols are unequally distributed. But unlike power and wealth, which show no signs of becoming more equally shared, the symbols of prestige have become available to an increasing number of Americans. These symbols are mainly of a material nature—houses, cars, color TV sets, designer clothes, and respectable jobs. As we noted earlier, people's prestige seems to be determined mainly by their work. Occupations are valued largely in terms of the incomes they provide, although other factors can also be relevant—how much education the job requires, whether it involves manual labor, and how much autonomy it offers (Reiss et al., 1961; Coleman and Rainwater, 1978; Hope, 1982). The main reason for the more even distribution of the symbols of prestige lies in a radical change in the nature of jobs since the beginning of the century. In 1900, 38 percent of the labor force were farm workers, and only 18 percent held white-collar jobs. Today, less than 3 percent work on farms, and 52 percent have white-collar jobs. The United States has become a predominantly middle-class society, in which the bulk of the jobs make possible a broadly similar lifestyle and the prestige that goes with it. Additionally, there is a fundamental belief in America that every individual is, at least potentially, as good as anyone else—a belief less strongly and less widely held in many other stratified societies.

The American Class System

How many classes are there in the United States, and who belongs to them? There is no definitive answer to this question, for various observers may draw the boundaries of class in different ways. Just as we can create many ways of measuring off the length of a piece of wood—by inches, millimeters, and so on—so we can create many ways of categorizing an unequal population into classes.

Sociologists have used three basic methods of analyzing the American class system. One, the "reputational" method, is to ask people to describe stratification as they see it in their own community. The second, the "subjective" method, is to ask people what class they think they belong to. The third, the "objective" method, is to rank people into classes according to such measures of socioeconomic status as income and occupation. These methods all yield fairly similar results, and most sociologists would probably accept that the United States contains an upper class of about 1 to 3 percent of the population; an upper-middle class of 10 to 15 percent; a lower-middle class of about 30 to 35 percent; a working class of about 40 to 45 percent; and a lower class of about 20 to 25 percent (Rossides, 1976; Vanfossen, 1979; Gilbert and Kahl, 1982; Kerbo, 1983).

Portrait of the Classes

It is possible to give a general portrait of the classes that make up the American system, but with this important caution: the descriptions are, of necessity, broad ones, and there are many individual exceptions to the overall patterns.

The Upper Class

The upper class is a tiny one, containing the richest and most powerful people in the land. Its most prestigious members (the "upper-upper class") are an old aristocracy of birth and wealth—for to be fully respectable in America, money, like wine, must age a little. The names of families in this group are familiar ones: the Rockefellers, Roosevelts, Kennedys, Vanderbilts, du Ponts, Astors, and others whose fortunes were founded at least a couple of generations ago. These people tend to know one another personally, to attend the same schools, to visit the same resorts, and to intermarry. The less prestigious members (the "lower-upper class") are those with "new" money—the real-estate developers, fast-food tycoons, computer whizzes, lottery winners, and others who have struck it rich. Although these newcomers may have more money, better houses, and larger automobiles than possessors of older money, they lack the right "breeding" to be accepted into the very highest social circles. Taken together, however, the members of this class are disproportionately

represented at the highest levels of power. As the dominant group in the most powerful and prosperous nation on earth, the upper class influences not only domestic issues but also the foreign, trade, and defense policies that affect the lives of people all over the world.

The Upper-Middle Class

The upper-middle class consists primarily of high-income business and professional families. Like the upper class, this group contains a disproportionate number of people from white, Protestant, Anglo-Saxon backgrounds. Members of this class are highly "respectable," but they are not "society." They tend to live in comfortable suburban homes, to enjoy a stable family life, and to participate actively in political and community life. They are concerned with personal career advancement and have high aspirations for their children, who are expected to receive a college education as a matter of course.

The Lower-Middle Class

The lower-middle class shares most of the values of the upper-middle class, but its members lack the educational or economic advantages that would let them enjoy the same lifestyle. This class consists of average-income people whose diverse jobs do not involve manual labor. It includes small-business operators and sales representatives, teachers and nurses, technicians and middle-management personnel. The lower-middle class is very concerned about "proper" behavior, decency, and the value of hard work. Members of this class, who usually have to work hard to achieve and retain what they have, are in many ways politically and economically conservative.

The Working Class

Strictly speaking, the class that falls below the middle class should be designated as the upper level of the "lower class." Polls have shown, however, that people in this stratum intensely dislike that phrase but are proud to call themselves "working class," so that is the term sociologists use. The working class contains a higher proportion of nonwhites and less-educated people than the middle and upper classes. It consists primarily of blue-collar workers—tradespeople, service personnel, and semiskilled workers of various kinds. Their jobs typically involve manual labor, have

Figure 10.15 *The economic distinctions among Americans translate into significant differences in lifestyles and life chances. Because people tend to transmit their social statuses to their children, inequalities are generally passed on from one generation to the next.*

little prestige, and often lack such "fringe benefits" as pensions, health insurance, sick leave, paid vacations, and job security. But the members of this class take great pride in being "respectable," a self-image they derive largely from the sense that they work hard—at "real" work done with the hands. They are sharply aware of the differences between themselves and the stratum below—fearing, perhaps, that some misfortune will thrust them into the lower class.

The Lower Class

The lower class consists of the "disreputable poor." Its members live in decaying urban neighborhoods or distressed rural areas. This class includes the chronically unemployed, the unskilled, the homeless, the illiterate, the "junkies" and the "bums," the welfare dependents, and other impoverished people. Being considered virtually worthless on the labor market, they are virtually worthless in terms of power and prestige as well. Indeed, the contrast between their "leverage" in society and that of the upper class could not be starker.

Members of this class are regarded with distaste by most other Americans. Their supposed laziness, promiscuity, and reliance on public handouts are contrasted with the proclaimed industriousness, morality, and sturdy independence of the middle class. Tending to lack a common consciousness, members of the lower class are often alienated from and cynical about society, and fatalistic about their own and their children's chances in life.

The American class system tends to reproduce itself from generation to generation. It is easy to see why. A child raised in a high-status family has a good opportunity to acquire the values, attitudes, personal contacts, education, and skills that make for success in American life. A child from a low-status family is raised in an atmosphere of poverty, interacts only with low-status peers, and lacks the models and opportunities that children in other classes take for granted. The upper-status child has a head start in life, the lower-status child, a handicap. As a result of these social influences on the individual, most Americans remain for a lifetime in their class of origin.

Class and Life Chances

Class membership correlates closely with many social characteristics, suggesting the impact of social class on life chances and lifestyles.

1. *Political behavior.* The higher a person's class, the more likely he or she is to take an interest in politics and to vote. People further up in the hierarchy are more likely to be Republican; those lower are more likely to be Democrats. On economic issues, high-income people are generally more conservative than lower-income people. On social issues, however, the reverse is the case; the higher their social class, the more tolerant people tend to be in their attitudes (Alford and Friedland, 1975; Nunn et al., 1978; Hyman and Wright, 1979; Wolfinger and Rosenstone, 1980).

2. *Marital stability.* Divorce is more common in the lower than in the higher classes, perhaps because economic problems generate friction between the spouses. Higher rates of illegitimate birth and of single-parent families headed by a woman are found lower in the social hierarchy. Gender roles for both men and women tend to be more rigid and traditional at lower socioeconomic levels (Rubin, 1976; Sidel, 1986).

3. *Religious affiliation.* The highest-status Americans tend to be Protestant. Within the Protestant churches there is a fairly close correlation between class and membership in a particular denomination. People of higher socioeconomic levels prefer denominations that offer quiet and restrained services, while those of lower status are disproportionately represented in evangelistic and fundamentalist sects, which tend to be more rousing in their worship (Gockel, 1969; Lauer, 1975; Nelsen, 1976; Newport, 1979).

4. *Educational achievement.* Social class has a strong influence on IQ scores and on educational achievement: the higher the social class of the parents, the better the children are likely to do in school. The offspring of upper-status families are therefore disproportionately represented in college—and hence in the best jobs (Sewell and Hauser, 1975, 1976; Griffin and Alexander, 1978; Jencks et al., 1979).

5. *Health.* The higher one's socioeconomic status, the better one's health is likely to be and the longer one is likely to live. Mental disorder is more common in the lower class than in other classes. The incidence of most diseases, including major killers such as heart disease and cancer, is significantly higher in the lower social classes. The reasons include safer work conditions and better standards of nutrition and health care in the higher classes. Also, the United States, unlike all other industrialized societies, offers health care primarily as a commercial enterprise rather than as a social service equally available to all; so the wealthier one is, the better the quantity and quality of care one can buy (Krause, 1977; Conrad and Kern, 1981; Califano, 1985).

6. *Values and attitudes.* Middle- and upper-class people feel a relatively strong sense of control over, and responsibility for, their lives. They are generally prepared to defer immediate gratification in the hope of greater future rewards. Members of the working and lower classes are more likely to believe that their lives are shaped primarily by luck and other forces beyond their control. They are generally less likely to defer gratification and more likely to focus on present needs and wants.

7. *Child-rearing practices.* Parents in each class tend unconsciously to socialize their children according to the norms of their own work world. Jobs at the upper levels of the hierarchy usually offer autonomy, while those at the lower levels involve close supervision. Accordingly, the child-rearing practices of the middle and upper classes focus on teaching principles of behavior that encourage children to shape their own conduct, whereas those of the working and lower classes tend to focus on teaching children to obey the rules and stay out of trouble. These child-rearing practices may color the later personalities of people in different classes (Walters and Stinnet, 1971; Kohn, 1963, 1977).

8. *Criminal behavior.* Although almost every American has committed some kind of criminal offense, people in the lower classes are the most likely to be arrested, denied bail, found guilty, and imprisoned. They do not necessarily commit more crimes, but they are more likely to commit the "street crimes" that are of most concern to society. Typical lower-class crimes, such as robbery and auto theft, are regarded as more serious than typical middle- or upper-class crimes, such as tax evasion and fraud.

Social Mobility in the United States

Abraham Lincoln was born in a log cabin but made it to the White House. Andrew Carnegie, John D. Rockefeller, and J. P. Morgan started life in poverty but became millionaires. These tales are a treasured part of American folklore, seeming to confirm the ideology of the American dream: that it is possible for anyone to reach the top, no matter how humble the person's origins. This belief is pervasive in American society: a 1981 poll, for example, found 69 percent agreeing with the statement that "it is possible nowadays for someone in this country to start out poor and become rich by working hard." But what about the countless would-be presidents and millionaires who, despite all their efforts, remained in poverty and obscurity—or the great mass of ordinary, hard-working Americans who never seem to make it anywhere near the top?

The reality is different, and more subtle, than the image of the dream. Extensive research on social mobility shows that most Americans do, indeed, enjoy higher statuses than their parents did—but most of this mobility consists of short-distance gains *within* a social class, not long-distance jumps *between* social classes. In reality, Americans have little chance of getting rich, and hard work is not the crucial factor in whether they get rich or not. Moreover, social factors have a powerful influence on individual mobility.

To measure intergenerational mobility, re-

Figure 10.16

"My family was very poor, and I never finished school. But in this great land of ours you don't have to be defeated by such things, even though I was."

Drawing by Handelsman; © 1979
The New Yorker Magazine, Inc.

searchers compare men's occupational status with that of their fathers. (There has been little research on female mobility: most women did not have independent careers until fairly recently, so their status was assumed to be the same as their husbands'.) In a classic study, Peter Blau and Otis Dudley Duncan (1967) found that about a third of the sons of working-class fathers entered the middle class, while two-thirds remained behind. Only 10 percent of the sons of manual laborers reached professional jobs, although more than 70 percent of the sons of professionals held such jobs. Most people, then, remain in their class of origin, never achieving great leaps (or suffering great falls) in status from one class to another.

Why should mobility to high statuses present such a formidable challenge? The answer is one of simple logic: too many people are seeking too few statuses. Consider specific high-status jobs. Even if "everybody" had an equal chance to become a U.S. senator, only 100 people in the entire society can occupy that status at the same time. Even if "anybody" could become president of one of the leading 10,000 corporations, only 10,000 out of tens of millions of Americans could have the jobs. Or consider the prospects of getting rich. If we define the "rich" as, say, the top 30 percent or so of taxpayers (currently those making more than $25,000 a year), then, automatically, over 70 percent cannot be rich. Or, if "rich" means only the top 5 percent of taxpayers (those making more than $50,000 a year), there will be no room in this category for the remaining 95 percent. And if we confine "rich" to the top 1 percent (those earning over $100,000), more than 99 percent are excluded. Few gamblers would be impressed with such odds. In fact, the prospects are worse than these numbers suggest, because many of the high-status positions are already "reserved" for the children and heirs of the wealthy. People do not all have equal opportunity to rise to the top: those already close to the heights have but a short way to travel; those nearer the bottom face a longer and harder journey.

By contrast, short-distance mobility within a particular class is much more common: over half the men in the United States are upwardly mobile within their class of origin. In most cases, however, they move to a status only somewhat above their fathers'—for example, from factory worker to factory supervisor, or from high school teacher to college professor. So, although the chances of streaking ahead and leaving others behind are small, the chances for rising together with most of the people at one's own level are quite good. Why should this be the case?

Figure 10.17 *Although "hard work" is supposed to be the key to success in American society, many people achieve success not by working harder than others but by having better ideas. Henry Ford made a fortune when he mass-produced the Model-T Ford; Steven Jobs achieved wealth by creating the Apple, the first personal computer.*

It seems that the United States has a great deal of upward structural mobility—the kind where economic growth creates a higher proportion of upper-status jobs from one generation to the next, ensuring that most people will be upwardly mobile to some degree. Over the course of this century the middle class has expanded, radically changing the shape of stratification in America—from a pyramid, with most statuses at the bottom, to an egg, with most bunched in the middle. Moreover, increasing prosperity has affected almost every job. An auto mechanic, for example, has much the same relative social status as a blacksmith had a couple of generations ago—but enjoys an incomparably higher standard of living. (Changes in the occupational structure of the United States are discussed in more detail in Chapter 17, "The Economic Order.")

Some people, however, are more upwardly mobile than others. What are their characteristics? Two factors have overriding importance. The first is social-class background: the higher the social class of your parents, the higher your ultimate position is likely to be. The second factor is education. The higher your level of education, the better your prospects for upward mobility—especially if you have a college degree. Of course, social class

influences educational achievement—more than 60 percent of white-collar sons have at least a year of college, compared with 32 percent of blue-collar sons. But those blue-collar sons who can overcome this hurdle are able to use their education to "cancel" the effects of their social-class background (Blau and Duncan, 1967; Duncan, Featherman, and Duncan, 1972; Sewell and Hauser, 1976; Sewell, Hauser, and Wolf, 1980; J. Davis, 1982).

What else, beyond class and education, affects individual mobility? Several factors have been identified—some under the control of the individual, some not. These include childhood nutrition, health, big-city residence, age at marriage, the status of one's spouse, willingness to postpone gratification, race, sex, height, physical appearance (especially among women), intelligence, and career field. Character traits are presumably important, too, and might include shrewd judgment, willingness to take risks, innovative imagination, skill at negotiating, and so on. In most successful careers, too, there is a random element of luck—basically, of happening to be in the right place at the right time (Blau and Duncan, 1967; Lipset and Bendix, 1959; Porter, 1968; Hauser and Featherman, 1978; Jencks et al., 1979.)

How does intergenerational mobility in the United States compare with rates in other Western industrialized societies? Studies have repeatedly found that there is very little difference among these societies—no matter what their ideologies on the subject may be. All these nations have been undergoing roughly similar changes in occupational structure, so rates of structural mobility are much the same from one country to another, with Israel, Canada, and the United States enjoying rather higher rates than the others (Lipset and Bendix, 1959; Tyree, Semyonov, and Hodge, 1979; McLendon, 1980; McRoberts and Selbee, 1981; Grusky and Hauser, 1984). The United States differs from most other societies in one principal respect: a much higher proportion of people from working-class backgrounds manage to reach professional status. Although only 1 working-class American male in 10 rises this far, the rates in other industrial societies are much more dismal—1 Japanese in 14, 1 Swede in 30, 1 Frenchman in 67, 1 Dane in 100, 1 Italian in 300. The reason for the contrast is that a far higher percentage of working-class children graduate from high school and college in the United States than anywhere else in the world, enabling them to use education as a passport to better jobs and higher statuses (Fox and Miller, 1965, 1966; Blau and Duncan, 1967; Lipset, 1972, 1982).

Of course, intergenerational mobility is not always upward. About a quarter of American men are downwardly mobile relative to their fathers, usually by only a short distance. Again, the class system works in favor of the upper classes: people starting out near the top have plenty of cushioning for a fall, while those starting out near the bottom must struggle just to make ends meet. During the 1980s, Nelson Bunker Hunt, heir to a vast oil fortune, lost several billion dollars as a result of some rash speculation in silver. That is downward mobility of a sort—yet even after these losses, Mr. Hunt remained a multimillionaire, one of the richest people in the United States. For tens of millions of other working Americans, the loss of a few thousand dollars of income—perhaps caused by the illness, unemployment, or death of a breadwinner—can plunge an entire family into grinding hardship. In the recession period of 1979–1980, over 5 million American workers were laid off from jobs they had held for at least three years. In a classic example of downward structural mobility, only 60 percent of them found new jobs, and of these, nearly half had to accept lower incomes. Some laid-off workers joined the large but almost invisible group of Americans who live in poverty.

What does all this mean for your own chances of upward mobility? If economic growth persists, you can expect the following. You, and most people similar to you, will enjoy upward mobility as the developing postindustrial economy improves living standards and creates new, higher-status jobs—including, no doubt, positions nobody has yet thought of, in industries that do not yet exist. You will probably experience occasional negative patches, when recessions threaten downward mobility. You will have to work hard to keep up with people at your own level, because most of them will be working hard, too. For whatever reasons, a few of you will be downwardly mobile relative to the group, and a few of you will be upwardly mobile relative to the group, moving by one means or another into the small number of very high statuses that are available. Overall, you will benefit not just from your own efforts but also from each others', because in the final analysis the whole economy is driven by the energy of the individuals who sustain it. Collectively, you will help shape the social forces which, in turn, will help shape your own careers.

Poverty

Millions of American adults and children live in poverty. For these impoverished people, life may be marked by illiteracy and ignorance, insecurity and homelessness, disease and early death, the stunting of human lives and potential. Yet many Americans, accustomed to life in a generally affluent, optimistic society, tend to ignore the existence of poverty or even to blame the poor themselves for their plight. To people in other nations, however, the existence of so much poverty in the midst of such wealth may seem to undermine America's claim to the superiority of its system and to moral leadership in the world.

What Is Poverty?

There are two ways to define poverty. The first is in terms of *relative deprivation,* the inability to maintain the living standards customary in the society. This approach assumes that people are poor only in relation to others who are not poor. Accordingly, the poor are simply defined as the lowest income-earners in society—say, the bottom fifth or the bottom tenth. The implication is that poverty cannot be eliminated as long as some people are significantly deprived in comparison with most others. The second way to define poverty is in terms of **absolute deprivation,** the inability to afford minimal standards of food, clothing, shelter, and health care. Under this definition, the proportion of the population that is poor depends on how many people lack these necessities. The implication is that poverty can be totally eliminated as soon as everyone is able to afford basic essentials.

In the United States poverty is usually defined in terms of absolute deprivation. Each year, the federal government establishes an annual income known as the "poverty line," and regards everyone living below that level as poor. The poverty line is determined by calculating the current cost of adequate nutrition under "emergency or temporary conditions," and then trebling that amount to cover other necessities. In 1985 the poverty line was $10,989 per year for a family of four—about $211 per week, or $53 for each family member. That income represents the official upper limit of poverty; most poor people, of course, earn less. Some 33 million Americans—14 percent of the total population—have incomes below the poverty line.

Who Are the Poor?

As we might expect, poverty is not randomly distributed among the population. Instead, it is concentrated, with some overlap, in three groups (Bureau of the Census, 1986c; Pear, 1986).

1. *Female-headed homes.* Poverty is becoming "feminized." Some 48 percent of the families that live in poverty have a female householder with no adult male present. In fact, over 34 percent of all families headed by a woman are in poverty—27 percent of those headed by white women, 52 percent of those headed by black women, and 53 percent of those headed by Hispanic women. One reason is that women generally earn less than men, but the major factor is a sharp increase in the number of unmarried mothers, who frequently lack job skills and may have to stay home to take care of their children.

2. *Children.* The highest poverty rates in the nation are among its children. Some 20.5 percent of all Americans under the age of eighteen live in poverty—16 percent of white children, 39 percent of Hispanic children, and 46 percent of black children. For children under the age of six, the rates are even higher: 41 percent of these Hispanic children and 51 percent of these black children live in poverty. More than half of all poor children live in female-headed households.

3. *Minorities.* Minority-group members are disproportionately likely to be in poverty. Some 11 percent of whites are poor, compared with 29 percent of Hispanics and 31 percent of blacks. The reasons include the relatively low incomes and high unemployment rates of minority-group members; subtle discrimination in hiring and promotion practices; and the sharp rise in female-headed households in the black community. Over 40 percent of black families are headed by a woman, and more than half of all black births are now to unmarried mothers, compared to a tenth of white births.

The poor actually form a highly diverse group. Many poor people work full time at unskilled jobs that will never pay much—as shoe shiners, domestic cleaners, dishwashers, parking-lot attendants, sweatshop laborers. Many live in areas of chronic unemployment, such as depressed rural regions or decaying urban neighborhoods where industries are in decline. Many have only recently become poor, and most do not stay poor for long: each year, about one-third of the nation's poor families manage to climb out of poverty, only to be replaced

U.S. POVERTY RATE

Percentage of the population living below the poverty line

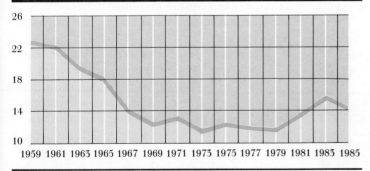

SOURCE: U.S. Bureau of the Census.

Figure 10.18 *The poverty rate has fluctuated a great deal over the years in response to changes in economic conditions and in government policies toward the poor. Antipoverty programs in the 1960s brought about a sharp drop in the poverty rate, but a recession and federal budget cuts around the beginning of the decade led to an increase in poverty. Thereafter, economic recovery produced a decline in the rate once more.*

by newcomers. Some of the poor, however, form an "underclass"—a group of about 5 to 10 million people who are trapped in long-term poverty. Their numbers are drawn from such groups as undocumented aliens, drug addicts, "skid row" alcoholics, panhandlers, illiterates, drifters, and the mentally disordered. Some of these become semipermanent welfare recipients, and as many as 3 million are homeless—sleeping for most of the year on park benches, under bridges, and in abandoned cars and buildings, and crowding into emergency shelters to avoid freezing in winter (Patterson, 1982; Auletta, 1982; Harrington, 1984).

Attitudes Toward Poverty

The United States could easily eliminate absolute poverty, at a cost roughly equivalent to the nation's annual expenditure on a single dangerous drug, tobacco. In fact, if the money currently spent on federal poverty programs were given directly to the poor, instead of to federal and state bureaucracies, it would raise the incomes of all the poor above the poverty line, and still leave a surplus of $25 billion (Seligman, 1984). Why, given that poverty is undesirable and that the costs of eradicating it are so small, is this not done? The reason lies in a peculiarly American belief: that the poor are in

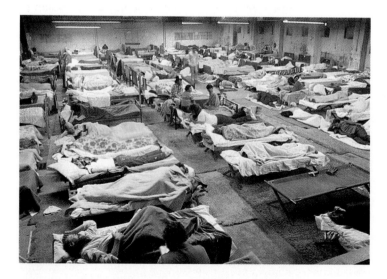

Figure 10.19 *Most Americans never have to confront poverty, for it is isolated from the mainstream of American life. Yet as many as 3 million Americans are so poor that they have no homes. This photograph shows a shelter for homeless men in Salt Lake City, Utah.*

poverty because they are idle and prefer to live on "handouts." This view is fervently held, even by millions of Americans who do not know poor people, have never tried to raise a family on welfare payments, and have not the vaguest idea what poverty is really like. Opinion polls repeatedly show large sections of the population favoring cuts in welfare spending, or favoring plans to "make welfare recipients go to work" (Huber and Form, 1973; Feagin, 1975; Gronjberg et al., 1978; Dalphin, 1981).

These attitudes bear little relationship to reality. More than 60 percent of welfare recipients are children, aged people, or disabled; most of the rest are mothers with young children, and less than 5 percent are able-bodied men, most of them unskilled workers in areas of high unemployment. Other myths abound: that welfare recipients are mostly black (nearly two-thirds are white); that they have many children (most have two or fewer); that they are on welfare indefinitely (most receive it for less than two years); and that welfare is a terrible burden on the taxpayer (welfare represents 2 percent of the federal budget).

Why do these curious myths about the poor persist? As we noted earlier, the ideology that legitimates stratification in America holds that everyone has the same chance to get ahead, and that inequality provides rewards for personal effort. As Figure 10.20 indicates, most Americans believe that the class system "shows what people made of their opportunities." If those who get ahead can claim credit for their success, then those who fall behind must, logically, be blamed for their failures. The poor are therefore supposed to need incentives to work, rather than help at the expense of the taxpayer.

There are few complaints, however, about how the United States pays out far more in "handouts" to the nonpoor than to the poor—in forms ranging from farmers' agricultural price supports to students' federally subsidized loans and grants. A large majority of nonpoor Americans receive such benefits in one form or another, to the tune of around $4,000 per year each. This fact generally escapes attention because these benefits take the indirect form of hidden subsidies or tax deductions rather than the direct form of cash payments. For example, if you rent your home, you cannot deduct the cost from your taxes. But if you own it (and even if you own a second home), you can deduct the cost of your property taxes and your mortgage interest from your taxable income. In effect, this is a subsidy by all taxpayers to help homeowners buy their property—and the more expensive the home,

AMERICAN OPINIONS ON CLASS DIFFERENCES

Statement: "Differences in social standing between people are acceptable because they basically reflect what people made out of the opportunities they had."

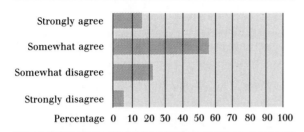

SOURCE: National Opinion Research Center, 1984.

Figure 10.20 *As this figure suggests, most Americans accept the ideology that legitimates the stratification system: that inequality is justified as a means of rewarding achievement—and, implicitly, of penalizing failure. This attitude tends to encourage negative attitudes toward the poor, who are blamed for their plight.*

the bigger this handout is. A 1983 Treasury Department study found that a third of the benefits from these and other hidden subsidies went to the top 5 percent of income earners in the United States (Page, 1983).

Even so, welfare expenditures remain highly controversial. In a typical argument, Charles Murray (1984) actually blames a great deal of poverty on welfare, which, he claims, becomes a way of life for the poor until they lose any incentive to escape their plight. There may well be some truth to this view, but welfare can hardly explain most poverty. After all, there was far more poverty in the days when there was no welfare; many impoverished people hold full-time jobs; and most welfare recipients are too young, old, or sick to work anyway. Also, the elimination of welfare payments (which Murray recommends) would in effect punish the millions of poor children who are in no way responsible for their parents' situations.

William Ryan (1976, 1982) warns against explanations of poverty that try to "blame the victim"—to focus on the supposed faults of the poor rather than on the social forces that create poverty. This does not mean, of course, that poverty is "all society's fault." Some poor people undoubtedly contribute to their deprived circumstances. But poverty, like wealth or indeed any other social characteristic, is the outcome of a complex interaction between individual human beings and the social environment in which they find themselves. In an unequal society, there will always be some poor people, just as there will always be some rich ones.

Over the generations, the human population has constructed castes and classes in society after society. Like other stratification systems, social class in the United States arises out of specific historical and social conditions. Since social stratification is socially constructed it must, in principle, be socially modifiable as well—provided only that people are conscious of their own ability to change what they have created. Whether they preserve, modify, or change the system is ultimately up to the people themselves.

Summary

1.   All societies treat their members differently, and social inequality may result. In most societies inequality becomes built into the social structure. The consequence is social stratification, in which entire categories of the population have different life chances.

2.   Stratification systems may be closed (caste) or open (class). In caste systems, such as that of India, the boundaries between strata are fixed, and status is lifelong and ascribed. In class systems, such as that of Great Britain, the boundaries are flexible, and new statuses can be achieved. Some countries, such as the Soviet Union, claim to be classless but still have great inequality.

3.   The amount of social mobility, especially intergenerational mobility, tells us how open a system is. Exchange mobility involves individuals displacing one another in the hierarchy; structural mobility in-

volves general movement as a result of changing economic conditions. In all modern societies, most mobility is structural mobility, and mobility from one class to another is rare.

4.   Marx argued that those who own and control the means of production are the dominant class; those who do not, and are exploited, are the subordinate class. Weber argued that class has three dimensions: wealth, power, and prestige. In practice, these three variables correlate strongly, and may be measured as socioeconomic status.

5.   Stratification is maintained through control of resources and through ideology. The upper stratum controls the resources necessary to uphold the system, but may be dislodged if the lower strata mobilize superior resources. An ideology legitimates inequality by making it seem right or natural, and is often accepted by the subordinate group. If that group rejects the ideology, class conflict will follow.

6.   Functionalists argue that stratification serves the function of matching important roles with scarce talents. Conflict theorists argue that stratification arises from a struggle to control scarce resources. Lenski's synthesis sees merit in both views, but holds that inequality at first increases during the course of sociocultural evolution, and then declines in advanced industrialized societies.

7.   The United States is a highly unequal society. Wealth, in the form of both income and assets, is very unequally shared. Power appears to be mostly concentrated at the upper levels of government and the corporate economy. Prestige is more equally distributed, as its symbols are more widely available.

8.   The American class system contains five basic strata: an upper class, an upper-middle class, a lower-middle class, a working class, and a lower class. Each has a distinctive lifestyle. Class membership correlates with a variety of other characteristics, such as political behavior, marital stability, religious affiliation, educational achievement, health, values and attitudes, child-rearing practices, and types of criminal behavior.

9.   There is a fair amount of upward mobility in the United States, but most mobility is within rather than between classes. Access to the highest statuses is limited because these statuses are so few. Most upward mobility occurs because structural changes in the economy create a higher proportion of well-paid, white-collar jobs. The main influences on ultimate class status are family background and educational achievement. The amount of social mobility is much the same in all industrial societies, except that working-class Americans have a better chance of reaching professional status.

10. Poverty may be defined in terms of relative deprivation (inability to maintain customary standards) or absolute deprivation (lack of basic necessities). Some 14 percent of Americans earn incomes below the poverty line. Poverty is concentrated among female-headed households, children, and minorities. Many people have negative attitudes toward the poor and resent public assistance for them, although government assistance to the affluent, in such forms as tax deductions, is much more generous. Social factors influence who becomes poor, and poverty may be an inevitable part of a stratification system that presupposes inequality.

Important Terms

social inequality (253)

social stratification (254)

life chances (254)

caste system (254)

ascribed status (254)

endogamy (254)

ritual pollution (254)

class system (255)

achieved status (255)

classless society (256)

social mobility (257)

intergenerational mobility (257)

exchange mobility (258)

structural mobility (258)

surplus wealth (259)

socioeconomic status (SES) (261)

social networks (261)

legitimacy (262)

ideology (262)

false consciousness (262)

class consciousness (263)

sociocultural evolution (266)

relative deprivation (276)

absolute deprivation (277)

Suggested Readings

ADAM, BARRY B. *The Survival of Domination: Inferiorization and Everyday Life.* New York: Elsevier, 1978.

An interesting analysis of how dominant groups use ideologies to convince subordinate groups that they are indeed inferior, and that inequality is thus justified.

DALPHIN, JOHN. *The Persistence of Social Inequality in America.* Cambridge, Mass.: Schenkman, 1981.

A short and readable discussion of the American class system and the reasons for its continued existence.

DOMHOFF, WILLIAM G. *Who Rules America Now?* Englewood Cliffs, N.J.: Prentice-Hall, 1983.

A good summary of research on the concentration of political power in the United States.

GILBERT, DENNIS, and JOSEPH A. KAHL. *The American Class Structure: A New Synthesis.* Homewood, Ill.: Dorsey, 1982.

A good portrait of social class in the United States. The book incorporates the results of extensive sociological research on the subject.

JENCKS, CHRISTOPHER, et al. *Who Gets Ahead? The Determinants of Economic Success in America.* New York: Basic Books, 1979.

An important analysis of available information on social mobility in the United States. Jencks emphasizes the importance of family background, education, and such apparently random events as "being in the right place at the right time."

LENSKI, GERHARD. *Power and Privilege: A Theory of Social Stratification.* New York: McGraw-Hill, 1966.

Lenski outlines his influential theory of social stratification. The book contains much interesting detail about social inequalities in preindustrial as well as industrial societies.

MURRAY, CHARLES. *Losing Ground: American Social Policy, 1950–1980.* New York: Basic Books, 1984.

An influential statement of the position that welfare contributes to the problem of poverty, rather than helps solve it.

VOSLENSKY, MICHAEL. *Nomenklatura: The Soviet Ruling Class.* New York: Doubleday, 1984.

An interesting and detailed account of social inequalities in the Soviet Union.

CHAPTER 11

Inequalities of Race and Ethnicity

One of the most fascinating aspects of our species is the extraordinary physical and cultural diversity of its members. Yet this diversity is often a source of conflict and inequality, because human relationships are all too often shaped by the differences rather than the similarities between groups.

As we saw in Chapter 10 ("Social Stratification"), all societies differentiate among their members, and these distinctions may be translated into social inequalities. Often people are distinguished on the basis of their inherited physical characteristics or their learned cultural traits. As a result of these social distinctions, the groups in question come to regard themselves, and to be regarded and treated by others, as "different." Those people who share similar physical characteristics are socially defined as a "race," and those who share similar cultural traits are socially defined as an "ethnic group."

Throughout history, relationships among racial and ethnic groups have been marked by antagonism, inequality, and violence. Over the course of the twentieth century alone, millions of people have been slaughtered, and many millions more subjected to humiliation, cruelty, and injustice, for no apparent reason other than their membership in some despised group. In the United States, a country formally committed to human equality, the physical and cultural differences among various groups still have a strong influence on their members' social status.

Race and Ethnicity as Social Facts

The words "race" and "ethnicity" are often misused in ordinary speech, and we must examine their meaning more closely.

Figure 11.1 *As a result of their adaptations to the particular environments in which they have lived, different human populations display a fascinating variety of physical characteristics. But if you traveled by land around the world, you would not suddenly come upon different "races." Instead, you would find a continuum of physical types, gradually blending into one another from one area to the next. The physical distinctions among people are a biological fact, but "race" is a social concept—a category that people impose on reality. Different peoples, in fact, have very different ideas about what a "race" is, or who belongs to any particular one.*

Race

There are about 5 billion people in the world, and they display a wide variety of skin colors, hair textures, limb-to-trunk ratios, and other characteristics, such as distinctive nose, lip, and eyelid forms (see Figure 11.1). Although the human animal can be traced back in the fossil record for well over 3 million years, the racial differences that we see today are of comparatively recent origin—50,000 years at the most.

These physical differences have resulted from the adaptations that human groups have made to the environments in which they lived. For example, populations in tropical areas tend to have dark skin, which protects them against harmful rays from the sun. Populations in high altitudes tend to have large lung capacity, which makes breathing easier for them. Populations in very cold climates tend to have relatively short limbs, which enable them to conserve body heat. So far as is known, these evolutionary differences affect only physical characteristics. There is no convincing evidence that different groups inherit psychological characteristics, whether these be general traits such as intelligence or more specific ones such as artistic ability.

As a biological concept, the word "race" is almost meaningless. There is certainly no such thing as a "pure" race. Different populations have been interbreeding for thousands of years, and a continuum of human types has resulted. Various societies slice up this continuum in different ways,

so that the same person might belong to one "race" in one society, but another "race" in a second society. In Brazil, for example, the continuum from "black" to "white" is loosely divided into several socially recognized categories, such as *branco*, *cabra*, *moreno*, *mulato*, and *escuro*. In South Africa, on the other hand, the same continuum is divided by law into three rigid racial categories: white, colored, and black. In the United States, only two basic categories on this continuum are recognized—black and white—even though most "black" Americans actually have white ancestry. And although all Americans who are not black are never referred to as "nonblacks," all Americans who are not white are collectively referred to as "nonwhites." In short, categories of race are a creation of the observer, not of nature.

For decades, anthropologists did try to create some kind of conceptual order out of this confusion by dividing the human species into races and subraces on the basis of physical features. The number of races that was discovered, however, depended very much on who was doing the discovering: estimates ranged from three races to over one hundred. The anthropological classification that won broadest acceptance divided the human species into three major categories: the Caucasoids, with fair skin and straight or wavy hair; the Mongoloids, with yellowish skin and a distinctive fold around the eyes; and the Negroids, with dark skin and woolly hair. However, there are many people who cannot be neatly fitted into this classification. The East Indians of Asia have Caucasoid features but dark skin. The Ainu of Japan have Mongoloid facial features but Caucasoid hair and skin color. The aborigines of Australia have dark skin, but their wavy hair is often blond. The San of Africa have coppery skin, woolly hair, and Mongoloid facial features. There are also hundreds of millions of people, such as those of Indonesia, whose ancestry is so mixed that they cannot possibly be fitted into one of the main categories. Most anthropologists have now abandoned the attempt to classify the human species into races and consider the term "race" to have no scientific meaning at all (Montagu, 1975; Kuper, 1975; van den Berghe, 1978).

Thus, the physical differences among human groups are no more than a biological fact. As such, they are of no particular concern to the sociologist. The intense sociological interest in race derives from its significance as a *social* fact, because people attach meanings to the physical differences, real or imagined, between human groups. If people believe that a certain group forms a biological unity, they will act on the basis of that belief. The members of the group will tend to develop a common loyalty and to intermarry with one another, and members of other groups will regard them as "different." From the sociological point of view, then, a *race* is a category of people who are regarded as socially distinct because they share genetically transmitted physical characteristics.

In Chapter 6 ("Social Interaction in Everyday Life"), we noted the important truth of the *Thomas theorem:* "If people define situations as real, they are real in their consequences." Applied to race relations, the theorem implies that it matters little whether social beliefs about race have any biological basis. It is people's *beliefs* about race rather than the *facts* about race that influence race relations, for better or worse. Many people, for example, consider the Jews a race. In biological terms, this view is nonsense. Jews have always interbred to some extent with their host populations, and many Jewish people are blond and blue-eyed in Sweden, small and swarthy in Eastern Europe, black in Ethiopia, or Mongoloid in China. Even in Nazi Germany, which attached such great importance to the distinctions between Jews and non-Jews, Jewish citizens were obliged to wear yellow stars so that their persecutors could distinguish them from the rest of the population. Yet when any group is arbitrarily defined as a race, as Jews were in Nazi Germany, important social consequences may follow.

Ethnicity

Whereas race refers only to physical characteristics, the concept of ethnicity refers to cultural features that may be handed down from one generation to the next. These features may include language, religion, national origin, dietary practices, a sense of common historical heritage, or any other distinctive cultural trait. Many groups, such as American blacks or Indians, are both racially and ethnically distinct from most people in their society. Such groups are regarded as doubly "different." In other cases, ethnic groups cannot be distinguished from the bulk of the population by their physical characteristics. German- and Polish-Americans, for example, are physically indistinguishable, but members of the two groups may form distinct subcultures based on their different ethnic backgrounds.

From the sociological viewpoint, then, an *ethnic group* is a category of people who, as a result of their shared cultural heritage, are regarded as socially distinct. Unlike racial differences, ethnic differences are culturally learned and not genetically inherited—a point that seems obvious enough, until we remember how often the supposed "intelligence," "industriousness," "warlikeness," "inscrutability," "laziness," or other characteristic of some group is assumed to be an inborn trait of its members. But no ethnic group has any inborn cultural traits; it acquires them through socialization in its particular environment. The Japanese of Japan and Americans of Japanese ancestry share the same genetic heritage, yet they display many different cultural norms and values.

Minority Groups

Within the small and homogeneous preindustrial societies of the past, everyone spoke the same language, shared the same values and beliefs, worshiped the same gods, and had very similar physical characteristics.

In the modern world, however, many societies are large and heterogeneous. As a result of colonial settlements, missionary work, migrations, and the flight of refugees from famine, poverty, and persecution, these societies frequently contain *minority groups*—peoples whose physical appearance or cultural practices are unlike those of the dominant group, making them susceptible to different and unequal treatment. In such cases, the dominant group may deny the minority equal access to the wealth, power, and prestige that its own members enjoy. If this happens, social stratification along racial or ethnic lines may result.

Unequal treatment (and not mere numbers) is an essential aspect of the sociological concept of a minority group. There are many numerical minorities in American society today—such as blue-eyed people, people of Scottish extraction, or Episcopalians—but these are not minority groups, for they do not suffer group deprivation. Generally, a minority group has the following distinguishing features (Wirth, 1945; Wagley and Harris, 1964; Vander Zanden, 1972).

1. *The members of a minority group suffer various disadvantages at the hands of another group.* The dominant group exploits the minority, keeping its members in low-status positions and draining off their labor and resources. And the members of the minority group are not merely exploited: they are the victims of abuse, humiliation, and deeply held social beliefs that they are somehow innately "inferior."

2. *A minority group is identified by characteristics that are socially visible.* All people sharing some visible or noticeable characteristic, such as skin color, religion, or language, are lumped together into a single category. No matter what characteristic is used to make this identification, it is believed to be of great social importance. Individual characteristics of a minority-group member are regarded as less significant than the supposed characteristics of the group to which the individual belongs.

3. *A minority group is a self-conscious group with a strong sense of "oneness."* Members of a minority, such as Jews in the Soviet Union, blacks in America, or Sikhs in India, tend to feel a strong affinity with one another. Their "consciousness of kind," or sense of common identity, is often so strong that differences within the group become submerged in a common loyalty to "the people." The more a minority group is persecuted, the more intense its group solidarity is likely to become.

4. *Membership in a minority group is an ascribed status.* People usually do not become members of a minority group voluntarily; they are born into it. It is often difficult for them to leave the group, for the reason that the dominant group regards anyone with minority-group ancestry as a permanent member of that minority. Thus, in the United States, a person with one black parent—or even with one black grandparent—still tends to be regarded as black rather than white.

Figure 11.2 *American military involvement in Southeast Asia led to the birth of many thousands of Amerasian children. In Vietnam especially, these children—fatherless and physically different from their peers—are treated with contempt by much of the population. Minority groups in countries all over the world face similar difficulties.*

5. *By choice or necessity, members of a minority group generally marry within the group.* This practice (called endogamy) may be encouraged by the dominant group, by the minority group, or by both. Members of the dominant group are typically reluctant to marry members of the stigmatized minority group, and the minority group's consciousness of kind predisposes its members to look for husbands or wives within the group. As a result, minority status within a society tends to be passed on from generation to generation.

There is one aspect of the sociological use of the term "minority group" that may seem rather peculiar at first: a minority group can sometimes be a numerical majority. In practice, of course, such a situation is rare, but examples do exist. In the African country of Burundi, the small Tutsi tribe dominates the large Hutu tribe; in Guatemala, the Hispanic inhabitants dominate the Indians who outnumber them; in South Africa, the white population dominates the much larger black population.

Patterns of Race and Ethnic Relations

Race and ethnic relations may follow many different patterns, ranging from harmonious coexistence to outright conflict. George Simpson and Milton Yinger (1985) have identified six basic patterns of intergroup hostility or cooperation. Their list covers virtually all the possible patterns of race and ethnic relations, and each pattern exists or has existed in some part of the world.

1. *Assimilation.* In some cases a minority group is simply eliminated by being assimilated, or absorbed, into the dominant group. This process may involve cultural assimilation, racial assimilation, or both. Cultural assimilation occurs when the minority group loses its distinctive cultural traits and adopts those of the dominant culture; racial assimilation occurs when the physical differences between the groups disappear as a result of interbreeding. Sometimes assimilation takes place voluntarily: in Hawaii, for example, various racial and ethnic groups from the Pacific, Asia, and Europe have blended fairly freely over many years. But sometimes assimilation is forced. Bulgaria, for example, is currently trying to eliminate the ethnic identity of the Turks who form 12 percent of the country's population. The Turks have been forced to change their Islamic names to Slavic ones; Turkish-language newspapers and broadcasts have been switched to Bulgarian; and history texts are being rewritten to obliterate all mention of the Turkish minority.

2. *Pluralism.* Some minorities do not want to lose their group identity; their members have a strong consciousness of, and pride in, their heritage, and are loyal to their own group. In response, a society may practice pluralism, or recognition and tolerance of diversity. Tanzania, for example, is a pluralistic society that respects the cultural distinctions among its African, Asian, European, and Middle Eastern peoples. In Switzerland, four ethnic groups, speaking German, French, Italian, and Romanche, retain their sense of group identity while living together amicably in the society as a whole.

3. *Legal protection of minorities.* In some societies, significant sections of the dominant group may have hostile attitudes toward minority groups. In such cases the government may enforce legal measures that protect the interests and rights of the minorities. In Great Britain, for example, the Race Relations Act of 1965 makes it illegal to discriminate on racial grounds in employment or housing. It is also a criminal offense to publish or even to utter publicly any sentiments that might encourage hostility between racial and ethnic groups in the population.

4. *Population transfer.* In some situations of intense hostility between groups, the problem is "solved" by removing the minority from the scene altogether. In 1972, for example, the entire Asian population was ordered to leave the African country of Uganda, in which they had lived for generations. In a few cases, population transfer may involve outright partition of a territory. Hostility between Hindus and Muslims in India was so intense that in 1947 the entire subcontinent was divided between them, creating a new Muslim state, Pakistan. Today, Cyprus is becoming divided into Greek and Turkish territories, and Lebanon into Muslim and Christian territories. Voluntary and forced population transfers have been taking place in both countries.

5. *Continued subjugation.* In some cases the dominant group has every intention of maintaining its privilege over the minority group indefinitely. It may be fully willing to use force to achieve this objective, and it may even physically segregate the members of the various groups. Historically, continued subjugation has been a very common policy. The climate of world opinion is now such that few countries dare to openly endorse indefinite repression, but the pattern does persist in some cases. The outstanding example is South Africa, where, under various versions of the policy of apartheid, or racial segregation, the white minority regime proposes to keep its power over the black majority forever, and has made clear its willingness to use all necessary force to achieve this goal. Less overt policies of continued subjugation are found in several Latin American countries, where dominant Hispanic groups continue to oppress the indigenous Indian minorities.

6. *Extermination.* In several parts of the world *genocide*—the extermination of entire populations—has been attempted and even achieved. The methods of genocide range from systematic slaughter by force of arms to the deliberate spreading of infectious diseases, particularly smallpox, among peoples who have no natural immunity to them. Dutch settlers in South Africa entirely exterminated the Hottentots and came close to exterminating the San, who at one point in South African history were actually classified as "vermin." English settlers on the island of Tasmania wiped out the local population, whom they hunted for

Figure 11.3 *Population transfer—often involving the expulsion of the unwanted group—is a drastic but not uncommon event in race and ethnic relations. In 1838, some 16,000 Cherokee were forced to march a thousand miles in winter from their homeland in Carolina and Georgia to be "resettled" in Oklahoma. Some 4,000 of them died during the ordeal. The American artist Robert Lidneux depicted their journey in this picture, Trail of Tears.*

sport and even for dog food. In 1915, Turks killed over 1 million Armenians who lived in their territory. Between 1933 and 1945, the Nazis murdered at least 6 million Jews in Europe. In 1972, the Tutsi tribe massacred nearly 100,000 members of the Hutu tribe in Burundi. And there is strong evidence that economic interests in Brazil, at times with the connivance of the Brazilian government, have slaughtered the Indian occupants of land that is wanted for agricultural development.

These patterns are not necessarily mutually exclusive, and more than one of them can exist in a society at the same time. It is interesting to note that at some point in their history, both the United States and Canada have made use of every single one of these six strategies. Immigrant groups, particularly those from northern European countries like Germany and Holland, have been *assimilated* into the mainstream of North American life. There is a strong trend toward *pluralism* at present, with different groups, such as American Hispanics and French Canadians, asserting pride in their own cultural traditions. *Legal protection of minorities* has been entrenched in the laws of both countries through civil-rights and similar legislation. *Population transfer* was used extensively against the Indians of North America, who were often forced to leave their traditional territories and to settle on remote reservations. The United States and Canada both practiced *continued subjugation* of their minorities, with the most extreme example being that of slavery in the Southern states. *Extermination* was used against American Indians in both countries, and tribes such as the Mohicans, Pequots, and Yana were in fact hounded out of existence.

Figure 11.4 *During World War II, the Nazis attempted the systematic genocide of the Jewish population of Germany and of several countries that German forces occupied. This photograph, taken in the final days of the war in Europe, shows American officials visiting the concentration camp at Buchenwald, one of several centers where Jews were sent to be murdered.*

Some racial and ethnic groups, then, are able to live together in conditions of equality and mutual respect, but others are in a state of constant inequality and conflict. Clearly, there is no inherent reason why different groups should be hostile to one another. Stratification along racial and ethnic lines has social causes. But what are these causes? How and why do racial and ethnic inequalities develop?

Intergroup Relations: A Functionalist View

Functionalist theorists generally try to explain persistent social features in terms of their positive effects on society as a whole. As we saw in Chapter 10 ("Social Stratification"), functionalists argue that social inequality can serve the function of rewarding scarce talents. We might expect, then, that since racial and ethnic inequalities are a common feature of societies, functionalists would look for some resulting social benefits. In practice they have rejected such reasoning, and have concentrated instead on the dysfunctions, or negative effects, that racial and ethnic antagonisms have on society.

The functionalist theorist Robert Merton (1971) points out that a social feature can be functional for one group but dysfunctional for others. A case could be made, for example, that racial slavery was functional for whites in the South before the Civil War, in the sense that it was the mainstay of their social and economic system. However, as functionalists acknowledge, slavery was highly dysfunctional for the slaves—and, ultimately, for the South as a whole, for it provoked antagonisms that ultimately led to the collapse of the entire social system. In the long run, racial and ethnic inequality will always tend to be dysfunctional for a society—partly because it prevents the society from making full use of the talents of all its members, and partly because, sooner or later, it inevitably generates hostility and even violence.

Functionalists also point out that a certain degree of group consciousness and loyalty can be functional under certain conditions. As we saw in Chapter 3 ("Culture"), most human groups tend to display **ethnocentrism**, the tendency to judge other cultures by the standards of one's own. Some measure of ethnocentrism is almost unavoidable in any racial or ethnic group. To most people, it is self-evident that their own norms, religion, attitudes, values, and cultural practices are right and proper, while those of other groups may seem inappropriate, peculiar, bizarre, or even immoral. Within limits, such ethnocentrism can be functional for the group's survival, for these attitudes ensure its members' solidarity and cohesion. People who believe that their group and its way of life are "best" will have faith and confidence in their own cultural tradition, will discourage penetration by outsiders, and will unite to work for their common goals (Coser, 1956; Levin and Levin, 1982). The difficulty is, of course, that under certain conditions, ethnocentric attitudes can lead to the exploitation and oppression of other groups.

In general, a functionalist theory of race and ethnic relations is poorly developed: it can show why hostile relations may be dysfunctional, but it does not really explain why racial and ethnic inequalities develop in the first place.

Intergroup Relations: A Conflict View

Most sociological analyses of racial and ethnic inequality have relied on conflict theory. From this perspective, these inequalities have the same source as any other form of social stratification: they stem from competition among different groups for the same scarce resources—wealth, power, and prestige. The victorious group in this conflict becomes the dominant group, while any other contenders become minority groups.

For racial or ethnic antagonisms and inequalities to develop, three basic conditions must usually be met (Noel, 1968; Cox, 1976; Vander Zanden, 1983):

1. *Identifiable groups.* There must be two or more social groups, identifiable by their visible physical characteristics or cultural practices. Unless people are aware of differences between the groups and are able to identify people as belonging to one group rather than another, conflict between them cannot develop.

2. *Competition for resources.* There must be competition between the groups for valued resources, such as power, land, or jobs. In this situation, members of one group will be inclined to secure their own interests by denying members of other groups full access to these resources.

3. *Unequal power.* The groups must be unequal in power, enabling one of them to make good its claim over scarce resources at the expense of the other group or groups. At this stage inequalities become structured into the society.

From this point on, events follow a fairly predictable course. The more the groups compete, the more negatively they view one another. The dominant group develops contemptuous beliefs about the supposed inferiority of the minority group or groups and uses these beliefs to justify its continued supremacy. Attempts by the minority group to assert its own interests are likely to be regarded as threatening by the dominant group, and further oppression may follow.

From the conflict perspective, the disputes among racial and ethnic groups are not really about racial or ethnic differences; they are about the use of such differences to create and preserve inequality in the competition for scarce resources. Thus, wherever different groups compete for the same resources—blacks and whites for power and wealth in South Africa, settlers and indigenous tribes for possession of the Brazilian hinterland, Israelis and Palestinians for the same piece of territory—intergroup hostility is the result, particularly if the groups remain unequal and one of them is able to exploit or victimize the other.

In fact, conflict theory predicts that hostilities may subside if the subordinate group is able to gain greater equality with the dominant group. The history of American race relations supports this view: the strong hostilities that originally existed against Japanese, Irish, Italian, and other immigrants has gradually lessened as these groups have gained entry to the broad American middle class, where they are seen as equals rather than as rivals. Antipathy is now greatest against those groups, such as blacks or Chicanos, who remain relatively impoverished—and this sentiment is strongest among low-status whites who feel most threatened by the economic progress and competition of the minorities. The evidence from other countries also shows a consistent pattern of racial intolerance among low-status members of the dominant group.

Racism

As we noted in Chapter 10 ("Social Stratification"), a dominant group always tries to legitimate its interests by means of an *ideology,* a set of beliefs that explains and justifies some actual or potential social arrangements. One such form of ideology is *racism*—the belief that one racial or ethnic group is inferior to another and that unequal treatment is therefore justified. The characteristic feature of racist ideologies is that they try to make social and economic inequalities among racial and ethnic groups seem "natural" or "right."

A good illustration of the relationship between racist ideology and economic interests comes from the European colonial period, which lasted from the fifteenth century until the middle of the twentieth century. *Colonialism* is the formal political and economic domination of one nation by a more powerful nation: in effect, the subordinate country is "owned" by the dominant one. Before countries like England, France, Spain, Portugal, Holland, and Belgium started building their respective colonial empires, there was very little racism in Europe. In fact, occasional visitors from exotic foreign lands were often treated with honor, and when European explorers discovered previously unknown indigenous peoples in Africa, Asia, the Americas, and the South Pacific, the initial contacts were usually friendly. But as travel and trade increased, the European powers came to rely on these foreign lands for labor, raw materials, markets for finished goods, and strategic bases. To secure these interests, they conquered the local peoples—eventually seizing control of almost half the land area and population of the world. Tiny minorities of white settlers formed the elite in the colonies, while the hard and dirty work was given to the local inhabitants. A system of rigid stratification, enforced by the settlers' superior military technology, was used to prevent the indigenous peoples from overwhelming their new rulers.

This era of colonial expansion was marked by an intense racism among European peoples, for they needed an ideology that would legitimate the system they had created. In particular, colonialism posed a severe moral dilemma for the European powers, especially those that practiced slavery. Their treatment of the subject peoples was clearly incompatible with their avowed Christian beliefs. Since no Christian could legitimately make a slave of another human being, an obvious justification presented itself—to classify the colonial peoples as subhuman. By the 1840s, one anthropologist, James Pritchard, was exploring the question of how relations between whites and nonwhites ought to differ from those between humans and orangutans. By the 1860s, Darwin's theory of evolution was being misused to "prove" the biological inferiority of the subject peoples: some argued that nonwhites were at a lower point on the evolutionary ladder than whites; others contended that they were products of a completely separate process of evolution and were thus half animal.

These attitudes became deeply embedded in Western European culture and were transported by white settlers to North America, where many traces of them remain to this day. Racist beliefs provided a convenient justification for slavery in the South and for the slaughter and dispossession of American Indians. Blacks were considered suitable for slavery "by nature," and the destruction of Indian societies by a "superior" white civilization was seen as a matter of a "manifest destiny" in which "the only good Indian is a dead one."

Although racism is found among different peoples in societies all over the world, the racism of the Western powers was notable for its international scale and systematic theoretical justification by theologians and scientists alike (Mosse, 1978). This racism reached its most extreme form during the course of this century in the rantings of Adolf Hitler, a short, dark man who believed that the tall, blond, blue-eyed "Aryan" race was infinitely superior to all others, destined to rule the world, and had to maintain its racial purity. In spite of the fact that there is no such thing as an "Aryan" race, Hitler's theories fired Germany with a sense of national identity—and led to concentration camps, gas chambers, and a global war. (Ironically, the American forces that helped destroy Nazi Germany fought Hitler with a racially segregated army, and fed German prisoners of war in canteens where black American soldiers were refused service.) Today, racist ideology is considered so disreputable that few people or governments, whatever their private attitudes, dare to openly endorse a racist attitude. Yet racism, often subtle in form, is still commonplace in the modern world.

The ideology of racism not only justifies existing inequalities; it also reinforces them by the process of the *self-fulfilling prophecy*—a prediction that leads to behavior that makes the prediction come true (Merton, 1968). For example, if people believe a prediction that their bank will go bankrupt, they will rush to withdraw their money—with the result that the bank *will* go bankrupt. In the field of race and ethnic relations, the self-fulfilling prophecy works as follows. The racist ideology of the dominant group defines the minority as inferior. Because the members of the minority group are considered inferior, they are believed to be unsuited for high-status jobs, advanced education, or responsible positions in society. Accordingly, they are not given access to these opportunities. Consequently, they hold low-status jobs, are poorly educated, and fill few responsible positions in society. The minority group's lack of achievement is then cited to "prove" its inferiority, and the racist ideology is confirmed.

It often happens, too, that an oppressed group accepts the ideology that justifies its oppression. There is little doubt, for example, that colonial peoples often accepted the colonizers' view of their inferiority, at least until the surge of nationalism in these countries after World War II. In such cases the minority is in a state of what Karl Marx called *false consciousness,* a subjective understanding of one's situation that does not accord with the objective facts. This situation parallels the tendency, discussed in Chapter 10 ("Social Stratification"), for subordinate social classes to believe in the ideology that justifies stratification in their own society. But once the members of any subordinate group gain an objective awareness of their own plight and shared interests as an oppressed group, they begin to challenge the legitimacy of the system—and social conflict follows.

Prejudice and Discrimination

Prejudice and discrimination are found in any situation of hostility and inequality between racial and ethnic groups. The two words are often used interchangeably in ordinary speech, but in fact they refer to two different, though related, phenomena: attitudes and behavior.

Prejudice is an irrational, inflexible attitude toward an entire category of people. (The word literally means "prejudged.") Although it is possible to be prejudiced in favor of a group, "prejudice" usually implies negative feelings—antipathy, hostility, even fear. The key feature of prejudice is that it is always rooted in generalizations and so ignores the differences among individuals. Thus, someone who is prejudiced against Arabs will tend to have a negative attitude toward any individual Arab, in the belief that all Arabs share the same supposed traits.

Discrimination is unequal treatment of people on the grounds of their group membership. Again, although it is possible to discriminate in favor of any specific group, "discrimination" usually implies negative actions. In particular, discrimination involves the refusal to give members of one group the opportunities that would be granted to similarly qualified members of another group. Discrimination occurs, for example, if an employer refuses to hire or promote someone solely because of that person's racial or ethnic background.

In a classic study, Richard LaPiere (1934) illustrated the practical difference between the two concepts. He traveled around the United States with a Chinese couple, stopping at over 250 restaurants and hotels on the way. In only one instance were they refused service—that is, discriminated against. Six months later, LaPiere wrote to each of the establishments he had visited and asked if they were willing to serve "members of the Chinese race." Over 90 percent of the replies indicated that Chinese would not be welcome—that is, there was prejudice against them. Yet the prejudice was not necessarily translated into discrimination. LaPiere's study is one of many examples of sociological research that reveal a marked discrepancy between what people say and what they do (Deutscher, 1973).

Robert Merton (1949) pointed out that prejudice and discrimination can actually be combined in four different ways. His model may not neatly accommodate a particular individual, but it does cover all the possibilities.

Figure 11.5 *Racial prejudice is widespread in societies all over the world, and in the United States takes many forms ranging from the subtle to the extreme. Social-science research can now give important insights into the sources, and irrational character, of this prejudice.*

1. *The unprejudiced nondiscriminator* adheres to the ideal of equality in both theory and practice. Such a person is not prejudiced and does not discriminate against others on racial or ethnic grounds.

2. *The unprejudiced discriminator* has no racial or ethnic prejudices, but may discriminate when it is convenient to do so. For example, an employer may have no personal hostility toward members of another group, but may not hire them for fear of offending customers.

3. *The prejudiced nondiscriminator* is a "timid bigot" who is prejudiced against other groups but who, because of legal or social pressures, is reluctant to translate attitudes into action.

4. *The prejudiced discriminator* does not genuinely believe in the values of freedom or equality and discriminates on the basis of prejudiced attitudes. Such a person may, however, attempt to disguise discriminatory acts—for example, by refusing to rent a room to a minority-group member on the grounds that "it's already been taken."

Sources of Prejudice

A major focus of the work of social scientists, particularly in the decade after World War II, has been the sources of prejudice. What are the characteristic features of prejudiced thought, and how and why do people become prejudiced?

Stereotypes

Prejudiced thought always involves the use of a *stereotype*—a rigid mental image that summarizes whatever is believed to be typical about a group. (The word originally referred to a printing plate, used for stamping the identical image over and over.)

Like ethnocentrism, stereotyped thinking is an almost unavoidable feature of social life. People tend to think in terms of general categories, if only to enable them to make sense of the world by simplifying its complexity. You probably have your own stereotype, for example, of what an Australian aborigine or an Eskimo is like. The essence of prejudiced thinking, however, is that the stereotype is not checked against reality. It is not modified by experiences that contradict the rigid image. If a prejudiced person finds that an individual member of a group does not conform to the stereotype for the group as a whole, this evidence is simply taken as "the exception that proves the rule" and not as grounds for questioning the original belief. Robert Merton (1968) shows how readily the same behavior can be interpreted differently to fit an existing stereotype:

> Did Lincoln work far into the night? This testifies that he was industrious, resolute, perseverant, and eager to realize his capacities to the full. Do the out-group Jews or Japanese keep the same hours? This only bears witness to their sweatshop mentality, their ruthless undercutting of American standards, their unfair competitive practices. Is the in-group hero frugal, thrifty, and sparing? Then the out-group villain is stingy, miserly, and penny-pinching. All honor is due to the in-group Abe for his having been smart, shrewd, and intelligent, and, by the same token, all contempt is owing the out-group Abes for their being sharp, cunning, crafty, and too clever by far.

The "Authoritarian Personality"

Do some people have personality patterns that make them more prone to prejudice than others? A classic study by Theodore Adorno and his associates (1950) tried to answer this question. To explore the nature of prejudice, Adorno tested his subjects on three different sets of attitudes: anti-Semitism, fascism, and ethnocentrism. His method was to ask the subjects to indicate their agreement or disagreement with a series of statements that were anti-Jewish, authoritarian, or hostile to different or unfamiliar ways of life. Adorno's significant finding was that people who agreed strongly with any one set of statements tended also to agree strongly with the others. In other words, those who were prejudiced against Jews were also likely to favor strong, authoritarian leadership, and to have a very ethnocentric view of their own group and its customs.

Adorno concluded that some people have a psychological makeup that he referred to as the *authoritarian personality*—a distinctive set of traits, including conformity, intolerance, and insecurity, that seem typical of many prejudiced people. Those who have this personality pattern, he found, are submissive to superiors and bullying to inferiors. They tend to have anti-intellectual and antiscientific attitudes; they are disturbed by any ambiguity in sexual or religious matters; and they see the world in very rigid and stereotyped terms. The authoritarian personality, Adorno claimed, is primarily a product of a family environment in which the parents were cold, aloof, disciplinarian, and themselves bigoted.

Adorno's work has since inspired over a thousand pieces of research and critical articles. Some writers have pointed out that Adorno's methodology was weak in certain respects; others that he neglected the possibility of an authoritarian personality among radicals as well as conservatives; others that his concept is too vague and sweeping in its scope. Despite these and other criticisms, however, it is now generally accepted that some people are psychologically more prone to prejudiced thinking than others.

Irrationality

Another consistent feature of prejudiced thought is that it is irrational—illogical and inconsistent. Adorno found, for example, that prejudiced people often believe mutually contradictory statements about groups they dislike. For example, most subjects who disliked Jews for keeping to themselves also disliked them for intruding too much. Similarly, those who disliked them for being too capitalistic and for controlling business also disliked them for being too communistic and subversive of business. Those who disliked them for being too miserly also disliked them for giving money to charity as a means of gaining prestige, and so on. Clearly, prejudiced people are not concerned about genuine group characteristics; they simply accept any negative statement that feeds their existing hostility.

In one study, Eugene Hartley (1946) found that people who were prejudiced against one minority group tended to be prejudiced against others. Nearly three-quarters of those who disliked Jews and blacks also disliked such people as the Wallonians, the Pireneans, and the Danireans. Some prejudiced people even urged that members of the latter three groups be expelled from the United States. As it happens, however, the Wallonians, the Pireneans, and the Danireans were fictitious names concocted by Hartley! His study convincingly demonstrates the irrationality of prejudice, for it shows that prejudiced people may be hostile toward groups they could never have met or even have heard of.

Scapegoating

Another factor that can contribute to prejudice is *scapegoating*—placing the blame for one's troubles on some relatively powerless individual or group. (The word comes from a custom recounted in the Old Testament—the laying of the people's sins on a goat, which was then allowed to escape into the wilderness.) Scapegoating typically occurs when the members of one group feel threatened but are unable to retaliate against the real source of the threat. Instead, they vent their frustrations on some weak and despised group—and thereby gain the sense that they are superior to someone at least.

The outstanding example of a scapegoated group is the Jews in Nazi Germany, who were conveniently blamed for the country's economic troubles after World War I. A more contemporary example comes from Great Britain, where prolonged recession has caused chronic unemployment among working-class white youths. Unable to strike at the real source of their problem—the "system"—some of these youths have taken to assaulting Pakistani immigrants, whom they believe to be competing for the few available jobs at the same level. Such attacks have become so common that there is now a word for them: "Paki-bashing."

Social Environment

The sources of prejudice mentioned thus far appear to be primarily psychological. But as we noted in Chapter 5 ("Socialization"), people's personalities—including their thoughts and feelings—develop in, and are shaped by, their social context.

Figure 11.6 *A century ago, Chinese immigrants to the western United States often served as scapegoats for the frustrations of low-status whites, who saw them as competitors for jobs. This engraving shows an anti-Chinese riot in Denver, Colorado, in 1880.*

Certain environments, therefore, may tend to encourage or discourage prejudice. In general, if groups interact regularly on terms of equality and cooperation, there is likely to be little prejudice among their members. Conversely, if there is inequality, competition, and minimal contact between groups, prejudice can develop unchecked.

Cross-cultural research by Thomas Pettigrew (1958, 1959) clearly reveals how social conditions can influence people's racial views. Pettigrew surveyed racial attitudes among whites in three regions—South Africa, a highly segregated society; the southern United States, a relatively less segregated society at the time; and the northern United States, which was the least segregated of the three. Not too surprisingly, he found a strong correlation between the degree of segregation in the society and the dominant group's racial attitudes: prejudice was strongest among the South African whites, less strong among white Southerners, and weakest among white Northerners. Prejudice, therefore, cannot be attributed solely to the psychological quirks of individuals, for it is often simply a matter of conformity to the norms of one's own group.

Forms of Discrimination

Discrimination occurs when the dominant group regards itself as entitled to social advantages and uses its power to secure them at the expense of minority groups. These advantages may be of many different kinds. The dominant group may, for example, reserve positions of political power for itself; it may establish a claim over desirable residential areas; it may demand the exclusive use of certain recreational facilities and schools; it may claim a right to high-status jobs. In extreme cases, as we have seen, it may even enforce the physical segregation of the minority group from the rest of society.

Discrimination takes two basic forms. The first is *legal discrimination*—unequal treatment, on the grounds of group membership, that is upheld by law. In the past, this form of discrimination was very common. It existed, for example, in all the colonies established by the European powers, where the laws reserved for the dominant group certain privileges, such as the right to vote. Similar laws existed in many parts of the United States until the 1960s, when they were gradually repealed or were struck down by the Supreme Court. The second form of discrimination is *institutionalized discrimination*—unequal treatment, on the grounds of group membership, that is entrenched in social customs. Such customs might include a pattern of segregated housing, or a tendency for minority-group members to be concentrated in low-paying jobs. Institutionalized discrimination is present wherever one racial or ethnic group maintains advantages over another, regardless of whether it also uses the law to secure its position.

At first sight, it might seem that legal discrimination is the more severe form: legal discrimination is certainly blatant, and it is often harsh in its consequences. But because it is established by law, legal discrimination can also be eliminated by law—abolished in a single stroke by the repeal of the discriminatory legislation. Institutionalized discrimination, on the other hand, being more indirect and often quite subtle in its effects, is very difficult to eradicate. Its elimination would require pervasive cultural changes, including alterations in people's informal conduct and private attitudes.

With these considerations in mind, let us examine American racial and ethnic relations in more detail.

Race and Ethnic Relations in the United States

The Declaration of Independence, signed on July 4, 1776, proclaimed to the world:

> We hold these truths to be self-evident, that all men are created equal, that they are endowed by their Creator with certain inalienable rights, that among these are life, liberty, and the pursuit of happiness.

Thomas Jefferson, who wrote these words of stirring idealism, was a slaveholder, and so were many others who appended their signatures to the document.

As the Swedish sociologist Gunnar Myrdal pointed out in 1944 in his classic study of American race relations, *An American Dilemma,* there has always been a deep tension between the expressed values on which the United States was founded and the actual treatment that minorities have received at the hands of the dominant group. This tension between ideal and real culture, Myrdal predicted, would ultimately have to be resolved, but the nation is still a long way from a final resolution. American society remains one in which inequalities of power, wealth, and prestige tend to follow the lines of racial and ethnic divisions.

Unlike most societies, the United States is primarily a nation of relatively recent immigrants; the forebears of most Americans arrived as explorers, adventurers, colonizers, captive slaves, deported criminals, or refugees. It is a cherished American belief that the society has served as a "melting pot" for these diverse peoples. The essence of this credo was captured in *The Melting Pot,* a popular Broadway play of 1908 (Zangwill, 1933):

> America is God's crucible, the great Melting Pot, where all the races of Europe are melting and reforming! Here you stand, good folk, think I, when I see them at Ellis Island, here you stand in your fifty groups, with your fifty languages and histories, and your fifty blood hatreds and rivalries. But you won't long be like that, brothers, for these are the fires of God you've come to . . . Germans, and Frenchmen, Irishmen and Englishmen, Jews and Russians—into the Crucible with you all! . . . God is making the American.

The truth, however, is very different. The first settlers came mostly from "Anglo-Saxon" northern Europe, and they quickly gained control of political and economic power. To a considerable extent, their descendants have managed to keep this power ever since, and their cultural values have become the dominant ones of the entire nation. Successive waves of immigrants have often had to struggle long and hard to be assimilated into the American mainstream, and some, thus far, have failed.

Two factors seem to have shaped the destinies of the various minorities. The first is simply their degree of similarity to the dominant "WASP" (white, Anglo-Saxon, Protestant) group. Those who were racially or ethnically akin to this group, such as the Scandinavians and Germans, were accepted fairly readily. Those who were racially akin but ethnically different, such as the Catholic Irish and Poles, faced much more prejudice and discrimination. Those who were both racially and ethnically dissimilar to the dominant group, such as blacks and Chicanos, have been excluded by formal and informal barriers from equal participation in American society. In the past, most sociological attention focused on this "similarity" factor and the

effects of the prejudice and discrimination that are linked to it.

The second factor is the unique historical circumstances surrounding each group's arrival in the United States and its entry into particular labor markets. For example, a group that is small and highly skilled (such as the Cuban professionals who fled their country's revolution in 1959) is likely to achieve acceptance and success more quickly than a group that is large and unskilled (such as today's illegal immigrants from Mexico). This is especially true if lower-status members of the dominant group fear competition for jobs and undercutting of wages. Many modern social scientists are making greater use of this historical factor to explain the variation in the progress of different minority groups toward equality (Bonacich, 1972; Lieberson, 1980; Steinberg, 1981; Sowell, 1981, 1983; Rollins, 1982).

We can trace the influence of both sets of factors by looking at the background, experience, and contemporary situation of the main minority groups: blacks, Hispanics, Indians, Asians, and "white ethnics" (Rose, 1981; McLemore, 1983; Schaefer, 1984; Parrillo, 1985).

Figure 11.7 *The American response to any immigrant group depends partly on that group's racial and ethnic similarity to the dominant group, and partly on the prevailing labor-market conditions. In the booming economy of the late nineteenth century, the United States accepted large numbers of immigrants from Europe, although Protestants were preferred to Catholics. In contrast, immigration from Mexico is currently discouraged, for there is little demand for the labor of these mostly unskilled workers. These photographs show European immigrants arriving in New York a century ago, and some of today's illegal migrants from Mexico being rounded up by the border patrol. Members of each group received a very different welcome.*

Blacks

After Nigeria, Ethiopia, and Zaire, the United States has the largest black population in the world. Black Americans are the largest minority group within the country; they number over 28.5 million and represent almost 12 percent of the population. Their history in the United States has, for the most part, been one of sustained oppression and discrimination (Elkins, 1963; Cheek, 1970; Litwak, 1980; Sitkoff, 1982).

The first Africans were brought in shackles to North America in 1619, and within a few decades the demand for their labor had created a massive slave trade that ultimately transported some 400,000 captives across the Atlantic. Contrary to common belief, few slaves were seized by whites on the West African coast. Most were captured by other Africans from the slave-owning kingdoms of the interior and sold to white traders at the coastal ports, from which they were shipped across the Atlantic under appalling conditions. On arrival in the United States, the slaves were sold at public auction and set to work, mostly on plantations. The original culture of these African people had little relevance in this new situation, and their old traditions, language, and religion soon fell into disuse and eventually disappeared. (One cultural feature that did survive in modified form, however, was the rhythm of West African traditional music. Transformed over the generations into blues, jazz, soul, rhythm and blues, and ultimately rock music, it has become a major contribution to contemporary American and world culture.)

At first, the slaveholders justified slavery, not by racist attitudes, but rather by their frankly admitted need for cheap labor in the cotton and tobacco fields. In time, however, the practice of slavery led to the creation of a racist ideology that justified the continued subjugation of the slaves by depicting blacks as subhuman: they were said to be innately irresponsible, promiscuous, stupid, lazy—and happy with their subordinate status. The experience of slavery set the stage for the subsequent interaction between black and white in the United States.

The Northern states began to outlaw slavery in 1780, but it persisted in the South until it was ended by the Civil War and legislation that followed Lincoln's emancipation of slaves in 1863. During the period of Reconstruction, which lasted for just over a decade after Lincoln's declaration, there was a concerted attempt to ensure that the newly freed slaves would indeed enjoy equality.

Figure 11.8 *This old print shows the "cargo" layout on one of the decks of a slave ship that plied the Africa-America route before the Civil War. On board, the slaves were chained wrist to wrist and ankle to ankle for the two-month voyage. To prevent the risk of mutiny and suicide among the captives, they were frequently kept in this position for days or weeks on end, lying in their own blood and excrement and unable even to sit up. Many of the slaves tried to starve themselves to death, but were force-fed through metal funnels that were jammed into their mouths. For years an intense debate raged between two groups of slave-traders: the "tight packers," who held that profits would be greater if as many slaves as possible were crammed aboard, and the "loose packers," who argued that so many slaves died during the voyages that it would be better to allow the captives a little more space. Dragged to America in chains to be subjected to slavery and then to decades of segregation and legal discrimination, black Americans have had an experience utterly different from that of any other racial or ethnic group in the society.*

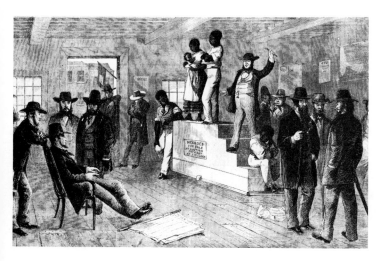

However, white political dominance was soon re-asserted by depriving the blacks of the vote and by the use of such terror tactics as lynching. Segregation remained the norm, and was gradually en-coded into law. Throughout the country, including supposedly liberal metropolitan areas of the North, segregation in hotels, restaurants, and other public facilities was common. In 1954, however, the Su-preme Court ruled in the historic *Brown* v. *Board of Education* case that segregated schools were inherently unequal and ordered nationwide school desegregation "with all deliberate speed." From that time on, the courts and the federal govern-ment began to dismantle the system of racial seg-regation and discrimination. Yet progress toward greater equality was painfully slow until the emer-gence of a powerful civil rights movement and a series of violent and costly riots in Northern cities during the 1960s. As conflict theory would suggest, this heightened tension between the competing groups generated rapid changes. In particular, the principle of racial equality was enshrined in the law of the land through a series of civil rights acts that prohibited legal discrimination.

One of the most important outcomes of the racial turmoil of the 1960s was a change in both black goals and black self-image. From the early days of slavery onward, many blacks and their white liberal sympathizers had hoped for an inte-grated society—in effect, one in which blacks would be accepted into the WASP middle-class cul-ture. The rise of a "black power" movement, with an emphasis on black pride and the validity of black culture, marked an important change of di-rection. The self-image of blacks was radically re-

Figure 11.9 *Some stages in the changing relation-ships of the black and white groups in the United States: a slave auction during the 1860s; legal dis-crimination in the 1950s; Martin Luther King, Jr., at a civil rights demonstration in the 1960s; and a black presidential candidate in the 1980s.*

vised, and the black community showed signs of unprecedented self-confidence. As a result, many blacks began to demand a plural society, rather than assimilation into the dominant culture—a demand that had profound effects on the way many other minorities have come to view themselves as well.

How has the black minority fared since the changes of the 1960s? In some respects there have been important gains. The gap between blacks' and whites' average years of schooling has narrowed rapidly—from three years in 1960 to less than half a year today. More than 5,000 blacks now hold local elective office; among them are over 250 mayors, including those of several of the nation's largest cities. Black workers are no longer concentrated in a handful of menial jobs: in the early 1960s, for example, one of every three working black women was a maid, but today, only one in twenty does that job. In fact, a substantial part of the black population—perhaps a third—has "made it" to the American middle class, and their jobs, incomes, family structure, and general lifestyle are similar to those of their white counterparts. Over 6 million blacks now live in suburban areas (Davis and Watson, 1982; L. Williams, 1985).

But in other respects blacks have made little progress, or have even lost ground. Institutionalized discrimination still persists throughout the United States—perhaps more so in the North (where about half the black population now lives, mostly in urban ghettos) than in the South, which in many ways has adjusted more readily to the changing relationships between the races. As a result of informal social and economic barriers to residential integration, most blacks live in neighborhoods that are overwhelmingly black, and most black children, despite busing programs, still attend predominantly black schools. Although black college enrollment doubled between 1960 and 1980, the percentage of blacks in college is beginning to slip once more. Blacks remain underrepresented, too, at the higher levels of the political system: in 1986 only 3 percent of members of Congress were black, and there was no black senator or governor. Most important of all, the economic position of blacks has actually worsened relative to that of whites. In 1970, the median black family income was 61 percent that of whites. In the recession years of the late 1970s and early 1980s, it actually shrank as low as 55 percent that of whites, before climbing back to 60 percent in 1985 (Reid, 1983; Farley, 1984; Bureau of the Census, 1986a, 1986c; Pear, 1986).

The fact is that despite the success of many blacks, the great majority have been left behind, and a hard core of these form an "underclass" of impoverished people who have little hope that their lives will ever improve. Almost one-third of all blacks live below the poverty line—a rate three times that of the white population. Many of these people are trapped in an unending cycle of broken homes, welfare, joblessness, violence, crime, and drug abuse. Half of the black births in America today are to unmarried women. One in every two black children lives in poverty, and one in every two lives in a home without a father. One in six black males is arrested by the age of nineteen, and homicide is the leading cause of death of black males between the ages of fifteen and nineteen. Unemployment rates for blacks are typically double those of whites, and in some urban areas the rate for black teenagers is over 50 percent. The persistence of this underclass seems a constant reproach to the proclaimed ideals of the United States, and it remains a powderkeg in the society's future. (Trends in the black family are discussed in more detail in Chapter 13, "The Family.")

Given that there is less prejudice and discrimination in the United States now than there was two decades ago, why has a significant part of the black population remained trapped at the bottom of the stratification system? And why has the overall position of black Americans shown little relative improvement and in some respects even worsened? To explain this phenomenon, some writers are now emphasizing the historical factors that have resulted in the intertwining of race and class in the United States.

Thomas Sowell (1981, 1983) points out that blacks are unique among minorities in that they came to the United States as slaves and were denied basic civil rights until the 1960s. Moreover, they have traditionally been a people of the rural South who began to migrate to large cities, mostly in the North, only a generation or so ago. Blacks have thus been isolated from the economic mainstream for most of their history in the United States, and in this sense are relatively "recent," unskilled immigrants to the industrialized areas of the nation. But unlike immigrants earlier in this century, blacks arrived at a time when the manufacturing base of the cities was disappearing as some blue-collar jobs vanished altogether and others were relocated to the suburbs. Informal barriers, such as racial prejudice and a lack of skills, kept most of the new arrivals from the opportunities beyond the ghettos.

Figure 11.10 *In a sense, black Americans are "recent" migrants to mainstream America, because until the middle of this century they were primarily a rural people living under segregation laws in the South. But unlike previous immigrants from Europe, black Americans arrived in the large Northern cities at a time when their industrial base was shrinking and jobs were disappearing to the suburbs. As a result, many blacks have become trapped in a ghetto "underclass." This painting of the black exodus from the South,* Migration of the Negro, No. 1, *is by the American artist Jacob Lawrence.*

Sowell is one of several relatively conservative black social scientists who insist that prejudice and discrimination are no longer sufficient to explain the plight of the black underclass. For example, William Junius Wilson (1980) argues that race is of "declining significance" in explaining inequality, for much of the gap that remains is based on class rather than color. Wilson concedes that past patterns of discrimination helped create the underclass, but he claims that this subculture has now taken on a life of its own, independent of the reasons for its origins. As we noted in Chapter 10 ("Social Stratification"), there is actually relatively little social mobility between classes in all societies, so stratification tends to reproduce itself from one generation to the next. Because the ghetto underclass is enmeshed in a tangle of economic, family, and other problems, its members are at a severe, self-perpetuating disadvantage.

This argument is controversial because it implies that current means of tackling racial inequality—financial assistance, preferential hiring, and the like—may not work for the ghetto underclass. Increased welfare benefits, for example, may only help perpetuate illegitimacy and dependency among people who have few employment prospects and little hope that things will improve; preferential employment can help those with the educational credentials necessary for good jobs, but is useless for those without them. According to this view, a different approach is needed, one that would involve the black community's taking responsibility to reverse the breakdown of the ghetto family structure and values. Other blacks reject this approach, which they see as an example of "blaming the victim" for faults that originate in the society beyond. They see the underclass as being created and maintained by institutionalized discrimination in the wider society, and aggravated by the Reagan administration's cuts in social spending (Staples, 1986).

Hispanic-Americans

The Spanish-speaking population of the United States contains around 15 million people, or 6 percent of the total population, and perhaps considerably more. The exact size of this category is not known because a significant proportion of Hispanics are "undocumented aliens"—immigrants who entered the United States illegally. These people avoid contact with public officials and do not complete census forms.

As a Spanish-speaking, Catholic, and generally poor people in an English-speaking, predominantly Protestant, and generally affluent society, the Hispanic population shares certain common characteristics. Yet these shared features should not obscure the fact that there is considerable diversity among the various Hispanic groups. The largest group are the Chicanos, or Mexican-Americans (about 8.7 million); the next largest, the Puerto Ricans (about 2 million); and the third largest, the Cubans (about 900,000). In addition, there are over 3 million other Spanish-speaking residents from various nations of Central and South America. The Hispanic population is growing very rapidly indeed—partly because it contains a disproportionate number of people in the early childbearing years, partly because of a cultural reluctance to practice birth control, and partly because there is a constant flow of new immigrants, legal and illegal, from Mexico and elsewhere. As a result, the Hispanic population could become larger than the black population before the end of the century, making Hispanics the nation's largest minority group. This fact has not been lost on some black Americans, who realize that they may have to compete with Hispanics for whatever benefits the larger society bestows on its minorities.

The Chicano population is primarily concentrated in five states—Texas, New Mexico, Colorado, Arizona, and California. Some Hispanics are descendants of people who have occupied these territories for over four centuries, and who were involuntarily made residents of the United States in 1848 when Mexico was forced to give up almost half its territory to its victorious neighbor after the Mexican-American War. Others have come as immigrants—legal or illegal, temporary or permanent. Migrant workers from Mexico have always been viewed as a convenient source of labor for the United States, and they have been encouraged or discouraged from crossing the border according to how great the need for their labor has been from time to time. Earlier in this century, Mexicans were imported in large numbers to help build the railroads and industries of the Southwest; during the Great Depression, when jobs were scarce, half a million Chicanos were deported to Mexico (often illegally, since some had been born in the United States and were citizens); between the 1940s and the early 1960s, Chicano workers were again in demand and were systematically imported; since then, there have been active campaigns to restrict the number of immigrants and to deport any illegal aliens among them. Illegal immigration is now a virtual torrent: immigration officials catch over 1.8 million would-be immigrants each year, but for each one that is intercepted, at least four cross the border undetected. There is little prospect that this flow of immigrants will cease, or even decline: Mexico has an unemployment rate of well over 30 percent, and the country is so poor that a fifth of the population earns less than $100 a year. Moreover, there is a continuing demand in the Southwest for the services of illegal aliens, who are willing to do jobs that "Anglos" will not touch, for pay that is often below the national minimum wage.

Although Chicanos have traditionally worked as migrant farm laborers, the mechanization of agriculture has steadily driven them into urban

Figure 11.11 *Mexico has a long tradition of public mural painting, a cultural trait that has diffused to the United States as a result of Chicano migration. Murals like this one are a common sight in parts of Los Angeles and other Southwestern cities.*

areas, where over 80 percent now live in barrios, or ghettos. The median family income in 1985 was about 68 percent that of whites, and 29 percent of Chicanos live below the poverty line. Only one-quarter of the population has completed high school, and, in fact, low educational achievement and a poor command of English are continuing barriers against better job opportunities for many Chicanos. Unlike other minorities, Chicanos are able to retain close ties with their country of origin because of its proximity—and so have easily maintained their language and ethnic identification. The time-honored use of the schools to "anglicize" and assimilate minority children has resulted in a backlash of resentment among Chicanos. As a result, they have successfully demanded Spanish or bilingual education for their children—a step that will undoubtedly enhance pride in Chicano culture, but which may do little to improve the command of English that is so necessary for social mobility in an English-speaking country. In any event, it seems that many Chicanos are reluctant to be assimilated into the mainstream culture. To some extent this reluctance is encouraged by political leaders in the Chicano community, who are increasingly aware of the political muscle that their numbers will give them in the future (Hernandez et al., 1976; Acuña, 1980; Rosaldo and Calvert, 1981; Rodriguez, 1983; Davis, Haub, and Willette, 1983; Bureau of the Census, 1986a).

The Puerto Ricans are a people of mixed Spanish, Indian, and African origins. The Island of Puerto Rico has been an American possession since the Spanish-American War, and Puerto Ricans have been United States citizens since 1917. Many of them have immigrated to the continental United States in search of better jobs, with more than half of them settling in New York City. Living primarily in ghetto areas, Puerto Ricans are one of the most impoverished groups in the nation: their median family income in 1985 was about 46 percent that of whites, and some 43 percent live below the poverty line. Perhaps because of these poor economic conditions, Puerto Ricans have done something that no other immigrant group has done before: in almost every year since 1972, Puerto Ricans have returned home in greater numbers than they have immigrated in (Wagenheim, 1975; Stockton, 1978; Davis, Haub, and Willette, 1983; Carr, 1984; Bureau of the Census, 1986a).

The Cuban population differs significantly from the other major Hispanic groups. After the Cuban revolution in 1959, nearly 500,000 Cubans fled the Castro regime and came to live in the United States, where most have now settled permanently. Unlike Chicano and Puerto Rican migrants, however, the bulk of these Cuban refugees were middle-class people, usually well-educated and often with skills and experience in the professions, business, and allied fields. These Cubans adapted remarkably quickly to their new environment, and their average income is much closer to the national average than to the income of other Hispanic immigrant groups. Miami, where the bulk of the Cubans settled, has been transformed from a fading resort town to a thriving commercial center largely through Cuban enterprise. In 1980, however, there was a second wave of Cuban immigration when over 110,000 "boat people" were allowed to depart for the United States. These new immigrants have posed a significant problem for their new country, for most of them are unskilled, and several thousand criminal and mentally disordered people were included among them.

Figure 11.12 *This photograph shows a large crowd of Cuban-Americans being formally sworn in as citizens of the United States. On the whole, Cuban-Americans have become one of the most successful of the Hispanic immigrant groups, and their presence has added a new dynamism and diversity to the areas where they have settled, particularly in South Florida.*

American Indians

Few groups in the United States have been as cruelly treated or as absurdly stereotyped as the original inhabitants of the country. When the first settlers arrived from Europe, there were at least 1.5 million Native Americans, but by 1850 their numbers had been reduced to a mere 250,000. There are now around 1.4 million Indians, about a third of whom are in urban areas, with the remainder living on or near 267 reservations, most of which are in the western half of the country. The Indians comprise nearly 500 diverse tribal groups, and about fifty of their original languages are still in use.

When the first white settlers arrived on the northeast coast, the native inhabitants befriended them. But the two groups were soon in open conflict as the settlers, armed with a superior military technology, started their relentless drive westward. On any objective analysis of the facts, the invading whites were morally in the wrong in their dispossession of the Indians, but since American history has been written primarily by whites, a grossly distorted picture of the events has been handed down as the true story. The ethnocentrism of the standard historical accounts is remarkable:

the whites are described as "pioneers," not "invaders"; the native peoples' defense of their way of life and economic assets is "treacherous," not "courageous"; the military successes of the whites are "victories," but those of the Indians are "massacres."

The policy toward the Native Americans was frequently one of outright genocide. As early as 1755 the following proclamation was issued in Boston against the Penobscot Indians:

> At the desire of the House of Representatives . . . I do hereby require his majesty's subjects of the Province to embrace all opportunities of pursuing, captivating, killing and destroying all and every of the aforesaid Indians. . . . The General Court of this Province have voted that a bounty . . . be granted: For the capture of every male Penobscot Indian above the age of twelve and brought to Boston, fifty pounds. For every scalp of a male Indian above the age aforesaid, brought in as evidence of their being killed as aforesaid, forty pounds. . . . For every scalp of such female Indian or male Indian under the age of twelve years that shall be killed and brought in as evidence of their being killed as aforesaid, twenty pounds. [Quoted in Paine, 1897]

It is a curious fact of history that settlers who were willing to pay large sums for the scalp of a murdered child under the age of twelve were able to successfully portray the Indians as savages and themselves as entirely righteous. Yet this stereotype, much reinforced during the present century by Western movies, has persisted almost unchallenged until very recently.

The westward advance of the whites shattered the cultures of the Indian peoples. The federal government broke treaty after treaty, and entire tribes were hounded from one area to another as new waves of settlers arrived and coveted the land the Indians had been promised. After 1871 all the Indians were made "wards" of the federal government—a legal status usually given to people, such as minors and imbeciles, who must have a guardian because they are incompetent to fulfill normal adult responsibilities. Not until 1924 were the descendants of the original inhabitants of the land granted the right of citizenship in it.

The current social and economic position of the Indians is probably worse than that of any other minority group in the United States. Nearly 60 percent of Indian children drop out of school before completing the eighth grade. Unemployment generally averages around 50 percent, but reaches 80 percent in some areas and seasons. Almost half the Indians who live on the reservations are unemployed, and of those who do have a job, nearly half work in some capacity for government agencies. Not surprisingly, almost half the reservation population lives below the poverty line, and many, if not most, reservation dwellings are far below the standards other Americans would consider tolerable. The suicide rate for American Indians is double the national average, and the alcoholism rate is nearly eight times as high.

In recent years, Indians have become better organized and more militant in their demands for equality. One of their most significant steps has been to demand that lands illegally seized from them in the past be returned. Some of this land, like much the Indians already own, has valuable water and mineral rights. More than a hundred of these legal claims, involving millions of acres in states from New England to the Southwest, are pending, and in several cases the courts have granted tribes large cash awards in compensation for the loss of their territories. The most prominent Indian leaders and organizations are now demanding not assimilation but respect for their own culture, and with it the right to self-determination on their reservations (American Indian Policy Review Commission, 1976; Raines, 1979; Spicer, 1980; Josephy, 1982).

Figure 11.13 *The Taos Pueblo in New Mexico is one of the oldest American Indian settlements in existence. Most Indians still live on the reservations, although their housing is rarely as picturesque.*

Asian-Americans

Asian-Americans are, with some exceptions, the only racial minority that has approached any real degree of equality with the whites, although they are still often regarded as intruders into American life. There are about 5 million Americans of Asian origin, representing some 2 percent of the total population. This minority includes over twenty ethnic groups. The largest are the Chinese, Filipinos, and Japanese, but there are also significant numbers of Asian-Indians, Koreans, and Vietnamese (one effect of American military involvement in Indochina is that over 300,000 refugees from the area have settled in the United States). Asian-Americans are heavily concentrated in two states, California and Hawaii.

Over 300,000 Chinese settled in the United States between 1850 and 1880, most of them imported to California as laborers in the mining industry and in railroad construction. Their presence aroused violent anti-Chinese feelings, especially among low-status whites who feared job competition from them. Frequent anti-Chinese riots took place. There were a number of lynchings of Chinese in California and even a wholesale massacre of Chinese in Wyoming in 1885. Fears of the "yellow peril" led Congress to pass the discriminatory Chinese Exclusion Act of 1882 that restricted the number of Chinese immigrants, and the entry of Chinese laborers to the United States was totally prohibited between the turn of the century and World War II. The Chinese have retained their language and other cultural traditions and have remained largely isolated from the mainstream of American life ever since. Living in their own very closed and densely populated communities, the Chinese-American population of 1 million remains largely inconspicuous to other Americans, who seem to value its members primarily for their cuisine (Li, 1982; Wong, 1982; Chang, 1983; Gardner, Robey, and Smith, 1985).

The Philippines became a U.S. possession when American troops intervened in that country's revolt against Spain in 1898. From then until 1935, when the Philippines finally gained independence, Filipinos were considered American subjects and so, unlike aliens, they were not subject to immigration quotas. Filipinos began to arrive in Hawaii early in this century, but there was no significant influx to the continental United States until 1923, when California fruit-growers, faced with new restrictions on migrants from Mexico, turned to Filipinos as an alternative labor source. The Filipinos soon encountered prejudice, which was aggravated by tales of their supposed lust for white women and their extraordinary sexual prowess. Several Western states passed laws prohibiting marriage between Filipinos and Caucasians, and very strict immigration quotas were imposed as soon as the Philippines became independent. Changes in the immigration laws in 1965 saw a sharp increase in Filipino immigration: the population more than doubled between 1970 and 1980. There are now about 1 million Filipino-Americans, and at current growth rates they will soon be the largest ethnic group in the Asian population (Gardner, Robey, and Smith, 1985).

Japanese began to immigrate to the United States somewhat later than the Chinese, and most of them settled in the Pacific states. During World War II the entire Japanese-American population of the West Coast, including tens of thousands of second-generation United States citizens, was interned in "security camps" (actually, concentration camps, complete with barbed wire and gun

Figure 11.14 *The entire Japanese population of the West Coast was interned during World War II—a remarkable and unparalleled violation of civil rights. The photograph shows Japanese residents at one of these guarded camps as they salute the American flag. Not a single Japanese-American was ever found guilty of any disloyalty to the United States before or during the war. The internment was clearly unconstitutional.*

turrets) in the Western deserts and the Rocky Mountains. Many of them suffered economic ruin as a result. The reasoning behind this drastic infringement of civil liberties was that the Japanese-Americans might be disloyal to the United States, but the racist implications of the step can be gauged by the fact that no discriminatory action was taken against Italian- and German-Americans at the time. Today, however, the Japanese-American population of nearly 800,000 has been relatively well assimilated into American society. Its members have the highest per capita income and educational achievements of any racial minority and are the only one that does not live mainly in neighborhood ghettos (Kitano, 1976; Wilson and Hosokawa, 1980; Woodrum, 1981).

With the exception of recent immigrants from Indochina, who, for the most part, still have relatively low social and economic status, Asian immigrant groups have been highly successful in America. After initially encountering prejudice and discrimination, they have gradually achieved economic equality, and with it, acceptance, or at least tolerance. An important source of the Asians' success is their remarkable achievements in education, where they outperform all other racial and ethnic groups, including whites. Why do the Asians do so well in school? The reason seems to lie in the tight-knit Asian family, which offers a level of domestic pressure, support, and discipline that other ethnic groups generally lack.

White Ethnics

Sociologists use the term "white ethnics" to refer to non-"WASP" groups of European origin. According to the 1980 census, the largest of these groups is the Irish (40.2 million), followed by the French (12.9 million), the Italians (12.2 million), and the Poles (8.2 million); and there are also significant numbers of other minorities such as Slavs and Greeks. Of course, not all Americans with white-ethnic ancestry identify with their ancestral group, and many are of mixed ethnic ancestry in any case.

As predominantly Catholic peoples with limited skills, these new arrivals from Europe were not as readily assimilated as other European immigrants from the Protestant countries of Northern Europe. In fact, when these various groups first came to the United States, they encountered a degree of hostility that is difficult to comprehend today. Anti-Catholic riots occurred again and again in the cities where the new immigrants settled; Italians were lynched by mobs in several states;

Irish laborers—if employers would hire them at all—were offered lower wages than blacks. In a fairly typical example of this prejudice, one editorial writer commented in 1886:

> These people are not Americans, but the very scum and offal of Europe . . . long-haired, wild-eyed, bad-smelling, atheistic—reckless foreign wretches, who never did an honest hour's work in their lives. . . . Crush such snakes . . . before they have time to bite. [Quoted in Parrillo, 1985]

The response of many of these European ethnics was to try as far as possible to be assimilated into

Figure 11.15 *This anti-immigrant cartoon, published half a century ago, is typical of the prejudiced and often vicious attitude that many established inhabitants had toward new immigrants from Poland, Ireland, Russia, Italy, and elsewhere. Today, descendants of these same groups are sometimes found decrying the arrival of Cambodians, Haitians, Mexicans, Cubans, and other new immigrants, and using exactly the same arguments to do so: that there are not enough jobs, that priority should be given to existing residents, that immigrants are a burden on society, and so on. Yet, in time, the United States may have a Vietnamese-American president or a Cuban-American secretary of state, just as it has already produced an Irish-American president and a Polish-American secretary of state—something the cartoonist and many of his contemporaries would never have believed possible.*

the mainstream culture; frequently, for example, they anglicized their last names, and they often insisted that their children speak only English, even in the home. At first it seemed a foregone conclusion that their ethnic identity would soon disappear, but social scientists increasingly questioned this assumption. The historian Marcus Hansen (1952) advanced the "third generation principle": that the first immigrant generation would remain largely "alien"; the second generation would become fully Americanized; but the third generation, feeling more secure than its predecessors, would display renewed interest in its ethnic heritage. As Hansen expressed it, "What the son wishes to forget, the grandson wishes to remember."

Subsequent research has shown that the white ethnics do not conform to this tidy principle: sometimes ethnic identification surges in later generations; sometimes it does not. Middle- and upper-class ethnics have been fairly readily assimilated into WASP society, but working-class ethnics, particularly in the large urban areas of the East, have tended to live in close-knit communities and to retain traditional loyalties. In these cities, Italian, Irish, Ukrainian, and other national holidays are often publicly celebrated with colorful marches and street fairs—often by third- or even fourth-generation Americans who have minimal contact with the culture of their forebears.

In the 1960s, however, sociologists did detect a resurgence of ethnic feeling of a sort—a sentiment among working-class white ethnics that seemed to express a backlash to the apparently preferential treatment that the WASP-dominated political authorities gave to other minorities. These advantages were offered to blacks, Hispanics, Indians, and Asians—but not to white ethnics, who are often in competition with these groups for jobs and other benefits (Novak, 1971; Patterson, 1977; Hill, 1977). There may be some truth to this picture, but there is considerable evidence that the stereotype of many white ethnics as blue-collar bigots has little basis in reality; in fact, many white ethnics are now in the middle class, and in some respects the ethnics are more tolerant and liberal than the WASP majority.

Currently, white ethnics seem to retain a considerable sense of their cultural identity, and they are often perceived to be distinct groups by the rest of society—a perception that is sometimes expressed, none too flatteringly, in "Polish" jokes, in stereotypes of drunken, priest-ridden Irish, or in popular misconceptions of Italians' overweight mothers or their links to organized crime. Addi-

tionally, white ethnics are generally underrepresented at the upper levels of the educational, economic, and political worlds; the most progress seems to have been made by the Irish, perhaps because they spoke English as a native language from the first generation (Greeley, 1976, 1977; Alba and Moore, 1982). Even so, white ethnic groups now perceive their identity as a potential source of pride and strength, and this has lent further impetus to the society's growing acceptance of pluralism as a whole.

Affirmative Action

In the United States, the removal of legal discrimination did not eliminate other patterns of discrimination which, over the generations, have become structured into social and economic life. Federal and local governments have therefore turned to other means to correct these historical imbalances. One important approach is the attempt to integrate education by busing black children into the schools of predominantly white areas. (This issue is discussed in more detail in Chapter 14, "Education.") Another major tool is "affirmative action," or positive steps to ensure that racial minorities (and women) are not informally discriminated against in access to higher education, employment, or promotion.

Affirmative action does not mean that unqualified people must be given preference over others simply because of their minority-group status; nor does it mean that specific numerical quotas are set. Essentially, the program sets goals and timetables for the hiring of minorities in government agencies and other large organizations that receive federal contracts or funds. For example, an affirmative-action goal for a particular factory might be to hire more minority workers until the composition of its work force more or less reflects that of the surrounding neighborhoods from which the workers are drawn. Such goals serve only as targets, and there are no sanctions against employers as long as they can demonstrate good-faith efforts to meet them. Actually, very few affirmative-action goals are fully reached, but even so, the program has greatly expanded opportunities for minorities and women.

Affirmative-action programs are controversial for the obvious reason that what is "affirmative action" to one group is "reverse discrimination" to another—the white males who must face new, government-mandated competition for jobs and other privileges. When a 1984 *New York Times/CBS News* poll asked "Where there was job discrimination against blacks in the past, should preference in hiring and promotion be given to blacks today?" only 37 percent of whites answered yes, compared to 74 percent of blacks. Blacks are often cynical of the white worker's concern for this "reverse discrimination," pointing out that there was little such concern when discrimination operated in the opposite direction in the past.

The New Immigration

The United States remains a magnet to people all over the world who are willing to risk the wrenching step of changing one homeland for another in order to better their lives. But patterns of immigration to the United States have altered markedly in the past two decades, and this change will have pervasive effects on the racial and ethnic composition of the American people (Keeley, 1982; Cafferty et al., 1983; Parrillo, 1985).

Immigration into the United States was largely unregulated until 1882, when Chinese were excluded. In the 1920s, further restrictions were introduced in the form of a quota system, which gave preference to immigrants from European countries, particularly those from which the WASP ma-

jority originally came. This system lasted until 1965 when, under the influence of the civil rights movement, Congress eliminated the discriminatory national-origin quotas. For some years thereafter there were separate ceilings on immigration from the eastern and western hemispheres, but even this restriction was eventually abandoned. Immigrants are now accepted from all over the world, under a complicated system that gives preference to close relatives of existing American residents and to people with essential or exceptional skills. Additionally, the United States accepts refugees from political persecution, although in practice people fleeing from communist regimes are far more readily welcomed than refugees from right-wing dictatorships and other tyrannies. In all, around 400,000 legal immigrants arrive in the United States each year. This number, though not especially large in relation to the total American population of about 240 million, represents about two-thirds of all the immigration in the entire world.

Additionally, there is a good deal of illegal immigration to the United States. Some of this occurs through foreign visitors and students who deliberately overstay their visas; some takes the form of stealthy landings by sea or air, primarily from the Caribbean and Central America; but most consists of the illegal border crossings from Mexico. Several million people make that hopeful

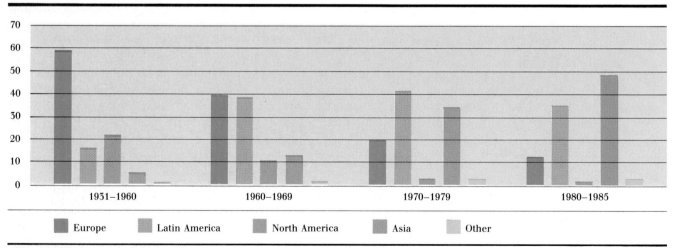

LEGAL IMMIGRANTS ADMITTED TO THE UNITED STATES, BY REGION OF BIRTH: 1931–1985
Percentage of total legal immigration

Legend: Europe | Latin America | North America | Asia | Other

SOURCE: U.S. Immigration and Naturalization Service.

Figure 11.16 *Immigration patterns have changed radically in the course of recent decades. Until the 1960s, most immigrants were from Europe, but today, most come from Asia and Latin America.*

journey every year, but most of them become temporary sojourners in the United States and eventually return to Mexico and their families. Others stay, joining a pool of permanent undocumented aliens whose number the Bureau of the Census estimates at anywhere from 3.5 million to 6 million people. In 1986, Congress passed legislation that allows aliens to claim legal residence if they lived in the United States continuously since 1981—even if they entered or stayed illegally.

As a result of all these new immigration patterns, Asians and Hispanics now account for more than 80 percent of all immigration to the United States. The effects are already noticeable in many American cities, where distinctive communities of Hispanics and the various Asian ethnic groups are now well established. If current migration patterns and birth rates continue, the United States could be one-quarter Asian and one-third Hispanic within a century, with its composition and perhaps culture significantly altered as a result. As has always been the case in American history, the prospect of "alien" immigration is provoking some anxiety among the existing population. A good deal of local prejudice and sometimes outright hostility are directed toward Hispanics and Asians, particularly the most recent arrivals (Butterfield, 1985). Opinion polls, too, show wariness about the new immigration. A 1984 *Newsweek* poll found that 53 percent of a national sample thought there were too many Hispanic immigrants, while 49 percent thought there were too many Asians. In a 1986 Roper poll, 51 percent thought immigration "should be decreased," 35 percent thought it "is about right now," and only 8 percent thought it "should be increased." It is ironic that, if such attitudes had prevailed in the past, the ancestors of many of today's Americans would never have been able to immigrate to the United States in the first place.

The Future

There is some indication that American intergroup relations are improving, but the process still has a long way to go. According to Milton Gordon (1961, 1977), there are three main options that are open to the United States in race relations.

1. *Anglo-conformity* assumes that it is desirable to maintain modified English institutions, language, and culture as the dominant standard in American life. In practice, "assimilation" in the United States has, historically, always meant Anglo-conformity.

2. *Melting pot* is a rather different concept, involving a totally new blend, culturally and biologically, of all the racial and ethnic groups in the United States. Given enough time, the melting pot may be the society's ultimate destiny, but in practice, it has been of limited significance in the American experience.

3. *Cultural pluralism* assumes a series of distinct but coexisting groups, each preserving its own tradition and culture, but each loyal to broader national unity. In practice, there has always been a high degree of cultural pluralism in the United States, but this pluralism has been based on inequality rather than equality.

Current indications are that, for the foreseeable future at least, American race and ethnic relations will be conducted primarily within a pluralist framework. Pursuit of cultural pluralism can be a dangerous course, however, for it presumes some degree of ethnocentrism on the part of the participating groups, and it can provide a workable solution only if it is based on equality, respect, and interdependence. But if Americans can achieve that, then finally, after three centuries, the "American dilemma" may be resolved.

Summary

1. Social inequality sometimes follows lines of race and ethnicity. A race is regarded as socially distinct because its members inherit common physical characteristics; an ethnic group is regarded as socially distinct because its members share a common cultural heritage.

2. A minority group is one that is differentiated from the rest of the population and treated unequally. Minorities suffer social disadvantages; are socially visible; have a consciousness of kind; are generally born into the group; and generally marry within the group.

3. Six possible patterns of race and ethnic relations are assimilation; pluralism; legal protection of minorities; population transfer; continued subjugation; and extermination. All have been attempted in North America.

4. Functionalists point out that while racial and ethnic inequality and ethnocentrism may be functional from the point of view of the groups that benefit from them, they may be dysfunctional in the long run if they lead to hostility and violence.

5. Conflict theorists see racial and ethnic inequalities as a form of social stratification based on competition for scarce resources, with the most powerful group becoming the dominant one. Conflict may also be a source of social change in this situation.

6. Racial and ethnic inequalities are justified by the ideology of racism, which holds that some groups are inferior to others. As the European colonial experience shows, racism arises when one group wants to justify its dominance or exploitation of another.

7. Prejudice is an inflexible attitude, usually negative, toward other groups; discrimination is unequal treatment of others on the grounds of group membership. Prejudice is not necessarily translated into discrimination. Sources of prejudice include stereotyping, authoritarian personality, irrationality, scapegoating, and certain social contexts. Discrimination can be legal or institutionalized, the latter being the more difficult to eliminate.

8. The United States has never been a "melting pot" for all its peoples. Some minorities have been treated unequally because they were unlike the majority or because of the historical and economic circumstances of their arrival and settlement. Important minorities in the modern United States are blacks, Hispanics, Indians, Asians, and "white ethnics." The groups have progressed at different rates, although a minority of blacks remain trapped in an "underclass."

9. The United States has, with some success, tried to eliminate institutionalized discrimination through such tools as affirmative action.

10. As a result of changing immigration regulations and illegal immigration, a much higher proportion of immigrants than ever before are Hispanic and Asian.

11. There are signs that American race and ethnic relations are improving. The most likely trend in the foreseeable future is cultural pluralism, in which different groups preserve their own culture.

Important Terms

race (286)	false consciousness (292)
Thomas theorem (286)	prejudice (293)
ethnic group (286)	discrimination (293)
minority group (286)	stereotype (294)
genocide (288)	authoritarian personality (294)
ethnocentrism (290)	scapegoating (295)
ideology (291)	legal discrimination (296)
racism (291)	institutionalized discrimination (296)
colonialism (291)	
self-fulfilling prophecy (292)	

Suggested Readings

DAVIS, CARY, CARL HAUB, and JOANNE WILLETTE. *U.S. Hispanics: Changing the Face of America.* Washington, D.C.: Population Reference Bureau, 1983.

A short but comprehensive overview of the various Hispanic minorities in the United States.

GARDNER, ROBERT W., BRYANT ROBEY, and PETER C. SMITH. *Asian Americans: Growth, Change, and Diversity.* Washington, D.C.: Population Reference Bureau, 1985.

A concise overview of the history, present status, and prospects for the growing Asian minority in the United States.

JOSEPHY, ALVIN M. *Now That the Buffalo's Gone: A Study of Today's American Indians.* New York: Knopf, 1982.

A good account of the current situation of the American Indian population, with useful historical background included.

PARRILLO, VINCENT N. *Strangers to These Shores: Race and Ethnic Relations in the United States.* 2nd ed. New York: Macmillan, 1985.

An excellent and comprehensive survey of the relationships among the various groups that have made the United States their home. The book includes material on prejudice, discrimination, and intergroup relations, and also on theoretical analysis of race relations.

PETTIGREW, THOMAS F., et al. *Prejudice.* Cambridge, Mass.: Harvard University Press, 1982.

A concise summary of the social and psychological aspects of prejudice and its relationship to discriminatory practices.

REID, JOHN. *Black America in the 1980s.* Washington, D.C.: Population Reference Bureau, 1982.

A concise and useful survey of the social and economic status of black Americans.

ROSALDO, RENATO, and R. A. CALVERT (eds.). *Chicanos: The Evolution of a People.* Huntington, N.Y.: Krieger, 1982.

A good selection of articles covering various aspects of Chicano history and contemporary experience.

SITKOFF, HARVARD. *The Struggle for Black Equality.* New York: Hill and Wang, 1982.

An account of the civil rights and subsequent movements for racial equality in the United States.

SKLARE, MARSHALL (ed.). *Understanding American Jewry.* New Brunswick, N.J.: Transaction Books, 1982.

A useful collection of sociological articles about the American Jewish community.

WILSON, WILLIAM J. *The Declining Significance of Race: Blacks and Changing American Institutions.* 2nd ed. Chicago: University of Chicago Press, 1980.

Wilson presents a controversial argument: that differences of social class are becoming more significant than differences of race in their effect on the status of black Americans.

CHAPTER 12

Inequalities of Gender and Age

Societies can distinguish among their members in many different ways—according to caste, class, race, language, religion, and a host of other features. Yet only two such characteristics are used in all societies: sex and age. These distinctions are universal, for they are based on ascribed statuses that arise inevitably from the human condition: our species contains males and females, and we all grow older from the time of birth to the moment of death.

Every society categorizes its members according to sex, treating men and women in different ways and expecting different patterns of behavior from them. Throughout history, men have generally been the dominant sex and women have been subordinate to them. Both men and women have usually taken this inequality for granted as a "natural" state of affairs, passing it down from generation to generation as part of their culture.

Similarly, all societies distinguish among their members on the grounds of age, giving different rights and responsibilities to people of various age categories and requiring them to play different social roles. Here, however, the patterns of inequality are not so consistent. Traditional societies are usually dominated by the old, but in modern societies, the middle-aged become the dominant category, and the old sometimes take on the characteristics of a disadvantaged minority.

Sex and age inequalities may affect your lives in profound ways. For example, a male college graduate in the United States can expect to enjoy lifetime earnings of about $1.5 million more than a female graduate. And a young person can expect that his or her income (and the power and prestige that go with it) will be relatively low in early adulthood, will rise through middle age, and will then decline markedly in later life. In this chapter we will examine these inequalities, using the general principles that we have already applied to other forms of structured social inequality.

Gender and Society

Throughout the world, the first question parents ask at the birth of a child is always the same: "Is it a boy or a girl?" The urgency of the question reveals the great importance that all human societies attach to the differences between men and women.

This division of the human species into two fundamental categories is based on *sex*—the biological distinction between males and females. All societies, however, elaborate this biological fact into secondary, nonbiological notions of "masculinity" and "femininity." These concepts refer not to sex but to *gender*—the culturally learned differences between men and women. In other words, male or female is what, by birth, you *are;* but masculine or feminine is what, with appropriate socialization, you may *become.* Gender thus refers to purely social characteristics, such as differences in hair styles, clothing patterns, occupational roles, and other culturally learned activities and traits.

The members of any society tend to assume that their particular version of masculinity and femininity is as much a part of "human nature" as the biological distinctions between males and females. Each society expects men and women to play specific *gender roles*—the behavior patterns, obligations, and privileges that are considered appropriate for each sex. And because the social statuses of the sexes are generally unequal, these gender roles tend to reflect (and to reinforce) whatever sexual stratification already exists.

Over the past quarter century or so, however, millions of people have challenged the traditional relationship of the sexes, particularly in the emerging postindustrial societies of North America and Western Europe. Growing numbers of women in these societies have been entering economic life, and in doing so have earned not just income but also independence. The result of this shift has been important changes in the status of women—changes that have opened up new risks as well as new possibilities.

How Different Are the Sexes?

Over 2,000 years ago, the Greek philosopher Aristotle declared that women are weaker and more passive than men because the female sex is "a deformity." Aristotle was one of the many male observers who, over the centuries, have tried to find evidence to prove that men and women are not only naturally dissimilar, but also naturally unequal. Women's supposed inferiority has been attributed to such unalterable influences as a divine plan, menstruation, the malign influence of the womb, raging hormones, cranium size, and even brain structure (Lowe and Hubbard, 1983; Beier, 1984; Fausto-Sterling, 1985).

Just how different are the sexes? Any analysis of sexual inequalities must confront the question of whether there are any inborn behavioral differences between men and women and, if so, how

Figure 12.1 *Unlike sex, which is a biological given, gender can be expressed in many different ways. Most Americans would regard this female body builder as being "masculine"; conversely, these Fulani tribesmen of North Africa have a manner and appearance that most Americans would consider "feminine." A wide range of gender roles is possible, for these roles are culturally created.*

significant these differences are. Are gender roles completely flexible, or are there some natural, genetically determined boundaries beyond which change is impossible?

To answer this question, sociologists have drawn on evidence from three other disciplines: biology, which tells us about the physical differences between men and women and their possible effects on behavior; psychology, which tells us about the nature and origins of possible personality differences between the sexes; and anthropology, which tells us about variations in gender roles among the many cultures of the world.

Biological Evidence

Men and women are different in their *genes,* which provide the inherited blueprint for their physical development. Females have two similar chromosomes (XX), while males have two dissimilar chromosomes (XY). Except in the area of short-term feats of physical strength, the male's lack of a second X chromosome makes him in many respects the weaker sex. Male infants are more likely than females to be stillborn or malformed. Over thirty hereditary disorders, such as hemophilia and webbing of the toes, are found only in men. Throughout the life course, the death rate for men is higher than it is for women. Although in the United States about 106 males are born for every 100 females, the ratio of the sexes is equal by the time a generation has reached its mid-twenties, and among people over sixty-five there are only 85 males for every 100 females. Women are more resistant than men to most diseases and seem to have a greater tolerance for pain and malnutrition.

Men and women also have differences in their *hormones,* chemical substances that are secreted by the body's various glands. The precise effects of hormones have not been fully determined, but it is known that they can influence both physical development and emotional arousal. Both sexes have "male" as well as "female" hormones, but the proportion of male hormones is greater in men and that of female hormones is greater in women. Experiments with some animals have shown that artificially increased levels of male hormones can heighten aggressiveness and sex drive, even in females. This evidence cannot be uncritically applied to human beings, however, for the increase in brain size during the course of our evolution has been accompanied by a corresponding decrease in the influence of hormones and other inborn factors on our behavior. The present consensus among natural and social scientists is that hormonal differences probably do have some influence on the behavior of men and women but that this influence varies greatly—not only among individuals, but also within the same person over time (Teitelbaum, 1976; Weitz, 1977; Shaffer, 1981).

Additionally, there are obvious differences in the sexes' *anatomy,* or physical structure and appearance. The most important of these distinctions, of course, is in the reproductive systems and their consequences. A man's biological involvement in reproduction begins and ends with a brief act of insemination. Women, on the other hand, bear and suckle children, and as a result their personal, social, and economic activities may be periodically restricted. There are also other anatomical dissimilarities in such characteristics as height, weight, amount of body hair, distribution of body fat, and musculature. These distinctions are socially important, both because they make it easy for others to recognize an individual's sex and because they make men more physically powerful than women, at least in short-term feats of exertion. Their greater strength gives men the potential to dominate women by force, a fact that helps to explain why there has never been a society in which women have had political status superior to that of men.

Psychological Evidence

Although there are many differences among both individual men and individual women, the typical personality patterns of adult men and women are clearly dissimilar in many ways. For example, men tend to be more aggressive and to have greater mathematical ability; women tend to be more nurturant and more emotional. But are these differences inborn or learned? In the case of adults, this question cannot be answered, since it is impossible to untangle the effects of biological and social influences on personality. For this reason, psychologists have focused much of their research on very young infants. Babies have had very little exposure to learning situations, and the earlier sex-linked differences in behavior appear, the more likely it is that they are the result of inborn factors.

Many studies of young infants have found sex-linked personality differences early in life. Even in the cradle, for example, male babies are more active than females; female babies smile more readily and are more sensitive to warmth and touch than males. These are only general tendencies, however. Many male babies show traits that are more typical of female babies, and vice versa. These and other findings seem at first sight to indicate some inborn personality differences between the sexes, but the case is not proved. It remains possible that even these early variations are learned. From the time children are born, the parents treat them in subtly different ways according to their sex: girl babies are cooed over; boy babies are bounced on the knee. Parents handle infant girls more affectionately and tenderly and are more tolerant of restlessness and aggression in boys. In fact, experiments have shown that if adults are told that a girl infant is a boy, they will respond to it as if it were a boy—for example, by commenting on its sturdiness and playing with it vigorously. But if they are told the same child is a girl, they are likely to remark on its prettiness and to touch it more gently. Infants may therefore learn to behave differently even in the first few weeks of life (Condry and Condry, 1979; Unger, 1979; Shaffer, 1981).

Some of the most important research on the psychology of gender concerns children who for some reason have been reared as a member of the opposite sex. (This situation may arise when mentally disturbed parents raise a boy as a girl or vice versa; or when genital deformities result in a baby's being mistakenly assigned to the wrong sex; or when, on the recommendation of psychiatrists, a boy who lacks a penis—usually as a result of a circumcision accident—is raised as a transsexual female.) If a child is biologically a boy but is raised as a girl, what happens? If gender were determined by biological factors, it should be impossible to socialize a child into the "wrong" role. But research by John Money and his associates indicates that children can easily be raised as a member of the opposite sex. In fact, beyond the age of about three or four, they strongly resist attempts to change their "false" gender and have great difficulty making the adjustment, in exactly the same way as a girl or boy raised in the "right" role would do. Money concludes that the human species is "psychosexually neuter at birth" and that gender is independent of biological sex (Money, 1977; Green, 1975).

Over the past two decades, psychologists have published more than 16,000 articles on the psychology of the sexes. The present consensus among researchers is that there are probably some predispositions toward differences in the behavior of the sexes at birth, but that these differences are not clear-cut and can be overridden by cultural learning. Also, the differences so far discovered are relatively insignificant, and hardly justify the elaborate gender-role distinctions or sexual inequalities found in many societies (Sherman, 1978; Maccoby, 1980; Hyde, 1985).

Cross-Cultural Evidence

If anatomy were destiny and if gender were largely determined by inborn differences, then we would expect the statuses and roles of men and women to be much the same in all cultures. On the other hand, if these social characteristics vary a great deal from one culture to another, then gender must be much more flexible than has usually been assumed in the past.

Anthropologists have reported on a number of societies whose gender characteristics diverge from our own. In an early study, Margaret Mead (1935) investigated three tribes in New Guinea. This large South Pacific island contains hundreds of small societies which, because they have been isolated from one another and the rest of the world by almost impassable jungle and mountain terrain, have sometimes evolved strikingly different cultural practices. In one tribe, the Arapesh, both men and women seemed gentle, passive, and emotionally warm. In contrast, the neighboring Mundugumor tribe were a headhunting people who expected both sexes to be aggressive and even violent. In the third tribe, the Tchambuli, the women were domineering and wore no ornaments, while the men were gossipy, artistic, and nurturant toward children. Since then, other anthropologists have described societies in which women seem aggressive, men seem passive, or there appear to be minimal differences in the roles of men and women (Barry et al., 1957; D'Andrade, 1966; Friedl, 1975; Shlegel, 1972, 1977).

Such cases, however, are exceptional, and the overall cross-cultural tendency points to a very strong pattern of male dominance. Despite mythic tales of societies ruled by Amazons or other warrior females, there is no record of any society in which women were the politically dominant sex, although in some cases individual women may achieve prominence. Even in those modern industrialized societies that have formal commitments to sexual equality, male dominance persists (Epstein and Coser, 1981). The Soviet Union, for example, has entrenched sexual equality in its constitution for over half a century, but high political status is still almost exclusively a male preserve. The same pattern applies even to the democratic nations of the Western world. In Scandinavia, only 23 percent of the members of the national legislatures are women; in West Germany, 10 percent; in Italy, 7 percent; in France, 5 percent; in the United States, 5 percent; in New Zealand, 4 percent; in Britain, 4 percent.

The fact that politics is primarily "man's work" points to another cross-cultural feature. All societies have at least some *division of labor,* the specialization by individuals or groups in particular economic activities. There are many ways that labor can be divided, but one method is universal—to allocate tasks according to sex. Around the world, child-rearing and home maintenance are usually considered a woman's task, while hunting and fighting are almost always reserved for the man. Men generally take on tasks that require vigorous physical activity or travel away from the home, such as hunting or herding. Women, on the other hand, are responsible for tasks that require less concentrated physical effort and can be performed close to home. Beyond these basic patterns,

however, there is great cross-cultural variation in the kind of labor that is considered appropriate for men and the kind considered appropriate for women (see Figure 12.2).

The general conclusion from the cross-cultural evidence is that there is a strong general pattern in dominance, personality, and work—but this pattern is not inevitable, for there are enough exceptions to prove that gender roles are potentially quite flexible. The specific content of "masculinity" and "femininity" is primarily a social product, learned anew by each generation. No society relies on "nature" to produce its particular gender roles, whatever they may be; in every culture, children are systematically socialized into acceptance of the prevailing assumptions.

Despite the fact that the biological, psychological, and anthropological evidence clearly shows that humans can be socialized into a wide range of gender roles, most societies are marked by striking inequalities between men and women. Why is this so?

Figure 12.2 *There is great cross-cultural variation in the tasks that are considered appropriate for men and women. In many cases, in fact, the division of labor is quite unlike our own. The general tendency, however, is for men to be responsible for tasks involving strenuous effort or travel, and for women to be responsible for tasks that can be performed near the home. The data in this table come from a survey of 224 traditional, preindustrial societies.*

THE DIVISION OF LABOR BY SEX: A CROSS-CULTURAL COMPARISON

Activity	Number of Societies in Which Activity Is Performed by:				
	Men Always	Men Usually	Either Sex Equally	Women Usually	Women Always
Pursuing sea mammals	34	1	0	0	0
Hunting	166	13	0	0	0
Trapping small animals	128	13	4	1	2
Herding	38	8	4	0	5
Fishing	98	34	19	3	4
Clearing land for agriculture	73	22	17	5	13
Dairy operations	17	4	3	1	13
Preparing and planting soil	31	23	33	20	37
Erecting and dismantling shelter	14	2	5	6	22
Tending fowl and small animals	21	4	8	1	39
Tending and harvesting crops	10	15	35	39	44
Gathering shellfish	9	4	8	7	35
Making and tending fires	18	6	25	22	62
Bearing burdens	12	6	35	20	57
Preparing drinks and narcotics	20	1	13	8	57
Gathering fruits, berries, nuts	12	3	15	13	63
Gathering fuel	22	1	10	19	89
Preserving meat and fish	8	2	10	14	74
Gathering herbs, roots, seeds	8	1	11	7	74
Cooking	5	1	9	28	158
Carrying water	7	0	5	7	119
Grinding grain	2	4	5	13	114

SOURCE: Adapted from George P. Murdock, "Comparative Data on the Division of Labor by Sex," *Social Forces,* 15 (May 1935), pp. 551–553.

Figure 12.3 *In the functionalist view, gender distinctions result from a sex-based division of labor. The family and society operate most efficiently if the sexes play different roles and are socialized into contrasting gender characteristics—even if the* result is sexual inequality. Such a sex-based division of labor, which has always been typical of preindustrial societies, is captured in this painting, Dinner for the Threshers, *by the American artist Grant Wood.*

Gender Inequality: A Functionalist View

Functionalist theorists start from the assumption that if all societies encourage gender differences, then these distinctions must have some positive effects for society as a whole. They point out that (at least in traditional, preindustrial societies) it was highly functional for men and women to play different roles. A society operates much more efficiently if duties are allocated to particular people who are socialized to play the specific roles involved. This division of labor need not necessarily be along sex lines—but sexual differences, being rooted in our biology, do offer an obvious and convenient means of achieving it.

The human infant is helpless for a longer period after birth than any other animal, and it has to be looked after. It is convenient if the mother, who bears and suckles the child and who may soon become pregnant with another, stays home and takes care of it. To the extent that she stays at home, domestic duties tend to fall on her as well. Likewise, it is convenient if the male, who is physically more powerful and who is not periodically pregnant or suckling children, takes on such tasks as hunting, defending the family against enemies or predators, and taking herds to distant pastures.

Because the female is largely dependent on the male for protection and because the male is physically capable of enforcing his will on the female, he inevitably becomes the dominant partner in this relationship. As a result of his domi-

nance, his activities and personality patterns become more highly regarded and rewarded. Over time, these arrangements become deeply structured into the society. Men accept their status as "natural," and women submit because sexual inequality has become the custom. The social origins of gender differences are lost to human consciousness, and the roles of men and women are regarded instead as being dictated by biological sex.

Are these traditional gender roles still functional in a modern industrialized society? Two functionalist theorists, Talcott Parsons and Robert Bales (1954), argued that they are. Parsons and Bales claimed that a modern family needs two adults who will specialize in particular roles. The "instrumental" role, which is usually taken by the father, focuses on relationships between the family and the outside world. The father, for example, is responsible for earning the income that supports the family. The "expressive" role, which is usually taken by the mother, focuses on relationships within the family. The mother is thus responsible for providing the love and support that is needed to hold the family together. The male's instrumental role requires that he be dominant and competent; the female's expressive role requires that she be passive and nurturant. In this way, the family unit functions more effectively than it would if gender differences were not so sharply defined. The whole society, too, benefits from these practical arrangements, despite the inequality they create.

This approach was accepted uncritically by most sociologists in the 1950s, but in the changing climate of later years, many critics came to see it as just an example of functionalism defending the status quo. They argued that traditional gender roles may well have been functional in preindustrial societies, but they make less sense in a modern society where the daily activities of men and women are far removed from these simple origins. Two centuries ago, the average American woman had a life expectancy of about forty-five years, and she had eight children between her twentieth and fortieth birthdays. Today, female life expectancy is seventy-eight years, and the average woman has two children during a five-year period in her twenties. Historical roles that keep a woman housebound seem increasingly irrelevant when she may live for half a century after her last child is born. Also, functionalist theory says nothing about the strains placed on modern women who want to play an "instrumental" role, or on men who would prefer to play an "expressive" one. Indeed, the theory overlooks the dysfunctions to society of preventing half the population from participating fully in economic life. However, a functionalist analysis does offer a plausible explanation of how traditional gender roles and sexual inequalities arose in the first place.

Gender Inequality: A Conflict View

A conflict analysis, on the other hand, may offer a better explanation of why sexual inequalities still persist today. To conflict theorists, the inequality of men and women is simply another form of social stratification. The stratification of the sexes takes an unusual form, however, for men and women are found in equal proportion at every level of the social-class hierarchy—but at any given position, women generally have inferior status to men who are at the same position. Thus, an upper-class woman may have superior status to a lower-class woman, but in many respects she has inferior status to an upper-class man.

Modern conflict theorists argue that men can enjoy superior status only if women have inferior status, and the existing gender-role patterns allow them to maintain their political, social, and economic privileges. This does not mean, of course, that there is a deliberate, conscious conspiracy by men to maintain the prevailing inequalities. It simply means that the dominant group benefits from the existing arrangements and has little moti-

vation to change them. Since the cultural arrangements of any society always reflect the interests of the dominant group, gender roles continue to reinforce the pattern of male dominance (Shlegel, 1977; Sanday, 1981b; Chafetz, 1984; Collins, 1985).

The underlying source of sexual inequality, in the view of conflict theorists, is the *economic* inequality between men and women. As we noted in Chapter 10 ("Social Stratification"), wealth is a prime source of social status; moreover, it can readily be converted into power and prestige as well. It follows that if men make a greater economic contribution to the family and the society than women, then men are likely to have superior social status in both. Conversely, if the economic contribution of women increases relative to that of men, then the inequalities between the sexes should diminish.

In fact, the cross-cultural evidence does suggest that when women are less economically productive than men, or when they stay at home while men work in the world beyond, their status is significantly lower than men's. In *hunting and gathering* societies meat is highly prized, and men tend to do the hunting, though with infrequent success: they may hunt with their primitive weapons for days on end and catch nothing. The women, on the other hand, do the gathering of fruits, vegetables, insects, and other items, and so provide the bulk of the society's food. In these societies, there is remarkably little sexual inequality. In *horticultural* and *pastoral* societies, on the other hand, men make a greater economic contribution: it is they who are usually responsible for clearing the land, tending the herds, or raiding neighboring tribes, and this fact is reflected in the greater sexual inequality that is usually a feature of these societies. In *agricultural* societies, men produce an even greater proportion of the society's wealth, for they are typically responsible for heavy agriculture, craft work, military plundering, and the other mainstays of the economy. In these societies, inequalities between men and women become even greater. This situation persists in early *industrial* societies, in which the bulk of the labor force is male and in which the few women who do work outside the home are paid very low wages. Entirely dependent on men for their livelihoods, the women in these societies are hardly in a position to assert their equality. But in the more advanced industrial societies, and especially in the emerging *postindustrial* societies, the picture begins to change. Women play an increasing role in the labor force, and as they do so, they gradually

PERCENTAGE OF LABOR FORCE PARTICIPATION, BY SEX

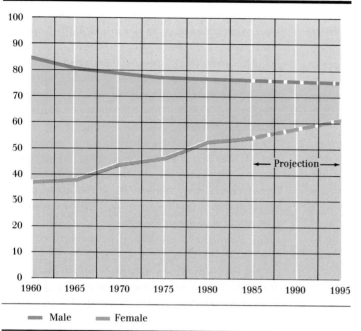

——— Male   ——— Female

SOURCE: U.S. Bureau of the Census.

Figure 12.4 *Particularly since World War II, women have played an increasing part in the American economy, and in the process, they have achieved more equality with men. Conflict theorists argue that economic inequality underlies the social inequality of men and women, and predict that the status of women will continue to improve only if they play an increasingly greater part in the economy.*

demand and gain more equality with men. In 1900, for example, only 5 percent of married American women held a job; in 1940, only 15 percent did so; but today, over 50 percent do. During this period, the sexes have grown steadily more equal in social as well as economic life—and if women increase their economic power further in the future, then their status in other respects should continue to rise accordingly.

Conflict and functionalist theories are not as contradictory on this issue as they might initially seem to be. Many conflict theorists accept that sex inequalities may have arisen because they were functional, even if they are functional no longer. Many functionalist theorists would also accept that traditional gender roles are becoming dysfunctional in the modern world.

Sexism

As we saw in our earlier discussions of inequalities of class, race, and ethnicity, the domination of one social group by another is always endorsed by an *ideology,* a set of beliefs that explains and justifies some actual or potential social arrangements. Just as the Indian caste system is legitimated by Hindu doctrine or just as racial discrimination is legitimated by racism, so the inequality of the sexes is made to seem legitimate by *sexism*—the belief that one sex is inferior to another and that unequal treatment is therefore justified.

Sexism is based on the deeply engrained view that gender characteristics and sexual inequalities are rooted in the natural order. Even our language, like many others, reflects male dominance. Whenever we talk about people in general, the language predisposes us to talk only of men: for example, we often speak of "man" and "mankind" when we really mean human beings and humanity. The English language does not even have a pronoun to cover cases of "he or she," and so we generally use "he" when referring to someone whose sex is not specified.

Like most ideologies that justify social inequality of various kinds, the ideology of sexism is everywhere endorsed to some extent by religion. For example, the sacred text of Islam, the Koran, declares:

> Men are superior to women on account of the qualities in which God has given them pre-eminence.

In all Islamic countries, such teachings are used to justify the virtual exclusion of women from high political, economic, or religious statuses. The more fundamentalist Islamic nations, in fact, make women almost invisible in public: in Saudi Arabia, for example, women may not appear without veils, may not drive cars, may not work in the same office with men, and do not even have the right to vote. In the Islamic nation of Oman, women are permitted to attend the country's only college—but they have to enter segregated classes through their own back door, and the entire campus has a system of overhead walkways for the exclusive use of women, so that contact with men can be avoided at all times (Altorki, 1986).

The Judeo-Christian religious tradition of the West also seems to value men above women. According to the Genesis story, God made man in His own image, with woman as a subsequent and secondary act of creation. The ancient Israelites were a strongly patriarchal people, and even today a male orthodox Jew is expected to say this prayer every morning:

> Blessed art thou, oh Lord our God, King of the Universe, that I was not born a gentile. Blessed art thou, oh Lord our God, King of the Universe, that I was not born a slave. Blessed art thou, oh Lord our God, King of the Universe, that I was not born a woman.

This bias was transmitted to Christianity, not through Jesus, but through the later teachings of Saint Paul, who explicitly saw the inferior role of women as part of a divinely ordained natural order:

> A man . . . is the image of God and reflects God's glory; but woman is the reflection of man's glory. . . . Man was not created for the sake of woman, but woman was created for the sake of man. [I Corinthians 11:7–9]

And elsewhere in the New Testament we find:

> Wives should regard their husbands as they regard the Lord, since as Christ is head of the church and serves the whole body, so is a husband the head of his wife; and as the Church submits to Christ, so should wives submit to their husbands, in everything. [Ephesians 5:22–23]

Even today many denominations reserve their priesthoods or equivalent positions for men—although, as women gain greater equality elsewhere in society, they are achieving higher statuses in religion also.

The sexist belief in the superiority of men pervades many areas of social life. Both men and women tend to incorporate prevailing stereotypes about femininity and masculinity into their self-concepts, and these understandings shape their personalities and the way they relate to one another. As we noted in Chapter 9 ("Sexuality and Society"), for example, women are widely viewed as being in some sense the sexual property of men, and so are expected to be suitably submissive and deferential. A striking illustration of this submission is the way women learn to hide, reveal, or distort their bodies in accordance with the prevailing male notions of how women should appear. In traditional China, men admired tiny female feet—so girls' feet were permanently deformed through footbinding, a painful practice that left them barely able to walk. In some West African tribes where men admire very plump women, young girls deliberately fatten themselves into obesity in order to attract a husband. Among some North African peoples, women have for generations submitted to brutal surgery to remove their clitoris—supposedly to reduce their sexual appetites and thus keep them faithful to their husbands. In North America, where large, firm breasts have been admired for most of this century, millions of women have had their breasts surgically reshaped or enlarged. Now that men's ideal for womanhood is shifting to a leaner and more athletic look, dieting has become a female obsession, with over a third of American women considering themselves too fat. Every year, in fact, over a quarter million young American women starve themselves to the point of anorexia, no less compulsively than some of their West African counterparts gorge themselves to plumpness. Men, in contrast, are rarely expected to shape their bodies to conform to women's notions of how they should look—for men rely rather on their power, wealth, or prestige to attract the opposite sex.

Throughout history, most women—whether in medieval Europe, nineteenth-century America, or modern Saudi Arabia—have accepted their society's system of sexual stratification, despite its consequences for their own relatively low wealth, power, and prestige. Why have they done so? As we noted in the previous two chapters, the members of a subordinate stratum tend to accept the ideology that justifies their own low statuses, because they see the existing arrangements as "natural" and proper, and do not question them. Marx called this kind of attitude ***false consciousness,*** a subjective understanding of one's situation that does not accord with the objective facts. As long as the

Figure 12.5

"Sexism! *For heaven's sake, Nancy, I'm not even over* racism *yet.*"

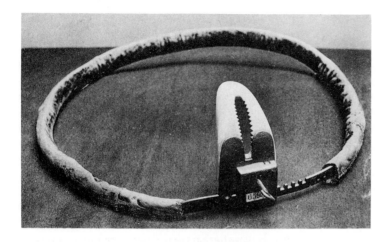

Figure 12.6 *Over the centuries, women have submitted to extraordinary physical restraints demanded by men. The top-left photograph shows a thirteenth-century chastity belt, designed to keep women faithful while their husbands were away. The top-right photograph shows the consequences of early twentieth-century footbinding in China, where men admired dainty female feet. The third picture shows a late-nineteenth-century advertisement for the rigid corsets that produced the wasplike waist that men expected in that era.*

members of the subordinate stratum continue to take the status quo for granted, it will persist. But if they come to see their situation as socially created—and unjust besides—they are likely to demand change. This is precisely what has happened in the United States since the early 1960s, when a women's movement arose and challenged traditional gender roles. The results were profound, and still reverberate through American society today.

Gender Roles in America

As America was transformed in the nineteenth century from a predominantly agricultural to a largely industrial society, men's work moved out of the family homestead and into the factory—leaving women isolated from the economic mainstream and utterly dependent on their menfolk for the essentials of life. In this environment, the inferior status of American women was widely accepted as an unalterable fact of life. The idea that females could contribute significantly to public life (or even benefit from higher education) was considered preposterous. In fact, for most legal purposes, women were treated much like children: they were not allowed to vote, to make contracts, or even to own property.

Despite this restrictive climate, a few women took an active part in various social movements, campaigning for the abolition of slavery, for temperance, and for children's rights—and inevitably for women's rights as well. In fact, many feminists at the turn of the century were radical even by today's standards: they advocated free-love communes, the abolition of marriage, and a new translation of the Bible to eliminate masculine bias. After a long and bitter struggle—sometimes involving violence, imprisonment, and hunger strikes—women won the right to vote in 1920. After this victory, however, the feminist movement lost much of its impetus.

Traditional gender roles continued largely unchanged until the early 1940s, when many American women were temporarily employed in "masculine" jobs left behind by men who were in military service during World War II. This experience showed that women could fill men's roles in an industrial economy—even in jobs that required a good deal of physical strength. After the war, women began to enter the work force in larger numbers. Yet social norms were slow to adjust: most states retained laws to "protect" women by limiting the amount of weight they might lift at work, and some states made women's earnings the legal property of their husband or father. Additionally, women were unable to get financial credit or to make contracts without a man's cosignature.

The era of the 1950s established the stereotypes that some Americans still regard with lingering nostalgia: the father as dutiful provider to his wife and family, playing his daily part in a booming economy; the mother as contented housewife, cheerfully doing the laundry and making peanut-butter sandwiches for the kids. Men held about 70 percent of the jobs in this economy, and most women stayed at home—on the surface, a harmonious social arrangement. Yet, as Betty Friedan (1963) first reported, many middle-class women were enmeshed in a "problem that had no name." They felt themselves to be prisoners in gilded cages, unfulfilled by their limited domestic roles and yearning for something beyond, something more.

In the turbulent 1960s a new social movement emerged, demanding women's liberation. Growing numbers of women in the work force resented the fact that they were automatically treated as adjuncts and subordinates rather than as equals—and in particular, that they were paid less than men for doing the same job. Even so, the campaign for sexual equality encountered resistance not only from many men, but also from many women. Through "consciousness-raising" and other techniques, however, the new movement began to make women aware that they were losers under the traditional arrangements—and that these arrangements were not biological imperatives, but were merely cultural artifacts that could be changed. In 1963 Congress passed the Equal Pay Act, which provided that equally qualified men and women be paid the same for doing the same job. In 1972 Congress approved the Equal Rights Amendment to the Constitution, which stated simply that "equality of rights under the law shall not be denied or abridged by the United States or any state on account of sex." Ten years later, however, the amendment died, having won ratification by only 35 of the needed 38 states—even though opinion polls at the time showed that over 60 percent of the public supported the amendment. But by then American gender roles were irreversibly altered, so much so that by 1984 a woman, Geraldine Ferraro, became a candidate for vice president of the United States.

American gender roles are now far more flexible than those in most other societies. Many traditional norms still exist, however, that structure the experience of most men and women and their basic options in life. Some deviance from these norms is permitted, but the woman who is "too masculine," and more particularly, the man who is "effeminate" in manner or interests, still invite ridicule. The strength of the reaction to deviance from the norms is a good indication of the strength of the norms themselves. Clearly defined gender roles exist, and they are reflected in the personalities, interpersonal relationships, and workplace experiences of men and women.

Because everything in her home is waterproof, the housewife of 2000 can do her daily cleaning with a hose.

Figure 12.7 *This image of the future, from a 1950s magazine, is interesting not only for its fanciful notion of housecleaning but also for its unquestioned assumption that the woman of the year 2000 would still be a "housewife."*

Sex and Personality

In the United States—perhaps more so than in any other society—there are vast individual differences in the way men and women interpret their roles. This is to be expected in a postindustrial society whose hallmarks are choice and diversity. But despite these differences, and despite the gender-role changes of recent years, there is still some consensus about what "masculinity" and "femininity" involve, and it is possible to outline these characteristics in a very general way. The personality traits of men and women tend to be complementary, so each sex may bring to a relationship qualities that the other may lack (Tavris and Wade, 1984; Lengerman and Wallace, 1985).

The American woman is widely expected to be sensitive, caring, and affectionate, but also relatively passive, conformist, and dependent. She is not supposed to be too knowledgeable about sports, mechanics, electronics, and similar "masculine" topics. In her relationships with men, she does not take the initiative, but instead allows the male to set the pace, while being careful not to threaten his often fragile ego. She often places more emphasis on romantic involvement than on sexual gratification. Her physical appearance is of great importance to her, and she may be obsessed about details of diet, makeup, and clothing. Although she may actively pursue a career, she is more likely than a man to be primarily interested in her home and family. Frequently, her self-image comes not from achievements in the outside world, but rather from her fulfillment of nurturant roles for her husband and children.

The American man, on the other hand, is expected to be self-reliant, competent, independent, and in some circumstances, competitive and aggressive. He typically keeps his emotions under stricter control than a woman, and in particular tries to hide signs of weakness. He is not supposed to be too knowledgeable about baby care, clothesmaking, floral arrangements, and similar "feminine" topics. In his relationships with the opposite sex he is expected to take the initiative, and he is often more interested in sexual gratification than in romantic involvement. He may share some authority in the home with his wife, but on major domestic issues, such as relocating to a different region, his wishes carry more weight. His self-image comes mainly from his achievements in the outside world, and work is a major focus of his life. This image may be undermined if his wife becomes the family breadwinner, or even if she earns more than he does.

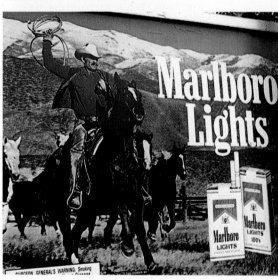

Figure 12.8 *Although "baby" may have come a long way, clearly defined gender roles still exist in America, and are well illustrated by these advertisements. Notice, incidentally, how gender images are used for marketing purposes: the advertisements contain virtually no information about the products themselves.*

These gender-linked personality traits each have their own advantages and disadvantages. Women, for example, are more easily able to develop a personality that is warm, intimate, and sympathetic, without worrying about constant competition in the "rat race." Their role also offers them the prospect of not having to earn a living, if they should marry a man who is willing and able to support them. However, women face the disadvantage of being largely cut off from the many political, economic, and cultural opportunities that remain a male preserve, such as high corporate or governmental office. Also, the role of a dependent person is not a socially valued one: those who rely on others for support—such as children, invalids, welfare recipients, or housewives—are expected to submit to the wishes of those who provide for them.

To a man, the main advantage is that he has relatively greater access to wealth, power, and prestige. He can earn more money, control more of his environment, and experience a range of career and other opportunities that are beyond the reach of most women. The main disadvantage is the tremendous stress associated with a life of competition, repressed feelings, and fear of failure. The statistics tell the story. Compared to women, men have three times the suicide rate, three times the rate for severe mental disorders, and six times the alcoholism rate. Men commit over 80 percent of all serious crimes and constitute over 90 percent of prison inmates. They are far more likely than women to suffer stress-related diseases such as ulcers, hypertension, and asthma. The bleakest statistic is life expectancy: the average American male dies seven years sooner than the average American female. It is hard at times to believe that this catalog of woes applies to the group that is supposed to be in the *upper* stratum in sexual stratification.

Of course, American gender roles are in a state of flux, with some people adhering to much more traditional patterns than those outlined here, and others exploring new and sometimes radical alternatives. There are also important subcultural variations. Generally speaking, the lower a person's social class, the more likely he or she is to conform to traditional stereotypes. The reason is probably that lower-status people have less freedom and effective choice in their lives, and so are slower to change established patterns. Hispanic-Americans, too, tend to conform more closely to traditional ways, partly because they tend to be relatively conservative on family issues and partly because a good deal of "machismo" is still entrenched in their culture. Black Americans, on the other hand, are the least male-dominated of the racial and ethnic groups in the United States because so many family breadwinners in the black community are female. But despite such variations, the prevailing patterns generally provide the standard against which all others are measured.

Male-Female Interaction

As we noted in Chapter 6 ("Social Interaction in Everyday Life"), many routine interactions between men and women carry symbolic meanings that may not be immediately obvious. For example, the "door ceremony," in which men open doors for women, symbolically reinforces the idea of female dependency and delicacy, while asserting men's paternalism and control. Although on the surface it seems no more than a courtesy, the ceremony helps underscore existing patterns of inequality—which is one reason why a woman who opened doors for men would draw reactions of discomfort rather than gratitude. As feminists point out, just as interesting as the question of *why* men open doors for women is the question of *which* doors they open for women: certainly not the symbolic doors that lead to positions of power, wealth, and influence (Sapiro, 1986).

Many other aspects of daily interaction reveal and reinforce the inequality of the sexes. Most obvious, perhaps, are the names by which people are known and the titles by which they address each other. A married woman replaces her last name with that of her husband, rather than the other way around; you can see the symbolic implications more clearly if you imagine the reverse situation, the groom taking the bride's name. Married or not, a man is known only as Mr., but until recently a woman had to be known as either Miss or Mrs.—a public indication of whether or not she was already a man's property. However, as women have gained more equality with men, the title Ms. has become established as the female equivalent of Mr., particularly among younger professionals.

The physical interaction of the sexes also reflects and reinforces their relationships. It is generally true that higher-status people take up more space than lower-status people. This is very much the case with the sexes: men typically require more personal space than women, and spread their arms or their legs sideways and outward much more than women do. Higher-status people are also permitted more liberty in touching lower-status people: the boss, for example, can pat a subordinate on the back, but the employee cannot do the same to the boss. Similarly, men touch women much more than women touch men, even when they are not on intimate terms. And if a pair is cuddling in public, the man assumes a controlling position by putting his arms around the woman; he will rarely allow a woman to hold him the same way if others are watching, for fear of appearing dependent (Henley, 1977).

Figure 12.9 *In their social interaction with men, women rarely take the initiative and instead play a passive role—supporting the men's conversation, waiting for them to call, and so on. This characteristic is well captured by Roy Lichtenstein's satirical pop-art image of a stood-up starlet, M-maybe (1965).*

Conversation between men and women is also a revealing form of social interaction. Any polite conversation follows the principle that only one person should speak at a time, but that both participants should have an equal chance to contribute. During the conversation, a speaker should watch for cues that the other party wishes to say something, and a listener should anticipate when a sentence will come to an end, so that an opportunity is created for the roles of speaker and listener to be swapped. Ideally, this transition should occur smoothly, without overlapping or interruption. Several studies have shown, however, that conversations involving a man and woman routinely violate this implicit understanding.

Despite the stereotype that women talk too much—that men "can't get a word in edgewise"—the fact is that when men and women are talking, men dominate the conversation. They not only speak for a disproportionate amount of time; they are also responsible, on average, for more than 95 percent of the interruptions that occur. Women, on the other hand, rarely try to interrupt; instead, they tend to treat men's contributions as more worthwhile than their own, and frequently abandon a

subject that interests them in favor of whatever men wish to talk about. Women also smile more frequently while listening, and they ask between two and three times as many questions as men— tactics that support the conversation by encouraging men to continue talking. When women do manage to make a lengthy statement, they are apt to be greeted by a series of "uh huh" sounds, rather than questions or other positive invitations to keep talking. These routine forms of social interaction between men and women reflect and enhance the inequality that is built into gender roles (Zimmerman and West, 1975; Fishman, 1978, 1980; Kramarae, 1980; Kollock, Blumstein, and Schwartz, 1985).

Gender Socialization

The basic gender characteristics expected of the sexes are learned in the family environment very early in life, and are then reinforced in the schools, in peer groups, in the mass media, and in many other specific agencies, ranging from sports teams to workplaces (Stockard and Johnson, 1980).

From the time that children are born, their parents treat them differently on the basis of their sex. Little boys are dressed in blue, little girls in pink. Girls are treated protectively, boys are given more freedom. Girls are valued for their docile and pleasing behavior and are not required to be achieving or competitive; charm and attractiveness are apt to receive more approval than intelligence. Boys, on the other hand, are given much more rigorous gender-role training. The little girl may be allowed some tomboyish behavior, but the little boy cannot be allowed to be a sissy. Parents usually view any "effeminate" behavior or interests with great alarm, and if these tendencies persist, they may be seen as a sign of psychological disturbance. The boy is repeatedly expected to prove his masculinity, particularly by performing well at sports. He is taught to "act like a man"—in other words, to suppress his emotions and particularly his tears. The requirement that the boy avoid anything "sissy" can breed a hostility toward femininity that may later develop into an unconscious contempt for the opposite sex.

As a result of this training, children learn their gender roles quickly and effectively. In fact, they are certain of the existence of two sexes and of their own identification with one of them long before they are aware of the biological basis for these distinctions. By the age of three, nearly all children know whether they are male or female, and by the age of four, they have very definite, even exaggerated, ideas of what masculinity and femininity should involve.

The psychological process by which children learn their gender roles is a complex one, but it contains three main elements. The first is *conditioning* through rewards and punishments, usually in the form of parental approval or disapproval. The child who behaves in the "right" way is encouraged, but the boy who plays with dolls or the girl who plays with mud is strongly discouraged. Sometimes parents deliberately arrange conditioning experiences for their children—for example, by giving them gender-related toys. But much conditioning is unconscious; as Virginia Sapiro (1986) points out, "If mommy and daddy are equally capable of driving, but mommy never drives if daddy is in the car, children nevertheless learn who is 'supposed' to drive the car." The second element in the learning process is *imitation.* Young children tend to imitate older children and adults, and are particularly inclined to imitate those whom they regard as most like themselves. Young children thus use other people of the same sex as models for their own behavior. The third and perhaps the most important element is *self-definition.* Through social interaction with others, children learn to categorize the people around them into two sexes and to label themselves as belonging to one sex rather than the other. They then use this self-definition to select their future interests and to construct their personalities and social roles (Kohlberg, 1966). (This is why children who have been assigned to the wrong sex at birth have such difficulty in identifying with the correct sex after the age of about three or four. The boy who has been raised as a girl "knows" that he is not a boy and naturally resists attempts to make him into one.)

The basic gender roles that children learn in the home are later reinforced, in various ways, by the school. Studies of school textbooks show that males and "masculine" activities are emphasized more than females and "feminine" activities—in readers, for example, male characters have long outnumbered female characters and have played much more diverse and significant social roles (Weitzman, 1979; Best, 1983). Additionally, many curricular and extracurricular activities—academic courses, hobbies, sports, and so on—tend to be segregated by sex. Girls are channeled into the cooking class, boys into the mechanics class; girls play softball, boys play hardball. Indeed, there is strong evidence that some girls refrain from studying mathematics and other subjects they consider "masculine," because they lack confidence in their

abilities in such fields—or even because they think boys will not like girls who do well in math (Sherman, 1980; Tobias and Weisbrod, 1980). But boys, too, are under strong social pressure to conform. Today, a girl might gain entry to the printing workshop without too much difficulty, but the boy who wants to take sewing classes faces the likelihood of discouragement from his teachers and ridicule from his peers. The girl who aspires to "masculine" pursuits is behaving in a way that is at least understandable to others, for she is seeking a status that is acknowledged to be superior, if inappropriate. But the boy who has "effeminate" interests is likely to be seen as behaving incomprehensibly, for he is deliberately seeking an inferior status.

Beyond the home and the school, social life is saturated with messages about which sex is dominant and about how men and women ought to behave. In particular, all forms of the mass media, from television soap operas to the lyrics of popular songs, tend to emphasize fairly traditional gender stereotypes.

Perhaps the most insidious of these media presentations is the one commonly offered in advertising. Women are typically portrayed either as sex objects, in an attempt to market various products to men, or as domesticated housewives, in order to market home-maintenance products to women. Market research has shown that one of the most effective ways for advertisers to reach a male audience is to associate a product, however remotely, with a seductive or smiling female. The sexuality of women is thus exploited by having glamorous models stroking new automobiles, cradling bottles of whiskey, or being sent into raptures by the odor of a particular after-shave. Advertising directed at women, on the other hand, shows females delighted beyond measure at the discovery of a new instant soup, or thrilled into ecstasy by the blinding whiteness of their wash. In fact, the vast majority of television advertisements that use women models are for kitchen or bathroom products (Tuchman, 1978).

Erving Goffman (1976) points out that when men and women appear together in advertisements, the men are always shown as taller than the women. The women never hold the advertised product in a firm grasp, and are rarely seen giving the men instructions. The eyes of the men in advertisements focus on the product or on important people, but the eyes of the women focus on men, whom they gaze at or cling to in apparent admiration. In fact, what is remarkable about advertising is how little its gender stereotypes have changed over the past quarter century. Men are the voice of authority on 80 percent of television commercials, including those directed at women. A barrage of advertisements still portray females as simple-minded creatures, bickering endlessly over which toothpaste or fabric softener is better (Klemesrud, 1981). (To fully appreciate the implications of these stereotypes, try mentally substituting men for the women on the screen the next time you watch TV advertisements, and note how utterly demeaning the portrayals would be.)

Men, Women, and Jobs

At the core of the inequality of men and women is the difference in their earnings. It is crucial to most people's sense of self-worth and independence that they have their own income. Unequal earnings are therefore a constant reminder of broader social inequality of the sexes. Moreover, in any intimate relationship, the partner with the higher income is likely to be in charge, for the other partner tends to become, at least in some sense, a dependent. As the old adage puts it, "He who pays the piper calls the tune."

Despite the fact that large numbers of women have taken jobs outside the home, a significant gap has persisted in the incomes of full-time male and female workers, with women generally earning around 60 percent of what men have earned (see Figure 12.10). Thus far, there is no job in which the average woman earns as much as the average man—not even among the jobs (such as nursing) where women far outnumber men. Even on the most optimistic estimates, the difference in incomes is unlikely to disappear any time soon. By the year 2000, the average woman is expected to be earning only 74 cents for every dollar earned by the average man.

Why, when women have flooded into the work force, does this gap persist? Several factors seem to be responsible. One is that women, on the whole, have less education and job experience than men, and so bring fewer skills to the labor market. Another is that women's traditional family responsibilities may affect their careers if pregnancy and child-raising cause them to drop out of the labor market for long periods. Additionally, there is strong evidence that employers perceive women as less able than men, and do not take them as serious candidates for promotion unless they perform exceptionally well. In fact, women occupy very few high-paying positions: only 8 of every 1,000 employed women holds a high-level executive, managerial, or administrative job. Even when men and women do similar jobs, they sometimes have different titles and pay scales: the male becomes an "administrative assistant"; the female, merely an "executive secretary" (Ilchman, 1985; Bergman, 1986; Reskin, 1985).

MEDIAN INCOME OF FULL-TIME MALE AND FEMALE WORKERS

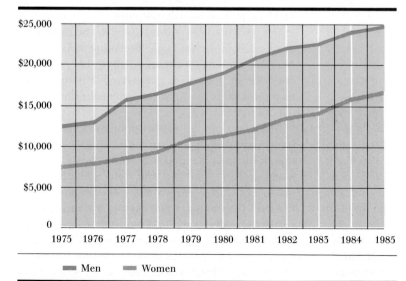

Figure 12.10 *As this graph shows, women's earnings have changed little in relation to those of men, despite the growing number of women in the work force. One reason is that most women work in a handful of low-paying "pink-collar" jobs, such as secretary, nurse, or receptionist.*

SOURCE: U.S. Bureau of the Census.

As a result of such factors, most women workers have become trapped in a handful of "pink collar" jobs—low-paying, female-dominated occupations. In fact, some 80 percent of all working women are concentrated in just 20 of the 427 major job categories recognized by the U.S. Department of Labor. Women represent 85 percent of elementary school teachers, 86 percent of librarians, 84 percent of cashiers, 96 percent of nurses, 97 percent of receptionists, 96 percent of typists, and 98 percent of secretaries (Bureau of the Census, 1986a).

In short, social arrangements have evolved in such a way that female-dominated jobs command less income than male-dominated jobs: librarians earn less than carpenters, cashiers less than trash collectors, nurses less than accountants. As a result, "equal pay for equal work" offers little benefit to most female workers: it does not help much if male secretaries are paid the same as female secretaries, when most secretaries are female and the job is a poorly paid one. Consequently, some people have demanded a radically different system: "equal pay for comparable work." The idea is that every job could be given a numerical rating of its practical worth, which would in turn be used to compare the intrinsic value of different jobs and to set salaries accordingly (Hartmann, 1985).

The federal government and employers have generally been hostile to the "comparable worth" suggestion. They claim that comparing different jobs is like comparing apples and oranges; that the proposal would lead to wage increases and therefore rising prices; that it could encourage employers to hire men instead of women; that it would encourage women to stay in their existing jobs rather than strike out into new fields; and that it might undercut the incomes of men who are family breadwinners (Samuelson, 1985). Certainly, any move that might equalize the incomes of men and women is likely to have a profound impact beyond the workplace. In any event, several state and local authorities are applying comparable-worth programs, and over a hundred additional city and state authorities have also begun preliminary studies of the issue. The proposal will certainly meet a good deal of resistance, but it is difficult to see how else the economic inequalities between men and women might be significantly reduced in the foreseeable future.

A minority of women have escaped from the "pink collar" jobs, and some have entered the professions. Women now represent 6 percent of engineers, 16 percent of physicians, 11 percent of ar-

Figure 12.11

"Very pleased to meet you. What does your husband do?"

Copyright Wm. Hamilton

chitects, 6 percent of dentists, 16 percent of lawyers and judges, 30 percent of computer scientists, 41 percent of accountants, and 37 percent of college teachers. Yet these women frequently encounter a different problem: the "invisible ceiling." In corporate and other workplaces, women may find themselves promoted—up to a point. Despite impressive gains at the entry level and middle management, women are having trouble rising to the top. Of the country's leading 500 corporations, only two have female chief executives—and one of them inherited control of the company from her father. Not one of these corporations has a woman executive on the "fast track" to the chief executive's job. This pattern is repeated throughout the economy: women may be 44 percent of the work force, but they are less than 5 percent of senior executives; they may be 71 percent of classroom teachers, but they are only 2 percent of school superintendents; they may be more than half the population, but they have only about 400 of the 16,000 seats on boards of the nation's thousand leading corporations (Fraker, 1984).

Why do women stop short of the top? One reason, no doubt, is the attitude of many men. Corporate leadership in America is a kind of old-boy network; there is no old-girl network to speak of. There are still many men who feel a woman should be at home, or in bed, or having babies—rather than hiring, firing, and ordering men around. In an atmosphere of often earthy male camaraderie, the combination of female competence and sexual attractiveness can be unsettling and even threatening. Another reason may be that the socialization process tends to produce women who lack the self-confidence and determination to compete with men for career goals. As we have seen, women are taught from childhood to be nice, to defer to men, to listen to them without interrupting, to be supportive rather than competitive. The few women who do rise toward the top tend to be those who have learned to behave in some respects in a "masculine" and assertive way, for this is the style that the corporate world understands. Other women, whose management style is less abrasive and more caring, are—thus far—less appreciated at the higher levels of the corporate culture.

Gender Roles Today

Every revolution has its consequences, its benefits and its costs. The revolution in gender roles has helped to reshape the workplace, the family, and the relationships of the sexes—but the feminist ideals of the 1960s have not always been fulfilled by the reality of the 1980s.

A great deal has changed in a quarter of a century. New economic roles have brought women greater equality with men and also many fresh opportunities, particularly the chance to experience careers and achievement in the world beyond the home. But working women have not simply traded their housework for a career: rather, they have taken on two jobs—one at home, one at work. The average American man spends about 4 hours a week in household chores; the average American woman, about 30 hours. In short, men are willing to "help out," but not to "do their share." One reason, of course, is that men simply do not want to do housework, which they consider trivial and even degrading; another reason, perhaps, is that many women are reluctant to give up an area of expertise on which their self-esteem has traditionally depended. So men still avoid the problem of coordinating two jobs as worker and homemaker, while women are often forced to face it squarely (Berk, 1985).

Surveys show that most working women enjoy their job, and for economic and other reasons would not wish to be "only a housewife." Yet for many women, the experience of a career has involved puzzlement and even pain. Women who looked forward to "having it all" are finding that the rigors of pursuing their careers, maintaining intimate relationships, and raising children are difficult to balance. Some, who put their career before marriage only to find that they have hit the "invisible ceiling," feel deeply betrayed. Now in

their forties, they regard themselves as casualties of their own revolution—especially if they did not marry and now face the prospect of never finding a husband or having children. Also, the postfeminist generation of women today takes the benefits of women's liberation for granted, yet is dubious about the burdens of being the perfect wife, mother, and executive. For the time at least, many women feel themselves stuck midway in a revolution that has run out of steam (Brownmiller, 1984; Hardesty and Jacobs, 1986).

Changes in women's roles have had an immense impact on the family. A generation of American children is now being raised by working mothers, who leave them in some form of day care from an early age—something unprecedented on this scale in the American experience. Additionally, women's new independence has made it possible for them to contemplate leaving unhappy marriages or raising children on their own. Partly as a result, there has been a sharp increase in the number of divorces, of births to unwed women, and of female-headed households. One in every two married women is now likely to get divorced, and one of every five mothers is single. Yet many of these women have found themselves highly vulnerable. An indirect and largely unforeseen effect of women's drive for independence has been a "feminization of poverty": one of every four divorced or separated women is on welfare, and one in every three families headed by women is in poverty. Overall, 57 percent of the poor are female. The main reason, of course, is that women have less earning power than men—although courts tend to award divorced women less alimony or child support than previously, on the grounds that they can now earn their own living (Rodgers, 1986; Weitzman, 1985). (These issues are discussed in more detail in Chapter 13, "The Family.")

For their part, American men, after some hesitancy, have generally reacted positively to the growing equality of women. In fact, their own roles, being complementary to those of women, are inevitably in some flux also. Men are now permitted a more gentle and expressive personality than would have been considered appropriate a few decades ago; the 1950s "John Wayne" image of American manhood has less and less appeal to both sexes. Like the feminine role, the masculine role is now more ambiguous, more flexible, more subject to interpretation by the individual. Resolving this kind of ambiguity is part of the challenge of social and cultural change. Under the old system, everyone knew what their roles were, and most people unquestioningly behaved as they were sup-posed to. The system constrained people, but it freed them from the need to make choices. There are fewer constraints today, but the individual now has the liberty—or the burden—to choose his or her own path to self-fulfillment (Pleck, 1981; Gerzon, 1982; Doyle, 1983; Franklin, 1984).

What will the final shape of American gender roles be? Sexual equality does not necessarily mean gender similarity or a "unisex" society. It does not necessarily mean that women will gradu-ally adopt the characteristics of men or that the two existing genders will converge on some happy medium. The most probable pattern is one in which many alternative lifestyles and roles will be acceptable for both men and women. Postindus-trial American society is individualistic and highly open to change and experimentation, and it is likely that men and women will explore a wide variety of possible roles. True liberation from the restrictions of gender would mean that all possible options would be open and equally acceptable for both sexes. Then a person's individual human qualities, rather than his or her biological sex, would be the primary measure of that person's worth and achievement.

Age and Society

As we saw in Chapter 5 ("Socialization"), the human life course is both a social and a biological process. Even the rate at which our bodies mature is influenced by social factors. In the nineteenth century, for example, the average American girl began to menstruate (and became a potential mother) at the age of seventeen, but today, largely as a result of the society's improved standards of nutrition, the average girl begins menstruation at the age of twelve. Similarly, our life expectancy is influenced by such social factors as the presence (or absence) of competent medical care, adequate sanitation, environmental pollution, warfare, or widespread access to such potentially lethal instru-ments as handguns and automobiles. A person born in the United States today can expect to live, on average, for seventy-five years, but a person born in the social setting of the United States of 1900 could expect to live, on average, for only forty-seven years.

The content of the life course, too, is affected by social factors, for each society imposes its own culturally defined "stages" on the continuous proc-ess of human aging. Most traditional societies rec-ognized three basic stages—childhood, maturity, and old age. Modern societies, such as the United States, generally recognize six—infancy, child-hood, adolescence, "youth" or young adulthood, middle age, and old age. Age is an important social status, for it affects the individual's relationship with others of similar, older, or younger statuses. For this reason, many societies, particularly tradi-tional ones, celebrate *rites of passage*—formal ceremonies that mark an individual's transition from one age status to another. There are traces of these rites in the modern United States, such as the high school graduation ceremony (marking the transition from adolescence to young adulthood) or the office retirement party (marking the transi-tion from middle age to old age).

All societies distribute different rights and re-sponsibilities to people on the basis of their age status. In the United States, for example, a person aged eight must attend school, but a person of eighty need not do so; a person of seventy can become president or can collect Social Security

Figure 12.12 *All societies distribute different rights and responsibilities to people of different ages—in one society, perhaps, expecting the young and the old to work; in another, expecting the young to go to school and the old to retire.*

retirement benefits, but a person of twenty-five is not entitled to do either; a person of twenty-one can drink in a bar, but a person of seventeen cannot. In addition to these formal rights and duties, there are also informal age-related expectations as well. We demand that people should "grow up" at some point, and no longer be "childish"; we insist that people should "act their age" when appropriate; we warn that they should not "behave like an old fool," and so on. People who violate the norms—whether by marrying "too early," staying in graduate school "too long," or retiring "too late"—risk being treated, in some sense, as deviants.

As a general rule, preindustrial societies granted the greatest power and prestige to the old; industrialized societies, on the other hand, accord the most valued rewards to the middle-aged and offer the old virtually no roles at all (Cowgill, 1974; Fischer, 1978; Kett, 1979; Atchley, 1985).

In most preindustrial societies, the aged were, in fact, so respected that younger people sometimes looked forward to old age. The old were the repository of the community's folklore, knowledge, experience, and wisdom, and younger people looked to them for guidance. In these preliterate societies, there was no other source of information about the past—yet that information was highly relevant to the daily life and recurrent problems of the community. How long might a drought last? Were there distant kinfolk in a community elsewhere? How could a certain disease be cured? What weapons and tactics could best defeat an enemy? It is hardly surprising, then, that in most preindustrial societies power was vested in older people: often, in fact, a "council of the elders" regulated the affairs of the community. Ownership of wealth, too, was linked to age, for the primary source of wealth in most preindustrial societies was land, which was typically held by the oldest male in the family until it passed, on his death, to his eldest son. The elderly also dominated the family. The large *extended family*—one in which more than two generations of the same kinship line live together—was quite common, and it was typically headed by the oldest male. And because nearly all preindustrial societies were relatively unproductive and needed every hand they could get for labor in the fields, the aged played an active economic role until they were too infirm to work any longer.

In industrialized societies, on the other hand, the status of the aged is very different. In these highly technological and rapidly changing socie-

Figure 12.13 *In most traditional societies, the aged have an honored and respected place in the community, and old men typically have the greatest wealth and political authority. Decisions are often made by a council of elders or some other body of older men, like this one in Senegal.*

ties, the store of relevant knowledge constantly alters and expands. Access to much of this knowledge comes through formal education, yet the schools are centered almost exclusively on the young and make very little provision for the aged. The accumulated experience of the old is no longer respected; rather, their knowledge is regarded as outmoded. Adolescents may know more (or believe they know more) about the modern world than their grandparents know. The economic status of the aged also changes as the ownership of land becomes a less significant source of wealth. In an industrialized society, new sources of wealth are created, and the main beneficiaries are middle-aged executives and other professionals.

The role of old people in the family also changes: instead of heading the unit, the aged are increasingly isolated from it, for the extended family gives way, in virtually all industrialized societies, to the **nuclear family**—one in which the family group consists only of the parents and their dependent children, living apart from other relatives. To make matters worse, the old usually have no jobs, and so are deprived of the political and social influence that economic power implies.

Age Inequality: A Functionalist View

The shifting rights and responsibilities of different age categories clearly result from the changes that are caused by industrialization. But the unequal status of the elderly is not an inevitable outcome of this situation: in other words, the rest of society could still find other ways of keeping old people actively involved in useful roles if there were good reason to do so. Some functionalist theorists have tried to explain the situation of the aged by suggesting that their "disengagement" from society is to everyone's benefit, including that of the old.

The principal statement of this view is that of Elaine Cumming and William Henry (1961), who are strongly influenced by the general functionalist assumption that society is a balanced system in which various elements function smoothly to maintain overall stability. The status of the elderly, they argue, is the result of a mutual process of disengagement, in which society gradually withdraws roles from the old, while the old gradually surrender their roles to other, younger, members of society. Cumming and Henry point out that since everyone will eventually die, a society must, if it is to outlive its individual members, arrange an orderly transition from the aged to those who are younger. As people grow older, the probability that they will soon die increases; hence, society phases out those individuals whose future contributions are problematic. For their part, people slowly relinquish their roles as they grow older, for they want to conserve their energies and devote more of their time to themselves. Social norms evolve to provide the guidelines for this disengagement process: for example, it becomes the standard practice to retire at about sixty-five, and the event is often marked by some rite of passage (such as the ceremonial gift of a gold watch) that signals the changed status of the individual. The net result is a decreased interaction between the aging person and the surrounding society, to the mutual satisfaction of both, for the elderly willingly accept their new but unequal status.

Functionalists explain changes in the status of the young, too, in terms of the need for overall social stability. Less than a century ago, American adolescents were often full-time workers, with their own incomes and with many adult rights. Today, it is generally illegal for them to work full-time, for they are required to be in school at least until the age of sixteen—even though their attendance keeps them in a dependent status in both the family and society. In the functionalist view, the reason for compulsory education is that the young need to learn the skills necessary to contribute to an industrialized economy. So, rather than assign social and economic statuses by letting the young, the middle-aged, and the old compete for them in the job market, society allocates the various statuses more efficiently—according to age.

Figure 12.14 *Functionalist theory explains the status of different age groups in terms of society's overall convenience. When child labor was socially useful, it was encouraged; now that child workers are no longer needed, children are expected to be in school. Similarly, the aged now lose many roles because their economic contribution is no longer socially necessary.*

Age Inequality: A Conflict View

Conflict theorists argue that the various age categories are really social strata. As such, they are ranked in a hierarchy of power, prestige, and wealth, and are in constant competition for scarce social resources. There is one major difference, though, between age stratification and other forms of stratification. Men do not spend part of their lives as women, nor do blacks spend part of their lives as whites—but anyone who lives long enough will belong to every age stratum at some point. Any given stratum, however, has its own interests to defend: the young, for example, are apt to think that cheaper and better college education is a top priority; the middle-aged are more likely than the young to be concerned that income taxes should not increase; the aged have a vested interest in better Social Security benefits. But society has only limited financial and other resources to distribute among its age strata, so one stratum's gain may be another stratum's loss (Riley et al., 1972; Foner, 1984).

Conflict theorists reject the functionalist explanation of why the status of both the elderly and the young has changed in the modern world. They point out that in a preindustrial society, the elderly and the young are expected to work because there is a labor shortage. But in a productive modern economy, the problem is not a shortage of labor but a surplus: industrialized societies have a chronic problem of unemployment and underemployment. In response to this difficulty, industrialized societies arbitrarily exclude two categories of the population from the competition for jobs: the young and the old. A new social invention, compulsory schooling, keeps the very young out of the work force, and another new invention, compulsory retirement, ensures that the old give up their jobs. Earlier in this century, in fact, much of the pressure to abolish child labor and to introduce mandatory retirement came from organized labor, which was intent on reducing the pool of the unemployed in order to improve workers' wages and bargaining position.

In the conflict view, the most powerful age stratum in any society is able to secure a disproportionate share of the society's resources for itself. The declining status of the aged in industrial societies results from the profound social changes that have enabled the middle-aged to wrest control of social resources from their elders. Any improvement in the situation of the aged would have to come about through a change in the power relationships of the strata. For example, if the proportion of the population that is old increases, or if the aged organize powerful social movements to press their case, they might effectively challenge the structured inequality between themselves and the other strata. The same principle would apply to the young, or any other age category.

Ageism

As we have seen, the dominant stratum in any unequal society uses an ideology to justify its position. Employing the analogy of racism and sexism, sociologists have coined the word *ageism,* the belief that one age category is in some respects inferior to other age categories and that unequal treatment of them is therefore justified.

The ideology of ageism, in fact, is remarkably similar to the ideologies that justify inequalities of race and gender. For example, the subordinate status of the old, like that of racial minorities or women, has been assumed to be rooted in biological characteristics: specifically, it is held that the mental or physical abilities of the aged are so diminished that they are unable to play a full role in society and may therefore be excluded from significant participation. Similarly, the ideology of ageism takes no account of individual differences, and instead treats all old people as though age were their single most important characteristic. And, like sexism or racism, the ageist ideology ignores the fact that many of the differences between the strata are caused by social factors—including differences that result from discrimination and unequal opportunity (Palmore and Manton, 1973; Butler, 1975; Levin and Levin, 1980).

Figure 12.15

Drawing by Modell; © 1986
The New Yorker Magazine, Inc.

An important feature of ageism, as with racism and sexism, is its reliance on negative stereotypes about the minority concerned. For example, it is widely believed that the old are not such productive workers as the young (actually, they have better job-attendance and productivity records); that many or most of them are infirm (more than 80 percent of the population over sixty-five are fully capable of getting around on their own); that a high proportion of the aged are senile (less than 10 percent of the aged under seventy-five display symptoms of senility); or that many of the elderly are confined to nursing homes or old-age homes (only 4 percent of those over sixty-five are in this situation). In addition, there are a variety of beliefs about the typical personalities of the aged—that they are cranky, forgetful, sexless, highly conservative, and the like—beliefs that either ignore the vast differences among old people (for, after all, individuals grow more different, not more similar, as they age), or have no basis in fact whatever. But no matter how inaccurate the public stereotype of the aged may be, it provides an implicit justification for excluding them from significant roles in the economy, the family, and other areas of society.

Ageism against the elderly is often subtle, but it is pervasive. Take a simple example, television commercials. These advertisements almost always present youthful, attractive, active people. When older characters appear, they are likely to have health problems and to be promoting health-related devices; old people are almost totally absent from commercials about cars, appliances, clothing, or home-care products. Advertising, like so many other aspects of the media, often reflects the "fountain of youth" theme that courses through a culture in which people are encouraged to believe that creams, soaps, lotions, colorings, vitamins, diet pills, exercise machines, sports cars, or whatever, will make them look like a young adult forever.

Ageist bias is revealed in people's attitudes toward their own age. Children and adolescents often wish they were older and sometimes overstate their age, for they correctly perceive that their own age status is a low one. Middle-aged people, on the other hand, often understate their ages, for they know that the years devalue people the older they get. This is especially true for women, who, because they are socialized to place so much importance on their youthful looks, are more devalued by advancing age than men are. In "lying about their age," people demonstrate their own ageism. Beneath this attitude lies not just a fear of aging, but the fear of death. In preindustrial societies, death regularly occurred at every stage of the life course and was especially common in children. In industrialized societies, where dying has become almost a taboo subject, death is primarily a phenomenon of old age.

Ageism, incidentally, need not necessarily apply only to old people, although in modern societies it is directed mainly against them. An ageist ideology could be unjustly applied to any age category, including the young or the middle-aged. In the 1960s, when the youth movement was challenging a war instigated by leaders from an older generation, the cry of many of the young was "Don't trust anyone over thirty!" Needless to say, that ageist slogan carried an unavoidable booby trap for those who proclaimed it.

Social Gerontology

For practical purposes, sociologists regard the aged in America as those who are at least sixty-five years old—the point in the life course at which a person can begin to draw Social Security benefits. This specific boundary between middle age and old age is, of course, an arbitrary one. In fact, it was not chosen on the basis of any medical, psychological, sociological, or other evidence, but on the personal whim of one man in 1889. Germany introduced the first social-security laws in that year, and the German chancellor, Bismarck, in his subjective wisdom, selected sixty-five as the age at which benefits could be drawn. Legislation in the United States and most other industrialized societies simply followed that precedent.

Social gerontology is the study of the social aspects of aging. This subdiscipline of sociology examines the influence of social forces on the aged and the aging process, and the impact of the aged and their needs on society. As social gerontologists point out, aging actually involves three related processes. One is *physical* aging, the maturation and other age-related changes that take place over time in the body. A second process is *psychological* aging, the developmental and other changes that occur in the personality, including its emotional, cognitive, and behavioral components. The third process is *social* aging, involving the various transitions from one social status to another that the individual experiences over the life course. These processes do not necessarily occur in unison. For example, an old novelist may produce a masterpiece despite failing eyesight; an aging athlete may remain physically strong yet suffer lapses of confidence and concentration; an airline pilot may be expected to give up flying at sixty, yet go on to become a politician whose skills are admired at seventy-five. Because all three aging processes can occur at different and uneven rates in any individual, generalizations about the abilities of the aged are very risky (Atchley, 1985; Kart, 1985).

The experience and the meaning of aging differ not only from individual to individual, but also from one social and historical context to another. Being an adolescent today is very different from being an adolescent fifty or a hundred years ago. In fact, being an adolescent right now is a different experience in some respects than it was even a few years ago, for people who are born at roughly the same time have a common history that is unlike that of all others in their society. To analyze this phenomenon, sociologists use the concept of a **cohort,** a category of people who are born during the same time period, such as a period of one, five, or ten years.

The members of a given cohort experience the same events differently than do those of other cohorts who were born earlier or later. Glen Elder (1974, 1975) illustrated this "cohort effect" in a study of how people reacted, later in life, to their experience of hardship during the Great Depression. He found that those who were very young during the depression had no memory of earlier prosperity, so they regarded the economic improvements of later years as a steady progress from adversity to affluence. But their elders, who had known better times before the depression, saw the new prosperity differently; to them, it was a sign of a possible cycle in which good and bad times might follow one another. So, decades after the depression, the younger cohort assumed that the bad times were gone forever; but the older cohort was still wary of the economic future and inclined to "save for a rainy day." The actual meaning of any stage in the life course, therefore, is a fluid one, in which people's expectations for themselves at a particular age depend on social assumptions unique to that time and place.

Another influence on the meaning of aging—and on the relationships among different age categories—is a society's **age structure,** the relative proportion of different age categories in a population. Because birth and death rates vary from time to time, different societies have different proportions of people at various ages. The age structure of any particular population gradually changes, of course, as new members are born and old members die. But if a society happens to have a high proportion of nonworking children or old people, then an extra burden is laid on the working population, for its members are expected to share much of what they produce with a large number of dependents. Naturally, this situation can increase the likelihood of competition among different age strata for their share of society's resources. Children, however large their numbers, have little direct political influence; but a large aged population may be better able to protect its interests.

The Aged in America

Until relatively recently, most accounts of the life of the American elderly painted an extremely negative picture. For example, Robert Butler (1975) described aging as a tragedy, in which "at best, the living old are treated as though they were already half dead." Today, social gerontologists take a rather more positive view, one that stresses diversity among the elderly and recognizes that many of them draw great satisfaction from the final stage of the life course. Gerontologists point out that most of the aged have modest but adequate incomes, own their own homes, drive their own cars, are fully capable of getting about on their own, and need relatively little in the way of social services.

Indeed, American society is now treating its aged members much better than before. One indication of this change is the declining poverty rate of the aged. In 1959, an astonishing 35 percent of

Figure 12.16 *People in different age cohorts experience the same stage of the life course differently. Two decades ago, American college students were often involved in demonstrations and protests against college administrations and national policies. Today's students, although they are of the same age, have a college experience that is different in many respects.*

THE BEST YEARS OF OUR LIVES

Question: People feel differently about what years are the best time of a person's life. Which of these do you think are the best time of life?

By age:	Childhood years	Teenage years	The twenties	The thirties	The forties	The fifties	Retirement years
18–29 years	22%	29%	42%	9%	4%	1%	3%
30–44 years	22%	21%	28%	31%	13%	4%	5%
45–59 years	17%	16%	24%	22%	20%	13%	8%
60+	14%	14%	19%	20%	16%	11%	31%

SOURCE: Roper Organization, 1984.

Figure 12.17 *People of different ages have quite different ideas about when the "best years" of their lives are. It may come as a surprise to young people that their elders look back on the teenage years with little enthusiasm—and that among older people, the single most popular period is the retirement years.*

people aged sixty-five or over lived below the poverty line, a situation that came to be regarded as a national disgrace. For the first time, the aged began to form an effective political force, and through organizations like the American Association of Retired Persons, they pressed for improved Social Security and other benefits. By the beginning of the 1970s, the poverty rate among the aged had dropped to 25 percent, and since then it has declined to 12.5 percent—a rate slightly lower than that for the population as a whole.

Even so, the aged still have some distinctive problems, the most obvious being the possibility of poor health. Advancing age inevitably brings with it a series of health problems, for the human body gradually degenerates with the passage of the years. Of course, the rate at which people appear to age varies a great deal, and people of seventy or eighty may be healthier, and even seem younger, than people twenty years their junior. Nonetheless, more than three-quarters of those over the age of sixty-five suffer from some chronic health problem, and although the aged represent only 12 percent of the total population, they fill a third of all hospital beds and use a quarter of the drugs prescribed each year. The most common ailments suffered by the aged include arthritis, diabetes, glaucoma, cancer, heart disease, and senility—diseases that can usually be treated, but not cured. Senility is perhaps the most notorious disability of the aged as far as the rest of the population is concerned, but the condition is rare among people under seventy-five; only thereafter does it become more common. Some senility involves the gradual loss of brain cells with advancing age, but much of it results from Alzheimer's disease, which is believed to be caused by a slowly developing viral infection. Many aged people are labeled as senile,

however, when they are really suffering from depression, from the side effects of medication, or from undiagnosed respiratory or cardiovascular problems that impede the flow of blood and oxygen to the brain.

The high incidence of poor health among the aged is compounded by the fact that the aged have much higher medical expenses than the nonaged—six times greater than the expenses of young adults, and three times greater than those of the middle-aged. The old often face these expenses at a time when they have lost their job-related medical insurance as a result of retirement. Although it is widely supposed that Medicaid and Medicare cover most of the medical bills of old people, this is far from the case; these programs assume only about 45 percent of the financial burden, and their coverage specifically excludes drugs prescribed outside hospitals as well as items that the old are disproportionately likely to need, such as hearing aids and eyeglasses.

Another problematic issue for the aged is work and retirement. We spend most of our lives working, and work is important for our sense of who and what we are: it enables us to provide for ourselves, to enjoy achievement and success, to express our worth, to earn social and economic independence. Workers who are approaching retirement age are especially vulnerable if they lose their jobs. The Age Discrimination in Employment Act protects workers who are over forty from discrimination on the grounds of age, but it is often difficult to prove such discrimination. When people are fired or laid off in their late fifties or early sixties, they are at a severe disadvantage, for if they can find a new job at all, it almost always involves downward social mobility and lower earnings.

Retirement, for most people, is an ambiguous but not an unwelcome event. The concept of retiring is actually a relatively new one, which began to emerge only in the late nineteenth century. In fact, few people could afford to retire before the Great Depression, for there was no system of social security to fall back on. Instead, people worked as long as they were physically able to do so, and then relied on their own savings and their family's support thereafter. But the Social Security Act of 1935 introduced old-age pensions and unemployment benefits, and encouraged not only retirement, but mandatory retirement. For several decades, most American workers were legally obliged to retire from their jobs at the age of sixty-five, no matter how well they were performing their work or how much they needed the income.

This system was clearly discriminatory, and, under pressure from the aged, Congress raised the mandatory retirement age to seventy in 1978, and then abolished it in 1986, except for a few categories of workers such as airline pilots, firefighters, and tenured college professors. In practice, the vast majority of workers—over 80 percent of men and 90 percent of women—still retire at sixty-five. Whether their retirement is a happy one seems to depend largely on how financially secure they are. And despite the myth that people are more likely to die if they retire than if they "keep busy," there is no difference, on average, between the health of those who go on working and those who do not.

Most of the elderly retain an active social life after retirement, but some find themselves increasingly isolated from the ongoing life of the society. Their social networks are steadily decimated by the disability and deaths of their contemporaries, and many of the elderly are, or soon become, widowed. If you are a woman, you will probably live without a husband for the final years of your life. From the age of sixty-five to seventy-four, about 80 percent of men live with a spouse, but less than 50 percent of the women do. From the age of seventy-five onward, more than 70 percent of the men are still with a wife, but only 20 percent of the women still have a husband. For the quarter of the aged who live alone, social isolation can be a serious and growing problem, and they may experience feelings of uselessness, boredom, frustration, and depression.

Isolation is not to be confused with independence, which involves the ability to control one's own life. Many of the elderly fear losing that independence as a result of ill health or financial problems. We are taught from birth to be self-sufficient and autonomous, and understandably fear the shift from the role of an independent person to a dependent one. In American society, dependent people—such as children, welfare recipients, and housewives with no income of their own—are expected to defer to the wishes of their benefactors, to give up their right of self-determination, and to be grateful for what they receive. Older people may have to fall back on their children, perhaps even moving in with them—a transition that involves a difficult reversal of roles and may arouse feelings of guilt in the parent and resentment in the offspring, not to mention any in-laws.

Yet, if people live long enough, dependence becomes inevitable. Extreme old age, beginning around the eighties, is accompanied, sooner or later, by a slowing or even crippling of mental and physical processes. Unable or unwilling to take care of an elderly relative, younger family members may arrange for the aged person to move to a nursing or old-age home. This prospect is hardly an appealing one, however: at best, it means living in an unfamiliar environment where one relies for medical and other needs on a professional staff rather than on friends or relatives. Some homes offer superb facilities, but many are dreary, shabby, and ill-equipped places, run by people whose concern is not the best interests of the elderly but rather whatever profit they can wring from the enterprise. Although only about 4 percent of the elderly are in a nursing or old-age home at any given time, most conclude their lives in that kind of setting. In 1900, nearly all old Americans died at home. Today, fewer than one in five dies in that familiar context; most of the rest meet death in a hospital or nursing home.

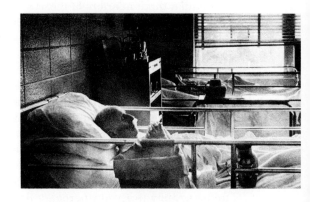

Figure 12.18. *A few generations ago, the aged were cared for by the family until the time of death; today they are more likely to face their end in a hospital or nursing home, isolated from their kin except, perhaps, during visiting hours.*

The New Poor: Children

Although America's aged have the lowest overall poverty rate in the country's history, they also have much lower average incomes than other adults. In fact, without Social Security benefits, more than half of the aged would be poor. Many aged people actually live just above the poverty line, and a significant minority live below it. Poverty among the aged is usually a continuation of poverty earlier in life, so the brunt of this hardship is born by women and minorities. About 17 percent of aged women are poor, compared with about 10 percent of aged men. Moreover, some 38 percent of elderly blacks —and nearly 43 percent of aged black women— live in poverty. And because there are few ways for old people to earn an income, their poverty is a permanent matter: once poor, they are likely to remain that way until the end of their days.

Today, however, America's real poor are its children. Over the past two decades, a complex of factors has created a new generation of impoverished children and adolescents. About 22 percent of Americans under the age of eighteen live in poverty—a sharp increase from just over 14 percent in 1970. Although poor white children outnumber poor black children by two to one, almost half the black children in America today are being raised in poverty. This trend is linked to the "feminization" of poverty that has resulted, in turn, from changes in the American family structure and the economic vulnerability of women. As a result of increased numbers of divorces and of births to unwed mothers, the number of households headed by a single female has risen rapidly. Children in these homes are four times more likely to be impoverished as children in two-parent homes. These young people, too, tend to be poorly educated and to become parents themselves at an early age, meaning that the problem of childhood poverty may be perpetuated, and perhaps worsened, for yet another generation (Sidel, 1986).

This mass of poor, ill-educated, politically silent young people is a phenomenon that, so far, is receiving little attention. Why does American society neglect this problem, even when it is finally beginning to attend to the needs of the aged? One reason, no doubt, is that children and adolescents are in the age stratum that has least power of all, whereas the elderly have at least some influence. In fact, the rest of society has a vested interest in taking care of the old, since everyone expects to be old one day and to reap the benefit of earlier generosity; but none of us will ever be a child again. A second reason, discussed in Chapter 10 ("Social

Figure 12.19. *As a result of the social changes of the past quarter century, American children now have the highest poverty rate of any age group. One child in five lives in poverty.*

Stratification"), is the distinctive American attitude toward the poor: that poverty is essentially the poor's own fault. Most people accept that the aged have a legitimate claim on society's resources, for they have contributed to the economy in the past. But many people are less favorably disposed to an unwed teenage mother's claims, for herself or even for her children.

Indeed, more than 30 percent of the total federal budget is spent on older Americans, whereas only 3 percent is devoted to the nation's children (Malcolm, 1985). For example, there is Medicare for older people, but no comparable program for children—even though, given the fact that medical insurance is usually linked to employment, the unemployed mother and her child are at an immediate disadvantage in the health care system. And, although nearly all other modern industrialized societies provide some form of free preschool day care, the United States does not. Again, the single mother is disadvantaged by a system that still seems to assume that women stay home and raise their children while men go to work to support them. In any event, in the competition among the dependent age strata for society's generosity, the children of the poor are the greatest losers.

The Graying of America

The United States is in the midst of a profound change in the age structure of its population, one that will affect virtually every area of national life over the next half century. The American population has been growing older for some time, at least since 1800. Back then, half the population was under sixteen. But by 1900, the median age had risen to nearly twenty-three; by 1970, to almost twenty-eight; and by 1985, to over thirty. The median age is expected to reach thirty-five by the year 2000 and may go as high as thirty-seven by the year 2030. At present there are over 28 million aged Americans, representing just over one in ten of the population. By the year 2030 there will be

over 50 million aged people representing approximately one in every five Americans. Conversely, the proportion of the population that is under sixteen has been shrinking, from 50 percent of the population in 1800 to 35 percent in 1900 to 22 percent today. The impact of these changes on the society's population structure is indicated in Figure 12.20.

Why has this dramatic change taken place? One reason is that people are living longer: since the beginning of the century, average life expectancy at birth has increased by twenty-eight years. But the main reason is an enormous bulge in the population structure as a result of America's post-World War II "baby boom." In two decades from about 1946 to 1964, some 76 million children were

AGE DISTRIBUTION OF THE U.S. POPULATION
Population in Millions

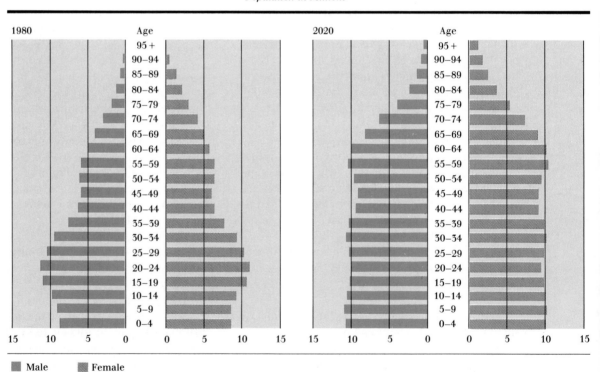

SOURCE: U.S. Bureau of the Census.

Figure 12.20. *This chart shows how the American age structure is changing. The age structure for 1980 is on the left, and the expected age structure for 2020 on the right. Each structure is illustrated in the form that sociologists call a "population pyramid": successive age cohorts are shown as* *horizontal bars, with the youngest at the bottom and the oldest at the top (males are shown on the left and females on the right). The bulge in each structure is the "baby boom" generation, whose progress through the life course is steadily increasing the society's median age.*

born, representing a third of the total present population. After 1964 the birth rate dropped, creating a "birth dearth," and the rate has remained at a relatively low level since then. (These and other aspects of population change are discussed in more detail in Chapter 21, "Population and Urbanization.")

As it proceeds through the life course, the huge "baby boom" generation is creating a moving bulge in the age structure of the society, rather like a pig gradually passing through a boa constrictor. The result is a whole range of multiple and successive impacts on almost every area of American life. During the 1950s and 1960s, this generation flooded the schools and colleges, necessitating a vast expansion of educational facilities and creating a youth culture that challenged many of the political and social conventions of the time. Throughout the 1970s, the children of the baby boom crowded the job market, adding to unemployment and forcing many college graduates to take jobs below their level of qualification. By the 1980s, much of this generation had settled down and married, pushing up the costs of rent and home ownership. During the 1990s, there will be a middle-aged bulge in the population structure. And finally, when this baby-boom generation retires early in the next century, American society will be largely oriented toward a huge dependent group of the elderly. Providing for their support, housing, and health care will be one of the biggest challenges American society has ever faced—and the responsibility, however it is exercised, will fall squarely on the generation containing most readers of this book (Pifer and Bronte, 1986; Wynne, 1986).

The graying of America will bring about a variety of changes, some of which are already apparent. To begin with, elementary schools and even high schools all over the nation have closed their doors, and teachers have been thrown out of work. Changes in population structure are being reflected in marketing trends as well: for example, Gerber baby foods now sells life insurance; Levi's jeans are now designed with more generous proportions for a market that is steadily tending toward middle-aged spread; models in TV advertisements appear to be somewhat older than they were a few years ago, for their appeal, in large measure, must be directed to an audience that is in its thirties.

Other changes are clearly in the offing. Educational facilities will have to offer more courses in continuing education for older people, or they may

have so few students that they will not survive. The medical problems of the aged will become a major growth area in medicine, for American physicians, despite their lack of enthusiasm for this field in the past, are likely to specialize where the greatest market is. Nursing homes, funeral homes, and crematoriums will proliferate. And in all likelihood, the aged will achieve a more respected status in society.

There are many signs that this process is well under way. The elderly are now established as a highly effective political lobby, and are staking their claim to a greater share of the society's resources. The possible implications of this trend—which include a potential for fresh conflict among the age strata—are most clearly seen in the Social Security system, under which benefits for those who are retired are paid for by those who are working. In 1945 there were thirty-five workers to one Social Security recipient; by 1955 the ratio was seven to one; by 1985, about three to one. Within the foreseeable future there may be two workers supporting every retiree, and the burden may be heavier still if the retired people of the future are able to secure more generous benefits—and if they live longer. To ease this financial burden somewhat, the age at which people will be entitled to draw their Social Security benefits will be raised to sixty-seven years by the end of the century.

Today's elderly people were born before the Great Depression; they grew up without television; they went to school in an era when an eighth-grade education was considered sufficient for most people; they experienced a world war; they generally did not have high expectations of aging and retirement. Even so, people of sixty-five today are much "younger" in their outlook and activities than were their counterparts of even a few decades ago. The cohorts of the baby boom are likely to continue this trend, and early in the next century they are likely to try to redefine what it means to be old. Well-educated, used to affluence, committed to self-fulfillment, they will anticipate a longer life, better health, more generous benefits, a more satisfying retirement. Already, members of this generation are moving into positions of economic and political power and influence, and the sheer weight of their numbers will influence decisions about the allocation of resources among different age groups, from now until well after the year 2000. The challenge for the entire society will be to ensure that no major age stratum—the young, working adults, or the aged—is denied a fair share of those resources.

Summary

1.   All societies treat their members unequally according to ascribed statuses of sex and age. These structured social inequalities are specific forms of the general phenomenon of social stratification.

2.   Sex refers to the biological distinctions between men and women; gender refers to culturally learned notions of masculinity and femininity. Gender roles are the learned patterns of behavior expected of the sexes in a specific society.

3.   The biological differences between the sexes are anatomical, genetic, and hormonal. Apart from reproductive functions, these differences have few inevitable implications for gender roles. There is probably some predisposition toward minor psychological differences in the sexes at birth, but people can be socialized into a variety of gender roles. The general cross-cultural trend is toward male dominance and female subordination, although some cultures are unlike our own.

4.   In the functionalist view, gender-role differences were useful in traditional societies, and some theorists argue that this is still the case. In the conflict view, traditional gender roles reflect a conflict of interest between men and women, and will change as women gain more power by playing economic roles beyond the home. Sexism is an ideology that upholds sexual stratification. Both men and women are inclined to regard sexual inequalities as being rooted in biology. Members of the subordinate stratum are in a state of false consciousness in this respect.

5.   There are distinct gender-role differences in the United States, expressed in personality traits and in the division of labor. Although gender roles have changed in recent decades, men are expected to have more dominant personalities and to play the more important economic roles. Routine patterns of male-female interaction, such as conversation, uphold traditional relationships. Agencies of socialization such as the family, the schools, and the mass media, reinforce the existing patterns. Although most women now work, they are concentrated in "pink collar" jobs and hit an "invisible ceiling" in promotions. One proposed remedy is to pay different jobs according to their "comparable worth."

6.   Gender roles have changed, but with some unforeseen consequences. In particular, women find themselves with two jobs, at home and at work, and poverty has become "feminized" as a result of changes in family structure and low female earnings.

7.   The life course is a social as well as a biological process; all societies define stages of life and assign different rights and responsibilities to people in various age categories. In general, preindustrial societies gave high status to the aged; industrial societies give them low status.

8.   In the functionalist view, the status of the elderly results from a process of mutual disengagement. In the conflict view, the status of the elderly results from competition among different age strata for valued social rewards. Ageism is the ideology that justifies the unequal treatment of different age groups, particularly the elderly.

9.   Social gerontology studies the relationship between aging and society. The meaning of aging may vary from one cohort to another,

and relationships among age strata are affected by a society's age structure.

10. The position of the aged in the United States has improved in recent years, although they may still have such problems as ill health, isolation, and loss of dependence. Poverty was once a significant problem for the aged, but is now predominantly a problem of children. America is "graying" as a result of changes in population structure. The result may be renewed competition among age strata for society's resources.

Important Terms

sex (314)

gender (314)

gender roles (314)

division of labor (317)

ideology (320)

sexism (320)

false consciousness (321)

rites of passage (331)

extended family (332)

nuclear family (333)

ageism (334)

social gerontology (335)

cohort (336)

age structure (336)

Suggested Readings

ATCHLEY, ROBERT C. *Social Forces and Aging.* 4th ed. Belmont, Calif.: Wadsworth, 1985.

An excellent introduction to social gerontology, the study of the social aspects of aging.

BERNARD, JESSIE. *The Female World.* New York: Free Press, 1981.

An interesting examination of the social world from a woman's perspective. The book makes informative reading for both sexes.

ELDER, GLEN. *Children of the Great Depression.* Chicago: University of Chicago Press, 1974.

A classic study of the "cohort effect" on people who experienced the Great Depression at different ages.

FONER, NANCY. *Ages in Conflict.* New York: Columbia University Press, 1984.

A good statement of the conflict approach to inequality among age strata.

FRANKLIN, CLYDE W. *The Changing Definition of Masculinity.* New York: Plenum, 1984.

The author examines how concepts of masculinity are developing in response to changing social conditions, particularly the new roles of women.

HESS, BETH B., and ELIZABETH MARKSON (eds.). *Growing Old in America.* 3rd ed. New Brunswick, N.J.: Transaction Books, 1984.

A selection of sociological articles on various aspects of aging in America.

SAPIRO, VIRGINIA. *Women in American Society.* Palo Alto, Calif.: Mayfield, 1986.

An excellent survey of social science knowledge about women and sexual inequality in the modern United States.

TAVRIS, CAROL, and CAROLE WADE. *The Longest War: Sex Differences in Perspective.* 2nd ed. New York: Harcourt Brace Jovanovich, 1984.

A good overview of the differences between men and women and their implications for social and economic life.

UNIT 4

Social Institutions

*Every society must meet certain basic social needs if it is to survive
and to offer a satisfying life to its members. In each society, therefore, people create social institutions to meet these needs.*

*As we noted in our discussion in Chapter 4 ("Society"), an insti-
tution is a fairly stable cluster of norms, values, statuses, and roles,
all of them centered on some social need. The family, for example, is
an institution built around the needs to regulate sexual activity and
to provide care and protection for the young. The educational institution focuses on the need to give young people formal training in
the skills that they will require later in life. The economic institution
centers on the social need for an orderly way of producing and distributing goods and services. Within these broad social institutions
there are, of course, many smaller units: for example, high schools
within the educational institution, churches within the wider religious institution.*

*The study of social institutions is important because they are a
central part of social structure, and there is an intimate relationship
between a society's institutional framework and the private experience of its members. In this unit we will focus on several of the most
important institutions in modern society: the family, education,
religion, medicine, the economic order, and the political order. As
you will see, social institutions are currently in a state of considerable flux as they are subjected to new demands and constant social
change.*

*The illustration opposite—which stoutly evokes the solidity and
interrelationships of such institutions as the family, religion, and the
political order—is* The Presidential Family, *by the contemporary
Latin American artist Fernando Botero.*

CHAPTER 13

The Family

The family is the most basic and ancient of all institutions, and it remains the fundamental social unit in every society. Yet there are many people today who predict the end of the family system as we know it. The family, it is contended, is breaking down, the victim of moral decay, sexual permissiveness, changing gender roles, or irresistible social forces.

Such predictions are heard in all industrialized societies, but the statistics suggest that the family system of the world's leading postindustrial society, the United States, is under the most pressure. The great majority of both American men and women begin sexual activity before marriage. One in every five American births is to an unmarried mother, usually a teenager. One in every four pregnancies ends in abortion. The number of unmarried couples living together has tripled in less than two decades. Americans are staying single longer than ever, and more than one adult in five now lives alone. About half of American marriages are expected to end in divorce. New alternatives to traditional marriage, such as the single-parent household, are becoming steadily more common. And to complicate matters further, children can now be conceived through artificial means, sometimes in a laboratory dish—an issue we will discuss in more detail in Chapter 22 ("Technology and Environment").

What does all this mean? Is the family threatened with collapse, or can it thrive under the changing social conditions of the modern world? In this chapter, we will begin with a sociological analysis of the institution, and then apply the insights of the discipline to the situation of the modern family. (To review the features of institutions in general, you can refer back to the discussion in Chapter 4, "Society.")

What exactly is a family? Our ideas on the subject may tend to be ethnocentric, for they are often based on the middle-class "ideal" family so relent-lessly portrayed in TV commercials, one that consists of a husband, a wife, and their dependent children. This particular family pattern, however, is far from typical. A more accurate conception of the family must take account of the many different family forms that have existed or still exist both in America and in other cultures.

What characteristics, then, are common to all family forms? First, the family consists of a group of people who are in some way related to one another. Second, its members live together for long periods. Third, the adults in the group assume responsibility for any offspring. And fourth, the members of the family form an economic unit—often for producing goods and services (as when all members share agricultural tasks) and always for consuming goods and services (such as food or housing). We may say, then, that the *family* is a relatively permanent group of people related by ancestry, marriage, or adoption, who live together, form an economic unit, and take care of their young. If this definition seems a little cumbersome, it is only because it has to include such a great variety of family forms.

Marriage and Kinship

Every human society institutionalizes some family system, for the family is a social arrangement that arises from biological features unique to our species. Human sexual relations, unlike those of other animals, are not restricted to brief breeding seasons. This fact encourages human mates to form stable, long-lasting bonds. In other species, moreover, the offspring are generally able to fend for themselves quite soon after being born or hatched. In contrast, the human infant is helpless and in need of constant care and protection for several years after birth—a far longer period of dependency than that found in any other animal. The fact that women bear and suckle infants restricts their activity during this period, making them at least temporarily dependent on the protection and economic support of males. In the past, every society has also found it convenient (or at least the men in every society have found it so) to assign responsibility for child-rearing to women, leaving the men to concentrate on such activities as hunting, heavy agriculture, or fighting. The result has been a universal pattern in which men and women establish

Figure 13.1 *Every society insists that a marriage be marked by a wedding or other socially recognized ritual. Such a ritual offers a public indication of the new status of the marital partners, and of their responsibility for any offspring.*

permanent bonds that maximize the efficiency of their child-rearing and economic activity: hence, the family.

Most of us spend our lives in two families in which we play quite different roles: a *family of orientation,* the one into which we are born, and a *family of procreation,* the one which we create ourselves. In every society, a family is expected to be formed through *marriage,* a socially approved mating arrangement between two or more people. Social recognition of a marriage is usually marked through some culturally prescribed ritual, such as a wedding by a religious official, a registration of the union by a judge or other government servant, or a formal exchange of gifts between the families of the partners. The partners in a marriage are expected to have a sexual relationship; indeed, many societies require that all sexual intercourse take place within this context. Additionally, marriage imposes certain economic rights and duties on the partners, for it implies the sharing of a household.

Every society distinguishes between offspring born in wedlock and those born out of wedlock. *Legitimate birth* is birth to a mother and father who are married to each other; *illegitimate birth* is birth to a mother who is not married to the father. All societies encourage legitimacy, because it enables them to automatically allocate the social roles of mother and father to specific persons who are then responsible for the care and protection of the young. Illegitimacy, on the other hand, can present a social problem, because although the mother is known, there may be nobody to take on the social role of father. As a result, illegitimate children tend to be more socially and economically vulnerable than legitimate children. Different social arrangements must then be made to provide for their needs: in some societies, for example, the mother's eldest brother is required to play the social role of father; in other societies, welfare agencies provide the necessary economic support. To discourage illegitimacy, many societies treat the unmarried mother as a deviant, and may even stigmatize her child as well.

The family is a unit within a much wider group of relatives, or kin. *Kinship* is a social network of people related by common ancestry, adoption, or marriage. In many traditional societies, kinship is the basis of social organization, but in modern societies the family tends to become isolated from all but the closest kin. Many of us do not even know the names of our second cousins or similarly distant relatives. Frequently, even close kin gather only for a few ceremonial occasions such as Thanksgiving or funerals.

A kinship network is a highly complicated affair, as you will know if you have ever tried to construct your own family tree. Your closest, or primary, relatives—mother, father, brother, sister, spouse, daughter, son—give a total of 7 possible types. Your secondary relatives—the primary relatives of your primary relatives—provide 33 additional types, ranging from mothers-in-law to nephews. If you further include tertiary relatives—the primary relatives of your secondary relatives—you have 151 more types, giving a grand total of 191. Since many of these positions can be occupied by several people, the number of primary, secondary, and tertiary relatives can easily run to several hundred. A kinship network of this size is more than people can deal with, socially or even conceptually, so every society finds a way of arbitrarily excluding some categories of relatives from its notion of kin. The most common way of doing this in traditional societies, odd as it may seem to us, is simply to acknowledge as kin only the relatives on either the father's or the mother's side of the family. In North America we consider the relatives of both father and mother as kin, and generally solve the problem of numbers by regarding nearly all tertiary and many secondary relatives as too distant to be considered real kinfolk.

The Family: A Functionalist View

Although the family institution arose from our characteristics as a species, we are not merely biological animals; we are social animals as well. A full understanding of the universality of the family must take into account the functions that the institution performs in all societies (Murdock, 1949; Parsons and Bales, 1955).

1. *Regulation of sexual behavior.* No society allows people to mate at random, and no society regards sexual behavior purely as a matter of private choice. The marriage and family system provides a means of regulating sexual behavior by specifying who may mate with whom and under what circumstances they may do so.

2. *Replacement of members.* A society cannot survive unless it has a system for replacing its members from generation to generation. The family provides a stable, institutionalized means

through which this replacement can take place, with specific individuals occupying the social roles of mother and father and assuming defined responsibilities.

3. *Socialization.* People do not become fully human until they are socialized, and the primary context for this socialization is the family, starting at birth. Because the child is theirs, the parents normally take particular care to monitor his or her behavior and to pass on the language, values, norms, and beliefs of the culture. Although in modern society many of these socialization functions have been taken over by other institutions—such as the schools, the churches, or the media—the family remains the earliest and most significant agency of socialization.

4. *Care and protection.* People need warmth, food, shelter, and care. The family provides an environment in which these needs can be met—a household where people share the material and other supports that cannot be readily obtained outside the family context. In particular, the productive members of the family can take care of those who, by reason of their youth, age, or infirmity, are unable to take care of themselves.

5. *Social placement.* Legitimate birth into a family gives the individual a stable place in society. We inherit from our family of orientation not only material goods but also our social status. We belong to the same racial or ethnic group and usually to the same religion and social class that our parents belong to. Our family background is the most significant single determinant of our status in society.

6. *Emotional support.* Human beings have a need for affection, nurturance, intimacy, and love. The family is the primary social context in which emotional needs can be fulfilled and the deepest personal feelings can be expressed. In this sense the family may function as "a haven in a heartless world," the place of ultimate emotional refuge and comfort (Lasch, 1977).

All these functions are necessary. As many critics have suggested, however, the family is not the only conceivable means through which they could be fulfilled. Yet the family fulfills them so effectively that it takes primary responsibility for them in every human culture.

The Family: A Conflict View

While conflict theorists do not dispute that the family has important social functions, they believe that the functionalist analysis does not tell the whole story. In particular, they note that the family is the principal institution in which the dominance of men over women has been expressed.

Karl Marx's colleague, Friedrich Engels (1942, orig. 1884), argued that marriage represents "the first class antagonism which appears in history . . . in which the well-being and development of the one group are attained by the misery and repression of the other." The relationship between the spouses in marriage, he claimed, provided the model on which later forms of oppression were based, especially that between capitalist and

Figure 13.2 *The family fulfills several important social functions, including the care, protection, and emotional support of its members.*

worker. Several conflict theorists continue to assert that marital relationships reflect and reinforce gender inequalities (Degler, 1980; Smart, 1984; Collins, 1985).

It is true that in many societies women have been treated for practical and legal purposes as the property of their husbands (or, if unmarried, of their fathers). As recently as the late 1960s, many American statutes made married women legally incompetent to enter into contracts, rent cars, or get credit without their husband's signature—in much the same way that minors cannot exercise certain privileges without the approval of a parent or guardian. Even more strikingly, husbands had absolute sexual rights over their spouses, and it is only in the present decade that some states have made it illegal for a husband to rape his wife. Traces of the old traditions are also to be found in our contemporary wedding ceremony: in the standard form of vows, the bride solemnly promises to "obey" the groom, and it is her father who "gives her away" to her new husband, as though some piece of property were being transferred. (We can see the implications of this symbolic interaction more clearly if we imagine its opposite—the mother of the groom giving him away to the bride, and he then vowing to obey his wife for the rest of his life.)

Nonetheless, the fact that women have been subordinate in all family systems in the past does not necessarily mean that there is something inherently wrong with the whole idea of the family, for it is entirely possible that utterly different family forms might emerge in the future. Particularly in some of the emerging postindustrial societies, in fact, there is a strong trend toward equality between the spouses.

Tension over gender roles is only one aspect of conflict in the family. The sociological research of the past two decades has revealed an astonishing amount of family violence—between spouses, between parents and offspring, and among the offspring themselves. Leading researchers on violence among family members have observed that "the American family and the American home are perhaps as or more violent than any single American institution (with the exception of the military, and only then in time of war)" (Straus, Gelles, and Steinmetz, 1981).

About a fifth of all murders in the United States are committed by a relative of the victim—in half of the cases, by the spouse. The police detest "disturbance calls"—usually family fights—because of the vicious and dangerous nature of so many of these conflicts; indeed, more police are killed in-

Figure 13.3

"Just remember: Your mother was a Van Puyster and your father was a rat."

Copyright Wm. Hamilton

tervening in these disputes than in almost any other type of situation they face. Surveys suggest that each year around 7 million couples go through a violent episode in which one spouse tries to cause the other serious pain or injury. Wives assault their husbands as often as husbands assault their wives, and spouses are equally likely to kill each other. Although wives are rarely a match for their husbands in a fistfight, they are more likely to use lethal weapons (notably kitchen knives). In most nonfatal physical violence between the spouses, however, wives are very much the victims, for wife-beating is a widespread and very serious problem. Each year, too, some 2 million children wield a gun or knife against a brother or sister, and parents kick, punch, bite or batter at least 2 million children. Child abuse—involving such acts as burning children with cigarettes, locking them up in closets, tying them up for hours or days, or breaking their bones—is alarmingly common, and probably causes many of the 2 million runaways that happen each year (Straus et al., 1979; Gelles and Cornell, 1983, 1985). And the sexual abuse of children—now recognized as a national epidemic—is rarely a matter of molestation by a stranger. It is usually perpetrated by one family member on another (Finkelhor, 1983, 1984; Russell, 1984, 1986).

One source of this violence may lie in the dynamics of the family as an intimate environment: close relationships are likely to involve more conflict than less intimate ones, since there are more occasions for tension to arise and more likelihood that deep emotions will be provoked. Another source may lie outside the family, for violence is frequently a response to frustration. If the person affected cannot strike back at the source of the problem—the arrogance of an employer, say, or the lack of a job—the aggression may be readily redirected at family members. Perhaps most important, violence between husband and wife takes place in a general social context that has traditionally emphasized male dominance and female subservience (Straus and Hotaling, 1980). In any event, the extent of violence in groups whose members are supposed to love and care for one another is not easily explained by functionalist theory, and suggests that the modern family may sometimes be under greater pressures than it can easily bear.

Family Patterns

Each society views its own patterns of marriage, family, and kinship as self-evidently right and proper, and usually as God-given as well. Much of the current concern about the fate of the modern family stems from this kind of ethnocentrism. If we assume that there is only one "right" family form, then naturally any change will be interpreted as heralding the doom of the whole institution. It is important to recognize, therefore, that there is an immense range in marriage, family, and kinship patterns; that each of these patterns may be, at least in its own context, perfectly viable; and above all, that the family, like any other social institution, must inevitably change through time, in our own society as in all others.

A Cross-Cultural Perspective

The family patterns of other cultures challenge many of our assumptions about the nature of marriage, family, and kinship (Murdock, 1949; Ford and Beach, 1955; Stephens, 1963; Fox, 1965; Murstein, 1974).

As we saw in Chapter 9 ("Sexuality and Society"), every society has an *incest taboo,* a powerful moral prohibition against sexual contact between certain categories of relatives. But although no society allows people to mate with anyone they choose, different societies have quite different ideas about who might be a prohibited marriage partner. In the United States, all fifty states prohibit marriage between a person and his or her parent, grandparent, uncle or aunt, brother or sister, and niece or nephew; an additional twenty-nine states regard marriage between first cousins as incestuous, but the remainder do not. Many societies, however, do not make any distinction between siblings (brothers and sisters) and cousins. In these societies there are usually no separate words for "brother" and "cousin": they are regarded as the same kind of relative, and the incest taboo is therefore extended to first, second, third, and even more distant cousins as well. A few societies actually extend the taboo to social as well as sexual behavior. Among the Nama Hottentots, an adult brother and sister could not be alone together or even speak to one another, and a Crow husband could not talk to or even look at his mother-in-law.

Some cultures, on the other hand, are very specific about whom people may or should marry, as well as whom they may not. Thus, although certain societies consider it incestuous to marry a child of one's mother's sister, or of one's father's brother, they may expect—or even require—that one should marry a child of one's mother's brother, or of one's father's sister. Biologically, of course, each type of cousin is equally close; but social norms define one union as revolting, the other as desirable.

In modern, industrialized societies it is generally assumed that marriage is founded on romantic love between the partners and that the choice of a mate should be left to the individual. But this concept of romantic love is entirely unknown in many societies and is considered laughable or tragic in many others. In most traditional societies, marriage is regarded as a practical economic arrangement or a matter of family alliances, not a love match. (Throughout history, in fact, alliances between entire societies have been sealed by marrying a prince of one royal family to a princess of another. Earlier in this century, for example, Ibn Saud, a local Arabian chieftain, married over 300 women from various tribes, binding these groups into the country now called Saudi Arabia.) In many traditional societies, therefore, marriage is negotiated by the parents of the partners, often with little or no consideration of their children's wishes. If love is a feature of these marriages at all, it is expected to be a result and not a cause of the union.

The economic aspect of these marriages is especially apparent in those societies in which an intending groom must pay a bride-price to his prospective father-in-law. This practice is especially widespread in sub-Saharan Africa, where nearly all the tribes expect a groom to exchange cattle for the bride.

In all Western nations, the law insists that a man have only one wife at a time and a woman, only one husband, but this ideal is held by a minority of the societies of the world. In a survey of evidence from 238 mostly preindustrial societies, George Murdock (1949) found that only 43 insisted on restriction to one mate at a time. In 4 of the remaining societies a woman was permitted to have more than one husband, and in all the rest a man was allowed to have more than one wife, a ratio that reflects the superior power and privileges of the male partner in the family institution.

Another traditional Western assumption has been that people should not have premarital or extramarital sexual experience, a value still very strongly held by many people in industrialized societies. In cross-cultural terms, however, this belief is something of an exotic curiosity, and the idea of virgin marriage is considered ludicrous. In fact, in a few societies, such as the Mentawei of Indonesia, a woman must give birth before she can marry, for she is expected to prove her fertility to her intending husbands. Many societies also allow extramarital sex, although the privilege is far more often granted to the husband than to the wife. After surveying the cross-cultural evidence, Murdock concluded: "It seems unlikely that a general prohibition of sexual relations outside marriage occurs in as many as five percent of the peoples of the earth."

In modern industrialized societies, we generally assume that married partners should be adults of much the same age, although certain exceptions are made for an older man and a younger woman. Some societies offer strikingly contrasting patterns. The Kadara of Nigeria marry infants to one another. The Chuckchee of Siberia, believing that parental care is the best way of cementing the marriage bond, allow adult women to marry males of only two or three years of age; the new wives then look after the boys until they are old enough to assume their husbandly duties. And among the Tiwi of Australia, adult males marry females even before they are conceived, annulling the marriage if the newborn turns out to be the wrong sex. (See the reading "Courtship and Marriage Among the Tiwi" at the end of this chapter.)

The Analysis of Family Patterns

Is there any underlying regularity in this extraordinary range of cultural practices centered on the family? Actually, family patterns are not quite as random or capricious as they might seem, and sociologists are able to analyze all family types in terms of six basic dimensions.

Figure 13.4 *The ideal that a husband should have more than one wife is still widely held in many parts of the world, and historically it has been the favored marriage form in most societies. This photograph, from the Maldive Islands of the Indian Ocean, shows a family consisting of one husband, two wives, and their children. In most traditional societies, a large family is considered an economic asset.*

Number of Partners

A marriage may include two or more partners. *Monogamy* is marriage involving one spouse of each sex; *polygamy* is marriage involving a spouse of one sex and two or more spouses of the opposite sex. A polygamous union may take the form of either *polygyny,* marriage between one husband and more than one wife, or *polyandry,* marriage between one wife and more than one husband. Although most societies favor polygyny rather than monogamy, most men in the world have only one wife—partly because the societies that insist on monogamy contain the bulk of the world's population, and partly because there are not enough women to permit widespread polygyny even in societies that favor the arrangement. In practice, it is usually the more wealthy and power-ful men in these societies who have more than one wife. Polyandry occurs only under exceptional conditions. The Toda of India, for example, prac-ticed female infanticide, so they had a large sur-plus of males. When a Toda woman married a man, she became wife to all his brothers as well.

Partner Preference

Some social groups prefer or require their mem-bers to marry outside the group, while other groups expect that their members marry within the group. *Exogamy* is marriage outside a particu-lar social category. The Aranda of Australia, for example, divide their entire society into two sec-tions, and an individual may marry only someone from the opposite section. Exogamy is generally preferred by groups that want to build alliances with others by exchanging kin through marriage. On the other hand, *endogamy* is marriage within the same social category. Religious, racial, and ethnic groups generally practice endogamy, either because of prejudice or lack of contact with other groups, or as a means of maintaining their group solidarity. Many groups, such as American blacks and Jews, are primarily endogamous but accept some exogamous marriages.

Residence Pattern

Where should newly married people live? The answer to that question depends very much on the norms of their society. Because marriage in tradi-tional societies is essentially an alliance of kinship groups, the partners are usually expected to reside with their kin. *Patrilocal residence* is the custom in which marriage partners settle in or near the

Figure 13.5 *Black Americans are one of many groups that generally practice endogamy, or marriage within their own social category.*

household of the husband's father; *matrilocal residence* is the custom in which married partners settle in or near the household of the wife's father. In modern societies, where marriage is conceived as a love-match between individuals, the predomi-nant practice is *neolocal residence,* the custom in which marriage partners establish a new resi-dence separate from the kin of either spouse.

Authority Relationships

Patterns of authority between husband and wife are always affected by the personalities of the spouses, but they generally follow the norms of the surrounding society. In nearly all societies the pre-vailing pattern is *patriarchy,* a system in which the husband has the greater authority in family matters. No society has a *matriarchy,* a system in which the wife has the greater authority in family matters, although several societies give the wife more influence than the husband in some domestic areas. Some female-dominated families are found in many societies, however, although never as the norm: they usually occur by default, through the death or desertion of the husband. A third and newly emerging pattern is that of the *egalitarian marriage,* a system in which husband and wife have a more or less equal say in family matters.

Descent and Inheritance

If an ancestor dies, who is entitled to inherit any property that is left? Descent may be traced, and property passed on, in one of three basic ways. The *patrilineal system* is one in which descent and inheritance pass through the male side of the family. The mother's relatives are not considered kin, and females do not inherit property rights. The reverse is the case under the *matrilineal system,* one in which descent and inheritance pass through the female side of the family. Under this system, it is the father's relatives who are not regarded as kin. The third method—more familiar to us, but practiced by less than half the peoples in the world—is the *bilateral system,* one in which descent and inheritance are traced through both sides of the family. The relatives of both parents are considered kin, and property may pass to both males and females.

Family Form

All family systems can be roughly categorized into one of two types. The *extended family* is one in which more than two generations of the same kinship line live together, either in the same house or in adjacent dwellings. The head of the entire family is usually the eldest male, and all adults share responsibility for child-rearing and other tasks. The extended family, which is quite commonly found in traditional, preindustrial societies, can be very large: sometimes it contains several adult offspring of the head of the family, together with all their spouses and children. In contrast, the *nuclear family* is one in which the family group consists only of the parents and their dependent children, living apart from other relatives. The nuclear family occurs in some preindustrial societies, and is the usual type in virtually all modern industrialized societies. In fact, the growing dominance of the nuclear family is transforming family life all over the world.

The Transformation of the Family

As one society after another has industrialized over the course of the past two centuries, there has been a major, global change in family patterns—a change that involves a fundamental shift in people's loyalties. Essentially, people have come to focus less on their responsibilities toward their kin and their families, and more on their desires for self-fulfillment as individuals. As Betty Yorburg (1983) observes:

> Adults will follow job opportunities even if it means breaking ties with relatives. Married women will go out to work even against opposition from their husbands. They will leave unhappy marriages, sometimes without their children, especially in the middle or upper classes. Husbands will leave their economically dependent wives. . . . The presence of children no longer preserves marriages. . . . The oldest child will no longer give up educational or other personal goals to support needy brothers and sisters or aged parents and grandparents. Young people will choose marital partners or live together in heterosexual or homosexual relationships with or without the approval of parents.

This shift in loyalties has had dramatic effects on family life. The extended family has tended to be replaced by the nuclear family; the ideal of polygamy has steadily given way to the ideal of monogamy; neolocal residence has rapidly replaced patrilocal or matrilocal residence; and patriarchal unions have become more egalitarian. Above all, people's entire way of thinking about marriage has changed: it is now viewed less as an economic arrangement or a kinship alliance, and more as a companionship based on the emotional commitment of two individuals.

This transformation is, of course, a general trend, not a hard and fast rule. Except among some Indian tribes, the extended family was never common in the United States or Canada, even in the days when they were agricultural societies. The nuclear family was fairly widespread in preindustrial Europe, and some extended families are still to be found in even the most advanced industrial societies, particularly Japan. In some parts of the world, the emergence of the nuclear family preceded and probably facilitated industrialization; in some, the two processes took place more or less simultaneously; in others, industrialization seems to have provoked the later collapse of the extended family. Nevertheless, the overall pattern is unmistakable: in industrialized societies, tradi-

tional family forms have given way to others that are better adapted to the changed conditions of social and economic life (Laslett, 1971, 1977; Laslett and Wall, 1972; Shorter, 1975; Stone, 1977; Gordon, 1983).

Why has the nuclear family become the dominant type? The answer is that the extended family is well suited to the conditions of preindustrial society, where every able-bodied family member is an economic asset. But the nuclear family is far better adapted to the conditions of the modern world, for several reasons.

1. *Geographic mobility.* Life in a modern society offers and sometimes requires geographic mobility—workers are expected to go where the jobs and promotions are. They cannot do so if obligations to various kin (such as a custom of patrilocal residence) tie them to a particular area and prevent prolonged separation from relatives.

2. *Social mobility.* Unlike traditional, preindustrial societies, modern societies offer people the chance to achieve new and often higher social statuses. Socially mobile people have education, interests, values, and incomes that are very different from those of people whose status is traditional and static. As a result of social mobility, various family members may eventually come to have lifestyles that are quite different from one another. Consequently, the bonds of common interests and shared experience that once bound the extended family together are loosened or, in some cases, even shattered.

3. *Loss of family functions.* In an industrialized, urban environment, formal organizations and institutions—corporations, schools, hospitals, welfare agencies, day-care centers, and the media—assume many of the functions that were once the prerogative of the family. In this sense, the extended family simply has less to offer. People no longer have to rely on the support network provided by their kin, and instead seek a new foundation for married life—close companionship with a single spouse.

Figure 13.6 *These two paintings illustrate the dramatic transformation that has taken place in the family. The first picture is* The Hatch Family, *painted in 1871 by the American artist Eastman Johnson. It shows a typical extended family of the time, with several generations living in the same household and with the family members evidently sharing a strong sense of mutual involvement. The second picture is* Meet the Megabytes, *painted in 1986 by the American artist Kinuko Craft. It portrays a nuclear family of the modern age, consisting of parents and their dependent offspring— and with each member obviously "into" his or her own interests as an individual. This shift in loyalties—from obligations to kin toward self-fulfillment as individuals—has profoundly changed the nature of family life.*

4. *Advantages of small families.* In a modern society, children become an economic liability rather than an asset. The parents get no financial benefits from the vast expense of clothing, feeding, and educating their offspring: almost as soon as the young are able to earn a living, they leave home and prepare to form their own separate families. People therefore find it convenient to restrict the size of their households, preferring to live in independent units away from other relatives.

5. *Individualism.* An outstanding feature of industrial societies, and especially of the emerging postindustrial societies, is individualism. As we noted in Chapter 3 ("Culture"), people in these societies are increasingly concerned with self-fulfillment as a personal goal. Individual desires become more important than traditional obligations, and people expect personal freedom in their choice of mate or place of residence. Whether the issue is marriage or divorce, they ask: "What's in it for me?" rather than "What does my kin group expect me to do?"

Yet although the nuclear family is functional in modern society, it suffers from a number of dysfunctions as well—and this is the key to understanding some of its present difficulties. In the extended family, the individual could turn for support to an array of relatives. Today the married partners can turn only to each other, and sometimes demand more from one another than either can provide. If members of an extended family were for some reason unable to play their roles, other members could take them over. In the nuclear family, on the other hand, the death, prolonged illness, or unemployment of a breadwinner can throw the entire family into severe crisis. In the extended family, people rarely had expectations of romantic love with their spouses; marriage was a practical, common-sense affair. In the nuclear family, far higher expectations exist, and if they are not fulfilled—and often they cannot be— discontent and unhappiness may result. In the extended family, the old had a meaningful role, but they may have no role at all in the nuclear family.

Marriage and Family in America

"Love and marriage," an old popular song tells us, "go together like a horse and carriage." A compelling assumption in American society is that everyone will fall in love, will marry, will have children, and will have an emotionally satisfying lifetime relationship with the chosen partner. It is probably true that most of us fall in love at some point; it is certainly true that nearly all of us marry and have children; but it is likely that a great many of us—perhaps the majority—find that married life falls below our expectations. To find out what can go wrong and why, we must look in more detail at American family patterns and at romantic love, courtship, marriage, and marital breakdown and divorce.

The American Family

How does the "typical" American family fit into the patterns we outlined earlier? First, it is *monogamous:* Americans may marry only one person at a time. Second, it is generally *endogamous:* most people marry within their own racial, ethnic, religious, and class group. Third, the system is *neolocal,* with newlyweds almost always establishing a home of their own away from their families of orientation. Fourth, it is increasingly *egalitarian;* there are still strong patriarchal tendencies, but

wives are becoming much more assertive, and husbands more flexible, than they were even a decade ago. Fifth, the American family is *bilateral;* relatives of both husband and wife are regarded as kin, and property generally passes to both sons and daughters. There is one strong patrilineal element, however: both wife and children usually take the last name of the husband. And finally, the system is *nuclear,* although occasionally a grandparent or other relative may live with the family group.

There have always been exceptions to this typical pattern, however. Before the Civil War, for example, slaves were not allowed to marry, although they were encouraged to mate in order to breed future slaves. The Mormons practiced polygamy until 1896, when their home territory of Utah was admitted to the Union on condition that they accept monogamy as the only permissible marriage form. In the nineteenth century, several communes advocated and practiced free love, and similar communes proliferated for a while in the 1960s and early 1970s, when this lifestyle enjoyed popularity among young members of the "hippie" counterculture. Today, there remain many ethnic and social-class differences among American families. For example, lower-class families are more likely to have a female householder with no adult male present than are middle-class families; higher-income couples tend to have more egalitarian marriages than lower-income couples; Hispanic families tend to be more patriarchal than comparable non-Hispanic families. And, as we will see later, the black ghetto family has extraordinarily

Figure 13.7 *There have always been exceptions to the general American pattern of the monogamous nuclear family. The first illustration shows the separation of a mother and child during the days of slavery; the second, a satirical cartoon of the time, supposedly shows a Mormon husband bringing home an additional wife during the days when Mormons practiced polygamy.*

high rates of single-parent households, due largely to high rates of births to unwed mothers (Mindel and Habenstein, 1978; Schneider and Smith, 1978; Willie, 1981).

Romantic Love

The American family is supposed to be founded on the romantic love of the marital partners. Traces of a more pragmatic attitude persist in the American upper classes, where daughters are expected to marry "well"—that is, to a male who is eligible by reason of family background and earning potential. Most Americans, however, tend to look askance at anyone who marries for money or some other practical reason in which love plays no part.

Happily enough, romantic love defies a clinical definition. It is a different kind of love, though, from the love you have for your parents or your dog. It involves physical symptoms, such as pounding heart and sexual desire, and psychological symptoms, such as obsessive focus on one person and a disregard for any resulting social or economic risks. Our culture encourages us to look for this love—to find that "one and only," perhaps even through "love at first sight." The phenomenon of romantic love occurs when two people meet and find one another personally and physically attractive. They become mutually absorbed, start to behave in what may appear to be a flighty, even irrational manner, decide that they are right for one another, and may then enter a marriage whose success is expected to be guaranteed by their enduring passion. Behavior of this kind is portrayed and warmly endorsed throughout American popular culture, by books, magazines, comics, records, popular songs, movies, and TV.

Romantic love is a noble ideal, and it can certainly help provide a basis for the spouses to "live happily ever after." But since marriage can equally well be founded on much more practical considerations, why is romantic love of such importance in the modern world? The reason seems to be that it has the following basic functions in maintaining the institution of the nuclear family (Goode, 1959):

1. *Transfer of loyalties.* Romantic love helps the young partners to loosen their bonds with their family of orientation, a step that is essential if a new neolocal nuclear family is to be created. Their total absorption in one another facilitates a transfer of commitment from existing family and kin to a new family of procreation, something that would be unlikely to happen under the extended family system.

Figure 13.8 *Romantic love, captured in this idealized painting, is a culture trait found primarily in the industrialized societies of the world. Although Westerners take romantic love for granted, it is unknown in many other societies, where far more practical considerations determine who will marry whom. The painting is* The Storm *(1880), by the French artist Pierre Auguste Cot.*

2. *Emotional support.* Romantic love provides the couple with emotional support in the difficulties that they face in establishing a new life on their own. This love would not be so necessary in an extended family, where the relatives are able to confront problems cooperatively. In an extended family, in fact, romantic love might even be dysfunctional, for it could distract the couple from their wider obligations to other kin.

3. *Incentive to marriage.* Romantic love serves as a bait to lure people into marriage. In the extended family system of traditional societies, it is automatically assumed that people will marry, but in the modern world, people have considerable choice over whether they will get married or not. A contract to form a lifelong commitment to another

person is not necessarily a very tempting proposition, however: to some, the prospect may look more like a noose than like a bed of roses. Without feelings of romantic love, many people might have no incentive to marry.

To most of us, particularly to those who are in love, romantic love seems to be the most natural thing in the world, but sociological analysis shows that it is a purely cultural product, arising in certain societies for specific reasons. In a different time or in a different society, you might never fall in love, nor would you expect to.

Courtship and Marriage

A courtship system is essentially a marriage market. (The metaphor of the "market" may seem a little unromantic, but, in fact, the participants do attempt to "sell" their assets—physical appearance, personal charms, talents and interests, and career prospects.) In the matter of mate selection, different courtship systems vary according to how much choice they permit the individual. The United States probably allows more freedom of choice than any other society. A parent who attempts to interfere in the dating habits or marriage plans of a son or daughter is considered meddlesome and is more likely to alienate than persuade the young lover.

In this predominantly urban and anonymous society, young people—often with access to automobiles—have an exceptional degree of privacy in their courting. The practice of dating enables them to find out about one another, to improve their own interpersonal skills in the market, to experiment sexually if they so wish, and finally to select a marriage partner.

Who marries whom, then? Cupid's arrow, it turns out, does not strike at random. Despite the cultural emphasis on love as something mysterious and irrational, the selection of marital partners is more orderly and predictable than romantics might like to think. In general, the American mate-selection process produces **homogamy,** marriage between partners who share similar social characteristics. Among the characteristics that seem to attract people to one another are the following:

1. *Similar age.* Married partners tend to be of roughly the same age. Husbands are usually older than their wives, but this difference in age has been gradually declining throughout the century, from about 4 years in 1900 to about 2.1 years today.

2. *Social class.* Most people marry within their own social class. The reasons are obvious: we tend to live in class-segregated neighborhoods, to meet mostly people of the same class, and to share class-specific tastes and interests. Interclass marriages are relatively more common, however, among college students. When there are class differences in a marriage, it is most often the wife who marries upward.

3. *Religion.* Most marriages are between people sharing the same religious faith, although Protestant interdenominational marriages are fairly common. Many people change their religion to that of their partner before marriage.

4. *Education.* Husbands and wives generally have a similar educational level. The college campus is, of course, a marriage market in its own right, and college-educated people are especially likely to marry people who have a similar educational achievement.

5. *Racial and ethnic background.* Members of racial and ethnic groups are more likely to marry within their own group than outside it. In particular, interracial marriages are extremely rare. Until the 1960s, several states had laws prohibiting interracial marriages, and such marriages still attract some social disapproval. Interracial marriages between blacks and whites are particularly unusual; in the majority of these cases, the husband is black and the wife white.

6. *Propinquity.* Spatial nearness is a common feature of those who marry one another, for the obvious reason that people are likely to have more social interaction and similarities with neighbors, coworkers, or fellow students than with others who are physically more distant.

Marital Breakdown

The divorce rate in the United States is believed to be the highest in the world, and statistics on the subject are often quoted as conclusive evidence of the decay of the family. This evidence indicates that about 50 percent of recent marriages will end in divorce, the average duration of these ill-fated unions being around 7 years.

Divorce constitutes official social recognition that a marriage has failed, and it can be a traumatic experience for all concerned. Most states now offer a "no fault" divorce on grounds of simple incompatibility, but there is still room for fierce resentment over the custody of offspring and child-support payments. Children are present in over 70 percent of the families that break up through divorce: more than a million children are involved every year. The children inevitably suffer through the divorce of their parents—particularly during the first year or two—but many people believe that it may be even more emotionally disturbing for them to remain in a home where the marriage is deeply unhappy. Emotionally, both divorcing parties may be in for a difficult time. American social life is tailored to the needs of couples, and divorced partners may experience great loneliness, isolation, and feelings of inadequacy. Divorce ruptures one's personal universe; it is no coincidence that men are much more likely to be fired from their jobs after divorce, nor that the death rate for divorced people is significantly higher than that for married people, at all age levels (Weiss, 1975; Emery et al., 1984).

The ex-wife may face severe economic problems, especially if she has to raise young children. In the past, when most wives were not expected to work outside the home, courts frequently awarded alimony to divorced women; but now that women are considered capable of earning their own living, they receive alimony in only about 15 percent of divorce settlements. Courts award child custody to mothers rather than to fathers in 90 percent of cases, however, and usually require that the fathers provide child support. But many divorced women find that they have low earning power—particularly if they have spent their entire married lives as housewives and have no job skills or experience—and more than half of all divorced fathers default on their child-support payments. In one study, Lenore Weitzman (1985) found that divorced women with dependent children suffered a 73 percent drop in living standards after the divorce, while divorced men experienced a 42 percent increase. More than half of American children in families where the father is absent live below the poverty line, and many single mothers become long-term welfare recipients.

Who gets divorced? The social characteristics of divorce-prone partners have been well established. Divorces are especially common among urban couples, among those who marry very young, among those who marry after only short or shallow acquaintance, and among those whose relatives and friends disapprove of the marriage. In general, the people who are most likely to get divorced are those who, statistically, would be considered the least likely to marry. And the greater the wife's ability to support herself, the more likely

MARRIAGE AND DIVORCE RATES: 1940 – 1985
Per 1,000 population

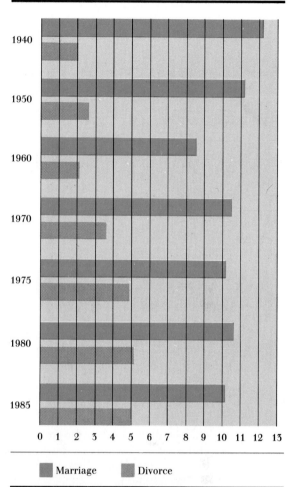

SOURCE: U.S. Bureau of the Census, 1986.

Figure 13.9 *As this chart shows, the rate of divorce has increased steadily since 1940, while the rate of marriage has fluctuated during this time. The divorce rate is now one-half the marriage rate. This ratio is distorted, however, by the fact that the population that is eligible for divorce is a huge one, containing everybody who is married, while the population that is eligible for marriage is much smaller, consisting primarily of unmarried people between the ages of eighteen and thirty. The ratio is therefore not as alarming as it seems to be.*

Different social factors influence the marriage and divorce rate. The divorce rate may be pushed up, for example, by laws that make divorces easier to get, or by better employment opportunities for women. The marriage rate, on the other hand, may be influenced by such factors as the proportion of young adults in the population, or by current social attitudes toward alternatives to marriage, such as living together.

she is to leave an unhappy marriage. Partners who have been married before are more likely to become involved in subsequent divorce. Most divorces take place within the first few years of marriage—half within the first seven years—and the longer a marriage has lasted, the less likely it is to end in divorce (Carter and Glick, 1976; Goode, 1982).

Causes of Marital Breakdown

There are many causes for the collapse of modern American marriages, but the following seem to be the main ones.

Stress on the Nuclear Family

As we have seen, the nuclear family is highly vulnerable if the breadwinner is for any reason unwilling or unable to meet economic obligations. This is especially true in the United States; in most other advanced industrialized societies the state offers much more support to the family in the form of family allowances, preferential housing, child-care programs, free childhood medical and dental care, and free college education. In addition, the spouses in a nuclear family have a very strong mutual dependency and may make heavy demands on one another for emotional support. The failure of one partner to meet the expectations of the other jeopardizes the marriage in a way that would hardly be possible under the extended family system.

The Fading of Romantic Love

Americans are thoroughly socialized into the expectation that romantic love will "conquer all" and make their marriage happy ever after. But the heady joys of romantic love are usually short-lived, and the excitement of the earlier relationship is lessened or even lost in the daily routines of job and housework, diapers and dishwashing, mortgages and bills. This does not mean that the partners no longer love one another; it is just that their love is likely to be of a different kind. It can be mature, companionable, intimate, committed, and deeply fulfilling—but Americans are not socialized to recognize or appreciate this change. Believing that romantic love is the only possible basis for a successful marriage, many people lose faith in their marriages and may start looking for romance elsewhere.

Figure 13.10

"Lost in the magic of your kiss, I forgot about the potato salad. Bring home a quart."

Drawing by Geo. Price; © 1976
The New Yorker Magazine, Inc.

The Changing Role of Women

In the past, the role of the wife in an American marriage was assumed to be that of housekeeper, child-rearer, and nurturant supporter of a husband who was active in the world beyond the home. More and more American women are rejecting this role, and in doing so are challenging the established structure of the nuclear family. Women are no longer confined to the home for much of their lives through pregnancy and the care of infants. The average family now has only two children, and the average woman now has her last child in her late twenties. Traditional family norms make little provision for the woman who wants an independent career, and even less for the family in which the wife earns more than the husband and becomes the primary breadwinner. The growing economic independence of women makes it much easier for them to divorce their mates, and it challenges the role relationship on which the nuclear family has been based (Kanter, 1978; Rubin, 1979).

Sexual Permissiveness

The development and widespread availability of contraceptives have potentially separated two quite different functions of sexual relations—procreation and recreation. In the days when intercourse was likely to lead to pregnancy, there was a strong practical incentive for sex to be restricted to marital partners, for our society makes little provision for the proper care of children born to unmarried mothers. But if the prospect of pregnancy is removed, many of the inhibitions against the use of sex for recreation disappear also. The nuclear family is founded on an assumption of monogamous fidelity, but permissiveness encourages many people to look outside their marriages for sexual satisfaction or, if they are unmarried, to have sexual experience before marriage. This experience gives the partners a standard by which to measure the performance of their spouses—an opportunity that the partners in a traditional virgin marriage did not have—and the spouses may be found wanting. Changing sexual norms inevitably threaten a family system based on the assumption that the partners will have an exclusive and mutually gratifying sexual relationship.

Current Issues

The American family is changing in response to changes in such areas as the economy and personal morality. The impact of these changes is illustrated in two issues of current concern: the black family, and abortion.

The Black Family

The sharpest divergence from the standard American family pattern is undoubtedly among poorer black people. In 1965, when more than a quarter of black families were headed by women, Daniel Patrick Moynihan (a sociologist who later became a U.S. senator) wrote a report on the plight of the black family. Moynihan claimed that an unstable black family structure was creating a "tangle of pathology" that perpetuated welfare dependency and other problems. The report caused immediate controversy, and Moynihan was widely accused of "blaming the victim" for faults that lay in the racism of the wider society. For years thereafter, both black and white observers were reluctant to raise the issue for fear of reviving the furor.

Yet in the two decades that have passed since then, the situation of the black family has grown worse—so much so that black leaders now regard it as one of the most serious challenges to their community's future. The percentage of black children living in homes with a single parent (usually the mother) rose from 36 percent in 1970 to 51 percent in 1980 and then to 59 percent in 1985. In that year, just over half of the black births in the United States were illegitimate, and in some ghetto areas the rate was much higher. As we noted in Chapter 10 ("Social Stratification"), families headed by women, and particularly by minority women, are especially vulnerable to poverty. Today, more than half of all black births are to teenage mothers, who frequently drop out of school and become welfare dependents in order to raise their children. As a result of these trends, one out of every two black children was living in poverty in 1985.

Of course, this predicament is not typical of all black families. The family pattern of a substantial part of the black population—particularly the third that has now entered the middle class—conforms to the American standard. The real problem lies in the self-perpetuating desolation of the ghetto, among people who are separated culturally, socially, and economically from the black mainstream, as well as from the wider society. This breakdown seems to have begun relatively recently; the black family was intact well into this century, and even when Moynihan wrote his report, 70 percent of black children were living in two-parent households.

The plight of the ghetto family occurs in the context of wider patterns of racial and class inequality. When, earlier in this century, rural blacks in the South were displaced from their jobs by the mechanization of agriculture, they moved to the industrial cities of the North in search of work. But in the years that followed, unskilled manufacturing jobs gradually disappeared from the inner cities, while barriers of prejudice, discrimination, and poor education kept the ghetto residents and their children from higher-level jobs and from the suburbs. Unemployment rates among blacks have consistently been over twice as high as for whites, and this joblessness is concentrated in the urban ghettoes. The contemporary result is an "underclass" of chronically jobless black men and youths, many of whom fall into a subculture of despair centered on crime, drug abuse, and promiscuity. In this context, children are having children, and thus perpetuating the cycle of educational and economic disadvantage for yet another generation.

Figure 13.11 *Although millions of black families are intact, a large and growing proportion consist of a single mother with her dependent children. Because such families are economically and socially vulnerable, this trend has become a major social problem in the black community.*

Although the breakdown of the ghetto family is unquestionably rooted in a history of racism and repression, it seems to have taken on a life of its own. Most black leaders now recognize that these problems must be talked about and openly confronted—and that solutions will require more than government intervention, for they must be based on the involvement and commitment of the black community itself (Willie, 1981; Cummings, 1983; Loury, 1985; Holman, 1985; Norton, 1985).

The Abortion Dilemma

Few issues in recent years have so divided Americans as has the morality of abortion. Until 1973, the practice was generally illegal in the United States except under limited conditions—primarily where the health of the mother or the unborn child was at serious risk. However, "backstreet" abortions by private physicians or even by untrained practitioners were fairly common. In that year the Supreme Court decided, in the case of *Roe* v. *Wade,* that American women do have the right to abortion if, for whatever reason, they do not wish to bear the child. This right is not absolute, however, for the court recognized that the unborn child seems to become more human as it develops, over the course of pregnancy, from a cluster of cells to an embryo and then to a fetus. On the basis of the medical evidence available at the time, the court divided pregnancy into three periods of three months each, or trimesters. In the first trimester, the mother is entitled to abortion on demand. In the second trimester, the right to abortion remains, but is subject to regulation by each state. In the third trimester—when abortions are more difficult to perform and when the fetus is potentially viable, or capable of independent life—all abortions are barred unless the health or life of the mother is in danger.

Far from ending the controversy over abortion, the Supreme Court decision inflamed it. The aftermath of the decision was an explosion in the number of abortions in the United States: over 15 million have been performed since 1973. By 1985, abortions were being performed at the rate of about 1.6 million a year, or more than 4,000 a day. About one in every four pregnancies in America is now terminated through abortion, and in some areas, like New York State, there are almost as many abortions as live births. In short, abortion is being used as a means of after-the-fact birth control. To some people, this is a matter of no particular significance; to others, it is little short of mass murder.

At the root of the controversy is a basic value judgment about the human status of the fetus. If the fetus is considered a baby, then abortion is a form of killing; if it is considered a mere collection of cells and tissue, then abortion is a morally neutral surgical procedure. But the status of the fetus is inherently ambiguous: it is neither self-evidently a human being nor self-evidently just tissue (for if these matters were self-evident, there would be little disagreement about abortion). On the one hand, the fetus is not a human being in the usual sense, for it is generally not viable. Indeed, no society treats the fetus as human; for example, if the mother accidentally miscarries, the fetus is not given a funeral, but is simply disposed of like any other tissue. On the other hand, the fetus is not like just any other tissue, such as discarded nail or hair clippings. The fetus is potentially a human being, one that might become as alive and unique as you who read this page now. The conflicting value judgments about abortion stem from this fundamental ambiguity in the status of the fetus.

The question is compounded by a related issue, the right of a woman to control her own body. Many women feel that a decision about abortion should be a strictly personal one, and they deeply resent other people insisting that they should bear a child they do not want to have. But here, too, there are ambiguities. Half the genes in the fetus were contributed by the father, and although the woman must bear the child, society may make the father responsible for the child's support for nearly two decades thereafter. If the father waives his responsibilities—for example, by

deserting the mother—then of course he has no further rights in the matter. But if he accepts his responsibilities and wants the child born, what are his rights in relation to the mother's right to control her body? And, for those who believe that the fetus is human, there is a third party present: the mother is controlling not only her own body, but somebody else's potential body and life (Shostak et al., 1983).

Other abortion-related issues go beyond the immediate concerns of the parents. Some see abortion as the thin end of a wedge leading to euthanasia, or the "mercy killing" of defective newborns and infirm old people. Some point out that the global population is soaring uncontrollably at a time when we cannot adequately feed hundreds of millions of people already alive. Some argue that because abortion will occur whether it is legal or not, it is better that it take place legally and under proper medical supervision. Some claim that the welfare expenditures and other costs of raising millions of unwanted and often illegitimate children must be taken into account in any decisions about abortion. Some have firm personal opinions about abortion, but are unwilling to impose their views on others who may have different views. And as time goes on, the legal, ethical, and medical complexities have not abated. New medical technology is making it possible to keep fetuses alive ever earlier in the course of pregnancy, while at

Figure 13.12 *The question of whether a woman should have the right to an abortion—and if so, under what conditions she should have that* *right—has become one of the most emotional and divisive issues in American society, with no end to the controversy in sight.*

the same time making it safer for a woman to have an abortion ever later in pregnancy—raising such difficult questions, for example, as what to do with an aborted fetus that turns out to be viable but probably defective.

In a study of people who actively campaign for or against the right to abortion, Kristen Luker (1985) found sharp differences between the social characteristics of "prolife" and "prochoice" women. The prolife activists generally had less education and income than the prochoice activists, but were more likely to be married and to have more children. Prolife women believed that traditional gender roles reflect deep natural differences between men and women and that parenthood is a natural function rather than a social choice. The prochoice women believed that gender roles are more flexible, were more permissive in their attitudes toward sexuality, and felt that choice over abortion was a basic freedom that was important for the quality of their lives.

Not surprisingly, opinion polls show public confusion on the issue of abortion. The great majority of the population supports abortion in cases of rape, incest, or a threat to the mother's health, but support for a mother's right to abortion on demand fluctuates between just over and just under half of the population. Even so, a 1985 *Newsweek* poll found that 40 percent of Americans wonder whether their own position on abortion is right—regardless of whether they oppose or approve it. In any event, the American abortion rate, which is believed to be the highest in the Western world, must be seen in the context of social changes in American premarital, marital, and family life—particularly the climate of sexual permissiveness and the sense of individualism that leads people to make decisions primarily in terms of their personal desires rather than of traditional norms (Wennberg, 1985; Paige, 1985; Harrison, 1985).

The Future of the Family

The alterations that the American family is undergoing cannot be halted by laws or sermons, for they are the products of much more encompassing social and economic developments. The changes in the family are perhaps even more extensive than is generally realized. For example, not only is the family consisting of a husband who works and a wife who stays home to care for their two dependent children no longer the norm; it exists in fewer than one of every ten households in the United States. One reason for the demise of that family is the sharp increase in the number of women in the work force. In 1940, only 27 percent of adult women worked; today, over 50 percent do, and most of these have children under the age of eighteen. The two-paycheck, dual-career marriage is now typical (Pepitone-Rockwell, 1980; Bergman, 1986).

In this climate of change, what may become of the American family? We can gain some insights into its future by looking at trends in the institution, and particularly at some alternatives to the established nuclear pattern that already exist. Some of these alternatives are relatively frequent; some are quite rare; and several overlap one another (Stinnet and Birdsong, 1978; Murstein, 1978; Levitan and Belous, 1981).

Single-Parent Families

The single-parent family is now emerging as the most common alternative to the nuclear unit. In 1960, 8 percent of families had one parent; in 1970, 13 percent; in 1980, 21 percent; in 1985, 26 percent. High divorce and illegitimacy rates are likely to push this figure up even further, and it is expected that half the children born in the 1980s will spend part of their childhood living with one parent. The main source of the rapid increase in single-parent families is a soaring illegitimacy rate, which has leaped from 4 percent of all births in 1950 to over 20 percent today—representing some 700,000 babies annually. About three-quarters of unmarried women are now sexually active—and most do not regularly practice birth control. Not too surprisingly, one in every four American women gets pregnant by the age of nineteen, and 80 percent of these pregnancies are premarital—a statistic without parallel in the modern world. Twenty years ago, most unmarried mothers either entered a "shotgun" wedding with the father or gave their babies away for adoption. Today, fewer women are willing to enter such marriages (although a quarter of all brides are either pregnant or already mothers by the time they reach the altar), and over 90 percent of those who have illegitimate babies keep and raise them. About 90 percent of all one-parent households are headed by women, and more than half of them live below the poverty line—compared with only 18 percent of families with both parents present. If current trends persist in the future, half of all the households in America could be headed by a single parent by the end of this century.

Cohabitation

Although it might have caused a minor neighborhood scandal a few decades ago, cohabitation, or openly "living together," is now a relatively common type of domestic and sexual arrangement, particularly among young people. The number of unmarried people of opposite sex sharing a household tripled between 1970 and 1983 and now comprises nearly 2 million adults, 60 percent of them under thirty-five years of age (Bureau of the Census, 1984). Cohabitation is particularly popular among college students; surveys have shown that about a quarter of undergraduates have tried this arrangement, and that under suitable conditions the great majority of college students would be willing to live together with someone of the opposite sex. Cohabitation has some similarities with marriage in that the partners have considerable affection for, and commitment to, one another, and their sexual relationship is usually an exclusive one. For whatever reason, however, they are wary of making the formal commitment of marriage. In some cases cohabitation seems to be a modern form of "going steady"; in others it is more like a "trial marriage," in which the partners explicitly decide to test their compatibility before taking the plunge into married life. (In fact, about a third of cohabiting couples eventually do marry; most of the rest separate within two or three years.) Since 1977, courts in several states have ruled that an agreement by unmarried partners to share their property is valid; if the arrangement breaks up, one partner can sue the other for part of the property and even for maintenance (Clayton and Voss, 1977; Simenauer and Carroll, 1982; Blumstein and Swartz, 1983).

Serial Monogamy

A growing number of people marry more than once; in fact, the great majority of divorced partners marry someone else within a few years of divorcing. Now that divorces are easier to get and provoke less social disapproval than ever before, many people embark on a career of "serial" marriages, marrying, divorcing, remarrying, perhaps divorcing again. Indeed, the more often people have been divorced, the more likely it is that their subsequent marriage will end in the same way. Jessie Bernard (1973) suggests that serial marriage makes having several spouses more common in America than polygamy does in other societies. Serial monogamy allows the partners to maintain a commitment to marriage, if not to one spouse.

Reconstituted Families

Divorce and remarriage may create a "reconstituted family"—one that is put together, as it were, from the fragments of previous families. These families, which are becoming increasingly common, face special difficulties, most obviously that of establishing appropriate relationships among step-parents and step-children, between the children of one spouse and the children of the other spouse, and, eventually perhaps, between various new half-brothers and half-sisters and the existing children. With a certain effort of the imagination, we can see that serial monogamy, leading to two or even more reconstituted marriages of two or more different sets of partners, can produce a very complex family tree indeed, and can create classes of relatives for which our language does not even have words (Duberman, 1975; Cherlin, 1981).

Figure 13.13

'Dearly beloved, we are gathered here yet again . . .'

Drawing by Opie; © 1980
The New Yorker Magazine, Inc.

Childless Couples

In the postindustrial United States, with its growing emphasis on personal self-fulfillment, an increasing number of married couples are deliberately choosing not to have children. On the whole, these couples are more likely than other couples to be first-born, highly educated, and career-oriented. Often they have married late, or have been married before, and are less traditional about sharing household chores. It seems that the decision not to have children is usually a gradual one, rather than a firm commitment at the time of marriage. A series of postponements ends with a final determination that having children would interfere too much with other goals and interests. Currently, about 5 percent of the married women in the United States have decided not to have children. Many more couples, of course, are childless because of infertility (Yorburg, 1983).

Communes

There have been many experiments in the United States aimed at establishing communal groups whose members may share both sexual relations and the task of raising children. There is great variation in the norms that operate within these communes. A few insist on free love, but in most of them the adults tend to pair off with one another, at least for periods of a few weeks or months. The limited evidence available suggests that "group marriages" are highly unstable (Ellis, 1970; Constantine, 1978), and despite the range of family systems in other cultures, anthropologists have never found a society that has institutionalized such a system. Communes with rather more restrictive sexual patterns have persisted for years and even decades, however. Although the appeal of communes seems to be rather limited, there is little doubt that they do represent an alternative family system (Melville, 1972; Muncy, 1974).

"Open" Marriage

Some spouses want to make many of the mutual commitments implied by marriage, but are unwilling to accept certain of the obligations that marriage traditionally imposes. Their response is the "open" marriage—essentially, one in which the partners agree to certain flexible arrangements, sometimes including the right of each to have extramarital sexual relationships. In some cases the spouses draw up a formal contract specifying what the various rights and responsibilities of the part-

ners are to be—a self-consciously "do-it-yourself" approach to the problem of how to modify existing family patterns to meet the needs of changing lifestyles. A few spouses in "open" marriages participate in "swinging," the mutually-agreed-to exchange of partners for the purposes of periodic extramarital sex. This practice, which is organized through networks that advertise in specialized magazines, seems to appeal to people who wish to preserve their marriage, but who are dissatisfied with the sexual exclusiveness of their relationship (Murstein, 1978a; Knapp and Whitehurst, 1978).

Gay Couples and Gay-Parent Families

About 10 percent of the population is believed to be predominantly homosexual, although most of these people also have some heterosexual experience and many actually marry. The great majority of gay men and lesbian women, however, form stable, long-lasting relationships with a person of the same sex at some time in their lives. Changing attitudes have made these unions far more socially acceptable than in the past, and, in fact, some churches are now performing weddings for gay couples, although these marriages have no legal force. A more significant change, perhaps, is the willingness of many courts to grant custody of children to a gay parent—usually the mother. In some cases, families with two gay adults are created, usually when a divorced lesbian mother forms a relationship with another woman. For several years, moreover, social welfare agencies in New York and other large cities have been placing orphaned or runaway gay teenage boys—who are unwelcome in heterosexual foster homes—in the custody of gay males, usually couples. One interesting possibility, incidentally, is suggested by the rapid advances in the availability and technology of artificial insemination: if they so choose, lesbian women may be able to become mothers without having had any heterosexual relationships at all (Frank, 1974; Tanner, 1978; Bell and Weinberg, 1978).

Remaining Single

A growing number of people are choosing to remain single. By 1985, more than a quarter of all American households consisted of people living alone or with nonrelatives. In that year, over 20 million people were living alone—a 90 percent increase in fifteen years. A major reason for this increase, in addition to the divorce rate, is a growing tendency for young adults to postpone marriage. The average age of first marriage is now 25.5 for men—the highest age since the turn of the century—and 23.3 for women—the highest age on record. Couples are now taking their vows, on average, two years later than they did fifteen years ago. Although a majority of single adults will eventually marry or remarry, it seems likely that there will be an increase in the proportion of the population remaining single throughout life, from about 5 percent today to perhaps 10 percent or more by the end of the century. For those who do not want children and do not see marriage as a prerequisite for sexual experience, married life may seem to offer few advantages, and in fact most young people who live alone cite freedom and independence as the main reasons for their choice. It is important to recognize that remaining single is not necessarily a matter of never having found the "right" partner; for many people, it is a deliberate decision about personal lifestyle (Libby, 1978; P. Stein, 1981; Cargan, 1982).

What conclusions can we draw from our survey of the American family? The existence of alternative patterns does not mean that the nuclear family is about to disappear. After all, three-quarters of the population aged 25 to 65 is married,

and about 90 percent of all Americans are expected to marry at some time. Even the divorced are still deeply committed to marriage—their marriage rates at all ages is higher than that for single or widowed persons. Four out of five children are still born in wedlock, and four out of five still live in a two-parent nuclear family. Divorce rates seem to have stopped rising, and birth rates seem to have stopped dropping. Clearly, the nuclear family is not about to disappear (Levitan and Belous, 1981; Bernard, 1982; Masnick and Bane, 1983).

What is happening, though, is that the United States is increasingly tolerating a variety of alternative marriage and family styles. The reasons are linked, primarily, to the nature of modern America as a postindustrial society. As we noted in Chapter 4 ("Society"), a hallmark of such a society is its economic and cultural diversity, combined with a highly developed sense of individualism. In this environment, people tend to make decisions about marriage, divorce, abortion, child-rearing, and the like in terms of what they, personally, want—rather than in terms of traditional moralities, obligations to kin, or the other impersonal pressures that previous generations unquestioningly accepted. Pursuing their own vision of self-fulfillment, or responding to the social and economic predicament in which they find themselves, many Americans are modifying the family system to suit their individual needs.

Significantly enough, some of the variant family patterns are becoming recognized, formally or informally, by such official agencies as the Bureau of the Census, the state and federal courts, the Internal Revenue Service, and government welfare departments. It could be, then, that the United States is moving to a situation in which variants on the nuclear family simply come to be taken for granted. No other society has ever endorsed more than one family form at a time, but no other society has been both as heterogeneous and as rapidly changing. Yet the family in the sense that we defined it earlier—a relatively permanent group of related people, living together, forming an economic unit, and sharing responsibility for the offspring—is here to stay as a permanent part of human society. Of the 87 million households in America in 1985, three-quarters contained families of one kind or another. As the social and economic factors that affect all institutions continue to change, the nuclear family will doubtless respond with further adaptations, but it seems destined to remain the preferred and dominant system in the societies of the modern world.

THE CHANGING AMERICAN FAMILY

	1965	1980	1985
Women working outside the home (percentage of all woman 16 and over)	36.7	51.1	54.7
Fertility rate (number of children per average woman)	2.9	1.8	1.8
Single-parent families (percentage of all families with children under 18)	10.1	19.5	22.2
Premarital births (percentage of all births)	7.7	18.4	21.5
Living alone (percentage of all households occupied by single person)	15.0	22.6	23.7

SOURCE: U.S. Bureau of the Census; National Center for Health Statistics.

Figure 13.14 *This table highlights some of the trends that are changing the American family as the end of the century approaches.*

Summary

1.   The family is the most basic of all social institutions. It consists of a relatively permanent group whose members are related by ancestry, marriage, or adoption, who live together and form an economic unit, and whose adult members assume responsibility for the young. The family is expected to be formed through a marriage which legitimates any offspring. The family is part of a wider network of relatives, or kin.

2.   The family is universal partly because it is highly functional. The main functions of the family are the regulation of sexual behavior, the replacement of members, socialization, care and protection, social placement, and emotional support.

3.   Conflict theorists emphasize that the family is the main institution in which male dominance of females is expressed, and they argue that the extraordinary degree of violence in the family is a symptom of its underlying tension.

4.   Family patterns vary widely from one society to another. All these patterns can be analyzed in terms of their variation along six basic dimensions: number of partners, partner preference, residence pattern, authority relationships, descent and inheritance, and family form.

5.   Industrialism and urbanization have been accompanied by a worldwide transformation of the family; the extended family is dysfunctional in the modern environment and has given way to the nuclear form. The nuclear family, however, experiences distinctive problems resulting from the intense reliance that the husband and wife have on one another.

6.   The American family is monogamous, endogamous, neolocal, increasingly egalitarian, bilateral, and nuclear, although there are some class and racial variations on this pattern. Americans place high emphasis on romantic love, which is functional for a nuclear family system. American marriage tends to be homogamous: people generally marry others with similar social characteristics.

7.   The American divorce rate is very high; the partners most likely to get divorced are those whose social characteristics differ markedly. The main causes of divorce are stress on the nuclear family, the fading of romantic love after marriage, the changing role of women, and certain effects of sexual permissiveness.

8.   Current issues in American family life are the plight of the black ghetto family, which suffers high rates of illegitimacy and poverty, and the moral dilemma over abortion.

9.   There are a number of existing alternatives to traditional marriage and family arrangements, such as single-parent families, cohabitation, serial monogamy, reconstituted families, childless couples, communes, "open" marriage, gay couples and gay-parent families, and remaining single. The great majority of Americans continue to marry, however, and although a range of alternatives is likely to be tolerated in the context of the growing individualism of postindustrial America, the nuclear family seems to be here to stay.

Important Terms

family (348)	endogamy (354)
family of orientation (349)	patrilocal residence (354)
family of procreation (349)	matrilocal residence (354)
marriage (349)	neolocal residence (354)
legitimate birth (349)	patriarchy (354)
illegitimate birth (349)	matriarchy (354)
kinship (349)	egalitarian marriage (355)
incest taboo (352)	patrilineal system (355)
monogamy (354)	matrilineal system (355)
polygamy (354)	bilateral system (355)
polygyny (354)	extended family (355)
polyandry (354)	nuclear family (355)
exogamy (354)	homogamy (360)

Suggested Readings

BERNARD, JESSIE. *The Future of Marriage.* 2nd ed. New Haven: Yale University Press, 1982.

A lively discussion of current and future changes in marriage and the family.

BLUMSTEIN, PHILIP, and PEPPER SCHWARTZ. *American Couples.* New York: Morrow, 1983.

An interesting survey of contemporary American couples—straight and gay, married and cohabitating—structured around the role of money, work, and sex in their lives.

GELLES, RICHARD J., and CLAIRE PEDRICK CORNELL. *Intimate Violence in Families.* Beverly Hills, Calif.: Sage, 1985.

A good overview of current theory and research on family violence, written by two of the leading researchers in the field.

HENSLIN, JAMES M. (ed). *Marriage and Family in a Changing Society.* New York: Free Press, 1985.

An excellent collection of short sociological articles covering all aspects of marital and family life.

LASCH, CHRISTOPHER. *Haven in a Heartless World: The Family Besieged.* New York: Basic Books, 1977.

A controversial book in which the author attributes many problems of modern society to the breakdown of the family.

SAXON, LLOYD. *The Individual, Marriage, and the Family.* 6th ed. Belmont, Calif.: Wadsworth, 1985.

A useful general introduction to the sociology of marriage and family.

WANNBERG, ROBERT N. *Life in the Balance: Exploring the Abortion Controversy.* New York: Eerdmans, 1985.

A reasoned analysis of some of the issues raised by the abortion dilemma.

YORBURG, BETTY. *Families and Societies: Survival or Extinction?* New York: Columbia University Press, 1983.

An excellent portrait and analysis of the changes that are taking place in family life, both around the world and in the United States.

Courtship and Marriage Among the Tiwi

CHERRY AND CHARLES LINDHOLM

The Tiwi are a hunting and gathering people living on a remote island off the Australian coast. This account of their norms of sexual behavior, courtship, and marriage points to the extraordinary contrast between our own family norms and those of preindustrial peoples.

Moving quickly between the trees, the women lead the young girl away from the bush camp, where they have been staying in isolation during her first menstruation, and wend their way to another camp in a small clearing. . . .

Soon the women and the girl reach the second campsite and emerge from the bush. The men are waiting. The girl at once lies down on the ground, feigning sleep. Her father, a dignified man in his fifties, steps forward and places an intricately carved ceremonial spear between her legs. He then hands the spear to another man who embraces it as though it were a woman and addresses it as "wife." This man, only a few years younger than her father, has become by this ritual the girl's son-in-law, the legal husband of all her future daughters!

This unique rite, which combines a puberty ceremony with a marriage contract for the pubescent girl's as-yet-unborn daughters (there is no other marriage ceremony), is enacted by the Tiwi people of Melville Island . . . Separated from Australia by a dangerous strait, the Tiwi have pursued their own separate evolution since they came or were blown here, perhaps from Southeast Asia, at least 17,000 years ago.

Until very recently, the Tiwi lived as hunters and gatherers in a region of relative plenty. Originally, they were divided into nine bands of 100 to 300 persons, each controlling a part of the 2,240 square miles of Melville Island. But although people identify with their territorial band, the main unit of cooperation and daily activity is the household. This is the group that lives together, forages together and shares food. The larger households may consist of an elder man with his wives, children and various relatives, perhaps 25 people in all. Women dig yams with their sticks and collect the plentiful nuts of palm trees. Together with the young men, they forage for oysters, cockles, eggs, snails, and hunt bandicoots, lizards, tree rats and carpet snakes. By custom, the men hunt the creatures of the sea and air, such as geese and crocodiles. The work of women and young men provides by far the largest part of the food supply, and the elder men, who have many wives—the record, 29—as well as daughters and sons-in-law, can live in leisure on what they provide. Thus, as many as 50 people may camp together. But a small household need not live within such a camp to survive, and even a man alone can easily forage enough to provide for himself. None need fear starvation on Melville.

Within [their] . . . simple and almost arcadian setting, an amazingly complex family system has developed, which unites matrilineal descent (tracing the lineage through the mother only) with cross-generational marriage, and which revolves around one very straightforward premise: All the women, regardless of age, must be married. Because of this fundamental rule, the newly menstruating girl is introduced to her son-in-law. His presence is guarantee of his intentions, and he henceforth becomes a constant presence in his mother-in-law's camp, where his duty is to provide her with food and support. In return, all her daughters are pledged to him as future wives. The relationship between the two is lifelong, but should he fail in his duties, he may be stripped of his rights.

The new mother-in-law was, of course, also married before she was born, as her mother went through the same puberty-betrothal rites. The young girl's husband, an elderly man, is at her menstrual ceremony. He now pursues his wife, catches her and sits her down beneath a tree. He and his brothers hurl spears at the tree, which represents her, perhaps in imitation of the sexual act that will lead to her impregnation. The brothers, by participating in this rite, stake their claim over the girl should her husband die.

The ritual ends and the girl returns to the main camp. In the flickering firelight, she contemplates the sleeping form of her husband on the opposite side of the campfire. They will sleep apart in this way and have no sexual relations until after her fourth menstrual period; at that time, she will no longer be regarded as a girl but as a young woman. She remembers the night, two years before, when her father took her to her husband's campfire and informed her that this man was her husband and she would sleep there from now on. She was not afraid. Her three older sisters were also his wives and had been sleeping with him for some time. They had told her that he was a kind and gentle old man. According to custom, her husband had deflowered her with his finger and then, gradually and patiently, had initiated her into sex; it had been a whole year before they had actual intercourse. The girl believes that the sexual activity with her husband is the sole cause of her present transformation from girlhood to womanhood; her menstruation and the development of her breasts and bodily hair are all the result of sexual intercourse with this man. "He grew me up," she thinks with gratitude.

Her fourth period ends and she

officially becomes a young woman. One stage of her life is over. Now she is held totally responsible for her own actions. She is no longer a pupil, neither economically nor sexually, and is expected to contribute as an adult to the camp's food supplies and take an active part on ceremonial occasions. Her position within the household, however, is not one of much prestige; she has as yet produced no children. Her husband's senior wife, who is old enough to be her mother and who in fact fulfills the role of mother-teacher to the younger wives, runs the household with a practiced expertise, organizing the gathering of food, delegating jobs and generally supervising all domestic activities, including the rearing of the children. The children themselves make no distinction between their actual mothers and their mothers' co-wives, calling every woman "mother." If one woman has too little milk to feed her infant, another woman (often a sister co-wife) will also feed the child.

After some time, the young woman realizes that she is pregnant. . . . [When] she has produced a child, the young mother is regarded as an equal among the other women in the camp. She may now express her opinions and give advice. Moreover, she has given birth to a girl and thus gained esteem in the eyes of both her husband and son-in-law. The latter is pleased because his mother-in-law has fulfilled her part of the contract made at her puberty ceremony and has provided him with a wife. Her husband is glad because when his daughter reaches puberty he will have the right to make the marriage contract between her unborn daughters and the man of his choice. The young mother herself is also happy, because now she has begun to gain status within the community and can look forward to her power increasing as she produces more children.

Her future will include a succession of husbands, since there is a wide age gap between men and their young wives. These new marriages of the young widow with other husbands bring to the fore the basic concern of Tiwi society: the prestige and honor gained through the control of women's marriages. The central issue in Tiwi marriages is not sex but the establishment of a man's authority over his wives and the regulation of the marriages of their daughters and daughters' daughters. At each successive marriage, various individuals dispute about their rights to the girl; the girl's "father" (the man married to her mother) negotiates with her brothers over whom she should be given to; her dead husband's brothers enter in as well, demanding she be given to them. Each seeks advantage for his own prestige. A man who is able to control the marriages of many women will, in turn, be rewarded with many wives from the grateful recipients, for women are not given without a promise of a return. He will then begin accumulating wives and will become a great man, a man of renown. The woman, too, as she becomes older and more respected, acquires some voice in her marriages; no woman can be married to someone she dislikes.

In their efforts to gain wives and indebted in-laws, the Tiwi exemplify a phenomenon that is characteristic of people at this level of development: the use of marriage exchange as a tool for gaining prestige, leadership and political authority. The Tiwi produce no surplus; have no essential manufacture; no scarce resources occur naturally. The products of the island are available to all and everyone is capable of utilizing them. There is nothing an ambitious Tiwi can try to monopolize except women. In nature, the number of men is approximately equal to the number of women, but the institution of marriage means that an artificial scarcity of women can be created. . . .

Two factors operate in this process by which women seem to become poker chips in male games of prestige. The first is age. The second is individual ability to manipulate the marriage exchange.

The Tiwi, like many other people with simple technologies, view age and authority as equivalent. Among men, the increment in status that comes with age is indicated concretely by their control over an increasing number of women. A man will be at least in his mid-thirties before the girl he has been promised becomes old enough to live with him. Until then, affairs with older men's wives satisfy his sexual needs. But after the first wife arrives more wives will follow, since a man's contract with his mother-in-law calls for marriage to all of her daughters, and one man may have contracts with several mothers-in-law.

In general, the younger men acquiesce to the system because they hope to gain by it eventually. They, too, will become elders and control wives. However, young men do not remain chaste nor are young wives satisfied with the attentions of their husbands, especially if the husband is very old and has many wives. As long as illicit sexual liaisons are kept secret, they do not threaten the power structure of the Tiwi society, and most women manage a number of affairs during their lives. Nevertheless, elder men are leery of strong romantic relationships between a young wife and her lover, for such a relationship may evolve into an elopement, an act that is the most reprehensible in Tiwi culture.

SOURCE: Cherry Lindholm and Charles Lindholm, "Mating Power Among the Tiwi," *Science Digest* (Sept./Oct. 1980), pp. 79–83, 114.

CHAPTER 14

Education

The word "school" comes from an ancient Greek word meaning "leisure." The link between the two words may not seem obvious today, but in preindustrial societies schooling had little practical use and was undertaken only by those with the time and money to pursue the cultivation of the mind for its own sake. The rest of the population began their working lives at adolescence or even earlier. Most people acquired all the knowledge and skills they needed through ordinary, everyday contacts with parents and other kin.

With the rise of industrialism, however, mass schooling came to be seen as desirable—and eventually, as necessary. Children and adolescents were gradually eased out of the labor force and into schools, where they were expected to learn, at a minimum, the basic literacy and numeracy that most jobs in an industrial society require. By the late nineteenth century, elementary education was widely available in the industrial societies of the time; by the 1930s, secondary education was becoming common and even compulsory; and in the years since World War II there has been a sharp increase in the proportion of high school graduates who proceed to college, particularly in the emerging postindustrial societies. Most people in the modern world accept that if citizens are to play their adult roles competently, their education cannot be left to chance: it requires attendance at formal educational organizations, from elementary schools to graduate schools. In all industrialized societies, education has become a central social institution (Boocock, 1980; Ballantine, 1983).

In its broadest sense, "education" is almost synonymous with "socialization," since both involve the passing on of culture from one person or group to another. The distinguishing feature of education in modern societies, however, is that it has become an institutionalized, formal activity.

These societies deliberately organize the educational experience, make it compulsory for people in certain age groups, train specialists to act as educators, and provide locations and equipment for the teaching and learning process. For our present purposes, then, *education* is the systematic, formalized transmission of knowledge, skills, and values.

In terms of the number of people involved, education is the largest single industry in the United States. If we include students, teachers, and administrators and other staff, more than one American in five currently participates in the institution—a figure without parallel anywhere else in the world. The several reasons for this remarkable emphasis on education lie in a peculiarly American attitude toward, and use of, the institution.

Characteristics of American Education

American education has several characteristics not found in the same combination in any other society. Many of the virtues and problems of the educational system stem from this unique blend of features.

Commitment to Mass Education

Americans take it for granted that everyone has a basic right to at least some formal education, and that the state should therefore provide free elementary and high school education for the masses. The United States pioneered this concept, and by the time of the Civil War most states were offering free education to their white residents. This development took place long before similar systems were introduced in Europe. European countries were much less inclined to regard mass education as a virtue in itself; instead, they have always tended to tailor their educational planning to the needs of their job markets.

The expansion of mass education in the United States in the course of this century has been unequaled anywhere. In 1900, about 7 percent of Americans in the appropriate age group were graduated from high school; by 1920 this figure had risen to 17 percent; by 1940, to 50 percent; and it stands today at nearly 80 percent. More than two-thirds of the present American population has a high school diploma, and the adult population has a median of 12.6 years of education. The propor-

tion of high school graduates attending college has also risen steeply, from 4 percent in 1900 to 16 percent in 1940 to about 40 percent by the late 1980s. By comparison, in Canada less than 20 percent of the people between the ages of eighteen and twenty-one attend college. In Western Europe, opportunities for advanced education are even more scarce: only about 20 percent of the sixteen- and seventeen-year-olds are still in school, and only about 10 percent of all children proceed to college. The less developed nations of the world present an even greater contrast. Although they try to provide all children with a few years of elementary education, only a small minority obtain secondary education, and a person's chances of attending a college are minimal. More than half of the world's population can neither read nor write, and the absolute number of illiterates is actually increasing.

This extension of educational opportunities in America has not been without its price, for mass education on this scale inevitably means some lowering of academic standards. Other industrialized countries have generally insisted on high standards, even though this meant denying educational opportunities to the less academically able.

Figure 14.1 *Like most children in the less developed nations of the world, these elementary school pupils in Somalia have little chance of attending high school, and virtually no chance of going to college. Compulsory education through the secondary school years is found only in the industrialized nations of the world, where teenagers are not needed in the labor force and where there are sufficient resources to maintain an extensive educational system.*

In fact, throughout most of this century, Western European countries like Great Britain and France have had separate schools for their brighter and their not-so-bright pupils. Until the late 1960s, for example, British schoolchildren were required to take a rigorous examination at the age of eleven, and on the basis of the results were sent to one of two quite different kinds of schools. Most British children went to schools that offered vocational training and only a basic academic curriculum, and they finished their education by the age of sixteen. A small minority went to "grammar" schools that had high academic standards, emphasized such subjects as Latin and physics, and prepared their students for the university. Even today, countries such as Britain and Japan use a uniform, national examination to select the small minority of high school seniors who are deemed qualified to apply for college admission.

Formal education in the United States is not merely freely available: it is actually compulsory. There are still many societies where this is not the case, or where schooling is compulsory for only the first few grades. American parents are legally obliged to send their children to school, although they may choose between public and private (including religious) education—choices that are not offered in many other countries. Education in the United States is financed by taxing everyone, including people without children and people whose children attend private schools. The implication is that public education benefits the entire society, not merely those who happen to receive it. Every child is thus entitled to at least twelve years of schooling at public expense, and we even expect some skilled professionals to spend twenty years or more in school—a period equal to almost half the life expectancy in some of the less developed countries of the world.

Utilitarian Emphasis

The American commitment to mass education arises partly from a historic belief not only that education is valuable and desirable in itself but also that it can serve a variety of social goals. At the founding of the Republic, Thomas Jefferson maintained that the schools should be used to ensure the success of democracy. If the voters were merely an ignorant rabble, Jefferson believed, the American experiment was probably doomed.

Since the nineteenth century, there has been a growing conviction that the schools can be used for a wide range of utilitarian purposes, including the solving of social problems that were once considered a more appropriate concern for the family or the church. Education was first used as a tool for social engineering in attempts to "Americanize" immigrants and to "civilize" Indian children. Since then, the society has continued to lay new burdens on its schools. In the 1960s, a "war on poverty" placed great emphasis on education, in the belief that the culture of the poor, not their lack of money, was the source of their problem. Today, when the teenage pregnancy rate soars, the schools are expected to reduce it through effective sex education. When drug addiction spreads, the public demands drug-education programs. When young drivers cause too many accidents, the schools are supposed to teach them to drive safely.

There is little evidence that these and similar programs have had much effect, and a good deal of evidence that they have not. For example, sex education has been accompanied by a rise in the teenage pregnancy rate; drug education has made no discernible impact on teenage drug abuse; driver education has not reduced the accident rate for teenage drivers. The "let's-solve-it-through-the-schools" approach is based on the fallacy that children learn what they are taught, remember what they learn, and behave accordingly. The dismal fact of the matter is that students fail to learn a good deal of what they are taught, and very quickly forget most of the rest. How much do you remember of your sixth-grade English, your ninth-grade math, or indeed of the college textbooks you studied last month? Also, even when students do learn and remember some of the values that the school teaches—such as those concerning sex, drugs, or hard work—there is no guarantee that their behavior will actually be guided by those values. The school is only one of many different agents of socialization, and the peer group or the latest rock lyrics may proclaim quite different—but more influential—values.

Despite the evidence, the American faith in education as a cure-all persists anyway. Other societies, of course, have used the schools to change attitudes and behavior—the outstanding examples are probably Nazi Germany and modern China—but they have done so in conjunction with sweeping changes in other social institutions at the same time. The faith that the schools *alone* can bring about social change is distinctively American. As sociologists of education are increasingly pointing out, there seems to be very little empirical justification for this faith, and it may be that we have cherished expectations of the institution that it cannot fulfill alone (Hurn, 1985).

Community Control

Most other countries regard education as a national enterprise, and many have uniform national curriculums, teacher salaries, funding policies, and examinations. Not long ago it was said, a little cynically, that the minister of education in France could state exactly which book every child at a given grade was using during a particular hour of any schoolday. In the United States, however, the schools are regarded as the concern of the community they serve, and most decisions—ranging from the hiring of teachers to the selection or even banning of school library books—are in the hands of a local school board elected by the voters of the community. In effect, America's local school systems have their own individual curricula, and they evaluate students according to a course credit system—even though courses may differ greatly from one community to another. The local community's ability to shape the content of education leads to extraordinary diversity in what is taught in American schools, and many subjects appear (such as typing, driving, or women's studies) that would never be taught in the more traditionally inclined schools of most other countries. American schools are also more apt to become involved in debate over such potentially controversial issues as sex education or the teaching of the theory of evolution, for local activists correctly perceive that they can influence what is taught to the children of the community.

Another implication of community control is that schools in wealthy neighborhoods are being far more lavishly funded than schools in poorer areas. At present the individual states provide about 48 percent of the funding for the schools, the federal government provides about 7 percent, and the remainder comes from local school districts—some of which have many times the potential income of others. As we will see, differences in educational expenditures have surprisingly little impact on students' academic achievement, but they do affect the physical quality of the school environment.

Compared with control from a distant national government, community control has many advantages, and it is a tradition that is highly valued and zealously guarded. The system has the drawback, however, that the nature of a child's educational experience may depend on the neighborhood in which he or she happens to live.

Education: A Functionalist View

The functionalist perspective explains the central importance of the schools in maintaining the social order as a whole. Several distinct functions of education can be identified.

1. *Cultural transmission.* If society is to survive, its culture must be handed down from one generation to the next. The schools provide young people with knowledge, skills, and values that a complex modern society considers especially important. Thus they learn about history, geography, and language. They learn how to read, write, and manipulate numbers. They learn about patriotism, the virtues of their political system, and their cul-

PER CAPITA PUBLIC SCHOOL EXPENDITURE, BY STATES, 1985

State	Average per Pupil	Rank	State	Average per Pupil	Rank
Alabama	2,241	49	Missouri	2,993	35
Alaska	6,867	1	Montana	3,968	11
Arizona	2,801	40	Nebraska	3,128	31
Arkansas	2,344	47	Nevada	2,998	34
California	3,291	26	New Hampshire	2,964	36
Colorado	3,398	24	New Jersey	5,220	3
Connecticut	4,477	6	New Mexico	3,278	28
Delaware	4,155	7	New York	5,226	2
District of			North Carolina	2,588	45
Columbia	4,753	5	North Dakota	3,249	30
Florida	3,409	21	Ohio	3,315	25
Georgia	2,692	42	Oklahoma	3,264	29
Hawaii	3,596	17	Oregon	3,963	12
Idaho	2,290	48	Pennsylvania	4,002	10
Illinois	3,517	18	Rhode Island	4,097	9
Indiana	2,638	44	South Carolina	2,650	43
Iowa	3,409	21	South Dakota	2,813	39
Kansas	3,668	16	Tennessee	2,349	46
Kentucky	2,792	41	Texas	3,287	27
Louisiana	2,821	38	Utah	2,182	51
Maine	3,038	33	Vermont	3,783	15
Maryland	4,101	8	Virginia	3,043	32
Massachusetts	3,889	13	Washington	3,437	19
Michigan	3,434	20	West Virginia	2,866	37
Minnesota	3,408	23	Wisconsin	3,880	14
Mississippi	2,205	50	Wyoming	4,809	4

SOURCE: U.S. Bureau of the Census, *Statistical Abstract of the United States, 1986* (Washington, D.C.: U.S. Government Printing Office, 1986).

Figure 14.2 *As this table shows, there is considerable variation from one state to another in the average amount of money that is spent on pupils in the public schools. The physical quality of the school environment—including such facilities as laboratories and athletic accommodations—may therefore be influenced by the specific state in which the school is located. There are much greater variations among local communities.*

ture's norms of behavior and morality. This function of education is an essentially conservative one, for the schools are transmitting the culture of the past, or, at best, the present. In a traditional society, this conservatism may not matter much, because culture changes very slowly. In a modern society, however, teachers of the older generation may find it impossible to equip students to face a future that can never be fully anticipated. In their transmission of cultural values, too, schools in all societies engage, deliberately or otherwise, in indoctrination. Americans are well aware of this practice in certain other societies whose values are different from theirs, but they tend to overlook it in their own because the values they are taught seem so "natural" to them. But if a schoolteacher deals with controversial values—if, for example, he or she tries to present the life and thought of Karl Marx in a favorable light, or discusses sexual practices that are accepted in other societies but are considered highly deviant in American society—a community furor is likely to result.

2. *Social integration.* Modern societies frequently contain many different ethnic, racial, religious, or other subcultures. Education can help to integrate the young members of these minorities into a common culture, encouraging the development of a relatively homogeneous society with shared values. In the United States the schools have always been considered an important factor in the "melting pot" process. Children of immigrants may arrive in the first grade unable to speak more than a few words of English, but they are supposed to emerge from school able to take their place in the mainstream of American life. This social-integration function is particularly important in many of the less developed nations. The borders of these countries were often established by European colonial powers without any regard to tribal, linguistic, or ethnic barriers. Consequently, some new nations contain literally hundreds of different language groups that lack a common cultural tradition and often have a history of mutual hostility—Zambia, for example, contains 73 ethnic groups; Zaire contains 270. These countries explicitly use the schools to teach a common language and to generate a common sense of national loyalty among the young.

3. *Personal development.* The schools teach a variety of facts and skills, most of which are expected to be of some practical use to the students later in their lives. They also provide the students with the opportunity to acquire something more subtle, but at least as important: the habits of

Figure 14.3 *Every society uses the schools to socialize its children into appropriately patriotic attitudes. To an American audience, the picture of Soviet children standing at attention in front of a portrait of Lenin immediately suggests "indoctrination." But is the American practice of standing at attention to pledge allegiance to the flag (often beneath portraits of national heroes) really any different?*

thought, the broader perspectives, that are the mark of an educated person. The schools cannot guarantee what their pupils will learn or how well they will learn it. But in both the formal curriculum and in informal interaction with peers and teachers, students inevitably learn a good deal about themselves and about the world that surrounds them. Some of this learning is relevant to their future occupational roles, but much of it is more valuable for personal emotional, social, and intellectual development. To take but one example, level of education has a strong impact on attitudes and opinions. A "don't know" response to questions in national opinion polls is consistently linked to low educational attainment, irrespective of the subject of the poll. The higher people's level of education, the more likely they are to reject prejudice and intolerant thinking. Each additional year of college appears to make a student more democratic in outlook and more tolerant toward civil liberties issues (Astin, 1977; Nunn et al., 1978; Hyman and Wright, 1979).

4. *Screening and selection.* Education is an important avenue to occupational and financial success in industrialized societies because the schools screen and select students for different kinds of jobs. The more rewarding a job, the larger the number of people who would like to have it, and an important function of the schools is to limit access to various occupations by granting the necessary diplomas, degrees, or other credentials to some students but not to others. From the elementary years onward, the schools constantly test students and evaluate their achievements, channeling some toward technical vocations, some toward academic subjects, and some straight into the job market. The credentials that people possess at the end of their education have a strong influence on their life chances.

5. *Innovation.* Educational institutions do not merely transmit existing knowledge; they add to the cultural heritage by developing new knowledge and skills as well. This function arises partly because the experience of education stimulates intellectual curiosity and critical thought, and partly because college and university teachers are usually expected to conduct research that will increase scientific knowledge. A good deal of research now takes place outside the schools—in government, industry, and specialized research institutes—but the college professor has a double role as teacher and researcher. (This role can generate tensions; in fact, many professors complain that they face the choice of neglecting either their research or their students.) The colleges and universities remain primarily responsible for **basic research,** systematic inquiry that is concerned with establishing new knowledge. But **applied research,** systematic inquiry that tries to find practical uses for existing knowledge, is increasingly pursued outside the college context.

6. *Latent functions.* The effects discussed so far are of the type that sociologists call a **manifest** *function*—a consequence that is recognized and intended. But education also has effects of the type called a **latent function**—a consequence that is unrecognized and unintended (Merton, 1968). For example, schools serve as "babysitting" agencies. They free parents from child-rearing tasks and permit them to work outside the home. Colleges and even high schools function as a "marriage market," by giving young people of fairly similar background a chance to interact with one another in a way that would not be possible if their social orbits were restricted to the home and workplace. By isolating the young from the rest of society, the schools also have the latent function of permitting distinctive youth cultures to form. The schools may also serve the latent function of keeping adolescents—who are not expected to have full-time jobs—occupied and out of trouble. In addition to their formal curricula, the schools also teach habits of punctuality, docility, and obedience to authority, a latent function that has a useful payoff when young people move on to offices and factories.

Education: A Conflict View

A functionalist analysis of education gives a useful understanding of the role this institution has in society. But the analysis does not tell the whole story, for it tends to ignore the fact that education can become deeply involved in social conflict. Debates about national or local educational policies, for example, are rarely about mere technicalities: they are about *whose* values will be taught, *whose* children will be bused, *whose* offspring will benefit from specific admissions policies, *whose* language will be used for instruction, *whose* sons and daughters will get the best education.

The conflict perspective focuses on the ways different social groups use education as a means of getting or keeping power, wealth, and prestige. As we noted in Chapter 10 ("Social Stratification"), there is a close link between education and social inequality. Schooling is an important influence on **social mobility,** or movement from one status to another, for in all modern societies, educational credentials are crucial in gaining access to superior jobs and the higher incomes that go with them. Understandably, people try to ensure the best possible education for their own children, hoping thereby to secure social and economic advantages for them. In Britain, for example, the sons of the upper class are likely to attend the handful of private boarding schools whose graduates have disproportionate influence in national life; in the Soviet Union, senior bureaucrats use their influence to ensure that their children gain entry to the elite schools from which the next generation of high officials is selected. In the United States, too, children of different social classes often attend different schools—the upper class, elite private schools; the middle class, suburban public schools; the working and lower classes, inner-city public schools. At every level, there is competition among groups and individuals for grades and other tokens of educational success.

Conflict theorists emphasize that the schools do not so much help to create the class system as to reproduce it from one generation to the next. In all societies, there is a direct relationship between the social class of the parents and the educational achievement of their children: the higher the social class, the better the offspring are likely to do in school. In effect, then, the schools' screening and selecting of students follows class lines: children of working- and lower-class parents tend to be eased out of the system and into the work force early in their academic careers, whereas children of the middle and upper classes are far more likely to continue their education at colleges and univer-

sities. In fact, the schools help to maintain not only the class system but also its legitimacy. People consider social inequality legitimate only if they are convinced it is fair—that the people at the top are really harder-working and more talented than other people, as evidenced by their greater educational success. Yet the system is not really fair at all, since children of upper-status families start out with advantages that guarantee them, on average, greater educational success than children of lower-status families. As we will see, much of the controversy that surrounds American schools derives from the fact that education is not just a learning process—it is a valued resource in the competition for society's prizes (Bowles and Gintis, 1976; Collins, 1979; Apple, 1982).

Inside the School

Every school is a miniature social system, with its own statuses and roles, subcultures, values and traditions, and rituals and ceremonies. Each school, classroom, and clique is an interacting social unit. The study of what actually goes on inside the school has been an important focus of sociological research (P. Jackson, 1968; Barr and Dreeben, 1983).

The Formal Structure of the School

Perhaps the most obvious feature of the school is that it is a formal, bureaucratic organization. Long gone is the school housed in a single room and staffed by a schoolmarm who teaches all pupils and all subjects; the educational process has been rationalized in the interests of efficiency. Pupils are grouped according to age, subject, and, in many schools, according to ability; teachers are specialists, with some of them, such as department heads, having formal authority over others; and an administrative staff supervises the entire operation.

Procedures within the school are kept as uniform as possible so that the organization can be run in an orderly and predictable way. This is no small task, given that the schools are expected to prevent pupils from doing things they would rather do, and to make them do things they would rather not do. A result of this bureaucratization is that the school atmosphere is necessarily repressive to some extent. Pupils may be obliged to remain

MEDIAN MONEY INCOME OF FAMILIES, BY
EDUCATION OF HEAD OF HOUSEHOLD
In thousands of dollars

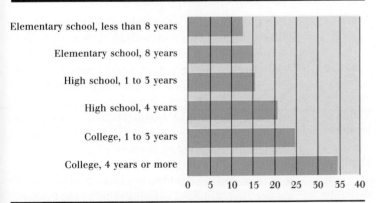

Elementary school, less than 8 years								
Elementary school, 8 years								
High school, 1 to 3 years								
High school, 4 years								
College, 1 to 3 years								
College, 4 years or more								

0 5 10 15 20 25 30 35 40

SOURCE: U.S. Bureau of the Census, *Statistical Abstract of the United States, 1986*
(Washington, D.C.: U.S. Government Printing Office, 1986).

Figure 14.4 *As this chart indicates, there is a strong link between the length of one's education and the amount of one's income. Conflict theorists point out that education has become a significant social resource because it is an avenue to social mobility. Different individuals and groups compete for educational credentials.*

Figure 14.5 *As the educational institution has expanded, schools have become large formal organizations, with a characteristic architecture and atmosphere—features instantly recognizable in Oskar Schlemmer's* Bauhaus Stairway *(1932).*

silent, to line up and march on command, to sit still for hours, to be punctual, and to request permission to use the toilet. In elementary schools and high schools, the degree of regimentation is greater than any that the students, except those who later enter the military or the prisons, will encounter again in their lifetime. The college atmosphere is much more permissive, but no student who has been through the veritable circus of form-filling known as "registration" can doubt the basically bureaucratic nature of college organization.

To be efficient, a bureaucracy must fit individuals to its own administrative needs, rather than fit its procedures to the needs of individuals. As a result, the elementary schools and high schools tend to emphasize conformity and obedience, and they have difficulty dealing with spontaneity,

energy, excitement, and individual creativity. Although the schools pay lip service to the ideal of encouraging students to think critically, they are generally authoritarian; although they preach the value of democratic participation, they are reluctant to practice it in the classroom. But despite this regimentation, American classrooms are, on the whole, a much more easy-going and informal environment than those in most other societies—where all pupils may have to wear uniforms, where desks may be bolted to the floor, and where discipline, sometimes including corporal punishment, is far sterner than most American students can readily imagine.

Like all formal organizations, the school contains many informal groups. Peer groups and cliques, for example, are of great importance in the culture of a school (or college), and may exert far more influence over the behavior and attitudes of individual students than do the efforts of teachers, counselors, or administrators. In fact, academic goals are usually not highly valued within pupil peer groups; individuals are likely to be admired for their athletic abilities, good looks, or popularity rather than their scholarly prowess. Students who are not gifted at, or interested in, schoolwork can find alternative sources of gratification in their peer group, where their acceptance may compensate for academic failure (J. S. Coleman, 1961; Goodlad, 1984).

Competitiveness

Like the American economic system, the educational system prizes competition. The use of grading encourages students to compete with one another for academic achievement, and the losers are gradually eliminated from the system altogether and sent into the work force. In many other cultures, this kind of competitive behavior is unknown or considered antisocial. In China, for example, the more able members of a class are expected to help the slower learners—an obligation that implicitly teaches the students of this socialist society that it is their responsibility to help others, particularly those who are less fortunate. In American schools, however, mutual assistance may be regarded as cheating. Jules Henry (1963) points to the implications of this competitiveness:

> Boris had trouble reducing "$\frac{12}{16}$" to the lowest terms, and could only get as far as "$\frac{6}{8}$." The teacher asked him quietly if that was as far as he could reduce it. She suggested he "think." Much heaving up and down and waving of hands by the other chil-

dren, all frantic to correct him. Boris pretty unhappy, probably mentally paralyzed. The teacher, quiet, patient, ignores the others and concentrates with looks and voice on Boris. . . . After a minute or two, she becomes more urgent, but there is no response from Boris. She then turns to the class and says, "Well, who can tell Boris what the number is?" A forest of hands appears, and the teacher calls Peggy. Peggy says that four may be divided into the numerator and the denominator. Thus Boris's failure has made it possible for Peggy to succeed; his depression is the price of her exhilaration; his misery the occasion of her rejoicing. This is the standard condition of the American elementary school. . . . So often somebody's success has been bought at the cost of our failure. To a Zuni, Hopi, or Dakota Indian, Peggy's performance would seem cruel beyond belief, for competition, the wringing of success from somebody else's failure, is a form of torture foreign to those noncompetitive redskins.

Competition within the school is, in fact, an essential part of the American socialization process. By being taught to compete with others for rewards, the children are, in effect, being prepared for economic roles in a capitalist society (Bowles and Gintis, 1976).

The competition for good grades can become so intense that it may actually begin to defeat the academic goals of education. As Ronald Dore (1976) points out, "Not all schooling is educational. Much of it is mere qualification-earning . . . ritualistic, tedious, suffused with anxiety and boredom,

destructive of curiosity and imagination; in short, anti-educational." In classic studies that still seem relevant today, Howard Becker and his associates found that college students concentrated more on strategies to get good grades than on acquiring the knowledge the grades supposedly represent. For example, students are more likely to take a "soft" course that offers an assured credit, but little else, rather than take an intellectually stimulating seminar that offers no credit at all. They often seek out "easy" teachers rather than those known to be tough graders. They tend to avoid reading that seems irrelevant to their tests, and they pump professors for hints about upcoming exams. Some enterprising students try to bluff and flatter their professors in the hope that this will improve their grades, and in some cases students resort to various methods of cheating in order to "make the grade" (Becker et al., 1968).

The Self-Fulfilling Prophecy

The result of academic competition—the success or failure of individual students—becomes part of an official record: individuals become labeled as bright or dull and are treated accordingly. This differential treatment is most obvious in the tracking system, which segregates students in the belief that they will learn better if they are grouped with others of similar ability. This assumption is widely held, but the evidence for its validity is doubtful at best: some studies find favorable results from tracking; but others report either mixed or unfavorable results (National Education Association, 1968; Schafer and Blexa, 1971; Hurn, 1985).

The labeling of students as "bright" or "dull" can have important effects on their later academic careers. Teachers' expectations and attitudes are influenced by these labels, and so are the self-concepts of the students themselves. The process of labeling may involve a *self-fulfilling prophecy* —a prediction that leads to behavior that makes the prediction come true. Believing that certain children will fail, the school treats them as failures, with the result that they do fail.

A classic experiment by the psychologist Robert Rosenthal (1969) suggests the possible effects of this kind of labeling. Rosenthal told a group of elementary school teachers that he had developed a new test to identify children whose learning abilities were likely to spurt ahead during the coming school year. The children were duly tested and the teachers were given a list of "spurters" with instructions to watch their progress without

Figure 14.6 *A characteristic feature of American education is competitiveness. From the earliest school years, children are taught to compete against one another—and are thus prepared for the competition against their fellows that they will experience throughout their lives.*

revealing their expectations to the children or the children's parents in any way. In actual fact, the test was a fake, and Rosenthal had merely chosen the names of the "spurters" at random. The only characteristic that distinguished these children from their classmates, then, was the teachers' expectation that their work would improve. A year later, Rosenthal found that the "spurters," particularly in the early grades, had made significantly greater academic gains than a control group of "nonspurters." He concluded that the teachers had changed their attitudes toward the children in subtle ways that had influenced the pupils' progress. Rosenthal's findings have remained controversial, however, as later attempts to replicate his experiment have produced varying results: his findings have been supported by some studies but not by others (Rist, 1970; Ritchie, 1977).

Grading, tracking, and counseling all gradually eliminate from the educational system those students who are not considered bright enough to benefit from further schooling. Unlike other educational systems, such as the former British one discussed earlier, the American system does not abruptly separate the academic sheep from the goats. Instead, it uses a more subtle process of "cooling out" unwanted students (Clark, 1960; London, 1978). Students thus learn slowly that a good education and the social prizes it brings are restricted to the few, and that hard work is not enough to ensure success. Since the vast majority of the students who are "cooled out" are from the lower social classes, the educational system helps to legitimate social inequality by making academic failure seem the result of individual inadequacies alone. The idea is that everyone is supposed to have the same chance, but that only some are able to make use of it.

Social Inequality and the Schools

People do not have equal opportunity to achieve educational success, for their chances are strongly influenced by the social class of the family into which they were born. Social stratification distributes educational opportunities as unequally as it distributes wealth, power, and prestige. By reinforcing the advantages that some people already have over others as a result of an accident of birth, the schools preserve the social inequalities that already exist (Rist, 1973; Squires, 1979; Apple, 1982).

Class, Race, and Education

It is obvious that educational achievement brings higher income, but it is not always so obvious that social class influences educational achievement. The fact is, however, that the average higher-status child stays in school longer and does better while there than the average lower-status child. The superior educational achievement of the upper-status person is then translated into further social and economic advantages.

There is no shortage of evidence on the different achievements of American children from different social classes. In a major study, for example, William Sewell (1971) followed the fortunes of some randomly selected high school pupils for fourteen years. He divided his sample into four groups on the basis of their socioeconomic status and found that those in the highest group were four times more likely to attend college, six times more likely to graduate, and nine times more likely to receive graduate or professional training than those in the lowest-status group. Research has repeatedly shown that intelligence is not the only or even the main determinant of who goes to college and finally gets a degree. Less than a tenth of students with high incomes and high abilities fail to enter college, whereas a quarter of low-income students with comparable abilities do not continue their education beyond high school (Jencks, 1972). And because race and class overlap to a great extent in the United States, minority groups also have a lower average educational achievement than whites.

How does the typical pupil's social class background affect his or her chances of educational success? It seems that several different factors may be responsible.

1. *Cost of education.* To keep a child in high school and especially to put a student through college is an expensive undertaking, particularly when indirect costs, such as the loss of the student's potential earnings, are taken into account. The more wealthy a family is, the more able it is to bear these costs.

2. *Family expectations.* If the family expects that a child will remain in high school and attend college, the expectation will influence the motivation of the student. Middle- and upper-class parents are inclined to take it for granted that their children will do well academically. Lower-class parents are much less likely to make the same assumption; they may instead hope that their child will become apprenticed to a trade.

Figure 14.7

*"Son, you're all grown up now. You owe me two
hundred and fourteen thousand dollars."*

Drawing by Weber; © 1983
The New Yorker Magazine, Inc.

3. *Cultural background.* Middle- and upper-class children are socialized in a way that maximizes their learning potential. Compared with lower-class children, for example, they grow up in smaller families, live in homes that are more likely to be stocked with books, are more likely to be given educational toys, are more encouraged to defer immediate gratification in favor of long-term goals, and are more exposed to the values needed for educational success.

4. *Language problems.* Schools teach pupils in the "standard" version of middle-class American English. Some students from minority groups—particularly Hispanic-Americans—enter school scarcely able to speak any English. The result can be an early setback from which the children may never recover. Black English and lower-class white English also differ in important respects from "standard" American English, and the pupils may be penalized or considered unintelligent because their language appears ungrammatical. (In fact, these variants of English have a perfectly regular system of grammatical rules and are simply dialects of the language, just like those of the Australians, the Irish, the queen of England, or, for that matter, middle-class Americans. The "correct" grammar and pronunciation of any language is merely the dialect of the upper classes in the society where it is spoken.)

5. *Teacher attitudes.* Most teachers have middle-class values and attitudes and may become biased against students who fail to display them. Understandably, teachers tend to appreciate students who are punctual, clean, neat, hard-working, obedient, and ambitious. Pupils who do not behave according to middle-class norms risk being considered "bad" students, regardless of their intelligence and ability.

6. *Labeling.* As we have seen, once a child is labeled a dull student, a self-fulfilling prophecy may follow. Lower-ability children are often put in slower tracks, or ability groups, and counseled to make "realistic" career choices. If these children internalize the self-concept that the school offers, their academic motivation may be undermined. There is also evidence that the quality of counseling in school is directly related to the social class of the pupil, irrespective of individual talent, and that class and race strongly affect the high school track to which a student is assigned, regardless of IQ or earlier achievement.

7. *Peer-group influence.* Peer groups in schools and colleges tend to influence the academic motivation and career plans of their members. These peer groups are usually composed of people of similar social background. Especially in high school, the importance of college plans to individual students is closely linked to the aspirations of their friends. In working-class peer groups, the norm may be to enter the work force at high school graduation or even before.

Class, Race, and Intelligence

Educational achievement is highly correlated with intelligence as measured on IQ (intelligence quotient) tests. Again, however, it seems that class, not measured intelligence, is the critical factor influencing achievement, for IQ scores are strongly influenced by social-class background. Lower-class whites score less well on IQ tests than middle- and upper-class whites, as do members of disadvantaged minority groups. Blacks, for example, score on the average 10 to 15 points below whites on these tests. However, individual members of both races are found at every point on the entire ability range, and middle-class Northern blacks generally do better than lower-class Southern whites. The issue of race and intelligence became highly controversial when the psychologist Arthur Jensen (1969, 1979) implied that the overall differences in IQ between blacks and whites could be partially explained by hereditary factors—a view that has been strongly refuted by scientists from several disciplines.

To evaluate this issue we must look at both "intelligence" and at IQ tests. Exactly what "intelligence" is, nobody knows. Psychologists have been trying to define the concept throughout this century without much success. It is generally agreed, however, that intelligence involves a combination of two factors: an innate, *inherited* element that sets a limit on a person's intellectual potential, and a learned, *environmental* element that determines how far that potential will be fulfilled. Since there is no such thing as a person who has not been exposed to socialization in some environment, there is no way to measure either the innate or the learned component alone. Both are inextricably mixed in any individual.

An IQ test measures "intelligence" by comparing the subject's performance on a number of specific tasks with the performance of the rest of his or her age group. The IQ test is misnamed, however, for it is not really a test of "intelligence" at all, whatever intelligence may be. It is actually a test of skills in a very limited range of fields, primarily in linguistic, spatial, symbolic, and mathematical knowledge and reasoning. The tests ignore many other intellectual capacities that are not directly relevant to the school curriculum—such as creativity (for example, literary imagination, art appreciation, or the ability to compose music), or social skills (for example, persuasiveness, wit, or the ability to be "street-wise"). In short, the IQ test focuses on academic aptitude, not on intelligence as a whole (Gardner, 1983).

Because IQ tests use language and assume basic information on the part of the person being tested, they are "culture-bound." That is, they require a familiarity with knowledge and assumptions more likely to be shared by one group than by another. Children reared in a culture or subculture other than that of the white middle-class America assumed by the tests are consequently at a disadvantage. The fact that a child who has never seen or heard of an eggplant cannot select it as the "odd one out" in a series of fruits does not mean that the child is unintelligent. An American child would not do well on a test that required the subject to select the poisonous insect from a series of four scorpions, but a child reared in the Sahara desert would have little difficulty in getting the answer right. What is often tested in IQ tests, then, is not "intelligence" but rather culturally acquired knowledge, which is a very different thing. The middle-class child has greater access to the kind of knowledge, experience, and skills demanded by these tests.

The current link between race, class, and average IQ scores is an example of a general pattern that has existed among various racial and ethnic groups ever since IQ tests were introduced at the beginning of this century. During the 1920s, for example, the working and lower classes in the big cities of the United States were made up of "white ethnic" groups. The IQ tests that were administered at the time showed that these Italian-, Greek-, Polish-, and Portuguese-Americans scored at least 15 points below the national average. And when IQ tests were administered to immigrant groups at Ellis Island, they supposedly showed that Jews exceeded all other groups in the frequency of "mental defect." Today, these various groups score at or above the national average—an improvement that reflects their enhanced socioeconomic status (Sowell, 1977). But, despite the fact that IQ is so strongly influenced by cultural factors, IQ tests are widely used for labeling and tracking students, providing another opportunity for the self-fulfilling prophecy of academic success or failure to occur (H. Taylor, 1980).

Figure 14.8 *Intelligence is the outcome of an interaction between heredity and environment. Genetic makeup may provide the individual's basic potential, but how that potential is fulfilled depends on the person's learning experiences—which in turn are influenced by social class.*

Equality of Educational Opportunity

In a situation of equal educational opportunity, we would expect that a random member of any given social class or racial group would have the same probability of entering college that a random member of any other group would have. Accidental factors such as sex, race, or class would not affect educational achievement.

Yet earlier in this century, there were striking differences in educational opportunities within virtually all the nations of the world: typically, lower-status children were channeled into public vocational schools, while upper-status children were encouraged, often via private, fee-paying schools, to study an academic curriculum in preparation for college. This situation came to be seen as a grave injustice, for it clearly reinforced the impact of social class on the life chances of the individual. Consequently, most modern societies have reorganized their schools in order to create equal educational opportunity for children of different social-class backgrounds—typically, by redrawing the lines of school districts and by combining the previously separate vocational and academic schools, so that children of different classes attend the same schools and have a similar educational experience (Boudon, 1977).

The United States, too, has long lacked equal educational opportunity, largely as a result of racial segregation in the schools. In the South, this segregation was enshrined in state laws, while elsewhere in the country it resulted primarily from residential segregation, which almost automatically produced segregated local school systems. Since the 1950s, however, a major thrust of American domestic policy has been to equalize educational opportunity between white and minority-group children, so as to provide minority members with the educational channels to social mobility that they were denied in the past.

By the 1950s, the elimination of racial inequality was becoming a pressing national concern—and, true to form, Americans looked to the schools to do the job. A crucial blow to segregation came in 1954, when the Supreme Court ruled that racially segregated schools were inherently unequal and that school systems must desegregate "with all deliberate speed." But progress was painfully slow until the civil rights movement and the racial disturbances of the 1960s finally provoked the federal government into action. The 1964 Civil Rights Act called for an investigation into racial inequalities in educational opportunities, and a team of sociol-

ogists led by James Coleman was asked to conduct a major study on the subject. The researchers gathered data from nearly 4,000 schools and surveyed some 570,000 students and 60,000 teachers. It was generally expected that the study would find important differences in the quality of education offered to whites and blacks.

The popular assumption was soon challenged. Coleman (1966) did find that the average white pupil performed better than the average black pupil. But to his astonishment, he found relatively little difference between predominantly black and predominantly white schools in virtually every factor he analyzed, including age of buildings, library facilities, laboratory facilities, number of books, class size, and measurable teacher characteristics. In fact, most of the variation in pupil achievement was not between one school or another but between pupils within the same schools. The facilities a school had at its disposal and the amount of money spent per pupil did not seem to have any significant effect on pupil performance. The cause-and-effect relationship between input of resources and output of achievement, so long taken for granted, hardly existed.

What, then, accounted for the differences in black and white academic achievement? Coleman's crucial finding was that achievement in all schools is principally related, not to the characteristics of the schools, but to the social-class background of the pupils themselves. He concluded that black students were underachieving mainly because they came from predominantly lower-class homes. White students were doing better because they came from predominantly middle-class homes, where they were better prepared and motivated for the academic demands of school life. Coleman also found some evidence to show that when blacks attended desegregated schools, their performance improved, presumably because these schools had a more "middle-class" atmosphere.

Coleman's findings had a profound impact on national policy. Educators held that many members of minority groups suffered from "cultural deprivation," or deficiencies in home, family, and neighborhood background that hinder the ability to compete in the larger culture. The remedy was "compensatory" education—programs designed to teach the knowledge and skills that would make up for supposed cultural deprivation. Some of these programs have been successful in the short term, but most have proved disappointing, perhaps because they were not sufficiently intensive or prolonged. The idea that minority groups are "culturally deprived" has also been criticized in more recent years as a case of white, middle-class ethnocentrism toward subcultures whose characteristics are assumed to be inferior simply because they are different.

The Coleman report also provided a strong incentive for the busing of pupils from one neighborhood to another to correct racial imbalances within school systems. The Supreme Court has reasoned that if it is unconstitutional to segregate schoolchildren, it must be constitutional to ensure that they are desegregated. But while the courts have been prepared to order busing within school districts, they have been reluctant to order it between central cities, where the ghettoes are located, and the surrounding suburbs, which are predominantly white; for this reason, many metropolitan-area schools remain as segregated as before. Even where busing does take place, it is usually "one-way"—that is, minority students are bused to white schools, but whites rarely are bused to schools with a nonwhite majority.

Figure 14.9 *In most American communities, the busing of children to ensure racial balance has passed without incident. In some cases, however, the white community has reacted with hostility. Americans overwhelmingly favor racially integrated schools, but have little enthusiasm for busing to achieve integration.*

The great majority of school systems that have been desegregated through busing have undergone the process with little difficulty. In some areas, however, strong resentment and even outright violence have resulted, and busing has become a highly controversial issue. Opinion polls since the 1970s have shown that a large majority of the public favors school integration, but also that a significant majority opposes busing, the only practicable way to achieve that goal. Although much of this opposition stems from outright racism, it is clear that there are other reasons for questioning the merits of busing. First, many people—nonwhite as well as white—resent interference in local community control over education and feel that their sense of neighborhood identity is violated by busing. Second, busing, particularly where it is imposed on reluctant communities, may yield few if any benefits for the minority children concerned. School desegregation has generally failed to have much effect on minority children's achievement, probably because it has so often taken place in an atmosphere of hostility, resentment, or indifference (St. John, 1975, 1981; Rist, 1979; Orfield, 1983). Third, there is some evidence that busing may actually be counterproductive. Coleman himself (1975) became a strong opponent of busing, because he believed that it was hastening a "white flight" from the central cities to the suburbs and was thus making integration even more difficult to achieve. The fact is that most big-city schools are now *more* segregated than they have ever been: there are simply not enough white children to integrate them. Indeed, more than three decades after the Supreme Court ordered school desegregation, one-third of black children attend schools that are over 90 percent black, and almost all white children attend schools that are predominantly white.

Can Education Create Equality?

The faith that social inequality can be reduced by equalizing educational opportunity was further shaken when Christopher Jencks (1972) published his controversial book *Inequality*. After a careful analysis of the available data, Jencks came to the conclusion that changing the schools would have hardly any effect on social inequality. He points out that social inequality is related to educational achievement—but it is not *caused* by it. The source of the inequality lies beyond the schools, which merely reflect the situation in the wider society. Americans, Jencks charges, have a "recurrent fantasy" that schools can solve their problems: they are guilty of "muddleheaded ideas about the various causes and cures of poverty and inequality."

Equality of opportunity cannot ensure social and economic equality, because people are differently equipped to take advantage of opportunities. It is like giving everyone an equal chance to run in a footrace, even though some are lame or have never trained for an athletic event. The "equal" chance merely ensures that those who are already better equipped are able to maintain their advantage. Jencks suggests that a fairer conception of equality would involve equality of social and economic results, which would require a major redistribution of the nation's wealth. But this is not a conception to which, as a people, Americans have very much inclination. Americans prefer to see life as a race to be won by the "fittest"—and the educational system reflects these values.

The findings of Coleman and of Jencks noticeably dampened enthusiasm for using the schools to bring about social change. Their work echoes that of Emile Durkheim, who made the first systematic sociological analysis of education around the turn of the century. The schools, Durkheim pointed out, are primarily concerned with transmitting the culture of the past and perhaps of the present. They are shaped by existing forces in society and therefore cannot be a significant instrument of social change in themselves. The schools will change as other institutions change, and if change is to be brought about, policy makers must focus on altering other areas of society, particularly the political and economic institutions. The schools will then change, faithfully reflecting and reinforcing the social and cultural changes that have taken place in the wider society.

A Crisis of Quality?

Since the mid-1980s, the American school system has come under a different kind of attack. This time, critics have accused the schools of failing in their most basic educational tasks. For example, the National Commission on Excellence in Education (1983) has warned that the schools are threatened with a "rising tide of mediocrity"; the Education Commission of the States (1984) has declared that "a real emergency is upon us"; and the Twentieth Century Fund (1983) has forecast "disaster" if steps are not taken to improve academic standards.

As Christopher Hurn (1985) observes, these dire warnings about the condition of the schools have a rather familiar ring, for such complaints recur quite regularly every decade or two. In the late 1950s, for example, Americans were disturbed to learn that the Soviet Union had launched the first space satellite, the sputnik. The United States, it seemed, was losing the "space race"—and the only remedy seemed to be better education, especially science education. As a result of public pressure, school curricula were reformed to include more math, physics, and chemistry. Additionally, the very latest technology was also brought to bear on the classroom—including closed-circuit TV and experimental "teaching machines," mechanical devices that tested students on their knowledge and seemed to represent the wave of the future. Actually, most pupils did not take well to the emphasis on science and the new technology proved to be an impractical fad, but the United States overtook the Soviet Union in the "space race" anyway—so quickly that the graduates of the reformed schools had not yet had a chance to become scientists and contribute to the victory. It was not long, however, before the educational system came in for another kind of criticism. In the late 1960s and early 1970s, critics charged that the schools were authoritarian; that they repressed individuality; that they stifled intellectual and emotional growth; that they failed to provide opportunities for disadvantaged and minority youth. This time, the response was to individualize instruction, to introduce a variety of electives into the curricula, to create a more "open" classroom environment, and—as we have seen—to attend to the needs of minorities and less privileged pupils (Silberman, 1979; Ravitch, 1983).

Today, the crisis in the classroom is diagnosed differently: indeed, many current problems are held to be the direct result of the "solutions" that were adopted in the 1960s and 1970s. The schools are now attacked for encouraging mediocrity rather than excellence; for wasting time on trivial electives that interfere with the learning of basic subject matter; for failing to create a sufficiently disciplined learning environment; and for abandoning academic standards in a misguided attempt to bring about fairness or equality.

In part, the changing criticisms of the schools reflect broader social fashions. When social values change, education, being focused as it is on past concerns, inevitably seems out of date and inadequate to the demands of the day. But the actual condition of the educational system may provoke legitimate criticisms, and there are good grounds

AVERAGE SCHOLASTIC APTITUDE TESTS

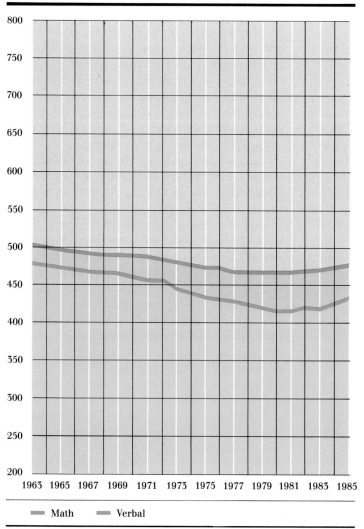

SOURCE: The College Board, 1986.

Figure 14.10 *Scores on the Scholastic Aptitude Test (SAT) range from a minimum of 200 to a maximum of 800. As this graph shows, average scores—which were none too impressive to begin with—declined from the early 1960s until the early 1980s. Other measures of pupil achievement, such as tests of reading abilities, have shown a similar trend. As a result of this decline, there is now a strong "back-to-basics" movement among American educators.*

for believing that American schools are failing in their academic responsibilities. Scores on Standard Achievement Tests and other measures declined steadily from 1967 to the early 1980s. Standards of reading and writing have sagged, and to compensate for this trend many textbooks are now written at two grade levels below the grade for which they are intended. The high schools have produced many graduates who are, for most practical purposes, unable to read or write. Overall, between 17 and 21 million Americans are illiterate in English, and tens of millions more are unable to complete a job application form or balance a checkbook. Most of the nation's colleges now offer courses in remedial English and math to their incoming freshmen—a provision that would have been almost inconceivable a few decades ago, and that has few parallels in the colleges of other nations. Surveys show that incoming freshmen have less academic knowledge than their predecessors had two decades ago, and that their professors consider them less prepared for the experience of college (Boyer, 1983; Astin, 1985).

Why have academic standards declined? The question has been much debated, and several potential factors have been identified.

1. *Permissive child-rearing.* Modern child-rearing practices are comparatively permissive, and this, some people believe, may have left the young without the self-discipline necessary for academic success, particularly when the subject matter seems boring or irrelevant.

2. *Changing family patterns.* The traditional family structure is changing under the impact of such factors as easy divorces and a high rate of illegitimacy. Many young people therefore lack the stable home background that would otherwise complement the efforts of the schools.

3. *Impact of television.* Television has immense influence on the young: the average child spends far more time in front of a TV set than in school. Television encourages a passive orientation: viewers expect to be entertained, and can switch channels as soon as unwelcome demands are made on their powers of concentration. Many teachers feel that TV has sharply reduced the average pupil's attention span.

4. *Overburdened curriculum.* Conflicting demands have been placed on the school system, ranging from teaching about drugs and sex to correcting past social injustices, and these new functions may interfere with the school's traditional tasks.

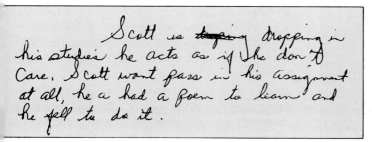

Scott is ~~teaching~~ dropping in his studies he acts as if the don't Care. Scott want pass in his assignment at all, he a had a poem to learn and he fell to do it.

SOURCE: *Time*, June 16, 1980, p. 59.

Figure 14.11 *This is part of a note written by a teacher with a master's degree. It has become apparent that many teachers are utterly incompetent, not only at teaching but also in commanding their own subjects. Many communities are now raising teacher salaries in order to attract more talented people to the profession.*

5. *Inferior teachers.* The quality of teaching is poor in many schools. The average high school teacher earns less than the average plumber, and the profession does not attract the most able people. Overall, high school graduates who intend to go into teaching score far lower on SAT measures than the average college-bound student.

6. *Discipline problems.* Authority is precarious in urban schools, and teachers are often less concerned with teaching than with merely maintaining some semblance of order. Over 100,000 teachers are assaulted by their pupils each year, and disciplinary problems undermine the educational effort in many classrooms. Opinion polls consistently find that the public rates "lack of discipline" as the most important problem of the schools.

7. *Fads and frills.* New and inadequately tested teaching fads have disrupted the learning process. The introduction of the much-vaunted "new math," for example, was followed by a sharp decline in math skills. The "open classroom," with its various "learning centers," easily degenerated into a shambles. And trendy, elective curricula may have left many students short on fundamentals.

8. *Greater educational access.* Attempts to broaden access to education may, at least initially, lead to a lowering of average standards. Automatic promotion may ensure that more people graduate from high school, but they will have lower average abilities than before; open admissions may give more people access to college, but the average freshman will be less gifted than when admission was more selective.

The cause of the decline in student abilities probably lies in some combination of these factors. Exactly how to reverse the decline is not immediately obvious, for despite decades of research, educators have achieved no real consensus on how to improve academic performance—other than to demand more work from students (Lightfoot, 1983; Boyer, 1983; Rutter, 1979; 1983; Coleman, Hoffer, and Kilgore, 1982). However, policy makers seem to have seized on two factors as offering the greatest promise for reform—the curriculum and the teachers. Throughout the United States, curricula are being reformed in a "back to basics" direction— that is, toward a thorough grounding in essential reading, writing, and mathematical skills. Additionally, state and local authorities are trying to improve the quality of teaching, by such means as improving teacher salaries and requiring teachers to be evaluated through periodic tests of their skills and knowledge. In general, school systems are increasingly demanding that students work harder and learn more—which, after all, is what academic excellence must inevitably entail.

The "Credential Society"

Actually, if we were to judge by grades alone, we would have to conclude that academic standards in American schools are soaring: today's students get at least 25 percent more As and Bs than the students of twenty years ago did. Yet surveys repeatedly show that they know far less than their predecessors—so why do their grades seem so promising? The reason, quite clearly, is that parents and pupils have applied irresistible pressure on the schools to improve student "achievement," and the result has been "grade inflation." This demand for higher grades reveals a crucial fact about American education: the entire system has been distorted away from the search for knowledge and toward the acquisition of credentials, such as diplomas and degrees.

Randall Collins (1979) describes the United States as a "credential society"—one in which overwhelming importance is attached to educational qualifications of various kinds. During this century, and particularly since World War II, the proportion of the population with high school diplomas, bachelor's and master's degrees, and even doctorates has increased at an astonishing pace. Why has this happened? The functionalist answer would be that education has expanded in response to economic growth: that new and more challeng-

Figure 14.12. *E. L. Henry's portrait of a traditional American schoolhouse reminds us of how far the educational institution has come in the course of the past century. But how much of that educational expansion is really necessary to meet the demands of the economy?*

ing jobs have demanded higher levels of skill, and that the schools have helped to keep the social system in balance by producing the necessary trained workers.

Until recently this explanation was almost unquestioned. The evidence, however, gives it surprisingly little support. Obviously, some new jobs that require advanced knowledge and skills have appeared (like that of the atomic physicist). But the content of most jobs has not changed in the course of this century. The level of skills required of file clerks, typists, cashiers, receptionists, assembly-line workers, lawyers, teachers, sales representatives, or managers is generally little different than it was decades ago. Yet the same kinds of jobs now demand more advanced qualifications. In fact, this kind of upgrading accounts for most of the increased educational requirements for jobs during this century. Only about 15 percent of the increase results from the appearance of new, high-skill jobs (Berg, 1970; Freeman, 1976; Collins, 1971b, 1979).

Why do employers demand ever higher educational credentials from their workers? There seem to be two reasons. First, employers use formal qualifications to make their task of screening and selecting job applicants easier; and when there is an oversupply of job candidates with the necessary credentials, employers simply increase the re-

quired qualifications. Second, employers share the widespread belief that better-educated workers are more productive than those who are less educated. Yet numerous studies have shown that there is little or no relationship between educational achievement and job performance or productivity. For example, good grades in a graduate school of medicine or education are poor predictors of whether someone will become a good doctor or teacher (Gintis, 1971; Collins, 1979; Fallows, 1985).

Why should this be the case? The fact is that the skills required to get an A grade in a college course on anatomy or educational philosophy are not the same as the skills needed to deal with a medical emergency or an unruly junior high school class. The schools and colleges teach very little (other than basic literacy and numeracy) that is directly relevant to the world of work. Most people pick up the necessary skills on the job, not in the classroom, and the characteristics that make for a successful career (such as initiative, leadership, drive, negotiating ability, willingness to take risks, and persuasiveness) are not even taught in the schools. It seems that the schools produce graduates with any number of educational credentials but with few specifically job-related skills. In fact, millions of people never put the specific content of their college education to direct use in their jobs, and nearly half of the country's college graduates actually work in fields they consider unrelated to their major subjects (Solomon et al., 1977).

On the whole, however, a higher credential means higher earnings, simply because of the value the job market places on it. If you turn back to Figure 10.6 on page 260, where the prestige rankings of various occupations are listed, you will notice that the most prestigious jobs tend to be those that are known not only to yield the highest incomes but also to require the longest education. In their landmark study of American social mobility, Peter Blau and Otis Duncan (1967) found that the most important factor affecting whether a son achieved a higher status than his father's was the amount of education the son attained. A high level of education is a scarce and valued resource, for which people compete vigorously. According to conflict theorists, the remarkable expansion of American education in recent decades has less to do with the demands of the economy than with competition for power, wealth, and prestige. In their view, the pressure for ever increasing credentials comes from two main sources: the professions, which insist on high membership qualifications as a means of protecting their own interests, and the consumers of education, who want credentials to enhance their career opportunities.

A **profession** is an occupation requiring extensive, systematic knowledge of, or training in, an art or science. Professionals try to maintain a clear distinction between themselves and lay persons, typically by the use of some form of licensing or certification, which is usually awarded only after a long socialization process involving a college degree or other advanced credential. A major purpose of this requirement is to limit entrance into the profession, thereby increasing its prestige, autonomy, and earning power. As hundreds of occupations have tried to become professionalized—first those of the physician and the lawyer, then of the engineer and the accountant, and now those of the social worker and the real estate broker—the demands on the schools for more and higher credentials have increased (Bledstein, 1976; Larson, 1977). (Professions are discussed in more detail in Chapter 17, "The Economic Order.")

The consumers of education, too, are well aware that educational credentials are the key to social mobility. Traditionally, people went to college to study academic subjects that interested them, in order to develop and broaden their minds. Today, many people go to college to study vocational subjects that frequently bore them, in the hopes of enhancing their job prospects. Even in the course of the past two decades, there has been a sharp decline in the percentage of freshmen who intend to major in such subjects as English, foreign languages, literature, history, and philosophy—fields that demand reading ability, critical and analytic thinking, and writing skills, but which do not lead directly to specific jobs. Twenty years ago, half the freshmen in America intended to major in the liberal arts—the natural sciences, social sciences, and humanities—but today less than a quarter do so. The most popular field currently is business: a quarter of freshmen now choose this single field for their major, and graduate business schools have shown a tenfold increase in enrollments since the mid-1960s. In 1985, some 70 percent of freshmen, compared with less than 50 percent in the early 1970s, said that a major reason for attending college is "to be able to make more money" (Astin and Green, 1986).

It is certainly true that the higher people's educational credentials, the higher their incomes are likely to be. In this respect, the pursuit of credentials may be a rational course of action for the individual. As Randall Collins points out, however, the obsession with credentials may be irrational from society's point of view. Even in the postindustrial United States, work is not so complex that it re-

Figure 14.13 *A college degree has become an almost essential credential for entry to better-paying jobs in America, and most students choose major subjects that they think will best serve them in the job market.*

quires a quarter of the population to have a college degree. The insistence on needlessly high qualifications means, first, that some people are denied jobs they could do, simply because they lack the credentials; and, second, that other people are spending unnecessary time and money on college, just to get credentials that are essentially irrelevant to the actual work that they will do for most of their lives. Also, the focus on currently "safe" majors in such vocational fields as business administration could prove to be ill-advised if, as has happened so often in the past, fashions in the public evaluation of education change yet again. It is possible, for example, that employers may tire of a glut of graduates who have indistinguishable entry-level vocational skills, but who are ignorant of cultural trends, unable to write a literate report, and incapable of sustaining an intelligent conversation on current affairs. There are already signs, in fact, that some employers are beginning to favor liberal arts graduates once more, on the grounds that they are more likely to have well-rounded skills and the ability to think creatively. Ideally, a college education should offer not only the prospects of a pleasant and rewarding career, but also the opportunity to grow and be challenged in ways that cannot be measured in dollars and cents (Bowen, 1977; Drew, 1978; Astin, 1977, 1985).

Summary

1.   Education is the systematic, formalized transmission of knowledge, skills, and values. Mass education is a recent historical development that has accompanied industrialization.

2.   American education has a unique combination of characteristics: commitment to elementary and high school education for all, a utilitarian emphasis on education, and a strong tradition of community control.

3.   Education has several important social functions: cultural transmission, social integration, personal development, screening and selection, innovation, and a number of latent functions.

4.   The conflict perspective emphasizes that educational credentials are a valuable resource in the competition for jobs. Individuals' educational achievement is strongly influenced by their social-class background. The schools thus reinforce existing inequalities.

5.   American schools are organized as formal, bureaucratic structures. They place great emphasis on competition for such rewards as grades. By treating pupils differently according to their supposed abilities, teachers may cause a self-fulfilling prophecy under which pupils perform according to the teacher's expectations.

6.   There are discrepancies in the average educational achievement of people from different social classes and races. Class and race distinctions overlap, and the racial differences are the product of class differences. Several specific factors account for these class differences: costs of education, family expectations, cultural background, childhood nutrition, language problems, teacher attitudes, labeling of students, and peer-group influence.

7.   Measured intelligence is also to some extent correlated with the class and race or ethnicity of the individual. IQ tests are an unsatisfactory way of measuring intelligence, because they are culture-bound and tend to test a narrow range of learned knowledge, not innate ability. Racial and ethnic differences in IQ vary according to the social statuses of the groups in question at the time in question.

8.   Attempts have been made to equalize educational opportunity in the belief that this will lead to greater social equality. The Coleman report, however, found that student achievement is primarily determined by class background. Minority students may do better in desegregated schools because these schools have a more "middle-class" atmosphere. Partly for this reason, controversial measures such as busing have been used to integrate the schools. Jencks argues that the schools cannot be used to change society because they merely reflect existing political and economic arrangements.

9.   American schools are regularly criticized for various failings; currently, they are charged with allowing academic standards to decline. There are several reasons for this decline, and reform efforts are now focused on curricula and teachers.

10. The United States is becoming a "credential society," in which competition for jobs has raised the required qualifications to unnecessarily high levels.

Important Terms

education (376)

basic research (380)

applied research (380)

manifest function (380)

latent function (380)

social mobility (380)

self-fulfilling prophecy (383)

profession (393)

Suggested Readings

CLARK, REGINALD M. *Family Life and School Achievement.* Chicago: University of Chicago Press, 1983.

A study of the factors that can cause poor black children to fail—or succeed—in school.

COLLINS, RANDALL. *The Credential Society: An Historical Sociology of Education and Stratification.* New York: Academic Press, 1979.

A carefully documented analysis of the reasons for expansion of American education.

GOODLAD, JOHN I. *A Place Called School: Prospects for the Future.* New York: McGraw-Hill, 1984.

A good overview of research on the American school system.

HURN, CHRISTOPHER J. *The Limits and Possibilities of Schooling.* 2nd ed. Boston: Allyn and Bacon, 1985.

A thoughtful introduction to the sociology of education, with a realistic assessment of the schools' potential to change society.

ILLICH, IVAN. *Deschooling Society.* New York: Harper and Row, 1971.

A provocative argument for abandoning formal schooling, which, the author claims, turns education into a commodity and stifles personal development and creativity.

LOEHLIN, JOHN C., et al. *Race Differences in Intelligence.* San Francisco: Freeman, 1975.

A clear discussion of race (and class) differences in IQ. The authors reject the view that these differences are genetically determined and present formidable evidence to support their conclusion.

LONDON, HOWARD B. *The Culture of a Community College.* New York: Praeger, 1978.

An interesting study of community college students' attitudes toward their educational experience.

RAVITCH, DIANNE. *The Troubled Crusade: American Education, 1945–1980.* New York: Basic Books, 1983.

An interesting and provocative analysis of attempts at educational reform in the United States.

ROSENTHAL, ROBERT, and LENORE JACOBSON. *Pygmalion in the Classroom.* New York: Holt, Rinehart and Winston, 1968.

An account of Rosenthal's experiments on the self-fulfilling prophecy in education.

SIZER, THEODORE R. *Horace's Compromise: The Dilemma of the American High School.* Boston: Houghton Mifflin, 1984.

A well-written and interesting account of what actually happens in American high schools.

CHAPTER 15

Religion

Some form of religion has existed in every society that we know of. Religious beliefs and practices are so ancient that they can be traced into prehistory, perhaps as far back as 100,000 years ago. Even the primitive Neanderthal people of that time, it seems, had some concept of a supernatural realm that lay beyond everyday reality. Among the fossilized remains of these cave dwellers, anthropologists have found evidence of funeral ceremonies in the form of flowers and artifacts that were buried with the dead, presumably to accompany them on the journey to an afterlife.

Although religion is a universal social institution, it takes a multitude of forms. Believers may worship gods, ancestors, or totems; they may practice solitary meditation, frenzied rituals, or solemn prayer. The great variety of religious behavior and belief makes it very difficult to say exactly what "religion" is. Many definitions have been offered in the past, but most of the ones we are familiar with have been biased by ethnocentric Judeo-Christian ideas about religion. These ideas are based on a number of central beliefs: that there exists one supreme being or God; that God created the universe and all life and takes a continuing interest in the creation; that there is a life hereafter; and that our moral behavior in this life influences our fate in the next. In cross-cultural terms, however, this particular combination of beliefs is unusual. Many religions do not recognize a supreme being, and a number do not believe in gods at all. Several religions ignore questions about the origins of the universe and life, leaving these problems to be dealt with instead by nonreligious myth. Many religions assume that the gods take little interest in human affairs. Some have almost nothing to say about life after death, and many—perhaps most—do not link our earthly morality with our fate beyond the grave. Obviously, religion cannot be defined in terms of the Western religious tradition alone. What, then, are its essential features?

Figure 15.1 *Believers in every religion practice some form of ritual when they approach the boundary between the profane and the sacred. In Indonesia, the ritual involves removing the shoes before entering a place of worship, and then* *kneeling on the floor to pray. But in a special ceremony of an Indian sect, the ritual may involve puncturing the fleshy parts of the body with knives and hooks as a way of proving one's faith and entering the realm of the sacred.*

Emile Durkheim, one of the first sociologists to study religion, pointed out that a single feature is common to all religions: a sharp distinction between the sacred and the profane. The **sacred** is anything that is regarded as part of the supernatural rather than the ordinary world; as such it inspires awe, reverence, and deep respect. Anything can be considered sacred: a god, a rock, the moon, a king, a symbol such as a cross. On the other hand, the **profane** is anything that is regarded as part of the ordinary rather than the supernatural world; as such it may be considered familiar, mundane, even corrupting. Of course, the profane, too, may be embodied by a rock, the moon, a king, or a symbol. Something becomes either sacred or profane only when it is socially defined as such by a community of believers. Durkheim also observed that a religious community always approaches the sacred through a **ritual**—a formal, stylized procedure, such as prayer, incantation, or ceremonial cleansing. Ritual is a necessary part of religion because the sacred has extraordinary and even dangerous qualities, and must be approached in a carefully prescribed, reverential manner.

We can say, then, that **religion** is a system of communally shared beliefs and rituals that are oriented toward some sacred, supernatural realm. The phenomenon is of such universal social importance that it has long been, and remains, a major focus of sociological interest (Berger, 1969; J. Wilson, 1978; McGuire, 1981; R. Johnstone, 1983; Chalfant, Beckley, and Palmer, 1986).

The Sociological Approach to Religion

Mr. Thwackum, a character in Henry Fielding's novel *Tom Jones*, declares: "When I mention religion, I mean the Christian religion; and not only the Christian religion, but the Protestant religion; and not only the Protestant religion, but the Church of England." Most people are like Mr. Thwackum: when they mention religion, they have their own in mind.

Whatever our religious beliefs may be, we usually learn them from other people through socialization into a particular faith (or through reso-cialization, if we convert from one faith to an-other). The religious convictions that anyone holds are thus influenced by the historical and social context in which that person happens to live. Someone born in ancient Rome would probably have believed that Jupiter is father of the gods; at any rate, he or she would certainly not have been a Southern Baptist or a Hindu. Similarly, if your par-ents are Catholic, you are probably Catholic; if they are Mormon, you too are probably a Mormon. We are not the passive prisoners of our upbringing, of course, but even people who decide to convert from one religion to another must almost inevita-bly select their new faith from the unique range of options that their particular culture happens to offer at a particular point in its history.

The fact that a religious doctrine is culturally learned does not necessarily put its "truth" in question: it might be the case, for example, that the learning process is inspired by some divine plan or purpose. What this cultural variety does mean, however, is that there are a large number of reli-gions, many of whose members are convinced that theirs is the one true faith and that all others are misguided, superstitious, even wicked. Where does this leave sociologists who study religion? Can and should they make judgments in these matters?

The answer is that sociology is not and cannot be concerned with the truth or falsity of any reli-gion. Like other empirical sciences, such as eco-nomics or chemistry, sociology is simply not com-petent to investigate the supernatural or to play umpire between competing faiths. Individual soci-ologists may be personally committed to a reli-gious viewpoint—as indeed many of the leading contemporary sociologists of religion are. But soci-ological research is necessarily directed at the social rather than the theological aspects of reli-gion. Regardless of whether or not a supernatural power exists, religion, like any other institution, has social characteristics that can be studied by the methods of social science.

Sociologists of religion focus on such issues as the relationship between society and religion. The sociologist can show, for example, that all religions reflect the cultural concerns of the societies in which they arise: war-prone societies tend to have gods of war; agricultural societies, gods of fertility. Societies that accord much greater power and prestige to men likewise tend to have male gods and religions dominated by male officials; it is therefore not surprising that priests, rabbis, and other clergy have been exclusively male in the past, or that this situation is gradually changing as gender roles become more flexible in other areas of society. Another example is that most Western Christians, being white, tend to think of both God and Jesus as white. The idea of a black God is almost unimaginable to them, and portraits of Jesus frequently present him as a blond Caucasian rather than as the person of Semitic features he no doubt was. In many African churches, on the other hand, statues and portraits of Jesus show him with dark, Negroid features.

Types of Religion

Sociologists who study religion have tried to bring some conceptual order to their field by classifying different religions into a series of basic types. One useful classification is that of Reece McGee (1975), who divides religions into four main categories according to their central belief: simple supernatu-ralism, animism, theism, and transcendent ideal-ism. These are merely artificial categories, of course, and not all religions will fit neatly into this classification.

Simple supernaturalism is a type of religion that does not recognize specific gods or spirits, but does assume that supernatural forces influence human events for better or worse. This type of reli-gion is fairly common in very simple preindustrial societies. The Melanesian Islanders of the South Pacific, for example, believe in "mana," a diffuse, impersonal force that may exist in both people and natural objects. A person does not necessarily have mana but can sometimes gain it by performing the appropriate rituals. Mana can be good or bad, per-haps causing arrows to fly straight or to miss their target. Some forms of simple supernaturalism still linger in the Western world: for example, the gam-bler's belief in "luck," a soldier's reliance on a pro-tective charm such as a rabbit's foot, or a baseball player's adherence to particular rituals to ensure a winning streak.

Animism is a type of religion that recognizes active, animate spirits operating in the world. These spirits may be found both in people and in natural phenomena such as rivers, mountains, and the weather. The spirits of animistic religion may be benevolent or evil, or they may even be indiffer-ent to human beings, but they are not gods, for they are not worshiped. People must take account of these spirits, however, and may try to influence them by the use of *magic*, or rituals intended to harness supernatural power for human ends. Animistic religions have been particularly common among the tribes of Africa and the Americas. In these communities there is typically a part-time specialist in the use of religious rituals, the shaman or "witch doctor." Some animism persists in the Western world in rituals such as exorcism, and in such occult forms as spiritualism and black magic.

Theism is a type of religion that centers on a belief in gods. A god is presumed to be powerful, to have at least some interest in human affairs, and to be worthy of worship. In cross-cultural terms the most common form of theism is *polytheism*, a belief in a number of gods. There is usually a "high god," who is often the "father" of the other gods and somewhat more powerful than they are. The lesser gods generally have specific spheres of influence, such as war, harvests, earthquakes, athletics, rain, and so on. A second form of theism is *monotheism*, the belief in a single supreme being. Although there are only three monotheistic religions in the modern world—Judaism, Christianity, and Islam—they have the greatest number of adherents. Actually, none of these three closely related faiths is purely monotheistic. Different versions of Christianity, for example, contain a number of semidivine lesser figures who in prac-

tice are sometimes prayed to or even worshiped, such as angels, saints, and the Virgin Mary. All three religions place such great emphasis on one supreme being, however, that for most purposes they can be considered monotheistic.

Transcendent idealism is a type of religion that centers not on the worship of a god but rather on sacred principles of thought and conduct. Its goal is to reach an elevated state of consciousness, and in this way to fulfill one's human potential to the utmost. Religions of transcendent idealism are characterized by reverence for such principles as life, truth, and tolerance of other beliefs. This type of religion is found predominantly in Asia; the best-known example is Buddhism, which is concerned with the attempt to become "at one with the universe" through many years of meditation. During the past two decades, some versions of these Eastern religions have attracted interest in the West, especially among young people.

Most religions do not try to win converts, and their adherents are usually indifferent toward the religions of others. Several of the major world religions, however, have tried to win converts at some point in their history. A common feature of these world religions is that they provide a convincing *theodicy*, an emotionally satisfying explanation for such great problems of earthly existence as human origins, suffering, and death (Berger, 1967, 1969).

Figure 15.2 *The title of this painting,* Where Do We Come From? What Are We? Where Are We Going? *suggests the universal questions that the theodicies of the major world religions try to* *answer. The painting is by Paul Gauguin (1897), the French artist who made his home in the islands of the South Pacific, where he was struck by the religious practices of the natives.*

We are born, live a brief span of years, often suffer, and then die. This universal sequence can easily seem purposeless and bleak, but a theodicy gives it meaning by explaining or justifying the presence of evil and misfortune in the world.

Theodicies can explain human problems in many ways. The Hindu doctrine of reincarnation deals with suffering and evil by extending the life span indefinitely: one's present existence becomes merely a tiny link in an endless chain, in which death and misery seem only temporary and insignificant. The mysticism of Buddhism or Taoism offers the believer salvation at a spiritual level, where earthly cares become unimportant. Christian theodicy holds out the hope of eternal salvation in heaven in recompense for ordeals on earth. The Zoroastrian theodicy sees the universe as a battleground between the evenly balanced forces of good and evil, with the misfortunes of humans stemming from their failure to throw their weight on the side of good. In Shintoism, which focuses on ancestor worship, one's sorrows and the idea of death are made more tolerable by the knowledge that one's life will be remembered and celebrated by one's descendants forever (Berger, 1969; Parkin, 1985).

Religion: A Functionalist View

Our discussion of theodicies implies that religion has some function in social life; and, in fact, the functionalist perspective offers many insights into the role of religion in society.

Durkheim: Religion and Social Cohesion

Emile Durkheim, one of the earliest functionalist theorists, was the first sociologist to apply the perspective to religion in a systematic way. His study *The Elementary Forms of Religious Life* was first published in 1912 and has since become a classic. Many of Durkheim's contemporaries saw religion as nothing more than a primitive relic that would soon disappear in the more sophisticated modern world. But Durkheim was impressed by the fact that religion is universal in human society, and he wondered why this should be so. His answer was that religion has a vital function in maintaining the social system as a whole.

Durkheim believed that the origins of religion were social, not supernatural. He pointed out that, whatever their source, the rituals enacted in any religion enhance the solidarity of the community as well as its faith. Consider such religious rituals as baptism, bar mitzvah, weddings, Sabbath services, Christmas mass, and funerals. Rituals like these serve to bring people together; to remind them of their common group membership; to reaffirm their traditional values; to maintain prohibitions and taboos; to offer comfort in times of crisis; and, in general, to help transmit the cultural heritage from one generation to the next. In fact, Durkheim argued, shared religious beliefs and the rituals that go with them are so important that every society needs a religion, or at least some belief system that serves the same functions. The cause of much of the social disorder in modern societies, he contended, is that "the old gods are growing old or are already dead, and others are not yet born." In other words, people no longer believe deeply in traditional religion, but they have found no satisfying substitute. Lacking commitment to a shared belief system, they tend to pursue their private interests without regard for their fellows.

The Functions of Religion

Modern sociologists have elaborated on Durkheim's ideas, and several of these social functions have been identified.

1. *Social solidarity.* Religion functions as a form of social "cement." It unites the believers by regularly bringing them together to enact various rituals, and by providing them with the shared values and beliefs that bind them into a community. An outstanding example of this function is the way the Jewish people, scattered for centuries across various cultures, have maintained their identity and cohesion simply through their religious commitment.

2. *Provision of meaning.* Religion provides a theodicy that gives meaningful answers to ultimate and eternal questions about existence. It offers explanations of human predicaments and gives purpose to a universe that might otherwise seem meaningless. People everywhere feel a need for these ultimate meanings to give coherence to their lives, and in most societies religion has almost a monopoly over the available answers.

3. *Social control.* The more important values and norms of a society—for example, those relat-

Figure 15.3 *Religion plays important functions in social life—binding people together, explaining the human predicament, helping to control social behavior, and providing individuals with emotional support in the uncertainties of life.*

ing to human life, sexual behavior, and property—tend to be incorporated not only in law but also in religious doctrine. The teachings found in such sacred scriptures as the Bible and the Koran would have far less force if they were regarded as the work of ordinary mortals. By powerfully reinforcing crucial values and norms, religion helps to maintain social control over individual behavior.

4. *Psychological support.* Religion provides individuals with emotional support in the uncertainty of the world. For example, it helps people during major events of the life course. Although puberty rites are no longer practiced in the United States (the nearest equivalent is the Jewish bar, or bat, mitzvah), birth, marriage, and death are almost always marked by religious rituals such as baptisms, weddings, and funerals.

Functional Equivalents of Religion

As Durkheim emphasized, a society requires some shared set of beliefs to ensure its cohesion. But do these beliefs have to be religious? Functionalist theory recognizes the concept of a ***functional equivalent***—a social or cultural feature that has the same effect as another, and may in that sense serve as a substitute for it. Actually, many other belief systems have been suggested as functional equivalents of religion, including psychotherapy, science, humanism, fascism, and communism. Some people argue that these and other belief systems fulfill the functions of religion so well that they can actually be regarded as "religions."

It is true that some of these belief systems have features similar to those of traditional Western religion. Consider the case of modern communism. It has its founding prophet, Karl Marx. It has sacred texts, the works of Marx, Engels, or, in different versions, Mao or Trotsky. It has its saints among those who were martyred in the cause of socialist revolution, such as the Cuban revolutionary Che Guevara; and it has its shrines, such as the tomb of Lenin in Moscow's Red Square. Like traditional religion, communism claims to have access to ultimate truth, and regards all alternative views as false. Similarly, it attempts to explain suffering in the world, and it offers a vision of a better life based on a moral command—"from each according to his ability, to each according to his needs." Like some religions, it has a missionary zeal to convert the world to its principles. The experience of conversion to communism can be similar to conversion to a new religion; the writer Arthur Koestler, for example, described his own conversion (which he later recanted) in these terms:

> Something had clicked in my brain which shook me like a mental explosion. To say that one had "seen the light" is a poor description of the mental rapture which only the convert knows (regardless of what faith he has been converted to). The new light seems to pour from all directions across the skull; the whole universe falls into pattern like the stray pieces of a jigsaw puzzle assembled by magic at one stroke. There is now an answer to every question, doubts and conflicts are a matter of the tortured past—a past already remote, when one had lived in dismal ignorance in the tasteless, colorless world of those who *don't know.* [Quoted in Crossman, 1952]

The essential difference between such belief systems and religion is, of course, that though the former serve some of the same functions as religion, they are not oriented toward the supernatural, a distinction that should not be disregarded.

Religion: A Conflict View

Although religion may often be functional for society, it can also be deeply implicated in social conflict. A full understanding of the role of religion in society must take account of this fact.

Marx: Religion as "Opium of the People"

The conflict approach to religion derives largely from the writings of Karl Marx, who saw religion as a form of false consciousness and as a tool of the powerful in the struggles between competing social classes.

To Marx, belief in religion was a profound form of human **alienation,** the situation in which people lose their control over the social world they have created, with the result that they find themselves "alien" in a hostile social environment. Thus, people create systems of government, law, marriage, feudalism, industrialism, or slavery, then lose the sense of their authorship of these products, taking them for granted as though they were part of an unchanging natural order. Nowhere is this process more poignant than in the field of religion: people create gods, lose their awareness that they have done so, and then worship or fear the very gods they created.

Moreover, Marx claimed, the *dominant* religion in any society is always the religion of its economically and politically dominant class, and it always provides a justification for existing inequalities and injustices. The dominant religion legitimates the interests of the ruling class and, like a narcotic, lulls the oppressed into acceptance of their lot. Marx proclaimed passionately:

> Man makes religion, religion does not make man. . . . Religious suffering is at the same time an expression of real suffering and a protest against real suffering. Religion is the sigh of the oppressed creature, the sentiment of a heartless world, and the soul of soulless conditions. It is the opium of the people. [1964b, orig. 1848]

Marx conceded that in very simple, preindustrial societies that have no class divisions, religion is simply a matter of superstition. In all other societies, he insisted, the dominant religion supports the status quo and diverts the attention of the oppressed from their real problems. (Inspired by Marx's critique, all communist-ruled societies tolerate religion only reluctantly, and are officially atheistic. This is a point their leaders occasionally overlook: at a Vienna summit meeting in 1979, the Soviet leader Leonid Brezhnev commented that "God will not forgive us if we fail"; and in 1985 the current leader, Mikhail Gorbachev, told Western reporters, "Surely God on high has not refused to give us enough wisdom to find ways to bring an improvement in our relations." Neither remark was reported in the Soviet media.)

Inequality and Religion

There is no shortage of historical evidence to support Marx's view that the dominant religion in any society legitimates the interests of the ruling class. In fact, it is difficult to find a contrary example.

The most striking instances occurred in those ancient societies in which the rulers were believed to be divine, or at least descended from gods. The pharaohs of ancient Egypt, for example, were regarded by their subjects as sacred—which made rebellion against them virtually unthinkable. Somewhat more subtle, though just as effective, were the religious ideologies that upheld the Indian caste system or the late European feudal system. As we saw in Chapter 10 ("Social Stratification"), Hindu doctrine threatens that Indians who try to change their caste status will be reincarnated as a member of a lower caste, or even as an animal, while the feudal system drew legitimacy from the notion of the "divine right" of kings to rule as God's representatives on earth.

Religion often serves to legitimate political authority when one society conquers and then rules another society whose people have a different religion. In such cases, the conquered people often assume (and are usually taught) that their new rulers have a superior god or gods. In time, the subject people tend to change their allegiance to the religion of their conquerors. Both of the two largest world religions, Christianity and Islam, were spread largely through conquest. Christianity was originally disseminated through western

Figure 15.4

"It's called 'the divine right of kings.' You should have your people look into it."

Europe as the official religion of the Roman empire, and then was carried to other continents when Europeans seized and colonized vast territories elsewhere in the world, particularly in Africa and the Americas. Similarly, Islam was spread around the Mediterranean, the Middle East, and the Near East through wars of conquest. Indeed, both religions have enjoyed immense success in societies that their adherents have dominated politically, while making relatively little headway elsewhere.

A striking contemporary example of religious beliefs serving to legitimate inequality occurs in South Africa, which, as we saw in Chapter 3 ("Culture"), is a caste system based on race. As descendants of early Dutch settlers, most members of the ruling white minority in South Africa belong to the local Dutch Reformed Church, which preaches that God placed them in South Africa to rule as part of a divine plan, and, furthermore, that racial mixing is a sin. Many white South Africans therefore appear convinced that their rule over the majority population of voteless blacks is God's will and is therefore morally right. Moreover, as a result of missionary work, millions of black South Africans also belong to segregated branches of this church, and to other churches that preach a similar message. Some of them still accept religious teachings about the status quo: as recently as 1985, a throng of over 1 million black members of the Zion Christian Church cheered the country's white president when he told them that it was their duty not to question the law, but to obey it. This is the kind of situation Friedrich Engels had in mind when he caustically remarked that religion tends to make the masses "submissive to the behests of the masters it had pleased God to place over them." (Incidentally, in 1981 the Gallup International Research Institutes asked respondents in fifteen countries to rate, on a scale of 1 to 10, how important God is in their lives. South Africans scored highest of all—whites, 8.5, and blacks, 8.4. Second highest were Americans, at 8.2.)

Social Conflict and Religion

Marx's view of religion as the "opium of the people" may have been too narrow, for religion can be involved in social conflict in other ways as well—including ways that challenge the status quo. This is so because communities or even societies that are hostile to one another often *use* religion as an ideological weapon, emphasizing differences in faith in order to justify conflict.

A nation at war invariably assumes that its gods are on its side—even when, as in the case of the two world wars of this century, several of the warring nations worship the same deity. Wars fought on ostensibly religious grounds are often marked by extreme bloodiness and fanaticism, but religious differences are not necessarily the *causes* of the wars, even though the participants themselves may think they are. The medieval Crusades, for example, appear at first sight to have been a purely religious conflict in which European Christians were trying to recover the Holy Land from Muslims. A closer analysis suggests an additional reason, however: the European nobility launched the Crusades partly to gain control of the trade routes to the East and partly to divert widespread unrest among their peasantry.

Similarly, contemporary conflict between Jews and Muslims in the Middle East may seem to arise from religious differences, but the tension is really over competing claims by two different ethnic groups, the Israelis and the Palestinians, for the same homeland. In much the same way, the continuing conflict in Northern Ireland seems on the surface to be one between Catholics and Protestants, but its roots lie much deeper in ethnic and class divisions between Irish of native descent and those descended from British settlers.

Sometimes a group may actually be inspired by religion to challenge the existing order. Religion plays this part in social conflict because religious doctrines can provide a moral standard against which existing social arrangements may be judged—and perhaps found wanting. These challenges rarely come from the dominant religious organizations, for they and their leaders are usually too closely linked to the social and political establishment. Instead, the challenges tend to come from religious movements near the fringes of society, or from dissident groups within the dominant religion. In many of the highly unequal and impoverished societies of Central and South America, for example, the Catholic Church has long been associated with the military, social, and economic elite. Yet in recent years a minority of priests and nuns has embraced "liberation theology," which blends Christian compassion for the poor with an explicit commitment to political change through class struggle. Most Church leaders view "liberation theology" with dismay, but the movement poses a significant challenge to the status quo. As we will see later, religion has persistently inspired criticism of the existing order in the United States, too—sometimes by liberals, sometimes by conservatives.

Figure 15.5 *Religion can become deeply involved in social conflict, particularly when the dominant religion is closely allied to the state. Between the thirteenth and the seventeenth centuries, the European clergy caused as many as half a million people to be tortured and murdered on the grounds of witchcraft or heresy. The victims ranged from old, widowed women to political and social deviants—Jews, Muslims, heretics, and critics of the political and religious leaders of the time. Typically, the "witches" were tortured until they confessed, after which they were burned to death. The* accused *were also forced to name their supposed accomplices—who were tortured in turn until even more witches were named. Naturally, the number of witches seemed to multiply. Fear of witchcraft helped to divert the attention of the wretched peasantry from the real source of many of their problems—corrupt popes and tyrannical princes— by shifting the responsibility to imaginary demons in human form. Much has changed in the centuries since then—but there are still zealots, in every faith, who create God in the image of their own bigotry.*

Religion and Social Change

The relationship between religion and social change involves the often subtle interplay between beliefs and behavior. This process can be illustrated by two important cases—one historical, one contemporary. The historical case concerns the "Protestant ethic," which some sociologists regard as a vital influence on the development of capitalism, and thus of much of our social and cultural environment today. The contemporary case concerns Islamic fundamentalism, a significant social movement that may have far-reaching international implications. In each case, these religious influences arose from communities that were mar-

ginal to their own faiths—the "Protestant ethic," from early Calvinists whose doctrines differed markedly from the traditional values of Western society; Islamic fundamentalism, from the Shiites, an often-despised minority group within their own religion.

The "Protestant Ethic"

According to Max Weber (1958a, orig. 1904), the ***Protestant ethic*** is a disciplined, moral commitment to regular, conscientious work and deferred gratification. Weber undertook his classic study of the Protestant ethic partly because of his great in-

Figure 15.6 *Grant Wood's famous painting American Gothic (1930) captures perfectly the "Protestant ethic" of disciplined commitment to regular, conscientious work and deferred gratification. Although the painting seems at first glance to portray a secular setting, it has strong religious overtones: the shape of the window recalls church architecture, and the form is echoed again in the man's pitchfork and the stitching on his garment. Weber argued that the historical "Protestant ethic" had a profound influence on the development of capitalism.*

terest in a controversial sociological question: Do ideas and beliefs shape changes in society and culture, or do social and cultural conditions shape the content of ideas and beliefs? Karl Marx, one of the first social theorists to deal with this issue, asserted that philosophy or religion merely reflects material conditions, and generally supports and justifies them. Religious changes therefore reflect social changes, not the other way around.

Weber, in contrast, maintained that under certain circumstances religious or other ideas could influence social change. Weber was fascinated by the growth of modern capitalism, which was rapidly transforming the European and American societies of his time. But why had capitalism first developed in Europe rather than in, say, China or India? Weber undertook a massive study of the

major world religions and the societies in which they are found, and concluded that the answer lay in the emergence in Europe of a specific type of religious belief—Protestant puritanism, especially Calvinism.

Modern capitalism, as Weber pointed out, is unlike traditional commercial activity. Formerly, merchants earned money in a haphazard way, spent it at once in luxurious living, and placed a higher value on consuming wealth than on earning it. The spirit of modern capitalism is quite different: it emphasizes the methodical accumulation of wealth through rational, calculated procedures, such as accounting and long-range planning. Hard work and making money are highly valued for their own sake. To spend money on idle luxury is considered disreputable; instead, the capital must be reinvested to earn yet more capital.

Weber argued that this new approach arose out of the Protestant ethic of regular work and a frugal lifestyle. The early Calvinists believed that God had predestined them to salvation in heaven or damnation in hell since the beginning of time. There was nothing they could do to change their fates, and their duty was simply to abstain from pleasure and to work for the glory of God. But because of their great psychological anxiety about their ultimate destiny, the Calvinists looked for "signs" that they were among the chosen—and they took worldly success as just such a sign. The more successful they were, the more likely it seemed that they were destined for heaven—and since profits could not be spent on pleasure, they had to be reinvested. Thus, argued Weber, modern capitalism was born. Ironically, the very people who rejected material comforts unwittingly created industrial capitalism, the foundation of modern affluence. By a further irony, industrialism in turn encouraged the rational-scientific world view, which undermines traditional religion. Modern capitalists, although they are no longer puritanical Calvinists, have retained traces of the Protestant ethic of diligent work, thrift, and deferred gratification.

Other religions, Weber argued, did not provide the same incentive for this kind of social and economic change. Catholicism stresses rewards in heaven and encourages its followers to be satisfied with their lot on earth. Hinduism threatens reincarnation in a lower form of life to anyone who tries to attain a higher caste status. Buddhism stresses mysticism, far removed from earthly goals. Taoism requires the believer to withdraw from worldly temptations. Confucianism emphasizes a static social structure as a part of the natural order. Although Islam is an activist religion, it lacks the emphasis on thrift and hard work. All these religions served to discourage the growth of capitalism (Weber, 1951, 1952, 1958b, 1963).

Weber did not intend to prove that the Protestant ethic was the *cause* of capitalism—merely that it was an important influence. Some critics have suggested that his analysis was wrong. For one thing, capitalism did not arise in some Calvinist societies (like Scotland); and England, which was not Calvinist, was the birthplace of the Industrial Revolution. Moreover, there is no way of showing that the "salvation panic" of the Calvinists led them to become capitalists. They may have done so for other reasons, such as the fact that they were more likely than Catholics to live in urban areas, or that their religion encouraged hard work, or even that they were not so wedded to tradition as were Catholics of the time. Weber's hypothesis is one of the most provocative in all sociology, but its subject is so vast and complex that his argument is probably unverifiable. Weber simply bit off more than he or anyone else could chew.

Most Western sociologists probably accept Weber's hypothesis as being at least plausible, and they generally agree that religion or other belief systems can influence society. The material and nonmaterial components of culture are best seen as parts of an interacting system, each influencing the other in different ways at different times.

Islamic Fundamentalism

Islam is one of the world's major religions; it claims the allegiance of a fifth of the entire human population. Although Westerners often think of Islam as an Arab religion, most Muslims are not Arabs. The largest Muslim populations are in Indonesia (153 million) and India (82 million), and there are even large concentrations of Muslims in China (31 million) and the Soviet Union (25 million). Islam is the second-largest faith in Europe after Christianity, and it competes with Christianity in many black African countries. Trends in Islamic societies, therefore, are potentially of global importance.

Over the past decade, religious fervor has erupted in the Islamic world in general and in the Middle East in particular. It has led, for example, to a revolution in Iran, to the assassination of Anwar Sadat, the president of Egypt, and to fierce resistance to the Soviet invasion of Afghanistan. This fervor has been inspired by *fundamentalism,* a commitment to, and reliance on, the traditional basics of religious doctrine. To many Westerners, Islamic fundamentalism seems like an almost scandalous return to a medieval morality. It conjures forth images of women behind veils, of adulterers being stoned, of thieves having their hands cut off, of public floggings and executions, of martyrdom in holy wars, and, in extreme cases, of political fanaticism exemplified in aircraft hijackings and terrorist bombings. This picture is rather distorted, for it is based on what is newsworthy rather than what is typical. In a way that is difficult for most Westerners to comprehend, Islam is a comprehensive way of life, continuously and intensely pervading belief and behavior, public conduct and private experience. The very word "Islam" means "submission" to the will of Allah, who demands personal integrity, social justice, and brotherhood among believers, and who has revealed the appropriate codes of conduct in virtually every field of life, from religious ritual to personal hygiene.

Why has Islamic fundamentalism intensified at all—especially at a time when we might expect the societies involved to be moving forward, toward modernization, rather than backward, toward tradition? Sociologists have observed that fundamentalist revivals, in whatever religion, take place in times when social changes have led to turmoil, uncertainty, and the erosion of familiar values. When people find themselves confused, threatened, or even appalled at changing conditions, they may see a "return to basics" as a solution. It is not surprising, therefore, that Islamic fundamentalism has surged in societies like Iran, which have experienced wrenching social change as a result of their new oil wealth. Some of these societies had previously remained culturally fairly static for generations—in some cases, for centuries. Then, in less than the space of a single life span, they were thrust into a world of airports and highways, schools and television, factories and power plants. As part of this process, some of the Islamic societies have been flooded with foreign advisers, officials, and entrepreneurs. These newcomers behave in a variety of ways that deeply offend the locals—Muslims, for example, use only the right hand for eating and only the left hand for cleaning the body after defecating, and the sight of Westerners placing food in the mouth with the left hand is utterly revolting to them. In the view of the fundamentalists, foreigners, especially from the West, are a profoundly immoral and corrupting influence.

Figure 15.7 *Largely as a result of unsettling social changes in Islamic countries, there is currently a surge of fundamentalist feeling in these societies. The photograph shows pilgrims in Mecca, the most sacred place in the Islamic world.*

The principal foreign enemy of the fundamentalists is the "Great Satan," the United States. One reason is that the fundamentalists find it politically helpful to have an alien enemy; as we noted in Chapter 7 ("Groups"), the solidarity of any community is enhanced if it perceives a common outside threat. A second reason is that the United States provides crucial support for Israel, whose presence in an otherwise Islamic area is seen as a continuing wound to all Muslims. The main cause of the fundamentalists' hostility to the United States, however, is that they fear the impact of American culture and political interference in their societies. Muslims look with horror at America's sexual permissiveness, at the relative assertiveness and immodesty of American women, at the high rates of illegitimacy, abortion, and divorce, at the preoccupation with pleasure, drugs, alcohol, pornography, and material possessions, and at the search for individual self-fulfillment at the expense of obligations to kin and community. The fundamentalists regard Americans essentially as barbarians—but as barbarians whose economic, technological, and military influence threatens the integrity of Muslim societies and traditions. Their own governments, they claim, are often used as mere pawns in America's geopolitical strategy against the Soviet Union, a strategy in which the interests of ordinary Muslims count for nothing.

Despite their antipathy to the United States, the fundamentalists are concerned mainly with conditions in their own countries. Most Muslims are desperately poor, for their nations' oil wealth has often been unequally shared, creating a new elite whose extravagant lifestyle arouses deep resentment in the populace. The fundamentalists aim at nothing less than the replacement of their rulers by Islamic governments, in which the distinction between the religious and the secular would disappear. Their inspiration comes from the 1979 Iranian revolution, in which the shah, a deeply unpopular ruler who was perceived as an American puppet, was deposed through a movement led by Shiite Muslim clergy. In many Islamic societies, Shiite fundamentalists now form an unofficial opposition to the political and social establishment. Islamic fundamentalism, like the Protestant ethic, thus arises out of specific social and cultural conditions and may then, in turn, influence the subsequent course of social change (Said, 1979; Rubin, 1983; Mottahedeh, 1985).

Religious Organizations

The "Protestant ethic" arose in a religious movement that had broken away from a larger and more established body, the Catholic Church, which, in turn, had originated centuries earlier as an offshoot of Judaism. The Shiites, similarly, are an offshoot of the main body of Islam. These are just some examples of a constant process by which new and different religious organizations are formed.

Religious organizations can be conveniently divided into one of four basic types: the ecclesia, the denomination, the sect, and the cult. These types apply best to organizations within the Western religious tradition, although some sociologists have tried to apply them to other religions as well. The classification represents only artificial categories designed to fit most situations, but it does help draw our attention to important differences in beliefs, practices, and membership (Weber, 1963; Niebuhr, 1929; Troeltsch, 1931; Johnstone, 1983).

The *ecclesia* is a religious organization that claims the membership of everyone in a society or even in several societies. One does not "join" an ecclesia; one is a member by virtue of one's citizenship. A powerful, bureaucratized organization with a hierarchy of full-time officials, it gives complete support to the state authorities and expects the same from them in turn. People who are born into a society with such an "official" religion become members almost automatically. The Roman Catholic Church was such an organization for centuries until Protestantism began to compete with it in several countries. Strictly speaking, there is probably no true ecclesia in the modern world, but there are some religious organizations that approximate one in varying degrees, such as Islam in Iran and Saudi Arabia, and the Catholic Church in Ireland and Spain.

The *denomination* (or "church") is one of two or more well-established, relatively tolerant religious organizations that claim the allegiance of a substantial part of the population. The denomination does not demand official support from the state and may even be at odds with it on occasion. Like the ecclesia, it has a formal, bureaucratic structure, with trained clergy and other officials. A given denomination will have been around a long time—certainly for many decades—and is "respectable," drawing its members primarily from the middle and upper classes. Many of the members are born into the faith, but the denomination usually accepts almost anyone who wants to join. Although they may compete for recruits, denominations are generally tolerant of one another. In North America, this type of organization includes the Greek Orthodox, Russian Orthodox, and Roman Catholic churches; the Methodist, Episcopal, and similar large Protestant churches; and, in most respects, the Orthodox, Conservative, and Reform branches of mainstream Judaism.

The *sect* is an exclusive and uncompromising religious organization, usually one that has split off from a denomination for doctrinal reasons. Particularly in the period soon after the founding of a sect, its adherents are generally recruited by conversion, with membership restricted to those who give continuing proof of their commitment. The sect is less socially "respectable" than the denomination, and its members are usually of lower socioeconomic status. Intolerant of other religious organizations, it is dogmatic and fundamentalist, believing that its particular interpretation of the Scriptures is the literal and only route to salvation. The sect also tends to be indifferent or even hostile to political authority, which it often regards as too worldly and corrupt. Sects usually have no trained clergy, and rituals of worship emphasize emotion, spontaneity, and extensive participation by the congregation. Most sects tend to be short-lived, but some gradually become denominations—always with an accompanying loss of fervor and a gain in social respectability. Contemporary North American sects include the Jehovah's Witnesses, the Assembly of God, the Amish, and Hassidic Jews.

RELIGIOUS ORGANIZATIONS IN THE UNITED STATES

Roman Catholic	52,392,934
Baptist	28,460,242
Methodist	13,696,951
Lutheran	8,382,610
Jewish	5,728,075
Pentecostal	4,696,457
Eastern Orthodox	4,033,668
Latter-Day Saints (Mormon)	3,799,884
Presbyterians	3,705,162
Episcopal	2,794,690
Muslim	2,000,000
United Church of Christ	1,701,513
Churches of Christ	1,600,000
Christian Church (Disciples of Christ)	1,145,918
Christian Churches & Churches of Christ	1,043,642
Christian Methodist Episcopal	718,922
Jehovah's Witness	649,697
Seventh-Day Adventist	623,563
Reformed	586,322
Church of the Nazarene	498,491
Salvation Army	419,475
Brethren (German Baptist)	289,649
Mennonite	286,226
Polish National Catholic	282,411
Churches of God	229,163
Christian & Missionary Alliance	204,713

SOURCE: *Yearbook of American and Canadian Churches*, 1985.

Figure 15.8 *Americans' religious preferences are overwhelmingly Christian. In practice, however, many hundreds of different religious organizations compete for people's loyalty, especially among Protestants. This table shows American religious organizations that have over 200,000 members; in addition, there are a variety of smaller denominations and sects.*

Figure 15.9 *Cults tend to be short-lived, for they are often centered on a single prophet and usually do not demand a great deal of commitment from their supporters. Between 1981 and 1986, Bhagwan Shree Rajneesh operated a commune in Oregon that attracted many thousands of mainly middle-class Americans. The guru quickly gained a reputation as the "swami of sex" because of the group's strong emphasis on free love as the route to enlightenment, which seemed to be conceived as a kind of cosmic orgasm. This photograph shows some of the red-clad devotees applauding Rajneesh as he passed by in one of dozens of Rolls-Royces that he owned. Soon after this picture was taken, the commune collapsed amid lawsuits and criminal investigations, and the guru hurriedly left the United States.*

The ***cult*** is a loosely organized religious movement that is independent of the religious tradition of the surrounding society. Unlike the sect, which attempts to revive or reinterpret older doctrines, the cult emphasizes the new, drawing symbols and rituals from beyond the religious mainstream. The cult tends to be the most temporary of all forms of religious organization. It usually has few coherent doctrines and imposes minimal demands on believers: like the denomination but unlike the sect, it is open to almost anyone who wishes to participate. The members tend to have relatively low commitment to the organization, and people drift in and out of the group. Cults are often centered on specific prophets or other leaders and generally lack trained officials. They appeal to people who, disenchanted with traditional religion, participate primarily for the personal benefits or experiences the cult offers them. In North America, contemporary cults currently include such loosely structured groups as Rosicrucians, spiritualists, and believers in astrology or transcendental meditation.

Since the ecclesia hardly exists and cults have relatively few adherents in modern societies, sociologists usually focus on denominations and sects. Although there is immense variety within each category, the overall differences between the two types of organization seem more significant. Denominations and sects are not static, however: their membership, rituals, and beliefs are in a constant flux, and this process is a vital element in religious change. Sects are continually formed as groups break off from denominations in search of doctrinal purity that the parent body seems to have lost. Most of these new sects wither and die; a few retain the intensity of conviction that first inspired them; and some survive over the generations, only to grow steadily more prosperous but less committed to the faith—occasionally, in fact, to become denominations from which new sects break off.

The Methodists, for example, started out as a spontaneous, unrestrained sect of the poor, but today they are among the most affluent and respectable of all Protestant denominations. Similarly, the Mormons were once an oppressed sect, persecuted in state after state until they settled in the area that became Utah. But as the Mormons became more prosperous and successful, they abandoned some earlier fundamentalist teachings (notably that permitting polygamy, which they gave up in order to gain statehood for Utah). The status of the organization now seems to be transitional between that of a sect and a denomination. The Seventh-Day Adventists, too, began as a sect prophesying the end of the world on a specific date. That day having come and gone, they are presently developing from a sect into a denomination with an increasingly middle-class membership and a trained clergy.

Religion in the United States

At the time of its founding, the United States seemed to be an infertile ground for religion. Many of the nation's leaders—including George Washington, Thomas Jefferson, and Benjamin Franklin—were not Christians, did not accept the authority of the Bible, and were hostile to organized religion. The attitude of the general public was one of apathy: in 1776, only about 5 percent of the population were participating members of churches. Yet, in the two centuries since then, religion has come to be one of the most highly regarded of all American institutions, claiming the adherence of the vast majority of the people.

Some Characteristics

The part played by religion in American life is different in many respects from that of religion in other societies, for the American institution has several distinctive characteristics.

1. *Freedom of religion.* The United States has no official, "established" religion; indeed, the Constitution forbids any formal or legal assumption that any particular faith is more or less "true" than any other. Of course, the line between government and religion is not always clearly drawn, and in some cases (particularly involving minors), the state does interfere in the exercise of religious freedom. Courts, for example, have shown little sympathy for sects that claim biblical authority to give children a purely religious education, to deny them vaccinations or medical treatment, or to severely beat them. No religion, however, can be declared illegal simply because of its beliefs and practices.

2. *Breadth of religious commitment.* The overwhelming majority of Americans appear to have some commitment to religion. Seven out of ten Americans belong to a religious organization, and in an average week about 40 percent of the population attends a church or synagogue. Other data yield a similar impression of widespread religious commitment. Over 70 percent of Americans—compared with only a minority of Europeans—believe in life after death. But whether this commitment is deep as well as broad is another matter. Thus, a 1982 Gallup poll found that only a quarter of those professing Christianity claim to lead a very Christian life. A 1985 Gallup poll found that although eight out of ten teenagers say they consider the Ten Commandments to be "valid rules for living today," two-thirds of them are unable to name more than half of the commandments. And although about 90 percent of the population claim to be Christian, most of them cannot even name the four gospels that contain Jesus's message, and most have no idea that it was Jesus who delivered that central Christian statement, the Sermon on the Mount.

3. *Religiosity as a value.* President Eisenhower once commented that it did not matter what religion a person believed in, as long as he or she had one. This is a characteristically American view, reflecting the high value placed on religiosity itself. Many Americans tend to use religion primarily for social rather than religious purposes, finding in their church a source of community and in its beliefs a justification for the American values of good neighborliness, self-help, individualism, hard work, and anticommunism. There is an implicit cultural assumption that Americans should be religious—not necessarily by attending church or synagogue, but at least by expressing a belief in God and in religious principles. A 1983 Gallup poll found that only 42 percent of Americans would be willing to vote for an atheist for president (compared with 66 percent who would vote for a Jew, 77 percent for a black, 80 percent for a woman, and 92 percent for a Catholic).

BELIEF IN GOD OR UNIVERSAL SPIRIT

Figure 15.10 *As this graph suggests, Americans are especially likely to believe in God or a universal spirit.*

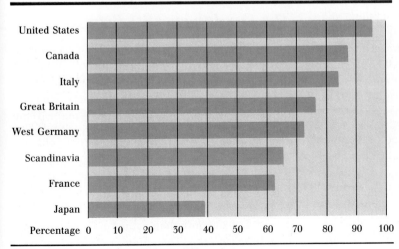

SOURCE: Princeton Religious Research Center, 1986.

4. *Religious pluralism.* The United States is probably the most religiously diverse society in history. In most societies there are only a handful of significant religious organizations. In Canada, for example, 90 percent of the population is Christian; half of them are Catholic and half are Protestant, and three-quarters of the Protestants belong to two denominations, the Anglican Church and the United Church of Canada. The United States is also about 90 percent Christian, but the largest denomination, the Catholic Church, has only about 28 percent of total church allegiance. Some 57 percent of Americans are Protestant, but they are fragmented into so many denominations and sects that none of them can claim even a tenth of the total religiously affiliated population. Although about two dozen organizations account for the preference of almost the entire religious population, there are currently over 1,300 distinct denominations, sects, and cults (Stark and Bainbridge, 1985).

5. *Tolerance of diversity.* Americans are, on the whole, tolerant of religious diversity, particularly among the main denominations. These organizations generally avoid public debates over controversial theological issues, and rarely try to convert one another's adherents. Sects and cults do not receive quite the same public tolerance as denominations, and there may be some personal prejudice against their members: when people were asked in a 1983 Gallup poll what groups they did not want as neighbors, 30 percent mentioned sects and cults and 11 percent mentioned fundamentalists, while only 2 percent mentioned Jews and only 1 percent, Catholics or Protestants. Nevertheless, the right of even the most exotic-seeming religious groups to exist and propagate their beliefs is rarely seriously questioned.

6. *Religion and ethnic characteristics.* Religion in the United States is not merely a set of beliefs and rituals. It can also be a source of personal and group identity. The most obvious example is the American Jewish community, an ethnic group held together by its common religion (Sklare, 1971, 1974). Catholicism, too, is one of the most important features distinguishing ethnic groups such as the Poles from other Americans (Greeley, 1977). The use of church schools by these groups enhances ethnic identification among younger members who might otherwise be assimilated more readily into the American mainstream. Churches are also an important institution in the black community, where they have been a significant source of group solidarity and identity from the time of slavery up to the present (Frazier, 1963; Lincoln, 1974). Religion remains one of the most racially segregated of all American institutions: most congregations are virtually all-white or all-black.

7. *Religion and social characteristics.* Membership in a particular religious organization tends to correlate with certain other social characteristics. For example, Jews have the highest income of the major religious groups, followed by the Episcopalians, Presbyterians, Lutherans, Catholics, Methodists, and Baptists. As the most highly educated group, Jews play a disproportionate role in the nation's intellectual life, but they are virtually excluded from the highest positions of corporate leadership except in the retail trade. Catholics' educational achievements, which once lagged behind those of Protestants, are now at the national level, but the upper echelons of foundations, corporations, politics, the media, and the arts are still dominated by white, Anglo-Saxon Protestants.

Political and social attitudes also correlate with religious affiliation. Jews, Catholics, and black Protestants have traditionally been predominantly Democratic, while white Protestants have been evenly divided between the Democrats and the Republicans. Jews are generally the most liberal on social issues, followed by the Catholics and then the Protestants. Two decades ago, Catholics were more conservative than Protestants on most issues of sexual morality, but today the situation is reversed: in 1985, for example, the Gallup poll found that 59 percent of Catholics thought premarital sex was "not wrong," compared to 46 percent of Protestants. On the issue of abortion, however, Catholics take the most conservative position. Overall, polls indicate that people who have high religious involvement are more conservative, and also happier in their personal lives, than those who lack this involvement.

The Fundamentalist Revival

Religion in America is in a state of constant flux, and the period since the early 1960s has been a time of unusual religious innovation. One of the most striking features has been the decline in commitment to traditional organizations—mainstream Judaism, the Roman Catholic Church, and the established Protestant denominations.

Judaism has been under pressure from an increasing trend toward interfaith marriages, something the religion has always strongly disapproved. In 1960, less than 5 percent of Jews married non-Jews; by 1980, more than a third married someone of a different faith. The children of many of these unions are likely to be raised outside the Jewish

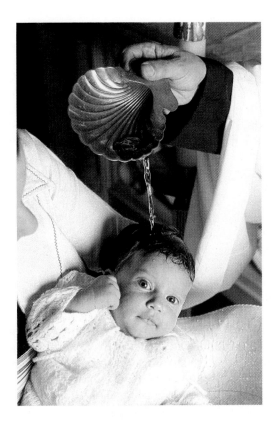

Figure 15.11 *Although there are great differences among both denominations and sects, denominations generally accept as members anyone born into the group, while sects draw much of their* *membership from adult converts. At present, sects and other fundamentalist organizations are gaining members, while the membership of denominations is stable or even declining.*

religion—an ominous trend for a group that gains members almost entirely through birth and does not encourage conversion. The Catholic Church has lost credibility among its supporters since the 1968 papal ban on birth control. The great majority of American Catholics reject the Church's position on this issue, and in doing so, have come to question it on many others. For example, a 1985 *New York Times*/CBS News poll found that a majority of Catholics were in favor of having women as priests, of letting priests marry, and of permitting Catholics to divorce and remarry. In fact, Catholics are more likely than Protestants or Jews to enter interfaith marriages and to get divorced. There has also been a sharp drop in average weekly attendance at mass—from a high of 72 percent in 1954 to only 51 percent in 1985. And the membership of most of the relatively liberal mainstream Protestant denominations—such as the Episcopalians, Methodists, Presbyterians, and Lutherans—has either leveled off or has actually dwindled.

In contrast, Protestant fundamentalism has shown every sign of vitality and growth. In the United States, fundamentalism represents the conservative wing of a larger Protestant movement, evangelism—the fervent belief in, and promulgation of, the Scriptures. In particular, the fundamentalists hold that every word of the Bible is literally true; they advance the belief that the individual can be saved only by being "born again" through a personal relationship with Jesus Christ; and they vigorously oppose permissive trends in personal morality and in the society at large. A subgroup of the fundamentalists, the Pentecostals, believe in the infusion of the Holy Spirit into religious experience and rituals—typically through such phenomena as faith healing and speaking in tongues. There are fundamentalists in all the Protestant organizations, but they are generally a minority in the denominations (except perhaps the Southern Baptists) and usually form a majority in the sects. Many predominantly fundamentalist organizations—such as the Assembly of God, the Church of the Nazarene, the Seventh-Day Adventists, and the Mormons—have enjoyed rapid growth over the past decade or so (Marty, 1976; Madden, 1981; Ostling, 1985).

One source of the fundamentalists' new strength is their domination of the "electronic church" (Hadden and Swan, 1981). Nearly a thousand American radio stations and eighty television stations are devoted to religious programming, most of which promotes the fundamentalist message. Prime-time preachers such as Jerry Falwell, Oral Roberts, Pat Robertson, and Jimmy Swaggart have become national celebrities whose messages are heard in millions of homes. The established churches tend to look askance at these presentations, claiming that they give a narrow, emotional, and superficial view of complex moral and political issues. Fund-raising appeals in the electronic church generate huge sums of money for the fundamentalist cause, sometimes through techniques that make other theologians wince: Oral Roberts, for example, has described his conversations with a 900-foot-tall Jesus—who promised that Roberts's medical center will discover the cure for cancer, provided supporters send a specific monthly contribution.

Each denomination or sect gives priority to different aspects of the Christian faith—the Quakers, for example, stress peace; the Jehovah's Witnesses emphasize the end of the world. The fundamentalists focus primarily on sin. This emphasis derives from the historically strong Southern influence on fundamentalism. Before the Civil War, all the major religious groups in the South supported slavery, and, indeed, actually taught the slaves that the Bible required them to obey their masters (Stampp, 1956). Well into this century, in fact, most of the Protestant groups in the South supported racial segregation. Inevitably, therefore, these organizations tended to downplay those aspects of the Christian message that deal with social justice, human equality, and love of one's fellows. Instead, they concentrated on issues that did not directly challenge the social order—personal vices such as drinking, gambling, lust, and wavering faith. Modern fundamentalists are still primarily concerned to combat such social phenomena as abortion, sexual equality, gay rights, the theory of evolution, alcohol and drug abuse, lewd rock lyrics, pornography, and the like. The fundamentalists label their main enemies "secular humanists," apparently a network of unidentified but conspiratorial liberals and atheists who propagate every-

thing the fundamentalists oppose and who are seen as weakening the moral fiber of society.

The fundamentalist revival seems to be broadly based. The Gallup poll found in 1983 that 42 percent of the population believe the Bible is literally the word of God, and in 1984, that 38 percent claim to have been "born again." Clearly, fundamentalism is able to draw on a large reservoir of dissatisfaction with the permissive trends that began in the 1960s. Indeed, the very appeal of the fundamentalist sects lies in their strictness, exclusivity, and definitive answers to the problems of the world (Horowitz, 1982; Liebman and Wuthnow, 1983; Flake, 1984).

Religion and Politics

It is widely believed that the American Constitution builds a "wall of separation" between church and state, but this view is largely a myth. The actual wording of the First Amendment to the Constitution is "Congress shall make no laws respecting an establishment of religion, or prohibiting the free exercise thereof." This sentence merely implies that the state, out of respect for the principle of freedom of religion, may not favor or penalize one belief relative to another. However, although the state may not become involved in religion, there is absolutely no prohibition against religious participation in the affairs of the state.

In practice, civic affairs and religion have long been closely intertwined in America, leading Robert Bellah (1970) to speak of the society's "civil religion"—a vague, nondenominational conviction that Americans are a godly people and that God favors America. In this "civil religion," various sacred elements are used to sanctify the secular American way of life.

For example, the Pledge of Allegiance declares that the country is one nation "under God." Its coins declare, "In God we trust." Religion is an element in oaths of office, party conventions, courtroom procedures, and indeed nearly all formal public occasions. Even the Boy Scouts give a "God and country" award, a phrase that implies, to say the least, a compatibility of interest between the two. Many of the nation's secular symbols also have a sacred quality—the flag, the eagle, the Constitution, the Bill of Rights, the Statue of Liberty, "America the Beautiful," "The Star-Spangled Banner," Washington, Jefferson, and Lincoln. Political leaders must always pay at least lip service to religious belief; in fact, every presidential inaug-

Figure 15.12 *The fundamentalist television evangelist Pat Robertson has sought the presidency of the United States—an unusually explicit indication of how politics and religion can become intertwined.*

ural address except one (Washington's second) makes mention of God—but only rhetorically, at the beginning or end of the speech. John F. Kennedy's inaugural, for example, captures the idea that America's social order and historical mission are specifically sanctioned by God:

> With a good conscience our only sure reward, with history the final judge of our deeds, let us go forth to lead the land we love, asking His blessing and His help, but knowing that here on earth God's work must truly be our own.

Such sentiments are not allied to any specific faith or political program; they are sufficiently broad to be acceptable to almost anyone.

But when specific religious doctrines or government policies are at stake, the relationship between church and state can be antagonistic. Throughout American history there have always been some religious groups and leaders who have found moral grounds to oppose government policies: opposition to slavery, for example, was based on the Christian ideal of universal brotherhood. After the Civil War, the churches in the South generally supported racial segregation, while those in the North were mostly silent on the issue. But as the political climate began to change over the years, so did the attitude of the churches. Led by reformers like Rev. Martin Luther King, Jr., the churches of the 1960s were in the forefront of the campaign for civil rights. Around the same period, some clergy from the Catholic Church and from some of the major Protestant denominations

became leading opponents of American involvement in the Vietnam war.

This religious involvement in the civil rights and antiwar movements was not always popular. The congregations often did not appreciate the activities of their religious leaders, and fundamentalist groups were often critical of the position of the more liberal denominations. Jerry Falwell, a former segregationist, spoke out fervently against religious participation in politics. Yet, two decades later, his movement—the now inactive "Moral Majority"—was campaigning against abortion, gay rights, and the Equal Rights Amendment, and he was endorsing the 1984 presidential candidacy of Ronald Reagan—who declared that "religion and politics are inseparable." On this occasion, it was some clergy of the more liberal denominations who protested vehemently.

The current political involvement of religious organizations presents a complicated picture, for each group tends to regard its own political activity as legitimate, but other groups' activities in favor of contrasting goals as unjustified interference. Some religious leaders have effectively told people who to vote for; others have merely implied that they should not vote for candidates who favor certain policies, such as abortion. One prominent "tele-evangelist," Pat Robertson, has even had presidential aspirations. There are also some uneasy alliances: fundamentalists and Catholics, for example, are in basic agreement on the issue of abortion, but little else. In practice, religious involvement in politics tends to be self-limiting, for it eventually antagonizes the public, including lay members of the religious organizations concerned. A 1984 *New York Times*/CBS News poll found that only 22 percent of the public believe political candidates should discuss religion, and only 17 percent believe that members of the clergy should use religion for political endorsements (Herbers, 1984; Demerath and Williams, 1984; Kennedy, 1984; Flake, 1984).

Two controversial issues involving the relationship between church and state do seem likely to endure, however. One is the question of abortion, which we discussed in detail in Chapter 13 ("The Family"). The other is school prayer, which the Supreme Court declared unconstitutional in 1962. Some groups, primarily the fundamentalists, have urgently campaigned for a constitutional amendment to permit prayer in the schools. They argue that the nation is predominantly Christian, that children should not be prohibited from exercising freedom of religion in the classroom, and that the ban on school prayer is intolerant. The counterargument, offered by most of the denominations and by minority religions such as Judaism, is that school prayer would effectively give government support to the majority religion, would make deviants of children who refused to participate, and is unnecessary since there are many other opportunities for prayer outside the public schools. Opinion polls consistently show large public majorities—usually around 70 percent—in favor of school prayer.

New Religions

An astonishing variety of new sects and cults has appeared in the United States in the past quarter century, some with beliefs and names—ranging from the Divine Light Mission and the Self-Revelation Church of Absolute Monism to the Church of the Psychedelic Venus—that seem alien or exotic to most Americans. Many of these organizations have vanished almost as rapidly as they emerged; some linger on as local, one-congregation groups with only a handful of members; but a few have flourished, sometimes attracting publicity that is out of all proportion to their size.

Hare Krishna

One of the most visible of the newer religions is the Hare Krishna movement, whose members, clad in saffron robes and often with heads shaved, may be seen dancing, chanting, and begging in such public places as urban streets and airports. The movement centers around a Hindu sect, the International Society for Krishna Consciousness, which was imported from India in 1965. Members are expected to associate only with other devotees to practice an ascetic, celibate lifestyle. Science, rationality, education, aggression, and competition are all negatively valued. The sect offers its members a complete personal transformation, based on the adoption of both new beliefs and new body imagery such as hairstyles and clothing. Although this religion rejects many core American values, its

Figure 15.13 *The Hare Krishna movement combines elements from both the Eastern and Western traditions—including Indian chants and American musical instruments.*

recruits come from the American mainstream: they are mainly middle-class white Americans in their early twenties, many of them college drop-outs and many of them former drug abusers. The religion has been considerably modified for its American participants, however. In original Indian doctrine, the achievement of Krishna conscious-ness requires many years of study and contempla-tion. In the American version, some Krishna con-sciousness can be achieved merely by performing the appropriate rituals, particularly chanting—an innovation which, though unorthodox, recognizes the American concern with technical means and immediate results (Judah, 1974; Daner, 1976; Cox, 1977; Rockford, 1985).

Unification Church

Another new religion is the Unification Church, founded by Sun Myung Moon, a Korean industrial-ist. When the sect was imported to the United States in the early 1960s, it was predicting the end of the world in 1967. As is usual in such cases, the prophecy was not fulfilled. (A failed prediction does not necessarily mean a failed sect, however: the Jehovah's Witnesses have awaited the apoca-lypse on five specific dates since 1914, during which time their membership has grown from a few thousand to more than 2 million people in 210 countries.) Moon has since developed a much more elaborate doctrine, containing elements of anticommunism, Eastern religions, and funda-mentalist Christianity: in essence, he claims that

the Koreans are the Chosen People; that a transfor-mation of the world will occur within the foresee-able future; and that he himself is Lord of the Second Advent—a successor to Jesus, who failed in his mission. The sect claims over 40,000 members in the United States, although the actual number is probably much lower. Most members are middle-class whites in their late teens or early twenties, often with some college education, and they fre-quently join the sect at a time of personal crisis or loneliness. Members are expected to give all their property to the sect, to associate only with one an-other, to remain celibate until they marry a partner personally selected for them by Moon, and to spend much of their time collecting money for the organization. Indeed, both the church and Moon have amassed a considerable financial empire—though under circumstances that led in 1984 to Moon's imprisonment for eighteen months on tax-evasion charges (Lofland, 1966, 1977; Edwards, 1979; Bromley and Shupe, 1979; Barker, 1984).

Scientology

Scientology is unusual among the new faiths in that it began, not as a religion, but rather as a lay psychotherapy called "dianetics." Conceived in 1950 by a science-fiction writer named L. Ron Hub-bard, the therapy was based on the idea that pain-ful memories, or "engrams," can be traced and extinguished through "auditing," or counseling sessions with a trained "auditor." This expert is equipped with an "E-meter," a device invented by

Figure 15.14 *The Reverend Sun Myung Moon and his wife preside over the mass wedding of some 5,000 members of his church. The marriages were arranged by Moon, who was reported to have per-sonally selected the spouses for each union.*

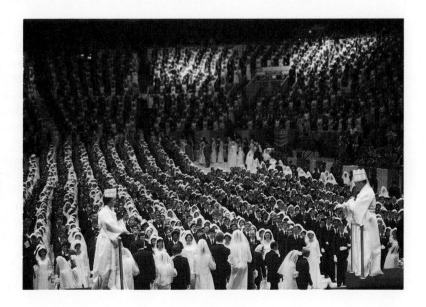

Hubbard that consists, essentially, of a tin can that is wired to a galvanometer and then held in the hand to provide a rough measure of emotional stress. After a series of these sessions—which can cost hundreds, thousands, or even tens of thousands of dollars—the subject may be declared "clear," or in command of the rational self. Dianetics was an immediate success, and within two years Hubbard registered it as a religion under the name of the Church of Scientology. New doctrinal elements were then added. Human beings, Hubbard revealed, are merely incarnations and reincarnations of spiritual beings, called Thetans; indeed, he claimed to be 74 trillion years old himself. Emphasizing its "scientific" nature in contrast to the "superstitious" traditional religions, Scientology enjoyed a degree of success that is unusual among cults. It spread to several countries and may have gained over 1 million members, all of whom joined by paying to be audited; church funds are believed to have totaled hundreds of millions of dollars. In several countries, however, allegations of fraud and quackery led to official investigations of Scientology, and the organization responded with its own campaign of infiltration, bugging, and burglary, directed at a number of foreign governments and at over one hundred government agencies in the United States. After disappearing in 1980 in the face of several investigations, Hubbard was alleged dead in 1986. Many millions of dollars of church funds have also disappeared, leading to speculation that the entire religion may have been a hoax all along. Membership appears to have declined substantially, but Scientology still has many thousands of adherents (Whitehead, 1974; Wallis, 1977; Lindsey, 1984).

Evaluation

Many of the new sects and cults have strained the American tolerance for freedom of religion. Why do these groups not enjoy the same tolerance as denominations? One charge is that some of the new movements seem like fraudulent enterprises, whose leaders live in luxury on the contributions of their ordinary members. There may be some truth to this claim, but the same might be said of some established churches, too: for centuries, bishops and cardinals lived in splendor while their followers suffered penury, and there are some very wealthy modern evangelists. Another charge is that some of the new religions "brainwash" recruits by isolating them from society and immersing them in their doctrines. There may be some

truth to this claim, too, but again, the same criticism may apply to some established churches—which, after all, may use monasteries, nunneries, and even religious schools to instill their doctrines.

The real reason for hostility to the new religions, it seems, is simply their apparently alien character. As we noted in Chapter 3 ("Culture"), new elements of nonmaterial culture, like religion, are much less readily accepted into a society than new artifacts, like cars or can openers; and the more exotic or outlandish a religion seems, the more resistance it is likely to meet. Of course, *any* religion may seem bizarre to believers of another faith: if you had never heard of Christianity, for example, you might be incredulous to hear claims that someone was born of a virgin, walked on water, and rose from the dead. But to Americans who are accustomed to the dominant religious tradition, it is doctrines on such topics as the divinity of Sun Myung Moon or the reincarnation of Thetans that seem highly implausible. In fact, some parents, concerned at the defection of their sons or daughters to cults and sects, have hired professional "deprogrammers" who kidnap the converts and submit them to intense psychological and even physical pressure to reject their new faith. The whole issue raises serious questions about religious freedom and civil liberties (Patrick, 1976; Enroth, 1977; Anthony et al., 1980; Bromley and Richardson, 1984).

What are we to make of the appearance of so many new religions? As sociologists point out, this phenomenon is not as novel or unprecedented as it might seem. In fact, the United States has long served as the birthplace of new religious organizations—for example, the Jehovah's Witnesses, the Mormons, the Seventh-Day Adventists, the Spiritualists, and the Christian Scientists. Nor is hostility toward new religions unprecedented in the American experience: Quakers, Mennonites, Hutterites, Mormons, Christian Scientists, and others have been subjected to attempts at repression, ranging from subtle discrimination to violence, arson, and murder (J. Wilson, 1978).

What is new is the extent of religious pluralism in the United States, as reflected in the extraordinary range of contemporary faiths—from long-established denominations to ephemeral cults, from groups that demand self-denial to those that offer self-indulgence, from those that search for a way back to those that offer a way out. This variety is hardly surprising, for it arises in an emerging postindustrial society whose hallmark is social diversity and whose citizens exhibit an unprece-

Precalculus Mathematics

A GRAPHING APPROACH

SECOND EDITION

Franklin Demana
Bert K. Waits
The Ohio State University
Stanley R. Clemens
Bluffton College

with the assistance of

Alan Osborne
The Ohio State University

Gregory D. Foley
Sam Houston State University

ADDISON-WESLEY PUBLISHING COMPANY

Reading, Massachusetts • Menlo Park, California • New York • Don Mills, Ontario • Wokingham, England
Amsterdam • Bonn • Sydney • Singapore • Tokyo • Madrid • San Juan • Milan • Paris

Sponsoring Editor	Bill Poole
Associate Editor	Kathleen A. Manley
Developmental Editor	Stephanie Botvin
Managing Editor	Karen M. Guardino
Production Supervisor	Jennifer Brownlow Bagdigian
Production Technology Consultant	Laurie Petrycki
Text Designer	Nancy Blodget/Books By Design
Copyeditor	Susan Middleton
Proofreader	Laura K. Michaels/Michaels Communications
Manufacturing Supervisor	Roy Logan
Cover Designer	Marshall Henrichs
Compositor	ETP Services, Inc.
Illustrator	Tech Graphics
Printer	Murray Printing

This book was produced with $\TeX$.

Reprinted with corrections, June 1992.

Library of Congress Cataloging-in-Publication Data

Demana, Franklin D., 1938-
    Precalculus : **A Graphing Approach** / Franklin Demana, Bert K.
Waits, Stan R. Clemens ; with the assistance of Alan Osborne,
Gregory D. Foley. -- [2nd ed.]
        p.   cm.
    Includes index.
    ISBN 0-201-52626-3
    1. Algebra. 2. Trigonometry.   I. Waits, Bert K.   II. Clemens,
Stanley R.   III. Title.
QA154.2.D43   1992
512--dc20   91-37507
                                                                 CIP

2 3 4 5 6 7 8 9 10-MU-95949392

Dedication

The authors dedicate this book to their wives, Christine Demana, Barbara Waits, and Joenita Clemens, without whose patience, love, and understanding this book would not have been possible.

Preface

Precalculus Mathematics: A Graphing Approach grew out of our strong conviction that incorporating graphing technology into the precalculus curriculum better prepares students for further study in mathematics and science. Before revising this text, we spoke to hundreds of teachers about their experiences using this approach in order to make this truly a user's revision. Our aim in preparing this second edition was to strengthen the technology-based approach while refining the organization and format of the text.

Our own research at The Ohio State University and at dozens of other test sites shows that the use of a calculator- or computer-based graphing approach dramatically changes results in the classroom. Instead of being bored and discouraged by conventional contrived problems, students suddenly grow excited by their ability to explore problems that arise from real world situations and learn from their experiences. The mathematics classroom is transformed into a mathematics laboratory, with a new interactive instructional approach that focuses on problem-solving. As a natural outgrowth of this excitement, students complete the course with a better understanding of mathematics and a solid intuitive foundation for calculus.

The Graphing Approach

As in the first edition, this text is designed to be used in a one year precalculus course. We take advantage of the power and speed of modern technology to apply a graphing approach to the course. The characteristics of this approach are described below.

Integration of Technology   Use of a graphing utility—whether a hand-held graphing calculator or computer graphing software—is not optional. Technology allows the focus of the course to be on problem solving and exploration, while building a deeper understanding of algebraic techniques. Students are expected to have regular and frequent access to a graphing utility for class activities as well as homework.

Problem Solving   The ultimate power of mathematics is that it can be used to solve problems. Technology removes the need for contrived problems and opens the door for realistic and interesting applications. Throughout this text, we focus on what we call problem situations—situations from the physical world, from our social environment, or from the quantitative world of mathematics. Using real life situations makes the math understandable to the students, and students come to value mathematics because they appreciate its power.

Throughout this text, we use a three step problem solving process. Students will be asked to:

1. Find an algebraic representation of the problem;
2. Find a complete graph of the algebraic representation; and
3. Find a complete graph of the problem solving situation.

These three steps prepare the student to find either a graphical or algebraic solution to the problem. Problem situations are highlighted in the exercise sets, and we encourage students to complete all the exercises which deal with that problem. See page 157, exercises 107–111.

Multiple Representations   A quantitative mathematical problem can often be approached using multiple representations. In a traditional precalculus course, problems are analyzed using an algebraic representation, and perhaps a numerical representation. However, modern technology allows us to take full advantage of a graphical, or geometric, representation of a problem. Our understanding of the problem is enriched by exploring it numerically, algebraically, and graphically. See pages 61 and 62.

Exploration   We believe that a technology-based approach enriches the students' mathematical intuition through exploration. With modern technology, accurate graphs can be obtained quickly and used to study the properties of functions. Students learn to decide for themselves what technique should be used. The speed and power of graphing technology allows an emphasis on exploration. See page 125.

Geometric Transformations   The exploratory nature of graphing helps students learn how to transform a graph geometrically by horizontal or vertical shifts, horizontal or vertical stretchs and shrinks, and reflection with respect to the axes. This develops students' abilities so that they can sketch graphs of functions quickly and understand the behavior of graphs. See page 131.

Foreshadowing Calculus   We foreshadow important concepts of calculus through an emphasis on graphs. Using graphs, students can find maxima and minima of functions, and intervals where functions are increasing or decreasing and limiting behavior of functions are determined graphically. We do not borrow the techniques of calculus—rather we lay the foundation for the later study by providing students with rich intutitions about functions and graphs. See page 165.

Approximate Answers Technology allows a proper balance between exact answers that are rarely needed in the real world and accurate approximations. Graphing techniques such as zoom-in provide an excellent geometric vehicle for discussion about error in answers. Students can read answers from graphs with accuracy up to the limits of machine precision. See page 57.

Visualization Graphing helps students to gain an understanding of the properties of graphs and makes the addition of geometric representations to the usual numeric and algebraic representations very natural. Exploring the connections between graphical representations and problem situations deepens student understanding about mathematical concepts and helps them appreciate the role of mathematics.

About the Second Edition

This second edition of *Precalculus Mathematics: A Graphing Approach* grew out of the experiences of hundreds of classrooms. We have carefully listened to comments and suggestions of both teachers and students, and incorporated them fully into the text. The entire text has been extensively revised and rewritten.

Development of Functions In this edition, the topics of functions—including operations on functions, composition of functions, and inverse functions—have been combined in Chapter 3. Polynomial functions and their graphs remain in a separate chapter (Chapter 4).

Rational Functions Coverage of rational functions and functions involving radicals (Chapter 5) has been streamlined from seven sections to four.

Trigonometry Chapters The three chapters on trigonometry (Chapters 7–9) have been developed to make concepts even more accessible, and now contain an even greater emphasis on graphing. A more complete development of trigonometric identities and solving trigonometric equations has been included since students need to practice these skills to be successful in calculus.

Polar Coordinates and Parametric Equations These topics are now covered in a separate chapter (Chapter 11) together with conic sections. The material on conics is treated in two sections. Topics from this chapter may be incorporated earlier if the instructor chooses.

Systems of Equations Sections on solving systems of equations algebraically and graphically are now combined with material on matrices. This material is now found in Chapter 10. We develop conceptual understanding of systems of equations in Chapter 2. For those instructors who want to cover all of this material earlier, Chapter 10 is designed to be usable at any place after Chapter 2.

Permutations, Combinations, and Probability We now include treatment of these important topics in Chapter 12. In addition, we treat mathematical induction and the binomial theorem in separate sections.

Algebra Skills New sections in Chapter 1 have been added to review concepts of algebra while at the same time building familiarity with the graphing utility. Sections added include the real number line, exponents, algebraic expressions, and fractional expressions. Use of this material as reference or review is optional.

Features

New pedagogical features have been incorporated into this text. It is our hope that these features will make the the text a stronger teaching and learning tool. The pedagogy now includes:

Explore with a Graphing Utility   This recurring box places the student in the role of participant in the development of the mathematics. By introducing topics through this experience-based process, the book literally interacts with the student. Students develop their critical thinking skills, and form generalizations about the behavior of functions.

Sidelight Boxes   Shaded boxes placed in the margin provide commentary on the mathematical development, and include problem solving tips, calculator hints, and reminders.

Color   A functional use of color has been introduced to help the reader better navigate through the text. In addition to using color to mark beginnings and ends of examples, and to identify definitions and theorems, the text uses color in the artwork to help the student correctly identify the concept being illustrated.

Artwork   We have made a visual distinction between graphs generated with a graphing utility and hand-sketched art. Art which has been derived from a grapher is outlined with a colored box; while the graphs have been drawn more smoothly we still try to emulate what the student sees on their grapher. Traditional art uses color within the graphs but is not boxed. The distinction between types of artwork underscores the difference between a sketch and a grapher-drawn complete graph.

Examples   As in the first edition, we have included many examples to develop the concepts. Titled examples help the student focus on the purpose of the example.

Exercises   We have closely focused on correlating end of section exercises to examples, and added many new exercieses. Writing to Learn and Discussion exercises have also been included in nearly every exercise set.

Supplements

Graphing Calculator and Computer Graphing Laboratory Manual   This edition of the lab manual has been updated to include instructions for the latest calculators from Casio, Texas Instruments, Sharp, and Hewlett-Packard. As with previous versions, the lab manual provides the student with keystroke-level descriptions for using the technology in precalculus.

Instructor's Resource Guide   Included in this guide for teachers are essays discussing the implementation of technology in the classroom, two forms of tests for each chapter, and section-by-section overviews with teaching goals.

Instructor's Solutions Manual   The Instructor's Solutions Manual contains worked out solutions to every problem in the text.

Student's Solutions Manual   This supplement contains worked out solutions to every odd-numbered problem in the text.

Answer Book Even and odd answers are provided in this supplement for instructors to make available to their students.

Master Grapher and 3D Grapher Software This software is available in versions for the IBM, MacIntosh, and Apple computers, and may be used for in-class demonstrations or laboratory use.

OmniTest II A unique algorithm-based test generator for Demana, Waits, Clemens, **Precalculus Mathematics**, produces virtually unlimited versions of problems appropriate for the graphing calculator. These printed problems include graphic representation of the images which appear on the graphing calculator. This provides a permanent record of the calculator image with which teachers and students may annotate instructional notes and illustrative comments. These printed problems are also useful in a cooperative learning environment.

Acknowledgments

We would like to thank the many wonderful teachers who participated in the development of this text. Their dedication and enthusiasm made this revision possible. Very important contributions to the book were made by our high school teaching partners Bruce Blackston and Dan Rohrs (*Upper Arlington High School*), Pamela Dase and Patricia Borys (*Centennial High School*), Fred Koenig (*Walnut Ridge High School*), and Ron Meyer (*Franklin Heights High School)* during the 1987–88 pilot year.

Creative suggestions for this edition came from so many of our family of teachers that it would be impossible to name them all here. However, we particularly want to thank: **Ohio:** Carolyn Anderson, *Gallia Academy High School*; Teri Ayotte, *Battelle Youth Science Program*; Bruce Blackston, *Upper Arlington High School*; Lisa Blakely, *Dixie High School*; Tris Borys, *Centennial High School*; Ron Brahler, *John Adams High School*; John Brooks, *John Glenn High School*; Jeff Cassell, *Franklin Monroe High School*; Judy Clovis, *Columbus School for Girls*; Jackie Craigo, *Mount Vernon High School*; Allen Curry, *Jackson High School*; Paul Dahnke, *Sandusky High School*; Pam Dase, *Centennial High School*; John DeMarco, *Lake High School*; John Detrick, *The Columbus Academy*; Sandra Dobberstein, *Brookville High School*; Tom Elfers, *New Richmond High School*; Donald Ellsworth, *Shawnee High School*; Vaughn Engle, *Princeton High School*; Claudia Evans, *Ottawa Hills High School*; Phil Everett, *Circleville High School*; Katherine Falcone, *Walnut Hills High School*; Mike Farmer, *J. R. Buchtel High School*; Paula Fistick, *West High School*; Sr. Sheila Gallagher, *Holy Name High School*; Don Grady, *Elyria High School*; Jim Hassel, *Berea High School*; Elmer Heinsius, *Upper Arlington High School*; Bob Hughes, *Heath High School*; Bill Hunt, *Mayfield High School*; Carl Jones, *Ansonia High School*; Jesse Kidd, *Kettering Fairmont High School*; Donn Klingler, *Cincinnati Country Day School*; Fred Koenig, *Walnut Ridge High School*; Ken Kubach, *John Marshall High School*; Tom Lanning, *Olmsted Falls High School*; Andrew Lingler, *Lorain Catholic High School*; Mattie McCloria, *Belmont High School*; Bill McGhee, *Grandview Heights High School*; Ron

Meyer, *Franklin Heights High School*; Gretchen Miller, *Turpin High School*; Teresa Monnett, *Briggs High School*; Susan Myers, *Washington Senior High School*; Kathy Neag, *Central-Hower High School*; Mark Pierce, *Keystone High School*; Fred Raisbeck, *Upper Arlington High School*; Ralph Rapp, *Marion Harding High School*; Ann Robinson, *Southview High School*; Ron Rogacki, *Dunbar High School*; Dan Rohrs, *Upper Arlington High School*; Carol Rzodkiewicz, *Columbus School for Girls*; Dan Scott, *River View High School*; Bob Shanks, *Northridge High School*; Doug Smeltz, *Northland High School*; Jan Stoudinger, *Lakota High School*; Jackie Tagg, *Washington Senior High School*; Jim Tawney, *Lake High School*; Ray Trenta, *Firestone Senior High School*; Ken Vassily, *North Olmsted High School*; Carolyn Vitak, *Bexley High School*; Wilma Wilson, *Whetstone High School*; Angie Windau, *St. Francis de Sales High School*; Carl Yeager, *Whitmer High School*; Lee Zeches, *Reynoldsburg High School*. **Alaska:** Hanna Schott, *Soldotna High School*. **California:** Evelyn O'Prey, *Redlands High School*. **Illinois:** Kathleen Murzyn, *Bogan Computer Technical High School*. **Michigan:** Ronda Cox, *Battle Creek Central High School*; George Kitchen, *Portage Northern High School*; Cameron Nichols, *Kalamazoo Area Math and Science Center*; Linda Robinson, *Andover High School*. **Montana:** Pam Koterba, *Ryegate High School*; Karen Longhart, *Flathead High School*; Ron Shumway, *Glasgow High School*. **New Mexico:** Coleen Ferguson, *Highland High School*. **New York:** Gene Olmstead, *Elmira Free Academy*. **North Dakota:** Gary Froelich, Bismarck High School. **Oregon:** Russ Geiseman, *South Eugene High School*; Sue McGraw, *Lake Oswego High School*; Gwen Waite, *Hermiston High School*. **Pennsylvania:** Bob Dilts, *Schenley High School Teacher Center*. **Texas:** Tommy Eads, *North Lamar High School*; Judy West, *Temple High School*. **Utah:** Pam Giles, *Brighton High School*. **Virginia:** Ellen Hook, *Granby High School*. **Washington:** Mike Dirks, *North Central High School*; Don Peterson, *Hudson's Bay High School*. **Wisconsin:** Arne Engebretsen, *Greendale High School*; Gary Luck, *Greendale High School*; Babs Merkert, *Waukesha South High School*.

We thank our colleagues, Greg Foley and Alan Osborne, for their constructive suggestions and their work on the Instructor's Guide. Special thanks are due to Penny Dunham, who coordinated the revision of the answer section and managed a team of teachers to solve and check the answers. We would like to thank the entire team for their valued contribution: Arne Engebretson, Babs Merkert, Tommy Eads, Pam Giles, Ray Barton, Karen Longhart, Betty Roseborough, and Jeri Nichols. We also thank Gerald White, of Western Illinois University, and Gloria Dion, of Penn State—Ogontz Campus, for their assistance in checking the mathematical accuracy of the manuscript.

We would also like to thank Jenny Bagdigian, Stephanie Botvin, Kathy Manley, Laurie Petrycki, and Bill Poole of Addison-Wesley for their hard work in making this second edition a reality.

Bert K. Waits
Franklin Demana
Stan Clemens

Contents

Fundamental Concepts of Algebra

1.1

Real Numbers and the Coordinate Plane

The set of numbers used most frequently in algebra is known as the **real numbers**. Real numbers are either **rational** or **irrational**. The set of **integers** is a subset of the set of rational numbers, since for each integer a, $a = a/1$ (see Fig. 1.1). Following are some examples:

$$\text{integers:} \quad 3, \quad -5, \quad 48$$

$$\text{rational numbers:} \quad \frac{3}{8}, \quad -\frac{2}{3}, \quad \frac{22}{7}$$

$$\text{irrational numbers:} \quad \pi, \quad \sqrt{2}, \quad \sqrt{17}.$$

Real numbers can be represented as decimal numbers. Integers have all zeros to the right of the decimal point. Rational numbers always have a block of numbers that repeat, and irrational numbers have no repeating blocks of digits. Some examples of rational and irrational numbers are:

$$\pi = 3.141592654\cdots, \quad \tfrac{5}{8} = 0.625, \quad \sqrt{2} = 1.414213562\cdots, \quad \tfrac{1}{3} = 0.33333\cdots.$$

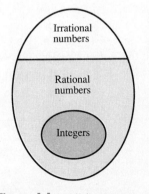

Figure 1.1 All integers are rational numbers, and all rational numbers are real numbers. A real number is either rational or irrational but not both.

1

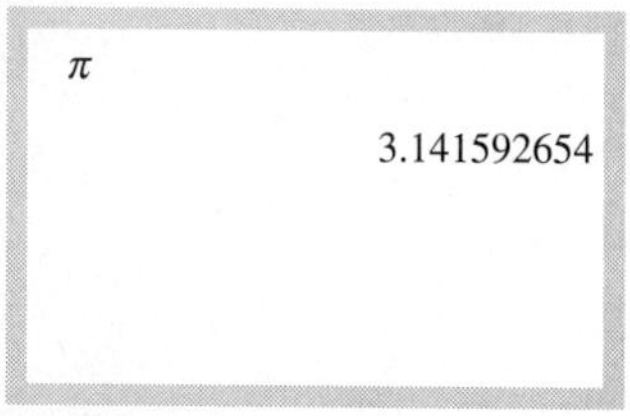

π

3.141592654

Figure 1.2   When an irrational number is keyed into one calculator, the digits to the right of the ten digits displayed and the three additional check digits are usually interpreted to be zero. Thus the number displayed is a rational number approximation to the exact value of the number. What does your calculator give for π?

Since a calculator or computer display of a decimal number can show only a finite number of digits, usually 7 to 10, many displays represent only approximations to the number keyed in. However, they are very accurate approximations (Fig. 1.2).

Arithmetic Operations

There are four binary operations for numbers: addition, subtraction, multiplication, and division, represented by the symbols $+$, $-$, $\times$ (or $\cdot$), $\div$.

Addition and multiplication satisfy a set of properties that can be used to change the form of a mathematical expression into an equivalent form. These properties are summarized as follows.

Real Number Properties of Addition and Multiplication

Let a, b, and c represent real numbers. Then all of the following are true:

	Addition	*Multiplication*
Closure:	$a + b$ is real.	$a \cdot b$ is real.
Commutative:	$a + b = b + a$	$a \cdot b = b \cdot a$
Associative:	$a + (b + c) = (a + b) + c$	$a \cdot (b \cdot c) = (a \cdot b) \cdot c$
Identity:	$a + 0 = 0 + a = a$	$a \cdot 1 = 1 \cdot a = a$
Inverse:	$a + (-a) = (-a) + a = 0$	$a \cdot \left(\dfrac{1}{a}\right) = \left(\dfrac{1}{a}\right) \cdot a = 1 \quad (a \neq 0)$
Distributive:	$a(b + c) = ab + ac$	

An **equation** is a statement of equality between two expressions. For example, $3 + 4$ and $2 + 5$ both represent 7. We write the equation $3 + 4 = 2 + 5$. We can use the commutative property of addition to conclude that for any real number x, $x + 5 = 5 + x$. In solving problems involving equations, three important properties of equality will be useful.

Real Number Properties of Equality

Let a, b, and c be real numbers. Then the following properties are true:

Reflexive: $a = a$
Symmetric: If $a = b$, then $b = a$
Transitive: If $a = b$ and $b = c$, then $a = c$.

EXAMPLE 1   Using Properties of Real Numbers

If x is any real number, show that $2 \cdot (x + 3) = 6 + 2 \cdot x$.

Solution

$$2 \cdot (x + 3) = 2 \cdot x + 2 \cdot 3 \qquad \text{distributive property}$$

$$2 \cdot x + 2 \cdot 3 = 6 + 2 \cdot x \qquad \text{commutative property}$$

so $\qquad 2 \cdot (x + 3) = 6 + 2 \cdot x. \qquad \text{transitive property of equality}$ ▤

Real Number Line

The set of all real numbers is often represented as points on a line (Fig. 1.3). To construct a **coordinate system** on a line, draw a line and label one point 0. This point is called the **origin**. Then mark equally spaced points on each side of 0. Label points to the right of zero 1, 2, 3, ... and to the left of zero $-1, -2, -3, \ldots$. The properties of *order* in Definition 1.1 describe the placement of all other numbers on the line. Figure 1.3 is called a **number line**.

Origin

$$\begin{array}{ccccccccccc} -5 & -4 & -3 & -2 & -1 & 0 & 1 & 2 & 3 & 4 & 5 \end{array}$$

Figure 1.3   Each real number corresponds to one and only one point on the number line, and each point on the number line corresponds to one and only one real number.

The number associated with a point P is called the **coordinate** of point P.

$a \qquad\qquad b$

Figure 1.4 a is less than b.

Definition 1.1   Order on the Real Number Line

If a and b are any two real numbers, then **a is less than b** if $b - a$ is a positive number. In this case, a is to the left of b on the number line (Fig. 1.4). This order relation is denoted by the **inequality $a < b$**. In all, there are four inequality symbols that express order relationships:

$$a < b \qquad a \text{ is less than } b$$

$$a \le b \qquad a \text{ is less than or equal to } b$$

$$a > b \qquad a \text{ is greater than } b$$

$$a \ge b \qquad a \text{ is greater than or equal to } b$$

EXAMPLE 2   Solving Inequalities

On the number line draw all numbers that are solutions to these inequalities:

a) $x \leq 3$;

b) $-3 \leq x < 2$.

Solution

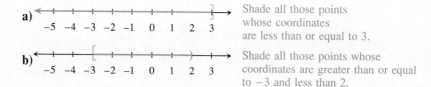

a)   Shade all those points whose coordinates are less than or equal to 3.

b)   Shade all those points whose coordinates are greater than or equal to -3 and less than 2.   ▤

Note in the number lines above the use of a square bracket to show inclusions, and the rounded parenthesis to show exclusions of particular endpoints.

The numbers 5 and -5 are the same distance from zero (0) on the number line (Fig. 1.5). So are π and $-\pi$, and $\sqrt{2}$ and $-\sqrt{2}$. To communicate this idea of distance from the origin of the coordinate line, we introduce a symbol. The **absolute value** of a number c, denoted $|c|$, represents the distance of c from zero on the number line. For example, $|-3| = 3$. A more formal definition follows.

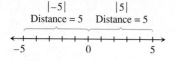

Figure 1.5   Both -5 and 5 are a distance of 5 from 0.

Definition 1.2   Absolute Value

If a is a real number, then the **absolute value of a** is given by

$$|a| = \begin{cases} a & \text{if } a \geq 0; \\ -a & \text{if } a < 0. \end{cases}$$

EXAMPLE 3   Evaluating Absolute Value

Write the expression $|\sqrt{3} - 2|$ without using absolute value notation.

Solution

$$|\sqrt{3} - 2| = -(\sqrt{3} - 2).$$ Because $\sqrt{3}$ is less than 2, $\sqrt{3} - 2$ is negative   ▤

We can use absolute value notation to describe the distance between any two points on the real number line. Notice that the distance between the points with coordinates 3 and 8 is $|3 - 8|$. Consider the general situation.

Definition 1.3   Distance between Points on a Line

Suppose A and B are two points on a number line with coordinates a and b, respectively. The **distance between A and B**, denoted $d(A, B)$, is given by

$$d(A, B) = |a - b|.$$

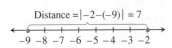

Distance $= |-2-(-9)| = 7$

$-9\ -8\ -7\ -6\ -5\ -4\ -3\ -2$

Figure 1.6   Distance between -2 and -9.

E X A M P L E   4   Finding the Distance between Points on the Number Line

Find the distance between the points with the coordinates -2 and -9.

Solution   (See Fig. 1.6.)

$$d(-2, -9) = \ |-2 - (-9)| \ = \ |7| \ = 7. \quad \text{Notice that } d(-2, -9) = d(-9, -2). \ \blacksquare$$

Notice in the solution to Example 4 that -2 and -9 are used as both the coordinate and the name of a point on the number line. It is common to simplify notation this way.

Cartesian Coordinate System

Just as each point on the line is associated with a real number, each point of the plane is associated with an ordered pair of real numbers. To determine which pairs of numbers get associated with which points, we will use the **Cartesian coordinate system** (also called the **rectangular coordinate system**). To construct a coordinate system, draw a pair of perpendicular real number lines, one horizontal and the other vertical with the lines intersecting at their respective origins (Fig. 1.7). The horizontal line is usually called the **x-axis** and the vertical line is usually called the **y-axis**. The positive direction on the x-axis is to the right, and the positive direction on the y-axis is up.

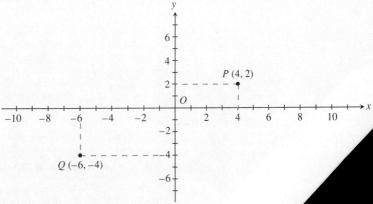

Figure 1.7 The Cartesian coordinate plane.

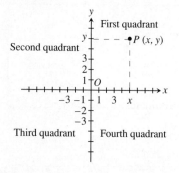

Figure 1.8   The four quadrants.

The intersection of the two coordinate axes, point O, is called the **origin**. The coordinate axes divide the plane into four **quadrants**, as shown in Fig. 1.8. Each point P of the plane is associated with an **ordered pair** (x, y) of real numbers called the **coordinates** of the point. The **x-coordinate** represents the directed distance from the y-axis to P, and the **y-coordinate** represents the directed distance from the x-axis to P.

Graphing calculators and graphing software for personal computers can be used to generate **graphical representations** of the Cartesian coordinate plane. The terms **grapher** and **graphing utility** will be used interchangeably to refer to a graphing calculator or a desktop computer with graphing software.

E X A M P L E   5   Displaying the Coordinate Plane on a Grapher

Display the coordinate plane on your grapher.

Solution   Use the keystrokes appropriate to a grapher to show the coordinate plane. Use appropriate keys to move the cursor up and down and to the right and left. As the cursor moves around, note that the displayed **screen coordinates** of the point represented by the cursor also change.   ≣

It is important to understand how graphers work. Only a portion of the entire plane can be displayed. The portion that is displayed at any one time is called a **viewing rectangle**. In particular, the viewing rectangle [Xmin, Xmax] by [Ymin, Ymax] is the set of all points in the plane satisfying the relationships Xmin $\leq x \leq X$max and Ymin $\leq y \leq Y$max (Fig. 1.9).

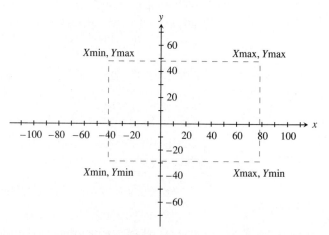

Figure 1.9   The viewing rectangle [Xmin, Xmax] by [Ymin, Ymax].

You can change the size of a viewing rectangle by giving the grapher the appropriate commands. The coordinates of the points (x, y) in a particular viewing rectangle satisfy the following inequalities:

$$X\text{min} \leq x \leq X\text{max} \qquad Y\text{min} \leq y \leq Y\text{max}.$$

Notice the large "gaps" in the screen coordinates as the cursor moves point by point.   On one model grapher the origin $(0,0)$ has screen coordinates $x = 0.10526316$ and $y = 0.15873016$ for the viewing rectangle $[-10, 10]$ by $[-10, 10]$. If the viewing rectangle is changed, the screen coordinates of the origin change. Can you figure out why?*

GAPS IN SCREEN COORDINATES

On a graphing utility display, a **pixel** is the smallest dot that can be lighted. One model grapher uses 96 columns of pixels and 64 rows of pixels. That means that for the $[-10, 10]$ by $[-10, 10]$ viewing rectangle, the "gap" in the horizontal screen coordinates will be $(10 - (-10)) \div 95 = 0.2105$ and the "gap" in the vertical screen coordinates will be $10 - (-10)) \div 63 = 0.3175$. (In a numerical situation it is understood that = means approximately equals.)

E X A M P L E   6   Changing the Viewing Rectangle

Set your grapher for the viewing rectangle: $[-20, 20]$ by $[-20, 20]$. Display the coordinate plane and move the cursor to the bottom-left and top-right corners of the screen to verify the coordinates of these points are correct. Approximate the widths of the "gaps" in both of the screen x- and y-coordinates for the viewing rectangle $[-20, 20]$ by $[-20, 20]$ on your grapher.

Solution   Set the range screen of a graphing utility as follows:

$$X\text{min} = -20$$
$$X\text{max} = 20$$
$$X\text{scl} = 1$$
$$Y\text{min} = -20$$
$$Y\text{max} = 20$$
$$Y\text{scl} = 1.$$

For the viewing rectangle $[-20, 20]$ by $[-20, 20]$ on one model grapher, the x-gap $= 0.42$ and the y-gap $= 0.63$.   ▤

E X A M P L E   7   Adjusting the Xscl and Yscl values

How does your grapher's viewing rectangle change if you change the range values used in Example 6 so that $X\text{scl} = 5$ and $Y\text{scl} = 5$?

Solution   The size of the viewing rectangle does not change. The tick marks on the coordinate axes are five units apart instead of one unit apart.   ▤

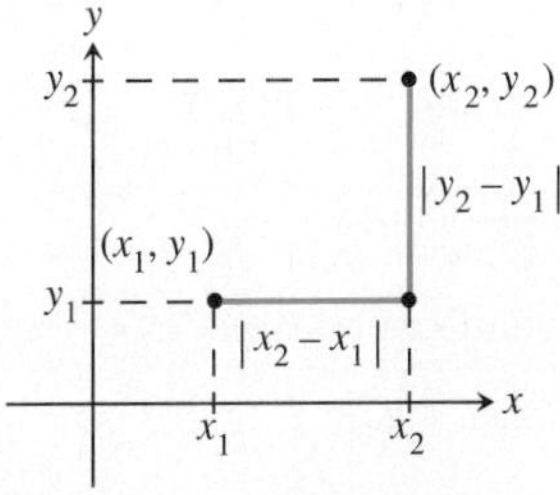

Distance between Two Points in the Plane

To find the distance between two points on a vertical or horizontal line on the coordinate plane, use the method illustrated in Fig. 1.10 and described in Example 4.

Figure 1.10   Finding the distance between points on a vertical or a horizontal line.

---

* Consult the accompanying *Graphing Calculator and Computer Graphing Laboratory Manual* to see how to use a graphing utility.

E X A M P L E   8   Distance between Points on a Horizontal Line

Find the distance between the following pairs of points:

a) $P(1, 3)$ and $Q(5, 3)$;

b) $P(1, 3)$ and $R(1, 4)$.

Solution   Refer to Fig. 1.10.

a) $d(P, Q) = |5 - 1|$ Since the y-coordinates of these points are equal, find this distance using only the x-coordinates.

$\qquad = 4$

b) $d(P, R) = |3 - 4|$ Since the x-coordinates of the points are equal, find this distance using only the y-coordinates.

$\qquad = 1$ ▤

Consider the general situation of two points $P(x_1, y_1)$ and $Q(x_2, y_2)$, and let the point $R(x_2, y_1)$ be the vertex of a right triangle, $\triangle PRQ$. Then $d(P, R) = |x_1 - x_2|$ and $d(R, Q) = |y_1 - y_2|$ (Fig. 1.11).

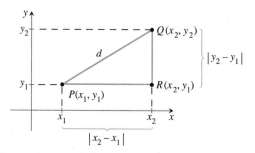

Figure 1.11 $d(P, Q)^2 = d(P, R)^2 + d(R, Q)^2$.

Apply the Pythagorean theorem (Fig. 1.12) to find the distance $d(P, Q)$:

$$d(P, Q) = \sqrt{|x_1 - x_2|^2 + |y_1 - y_2|^2}.$$

By replacing $|x_1 - x_2|^2$ and $|y_1 - y_2|^2$ with the equivalent expressions $(x_1 - x_2)^2$ and $(y_1 - y_2)^2$, we arrive at the following general rule.

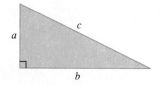

Figure 1.12   Recall the **Pythagorean theorem:** $a^2 + b^2 = c^2$.

Distance Formula

The distance $d(P, Q)$ between points $P(x_1, y_1)$ and $Q(x_2, y_2)$ in the coordinate plane is

$$d(P, Q) = \sqrt{(x_1 - x_2)^2 + (y_1 - y_2)^2}.$$

You should be able to

- show the x-axis and y-axis on a viewing rectangle;
- use the range key to set and change the viewing rectangle and axis scaling;
- move the cursor around the screen and observe the screen coordinates of the points;
- clear any drawing.

EXAMPLE 9   Find the Distance between Two Points in a Plane

Find the distance between the points $P(1, 5)$ and $Q(6, 2)$.

Solution

$$d(P, Q) = \sqrt{(1 - 6)^2 + (5 - 2)^2} \quad \text{Apply the distance formula.}$$
$$= \sqrt{(-5)^2 + 3^2}$$
$$= \sqrt{25 + 9}$$
$$= \sqrt{34}$$

Exercises for Section 1.1

Identify the real-number properties that explain why each of the following are valid equations.

1. $(3 + \sqrt{2}) + 7 = 3 + (\sqrt{2} + 7)$

2. $2(\sqrt{3} + 4) = 2 \cdot \sqrt{3} + 8$

3. $2 + (x + 5) = (5 + x) + 2$

4. $\frac{1}{2} \cdot (4 \cdot x) = \left(\frac{1}{2} \cdot 4\right) \cdot x = 2x$

On the real number line, draw all numbers that are solutions to these inequalities.

5. $-2 \le x < 3$ **6.** $4 \le x \le 5$

7. $5 \ge x$ **8.** $-3 < x < -1$

9. $x \le \sqrt{2}$ **10.** $-4 \le x \le 5$

Write an exact value for each expression without using absolute value bars.

11. $|-8|$ **12.** $|4 - 9|$

13. $|5 - \sqrt{3}|$ **14.** $|2 - \sqrt{5}|$

Find the distance between the points on the real-number line with each of the given coordinates.

15. 5, 17   **16.** -3, 4

17. -7, -3 **18.** 2, -6

19. x, 4   **20.** x, -3

21. Graph the points in (a) to (f) on the same coordinate plane. Identify the quadrant containing each point.

a) $(2, 4)$ **b)** $(0, 3)$ **c)** $(3, 0)$

d) $(-1, -4)$ **e)** $(-2, 3)$ **f)** $\left(-\frac{1}{2}, -5\right)$

Set your grapher for each of the following viewing rectangles. In each case move the cursor to the bottom-left and top-right corners of the viewing rectangle to confirm that you have the correct rectangle. Also, set the Xscl and Yscl on the range menu so that the tick marks are reasonably spaced on each axis.

22. $[-10, 20]$ by $[-20, 10]$

23. $[-5, 5]$ by $[-3, 4]$

24. $[-100, 100]$ by $[-50, 50]$

25. $[-20, 20]$ by $[-2, 2]$

Find the distance between the points in the plane with the following coordinates.

26. $(0, 0)$, $(3, 4)$ **27.** $(-1, 2)$, $(2, 3)$

28. $(-3, -2)$, $(6, -2)$ **29.** $(-4, 6)$, $(2, 3)$

30. Show that the points $(1, 3)$, $(4, 7)$, and $(8, 4)$ are the vertices of an isosceles triangle.

31. Show that the points $(2, 5), (5, 9), (9, 6)$, and $(6, 2)$ are the vertices of a rhombus.

Write an expression that gives the distance between the following points in a coordinate plane.

32. (a, b), $(2, 3)$ **33.** $(0, y)$, $(4, 0)$

34. $(0, y)$, $(-4, 0)$ **35.** $(x, 0)$, $(-1, 3)$

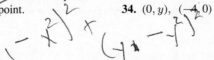

Find x so that the distance between the following points is 10.

36. $(x, 5),\ (1, -3)$ **37.** $(2, -1),\ (x, 7)$

38. Suppose the viewing rectangle on a grapher is $[-20, x]$ by $[-20, y]$. What are the values of x and y if each pixel represents "one unit"? (Answers may vary depending on the type of grapher being used.)

39. Find a viewing rectangle for your grapher for which a single move of the cursor causes a change, or gap, of two units.

40. Set the viewing window of your grapher so that the coordinate axes are centered (or nearly centered) and such that the cursor as you move it around the screen always has integer values.

41. Show that $|a| \geq 0$.

42. Show that $|a \cdot b| = |a| \cdot |b|$.

43. *Writing to Learn.* Write several sentences that explain the difference between the *coordinates of points* in the Cartesian coordinate plane (math coordinates) and the *screen coordinates* in a computer graphical representation of the coordinate plane. Give an example of a point that lies in a particular viewing rectangle whose (x, y) math coordinates do not appear as screen coordinates. (Suggestion: First consider Exercises 38 and 39.)

1.2 _____

Graphing Utilities and Complete Graphs
Problem Solving

Mathematics is used frequently as a tool for solving scientific and economic problems.

George Pólya is sometimes called the father of modern problem solving because of his significant writing and analysis of the mathematical problem solving process. Pólya was born in Hungary in 1887 and completed his Ph.D. at the University of Budapest. In 1940 he came to Brown University before joining the faculty at Stanford University in 1942. He died at the age of 97 in 1985. His four-step process continues to be valid and helpful in this age of computers and graphing utilities.

In Step 1 of this four-step process, you might need to do all of the following: reading the problem as stated, several times if necessary; restating the problem in your own words; writing down a statement or variable name that identifies what the problem asks you to find or solve for; and identifying clearly what information is given and what you need to find. Many people find it helpful to discuss their understanding of a problem out loud.

In Step 2 you devise a plan for solving the problem. Your plan will usually consist of identifying which strategy or combination of strategies can be used to solve the problem. Each of the strategies listed in the margin suggests a **problem-solving process**. Successful problem solvers learn how to match a strategy or several strategies with the problem that needs to be solved.

In Step 3 you carry out the plan that has been devised while completing Steps 1 and 2. Sometimes Step 3 will take less time than a careful completion of Steps 1 and 2. *Most beginning problem solvers skip over Steps 1 and 2 and begin pushing a pencil or punching a calculator too soon. Taking time to follow Steps 1 and 2 will generally lead to more success in Step 3 activities.*

PÓLYA'S FOUR-STEP PROCESS

Pólya identified four steps in problem solving:

1. Understand the problem.
2. Devise a plan.
3. Carry out the plan.
4. Look back.

In Step 4 you look back and analyze the process that you have completed. You may reflect on the relationship between this problem and others you have solved in the past and see a pattern. Then you identify what characteristics of the problem might provide clues for strategies most likely to succeed as you encounter similar problems in the future.

EXAMPLE 1   Observing the Pattern and Generalizing

A Problem Situation   Consider this economic situation.   Quality Rent-a-Car charges $15 plus $0.20 per mile to rent a car. There are many questions one can ask about this situation that pose a mathematical problem. Consequently, we call this situation a **problem situation**.

Quality Rent-a-Car charges $15 plus $0.20 per mile to rent a car. How much does Quality Rent-a-Car charge if a rented car is driven

a) 50 miles?

b) 75 miles?

c) 100 miles?

d) 200 miles?

e) x miles?

Solution   Use the problem-solving strategies of "Look for a Pattern" and "Use a Variable".

a) $0.20(50) + 15 = \$25.00$ cost/mile times 50 miles plus 15 dollars

b) $0.20(75) + 15 = \$30.00$

c) $0.20(100) + 15 = \$35.00$

d) $0.20(200) + 15 = \$55.00$

Generalization   To answer part (e), for x miles, the cost y is found by using the equation

$$y = 0.20 \cdot x + 15.$$

The equation $y = 0.2x + 15$ is called an **algebraic representation** or a **mathematical model** of the problem situation. The power of mathematics is that this model equation can now be used to find the cost (y) for any other number of miles driven (x).

Drawing a graph is one way to picture this relationship. Draw a pair of axes and label them as in Fig. 1.13. (Since distance is represented by positive values, only the positive axes appear.) Then plot the five points whose coordinates are the **data pairs** listed in the following table. (This kind of table is often called a **table of values** or **data table**.) These points satisfy the equation $y = 0.2x + 15$.

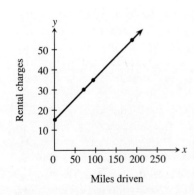

Figure 1.13 Relationship between miles driven and rental charges: $y = 0.2x + 15$.

x	0	50	75	100	200	x
y	15	25	30	35	55	$0.2x + 15$

Note that these points appear to lie on a line. Draw a ray beginning at point $(0, 15)$ and continuing through the other four points. This ray is a graphical representation of the Quality Rent-a-Car problem situation. To summarize, in a given problem situation there may be both an algebraic representation and a graphical representation of the problem situation.

In Example 1 we collected data and found an algebraic representation for the data. Next we consider the converse situation, where an equation is used to generate data.

E X A M P L E 2   Using an Equation to Find Data

Suppose Sarah is charged $50 for renting a car from Quality Rent-a-Car. How many miles did she drive the car?

Solution   **Algebraic Method** $y = 0.2x + 15$ and the cost y is 50.

$$50 = 0.2x + 15 \qquad \text{Substitute 50 for } y \text{ and solve the resulting equation for } x.$$

$$50 - 15 = 0.2x$$

$$\frac{35}{0.2} = x$$

so

$$x = 175 \qquad \text{Sarah drove 175 miles.}$$

Graphical Method   Apply the following steps:

1. Draw a graph of the model $y = 0.2x + 15$ (Fig. 1.14).
2. Begin at the point $(0, 50)$ on the y-axis and move horizontally to the graph.
3. Read the x-coordinate of this point to find an *estimate* to the solution to the problem.

Solutions found graphically will be approximations with the accuracy depending on the viewing rectangle used.*

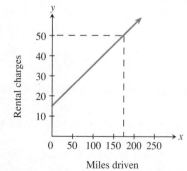

Figure 1.14 Finding the number of miles for a $50 fee.

---

* Consult the accompanying *Graphing Calculator and Computer Graphing Laboratory Manual* to expand on this aspect of using a graphing utility.

When doing this Exploration you may have discovered that the first viewing rectangle you chose was not large enough to include the point $(175, 50)$, which is needed to solve the problem graphically. The viewing rectangle $[0, 200]$ by $[0, 100]$ will contain the point $(175, 50)$. What viewing rectangle did you use?

This situation illustrates the importance of choosing an appropriate viewing rectangle when graphing an equation. What is appropriate in one situation may not be appropriate in the next situation. Deciding which viewing rectangle to use is a judgment skill required to use a graphing utility.

Related to this discussion is the concept of complete graph. A graph of an equation is a **complete graph** if it suggests all points of the graph and all of the important features of the graph. Once you find a viewing rectangle that shows a complete graph, a slightly larger or smaller viewing rectangle usually produces a complete graph also. Thus a given equation generally has *many* complete graphs.

The next example illustrates several of the kinds of things that can happen if the selected viewing rectangle does not show a complete graph.

E X A M P L E 3   Finding a Complete Graph with a Grapher

Graph $y = x^2 + 10$ in each of the viewing rectangles:

a) $[-5, 5]$ by $[-5, 5]$

b) $[-10, 10]$ by $[-10, 10]$

c) $[-10, 10]$ by $[-50, 50]$.

Choose which viewing rectangle gives a complete graph.

Solution   The best viewing rectangle is $[-10, 10]$ by $[-50, 50]$ (see Fig. 1.15). The viewing rectangle $[-5, 5]$ by $[-5, 5]$ includes no points of a graph, and the $[-10, 10]$ by $[-10, 10]$ rectangle includes only one point of a graph.

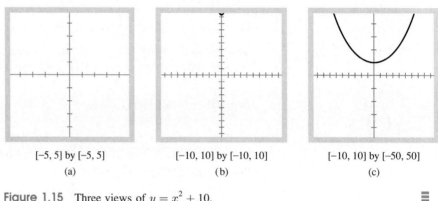

$[-5, 5]$ by $[-5, 5]$	$[-10, 10]$ by $[-10, 10]$	$[-10, 10]$ by $[-50, 50]$
(a)	(b)	(c)

Figure 1.15   Three views of $y = x^2 + 10$.

The curve given by a complete graph of $y = x^2 + 10$ is called a **parabola**.

Notice that in Fig. 1.15(a, b) the scale marks on both coordinate axes are one unit apart. However, in Fig. 1.15(c), the scale marks on the x-axis are one unit apart and the scale marks on the y-axis are 10 units apart. When changing the viewing rectangle on a grapher, it is often helpful to change the scale marks on the two axes.

Many of the keys on your calculator can be used to generate a table of (x, y) data pairs that can be graphed. Consider for example the $\sqrt{x}$ key, where $\sqrt{x}$ stands for the nonnegative square root of x. This function key can be used to generate the pairs $(x, \sqrt{x})$. A picture of the graph of all these pairs can be obtained by graphing the equation $y = \sqrt{x}$.

EXAMPLE 4   Find a Complete Graph

Find the graph of the equation $y = \sqrt{x} + 20$. Which of these rectangles shows a complete graph?

a) $[-10, 10]$ by $[-10, 10]$

b) $[-50, 50]$ by $[-10, 10]$

c) $[-10, 10]$ by $[-50, 50]$

Solution   See Fig. 1.16.

STANDARD VIEWING RECTANGLE

The **standard viewing rectangle** is the rectangle $[-10, 10]$ by $[-10, 10]$. As you attempt to find a complete graph of an equation, begin with the standard viewing rectangle and change to an alternate viewing rectangle as needed.

GRAPHER SKILLS UPDATE

You should be able to

■ graph an equation that begins $y =$;

■ experiment with viewing rectangles until a complete graph can be determined;

■ use the trace feature to move along the graph.

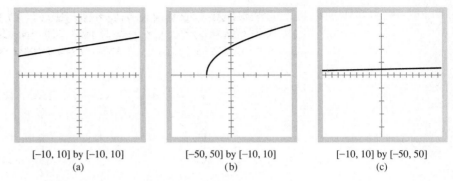

[−10, 10] by [−10, 10]   [−50, 50] by [−10, 10]   [−10, 10] by [−50, 50]
(a)   (b)   (c)

Figure 1.16   Three views of $y = \sqrt{x + 20}$.

The viewing rectangle in Fig. 1.16(b) shows a complete graph. The viewing rectangles in Fig. 1.16(a,c) do not show a significant portion of the graph or properly indicate the behavior of the graph.

Examples 3 and 4 show that finding a complete graph depends on choosing an appropriate viewing rectangle. It is important to realize that a given function does not have a unique, complete graph. Consequently, we speak of a complete graph rather than the complete graph of a function.

As you progress in this course, there will be occasions when you cannot find a complete graph in a single viewing rectangle. You may need to use a large rectangle to obtain a global view, and to zoom-in on some small piece of the graph to see necessary detail.

On the other hand, when collecting and plotting data points for a hand-drawn graph, the task of finding a complete graph is different. Here the question may be, What is the correct way to connect the data points?

Since the four points graphed in the Quality Rent-a-Car problem fell on a line, it was relatively easy to determine the graph. When the points do not lie on a straight line, a hand-drawn graph is less reliable.

Special Agreement about Graphs

This text illustrates graphs produced by hand and on a grapher. Note that figures of grapher-produced graphs (for example Figs. 1.15 and 1.16) have a color border, while those representing hand-drawn graphs (such as Fig. 1.17) do not.

In the text and exercises the words *draw* and *sketch* refer to hand-drawn graphs, and the word *find* indicates use of the grapher. Sometimes you will be asked to "draw a complete graph," as in Example 5. Usually, however, you will be asked to "find a complete graph."

EXAMPLE 5   Drawing Sketches of Complete Graphs

The following data table shows the (x, y) pairs for some relationship.

x	-3	-2.5	-2	-1.5	-1	-0.5	0	0.5	1	1.5	2	2.5	3
y	-15	-5.625	0	2.625	3	1.875	0	-1.875	-3	-2.625	0	5.625	15

a) On a rectangular coordinate system graph the data from this table.

b) Draw three different complete graphs of this relationship between x and y. (Recall the agreement about the use of the word *draw*.)

Solution   A complete graph must contain the data from the table. The graph also must suggest the *pattern* of the data.

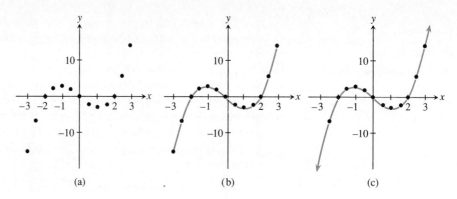

(a)   (b)   (c)

Figure 1.17   Three complete graphs of the data.

Figure 1.17(a) is strictly the graph of the data and so by definition is a complete graph. It is not the only possible complete graph; Fig. 1.17(b, c) show two other complete graphs. ≡

EXAMPLE 6   Finding an Equation to Model the Data

Show that the equation $y = x^3 - 4x$ is a model for the data table given in Example 5.

Solution

$$(-3)^3 - 4(-3) = -15$$ Substitute -3 for x and solve for y.

$$(-2.5)^3 - 4(-2.5) = -5.625$$ Substitute -2.5 for x.

$$\vdots$$

$$(2.5)^3 - 4(2.5) = 5.625$$

$$(3)^3 - 4(3) = 15$$

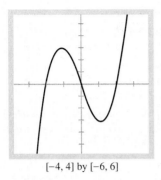

[−4, 4] by [−6, 6]

Figure 1.18 Complete graph of $y = x^3 - 4x$.

Figure 1.18 shows a complete graph of the equation $y = x^3 - 4x$.

One possible complete graph through the data points found in Example 5 is precisely the graph of $y = x^3 - 4x$. In a real sense it is also the best complete graph because it is a smooth curve that contains the given data. If more data points were given following the same pattern, this choice of model equation would continue to be appropriate.

Graphers work by creating a finite table of values from a given equation (model), plotting the data points, and connecting the points with a smooth curve. One model grapher uses 96 data points from Xmin to Xmax to create its graphs. Some computer graphing utilities use 500 or more points between Xmin and Xmax. Graphers do the tedious computation and allow us to view graphs today that would have been too time-consuming to produce in the past.

Exercises for Section 1.2

On a rectangular coordinate system graph the (x, y) pairs from the given data. In each case estimate a complete graph.

1.

x	−4	−1	1	4	9
y	−2	1	3	6	11

2.

x	1	2	3	4	5
y	1	4	9	16	25

3. Use a graphing utility to graph $y = 100\sqrt{x}$. Then use the technique that you used in the Exploration activity to complete the following table of values.

x	?	?	?	?	?
y	10	20	30	40	50

4. Show that the equation $y = x + 2$ is a model for the data in Exercise 1.

5. Show that the equation $y = x^2$ is a model for the data in Exercise 2.

6. Which of the following equations is a model for the following set of data?

x	1	2	3	4
y	0	4	10	18

a) $y = x^2$ **b)** $y = x^2 + x - 2$ **c)** $y = x^3$

Exercises 7 to 10 refer to the following problem situation. A school club pays $35.75 to rent a video cassette player to show a movie for a fund-raising project. The club charges $0.25 per ticket for the movie.

7. How much profit does the club make if it sells
   a) 100 tickets?   **b)** 175 tickets?
   c) 250 tickets?   **d)** 425 tickets?

8. Find the pattern and generalize. What is the profit y if the club sells x tickets?

9. Draw a complete graph of the equation that describes the profit y for selling x tickets.

10. Use the graph you completed in Exercise 9 to determine the minimum number of tickets that must be sold for the club to
   a) break even;   **b)** realize a profit.

Which of the following points lie in the viewing rectangle $[-2, 3]$ by $[1, 10]$?

11. $(0, 0)$ **12.** $(0, 5)$ **13.** $(5, 0)$

14. $(3, 2)$ **15.** $(1, 6)$ **16.** $(1, -1)$

17. Choose a viewing rectangle $[X\min, X\max]$ by $[Y\min, Y\max]$ that includes all of the indicated points:
   a) $(-9, 10)$, $(2, 8)$, and $(3, 12)$;
   b) $(20, -3)$, $(13, 56)$, and $(-11, 2)$.

18. Which viewing rectangles show a complete graph of $y = x^2 - 30x + 225$?

a) $[-5, 5]$ by $[-5, 5]$ **b)** $[-10, 10]$ by $[-10, 10]$
c) $[15, 30]$ by $[-50, 50]$ **d)** $[5, 25]$ by $[-100, 100]$
e) $[10, 20]$ by $[-1000, 1000]$

19. Which viewing rectangles show a complete graph of $y = 20 - 30x + x^3$?

a) $[-10, 10]$ by $[-10, 10]$ **b)** $[-50, 50]$ by $[-10, 10]$
c) $[-10, 10]$ by $[-50, 50]$ **d)** $[0, 10]$ by $[-100, 100]$
e) $[-10, 10]$ by $[-50, 100]$

For Exercises 20 to 29 use your grapher to draw a complete graph of each of these equations. Begin with the standard viewing rectangle, and modify the rectangle until you arrive at a satisfactory viewing rectangle.

20. $y = 6 - x$ **21.** $y = 2x^2 + 1$

22. $y = x^3 + x$ **23.** $y = 2x^2 - 3x + 5$

24. $y = 4 - x - x^3$ **25.** $y = \dfrac{(x+3)^2}{5} + 2x + 4$

26. $y = 200x - 10$ **27.** $y = 10x^2 + 500$

28. $y = \sqrt{x - 2}$ **29.** $y = \sqrt{2x + 10}$

Find a complete graph of each equation on the same coordinate system.

30. $y = x^2$, $y = (x - 1)^2$, $y = (x - 2)^2$, $y = (x + 3)^2$.

31. $y = -1 + x^2$, $y = 2 + x^2$, $y = -2 + x^2$, $y = x^2 - 4$.

For Exercises 32 to 34, complete a table of (x, y) pairs for the given values of x. Round your y-values to the second decimal place.

32. $y = \sqrt{x + 4}$ for $x = -3, -2, -1, 0, 1, 2, 3, 4, 5, 6$.

33. $y = \log x$ for $x = 0.25, 0.5, 1, 1.5, 2, 3, 4, 5$.

34. $y = \sin x$ for $x = 0, 0.52, 1.05, 1.57, 2.09, 2.62, 3.14, 3.67, 4.19, 4.71$.

35. Graph the (x, y) pairs from the data table you completed for Exercise 32, and make a sketch of your best estimate of a complete graph for this data.

36. Graph the (x, y) pairs from the data table you completed for Exercise 33, and make a sketch of your best estimate of a complete graph for this data.

37. Graph the (x, y) pairs from the data table you completed for Exercise 34, and make a sketch of your best estimate of a complete graph for this data.

38. If the point (a, b) is on the graph of $y = 100/x$, find the product ab.

39. **Collect Data** Find an algebraic and a graphical representation that shows the relationship between gallons of gasoline used and miles driven for your personal or family (or a friend's) car.

40. **Writing to Learn** Write a paragraph that explains your answer to this question. The two equations $y = x + 1$ and $y = x + 1.01$ have what appear to be identical graphs in the standard viewing rectangle, even though their equations are not identical. (Check that this is true.) Why does this happen? Does this happen for all viewing rectangles?

41. **Writing to Learn** Why does the graph of the straight line $y = 0.5x$ appear jagged when using a grapher?

42. **Writing to Learn** Why does the graph of $y = \sqrt{x + 20}$ appear to be a straight line in some viewing rectangles? (See Example 4.)

1.3 _____ Graphing $y = x^n$ and Properties of Exponents

Complete an experiment: Graph both of these equations, one after another, on the same coordinate system: $y = (x + 3)(x - 2)$ and $y = x^2 + x - 6$. Notice that the grapher seems to be drawing only one graph. As the grapher draws the second graph, it retraces the graph of the first equation. This exercise demonstrates visually that the two equations may be equivalent.

Complete the Exploration activity, and formulate generalizations about equations that may be equivalent.

GRAPHER SKILLS UPDATE

Here are some methods you can use that provide evidence that the grapher is retracing the graph.

- On one model grapher there is a small black square in the upper right corner of the display when the grapher is busy tracing a graph.
- While the grapher is retracing the graph, push the range key and observe that the grapher does not respond—evidence that it is busy doing something.

🔎 EXPLORE WITH A GRAPHING UTILITY

On the same coordinate system and viewing rectangle, graph each of the following pairs of equations:

- $y = x(x^2)$ and $y = x^3$
- $y = (x^3)(x^2)$ and $y = x^5$
- $y = x^5 \div x^3$ and $y = x^2$.

Study the patterns and generalize. Write some equations of your own that you think might be equivalent, and check your guess with a graphing utility.

Questions

1. Which pairs of equations appear to be equivalent?
2. What generalizations can you make regarding exponents?

Exploring with the graphing utility can show visually some relationships about exponents in equations, for example, as in $(x^2)(x^3) = x^5$. On the other hand, it is important to realize that the properties of exponents discussed in this section are not true because of evidence produced by the grapher; they are true for logical reasons, as discussed in this section. The grapher is not automatically intelligent; it is programmed by engineers to reflect mathematical properties. Furthermore, although two graphs may appear to be the same, they are not necessarily the same.

Positive Integer Exponents

An exponent is a notational convenience—a type of mathematical shorthand. It is conventional to agree that when n is a positive integer, a^n means that n factors of a have been multiplied together.

Definition 1.4 Exponential Notation

Let n be a positive integer. Then we read a^n as **a to the nth power**, and

$$a^n = \underbrace{a \cdot a \cdot \,\cdots\, \cdot a}_{n \text{ factors}}$$

where n is called the **exponent** and a is called the **base**.

We use this definition to find an equivalent form for an expression like $(a^3)(a^5)$:

$$(a^3)(a^5) = \underbrace{a \cdot a \cdot a}_{3 \text{ factors}} \cdot \underbrace{a \cdot a \cdot a \cdot a \cdot a}_{5 \text{ factors}} = \underbrace{a \cdot a \cdot a \cdot a \cdot a \cdot a \cdot a \cdot a}_{8 \text{ factors}} = a^8.$$

Verify this relationship for positive-integer exponents other than 3 and 5, and discover the following generalization:

$$(a^n)(a^m) = a^{n+m}.$$

Notice a^0 must be interpreted as 1 in order for the next equation to be true:

$$a^{n+0} = a^n a^0.$$

Likewise, each of the following properties of exponents can be shown to be true.

Properties of Exponents

Let a, b, x, and y be real numbers, and let n and m be positive integers. Then each of the following properties is true.

Properties	Example
1. $a^m a^n = a^{m+n}$	$5^3 5^6 = 5^{3+6} = 5^9$
2. $\dfrac{a^n}{a^m} = a^{n-m}$	$\dfrac{x^9}{x^4} = x^{9-4} = x^5$
3. $a^0 = 1$	$8^0 = 1$
4. $(ab)^m = a^m b^m$	$(2y)^5 = 2^5 y^5 = 32y^5$
5. $(a^m)^n = a^{mn}$	$(u^2)^3 = u^{2 \cdot 3} = u^6$
6. $\left(\dfrac{a}{b}\right)^m = \dfrac{a^m}{b^m}$	$\left(\dfrac{x}{y}\right)^7 = \dfrac{x^7}{y^7}$

EXAMPLE 1   Simplifying Expressions with Positive Exponents

Simplify each of these expressions:

a) $(2ab^3)(5a^2 b^5)$,   **b)** $\left(\dfrac{x}{2}\right)^2 (2y)^3$,   **c)** $\dfrac{(u^2 v)^3}{v^2}$,   **d)** $\left(\dfrac{x^3}{y^2}\right)^4$.

Solution

a) $(2ab^3)(5a^2 b^5) = 10\,(a \cdot a^2)(b^3 \cdot b^5) = 10a^3 b^8$

b) $\left(\dfrac{x}{2}\right)^2 (2y)^3 = \dfrac{x^2}{2^2}(2^3 y^3) = 2x^2 y^3$

c) $\dfrac{(u^2v)^3}{v^2} = \dfrac{(u^2)^3v^3}{v^2} = \dfrac{u^6v^3}{v^2} = u^6v$

d) $\left(\dfrac{x^3}{y^2}\right)^4 = \dfrac{(x^3)^4}{(y^2)^4} = \dfrac{x^{12}}{y^8}$

■

Negative-Integer Exponents

If we agree that $a^{-n} = 1/a^n$ when n is a positive integer, then the six properties of exponents remain true when the exponent is a negative integer. The next example illustrates this fact.

E X A M P L E   2   Simplifying Expressions with Negative Exponents

Simplify each of these expressions:

a) $\dfrac{x^2}{x^{-3}}$,   **b)** $\dfrac{u^2v^{-2}}{u^{-1}v^3}$,   **c)** $[(4)^{-2}]^3$,   **d)** $\left(\dfrac{x^2}{2}\right)^{-3}$.

Solution

a) $\dfrac{x^2}{x^{-3}} = x^2 \cdot \dfrac{1}{x^{-3}} = x^2 \cdot x^3 = x^{2+3} = x^5$

b) $\dfrac{u^2v^{-2}}{u^{-1}v^3} = \dfrac{u^2u^1}{v^2v^3} = \dfrac{u^{2+1}}{v^{2+3}} = \dfrac{u^3}{v^5}$

c) $[(4)^{-2}]^3 = 4^{(-2)(3)} = 4^{-6} = \dfrac{1}{4^6} = \dfrac{1}{4096}$

d) $\left(\dfrac{x^2}{2}\right)^{-3} = \dfrac{(x^2)^{-3}}{2^{-3}} = \dfrac{x^{-6}}{2^{-3}} = \dfrac{2^3}{x^6} = \dfrac{8}{x^6}$

■

Rational-Number Exponents

What does the symbol $a^{1/2}$ mean? Meaning has been assigned to this notation in such a way that the properties of exponents remain true. For example, according to property 5,

$$(a^{1/2})^2 = a^{(1/2)(2)} = a^1 = a.$$

So $a^{1/2}$ is a solution of the equation $x^2 = a$. That means that $a^{1/2} = \sqrt{a}$ or $a^{1/2} = -\sqrt{a}$. By convention $a^{1/2} = \sqrt{a}$, the **principal square root**.

In general, if a is a real number and n is a positive integer, then

$$(a^{1/n})^n = a^{(1/n)n} = a^1 = a.$$

So $a^{1/n}$, called the **principal nth root** of a, is a solution to the equation $x^n = a$. In particular, $a^{1/2}$ is called the principal square root of a (as just shown), and $a^{1/3}$ is known as the **principal cube root** of a. Similarly, $a^{1/4}$, $a^{1/5},\ldots$ are the principal fourth and fifth roots of a, and so on.

🔍 EXPLORE WITH A GRAPHING UTILITY

Use the viewing rectangle $[-100, 100]$ by $[-10, 10]$ and graph on the same coordinate system the following pairs of equations:

- $y = \sqrt{x}$ and $y = x^{1/2}$
- $y = \sqrt[3]{x}$ and $y = x^{1/3}$.

Questions

1. Do the equations in each pair appear to be equivalent? Does your experiment support the meaning we have given to fractional exponents?

2. Why did the graph of the first pair fall entirely to the right of the y-axis, whereas the graph of the second pair appeared on both sides of the y-axis?

3. What generalization can you make for $x^{1/n}$ that depends on whether n is odd or even?

Recall that the square root of a negative number, for example $\sqrt{-3}$, does not represent a real number since any number times itself must be positive. In other words, in the expressions $\sqrt{x}$ and $x^{1/2}$, x cannot be a negative number. The same is true for $x^{1/n}$ when n is any even integer. This observation gives a partial answer to Question 2 of the Exploration.

In contrast, $\sqrt[3]{-8}$ is defined. Why? Because $\sqrt[3]{-8} = -2$, since $(-2)^3 = -8$. So when n is odd and x is negative, $x^{1/n}$ is defined and is negative. This finding is summarized with a definition.

> **Definition 1.5** $a^{1/n}$ *n*th Root of a Number
>
> Let n be a positive integer and a a real number. Then
>
> $$a^{1/n} = \begin{cases} \text{the } n\text{th root of } a \text{ if } n \text{ is odd;} \\ \text{the nonnegative } n\text{th root of } a \text{ if } n \text{ is even and } a \geq 0. \end{cases}$$

We next turn attention to deciding what symbols like $x^{2/3}$ mean. It can be shown that whenever m is an integer and n is a positive integer, then

$$\left(a^{1/n}\right)^m = \left(a^m\right)^{1/n}$$

where a is a nonzero real number for which the indicated powers exist. It makes sense to replace each expression in this equation with the single symbol $a^{m/n}$.

GRAPHER SKILLS UPDATE

When you want to graph $y = x^{m/n}$, use one of the two forms from Definition 1.6: $y = \left(x^{1/n}\right)^m$ or $y = \left(x^m\right)^{1/n}$. For example, if you key into a grapher $y = x^{2/3}$, you may not get the correct graph. The graphing utility does not store the definition of $x^{2/3}$; you have to tell it the definition.

> **Definition 1.6 $a^{m/n}$ Rational Number Exponents**
>
> For all integers m and all positive integers n, m/n is in lowest terms, and for all nonzero real numbers a for which all the indicated powers exist, then
> $$a^{m/n} = \left(a^{1/n}\right)^m = \left(a^m\right)^{1/n}.$$

Our development of the concept *exponent* began with positive-integer exponents. We then extended that meaning to include negative-integer exponents, exponents of the form $1/n$, and finally exponents of the form m/n. This discussion leads to the following theorem.

> **Theorem 1.1   Properties of Rational Exponents**
>
> Exponent properties 1 to 6 listed earlier in Section 1.3 are true when the exponents represent rational numbers.

COMMON ERROR

Students often make the mistake of assuming that $(\sqrt{x^2}) = x$. In fact, the correct equation is $(\sqrt{x^2}) = |x|$. Notice that $\sqrt{(-3)^2} \neq -3$. For similar reasons, whenever n is even, $(a^{1/n})^n = |a|$.

We use this theorem to complete the following example.

E X A M P L E   3   Simplifying Expressions with Fractional Exponents

Simplify each of these expressions:

a) $8^{2/3}$,   b) $x^{1/4}x^{1/3}$,   c) $\left(x^3y^{2/3}\right)^{1/2}$,   d) $\left(\dfrac{x^2}{y^3}\right)^{-1/2}$.

Solution

a) $8^{2/3} = \left(8^{1/3}\right)^2 = 2^2 = 4$

b) $x^{1/4}x^{1/3} = x^{(1/3+1/4)} = x^{7/12}$

c) $\left(x^3y^{2/3}\right)^{1/2} = \left(x^3\right)^{1/2}\left(y^{2/3}\right)^{1/2} = x^{3/2}y^{1/3}$

d) $\left(\dfrac{x^2}{y^3}\right)^{-1/2} = \left(\dfrac{y^3}{x^2}\right)^{1/2} = \dfrac{(y^3)^{1/2}}{(x^2)^{1/2}} = \dfrac{y^{3/2}}{|x|}$.

Exercises for Section 1.3

In Exercises 1 to 14, evaluate the given numerical expression:

1. $(2^3) \cdot (3^2)$

2. 3^{-1}

3. $3^4 \cdot 3^{-6}$

4. $\left(\dfrac{4}{9}\right)^{1/2}$

5. $7^{-2} \cdot 7^5$

6. $\dfrac{4 \cdot 5^{-4}}{5^{-2} \cdot 4^{-2}}$

7. $9^{1/2}$

8. $16^{1/4}$

9. $8^{2/3}$

10. $16^{3/4}$

11. $16^{-1/2}$

12. $8^{-1/3}$

13. $27^{2/3}$

14. $32^{-3/5}$

Use a calculator for Exercises 15 to 18:

15. $(3.2)^{1/3}$

16. $(0.015)^{3.125}$

17. $(1.25)^{-2/3}$

18. $(3.14)^{3.1}$

Use a calculator to answer Exercises 19 to 21:

19. Which number is larger, $2^{2/3}$ or $3^{3/4}$?

20. Which number is smaller, $4^{-2/3}$ or $3^{-3/4}$?

21. Order these numbers from smallest to largest: $3^{3/4}$, $4^{5/8}$, $12^{3/10}$.

22. As you completed Exercises 9 to 14, which of these forms did you find easier to use: $y = \left(x^m\right)^{1/n}$ or $y = \left(x^{1/n}\right)^m$?

23. Graph these equations on a grapher: $y = \left(x^2\right)^{1/3}$ and $y = \left(x^{1/3}\right)^2$. Does your grapher suggest that these equations are equivalent?

24. Graph these equations on a grapher: $y = \left(x^5\right)^{1/3}$ and $y = \left(x^{1/3}\right)^5$. Does your grapher suggest that these equations are equivalent?

25. Graph these equations on a grapher: $y = \left(x^3\right)^{1/4}$ and $y = \left(x^{1/4}\right)^3$. Does your grapher suggest that these equations are equivalent?

26. Graph these equations on a grapher: $y = x^{2/3}$ and $y = \left(x^{1/3}\right)^2$. Are the graphs identical? Which one allows negative values of x?

27. Experiment with a grapher and find a generalization. Under what conditions does the graph of $y = \left(x^{1/n}\right)^m$, where m and n are integers, lie entirely in the first quadrant? (Note: Not all graphers produce identical results.)

In Exercises 28 to 43, simplify the expression:

28. $\dfrac{x^4 \cdot y^3}{x^2 \cdot y^5}$

29. $\dfrac{(u \cdot v^2)^3}{v^2 \cdot u^3}$

30. $\dfrac{(3x^2)^2 \cdot y^4}{3y^2}$

31. $\left(\dfrac{4}{x^2}\right)^2$

32. $\dfrac{(2x^2y)^{-1}}{xy^2}$

33. $(3x^2y^3)^{-2}$

34. $\dfrac{x^{-3}y^3}{x^{-5}y^2}$

35. $\left(\dfrac{2}{xy}\right)^{-3}$

36. $\left(\dfrac{1}{x} + \dfrac{1}{y}\right)(x+y)^{-1}$

37. $\dfrac{(x+y)^{-1}}{(x-y)^{-1}}$

38. $\left(x^2y^4\right)^{1/2}$

39. $\left(x^{2/3}\right)^{1/2}$

40. $\left(\dfrac{x^{1/2}}{y^{2/3}}\right)^6$

41. $\left(x^2y^3\right)^{3/4}$

42. $\dfrac{\left(p^2q^4\right)^{1/2}}{\left(27q^3p^6\right)^{1/3}}$

43. $\dfrac{\left(x^{-3}y^2\right)^{-4}}{\left(y^6x^{-4}\right)^{-2}}$

Exercises 44 and 45 refer to the following **problem situation**. The amount A after t years in a savings account earning an annual interest rate r compounded n times per year is

$$A = P\left(1 + \frac{r}{n}\right)^{nt},$$

where P is the **principal** (the original amount saved).

44. How much will be in a savings account after 5 years if $5,500 is deposited in a savings account that earns 8% per year compounded quarterly?

45. Which is the better deal, a savings account that pays 8.25% compounded annually or one that pays 8% compounded monthly?

46. Suppose you place a single penny on a checkerboard's corner square, two pennies on the next square, four pennies on the next square, and so on. How many pennies will there be on the 64th square?

47. Estimate Mentally   In Exercise 46, approximately how high will the stack of pennies on the last square of the checkerboard be?
a) the height of a four-story building;
b) the height of a skyscraper;
c) the height of a space needle reaching to the moon;
d) a height greater than all of the above.

48. Use the definition of exponential notation to show that $a^7/a^2 = a^{7-2}$.

49. Use the definition of exponential notation to show that $(a^3)^4 = a^{3 \cdot 4}$.

1.4 _____ Algebraic Expressions

In algebra, we often use letters to represent numbers. Sometimes we use letters to represent fixed numbers (called **constants**) like $\pi \approx 3.14$ or e ≈ 2.718. But more often, we let letters stand for a collection of numbers, as in $y = .25x + 15$, in which case we call the letters **variables**. An **algebraic expression** is a collection of variables and constants; these are combined by using addition, subtraction, multiplication, division, and radicals or fractional exponents. Here are some examples:

$$3x^2 + 4x - 5, \qquad \frac{(x-3)^{1/2}}{x^2}, \qquad \sqrt{x^2 + y^2}, \qquad 3x^2y + 4x + 7y.$$

A **term** in an algebraic expression is a number or the product of a number and one or more variables. For example, $3x^2 + 4x - 5$ has three terms: $3x^2$, $4x$, and 5. The real numbers in each term are called the **coefficients** of the term. The coefficient of the second term of $3x^2 + 4x - 5$ is 4.

To **evaluate** an algebraic expression means that a specific number value is substituted for each variable and the result is then calculated.

E X A M P L E 1   Evaluating an Expression

The volume and surface area of a box with length l, height h, and width w (Fig. 1.19) are given by the expressions

$$\text{volume} = lwh \qquad \text{and} \qquad \text{surface area} = 2lw + 2lh + 2wh.$$

Find the volume and surface area of a box with $l = 18$ cm, $w = 9$ cm, and $h = 5$ cm.

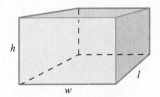

Figure 1.19 Box dimensions.

Solution   See Fig. 1.19.

Volume $= lwh$

$= 18 \cdot 9 \cdot 5$ Substitute $18, 9$, and 5 for l, w, and h respectively.

$= 810.$

Surface area $= 2lw + 2lh + 2wh$

$= 2 \cdot 18 \cdot 9 + 2 \cdot 18 \cdot 5 + 2 \cdot 9 \cdot 5$ Substitute $18, 9$, and 5 for l, w, and h respectively.

$= 594.$

The volume is 810 cm^3, and the surface area is 594 cm^2.

Two expressions are **equivalent** when they yield the same numerical value for all values of the variables.

A **polynomial** is an algebraic expression defined as the sum of a finite number of terms with only nonnegative integer exponents permitted. Some examples are

$$2x^3 + 2x - 3, \qquad y^4 + 3y^2 + y + 5, \qquad 3x^2y + xy^3 - 14.$$

The first is a polynomial in x, the second is a polynomial in y, and the third is a polynomial in x and y. A polynomial containing exactly three terms is called a **trinomial**, and one with exactly two terms is called a **binomial**.

Here is a formal definition.

Definition 1.7   Polynomial

A **polynomial in x** is an expression of the form

$$a_n x^n + a_{n-1} x^{n-1} + \cdots + a_1 x^1 + a_0,$$

where a_n, a_{n-1}, ..., and a_0 are real numbers and n is an integer such that $n \geq 0$. n is the **degree** of the polynomial, and a_n (read "a sub n") is called the **leading coefficient**.

Operations with Polynomials

Polynomials are added and subtracted by using commutative, associative, and distributive properties and by combining like terms. Study this example.

E X A M P L E   2   Adding and Subtracting Polynomials

Perform the indicated operations and simplify:

a) $(2x^3 - 3x^2 + 4x - 1) + (x^3 + 2x^2 - 5x + 3)$

b) $(4x^2 + 3x - 4) - (2x^3 + x^2 - x + 2)$.

Solution

a) $(2x^3 - 3x^2 + 4x - 1) + (x^3 + 2x^2 - 5x + 3)$

$\qquad = (2x^3 + x^3) + (-3x^2 + 2x^2) + (4x - 5x) + (-1 + 3)$ Group like terms.

$\qquad = 3x^3 + (-1)x^2 + (-1)x + 2$ Combine like terms.

$\qquad = 3x^3 - x^2 - x + 2$

b) $(4x^2 + 3x - 4) - (2x^3 + x^2 - x + 2)$

$\qquad = -2x^3 + (4x^2 - x^2) + (3x - (-1x)) + (-4 - 2)$ Group like terms.

$$= -2x^3 + 3x^2 + (3 - (-1))x + (-6) \qquad \text{Combine like terms.}$$

$$= -2x^3 + 3x^2 + 4x - 6$$

To find the **product** of two polynomials, use the distributive properties and the properties of exponents. For example, the product of the two binomials $x^2 + 3$ and $x - 7$ can be completed as follows:

$$(x^2 + 3)(x - 7) = x^2(x - 7) + 3(x - 7) \qquad \text{Use the distributive property.}$$

product of   product of   product of   product of
first terms   outer terms   inner terms   last terms

$$= x^2 \cdot x - 7x^2 + 3x - 21 \qquad \text{Use the distributive property again.}$$

$$= x^3 - 7x^2 + 3x - 21.$$

Notice that after using the distributive property the second time there are four terms. The first term is the product of the first terms of the two binomials. The second is the product of the outer terms of the two binomials. The third and fourth terms are the products of the inner and last terms of the two binomials, respectively. This procedure is often called the FOIL method of multiplying two binomials, where FOIL stands for *F*irst, *O*uter, *I*nner, and *L*ast.

E X A M P L E 3   Multiplying Two Binomials with the FOIL Method

Find the product of $x^7 + 3x^2$ and $x^3 - 5x$.

Solution

$$(x^7 + 3x^2)(x^3 - 5x) = x^7 \cdot x^3 + x^7 \cdot (-5x) + 3x^2 \cdot x^3 + 3x^2 \cdot (-5x)$$

$$= x^{10} - 5x^8 + 3x^5 - 15x^3$$

Sometimes the product of the outer and inner terms have the same degree. In that case these two terms are combined into a single term called the **middle term**. With practice these two terms can be combined mentally to find the middle term.

E X A M P L E 4   Multiplying Binomials Yielding One Middle Term

Find the product of $x + 4$ and $x - 5$.

Solution

$$(x + 4)(x - 5) = x^2 + \, ? \, - 20 \qquad \text{Think: } -5x + 4x = -x \text{ is the middle term.}$$

$$= x^2 - x - 20$$

The FOIL method can also be used to multiply nonpolynomial expressions that each have two terms.

E X A M P L E   5   Multiplying Expressions with the FOIL Method

Find the product of $1/x^2 + 3$ and $x + 6/x^3$, and express the answer using positive exponents.

Solution

$$\left(\frac{1}{x^2} + 3\right)\left(x + \frac{6}{x^3}\right) = (x^{-2} + 3)(x + 6x^{-3})$$

$$= x^{-2}x + x^{-2} \cdot 6x^{-3} + 3x + 3 \cdot 6x^{-3}$$

$$= x^{-1} + 6x^{-5} + 3x + 18x^{-3}$$

$$= \frac{1}{x} + \frac{6}{x^5} + 3x + \frac{18}{x^3}. \qquad \equiv$$

A grapher can be used to support that the algebraic manipulations are correct. Attempts to graph the equations $y = (x^2 + 3)(x - 7)$ and $y = x^3 - 7x^2 + 3x - 21$ in the same viewing rectangle will produce identical graphs. Note that this method is *not a proof*; it is merely suggestive. What happens when $y = x$ and $y = x + 0.01$ are graphed in the standard viewing rectangle?

However, a grapher can be used to determine that two expressions have been multiplied incorrectly. For example, to show that the statement

$$(x^2 - 3)(x + 4) = x^3 + 4x^2 - 12$$

is false, graph $y = (x^2 - 3)(x + 4)$ and $y = x^3 + 4x^2 - 12$ and observe that these graphs are not identical (Fig. 1.20).

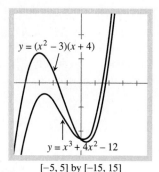

$y = (x^2 - 3)(x + 4)$

$y = x^3 + 4x^2 - 12$

[−5, 5] by [−15, 15]

Figure 1.20 Graphs of $y = x^3 + 4x^2 - 12$ and $y = (x^2 - 3)(x + 4)$.

🔍 **EXPLORE WITH A GRAPHING UTILITY**

Use a grapher to find which of these statements is false.

1. $(x + 2)^2 = x^2 + 4$
2. $(x - 3)^2 = x^2 - 6x - 9$
3. $(x - 1)(x + 4) = x^2 + 3x - 4$
4. $x^4 - 1 = (x - 1)^4$

For each of the false statements write several other false statements that have the same type of error. Support your work with a grapher.

In Examples 3 and 4 two binomial expressions were multiplied together to obtain an expression. How can this process be reversed? That is, given a polynomial, how can we find two factors whose product is that given polynomial? The process of writing one polynomial as a product of two polynomials is called **factoring**.

Notice that $x^2 + x - 6 = (x + 3)(x - 2)$. We say that $x^2 + x - 6$ is a **factored polynomial** and that $x + 3$ and $x - 2$ are **factors** of $x^2 + x - 6$. It is easy to observe that $y = (x + 3)(x - 2)$ has a value of 0 when $x = -3$ or $x = 2$. It is not as obvious when this same polynomial is written in the form $y = x^2 + x - 6$. Important properties of a polynomial are thus sometimes more observable in factored form. Later in this book computer graphing will prove to be a powerful aid to factoring.

Common Factors

Often it is not obvious how to factor a polynomial. However, there are patterns of coefficients in certain polynomials that make factors more recognizable. One pattern involves sharing a common factor. In an expression of the form $ab + ac$, the terms ab and ac have a common factor of a. So

$$ab + ac = a(b + c).$$

E X A M P L E 6   Removing Common Factors

Factor the following:

a) $3x^4 + 6x^2 - 24x$

b) $4x^2y^3 + 12x^4y^2$.

Solution

a) $3x^4 + 6x^2 - 24x = 3x(x^3 + 2x - 8)$

b) $4x^2y^3 + 12x^4y^2 = 4x^2y^2(y + 3x^2)$

$\equiv$

Difference of Squares

A second pattern called the **difference of two squares** has a factorization that is easily recognizable. For example,

$$u^2 - v^2 = (u - v)(u + v).$$

The correctness of this pattern can be verified by multiplying the factors together. We agree not to factor an expression that requires the introduction of irrational numbers. For example, even though $x^2 - 2 = (x - \sqrt{2})(x + \sqrt{2})$, we will not factor $x^2 - 2$.

Sometimes after an expression has been factored, one or both of the factors can be factored again. Once each new factor has been been factored as often as possible, the expression has been **factored completely**.

E X A M P L E 7   Factoring the Difference of Squares

Factor the following as completely as possible without introducing radicals:

a) $25x^2 - 36$;

b) $4y^4 - 64$.

Solution

a) $25x^2 - 36 = (5x - 6)(5x + 6)$.   Think: $25x^2 = (5x)^2$.

b) $4y^4 - 64 = 4(y^2 - 4)(y^2 + 4)$ Remove common factors.

$$= 4(y - 2)(y + 2)(y^2 + 4).$$

≡

Factoring Trinomials into Binomial Factors

The final method of factoring requires reversing the thought process used when multiplying by the FOIL method. First recall the FOIL method used to multiply $(x + 2)(x - 3)$:

$$(x + 2)(x - 3) = x^2 + \ ? \ + (-6)$$ Think: outer is $-3x$, inner is $2x$ for a sum of $-x$, and last is -6.

$$= x^2 - x - 6.$$

To factor $x^2 - x - 6$, reverse the thought process:

$$x^2 - x - 6 = (x + ?)(x + ?)$$ Think: Find two numbers with the sum of -1 and the product of -6.

$$= (x - 3)(x + 2)$$ Is it -2 and 3, or 2 and -3 ? It is -3 and 2.

E X A M P L E 8   Factoring Trinomials

Factor the following trinomials:

a) $x^2 + 3x - 10$

b) $x^2 + 11xy + 28y^2$

c) $6x^2 - x - 12$.

Solution

a) $x^2 + 3x - 10 = (x + ?)(x + ?)$ Think: factors of -10 whose sum is 3.

$$= (x + 5)(x - 2).$$

b) $x^2 + 11xy + 28y^2 = (x + ?y)(x + ?y)$ Think: factors of 28 whose sum is 11.

$$= (x + 4y)(x + 7y).$$

c) $6x^2 - x - 12 = (3x + ?)(2x + ?)$ Think of factors of -12 which lead to a middle term of $-x$.

$$= (2x - 3)(3x + 4).$$

Exercises for Section 1.4

1. Write three different expressions using all of the following expressions in each one: x^2, $\sqrt{x-1}$, and $9x$.

2. Is $\sqrt{2x^3 + 4x^2 - 5x + 7}$ a polynomial? Why?

3. Write an expression that is not a polynomial, and state why it fails to be a polynomial.

4. An object in free-fall (ignoring air friction) falls approximately D feet in t seconds where $D = 16t^2$. How far does a skydiver fall during the first 5 seconds of free-fall?

5. Jon found that his cost C for a telephone call was \$0.85 per minute, so the cost for t minutes can be found using the relationship $C = 0.85t$. What is the cost of a 45-minute call?

6. The volume V of a cylinder can be found by using $V = \pi r^2 h$, where r is the radius of the base and h is the height. Find the volume of a soup can that is 12 centimeters tall with a radius of 4 centimeters.

For Exercise 6

7. What is the degree and leading coefficient of the polynomial $3x^4 - 5x + 3$?

8. What is the degree and leading coefficient of the polynomial $3x^2 + 5x^3 - 2x + 1$?

In Exercises 9 to 18, perform the indicated operations and simplify.

9. $(3x^2 + 4) + (5x - 2)$

10. $(x^2 - 3x + 7) + (3x^2 + 5x - 3)$

11. $(-3x^2 - 5) - (x^2 + 7x + 12)$

12. $(4x^3 - x^2 + 3x) - (x^3 + 12x - 3)$

13. $(2x + x^2 - 3) + (5x^2 + 3x + 4)$

14. $3x - [7 - (3x + 5)]$

15. $(12x^2 - 5x + 2) - (-x^2 - 2x + 3)$

16. $3x + (x^2 + 4x - 3) - (x^2 + 7)$

17. $(7 - 3x + x^2) - (4x + 2x^2 - 8)$

18. $(4x - 7 + x^2) - (-3x^2 + 4 - 7x)$

In Exercises 19 to 36, find the given product (check with a grapher).

19. $(x + 3)(x + 5)$ 20. $(x - 2)(x + 5)$

21. $(x + 7)(x - 2)$ 22. $(2x - 1)(x + 3)$

23. $(x - 3)(x - 1)$ 24. $(x - 9)(x - 3)$

25. $(2x + 3)(4x + 1)$ 26. $(3x - 5)(x + 2)$

27. $(5 - x)(2 + x)$ 28. $2x(x + 3)$

29. $(x^2 + 1)(x^2 - 3)$ 30. $(x + 4)(x^2 + 2)$

31. $(x^2 + 1)(x^3 + 4)$ 32. $x^5(x^2 - 3)$

33. $(x^{-2} + 1)(x^{-1} + 3)$ 34. $(x^{-2} + 4)(x^3 - 3)$

35. $(x^2 + 2x + 3)(x + 4)$

36. $(x^2 + x - 3)(x^2 + 3x + 1)$

For Exercises 37 to 43, use a grapher to determine which equations are false.

37. $(x + 4)^2 = x^2 + 16$

38. $(x - 1)^3 = x^3 - 1$

39. $(x - 3)(x - 1) = x^2 - 3x + 3$

40. $(x^2 + 2)(x^2 - 2) = x^4 - 4^2$

41. $(x^2 + 3)(x - 1) = (x^2 + 2x - 3)$

42. $x^3 - 1 = (x - 1)(x^2 - 1)$

43. $x^3 - 1 = (x - 1)(x^2 + 1)$

Use your grapher for Exercises 44 to 46. Then confirm by multiplying or expanding.

44. Graph the (a) sum, (b) difference, and (c) product of $x^2 - 3$ and $x + 2$.

45. Which is the correct factorization of $12x^2 + x - 6$?
   a) $(3x + 1)(x - 6)$ **b)** $(3x - 2)(4x + 3)$

46. Which is the correct factorization of $x^3 + 2x^2 + 4x + 8$?
   a) $(x^2 + 4)(x + 2)$ **b)** $(x^2 + 2)(x + 4)$

Factor Exercises 47 to 71 completely (support with a grapher when possible).

47. $4x - 64$ **48.** $2x^3 - 4x^2$

49. $x^3 - 5x^2 + 7x$ **50.** $y^4 - 3y^3 + y$

51. $(x - 3)(x + 2)^2 + (x - 3)^2(x + 2)$

52. $x^2 - 16$ **53.** $y^2 - 4x^2$

54. $x^2y^2 - 25$ **55.** $x^4 - 81$

56. $(x + 9)^2 - 16$ **57.** $(x - 1)^4 - 9$

58. $x^2 - 6x + 9$ **59.** $x^2 + 6x + 9$

60. $x^2 - 3x - 4$ **61.** $x^2 + x - 6$

62. $x^2 + 3x - 4$ **63.** $x^2 + 8x + 12$

64. $x^2 - 8x + 12$ **65.** $x^2 + 5xy + 6y^2$

66. $2x^2 - x - 6$ **67.** $8x^2 - 8x - 6$

68. $x^2 + 3xy - 10y^2$ **69.** $4x^2 - 2x - 12$

70. $x^4 - x^2 - 12$ **71.** $x^4 - 14x^2 - 32$

72. Writing to Learn   Write a few paragraphs that explain your answer to the following question. In the Exploration you used a grapher to decide that two expressions were not equal. When you want to conclude that two expressions are equal, which is more convincing, using an algebraic argument or a grapher?

1.5   _____   Fractional Expressions

A **fractional expression** is a quotient of two algebraic expressions. If the expression is written in the fraction form a/b, then a is the **numerator** and b is the **denominator**. Here are several examples:

$$\frac{\sqrt{x^2 + 1}}{x + 2}, \qquad \frac{4x^3 - 3x^2 + 5}{x^2 + 1}, \qquad \frac{5}{\sqrt{x^3 - 3x}}. \qquad \textbf{(1)}$$

If both numerator and denominator are polynomials, then the fractional expression is called a **rational expression**. The middle expression in line (1) above is a rational expression. The first expression fails to be rational because the numerator has a radical. The third expression is not rational because of the radical in the denominator. Here are several other rational expressions:

$$\frac{x^4 + 3x^3 - x + 5}{x^2 - 7}, \qquad \frac{x + 3}{x^2 - 4x + 3},$$

$$\frac{x^{17} - 5x^4 + 1}{x^2 - 2x + 1}, \qquad \frac{x^4 - 3x^2 + 2}{x^7 - 5}. \qquad \textbf{(2)}$$

Recall that a fraction is undefined if the denominator equals zero. So you cannot substitute a value of x into the expression that makes the denominator have the value of zero. For example, in the first expression in line (1), -2 cannot replace x, while in the first expression in line (2), $\sqrt{7}$ cannot replace x.

Simplifying Rational Expressions

🔍 EXPLORE WITH A GRAPHING UTILITY

Use a grapher to find which of the two expressions may be equivalent to the given expression.

1. Is $\dfrac{2x+8}{4}$ equivalent to (a) $\dfrac{x+4}{2}$, or (b) $\dfrac{x+8}{2}$?

2. Is $\dfrac{x^2+x}{x}$ equivalent to (a) $x+1$, or (b) x^2+1?

3. Is $\dfrac{x^2+x-2}{x-1}$ equivalent to (a) $x+2$, or (b) $-(x^2-2)$?

Conjecture a Generalization   For each of these expressions write an equivalent expression and support your solution with a graphing utility:

$$\frac{x^2+x}{x^2}, \qquad \frac{4x^2+3x}{x}, \qquad \frac{x^2-1}{x+1}.$$

What algebraic property can be used to confirm the answers in this Exploration? Recall that numerical fractions can be simplified by dividing out common factors and **reducing to lowest terms**:

$$\frac{ac}{bc} = \frac{a}{b} \qquad (b, c \neq 0).$$

This same property can be used when a, b, and c represent algebraic expressions. We illustrate this property in the next two examples.

E X A M P L E   1   Reducing to Lowest Terms

Reduce to lowest terms the rational expression $\dfrac{3x^3 - 9x^2 + 27x}{6x}$.

Solution

$$\frac{3x^3 - 9x^2 + 27x}{6x} = \frac{3x(x^2 - 3x + 9)}{2 \cdot 3x}$$

$$= \frac{x^2 - 3x + 9}{2}$$

$$= \frac{1}{2}x^2 - \frac{3}{2}x + \frac{9}{2}$$

■

Often, before an algebraic expression can be simplified, it must be factored completely, as the next example illustrates.

E X A M P L E   2   Simplifying Rational Expressions

Reduce to lowest terms the rational expression

$$\frac{(x^2 - 9)(x^2 + 2x + 1)}{(x + 3)(x + 1)^2}.$$

Solution

$$\frac{(x^2 - 9)(x^2 + 2x + 1)}{(x + 3)(x + 1)^2} = \frac{(x - 3)(x + 3)(x + 1)^2}{(x + 3)(x + 1)^2} \qquad \text{Factor the numerator.}$$

$$= x - 3, (x \neq 3), (x \neq -1) \quad \text{Cancel common factors.} \quad \blacksquare$$

You can use a grapher to support the algebraic conclusion of the above example. Graph both

$$y = \frac{(x^2 - 9)(x^2 + 2x + 1)}{(x + 3)(x + 1)^2} \qquad \text{and} \qquad y = x - 3$$

in $[-5, 5]$ by $[-5, 5]$. What do you observe?

Multiplying and Dividing Rational Expressions

Algebraic rational expressions are multiplied and divided in the same way as numerical rational expressions. For example, if $a, b, c,$ and d represent polynomial expressions, the **product of a/b and c/d** is given by

$$\frac{a}{b} \cdot \frac{c}{d} = \frac{a \cdot c}{b \cdot d} = \frac{ac}{bd}.$$

To explain the quotient of rational expressions, recall that a quotient of whole numbers can be thought of as a **missing factor**. For example, $8 \div 2 = x$ where x is the missing factor in $8 = 2 \cdot x$. In the same way,

$$\frac{a}{b} \div \frac{c}{d} = x \qquad \text{where} \qquad \frac{a}{b} = \frac{c}{d} \cdot x.$$

Solving for x yields the **quotient of a/b and c/d**:

$$\frac{a}{b} \div \frac{c}{d} = \frac{a}{b} \cdot \frac{d}{c}.$$

This definition for division is sometimes described with the phrase "invert and multiply."

E X A M P L E   3   Dividing Rational Expressions

Perform the indicated division and simplify:

$$\frac{x^2 - y^2}{2y} \div \frac{x + y}{4}.$$

Solution

$$\frac{x^2 - y^2}{2y} \div \frac{x + y}{4} = \frac{(x - y)(x + y)}{2y} \cdot \frac{4}{x + y} \qquad \text{Factor expressions and invert and multiply.}$$

$$= \frac{4(x - y)(x + y)}{2y(x + y)} \qquad \text{Complete the multiplication and simplify.}$$

$$= \frac{2(x - y)}{y}.$$

≡

Notice that in Examples 1 to 3 the rational expressions were simplified by factoring numerator and/or denominator and dividing out common factors. If multiplication is changed to addition or subtraction, there are no common factors to divide out.

Warning   In general,

$$\frac{a + c}{b + c} \neq \frac{a}{b}.$$

🔎 **EXPLORE WITH A GRAPHING UTILITY**

Use a grapher to find which of the two expressions may be equivalent to the given expression.

1. Is $\dfrac{x}{2} + \dfrac{1}{4}$ equivalent to (a) $\dfrac{2x + 1}{4}$, or (b) $\dfrac{x + 2}{4}$?

2. Is $\dfrac{1}{x} + \dfrac{1}{4}$ equivalent to (a) $\dfrac{x + 4}{4x}$, or (b) $\dfrac{1}{4 + x}$?

3. Is $\dfrac{2}{x} + \dfrac{4}{3x}$ equivalent to (a) $\dfrac{10}{3x}$, or (b) $\dfrac{6}{4x}$?

Conjecture a Generalization   For each of these expressions write an equivalent expression and check your solution with a graphing utility:

$$\frac{x}{3} + \frac{1}{5}, \qquad \frac{1}{x} + \frac{2}{7}, \qquad \frac{1}{4x} + \frac{1}{6x}.$$

Adding and Subtracting Rational Expressions

To add or subtract two rational expressions, apply the same definition used for numerical fractions. That is, if the denominators are identical, simply add or subtract the numerators. If $a, b,$ and c represent expressions, then

$$\frac{a}{c} + \frac{b}{c} = \frac{a+b}{c} \qquad \text{and} \qquad \frac{a}{c} - \frac{b}{c} = \frac{a-b}{c}. \tag{3}$$

E X A M P L E 4 Adding Expressions with Like Denominators

Perform the addition

$$\frac{(x^2 - 6)}{x - 2} + \frac{x}{x - 2}$$

and simplify. Support using a grapher.

Solution

$$\frac{(x^2 - 6)}{x - 2} + \frac{x}{x - 2} = \frac{x^2 + x - 6}{x - 2} \qquad \text{Add the numerators.}$$

$$= \frac{(x - 2)(x + 3)}{x - 2} \qquad \text{Factor and cancel the common factor.}$$

$$= x + 3, \qquad (x \neq 2)$$

The check with a grapher is shown in Figure 1.21.

REMINDER

The two graphs in Fig. 1.21 appear identical on graphing utilities. However, it is important to observe that one of the expressions is undefined for $x = 2$, so the graphs are really not identical.

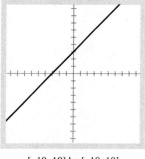

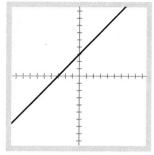

$[-10, 10]$ by $[-10, 10]$ $[-10, 10]$ by $[-10, 10]$

(a)   (b)

Figure 1.21 (a) $y = \dfrac{(x^2 - 6)}{(x - 2)} + \dfrac{x}{(x - 2)}$; (b) $y = x + 3$.

If the denominators are not identical, there are two strategies: Either multiply the numerator and denominator of each term by the appropriate expression to obtain the **lowest common denominator (LCD)**, or use the following definition:

$$\frac{a}{b} + \frac{c}{d} = \frac{ad + bc}{bd} \qquad \text{and} \qquad \frac{a}{b} - \frac{c}{d} = \frac{ad - bc}{bd}. \tag{4}$$

Recall that the LCD of several fractions consists of the product of all prime factors in the denominators, with each factor given the highest power of its occurrence in any denominator.

E X A M P L E   5   Finding the LCD and Subtracting

Perform the indicated subtraction and simplify:

$$\frac{5}{2x} - \frac{2x - 3}{3x} = \frac{3 \cdot 5}{3 \cdot 2x} - \frac{2(2x - 3)}{2 \cdot 3x}$$

Multiply numerator and denominator by the appropriate factor to obtain the common denominator $6x$.

$$= \frac{15 - 2(2x - 3)}{6x}$$

$$= \frac{15 - 4x + 6}{6x}$$

Subtract numerators, use the distributive property, and combine terms.

$$= \frac{21 - 4x}{6x}.$$

≡

E X A M P L E   6   Adding and Simplifying Fractional Expressions

Perform the indicated addition and simplify:

$$\frac{3}{x - 3} + \frac{4}{x + 2}.$$

Solution

$$\frac{3}{x - 3} + \frac{4}{x + 2} = \frac{3(x + 2) + 4(x - 3)}{(x - 3)(x + 2)}$$

Use the definition in Eq. (4).

$$= \frac{3x + 6 + 4x - 12}{(x - 3)(x + 2)}$$

Use the distributive property.

$$= \frac{7x - 6}{(x - 3)(x + 2)}$$

Combine terms.

≡

The results of Examples 5 and 6 can be supported using a grapher.

Negative exponents have the same meaning with algebraic expressions as they do with numerical expressions. Study this example.

EXAMPLE 7   Using Negative Exponents

Perform the indicated addition and simplify:

$$3 + x^{-1} + x.$$

Solution

$$3 + x^{-1} + x = 3 + \frac{1}{x} + x \qquad \text{Note that } 3 + x^{-1} \neq (3 + x)^{-1}$$
$$\text{and } x^{-1} + x \neq x^0.$$

$$= \frac{3x + 1 + x^2}{x}$$

$$= \frac{x^2 + 3x + 1}{x}.$$

Exercises for Section 1.5

In Exercises 1 to 6, find the missing numerator or denominator so that the two rational expressions are equal:

1. $\dfrac{2}{3x} = \dfrac{?}{6x^2}$

2. $\dfrac{4y}{3x} = \dfrac{12xy}{?}$

3. $\dfrac{9x^2}{27xy} = \dfrac{?}{3y}$

4. $\dfrac{14x^3y^2}{2x^2y} = \dfrac{7xy}{?}$

5. $\dfrac{x^2 - 3x}{x^3} = \dfrac{?}{x^2}$

6. $\dfrac{(x-1)(x+3)}{x^2 + 5x + 6} = \dfrac{x-1}{?}$

In Exercises 7 to 16, reduce each of the following to lowest terms. Support your work with a graphing utility.

7. $\dfrac{4x^2}{12x}$

8. $\dfrac{15xy^2}{3xy}$

9. $\dfrac{(x-1)(3x+2)}{(x-1)^2}$

10. $\dfrac{(x-1)(x+3)}{x^2 - 2x + 1}$

11. $\dfrac{(x+2)(x-3)}{x^2 + x - 2}$

12. $\dfrac{x^2 + 3x - 4}{(x-1)(x-2)}$

13. $\dfrac{x^3 - x^2}{x - 1}$

14. $\dfrac{9 - x^2}{x - 3}$

15. $\dfrac{x^2 - y^2}{3x + 3y}$

16. $\dfrac{x^2 - x - 1}{x^2 + 3x + 2}$

For Exercises 17 to 20, use a grapher to identify and then confirm algebraically:

17. Is $\dfrac{x^2 - 1}{x - 1}$ equivalent to

a) x, or

b) $x + 1$?

18. Is $\dfrac{3x^3 + 12x}{9x}$ equivalent to

a) $\dfrac{x^2 + 4}{3}$, or

b) $x + 4$?

19. Is $\dfrac{x^3 - 2x^2 + 2x - 1}{x - 1}$ equivalent to

a) $x^2 + 2$, or

b) $x^2 - x + 1$?

20. Is $\dfrac{x^2 - 3}{x^2 + 2\sqrt{3}x + 3}$ equivalent to

a) $\dfrac{x - \sqrt{3}}{x + \sqrt{3}}$, or

b) $\dfrac{-3}{2\sqrt{3} + 3}$?

In Exercises 21 to 34, perform the indicated operations and simplify. Support your work with a grapher.

21. $\dfrac{3}{x - 1} \cdot \dfrac{x^2 - 1}{9}$

22. $\dfrac{x + 3}{7} \cdot \dfrac{14}{2x + 6}$

23. $\dfrac{x + 3}{x - 1} \cdot \dfrac{1 - x}{x^2 - 9}$

24. $\dfrac{1}{2x} \div \dfrac{1}{4}$

25. $\dfrac{18x^2 - 3x}{3xy} \cdot \dfrac{12y^2}{6x - 1}$

26. $\dfrac{4x}{y} \div \dfrac{8y}{x}$

27. $\dfrac{x^2 - 3x}{14y} \div \dfrac{2xy}{3y^2}$

28. $\dfrac{7(x - y)}{4} \div \dfrac{14(x - y)}{3}$

29. $\dfrac{2x^2y/(x - 3)^2}{8xy/(x - 3)}$

30. $\dfrac{(x + 2)^2(x - 1)/(x + 4)^2}{(x - 1)^3/(x + 2)^2(x + 4)}$

31. $\dfrac{x^2 + 3x + 2}{x^2 - 1} \cdot \dfrac{x^2 + 2x + 1}{x^2 + x - 2}$

32. $\dfrac{x^2 - y^2}{2xy} \cdot \dfrac{4x^2y}{y^2 - x^2}$

33. $\dfrac{(3x - 2)(x + 5)}{2x - 1} \div \dfrac{(x + 5)(2x - 1)}{(3x - 2)^2}$

34. $\dfrac{2x^2 + 3x - 3}{x + 4} \div \dfrac{x^2 + x - 2}{x^2 + 5x + 4}$

In Exercises 35 to 38, use a grapher to identify and then confirm algebraically:

35. Is $\dfrac{x}{7} + \dfrac{1}{x}$ equivalent to

   a) $\dfrac{x + 1}{7 + x}$, or   **b)** $\dfrac{x^2 + 7}{7x}$?

36. Is $\dfrac{1}{3x} + \dfrac{1}{4x}$ equivalent to

   a) $\dfrac{1}{12x^2}$, or   **b)** $\dfrac{7}{12x}$?

37. Is $\dfrac{x}{3} + \dfrac{x}{7}$ equivalent to

   a) $\dfrac{2x}{10}$, or   **b)** $\dfrac{10x}{21}$?

38. Is $x^{-1} + 4$ equivalent to

   a) $\dfrac{4x + 1}{x}$, or   **b)** $(x + 4)^{-1}$?

Perform the indicated operations and simplify.

39. $\dfrac{1}{x} + \dfrac{2}{5}$

40. $\dfrac{1}{2x} - \dfrac{1}{y}$

41. $\dfrac{4}{x - 1} + \dfrac{3}{x - 2}$ **42.** $\dfrac{7}{x + 3} + \dfrac{1}{x - 2}$

43. $\dfrac{5x}{x + 5} - \dfrac{3}{x + 2}$ **44.** $\dfrac{3x}{x - 1} + \dfrac{x}{x + 3}$

In Exercises 45 to 48, perform the indicated operations and simplify. Support your work with a grapher if possible.

45. $\dfrac{4}{(x - 1)(x + 2)} - \dfrac{7}{(x - 1)(x + 4)}$

46. $\dfrac{2}{(x - 7)(x + 3)} + \dfrac{5x}{(x - 2)(x + 3)}$

47. $\dfrac{5x}{x^2 + x - 2} + \dfrac{2x}{x^2 + 3x + 2}$

48. $\dfrac{x - 3}{x^2 - 2x - 8} + \dfrac{x + 2}{x^2 - x - 6}$

In Exercises 49 to 54, perform the indicated operation and simplify. When exponents are needed, write answers with positive-integer exponents.

49. $\dfrac{2^{-1} + 4^{-1}}{8^{-1}}$ **50.** $\dfrac{3^{-1} + 6^{-1}}{5^{-1}}$

51. $x^{-1} + y^{-1}$ **52.** $\left(x^{-1} + y^{-1}\right)^{-1}$

53. $\dfrac{1}{(x + 1)^{-1}} + \dfrac{1}{(x - 1)^{-1}}$ **54.** $\dfrac{x^{-1}}{x + y} + \dfrac{y^{-1}}{x + y}$

55. Use the problem-solving strategies of "Use Reasoning" and "Consider a Special Case" to show that the expressions $(x^2 - 1)/(x + 1)$ and $x - 1$ are equal for all values of x except one.

Chapter 1 Review

KEY TERMS

absolute value	coefficients	equivalent expressions	graphical representation
algebraic expression	commutative property	equation	graphing utility
algebraic representation	complete graph	evaluate	identity property
associative property	coordinate system	exponent	inequality
base	degree	factor	integers
binomial	denominator	factors	inverse property
Cartesian coordinate system	difference of two squares	FOIL method	irrational numbers
closure property	distance	fractional expression	leading coefficient
	distributive property	grapher	less than

lowest common denominator (LCD)	polynomial	quadrants	reflexive property
mathematical model	power	rational expression	screen coordinate
number line	principal cube root	rational numbers	term
numerator	principal nth root	real numbers	transitive property
ordered pair	principal square root	rectangular coordinate system	trinomial
origin	problem-solving process	reduce to lowest terms	variables
	Pythagorean theorem		viewing rectangle

REVIEW EXERCISES

Identify the real-number properties that are used to explain why each of the following are valid equations.

1. $2(3 + \sqrt{5}) = 2 \cdot \sqrt{5} + 2 \cdot 3$

2. $x + (2 + y) = (x + y) + 2$

In Exercises 3 to 8, draw on a number line all numbers that are solutions to these inequalities.

3. $-3 \leq x < 4$ **4.** $1 \leq x \leq 4$

5. $-5 < x \leq -3$ **6.** $x \leq 2$

7. $5 < x$ **8.** $x < 3$

In Exercises 9 to 16, evaluate each numerical expression.

9. $|-2.5|$ **10.** 2^{-3}

11. $27^{2/3}$ **12.** $8^{-2/3}$

13. $|-(5-2)|$ **14.** $|2-6|$

15. $16^{3/4}$ **16.** $4^2 \cdot 8^3$

17. Write the exact value of the indicated expression without using absolute-value notation.
  a) $|\sqrt{7} - 2.6|$
  b) $|2.6 - \sqrt{7}|$
  c) $|\pi - 3|$
  d) $|x - 5|$ where $x > 5$

In Exercises 18 and 19, consider the points $P(-2, 4)$ and $Q(3, -1)$ in the coordinate plane.

18. Find the coordinates of the point in the first quadrant that is on the vertical line through Q and on the horizontal line through P.

19. Find the coordinates of the point in the third quadrant that is on the horizontal through Q and on the vertical line through P.

20. Find the distance between the two points on the number line with the given coordinates.
  a) $-2, 4$ **b)** $5, -2$ **c)** $-\pi, -1$

In Exercises 21 to 24, find the distance between the points in the plane with the given coordinates.

21. $(1, 1), (3, 4)$ **22.** $(-3, -8), (2, 3)$

23. $(2, -1), (1, -3)$ **24.** $(-3, -1), (-5, -4)$

For Exercises 25 and 26, the accompanying graph shows a line that goes through the origin and the upper right corner of the display. For the given viewing rectangles select the equation whose graph has this characteristic.

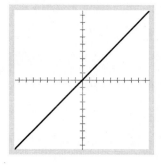

For Exercises 25 and 26

25. For viewing rectangle $[-10, 10]$ by $[-10, 10]$, the figure shows a complete graph of which equation?
  a) $y = x$
  b) $y = 5x$
  c) $y = \frac{1}{2}x$

26. For viewing rectangle $[-10, 10]$ by $[-50, 50]$, the figure shows a complete graph of which equation?
  a) $y = x$
  b) $y = 5x$
  c) $y = 50x$

For Exercises 27 and 28, write an expression that gives the distance in the plane between each pair of points.

27. $(0, y)$, $(-2, 3)$ **28.** $(x, 0)$, $(0, -4)$

29. Which of the following viewing rectangles gives the best complete graph of $y = x^2 - 30x - 100$?
   a) $[-10, 5]$ by $[-10, 5]$
   b) $[-10, 10]$ by $[-10, 10]$
   c) $[25, 50]$ by $[-500, 1000]$
   d) $[-10, 50]$ by $[-400, 800]$
   e) $[-100, 100]$ by $[-10, 10]$

30. Which of the following viewing rectangles gives the best complete graph of $y = 200 - 10x - x^3$?
   a) $[-10, 10]$ by $[-10, 10]$
   b) $[-50, 50]$ by $[-10, 10]$
   c) $[-10, 10]$ by $[-50, 50]$
   d) $[-10, 10]$ by $[-1000, 1000]$
   e) $[-100, 100]$ by $[-10, 10]$

In Exercises 31 and 32, choose a viewing rectangle $[X\min, X\max]$ by $[Y\min, Y\max]$ that will include all of the indicated points.

31. $(-9, 12)$, $(2, -8)$, $(3, 20)$

32. $(20, -11)$, $(18, 156)$, $(-11, 2)$

In Exercises 33 to 40, find a complete graph of each of the following equations. Begin with the standard viewing rectangle, and modify until an appropriate viewing rectangle is found. Transfer your graph to paper and record the viewing rectangle and scale used.

33. $y = 5 - 3x^2$ **34.** $y = x^3 - 4x^2 + 3x - 2$

35. $y = 17x^2 - 48$ **36.** $y = \sqrt{x + 21}$

37. $y = 13x - 5x^2$ **38.** $y = 2x + x^3 - 28$

39. $y = 5(x - 12)^2 - 17$ **40.** $y = -(9x - 12)$

41. For the equation $y = \sqrt{x + 3}$, complete a table of (x, y) pairs for $x = -3, -2, -1, 0, 1, 2, 3, 4,$ and 5. Round your y-values to the third decimal place.

In Exercises 42 to 50, perform the indicated operation and simplify:

42. $\dfrac{x^2 y^{-3}}{x^4 y^2}$ **43.** $\dfrac{(3x^2)^4}{9x^3}$

44. $\dfrac{(2x)^{-1} y^2}{xy^3}$ **45.** $\dfrac{(2z^2 b)^3}{a^5 b}$

46. $\dfrac{(4x^6 y^3)^{1/2}}{(9xy^2)^2}$ **47.** $\dfrac{(3u^2 v^{-1})^{-2}}{(9uv^2)^{-3}}$

48. $(5x^2 - 3x + 2) + (-7x + x^2 + 3)$

49. $(5 - 3x^2 + x^3) - (x^2 - 3x + 2)$

50. $(x^4 + 3x^2 - 5x^3) + (3x - 2x^3)$

In Exercises 51 to 60, find the given product.

51. $(x - 5)(x + 3)$ **52.** $(x + 2)(x - 3)$

53. $(2x - 3)(7 - 3x)$ **54.** $5(3x - 4)(\frac{1}{2}x - 1)$

55. $(9 - 2x)(5 - x)$ **56.** $(3x - 1)(6 - x)$

57. $(5 - 3x)(2 - 3x)$ **58.** $(3x^2 - x)(5x^3)$

59. $(2x + y)(y - 3x)$ **60.** $\left(\dfrac{1}{x} + 3\right)\left(5 + \dfrac{2}{x^2}\right)$

In Exercises 61 to 67 perform the indicated operation and simplify:

61. $\dfrac{1}{x} + \dfrac{3}{x^2}$ **62.** $\dfrac{1}{x - 3} - \dfrac{4}{x + 2}$

63. $\dfrac{x}{x - 3} - \dfrac{4}{x + 2}$ **64.** $x + 3 + \dfrac{1}{x - 2}$

65. $\dfrac{x + 3}{x^2 + 4x + 1} \div \dfrac{x^2 + 2x - 3}{x + 3}$

66. $\dfrac{1}{x^2 + 3x + 2} + \dfrac{2x - 1}{(x - 3)(x + 1)}$

67. $2x + 1 + \dfrac{2}{x + 3} + \dfrac{x + 1}{(x + 3)^2}$

68. The perimeter P of a rectangle is given by the equation $P = 2L + 2W$, where L is the length and W is the width. If the width is 220 units, then write an equation for the perimeter P as a function of the length. Find a complete graph showing how P varies with length.

69. The area A of a rectangle is given by the equation $A = \ell w$. If the length is 125 units, write the area A in terms of the width. Find a complete graph of A showing how A varies with width.

70. Jerry runs at a constant speed of 4.25 mph. Find the algebraic representation for distance d in terms of time t. Use a complete graph of this algebraic representation to find how long it takes Jerry to run a 26-mile marathon.

71. $A = \pi r^2$ is an equation for the area of a circle with a radius of r units. Find a complete graph of this algebraic representation, and use it to find the radius of a circle whose area is 150 square units.

Exercises 72 to 75 refer to this **problem situation**. A school club buys a scientific calculator for \$18.25 to use as a raffle prize for a fund-raising project. The club charges \$0.50 per raffle ticket.

72. Find an algebraic representation that gives the club's profit or loss, P, in terms of the number of tickets sold, n.

73. Find a complete graph of the algebraic representation. What part of this graph represents the problem situation? Hint: You cannot sell half a ticket.

74. What are the possible values of n in the algebraic representation?

75. Use your graph from Exercise 73 to determine the minimum number of tickets that must be sold for the club to realize a profit.

Exercises 76 to 78 refer to the following problem situation. A bike manufacturer determines the annual cost C of making x bikes to be $85 per bike plus $75,000 in fixed overhead costs.

76. Find an algebraic representation of the total annual cost as a function of the number of bikes made. Find a complete graph of this algebraic representation.

77. What portion of your graph from Exercise 76 represents possible total annual costs of producing the bikes?

78. Use the graph in Exercise 76 to determine the number of bikes made if the total cost is $143,000.

Exercises 79 to 81 refer to the following problem situation. Consider all rectangles whose length plus width equals 150 inches, and let x be the length of such a rectangle.

79. Show that $A = x(150 - x)$ is an algebraic representation that gives the area A of a rectangle in the collection in terms of its length.

80. Find a complete graph of the algebraic representation in Exercise 79.

81. What values of x make sense in this problem situation? Find a graph of the problem situation.

For Exercises 82 to 84 consider the following problem situation. The annual profit P of a baby food manufacturer is determined by the formula $P = R - C$, where R is the total revenue generated from selling x jars of baby food and C is the total cost of making and selling x jars of baby food. Each jar sells for $0.60 and costs $0.45 to make. The fixed costs of making and selling the baby food are $83,000 annually.

82. Find the algebraic representation for the company's annual profit in terms of x.

83. How many jars of baby food must be sold for the company to break even?

84. How many jars of baby food must be sold for the company to make a profit of $10,000$?

Exercises 85 to 87 refer to this problem situation. A trucker averages 48 mph on a cross-country trip from Boston to Seattle. Let t be the time since the trucker left Boston.

85. Find a complete graph of an algebraic representation for the distance the trucker travels in terms of time.

86. What part of the graph in Exercise 85 represents a graph of the problem situation?

87. Use the graph in Exercise 85 to find how many hours have elapsed since the trucker left Boston if the distance traveled is 1200 miles.

2

Solving Equations and Inequalities

2.1

Solving Linear and Quadratic Equations Algebraically

The concept of problem situation was introduced in Section 1.2. A problem situation can be described in both an algebraic and a graphical representation. We use both algebraic and graphical representations of a problem situation in pursuit of its solution. In so doing, we explore the connections among the model (often an equation or an inequality), its associated graphs, and the problem situation.

Recall that an equation is a statement equating two expressions. If at least one of the expressions is an algebraic expression in a variable x, the statement is called **an equation in x**. To **solve** an equation in x means that you find all the values of x for which the equation is true.

There are two types of equations. An **identity** is an equation that is true for all values of the variable for which the expressions are defined. On the other hand, an equation in x that is true for only certain values of x is called a **conditional equation**. Here are some examples of each:

Identities: $\qquad\qquad\qquad x + 3 = 3 + x, \qquad x(x - 3) = x^2 - 3x$

Conditional equations: $\qquad x + 2 = 5, \qquad\qquad\qquad x^2 = 25$

In this chapter you will study certain types of conditional equations.

A number a is a **solution to an equation in** x if a true statement results when x is replaced by a everywhere in the equation.

E X A M P L E 1   Verifying a Solution

Show that $x = -2$ is a solution to the equation $x^3 - x + 6 = 0$.

Solution

$$x^3 - x + 6 = 0 \qquad\qquad \text{Begin with the equation.}$$
$$(-2)^3 - (-2) + 6 = -8 + 2 + 6 \qquad \text{Substitute } -2 \text{ for } x.$$
$$= 0$$

Solution Agreement   Once all the real number solutions for a given equation have been found, the equation is considered solved. In this section the focus is on algebraic techniques for solving equations.

Perhaps the simplest type of conditional equation is a linear one.

Definition 2.1   Linear Equation

A **linear equation in** x is an equation that can be written in the form $ax + b = 0$, where a and b are real numbers and $a \neq 0$.

Solving Linear Equations by Writing Equivalent Equations

Equivalent equations are two or more equations with exactly the same set of solutions. One important method of solving a linear equation requires transforming it into an equivalent equation whose solutions are obvious. For example, the equations $2x - 4 = 0$, $x - 2 = 0$, and $x = 2$ are all equivalent, and the solution to the last one is obvious.

Obtaining Equivalent Equations

An equivalent equation is obtained if any one of the following operations is performed:

	Given Equation	Equivalent Equation
Combine like terms or reduce fractions.	$2x + x = \frac{3}{9}$	$3x = \frac{1}{3}$
Add or subtract the same real number to each side of the equation.	$x + 3 = 7$	$x = 4$
Add or subtract the same polynomial to each side of the equation.	$4x^2 - 2x = x$	$4x^2 - 3x = 0$
Multiply or divide each side of the equation by the same nonzero number.	$3x = 12$	$x = 4$

These methods of obtaining equivalent equations will be used in the next several examples.

E X A M P L E 2   Combining Like Terms

Solve $2(2x - 3) + 3(x + 1) = 5x + 2$.

Solution

$$2(2x - 3) + 3(x + 1) = 5x + 2$$

$$4x - 6 + 3x + 3 = 5x + 2 \qquad \text{Use the distributive property.}$$

$$7x - 3 = 5x + 2 \qquad \text{Combine like terms.}$$

$$2x - 3 = 2 \qquad \text{Subtract } 5x \text{ from both sides of the equation.}$$

$$2x = 5 \qquad \text{Add 3 to both sides.}$$

$$x = 2.5 \qquad \text{Divide each side by 2.}$$

Check the Solution

$$2\big(2(2.5) - 3\big) + 3(2.5 + 1) \overset{?}{=} 5(2.5) + 2$$

Substitute $x = 2.5$ into both sides of the equation.

$$2(2) + 3(3.5) \overset{?}{=} 14.5$$

$$14.5 = 14.5$$

It checks. The solution $x = 2.5$ is correct.

This method can be extended to equations that involve expressions of the form $|ax + b|$. Recall that $|a|$ represents the distance on the real number line from the origin to the point with coordinate a.

E X A M P L E   3   Linear Equation with Absolute Value

Solve $|2x + 3| = 5$.

Solution   The expression inside the absolute value symbols must be either 5 or -5, so $2x + 3$ equals 5 or -5. Solving for both values of the expression yields two values for x.

$$2x + 3 = -5 \qquad 2x + 3 = 5$$
$$2x = -8 \qquad\qquad 2x = 2$$
$$x = -4 \qquad\qquad x = 1$$

Check the Solution

$$|2(-4) + 3| = 5 \qquad \text{and} \qquad |2(1) + 3| = 5$$

The solutions to $|2x + 3| = 5$ are -4 and 1.

E X A M P L E   4   APPLICATION: Mixture Problem

Sparks Drug Store keeps two acid solutions on hand to fill orders for its customers. One solution is 10% acid and the other is 25% acid. An order is received for 15 liters of 12% acid solution. How much 10% acid solution and how much 25% acid solution should be combined to fill this order?

Solution   Let x represent the number of liters of 10% acid solution needed to make the 12% mixture. There will be 15 liters of the mixture, so $15 - x$ represents the number of liters of 25% acid solution.

An acid solution is made by taking pure acid and diluting it with water. A 10% solution means that 10% of the mixture is pure acid. Therefore,

$$0.1x = \text{amount of pure acid in the 10\% solution}$$

$$0.25(15 - x) = \text{amount of pure acid in the 25\% solution}$$

$$0.12(15) = \text{amount of pure acid in the final 15-liter solution.}$$

The total amount of acid in the mixture is the sum of the acid in the 10% and 25% solutions. The equation is:

$$0.1x + 0.25(15 - x) = 0.12(15)$$

$$0.1x + 3.75 - 0.25x = 1.8$$

$$-0.15x + 3.75 = 1.8$$

$$-0.15x = -1.95$$

$$x = 13. \qquad \text{13 liters of 10% solution are combined with 2 liters of 25% solution.}$$

Check the Solution

$$\frac{0.1(13) + 0.25(2)}{15} = 0.12$$

Many problem situations can be solved by using linear equations. Another important class of equations is the quadratic equation.

Definition 2.2 Quadratic Equations

A **quadratic equation in x** is an equation that can be written in the form $ax^2 + bx + c = 0$, where a, b, and c are real numbers and $a \neq 0$.

Solving Quadratic Equations by Factoring

Linear equations are solved by finding equivalent equations which have obvious solutions. In a similar fashion, quadratic equations can be solved by using the method of factoring to find equivalent equations.

E X A M P L E   5   Solving a Quadratic by Factoring

Solve $2x^2 + 5x - 3 = 0$.

Solution

$$2x^2 + 5x - 3 = 0$$

$$(2x - 1)(x + 3) = 0$$

$$2x - 1 = 0 \qquad \text{or} \qquad x + 3 = 0 \qquad \text{A product is zero only if at least one factor is zero.}$$

The solutions are $x = \frac{1}{2} = 0.5$ and $x = -3$.

Often the linear factors of a quadratic equation cannot be quickly seen. In that case you can solve the equation by using the quadratic formula.

Quadratic Formula

The solutions to a quadratic equation in x in the standard form $ax^2 + bx + c = 0, (a \neq 0)$ are given by the **quadratic formula**

$$x = \frac{-b \pm \sqrt{b^2 - 4ac}}{2a}.$$

Consider the general quadratic equation $ax^2 + bx + c = 0$. The quadratic formula is derived from this equation using a technique called **completing the square**. This technique calls for changing the equation to a form that includes a perfect square—an expression of the form $(x + k)^2$.

$$ax^2 + bx + c = 0$$

$$ax^2 + bx = -c \qquad \text{Subtract } c \text{ from each side.}$$

$$x^2 + \frac{b}{a}x = -\frac{c}{a} \qquad \text{Divide each side by } a.$$

$$x^2 + \frac{b}{a}x + \left(\frac{b}{2a}\right)^2 = -\frac{c}{a} + \left(\frac{b}{2a}\right)^2 \qquad \text{Add } (b/2a)^2 \text{ to each side.}$$

$$\left(x + \frac{b}{2a}\right)^2 = -\frac{c}{a} + \left(\frac{b}{2a}\right)^2 \qquad \text{Factor the left-hand side to get a perfect square.}$$

$$\left(x + \frac{b}{2a}\right)^2 = \frac{b^2 - 4ac}{4a^2} \qquad \text{Combine fractions on the right-hand side.}$$

$$x + \frac{b}{2a} = \pm\sqrt{\frac{b^2 - 4ac}{4a^2}} \qquad \text{Take the square root of both sides.}$$

$$x = \frac{-b \pm \sqrt{b^2 - 4ac}}{2a} \qquad \text{Solve for } x.$$

E X A M P L E   6   Using the Quadratic Formula

Solve $2x^2 + 2x - 1 = 0$ using the quadratic formula.

Solution   In this case $a = 2, b = 2$, and $c = -1$. Thus

$$x = \frac{-b \pm \sqrt{b^2 - 4ac}}{2a} \qquad \text{quadratic formula}$$

$$= \frac{-2 \pm \sqrt{2^2 - 4(2)(-1)}}{2(2)} \qquad \begin{array}{l} \text{Substitute into the quadratic formula} \\ a = 2, b = 2, \text{ and } c = -1. \end{array}$$

$$= \frac{-2 \pm \sqrt{12}}{4}$$

$$= \frac{-1 \pm \sqrt{3}}{2}. \qquad \text{Recall that } \sqrt{12} = \sqrt{4 \cdot (3)} = 2\sqrt{3}.$$

Verify with a calculator that

$$x = \frac{-1 + \sqrt{3}}{2} = 0.3660254038 \qquad \text{and} \qquad x = \frac{-1 - \sqrt{3}}{2} = -1.366025404$$

are accurate to the number of displayed decimal places.

EXPRESSING IRRATIONAL NUMBERS AS DECIMALS

In this text we will write $\sqrt{3} = 1.732050808$ (instead of $\sqrt{3} \approx 1.732050808$) with the understanding that the right side is a decimal approximation for the irrational number on the left side, accurate to the number of decimal places displayed.

EXAMPLE 7   Using the Quadratic Formula

Solve $3x - x^2 = 1$.

Solution   Rewrite the given equation into the following standard form: $-x^2 + 3x - 1 = 0$. Then it is clear that $a = -1, b = 3$, and $c = -1$. The quadratic formula then yields

$$x = \frac{-b \pm \sqrt{b^2 - 4ac}}{2a}$$

$$= \frac{-3 \pm \sqrt{3^2 - 4(-1)(-1)}}{2(-1)}$$

$$= \frac{-3 \pm \sqrt{9 - 4}}{-2}$$

$$= \frac{3 \mp \sqrt{5}}{2}.$$

REMINDER

When a quadratic equation is not in standard form, be sure you choose the correct values for a, b, and c.

$$x = \frac{-b \pm \sqrt{b^2 - 4ac}}{2a}$$

The expression under the **radical** (square root sign) in the quadratic formula, $b^2 - 4ac$, is called the **discriminant** of the quadratic equation $ax^2 + bx + c = 0$. The discriminant is important because it determines whether there are any real number solutions and if so how many. If $b^2 - 4ac$ is positive, there are two real solutions. If it is zero, the equation has exactly one solution. If it is negative, there are no

$$\frac{-b \pm \sqrt{b^2 - 4ac}}{2a}$$

real number solutions. (Recall that the square root of a negative number is not a real number.)

E X A M P L E   8   APPLICATION: Finding Box Dimensions

A Problem Situation   Squares with a side length of 5 inches are cut from each corner of a rectangular piece of cardboard with width w and length ℓ (Fig. 2.1). By folding along the dashed lines in Fig. 2.1(a), a box is formed whose height is 5 inches, width is $(w - 10)$ inches, and length is $(\ell - 10)$ inches.

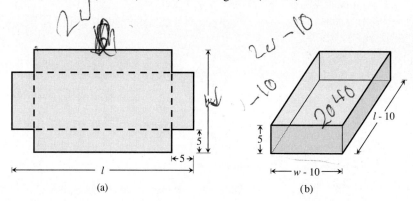

(a)   (b)

Figure 2.1   Box dimensions and completed box for the problem situation.

Suppose the length of the cardboard in Fig. 2.1 is twice its width. Find the dimensions of the cardboard if the volume of the resulting box is 2040 cubic inches.

Solution   Let V be the volume of the box. Since $V = \ell w h$,

$$5(w - 10)(\ell - 10) = V$$

$$5(w - 10)(2w - 10) = 2040 \qquad \ell = 2w \text{ and } V = 2040.$$

$$(w - 10)(w - 5) = 204 \qquad \begin{array}{l}\text{Factor 2 from } 2w - 10 \text{ and divide} \\ \text{both sides by 10.}\end{array}$$

$$w^2 - 15w - 154 = 0 \qquad \begin{array}{l}\text{Multiply the left-hand side} \\ \text{and combine terms.}\end{array}$$

$$(w - 22)(w + 7) = 0. \qquad \begin{array}{l}\text{Use the quadratic formula} \\ \text{if this factorization is not evident.}\end{array}$$

Although -7 and 22 are both solutions to this equation, only 22 is a solution to the problem since width must be positive. The dimensions of the cardboard are 22 inches by 44 inches.   ▤

Exercises for Section 2.1

In Exercises 1 to 6, determine whether each equation is a *conditional equation* or an *identity*:

1. $x + 3 = -1$

2. $x + 3 = -1 + x + 4$

3. $3(x + 2) = 3x + 6$

4. $5/x = 35$

5. $5 - x = 18$

6. $x^2 + 4x + 3 = (x + 3)(x + 1)$

7. Is $x = 2$ a solution to $x^3 - 3x - 2 = 0$?

8. Is $x = 3$ a solution to $x^5 - 4x^3 - 6x + 117 = 0$?

In Exercises 9 and 10, decide which of the given values of x are solutions to the equation.

9. $x^3 + 2x^2 - 5x - 6 = 0$

   a) $x = -3$ **b)** $x = -2$ **c)** $x = -1$

10. $x^3 + 2x^2 - 5x - 6 = 0$

   a) $x = 1$ **b)** $x = -3$ **c)** $x = 2$

In Exercises 11 to 21, use an algebraic method to solve each equation. Check by substitution into the original equation.

11. $2x - 3 = 4x - 5$

12. $4(x - 2) = 5x$

13. $\frac{1}{2}x - \frac{2}{3} = 2x + 7$

14. $-3x + 4 = 2(x + 4)$

15. $2(3 - 4x) - 5(2x + 3) = x - 17$

16. $\dfrac{t - 1}{3.5} = 8$

17. $|x + 1| = 4$

18. $|x - 2| = -5$

19. $|2t - 3| - 1/2 = 0$

20. $|3 - 5x| = |-4|$

21. $|x - 3| = |2x + 1|$

In Exercises 22 to 29, solve each equation by factoring.

22. $x^2 + x - 2 = 0$

23. $x^2 - 5x + 6 = 0$

24. $x^2 - x - 20 = 0$

25. $x^2 - 4x + 3 = 0$

26. $2x^2 + 5x - 3 = 0$

27. $4x^2 - 8x + 3 = 0$

28. $x^2 - 8x = -15$

29. $x^2 + 4x - 3 = 2$

In Exercises 30 to 37, solve each equation by using the quadratic formula.

30. $x^2 + x - 1 = 0$

31. $x^2 - 4x + 2 = 0$

32. $x^2 + 8x - 2 = 0$

33. $2x^2 - 3x + 1 = 0$

34. $x^2 - 2x = 7$

35. $3x + 4 = x^2$

36. $5 - x^2 = 8x$

37. $x^2 - 5 = \sqrt{3}x$

In Exercises 38 to 41, use any methods to solve the equation.

38. $x^2 - 5x + 6 = 30$

39. $3y^3 - 2y^2 + y = 0$

40. $|x^2 + 4| = 8$

41. $x^4 + 4x^2 - 5 = 0$

In Exercises 42 to 45, determine the number of real solutions to each equation.

42. $x^2 + 3x + 2 = 0$

43. $2x^2 - 3x + 2 = 0$

44. $x^2 - \pi x + \sqrt{3} = 0$

45. $x^2 - 1 = 0$

Exercises 46 and 47 refer to the formula $F = \frac{9}{5}C + 32$, which gives the Fahrenheit temperature F as a function of the Celsius temperature C.

46. Normal body temperature is $98.6°$F. How many degrees Celsius is this?

47. Solve the formula for C.

Exercises 48 to 50 refer to the following **problem situation**: The perimeter of a rectangle is 360 inches and its width is 20 inches.

48. Write an equation that includes the variable l representing length.

49. Find the area of the rectangle.

50. If the width of the rectangle is changed so that its length is twice its width, what is its length and width?

Exercises 51 to 53 refer to the following **problem situation**: A storage box with a rectangular base has a height of 30 cm (centimeters) and a volume of 5400 cm^3.

51. If x represents the length of the box in centimeters and y represents the width in centimeters, write an equation in the form $y = ?$ where the right-hand side of the equation is an expression in x.

52. Find the width of the box if its length is 24 cm.

53. Find the length of the box if its width is 12 cm.

Exercises 54 and 55 refer to the following **problem situation**: A laboratory keeps two acid solutions on hand. One is 20% acid and the other is 35% acid.

54. How much 20% acid solution and how much 35% acid solution should be used to fill an order for 25 liters of a 26% acid solution?

55. How many liters of distilled water should be added to a liter of the 35% acid solution in order to dilute it to a 20% acid solution?

Exercises 56 and 57 refer to the following **problem situation**: An investment pays simple interest. If P dollars are invested at an interest rate r per year, the value S after n years is given by the algebraic representation $S = P(1 + rn)$.

56. Solve this equation for n.

57. How many years are required for an investment earning 8% simple interest to triple in value?

58. The formula for the area of a trapezoid is $A = \frac{1}{2}h(b_1 + b_2)$. Solve this equation for b_1.

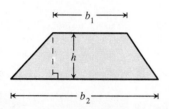

For Exercise 58

59. A semicircle is placed on one side of a square so that its diameter coincides with a side of the square. Find the side length of the square if the total area of the square plus the semicircle is 200 square units.

Exercises 60 to 62 refer to the following **problem situation**: A single-commodity open market is driven by the supply-and-demand principle. Economists have determined that supply curves are usually increasing; that is, as the price increases, the sellers increase production. Use the algebraic representation relating the price p and the number of units produced, x.

60. If $p = 12 + 0.025x$ is an algebraic representation of this problem situation, find the price if the production level is 120 units.

61. Using the same algebraic representation as in Exercise 60, find the production if the price is $23.00.

62. Repeat Exercises 60 and 61 assuming the algebraic representation is $p = 5 + 0.01x^2$.

Exercises 63 to 65 refer to the following **problem situation**: A real estate company has two agents. Company profits P depend on the number of weekly listings x, and are described by the algebraic representation $P = -5x^2 + 100x + 20$.

63. How many weekly listings are necessary to realize a profit of $300?

64. Is there a maximum possible profit in this situation?

65. What can you say about the weekly profit as the number of listings increases? Explain why this might be reasonable.

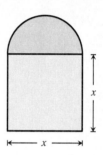

For Exercise 59

2.2 _____ Solving Equations Graphically

The algebraic techniques demonstrated in Section 2.1 resulted in exact solutions that often involved radicals. For example, in Example 6 the solutions were

$$x = \frac{-1 + \sqrt{3}}{2} \quad \text{and} \quad x = \frac{-1 - \sqrt{3}}{2}. \tag{1}$$

If these solutions were applied to a real-world problem, $\sqrt{3}$ would be replaced by an approximation. And since real-world problems usually require taking measurements, which is an inexact process, no further accuracy will be lost if the exact solutions in line (1) are replaced with approximations having a prescribed accuracy. So approximation methods are appropriate.

Linear and quadratic equations belong to a larger family of equations called polynomial equations. A graphing utility can be used to find very accurate solutions to polynomial equations. Graphs sometimes suggest exact answers; often a graphical method can be used to solve an equation that cannot be solved algebraically.

Definition 2.3   Polynomial Equation

A **polynomial equation in x** is an equation that can be written in the form

$$a_n x^n + a_{n-1} x^{n-1} + \cdots + a_1 x + a_0 = 0,$$

where n is a positive integer. If $a_n \neq 0$, the equation is called a **polynomial equation in x of degree n.**

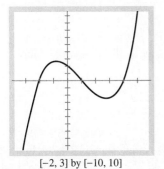

[−2, 3] by [−10, 10]

Figure 2.2
$y = 2x^3 - 3x^2 - 3x + 2.$

Finding a Solution from the Graph

To learn how to find solutions from graphs, begin by exploring the relationship between the graph of the equation $y = 2x^3 - 3x^2 - 3x + 2$ and solutions to the equation $2x^3 - 3x^2 - 3x + 2 = 0$.

⌕ EXPLORE WITH A GRAPHING UTILITY

Graph $y = 2x^3 - 3x^2 - 3x + 2$ using the viewing rectangle $[-2, 3]$ by $[-10, 10]$. See Fig. 2.2.

Questions

1. How many times does the graph cross the x-axis?

2. What seems to be true about the y-coordinate of the points where the graph crosses the x-axis? (Use the trace key on your grapher.)

3. How do the x-coordinates of these points compare with the solutions to the equation $2x^3 - 3x^2 - 3x + 2 = 0$?

Generalize   Make some general statements that you think will always be true about the coordinates of the points where the graph crosses the x-axis.

Summary of Your Experience   From the Exploration you should have come to these conclusions:

1. A solution to $2x^3 - 3x^2 - 3x + 2 = 0$ corresponds to the x-coordinate of a point where the graph of $y = 2x^3 - 3x^2 - 3x + 2$ crosses the x-axis.

2. If $x = a$ is a real solution to $2x^3 - 3x^2 - 3x + 2 = 0$, then $(a, 0)$ is a point on the graph of $y = 2x^3 - 3x^2 - 3x + 2$.

Such a point $(a, 0)$ is called an **x-intercept** of $y = 2x^3 - 3x^2 - 3x + 2$. The value a is also called a **root** or **zero**, since it is the x-value that makes y equal to zero. Sometimes the x-intercept is called a rather than $(a, 0)$.

Linear Equations

The linear equation $ax + b = 0$ has a unique solution, namely $-b/a$, (where $a \neq 0$). The graph of the equation $y = ax + b$ is a straight line that crosses the x-axis at the point $(-b/a, 0)$.

E X A M P L E   1   Solving a Linear Equation Graphically

Solve $2x + 3 = 0$.

Solution   See Fig. 2.3. The x-intercept appears to be $-\frac{3}{2}$, so reading from the graph gives an approximate solution of -1.5. The exactness of this approximation can be confirmed by substitution.   ≡

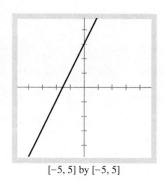

[−5, 5] by [−5, 5]

Figure 2.3 $y = 2x + 3$.

Quadratic Equations

The graphs of quadratic equations of the form $y = ax^2 + bx + c$ are called **parabolas**. In Chapter 4 we will study these graphs in more detail, but for now assume that a complete graph of $y = ax^2 + bx + c$ looks like one of the two parabolas in Fig. 2.4.

Figure 2.5 illustrates that the number of x-intercepts for a quadratic equation can be zero, one, or two depending on whether the discriminant $b^2 - 4ac$ is negative, zero, or positive.

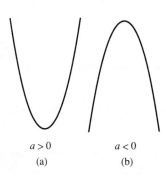

$a > 0$ $a < 0$

(a)   (b)

Figure 2.4   The two possible graphs of $y = ax^2 + bx + c$.

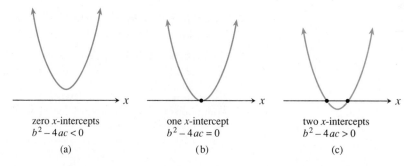

zero x-intercepts   one x-intercept   two x-intercepts
$b^2 - 4ac < 0$ $b^2 - 4ac = 0$ $b^2 - 4ac > 0$

(a)   (b)   (c)

Figure 2.5   Graphs of $y = ax^2 + bx + c$, $(a > 0)$. Notice how the sign of the discriminant affects the number of x-intercepts.

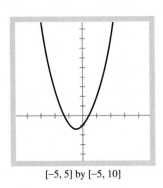

[−5, 5] by [−5, 10]

Figure 2.6 $y = 2x^2 + 2x - 1$.

E X A M P L E   2   Solving a Quadratic Equation Graphically

Solve $2x^2 = 1 - 2x$.

Solution

1. Rewrite the equation $2x^2 = 1 - 2x$ to the equivalent form $2x^2 + 2x - 1 = 0$.
2. Graph the equation $y = 2x^2 + 2x - 1$ in the viewing rectangle $[-5, 5]$ by $[-5, \; 10]$ (Fig. 2.6).
3. The x-intercepts appear to be approximately 0.3 and -1.3.

   Compare these estimates with the 10–digit approximations found in Example 6, Section 2.1.   ≡

Finding Solutions Graphically Using Zoom-In

A graphing utility can be used to find solutions to a high degree of accuracy with a procedure called **zoom-in**.* This is accomplished by "trapping" the x-intercept in a sequence of viewing rectangles, each new one contained within the previous one (Fig. 2.7). Zoom-in continues until the viewing rectangle has enlarged a small enough portion of the graph that the user can read the value of x to the level of accuracy desired. However, it is important to note that solutions cannot be read more accurately than the graphing utility permits. Most computers and graphing calculators allow answers to be read to at least 9 or 10 significant digits.

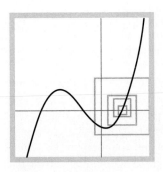

Figure 2.7   Zoom-in creates a nested sequence of viewing rectangles decreasing in size.

E X A M P L E   3   Solving Graphically with Zoom-in

Use a complete graph to show that $x^3 + 2x = 1$ has only one solution, then find an approximation of that solution.

Solution   Rewrite the equation as $x^3 + 2x - 1 = 0$, and complete the following steps:

1. Graph $y = x^3 + 2x - 1$ in the standard viewing rectangle (Fig. 2.8a). The graph crosses the x-axis between $x = 0$ and $x = 1$ (scale marks are 1 unit apart).
2. Find a new graph using the viewing rectangle $[0, 1]$ by $[-1, 1]$ with scale marks 0.1 unit apart (Fig. 2.8b). The graph crosses the x-axis between $x = 0.4$ and $x = 0.5$.
3. Find a new graph using the viewing rectangle $[0.4, 0.5]$ by $[-0.1, 0.1]$ with scale marks 0.01 unit apart (Fig. 2.8c).

---

* Consult the accompanying *Graphing Calculator and Computer Graphing Laboratory Manual* to see how to use a graphing utility.

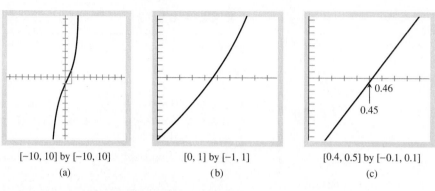

[−10, 10] by [−10, 10]   [0, 1] by [−1, 1]   [0.4, 0.5] by [−0.1, 0.1]

(a)   (b)   (c)

Figure 2.8   Three views of $y = x^3 + 2x - 1$.

Read the graph and report that an approximate solution is 0.453.

Analysis of Error

Study Example 3 in more detail. The (exact) solution of $x^3 + 2x - 1 = 0$ is between 0.45 and 0.46, a fact that can be read from the graph in Fig. 2.8(c). Furthermore, since the difference between 0.45 and 0.46 is 0.01, *any* number in the interval $[0.45, 0.46]$ is the solution with an error of at most 0.01.

Which number should be reported as the solution with an error of at most 0.01? One reader might read the graph in Fig. 2.8(c) as crossing the x-axis about $\frac{3}{10}$ of the way between two tick marks and could report 0.453 as a solution (with an error of at most 0.01). A second reader might read the graph as crossing the x-axis about $\frac{4}{10}$ of the way between two tick marks and could report the solution as 0.454 (with an error of at most 0.01). Both conclusions would be correct.

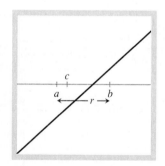

Figure 2.9   A typical graph.

Definition 2.4   Error of a Solution

Suppose a graph crosses the x-axis between two consecutive scale marks a and b and $b - a = r$ (Fig. 2.9). If c is any number in the interval $[a, b]$ determined by the scale marks, c is a **solution with error of at most** r.

Suppose the graph of an equation crosses the x-axis in viewing rectangle $[X\min, X\max]$ by $[Y\min, Y\max]$ in which no scale marks are displayed. Then any number between $X\min$ and $X\max$ would be a solution with an error of at most $r = X\max - X\min$.

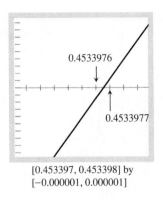

0.4533976

0.4533977

[0.453397, 0.453398] by
[−0.000001, 0.000001]

Figure 2.10 $y = x^3 + 2x - 1.$

E X A M P L E   4   Using Zoom-in for a Very Accurate Solution

Solve the equation $x^3 + 2x = 1$ with an error of at most 0.0000001.

Solution

1. Continue the process begun in Example 3 by graphing the equation using viewing rectangle [0.45, 0.46] by [−0.01, 0.01] with scale marks 0.001 unit apart.

2. Using smaller and smaller viewing rectangles, zoom in until you see viewing rectangle [0.453397, 0.453398] by [−0.000001, 0.000001] (Fig. 2.10).

3. Notice that the graph crosses the x-axis about halfway between $x = 0.4533976$ and $x = 0.4533977$. Thus the solution is $x = 0.4533976 + 0.00000005 = 0.45339765$ with an error of at most $0.4533977 - 0.4533976 = 0.0000001.$
≡

Ordinarily it is not necessary to approximate solutions as accurately as in Example 4. However, the example illustrates that accuracy is limited only by machine precision.

Accuracy Agreement

Throughout the rest of this text we shall adhere to the following convention: Unless stated to the contrary, to *solve an equation* means "to approximate all real solutions of the equation with an error of at most 0.01" or "to state the exact solution." Assume that numbers provided in examples and exercises are exact unless otherwise specified.

Third-Degree Polynomial Equations

A **third-degree polynomial equation** has the form

$$ax^3 + bx^2 + cx + d = 0.$$

Solving this equation graphically requires first finding the complete graph of the equation $y = ax^3 + bx^2 + cx + d$, and then using zoom-in as illustrated in Examples 3 and 4.

It is essential to begin with a complete graph to determine how many real solutions exist. For example, the graph of $x^3 + 2x = 1$ in Example 3 crossed the x-axis once; therefore it has only one real solution.

When completing exercises, assume that a complete graph of a third-degree polynomial looks like one of the graphs in Fig. 2.11. These forms will be confirmed in Chapter 5.

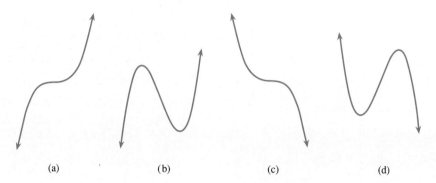

(a)   (b)   (c)   (d)

Figure 2.11   The graph of $y = ax^3 + bx^2 + cx + d$ will always have one of these shapes.

E X A M P L E   5   Finding the Number of Solutions

How many real number solutions are there to the equation $x^3 - 5x^2 + 6x - 1 = 0$?

Solution   Find the complete graph as shown in Fig. 2.12.   Read from the graph that there are three real number solutions.   ≡

E X A M P L E   6   Approximating One of Several Solutions

Find the middle of the three real number solutions to $x^3 - 5x^2 + 6x - 1 = 0$ with an error of at most 0.01.

Solution

1. Graph $y = x^3 - 5x^2 + 6x - 1$ in the standard viewing rectangle (see Fig. 2.12). Observe that the middle solution is between $x = 1$ and $x = 2$.

2. Use zoom-in several times to arrive at viewing rectangle [1.5, 1.6] by [−0.1, 0.1] with scale marks 0.01 units apart.

3. Note that the solution is $x = 1.555$.   ≡

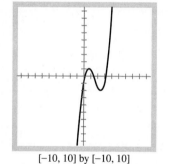

[−10, 10] by [−10, 10]

Figure 2.12
$y = x^3 - 5x^2 + 6x - 1$.

The equations in Examples 4, 5, and 6 can be solved with very complicated algebraic techniques that go beyond the scope of this book. With a grapher the solutions are manageable. Furthermore, for polynomial equations of degrees 5, and greater, an algebraic method is usually impossible whereas the graphical method is always possible.

Summary of the Graphical Method for Solving Equations

▪ Write an equation in the form $y = \ldots$ whose x-intercepts are the solutions to the original equation.

▪ Find a complete graph of the equation in the previous step so that all solutions are visible. Two or more viewing rectangles may be necessary.

▪ Use zoom-in to approximate each solution to an error at most 0.01 unless otherwise stated.

Exercises for Section 2.2

In Exercises 1 to 6, use an algebraic method to solve each equation. Support your answer with a graphing utility.

1. $(x - 3)(x + 2) = 0$ **2.** $x^2 = 14$

3. $x^2 - 3x + 2 = 0$ **4.** $x^2 - 2x + 3 = 0$

5. $x^3 - x = 0$ **6.** $|x - 2| = 6$

In Exercises 7 to 14, find a complete graph whose x-intercepts are solutions to the given equation. In each case, state how many real solutions there are and record the viewing rectangle that you used.

7. $x^2 - 3x - 10 = 0$ **8.** $x^2 + 10x - 119 = 0$

9. $1000 - 15x - x^2 = 0$ **10.** $x^2 - 14x - 10 = 3$

11. $x^3 - 25x = 0$

12. $x^3 + 2x^2 - 109x - 110 = 0$

13. $x^3 - 2x^2 + 3x - 5 = 0$ **14.** $x^3 - 65x + 10 = 0$

In Exercises 15 and 16, find a complete graph whose x-intercepts are solutions to the given equation. Explain why you may need to use both a complete graph and zoom-in to determine how many solutions there are to these equations.

15. $\frac{1}{8}x^4 - 5x^2 + 2 = 0$ **16.** $\frac{1}{2}x^3 - 7x^2 = -3$

In Exercises 17 to 24, assume that the graph of an equation crosses the x-axis in the interval given. Find the value of r such that any number in this interval is a solution to the corresponding equation with an error of at most r.

17. $[3.25, 3.26]$ **18.** $[4.8, 4.9]$

19. $[-3.5, -3.0]$ **20.** $[6.213, 6.214]$

21. $[1.32, 1.33]$ **22.** $[-2.008, -2.007]$

23. $[0.036, 0.362]$ **24.** $[1.5, 1.55]$

In Exercises 25 and 26, find a sequence of four viewing rectangles containing each solution. Choose each sequence to permit the solutions to be read with errors of at most 0.1, 0.01, 0.001, and finally 0.0001.

25. $x^3 - x^2 + x - 3 = 0$.   **26.** $x^3 - 2x + 3 = 0$.

In Exercises 27 to 30, find one positive solution to each equation with an error of at most 0.01.

27. $x^3 - x - 2 = 0$ **28.** $\frac{1}{100}x^3 - x - 2 = 0$

29. $\frac{1}{10}x^3 - x^2 - 2 = 0$ **30.** $x^3 - \frac{1}{10}x = 0$

In Exercises 31 to 36, solve the equation.

31. $3x^2 - 15x + 8 = 0$ **32.** $x^3 - 2x^2 + 3x - 1 = 0$

33. $x(x - 25)(x - 35) = 3000$

34. $x^4 - 5x^3 + x^2 - 3x = 2$

35. $|x| + |x - 3| = 6$ **36.** $|x| - |x - 6| = 0$

37. Find three distinct approximations to the one real number solution to $x^3 - 10 = 0$ with an error of at most 0.01. What is the exact solution?

38. Find three distinct approximations to the one real number solution to $x^3 + 4 = 0$ with an error of at most 0.01. What is the exact solution?

In Exercises 39 to 42, solve for x in the given interval with error of at most 0.01.

39. $x^4 - 3x^3 - 6x + 5 = 0$, where $0 \le x \le 10$.

40. $\dfrac{x^3 - 10x^2 + x + 50}{x - 2} = 0$, where $-10 \le x \le 10$.

41. $3\sin(x-5) = 0$, where $0 \le x \le 10$.

42. $\sqrt[3]{x^2 - 2x + 3} = 0$, where $-10 \le x \le 10$.

43. The owner of the Olde Time Ice Cream Shoppe pays $1000 per month for fixed expenses such as rent, electricity, and wages. Ice cream cones are sold at $0.75 each, of which $0.40 goes for ice cream, cone, and napkin. How many cones must be sold to break even?

Exercises 44 to 47 refer to the following **problem situation**: There are many rectangles whose perimeters are 320 inches. Consider all these rectangles.

44. Illustrate the problem-solving strategy Draw a Picture by drawing a picture of this problem situation. Label the length x. What values of x make sense in this problem situation?

45. Find an algebraic representation of the area of the rectangles in this collection.

46. Find a graphical representation of the area of the rectangles in this collection.

47. Verify that $(-40, -8000)$ is a point on a complete graph of the algebraic representation of this problem situation. What meaning do these coordinates have?

48. For a certain car, it has been determined that $D = r + r^2/19.85$ is an algebraic representation that approximates the stopping distance D (in feet) when a car is traveling at a speed of r mph. Use a graphical representation of this problem situation to estimate the speed of a car if the stopping distance is 300 feet.

49. The rate at which a blood cell flows depends on the distance of the cell from the center of the artery. Research has determined that a mathematical model of this problem situation is the equation $v = 1.19 - (1.85 \times 10^4)r^2$, where r is the distance (in centimeters) of the blood cell from the center of the artery and v is the velocity (in centimeters per second). If a blood cell is traveling at 0.975 cm/sec, use a graphical representation of the model equation to estimate the distance of the blood cell from the center of the artery.

Exercises 50 and 51 refer to the following **problem situation**: A graphic artist designs pages $8\frac{1}{2}$ by 11 inches with a picture centered on the paper. Suppose the distance from the outer edge of the paper to the picture is x inches on all sides.

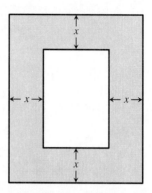

For Exercises 50 and 51

50. Find an algebraic representation that describes the area A of the picture when the width of the border is x inches on all sides.

51. Use a graphical representation on a grapher to estimate the width of the uniform border if the area of the picture is 50 square inches.

Exercises 52 and 53 refer to the following **problem situation**: A single-commodity open market is driven by the supply-and-demand principle. Economists have determined that supply curves usually increase (that is, as the price increases, the sellers increase production), and demand curves usually decrease (as the price increases, the consumer buys less).

52. Suppose $p = 15 - 0.023x$. Find the price p if the production level x is 120 units, and find the production level x if the price p is 2.30.

53. Suppose $p = 100 - 0.0015x^2$. Find the price p if the production level x is 120 units, and find the production level x if the price p is 2.30.

54. Writing to Learn A student writes that $-1, 2$, and 3 are solutions to the equation $x^3 + 2x^2 - 5x - 6 = 0$. Write several paragraphs explaining whether you agree. Include in your response how you could determine if this equation has any real solutions, and how graphing can help determine all real solutions.

Two or more viewing windows may be needed to show a complete graph of an equation. Take that into account in these next two exercises.

55. Find a complete graph of $y = x^3 - 8x^2 + 12.99x - 5.94$

56. Solve $x^3 - 8x^2 + 12.99x - 5.94 = 0$

2.3 _____

Applications and Mathematical Models

Recall the Quality Rent-a-Car problem situation studied in Section 1.2. Here the equation $y = 0.2x + 15$ is an algebraic representation of the problem situation, and Fig. 2.13 is a graphical representation of the problem situation. The equation, its graph, or both together are often referred to as a mathematical model of the problem situation since the data given in the problem satisfy this equation.

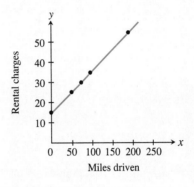

Figure 2.13   Graph of the Quality Rent-a-Car Problem Situation: $y = 0.2x + 15$.

When solving a problem posed for some problem situation, first make sure you understand the problem situation and the problem. Then find an algebraic or graphical representation.

Strategy: Analyzing a Problem Situation

Understand the problem situation and the problem before trying to develop a model. Then follow this two-step process:

- Find an algebraic representation of the problem situation.
- Find and analyze a complete graph of the problem situation.

E X A M P L E 1   Finding an Algebraic Representation

Bill invests $20,000, a portion of this at 6.75% simple interest and the remainder at 8.6% simple interest. Find an algebraic representation for the total interest earned assuming that Bill invests x dollars at 6.75% and the rest at 8.6%.

Solution   Let x represent the amount invested in the 6.75% account and y represent the total interest Bill earns in 1 year.

$$y = (6.75)(x) +$$

The problem-solving strategy "Completing a Table" is helpful for this problem:

Interest Rate	Dollars Invested	Interest Earned
6.75%	x	$0.0675x$
8.6%	$20{,}000 - x$	$0.086(20{,}000 - x)$

Total interest = interest from the 6.75% account + interest from the 8.6% account.

Thus an algebraic representation is

$$y = 0.0675x + 0.086(20{,}000 - x).$$

This equation can be simplified as follows:

$$y = 0.0675x + 0.086(20{,}000 - x)$$
$$= 0.0675x + 1720 - 0.086x$$
$$= -0.0185x + 1720.$$

The context of the problem shows that the only values of x that make sense are *nonnegative values that do not exceed* 20,000. Consequently the graph of nonnegative $y = -0.0185x + 1720$ in the viewing rectangle [0, 20,000] by [0, 1720] is a **complete graph of the problem situation** (shaded portion of Fig. 2.14).

In a different context from the problem situation in Example 1, a graph of the equation $y = -0.0185x + 1720$ could include values for x that are negative or greater than 20,000. Thus the whole graph shown in Fig. 2.14 (ignoring the shading) is called a **complete graph of the algebraic representation** $y = 0.0675x + 0.086(20{,}000 - x)$.

In other words, the complete graph of a problem situation is often *only a part* of a complete graph of the algebraic representation.

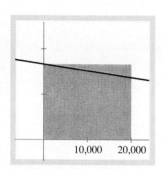

[−6000, 24,000] by [−600, 2,400]

Figure 2.14
$y = -0.0185x + 1720$. Shaded area shows viewing rectangle [0, 20,000] by [0, 1720].

EXAMPLE 2   Solving the Problem: Graphically

Use a graphing utility and the problem situation in Example 1 to estimate the amount invested at each rate if Bill receives $1,509.10 in interest in 1 year.

Solution

1. Find a graph of $y = -0.0185x + 1720$ with viewing rectangle [0, 20,000] by [0, 1720] (Fig. 2.14).

2. Locate the point on the graph whose y-coordinate is closest to $1509.10.

3. Read the x-coordinate of the point.

The x-coordinate of the point indicates that Bill invests about $11,400 at 6.75% and $20,000 − $11,400 = $8,600 at 8.6%.

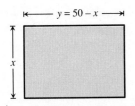

Figure 2.15 Rectangle with a perimeter of 100 inches, where x = width.

EXAMPLE 3   Finding an Algebraic Representation

Consider the collection of all rectangles having a perimeter of 100 inches. Find an algebraic representation that describes the area of these rectangles in terms of their width.

Solution   The problem-solving strategies "Drawing a Picture" and "Using Variables" are helpful in this problem situation (Fig. 2.15). Let x = width and y = length in inches. Then

$$100 = 2x + 2y \quad \text{or} \quad 50 = x + y. \quad \text{The perimeter is 100 inches.}$$

$$\text{Area} = xy \quad \text{where} \quad y = 50 - x.$$

Therefore the equation $A = x(50 - x)$ is an algebraic representation of the problem situation. ▤

EXAMPLE 4   APPLICATION: Area of a Rectangle

Find a complete graph of the problem situation of Example 3.

Solution

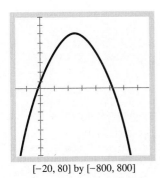

[−20, 80] by [−800, 800]

Figure 2.16 $A = x(50 - x)$: complete graph of the *algebraic representation*.

1. Find a complete graph of the algebraic representation $A = x(50 - x)$ using the viewing rectangle $[-20, 80]$ by $[-800, 800]$.

2. Notice that this viewing rectangle allows the observation that, in the complete graph of the algebraic representation, x can represent any real number (Fig. 2.16).

3. Also notice, however, that in the context of the problem situation, x is positive and cannot exceed 50 because the area of a rectangle is always positive.

   Thus the complete graph of the problem situation includes *only* the portion of the graph of $A = x(50 - x)$ between $x = 0$ and $x = 50$, as shown in Fig. 2.17. ▤

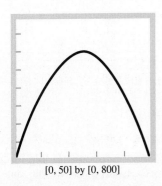

[0, 50] by [0, 800]

Figure 2.17 $A = x(50 - x)$: complete graph for the *Problem Situation* in Example 4. Compare with Fig. 2.16.

EXAMPLE 5   APPLICATION: Finding Manufacturing Costs

A Problem Situation   Companies that produce goods have fixed costs and variable costs. Fixed costs include salaries, benefits, equipment maintenance, utilities, and so forth. Quick Manufacturing Company produces T-shirts and has fixed annual costs of $200,000. The variable cost to produce one T-shirt is $1.50, and each shirt sells for $4.

Find complete graphs of the algebraic representations of the total cost C, and the revenue R in this problem situation.

Solution

Total cost = variable cost × number produced + fixed costs.
Let x be the number of T-shirts produced in 1 year. Then

$$C = 1.5x + 200{,}000 \qquad \text{1.5x is the cost of producing } x \text{ T-shirts.}$$
Add the fixed cost of $200,000.

$$R = 4x. \qquad \text{4x is the revenue generated by selling } x \text{ T-shirts.}$$

Complete graphs are shown in Fig. 2.18.

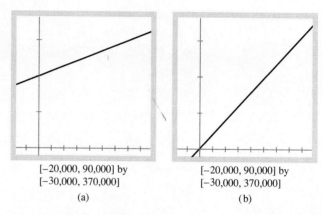

[−20,000, 90,000] by   [−20,000, 90,000] by
[−30,000, 370,000]   [−30,000, 370,000]
(a)   (b)

Figure 2.18 (a) $y = 1.5x + 200{,}000$; (b) $y = 4x$.

Note that Fig. 2.18 shows complete graphs of the algebraic representations. Since the only values of x that make sense in this problem situation are whole numbers, complete graphs of the problem situation would consist of only the points on the lines in Fig. 2.18 whose x-coordinates are positive whole numbers.

EXAMPLE 6   APPLICATION: Breaking Even

In order to break even, total revenue R from a product must equal the total cost C of production. How many T-shirts must Quick Manufacturing Company sell so that their total revenue equals their total cost?

Solution

Graphical Method

1. Find complete graphs of both $R = 4x$ and $C = 1.5x + 200{,}000$ in the same viewing rectangle $[-20{,}000, 90{,}000]$ by $[-30{,}000, 370{,}000]$ (Fig. 2.19).

2. To the left of the point where the two graphs intersect, R is less than C. To the right, R is greater than C. Therefore cost and revenue are equal when x equals the x-coordinate of this point of intersection.

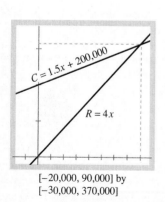

[−20,000, 90,000] by
[−30,000, 370,000]

Figure 2.19 Complete graphs of C and R for Example 5.

3. Use trace to estimate the x-coordinate of this point as 80,000.

Algebraic Method   To solve this problem algebraically, express C and R in terms of x, and then write and solve the equation $R = C$.

$$R = C$$

$$4x = 1.5x + 200{,}000$$

$$2.5x = 200{,}000$$

$$x = 80{,}000$$

The graphical and algebraic methods agree. The breakeven point for Quick Manufacturing Company is $x = 80{,}000$ shirts.

≡

Exercises for Section 2.3

In Exercises 1 to 4, assume that the equations are algebraic representations of some problem situation. Find a complete graph of each algebraic representation.

1. $P = 2N + 50$ **2.** $V = 5L^2$

3. $S = 1105 + 1105(0.08)N$ **4.** $E = 1000C^2$

Exercises 5 to 8 use the following information. The area A of a rectangle is given by the equation $A = LW$, where L is the length and W is the width.

5. If the width is 50 units, then write the area A in terms of the length L.

6. If the length is 200 units, then write the area A in terms of the width W.

7. Find a complete graph of the algebraic representation in Exercise 5.

8. Find a complete graph of the algebraic representation in Exercise 6.

Exercises 9 to 12 use the following information: The perimeter P of a rectangle is given by the equation $P = 2L + 2W$, where L is the length and W is the width.

9. If the width is 100 units, then write the perimeter P in terms of the length L.

10. If the length is 40 units, then write the perimeter P in terms of the width W.

11. Find a complete graph of the algebraic representation in Exercise 9.

12. Find a complete graph of the algebraic representation in Exercise 10.

In Exercises 13 to 16, consider the collection of all rectangles having a length of twice their width.

13. Write the area A in terms of the width W of the rectangle.

14. Write the area A in terms of the length L of the rectangle.

15. Write the perimeter P in terms of the width W of the rectangle.

16. Write the perimeter P in terms of the length L of the rectangle.

17. Refer to the problem situation in Example 3. Use a graph to find the dimensions of one of the rectangles if its area is 500 square inches.

For Exercises 18 to 20, consider the collection of all rectangles the sum of whose length and width is 75 inches. Let x be the length of such a rectangle, and consider the area of these rectangles.

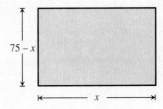

For Exercise 18

18. Show that $A = x(75 - x)$ is an algebraic representation for the area of one of these rectangles in terms of its length x.

19. Verify graphically that $(-10, -850)$ is a point on the graph of the algebraic representation in Exercise 18. What meaning do these coordinates have in this problem situation?

20. Is the graph used in Exercise 19 a complete graph of the algebraic representation, or a complete graph of the problem situation?

For Exercises 21 to 23, consider the collection of all rectangles whose perimeter is 360 inches. Let x be the length of such a rectangle, and consider the area A of all these rectangles.

21. Find an algebraic representation of this problem situation.

22. What values of x make sense in this problem situation? Why?

23. What is the smallest viewing rectangle that will show a complete graph of the problem situation? Find this graph.

24. $A = \pi x^2$ is an equation that gives the area A of a circle with radius x. How might a complete graph of this algebraic representation differ from a complete graph of this problem situation?

For Exercises 25 to 27, consider this **problem situation**: Janet is making a rectangular end table for her living room. She has decided the tabletop should have a surface area of 625 square inches. Let L be the length of the tabletop in inches and W be the width in inches.

25. Write an equation that relates the length L and the width W.

26. Solve the equation you found in Exercise 25 for L, and find a complete graph of this equation.

27. What portion of the graph in Exercise 26 represents the problem situation?

Exercises 28 to 30 refer to the following **problem situation**: A bag of lawn fertilizer can cover a rectangular lawn with an area of 6000 square feet. Let x be the length of the lawn (in feet) and y the width (in feet).

28. Write an equation that relates the length and the width of the lawn.

29. Find a complete graph of this problem situation.

30. Use the graph in Exercise 29 to find the length of the lawn covered by fertilizer if the width is 45 feet.

Exercises 31 to 34 refer to the following **problem situation**: Reggie invests $12,000, part at 7% simple interest and the remainder at 8.5% simple interest.

31. Write the total interest Reggie receives in one year in terms of the amount he invests at 7%.

32. Find a complete graph of the algebraic representation in Exercise 31.

33. What portion of the graph in Exercise 32 represents this problem situation?

34. Use the graph in Exercise 32 to find the amount invested at each rate if Reggie receives $900 interest in one year.

Exercises 35 to 39 refer to the following **problem situation**: A shoe manufacturer determines that the annual cost C of making x pairs of shoes is $30 per pair plus $100,000 in fixed overhead costs. Each pair of shoes that is manufactured is sold for $50 per pair.

35. Write an algebraic representation for the total cost C in terms of the number of pairs x produced.

36. Find a complete graph of this problem situation.

37. Use the graph in Exercise 36 to find the number of shoes produced if the total cost is $340,000.

38. Write an algebraic representation for revenue R in terms of the number of pairs x produced.

39. How many shoes must be sold before revenue exceeds annual cost?

40. Discussion   Exercises 1 to 4 asked you to find complete graphs of algebraic representations of problem situations without knowing any details about them. Could you also find the complete graphs of the problem situations without knowing more about them?

41. Writing to Learn   Write several paragraphs that explain the difference between a complete graph of a problem situation and a complete graph of an algebraic representation of the problem situation.

42. Solve Example 2 algebraically.

43. Solve Exercise 34 algebraically.

2.4 _____ Solving Linear Inequalities

Here is a good place to review the concept of *inequality* introduced in Section 1.1. Simple inequalities were defined in the context of order on the real-number line. Definition 1.1 defined the concept *less than*, represented by the symbol $<$: For real numbers a and b, $a < b$ if $b - a$ is a positive number. Similarly, we defined the relations represented by the symbols $\leq$, $>$, and $\geq$. The symbols $<$, $\leq$, $>$, and $\geq$ are inequality signs, and the expressions $a < b$, $a \leq b$, $a > b$, and $a \geq b$ are called inequalities.

Inequalities may include variables just as equations do. For example, consider the inequality

$$-4 \leq x.$$

A number a is called a solution to an inequality if replacing the variable x with a results in a true statement.

E X A M P L E 1   Verifying a Solution to an Inequality

Show that $x = 120$ is a solution to the inequality $0.2x + 15 \leq 100$.

Solution

$$0.2x + 15 \leq 100$$

$$0.2(120) + 15 \leq 100 \quad \text{Substitute } x = 120 \text{ into the inequality.}$$

$$39 \leq 100 \quad \text{39 is to the left of 100 on the number line.}$$

This confirms that $x = 120$ is a solution to the inequality. ▬

Sometimes it is convenient to combine two inequalities into one statement. For example, if $-1 \leq x$ and $x < 3$, we can write this information as the single statement

$$-1 \leq x < 3.$$

We call the set of all solutions to this double inequality an **interval** on the real-number line. Notice that -1 is included in the interval but 3 is not. This interval is said to be "closed on the left and open on the right" and is thus called a half-open interval. There are four types of **bounded intervals,** each with its own notation.

Interval Notation for Bounded Intervals

Notation	Interval Type	Inequality	Graph
$[a, b]$	Closed	$a \leq x \leq b$	
(a, b)	Open	$a < x < b$	
$[a, b)$	Half-open: closed-left, open-right	$a \leq x < b$	
$(a, b]$	Half-open: open-left, closed-right	$a < x \leq b$	

REMINDER

It is not correct to write the two inequalities $x \leq -1$ and $x > 3$ in the single statement

$$-1 \geq x > 3$$

because no real number is less than or equal to -1 and at the same time greater than 3.

An **unbounded interval** is indicated by the symbols $-\infty$ and ∞ in interval notation. For example, $(-\infty, 3]$ stands for all the numbers less than or equal to 3. In other words, $(-\infty, 3]$ represents the set of all solutions to the inequality $x \leq 3$. It is unbounded on the left and closed on the right. There are four kinds of unbounded intervals.

Interval Notation for Unbounded Intervals

Notation	Interval Type	Inequality	Graph
$(-\infty, b]$	Unbounded-left, closed	$x \leq b$	
$(-\infty, b)$	Unbounded-left, open	$x < b$	
$[a, \infty)$	Closed, unbounded-right	$a \leq x$	
(a, ∞)	Open, unbounded-right	$a < x$	

E X A M P L E   2   Writing Inequalities

Write an inequality represented by each of the following intervals:
(a) $(-3, 5]$, (b) $[-4, \infty)$ and (c) $[-8, -3]$.

Solution

a) $(-3, 5]$ represents $-3 < x \leq 5$

b) $[-4, \infty)$ represents $-4 \leq x$

c) $[-8, -3]$ represents $-8 \leq x \leq -3$

E X A M P L E   3   Number-line Graphs of Intervals

The graphs shown in the previous two boxes on interval notation are called number-line graphs. Draw number-line graphs of the solutions to the following inequalities:

(a) $x \geq 2$, (b) $x < 5$, and (c) $-1 \leq x < 3$.

Solution

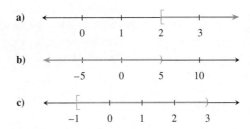

Equivalent Inequalities

To solve an inequality means to find all numbers that are solutions to the inequality. Inequalities can be solved using either algebraic or graphical methods. However, a much wider range of inequalities can be solved using a graphical method.

🔍 EXPLORE WITH A GRAPHING UTILITY

1. Find the graphs of both $y = -x^2 + 5x + 2$ and $y = 6$ in the viewing rectangle $[-2, 8]$ by $[-2, 10]$.

2. Are there any values of x for which $-x^2 + 5x + 2 \geq 6$? What characteristic of these graphs gives you an answer?

3. Trace the graph to estimate values of x that satisfy this inequality.

4. Graph $y = -x^2 + 5x - 4$ on the same viewing rectangle. How do the solutions to the inequality $-x^2 + 5x + 2 \geq 6$ compare with the interval associated with where this third graph lies above the x-axis?

Generalize   Can you formulate a procedure for solving an inequality by a graphical method that would always work?

Methods for solving inequalities algebraically are similar to those used for solving equations algebraically: Two inequalities are said to be **equivalent** if they have exactly the same set of solutions. To solve an inequality algebraically, replace the given inequality with an equivalent one that is simpler. Use any of the properties listed in Theorem 2.1 to change a given inequality to an equivalent one.

Theorem 2.1 Properties of Inequalities

Let a, b, and c be real numbers.

Addition of a number If $a < b$, then $a + c < b + c$.
Multiplication by a positive number If $a < b$ and $c > 0$, then $ac < bc$.
Multiplication by a negative number If $a < b$ and $c < 0$, then $ac > bc$.
Transitive property If $a < b$ and $b < c$, then $a < c$.

These four properties remain true when $<$ is replaced by any of the other three inequality symbols: $\leq, >$, or $\geq$.

Proof We shall prove multiplication by a negative number:

$$a < b \text{ implies that } b - a > 0 \qquad \text{Definition of } \textit{less than}$$

$$(b - a)c < 0 \qquad \text{The product of a positive and a negative is negative.}$$

$$bc - ac < 0 \qquad \text{Distributive property}$$

$$ac > bc \qquad \text{Definition of } \textit{less than}$$

Proofs of the other three properties are similar and are left as an exercise.

Definition 2.5 Linear Inequality

A **linear inequality** in x is an equality that can be written in the form

$$ax + b > 0, \qquad ax + b \geq 0, \qquad ax + b < 0, \qquad \text{or} \qquad ax + b \leq 0,$$

where a and b are real numbers and $a \neq 0$.

Examples 4 to 8 show how to solve a linear inequality.

E X A M P L E 4   Solving Inequalities Algebraically

Solve $4x - 1 < 2$ algebraically, and draw a number-line graph of the solution interval.

Solution

$$4x - 1 < 2$$

$$4x < 3 \qquad \text{Add 1 to each side.}$$

$$x < \tfrac{3}{4} \qquad \text{Divide each side by 4.}$$

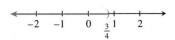

Figure 2.20 $(-\infty, \frac{3}{4})$.

The solution interval is $(-\infty, \frac{3}{4})$ which contains all real numbers less than $\frac{3}{4}$. Figure 2.20 shows the number-line graph of the solution interval. ≡

EXAMPLE 5   Solving Inequalities Algebraically (Continued)

Solve the inequality $3(x - 1) + 2 \le 5x + 6$ algebraically and draw a number-line graph of the solution.

Solution

$$3(x - 1) + 2 \le 5x + 6$$

$$3x - 3 + 2 \le 5x + 6 \quad \text{Distributive property}$$

$$3x - 1 \le 5x + 6$$

$$-2x \le 7 \quad \text{Subtract } 5x \text{ from both sides.}$$

$$x \ge -\frac{7}{2} \quad \text{Divide both sides by } -2.$$

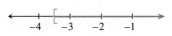

Figure 2.21 $[-3.5, \infty)$

The solution interval is $[-\frac{7}{2}, \infty)$ which contains all real numbers greater than or equal to $-\frac{7}{2}$. Figure 2.21 is the number-line graph for the solution inequality. ≡

Most linear inequalities can be solved by using the algebraic method illustrated in Examples 4 and 5.

When inequalities cannot be solved algebraically, a graphical approach can be used. One method requires rewriting the inequality so that only a zero remains on one side of the inequality. For example, rewrite $4x - 1 < 2$ as follows:

$$4x - 1 < 2 \iff 4x - 3 < 0.$$

Now graph the equation $y = 4x - 3$ and determine where the graph is *below* the x-axis.

To solve the inequality $4x - 3 > 0$ determine where the graph is *above* the x-axis.

EXAMPLE 6   Solving Inequalities Graphically: Method 1

Solve $4x - 1 < 2$ graphically.

Solution

1. Rewrite $4x - 1 < 2$ as $4x - 3 < 0$.

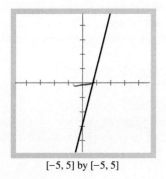

[-5, 5] by [-5, 5]

Figure 2.22 $y = 4x - 3$.

2. Find the graph of $y = 4x - 3$ in the viewing rectangle $[-5, 5]$ by $[-5, 5]$ (Fig. 2.22).

3. Determine the values of x when the graph of $y = 4x - 3$ is below the x-axis.

4. Notice that the graph of $y = 4x - 3$ appears to cross the x-axis at about $x = \frac{3}{4}$. This is easily confirmed algebraically: ($4x - 3 = 0$, so $x = \frac{3}{4}$).

5. Thus the graph of $y = 4x - 3$ lies below the x-axis when $x < \frac{3}{4}$.

The solution is the interval $(-\infty, 3/4)$.   ☰

Example 7 illustrates a second method of solving the same inequality graphically.

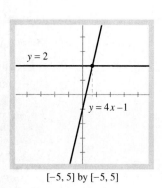

$y = 2$

$y = 4x - 1$

$[-5, 5]$ by $[-5, 5]$

Figure 2.23 $y = 2$ and $y = 4x - 1$.

SUGGESTION

Of the two graphical methods shown in Examples 6 and 7, sometimes Method 1 is preferred, and at other times Method 2 is more natural. Practice using both methods. With experience you may develop a preference.

E X A M P L E 7   Solving Inequalities Graphically: Method 2

Solve $4x - 1 < 2$ graphically by graphing both $y = 4x - 1$ and $y = 2$ on the same coordinate system.

Solution

1. Draw graphs of both $y = 4x - 1$ and $y = 2$ in the same viewing rectangle $[-5, 5]$ by $[-5, 5]$ (Fig. 2.23).

2. Identify the x-coordinates of points on the graph of $y = 4x - 1$ that lie *below* the graph of $y = 2$.

3. Note that the two graphs appear to intersect at point $(0.75, 2)$.

4. Thus the values of x where the graph of $y = 4x - 1$ is below the graph of $y = 2$ is when $x < \frac{3}{4}$.

The solution interval is $(-\infty, \frac{3}{4})$.   ☰

For a simple inequality an algebraic method may be quicker than a graphical method. However, when the inequalities are more complicated, a graphical solution is easier. Section 2.6 will show examples of situations in which a graphical solution is the only reasonable method.

E X A M P L E 8   Solving Double Inequalities

Solve

$$-3 < \frac{2x + 5}{3} \le 5$$

both algebraically and graphically.

Solution   The algebraic solution is found by applying the properties of real numbers and of inequalities until the variable remains alone in the middle expression. Note that each property or operation must be applied to all three expressions in a

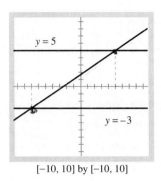

[−10, 10] by [−10, 10]

Figure 2.24 $y = (2x + 5)/3$, $y = 5$, and $y = -3$.

double inequality, not just the left-hand and right-hand sides.

$$-3 < \frac{2x + 5}{3} \leq 5$$

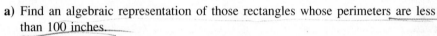

$-9 < 2x + 5 \leq 15$ Multiply each expression by 3.

$-14 < 2x \leq 10$ Add -5 in each expression.

$-7 < x \leq 5$ Multiply each expression by 1/2.

A graphical solution can be found by reproducing and analyzing the graph in Fig. 2.24. However, the fact that the endpoint $x = 5$ is a solution cannot be deduced from a graph.

E X A M P L E 9   APPLICATION: Finding a Rectangle Perimeter

Consider the set of all rectangles whose length is one unit more than twice its width.

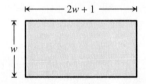

Figure 2.25   Rectangles with a length 1 unit more than twice the width w.

a) Find an algebraic representation of those rectangles whose perimeters are less than 100 inches.

b) Find the possible widths of these rectangles.

Solution   If w is the width of a rectangle, then its length is $2w + 1$ (Fig. 2.25).

a) The perimeter is $2w + 2(2w + 1)$, and an algebraic representation of the problem situation is

$$2w + 2(2w + 1) < 100.$$

b) Solve the algebraic representation to get the width.

$$2w + 4w + 2 < 100$$
$$6w + 2 < 100$$
$$6w < 98$$
$$w < \frac{49}{3}$$

The width can be any positive number less than $\frac{49}{3}$ inches. That is, it can be any number in the open interval $(0, \frac{49}{3})$.

A graphical solution can be obtained by graphing $y = 2x + 2(2x + 1)$ and $y = 100$ on the same viewing rectangle $[-20, 50]$ by $[-50, 150]$.

Exercises for Section 2.4

In Exercises 1 to 8, use the problem-solving strategy "Guessing and Testing" to find three specific values of x that are solutions to each inequality.

1. $2x - 3 < 7$ **2.** $3 - x \geq 5$

3. $0.1x + 3 < 10$ **4.** $8 \leq 2x + 4$

5. $1 \leq 2x < 5$ **6.** $1 < 3x < 9$

7. $5 \geq x - 3 \geq -1$ **8.** $12 < 4x + 3 \leq 25$

In Exercises 9 to 16, write an inequality that represents each interval.

9. $[-3, 5)$ **10.** $(-3, 7)$

11. $[2, 5]$ **12.** $(-3, -1]$

13. $(-\infty, 4)$ **14.** $[3, \infty)$

15. $(-\infty, -2]$ **16.** $(-\infty, \infty)$

In Exercises 17 to 21, use interval notation to name the intervals depicted graphically.

17.

18.

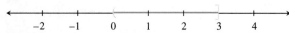

19.

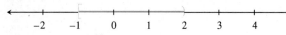

20.

21.

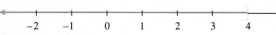

In Exercises 22 to 27, graph each interval on a number line.

22. $(-2, 5)$ **23.** $[-1, 0)$

24. $(3.5, 7]$ **25.** $(-\infty, 5)$

26. $[\frac{5}{4}, 7]$ **27.** $[-2, \infty)$

In Exercises 28 to 31, translate each English phrase into interval notation and inequality notation.

28. The set of all real numbers less than or equal to 5 and greater than 2.

29. The set of all numbers greater than 3 and less than 7.

30. The set of all numbers greater than 8.

31. The set of all numbers less than or equal to -4.

In Exercises 32 to 39, use an algebraic method to solve the inequality.

32. $2x - 1 > 4x + 3$

33. $\frac{1}{2}(x - 4) - 2x \leq 5(3 - x)$

34. $\frac{3x - 2}{5} > -1$

35. $\frac{1}{2}(x + 3) + 2(x - 4) < \frac{1}{3}(x - 3)$

36. $\frac{3 - x}{2} + \frac{5x - 2}{3} < -1$

37. $2 \leq x + 6 < 9$

38. $-1 < 3x - 2 < 7$

39. $4 \geq \frac{2x - 5}{3} \geq -2$

40. Solve the inequality $3x + 4 < 19$ graphically using Method 1 (see Example 6). That is, graph $y = 3x - 15$, and find the values of x for which the graph lies below the x-axis.

41. Solve the inequality $2x - 1 > 6$ graphically using Method 2 (Example 7). That is, graph $y = 2x - 1$ and $y = 6$ in the same viewing rectangle. Find the values for x for which the graph of $y = 2x - 1$ is *above* the graph of $y = 6$.

In Exercises 42 to 47, use an algebraic method to solve the inequality. Write your answer in interval notation. Support your solutions with a graphing utility.

42. $\frac{1}{2} < \frac{5x - 2}{6} \leq \frac{8}{3}$ **43.** $\frac{3}{x - 2} > 0$

44. $-\frac{3}{4} < \frac{3 - x}{2} < 8$ **45.** $-2(4 - \frac{x}{3}) < 3 + 5x$

46. $\frac{x + 5}{3} < 2$ **47.** $0 < \frac{2}{x + 5} < 6$

Exercises 48 to 50 refer to the following **problem situation**. Sarah has $45 to spend and wishes to take as many friends as possible to a concert. Parking is $5.75 and concert tickets are $7.50 each.

48. Let x represent the number of friends Sarah takes to the concert. Write an inequality that is an algebraic representation for this problem situation.

49. Solve the inequality in Exercise 48.

50. How many friends can Sarah take to the concert?

51. Barb wants to drive to a city 105 miles from her home in no more than 2 hours. What average speed must she drive?

52. An electrician charges $18 per hour plus $25 per service call for home repair work. How long did she work if her charges were less than $100? Assume she rounds off her time to the nearest quarter hour.

53. Consider the collection of all rectangles that have a length 2 inches less than twice the width (in inches). Find the possible widths of these rectangles if their perimeters are less than 200 inches. Solve this problem algebraically and with a graphing utility.

54. A candy company finds that the cost of making a certain candy bar is $0.23 per bar plus fixed costs of $2000 per week. If each bar sells for $0.25, find the minimum number of candy bars that must be made and sold in order for the company to make a profit.

55. *Boyle's law* for a certain gas states that $PV = 400$, where P is pressure and V is volume. If $20 \leq V \leq 40$, what is the corresponding range for P?

56. A company has current assets (cash, property, inventory, and accounts receivable) of $200,000 and current liabilities (taxes, loans, accounts payable) of $50,000. How much can they borrow if they want their ratio of assets to liabilities to be less than 2? Assume the amount borrowed is added to both current assets and current liabilities.

57. Complete a formal definition of the relation *greater than*. *Hint:* Model your definition after the definition given for *less than* in Section 1.1.

58. Prove the first, second, and fourth parts of Theorem 2.1.

59. Writing to Learn Write several paragraphs that explain how to use graphical Methods 1 and 2 to solve the inequality $3(x - 1) + 2 \leq 5x + 6$ from Example 5.

2.5 _____ Solving Inequalities Involving Absolute Value

In Section 1.1 the absolute value of a real number a, denoted $|a|$, was defined to be its distance from 0 on the real-number line. Thus a real number x is a solution to the inequality $|x| \leq 2$ if and only if the distance from the point to the origin is less than or equal to 2 (Fig. 2.26). This set of numbers is precisely all those between (and including) -2 and 2. Typically the set of all solutions to the inequality $|x| \leq 2$ can be described using either a double inequality or interval notation.

It is convenient to use the symbol $\cup$, called the **union** symbol. The notation $(a, b) \cup (c, d)$ indicates the collection of all real numbers that belong to (a, b) or (c, d) or both.

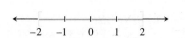

Figure 2.26 $|x| \leq 2$.

Inequalities with Absolute Value		
Inequality	**Solution Described by an Inequality**	**Solution Described in Interval Notation**
$\|x\| < a$	$-a < x < a$	$(-a, a)$
$\|x\| \leq a$	$-a \leq x \leq a$	$[-a, a]$
$\|x\| > a$	$x < -a$ or $x > a$	$(-\infty, -a) \cup (a, \infty)$
$\|x\| \geq a$	$x \leq -a$ or $x \geq a$	$(-\infty, -a] \cup [a, \infty)$

Communication in mathematics occurs with words, symbols, and pictures. Often a single idea is communicated in all three ways. The examples in this section provide practice in recognizing when words, symbols, and pictures are all communicating the idea of interval.

E X A M P L E   1   Changing Inequalities to Graphs

On a real-number line, draw the interval represented by each inequality: (a) $-3 < x < 8$, (b) $|x| \geq 2$, and (c) $|x - 3| < 3$.

Solution

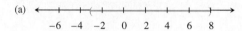

(a)
$$-6 \quad -4 \quad -2 \quad 0 \quad 2 \quad 4 \quad 6 \quad 8$$

(b)
$$-3 \quad -2 \quad -1 \quad 0 \quad 1 \quad 2 \quad 3 \quad 4$$

(c)
$$0 \quad 1 \quad 2 \quad 3 \quad 4 \quad 5 \quad 6 \quad 7$$

E X A M P L E   2   Translating from Words into Math

Use absolute value to write an inequality that represents each of the following statements:

a) x is within 4 units of the origin on the real-number line.

b) x is less than 3 units from the point 2 on the real-number line.

c) x is at least 5 units from the point -3 on the real-number line.

Solution

a) $|x| \leq 4$

b) $|x - 2| < 3$ $|x - 2|$ describes the distance between x and 2 on the real-number line.

c) $|x - (-3)| \geq 5$ $|x - (-3)|$ is the distance between x and -3.

Section 2.4 described ways to solve inequalities using both algebraic and graphical methods. Examples 3 and 4 illustrate both methods. A goal is to learn how to judge when an algebraic method is preferable to a graphical one and vice versa.

EXAMPLE 3 Comparing Algebraic and Graphical Methods

Solve $|x - 2| < 3$ both algebraically and graphically.

Solution

Algebraic Method

$$|x - 2| < 3$$

$$-3 < x - 2 < 3 \qquad \text{Convert to a double inequality to remove the absolute value symbols.}$$

$$-1 < x < 5$$

The solution is the interval $(-1, 5)$.

Graphical Method

1. Since $|x - 2| < 3$ is equivalent to $|x - 2| - 3 < 0$, find a complete graph of the equation $y = |x - 2| - 3$ (Fig. 2.27).

2. Notice that the graph appears to lie below the x-axis between the x-coordinates of -1 and 5.

3. Confirm by direct substitution that the graph crosses the x-axis at $x = -1$ and $x = 5$.

Again the solution interval is $(-1, 5)$.

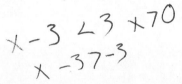

[−3, 7] by [−5, 5]

Figure 2.27 $y = |x - 2| - 3$.

EXAMPLE 4 Comparing Algebraic and Graphical Methods

Solve $|3x - 2| > 1$ both algebraically and graphically.

Solution

Algebraic Method

$$|3x - 2| > 1$$

$$3x - 2 < -1 \qquad \text{or} \qquad 3x - 2 > 1$$

$$3x < 1 \qquad \text{or} \qquad 3x > 3$$

$$x < \tfrac{1}{3} \qquad \text{or} \qquad x > 1$$

The solution is $(-\infty, \tfrac{1}{3}) \cup (1, \infty)$.

Graphical Method

1. Since $|3x - 2| > 1$ is equivalent to $|3x - 2| - 1 > 0$, find a complete graph of $y = |3x - 2| - 1$ (Fig. 2.28).

[−3, 3] by [−3, 3]

Figure 2.28 $y = |3x - 2| - 1$.

2. Notice that the graph appears to be above the x-axis when $x < \frac{1}{3}$ and also when $x > 1$.

3. Confirm by direct substitution that the graph crosses the x-axis at $x = \frac{1}{3}$ and $x = 1$.

Again the solution is $(-\infty, \frac{1}{3}) \cup (1, \infty)$.   ≡

EXAMPLE 5   Choosing the Method

Solve $|1 - 2x| \le 4$, and draw a number-line graph of the solution.

Solution   Examples 3 and 4 should convince you that the algebraic method is easier for this type of inequality.

$$|1 - 2x| \le 4$$

$$-4 \le 1 - 2x \le 4$$

$$-5 \le -2x \le 3$$

$$\frac{5}{2} \ge x \ge -\frac{3}{2} \qquad \text{Multiplying an inequality by a negative number reverses the inequality.}$$

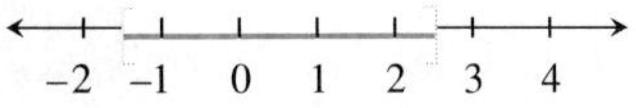

The solution is $[-\frac{3}{2}, \frac{5}{2}]$, and a number-line graph is shown in Fig. 2.29.

Although the double inequality is correct as expressed above, it is customary and helpful to reverse the signs:

$$-\frac{3}{2} \le x \le \frac{5}{2}.$$

Now the left-hand side corresponds to the left of the two numbers given in the solution interval and also to the left-hand side of the number-line graph. It is easier to avoid mistakes in both reading and constructing graphs if left and right sides of the algebraic and graphic representations match.   ≡

When faced with an unfamiliar or difficult inequality, it may not be clear how to proceed with an algebraic approach. In these cases the graphical approach may be easier. Examples 6 and 7 illustrate two, more complex inequalities.

EXAMPLE 6   Solving a More Difficult Inequality

Solve $\dfrac{x + 3}{|x - 2|} > 0$. -3

Solution   For this inequality it may be easier to begin with a graphical approach.

Graphical Method

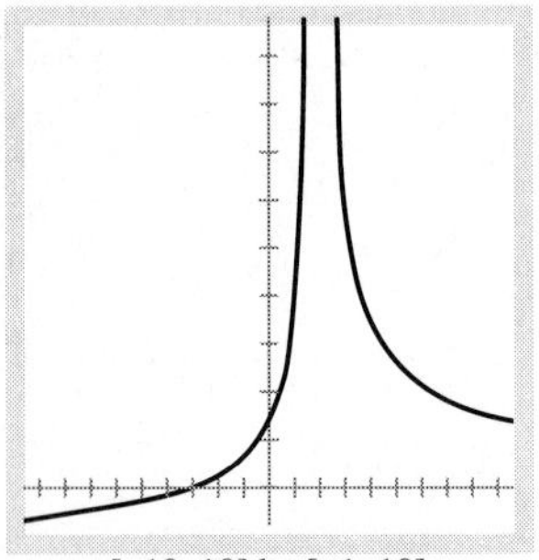

1. Graph $y = (x + 3)/|x - 2|$ in the $[-10, 10]$ by $[-1, 10]$ viewing rectangle (Fig. 2.30).

Figure 2.29 $-\frac{3}{2} \le x \le \frac{5}{2}$.

$[-10, 10]$ by $[-1, 10]$

Figure 2.30 $y = \dfrac{x + 3}{|x - 2|}$.

2. Study the graph to determine where it lies *above* the x-axis. Notice that $x = 2$ results in a zero in the denominator of the inequality, so $x = 2$ cannot be a part of the solution.

3. Notice that the graph appears to cross the x-axis at $x = -3$. Confirm this by substituting $x = -3$ into the inequality. The grapher does not visually distinguish between $>$ and $\geq$; this substitution does that.

The solution consists of all values of x greater than -3 except $x = 2$. Write this solution in interval notation as $(-3, 2) \cup (2, \infty)$.

Algebraic Method   Since the denominator of $(x + 3)/|x - 2|$ is always nonnegative, the quotient is greater than zero whenever the numerator is greater than zero and the denominator is not zero. That is, the solution to the inequality consists of all values of x such that

$$x + 3 > 0 \qquad \text{and} \qquad x - 2 \neq 0,$$

that is, $x > -3, x \neq 2$.

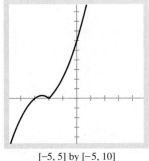

[−5, 5] by [−5, 10]

Figure 2.31 $y = (x+3)|x+2|$.

EXAMPLE 7   Using a Graphical Method

Solve $(x + 3)|x + 2| \geq 0$.

Solution

1. Find a complete graph of $y = (x + 3)|x + 2|$ in the $[-5, 5]$ by $[-5, 10]$ viewing rectangle (see Fig. 2.31).

2. Notice that the graph appears to be above the x-axis for $-3 < x < -2$ and for $x > -2$.

3. Verify by substitution that $x = -3$ and $x = -2$ are solutions to the inequality. The solution to the inequality is $[-3, \infty)$.

In this section we have seen that some inequalities can be solved by either an algebraic method or a graphical method. Even when the algebraic method is easier, the graphical method may provide additional insight.

Exercises for Section 2.5

In Exercises 1 to 8, graph each interval on a real-number line.

1. $[-4, 2)$

2. $[3, 7)$

3. $(-\infty, 3]$

4. $(-\infty, 2) \cup [5, 8)$

5. $x \leq 2$ or $x > 5$

6. $x > -3$ or $x \leq -6$

7. $x \geq -3$ and $x < 5$

8. $x \leq -1$ and $x > -3$

In Exercises 9 to 14, draw the solution to each inequality on a real-number line.

9. $|x| < 3$

10. $|x| \geq 2$

$-x < -2$
X

$x - (-2) \le 1$

11. $|x - 2| < 5$

12. $|x + 3| \le 7$

13. $|3 - x| < 1 - 3$

14. $|x - 1| > 2$

In Exercises 15 to 19, use absolute value to write an inequality that represents each statement.

15. x is within 4 units of 0 on the real-number line.

16. x is less than 2 units from 3 on the real-number line.

17. x is less than 1 unit from -2 on the real-number line.

18. x is within 5 units of 1 on the real-number line.

19. x is at least 3 units from 4 on the real-number line.

In Exercises 20 to 23, use interval notation to describe the intervals depicted graphically. You may need to use the $\cup$ symbol.

$x \le |x + (+2)|$
$x \le 3$ $|x - 1| \le 2$

20.

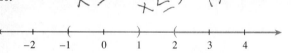

21.

22.

23.

In Exercises 24 to 27, use absolute value notation to describe the intervals depicted graphically. *Hint:* Find numbers a and b so that the solutions to $|x - a| < b$ (or similar expressions using $\le$, $>$, or $\ge$) are the indicated interval or intervals.

24.

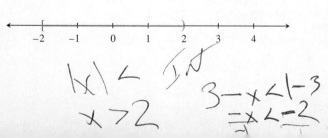

25.

$x - (-2) \le 1$

26.

27.

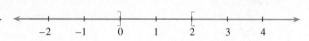

In Exercises 28 to 37, use both algebraic and graphical methods to solve the inequalities.

28. $2x - 3 \le 4$ or $x + 3 > -4$

29. $\dfrac{2x - 3}{2} < 8$ or $\dfrac{2x + 4}{3} \ge 2$

30. $|x - 3| < 2$ **31.** $|x + 3| \le 5$

32. $|x - 5| > 3$ **33.** $|x - 3| \ge 5$

34. $|3 - x| < 8$ **35.** $|2x - 8| < 20$

36. $\dfrac{3x - 8}{2} > 6$ **37.** $3|x| - 4 > 0$

In Exercises 38 to 41, choose between an algebraic method and a graphical method, and solve the inequality.

38. $x|x - 2| > 0$ **39.** $\dfrac{x - 3}{|x + 2|} < 0$

40. $\left|\dfrac{1}{x}\right| < 3$ **41.** $|x| < |x - 3|$

Exercises 42 and 43 refer to the following **problem situation**: The Celsius-to-Fahrenheit temperature conversion formula is $F = \frac{9}{5}C + 32$. Water boils when its temperature is greater than or equal to 212°F.

42. Write an inequality that describes algebraically the temperature Celsius at which water will boil.

43. Solve the inequality found in Exercise 42.

Exercises 44 to 46 refer to the following **problem situation**: The annual profit P of a candy manufacturer is determined by the formula $P = R - C$, where R is the total revenue generated from selling x pounds of candy, and C is the total cost of making and distributing x pounds of candy. Each

$|x| < \text{JN}$
$x > 2$

$3 - x < 1 - 3$
$-x < -2$

$-3 + x < 1$
$3 - x > -1$
$-x > -4 \quad x < 4$

pound of candy sells for $1.80 and costs $1.38 to make. The fixed costs of making and distributing the candy are $20,000 annually.

44. Write an algebraic representation of the company's annual profit in terms of x.

45. Write an algebraic representation for the number of pounds of candy that must be produced and sold for the company to make a profit.

46. Use a graphing utility to find the production level that will yield a profit for the year.

In Exercises 47 to 49, use any method to solve the inequality:

47. $|x| - |8 - x| > 0$

48. $|x + 3| < |x|$

49. $|x + 5| > |x|$

Exercises 50 to 53 refer to the equation $y = 3x - 5$.

50. Write intervals equivalent to the following inequalities:
 a) $|x - 2| < 0.1$ b) $|y - 1| < 0.3$

51. On the x-axis draw a number-line graph of the solution to $|x - 2| < 0.1$.

52. On the y-axis draw a number-line graph of the solution to $|y - 1| < 0.3$.

53. Find all values of $d > 0$ such that, if $|x - 2| < d$, then $|y - 1| < 0.01$.

2.6 _____

Solving Higher-Order Inequalities Algebraically and Graphically

In this section we illustrate that a graphing method with a graphing utility is nearly always more reasonable than using an algebraic method for solving higher-order inequalities.

Projectile motion is a frequently studied problem situation in physical science. Consider the following common problem situation and its algebraic representation.

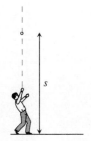

Figure 2.32 Distance s of an object above ground level at time t.

Projectile Motion

An object is thrown straight up from a point s_0 feet above ground level with an initial velocity of v_0. If s represents the distance in feet of the object above ground level t seconds after it is thrown, then we know from physics that $s = -16t^2 + v_0 t + s_0$. See Fig. 2.32.

E X A M P L E   1   Solving Projectile Motion Problems Graphically

Suppose a baseball is thrown straight up from ground level with an initial velocity of 80 feet per second. When will the baseball be at least 64 feet above the ground?

Solution   Since the ball is thrown from the ground, $s_0 = 0$. The initial velocity is $v_0 = 80$. The algebraic representation of this problem is

$$s = -16t^2 + 80t.$$

Since we want to find out when $s \geq 64$, we must solve the inequality $-16t^2 + 80t \geq 64$.

1. Graph $s = -16t^2 + 80t$ and $s = 64$ in the same viewing rectangle and determine the values of t for which the graph of $s = -16t^2 + 80t$ lies above the graph of $s = 64$.

2. Figure 2.33(a) shows complete graphs of both algebraic representations of s. Figure 2.33(b) shows a complete graph of the problem situation since t is non-negative and t cannot be greater than 5. Can you explain why t cannot be greater than 5?

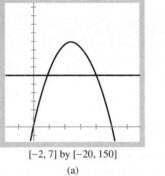
[−2, 7] by [−20, 150]
(a)

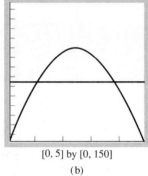
[0, 5] by [0, 150]
(b)

Figure 2.33   Two views of $s = -16t^2 + 80t$ and $s = 64$.

3. It appears that $s \geq 64$ (in other words, that the baseball is at least 64 feet above the ground) when $1 \leq t \leq 4$.

4. We can verify by direct substitution that $s = 64$ when $t = 1$ or $t = 4$.

$$\text{For } t = 1: \quad -16(1)^2 + 80(1) = -16 + 80 = 64.$$

$$\text{For } t = 4: \quad -16(4)^2 + 80(4) = -16(16) + 80(4)$$

$$= -256 + 320 = 64.$$

For the sake of comparing methods, Example 2 uses an algebraic method.

E X A M P L E   2   Solving Projectile Motion Problems Algebraically

Use an algebraic method to answer these questions:

a) How long does the baseball in Example 1 stay in the air?

b) When is the ball at least 64 feet off the ground?

Solution

a)
$$-16t^2 + 80t \geq 0$$

$$-16t(t - 5) \geq 0$$

$t \geq 0$ and $t - 5 \leq 0$ From the context of the problem $t > 0$, in order for the product to be positive, $t - 5 < 0$.

The baseball is in the air when $0 < t < 5$, so it is in the air **5 seconds**.

b)
$$-16t^2 + 80t \geq 64$$

$$-16t^2 + 80t - 64 \geq 0$$

$t^2 - 5t + 4 \leq 0$ Multiplying the inequality by $-\frac{1}{16}$ reverses the inequality.

$(t - 1)(t - 4) \leq 0$ This product is less than or equal to zero whenever it is not positive, that is, whenever $t \leq 4$ and $t \geq 1$. So the solution to this inequality is $[1, 4]$.

The baseball is at least 64 feet off the ground if $1 \leq t \leq 4$.   ≡

Sign Pattern

The problem-solving strategy "Study the Pattern" can be used to advantage to solve algebraically an inequality like $(t - 1)(t - 4) \leq 0$. Every linear factor is zero for exactly one value. For example, $t - 1$ is zero for $t = 1$. So when $t < 1$, the factor $t - 1 < 0$ is negative, and when $t > 1$, the factor $t - 1 > 0$ is positive.

It is convenient to record this information in a **sign-pattern picture**:

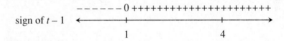

In a similar fashion we determine the sign of $t - 4$. Since the product $(t - 1)(t - 4)$ is positive whenever both factors are positive or both negative, we can see with a glance at the following graphic when $(t - 1)(t - 4)$ is positive. Similarly we can see when the product is negative.

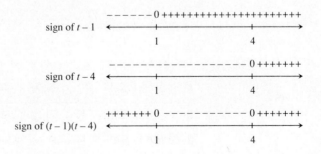

We see from this sign-pattern picture that $(t-1)(t-4) \leq 0$ when $1 \leq t \leq 4$. We say that a solution to the inequality is the interval $[1, 4]$. A sign-pattern picture like the one illustrated here can be used *whenever an expression can be factored into factors with known signs*.

The next three examples illustrate the use of sign-pattern pictures to solve an inequality algebraically.

E X A M P L E   3   Using a Sign Pattern for Two Factors

Use a sign-pattern picture to solve $2x^2 + 9x - 5 > 0$. Support your solution graphically.

Solution $2x^2 + 9x - 5 = (2x - 1)(x + 5) = 0$ if and only if $x = \frac{1}{2}$ or $x = -5$.

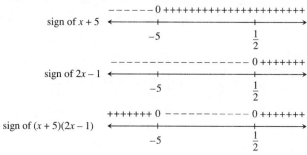

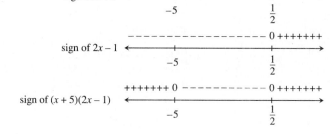

The solution to the inequality $2x^2 + 9x - 5 > 0$ is $(-\infty, -5) \cup (\frac{1}{2}, \infty)$. This is supported graphically by finding a complete graph of $y = 2x^2 + 9x - 5$ (see Fig. 2.34). ≣

[−10, 10] by [−50, 100]

Figure 2.34 $y = 2x^2 + 9x - 5$.

This method of using sign-pattern pictures can also be used when there are more than two factors. As the number of factors increases, the number of intervals in the picture increases.

E X A M P L E   4   Using a Sign Pattern for Three Factors

Solve $x(x + 3)(x - 1) \geq 0$ algebraically. Check your answer graphically.

Solution $x(x + 3)(x - 1) = 0$ when $x = 0, -3$, or 1.

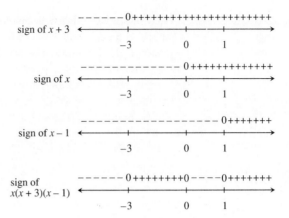

$$-------0+++++++++++++++++++++++$$
sign of $x + 3$ ⟵ ——————|——————|——————|——————⟶
$\qquad\qquad\qquad\qquad\quad -3 \qquad\quad 0 \qquad\quad 1$

$$--------------0++++++++++++++$$
sign of x ⟵ ——————|——————|——————|——————⟶
$\qquad\qquad\qquad\qquad\quad -3 \qquad\quad 0 \qquad\quad 1$

$$----------------- 0+++++++$$
sign of $x - 1$ ⟵ ——————|——————|——————|——————⟶
$\qquad\qquad\qquad\qquad\quad -3 \qquad\quad 0 \qquad\quad 1$

sign of
$x(x + 3)(x - 1)$
$$------0++++++++0----0+++++++$$
⟵ ——————|——————|——————|——————⟶
$\qquad\qquad\qquad\qquad\quad -3 \qquad\quad 0 \qquad\quad 1$

The solution to $x(x + 3)(x - 1) \geq 0$ is $[-3, 0] \cup [1, \infty)$. This conclusion is supported graphically by finding a complete graph of $y = x(x + 3)(x - 1)$ (see Fig. 2.35). The graph is on or above the x-axis when $-3 \leq x \leq 0$ or $x \geq 1$.

This next example illustrates that the method of a sign-pattern picture can be used for quotients of polynomials also.

E X A M P L E   5   Using a Sign Pattern for a Quotient

Use a sign-pattern picture to solve

$$\frac{x - 4}{2x + 5} \leq 0.$$

Solution   The numerator equals zero when $x = 4$, and the denominator equals zero when $x = -\frac{5}{2}$.

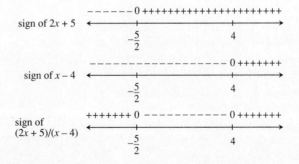

$$------0 ++++++++++++++++++++++$$
sign of $2x + 5$ ⟵ ——————|——————|——————⟶
$\qquad\qquad\qquad\qquad -\frac{5}{2} \qquad\qquad 4$

$$---------------- 0+++++++$$
sign of $x - 4$ ⟵ ——————|——————|——————⟶
$\qquad\qquad\qquad\qquad -\frac{5}{2} \qquad\qquad 4$

sign of
$(2x + 5)/(x - 4)$
$$+++++++ 0 ----------- 0+++++++$$
⟵ ——————|——————|——————⟶
$\qquad\qquad\qquad\qquad -\frac{5}{2} \qquad\qquad 4$

The solution to the inequality is $(-2.5, 4]$. Notice that -2.5 is not included in the solution. Why?

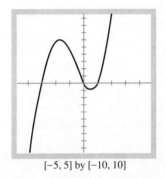

[-5, 5] by [-10, 10]

Figure 2.35 $y = x(x+3)(x-1)$.

This next example is an important one in the section since the expression cannot be factored over the rationals. It illustrates both the power of the graphical method and the limitation of an algebraic method. In solving real-world problems, it is extremely rare to find an inequality in which the expression can be factored algebraically; hence there will be few opportunities to apply the sign-pattern method. The graphical method is the most universal means of solving inequalities.

Example 6 uses zoom-in to determine the endpoints of the intervals in the solution. Recall that a grapher cannot distinguish between the signs $>$ and $\geq$ when solving an inequality. Therefore it is important to include the endpoints of intervals when solving a $\geq$ inequality and to omit the endpoints when solving a $>$ inequality.

EXAMPLE 6   Using a Graphical Method

Solve $x^3 - 2x^2 - 5x + 7 \geq 2x + 1$.

Solution

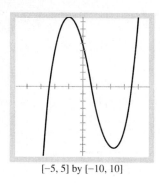

[−5, 5] by [−10, 10]

Figure 2.36 $y = x^3 - 2x^2 - 7x + 6$.

1. The inequalities
$$x^3 - 2x^2 - 5x + 7 \geq 2x + 1 \qquad \text{and} \qquad x^3 - 2x^2 - 7x + 6 \geq 0$$
are equivalent. So find a complete graph of $y = x^3 - 2x^2 - 7x + 6$ (see Fig. 2.36).

2. Use zoom-in to find the three x-intercepts, which are $-2.263, 0.756$, and 3.507. The solutions to the equation with an error of at most 0.01 are $-2.26, 0.76$, and 3.51.

3. Solutions to the inequality coincide with intervals on which the graph is above the x-axis. Therefore the solution is $[-2.26, 0.76] \cup [3.51, \infty)$. ▤

Exercises for Section 2.6

Exercises 1 to 3 refer to the baseball throw described in Example 1, whose algebraic representation is $s = -16t^2 + 80t$.

1. For how many seconds will the ball be at least 64 feet above the ground?

2. Write an equation that could be used to find how long (in seconds) the ball is in the air.

3. Write an inequality that could be solved to find when the ball is
   a) more than 10 feet off the ground;
   b) at least 10 feet off the ground.

4. If a baseball is thrown straight up from ground level at an initial velocity of 48 feet per second, what is the algebraic

representation for the distance above the ground?

5. If a baseball is thrown straight up from a platform that is 120 feet above the ground with an initial velocity of 32 feet per second, what is the algebraic representation for the distance above the ground?

In Exercises 6 to 15, write the intervals that should be used when completing a sign-pattern picture for each inequality.

6. $(x - 3)(x + 2) \geq 0$ 7. $(x + 5)(x + 6) < 0$

8. $x^2 + 4x + 3 > 0$ 9. $(x + 3)(x - 2)(x + 5) < 0$

10. $(x - 4)(x^2 - x - 6) \leq 0$ 11. $x^2 - 6x + 10 \geq 2$

12. $(3 - x)(x + 2)(x - 5) \geq 0$

13. $(x^2 - 1)(x^2 - 4) > 0$

14. $(x - 2)(x + 3)^2 < 0$

15. $(x - 3)(x^2 + 2x - 1) \geq 0$

In Equations 16 to 19, write an equation that you could graph in order to solve the given inequality graphically.

16. $x^2 - 3x + 2 \geq -3$

17. $7x^3 - 2x^2 > 5x - 3$

18. $x^2 - 5x - 17 \geq -2x + 1$

19. $x^5 - 4x^2 > 2x^2 + x + 3$

In Exercises 20 to 27, use a sign-pattern picture to solve each inequality. Write the solution in interval notation.

20. $(x - 1)(x + 2) < 0$ **21.** $x(x - 3) \leq 0$

22. $x^2 - 5x + 6 \geq 0$ **23.** $x^2 - 4x - 21 < 0$

24. $2x^2 + 5x \geq 3$ **25.** $x^2 < x$

26. $\dfrac{x + 3}{x - 1} \geq 0$ **27.** $x(x - 4)(x + 2) \geq 0$

In Exercises 28 to 31, use a graphical method to solve each inequality.

28. $3x^3 - 8x^2 - 5x + 6 \leq 0$

29. $x^3 - 9x^2 + 6x + 55 < 0$

30. $|x^2 - 1|(x - 2) \geq 3$

31. $5 \sin x < 2$ for $0 \leq x \leq 10$

In Exercises 32 to 39, decide whether you prefer the sign-pattern method or a graphical method and solve each inequality.

32. $(x - 2)^3 > 0$ **33.** $(x + 1)(x - 2)(x + 4) < 0$

34. $x^4 + 3x^2 < 4$ **35.** $\dfrac{x + 3}{x - 1} < 0$

36. $x^2 - 5x + 3 > 0$ **37.** $2 - 8x + 3x^2 \leq 0$

38. $3x^2 - x + 6 \leq 2x^3 - x^2 + 3x - 4$

39. $2x + 1 > x^3 + 2x^2 - 3x + 5$

Exercises 40 to 43 refer to the following projectile-motion **problem situation**, whose algebraic representation is $s = -16t^2 + v_0t + s_0$. Suppose an object is propelled upward from a tower 200 feet tall with an initial velocity of 100 feet per second.

40. Write an equation that is an algebraic representation for the question, When will the object hit the ground?

41. Find a complete graph of the problem situation. How does this graph compare with a complete graph of the algebraic representation in Exercise 40?

42. For how long will the object be above the ground?

43. When will the object hit the ground?

44. Answer the questions of Exercises 40 to 43 if the object is propelled straight upward from a tower 155 feet tall with an initial velocity of 275 feet per second.

Exercises 45 to 47 refer to the following **problem situation**: A swimming pool with dimensions of 20 feet by 30 feet is surrounded by a sidewalk of uniform width x. Find the possible widths of the sidewalk if the total area of the sidewalk is to be greater than 200 square feet but less than 360 square feet.

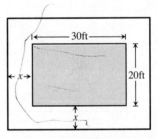

For Exercises 45 to 47

45. Write an equation that gives the area of the sidewalk in terms of x.

46. Write an inequality that is an algebraic representation of this problem situation.

47. Choose a method and find a solution to the problem situation.

Exercises 48 and 49 refer to the following **problem situation**: An investor can earn interest using the simple interest formula $S = P(1 + rn)$, where r is the interest rate, n is the number of years, P is the amount invested, and S is the total amount in the account. The investor wants to accumulate at least $30,000 in 18 years by investing $5,000 today. What interest rate is required for the investor to meet his goal?

48. Write an inequality that describes this problem situation.

49. Find a complete graph of each side of the inequality in Exercise 48 in the same viewing rectangle, and determine a solution to the problem situation.

50. Equal squares are removed from the four corners of a 22-by-29-inch rectangular sheet of cardboard. The sides are turned up to make a box with no lid. Find the possible lengths of the sides of the removed squares if the volume of the box is to be less than 2000 cubic inches.

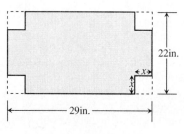

29in.

For Exercise 50

Exercises 51 and 52 refer to the following **problem situation**: Sam makes two initial investments of $1,000 each. The first

earns 10% simple interest: after n years its value is $S = 1000(1 + 0.10n)$. The second investment earns interest using 5% *simple discount*: after n years its value is $S = 1000/(1 - 0.05n)$.

51. Find a complete graph of each algebraic representation in the viewing rectangle $[0, 30]$ by $[0, 6000]$ and determine whether there is a time when both investments are equal.

52. Is there a period of time when the value of the simple-interest investment is less than the value of the simple-discount investment?

In Exercises 53 to 55, decide if each inequality is true for (a) some values of x, (b) all values of x, or (c) no values of x:

53. $|x + (5)| \leq |x| + |5|$

54. $|x + (-3)| \leq |x| + |-3|$

55. $|x + (-7)| \leq |x| + |-7|$

56. Generalize   Decide whether $|a + b| \leq |a| + |b|$ is true for all real-number values of a and b.

Chapter 2 Review

KEY TERMS

bounded interval	equivalent equations	quadratic equation in x	solution with error of
complete graph of	equivalent inequalities	quadratic formula	at most r
the algebraic	identity	radical	third-degree polynomial
representation	interval	root	unbounded interval
complete graph of the	linear equation in x	sign-pattern picture	union
problem situation	linear inequality	solution to an equation	x-intercept
completing the square	parabola	in x	zero
conditional equation	perfect square	solution to an inequality	zoom-in
discriminant	polynomial equation		

REVIEW EXERCISES

In Exercises 1 to 6, use an algebraic method to solve each equation. Check your answers by substitution into the original equation.

1. $\frac{1}{3}x + 2 = 3x + \frac{1}{5}$

2. $3(2 - x) - 2(3x + 7) = x + 2$

3. $x^2 - 4x - 21 = 0$ **4.** $x^2 - 3x - 28 = 0$

5. $2x^4 - 4x^2 - 6 = 0$ **6.** $|2 - 3x| = 7$

In Exercises 7 to 10, use a number line to graph each interval.

7. $(-3, 5]$ **8.** $[-5, -2]$

9. $-2 \leq x < 7$ **10.** $(-\infty, -3)$

In Exercises 11 to 18, use a number line to graph solutions to each inequality.

11. $|x - 3| < 5$ **12.** $|4 - x| < 7$

13. $|2x - 3| < 1$ **14.** $|3x + 2| \leq 3$

15. $|x + 4| \geq 2$

16. $|2x - 3| > 5$

17. $|5x - 1| < |-3|$

18. $|2x - \sqrt{3}| < \sqrt{7}$

In Exercises 19 to 22, use an algebraic method to solve each equation. Support each answer with a graphing utility.

19. $x^2 = 6$

20. $x^2 - 2x - 8 = 0$

21. $2x^2 - 3x - 7 = 0$

22. $x^2 + 3x - 8 = 0$

In Exercises 23 to 26, use a graphical method to solve each equation.

23. $4x^2 - 5x - 3 = 0$

24. $2x - 3x^2 + 15 = 0$

25. $x^2 - 3 - \sqrt{x} = 0$

26. $3x^2 - 17x - 39 = 0$

In Exercises 27 to 36, solve each equation. Use whatever method is preferred.

27. $3x^2 - 4x + 2 = 0$

28. $2x^3 - 4x + 7 = 0$

29. $4x^3 - 3x + 1 = 0$

30. $2x^3 - 6x^2 + 7x - 5 = 0$

31. $2x^3 - 4x^2 + 3x - 9 = 0$

32. $x^3 - 31x + 2 = 0$

33. $x^3 - 5x = 1/x$

34. $x^2 - 3x = \sqrt{x}$

35. $x^3 + 5x - 3 = 2\sqrt{x}$

36. $4x^3 + 60x^2 - 103x - 65 = 0$

In Exercises 37 to 42, use an algebraic method to solve each inequality. Write your answers in interval notation, and support your answers with a graphing utility.

37. $3x + 5 \leq x - 4$

38. $\dfrac{x - 1}{2} - \dfrac{2x + 1}{5} > 1$

39. $\dfrac{1}{4} \leq \dfrac{4x - 1}{12} < \dfrac{11}{6}$

40. $|3x - 2| \geq 7$

41. $5|x| + 3 < 2$

42. $\dfrac{3x + 6}{|x + 1|} \geq 0$

In Exercises 43 to 54, use a sign-pattern picture to solve each inequality. Write the solution in interval notation, and support your answers with a graphing utility.

43. $(x - 4)(x + 1) \geq 0$

44. $(x - 2)(x + 3) < 0$

45. $(x + 3)(x + 7) \geq 0$

46. $(x - 8)(x + 5) > 0$

47. $x^2 - 5x + 6 \geq 0$

48. $x^2 + 20 < x$

49. $x(x + 2)(2x - 3) > 0$

50. $\dfrac{4x + 8}{x + 5} > 0$

51. $10 + x - 2x^2 < 0$

52. $|x - 1|(2x - 4) \leq 0$

53. $\dfrac{4x - 8}{x + 5} < 0$

54. $\dfrac{5 - 3x}{x - 1} \geq 0$

In Equations 55 to 58, solve each inequality. Use whatever method is preferred.

55. $3x^2 - 5x + 1 \geq 0$

56. $x^3 - 4x^2 - 2x + 3 < 0$

57. $2x^2 + x - 6 \leq x^3 - x^2 + 4x$

58. $\sqrt{x + 2} > 1 - x$

59. Consider the equation $3x^3 + 8x^2 + 24x - 9 = 0$. It has one real-number solution. Find a sequence of four viewing rectangles containing the solution. The first viewing rectangle should permit the solution to be read with error of at most 0.1, the second 0.01, the third 0.001, and the last 0.0001.

60. The owner of Christine's Crewel Craft Center pays $1500 per month for fixed expenses such as rent, lights, and wages. Craft kits are sold at $22 each, and $15 is required for material, floss, needle, and instructions for each kit. How many kits must be sold to break even?

61. A storage box with a height of 25 cm has a volume of 10,500 cm³. Let x be the length of the box in centimeters and y the width in centimeters. Find the algebraic representation for the width y in terms of the length x. What is the length when the width is 12 cm?

62. Three-hundred twenty-five tickets were sold for a movie. There were two ticket prices: adults at $5.50 and children at $3.00. How many tickets of each type were sold if the total proceeds from the sale of the tickets were $1500?

63. The total value of 23 coins consisting of pennies, nickels, and dimes is $1.51. If there are twice as many dimes as pennies, determine the number of pennies, nickels, and dimes.

64. Sandy can swim 1 mile upstream (against the current) in 20 minutes. She can swim the same distance downstream in 9 minutes. Find Sandy's swimming speed and the speed of the current, if both speeds are constant.

65. The length of a certain rectangle is 5 inches greater than its width. Find the possible widths of the rectangle if its perimeter is less than 300 inches.

66. A single-commodity open market is driven by the supply-and-demand principle. Economists have determined that supply curves are usually increasing (that is, as the price increases, the sellers increase production). For the supply equation $p = 0.003x + 2$, find the price p if the production level is 2000 units.

Exercises 67 to 69 refer to the following **problem situation**: A farmer has 530 yards of fence to use to make a rectangular corral.

67. If x is the length of such a rectangle, show that $A = x(265 - x)$ is an algebraic representation of the area in terms of x. Find a complete graph of this model.

68. Verify that $(100, 16{,}500)$ is a point on the graph found in Exercise 67. What meaning do these coordinates have in this problem situation?

69. Verify that $(-100, -36{,}500)$ is a point on the graph in Exercise 67. What meaning do these coordinates have in this problem situation?

Exercises 70 to 72 refer to the following **problem situation**: A picture frame's outside dimensions measures 16 inches by 20 inches. The picture will be surrounded by a mat with a uniform border. The distance from the edge of the frame to the picture is x inches on all sides.

70. Find an algebraic representation for the area A of the picture in terms of x, and find a complete graph of this algebraic representation.

71. What values of x make sense in this problem situation?

72. Use a graphing utility to estimate the width of the uniform border if the area of the picture is 250 square inches.

Exercises 73 and 74 refer to the following **problem situation**: Chris has \$36 to spend on a pizza party for herself and her friends. Each pizza costs \$8.50 and serves two.

73. Let x represent the number of friends Chris can invite. Write an inequality that is an algebraic representation for this problem situation.

74. Solve the inequality found in Exercise 73 and find how many friends Chris can invite.

Exercises 75 to 77 refer to the following **problem situation**: A publishing company prints x books each week at a total cost $C = (x - 100)^2 + 400$ (in dollars). The company receives \$15.25 for each book sold. Assume all books printed are sold.

75. Find an algebraic representation expressing the weekly profit of the company as a function of x, and find a complete graph of this algebraic model.

76. What portion of the graph in Exercise 75 is a graph of the problem situation?

77. Use the graph in Exercise 75 to determine what level of weekly production the company must maintain to break even.

Exercises 78 to 80 refer to the following **problem situation**: The annual profit P of a candy manufacturer is determined by the formula $P = R - C$, where R is the total revenue generated from selling x pounds of candy, and C is the total cost of making and selling x pounds of candy. Each pound of candy sells for \$5.15 and costs \$1.26 to make. The fixed costs of making and selling the candy are \$34,000 annually.

78. Find an algebraic representation for the company's annual profit in terms of x, the number of pounds of candy made and sold.

79. Write an inequality that represents a company profit of at least \$42,000 per year. Solve this problem both algebraically and graphically.

80. How many pounds of candy must be produced and sold for the company to make a profit of at least \$42,000 for the year?

Exercises 81 to 83 refer to the following **problem situation**: A park with dimensions of 125 feet by 230 feet is surrounded by a sidewalk of uniform width x.

81. Find an algebraic representation for the area of the sidewalk in terms of the width x of the sidewalk.

82. Write an inequality that describes the situation in which the area of the sidewalk is greater than 2900 square feet but less than 3900 square feet.

83. Solve the inequality in Exercise 82 graphically to determine possible sidewalk widths that meet the conditions of this problem situation.

Exercises 84 to 86 refer to the following **problem situation**: An object 30 feet above level ground is shot straight up with an initial velocity of 250 feet per second.

84. Find an algebraic representation for the height of the object above the ground in terms of t.

85. Draw a complete graph of the algebraic representation in Exercise 84, and indicate what portion of the graph represents the problem situation.

86. At what time t will the object be 550 feet above the ground?

87. Use the distance-formula representation of absolute values to solve $|x - 6| - |x| > 0$.

3

Functions and Graphs

$C = ($

Graphs of Relations

An equation or an inequality in x and y defines a **relation in x and y.** If a pair of numbers (x, y) satisfies the equation or the inequality, we say that the numbers are **related** or are **in the relation**. Otherwise they are not related or are not in the relation.

For example, the equations below show that the pair $(-3, 4)$ is in the relation $x^2 + y^2 = 25$ whereas the pair $(2, 7)$ is not.

$$(-3)^2 + (4)^2 = 9 + 16 = 25 \qquad \text{The pair } (-3, 4) \text{ satisfies the equation.}$$

$$2^2 + 7^2 = 4 + 49 \neq 25 \qquad \text{The pair } (2, 7) \text{ does not satisfy the equation.}$$

Similarly, the pair $(2, \sqrt{3})$ is in the relation $x^2 - y^2 = 1$ and the pair $(3, 4)$ is not.

$$2^2 - (\sqrt{3})^2 = 4 - 3 = 1$$

$$3^2 - 4^2 = 9 - 16 \neq 1$$

EXAMPLE 1   Checking Number Pairs in a Relation

For $x^2y + y^2 = 5$, show (a) that $(2, -5)$ is in the relation and (b) that $(1, 3)$ is not in the relation.

Solution

a) Check $(2, -5)$:

$$x^2y + y^2 = 5$$

$$(2^2)(-5) + (-5)^2 \stackrel{?}{=} 5 \qquad \text{Substitute } x = 2 \text{ for } x \text{ and } y = -5 \text{ for } y.$$

$$-20 + 25 = 5. \qquad \text{The sum is 5. It checks.}$$

b) Check $(1, 3)$:

$$x^2y + y^2 = 5$$

$$(1)^2(3) + (3)^2 \stackrel{?}{=} 5 \qquad \text{Substitute } x = 1 \text{ and } y = 3 \text{ into the equation.} \\ \text{Check whether the equation is true.}$$

$$3 + 9 \neq 5.$$

Thus $(2, -5)$ is in the relation, but $(1, 3)$ is not.

Graph of a Relation

The **graph of a relation** consists of all points in the rectangular coordinate plane whose coordinates satisfy the condition that defines the relation.

To graph a relation by the traditional method of point plotting, complete a table of number pairs that satisfy the equation. Then graph these number pairs and connect the points with a smooth curve.

For example, consider the equation $y^2 = x$. Substitute values for x and find approximate corresponding y-values, as shown here:

x	0	0.5	1	1.5	2	2.5	3	4	5
y	0	±0.7	±1	±1.2	±1.4	±1.6	±1.7	±2	±2.2

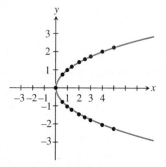

Figure 3.1   The relation $y^2 = x$ plotted from a table of (x, y)-values.

Then graph these points and connect them as shown in Fig. 3.1. The technology of graphing utilities reduces the importance of this traditional graphing method.

Figure 3.2 shows several relations and their graphs.

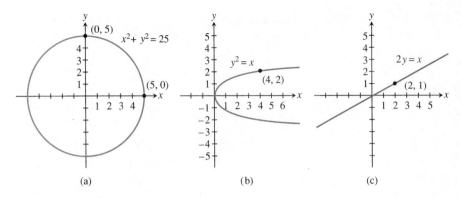

Figure 3.2   (a) A circle, (b) a parabola, and (c) a straight line.

GRAPHER UPDATE

1. To graph $y^2 = x$, graph the pair of equations $y = \sqrt{x}$ and $y = -\sqrt{x}$ in the same viewing rectangle.

2. To graph $x^2 + y^2 = 25$, graph $y = \sqrt{25 - x^2}$ and $y = -\sqrt{25 - x^2}$ together.

Intercepts of a Graph

Chapter 2 introduced the concept of x-intercept. An **intercept** of the graph of an equation is a point that lies on both the graph and one of the coordinate axes. Intercepts are among the easiest points on a graph to identify. Following is a more formal definition than the one given in Chapter 2.

Definition 3.1   Intercepts

A point $(a, 0)$ is called an **x-intercept** of the graph of an equation if the number pair $(a, 0)$ satisfies the equation.

A point $(0, b)$ is called a **y-intercept** of the graph of an equation if the number pair $(0, b)$ satisfies the equation.

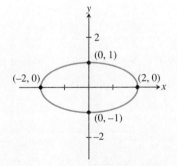

Figure 3.3 $x^2 + 4y^2 = 4$. Note the x- and y-intercepts.

In Fig. 3.3 the intercepts are highlighted. Strictly speaking the x- and y-intercepts refer to the *points* $(a, 0)$ and $(0, b)$, as given in Definition 3.1. However, it is convenient to abbreviate and speak of the x-intercept as a and the y-intercept as b. We will refer to intercepts both ways in this text.

E X A M P L E   2   Finding Intercepts

The graph of the relation $x^2 + 4y^2 = 4$ is shown in Fig. 3.3. Find the x and y intercepts of the graph.

Solution

a) Let $y = 0$ and solve for x.

$$x^2 + 4(0)^2 = 4$$

$$x^2 = 4$$

$$x = \pm 2$$

The points $(-2, 0)$ and $(2, 0)$ are x-intercepts.

b) Let $x = 0$ and solve for y.

$$(0)^2 + 4y^2 = 4$$

$$y = \pm 1$$

The points $(0, -1)$ and $(0, 1)$ are y-intercepts.   ≡

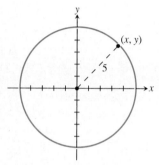

Figure 3.4   Circle with center $(0, 0)$ and a radius of 5.

Equations of Circles

Suppose that a point (x, y) in the coordinate plane has a distance 5 units from the origin (Fig. 3.4). From the distance formula we see that

$$\sqrt{(x - 0)^2 + (y - 0)^2} = 5$$

$$x^2 + y^2 = 25.$$

Consequently each point 5 units from the origin has coordinates (x, y), which are in the relation $x^2 + y^2 = 25$. So the graph of the relation $x^2 + y^2 = 25$ is the circle centered at the origin with a radius of 5.

Suppose the point (h, k) is the center of a circle of radius r (Fig. 3.5).   If (x, y) is a typical point on the circle, then the distance formula yields the equation

$$\sqrt{(x - h)^2 + (y - k)^2} = r.$$

By squaring both sides we obtain the following:

$$(x - h)^2 + (y - k)^2 = r^2.$$

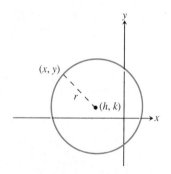

Figure 3.5   Circle with center (h, k) and radius r.

Standard Form of the Equation of a Circle

For a circle with center (h, k) and radius r, the standard equation is

$$(x - h)^2 + (y - k)^2 = r^2.$$

E X A M P L E   3   Finding the Standard Equation of a Circle

Find an equation of the circle with center $(-4, 1)$ and a radius of 8.

Solution

$$(x - h)^2 + (y - k)^2 = r^2$$

$$(x - (-4))^2 + (y - 1)^2 = 8^2 \qquad \text{To get the standard form,}$$
$$\text{substitute } h = -4, \ k = 1, \text{ and } r = 8.$$

$$(x + 4)^2 + (y - 1)^2 = 64$$

Symmetry of Graphs

The graphs of some relations possess **symmetry**. One type of symmetry is called reflectional symmetry. This means that one-half of the graph is a mirror image of the other half. Often a mirror image can be found by mentally folding the coordinate plane so that one-half of the graph folds to exactly coincide with the other half. The line where this fold occurs is called a **line of symmetry,** and the process of rotation about this line is called **reflection**.

A graph with reflectional symmetry may have only one line of reflectional symmetry, or it may have two or more. For example, in Fig. 3.1 the x-axis is the line of symmetry, in Fig. 3.3 the x- and y-axes are both lines of symmetry, and in Fig. 3.4 all the lines passing through the origin are lines of symmetry.

The graph in Fig. 3.6(a) is symmetric about the y-axis because the point $(-x, y)$ lies on the graph of $y = x^2$ whenever (x, y) does. Similarly, Fig. 3.6(b) is symmetric about the x-axis, since the point $(x, -y)$ lies on the graph of $y^2 = x$ whenever (x, y) does.

Figure 3.6(c) is an interesting case. Notice that there are no lines of symmetry. That is, there is no way to fold the coordinate plane and have one-half of the graph exactly coincide with the other half. However, there is another type of symmetry called symmetry about the origin. Algebraically we say that Fig. 3.6(c) is symmetric about the origin since the point $(-x, -y)$ lies on the graph of $y = x^3 + x$ whenever (x, y) does.

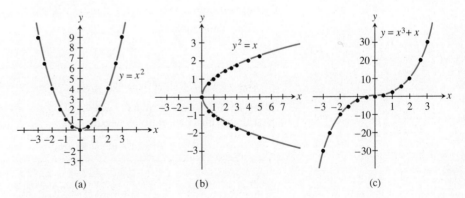

Figure 3.6 Three kinds of symmetry: (a) about the y-axis; (b) about the x-axis; (c) about the origin.

The three examples in Fig. 3.6 motivate the following algebraic definitions of symmetry:

Definition 3.2 Symmetry about Coordinate Axes and Origin

- A graph is **symmetric about the x-axis** if $(x, -y)$ is on the graph whenever (x, y) is on the graph.
- A graph is **symmetric about the y-axis** if $(-x, y)$ is on the graph whenever (x, y) is on the graph.
- A graph is **symmetric about the origin** if $(-x, -y)$ is on the graph whenever (x, y) is on the graph.

Because these three types of symmetry have been formulated in algebraic terms, it is possible to use an algebraic method to determine whether a relation has a symmetric graph. For example, to show that the graph of $y = x^4 + 3x^2$ is symmetric about the y-axis, verify that the point $(-x, y)$ satisfies the equation whenever (x, y) does.

E X A M P L E 4   Checking for Symmetry

Show that the graph of $y^2 = x^4 + 3x^2$ is symmetric about both the x-axis and y-axis.

Solution

x-**axis symmetry**   Replace y with $-y$ in the equation, and show that the result is an equivalent equation.

$$(-y)^2 = x^4 + 3x^2$$
$$y^2 = x^4 + 3x^2$$

y-**axis symmetry**   Replace x with $-x$ in the equation $y^2 = x^4 + 3x^2$ and show that the result is an equivalent equation.

$$y^2 = (-x)^4 + 3(-x)^2$$

$$y^2 = x^4 + 3x^2 \qquad \text{$(-x)^k = x^k$ whenever k is an even integer.}$$

There is a relationship between symmetry about the x and y axes and symmetry about the origin that is summarized in this theorem.

Theorem 3.1 Symmetry About the Origin

If a graph is symmetric about both the x-axis and the y-axis, then it is also symmetric about the origin.

Analysis of Example 4 shows that the graph of $y^2 = x^4 + 3x^2$ is symmetric about the origin.

EXAMPLE 5 Checking for Symmetry (Continued)

Determine the symmetry of the graph of the equation $y = 2x^3 + 5x$.

Solution y-axis symmetry

$$y = 2(-x)^3 + 5(-x)$$ Replace x with $-x$ and check whether the equations are equivalent.

$$y = -2x^3 - 5x$$

$$y = -(2x^3 + 5x)$$

The equations $y = 2x^3 + 5x$ and $y = -(2x^3 + 5x)$ are not equivalent, so the graph is not symmetric with respect to the y-axis.

Next, check for x-axis symmetry. In a similar fashion to the solution above, we can show that the graph is not symmetric with respect to the x-axis.

Symmetry with respect to the origin

$$(-y) = 2(-x)^3 + 5(-x)$$ Replace x with $-x$ and y with $-y$.

$$-y = -2x^3 - 5x$$

$$-y = -(2x^3 + 5x)$$ Multiply both sides of the equation by -1 to obtain an equivalent equation.

$$y = 2x^3 + 5x$$

The graph is symmetric about the origin. The graph in Fig. 3.7 supports the algebraic analysis. ▤

Observations about the symmetry of a graph can be used when trying to draw the graph. For example, once you know that a graph is symmetric about both the x- and y-axes, knowing the graph in the first quadrant is sufficient to determine the complete graph.

EXAMPLE 6 Finding and Drawing a Symmetric Graph

Use a graphing utility to find the complete graph of the equation $4x^2 + 9y^2 = 36$. Also sketch the complete graph of the same equation by hand.

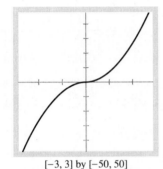

[−3, 3] by [−50, 50]

Figure 3.7 $y = 2x^3 + 5x$.

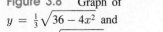

[−4, 4] by [−4, 4]

Figure 3.8 Graph of $y = \frac{1}{3}\sqrt{36 - 4x^2}$ and $y = -\frac{1}{3}\sqrt{36 - 4x^2}$. (See solution to Example 6.)

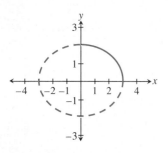

Figure 3.9   Graph of $4x^2 + 9y^2 = 36$ plotted in the first quadrant and then reflected through the x- and y-axes.

Solution

1. Verify that the graph is symmetric about both the x- and y-axes by using the algebraic methods illustrated in Examples 4 and 5.
2. Solve $4x^2 + 9y^2 = 36$ for y.
3. Graph $y = \frac{1}{3}\sqrt{36 - 4x^2}$ and $y = -\frac{1}{3}\sqrt{36 - 4x^2}$ (see Fig. 3.8).
4. To sketch this graph, first plot the graph in quadrant I and then reflect it in one axis to obtain half the ellipse. Then reflect this half ellipse in the other axis to obtain the complete ellipse (Fig. 3.9).   ■

Exercises for Section 3.1

1. Show that the point $(3, 8)$ is in the relation $2x - y = -2$ and that $(4, 2)$ is not.

2. Show that the point $(2, 5)$ is in the relation $2x^2 - y = 3$ and that $(5, 2)$ is not.

3. Show that the point $(-3, 6)$ is in the relation $x + y^2 = 33$ and that $(-2, 4)$ is not.

4. Show that the point $(1, 2)$ is in the relation $5x^3 - 2y = 1$ and that $(3, 2)$ is not.

In Exercises 5 to 12, determine whether the given number pairs are in the given relation.

5. $(3, 5)$; $x^2 + y^2 = 8$
6. $(7, 2)$; $x - 5y = -3$
7. $(1, 2)$; $x^3 + 3y = -1$
8. $(3, 1)$; $x - 4y^3 = 2$
9. $(2, 3)$; $x^2 - y = 3$
10. $(3, 4)$; $x^2 + y^2 = 25$
11. $(2, \sqrt{2})$; $x^3 - 3y^2 = 2$
12. $(\sqrt{3}, 2)$; $4x - 3y^2 = 5$

In Exercises 13 to 18, find the x- and y-intercepts of the graph of each equation.

13. $x^2 + 4y^2 = 4$
14. $4x^2 + 9y^2 = 36$
15. $4x^2 - y^2 = 4$
16. $x - 4 = y^2$
17. $3x^2 + 5y^2 = 15$
18. $x + 5 = -y^2$

In Exercises 19 to 22, find an equation of the circle with the given center and radius.

19. $(1, 2)$; $r = 5$
20. $(-3, 2)$; $r = 1$
21. $(-1, -4)$; $r = 3$
22. $(5, -3)$; $r = 8$

23. Find the center and radius of the circle whose equation is $(x - 3)^2 + (y - 1)^2 = 36$.

24. Find the center and radius of the circle whose equation is $(x + 4)^2 + (y - 2)^2 = 121$.

25. Suppose that the point $(2, 3)$ is on a graph. Determine a second point on the graph if the graph is symmetric with respect to
   a) the x-axis;   b) the y-axis;   c) the origin.

26. Suppose that the point $(a, -b)$ is on a graph. Determine a second point on the graph if the graph is symmetric about
   a) the x-axis;   b) the y-axis;   c) the origin.

27. Determine whether the following graphs are symmetric about the x-axis, the y-axis, or the origin.

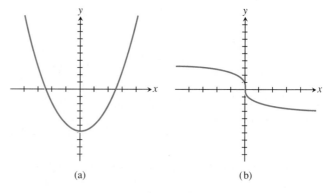

(a)   (b)

For Exercise 27

28. Determine whether the following graphs are symmetric about the x-axis, the y-axis, or the origin.

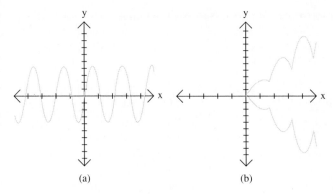

(a)   (b)

For Exercise 28

In Exercises 29 to 32, complete the following graph if you know that a complete graph is symmetric about the following:

29. x-axis only   **30.** y-axis only

31. origin only   **32.** y-axis and origin

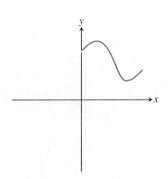

For Exercises 29 to 32

In Exercises 33 to 40, determine whether the graph of each equation is symmetric about the x-axis, the y-axis, or the origin.

33. $y = x^2 + 1$ **34.** $y^2 = x + 1$

35. $y^3 = x$ **36.** $x^2 y = 1$

37. $x^2 - y^4 = 8$ **38.** $y = (x - 2)^2$

39. $x^2 + y^3 = 1$ **40.** $y^2 + y = x$

In Exercises 41 and 42, use a graphing utility to determine whether the graph is symmetric about the x-axis, the y-axis, or the origin.

41. $y = -\sin x$ **42.** $y = 2\cos x$

43. Draw a complete graph of $y = (x - 2)^2$. Does the graph have a reflectional line of symmetry? If so, what is an equation of that line?

44. Draw a complete graph of $y = x^3 + 2$. Is the graph symmetric about some point? If so, what is the point of symmetry?

In Exercises 45 to 48, give an equation for a line whose graph is a line of symmetry for the graph of each function.

45. $y = |x + 2|$ **46.** $y = |x - 5|$

47. $y = |3 - x|$ **48.** $y = |x| + 2$

49. Use a graphing utility to find a complete graph of $y^2 = 2x^2 + 1$ by solving for y and then finding two complete graphs in the same viewing rectangle.

50. Use a graphing utility to find a complete graph of $y^2 = 3x + x^2$ by solving for y and then finding two complete graphs in the same viewing rectangle.

51. Graph the relation $y^2 = x^4 + 3x^2$ on a graphing utility by graphing $y = \sqrt{x^4 + 3x^2}$ and $y = -\sqrt{x^4 + 3x^2}$.

3.2 _____ Functions

Recall that any equation in x and y defines a relation. As observed in Example 6 in Section 3.1, a graphing utility can be used to graph relations that can be written in the form

$$y = \cdots \text{(an expression involving variable } x\text{)}.$$

A special type of relation that occurs frequently in mathematics is the function. The property that distinguishes a function of x from other types of relations is that for a given value of x there is exactly one value of y. Examples of functions are

$$y = x^3 - 4x^2 + 3, \qquad y = \sin x, \qquad \text{and} \qquad y = \sqrt{x - 3}.$$

Definition 3.3   Function

A **function of x** is a relation with the following property: If both (x, y_1) and (x, y_2) belong to the relation, then $y_1 = y_2$. The set of all x-values is called the **domain of the function**, and the set of all y values is called the **range of the function.**

E X A M P L E   1   Verifying a Relation is Not a Function

Show that $y^2 = x$ is a relation that is not a function.

Solution

x	0	0.5	1	1.5	2	2.5	3	4	5
y	0	±0.7	±1	±1.2	±1.4	±1.6	±1.7	±2	±2.2

Since there are two y-values corresponding to some x-values, this relation does not meet the condition for being a function. ≡

Notice that restricting the table of values in Example 1 to the positive y-values results in pairs for the function $y = \sqrt{x}$:

x	0	0.5	1	1.5	2	2.5	3	4	5
y	0	0.7	1	1.2	1.4	1.6	1.7	2	2.2

Functions are encountered routinely in our daily lives in tabular form: height and weight charts, time and temperature charts, price and sales tax charts, income tax tables, and so forth.

That functions are important in scientific applications is evident by the fact that functions abound on a scientific calculator. For example, the calculator keys

$$[\sqrt{}\,], \qquad [x^2], \qquad [\sin], \qquad [\log]$$

each represent a function because for each *input* value x, there is only one *output* value—the one shown on the screen. This output value represents the y-value. Figure 3.10 shows that for the function $y = \log x$, the input value 2 has the output value 0.3010299957. We will study many of the functions on a scientific calculator more thoroughly later in this book.

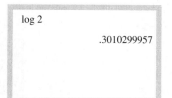

log 2

.3010299957

Figure 3.10   The input value 2 has the output value $\log 2$.

Examining the graph of $y^2 = x$ shows that this relation is not a function because the vertical line $x = 1$ intersects the graph at the two points $(1, 1)$ and $(1, -1)$ (see Fig. 3.11). In general, a relation is not a function if there exists one vertical line that intersects the graph of the relation in more than one point. This observation leads to the **vertical line test** for functions.

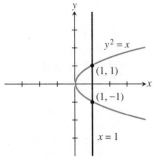

Figure 3.11 Testing whether $y^2 = x$ is a function using $x = 1$.

Definition 3.4 Vertical Line Test for a Function

If every vertical line intersects the graph of a relation in at most one point, then the relation is a function of x.

E X A M P L E   2   Using the Vertical Line Test

Which of the relations represented by the following graphs are functions?

Solution   All four graphs satisfy the vertical line test except part (b). Therefore only part (b) is not the graph of a function of x.

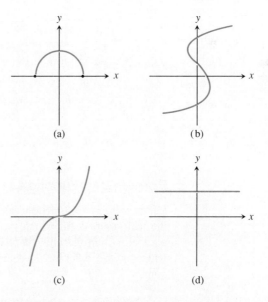

(a)

(b)

(c)

(d)

Function Notation

An equation like $y = 4x^2 + x - 2$ defines a function. Suppose we give this function the name f for function. We use the following **function notation**:

Input	Output	Equation or Rule
x	$f(x)$	$f(x) = 4x^2 + x - 2$

The symbol $f(x)$ is read "f of x" and is called the **value of f at x**. This value $f(x)$ is the y-value that corresponds to the value of x, so $y = f(x)$. To find the y-values for $x = -1$ and $x = 3$, replace the variable x with the given value of x and simplify:

$$f(-1) = 4(-1)^2 + (-1) - 2 = 1$$

$$f(3) = 4(3)^2 + (3) - 2 = 37.$$

The function $f(x) = 4x^2 + x - 2$ has now been **evaluated** at $x = -1$ and $x = 3$.

E X A M P L E 3   Evaluating a Function

Let f be the function defined by the equation $y = x^2 + 1$. Find $f(-2)$, $f(3)$, $f(a)$, and $f(x - 3)$.

Solution

$$f(-2) = (-2)^2 + 1 = 5 \qquad \text{Replace } x \text{ with } -2.$$

$$f(3) = (3)^2 + 1 = 10$$

$$f(a) = a^2 + 1 \qquad \text{Replace } x \text{ with } a.$$

$$f(x - 3) = (x - 3)^2 + 1 = x^2 + 2x(-3) + (-3)^2 + 1 \qquad \text{Replace } x \text{ with } x - 3 \text{ and simplify.}$$

$$= x^2 - 6x + 10 \qquad \blacksquare$$

Domain of a Function

Let $y = f(x)$ be a function. The **understood domain of f** is the largest subset of the real numbers for which the equation $y = f(x)$ makes sense. That is, the real number a is in the understood domain of f if and only if $f(a)$ is a real number. Unless stated otherwise, assume that the domain of a function is its understood domain.

E X A M P L E 4   Finding Domain and Range

Find a complete graph of the function $f(x) = \sqrt{x - 3}$. Also find its domain and range.

Solution See Fig. 3.12 for a complete graph.

$$x - 3 \geq 0 \qquad \text{The expression under a square root must be nonnegative.}$$

$$x \geq 3$$

The domain of f is the interval $[3, \infty)$. We read from the graph that the range is all numbers y such that $y \geq 0$. In other words, the range of f is the interval $[0, \infty)$. ▤

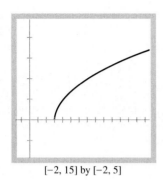

Figure 3.12 $f(x) = \sqrt{x - 3}$.

E X A M P L E 5   Finding Domain and Range

Compare complete graphs of $f(x) = x^2 - 4$ and $g(x) = |x^2 - 4|$. Determine the domain and range of each function.

Solution Figure 3.13 shows complete graphs. For each function, x can represent any real number. Therefore

$$\text{domain of } f = (-\infty, \infty) \qquad \text{and} \qquad \text{domain of } g = (-\infty, \infty).$$

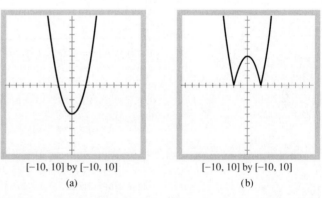

[−10, 10] by [−10, 10]   [−10, 10] by [−10, 10]
(a)   (b)

Figure 3.13 $f(x) = x^2 - 4$ and $g(x) = |x^2 - 4|$.

The range of f is the set of all numbers y such that $y \geq -4$; in other words, the range of f is the interval $[-4, \infty)$. The range of g is the interval $[0, \infty)$. ▤

Notice that, since the absolute value of an expression is always nonnegative, the graph of $g(x) = |x^2 - 4|$ can never go below the x-axis. The absolute value symbols in g have the effect of bringing the part of the graph of f that lies below the x-axis to above the x-axis.

This example leads to the following general principle.

Graph of Absolute Value

To obtain a complete graph of $y = |f(x)|$ from a complete graph of $y = f(x)$, reflect the portion of the graph of $y = f(x)$ that lies below the x-axis about the x-axis, and join this reflection with the portion of the graph of $y = f(x)$ that lies above the x-axis.

Built-in Functions

Computers and graphing calculators have special built-in functions that can be accessed by pushing a special key or typing a special code. For example, in graphing the equation in Example 5, the syntax of a graphing utility usually requires that $f(x) = |x^2 - 4|$ be written in the form $f(x) = \text{ABS}(x^2 - 4)$. Also, typing $\text{SQR}(x)$—or $\text{SQRT}(x)$ on some computers—will usually produce the **square root function** $f(x) = \sqrt{x}$.

E X A M P L E 6   Finding Domain and Range

Find a complete graph of $f(x) = \sqrt{x}/(2x - 4)$, and find its domain and range.

Solution   Figure 3.14 shows a complete graph of the function. Notice that 2 is not in the domain since the denominator $2x - 4$ cannot equal zero. Also, x cannot be less than zero because of the $\sqrt{x}$ in the numerator. Thus the domain of f is $[0, 2) \cup (2, \infty)$.

Notice that $f(0) = 0$, so 0 is in the range of f. Investigate further to conclude from the graph that the range of f is the set of all real numbers.   ▤

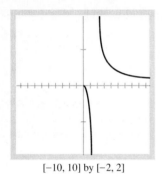

[−10, 10] by [−2, 2]

Figure 3.14
$f(x) = \sqrt{x}/(2x - 4)$.

The **greatest integer function** is another function that is built in on many graphers and is denoted by $[\![x]\!]$ or $\text{INT}(x)$. $[\![x]\!]$ is defined to be the greatest integer less than or equal to x. For example, $[\![3.7]\!] = 3$, $[\![-1.2]\!] = -2$, and $[\![6]\!] = 6$.

E X A M P L E 7   Graphing the Greatest Integer Function

Find a complete graph of $f(x) = \text{INT}(x)$ and determine its domain and range.

Solution   See Fig. 3.15.*

Domain of $f = (-\infty, \infty)$

There is a unique largest integer less than or equal to any number x.

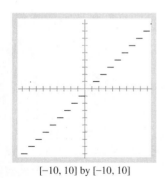

[−10, 10] by [−10, 10]

Figure 3.15 $f(x) = \text{INT}(x)$.

* Consult the accompanying *Graphing Calculator and Computer Graphing Laboratory Manual* to see whether your graphing utility is capable of duplicating Fig. 3.15.

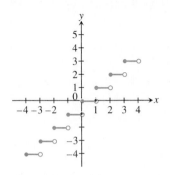

Figure 3.16 Sketch of $f(x) = \text{INT}(x)$.

Range of $f = \{\ldots, -3, -2, -1, 0, 1, 2, 3, \ldots\}$ The value of the function is always an integer. ≡

Notice that the graph of $f(x) = \text{INT}(x)$ coincides with the x-axis when x is between 0 and 1 since $\text{INT}(x) = 0$ in that interval. Moreover, a grapher with the standard viewing rectangle does not show whether $\text{INT}(3)$ is 2 or 3 (see Fig. 3.15). The detail at each integer value is shown better in a hand-drawn sketch (Fig. 3.16). A solid circle is placed at the left end of each segment to show the function value for each integer, and an open circle is placed at the right of each segment to show that the endpoint is missing on the right of each line segment. This illustrates, for example, that $\text{INT}(1) = 1$ and $\text{INT}(3) = 3$.

The function $f(x) = \text{INT}(x)$ is sometimes called a **step function** because its completed graph looks like a series of steps.

E X A M P L E 8   Finding an Appropriate Viewing Rectangle

Find a complete graph of the function $f(x) = 16x - x^3$. Determine the domain and range of f.

Solution   Begin with the standard viewing rectangle $[-10, 10]$ by $[-10, 10]$. Figure 3.17 illustrates that the graph of $f(x) = 16x - x^3$ in the standard rectangle goes off the screen vertically. That means that the values for Ymin and Ymax must be increased. Experiment until you find an acceptable viewing rectangle. See Figure 3.18. Conclude that the domain and range are $(-\infty, \infty)$, the set of real numbers. ≡

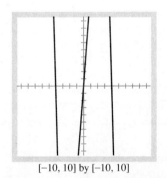

$[-10, 10]$ by $[-10, 10]$

Figure 3.17 $f(x) = 16x - x^3$.

E X A M P L E 9   Determining Functions from a Relation

Write two functions that are determined by the relation $x^2 + y^2 = 9$. Graph the relation using a grapher.

Solution

$$x^2 + y^2 = 9$$

$$y^2 = 9 - x^2$$

$$y = \pm\sqrt{9 - x^2}$$

This relation determines the two functions $f(x) = \sqrt{9 - x^2}$ and $g(x) = -\sqrt{9 - x^2}$. The graphs of f and g together represent the relation $x^2 + y^2 = 9$ (see Fig. 3.19). On the graphing utility, do these graphs cross the x-axis? Explain. ≡

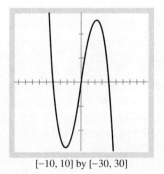

$[-10, 10]$ by $[-30, 30]$

Figure 3.18 $f(x) = 16x - x^3$.

Functions can be used to model many problem situations. Often a graphing utility can be used to help understand the problem. Example 10 considers the area

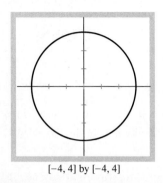

[−4, 4] by [−4, 4]

Figure 3.19 $x^2 + y^2 = 9$.

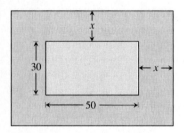

Figure 3.20   Diagram of swimming pool with a sidewalk of uniform width x.

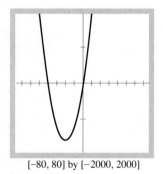

[−80, 80] by [−2000, 2000]

Figure 3.21
$A(x) = 4x^2 + 160x$.

of a sidewalk around a pool, and Example 11 again examines the projectile-motion Problem Situation first introduced in Section 2.6.

E X A M P L E   10   APPLICATION: Area of a Sidewalk

A rectangular swimming pool with dimensions 30 by 50 feet is surrounded by a sidewalk of uniform width x (see Fig. 3.20). What is the width of the sidewalk when the sidwalk area is 600 square feet?

Solution

1. First find the area of the sidewalk, A, as a function of x.

$$\text{total length} = 50 + 2x$$
$$\text{total width} = 30 + 2x$$
$$\text{total area} = (50 + 2x)(30 + 2x)$$
$$\text{swimming pool area} = 50(30)$$
$$A(x) = (50 + 2x)(30 + 2x) - (50)(30)$$
$$= 4x^2 + 160x$$

2. Next determine what portion of the complete graph of $A(x) = 4x^2 + 160x$ (Fig. 3.21) represents the Problem Situation. Only the positive values of x make sense in this Problem Situation, so the domain of $A(x)$ for the Problem Situation is $(0, \infty)$.

3. Graph both $A(x) = 4x^2 + 160x$ and $y = 600$ in the viewing rectangle $[0, 10]$ by $[0, 1000]$ (see Fig. 3.22). The x-coordinate a of the point of intersection is approximately 3.5. Thus when the area of the sidewalk is 600 square feet the width is about 3.5 feet.   ▤

E X A M P L E   11   APPLICATION: Projectile Motion

A model rocket is shot straight up from ground level with an initial velocity of 64 feet per second.

a) At what time will the object be 50 feet above the ground?

b) What is the maximum height reached by this object, and how long does it take to reach this height?

Solution   Recall from Section 2.6 that the height $s(t)$ after t seconds is given by $s(t) = -16t^2 + v_0 t + s_0$. So in this problem $s(t) = -16t^2 + 64t$.

a) Graph the functions $s(t) = -16t^2 + 64t$ and $s = 50$ (see Fig. 3.23). Why is $[0, 4]$ the appropriate domain for this problem situation? Zoom in on the points of intersection, and discover that the object is 50 feet above the ground at 1.06 seconds and 2.94 seconds after the object is thrown.

b) Zoom in on the highest point, and confirm that it is $(2, 64)$. This means that the object reaches a maximum height of 64 feet after 2 seconds. ▄

Piecewise-Defined Functions

In a **piecewise-defined function** the domain of the function is divided into several parts and a different function rule is applied to each part. For example, consider the following function:

$$f(x) = \begin{cases} 3 - x^2 & \text{if } x < 1 \\ x^3 - 4x & \text{if } x \geq 1 \end{cases} \qquad (1)$$

The rule $f(x) = 3 - x^2$ applies only when x falls in the interval $(-\infty, 1)$, and the rule $f(x) = x^3 - 4x$ applies only when x falls in the interval $[1, \infty)$. To find a complete graph of this function, piece together the unshaded portion of the graph in Fig. 3.24(a) with the unshaded portion of the graph in Fig. 3.24(b).

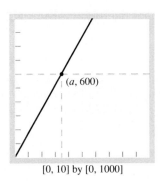

[0, 10] by [0, 1000]

Figure 3.22
$A(x) = 4x^2 + 160x$.

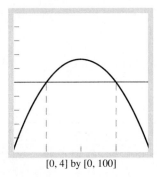

[0, 4] by [0, 100]

Figure 3.23
$s(t) = -16t^2 + 64t$.

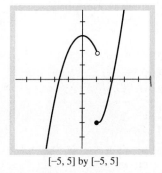

[−5, 5] by [−5, 5]

Figure 3.25   The graph of the piecewise function defined in Example 12.

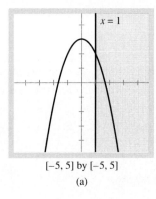

[−5, 5] by [−5, 5]

(a)

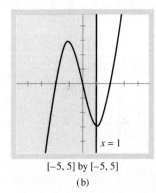

[−5, 5] by [−5, 5]

(b)

Figure 3.24   (a) $y = 3 - x^2$; (b) $y = x^3 - 4x$. Combining the unshaded portions results in the piecewise function in Eq. (1).

E X A M P L E   12   Piecewise-Defined Function

Sketch a complete graph of the function

$$f(x) = \begin{cases} 3 - x^2 & \text{if } x < 1 \\ x^3 - 4x & \text{if } x \geq 1 \end{cases}$$

Solution   See Fig. 3.25.* ▄

---

* Consult the accompanying *Graphing Calculator and Computer Graphing Laboratory Manual* to see whether your graphing utility is capable of duplicating Fig. 3.25.

Exercises for Section 3.2

The functions $f(x) = x^2 - 1$ and $g(x) = 1/(x+1)$ apply to Exercises 1 to 6.

1. Find $f(0)$ and $f(1)$.   **2.** Find $f(3)$ and $f(-5)$.

3. Find $g(0)$ and $g(1)$.   **4.** Find $g(3)$ and $g(-5)$.

5. Find $g(2/t)$.   **6.** Find $f(x+2)$.

In Exercises 7 to 10, consider the graph of the function $y = f(x)$ given in the accompanying figure. Estimate the indicated values. (Each tick mark represents a value of 1.)

7. $f(0), f(-1)$, and $f(4)$ **8.** x if $f(x) = 0$

9. x if $f(x) = 1$ **10.** x if $f(x) = -8$

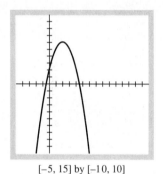

[−5, 15] by [−10, 10]

For Exercises 7 to 10

In Exercises 11 to 13, use the vertical line test to decide which are graphs of functions of x.

11.

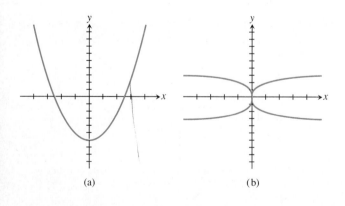

(a)   (b)

12.

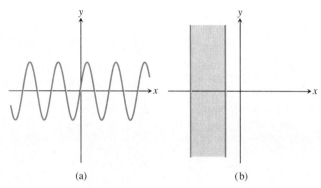

(a)   (b)

13.

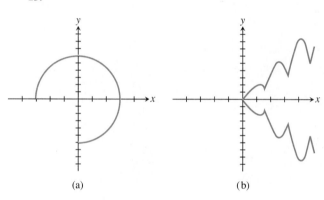

(a)   (b)

In Exercises 14 to 23, determine the domain and range of each function. Use a grapher if necessary.

14. $f(x) = \sqrt{x}$ **15.** $f(x) = \dfrac{2}{x-3}$

16. $f(x) = x^2 - 3$ **17.** $g(x) = |x+5|$

18. $h(x) = \dfrac{x}{|x+4|}$ **19.** $f(x) = \sqrt{8-x}$

20. $g(x) = \dfrac{x-2}{x^2+5}$ **21.** $h(x) = \sqrt{\dfrac{1}{x+1}}$

22. $h(x) = \sqrt{x^3 - 8x}$ **23.** $f(x) = x^2 - 5x - 10$

24. Which viewing rectangle gives the best complete graph of $f(x) = x^3 + 10x + 100$?
a) $[-10, 10]$ by $[-10, 10]$
b) $[-10, 10]$ by $[-100, 100]$

c) $[-10, 10]$ by $[0, 100]$

d) $[-10, 10]$ by $[-100, 0]$

e) $[-10, 10]$ by $[-1000, 1000]$

25. Which viewing rectangle gives the best complete graph of $f(x) = 12x^2 - 5x + 19$?

a) $[-10, 10]$ by $[-10, 10]$

b) $[10, 10]$ by $[-100, 100]$

c) $[-50, 50]$ by $[-5, 5]$

d) $[-5, 5]$ by $[-50, 50]$

e) $[-10, 0]$ by $[0, 50]$

26. Which viewing rectangle gives the best complete graph of $f(x) = 0.005x^3 - 5x^2 - 60$?

a) $[-10, 10]$ by $[-100, 100]$

b) $[-100, 100]$ by $[-100,000, 100,000]$

c) $[-1000, 2000]$ by $[-1,000,000, 1,000,000]$

d) $[0, 2000]$ by $[0, 1,000,000]$

e) $[-1000, 1000]$ by $[-1000, 1000]$

In Exercises 27 to 42, find a complete graph of each function.

27. $g(x) = \dfrac{x - 4}{5}$

28. $f(x) = x^2 - 4$

29. $f(x) = 2x^2 - 3x + 5$

30. $f(x) = x^3 - x + 1$

31. $g(x) = (x + 3)^2 + 2x + 4$

32. $h(x) = 4 - x - x^3$

33. $h(x) = \sqrt{x + 1}$

34. $g(x) = -1 - \sqrt{x - 1}$

35. $k(x) = 1 + |x - 2|$

36. $f(x) = -|2x^3|$

37. $g(x) = \text{INT}(x + 2)$

38. $f(x) = (x - 30)(x + 20)$

39. $k(x) = |x^2 - 6x - 12|$

40. $h(x) = 2x^3 - x + 3$

41. $f(x) = x^3 - 8x$

42. $g(x) = 10x^3 - 20x^2 + 5x - 30$

In Exercises 43 and 44, find a complete graph of each function. Record each series of graphs on the *same* coordinate system.

43. $f(x) = x^2$, $g(x) = (x - 1)^2$, $h(x) = (x - 2)^2$, $k(x) = (x + 3)^2$.

44. $f(x) = -1 + x^2$, $g(x) = 2 + x^2$, $h(x) = 4 - x^2$, $k(x) = x^2 - 4$.

In Exercises 45 to 47, sketch a complete graph of each piecewise-defined function. Support your work with a graphing utility.

45. $f(x) = \begin{cases} x^2 & \text{if } x < 3 \\ x - 4 & \text{if } x \geq 3 \end{cases}$

46. $g(x) = \begin{cases} -x & \text{if } 0 \leq x < 4 \\ \sqrt{x - 3} & \text{if } x \geq 4 \end{cases}$

47. $h(x) = \begin{cases} 4 - x + x^2 & \text{if } x < 2 \\ 1 - 2x + 3x^2 & \text{if } x \geq 2 \end{cases}$

48. Jerry runs at a constant rate of 4.125 mph. Describe the distance that Jerry runs as a function $y = d(t)$, and find a complete graph of this function.

49. Use the graph in Exercise 48 to determine the time it takes Jerry to run a 26-mile marathon.

Exercises 50 to 52 refer to the following **problem situation:** A 4- by 6.5-inch picture pasted on a cardboard sheet is surrounded by a border of uniform width x and area A.

50. Determine the area A of the border region as a function $y = A(x)$, and find a complete graph of this function.

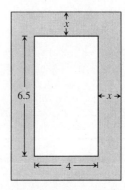

For Exercises 50 to 52

51. In the function $A(x)$ found in Exercise 50, what values of x are possible in this problem situation?

52. Use the graph in Exercise 50 to determine the width of the border if its area is 20 square inches.

Exercises 53 and 54 refer to the following **problem situation:** 80 feet of fencing are cut into two unequal lengths, and each piece is used to make a square enclosure. Let x be the perimeter of the smaller enclosure.

53. Express the total area A of both enclosures as a function $y = A(x)$. What domain values are possible in this problem situation?

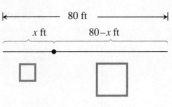

For Exercises 53 and 54

54. Find a complete graph of the function found in Exercise 53 and use it to approximate the smaller length of fence when $A = 300$ square feet.

Exercises 55 to 57 refer to the following **problem situation**: The regular long-distance telephone charges C from Columbus, Ohio, to Lancaster, Pennsylvania, are $0.48 for the first minute or fraction of a minute, and $0.28 for each additional minute.

55. Express the cost C of calling Lancaster from Columbus as a function $y = C(t)$, and sketch a complete graph. What are the possible range values of this function?

56. What part of the domain of the function in Exercise 55 represents this problem situation?

57. Use the graph of the function in Exercise 55 to determine how long Bill talked to his girlfriend if he spent $1.88.

Exercises 58 to 60 refer to a projectile motion **problem situation** in which an object 10 feet above ground level is shot straight up with an initial velocity of 150 feet per second. See the description of the projectile motion problem situation in Section 2.6.

58. Determine the height s of the object above the ground as a function $s = f(t)$, and find a complete graph.

59. What portion of the graph of the function found in Exercise 58 represents the problem situation?

60. At what time t will the object be 300 feet above the ground?

3.3 _____ Linear Functions and Linear Inequalities

A primary reason for studying mathematics is to solve everyday problems. Section 1.2 introduced the Quality Rent-a-Car problem. The function $f(x) = 0.2x + 15$, which was a mathematical model for that problem, is an example of a linear function.

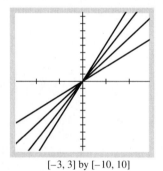

[−3, 3] by [−10, 10]

Figure 3.26 $f_1(x) = 2x$, $f_2(x) = 3x$, $f_3(x) = 4x$, and $f_4(x) = 5x$.

EXPLORE WITH A GRAPHING UTILITY

Graph the four functions $f_1(x) = 2x$, $f_2(x) = 3x$, $f_3(x) = 4x$, and $f_4(x) = 5x$, one after another without erasing (Fig. 3.26).

Questions

1. How are the four graphs the same? How do they differ as the coefficient of x changes from 2 to 3 to 4 to 5?

2. Predict how the graphs of $f_1(x) = -2x$, $f_2(x) = -3x$, $f_3(x) = -4x$, and $f_4(x) = -5x$ will look. Check your prediction.

Generalize   How would you describe the graph of $f(x) = mx$, where m is a constant?

You have probably discovered that the graph of $f(x) = mx$ is always a straight line. When m is a positive number, the line rises as it moves from left to right, and when m is negative, the line falls in moving from left to right.

The equation $y = 2x + 3$ is also a line. Experiment with other equations of the form $y = mx + b$, where m and b are constants.

Definition 3.5   Linear Function

A **linear function** is a function that can be written in the form $f(x) = mx + b$, where m and b are real numbers and $m \neq 0$.

When the equation for a line is written as a linear equation, the numbers m and b give useful information about the graph. First let us consider m.

Suppose that (x_1, y_1) and (x_2, y_2) are two distinct points on the graph of $y = mx + b$ (see Fig. 3.27). Then $y_1 = mx_1 + b$ and $y_2 = mx_2 + b$. (Why?) We can isolate m by subtracting one equation from the other:

$$y_2 - y_1 = (mx_2 + b) - (mx_1 + b)$$

$$= m(x_2 - x_1)$$

$$m = \frac{y_2 - y_1}{x_2 - x_1}.$$

The number m thus describes the steepness, or slope, of the line.

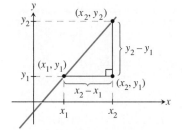

Figure 3.27 $m = \dfrac{y_2 - y_1}{x_2 - x_1}.$

Definition 3.6   Slope

The **slope** of the graph of $y = mx + b$ is the quotient

$$m = \frac{y_2 - y_1}{x_2 - x_1},$$

where (x_1, y_1) and (x_2, y_2) are any two points on the line $y = mx + b$ such that $x_1 \neq x_2$.

The slope tells us two things about the line. The sign of m determines whether the line rises or falls in moving from left to right: When m is positive, the line rises, and when m is negative, the line falls. The absolute value of m determines the steepness of that rise or fall.

E X A M P L E   1   Calculating the Slope

Find the slope of the line passing through the points $(-1, 2)$ and $(4, -2)$.

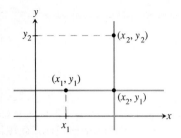

Figure 3.28   Vertical line $x = x_2$ and horizontal line $y = y_1$.

Solution   Let $(x_1, y_1) = (-1, 2)$ and $(x_2, y_2) = (4, -2)$. Then

$$m = \frac{y_2 - y_1}{x_2 - x_1} = \frac{-2 - 2}{4 - (-1)} = -\frac{4}{5}.$$ Substitute into the slope definition the values of the coordinates of the given points.

Figure 3.28 shows that the slope of the horizontal line is $(y_1 - y_1)/(x_2 - x_1) = 0$. The slope of a horizontal line is always zero because the numerator in the slope fraction is always $y_1 - y_1 = 0$. The slope of the vertical line is $(y_2 - y_1)/(x_2 - x_2)$. However, since division by zero is not defined, *the slope of a vertical line is not defined.*

Slope is one characteristic of the equation of a line. Another characteristic relates to where the line crosses the y-axis.

🔍 EXPLORE WITH A GRAPHING UTILITY

Graph the following four functions, one after another, without erasing: $f_1(x) = mx - 2$, $f_2(x) = mx + 1$, $f_3(x) = mx + 3$, and $f_4(x) = mx + 5$ for $m = 1, m = 3$, and $m = -2$.

Questions

1. For a particular value of m, how are these graphs the same?
2. For a particular value of m, how are they different?

Generalize   How would you describe the graph of $f(x) = mx + b$?

From the Exploration you have seen that if several equations of the form $y = mx + b$ have the same coefficient of x, then their graphs are parallel lines.

Recall from Definition 3.1 that if the graph of an equation crosses the y-axis at $(0, b)$, then $(0, b)$ (or simply b) is the y-intercept of the graph. We conclude with the following generalization.

The graph of $y = mx + b$ is a straight line with slope m and y-intercept b.

E X A M P L E   2   Finding Slope and y-Intercept

Find the slope and the y-intercept for the equation $3y - \sqrt{20}x = 9$. Sketch a complete graph.

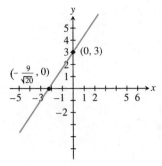

Figure 3.29 $y = (\sqrt{20}/3)x + 3$.

Solution

$$3y - \sqrt{20}x = 9$$

$$3y = \sqrt{20}x + 9$$

$$y = \frac{\sqrt{20}}{3}x + 3 \quad \text{Solve for } y.$$

The slope of this line is $\sqrt{20}/3$, and its y-intercept is 3. Use this information to sketch a correct graph (Fig. 3.29). ≡

There are many applied problems whose solutions can be modeled by graphing a line, as illustrated by the next example.

E X A M P L E 3   APPLICATION: Value of a House

A house was purchased 10 years ago for $60,000. This year it was appraised at $85,000. Assume the value V of the house is $V(t) = mt + b$ for some real numbers m and b where t represents the time in years. When was the house worth $71,250?

Solution

1. First find the value of b.

$60,000 = m\emptyset + b$

$$V = mt + b$$

$$60,000 = m(0) + b \quad \text{When } t = 0, V = 60,000.$$

$$60,000 = b$$

$8500\,\emptyset m + 60{,}000$

Therefore $V = mt + 60,000$ for some value of m. Next find the value of m.

$$85,000 = m(10) + 60,000 \quad \begin{array}{l}\text{Substitute } t = 10 \text{ and } V = 85,000 \\ \text{into the equation } V = mt + 60,000.\end{array}$$

$$85,000 - 60,000 = 10m + 60,000 - 60,000$$

$$25,000 = 10m$$

$$2500 = m \quad m = 2500$$

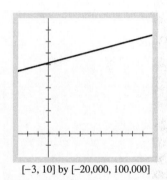

[−3, 10] by [−20,000, 100,000]

Figure 3.30
$V(t) = 2500t + 60,000$.

The linear function that models this problem is $V(t) = 2500t + 60,000$ (see Fig. 3.30).

$2500t$

2. To find t when $V = 71,250$, substitute $V = 71,250$ and solve for t.

$$V = 2500t + 60,000$$

$$71,250 = 2500t + 60,000$$

$$11,250 = 2500t$$

$$4.5 = t$$

Therefore the house was worth $71,250, 4.5 years after its purchase. ≡

Linear Inequalities

Suppose that a linear equation or a linear function is changed to an inequality. How do the graphs of the equality and the inequality relate?

🔍 EXPLORE WITH A GRAPHING UTILITY

Graph $y = 2x + 3$. Move the cursor to a point on the graph. Then move the cursor up and down.

Questions

1. Does the x-coordinate of the moving point change as you move the cursor up and down?
2. What happens to the y-coordinate of the moving point?
3. Would the coordinates of this moving point satisfy the inequality $y < 2x + 3$ or the inequality $y > 2x + 3$? How do you know?

Generalize   If you would shade in all points that satisfy $y > 2x + 3$, what points would be shaded?

This Exploration has motivated the following definition.

Definition 3.7   Linear Inequality

A **linear inequality** in the two variables x and y is an inequality that can be written in one of the following forms:

$$y < mx + b, \qquad y \le mx + b, \qquad y > mx + b, \qquad y \ge mx + b.$$

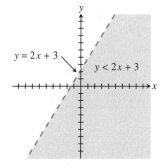

Figure 3.31 $y = 2x + 3$ (dashed line) and $y < 2x + 3$ (shaded area). The line is dashed to indicate it is *not* part of the solution to $y < 2x + 3$.

Consider the linear equation $y = 2x + 3$. The point $(1, 5)$ is on this line since $5 = 2(1) + 3$. Suppose c is a number such that $c < 2(1) + 3$. Will the point $(1, c)$ lie below or above the line $y = 2x + 3$? For example, $(1, 3)$ and $(1, -1)$ both lie below the line. These points also satisfy the inequality $y < 2x + 3$.

The graph of an inequality consists of all points whose coordinates satisfy the inequality. So, among the points on the vertical line $x = 1$, the points below the graph of $y = 2x + 3$ are solutions to $y < 2x + 3$, and the points above the graph of $y = 2x + 3$ are *not* solutions to $y < 2x + 3$. Since a similar argument can be

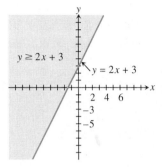

Figure 3.32 $y \geq 2x + 3$.

made for each vertical line, a complete graph of $y < 2x + 3$ consists of all the points below the graph of $y = 2x + 3$ (see Fig. 3.31).

E X A M P L E 4   Graphing an Inequality

Draw the graph of $y \geq 2x + 3$.

Solution

1. Plot the line $y = 2x + 3$. Make the line solid to indicate that it will be part of the solution to $y \geq 2x + 3$.
2. Shade the region above the line.

The result is shown in Fig. 3.32.

E X A M P L E 5   Graphing Another Inequality

Draw the graph of $2x + 3y < 4$.

Solution

$$2x + 3y < 4$$
$$3y < -2x + 4$$
$$y < -\frac{2}{3}x + \frac{4}{3} \quad \text{Solve for } y.$$

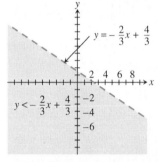

Figure 3.33 $y < -\frac{2}{3}x + \frac{4}{3}$.
Why is the line dashed?

Draw the graph of $y = -\frac{2}{3}x + \frac{4}{3}$, and shade the region below this line (see Fig. 3.33).

Exercises for Section 3.3

In Exercises 1 to 4, which equations have graphs that rise (going from left to right), and which ones fall? Support your answers by graphing each equation on a graphing utility.

1. $y = 3x, \quad y = \frac{1}{3}x, \quad y = -3x$

2. $y = -3x, \quad y = 2x, \quad y = -\frac{1}{4}x$

3. $y = -2x - 1, \quad y = -4x + 3, \quad y = 2x + 5$

4. $y = 3 - 2x, \quad y = -2x + 3, \quad y = 5 + 3x$

In Exercises 5 to 8, find the slope of the line through each pair of points.

5. $(-1, 2); \quad (2, -6)$

6. $(0, -6); \quad (-4, 7)$

7. $(-1, -3); \quad (4, 1)$

8. $(-3, 1); \quad (-1, -5)$

In Exercises 9 to 14, determine the slope and y-intercept of the graph of each equation.

9. $y = 2x - 4$

10. $y = 1 - 3x$

11. $2x + 3y = 2$

12. $-x + 3y + 2 = 0$

13. $x + 2y = 3$

14. $-x - 3y = 8$

In Exercises 15 to 18, draw the line that contains point P and has slope m.

15. $P(1, 2); \quad m = 2$

16. $P(2, -1); \quad m = \frac{1}{3}$

17. $P(0, 3)$; $m = 0$ **18.** $P(3, -1)$; $m =$ undefined

In Exercises 19 to 22, find an equation of the line through the given pair of points. (*Hint:* Find the slope of the line, and apply the approach used in Example 2.)

19. $(0, 3)$; $(2, 6)$ **20.** $(1, 1)$; $(0, 2)$

21. $(0, 300)$; $(10, 365)$ **22.** $(5, 200)$; $(35, 1050)$

23. When the x- and y-axes have the same scale, a line with a slope of 1 appears to be a $45°$ line. Find a *square viewing rectangle*, that is, a viewing rectangle on which $y = x$ looks like a $45°$ line.

24. Find a graph of the following linear equations. Which one appears steeper? Which one has the greater slope?
   a) $y = 3x + 1$, viewing rectangle of $[-10, 10]$ by $[-10, 10]$
   b) $y = 5x - 1$, viewing rectangle of $[-10, 10]$ by $[-50, 50]$.

25. Suppose the equation $y = 5x - 2$ is graphed using the following viewing rectangles. Which graph will appear steeper? Is the slope the same or different in the two cases?
   a) $[-10, 10]$ by $[-10, 10]$
   b) $[-2, 2]$ by $[-10, 10]$

26. Suppose the equation $y = 5x - 2$ is graphed using the following viewing rectangles. Which graph will appear steeper? Is the slope the same or different in the two cases?
   a) $[-10, 10]$ by $[-10, 10]$
   b) $[-25, 25]$ by $[-10, 10]$

27. The graph of the function $f(x) = x$ drawn with a viewing rectangle $[-10, 10]$ by $[-10, 10]$ will appear identical to the graph of $g(x) = 5x$ on which viewing rectangle?

28. Use a graphing utility to complete Example 3. Change the viewing rectangle until you are able to get an approximation for the solution to within the nearest hundredth.

29. Explain why either point can be labeled (x_1, y_1) or (x_2, y_2) when applying the slope formula.

30. What do a and b represent in the equation $x/a + y/b = 1$? (*Hint:* Draw a complete graph of the equation for a few specific values of a and b.)

31. Use the concept of slope to determine whether the three points $(-1, 2), (2, 4)$, and $(6, 9)$ are *collinear*, that is, whether they all lie on the same line.

32. Candy worth $0.95 per pound is mixed with candy worth $1.35 per pound. Determine an inequality that expresses the requirement that the value of the new mixture not exceed $1.15 per pound. Find its complete graph.

Exercises 33 to 35 refer to the following **problem situation**: A house was purchased 8 years ago for $42,000. This year it was appraised at $67,500. Assume that the value V of the house changes linearly with time (t).

33. Find a linear equation that models this problem situation.

34. Use a graph to estimate when this house will be worth $90,000.

35. Determine algebraically when this house will be worth $90,000.

Exercises 36 to 38 refer to the following **problem situation**: Mary Ellen intends to invest $18,000, putting part of the money in one savings account that pays 5% annually (which can be withdrawn without penalty) and the rest in another account that pays 8% annually.

36. Write an equation that describes the total interest I received at the end of one year in terms of the amount A invested at 8%.

37. Find a complete graph of the equation in Exercise 36.

38. If Mary Ellen's annual interest is $1020, how much of her original $18,000 did she invest at 8%?

39. The equation describing home appreciation in Example 3 was $V = 2500t + 60,000$. The percent appreciation in year 1 is

$$\frac{\text{change in value during year}}{\text{value at beginning of year}} = \frac{2500}{60,000} = 4.17\%$$

What is the percent appreciation during year 2? During year 3? During year 4? During year 5?

In Exercises 40 to 47, find a complete graph of each equation or inequality.

40. $y = 3x - 6$ **41.** $y < x - 2$

42. $x - 2y \geq 6$ **43.** $2x + y = 8$

44. $2x - 6y = 8$ **45.** $y \geq x$

46. $5x - 2y < 8$ **47.** $2x + 3y - 5 \geq 0$

48. Is there a line that cannot be graphed with a function grapher? Are there any lines whose equation cannot be written in the form $y = mx + D$?

49. Tickets to a concert cost $2.50 for students and $3.75 for adults. Suppose x represents the number of student tickets sold, and y represents the number of adult tickets sold. Write an inequality that describes the condition that total receipts must exceed $1500.

50. Discussion Form groups of two or three students, and discuss with each other the following situation. Suppose you plan to graph the inequality in Exercise 49. Recall that this is a graphical representation of the **problem situation**: Discuss whether your graph should include all the points above a certain line or only a square grid of points above a certain line. Defend your decision.

51. Discussion Do you think that a linear model of economic

growth is a good one to explain economic activity as you have experienced it? For example, consider the value of a house in Example 3. Is house value likely to change linearly? Consider Exercise 39.

52. Writing to Learn Write several sentences that explain how the solution to the inequality $0 < 3x + 5$ differs from the solution to the inequality $y < 3x + 5$.

53. Writing to Learn Read in a reference manual about aspect ratio. Then write a paragraph explaining how aspect ratio is related to Exercise 24.

3.4 _____ Analytic Geometry of Lines

In Section 3.3 we found that the graph of an equation of the form $f(x) = mx + b$ or $y = mx + b$ was a line. It was also shown that the graph of an equation of this form had slope m and y-intercept b. Consequently any equation of the form $y = mx + b$ is called the **slope-intercept form** for an equation of the line.

E X A M P L E 1   Finding the Slope-Intercept Form

Write an equation of the line with slope -3 and y-intercept 2.

Solution   The slope is $m = -3$ and the y-intercept is $(0, 2)$. Therefore the equation of the line is $y = -3x + 2$. ≡

Example 1 shows that knowing the slope and the y-intercept of a line allows you to use the slope-intercept form to write the equation of the line. Conversely, if you know the slope-intercept form of a line, you can read from it the slope and the y-intercept of the line.

Sometimes it is advantageous to change an equation of a line and write it in the slope-intercept form. For example, $2x + 3y = 6$ can be written in the equivalent form $y = (-2/3)x + 2$. In this slope-intercept form we conclude that the slope of the line is $-2/3$ and that its y-intercept is 2.

Horizontal and vertical lines are special cases. A horizontal line has a slope $m = 0$, so the slope-intercept form is $y = 0x + b$, or simply $y = b$.

All points on the vertical line through the point (a, b) have the same x-coordinate, so its equation would be $x = a$. Vertical lines are the only lines whose equations cannot be expressed in the form $y = mx + b$.

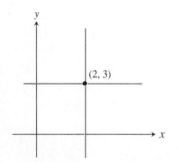

Figure 3.34 $x = 2$ and $y = 3$.

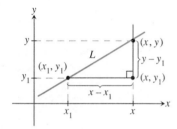

Figure 3.35   Finding the equation of a line given the slope and a point (x_1, y_1) on the line.

E X A M P L E   2   Finding Horizontal and Vertical Lines

Write equations for the horizontal and vertical lines through the point $(2, 3)$.

Solution   See Fig. 3.34. The horizontal line is $y = 3$, and the vertical line is $x = 2$.   ≡

Suppose we know that the slope of a line L is m and are given a point (x_1, y_1) on L that is not necessarily the y-intercept. How do we find an equation of that line?

To figure this out, suppose that (x, y) is *any other* point on line L (see Fig. 3.35). Then the slope m of line L satisfies the following equations:

$$m = \frac{y - y_1}{x - x_1}$$

$$y - y_1 = m(x - x_1).$$

This observation is summarized in Theorem 3.2.

Theorem 3.2   Point-Slope Form

If L is the line through the point (x_1, y_1) with slope m, then the equation

$$y - y_1 = m(x - x_1)$$

is an equation of line L. An equation in this form is called the **point-slope form** for the equation of line L.

E X A M P L E   3   Point-Slope Form

Write an equation for the line that has a slope of 0.5 and contains the point $(-2, 3)$.

Solution $m = 0.5$, and $(x_1, y_1) = (-2, 3)$. Therefore

$$y - y_1 = m(x - x_1)$$

$$y - 3 = 0.5(x + 2) \quad \text{Substitute into the slope-intercept form.}$$

$$y = 0.5x + 1 + 3$$

$$y = 0.5x + 4.$$ ≡

E X A M P L E   4   Writing an Equation Given Two Points

Write an equation for the line that contains the two points $(-3, 1)$ and $(4, -3)$.

Solution

$$m = \frac{-3 - 1}{4 - (-3)} = -\frac{4}{7}$$ First find the slope, and
then use the point-slope form.

$$y - 1 = -\frac{4}{7}(x + 3)$$ Substitute $(-3, 1)$ into the point-slope form.

$$y = \frac{4}{7}x - \frac{12}{7} + 1$$

$$y = -\frac{4}{7}x - \frac{5}{7}$$

$$4x + 7y = -5$$

$(y - x_1) = m(x - x_1)$

If we had chosen to use the point $(4, -3)$, we would have obtained the same
equation. Notice that $4(4) + 7(-3) = -5$, which demonstrates that $(4, -3)$ is on
this line.

The equation of the line in Example 4 can also be written as $4x + 7y + 5 = 0$.
This form $Ax + By + C = 0$ is called the **general form** of a linear equation,
A and B not both zero. Every line has an equation that can be written in this
form. However, equations for vertical lines, $x = a$, cannot be written in the
slope-intercept form.

Following is a summary of the several forms for equations of lines that have
been discussed.

Forms for Linear Equations

General form:	$Ax + By + C = 0, A$ and B not both zero.
Vertical line:	$x = a$
Horizontal line:	$y = b$
Slope-intercept form:	$y = mx + b$
Point-slope form:	$(y - y_1) = m(x - x_1)$

Parallel and Perpendicular Lines

If two lines are parallel, then either they are both vertical (slope undefined) or they
have equal slopes. You discovered this in one of the Explorations in Section 3.3.
For example, the lines with equations $y = 3x - 4$ and $y = 3x + 7$ both have a
slope of 3, and so the lines are parallel.

The next exploration concerns perpendicular lines.

🔍 EXPLORE WITH A GRAPHING UTILITY

Using the viewing rectangle $[-15, 15]$ by $[-10, 10]$ graph each pair of equations. Do they appear to be perpendicular?

1. $y = x - 3$ and $y = -x + 2$

2. $y = \frac{1}{3}x + 7$ and $y = -3x + 2$

3. $y = 2x - 3$ and $y = \frac{1}{2}x + 1$

4. $y = \frac{5}{4}x + 1$ and $y = -\frac{4}{5}x - 3$

5. $y = -2x + 1$ and $y = \frac{1}{5}x - 2$

6. $y = -\frac{2}{3}x + 2$ and $\frac{3}{2}x - 3$

Generalize   How are the slopes of lines related when they are perpendicular?

The following theorem is given without proof.

Theorem 3.3   Parallel and Perpendicular Lines

Let ℓ_1 be a line with equation $y = m_1 x + b_1$ and ℓ_2 be a line with equation $y = m_2 x + b_2$. Then

- the lines ℓ_1 and ℓ_2 are parallel if and only if $m_1 = m_2$, and

- the lines ℓ_1 and ℓ_2 are perpendicular if and only if $m_1 = -\dfrac{1}{m_2}$.

E X A M P L E   5   Determining a Line

Write an equation for the line passing through $(1, -2)$ and parallel to the line $3x - 2y = 1$.

Solution   First change the equation to the slope-intercept form to find its slope.

$$3x - 2y = 1$$

$$-2y = -3x + 1$$

$$y = \tfrac{3}{2}x - \tfrac{1}{2}$$

Next use the point-slope form with $m = \frac{3}{2}$ and the point $(1, -2)$.

$$y + 2 = \tfrac{3}{2}(x - 1) \qquad \text{or} \qquad 3x - 2y = 7$$

■

Notice that the given equation $3x - 2y = 1$ in Example 5 and the solution equation $3x - 2y = 7$ both begin with the expression $3x - 2y$. Why is this the case?

Midpoint

The coordinates of the midpoint of a segment can be found if the coordinates of the endpoints are known.

Theorem 3.4   Midpoint Formula $X + X$

The **midpoint** of the line segment with endpoints (a, b) and (c, d) is the point with coordinates $\left(\dfrac{a+c}{2}, \dfrac{b+d}{2}\right)$.

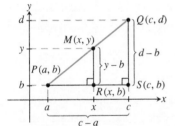

Figure 3.36   For proof of the midpoint formula.

Proof   Let $M(x, y)$ be the midpoint of the line segment determined by the points $P(a, b)$ and $Q(c, d)$ (see Fig. 3.36). Then the following proportions hold since triangles PRM and PSQ are similar. Solve each proportion for x and y.

$$\frac{x-a}{c-a} = \frac{1}{2} \qquad\qquad \frac{y-b}{d-b} = \frac{1}{2}$$

$$x - a = \frac{c-a}{2} \qquad\qquad y - b = \frac{d-b}{2}$$

$$x = \frac{a+c}{2} \qquad\qquad y = \frac{b+d}{2}$$

An easy way to remember the conclusion of this theorem is to observe that the coordinates of the midpoint are found by averaging the x- and y-coordinates of the two points.

E X A M P L E 6   Finding Midpoint Coordinates

Find the midpoint of the segment with endpoints $(-5, 2)$ and $(3, 7)$.

Solution   From Theorem 3.4 we have

$$x = \frac{-5 + 3}{2} \qquad\qquad y = \frac{2 + 7}{2}$$

$$x = -1 \qquad\qquad y = 4.5.$$

The midpoint is $(-1, 4.5)$.

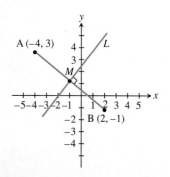

Figure 3.37   The slopes of a line segment and its perpendicular bisector are negative reciprocals.

E X A M P L E   7   Finding a Perpendicular Bisector

Write an equation for the perpendicular bisector of the line segment determined by points $A(-4, 3)$ and $B(2, -1)$.

Solution   Let $m =$ the slope of segment AB, and let $M =$ the midpoint of segment AB. Then

$$M = \left(\frac{-4+2}{2}, \frac{3-1}{2}\right) = (-1, 1) \quad \text{and} \quad m = \frac{-1-3}{2-(-4)} = -\frac{2}{3}.$$

The slope of the perpendicular bisector L is the negative reciprocal of m and contains the point M (see Fig. 3.37).

$$y - 1 = \frac{3}{2}(x + 1) \quad \text{Use the point-slope form.}$$
$$3x - 2y + 5 = 0$$

Examples 8 and 9 show that we can use the theorems from this section to verify the truth of some relationships in geometry.

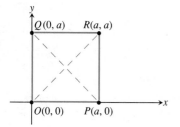

Figure 3.38   Square $OQRP$.

E X A M P L E   8   Diagonals of a Square

Show that the diagonals of a square are perpendicular.

Solution   Draw a diagram like Fig. 3.38. Assign a coordinate system to the figure so that the coordinates of the vertices of the square are $(0, 0), (a, 0), (0, a)$, and (a, a). Then

$$\text{slope of } OR = \frac{a-0}{a-0} = 1 \quad \text{and} \quad \text{slope of } QP = \frac{0-a}{a-0} = -1.$$

These slopes are negative reciprocals, so the diagonals are perpendicular.

E X A M P L E   9   Diagonals of a Parallelogram

Show that the diagonals of a parallelogram bisect each other.

Solution   Draw a diagram of a parallelogram. Recall from your study of geometry that opposite sides of a parallelogram are parallel. Use this fact to assign a coordinate system to your figure so that the vertices of the parallelogram are $(0, 0), (a, b), (a + c, b)$, and $(c, 0)$ (see Fig. 3.39).

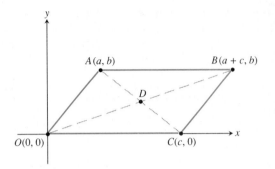

Figure 3.39 Parallelogram $OABC$.

Then

$$\text{midpoint of } OB = \left(\frac{0+a+c}{2}, \frac{0+b}{2}\right) = \left(\frac{a+c}{2}, \frac{b}{2}\right),$$

$$\text{midpoint of } AC = \left(\frac{a+c}{2}, \frac{b+0}{2}\right) = \left(\frac{a+c}{2}, \frac{b}{2}\right).$$

Since these midpoints are the same point, conclude that the diagonals of parallelogram $OABC$ bisect each other.   ≡

Exercises for Section 3.4

In Exercises 1 to 4, write an equation for the line with the given slope m and y-intercept b.

1. $m = \frac{3}{2}$, $b = 2$

2. $m = -\frac{3}{4}$, $b = -3$

3. $m = \frac{1}{5}$, $b = -\frac{2}{3}$

4. $m = 6$, $b = \frac{1}{2}$

In Exercises 5 to 8, write an equation for the line with the given slope m that contains the given point.

5. $m = \frac{3}{2}$; $(-1, 0)$

6. $m = -\frac{2}{3}$; $(2, -4)$

7. $m = 0$; $(2, 5)$

8. $m = 10$; $(-1, 3)$

In Exercises 9 to 12, write an equation for the line determined by each pair of points.

9. $(0, 0)$; $(2, 3)$

10. $(2, -1)$; $(-3, 4)$

11. $(-1, 0)$; $(3, 1)$

12. $(8, 1)$; $(8, -4)$

In Exercises 13 and 14, write an equation of both the vertical and the horizontal line through each point.

13. $P(-2, 3)$

14. $Q(0, -2)$

In Exercises 15 to 18, find the midpoint of the line segment determined by the pair of points.

15. $(-1, 3)$; $(5, 9)$

16. $(2, -3)$; $(-1, -1)$

17. $(3, \sqrt{2})$; $(6, 2)$

18. (a, b); $(3, -6)$

In Exercises 19 and 20, write an equation for the perpendicular bisector of the line segment determined by each pair of points.

19. $(-1, 3)$; $(5, -3)$

20. $(3, -5)$; $(-6, 10)$

In Exercises 21 to 24, write an equation for the line determined by the given conditions:

21. It contains the point $(-2, 4)$ and is parallel to the line $x - 4y = 8$.

22. It contains the point $(4, -1)$ and is perpendicular to the line $2x - y = 4$.

23. It contains the point $(0, 2)$ and is parallel to the line $y = 8$.

24. It contains the point $(-2, 0)$ and is parallel to the line $x = 4$.

25. Show that the triangle with vertices $(-1, 2), (-6, -2)$, and $(2, -12)$ is a right triangle.

26. Show that the midpoint of the hypotenuse of a right triangle with vertices $(0, 0), (5, 0)$, and $(0, 7)$ is equidistant from all three vertices.

27. Do the midpoints of the sides of the quadrilateral with vertices $(-1, 2), (2, 6), (-3, 7)$, and $(8, -2)$ form a rectangle?

21-27

28. Determine D so that $A = (1, 2)$, $B = (3, 5)$, $C = (7, 7)$, and D are vertices of a parallelogram. (There are three answers.)

For Exercises 29 and 30, let $A = (3, 0)$, $B = (-1, 2)$, and $C = (5, 4)$.

29. Prove that the triangle determined by A, B, and C is isosceles but not equilateral.

30. Prove that the line through A and the midpoint of BC is perpendicular to BC.

31. Triangle ABC has vertices $A(0, 0)$, $B(2, 6)$, and $C(5, 0)$. Write an equation for each of the three lines determined by a vertex and the midpoint of the opposite side of the triangle.

32. Show that in any triangle, the line segment joining the midpoints of two sides is parallel to the third side.

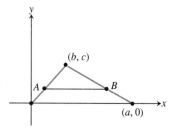

For Exercise 32

33. Show that if the midpoints of consecutive sides of any quadrilateral are connected, the result is a parallelogram.

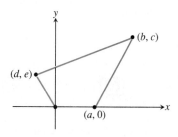

For Exercise 33

34. Prove that the line segments joining the midpoints of the opposite sides of any quadrilateral bisect each other.

35. Prove that the diagonals of a rectangle are equal in length.

36. Prove that if the diagonals of a rectangle are perpendicular, then the rectangle is a square.

37. Prove that the midpoint of the hypotenuse of a right triangle is the same distance from each of the three vertices.

38. Let $A = (-1, 3)$ and $B = (9, 6)$. Find the coordinates of the two points on the line AB that divide the segment AB into three equal segments.

39. Let $A = (-1, 3)$ and $B = (9, 6)$. Find the coordinates of the three points on the line AB that divide the segment AB into four equal segments.

For Exercises 40 to 42, refer to the following figure.

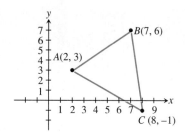

For Exercises 40 to 42

40. Find an equation for the line through A and B.

41. Find an equation for the line through A and the midpoint of BC. This segment is called a **median**.

42. Find an equation for the line through A and perpendicular to BC. This segment is called an **altitude**.

43. Show that the altitudes of a triangle are *coincident* (that is, intersect in a common point). *Hint:* Show that the three altitudes ℓ_1, ℓ_2, and ℓ_3 intersect at the point $\left(a, a(c - a)/b\right)$.

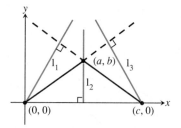

For Exercise 43

44. Prove that if $c \neq d$, and a and b are not both zero, $ax + by = c$ and $ax + by = d$ are parallel lines.

3.5 _____ Graphs of Quadratic Functions

This section focuses on a family of functions known as the quadratic functions.

Definition 3.8   Quadratic Function

A function f is called a **quadratic function** if it can be written in the form $f(x) = ax^2 + bx + c$, where a, b, and c are real numbers, called coefficients, and $a \neq 0$.

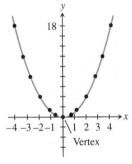

Figure 3.40 $y = x^2$.

The simplest and most basic quadratic function is $f(x) = x^2$ (Fig. 3.40). Observe that $f(-x) = f(x)$, which means that if (x, y) is a point of the graph, $(-x, y)$ is also. The y-axis is a line of symmetry. Recall that the graph of this function is called a parabola. The point $(0, 0)$ is the lowest point of the graph and is called the **vertex** of the parabola.

Transforming the Graph of $y = x^2$

We shall show that the graph of any quadratic function can be obtained from $y = x^2$ by stretching or shrinking, shifting the whole graph horizontally or vertically, reflecting the graph through the x-axis, or some combination of these **transformations**.

🔍 **EXPLORE WITH A GRAPHING UTILITY**

Find graphs for the following four functions, one after another, without erasing: $f_1(x) = x^2$, $f_2(x) = \frac{1}{3}x^2$, $f_3(x) = 2x^2$, and $f_4(x) = 4x^2$.

Questions:

1. Which graphs lie below the graph of $f(x) = x^2$?

2. Which graphs lie above the graph of $f(x) = x^2$?

3. Propose an equation of a quadratic function whose graph is between the graphs of $f(x) = 2x^2$ and $f(x) = 4x^2$. Support your guess graphically.

Generalize   Describe the graph of $f(x) = ax^2$ for various positive values of the coefficient a.

Conjecture   How will these graphs change if a is negative?

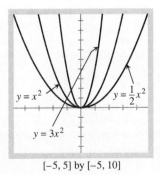

[−5, 5] by [−5, 10]

Figure 3.41   Three parabolas.

The graphs in Fig. 3.41 add additional evidence to support your generalizations. Notice that all these graphs pass through the point $(0, 0)$, that all of them lie above the x-axis, and that the y-axis is a line of symmetry for all of them.

If x is any nonzero number, then $\frac{1}{2}x^2 < x^2$, and the graph of $y = \frac{1}{2}x^2$ lies below the graph of $y = x^2$. Similarly, $x^2 < 3x^2$, and the graph of $y = x^2$ lies below the graph of $y = 3x^2$. These general relationships can be summarized:

Value of a	Comparison of Graphs
$a > 1$	$y = ax^2$ is above $y = x^2$.
$0 < a < 1$	$y = ax^2$ is below $y = x^2$.

The graph of $y = x^2$ can be *stretched up* to the graph of $y = 3x^2$ or *shrunk down* to the graph of $y = \frac{1}{2}x^2$.

Definition 3.9   Vertical Stretch and Shrink

If $a > 1$, the graph of $f(x) = ax^2$ can be obtained from the graph of $y = x^2$ with a **vertical stretch** of the graph of $y = x^2$ by a factor of a.

If $0 < a < 1$, the graph of $f(x) = ax^2$ can be obtained from the graph of $y = x^2$ with a **vertical shrink** of the graph of $y = x^2$ by the factor a.

The graph of f has vertex $(0, 0)$, and the y-axis is a line of symmetry.

The next example confirms whether your conjecture in the Exploration was correct.

EXAMPLE 1   Obtaining a Graph by Reflection

Find complete graphs of the functions $y = -x^2$, $y = -3x^2$, and $y = -\frac{1}{2}x^2$, one after the other in the same viewing rectangle. How do these graphs differ from those in Fig. 3.41?

Solution   Figure 3.42 shows that all the graphs are parabolas that open downward, whereas in Fig. 3.41 all the parabolas open upward.

If the coordinate plane in Fig. 3.41 is folded along the x-axis, the resulting graphs would coincide with the graphs in Fig. 3.42.

In general, any graph of the form $y = -ax^2$ can be obtained by reflecting the graph of $y = ax^2$ through the x-axis.

EXAMPLE 2   Combining Two Transformations

Describe how a complete graph of $y = -5x^2$ can be obtained from the graph of $y = x^2$ by stretching, shrinking, and/or reflection.

Solution   There are two solutions. You can vertically stretch the graph of $y = x^2$ by a factor of 5, and then reflect the result through the x-axis. Or you can reflect

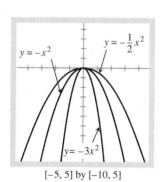

[−5, 5] by [−10, 5]

Figure 3.42   Three downward-opening parabolas.

the graph of $y = x^2$ through the x-axis, and then stretch the graph of $y = -x^2$ by a factor of 5. ≡

In Example 2 the order in which the two transformations are performed does not matter. That will not always be the case, however. Let us summarize the transformations explored so far.

Transformations of Stretching/Shrinking and Reflection

Condition on coefficient a   **To obtain $y = ax^2$ from $y = x^2$**

$a > 1$	Stretch by a factor of a.
$0 < a < 1$	Shrink by a factor of a.
$-1 < a < 0$	Shrink by factor $|a|$ and reflect through the x-axis.
$a < -1$	Stretch by factor $|a|$ and reflect through the x-axis.

E X A M P L E   3   *Obtaining a Graph by a Vertical Shift*

Describe how complete graphs of $y = x^2 + 2$ and $y = x^2 - 3$ can be obtained from the graph of $y = x^2$.

Solution   The graph of $y = x^2 + 2$ can be obtained from the graph of $y = x^2$ by shifting it up 2 units (Fig. 3.43a).

Similarly the graph of $y = x^2 - 3$ can be obtained from the graph of $y = x^2$ by shifting it down 3 units (Fig. 3.43b). When shifting a graph up or down, the y-axis remains a line of symmetry.

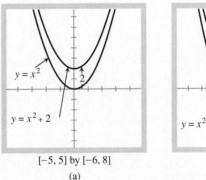

[−5, 5] by [−6, 8]

(a)

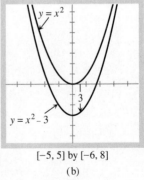

[−5, 5] by [−6, 8]

(b)

Figure 3.43   Vertical-shift transformations of $y = x^2$ (a) to $y = x^2 + 2$ and (b) to $y = x^2 - 3$. ≡

Example 3 can be generalized to the following definition.

Definition 3.10   Vertical Shift

The graph of $f(x) = x^2 + k$ is said to be obtained from the graph of $y = x^2$ by a **vertical shift**.

- If $k > 0$, the shift is *up* k units.
- If $k < 0$, the shift is *down* $|k|$ units.

For any k, the graph of f has the vertex $(0, k)$, and the y-axis is the line of symmetry.

The vertical-shift transformation is a rigid motion because it preserves both the size and shape of the graph. In contrast, the transformations vertical stretch and vertical shrink are not rigid motion transformations.

E X A M P L E   4   Obtaining a Graph by a Horizontal Shift

Describe how complete graphs of $y = (x - 3)^2$ and $y = (x + 2)^2$ can be obtained from the graph of $y = x^2$.

Solution   The graph of $y = (x - 3)^2$ can be obtained from the graph of $y = x^2$ by shifting it to the right 3 units (Fig. 3.44a). Similarly the graph of $y = (x + 2)^2$ can be obtained from the graph of $y = x^2$ by shifting it left 2 units (Fig. 3.44b). When a graph is shifted right or left, the line of symmetry of the graph slides in the same direction.

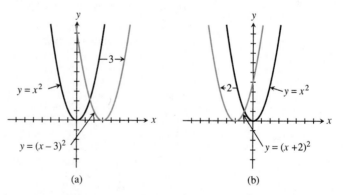

(a)   (b)

Figure 3.44   Two horizontal-shift transformations of $y = x^2$. (a) to $y = (x - 3)^2$; (b) to $y = (x + 2)^2$.

From Example 4 we can generalize the following definition.

Definition 3.11   Horizontal Shift

The graph of $f(x) = (x - h)^2$ is said to be obtained from the graph of $y = x^2$ by a **horizontal shift**.

- If $h > 0$, the shift is *to the right* h units.
- If $h < 0$, the shift is *to the left* $|h|$ units.

For any h, the graph of f has the vertex $(h, 0)$ and the line of symmetry $x = h$.

In summary, we have considered four types of transformations:

a) vertical stretch or shrink,

b) vertical shift,

c) horizontal shift, and

d) reflection through the x-axis.

As these transformations are performed on the parabola $y = x^2$, it is often helpful to keep track of the vertex and the line of symmetry.

Examples 5 to 7 illustrate how these transformations can be combined.

E X A M P L E   5   Combining Two Shift Transformations

Find the vertex and line of symmetry of the graph of $f(x) = (x + 2)^2 - 3$. Describe how its complete graph can be obtained from the graph of $y = x^2$.

Solution   Study the algebraic form of the equation $y = (x + 2)^2 - 3$. Rewriting the factor $(x + 2)^2$ as $(x - (-2))^2$ shows that a horizontal shift left 2 units is required. The "-3" indicates a shift down 3 units (see Fig. 3.45). The new vertex is $(-2, -3)$, and the new line of symmetry is $x = -2$.

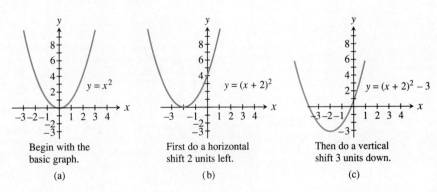

Begin with the basic graph. (a)

First do a horizontal shift 2 units left. (b)

Then do a vertical shift 3 units down. (c)

Figure 3.45   Transforming $y = x^2$ to $y = (x + 2)^2 - 3$.

A look at the graphs in Fig. 3.45 shows that the order of the transformations in the solution could have been reversed. The vertical shift could have been completed first, followed by the horizontal shift.

EXAMPLE 6   Combining Stretch and Shift Transformations

Describe how the complete graph of $f(x) = 5x^2 + 4$ can be obtained from the graph of $y = x^2$. Find the vertex and line of symmetry of f.

Solution   See Fig. 3.46.

1. Begin with the basic graph of $y = x^2$.
2. Stretch vertically 5 units to get $y = 5x^2$.
3. Then shift up 4 units to get $y = 5x^2 + 4$.

The vertex is $(0, 4)$, and the line of symmetry is $x = 0$.

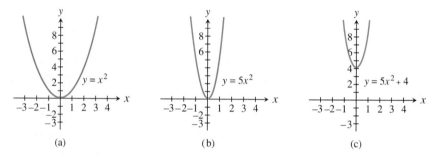

(a)   (b)   (c)

Figure 3.46   Transforming $y = x^2$ to $y = 5x^2 + 4$.

REMINDER

When combining several transformations, the order in which they are performed often makes a difference. In general, when a sequence of transformations includes vertical stretch or shrink, or a reflection through the x-axis, the order may make a difference.

Notice that in Example 6 a vertical stretch followed by a vertical shift does not result in the same graph as the reverse order of transformations. To shift up first and then do a vertical stretch would yield the following sequence of equations:

$$y = x^2, \qquad y = x^2 + 4, \qquad y = 5(x^2 + 4) = 5x^2 + 20.$$

Note that this final equation is not the same as $y = 5x^2 + 4$.

EXAMPLE 7   Combining Several Transformations

Describe how the complete graph of $f(x) = -3(x - 1)^2 + 4$ can be obtained from the graph of $y = x^2$, and find its vertex and line of symmetry.

Solution

1. Begin with the basic graph of $y = x^2$.
2. Shift right 1 unit to find $y = (x - 1)^2$.

3. Stretch vertically by a factor of 3 to get $y = 3(x - 1)^2$.

4. Reflect through the x-axis to arrive at $y = -3(x - 1)^2$.

5. Shift up 4 units to get $y = -3(x - 1)^2 + 4$.

The vertex is $(1, 4)$, and the line of symmetry is $x = 1$.

    Thus far in this section all the quadratic functions have been written in a particular form called standard form. This has been helpful for finding the right combination of transformations asked for in the examples. Later in the section we will see how to convert other quadratic equation forms into standard form in order to find the right transformations.

Definition 3.12 Standard Form of a Quadratic Function

The **standard form of a quadratic function** $y = f(x)$ is
$f(x) = a(x - h)^2 + k$, where a, h, and k, are real-number constants.

    We summarize how the graph of a quadratic function in standard form can be obtained by transforming the graph of the function $y = x^2$.

Transforming $y = x^2$ to $f(x) = a(x - h)^2 + k$

The graph of a quadratic function in standard form $f(x) = a(x - h)^2 + k$ can be obtained from the graph of $y = x^2$ through the following sequence of transformations, performed in the indicated order.

1. *Horizontal shift h units:* Shift right if $h > 0$ and left if $h < 0$.
2. *Vertical stretch/shrink by factor $|a|$.* Stretch if $|a| > 1$ and shrink if $0 < |a| < 1$.
3. *Reflect in x-axis only if $a < 0$.*
4. *Vertical shift k units:* Shift up if $k > 0$, and down if $k < 0$.

The vertex of the graph of f is the point (h, k), and its line of symmetry is $x = h$.

Finding the Graph of $f(x) = ax^2 + bx + c$

To find the vertex and line of symmetry of a general quadratic function and to identify the transformations used to transform $y = x^2$, use the technique of completing the square to change the function to standard form.

E X A M P L E   8   Writing a Quadratic Function in Standard Form

Describe how the complete graph of $f(x) = -2x^2 - 12x - 13$ can be obtained from the graph of $y = x^2$. Find the vertex and line of symmetry of f.

Solution

$$f(x) = -2x^2 - 12x - 13 \quad \text{First complete the square.}$$

$$= -2(x^2 + 6x) - 13$$

$$= -2(x^2 + 6x + 9) - 13 + 18$$

$$= -2(x + 3)^2 + 5$$

The graph of this function (Fig. 3.47) can be obtained from the graph of $y = x^2$ as follows: Shift left 3 units, stretch vertically by a factor of 2, reflect through the x-axis, and finally shift up 5 units.

The vertex is $(-3, 5)$, and the line of symmetry is $x = -3$.

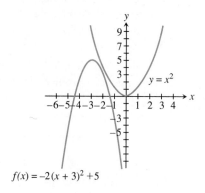

$$f(x) = -2(x + 3)^2 + 5$$

Figure 3.47   Notice how much easier it is to graph $f(x) = -2x^2 - 12x - 13$ once it is written in the form $f(x) = -2(x + 3)^2 + 5$.   ▤

This following theorem describes the coordinates of the vertex and the line of symmetry for a general quadratic function.

Theorem 3.5   Symmetry and Vertex of $f(x) = ax^2 + bx + c$

For the graph of the function $f(x) = ax^2 + bx + c$

▪ the vertex is $\left(-\dfrac{b}{2a}, c - \dfrac{b^2}{4a}\right)$;

▪ the line of symmetry is $x = -\dfrac{b}{2a}$.

Proof

$$f(x) = ax^2 + bx + c$$

$$= a\left(x^2 + \frac{b}{a}x\right) + c$$

$$= a\left(x^2 + \frac{b}{a}x + \frac{b^2}{4a^2}\right) + c - \frac{b^2}{4a}$$

$$= a\left(x + \frac{b}{2a}\right)^2 + \left(c - \frac{b^2}{4a}\right)$$

So the line of symmetry is $x = -b/2a$. This means that the x-coordinate of the vertex is also $-b/2a$ and the y-coordinate is $f(-b/2a) = c - b^2/4a$. ∎

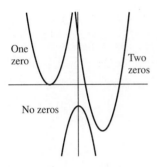

Figure 3.48 Examples of quadratic graphs with different numbers of zeros.

Zeros of a Quadratic Function

Recall from Section 2.2 that a number k is called a zero of an equation if $(k, 0)$ is an x-intercept for the graph of the equation. In other words, k is a zero for a function f if $f(k) = 0$. Consequently, a number k is a zero for a quadratic function $f(x) = ax^2 + bx + c$ if and only if it is a solution to the equation $ax^2 + bx + c = 0$. A quadratic function can have zero, one, or two zeros (see Fig. 3.48). The discriminant $b^2 - 4ac$ can be used to determine the number of real-number zeros for a quadratic function.

Theorem 3.6   Discriminant and Zeros

Let $f(x) = ax^2 + bx + c$.

- If $b^2 - 4ac < 0$, then f has no real-number zeros, and the graph of f does not cross the x-axis.

- If $b^2 - 4ac = 0$, then f has exactly one real-number zero, and the graph of f is tangent to the x-axis.

- If $b^2 - 4ac > 0$, then f has two real-number zeros, and the graph of f crosses the x-axis twice.

Proof   Recall that zeros to the quadratic equation $ax^2 + bx + c = 0$ are given by the quadratic formula:

$$x = \frac{-b \pm \sqrt{b^2 - 4ac}}{2a}.$$

If $b^2 - 4ac < 0$, this expression is not defined and the equation has no real solutions. If $b^2 - 4ac = 0$, the quadratic equation has only one real solution; and if $b^2 - 4ac > 0$, there are both positive and negative square roots, which means the equation has two real solutions. ≡

E X A M P L E   9   APPLICATION: Maximum Enclosed Area

If 200 feet of fence are used to enclose a rectangular plot of land using an existing wall as one side of the plot, find the dimensions of the rectangle with maximum enclosed area.

Solution   Let x represent the width of the rectangle. Then $200 - 2x$ represents its length, and $A(x) = x(200 - 2x)$ is an algebraic representation for the area of the rectangular plot. Figure 3.49(a) suggests that the maximum area is about 5000 when x is about 50.

Apply zoom-in to obtain Fig. 3.49(b). This graph permits us to read that the maximum area is 5000 and occurs for $x = 50$ with an error of at most 0.01.

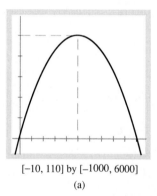
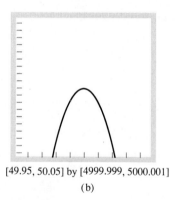

[−10, 110] by [−1000, 6000]   [49.95, 50.05] by [4999.999, 5000.001]

(a)   (b)

Figure 3.49   Two views of $A(x) = x(200 - 2x)$.

The zeros of $A(x) = x(200 - 2x)$ are 0 and 100. Thus, by symmetry, the x-coordinate of the vertex is 50 and the y-coordinate of the vertex is $A(50) = 5000$. This confirms that the dimensions of the maximum enclosed area are 50 feet by 100 feet. ≡

Exercises for Section 3.5

In Exercises 1 to 6, find complete graphs of the three functions in the same viewing rectangle.

1. $y = 3x^2$, $y = 3(x - 2)^2$, $y = 3(x + 2)^2$

2. $y = -x^2$, $y = -(x + 4)^2$, $y = -(x - 4)^2$

3. $y = 2x^2$, $y = 2(x - 1)^2$, $y = 2(x + 1)^2$

4. $y = -x^2$, $y = -x^2 - 4$, $y = -x^2 + 4$

5. $y = x^2 + 3$, $y = (x + 2)^2 + 3$, $y = (x - 3)^2 + 3$

6. $y = x^2 - 2$, $y = 3x^2 - 2$, $y = -2x^2 - 2$

In Exercises 7 to 9, when both functions are graphed in the same viewing rectangle, which graph is "above" the other?

7. $y = 3x^2$ or $y = 4x^2$ **8.** $y = \frac{2}{3}x^2$ or $y = \frac{3}{4}x^2$

9. $y = 3.21x^2$ or $y = 3.021x^2$

In Exercises 10 to 13, describe a transformation that can be used to transform the graph of the first function to the graph of the second function.

10. $y = (x - 3)^2$ and $y = (x + 3)^2$

11. $y = (x - 2)^2$ and $y = (x - 3)^2$

12. $y = (x + 5)^2$ and $y = (x + 2)^2$

13. $y = (x + 3.2)^2$ and $y = (x + 0.2)^2$

In Exercises 14 to 18, describe how each graph can be obtained from the graph of $y = x^2$. Support your work with a grapher.

14. $f(x) = 4x^2$ **15.** $f(x) = -3x^2$

16. $f(x) = (x - 5)^2$ **17.** $f(x) = (x + 1)^2$

18. $f(x) = 2x^2 - 3$ **19.** $f(x) = -3x^2 + 2$

In Exercises 20 to 25, find the vertex and the line of symmetry for each parabola.

20. $f(x) = 3(x - 1)^2 + 5$ **21.** $f(x) = -3(x + 2)^2 - 3$

22. $f(x) = 5(x - 3)^2 - 7$ **23.** $f(x) = 2(x - \sqrt{3})^2 + 4$

24. $f(x) = (x - 5)^2 + \sqrt{2}$ **25.** $f(x) = \sqrt{5}(x + 4)^2 + 3$

In Exercises 26 to 31, draw a complete graph of each function. Support your sketch with a grapher.

26. $f(x) = (x - 4)^2 + 3$ **27.** $f(x) = -(x + 3)^2 - 2$

28. $f(x) = 2(x - 1)^2 + 3$ **29.** $f(x) = -3(x + 4)^2 - 5$

30. $f(x) = 3(x - 4)^2 + 7$ **31.** $f(x) = (x - \sqrt{2})^2 - \sqrt{3}$

32. Write an equation whose graph can be obtained from the graph of $y = x^2$ by vertically stretching by a factor of 3 and then shifting right 4 units.

33. Write an equation whose graph can be obtained from the graph of $y = x^2$ by shifting right 4 units and then vertically stretching by a factor of 3.

34. Are the graphs of the equations found in Exercises 32 and 33 the same? Explain any differences.

35. Write an equation whose graph can be obtained from the graph of $y = x^2$ by vertically stretching by a factor of 3 and then vertically shifting up 4 units.

36. Write an equation whose graph can be obtained from the graph of $y = x^2$ with a vertical shift up 4 units followed by a vertical stretch by a factor of 3.

37. Are the graphs of the equations found in Exercises 35 and 36 the same? Explain any differences.

38. Write an equation whose graph can be obtained from the graph of $y = x^2$ by shifting left 2 units, then vertically stretching by a factor of 3, and finally shifting down 4 units.

39. Write an equation whose graph is obtained from the graph of $y = x^2$ by shifting right 4 units, then vertically stretching by a factor of 2, followed by a reflection through the x-axis, and ending with a shift up 3 units.

In Exercises 40 to 43, complete the square for each function. Then write a sequence of transformations that will produce its graph from the graph of $y = x^2$. In each case find the vertex and the line of symmetry of the parabola. Support your work with a grapher.

40. $f(x) = x^2 - 4x + 6$ **41.** $f(x) = x^2 - 6x + 12$

42. $f(x) = 2x^2 - 8x + 20$ **43.** $f(x) = 10 - 16x - x^2$

In Exercises 44 to 49, use the discriminant to determine how many real-number zeros each quadratic function has. Support your work with a grapher.

44. $f(x) = 2x^2 + 5x + 1$ **45.** $f(x) = x^2 - 2x + 1$

46. $f(x) = x^2 + x + 1$ **47.** $f(x) = 2x^2 - 4x + 1$

48. $f(x) = 3x^2 - 7x - 3$ **49.** $f(x) = 2x^2 - x + 3$

50. Find the midpoint of the real zeros of $f(x) = (x - 8)(x + 2)$.

51. Find the midpoint of the real zeros of $f(x) = x^2 - x - 1$.

52. Show that the line of symmetry for the graph of $f(x) = (x - a)(x - b)$ is $x = (a + b)/2$, where a and b are any positive real numbers.

53. Find the vertex of $f(x) = (x - a)(x - b)$, where a and b are any positive real numbers.

54. Let f be the function given by the following graph. Determine the points on the graph of $y = 2 + 3f(x + 1)$ corresponding to the points $(-2, f(-2))$, $(0, f(0))$, and $(4, f(4))$.

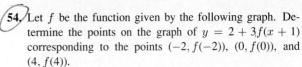

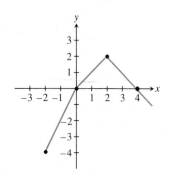

For Exercise 54

In Exercises 55 to 57, $f(x) = |x|$.

55. Complete the equation $f(x-2) = ?$ Explain how the graph of $f(x-2)$ can be obtained from the graph of $f(x)$.

56. Complete the equation $3f(x) = ?$ Explain how the graph of $3f(x)$ can be obtained from the equation of $f(x)$.

57. Complete the equation $2f(x+3)-1 = ?$ Explain how the graph of $2f(x+3)-1$ can be obtained from the graph of $f(x)$.

58. A rectangle is 3 feet longer than it is wide. If each side is increased by 1 foot, the area of the new rectangle is 208 square feet. Find the dimensions of the original rectangle.

59. A rectangular pool with dimensions of 25 by 40 feet is surrounded by a walk with a uniform width. If the area of the walk is 504 square feet, find the width of the walk.

60. Among the rectangles with perimeters of 100 feet, find the dimensions of the one with the maximum area.

61. A piece of wire 20 feet long is cut into two pieces so that the sum of the squares of the length of each piece is 202 square feet. Find the length of each piece.

62. A long rectangular sheet of metal 10 inches wide is to be made into a gutter by turning up sides of equal length perpendicular to the sheet. Find the length that must be turned up to produce a gutter with maximum cross-sectional area.

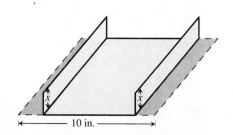

For Exercise 62

63. A rectangular fence is to be constructed around a field so that one side of the field is bounded by the wall of a large building. Determine the maximum area that can be enclosed if the total length of fencing to be used is 500 feet.

64. **Writing to Learn**   Suppose the graph of a function f is obtained from the graph of a function g by performing a sequence of transformations. Write several sentences that explain when the sequence of transformations can be performed in any order and when the order makes a difference.

65. **Writing to Learn**   Find a complete graph of $y = x^2$ in $[-10, 10]$ by $[-10, 10]$ and $y = 3x^2$ in $[-10, 10]$ by $[-50, 50]$. Write several paragraphs that describe which graph appears to be the steepest, and describe what you mean by that phrase. But which graph really is the steepest and why?

3.6 _____ Operations on Functions and Composition of Functions

A function consists of a domain and a **rule**. The rule is often described by using an algebraic formula. A new function can be defined by combining several other functions using addition, subtraction, multiplication, or division. For example, consider the functions $f(x) = x^2$ and $g(x) = \sqrt{x + 1}$:

$$f(x) + g(x) = x^2 + \sqrt{x+1} \qquad \text{Sum of } f \text{ and } g$$

$$f(x) - g(x) = x^2 - \sqrt{x+1} \qquad \text{Difference of } f \text{ and } g$$

$$f(x)g(x) = x^2\sqrt{x+1} \qquad \text{Product of } f \text{ and } g$$

$$\frac{f(x)}{g(x)} = \frac{x^2}{\sqrt{x+1}} \; \left(x \neq -1\right) \quad \text{Quotient of } f \text{ and } g$$

The domain of the new function consists of all numbers x that belong to the domains of *both* f and g.

Definition 3.13   Sum, Difference, Product, and Quotient of Functions

Let f and g be two functions. We define the **sum, difference, product**, and **quotient** of f and g to be the functions whose domains are the set of all numbers common to the domains of f and g, and which are defined as follows:

$$(f + g)(x) = f(x) + g(x)$$

$$(f - g)(x) = f(x) - g(x)$$

$$(fg)(x) = f(x)g(x)$$

$$\left(\frac{f}{g}\right)(x) = \frac{f(x)}{g(x)} \qquad \left(g(x) \neq 0\right).$$

Notice that in the quotient function the denominator cannot be zero.

EXAMPLE 1   Combining Functions

Let $f(x) = \sqrt{x+3}$ and $g(x) = \sqrt{x-2}$. Find the domains and rules for $f+g$ and f/g.

Solution

$$(f + g)(x) = f(x) + g(x)$$

$$= \sqrt{x+3} + \sqrt{x-2}, \quad x+3 \geq 0 \text{ and } x-2 \geq 0$$

$$\left(\frac{f}{g}\right)(x) = \frac{f(x)}{g(x)} = \frac{\sqrt{x+3}}{\sqrt{x-2}}. \quad x+3 \geq 0 \text{ and } x-2 > 0$$

The domain of $f = [-3, \infty)$, and the domain of $g = [2, \infty)$. Therefore the domain of $f + g$ is $[2, \infty) \cap [-3, \infty) = [2, \infty)$.

Since the denominator of (f/g) cannot be zero, its domain is $(2, \infty)$.

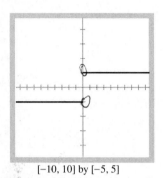

[−10, 10] by [−5, 5]

Figure 3.50 $f(x) = |x|/x$. Note that $f(0)$ is not defined but the grapher cannot indicate this fact.

EXAMPLE 2   Combining Functions

Let $f(x) = |x|$ and $g(x) = x$. Find a complete graph of $(f/g)(x) = f(x)/g(x)$.

Solution   Figure 3.50 shows the graph found with a graphing utility. However, the grapher does not show that fact that $f(0)$ is not defined. This fact can be conveyed when sketching this graph by adding small open circles to the endpoints of the horizontal pieces of the graph (see Fig. 3.51). ≡

Composition of Functions

The function $h(x) = \sqrt{x^2 + 3}$ can be thought of as built from two previously defined functions. Suppose that $g(x) = \sqrt{x}$ and $f(x) = x^2 + 3$. Observe that

$$g(f(x)) = g(x^2 + 3) \quad \text{Replace } f(x) \text{ by } x^2 + 3.$$

$$= \sqrt{x^2 + 3}.$$

With this process a new function, called the composition of f by g, is formed from two given functions f and g. For example, we say that $h(x) = \sqrt{x^2 + 3}$ is the composition of $x^2 + 3$ by $\sqrt{x}$.

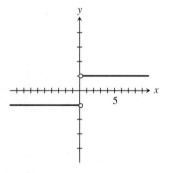

Figure 3.51   Complete graph of $|x|/x$.

Definition 3.14   Composition of Functions *f* by *g*

The **composition of functions f by g**, denoted $g \circ f$, is given by

$$g \circ f(x) = g(f(x)).$$

The domain of $g \circ f$ is the set of all x in the domain of f such that $f(x)$ is in the domain of g.

Since we read from left to right, it is easy to make the error of thinking that, in the composition $g \circ f$, function g is performed first. In fact, the opposite is true (see Fig. 3.52).

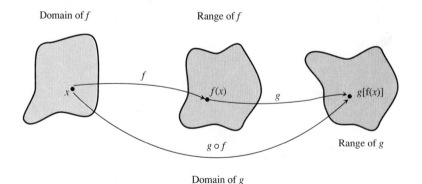

Figure 3.52

Notice that in order for a value of x to be in the domain of $g \circ f$, two conditions must be met:

a) x must be in the domain of f, and

b) $f(x)$ must be in the domain of g.

In other words, the range of f must be a subset of the domain of g.
    The next several examples illustrate finding the composition.

E X A M P L E 3   Forming the Composition

Let $f(x) = x + 1$ and $g(x) = \sqrt{x}$. Find (a) $f(g(9))$, (b) $g(f(3))$, (c) $f(g(x))$, and (d) $g(f(x))$.

Solution

a) $f(g(9)) = f(\sqrt{9}) = f(3) = 4$ Substitute $\sqrt{9}$ for $g(9)$, and evaluate $\sqrt{9}$.

b) $g(f(3)) = g(4) = \sqrt{4} = 2$

c) $f(g(x)) = f(\sqrt{x}) = \sqrt{x} + 1$ Substitute $\sqrt{x}$ for $g(x)$.

d) $g(f(x)) = g(x + 1) = \sqrt{x + 1}$

Example 3 illustrates that $f(g(x))$ and $g(f(x))$ are generally not equal functions.

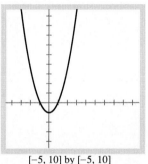

[−5, 10] by [−5, 10]

Figure 3.53 $f(x) = x^2 - 1$.

E X A M P L E 4   Finding the Domain of the Composition

Let $f(x) = x^2 - 1$ and $g(x) = \sqrt{x}$. Find $(g \circ f)(x)$ and $(f \circ g)(x)$ and the domain of each.

Solution   See Figs. 3.53 and 3.54 to see the domain and range of functions f and g.

$$(g \circ f)(x) = g(f(x)) \qquad (f \circ g)(x) = f(g(x))$$
$$= g(x^2 - 1) \qquad\qquad = f(\sqrt{x}), \quad x \geq 0,$$
$$= \sqrt{x^2 - 1} \qquad\qquad = (\sqrt{x})^2 - 1$$
$$= x - 1.$$

Domain of $g \circ f$

$$(g \circ f)(x) = g(x^2 - 1),$$
$$x^2 - 1 \geq 0 \quad x^2 - 1 \text{ must be in the domain of } g.$$
$$x^2 \geq 1.$$

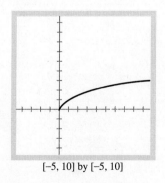

[−5, 10] by [−5, 10]

Figure 3.54 $g(x) = \sqrt{x}$.

So $x \le -1$ or $x \ge 1$. Therefore the domain of $g \circ f = (-\infty, -1] \cup [1, \infty)$.

Domain of $f \circ g$

$$(f \circ g)x = f(\sqrt{x}),$$

$x \ge 0$. $\sqrt{x}$ must be defined for x to be in the domain of $f \circ g$.

Therefore the domain of $f \circ g = [0, \infty)$.   ≣

We see from Example 4 that in general the domains of $f \circ g$ and $g \circ f$ are not equal. This example also underscores the fact that x is in the domain of $(g \circ f)(x)$ only if $f(x)$ is in the domain of g.

A similar consideration must be made when determining the range. In Example 4 we found that $(f \circ g)(x) = x - 1$ when $x \ge 0$. We must be cautious and not simply look at $x - 1$ and conclude that the range of $f \circ g$ is all real numbers. In fact $(f \circ g)(x)$ is in the range of $f \circ g$ only if x is in the domain of $f \circ g$.

E X A M P L E 5   Domain and Range of a Composition

Let $f(x) = \sqrt{x}$ and $g(x) = x - 3$. Find $g \circ f$ and $f \circ g$ and the domain and range of each.

Solution   See Fig. 3.55.

$$(g \circ f)(x) = g(f(x)) = g(\sqrt{x}) \qquad\qquad (f \circ g)(x) = f(g(x)) = f(x - 3)$$

$$= \sqrt{x} - 3. \quad \text{So } x \ge 0. \qquad\qquad = \sqrt{x - 3}. \quad \text{So } x \ge 3.$$

domain of $g \circ f = [0, \infty)$,   domain of $f \circ g = [3, \infty)$,

range of $g \circ f = [-3, \infty)$.   range of $f \circ g = [0, \infty)$.

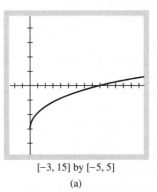

[−3, 15] by [−5, 5]

(a)

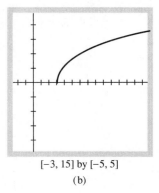

[−3, 15] by [−5, 5]

(b)

Figure 3.55   (a) $(g \circ f)(x) = \sqrt{x} - 3$; (b) $(f \circ g)(x) = \sqrt{x - 3}$.   ≣

In Section 3.5 the graphs of functions $h_1(x) = ax^2$, $h_2(x) = x^2 + k$, and $h_3(x) = (x - h)^2$ were found to be transformations of the graph of $f(x) = x^2$. The next example shows that for each of these functions it is possible to find a function g so that these functions can be represented as composites of f and g.

E X A M P L E 6 Transformations as Compositions of Two Functions

Let $f(x) = x^2$.

Find the functions $g(x)$ such that

a) $h_1(x) = ax^2 = g(f(x))$,

b) $h_2(x) = x^2 + k = g(f(x))$, and

c) $h_3(x) = (x - h)^2 = f(g(x))$.

Solution

a) If $g(x) = ax$, then $(g \circ f)(x) = g(f(x)) = g(x^2) = ax^2 = h_1(x)$.

b) If $g(x) = x + k$, then $(g \circ f)(x) = g(f(x)) = g(x^2) = x^2 + k = h_2(x)$.

c) If $g(x) = x - h$, then $(f \circ g)(x) = f(g(x)) = f(x - h) = (x - h)^2 = h_3(x)$. ▰

Transformations can be performed on a general function $y = f(x)$ as well as on the function $y = x^2$.

Transformation Equations for $y = f(x)$

Suppose that a, k, and h are positive real numbers. Then transformations of the graph of $y = f(x)$ are represented as follows:

Transformation Performed on $y = f(x)$	Transformation Function
Vertical stretch or shrink	$h(x) = af(x)$
Vertical shift k units upward	$h(x) = f(x) + k$
Vertical shift k units downward	$h(x) = f(x) - k$
Horizontal shift h units to the right	$h(x) = f(x - h)$
Horizontal shift h units to the left	$h(x) = f(x + h)$
Reflection through the x-axis	$h(x) = -f(x)$
Reflection through the y-axis	$h(x) = f(-x)$

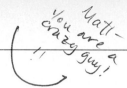

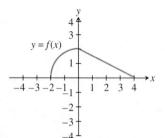

$y = f(x)$

Figure 3.56 Graph of function for Example 7.

EXAMPLE 7   Transforming the Graph of $f(x)$

A graph of a function f is given in Fig. 3.56. Sketch the graph of $y = 2f(x+1)-3$.

Solution   First do a vertical stretch by factor 2 to get $y = 2f(x)$ (Fig. 3.57a). Then do a horizontal shift left 1 unit to get $y = 2f(x + 1)$ (Fig. 3.57b). Finally, do a vertical shift down 3 units to get $y = 2f(x + 1) - 3$ (Fig. 3.57c).

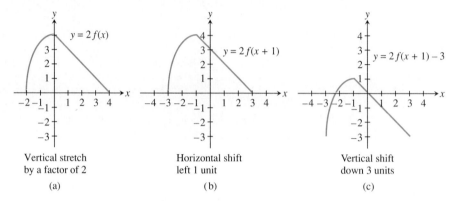

Vertical stretch by a factor of 2	Horizontal shift left 1 unit	Vertical shift down 3 units
(a)	(b)	(c)

Figure 3.57 Transformations performed on the graph of $y = f(x)$ in Fig. 3.56 to get $y = 2f(x + 1) - 3$.

Composition of functions is important in applications. Suppose that a spherical balloon is being inflated. This means that both the radius r and volume V of the sphere change as time changes. That is, r and V are both functions of t. Recall that $V = \frac{4}{3}\pi r^3$. Thus if $r = f(t)$, then $V(t)$ can be expressed as the composition

$$V(t) = \frac{4}{3}\pi(f(t))^3.$$

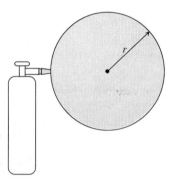

Figure 3.58 Inflation of a balloon with radius r.

EXAMPLE 8   APPLICATION: Volume of a Balloon

A spherically-shaped balloon is being inflated so that the radius r is changing at the constant rate of 2 inches per second (Fig. 3.58). Assume that $r = 0$ at time $t = 0$. Find an algebraic representation $V(t)$ for the volume as a function of t, and determine the volume of the balloon after 5 seconds.

Solution

$$r = 2t$$ *r changes at 2 inches per second, so after t seconds $r = 2t$ inches.*

$$V = \frac{4}{3}\pi r^3$$

$$= \frac{4}{3}\pi(2t)^3$$ *This equation expresses V as a composition of functions.*

$$V(t) = \frac{32}{3}\pi t^3.$$

Substitute $t = 5$ into the algebraic representation $V(t) = \frac{32}{3}\pi t^3$:

$$V(5) = \frac{32}{3}\pi(5)^3$$

$$= \frac{4000}{3}\pi \qquad \text{Completing this calculation on a calculator yields an approximation for } V.$$

The volume V is approximately 4188.79 cubic inches after 5 seconds of inflation.

≡

EXAMPLE 9   APPLICATION: Length of a Shadow

Anita is 5 feet tall and walks at the rate of 4 feet per second away from a streetlight with its lamp 12 feet above level ground. Find an algebraic representation for the length of Anita's shadow as a function of time t, and find the length of the shadow after 7 seconds.

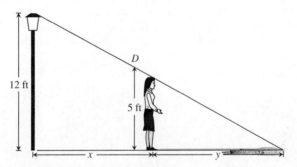

Figure 3.59   A 12-foot streetlight casts a shadow y feet long as Anita walks away from the streetlight.

Solution   Refer to Fig. 3.59.
Given:

> y: length of Anita's shadow
> x: distance from Anita to the streetlight
> $x = 4t$: distance from Anita to the streetlight after t seconds ...

Find: y as a function of t.

Use the fact that the two right triangles are similar to obtain the following proportion.

$$\frac{12}{5} = \frac{x + y}{y} \qquad \text{This proportion works because two right triangles are similar.}$$

$$12y = 5x + 5y$$

$$7y = 5x$$

$$y = \frac{5}{7}x \qquad \text{Substitute } x = 4t \text{ into this equation.}$$

$$y = \frac{5}{7}(4t)$$

$$y = \frac{20}{7}t$$

Substitute $t = 7$ into the algebraic representation $y = \frac{20}{7}t$, to find that the length of the shadow after 7 seconds is 20 feet. ▤

EXAMPLE 10   APPLICATION: Area of a Rectangle

The initial dimensions of a rectangle are 3 by 4 cm, and the length and width of the rectangle are increasing at the rate of 1 cm per second. How long will it take for the area to be at least 10 times its initial size?

Solution

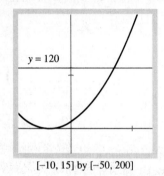

$y = 120$

[−10, 15] by [−50, 200]

Figure 3.60 $A(t) = (3 + t)(4 + t)$.

length ℓ:	$\ell = 3 + t$,	length after t seconds
width w:	$w = 4 + t$,	width after t seconds
area:	$A(t) = (3 + t)(4 + t)$.	area after t seconds

When the area is 10 times its initial size, $A = 10(3)(4) = 120$. Thus we want to solve the inequality $A(t) \geq 120$ or $(3 + t)(4 + t) \geq 120$. Find complete graphs of the algebraic representations $y = 120$ and $A(t) = (3 + t)(4 + t)$ in the same viewing rectangle. (Fig. 3.60). Then use zoom-in to determine that the value of t at this point of intersection is $t = 7.47$ with an error of at most 0.01.

The area will be at least ten times its initial size when $t \geq 7.47$. ▤

Exercises for Section 3.6

In Exercises 1 to 5, determine the domain and a rule for $f + g, f − g, fg,$ and f/g.

1. $f(x) = 2x − 1$; $g(x) = x^2$

2. $f(x) = (x − 1)^2$; $g(x) = 3 − x$

3. $f(x) = x^2$; $g(x) = 2x$

4. $f(x) = \sqrt{x}$; $g(x) = x − 2$

5. $f(x) = x + 3$; $g(x) = \dfrac{2x − 1}{3}$

In Exercises 6 and 7, determine the domain and range and find a complete graph.

6. $f(x) = \dfrac{|x − 5|}{x − 5}$

7. $f(x) = \dfrac{x + 4}{x + 4}$

In Exercises 8 to 11, find $(f \circ g)(3)$ and $(g \circ f)(−2)$:

8. $f(x) = 2x − 3$; $g(x) = x + 1$

9. $f(x) = x^2 − 1$; $g(x) = 2x − 3$

10. $f(x) = x^2$; $g(x) = \sqrt{x − 1}$

11. $f(x) = 2x − 3$; $g(x) = x^2 − 2x + 3$

In Exercises 12 to 17, find both $f \circ g$ and $g \circ f$ and the domain and range for each composite.

12. $f(x) = 3x + 2$; $g(x) = x - 1$

13. $f(x) = x^2 - 1$; $g(x) = \dfrac{1}{x - 1}$

14. $f(x) = 2x - 5$; $g(x) = \dfrac{x + 3}{2}$

15. $f(x) = x^2 - 2$; $g(x) = \sqrt{x + 1}$

16. $f(x) = \dfrac{1}{x - 1}$; $g(x) = (x + 1)^2$

17. $f(x) = x^2 - 3$; $g(x) = \sqrt{x + 2}$

In Exercises 18 and 19, find a complete graph of $f, g, f \circ g$, and $g \circ f$ in the same viewing rectangle. Add the line $y = x$. What symmetry do you see?

18. $f(x) = \dfrac{2x - 3}{4}$; $g(x) = \dfrac{4x + 3}{2}$

19. $f(x) = \sqrt{x + 3}$; $g(x) = x^2 - 3$, $x \geq 0$

In Exercises 20 and 21, let $f(x) = x^2$. Find $g(x)$ so that $g \circ f$ produces the specified transformation.

20. Shift the graph of f up 6 units.

21. Shift the graph of f down 3 units.

In Exercise 22 to 27, determine functions g and h so that $f(x) = h(g(x))$.

22. $f(x) = (x + 3)^2$

23. $f(x) = \left(\dfrac{1}{x + 1}\right)^3$

24. $f(x) = \sqrt{x + 3}$

25. $f(x) = \dfrac{2}{(x - 3)^2}$

26. $f(x) = (x - 3)^4 - 2$

27. $f(x) = 3 - \sqrt{x}$

In Exercises 28 and 29, let $f(x) = x^2$. Find $g(x)$ so that $f \circ g$ produces the specified transformation.

28. Shift the graph of f right 4 units.

29. Shift the graph of f left 8 units.

In Exercises 30 and 31, express each function as a composition of $f(x) = x^2, g(x) = 3x, h(x) = x + 4$, and $k(x) = x - 2$.

30. $y = 3(x + 4)^2 - 2$

31. $y = 3(x - 2)^2 + 4$

32. Verify that $(f \circ g) \circ h = f \circ (g \circ h)$ for the functions $f(x) = x^2 - 1, g(x) = 1/x$, and $h(x) = \sqrt{x - 2}$.

For Exercises 33 to 36, let f be given by the following figure. Sketch a complete graph of each composite function.

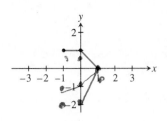

For Exercises 33 to 36

33. $y = -1 + f(x)$ **34.** $y = f(x + 1)$

35. $y = -2f(x)$ **36.** $y = 2f(x - 1)$

In Exercises 37 to 40, let f be given by the following figure. Sketch a complete graph of each composite function.

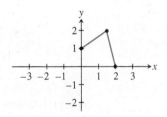

For Exercises 37 to 40

37. $y = 1 + f(x)$ **38.** $y = -2 + f(x)$

39. $y = 2f(x)$ **40.** $y = -2f(x)$

In Exercises 41 to 44, let f be given by the following figure. Sketch a complete graph of each composite function.

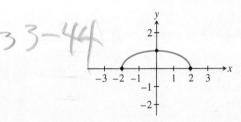

For Exercises 41 to 44

41. $g(x) = 3 + f(x)$ **42.** $g(x) = 3f(x)$

43. $g(x) = f(x - 3)$ **44.** $g(x) = f(x + 3)$

In Exercises 45 to 50, let f be given by the following figure. Sketch a complete graph of each composite function.

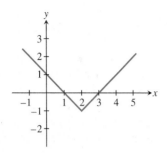

For Exercises 45 to 50

45. $g(x) = -3f(x)$ **46.** $g(x) = -1 + 2f(x)$

47. $g(x) = 1 - 2f(x-1)$ **48.** $g(x) = 1 + 2f(-x)$

49. $y = f(x+2)$ **50.** $y = -1 + 2f(x-1)$

In Exercises 51 to 54, list the transformations that can be applied, in order, to obtain the graph of $f(x)$ from the graph of $y = |x|$. Draw a complete graph of the given function without using a graphing utility.

51. $f(x) = |x-3|$ **52.** $f(x) = -2|x+3|$

53. $f(x) = 2 + 3|x-4|$ **54.** $f(x) = 3 - |x-2|$

In Exercises 55 to 58, assume that the point $(3,4)$ is on the graph of $y = f(x)$. What point is on the graph of the following composites?

55. $y = 2f(x)$ **56.** $y = 4f(x)$

57. $y = 2 + f(x)$ **58.** $y = -2 - 3f(x)$

59. Assume that point $(4,3)$ is on the graph of $y = f(x)$. Find b so that $(2,b)$ is on the graph of $y = f(x+2)$.

60. Assume that point $(-1,5)$ is on the graph of $y = f(x)$. Find b so that $(2,b)$ is on the graph of $y = f(x-3)$.

In Exercises 61 to 64, assume that points $(2,5)$ and $(0,3)$ are on the graph of $y = f(x)$. Name two points that are on the graph of each function.

61. $y = f(x-2)$ **62.** $y = f(x) + 2$

63. $y = -3f(x-2)$ **64.** $y = 3 + 2f(x-2)$

65. Suppose the balloon in Example 8 will burst when its volume is 10,000 cubic inches. When will the balloon burst?

66. Express the distance D between the lamp and the tip of Anita's shadow (in Example 9) as a function of t. When will that distance D be 100 feet?

67. The initial dimensions of a rectangle are 5 by 7 cm, and the length and width of the rectangle are increasing at the rate of 2 cm per second. How long will it take for the area to be at least 5 times its initial size?

68. Leon is 6 feet 8 inches tall and walks at the rate of 5 feet per second away from a streetlight with a lamp 15 feet above ground level. Determine an algebraic representation for the length of Leon's shadow, and find the length of the shadow after 5 seconds.

69. A spherical balloon is inflated so that the radius r is increasing at the rate of 3 inches per second such that $r = 0$ at time $t = 0$. Determine an algebraic representation for the volume of the balloon, and find the volume when $t = 3$ seconds.

70. A rock is tossed into a pond. The radius of the first circular ripple (wave) increases at the rate of 2.3 feet per second. Determine an algebraic representation for the area of the ripple, and find the area when $t = 6$ seconds.

71. The surface area of a sphere of radius r is given by $S = 4\pi r^2$. A hard candy ball of radius 1.6 cm is dropped into a glass of water. Its radius decreases at the rate of 0.0027 cm per second. Determine an algebraic representation for the surface area of the candy ball as a function of t. When will the candy be completely dissolved?

72. The initial dimensions of a computer image of a box are 5 by 7 by 3 cm. If each of the three side lengths is increasing at a rate of 2 cm per second, how long will it take for the volume of the box to be at least 5 times its initial size?

Exercises 73 to 75 refer to the following **problem situation**: A certain long-distance phone company charges the following amounts for calls placed after 6 P.M. and before 8 A.M. from Columbus, Ohio to San Francisco, California. For the first 5 minutes (up to but less than 5 minutes), the charge is $.72 per minute or fraction of a minute. For the next 10 minutes (beginning at 5 minutes but less than 15 minutes), the charge is $.63 per minute or fraction of a minute. After 15 minutes the charge is $.51 per minute or fraction of a minute.

73. Determine a piecewise function that is an algebraic representation of the cost of a call placed from 6 P.M. to 8 A.M.

74. Determine the domain and range of the function in Exercise 73.

75. Sketch a graph of this problem situation without using a graphing utility.

3.7 _____ Inverse Functions

Roughly speaking, *inverse* means "undoing." Suppose that we know the effect of a certain process on an object. For example, if heat is removed from water at 32°F, it becomes ice. The inverse process, if there is one, is what has to be done to return to the starting point. In our example the inverse process would be to add heat to convert the ice back to water.

Cubing is a process that is undone by taking the principal cube root:

$$2 \quad \overset{\substack{cubing \\ (do)}}{\longrightarrow} \quad 8 \quad \overset{\substack{cube\ root \\ (undo)}}{\longrightarrow} \quad 2$$

In Section 3.1 we saw that a relation can be defined by an equation and that an ordered pair (x, y) is in the relation if it satisfies the equation.

Using equations, as done in Section 3.1, we can say that

$$(2, 8) \text{ is in the relation } y = x^3 \text{ since } 8 = 2^3, \text{ and}$$

$$(8, 2) \text{ is in the relation } x = y^3 \text{ since } 8 = 2^3.$$

In other words, $(2, 8)$ is in the relation "cubing" and $(8, 2)$ is in the relation "cube root." Notice that the relation $x = y^3$ and $\sqrt[3]{x} = y$ are identical.

Inverse Relations

Suppose that R represents a relation defined by an equation or inequality in x and y. In other words R consists of all ordered pairs (x, y) which satisfy the defining equation or inequality. For example, the relation $R : x^2 + y^2 = 1$ consists of the points on a circle of radius 1.

Whenever a relation R is defined, a second relation called its inverse is also defined. That definition follows.

Definition 3.15   Inverse Relation

Suppose that a relation R is given by an equation. The **inverse relation of R**, denoted R^{-1}, consists of all those ordered pairs (b, a) for which (a, b) belong to R.

In other words, (a, b) is in the relation R if and only if (b, a) is in the relation R^{-1}.

REMINDER

The -1 in R^{-1} is not to be interpreted as an exponent. That is, $R^{-1} \neq 1/R$. R^{-1} is simply a symbol used to name the inverse relation of R.

An important relationship between the domain and range of a relation and its inverse is that the following sets are equal:

$$\text{domain of } f = \text{range of } f^{-1} \quad \text{and} \quad \text{domain of } f^{-1} = \text{range of } f.$$

E X A M P L E 1 Verifying Inverse Relations

Show that $y = x^2$ and $x = y^2$ are inverse relations. Find complete graphs of each.

Solution

$y = x^2$ This equation defines a relation R. Suppose (a, b) is in this relation.

$b = a^2$ This equation shows that (b, a) satisfies the equation $x = y^2$.

This shows that, if (a, b) is in the relation $y = x^2$, then (b, a) is in the relation $x = y^2$. By reversing these arguments we could show that the converse is also true. So $y = x^2$ and $x = y^2$ are inverse relations (see Fig. 3.61).

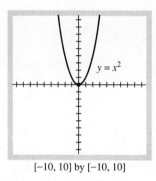
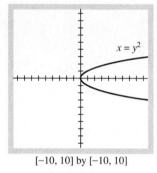

[−10, 10] by [−10, 10]   [−10, 10] by [−10, 10]

Figure 3.61 Inverse relations (a) $y = x^2$ and (b) $x = y^2$.

The relation $y = x^2$ is a function since there is only one y-value associated with each x-value. Notice that the vertical line test of Definition 3.4 is not met for the inverse relation $x = y^2$. So the inverse relation $x = y^2$ is not a function.

E X A M P L E 2 Verifying Inverse Relations

Show that $y = 2x + 3$ and $y = (x - 3)/2$ are inverse relations.

Solution See Fig. 3.62.

$y = 2x + 3$ This equation defines a relation R.

$b = 2a + 3$ Suppose (a, b) is in this relation.

$b - 3 = 2a$

$a = \dfrac{b - 3}{2}$ This equation shows that (b, a) satisfies the equation $y = (x - 3)/2$.

Since these steps can be reversed we conclude that $y = 2x + 3$ and $y = (x - 3)/2$ are inverse relations (see Fig. 3.62).

Figure 3.62 A function and its inverse relation.

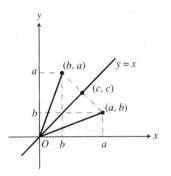

Figure 3.63 (a, b) and (b, a) are symmetric with respect to the line $y = x$.

The points (a, b) and (b, a) are symmetric with respect to the line $y = x$ (see Fig. 3.63). So the graph of a function and its inverse relation are symmetric with respect to this line. This observation is confirmed by Examples 1 and 2. This observation leads to the following theorem.

Theorem 3.7   Graph of a Relation and Its Inverse

The graph of the inverse of a relation can be obtained by reflecting the graph of the relation through the line $y = x$.

Inverse Functions

From Examples 1 and 2 we see that some functions have inverse relations that are also functions and others have inverse relations that are *not* functions.

Definition 3.16   Inverse Function

If the inverse relation of a function f is also a function, it is called the **inverse function of f**, denoted f^{-1}. A function and its inverse are related by the following two equations:

$$f(f^{-1}(x)) = x \quad \text{for all values of } x \text{ in the domain of } f^{-1} \text{ and}$$

$$f^{-1}(f(x)) = x \quad \text{for all values of } x \text{ in the domain of } f.$$

If either $f(f^{-1}(x)) = x$ or $f^{-1}(f(x)) = x$ fails for some value of x, the inverse relation of f is not a function.

E X A M P L E   3   Demonstrating Inverse Functions

Show that functions $f(x) = x^2$, where $x \geq 0$, and $f^{-1}(x) = \sqrt{x}$ are inverse functions. Find complete graphs of each.

Solution   We must show that $f(f^{-1}(x)) = x$ and $f^{-1}(f(x)) = x$ for all $x \geq 0$.

$$f(f^{-1}(x)) = f(\sqrt{x})$$

$$= (\sqrt{x})^2$$

$$= x \quad \text{All } x\text{-values are positive.}$$

$$f^{-1}(f(x)) = \sqrt{f(x)}$$

$$= \sqrt{x^2}$$

$$= x \quad \text{All } x\text{-values are positive.} \qquad \blacksquare$$

[–10, 10] by [–10, 10]

Figure 3.64 $f(x) = x^2$, $x \geq 0$.

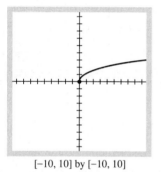

[–10, 10] by [–10, 10]

Figure 3.65 $f^{-1}(x) = \sqrt{x}$.

Figures 3.64 and 3.65 are complete graphs of f and f^{-1}. The remainder of this section deals with two questions:

1. When is the inverse relation of the function $y = f(x)$ also a function?

2. Given a function whose inverse is also a function, how can one find a rule for the inverse?

The function $y = x^2$ with domain $(-\infty, \infty)$ is graphed in Fig. 3.61, and $y = x^2$ with domain $[0, \infty)$ is graphed in Fig. 3.64. There is a major difference in these two examples. In the first case, there are horizontal lines that intersect the graph of $y = x^2$ in more than one point. That means the *inverse* relation of $y = x^2$ is not a function because its graph does not satisfy the vertical line test. However, every horizontal line intersects the graph of $y = x^2$ with the restricted domain in at most one point. That means that its inverse satisfies the vertical line test and is a function. (See Fig. 3.65.)

Theorem 3.8   Horizontal Line Test and f^{-1}

The inverse relation R^{-1} of a function $y = f(x)$ is also a function if and only if f passes the **horizontal line test**; that is, every horizontal line intersects the graph of f in at most one point.

There is another way to describe those functions whose inverses are also functions. A function f is said to be **one-to-one** if, for every pair of distinct values in the domain, x_1 and x_2, it is also true that $f(x_1)$ and $f(x_2)$ are distinct. In other words, if $x_1 \neq x_2$, then $f(x_1) \neq f(x_2)$. This condition is satisfied only if the horizontal line test is met.

Theorem 3.9   A One-to-one Function and f^{-1}

The inverse f^{-1} of f is a function if and only if f is a one-to-one function. Furthermore, f is one-to-one if and only if every horizontal line intersects the graph of f in at most one point.

E X A M P L E   4   Determining One-to-one Functions

Determine whether the following functions are one-to-one: (a) $f(x) = -3x + 4$, (b) $g(x) = x^3 - 4x$.

Solution   Find complete graphs of each function. The graph of $f(x) = -3x + 4$ (Fig. 3.66a) meets the horizontal line test and hence is one-to-one. The graph of $g(x) = x^3 - 4x$ (Fig. 3.66b) does not meet the horizontal line test and so is not one-to-one.

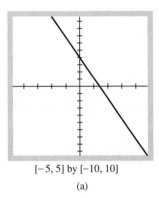
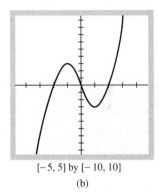

$[-5, 5]$ by $[-10, 10]$ $[-5, 5]$ by $[-10, 10]$

(a)   (b)

Figure 3.66   (a) $f(x) = -3x + 4$; (b) $g(x) = x^3 - 4x$. The inverse of f is a function while the inverse of g is not.

Finding Inverse Functions

In addition to determining when an inverse relation is also a function, it is often necessary to find a rule that describes the inverse function.

Finding an Inverse Function

Find the inverse function f^{-1} of a function f by following these steps:

1. Show that f is one-to-one.
2. Interchange x and y in the equation $y = f(x)$.
3. Solve for y.
4. Confirm that the domain of f^{-1} is equal to the range of f.

Math Help

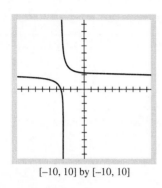

[−10, 10] by [−10, 10]

Figure 3.67
$f(x) = (2x + 7)/(x + 3)$.

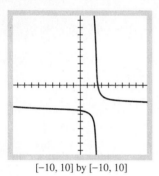

[−10, 10] by [−10, 10]

Figure 3.68
$f^{-1}(x) = (-3x + 7)/(x - 2)$

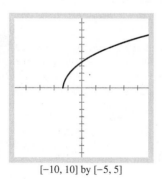

[−10, 10] by [−5, 5]

Figure 3.69 $y = \sqrt{x + 3}$.

E X A M P L E   5   Finding an Inverse Function

Show that $f(x) = (2x + 7)/(x + 3)$ is one-to-one, and find a rule for its inverse.

Solution f is one-to-one by the horizontal line test (Fig. 3.67).

$$y = \frac{2x + 7}{x + 3}$$

$$x = \frac{2y + 7}{y + 3} \qquad \text{Interchange } x \text{ and } y.$$

$$x(y + 3) = 2y + 7 \qquad \text{Solve for } y.$$

$$xy + 3x = 2y + 7$$

$$xy - 2y = -3x + 7$$

$$y(x - 2) = -3x + 7$$

$$y = \frac{-3x + 7}{x - 2}$$

The inverse function is $f^{-1}(x) = (-3x + 7)/(x - 2)$. See Fig. 3.68.   ▤

E X A M P L E   6   Finding an Inverse Function (Continued)

Let $f(x) = \sqrt{x + 3}$. Show that the inverse of f is a function, find a rule for f^{-1}, and determine the domain and range of f^{-1}.

Solution   Figure 3.69 shows that f satisfies the horizontal line test. Consequently f^{-1} is a function.

$$y = \sqrt{x + 3}$$

$$x = \sqrt{y + 3} \qquad \text{Interchange } x \text{ and } y.$$

$$x^2 = y + 3 \qquad \begin{array}{l} \text{Square both sides in order to solve for } y. \\ \text{This step may introduce extraneous solutions.} \end{array}$$

$$y = x^2 - 3$$

The rule $y = x^2 - 3$ does not represent f^{-1} unless x is restricted to the interval $[0, \infty)$. This restriction must be done because the squaring process introduced extraneous solutions.   ▤

Exercises for Section 3.7

In Exercises 1 to 4, verify that each pair of equations are inverse relations.

1. $y = x^3;\ x = y^3$

2. $y = x^2 + 1;\ x = y^2 + 1$

3. $y = x^2 - 4;\ x = y^2 - 4$

4. $y = x^3 + x^2 - 6x;\ x = y^3 + y^2 - 6y$

In Exercises 5 to 8, show that the given functions f and g are inverses of each other by showing that $f(g(x)) = x$ and the $g(f(x)) = x$ for all x in the respective domains.

5. $f(x) = 3x - 2;\ g(x) = \dfrac{1}{3}(x + 2)$

6. $f(x) = \dfrac{x + 3}{4};\ g(x) = 4x - 3$

7. $f(x) = x^3 + 1;\ g(x) = (x - 1)^{1/3}$

8. $f(x) = \dfrac{1}{x};\ g(x) = \dfrac{1}{x}.$

In Exercises 9 to 14, find a complete graph of each function and decide whether it is one-to-one.

9. $y = x^2 - 5$ **10.** $y = x^3 - 4x + 5$

11. $y = x^4 - 5x^2 + 1$ **12.** $y = 0.001x^3$

13. $f(x) = 4 - x^3$ **14.** $g(x) = \sqrt{x - 4}$

In Exercises 15 to 17, consider the relation $y = 2x + 4$.

15. Is point $(0, 4)$ on the graph of the inverse of the relation?

16. Is point $(4, 0)$ on the graph of the inverse of the relation?

17. Find a point (a, b) that is on both the graph of the relation and the graph of its inverse.

In Exercises 18 and 19, sketch a complete graph of the inverse of each relation.

18.

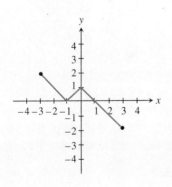

19.

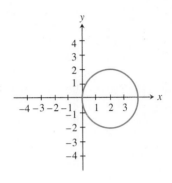

20. Let the domain of f be $(-\infty, 0]$ and let $f(x) = x^2$ when $x \le 0$. Find a rule for f^{-1}.

21. Find a rule for the inverse of $f(x) = \sqrt{x - 2}$. Determine the domain and range of both f and f^{-1}.

In Exercises 22 to 27, show that each function f is one-to-one and find a rule for f^{-1}.

22. $f(x) = 3x - 6$

23. $f(x) = 2x + 5$

24. $f(x) = x^3$

25. $f(x) = \dfrac{x + 3}{x - 2}$

26. $f(x) = \dfrac{2x - 3}{x + 1}$

27. $f(x) = \sqrt{x + 2}$

In Exercises 28 to 32, use a graphing utility to find a complete graph of each function. Sketch the inverse relation of each function without the aid of a graphing utility. Identify those functions whose inverses are also functions.

28. $f(x) = x^3 - 8x$

29. $f(x) = x^4 - 2x + 3$

30. $f(x) = \dfrac{x^2 - 2x + 3}{x + 2}$

31. $f(x) = x^3 - 2x - 6$

32. $f(x) = x^3 + 2x + 2$

Chapter 3 Review

KEY TERMS

composition of f with g
difference of f and g
domain of a function
evaluating a function
function
function notation
general form of
   a linear equation
graph of a relation
horizontal line test
horizontal shift (slide)
intercept

inverse function
inverse function of f
inverse relation of R
linear function
linear inequality
line of symmetry
midpoint of a line
   segment
one-to-one function
parallel lines
perpendicular bisector
perpendicular lines

piecewise function
point-slope form
product of f and g
quadratic function
quotient of f and g
range
reflection
relation
rule of a function
slope
slope-intercept form
step function

sum of f and g
symmetry
transformation
understood domain
vertex of a parabola
vertical line test
vertical shift (slide)
vertical shrink or stretch
x-intercept
y-intercept

REVIEW EXERCISES

In Exercises 1 to 4, find a complete graph of each equation without using a graphing utility. Choose an appropriate scale for each axis.

1. $y - 5 = \dfrac{1}{2}x$

2. $x - y = 6$

3. $y = 200x - 10$

4. $y = 2x^2 + 1000$

5. Complete the following graph if a complete graph is symmetric with respect to (a) the x-axis, (b) the y-axis, and (c) the origin.

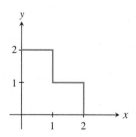

For Exercise 5

In Exercises 6 to 11, determine whether the graph of the equation is symmetric with respect to the x-axis, the y-axis, the origin, or none of these.

6. $x^2 y = 1$

7. $x^2 - xy^4 = 2$

8. $x^2 y^3 + 3xy = 1$

9. $xy^3 + x^3 y = 25$

10. $y^2 = x^2 + 4$

11. $y = x^3 - 5x$

12. Find a complete graph of $y = (x + 5)^2$. Is the graph symmetric about some line? If so, what is an equation of that line of symmetry?

In Exercises 13 to 18, sketch a complete graph of each equation and specify its domain and range. Give an equation of the line of symmetry, and indicate which equations define y as a function of x.

13. $y = |x - 3|$

14. $y = 5 - |x|$

15. $|y - 4| = x$

16. $y = |x^3 - 8x|$

17. $x|y| = 3$

18. $y = \left| \dfrac{3}{x - 2} \right|$

19. Let $f(x) = x^2 + 2$. Find $f(0)$, $f(1)$, $f(3)$, $f(-5)$, $f(t)$, $f(-t)$, $f(-1/t)$, $f(a + h)$, and $[f(a + h) - f(a)]/h$.

20. Let $g(x) = 1/(2 - x)$. Find $g(2)$, $g(0)$, $g(-2)$, $g(a)$, $g(1/a)$, and $g(a + h)$.

21. Consider the graph of the function $y = f(x)$ in the following figure and estimate the indicated values.
   a) $f(0)$, $f(-1)$, $f(2)$
   b) x if $f(x) = 0$
   c) x if $f(x) = 2$

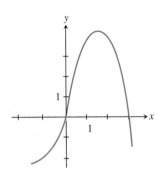

For Exercise 21

22. Determine whether each graph in the following figure is symmetric with respect to the x-axis, the y-axis, or the origin. Justify your answers.

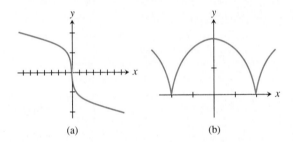

(a)   (b)

For Exercise 22

In Exercises 23 to 28, find a complete graph of each function. Explain why the graph is a complete graph.

23. $g(x) = x^2 - 40$ **24.** $f(x) = 10x^3 - 400x$

25. $h(x) = 2 - x$ **26.** $f(x) = \sqrt{x - 3}$

27. $t(x) = \left(\dfrac{x}{4}\right)^2 + \left(\dfrac{200 - x}{4}\right)^2$

28. $g(x) = -2 - \sqrt{x + 3}$

29. Determine the domain and range of the function in Exercise 26.

30. Determine the domain and range of the function in Exercise 27.

31. Determine the domain and range of the function in Exercise 28.

In Exercises 32 to 37, sketch a complete graph of the function without using a graphing utility. Determine the domain and range.

32. $f(x) = \begin{cases} x + 7, & x \le -3 \\ x^2 + 1, & x > -3 \end{cases}$

33. $f(x) = \begin{cases} 4 - x^2, & x < 1 \\ \sqrt{x + 2}, & x \ge 1 \end{cases}$

34. $f(x) = \begin{cases} -2x, & x < 1 \\ \sqrt{x + 5}, & x \ge 1 \end{cases}$

35. $f(x) = \begin{cases} 3 - x, & x < -3 \\ (x - 2)^2, & -3 \le x < 2 \\ x^3, & x \ge 2 \end{cases}$

36. $f(x) = \dfrac{2|x - 3|}{x - 3}$

37. $g(x) = \begin{cases} 2x + x^5, & x < 2 \\ x^3 - x - 1, & x \ge 2 \end{cases}$

38. Draw a line through the point $(3, 4)$ with a slope of $-\frac{1}{2}$.

39. Draw a line through the point $(-1, 3)$ with a slope of 2.

40. Draw graphs of the functions $y = 2x^2 + 3$, $y = 2x^2 - 1$, and $y = 2x^2 - 3$ on the same coordinate system. Do not use a graphing utility.

41. Determine the slope of the line through the points $(0, 3)$ and $(-2, 6)$.

42. Determine the y-intercept of the graph of the function $3x - 2y + 8 = 0$. Graph the function.

In Exercises 43 and 44, determine a formula for the linear function f that satisfies the given conditions.

43. $f(2) = 0$, $f(0) = 4$ **44.** $f(0) = 250$, $f(-10) = 200$

In Exercises 45 to 48, sketch a complete graph of each equation or inequality.

45. $2x + y \le 3$ **46.** $3x - 4y = 12$

47. $x + 3y = 9$ **48.** $y \le x$

49. Write an equation for the line with a slope of $-\frac{2}{3}$ and a y-intercept at $(0, 4)$.

50. Write an equation for the line with a slope of $\frac{3}{4}$ that contains the point $(1, 2)$.

51. Write an equation for the line determined by the points $(-3, 4)$ and $(2, 5)$.

52. Given the point $A = (5, 7)$, write an equation for the following:
a) the vertical line through A
b) the horizontal line through A.

53. Find the midpoint of the line segment determined by the two points $(2, -3)$ and $(-4, 6)$.

54. Write an equation for the perpendicular bisector of the line segment determined by the two points $(1, 3)$ and $(-3, 7)$.

In Exercises 55 and 56, write an equation for the line determined by the given conditions.

55. The line contains the point $(6, 1)$ and is perpendicular to the line $3x - 2y = 4$.

56. The line contains the point $(5, -8)$ and is perpendicular to the line $y = 31$.

57. Let $A = (-2, 3)$, $B = (3, -4)$, and $C = (-4, 1)$.
   a) Prove that triangle ABC is isosceles but not equilateral.
   b) Prove that the line passing through B and the midpoint of AC is perpendicular to AC.

58. Let $A = (0, 0)$, $B = (4, 2)$, and $C = (6, -2)$.
   a) Write an equation for each of the three lines determined by a vertex and the midpoint of the opposite side of triangle ABC.
   b) Prove that the three lines in part (a) intersect in one point.

59. Prove that the diagonals of a square are perpendicular.

For Exercises 60 to 62, consider the triangle ABC shown in the following figure:

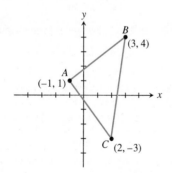

For Exercises 60 to 62

60. Find an equation of the line through B and C.

61. Find an equation of the line through A and the midpoint of BC (median).

62. Find an equation of the line through A and perpendicular to BC (altitude).

In Exercises 63 to 70, sketch a complete graph of $y = f(x)$ without using a graphing utility. Describe how each graph is obtained from the graph of $y = x^2$.

63. $y = -x^2$

64. $y = (x - 3)^2$

65. $y = -2(x + 3)^2 + 4$

66. $y = (x + 1)^2 - 4$

67. $y = 4(x - 2)^2$

68. $y = 4(x + 4)^2$

69. $y = -2(x + 3)^2$

70. $y = 2(x - 3)^2$

In Exercises 71 and 72, find a complete graph of $y = f(x)$. Describe how each graph is obtained from the graph of $y = |x|$.

71. $y = 2|x - 3|$

72. $y = -3 - |x + 4|$

73. Assume the point $(4, 3)$ is on the graph of $y = f(x)$. Find b so that $(1, b)$ is on the graph of $y = f(x + 3)$.

74. Assume the points $(-3, 2)$ and $(1, 0)$ are on the graph of $y = f(x)$. Find b so that
   a) $(-1, b)$ is on the graph of $y = f(x - 2)$.
   b) $(3, b)$ is on the graph of $y = f(x - 2)$.
   c) $(-1, b)$ is on the graph of $y = -3f(x - 2)$.
   d) $(3, b)$ is on the graph of $y = 2 + 2f(x - 2)$.

75. Consider the graph of $y = x^2$.
   a) Vertically stretch this graph by a factor of 2 followed by a vertical shift up 1 unit. What is an equation of this new graph? Sketch a complete graph.
   b) What is an equation of the transformed graph if the order of the two transformations in part (a) is reversed?
   c) Are the two graphs the same? Explain the effect of reversing the order of the transformations.

In Exercises 76 and 77, write a sequence of transformations that will produce a complete graph of each function from the graph of $y = x^2$. Specify an order in which the transformations should be applied.

76. $f(x) = 2x^2 - 12x + 4$

77. $f(x) = 14 - 6x - x^2$

In Exercises 78 and 79, list the transformations that will produce a complete graph of each function from the graph of $y = x^3$. Specify the order in which the transformations should be applied, and then sketch a complete graph of the function without using a graphing utility. Use a graphing utility to support your work.

78. $y = (x + 2)^3$

79. $y = -2(x - 3)^3 - 5$

In Exercises 80 to 83, draw a complete graph of each inequality.

80. $y > x^2 - 3x + 2$

81. $y \le x^5 - 40x$

82. $y \ge 1 - (x - 2)^2$

83. $y < 3x^3 - 2x^2 + x - 1$

In Exercises 84 to 86, consider the complete graphs of $y = f(x)$ and $y = g(x)$ shown in the following figure:

[−4, 4] by [−4, 4]

For Exercises 84 to 86

84. Compare the following:
a) $f(1)$ and -3
b) $g(4)$ and 1

85. Compare $f(a)$ and $g(a)$
a) if $a = -2$;
b) if $a = 2$.

86. Is $x = -1$ a solution to
a) $f < g$?
b) $f = g$?
c) $f > g$?

87. List the transformations that will produce a complete graph of the function $y = (x+3)^4 + 2$ from the graph of $y = x^4$. Specify the order in which the transformations should be applied, and sketch a complete graph of the function. Then use a graphing utility to check your answer.

88. Consider $f(x) = 1/(x-1)$ and $g(x) = (x+2)^2$. Determine the domain and a rule for $f + g$, $f - g$, fg, and f/g.

In Exercises 89 and 90, determine $(f \circ g)(-3)$ and $(g \circ f)(2)$.

89. $f(x) = 5x + 7$; $g(x) = x - 4$

90. $f(x) = x^2 + 4$; $g(x) = \sqrt{1-x}$

91. Determine $f \circ g$ and $g \circ f$ if $f(x) = x^2 + 2$ and $g(x) = (x+3)/2$.

92. Find the domain and range of f, g, $f \circ g$, and $g \circ f$ if $f(x) = (2x - 3)/4$ and $g(x) = x^2 - 2$.

93. Let $f(x) = x^2$. Find $g(x)$ so that $g \circ f$ produces the specified transformation.
a) Vertically shift the graph of f down 5 units.
b) Vertically shift the graph of f up 4 units.

94. Let $f(x) = x^2$. Find $g(x)$ so that $f \circ g$ produces the specified transformation.

a) Horizontally shift the graph of f left 5 units.
b) Horizontally shift the graph of f right 6 units.

95. Express $y = 2(x+3)^2 - 4$ as a composition of $f(x) = x^2$, $g(x) = 2x$, $h(x) = x + 3$, and $k(x) = x - 4$.

In Exercises 96 and 97, find functions g and h so that $f(x) = (h \circ g)(x) = h(g(x))$.

96. $f(x) = (x + 5)^2$ **97.** $f(x) = \dfrac{3}{(x-2)^2}$

In Exercises 98 and 99, sketch a complete graph of $y = f(x)$. Then check your answer with a graphing utility.

98. $y = 2(x - 2)^2 + 3$ **99.** $y = 4 - 3\sqrt{x+1}$

In Exercises 100 and 101, draw a complete graph of each relation and its inverse without using a graphing utility. Determine an equation for the inverse and specify whether it is a function.

100. $y = 5 - 3x$ **101.** $y = x^2 - 2$

In Exercises 102 and 103, determine whether each function is one-to-one, and find an equation for the inverse relation of each function. Is the inverse a function? If so, find a function rule $y = f^{-1}(x)$ for the inverse. Draw a graph of f and its inverse relation. Then support your answer with a graphing utility.

102. $f(x) = (x + 2)^2$ **103.** $f(x) = 2\sqrt{x-4}$

104. Determine the domain and range of both the function and its inverse in Exercise 102.

105. Ethanol worth $0.75 per gallon is mixed with gasoline worth $1.10 per gallon. The value of the new mixture cannot exceed $0.999 per gallon. (At a gas station this would be written as $0.99\frac{9}{10}$ per gallon.) Write an inequality expressing this requirement, and sketch its complete graph.

106. A fast-food restaurant makes $0.40 profit on a medium-sized soft drink, $0.15 profit on a taco, and breaks even on the other items. If the weekly overhead is $700, write an inequality that expresses the requirement that the weekly profits must exceed $500. Sketch its complete graph.

Exercises 107 to 111 refer to the following **problem situation:** An object is shot straight up (launched) from the top of a building 200 feet tall with an initial velocity of 70 feet per second. Let t be the time in seconds since the object was launched.

107. Determine an algebraic representation that gives the height of the object above ground level as a function of t.

108. Draw a complete graph of the algebraic representation.

109. What portion of the graph of the algebraic representation represents this problem situation?

110. Determine the time when the object is 225 feet above the ground.

111. Determine the time when the object is more than 225 feet above the ground.

CHAPTER 4

Polynomial Functions

4.1 Graphs of Polynomial Functions

Polynomial functions are related to the polynomial equations studied in Chapter 2. We define them here.

Definition 4.1   Polynomial Function

A **polynomial function** is one that can be written in the form

$$f(x) = a_n x^n + a_{n-1} x^{n-1} + \ldots + a_1 x + a_0,$$

where n is a nonnegative integer and the coefficients $a_0, a_1, \ldots, a_n$ are real numbers. If $a_n \neq 0$, then n is the **degree of the polynomial function**.

Linear and quadratic functions are special cases of polynomial functions. They are polynomial functions of degree 1 and 2 respectively.

Functions f, g, and h are polynomial functions, whereas k is not a polynomial function.

$$f(x) = 3x - 2, \qquad\qquad g(x) = 5x^2 - 3x + 1$$

$$h(x) = 3x^4 + 5x^2 - 3x + 2, \quad k(x) = \sqrt{x^2 + 3}$$

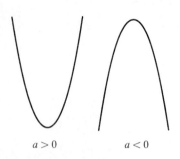

$a > 0$ $a < 0$

Figure 4.1 (a) Upward parabola; (b) downward parabola.

If $f(x)$ is a polynomial function, x can represent any value. So the domain of a polynomial function is the set of all real numbers. The range varies and depends on the characteristics of the specific polynomial.

This chapter focuses on two major themes concerning the behavior of polynomial functions.

1. What are the main characteristics of the graphs of polynomial functions?
2. How many zeros does a given polynomial function have and how can they be found?

In Chapter 2 we saw that the graph of a degree 2 function $f(x) = ax^2 + bx + c$ is called a parabola and has one of the shapes represented in Fig. 4.1. A third-degree polynomial function $f(x) = ax^3 + bx^2 + cx + d$ is sometimes called a **cubic** function. Graphs of cubic polynomial functions fall into one of the four types illustrated in Fig. 4.2.

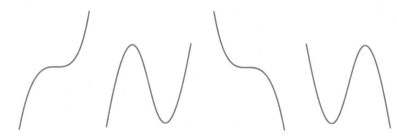

Figure 4.2 The graphs of $f(x) = ax^3 + bx^2 + cx + d$.

The visual information found in Fig. 4.2 helps as you try to find a complete graph of a cubic function.

🔍 EXPLORE WITH A GRAPHING UTILITY

Graph each of these functions in the standard viewing rectangle. Then continue to modify the viewing rectangle until you have found a complete graph. Record the sequence of viewing rectangles you tried.

1. $f(x) = x^3 + 13x^2 + 10x - 4$
2. $g(x) = x^3 + x^2 - 132x$

Write a paragraph explaining how the information from Fig. 4.2 helped you find complete graphs of these functions.

Fourth- and Fifth-Degree Polynomial Functions

Graphs of degree 4 polynomial functions fall into one of four types as indicated in Fig. 4.3.

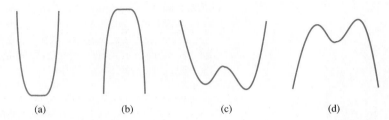

(a)   (b)   (c)   (d)

Figure 4.3 A graph of $f(x) = ax^4 + bx^3 + cx^2 + dx + e$ is one of four types.

E X A M P L E   1   Graphing of a Degree 4 Polynomial Function

Find a complete graph of $f(x) = x^4 + 5x^3 + 2x^2 - 8x + 1$. Which one of the four graphs in Fig. 4.3 most closely matches this one? Describe the domain and range of f.

Solution   Begin by graphing f in the standard viewing rectangle. Notice that the resulting graph covers a fairly narrow portion of the viewing rectangle.

Try a smaller interval for x and a larger interval for y, as shown in Fig. 4.4. This graph is like Fig. 4.3(c).

Domain of f $(-\infty, \infty)$.

Range of f   All $y \geq k$, where k appears to be approximately -12.

In the same fashion, to find a complete graph of a degree 5 polynomial function it is important to know the general shapes of these graphs. Figure 4.5 shows the six types of graphs for degree 5 polynomial functions. With calculus it can be shown that these shapes are the only possible types of degree 5 polynomial functions.

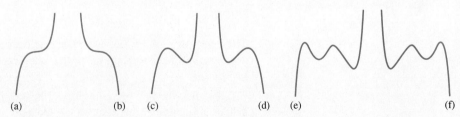

(a)   (b)   (c)   (d)   (e)   (f)

Figure 4.5 A graph of $f(x) = ax^5 + bx^4 + cx^3 + dx^2 + ex + k$ is one of six types.

Local Maximum and Minimum Values

Suppose that Ryne Sandberg hits an infield fly ball straight up in the Houston Astrodome with an initial velocity of 84 feet per second. Will the baseball hit the

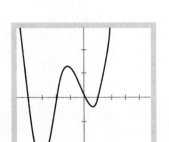

[−5, 5] by [−15, 15]

Figure 4.4
$f(x) = x^4 + 5x^3 + 2x^2 - 8x + 1$.

ceiling of the dome? To answer this question we need to know how high the ball will fly, in other words, its maximum height. One way to answer this question would be to graph an algebraic representation $y = f(x)$ and find the maximum value of y.

Study Fig. 4.6. Notice that often you can identify a portion of a complete graph of a polynomial function that could be characterized as a peak or a valley. The mathematical terminology is local maximum value or local minimum value. Figure 4.6 shows a complete graph of the cubic function $f(x) = x^3 - 4x$ on which the local maximum and local minimum have been labeled.

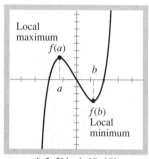

[−5, 5] by [−10, 10]

Figure 4.6 $f(x) = x^3 - 4x.$

Definition 4.2   Local Maximum and Local Minimum

A value $f(a)$ is a **local maximum** of f if there is an open interval (c, d) containing a such that $f(x) \le f(a)$ for all values of x in (c, d).
A value $f(b)$ is a **local minimum** of f if there is an open interval (c, d) containing b such that $f(x) \ge f(b)$ for all values of x in (c, d).

Local maximum and minimum values together are called **local extremum values**, or simply, **local extrema**.

Notice that the maximum and minimum values of a function, if they exist, are "output" values of the function. In Fig. 4.6 the local maximum value is $f(a)$, not a.

E X A M P L E   2   Finding a Local Minimum

Find the local minimum value of the function $f(x) = x^3 - 4x$, and find where it occurs.

Solution

1. The graph in Fig. 4.6 suggests that the local minimum occurs between $x = 0$ and $x = 2$. Find the graph in the viewing rectangle $[0, 2]$ by $[-4, -2]$ shown in Fig. 4.7.

2. Estimate that the low point in Fig. 4.7 has its x-coordinate between 1.1 and 1.2 and its y-coordinate between -3.1 and -3.0. Find the graph in the viewing rectangle $[1.1, 1.2]$ by $[-3.1, -3.0]$ (Fig. 4.8a).

3. Move the cursor to the valley point (Fig. 4.8a). The y-coordinate of this point is -3.079, but the x-coordinate is difficult to identify because the graph is too flat to determine when the cursor is at the lowest point. To alleviate this problem change the viewing rectangle so that its width is 10 times its height (Fig. 4.8b).

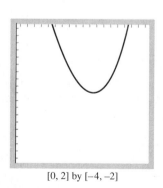

[0, 2] by [−4, −2]

Figure 4.7 $f(x) = x^3 - 4x.$

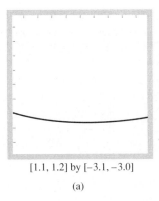

[1.1, 1.2] by [−3.1, −3.0]

(a)

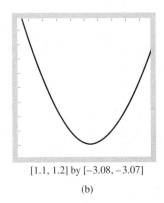

[1.1, 1.2] by [−3.08, −3.07]

(b)

Figure 4.8   Two views of $f(x) = x^3 - 4x$.

4. Using the viewing rectangle [1.1, 1.2] by [−3.08, −3.07], and move the cursor to the low point. Its coordinates are (1.155, −3.0792).

Therefore f achieves a local minimum value of −3.0792 when x is 1.155. The error of the x-coordinate is at most 0.01 and of the y-coordinate is at most 0.001. The y-coordinate was found to a greater precision than the x-coordinate so that the error in x would be at most 0.01.   ≡

E X A M P L E   3   Finding the Local Maximum Value

Find the local maximum of $f(x) = x^3 - 4x$.

Solution   Use information from Example 2 together with the fact that the graph of f is symmetric about the origin.

1. The graph of f is symmetric about the origin:

$$f(-x) = (-x)^3 - 4(-x)$$

$$= -x^3 + 4x$$

$$= -(x^3 - 4x) = -f(x)$$

2. In Example 2 we found that the valley point of the graph is (1.155, −3.0792). Since the graph of f is symmetric about the origin, we can conclude that the peak point of the graph is the point (−1.155, 3.0792).

Therefore, f achieves a local maximum value of 3.0792 when x is −1.155.

≡

Often we are able to use the method of Example 2 to solve applied problems. Here are several examples.

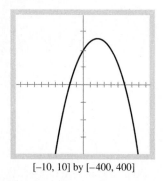

[−10, 10] by [−400, 400]

Figure 4.9
$s = -16t^2 + 64t + 200$.

E X A M P L E   4   APPLICATION: Finding the Maximum Height

A baseball is thrown straight up from the top of a building 200 feet tall with an initial velocity of 64 feet per second. When does the baseball reach its maximum height above ground, and what is this maximum height?

Solution   This is a projectile motion problem situation. The height of the object t seconds after launch is

$$s = -16t^2 + 64t + 200.$$

Review the Projectile Motion Problem Situation in Section 2.6. We learned that $y = -16t^2 + v_0 t + s_0$.

Graphical Solution   Find the graph of $s = -16t^2 + 64t + 200$ (see Fig. 4.9) and use zoom-in to find the coordinates of the highest point. The highest point is $(2, 264)$ with an error of at most 0.01. The maximum height that the object achieves is 264 feet, as shown by the algebraic solution.

Algebraic Solution   Complete the square of $s = -16t^2 + 64t + 200$ and obtain the form $y = -16(t - 2)^2 + 264$. We know that the coordinates of the vertex are exactly $(2, 264)$. The maximum height that the baseball achieves is exactly 264 feet. This maximum height occurs exactly 2 seconds after the baseball is thrown.

E X A M P L E   5   APPLICATION: Find the Maximum Volume

Squares are cut from the corners of a 20- by 25-inch piece of cardboard, and a box is made by folding up the flaps (Fig. 4.10). Determine the graph of the problem situation and find the dimensions of the squares so that the resulting box has the maximum possible volume.

Solution

x = width of square and height of the resulting box in inches

$20 - 2x$ = width of the base in inches

$25 - 2x$ = length of the base in inches

$V(x) = x(20 - 2x)(25 - 2x)$ Volume is equal to length × width × height.

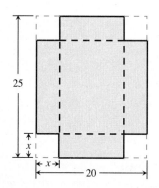

Figure 4.10   Squares cut from a piece of cardboard measuring 20 by 25 inches.

Find a complete graph of $V(x) = x(20 - 2x)(25 - 2x)$ (see Fig. 4.11a). In this problem situation $0 < x < 10$, so the complete graph of the problem situation is shown in Fig. 4.11(b).

Use zoom-in to find the coordinates of the local maximum (Fig. 4.11c). Read the coordinates of the high point as $(3.68, 820.5282)$ with an error of at most 0.01. Thus the maximum volume is 820.5282 cubic inches and this volume occurs when $x = 3.68$ inches.

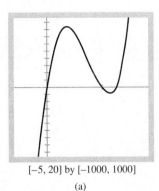

[−5, 20] by [−1000, 1000]

(a)

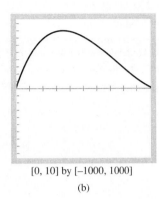

[0, 10] by [−1000, 1000]

(b)

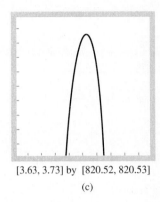

[3.63, 3.73] by [820.52, 820.53]

(c)

Figure 4.11 Three views of $V(x) = x(20 - 2x)(25 - 2x)$.

Increasing and Decreasing Functions

This next Exploration introduces the concepts *increasing function* and *decreasing function*.

🔍 EXPLORE WITH A GRAPHING UTILITY

Find a complete graph of each of the following functions:

1. $f(x) = 1 - x^3$

2. $f(x) = x^3 - x^2 - 6x$

3. $f(x) = x^3 - 4$

4. $f(x) = -x^3 - 2x^2 + 8x + 2$

Note that as the trace cursor moves along the graph from the extreme left to the extreme right, the *x-coordinate of the cursor continually increases.* In each case ask yourself, does the *y*-coordinate

a) continually increase?

b) increase for a while, then decrease, and then increase?

c) decrease for a while, then increase, and then decrease?

d) continually decrease?

Generalize What do you think it means to call a function *an increasing function on an interval,* and what do you think it means to call a function *a decreasing function on an interval*?

Study Fig. 4.12(a). Notice that the function f decreases on the intervals $(-\infty, a)$ and (b, ∞) and increases on the interval (a, b). The function g in Fig. 4.12(b) increases on the intervals $(-\infty, a)$ and (b, ∞) and decreases on the interval (a, b). Further notice that a function changes from increasing to decreasing at a local maximum, and from decreasing to increasing at a local minimum.

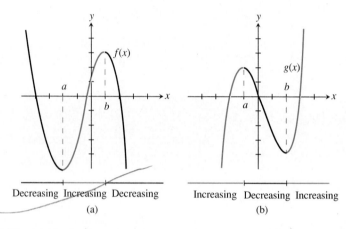

Figure 4.12   (a) The local maximum and minimum of f are $f(b)$ and $f(a)$ respectively.
(b) The local maximum and minimum of g are $g(a)$ and $g(b)$ respectively.

Definition 4.3   Increasing and Decreasing Functions

A function f is **increasing on an interval J** if the values $f(x)$ increase as x increases in J. A function f is **decreasing on an interval J** if the values $f(x)$ decrease as x increases in J.

This intuitive definition is stated with more precision in a calculus course.

EXAMPLE   6   Finding Increasing and Decreasing Intervals

Find the intervals on which $f(x) = x^3 - 4x$ is increasing and decreasing.

Solution   In Examples 2 and 3 we found the following information:

$$(-1.155, 3.0792) = \text{point where a local maximum occurs}$$

$$(1.155, -3.0792) = \text{point where a local minimum occurs}$$

Use this information to conclude the following about this function:

- f is increasing on the intervals $(-\infty, -1.155)$ and $(1.155, \infty)$.
- f is decreasing on the interval $(-1.155, 1.155)$.

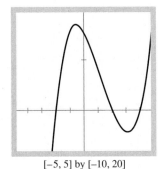

[−5, 5] by [−10, 20]

Figure 4.13
$f(x) = x^3 - 4x^2 - 4x + 16$.

E X A M P L E 7   Finding Increasing and Decreasing Intervals

Find the intervals on which $f(x) = x^3 - 4x^2 - 4x + 16$ is increasing and decreasing.

Solution

1. Find a complete graph of f (see Fig. 4.13).
2. Use zoom-in to show that a local maximum occurs when $x = -0.43$ and that a local minimum occurs when $x = 3.10$.

The function f is increasing on the intervals $(-\infty, -0.43)$ and $(3.10, \infty)$. The function f is decreasing on the interval $(-0.43, 3.10)$.

Exercises for Section 4.1

In Exercises 1 to 8, find a complete graph of each polynomial function. Specify the viewing rectangle you used.

1. $f(x) = x^2 - x + 3$
2. $y = 12x^2 - 20x + 60$
3. $A = \left(\dfrac{x}{4}\right)^2 + \left(\dfrac{500 - x}{4}\right)^2$
4. $A = x(8 - x^2)$
5. $V = x(30 - 2x)(40 - 2x)$
6. $g(x) = 2x^3 - 6x^2 + 3x - 5$
7. $V(x) = 200 - 20x^2 + 0.01x^3$
8. $f(x) = 2x^5 - 10x^4 + 3x^3 + 2x^2 - 10x + 5$

In Exercises 9 to 12, determine the *exact* values of all local maximum and minimum values and the corresponding values of x that give these values:

9. $y = x^2 - 4x + 5$
10. $f(x) = 30 - 3x + 7x^2$
11. $g(x) = |10 - 7x + x^2|$
12. $f(x) = 3 - 2|4x + 7|$

In Exercises 13 to 24, draw a complete graph of the function. Find the points where the graphs cross the x-axis. Determine all local maximum and minimum values and the corresponding values of x that give these extremum values.

13. $y = 10 - x^2$
14. $f(x) = 2x^2 - 6x + 10$
15. $g(x) = x^3 - 10x^2$
16. $y = 2x^3 - x^2 + x - 4$
17. $f(x) = x^4 - 4x^2 - 3x + 12$
18. $y = |2x^3 - 4x^2 + x - 3|$
19. $f(x) = x^3 - 2x^2 + x - 30$
20. $V(x) = x(34 - 2x)(53 - 2x)$
21. $T(x) = |20x^3 + 2x^2 - 10x + 5|$
22. $V(x) = x(22 - 2x)(8 - 2x)$
23. $f(x) = 12 - x + 3x^2 - 2x^3$
24. $y = x^5 - 3x^2 + 3x - 6$

In Exercises 25 to 30, find the intervals on which each function is increasing and decreasing:

25. $g(x) = x(x - 3)$ **26.** $t(x) = x(x - 2)(x + 3)$

27. $g(x) = x^3 - 4x^2 + 4x$ **28.** $f(x) = x^3 + 7x^2 + 7x - 15$

29. $h(x) = x^4 - 2x^2 - 5x + 6$

30. $k(x) = -x^4 + x^3 + 4x^2 - 4x - 2$

In Exercises 31 and 32, find the intervals on which each function is increasing and decreasing. (Expect to find *hidden* behavior.)

31. $f(x) = x^3 - 2x^2 + x - 30$

32. $f(x) = 20x^3 + 2x^2 - 10$

33. Describe how $y = -2(x + 3)^3 + 1$ can be obtained from $y = x^3$ by a sequence of one or more of the following transformations: horizontal or vertical shift, vertical stretch or shrink, reflection through an axis, and/or stretch.

34. Sketch a complete graph of $y = -2(x + 3)^3 + 1$, and identify the intervals on which the function is increasing or decreasing.

35. Describe conditions on constants a, h, and k under which $y = a(x - h)^3 + k$ is (a) an increasing function and (b) a decreasing function.

36. Writing to Learn   Write a paragraph explaining how Example 7 together with the results of Exercise 35 can be used to show that $y = x^3 - 4x^2 - 4x + 16$ *cannot* be obtained from $y = x^3$ using vertical stretching or shrinking, reflection, horizontal shifting or vertical shifting.

37. A rectangular area is to be fenced against an existing wall. The three sides of the fence must be 1050 feet long. Find the dimensions of the maximum area that can be enclosed. What is the maximum area?

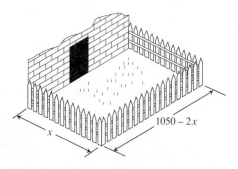

For Exercise 37

Exercises 38 to 40 refer to the following **problem situation**: A ball is thrown straight up from the top of a building 300 feet tall with an initial velocity of 40 feet per second.

38. Find an algebraic representation of the height above ground of the ball as a function of time.

39. When does the object reach its maximum height above ground, and what is this maximum height?

40. When will the ball hit the ground? Assume it does not land on the building.

41. A rectangular sheet of metal 37 inches wide is to be made into a trough to feed hogs by turning up sides of equal length perpendicular to the sheet. Find the length of the turned-up sides that gives the trough the maximum cross-sectional area. What is the maximum cross-sectional area?

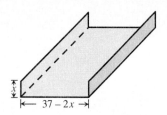

For Exercise 41

Exercises 42 to 44 refer to the following **problem situation**: A large apartment rental company has 2500 units available, and 1900 are currently rented at an average of $450 per month. A market survey indicates that each $15 decrease in average monthly rent will result in 20 new tenants.

42. Let x represent the number of $15 decreases in monthly rent. (That is, if $x = 3$, the rent is $405. Write expressions that represent (a) the resulting rent per unit and (b) the resulting number of tenants.

43. Let R represent the total rental income and x represent the number of $15 decreases in monthly rent. Use what you found in Exercise 42 to find an algebraic representation of R as a function of x. What is the domain of this function for this problem situation?

44. Find the rent that will yield the rental company the maximum monthly income.

Exercises 45 to 49 refer to the following **problem situation**: A 300-inch piece of wire is cut into two pieces. Each piece of wire is used to make a square wire frame. Let x be the length of one piece of the wire.

45. Find an algebraic representation that gives the total area of the two squares as a function of x.

46. Find a complete graph of this algebraic representation.

47. What portion of the graph of the algebraic representation represents the problem situation?

48. Find the lengths of the two pieces of wire that produce two squares of minimum total area.

49. Is there a way to cut the wires so that the area of the two squares is a maximum total area?

Exercises 50 to 53 refer to the following **problem situation**: An apartment building is built in the shape of a box with square cross section and a triangular prism forming the roof. The total height of the building is 30 feet, and the sum of the length and width of this building is 100 feet.

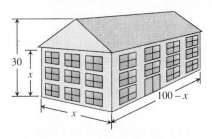

For Exercises 50 to 53

50. Find an algebraic representation for the volume V of the building as a function of x.

51. Find a complete graph of this algebraic representation.

52. What portion of this complete graph represents this problem situation?

53. What are the dimensions of the building with maximum volume, and what is this maximum volume?

Exercises 54 to 57 refer to the following **problem situation**: The total daily revenue of a lemonade stand at a state fair is given by the equation $R = xp$, where x is the number of glasses of lemonade sold daily and p is the price of one glass of lemonade. Assume that the price of the lemonade is given by the "supply" equation $p = 2 + 0.002x - 0.0001x^2$.

54. Find an algebraic representation that gives the total daily revenue as a function of x.

55. Find a complete graph of this algebraic representation. What portion of this graph represents this problem situation?

56. Find the number of glasses of lemonade to be sold to produce maximum daily revenue. What is the maximum daily revenue?

57. Writing to Learn   Conventional wisdom says that management should work to continually increase sales. Write a paragraph that either supports or refutes this point of view in the case of this problem situation.

4.2 _____ Continuity, the Intermediate Value Property, and End Behavior

Section 4.1 explored the increasing and decreasing patterns of polynomial functions. In this section we study several other properties of polynomials, beginning with one called continuity.

Most graphers are designed to plot points and then connect the points with an unbroken curve. In other words, outputs are assumed to vary continuously with the inputs and do not jump from one value to another without taking on all the values in between. For example, graphers will sometimes connect the two branches of the graph of $y = 1/(x - 1)$ suggesting that the function is defined and continuous at $x = 1$. This is why some graphers allow the user to turn off the connecting feature in order to view the plotted points and decide if the function graphed is really continuous.

Graph each of these functions in the viewing rectangle $[-5, 5]$ by $[-5, 5]$:

1. $f(x) = \dfrac{1}{x - 3}$

2. $g(x) = \sqrt{x + 4}$

3. $f(x) = x^3 - x^2 - 6x + 1$

4. $h(x) = \text{INT}(x)$ (If your grapher allows it, set the mode on "dot" rather than "connected" for this function.)

Also sketch each graph by hand. Once you begin the sketch, can you complete it without lifting the pencil from the paper?

Continuous Functions

Which of the functions in this exploration could be sketched by drawing one continuous curve? These are called continuous functions. Which ones required you to lift your pencil from the paper at least once? These are discontinuous functions.

Continuous Function Over an Interval *J*

A function f is **continuous on the interval *J*** if, for all a and b in *J*, it is possible to trace the graph of the function between a and b without lifting the pencil from the paper. If f fails to be continuous on an interval *J*, then it is **discontinuous on interval *J***.

A function may be continuous over one interval and discontinuous over another interval.

E X A M P L E   1   Finding Continuity and Discontinuity

Find three intervals over which $f(x) = 1/x$ is continuous and three over which it is discontinuous.

Solution   Find a complete graph of $f(x) = 1/x$ (see Fig. 4.14). If you were to sketch this graph, you would have to lift your pencil at $x = 0$. So the function is

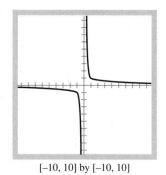

$[-10, 10]$ by $[-10, 10]$

Figure 4.14 $f(x) = 1/x$.

discontinuous on any interval that includes $x = 0$. Consequently there are many intervals on which f is continuous and many on which it is discontinuous. Here are two cases:

- f is continuous on the intervals $(2, 5)$, $[-4, -1]$, and $(\sqrt{2}, 3)$.
- f is discontinuous on the intervals $[-2, 3)$, $(-1, 4)$, and $(-0.2, 5]$.

Some functions fail to be continuous at many points. The following example shows one of these: the step function introduced in Section 3.2. It fails to be continuous at each integer value of x.

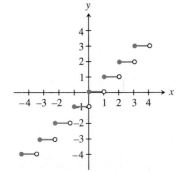

Figure 4.15 $f(x) = \text{INT}(x)$.

E X A M P L E 2   Finding Continuity in a Step Function

Determine the length of the longest interval on which the function $f(x) = \text{INT}(x)$ is continuous.

Solution   See Fig. 4.15. The longest interval on which f is continuous is 1 unit long. Here's why. Read from the graph that $f(2) \neq 1$ but that $f(2) = 2$. In general, if x is in the interval $[n, n+1)$, where y is an integer, then $f(x) = n$. So f is continuous on the interval $[n, n+1)$ for each n.

Any interval that contains an integer as an interior point includes a break point for the graph, and f is not continuous on such an interval.

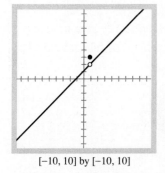

$[-10, 10]$ by $[-10, 10]$

Figure 4.16

$$f(x) = \begin{cases} \dfrac{x^2 - 1}{x - 1} & \text{for } x \neq 1 \\ 3 & \text{for } x = 1 \end{cases}.$$

Understanding: Point of Discontinuity

A function f has a **point of discontinuity** at $x = a$ if one of the following three conditions hold:

1. The function is not defined at $x = a$. An example is $f(x) = 1/x$ at $x = 0$ (Fig. 4.14).
2. The graph of the function has a break at $x = a$. An example is $f(x) = \text{INT}(x)$ at any integer value of x (Fig. 4.15).
3. The graph of the function has a hole in it at $x = a$. For example,

$$f(x) = \begin{cases} \dfrac{x^2 - 1}{x - 1} & \text{for } x \neq 1 \\ 3 & \text{for } x = 1 \end{cases}$$

has a discontinuity at $x = 1$ (see Fig. 4.16).

Notice that the graphs in Figures 4.14, 4.15, and 4.16 illustrate the three different types of discontinuity at a point.

Have you noticed that the graphs of polynomial functions contrast sharply with the graphs of the functions in Examples 1 and 2? One major difference is that these two functions are discontinuous on at least one point, whereas polynomial functions are not.

The theory of calculus will allow a more thorough discussion of continuity. For the time being we state an important theorem.

Theorem 4.1   Continuity of Polynomial Functions

Every polynomial function is continuous on the interval $(-\infty, \infty)$.

A function that is continuous on the interval $(-\infty, \infty)$ is called a **continuous function**. Notice that there is an important distinction between a function that is continuous on an interval J and a continuous function. Theorem 4.1 tells us that all polynomial functions are continuous.

Intermediate Value Property

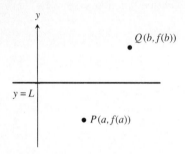

Figure 4.17   Trace the figure. Can you draw a continuous curve from P to Q that does not cross the line $y = L$?

Continuous functions satisfy a very important property called the **intermediate value property.** To help understand it, trace Fig. 4.17 and draw a continuous curve from P to Q. Can this be done without crossing the line $y = L$? No, any continuous curve from P to Q must cross the line $y = L$. This observation is the essence of the intermediate value property.

Theorem 4.2   Intermediate Value Property

If a function is continuous on $[a, b]$, then f assumes every value between $f(a)$ and $f(b)$. In other words, if $f(a) < L < f(b)$, then there is a number c in $[a, b]$ such that $f(c) = L$. See Fig. 4.18.

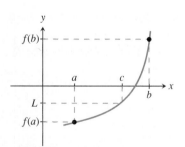

Figure 4.18   If L is between $f(a)$ and $f(b)$, then f assumes the value L in the interval (a, b), that is, $f(c) = L$.

The next two examples involve the intermediate value property.

E X A M P L E   3   Applying the Intermediate Value Property

Let $f(x) = 3x - 4$. Determine c on $[-10, 10]$ so that $f(c) = 15$.

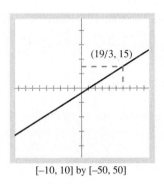

$[-10, 10]$ by $[-50, 50]$

Figure 4.19 $f(x) = 3x - 4$.

Solution (See Figure 4.19)

$$f(-10) = 3(-10) - 4 = -34 \qquad \text{f is a degree 1 polynomial and hence is continuous.}$$

$$f(10) = 3(10) - 4 = 26$$

$$-34 < 15 < 26$$

$$f(-10) < 15 < f(10) \qquad \text{The intermediate value property can be applied, since f is continuous on $[-10, 10]$.}$$

The intermediate value property assures us that there is a number c between -10 and 10 such that $f(c) = 15$. That is:

$$f(c) = 15$$

$$3c - 4 = 15 \qquad \text{Solve for c.}$$

$$3c = 19$$

$$c = \frac{19}{3} \qquad \text{Note that c is in $[-10, 10]$}$$

Finally, confirm that $f\left(\frac{19}{3}\right) = 15$. ▤

We sometimes describe the situation of Example 3 by saying that $f(x) = 3x - 4$ assumes the value 15.

E X A M P L E 4 Applying the Intermediate Value Property

Let $f(x) = x^2 + 3x - 4$. Determine c on $[-2, 3]$ so that $f(c) = -3$.

Solution See Fig. 4.20.

$$f(-2) = (-2)^2 + 3(-2) - 4 = -6$$

$$f(3) = 3^2 + 3(3) - 4 = 14$$

$$-6 < -3 < 14$$

$$f(-2) < -3 < f(3) \qquad \text{f is a degree 2 polynomial, so the intermediate value property applies.}$$

Since f is a continuous function, the intermediate value theorem assures us that there is a c between -2 and 3 for which $f(c) = -3$. That is,

$$f(c) = -3$$

$$c^2 + 3c - 4 = -3$$

$$c^2 + 3c - 1 = 0.$$

Apply the quadratic formula to get c accurate to hundredths.

$$c = \frac{-3 \pm \sqrt{13}}{2} = -3.30 \text{ and } 0.30$$

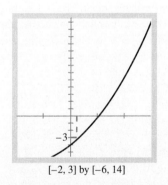

$[-2, 3]$ by $[-6, 14]$

Figure 4.20 $f(x) = x^2 + 3x - 4$.

Since -3.3 is not between -2 and 3, $(-3 + \sqrt{13})/2$ is the only number between -2 and 3 such that

$$f\left(\frac{-3 + \sqrt{13}}{2}\right) = -3.$$ ≣

The importance of the intermediate value property is that it guarantees the existence of a real number that may be difficult or impossible to compute. The intermediate value property is perhaps most commonly used to locate where a function value is zero.

E X A M P L E 5   Approximating the Zero of a Function

Show that $f(x) = x^5 + 2x - 1$ has a zero in the interval $[0.25, 0.75]$.

Solution   We want to find c so that $f(c) = 0$ where c is in $[0.25, 0.75]$.

$$f(0.25) = (0.25)^5 + 2(0.25) - 1 = -0.499$$

$$f(0.75) = (0.75)^5 + 2(0.75) - 1 = 0.737$$

Since f is continuous and $f(0.25) < 0 < f(0.75)$, conclude from the intermediate value property that there is a value c in $[0.25, 0.75]$ such that $f(c) = 0$. That is, there is a zero between 0.25 and 0.75.   ≣

Example 5 provides the basis for a numerical zoom-in procedure for estimating a zero of a function. (The **bisection method** involves continually bisecting the interval in the previous viewing rectangle considered.) At each new midpoint the function is evaluated to see whether it is positive or negative. By using the intermediate value property you can then determine in which of the two intervals resulting from the bisection the graph of the function crosses the x-axis.

Example 5 shows that $f(0.25)$ is negative and $f(0.75)$ is positive. Theorem 4.2 tells us there is a zero between 0.25 and 0.75. Bisecting the interval (0.25, 0.75) results in the midpoint 0.5. The new interval will thus have 0.5 as one endpoint and one of the two previous endpoints as the other endpoint. How is the other endpoint chosen? It must be the point whose sign is opposite to that of the midpoint. Since both $f(0.5)$ and $f(0.75)$ are positive, we do not choose 0.75 as the new endpoint. However, $f(0.5)$ and $f(0.25)$ have opposite signs, so the new interval for bisection is (0.25, 0.5).

This second interval is bisected to get a second midpoint. The process is repeated until an interval small enough to provide the desired accuracy is reached. In this case we continue the method for two more rounds until the zero is found to be in the interval (0.4375, 0.5). The following table records the process; notice that the midpoints are boldfaced. See also Fig. 4.21.

	Starting Interval	Step 1	Step 2	Step 3
Positive values	$f(0.75)$	$\boldsymbol{f(0.5)}$	$f(0.5)$	$f(0.5)$
Negative values	$f(0.25)$	$f(0.25)$	$\boldsymbol{f(0.375)}$	$\boldsymbol{f(0.4375)}$

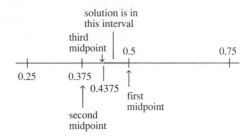

Figure 4.21 Bisection method for approximating a zero of $f(x) = x^5 + 2x - 1$.

End Behavior of a Polynomial Function

What happens to the graph of a function on the extreme right and left ends of the x-axis? This is the same as asking about the **end behavior** of the function: What happens to the $f(x)$ values when $|x|$ is large?

Consider the graph of $f(x) = x^3$ (Fig. 4.22).

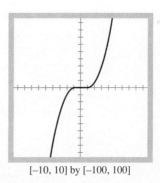

[–10, 10] by [–100, 100]

Figure 4.22 $f(x) = x^3$ has end behavior type ($\diagup$, $\diagup$).

We say: as x approaches infinity, $f(x)$ approaches infinity.

We write: as $x \to \infty$, $f(x) \to \infty$.

We mean: as x gets very large, $f(x)$ also gets very large.

Similarly, we write: as $x \to -\infty$, $f(x) \to -\infty$. When $f(x) \to +\infty$ at the extreme right of the graph and $f(x) \to -\infty$ at the extreme left of the graph, we describe the **end behavior type** of f as $(\swarrow, \nearrow)$. So $(\swarrow, \nearrow)$ is a notational abbreviation for the two statements:

$$\text{as } x \to -\infty, f(x) \to -\infty \qquad \text{and} \qquad \text{as } x \to \infty, f(x) \to \infty.$$

There are four end behavior types for polynomial functions. These four types are $(\nwarrow, \nearrow), (\swarrow, \nearrow), (\nwarrow, \searrow), (\swarrow, \searrow)$ and are illustrated in Figure 4.23.

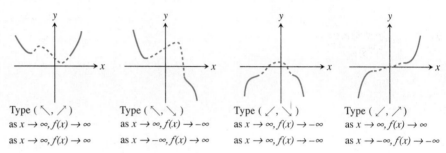

Type $(\nwarrow, \nearrow)$
as $x \to \infty, f(x) \to \infty$
as $x \to \infty, f(x) \to \infty$

Type $(\nwarrow, \searrow)$
as $x \to \infty, f(x) \to -\infty$
as $x \to -\infty, f(x) \to \infty$

Type $(\swarrow, \searrow)$
as $x \to \infty, f(x) \to -\infty$
as $x \to \infty, f(x) \to -\infty$

Type $(\swarrow, \nearrow)$
as $x \to \infty, f(x) \to \infty$
as $x \to -\infty, f(x) \to -\infty$

Figure 4.23   The four possible end behaviors for polynomial functions.

E X A M P L E   6   Identifying the End Behavior Type

Identify the end behavior type for $f(x) = x^4$ and $g(x) = -x^4$.

Solution   Study Figs. 4.24 and 4.25.

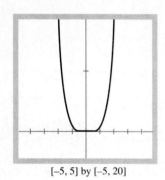

[–5, 5] by [–5, 20]

Figure 4.24 $f(x) = x^4$.

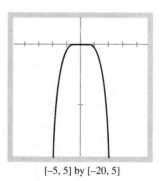

[–5, 5] by [–20, 5]

Figure 4.25 $g(x) = -x^4$.

The end behavior type of f is $(\nwarrow, \nearrow)$, and the end behavior type of g is $(\swarrow, \searrow)$.

🔍 **EXPLORE WITH A GRAPHING UTILITY**

Find the end behavior type for each of these functions. Record your results.

$$f(x) = 3x^4 \qquad\qquad f(x) = 2x^3$$

$$f(x) = -2x^4 \qquad\qquad f(x) = -4x^5$$

$$f(x) = -5x^2 \qquad\qquad f(x) = -2x^3$$

$$f(x) = 2x^6 \qquad\qquad f(x) = 2x^7$$

Generalize Describe the end behavior type of a function $f(x) = a_n x^n$.

The following box summarizes the generalization that you may have discovered in this Exploration.

End Behavior of $f(x) = a_n x^n$

The polynomial functions of the form $f(x) = a_n x^n (n \geq 1)$ have the following types of end behavior:

	n **even**	n **odd**
$a_n > 0$	$(\searc" , \nearrow)$ end behavior	$(\nearrow , \nearrow)$ end behavior
$a_n < 0$	$(\nearrow , \searrow)$ end behavior	$(\searrow , \searrow)$ end behavior

---

Using Zoom-Out to Find a Model of End Behavior

Each polynomial function belongs to one of four categories of end behavior type as shown in Fig. 4.23. For example, the polynomial $f(x) = 2x^3 - 7x^2 - 8x + 16$ has end behavior type $(\nearrow , \nearrow)$. In particular, as $x \to \infty$, $f(x) \to \infty$ and as $x \to -\infty$, $f(x) \to \infty$. But how fast does $f(x)$ increase as x increases?

The term having the highest degree in a polynomial is called the **leading term**. For $f(x) = 2x^3 - 7x^2 - 8x + 16$ the leading term is $2x^3$. In the following table notice that the values of $2x^3$ are very large in absolute value compared with the absolute values of $-7x^2 - 8x + 16$. We describe this by saying that the leading term dominates the polynomial f.

Comparing the Leading Term $2x^3$ and $f(x)$

x	$2x^3$	$-7x^2 - 8x + 16$	$f(x)$
20	16,000	$-2,944$	13,056
50	250,000	$-17,884$	232,116
100	2,000,000	$-70,784$	1,929,216
-20	$-16,000$	$-2,624$	$-18,624$
-50	$-250,000$	$-17,084$	$-267,084$
-100	$-2,000,000$	$-69,184$	$-2,069,184$

Another way of saying it is that $2x^3$ models how rapidly $f(x) = 2x^3 - 7x^2 - 8x + 16$ increases; that is, $2x^3$ is the end behavior model of $f(x) = 2x^3 - 7x^2 - 8x + 16$. This leads to the following definition.

Definition 4.4   End Behavior Model

The **end behavior model** of a polynomial

$$f(x) = a_n x^n + a_{n-1} x^{n-1} + \cdots + a_1 x + a_0 \quad (a_n \neq 0)$$

is the polynomial $g(x) = a_n x^n$.

A grapher can provide visual evidence to support this numerical evidence of end behavior. The process of viewing a graph in increasingly larger viewing rectangles is called **zoom-out**. We can use zoom-out to find functions that model the end behavior of a polynomial.

E X A M P L E   7   Visualizing End Behavior

Graph both $f(x) = 2x^3 - 7x^2 - 8x + 16$ and $g(x) = 2x^3$ in viewing rectangle $[-8, 8]$ by $[-100, 100]$. Then zoom out to the viewing rectangle $[-40, 40]$ by $[-10,000, 10,000]$.

Solution   In Fig. 4.26(a) the differences between the two functions are evident. In Fig. 4.26(b), which is a zoom-out version of Fig 4.26(a), the end behaviors of the two functions appear alike.

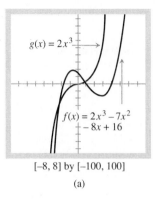
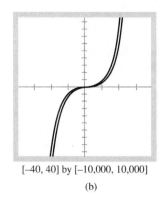

[–8, 8] by [–100, 100]   [–40, 40] by [–10,000, 10,000]

(a)   (b)

Figure 4.26   Two views of $f(x) = 2x^3 - 7x^2 - 8x + 16$ and $g(x) = 2x^3$.

Example 7 gives a visual justification for the concept *end behavior model*. We see that $2x^3$ does model the function $f(x) = 2x^3 - 7x^2 - 8x + 16$ when $|x|$ is large.

E X A M P L E   8   Finding the End Behavior Model

Find the end behavior model for $f(x) = -0.5x^4 + 5x^3 - 10x + 1$. Also determine the end behavior type of f.

Solution   The function $g(x) = -0.5x^4$ is the end behavior model of $f(x) = -0.5x^4 + 5x^3 - 10x + 1$. f has end behavior type ($\nearrow$, $\searrow$).

E X A M P L E   9   Find the Maximum Possible Area

Find the maximum possible area of a rectangle that has its base on the x-axis and its upper two vertices on the graph of the equation $y = 4 - x^2$ (see Fig. 4.27).

Solution

$$\text{width of rectangle:} \qquad 2x$$

$$\text{height of rectangle:} \qquad y = 4 - x^2$$

$$\text{area of rectangle:} \qquad A(x) = 2x(4 - x^2)$$

The only values of x that make sense in the problem situation are those such that $0 < x < 2$. Why?

Find a complete graph of $A(x)$, and observe that there is a local maximum between 0 and 2. Use zoom-in to find the local maximum.

The value of x, with error of at most 0.01, producing the largest value for the area of the rectangle, is 1.155. The area for $x = 1.155$ is 6.16 square units.

[–3, 3] by [–1, 5]

Figure 4.27 $y = 4 - x^2$.

Exercises for Section 4.2

In Exercises 1 to 8, assume that each graph is complete. Identify the function as continuous or discontinuous. If it is discontinuous, name two intervals on which it is continuous and two intervals on which it is discontinuous.

1.

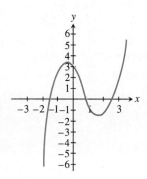

2.

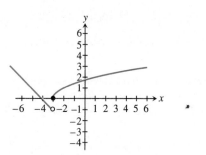

3.

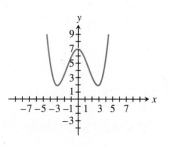

4.

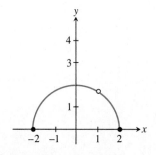

5.

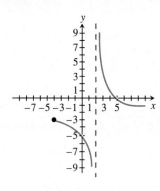

6.

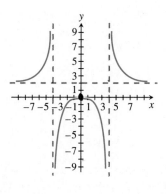

7.

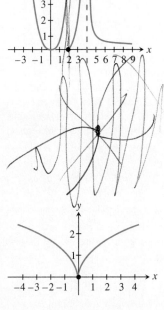

8.

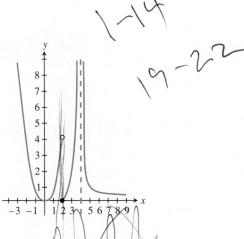

In Exercises 9 to 14, determine the points of discontinuity of each function.

9. $f(x) = \text{INT}(x + 2)$

10. $g(x) = 2x^2 - 3x + 6$

11. $V(x) = 4x^3 - 200x^2 + 30x$

12. $f(x) = \begin{cases} -\dfrac{1}{x} & \text{for } x < 0 \\ x^2 + 1 & \text{for } x \geq 0 \end{cases}$

13. $y = \dfrac{2}{x - 3}$

14. $f(x) = \begin{cases} |x - 2| & \text{for } x < -1 \\ 2x & \text{for } x \geq -1 \end{cases}$

15. Consider the function $f(x) = 3x - 12$. Verify that 5 is a number between $f(-10)$ and $f(10)$. Determine a value of c so that $f(c) = 5$ and $-10 \leq c \leq 10$.

16. Consider the function $f(x) = 4x - 7$. Verify that 0 is a number between $f(1)$ and $f(2)$, and determine a value of c so that $f(c) = 0$ and $1 \leq c \leq 2$.

17. Consider the quadratic function $f(x) = 2x^2 + 4x - 10$. Verify that 50 is a number between $f(0)$ and $f(10)$. Determine a value of c so that $f(c) = 50$, and $0 \leq c \leq 10$.

18. Consider the linear function $f(x) = ax + b$. Let L be a number between $f(-10)$ and $f(10)$, and determine a value of c so that $f(c) = L$ and $-10 \leq c \leq 10$.

For Exercises 19 and 20, assume the graph of $y = f(x)$ is complete, and complete each statement.

19. As $x \to \infty, f(x) \to ?$ **20.** As $x \to -\infty, f(x) \to ?$

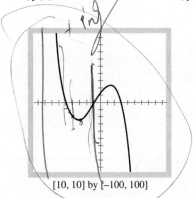

[10, 10] by [–100, 100]

For Exercises 19 and 20

In Exercises 21 and 22, assume the graph of $y = f(x)$ is complete, and complete each statement.

21. As $x \to \infty, f(x) \to ?$ **22.** As $x \to -\infty, f(x) \to ?$

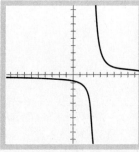

[–10, 10] by [–10, 10]

For Exercises 21 and 22

Exercises 23 to 25 refer to the following **problem situation**: The total daily revenue of Chris's Cookie Shop is given by the equation $R = xp$, where x is the number of pounds of cookies sold and p is the price of 1 lb of cookies. Assume the price per pound of cookies is given by the supply equation $p = 0.2 + 0.01x - 0.00001x^2$.

23. What values of x make sense in this problem situation?

24. Find a complete graph of the revenue function R, and determine for what values of x the revenue function is increasing.

25. Find the number of pounds of cookies Chris's Cookie Shop needs to sell to achieve maximum revenue. What is this maximum revenue?

26. A box is made by cutting equal squares from the four corners of a 16- by 28-inch piece of material. Determine the size of the square that must be cut out to produce a box with maximum volume. What is the corresponding maximum volume?

27. Consider the following figure, which represents a rectangular piece of fabric 3 feet wide. Suppose one corner E is folded over along the line DF until the corner E touches the opposite edge at B. Let A be the area of the shaded triangle BCD. Let x be the distance between the vertex C and point B. It can be shown that the area of triangle BCD is $A = \frac{3}{4}x - \frac{1}{12}x^3$. What is the largest possible area A?

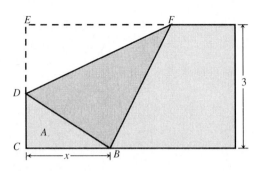

For Exercise 27

Exercises 28 and 29 refer to the following algebraic situation: Given $n + 1$ points in the coordinate plane, it can be shown that there is a unique polynomial of a degree less than or equal to n whose graph passes through these $n + 1$ points. Such a polynomial is said to *interpolate* these data points. (Such interpolating polynomials are important tools in understanding data generated from many kinds of scientific experiments and statistical analyses.)

28. Show that $L(x) = 2x^3 - 11x^2 + 12x + 5$ interpolates the data points $(-1, -20), (0, 5), (1, 8)$, and $(2, 1)$.

29. Assume that $L(x) = 2x^3 - 11x^2 + 12x + 5$ interpolates a set of data points from some experiment. Suppose that $(1.5, 6)$ is another data point generated by the same experiment. What is the predicted outcome if $x = 1.5$ is used in the interpolating polynomial $L(x)$?

30. Writing to Learn   Write several paragraphs that explain the difference between the concepts *end behavior type* and *end behavior model*.

31. Writing to Learn   Write several paragraphs describing a few motions or activities that can be represented by one quantity varying continuously as another variable changes.

4.3

Real Zeros of Polynomials: The Factor Theorem

The words *zero* and *root*, introduced in Section 2.2, are used interchangeably when discussing functions. The zeros or roots of a function f are the solutions to the equation $f(x) = 0$. A number a is a zero or a root if and only if $f(a) = 0$.

Section 2.1 showed how to find exact zeros for linear and quadratic functions. In this section and Section 4.4 we focus on special techniques that can be used to find real zeros algebraically for polynomial functions of degrees greater than or equal to 3.

Factors and Long Division

The zeros of a polynomial function can be found by finding its factors. For example, if $x - 2$ is a factor of f, long division can be used to find a quotient $q(x)$. We can then write $f(x)$ as

$$f(x) = (x - 2)q(x).$$

Since

$$f(2) = (2 - 2)q(2) = 0,$$

2 is a zero of f. So if a linear factor can be found, a zero has also been found.

Whether $x - c$ is a factor of a polynomial can be determined by dividing the polynomial by $x - c$ by using long division and checking to see if the remainder is zero.

EXAMPLE 1   Completing Polynomial Long Division

Divide the polynomial $x^3 - 8x - 3$ by $x - 3$, and find a zero of $x^3 - 8x - 3$.

Solution   When dividing $x - 3$ into $x^3 - 8x - 3$, first find a partial quotient of x^2 by dividing x into the first term x^3 to obtain x^2. Then multiply x^2 by $x - 3$ and subtract the product $x^3 - 3x^2$ from the dividend. Repeat the process until you reach a remainder.

$$
\begin{array}{r}
x^2 + 3x + 1 \quad\longleftarrow \text{Quotient} \\
x - 3 \,\overline{)\, x^3 + 0x^2 - 8x - 3} \quad\longleftarrow \text{Dividend} \\
\underline{x^3 - 3x^2} \qquad\qquad\quad \longleftarrow x^2 \text{ multiplied by } x - 3 \\
3x^2 - 8x - 3 \quad\longleftarrow \text{Result of first subtraction} \\
\underline{3x^2 - 9x} \qquad\quad \longleftarrow 3x \text{ multiplied by } (x - 3) \\
x - 3 \\
\underline{x - 3} \\
0 \quad\longleftarrow \text{Remainder}
\end{array}
$$

Divisor $\longrightarrow$

Since the remainder is zero, we can conclude that

$$x^3 - 8x - 3 = (x - 3)(x^2 + 3x + 1)$$

and 3 is a zero of $x^3 - 8x - 3$.   ≡

Notice that the terms *dividend, divisor, quotient,* and *remainder* are used here exactly as they are in the division of integers.

E X A M P L E   2   Completing Long Division (Continued)

Find the quotient and remainder when $2x^4 - x^3 - 2$ is divided by $2x^2 + x + 1$.

Solution

Notice that the degree of the remainder is less than the degree of the divisor.

≡

We can write the dividend as the product of the divisor and the quotient plus the remainder.

Dividend   =   Divisor × Quotient + Remainder

$$2x^4 - x^3 - 2 = (2x^2 + x + 1)(x^2 - x) + (x - 2)$$

Examples 1 and 2 illustrate the general process called the **division algorithm for polynomials**, which can be stated more formally as follows.

Division Algorithm for Polynomials

If $f(x)$ and $h(x)$ are polynomials, then there are polynomials $q(x)$ and $r(x)$, called the **quotient** and **remainder**, such that

$$f(x) = h(x)q(x) + r(x).$$

Either $r(x) = 0$ or the degree of $r(x)$ is less than the degree of $h(x)$.

Factors and Zeros

The division algorithm tells us that the degree of the remainder is less than the degree of the divisor. That means that whenever a given polynomial is divided by a linear polynomial (degree 1), the remainder must be a zero-degree polynomial, in other words, a constant.

So if $f(x)$ is divided by $x - c$, it is true for all values of x that

$$f(x) = (x - c)q(x) + r,$$

where r is a constant. In particular, for $x = c$,

$$f(c) = (c - c)q(c) + r$$

$$f(c) = r.$$

where r is a constant. In particular, for $x = c$,

$$f(c) = (c - c)q(c) + r$$

$$f(c) = r.$$

This proves the following theorem.

Theorem 4.3   Remainder Theorem

If a polynomial $f(x)$ is divided by $x - c$, then the remainder is $f(c)$. Thus

$$f(x) = (x - c)q(x) + f(c)$$

where $q(x)$ is the quotient.

E X A M P L E   3   Applying the Remainder Theorem

Find the remainder when the polynomial $f(x) = x^3 - 2x^2 + x - 5$ is divided by (a) $x - 3$ and (b) $x + 1$.

Solution

a) $f(x) = x^3 - 2x^2 + x - 5$

$$f(3) = (3)^3 - 2(3)^2 + 3 - 5 \qquad \begin{array}{l}\text{The remainder theorem says that}\\ \text{the remainder is } f(3) \text{ when}\\ f(x) \text{ is divided by } x - 3.\end{array}$$

$$= 7$$

The remainder when $f(x)$ is divided by $x - 3$ is $f(3) = 7$.

b) $f(-1) = (-1)^3 - 2(-1)^2 + (-1) - 5 \qquad \begin{array}{l}\text{The remainder theorem says that}\\ \text{the remainder is } f(-1) \text{ when}\\ f(x) \text{ is divided by } x + 1.\end{array}$

$$= -9$$

The remainder when $f(x)$ is divided by $x + 1$ is $f(-1) = -9$.   ≡

Suppose that a polynomial function $f(x)$ is divided by $x - c$. Then the remainder theorem says that, for all values of x,

$$f(x) = (x - c)q(x) + f(c).$$

Suppose that $x - c$ is a factor of $f(x)$. Then the remainder is zero and $f(c) = 0$. This means that c is a zero of f.

Conversely, suppose that c is a zero of f. Then $f(c) = 0$ and by the remainder theorem we can conclude that

$$f(x) = (x - c)q(x).$$

Thus $x - c$ is a factor. This discussion proves the following theorem.

Theorem 4.4   Factor Theorem

Let $f(x)$ be a polynomial. Then $x - c$ is a factor of $f(x)$ if and only if c is a zero of $f(x)$.

E X A M P L E   4   Applying the Factor Theorem

Use the factor theorem to show that $x + 2$ is a factor of $x^3 + 5x^2 + 5x - 2$.

Solution   Show that -2 is a zero of $f(x) = x^3 + 5x^2 + 5x - 2$:

$$f(-2) = (-2)^3 + 5(-2)^2 + 5(-2) - 2$$
$$= -8 + (20) + (-10) - 2$$
$$= 0$$

So -2 is a zero, which means that $x - (-2) = x + 2$ is a factor.   ▤

There are many equivalent ways to formulate a statement using the terms *factor, root,* and *intercept.* These various formulations are based on equivalent statements about roots and zeros.

Equivalent Statements about Roots and Zeros

The following statements are equivalent for a polynomial $f(x)$ and a real number c.

- c is a solution to the equation $f(x) = 0$.
- c is a zero of $f(x)$.
- c is a root of $f(x)$.
- $x - c$ is a factor of $f(x)$.
- When $f(x)$ is divided by $x - c$, the remainder is 0.
- c is an x-intercept of the graph of $y = f(x)$.

These equivalent statements show that whenever you know a root of a polynomial function, you also know a factor. Conversely, whenever you know a factor, you also know a root.

E X A M P L E   5   Finding a Polynomial with Certain Zeros

Find a polynomial of degree 3 whose coefficients are real numbers and whose zeros are $-2, 1, 3$.

Solution

-2 is a zero of f $\Longleftrightarrow$ $x + 2$ is a factor of f.

1 is a zero of f $\Longleftrightarrow$ $x - 1$ is a factor of f. These statements are true by the factor theorem.

3 is a zero of f $\Longleftrightarrow$ $x - 3$ is a factor of f.

Therefore $(x + 2)(x - 1)(x - 3) = x^3 - 2x^2 - 5x + 6$ is a polynomial of degree 3 with zeros $-2, 1$, and 3.   ▤

When the factors of a polynomial are recognized or can otherwise be found, the factors can be used to find zeros of the polynomial algebraically. Example 6 illustrates this method.

E X A M P L E   6   Factoring to Find Zeros of a Polynomial

Use factoring to find the real zeros of $f(x) = x^3 + 2x^2 - 4x - 8$.

Solution   Factor by grouping the first two terms and the last two terms together.

$$x^3 + 2x^2 - 4x - 8 = x^2(x + 2) - 4(x + 2)$$

$$= (x + 2)(x^2 - 4) \quad \text{Factor out the common factor } x + 2.$$

$$= (x + 2)(x - 2)(x + 2)$$

$$= (x + 2)^2(x - 2)$$

The real zeros of f are 2 and -2.   ▤

Although factoring can be used to find the zeros of a polynomial, it is often difficult to recognize the factors of a polynomial, particularly if the polynomial is of degree 3 or greater. Sometimes a grapher can be used to help find one zero and hence a corresponding linear factor.

E X A M P L E   7   Using a Grapher to Find Factors

Use the graph of $f(x) = 2x^3 - 4x^2 + x - 2$ to find the real zeros of $f(x)$.

Solution   The graph shown in Fig. 4.28 suggests that f has a zero at $x = 2$. Indeed,

$$f(2) = 2(2^3) - 4(2^2) + 2 - 2 = 0. \quad \begin{array}{l}\text{Conclude from the factor theorem}\\ \text{that } x - 2 \text{ is a factor.}\end{array}$$

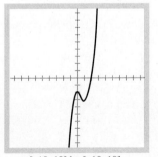

[-10, 10] by [-10, 10]

Figure 4.28
$f(x) = 2x^3 - 4x^2 + x - 2$.

To find the other factor, complete the following long division:

$$\begin{array}{r} 2x^2 + 1 \\ x-2 \overline{\smash{)}\, 2x^3 - 4x^2 + x - 2} \\ \underline{2x^3 - 4x^2 } \\ x - 2 \\ \underline{x - 2 } \\ 0 \end{array}$$

Thus $f(x) = (x-2)(2x^2 + 1)$. From this, conclude that 2 is the only real zero of f. (Why?)

Even with the help of a graph to suggest roots, in most cases the zeros of a polynomial function cannot be found by algebraic means. In that case the zoom-in method is used to find a numerical root.

To illustrate this situation consider the following application.

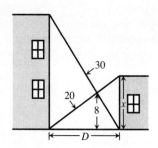

Figure 4.29   Diagram for Example 8.

EXAMPLE 8   APPLICATION: Crossing Ladders

Suppose two ladders, one 20 feet long and one 30 feet long, are placed between two buildings as shown in Fig. 4.29. How far apart are the buildings if the ladders cross at a height of 8 feet?

Solution   In Exercise 40 you will verify that the value of x in Fig. 4.29 satisfies the equation $x^4 - 16x^3 + 500x^2 - 8000x + 32,000 = 0$. Once x is known, D can be found because $20^2 = D^2 + x^2$.

To find a solution to this fourth-degree equation, find a complete graph of $f(x) = x^4 - 16x^3 + 500x^2 - 8000x + 32,000$ (see Fig. 4.30).

There is one solution near 6 and another near 12. Use zoom-in to find that the zeros are 5.944 and 11.712 with an error of at most 0.01.

Studying Fig. 4.29 shows that in this problem situation, the value of x must be between 8 and 20. (Why?) So let $x = 11.712$ in the equation $20^2 = D^2 + x^2$. Then

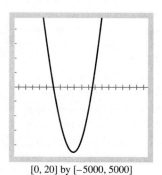

[0, 20] by [−5000, 5000]

Figure 4.30 $f(x) = x^4 - 16x^3 + 500x^2 - 8000x + 32,000$. Knowing that the y-intercept is 32,000 and that $y = x^4$ is a model of end behavior are clues that a large viewing rectangle is needed.

$$D^2 = 20^2 - (11.712)^2$$
$$D = \sqrt{(20)^2 - (11.712)^2}$$
$$= 16.212.$$

The buildings are 16.21 feet apart.

(handwritten: 3, 4, 7-8, 10, 11, 16-18, 20, 21, 24, 25, 27, 38)

Exercises for Section 4.3

In Exercises 1 to 4, find the quotient $q(x)$ and remainder $r(x)$ when $f(x)$ is divided by $h(x)$. Then compute $q(x)h(x) + r(x)$ and compare the result with $f(x)$.

1. $f(x) = x^2 - 2x + 3$; $h(x) = x - 1$
2. $f(x) = x^3 - 1$; $h(x) = x + 1$
3. $f(x) = 4x^3 - 8x^2 + 2x - 1$; $h(x) = 2x + 1$
4. $f(x) = x^4 - 2x^3 + 3x^2 - 4x + 6$; $h(x) = x^2 + 2x - 1$

In Examples 5 to 8, use the remainder theorem to determine the remainder when $f(x)$ is divided by $x - c$. Check by using long division.

5. $f(x) = 2x^2 - 3x + 1$; $c = 2$
6. $f(x) = x^4 - 5$; $c = 1$
7. $f(x) = 2x^3 - 3x^2 + 4x - 7$; $c = 2$
8. $f(x) = x^5 - 2x^4 + 3x^2 - 20x + 3$; $c = -1$

In Exercises 9 to 12, use the factor theorem to determine whether the first polynomial is a factor of the second polynomial.

9. $x + 2$; $x^2 - 4$ 10. $x - 1$; $x^3 - x^2 + x - 1$
11. $x - 3$; $x^3 - x^2 - x - 15$
12. $x + 1$; $2x^{10} - x^9 + x^8 + x^7 + 2x^6 - 3$

In Exercises 13 to 18, find all real zeros of each polynomial by factoring. Use a graphing utility to support your answer.

13. $f(x) = x^2 - 5x + 6$ 14. $f(x) = 6x^2 + 8x - 8$
15. $f(x) = x^3 - 9x$
16. $g(x) = x^3 - 1$
17. $T(x) = 2x^4 + x^2 - 15$
18. $g(x) = x^3 - x^2 - 2x + 2$

In Exercises 19 to 22, draw a complete graph of each function. Use the graph as an aid in factoring the polynomial, and then determine all real zeros.

19. $f(x) = 5x^2 - 2x - 51$
20. $f(x) = x^3 - 2x^2 - 3x + 6$
21. $f(x) = x^3 - 11x^2 + x - 11$
22. $g(x) = x^4 - 16$

In Exercises 23 to 26, determine all real zeros.

23. $f(x) = x^3 + 3x^2 - 10x - 1$
24. $g(x) = 2 - 15x + 11x^2 - 3x^3$

25. $f(x) = 100x^3 - 403x^2 + 406x + 1$
26. $f(x) = 100x^3 - 403x^2 + 406x - 1$
27. A toy rocket is shot straight up into the air with an initial velocity of 48 feet per second. Its height $s(t)$ above the ground after t seconds is given by $s(t) = -16t^2 + 48t$. What is the maximum height attained by the rocket?
28. An object is shot straight up from the top of a 260-foot tall tower with an initial velocity of 35 feet per second.
    a) When will the object hit the ground?
    b) When does the object reach its maximum height above the ground, and what is this maximum height?
29. Draw the graph of $f(x) = 100x^3 - 203x^2 + 103x - 1$ in the $[-5, 5]$ by $[-100, 100]$ viewing rectangle.
    a) How many real zeros are evident from this graph?
    b) How many actual real zeros exist in this case?
    c) Find all real zeros.

In Exercises 30 to 33, find a polynomial with real coefficients satisfying the given conditions.

30. Degree 2, with 3 and -4 as zeros.
31. Degree 2, with 2 as the only real zero.
32. Degree 3, with -2, 1, and 4 as zeros.
33. Degree 3, with -1 as the only real zero.

Exercises 34 and 35 refer to the following **problem situation**: NICE-CALC Company manufactures the only calculator with the ZAP feature. Use the monthly supply function $P = S(x)$ and monthly demand function $P = D(x)$ to find the equilibrium price (breakeven price) and the associated production level needed to achieve equilibrium.

34. $S(x) = 6 + 0.001x^3$ and x is in thousands; $D(x) = 80 - 0.02x^2$ and x is in thousands.
35. $S(x) = 20 - 0.1x + 0.00007x^4$ and x is in thousands; $D(x) = 150 - 0.004x^3$ and x is in thousands.
36. If $f(x) = 2x^3 - 3kx^2 + kx - 1$, find a number k so that the graph of f contains the point $(1, 9)$.
37. Determine a linear factor of $f(x) = (x - 1)^6 - 64$.
38. Determine the remainder when
    a) $x^{40} - 3$ is divided by $x + 1$;
    b) $x^{63} - 17$ is divided by $x - 1$.
39. The hypotenuse of a right triangle is 2 inches longer than one of its legs and the triangle has an area of 50 square inches.

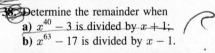

a) Show that, if x denotes the length of this leg, then $10,000 - 4x^3 - 4x^2 = 0$.

b) Determine the solutions to the equation in part (a).

40. Challenge   Derive the fourth-degree polynomial that gives the solution to the ladder problem of Example 8. *Hint:* Consider the following figure. Notice that $x^2 + z^2 = 20^2$ and $y^2 + z^2 = 30^2$. Write one equation that involves only x and y. Now show that the length of $AF = 8z/x$, and the length of $BF = 8z/y$. (Supply only the reasons.) Next, use the fact that the length of AF plus the length of BF is equal to z to determine a second equation in terms of x and y only. Solve the second equation for y and substitute it into the first equation.

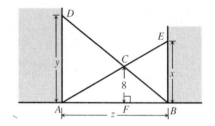

For Exercise 40, $AE = 20$, $DB = 30$

4.4

Rational Zeros and Horner's Algorithm

Some polynomial functions have zeros that are irrational numbers. For example,

$$f(x) = x^2 - 2 = (x - \sqrt{2})(x + \sqrt{2}).$$

The factor theorem shows that the function $f(x) = x^2 - 2$ has zeros $\sqrt{2}$ and $-\sqrt{2}$. Since these numbers are irrational numbers, the function f is said to have **irrational zeros**. On the other hand, the function $g(x) = 4x^2 - 9$ has zeros $\frac{3}{2}$ and $-\frac{3}{2}$. Since these numbers are rational numbers, g has **rational zeros.**

A polynomial function can have rational zeros, or irrational zeros, or it can have some of each. In this section we learn some techniques that can be used to find rational zeros if they exist.

We begin with a theorem that tells what the possible rational zeros are for polynomial functions whose coefficients are integers.

Theorem 4.5   Rational Zeros Theorem

Suppose all the coefficients in the polynomial

$$f(x) = a_n x^n + a_{n-1} x^{n-1} + \cdots + a_0 \qquad (a_n \neq 0, a_0 \neq 0)$$

are integers.

If $x = p/q$ is a rational zero, where p and q have no common factors, then

- p is a factor of the constant term a_0, and

- q is a factor of the leading coefficient a_n.

E X A M P L E   1   Finding All the Rational Zeros

Make a complete list of possible rational number zeros of $f(x) = 10x^5 - 3x^2 + x - 6$.

Solution   Suppose p/q is a rational zero. Then

$$p : \pm 1, \pm 2, \pm 3, \pm 6 \qquad \begin{array}{l} p \text{ must be a factor} \\ \text{of the constant term } -6. \end{array}$$

$$q : \pm 1, \pm 2, \pm 5, \pm 10. \qquad \begin{array}{l} q \text{ must be a factor of the} \\ \text{leading coefficient 10.} \end{array}$$

To write a complete list of possible rational zeros, choose a numerator from the p list and denominator from the q list and write the rational number in reduced form. The complete list is

$$\frac{p}{q} : \pm 1, \pm 2, \pm 3, \pm 6, \pm \frac{1}{2}, \pm \frac{1}{5}, \pm \frac{1}{10}, \pm \frac{2}{5}, \pm \frac{3}{2}, \pm \frac{3}{5}, \pm \frac{3}{10}, \pm \frac{6}{5}. \qquad \equiv$$

The complete list in Example 1 includes 24 rational numbers. To verify algebraically which ones, if any, are zeros you could use one of these techniques:

1. Calculate $f(p/q)$ in each case to see whether the remainder is zero.

2. Divide $10x^5 - 3x^2 + x - 6$ by $(x - p/q)$ in each case to see whether the remainder is zero.

Either method is time-consuming and tedious, even if a calculator is used. Once again, the work can be shortened by using a graphing utility.

E X A M P L E   2   Using a Grapher to Support an Algebraic Approach

Show that $f(x) = 10x^5 - 3x^2 + x - 6$ has exactly one real number root, and that it is an irrational number.

Solution   Find a complete graph of f and observe that there is only one real number zero and that it appears to be 1 (see Fig. 4.31).

$$f(1) = 10(1)^5 - 3(1)^2 + 1 - 6 = 2 \neq 0 \qquad \begin{array}{l} \text{Conclude from the remainder theorem} \\ \text{that } x = 1 \text{ is not a zero.} \end{array}$$

Use zoom-in to observe that the zero is approximately $x = 0.95$. Using information from Example 1, notice that the nearest rational zero less than 1 is $x = 3/5$. Then

$$f\left(\frac{3}{5}\right) = 10\left(\frac{3}{5}\right)^5 - 3\left(\frac{3}{5}\right)^2 + \frac{3}{5} - 6 \neq 0. \qquad \begin{array}{l} \text{Conclude from the remainder theorem} \\ \text{that } x = 3/5 \text{ is not a zero.} \end{array}$$

Thus there are no rational zeros and there is one irrational zero. $\equiv$

[−5, 5] by [−20, 20]

Figure 4.31
$f(x) = 10x^5 - 3x^2 + x - 6.$

Because a grapher cannot usually distinguish between rational and irrational zeros, it is often necessary to use algebraic methods if you specifically want to find the rational zeros.

Horner's Algorithm (Synthetic Division)

Suppose you want to evaluate $f(x) = 4x^3 - 3x^2 + x - 4$ for $x = 2$. It appears that 2 must be raised to powers since

$$f(2) = 4(2)^3 - 3(2)^2 + 2 - 4.$$

However, Horner's algorithm provides a method of evaluating polynomials that uses only multiplication and addition. Consider this expression:

$$f(x) = 4x^3 - 3x^2 + x - 4$$
$$= x[4x^2 - 3x + 1] - 4$$
$$= x[x(4x - 3) + 1] - 4.$$

The basis for Horner's algorithm is the last line of nested parentheses. For $f(2)$ this expression becomes

$$
\begin{array}{c}
\qquad\qquad\qquad\qquad\qquad \text{6. Add } -4 \\
\qquad\qquad\qquad\quad \text{4. Add } 1 \qquad\Big| \\
\qquad\qquad \text{2. Add } -3 \quad\Big|\downarrow\quad \Big|\downarrow \\
\qquad\qquad\qquad \downarrow \\
f(2) = 2[2(4 \cdot 2 - 3) + 1] - 4. \\
\qquad\quad \uparrow\uparrow \quad \uparrow \\
\qquad\quad \Big|\Big|\quad \text{1. Multiply by 2} \\
\quad \text{3. Multiply by 2} \\
\text{5. Multiply by 2}
\end{array}
$$

We evaluate from the innermost set of parentheses and work towards the outside. Multiply 4×2, add -3, mulitiply by 2, add 1, multiply by 2, and add -4.

This computation can be arranged in a 3-row format as follows. List the coefficients in the first row. Each number in the second row is obtained by multiplying the entry in row 3 of the previous column by 2. Each number in the third row is obtained by adding the corresponding entries in rows 1 and 2. This procedure is known as **Horner's algorithm.***

---

* William Horner, 1786–1837, was an English mathematician who developed this method for finding zeros of polynomials. This procedure is often referred to in algebra books as *synthetic division* or *synthetic substitution*. However, in recent years computer scientists have revived this method and use it as the basis of a recursive algorithm.

$$(x = 2) \quad 2 \,\big|\, \begin{array}{rrrr} 4 & -3 & 1 & -4 \end{array} \quad \longleftarrow \text{Coefficients of } f(x)$$

$$\begin{array}{rrrr} & 8 & 10 & 22 \\ \hline 4 & 5 & 11 & 18 \end{array}$$

$$\underbrace{}_{\substack{\text{Coefficients} \\ \text{of quotient}}} \qquad \underset{f(2)}{\uparrow}$$

Notice that the last entry in the last row is precisely $f(2)$. So $f(2) = 18$. It can be shown that the remaining numbers in row 3 are the coefficients of the polynomial that results when $4x^3 - 3x^2 + x - 4$ is divided by $x - 2$. In other words,

$$4x^3 - 3x^2 + x - 4 = (x - 2)(4x^2 + 5x + 11) + 18.$$

If $x = 2$ were a zero of this polynomial, then the last entry in row 3 would be zero and a factorization would have been obtained.

E X A M P L E 3   Using Horner's Algorithm

Show that $3/2$ is a zero of $f(x) = 2x^3 - 5x^2 + x + 3$, and write $2x^3 - 5x^2 + x + 3$ in factored form.

Solution   First use Horner's algorithm:

$$\tfrac{3}{2} \,\big|\, \begin{array}{rrrr} 2 & -5 & 1 & 3 \end{array}$$

$$\begin{array}{rrrr} & 3 & -3 & -3 \\ \hline 2 & -2 & -2 & 0 \end{array}$$

Since the last entry in the last row is 0, $f(\tfrac{3}{2}) = 0$ and $\tfrac{3}{2}$ is thus a zero.

Also, $2x^2 - 2x - 2$ must be a factor, so

$$2x^3 - 5x^2 + x + 3 = \left(x - \tfrac{3}{2}\right)(2x^2 - 2x - 2)$$

$$= \left(x - \tfrac{3}{2}\right)2(x^2 - x - 1)$$

$$= (2x - 3)(x^2 - x - 1). \qquad \blacksquare$$

We can find the remaining zeros of f by applying the quadratic formula to $x^2 - x - 1$ to obtain the irrational zeros

$$x = \frac{1 + \sqrt{5}}{2}, \qquad x = \frac{1 - \sqrt{5}}{2}.$$

Notice that the factor theorem tells us that $x^2 - x - 1$ can be factored as

$$x^2 - x - 1 = \left(x - \frac{1 + \sqrt{5}}{2}\right)\left(x - \frac{1 - \sqrt{5}}{2}\right).$$

The complete factorization of $2x^3 - 5x^2 + x + 3$ is

$$2x^3 - 5x^2 + x + 3 = (2x - 3)\left(x - \frac{1 + \sqrt{5}}{2}\right)\left(x - \frac{1 - \sqrt{5}}{2}\right).$$

However, we will not ordinarily factor expressions into linear terms that involve irrational numbers. The exception is when we specifically want to display the irrational zeros.

E X A M P L E   4   Using Horner's Algorithm (Continued)

Use Horner's algorithm to find the quotient and remainder when $3x^4 + 7x^3 + x - 11$ is divided by $x + 3$.

Solution

$$
\begin{array}{r|rrrrr}
-3 & 3 & 7 & 0 & 1 & -11 \\
   &   & -9 & 6 & -18 & 51 \\
\hline
   & 3 & -2 & 6 & -17 & 40 \\
   & \downarrow & \downarrow & \downarrow & \downarrow & \\
   & 3x^3 & -2x^2 + & 6x & -17 &
\end{array}
$$

The quotient is $3x^3 - 2x^2 + 6x - 17$, and the remainder is 40.   ≣

E X A M P L E   5   Using Horner's Algorithm (Continued)

Use Horner's algorithm to show that 3 is *not* a zero of $f(x) = 2x^3 + 5x^2 - 2x - 3$.

Solution

$$
\begin{array}{r|rrrr}
3 & 2 & 5 & -2 & -3 \\
  &   & 6 & 33 & 93 \\
\hline
  & 2 & 11 & 31 & 90 \\
\end{array}
$$

Since $f(3) = 90$, conclude from the remainder theorem that 3 is not a zero of f.   ≣

Finding Zeros of a Polynomial Function

By combining the methods of graphing, the rational zeros theorem, Horner's algorithm, and factoring, we can find the rational zeros of polynomials. We summarize the procedure.

Strategy for Finding Zeros

Given a polynomial function

$$f(x) = a_n x^n + \cdots + a_0 \qquad (a_n \neq 0)$$

with integer coefficients, the real zeros can be found by following these steps:

1. List all potential rational zeros by using the rational zeros theorem.
2. Find a complete graph of f with a graphing utility to decide which rational numbers in this list are most likely to be zeros. Use Horner's algorithm and the remainder theorem to determine whether any of these rational numbers is a zero.

   a) If one is, the numbers in the last row of Horner's algorithm are the coefficients of the degree $(n-1)$ factor. Repeat Steps 1 and 2 with that factor.

   b) If no rational zero is found, use the graphing utility to find zeros to whatever degree of precision is desired.

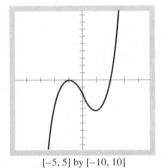

[−5, 5] by [−10, 10]

Figure 4.32 $f(x) = x^3 - 3x - 2$.

EXAMPLE 6   Finding All Rational Zeros

Find all rational zeros of $f(x) = x^3 - 3x - 2$ and find a complete graph.

Solution   See Fig. 4.32.

$$p: \pm 1, \pm 2 \quad p \text{ must be a factor of } -2.$$

$$q: \pm 1 \qquad q \text{ must be a factor of } 1.$$

The only possible rational zeros are ± 1 and ± 2. The graph in Fig. 4.32 suggests that -1 and 2 are the most likely zeros. Check -1 using Horner's algorithm:

$$
\begin{array}{r|rrrr}
-1 & 1 & 0 & -3 & -2 \\
   &   & -1 & 1 & 2 \\
\hline
   & 1 & -1 & -2 & 0
\end{array}
$$

Note that $x^2 - x - 2$ is a factor of f. Therefore

$$x^3 - 3x - 2 = (x+1)(x^2 - x - 2)$$

$$= (x+1)(x+1)(x-2)$$

$$= (x+1)^2(x-2).$$

The zeros of f are -1 and 2.

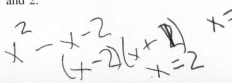

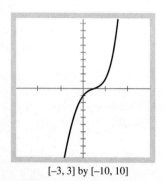

[-3, 3] by [-10, 10]

Figure 4.33
$f(x) = 6x^3 - 5x^2 + 3x - 1.$

E X A M P L E   7   Finding All Rational Zeros (Continued)

Find all rational zeros of $f(x) = 6x^3 - 5x^2 + 3x - 1.$

Solution

$$p: \pm 1$$

$$q: \pm 1, \pm 2, \pm 3, \pm 6$$

The only possible rational zeros are $\pm 1, \pm \frac{1}{2}, \pm \frac{1}{3}, \pm \frac{1}{6}$. The graph of f in Fig. 4.33 suggests that we check $\frac{1}{2}$.

$$
\begin{array}{r|rrrr}
\frac{1}{2} & 6 & -5 & 3 & -1 \\
   &   & 3 & -1 & 1 \\
\hline
   & 6 & -2 & 2 & 0
\end{array}
$$

$$6x^3 - 5x^2 + 3x - 1 = (x - \tfrac{1}{2})(6x^2 - 2x + 2)$$

$$= (x - \tfrac{1}{2})(2)(3x^2 - x + 1)$$

$$= (2x - 1)(3x^2 - x + 1)$$

Check the discriminant $b^2 - 4ac$ for $(3x^2 - x + 1)$:

$$b^2 - 4ac = (-1)^2 - 4(3)(1) = -11$$

Since the discriminant is less than zero, $3x^2 - x + 1$ does not have real zeros, and $\frac{1}{2}$ is the only real zero for f.   ≡

E X A M P L E   8   Finding and Classifying Zeros

Find all real number zeros of $f(x) = 3x^3 - 8x^2 + x + 2$. Classify them as integer, noninteger, rational, or irrational.

Solution   The possible rational zeros are as follows:

$$\frac{p}{q}: \pm \frac{1}{3}, \pm \frac{2}{3}, \pm 1, \pm 2.$$

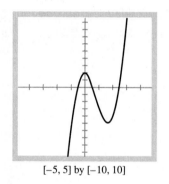

[-5, 5] by [-10, 10]

Figure 4.34
$f(x) = 3x^3 - 8x^2 + x + 2.$

The graph in Fig. 4.34 suggests that there are three real zeros, one close to $\frac{2}{3}$; use Horner's algorithm to confirm.

$$
\begin{array}{r|rrrr}
\frac{2}{3} & 3 & -8 & 1 & 2 \\
   &   & 2 & -4 & -2 \\
\hline
   & 3 & -6 & -3 & 0
\end{array}
$$

Therefore

$$3x^3 - 8x^2 + x + 2 = (x - \frac{2}{3})(3x^2 - 6x - 3)$$

$$= (3x - 2)(x^2 - 2x - 1)$$

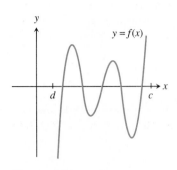

Figure 4.35 c is an upper bound and d is a lower bound for the set of zeros.

Use the quadratic formula to find the zeros of $x^2 - 2x - 1$:

$$x = \frac{2 \pm \sqrt{(-2)^2 - 4(-1)}}{2} \quad \text{or} \quad 1 \pm \sqrt{2}.$$

Thus $\frac{2}{3}$ is a noninteger rational zero and $1 + \sqrt{2}$ and $1 - \sqrt{2}$ are irrational zeros.

≡

Upper and Lower Bounds for Real Zeros

A number c is an **upper bound** for the set of real zeros of a function f if $f(x) \neq 0$ whenever $x > c$. Likewise, a number d is a **lower bound** for the set of real zeros of f if $f(x) \neq 0$ whenever $x < d$ (see Fig. 4.35).

Horner's algorithm can be used to find upper and lower bounds as described in the next two theorems.

Theorem 4.6   Upper Bound for Zeros

Let f be a polynomial with $\begin{Bmatrix} \text{positive} \\ \text{negative} \end{Bmatrix}$ leading coefficient, and let c be a positive number. If the last line of Horner's algorithm contains no $\begin{Bmatrix} \text{negative} \\ \text{positive} \end{Bmatrix}$ numbers using c as a potential zero, then c is an upper bound.

E X A M P L E   9   Checking for Upper Bounds

Show that 3 is an upper bound for the real number zeros of $f(x) = x^3 - 3x^2 + x - 1$.

Solution

$$
\begin{array}{r|rrrr}
3 & 1 & -3 & 1 & -1 \\
  &   & 3 & 0 & 3 \\
\hline
  & 1 & 0 & 1 & 2 \\
\end{array}
$$

The last line of Horner's algorithm has no negative numbers, so 3 is an upper bound.

Here's why. Horner's algorithm gives the factorization

$$f(x) = x^3 - 3x^2 + x - 1 = (x - 3)(x^2 + 1) + 2.$$

Note that $x^2 + 1$ is a positive number for each value of x. So, when $x > 3$, then $x - 3 > 0$ and $f(x) > 2$. Therefore f has no zero greater than 3.

≡

To find lower bounds we convert the problem to one of finding upper bounds. Figure 4.36 shows the graph of a function f and its reflection about the y-axis.

Notice that a negative number c is a lower bound for the set of zeros of $f(x)$ if the positive number $-c$ is an upper bound for the zeros of the function $f(-x)$. This observation leads to Theorem 4.7.

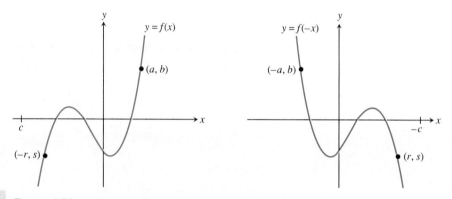

Figure 4.36   A function $f(x)$ and the related function $f(-x)$. These graphs are related by symmetry with respect to the y-axis. Notice that whenever (a, b) is on the graph of $f(x)$, $(-a, b)$ is on the graph of $f(-x)$.

FINDING THE VIEWING RECTANGLE

When finding a complete graph of a polynomial, you must choose a viewing rectangle that includes all the zeros. If c is an upper bound and d is a lower bound for zeros, then you know to choose a viewing rectangle so that $X\min < d < c < X\max$.

Theorem 4.7   Lower Bound for Zeros

The negative number d is a lower bound for the real zeros of $f(x)$ if and only if the positive number $-d$ is an upper bound for the real zeros of $f(-x)$.

E X A M P L E   10   *Checking for Lower Bounds*

Show that -6 is a lower bound for $f(x) = x^3 + 2x^2 - 21x + 16$.

Solution   According to Theorem 4.7, this problem is equivalent to showing that 6 is an upper bound for $f(-x)$.

$$f(-x) = (-x)^3 + 2(-x)^2 - 21(-x) + 16$$
$$= -x^3 + 2x^2 + 21x + 16$$

$$
\begin{array}{r|rrrr}
6 & -1 & 2 & 21 & 16 \\
  &   & -6 & -24 & -18 \\
\hline
  & -1 & -4 & -3 & -2 \\
\end{array}
$$

Since all the numbers in the third row are negative, we see that 6 must be an upper bound for $f(-x)$. Therefore -6 is a lower bound for $f(x)$. ≡

We end this section with an application.

E X A M P L E   11   APPLICATION: Floating Buoy

Suppose a spherical floating buoy has a radius of 1 meter and a density $\frac{1}{4}$ that of seawater. Find the depth that the buoy sinks in seawater (see Fig. 4.37).

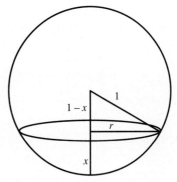

Figure 4.37   Spherical buoy.

Solution   By Archimedes' law the volume of the displaced water is equal to the volume of the submerged portion of the buoy. Choose variables:

$x =$ depth that the buoy sinks
$r =$ radius of the submerged spherical segment
$V =$ volume of the submerged spherical segment.

Then

$$V = \frac{\pi}{6}x(3r^2 + x^2)$$ This formula comes from solid geometry.

$$(1 - x)^2 + r^2 = 1.$$ Apply the Pythagorean theorem to obtain a relationship between x and r.

Solve for r^2 and substitute into the volume formula to obtain

$$V = \frac{\pi}{6}x(3r^2 + x^2)$$

$$= \frac{\pi}{6}x[3(1 - (1 - x)^2) + x^2]$$

$$= \frac{\pi}{3}(3x^2 - x^3).$$

On the other hand, since the density of the buoy is $\frac{1}{4}$ that of water, $\frac{1}{4}$ of the volume of the buoy is submerged. The volume of this sphere is $4\pi/3$ (since the volume of a sphere is $4\pi r^3/3$). Therefore the volume of the submerged spherical segment is $\pi/3$.

Setting these two volumes equal to each other, we obtain

$$\frac{\pi}{3} = \frac{\pi}{3}(3x^2 - x^3)$$

$$1 = 3x^2 - x^3$$

$$0 = x^3 - 3x^2 + 1.$$

The problem will be solved by finding a zero for $f(x) = x^3 - 3x^2 + 1$ that is between 0 and 1.

Exercise 56 asks you to show that there are no rational zeros to this function, so a graphical method must be used.

Figure 4.38 shows a complete graph of f. Notice that $x < 1$. Using zoom-in, show that $x = 0.653$ is a solution with an error of less than 0.01. The buoy sinks 0.653 meter into the sea.

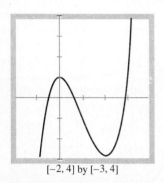

$[-2, 4]$ by $[-3, 4]$

Figure 4.38
$f(x) = x^3 - 3x^2 + 1.$

Exercises for Section 4.4

In Exercises 1 to 4, use the rational zeros theorem to list all possible rational zeros of each function.

1. $f(x) = x^3 - 2x^2 + 3x - 4$

2. $g(x) = 2x^3 - x + 1$

3. $f(x) = 2x^3 - 4x^2 - 5x + 10$

4. $g(x) = 4x^3 - x^2 + 2x - 6$

In Exercises 5 to 8, show that each function has no rational zeros.

5. $f(x) = x^3 + 2x^2 + x - 1$

6. $f(x) = x^3 - x + 2$

7. $f(x) = 2x^4 - x^3 + 1$

8. $f(x) = 3x^3 + x^2 - 2x + 1$

In Exercises 9 to 12, use Horner's algorithm to show that the indicated number is a zero of $f(x)$. Then factor f.

9. $f(x) = x^3 + x^2 - 10x + 8;\ 2$

10. $f(x) = x^4 + 3x^3 - 4x^2 - 11x + 3;\ -3$

11. $f(x) = 2x^3 + x^2 - 6x - 3;\ -\frac{1}{2}$

12. $f(x) = 3x^3 - 7x^2 + 10x - 8;\ \frac{4}{3}$

In Exercises 13 to 16, use Horner's algorithm to find the quotient and remainder when the first polynomial is divided by the second polynomial.

13. $x^3 + 2x^2 - 3x + 1;\ x + 2$

14. $-2x^3 - x^2 - 4;\ x - 1$

15. $x^4 - 2x^3 + x^2 - x + 2;\ x + 1$

16. $2x^4 - 3x^2 + x + 5;\ x + 3$

In Exercises 17 to 20, find all rational zeros of each function using an algebraic method.

17. $f(x) = x^2 - 3x + 4$ **18.** $g(x) = x^3 - 4x$

19. $g(x) = x^3 - 5x$ **20.** $f(x) = x^3 + x$

In Exercises 21 to 24, draw a complete graph of each polynomial. Confirm that there is at least one rational root in each case. Use Horner's algorithm to find the other quadratic factor, and then determine all real zeros. Classify each real number zero as rational or irrational.

21. $f(x) = x^3 + 4x^2 - 4x - 1$

22. $f(x) = 6x^3 - 5x - 1$

23. $f(x) = 3x^3 - 7x^2 + 6x - 14$

24. $f(x) = 2x^3 - x^2 - 9x + 9$

In Exercises 25 to 30, determine the real number zeros of each polynomial and classify each as rational or irrational. Carefully outline why you are sure of your results.

25. $f(x) = 2x^4 - 7x^3 - 2x^2 - 7x - 4$

26. $f(x) = 3x^4 - 2x^3 + 3x^2 + x - 2$

27. $f(x) = 2x^3 - x^2 - 18x + 9$

28. $g(x) = 3x^3 - x^2 + 27x - 9$

29. $f(x) = x^4 + x^3 - 3x^2 - 4x - 4$

30. $f(x) = x^4 + 3x^2 + 2$

In Exercises 31 to 34, use Horner's algorithm to find upper and lower bounds for the real number zeros of each polynomial function.

31. $f(x) = x^2 - 2x - 5$

32. $f(x) = x^3 - x^2 + 2x - 5$

33. $g(x) = x^3 + 2x^2 - 3x - 1$

34. $f(x) = x^4 + 2x^3 - 7x^2 - 8x + 12$

35. Does $f(x) = 3x^4 - 2x^2 + x - 1$ have any rational zeros? Any irrational zeros? If so, how many of each? Give both graphical and algebraic reasons for your answer.

36. The function $f(x) = 6x^3 + x^2 - 3x + 12$ has 24 possible rational roots. How many of them can be eliminated as candidates by showing that 1 is an upper bound of all the zeros?

Exercises 37 to 39 are about the following **problem situation**: A 172-foot-long steel beam is anchored at one end of a piling 20 feet above the ground. It is known that the steel beam bends s feet (vertical distance) if a 200-pound object is placed d feet from the anchored end and that s is given by

$$s = (3 \times 10^{-7})d^2(550 - d).$$

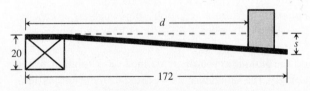

For Exercises 37 to 39

37. Draw a complete graph of the algebraic representation of this problem situation. What is the domain of this model of the problem? What values of d make sense in this problem situation?

38. How far is the 200-pound object from the anchored end if the vertical deflection is 1.25 feet?

39. What is the greatest amount of vertical deflection, and where does it occur?

Exercises 40 to 43 refer to the following **problem situation**: Biologists have determined that the polynomial function $P(t) = -0.00001t^3 + 0.002t^2 + 1.5t + 100$ approximates the population t days later of a certain group of wild turkeys left to reproduce on their own with no predators.

40. Draw a complete graph of the algebraic model $y = P(t)$ of this problem situation.

41. Find the maximum turkey population and when it occurs.

42. When will this turkey population be extinct?

43. Create a scenario that could explain the "growth" exhibited by this turkey population.

Exercises 44 to 49 refer to the complete graph of $y = f(x)$ given in the following figure. Draw a complete graph of each function, and describe the transformations needed to obtain its graph from the graph of $y = f(x)$.

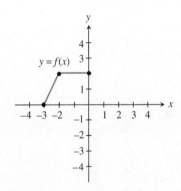

For Exercises 44 to 49

44. $y = 1 + 2f(x)$ 45. $y = -f(x)$

46. $y = -\frac{1}{2}f(x)$ 47. $y = -1 + 2f(-x)$

48. $y = -2f(x - 2)$ 49. $y = 2 - f(x + 1)$

Exercises 50 to 55 refer to the complete graph of $y = f(x)$ given in the following figure. Draw a complete graph of each function, and describe the transformations needed to obtain its graph from the graph of $y = f(x)$.

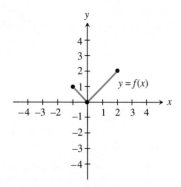

For Exercises 50 to 55

50. $y = f(-x)$ **51.** $y = -f(x)$

52. $y = -f(x - 3)$ **53.** $y = -f(3 - x)$

54. $y = 2 - 3f(x + 1)$ **55.** $y = -1 + 2f(1 - x)$

Exercises 56 to 59 refer to the floating-buoy **problem situation** of Example 11.

56. Show that the equation solved in Example 11 does not have any rational roots.

57. Use zoom-in to show that $x = 0.653$ is a solution to Example 11.

58. Find the depth that the buoy sinks in seawater if its density is $\frac{1}{3}$ that of sea water.

59. Find the depth that the buoy sinks in seawater if its density is $\frac{1}{5}$ that of seawater.

60. **Writing to Learn**   Write several paragraphs that describe how the zeros of $f(x) = \frac{1}{3}x^3 + x^2 + 2x - 3$ are related to the zeros of $g(x) = x^3 + 3x^2 + 6x - 9$. In what ways does this example illustrate how the rational zeros theorem can be generalized to include all polynomials with rational number coefficients?

4.5   Complex Numbers as Zeros

In the last two sections we have focused on the task of finding zeros of polynomial functions. We have seen that a real number c is a zero of a polynomial function f if $f(c) = 0$. This is equivalent to saying that $(c, 0)$ is an x-intercept of the graph of f, which implies that if the graph of a polynomial function does not cross the x-axis, it cannot have any real number zeros.   Figure 4.39 shows that the function $f(x) = x^2 + 1$ does not have any real number zeros. Equivalently, $x^2 + 1 = 0$ has no solutions that are real numbers. There are applications in mechanics, electricity, and other areas of physics in which it is helpful for each polynomial equation to have a solution.

A new symbol i, called the **imaginary unit**, is defined as a solution to the equation $x^2 + 1 = 0$. Accordingly, the imaginary unit i satisfies these properties:

$$i^2 + 1 = 0$$

$$i^2 = -1$$

$$i = \sqrt{-1}.$$

Since there is no real number equal to $\sqrt{-1}$, i cannot be a real number. Notice that

$$(-i)^2 + 1 = -1 + 1 = 0,$$

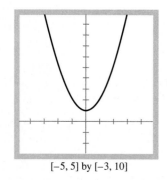

[−5, 5] by [−3, 10]

Figure 4.39 $f(x) = x^2 + 1$.

which means that $-i$ is also a solution to $x^2 + 1 = 0$.

A new system of numbers, called the complex numbers, is based on the symbol i. This new system includes real number multiples of i as well as sums of real numbers and real number multiples of i. The following expressions are all complex numbers:

$$3i \qquad 5i \qquad -7i \qquad \frac{5}{2}i \qquad 7.3i$$

$$2 + 3i \qquad 5 - i \qquad \frac{1}{3} + \frac{4}{5}i.$$

Definition 4.5   Complex Numbers

For real numbers a and b, the expression

$$a + bi$$

is called a **complex number**. The real number a is called the **real part**, and the real number b is called the **imaginary part** of the complex number $a + bi$.

Note that all real numbers are also complex numbers, since any real number a can be expressed in the form $a + bi$ where $b = 0$.

Two complex numbers $a + bi$ and $c + di$ are equal if their real parts are equal and their imaginary parts are equal. That is

$$a + bi = c + di$$

if and only if

$$a = c \text{ and } b = d.$$

Operations with Complex Numbers

Adding two complex numbers involves adding the real parts and the imaginary parts separately. Two complex numbers can be subtracted in a similar fashion.

Definition 4.6   Addition and Subtraction of Complex Numbers

Let $a + bi$ and $c + di$ be any two complex numbers. The sum and the difference of these two complex numbers are given as follows:

Addition: $(a + bi) + (c + di) = (a + c) + (b + d)i$
Subtraction: $(a + bi) - (c + di) = (a - c) + (b - d)i$.

E X A M P L E   1   Adding and Subtracting Complex Numbers

Complete each of these operations: a) $(7 - 3i) + (4 + 5i)$ and b) $(4 - 2i) - (6 + i)$.

Solution

a) $(7 - 3i) + (4 + 5i) = (7 + 4) + (-3 + 5)i$

$$= 11 + 2i$$

b) $(4 - 2i) - (6 + i) = (4 - 6) + (-2 - 1)i$

$$= -2 + (-3)i$$

$$= -2 - 3i$$

Two complex numbers can be multiplied by thinking of them as binomials and multiplying them using the FOIL method (see Section 1.4). To simplify the resulting expression use the fact that $i^2 = -1$.

E X A M P L E   2   Multiplying Complex Numbers

Multiply $2 + 3i$ and $5 - i$.

Solution

$$(2 + 3i)(5 - i) = 2(5) + 2(-i) + 5(3i) + (3i)(-i)$$

$$= 10 - 2i + 15i - 3i^2$$

$$= 10 + 13i + 3 \quad \text{Use the relation } i^2 = -1.$$

$$= 13 + 13i.$$

To find a general rule for the product of two complex numbers, multiply $a + bi$ and $c + di$ using the same method as in Example 2.

$(a + bi)(c + di) = a(c + di) + (bi)(c + di)$ Use the distributive property.

$\quad\quad = ac + (ad)i + (bc)i + (bd)i^2$ Use the distributive property.

$\quad\quad = ac + (ad + bc)i + (bd)(-1)$ Use $i^2 = -1$, and factor i from the middle two terms.

$\quad\quad = (ac - bd) + (ad + bc)i$

Complex Conjugates

Understanding the division of complex numbers requires introducing a new concept. The complex number pairs $a + bi$ and $a - bi$ are **complex conjugates**. Notice that the product of complex conjugates $a + bi$ and $a - bi$ is the real number $a^2 + b^2$:

$$(a + bi)(a - bi) = a^2 - abi + abi - b^2 i^2$$

$$= a^2 + b^2.$$

Complex conjugates are used to complete division of complex numbers, as illustrated in this next example.

E X A M P L E   3   Dividing Complex Numbers

Find $(5 + i) \div (2 - 3i)$, and write the quotient in the form $a + bi$.

Solution

$$\frac{5 + i}{2 - 3i} = \frac{(5 + i)(2 + 3i)}{(2 - 3i)(2 + 3i)}$$ Multiply the numerator and denominator by the complex conjugate of the denominator.

$$= \frac{10 + 15i + 2i - 3}{4 + 9}$$

$$= \frac{7}{13} + \frac{17}{13} i$$

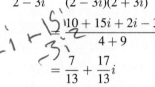

These last two examples illustrate how complex numbers are multiplied and divided. A general definition of these two operations follows.

Definition 4.7   Multiplication and Division of Complex Numbers

Let $a + bi$ and $c + di$ be any two complex numbers.

Multiplication: $(a + bi)(c + di) = (ac - bd) + (ad + bc)i$

Division: $\dfrac{a + bi}{c + di} = \dfrac{ac + bd}{c^2 + d^2} + \dfrac{bc - ad}{c^2 + d^2} i \quad (c^2 + d^2 \neq 0)$

Finding Complex Zeros of a Polynomial Function

Some polynomials have only real number zeros. Other polynomials have both real number zeros and nonreal complex zeros, and still others have only nonreal complex zeros. We begin with an example.

E X A M P L E   4   Complex Zeros

Find the zeros of $f(x) = x^2 + x + 1$.

Solution   Use the quadratic formula to solve the equation $x^2 + x + 1 = 0$:

$$x = \frac{-1 \pm \sqrt{1-4}}{2} \qquad \text{Simplify by using } \sqrt{-3} = \sqrt{-1}\sqrt{3} = i\sqrt{3}.$$

$$= \frac{-1}{2} \pm \frac{\sqrt{3}}{2}i$$

Thus the two zeros are $-\frac{1}{2} + \frac{\sqrt{3}}{2}i$ and $-\frac{1}{2} - \frac{\sqrt{3}}{2}i$.   ∎

Notice that the two zeros of $x^2 + x + 1$ are complex conjugates. It can be shown that complex zeros always occur in conjugate pairs for polynomials with real coefficients. The following theorem is stated without proof.

Theorem 4.8   Complex Conjugate Zeros

If $a + bi$ with $b \neq 0$ is a zero of a polynomial function f with real coefficients, then its complex conjugate $a - bi$ is also a zero of f.

It is important to observe that the remainder and factor theorems hold for both real and nonreal complex roots. Consequently Horner's algorithm can also be used with nonreal complex zeros, as illustrated in the next example.

E X A M P L E   5   Finding Complex Zeros

Show that $1 - 2i$ is a zero of $f(x) = 4x^4 + 17x^2 + 14x + 65$, and find all other zeros of f.

Solution   Use Horner's algorithm to show that $f(1 - 2i) = 0$.

$$
\begin{array}{r|ccccc}
1-2i & 4 & 0 & 17 & 14 & 65 \\
 & & 4-8i & -12-16i & -27-26i & -65 \\
\hline
 & 4 & 4-8i & 5-16i & -13-26i & 0
\end{array}
$$

Thus $1 - 2i$ is a zero of f. By Theorem 4.8, $1 + 2i$ is also a zero. Use Horner's algorithm again to find the remaining quadratic factor.

$$
\begin{array}{r|cccc}
1+2i & 4 & 4-8i & 5-16i & -13-26i \\
 & & 4+8i & 8+16i & 13+26i \\
\hline
 & 4 & 8 & 13 & 0
\end{array}
$$

Therefore,

$$f(x) = \left[x - (1 - 2i) \right] \left[x - (1 + 2i) \right] (4x^2 + 8x + 13).$$

Finally, use the quadratic formula to find the two zeros of $4x^2 + 8x + 13$:

$$x = \frac{-8 \pm \sqrt{64 - 208}}{8}$$

$$= \frac{-8 \pm \sqrt{-144}}{8}$$

$$= \frac{-8 \pm 12i}{8}$$

$$= -1 \pm \frac{3}{2}i.$$

Thus the four zeros of f are $1 - 2i$, $1 + 2i$, $-1 + \dfrac{3}{2}i$, and $-1 - \dfrac{3}{2}i$.

A complete graph of the fourth-degree polynomial $f(x) = 4x^4 + 17x^2 + 14x + 65$ in Example 5 would show that it does not cross the x-axis anywhere. This is visual evidence that there are no real roots.

Consider the case of an odd-degree polynomial. Any odd-degree polynomial has end behavior type either $(-\infty, +\infty)$ or $(+\infty, -\infty)$. It follows from the intermediate value theorem that such a polynomial has at least one real zero.

Theorem 4.9   Polynomial Function of Odd Degree

A polynomial function f of odd degree has at least one real number zero. The domain and range of f are each $(-\infty, \infty)$.

Finding a complete graph of f will help identify when a polynomial has complex zeros.

E X A M P L E   6   Finding Complex Zeros

Find a complete graph of $f(x) = x^3 - 1$ to show that it has only one real number zero. Find all zeros.

Solution   The complete graph of $f(x) = x^3 - 1$ in Fig. 4.40 suggests that 1 is a real zero of $x^3 - 1$. Use Horner's algorithm to confirm that 1 is a zero and that f can be factored as follows:

$$x^3 - 1 = (x - 1)(x^2 + x + 1).$$

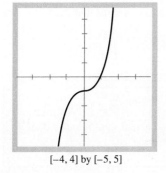

$[-4, 4]$ by $[-5, 5]$

Figure 4.40 $f(x) = x^3 - 1.$

In Example 4 we found that $-\frac{1}{2} + (\sqrt{3}/2)i$ and $-\frac{1}{2} - (\sqrt{3}/2)i$ are the two zeros of $x^2 + x + 1$. Thus $x^3 - 1$ has three zeros:

$$1, \qquad -\frac{1}{2} + \frac{\sqrt{3}}{2}i, \qquad -\frac{1}{2} - \frac{\sqrt{3}}{2}i.$$

■

Notice that the zeros of $x^3 - 1$ are solutions to the equivalent equations

$$x^3 - 1 = 0 \iff x^3 = 1.$$

So these zeros are often called the cube roots of 1 or the cube roots of unity. In general, a solution to the equation $x^n - 1 = 0$ is called an ***nth root of unity***.

E X A M P L E 7   Roots of Unity

Find the fourth roots of unity.

Solution   Find solutions to $x^4 - 1 = 0$, or equivalently find the zeros of $f(x) = x^4 - 1$.

$$x^4 - 1 = (x^2 - 1)(x^2 + 1) \qquad \text{Factor the difference of squares.}$$

$$x^4 - 1 = (x - 1)(x + 1)(x^2 + 1)$$

$$= (x - 1)(x + 1)(x - i)(x + i) \quad \text{i and $-i$ are zeros of $x^2 + 1$.}$$

The four fourth roots of unity are 1, -1, i, and $-i$.

■

Notice that in Examples 4 through 7 the number of zeros, real plus complex, equals the degree of the given polynomial. The next two theorems and the following discussion will clarify this observation.

Theorem 4.10   Fundamental Theorem of Algebra

If f is a polynomial function of degree $n > 0$ with real coefficients, then f has at least one zero in the set of complex numbers.

Note that the zero mentioned in Theorem 4.10 may be a real number since any real number r can be expressed as the complex number $r + 0i$.

The fundamental theorem of algebra is used in the proof of this theorem.

> **Theorem 4.11 Linear Factorization Theorem**
>
> If $f(x)$ is a polynomial of degree $n > 0$ with real coefficients, then f has precisely n linear factors
>
> $$f(x) = a(x - c_1)(x - c_2) \cdots (x - c_n)$$
>
> where $c_1, c_2, \ldots, c_n$ are complex numbers and a is the leading coefficient of $f(x)$.

Here is the idea behind the proof for the case that the roots are all real numbers. If c_1 is a real number zero of f, then $x - c_1$ is a factor of f; that is,

$$f(x) = (x - c_1)f_1(x),$$

where $f_1(x)$ is a polynomial of degree $n - 1$. Repeat this argument for $f_1(x)$ to obtain the factorization

$$f(x) = (x - c_1)(x - c_2)f_2(x)$$

where $f_2(x)$ is a polynomial of degree $n - 2$. Continue this process to eventually obtain a factorization of linear factors. This argument can be modified when there are nonreal complex roots.

It is important to observe that the c_i's in Theorem 4.11 need not be distinct. For example, we could have

$$f(x) = (x - 2)(x - 2)(x - 2)(x + 1)(x + 1)$$
$$= (x - 2)^3(x + 1)^2$$

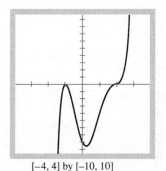

[−4, 4] by [−10, 10]

Figure 4.41
$f(x) = (x - 2)^3(x + 1)^2.$

(see Fig. 4.41). In this case we say that for f, 2 is a **zero of multiplicity 3** and -1 is a **zero of multiplicity 2**. Counting multiplicities, we can conclude from Theorem 4.11 that a polynomial of degree n has n zeros.

E X A M P L E 8   Finding Linear Factors

Write $f(x) = 3x^5 - 2x^4 + 6x^3 - 4x^2 - 24x + 16$ as a product of linear factors. Classify the zeros of f as rational, irrational, or nonreal complex.

Solution   From the rational zeros theorem, the only possible rational zeros are

$$\pm 1, \pm 2, \pm 4, \pm 8, \pm 16, \pm\frac{1}{3}, \pm\frac{2}{3}, \pm\frac{4}{3}, \pm\frac{8}{3}, \pm\frac{16}{3}.$$

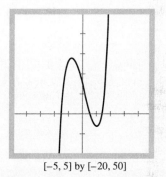

[−5, 5] by [−20, 50]

Figure 4.42 $f(x) =$
$3x^5 - 2x^4 + 6x^3 - 4x^2 - 24x + 16.$

The complete graph of f in the $[-5, 5]$ by $[-20, 50]$ viewing rectangle (Fig. 4.42) suggests that the list of possible rational zeros can be reduced to $-\frac{4}{3}, \frac{2}{3}, \frac{4}{3}$.

Use Horner's algorithm to check $\frac{2}{3}$.

$$
\begin{array}{r|rrrrrr}
\frac{2}{3} & 3 & -2 & 6 & -4 & -24 & 16 \\
  &   & 2 & 0 & 4 & 0 & -16 \\
\hline
  & 3 & 0 & 6 & 0 & -24 & 0
\end{array}
$$

Thus, $f(\frac{2}{3}) = 0$ and f factors as follows:

$$
\begin{aligned}
f(x) &= (x - \tfrac{2}{3})(3x^4 + 6x^2 - 24) \\
&= (x - \tfrac{2}{3})(3)(x^4 + 2x^2 - 8) \\
&= (3x - 2)(x^4 + 2x^2 - 8) \\
&= (3x - 2)(x^2 - 2)(x^2 + 4).
\end{aligned}
$$

The zeros of $x^2 - 2$ are $\pm\sqrt{2}$, and the zeros of $x^2 + 4$ are $\pm 2i$. Therefore

$$
f(x) = (3x - 2)(x - \sqrt{2})(x + \sqrt{2})(x - 2i)(x + 2i).
$$

The two real zeros $\sqrt{2}$ and $-\sqrt{2}$ are irrational, and the real zero $\frac{2}{3}$ is rational. Finally, the zeros $2i$ and $-2i$ are nonreal complex numbers. ∎

Exercises for Section 4.5

In Exercises 1 to 8, write each expression in the form $a + bi$ where a and b are real numbers.

1. $2 - 3i + 6$

2. $2 - 3i + 6 - 4i$

3. $(2 + 3i)(2 - i)$

4. $(2 - i)(1 + 3i)$

5. $2(1 + i) - 1 - i$

6. $3(6 - i) - 2(-1 - 3i)$

7. $3(2 + i)^2 - 4i$

8. $(1 - i)^3$

In Exercises 9 to 12, determine the complex conjugate of each complex number.

9. $2 - 3i$

10. $-6i$

11. $-3 + 4i$

12. $-1 - \sqrt{2}i$

In Exercises 13 to 18, write each expression in the form $a + bi$ where a and b are real numbers.

13. $\dfrac{1}{2 + i}$

14. $\dfrac{i}{2 - i}$

15. $\dfrac{2 + i}{2 - i}$

16. $\dfrac{2 + i}{3i}$

17. $\dfrac{(2 + i)^2(-i)}{1 + i}$

18. $\dfrac{(2 - i)(1 + 2i)}{5 + 2i}$

In Exercises 19 to 24, determine the number of real number zeros and the number of nonreal complex zeros of each function.

19. $f(x) = x^2 - 2x + 7$

20. $f(x) = x^3 - 3x^2 + x + 1$

21. $f(x) = x^3 - x + 3$

22. $f(x) = x^4 - 2x^2 + 3x - 4$

23. $f(x) = x^4 - 5x^3 + x^2 - 3x + 6$

24. $f(x) = x^5 - 2x^2 - 3x + 6$

In Exercises 25 to 28, find all the zeros of each polynomial. Classify each zero as integer, noninteger rational, irrational, or nonreal complex.

25. $f(x) = x^3 + 4x - 5$

26. $g(x) = x^3 - 10x^2 + 44x - 69$

27. $f(x) = x^4 + x^3 + 5x^2 - x - 6$

28. $g(x) = 3x^4 + 8x^3 + 6x^2 + 3x - 2$

29. Show that $1 + i$ is a zero of $f(x) = 3x^3 - 7x^2 + 8x - 2$, and find all other zeros of f.

30. Show that $3 - 2i$ is a zero of $f(x) = x^4 - 6x^3 + 11x^2 + 12x - 26$, and find all the other zeros of f.

In Exercises 31 to 34, write each polynomial as a product $f(x) = k(x - c_1)(x - c_2) \cdots (x - c_n)$, where n is the degree of the polynomial, k is a real number, and each c_i is a zero of f.

31. $f(x) = x^3 - x^2 + x - 1$

32. $f(x) = x^4 - 6x^2 + 5$

33. $f(x) = 2x^3 - x^2 + 3x - 4$

34. $f(x) = x^4 + 6x^3 + 7x^2 - 12x - 18$

In Exercises 35 to 38, find a polynomial with real number coefficients satisfying the given conditions.

35. degree 2; zero $2 - 3i$ **36.** degree 3; zeros 1 and i

37. degree 3; zeros 3 and $1 - i$

38. degree 4; zeros $-2 + i$ and $1 - i$

39. Can you find a polynomial of degree 3 with real number coefficients that has -2 as its only real number zero?

40. Can you find a polynomial of degree 3 with real number coefficients that has $2i$ as its only nonreal zero?

41. Find a polynomial $f(x)$ of degree 4 with real number coefficients that has -3, $1 + i$, and $1 - i$ as its only zeros.

42. Find a polynomial $f(x)$ of degree 4 with real number coefficients that has -3, $1 + i$, and $1 - i$ as its only zeros, and also satisfies $f(0) = 1$.

Exercises 43 to 45 refer to the following **problem situation**: *Archimedes' law* states that when a sphere of radius r with density d_S is placed in a liquid of density $d_L = 62.5$ lb/ft^3, it will sink to a depth h where

$$\frac{\pi}{3}(3rh^2 - h^3)d_L = \frac{4}{3}\pi r^3 d_S.$$

43. If $r = 5$ feet and $d_S = 20$ lb/ft^3, use zoom-in to determine h with an error of less than 0.01.

44. If $r = 5$ feet and $d_S = 45$ lb/ft^3, use zoom-in to determine h with an error of less than 0.01.

45. If $r = 5$ feet and $d_S = 70$ lb/ft^3, use zoom-in to determine h with an error of less than 0.01.

46. Find the two square roots of unity; that is, solve the equation $x^2 = 1$.

47. Find the three cube roots of 8; that is, solve the equation $x^3 = 8$.

48. We denote $\bar{z}$ as the conjugate of $z = a + bi$. Prove that $z + \bar{z}$ is a real number for any complex number z.

49. Prove that $z \cdot \bar{z}$ is a real number for any complex number z.

50. Verify that the complex number i is a zero of the polynomial $f(x) = x^3 - ix^2 + 2ix + 2$.

4.6   Polynomial Functions and Inequalities

Recall that the solution to an inequality is usually reported in interval notation as one or more intervals. In this section we are interested in solving inequalities like $x^4 \geq x^2$. Notice that solving $x^4 \geq x^2$ is equivalent to solving $x^4 - x^2 \geq 0$.

When using an algebraic method of solution, the form $x^4 - x^2 \geq 0$ is the preferred form. We can solve this form in a manner similar to the one used in finding the zeros of $f(x) = x^4 - x^2$ in the last several sections.

Chapter 2 showed that a graphical approach to solving equations and inequalities is often quicker and more general than an algebraic approach. Consequently we will use a graphical method in this section. The graphical method allows either the form $x^4 \geq x^2$ or the form $x^4 - x^2 \geq 0$ to be used. When using the form $x^4 \geq x^2$, we are making comparisons between the graphs of $y = x^n$ for various values of n.

Your experiences in the following Exploration will help you understand how the graphs of $y = x^2, y = x^3, y = x^4,$ and $y = x^5$ compare for values of x near 1.

🔍 EXPLORE WITH A CALCULATOR

What happens when you raise a number to a power? Does it get larger or smaller? Use a calculator to find all values for the following table:

x	x^2	x^3	x^4	x^5
0.5	0.25	0.125	0.0625	
0.9				
0.99				
1				
1.01				
1.1				

Complete a Generalization   For what values of x do the powers of x get larger? For what values of x do the powers of x get smaller?

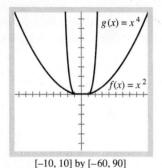

[−10, 10] by [−60, 90]

Figure 4.43 $f(x) = x^2$ and $g(x) = x^4$.

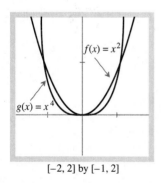

[−2, 2] by [−1, 2]

Figure 4.44 $f(x) = x^2$ and $g(x) = x^4$ in a smaller viewing rectangle.

Graphs of $y = x^n$ When n Is Even

We begin by comparing the graphs of $y = x^n$ when n is even. For example, compare $f(x) = x^2$ and $g(x) = x^4$. Figure 4.43 shows the graphs in the viewing rectangle $[-10, 10]$ by $[-60, 90]$. The graph of g seems to be *above* the graph of f. But is it? Recall from the Exploration that if $0 < x < 1$, powers of x get smaller. So for a complete comparison, we must also consider the viewing rectangle $[-2, 2]$ by $[-1, 2]$ shown in Fig. 4.44.

The points of intersection of these graphs seem to be $(-1, 1), (0, 0),$ and $(1, 1)$. To confirm this claim algebraically, consider the following equations:

$$x^4 = x^2$$

$$x^4 - x^2 = 0$$

$$x^2(x^2 - 1) = 0$$

$$x^2(x - 1)(x + 1) = 0.$$

The solutions are $x = -1,$ $x = 0,$ and $x = 1$.

To summarize what we have learned:

$$x^4 < x^2 \quad \Longleftrightarrow \quad x \text{ is in intervals } (-1, 0) \cup (0, 1),$$

$$x^4 = x^2 \quad \Longleftrightarrow \quad x = -1, x = 0, \text{ or } x = 1,$$

$$x^4 > x^2 \quad \Longleftrightarrow \quad x \text{ is in intervals } (-\infty, -1) \cup (1, \infty).$$

EXAMPLE 1   Solving Inequalities

Solve the inequality $x^6 \leq x^2$.

Solution   Let $f(x) = x^2$ and $g(x) = x^6$. For what values of x does $g(x) = f(x)$, and when is $g(x) < f(x)$? Consider the graphs of $f(x) = x^2$ and $g(x) = x^6$ shown in Fig. 4.45.

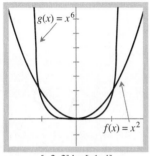

$$x^6 \leq x^2 \quad \Longleftrightarrow \quad x \text{ is in the interval } [-1, 1]$$

Notice the use of square brackets to indicate that the endpoints are included in the interval (that is, the solution is a closed interval).   ≡

Using the method of Example 1, we can solve any inequalities of the form $x^n \leq x^m$, where n and m are even integers.

[−2, 2] by [−1, 4]

Figure 4.45 $f(x) = x^2$ and $g(x) = x^6$.

Graphs of $y = x^n$ When n Is Odd

We now turn our attention to comparing graphs of $y = x^n$ when n is odd. For example, compare $f(x) = x^3$ and $g(x) = x^5$ as shown in Fig. 4.46.

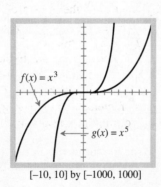

[−10, 10] by [−1000, 1000]

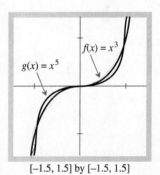

[−1.5, 1.5] by [−1.5, 1.5]

Figure 4.46 Two views of $f(x) = x^3$ and $g(x) = x^5$.

At least two viewing rectangles must be considered to support the behavior of these two graphs. These two graphs appear to intersect at the points $(-1, -1), (0, 0)$, and $(1, 1)$. The graph of $f(x) = x^3$ is above the graph of $g(x) = x^5$ when x is in

the intervals $(-\infty, -1)$ and $(0, 1)$ and below the graph of $g(x) = x^5$ when x is in the intervals $(-1, 0)$ and $(1, \infty)$.

EXAMPLE 2   Solving Inequalities

Solve the inequality $x^5 - x^3 > 0$ algebraically and graphically.

Solution

Method 1   Rewrite the inequality in the form $x^5 > x^3$. Read the solution from the graphs in Fig. 4.46 by observing where the graph of $g(x) = x^5$ is above the graph of $f(x) = x^3$.

$$x^5 > x^3 \quad \Longleftrightarrow \quad x \text{ is in } (-1, 0) \cup (1, \infty)$$

Method 2   Find a complete graph of $h(x) = x^5 - x^3$, find the zeros, and determine where the graph is above the x-axis (see Fig. 4.47).

$$x^5 - x^3 = 0$$
$$x^3(x^2 - 1) = 0$$
$$x^3(x - 1)(x + 1) = 0$$

The zeros of h are $-1, 0,$ and 1.

$$x^5 - x^3 > 0 \quad \Longleftrightarrow \quad x \text{ is in } (-1, 0) \cup (1, \infty).$$

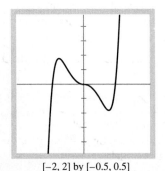

[−2, 2] by [−0.5, 0.5]

Figure 4.47 $h(x) = x^5 - x^3$.

In Example 2 it was possible to determine the zeros algebraically since $x^5 - x^3$ could be factored. Usually the algebraic technique is very hard or impossible. In that case the zeros can be determined graphically by using zoom-in. This next example illustrates the zoom-in method.

EXAMPLE 3   Solving Inequalities

Solve the inequality $x^3 < 4x - 1$.

Solution   Write the inequality in the form $x^3 - 4x + 1 < 0$, and find the values of x for which the complete graph of $f(x) = x^3 - 4x + 1$ lies below the x-axis. Use zoom-in to find

$$\text{zeros of } f: -2.11, 0.25, 1.86$$

with an error of less than 0.01 (see Fig. 4.48).
Therefore

$$x^3 - 4x + 1 < 0 \quad \Longleftrightarrow \quad x \text{ is in } (-\infty, -2.11) \cup (0.25, 1.86).$$

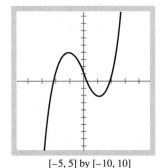

[−5, 5] by [−10, 10]

Figure 4.48 $f(x) = x^3 - 4x + 1$.

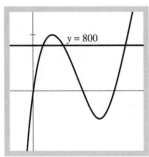

[−5, 20] by [−1000, 1500]

Figure 4.49 $y = 800$ and
$V(x) = x(20 - 2x)(30 - 2x)$.

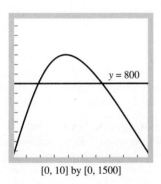

[0, 10] by [0, 1500]

Figure 4.50 $y = V(x)$ and
$y = 800$.

Endpoint Agreement

Even though the endpoints reported in solutions are approximations, we treat
them as if they are exact. Consequently we will continue to use parentheses
( ) to communicate the open intervals for the relations $<$ and $>$ and square
brackets [ ] to communicate the closed intervals for the relations $\leq$ and $\geq$.

EXAMPLE 4   APPLICATION: Minimum Box Volume

A box is formed by removing squares of side length x from each corner of a
rectangular piece of cardboard 20 inches wide by 30 inches long. Determine x so
that the volume of the resulting box is at least 800 cubic inches.

Solution   Let x = width of square = height of the resulting box, and $V(x)$ = the
volume of the resulting box. Then

$$20 - 2x = \text{width of the base}$$

$$30 - 2x = \text{length of the base}$$

$$V(x) = x(20 - 2x)(30 - 2x).$$ Volume is equal to length $\times$ width $\times$ height.

Figure 4.49 shows a complete graph of $V(x)$ and $y = 800$. However, the
problem situation allows only values of x between $x = 0$ and $x = 10$. (Why?)
Consequently the graph in Fig. 4.50 is a graphical representation of the problem
situation.

We must find the values of x for which the graph of V is on or above the
graph of $y = 800$. Using zoom-in the x-coordinates of the points of intersection
are

$$x = 1.88, x = 6.36$$

with an error of less than 0.01. Therefore the resulting box has a volume of at
least 800 cubic inches provided x is in the interval $[1.88, 6.36]$.   ≡

Exercises for Section 4.6

In Exercises 1 to 14, solve the inequality.

1. $x^4 < 2x^2$

2. $x^3 > 3x$

3. $x^6 < x^4$

4. $5x^2 \geq x^4$

5. $x^2 > x^3$

6. $x^7 < x^9$

7. $x^3 < x^5$

8. $2x^3 > 4x^5$

9. $x^3 + 8 > 0$

10. $x^3 - 8x + 1 \leq 0$

11. $x^3 - 2x^2 + 3 > 0$

12. $2x^3 - 3x^2 + 2x - 5 \geq 0$

13. $x^3 - 2x + 3 < 2x^2 - 3x + 5$

14. $x^4 \geq x^3 - 1$

In Exercises 15 to 20, use the sign-pattern method shown in Section 2.6 to solve each inequality algebraically. Support your answer with a graphing utility.

15. $x^2(x-1) > 0$ **16.** $x(x-1)(x+3) \le 0$

17. $x^3 > x$ **18.** $x^3 - x^2 - 2x > 0$

19. $x^3 - 4x^2 - x + 4 \ge 0$ **20.** $|x^3 - 8x| \le 0$

In Exercises 21 and 22, draw a complete graph of each inequality.

21. $y < x^3 - 5x^2 - 3x + 15$

22. $y \ge |x^2 + 2x - 3|$

23. Squares of side length x are removed from a 15- by 60-inch piece of cardboard, and a box with no top is formed. Determine x so that the volume of the resulting box is at most 450 cubic inches.

24. Squares of side length x are removed from a 10- by 25-cm piece of cardboard, and a box with no top is formed. Determine x so that the volume of the resulting box is at least 175 cm^3.

25. The function $V = 2666x - 210x^2 + 4x^3$ represents the volume of a certain box that has been made by removing equal squares of side length x from each corner of a rectangular sheet of material and then folding up the sides. What are the possible values of x for the height of the box?

Exercises 26 to 28 refer to the following **problem situation**: A rectangular area, with one side against an existing wall, is to be enclosed by three sides of fencing totaling 335 feet in length. Let x be the length of the side of the fence perpendicular to the existing wall.

26. Find an algebraic representation that gives the area enclosed as a function of x.

27. Find a complete graph of this problem situation. (Recall that the complete graph of a problem situation is only a portion of the complete graph of the algebraic representation.)

28. Find x so that the area is less than or equal to 11,750 square feet.

Exercises 29 and 30 refer to the following **problem situation**: The profit P of a business is determined by the formula $P = R - C$, where R is the total revenue generated by the business, and C is the total cost of operating the business. Suppose $R(x) = 0.0125x^2 + 412x$ is the total annual revenue of the business where x is the number of customers patronizing the business. Further, suppose $C(x) = 12{,}225 + 0.00135x^3$ is the total annual cost of doing business.

29. Find the number of customers that the business must have in 1 year for it to make a profit.

30. How many customers must the business have for it to realize an annual profit of $60,000?

Exercises 31 and 32 relate to finding hidden behavior of a function.

31. Draw the graph of $f(x) = 33x^3 - 100x^2 + 101x + 5$ in each viewing rectangle.
a) $[-10, 10]$ by $[-1000, 1000]$
b) $[-1, 1]$ by $[-100, 100]$
c) $[0.9, 1.1]$ by $[20, 50]$

32. The function f in Exercise 31 appears to be increasing on any interval. *It is not.* There is *hidden behavior* that can be determined by zooming in near the point $(1, f(1))$. Find a viewing rectangle that exhibits the hidden behavior.

In Exercises 33 to 36, draw a complete graph. Determine all local maximum and minimum values. Determine all real number zeros. Determine the intervals on which the function is increasing and the intervals on which the function is decreasing.

33. $f(x) = 2 - 3x + x^2 - x^3$

34. $f(x) = (x-1)^2 x^3$

35. $g(x) = 3x^4 - 5x^3 + 2x^2 - 3x + 6$

36. $T(x) = 2x^5 - 3x^4 + 2x^3 - 3x^2 + 7x - 4$

Chapter 4 Review

KEY TERMS

addition of complex numbers	bisection method complex conjugates	complex number continuous function	continuous on an interval J

cubic function
decreasing on an
    interval J
degree of a polynomial
    function
discontinuous on an
    interval J
division algorithm
    for polynomials
division of
    complex numbers
end behavior model
end behavior of
    a function

end behavior type
    $(-\infty, +\infty)$
factor
factor theorem
fundamental theorem
    of algebra
Horner's algorithm
imaginary part of a
    complex number
imaginary unit
increasing on an
    interval J
intermediate value
    property

irrational zeros
leading term
local extrema
local maximum value
local minimum value
lower bound
multiplication of
    complex numbers
nth root of unity
point of continuity
point of discontinuity
polynomial function
quotient polynomial
rational zeros

real part of a
    complex number
remainder polynomial
root
subtraction of
    complex numbers
synthetic division
upper bound
zoom-out
zero
zero of multiplicity 2
zero of multiplicity 3

REVIEW EXERCISES

In Exercises 1 to 4, graph the two functions in the same viewing rectangle.

1. $y = (x + 1)(x - 3)$; $y = -2(x + 1)(x - 3) + 4$

2. $y = (x - 1)(x + 2)(x - 3)$; $y = 3(x - 1)(x + 2)(x - 3) - 5$

3. $y = (x + 2)(x - 3)^2$; $y = 3(x + 2)(x - 3)^2 - 5$

4. $y = (x - 1)(x - 2)(x - 3)(x - 4)$;
   $y = 3(x - 1)(x - 2)(x - 3)(x - 4) - 8$

In Exercises 5 to 12, draw a complete graph for each function. Find all the real number zeros, and find all local extrema.

5. $f(x) = x^3 - 3x - 2$

6. $f(x) = x^3 - 6x^2 + 9x + 1$

7. $f(x) = 3x^4 - 4x^3 + 3$

8. $f(x) = x^4 + 8x^3 - 270x^2 + 10$

9. $f(x) = x^5 + 2x^4 - 6x^3 + 2x - 3$

10. $f(x) = 1000x^3 + 780x^2 - 5428x + 3696$

11. $f(x) = x^4 - 5x^3 + 2x - 10$

12. $f(x) = 100x^5 - 270x^4 + 36x^3 + 400x^2 - 280x + 460$

In Exercises 13 to 16, draw a complete graph of the function $y = f(x)$ in an appropriate viewing rectangle. Then find two values for c for which $f - c$ has three real zeros.

13. $f(x) = x^3 - 6x^2 + 9x + 6$

14. $f(x) = x^3 + 2x^2 + 2x - 5$

15. $f(x) = x^3 + x^2 - 4x - 9$

16. $f(x) = -x^3 - x^2 + 2x - 10$

In Exercises 17 and 18, draw a complete graph of the function $y = f(x)$ in an appropriate viewing rectangle. Then find two values for c for which $f - c$ has four real zeros.

17. $f(x) = x^4 - 4x^3 + 3x^2 + 2$

18. $f(x) = x^4 - 2x^2 - 4$

In Exercises 19 to 21, draw a complete graph for each function. Find all the real number zeros, and find all the local extrema.

19. $f(x) = 2x^3 - 3x^2 - 72x + 76$

20. $f(x) = 3x^4 - 4x^3 - 12x^2 + 13$

21. $f(x) = x^5 + 2x^4 - 6x^3 + 2x + 3$

In Exercises 22 to 25, determine the domain, range, and the points of discontinuity of each function.

22. $g(x) = \begin{cases} x^2 - 1 & x < 2 \\ \dfrac{3x}{2} & x \geq 2 \end{cases}$

23. $V(x) = 5x^3 - 25x^2 + 30x + 9$

24. $y = \dfrac{1}{x + 5}$

25. $f(x) = \text{INT}(x + 2)$

In Exercises 26 and 27, determine the domain, range, and values of x for which the function given by the graph is discontinuous. Assume the graph is complete.

26.

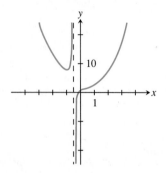

27.

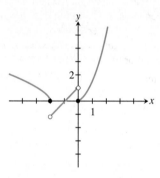

28. Graph the polynomial functions $f(x) = 5x^5 + 2x^2 - 4x + 7$ and $g(x) = 5x^5$ in a viewing rectangle that graphically illustrates that the end behavior of the two functions are the same. That is, a viewing rectangle in which the two graphs are nearly identical.

In Exercises 29 and 30, assume that the graph of $y = f(x)$ is complete.

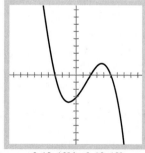

[−10, 10] by [−10, 10]

For Exercises 29 and 30

29. As $x \to \infty$, $f(x) \to ?$

30. As $x \to -\infty$, $f(x) \to ?$

In Exercises 31 and 32, assume that the graph of $y = f(x)$ is complete.

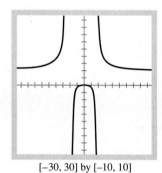

[−30, 30] by [−10, 10]

For Exercises 31 and 32

31. As $x \to \infty$, $f(x) \to ?$

32. As $x \to -\infty$, $f(x) \to ?$

In Exercises 33 and 34, find the quotient $q(x)$ and remainder $r(x)$ when $f(x)$ is divided by $h(x)$.

33. $f(x) = 3x^2 - 2x + 7$; $h(x) = x + 2$

34. $f(x) = 6x^3 - x^2 + 9x + 1$; $h(x) = 3x + 2$

35. Use the remainder theorem to determine the remainder when $f(x) = 3x^3 - 2x + 17$ is divided by $x - 1$. Check by using division.

36. Determine the remainder when $f(x) = 3x^{38} - 2x^{15} + 17x^2 - 3x + 12$ is divided by $x - 1$.

37. Use the factor theorem to determine whether $x - 3$ is a factor of $x^3 - 2x^2 - 4x + 3$.

38. Determine the coordinates of a point (a, b) that must be added to the graph of

$$f(x) = \frac{x^2 - 4}{x + 2}$$

to make the function continuous for every real number.

In Exercises 39 and 40, find all real number zeros of each polynomial by factoring. Use a graphing utility to support your answer.

39. $f(x) = 8x - x^3$ **40.** $T(x) = x^4 - 13x^2 + 36$

41. Draw a complete graph of $f(x) = x^3 - x - 6$. Use the graph as an aid in factoring the polynomial, and then determine all real number zeros.

42. Determine *all* the zeros, real and nonreal, of the polynomial in Exercise 41.

43. Determine all the real number zeros of $f(x) = x^5 - 5x^4 - x^3 + 5x^2 + 16x - 80$.

44. Draw the graph of $f(x) = 800x^3 + 780x^2 - 21x - 1$ in the $[-5, 5]$ by $[-150, 150]$ viewing rectangle.
  a) How many real number zeros are evident from this graph?
  b) How many actual real number zeros exist in this case?
  c) Find all real number zeros.

45. How many real zeros does $f(x) = 2x^4 + 2x^3 + 3x^2 + 2x + 1$ have? Why?

46. Draw the graph of $f(x) = 33x^3 - 300.5x^2 + 903x + 500$ in the $[-10, 10]$ by $[-3000, 3000]$ viewing rectangle.
  a) Where does the function appear to be increasing based on this graph?
  b) How many local extrema does the function have based on this graph?
  c) Determine the actual number of local extrema of the function.

47. Draw a complete graph of $f(x) = 4x^3 + mx$ for $m = -3$, -2, 0, 2, and 4. For each value of m, determine
  a) the number of real number zeros of f;
  b) the number of local extrema of f.
  c) the intervals on which f is increasing and the intervals on which f is decreasing.

48. Determine a polynomial of degree 3 with real number coefficients that has
  a) 2 and -3 as zeros;
  b) 2 and -3 as the *only* zeros;
  c) 2 and $2 - i$ as zeros.

49. If $f(x) = 3x^3 + 2kx^2 - kx + 2$, find a number k so that the graph of f contains the point $(1, 3)$.

In Exercises 50 and 51, determine all real number zeros of each function by algebraic methods. Classify them as integer, noninteger rational, or irrational. Support your work with a graphing utility.

50. $f(x) = x^3 + 3x^2 - 5x - 15$

51. $f(x) = x^4 - 8x^2 - 9$

In Exercises 52 and 53, use the rational zeros theorem to list all possible rational zeros of each function. Find the graph of each function in an appropriate viewing rectangle, and indicate which of the possible rational zeros are actual zeros. Determine all real number zeros (both rational and irrational) of each function.

52. $f(x) = x^3 - 5x^2 + 2x - 10$

53. $f(x) = 3x^3 + 3x^2 - 4x - 2$

54. Use synthetic division to find the quotient and remainder when $2x^3 + x^2 - 4x + 5$ is divided by $x + 5$.

55. Draw a complete graph of $f(x) = x^3 + 7x^2 + 6x - 8$. Confirm that there is at least one rational root. Use synthetic division to find the other quadratic factor, and then determine all real number zeros. Classify each real number zero as rational or irrational.

56. Determine the real number zeros of $f(x) = x^4 + 3x^3 - 3x^2 - 3x + 2$. Classify them as rational or irrational. Carefully outline why you are sure of your results.

In Exercises 57 and 58, use synthetic division to find upper and lower bounds for the zeros of each polynomial function.

57. $f(x) = x^3 + 3x - 1$

58. $g(x) = x^3 - x^2 - 2x + 1$

59. Show that $x + 3$ is a factor of $g(x) = x^6 - 729$.

In Exercises 60 to 63, write each expression in the form $a + bi$ where a and b are real numbers.

60. $(5 - 2i)(1 - i)$ **61.** $3(2 + 3i) - 4 + 2i$

62. $\dfrac{3 + i}{5 + 4i}$ **63.** $(i^{93})^4$

In Exercises 64 and 65, determine the number of real zeros and the number of nonreal complex zeros of each function.

64. $f(x) = 2x^3 + 3x^2 + 3x + 1$

65. $f(x) = x^3 - 2x^2 + 2x - 2$

66. Use computer graphing, the rational zeros theorem, synthetic division, and the fundamental theorem of algebra to find all the zeros of $f(x) = x^4 - 3x^3 - 12x - 16$. Classify each zero as integer, noninteger rational, irrational, or nonreal complex.

In Exercises 67 and 68, find a polynomial with real number coefficients satisfying the given condition.

67. degree 2; zero $1 - 2i$

68. degree 3; zeros $2 + 5i$ and 2

69. Find a polynomial $f(x)$ of degree 4 with real number coefficients that has 2, $3 + i$, and $3 - i$ as its only zeros.

70. Find a polynomial $f(x)$ of degree 4 with real number coefficients that has 2, $3 + i$, and $3 - i$ as its only zeros and that also satisfies $f(0) = 1$.

Exercises 71 to 75 refer to the following **problem situation**: The temperature in a certain town for a 24-hour period is given by the algebraic representation $f(t) = 0.04t(t - 24)(t - 22) + 30$. Assume $t = 0$ is 6 A.M.

71. Without using a graphing utility, sketch a complete graph of the model. What is the domain of the model? What values of t make sense in this problem situation?

72. Use a graphing utility to draw a complete graph of the model, and compare it with your sketch in Exercise 71.

73. When will the temperature be $45°$F?

74. What is the highest temperature, and when is it achieved?

75. What is the lowest temperature, and when is it achieved?

A good deal of real-world mathematics involves interpreting concrete data generated from experiments, observations, or computer simulations. Polynomials are frequently used to create functions that approximate the observed data and then used as algebraic representations of the real-world problem. Exercises 76 to 80 explore the nature of *Chebyshev polynomials*, which are useful in this type of investigation.

76. Draw a complete graph of the third-degree Chebyshev polynomial $C_3(x) = 4x^3 - 3x$.

77. Draw a complete graph of the fourth-degree Chebyshev polynomial $C_4(x) = 8x^4 - 8x^2 + 1$.

78. Draw a complete graph of the fifth-degree Chebyshev polynomial $C_5(x) = 16x^5 - 20x^3 + 5x$.

79. What are the local extrema of each of the Chebyshev polynomials in Exercises 76 to 78?

80. Can you predict the graph of the sixth-degree Chebyshev polynomial?

81. The polynomial function $M(x) = x^m(1 - x)^{n-m}$ is used in applied statistics to determine *maximum likelihood estimates*. For the indicated values of m and n, draw the graph of the function $y = M(x)$ in the $[-2, 2]$ by $[-2, 2]$ viewing rectangle.
a) $m = 2, n = 5$
b) $m = 4, n = 8$
c) $m = 3, n = 10$

Exercises 82 to 85 refer to the following **problem situation**: A 255-foot-long steel beam is anchored between two pilings 50 feet above the ground. An algebraic representation for the amount of vertical deflection s caused by a 250-pound object placed d feet from the west piling is $s = (8.5 \times 10^{-7})d^2(255 - d)$.

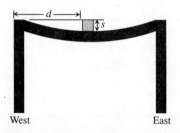

West   East

For Exercises 82 to 85

82. Draw a complete graph of the model. What is the domain of the model? What values of d make sense in this problem situation?

83. Where is the object placed if the amount of vertical deflection is 1 foot?

84. What is the greatest amount of vertical deflection, and where does it occur?

85. Give a possible scenario explaining why the solution to Exercise 84 does not occur at the halfway point.

Exercises 86 to 89 refer to the following **problem situation**: A liquid storage container on a truck is in the shape of a cylinder with hemispheres on each end. The cylinder and hemispheres have the same radius. The total length of the container is 140 feet.

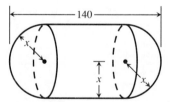

For Exercises 86 to 89

86. Determine the volume V of the container as a function of the radius x.

87. Draw a complete graph of the volume function $y = V(x)$.

88. What are the possible values of the radius determined by this problem situation?

89. What is the radius of the container with largest possible volume?

Exercises 90 to 93 refer to the following problem situation: The total daily revenue of Henrietta's Hamburger Haven is given by the equation $R = x \cdot p$, where x is the number of hamburgers sold, and p is the price of one hamburger. Assume the price per hamburger is given by the supply equation $p = 0.3x + 0.05x^2 + 0.0007x^3$.

90. Determine for what positive values of x the supply function is increasing.

91. Draw a complete graph of the revenue function R.

92. What values of x make sense in the problem situation?

93. Determine the maximum possible daily revenue of Henrietta's Hamburger Haven and the number of hamburgers she needs to sell to achieve maximum revenue.

Exercises 94 to 97 refer to the following problem situation: Biologists have determined that the polynomial function $P(t) = -0.00005t^3 + 0.003t^2 + 1.2t + 80$ approximates the population t days later of a certain group of wild pheasants left to reproduce on their own with no predators.

94. Draw a complete graph of $y = P(t)$.

95. Find the maximum pheasant population and when it occurs.

96. When will this pheasant population be extinct?

97. Create a scenario that could explain the "growth" exhibited by this pheasant population.

CHAPTER 5

Rational Functions and Functions Involving Radicals

5.1   Rational Functions and Asymptotes

Chapter 4 examined the class of functions known as the polynomials. Recall that polynomial functions are continuous functions that often have local maximums and minimums. Also recall the exploration of end behavior models and zeros of polynomial functions.

Knowledge of these characteristics of polynomial functions will be useful in learning about a class of functions known as rational functions—functions that are a quotient of two polynomial functions.

Definition 5.1   Rational Functions

A **rational function** is one that can be written in the form

$$f(x) = \frac{p(x)}{q(x)}$$

where $p(x)$ and $q(x)$ are polynomial functions, $q(x) \neq 0$.

The following are examples of rational functions:

$$f(x) = \frac{x^2 + 1}{x - 3}, \qquad g(x) = \frac{3x^2 - 4x + 1}{x^2 + x - 2}, \qquad h(x) = \frac{4x^3 + 7x^2 - 3}{(x - 2)(x + 4)}.$$

The domain of a rational function is the set of all real numbers except those for which the denominator is zero.

EXAMPLE 1   Finding Domains of Rational Functions

Find the domains of the following rational functions:

a) $f(x) = \dfrac{x^2 + 1}{x - 3}$

b) $g(x) = \dfrac{3x^2 - 4x + 1}{x^2 + x - 2}$

c) $h(x) = \dfrac{4x^3 + 7x^2 - 3}{(x - 2)(x + 4)}.$

Solution

a) Domain of $f = (-\infty, 3) \cup (3, \infty)$.

b) Domain of $g = (-\infty, -2) \cup (-2, 1) \cup (1, \infty)$ $x^2 + x - 2 = (x + 2)(x - 1)$

c) Domain of $h = (-\infty, -4) \cup (-4, 2) \cup (2, \infty)$

Horizontal Asymptotes

Perhaps the simplest rational function is the **reciprocal function,** $f(x) = 1/x$, which is graphed in Fig. 5.1. The following table gives numerical evidence that as $|x|$ gets larger, $f(x)$ gets closer and closer to zero.

x	± 1	± 2	± 3	± 4	$\cdots$	± 1000
$f(x)$	± 1	$\pm 1/2$	$\pm 1/3$	$\pm 1/4$	$\cdots$	$\pm 1/1000$

The following Exploration will give visual evidence of the same thing.

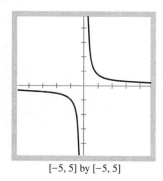

[−5, 5] by [−5, 5]

Figure 5.1 $f(x) = \dfrac{1}{x}$.

🔎 EXPLORE WITH A GRAPHING UTILITY

Find the graph of $f(x) = 1/x$ in each of the following viewing rectangles. In each case observe the values of the x- and y-coordinates as you move the cursor along the graph to the right using the trace key.

a) $[-10, 10]$ by $[-2, 2]$

b) $[-100, 100]$ by $[-0.1, 0.1]$

c) $[-1000, 1000]$ by $[-0.01, 0.01]$

For the function $f(x) = 1/x$ used in the Exploration we say, "as x approaches positive or negative infinity, $f(x)$ approaches 0." We write

$$\text{as } x \to \infty \text{ or as } x \to -\infty, f(x) \to 0.$$

The horizontal line $y = 0$ is called a horizontal asymptote of $f(x) = 1/x$.

Figure 5.2 shows several other cases of horizontal asymptotes. In each case the graph approaches the horizontal line $y = L$ as $|x| \to \infty$.

REMINDER

In Fig. 5.3, and other figures that follow, a dashed line has been added to indicate a horizontal or vertical asymptote. This dashed line is not part of the graph.

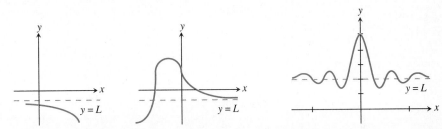

Figure 5.2   Examples of graphs and their horizontal asymptotes.

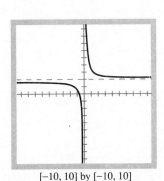

[−10, 10] by [−10, 10]

Figure 5.3 $g(x) = 1/x + 2$.

Definition 5.2   Horizontal Asymptote

The horizontal line $y = L$ is a **horizontal asymptote** of a function f if

$$f(x) \to L \text{ as } x \to \infty \qquad or \qquad f(x) \to L \text{ as } x \to -\infty.$$

E X A M P L E   2   Finding Horizontal Asymptotes

Find the horizontal asymptotes of $g(x) = 1/x + 2$ and $h(x) = 1/x - 3$.

Solution

$$\frac{1}{x} \to 0 \text{ as } |x| \to \infty$$

Therefore

$$g(x) \to 2 \qquad \text{and} \qquad h(x) \to -3, \text{ as } |x| \to \infty.$$

The line $y = 2$ is a horizontal asymptote for g, and the line $y = -3$ is a horizontal asymptote for h.

The graphs of g and h are shown in the standard viewing rectangle in Figs. 5.3 and 5.4. Try other viewing rectangles where $|X\text{max}|$ and $|X\text{min}|$ are large.

≡

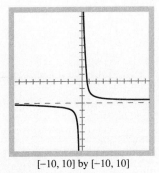

[−10, 10] by [−10, 10]

Figure 5.4 $h(x) = 1/x - 3$.

The graphs of g and h provide visual support for these conclusions. These graphs can be found either by using a graphing utility or by using the horizontal and vertical shift transformations studied in Section 3.6. These transformations are illustrated in Example 3.

EXAMPLE 3   Sketching Graphs Using Transformations

Sketch the graphs of functions g and h defined in Example 2 by applying transformations studied in Section 3.6 to the graph of $f(x) = 1/x$.

Solution

$$g(x) = \frac{1}{x} + 2 = f(x) + 2$$

$$h(x) = \frac{1}{x} - 3 = f(x) - 3$$

Therefore the graph of g is obtained from the graph of f by a vertical shift up 2 units. Similarly, the graph of h is obtained from the graph of f by a vertical shift down 3 units. ≡

Example 4 shows that a function may have two horizontal asymptotes.

EXAMPLE 4   Two Horizontal Asymptotes

Find a complete graph of

$$f(x) = \frac{x - 2}{|x| + 3}$$

and show algebraically that f has two horizontal asymptotes.

Solution   A complete graph appears in Fig. 5.5.

Because $|x| \geq 0$, we see that $|x| + 3 > 0$. Consider two cases:

Case 1   Suppose $x \geq 0$. Then $|x| = x$. Using division, f can be written as follows:

$$f(x) = \frac{x - 2}{x + 3} = 1 - \frac{5}{x + 3} \qquad (x \geq 0).$$

As $x \to \infty$, $f(x) \to 1$, which means that the line $y = 1$ is a horizontal asymptote.

Case 2   Suppose $x < 0$. Then $|x| = -x$. Using division f can be written as follows:

$$f(x) = \frac{x - 2}{-x + 3} = -1 + \frac{1}{-x + 3} \qquad (x < 0).$$

As $x \to -\infty$, $f(x) \to -1$, which means that the line $y = -1$ is a horizontal asymptote.

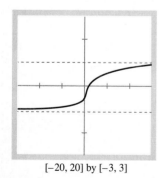

[−20, 20] by [−3, 3]

Figure 5.5 $f(x) = \dfrac{x - 2}{|x| + 3}$.

Vertical Asymptotes

Again consider the reciprocal function $f(x) = 1/x$ shown in Fig. 5.1. The following table shows that as x approaches 0 from the positive side, $f(x)$ increases without bound. That is,

$$f(x) \to +\infty \quad \text{as} \quad x \to 0^+.$$

The plus sign in 0^+ means that x assumes only values greater than zero. Likewise, 0^- means x assumes only values less than zero.

x	1	1/2	1/3	1/4	$\cdots$	1/1000	$x \to 0^+$
$f(x)$	1	2	3	4	$\cdots$	1000	$f(x) \to \infty$

A similar table with x approaching 0 through values less than zero would show that

$$f(x) \to -\infty \text{ as } x \to 0^-.$$

We say that the vertical line $x = 0$ is a vertical asymptote. Figure 5.6 shows some additional examples of vertical asymptotes.

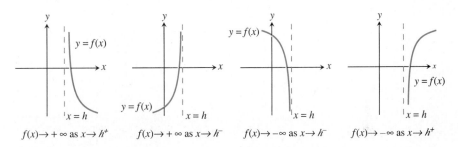

$f(x) \to +\infty$ as $x \to h^+$ $f(x) \to +\infty$ as $x \to h^-$ $f(x) \to -\infty$ as $x \to h^-$ $f(x) \to -\infty$ as $x \to h^+$

Figure 5.6 Examples of graphs and their vertical asymptotes.

Definition 5.3   Vertical Asymptotes

The vertical line $x = h$ is called a **vertical asymptote** of a function f if

$$f(x) \to +\infty \qquad \text{or} \qquad f(x) \to -\infty$$

as $x \to h$ from the right or from the left.

If the numerator and denominator of a rational function have no common factors, a vertical asymptote will occur whenever the denominator is zero.

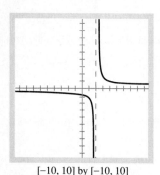

[−10, 10] by [−10, 10]

Figure 5.7 $f(x) = \dfrac{1}{x-2}$.

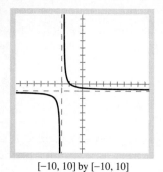

[−10, 10] by [−10, 10]

Figure 5.8 $g(x) = \dfrac{1}{x+3} - 1$.

REMINDER

Notice that there are no vertical asymptotes for

$$f(x) = \frac{4-2x}{x-2}$$

because this numerator and denominator have a common factor of $x - 2$, leaving $f(x) = -2$.

EXAMPLE 5   Finding Vertical Asymptotes

Find the vertical asymptotes of (a) $f(x) = 1/(x-2)$ and (b) $g(x) = 1/(x+3) - 1$.

Solution

a) Consider where the denominators are zero.

$$x - 2 = 0 \iff x = 2$$

Therefore the vertical line $x = 2$ is a vertical asymptote for f (see Fig. 5.7).

b) The function g is undefined if $x + 3 = 0$:

$$x + 3 = 0 \iff x = -3.$$

Therefore the vertical line $x = -3$ is a vertical asymptote for g.   ≡

EXAMPLE 6   Sketching Graphs Using Transformations

Sketch the graphs of (a) $f(x) = 1/(x-2)$ and (b) $g(x) = 1/(x+3)-1$ by applying transformations to the graph of $h(x) = 1/x$.

Solution

a) $$f(x) = h(x-2) = \frac{1}{x-2}$$

Therefore the graph of f is obtained from the graph of $1/x$ by a horizontal shift 2 units to the right (see Fig. 5.7).

b) $$g(x) = \frac{1}{x+3} - 1 = h(x+3) - 1$$

The graph of g is obtained from the graph of $1/x$ by a horizontal shift to the left 3 units followed by a vertical shift down 1 unit (see Fig. 5.8).   ≡

EXAMPLE 7   Sketching Graphs Using Long Division

Determine the horizontal and vertical asymptotes for

$$f(x) = \frac{2x-13}{x-5}.$$

Also describe how a graph of f can be obtained from $y = 1/x$.

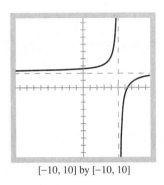

Figure 5.9 $f(x) = 2 - \dfrac{3}{x-5}$.

Solution   Begin by finding a vertical asymptote:

$$x - 5 = 0 \Longleftrightarrow x = 5 \qquad \text{and} \qquad 2x - 13 \neq 0 \text{ when } x = 5.$$

Since the numerator is not also zero when $x = 5$, the vertical line $x = 5$ is a vertical asymptote for f. Since the numerator is not a constant, complete the following long division to find that the quotient is 2 and the remainder is -3:

$$x - 5 \overline{\smash{\big)}\ 2x - 13} \atop {\ \underline{2x - 10}} \atop {\ -\ 3}$$

$$\begin{array}{r} 2 \\ x-5 \overline{\smash{\big)}\ 2x - 13} \\ \underline{2x - 10} \\ -\ 3 \end{array}$$

Therefore $f(x) = \dfrac{2x - 13}{x - 5} = 2 - \dfrac{3}{x - 5}.$

The horizontal line $y = 2$ is a horizontal asymptote.

The graph of f shown if Fig. 5.9 can be obtained from $y = 1/x$ by applying the following transformations:

1. Horizontal shift 5 units to the right;

2. Vertical stretch by a factor of 3;

3. Reflection through the x-axis;

4. Vertical shift up 2 units.   ▤

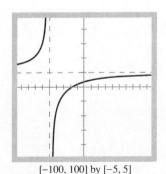

50 oz. of a 35% acid solution

Figure 5.10   Mixing pure and diluted acid solutions.

Rational functions often occur as algebraic models of problem situations like the mixture problem in the next example. Recall from an earlier mixture problem that if you have 50 ounces of a 35% acid solution, there are $50(0.35) = 17.5$ ounces of pure acid in the solution.

If 10 ounces of pure acid are added to this 50-ounce solution, the resulting 60-ounce solution contains 27.5 ounces of pure acid. In this mixture the ratio of pure acid to total solution is $27.5/60 = 0.458$, resulting in a 45.8% solution.

$[-100, 100]$ by $[-5, 5]$

Figure 5.11   A complete graph of the algebraic representation of $C(x)$.

E X A M P L E   8   APPLICATION: Mixture Problem Situation

Suppose that x ounces of pure acid is added to 50 ounces of a 35% acid solution (Fig. 5.10).

a) Find a complete graph of the algebraic representation $C(x)$ that represents the concentration of the new mixture as a function of x.

b) Find a complete graph of the problem situation. (That is, what values of x make sense?)

c) How much pure acid should be added to the 35% acid solution to produce a mixture that is at least 75% acid?

Solution

a) Let x = ounces of acid added. Then

$$x + 50(0.35) = \text{ounces of pure acid in the new solution}$$

$$x + 50 = \text{ounces of new solution}$$

$$\frac{\text{ounces of pure acid}}{\text{ounces of total solution}} = \text{concentration of acid in the new solution}$$

$$C(x) = \frac{x + 17.5}{x + 50}.$$

Notice that the domain of the algebraic representation $C(x)$ is all the real numbers except -50. However, in this problem only $x \geq 0$ makes sense.

A complete graph of $C(x)$ is found in Fig. 5.11. Notice that the line $x = -50$ is a vertical asymptote. It appears that line $y = 1$ is a horizontal asymptote.

b) The portion of the graph in Fig. 5.11 where $x \geq 0$ is a complete graph of the problem situation. This portion is shown in Fig. 5.12.

c) Since the mixture is a 75% solution when $C(x) = 0.75$, the line $y = 0.75$ is also shown in Fig. 5.12. Use zoom-in to see that the two graphs intersect at the point $(80, 0.75)$. At least 80 ounces of pure acid must be added.   ▤

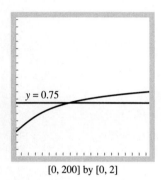

$y = 0.75$

[0, 200] by [0, 2]

Figure 5.12   A complete graph of the problem situation in Example 8.

Exercises for Section 5.1

In Exercises 1 to 10, find the domain of each rational function. Support your answer with a graphing utility.

1. $f(x) = \dfrac{x}{(x-2)(x+1)}$

2. $g(x) = \dfrac{5}{x^2 - 1}$

3. $h(x) = \dfrac{x+2}{(x+3)(x-1)}$

4. $f(x) = \dfrac{2}{x^2 + 4x + 3}$

5. $f(x) = \dfrac{x^2 + 1}{x^2 - 1}$

6. $t(x) = \dfrac{2}{2x^2 - x - 3}$

7. $f(x) = \dfrac{x^2 - 4}{x^2 - 4x - 1}$

8. $P(x) = \dfrac{4x - 2}{x^2 + 5x + 8}$

9. $f(x) = \dfrac{x^4 - 3x^2 - 5}{x^5 - x}$

10. $f(x) = \dfrac{2x^2 + 5}{x^3 - 2x^2 + x}$

In Exercises 11 to 16, find a horizontal asymptote for each of these functions.

11. $f(x) = -\dfrac{1}{x}$

12. $g(x) = \dfrac{1}{x} + 3$

13. $h(x) = \dfrac{1}{x} - 4$

14. $f(x) = 2 - \dfrac{1}{x}$

15. $g(x) = -12 + \dfrac{1}{x}$

16. $h(x) = 17 + \dfrac{1}{x}$

In Exercises 17 to 22, find the horizontal and vertical asymptotes for each of these functions.

17. $y = \dfrac{2}{x+1}$

18. $y = -\dfrac{1}{x-2}$

19. $y = 4 + \dfrac{1}{x+1}$

20. $y = -2 + \dfrac{2}{x+3}$

21. $y = \dfrac{2}{4-x}$

22. $f(x) = -1 - \dfrac{3}{x+1}$

In Exercises 23 to 30, list the geometric transformations needed to produce a complete graph of the function f from a complete graph of $y = 1/x$. Specify the order in which the transformations should be applied. In each case, draw a graph of the function without the aid of a graphing utility and write the equations of any vertical or horizontal asymptotes. Support your answer with a graphing utility.

23. $f(x) = \dfrac{1}{x - 3}$

24. $f(x) = \dfrac{2}{x + 2}$

25. $y = -\dfrac{2}{x + 5}$

26. $y = \dfrac{1}{x + 3}$

27. $y = -3 + \dfrac{1}{x + 1}$

28. $y = -2 + \dfrac{1}{x + 3}$

29. $y = \dfrac{5}{1 - x}$

30. $f(x) = -1 - \dfrac{1}{x + 1}$

In Exercises 31 to 36, find the horizontal and vertical asymptotes of each function. Use long division first if necessary.

31. $g(x) = \dfrac{3x - 1}{x + 2}$

32. $f(x) = \dfrac{8x + 6}{2x - 4}$

33. $f(x) = \dfrac{2x + 4}{x - 3}$

34. $h(x) = \dfrac{x - 3}{2x + 5}$

35. $t(x) = \dfrac{x - 1}{x + 4}$

36. $k(x) = \dfrac{2x - 3}{x + 2}$

Exercises 37 and 38 are based on the following computer-generated graph of $y = f(x)$.

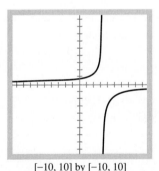

[−10, 10] by [−10, 10]

For Exercises 37 and 38

37. As $x \to \infty$, $f(x) \to$?

38. As $x \to 3^-$, $f(x) \to$?

Exercises 39 and 40 are based on the following computer-generated graph of $y = g(x)$ with a vertical asymptote at $x = -3$ and a horizontal asymptote at $y = 4$.

[−20, 20] by [−20, 20]

For Exercises 39 and 40

39. As $x \to -\infty$, $g(x) \to$?   **40.** As $x \to -3^+$, $g(x) \to$?

In exercises 41 and 42, draw a complete graph of each function. Give the domain and range, and write equations of any asymptotes.

41. $y = \dfrac{x - 1}{2x - 2}$

42. $y = \dfrac{3x - 9}{6 - 2x}$

43. Describe how the graph of $y = 3 - 2/(x - 1)$ is obtained from the graph of $y = 1/x$.

44. Describe how the graph of $f(x) = r/(x - h) + k$ is obtained from the graph of $y = 1/x$.

45. Consider the function $f(x)$ with $c \neq 0$ and $bc > ad$:

$$f(x) = \frac{ax + b}{cx + d}.$$

List the transformations that will produce a complete graph of f from a complete graph of $y = 1/x$, and specify an order in which they should be applied. (*Hint:* Use long division.)

46. Consider the following **problem situation**: The area of a rectangle is 300 square units. Determine an algebraic representation that gives the length of this rectangle as a function of its width x. Sketch a complete graph of both this algebraic representation and of this problem situation. What is the width of the rectangle if the length is 2000 units?

47. Solve Example 8 algebraically.

48. Consider the following **problem situation**: x ounces of pure acid are added to 125 ounces of a 60% acid solution.

a) Find a complete graph of this problem situation where $C(x)$ represents the concentration of the new mixture as a function of x.

b) Use a computer-drawn graph to determine how much pure acid should be added to the 60% solution to produce a new mixture that is at least 83% acid.

c) Solve part (b) algebraically.

49. Sally wishes to obtain 100 ounces of a 40% acid solution by combining a 60% acid solution and a 10% acid solution. How much of each solution should Sally use? Solve both

algebraically and graphically.

50. Find the domain and range of $f(x) = r/(x - h) + k$.

51. Find the domain and range of $f(x)$ where $c \neq 0, d \neq 0$:

$$f(x) = \frac{ax + b}{cx + d}.$$

5.2 _____ Rational Functions and Their Graphs

All the rational functions in Section 5.1 met the special condition that the numerator and denominator were both linear polynomials.

In the rational functions in this section, either the numerator or the denominator (or both) are polynomials of degree 2 or higher.

Numerator and Denominator with Common Factors

When the numerator and denominator of a rational function have a common factor, the function has a discontinuity that may not be noticed when using a graphing utility. Consider the following two rational functions:

$$f(x) = \frac{x - 1}{x - 1}, \qquad g(x) = \frac{(x - 1)^2}{x - 1}.$$

The domain of each function consists of all the real numbers except $x = 1$. These functions can be simplified algebraically as follows:

$$f(x) = \frac{x - 1}{x - 1} = 1 \qquad (x \neq 1)$$

$$g(x) = \frac{(x - 1)^2}{x - 1} = x - 1 \qquad (x \neq 1).$$

E X A M P L E   1   Common Factors in Rational Functions

Sketch complete graphs of the functions:

$$f(x) = \frac{x - 1}{x - 1} \qquad \text{and} \qquad g(x) = \frac{(x - 1)^2}{x - 1}.$$

Solution   The graph of f and the line $y = 1$ are identical except at $x = 1$. Since f is undefined at $x = 1$, the graph of f is the horizontal line $y = 1$ with a missing point at $(1,1)$ (see Fig. 5.13).

The graph of g and the line $y = x - 1$ are identical except for $x = 1$. So the graph of g is the line $y = x - 1$ with a missing point at $(1,0)$ (see Fig. 5.14). (*Note:* The open circles in Figs. 5.13 and 5.14 may not appear on a graphing utility.)   ▣

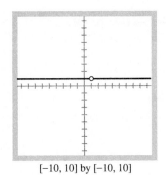

[−10, 10] by [−10, 10]

Figure 5.13 $f(x) = \dfrac{x-1}{x-1}$.

There are several important observations to make about the graphs in Example 1.

1. Even though the denominator is zero for $x = 1$, there is no vertical asymptote because the numerator is also zero for $x = 1$.

2. Both functions are discontinuous since their graphs have a missing point. This discontinuity is called a **removable discontinuity** because the discontinuity can be removed by redefining the function at $x = 1$.

3. It is usually impossible to see a single-point discontinuity on graphs produced by graphing utilities. Be alert to the possibility of these discontinuities, and find them algebraically.

Because of these conditions, the rational functions in the remainder of this section, except $g(x)$ in Example 2, have been chosen to be without common factors in the numerator and the denominator. No loss of generality in the discussion will occur in making this assumption.

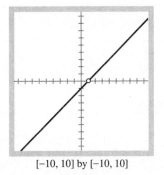

[−10, 10] by [−10, 10]

Figure 5.14 $g(x) = \dfrac{(x-1)^2}{x-1}$.

End Behavior Models for Rational Functions

Suppose that f is a rational function defined as follows:

$$f(x) = \frac{a_n x^n + a_{n-1} x^{n-1} + \cdots + a_0}{b_m x^m + b_{m-1} x^{m-1} + \cdots + b_0}.$$

Recall these two facts studied in Section 4.2 about end behavior models for polymonials:

1. $a_n x^n$ is the end behavior model for $a_n x^n + a_{n-1} x^{n-1} + \cdots + a_0$ $(a_n \neq 0)$.

2. $b_m x^m$ is the end behavior model for $b_m x^m + b_{m-1} x^{m-1} + \cdots + b_0$ $(b_m \neq 0)$.

In other words, when $|x|$ is very large, the following approximation is true:

$$f(x) \approx \frac{a_n x^n}{b_m x^m} = \left(\frac{a_n}{b_m} \right) x^{n-m}.$$

Definition 5.4   End Behavior for a Rational Function

The function

$$g(x) = \frac{a_n x^n}{b_m x^m} = \left(\frac{a_n}{a_m}\right) = x^{n-m}$$

is the **end behavior model** for the rational function

$$f(x) = \frac{a_n x^n + a_{n-1} x^{n-1} + \cdots + a_0}{b_m x^m + b_{m-1} x^{m-1} + \cdots + b_0}.$$

Definition 5.4 is applied in this next example.

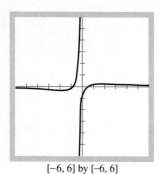

[−6, 6] by [−6, 6]

Figure 5.15

$$f(x) = \frac{2x^2 - 1}{3x^3 + 2x + 1}.$$

E X A M P L E   2   Finding an End Behavior Model

Find an end behavior model and any horizontal asymptotes for functions f and g, where

$$f(x) = \frac{2x^2 - 1}{3x^3 + 2x + 1} \qquad \text{and} \qquad g(x) = \frac{2x^4 - 3x^2 + 1}{3x^4 - x^2 + x - 1}.$$

Solution   The end behavior model for f is $2x^2/3x^3 = 2/3x$; the horizontal asymptote for f is $y = 0$.

The end behavior model for g is $2x^4/3x^4 = \frac{2}{3}$; the horizontal asymptote for g is $y = \frac{2}{3}$. The graphs in Figs. 5.15 and 5.16 support these conclusions.

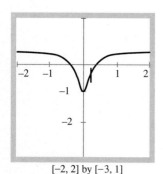

[−2, 2] by [−3, 1]

Figure 5.16

$$g(x) = \frac{2x^4 - 3x^2 + 1}{3x^4 - x^2 + x - 1}.$$

Sketching a Graph of a Rational Function when $n \leq m$

We now turn to rational functions, in which the degree of the numerator does not exceed the degree of the denominator.

Often in graphing a rational function with a graphing utility, there are not enough pixels on the display to give a detailed view of the graph, particularly when the graph has several vertical asymptotes. The graphing utility user must have a general understanding of what the graphs of rational functions might look like in order to find a complete graph. For example, a computer graphing utility user must be able to interpret the sharp spike that appears in Fig. 5.16 and to decide which viewing rectangle to choose.

In other words, the computer graphing utility and the user complement each other. Between the two an accurate sketch should be possible.

To find a complete graph, first find the x- and y-intercepts and the horizontal and vertical asymptotes if there are any. If there are, find values of the function for x near the vertical asymptotes.

E X A M P L E   3   Graphing a Rational Function

Sketch a complete graph of the rational function

$$f(x) = \frac{x-1}{x^2 - x - 6}.$$

Solution   First find x- and y-intercepts:

$$y\text{-intercept:} \qquad f(0) = \frac{1}{6}$$

$$x\text{-intercept:} \qquad f(1) = 0.$$

To find vertical asymptotes, factor the denominator:

$$x^2 - x - 6 = (x-3)(x+2) = 0.$$

Thus the vertical asymptotes are the lines $x = -2$ and $x = 3$. The end behavior for f is

$$g(x) = \frac{x}{x^2} = \frac{1}{x}$$

so the horizontal asymptote for f is $y = 0$.

Use a calculator to find values of f for x near $x = -2$ and $x = 3$ on either side of these asymptotes:

x	-2.1	-1.9		x	2.9	3.1
$f(x)$	-6.08	5.92		$f(x)$	-3.88	4.12

These values confirm the following:

$$f(x) \to -\infty \text{ as } x \to -2^-, \qquad f(x) \to -\infty \text{ as } x \to 3^-$$

$$f(x) \to \infty \text{ as } x \to -2^+, \qquad f(x) \to \infty \text{ as } x \to 3^+.$$

The final graph shown in Fig. 5.17 supports these results.   ▤

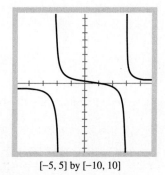

[−5, 5] by [−10, 10]

Figure 5.17

$f(x) = \dfrac{x-1}{x^2 - x - 6}.$

The solution to Example 3 follows the following guidelines for graphing rational functions.

Strategy for Graphing a Rational Function f when $n \leq m$.

1. Find the y-intercept by finding $f(0)$.
2. Find the x-intercepts by finding the zeros of the numerator. (Remember to consider symmetry.)
3. Find vertical asymptotes by finding the zeros of the denominator.
4. Find an end behavior model (Definition 5.4) for f, and identify the horizontal asymptotes.
5. Evaluate f near and on either side of each vertical asymptote.
6. Combine the information derived from Steps 1 to 5 with what you observe using a graphing utility.

E X A M P L E   4   Graphing Another Rational Function

Sketch a graph of

$$f(x) = \frac{3x^2 + x - 4}{2x^2 - 5x}.$$

Solution

y-intercept: $f(0)$ is undefined, so there is no y-intercept.

x-intercepts: $3x^2 + x - 4 = (x-1)(3x+4) = 0 \iff x = 1, x = -4/3$

Vertical asymptotes: $2x^2 - 5x = x(2x - 5) = 0 \iff x = 0, x = 5/2$

So the vertical asymptotes are the lines $x = 0$ and $x = \frac{5}{2}$. End behavior model for f: $\frac{3x^2}{2x^2} = \frac{3}{2}$. The horizontal asymptote is $y = \frac{3}{2}$.

Evaluate f for x near the vertical asymptotes to support these conclusions:

$$f(x) \to -\infty \text{ as } x \to 0^-, \qquad f(x) \to -\infty \text{ as } x \to \frac{5^-}{2}$$

$$f(x) \to \infty \text{ as } x \to 0^+, \qquad f(x) \to \infty \text{ as } x \to \frac{5^+}{2}$$

After sketching the coordinate axes and those asymptotes that are not axes, draw a smooth curve satisfying all of the information listed above (see Fig. 5.18). Support your sketch with a graphing utility. ▤

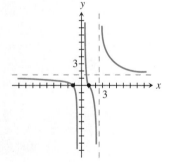

Figure 5.18
$f(x) = \dfrac{3x^2 + x - 4}{2x^2 - 5x}.$

Sketching a Graph of a Rational Function when $n > m$

So far in this section the degree of the numerator was less than or equal to the degree of the denominator. Next we consider rational functions in which the degree of the numerator is greater than the degree of the denominator. To understand the graphs of this group of rational fractions requires introducing the concept **end behavior asymptote**. Before defining this concept formally, we illustrate the process of determining the end behavior asymptote with an example. Long division is an algebraic technique that can be used to find the end behavior asymptote.

E X A M P L E 5   Finding an End Behavior Asymptote

Use long division to determine the quotient and remainder when the indicated division for

$$f(x) = \frac{2x^3 - 4x^2 + 3}{x - 2}$$

is completed.

Solution   Divide $2x^3 - 4x^2 + 3$ by $x - 2$ using long division.

$$
\begin{array}{r}
2x^2 \\
x - 2 \,\overline{)\, 2x^3 - 4x^2 + 3} \\
\underline{2x^3 - 4x^2 } \\
3
\end{array}
$$

Quotient $= 2x^2$.
Remainder $= 3$.

$f(x)$ can be written as follows:

$$f(x) = \frac{2x^3 - 4x^2 + 3}{x - 2} = 2x^2 + \frac{3}{x - 2}.$$

Notice that as $|x|$ gets larger, $|x - 2|$ also gets larger. When 3 is divided by a large number, the result is a number close to zero. To summarize,

$$\text{as } |x| \to \infty, \frac{3}{x - 2} \to 0.$$

Definition 5.5   End Behavior Asymptote

Suppose $h(x)$ and $g(x)$ are polynomial functions that are the numerator and denominator, respectively, of the rational function

$$f(x) = \frac{h(x)}{g(x)}.$$

Suppose $q(x)$ and $r(x)$ are the quotient and remainder resulting from this division and that

$$f(x) = q(x) + \frac{r(x)}{g(x)}.$$

Then the function $q(x)$ is the **end behavior asymptote of f**.

There are several points to note about this concept. The first is the distinction between end behavior model and end behavior asymptote. An end behavior *model* is found by using the leading terms of both numerator and denominator (see Definition 5.4), whereas the end behavior *asymptote* is the quotient $q(x)$ as given in Definition 5.5.

Secondly, the end behavior model and the end behavior asymptote are sometimes the same and sometimes not. In Example 5 and in the next example, the end behavior model and the end behavior asymptote of f are both $2x^2$. Example 7 will examine a function in which the end behavior model differs from the end behavior asymptote.

And third, until now all asymptotes have been defined as straight lines. For rational functions where $n \leq m$ (which we explored earlier in this section), this continues to be true: the end behavior asymptote is simply the horizontal asymptote. However, for cases where $n > m$, the end behavior asymptote may be a curve. In Examples 5 and 6, for example, it is a parabola.

Section 4.2 showed how to use zoom-out as a way of supporting a claim of an end behavior model. The same can be done for rational functions.

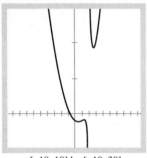

[−10, 10] by [−10, 30]

Figure 5.19
$$f(x) = \frac{2x^3 - 4x^2 + 3}{x - 2}.$$

E X A M P L E 6   Using Zoom-out to Support End Behavior

Use zoom-out to support a claim that $g(x) = 2x^2$ is an end behavior model of

$$f(x) = \frac{2x^3 - 4x^2 + 3}{x - 2}.$$

Solution   Find the graph of f in the viewing rectangle $[-10, 10]$ by $[-10, 30]$, (Fig. 5.19). There appears to be a vertical asymptote at $x = 2$, which is just as expected with a denominator of $x - 2$.

Next zoom out for the graphs of both f and $g(x) = 2x^2$ in the viewing rectangle $[-100, 100]$ by $[-1000, 1000]$ (Fig. 5.20). It is no longer possible to see that f has a vertical asymptote at $x = 2$. However, the graphs of f and g look identical, which supports the claim that $2x^2$ is the end behavior model of f. Example 5 shows that $y = 2x^2$ is an end behavior asymptote of f.   ≡

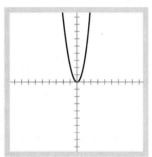

[−100, 100] by [−1000, 1000]

Figure 5.20 $g(x) = 2x^2$ and
$$f(x) = \frac{2x^3 - 4x^2 + 3}{x - 2}.$$

The information gathered about end behavior in Examples 5 and 6 can be used to complete a rough sketch of the graph of f, as shown in Fig. 5.21.

Follow these three steps.

1. Sketch a graph of $y = 2x^2$, the end behavior asymptote of f, and then erase a portion near $x = 2$.

2. Sketch the vertical asymptote $x = 2$.

3. Complete the graph using the facts that $f(x) \to \infty$ as $x \to 2^+$ and $f(x) \to -\infty$ as $x \to 2^-$.

Step 1
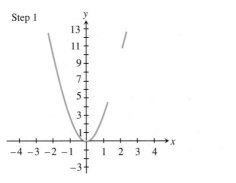

Steps 2 and 3
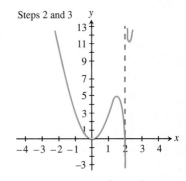

Figure 5.21   Three-step process for sketching the graph of $f(x) = \dfrac{2x^3 - 4x^2 + 3}{x - 2}$.

E X A M P L E 7   Graphing a Rational Function

Determine the end behavior asymptote, the vertical asymptotes, and sketch a complete graph of

$$f(x) = \frac{2x^3 + 7x^2 - 4}{x^2 + 2x - 3}.$$

Solution   Complete long division to find the end behavior asymptote.

$$
\begin{array}{r}
2x \ + 3 \\
x^2 + 2x - 3 \overline{\smash{\big)}\ 2x^3 + 7x^2 - 4} \\
\underline{2x^3 + 4x^2 - 6x } \\
3x^2 + 6x - 4 \\
\underline{3x^2 + 6x - 9} \\
5
\end{array}
$$

The end behavior asymptote is thus the line $y = 2x + 3$.

The vertical asymptotes are the lines $x = -3$ and $x = 1$. This claim is confirmed by the following equation:

$$x^2 + 2x - 3 = (x + 3)(x - 1).$$ Factor the denominator to look for vertical asymptotes.

To sketch the complete graph, follow the same three steps as in Example 6. Sketch a graph in which the end behavior asymptote is drawn, and then draw the vertical asymptotes (see Fig. 5.22a). Finally, use a calculator to gather the following information about the behavior of f near the vertical asymptotes:

$$f(x) \to \infty \quad \text{as } x \to -3^-, \qquad f(x) \to -\infty \quad \text{as } x \to 1^-$$
$$f(x) \to -\infty \quad \text{as } x \to -3^+, \qquad f(x) \to \infty \quad \text{as } x \to 1^+.$$

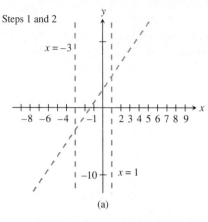

Steps 1 and 2

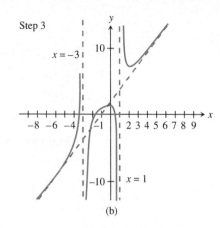

Step 3

(a)   (b)

Figure 5.22 $f(x) = \dfrac{2x^3 + 7x^2 - 4}{x^2 + 2x - 3}$.

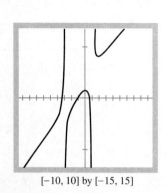

[−10, 10] by [−15, 15]

Figure 5.23

$$f(x) = \dfrac{2x^3 + 7x^2 - 4}{x^2 + 2x - 3}.$$

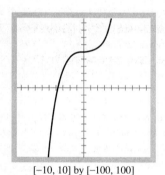

[−10, 10] by [−100, 100]

Figure 5.24 $y = x^3 - x + 50$.

Use all of the above information to complete a sketch (see Fig. 5.22b). A graphing utility graph will support your work (see Fig. 5.23).   ☰

Hidden Behavior of Rational Functions

The following rational function is more complicated than the others that have been graphed so far:

$$f(x) = \frac{2x^4 + 7x^3 + 7x^2 + 2x}{x^3 - x + 50}.$$

In particular, the zeros of the denominator cannot be found by factoring. However, a complete graph of the denominator $x^3 - x + 50$ (Fig. 5.24) shows that there is one zero; hence f has one vertical asymptote between $x = -3$ and $x = -4$.

Knowing that the denominator of f has one zero helps in understanding the complete graph of f, although Example 8 will show there are some hidden surprises. In fact, sometimes more than one viewing rectangle is needed to gain a complete understanding about the nature of the graph of a rational function.

EXAMPLE 8   Finding Hidden Behavior

IMPORTANT OBSERVATION

The theory of calculus can be used to predict where hidden behavior will occur. A graphing utility cannot predict this behavior. It must be found by an inquiring mind, as illustrated in Example 8.

Find a complete graph of

$$f(x) = \frac{2x^4 + 7x^3 + 7x^2 + 2x}{x^3 - x + 50}$$

including the hidden behavior between $x = -2$ and $x = 1$.

Solution   The end behavior model for $f(x)$ is

$$g(x) = \frac{2x^4}{x^3} = 2x.$$

This observation may contribute to a belief that the graph in figure 5.25(a) is a complete graph of f. However, this graph looks suspiciously flat around the origin. Use zoom-in to investigate the graph near the origin (Fig. 5.25b).

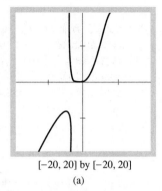

[−20, 20] by [−20, 20]

(a)

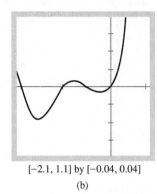

[−2.1, 1.1] by [−0.04, 0.04]

(b)

Figure 5.25 Two views of $f(x) = \dfrac{2x^4 + 7x^3 + 7x^2 + 2x}{x^3 - x + 50}$.

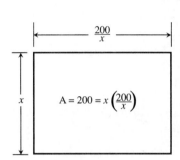

Figure 5.26 $P(x) = 2x + 400/x$.

We close this section with a problem situation that has a rational function for an algebraic model.

E X A M P L E   9   APPLICATION: Minimum Perimeter

Problem Situation   An architect might be interested in finding what shape of rectangle has the minimum perimeter for a given area. A minimum perimeter would reduce the construction cost.

Consider all rectangles with an area of 200 square feet. Let x be the width in feet of one such rectangle. Find an algebraic representation and a complete graph for $P(x)$, the perimeter as a function of x. Find the dimensions of the rectangle with the least possible perimeter.

Solution   If the width of a rectangle with an area of 200 is x feet, then its length must be $200/x$ feet (see Fig. 5.26). Then

$$P(x) = 2x + 2\left(\frac{200}{x}\right) = 2x + 400/x.$$

Notice that $y = 2x$ is the end behavior asymptote of $P(x)$, and that line $x = 0$ is a vertical asymptote of $P(x)$. A complete graph of P is shown in Fig. 5.27. Notice that only the portion of the graph for $x > 0$ applies to this problem situation. Using zoom-in the local minimum near $x = 15$ is found to be $x = 14.14$. Therefore the dimensions of a rectangle with minimum perimeter are

$$x = 14.14 \qquad \text{and} \qquad P(x) = \frac{200}{14.14} = 14.14.$$

Notice that the minimum perimeter occurs when the rectangle is a square.

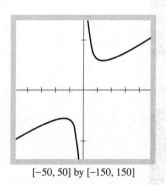

[−50, 50] by [−150, 150]

Figure 5.27 $P(x) = 2x + 400/x$.

Exercises for Section 5.2

In Exercises 1 to 8, find the domain of each function alge-braically. Support your answer with a graphing utility.

1. $f(x) = \dfrac{x^2 + 1}{x^2 - 1}$

2. $f(x) = \dfrac{x^2 - 4}{x^2 - 4x - 1}$

3. $f(x) = \dfrac{x^2 + 1}{x}$

4. $f(x) = \dfrac{x^2 - 1}{x}$

5. $f(x) = \dfrac{x^3 + 1}{x^2 - 1}$

6. $f(x) = \dfrac{x^3 - 1}{x^2 + 1}$

7. $t(x) = \dfrac{2}{2x^2 - x - 3}$

8. $P(x) = \dfrac{4x - 2}{x^2 + 5x + 8}$

In Exercises 9 to 14, find the end behavior model for each rational function.

9. $f(x) = \dfrac{x^4 - 3x^2 - 5}{x^5 - x}$

10. $f(x) = \dfrac{2x^2 + 5}{x^3 - 2x^2 + x}$

11. $f(x) = \dfrac{3x^2 - 2x + 4}{x^2 - 4x + 1}$

12. $f(x) = \dfrac{4x^2 + 2x}{x^2 - 4x + 8}$

13. $f(x) = \dfrac{x^3 - 1}{x^2 + 4}$

14. $f(x) = \dfrac{x^3 - 1}{x^2 - 4}$

In Exercises 15 to 18, use algebraic means to sketch the graph of each rational function. Find all vertical and horizontal asymptotes. Determine the end behavior model for each func-tion. Support your answer with a graphing utility.

15. $f(x) = \dfrac{2}{x - 3}$

16. $g(x) = \dfrac{x - 2}{x^2 - 2x - 3}$

17. $f(x) = \dfrac{x - 1}{x^2 + 3}$

18. $h(x) = \dfrac{3x^2 - 12}{4 - x^2}$

For Exercises 19 and 20,

$$f(x) = \frac{x - 1}{x^2 - x - 6},$$

the function from Example 3. Use a calculator to complete each of the following tables.

19.

x	-1	-10	-100	-1000	$-10,000$
$f(x)$	?	?	?	?	?

20.

x	3	2.9	2.99	2.999	2.9999
$f(x)$	?	?	?	?	?

21. Use the table in Exercise 19 to determine numerically what happens to $f(x)$ as $x \to -\infty$.

22. Use the table in Exercise 20 to determine numerically what happens to $f(x)$ as $x \to 3^-$.

In Exercises 23 to 28, find a complete graph of each function. Also find the domain, range, asymptotes, and end behavior model for each.

23. $f(x) = \dfrac{x + 1}{x^2}$

24. $f(x) = \dfrac{1}{x - 1} + \dfrac{2}{x - 3}$

25. $g(x) = \dfrac{x + 1}{x^2 - 1}$

26. $f(x) = \dfrac{x^2 + 1}{x^4 + 1} + \dfrac{2}{x - 3}$

27. $T(x) = \dfrac{x - 1}{x^2 + 3x - 1}$

28. $g(x) = \dfrac{2x}{(x - 3)(x + 2)}$

In Exercises 29 to 32, let $g(x) = 3/(x - 2)$ and

$$f(x) = 2x^2 + \frac{3}{x - 2} = \frac{2x^3 - 4x^2 + 3}{x - 2},$$

the function of Example 6. Use a calculator to complete each of the following tables.

29.

x	3	2.1	2.01	2.001	2.0001
$f(x)$	?	?	?	?	?
$g(x)$	?	?	?	?	?

30.

x	1	1.9	1.99	1.999	1.9999
$f(x)$	?	?	?	?	?
$g(x)$	?	?	?	?	?

31.

x	1	10	100	1,000	10,000
$f(x)$	?	?	?	?	?
$g(x)$	?	?	?	?	?

32.

x	-1	-10	-100	$-1,000$	$-10,000$
$f(x)$	?	?	?	?	?
$g(x)$	?	?	?	?	?

33. Use the table in Exercise 29 to determine numerically what happens to $f(x)$ as $x \to 2^+$.

34. Use the table in Exercise 30 to determine numerically what happens to $f(x)$ as $x \to 2^-$.

35. Use the table in Exercise 31 to determine numerically what happens to $f(x)$ as $x \to \infty$.

36. Use the table in Exercise 32 to determine numerically what happens to $f(x)$ as $x \to -\infty$.

In Exercises 37 to 44, use long division to find the end behavior asymptote of each function. Sketch a complete graph including all asymptotes. Support your answer with a graphing utility.

37. $f(x) = \dfrac{x^2 - 2x + 3}{x + 2}$

38. $g(x) = \dfrac{3x^2 - x + 5}{x^2 - 4}$

39. $f(x) = \dfrac{x^3 - 1}{x - 1}$

40. $h(x) = \dfrac{x^3 + 1}{x^2 + 1}$

41. $f(x) = \dfrac{x^2 - 3x - 7}{x + 3}$

42. $g(x) = \dfrac{2x^3 - 2x^2 - x + 5}{x - 2}$

43. $f(x) = \dfrac{2x^4 - x^3 - 16x^2 + 17x - 5}{2x - 5}$

44. $g(x) = \dfrac{2x^5 - 3x^3 + 2x - 4}{x - 1}$

In Exercises 45 to 50, use a graphing utility to find a complete graph of each function. Find the domain, range, asymptotes, and end behavior model for each.

45. $f(x) = \dfrac{x^2 - 2x + 5}{x + 1}$

46. $g(x) = \dfrac{x^2 - 2x + 1}{x - 2}$

47. $f(x) = \dfrac{2x^3 - x^2 + 3x - 2}{x^3 + 3}$

48. $g(x) = \dfrac{x^3 - 2x + 1}{x - 2}$

49. $f(x) = \dfrac{x^4 - 2x^2 - x + 3}{x^2 + 4}$

50. $g(x) = \dfrac{x^4 - 2x^2 - x + 3}{x^2 - 4}$

In Exercises 51 to 54, determine the intervals on which each function is increasing and the intervals on which each function is decreasing.

51. $f(x) = \dfrac{x^2 + 1}{x}$

52. $g(x) = \dfrac{2x^3 - 3x + 1}{x^2 + 4}$

53. $f(x) = \dfrac{x^3 - 2x - 1}{3x + 5}$

54. $g(x) = \dfrac{2x^3 - x^2 + 1}{2 - x}$

In Exercises 55 to 59, determine all local extrema, intervals when the function is increasing and decreasing, and all zeros of the function. Determine the end behavior model, and look for any hidden behavior.

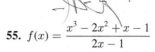

55. $f(x) = \dfrac{x^3 - 2x^2 + x - 1}{2x - 1}$

56. $f(x) = \dfrac{2x^3 + x^2 - 24x - 12}{x^2 + x - 12}$

57. $f(x) = \dfrac{2x^4 + 3x^3 + x^2 + 2}{x^3 - x^2 + 20}$

58. $f(x) = \dfrac{x^3 + 1}{x}$

59. $g(x) = \dfrac{2x^4 - 2x^2 + x + 5}{x^2 - 3x - 4}$

60. Let $f(x) = \dfrac{2x^4 - 3x^2 + 1}{3x^4 - x^2 + x - 1}$. Find the graph of f in the standard viewing rectangle. Is a vertical asymptote apparent? Now find the graph in the $[-0.5, 1.0]$ by $[-1.5, 1.5]$ viewing rectangle. What changes do you see?

61. Use zoom-out to find the end behavior model for
$$f(x) = \dfrac{3x^5 - 2x^4 + 3x^2 + 5x - 6}{x^2 - 3x + 6},$$
and find the end behavior asymptote of f.

62. Consider all the rectangles with an area of 182 square units. Let x be the width of one such rectangle. Find an algebraic representation and a complete graph of $P(x)$, the perimeter as a function of x. Find the dimensions of a rectangle that has the least possible perimeter.

63. Consider all rectangles with an area of 375 square feet. Let x be the width of such a rectangle. Find an algebraic representation and a complete graph of $P(x)$, the perimeter as a function of x. Find the dimensions of a rectangle that has the least possible perimeter.

64. Consider the following **problem situation**: Pure acid is added to 78 ounces of a 63% acid solution. Let x be the amount (in ounces) of pure acid added. Find an algebraic representation for $C(x)$, the concentration of acid as a function of x, and find a complete graph of this problem situation on a graphing utility. Use this graph to determine how much pure acid should be added to the 63% solution to produce a new mixture that is at least 83% acid.

65. A certain amount x of a 100% pure barium solution is added to 135 ounces of a 35% barium solution to obtain a 63% barium solution. Use a graphing utility graph and zoom in to determine x.

5.3 _____ Equations and Inequalities with Rational Functions

This section uses both graphical and algebraic techniques to solve equations and inequalities that involve rational functions. We shall also investigate problem situations that have such equations and inequalities as models.

E X A M P L E 1   APPLICATION: Time-Rate Problem

A Problem Situation   Sue drove 30 miles to a train station and then completed her trip by train. In all she traveled 120 miles. The average rate of the train was 20 mph faster than the average rate of the car.

Find an algebraic representation that gives the total time T required to complete the trip as a function of the rate x of the car.

Solution   Choose variables as suggested by Fig. 5.28.

$$t_1 = \text{time in hours to travel distance } d_1 = 30 \text{ miles}$$

$$t_2 = \text{time in hours to travel distance } d_2 = 90 \text{ miles}$$

$$t_1 + t_2 = \text{total time in hours to travel the 120 miles}$$

$$d = rt \quad \text{Remember that } r \text{ represents average rate.}$$

Let x be the average rate in mph of the car; then $x + 20$ is the average rate of the train.

$$d_1 = xt_1 \quad \text{and} \quad d_2 = (x + 20)t_2$$

$$\frac{d_1}{x} = t_1 \quad \text{and} \quad \frac{d_2}{x + 20} = t_2$$

$$T(x) = t_1 + t_2 = \frac{d_1}{x} + \frac{d_2}{x + 20}$$

$$T(x) = \frac{30}{x} + \frac{90}{x + 20}$$

> **TIME-RATE PROBLEMS**
>
> A time-rate problem involves an object that moves a certain distance (d) at a certain average rate (r) for a certain period of time (t). The equation relating these variables is: $d = rt$.

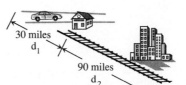

30 miles
d_1

90 miles
d_2

Figure 5.28   Diagram for Example 1.

E X A M P L E   2   Analyzing an Algebraic Representation

Find the real zeros, the vertical asymptotes, and the end behavior model for

$$T(x) = \frac{30}{x} + \frac{90}{x + 20}.$$

Also determine a complete graph.

Solution   First rewrite $T(x)$ by finding a common denominator.

$$
\begin{aligned}
T(x) &= \frac{30}{x} + \frac{90}{x + 20} \\
&= \frac{30(x + 20) + 90x}{x(x + 20)} \\
&= \frac{120x + 600}{x(x + 20)}
\end{aligned}
$$

The vertical asymptotes are thus $x = 0$ and $x = -20$. To find the x-intercept, determine where the numerator is zero.

$$120x + 600 = 0 \iff x = \frac{-600}{120} = -5$$

A rational function is zero only when the numerator is zero provided the denominator is not zero for the same value.

The end behavior model is

$$y = \frac{120x}{x^2} = \frac{120}{x},$$

and the horizontal asymptote is $y = 0$.

All of this information is combined in the complete graph shown in Fig. 5.29.

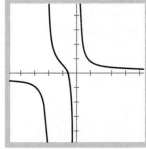

[−50, 50] by [−50, 50]

Figure 5.29
$$T(x) = \frac{120x + 600}{x(x + 20)}.$$

With this analysis of the time-rate problem situation, we are ready to solve the following problem.

E X A M P L E   3   Solving the Time-Rate Problem

Sue has 2 hours to complete the 120-mile trip described in Example 1. Use both a graphical and an algebraic method to find the rate she must travel by car.

Solution   Examples 1 and 2 showed that

$$T(x) = \frac{30}{x} + \frac{90}{x + 20} = \frac{120x + 600}{x(x + 20)}.$$

We need to find a value of x such that $T(x) = 2$.

Graphical Method   Figure 5.30 shows a graphical representation of the problem situation together with the line $y = 2$. Use zoom-in to show that the x-coordinate

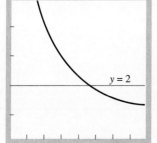

[0, 80] by [0, 5]

Figure 5.30
$$T(x) = \frac{120x + 600}{x(x + 20)}.$$

of the point of intersection is $x = 46.46$ with an error of at most 0.01. This is the value of x that solves the problem.

Algebraic Method   Solve the equation:

$$\frac{120x + 600}{x(x + 20)} = 2.$$

Begin by multiplying both sides of the equation by $x(x + 20)$ and simplifying.

$$120x + 600 = 2x(x + 20)$$

$$120x + 600 = 2x^2 + 40x$$

$$0 = 2x^2 - 80x - 600$$

$$0 = x^2 - 40x - 300$$

Use the quadratic formula to get

$$x = 20 + 10\sqrt{7} \qquad \text{and} \qquad x = 20 - 10\sqrt{7}.$$

Since $x = 20 - 10\sqrt{7}$ is a negative number, the only solution relevant to the problem situation is $20 + 10\sqrt{7} = 46.46$. Sue must travel an average of 46.46 mph. ▤

Analysis of This Algebraic Solution

In the algebraic solution to the problem in Example 3, both sides of the original equation were multiplied by an expression containing the variable x. Whenever this is done, the resulting equation may not be equivalent to the original equation. That is, there may be solutions to the resulting equation that were not solutions to the original equation.

Any solution to the resulting equation that is not a solution of the original equation is called an **extraneous solution.**

Consider the following simple example:

$$x - 1 = 0. \quad \text{This equation has one solution: } x = 1.$$

Multiply both sides of the equation by x:

$$x(x - 1) = x \cdot 0 = 0. \quad \text{This equation has two solutions, } x = 0 \text{ and } x = 1.$$

So $x = 0$ is an extraneous solution to the original equation $x - 1 = 0$.

Equation-solving Principle

When each side of an equation is multiplied by an expression containing the variable, each solution of the resulting equation must be checked to make sure it is a solution of the original equation.

E X A M P L E   4   Solving a Rational Equation

Solve the following rational equation for x: $\dfrac{2x}{x-1} + \dfrac{1}{x-3} = \dfrac{2}{x^2 - 4x + 3}$.

Solution

Algebraic Method   Notice that $x^2 - 4x + 3 = (x-1)(x-3)$. Thus the least common denominator of the three fractions in the equation is $(x-1)(x-3)$. Multiply both sides of the equation by this common denominator:

$$(x-1)(x-3)\left[\frac{2x}{x-1} + \frac{1}{x-3}\right] = (x-1)(x-3)\frac{2}{x^2 - 4x + 3}$$

$$\frac{2x(x-1)(x-3)}{x-1} + \frac{(x-1)(x-3)}{x-3} = \frac{2(x-1)(x-3)}{x^2 - 4x + 3} \qquad \text{Distributive property}$$

$$2x(x-3) + (x-1) = 2 \qquad \begin{array}{l}\text{Simplify numerator}\\ \text{and denominator}\\ \text{that have equal factors.}\end{array}$$

$$2x^2 - 6x + x - 1 = 2$$

$$2x^2 - 5x - 3 = 0$$

$$(2x + 1)(x - 3) = 0$$

$$x = 3, \qquad x = -\frac{1}{2}$$

Check each solution: Substitute $x = 3$ and $x = -\frac{1}{2}$ into the original equation.

$$\frac{2(3)}{3-1} + \frac{1}{3-3} \neq \frac{2}{3^2 - 4\cdot(3) + 3} \qquad \begin{array}{l}\text{These expressions are not defined}\\ \text{because they involve division by zero.}\end{array}$$

$$\frac{2(-\frac{1}{2})}{(-\frac{1}{2})-1} + \frac{1}{(-\frac{1}{2})-3} = \frac{2}{(-\frac{1}{2})^2 - 4(-\frac{1}{2}) + 3}$$

$$\frac{8}{21} = \frac{8}{21}$$

So we see that $x = 3$ is not a solution whereas $x = -\frac{1}{2}$ is a solution.

Graphical Method   Solve the equation graphically by finding the zeros of the function

$$f(x) = \frac{2x}{x-1} + \frac{1}{x-3} - \frac{2}{x^2 - 4x + 3}.$$

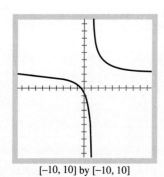

[−10, 10] by [−10, 10]

Figure 5.31 $f(x) = \dfrac{2x}{x-1} + \dfrac{1}{x-3} - \dfrac{2}{x^2 - 4x + 3}$.

A complete graph of f that supports the $-\frac{1}{2}$ solution found algebraically appears in Fig. 5.31. Notice that line $x = 3$ is not a vertical asymptote even though the function is not defined for $x = 3$. We see why this is true algebraically by combining the three fractions of f to show that:

$$f(x) = \frac{2x^2 - 5x - 3}{(x-1)(x-3)} = \frac{(2x+1)(x-3)}{(x-1)(x-3)}$$

So, f has a removeable discontinuity at $x = 3$.

The next example illustrates that *all* solutions of a rational equation may turn out to be extraneous solutions.

E X A M P L E   5   Solving a Rational Equation

Find an algebraic solution to the equation

$$\frac{x-3}{x} + \frac{3}{x+2} + \frac{6}{x^2 + 2x} = 0.$$

Solution   Multiply both sides of the equation by the least common denominator of $x(x+2)$, and simplify.

$$\frac{x-3}{x} + \frac{3}{x+2} + \frac{6}{x^2+2x} = 0$$

$$(x-3)(x+2) + 3x + 6 = 0$$

$$x^2 - x - 6 + 3x + 6 = 0$$

$$x^2 + 2x = 0$$

$$x(x+2) = 0$$

$$x = 0, \qquad x = -2$$

Notice that neither of these solutions is a solution of the original equation since both values result in division by zero.

Knowing that multiplying both sides of an equation sometimes introduces extraneous solutions, we return to the problem of Sue's trip by car and train.

E X A M P L E   6   APPLICATION: Time-Rate Problem Revisited

At what possible rates could Sue travel by car to be sure that the total time for her to complete the trip is less than 2.5 hours?

Solution   We must find the positive values of x for which $T(x) < 2.5$, where

$$T(x) = \frac{30}{x} + \frac{90}{x+20}.$$

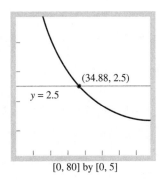

[0, 80] by [0, 5]

Figure 5.32
$$T(x) = \frac{30}{x} + \frac{90}{x + 20}$$
and $y = 2.5$.

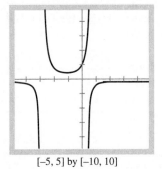

[−5, 5] by [−10, 10]

Figure 5.33
$$f(x) = \frac{2x^2 + 6x - 8}{2x^2 + 5x - 3} - 1.$$

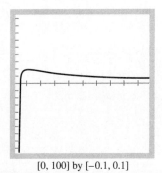

[0, 100] by [−0.1, 0.1]

Figure 5.34
$$f(x) = \frac{2x^2 + 6x - 8}{2x^2 + 5x - 3} - 1.$$

Figure 5.32 shows a graph of the line $y = 2.5$ and the complete graph of Sue's trip. To solve the inequality $T < 2.5$, find the positive values of x for which the graph of T lies *below* the graph of $y = 2.5$.

Use zoom-in to find that the coordinates of the point of intersection are $(34.88, 2.5)$ with an error of at most 0.01. Therefore the graph of $T(x)$ lies below the line $y = 2.5$ when $x > 34.88$.

So Sue must travel at an average speed greater than 34.88 mph to complete her trip in time. ≡

We have seen in Examples 3 and 4 that equations involving rational expressions can often be solved by either algebraic or graphical methods. This is also true for inequalities involving rational expressions.

The next example illustrates that the graphical method, which is a more general method, also has the potential to hide information.

E X A M P L E 7 Solving a Rational Inequality

Use both graphical and algebraic methods to solve

$$\frac{2x^2 + 6x - 8}{2x^2 + 5x - 3} < 1.$$

Solution

Graphical Method Begin by graphing

$$f(x) = \frac{2x^2 + 6x - 8}{2x^2 + 5x - 3} - 1$$

in a standard viewing rectangle (Fig. 5.33). Notice that f has vertical asymptotes at $x = -3$ and $x = \frac{1}{2}$, which can be confirmed algebraically by factoring the denominator $2x^2 + 5x - 3 = (2x - 1)(x + 3)$.

It appears that the graph is below the x-axis over the interval $(-\infty, -3)$. We might be tempted to conclude the same for when x is positive. However, there is hidden behavior for $x > 0$.

To see this, it is necessary to zoom in along the y-axis where $x > 0$. Figure 5.34 shows the graph in the viewing rectangle $[0, 100]$ by $[-0.1, 0.1]$. In this viewing rectangle it becomes clear that the graph of f crosses the x-axis at $x = 5$. Thus the interval $(\frac{1}{2}, 5)$ is part of the solution.

Algebraic Method In Fig. 5.34 the graph appears to be below the x-axis when $0 < x < 5$. However, this is not correct because there is a vertical asymptote at $x = \frac{1}{2}$.

To proceed with an algebraic solution to the inequality, subtract 1 from each side of the inequality, combine terms, and simplify:

$$\frac{2x^2 + 6x - 8}{2x^2 + 5x - 3} - 1 < 0$$

$$\frac{2x^2 + 6x - 8}{2x^2 + 5x - 3} - \frac{2x^2 + 5x - 3}{2x^2 + 5x - 3} < 0 \qquad \text{Find a common denominator}$$
and subtract.

$$\frac{2x^2 + 6x - 8 - 2x^2 - 5x + 3}{2x^2 + 5x - 3} < 0$$

$$\frac{x - 5}{2x^2 + 5x - 3} < 0 \qquad \text{Simplify the numerator.}$$

$$\frac{x - 5}{(2x - 1)(x + 3)} < 0. \qquad \text{Factor the denominator.}$$

Since the numerator and denominator polynomials can be factored, a sign-pattern method can be used for solving this inequality.

We see that the three linear factors are zero for $x = 5, x = \frac{1}{2}$, and $x = -3$. These three numbers divide the real number line into four intervals, as shown in the following sign-pattern pictures. Each of the three factors $(x - 5), (2x - 1)$, and $(x + 3)$ is either positive or negative throughout each interval.

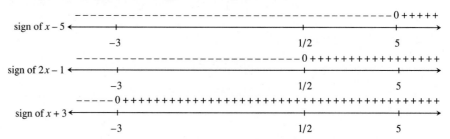

Since $f(x) < 0$ when an odd number of factors is negative (in this case all three factors or only one), the complete solution to

$$f(x) = \frac{2x^2 + 6x - 8}{2x^2 + 5x - 3} - 1 < 0$$

is $(-\infty, -3) \cup (\frac{1}{2}, 5)$. A graphical analysis supports this solution.   ▤

That the graphical method is more general than the algebraic method is underscored with the last example.

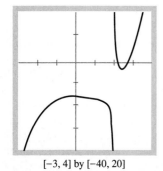

[−3, 4] by [−40, 20]

Figure 5.35   A complete graph of $f(x) = \dfrac{x^4 - 3x^3 + 2x^2 + 2}{x - 2} - 15.$

E X A M P L E   8   *Solving Another Rational Inequality*

Solve the following inequality for x:

$$\frac{x^4 - 3x^3 + 2x^2 + 2}{x - 2} \geq 15.$$

Solution Find a complete graph of

$$f(x) = \frac{x^4 - 3x^3 + 2x^2 + 2}{x - 2} - 15.$$

See Fig. 5.35. Look for values of x corresponding to where the graph of f lies above the x-axis. Note from the denominator of f that $x = 2$ is a vertical asymptote.

Use zoom-in to determine that the two x-intercepts are 2.223 and 2.679 with an error of at most 0.01.

The solution to the inequality is $(2, 2.223] \cup [2.679, \infty)$.   ▤

Exercises for Section 5.3

In Exercises 1 to 10, solve each equation algebraically. Support your answer with a graphing utility.

1. $\dfrac{x - 1}{x + 2} = 3$

2. $\dfrac{2}{x - 1} + x = 5$

3. $\dfrac{1}{x} - \dfrac{2}{x - 3} = 4$

4. $\dfrac{3}{x - 1} + \dfrac{2}{x} = 8$

5. $\dfrac{x^2 - 2x + 1}{x + 5} = 0$

6. $\dfrac{x^2 - 6x + 5}{x^2 - 2} = 3$

7. $\dfrac{x^3 - x}{x^2 + 1} = 0$

8. $\dfrac{2x^4 + x^2 - 1}{x^2 - 9} = 0$

9. $\dfrac{3x}{x + 2} + \dfrac{2}{x - 1} = \dfrac{5}{x^2 + x - 2}$

10. $\dfrac{x - 3}{x} - \dfrac{3}{x + 1} + \dfrac{3}{x^2 + x} = 0$

In Exercises 11 to 19, solve each inequality algebraically using the sign-pattern picture method. Support your answer with a graphing utility.

11. $\dfrac{1}{x - 3} + 4 > 0$

12. $\dfrac{x - 3}{x + 5} - 6 \le 3$

13. $\dfrac{x + 3}{2x - 7} < 5$

14. $\dfrac{x - 1}{x + 4} < 0$

15. $\dfrac{x - 1}{x + 4} > 3$

16. $\dfrac{x - 1}{x^2 - 4} < 0$

17. $\dfrac{x^2 - 1}{x^2 + 1} \ge 0$

18. $\dfrac{x^2 - 3x - 2}{x^2 - 4x + 4} \le 0$

19. $\dfrac{x^2 - x + 1}{x + 2} < 3$

In Exercises 20 to 23, solve the equation or the inequality.

20. $\dfrac{x^4 - 2x^2 - 3}{x^2 - 5} = -3$

21. $\dfrac{x^6 - x^4 + x^3 - 2x - 4}{x^2 - 2x + 1} = 5$

22. $\dfrac{x^5 - 2x^2 + 4}{x^3 + 5} < 3$

23. $\dfrac{x^4 - 3x^2 + 4x - 2}{x - 3} \ge 2$

In Exercises 24 to 27, find the zeros, y-intercepts, vertical asymptotes, and end behavior asymptotes of each rational function. Find a complete graph that shows all of this behavior. (More than one viewing rectangle may be needed.)

24. $f(x) = \dfrac{x^3 - 2x + 3}{x^2 - x + 4}$

25. $f(x) = \dfrac{x^4 - 2x^2 + 1}{x^2 + x - 1}$

26. $f(x) = \dfrac{x^4 - 2x^3 + 3x^2 + x - 4}{x^2 - 5x + 4}$

27. $f(x) = \dfrac{x^5 - x^3 + x - 5}{x^2 - 3x - 1}$

Exercises 28 to 31 refer to the following **problem situation**: Josh rode his bike 17 miles from his home to Columbus, Ohio, and then completed a 53-mile trip by car from Columbus to Mansfield. Assume the average rate of the car was 43 mph faster than the average rate of the bike.

28. Find an algebraic representation for the total time T required to complete the 70-mile trip (bike and car) as a function of the average rate x of the bike.

29. Find a complete graph of the algebraic representation of this problem situation indicating any vertical and horizontal asymptotes and any zeros.

30. Make a complete graph of this problem situation, showing only the values of x that make sense in this problem situation.

31. Use a graphical method to find the rate of the bike if the total time of the trip was 1 hour and 40 minutes.

Exercises 32 to 34 refer to the following **problem situation**: Drains A and B are used to empty a swimming pool. Drain A alone can empty the pool in 4.75 hours. Let t be the time it takes for drain B alone to empty the pool. (Assume the pool drains at a constant rate.)

32. Find an algebraic representation that gives the part of the drainage that can be done in 1 hour with both drains open at the same time as a function of t.

33. Find a complete graph of this problem situation.

34. Use a graphical method to find the time it takes for drain B alone to empty the pool if both drains, when open at the same time, can empty the pool in 2.60 hours.

Exercises 35 to 37 refer to the following **problem situation**: The total electrical resistance R of two resistors connected in parallel with resistance R_1 and R_2 is given by

$$R = \frac{R_1 R_2}{R_1 + R_2}.$$

One resistor has a resistance of 2.3 ohms. Let x be the resistance of the second resistor.

35. Find an algebraic representation for $R(x)$, the total resistance of the pair of resistors connected in parallel.

36. Draw a complete graph of this problem situation.

37. Use a graphical method to find the resistance of the second resistor if the total resistance of the pair is 1.7 ohms.

Exercises 38 to 40 refer to the following **problem situation**: A cylindrical soda-pop can of radius r and height h is to hold exactly 355 ml (milliliters) of liquid when completely full. A manufacturer wishes to find the dimensions of the can with the minimum surface area.

For Exercises 38 to 40

38. Find the algebraic representation for the surface area S as a function of r. (*Hint*: Show that the surface area of the can is $S = 2\pi r^2 + 2\pi rh$. Then use the fact that the volume of the can is $355 = \pi r^2 h$.)

39. What are the restrictions on r for this problem situation? Find a complete graph of this problem situation.

40. Use zoom-in to determine the radius r and height h that yield a can of minimal surface area. What is the minimal surface area?

Exercises 41 to 43 refer to the following **problem situation**: A single-story house with a rectangular base is to contain 900 square feet of living area. Local building codes require that both the length L and the width W of the base of the house be greater than 20 feet. To minimize the cost of the foundation, the builder wants to minimize the perimeter of the foundation.

For Exercises 41 to 43

41. Find an algebraic representation for the perimeter P as a function of L, the length of the base.

42. Find a complete graph of this problem situation showing only the values of L that make sense.

43. Use a graphical method to find the value of L that minimizes the perimeter. What is the minimum perimeter?

5.4 _____ Radical Functions

In this section we investigate the graphs of functions that involve radicals, for example,

$$y = \sqrt{x - 2} \quad \text{and} \quad y = \sqrt[3]{x^2 - 1} + x.$$

Before proceeding further it will be useful to review what the radical symbol means.

Radical Symbol

Recall from Chapters 1 and 2 that any expression of the form $\sqrt[n]{a}$, where n is an integer greater than 1, is called a radical. The integer n is the **index** of the radical, and a is the **radicand**. The symbol $\sqrt{}$ is the **radical sign**. If no index appears over the radical sign, n is understood to equal 2.

Radical expressions can also be written using fractional exponents, as illustrated by the following expressions:

$$\sqrt{x - 2} = (x - 2)^{1/2}, \qquad \sqrt[3]{x^2 - 1} = (x^2 - 1)^{1/3}, \qquad \sqrt[5]{x^4} = x^{4/5}.$$

We restate more formally what the radical symbol means.

Definition 5.6   Radical Symbol

Let n be an integer greater than 1 and let a be a real number. Then the **principal nth root of a**, denoted $\sqrt[n]{a}$, is:

1. The real solution to $x^n = a$, if n is odd;
2. The nonnegative real solution to $x^n = a$, if n is even and $a \geq 0$.

When n is even, a must be nonnegative because an even power of x is always a nonnegative number.

$\sqrt{a}$ is the principal square root, and $\sqrt[3]{a}$ is the principal cube root of a.

🔍 **EXPLORE WITH A CALCULATOR**

What happens when you find the root of a number? Is the root larger or smaller than the number? Use a calculator to complete the following table of values:

x	0.5	0.9	0.99	1	1.01	1.1
$\sqrt{x}$						
$\sqrt[3]{x}$						
$\sqrt[4]{x}$						
$\sqrt[5]{x}$						

Complete a Generalization   For what values of x is the root of x larger than x? For what values of x is the root of x smaller than x?

Graphs of $y = \sqrt[n]{x}$ When n Is Even

You discovered in the above Exploration that when $0 < x < 1$, $\sqrt[n]{x}$ is larger than x, and that when $x > 1$, $\sqrt[n]{x}$ is smaller than x. What impact does this observation have on the graphs of $y = \sqrt[n]{x}$?

E X A M P L E   1   Comparing Graphs of Radical Functions

Find and compare complete graphs of $y = \sqrt{x}$, $y = \sqrt[4]{x}$, and $y = \sqrt[6]{x}$. Determine the domain and range of each function.

Solution   The domain of each function is $[0, \infty)$. The graphs of all three functions are seen using viewing rectangle $[-5, 30]$ by $[-5, 10]$ (Fig. 5.36a). These graphs appear to overlap near the origin. Choose the smaller viewing rectangle shown in Fig. 5.36(b) to investigate the detail near the origin.

The range of each function is the interval $[0, \infty)$.   ▤

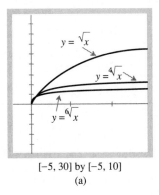

[−5, 30] by [−5, 10]

(a)

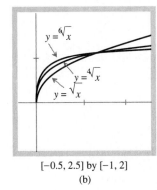

[−0.5, 2.5] by [−1, 2]

(b)

Figure 5.36 Three radical functions with even indexes.

Figure 5.36 suggests the following summarizing points about the graphs of radical functions with even indexes:

- Points common to all graphs: $(0, 0)$ and $(1, 1)$.
- For values of x in the interval $(0, 1)$, the graph of $y = \sqrt{x}$ lies below the graph of $y = \sqrt[4]{x}$, which in turn lies below the graph of $y = \sqrt[6]{x}$. That is

$$\sqrt{x} < \sqrt[4]{x} < \sqrt[6]{x} < \cdots < \sqrt[2n]{x} \qquad (0 < x < 1).$$

- For values of x in interval $(1, \infty)$, the graph of $y = \sqrt{x}$ lies above the graph of $y = \sqrt[4]{x}$, which in turn falls above the graph of $y = \sqrt[6]{x}$. That is,

$$\sqrt{x} > \sqrt[4]{x} > \sqrt[6]{x} > \cdots > \sqrt[2n]{x} \qquad (x > 1).$$

- The domain of each function is $[0, \infty)$.
- The range of each function is $[0, \infty)$. On some graphing utilities the range may appear to be $[a, \infty)$ for some $a > 0$ because of the steepness of the graph near the origin.

Graphs of $y = \sqrt[n]{x}$ When n is Odd

We begin with an example that compares the graphs of radical functions with odd indexes.

E X A M P L E 2   *Comparing Graphs of Radical Functions*

Find and compare complete graphs of $y = \sqrt[3]{x}$, $y = \sqrt[5]{x}$, and $y = \sqrt[7]{x}$. Determine the domain and range of each function.

Solution   All domains are $(-\infty, \infty)$. All ranges as observed from the graphs in Fig. 5.37 are also $(-\infty, \infty)$.

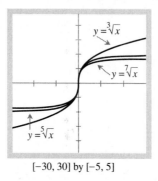

[−30, 30] by [−5, 5]

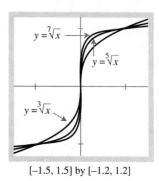

[−1.5, 1.5] by [−1.2, 1.2]

Figure 5.37   Three radical functions with odd indexes.

Both the domain and range for all these functions is $(-\infty, \infty)$. Figure 5.37 suggests the following summarizing points about radical functions with odd indexes:

- Points common to all graphs: $(-1, -1), (0, 0)$, and $(1, 1)$.
- For values of x in the interval $(-\infty, -1) \cup (0, 1)$, the graph of $\sqrt[3]{x}$ lies below the graph of $\sqrt[5]{x}$, which in turn is below the graph of $\sqrt[7]{x}$. That is,

$$\sqrt[3]{x} < \sqrt[5]{x} < \sqrt[7]{x} < \cdots < \sqrt[2n+1]{x} \qquad (x < -1 \text{ or } 0 < x < 1).$$

- For values of x in the interval $(-1, 0) \cup (1, \infty)$, the graph of $\sqrt[3]{x}$ falls above the graph of $\sqrt[5]{x}$, which is above the graph of $\sqrt[7]{x}$. That is,

$$\sqrt[3]{x} > \sqrt[5]{x} > \sqrt[7]{x} > \cdots > \sqrt[2n+1]{x} \qquad (-1 < x < 0 \text{ or } x > 1).$$

Transformations of $y = \sqrt[n]{x}$

In earlier sections of this text we graphically transformed $y = x^2$ into the graph of $f(x) = 2(x - 3)^2 - 4$, and the graph of $y = 1/x$ into the graph of $f(x) = 1/(x + 3) - 2$.

In a similar spirit, in this section we examine how the graph of $y = a\sqrt[n]{bx + c} + d$ can be obtained from the graph of $y = \sqrt[n]{x}$. As before, the answer involves transformations of vertical and horizontal shifts and stretches and reflection through the x- or y-axis.

E X A M P L E   3   Using Transformations with Radicals

Explain how to sketch each of the following functions from the graph of $f(x) = \sqrt{x}$ using transformations: (a) $g(x) = \sqrt{x - 2}$, (b) $h(x) = \sqrt{x + 3}$, and (c) $k(x) = \sqrt{3 - x}$.

Solution   See Fig. 5.38.

a) $g(x) = \sqrt{x-2} = f(x-2)$ A horizontal shift 2 units right

b) $h(x) = \sqrt{x+3} = f(x+3)$ A horizontal shift 3 units left

c) $k(x) = \sqrt{(3-x)} = \sqrt{-(x-3)}$

$\qquad\qquad = f(-(x-3))$ A reflection through the y-axis followed by a horizontal shift 3 units right

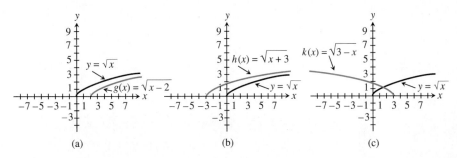

(a)   (b)   (c)

Figure 5.38   Transformations applied to the graph of $y = \sqrt{x}$.

Applying Transformations to $y = \sqrt[n]{x}$

It can be shown that the graph of any radical function of the form

$$y = a\sqrt[n]{bx+c} + d$$

can be obtained by applying transformations to the graph of $y = \sqrt[n]{x}$.

Knowing that the graph of $f(x) = a\sqrt[n]{bx+c}+d$ can be obtained as the result of transformations applied to the graph of $y = \sqrt[n]{x}$ tells us what the overall shape of f is going to be. The location and general orientation of the graph of f can be found by plotting two or three points. When doing so, always be careful to include the point of $f(x) = a\sqrt[n]{bx+c}+d$ that corresponds to the point $(0,0)$ of $y = \sqrt[n]{x}$. Examples 4 and 5 illustrate this method.

E X A M P L E   4   Sketching a Graph by Plotting Several Points

Sketch a complete graph of $f(x) = 2\sqrt[3]{3-2x}+1$.

Solution   If $x = \frac{3}{2}$, then $\sqrt[3]{3-2x} = 0$. Therefore $f\left(\frac{3}{2}\right) = 1$. So the point $\left(\frac{3}{2}, 1\right)$ corresponds to the point $(0,0)$ of $y = \sqrt[3]{x}$ under the transformations that convert $y = \sqrt[3]{x}$ to $f(x) = 2\sqrt[3]{3-2x}+1$.

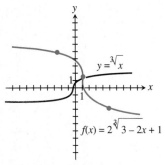

Figure 5.39 $f(x) = 2\sqrt[3]{3-2x} + 1.$

Find a point on the graph of f to the left and to the right of $\left(\frac{3}{2}, 1\right)$.

$$f\left(\frac{11}{2}\right) = 2\sqrt[3]{3-(11)} + 1 \qquad f\left(-\frac{5}{2}\right) = 2\sqrt[3]{3-(-5)} + 1$$

$$= 2\sqrt[3]{-8} + 1 \qquad\qquad\qquad = 2\sqrt[3]{8} + 1$$

$$= -4 + 1 = -3 \qquad\qquad\qquad = 4 + 1 = 5$$

Points $\left(\frac{11}{2}, -3\right)$ and $\left(-\frac{5}{2}, 5\right)$ are on the graph of f. These three points are sufficient to determine the graph of f (see Fig. 5.39). ≡

E X A M P L E   5   Sketching a Graph by Plotting Two Points

Sketch a complete graph of $f(x) = 3\sqrt[4]{4 - 3x} - 2$.

Solution   If $x = \frac{4}{3}$, then $\sqrt[4]{4-3x} = 0$. Therefore $f\left(\frac{4}{3}\right) = -2$. So the point $\left(\frac{4}{3}, -2\right)$ corresponds to the point $(0,0)$ of $y = \sqrt[4]{x}$ under the transformations that convert $y = \sqrt[4]{x}$ to $f(x) = 3\sqrt[4]{4-3x} - 2$.

$$f(-4) = 3\sqrt[4]{4 - (-12)} - 2$$

$$= 3\sqrt[4]{16} - 2$$

$$= 6 - 2 = 4$$

Thus the points $(-4, 4)$ and $\left(\frac{4}{3}, -2\right)$ are on the graph of f. A complete graph is shown in Fig. 5.40. ≡

Solving Equations and Inequalities Involving Radicals

As before, you can sometimes use either a graphical or an algebraic method to solve an equation that involves a radical.

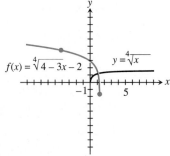

Figure 5.40 $f(x) = 3\sqrt[4]{4 - 3x} - 2$.

E X A M P L E   6   Solving an Equation Involving a Square Root

A real number plus its principal square root equals 1. Find all such numbers using both a graphical and an algebraic method.

Solution   If x is such a number, then $x + \sqrt{x} = 1$. To find all solutions to this equation, begin with the graphical method since it is easier.

Graphical Method   Find a complete graph of $y = x + \sqrt{x}$ and $y = 1$ (Fig. 5.41). We see that there is exactly one solution, and it is between 0 and 1. Use zoom-in to find that the solution is $x = 0.38$ with an error of at most 0.01.

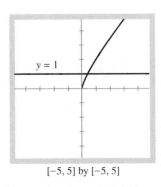

[−5, 5] by [−5, 5]

Figure 5.41 $y = x + \sqrt{x}$ and $y = 1$.

Algebraic Method

$$x + \sqrt{x} = 1$$

$$\sqrt{x} = 1 - x \qquad \text{Isolate the radical on one side of the equation and then square each side of the equation.}$$

$$x = 1 - 2x + x^2 \qquad \text{Squaring both sides may introduce extraneous solutions.}$$

$$0 = x^2 - 3x + 1 \qquad \text{This equation is not equivalent to the original equation.}$$

$$x = \frac{3 + \sqrt{5}}{2} = 2.62 \quad \text{and} \quad x = \frac{3 - \sqrt{5}}{2} = 0.38$$

Check each of these solutions to see if they are also solutions of the original equation.

$$2.62 + \sqrt{2.62} = 4.24 \qquad \text{2.62 is not a solution.}$$

$$0.38 + \sqrt{0.38} = 1.00 \qquad\qquad\qquad\qquad \blacksquare$$

E X A M P L E   7   Solving an Equation Involving Square Root

Find all real numbers that are solutions to $\sqrt{6x + 12} - \sqrt{4x + 9} = 1$ using both graphical and algebraic methods.

Solution

Graphical Method   Find the x-intercepts of a complete graph of $f(x) = \sqrt{6x + 12} - \sqrt{4x + 9} - 1$ (see Fig. 5.42). It appears that $x = 4$ is the only solution.

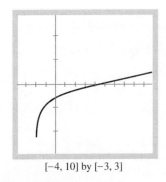

[−4, 10] by [−3, 3]

Figure 5.42 $f(x) = \sqrt{6x + 12} - \sqrt{4x + 9} - 1$.

Algebraic Method

$$\sqrt{6x + 12} - \sqrt{4x + 9} = 1$$

$$\sqrt{6x + 12} = \sqrt{4x + 9} + 1 \qquad \text{Prepare to square both sides of the equation.}$$

$$6x + 12 = 4x + 9 + 2\sqrt{4x + 9} + 1 \qquad \text{Square both sides.}$$

$$2x + 2 = 2\sqrt{4x + 9}$$

Collect terms and simplify.

$$x + 1 = \sqrt{4x + 9}$$

$$x^2 + 2x + 1 = 4x + 9$$

Square both sides of the equation a second time.

$$x^2 - 2x - 8 = 0$$

$$(x - 4)(x + 2) = 0$$

So $x = 4$ or $x = -2$. Checking for extraneous solutions shows that $x = 4$ is a solution whereas $x = -2$ is not.

If radicals other than square roots are involved, then an algebraic solution requires that each side of the equation be raised to higher powers.

E X A M P L E   8   A Radical with an Index Greater Than 2

Find all real numbers x that are solutions to $\sqrt[3]{x^2 - 2x + 2} = x$.

Solution

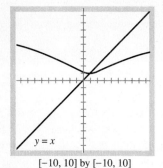

$y = x$

$[-10, 10]$ by $[-10, 10]$

Figure 5.43

$y = \sqrt[3]{x^2 - 2x + 2}$ and $y = x$.

Graphical Method   Find the zeros of the function $y = \sqrt[3]{x^2 - 2x + 2} - x$ or find where the graphs of $y = \sqrt[3]{x^2 - 2x + 2}$ and $y = x$ intersect. Either method works; we choose the latter. Find a complete graph (see Fig. 5.43). Use zoom-in to find that the solution is 1.00 with an error of at most 0.01.

Algebraic Method   Cube both sides of the equation to eliminate the radical.

$$x = \sqrt[3]{x^2 - 2x + 2}$$

$$x^3 = x^2 - 2x + 2 \quad \text{Cube both sides.}$$

$$x^3 - x^2 + 2x - 2 = 0$$

$$x^2(x - 1) + 2(x - 1) = 0$$

$$(x - 1)(x^2 + 2) = 0$$

$x = 1$ is the only real solution. Check that it is a solution.

The solution is $x = 1$.

Examples 6 to 8 show that an equation can often be solved using either a graphical method or an algebraic method. The graphical method is more general and usually easier. On the other hand, some things, like proving there is a vertical asymptote, require an algebraic method for verification. It is essential to be comfortable using both methods.

The next example requires a graphical method since it cannot be solved algebraically.

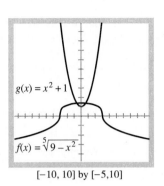

[−10, 10] by [−5,10]

Figure 5.44 $f(x) = \sqrt[5]{9 - x^2}$ and $g(x) = x^2 + 1$.

EXAMPLE 9   Solving an Inequality with a Radical

Solve the following inequality for x: $\sqrt[5]{9 - x^2} \geq x^2 + 1$.

Solution   There are two approaches to a graphical method:

1. Find the values of x for which the graph of $h(x) = \sqrt[5]{9 - x^2} - x^2 - 1$ lies on or above the x-axis.

2. Find the values of x for which the graph of $f(x) = \sqrt[5]{9 - x^2}$ lies above or intersects the graph of $g(x) = x^2 + 1$.

With the second approach the problem can be visualized better since complete graphs of both functions are shown. Figure 5.44 shows both graphs. Use zoom-in to find that the x-coordinates of the points of intersection are -0.73 and 0.73 with an error of at most 0.01.

The solution to the inequality is the interval $[-0.73, 0.73]$.   ▤

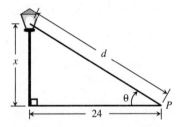

Figure 5.45   Diagram for the maximum illumination problem situation.

EXAMPLE 10   APPLICATION: Maximum Illumination

A streetlight is situated on a pole x feet above the ground. The intensity of illumination I at a point P that is 24 feet from the base of the pole is known to vary according to the equation $I = kx/d^3$, where d is the distance from P to the light, and k is some positive real number (see Fig. 5.45). How high above the ground should a security light be placed to provide maximum illumination at the point P on the ground.

Solution   Describe d in terms of x, and substitute the expression into the equation $I = kx/d^3$.

$$d = \sqrt{x^2 + 24^2} = \sqrt{x^2 + 576}$$

and therefore

$$I(x) = \frac{kx}{(x^2 + 576)^{3/2}}.$$

Figure 5.46 shows a complete graph of

$$I(x) = \frac{x}{(x^2 + 576)^{3/2}}.$$

Notice we set $k = 1$. The graph of I for any other value of k is a vertical stretching or shrinking of

$$y = \frac{x}{(x^2 + 576)^{3/2}}$$

by the factor k.

The value of x that gives the maximum value of I (when k is positive) is the same no matter what the actual value of k is. (Why?)

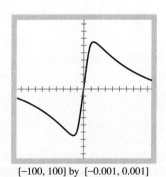

[−100, 100] by [−0.001, 0.001]

Figure 5.46
$I(x) = \dfrac{x}{(x^2 + 576)^{3/2}}.$

Figure 5.46 shows a complete graph of the algebraic representation. Use zoom-in to see that $x = 16.97$ with an error of at most 0.01 gives the maximum value of I.

The light should be placed on the pole 16.97 feet above the ground for maximum illumination.   ≡

Exercises for Section 5.4 _____

In Exercises 1 to 4, use a graphing utility to solve each inequality for x.

1. $\sqrt[3]{x} > \sqrt[4]{x}$ **2.** $\sqrt[4]{x} > \sqrt[5]{x}$

3. $\sqrt{x} < 2\sqrt[4]{x}$ **4.** $\sqrt{x} > 4\sqrt[3]{x}$

In Exercises 5 to 10, list the transformations that can be applied to the graph of $y = \sqrt{x}$, $y = \sqrt[3]{x}$, or $y = \sqrt[4]{x}$ to obtain sketches of each function.

5. $y = -2\sqrt{x+3}$ **6.** $y = 4 + (x+2)^{1/2}$

7. $y = -3 + \sqrt{x-5}$ **8.** $y = 3 - 2(x-3)^{1/3}$

9. $y = 2\sqrt[3]{3x-5}$ **10.** $y = -2 + 3(2-5x)^{1/3}$

In Exercises 11 to 18, sketch a complete graph of each function. Support your answer with a graphing utility.

11. $y = 3\sqrt{x-2}$ **12.** $y = -1 + (x+5)^{1/2}$

13. $y = -1 + \sqrt{x+2}$ **14.** $y = 3 - 2(x+1)^{1/3}$

15. $y = 2\sqrt[3]{x+3}$ **16.** $y = 2 - 3(1+2x)^{1/3}$

17. $y = 1 - \sqrt[4]{2-4x}$ **18.** $y = 2 + 3\sqrt[4]{2x+8}$

In Exercises 19 to 28, solve each equation algebraically. Support your answer with a graphing utility.

19. $\sqrt{x-2} = 6$ **20.** $(2x-1)^{1/2} = 2$

21. $(2x-1)^{1/3} = 2$ **22.** $2\sqrt{3-x} = -1$

23. $\sqrt[3]{x^2-1} = 3$ **24.** $(x^2-1)^{1/3} = -\dfrac{1}{2}$

25. $x - \sqrt{x} = 1$ **26.** $\sqrt{x-1} = \dfrac{x}{5} + 1$

27. $\sqrt{x-3} - 3\sqrt{x+12} = -11$

28. $\sqrt{x-5} - \sqrt{x+3} = -2$

In Exercises 29 and 30, solve each inequality algebraically. Support your answer with a graphing utility.

29. $\sqrt{x+3} > 6$ **30.** $\sqrt{x^2-4x-5} > x+2$

In Exercises 31 to 34, solve each equation or inequality.

31. $\sqrt{x^3+2} = 5$ **32.** $\sqrt[3]{x^2-2x+1} = 3x$

33. $\sqrt{9-x^2} > x^2+1$ **34.** $2x+5 < 10 + 4\sqrt{3x-4}$

In Exercises 35 and 36, sketch a complete graph of the region satisfying the inequality without using a graphing utility. Then support the boundary of your answer with a graphing utility.

35. $y < \sqrt{x-2}$ **36.** $y > 4 - \sqrt[3]{x+3}$

37. Draw a graph of $y = |x|/x$ without using a graphing utility. (*Hint:* Consider two cases, $x \geq 0$ and $x < 0$. What are the domain and range of each?)

38. Show how to determine the number of real number solutions to $\sqrt[3]{x-1} = 4 - x^2$. Do not use a graphing utility.

39. Use zoom-out to determine the end behavior of $f(x) = \sqrt{x^2 - 4x - 5}$.

40. Determine the end behavior of $f(x) = \sqrt{ax^2 + bx + c}$.

41. A number plus twice its square root equals 2. Find the initial and resulting numbers using an algebraic method. Support your solution with a graphing utility.

42. This **problem situation** is similar to the one in Example 10. A pole is situated 30 feet from the front of a store. How high above the ground should a security light bulb be placed in order to provide maximum illumination at point P on the base of the storefront?

43. Determine the minimum *vertical* distance between the parabola $y = \dfrac{1}{10}(x-4)^2 + 28$ and the line $y = 2x - 11$. At what point on the parabola does it occur?

Exercises 44 to 47 refer to the following **problem situation**: Penny is boating 20 miles offshore. She wishes to reach a coastal city 60 miles further down the shore by steering the boat to a point P along the shore, and then driving the remaining distance.

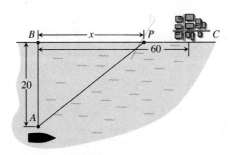

For Exercises 44 to 47

Let A denote the position of the boat, C that of the city, and AB the perpendicular to the shoreline. Furthermore, let x be the distance between B and P, and let T be the total time (in hours) for the trip.

44. If Penny's boat speed is 30 mph and her driving speed is 50 mph, where should she steer her boat to arrive at the city in the least amount of time?

45. Express T as a function of x, and compute $T(0)$ and $T(60)$. Interpret these values in terms of the problem situation.

46. Find a complete graph that includes only those values of x that make sense in the problem situation.

47. What value of x results in the least amount of time for the trip?

Exercises 48 to 51 refer to the following problem situation: The surface area S of a (right circular) cone excluding the base is given by the equation $S = \pi r \sqrt{r^2 + h^2}$, where r is

the radius and h is the height. The volume of the cone is $V = \dfrac{1}{3}\pi r^2 h$.

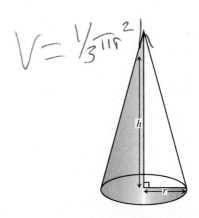

For Exercises 48 to 51

48. Suppose the height of the cone is 21 feet. Find an algebraic representation and a complete graph of the surface area S as a function of the radius r.

49. If the height of the cone is 21 feet, what radius produces a surface area of 155 square feet?

50. Suppose the volume is 380 cubic feet. Find an algebraic representation and a complete graph of S as a function of r. (*Hint:* Solve for h in the volume equation, and substitute into the surface area equation.)

51. Find the dimensions of a cone with volume 380 cubic feet that has the minimum surface area.

Chapter Review

KEY TERMS

end behavior asymptote
  for a rational
    function
end behavior model for a
  rational function

extraneous solution
horizontal asymptote
index
principal nth root of a

radical function
radical sign
radicand
rational function

reciprocal function
removable discontinuity
vertical asymptote

REVIEW EXERCISES

In Exercises 1 to 6, find the domain of each function by algebraic means. Then support your answer with a graphing utility.

1. $f(x) = \dfrac{x+1}{(x-1)(x+2)}$

2. $g(x) = \dfrac{(x+3)(x-2)}{x+1}$

3. $h(x) = \dfrac{3}{x^2 - 2x - 3}$

4. $f(x) = \dfrac{3x-5}{x^2 + x - 6}$

5. $g(x) = \dfrac{5}{x^2 - 3x + 1}$

6. $f(x) = \dfrac{x^3 + 1}{x^2 + 5}$

In Exercises 7 to 10, sketch a complete graph of each function without using a graphing utility. Find all the vertical and horizontal asymptotes. Then support your answer with a graphing utility.

7. $f(x) = \dfrac{7}{x+5}$

8. $g(x) = \dfrac{2x^2 - 6}{3 - x^2}$

9. $y = \dfrac{5x}{x-3}$

10. $y = \dfrac{2 + |x|}{x+1}$

11. Find the domain and range of the function in Exercise 9.

12. Write the function in Exercise 10 as a piecewise function without using absolute value symbols.

Exercises 13 and 14 refer to the following complete graph of $y = f(x)$.

13. As $x \to \infty$, $f(x) \to$?

14. As $x \to -4^+$, $f(x) \to$?

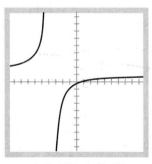

[−10, 10] by [−10, 10]

For Exercises 13 and 14

In Exercises 15 to 18, list the geometric transformations needed to produce the graph of f from the graph of $y = 1/x$ or $y = x^2$ or $y = \sqrt{x}$. Specify the order in which the transformations

should be applied. In each case sketch a complete graph of the function without the aid of a graphing utility. Write an equation for any vertical or horizontal asymptotes. Then support your answer with a graphing utility.

15. $f(x) = \dfrac{5}{x-2}$

16. $f(x) = 2 - \dfrac{3}{x+5}$

17. $g(x) = 2(x-2)^2 + 3$

18. $h(x) = 4 - 3\sqrt{x+1}$

In Exercises 19 to 21, draw a complete graph of each function and determine its domain and range. Find all the vertical asymptotes and the end behavior asymptote. Find all the zeros of the function.

19. $g(x) = \dfrac{3x^2}{(x-5)(x+4)}$

20. $f(x) = \dfrac{x^2 - 4}{x^2 + 4}$

21. $g(x) = \dfrac{2x^3 + 3x^2 - 6x - 1}{x^3 + 2}$

In Exercises 22 and 23, determine the intervals on which each function is increasing and the intervals on which each function is decreasing.

22. $f(x) = \dfrac{x^3 + 1}{x^2}$

23. $g(x) = \dfrac{-1}{x^3 + x}$

In Exercises 24 and 25, draw a complete graph of each function. Determine all local minima and maxima.

24. $f(x) = \dfrac{3x^2 + 10}{x}$

25. $f(x) = \dfrac{x^4 + 3x^3 + 2x^2 - 7}{x^2 + 2x - 1}$

In Exercises 26 and 27, sketch a complete graph. Determine the end behavior model. Find all vertical and horizontal asymptotes. Determine all zeros. Determine all extrema and the intervals where the function is increasing and decreasing.

26. $g(x) = \dfrac{x^3 + 1}{x^2 - 9}$

27. $f(x) = \dfrac{x^2 - 4x + 13}{x+2}$

In Exercises 28 to 31, find the end behavior model and the end behavior asymptote of each function. Support your answer with a graphing utility.

28. $f(x) = \dfrac{x^3 - 5x^2 - 7x - 1}{x+2}$

29. $g(x) = \dfrac{x^3 - 8}{x-2}$

30. $f(x) = \dfrac{x^2 - x - 2}{x^3 + 1}$

31. $f(x) = \dfrac{x^4 - 2x^3 - 8x^2 + 2x + 3}{x+1}$

32. Let $g(x) = 5/(x+1)$ and

$$f(x) = x^2 + \dfrac{5}{x+1} = \dfrac{x^3 + x^2 + 5}{x+1}.$$

Complete the following table using a calculator.

x	-0.9	-0.99	-0.999	-0.9999
$f(x)$	?	?	?	?
$g(x)$	?	?	?	?

33. Use the table in Exercise 32 to numerically determine what happens to the function values $f(x)$ as $x \to -1^{+}$.

Let

$$f(x) = \frac{x + 5}{x^2 - 2x - 8}.$$

Use a calculator to create tables of values that can be used for Exercises 34 and 35.

34. Determine numerically what happens to the values of the function $f(x)$ as $x \to -\infty$.

35. Determine numerically what happens to the values of the function $f(x)$ as $x \to 4^{-}$.

In Exercises 36 to 39, solve each equation algebraically. Support your answer with a graphing utility.

36. $\dfrac{2}{x} - \dfrac{3}{x + 5} = 0$ **37.** $\dfrac{1}{x - 3} + \dfrac{5}{x} = 2$

38. $\dfrac{x^3 + x}{x^2 + 1} = 0$ **39.** $\dfrac{2}{x} - \dfrac{3}{x - 1} = 6$

In Exercises 40 to 43, solve each inequality algebraically using the sign-pattern picture method. Support your answer with a graphing utility.

40. $\dfrac{x - 2}{x + 5} < 0$ **41.** $\dfrac{x^2 - 4}{x + 4} \geq 0$

42. $\dfrac{2}{x - 3} + 6 < 0$ **43.** $\dfrac{x + 3}{x - 2} < 5$

In Exercises 44 to 47, solve each equation or inequality.

44. $\dfrac{x^2 - x - 7}{x^2 + 1} = -1$ **45.** $\dfrac{x^4 + x^2 - 12}{x^2 - 3} = -5$

46. $\dfrac{x^4 + 3x^2 - x - 1}{x^2 + 3} < 0$ **47.** $\dfrac{x^5 - 3x^2 + 1}{x^3 + 7} < 3$

48. Find the zeros, y-intercept, vertical asymptotes, and end behavior asymptote of the following function:

$$f(x) = \frac{x^4 - 2x^3 + 3x^2 + x - 4}{x^2 - 5x - 14}$$

Find a complete graph that shows all of this behavior. (More than one viewing rectangle may be needed.)

In Exercises 49 to 52, solve each equation algebraically. Support your answer with a graphing utility.

49. $2(x - 1)^{1/2} = 2$ **50.** $\sqrt[3]{x^2 + 3x + 1} = 2$

51. $\sqrt{3x - 5} = 2$ **52.** $(x^2 + 2x - 3)^{1/3} = 5$

53. Use a graphical argument to show that if $x < 5$, then x is *not* a solution to the inequality $\sqrt{x + 5} > 5 - x/3$. Solve the inequality.

In Exercises 54 and 55, sketch a complete graph of each function. Then support your answer with a graphing utility. List the transformations that can be applied to $y = \sqrt{x}$ or $y = \sqrt[3]{x}$ to obtain the given graph. Specify the order in which transformations should be applied.

54. $f(x) = \sqrt[3]{x - 3}$ **55.** $g(x) = -3 + 2\sqrt{5 - x}$

56. The area of a triangle is to be 150 square units.
   a) Express the height of this triangle as a function of the length x of its base, and draw a complete graph of the function.
   b) Find the domain and range of the function found in part (a). What values of x make sense in the context of this problem?
   c) Use a graphical method to find the length of the base of the triangle if the height is 800 units.

57. The area of a rectangle is to be 500 square feet. Let x be the width of such a rectangle.
   a) Express the perimeter P as a function of x.
   b) Determine the vertical asymptotes and the end behavior asymptote, and find a complete graph of the function in part (a).
   c) Find the dimensions of a rectangle with an area of 500 square feet and the least possible perimeter. What is this perimeter?

Exercises 58 to 61 refer to the following **problem situation**: Judy is 5 feet 6 inches tall and walks at the rate of 4 feet per second away from a streetlight with a lamp 14.5 feet above level ground.

58. Find an algebraic representation of the length of Judy's shadow.

59. At what rate is the length of Judy's shadow increasing?

60. Express the distance D between the lamp and the tip of Judy's shadow as a function of time t.

61. When will the distance D be 100 feet?

Exercises 62 to 64 refer to the following **problem situation**: A balloon in the shape of a sphere is being inflated. Assume the radius r of the balloon is increasing at the rate of 3 inches per second and is zero when $t = 0$.

62. Express the volume V of the balloon as a function of time t.

63. Determine the volume of the balloon at $t = 5$ seconds.

64. Suppose the balloon will burst when its volume is 15,000 cubic inches. When will the balloon burst?

Exercises 65 to 67 refer to the following **problem situation**: Pure acid is added to 150 ounces of a 50% acid solution. Let x be the number of ounces of pure acid added.

65. Determine an algebraic representation of the acid concentration of the mixture.

66. Draw a complete graph of both the algebraic representation and of the problem situation.

67. Use a graphical method to find how much pure acid should be added to the 50% solution to produce a new mixture that is at least 78% acid.

68. Lisa wishes to obtain 85 ounces of a 40% acid solution by combining a 72% acid solution with a 25% acid solution. How much of each solution should Lisa use?

Exercises 69 to 72 refer to the following **problem situation**: Eric is boating 15 miles offshore. He wishes to reach a coastal city 55 miles further down the shore by steering the boat to a point P along the shore, and then driving the remaining distance. Assume that his boat speed is 25 mph and his driving speed is 40 mph. Let A denote the position of the boat, C that of the city, and AB the perpendicular to the shoreline. Furthermore, let x be the distance between B and P, and let T be the total time (in hours) for the trip.

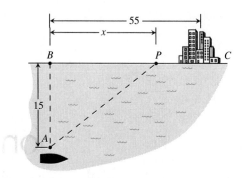

For Exercises 69 to 72

69. Determine an algebraic representation for the total time T of the trip. Find $T(0)$ and $T(55)$, and interpret these values in the problem situation.

70. Draw a complete graph of the algebraic representation function T. Also find the graph of the problem situation.

71. Where should he steer his boat in order to arrive at the city in the least amount of time?

72. What is the least amount of time?

Exercises 73 to 75 refer to the following **problem situation**: Jeri rode her bike 11 miles from her home to Columbus and then completed a 45-mile trip by car from Columbus to Marysville. Assume the average rate of the car was 41 mph faster than the average rate of the bike.

73. Find an algebraic representation for the total time T required to complete the trip (bike and car) as a function of the rate x of the bike.

74. What values of x make sense in this problem situation?

75. Use a graphical method to find the rate of the bike if the total time of the trip was 55 minutes.

6

Exponential and Logarithmic Functions

6.1 Exponential Functions

So far in this text three categories of functions have been discussed: polynomial functions, rational functions, and functions with radicals. This chapter introduces two more categories of functions: exponential and logarithmic functions.

We begin our study of exponential functions by comparing two notational conventions that represent two different functions. Both x^2 and 2^x have a **base number** and an **exponent**.

x^2: The base is x, and the exponent is 2.

2^x: The base is 2, and the exponent is x.

In the first case the variable x is the base, and in the second case x is the exponent. When the variable is in the base position, and the exponent is a nonnegative integer, as in x^2, the function is a polynomial, as we saw earlier. However, when the variable is in the exponent position and the base is a positive real number $\neq 1$, as in 2^x, the function is called an exponential function.

Definition 6.1   Exponential Function

Let a be a positive real number other than 1. The function $f(x) = a^x$ whose domain is the set of all real numbers is the **exponential function with base a**.

The following are examples of exponential functions:

$$f(x) = 10^x, \qquad g(v) = 4^v, \qquad h(x) = \pi^x, \qquad y = 2^x.$$

These next functions are not exponential functions:

$$f(x) = x^3, \qquad g(x) = \frac{x^4}{2}, \qquad y = \frac{\sqrt{x}}{x^2 + 3}, \qquad y = 3^5.$$

When studying calculus, you will learn a more complete definition of exponential functions. In this text you will become familiar with exponential functions by studying their graphs using a graphing utility.

🔍 EXPLORE WITH A GRAPHING UTILITY

Graph the following functions together in the same viewing rectangle:

$$y = 2^x, \qquad y = 3^x, \qquad y = 5^x.$$

1. Find a viewing rectangle that clearly distinguishes the complete graphs of these three functions.
2. For what values of x is it true that $2^x > 3^x > 5^x$?
3. For what values of x is it true that $2^x < 3^x < 5^x$?

Answer the same three questions for these functions:

$$y = 2^{-x}, \qquad y = 3^{-x}, \qquad y = 5^{-x}.$$

Generalize   How do the graphs of $y = a^x$ and $y = a^{-x}$ compare? How do the graphs of $y = a^x$ compare for various values of a?

Graphs of Exponential Functions

Using the properties of exponents studied in Section 1.3 we know that $a^{-1} = 1/a$. Therefore

$$a^{-x} = \left(a^{-1}\right)^x = \left(\frac{1}{a}\right)^x.$$

So, in particular,

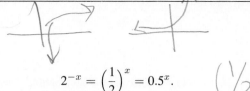

$$2^{-x} = \left(\frac{1}{2}\right)^x = 0.5^x.$$

You may have made the following observation about the behavior of exponential functions while completing the Exploration.

Generalization about Exponential Functions

- If $a > 1$, the graph of $f(x) = a^x$ has a shape like the graph of $y = 2^x$.
- If $0 < a < 1$, the graph of $f(x) = a^x$ has a shape like the graph of $y = 0.5^x$.
- For all base values $a > 0$, $f(0) = 1$.

[−5, 5] by [−5, 20]

Figure 6.1 $f(x) = 2^x$.

E X A M P L E 1 Graphing Exponential Functions

Find and compare complete graphs of $f(x) = 2^x$ and $g(x) = 0.5^x = 2^{-x}$. Find the domain and range of each function.

Solution Observe the following properties of f and g by studying Figs. 6.1 and 6.2:

$$\text{domain for both:} \quad (-\infty, \infty)$$
$$\text{range for both:} \quad (0, \infty).$$

[−5, 5] by [−5, 20]

Figure 6.2
$g(x) = 0.5^x = 2^{-x}$.

Several other general properties of the functions f and g are illustrated in Example 1. The x-axis is a horizontal asymptote for each. Also, f is an increasing function, while g is a decreasing function.

We can make two additional generalizations about the end behavior of f and g.

$$f(x) \to \infty \text{ as } x \to \infty \qquad \qquad f(x) \to 0 \text{ as } x \to -\infty$$
$$\text{and}$$
$$g(x) \to 0 \text{ as } x \to \infty \qquad \qquad g(x) \to \infty \text{ as } x \to -\infty$$

Finally, it is important to observe that

$$f(-x) = 2^{-x} = g(x) \qquad \text{and} \qquad g(-x) = 2^{-(-x)} = f(x),$$

which means that the graph of each function is the reflection about the y-axis of the other.

As with other categories of functions, exponential functions may be transformed by vertical and horizontal shifts and by vertical stretches.

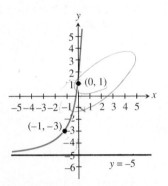

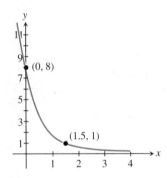

Figure 6.3 $g(x) = 2(3^{x+1}) - 5$.

Figure 6.4 $f(x) = 2^{3-2x}$ and $g(x) = 0.25^{x-1.5}$.

E X A M P L E   2   Transforming Exponential Functions

List the transformations used to obtain a complete graph of

$$g(x) = 2(3^{x+1}) - 5$$

from $f(x) = 3^x$. Sketch a complete graph of g.

Solution   Apply the following transformations, in order, to $f(x) = 3^x$:

1. Vertical stretch by a factor of 2 to obtain $y = 2(3^x)$.

2. Horizontally shift left 1 unit to obtain $y = 2(3^{x+1})$.

3. Vertically shift down 5 units to obtain $y = 2(3^{x+1}) - 5$.

See Fig. 6.3.

Often the properties of exponents are necessary to graph an exponential function.

E X A M P L E   3   Using Properties of Exponents

Use the properties of exponents to show that $f(x) = 2^{3-2x}$ and $g(x) = 0.25^{x-1.5}$ are the same function. Sketch the graph of each.

Solution

$$2^{3-2x} = 2^{-2(x-3/2)} = (2^{-2})^{x-1.5} = 0.25^{x-1.5}$$

Since $0 < 0.25 < 1$, we see that g is a decreasing function. It can be obtained from the graph of $y = 0.25^x$ by a horizontal shift right 1.5 units (see Fig. 6.4).

Natural Base e

For the exponential functions of the form $f(x) = a^x$ considered so far, a has had integer or rational number values such as $2, 3, 5, 10, 0.5$, and 0.25.

There is one particular exponential function that is especially important because it models many phenomena in both the natural world and the world of manufacturing. We begin the development of this special exponential function by considering the graph of the function $f(x) = (1 + 1/x)^x$.

Recall that the base of an exponential function must be positive. Therefore

$$1 + \frac{1}{x} > 0 \iff x > 0 \text{ or } x < -1.$$

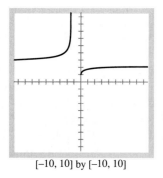

[−10, 10] by [−10, 10]

Figure 6.5 $f(x) = \left(1 + \dfrac{1}{x}\right)^{x}$.

In other words, the domain of the function f is $(-\infty, -1) \cup (0, \infty)$.

More importantly, however, the graph of f in Fig. 6.5 suggests that there is a horizontal asymptote. You can approximate the y-coordinate of the horizontal asymptote by a careful selection of viewing rectangles. It turns out that this asymptote is the line $y = k$ where k is an irrational number that can be approximated accurately to nine decimal places as $k = 2.718281828\cdots$.

Recall that the Greek letter π is used to represent the irrational ratio C/d of a circle (where C is the circumference and d is the diameter). Similarly, the special number $k = 2.718281828\cdots$ is represented by a particular symbol, e. This number e is the base of the natural exponential function.

Definition 6.2   Natural Exponential Function

The **natural exponential function** is the function

$$f(x) = e^{x},$$

where $e =$ the irrational number $2.718281828\cdots$.

Applications of Exponential Functions to Growth and Decay Problems

Suppose that the population P of a certain town is increasing at constant rate r each year, where r is in decimal form.

$$P + Pr = P(1 + r) \qquad \text{Population one year later}$$

$$P(1 + r) + P(1 + r)r = P(1 + r)^{2} \qquad \text{Population two years later}$$

$$\vdots$$

$$P(1 + r)^{t-1} + P(1 + r)^{t-1}r = P(1 + r)^{t} \qquad \text{In general, the population } t \text{ years later}$$

If the population is *decreasing*, the population at the end of t years would be $P(1 - r)^{t}$. These are examples of problems of **exponential growth** and **exponential decay**, which are found in biology, chemistry, business, and other social and physical sciences.

EXAMPLE 4   APPLICATION: Population Growth

A town has a population of 50,000 that is increasing at the rate of 2.5% each year. Use a complete graph of $f(t) = (50,000)(1 + 0.025)^{t}$ to find when the population of the town will be 100,000.

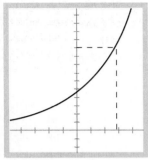

[−50, 50] by [−30,000, 150,000]

Figure 6.6
$f(t) = (50,000)(1 + 0.025)^t$.
Notice that when
$y = f(t) = 100,000$, the value for
t is about 28.

Solution   Begin by finding a complete graph of f (Fig. 6.6).
You need to find the value of t that makes $f(t) = 100,000$. Use zoom-in to find that $t = 28.07$ with an error of at most 0.01.   ▤

Is Fig. 6.6 a complete graph of the problem situation? It depends on how the situation is interpreted. If $t = 0$ represents present time and the 2.5% growth rate extends only into the future, then the complete graph would only include the portion where $t \geq 0$, or points to the right of the y-axis. On the other hand, if the 2.5% rate also applies to prior years, then the graph to the left of the y-axis describes the problem situation in prior years.

The word *population* is used broadly. In addition to humans it can refer to some species of animal or plant, to bacteria or molecules. It could even refer to currency such as the dollar.

For example, assume that the number of bacteria in a certain bacterial culture doubles every hour and that there are 100 present initially. Study the following pattern, and generalize to find a description of the population P after t hours:

$$200 = 100(2) \qquad \text{Total bacteria after 1 hour}$$

$$400 = 100(2^2) \qquad \text{Total bacteria after 2 hours}$$

$$800 = 100(2^3) \qquad \text{Total bacteria after 3 hours}$$

$$\vdots$$

$$P = 100(2^t). \qquad \text{Total bacteria after } t \text{ hours}$$

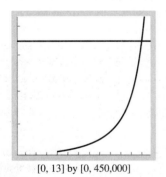

[0, 13] by [0, 450,000]

Figure 6.7 $P(t) = 100(2^t)$ and
$y = 350,000$.

E X A M P L E   5   Graphical Method for Biological Growth

Suppose a culture of 100 bacteria are put in a petri dish and the culture doubles every hour. Find when the number of bacteria will be 350,000.

Solution   From the discussion prior to this example we see that the population P of the petri dish after t hours is $P(t) = 100(2^t)$. Find a complete graph of this function.

We must find an appropriate viewing rectangle. Observe that $100(2^{13}) = 819,200$. So consider the graph of $P(t) = 100(2^t)$ in the viewing rectangle $[0, 13]$ by $[0, 450,000]$ (see Fig. 6.7).

The solution is found at the point of intersection of the graphs of $P(t) = 100(2^t)$ and $y = 350,000$. The graph of f shows that t at the point of intersection is a little less than 12. Use zoom-in to find that t is 11.77 with an error of at most 0.01.

Thus after 11 hours and 46.2 minutes the number of bacteria is approximately 350,000.   ▤

Exponential functions also model radioactive decay. The **half-life** of a radioactive substance is the amount of time it takes for half of the substance to decay. Suppose that the half-life of a certain radioactive substance is 20 days and that there are 5 grams initially. Study the following pattern, and generalize to find a description of the number of grams $f(t)$ present after t days:

$$\frac{5}{2} = 5\left(\frac{1}{2}\right) \qquad \text{Grams remaining after 20 days}$$

$$\frac{5}{4} = 5\left(\frac{1}{2}\right)^2 \qquad \text{Grams remaining after 40 days}$$

$$\vdots$$

$$f(t) = 5\left(\frac{1}{2}\right)^{t/20}. \qquad \text{Grams present after } t \text{ days}$$

We use this generalization in Example 7.

EXAMPLE 6   APPLICATION: Radioactive Decay

Suppose the half-life of a certain radioactive substance is 20 days and there are 5 grams present initially. Draw a complete graph of an algebraic representation of this problem situation, and find when there will be less than 1 gram of the substance remaining.

Solution   Based on the discussion prior to the example, an algebraic representation of this problem situation is

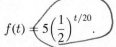
$$f(t) = 5\left(\frac{1}{2}\right)^{t/20}.$$

Since $f(0) = 5$ and we want to find t such that $f(t) = 1$, a viewing rectangle with $Y\min = -5$ and $Y\max = 10$ should be reasonable for the initial view (see Fig. 6.8). Use zoom-in to find that two graphs intersect at $t = 46.44$.

Thus there will be less than 1 gram of the radioactive substance left after 46.44 days.   ≡

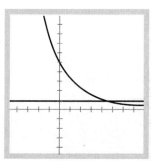

[−50, 80] by [−5, 10]

Figure 6.8 $f(t) = 5\left(\frac{1}{2}\right)^{t/20}$
and $y = 1$.

We close this section by investigating an important graph that occurs in the study of statistics; the **normal distribution curve**, sometimes called a **bell curve** because of its shape.

EXAMPLE 7   APPLICATION: Normal Distribution Curve

Let

$$f(x) = \frac{1}{\sqrt{2\pi}}e^{-x^2/2}.$$

Find a complete graph of f, and find its maximum value.

Solution   No graph is evident in the standard viewing rectangle. So the graph either lies outside the standard viewing rectangle or is hidden within it.

$$\frac{x^2}{2} \geq 0 \implies 0 < e^{-(x^2/2)} \leq 1$$

$$\implies 0 < \frac{1}{\sqrt{2\pi}}e^{-(x^2/2)} < \frac{1}{\sqrt{2\pi}}$$

$$0 < f(x) \leq \frac{1}{\sqrt{2\pi}} \approx 0.399$$

Try the viewing rectangle $[-5, 5]$ by $[-0.5, 0.5]$ (Fig. 6.9).

The maximum value is $f(0) = \dfrac{1}{\sqrt{2\pi}} = 0.399$ with an error of at most 0.01. ∎

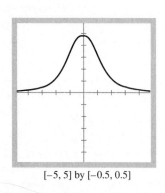

$[-5, 5]$ by $[-0.5, 0.5]$

Figure 6.9 $f(x) = \dfrac{1}{\sqrt{2\pi}}e^{-x^2/2}$.

Exercises for Section 6.1

1. Find complete graphs of

$$y_1 = 3^x, \quad y_2 = 5^x, \quad \text{and} \quad y_3 = 10^x$$

in the same viewing rectangle and show that all three graphs pass through the point $(0, 1)$.

2. The graph of $y = 3^{-x}$ is symmetric about the y-axis with which one of the following curves?

a) $y_1 = -3^x$ b) $y_2 = 3^x$ c) $y_3 = \dfrac{1}{3^x}$

In Exercises 3 and 4, determine which of the three functions are decreasing functions without using a graphing utility. Then support your answer with a graphing utility.

3. a) $y_1 = 4^{-x}$ b) $y_2 = 6^x$ c) $y_3 = 0.5^x$
4. a) $y_1 = 0.25^x$ b) $y_2 = 0.8^x$ c) $y_3 = 1.3^x$

In Exercises 5 to 10, list the transformations that can be used to obtain a complete graph of the given function from the graph of $y = 2^x$.

5. $y = 2^x - 4$ 6. $y = 3(2^x)$
7. $y = 2^{x-3}$ 8. $y = -2^{-x}$
9. $y = 2^{x+1} + 7$ 10. $y = -2 \cdot 2^{x+2} - 1$

In Exercises 11 to 14, draw the graphs of $y = \left(\frac{1}{4}\right)^x$, $y = \left(\frac{1}{3}\right)^x$, $y = \left(\frac{1}{2}\right)^x$ in the same $[-2, 4]$ by $[-1, 2]$ viewing rectangle. Solve each inequality.

11. $\left(\frac{1}{4}\right)^x > \left(\frac{1}{3}\right)^x$ 12. $\left(\frac{1}{3}\right)^x > \left(\frac{1}{2}\right)^x$
13. $\left(\frac{1}{4}\right)^x < \left(\frac{1}{3}\right)^x$ 14. $\left(\frac{1}{3}\right)^x < \left(\frac{1}{2}\right)^x$

In Exercises 15 to 18, use properties of exponents to select the pair of functions that are equal.

15. a) $y_1 = 3^{2x+4}$ b) $y_2 = 3^{2(x)} + 4$ c) $y_3 = 9^{x+2}$
16. a) $y_1 = 2^{3x-1}$ b) $y_2 = 8^{x-1/2}$ c) $y_3 = 2^{3x-3/2}$
17. a) $y_1 = 4^{3x-2}$ b) $y_2 = 2 \cdot 2^{3x-2}$ c) $y_3 = 2^{3x-1}$
18. a) $y_1 = 2^{-(x-4)}$ b) $y_2 = (0.5)^{x-4}$ c) $y_3 = (0.25)^{2x-8}$

In Exercises 19 to 24, sketch a complete graph of each function without using a graphing utility. Then support your answer with a graphing utility.

19. $f(x) = 1 + 2^x$ 20. $f(x) = 1 - 3^x$
21. $f(x) = 2^{x-3}$ 22. $y = 3 \cdot 2^{x+2}$
23. $g(x) = -2 - 2^{x+3}$ 24. $D(x) = -2 + \left(\frac{1}{2}\right)^{x+1}$

25. Determine the domain and range of the function in Exercise 19.

26. Determine the domain and range of the function in Exercise 20.

In Exercises 27 to 30, use the rules of exponents to solve each equation.

27. $2^x = 4^2$

28. $x^4 = 16$

29. $8^{x/2} = 4^{x+1}$

30. $(-8)^{5/3} = 2(4^{x/2})$

In Exercises 31 to 34, sketch a complete graph and determine the domain of each function.

31. $f(x) = e^{2x-1}$

32. $g(x) = 2^{x^2-1}$

33. $f(x) = x(3^x)$

34. $f(x) = xe^{-x}$

In Exercises 35 to 40, determine where each function is increasing and decreasing. Determine all local maximum and minimum values and the range of each function.

35. $f(x) = e^{2x-1}$

36. $g(x) = 2^{x^2-1}$

37. $f(x) = x(3^x)$

38. $f(x) = xe^{-x}$

39. $f(x) = x(2^{-x^2})$

40. $g(x) = -x(10^{x^2/50})$

In Exercises 41 and 42, sketch a complete graph of each inequality.

41. $y < e^x - 1$

42. $y \geq 2e^{x-3}$

43. Find the points that satisfy the equations $y = x^2$ and $y = 2^x$ simultaneously. Use both of these methods, and compare the two methods. Which one do you prefer?

Method 1 Find a complete graph of each equation in the same viewing rectangle; then use zoom-in to find the points where the two graphs intersect.

Method 2 Find the zeros of the function $y = 2^x - x^2$. Use the zeros to find where the graphs cross.

44. Use the two methods outlined in Exercise 43 to find the points that satisfy each of these equations simultaneously: $y = 3^x$ and $y = x^3$.

45. Investigate graphically the end behavior of $y = (1+2/x)^x$ by drawing the graph of $y = (1+2/x)^x$ and the line $y = e^2$ in the $[0, 100]$ by $[0, 10]$ viewing rectangle. Repeat in the $[100, 1000]$ by $[7, 8]$ viewing rectangle. Find an equation for a horizontal asymptote.

46. Investigate graphically the end behavior of $y = (1+3/x)^x$ by drawing the graph of $y = (1 + 3/x)^x$ and the line $y = e^3$ in the $[0, 100]$ by $[0, 25]$ viewing rectangle. Repeat in the $[100, 1000]$ by $[19, 21]$ viewing rectangle. Find an equation for a horizontal asymptote.

Exercises 47 to 49 refer to the following **problem situation**: The number of bacteria in a petri dish culture doubles every 3 hours. Initially there are 2500 bacteria present.

47. Find the number of bacteria present after (a) 3 hours, (b) 6 hours, and (c) t hours.

48. Find a complete graph that shows the number of bacteria present during the first 24-hour period.

49. Find when the number of bacteria will be 100,000.

Exercises 50 to 53 refer to the following **problem situation**: The number of rabbits in a certain population doubles every month, and there are 20 rabbits present initially.

50. How many rabbits are present after 1 year? After 5 years?

51. Find a graph that shows the number of rabbits present during the first year.

52. When will the number of rabbits be 10,000?

53. Writing to Learn Write a paragraph that explains why this exponential growth model is not a good model for rabbit population growth over a long period of time. What factors influence population growth?

54. The population P of a town is 475,000 and is increasing at the rate of 3.75% each year. Find an algebraic representation for P as a function of time. When will the population of the town be 1 million?

55. The population of a small town in the year 1890 was 6250. Assume that the population increased at the rate of 3.75% per year. What was the population in 1915? What was it in 1940?

56. The population P of a town is 123,000 and is decreasing at the rate of 2.375% each year. Find an algebraic representation for P as a function of time. Determine when the population of the town will be 50,000.

57. The half-life of a certain radioactive substance is 14 days, and there are 6.58 grams present initially. Find an algebraic representation for P as a function of time. When will there be less than 1 gram of the substance remaining?

58. The half-life of a certain radioactive substance is 65 days, and there are 3.5 grams present initially. Draw a complete graph of this problem situation where A is the amount and is a function of t. When will there be less than 1 gram remaining?

Exercises 59 to 61 refer to the following **problem situation**: The half-life of a certain radioactive substance is 1.5 seconds, and S represents the amount of the substance initially (in grams).

59. How much of the substance is left after 1.5 seconds? After 3 seconds? After t seconds?

60. Sketch a complete graph of an algebraic representation if there are 2 grams of the substance initially.

61. What is the initial amount of the substance needed if there is to be 1 gram left after 1 minute?

6.2 _____

Simple and Compound Interest

Many people pay rent for the use of an apartment that is owned by someone else. Interest paid on a savings deposit or charged for a loan works essentially in the same way. It is "rent" for the use of someone else's money. Interest can be calculated in two ways: simple and compound. We will see that interest is an economic application of exponential functions.

Simple Interest

Suppose you deposit $200 in a bank savings account that pays 7% for one year. The interest earned (the rent the bank pays you for the use of your money) is $200(0.07), or $14. We say that $200 is invested at a simple annual interest rate of 7%.

Definition 6.3   Simple Interest

Suppose P dollars are invested at a **simple interest rate** r, where r is a decimal, then P is called the **principal** and $P \cdot r$ is the **interest** received at the end of one interest period.

The following pattern, which results from applying Definition 6.3, leads to a general formula for the total amount after n interest periods:

$$P + Pr \quad \text{principal plus the interest for one period}$$

$$P + 2Pr \quad \text{total amount after two interest periods}$$

$$P + 3Pr \quad \text{total amount after three interest periods}$$

$$\vdots$$

$$P + Pnr = P(1 + nr) \quad \text{total amount after } n \text{ interest periods}$$

Simple Interest Formula

Suppose P dollars are invested at a simple interest rate r, then the **simple interest formula** for the total amount T after n interest periods is

$$T = P(1 + nr).$$

E X A M P L E 1   Calculating Simple Interest

Silvia deposits $500 in an account that pays 7% simple annual interest. How much will she have saved after 10 years?

Solution   Let $P = 500$, $n = 10$, and $r = 7\%$ (or 0.07); let T be the total saved after 10 years. Applying the simple interest formula, we get

$$T = P(1 + nr)$$

$$T = 500\big[1 + 10(0.07)\big] \quad \text{Substitute values for } P, r, \text{ and } n.$$

$$= 850$$

The value of the investment after 10 years is $850.

Compound Interest

Financial institutions commonly allow interest to compound; that is, they pay *interest on the interest*. Suppose P dollars are invested at rate r with interest compounded at the end of each year. Then P_n is the total amount after year n:

$$P_1 = P(1 + r)$$

$$P_2 = P_1(1 + r) = P(1 + r)(1 + r) = P(1 + r)^2$$

$$P_3 = P_2(1 + r) = P(1 + r)^2(1 + r) = P(1 + r)^3$$

$$\vdots$$

$$P_n = P(1 + r)^n$$

Interest accumulated in this way is called **compound interest**, and the total amount S at the end of n interest periods is given by the formula

$$S = P(1 + r)^n.$$

When the interest period is 1 year, we say that the interest is **compounded annually**.

Notice that the compound interest formula is an exponential function with a base of $1 + r$. Compare this formula with the model of exponential growth in Section 6.1.

E X A M P L E 2   Calculating Compound Interest

Suppose $500 is invested at 7% interest compounded annually. Find the value of the investment 10 years later.

Solution   Let $P = 500$, $n = 10$, and $r = 7\%$ (or 0.07). Let S be the total amount after 10 years. Then

REMINDER ABOUT ROUNDING

Do not round off until the final step has been completed. In Example 2, if the intermediate rounded value 1.967 had actually been used in the calculation, the result would be $983.50 instead of $983.58. Intermediate rounding can be avoided by entering the original numerical expression on your calculator.

$S = P(1 + r)^n$

$= 500(1 + .07)^{10}$ Substitute values for $P, r,$ and n.

$= 500(1.07)^{10}$ Use a calculator to evaluate 1.07^{10}.

$= 500(1.967)$ This intermediate result is not necessary when using a calculator; you can find the final answer $983.58 directly from calculating the line above.

$= 983.58$

The value of the investment after 10 years is $983.58.   ☰

Often interest is compounded more often than once a year. Suppose $500 is invested at 7% compounded quarterly, that is, four times a year. In each quarter you would expect to receive $\frac{1}{4}$ as much interest as you do for an entire year. In this case the simple interest rate for each quarter is $0.07/4$. On the other hand, in 10 years there are 40 interest periods. The formula for compound interest is

$S = P(1 + r)^n$ In this formula r is the interest rate for the interest period. Since interest is compounded quarterly, $r = 0.07/4$.

$= 500\left(1 + \dfrac{0.07}{4}\right)^{40}$ There are 40 interest periods in 10 years.

$= 500(1.0175)^{40}$ Use a calculator to evaluate this expression.

$= 1000.80.$

At the end of 10 years the total value of the investment would be $1000.80.

We say that the 7% is the annual percentage rate and the $\frac{7}{4}$% is the interest rate per quarter.

In general, suppose that P dollars are invested at an annual rate r per year compounded k times a year. Then r is called the **annual percentage rate (APR),** and (r/k) the **interest rate per period.**

Compound Interest Formula

Suppose that P dollars are invested at annual percentage rate (APR) r (where r is given in decimal form) compounded k times per year. Then the **compound interest formula** for the value S of the investment at the end of n interest periods is given by

$$S = P\left(1 + \frac{r}{k}\right)^n.$$

The next example illustrates another compound interest problem.

EXAMPLE 3   Using the Compound Interest Formula

Suppose $500 is invested at 9% APR compounded monthly. Find the value of the investment after 5 years.

Solution   Let $P = 500$, $r = 0.09$, $k = 12$, and $n = 12(5) = 60$. Let S be the quantity to be found. Then

$$S = P\left(1 + \frac{r}{k}\right)^{n}$$

$$= 500\left(1 + \frac{0.09}{12}\right)^{60} \qquad \text{Substitute values for } P, r, k, \text{ and } n.$$

$$= 500(1.0075)^{60}$$

$$= 782.84.$$

The value of the investment after 5 years is $782.84.   ▤

The compound interest formula is an important application of the exponential function. For instance, in Example 3, $500 was invested at 9% compounded monthly. An algebraic representation for the total value of the investment after t interest periods is

$$S(t) = 500(1.0075)^{t}.$$

The graphical representation shown in Fig. 6.10 shows how the investment grows.

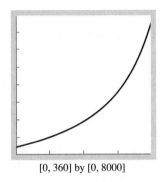

[0, 360] by [0, 8000]

Figure 6.10
$S(t) = 500(1.0075)^{t}$.

EXAMPLE 4   Calculating Compound Interest

How long will it take for the investment described in Example 3 to grow to $3000?

Solution   This problem can be solved graphically by determining where the complete graphs of $S(t) = 500(1.0075)^{t}$ and $y = 3000$ intersect (see Fig. 6.11). Use zoom-in to find that $t = 239.796$ with an error of at most 0.01. Thus the value of the investment will slightly exceed $3000 in 240 months, or 20 years.   ▤

What if we want to reverse the process? That is, if we know how much interest we want to earn, how much do we need to invest to meet our goal?

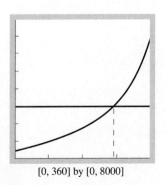

[0, 360] by [0, 8000]

Figure 6.11 $S(t) =$
$500(1.0075)^{t}$ and $y = 3000$.

EXAMPLE 5   Calculating Compound Interest

How much must be invested at 8% APR compounded daily so that the value of the investment 5 years later is $5000? (Assume 365 days in each year.)

Solution   For the compound interest formula $S = P\left(1 + \dfrac{r}{k}\right)^n$ we are given that $r = 0.08$, $k = 365$, $n = 365 \cdot 5 = 1825$, and $S = 5000$. We need to find P.

$$S = P\left(1 + \frac{r}{k}\right)^n$$

$$5000 = P\left(1 + \frac{0.08}{365}\right)^{1825} \qquad \text{Substitute values for } S, r, k, \text{ and } n, \text{ and} \atop \text{solve for } P.$$

$$P = \frac{5000}{(1 + 0.08/365)^{1825}}$$

$$P = 3351.75$$

An investment of \$3351.75 at 8% APR compounded daily will have a value of \$5000 after 5 years.   ≣

The next example assumes that the original investment amount and the final goal are both known. We ask what APR is needed to meet the goal. It also illustrates that some interest-rate problems can be solved either graphically or algebraically.

[0, 0.02] by [0, 4]

Figure 6.12 $y = (1 + x)^{84}$ and $y = 2$.

E X A M P L E   6   Calculating Compound Interest

What APR compounded monthly is required for a \$2000 investment to accumulate to \$4000 in 7 years?

Solution   We need to solve the compound interest formula for r:

$$4000 = 2000\left(1 + \frac{r}{12}\right)^{84}$$

$$2 = (1 + x)^{84}. \quad \text{Let } x = r/12.$$

Graphical Method   Find where complete graphs of $y = (1 + x)^{84}$ and $y = 2$ intersect (Fig. 6.12). Use zoom-in to find that $x = 0.0082$.

Algebraic Method   Solve the following equation for x:

$$2 = (1 + x)^{84}$$

$$2^{1/84} = \left[(1 + x)^{84}\right]^{1/84} \qquad \text{Take the 84th root of both sides of the equation.}$$

$$2^{1/84} = 1 + x \qquad \text{Solve the equation for } x.$$

$$x = 2^{1/84} - 1 \qquad \text{Evaluate this expression with a calculator.}$$

$$x = 0.0082858917$$

Finally, solve for r:

$$x = \frac{r}{12}$$

$$r = 12x$$

$$r = 12(0.0082858917) = 0.099430703$$

Rounding we get $r = 0.09943.$

An APR of 9.943% compounded monthly will produce \$4000 in 7 years.   ≡

Suppose \$1000 is invested at 8%. How much difference is there in the total value of the investment after 1 year based on different compounding periods? The following calculations show that this value increases as the number of compounding periods increases. The value appears to be approaching a little less than \$1083.30.

Compounding Period	Total Value after 1 Year	
Annually	$S = 1000(1 + 0.08)$	$= \$1080.00$
Quarterly	$S = 1000\left(1 + \dfrac{0.08}{4}\right)^4$	$= \$1082.43$
Monthly	$S = 1000\left(1 + \dfrac{0.08}{12}\right)^{12}$	$= \$1083.00$
Weekly	$S = 1000\left(1 + \dfrac{0.08}{52}\right)^{52}$	$= \$1083.22$
Daily	$S = 1000\left(1 + \dfrac{0.08}{365}\right)^{365}$	$= \$1083.28$
Hourly	$S = 1000\left(1 + \dfrac{0.08}{8760}\right)^{8760}$	$= \$1083.29$

Notice that what we really want to know is the end behavior of the function

$$f(x) = 1000\left(1 + \frac{0.08}{x}\right)^x.$$

It can be shown that

$$\left(1 + \frac{0.08}{n}\right)^n \longrightarrow e^{0.08} \text{ as } n \to \infty.$$

See Fig. 6.13. In general, if P dollars are invested at compound interest rate r for t years and the number of compounded periods approaches infinity, then the value of the investment approaches Pe^{rt}. This is called **continuous interest**.

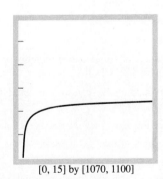

[0, 15] by [1070, 1100]

Figure 6.13
$y = 1000\left(1 + \dfrac{0.08}{x}\right)^x.$

Continuous Interest Formula

If P dollars are invested at APR r (in decimal form) and **compounded continuously**, then the value of the investment after t years is given by $S = Pe^{rt}$, where e is 2.718281828 (calculated to 9 places).

E X A M P L E   7   Calculating Continuous Interest

Suppose Noah invests $1000 at an 8% APR compounded continuously. After 5 years, what will his account be worth?

Solution   Let $P = 1000$, $r = 0.08$, and $t = 5$. Then

$$S = Pe^{rt}$$

$$S = 1000e^{0.08(5)}$$

Most calculators have e built in, so that this value can be computed with a calculator. You can also enter 2.718281828 for e and compute the value of S.

$$= 1491.82.$$

The value of the investment after 5 years is $1491.82.

Exercises for Section 6.2

1. Suppose you invest $1250 at 8% simple interest for 2 years. How much interest will you earn? What will be the value of your investment after 2 years?

2. Suppose you invest $5000 at 9% simple interest for 5 years. At the end of 5 years you use part of the investment to make a $7000 down payment for a house. How much of your investment remains?

3. Suppose you borrow $575 at 11.5% simple interest. The note needs to be repaid in a single payment at the end of 1 year. What is the total payoff?

4. A certain investment earns 7% simple interest. If you invest $500, how long will it take until your investment has grown to $600?

In Exercises 5 to 11, find the value of the investment for each initial amount, invested at the given rate, after the stated elapsed time.

5. $700, 7% compounded annually, 5 years

6. $1200, 9% compounded annually, 8 years

7. $7000, 11% compounded annually, 15 years

8. $5000, 8% compounded quarterly, 5 years

9. $20,000, 7.5% compounded monthly, 8 years

10. $8000, 8.3% compounded daily, 4 years

11. $3540, 9% compounded monthly, 12 years

12. Would you rather invest at 11.1% compounded monthly or at 11.2% compounded quarterly? Why?

13. Would you rather invest money for 10 years at 11% simple interest or at 8% compounded annually?

14. Draw a complete graph in the same viewing rectangle for $0 \le x \le 10$ of both

$$y = 1000(1 + 0.06x) \quad \text{and} \quad y = 1000(1 + 0.09x).$$

What value of Ymax did you use to make these graphs clearly distinguishable?

15. Draw a complete graph in the same viewing rectangle for

$0 \leq x \leq 10$ of both

$$y = 1000(1 + 0.05x) \quad \text{and} \quad y = 1000(1.05)^x.$$

What value of Ymax did you use to make these graphs clearly distinguishable?

16. The functions in Exercise 14 are algebraic representations for simple interest. What is the annual percentage rate (APR) in each case?

17. One function in Exercise 15 is an algebraic representation for simple interest and the other one is an algebraic representation for compound interest. Which one is which, and what is the APR in each case?

18. Draw a complete graph in the same viewing rectangle for $0 \leq x \leq 10$ of both $y = 1000(1.06)^x$ and $y = 1000(1.09)^x$. What value of Ymax did you use to make these graphs clearly distinguishable?

Exercises 19 to 24 involve equations that occur in either simple or compound interest problems. Solve each of these equations algebraically.

19. Find r if $2500 = 1000(1 + 12r)$.

20. Find t if $2500 = 1000(1 + 0.07t)$.

21. Determine P if $2500 = P[1 + 0.08(16)]$

22. Find r if $2500 = 1000(1 + r)^{12}$.

23. Find P if $2500 = P(1.08)^{16}$.

24. Find S if $S = \dfrac{(1 + i)^{120} - 1}{i}$ and $i = 0.06$.

25. Use a graphical method to solve the equation $2500 = 1000(1.07)^n$ for n.

26. Find S if $S = 500\dfrac{(1 + i)^{48} - 1}{i}$ and $i = 0.08$.

Exercises 27 to 31 refer to the following problem situation: Sally deposits $500 in a bank that pays 6% annual interest. Assume that she makes no other deposits or withdrawals. Determine how much she has accumulated after 5 years if the bank pays interest compounded as follows:

27. annually   **28.** quarterly

29. monthly   **30.** daily

31. continuously

Exercises 32 to 36 refer to the following problem situation: Escobar deposits $4500 in a bank that pays 7% annual interest. Assume that he makes no other deposits or withdrawals. Find out how much he has accumulated after 8 years if the bank pays interest compounded as follows:

32. annually   **33.** quarterly

34. monthly   **35.** daily

36. continuously

37. Find when an investment of $2300 accumulates to a value of $4150 if the investment earns interest at the rate of 9% compounded quarterly.

38. Find when an investment of $1500 accumulates to a value of $3750 if the investment earns interest at the rate of 8% compounded monthly.

39. A $1580 investment earns interest compounded annually. Determine the annual interest rate if the value of the investment is $3000 after 8 years.

40. A $22,000 investment earns interest compounded monthly. Determine the annual interest rate if the value of the investment is $36,500 after 5 years.

41. What is the value of an initial investment of $2575.00 at 8% compounded continuously for 6 years?

42. Find when an investment doubles in value at 6% compounded continuously.

43. Find r if $2300 = 1500\, e^{10r}$. Make up a problem situation for which the equation is a model.

44. Determine how much time is required for an investment to double in value if interest is earned at the rate of 5.75% compounded quarterly.

45. Determine how much time is required for an investment to triple in value if interest is earned at the rate of 6.25% compounded monthly.

Exercises 46 to 49 refer to the following problem situation: The formula $S = C(1 + r)^n$ is frequently used to model inflation. In such a case, r is the annual inflation rate, C is the value today, and S is the *inflated* value n years from now. The *purchasing power* of $1 n years from now (assuming an annual inflation rate of r is $C = 1/(1 + r)^n$.

46. What is the purchasing power of $1 in 10 years if the annual inflation rate is 3%?

47. What is the purchasing power of $1 in 10 years if the annual inflation rate is 8%?

48. What is the purchasing power of $1 in 10 years if the annual inflation rate is 15%?

49. Assume an inflation rate of 8%. Use a graph to determine the value of a $55,000 house in 7 years. (Assume no other factors affect the value of the house.)

50. **Writing to Learn**   Write a paragraph explaining the difference between simple interest and compound interest. Include in your discussion a calculation that shows what interest rate is required for simple interest to yield the same as 8% compounded quarterly for 10 years.

6.3 _____   Effective Rate and Annuities

Effective Annual Rate

How does one compare investment options when there are so many ways that interest can be compounded? For example, would you invest in an account that pays 8.75% APR compounded quarterly or one that pays 8.7% compounded monthly?

One way to make comparisons is to compare a given method of compounding to the simple interest rate that would yield the same balance at the end of 1 year. This simple interest rate is called the effective yield or the effective annual rate (i_{eff}).

Definition 6.4   Effective Annual Rate

The **effective annual rate i_{eff}** of APR r compounded k times per year is given by the equation

$$i_{\text{eff}} = \left(1 + \frac{r}{k}\right)^k - 1.$$

Another name for effective annual rate is **effective yield**.

Example 1 illustrates how the effective-annual-rate formula can be used.

E X A M P L E   1   Comparing Effective Annual Rates

Compare the effective annual rates of an account paying 8.75% compounded quarterly with an account paying 8.75% compounded monthly.

Solution   For 8.75% compounded quarterly the effective annual rate is

$$i_{\text{eff}} = \left(1 + \frac{r}{k}\right)^k - 1$$

$$= \left(1 + \frac{0.0875}{4}\right)^4 - 1$$

$$= 0.0904$$

or 9.04%. For 8.75% compounded monthly the effective annual rate is

$$i_{\text{eff}} = \left(1 + \frac{r}{k}\right)^k - 1$$
$$= \left(1 + \frac{0.0875}{12}\right)^{12} - 1$$
$$= 0.0911$$

or 9.11%, which is just slightly better than the effective rate of 8.75% compounded quarterly. ≡

Ordinary Annuity

So far in Sections 6.2 and 6.3 we have focused on finding the value of a single investment as a result of either simple or compound interest. In this section we consider investments that involve regular equal deposits into the investment over regular time intervals. An investment program of this type is called an annuity.

> **Definition 6.5   Annuity**
>
> An **ordinary annuity** is a sequence of equal regular periodic payments to be made in the future (see Fig. 6.14).

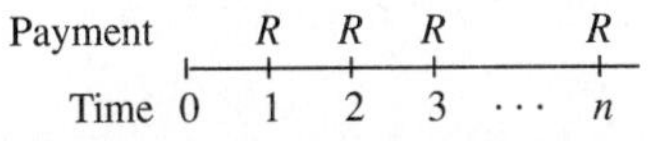

Payment R R R R

Time   0   1   2   3 $\cdots$ n

Figure 6.14 In an ordinary annuity, equal payments of R dollars are invested each payment period.

E X A M P L E   2   Calculating Ordinary Annuity

Sarah makes $500 payments each quarter into a retirement account that pays interest at the end of each quarter of the year. If the account pays 8% compounded quarterly, how much will be in Sarah's account at the end of the first year.

Solution   At the end of the first quarter the value is only equal to the original $500 payment. At the end of the second quarter the value includes the first payment plus interest, 500(1.02), plus a second $500 payment. The pattern continues as shown in this table.

	TotalValue
End of 1st quarter	$500
End of 2nd quarter	$500(1.02) + 500 = \$1010$
End of 3rd quarter	$1010(1.02) + 500 = \$1530.20$
End of 4th quarter	$1530.20(1.02) + 500 = \$2060.80$

At the end of the year the value of the account will be $2060.80. ≡

When you calculate the value S of an account in the future, you have found what is called the future value of S. In Example 2 we found the future value of Sarah's account at the end of 1 year.

It is not practical to try to find the future value of Sarah's account at the end of 35 years using the step-by-step solution method of Example 2. Instead we will use a formula that will be verified in Chapter 12.

Future Value of an Ordinary Annuity

The **future value S of an annuity** consisting of n equal payments of R dollars, each with the interest rate i per period (payment interval), is given by

$$S = R\frac{(1 + i)^n - 1}{i}. \tag{1}$$

EXAMPLE 3   Finding the Future Value of an Annuity

Suppose you deposit $25 each month into a retirement account that pays an APR of 9% or 0.75% each month. What is the value S of this annuity at the end of 47 years?

Solution   Let $R = \$25$, $i = 0.0075$, and $n = 12(47) = 564$. Use Eq. (1) to find the value S:

$$S = R\frac{(1 + i)^n - 1}{i}$$

$$= 25\left(\frac{(1.0075)^{564} - 1}{0.0075}\right)$$

$$= \$222{,}137.13.$$

The value S of the annuity after 47 years is $222,137.13.   ≣

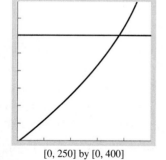

[0, 250] by [0, 400]

Figure 6.15

$S(x) = \dfrac{(1.005)^x - 1}{0.005}$ and $y = 300$.

Notice that 47 years is approximately the length of time between high school graduation and retirement. Example 3 shows that investing $25 per month will yield a good start at building a retirement fund.

If we replace the variable n in Eq. (1) with x, we have a function $S(x)$ that describes the future value of an annuity x payment intervals into the future. The function in Fig. 6.15,

$$S(x) = \frac{(1.005)^x - 1}{0.005},$$

describes the value of depositing $1 each month into an account that pays 6% APR.

E X A M P L E   4   Finding the Future Value of an Annuity

Use the graph shown in Fig. 6.15 to find how many months it will take to accumulate $300 when $1 is deposited each month at an interest rate of 0.5%.

Solution   Find the x-coordinate of the point of intersection of the graphs of

$$y = \frac{(1.005)^x - 1}{0.005} \quad \text{and} \quad y = 300.$$

Use zoom-in to show that $x = 183.72$ with an error of at most 0.01. The value of the annuity will exceed $300 for the first time after 184 months.   ≡

In Example 3 we knew the amount of each equal periodic payment, and we used the future-value-of-an-annuity formula to project the accumulated value into the future.

Consider this question: Ellie has received an inheritance. How much of her inheritance should she save today in order for this one-time investment to accumulate at retirement the same amount as Carlos, who is saving $50 each month?

The same question can be asked in general terms. What is the total amount A that should be invested today as a single lump sum in order to accumulate the same amount as an annuity of equal periodic payments, where each has the same interest rate?

In other words, we want to solve the following equation for A:

$$A(1 + i)^n = R\frac{(1 + i)^n - 1}{i}$$

$$A = R\frac{1 - (1 + i)^{-n}}{i}. \quad \text{Divide both sides of the equation by } (1 + i)^n.$$

We call this amount A the present value of an annuity.

Present Value of an Ordinary Annuity

The **present value A of an annuity** consisting of n equal payments or deposits of R dollars, each with an interest rate i per payment interval, is given by the formula

$$A = R\frac{1 - (1 + i)^{-n}}{i}.$$

Loan payments to a bank are regular periodic payments characteristic of an annuity. If a bank lends you $9000 for the purchase of a car, the monthly payments represent the equal payments of the annuity and the $9000 represents the present value of the annuity.

EXAMPLE 5   Finding the Present Value of an Annuity

What monthly payments are required for a 5-year, $9000 car loan at 12.5% APR compounded monthly?

Solution   This is an example of a 5-year annuity with a present value of $9000. (Why?) So use the present-value-of-an-annuity formula

$$A = R\frac{1 - (1 + i)^{-n}}{i}.$$

Substitute in $i = 0.125/12$, $n = 5(12) = 60$, and $A = 9000$, and solve for R:

$$9000 = R\frac{1 - \left(1 + \frac{0.125}{12}\right)^{-60}}{\left(\frac{0.125}{12}\right)}$$

$$R = \frac{9000\left(\frac{0.125}{12}\right)}{1 - \left(1 + \frac{0.125}{12}\right)^{-60}}.$$

Use a calculator to find that $R = 202.48$. The payments would be $202.48 per month. ∎

Exercises for Section 6.3

In Exercises 1 to 4, determine which investment yields the greatest return.

1. 6% compounded quarterly or 5.75% compounded daily

2. 8.25% compounded monthly or 8% compounded daily

3. 7% compounded quarterly or 7.20% compounded daily

4. 8.5% compounded quarterly or 8.40% compounded monthly

5. Amy contributes $50 per month into an IRA (Individual Retirement Account) annuity for 25 years. Assuming that the IRA earns 6.25% annual interest, what is the value of Amy's IRA account after 25 years?

6. Frank contributes $50 per month into an IRA annuity for 15 years. Assuming that the IRA earns 5.5% annual interest, what is the value of Frank's IRA account after 15 years?

7. Betsy contributes to a retirement annuity in which she earns 8.5% annual interest compounded quarterly. If she wants to accumulate $125,000 by the end of 18 years, how much should she invest each quarter?

In Exercises 8 to 11, each function is an algebraic representation for the future value of a certain annuity. In each case determine, from the form of the function, the annual interest rate and the number of payments per year.

8. $f(x) = 100\dfrac{(1 + 0.08/12)^x - 1}{0.08/12}$

9. $f(x) = 100\dfrac{(1 + 0.09/4)^x - 1}{0.09/4}$

10. $g(x) = \dfrac{(1.05)^x - 1}{0.05}$ 11. $g(x) = \dfrac{(1.01)^x - 1}{0.01}$

In Exercises 12 and 13, find a complete graph of each function in the viewing rectangle for $0 \leq x \leq 240$.

12. $y = 100\dfrac{(1.005)^x - 1}{0.005}$

13. $y = 100\dfrac{(1 + 0.08/12)^x - 1}{0.08/12}$

14. How are the graphs in Exercises 12 and 13 related to a retirement annuity requiring payments of $100 per month?

15. What monthly payments are required for a 4-year, $9000 car loan at 10.5% APR compounded monthly?

16. What monthly payments are required for a 3-year, $4500 car loan at 13% APR compounded monthly?

17. An $86,000 mortgage loan at 12% APR requires monthly payments. Find the required monthly payment if the loan has a term of 30 years.

18. An $86,000 mortgage loan at 12% APR requires monthly payments. Find the required monthly payment if the loan has a term of 15 years.

19. A $100,000 mortgage requires monthly payments for 30 years at 12% APR. How much is each payment?

20. An $86,000 mortgage for 30 years at 12% APR requires monthly payments of $884.61. Suppose you decided to make monthly payments of $1050.00. When would the mortgage loan be completely paid?

21. Suppose you make payments of $884.61 for the $86,000 mortgage in Exercise 20 for 10 years and then make payments of $1050 until the loan is paid. When will the mortgage loan be completely paid under these circumstances?

In Exercises 22 to 25, each function is an algebraic representation for the present value of a certain annuity. In each case determine, from the form of the function, the annual interest rate and the number of payments per year.

22. $f(x) = 200\dfrac{1 - \left(1 + 0.08/12\right)^{-x}}{0.08/12}$

23. $g(x) = 200\dfrac{1 - \left(1 + 0.11/4\right)^{-x}}{0.11/4}$

24. $f(x) = 200\dfrac{1 - (1.01)^{-x}}{0.01}$

25. $g(x) = 500\dfrac{1 - (1.0075)^{-x}}{0.0075}$

26. Draw a complete graph of the following functions in the same viewing rectangle for $0 \leq x \leq 60$.

a) $y = 200\dfrac{1 - \left(1 + 0.08/12\right)^{-x}}{0.08/12}$

b) $y = 200\dfrac{1 - (1.01)^{-x}}{0.01}$

27. Explain how the graphs in Exercise 26 are related to financing a car requiring monthly payments of $200.

28. Consider the following equation:
a) Solve for R.

$$86,000 = R\dfrac{1 - (1.01)^{-x}}{0.01}$$

b) Draw a complete graph of $R = f(x)$ for $0 \leq x \leq 360$.
c) Explain how the graph in part (b) relates to an $86,000 mortgage loan at 12% APR.

29. Solve the following equation for t using a graphing utility:

$$10,000 = 200\dfrac{1 - (1.01)^{-t}}{0.01}.$$

Explain how this problem relates to a car loan of $10,000 requiring monthly payments of $200.00.

30. Solve the following equation for i using a graphing utility:

$$10,000 = 238\dfrac{1 - (1 + i)^{-60}}{i}.$$

Explain how this problem relates to a car loan of $10,000 requiring monthly payments of $238.00.

Exercises 31 to 35 refer to the following Constant Percentage Depreciation **problem situation**: A building, item of equipment, or other capital improvement investment that a business might make has a useful life. The item *depreciates* from the time it is new (original cost C) until it reaches the end of its useful life (salvage value S). A continuous model for *book value B* at any time t using the *constant percentage method* is

$$B = C(1 - r)^t \quad \text{where} \quad S = C(1 - r)^n, \quad 0 \leq t \leq n$$

n is the length of the useful life, and r is the presumed interest rate. Suppose that a machine costing $17,000 has a useful life of 6 years and a salvage value of $1200.

31. Assume that the machine is depreciated using the constant percentage method. Use the fact that $S = C(1 - r)^n$ to determine r.

32. Draw a complete graph of the book value model $y = B(t)$.

33. What values of t make sense in this problem situation?

34. What is the book value in 4 years, 3 months?

35. Draw the graph of book value of the machine using both the straight-line method (where the depreciation is linear) and the constant percentage method in the same viewing rectangle for $0 \leq t \leq 6$.

Exercises 36 to 38 refer to this appreciation/depreciation **problem situation**: A precision computer-assisted design (CAD) machine purchased from Japan costs $22,600. It appreciates in value for 3 years to $26,400 (due to the fall in the value of the dollar) and then depreciates in value for 4 years (when the age of the machine overshadows the fall in the value of the dollar) and has a salvage value of $4700. Assume straight line appreciation and depreciation for computing book value.

36. Write a piecewise-defined function of time that is a model

of the book value for this problem situation.

37. Draw a complete graph of the model of the book value of the machine.

38. What is the book value of the machine after 5 years, 6 months?

In Exercises 39 and 40, the constant percentage depreciation method is closely related to a very common method of determining appreciation (inflation or growth).

39. Show that if $r < 0$, then $C(1 - r)^n = S$ becomes $C(1 + r)^n = S$ with $r > 0$. Further show that $S > C$, which means that the asset has *appreciated* over time.

40. Let $C = \$55,000$ and $r = -0.08$. Draw a complete graph of $y = S(n) = C(1 - r)^n$.

6.4 _____ Logarithmic Functions and Their Properties

The final family of functions we will discuss in this chapter are the logarithmic functions. Each logarithmic function is the inverse of an exponential function.

   Section 3.7 introduced the horizontal line test for determining whether the inverse relation of a function was again a function. We review this test here.

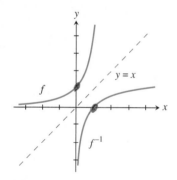

Figure 6.16 An exponential function and its inverse.

Horizontal Line Test

If every horizontal line intersects the graph of f in at most one point, then the inverse relation of f is a function denoted by f^{-1}.

   In section 6.1 you learned that the graphs of exponential functions look essentially like the graph of f shown in Fig. 6.16.

   It is evident that every horizontal line either intersects the graph of f at exactly one point or it does not intersect it at all. This observation leads to the following theorem.

Theorem 6.1   Inverse of Exponential Functions

Let $a > 0$ and $a \neq 1$. Then the inverse of the exponential function $y = a^x$ is a function.

Recall that the graph of a function f and the graph of its inverse f^{-1} are symmetric about the line $y = x$, as shown in Fig. 6.16. Note that an inverse of any exponential function $y = a^x$, where $a > 1$, is an increasing function whose graph lies in the first and fourth quadrants.

Logarithmic Functions

We begin with the formal definition.

Definition 6.6   Logarithmic Functions

The inverse of the exponential function $y = a^x$ is called the **logarithmic function with base a** and is denoted by $y = \log_a x$.

The value of $\log_a x$ is called the **logarithm of x with base a**.

CALCULATOR UPDATE

Most calculators have a key to evaluate the functions $y = \log x$ and $y = \ln x$. Computers generally have only $y = \ln x$ built in. Unfortunately it is a notational inconsistency that the function $y = \ln x$ is often accessed on the computer by entering $y = \log x$.

In the next section you will learn how to use a calculator to calculate values $y = \log_a x$ for base values other than 10 and e.

Logarithmic functions with bases 10 and e are given special names. The function $y = \log_{10} x$ is called the **common logarithmic function**, and the function $y = \log_e x$ is called the **natural logarithmic function**.

Often for common and natural logarithms, their bases, (10 and e, respectively) are omitted from the notation. Instead we write

$$y = \log x \quad \text{for} \quad y = \log_{10} x \qquad \text{and} \qquad y = \ln x \quad \text{for} \quad y = \log_e x.$$

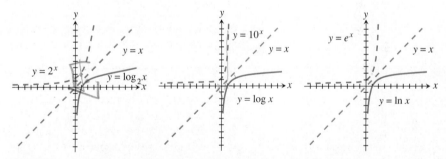

Figure 6.17   Three exponential functions and their logarithmic inverses.

Figure 6.17 supports the following generalization for logarithmic functions:

$$\textbf{domain} \quad (0, \infty) \qquad \textbf{range} \quad (-\infty, \infty).$$

We can compute the values of a logarithmic function by computing the values of the corresponding exponential function. This is also consistent with the general relationship between the domains and ranges of functions and their inverses.

EXAMPLE 1   Evaluating a Logarithm

Use the definition of logarithms to show that $\log_2 8 = 3$.

Solution

$$8 = 2^3 \implies (3, 8) \text{ is a solution to } y = 2^x.$$
$$\implies (8, 3) \text{ is a solution to the inverse } y = \log_2 x$$

Therefore $3 = \log_2 8$.

Try this:

1. Select parametric graphing mode.
2. Let $X_1(T) = T$,
   $Y_1(T) = e^T$,
   $X_2(T) = e^T$, $Y_2(T) = T$.
3. Find the graph in the standard viewing rectangle for $-10 \leq T \leq 10$.
4. Use the trace key to see the function and inverse function values.
5. Add $X_3(T) = T$ and $Y_3(T) = T$, and explain your visualization.

The reasoning used in Example 1 can be used for logarithmic functions of all bases. If we replace the pair $(3, 8)$ with the pair (x, y), we obtain the following generalization.

Generalization for Logarithmic and Exponential Equations

If $a > 0$ and $a \neq 1$, then

$$y = \log_a x \qquad \text{if and only if} \qquad x = a^y. \tag{1}$$

Notice that $\log_a x$ is an exponent. It is the exponent y such that $a^y = x$. We use this generalization in the following examples.

EXAMPLE 2   Evaluating a Logarithm

Use the above generalization to compute $\log_5(\frac{1}{25})$.

Solution

$$\log_5 \frac{1}{25} = x \quad \Longleftrightarrow \quad 5^x = \frac{1}{25} \qquad \begin{array}{l} \text{Notice that } x = -2 \text{ is a solution to this} \\ \text{equation since } 5^{-2} = (\frac{1}{25}). \end{array}$$
$$= \frac{1}{5^2}$$
$$= 5^{-2}$$

Therefore $x = -2$ and $\log_5(\frac{1}{25}) = -2$.

This same generalization can be used to solve equations involving logarithms.

EXAMPLE 3   Solving Logarithmic Equations

Use exponents to solve the following equations for x:
(a) $\log_5 x = 1.5$;   (b) $\log_2(x - 3) = 4$;   (c) $\log_x 3 = 2$;   (d) $\log_x(\frac{1}{8}) = -3$.

Solution

a) $\log_5 x = 1.5 \iff x = 5^{1.5}$ Use a calculator to evaluate
x accurate to hundredths.

$$x = 11.18$$

b) $\log_2(x - 3) = 4 \iff x - 3 = 2^4$

$$x = 19$$

c) $\log_x 3 = 2 \iff x^2 = 3$

$$x = \sqrt{3}$$ The base of a logarithm must be positive.

d) $\log_x \left(\dfrac{1}{8}\right) = -3 \iff x^{-3} = \left(\dfrac{1}{8}\right) = 2^{-3}$

$$x = 2$$

Properties of Logarithms

The graphs of the logarithmic functions give us visual information about the nature of these functions. But information about the nature of these functions can also be gained by exploring some of the properties that they satisfy. The next Exploration provides a visual way to discover whether two expressions are equal.

🔍 EXPLORE WITH A GRAPHING UTILITY

Written below are equations that *may or may not* be true. Find the graph of each side of each equation in the viewing rectangle $[-3, 10]$ by $[-2, 3]$, and decide whether you think the equation is true for all values of x.

1. $\log(x + 2) = \log x + \log 2$

2. $\log x^2 = (\log x)^2$

3. $\log \dfrac{x}{4} = \dfrac{\log x}{\log 4}$

Which of these equations are true?

In this Exploration you may have discovered several expressions you guessed to be true that turned out to be false. It is also important to learn those properties that *are* true. The next two theorems describe such properties. A graphing utility can be used to support and demonstrate these properties.

> **Theorem 6.2   Properties of Logarithms**
>
> Let $a > 0$ and $a \neq 1$. Then, the following statements are true:
>
> **a)** $a^{\log_a x} = x$ for every positive real number x
> **b)** $\log_a a = 1$
> **c)** $\log_a 1 = 0$.

Proof

a) $y = \log_a x \iff x = a^y$ Use statement (1).

$x = a^y = a^{\log_a x}$

b) $a^1 = a \iff \log_a a = 1$ This directly follows statement (1).

c) $a^0 = 1 \iff 0 = \log_a 1$

> **Theorem 6.3   Properties of Logarithms**
>
> Let a, r, and s be positive real numbers such that $a \neq 1$. Then the following statements are true:
>
> **a)** $\log_a rs = \log_a r + \log_a s$
> **b)** $\log_a \dfrac{r}{s} = \log_a r - \log_a s$
> **c)** $\log_a r^c = c \log_a r$ for every real number c
> **d)** $\log_a a^x = x$ for every real number x.

Proof   Let $\log_a r = u$ and $\log_a s = v$. Then, using the exponential form, we have $a^u = r$ and $a^v = s$.

a) $rs = a^u a^v = a^{u+v}$. The logarithmic form of $rs = a^{u+v}$ is $\log_a rs = u + v$. Substituting for u and v results in the relation

$$\log_a rs = u + v = \log_a r + \log_a s.$$

b) $r/s = a^u/a^v = a^{u-v}$. The logarithmic form of the equation $r/s = a^{u-v}$ is $\log_a(r/s) = u - v$. Substituting for u and v we find that

$$\log_a \frac{r}{s} = \log_a r - \log_a s.$$

c) $r^c = (a^u)^c = a^{uc}$. Thus, $\log_a r^c = uc = cu$. Substituting for u yields

$$\log_a r^c = c \log_a r.$$

d) Substitute $r = a$ and $c = x$ in Theorem 6.3(c) to obtain $\log_a a^x = x \log_a a$. By Theorem 6.2(b), we know that $\log_a a = 1$. Thus $\log_a a^x = x$.   ▪

Theorem 6.3 is used to express the logarithm of a complicated expression in terms of the logarithms of its simpler components. The basic idea is illustrated in the next example.

E X A M P L E   4   Using the Properties of Logarithms

Express $\log_a[(x^3 y^{3/2})/\sqrt{z}]$ in terms of $\log_a x$, $\log_a y$, and $\log_a z$.

Solution   Use Theorem 6.3 to obtain the following:

$$\log_a \frac{x^3 y^{3/2}}{\sqrt{z}} = \log_a(x^3 y^{3/2}) - \log_a \sqrt{z} \qquad \text{Theorem 6.3(b)}$$

$$= \log_a x^3 + \log_a y^{3/2} - \log_a z^{1/2} \qquad \text{Theorem 6.3(a)}$$

$$= 3 \log_a x + (3/2) \log_a y - (1/2) \log_a z. \qquad \text{Theorem 6.3(c)} \quad ▪$$

Example 4 shows that the logarithm of an expression involving products, quotients, and exponents can be expressed as sums and differences of products of logarithms and numbers. On the other hand, Example 5 shows that an exponential function with an exponent involving sums and differences can be expressed as a product and quotient of exponential expressions.

E X A M P L E   5   Using the Properties of Exponents

Express $a^{2x+3y-z}$ in terms of a^x, a^y, and a^z.

Solution   Use properties of exponents to obtain the following:

$$a^{2x+3y-z} = a^{2x} a^{3y} a^{-z}$$

$$= \frac{(a^x)^2 (a^y)^3}{a^z}. \qquad ▪$$

In Example 4 of Section 6.1 a graphical method was used to find how long it would take a town with a population of 50,000, increasing at the rate of 2.5% per year, to reach a population of 100,000. In this next example we see how logarithms can be used to solve the same problem algebraically.

E X A M P L E   6   Problem Solving with Logarithms

Use an algebraic method to find how long it would take a town with a population of 50,000, increasing at the rate of 2.5% per year, to reach a population of 100,000.

Solution   The population of the town at any time t is $P(t) = 50,000(1.025)^t$. Thus we need to solve the following equation for t:

$$50,000(1.025)^t = 100,000$$

$$1.025^t = 2 \qquad \text{Divide both sides of the equation by 50,000.}$$

$$\log(1.025^t) = \log 2 \qquad \text{For any function } f, \text{ if } a = b, \text{ then } f(a) = f(b). \text{ In particular, } \log a = \log b.$$

$$t\log(1.025) = \log 2$$

$$t = \frac{\log 2}{\log 1.025} = 28.071.$$

Thus $t = 28.07$ is accurate to 0.01.

The population of the town will reach 100,000 in 28 years and a few days.

≡

Data Analysis

Scientists working in a laboratory collect enough experimental data to establish that a given rule is plausible. The data points are graphed, and the scientist tries to find the **curve of best fit**. The relationship may be linear. In that case the data points will nearly lie on a line, taking into account experimental error. The line of best fit is relatively easy to find.

However, if the relationship is not linear, the data points may look something like the graph is Fig. 6.18, and the curve of best fit may not be obvious.

Often it is possible to use a logarithmic function to convert the data from a nonlinear relationship to a linear one, making it easier to find the experimental relationship.

For example, suppose that the actual relationship is described by a **power** function $y = ax^m$, where a is a positive constant and x is a positive independent variable. Then the following equations are equivalent:

$$y = ax^m$$

$$\ln y = \ln ax^m$$

$$\ln y = \ln a + \ln x^m$$

$$\ln y = \ln a + m \ln x.$$

Notice that $\ln y$ is the *linear* function of $\ln x$ with slope m and y-intercept $\ln a$.

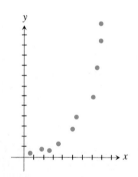

Figure 6.18   What is the best-fit curve for these data points.

Theorem 6.4   Converting a Power Function Relationship to a Linear Function Relationship

Let a, x, and y be positive. Then $y = ax^m$ if and only if $\ln y$ is a linear function of $\ln x$.

Proof   We have already shown that when $y = ax^m$, $\ln y = \ln a + m \ln x$. Thus $\ln y$ is a linear function of $\ln x$.

Conversely, suppose $\ln y$ is a linear function of $\ln x$. Then there are real numbers m and c so that $\ln y = m \ln x + c$. The natural logarithm function is one-to-one, and has the range $(-\infty, \infty)$. Thus there is a unique positive real number a such that $\ln a = c$. We substitute this form for c in the expression for $\ln y$:

$$\ln y = m \ln x + c$$

$$\ln y = m \ln x + \ln a$$

$$\ln y = \ln x^m + \ln a$$

$$\ln y = \ln ax^m$$

$$y = ax^m.$$

This next example applies Theorem 6.4 to a set of data in order to conclude that the data satisfy a power function relationship.

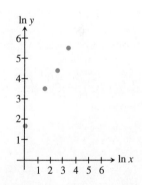

Figure 6.19 Plot of the data points $(\ln x, \ln y)$ for Example 7.

E X A M P L E   7   *Finding a Relationship for Data*

Determine a power rule model for y in terms of x for the following data:

x	1	3	5	8
y	5	31.2	73.1	160

Solution   According to Theorem 6.4 we can show that y is a power function of x by showing that $\ln y$ is a linear function of $\ln x$. Calculate and graph the data points $(\ln x, \ln y)$ (see Fig. 6.19).

$\ln x$	0	1.10	1.61	2.08
$\ln y$	1.61	3.44	4.29	5.08

The plotted data appear to have a linear relationship. Use two of the data points to find an equation of a line. This line should be close to the line of best fit.

Use the points $(\ln 1, \ln 5)$ and $(\ln 8, \ln 160)$ to determine m and b in $\ln y = m \ln x + b$.

$$\ln 5 = m \ln 1 + b \qquad \text{Substitute } (1, 5) \text{ into the equation } \ln y = m \ln x + b.$$

$$\ln 5 = m \cdot 0 + b$$

$$\ln 5 = b$$

$$\ln 160 = m \ln 8 + \ln 5 \qquad \text{Substitute } (8, 160) \text{ and } b = \ln 5 \text{ into the equation } \ln y = m \ln x + b.$$

$$\ln 160 = \ln(8^m)(5) \qquad \text{Use properties from Theorem 6.3.}$$

$$160 = 5(8^m)$$

$$32 = 8^m \qquad \text{Express both sides of the equation as a power of 2.}$$

$$2^5 = 2^{3m}$$

$$m = \frac{5}{3}$$

We can use the values of m and b to write y as a power function of x:

$$\ln y = m \ln x + b$$

$$\ln y = \frac{5}{3} \ln x + \ln 5$$

$$\ln y = \ln(5x^{5/3})$$

$$y = 5x^{5/3}.$$

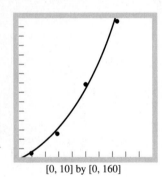

[0, 10] by [0, 160]

Figure 6.20 $y = 5x^{5/3}$.

See Fig. 6.20.

Even though in Example 7 the exact values for b and m were found, often we would simply approximate their values. In the past, before calculators became common, the values would be plotted on log-log graph paper.

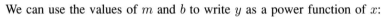

Exercises for Section 6.4

Compute Exercises 1 to 8 without using a calculator.

1. $\log_4 16$

2. $\log_{10} 10$

3. $\log_2 8$

4. $\log_3 81$

5. $\log_{1/2} 16$

6. $\ln 1$

7. $\log_2(-8)$

8. $\log_4(-2)^4$

In Exercises 9 to 12, sketch a complete graph without using a graphing utility. Use the inverse property.

9. $f(x) = \log_3 x$

10. $g(x) = \log_5(x)$

11. $y = \log_{1/4} x$

12. $y = \log_2(-x)$

In Exercises 13 to 20, solve each equation without using a calculator.

13. $\log_9 x = 2$ **14.** $\log_2 x = 5$

15. $\log_x(\frac{1}{125}) = -3$ **16.** $\log_3(x + 1) = 2$

17. $\log_x 81 = 9$ **18.** $\log_2 x^2 = -2$

19. $\log_3 |x| = 1$ **20.** $\log_6(x^2 - 2x + 1) = 0$

Express Exercises 21 to 24 in logarithmic form.

21. $y = 7^x$ **22.** $xy = 3^4$

23. $x + y = 2^8$ **24.** $(1 + r)^n = P$

Express Exercises 25 to 28 in exponential form.

25. $\log_3 x = 5$ **26.** $\log_2 x = y$

27. $\log_3 \dfrac{x}{y} = -2$ **28.** $\dfrac{\ln P}{\ln(1 + r)} = n$

In Exercises 29 to 34, use properties of logarithms to write the expression as a sum, difference, or product of simple logarithms (that is, logarithms without sums, products, quotients, or exponents).

29. $\log_2(x^3 y^2)$ **30.** $\ln(xy^3)$

31. $\log_a \left(\dfrac{x^2}{y^3} \right)$ **32.** $\log_{10} 1000x^4$

33. $\log[5000x(1 + r)^{360}]$ **34.** $\log(\sqrt[5]{216z^3})$

In Exercises 35 to 38, find an appropriate viewing rectangle that shows a complete graph of each function.

35. $f(x) = e^{1/x}$ **36.** $f(x) = \dfrac{\ln x}{x}$

37. $f(x) = x^{1/x}$ **38.** $f(x) = \dfrac{x}{\ln x}$

In Exercises 39 to 42, use a calculator to investigate numerically the end behavior of each function.

39. $f(x) = e^{2/x}$ **40.** $f(x) = \dfrac{\ln x^2}{x}$

41. $f(x) = x^{1/x}$ **42.** $f(x) = \dfrac{3x}{\ln x}$

In Exercises 43 to 47, use logarithms, if needed, to solve each problem algebraically.

43. The population of a town is 475,000 and is increasing at the rate of 3.75% each year. Determine when the population of the town will be 1 million.

44. The population of a town is 123,000 and is decreasing at the rate of 2.375% each year. Determine when the population of the town will be 50,000.

45. The population of a small town in the year 1890 was 6250. Assume the population increased at the rate of 3.75% each

year. Determine the population of the town in 1915 and in 1940.

46. The half-life of a certain radioactive substance is 14 days, and there are 6.58 grams present initially. When will there be less than 1 gram of the substance remaining?

47. The half-life of a certain radioactive substance is 65 days, and there are 3.5 grams present initially. When will there be less than 1 gram of the substance remaining?

48. Determine a specific power rule algebraic representation for the data in this table.

x	4	6.5	8.5	10
y	2816	31908	122,019	275,000

49. Consider the two sets of data given below. Which one has an algebraic representation that is a power rule? Determine the specific power rule.

x	2	3	7.5	7.7
y	7.48	7.14	6.43	6.41
x	8	12	15	40
y	23.84	58.2	113.69	162.13

In Exercises 50 to 52, use an algebraic method to solve the equation for t. Support your answer with a graphing utility.

50. $2500 = 1000(1.08)^t$

51. $6000 = 4600(1.05)^t$

52. $10,000 = 3500(1.07)^t$

53. Explain how Exercises 50 to 52 relate to interest-bearing savings accounts.

54. Solve for t: $S = P(1 + r)^t$.

55. Use an algebraic method to determine how long it will take for an initial deposit of \$1250 to double in value at 7% compounded monthly.

56. Use an algebraic method to determine how long it will take for an initial deposit of \$1250 to triple in value at 7% compounded monthly.

Exercises 57 to 59 refer to the following **problem situation**: The table below gives the period of one complete revolution about the sun for the listed planets along with the length of the semimajor orbit axes. Let P be the orbit period and x the length of the semimajor axis.

Planet	Period (Days)	Semimajor Axes (Miles)
Earth	365	92,600,000
Mercury	88	36,000,000
Venus	225	67,100,000
Mars	687	141,700,000
Jupiter	4330	483,000,000
Saturn	10,750	886,100,000

57. Plot $\ln P$ against $\ln x$. That is, plot the pairs $(\ln x, \ln P)$. Verify that the relationship is linear, and estimate the slope m and y-intercept.

58. Use Exercise 57 to show that $P = ax^m$ for constants a and m. This result was discovered by Kepler in the early 1700s and is known as *Kepler's third law of planetary motion.*

59. Predict the period of Pluto's orbit if its semimajor orbit axis length is 3,660,000,000 miles.

Exercises 60 and 61 refer to the following **problem situation**: The *at-rest blood pressure* P and weight x of various primates were measured as shown in this table:

Weight, x (lbs)	20	50	80	110	125	140
Blood pressure P	106	133	150	162	167	172

60. Plot $\ln P$ against $\ln x$. That is, plot the pairs $(\ln x, \ln P)$. Verify that the relationship is linear. Determine the slope m and y-intercept.

61. Use Exercise 60 to find a formula expressing the blood pressure as a function of weight.

6.5   Graphs of Logarithmic Functions

In Section 6.4 the only logarithmic functions graphed with a graphing utility were the *common logarithm function* $y = \log x$ and the *natural logarithm function* $y = \ln x$. These may be graphed using the built-in function keys for $y = \log x$ and $y = \ln x$ found in most graphing utilities.

However, to graph other logarithmic functions such as $y = \log_2 x, y = \log_5 x$, and $y = \log_8 x$, a formula called the **change-of-base formula** is used to transform the function. This formula can be used to compute logarithms with any base on a calculator and to obtain a complete graph of any logarithmic function with a graphing utility.

Theorem 6.5   Change-of-Base Formula

Let a and b be positive real numbers, with $a \neq 1, b \neq 1$. Then

a) $\log_b x = \dfrac{\log_a x}{\log_a b}$

b) $\log_b a = \dfrac{1}{\log_a b}$.

In these formulas a is sometimes called the **given base** and b the **desired base**.

Proof

a)
$$y = \log_b x \iff x = b^y$$

Apply the logarithm base a to both sides of the equation $x = b^y$.

$$\log_a x = \log_a b^y$$

$$\log_a x = y \log_a b$$

$$y = \frac{\log_a x}{\log_a b}.$$

b)
$$\log_b x = \frac{\log_a x}{\log_a b}$$
Substitute $x = a$ into Theorem 6.5 (a).

$$\log_b a = \frac{\log_a a}{\log_a b}.$$
Substitute $\log_a a = 1$ (Theorem 6.2b).

$$\log_b a = \frac{1}{\log_a b}$$

To apply the change-of-base formula, let $a = 10$ or $a = e$. Then the logarithm of any base b can be represented in terms of either common logarithms or natural logarithms. For example,

$$\log_3 x = \frac{\log x}{\log 3}, \qquad \log_7 x = \frac{\ln x}{\ln 7}, \qquad \log_5 x = \frac{\log x}{\log 5}, \qquad \log_9 x = \frac{\ln x}{\ln 9}.$$

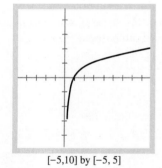

[−5,10] by [−5, 5]

Figure 6.21 $f(x) = \log_3 x$.

E X A M P L E   1   Graphing a Logarithmic Function

Use a graphing utility to find a complete graph of $f(x) = \log_3 x$. Also find its domain and range.

Solution   Use the change-of-base formula found in Theorem 6.5(a).

$$f(x) = \log_3 x = \frac{\log x}{\log 3} = \frac{\ln x}{\ln 3}.$$

To find the complete graph of f, graph either $y = \log x / \log 3$ or $y = \ln x / \ln 3$. See Fig. 6.21. The domain and range of f are the same as for logarithmic functions with other bases; that is, the domain is $(0, \infty)$ and the range is $(-\infty, \infty)$.

The method shown in Example 1 can be used to find the graphs of logarithmic functions with other bases.

The standard transformations of vertical and horizontal shift, vertical stretch, and reflection about the x- and y-axes can be used to find the graphs of logarithms.

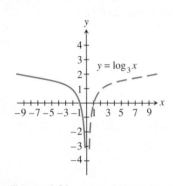

Figure 6.22 $g(x) = \log_3(-x)$ reflecting the graph of $f(x) = \log_3 x$ about the y-axis results in $g(x) = \log_3(-x)$.

Applying Transformations to $y = \log_b x$

The graph of any logarithmic function of the form $y = a \log_b(cx + d) + k$ can be obtained by applying geometric transformations to the graph of $y = \log_b x$.

EXAMPLE 2   Using Transformations to Graph Logarithms

Explain how a sketch of the graph of $g(x) = \log_3(-x)$ can be obtained from the graph of $f(x) = \log_3 x$. Also determine the domain, range, and vertical asymptote of g.

Solution   See Fig. 6.22.

$$g(x) = \log_3(-x) = f(-x)$$ A graph of g can be obtained from a graph of f by reflection through the y-axis.

$$-x > 0 \iff x < 0$$ This means that the domain of g is $(-\infty, 0)$.

Domain of g $(-\infty, 0)$.

Range of g $(-\infty, \infty)$.

Vertical Asymptote of g $x = 0$.

EXAMPLE 3   Using Transformations to Graph Logarithms

Explain how a sketch of the graph of $g(x) = \log_5(3 - x)$ can be obtained from a sketch of $f(x) = \log_5 x$. Also, find the domain, range, and asymptotes of g.

Solution

$$g(x) = \log_5(3 - x) = \log_5[(-1)(x - 3)]$$

$$= f[-(x - 3)]$$ Recall that the -1 signifies a reflection through the y-axis.

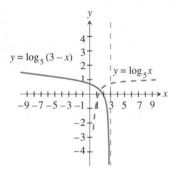

Figure 6.23 $f(x) = \log_5(3 - x)$.

The graph of f can be obtained from the graph of $y = \log_5 x$ through the following sequence of transformations:

1. A reflection about the y-axis.

2. A horizontal shift right 3 units (see Fig. 6.23). The vertical asymptote of f also shifts 3 units right.

$$3 - x > 0 \iff x < 3$$ This means that the domain of f is $(-\infty, 3)$.

Domain of g $(-\infty, 3)$.

Range of g $(-\infty, \infty)$.

Vertical Asymptote of g $x = 3$.

The next example illustrates that since we know the general shape of the graph of a logarithmic function, we can find its position and orientation by plotting a few specific points. At the same time we investigate the effect of the coefficient a in $y = \log_b(ax + c)$.

EXAMPLE 4   Sketching a Graph by Plotting Several Points

Sketch a complete graph of $g(x) = \log_2(3x+5)$ by plotting several points and taking into account the transformations that can be applied to the graph of $f(x) = \log_2 x$. Also find its domain, range, and asymptotes.

Solution   Suppose that we rewrite $g(x)$ as follows:

$$g(x) = \log_2(3x + 5)$$

$$= \log_2[3(x + \tfrac{5}{3})]$$

$$= \log_2 3 + \log_2(x + \tfrac{5}{3})$$

$$= f(x + \tfrac{5}{3}) + \log_2 3. \quad \text{The graph of } y = \log_2 x \text{ shifts left } \tfrac{5}{3} \text{ units then up } \log_2 3 \text{ units.}$$

To help locate the position of the graph, find its x- and y-intercepts.

$$\log_2(3x + 5) = 0 \iff 3x + 5 = 2^0 = 1$$

$$x = -\frac{4}{3}$$

$$g(0) = \log_2 5$$

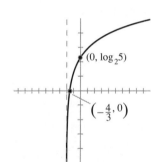

Figure 6.24
$g(x) = \log_2(3x + 5)$.

The points $(-\tfrac{4}{3}, 0)$ and $(0, \log_2 5)$ are on the graph of g. See Fig. 6.24.

$$3x + 5 > 0 \iff 3x > -5 \quad \text{\small $3x + 5$ must be positive to be in the domain of g.}$$

$$\iff x > -\frac{5}{3} \quad \text{\small This means that the domain of g is $\left(-\tfrac{5}{3}, \infty\right)$.}$$

Domain of g $\left(-\tfrac{5}{3}, \infty\right)$.

Range of g $(-\infty, \infty)$.

Vertical Asymptote of g $x = -\tfrac{5}{3}$.

EXAMPLE 5   Combining Methods to Find a Graph

Find a complete graph of $g(x) = -3\log_4(2x-5)+1$. Determine its domain, range, and asymptote.

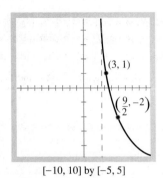

[−10, 10] by [−5, 5]

Figure 6.25 $g(x) = -3\log_4(2x - 5) + 1$.

Solution   Combine all the methods of the last several examples.

To find a complete graph of g with a graphing utility, enter g in the form

$$g(x) = -3\frac{\log(2x - 5)}{\log 4} + 1.$$

See Fig. 6.25.

Using properties of logarithms, we obtain the following:

$$g(x) = -3\log_4(2x - 5) + 1$$

$$= -3\log_4[2(x - \tfrac{5}{2})] + 1$$

$$= -3[\log_4 2 + \log_4(x - \tfrac{5}{2})] + 1$$

$$= -3\log_4 2 - 3\log_4(x - \tfrac{5}{2}) + 1$$

$$= -3\log_4(x - \tfrac{5}{2}) + (1 - 3\log_4 2)$$

$$= -3f(x - \tfrac{5}{2}) + (1 - 3\log_4 2)$$

The graph of $f(x) = \log_4 x$ shifts right $\tfrac{5}{2}$ units, reflects through the x-axis, stretches by a factor of 3, and then shifts up $(1 - 3\log_4 2)$ units.

$$2x - 5 > 0 \Longleftrightarrow x > \frac{5}{2}.$$

The domain of g is $(\tfrac{5}{2}, \infty)$ and the vertical asymptote is $x = \tfrac{5}{2}$.

Confirm that the points $(3, 1)$ and $\left(\tfrac{9}{2}, -2\right)$ are on the graph of g.

Domain of g $\left(\tfrac{5}{2}, \infty\right)$.

Range of g $(-\infty, \infty)$.

Vertical Asymptote of g $x = \tfrac{5}{2}$.   ≡

We close this section by applying our knowledge of logarithms to a couple of applications. Example 6 examines the effect of the monthly payment on the term (length) of a loan, and Example 7 considers the Richter scale, a common way to measure earthquakes.

E X A M P L E   6   APPLICATION: Loan Repayment

A Problem Situation

Suppose that to buy a house, Alicia takes out an $86,000 loan at APR 12% compounded monthly. She wants to pay off the loan as quickly as possible. The interest payment required the first month is $0.01(86,000) = \$860$. Thus monthly payments must exceed \$860 in order to pay off the loan. Assume that the interest rate and payment are fixed.

a) Find a complete graph of an algebraic representation that shows how the number of months t for the loan depends on the amount of the monthly payment x.

b) What are the monthly payments if the loan is paid in 25 years?

c) If the amount in part (b) is increased by \$50, how long will it take to pay off the loan?

Solution   This problem is a present-value-of-an-annuity problem. Use the formula introduced in Section 6.3:

$$A = R\frac{1 - (1 + i)^{-n}}{i}$$

and let $A = \$86{,}000$ and $i = 0.01$. Let x represent the unknown monthly payment, and let t represent the time of the loan. Then

a)
$$86{,}000 = x\frac{1 - 1.01^{-t}}{0.01}.$$

Next, solve this equation for t:

$$86{,}000 = x\frac{1 - 1.01^{-t}}{0.01}$$

$$860 = x(1 - 1.01^{-t})$$

$$\frac{860}{x} = 1 - 1.01^{-t}$$

$$1.01^{-t} = 1 - \frac{860}{x}$$

$$1.01^{-t} = \frac{x - 860}{x}$$

$$1.01^{t} = \frac{x}{x - 860}$$

$$\ln(1.01^{t}) = \ln\left(\frac{x}{x - 860}\right)$$

$$t = \frac{1}{\ln 1.01}\ln\left(\frac{x}{x - 860}\right).$$

This is an algebraic representation for time t (in months) as a function of the amount of the monthly payment x. Fig. 6.26 shows a complete graph of this representation.

b) Let $t = 300$ months, and use zoom-in to find the point of intersection of the graph of t and the horizontal line $t = 300$. The x-coordinate of that point of intersection is 905.77, which means that the monthly payments are \$905.77 to pay off the loan in 25 years.

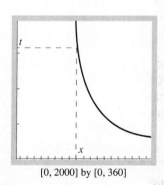

[0, 2000] by [0, 360]

Figure 6.26
$$t = \frac{1}{\ln 1.01}\ln\left(\frac{x}{x - 860}\right).$$

c) Substitute $x = 955.77$ into the algebraic representation of part (a) to find t:

$$t = \frac{1}{\ln 1.01} \ln \left(\frac{955.77}{955.77 - 860} \right) = 231.21.$$

Thus $t = 231.21$ months, which is equal to 19.27 years. If the payments are increased by $50, the loan will be paid off about 5.73 years sooner. ▄

The intensity of an earthquake is rated by its measurement on the Richter scale. This scale is actually the logarithmic function

$$R = \log \left(\frac{a}{T} \right) + B,$$

where R is the magnitude of the intensity, a is the amplitude (in micrometers) of the vertical ground motion at the receiving station, T is the period of the seismic wave (in seconds), and B is a factor that accounts for the weakening of the seismic wave with increasing distance from the epicenter of the earthquake.

EXAMPLE 7   APPLICATION: The Richter Scale

At the early stages of a particular earthquake, the amplitude of vertical ground motion was a, and at later stages the amplitude became $10a$. How much did the intensity R change as the earthquake progressed?

Solution Let R_1 be the intensity when the amplitude was a and R_2 be the intensity when the amplitude was $10a$. So $R_1 = \log(a/T) + B$ and $R_2 = \log(10a/T) + B$. Combine these two equations and solve for either R_1 or R_2.

$$R_2 - R_1 = \left[\log \left(\frac{10a}{T} \right) + B \right] - \left[\log \left(\frac{a}{T} \right) + B \right]$$

$$= \log \left(\frac{10a}{T} \right) - \log \left(\frac{a}{T} \right)$$

$$= (\log 10a - \log T) - (\log a - \log T)$$

$$= \log 10a - \log a$$

$$= \log \frac{10a}{a} = \log 10 = 1$$

$$R_2 = R_1 + 1$$

The intensity increased by 1 Richter scale unit. ▄

Thus, for example, an earthquake with a Richter scale intensity of 6 is 10 times greater than one with an intensity of 5.

Exercises for Section 6.5

In Exercises 1 to 6, use a graphing utility to find a complete graph for each function. State the viewing rectangle that you used for each, and each function's domain and range.

1. $f(x) = \log_4 x$ **2.** $g(x) = \log_8 x$

3. $h(x) = \log_5 x + 3$ **4.** $f(x) = \log_2 x - 10$

5. $k(x) = \log_3 x + \log_2 64$ **6.** $f(x) = \log_7 x + 25$

7. Use a graphing utility to draw complete graphs of $y = \log_2 x$, $y = \ln x$, $y = \log_3 x$, $y = \log_5 x$, and $y = \log x$ in the same viewing rectangle.

In Exercises 8 to 15, explain how a sketch of a complete graph of each function can be obtained from the graph of $y = \log_a x$ for the appropriate value of a. In each case identify the vertical asymptote.

8. $f(x) = \log_3(x - 2)$ **9.** $g(x) = \log_4(x + 5) - 1$

10. $g(x) = \log(5 - x)$ **11.** $f(x) = \log_5(2 - x)$

12. $k(x) = \log_2(3x - 4)$ **13.** $j(x) = \ln(2x + 3) + 2$

14. $f(x) = -\log(x + 3) - 2$ **15.** $g(x) = -\log(4 - x) - 2$

In Exercises 16 to 19, sketch a complete graph of each function by plotting a pair of points. State the domain and range of each function.

16. $f(x) = \log_2(x + 3)$ **17.** $k(x) = \log_3(2x - 1)$

18. $g(x) = 2\log(-x)$ **19.** $f(x) = \log(3 - x)$

In Exercises 20 to 27, use any method to sketch a complete graph of each function. Support your answer with a graphing utility.

20. $f(x) = 2\ln(x + 3)$ **21.** $g(x) = -1 - \ln(x - 1)$

22. $h(x) = 1 + \log_3(x - 2)$ **23.** $f(x) = 2 - \log_2(2x + 6)$

24. $k(x) = \log_5 \sqrt{x - 3}$ **25.** $f(x) = \log_2(x + 3)^2$

26. $g(x) = \ln(5 - 2x)$ **27.** $f(x) = 4 + \log_5 \sqrt{x - 3}$

In Exercises 28 to 31, solve each inequality graphically.

28. $\log_2 x < \log_3 x$ **29.** $\log_2 x > \log_3 x$

30. $\ln x < \log_3 x$ **31.** $\ln x > \log_3 x$

In Exercises 32 to 35, determine the end behavior of each function. That is, determine what $f(x)$ approaches as $|x| \to \infty$.

32. $f(x) = x \ln x$ **33.** $f(x) = x^2 \ln x$

34. $f(x) = x^2 \ln |x|$ **35.** $f(x) = \dfrac{\ln x}{x}$

In Exercises 36 to 39, find a complete graph of each function. Determine where the function is increasing and decreasing. Determine all local maximum and minimum values.

36. $f(x) = x \ln x$ **37.** $g(x) = x^2 \ln x$

38. $f(x) = x^2 \ln |x|$ **39.** $g(x) = \dfrac{\ln x}{x}$

In Exercises 40 and 41, sketch the graph of each inequality without using a graphing utility.

40. $y < \ln(3 - x)$ **41.** $y \geq 2 - \ln(x + 2)$

In Exercises 42 and 43, find the points of intersection of each equation.

42. $y = 6 - x$ and $y = \ln(x - 2)$

43. $y = x^2 - 2$ and $y - 1 = \ln |x + 5|$

44. Show that $y = \frac{1}{2}(e^x - e^{-x})$ and $y = \ln(x + \sqrt{x^2 + 1})$ are inverses of each other. Give a graphical argument.

In Exercises 45 to 50, for each pair of functions f and g, find the solutions to $f(x) > g(x)$, $f(x) < g(x)$, and $f(x) = g(x)$ graphically.

45. $f(x) = 3^x$; $g(x) = x^3$

46. $f(x) = e^x$; $g(x) = x^e$

47. $f(x) = 10^x$; $g(x) = x^x$

48. $f(x) = e^x$; $g(x) = (\ln x)^x$

49. $f(x) = \ln x$; $g(x) = \ln(\ln x)$

50. $f(x) = \ln x$; $g(x) = x^{1/3}$

51. How would you graph $y = \log_x 4$ using a graphing utility?

Exercises 52 to 54 refer to the Richter scale **problem situation** in Example 7.

52. What is the magnitude on the Richter scale of an earthquake if $a = 250$, $T = 2$, and $B = 4.250$?

53. Explain why an earthquake of magnitude 6 on the Richter scale is 100 times more intense than one with the same epicenter of magnitude 4 on the Richter scale. Assume that T and B in the formula for the Richter scale are constant. The change in the vertical ground motion (amplitude) is directly related to the *intensity* of the earthquake.

54. Draw a complete graph of the Richter scale model (magnitude R as a function of amplitude a). Assume that $T = 2$ and $B = 4.250$. What are the values of a that make sense in this problem situation?

Exercises 55 to 58 refer to the following problem situation: The *Beer-Lambert law of light absorption* is given by

$$\log\left(\frac{I}{I_0}\right) = Kx,$$

where I_0 and I denote the intensity of light of a particular type before and after passing through a body of material, respectively, and x denotes the length of the path followed by the beam of light passing through the material. K is a constant.

55. Let $I_0 = 12$ lumens, and assume that $K = -0.00235$. Express I as a function of x.

56. Draw a complete graph of $I = f(x)$.

57. Suppose I_0 represents the intensity of light measured at the surface of a lake. The Beer-Lambert law can be used to determine the intensity I of the light measured at a depth of x feet from the surface. Assume the constants given in Exercise 55 are correct for Lake Erie. What is the intensity of the light at a depth of 30 feet?

58. Suppose that, for Lake Superior, $K = -0.0125$ and the surface intensity of the light is 12 lumens. What is the intensity at a depth of 30 feet?

Exercises 59 to 62 refer to the table of data given below. Exponential relations appear to be linear when plotted on *semilogarithmic graph paper*. Before calculators and computers were readily available, techniques for data analysis frequently involved semilogarithmic graph paper. The same analysis can be carried out using ordinary graph paper and a scientific or graphing calculator.

x	2.3	4	5.5	7	9
y	43.8	283.5	1473.1	7654.5	68,890.5

59. Plot the data pairs $(x, \log y)$ on regular graph paper using the values for x and y given above. Verify that the points are *collinear* (fall on the same line).

60. Compute the slope m and the y-intercept y_0 of the line in Exercise 59. Verify that the data can be represented by the exponential relationship $y = ab^x$, where $m = \log b$ and $\log a = y_0$.

61. Prove that if f is the exponential function $f(x) = ab^x$ then $\log f(x)$ varies linearly with x. That is, show that $\log f(x) = mx + y_0$ for some constants m and y_0.

62. Determine the actual exponential function which provides a model of the data in Exercise 59. (*Hint:* Use Exercise 61.)

63. Consider a $75,000 mortgage loan at 10.50% APR compounded monthly.
a) Draw a graph that shows how the term of the loan depends on the amount of the monthly payment.
b) What monthly payments are required to pay off the loan in 25 years?
c) If the amount in part (b) is increased by $50, how long will it take to pay off the loan?

64. Consider a $110,000 mortgage loan at 9% APR compounded monthly.
a) Draw a graph that shows how the term of the loan depends on the amount of the monthly payment.
b) What monthly payments are required to pay off the loan in 25 years?
c) If the amount in part (b) is increased by $50, how long will it take to pay off the loan?

6.6   Equations, Inequalities, and Extreme Value Problems

In this section we solve equations and inequalities that involve exponential or logarithmic functions. Both graphical and algebraic methods will be used. The algebraic method generally involves moving from the exponential form to the logarithmic form and vice versa. Sometimes the solution of the problem requires finding a local maximum or minimum of a function.

E X A M P L E 1   Solving a Logarithmic Equation with a Calculator

Solve $\log x = -2.5$.

Solution

$$\log x = -2.5 \Longleftrightarrow x = 10^{-2.5}$$ Apply statement (1) from Section 6.4.

Use the exponentiation key to show that $x = 0.0031623$.

Using Properties of Logarithms to Solve Equations

Suppose we want to solve the equation

$$\log x - \log(x - 2) = -2 \tag{1}$$

using algebraic methods. The properties summarized in Theorem 6.3 can be used.

Caution: Extraneous solutions are sometimes introduced when both sides of an equation are squared, as seen in Section 5.3. The same thing can happen when using the properties of logarithms. For example, suppose Theorem 6.3(b) is used to conclude that

$$\log x - \log(x - 2) = \log \frac{x}{x - 2}.$$

The fact that extraneous roots are introduced can be seen by comparing the domains of $f(x) = \log[x/(x - 2)]$ and $g(x) = \log x - \log(x - 2)$:

$$f(x) = \log \frac{x}{x - 2} \text{ is defined} \iff \frac{x}{x - 2} > 0$$

$$\iff x \text{ is in } (-\infty, 0) \cup (2, \infty)$$

$$g(x) = \log x - \log(x - 2) \text{ is defined} \iff x > 0 \text{ and } x - 2 > 0$$

$$\iff x \text{ is in } (2, \infty).$$

This illustrates that the domains are not identical. It is evident from the graphs of these two functions (Figs. 6.27 and 6.28) that

$$\log \frac{x}{x - 2} = -2$$

has a solution but that

$$\log x - \log(x - 2) = -2$$

does not have a solution.

This comparison suggests the following **principle about extraneous solutions.**

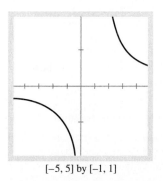

[−5, 5] by [−1, 1]

Figure 6.27 $f(x) = \log \dfrac{x}{x - 2}$.

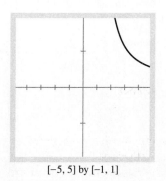

[−5, 5] by [−1, 1]

Figure 6.28
$g(x) = \log x - \log(x - 2)$.

Principle of Extraneous Solutions

To find all solutions, we can replace

$$\log_a f(x) - \log_a g(x) \quad \text{by} \quad \log_a \frac{f(x)}{g(x)}$$

or

$$\log_a f(x) + \log_a g(x) \quad \text{by} \quad \log_a \left[f(x) \cdot g(x) \right].$$

However, extraneous solutions may be introduced through these replacements.

The algebraic solution in this next example illustrates how to use the principle on extraneous solutions.

E X A M P L E   2   Solving a Logarithmic Equation

Solve $\frac{1}{2} \log_5(x + 6) - \log_5 x = 0$.

Solution

Graphical Method   A complete graph of $y = \frac{1}{2} \log_5(x + 6) - \log_5 x$ (Fig. 6.29) suggests that $x = 3$ is the one zero of this function. Use zoom-in or direct numerical substitution to support this claim, or use the following algebraic solution.

Algebraic Method   Use the properties of Theorem 6.3:

$$\frac{1}{2} \log_5(x + 6) - \log_5 x = 0$$

$$\log_5(x + 6)^{1/2} - \log_5 x = 0$$

$$\log_5 \sqrt{x + 6} - \log_5 x = 0$$

$$\log_5 \frac{\sqrt{x + 6}}{x} = 0 \qquad \text{\small This step might introduce extraneous solutions.}$$

$$\frac{\sqrt{x + 6}}{x} = 5^0$$

$$\frac{\sqrt{x + 6}}{x} = 1.$$

Next, solve $\sqrt{x + 6}/x = 1$ in the usual way:

$$\frac{\sqrt{x + 6}}{x} = 1$$

$$\sqrt{x + 6} = x$$

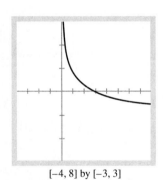

[−4, 8] by [−3, 3]

Figure 6.29
$y = \frac{1}{2} \log_5(x + 6) - \log_5 x.$

$$x + 6 = x^2$$

$$0 = x^2 - x - 6$$

$$0 = (x - 3)(x + 2)$$

$$x = 3, \qquad x = -2.$$

Check   Let $x = 3$. Then

$$\frac{1}{2}\log_5(3 + 6) - \log_5 3 = 0.$$ Use a calculator to evaluate this expression.

The expression $\log_5(-2)$ is not defined, so $x = -2$ is not a solution. ≡

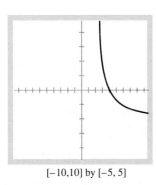

[−10,10] by [−5, 5]

Figure 6.30 $f(x) = \log_2(2x+1)-\log_2(x-3)-2\log_2 3.$

E X A M P L E 3   Solving a Logarithmic Equation

Solve $\log_2(2x + 1) - \log_2(x - 3) = 2\log_2 3$.

Solution

Graphical Method   A complete graph of $f(x) = \log_2(2x + 1) - \log_2(x - 3) - 2\log_2 3$ (Fig. 6.30) suggests that $x = 4$ is the one zero of f. Use zoom-in to support this claim, or use the following algebraic solution.

Algebraic Method

$$\log_2(2x + 1) - \log_2(x - 3) = 2\log_2 3$$

$$\log_2 \frac{2x + 1}{x - 3} = \log_2 9$$

$$\frac{2x + 1}{x - 3} = 9$$ Since $f(x) = \log_2 x$ is a one-to-one function, $\log a = \log b$ implies that $a = b$.

$$9x - 27 = 2x + 1$$

$$7x = 28$$

$$x = 4.$$

Check   Let $x = 4$. Then

$$\log_2(2 \cdot 4 + 1) - \log_2(4 - 3) = 2\ \log_2 3$$

$$\log_2 9 - \log_2 1 = 2\ \log_2 3$$

$$\log_2 3^2 - 0 = 2\ \log_2 3$$

$$2\ \log_2 3 = 2\ \log_2 3.$$

So $x = 4$ is a solution to the equation. ≡

E X A M P L E   4   Solving an Exponential Equation

When will your money triple in value at 8% compounded annually?

Solution   To answer this question, solve the equation $3P = P(1 + 0.08)^x$ which is equivalent to $3 = 1.08^x$:

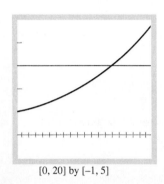

[0, 20] by [−1, 5]

Figure 6.31 $y = 1.08^x$ and $y = 3$.

$$1.08^x = 3 \qquad \text{Take the base 10 logarithm of both sides of the equation.}$$

$$\log 1.08^x = \log 3$$

$$x \log 1.08 = \log 3$$

$$x = \frac{\log 3}{\log 1.08}. \qquad \text{Use a calculator to evaluate this expression.}$$

$$x = 14.27$$

You can use zoom-in to support this solution by graphing $y = 1.08^x$ and $y = 3$ (Fig. 6.31). ≡

E X A M P L E   5   Solving an Exponential Equation

Solve the equation $(3^x - 3^{-x})/2 = 5$.

Solution

Graphical Method   Figure 6.32 shows a complete graph of $y = 5$ and $y = (3^x - 3^{-x})/2$. Since these graphs are complete, there appears to be one solution. Use zoom-in to find the x-coordinate of the point of intersection, or use the following algebraic solution.

Algebraic Method

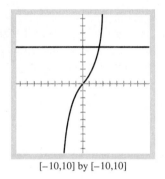

[−10,10] by [−10,10]

Figure 6.32 $y = \dfrac{3^x - 3^{-x}}{2}$ and $y = 5$.

$$\frac{3^x - 3^{-x}}{2} = 5$$

$$3^x - 3^{-x} = 10$$

$$(3^x)^2 - 1 = (10)3^x \qquad \text{Multiply each side by } 3^x.$$

$$(3^x)^2 - (10)3^x - 1 = 0$$

This equation is a quadratic in 3^x. Therefore, the quadratic formula yields

$$3^x = \frac{10 \pm \sqrt{104}}{2} = 5 \pm \sqrt{26}.$$

$5 - \sqrt{26}$ is negative and so does not result in a solution.

$$3^x = 5 + \sqrt{26}$$

$$\log_3 3^x = \log_3(5 + \sqrt{26}) \qquad \text{Use a calculator to evaluate this expression.}$$

$$x = 2.10$$

≡

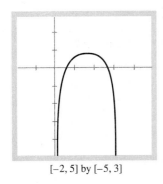

[−2, 5] by [−5, 3]

Figure 6.33
$f(x) = \ln[x(3 − x)]$.

The next example asks you to find any local extrema.

E X A M P L E   6   Finding Maximum and Minimum Values

Find the domain, range, and local extrema of $f(x) = \ln\big[x(3 − x)\big]$, and draw a complete graph.

Solution f is defined if

$$x(3 − x) > 0 \Longleftrightarrow x \text{ is in } (0, 3).$$

Figure 6.33 shows a complete graph of f. Use zoom-in to show that the local maximum value is 0.81 with an error of at most 0.01.

Domain of f $(0, 3)$.

Range of f $(−\infty, 0.81]$.

The next example introduces another application with an exponential function for a model.

E X A M P L E   7   APPLICATION: Atmospheric Pressure

Scientists have established that standard atmospheric pressure of 14.7 pounds per square inch is reduced by half for each 3.6 miles of vertical ascent. This rule for atmospheric pressure holds for altitudes up to 50 miles. Express the atmospheric pressure P as a function of altitude, and determine when the atmospheric pressure will be 4 lb/in².

Solution   Use the given information to conclude that

$$P = 14.7(0.5)^{h/3.6}$$

is an algebraic representation of atmospheric pressure as a funciton of h. Solve this equation for h with $P = 4$.

$$14.7(0.5)^{h/3.6} = 4$$

$$(0.5)^{h/3.6} = \frac{4}{14.7}$$

$$\frac{h}{3.6} \log(0.5) = \log\left(\frac{4}{14.7}\right)$$

$$h = \frac{3.6 \log(4/14.7)}{\log(0.5)} \qquad \text{Use a calculator to evaluate this expression.}$$

$$= 6.7598793.$$

Thus the atmospheric pressure will be 4 lb/in² at an altitude of approximately 6.76 miles.   ∎

EXAMPLE 8   APPLICATION: Probability Theory

An important function in probability theory is the **normal distribution function**

$$f(x) = \left(\frac{c}{r\sqrt{2\pi}}\right)e^{-(x-u)^2/2r^2},$$

where u represents the mean and r^2 is the variance. If $u = 0$, $c = 25$, and $r^2 = 2.35$, what is the maximum of the function f?

Solution   If $u = 0$ and $r^2 = 2.35$, the function $f(x)$ becomes

$$f(x) = \left(\frac{25}{\sqrt{2\pi \cdot (2.35)}}\right)e^{-x^2/4.7}.$$

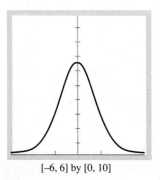

[–6, 6] by [0, 10]

Figure 6.34 $f(x) = \left(\dfrac{25}{\sqrt{2\pi \cdot (2.35)}}\right)e^{-x^2/4.7}.$

Figure 6.34 shows a complete graph of f. Use zoom-in to find that the maximum is 6.51 with an error of at most 0.01.   ∎

Exercises for Section 6.6

In Exercises 1 to 14, solve each equation algebraically. Support your answer with a graphing utility.

1. $\log x = 4$
2. $\ln x = -1$
3. $\log_4(x - 5) = -1$
4. $\log_x(1 - x) = 1$
5. $\log(x + 3) = 2$
6. $\log(x - 1) = 3$
7. $\log_2 x = 4$
8. $\log_3(x + 7) = 12$
9. $\log_x(12 - x) = 2$
10. $3\log_2 x = 4$
11. $\ln x + \ln 2 = 3$
12. $\frac{1}{2}\log_3(x + 1) = 2$
13. $\log_2 x + \log_2(x + 3) = 2$
14. $\log_4(x + 1) - \log_4 x = 1$

In Exercises 15 to 18, compare the domain and range of each pair of functions.

15. $y = 2\log x$; $y = \log x^2$
16. $y = \log x + \log(x + 1)$; $y = \log[x(x + 1)]$
17. $y = \log_5 \sqrt{x + 6} - \log_5 x$; $y = \log_5 \dfrac{\sqrt{x + 6}}{x}$
18. $y = \log_2 x - \log_2(x + 1)$; $y = \log_2\left(\dfrac{x}{x + 1}\right)$

In Exercises 19 to 24, find the exact solutions to each equation.

19. $(1.06)^x = 4.1$
20. $(0.98)^x = 1.6$
21. $(1.09)^x = 18.4$
22. $(1.12)^x = 3.2$
23. $\dfrac{2^x - 2^{-x}}{3} = 4$
24. $\dfrac{2^x + 2^{-x}}{2} = 3$
25. Use a calculator to find a decimal approximation to each solution in Exercises 19 to 24.

In Exercises 26 to 31, find a complete graph of each function. Determine the domain and range, and find where the function is increasing or decreasing. Find all local extrema.

26. $y = xe^x$
27. $y = x^2 e^{-x}$
28. $y = \dfrac{3^x - 3^{-x}}{3}$
29. $y = \dfrac{3^x + 3^{-x}}{3}$
30. $y = \ln(x^2 + 2x)$
31. $y = \ln\left(\dfrac{x}{2 + x}\right)$

In Exercises 32 and 33, solve each inequality.
32. $2\log_2 x - 4\log_2 3 > 0$
33. $2\log_3(x + 1) - 2\log_3 6 < 0$

In Exercises 34 to 37, solve each equation or inequality.
34. $e^x + x = 5$
35. $\ln|x| - e^{2x} \geq 3$
36. $e^x < 5 + \ln x$
37. $e^{2x} - 8x + 1 = 0$

In Exercises 38 and 39, solve each equation using a method of your choice.

38. $\dfrac{\ln x}{x} = \dfrac{1}{10}\ln 2$ **39.** $2^x = x^{10}$

40. Explain why Exercises 38 and 39 have the same *positive* solutions.

Exercises 41 to 44 refer to the normal probability density function problem situation introduced in Example 8 with a mean of $u = 11.6$, a variance $r^2 = 2.35$ and $c = 25$.

41. Find a complete graph of f.

42. Determine the domain of f.

43. Show that the graph of f is symmetric with respect to the line $x = u$.

44. Determine all x where $f(x) = 2$.

45. Using the model for atmospheric pressure from Example 7, find the pressure at an altitude of 50 miles.

Exercises 46 to 48 refer to the following **problem situation**: In a certain molecular structure, the total *potential energy E* between two ions is given by

$$E = \frac{-5.6}{r} + 10e^{-r/3},$$

where r is the distance separating the nuclei.

46. Draw a complete graph of E as a function of r. Determine the domain of E.

47. What values of r make sense in the problem situation?

48. Find any relative extrema of the total potential energy on $(0, \infty)$ and the number r for which they occur.

For the mortgage interest problems in Exercises 49 and 50, there is no known method to determine an exact, explicit solution. Use a graphing zoom-in method.

49. Carlos and Maria can afford to make monthly mortgage payments of $800. They want to purchase a home requiring a 30-year, $92,000 mortgage. What APR interest rate will be required?

50. Jill and Benny can afford to make monthly mortgage payments of $1200. They want to purchase a home requiring a 30-year $130,000 mortgage. What APR interest rate will be required?

Exercises 51 and 52 refer to the following **problem situation**: From the time an item is new (original cost C) until it reaches the end of its useful life (salvage value S), it depreciates. A continuous model for book value B at any time t using the *sinking fund method of depreciation* is

$$B = C - \left[\frac{C - S}{[(1 + i)^n - 1]/i}\right]\left[\frac{(1 + i)^t - 1}{i}\right],$$

n, the useful life, where $0 \le t \le n$ and i is an annual interest rate. In this case the annual depreciation charge is assumed to earn interest at the rate i per year, and the annual depreciation charges accumulate to the total depreciation $D = C - S$.

51. A machine costs $17,000, has a useful life of 6 years, and has a salvage value of $1200. Draw a complete graph of the book-value model $y = B(t)$. What values of t make sense in the problem situation? Assume $i = 5\%$.

52. Consider the machine in Exercise 51. What is the book value of the machine in 4 years, 3 months?

The exponential function $y = e^x$ is an important function because it models such a variety of phenomena. A significant theory in calculus shows that $y = e^x$ can be approximated by polynomials. Consider this list of polynomial functions of increasing degree.

$$f_1(x) = x + 1$$

$$f_2(x) = \frac{x^2}{2!} + x + 1$$

$$f_3(x) = \frac{x^3}{3!} + \frac{x^2}{2!} + x + 1$$

$$f_4(x) = \frac{x^4}{4!} + \frac{x^3}{3!} + \frac{x^2}{2!} + x + 1$$

$$\vdots$$

$$f_n(x) = \frac{x^n}{n!} + \frac{x^{n-1}}{(n-1)!} + \ldots + x + 1$$

$$\vdots$$

$$n! = n(n-1)(n-2)\cdots 3 \cdot 2 \cdot 1$$

Exercises 53 to 56 give a glimpse of that result.

53. Show algebraically that $f_n(x) = \dfrac{x^n}{n!} + f_{n-1}(x)$.

54. Draw the graphs of $y = f_1(x)$, $y = f_2(x)$, $y = f_3(x)$, $y = f_4(x)$, and $y = e^x$ in the $[-5, 5]$ by $[-25, 25]$ viewing rectangle.

55. For what values of x does $f_3(x)$ approximate e^x with an error of less than 0.1?

56. For what values of x does $f_5(x)$ approximate e^x with an error of less than 0.1?

Chapter Review

KEY TERMS

annual percentage
    rate (APR)
base number
bell curve
change-of-base formula
common logarithmic
    function
compounded annually
compounded continuously
compound interest
compound interest
    formula

continuous interest
continuous interest formula
desired base
effective annual rate i_{eff}
effective yield
exponent
exponential function with
    base a
exponential decay
exponential growth
given base

future value S of
    an annuity
half-life
interest
interest rate per period
logarithm of x with
    base a
logarithmic function with
    base a
natural exponential
    function

natural logarithmic
    function
normal distribution curve
normal distribution
    function
ordinary annuity
present value A of
    an annuity
principal
simple interest formula
simple interest rate r

REVIEW EXERCISES

In Exercises 1 to 6, sketch a complete graph of each function without using a graphing utility. Then support your answer with a graphing utility.

1. $f(x) = 2 + 3^x$

2. $f(x) = 3 - 2^{x+2}$

3. $y = 2 + \ln(x - 3)$

4. $y = \ln(x - 2) - 1$

5. $y = 3 \ln x$

6. $y = 2 \ln(x + 4)$

7. Use rules of exponents to solve $2^{x+1} = 4^3$.

In Exercises 8 to 12, use a graphing utility to find a complete graph of each function. Determine the domain and range. Find all local extrema if they exist.

8. $f(x) = (8x)2^{-x}$

9. $g(x) = \dfrac{\ln \sqrt{x + 2}}{x - 2}$

10. $h(x) = \log_3(x - 5)^2$

11. $f(x) = \ln\left(\dfrac{x}{x - 3}\right)$

12. $g(x) = \dfrac{2^x + 2^{-x}}{3}$

In Exercises 13 and 14, determine where each function is increasing and decreasing, and find all local extrema.

13. $f(x) = e^{-2x}$ **14.** $g(x) = (8x)2^{-x}$

Compute Exercises 15 and 16 without using a calculator.

15. $\log_5 125$ **16.** $\log_3(-9)$

In Exercises 17 and 18, solve each equation. Do not use a calculator.

17. $\log_x \frac{1}{9} = -2$ **18.** $\log_4 x = 3$

19. Use the properties of logarithms to write the expression $\log[(1 + r)^{12}/r]$ as a sum, difference, and/or product of simple logarithms.

20. Use the properties of logarithms to solve $z = (23 + x)^M$ for M.

21. Use a calculator to investigate numerically the end behavior of the function $f(x) = x^2/\ln x$. That is, find what $f(x)$ approaches as $x \to \infty$.

22. Use a calculator to investigate the behavior of $g(x) = x/\ln(x - 2)$ as $x \to 2^+$.

23. Use a calculator to investigate the behavior of $f(x) = x/\ln x^2$ as $x \to 1^-$.

24. Solve $\ln x > \log_2 x$ graphically.

25. Determine the end behavior of $f(x) = x^3 \ln x$. That is, determine what $f(x)$ approaches as $x \to \infty$.

26. Draw a complete graph of $y = x^3 \ln x$. Determine where the function is increasing and decreasing. Determine all local extrema.

In Exercises 27 and 28, solve each equation algebraically. Support your answer with a graphing utility.

27. $5\log_3 x = 2$

28. $\log_5 x + \log_5(x-4) = 1$

29. Compare the domain and range of the functions $y = \log_3 x - \log_3(x+2)$ and $y = \log_3[x/(x+2)]$.

30. Find the exact solution to the equation $(1.5)^x = 0.90$.

31. Use a calculator to find a decimal approximation to the solution in Exercise 30. Then use a graphing utility to check the solution.

Solve Exercises 32 to 34 algebraically. Check with a graphing utility.

32. $3\log_5(x-1) - 2\log_5 4 > 0$

33. $\log_2(x-1) + \log_2(x+2) = 2$

34. $\log_3(x+5) + 2\log_3 x > 1$

In Exercises 35 to 38, use a graphing utility to solve each equation or inequality.

35. $e^x + \ln x = 5$

36. $2\log x - e^x = -3$

37. $e^{2x} + 3e^x \le 10$

38. $75\log x - e^{2x} \ge -10$

39. Find the simultaneous solution to the system
$$\begin{cases} y = x^2 \\ y = 2^x \end{cases};$$
that is, solve $x^2 = 2^x$. For what values of x is $2^x > x^2$? For what values of x is $x^2 > 2^x$?

40. Find the simultaneous solution to the system
$$\begin{cases} y = x^3 \\ y = 3^x \end{cases};$$
that is, solve $x^3 = 3^x$. For what values of x is $3^x > x^3$? For what values of x is $x^3 > 3^x$?

Exercises 41 to 46 refer to the following problem situation: Linda deposits $500 in a bank that pays 7% annual interest. Assume that she makes no other deposits or withdrawals. How much has she accumulated after 5 years if the bank pays interest compounded as indicated?

41. annually

42. quarterly

43. monthly

44. daily

45. semiannually

46. continuously

47. Determine when an investment of $1500 accumulates to a value of $2280 if the investment earns interest at the rate of 7% compounded monthly.

48. Determine how much time is required for an investment to double in value if interest is earned at the rate of 6.25% compounded quarterly.

49. Draw a graph that shows the value at any time t of a $500 investment that earns 9% simple interest. In the same viewing rectangle, draw the graph that shows the value at any time t of a $500 investment that earns 9% interest, compounded monthly.

Exercises 50 to 52 refer to the following problem situation: The population of a town is 625,000 and is increasing at the rate of 4.05% each year.

50. Find an algebraic representation of the population P as a function of time.

51. Draw a complete graph of the function P in Exercise 50. What portion of the graph represents the problem situation?

52. Determine when the population of the town is 1 million.

Exercises 53 and 54 are the basis for what is called the *rule of 72*.

53. Graph $y = r$ and $y = \ln(1+r)$ for $0 \le r \le 1$ in the same viewing rectangle. When is $\ln(1+r)$ approximately equal to r?

54. Show how, using 0.72 as an approximate value for $\ln 2$, you can derive an easy-to-remember "rule" that says money invested at annual rate r compounded annually will double in value after $72/100r$ years. For example, at 6% interest compounded annually, you would expect money to double in value after $72/[100(0.06)] = 72/6 = 12$ years. Is this a good rule of thumb?

Exercises 55 to 57 refer to the following problem situation: The half-life of a certain radioactive substance is 21 days, and there are 4.62 grams present initially.

55. Find an algebraic representation for the amount A of substance remaining as a function of time.

56. Find a complete graph of the function in Exercise 55.

57. When will there be less than 1 gram of the substance remaining?

Exercises 58 and 59 refer to the Richter scale problem situation described in Section 6.5.

58. What is the magnitude on the Richter scale of an earthquake if $a = 275$, $T = 2.5$, and $B = 4.250$?

59. Draw a complete graph of the Richter scale model (magnitude R as a function of amplitude a). Assume $T = 2.5$ and $B = 4.250$. What are the values of a that make sense in this problem situation?

Exercises 60 and 61 refer to the following **problem situation**: It is known from the theory of electricity that in an RL *circuit*, the current I in the circuit is given by

$$I = \frac{V}{R}(1 - e^{-(Rt)/L})$$

as a function of time t. Here V, R, and L are constants for voltage, resistance, and self-inductance, respectively.

60. Assume $V = 10$ volts, $R = 3$ ohms, and $L = 0.03$ henries. Draw a complete graph of $I = f(t)$.

61. Show that $I \to V/R = 10/3$ as $t \to \infty$. Give a graphical argument.

62. Find the present value of an ordinary annuity for $100 payments in each of 30 payment intervals where the interest rate is 4% per payment interval.

63. Use a graphing utility to solve

$$10{,}000 = 250[1 - (1 + i)^{-60}]/i$$

for i. (*Note:* Think about solving this equation algebraically. There is no known method of explicitly solving this equation for i!)

64. Explain why the formula

$$B(n) = R\frac{1 - (1 + i)^{-(360-n)}}{i}$$

gives the outstanding loan balance of a 30-year mortgage loan requiring monthly payments of R dollars with an APR of $12i$ as a function of the number n of payments made.

65. Let $f(x) = ab^x$. Show that

$$\log b = \frac{\log f(x_2) - \log f(x_1)}{x_2 - x_1}$$

for any pair of real numbers x_1 and x_2 such that $x_1 \neq x_2$. Assume that $a > 0$ and $b > 1$.

66. Consider the equation

$$y = \$884.61\frac{1 - (1.01)^{-(360-x)}}{0.01}.$$

a) Draw a complete graph.
b) Explain how this graph relates to the outstanding loan balance of an $86,000 mortgage loan with a 30-year term requiring monthly payments of $884.61.

67. Some mortgage loans are available that require payments every 2 weeks (26 times each year). Consider a mortgage loan of $80,000 for a 30-year term at 10% APR requiring monthly payments.

a) Determine the monthly payment.
b) Suppose one-half of the monthly payment was made every 2 weeks. When would the mortgage loan be completely paid? Assume the interest rate per 2-week interval is one-half of the monthly interest rate.

CHAPTER 7

The Trigonometric Functions

7.1   Angles and Their Measure

So far in this book we have studied several types of functions: polynomial functions, rational functions, exponential and logarithmic functions, and functions involving radicals. In this chapter you will learn of another collection of functions called the **trigonometric functions**.

    Trigonometric functions are important because they model a wide variety of cyclical phenomena—from pendulum swings to alternating electrical current. Our development in this text takes into account both historical and modern approaches to this subject.

    In geometry an **angle** is defined as the union of two rays (half lines) with a common endpoint called the **vertex of the angle**. Trigonometry takes a more dynamic view by describing an angle in terms of a rotating ray. The beginning ray, called the **initial side of the angle**, is rotated about its endpoint. The final position is called the **terminal side of the angle**, and the endpoint of the ray is again called the vertex of the angle (see Fig. 7.1). Notice that the initial and terminal sides of an angle divide a plane into two different angles, one clockwise and the other counterclockwise.

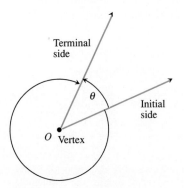

Figure 7.1   A clockwise and a counterclockwise angle.

319

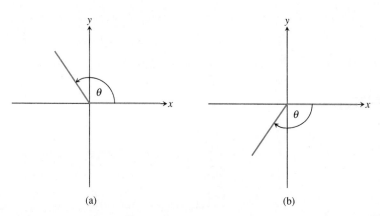

(a)   (b)

Figure 7.2 Two angles in standard position: (a) counterclockwise and (b) clockwise.

An angle is usually named with a single Greek letter, such as α (alpha), β (beta), γ (gamma), or θ (theta), or by an uppercase letter such as A, B, or C. We also use the symbol $\angle$ (angle), so that $\angle A$ is read "angle A."

An angle is called an **angle in standard position** when it is positioned on a rectangular coordinate system with its vertex at the origin and its initial side on the positive x-axis. Figure 7.2 shows two examples of angles in standard position.

Degree Measure

Angles are often measured using units called **degrees**. The measure of an angle determined by one complete counterclockwise rotation is defined to be 360 degrees, denoted 360°. So the measure of one-half and one-quarter of a complete counter-clockwise rotation would be 180° and 90° respectively (see Fig. 7.3). When the angle is rotated counterclockwise, the measure in degrees is positive, and when the angle is rotated clockwise, its measure in degrees is negative. Figure 7.4 shows both positive and negative angles. Notice that an angle will be more than 360° if it makes more than one complete revolution (Fig 7.4a,c).

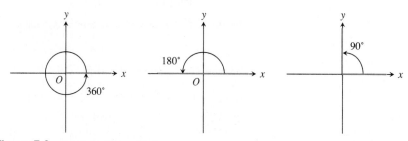

Figure 7.3 Angles with positive measure.

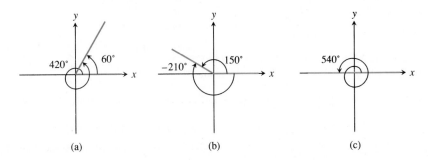

Figure 7.4   Examples of positive, negative, and coterminal angles.

Two angles are **coterminal** if they have the same initial side and the same terminal side. Coterminal angles can be found by adding or subtracting an integer multiple of 360°. For example, Fig. 7.4 (a) shows that a 60° angle and a 420° angle are coterminal angles; notice that $420 - 360 = 60$. Similarly, angles of $-210°$ and 150° are also coterminal: $-210 + 360 = 150$ (see Fig. 7.4b).

E X A M P L E   1   Finding Coterminal Angles

Sketch each of the following angles in standard position, and find one negative and one positive angle coterminal with each: (a) $\theta = 30°$,   (b) $\theta = 145°$, and   (c) $\theta = -45°$.

Solution   See Fig. 7.5.

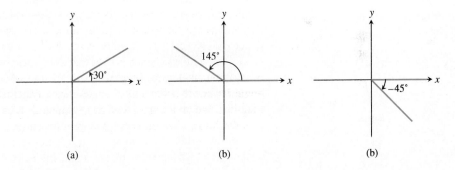

Figure 7.5   Three angles in standard position.

a) $\theta = 30°$ is coterminal with

$$\alpha = 30° + 360° = 390° \quad \text{and} \quad \beta = 30° + (-360°) = -330°.$$

b) $\theta = 145°$ is coterminal with

$$\alpha = 145° + 360° = 505° \quad \text{and} \quad \beta = 145° + (-360°) = -215°.$$

c) $\theta = -45°$ is coterminal with

$$\alpha = -45° + 360° = 315° \qquad \text{and} \qquad \beta = -45° + (-360°) = -405°.$$

Since a coterminal angle can be obtained by adding or subtracting an integer multiple of $360°$, there are an infinite number of correct answers.   ▤

Certain angles are given special names because they occur so frequently in trigonometric relations, as we shall see later in the chapter. A **right angle** is a $90°$ angle. An angle θ is an **acute angle** if $0° < \theta < 90°$, and an angle α is an **obtuse angle** if $90° < \alpha < 180°$. Two positive angles α and β are **supplementary angles** if their sum is $180°$, and they are **complementary angles** if their sum is $90°$. Negative angles do not have complements or supplements, and positive angles greater than $90°$ do not have complements.

EXAMPLE 2   Finding Complements and Supplements

Find the supplement and the complement of each of the following angles: (a) $48°$, (b) $135°$, (c) $-18°$, and (d) $x°$ where $0 < x < 90$.

Solution   To find the complement of the angle, subtract the angle from $90°$, and to find the supplement, subtract the angle from $180°$:

a) $\theta = 48°$: $180° - \theta = 132°$ (supplement); $90° - \theta = 42°$ (complement).

b) $\theta = 135°$: $180° - \theta = 45°$ (supplement); the complement of θ does not exist.

c) $\theta = -18°$ has no supplement or complement.

d) $\theta = x°$: $180° - x°$ (supplement); $90° - x°$ (complement).   ▤

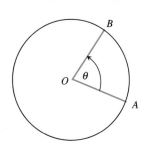

Figure 7.6   Central angle θ with intercepted arc AB.

Radian Measure

In addition to degree there is a second unit of angle measure called the radian. Radian measure is the unit of angle measure that is used frequently in trigonometry, calculus, and more advanced mathematics. It is important to understand radian measure and its relationship to degree measure.

If the vertex of an angle θ is the center of a circle, θ is called a **central angle** of the circle. If the sides of the angle intersect the circle at points A and B, the angle has an **intercepted arc AB** (see Fig. 7.6). If the length of this arc AB is equal to the radius r of the circle, then θ has a measure of 1 radian.

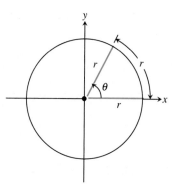

Figure 7.7   An angle of 1 radian.

Definition 7.1   Radian Measure

One **radian** is the measure of a central angle θ whose intercepted arc has a length equal to the radius of the circle. See Fig. 7.7.

To explore the relationship of radian measure to degree measure, we begin by considering a circle with radius $r = 1$. Such a circle is called a **unit circle**.

The radian measure of a central angle of a unit circle is equal to the length of the intercepted arc. Since the degree measure of a straight angle is $180°$ and half of the circumference of a unit circle is π, we conclude that an angle of $180° = \pi$ radians (see Fig. 7.8). This fact can be used to convert radians to degrees and vice versa.

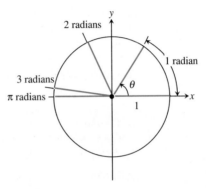

Figure 7.8 π radians $= 180°$.

RADIAN MEASURE
CONVENTION

From now on the word *radian* will be omitted when giving the measure of an angle in radians. For example, an angle of 2 radians will be reported as an angle whose measure is 2. We continue to use the established abbreviation for degree measure. That is, $2°$ stands for an angle that measures 2 degrees.

Conversion between Radians and Degrees

Since π radians $= 180°$, it follows that

$$1 \text{ radian} = \frac{180°}{\pi} \qquad \text{and} \qquad 1° = \frac{\pi}{180} \text{ radians.}$$

E X A M P L E   3   Converting from Degrees to Radians

Change each of these common angles from degrees to radians: $30°$, $45°$, $60°$, and $90°$.

Solution

$$30° = 30° \left(\frac{\pi \text{ rad.}}{180°} \right) = \frac{\pi}{6} \text{ rad.} \qquad 45° = 45° \left(\frac{\pi \text{ rad.}}{180°} \right) = \frac{\pi}{4} \text{ rad.}$$

$$60° = 60° \left(\frac{\pi \text{ rad.}}{180°} \right) = \frac{\pi}{3} \text{ rad.} \qquad 90° = 90° \left(\frac{\pi \text{ rad.}}{180°} \right) = \frac{\pi}{2} \text{ rad.}$$

EXAMPLE 4   Converting from Radians to Degrees

Change each of these angles from radians to degrees: $3\pi/2$, $2\pi/3$, $5\pi/4$, and $7\pi/12$.

Solution

$$\frac{3\pi}{2} = 3\left(\frac{\pi}{2}\right) = 3(90°) = 270° \qquad \frac{2\pi}{3} = 2\left(\frac{\pi}{3}\right) = 2(60°) = 120°$$

$$\frac{5\pi}{4} = 5\left(\frac{\pi}{4}\right) = 5(45°) = 225° \qquad \frac{7\pi}{12} = \frac{7\pi}{12}\left(\frac{180°}{\pi}\right) = 105°$$ ▤

GRAPHER UPDATE

Scientific calculators and graphing calculators have both a degree mode and a radian mode. Make sure the mode setting for angle measure is correct.

The angles $30°, 45°, 60°$, and $90°$ are frequently used in trigonometry. Since they are factors of $180°$, their radian measure equivalents, $\pi/6, \pi/4, \pi/3$, and $\pi/2$, and their integer multiples, are usually expressed in this fractional form. The radian measure of other angles are commonly expressed in decimal form.

EXAMPLE 5   Converting from Degrees to Radians

Find the radian measure of an angle whose measure is (a) $500°$ or (b) $-200°$.

Solution

a) $500° = 500°\left(\dfrac{\pi}{180°}\right) = 8.72664626$

b) $-200° = -200°\left(\dfrac{\pi}{180°}\right) = -3.490658504$ ▤

In a unit circle the length of an arc and its subtended central angle measured in radians have the same measure. However, this is not true when the radius of the circle is not 1. Figure 7.9 shows a central angle with radian measure θ. The length x of arc AB determined by this angle is a fraction of the circumference $C = 2\pi r$ of the circle and can be determined from the following proportion:

$$\frac{\theta}{2\pi} = \frac{x}{2\pi r}$$

$$x = \frac{\theta}{2\pi}(2\pi r) = \theta r.$$

In this proportion, angle θ must be measured in radians.

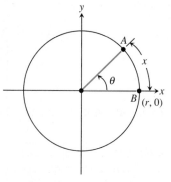

Figure 7.9   Length x of arc AB subtends the central angle θ.

Theorem 7.1   Arc Length

Given a circle of radius r. If x is the length of the intercepted arc of a central angle θ, then

$$x = r\theta.$$

Notice that the formula in Theorem 7.1 is correct for θ expressed in radians only.

EXAMPLE 6   Finding Arc Length

Find the length x of the arc of a circle of radius 2 intercepted by a central angle measuring $\pi/4$.

Solution   Use Theorem 7.1.

$$x = r\theta = 2\left(\frac{\pi}{4}\right)$$

$$= \frac{\pi}{2}$$

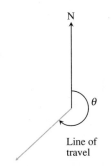

N

θ

Line of
travel

Figure 7.10   A certain angle west of north.

Applications

Many real-world application situations use degrees for angle measure, while many scientific applications use radians.

In navigation, the **course**, or **path**, of an object is sometimes given as the measure of the clockwise angle θ that the **line of travel** makes with due north (see Fig. 7.10). That is, the due-north ray is the initial side, and the line of travel is the terminal side of the angle of the path. By convention, the angle measure θ is positive even though the angle rotation is clockwise.

We also say that the line of travel has **bearing θ**.

EXAMPLE 7   APPLICATON: Navigation

The captain of a boat steers a course 35° from home port. Use a drawing to illustrate the path of the boat.

Solution   Draw a ray from home port in the due-north direction. Rotate the north ray 35° clockwise (see Fig. 7.11). The boat travels in the direction of this second ray. We say that the bearing of the boat is 35°.

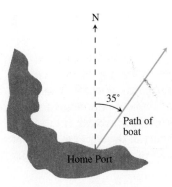

N

35°

Path of
boat

Home Port

Figure 7.11   East of north.

In navigation and other situations, it is often necessary to measure angles smaller than 1°. The degree is divided into 60 equal parts, called **minutes** (denoted by ′), and each minute is divided into 60 equal parts, called **seconds** (denoted by ″). So an angle of 23° 15′ 45″ is equal to

$$23 + \frac{15}{60} + \frac{45}{3600} = 23 + \frac{900}{3600} + \frac{45}{3600} \qquad \text{One second is 1/60th of 1/60th or 1/3600th of a degree.}$$

$$= 23.2625°.$$

Figure 7.12 If $\angle AOB$ is $1/60°$, then the length of AB is 1 nautical mile.

The measure of distance used by navigators is the nautical mile. It is defined in terms of the earth itself with point O located at the center of the earth. If $\angle AOB$ has measure 1 minute (1/60 of a degree), then the distance between A and B on the circumference of the circle is *1* **nautical mile** (see Fig. 7.12). The diameter of the Earth averages 7912.176 statute miles where a **statute mile** is a standard mile of 5280 feet.

E X A M P L E   8   APPLICATON: Nautical Miles

How many feet are in 1 nautical mile?

Solution   We need to find the length x of arc AB in Fig. 7.12.

$$\text{radius } r \text{ of earth} = \frac{7912.176}{2} \text{ miles and 5280 feet/mile}$$

$$x = r\theta$$

$$= \frac{7912.176}{2}\left(\frac{1}{60}\right)^{\circ}(5280)$$

$$= \frac{7912.176}{2}\left(\frac{\pi}{60 \cdot 180}\right)5280$$

$$= 6076.115 \text{ feet}$$

There are 6076.115 feet in 1 nautical mile.

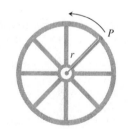

Figure 7.13 A rotating wheel.

Radian measure can also be used to analyze the motion of a point moving at a constant speed along a circular path. Suppose for example, a wheel of radius r is rotating at a constant rate (see Fig. 7.13). Let P be a point on the circumference of the wheel. The **angular speed** of the wheel, in radians per second, is the angle swept out in 1 second by the line segment from the center of the wheel to the point P on the circumference of the wheel. The **linear speed** of the point P, in feet per second, is the distance P travels in 1 second.

$$\text{angular speed:} \quad \theta \text{ rad/sec} = \frac{s}{r} \text{ rad/sec}$$

$$\text{linear speed:} \quad s \text{ ft/sec} = r\theta \text{ ft/sec}$$

E X A M P L E   9   APPLICATION: Angular Speed

A wheel with a radius of 18 inches is rotating at 850 rpm (revolutions per minute). Determine (a) the angular speed of the wheel in radians per second, and (b) the linear speed in feet per second of a point on the circumference of the wheel (see Fig. 7.13). *Hint*: 1 rpm = 2π rad/minute

Solution

a) First, change revolutions per minute to radians per second:

$$850 \text{ rpm} = \frac{850(2\pi)}{60} \text{ rad/sec} = \left(\frac{85}{3}\right)\pi \text{ rad/sec}.$$

The angular speed of the wheel is $85/3\pi$ rad/sec.

b) From Theorem 7.1 we know that if x represents arc length, $x = r\theta$, and from part (a) that $\theta = \left(\frac{85}{3}\right)\pi$.

$$x = r\theta$$

$$= 1.5\left(\frac{85}{3}\right)\pi \qquad \text{18 inches} = 1.5 \text{ feet}$$

$$= 133.52 \text{ ft/sec.}$$

The linear speed of a point on the wheel is 133.52 ft/sec.

Exercises for Section 7.1

In Exercises 1 to 6, determine the quadrant of the terminal side of each angle in standard position.

1. $-160°$ **2.** $280°$ **3.** $452°$

4. $-827°$ **5.** $1150°$ **6.** $-455°$

In Exercises 7 to 10, determine the measure of an angle θ coterminal with the given angle that satisfies the specified condition.

7. $48°$; $360° \leq \theta \leq 720°$ **8.** $110°$; $-360° \leq \theta \leq 0°$.

9. $-15°$; $180° \leq \theta \leq 540°$ **10.** $-250°$; $360° \leq \theta \leq 720°$

In Exercises 11 to 20, draw a sketch of each angle and determine four different coterminal angles, two with positive and two with negative measures.

11. $55°$ **12.** $-22°$ **13.** $410°$

14. $-150°$ **15.** $\dfrac{\pi}{4}$ **16.** $\dfrac{3\pi}{2}$

17. $\dfrac{\pi}{6}$ **18.** $\dfrac{5\pi}{6}$ **19.** $-\dfrac{\pi}{3}$

20. $-\dfrac{7\pi}{4}$

In Exercises 21 to 28, find the complement and supplement of each angle. Use the same unit of angle measure as in the given angle.

21. $35°$ **22.** $23°$ **23.** $68°$

24. $12°$ **25.** $\pi/3$ **26.** $\pi/12$

27. $\dfrac{5\pi}{13}$ **28.** $\dfrac{3\pi}{7}$

In Exercises 29 to 34, assume the given point is on the terminal side of an angle θ in standard position where $0° \leq \theta \leq 360°$. Determine θ in both degrees and radians.

29. $(-1, 0)$ **30.** $(0, 5)$ **31.** $(3, 3)$

32. $(-2, 2)$ **33.** $(5, -5)$ **34.** $(10, 0)$

In Exercises 35 to 40, determine the measure in both degrees and radians, and draw the angle in standard position.

35. one-half counterclockwise rotation

36. one-third clockwise rotation

37. four-thirds counterclockwise rotation

38. five-thirds clockwise rotation

39. 2.5 counterclockwise rotations

40. 3.5 clockwise rotations

In Exercises 41 to 46, find the equivalent radian measure for each angle.

41. $45°$ **42.** $60°$ **43.** $135°$

44. $210°$ **45.** $120°$ **46.** $330°$

In Exercises 47 to 50, find the equivalent radian measure for each angle.

47. $23°$ **48.** $118°$

49. $72°$ **50.** $249°$

In Exercises 51 to 54, find the equivalent degree measure for each angle.

51. $\dfrac{5\pi}{12}$ **52.** 4.5

53. 3.75 **54.** 12.9

In Exercises 55 to 58, determine the length of the arc of a circle with the specified radius subtended by a central angle of the given measure.

55. $r = 2$; $\theta = 30°$ **56.** $r = 3.75$; $\theta = 122°$

57. $r = 5.76$; $\theta = 155°$ **58.** $r = 20.55$; $\theta = 72°$

In Exercises 59 to 62, let θ be a central angle of a circle of radius r and s the length of the subtended arc. Find the arc length s.

59. $\theta = 22°$, $r = 15$ inches   **60.** $\theta = 3$, $r = 5.6$ feet

61. $\theta = 1.75$, $r = 3.5$ cm   **62.** $\theta = \dfrac{\pi}{12}$, $r = 5.1$ inches

63. The captain of a boat follows a $38°$ course for 2 miles and then changes to a $47°$ course, which he follows for the next 4 miles. Draw a sketch of this trip.

64. Find the angles that describe the following compass directions: (a) NE (northeast), (b) NNE (north-northeast), and (c) ENE (east-northeast).

65. A ship's captain traveling east discovers that he is traveling on a course that is $5°$ north of the correct direction of his destination. If the captain makes a single midcourse correction when he is exactly halfway to his destination, will he make a course correction of (a) $5°$, (b) $10°$, (c) $-5°$, or (d) $-10°$?

66. Points A and B are 257 nautical miles apart. How far apart are A and B in *statute* miles?

67. Draw diagrams to illustrate navigational courses of $35°$, $128°$, and $310°$.

68. At a certain time an airplane is between two signal towers that lie on an east–west line. The bearing from the plane to each tower is $340°$ and $37°$, respectively. Use a drawing to show the exact location of the plane.

69. Let A be the origin of a coordinate plane. Draw a diagram showing the location of point B if the bearing from A to B is (a) $22°$, (b) $185°$, and (c) $292°$.

Exercises 70 and 71 refer to the following **problem situation:** A wheel with a radius of 5 feet rotating at 1200 rpm.

70. Determine the angular speed of the wheel.

71. Determine the linear speed of a point on the circumference of the wheel.

Exercises 72 and 73 refer to the following **problem situation:** A wheel with a radius of 2.8 feet is rotating at 600 rpm.

72. Determine the angular speed of the wheel.

73. Determine the linear speed of a point on the circumference of the wheel.

74. Elena can obtain a speed of 42 mph on her exercise bike in high gear. The bike wheels are 30 inches in diameter, the pedal sprocket is 16 inches in diameter, and the wheel sprocket is 5 inches in diameter (in high gear). Find the angular speed of the wheel and of both sprockets. *(Note: The linear speed of a point on the circumference of the wheel is also 42 mph.)*

Exercises 75 and 76 refer to the following **problem situation:** A simple winch used to lift heavy objects is positioned 10 feet above ground level. Assume that the radius of the winch is r feet. For the given radius r and winch rotation θ, determine the distance that the object is lifted above ground.

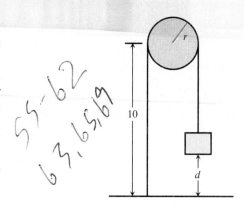

For Exercises 75 and 76

75. $r = 4$ inches, $\theta = 720°$ **76.** $r = 1$ foot, $\theta = 720°$

7.2 _____

Trigonometric Functions of an Acute Angle

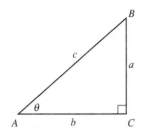

Figure 7.14   In a right triangle one angle (here $\angle C$) is a right angle and angles A and B are acute.

The Greeks developed trigonometry over 2000 years ago to measure angles and sides of triangles, particularly for land measurement. In fact the word *trigonometry* is derived from two Greek words that mean "triangle measurement." Since the Greeks based their calculations on the lengths of sides of a right triangle, the historical development of trigonometry is based on the right triangle. A more modern development, based on the unit circle, will be developed in Section 7.3.

We begin with some terminology regarding right triangles.

For triangle ABC, denoted $\triangle ABC$, in Fig. 7.14 side a is opposite $\angle A$, side b is opposite $\angle B$, and side c is opposite $\angle C$. The side c opposite the right angle is the **hypotenuse**, and a and b are the **legs**.

Side a is called the **side opposite** $\angle A$ and b is called the **side adjacent to** $\angle A$. Likewise, side b is opposite $\angle B$ and side a is adjacent to $\angle B$.

We define the six trigonometric functions of an angle θ in terms of the lengths of the sides of a right triangle with an acute angle θ.

Definition 7.2   Trigonometric Functions

The six trigonometric functions of any angle $0° < \theta < 90°$ are defined as follows. (Refer to Fig. 7.14.) The abbreviations opp, adj, and hyp represent the lengths of the sides opposite and adjacent to angle θ and the length of the hypotenuse.

$$\text{sine } \theta = \frac{a}{c} = \frac{\text{opp}}{\text{hyp}} \qquad \text{cosecant } \theta = \frac{c}{a} = \frac{\text{hyp}}{\text{opp}}$$

$$\text{cosine } \theta = \frac{b}{c} = \frac{\text{adj}}{\text{hyp}} \qquad \text{secant } \theta = \frac{c}{b} = \frac{\text{hyp}}{\text{adj}}$$

$$\text{tangent } \theta = \frac{a}{b} = \frac{\text{opp}}{\text{adj}} \qquad \text{cotangent } \theta = \frac{b}{a} = \frac{\text{adj}}{\text{opp}}$$

AGREEMENT

The symbol θ will be used to represent both the name of the angle and the measure of the angle. Thus, in Fig. 7.14 the measure of $\angle B$ is $\pi/2 - \theta$ or $90° - \theta$, whichever unit of angle measure is used.

We often use the abbreviation *trig* for *trigonometry* or *trigonometric*. Also the following are standard abbreviations for the trig functions:

$$\sin \theta = \text{sine } \theta \qquad \csc \theta = \text{cosecant } \theta$$

$$\cos \theta = \text{cosine } \theta \qquad \sec \theta = \text{secant } \theta$$

$$\tan \theta = \text{tangent } \theta \qquad \cot \theta = \text{cotangent } \theta$$

In order for the trig functions to be well defined, their values for a given acute angle θ must be the same no matter which right triangle with acute angle θ is used in the definition.

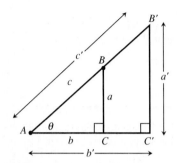

Figure 7.15 $\triangle ABC$ and $\triangle AB'C'$ are similar, so ratios of corresponding sides are equal.

Recall from your study of geometry that **similar triangles** are triangles whose corresponding angles are **congruent**. Figure 7.15 shows that any two right triangles with the same acute angle θ are similar. (Why?) Consequently, corresponding ratios of the two triangles are equal. From this we see that the trig functions have the same value no matter what right triangle is used with $\angle\theta$.

Since the angles $30°, 45°$, and $60°$ occur frequently, it is convenient to know their trig values without having to use a calculator to figure them. Example 1 gives you these values.

E X A M P L E   1   Finding Trig Values of 30° and 60° Angles

Find the values of the trig functions at $30°$ and $60°$.

Solution   In the equilateral triangle ABC shown in Fig. 7.16, altitude BD is the angle bisector of $\angle B$ and is also the perpendicular bisector of AC. It follows that $\triangle ABD$ has angles of $30°$, $60°$, and $90°$, so if $AB = 2$, then $AD = 1$, and $BD = \sqrt{3}$. Apply the definitions of the trig functions to the triangles in Fig. 7.16:

$$\sin 30° = \frac{1}{2} \qquad \csc 30° = \frac{2}{1} \qquad \sin 60° = \frac{\sqrt{3}}{2} \qquad \csc 60° = \frac{2}{\sqrt{3}}$$

$$\cos 30° = \frac{\sqrt{3}}{2} \qquad \sec 30° = \frac{2}{\sqrt{3}} \qquad \cos 60° = \frac{1}{2} \qquad \sec 60° = \frac{2}{1}$$

$$\tan 30° = \frac{1}{\sqrt{3}} \qquad \cot 30° = \frac{\sqrt{3}}{1} \qquad \tan 60° = \frac{\sqrt{3}}{1} \qquad \cot 60° = \frac{1}{\sqrt{3}}$$

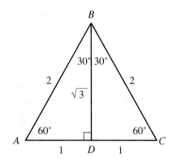

Figure 7.16   A $30°$-$60°$-$90°$ triangle is half of an equilateral triangle.

E X A M P L E   2   Finding Trig Values of a 45° Angle

Find the values of the trig functions at $45°$.

Solution   Consider an isosceles right triangle with a $45°$ angle and legs of length 1 (see Fig. 7.17).

$$\sin 45° = \frac{1}{\sqrt{2}} = \frac{\sqrt{2}}{2} \qquad \csc 45° = \frac{\sqrt{2}}{1} = \sqrt{2}$$

$$\cos 45° = \frac{1}{\sqrt{2}} = \frac{\sqrt{2}}{2} \qquad \sec 45° = \frac{\sqrt{2}}{1} = \sqrt{2}$$

$$\tan 45° = \frac{1}{1} = 1 \qquad \cot 45° = \frac{1}{1} = 1$$

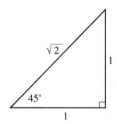

Figure 7.17   A right triangle with a $45°$ angle.

When we write a trig function of a number, for example $(\sin \pi/6)$, the number represents the radian measure of an angle.

The sine, cosine, and tangent values for angles with radian measure $\pi/6, \pi/4,$ and $\pi/3$ are summarized in the next table. Recall that these radian measures are equivalent to $30°, 45°,$ and $60°$ angles.

Sine, Cosine, and Tangent for Angles of $\dfrac{\pi}{6}, \dfrac{\pi}{4},$ and $\dfrac{\pi}{3}$ Radians

$$\sin\frac{\pi}{6} = \frac{1}{2} \qquad \sin\frac{\pi}{4} = \frac{\sqrt{2}}{2} \qquad \sin\frac{\pi}{3} = \frac{\sqrt{3}}{2}$$

$$\cos\frac{\pi}{6} = \frac{\sqrt{3}}{2} \qquad \cos\frac{\pi}{4} = \frac{\sqrt{2}}{2} \qquad \cos\frac{\pi}{3} = \frac{1}{2}$$

$$\tan\frac{\pi}{6} = \frac{1}{\sqrt{3}} \qquad \tan\frac{\pi}{4} = 1 \qquad \tan\frac{\pi}{3} = \frac{\sqrt{3}}{1}$$

Finding Values of Trig Functions

Examples 1 and 2 illustrate how to find the values of the trig functions for several common angles. How are values of the trig functions found for other angles?

Historically, tables of values were published for mathematicians, engineers, and students to use. Now, however, scientific calculators have taken their place.

USING A CALCULATOR

Make sure the mode setting is correct when using a calculator with trig functions. Check the owner's manual of your calculator to see how the trig keys work.

E X A M P L E   3   Finding Trig Values with a Calculator

Find $\sin\theta, \cos\theta,$ and $\tan\theta$ for (a) $\theta = 42°$ and (b) $\theta = \pi/12$.

Solution   Use a scientific calculator.

a) $\sin 42° = 0.6691306064$ **b)** $\sin\dfrac{\pi}{12} = 0.2588190451$

$\cos 42° = 0.7431448255$ $\cos\dfrac{\pi}{12} = 0.9659258263$

$\tan 42° = 0.9004040443$ $\tan\dfrac{\pi}{12} = 0.2679491924$

Most calculators have function keys for $\sin\theta, \cos\theta,$ and $\tan\theta$ but not for $\cot\theta, \sec\theta,$ or $\csc\theta$. In order to use a calculator to find values for these latter three functions, use the following reciprocal trig relationships. They follow directly from the six trig functions given in Definition 7.2 and are valid for all acute angles. Consequently these equations are called identities.

Reciprocal Identities

If θ is an acute angle, then

$$\csc \theta = \frac{1}{\sin \theta}, \qquad \sec \theta = \frac{1}{\cos \theta}, \qquad \cot \theta = \frac{1}{\tan \theta}.$$

E X A M P L E   4   Finding Trig Values with a Calculator

Find (a) cot 0.29, (b) sec 0.29, and (c) csc 0.29 .

Solution   Use the reciprocal identities and a scientific calculator in radian mode.

a) $\cot 0.29 = \dfrac{1}{\tan 0.29} = 3.35106284$

b) $\sec 0.29 = \dfrac{1}{\cos 0.29} = 1.043575676$

c) $\csc 0.29 = \dfrac{1}{\sin 0.29} = 3.497087668$

Sine and cosine are called **cofunctions**, as are tangent and cotangent, and secant and cosecant. Basic identities between each of the cofunctions using radian measure are summarized next.

Notice that in Fig. 7.18 angles A and B are complementary.

$$\sin \theta = \sin A = \frac{a}{c}$$

$$\cos \left(\frac{\pi}{2} - \theta\right) = \cos B = \frac{a}{c}$$

Therefore $\sin \theta = \cos(\pi/2 - \theta)$. The identities for the other cofunctions can be established in a similar fashion.

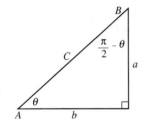

Figure 7.18   The two acute angles in a right triangle are complementary.

Cofunctions of Complementary Angles

If θ is any acute angle, a trig function value of θ is equal to the cofunction of the complement of θ. That is,

$$\sin \theta = \cos \left(\frac{\pi}{2} - \theta\right) \qquad \cot \theta = \tan \left(\frac{\pi}{2} - \theta\right)$$

$$\cos \theta = \sin \left(\frac{\pi}{2} - \theta\right) \qquad \sec \theta = \csc \left(\frac{\pi}{2} - \theta\right)$$

$$\tan \theta = \cot \left(\frac{\pi}{2} - \theta\right) \qquad \csc \theta = \sec \left(\frac{\pi}{2} - \theta\right)$$

If you know the value of one trig function for an acute angle θ, you can find the values for the other five functions as illustrated in Example 5.

E X A M P L E   5   Finding Trig Values

Let θ be an acute angle such that $\sin\theta = \frac{5}{6}$. Find the values of all the trig functions of θ.

Solution   Using the information $\sin\theta = \frac{5}{6}$, label a right triangle as shown in Fig. 7.19. From the Pythagorean theorem it follows that

$$b^2 + 5^2 = 6^2$$

$$b^2 = 6^2 - 5^2 = 11$$

$$b = \sqrt{11}.$$

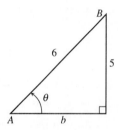

Figure 7.19   In Example 5 the hypotenuse and one leg are known.

Use the value $b = \sqrt{11}$ to find the remaining trig functions:

$$\sin\theta = \frac{5}{6} \qquad \csc\theta = \frac{6}{5}$$

$$\cos\theta = \frac{\sqrt{11}}{6} \qquad \sec\theta = \frac{6}{\sqrt{11}}$$

$$\tan\theta = \frac{5}{\sqrt{11}} \qquad \cot\theta = \frac{\sqrt{11}}{5}$$

Solving Right Triangles

One of the earliest uses of trigonometry was to find unknown parts of a triangle. The ancient Greeks established that if the measure of two sides of a right triangle, or the measure of one side and one angle, are known, then the measure of the other sides or angles of the right triangle can be determined. Determining the measures of the missing parts of a right triangle is often referred to as **solving a right triangle**. The next two examples illustrate the procedure for solving a right triangle.

E X A M P L E 6   Solving a Right Triangle

One angle of a right triangle measures $37°$, and the hypotenuse has a length of 8. Find the measure of the remaining sides of the right triangle (see Fig. 7.20).

Solution

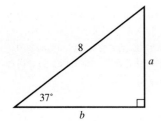

$$\sin 37° = \frac{a}{8} \qquad\qquad \cos 37° = \frac{b}{8}$$

$$a = 8 \sin 37° \qquad\qquad b = 8 \cos 37°$$

$$= 4.814520185 \qquad\qquad = 6.38908408$$

Rounded to the nearest hundredths, $a = 4.81$ and $b = 6.39$.

Figure 7.20 In Example 6 the hypotenuse and one acute angle are known.

We can use the Pythagorean theorem as a check on the trig calculations in Example 6. In Fig. 7.20, $a^2 + b^2 = 8^2$, or $8 = \sqrt{a^2 + b^2}$.

$$\sqrt{a^2 + b^2} = \sqrt{(4.81)^2 + (6.39)^2} \quad \text{Substitute } a = 4.81 \text{ and } b = 6.39.$$

$$= \sqrt{23.1361 + 40.8321}$$

$$= 7.998012253$$

This calculation will not be exactly 8 since a and b were rounded to the nearest hundredth. However, the result is close enough to 8 to be confident that 4.81 and 6.39 are correct. If the complete expressions for $8 \sin 37°$ and $8 \cos 37°$ had been used, the result would be 8. Confirm with a calculator that

$$\sqrt{a^2 + b^2} = \sqrt{(8 \sin 37°)^2 + (8 \cos 37°)^2}$$

$$= 8.$$

E X A M P L E 7   Solving a Right Triangle

The hypotenuse and one leg of a right triangle measure 12.7 and 6.1, respectively. Find the measures of the angle θ formed by these three sides.

Figure 7.21 In Example 7 only the lengths of two sides are known.

Solution   From Fig. 7.21 notice that

$$\cos \theta = \frac{6.1}{12.7} = 0.4803149606.$$

AGREEMENT ON NOTATION

We use the notation
$\cos^{-1}(6.1/12.7)$ to denote the
angle θ (in degree mode) or
the number θ (in radian mode)
for which $\cos\theta = 6.1/12.7$.
We will use $\cos^{-1}$ to denote
the calculator keys $\boxed{\text{INV}}$
$\boxed{\text{COS}}$, or $\boxed{\text{2nd}}$ $\boxed{\text{COS}}$, or
$\boxed{\text{SHIFT}}$ $\boxed{\text{COS}}$. The symbols
$\sin^{-1}$ and $\tan^{-1}$ are used in a
similar way.

We want to find an angle (in degrees) whose cosine is 0.4803149606. That is, we want to find $\cos^{-1}(6.1/12.7)$. (See the Agreement on Notation.)

$$\cos^{-1}\left(\frac{6.1}{12.7}\right) = \boxed{\text{2nd}}\ \boxed{\text{COS}}\left(\frac{6.1}{12.7}\right) = 61.29°$$

The answer to Example 7 can be confirmed by evaluating the trig value on a calculator. For example, cos 61.29° = 0.48037, which is sufficiently close to 6.1/12.7 to confirm the solution.

Applications for Solving Right Triangles

Since the time of the ancient Greeks, people have used the principles of solving a right triangle to measure and survey the landscape. Finding these measurements requires finding the measure of sides or angles of the right triangle that models the problem. The terms **angle of elevation** or **angle of depression** are used to describe the angle between the line of sight and the horizontal (see Fig. 7.22).

ACCURACY AGREEMENT

In Example 7 lengths 12.7 and
6.1 were assumed to be exact.
Some textbooks assume that
numbers like 12.7 and 6.1
are accurate only to 0.1. In
this textbook, assume given
information is exact unless
otherwise specified. Carry
full calculator approximations
until all computations are
completed. Then round off all
answers so they have an error
of at most 0.01.

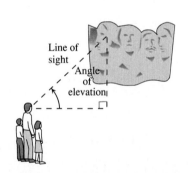 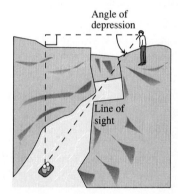

Figure 7.22   A right triangle is used in figuring the angle of elevation or the angle of depression.

E X A M P L E   8   APPLICATION: Unknown Height

The angle of elevation of the top of a building from a point 100 feet away from the building on level ground is 65° (see Fig. 7.23). Find the height h of the building.

Solution   Notice from Fig. 7.23 that

$$\tan 65° = \frac{h}{100}$$

$$h = 100\tan 65°\qquad \text{Enter the right-hand side on your calculator.}$$

$$= 214.45.$$

The height of the building is 214.45 feet.

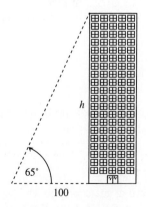

Figure 7.23   Sketch for Example 8.

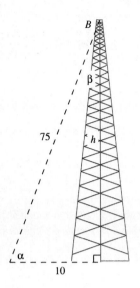

75

β

h

B

α

10

Figure 7.24 Sketch for Example 9.

EXAMPLE 9 APPLICATION: Angle of Elevation

A guy wire 75 feet long runs from a radio tower to a point on level ground 10 feet from the center of the base of the tower (see Fig. 7.24). Determine the angle α the guy wire makes with the horizontal, the angle β the guy wire makes with the tower, and the distance h between the ground and the point B where the guy wire is attached to the tower.

Solution

$$\cos \alpha = \frac{10}{75} = 0.1333333$$

Use the calculator keys $\boxed{\text{INV}}$ $\boxed{\text{COS}}$, $\boxed{\text{2nd}}$ $\boxed{\text{COS}}$, or $\boxed{\text{SHIFT}}$ $\boxed{\text{COS}}$ to determine that

$$\alpha = 82.34° \qquad \text{and} \qquad \beta = 90° - 82.34° = 7.66°.$$

To find h use either the Pythagorean theorem or the tangent function, as follows.

$$75^2 = 10^2 + h^2 \qquad\qquad \tan \alpha = \frac{h}{10}$$

$$h^2 = 5625 - 100 \qquad\qquad h = 10 \tan 82.34°$$

$$h = \sqrt{5525} = 74.33 \qquad\qquad = 74.35$$

Thus the guy wire makes a 82.34° angle with the horizontal and a 7.66° angle with the tower, and the guy wire is attached to a point 74.33 feet above ground.

≡

What explains the discrepancy in the two solutions for h in Example 9? Which value for h is the most reliable? (See Exercise 84.)

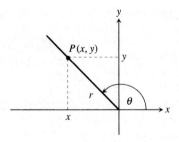

y

$P(x, y)$

y

r

θ

x

x

Figure 7.25 An angle in standard position.

Defining Trig Functions for Angles in Standard Position

Up to this point we have defined each trig function as the ratio of the lengths of two sides in a right triangle. In this section we extend the definitions of the trig functions as follows.

Suppose that θ is any angle in standard position and that point $P(x, y)$ is on the terminal side of the angle (see Fig. 7.25). Notice that θ can have any value either positive or negative. Angles are no longer restricted to acute angles. The trig functions will now be defined in terms of the coordinates of P and the distance r between P and the origin.

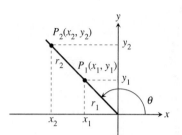

Figure 7.26 Choosing different points on the same terminal side results in the same ratios.

Definition 7.3 Trigonometric Functions of Any Angle

Let θ be an angle in standard position, $P(x, y)$ a point other than the origin on the terminal side of P, and $r = \sqrt{x^2 + y^2}$. See Fig. 7.25. The six trig function values of θ are defined as follows:

$$\sin \theta = \frac{y}{r} \qquad\qquad \csc \theta = \frac{r}{y} \quad (y \neq 0)$$

$$\cos \theta = \frac{x}{r} \qquad\qquad \sec \theta = \frac{r}{x} \quad (x \neq 0)$$

$$\tan \theta = \frac{y}{x} \quad (x \neq 0) \qquad \cot \theta = \frac{x}{y} \quad (y \neq 0)$$

Notice that the ratios in this definition do not depend on the choice of the point P on the terminal side of the angle. Figure 7.26 shows that if point P_2 is chosen rather than P_1, the two triangles formed are similar and the ratios of corresponding sides are equal. Also, these definitions are consistent with all previous definitions in this chapter.

E X A M P L E   10   Finding Trig Values

Find the values of the trig functions at an angle θ in standard position with point $P(2, 3)$ on its terminal side (see Fig. 7.27).

Solution   Apply Definition 7.3 where $x = 2, y = 3$, and $r = \sqrt{2^2 + 3^2} = \sqrt{13}$.

$$\sin \theta = \frac{3}{\sqrt{13}} \qquad \csc \theta = \frac{\sqrt{13}}{3}$$

$$\cos \theta = \frac{2}{\sqrt{13}} \qquad \sec \theta = \frac{\sqrt{13}}{2}$$

$$\tan \theta = \frac{3}{2} \qquad \cot \theta = \frac{2}{3}$$

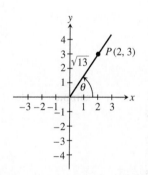

Figure 7.27 Angle in standard position with point $P(2, 3)$ on its terminal side.

E X A M P L E   11   Finding Angle Measure

Find the measure of the angle described in Example 10 assuming that it is an acute angle.

Solution   We have seen in Example 10 that $\tan \theta = 1.5$. Therefore

$$\theta = \tan^{-1}(1.5) = 56.31°.$$

Recall the agreements on inverse notation and accuracy that followed Example 7.

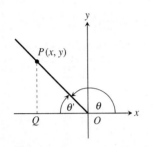

Figure 7.28 Angle θ in standard position with reference angle θ'.

When the terminal side of an angle falls in quadrants II, III, or IV, the angle is not an acute angle as was assumed in Example 11. For example, in Fig. 7.28 the angle θ satisfies the inequality $90° < \theta < 180°$. Whenever point P is selected on the terminal side of a nonacute angle, drop a perpendicular from P to the x-axis to form a right triangle ($\triangle POQ$ in Fig. 7.28). This triangle is called the **reference triangle** of angle θ, and the acute angle θ' in this reference triangle is called the **reference angle**.

An acute angle can serve as the reference angle for four different terminal sides, as shown in Fig. 7.29.

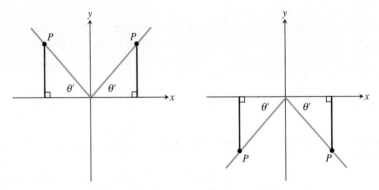

Figure 7.29 Four different angles with the same reference angle θ'.

EXAMPLE 12   Finding Trig Values and Angle Measure

Find the values of all the trig functions and the angle measure of angle θ where $P(-2, 3)$ is a point on the terminal side of θ.

Solution $r = \sqrt{(-2)^2 + 3^2} = \sqrt{13}$.

$$\sin \theta = \frac{3}{\sqrt{13}} \qquad \csc \theta = \frac{\sqrt{13}}{3}$$

$$\cos \theta = -\frac{2}{\sqrt{13}} \qquad \sec \theta = -\frac{\sqrt{13}}{2}$$

$$\tan \theta = -\frac{3}{2} \qquad \cot \theta = -\frac{2}{3}.$$

To find angle θ, first find the reference angle $\theta' = \tan^{-1}(1.5) = 56.31°$ (see Fig. 7.28). Therefore

$$\theta = 180° - 56.31° = 123.69°.$$

Exercises for Section 7.2

Consider the following right triangle, and complete each equation in Exercises 1 to 6.

1. $\sin A = ?$ **2.** $\cos A = ?$ **3.** $\tan A = ?$

4. $\cot A = ?$ **5.** $\sec A = ?$ **6.** $\csc A = ?$

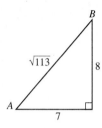

For Exercises 1 to 7

7. Complete the same six equations given in Exercises 1 to 6 for $\angle B$.

Consider the following right triangle and complete each equation in Exercises 8 to 13.

8. $\sin A = ?$ **9.** $\cos A = ?$ **10.** $\tan A = ?$

11. $\cot A = ?$ **12.** $\sec A = ?$ **13.** $\csc A = ?$

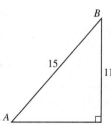

For Exercises 8 to 14

14. Complete the same six equations for $\angle B$.

In Exercises 15 to 20, write out the values $\sin \theta$, $\cos \theta$, $\tan \theta$, $\cot \theta$, $\sec \theta$, and $\csc \theta$ without looking at a reference for the following angles. (That is, refigure these function values if they are not already memorized.)

15. $\theta = 30°$ **16.** $\theta = 45°$ **17.** $\theta = \dfrac{\pi}{3}$

18. $\theta = \dfrac{\pi}{6}$ **19.** $\theta = 60°$ **20.** $\theta = \dfrac{\pi}{4}$

Use a calculator to find the values of $\sin \theta$, $\cos \theta$, and $\tan \theta$ for each of the acute angles in Exercises 21 to 28. In each case decide whether to use the degree or radian mode.

21. $\theta = 21°$ **22.** $\theta = 49°$

23. $\theta = 1.23$ **24.** $\theta = 0.78$

25. $\theta = 82°$ **26.** $\theta = 19°$

27. $\theta = 0.27$ **28.** $\theta = 0.95$

Use a calculator to find the values of $\cot \theta$, $\sec \theta$, and $\csc \theta$ for each of the acute angles in Exercises 29 to 36. In each case decide whether to use the degree or radian mode.

29. $\theta = 38°$ **30.** $\theta = 72°$

31. $\theta = 0.83$ **32.** $\theta = 0.12$

33. $\theta = 46°$ **34.** $\theta = 62°$

35. $\theta = 1.35$ **36.** $\theta = 1.03$

In Exercises 37 to 40, use a right triangle to determine the values of all the trig functions at θ.

37. $\sin \theta = \dfrac{3}{5}$ **38.** $\tan \theta = \dfrac{1}{3}$

39. $\cos \theta = \dfrac{\sqrt{3}}{2}$ **40.** $\sin \theta = \dfrac{12}{13}$

In Exercises 41 to 54, use a calculator to determine θ. Report answers in both degrees and radians.

41. $\sin \theta = \dfrac{1}{2}$ **42.** $\sin \theta = 0.8245$

43. $\cos \theta = \dfrac{4}{5}$ **44.** $\cos \theta = 0.125$

45. $\tan \theta = 1$ **46.** $\tan \theta = 3$

47. $\tan \theta = 0.423$ **48.** $\tan \theta = 2.80$

49. $\csc \theta = 2$ **50.** $\sec \theta = 3.81$

51. $\cot \theta = \dfrac{3}{5}$ **52.** $\cot \theta = 1.875$

53. $\theta = \sin^{-1}\left(\dfrac{2}{3}\right)$ **54.** $\theta = \tan^{-1}(2)$

In Exercises 55 to 64, solve the following right triangle.

55. $\angle A = 20°$; $a = 12.3$ **56.** $a = 3$; $b = 4$

57. $\angle A = 41°$; $c = 10$ **58.** $\angle A = 55°$; $b = 15.58$

59. $b = 5$; $c = 7$ **60.** $a = 20.2$; $c = 50.75$

61. $a = 2$; $b = 9.25$ **62.** $a = 5$; $\angle B = 59°$

63. $c = 12.89$; $\angle B = 12.55°$

64. $\angle A = 10.2°$; $c = 14.5$

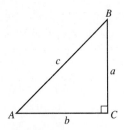

For Exercises 55 to 64

For Exercises 65 to 72, let θ be an angle in standard position with the point P on the terminal side of θ. Sketch the reference triangle and the reference angle θ' determined by each angle θ. Find the values of the six trig functions at θ, and determine the measures of θ' and θ.

65. $P(-3, 0)$ **66.** $P(0, 5)$

67. $P(4, 3)$ **68.** $P(-1, 2)$

69. $P(-4, -6)$ **70.** $P(5, -2)$

71. $P(22, -22)$ **72.** $P(-8, -1)$

In Exercises 73 to 76, sketch the angle θ and the reference angle θ' and a reference triangle. Determine the trig function values of θ and θ'.

73. $156°$ **74.** $-305°$

75. $614°$ **76.** $213°$

For Exercises 77 to 83 sketch a picture of each **problem situation**, and solve the problem.

77. The angle of elevation of the top of a building from a point 100 feet away from the building on level ground is 45°. Determine the height of the building.

78. The angle of elevation of the top of a building from a point 80 feet away from the building on level ground is 70°. Determine the height of the building.

79. The angle of depression of a buoy from a point on a lighthouse 120 feet above the surface of the water is 10°. Find the distance from the lighthouse to the buoy.

80. The angle of depression of a buoy from a point on a lighthouse 100 feet above the surface of the water is 3°. Find the distance from the lighthouse to the buoy.

81. The angle of elevation of the top of a building from a point 250 feet away from the building on level ground is 23°. Determine the height of the building.

82. A guy wire 30 meters long runs from an antenna to a point on level ground 5 meters from the base of the antenna. Determine the angle the guy wire makes with the horizontal, the angle the guy wire makes with the antenna, and the distance between the ground and the point where the guy wire is attached to the antenna.

83. A building casts a shadow 130 feet long when the angle of elevation of the sun (measured from the horizon) is 38°. How tall is the building?

84. Writing to Learn   Write a paragraph that explains the discrepancy in the two solutions for h in Example 9. In particular, which value do you think is the most reliable: $h = 74.33$ or $h = 74.35$?

7.3 _____   The Unit Circle

At the beginning of Section 7.2 the six trig functions were defined as ratios of the lengths of the sides of a right triangle. In particular, the trig functions were initially defined only for positive, acute angles. In this section we take a more modern approach based on the unit circle and define the trig functions for all angles, positive and negative.

Real Number Line and the Unit Circle

The unit circle is the circle with a radius of 1 defined by the relation $x^2 + y^2 = 1$ (see Fig. 7.30). Imagine that a flexible string with infinite length represents the real number line. The origin of this number line is attached to the circle at point $(1, 0)$ and wraps around the circle such that the positive real numbers wrap counterclockwise and the negative ones wrap clockwise (see Fig. 7.31).

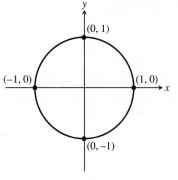

Figure 7.30 The unit circle.

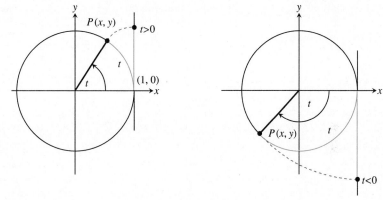

Figure 7.31 Wrapping the real number line around the unit circle.

As the string wraps around the unit circle, each real number t on the string is associated with a point $P(x, y)$ on the circle. Thus, the real number line from 0 to t makes an arc of length t beginning on the circle at $(1, 0)$ and ending at a point $P(t) = P(x, y)$ on the unit circle. Notice that this arc **subtends an angle** in standard position whose radian measure is t. To find the point on the unit circle associated with t requires finding the coordinates of the endpoint of an arc of length t that begins at $(1, 0)$.

EXAMPLE 1   Finding P(t)

Find the point $P(t)$ on the unit circle that matches each of the following numbers in the wrapping process: (a) $t = \pi/2$,   (b) $t = 3\pi/4$,   (c) $t = -2\pi/3$,   and (d) $t = 9\pi/4$.

Solution   Find the coordinates of P by finding the values of x and y for the right triangles in Fig. 7.32.

a) An arc of length $\pi/2$ beginning at $(1, 0)$ completes a one-quarter counterclockwise rotation ending at $(0, 1)$. Therefore

$$P\left(\frac{\pi}{2}\right) = (0, 1).$$

b) An arc of length $3\pi/4$ beginning at $(1,0)$ completes a three-eighths counterclockwise rotation ending at $\left(-\sqrt{2}/2, \sqrt{2}/2\right)$. Therefore

$$P\left(\frac{3\pi}{4}\right) = \left(-\frac{\sqrt{2}}{2}, \frac{\sqrt{2}}{2}\right).$$

c) An arc of length $-2\pi/3$ beginning at $(1,0)$ completes a one-third clockwise rotation ending at $\left(-1/2, -\sqrt{3}/2\right)$. Therefore

$$P\left(-\frac{2\pi}{3}\right) = \left(-\frac{1}{2}, -\frac{\sqrt{3}}{2}\right).$$

d) An arc of length $9\pi/4$ beginning at $(1,0)$ completes a one-and-one-eighth counterclockwise rotation ending at $\left(\sqrt{2}/2, \sqrt{2}/2\right)$. Therefore

$$P\left(\frac{9\pi}{4}\right) = \left(\frac{\sqrt{2}}{2}, \frac{\sqrt{2}}{2}\right).$$

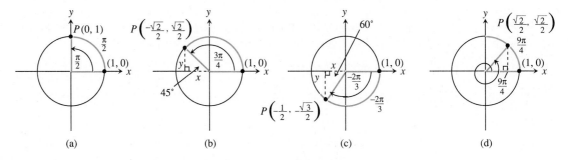

(a)   (b)   (c)   (d)

Figure 7.32   The four values for $P(t) = P(x,y)$ in Example 1.

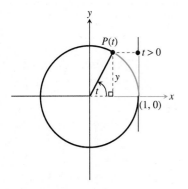

Figure 7.33   The arc from $(1,0)$ to $P(t)$ has a length t.

Trig Functions and the Unit Circle

We apply the definition of trig functions to the reference triangle in Fig. 7.33 to find the trig functions of the angle with radian measure t. For example,

$$\sin t = \frac{\text{opp}}{\text{hyp}} = \frac{y}{1} \qquad \text{and} \qquad \cos t = \frac{\text{adj}}{\text{hyp}} = \frac{x}{1}.$$

Notice that $\sin t$ and $\cos t$, as well as the remaining four trig functions, can be defined in terms of the coordinates of the point $P(x,y)$. The following definition is consistent with Definition 7.3.

Definition 7.4 Trig Functions in Radian Measure

Let $P(t) = (x, y)$ be the point on the unit circle corresponding to the real number t. Then for any angle the following is true:

$$\sin t = y \qquad\qquad \csc t = \frac{1}{y} \quad (y \neq 0)$$

$$\cos t = x \qquad\qquad \sec t = \frac{1}{x} \quad (x \neq 0)$$

$$\tan t = \frac{y}{x} \quad (x \neq 0) \qquad \cot t = \frac{x}{y} \quad (y \neq 0)$$

REMINDER

When the trig functions are defined in terms of a unit circle, *radian* measure is always used. Each real number t is associated with an arc length on the unit circle, and the arc length is also the radian measure of the central angle t.

Definition 7.4 does not require angles to be acute. Angles can be of any size and can be either positive or negative.

EXAMPLE 2   Using the Unit Circle for Sine and Cosine Values

REMINDER

- $\cos t$ is the x-coordinate of the point $P(x, y)$ associated with t.

- $\sin t$ is the y-coordinate of the point $P(x, y)$ associated with t.

Let $f(t) = \sin t$ and $g(t) = \cos t$. Use the unit circle to find the value of the functions f and g for (a) $t = 5\pi/6$ and (b) $t = 5\pi/3$.

Solution   See Fig. 7.34.

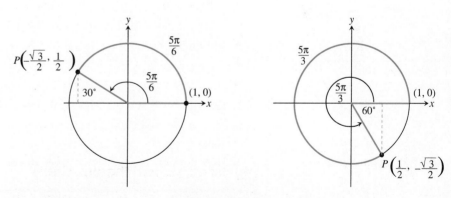

Figure 7.34   Two angles in standard position on a unit circle.

a) $f\left(\dfrac{5\pi}{6}\right) = \sin\dfrac{5\pi}{6} = \dfrac{1}{2}$ $\qquad g\left(\dfrac{5\pi}{6}\right) = \cos\dfrac{5\pi}{6} = -\dfrac{\sqrt{3}}{2}$

b) $f\left(\dfrac{5\pi}{3}\right) = \sin\dfrac{5\pi}{3} = -\dfrac{\sqrt{3}}{2}$ $\qquad g\left(\dfrac{5\pi}{3}\right) = \cos\dfrac{5\pi}{3} = \dfrac{1}{2}$

E X A M P L E   3   Using the Unit Circle for Other Trig Values

Let $f(t) = \tan t$ and $g(t) = \sec t$. Use the unit circle to find (a) $f\left(5\pi/6\right)$ and (b) $g\left(5\pi/3\right)$.

Solution   See Fig. 7.34.

a)
$$f\left(\frac{5\pi}{6}\right) = \tan\frac{5\pi}{6} = \frac{y}{x} \qquad \text{Substitute the coordinates of the point } P.$$

$$= \frac{\frac{1}{2}}{-\frac{\sqrt{3}}{2}} = -\frac{1}{\sqrt{3}} = -\frac{\sqrt{3}}{3}$$

b) $g\left(\dfrac{5\pi}{3}\right) = \sec\dfrac{5\pi}{3} = \dfrac{1}{x} = \dfrac{1}{\frac{1}{2}} = 2$

Properties of sin t and cos t

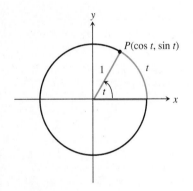

Figure 7.35   A unit circle.

🔍 EXPLORE WITH A GRAPHING UTILITY

Set a graphing calculator as follows:

- Radian mode,   parametric mode
- Range: $T\text{min} = 0$, $T\text{max} = 6.28$, $T\text{step} = 0.0314$
- Viewing rectangle: $[-1.5, 1.5]$ by $[-1, 1]$
- $X_1(T) = \cos T$ $Y_1(T) = \sin T$

1. Describe what you see when you press $\boxed{\text{GRAPH}}$.
2. As you use the $\boxed{\text{TRACE}}$ key, what is the meaning of the variables T, x, and y?
3. How does Fig. 7.35 relate to what you are seeing?

When you pressed the $\boxed{\text{TRACE}}$ key in this Exploration, the T variable represents the arc length from $(1, 0)$ counterclockwise around the circle to the cursor. The (x, y) coordinates of the cursor are $(\cos t, \sin t)$.

Experiment some more. Notice how the $\sin t$ and $\cos t$ functions vary as t varies.

Consider these observations and the resulting properties that follow.

1. Since the circle has a radius of 1, the coordinates of the cursor always fall between -1 and 1 inclusive. Therefore $\sin t$ and $\cos t$ are also both between -1 and 1 for all values of t (see Fig. 7.35).

2. If the cursor continues going around and around, an additional arc length of 2π is added with each revolution. The coordinates of $P(\cos t, \sin t)$ repeat their values.

Properties of sin *t* and cos *t*

1. The domain of $f(t) = \sin t$ and of $g(t) = \cos t$ is the set of all real numbers.
2. For each real number t,

$$-1 \leq \sin t \leq 1 \qquad \text{and} \qquad -1 \leq \cos t \leq 1.$$

3. For each real number t and for each integer n,

$$\sin t = \sin(t \pm 2\pi n) \qquad \text{and} \qquad \cos t = \cos(t \pm 2\pi n).$$

Definition 7.4 and experiences in the Exploration explain why the trig functions are often called **circular functions.**

Property 3 above says that the values of the sine and cosine repeat each time the cursor goes around the circle. This is called the **periodic property of sine and cosine.** Later we will define the concept *periodic function.*

E X A M P L E   4   Using the Periodic Property

Find $f(t) = \sin t$ and $g(t) = \cos t$ for (a) $t = 7\pi/3$ and (b) $t = 25\pi/6$ using the periodic properties of these functions.

Solution   See Fig. 7.36.

a)
$$\frac{7\pi}{3} = 2\pi + \frac{\pi}{3}$$

$$f\left(\frac{7\pi}{3}\right) = \sin\frac{7\pi}{3} = \sin\left(2\pi + \frac{\pi}{3}\right) = \sin\frac{\pi}{3} = \frac{\sqrt{3}}{2} \qquad \text{Use the periodic property of } \sin t.$$

$$g\left(\frac{7\pi}{3}\right) = \cos\frac{7\pi}{3} = \cos\left(2\pi + \frac{\pi}{3}\right) = \cos\frac{\pi}{3} = \frac{1}{2}$$

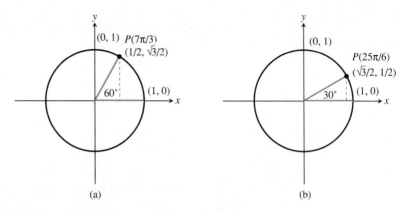

Figure 7.36   Using a unit circle definition in Example 4.

b)
$$\frac{25\pi}{6} = \frac{24\pi}{6} + \frac{\pi}{6} = 2 \cdot 2\pi + \frac{\pi}{6}$$

$$f\left(\frac{25\pi}{6}\right) = \sin\frac{25\pi}{6} = \sin\left(2 \cdot 2\pi + \frac{\pi}{6}\right) = \sin\frac{\pi}{6} = \frac{1}{2} \qquad \text{Use the periodic property of } \sin t.$$

$$g\left(\frac{25\pi}{6}\right) = \cos\frac{25\pi}{6} = \cos\left(2 \cdot 2\pi + \frac{\pi}{6}\right) = \cos\frac{\pi}{6} = \frac{\sqrt{3}}{2}$$

The results of Example 4 can be confirmed using a hand calculator. ▤

Values of the Trig Functions for Quadrantal Angles

A **quadrantal angle** is an angle in standard position whose terminal side coincides with a coordinate axis. The following are quadrantal angles:

$$t = \ldots, -2\pi, 0, 2\pi, 4\pi, \ldots, 2n\pi, \ldots$$

$$t = \ldots, -\frac{3\pi}{2}, \frac{\pi}{2}, \frac{\pi}{2} + 2\pi, \frac{\pi}{2} + 4\pi, \ldots, \frac{\pi}{2} + 2n\pi, \ldots$$

$$t = \ldots, -\pi, \pi, \pi + 2\pi, \pi + 4\pi, \ldots, \pi + 2n\pi, \ldots$$

$$t = \ldots, -\frac{\pi}{2}, \frac{3\pi}{2}, \frac{3\pi}{2} + 2\pi, \frac{3\pi}{2} + 4\pi, \ldots, \frac{3\pi}{2} + 2n\pi, \ldots$$

Using Definition 7.4 and Fig. 7.37, we can see at a glance that for the quadrantal angles the trig functions are either $1, -1, 0, 1/0$ (and hence undefined), or $-1/0$ (undefined).

E X A M P L E   5   Finding Trig Values for Quadrantal Angles

Find the values of the trig functions for the quadrantal angles (a) 0, (b) $\pi/2$, (c) π, and (d) $3\pi/2$.

Solution   Use Definition 7.4 and the coordinates of the points $(0,0), (0,1), (-1,0),$ and $(0,-1)$ (see Fig. 7.37).

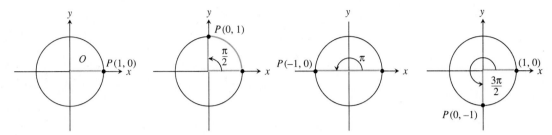

Figure 7.37   Quadrantal angles.

t	$\sin t$	$\cos t$	$\tan t$	$\cot t$	$\sec t$	$\csc t$
0	0	1	0	undefined	1	undefined
$\dfrac{\pi}{2}$	1	0	undefined	0	undefined	1
π	0	-1	0	undefined	-1	undefined
$\dfrac{3\pi}{2}$	-1	0	undefined	0	undefined	-1

≡

Fundamental Trigonometric Identities

Section 2.1 described the difference between a conditional equation and an identity. The equation $x + 3 = 5$ is a conditional equation since the equation is true only if x meets a certain condition. On the other hand, $x + 3 = 3 + x$ is an identity since the equation is true for all permissible values of x.

An equation that includes trigonometric functions and is true for all permissible values of the variable is called a **trigonometric identity**. This identity is verified on page 348.

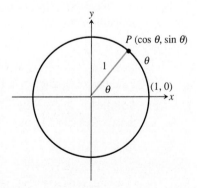

Figure 7.38   Unit circle.

Section 7.2 introduced the reciprocal identities. Definition 7.4 shows that the reciprocal identities are true not only for acute angles, but for all angles that do not cause either side of the equation to be undefined.

For any value θ, the point $P(\cos\theta, \sin\theta)$ lies on the unit circle (Fig. 7.38) and satisfies the equation $x^2 + y^2 = 1$, which defines the unit circle. That is,

$$x^2 + y^2 = 1 \quad \text{Defining equation for the unit circle.}$$

$$(\cos\theta)^2 + (\sin\theta)^2 = 1 \quad \text{Substitute } x = \cos\theta \text{ and } y = \sin\theta.$$

$$\cos^2\theta + \sin^2\theta = 1.$$

The 11 **fundamental trig identities** are summarized below. The remaining two Pythagorean identities can be verified by dividing both sides of the equation $\cos^2\theta + \sin^2\theta = 1$ by either $\sin^2\theta$ or $\cos^2\theta$.

Fundamental Trig Identities

Reciprocal Identities

$$\sin\theta = \frac{1}{\csc\theta}, \qquad \cos\theta = \frac{1}{\sec\theta}, \qquad \tan\theta = \frac{1}{\cot\theta}$$

$$\csc\theta = \frac{1}{\sin\theta}, \qquad \sec\theta = \frac{1}{\cos\theta}, \qquad \cot\theta = \frac{1}{\tan\theta}$$

Tangent and cotangent identities

$$\tan\theta = \frac{\sin\theta}{\cos\theta}, \qquad \cot\theta = \frac{\cos\theta}{\sin\theta}$$

Pythagorean identities

$$\sin^2\theta + \cos^2\theta = 1, \qquad 1 + \tan^2\theta = \sec^2\theta, \qquad 1 + \cot^2\theta = \csc^2\theta$$

Example 6 illustrates how identities can be used to find the value of one trig function if the value of another trig function is known.

E X A M P L E   6   Using Trig Identities

Find $\tan\theta$ if $\csc\theta = 1.25$ and $0 \leq \theta < 2\pi$.

Solution   Since $\csc\theta$ is positive in both quadrants I and II, θ can be in either of these quadrants. In quadrant I, $\tan\theta > 0$, and in quadrant II, $\tan\theta < 0$.

$$\sin\theta = \frac{1}{\csc\theta} = \frac{1}{1.25} = 0.8$$

$$\tan\theta = \frac{\sin\theta}{\cos\theta} = \frac{\sin\theta}{\pm\sqrt{1 - \sin^2\theta}} = \pm\frac{0.8}{\sqrt{1 - (0.8)^2}} = \pm\frac{0.8}{0.6} = \pm 1.33$$

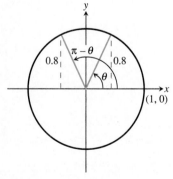

Figure 7.39   Two solutions to the equation $\sin\theta = 0.8$ for $0 < \theta < 2\pi$.

So $\tan \theta = 1.33$ when θ is in quadrant I, and $\tan \theta = -1.33$ when θ is in quadrant II.

Of course there is a more modern way to complete this problem. We can use a calculator to conclude that $\sin \theta = 0.8$ implies that $\theta = \sin^{-1}(0.8) = 0.927295218$ or $\theta = \pi - \sin^{-1}(0.8) = 2.214297436$ (see Fig. 7.39). Furthermore, $\tan 0.927295218 = 1.33$ and $\tan 2.214297436 = -1.33$. ▬

We will show in Section 7.4 that the equation $\sin \theta = 0.8$ has many solutions.

Exercises for Section 7.3

In Exercises 1 to 12, find the point $P(t) = P(x, y)$ on the unit circle that corresponds to each value of t.

1. $t = \dfrac{\pi}{2}$ **2.** $t = \dfrac{\pi}{4}$ **3.** $t = -\dfrac{\pi}{4}$

4. $t = \dfrac{5\pi}{6}$ **5.** $t = -\dfrac{3\pi}{2}$ **6.** $t = \dfrac{5\pi}{3}$

7. $t = -\dfrac{3\pi}{4}$ **8.** $t = \pi$ **9.** $t = \dfrac{11\pi}{6}$

10. $t = \dfrac{11\pi}{4}$ **11.** $t = \dfrac{8\pi}{3}$ **12.** $t = -\dfrac{5\pi}{6}$

In Exercises 13 to 20, let $f(t) = \sin t$ and $g(t) = \cos t$. Use the unit circle to find $f(t)$ and $g(t)$.

13. $t = \dfrac{\pi}{6}$ **14.** $t = \dfrac{\pi}{4}$ **15.** $t = \dfrac{\pi}{3}$

16. $t = \dfrac{2\pi}{3}$ **17.** $t = \dfrac{3\pi}{4}$ **18.** $t = \dfrac{5\pi}{6}$

19. $t = -\dfrac{2\pi}{3}$ **20.** $t = -\dfrac{\pi}{6}$

In Exercises 21 to 28, use the unit circle to find $\tan t$, $\cot t$, $\sec t$, and $\csc t$.

21. $t = \dfrac{\pi}{6}$ **22.** $t = \dfrac{\pi}{4}$ **23.** $t = \dfrac{\pi}{3}$

24. ∗$t = \dfrac{2\pi}{3}$ **25.** $t = \dfrac{3\pi}{4}$ **26.** $t = \dfrac{5\pi}{6}$

27. $t = -\dfrac{2\pi}{3}$ **28.** $t = -\dfrac{\pi}{6}$

In Exercises 29 to 34, determine which trig functions are undefined for each quadrantal angle θ.

29. $\theta = \dfrac{\pi}{2}$ **30.** $\theta = \pi$ **31.** $\theta = \dfrac{3\pi}{2}$

32. $\theta = 5\pi$ **33.** $\theta = \dfrac{5\pi}{2}$ **34.** $\theta = \dfrac{7\pi}{2}$

In Exercises 35 to 38, use the periodic properties to find $f(x) = \sin x$ and $g(x) = \cos x$.

35. $x = \dfrac{13\pi}{4}$ **36.** $x = \dfrac{13\pi}{6}$

37. $x = \dfrac{8\pi}{3}$ **38.** $x = \dfrac{23\pi}{6}$

Use the fundamental trig identities to complete Exercises 39 to 42. Check your answers with a calculator.

39. Find $\tan \theta$ if $\sin \theta = 0.32$.

40. Find $\tan \theta$ if $\cos \theta = 0.87$.

41. Find $\cot \theta$ if $\sec \theta = 1.29$.

42. Find $\sec \theta$ if $\sin \theta = 0.72$.

43. Prove that $1 + \tan^2 \theta = \sec^2 \theta$ by dividing both sides of $\sin^2 \theta + \cos^2 \theta = 1$ by $\cos^2 \theta$.

44. Prove that $1 + \cot^2 \theta = \csc^2 \theta$ by dividing both sides of $\sin^2 \theta + \cos^2 \theta = 1$ by $\sin^2 \theta$.

For Exercises 45 to 48, complete the table below by adding a $+$ or $-$ to record intervals on which $\sin x$, $\cos x$, and $\tan x$ are positive and negative.

	$\sin x$	$\cos x$	$\tan x$
45. $0 < x < \dfrac{\pi}{2}$	$+$		
46. $\dfrac{\pi}{2} < x < \pi$	$-$		
47. $\pi < x < \dfrac{3\pi}{2}$			
48. $\dfrac{3\pi}{2} < x < 2\pi$			

In Exercises 49 to 54, find $\sin \theta$, $\cos \theta$, and $\tan \theta$ for each angle. Wherever possible, find these values without using a calculator.

49. $\theta = \dfrac{7\pi}{3}$ **50.** $\theta = \dfrac{31\pi}{6}$ **51.** $\theta = \dfrac{5\pi}{12}$

52. $\theta = \dfrac{8\pi}{12}$ **53.** $\theta = \dfrac{11\pi}{24}$ **54.** $\theta = \dfrac{7\pi}{36}$

7.4 _____ Graphs of sin x and cos x

🔍 **EXPLORE WITH A GRAPHING UTILITY**

Set a graphing calculator as follows:

- Radian mode,   parametric mode,   simultaneous mode
- Range: $T\text{min} = 0$, $T\text{max} = 6.28$, $T\text{step} = 0.1$
- Viewing rectangle: $[-2, 6.28]$ by $[-2.5, 2.5]$
- $X_1(T) = -1 + \cos T$ $Y_1(T) = \sin T$
  $X_2(T) = T$ $Y_2(T) = \sin T$

1. Describe what you see when you press ⬚GRAPH⬚. How is this graph related to the graph in the Exploration in Section 7.3?

2. As you move the ⬚TRACE⬚ cursor from one curve to the other by using the ⬚UP⬚ or ⬚DOWN⬚ key, how do the y-coordinates of the cursor compare?

This Exploration provides a dynamic simulation of $y = \sin x$, while a textbook can only provide static figures as we do in the next several figures.

Consider the arc of the unit circle from $(1, 0)$ to P whose arc length is x. Then the value $f(x) = \sin x$ is the y-coordinate of P. See Fig. 7.40.

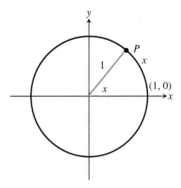

Figure 7.40   If an arc from $(1, 0)$ to P has length x, then the coordinates of P are $(\cos x, \sin x)$.

As x increases along the x-axis, the value of $f(x)$ is the y-coordinate of the corresponding point $P(x)$ on the unit circle (see Fig. 7.41a). As x varies from 0 to $\pi/2$, $\sin x$ varies from 0 to 1; as x varies from $\pi/2$ to π, $\sin x$ varies from 1 to 0 (see Fig. 7.41b).

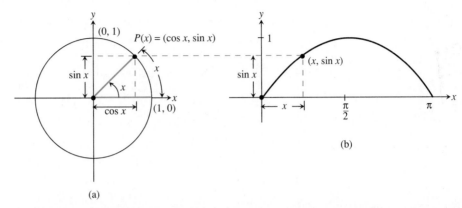

(a)

Figure 7.41 $f(x) = \sin x$ for $0 \le x \le \pi$. (a) Unit circle definition. (b) Graph of $f(x) = \sin x$.

In a similar fashion we see that, as x varies from 0 to $-\pi$, $\sin x$ varies from 0 to -1 and back to 0 as shown in Fig. 7.42. In particular,

$$f(-\pi) = 0, \qquad f\left(\frac{\pi}{2}\right) = -1, \qquad f(0) = 0, \qquad f\left(-\frac{\pi}{2}\right) = 1, \qquad f(\pi) = 0.$$

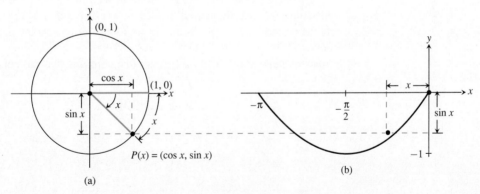

(a)

(b)

Figure 7.42 $f(x) = \sin x$ for $-\pi \le x \le 0$. (a) Unit circle definition. (b) Graph of $f(x)$.

The graphs in Figs. 7.41 and 7.42 are pieced together to form the graph of $f(x) = \sin x$ on the interval $[-\pi, \pi]$ shown on the next page in Fig. 7.43.

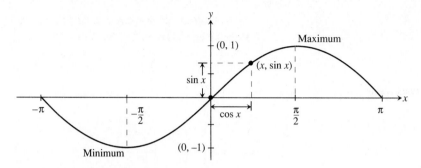

Figure 7.43   Graph of $y = \sin x$ for $-\pi \leq x \leq \pi$.

If $x > \pi$ or $x < -\pi$, there is a repetition of the values that $\sin x$ has over the interval $[-\pi, \pi]$. This is what is called a **periodic function**.

Definition 7.5   Periodic Function

A function f is said to be a **periodic function** if there is a positive real number h such that $f(x+h) = f(x)$ for every value of x in the domain of f. The smallest such positive number h is called the **period of f**. The period corresponds to the length of one cycle on the graph of f.

One of the properties of $\sin x$ listed in section 7.3 is that $\sin x = \sin(x \pm 2n\pi)$, which suggests that the period of $\sin x$ is 2π. The graph in Fig. 7.43 also suggests that the period of $y = \sin x$ is 2π. In addition, from the graph of $y = \sin x$ over the interval $[-3\pi, 3\pi]$ (Fig. 7.44), it is evident that the graph begins repeating itself as it extends beyond the interval $[0, 2\pi]$; this confirms that the period of $y = \sin x$ is 2π.

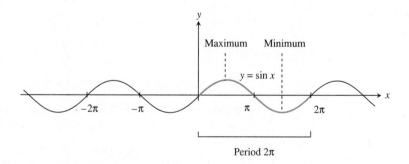

Figure 7.44   Complete graph of $f(x) = \sin x$.

As point P on the unit circle in Fig. 7.45 rotates the x-coordinate of P goes through the same cycle of values as the y-coordinate does. They simply begin at a different point in the cycle. Confirm this by checking the values $\cos(-\pi), \cos(-\pi/2), \cos 0, \cos(\pi/2)$, and $\cos \pi$. The graph of $y = \cos x$ is shown in Fig. 7.46.

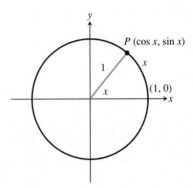

Figure 7.45   Unit circle definition.

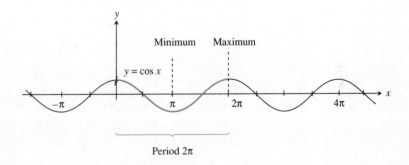

Figure 7.46   Complete graph of $y = \cos x$.

Symmetry of the Graphs of Sine and Cosine

Figure 7.47 shows that if (a, b) is the point on the unit circle associated with $P(x)$, then $(a, -b)$ is the point associated with $P(-x)$. This means that

$$\sin(-x) = -\sin x \qquad \text{for all real numbers } x.$$

In other words, the graph of $f(x) = \sin x$ is symmetric about the origin.

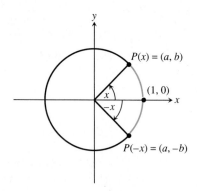

Figure 7.47   A counterclockwise arc of length x and a clockwise arc of length x.

In a similar manner it can be shown that

$$\cos(-x) = \cos x \qquad \text{for all real numbers } x.$$

In other words the graph of $f(x) = \cos x$ is symmetric about the y-axis.

Amplitude of Sine and Cosine

A graphing utility can be used to discover properties of the trig functions experimentally.

🔍 **EXPLORE WITH A GRAPHING UTILITY**

Find a complete graph of each of these functions in the same viewing rectangle.

- $y = 3 \sin x$
- $y = \sin x$
- $y = 2 \sin x$

1. How are these graphs the same? How are they different?

2. What are the maximum and minimum values for each function?

Generalize   What is the maximum and minimum value of the function $y = a \sin x$ where a is any positive real number?

This Exploration motivates the following definition.

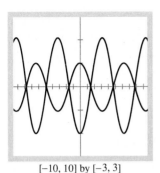

[−10, 10] by [−3, 3]

Figure 7.48 $y = -2\cos x$ and $y = \cos x$.

Definition 7.6   Amplitude of Sine and Cosine

The **amplitude** of functions $f(x) = a\sin x$ and $g(x) = a\cos x$ is the maximum value of y where a is any real number; **amplitude** $= |a|$.

EXAMPLE 1   Finding the Amplitude of a Cosine Function

Find a complete graph of $y = -2\cos x$. Also find its amplitude and describe how the negative factor affects the graph.

Solution   See Fig. 7.48.

Amplitude $|-2| = 2$.

We have seen in Chapter 3 that the graph of $y = -f(x)$ is obtained by reflecting the graph of $y = f(x)$ about the x-axis. Therefore the graph of $y = -2\cos x$ is obtained from the graph of $y = 2\cos x$ by reflection about the x-axis.

≡

Horizontal Stretch or Shrink for Sine and Cosine

The period for $y = \sin x$ and for $y = \cos x$ is 2π. Now consider the functions $y = \sin bx$ and $y = \cos bx$, where b is a positive constant coefficient of x. As in the graphs of earlier functions, b has the impact of horizontally stretching or shrinking the graph depending on the value of b. When b is a positive integer, the period will be some fraction of 2π.

🔍 **EXPLORE WITH A GRAPHING UTILITY**

Find a graph of each of the following functions in the viewing rectangle $[-3.14, 3.14]$ by $[-2, 2]$:

- $y = \sin 2x$
- $y = \sin x$
- $y = \sin 3x$
- $y = \sin 0.5x$

How many complete periods occur in the given viewing rectangle for each function?

Generalize   What is the period of $y = \sin bx$?

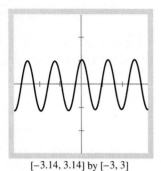

[−3.14, 3.14] by [−3, 3]

Figure 7.49 $y = \cos 5x$.

This Exploration may have led you to determine the effect of a constant on the period of a sine function. It is also possible to determine this relationship in a more algebraic way, as illustrated in the next example.

E X A M P L E   2   Finding the Period of $y = \cos 5x$

Find the period of the function $f(x) = \cos 5x$.

Solution

Graphical Method   Observe in Fig. 7.49 that $y = \cos 5x$ completes five complete cycles over the interval $[-\pi, \pi]$. That means that the period is $2\pi \div 5 = 2\pi/5$.

Algebraic Method   The function $y = \cos t$ completes one complete cycle as t varies from 0 to 2π. Likewise, as $5x$ varies from 0 to 2π, $y = \cos 5x$ completes one cycle.

Cycle begins: $5x = 0$ or $x = 0.$
Cycle ends: $5x = 2\pi$ or $x = 2\pi/5.$ ▤

This example can be generalized to any functions $y = \sin bx$ and $y = \cos bx$ as summarized here.

Theorem 7.2   Period of Sine and Cosine Functions

The period for $y = \sin bx$ or $y = \cos bx$ is $2\pi/|b|$.

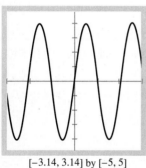

[−3.14, 3.14] by [−5, 5]

Figure 7.50 $f(x) = 4\sin 3x$.

Proof   If the period for $y = \sin bx$ or $y = \cos bx$ begins at $x = 0$, then it ends at $bx = 2\pi$, or $x = 2\pi/b$, so the period, or length of one cycle is $|2\pi/b| = 2\pi/|b|$ for each function.   ▤

E X A M P L E   3   Using a Graphing Utility

Find a complete graph of $f(x) = 4\sin 3x$ in the viewing rectangle $[-3.14, 3.14]$ by $[-5, 5]$. Find the domain, range, amplitude, and period of $f(x)$.

Solution

Graphical Method   Figure 7.50 shows a graph of $y = 4\sin 3x$. Using the $\boxed{\text{TRACE}}$ key, observe that the maximum value of f is shown on the screen display as 3.99 and the minimum value is reported as -3.99.

The graph supports the conclusion that the amplitude is 4 and the period is $2\pi/3$. This claim is confirmed by Definition 7.6 and Theorem 7.2.

Domain of f: $(-\infty, \infty)$.
Range of f: $[-4, 4]$.   ▤

Horizontal Shift Identities

Figure 7.51 shows graphically that $f(x) = \cos x$ (dashed line) can be obtained from $g(x) = \sin x$ by a horizontal shift left $\pi/2$ units. In other words, it appears from the graphs that $f(x) = g(x + \pi/2)$.

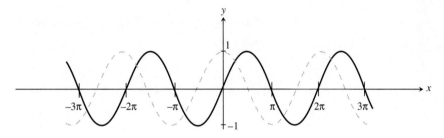

Figure 7.51 $f(x) = \cos x$ and $g(x) = \sin x$.

The following horizontal shift identities can be proved.

Theorem 7.3   Horizontal Shift Identities

For all values of x,

1. $\cos x = \sin\left(x + \dfrac{\pi}{2}\right)$

2. $\sin x = \cos\left(x - \dfrac{\pi}{2}\right).$

Proof   We shall prove the first of these two identities. Figure 7.52 will be referred to in the proof.

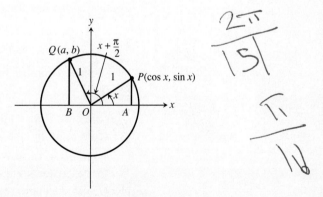

Figure 7.52 Angles x and $x + \pi/2$ in standard position.

$P(\cos x, \sin x)$ is the point associated with angle x, and $Q(a, b)$ is the point associated with angle $x + \pi/2$ (Fig. 7.52). Since $\triangle OAP$ is congruent with $\triangle QBO$, we see that $QB = OA$. That means that $b = \cos x$. But b, the y-coordinate of Q, is equal to $\sin(x + \pi/2)$. In other words,

$$\cos x = \sin\left(x + \frac{\pi}{2}\right).$$

The graph of $f(x + \pi/2)$ is obtained from the graph of $f(x)$ by a horizontal shift left $\pi/2$ units.   ▤

Section 8.4 will develop what it means to verify a trigonometric identity. In the meantime we will be content to use identities.

E X A M P L E 4   Using an Identity to Verify a Trig Equation

Verify that $\sin x = \cos(x - \pi/2)$.

Solution   Let $x = u + \pi/2$. Then

$$\sin x = \sin\left(u + \frac{\pi}{2}\right)$$

$$= \cos u \qquad \text{Use the first identity of Theorem 7.3.}$$

$$= \cos\left(x - \frac{\pi}{2}\right) \qquad \text{Substitute } (x - \pi/2) \text{ for } u. \qquad ▤$$

Solving Trig Equations

In Section 7.3, Example 6, you solved the equation $\sin x = 0.8$ for $0 \le x < 2\pi$. However, in that section you were limited to two solutions. In the next section you will learn that there are many other solutions to that equation as well.

Acute-angle solutions to trig equations like $\sin x = 0.8$ can be solved by evaluating $x = \sin^{-1}(0.8)$. In addition, a graphical method can be used that is identical to the one used with functions in previous chapters.

E X A M P L E 5   Solving a Trig Equation

Find both solutions of $\sin x = 0.4$ in the interval $0 \le x < 2\pi$.

Solution

Graphical Method   Find a complete graph of $f(x) = \sin x$ and $g(x) = 0.4$, and use zoom-in to find the solutions $x = 0.41$ and $x = 2.73$ (Fig. 7.53).   ▤

A calculator computation can be used to confirm the solutions in Example 5. For example, $x = \sin^{-1}(0.4) = 0.4115168461$. The other solution is $\pi - 0.4115168461 = 2.730075808$.

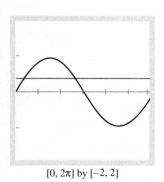

[0, 2π] by [−2, 2]

Figure 7.53 $f(x) = \sin x$ and $g(x) = 0.4$.

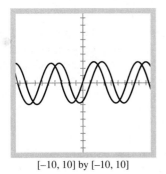

[−10, 10] by [−10, 10]

Figure 7.54 $f(x) = 3\sin(x-1)$ is shifted 1 unit right of $g(x) = 3\sin x$, which passes through the origin.

EXAMPLE 6   Finding Period and Amplitude

Find a complete graph of $f(x) = 3\sin(x-1)$. Determine the domain, range, period, and amplitude.

Solution   Compare the graph of f to the graph of $g(x) = 3\sin x$.

$$g(x-1) = 3\sin(x-1)$$

From this we see that the graph of f is obtained from the graph of g by a horizontal shift right 1 unit (Fig. 7.54).

Domain: $(-\infty, \infty)$.
Range: $[-3, 3]$.
Amplitude: 3.
Period: 2π.

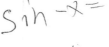

Exercises for Section 7.4

In Exercises 1 to 6, find a complete graph and the maximum value of each function. Also find its amplitude.

1. $y = 4\sin x$
2. $y = \cos 3x$
3. $y = 15\cos 2x$
4. $y = -3\sin x$
5. $y = -5\cos x$
6. $y = -12\sin 2x$

In Exercises 7 to 12, find a complete graph of each function. Also find the domain, range, and period of each.

7. $y = \cos 3x$
8. $y = \sin 7x$
9. $y = 4\sin 5x$
10. $y = -2\cos 9x$
11. $y = -3\cos 2x$
12. $y = 6\sin 9x$

In Exercises 13 to 20, sketch a complete graph without using a graphing utility. State the domain, range, and period. Check with a grapher.

13. $y = \sin 3x$
14. $y = 2 + \sin x$
15. $y = 2 + \sin(x - 4)$
16. $y = -1 - \cos(x - \pi)$
17. $y = -1 + 3\cos(x - 2)$
18. $y = 2 - 2\cos(x + 3)$
19. $y = -1 + 3\sin(x - 2)$
20. $y = 2 - 2\sin(x + 1)$

In Exercises 21 to 26, for each function find a viewing rectangle that displays exactly one period of the function.

21. $y = \sin 2x$
22. $y = \cos \frac{1}{2}x$
23. $y = 2\cos \frac{1}{2}x$
24. $y = \sin \frac{1}{3}x$
25. $y = 3\cos \frac{1}{5}x$
26. $y = 3\sin \frac{1}{4}x$

In Exercises 27 to 34, solve for $0 \le x < 2\pi$. Use both a graphical and a calculator method. Confirm that the two methods agree.

27. $\sin x = 0.5$
28. $\sin x = -0.6$
29. $\sin x = 0.8$
30. $\sin x = 0.3$
31. $\cos x = 0.6$
32. $\cos x = -0.4$
33. $3\sin x = 1.7$
34. $2\cos \frac{1}{2}x = 1.5$

Solve Exercises 35 to 38 for $0 \le x < 2\pi$ using a graphical method.

35. $\sin x = \cos x$
36. $\sin \frac{1}{2}x = \cos x$
37. $3\cos \frac{1}{2}x = 2\sin x$
38. $\sin x = -\cos x$

Solve the inequalities in Exercises 39 to 42 for $0 \le x < 2\pi$.

39. $\sin x < 0.6$
40. $3x\cos x < 4$
41. $2\cos x > -1.3$
42. $\sin x > 0.05$

43. Use identities from this section to verify that $\tan(-x) = -\tan x$.

44. Is applying a vertical stretch factor of 2 to the graph of $y = \sin x$ followed by a vertical shift up 3 units the same or different as applying a vertical shift up 3 units to the graph of $y = \sin x$ followed by a vertical stretch factor of 2?

45. Determine the two equations of the resulting graphs from Exercise 44. Confirm that they are different graphs.

46. A signal buoy bobs up and down so that at time t (in seconds), it is $\sin t$ feet above the average water level. A bell rings whenever the buoy is 0.5 feet above the average water level. What are the time intervals between bell rings in a sequence of six rings?

47. A ferris wheel 50 feet in diameter makes one revolution every 2 minutes. If the center of the wheel is 30 feet above the ground, how long after reaching the low point is a rider 50 feet above the ground?

48. Writing to Learn   In a certain video game a cursor bounces back and forth across the screen at a constant rate. Its distance d from the center of the screen varies with time t and hence can be described as a function of t. Write several sentences, including a graph, to explain that this horizontal distance d from the center of the screen *does not* vary according to an equation $d = a \sin bt$ where t represents seconds.

7.5 _____   Graphs of the Other Trig Functions

In this section we shall develop the graphs of the functions $y = \tan x, y = \cot x, y = \sec x$, and $y = \csc x$.

Graphs of Tangent and Cotangent Functions

Exercise 43 of Section 7.4 established that $\tan(-x) = -\tan x$. This means that the graph of $y = \tan x$ is symmetric about the origin.

Recall from Section 7.3 the tangent identity

$$\tan x = \frac{\sin x}{\cos x}.$$

This identity allows us to make the following observations:

1. $\tan x = 0$ whenever $\sin x = 0$. That is,

$$\tan x = 0 \iff x = \ldots, -2\pi, -\pi, 0, \pi, 2\pi, \ldots.$$

2. $\tan x$ is undefined whenever $\cos x = 0$. Consequently, the graph of $y = \tan x$ is expected to have a vertical asymptote whenever

$$x = \ldots, -\frac{3\pi}{2}, -\frac{\pi}{2}, \frac{\pi}{2}, \frac{3\pi}{2}, \ldots.$$

3. When x is very close to $\pi/2$ on the left, $\sin x$ is close to 1 and $\cos x$ is close to zero. *Therefore the quotient $\tan x$ is a large positive number.* Similarly, if x is very close to $\pi/2$ from the right, $\tan x$ is a large negative number. Figure 7.55(a) shows the graph of $y = \tan x$.

The identity $\cot x = 1/\tan x$ contributes to our understanding of the graph of $y = \cot x$. In particular,

$$\tan x = 0 \implies \cot x \text{ is undefined}$$

$$\tan x \to \pm\infty \implies \cot x \to 0$$

So we see that there are vertical asymptotes whenever $\tan x = 0$. See Fig. 7.55(b).

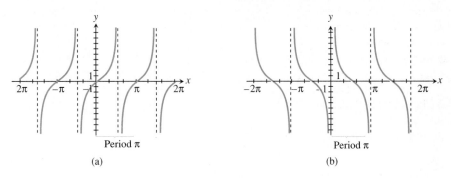

(a)   (b)

Figure 7.55   (a) $y = \tan x$. Note that $\tan x \to \infty$ as $x \to (\pi/2)^-$ and $\tan x \to -\infty$ as $x \to (\pi/2)^+$. (b) $y = \cot x$. Note that $\cot x \to \infty$ as $x \to \pi^+$, and $\cot x \to -\infty$ as $x \to \pi^-$.

Period of Tangent and Cotangent

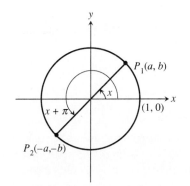

Figure 7.56   Unit circle showing the angles x and $x + \pi$.

The graph in Fig. 7.55 suggests that the period of $y = \tan x$ is π. In other words, $\tan(x + \pi) = \tan x$ for all values of x for which $\tan x$ is defined. To verify this equation analytically, consider Fig. 7.56. Here P_1 is the point on the unit circle associated with angle x, and P_2 is the point associated with angle $x + \pi$. Therefore

$$\tan x = \frac{b}{a} \quad \text{and} \quad \tan(x + \pi) = \frac{-b}{-a} = \frac{b}{a}.$$

A similar argument yields an identity for $y = \cot x$.

Identities Showing Period of Tangent and Cotangent

For all values of x, $\tan x = \tan(x + \pi)$ and $\cot x = \cot(x + \pi)$

We see from Fig. 7.55 that the periods of $y = \tan x$ and $y = \cot x$ are π. If a is a positive constant coefficient of x, a affects the period of the tangent function just as it does the period of $y = \sin ax$, that is, by horizontally stretching or shrinking the graph. It is helpful to recognize that one period in any tangent or cotangent function represents the width of the graph between adjacent vertical asymptotes.

E X A M P L E   1   Finding the Period of a Tangent Function

Find the period of $y = \tan 2x$. Also find a complete graph in a viewing rectangle that shows three complete periods.

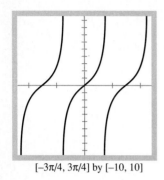

[−3π/4, 3π/4] by [−10, 10]

Figure 7.57 $y = \tan 2x$.

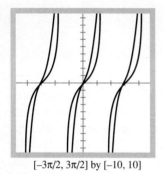

[−3π/2, 3π/2] by [−10, 10]

Figure 7.58 $y = 2 \tan x$ and $y = 5 \tan x$.

Solution It is convenient to consider a period of the tangent function from $-\pi/2$ to $\pi/2$.

One period begins: $2x = -\pi/2$ or $x = -\pi/4$.

One period ends: $2x = \pi/2$ or $x = \pi/4$.

The period of $y = \tan 2x$ is $\pi/2$. Use the viewing rectangle $[-3\pi/4, 3\pi/4]$ by $[-10, 10]$ to find a complete graph with three complete periods. See Fig. 7.57.

E X A M P L E 2   Comparing Graphs of Tangent Functions

Identify which graph in Fig. 7.58 is the graph of $y = 2 \tan x$ and which one is the graph of $y = 5 \tan x$.

Solution As a grapher traces out these graphs, it will be obvious which graph is which.

The graph of $y = 2 \tan x$ is obtained from $y = \tan x$ by stretching it vertically by a factor of 2, and the graph of $y = 5 \tan x$ is obtained from $y = \tan x$ by stretching it vertically by a factor of 5.

Graphs of Secant and Cosecant Functions

The reciprocal identities

$$\sec x = \frac{1}{\cos x} \qquad \text{and} \qquad \csc x = \frac{1}{\sin x}$$

contribute to our understanding of the graphs of $y = \sec x$ and $y = \csc x$. Since $y = \sin x$ and $y = \cos x$ are periodic functions, it follows that $y = \sec x$ and $y = \csc x$ are also. Whenever $\cos x$ is nearly zero, $|\sec x|$ is large. In particular, the graph of $y = \sec x$ has a vertical asymptote whenever $\cos x = 0$. Whenever $\cos x = 1$, then $\sec x$ is also 1. See Fig. 7.59(a).

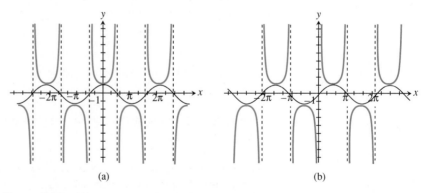

(a)   (b)

Figure 7.59 (a) $y = \sec x$ (color) and $y = \cos x$. (b) $y = \csc x$ (color) and $y = \sin x$.

EXAMPLE 3   Exploring the Secant Function

Find the domain, range, period, and vertical asymptotes of the function $f(x) = \sec x$.

Solution   The following information can be found in Fig. 7.59(a):
Domain: all x except $x = \pi/2 + k\pi$ for any integer k.
Range: $(-\infty, -1] \cup [1, \infty)$.
Period: 2π.
Vertical asymptotes: $x = \pi/2 + k\pi$ for any integer k.

The graph of $y = \csc x$ looks like the graph of $y = \sec x$ except that it has been shifted $\pi/2$ units right. See Fig. 7.59(b).

EXAMPLE 4   Exploring the Cosecant Function

Find the domain, range, period, and vertical asymptotes of the function $f(x) = \csc x$.

Solution   The following information can be found in Fig. 7.59(b):
Domain: all x except $x = k\pi$ for any integer k.
Range: $(-\infty, -1] \cup [1, \infty)$.
Period: 2π.
Vertical asymptotes: $x = k\pi$ for any integer k.

Finding the Period of a Function

Since the four trig functions $y = \tan x, y = \cot x, y = \sec x$, and $y = \csc x$ can be described in terms of $\sin x$ and $\cos x$, it is not surprising to find that the periods of these four functions are also related to the periods of $\sin x$ and $\cos x$.

EXAMPLE 5   Finding the Period of a Cosecant Function

Find the period of the function $y = \csc 3x$.

Solution   It is convenient to consider a period of $y = \csc x$ that begins at the vertical asymptote $x = -\pi$ and ends at $x = \pi$. In a similar fashion analyze $y = \csc 3x$.
One period begins: $3x = -\pi$ or $x = -\pi/3$.
One period ends: $3x = \pi$ or $x = \pi/3$.
    Therefore the period of $y = \csc 3x$ is $\pi/3 + \pi/3 = 2\pi/3$.

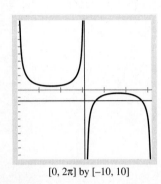

[0, 2π] by [−10, 10]

Figure 7.60 $y = \csc x$ and $y = -1.6$.

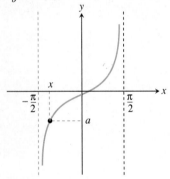

Figure 7.61
$y = \tan x$. $\tan x = a$ has a unique solution over $(-\pi/2, \pi/2)$.

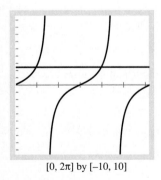

[0, 2π] by [−10, 10]

Figure 7.62 $y = \tan x$ and $y = 2.5$.

Theorem 7.4   Period of Tangent, Cotangent, Secant, and Cosecant Functions

For $y = \tan bx$ or $y = \cot bx$,

$$\text{period} = \frac{\pi}{|b|}.$$

For $y = \sec bx$ or $y = \csc bx$,

$$\text{period} = \frac{2\pi}{|b|}.$$

Solving Equations with Trig Functions

An equation $\sin x = a$ or $\cos x = a$ (where a is a constant) has two solutions or none over any interval of length 2π since the period of each function is 2π. The same is true for the equations $\sec x = a$ and $\csc x = a$. To find all solutions to an equation of any one of these four types, first find the two solutions over the interval of length 2π. Then add $2k\pi$ to each value for all integer values of k.

E X A M P L E   6   Solving csc x = a Graphically

Find all solutions to $\csc x = -1.6$.

Solution   Find a complete graph of $y = \csc x$ and $y = -1.6$ in the viewing rectangle $[0, 2\pi]$ by $[-10, 10]$ (see Fig. 7.60).

Use zoom-in to find the two solutions $x = 3.82$ and 5.61 in the interval $[0, 2\pi)$. Now add $2k\pi$ to each of these values for each integer value of k:

Solutions: $x = 3.82 + 2k\pi$ and $x = 5.61 + 2k\pi$

for all integer values of k.   ≡

An equation of the form $\tan x = a$ has a unique solution over the interval $(-\pi/2, \pi/2)$, as indicated in Fig. 7.61. After finding that unique solution, we can find all other solutions of the equation by adding $k\pi$ for all integer values of k.

E X A M P L E   7   Solving tan x = a Graphically

Find all solutions to $\tan x = 2.5$.

Solution   Find a complete graph of $y = \tan x$ and $y = 2.5$ in the same viewing rectangle, as shown in Fig. 7.62. Use zoom-in to find the solution $x = 1.19$.

Solutions: $x = 1.19 + k\pi$ for all integer values of k.   ≡

Exercises for Section 7.5

1. Use a graphing utility to draw the graph of $y = \tan x$ in each of the following viewing rectangles. (Use $\pi = 3.14159$.) What generalization do you observe?

   a) $\left[-\dfrac{\pi}{2}, \dfrac{\pi}{2}\right]$ by $[-10, 10]$

   b) $\left[\dfrac{7\pi}{2}, \dfrac{9\pi}{2}\right]$ by $[-10, 10]$

   c) $\left[-\dfrac{11\pi}{2}, -\dfrac{9\pi}{2}\right]$ by $[-10, 10]$

   d) $\left[\dfrac{71\pi}{2}, \dfrac{73\pi}{2}\right]$ by $[-10, 10]$

2. The following figure shows one period of the graphs of both $y = \csc x$ and $y = 2\csc x$. Identify each function.

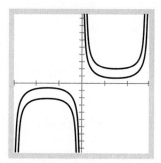

.786

For Exercise 2

3. The following figure shows two periods of the graphs of both $y = 0.5\tan x$ and $y = 5\tan x$. Identify each function.

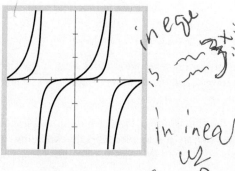

these

3×:3

is

in inea

us

For Exercise 3

2 π is per.

4. Identify three viewing rectangles that illustrate that portions of the graph of $y = \cot x$ are identical to each other as illustrated in Exercise 1 for $y = \tan x$.

5. Identify three viewing rectangles that illustrate that portions of the graph of $y = \sec x$ are identical to each other as illustrated in Exercise 1 for $y = \tan x$.

6. The figure shows graphs of two trig functions. Which of the following pairs correctly identifies them?

   a) $y = \tan x$ and $y = \sec x$

   b) $y = \cot x$ and $y = \csc x$

   c) $y = \tan x$ and $y = \csc x$

   d) $y = \cot x$ and $y = \sec x$

tan = 1.19 + Kπ   K is int

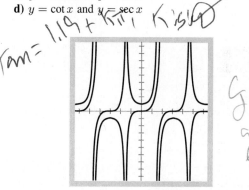

g
a
e
b

For Exercise 6

For each function in Exercises 7 to 12, find its period and a complete graph in a viewing rectangle that shows exactly three periods.

7. $y = \tan 2x$ 8. $y = \cot 3x$

9. $y = 2\sec 2x$ 10. $y = \csc \dfrac{x}{2}$

11. $y = \sec 3x$ 12. $y = 3\tan \dfrac{x}{2}$

In Exercises 13 to 28, sketch a graph of each function. Determine the domain, range, period, and asymptotes (if any).

13. $y = 3\tan x$ 14. $y = -\tan x$

15. $y = \dfrac{1}{2}\sec x$ 16. $y = \sec(-x)$

17. $y = 3\csc x$ 18. $y = 2\tan x$

19. $y = -3\tan\dfrac{1}{2}x$ 20. $y = 2\cot\dfrac{1}{2}x$

21. $y = 2\csc x$ 22. $y = -2\sec\dfrac{1}{2}x$

(.785 + 2 Kπ, 3.927 + 2(kπ)

K is an int

23. $y = 2\tan 3x$

24. $y = \sec\left(-\dfrac{1}{2}x\right)$

25. $y = -\tan\dfrac{\pi}{2}x$

26. $y = 2\tan \pi x$

27. $y = 3\sec 2x$

28. $y = 4\csc\dfrac{1}{3}x$

In Exercises 29 to 32, solve each equation for $-2\pi \leq x \leq 2\pi$.

29. $\tan x = 3.25$

30. $\cot x = -5.6$

31. $\sec x = 1.2$

32. $-\csc x = 3.1$

In Exercises 33 to 36, solve each equation for $-1 \leq x \leq 1$.

33. $\tan x = \cos x$

34. $\sin x = \cos x$

35. $\cot x = \sin x$

36. $\tan x = \cos 2x$

In Exercises 37 to 40, solve each inequality for $-\pi/2 < x < \pi/2$.

37. $5\tan x > \sec x$

38. $\tan x < \cot x$

39. $\tan x \geq \cos x$

40. $\sec x < \csc x$

Exercises 41 to 44 concern the equation $\sin x = 0.75$. All real solutions are given by $x + 2k\pi$, $k = 0, \pm 1, \pm 2, \ldots$ where x is 0.85 or 2.29. Use zoom-in to confirm this statement for each value of k.

41. $k = 0$

42. $k = 2$

43. $k = -3$

44. $k = 5$

In Exercises 45 to 54, find all real solutions.

45. $\sin x = 0.25$

46. $\tan x = 4$

47. $\cos x = 0.42$

48. $\sec x = 3$

49. $\sin x < 0.15$

50. $\tan x > 2$

51. $\sin 3x = 0.55$

52. $\cos 2x = 0.85$

53. $\csc\dfrac{1}{2}x \leq 4$

54. $3\sin\dfrac{1}{2}x > 2\cos x$

7.6 _____ Additional Applications Using Trig Functions

Our development of the trig functions has included three different approaches. Section 7.2 began by defining the trig functions in terms of ratios of sides of a right triangle. By the end of Section 7.2 the trig functions were defined in terms of the coordinates of any point on the terminal side of an angle in standard position. In Section 7.3 the trig functions were defined in terms of the unit circle.

Now that all three approaches have been developed, choose the one that seems most appropriate for the problem being analyzed.

This section begins by considering problems that are geometric in nature.

E X A M P L E   1   Finding Trig Function Values

The terminal side of θ is in the fourth quadrant and lies on the line $y = -2.5x$. Find all trig function values of θ and the measure of both angle θ and the reference angle θ'.

Solution   Any point on the line $y = -2.5x$ that falls in quadrant IV will be on the terminal side of θ and generate a reference triangle containing θ'. We choose the point $(2, -5)$ (see Fig. 7.63). Find the distance r from the origin to $(2, -5)$:

$$r = \sqrt{2^2 + (-5)^2} = \sqrt{29}.$$

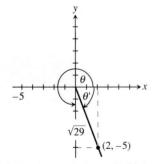

Figure 7.63 $y = -2.5x$.

Apply Definition 7.3 for $x = 2, y = -5,$ and $r = \sqrt{29}$:

$$\sin \theta = -\frac{5}{\sqrt{29}} \qquad \csc \theta = -\frac{\sqrt{29}}{5}$$

$$\sec \theta = \frac{\sqrt{29}}{2} \qquad \cos \theta = \frac{2}{\sqrt{29}}$$

$$\tan \theta = -\frac{5}{2} \qquad \cot \theta = -\frac{2}{5}.$$

Since $\tan \theta = -\dfrac{5}{2}$, we can tell using a calculator that the reference angle $\theta' = 68.2°$. Therefore

$$\theta = 360° - 68.2° = 291.8°.$$

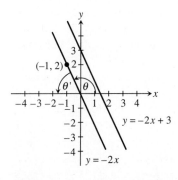

Figure 7.64   The intersection of two lines always creates two pairs of equal angles.

Angle between Intersecting Lines

When two lines intersect, they form four angles (see Fig. 7.64). The **angle between ℓ_1 and ℓ_2** is the smaller, acute angle between the lines. We can use the methods applied in Example 1 to find the angle measure between any two lines in the plane.

E X A M P L E 2   Finding Angles between Lines

Determine the angle between the x-axis and the line $y = -2x + 3$.

Solution   The line $y = -2x$ is parallel to $y = -2x + 3$ (see Fig. 7.65). We shall use $y = -2x$ in this solution since it goes through the origin and thus determines an angle in standard position.

Choose a point on the terminal side of θ: $P(-1, 2)$. Since $\tan \theta = -2$, we see that angle θ in Fig. 7.65 is $116.57°$, and the angle between the x-axis and graph of $y = 2x + 3$ is $66.43°$.

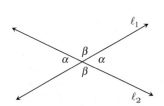

Figure 7.65   A pair of parallel lines.

Additional Applications

E X A M P L E 3   APPLICATION: Angle of Depression

The angle of depression of a buoy from a point on a lighthouse 130 feet above the surface of the water is $6°$. Find the distance x from the base of the lighthouse to the buoy.

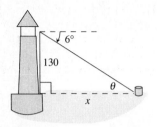

Figure 7.66   Diagram of the problem situation in Example 3.

Solution   See Fig. 7.66.

$$\tan \theta = \tan 6° = \frac{130}{x}$$

$$x = \frac{130}{\tan 6°} = 1236.87$$

The distance from the base of the lighthouse to the buoy is 1236.87 feet.   ≡

E X A M P L E   4   APPLICATION: Indirect Measurement

From the top of a 100-foot building a man observes a car moving toward him. If the angle of depression of the car changes from 22° to 46° during the period of observation, how far does the car travel?

Solution   See Fig. 7.67. $\alpha = 22°$ and $\beta = 46°$.

$$\tan \alpha = \frac{100}{x + d} \qquad \tan \beta = \frac{100}{d}$$

$$x + d = \frac{100}{\tan 22°} \qquad d = \frac{100}{\tan 46°}$$

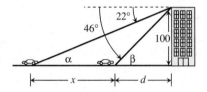

Figure 7.67   Diagram for Example 4.

Therefore

$$x = \frac{100}{\tan 22°} - d$$

$$= \frac{100}{\tan 22°} - \frac{100}{\tan 46°}$$

$$= 150.94.$$

The car travels 150.94 feet.   ≡

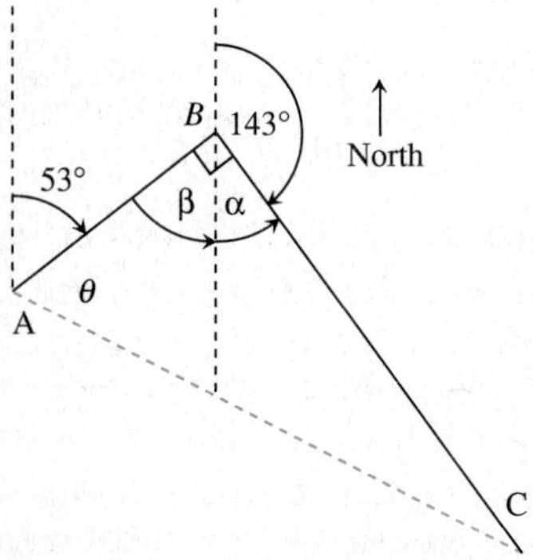

E X A M P L E   5   APPLICATION: Navigation

A naval boat travels at a speed of 35 mph for 2 hours on a course 53° east of north; then it changes to a course 143° east of north and travels for another 3 hours. Determine the distance from the boat to its home port (Fig. 7.68). What is the bearing from the boat's home port to its location at the end of 5 hours?

Figure 7.68   Diagram for Example 5.

Solution

A: boat's home port
B: position when boat changes course
C: position at end of trip
$\alpha = 37°$, $\beta = 53°$,   segment AC is the hypotenuse of right $\triangle ABC$.

$AB = (35 \text{ mi/hr})(2 \text{ hr}) = 70 \text{ mi}$
$BC = (35 \text{ mi/hr})(3 \text{ hr}) = 105 \text{ mi}$
$AC = \sqrt{70^2 + 105^2} = 126.19$ Use the Pythagorean theorem.

Bearing from A to C: $53° + \theta$ where

$$\tan \theta = \frac{BC}{AB} = \frac{105}{70} \qquad \text{or} \qquad \theta = \tan^{-1}(1.5).$$

The bearing from A to C is $53° + \tan^{-1}(1.5) = 109.31°$.

Exercises for Section 7.6

In Exercises 1 to 8, let θ be an angle in standard position with its terminal side as given by the equation. Find the values of the six trig functions at θ.

1. $y = x$, quadrant III

2. $y = 2x$, quadrant I

3. $y = x$, quadrant I

4. $y = 2x$, quadrant III

5. $y = \dfrac{3}{4}x$, quadrant I

6. $y = -x$, quadrant II

7. $y = \dfrac{2}{3}x$, quadrant III

8. $y = -\dfrac{3}{5}x$, quadrant IV

In Exercises 9 to 12, determine the angle between the x-axis and the line.

9. $y = 2x$

10. $2x - 3y = 4$

11. $y = -3x + 1$

12. $3x - 5y = -2$

In Exercises 13 to 16, find the quadrant containing the terminal side of θ, which is an angle in standard position.

13. $\sin \theta < 0$ and $\tan \theta > 0$

14. $\cos \theta > 0$ and $\tan \theta < 0$

15. $\tan \theta > 0$ and $\sec \theta < 0$

16. $\sin \theta > 0$ and $\cos \theta < 0$

17. A wire stretches from the top of a vertical pole to a point on level ground 16 feet from the base of the pole. If the wire makes an angle of $62°$ with the ground, determine the height of the pole and the length of the wire.

18. A lighthouse L stands 3 miles from the nearest point P on the shore. Point Q is located down the shoreline and $\overline{PQ} \perp \overline{PL}$. Determine the distance from P to a point Q along the shore if $\angle PQL = 35°$.

19. Using a sextant, a surveyor determines that the angle of elevation of a mountain peak is $35°$. Moving 1000 feet further away from the mountain the surveyor determines the angle of elevation to be $30°$. Determine the height of the mountain.

20. An observer on the ground is 1 mile from a building 1200 feet tall. What is the angle of elevation from the observer to the top of the building?

21. The angle of elevation from an observer to the base of the roof of a tower located 200 feet from the observer is $30°$. The angle of elevation from the observer to the top of the same roof is $40°$. What is the height AB? (Assume points A, B, and C are on the same perpendicular line to the ground.)

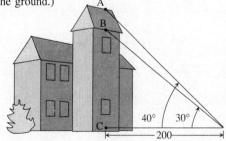

For Exercise 21

22. From the top of a 100-foot building a man observes a car moving toward him. If the angle of depression of the car changes from 15° to 33° during the period of observation, how far does the car travel?

23. A boat travels at a speed of 30 mph from its home port on a course of 95° for 2 hours and then changes to a course of 185° for 2 hours. Determine the distance from the boat to its home port and the bearing from the home port to the boat.

24. A boat travels at a speed of 40 mph from its home base on a course of 65° for 2 hours and then changes to course of 155° for 4 hours. Determine the distance from the boat to its home port and the bearing from the home port to the boat.

25. A point on the north rim of the Grand Canyon is 7256 feet above sea level. A point on the south rim directly across from the other point is 6159 feet above sea level. The canyon is 3180 feet wide (horizontal distance) between the two points. What is the angle of depression from the north-rim point to the south-rim point?

26. A ranger spots a fire from a 73-foot tower in Yellowstone National Park. She measures the angle of depression to be 1°20′. How far is the fire from the tower?

27. A footbridge is to be constructed along an east–west line across a river gorge. The bearing of a line of sight from a point 325 feet due north of the west end of the bridge to the east end of the bridge is 117°. What is the length ℓ of the bridge?

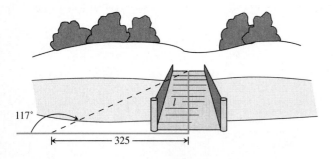

For Exercise 27

28. The angle of elevation of a space shuttle launched from Cape Canaveral is measured to be 17° relative to the point of launch when it is directly over a ship 12 miles down range. What is the altitude of the shuttle when it is directly over the ship?

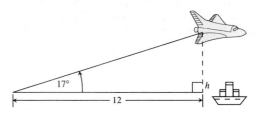

For Exercise 28

29. A truss for a barn roof is constructed as shown in the figure. What is the height of the vertical center span?

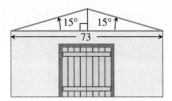

For Exercise 29

30. A hot-air balloon over Park City, Utah, is 760 feet above the ground. The angle of depression from the balloon to a small lake is 5.25°. How far is the lake from a point on the ground directly under the balloon?

31. The bearings of lines of sight from two points on the shore to a boat are 110° and 100°. Assume the two points are 550 feet apart. How far is the boat from the nearest point on the shore?

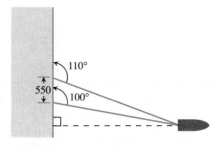

For Exercise 31

32. Boats A and B leave from ports on opposite sides of a large lake. The ports are on an east–west line. Boat A

steers a course of $105°$, and boat B steers a course of $195°$. Boat A averages 23 mph and collides with boat B (it was a foggy night). What was boat B's average speed?

33. **Writing to Learn** Write several paragraphs that explain how the three approaches to the trig functions represented by Definitions 7.2, 7.3, and 7.4 are consistent with one another.

Chapter 7 Review

KEY TERMS

acute angle
amplitude
angle
angle between ℓ_1 and ℓ_2
angle in standard position
angle of depression
angle of elevation
angular speed
bearing
central angle
circular functions
cofunctions

complementary angles
coterminal angles
course
degrees
fundamental trig identities
hypotenuse
initial side of an angle
intercepted arc AB
linear speed
line of travel
minutes
nautical mile

obtuse angle
path
periodic function
periodic property of sine
    and cosine
period of f
quadrantal angle
radian
reference angle
reference triangle
right angle
seconds

side adjacent to an angle
side opposite an angle
similar triangles
solving a right triangle
subtends an angle
supplementary angles
statute mile
terminal side of an angle
trigonometric functions
trigonometric identity
unit circle
vertex of an angle

REVIEW EXERCISES

In Exercises 1 to 8, determine the quadrant of the terminal side of each angle in standard position. If the angle is in degrees, give its radian equivalent; if it is in radians, give its degree equivalent.

1. $135°$
2. $-45°$
3. $\dfrac{5\pi}{2}$
4. $\dfrac{3\pi}{4}$
5. $78°$
6. $112°$
7. $\dfrac{\pi}{12}$
8. $\dfrac{7\pi}{10}$

In Exercises 9 and 10, determine the angle measure in both degrees and radians, and draw the angle in standard position if the terminal side of the angle is obtained as follows:

9. A three-quarters' counterclockwise rotation

10. Two and one-half counterclockwise rotations

In Exercises 11 to 16, the given point is on the terminal side of an angle in standard position. Give the smallest positive angle in both degrees and radians for this angle.

11. $(2, 4)$
12. $(-1, 1)$
13. $(-1, \sqrt{3})$
14. $(-3, -3)$
15. $(6, -12)$
16. $(\sqrt{3}, 1)$

In Exercises 17 to 28, find the exact values of each trig function.

17. $\sin 30°$
18. $\cos 270°$
19. $\tan 135°$
20. $\sin \dfrac{5\pi}{6}$
21. $\csc \dfrac{2\pi}{3}$
22. $\sec 135°$
23. $\csc \dfrac{\pi}{3}$
24. $\csc 210°$
25. $\cos \dfrac{2\pi}{3}$
26. $\sec 330°$
27. $\cot 135°$
28. $\cot \dfrac{5\pi}{4}$

In Exercises 29 to 34, use properties of a $30°$-$60°$ right triangle and a $45°$ right triangle to determine the exact values for all six trig functions for these angles.

29. 0
30. $-\dfrac{\pi}{6}$
31. $\dfrac{3\pi}{4}$
32. $60°$
33. $-135°$
34. $300°$

35. Find all six trig functions of $\angle A$ in $\triangle ABC$.

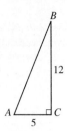

For Exercise 35

36. Use a right triangle to determine the values of all trig functions at θ with $\cos\theta = \frac{5}{7}$.

37. Use a right triangle to determine the values of all trig functions at θ with $\cos\theta = \frac{12}{13}$.

38. Use a calculator to solve $\cos\theta = \frac{3}{7}$ if $0° \le \theta \le 90°$. Make sure your calculator is set in degree mode. (Recall the meaning and use of $\cos^{-1}$.)

39. Use a calculator to solve $\cot\theta = \frac{1}{3}$ if $0° \le \theta \le 90°$.

40. Use a calculator to solve $\tan x = 1.35$ if $0 \le x \le \pi/2$. Make sure your calculator is set in radian mode.

41. Use a calculator to solve $\sin x = 0.218$ if $0 \le x \le \dfrac{\pi}{2}$.

In Exercises 42 to 47, solve the right triangle ABC for each of the given data.

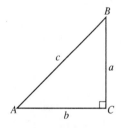

For Exercises 42 to 47

42. $\angle A = 35°, c = 15$ **43.** $b = 8, c = 10$

44. $\angle B = 48°, a = 7$ **45.** $\angle A = 28°, c = 8$

46. $b = 5, c = 7$ **47.** $a = 2.5, b = 7.3$

If x is an angle in standard position and $0 \le x \le 2\pi$, find the quadrant of x in Exercises 48 to 51.

48. $\sin x < 0$ and $\tan x > 0$

49. $\cos x < 0$ and $\csc x > 0$

50. $\tan x < 0$ and $\sin x < 0$

51. $\csc x > 0$ and $\sec x < 0$

52. Show that

$$\cot\theta = \frac{\cos\theta}{\sin\theta}$$

for all acute angles θ.

Use the fundamental trig identities to complete Exercises 53 and 54. Check your answers with a calculator.

53. $\tan\theta$ if $\sin\theta = 0.58$ **54.** $\tan\theta$ if $\cos\theta = 0.82$

In Exercises 55 to 58, let θ be an angle in standard position with the point P on the terminal side of θ. Find the values of each of all six trig functions if $0 < \theta \le \pi$ in each case.

55. $(-3, 6)$ **56.** $(12, 7)$

57. $(-5, -3)$ **58.** $(4, 9)$

In Exercises 59 to 66, sketch a complete graph without using a graphing utility. Check your answers with a graphing utility.

59. $y = \sin(x + 45°)$ **60.** $y = 3 + 2\cos x$

61. $y = -\sin(x + \pi/2)$ **62.** $y = -2 - 3\sin(x - \pi)$

63. $y = \tan 2x$ **64.** $y = 3\cos 2x$

65. $y = -2\sin 3x$ **66.** $y = \csc \pi x$

In Exercises 67 and 68, investigate graphically what happens to the values of $f(x)$ as $x \to 0$.

67. $f(x) = \dfrac{1}{x}\sin\left(\dfrac{1}{x}\right)$ **68.** $f(x) = \dfrac{\sin x}{x^2}$

In Exercises 69 to 72, use a calculator to evaluate each expression. Express your answers in both degrees and as real numbers.

69. $\sin^{-1}(0.766)$ **70.** $\sin^{-1}(0.479)$

71. $\sin^{-1}\left(\dfrac{\sqrt{3}}{2}\right)$ **72.** $\tan^{-1} 1$

Use a calculator to evaluate Exercises 73 to 76. Express your answer as a real number.

73. $\sin[\sin^{-1}(0.25)]$ **74.** $\cos^{-1}[\tan(0.2)]$

75. $\tan(\sin^{-1} 2)$ **76.** $\sin^{-1}[\sin(\sqrt{3}\cos 3)]$

77. Solve the inequality $3\cos x < x + 2$.

78. The angle of elevation of the top of a building from a point 100 meters away from the building on level ground is $78°$. Determine the height of the building.

79. A tree casts a shadow 51 feet long when the angle of elevation of the sun (measured from the horizon) is 25°. How tall is the tree?

80. From the top of a 150-foot building Flora observes a car moving toward her. If the angle of depression of the car changes from 18° to 42° during the observation, how far does the car travel?

81. A lighthouse L stands 4 miles from the closest point P along a straight shore. Find the distance from P to a point Q along the shore if $\angle PLQ = 22°$.

82. An airplane at a certain time is between two signal towers positioned on a line with bearing 0° (that is, along a north–south line). The bearings between the plane and the north and south towers are 23° and 128°, respectively. Use a drawing to show the exact location of the plane.

83. A shoreline runs north-south and a boat is due east of the shore line. The bearings of lines of sight from a boat to two points on the shore are 115° and 123°. Assume the two points are 855 feet apart. How far is the boat from the nearest point on shore if the shore is a straight line?

CHAPTER 8

Analytic Trigonometry

$$\sin^{-1} = \left[-\pi/2, \pi/2\right]$$

$$\tan^{-1} = \left(-\pi/2, \pi/2\right)$$

$$\cos^{-1} = \left[0, \pi\right]$$

use sin not csc.

$$\cos\left(\sin^{-1} -4/5\right)$$

5/5

-4 ⟋⟍ 5

3

8.1 _____ Transformations and Trigonometric Graphs

In Chapter 7 the trig functions were introduced as ratios of sides of right triangles. This chapter focuses on graphs of the trig functions, equation solving, and trig identities. These aspects of trigonometry, which are important in calculus, are often referred to as **analytic trigonometry**.

In Chapter 3 you learned to transform the graph of a function by horizontal and vertical shifts, by vertical stretching and shrinking, and by reflection through the x-axis. Following is a review of these transformations:

375

Review of Transformations

Suppose that $a, c,$ and d are positive real numbers.

To obtain the graph of:	**From the graph of $y = f(x)$:**
$y = af(x)$	Vertical stretch or shrink by a factor of a units.
$y = -f(x)$	Reflect through the x-axis.
$y = f(x + c)$	Shift left c units.
$y = f(x - c)$	Shift right c units.
$y = f(x) + d$	Shift up d units.
$y = f(x) - d$	Shift down d units.
$y = f(-x)$	Reflect through the y-axis.

These same transformations can be applied to the graphs of any of the trigonometric functions. These transformations are illustrated for the functions $y = \sin x$ and $y = \cos x$.

UNDERSTANDING NOTATION

Notice the difference in notation between $y = \sin x - 2$ and $y = \sin(x - 2)$. Writing $\sin x - 2$ means finding the sine of x and then subtracting 2. On the other hand, $\sin(x - 2)$ means first finding $x - 2$ and then finding the sine of $x - 2$. The two values, $\sin x - 2$ and $\sin(x - 2)$, are not equal.

E X A M P L E   1   Finding Sine Function Transformations

Describe how a complete graph of the following functions can be obtained from $y = \sin x$. Support your answer with a graphing utility.

a) $f(x) = 5 \sin x$

b) $g(x) = \sin x - 2$

Solution

a) A complete graph of $f(x) = 5 \sin x$ can be obtained from a graph of $y = \sin x$ by a vertical stretch by a factor of 5 (see Fig. 8.1a).

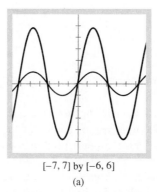

[−7, 7] by [−6, 6]

(a)

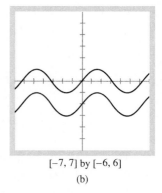

[−7, 7] by [−6, 6]

(b)

Figure 8.1 (a) $y = \sin x$ and $f(x) = 5 \sin x$, (b) $y = \sin x$ and $g(x) = \sin x - 2$.

b) A complete graph of $g(x) = \sin x - 2$ can be obtained from a graph of $y = \sin x$ by a vertical shift down 2 units (see Fig. 8.1b). ≡

Recall that the vertical stretch factor 5 in Example 1 is called the amplitude of $f(x)$. The amplitude of a sine or cosine function determines the local maximum and local minimum of that function.

This next example reviews how horizontal shift transformations can be used with cosine functions.

E X A M P L E   2   Finding Cosine Function Transformations

Describe how a complete graph of the following functions can be obtained from $y = \cos x$. Support your answer with a graphing utility.

a) $f(x) = \cos(x - 1.5)$

b) $g(x) = \cos(x + 0.5)$

Solution

a) A complete graph of $f(x) = \cos(x - 1.5)$ can be obtained from a graph of $y = \cos x$ by a shift to the right 1.5 units (see Fig. 8.2a).

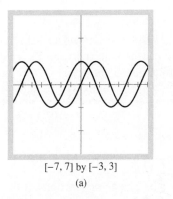 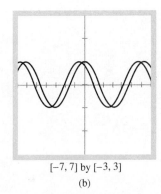

$[-7, 7]$ by $[-3, 3]$	$[-7, 7]$ by $[-3, 3]$
(a)	(b)

Figure 8.2   (a) $y = \cos x$ and $f(x) = \cos(x - 1.5)$; (b) $y = \cos x$ and $g(x) = \cos(x + 0.5)$.

b) A complete graph of $g(x) = \cos(x + 0.5)$ can be obtained from a graph of $y = \cos x$ by a shift left 0.5 units (see Fig. 8.2b). ≡

Trigonometry is important in electronics because the sine and cosine functions model alternating current. Physicists have developed their own terminology for this application. They would say that the graphs of $f(x) = \cos(x - 1.5)$ and $g(x) = \cos(x + 0.5)$ are obtained from the graph of $y = \cos x$ by a **phase shift.** Example 2(a) illustrated a phase shift to the right 1.5 units.

To summarize, so far we have considered the transformations of vertical and horizontal shifting and vertical stretching. The graph of $y = a\sin(x + c) + d$ can be obtained from the graph of $y = \sin x$ by using these transformations.

The following Exploration focuses on what impact the constant b has on the graph of $y = \sin bx$.

🔎 EXPLORE WITH A GRAPHING UTILITY

Graph each pair in the viewing rectangle $[-10, 10]$ by $[-4, 4]$. (The $+2$ and -2 are included so that the two graphs will not overlap.) Would the graph of the second function be obtained by compressing (that is, horizontally shrinking) or stretching the graph of the first function?

1. $y = \sin x + 2;\quad y = \sin 2x - 2$

2. $y = \sin x + 2;\quad y = \sin 3x - 2$

3. $y = \sin x + 2;\quad y = \sin \frac{1}{2}x - 2$

Try several other examples of your choice.

Generalize   Under what conditions do you think that the graph of $y = \sin bx$ can be obtained from the graph of $y = \sin x$ by a horizontal stretch? By a horizontal shrink?

Graphs of $y = \sin(bx + c)$

Consider the graphs of functions of the form $y = \sin(bx + c)$ where b is a positive real number and c is any real number, positive or negative. We saw in Chapter 7 that the trigonometric functions are periodic. The period of $f(x) = \sin bx$ is $2\pi/|b|$, so the constant b determines the period of f.

How do the constants b and c affect the graph of $y = \sin(bx + c)$? Figure 8.3 shows the beginning and end of one period of $y = \sin(bx + c)$. Since the sine function is a periodic function with a period of 2π, the beginning of the period shown occurs where $bx + c = 0$ and the end of the period occurs where $bx + c = 2\pi$.

We can use this information to find the x-intercepts at the beginning and the end of the period.

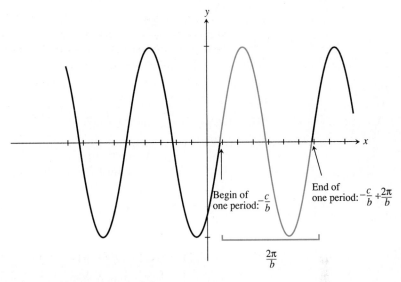

Figure 8.3 $y = \sin(bx + c)$.

Beginning of Period	**End of Period**
$bx + c = 0$	$bx + c = 2\pi$
$bx = -c$	$bx = 2\pi - c$
$x = -\dfrac{c}{b}$	$x = \dfrac{2\pi}{b} - \dfrac{c}{b}$

The constants b and c affect both the period and phase shift of the graph. The graph of $y = \sin(bx + c)$ has a phase shift of $-c/b$ and a period of $2\pi/|b|$. The same is true for any periodic function, a fact which leads to this generalization.

Theorem 8.1   Phase Shift and Period of $y = f(bx + c)$

Suppose that $y = f(x)$ is a trigonometric function with period P and that b is a positive number. Then

a) the number $-c/b$ is the phase shift of $y = f(bx + c)$, and
b) the period of $y = f(bx + c)$ is $P/|b|$.

We say that the graph of $y = f(bx)$ can be obtained from the graph of $y = f(x)$ by a horizontal shrink if $b > 1$ and by a horizontal stretch if $0 < b < 1$.

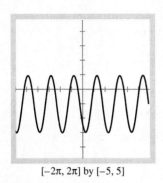

$[-2\pi, 2\pi]$ by $[-5, 5]$

Figure 8.4
$f(x) = 2\sin(3x + 4) - 1.$

E X A M P L E   3   *Analyzing a Complete Graph*

Find a complete graph and the domain, range, period, and phase shift of $f(x) = 2\sin(3x + 4) - 1$.

Solution
Domain: x can represent any real number, so the domain of f is $(-\infty, \infty)$.
Range: Consider the graph of $y = 2\sin(3x + 4) = f(x) + 1$. The amplitude of y is 2, which means that $-2 \leq y \leq 2$. Therefore $-2 - 1 \leq f(x) \leq 2 - 1$, and the range of f is the interval $[-3, 1]$.
Phase shift: It follows from Theorem 8.1 that the phase shift is $-\frac{4}{3}$.
Period: It follows from Theorem 8.1 that the period is $2\pi/3$. A complete graph is shown in Fig. 8.4.   ▤

We now summarize the characteristics of amplitude, period, phase shift, and maximum and minimum values for the completely general sine function $f(x) = a\sin(bx + c) + d$.

Summary: $f(x) = a\sin(bx + c) + d$

The function $f(x) = a\sin(bx + c) + d$, where a, b, c and d are any real numbers, is a periodic function with the following characteristics:

Amplitude: $|a|$ Period: $\dfrac{2\pi}{|b|}$ Phase shift: $-\dfrac{c}{b}$

Local maximum of $f(x)$: $d + |a|$

Local minimum of $f(x)$: $d - |a|$

The functions $f(x) = a\cos(bx + c) + d$, $f(x) = a\sec(bx + c) + d$, and $f(x) = a\csc(bx + c) + d$ have the same characteristics, except that the secant and cosecant functions do not have amplitudes and the local maximum and local minimum values are reversed from the cosine and sine functions.

Example 4 supports the claim that the functions $f(x) = a\tan(bx + c) + d$ and $f(x) = a\cot(bx + c) + d$ do not have amplitudes or a maximum or minimum and that their period is $\pi/|b|$.

E X A M P L E   4   Analyzing a Complete Graph

Describe how the function $f(x) = -4\cot(2x+\pi/3)$ can be obtained from $y = \cot x$ by applying transformations.

Solution   Notice that $f(x)$ can be rewritten as

$$f(x) = -4\cot\left(2x + \frac{\pi}{3}\right) = -4\cot\left[2\left(x + \frac{\pi}{6}\right)\right].$$

Apply the following transformations to the graph of $y = \cot x$ to obtain the graph of f as expressed by this equation.

1. A vertical stretch by a factor of 4 to obtain $y = 4\cot x$.
2. A reflection through the x-axis to obtain $y = -4\cot x$.
3. A horizontal shrink by a factor of $\frac{1}{2}$ to obtain $y = -4\cot 2x$.
4. A horizontal shift to the left $\pi/6$ units to obtain $f(x) = -4\cot\left[2\left(x + \frac{\pi}{6}\right)\right]$.

A complete graph is shown in Fig. 8.5.   ≡

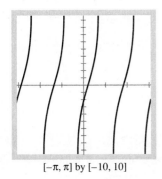

$[-\pi, \pi]$ by $[-10, 10]$

Figure 8.5
$f(x) = -4\cot(2x + \pi/3)$

Sinusoids

The functions discussed in Examples 1 to 3 belong to the category of functions called sinusoids.

Definition 8.1   Sinusoids

A **sinusoid** is a function that can be written in the form

$$f(x) = a\sin(bx + c) + d,$$

where $a, b, c,$ and d are real numbers.

Notice that the graph of a sinusoid can be obtained from the graph of $y = \sin x$ by a combination of horizontal stretching or shrinking, horizontal shifting, vertical stretching or shrinking, and vertical shifting. In the next few Explorations you will investigate what happens when you add or subtract sine and cosine functions.

A sum of the form $a\sin cx + b\cos dx$ where $a, b, c,$ and d are constants is called a **linear combination** of $\sin cx$ and $\cos dx$. In the next several explorations you will investigate the conditions under which a linear combination of $\sin cx$ and $\cos dx$ is also a sinusoid.

Experiment by graphing these functions. Which appear to be sinusoidal?

$$y = 3 \sin x + 2 \cos x \qquad y = 2 \sin x - 3 \cos x$$

$$y = 2 \sin 3x + 4 \cos 2x \qquad y = 3 \sin 5x - 5 \cos 5x$$

$$y = 4 \sin x - 2 \cos x \qquad y = 3 \cos 2x + 2 \sin 3x$$

Experiment with other sums and differences of sine and cosine functions.

Write a Conjecture   Under what conditions will these sums and differences be sinusoidal?

In this Exploration you have discovered that not all of the functions are sinusoidal. Your experience may have led you to guess that any linear combination of $\sin x$ and $\cos x$ is a sinusoid. This is the subject of a theorem.

Theorem 8.2   Sums That Are Sinusoidal

For all real numbers a and b the function

$$f(x) = a \sin x + b \cos x$$

is a sinusoid. In particular, there exist real numbers A and α such that

$$a \sin x + b \cos x = A \sin(x + \alpha)$$

where $|A|$ is the amplitude and α is the phase shift.

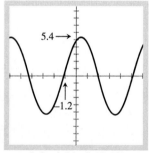

[-2π, 2π] by [-10, 10]

Figure 8.6 $f(x) = 2 \sin x + 5 \cos x$ has the same graph as $y = 5.4 \sin(x + 1.2)$.

E X A M P L E   5   Finding the Amplitude and Phase Shift

Show that $f(x) = 2 \sin x + 5 \cos x$ is a sinusoid. Also approximate A and α so that $A \sin(x + \alpha) = 2 \sin x + 5 \cos x$.

Solution   By Theorem 8.2 the function f is sinusoidal, which is confirmed by the graph in Fig. 8.6. Using the trace key and/or zoom-in, estimate the following values:

Amplitude: 5.4, or $A = 5.4$.

Phase shift: 1.2 units to the left, or $\alpha = 1.2$.

Period: 2π.

Support these estimates by overlaying the graph of $y = 5.4\sin(x + 1.2)$ with the graph of $f(x) = 2\sin x + 5\cos x$ (Fig. 8.6). (Example 5 of Section 8.5 gives an algebraic way to do this exercise.) ▤

Theorem 8.2 and Example 5 were about linear combinations of $\sin x$ and $\cos x$. The next Exploration broadens the investigation to include linear combinations of functions with phase shifts and periods other than 2π.

🔍 **EXPLORE WITH A GRAPHING UTILITY**

Experiment and decide which of these functions appear to be sinusoids:

$$y = 2\sin(3x + 1) - 5\cos(3x - 2) \qquad y = 3\sin(2x - 0.5) + \cos(2x + 1)$$
$$y = \sin(3x - 1) + 3\cos(3x + 2) \qquad y = 2\sin(x - 2) + 3\cos(4x + 1)$$
$$y = 3\sin(4x + 1) - 2\cos(2x - 3) \qquad y = 2\sin(3x - 2) + 3\cos(3x + 4)$$

Experiment with other sums and differences of sine and cosine functions of your own choice.

Write a Conjecture   Under what conditions will these linear combinations be sinusoidal?

$\sqrt{29}\,\sin\left(x +\right.$ This Exploration supports the following theorem.

Theorem 8.3   Sums That Are Sinusoidal

For all real numbers a, b, d, h, and k, the function

$$f(x) = a\sin(bx + h) + d\cos(bx + k)$$

is a sinusoid. In particular, there exist real numbers A and α such that

$$a\sin(bx + h) + d\cos(bx + k) = A\sin(bx + \alpha).$$

E X A M P L E   6   Finding the Amplitude and Phase Shift

Show that $f(x) = 3\sin(2x - 1) + 4\cos(2x + 3)$ is a sinusoid. Also estimate A and α so that $A\sin(2x + \alpha) = 3\sin(2x - 1) + 4\cos(2x + 3)$.

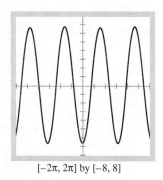

[−2π, 2π] by [−8, 8]

Figure 8.7 $f(x) =$
$3\sin(2x - 1) + 4\cos(2x + 3)$
has the same graph as
$y = 6.6\sin(2x - 1.42)$.

Solution   From Theorem 8.3 we know that f is sinusoidal, which is supported by the graph in Fig. 8.7. Using the trace key and/or zoom-in, estimate the following values:

Amplitude: 6.6.

Phase shift: 0.71 units to the right or $\alpha = -1.42$.

Period: π.

Support these estimates by overlaying the graph of $y = 6.6\sin[2(x - 0.71)]$ with the graph of $f(x) = 3\sin(2x - 1) + 4\cos(2x + 3)$ in Fig. 8.7.   ≣

Notice that in Theorem 8.2 as well as Theorem 8.3 both the sine and cosine terms in the linear combination have the same period. If the periods of the sine and cosine are different, then the linear combination is not a sinusoid.

A value $f(c)$ is an **absolute maximum** for a function f on an interval $[a, b]$ if $f(c) \geq f(x)$ for all x in $[a, b]$. Similarly, $f(c)$ is an **absolute minimum** if $f(c) \leq f(x)$ for all x in $[a, b]$.

A value $f(c)$ is an **absolute extremum** if it is either an absolute maximum or an absolute minimum.

E X A M P L E   7   Showing a Sum Is Not a Sinusoid

Show that the function $f(x) = \sin 2x + \cos 3x$ is not sinusoidal. Also find the domain, range, and period of f.

Solution   Figure 8.8(a) shows a complete graph of f. From this graph we conclude that f is not sinusoidal.

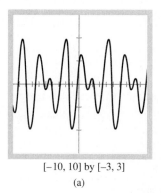   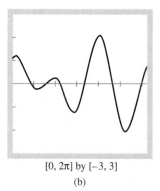

[−10, 10] by [−3, 3]   [0, 2π] by [−3, 3]

(a)   (b)

Figure 8.8   Two views of $f(x) = \sin 2x + \cos 3x$.

$1 \sin(x + .58)$

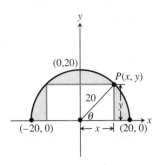

Figure 8.9 A semicircular tunnel has walls and ceiling forming a rectangular cross section.

Domain: $(-\infty, \infty)$. (Why?)

Period: The period of $\sin 2x$ is π, and the period of $\cos 3x$ is $2\pi/3$. The period of f must be a common multiple of these two periods, and the least common multiple is 2π.

Range: In order to determine the range of f we investigate a graph of the single period of f shown in the $[0, 2\pi]$ by $[-3, 3]$ viewing rectangle (Fig. 8.8b).

Use zoom-in to determine that the absolute maximum of f in $[0, 2\pi]$ is 1.91 and occurs when $x = 4.11$. The absolute minimum is -1.91 and occurs when $x = 5.32$. So the range is $[-1.91, 1.91]$. ≡

Applications of Trigonometric Functions

Analyzing the graphs of trigonometric functions is often the key to solving an applied problem. We illustrate with several examples.

E X A M P L E 8   APPLICATION: Building a Tunnel

The cross section of a tunnel is a semicircle with a radius of 20 feet. The interior walls of the tunnel form a rectangle as illustrated in Fig. 8.9. An engineer is asked to find the width and height of the tunnel opening with the maximum cross-sectional area.

Solution   We want to find an algebraic representation of the tunnel's cross-sectional area. Let $P(x, y)$ be the upper right corner point of the rectangle and θ the angle that OP makes with the positive x-axis. Then $\cos \theta = x/20$ and $\sin \theta = y/20$, or $x = 20 \cos \theta$ and $y = 20 \sin \theta$.

Since the area A of the rectangle is the quantity to be maximized, express A as a function of θ:

$$A = 2xy$$
$$= 2(20 \cos \theta)(20 \sin \theta)$$
$$= 800 \sin \theta \cos \theta.$$

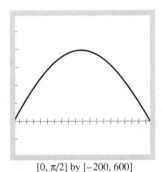

$[0, \pi/2]$ by $[-200, 600]$

Figure 8.10
$A = 800 \sin \theta \cos \theta.$

The context of the problem situation indicates that θ must be in the interval $[0, \pi/2]$. Figure 8.10 shows a graph of $A = 800 \sin \theta \cos \theta$ in $[0, \pi/2]$. Use zoom-in to find that the coordinates of the highest point of the graph are $(0.785, 400)$ with an error at most 0.01.

Since the maximum area occurs when $\theta = 0.785$, we see that

$$x = 20 \cos 0.785 = 14.14 \text{ feet} \quad \text{and} \quad y = 20 \sin(0.785) = 14.14 \text{ feet.} \quad ≡$$

REMINDER

Figure 8.10 shows a complete graph of the problem situation. But it is not a complete graph of the algebraic representation $A = 800 \sin \theta \cos \theta.$

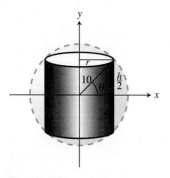

Figure 8.11   A hole is cut through the center of a sphere.

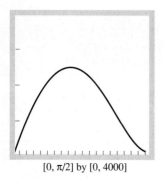

$[0, \pi/2]$ by $[0, 4000]$

Figure 8.12
$V = 2000\pi \sin \theta \cos^2 \theta.$

The next problem situation deals with a sphere with a hole drilled through it. From Fig. 8.11 it is evident that as the radius of the hole increases, the height of the hole decreases.

E X A M P L E   9   APPLICATION: Drilling a Hole in a Sphere

A hole is drilled through the center of a sphere of radius 10. The portion of the sphere drilled out is a right circular cylinder and two spherical caps. Find the dimensions of the cylindrical hole with the maximum volume that can be drilled out of a sphere.

Solution   Using the reference triangle in Fig. 8.11 we see that $h/2 = 10 \sin \theta$ and $r = 10 \cos \theta$. Since volume is the quantity to be maximized, express V as a function of θ.

$$V = \pi r^2 h$$
$$= \pi (10 \cos \theta)^2 (20 \sin \theta)$$
$$= 2000\pi \sin \theta \cos^2 \theta$$

Notice that in this problem situation, θ must be in the interval $[0, \pi/2]$. Fig. 8.12 shows a complete graph of the problem situation. Use zoom-in to determine that the coordinates of the highest point of the graph of V are $(0.615, 2418.399)$ with error at most 0.01.

The maximum volume is 2418.399 cubic units, and it occurs when $\theta = 0.615$ radians. Substituting this value of θ into the equations for h and r we find that the maximum volume occurs when $r = 8.17$ and $h = 11.54$.   ▤

Exercises for Section 8.1

In Exercises 1 to 4, list the transformations in the order of their application to transform $y = \sin x$ or $y = \tan x$ into the indicated graph.

1. $y = 3 - 4 \sin(2x - \pi)$ **2.** $y = 2 + 3 \sin\left(\frac{1}{2}x + \frac{\pi}{2}\right)$

3. $y = 2 - \tan(x - \pi)$ **4.** $y = 1 + 2 \tan(2x - \pi)$

In Exercises 5 to 14, sketch a complete graph of each function without using a graphing utility. Support your answer with a graphing utility if necessary.

5. $y = 2 + \sin\left(x - \frac{\pi}{4}\right)$ **6.** $y = -1 - \cos(x - \pi)$

7. $y = -1 + 3 \sin(x - 2)$ **8.** $y = 2 - 2 \sin(x + 3)$

9. $f(x) = 2 - 3 \sin(2x)$ **10.** $g(x) = -2 + \tan\left(\frac{1}{2}x\right)$

11. $y = 2 + 3 \cos\left(\frac{x-1}{2}\right)$ **12.** $y = -2 - 4 \sin(2x + 6)$

13. $T(x) = -3 + 2 \sin(2x - \pi)$

14. $y = 2 - 3 \cos(4x - 2\pi)$

In Exercises 15 to 18, determine the domain, range, period, and asymptotes (if any) of the function in each exercise.

15. Exercise 3   **16.** Exercise 5

17. Exercise 6   **18.** Exercise 8

In Exercises 19 to 24, find the period and phase shift for each function.

19. $f(x) = 3\sin(2x - \pi)$ **20.** $g(x) = \cos\left(5x - \dfrac{\pi}{2}\right)$

21. $k(x) = \tan\left(x - \dfrac{\pi}{4}\right)$ **22.** $h(x) = \cot(3x - 1.5)$

23. $f(x) = \sec(2x - 0.5)$ **24.** $g(x) = \cos\left(\dfrac{x}{2} - 3\right)$

In Exercises 25 to 28, write an equation of a sinusoidal function with the given amplitude A, phase shift B, and period P. Draw a complete graph.

25. $A = 3, B = \dfrac{\pi}{2}, P = \pi$

26. $A = \dfrac{1}{3}, B = 2, P = 4$

27. $A = 2, B = -\dfrac{\pi}{4}, P = 4\pi$

28. $A = 5, B = -1, P = 1$

In Exercises 29 to 34, find a complete graph and the domain, range, period, and phase shift of each function.

29. $y = 3\sin 2x$ **30.** $y = 1 + 2\cos(x - \pi)$

31. $y = -\cot(x - \pi)$ **32.** $y = 2\sec\left(x + \dfrac{\pi}{2}\right)$

33. $y = 2 - 3\sin(4x - \pi)$

34. $y = -3 + 2\cos\left(\dfrac{1}{3}x - \dfrac{\pi}{6}\right)$

In Exercises 35 to 38, find all real number solutions.

35. $2 = 4\sin 3x$ **36.** $3 = 2\sin 3x$

37. $\cos\dfrac{1}{2}x = 0.24$ **38.** $4\sin 2x < x$

In Exercises 39 to 42 find all real number solutions for x in $[0, 5]$.

39. $5\sin(x - \pi) = 3\cos\left(x + \dfrac{\pi}{2}\right)$

40. $\tan(x - \pi) = 3\sin 2x$

41. $3\sin x > 2\cos(x - 1)$

42. $3\sin^2 x > 2.65$

In Exercises 43 to 46, find a complete graph of each function. Show that each is a sinusoid in the form $y = A\sin(bx + \alpha)$ by estimating $A, b,$ and α. Overlay the complete graph with the graph of $y = A\sin(bx + \alpha)$ to check your estimated values.

43. $y = 3\sin x + 2\cos x$ **44.** $y = -5\sin x + 3\cos x$

45. $y = -\sin(x + \pi) + \cos x$

46. $y = 4\sin 2x - 3\cos 2x$

In Exercises 47 to 52, find a complete graph of each function. Find the domain, range, and period of each function. Determine all local and absolute extrema in the interval $[0, 2\pi]$.

47. $f(x) = \sin x + \cos 2x$

48. $g(x) = 2\sin x + 3\cos 2x$

49. $f(x) = \sin 3x + \cos x$ **50.** $t(x) = 3\sin 2x - \cos x$

51. $h(x) = 2\sin x + 5\cos x$ **52.** $k(x) = \sin\dfrac{x}{2} + \sin\dfrac{x}{3}$

Exercises 53 to 56 refer to the following **problem situation**: The *frequency* of a periodic function is the reciprocal of its period. One *cycle* of a periodic function is the graph in one period. It follows that the frequency represents the number of cycles of a periodic function that occur over an interval whose length is 1 unit. Determine the period and frequency.

53. $y = 2\sin 3x$ **54.** $y = -4\cos\dfrac{1}{2}x$

55. $y = 3\sin\dfrac{\pi}{2}x$ **56.** $y = 2\cos 2\pi x$

Exercises 57 and 58 refer to the following **problem situation**: A belt rotates around two wheels having radii r_1 and r_2 as shown.

57. If $r_1 = 22$ in. and $r_2 = 15$ in. and the centers of the wheels are 50 inches apart, find the length of the belt. (*Hint:* Compute d, then compute $\angle\alpha$).

58. Determine the length of a belt if $r_1 = 18$ inches and $r_2 = 11$ inches and the centers of the wheels are 36 inches apart.

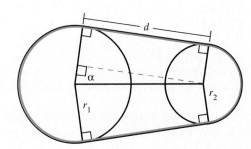

For Exercises 57 and 58

59. A playground merry-go-round 16 feet in diameter rotates at 20 rpm (revolutions per minute). Find the angular velocity in radians per second.

60. Determine the speed (in mph) of a boy located at a point 2 feet from the center of the merry-go-round in Exercise 59.

61. Determine the speed (in mph) of a girl located at the edge of the merry-go-round in Exercise 59.

62. A right circular cylinder is inscribed in a sphere of radius 20 (see Example 9). Find a complete graph of the problem situation for the volume V of the cylinder in terms of the angle θ. Find the dimensions of the cylinder of maximum volume that can be inscribed in the sphere.

63. A rocket is launched straight up from ground level at a rate of 200 ft/sec. An observation post is located at a point P located 2055 feet from the launch point. Describe θ as a function of t. Determine the angle θ 15 seconds after launch.

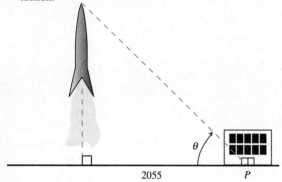

For Exercise 63

Exercises 64 and 65 refer to the following **problem situation**: The sinusoidal equation

$$T = A + B \sin\left\{\frac{\pi}{6}\left[360 - (360 - t)/30\right] + C\right\}$$

is a model for the mean daily temperature T as a function of time t measured in days. A is the mean yearly temperature, B is $\frac{1}{2}$ of the total mean temperature variation, and C is a phase-shift factor for the beginning of a temperature cycle.

64. In Columbus, Ohio, the mean yearly temperature is $58°$F and the total mean temperature variation is $56°$. Assume the temperature on April 1 is the mean yearly temperature, so $C = 0$, and t is the number of days past April 1. Find a complete graph of this problem situation.

65. About what month and day is it the hottest and coldest during the year in Columbus?

Exercises 66 to 69 refer to the following **problem situation**: The function $y = A \cos Bt$ is a sinusoidal model for *simple harmonic motion*, which describes the bouncing motion of an object hung from the end of a spring. Introduce a coordinate system so the vertical axis of the spring coincides with the y-axis and the rest position of the object is at the origin. Suppose

that at $t = 0$ the object has been stretched to a position $(0, A)$ where $A < 0$ and released (when $t > 0$). Let y be the vertical position of the object as a function of time t. (Assume there is no friction to stop the motion once it has started.)

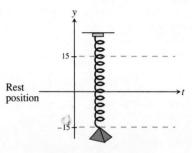

For Exercises 66 to 69

66. Suppose a spring oscillates between $y = -15$ and $y = 15$, and the frequency of oscillation is $\frac{1}{4}$ cycle per second. Determine the time interval of one complete cycle (that is, the period). Then determine A and B of the algebraic representation for the vertical position y at time t.

67. Find a complete graph of the algebraic representation in Exercise 66, and describe which part of the graph represents the problem situation.

68. At what times is the object in Exercise 67 5 units from the rest position?

69. Suppose an object on a spring oscillates between $y = -28$ and $y = 28$, and the *frequency* of oscillation is 3 cycles per second. Find the algebraic representation for the vertical position of this object and determine the times the object is 5 units from the rest position.

Exercises 70 and 71 refer to the following **problem situation**: Actual oscillatory motion of a object on a spring is affected by friction, so eventually the object returns to an at-rest position. This behavior is called *damped motion*.

70. Find a complete graph of $y = (20 - x)\cos(x - 3)$.

71. **Writing to Learn**   Write a paragraph that explains how a portion of the graph in Exercise 70 could be a model for the motion of an object hung from a stretched spring.

72. **Writing to Learn**   Write a paragraph that explains when a linear combination of sine and cosine functions is a sinusoid.

8.2 _____

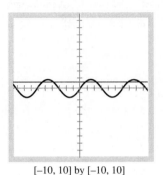

[–10, 10] by [–10, 10]

Figure 8.13 $y = \sin x$ intersects an arbitrary horizontal line $y = c$ more than once, thus indicating that the inverse of $y = \sin x$ will not be a function.

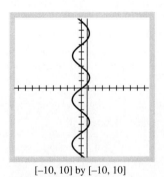

[–10, 10] by [–10, 10]

Figure 8.14 The inverse of $y = \sin x$ is not a function since it fails the vertical line test.

Inverse Trigonometric Functions

In Section 3.7 you learned that if (x, y) belongs to a relation R, then (y, x) belongs to the inverse relation R^{-1}. Theorem 3.6 established that the graph of an inverse relation can be obtained by reflecting the graph of the relation about the line $y = x$. Applying this result to the relation $y = \sin x$, we conclude that the graph in Fig. 8.14 is the inverse of the relation $y = \sin x$ shown in Fig. 8.13.

It is evident that the inverse relation of $y = \sin x$ (Fig. 8.14) does not satisfy the vertical line test and hence is not a function. This is what we expect to find, given that the graph of $y = \sin x$ does not satisfy the horizontal line test. (Recall that the horizontal line test states that the inverse of a function f is also a function if and only if every horizontal line intersects the graph of f at most once.) Therefore the inverse of the sine function over $(-\infty, \infty)$ is not a function.

Defining the Inverse Sine Function

Although there is no inverse function for the sine when it is defined over its whole domain, we can define the inverse sine function if we restrict the domain of $y = \sin x$ so that it satisfies the horizontal line test. Consider the function $f(x) = \sin x$ over the interval $[-\pi/2, \pi/2]$. The graph of this function f, shown in Fig. 8.15(a), is a small portion of the complete graph of $y = \sin x$.

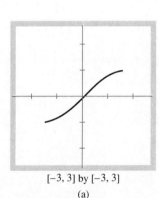

[–3, 3] by [–3, 3]

(a)

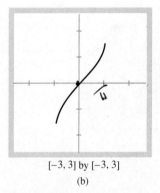

[–3, 3] by [–3, 3]

(b)

Figure 8.15 (a) $f(x) = \sin x$ for $-\pi/2 \le x \le \pi/2$ and (b) inverse of f.

Notice that the graph of the function f in Fig. 8.15(a) satisfies the horizontal line test. Thus the inverse of f shown in Fig. 8.15(b) is also a function. The inverse sine function can now be defined.

Definition 8.2   Inverse Sine Function

The **inverse sine function**, denoted $y = \sin^{-1} x$, or $y = \arcsin x$, is the function with a domain of $[-1, 1]$ and a range of $-\pi/2 \leq x \leq \pi/2$ that satisfies the relation $\sin y = x$.

The following theorem, stated without proof, confirms that the restricted sine and arcsine are inverse functions.

Theorem 8.4   Inverse Functions

Let $f(x) = \sin x$ such that $-\pi/2 \leq x \leq \pi/2$. Then $f^{-1}(x) = \sin^{-1} x$ and

a) $(f^{-1} \circ f)(x) = x$ [or $\sin^{-1}(\sin x) = x$] for all x in $[-\pi/2, \pi/2]$;
b) $(f \circ f^{-1})(x) = x$ [or $\sin(\sin^{-1} x) = x$] for all x in $[-1, 1]$.

Defining the Inverse Cosine and Tangent Functions

The inverse cosine function, denoted $y = \cos^{-1} x$, and the inverse tangent function, denoted $y = \tan^{-1} x$, can be defined by following a procedure similar to the one used for defining $y = \sin^{-1} x$. The complete graphs of $y = \cos x$ and $y = \tan x$ (Fig. 8.16) show that neither relation satisfies the horizontal line test.

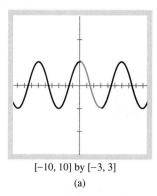
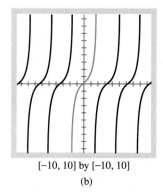

| [−10, 10] by [−3, 3] | [−10, 10] by [−10, 10] |
| (a) | (b) |

Figure 8.16   (a) $y = \cos x$, and (b) $y = \tan x$. Colored portion of each curve represents the portion of the function used to define the inverse.

However, if the domain of each is restricted to include only the colored portion of each graph, the graph satisfies the horizontal line test. The inverse cosine function and inverse tangent function can be defined when thus restricted.

Definition 8.3   Inverse Cosine Function

The **inverse cosine function**, denoted by $y = \cos^{-1} x$ or $y = \arccos x$, is the function with a domain of $[-1, 1]$ and a range of $[0, \pi]$, and which satisfies the relation $\cos y = x$.

Definition 8.4   Inverse Tangent Function

The **inverse tangent function**, denoted by $y = \tan^{-1} x$ or $y = \arctan x$, is the function with a domain of $(-\infty, \infty)$ and a range of $(-\pi/2, \pi/2)$, and which satisfies the relation $\tan y = x$.

Complete graphs of $y = \sin^{-1} x$, $y = \cos^{-1} x$, and $y = \tan^{-1} x$ are shown in Fig. 8.17.

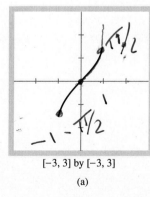
[-3, 3] by [-3, 3]

(a)

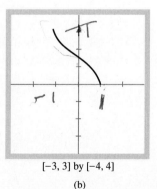
[-3, 3] by [-4, 4]

(b)

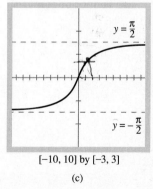
[-10, 10] by [-3, 3]

(c)

Figure 8.17   (a) $y = \sin^{-1} x$; (b) $y = \cos^{-1} x$; (c) $y = \tan^{-1} x$.

The lines $y = -\pi/2$ and $y = \pi/2$ are horizontal asymptotes of $y = \tan^{-1} x$. The inverse cotangent, secant, and cosecant functions are so rarely used that definitions will not be given for them here.

Transformations of Inverse Trig Functions

The graph of the inverse sine function can be transformed by stretch factors and vertical and horizontal shift constants just like other functions we have studied.

E X A M P L E   1   Finding Graphs of Inverse Sine Functions

Find the domain and range and a complete graph of the following:

a) $f(x) = \sin^{-1}(2x)$

b) $g(x) = \sin^{-1}\left(\frac{1}{3}x\right)$

Solution   Since the domain of the inverse sine function is $[-1, 1]$, conclude the initial inequality for both parts (a) and (b).

a) For f:

$$-1 \leq 2x \leq 1$$

$$-\frac{1}{2} \leq x \leq \frac{1}{2}$$

The domain of f is the interval $[-\frac{1}{2}, \frac{1}{2}]$. We say that f has been obtained from $y = \sin^{-1} x$ by a horizontal shrink by a factor of $\frac{1}{2}$.

b) For g:

$$-1 \leq \frac{1}{3}x \leq 1$$

$$-3 \leq x \leq 3$$

The domain of g is the interval $[-3, 3]$. We say that g has been obtained from $y = \sin^{-1} x$ by a horizontal stretch by a factor of 3.

The range of both f and g is $[-\pi/2, \pi/2]$. The complete graphs of f and g are seen in Fig. 8.18.

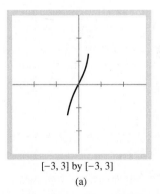

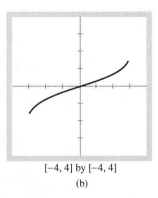

$[-3, 3]$ by $[-3, 3]$	$[-4, 4]$ by $[-4, 4]$
(a)	(b)

Figure 8.18   (a) $f(x) = \sin^{-1}(2x)$, and (b) $g(x) = \sin^{-1}\left(\frac{1}{3}x\right)$.

The graph in Fig. 8.18(a) can be obtained from $y = \sin^{-1} x$ by a horizontal shrink by a factor of $\frac{1}{2}$, and the graph in Fig. 8.18(b) can be obtained from $y = \sin^{-1} x$ by a horizontal stretch by a factor of 3.

E X A M P L E   2   Identifying Transformations

Identify transformations that can be used to obtain the graph of

$$f(x) = 3 \sin^{-1}\left[\frac{1}{4}(x+8)\right] - 5$$

from the graph of $y = \sin^{-1} x$. Then find the domain and range and sketch a complete graph of f.

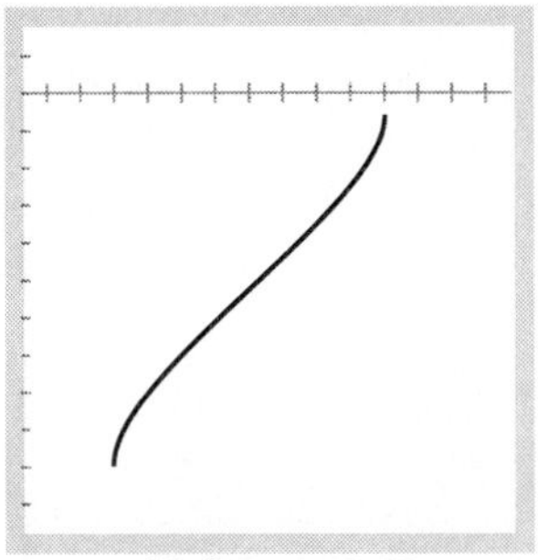

Solution   The graph of f (Fig. 8.19) can be obtained from the graph of $y = \sin^{-1} x$ by applying, in order, the following transformations:

1. A horizontal stretch by a factor of 4.

2. A horizontal shift to the left 8 units.

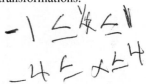

3. A vertical stretch by a factor of 3.

4. A vertical shift down 5 units.

The first two transformations change the domain of $y = \sin^{-1} x$ from $[-1, 1]$ to $[-12, -4]$, and the third and fourth transformations change the range of $y = \sin^{-1} x$ from $[-\pi/2, \pi/2]$ to $[-3\pi/2 - 5, 3\pi/2 - 5]$.   ■

[−15, 0] by [−12, 2]

Figure 8.19
$f(x) = 3 \sin^{-1}\left[\frac{1}{4}(x+8)\right] - 5$.

Evaluating Inverse Trigonometric Functions

In Section 7.2 when solving an equation like $\cos x = 0.28$, the notation $\cos^{-1} x$ was introduced to mean the angle whose cosine is x. The calculator keys $\boxed{\text{INV}}$ $\boxed{\text{COS}}$, $\boxed{\text{2nd}}$ $\boxed{\text{COS}}$, or $\boxed{\text{SHIFT}}$ $\boxed{\text{COS}}$ were used to find a unique angle solution to this equation. Similar calculator function keys can be used to solve other trig equations. For example, $\boxed{\text{INV}}$ $\boxed{\text{SIN}}$, $\boxed{\text{2nd}}$ $\boxed{\text{SIN}}$, or $\boxed{\text{SHIFT}}$ $\boxed{\text{SIN}}$ can be used for evaluating $\sin^{-1} x$. Thus we have implicitly been using inverse functions when solving some trig equations even before the concept of inverse function was formally defined.

E X A M P L E   3   Evaluating the Inverse Sine Function

Evaluate each of the following inverse sine functions at the given value: (a) $\sin^{-1}(0.5)$; (b) $\sin^{-1}(-0.7)$; (c) $\sin^{-1}(1.2)$.

Solution   The basis for doing these problems is the definition

$$y = \sin^{-1} x \qquad \text{if and only if} \qquad x = \sin y \text{ and } -\frac{\pi}{2} \le y \le \frac{\pi}{2}.$$

a) $y = \sin^{-1}(0.5)$ if and only if $\sin y = 0.5$ and $-\pi/2 \le y \le \pi/2$. The sine of what angle y is 0.5? Recall that $\sin \pi/6 = \sin 30° = 0.5$ and therefore

$$\sin^{-1}(0.5) = \pi/6. \qquad \text{If you do not remember this value, you can also use a calculator.}$$

b) Use a calculator set in radian mode to get $\sin^{-1}(-0.7) = -0.7753974966$.

c) A calculator gives an error message for $\sin^{-1}(1.2)$. The error message occurs because there is no angle whose sine equals 1.2. The sine of any angle or real number is a number in the interval $[-1, 1]$. ≡

Example 3 illustrates how to use a calculator to find numerical values of the inverse trig functions. In other situations an algebraic expression may be needed. Example 4 shows that when evaluating an expression like $\cos(\sin^{-1} v)$, it is helpful to think of $\sin^{-1} v$ as an angle.

EXAMPLE 4   Evaluating a Trig Expression

Write an algebraic expression in terms of v for $\cos(\sin^{-1} v)$ and $\tan(\sin^{-1} v)$.

Solution   It follows from the definition for $\sin^{-1} v$ that

$$\sin^{-1} v \text{ is an angle } \theta \text{ such that } \sin \theta = v \qquad \text{and} \qquad -\frac{\pi}{2} \le \theta \le \frac{\pi}{2}.$$

Figure 8.20   Picture $\sin^{-1} v$ as an angle.

Notice that θ can be in either the first or fourth quadrant depending on whether v is positive or negative. Fig. 8.20 shows that $v > 0$ if and only if θ is in the first quadrant. Likewise, $v < 0$ if and only if θ is in the fourth quadrant. Use the Pythagorean theorem to find the length of the side adjacent to θ to be $\sqrt{1 - v^2}$. Thus

$$\cos(\sin^{-1} v) = \sqrt{1 - v^2} \qquad \text{and} \qquad \tan(\sin^{-1} v) = \frac{v}{\sqrt{1 - v^2}}.$$

Notice that if $v > 0$, $\tan \theta > 0$, and if $v < 0$, $\tan \theta < 0$. However, the $\cos \theta$ is positive whether v is positive or negative. ≡

EXAMPLE 5   Finding Values without a Calculator

Without using a calculator, find the exact value of each expression:
(a) $\sin^{-1}(\tan 3\pi/4)$ and (b) $\cos[\tan^{-1}(\frac{1}{2})]$.

Solution

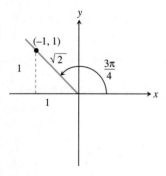

Figure 8.21   Reference triangle for Example 5, part (a): $\theta = 3\pi/4$.

a) The point $(-1, 1)$ is on the terminal side of angle $3\pi/4$ (see Fig. 8.21). Therefore

$$\tan \frac{3\pi}{4} = -1 \qquad \text{and} \qquad \sin^{-1}\left(\tan \frac{3\pi}{4}\right) = \sin^{-1}(-1).$$

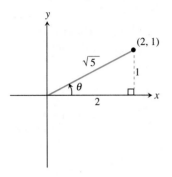

Figure 8.22 Reference triangle for Example 5, part b: $\tan\theta = \frac{1}{2}$.

Figure 8.15(b) is a reminder that the domain of $y = \sin^{-1}x$ is restricted to $[-1, 1]$ and the range is $[-\pi/2, \pi/2]$. So $\sin^{-1}(-1) = -\pi/2$.

b) Let θ be an angle between $-\pi/2$ and $\pi/2$ whose tangent is $\frac{1}{2}$. Then θ must be in the first quadrant since the tangent is negative in the fourth quadrant (Fig. 8.22).

$$\theta = \tan^{-1}\left(\frac{1}{2}\right)$$

$$\cos\theta = \cos\left[\tan^{-1}\left(\frac{1}{2}\right)\right] \qquad \text{Use Fig. 8.22.}$$

$$= \frac{2}{\sqrt{5}} \qquad\qquad\qquad ▣$$

We end this section by illustrating how to use a calculator to solve certain trigonometric equations.

EXAMPLE 6   Solving Equations

Solve each of the following equations for x: (a) $\sin x = 0.6$; (b) $\cot x = 2.5$.

Solution Because of the periodic nature of the trig functions, there are many solutions to each of these equations. The inverse trig functions can be used to find the solution in one period. The arguments that follow show how to find the rest.

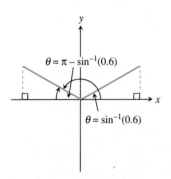

Figure 8.23 Reference triangles for the two solutions to Exercise 6, part a: $\sin x = 0.6$.

a) One solution to $\sin x = 0.6$ can be found by using a calculator to determine

$$\sin^{-1}(0.6) = 0.6435011.$$

A second solution is the angle in the second quadrant $\pi - 0.6435011 = 2.4980915$ (see Fig. 8.23). All other solutions are angles θ that are coterminal with one of these two solutions. Thus the solutions to $\sin\theta = 0.6$ are

$$0.6435011 + 2k\pi \qquad \text{and} \qquad 2.4980915 + 2k\pi \qquad \text{where } k \text{ is an integer.}$$

b) Since calculators do not have $\cot x$ as a built-in function, we can change this equation to one involving $\tan x$.

$$\cot x = 2.5 \qquad \text{if and only if} \qquad \tan x = \frac{1}{\cot x} = \frac{1}{2.5} = 0.4$$

$$\tan^{-1}(0.4) = 0.3805064$$

Since the tangent function is positive in both first and third quadrants, the other solutions to $\tan x = 0.4$ are

$$0.3805064 + k\pi \qquad \text{where } k \text{ is any integer.} \qquad ▣$$

E X A M P L E   7   Verifying an Identity

Show that $\sin^{-1} x + \cos^{-1} x = \pi/2$ for all x in $[-1, 1]$.

Solution   Let $\theta = \sin^{-1} x$. Then

$$x = \sin\theta \qquad \text{and} \qquad -\frac{\pi}{2} \le \theta \le \frac{\pi}{2}.$$

By the horizontal shift identities in Section 7.4 and the fact that $\cos(\theta - \pi/2) = \cos(\pi/2 - \theta)$ we see that

$$x = \sin\theta = \cos\left(\frac{\pi}{2} - \theta\right) \qquad \text{and} \qquad 0 \le \frac{\pi}{2} - \theta \le \pi.$$

It follows that

$$\cos^{-1} x = \frac{\pi}{2} - \theta$$

$$\theta + \cos^{-1} x = \frac{\pi}{2}$$

$$\sin^{-1} x + \cos^{-1} x = \frac{\pi}{2}. \qquad\qquad \blacksquare$$

Exercises for Section 8.2

In Exercises 1 to 6, find the domain, range, and a complete graph of each function.

1. $f(x) = \sin^{-1}(3x)$ **2.** $g(x) = \cos^{-1}(x) - \dfrac{\pi}{2}$

3. $h(x) = \arcsin(x + 1)$ **4.** $k(x) = 2\sin^{-1}\left(\dfrac{x}{3}\right)$

5. $f(x) = 3\arccos(2x - 4)$ **6.** $g(x) = \tan^{-1}(x - 1) + \pi$

In Exercises 7 to 12, identify transformations that can be used to draw the graph of each function. Then sketch a complete graph and find the domain and range of each.

7. $y = 1 - \arcsin x$ **8.** $y = 3 + \cos^{-1}(x - 2)$

9. $y = -0.25\tan^{-1}(x - \pi)$

10. $g(x) = 3\arccos\left(\dfrac{1}{2}x - \pi\right)$

11. $y = \sin(\sin^{-1} x)$ **12.** $y = \sin^{-1}(\sin x)$

In Exercises 13 to 16, use a calculator to evaluate each expression. Express your answer in degrees.

13. $\sin^{-1}(0.362)$ **14.** $\arcsin(-1.67)$

15. $\tan^{-1}(0.125)$ **16.** $\tan^{-1}(-2.8)$

In Exercises 17 to 20, use a calculator to evaluate each expression. Express your answer in radians.

17. $\sin^{-1}(0.46)$ **18.** $\cos^{-1}(-0.853)$

19. $\tan^{-1}(2.37)$ **20.** $\tan^{-1}(-22.8)$

In Exercises 21 to 26, compute the exact value in radians without using a calculator.

21. $\sin^{-1} 1$ **22.** $\tan^{-1}\sqrt{3}$

23. $\sin^{-1}\dfrac{\sqrt{2}}{2}$ **24.** $\cos^{-1}\left(-\dfrac{\sqrt{3}}{2}\right)$

25. $\tan^{-1}(-\sqrt{3})$ **26.** $\sin^{-1}(-1)$

In Exercises 27 to 36, use a calculator to evaluate each expression. Express your answer as a real number.

27. $\sin[\sin^{-1}(0.36)]$ **28.** $\sin[\arccos(0.568)]$

29. $\sin^{-1}(\cos 20)$ **30.** $\cos[\sin^{-1}(-0.125)]$

31. $\sin[\sin^{-1}(1.2)]$ **32.** $\sin^{-1}(\sin 1.2)$

33. $\sin[\sin^{-1}(2)]$ **34.** $\sin^{-1}(\sin 2)$

35. $\tan^{-1}(\sin 2)$ **36.** $\tan(\arctan 3)$

In Exercises 37 to 42, compute the exact value without using a calculator.

37. $\cos\left[\sin^{-1}\frac{1}{2}\right]$

38. $\sin[\tan^{-1}1]$

~~**39.** $\cos[(2\sin^{-1}\frac{1}{2})]$~~

40. $\cos[\tan^{-1}(\sqrt{3})] - \sin[\tan^{-1}(0)]$

41. $\cos[\sin^{-1}(0.6)]$

42. $\sin[\tan^{-1}(2)]$

In Exercises 43 to 46, solve for x. Find the exact solution(s) in each case.

43. $\sin(\sin^{-1}x) = 1$

44. $\cos^{-1}(\cos x) = 1$

45. $2\sin^{-1}x = 1$

46. $\tan^{-1}x = -1$

In Exercises 47 to 50, find an equivalent algebraic expression not involving trig functions.

47. $\sin(\tan^{-1}x)$

48. $\cos(\tan^{-1}x)$

49. $\tan(\sin^{-1}x)$

50. $\cot(\cos^{-1}x)$

In Exercises 51 to 54, solve for x with an error of at most 0.01. Find *all* solutions.

51. $\tan x = 2.3$

52. $\sin x = -0.75$

53. $\sec x = 3$

54. $\cot x = -5$

In Exercises 55 and 56, use a graphical method to find the solutions to each inequality over the interval $[-\pi, \pi]$.

55. $(\sin x)(\tan^{-1}x) \geq 0$

56. $\dfrac{\sin^{-1}(2x)}{\sin x} \geq 2$

In Exercises 57 to 60, verify each identity.

57. $\sin^{-1}(-x) = -\sin^{-1}x$ for $|x| \leq 1$

58. $\sin^{-1}x = \tan^{-1}\dfrac{x}{\sqrt{1-x^2}}$ for $|x| < 1$

59. $\arccos x + \arcsin x = 90°$

60. $\cos(\sin^{-1}x) = \sqrt{1-x^2}$ for $|x| \leq 1$

61. The length L of the shadow cast by a tower 50 feet tall depends on θ, the angle of elevation of the sun (measured from the horizontal). Express θ as a function of L. Draw a complete graph of the function. Which portion of the graph represents the problem situation?

62. Consider the following **problem situation**: A revolving light beacon L stands 3 miles from the closest point P along a straight shoreline. Express angle $PLQ = \theta$, as a function of the distance x from P to Q. Draw a complete graph of this function, and describe which portion of the graph represents the problem situation.

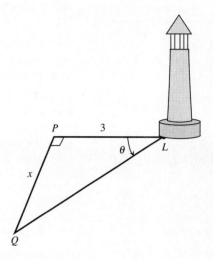

For Exercise 62

63. Suppose triangle ABC is isosceles with $a = b$ and $\angle C = \theta$. Show that the area of the triangle is given by $A = \frac{1}{2}a^2\sin\theta$.

64. Use a graphical method to find all values of x such that $\sin^{-1}\left(\dfrac{2x}{x^2+1}\right) = 2\tan^{-1}x$.

65. Writing to Learn Write a paragraph that explains how solving the equation $\sin y = 0.5$ is different from finding the value $\sin^{-1}(0.5)$.

8.3 _____ **Solving Trigonometric Equations and Inequalities Graphically**

Even though trigonometric functions differ in many respects from polynomial, logarithmic, and exponential functions, the graphical methods for solving equations used in previous chapters apply to trigonometric functions as well.

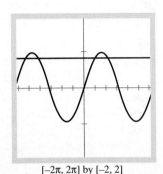

[−2π, 2π] by [−2, 2]

Figure 8.24 $y = \sin x$ and $y = 0.8$.

Solving Trigonometric Equations

Example 6 in Section 8.2 shows that there are an infinite number of solutions to trigonometric equations of the type that will be solved in this section. The procedure used in this section to solve trig equations is as follows. First use a graphical method to find all solutions for one period (excluding the right end point) of the trig function found in the equation. Then find all other solutions by taking into account the periodicity of the functions.

E X A M P L E   1   Solving an Equation with a Single Trig Function

Find all solutions to the equation $\sin x = 0.8$.

Solution   Complete graphs of functions $y = \sin x$ and $y = 0.8$ are shown in Fig. 8.24. Notice that these two graphs will have an infinite number of solutions in the domain $(-\infty, \infty)$.

Our method is to first find all solutions in one period of $y = \sin x$. Then we find all other solutions.

Solutions in $[0, 2\pi)$ From Fig. 8.24 estimate that $x = 0.9$ and $x = 2.2$ are solutions. The value $\sin^{-1}(0.8) = 0.927$, which by definition of the function $y = \sin^{-1} x$ is in the first quadrant.

The second-quadrant solution is $\pi - \sin^{-1}(0.8) = 2.214$. (Why?)

Complete Solution   The solution set consists of all real numbers of the form $0.927 + 2k\pi$ or $2.214 + 2k\pi$, where k is any integer.   ▤

If $y = f(x)$ is a trigonometric function, then solving the equation $f(x) = 0$ is equivalent to finding the zeros of the function $y = f(x)$. The method for finding all zeros of a trigonometric function is summarized next.

Zeros of Periodic Functions

If $y = f(x)$ is a periodic function with period P, the equation $f(x) = 0$ is called a **periodic equation**.

Suppose $x_1, x_2, \ldots, x_n$ are all the solutions to $f(x) = 0$ over an interval of length P.

Then the set of all solutions to $f(x) = 0$ over $(-\infty, \infty)$ consists of the numbers $x_i + kP$ where $i = 1, 2, \ldots, n$ and k is any integer.

This method of finding zeros of a trigonometric equation is illustrated in Examples 2 to 4.

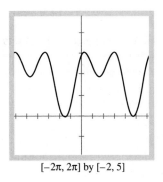

[-2π, 2π] by [-2, 5]

Figure 8.25 $y = 2\cos^2 t + \sin t + 1$.

E X A M P L E   2   Solving an Equation with Several Trig Functions

Find all solutions to the equation $2\cos^2 t + \sin t + 1 = 0$.

Solution   A complete graph of $y = 2\cos^2 t + \sin t + 1$ is given in Fig. 8.25. We see that this graph shows two complete periods and that there is only one solution in the single period interval $[0, 2\pi)$. Use zoom-in to determine this solution to be $x = 4.71$ with an error at most 0.01.

Complete Solution   The solution set consists of all real numbers of the form $4.71 + 2k\pi$ where k is any integer.   ≡

Section 8.6 will show that the solutions to the equation in Example 2 can be derived using an algebraic method. However, the graphical method is more general since it can be used when the algebraic methods fail. Examples 3 and 4 provide examples of such equations.

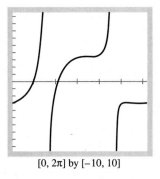

[0, 2π] by [-10, 10]

Figure 8.26   A complete graph of $f(x) = \tan x - 3\cos x$.

E X A M P L E   3   Solving an Equation with Several Trig Functions

Find all the solutions to the equation $\tan x = 3\cos x$.

Solution   We need to find the zeros of the function $f(x) = \tan x - 3\cos x$. The period of $y = \tan x$ is π, and the period of $3\cos x$ is 2π. So we first consider solutions in the interval $[0, 2\pi)$.

Solutions in $[0, 2\pi)$ Solutions to the equation $\tan x = 3\cos x$ can be found by finding zeros to the function $f(x) = \tan x - 3\cos x$. Figure 8.26 shows that there are two zeros in the interval $[0, 2\pi)$.

Use zoom-in to determine that the two solutions in this interval are $x = 1.01$ and 2.13 with errors of at most 0.01.

Complete Solution   The solution set consists of all real numbers of the form $1.01 + 2k\pi$ and $2.13 + 2k\pi$ where k is any integer.   ≡

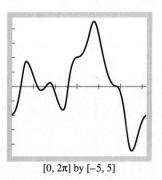

[0, 2π] by [-5, 5]

Figure 8.27   A complete graph of $f(x) = 3\sin^3 2x - 2\cos x$.

E X A M P L E   4   Solving an Equation with Several Trig Functions

Find all solutions to the equation $3\sin^3 2x - 2\cos x = 0$.

Solution   We first find all zeros in one period of the function $f(x) = 3\sin^3 2x - 2\cos x$. It can be shown that the period of $f(x) = 3\sin^3 2x - 2\cos x$ is 2π, and so we begin by finding all solutions in the interval $[0, 2\pi)$.

Solutions in $[0, 2\pi)$ Figure 8.27 shows that $f(x) = 3\sin^3 2x - 2\cos x$ has six zeros in the interval $[0, 2\pi)$. Use zoom-in to show that they are 0.50, 1.25, 1.57, 1.89, 2.65, and 4.71 with errors of at most 0.01.

Complete Solution   The solution set consists of all real numbers of the form $0.50 + 2k\pi$, $1.25 + 2k\pi$, $1.57 + 2k\pi$, $1.89 + 2k\pi$, $2.65 + 2k\pi$, and $4.71 + 2k\pi$.   ≡

Solving Inequalities

Examples 1 to 4 illustrated how trigonometric equations can be solved using a graphical method. The technique used was to first find all solutions in one period of the function and then find all other solutions by using the fact that functions are periodic. Inequalities can be solved graphically in much the same way. First we will find solutions to the corresponding equation, and then take into account the inequality.

E X A M P L E 5   Solving a Trigonometric Inequality

Solve $\sin x < \cot x$.

Solution   The inequality $\sin x < \cot x$ is equivalent to the inequality $\sin x - \cot x < 0$. Consider the graph of $f(x) = \sin x - \cot x$ (Fig. 8.28), and determine what portion lies below the x-axis.

Since it can be shown that the period of f is 2π, it is sufficient to consider the solution in the interval $[0, 2\pi)$. Furthermore, f has vertical asymptotes at $x = 0, x = \pi$, and $x = 2\pi$.

Use zoom-in to determine the two zeros of f in $[0, 2\pi)$ to be $x = 0.90$ and $x = 5.38$ with errors at most 0.01.

Solution in $[0, 2\pi)$ The solution to $\sin x < \cot x$ in $[0, 2\pi)$ consists of all numbers whose x-values lie in the intervals $(0, 0.90)$ or $(\pi, 5.38)$.

Complete Solution   The solution set consists of $R = (0, 0.90) \cup (\pi, 5.38)$ together with all horizontal shifts of R to the right and left through all integer multiples of 2π.   ≡

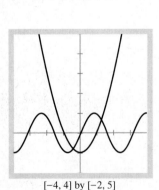

[0, 2π] by [−4, 4]

Figure 8.28   A complete graph of $f(x) = \sin x - \cot x$.

The power of the graphical method is perhaps most dramatically illustrated by using it to solve an equation or an inequality that combines trigonometric functions with nontrigonometric functions. Algebraic methods are generally not useful for this type of equation or inequality.

E X A M P L E 6   Solving a Trig and Polynomial Inequality

Find all solutions to $\sin 2x \geq x^2 - 1$.

Solution   Figure 8.29 shows the complete graphs of both $y = \sin 2x$ and $y = x^2 - 1$. Notice that the graph of $y = \sin 2x$ lies above the graph of $y = x^2 - 1$ for only one interval. Use zoom-in to find that the two curves intersect when $x = -0.46$ and $x = 1.26$, with errors at most 0.01.

The solution to $\sin 2x \geq x^2 - 1$ is the interval $[-0.46, 1.26]$. Notice that the end points are included since the inequality is $\geq$ rather than $>$.   ≡

[−4, 4] by [−2, 5]

Figure 8.29 $y = \sin 2x$ and $y = x^2 - 1$.

27

13

We end this section by considering several functions that have interesting and unusual behaviors.

🔍 **EXPLORE WITH A GRAPHING UTILITY**

Find a graph of $f(x) = \sin(1/x)$. Experiment with various viewing rectangles to gain an understanding of two things.

1) As $x \to \infty$, what is the behavior of $f(x)$? That is, what is the end behavior of $f(x)$?

2) As $x \to 0$, what is the behavior of $f(x)$?

The experience from this Exploration should help in your understanding of the next two examples.

E X A M P L E   7   Solving a Special Trig Equation

How many solutions are there to the equation $\sin(1/x) = 0$?

Solution   An exploration of the graph of $f(x) = \sin(1/x)$ in three different viewing rectangles reveals some interesting behavior.

Figure 8.30(a) shows the end behavior of the function. In particular, the x-axis is an asymptote, and there are no solutions to the equation when $|x|$ is large.

Figure 8.30(b) shows interesting behavior near $x = 0$, and Fig. 8.30(c) supports a claim that there are an infinite number of solutions to the equation.

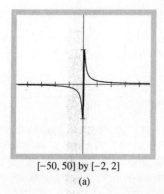

[−50, 50] by [−2, 2]

(a)

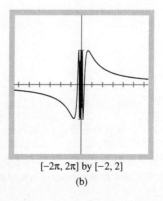

[−2π, 2π] by [−2, 2]

(b)

[−0.1, 0.1] by [−2, 2]

(c)

Figure 8.30   Three different views of $f(x) = \sin(1/x)$.

To analyze this behavior near $x = 0$ algebraically, observe that $\sin \alpha = 0$ whenever $\alpha = k\pi$ (where k is a nonzero integer). Therefore

$$\sin \frac{1}{x} = 0 \quad \text{if and only if} \quad \frac{1}{x} = k\pi$$

$$\text{if and only if} \quad x = \frac{1}{k\pi}.$$

As $|k|$ gets larger, each value $1/2k\pi$ is closer to zero. Therefore we see that $f(x) = \sin(1/x)$ has an infinite number of zeros, all in the interval $[-1, 1]$. ▣

E X A M P L E   8   Solving a Double Inequality

Use a graphical method to describe solutions for the following inequalities:

a) $-x \le x \sin x \le x$

b) $-|x| \le x \sin x \le |x|$

TRY THIS

1. Set your grapher mode to *simultaneous*.

2. Graph $y = x, y = x \sin x$, and $y = -x$ simultaneously in the viewing rectangle $[-30, 30]$ by $[-30, 30]$.

Solution   A typical method for solving an inequality is to graph the function on each side of the inequality sign in the same viewing rectangle. This will work with double inequalities also. Find graphs of the three functions $y = x, y = -x$, and $y = x \sin x$ in the viewing rectangle $[-30, 30]$ by $[-30, 30]$ (see Fig. 8.31). Notice that the graph of $y = x \sin x$ oscillates back and forth and always lies between the lines $y = x$ and $y = -x$.

At first glance you may be inclined to say that the two inequalities are satisfied for all values of x. However, that is not correct.

a) Notice that the graph of $y = x \sin x$ lies on or below the graph of $y = x$ for all x-values to the right of the y-axis. However, only for certain specific negative values of x is it true that $x \sin x \le x$.

Also, the graph of $y = x \sin x$ lies on or above the graph of $y = -x$ to the right of the y-axis. Again, only for certain specific negative values of x is it true that $x \sin x \ge -x$.

The negative values of x for which $x \sin x = x$ are not the same values of x for which $x \sin x = -x$, so we conclude that

the solution to the inequality $-x \le x \sin x \le x$ is the interval $[0, \infty)$.

b) The graph of $y = x \sin x$ lies on or below the graph of $y = |x|$ for all values of x and it lies on or above the graph of $y = -|x|$ for all values of x.

The solution to $-|x| \le x \sin x \le |x|$ is the interval $(-\infty, \infty)$. ▣

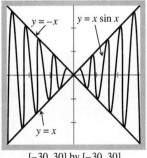

[−30, 30] by [−30, 30]

Figure 8.31 $y = x, y = -x$, and $y = x \sin x$.

Exercises for Section 8.3

In Exercises 1 to 4, use a graphing utility.

1. Solve the equation in Example 2 by considering the graphs of $y = 2\cos^2 t$ and $y = -\sin t - 1$.

2. Support the solution to the equation in Example 2 by comparing the graphs of $y = 2\cos^2 t + \sin t$ and $y = -1$. Does the solution agree with Example 2 and Exercise 1.

3. Find the solutions to the equation $\tan x = 3\cos x$ in Example 3 by finding the points of intersection of the graphs of $y = \tan x$ and $y = 3\cos x$.

4. Solve the equation in Example 4 by finding the points of intersection of the graphs of $y = 3\sin^3 2x$ and $y = 2\cos x$.

In Exercises 5 to 8, solve each equation.

5. $\sin x = 0.7$ **6.** $\cos x = 0.9$

7. $\sin x = 1.3$ **8.** $\tan x = 2.75$

In Exercises 9 to 18, solve each equation over the interval $[0, 2\pi)$.

9. $\sin 2x = 1$ **10.** $\sin 3t = 1$

11. $2\sin x = 1$ **12.** $2\sin 3x = 1$

13. $3\cos 2x = 1$ **14.** $\sin 2t = \sin t$

15. $\sin^2 x = 0$ **16.** $\sin x \tan x + \sin x = 0$

17. $(\cos x)(\sin x - 1) = 0$ **18.** $\sin^2 x - 1 = 0$

In Exercises 19 to 28, find the complete solution for each equation.

19. $\sin^2 \theta - 2\sin \theta = 0$ **20.** $2\cos 2t = 1$

21. $3\sin t = 2\cos^2 t$ **22.** $\cos(\sin x) = 1$

23. $1 = \csc x - \cot x$ **24.** $\sin 2t = \sin t$

25. $2\sin^2 x + 3\sin x - 2 = 0$

26. $2\cos^2 x + \cos x - 1 = 0$

27. $\cos 2x + \cos x = 0$

28. $\tan^2 x \cos x + 5\cos x = 0$

In Exercises 29 to 32, solve each inequality.

29. $\sin x < \dfrac{1}{2}$ for $0 \le x \le 2\pi$

30. $|\sin x| < \dfrac{1}{2}$ for $0 \le x \le 2\pi$

31. $\sin 2x < \cos 2x$ **32.** $\tan x > 0$

In Exercises 33 to 40, find the complete solution to each of these equations or inequalities.

33. $3\sin x = x$

34. $\tan x = x$ for $-\pi \le x \le \pi$

35. $3\sin 2x - x^2 = 0$

36. $\sin x < \cos(x - \pi)$

37. $5\sin 2x < 3\cos x$

38. $x \sin x \ge 1$ for $-10 \le x \le 10$

39. $\sin 3x + \cos x = 0$

40. $3\sin 2x = \cos x$

In Exercises 41 to 44 find the graph in the indicated interval. Determine all local extrema over the interval.

41. $g(x) = 2 - 3\sin\left(\dfrac{1}{2}x - \dfrac{\pi}{2}\right)$ for $0 \le x < 4\pi$

42. $f(x) = x^2 \sin x$ for $-\pi \le x < \pi$

43. $g(x) = -1 + 2\cos(\pi x - 2)$ for $0 \le x \le 3$

44. $f(x) = e^{-x/2}\sin 2x$ for $0 \le x \le 8$

45. Show that the function $f(x) = x \sin x$ is not a periodic function.

46. Prove or disprove that $g(x) = \sin 1/x$ is a periodic function.

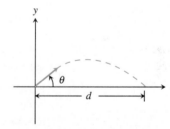

For Exercises 47 to 52

Exercises 47 to 49 refer to the following **problem situation**: A cannon shell is fired with an initial velocity V (in feet per second). If the cannon barrel makes an angle θ with the ground, then the horizontal distance d the shell travels before it hits the ground is given by $d = \dfrac{V^2}{16}\sin\theta \cos\theta$.

47. Suppose $V = 500$ ft/sec. Draw a complete graph of d as a function of θ. What portion of the graph represents the problem situation?

48. If the initial velocity is 500 ft/sec, at what angle should the cannon be aimed to hit a target 2350 feet away?

49. If the initial velocity is 500 ft/sec, what is the maximum distance the shell travels if the initial velocity is 500 ft/sec?

Exercises 50 to 52 refer to the following **problem situation** as shown by the preceding figure: The range d of a projectile shot at an angle of elevation θ and with an initial velocity v is given by:

$$d(\theta) = \frac{v^2}{g} \sin 2\theta$$

where g is the acceleration due to gravity (32 ft/sec). Assume $v = 85$ ft/sec.

50. Draw a complete graph of the trigonometric representation d, and discuss the values of θ that make sense in this problem situation.

51. At what angle should the projectile be aimed in order to

hit a target that is 215 feet down range?

52. For what value of θ is the range maximum?

53. Writing to Learn Find a complete graph of $f(x) = x \sin 1/x$ and then write a paragraph that describes the end behavior of f.

54. Writing to Learn Find a complete graph of $f(x) = x^{\sin x}$ and then write a paragraph that describes the end behavior of f.

55. Writing to Learn Write a paragraph or two that describes at least two graphical methods for solving the inequality $f(x) \leq g(x)$ where f and g are any two functions.

56. Writing to Learn Explain why in Example 1, when solutions in one period are found, the right end point in $[0, 2\pi)$ is excluded.

8.4 _____ Trigonometric Identities

You will recall from earlier work in solving equations that an identity is an equation that is true for all values of the variable for which the expressions are defined. We restate here for convenience the fundamental identities introduced in Section 7.3.

Fundamental Trig Identities

Reciprocal Identities

$$\sin \theta = \frac{1}{\csc \theta}, \qquad \cos \theta = \frac{1}{\sec \theta}, \qquad \tan \theta = \frac{1}{\cot \theta}$$

$$\csc \theta = \frac{1}{\sin \theta}, \qquad \sec \theta = \frac{1}{\cos \theta}, \qquad \cot \theta = \frac{1}{\tan \theta}$$

Tangent and Cotangent Identities

$$\tan \theta = \frac{\sin \theta}{\cos \theta}, \qquad \cot \theta = \frac{\cos \theta}{\sin \theta}$$

Pythagorean Identities

$$\sin^2 \theta + \cos^2 \theta = 1, \qquad 1 + \tan^2 \theta = \sec^2 \theta, \qquad 1 + \cot^2 \theta = \csc^2 \theta$$

Trig identities have a variety of uses. Example 4 in Section 7.2 illustrates that the reciprocal identities are applied whenever the cotangent, secant, or cosecant functions are evaluated using a calculator.

Often it is necessary to change the form of an equation before a solution can be found. In calculus trig identities will often be used to change a trigonometric expression to a different form, one more appropriate for solving the given problem.

Another important reason for learning to simplify trigonometric expressions is that they are helpful for interpreting certain computer output.

E X A M P L E   1   Simplifying a Trig Expression

Simplify the expression $(\cot\theta)/(\csc\theta)$.

Solution

$$\frac{\cot\theta}{\csc\theta} = \cot\theta \cdot \frac{1}{\csc\theta}$$

$$= \frac{\cos\theta}{\sin\theta} \cdot \frac{\sin\theta}{1} = \cos\theta \qquad \text{Use the fundamental identity for } \cot\theta \text{ and simplify algebraically.}$$

SUGGESTION

Often a trigonometric expression can be simplified if all functions are changed to expressions involving $\sin\theta$ and $\cos\theta$. That is the method used in the solution to Example 1.

The algebra in the solution of Example 1 shows that $(\cot\theta)/(\csc\theta) = \cos\theta$ is a trig identity. That is, this equation is true for all values of θ for which the expressions are defined.

An equation is not an identity if the equation fails to be true for at least one value of the variable for which the expressions are defined. Graphing the function represented by each side of the equation visually supports the conclusion that an equation is or is not an identity. This use of a graphing utility is illustrated in Example 2.

E X A M P L E   2   Demonstrating a Trig Nonidentity

Show that

$$\frac{1 + \sin^2\theta}{\cos\theta} = \cos\theta$$

is not an identity.

Solution   There are some solutions for this equation; in particular, $\theta = k\pi$ is a solution to the equation for any integer value of k.

Since some solutions exist, the question occurs, is this equation an identity? We see that the graphs of $y = (1 + \sin^2\theta)/\cos\theta$ and $y = \cos\theta$ in Fig. 8.32 show that the two sides of the equation are not identical. That is, this equation is not an identity.

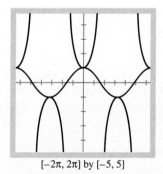

$[-2\pi, 2\pi]$ by $[-5, 5]$

Figure 8.32 $y = \dfrac{1 + \sin^2\theta}{\cos\theta}$ and $y = \cos\theta$.

SUGGESTIONS FOR VERIFYING
IDENTITIES

- If one side of the equation
  is more complicated, begin
  working on that side.
- Consider changing all
  terms to sines and cosines.
- Perform indicated
  operations: add fractions,
  find common factors, and
  perform multiplications
  and divisions.
- Use fundamental identities
  whenever possible.
- Multipy by a conjugate
  when appropriate.

Verifying Trigonometric Identities

To verify that a trig equation is an identity, we must show that the equation is true for all values of the variable for which all expressions in the equation are defined. Follow one of these steps.

Verifying an Identity

To verify that an equation is an identity, follow one of these two approaches.

1. Simplify the more complicated side until it is identical to the other side.
2. Simplify each side separately until both sides are identical.

E X A M P L E   3   Verifying an Identity

Verify that

$$\sin \theta = \frac{\sec \theta}{\tan \theta + \cot \theta}$$

is an identity.

Solution   We shall simplify the right side of the equation until it is identical to the left side.

$$\frac{\sec \theta}{\tan \theta + \cot \theta} = \frac{1}{\cos \theta}\left(\frac{\sin \theta}{\cos \theta} + \frac{\cos \theta}{\sin \theta}\right)^{-1}$$

$$= \frac{1}{\cos \theta}\left(\frac{\sin^2 \theta + \cos^2 \theta}{\sin \theta \cos \theta}\right)^{-1}$$

$$= \frac{1}{\cos \theta}\frac{\sin \theta \cos \theta}{1}$$

$$= \frac{\sin \theta \cos \theta}{\cos \theta}$$

$$= \sin \theta$$

When verifying that an equation is an identity, it is important not to perform a step that already assumes that the equation is valid for all values of the variable. In particular, *it is not valid to multiply both sides of an equation by an expression.*

≡

E X A M P L E   4   Multiplying Numerator and Denominator

Verify the identity

$$\frac{\cos t}{1 - \sin t} = \frac{1 + \sin t}{\cos t}.$$

Solution It may be tempting to begin by multiplying both sides of the equation by $\cos t$ and by $1 - \sin t$. However, that method presumes that the equation is an identity. That is, it assumes the equation is true before it has been verified.

A valid method is to simplify the right side of the equation until it is identical to the left.

$$\frac{1 + \sin t}{\cos t} = \frac{1 + \sin t}{\cos t} \cdot \frac{1 - \sin t}{1 - \sin t}$$ Multiply numerator and denominator by the conjugate of the numerator.

$$= \frac{1 - \sin^2 t}{(\cos t)(1 - \sin t)}$$

$$= \frac{\cos^2 t}{(\cos t)(1 - \sin t)}$$

$$= \frac{\cos t}{1 - \sin t}$$

Therefore

$$\frac{\cos t}{1 - \sin t} = \frac{1 + \sin t}{\cos t}$$

is an identity.

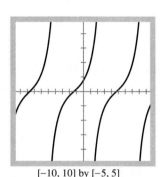

[−10, 10] by [−5, 5]

Figure 8.33 $y = \dfrac{\cos t}{1 - \sin t}$ and $y = \dfrac{1 + \sin t}{\cos t}$.

SUGGESTIONS FOR SUPPORTING IDENTITIES GRAPHICALLY

The graphs of $y_1 = \dfrac{\cos t}{1 - \sin t}$ and $y_2 = \dfrac{1 + \sin t}{\cos t}$ appear to be identical. Can you see the graph of $y_1 - y_2$? Why? Try graphing $y_1 - y_2 + 1 = y$.

The graph in Fig. 8.33 supports this algebraic verification.

In some cases it is easier to verify an identity by working with both sides of the equation. Work on one side until it has become simpler, and then work on the other side until it becomes identical.

EXAMPLE 5 Working on Each Side

Verify the identity

$$\frac{\tan^2 x - 1}{\sec^2 x} = \frac{\tan x - \cot x}{\tan x + \cot x}.$$

Solution First change the right side:

$$\frac{\tan x - \cot x}{\tan x + \cot x} = \frac{\tan x - \dfrac{1}{\tan x}}{\tan x + \dfrac{1}{\tan x}}$$

$$= \frac{(\tan x)\left(\tan x - \dfrac{1}{\tan x}\right)}{(\tan x)\left(\tan x + \dfrac{1}{\tan x}\right)}$$

$$= \frac{\tan^2 x - 1}{\tan^2 x + 1}$$

Then change the left side:

$$\frac{\tan^2 x - 1}{\sec^2 x} = \frac{\tan^2 x - 1}{\tan^2 x + 1}$$

The right side was simplified to $(\tan^2 x - 1)/(\tan^2 x + 1)$, and the left side was simplified to $(\tan^2 x - 1)/(\tan^2 x + 1)$.   ■

A graphing utility can be used to support a claim that an equation is an identity. After finding a complete graph of the function on the left side of the equation, overlay a graph of the right side of the equation in the same viewing rectangle. Check that the graphs appear to be identical.

E X A M P L E   6   Providing Visual Support for an Identity

Use a grapher to provide visual support for the claim that the equation

$$(\cos x)(1 + \tan x)^2 = \frac{1}{\cos x} + 2\sin x$$

is an identity.

Solution   Figure 8.34 shows a complete graph of $y = (\cos x)(1 + \tan x)^2$. The graph of

$$y = \frac{1}{\cos x} + 2\sin x$$

is overlaid and appears to be identical.   ■

Notice that the visual support provided in Example 6 is not a verification that the equation is an identity. Formal verification can only be done algebraically.

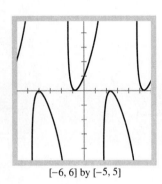

$[-6, 6]$ by $[-5, 5]$

Figure 8.34
$y = (\cos x)(1 + \tan x)^2$ and
$y = \dfrac{1}{\cos x} + 2\sin x.$

Exercises for Section 8.4

In Exercises 1 to 10, simplify each expression using the fundamental identities.

1. $\tan\theta\cos\theta$

2. $\cot x \tan x$

3. $\sec x \cos x$

4. $\cot\theta\sin\theta$

5. $\dfrac{1 + \tan^2 x}{\csc^2 x}$

6. $\dfrac{1 - \cos^2\theta}{\sin\theta}$

7. $(\sec^2 x + \csc^2 x) - (\tan^2 x + \cot^2 x)$

8. $\dfrac{\tan x \csc x}{\sec x}$

9. $\dfrac{1 + \tan x}{1 + \cot x}$

10. $\dfrac{\sec x + \tan x}{\sec x + \tan x - \cos x}$

In Exercises 11 to 16, reduce each expression to an equivalent expression involving only sines and cosines.

11. $\tan x + \cot x$

12. $\sin\theta + \tan\theta\cos\theta$

13. $(\sec t + \csc t)^2 \cot t$

14. $(\csc\theta - \sec\theta)\sin\theta\cos\theta$

15. $\dfrac{1}{\csc^2 x} + \dfrac{1}{\sec^2 x}$

16. $\dfrac{\sec x \csc x}{\sec^2 x + \csc^2 x}$

In Exercises 17 to 20, use a grapher to identify whether you think the equation is an identity. Notice that this method can be used to develop conjectures but not to verify proofs.

17. $\dfrac{\sin t - \cos t}{\cos t} + 1 = \tan t$

18. $\csc(x + \pi) = -\sec x$

19. $\cos(3\pi + x) = -\cos x$

20. $\dfrac{1}{\tan t} + \dfrac{\sin t}{\cos t - 1} = -\csc t$

In Exercises 21 to 24, use a grapher to provide visual support for a claim that each equation is an identity. Then verify the identity algebraically.

21. $1 + \cot^2\theta = \csc^2\theta$

22. $1 - 2\sin^2 x = 2\cos^2 x - 1$

23. $\cos^2\theta + 1 = 2\cos^2\theta + \sin^2\theta$

24. $\sin\theta + \cos\theta\cot\theta = \csc\theta$

In Exercises 25 to 38, verify that each of the following is an identity.

25. $\dfrac{\sin x}{\tan x} = \cos x$

26. $\sec^2\theta(1 - \sin^2\theta) = 1$

27. $(\cos t - \sin t)^2 + (\cos t + \sin t)^2 = 2$

28. $\sin^2\alpha - \cos^2\alpha = 1 - 2\cos^2\alpha$

29. $\dfrac{1 + \tan^2 x}{\sin^2 x + \cos^2 x} = \sec^2 x$

30. $\dfrac{1}{\tan\beta} + \tan\beta = \sec\beta\csc\beta$

31. $\dfrac{1 - \cos\theta}{\sin\theta} = \dfrac{\sin\theta}{1 + \cos\theta}$

32. $\dfrac{\tan x}{\sec x - 1} = \dfrac{\sec x + 1}{\tan x}$

33. $\dfrac{\sin t - \cos t}{\sin t + \cos t} = \dfrac{2\sin^2 t - 1}{1 + 2\sin t\cos t}$

34. $\dfrac{1 + \cos x}{1 - \cos x} = \dfrac{\sec x + 1}{\sec x - 1}$

35. $(x\sin\alpha + y\cos\alpha)^2 + (x\cos\alpha - y\sin\alpha)^2 = x^2 + y^2$

36. $\dfrac{\sin t}{1 - \cos t} + \dfrac{1 + \cos t}{\sin t} = \dfrac{2(1 + \cos t)}{\sin t}$

37. $\dfrac{\sin\theta}{1 + \cos\theta} + \dfrac{1 + \cos\theta}{\sin\theta} = 2\csc\theta$

38. $\dfrac{\sin A\cos B + \cos A\sin B}{\cos A\cos B - \sin A\sin B} = \dfrac{\tan A + \tan B}{1 - \tan A\tan B}$

39. Writing to Learn Explain why even though $\sin^2 x + \cos^2 x = 1$ is an identity, $\sin x = \sqrt{1 - \cos^2 x}$ is not.

40. Writing to Learn Graph both $y = \sin x$ and $y = x$ in the viewing rectangle $[-0.1, 0.1]$ by $[-0.1, 0.1]$. Write several paragraphs to explain whether this experience with the grapher is proof that $\sin x = x$.

8.5 _____ Sum and Difference Identities

Example 4 in Section 8.4 reminds us that graphical methods do not provide proof that an equation is really an identity. Algebraic and trigonometric methods continue to be important. Sections 8.5 and 8.6 develop some of the more important trig identities.

We begin this section with an Exploration.

🔍 **EXPLORE WITH A GRAPHING UTILITY**

Experiment with a graphing utility and decide which of these equations might be an identity:

1. $\sin(x + 3) = \sin x + \sin 3$
2. $\cos(x - 1) = \cos x - \cos 1$
3. $\tan(2 + x) = \tan 2 + \tan x$

You may have been tempted in this Exploration to apply the distributive property of algebra to trig functions and conclude that the equations in the Exploration are identities. In fact, all of the equations in the Exploration fail to be true for most values of x. The distributive property cannot be applied as suggested by the Exploration.

Next we shall establish trig identities about sums and differences of angles.

Difference and Sum Formulas

This section introduces equations known as the **sum and difference identities for sine and cosine**; these contain the expressions $\cos(\alpha - \beta), \cos(\alpha + \beta), \sin(\alpha - \beta)$, and $\sin(\alpha + \beta)$. We first develop an identity for $\cos(\alpha - \beta)$.

Figure 8.35(a) shows angles α and β in standard position, whereas the difference $\alpha - \beta$ is not; Fig. 8.35(b) shows the angle $\alpha - \beta$ in standard position. These two positions allow us to establish an equation and conclude some algebraic relationships.

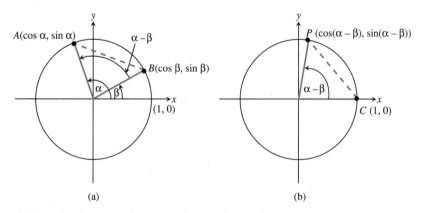

(a)   (b)

Figure 8.35   Angle $\alpha - \beta$ on the unit circle. (a) α and β are both in standard position but $\alpha - \beta$ is not and (b) $\alpha - \beta$ is in standard position.

Notice that triangle AOB in Fig. 8.35(a) is congruent to triangle POC in Fig. 8.35(b), which means that $d(A, B) = d(C, P)$. Therefore, $d^2(C, P) = d^2(A, B)$. First, we convert the left side of this equation into an equation involving trig functions.

$$
\begin{aligned}
[d(A, B)]^2 &= (\cos \alpha - \cos \beta)^2 + (\sin \alpha - \sin \beta)^2 \\
&= \cos^2 \alpha - 2 \cos \alpha \cos \beta + \cos^2 \beta + \sin^2 \alpha - 2 \sin \alpha \sin \beta + \sin^2 \beta \\
&= (\sin^2 \alpha + \cos^2 \alpha) + (\sin^2 \beta + \cos^2 \beta) - 2 \cos \alpha \cos \beta - 2 \sin \alpha \sin \beta \\
&= 2 - 2 \cos \alpha \cos \beta - 2 \sin \alpha \sin \beta
\end{aligned}
$$

Next we find a trig equation for $d^2(C, P)$.

$$
\begin{aligned}
[d(C, P)]^2 &= [1 - \cos(\alpha - \beta)]^2 + [0 - \sin(\alpha - \beta)]^2 \\
&= 1 - 2 \cos(\alpha - \beta) + \cos^2(\alpha - \beta) + \sin^2(\alpha - \beta) \\
&= 2 - 2 \cos(\alpha - \beta)
\end{aligned}
$$

Finally, we simplify the equation $[d(C, P)]^2 = [d(A, B)]^2$.

$$
\begin{aligned}
2 - 2 \cos(\alpha - \beta) &= 2 - 2 \cos \alpha \cos \beta - 2 \sin \alpha \sin \beta \\
-2 \cos(\alpha - \beta) &= -2(\cos \alpha \cos \beta + \sin \alpha \sin \beta) \\
\cos(\alpha - \beta) &= \cos \alpha \cos \beta + \sin \alpha \sin \beta
\end{aligned}
$$

This development verifies the identity for $\cos(\alpha - \beta)$ stated in the following theorem.

Theorem 8.5 Formula for Cosine of a Difference

For all angles α and β,

$$
\cos(\alpha - \beta) = \cos \alpha \cos \beta + \sin \alpha \sin \beta.
$$

Example 1 illustrates how to use this identity to find an exact value for $\cos 15°$.

E X A M P L E 1   Using the Identity for $\cos(\alpha - \beta)$

Find an exact value for $\cos 15°$.

Solution

$$
\begin{aligned}
\cos 15° &= \cos(45° - 30°) \\
&= \cos 45° \cos 30° + \sin 45° \sin 30°
\end{aligned}
$$

REMARK

An engineer would use a calculator to find cos 15°. Example 1 serves as practice in using Theorem 8.5.

$$= \frac{\sqrt{2}}{2} \cdot \frac{\sqrt{3}}{2} + \frac{\sqrt{2}}{2} \cdot \frac{1}{2}$$

$$= \frac{\sqrt{6} + \sqrt{2}}{4}$$

Theorem 8.5 is also important because it can be used to verify other trig identities, as Example 2 illustrates.

E X A M P L E   2   Verifying Identities with the $\cos(\alpha - \beta)$ Identity

Let θ be any angle. Use Theorem 8.5 to verify the following identities. Then use a grapher to provide visual support for your work.

a) $\cos(\pi/2 - \theta) = \sin\theta$

b) $\cos(\pi - \theta) = -\cos\theta$

Solution

a) Use Theorem 8.5 with $\alpha = \pi/2$ and $\beta = \theta$.

$$\cos\left(\frac{\pi}{2} - \theta\right) = \cos\frac{\pi}{2}\cos\theta + \sin\frac{\pi}{2}\sin\theta$$

$$= 0\cos\theta + 1\sin\theta$$

$$= \sin\theta$$

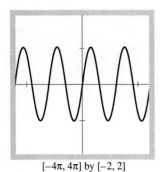

[−4π, 4π] by [−2, 2]

Figure 8.36 $y = \cos(\pi/2 - \theta)$ and $y = \sin\theta$.

Figure 8.36 provides visual support for this identity. Both $y = \cos(\pi/2 - \theta)$ and $y = \sin x$ are graphed in Fig. 8.36 and they coincide.

b) Use Theorem 8.5 with $\alpha = \pi$ and $\beta = \theta$.

$$\cos(\pi - \theta) = \cos\pi\cos\theta + \sin\pi\sin\theta$$

$$= (-1)\cos\theta + (0)\sin\theta$$

$$= -\cos\theta.$$

Figure 8.37 provides visual support for this identity.

The identity for the cosine of a difference is used to verify an identity for the cosine of a sum, which is the subject of Theorem 8.6.

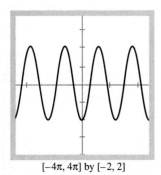

[−4π, 4π] by [−2, 2]

Figure 8.37 $y = \cos(\pi - \theta)$ and $y = -\cos\theta$.

Theorem 8.6   Formula for Cosine of a Sum

For all angles α and β,

$$\cos(\alpha + \beta) = \cos\alpha\cos\beta - \sin\alpha\sin\beta.$$

Proof   We use the fact that $\cos(-x) = \cos x$ and $\sin(-x) = -\sin x$ for all values of x. Then,

$$\cos(\alpha + \beta) = \cos[\alpha - (-\beta)]$$

$$= \cos \alpha \cos(-\beta) + \sin \alpha \sin(-\beta) \qquad \text{Recall that } \cos(-x) = \cos x \text{ and } \sin(-x) = -\sin x.$$

$$= \cos \alpha \cos \beta - \sin \alpha \sin \beta.$$

≡

E X A M P L E   3   Using the Identity for cos $(\alpha + \beta)$

Find the exact value of $\cos 75°$.

Solution

$$\cos 75° = \cos(45° + 30°)$$

$$= \cos 45° \cos 30° - \sin 45° \sin 30°$$

$$= \frac{\sqrt{2}}{2} \cdot \frac{\sqrt{3}}{2} - \frac{\sqrt{2}}{2} \cdot \frac{1}{2}$$

$$= \frac{\sqrt{6} - \sqrt{2}}{4}$$

≡

Since we could approximate the value of $\cos 75°$ directly with a calculator, we might expect to use this method. However, the identity remains important for solving theoretical applications, as illustrated in Example 2 and Theorem 8.7. Numerical examples, like Example 3, help you become familiar with these identities.

Theorem 8.7   Formulas for Sine of a Sum and Difference

For all angles α and β,

$$\sin(\alpha + \beta) = \sin \alpha \cos \beta + \cos \alpha \sin \beta$$

$$\sin(\alpha - \beta) = \sin \alpha \cos \beta - \cos \alpha \sin \beta$$

Proof

$$\sin(\alpha + \beta) = \cos\left[\frac{\pi}{2} - (\alpha + \beta)\right] \qquad \text{See Example 2(a).}$$

$$= \cos\left[\left(\frac{\pi}{2} - \alpha\right) - \beta\right]$$

$$= \cos\left(\frac{\pi}{2} - \alpha\right)\cos\beta + \sin\left(\frac{\pi}{2} - \alpha\right)\sin\beta$$

$$= \sin\alpha\cos\beta + \cos\alpha\sin\beta$$

Proof of the second identity is left as an exercise.   ▤

It was mentioned earlier that the identities for the sine and cosine of the sum and difference are needed in calculus. In particular, if $f(x) = \sin x$, the quotient

$$\frac{f(x + h) - f(x)}{h},$$

which is used in calculus in the definition of the derivative of f, uses the identity for the sine of a sum. Example 4 illustrates this application.

EXAMPLE 4   Using the Identity for $\sin(\alpha + \beta)$

Let $f(x) = \sin x$ and $h \neq 0$. Show that

$$\frac{f(x + h) - f(x)}{h} = \sin x\left(\frac{\cos h - 1}{h}\right) + \cos x\left(\frac{\sin h}{h}\right).$$

Solution

$$\frac{f(x + h) - f(x)}{h} = \frac{\sin(x + h) - \sin x}{h}$$

$$= \frac{\sin x \cos h + \cos x \sin h - \sin x}{h}$$

$$= \frac{\sin x(\cos h - 1) + \cos x \sin h}{h}$$

$$= \sin x\left(\frac{\cos h - 1}{h}\right) + \cos x\left(\frac{\sin h}{h}\right)$$ ▤

Theorems 8.2 and 8.3 stated that the sum of a sine function and a cosine function is a sinusoid. Example 5 shows how to find the period and phase-shift constants of the resulting sinusoid. The solution in Example 5 can be generalized to provide a proof of Theorem 8.3.

EXAMPLE 5   Finding a Sinusoid

Find constants A and α so that for every value of x, $2\cos 3x + 5\sin 3x = A\sin(3x + \alpha)$.

Solution

$$2\cos 3x + 5\sin 3x = A\sin(3x + \alpha)$$

$$= A\sin 3x\cos\alpha + A\cos 3x\sin\alpha$$

We conclude that

$$A\cos\alpha = 5 \quad \text{or} \quad \cos\alpha = 5/A,$$

$$A\sin\alpha = 2 \quad \text{or} \quad \sin\alpha = 2/A.$$

Therefore

$$\tan\alpha = \frac{\sin\alpha}{\cos\alpha} = \frac{2/A}{5/A} = \frac{2}{5} \quad \text{or} \quad \alpha = \tan^{-1}\left(\frac{2}{5}\right).$$

We can conclude from Fig. 8.38 that $A = \sqrt{2^2 + 5^2} = \sqrt{29}$.

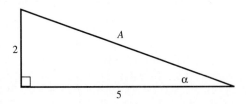

Figure 8.38 $\cos C = 5/A$ and $\sin C = 2/A$.

Graph $y = \sqrt{29}\sin(3x + \tan^{-1}(\frac{2}{5}))$ and overlay the graph of $y = 2\cos 3x + 5\sin 5x$.

Finally, there are two **sum and difference identities for tangent**, stated here in Theorem 8.8. The proofs are saved for Exercises 47 and 48.

Theorem 8.8   Tangent of a Sum and a Difference

For all angles α and β for which the expressions are defined,

$$\tan(\alpha + \beta) = \frac{\tan\alpha + \tan\beta}{1 - \tan\alpha\tan\beta}$$

$$\tan(\alpha - \beta) = \frac{\tan\alpha - \tan\beta}{1 + \tan\alpha\tan\beta}.$$

Double-angle Formulas

In this section we discuss identities for $\sin 2x, \cos 2x$, and $\tan 2x$. It is tempting to claim that the 2 can be factored out to give $\sin 2x = 2\sin x$. Students who manipulate symbols without thinking about what they mean often make this assertion. Is it true? The following Exploration should help you decide.

φ **EXPLORE WITH A GRAPHING UTILITY**

Experiment with a graphing utility, and decide which of these equations might be an identity.

1. $\sin 2x = 2 \sin x$

2. $\cos 3x = 3 \cos x$

3. $\tan 2x = 2 \tan x$

You should have discovered that none of the equations in the Exploration are valid. Notice that $\sin 2\theta$ is equal to $\sin(\theta + \theta)$. Consequently, the identity for $\sin(\alpha + \beta)$ can be used to develop an identity for $\sin 2\theta$, called a **double-angle identity**.

Theorem 8.9   Double-angle Identities

For all angles θ for which the expressions are defined,

$$\sin 2\theta = 2 \sin \theta \cos \theta$$

$$\cos 2\theta = \cos^2 \theta - \sin^2 \theta = 1 - 2\sin^2 \theta = 2\cos^2 \theta - 1$$

$$\tan 2\theta = \frac{2 \tan \theta}{1 - \tan^2 \theta}.$$

E X A M P L E   6   Verifying a Double-angle Identity

Verify that $\sin 2\theta = 2 \sin \theta \cos \theta$.

Solution   Use the identity for $\sin(\alpha + \beta)$ where $\alpha = \beta = \theta$. Then

$$\sin 2\theta = \sin(\theta + \theta) \qquad \text{\small Use the identity for } \sin(\alpha + \beta) \text{\small \ where } \alpha \text{\small \ and } \beta \text{\small \ are both } \theta.$$

$$= \sin \theta \cos \theta + \cos \theta \sin \theta$$

$$= 2 \sin \theta \cos \theta. \qquad\qquad\qquad\qquad \blacksquare$$

Proofs of the identities for $\cos 2x$ and $\tan 2x$ are saved for Exercises 49 to 51.

E X A M P L E   7   Using Double-angle Identities

Write $2 \cos x + \sin 2x$ as an expression involving only $\sin x$ and $\cos x$.

Solution

$$2\cos x + \sin 2x = 2\cos x + 2\sin x \cos x \qquad \text{Use the identity for } \sin 2x.$$

$$= (2\cos x)(1 + \sin x)$$

≡

EXAMPLE 8   Finding Zeros in a Double-angle Function

Use both graphical and algebraic methods to find all the zeros of the function $f(x) = \sin 2x + \cos 3x$ over the interval $[0, 2\pi)$.

Solution

Graphical Method   Figure 8.39 shows a complete graph of f for the interval $[0, 2\pi]$. Use zoom-in to show that the zeros of f are $0.94, 1.57, 2.20, 3.46, 4.71$, and 5.97.

Algebraic Method   To solve the equation $\sin 2x + \cos 3x = 0$ algebraically, rewrite the equation in terms of $\sin x$ and $\cos x$.

$$0 = \sin 2x + \cos 3x = \sin 2x + \cos(2x + x)$$

$$= \sin 2x + \cos 2x \cos x - \sin 2x \sin x$$

$$= 2\sin x \cos x + (1 - 2\sin^2 x)\cos x - 2\sin x \cos x \sin x$$

$$= 2\sin x \cos x + \cos x - 2\sin^2 x \cos x - 2\sin^2 x \cos x$$

$$= (\cos x)(2\sin x + 1 - 4\sin^2 x)$$

Therefore either $\cos x = 0$ or $2\sin x + 1 - 4\sin^2 x = 0$. We know that the solutions of $\cos x = 0$ in $[0, 2\pi)$ are $\pi/2$ and $3\pi/2$.

To find the solutions to $4\sin^2 x - 2\sin x - 1 = 0$, use the fact that the equation is a quadratic in $\sin x$ to obtain the following results:

$$\sin x = \frac{2 \pm \sqrt{4 + 16}}{8} = \frac{1 \pm \sqrt{5}}{4}$$

The solutions to $\sin x = (1 + \sqrt{5})/4$ in $[0, 2\pi)$ are 0.94 and 2.20. The solutions to $\sin x = (1 - \sqrt{5})/4$ in $[0, 2\pi)$ are 3.46 and 5.97.

Therefore the zeros of $f(x)$ are $0.94, 1.57, 2.20, 3.46, 4.71$, and 5.97.   ≡

Half-angle Formulas

The double-angle identities can be used to obtain formulas that permit us to write $\sin(\theta/2), \cos(\theta/2)$, and $\tan(\theta/2)$ in terms of $\sin\theta, \cos\theta$, and $\tan\theta$. For example, applying Theorem 8.9, for angle α

$$\cos 2\alpha = 2\cos^2 \alpha - 1$$

which is equivalent to

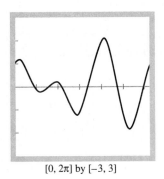

$[0, 2\pi]$ by $[-3, 3]$

Figure 8.39   A complete graph of $f(x) = \sin 2x + \cos 3x$.

$$\cos^2 \alpha = \frac{1 + \cos 2\alpha}{2}.$$

Let $2\alpha = \theta$, so that $\alpha = \theta/2$, and obtain

$$\cos \frac{\theta}{2} = \pm \sqrt{\frac{1 + \cos \theta}{2}}.$$

This identity is known as a **half-angle identity**.

Theorem 8.10   Half-angle Identities

For all angles θ

$$\sin \frac{\theta}{2} = \pm \sqrt{\frac{1 - \cos \theta}{2}}$$

$$\cos \frac{\theta}{2} = \pm \sqrt{\frac{1 + \cos \theta}{2}}$$

$$\tan \frac{\theta}{2} = \frac{\sin \theta}{1 + \cos \theta}$$

Exercises for Section 8.5

In Exercises 1 to 8, use the sum and difference identities to find exact values of each of the following.

1. $\sin 15°$

2. $\tan 15°$

3. $\sin 75°$

4. $\tan 75°$

5. $\cos \dfrac{\pi}{12}$

6. $\sin \dfrac{5\pi}{12}$

7. $\tan \dfrac{5\pi}{12}$

8. $\tan \dfrac{\pi}{12}$

In Exercises 9 to 12, express each of the following in terms of $\sin x$, $\cos x$, $\tan x$, or $\cot x$.

9. $\sin(x + 90°)$

10. $\tan(180° + x)$

11. $\cos\left(\dfrac{\pi}{2} + x\right)$

12. $\cot(x + 2\pi)$

In Exercises 13 to 16, prove each identity. Use a grapher to provide visual support for your work.

13. $\sin\left(\theta + \dfrac{\pi}{2}\right) = \cos \theta$

14. $\cos\left(\theta - \dfrac{\pi}{4}\right) = \dfrac{\sqrt{2}}{2}(\cos \theta + \sin \theta)$

15. $\tan\left(\theta + \dfrac{\pi}{4}\right) = \dfrac{1 + \tan \theta}{1 - \tan \theta}$

16. $\cos\left(\theta + \dfrac{\pi}{2}\right) = -\sin \theta$

In Exercises 17 to 22, write each of the following as an expression involving only $\sin \theta$ and $\cos \theta$.

17. $\sin 2\theta + \cos \theta$

18. $\sin 2\theta + \cos 2\theta$

19. $\sin 2\theta + \cos 3\theta$

20. $\sin 3\theta + \cos 2\theta$

21. $\sin 4\theta + \cos 3\theta$

22. $\tan 2\theta + \tan \theta$

In Exercises 23 to 26, use a grapher to find a complete graph of each equation. If it is a sinusoid, give the period, amplitude, and phase shift.

23. $y = \cos 3x + 2\sin 3x$

24. $y = 3\cos 2x - 2\sin 2x$

25. $y = 3\sin x + 5\sin(x + 2)$

26. $y = 3\sin(2x - 1) + 5\sin(2x + 3)$

In Exercises 27 to 30, find the domain, range, and a complete graph of each function.

27. $f(x) = \sec x^2$

28. $g(x) = x^2 \sin\left(x - \dfrac{\pi}{2}\right)$

29. $g(x) = 3 \sin^2 x$

30. $f(x) = \dfrac{\tan x}{x^2}$

In Exercises 31 and 32, let $\sin x = \dfrac{2}{3}$ and $\pi/2 < x < \pi$, and find the value of each expression.

31. (a) $\cos x$; (b) $\csc x$

32. (a) $\tan 2x$; (b) $\cos \dfrac{x}{2}$

In Exercises 33 to 36, let $\cos x = -\dfrac{1}{2}$ and $\pi < x < 3\pi/2$, and find the value of each expression.

33. $\sec x$ **34.** $\sin x$ **35.** $\tan 2x$ **36.** $\cos \dfrac{x}{2}$

In Exercises 37 to 44, solve each equation for x in the interval $[0, 2\pi)$. Find exact answers when possible. Check your answer using a graphing utility.

37. $\sin x = \dfrac{1}{2}$

38. $\cos x = 0$

39. $\sin x = \dfrac{\sqrt{3}}{2}$

40. $\tan x = 1$

41. $\sin^2 x - 1 = 0$

42. $2 \sin^2 x + \sin x - 1 = 0$

43. $\sin^2 x - 2 \sin x = 0$

44. $\cos 2x + \sin 3x = 0$

45. Use Example 2(a) to verify that $\sin(\pi/2 - \alpha) = \cos \alpha$ for all angles α.

46. Verify the identity
$$\sin(\alpha - \beta) = \sin \alpha \cos \beta - \cos \alpha \sin \beta.$$

47. Verify the identity

$$\tan(\alpha + \beta) = \frac{\tan \alpha + \tan \beta}{1 - \tan \alpha \tan \beta}.$$

48. Verify the identity $\tan(\alpha - \beta) = \dfrac{\tan \alpha - \tan \beta}{1 + \tan \alpha \tan \beta}$.

49. Verify the identity $\cos 2\theta = \cos^2 \theta - \sin^2 \theta$.

50. Verify the two alternate identities for $\cos 2\theta$:
   a) $\cos 2\theta = 1 - 2 \sin^2 \theta$ **b)** $\cos 2\theta = 2 \cos^2 \theta - 1$.

51. Verify the identity

$$\tan 2\theta = \frac{2 \tan \theta}{1 - \tan^2 \theta}.$$

52. Verify the identity

$$\sin \frac{\theta}{2} = \pm \sqrt{\frac{1 - \cos \theta}{2}}.$$

53. Verify the identity

$$\tan \frac{\theta}{2} = \frac{\sin \theta}{1 + \cos \theta}.$$

54. Use identities to verify that $f(x) = 2 \sin x \cos x$ and $g(x) = 1 - 2 \sin^2 x$ are both sinusoidal functions.

55. Writing to Learn   Explain how the graphs of $y = \cos(x + 4)$ and $y = \cos x + 4$ can be obtained from $y = \cos x$. Write a paragraph explaining how this graphical approach can be used to show that $\cos(x + 4) \neq \cos x + \cos 4$.

56. Use the fact that $\cos(\pi/2 - \theta) = \sin \theta$ to show that $\sin(\pi/2 - \alpha) = \cos \alpha$. (*Hint*: Let $\alpha = \pi/2 - \theta$.)

57. Verify the second identity stated in Theorem 8.7.

8.6 _____ Solving Trigonometric Equations and Inequalities Analytically

In Section 8.3 graphical methods were used to solve a variety of trig equations and inequalities. In this section we revisit equation and inequality solving using algebraic techniques. These methods are useful in situations where exact solutions are desired.

Example 1 deals with the equation $2\cos^2 t + \sin t + 1 = 0$, which we solved graphically in Example 2 of Section 8.3. Now we see how trig identities can be combined with general algebraic properties to solve the equation analytically.

EXAMPLE 1   Solving a Trig Equation with Factoring

Find all solutions to $2\cos^2 t + \sin t + 1 = 0$ in the interval $[0, 2\pi)$.

Solution   Rewrite the equation into an equivalent form that involves powers of $\sin x$ instead of combinations of $\sin x$ and $\cos x$.

$$2\cos^2 t + \sin t + 1 = 0$$

$$2(1 - \sin^2 t) + \sin t + 1 = 0$$

$$2 - 2\sin^2 t + \sin t + 1 = 0$$

$$-2\sin^2 t + \sin t + 3 = 0$$

$$2\sin^2 t - \sin t - 3 = 0 \qquad \text{This quadratic equation in } \sin t \text{ can now be factored.}$$

$$(2\sin t - 3)(\sin t + 1) = 0$$

So t is a solution to $2\cos^2 t + \sin t + 1 = 0$ if and only if

$$2\sin t - 3 = 0 \qquad\qquad \sin t + 1 = 0$$
$$\qquad\qquad\qquad \text{or}$$
$$\sin t = \frac{3}{2} \qquad\qquad \sin t = -1$$

There are no solutions for $\sin t = \frac{3}{2}$. (Why?) Thus it is sufficient to consider $\sin t = -1$. The solution to $\sin t = -1$ is $t = 3\pi/2$.

Therefore the solution to $2\cos^2 t + \sin t + 1 = 0$ in $[0, 2\pi)$ is $t = 3\pi/2$. Figure 8.40 shows this solution graphically.   ≡

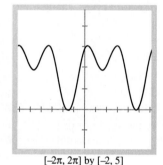

$[-2\pi, 2\pi]$ by $[-2, 5]$

Figure 8.40 $y = 2\cos^2 t + \sin t + 1.$

As discussed in Section 8.3, the complete set of solutions to an equation with period P can be found by adding multiples of P (where k is an integer) to the solutions found over an interval of length P. In this section we will ordinarily not list the complete set of solutions.

The next example again uses identities to change the original equation to a quadratic in $\sin x$ in order to solve the equation. The quadratic is factored if possible; otherwise we shall use the quadratic formula.

EXAMPLE 2   Using the Quadratic Formula

Find all solutions to $\tan x = 3\cos x$ over the interval $[0, 2\pi)$.

Solution   It is often helpful to rewrite a trig equation in terms of the sine and cosine. Then use identities and algebraic properties as necessary to change the form to a quadratic equation in $\sin x$.

$$\tan x = 3 \cos x$$

$$\frac{\sin x}{\cos x} = 3 \cos x$$

$$\sin x = 3 \cos^2 x \qquad \text{Since both sides of the equation are multiplied}$$

by $\cos x$, extraneous solutions may be introduced.

$$\sin x = 3(1 - \sin^2 x)$$

$$3 \sin^2 x + \sin x - 3 = 0$$

Since it is not evident how to factor this expression, use the quadratic formula to get

$$\sin x = \frac{-1 \pm \sqrt{37}}{6}.$$

The equation

$$\sin x = \frac{-1 - \sqrt{37}}{6}$$

has no solutions. However, the equation

$$\sin x = \frac{-1 + \sqrt{37}}{6}$$

has two solutions, one in the first quadrant and one in the second quadrant. The solution in the first quadrant is

$$\sin^{-1}\left(\frac{-1 + \sqrt{37}}{6}\right) = 1.01,$$

and the solution in the second quadrant is $\pi - 1.01 = 2.13$.

The graphical support seen in Fig. 8.41 shows that these solutions are not extraneous. Check that these values are solutions to the original equation. The solutions to $\tan x = 3 \cos x$ in $[0, 2\pi)$ are $x = 1.01$ and $x = 2.13$. ≡

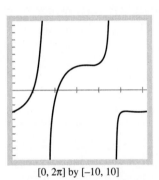

[0, 2π] by [−10, 10]

Figure 8.41 $f(x) = \tan x - 3 \cos x.$

EXAMPLE 3   Solving a Trig Equation with Factoring

Find all solutions in one period of the periodic equation $3 \tan^4 x = 1 + \sec^2 x$.

Solution   Since $\sec^2(x + \pi) = \sec^2 x$, $\sec x$ has period π, and since $\tan x$ also has period π, the period of $\sec^2 x$ is a divisor of π. The graph in Fig. 8.42 shows that the period is at least π, so we conclude that the period is π. We shall find all solutions in the interval $[-\pi/2, \pi/2)$.

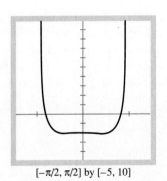

[−π/2, π/2] by [−5, 10]

Figure 8.42 $f(x) = 3 \tan^4 x - 1 - \sec^2 x.$

$$3 \tan^4 x = 1 + \sec^2 x$$

$$= 1 + 1 + \tan^2 x$$

$$3 \tan^4 x - \tan^2 x - 2 = 0$$

$$(3 \tan^2 x + 2)(\tan^2 x - 1) = 0$$

So we need to solve the following equations:

$$3 \tan^2 x + 2 = 0 \qquad\qquad \tan^2 x - 1 = 0$$

$$\tan^2 x = -\tfrac{2}{3} \qquad\qquad \tan^2 x = 1$$

$$\tan x = \pm 1$$

However, the equation $\tan^2 x = -\frac{2}{3}$ has no real number solutions.

A solution to $\tan x = 1$ is $\tan^{-1}(1) = \pi/4$, and a solution to $\tan x = -1$ is $\tan^{-1}(-1) = -\pi/4$.

It is clear from the graph in Fig. 8.42 that there are only two zeros to $f(x) = 3 \tan^4 x - 1 - \sec^2 x$ in $[-\pi/2, \pi/2)$.

So the solutions to $3 \tan^4 x = 1 + \sec^2 x$ in $[-\pi/2, \pi/2)$ are $x = \pi/4$ and $x = -\pi/4$.   ▤

E X A M P L E   4   Factoring by Grouping

Find all solutions in one period of the periodic equation $2 \cot x \cos x - 3 \cos x + 6 \cot x - 9 = 0$.

Solution   Since $\cos x$ has a period of 2π and $\cot x$ has a period of π, the period of $f(x) = 2 \cot x \cos x - 3 \cos x + 6 \cot x - 9$ is a divisor of 2π. It is evident from the graph in Fig. 8.43 that the period is at least 2π. So we look for all solutions in the interval $[0, 2\pi)$.

Group terms and factor as shown.

$$(2 \cot x \cos x - 3 \cos x) + (6 \cot x - 9) = 0$$

$$(\cos x)(2 \cot x - 3) + 3(2 \cot x - 3) = 0$$

$$(\cos x + 3)(2 \cot x - 3) = 0$$

The equation $\cos x + 3 = 0$ has no solution. So consider the equation $2 \cot x - 3 = 0$.

$$2 \cot x - 3 = 0 \qquad \text{is equivalent to} \qquad \cot x = \tfrac{3}{2}$$

$$\cot x = \tfrac{3}{2} \qquad \text{is equivalent to} \qquad \tan x = \tfrac{2}{3}$$

One solution to $\tan = \frac{2}{3}$ is $\tan^{-1}(\frac{2}{3}) = 0.59$, an angle in the first quadrant. Since the tangent function is positive in the third quadrant, $0.59 + \pi$ is also a solution.

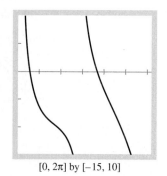

[0, 2π] by [−15, 10]

Figure 8.43 $f(x) = 2 \cot x \cos x - 3 \cos x + 6 \cot x - 9$.

The solutions to $2 \cot x \cos x - 3 \cos x + 6 \cot x - 9 = 0$ in $[0, 2\pi)$ are $x = 0.59$ and $x = 0.59 + \pi = 3.73$. ▤

Sometimes an analytical method for solving a trig equation depends on a double-angle identity.

E X A M P L E   5   Using a Double-angle Identity

Find all solutions in one period of the periodic equation $\sin 2x = \sin x$.

Solution   The period of the function $f(x) = \sin 2x - \sin x$ is 2π, so we shall find all solutions in $[0, 2\pi)$ (see Fig. 8.44)

$$\sin 2x - \sin x = 0$$

$$2 \cos x \sin x - \sin t = 0$$

$$(\sin x)(2 \cos x - 1) = 0$$

So we must solve the equations

$$\sin x = 0 \qquad \text{and} \qquad \cos x = \tfrac{1}{2}.$$

The solutions to $\sin x = 0$ are 0 and π, and the solutions to $\cos x = \tfrac{1}{2}$ are $\pi/3$ and $5\pi/3$. The solutions to $\sin 2x = \sin x$ in $[0, 2\pi)$ are $0, \pi/3, \pi$, and $5\pi/3$. ▤

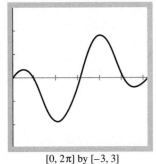

$[0, 2\pi]$ by $[-3, 3]$

Figure 8.44 $f(x) = \sin 2x - \sin x$.

E X A M P L E   6   Using Fundamental and Double-angle Identities

Find all solutions in one period of the periodic equation $\cos 2x - 2 \sin^2 x = 0$.

Solution   The period of this periodic equation is π. Therefore we shall find all solutions in $[0, \pi)$.

$$\cos 2x - 2 \sin^2 x = 0$$

$$(1 - 2 \sin^2 x) - 2 \sin^2 x = 0 \qquad \text{Use the identity for } \cos 2x.$$

$$1 - 4 \sin^2 x = 0$$

$$\sin^2 x = \tfrac{1}{4}$$

$$\sin x = \pm \tfrac{1}{2}$$

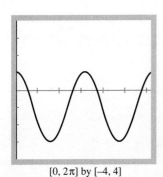

$[0, 2\pi]$ by $[-4, 4]$

Figure 8.45 $y = \cos 2x - 2 \sin^2 x$.

The solutions to $\sin x = \tfrac{1}{2}$ are $\pi/6$ and $5\pi/6$, and $\sin x = -\tfrac{1}{2}$ has no solution in $[0, \pi]$.

The solutions to $\cos 2x - 2 \sin^2 x = 0$ over $[0, \pi)$ are $x = \pi/6$ and $x = 5\pi/6$. Fig. 8.45 provides visual support for these solutions. ▤

Exercises for Section 8.6

In Exercises 1 to 6, find all solutions in one period of each periodic equation.

1. $\sin x = 0.3$ **2.** $\cos x = 0.75$

3. $\tan x = 1.5$ **4.** $\sin x = 1.25$

5. $\cos 2t = \frac{1}{2}$ **6.** $\tan 2\theta = 1$

In Exercises 7 to 10, find all solutions in one period of each periodic equation.

7. $(\sin x - 0.5)(\cos x + 0.3) = 0$

8. $(\sin x + 0.2)(\cos 2x - 1) = 0$

9. $(\cos x + 0.8)(\cos x - 0.5) = 0$

10. $(\sin x + 1.4)(\cos x - 0.1) = 0$

In Exercises 11 to 21, find all solutions in one period of each periodic equation.

11. $(\sin x)(\tan x - 1)(\cos x - 1) = 0$

12. $(\tan x - 1.5)(2\sin x + 1)(2\cos x - 1) = 0$

13. $(\sin^2 x - 1)(\cos x - 1) = 0$

14. $2\sin x \cos x = \sin x$ **15.** $2\sin^2 x = 1 + \cos x$

16. $4\sin^2 x = 3$ **17.** $2\tan^2 x = \sec x - 1$

18. $\sin 2x = \cos x$ **19.** $2\tan^2 x + 3\sec x = 0$

20. $2\cos^2 x = 1 - \sin x$ **21.** $2\sin^2 t - \sin t = 1$

In Exercises 22 and 23, find all solutions over the interval $[0, 2\pi)$ for each equation.

22. $\cos 2x - \sin x = \dfrac{1}{2}$

23. $\cos 2x + \cos x = 0$

Exercises 24 to 26 develop a formula for the area $\mathcal{A}$ of a triangle based on the figure below.

24. Show that

$$\mathcal{A} = \frac{1}{2}x_1 h + \frac{1}{2}x_2 h.$$

25. Use the formula in Exercise 24 to show that

$$\mathcal{A} = \frac{1}{2}ab \, \sin\theta_1 \cos\theta_2 + \frac{1}{2}ab \cos\theta_1 \sin\theta_2$$

26. Use the formula in Exercise 25 to show that

$$\mathcal{A} = \frac{1}{2}ab \sin C$$

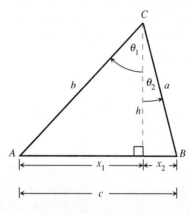

For Exercises 24 to 26

Exercises 27 to 30 refer to the following **problem situation**. When light passes through a medium, it changes direction, as shown in the figure. This bending is referred to as *light refraction*. If α is the angle of incidence and β is the angle of refraction, *Snell's law* states that for a given medium,

$$\frac{\sin\alpha}{\sin\beta} = C,$$

where the constant C is called the *index of refraction*.

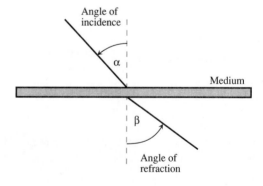

For Exercises 27 to 30

27. Suppose the index of refraction for a diamond is 2.42. Show that the trigonometric representation for β as a function of α is $\beta = \sin^{-1}(0.413 \sin\alpha)$. Find a complete graph of this problem situation and state the domain.

28. What is the maximum value for the angle of refraction for this diamond medium?

29. What angle of incidence should you choose if you want the angle of refraction to be 0.38 radians?

30. Find the angle of refraction when the angle of incidence

is $\pi/4$.

31. Writing to Learn Try to solve the equation $\tan x = \sec x$ both algebraically and graphically. Write a paragraph that explains which method is most convincing for you on this problem and why.

Chapter Review

KEY TERMS

analytic trigonometry
double-angle identity
half-angle identity
inverse cosine function

inverse sine function
inverse tangent function
linear combination
periodic equation

phase shift
sinusoid
sum and difference
   identities for sine

and cosine
sum and difference
   identities for tangent

REVIEW EXERCISES

In Exercises 1 to 6, determine the amplitude, period, phase shift, domain, and range for each function.

1. $f(x) = 2\sin 3x$

2. $g(x) = 3\cos 4x$

3. $f(x) = 1.5\sin\left(2x - \pi/4\right)$ **4.** $g(x) = 2\sin(3x + 1)$

5. $f(x) = 4\sin(2x - 1)$ **6.** $g(x) = -2\sin\left(3x - \pi/3\right)$

In Exercises 7 to 12, describe the transformations that can be used to obtain a graph of the given function from the graph $y = \sin x$.

7. $f(x) = 3\sin(2x - 1) + 7$

8. $g(x) = -2\sin(2x - 0.5) - 3$

9. $h(x) = 5\sin(3x + 1.5) + 2.3$

10. $f(x) = -3\sin(\pi x - 2) + 4$

11. $g(x) = 2\sin(2\pi x + 3) - 2$

12. $f(x) = -\sin(x - \pi/2) - 1$

In Exercises 13 to 16, sketch a graph of each function.

13. $f(x) = 2\cos(3x - \pi) + 1$

14. $h(x) = 3\sin\left(2\pi x - \dfrac{\pi}{4}\right)$

15. $g(x) = -2\cos(x + 1)$

16. $h(x) = 5\cos\left(4x + \dfrac{\pi}{3}\right) - 2$

In Exercises 17 to 20, find a complete graph of each function. Show that each is a sinusoid of the form $y = A\sin(bx + \alpha)$ and estimate the value of A, b, and α.

17. $y = 2\sin x - 4\cos x$ **18.** $y = 3\cos 2x - 2\sin 2x$

19. $y = 3\sin(2x - 1) + 5\cos(2x + 3)$

20. $y = 2\sin(3x + 1) + 3\cos(3x - 2)$

In Exercises 21 to 24, estimate values of A and C that solve each equation.

21. $2\cos 2x + 3\sin 2x = A\sin(2x + C)$

22. $3\sin 3x + 4\cos 4x = A\cos(3x + C)$

23. $5\sin 2x - 3\cos 2x = A\sin(2x + C)$

24. $7\cos 3x + 4\sin 3x = A\sin(3x + C)$

In Exercises 25 to 32, sketch a complete graph of each function. What transformations did you use, if any, in completing this graph?

25. $y = \sin^{-1} x$ **26.** $y = \cos^{-1} x$

27. $y = \sin^{-1} 2x$ **28.** $y = \tan^{-1} x$

29. $y = \tan^{-1} 2x$ **30.** $y = \sin^{-1}(2x - 1)$

31. $y = \sin^{-1}(3x - 1) + 2$ **32.** $y = \cos^{-1}(2x + 1) - 3$

In Exercises 33 to 42, use a calculator if necessary to find all solutions for each of these trigonometric equations.

33. $\sin 2x = 0.5$ **34.** $\cos x = \dfrac{\sqrt{3}}{2}$

35. $\tan x = -1$ **36.** $\sin x = 0.7$

37. $\cos 2x = 0.13$ **38.** $\cot x = 1.5$

39. $3\sin x = 0.9$ **40.** $2\cos 3x = 0.45$

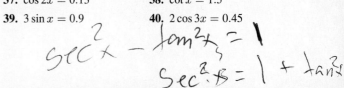

41. $2 \sin^{-1} x = \sqrt{2}$ **42.** $\tan^{-1} x = 1$

In Exercises 43 to 50, find a complete graph of each function and determine the domain and range of each.

43. $y = 3x \cos x + \sin 2x$ **44.** $y = 2 \sin 3x - 5 \cos 2x$

45. $y = \dfrac{2x - 1}{\tan x}$ **46.** $f(x) = x^2 \sin x$

47. $g(x) = 5 \cos^2 2x$ **48.** $y = \arccos x - 1$

49. $f(x) = (\sin^{-1} x)^2$ **50.** $g(x) = (\tan^{-1} x)^2$

In Exercises 51 to 58, prove each identity algebraically. Support these identities by graphing each side of the equation and comparing their graphs.

51. $\cos 3x = 4 \cos^3 x - 3 \cos x$

52. $\cos^2 2x - \cos^2 x = \sin^2 x - \sin^2 2x$

53. $\tan^2 x - \sin^2 x = \sin^2 x \tan^2 x$

54. $2 \sin \theta \cos^3 \theta + 2 \sin^3 \theta \cos \theta = \sin 2\theta$

55. $\csc x - \cos x \cot x = \sin x$

56. $\dfrac{\tan \theta + \sin \theta}{2 \tan \theta} = \cos^2 \left(\dfrac{\theta}{2} \right)$

57. $\dfrac{1 + \tan \theta}{1 - \tan \theta} + \dfrac{1 + \cot \theta}{1 - \cot \theta} = 0$

58. $\sin 3\theta = 3 \cos^2 \theta \sin \theta - \sin^3 \theta$

In Exercises 59 and 60, use a graphing utility to investigate whether the equation is an identity. If not, determine a *counterexample*.

59. $\sec x - \sin x \tan x = \cos x$

60. $(\sin^2 \alpha - \cos^2 \alpha)(\tan^2 \alpha + 1) = \tan^2 \alpha - 1$

In Exercises 61 to 64, write each expression in terms of $\sin x$ and $\cos x$ only.

61. $\sin 3x + \cos 3x$ **62.** $\sin 2x + \cos 3x$

63. $\cos^2 2x - \sin 2x$ **64.** $\sin 3x - 3 \sin 2x$

In Exercises 65 to 68, find an equivalent algebraic expression that does not involve trig functions.

65. $\sin(\cos^{-1} x)$ **66.** $\sin(\tan^{-1} x)$

67. $\cos(\sin^{-1} x)$ **68.** $\sin(2 \cos^{-1} x)$

In Exercises 69 to 72, solve each equation graphically.

69. $\sin^2 x - 3 \cos x = -0.5$

70. $\cos^3 x - 2 \sin x - 0.7 = 0$

71. $\sin^4 x + x^2 = 2$

72. $\sin 2x = x^3 - 5x^2 + 5x + 1$

In Exercises 73 to 78, solve each equation algebraically over the interval $[0, 2\pi)$. Support your conclusions with a graphing utility.

73. $2 \sin 2x = 1$ **74.** $2 \cos x = 1$

75. $\sin 3x = \sin x$ **76.** $\sin^2 x - 2 \sin x - 3 = 0$

77. $\cos 2t = \cos t$ **78.** $\sin(\cos x) = 1$

In Exercises 79 to 82, solve each inequality algebraically. Support your conclusions with a graphing utility.

79. $2 \cos 2x > 1$ for $0 \leq x < 2\pi$

80. $\sin 2x > 2 \cos x$ for $0 < x \leq 2\pi$

81. $2 \cos x < 1$ for $0 \leq x < 2\pi$

82. $\tan x < \sin x$ for $-\dfrac{\pi}{2} < x < \dfrac{\pi}{2}$

In Exercises 83 and 84, draw a complete graph and determine the end behavior of the function.

83. $y = \dfrac{1}{x} \sin \dfrac{1}{x}$ **84.** $y = x^3 \cos x$

Exercises 85 to 88 refer to the following **problem situation**. A single cell in a beehive is a regular hexagonal prism open at the front with a trihedral top at the back. It can be shown that the surface area of a cell is given by

$$S(\theta) = 6ab + \frac{3}{2}b^2 \left(-\cot \theta + \frac{\sqrt{3}}{\sin \theta} \right)$$

where θ is the trihedral angle, a is the depth of the cell, and $2b$ is the length of the line segment through the center connecting opposite vertices of the hexagonal front. Assume $a = 1.75$ (inches) and $b = 0.65$ (inches).

85. Draw a complete graph of the trigonometric representation for the surface area.

86. What values of θ make sense in the problem situation?

87. What value of θ gives the minimum surface area? (*Remark:* This answer is quite close to the observed angle in nature.)

88. What is the minimum surface area?

9

More Applications of Trigonometry

9.1   Law of Sines

Section 7.2 demonstrated how to use trigonometric functions to solve right triangles when an acute angle and one side are known, or when two sides are known. Recall that solving a triangle involves using known angle and side measures to find the remaining angles and side lengths.

In this section we generalize the technique for solving **oblique triangles**, that is, triangles that are not right triangles. Oblique triangles include **acute triangles**, in which all the angles measure less than 90°, and **obtuse triangles**, in which one angle is greater than 90° (see Fig. 9.1). The following notation will be used throughout this chapter. The vertices of a triangle will be denoted A, B, and C, and the angles at A, B, and C will be denoted α, β, and γ, respectively. The lengths of the sides opposite A, B, and C are denoted a, b, and c, respectively. So aside from its vertices, a triangle has six "parts": three sides and three angles (see Fig. 9.1).

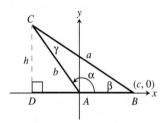

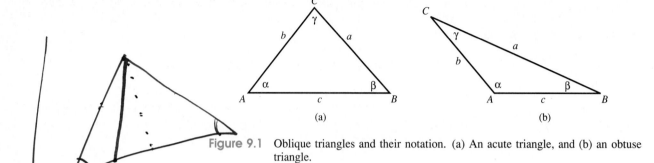

Figure 9.1   Oblique triangles and their notation. (a) An acute triangle, and (b) an obtuse triangle.

An important theorem that can be used to solve triangles is the **law of sines**. We begin by stating and proving this theorem.

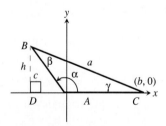

Figure 9.2   A triangle on the rectangular coordinate system used for proving the law of sines.

Theorem 9.1   Law of Sines

In any triangle ABC,

$$\frac{\sin \alpha}{a} = \frac{\sin \beta}{b} = \frac{\sin \gamma}{c}.$$

Proof   Without loss of generality assume that triangle ABC is an obtuse triangle. Position ABC on a rectangular coordinate system in such a way that A is at the origin and B lies on the positive x-axis at $(c, 0)$. Let D be the foot of the perpendicular from C to the x-axis (see Fig. 9.2).

Since α is in standard position, $\sin \alpha = h/b$, or $h = b \sin \alpha$. Likewise, $\sin \beta = h/a$, or $h = b \sin \beta$. Therefore

$$b \sin \alpha = a \sin \beta$$

$$\frac{\sin \alpha}{a} = \frac{\sin \beta}{b}.$$

Figure 9.3   Reposition the triangle in Fig. 9.2 so C is now on the x-axis.

By repositioning triangle ABC with A at the origin and vertex C on the x-axis at $(b, 0)$ (Fig. 9.3) and repeating the same argument, we can conclude that

$$\frac{\sin \alpha}{a} = \frac{\sin \gamma}{c}.$$

Therefore

$$\frac{\sin \alpha}{a} = \frac{\sin \beta}{b} = \frac{\sin \gamma}{c}.$$

Since this argument can be repeated in the case where α is acute, the proof is complete.   ≡

Two Angles and a Side Specified

The law of sines allows us to solve a triangle when two angles and a side are specified. Example 1 illustrates how we can find the length of the other two sides and the measure of the third angle using the law of sines.

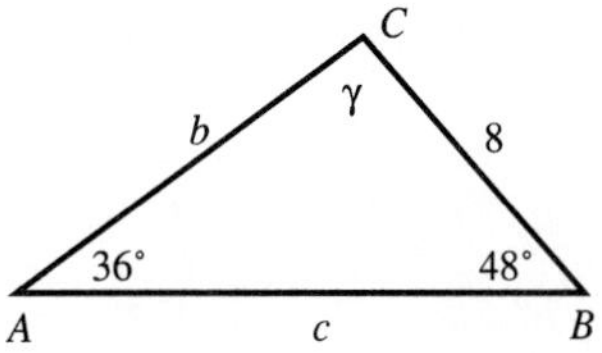

E X A M P L E   1   Finding Two Sides and One Angle

In triangle ABC, $\alpha = 36°, \beta = 48°$, and $a = 8$. Find the remaining sides and angle.

Solution   We need to find b, c, and γ (see Fig. 9.4).

$$\gamma = 180° - (36° + 48°) = 96°.$$

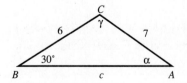

Figure 9.4   Triangle for Example 1.

$$\frac{\sin \alpha}{a} = \frac{\sin \beta}{b} \qquad \frac{\sin \alpha}{a} = \frac{\sin \gamma}{c} \quad \text{by the law of sines}$$

$$\frac{\sin 36°}{8} = \frac{\sin 48°}{b} \qquad \frac{\sin 36°}{8} = \frac{\sin 96°}{c}$$

$$b = \frac{8 \sin 48°}{\sin 36°} \qquad c = \frac{8 \sin 96°}{\sin 36°}$$

$$b = 10.11 \qquad c = 13.54 \qquad\qquad ≡$$

The method shown in Example 1 will work whenever you are given two angles, whose sum is less than 180°, and a side. It is generally true that a unique triangle is determined whenever two angles and a side are given.

Two Sides and an Angle Specified

The next example looks very similar to Example 1 except that the lengths of two sides and one angle are given.

E X A M P L E   2   Finding Two Angles and One Side

In triangle ABC, $\beta = 30°, a = 6$, and $b = 7$. Find the unknown side and angles.

Solution   Study Fig. 9.5. As illustrated by Example 1, to use the law of sines to find the length of a side, the angle opposite that side must be given. Therefore, before finding length c, you need to find γ. Since $\alpha + \beta + \gamma = 180°$, γ can be

Figure 9.5   Triangle for Example 2.

found once α is known. Use the law of sines to find α.

$$\frac{\sin \alpha}{a} = \frac{\sin \beta}{b}$$

$$\frac{\sin \alpha}{6} = \frac{\sin 30°}{7}$$

$$\sin \alpha = \frac{6 \sin 30°}{7}$$

$$\sin \alpha = \frac{3}{7}$$

There are two values of α in the interval $0 < \alpha < 180°$ that solve $\sin \alpha = \frac{3}{7}$, namely, $\alpha = \sin^{-1}\left(\frac{3}{7}\right) = 25.38°$ and $\alpha = 180° - 25.38° = 154.62°$. However, if $\alpha = 154.62°$, $\alpha + \beta = 184.62°$ which is not possible. Therefore

$$\alpha = 25.38° \qquad \text{and} \qquad \gamma = 180° - (25.38° + 30°) = 124.62°.$$

Now use the law of sines to find c:

$$\frac{\sin \beta}{b} = \frac{\sin \gamma}{c}$$

$$\frac{\sin 30°}{7} = \frac{\sin 124.62°}{c}$$

$$= \frac{7 \sin 124.62°}{\sin 30°}$$

$$c = 11.52$$

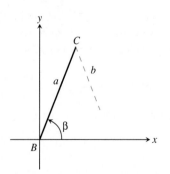

Figure 9.6   Two sides and their included angle.

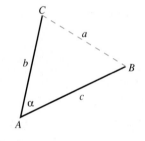

Figure 9.7 β is not an included angle.

Example 2 illustrates two important points. One is that the law of sines solution method worked because the given angle was *opposite* one of the given sides. If the given angle had been *included between* the given sides (see Fig. 9.6), the law of sines would not have been helpful. The law of cosines, to be introduced in Section 9.2, can be used to solve that situation.

A second aspect of Example 2 that must be discussed is that a unique triangle exists with the given angle $\beta = 30°$ and given sides, $a = 6$ and $b = 7$. But when two sides and a nonincluded angle are given, there are several other possibilities.

For example, suppose that angle β and side a are given and that β is placed on a coordinate system in standard position as shown (Fig. 9.7). There are several ways of completing a triangle by drawing side b from vertex C down to the x-axis, and these are shown in Fig. 9.8.

1. If b is too short, no triangle is formed (Fig. 9.8a).
2. If b represents the perpendicular distance from C to the x-axis, a right triangle is formed (Fig. 9.8b).

3. If b is just a bit longer than in Fig. 9.8(b) but still shorter than a, two triangles can be formed (Fig. 9.8c).

4. If b is as long as or longer than a, a unique triangle is formed (Fig. 9.8d).

Notice that Example 2 falls in the fourth category, Fig. 9.8(d).

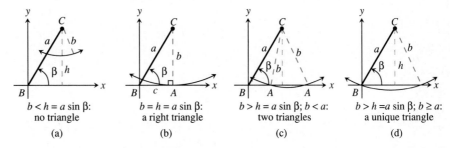

$b < h = a \sin\beta$: no triangle (a)

$b = h = a \sin\beta$: a right triangle (b)

$b > h = a \sin\beta; b < a$: two triangles (c)

$b > h = a \sin\beta; b \geq a$: a unique triangle (d)

Figure 9.8 Four ways to complete a triangle given an acute angle in standard position and one adjacent side.

E X A M P L E 3   Finding the Number of Triangles

Suppose in triangle ABC that $\beta = 30°$ and $a = 6$. How many triangles are formed if (a) $b = 2$, (b) $b = 3$, (c) $b = 5$, or (d) $b = 7$?

Solution

a) Since $b = 2 < 6\sin 30° = a\sin\beta$, no triangle is formed.

b) Since $b = 3 = 6\sin 30° = a\sin\beta$, a unique right triangle is formed.

c) Since $b = 5$ is greater than $a\sin\beta = 6\sin 30° = 3$ and less than $a = 6$, two triangles are formed.

d) Since $b = 7 \geq 6 = a$, a unique triangle is formed (see Example 2). ≡

When two sides and a nonincluded angle of a triangle are given, it is important to identify to which of the four cases shown in Fig. 9.8 the triangle belongs. That determines whether the triangle has no solution, a unique solution, or two solutions.

E X A M P L E 4   Solving Triangles with Nonincluded Angles

In triangle ABC, $\beta = 30°$ and $a = 6$. Find the unknown sides and angles if (a) $b = 3$, or (b) $b = 5$.

Solution

a) Since $b = 3 = a\sin\beta$, Example 3 shows that there is a unique right triangle formed (see Fig. 9.9). Therefore $\gamma = 90° - 30° = 60°$, and by the Pythagorean

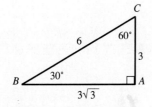

Figure 9.9 Triangle for Example 4, part a.

theorem $c = \sqrt{6^2 - 3^2} = \sqrt{36 - 9} = 3\sqrt{3}$.

b) Since $b = 5 > 6\sin 30° = a\sin\beta$ and $b = 5 < 6 = a$, Example 3 and Fig. 9.8 show that there are two possible values of α.

$$\frac{\sin\alpha}{a} = \frac{\sin\beta}{b} \quad \text{law of sines}$$

$$\frac{\sin\alpha}{6} = \frac{\sin 30°}{5}$$

$$\sin\alpha = \frac{6\sin 30°}{5}$$

$$\sin\alpha = \frac{3}{5}$$

The two solutions to this equation are $\alpha = \sin^{-1}\left(\frac{3}{5}\right) = 36.87°$ and $\alpha = 180 - 36.87° = 143.13°$.

If $\alpha = 36.87°$, then $\gamma = 180° - (36.87° + 30°) = 113.13°$, and we find c.

$$\frac{\sin\beta}{b} = \frac{\sin\gamma}{c} \quad \text{law of sines}$$

$$\frac{\sin 30°}{5} = \frac{\sin 113.13°}{c}$$

$$c = 9.20$$

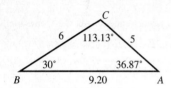

Figure 9.10   One solution to Example 4, part b.

One solution is $\alpha = 36.87°$, $\gamma = 113.13°$, and $c = 9.20$ (see Fig. 9.10).

If $\alpha = 143.13°$, then $\gamma = 180° - (143.13° + 30°) = 6.87°$, and we find c.

$$\frac{\sin\beta}{b} = \frac{\sin\gamma}{c} \quad \text{law of sines}$$

$$\frac{\sin 30°}{5} = \frac{\sin 6.87°}{c}$$

$$c = 1.20$$

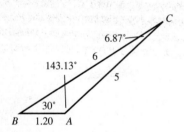

Figure 9.11   A second solution to Example 4, part b.

The second solution is $\alpha = 143.13°$ and $c = 1.20$ (see Fig. 9.11).   ▬

In Example 4, β was an acute angle. What happens if β is an obtuse angle? Figure 9.12 shows the four cases considered in Fig. 9.8 except that now β is obtuse. However, in this case there is either exactly one solution or no solution since A is on the positive x-axis.

Applications

Applications of the law of sines are illustrated in the next two examples.

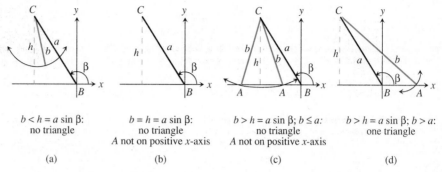

$b < h = a \sin \beta$:
no triangle

(a)

$b = h = a \sin \beta$:
no triangle
A not on positive x-axis

(b)

$b > h = a \sin \beta; b \leq a$:
no triangle
A not on positive x-axis

(c)

$b > h = a \sin \beta; b > a$:
one triangle

(d)

Figure 9.12 Ways to complete a triangle given an obtuse angle in standard position and one adjacent side.

E X A M P L E 5   APPLICATION: Fire Location

A forest ranger at an observation point A along a straight road sights a fire in the direction $32°$ east of north. Another ranger at a second observation point B 10 miles due east of A on the road sights the same fire $48°$ west of north. Find the distance from each observation point to the fire, and find the shortest distance CD from the road to the fire.

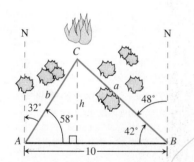

Figure 9.13 Triangle for Example 5.

Solution   In Fig. 9.13 vertex C represents the location of the fire. We are asked to find a, b, and h, the distance to the road.

The fire is $32°$ east of north, so $\alpha = 90° - 32° = 58°$. Similarly, $\beta = 90° - 48° = 42°$. So $\gamma = 180° - (58° + 42°) = 80°$.

$$\frac{\sin \alpha}{a} = \frac{\sin \gamma}{c} \qquad\qquad \frac{\sin \beta}{b} = \frac{\sin \gamma}{c}$$

$$\frac{\sin 58°}{a} = \frac{\sin 80°}{10} \qquad\qquad \frac{\sin 42°}{b} = \frac{\sin 80°}{10}$$

$$a = \frac{10 \sin 58°}{\sin 80°} \qquad\qquad b = \frac{10 \sin 42°}{\sin 80°}$$

$$a = 8.6113 \qquad\qquad b = 6.7945$$

The distance h is $b \sin 58° = a \sin 42° = 5.76$.

Thus the fire is 6.79 miles from A, 8.61 miles from B, and 5.76 miles is the shortest distance from the road AB.

E X A M P L E 6   APPLICATION: Height of a Pole

A road slopes at a $10°$ angle with the horizontal, and a vertical telephone pole stands by the road. When the angle of elevation of the sun is $62°$, the telephone pole casts a 14.5-foot shadow downhill parallel with the road. Find the height of the telephone pole.

$$\tan A = \frac{2.8}{5.3} \qquad\qquad \tan^{-1}\left(\frac{2.8}{5.3}\right) = A$$

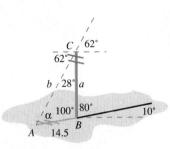

Figure 9.14   Diagram for Example 6.

Solution It helps to begin by drawing and labeling a figure (Fig. 9.14). Let BC represent the pole and let AB be the pole's shadow. Since the angle of elevation of the sun is $62°$, $\gamma = 90° - 62° = 28°$. Since the road makes a $10°$ angle with the horizontal, apply geometry to Fig. 9.14 to conclude that $\beta = 100°$ and $\alpha = 52°$.

The length of the shadow is $c = 14.5$. Now the law of sines can be used to find the height, a, of the telephone pole.

$$\frac{\sin \alpha}{a} = \frac{\sin \gamma}{c}$$

$$\frac{\sin 52°}{a} = \frac{\sin 28°}{14.5}$$

$$a = \frac{14.5 \sin 52°}{\sin 28°}$$

$$a = 24.34$$

Thus the height of the telephone pole is 24.34 feet.

Exercises for Section 9.1

1. Give the side lengths a, b, and c for two different triangles ABC whose interior angles are $\alpha = 32°$, $\beta = 75°$, and $\gamma = 73°$.

2. Give the side lengths a, b, and c of two different triangles ABC whose interior angles are $\alpha = 54°$ and $\gamma = 16°$.

Solve each triangle specified by the angles and sides given in Exercises 3 to 16.

3. $\alpha = 40°$, $\beta = 30°$, $b = 10$

4. $\alpha = 60°$, $a = 3$, $b = 4$

5. $\beta = 30°$, $a = 12$, $b = 6$

6. $\alpha = 50°$, $\beta = 62°$, $a = 4$

7. $\alpha = 33°$, $\beta = 79°$, $b = 7$

8. $\beta = 85°$, $a = 4$, $b = 6$

9. $\alpha = 50°$, $a = 4$, $b = 5$

10. $\beta = 38°$, $a = 16$, $b = 20$

11. $\beta = 38°$, $a = 16$, $b = 12$

12. $\beta = 116°$, $a = 11$, $b = 13$

13. $\beta = 116°$, $a = 11$, $b = 10$

14. $\beta = 116°$, $a = 11$, $b = 8$

15. $\beta = 152°$, $a = 8$, $b = 10$

16. $\gamma = 103°$, $\beta = 16°$, $c = 12$

17. If $a = 10$ and $\beta = 42°$, determine the values of b for which α has the following:

   a) two values   b) one value   c) no value

18. Two markers A and B on the same side of a canyon rim are 56 feet apart, and a third marker is located across the rim at point C. A surveyor determines that $\angle BAC = 72°$ and $\angle ABC = 53°$.

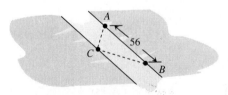

For Exercise 18

   a) What is the distance between C and point A?
   b) What is the distance between the two canyon rims? (Assume they are parallel.)

19. A weather forecaster at an observation point A along a straight road sights a tornado in the direction $38°$ east of

north. Another forecaster, at an observation point B on the road and 25 miles due east of A, sights the same tornado at $53°$ west of north. The tornado is moving due south. Find the distance from each observation point to the tornado. Also find the distance between the tornado and the road.

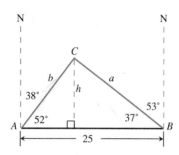

For Exercise 19

20. A vertical flagpole stands by the side of a road that slopes at an angle of $15°$ with the horizontal. When the angle of elevation of the sun is $62°$, the flagpole casts a 16-foot shadow downhill parallel to the road. Find the height of the flagpole.

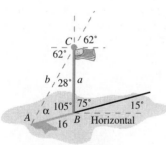

For Exercise 20

21. A hot-air balloon is seen over Park City, Utah, simultaneously by two observers at points A and B 2.32 miles apart. Assume that the balloon and the observers are in the same vertical plane and that the angles of elevation and the distances are as shown in the following figure. How high above ground is the balloon?

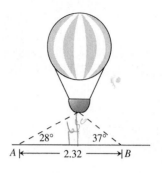

For Exercise 21

22. A 4-foot airfoil is attached to the cab of a truck to reduce wind resistance, as shown in the following figure. The angle between the airfoil and the cab top is $18°$. What is the length of a vertical brace positioned as shown in the figure if angle β is $10°$?

For Exercise 22

23. Solve triangle ABC shown here, given that $a = 5$, $b = 8$, and $\gamma = 22°$. (*Hint*: Draw a perpendicular from A to the line through B and C.)

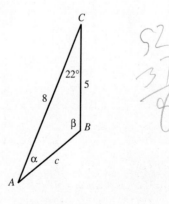

For Exercise 23

9.2 _____

Law of Cosines

In Section 9.1 the law of sines was used to find unknown parts of a triangle if two angles and a side were known or if two sides and a nonincluded angle were known. However, in the case where two sides and the included angle are given, as shown in Fig. 9.15, the law of sines does not apply. Instead we apply the **law of cosines** to find the length of the side opposite the given angle.

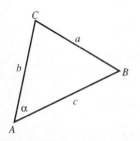

Figure 9.15   Two sides and the included angle.

Theorem 9.2   Law of Cosines

For any triangle ABC labeled in the usual way (see Fig. 9.15),

$$a^2 = b^2 + c^2 - 2bc\cos\alpha,$$

$$b^2 = a^2 + c^2 - 2ac\cos\beta, \text{ and}$$

$$c^2 = a^2 + b^2 - 2ab\cos\gamma.$$

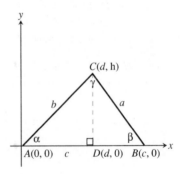

Figure 9.16   Triangle for Theorem 9.2.

Proof   Without loss of generality we place triangle ABC so that vertex A is at the origin and vertex B lies on the positive x-axis at $(c, 0)$. Choose D on the x-axis at $(d, 0)$ so that segment CD is perpendicular to the x-axis. If h is the altitude from C, then the coordinates of C are (d, h) (see Fig. 9.16). Because α is in standard position,

$$\cos\alpha = \frac{d}{b} \qquad \text{and} \qquad \sin\alpha = \frac{h}{b}$$

$$d = b\cos\alpha \qquad\qquad\qquad h = b\sin\alpha.$$

Using the Pythagorean theorem and substituting these values of d and h, we have

$$a^2 = (c - d)^2 + (0 - h)^2$$

$$a^2 = (c - d)^2 + h^2$$

$$= (c - b\cos\alpha)^2 + (b\sin\alpha)^2$$

$$= c^2 - 2bc\cos\alpha + b^2\cos^2\alpha + b^2\sin^2\alpha$$

$$= c^2 - 2bc\cos\alpha + b^2(\cos^2\alpha + \sin^2\alpha)$$

$$a^2 = b^2 + c^2 - 2bc\cos\alpha.$$

The other two equations follow by beginning with the angle β or γ in standard position and repeating the above argument.

OBSERVATION

Notice that the law of cosines can be thought of as a generalization of the Pythagorean theorem. The term $-2bc\cos\alpha$ becomes zero when $\alpha = 90°$ and the law of cosines reduces to the Pythagorean theorem.

Two Sides and the Included Angle Specified

If two sides and an angle opposite one of those sides are given, we found in Section 9.1 that zero, one, or two triangles were possible. In the case where two sides and an included angle of measure between $0°$ and $180°$ are specified, then precisely one triangle is determined. We use the law of cosines to find the remaining side and angles, as illustrated in Example 1.

E X A M P L E   1   Finding Two Angles and One Side

Solve triangle ABC if $a = 4, b = 7$, and $\gamma = 42°$.

Solution   First use the law of cosines to find the third side:

$$c^2 = a^2 + b^2 - 2ab\cos\gamma$$

$$c^2 = 4^2 + 7^2 - 2(4)(7)\cos 42°$$

$$c^2 = 23.383890$$

$$c = 4.8357.$$

The value of c was not rounded to hundredths because it will be used again.

Next use the law of sines to determine α:

$$\frac{\sin\alpha}{a} = \frac{\sin\gamma}{c}$$

$$\frac{\sin\alpha}{4} = \frac{\sin 42°}{4.8357}$$

$$\sin\alpha = \frac{4\sin 42°}{4.8357}$$

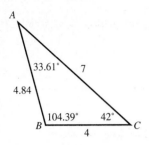

Figure 9.17   Triangle for Example 1.

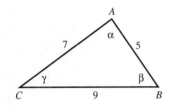

Figure 9.18   Triangle for Example 2.

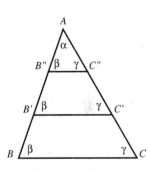

Figure 9.19   Three of the infinite number of triangles possible when three angles and no sides are specified.

$$\alpha = \sin^{-1}\left(\frac{4\sin 42°}{4.8357}\right)$$

$$\alpha = 33.61°.$$

Thus $\alpha = 33.61°, \beta = 104.39°, c = 4.84$, and we have determined the triangle in Fig. 9.17. ▄

Three Sides Specified

Suppose that the measures of the three sides of a triangle are specified. In order for there actually to be such a triangle, the sum of the measures of any two sides must exceed the measure of the third side. (Why?) The law of cosines can be applied in this case to find the measures of the angles.

E X A M P L E   2   Finding Three Angles

Solve triangle ABC if $a = 9, b = 7$, and $c = 5$.

Solution   First, use the law of cosines to find angle α (see Fig. 9.18).

$$a^2 = b^2 + c^2 - 2bc\cos\alpha$$

$$9^2 = 7^2 + 5^2 - 2(7)(5)\cos\alpha$$

$$\cos\alpha = \frac{7^2 + 5^2 - 9^2}{2(7)(5)}$$

$$\cos\alpha = -0.1.$$

The only solution to $\cos\alpha = -0.1$ where $0° < \alpha < 180°$ is $\cos^{-1}(-0.1) = 95.7392°$. Now use the law of cosines to find angle β:

$$b^2 = a^2 + c^2 - 2ac\cos\beta$$

$$7^2 = 9^2 + 5^2 - 2(9)(5)\cos\beta$$

$$\cos\beta = \frac{9^2 + 5^2 - 7^2}{2(9)(5)}$$

Thus $\beta = 50.7035°$. It follows that $\gamma = 180° - (95.7392° + 50.7035°) = 33.5573°$. So the three angles are $\alpha = 95.74°, \beta = 50.70°$, and $\gamma = 33.56°$. ▄

Three Angles Specified

We have considered all the possibilities for three parts of a triangle to be specified, except for one. Suppose all three angles are specified. Figure 9.19 illustrates that there are infinitely many different triangles with the same three angles. Consequently, it is not possible to solve for the three sides. They are not uniquely determined.

Following is a summary of the number of triangles determined when three parts of a triangle are given.

Summary: Solving an Oblique Triangle

Parts Given	Number of Possible Triangles
1. Three angles (sum equals 180°)	Infinitely many
2. Two angles (sum less than 180°), one side	One
3. One angle, two sides	Zero, one, or two
4. Three sides(sum of any two greater than the third)	One

Area of Triangles

The law of cosines allows us to calculate the length of one side of a triangle given the opposite angle and the other two sides. It is therefore possible to find the area of the resulting triangle also.

Theorem 9.3   Area of Triangles

Let ABC be a triangle labeled in the usual way. Then the area $\mathcal{A}$ of the triangle is given by

$$\mathcal{A} = \frac{1}{2}bc\sin\alpha = \frac{1}{2}ac\sin\beta = \frac{1}{2}ab\sin\gamma.$$

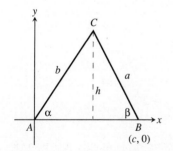

Figure 9.20   Triangle for Theorem 9.3.

Proof   Place triangle ABC in standard position and let h be an altitude of triangle ABC (see Fig. 9.20). Notice that $h = b\sin\alpha$. Then

$$\mathcal{A} = \frac{1}{2}ch$$

$$= \frac{1}{2}cb\sin\alpha$$

$$= \frac{1}{2}bc\sin\alpha.$$

The other two forms of the theorem follow by a similar argument. Notice that if $\beta = 90°$, then $\mathcal{A} = \frac{1}{2}ac\sin 90° = \frac{1}{2}ac$, so $\mathcal{A} = \frac{1}{2}$ base × height, as expected. ∎

EXAMPLE 3   Finding the Area of a Triangle

Find the area of triangle ABC if $a = 8, b = 5$, and $\gamma = 52°$.

Solution   Theorem 9.3 says that the area is given by

$$\mathcal{A} = \frac{1}{2}ab\sin\gamma$$

$$= \frac{1}{2}(8)(5)\sin 52°$$

$$= 15.76.$$

Thus the area is 15.76 square units.   ≡

If we know two sides and the included angle, we can find a base and altitude and thus the area of a triangle. Theorem 9.4 gives **Heron's formula**, which can be used to find the area of a triangle when all three sides are known.

Theorem 9.4   Heron's Formula

Let triangle ABC be labeled in the usual way. Then the area $\mathcal{A}$ of the triangle is given by

$$\mathcal{A} = \sqrt{s(s-a)(s-b)(s-c)},$$

where $s = \frac{1}{2}(a+b+c)$ is one-half of the perimeter, or **semiperimeter**.

Proof   We begin by rewriting the formula for area found in Theorem 9.3 in such a way that the law of cosines can be used to obtain an equation involving only sides $a, b,$ and c.

$$\mathcal{A} = \frac{1}{2}ab\sin\gamma$$

$$2\mathcal{A} = ab\sin\gamma$$

$$4\mathcal{A}^2 = a^2b^2\sin^2\gamma$$

$$= a^2b^2(1 - \cos^2\gamma)$$

$$= a^2b^2 - a^2b^2\cos^2\gamma \tag{1}$$

Next, we multiply each side of Eq. (1) by 4 again and then use the law of cosines to replace $2ab\cos\gamma$ by $a^2 + b^2 - c^2$:

$$16\mathcal{A}^2 = 4a^2b^2 - (2ab\cos\gamma)^2$$

$$= 4a^2b^2 - (a^2 + b^2 - c^2)^2 \tag{2}$$

It can be verified that the right-hand side of Eq. (2) is the same as $(a + b + c)(a + b - c)(b + c - a)(c + a - b)$. Thus

$$16\mathcal{A}^2 = (a + b + c)(a + b - c)(b + c - a)(c + a - b).$$

Notice that $a + b + c = 2s$, $a + b - c = 2s - 2c$, $b + c - a = 2s - 2a$, and $a + c - b = 2s - 2b$. Substituting these values we obtain

$$16\mathcal{A}^2 = 2s(2s - 2c)(2s - 2a)(2s - 2b)$$

$$16\mathcal{A}^2 = 16s(s - c)(s - a)(s - b)$$

$$\mathcal{A} = \sqrt{s(s - a)(s - b)(s - c)}.$$

EXAMPLE 4 Using Heron's Formula

Find the area of triangle ABC if $a = 9, b = 7$, and $c = 5$.

Solution First note that $s = \frac{1}{2}(a + b + c) = 10.5$. Then compute the area using Heron's formula:

$$\mathcal{A} = \sqrt{s(s - a)(s - b)(s - c)}$$

$$= \sqrt{10.5(1.5)(3.5)(5.5)}$$

$$= 17.41.$$

Applications of the Law of Cosines

EXAMPLE 5 APPLICATION: Distance Measured Indirectly

A surveyor wants to find the distance between two points A and B on opposite sides of a building (see Fig. 9.21). The surveyor locates a point C that is 110 feet from A and 160 feet from B. If $\gamma = 54°$, find distance AB.

Solution The distance from A to B in triangle ABC is c. Using the law of cosines,

$$c^2 = a^2 + b^2 - 2ab\cos\gamma$$

$$c^2 = 160^2 + 110^2 - 2(160)(110)\cos 54°$$

$$c = 130.42.$$

Thus the distance between A and B is 130.42 feet.

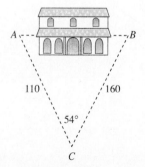

Figure 9.21 Points A and B are on opposite sides of a building.

EXAMPLE 6 APPLICATION: Baseball Diamond

In major league baseball the four bases form a square whose sides are 90 feet long. The front edge of the pitching rubber on which the pitcher stands is 60.5 feet from home plate. Find the distance from the front edge of the pitching rubber to first base.

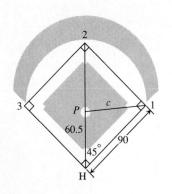

Figure 9.22   Baseball diamond for Example 6.

Solution   In Fig. 9.22 let P be the middle of the front edge of the pitching rubber, H be home plate, and c be the distance from P to the corner of first base. Since $\gamma = 45°$, distance c can be calculated as follows:

$$c^2 = (60.5)^2 + (90)^2 - 2(60.5)(90)\cos 45°$$

$$c = 63.72.$$

Thus the distance from the front edge of the pitching rubber to first base is 63.72 feet.   ≡

Recall that in Section 7.6 we defined the angle between two nonperpendicular lines to be the acute angle determined by the lines. Example 7 shows how to apply the law of cosines to find the angle between two lines.

E X A M P L E 7   Finding the Angle between Two Lines

Find the angle between the lines $y = 3x$ and $y = -x$.

Solution   Using the distance formula we see that in Fig. 9.23, segments $OP = \sqrt{10}, OQ = \sqrt{2},$ and $PQ = 4$. Applying the law of cosines to triangle POQ with $\alpha = \angle POQ$ yields the following:

$$4^2 = (\sqrt{10})^2 + (\sqrt{2})^2 - 2\sqrt{2}\sqrt{10}\cos\alpha$$

$$16 = 10 + 2 - 4\sqrt{5}\cos\alpha$$

$$-\frac{1}{\sqrt{5}} = \cos\alpha$$

$$\alpha = \cos^{-1}\left(-\frac{1}{\sqrt{5}}\right) = 116.57°$$

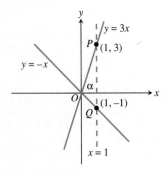

Figure 9.23   Two intersecting lines for Example 7.

Therefore the acute angle between these two lines is $180° - 116.57° = 63.43°$.   ≡

Exercises for Section 9.2

In Exercises 1 to 10, solve each triangle ABC.

1. $a = 1, b = 5, c = 4$

2. $a = 1, b = 5, c = 8$

3. $a = 3.2, b = 7.6, c = 6.4$

4. $\alpha = 21°, \beta = 17°, c = 15$

5. $\alpha = 55°, b = 12, c = 7$

6. $\beta = 125°, a = 25, c = 41$

7. $\beta = 103°, b = 13, a = 18$

8. $\alpha = 36°, b = 17, a = 14$

9. $\beta = 110°, b = 13, c = 15$

10. $a = 5, b = 7, c = 6$

11. If $a = 8$ and $\beta = 58°$, determine the values of b for which α has (a) two values, (b) one value, or (c) no value.

12. If $a = 12$ and $\beta = 32°$, determine the values of b for which α has (a) two values, (b) one value, or (c) no value.

In Exercises 13 to 18, find the area of each triangle ABC determined by the given information.

13. $b = 6$, $c = 8$, $\alpha = 47°$

14. $a = 17$, $c = 14$, $\beta = 103°$

15. $\alpha = 15°$, $\beta = 65°$, $a = 8$

16. $\alpha = 10°$, $\gamma = 110°$, $c = 12.3$

17. $a = 2$, $b = 6$, $c = 7$

18. $a = 20$, $b = 36$, $c = 50$

19. In order to determine the distance between two points A and B on opposite sides of a lake, a surveyor chooses a point C that is 860 feet from A and 175 feet from B. If the measure of the angle at C is 78°, find the distance between A and B.

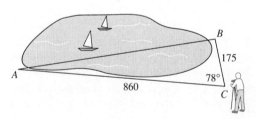

For Exercise 19

Exercises 20 to 22 refer to Fig. 9.22.

20. Find the distance from the center of the front edge of the pitching rubber to second base.

21. Find the angle created by home plate, the center of the front edge of the pitching rubber, and first base.

22. Find the angle formed by the center of the front edge of the pitching rubber, first base, and home plate.

23. In softball the four bases form a square whose sides are 60 feet in length. The front edge of the pitching rubber is 40 feet from home plate. Find the distance from the front edge of the pitching rubber to first base.

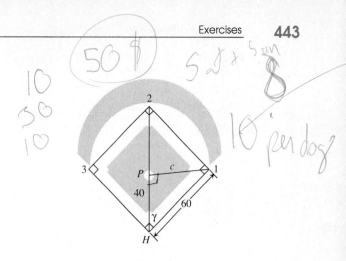

For Exercise 23

24. Find the radian measure of the largest angle in the triangle whose sides have lengths of 4, 5, and 6.

25. The sides of a parallelogram have lengths of 18 and 26 feet, and one angle is 39°. Find the length of the longer diagonal.

26. Two observers are 600 feet apart on opposite sides of a flagpole. The angles of elevation from the observers to the top of the pole are 19° and 21°. Find the height of the flagpole.

27. A blimp is sighted simultaneously by two observers: A at the top of a 650-foot tower and B at the base of the tower. Find the distance of the blimp from observer A if the angle of elevation (from the horizontal) as viewed by A is 32° and the angle of elevation as viewed by B is 56°. How high is the blimp?

28. In a parallelogram, two adjacent sides meet at an angle of 35° and are 3 feet and 8 feet in length. What is the length of the shorter diagonal of the parallelogram?

29. Two observers are 400 feet apart on opposite sides of a tree. If the angles of elevation from the observers to the top of the tree are 15° and 20°, how tall is the tree?

30. Suppose that ℓ_1 and ℓ_2 are two lines with slopes m_1 and m_2, respectively. Show that the angle α between the two lines is either

$$\alpha = \cos^{-1}\left(\frac{1 + m_1 m_2}{\sqrt{(1 + m_1^2)(1 + m_2^2)}}\right) \quad \text{if } \alpha < 90$$

or $180° - \alpha$ if $\alpha > 90°$.

Exercises 31 to 33 refer to the following **problem situation**: Let AOB be a sector of a circle of radius r with central angle θ.

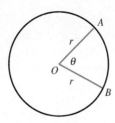

For Exercises 31 to 33

31. Show that the area $\mathcal{A}$ of the sector is $r^2\theta/2$.

32. Assume the perimeter $P = 2r + \theta r$ of the sector is fixed. What is the maximum area of the sector?

33. Explain how the function

$$f(x) = \frac{x}{2(2+x)^2}$$

is related to the solution of Exercise 32.

9.3 _____ Trigonometric Form of Complex Numbers

Complex numbers were introduced in Section 4.5. Recall that a complex number is written in the form $a + bi$ where a and b are real numbers. Also recall that

$$(a + bi) + (c + di) = (a + c) + (b + d)i.$$

In this section we introduce two additional ways to represent complex numbers. The first is geometric representation and the second is trigonometric.

Geometric Representation of Complex Numbers

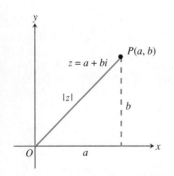

Figure 9.24 Complex numbers represented as points in the coordinate plane.

There is a natural one-to-one correspondence between the set of complex numbers and the points in the coordinate plane. The complex number $a + bi$ corresponds to the point $P(a, b)$. When the coordinate plane is viewed as a representation of the complex numbers, it is called the **complex plane** or the **Gaussian plane**. Figure 9.24 shows the complex numbers $2 + 3i$, $-3 - 2i$, and $2 - 3i$ on the complex plane. The x-axis of the complex plane is called the **real axis** and the y-axis is called the **imaginary axis.**

If we draw a segment from the origin to the point representing $a + bi$, the length of this segment is $\sqrt{a^2 + b^2}$ (see Fig. 9.25). This length is the concept defined in the following definition.

Figure 9.25 $|z| = \sqrt{a^2 + b^2}$.

Definition 9.1 Absolute Value of a Complex Number

The **absolute value** or **modulus** of the complex number $z = a + bi$ is given by

$$|a + bi| = \sqrt{a^2 + b^2}.$$

The absolute value of $a + bi$ is the length of the segment from the origin O to $a + bi$.

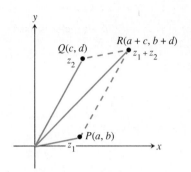

Figure 9.26 Geometric representation of complex addition.

Complex numbers have many of the algebraic properties of real numbers. In particular, they can be added and subtracted. A close association exists between complex number addition and vector addition that will be defined in Section 9.5. Consequently we use a geometric representation to introduce complex number addition.

If $z_1 = a + bi$ is represented by point $P(a, b)$ and $z_2 = c + di$ is represented by point $Q(c, d)$, then the complex number $z_1 + z_2$ is represented by the point $R(a + c, b + d)$. See Fig. 9.26. It can be shown that segment OR is the diagonal of the parallelogram determined by segments OP and OQ.

EXAMPLE 1 Finding Geometric Representations

Show a geometric representation for (a) $(2 + i) + (1 + 3i)$ and (b) $(3 + 5i) - (2 + i)$.

Solution

a) $(2 + i) + (1 + 3i)$ corresponds to the vertex R of the parallelogram $OPRQ$ in Fig. 9.27. To locate point R begin at $P(2,1)$ and move right 1 unit and up 3 units to the point with coordinates $(3, 4)$. The complex number that corresponds to the point with coordinate $(3, 4)$ is

$$(1 + 3i) + (2 + i) = (3 + 4i).$$

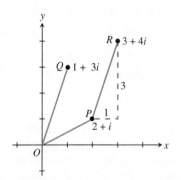

Figure 9.27 $(2 + i) + (1 + 3i)$.

b) $(3 + 5i) - (2 + i) = a + bi$, where $(a + bi) + (2 + i) = 3 + 5i$. Since $a + 2 = 3$ and $b + 1 = 5$, it is evident that $a = 1$ and $b = 4$. Therefore the complex number $a + bi$ is associated with point $(1, 4)$. See Fig. 9.28. ▧

Trigonometric Form for Complex Numbers

A common form for expressing complex numbers involves the trig functions $\sin \theta$ and $\cos \theta$. To develop this form we will use a geometric representation of complex numbers.

The complex number $a + bi$ corresponds to the point $P(a, b)$ in the complex plane. In Fig. 9.29 we see that for the right triangle determined by $z = a + bi$, the lengths of the three sides a, b, and r are given by

$$r = \sqrt{a^2 + b^2}, \qquad \cos \theta = \frac{a}{r}, \qquad \sin \theta = \frac{b}{r}.$$

Therefore we can write

$$a + bi = (r \cos \theta) + (r \sin \theta)i$$

$$= r(\cos \theta + i \sin \theta).$$

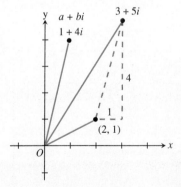

Figure 9.28 Finding $(3 + 5i) - (2 + i)$.

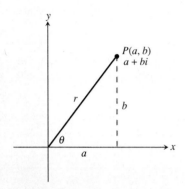

Figure 9.29   The complex number $a + bi$ determines a right triangle.

> **Definition 9.2   Trigonometric Form of a Complex Number**
>
> Let $z = a + bi \neq 0$ be a complex number. A **trigonometric form of** z is
>
> $$z = r(\cos\theta + i\sin\theta)$$
>
> where $a = r\cos\theta, b = r\sin\theta$, and $r = |z| = \sqrt{a^2 + b^2}$.

The angle θ can always be chosen so that $0 \leq \theta < 2\pi$, although any angle coterminal with θ could be used. Consequently the angle θ is not unique, and hence the trigonometric representation of z is not unique.

E X A M P L E   2   Finding Trigonometric Representations

Find the trigonometric representation with $0 \leq \theta < 2\pi$ for (a) $-2+2i$, (b) $3-3\sqrt{3}i$, and (c) $-3 - 4i$.

Solution   First calculate r, and then use that calculated value to find θ.

a) $r = |-2 + 2i| = \sqrt{(-2)^2 + 2^2} = \sqrt{8} = 2\sqrt{2}$. The angle θ formed by the positive x-axis and $-2 + 2i$ is $3\pi/4$ (Fig. 9.30a). Therefore

$$-2 + 2i = 2\sqrt{2}\left(\cos\frac{3\pi}{4} + i\sin\frac{3\pi}{4}\right).$$

b) $r = |3 - 3\sqrt{3}i| = \sqrt{9 + 27} = 6$. The angle θ formed by the positive x-axis and $3 - 3\sqrt{3}i$ is $5\pi/3$ (Fig. 9.30b). (Why?) Therefore

$$3 - 3\sqrt{3}i = 6\left(\frac{1}{2} - i\frac{\sqrt{3}}{2}\right) = 6\left(\cos\frac{5\pi}{3} + i\sin\frac{5\pi}{3}\right).$$

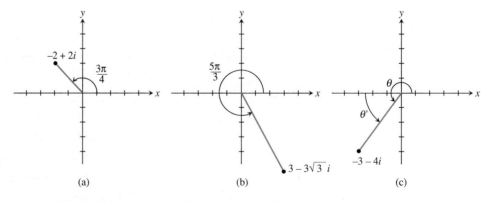

Figure 9.30   Graphs of the trigonometric representations for Example 2.

c) $r = |-3 - 4i| = \sqrt{(-3)^2 + (-4)^2} = 5$. Let θ be the angle that $-3 - 4i$ makes with the positive x-axis, and let θ' be the reference angle (Fig. 9.30c). Since $\tan\theta = (-4)/(-3)$,

$$\theta' = \tan^{-1}\left(\tfrac{4}{3}\right) = 0.9273.$$

It follows that $\theta = \pi + 0.9273 = 4.0689$. Therefore

$$-3 - 4i = 5(\cos 4.07 + i\sin 4.07).$$

The trigonometric representation of complex numbers is particularly convenient to use when multiplying or dividing complex numbers. The following theorem describes this method.

Theorem 9.5   Product and Quotient of Trig Representation

Let $z_1 = r_1(\cos\theta_1 + i\sin\theta_1)$ and $z_2 = r_2(\cos\theta_2 + i\sin\theta_2)$. Then

a) $z_1 z_2 = r_1 r_2\big[\cos(\theta_1 + \theta_2) + i\sin(\theta_1 + \theta_2)\big]$

b) $\dfrac{z_1}{z_2} = \dfrac{r_1}{r_2}\big[\cos(\theta_1 - \theta_2) + i\sin(\theta_1 - \theta_2)\big]$ $(r_2 \neq 0)$

Proof

a) Multiply z_1 and z_2 in the usual way and apply the identities for $\sin(\theta_1 + \theta_2)$ and $\cos(\theta_1 + \theta_2)$:

$$z_1 z_2 = [r_1(\cos\theta_1 + i\sin\theta_1)][r_2(\cos\theta_2 + i\sin\theta_2)]$$

$$= r_1 r_2[(\cos\theta_1\cos\theta_2 - \sin\theta_1\sin\theta_2) + i(\sin\theta_1\cos\theta_2 + \cos\theta_1\sin\theta_2)]$$

$$= r_1 r_2\big[\cos(\theta_1 + \theta_2) + i\sin(\theta_1 + \theta_2)\big]$$

b) To divide z_1 by z_2 first multiply the numerator and denominator by the complex conjugate of the portion of the denominator inside the parentheses:

$$\frac{z_1}{z_2} = \frac{r_1(\cos\theta_1 + i\sin\theta_1)}{r_2(\cos\theta_2 + i\sin\theta_2)}$$

$$= \frac{r_1}{r_2} \cdot \frac{(\cos\theta_1 + i\sin\theta_1)}{(\cos\theta_2 + i\sin\theta_2)} \cdot \frac{(\cos\theta_2 - i\sin\theta_2)}{(\cos\theta_2 - i\sin\theta_2)}$$

$$= \frac{r_1}{r_2} \cdot \frac{(\cos\theta_1\cos\theta_2 + \sin\theta_1\sin\theta_2) + i(\sin\theta_1\cos\theta_2 - \cos\theta_1\sin\theta_2)}{\cos^2\theta_2 + \sin^2\theta_2}$$

$$= \frac{r_1}{r_2}\big[\cos(\theta_1 - \theta_2) + i\sin(\theta_1 - \theta_2)\big] \quad \text{Use identities for the sine and cosine of the difference.}$$

E X A M P L E   3   Multiplying Complex Numbers

Suppose $z_1 = -2 + 2i$ and $z_2 = 3 - 3\sqrt{3}i$. Use the trigonometric form to find $z_1 z_2$, and confirm that your answer agrees with the product by using the definition of product.

Solution   In Example 2 we found that

$$-2 + 2i = 2\sqrt{2}\left(\cos\frac{3\pi}{4} + i\sin\frac{3\pi}{4}\right) \quad \text{and} \quad 3 - 3\sqrt{3}i = 6\left(\cos\frac{5\pi}{3} + i\sin\frac{5\pi}{3}\right).$$

We now compute $z_1 z_2$.

$$z_1 z_2 = (-2 + 2i)(3 - 3\sqrt{3}i)$$

$$= \left[2\sqrt{2}\left(\cos\frac{3\pi}{4} + i\sin\frac{3\pi}{4}\right)\right]\left[6\left(\cos\frac{5\pi}{3} + i\sin\frac{5\pi}{3}\right)\right] \qquad \text{Substitute the trig form.}$$

$$= 12\sqrt{2}\left[\cos\left(\frac{3\pi}{4} + \frac{5\pi}{3}\right) + i\sin\left(\frac{3\pi}{4} + \frac{5\pi}{3}\right)\right] \qquad \text{Apply Theorem 9.5.}$$

$$= 12\sqrt{2}\left(\cos\frac{29\pi}{12} + i\sin\frac{29\pi}{12}\right)$$

$$= 12\sqrt{2}\left(\cos\frac{5\pi}{12} + i\sin\frac{5\pi}{12}\right)$$

Use the definition for $z_1 z_2$ to obtain

$$(-2 + 2i)(3 - 3\sqrt{3}i) = (-6 + 6\sqrt{3}) + (6 + 6\sqrt{3})i.$$

Now use a calculator to confirm that $-6 + 6\sqrt{3}$ and $12\sqrt{2}\cos(5\pi/12)$ are equal, and that $6 + 6\sqrt{3}$ and $12\sqrt{2}\sin(5\pi/12)$ are equal. Therefore

$$(-6 + 6\sqrt{3}) + (6 + 6\sqrt{3})i = 12\sqrt{2}\left(\cos\frac{5\pi}{12} + i\sin\frac{5\pi}{12}\right). \qquad \blacksquare$$

E X A M P L E   4   Dividing Complex Numbers

Suppose $z_1 = -2 + 2i$ and $z_2 = 3 - 3\sqrt{3}i$. Use the trigonometric form to find z_1/z_2, and confirm that your answer agrees with the quotient using the definition of quotient.

Solution   Use Theorem 9.5 to find z_1/z_2:

$$\frac{z_1}{z_2} = \frac{-2 + 2i}{3 - 3\sqrt{3}i}$$

$$= \frac{2\sqrt{2}\left(\cos\frac{3\pi}{4} + i\sin\frac{3\pi}{4}\right)}{6\left(\cos\frac{5\pi}{3} + i\sin\frac{5\pi}{3}\right)}$$

$$= \frac{\sqrt{2}}{3}\left[\cos\left(\frac{3\pi}{4} - \frac{5\pi}{3}\right) + i\sin\left(\frac{3\pi}{4} - \frac{5\pi}{3}\right)\right]$$

$$= \frac{\sqrt{2}}{3}\left[\cos\left(-\frac{11\pi}{12}\right) + i\sin\left(-\frac{11\pi}{12}\right)\right]$$

$$= \frac{\sqrt{2}}{3}\left(\cos\frac{11\pi}{12} - i\sin\frac{11\pi}{12}\right)$$ Recall that $\cos(-x) = \cos x$ and $\sin(-x) = -\sin x$.

Another way to find the quotient is to multiply numerator and denominator by the conjugate of the denominator. Then

$$\frac{-2+2i}{3-3\sqrt{3}i} = \frac{-2+2i}{3-3\sqrt{3}i} \cdot \frac{3+3\sqrt{3}i}{3+3\sqrt{3}i}$$

$$= -\frac{1+\sqrt{3}}{6} + i\frac{1-\sqrt{3}}{6}.$$

Use a calculator to conclude that $-(1+\sqrt{3})/6$ and $(\sqrt{2}/3)\cos(11\pi/12)$ are equal, and that $(1-\sqrt{3})/6$ and $-(\sqrt{2}/3)\sin(11\pi/12)$ are equal. Therefore

$$-\frac{1+\sqrt{3}}{6} + \frac{1-\sqrt{3}}{6}i = \frac{\sqrt{2}}{3}\left(\cos\frac{11\pi}{12} - i\sin\frac{11\pi}{12}\right).$$ ∎

Exercises for Section 9.3

In Exercises 1 to 6, simplify and write in the form $a + bi$.

1. $(-1 + 2i) + (3 + 5i)$ **2.** $3(2 - 3i)$

3. $(2 - 4i)(3 + 2i)$ **4.** $(-1 + 2i)^2$

5. $\dfrac{1+i}{1-i}$ **6.** $\dfrac{2-3i}{4+5i}$

In Exercises 7 to 10, consider the complex numbers z_1 and z_2 as represented in the following figure.

7. If $z_1 = a + bi$, determine a, b, and $|z_1|$.

8. If $z_2 = a + bi$, determine a, b, and $|z_2|$.

9. Determine the trig form of z_1.

10. Determine the trig form of z_2.

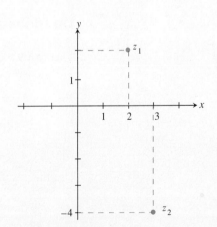

For Exercises 7 to 10

In Exercises 11 to 16, plot each of the following in the complex plane.

11. 3

12. $3i$

13. $4 - 4i$

14. $-4 + 3i$

15. $2(\cos 30° + i \sin 30°)$

16. $3\left(\cos \dfrac{\pi}{4} + i \sin \dfrac{\pi}{4}\right)$

In Exercises 17 to 28, find the trigonometric representation for each complex number such that $0 \le \theta < 2\pi$.

17. $1 + i$

18. $-1 + \sqrt{3}i$

19. $-2\sqrt{3} - 2i$

20. $3 - 4i$

21. $1 + 3i$

22. $-2 + 3i$

23. $3 - 4i$

24. $2i$

25. $2 + 3i$

26. $-4 + 4i$

27. $\sqrt{2} - 8i$

28. $-1 - 2i$

In Exercises 29 to 32, write the complex number in the form $a + bi$.

29. $2(\cos 60° + i \sin 60°)$

30. $5\left(\cos \dfrac{3\pi}{4} + i \sin \dfrac{3\pi}{4}\right)$

31. $3.4(\cos 5 + i \sin 5)$

32. $10(\cos 6\pi + i \sin 6\pi)$

In Exercises 33 to 36, complete each operation.

33. $2(\cos 30° + i \sin 30°) \cdot 3(\cos 60° + i \sin 60°)$

34. $\dfrac{2(\cos 30° + i \sin 30°)}{3(\cos 60° + i \sin 60°)}$

35. $\sqrt{2}(\cos 3 + i \sin 3) \cdot \sqrt{3}(\cos 5 + i \sin 5)$

36. $(2 - 3i)(-3 + 4i)$

In Exercises 37 to 40, use the trigonometric form to find the product and quotient of each pair of complex numbers.

37. $\dfrac{\sqrt{2}}{2} + \dfrac{\sqrt{2}}{2}i$ and $\dfrac{\sqrt{3}}{2} + \dfrac{1}{2}i$

38. $\dfrac{\sqrt{2}}{2} - \dfrac{\sqrt{2}}{2}i$ and $\dfrac{1}{2} + \dfrac{\sqrt{3}}{2}i$

39. $-3 + 3i$ and $\sqrt{3} - i$ **40.** $4 + 3i$ and $\sqrt{3} - i$

In Exercises 41 to 46, let $z_1 = -2 + 3i$, $z_2 = 3 + 4i$, and $z_3 = 2 - 5i$. Perform the indicated computation and write in the form $a + bi$.

41. $z_1 + z_2$

42. $4z_3$

43. $z_1 z_3$

44. $|z_1 - z_2|$

45. $|z_1 z_2|$

46. $\dfrac{z_2}{z_3}$

47. Determine $(1 + 3i) + (4 + 4i)$ using a geometric representation.

48. Determine $(-3 + i) - (4 + 2i)$ using a geometric representation.

9.4 _____   De Moivre's Theorem and *n*th Roots

Theorem 9.5 can be used to raise a complex number to a power. For example, let $z = r(\cos \theta + i \sin \theta)$. Then

$$z^2 = r(\cos \theta + i \sin \theta) \cdot r(\cos \theta + i \sin \theta)$$

$$= r^2[\cos(\theta + \theta) + i \sin(\theta + \theta)]$$

$$= r^2(\cos 2\theta + i \sin 2\theta)$$

Use this result to find z^3:

$$z^3 = z \cdot z^2 = r(\cos \theta + i \sin \theta) \cdot r^2(\cos 2\theta + i \sin 2\theta)$$

$$= r^3\left[\cos(\theta + 2\theta) + i \sin(\theta + 2\theta)\right]$$

$$= r^3(\cos 3\theta + i \sin 3\theta)$$

In a similar fashion we could find $z^4, z^5, \ldots$ and arrive at the generalization known as **De Moivre's theorem**.

Theorem 9.6   De Moivre's Theorem

Let n be any integer. Then

$$[r(\cos\theta + i\sin\theta)]^n = r^n(\cos n\theta + i\sin n\theta).$$

It is helpful to intepret De Moivre's theorem geometrically. When a complex number is squared, the angle in its trig form is doubled and its absolute value is squared. We see in Fig. 9.31 that drawing z^2 involves rotating z through an angle θ and stretching or shrinking it to its appropriate length. If z is outside the unit circle, then its absolute value is greater than 1 and z^2 is further away from the origin than z is (Fig. 9.31a). If z has an absolute value of 1 and is on the unit circle, then so is z^2 or any higher power of z (Fig. 9.31b). If z is inside the unit circle, then its absolute value is less than 1 and z^2 is closer to the origin than z is.

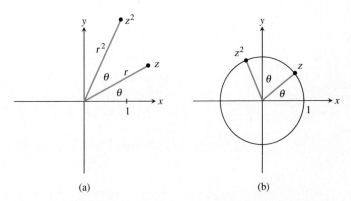

(a)   (b)

Figure 9.31   To find z^2, double the angle θ and square the modulus of z. (a) $|z| > 1$ and (b) $|z| = 1$.

E X A M P L E   1   Using De Moivre's Theorem

Find $(1 + \sqrt{3}i)^3$ using De Moivre's theorem.

Solution   Use the technique of Example 2 of Section 9.3 to write $1 + \sqrt{3}i$ in the trigonometric form $2[\cos(\pi/3) + i\sin(\pi/3)]$. Then

$$(1 + \sqrt{3}i)^3 = \left[2\left(\cos\frac{\pi}{3} + i\sin\frac{\pi}{3}\right)\right]^3$$

$$= 2^3\left[\cos\left(3\cdot\frac{\pi}{3}\right) + i\sin\left(3\cdot\frac{\pi}{3}\right)\right]$$

$$= 8(\cos\pi + i\sin\pi)$$

$$= 8(-1 + 0i) = -8.$$

$\blacksquare$

E X A M P L E   2   Using De Moivre's Theorem

Find $(-\sqrt{2}/2 + (\sqrt{2}/2)i)^8$ using De Moivre's theorem.

Solution   Begin by writing $-\sqrt{2}/2 + (\sqrt{2}/2i)$ in the trigonometric form $\cos(3\pi/4) + i\sin(3\pi/4)$. Then

$$\left(-\frac{\sqrt{2}}{2} + \frac{\sqrt{2}}{2}i\right)^8 = \left(\cos\frac{3\pi}{4} + i\sin\frac{3\pi}{4}\right)^8$$

$$= \cos\left(8\cdot\frac{3\pi}{4}\right) + i\sin\left(8\cdot\frac{3\pi}{4}\right)$$

$$= \cos 6\pi + i\sin 6\pi$$

$$= \cos 0 + i\sin 0$$

$$= 1 + 0i = 1$$

$\blacksquare$

Think how difficult it would be to compute $\left(-\sqrt{2}/2 + (\sqrt{2}/2)i\right)^8$ without using De Moivre's theorem.

Example 1 shows a complex number that satisfies the equation $z^3 = -8$, and Example 2 shows a complex number that satisfies the equation $z^8 = 1$. These equations suggest employing the terminology of *roots* used with real numbers.

Definition 9.3   nth Roots

Let a be a complex number and n be an integer greater than 1. An **nth root of a** is any complex number z satisfying the relation

$$z^n = a.$$

If z is a number satisfying $z^n = 1$, then z is called an **nth root of unity**.

From the definition of nth roots, we conclude that $1 + \sqrt{3}i$ in Example 1 is a third root of -8 and that $-\sqrt{2}/2 + (\sqrt{2}/2)i$ in Example 2 is an eighth root of unity.

E X A M P L E 3   Finding the Fourth Roots of Unity

Find and graph the fourth roots of unity, and give their trig forms in radians.

Solution   Find these roots by solving the equation $z^4 = 1$ algebraically:

$$z^4 = 1$$

$$z^4 - 1 = 0$$

$$(z^2 - 1)(z^2 + 1) = 0$$

$$(z - 1)(z + 1)(z^2 + 1) = 0$$

We conclude from these equations that the four fourth roots of unity are 1, -1, $-i$, and i, as shown in Fig. 9.32.

Next give their trig forms in radians:

$$1 = \cos 0 + i \sin 0 = 1 + 0i$$

$$i = \cos \frac{\pi}{2} + i \sin \frac{\pi}{2} = 0 + i$$

$$-1 = \cos \pi + i \sin \pi = 1 + 0i$$

$$-i = \cos \frac{3\pi}{2} + i \sin \frac{3\pi}{2} = 0 - i$$

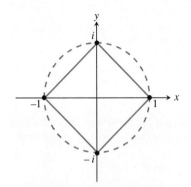

Figure 9.32   Fourth roots of unity.

Notice that the points representing the fourth roots of unity are evenly spaced $90°$ apart on the unit circle and therefore are the vertices of a square. This same geometric interpretation of De Moivre's theorem applies to all the roots of unity. Example 4 repeats this development for the eighth roots of unity.

E X A M P L E 4   Verifying Eighth Roots of Unity

Show that

$$z = \cos \frac{2\pi}{8} + i \sin \frac{2\pi}{8}$$

is an eighth root of unity. Also show that the kth power of z for any value k is an eighth root of unity.

Solution   According to De Moivre's theorem

$$z^8 = \left(\cos \frac{2\pi}{8} + i \sin \frac{2\pi}{8} \right)^8 = \cos \left(8 \cdot \frac{2\pi}{8} \right) + i \sin \left(8 \cdot \frac{2\pi}{8} \right)$$

$$= \cos 2\pi + i \sin 2\pi$$

$$= 1.$$

Therefore $z = \cos(2\pi/8) + i \sin(2\pi/8)$ is an eighth root of unity.

Next show that z^k is an eighth root:

$$(z^k)^8 = \left(\cos \frac{2k\pi}{8} + i \sin \frac{2k\pi}{8} \right)^8 = \cos \left(8 \cdot \frac{2k\pi}{8} \right) + i \sin \left(8 \cdot \frac{2k\pi}{8} \right)$$

$$= \cos 2k\pi + i \sin 2k\pi$$

$$= 1$$

Since there are eight distinct powers of z shown in Fig. 9.33, there are eight distinct eighth roots of unity, which are the vertices of a regular octagon.   ≣

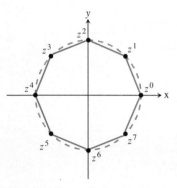

Figure 9.33   Eighth roots of unity.

The following Exploration will provide methods of visualizing the nth roots of unity.

🔍 EXPLORE WITH A GRAPHING UTILITY

Set your graphing utility as follows:

- Deg mode,   Param (parametric) mode

- Range: Tmin = 0, Tmax = 360, Tstep = 45

- Viewing rectangle: $[-1.5, 1.5]$ by $[-1, 1]$
- $X_1(T) = \cos T$ $Y_1(T) = \sin T$

1. Describe what you see when you press GRAPH.

2. Use the TRACE key to see the eighth roots of unity.

3. Change the Tstep value to show the fourth roots of unity.

4. Change the Tstep value to show the sixth roots of unity.

Generalize   What Tstep value is needed to obtain a picture of the nth roots of unity?

Examples 3 and 4 together with experiences from this Exploration should make it plausible that there are n nth roots of unity for each positive integer n.

Theorem 9.7 nth roots of Unity

Let n be an integer greater than 1. The complex number

$$z = \cos \frac{2\pi}{n} + i \sin \frac{2\pi}{n}$$

is an nth root of unity. The n nth roots of unity are

$$z^0, z^1, z^2, \ldots, z^{n-1}.$$

Using Theorem 9.7, we can apply the techniques used to find roots of unity to finding roots of other complex numbers.

EXAMPLE 5   Finding the Cube Roots of -1

Find and graph the cube roots of -1.

Solution   The cube roots of -1 are the solutions to $z^3 = -1$. Since $(-1)^3 = -1$, conclude that -1 is a cube root of -1.

It is reasonable to expect the cube roots of -1 to be evenly spaced on the unit circle. The geometry of Fig. 9.34 suggests that $\cos 60° + i \sin 60°$ and $\cos(-60)° + i \sin(-60)°$ should also be cube roots of -1. Use De Moivre's theorem to verify these claims.

$$(\cos 60° + i \sin 60°)^3 = \cos 180° + i \sin 180°$$
$$= -1 + 0i$$
$$= -1$$

$$[\cos(-60°) + i \sin(-60°)]^3 = \cos(-180°) + i \sin(-180°)$$
$$= -1 + 0i$$
$$= -1$$

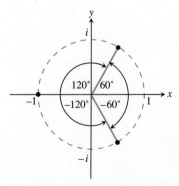

Figure 9.34   Cube roots of -1.

We have verified that

$$\cos 60° + i \sin 60° = \frac{1}{2} + i \frac{\sqrt{3}}{2}, \qquad \text{and}$$

$$\cos(-60°) + i \sin(-60°) = \frac{1}{2} - i \frac{\sqrt{3}}{2}.$$

Therefore,

$$\frac{1}{2} + i\frac{\sqrt{3}}{2} \qquad \text{and} \qquad \frac{1}{2} - i\frac{\sqrt{3}}{2}$$

are cube roots of -1.

E X A M P L E   6   Finding the Cube Roots of -8

Find and graph the cube roots of -8.

Solution   If $z = r(\cos\theta + i\sin\theta)$ is a cube root of -8, then

$$z^3 = -8$$

$$[r(\cos\theta + i\sin\theta)]^3 = -8$$

$$r^3(\cos 3\theta + i\sin 3\theta) = -8.$$

To complete the problem, write the complex number -8 in its trig form $-8 = 8(\cos\pi + i\sin\pi)$ and substitute into the right-hand side of the above equation to obtain

$$r^3(\cos 3\theta + i\sin 3\theta) = 8(\cos\pi + i\sin\pi).$$

This equation is satisfied if $r^3 = 8$ and 3θ is any angle coterminal with π. Thus

$$r = 2 \qquad \text{and} \qquad 3\theta = \pi + 2k\pi,$$

or equivalently,

$$r = 2 \qquad \text{and} \qquad \theta = \frac{\pi}{3} + \frac{2k\pi}{3}.$$

Notice that

$$\theta = \begin{cases} \pi/3 & \text{if } k = 0 \\ \pi & \text{if } k = 1 \\ 5\pi/3 & \text{if } k = 2. \end{cases}$$

Any other integer value of k produces an angle coterminal with one of these three angles, so the three distinct cube roots of -8 are

$$2\left(\cos\frac{\pi}{3} + i\sin\frac{\pi}{3}\right) = 2\left(\frac{1}{2} + i\frac{\sqrt{3}}{2}\right) = 1 + i\sqrt{3}$$

$$2\left(\cos\pi + i\sin\pi\right) = -2$$

$$2\left(\cos\frac{5\pi}{3} + i\sin\frac{5\pi}{3}\right) = 2\left(\frac{1}{2} - i\frac{\sqrt{3}}{2}\right) = 1 - i\sqrt{3}.$$

See Fig. 9.35.

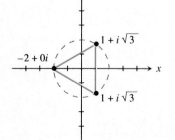

Figure 9.35   Cube roots of -8.

Examples 5 and 6 found the cube roots of numbers other than 1. In fact, it is possible to find nth roots of any complex number as described in the following theorem.

Theorem 9.8 nth Roots of a Complex Number

Let n be an integer greater than 1, and let $z = r(\cos\theta + i\sin\theta)$ be any complex number. Then z has n distinct nth roots as follows:

$$z_k = \sqrt[n]{r}\left[\cos\left(\frac{\theta + 2k\pi}{n}\right) + i\sin\left(\frac{\theta + 2k\pi}{n}\right)\right]$$

for $k = 0, 1, 2, \ldots, n-1$. The n distinct nth roots lie on the circle of radius $\sqrt[n]{r}$ centered at the origin and determine a regular polygon with n equal sides.

We use Theorem 9.8 to complete Example 7.

E X A M P L E 7   Finding the Fifth Roots of $1 + i$

Find the fifth roots of $1 + i$, and write these complex numbers in trig form.

Solution

$$1 + i = \sqrt{2}\left(\cos\frac{\pi}{4} + i\sin\frac{\pi}{4}\right)$$

Use Theorem 9.8 to conclude that the fifth roots of $1 + i$ are as follows:

$$z_1 = \sqrt[10]{2}\left(\cos\frac{\pi}{4} + i\sin\frac{\pi}{4}\right)$$

$$z_2 = \sqrt[10]{2}\left[\cos\left(\frac{\pi}{20} + \frac{2\pi}{5}\right) + i\sin\left(\frac{\pi}{20} + \frac{2\pi}{5}\right)\right] = \sqrt[10]{2}\left(\cos\frac{9\pi}{20} + i\sin\frac{9\pi}{20}\right)$$

$$z_3 = \sqrt[10]{2}\left[\cos\left(\frac{\pi}{20} + \frac{4\pi}{5}\right) + i\sin\left(\frac{\pi}{20} + \frac{4\pi}{5}\right)\right] = \sqrt[10]{2}\left(\cos\frac{17\pi}{20} + i\sin\frac{17\pi}{20}\right)$$

$$z_4 = \sqrt[10]{2}\left[\cos\left(\frac{\pi}{20} + \frac{6\pi}{5}\right) + i\sin\left(\frac{\pi}{20} + \frac{6\pi}{5}\right)\right] = \sqrt[10]{2}\left(\cos\frac{25\pi}{20} + i\sin\frac{25\pi}{20}\right)$$

$$z_5 = \sqrt[10]{2}\left[\cos\left(\frac{\pi}{20} + \frac{8\pi}{5}\right) + i\sin\left(\frac{\pi}{20} + \frac{8\pi}{5}\right)\right] = \sqrt[10]{2}\left(\cos\frac{33\pi}{20} + i\sin\frac{33\pi}{20}\right)$$

Exercises for Section 9.4

In Exercises 1 to 6, write each complex number in trig form such that $0 \le \theta < 2\pi$.

1. $3 - 4i$ **2.** $-2 + 2i$ **3.** $5 + 3i$

4. $8 - 5i$ **5.** $-2i$ **6.** -10

In Exercises 7 to 16, raise each complex number to the indicated power.

7. $\left(\cos \dfrac{\pi}{4} + i \sin \dfrac{\pi}{4} \right)^3$ **8.** $\left(\cos \dfrac{\pi}{3} + i \sin \dfrac{\pi}{3} \right)^4$

9. $2(\cos \pi + i \sin \pi)^6$ **10.** $3 \left(\cos \dfrac{3\pi}{2} + i \sin \dfrac{3\pi}{2} \right)^5$

11. $(1 + i)^5$ **12.** $(3 + 4i)^{20}$

13. $(1 - \sqrt{3}i)^3$ **14.** $-\left(\dfrac{\sqrt{2}}{2} + i \dfrac{\sqrt{2}}{2} \right)^4$

15. $\left(\dfrac{1}{2} + i \dfrac{\sqrt{3}}{2} \right)^3$ **16.** $(3 - 4i)^5$

17. Find $(2 + i)^2$ in two ways: (a) using De Moivre's theorem, and (b) using the definition of multiplication of complex numbers. Show that the results are the same with each method.

18. Use a hand-held graphing utility as in the preceding Exploration to show the cube roots of unity. Write these roots in the form $a + bi$ where a and b are decimals.

19. Use a hand-held graphing utility as in the preceding Exploration to show the fifth roots of unity. Write these roots in the form $a + bi$ where a and b are decimals.

20. If $z = \cos(\pi/4) + i \sin(\pi/4)$, write z^2, z^4, z^5, and z^7 in trig form such that $0 \le \theta < 2\pi$.

21. Show that each of these complex numbers is an eighth root of unity.

$$\frac{1}{\sqrt{2}} + \frac{1}{\sqrt{2}}i, \quad -\frac{1}{\sqrt{2}} + \frac{1}{\sqrt{2}}i,$$

$$-\frac{1}{\sqrt{2}} - \frac{1}{\sqrt{2}}i, \quad \frac{1}{\sqrt{2}} - \frac{1}{\sqrt{2}}i$$

In Exercises 22 to 24, express these roots of unity in the form $a + bi$ where a and b are real numbers expressed as exact values.

22. Sixth roots of unity

23. Eighth roots of unity

24. Cube roots of unity

In Exercises 25 to 30, find the nth roots of each complex number for the specified value of n. Graph each nth root in the complex plane.

25. $1, \quad n = 4$ **26.** $1, \quad n = 6$

27. $2 + 2i, \quad n = 4$ **28.** $-2 + 2i, \quad n = 4$

29. $-2 + 2i, \quad n = 6$ **30.** $32, \quad n = 5$

31. Determine z and the three cube roots of z if one cube root of z is $1 + \sqrt{3}i$. Graph the roots.

32. Determine z and the four fourth roots of z if one fourth root of z is $-2 - 2i$. Graph the roots.

33. Solve $z^4 = 5 - 5i$, and graph the solutions.

34. Solve $z^6 = 2i$, and graph the solutions.

35. Show that $(-1 + i)^{12} = -64$.

36. In Exercise 35 you found that $-1 + i$ was a 12th root of -64. Determine the other eleven 12th roots of -64, and graph each in the complex plane.

9.5 _____ Vectors

A **vector** is a directed line segment. For example, $\overrightarrow{AB}$ denotes the vector determined by the line segment AB with direction assigned from A to B (see Fig. 9.36).

A is called the **initial point of $\overrightarrow{AB}$**, and B is called the **terminal point** of $\overrightarrow{AB}$.

The **magnitude of $\overrightarrow{AB}$** is the length of line segment AB and is denoted $|\overrightarrow{AB}|$.

Notice that vectors $\overrightarrow{AB}$ and $\overrightarrow{BA}$ have the same magnitude but opposite directions.

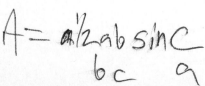

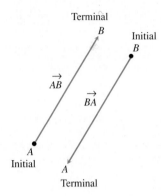

Figure 9.36   Vectors $\overrightarrow{AB}$ and $\overrightarrow{BA}$.

A coordinate system is necessary in order to calculate the magnitude and direction of a vector.

E X A M P L E   1   Finding Magnitude and Direction

Let $A = (1, 2)$ and $B = (5, 4)$. Find the following:

a) the magnitude of $\overrightarrow{AB}$;

b) the angle θ that $\overrightarrow{AB}$ makes with the positive x-axis (see Fig. 9.37);

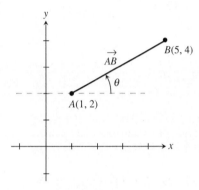

Figure 9.37   Graph for Example 1, part b.

c) the magnitude and direction of $\overrightarrow{BA}$.

Solution

a) By the distance formula the magnitude of $\overrightarrow{AB}$ is

$$\sqrt{(5 - 1)^2 + (4 - 2)^2} = \sqrt{20}.$$

b) If θ is the direction of $\overrightarrow{AB}$ with the positive x-axis, then $\tan\theta = \frac{2}{4}$. (Why?) Therefore

$$\theta = \tan^{-1}\left(\frac{1}{2}\right)$$

$$= 26.57°.$$

c) The magnitude of $\overrightarrow{BA}$ is also $\sqrt{20}$. Its direction is $26.57° + 180° = 206.57°$.

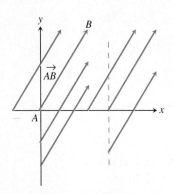

Figure 9.38   Some vectors equal to $\overrightarrow{AB}$.

In physics a **force** is a quantity that has both magnitude and direction, so a vector can be used to represent a force. Two vectors with the same direction and magnitude model the same force. Consequently, we call two such vectors equal. That is, two **vectors are equal** if and only if they have the same magnitude and direction.

Figure 9.38 shows several of the infinitely many vectors that are equal to vector $\overrightarrow{AB}$. Notice that any vector in the figure can be obtained from $\overrightarrow{AB}$ by horizontal or vertical shifts or by a combination of the two.

This observation leads to the following theorem.

Theorem 9.9   Equal Vectors

Vectors $\overrightarrow{AB}$ and $\overrightarrow{CD}$ are equal if and only if $\overrightarrow{AB}$ can be obtained from $\overrightarrow{CD}$ by applying an appropriate combination of horizontal and/or vertical shifts.

E X A M P L E   2   Demonstrating Vector Equivalence

Let $A = (-4, 2)$, $B = (-1, 6)$, $O = (0, 0)$, and $P = (3, 4)$. Show that $\overrightarrow{AB} = \overrightarrow{OP}$.

Solution

$$|\overrightarrow{AB}| = \sqrt{[-1 - (-4)]^2 + (6 - 2)^2} = \sqrt{3^2 + 4^2} = 5$$

$$|\overrightarrow{OP}| = \sqrt{3^2 + 4^2} = 5$$

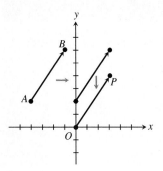

Figure 9.39 $\overrightarrow{AB}$ is equal to $\overrightarrow{OP}$.

We can obtain $\overrightarrow{OP}$ from $\overrightarrow{AB}$ by shifting right 4 units and then shifting the resulting vector down 2 units (see Fig. 9.39).   ≡

Theorem 9.9 and Example 1 allow us to draw the following conclusion. Given any vector $\overrightarrow{AB}$, there is a *unique* point P such that $\overrightarrow{AB} = \overrightarrow{OP}$ where O is the origin. Furthermore, any point P determines a unique vector $\overrightarrow{OP}$.

If (x, y) is the terminal point of a vector **v** whose initial point is $(0, 0)$, we will write $\mathbf{v} = (x, y)$ because **v** is completely determined by its terminal point. We call x the **x-component** and y the **y-component** of vector **v**. Notice that the magnitude $|\mathbf{v}|$ is equal to $\sqrt{x^2 + y^2}$.

AGREEMENT

We agree that from now on $\mathbf{v} = (x, y)$ represents the unique vector $\overrightarrow{OP}$ when $P = (x, y)$.

E X A M P L E   3   Finding Equal Vectors **v**

Let $A = (2, 5), B = (4, 6), C = (-3, 4)$, and $D = (-5, -2)$ be four points. Determine the vector $\mathbf{v} = (x, y)$ that is equal (a) to $\overrightarrow{AB}$ and (b) to $\overrightarrow{CD}$.

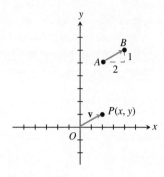

Figure 9.40 Equal vectors for Example 3, part a.

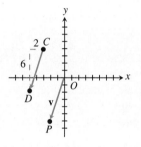

Figure 9.41 Equal vectors for Example 3, part b.

Solution

a) The terminal point B of $\overrightarrow{AB}$ is 2 units right and 1 unit up from the initial point A. So the terminal point P of $\overrightarrow{OP}$ must also be 2 units right and 1 unit up from the initial point $(0, 0)$. Thus $P = (2, 1)$ and $\mathbf{v} = (2, 1)$ (see Fig. 9.40).

b) P must be 2 units left and 6 units down from the origin, so $P = (-2, -6)$. Therefore $\mathbf{v} = (-2, -6)$ (see Fig. 9.41).   ≡

Notice in Example 3, part a, that the coordinates of vector $\mathbf{v} = (2, 1)$ can be obtained by subtracting the coordinates of point $A = (2, 5)$ from the coordinates of point $B = (4, 6)$. That is, $\mathbf{v} = (2, 1) = (4 - 2, 6 - 5)$. Similarly, for the vector of Example 3, part b, we have $\mathbf{v} = (-2, -6) = (-5 - (-3), -2 - 4)$. These are special cases of the following theorem.

Theorem 9.10   Finding the Terminal Point of a Vector

Let $A = (a_1, a_2)$ and $B = (b_1, b_2)$ be two points, and let $\mathbf{v} = (x, y)$ be the vector that is equal to $\overrightarrow{AB}$. Then

$$x = b_1 - a_1 \text{ and } y = b_2 - a_2.$$

That is, $\mathbf{v} = (x, y) = (b_1 - a_1, b_2 - a_2)$.

Addition and Subtraction of Vectors

Since vectors model force, vector addition should be defined so that it models the way forces add together. And forces add according to a parallelogram property.

The sum of vectors $\mathbf{u}$ and $\mathbf{v}$ is represented by the diagonal of the parallelogram whose sides are $\mathbf{u}$ and $\mathbf{v}$. Figure 9.42 shows that $\mathbf{u} + \mathbf{v}$ is equal to $\mathbf{v} + \mathbf{u}$.

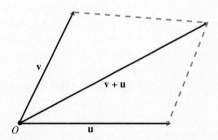

Figure 9.42 $\mathbf{u} + \mathbf{v} = \mathbf{v} + \mathbf{u}$.

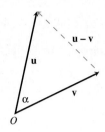

Figure 9.43 $\mathbf{v} + (\mathbf{u} - \mathbf{v})$.

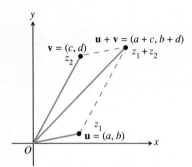

Figure 9.44 Complex number addition and vector addition.

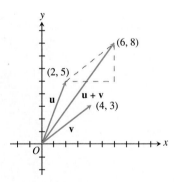

Figure 9.45 Figure for Example 4(b).

The difference of two vectors $\mathbf{u}$ and $\mathbf{v}$, denoted $\mathbf{u} - \mathbf{v}$, is the vector that when added to $\mathbf{v}$ gives $\mathbf{u}$ (see Fig. 9.43). That is, $\mathbf{v} + (\mathbf{u} - \mathbf{v}) = \mathbf{u}$. Notice that the initial point of vector $\mathbf{u} - \mathbf{v}$ is the terminal point of $\mathbf{v}$ and that the terminal point of $\mathbf{u} - \mathbf{v}$ is the terminal point of $\mathbf{u}$.

Vector addition and subtraction can also be defined in terms of vector components.

Definition 9.4 Vector Addition and Subtraction

Suppose $\mathbf{u} = (a, b)$ and $\mathbf{v} = (c, d)$. Then

$$\mathbf{u} + \mathbf{v} = (a, b) + (c, d) = (a + c, b + d)$$

$$\mathbf{u} - \mathbf{v} = (a, b) - (c, d) = (a - c, b - d).$$

Notice that the vectors $\mathbf{u} = (a, b)$ and $\mathbf{v} = (c, d)$ can also be represented by the complex numbers $z_1 = a + bi$ and $z_2 = c + di$. Figure 9.26 was used in Section 9.3 to represent addition of complex numbers. We duplicate it here as Fig. 9.44 to show that it also illustrates the vector sum $\mathbf{u} + \mathbf{v}$ where $\mathbf{u} = (a, b)$ and $\mathbf{v} = (c, d)$.

E X A M P L E 4   *Doing Vector Addition*

Let $\mathbf{u} = (2, 5)$ and $\mathbf{v} = (4, 3)$. Find $\mathbf{u} + \mathbf{v}$ using (a) component addition and (b) a geometric definition.

Solution

a) See Fig. 9.45.

$$\mathbf{u} + \mathbf{v} = (2, 5) + (4, 3)$$
$$= (2 + 4, 5 + 3)$$
$$= (6, 8)$$

b) Consider the vector equal to $\mathbf{v} = (4, 3)$ with initial point $(2, 5)$. Its terminal point is $(6, 8)$. Therefore

$$\mathbf{u} + \mathbf{v} = (6, 8).$$

Multiplication of a Vector by a Scalar

A vector can be multiplied by a real number, called a **scalar**, to obtain another vector. A geometric model for multiplication of a vector by a scalar is the following. If a vector $\mathbf{v}$ is multiplied by a positive scalar a, then $\mathbf{v}$ is stretched (if $a > 1$) or shrunk (if $0 < a < 1$) by the factor a. If $\mathbf{v}$ is multiplied by a negative scalar a, then the direction of $\mathbf{v}$ is reversed as well as being stretched or shrunk (see Fig. 9.46).

The multiplication of a vector by a scalar can also be defined in terms of the components of the vector.

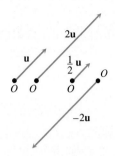

Figure 9.46 Examples of vector-scalar multiplication.

Definition 9.5   Multiplication of a Vector by a Scalar

Suppose that r is any real number and that $\mathbf{v} = (a, b)$ is any vector. Then the **scalar product** $r\mathbf{v}$ is defined to be

$$r\mathbf{v} = r(a, b) = (ra, rb).$$

Notice that a scalar product always yields a new *vector*, not a scalar.

E X A M P L E 5   Completing Vector-Scalar Computations

Let $r = 2, s = 3, \mathbf{u} = (-1, 3)$, and $\mathbf{v} = (2, -4)$. Find $r\mathbf{u} + s\mathbf{v}$ and $|r\mathbf{u} + s\mathbf{v}|$.

Solution

a) $r\mathbf{u} + s\mathbf{v} = 2(-1, 3) + 3(2, -4)$

$$= (-2, 6) + (6, -12)$$

$$= (-2 + 6, 6 + (-12))$$

$$= (4, -6)$$

b) $|r\mathbf{u} + s\mathbf{v}| = |(4, -6)|$

$$= \sqrt{4^2 + (-6)^2}$$

$$= \sqrt{16 + 36}$$

$$= \sqrt{52} = 2\sqrt{13}$$

Linear Combinations of Vectors

The vector $r\mathbf{u} + s\mathbf{v}$ in Example 5 is an example of a linear combination of vectors $\mathbf{u}$ and $\mathbf{v}$.

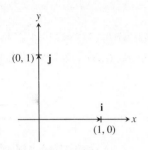

Figure 9.47 Unit vectors.

Definition 9.6 Linear Combination

The vector **w** is said to be a **linear combination of the vectors u and v** if there are scalars a and b such that

$$\mathbf{w} = a\mathbf{u} + b\mathbf{v}.$$

The two vectors $\mathbf{i} = (1, 0)$ and $\mathbf{j} = (0, 1)$ have magnitudes of 1 and consequently are called **unit vectors** (see Fig. 9.47). Every vector can be written as a linear combination of these two unit vectors in a very natural way. For example, let $\mathbf{v} = (a, b)$ be any vector. Then

$$\mathbf{v} = (a, b)$$
$$= (a, 0) + (0, b)$$
$$= a(1, 0) + b(0, 1)$$
$$= a\mathbf{i} + b\mathbf{j}.$$

Notice that the scalars in this case are the x- and y-components of the vector $\mathbf{v} = (a, b)$ (see Fig. 9.48).

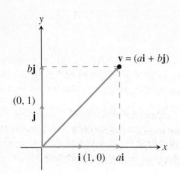

Figure 9.48 **v** as a linear combination of **i** and **j**.

Relationship between Vector Components and Vector Direction

The next theorem explains how the components of a vector **v** can be found if both the angle that **v** forms with the positive x-axis and its absolute value are known.

Theorem 9.11 Finding Vector Components

Let $\mathbf{v} = (a, b)$ be any vector and P be the point with coordinates (a, b). If θ is an angle in standard position with terminal side OP, then

$$a = |\mathbf{v}| \cos \theta \quad \text{and} \quad b = |\mathbf{v}| \sin \theta.$$

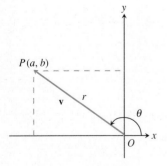

Figure 9.49 Finding the components of $\mathbf{v} = (a, b)$.

Proof We see from Fig. 9.49 that

$$|\mathbf{v}| = \sqrt{a^2 + b^2} = r, \qquad \cos \theta = \frac{a}{r}, \qquad \sin \theta = \frac{b}{r}.$$

Therefore

$$a = |\mathbf{v}| \cos \theta \quad \text{and} \quad b = |\mathbf{v}| \sin \theta. \qquad \blacksquare$$

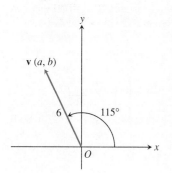

Figure 9.50   Vector **v** given for Example 6.

E X A M P L E   6   Finding the Components of a Vector

Find the components of the vector shown in Fig. 9.50.

Solution   We apply Theorem 9.11.

$$a = 6\cos 115° = -2.54 \quad \text{and} \quad b = 6\sin 115° = 5.44$$

Thus **v** $= (-2.54, 5.44)$.

In Example 6 we were given both the direction and magnitude of a vector and asked to find its components. Example 7 gives us the components of two vectors and asks us to find their directions.

E X A M P L E   7   Finding the Direction of a Vector

Let **u** $= (3, 2)$ and **v** $= (-2, 5)$. Find the following:

a) the angle each vector makes with the positive x-axis;

b) the angle with initial side **u** and terminal side **v**.

Solution   Study Fig. 9.51.

a)
$$\tan \alpha = \tfrac{2}{3} \text{ and therefore } \alpha = \tan^{-1}\left(\tfrac{2}{3}\right) = 33.6901°$$

$$\tan \beta = -\left(\tfrac{5}{2}\right) \text{ and } \tan^{-1}\left(-\tfrac{5}{2}\right) = -68.1986°$$

The angle β is in the second quadrant, and $\tan^{-1}\left(-\tfrac{5}{2}\right) = -68.1986°$ is in the fourth quadrant. Therefore $\beta = 180° + \tan^{-1}\left(-\tfrac{5}{2}\right) = 111.8014°$.

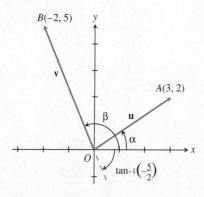

Figure 9.51   Solving **u** and **v** for Example 7.

b) Notice from Fig. 9.51 that the angle θ with initial side **u** and terminal side **v** is $\beta - \alpha$, or $78.11°$.

Using the Law of Cosines

In Example 7, part(b), the angle between two vectors was found. Example 8 shows an alternate way to complete this calculation.

E X A M P L E 8   Finding the Angle between Two Vectors

Find the angle $\beta - \alpha$ from vector $\mathbf{u} = (3, 2)$ to vector $\mathbf{v} = (-2, 5)$ shown in Fig. 9.51.

Solution Apply the law of cosines to triangle AOB.

$$d^2(A, B) = |\mathbf{u}|^2 + |\mathbf{v}|^2 - 2|\mathbf{u}||\mathbf{v}| \cos(\beta - \alpha)$$

$$34 = 13 + 29 - 2\sqrt{13}\sqrt{29} \, \cos(\beta - \alpha)$$

$$\beta - \alpha = \cos^{-1}\left(\frac{13 + 29 - 34}{2\sqrt{13}\sqrt{29}}\right)$$

$$\beta - \alpha = 78.11°$$

Applications of Vectors

We have already pointed out that vectors model forces in physics. The **velocity** of a moving object is another physical situation modeled by vectors because velocity has both magnitude and direction. Usually the magnitude of velocity is called **speed**.

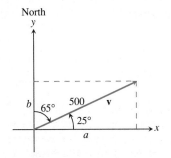

Figure 9.52 Model for the velocity of the plane in Example 9.

E X A M P L E 9   APPLICATION: Plane Velocity

A plane is flying on a bearing 65° east of north at 500 mph. Express the velocity of the plane as a vector.

Solution The vector $\mathbf{v}$ in Fig. 9.52 represents the velocity of the plane.

Direction: 65° east of north is 25° north of east.

Magnitude: $|\mathbf{v}| = 500$ since the plane is flying 500 mph.
     Apply Theorem 9.11 to get:

$$\mathbf{v} = (500 \cos 25°, 500 \sin 25°)$$

$$= (453.15, 211.31)$$

The next example illustrates the kind of problem that a flight engineer must solve on a daily basis.

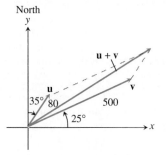

North

Figure 9.53 Model of the velocity of the plane described in Example 10.

EXAMPLE 10   APPLICATION: Actual Speed and Velocity

A plane is flying on a bearing of 65° east of north at 500 mph. A tail wind that adds to the plane's velocity is blowing in the direction 35° east of north at 80 mph. Express the actual velocity of the plane as a vector. Determine the actual speed of the plane.

Solution   Let **v** the velocity of the plane and let **u** be the velocity of the wind. See Fig. 9.53.

From Example 9 we know that $\mathbf{v} = (453.15, 211.31)$.

Since **u** has a direction 55° north of east,

$$\mathbf{u} = (80\cos 55°, 80\sin 55°) = (45.89, 65.53).$$

The actual velocity of the plane is $\mathbf{u} + \mathbf{v}$:

$$\mathbf{u} + \mathbf{v} = (45.89, 65.53) + (453.15, 211.31)$$

$$= (499.04, 276.84)$$

The speed of the plane is $|\mathbf{u} + \mathbf{v}| = \sqrt{499.04^2 + 276.84^2} = 570.69$ mph.   ▬

Usually pilots face a slightly different problem. The actual speed and direction $\mathbf{u} + \mathbf{v}$ are known as well as the tail-wind or head-wind vector **u**. The flight bearing must be established. This problem is explored in Exercises 43 and 44.

Exercises for Section 9.5

In Exercises 1 to 4, find the magnitude of vector $\overrightarrow{AB}$ and the angle that $\overrightarrow{AB}$ makes with the positive x-axis.

1. $A = (1, 2)$, $B = (4, 5)$ **2.** $A = (2, 3)$, $B = (-3, 2)$

3. $A = (-2, 5)$, $B = (1, 4)$ **4.** $A = (1, 3)$, $B = (2, 5)$

In Exercises 5 to 12, let $\mathbf{u} = (-1, 3)$, $\mathbf{v} = (2, 4)$, and $\mathbf{w} = (2, -5)$ be vectors. Calculate the following.

5. $\mathbf{u} + \mathbf{v}$ **6.** $\mathbf{u} - \mathbf{v}$

7. $\mathbf{u} - \mathbf{w}$ **8.** $3\mathbf{v}$

9. $2\mathbf{u} + 3\mathbf{w}$ **10.** $2\mathbf{u} - 4\mathbf{v}$

11. $|\mathbf{u} + \mathbf{v}|$ **12.** $|\mathbf{u} - \mathbf{v}|$

In Exercises 13 and 14, use the geometric definitions of addition and subtraction of vectors to find the sum $\mathbf{u} + \mathbf{v}$ and the difference $\mathbf{u} - \mathbf{v}$. Compare your answers with the results obtained using the respective componentwise definitions.

13. $\mathbf{u} = (1, 3)$, $\mathbf{v} = (3, 6)$ **14.** $\mathbf{u} = (-1, 2)$, $\mathbf{v} = (4, -2)$

In Exercises 15 to 20, let $A = (-1, 2)$, $B = (3, 4)$, $C = (-2, 5)$, and $D = (2, -8)$. Write each of the following in the form $\mathbf{v} = (x, y)$.

15. $\overrightarrow{AB}$ **16.** $\overrightarrow{CD}$

17. $3\overrightarrow{AB}$ **18.** $2\overrightarrow{AB} - \overrightarrow{BA}$

19. $\overrightarrow{AB} + \overrightarrow{CD}$ **20.** $2\overrightarrow{AB} + \overrightarrow{CD}$

In Exercises 21 to 24, compute the following:

21. $|\overrightarrow{AB}|$

22. $|2\overrightarrow{AB}|$

23. $|\overrightarrow{AB} + \overrightarrow{BA}|$

24. $|\overrightarrow{AB} + \overrightarrow{CD}|$

In Exercises 25 and 26, show geometrically that $\overrightarrow{AB} = \overrightarrow{OB} - \overrightarrow{OA}$.

25. $A = (2,3)$, $B = (5,2)$

26. $A = (-2,4)$, $B = (2,6)$

In Exercises 27 and 30, express $\overrightarrow{AB}$ as a linear combination of $\mathbf{i} = (1,0)$ and $\mathbf{j} = (0,1)$.

27. $A = (3,0)$, $B = (0,6)$ **28.** $A = (2,1)$, $B = (5,0)$

29. $A = (3,-2)$, $B = (2,6)$

30. $A = (-2,1)$, $B = (-3,-5)$

In Exercises 31 to 34, find the angle each vector makes with the positive x-axis. Then determine the angle between the vectors.

31. $\mathbf{u} = (3,4)$, $\mathbf{v} = (1,0)$ **32.** $\mathbf{u} = (-1,2)$, $\mathbf{v} = (3,2)$

33. $\mathbf{u} = (-1,2)$, $\mathbf{v} = (3,-4)$

34. $\mathbf{u} = (2,-3)$, $\mathbf{v} = (-3,-5)$

35. Let $\mathbf{r} = (1,2)$ and $\mathbf{s} = (2,-1)$. Show that the vector $\mathbf{v} = (5,7)$ can be expressed as a linear combination of $\mathbf{r}$ and $\mathbf{s}$. Explain what this means geometrically.

36. Let $\mathbf{r} = (1,2)$ and $\mathbf{s} = (2,-1)$. Show that *any* vector $\mathbf{v} = (x,y)$ can be expressed as a linear combination of $\mathbf{r}$ and $\mathbf{s}$.

37. Let $\mathbf{r} = (a,b)$ and $\mathbf{s} = (c,d)$. Show that any vector $\mathbf{v} = (x,y)$ can be expressed as a linear combination of $\mathbf{r}$ and $\mathbf{s}$ for almost all values of a, b, c, and d. For what values of a, b, c, and d is it *impossible* to express $\mathbf{v}$ as a linear combination of $\mathbf{r}$ and $\mathbf{s}$?

38. A plane is flying on a bearing $25°$ west of north at 530 mph. Express the velocity of the plane as a vector.

39. A plane is flying on a bearing $10°$ east of south at 460 mph. Express the velocity of the plane as a vector.

40. A plane is flying on a bearing $20°$ west of north at 325 mph. A tail wind is blowing in the direction $40°$ west of north at 40 mph. Express the actual velocity of the plane as a vector. Determine the actual speed and direction of the plane.

41. A plane is flying on a bearing $10°$ east of south at 460 mph. A tail wind is blowing in the direction $20°$ west of

south at 80 mph. Express the actual velocity of the plane as a vector. Determine the actual speed and direction of the plane.

42. A sailboat under auxiliary power is proceeding on a bearing $25°$ north of west at 6.25 mph in still water. Then a tail wind blowing 15 mph in the direction $35°$ south of west alters the course of the sailboat. Express the actual velocity of the sailboat as a vector. Determine the actual speed and direction of the boat.

43. A pilot must actually fly due west at a constant speed of 382 mph against a head wind of 55 mph blowing in the direction $22°$ south of east. What direction and speed must the pilot maintain to keep on course (due west)?

44. A jet fighter pilot must actually fly due north at a constant speed of 680 mph against a head wind of 80 mph blowing in the direction $10°$ west of south. What direction and speed must the pilot maintain to keep on course (due north)?

45. If possible find a way to illustrate the vector sum $(1,2) + (3,5) = (4,7)$ on your graphing utility.

Exercises 46 to 49 refer to the following **problem situation**: A ball is tossed up in the air at an angle of $70°$ with the horizontal and with an initial velocity of 36 ft/sec. Neglect air resistance and gravity.

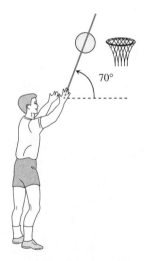

For Exercises 46 to 49

46. Specify the position of the ball as a vector 1, 2.5, and 4 seconds after the ball is released.

47. Express the position of the ball at time t, where t is the number of seconds after the ball is released.

48. Model this problem situation on a hand-held graphing computer using parametric graphs.

49. Explain why the description of this problem situation does not provide a realistic model of a thrown ball. For example, when does the ball return to the ground?

Exercises 50 and 51 refer to the following **problem situation**: Consider an object dropped with initial velocity *zero* (a so-called freely falling body) from a tower at point A. Let point B be the position of the object t seconds after it is released (neglecting air resistance and wind effects). It is a fact from elementary physics that on Earth the vector $\overrightarrow{AB}$ is equal to the *effect-of-gravity vector* $\mathbf{g} = (0, -16t^2)$. Assume point A is 220 feet above the ground.

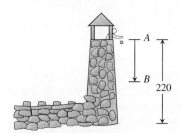

For Exercises 50 and 51

50. Determine a vector that describes the position of the object after 2, 3, and 4 seconds. Specify the coordinates of point B.

51. When will the object hit the ground?

Exercises 52 to 54 refer to the following **problem situation**: Consider the thrown ball described for Exercises 46 to 49, and modify that problem situation by accounting for the *effect of gravity*. (*Hint:* Let $\mathbf{u}$ be the vector describing the positions in Exercise 46 and $\mathbf{g}$ be the effect-of-gravity vector described for Exercises 50 and 51, and find $\mathbf{u} + \mathbf{g}$.)

52. Describe a vector $\mathbf{v}$ that gives the position of the ball at time t.

53. When will the ball hit the ground?

54. What maximum height above ground will the ball reach? How far will the ball travel in the horizontal direction?

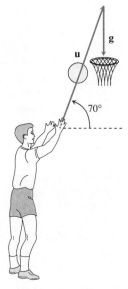

For Exercises 52 to 54

55. Suppose that β is the angle between vectors $\mathbf{u}$ and $\mathbf{v}$. Show that

$$\beta = \cos^{-1}\left(\frac{|\mathbf{u}|^2 + |\mathbf{v}|^2 - d^2}{2|\mathbf{u}||\mathbf{v}|}\right)$$

where d is the distance between the terminal points of $\mathbf{u}$ and $\mathbf{v}$.

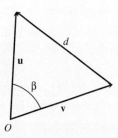

For Exercise 55

Chapter Review

KEY TERMS

absolute value of	Heron's formula	nth root of a	speed
a complex number	imaginary axis	a complex number	terminal point of a vector
acute triangle	initial point of a vector	nth root of unity	trigonometric form of
complex axis	law of cosines	oblique triangle	a complex number
complex plane	law of sines	obtuse triangle	unit vectors
De Moivre's theorem	linear combination	real axis	vector
equal vectors	of vectors	scalar	velocity
force	magnitude of a vector	scalar product	x-component of a vector
Gaussian plane	modulus	semiperimeter	y-component of a vector

REVIEW EXERCISES

In Exercises 1 to 8, solve the following triangle.

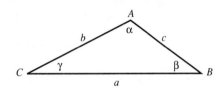

For Exercises 1 to 9

1. $\alpha = 79°, \beta = 33°, a = 7$ **2.** $a = 5, b = 8, \beta = 110°$

3. $a = 14.7, \alpha = 29.3°, \gamma = 37.2°$

4. $a = 8, b = 3, \beta = 30°$ **5.** $\alpha = 34°, \beta = 74°, c = 5$

6. $c = 41, \alpha = 22.9°, \gamma = 55.1°$

7. $a = 5, b = 7, c = 6$ **8.** $\alpha = 85°, a = 6, b = 4$

9. Refer to the figure above. If $a = 12$ and $\beta = 28°$, determine the values of b for which α has (a) two values, (b) one value, and (c) no values.

In Exercises 10 and 11, find the area of triangle ABC.

10. $a = 3, b = 5, c = 6$ **11.** $a = 10, b = 6, \gamma = 50°$

12. Two markers A and B on the same side of a canyon rim are 80 feet apart. A hiker is located across the rim at point C. A surveyor determines that $\angle BAC = 70°$ and $\angle ABC = 65°$.
a) What is the distance between the hiker and point A?
b) What is the distance between the two canyon rims? (Assume they are parallel.)

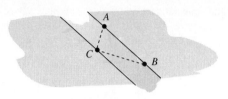

For Exercise 12

13. A hot-air balloon is seen over Tucson, Arizona, simultaneously by two observers at points A and B 1.75 miles apart. Assume the balloon and the observers are in the same vertical plane and the angles of elevation are as shown here. How high above ground is the balloon?

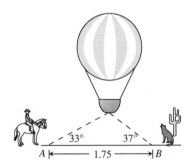

For Exercise 13

14. In order to determine the distance between two points A and B on opposite sides of a lake, a surveyor chooses a point C that is 900 feet from A and 225 feet from B (see the figure). If the measure of the angle at C is $70°$, find the distance between A and B.

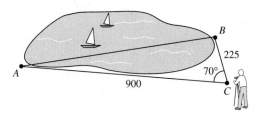

For Exercise 14

15. Find the radian measure of the largest angle of the triangle whose sides have lengths of 9, 8, and 10.

In Exercises 16 to 21, convert each expression to the form $a + bi$ where a and b are real numbers.

16. $(4 + 3i) - (2 - i)$ **17.** $(3 + 2i) + (-5 - 7i)$

18. $(1 - i)(3 + 2i)$ **19.** $(2 - 4i)(3 + i)$

20. $\dfrac{-2 + 4i}{1 - i}$ **21.** $\dfrac{-1 + 2i}{3 - 7i}$

Graph Exercises 22 to 25 in the complex plane.

22. $-5 + 2i$ **23.** $4 - 3i$

24. $2\left(\cos\dfrac{\pi}{3} + i\sin\dfrac{\pi}{3}\right)$

25. $3\left[\cos\left(-\dfrac{\pi}{6}\right) + i\sin\left(-\dfrac{\pi}{6}\right)\right]$

For Exercises 26 and 27, consider the complex number z_1 as represented in this figure.

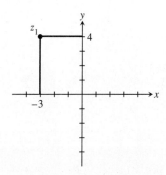

For Exercises 26 and 27

26. If $z_1 = a + bi$, determine $a, b,$ and $|z_1|$.

27. Determine the trig form of z_1.

In Exercises 28 to 31, let $z_1 = -1 + 4i, z_2 = 3 + 4i$ and $z_3 = 5 - 2i$. Perform the indicated computation, and write it in the form $a + bi$.

28. $z_1 - z_2$ **29.** $z_2 z_3$

30. $|z_1 z_3|$ **31.** $z_1(z_2 + z_3)$

In Exercises 32 to 35, write each complex number in the form $a + bi$.

32. $6(\cos 30° + i\sin 30°)$ **33.** $3(\cos 150° + i\sin 150°)$

34. $2.5\left(\cos\dfrac{4\pi}{3} + i\sin\dfrac{4\pi}{3}\right)$ **35.** $4(\cos 2.5 + i\sin 2.5)$

Write Exercises 36 to 39 in trig form where $0 \leq \theta \leq 2\pi$. Then give all possible trig forms.

36. $3 - 3i$ **37.** $-1 + \sqrt{2}i$

38. $3 - 5i$ **39.** $-2 - 2i$

In Exercises 40 to 43, use Theorem 9.5 to compute each expression.

40. $[3(\cos 30° + i\sin 30°)][4(\cos 60° + i\sin 60°)]$

41. $[2(\cos 30° + i\sin 30°)][5(\cos 30° + i\sin 30°)]$

42. $\dfrac{3(\cos 30° + i\sin 30°)}{4(\cos 60° + i\sin 60°)}$

43. $\dfrac{5(\cos 75° + i\sin 75°)}{2(\cos 30° + i\sin 30°)}$

44. Write the two complex numbers in Exercise 42 in the form $a+bi$, perform the division, and verify that the result is the same as that obtained using the trig form and Theorem 9.5.

45. Write the two complex numbers in Exercise 43 in the form $a+bi$, perform the division, and verify that the result is the same as that obtained using the trig form and Theorem 9.5.

In Exercises 46 to 49 use De Moivre's theorem to compute each of the following. Express the answer in the form $a + bi$.

46. $\left[3\left(\cos\dfrac{\pi}{4} + i\sin\dfrac{\pi}{4}\right)\right]^5$

47. $\left[2\left(\cos\dfrac{\pi}{12} + i\sin\dfrac{\pi}{12}\right)\right]^8$

48. $\left[5\left(\cos\dfrac{5\pi}{3} + i\sin\dfrac{5\pi}{3}\right)\right]^3$

49. $\left[7\left(\cos\dfrac{\pi}{24} + i\sin\dfrac{\pi}{24}\right)\right]^6$

Find and graph the nth roots of each complex number for the specified value of n in Exercises 50 and 51.

50. $3 + 3i, n = 4$ **51.** $8, n = 3$

52. Determine z and the three cube roots of z if one cube root is $2 + 2i$.

53. Solve $z^4 = 4 - 4i$, and graph the solutions.

In Exercises 54 to 57, let $\mathbf{u} = (2, -1), \mathbf{v} = (4, 2)$ and $\mathbf{w} = (1, -3)$ vectors, and determine each expression.

54. $\mathbf{u} - \mathbf{v}$ **55.** $2\mathbf{u} - 3\mathbf{w}$

56. $|\mathbf{u} + \mathbf{v}|$ **57.** $|\mathbf{w} - 2\mathbf{u}|$

58. Use the geometric definitions of addition and subtraction of vectors to find $\mathbf{u} + \mathbf{v}$ and $\mathbf{u} - \mathbf{v}$. Then compare these results with those obtained using the respective componentwise definitions for $\mathbf{u} = (2, 4)$ and $\mathbf{v} = (-1, 3)$.

In Exercises 59 to 62, let $A = (2, -1), B = (3, 1), C = (-4, 2)$, and $D = (1, -5)$. Write each expression as a vector whose initial point is at the origin. Also find the indicated magnitudes.

59. $3\overrightarrow{AB}$ **60.** $\overrightarrow{AB} + \overrightarrow{CD}$

61. $|\overrightarrow{AB} + \overrightarrow{CD}|$ **62.** $|\overrightarrow{CD} - \overrightarrow{AB}|$

In Exercises 63 and 64, express vector $\overrightarrow{AB}$ as a linear combination of $\mathbf{i} = (1, 0)$ and $\mathbf{j} = (0, 1)$.

63. $A = (4, 0), B = (2, 1)$ **64.** $A = (3, 1), B = (5, 1)$

In Exercises 65 and 66, find the angle each vector makes with the positive x-axis. Then determine the angle between the vectors.

65. $\mathbf{u} = (4, 3), \mathbf{v} = (2, 5)$ **66.** $\mathbf{u} = (-2, 4), \mathbf{v} = (6, 4)$

67. Let $\mathbf{r} = (1, 2)$ and $\mathbf{s} = (2, -1)$. Show that *any* vector $\mathbf{v} = (x, y)$ can be expressed as a linear combination of $\mathbf{r}$ and $\mathbf{s}$.

68. A plane is flying on a bearing $10°$ east of south at 460 mph. A tail wind is blowing in the direction $20°$ west of south at 80 mph. Express the actual velocity of the plane as a vector. Also determine the actual speed and direction of the plane.

69. A plane is flying on a bearing $10°$ east of south at 460 mph. A 30-mph head wind is blowing in the direction $20°$ east of north. Express the actual velocity of the plane as a vector. Determine the actual speed and direction of the plane.

70. A sailboat under auxiliary power is proceeding on a bearing $25°$ north of west at 6.25 mph in still water. Then a tail wind blowing 15 mph in the direction $35°$ south of west alters the course of the sailboat. Express the actual velocity of the sailboat as a vector. Also determine the actual speed and direction of the boat.

10

Matrices and Systems of Equations and Inequalities

10.1 _____ Solving Systems of Equations Algebraically

Sometimes a problem situation includes a set of conditions that must be satisfied simultaneously. Each condition results in an equation, and so the algebraic representation of the problem situation includes a set of equations, called a **system of equations.** For example, suppose we want to find the length L and width W of a rectangle with a perimeter of 100 units and an area of 300 square units (see Fig. 10.1). Then the algebraic representation of this problem situation is the following system of equations:

$$2L + 2W = 100$$

$$LW = 300$$

A solution to the problem requires finding values that satisfy both equations simultaneously.

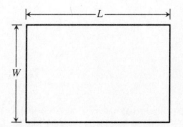

Figure 10.1 A rectangle with width W and length L.

As another example, recall that in Example 6 of Section 2.3 the Quick Manufacturing Company wanted to find their break-even point. A comparison of revenue and cost led to the system of equations

$$y = 1.5x + 200,000$$

$$y = 4x.$$

(1)

A solution of the Quick Manufacturing Company system of equations is the number pair (a, b) that satisfies both equations of the system. For instance, Example 6 of Section 2.3 found that a solution to system (1) is the number pair $(80,000, 320,000)$. We verify that claim here:

$$320{,}000 = 1.5(80{,}000) + 200{,}000$$

$$320{,}000 = 4(80{,}000)$$

Definition 10.1   Solution to a System of Equations

A pair of real numbers is a **solution to a system of equations** in two variables if and only if the pair of numbers is a solution to each equation. When we have found all solutions to the system of equations, we say that we have solved the system of equations.

Up to this point we have used graphical methods to solve a system of equations. That is, we found a point (a, b), usually through zoom-in, at which the graphs of the equations intersected. The coordinates of that point represented a solution to the system.

In this section we introduce two new algebraic methods, the **substitution method** and the **elimination method**.

Substitution Method

Consider the system

$$2y + 2x = 100$$

$$xy = 300.$$

To solve this system graphically, first solve each equation for y.

$$y = 50 - x$$

$$y = \frac{300}{x}$$

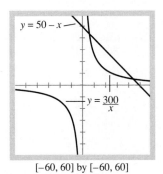

$[-60, 60]$ by $[-60, 60]$

Figure 10.2   Graphs of $y = 50 - x$ and $y = 300/x$.

Then find complete graphs of both equations in the same viewing rectangle (see Fig. 10.2). Use zoom-in to find the points of intersection.

We can solve this system algebraically using a somewhat similar technique. First, solve one equation for y and then substitute that expression for y into the other equation. The resulting equation in the single variable x can be solved. To illustrate this method Example 1 returns to the rectangle problem that opened this section.

E X A M P L E   1   Solving a System by Substitution

Solve the system

$$2y + 2x = 100$$
$$xy = 300.$$

Solution   Solve the first equation for y to get $y = 50 - x$. Then substitute this value of y into the second equation:

$$xy = 300$$
$$x(50 - x) = 300$$
$$x^2 - 50x + 300 = 0.$$

Use the quadratic formula to solve for x:

$$x = \frac{50 \pm \sqrt{(-50)^2 - 4(300)}}{2}$$
$$= \frac{50 \pm 10\sqrt{13}}{2}$$
$$= 25 \pm 5\sqrt{13}.$$

Substituting these values into the equation $y = 50 - x$ results in the following:

$$y = 50 - (25 + 5\sqrt{13}) = 25 - 5\sqrt{13}$$
$$y = 50 - (25 - 5\sqrt{13}) = 25 + 5\sqrt{13}.$$

Thus the two solutions are

$$(25 + 5\sqrt{13}, 25 - 5\sqrt{13}) \qquad \text{and} \qquad (25 - 5\sqrt{13}, 25 + 5\sqrt{13}). \qquad \blacksquare$$

E X A M P L E   2   Solving the Rectangle Problem

Find the exact dimensions of a rectangle with a perimeter of 100 units and an area of 300 square units.

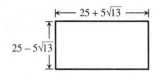

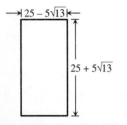

Figure 10.3   Rectangles corresponding to the two solutions of the system in Examples 1 and 2.

Solution   The system of equations in Example 1 is the algebraic representation for this problem, and that system has the two solutions:

$$(25 + 5\sqrt{13}, 25 - 5\sqrt{13}) \qquad \text{and} \qquad (25 - 5\sqrt{13}, 25 + 5\sqrt{13}).$$

The first solution represents a rectangle with a length and width of

$$\ell = 25 + 5\sqrt{13} \qquad \text{and} \qquad w = 25 - 5\sqrt{13},$$

and the second solution represents a rectangle with a length and width of

$$\ell = 25 - 5\sqrt{13} \qquad \text{and} \qquad w = 25 + 5\sqrt{13}.$$

But these two rectangles are congruent (see Fig. 10.3). Therefore there is a unique (one and only one) solution.

The dimensions of the rectangle are $25 - 5\sqrt{13}$ and $25 + 5\sqrt{13}$. In decimal form the dimensions are 6.97 and 43.03 with an error of at most 0.01.   ≡

Elimination Method

A system of two linear equations with two unknowns may also be solved by the elimination method. In this method you rewrite the pair of equations so that the coefficients of one of the variables, say x, have the same absolute value but are opposite in sign. Then add the two equations together. In the resulting equation, the coefficient of x becomes 0 and the variable x has been eliminated. You can then solve the resulting equation of one variable.

E X A M P L E   3   Solving a System by Elimination

Find the simultaneous solutions to

$$2x + 3y = 5$$
$$-3x + 5y = 21.$$

Solution   The least common multiple of the coefficients of x (2 and 3) is 6. So multiply the first equation by 3 and the second equation by 2.

$$6x + 9y = 15 \qquad \text{Multiply the first equation by 3.}$$
$$-6x + 10y = 42 \qquad \text{Multiply the second equation by 2.}$$

Then add the two equations together to obtain

$$6x + 9y + (-6x) + 10y = 15 + 42$$
$$19y = 57$$
$$y = 3.$$

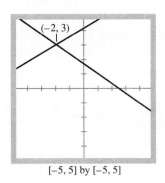

[−5, 5] by [−5, 5]

Figure 10.4 $y = -\frac{2}{3}x + \frac{5}{3}$ and $y = \frac{3}{5}x + \frac{21}{5}$.

Substituting $y = 3$ into either of the original equations gives $x = -2$.

Therefore the unique solution to this system is $x = -2, y = 3$, or more simply, $(-2, 3)$. ≡

Example 3 can also be solved graphically. First, write each equation in function form:

$$y = -\frac{2}{3}x + \frac{5}{3}$$

$$y = \frac{3}{5}x + \frac{21}{5}$$

Then find complete graphs of each and use zoom-in to find the point of intersection as shown in Fig. 10.4.

There is a major difference between the system in Example 1 and the one in Example 3. Notice that in Example 3 both equations in the system are linear while in Example 1 the second equation $xy = 300$ is not linear. The elimination method used in Example 3 can be used for any linear system of two equations in two variables. However, it may not work for nonlinear systems.

Types of Solutions to Systems of Equations

What types of solutions are there for systems of two linear equations with two variables? There are three possibilities. The graphs of the two equations may intersect in exactly one point, as in Example 3. A second possibility is that the two graphs may be parallel lines, in which case the system has no solutions. Finally, the two graphs may be the same line, in which case there are infinitely many solutions. Examples 4 and 5 illustrate these two possibilities.

E X A M P L E 4   Solving a System of Two Linear Equations

Find the simultaneous solutions to the system:

$$2x - 3y = 5$$

$$-6x + 9y = 10.$$

Solution Multiply each side of the first equation by 3 so that in both equations x has the same coefficient and opposite sign.

$$6x - 9y = 15$$

$$-6x + 9y = 10$$

Then add the two equations together and check the results:

$$6x - 6x - 9y + 9y = 0$$

$$0 = 25$$

The false statement $0 = 25$ tells us that the system of equations has no solutions; when we eliminate one variable, we also eliminate the other. ≡

Figure 10.5 confirms that the graphs of the two equations in the system of Example 4 are a pair of parallel lines. Since these lines do not cross, the system has no solutions.

Still another way to see that the lines are parallel is to observe that the slope of each line is $\frac{2}{3}$ but they have different y-intercepts.

E X A M P L E 5   Solving a System of Two Linear Equations

Find the simultaneous solutions to the system

$$x - 3y = -2$$

$$-2x + 6y = 4.$$

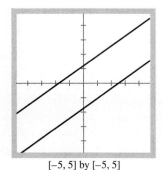

[−5, 5] by [−5, 5]

Figure 10.5 $2x - 3y = 5$ (lower) and $-6x + 9y = 10$ (upper).

Solution   Multiply the first equation by 2 to obtain the following system:

$$2x - 6y = -4$$

$$-2x + 6y = 4$$

Adding the two equations in the system yields the equation

$$0 = 0.$$

This means that the graphs of the two equations are the same line and that each point on that line is a solution to each equation. ≡

Extending the Elimination Method

The elimination method of solving a system of linear equations can be extended to systems of three linear equations in three variables, or to even larger systems.

The elimination method of solving a system of linear equations generalizes and can be applied to systems of m equations each with n variables, where n is not necessarily equal to m. Let $x_1, x_2, \ldots, x_n$ be variables, b be a real number, and $a_1, a_2, \ldots, a_n$ be real numbers not all of which are zero. Any equation of the form

$$a_1 x_1 + a_2 x_2 + \cdots + a_n x_n = b$$

is called a **linear equation in the variables $x_1, x_2, \ldots, x_n$.**

To solve a system of three or more linear equations, choose one variable to be eliminated. Then combine one equation with each of the remaining equations to eliminate the chosen variable from the system. Repeat this process with each of the remaining variables. Example 6 illustrates the method for three equations with three variables.

E X A M P L E 6   Solving a System of Three Linear Equations

Find the simultaneous solutions to the following system:

$$2x + 3y - \ z = -1 \tag{2a}$$

$$3x - 2y + 2z = 15 \tag{2b}$$

$$x + 4y - 3z = -8. \tag{2c}$$

Solution   Eliminate z by pairing the first equation with the other two.
Multiply Eq. (2a) by 2, and pair it with Eq. (2b) to obtain the system

$$4x + 6y - 2z = -2 \tag{3a}$$

$$3x - 2y + 2z = 15. \tag{3b}$$

Multiply Eq. (2a) by -3, and rewrite Eq. (2c) to obtain the system

$$-6x - 9y + 3z = 3 \tag{4a}$$

$$x + 4y - 3z = -8. \tag{4b}$$

Add Eqs. (3a) and (3b) to obtain $7x + 4y = 13$, and add Eqs. (4a) and (4b) to obtain $-5x - 5y = -5$ or $x + y = 1$.
So now consider the reduced system

$$7x + 4y = 13 \tag{5a}$$

$$x + \ y = 1. \tag{5b}$$

Multiply Eq. (5b) by -4, and add the resulting equation to Eq. (5a) to obtain

$$7x - 4x + 4y - 4y = 9 \tag{6a}$$

$$3x = 9 \tag{6b}$$

$$x = 3. \tag{6c}$$

Substitute $x = 3$ into either Eq. (5a) or (5b) to obtain $y = -2$, and substitute $x = 3$ and $y = -2$ into Eq. (2a), (2b), or (2c) to obtain $z = 1$.
The solution of the original system of three equations with three variables is

$$x = 3, \qquad y = -2, \qquad z = 1. \qquad \blacksquare$$

It turns out that systems of three linear equations in three variables also have either one solution, no solutions, or infinitely many solutions. However, the geometry in this case is more complicated than for systems of two linear equations in two variables. In Section 10.2 you will see that the graph of a linear equation in three variables is a plane in three-dimensional space. Considering the possible ways that three planes can intersect will reveal why only the three cases mentioned above occur for solutions of systems of three linear equations in three variables.

Exercises for Section 10.1

In Exercises 1 to 6, use the substitution method to find the simultaneous solutions to each system of equations.

1. $\begin{cases} x = 3 \\ x - y = 20 \end{cases}$

2. $\begin{cases} 2x - 3y = -23 \\ x + y = 0 \end{cases}$

3. $\begin{cases} 3x + y = 20 \\ x - 2y = 10 \end{cases}$

4. $\begin{cases} y = x^2 \\ y - 9 = 0 \end{cases}$

5. $\begin{cases} x - 3y = 6 \\ 6y - 2x = 4 \end{cases}$

6. $\begin{cases} x = y + 3 \\ x - y^2 = 3y \end{cases}$

In Exercises 7 to 12, use the elimination method to solve each system of equations.

7. $\begin{cases} x - y = 10 \\ x + y = 6 \end{cases}$

8. $\begin{cases} 2x + y = 10 \\ x - 2y = -5 \end{cases}$

9. $\begin{cases} 3x - 2y = 8 \\ 5x + 4y = 28 \end{cases}$

10. $\begin{cases} 2x - 4y = 8 \\ -x + 2y = -4 \end{cases}$

11. $\begin{cases} 2x - y = 3 \\ -4x + 2y = 5 \end{cases}$

12. $\begin{cases} x^2 - 2y = -6 \\ x^2 + y = 4 \end{cases}$

13. Consider the system

$$2x + 2y = 200$$

$$xy = 500.$$

  a) Which method, substitution or elimination, can be used to solve this system algebraically?

  b) Find complete graphs of both equations in the same viewing rectangle.

  c) How many solutions are there to the system?

  d) Solve the system.

In Exercises 14 and 15, find the simultaneous solutions to each system.

14. $\begin{cases} x - y + z = 6 \\ 2x - z = 6 \\ 2x + 2y - z = 12 \end{cases}$

15. $\begin{cases} 2x + y - 2z = 1 \\ 6x + 2y - 4z = 3 \\ 4x - y + 3z = 5 \end{cases}$

16. A candy recipe calls for 2.25 times as much brown sugar as white sugar. If 23 ounces of sugar are required, how much of each type is needed?

17. Find the dimensions of a rectangular cornfield with a perimeter of 220 yards and an area of 3000 square yards.

18. Hank can row a boat 1 mile upstream (against the current) in 24 minutes. He can row the same distance downstream in 13 minutes. If both the rowing speed and current speed are constant, find Hank's rowing speed and the speed of the current.

19. Four hundred fifty-two tickets were sold for a high school basketball game. There were two ticket prices: student at $0.75 and nonstudent at $2.00. How many tickets of each type were sold if the total proceeds from the sale of the tickets were $429?

20. An airplane flying from Los Angeles to New York with the wind takes 3.75 hours. Flying against the wind, the return trip takes 4.4 hours. If the air distance between Los Angeles and New York is 2500 miles and the plane speed and wind speed are both constant, find the plane speed and the wind speed.

21. At a local convenience store, the total cost of one small, one medium, and one large soft drink is $2.34. The cost of a large soft drink is 1.75 times the cost of a small soft drink. The difference in cost between a medium soft drink and a small soft drink is $0.20. Determine the cost of each size of soft drink.

22. Determine a and b so that the graph of $y = ax + b$ contains the two points $(-1, 4)$ and $(2, 6)$.

23. Jessica invests $38,000, part at 7.5% simple interest and the remainder at 6% simple interest. If her annual interest income is $2600, how much does she have invested at each rate?

24. A 5-pound nut mixture is worth $2.80 per pound. The mixture contains peanuts worth $1.70 per pound and cashews worth $4.55 per pound. How many pounds of each type of nut are in the mixture?

25. Writing to Learn Write several paragraphs explaining whether you prefer finding a graphical solution or an algebraic solution to the system

$$y = 0.2x + 2$$

$$y = 0.18x + 1.9.$$

Give reasons for your choice.

Exercises 26 and 27 refer to the following economic **problem** situation: Economists have determined that supply curves are usually increasing (as the price increases, sellers increase production) and the demand curves are decreasing (as the price increases, consumers buy less). Suppose that a certain single-commodity market situation is modeled by the system

$$\text{Supply:} \qquad P = 17 + 0.1x$$

$$\text{Demand:} \qquad P = 25 - 0.03x.$$

26. Graph both the supply and the demand equations on the same coordinate system in the *first* quadrant where p represents the price (vertical axis) and x represents the number of units of the commodity produced.

27. Determine the equilibrium price, that is, the price where the supply is equal to the demand.

28. Repeat Exercises 26 and 27 for a single-commodity market situation modeled by the system

$$\text{Supply:} \qquad P = 5 + 0.125x^2$$

$$\text{Demand:} \qquad P = 20 - 0.2x.$$

29. Use zoom-in on a graphing utility to support the solution to Example 1 graphically.

10.2 _____ Matrices and Systems of Equations

In Section 10.1 we solved systems of equations algebraically using the elimination or substitution method. In this section we streamline the elimination method of solving systems of linear equations by using matrices. We will define the concept *matrix* formally later in the section. Until then we explore the concept through some examples.

E X A M P L E   1   Solving a System of Equations

Solve the following system of equations:

$$x - 2y + z = -1 \tag{1a}$$

$$2x + 3y - 2z = -3 \tag{1b}$$

$$x + 3y - 2z = -2 \tag{1c}$$

Solution   Multiply Eq. (1a) by -2, and add the result to Eq. (1b) to obtain $7y - 4z = -1$. Replace Eq. (1b) by the new equation $7y - 4z = -1$ to obtain a new system equivalent to system (1):

$$x - 2y + z = -1 \tag{2a}$$

$$7y - 4z = -1 \tag{2b}$$

$$x + 3y - 2z = -2 \tag{2c}$$

Now repeat this process. Multiply Eq. (2a) by -1 and add the result to Eq. (2c) to obtain $5y - 3z = -1$:

$$x - 2y + z = -1 \tag{3a}$$

$$7y - 4z = -1 \tag{3b}$$

$$5y - 3z = -1 \tag{3c}$$

We have now eliminated the x-variable from two of the equations.

Next, multiply Eq. (3b) by -5 and Eq. (3c) by 7, and add the two new equations to obtain $-z = -2$. We obtain the following equivalent system of equations:

$$x - 2y + z = -1 \qquad \textbf{(4a)}$$

$$7y - 4z = -1 \qquad \textbf{(4b)}$$

$$-z = -2 \qquad \textbf{(4c)}$$

Finally, multiply Eq. (4b) by $\frac{1}{7}$ and Eq. (4c) by -1:

$$x - 2y + z = -1 \qquad \textbf{(5a)}$$

$$y - \tfrac{4}{7}z = -\tfrac{1}{7} \qquad \textbf{(5b)}$$

$$z = 2 \qquad \textbf{(5c)}$$

Substituting Eq. (5c) into Eq. (5b) gives $y = 1$. Then, substituting the values of y and z into Eq. (5a) yields $x = -1$. Thus the solution to system (1) is the ordered triple $(-1, 1, 2)$.   ≡

Using Matrices to Solve Systems of Equations

Example 1 provided a transition from the elimination method of Section 10.1 to a method that uses matrices. In solving Example 1, we added one equation to another to eliminate a variable and made the resulting equation a part of a new system of equations, equivalent to the preceding system. Notice that all the action took place with the coefficients. The primary role of the variables was to keep track of which columns the coefficients were written in.

This same solution is repeated below by arranging the coefficients into a rectangular array, called a **matrix**. A solution to the system in Example 1 begins with the following matrix:

$$\begin{pmatrix} 1 & -2 & 1 & -1 \\ 2 & 3 & -2 & -3 \\ 1 & 3 & -2 & -2 \end{pmatrix}$$

The first step in Example 1 was to multiply Eq. (1a) by -2 and add the result to Eq. (1b). When the system of equations is expressed as a matrix, that first step becomes "multiply row 1 by -2, add the result to row 2, and write the result in row 2." This step is symbolized as follows:

$$-2r_1 + r_2 \quad \text{Multiply row 1 by } -2 \text{ and add the result to row 2.}$$

Here then is a solution to Example 1 using matrix notation. Notice that the goal of this solution process is to obtain zeros in the bottom left part of the matrix with the first nonzero entry of each row a 1.

$$\begin{pmatrix} 1 & -2 & 1 & -1 \\ 2 & 3 & -2 & -3 \\ 1 & 3 & -2 & -2 \end{pmatrix} \xrightarrow{-2r_1+r_2} \begin{pmatrix} 1 & -2 & 1 & -1 \\ 0 & 7 & -4 & -1 \\ 1 & 3 & -2 & -2 \end{pmatrix}$$

$$\xrightarrow{-r_1+r_3} \begin{pmatrix} 1 & -2 & 1 & -1 \\ 0 & 7 & -4 & -1 \\ 0 & 5 & -3 & -1 \end{pmatrix} \xrightarrow{-5r_2+7r_3} \begin{pmatrix} 1 & -2 & 1 & -1 \\ 0 & 7 & -4 & -1 \\ 0 & 0 & -1 & -2 \end{pmatrix}$$

$$\xrightarrow{\frac{1}{7}r_2,\ -r_3} \begin{pmatrix} 1 & -2 & 1 & -1 \\ 0 & 1 & -\frac{4}{7} & -\frac{1}{7} \\ 0 & 0 & 1 & 2 \end{pmatrix}$$

The expressions $-r_1+r_3$, $-5r_2+7r_3$, $\frac{1}{7}r_2$, $-r_3$ explain how the third, fourth, and fifth arrays were obtained.

Notice that the last matrix represents the following system of equations, the final system (5) from the Example 1 solution:

$$x - 2y + z = -1$$
$$y - \frac{4}{7}z = -\frac{1}{7}$$
$$z = 2$$

As you might expect, modern technology can easily handle such matrix calculations.

We will use this matrix method in Example 2.

E X A M P L E 2   *Using Matrices to Solve a System*

Solve the following system:

$$x \quad + z = 4$$
$$2x + 2y + 4z = 10$$
$$x + 6y + 8z = 4$$

Solution   Perform operations on the rows of the matrix until 0s appear in the bottom left corner and the first nonzero entry of each row is 1. The leading 1s should move to the right as you look down the matrix.

$$\begin{pmatrix} 1 & 0 & 1 & 4 \\ 2 & 2 & 4 & 10 \\ 1 & 6 & 8 & 4 \end{pmatrix} \xrightarrow{-2r_1+r_2} \begin{pmatrix} 1 & 0 & 1 & 4 \\ 0 & 2 & 2 & 2 \\ 1 & 6 & 8 & 4 \end{pmatrix}$$

$$\xrightarrow{-r_1+r_3} \begin{pmatrix} 1 & 0 & 1 & 4 \\ 0 & 2 & 2 & 2 \\ 0 & 6 & 7 & 0 \end{pmatrix} \xrightarrow{-3r_2+r_3} \begin{pmatrix} 1 & 0 & 1 & 4 \\ 0 & 2 & 2 & 2 \\ 0 & 0 & 1 & -6 \end{pmatrix}$$

$$\xrightarrow{\frac{1}{2}r_2} \begin{pmatrix} 1 & 0 & 1 & 4 \\ 0 & 1 & 1 & 1 \\ 0 & 0 & 1 & -6 \end{pmatrix}$$

Note from the final matrix that $z = -6$. Substitute this value into the equation $y + z = 1$ to see that $y = 7$, and substitute these values into $x + z = 4$ to see that the solution for the system is

$$x = 10, \qquad y = 7, \qquad z = -6.$$

System of m Equations in n Variables

We now formalize some of the terminology and concepts used in the discussion for Examples 1 and 2.

Definition 10.2 $m \times n$ matrix

Let m and n be positive integers. An $m \times n$ **matrix** A is a rectangular array of numbers with m rows and n columns:

$$A = \begin{pmatrix} a_{11} & a_{12} & a_{13} & \cdots & a_{1n} \\ a_{21} & a_{22} & a_{23} & \cdots & a_{2n} \\ \vdots & \vdots & \vdots & & \vdots \\ a_{m1} & a_{m2} & a_{m3} & \cdots & a_{mn} \end{pmatrix}.$$

The numbers a_{ij} are called the **elements of the matrix**. The subscript i indicates that element a_{ij} is in the ith row, and the subscript j indicates that a_{ij} is in the jth column. If $m = n$, the matrix is called a **square matrix**.

In general, capital letters denote the matrix as a whole, and lowercase letters denote individual matrix elements.

It is common to refer to the unique matrix associated with a system of linear equations as the **matrix of the system**. For example,

$$A = \begin{pmatrix} 1 & 0 & 1 & 4 \\ 2 & 2 & 4 & 10 \\ 1 & 6 & 8 & 4 \end{pmatrix}$$

is the matrix of the system of equations in Example 2. The size of matrix A is determined by the fact that there were three equations with three variables. A is a 3×4 matrix. Notice that there is one more column than the number of variables.

Next consider the general situation with the following system of m linear equations in the n variables $x_1, x_2, \ldots, x_n$:

$$\begin{array}{ccccccccc}
a_{11}x_1 & + & a_{12}x_2 & + & \cdots & + & a_{1n}x_n & = & b_1 \\
a_{21}x_1 & + & a_{22}x_2 & + & \cdots & + & a_{2n}x_n & = & b_2 \\
\vdots & & \vdots & & & & \vdots & & \vdots \\
a_{m1}x_1 & + & a_{m2}x_2 & + & \cdots & + & a_{mn}x_n & = & b_m
\end{array} \tag{6}$$

The $m \times (n+1)$ matrix

$$\begin{pmatrix}
a_{11} & a_{12} & \cdots & a_{1n} & b_1 \\
a_{21} & a_{22} & \cdots & a_{2n} & b_2 \\
\vdots & \vdots & & \vdots & \vdots \\
a_{m1} & a_{m2} & \cdots & a_{mn} & b_m
\end{pmatrix} \tag{7}$$

is a **matrix model** of the system, whereas the unique matrix determined by the particular system is the matrix of the system.

Matrix Row Operations

The matrix method used to solve Example 2 involved arithmetic operations on the rows of a matrix. This method can be extended to any system of m linear equations in n variables. The row operations are summarized in Theorem 10.1.

Theorem 10.1   Matrix Row Operations

When any one of the following **elementary row operations** is applied to a matrix, the system of equations of the resulting matrix is equivalent to the original system of equations. (Shorthand notation is given for each row operation.)

a) Interchanging any two rows: $r_{i,j}$.
b) Multiplying all elements of a row by the nonzero number k: kr_i.
c) Multiplying k times the elements in one row and adding the result to the corresponding elements in another row: $kr_i + r_j$.

Row Echelon Form

In Example 2, notice that after the elementary row operations were applied, the final matrix had 0s in the bottom left corner of the matrix. These 0s resulted in the last equation being $z = -6$ and made the calculations relatively simple when values were substituted back to find the values for x and y. The next definition describes the final form that should result when using the row operations.

Definition 10.3 Row Echelon Form

A matrix is said to be in **row echelon form** if the following conditions are satisfied:

a) The first nonzero entry in each row is a 1.
b) The index j of the column in which the first nonzero entry of a row occurs is less than the column index of the first nonzero entry of the next row.
c) Any rows consisting entirely of 0s occur at the bottom of the matrix.

E X A M P L E 3   Solve a System of Equations—Echelon Form

Solve the system

$$
\begin{aligned}
x - 2y + z &= 7 \\
2x + 3y - w &= 0 \\
y + 2z - 3w &= 2 \\
-x - y + 3z - w &= 7.
\end{aligned}
\tag{8}
$$

Solution   Begin with the matrix of the system, and use row operations to bring it to row echelon form.

$$
\begin{pmatrix} 1 & -2 & 1 & 0 & 7 \\ 2 & 3 & 0 & -1 & 0 \\ 0 & 1 & 2 & -3 & 2 \\ -1 & -1 & 3 & -1 & 7 \end{pmatrix}
\xrightarrow{-2r_1+r_2}
\begin{pmatrix} 1 & -2 & 1 & 0 & 7 \\ 0 & 7 & -2 & -1 & -14 \\ 0 & 1 & 2 & -3 & 2 \\ -1 & -1 & 3 & -1 & 7 \end{pmatrix}
$$

$$
\xrightarrow{r_1+r_4}
\begin{pmatrix} 1 & -2 & 1 & 0 & 7 \\ 0 & 7 & -2 & -1 & -14 \\ 0 & 1 & 2 & -3 & 2 \\ 0 & -3 & 4 & -1 & 14 \end{pmatrix}
\xrightarrow{r_{2,3}}
\begin{pmatrix} 1 & -2 & 1 & 0 & 7 \\ 0 & 1 & 2 & -3 & 2 \\ 0 & 7 & -2 & -1 & -14 \\ 0 & -3 & 4 & -1 & 14 \end{pmatrix}
$$

$$
\xrightarrow{-7r_2+r_3}
\begin{pmatrix} 1 & -2 & 1 & 0 & 7 \\ 0 & 1 & 2 & -3 & 2 \\ 0 & 0 & -16 & 20 & -28 \\ 0 & -3 & 4 & -1 & 14 \end{pmatrix}
\xrightarrow{3r_2+r_4}
\begin{pmatrix} 1 & -2 & 1 & 0 & 7 \\ 0 & 1 & 2 & -3 & 2 \\ 0 & 0 & -16 & 20 & -28 \\ 0 & 0 & 10 & -10 & 20 \end{pmatrix}
$$

$$
\xrightarrow{\frac{1}{10}r_4}
\begin{pmatrix} 1 & -2 & 1 & 0 & 7 \\ 0 & 1 & 2 & -3 & 2 \\ 0 & 0 & -16 & 20 & -28 \\ 0 & 0 & 1 & -1 & 2 \end{pmatrix}
\xrightarrow{r_{3,4}}
\begin{pmatrix} 1 & -2 & 1 & 0 & 7 \\ 0 & 1 & 2 & -3 & 2 \\ 0 & 0 & 1 & -1 & 2 \\ 0 & 0 & -16 & 20 & -28 \end{pmatrix}
$$

$$
\xrightarrow{16r_3+r_4}
\begin{pmatrix} 1 & -2 & 1 & 0 & 7 \\ 0 & 1 & 2 & -3 & 2 \\ 0 & 0 & 1 & -1 & 2 \\ 0 & 0 & 0 & 4 & 4 \end{pmatrix}
\xrightarrow{\frac{1}{4}r_4}
\begin{pmatrix} 1 & -2 & 1 & 0 & 7 \\ 0 & 1 & 2 & -3 & 2 \\ 0 & 0 & 1 & -1 & 2 \\ 0 & 0 & 0 & 1 & 1 \end{pmatrix}
$$

The last matrix corresponds to the following system of equations:

$$x - 2y + z \qquad = 7 \tag{9a}$$

$$y + 2z - 3w = 2 \tag{9b}$$

$$z - w = 2 \tag{9c}$$

$$w = 1 \tag{9d}$$

System (9) is equivalent to system (8).

Substituting Eq. (9d) into Eq. (9c) gives $z = 3$. Continuing substitution yields $y = -1$ and $x = 2$. You can check that the ordered 4-tuple $(2, -1, 3, 1)$ is a solution to each of the four original equations.   ≡

With practice you will be able to perform two or more row operations on a matrix at the same time. We will often do this to save space.

Interpreting the Solution of a System of Linear Equations Geometrically

It can be shown that a complete graph of one linear equation with three variables, such as $x + y + 2z = -2$, is a plane in three-dimensional space. For a system of two equations and three variables, like the one considered in the next example, a solution exists if the two planes intersect in a line. In that case the system has an infinite number of solutions (see Fig. 10.6).

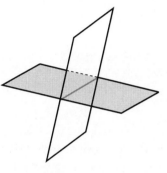

Figure 10.6   For a system of two linear equations with three variables, the solution can consist of the intersection of two planes.

E X A M P L E   4   A System with an Infinite Number of Solutions

Solve the system

$$\begin{aligned} x + y + z &= 3 \\ 2x + y + 4z &= 8. \end{aligned} \tag{10}$$

Solution   First reduce the matrix of the system to row echelon form:

$$\begin{pmatrix} 1 & 1 & 1 & 3 \\ 2 & 1 & 4 & 8 \end{pmatrix} \xrightarrow{-2r_1 + r_2} \begin{pmatrix} 1 & 1 & 1 & 3 \\ 0 & -1 & 2 & 2 \end{pmatrix} \xrightarrow{-r_2} \begin{pmatrix} 1 & 1 & 1 & 3 \\ 0 & 1 & -2 & -2 \end{pmatrix}.$$

Now simplify this system even more by completing the row operation $-r_2 + r_1$. The resulting matrix

$$\begin{pmatrix} 1 & 0 & 3 & 5 \\ 0 & 1 & -2 & -2 \end{pmatrix}$$

corresponds to the system

$$\begin{aligned} x + 3z &= 5 \\ y - 2z &= -2. \end{aligned}$$

Consequently, $x = -3z + 5$ and $y = 2z - 2$. The system consists of all ordered triples $(-3z + 5, \ 2z - 2, \ z)$, where z can be any real number. Vector addition as developed in Section 9.5 can be generalized to the three-dimensional case and ordered triples. Treat this triple as a vector and use vector addition to write this triple as

$$(-3z + 5, 2z - 2, z) = (5, -2, 0) + z(-3, 2, 1).$$

The set of solutions consists of points on the line L where L is obtained by translating the line of scalar multiples of the vector $(-3, 2, 1)$ by the vector $(5, -2, 0)$ (see Fig. 10.7). ▤

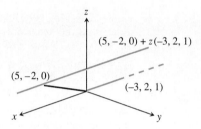

Figure 10.7   The line through the origin determined by $(-3, 2, 1)$ is translated by $(5, -2, 0)$.

A second possibility for a system of two equations with three variables is that the two planes representing the equations are parallel. In that case the system has no solutions since the two planes have no points in common.

A system with no solutions is called an **inconsistent system** (see Fig. 10.8).

Example 5 illustrates a system of three equations with three variables in which there are no solutions.

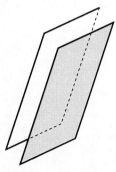

Figure 10.8   If a system of two equations and three variables is inconsistent, the planes representing the equations will be parallel.

E X A M P L E   5   A System with No Solutions

Solve the following system of equations:

$$\begin{aligned} x + \ y - 2z &= -2 \\ 2x - 3y + \ z &= \ \ 1 \\ 2x + \ y - 3z &= -2 \end{aligned}$$

Solution   Use elementary row operations to reduce the matrix of the system to echelon form.

$$\begin{pmatrix} 1 & 1 & -2 & -2 \\ 2 & -3 & 1 & 1 \\ 2 & 1 & -3 & -2 \end{pmatrix} \xrightarrow[-2r_1+r_3]{-2r_1+r_2} \begin{pmatrix} 1 & 1 & -2 & -2 \\ 0 & -5 & 5 & 5 \\ 0 & -1 & 1 & 2 \end{pmatrix}$$

$$\xrightarrow{r_{2,3}} \begin{pmatrix} 1 & 1 & -2 & -2 \\ 0 & -1 & 1 & 2 \\ 0 & -5 & 5 & 5 \end{pmatrix} \xrightarrow{-5r_2+r_3} \begin{pmatrix} 1 & 1 & -2 & -2 \\ 0 & -1 & 1 & 2 \\ 0 & 0 & 0 & -5 \end{pmatrix}$$

$$\xrightarrow[-0.2r_3]{-r_2} \begin{pmatrix} 1 & 1 & -2 & -2 \\ 0 & 1 & -1 & -2 \\ 0 & 0 & 0 & 1 \end{pmatrix}$$

The third row of the last matrix corresponds to the false equation $0 = 1$. This means the system has no solutions.   ≡

Reduced Row Echelon Form

In Examples 3 and 5 the matrix of the system was reduced to row echelon form. In Example 4 the matrix of the system was simplified even further to what is called reduced row echelon form.

A matrix is in **reduced row echelon form** if it is in row echelon form and all other entries are 0 in each column that contains a leading 1. Which one of these matrices is in reduced row echelon form?

$$\begin{pmatrix} 1 & 2 & 0 & -6 \\ 0 & 1 & 0 & 1 \\ 0 & 0 & 1 & -2 \end{pmatrix} \qquad \begin{pmatrix} 0 & 1 & 0 & 2 \\ 0 & 0 & 1 & -1 \\ 0 & 0 & 0 & 1 \end{pmatrix} \qquad \begin{pmatrix} 1 & 0 & 0 & -2 \\ 0 & 1 & 0 & 7 \\ 0 & 0 & 1 & 4 \end{pmatrix}$$

Once the matrix of a system of equations is in reduced row echelon form, the solutions to the system are even more immediate. This method is illustrated in Example 6.

E X A M P L E   6   *Solving a System-Reduced Row Echelon Form*

Solve the following system:

$$x + 2y - 3z \qquad = -1$$
$$2x + 3y - 4z + w = -1$$
$$3x + 5y - 7z + w = -2$$

Solution   First bring the matrix of the system to reduced row echelon form:

$$\begin{pmatrix} 1 & 2 & -3 & 0 & -1 \\ 2 & 3 & -4 & 1 & -1 \\ 3 & 5 & -7 & 1 & -2 \end{pmatrix} \xrightarrow[-3r_1+r_3]{-2r_1+r_2} \begin{pmatrix} 1 & 2 & -3 & 0 & -1 \\ 0 & -1 & 2 & 1 & 1 \\ 0 & -1 & 2 & 1 & 1 \end{pmatrix}$$

$$\xrightarrow[-r_2+r_3]{2r_2+r_1} \begin{pmatrix} 1 & 0 & 1 & 2 & 1 \\ 0 & -1 & 2 & 1 & 1 \\ 0 & 0 & 0 & 0 & 0 \end{pmatrix} \xrightarrow{-r_2} \begin{pmatrix} 1 & 0 & 1 & 2 & 1 \\ 0 & 1 & -2 & -1 & -1 \\ 0 & 0 & 0 & 0 & 0 \end{pmatrix}$$

The following system of equations corresponds to the last matrix above:

$$x + \quad\quad z + 2w = \quad 1$$
$$y - 2z - \quad w = -1$$

This is equivalent to

$$x = -z - 2w + 1$$
$$y = 2z + w - 1.$$

Thus the solutions to the system consist of all ordered 4-tuples of the form

$$(-z - 2w + 1, \ 2z + w - 1, \ z, \ w) = (1, -1, 0, 0) + z(-1, 2, 1, 0) + w(-2, 1, 0, 1)$$

where z and w can be any real numbers.   ≡

These 4-tuples are called a **two-parameter family of solutions** because the two variables z and w can be chosen independently.

E X A M P L E 7   APPLICATION: Mixture Problem

A chemist wants to prepare a 60-liter mixture that is 40% acid using three concentrations of acid. The first concentration is 15% acid, the second is 35% acid, and the third is 55% acid. Because of the amounts of acid solution on hand, the chemist wants to use twice as much of the 35% solution as the 55% solution. How much of each solution should be used?

Solution   Choose variables to represent the amounts of each solution to make a 60-liter 40% acid solution.

$$x : \text{number of liters of 15\% solution}$$
$$y : \text{number of liters of 35\% solution}$$
$$z : \text{number of liters of 55\% solution}$$

Then each of these equations must be satisfied:

$$x + \quad y + \quad z = 60$$
$$0.15x + 0.35y + 0.55z = 24 \quad \text{40\% of 60 is 24.}$$
$$y - \quad 2z = \quad 0$$

Reduce the matrix of this system to row echelon form.

$$\begin{pmatrix} 1 & 1 & 1 & 60 \\ 0.15 & 0.35 & 0.55 & 24 \\ 0 & 1 & -2 & 0 \end{pmatrix} \xrightarrow{-0.15r_1+r_2} \begin{pmatrix} 1 & 1 & 1 & 60 \\ 0 & 0.2 & 0.4 & 15 \\ 0 & 1 & -2 & 0 \end{pmatrix}$$

$$\xrightarrow{r_{2,3}} \begin{pmatrix} 1 & 1 & 1 & 60 \\ 0 & 1 & -2 & 0 \\ 0 & 0.2 & 0.4 & 15 \end{pmatrix} \xrightarrow{-0.2r_2+r_3} \begin{pmatrix} 1 & 1 & 1 & 60 \\ 0 & 1 & -2 & 0 \\ 0 & 0 & 0.8 & 15 \end{pmatrix}$$

$$\xrightarrow{\frac{1}{0.8}r_3} \begin{pmatrix} 1 & 1 & 1 & 60 \\ 0 & 1 & -2 & 0 \\ 0 & 0 & 1 & 18.75 \end{pmatrix}$$

The last matrix is equivalent to the following system of equations:

$$x + y + z = 60$$
$$y - 2z = 0$$
$$z = 18.75$$

Solving this system gives $z = 18.75, y = 37.50$, and $x = 3.75$. Consequently, 3.75 liters of 15% acid, 37.50 liters of 35%, and 18.75 liters of 55% acid are needed to make a 60-liter 40% acid solution. ▤

Exercises for Section 10.2

In Exercises 1 to 7, consider the matrix

$$A = \begin{pmatrix} -1 & 2 & 3 & -1 \\ 4 & 0 & 1 & 4 \\ 2 & 6 & -2 & 3 \end{pmatrix}.$$

1. What is the size of the matrix? How many rows are there? How many columns are there?

2. What is the value of each of these entries in the matrix? $a_{21}, a_{33}, a_{23}, a_{14}, a_{24}$

3. Find the matrix that results from applying the elementary row operation $r_1 + r_2$ to A.

4. Find the matrix that results from applying the elementary row operation $2r_1 + r_3$ to A.

5. Find the matrix that results from applying the elementary row operation $4r_1 + r_2$ to A.

6. Find the row echelon form of A.

7. Find the reduced row echelon form of A.

In Exercises 8 to 14, consider the matrix

$$A = \begin{pmatrix} 3 & 0 & -9 & 2 & 1 \\ 1 & 1 & -1 & 0 & 3 \\ -6 & 0 & 18 & -4 & -2 \end{pmatrix}.$$

8. What is the size of the matrix? How many rows are there? How many columns are there?

9. What is the value of each of these entries in the matrix? $a_{13}, a_{32}, a_{23}, a_{25}, a_{34}$

10. Find the matrix that results from applying the elementary row operation $\frac{1}{3}r_1$ to A.

11. Find the matrix that results from applying the elementary row operation $2r_1 + r_3$ to A.

12. Find the matrix that results from applying the elementary row operation $-\frac{1}{3}r_1 + r_2$ to A.

13. Find the row echelon form of A.

14. Find the reduced row echelon form of A.

15. Determine the reduced row echelon form of the matrix of system (1) of Example 1.

16. Determine the reduced row echelon form of the matrix of system (10) of Example 3.

In Exercises 17 to 30, write a matrix model for each system of equations. Solve the system by reducing the matrix of the system to row echelon form or reduced row echelon form.

17. $\begin{cases} x - 3y = 6 \\ 2x + y = 19 \end{cases}$

18. $\begin{cases} 1.3x - 2y = 3.3 \\ 5x + 1.6y = 3.4 \end{cases}$

19. $\begin{cases} x - y + z = 6 \\ x + y + 2z = -2 \end{cases}$

20. $\begin{cases} x + y = 3 \\ x - y = 5 \\ 2x + y = -1 \end{cases}$

21. $\begin{cases} x - y + z = 0 \\ 2x - 3z = -1 \\ -x - y + 2z = -1 \end{cases}$

22. $\begin{cases} 2x - y = 0 \\ x + 3y - z = -3 \\ 3y + z = 8 \end{cases}$

23. $\begin{cases} x + y - 2z = 2 \\ 3x - y + z = 4 \\ -2x - 2y + 4z = 6 \end{cases}$

24. $\begin{cases} 2x - y = 10 \\ x - z = -1 \\ y + z = -9 \end{cases}$

25. $\begin{cases} x + y - 2z = 2 \\ 3x - y + z = 1 \\ -2x - 2y + 4z = -4 \end{cases}$

26. $\begin{cases} 1.25x + z = 2 \\ y - 5.5z = -2.75 \\ 3x - 1.5y = -6 \end{cases}$

27. $\begin{cases} x + y - z = 4 \\ y + w = 4 \\ x - y = 1 \\ x + z + w = 4 \end{cases}$

28. $\begin{cases} \frac{1}{2}x - y + z - w = 1 \\ -x + y + z + 2w = -3 \\ x - z = 2 \\ y + w = 0 \end{cases}$

29. $\begin{cases} 2x + y + z + 2w = -3.5 \\ x + y + z + w = -1.5 \end{cases}$

30. $\begin{cases} 2x + y + 4w = 6 \\ x + y + z + w = 5 \end{cases}$

31. At a zoo in Pittsburgh, Pennsylvania, children ride a train for 25 cents, but adults must pay $1.00. On a given day, 1088 passengers paid a total of $545 for the rides. How many passengers were children? Adults?

32. One silver alloy is 42% silver, and another silver alloy is 30% silver. How many grams of each are required to produce 50 grams of a new alloy that is 34% silver?

33. Jimenez inherits $20,000. He is advised to divide the money into three amounts and then make three different investments. The first earns 6% APR, the second 8% APR, and the third 10% APR. How much is invested at 6%, 8%, and 10% if the amount of the first investment is twice that of the second investment and the total annual interest received in the first year is $1640.00?

34. A scientist observes that data derived from an experiment seem to be parabolic when plotted on ordinary graph paper. Three of the observed data points are $(1, 59), (5, 75)$, and $(10, 50)$. Determine an algebraic representation of the parabola that is a model for this problem situation.

35. A scientist observes that data derived from an experiment seem to be parabolic when plotted on ordinary graph paper. Three of the observed data points are $(1, 10), (2, 8)$ and $(3, 4)$. Determine an algebraic representation of the parabola that is a model for this problem situation.

36. Joe has three employees of different abilities. They are assigned to work together on a task. Susan can do the task by herself in 6 hours, Jim and Bill working together can do the task in 1.2 hours, and Susan and Bill working together can do the task in 1.5 hours. How long will it take Susan, Bill, and Jim working together to complete the task?

37. Writing to Learn A certain investor has $50,000 to invest and plans to invest some into a long-term investment that earns 9%, some in a short-term investment that earns 7%, and some in a money market account that earns 5%. The investor expects her interest income to be $3750 for the first year. Write several paragraphs explaining how this problem is related to finding a solution to a system of linear equations.

Solving a System of Equations with Matrix Multiplication

In Section 10.2 you learned a method for solving a system of linear equations that used row operations on the matrix of the system of equations. Reducing the matrix of a system to reduced row echelon form is a general method that applies to systems of any size.

A system of linear equations is a **square system** if there are the same number of equations as there are variables in the system. For example, the following system is a square system because there are three equations and three variables x, y, and z.

$$\begin{aligned} x - 2y + z &= -1 \\ 2x + 3y - 2z &= -3 \\ x + 3y - 2z &= -2 \end{aligned} \qquad \textbf{(1)}$$

The method of solving a square system of linear equations discussed in this section is made much easier by modern technology because of increased ease in completing matrix operations.

Matrix Multiplication

GRAPHER SKILLS UPDATE

Many graphing calculators and other scientific calculators have the capability of multiplying matrices. Learn how to multiply matrices with your calculator if it has that capability.

We begin this section by defining matrix multiplication for 2×2 matrices, that is, matrices with two rows and two columns. Consider the two matrices A and B defined as follows:

$$A = \begin{pmatrix} a_{11} & a_{12} \\ a_{21} & a_{22} \end{pmatrix} \qquad B = \begin{pmatrix} b_{11} & b_{12} \\ b_{21} & b_{22} \end{pmatrix}$$

The product of these two matrices, denoted AB, is defined as follows:

$$\begin{aligned} AB &= \begin{pmatrix} a_{11} & a_{12} \\ a_{21} & a_{22} \end{pmatrix} \cdot \begin{pmatrix} b_{11} & b_{12} \\ b_{21} & b_{22} \end{pmatrix} \\ &= \begin{pmatrix} a_{11}b_{11} + a_{12}b_{21} & a_{11}b_{12} + a_{12}b_{22} \\ a_{21}b_{11} + a_{22}b_{21} & a_{21}b_{12} + a_{22}b_{22} \end{pmatrix} \end{aligned} \qquad \textbf{(2)}$$

EXAMPLE 1   Finding a Product of Two Matrices

Find the product $A \cdot B$ where

$$A = \begin{pmatrix} 2 & -1 \\ 1 & -3 \end{pmatrix} \qquad \text{and} \qquad B = \begin{pmatrix} 1 & -1 \\ -2 & 0 \end{pmatrix}.$$

Solution

$$\begin{pmatrix} 2 & -1 \\ 1 & -3 \end{pmatrix} \cdot \begin{pmatrix} 1 & -1 \\ -2 & 0 \end{pmatrix} = \begin{pmatrix} 2 \cdot 1 + (-1)(-2) & 2(-1) + (-1)0 \\ 1 \cdot 1 + (-3)(-2) & 1(-1) + (-3)0 \end{pmatrix}$$

$$= \begin{pmatrix} 4 & -2 \\ 7 & -1 \end{pmatrix}$$

■

It is important to observe that matrix multiplication is not commutative. Example 1 found the product AB. Verify for yourself that $BA \neq AB$.

In general, any two $n \times n$ matrices can be multiplied. Sometimes it is possible to multiply pairs of matrices that are not square. The product AB can be defined if the number of *columns* of A equals the number of *rows* of B.

Definition 10.4   Matrix Multiplication

Let A be an $m \times r$ matrix and B be an $r \times n$ matrix. Then the **matrix product**, AB, is the $m \times n$ matrix C whose entries are found as follows. To find the entry c_{ij} in row i and column j, pair row i of A with column j of B and add products of corresponding entries:

$$c_{ij} = \begin{pmatrix} a_{i1} & a_{i2} & \cdots & a_{ir} \end{pmatrix} \cdot \begin{pmatrix} b_{1j} \\ b_{2j} \\ \vdots \\ b_{rj} \end{pmatrix} = a_{i1}b_{1j} + a_{i2}b_{2j} + \cdots + a_{ir}b_{rj}$$

Notice that the definition in Eq. (2) for the product of two 2×2 matrices agrees with the more general product in Definition 10.4.

E X A M P L E   2   Finding a Product of Two Matrices

Find the products AB and BA where

$$A = \begin{pmatrix} 2 & 1 & -3 \\ 0 & 1 & 2 \end{pmatrix} \quad \text{and} \quad B = \begin{pmatrix} 1 & -4 \\ 0 & 2 \\ 1 & 0 \end{pmatrix}.$$

Solution

$$AB = \begin{pmatrix} 2 & 1 & -3 \\ 0 & 1 & 2 \end{pmatrix} \cdot \begin{pmatrix} 1 & -4 \\ 0 & 2 \\ 1 & 0 \end{pmatrix} = \begin{pmatrix} -1 & -6 \\ 2 & 2 \end{pmatrix}$$

and

$$BA = \begin{pmatrix} 1 & -4 \\ 0 & 2 \\ 1 & 0 \end{pmatrix} \cdot \begin{pmatrix} 2 & 1 & -3 \\ 0 & 1 & 2 \end{pmatrix} = \begin{pmatrix} 2 & -3 & -11 \\ 0 & 2 & 4 \\ 2 & 1 & -3 \end{pmatrix}$$ ▤

Two matrices are equal if each pair of corresponding elements are equal. The next example uses equality of matrices to show that a system of linear equations can be expressed as a product of two matrices.

E X A M P L E 3 A System of Equations as a Matrix Equation
___

Express the system of linear equations

$$\begin{aligned} 2x + 3y &= 7 \\ -4x - y &= 3 \end{aligned}$$ **(3)**

as a product of matrices.

Solution Let A be the matrix $A = \begin{pmatrix} 2 & 3 \\ -4 & -1 \end{pmatrix}$. Then

$$A\begin{pmatrix} x \\ y \end{pmatrix} = \begin{pmatrix} 2 & 3 \\ -4 & -1 \end{pmatrix} \cdot \begin{pmatrix} x \\ y \end{pmatrix} = \begin{pmatrix} 2x + 3y \\ -4x - y \end{pmatrix}.$$

Therefore, the matrix equation

$$\begin{pmatrix} 2 & 3 \\ -4 & -1 \end{pmatrix} \cdot \begin{pmatrix} x \\ y \end{pmatrix} = \begin{pmatrix} 7 \\ 3 \end{pmatrix}$$

is equivalent to system (3). ▤

In a similar manner, any square system of linear equations can be expressed as a **matrix equation**. For example, system (1) is equivalent to the following matrix equation:

$$\begin{pmatrix} 1 & -2 & 1 \\ 2 & 3 & -2 \\ 1 & 3 & -2 \end{pmatrix} \cdot \begin{pmatrix} x \\ y \\ z \end{pmatrix} = \begin{pmatrix} -1 \\ -3 \\ -2 \end{pmatrix}$$

Identity Matrices and Inverse Matrices

The **identity matrix** I has the property that $AI = IA = A$ for all square matrices of a certain size. It can be shown that each of the following are identity matrices.

The subscript identifies the size of the matrix.

$$I_2 = \begin{pmatrix} 1 & 0 \\ 0 & 1 \end{pmatrix}, \qquad I_3 = \begin{pmatrix} 1 & 0 & 0 \\ 0 & 1 & 0 \\ 0 & 0 & 1 \end{pmatrix}, \qquad I_4 = \begin{pmatrix} 1 & 0 & 0 & 0 \\ 0 & 1 & 0 & 0 \\ 0 & 0 & 1 & 0 \\ 0 & 0 & 0 & 1 \end{pmatrix}$$

It is reasonable to call these matrices identity matrices. They play the same role for matrix multiplication that the number 1 plays for multiplication of real numbers. When you multiply an $n \times n$ matrix A by the identity matrix I_n, the product is the original matrix A.

The real numbers $\frac{1}{3}$ and 3 are called multiplicative inverses because $\frac{1}{3} \cdot 3 = 3 \cdot \frac{1}{3} = 1$. Inverse matrices are defined in a similar manner.

Definition 10.5   Inverse Matrices

Two $n \times n$ matrices A and B are **inverse matrices** if

$$AB = BA = I_n.$$

We say that A is the inverse of B, denoted $A = B^{-1}$, and that B is the inverse of A, denoted $B = A^{-1}$.

E X A M P L E   4   Verifying Inverse Matrices

Show that

$$A = \begin{pmatrix} 1 & 2 \\ 1 & 3 \end{pmatrix} \qquad \text{and} \qquad B = \begin{pmatrix} 3 & -2 \\ -1 & 1 \end{pmatrix}$$

are inverse matrices.

Solution

$$AB = \begin{pmatrix} 1 & 2 \\ 1 & 3 \end{pmatrix} \cdot \begin{pmatrix} 3 & -2 \\ -1 & 1 \end{pmatrix} = \begin{pmatrix} 1 & 0 \\ 0 & 1 \end{pmatrix}$$

and

$$BA = \begin{pmatrix} 3 & -2 \\ -1 & 1 \end{pmatrix} \cdot \begin{pmatrix} 1 & 2 \\ 1 & 3 \end{pmatrix} = \begin{pmatrix} 1 & 0 \\ 0 & 1 \end{pmatrix}$$ ≡

Not all matrices have inverses. A matrix that has an inverse is called an **invertible matrix**. That raises an important question: When does a square matrix have an inverse, and how can you find the inverse of a matrix if it exists? Theorem 10.2 gives an answer for 2×2 matrices.

Theorem 10.2   Inverses of 2 × 2 Matrices

Consider the 2×2 matrix $A = \begin{pmatrix} a & b \\ c & d \end{pmatrix}$. If $ad - bc \neq 0$, then the inverse of matrix A exists and is given by

$$A^{-1} = \frac{1}{ad - bc} \begin{pmatrix} d & -b \\ -c & a \end{pmatrix}.$$

The expression $ad - bc$ is called the **determinant** of the 2×2 matrix $\begin{pmatrix} a & b \\ c & d \end{pmatrix}$ and is denoted by either

$$\det A \qquad \text{or} \qquad \begin{vmatrix} a & b \\ c & d \end{vmatrix}.$$

GRAPHER SKILLS UPDATE

Calculators that have a matrix capability usually have a function DET that will calculate the determinant of a matrix. We suggest that you learn how to calculate the determinant of matrices with your calculator.

Theorem 10.2 tells us that a 2×2 matrix A has an inverse if $\det A \neq 0$. Although in this text we restrict our definition of the determinant to 2×2 matrices, it is also possible to calculate the determinant of larger square matrices. The situation described for 2×2 matrices generalizes to $n \times n$ matrices as described in this theorem.

Theorem 10.3   Inverse of an n × n Matrix

An $n \times n$ matrix has an inverse matrix if and only if $\det A \neq 0$.

We suggest using a calculator or a computer to find the determinant of a larger matrix.

EXAMPLE 5   Inverse Matrices

Determine whether each matrix is invertible. If so, find its inverse matrix.

a) $A = \begin{pmatrix} 3 & 1 \\ 4 & 2 \end{pmatrix}$

b) $B = \begin{pmatrix} -4 & 6 \\ -2 & 3 \end{pmatrix}$

Solution

a) Since det $A = ad - bc = 3 \cdot 2 - 1 \cdot 4 = 2 \neq 0$, conclude that matrix A has an inverse, and use Theorem 10.2 to find it:

$$A^{-1} = \frac{1}{2} \begin{pmatrix} 2 & -1 \\ -4 & 3 \end{pmatrix} = \begin{pmatrix} 1 & -\frac{1}{2} \\ -2 & \frac{3}{2} \end{pmatrix}$$

b) Since det $B = ad - bc = -12 - (-12) = 0$, B does not have an inverse. ■

GRAPHER SKILLS UPDATE

Calculators that have a matrix capability will calculate the inverse of a matrix. If a matrix does not have an inverse, an error message should occur. Experiment with your calculator. Will it calculate inverse matrices?

Solving Systems of Linear Equations

Consider the system of equations

$$\begin{aligned} x + 2y &= 7 \\ x + 3y &= 3. \end{aligned} \tag{4}$$

The matrix

$$A = \begin{pmatrix} 1 & 2 \\ 1 & 3 \end{pmatrix}$$

is called the **matrix of coefficients** for system (4). We have seen in Example 3 that this system can be written as the matrix equation

$$A \begin{pmatrix} x \\ y \end{pmatrix} = \begin{pmatrix} 7 \\ 3 \end{pmatrix}. \tag{5}$$

Example 4 shows that

$$A^{-1} = \begin{pmatrix} 3 & -2 \\ -1 & 1 \end{pmatrix}.$$

Multiplying both sides of equation (5) on the left by A^{-1} results in the following:

$$A^{-1} A \begin{pmatrix} x \\ y \end{pmatrix} = A^{-1} \begin{pmatrix} 7 \\ 3 \end{pmatrix}$$

$$\begin{pmatrix} x \\ y \end{pmatrix} = \begin{pmatrix} 3 & -2 \\ -1 & 1 \end{pmatrix} \cdot \begin{pmatrix} 7 \\ 3 \end{pmatrix}$$

$$= \begin{pmatrix} 15 \\ -4 \end{pmatrix}$$

Therefore the solution to this system is

$$x = 15 \quad \text{and} \quad y = -4.$$

Once the inverse of matrix A is found (which can be done with a calculator or computer), the solution to the system is found by matrix multiplication. The following theorem is stated for n equations with n variables.

Theorem 10.4 Solving a System of Equations

Suppose that a system of n equations and n variables is written as the matrix equation $AX = B$, where A is the matrix of coefficients of the system, and X and B are $n \times 1$ matrices of variables and constants respectively.

If det $A \neq 0$, then the system

$$AX = B$$

has the unique solution

$$X = A^{-1}B.$$

E X A M P L E 6   Solving a System of Equations

Use matrix multiplication to solve the following system.

$$3x - 3y + 6z = 20$$
$$x - 3y + 10z = 40$$
$$-x + 3y - 5z = 30$$

Solution   Let

$$A = \begin{pmatrix} 3 & -3 & 6 \\ 1 & -3 & 10 \\ -1 & 3 & -5 \end{pmatrix}$$

be the matrix of coefficients of the system of equations. Then

$$A \cdot \begin{pmatrix} x \\ y \\ z \end{pmatrix} = \begin{pmatrix} 20 \\ 40 \\ 30 \end{pmatrix} \quad \text{and} \quad \begin{pmatrix} x \\ y \\ z \end{pmatrix} = A^{-1} \begin{pmatrix} 20 \\ 40 \\ 30 \end{pmatrix}.$$

The unique solution to this system is $x = 18$, $y = 39.33$, and $z = 14$.   ≡

In the following exercises if the systems are larger than two equations and two variables, use a calculator or computer to find A^{-1} and to solve the system of equations.

Exercises for Section 10.3 _____

In Exercises 1 to 6, find the products $A \cdot B$ and $B \cdot A$ (if defined) for the given matrices.

1. $A = \begin{pmatrix} 2 & 3 \\ -1 & 5 \end{pmatrix}$; $B = \begin{pmatrix} 1 & -3 \\ -2 & -4 \end{pmatrix}$

2. $A = \begin{pmatrix} 1 & -4 \\ 2 & 6 \end{pmatrix}; B = \begin{pmatrix} 5 & 1 \\ -2 & -3 \end{pmatrix}$

3. $A = \begin{pmatrix} 2 & 0 & 1 \\ 1 & 4 & -3 \end{pmatrix}; B = \begin{pmatrix} 1 & 2 \\ -3 & 1 \\ 0 & -2 \end{pmatrix}$

4. $A = \begin{pmatrix} -1 & 4 \\ 0 & 6 \end{pmatrix}; B = \begin{pmatrix} 3 & -1 & 5 \\ 0 & -2 & 4 \end{pmatrix}$

5. $A = \begin{pmatrix} -1 & 0 & 2 \\ 4 & 1 & -1 \\ 2 & 0 & 1 \end{pmatrix}; B = \begin{pmatrix} 2 & 1 & 0 \\ -1 & 0 & 2 \\ 4 & -3 & -1 \end{pmatrix}$

6. $A = \begin{pmatrix} 1 & 0 & -2 & 3 \\ 2 & 1 & 4 & -1 \end{pmatrix}; B = \begin{pmatrix} 5 & -1 \\ 0 & 2 \\ -1 & 3 \\ 4 & 2 \end{pmatrix}$

In Exercises 7 to 10, write each system of equations as a matrix equation.

7. $\begin{cases} 2x + 5y = -3 \\ x - 2y = 1 \end{cases}$

8. $\begin{cases} x - 2y = 1 \\ 2x - 5y = 3 \end{cases}$

9. $\begin{cases} 5x - 7y + z = 2 \\ 2x - 3y - z = 3 \\ x + y + z = -3 \end{cases}$

10. $\begin{cases} 2x + 3y - z = 2 \\ 2x - 3y + 2z = -1 \\ -x - y + 3z = -4 \end{cases}$

In Exercises 11 to 14 write each matrix equation as a system of linear equations.

11. $\begin{pmatrix} 3 & -1 \\ 2 & 4 \end{pmatrix} \begin{pmatrix} x \\ y \end{pmatrix} = \begin{pmatrix} -1 \\ 3 \end{pmatrix}$

12. $\begin{pmatrix} 2 & 4 \\ -1 & -2 \end{pmatrix} \begin{pmatrix} x \\ y \end{pmatrix} = \begin{pmatrix} 5 \\ -2 \end{pmatrix}$

13. $\begin{pmatrix} 1 & 0 & -3 \\ 2 & -1 & 3 \\ -2 & 3 & -4 \end{pmatrix} \begin{pmatrix} x \\ y \\ z \end{pmatrix} = \begin{pmatrix} 3 \\ -1 \\ 2 \end{pmatrix}$

14. $\begin{pmatrix} 1 & -1 & 0 \\ 2 & 1 & -3 \\ -1 & 1 & 2 \end{pmatrix} \begin{pmatrix} x \\ y \\ z \end{pmatrix} = \begin{pmatrix} 3 \\ -1 \\ 4 \end{pmatrix}$

In Exercises 15 to 20, determine whether each matrix has an inverse and if so, find it. When the matrix is larger than 2×2, use a calculator or computer to answer the question.

15. $\begin{pmatrix} 2 & -3 \\ 4 & -1 \end{pmatrix}$

16. $\begin{pmatrix} 1 & -3 \\ 2 & 4 \end{pmatrix}$

17. $\begin{pmatrix} 6 & 3 \\ 4 & 2 \end{pmatrix}$

18. $\begin{pmatrix} -1 & -2 \\ -4 & -8 \end{pmatrix}$

19. $\begin{pmatrix} 2 & 0 & 1 \\ 4 & 1 & 2 \\ 2 & 0 & 4 \end{pmatrix}$

20. $\begin{pmatrix} 3 & -1 & 0 \\ 0 & 0 & 2 \\ -1 & 2 & 0 \end{pmatrix}$

In Exercises 21 to 26, solve each system of equations using matrix multiplication.

21. $\begin{cases} 2x - 3y = 7 \\ 4x + y = 2 \end{cases}$

22. $\begin{cases} x + 2y = 5 \\ -x + 3y = 6 \end{cases}$

23. $\begin{cases} 3x - 2y = 6 \\ x + y = 2 \end{cases}$

24. $\begin{cases} 7x - 5y = 12 \\ 2x + 3y = 4 \end{cases}$

25. $\begin{cases} x + 2y + z = -1 \\ x - 3y + 2z = 1 \\ 2x - 3y + z = 5 \end{cases}$

26. $\begin{cases} 2x + y + z - w = 1 \\ 2x - y + z + w = -2 \\ -x + y - z + w = -3 \\ x - 2y + z - w = 1 \end{cases}$

Exercises 27 to 31 refer to the following **problem situation**: For the 2×2 matrix

$$A = \begin{pmatrix} a & b \\ c & d \end{pmatrix},$$

the polynomial

$$C(x) = \begin{vmatrix} a - x & b \\ c & d - x \end{vmatrix} = (a - x)(d - x) - bc$$

is called the *characteristic polynomial* of matrix A. Let

$$A = \begin{pmatrix} 3 & 2 \\ 1 & 5 \end{pmatrix} \quad \text{and} \quad B = \begin{pmatrix} 2 & -1 \\ -5 & 2 \end{pmatrix}.$$

27. Find the characteristic polynomials for matrices A and B.

28. For each characteristic polynomial from Exercise 27 find a complete graph.

29. The roots of the characteristic polynomial of a matrix A are called the *eigenvalues* of the matrix. Find the eigenvalues of the matrices A and B.

30. Compare det A and det B with the y-intercept of the characteristic polynomial of each. What is your conjecture?

31. Add the numbers on the main diagonal of A and B ($a_{11} + a_{22}$ and $b_{11} + b_{22}$). Compare this sum with the eigenvalues of each matrix. What is your conjecture?

Exercises 32 to 37 refer to this **problem situation**: Each of the following sets of points represents data from some problem situation. Determine a polynomial $f(x) = a_n x^n + a_{n-1} x^{n-1} + \ldots + a_1 x + a_0$ that contains the points as follows:

a) Write a system of linear equations that determine the coefficients of the polynomial.

b) Write a matrix equation $AX = B$ that is equivalent to the system in a).

c) Determine the coefficients of the desired polynomial (by matrix methods $X = A^{-1}B$).

d) Graph the data points.

e) Support the solution in part c) by overlaying the graph of the polynomial with the graph of the data points in d).

32. (2, 3), (5, 8), (7, 2)

33. (2, 8), (6, 3), (9, 4)

34. (2, 3), (5, 8), (7, 2), (9, 4)

35. (2, 8), (4, 5), (6, 3), (9, 4)

36. (−2, −4), (1, 2), (3, 6), (4, −2), (7, 8)

37. (−1, 8), (1, 2), (4, −6), (7, 5), (8, 2)

38. Generalize The characteristic polynomial of an $n \times n$ matrix A is $C(x) = \det(A - xI_n)$. For the matrices in Exercises 19 and 20, graph $C(x)$ to find the eigenvalues.

10.4 — Solving Systems of Equations Graphically

In Sections 10.1 and 10.2 we have found that a solution to a system of equations is a point that lies on the complete graph of each of the equations in the system. The algebraic method of eliminating variables employed in Sections 10.1 and 10.2 generally does not work when the equations in the system are not linear.

When there are only two equations, each with the same one or two variables, a graphical approach can be used. Complete graphs of each equation are found and zoom-in is used to identify the solutions to the system where the graphs intersect. This method is particularly powerful when the equations are not linear.

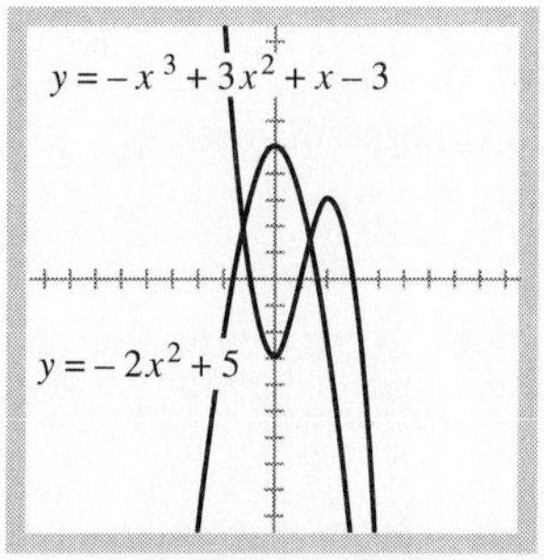

$y = -x^3 + 3x^2 + x - 3$

$y = -2x^2 + 5$

[−10, 10] by [−10, 10]

Figure 10.9 In this viewing rectangle there appear to be two points of intersection to system (1).

E X A M P L E 1 Finding the Number of Solutions to a System

Find the number of solutions to the system

$$y = -x^3 + 3x^2 + x - 3$$
$$y = -2x^2 + 5. \tag{1}$$

Solution Begin by finding the graph of each function in the standard viewing rectangle (Fig. 10.9). There appear to be two solutions. However, we should be suspicious enough to investigate the fourth quadrant more thoroughly: Notice that as x increases, the two graphs seem to be approaching each other and may intersect "offscreen." So it is appropriate to investigate the end behavior models of these two functions.

1. The end behavior model of $y = -x^3 + 3x^2 + x - 3$ is $y = -x^3$.

2. The end behavior model of $y = -2x^2 + 5$ is $y = -2x^2$.

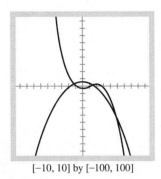

$[-10, 10]$ by $[-100, 100]$

Figure 10.10 System (1) seen in a different viewing rectangle.

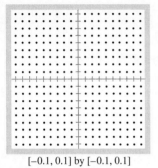

$[-0.1, 0.1]$ by $[-0.1, 0.1]$

Figure 10.11 The points suggest a grid of squares, each with a length and width of 0.01.

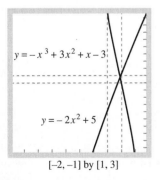

$y = -x^3 + 3x^2 + x - 3$

$y = -2x^2 + 5$

$[-2, -1]$ by $[1, 3]$

Figure 10.12 One solution to system (1) lies in the viewing rectangle $[-1.3, -1.2]$ by $[2.0, 2.1]$, which is indicated by the dashed lines.

Knowing that $y = -x^3$ decreases more rapidly than $y = -2x^2$ for large values of x confirms the suspicion that there may be a point of intersection in the fourth quadrant. Find graphs of the functions in system (1) in a viewing rectangle with greater vertical range, say $[-10, 10]$ by $[-100, 100]$. Figure 10.10 reveals that there is indeed a third point of intersection. Can you be sure there are no more? Why? ≡

Throughout the text we have been following the convention that graphical solutions be found with an error of at most 0.01. For systems of equations that means the solution for each variable must be found with an error of at most 0.01.

There is a geometric interpretation of this agreement. Consider the viewing rectangle $[-0.1, 0.1]$ by $[-0.1, 0.1]$ with the grid of small squares shown in Fig. 10.11. The length and width of each square is 0.01. This grid suggests the geometric interpretation to our error agreement.

Error Agreement for Solutions to Systems of Equations

If the solution of a system of equations falls within one of the squares of the grid shown in Fig. 10.11, then any ordered pair (a, b) that falls within the same small square is reported as a *solution with an error of at most* 0.01.

Example 1 explains that system (1) has three solutions. There is a difference between the two solutions that appear in the standard viewing rectangle and the third solution. So we consider them separately and explain the difference.

E X A M P L E   2   Solving a System of Equations: Two Points

Find all solutions, with errors of at most 0.01, that fall within the viewing rectangle $[-10, 10]$ by $[-10, 10]$ for the system

$$y = -x^3 + 3x^2 + x - 3$$

$$y = -2x^2 + 5.$$

Solution   We can estimate from Fig. 10.9 that there is one solution in the viewing rectangle $[-2, -1]$ by $[1, 3]$ and a second one in the viewing rectangle $[1, 2]$ by $[1, 2]$. We consider these solutions one at a time.

Case 1   Figure 10.12 shows the graphs in the viewing rectangle $[-2, -1]$ by $[1, 3]$. The vertical dashed lines in this figure are $x = -1.3$ and $x = -1.2$, and the horizontal dashed lines are $y = 2.0$ and $y = 2.1$. These values determine the viewing rectangle $[-1.3, -1.2]$ by $[2.0, 2.1]$ shown in Fig. 10.13. Notice that any

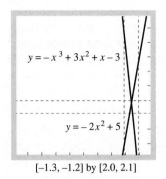

[−1.3, −1.2] by [2.0, 2.1]

Figure 10.13 Zooming in to [−1.22, −1.21] by [2.03, 2.04] (dashed lines) will generate a solution to system (1) with the desired degree of accuracy.

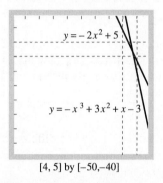

[4, 5] by [−50,−40]

Figure 10.14 The third solution to system (1) appears to be in the rectangle [4.8, 4.9] by [−43, −42].

point in the viewing rectangle [−1.22, −1.21] by [2.03, 2.04] will be a solution with an error of at most 0.01.

We report the solution as the point (−1.215, 2.038).

Case 2   By using a technique similar to the one in Case 1 we can show that the second solution is the point (1.350, 1.356) (not shown in a figure).   ≡

An important characteristic to note about the two solutions found in Example 2 is that we were able to have the scale marks represent the same horizontal and vertical intervals throughout the process of zooming in. This will *not* be possible for finding the remaining point of intersection.

E X A M P L E   3   Solving a System of Equations: Third Point

Find the solution, with an error of at most 0.01, that falls in the viewing rectangle [4, 5] by [−50, −40] for system (1) in Example 2.

Solution   Figure 10.14 shows the graphs of system (1) in the viewing rectangle [4, 5] by [−50, −40]. To find the third solution, continue to zoom in so that the length and width of each succeeding viewing rectangle is reduced by a factor of 1/10 from the previous one. Successive viewing rectangles will be [4.8, 4.9] by [−43, −42] and then [4.86, 4.87] by [−42.4, −42.3].

Finally, Fig. 10.15 shows the graphs in the viewing rectangle [4.864, 4.869] by [−42.42, −42.36]. We read the solution to be (4.868, −42.39) with an error of at most 0.01.

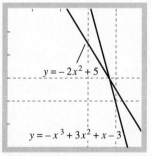

[4.864, 4.869] by [−42.42, −42.36]

Figure 10.15   The third solution is (4.868, −42.39) with an error of at most 0.01. This point must fall within the rectangle indicated by the dashed lines in order to have the desired accuracy.   ≡

Notice in Example 3 that we need an error of at most 0.001 in the x-coordinate in order to obtain an error of at most 0.01 in the y-direction. This is because the horizontal and vertical scales are not the same. Notice that in Fig. 10.14 the

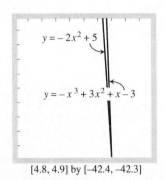

[4.8, 4.9] by [–42.4, –42.3]

Figure 10.16 The solution to the third point of intersection of system (1) can not be easily determined using this viewing rectangle.

horizontal scale marks represent 0.1 unit and the vertical scale marks represent 1 unit. In each of the successive viewing rectangles the horizontal and vertical scale marks represent different units. This is in contrast to the solutions in Example 2.

To understand visually why the horizontal and vertical scales are chosen differently, consider the viewing rectangle [4.8, 4.9] by [−42.4, −42.3] as shown in Fig. 10.16. Even though it appears that the solution falls in this rectangle, it is clear that it is not a good rectangle to use because the coordinates of the point of intersection will be hard to determine.

Box Problem Revisited

In Section 4.1, Example 5, we considered the volume of a box that was made by cutting a square of side length x from each corner of a cardboard rectangle 20 inches by 25 inches. See Fig. 10.17. That problem asked us to find the value of x that would maximize the volume of the box. The next example asks a slightly different question.

E X A M P L E   4   APPLICATION: Box Dimensions

Find the side length of the square that must be cut from a 20- by 25-inch piece of cardboard to form a box with a volume of 500 cubic inches.

Solution Use Fig. 10.17 to find that the volume of the box is described by $V(x) = x(20 - 2x)(25 - 2x)$. To solve the problem, set $y = V(x)$ and solve the following system of equations:

$$y = x(20 - 2x)(25 - 2x)$$
$$y = 500$$

(2)

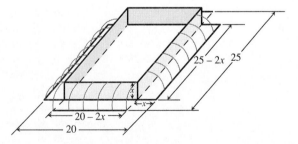

Figure 10.17 Squares cut from a piece of cardboard measuring 20 by 25 inches. Fold along the dotted lines to form a box.

Since the width of the rectangle is 20, x must be restricted to $0 < x < 10$. (Why?) Therefore consider the graph of this system in the viewing rectangle $[0, 10]$ by $[0, 1000]$ (Fig. 10.18a). There are two solutions.

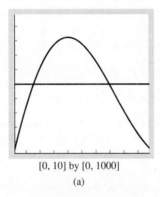
[0, 10] by [0, 1000]
(a)

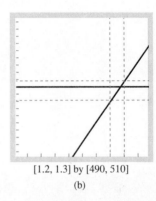
[1.2, 1.3] by [490, 510]
(b)

Figure 10.18 $y = x(20 - 2x)(25 - 2x)$ and $y = 500$. (a) Complete graph for the problem situation in Example 4. (b) Zoom in to a smaller viewing rectangle. Dashed lines indicate the viewing rectangle $[1.27, 1.28]$ by $[498, 501]$, which will yield a solution with an error of at most 0.01.

Zoom in to the viewing rectangle $[1.2, 1.3]$ by $[490, 510]$ (Fig. 10.18b). Now the graph of $V(x)$ appears to be a straight line from the bottom left corner to the top right corner of the viewing rectangle $[1.27, 1.28]$ by $[498, 501]$ and crosses the graph of $y = 500$ in this rectangle.

Since the width of this rectangle is 0.01, any point in this rectangle represents a solution whose x-coordinate has an error of at most 0.01. The length of x is 1.277 with an error of at most 0.01 when the volume is 500.   ≡

Notice that in Example 4 we did not find a solution for *both* x and $y = V(x)$ accurate to at least 0.01. While the x-coordinate had an error of at most 0.01, the value of y was found with an error of at most 2 (see Fig. 10.18b).

To find the value of y with greater accuracy than an error of at most 2, the accuracy of x must be increased also. To see this, try to increase the accuracy of $y = V(x)$ while keeping the accuracy of x the same. For example, consider the $[1.2, 1.3]$ by $[499.9, 500.1]$ viewing rectangle. Figure 10.19(a) shows that this viewing rectangle does not work because the graph of $y = V(x)$ is too near vertical. So the accuracy of x must be increased in order to increase the accuracy of $V(x)$. Figure 10.19(b) shows that $V = 500$ with an error of at most 0.03 when $1.2767 \leq x \leq 1.2768$.

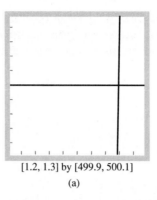
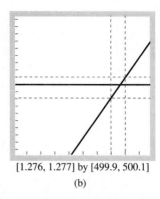

[1.2, 1.3] by [499.9, 500.1]   [1.276, 1.277] by [499.9, 500.1]

(a)   (b)

Figure 10.19 Two attempts to increase the accuracy of the y-coordinate of the solution to system (2). In (b), the horizontal dashed lines show that y has an error of at most 0.03.

We must find x with an error of at most 0.0001 in order to find $y = V(x)$ with an error of at most 0.03.

Although most nonlinear systems of equations with two variables are very difficult or impossible to solve algebraically, some may be possible. The next example illustrates a system whose exact solutions can be found algebraically.

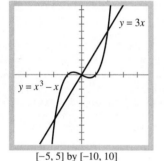

[−5, 5] by [−10, 10]

Figure 10.20 $y = x^3 - x$ and $y = 3x$.

E X A M P L E 5   Solving a System Graphically and Algebraically

Find the simultaneous solutions to the system

$$y = x^3 - x \tag{3a}$$

$$y = 3x. \tag{3b}$$

Solution Graphical Method Find the complete graph of this system in the viewing rectangle $[-5, 5]$ by $[-10, 10]$ (Fig. 10.20). The figure suggests that $(-2, -6), (0, 0)$, and $(2, 6)$ are solutions to this system. Verify directly by substitution that these three pairs are solutions to the system.

Algebraic Method Substitute the value of y from Eq. (3a) into Eq. (3b) and factor to find the zeros.

$$x^3 - x = 3x$$

$$x^3 - 4x = 0$$

$$x(x^2 - 4) = 0$$

$$x(x - 2)(x + 2) = 0$$

The x-values are -2, 0, and 2. The corresponding values of y are -6, 0, and 6, respectively. Thus the three solutions are $(-2, -6)$, $(0, 0)$, and $(2, 6)$. ▤

Although an algebraic approach was possible in Example 5, generally it will not be. However, a graphical approach will always work, provided the equations can be graphed with a graphing utility, as illustrated in the next example.

E X A M P L E 6   Solving a System Graphically

Find the simultaneous solution to the system

$$y = \cos x$$

$$y = x^2$$

such that $0 \le x \le 1$.

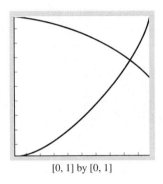

[0, 1] by [0, 1]

Figure 10.21 $y = \cos x$ and $y = x^2$.

Solution   Since x is between 0 and 1, find the graph of the system in the viewing rectangle [0, 1] by [0, 1]. Then zoom in to find the unique solution to be the pair $x = 0.82$ and $y = 0.68$ (see Fig. 10.21).   ≡

Exercises for Section 10.4

In Exercises 1 and 2, graph the equations E_1, E_2, and E_3 in the standard viewing rectangle [−10, 10] by [−10, 10].

$$x - 2y = 4 \tag{E_1}$$

$$4y - 2x = 12 \tag{E_2}$$

$$4y - 2x = -8 \tag{E_3}$$

1. Describe geometrically the simultaneous solution to the system of equations E_1 and E_2.

2. Describe geometrically the simultaneous solution to the system of equations E_1 and E_3.

In Exercises 3 to 6 use an algebraic method to determine the simultaneous solution to each system. Use a graphing utility and zoom-in to check your answer.

3. $\begin{cases} x - y = 4 \\ 2x + y = 14 \end{cases}$ 4. $\begin{cases} 2x - 3y = 33 \\ 5x + 2y = 35 \end{cases}$

5. $\begin{cases} 2x + 2y = 40 \\ xy = 100 \end{cases}$ 6. $\begin{cases} y = x^3 - x \\ y = x \end{cases}$

7. Consider the system of equations

$$y = x^3 - 2x^2 + 3x - 5$$

$$y = 5x.$$

Find each simultaneous solution (x, y) to the system, and determine what maximum error in x will ensure that the maximum error in y is at most 0.01. For each simultaneous solution, specify a viewing rectangle for which the solution can be read with an error of at most 0.01.

In Exercises 8 to 17, solve each system. (*Remember*: Both x and y must have an error of at most 0.01.)

8. $\begin{cases} 2x - 5y = 6 \\ y = 6 - x^2 \end{cases}$ 9. $\begin{cases} y = x^2 - 4 \\ y = 6 - x^2 \end{cases}$

10. $\begin{cases} y = x^3 \\ y = 4 - x^2 \end{cases}$ 11. $\begin{cases} y = 2x^2 - 3x - 10 \\ y = \dfrac{1}{x} \end{cases}$

12. $\begin{cases} y = 16x - x^3 \\ y = 10 - x^2 \end{cases}$ 13. $\begin{cases} y = 2x + 10 - x^2 \\ y = 2x^3 + 13x^2 - 9x + 1 \end{cases}$

14. $\begin{cases} y = \sin x \\ y = 2 - x^2 \end{cases}$ 15. $\begin{cases} y = 2 - \cos x \\ y = x^3 \end{cases}$

16. $\begin{cases} y = \sin x \\ y = x^3 - x \end{cases}$ 17. $\begin{cases} y = \dfrac{1}{x} \\ y = 1 + \cos x \end{cases}$

18. Let $H(x) = ax + b$ be a polynomial function of degree 1.

If $H(2) = -3$ and $H(-4) = -5$, determine a and b.

19. A function T describing the behavior of a certain physical phenomenon is known to be a polynomial function of degree 2; that is, $T(x) = ax^2 + bx + c$. It is also known that $T(0) = 5$, $T(1) = -2$, and $T(3) = 6$. Determine the function T.

20. A scholarship fund earns income from three investments at simple interest rates of 5%, 6%, and 10%. The annual income available for scholarships from the three investments is $1000. If the amount invested at 5% is 5 times the amount invested at 6%, and the total amount invested at 5% and 6% is equal to the amount invested at 10%, determine how much is invested at each rate.

21. The total value of 17 coins consisting of nickels, dimes, and quarters is $2.95. There are twice as many quarters as nickels. Determine the number of nickels, dimes, and quarters.

22. The sum of the digits of a certain two-digit number is 16. If the digits are reversed, the original number is increased by 18. What is the original number?

For Exercises 23 to 25, sketch the graphs of $x^2 + y^2 = 16$ and $x + y = 2$ on the same coordinate system.

23. Determine the number of simultaneous solutions to the system

$$x^2 + y^2 = 16$$

$$x + y = 2.$$

24. Determine the solutions with errors of at most 0.01 using zoom-in with a graphing utility. (*Hint:* Write $x^2 + y^2 = 16$ as $y = \sqrt{16 - x^2}$ or $y = -\sqrt{16 - x^2}$.)

25. Determine the simultaneous solutions algebraically.

For Exercises 26 to 28, sketch the graphs of $x^2 + y^2 = 25$ and $y = x^2 - 16$ on the same coordinate system.

26. Determine the number of simultaneous solutions to the system

$$x^2 + y^2 = 25$$

$$y = x^2 - 16.$$

27. Determine the solutions with errors of at most 0.01 using zoom-in with a graphing utility.

28. Determine the simultaneous solutions algebraically.

Exercises 29 to 31 refer to the following **problem situation**: Let x be the side length of the square that must be cut out from each corner of a 30- by 40-inch piece of cardboard to form a box with no top.

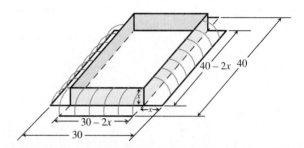

For Exercises 29 to 31

29. Express the volume $V(x)$ of the box as a function of x.

30. Write a system of equations to solve in order to find the size of the square that must be cut from each corner of the piece of cardboard to produce a box with a volume of 1200 cubic inches. Find a complete graph of the system on a grapher. How many solutions are there to this problem situation?

31. Use zoom-in to determine all values of x that produce a box whose volume is 1200 cubic inches. State the maximum error in x necessary to produce an error in the volume of at most 0.01 cubic inches.

Exercises 32 and 33 refer to the following economic **problem situation:** Economists have determined that supply curves are usually increasing (as the price increases, sellers increase production) and the demand curves are usually decreasing (as the price increases, consumers buy less). Suppose that a certain single-commodity market situation is modeled by the system

$$\text{Supply:} \quad P = 10 + 0.1x^2$$

$$\text{Demand:} \quad P = \frac{50}{1 + 0.1x}$$

32. Find the graph of both the supply and demand equations in the *first* quadrant; p is the price (vertical axis), and x represents the number of units of the commodity produced.

33. Determine the equilibrium price, that is, the price at which supply is equal to demand.

34. Repeat Exercises 32 and 33 for a single-commodity market situation modeled by the system

Supply: $P = 5 + 0.014x^2$

Demand: $P = \dfrac{133}{1 + 0.0251x}.$

Exercises 35 to 37 refer to the following investment **problem situation:** Sam makes two initial investments of $1000 each. The first earns 10% simple interest, and the second earns interest using 5% *simple discount*. After n years, the value of the first investment is $S = 1000(1 + 0.10n)$, and the value of the second investment is $S = 1000/(1 - 0.05n)$.

35. Find the graph of each of the above functions in the view-

ing rectangle $[0, 30]$ by $[0, 6000]$.

36. Is there a time when the future values of both investments are equal?

37. What happens to the value of the simple discount investment at the end of 19 years? 19.5 years? 19.9 years? 19.99 years? exactly 20 years? Could your results explain why the simple discount model is used only for short periods of time in actual practice? (*Note:* Normally interest is paid at the end of a term. In the case of simple discount, interest is paid in advance, at the beginning of the term.)

10.5

Systems of Equations and Inequalities with Nonlinear Relations

In Sections 10.1 to 10.3 the equations in the systems of equations considered were primarily linear. In Section 10.4 graphical methods were used to solve systems of equations that involved quadratic and cubic functions.

In this section we consider systems of equations like

$$4x^2 + 9y^2 = 36$$

$$2x - y = 0$$

whose first equation defines a relation that is not a function. A graphical method can be used to solve this type of system once you learn how to find the graph of the relation.

In Section 3.1 Example 6, the relation $4x^2 + 9y^2 = 36$ was graphed by finding the two functions

$$y = \left(\frac{1}{3}\sqrt{36 - 4x^2}\right) \quad \text{and} \quad y = -\left(\frac{1}{3}\sqrt{36 - 4x^2}\right)$$

in the same viewing rectangle. Example 1 uses this method.

EXAMPLE 1   Solving a Nonlinear System of Equations

Solve the system

$$4x^2 + 9y^2 = 36 \tag{1a}$$

$$2x - y = -1. \tag{1b}$$

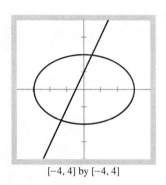

[−4, 4] by [−4, 4]

Figure 10.22 $4x^2 + 9y^2 = 36$ and $2x - y = -1$.

Solution   Begin by graphing $y = \frac{1}{3}\sqrt{36 - 4x^2}$, $y = -\frac{1}{3}\sqrt{36 - 4x^2}$, and $y = 2x + 1$ in the viewing rectangle $[-4, 4]$ by $[-4, 4]$ (Fig. 10.22).

Use zoom-in to find that the two solutions are $(0.487, 1.973)$ and $(-1.387, -1.773)$ with an error of at most 0.01.   ▤

Finding the Graph of a Second-degree Equation

Equation (1a) in Example 1 is a special case of the **general second-degree equation in two variables**.

$$Ax^2 + Bxy + Cy^2 + Dx + Ey + F = 0$$

where A, B, C, D, E, and F are real number constants. You will learn in Section 11.4 that the graph of an equation of this form is called a conic section. To find the graph of this general second-degree equation, for $C \neq 0$, we can rewrite the equation as a quadratic in y^2 and use the quadratic formula as follows:

$$Cy^2 + (Bx + E)y + (Ax^2 + Dx + F) = 0$$

$$y = \frac{-(Bx + E) \pm \sqrt{(Bx + E)^2 - 4C(Ax^2 + Dx + F)}}{2C} \qquad (2)$$

A complete graph of equation (2) can be obtained by finding the graphs of

$$f(x) = \frac{-(Bx + E) + \sqrt{(Bx + E)^2 - 4C(Ax^2 + Dx + F)}}{2C}$$

and

$$g(x) = \frac{-(Bx + E) - \sqrt{(Bx + E)^2 - 4C(Ax^2 + Dx + F)}}{2C}$$

in an appropriate viewing rectangle.

We can use these equations to complete a solution to Example 2.

E X A M P L E   2   Solving a Nonlinear System of Equations

Find the simultaneous solutions to the system

$$x^2 - 2xy + y^2 - 8x - 8y + 48 = 0 \qquad (3a)$$

$$5x^2 + xy + 6y^2 - 79x - 73y + 196 = 0. \qquad (3b)$$

Solution   We begin by rewriting each equation in system (3) using the quadratic formula:

$$y = \frac{2x + 8 \pm \sqrt{(2x + 8)^2 - 4(x^2 - 8x + 48)}}{2}$$

$$y = \frac{73 - x \pm \sqrt{(73 - x)^2 - 24(5x^2 - 79x + 196)}}{12}$$

Notice that four functions are represented here. They are shown in Fig. 10.23. The curve at the top of Fig. 10.23 is a parabola, a form introduced earlier in the text. The closed curve in the center is called an **ellipse**; Chapter 11 will examine both of these forms in greater detail.

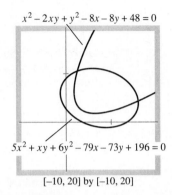

$$x^2 - 2xy + y^2 - 8x - 8y + 48 = 0$$

$$5x^2 + xy + 6y^2 - 79x - 73y + 196 = 0$$

[–10, 20] by [–10, 20]

Figure 10.23   System (3). The two equations yield four *functions* but only two distinct curves when graphed.

Use zoom-in to find that the solutions are $(3.26, 11.74)$ and $(15.05, 4.60)$.   ▤

Application: Locating a Position

Three observers are strategically located with synchronized watches. Person A is located relative to a large coordinate system at the origin $(0,0)$; Person B is at point $(0, 4000)$, and person C is at point $(7000, 0)$. Observer B hears the sound of a gun 2 seconds before observer A, and observer C hears the sound 4 seconds before observer A.

We are interested in finding the point $P(x, y)$ where the gun is located. See Fig. 10.24.

Using the information given in the problem situation and the fact that sound travels at the rate of 1100 ft/sec, we draw the following conclusions. Why?

$$d(P, A) - d(P, B) = 2200 \qquad \text{and} \qquad d(P, A) - d(P, C) = 4400 \qquad \textbf{(4)}$$

Using the distance formula we obtain the following:

$$d(P, A) - d(P, B) = 2200$$

$$\sqrt{(x - 0)^2 + (y - 0)^2} - \sqrt{(x - 0)^2 + (y - 4000)^2} = 2200 \qquad \textbf{(5)}$$

By completing the rather long and tedious algebraic simplification or by using a method that will be introduced in Section 11.4, we conclude that Eq. (5) simplifies to

$$\frac{(y - 2000)^2}{(1100)^2} - \frac{x^2}{2{,}790{,}000} = 1.$$

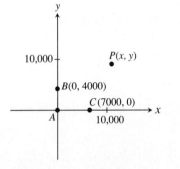

Figure 10.24   Observers are located at points A, B, and C. They want to find the location P of a gun.

In a similar fashion the equation $d(P, A) - d(P, C) = 4400$ simplifies to

$$\frac{(x - 3500)^2}{(2200)^2} - \frac{y^2}{7,410,000} = 1.$$

The gun is located at a point that lies on both of these curves, so we need to find the simultaneous solutions to this pair of equations.

E X A M P L E   3   Solving a Nonlinear System of Equations

Find the simultaneous solutions to

$$\frac{(x - 3500)^2}{(2200)^2} - \frac{y^2}{7,410,000} = 1 \qquad \textbf{(6a)}$$

$$\frac{(y - 2000)^2}{(1100)^2} - \frac{x^2}{2,790,000} = 1. \qquad \textbf{(6b)}$$

Solution   To find the graph of each of these equations, solve each one for y. Equation (6a) becomes

$$y = \pm\sqrt{7,410,000\left[\frac{(x - 3500)^2}{(2200)^2} - 1\right]},$$

and Eq. (6b) becomes

$$y = 2000 \pm 1100\sqrt{\frac{x^2}{2,790,000} + 1}.$$

From the graphs of these four functions (Fig. 10.25) it is apparent that there are four points of intersection and thus four simultaneous solutions.

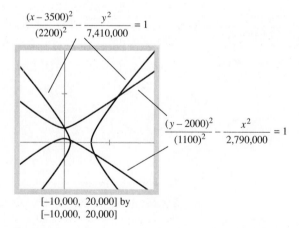

$$\frac{(x - 3500)^2}{(2200)^2} - \frac{y^2}{7,410,000} = 1$$

$$\frac{(y - 2000)^2}{(1100)^2} - \frac{x^2}{2,790,000} = 1$$

[−10,000, 20,000] by
[−10,000, 20,000]

Figure 10.25   System of equations (6). Note the four curves with four points of intersection.

Use zoom-in to determine that the four solutions are the points (162.63, 3105.20), (1241.99, 629.24), (6414.37, −2365.08), and (11,714.31, 9792.52). ▤

E X A M P L E   4   APPLICATION: Location of a Point

Determine the position of the gun in the problem that led to system of equations solved in Example 3.

Solution   The calculations in Example 3 resulted in four possible locations for the gun.

Figure 10.26 shows the original locations A, B, and C of the observers (from Fig. 10.24) and the curves of system (6) and their four points of intersection (from Fig. 10.25). The point P must be one of these four points.

Since $d(P, A) - d(P, C) = 4400 > 0$ (see Eq. 4), P must be farther from A than C. This indicates that the gun location must be either (6414.37, −2365.08) or (11,714.31, 9792.52). And since $d(P, A) - d(P, B) = 2200 > 0$ (see Eq. 4), the point P also must be farther from A than B. This condition narrows the choice to the point (11,714.31, 9792.52).

The gun is located at point (11,714.31, 9792.52). ▤

This same technique can be used in navigation using radio waves instead of sound waves to determine location.

Solving Systems of Inequalities

The technique for solving a system of inequalities is the same as that for solving equalities. First sketch the graph of the solution set for each individual inequality. Then overlay these solution sets, and identify the points that belong to each solution set of the system. This process is a graphical means of finding the intersection of the individual solution sets. This intersection is the solution to the system of inequalities.

E X A M P L E   5   Solving a System of Inequalities

Solve the system

$$y > x^2$$

$$2x + 3y < 4. \tag{7}$$

Solution   The graph of the equation $y = x^2$ is the boundary of the region that is the solution to the inequality $y > x^2$. Since $(0, 2)$ is a solution to the inequality, the solution must consist of all the points *inside* the parabola; the points on the boundary are not included. (Why?) See Fig. 10.27 (a).

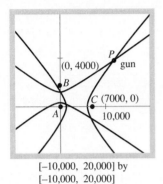

[−10,000, 20,000] by
[−10,000, 20,000]

Figure 10.26 The gun is located at one of the four points of intersection of system (6).

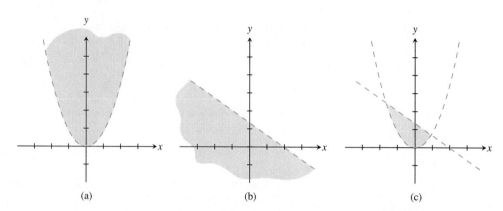

Figure 10.27   Steps in solving graphically the system of inequalities (7). (a) $y > x^2$, (b) $2x + 3y < 4$, and (c) graph of the system. Dashed lines indicate that the points on the line and parabola are not part of the solution.

The solution to the inequality $2x + 3y < 4$ is the region below the line $2x + 3y = 4$. The points on this line are not included in the solution. See Fig. 10.27(b).

Therefore the solution is the region below the line $2x + 3y < 4$ and above the parabola $y = x^2$ (Fig. 10.27c). Figure 10.28 shows the result of finding the solution directly on a graphing utility with a shade function.

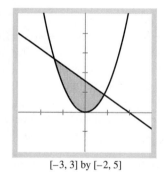

[−3, 3] by [−2, 5]

Figure 10.28
SHADE $(x^2, (1/3)(4 − 2x))$ is the solution to system (7).

E X A M P L E   6   Solving a System of Inequalities

Solve the system

$$x^2 - 2xy + y^2 - 8x - 8y + 48 \leq 0 \qquad \textbf{(8a)}$$

$$5x^2 + xy + 6y^2 - 79x - 73y + 196 > 0. \qquad \textbf{(8b)}$$

Solution   Complete graphs of $x^2 - 2xy + y^2 - 8x - 8y + 48 = 0$ and $5x^2 + xy + 6y^2 - 79x - 73y + 196 = 0$ were found in Example 2 (see Fig. 10.23). We complete the solution to system (8) by checking to see where the test point $(4, 4)$ falls.

Check (4, 4) in the first inequality:

$$4^2 - 2(4)(4) + 4^2 - 8(4) - 8(4) + 48 = -16$$

(4, 4) satisfies the first inequality and is therefore inside the parabola.

Check (4, 4) in the second inequality:

$$5(4^2) + (4)(4) + 6(4^2) - 79(4) - 73(4) + 196 = -220$$

(4, 4) does not satisfy the second inequality and is therefore outside the ellipse.

Since the point (4, 4) does not satisfy inequality (8*b*), the inside of the ellipse is not shaded. Therefore the solution is the region on or inside the parabola and outside the ellipse (see Fig. 10.29). ≡

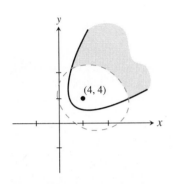

Figure 10.29   The shaded region is the solution to the system of inequalities (8).

The final example of this section involves a system of inequalities as an algebraic representation of a problem situation.

E X A M P L E 7   APPLICATION: Paint Mixtures

White paint at $1.00/cm^3 is mixed with red paint which costs $0.20/cm^3 in a container with a capacity of 1050 cm^3. If x is the number of cubic centimeters of red paint, and y is the number of cubic centimeters of white paint, color mixologists have determined that the product of x and y must be greater than 100,000 to produce eye-pleasing colors. What mixtures are possible that produce eye-pleasing colors and have a total cost less than or equal to $500?

a) Determine an algebraic representation of the problem situation.

b) Draw a graph of the algebraic representation, and shade the portion of the graph that represents a solution to the problem situation.

Solution

a) Choose variables as follows:

$$x: \text{ the number of cm}^3 \text{ of red paint}$$

$$y: \text{ the number of cm}^3 \text{ of white paint}$$

$$x + y \leq 1050 \qquad \text{The capacity of the container is 1050 cm}^3. \qquad \textbf{(9a)}$$

$$0.2x + y \leq 500 \qquad \text{The total cost must be no more than \$500.} \qquad \textbf{(9b)}$$

$$xy > 100{,}000 \qquad \text{This condition insures eye-pleasing colors.} \qquad \textbf{(9c)}$$

It is also true that $x \geq 0$ and $y \geq 0$. (Why?)

b) A complete graph of this system appears in Fig. 10.30. Notice that the shaded region includes the points on and below the lines $x + y = 1050$ and $0.2x + y = 500$ and above but not on the curve $xy = 100{,}000$. ≡

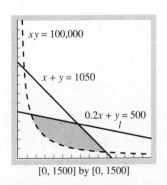

[0, 1500] by [0, 1500]

Figure 10.30   The solution to the system of inequalities (9).

Exercises for Section 10.5

In Exercises 1 to 10, find the simultaneous solutions to each system.

1. $\begin{cases} 4x^2 + 9y^2 = 36 \\ x + 2y = 2 \end{cases}$ 2. $\begin{cases} 4x^2 + 9y^2 = 36 \\ x - 2y = 2 \end{cases}$

3. $\begin{cases} 9x^2 - 4y^2 = 36 \\ x + 2y = 4 \end{cases}$ 4. $\begin{cases} 9x^2 - 4y^2 = 36 \\ x - 2y = 4 \end{cases}$

5. $\begin{cases} 9x^2 - 4y^2 = 36 \\ 4x^2 + 9y^2 = 36 \end{cases}$ 6. $\begin{cases} 9x^2 - 4y^2 = 36 \\ 9x^2 + 4y^2 = 36 \end{cases}$

7. $\begin{cases} x^2 + 4y^2 = 4 \\ y = 2x^2 - 3 \end{cases}$ 8. $\begin{cases} x^2 - 4y^2 = 4 \\ y = 2x^2 - 3 \end{cases}$

9. $\begin{cases} x^2 - 4y^2 = 4 \\ x = 2y^2 - 3 \end{cases}$ 10. $\begin{cases} x^2 + 4y^2 = 4 \\ x = 2y^2 - 3 \end{cases}$

In Exercises 11 to 14, draw a complete graph of each equation, and find the simultaneous solutions to each system.

11. $\begin{cases} x^2 + xy + y^2 + x + y - 6 = 0 \\ 2x^2 - 3xy + 2y^2 + x + y - 8 = 0 \end{cases}$

12. $\begin{cases} 5x^2 - 40xy + 20y^2 - 17x + 25y + 50 = 0 \\ xy - 3x = 0 \end{cases}$

13. $\begin{cases} 2x^2 - 3xy + 2y^2 + x + y - 8 = 0 \\ 2x^2 - 8xy + 3y^2 + x + y - 10 = 0 \end{cases}$

14. $\begin{cases} 3x^2 - 5xy + 6y^2 - 7x + 5y - 9 = 0 \\ x^2 + y^2 - 2x - 6 = 0 \end{cases}$

In Exercises 15 to 20, draw a graph representing the solution to each system of inequalities.

15. $\begin{cases} y \geq x^2 \\ x^2 + y^2 \leq 4 \end{cases}$ 16. $\begin{cases} y \leq x^2 + 4 \\ x^2 + y^2 \geq 4 \end{cases}$

17. $\begin{cases} x^2 - y^2 < 4 \\ x^2 + y^2 < 4 \end{cases}$

18. $\begin{cases} x^2 + 4y^2 - 2x + 4y - 6 > 0 \\ y < \frac{1}{2}x + 1 \end{cases}$

19. $\begin{cases} x^2 + 2xy - 5y^2 + 2x + 4y - 10 > 0 \\ 4x^2 + xy + 4y^2 - 5x + 5y - 15 < 0 \end{cases}$

20. $\begin{cases} x^2 + 2xy + 5y^2 + 2x + 4y - 10 > 0 \\ 5y^2 + 2x + 3y - 6 < 0 \end{cases}$

Exercises 21 to 23 refer to the following **problem situation**: Consider an acid solution of 84 ounces that is 58% pure acid. How many ounces of pure acid (x) must be added to obtain a solution that is 70% to 80% acid? Let y be the concentration of acid in the final solution.

21. Find an algebraic representation of this problem situation consisting of a system of two inequalities and one equation whose simultaneous solution can be used to solve the problem situation.

22. Find a complete graph of the system of equations in Exercise 21.

23. Find the values of x and y that make sense in this problem situation, and solve the system.

Exercise 24 refers to the following **problem situation**: Suppose three observers A, B, and C are listening for illegal dynamite explosions. They are positioned so the angle of the line between A and B and the line between B and C is $90°$. Further suppose that A and B are 6000 feet apart and that B and C are 2000 feet apart. A hears the explosion 4.06 seconds before B, and C hears the explosion 0.63 seconds before B.

24. The system of equations

$$\frac{(x - 3000)^2}{2233^2} - \frac{y^2}{4{,}013{,}711} = 1$$

and $\dfrac{(y - 1000)^2}{346.5^2} - \dfrac{x^2}{879{,}937.75} = 1$

are an algebraic representation of this problem situation. Find a complete graph of this problem situation. Find the location of the dynamite assuming that it is located in the first quadrant.

Exercises 25 and 26 refer to the following **problem situation**: "Hush Dog" shoes are made from two types of leather, A and B. Type A costs $0.25 per square inch, and type B costs $0.65 per square inch. The "Hush Dog" Company must buy at least 3000 square inches of A per day and 8600 square inches of B per day (or the supplier will not do business). However, the total square inches of material provided by the supplier per day must be less than 30,000 square inches. Experience has shown the president of the company that the total cost of the material must remain less than $10,000 per day or no one will buy "Hush Dogs" (because they would need to be priced too high).

25. Determine a system of inequalities whose solution models all possible combinations of the amounts of leather A and leather B that could be used in this problem situation.

26. Find the graph of the region that represents all possible combinations of the amounts of leather A and leather B that could be used in this problem situation.

In Exercises 27 and 28, use the shade feature of your grapher to solve the following systems.

27. $\begin{cases} y > x^3 - 4x \\ y < 6 - x^2 \end{cases}$

28. $\begin{cases} y > x + 2 \\ y < \sqrt{x + 3} \end{cases}$

Chapter Review

KEY TERMS

conic section
determinant
elementary row operations
elements of a matrix
elimination method
ellipse
general second-degree
   equation
identity matrix

inconsistent system
inverse of a matrix
invertible matrix
linear equation in the
   variables $x_1, x_2, \ldots, x_n$
matrix
matrix equation
matrix model

matrix of the coefficients
matrix of the system
matrix product $A \cdot B$
matrix row operations
$m \times n$ matrix
reduced row echelon form
row echelon form
solution to a system
   of equations

square matrix
square system
substitution method
system of equations
two-parameter family
   of solutions

REVIEW EXERCISES

In Exercises 1 and 2, use the substitution method to find the simultaneous solutions to each system of equations. Support your answer with a graphing utility.

1. $\begin{cases} 2x - y = 4 \\ y = 6 \end{cases}$

2. $\begin{cases} x + 5y = 16 \\ 2x + y = 5 \end{cases}$

In Exercises 3 and 4, use the elimination method to find the simultaneous solutions to each system of equations. Support your answer with a graphing utility.

3. $\begin{cases} 6x - 3y = 9 \\ -4x + 2y = -6 \end{cases}$

4. $\begin{cases} x^2 + 3y = 7 \\ x^2 - y = -1 \end{cases}$

5. Find the simultaneous solutions to the system

$$x + 2y + z = 1$$
$$2x - y + z = 2$$
$$x - 3y - z = 6.$$

In Exercises 6 to 11, write a matrix for each system of equations. Solve the system by reducing the matrix of the system to row echelon form or reduced row echelon form.

6. $\begin{cases} x + y = 3 \\ x - y = 1 \\ 2x + y = 1 \end{cases}$

7. $\begin{cases} x - y + z = 6 \\ x + y + 2z = -4 \end{cases}$

8. $\begin{cases} x - y + z = 0 \\ 2x - 3z = 4 \\ -x - y + 2z = -4 \end{cases}$

9. $\begin{cases} 4x - 2y \qquad = \quad 0 \\ x + 3y - \ z = -3 \\ \qquad 6y + 2z = \ 16 \end{cases}$

10. $\begin{cases} x + \ y - 2z = -4 \\ 3x - \ y + \ z = -7 \\ -2x - 2y + 4z = \ \ 8 \end{cases}$

11. $\begin{cases} 2x - 4y \qquad = \ 10 \\ x \qquad - z = -1 \\ \qquad 2y - z = -5 \end{cases}$

For Exercises 12 to 16 use the following matrices and find the matrix products indicated.

$$A = \begin{pmatrix} 3 & -2 & 1 \\ 0 & -1 & 2 \\ 1 & -3 & 1 \end{pmatrix}, \qquad B = \begin{pmatrix} -1 & 2 \\ 4 & 3 \end{pmatrix}$$

$$C = \begin{pmatrix} 1 & -3 & 2 \\ 0 & -2 & 4 \end{pmatrix}, \qquad D = \begin{pmatrix} 1 & 0 \\ -3 & 4 \\ 1 & 1 \end{pmatrix}$$

12. $A \cdot D$ **13.** $C \cdot A$ **14.** $D \cdot B$

15. $B \cdot C$ **16.** $(D \cdot C) \cdot A$

In Equations 17 to 22, solve each system using matrix multiplication.

17. $\begin{cases} 2x - 3y = 2 \\ 4x + \ y = 5 \end{cases}$

18. $\begin{cases} 5x - 17y = 42 \\ 9x + \ 6y = 19 \end{cases}$

19. $\begin{cases} 0.32x + \ 1.8y = 3.2 \\ 2.4x - 0.08y = 5.2 \end{cases}$

20. $\begin{cases} 3x - 4y + 5z = 7 \\ 2x + \ y - \ z = 2 \\ -x + 2y + 2z = 5 \end{cases}$

21. $\begin{cases} 0.02x - 5.1y + \ 2z = \ \ 6 \\ x + 2.3y + 0.7z = -1 \\ x - 0.5y + 1.1z = \ \ 2 \end{cases}$

22. $\begin{cases} 2x - \ 3y + \quad z - 1.5w = \ \ 3 \\ x + \ 2y - \ 3z + \quad w = -2 \\ -x - 1.3y + 2.5z - 0.7w = \ \ 4 \\ 3x + \ 7y - 4.2z + \ 5w = \ 17 \end{cases}$

In Exercises 23 to 33, solve each system.

23. $\begin{cases} 3x + 2y = 6 \\ y = x^2 - 2x + 5 \end{cases}$

24. $\begin{cases} y = |2x + 5| \\ y = 3x^2 - 2x + 1 \end{cases}$

25. $\begin{cases} x^2 - 2y - 4x + 10 = 0 \\ 5x - 4y + 24 = 0 \end{cases}$

26. $\begin{cases} x^2 - 2y - 4x + 10 = 0 \\ 5x - y + 24 = 0 \end{cases}$

27. $\begin{cases} y = 16 - x^2 \\ y = 9x - x^3 \end{cases}$

28. $\begin{cases} y = 6 - x^2 \\ y = 3\sin(x - 4) \end{cases}$

29. $\begin{cases} y = 115x - 3x^3 \\ y = 50\cos x \end{cases}$

30. $\begin{cases} 9x^2 + 25y^2 = 225 \\ x + 2y = 2 \end{cases}$

31. $\begin{cases} 9x^2 - 25y^2 = 225 \\ x + 2y = 4 \end{cases}$

32. $\begin{cases} 9x^2 - 25y^2 = 225 \\ 9x^2 + 25y^2 = 225 \end{cases}$

33. $\begin{cases} x^2 + 9y^2 = 9 \\ y = 2x^2 + 3 \end{cases}$

In Exercises 34 and 35, determine the number of simultaneous solutions to each system.

34. $\begin{cases} 2x^2 - 3xy + 2y^2 + x + y - 8 = 0 \\ 3x^2 - 8xy + 2y^2 + x + y - 10 = 0 \end{cases}$

35. $\begin{cases} 3x^2 - 5xy + 6y^2 - 7x + 5y - 9 = 0 \\ x^2 + y^2 - 2y - 6 = 0 \end{cases}$

36. Find the simultaneous solutions to the system in Exercise 34.

37. Find the simultaneous solutions to the system in Exercise 35.

In Exercises 38 and 39, draw a graph representing the solution to the system of inequalities.

38. $\begin{cases} x^2 + y^2 < 9 \\ y > x^2 \end{cases}$

39. $\begin{cases} x^2 - y^2 > 9 \\ x^2 + y^2 < 9 \end{cases}$

11

Parametric Equations and Polar Coordinates

11.1 _____ Parametric Equations and Graphs

In the Exploration in Section 7.3 you were asked to set a graphing utility to "param mode" and to key in two functions, for example, $X_1(t) = \cos t$ and $Y_1(t) = \sin t$. You were using a method of describing a curve that is known as parametric graphing.

In those Explorations once you pressed the **graph** key you watched the curve being generated over an interval of t-values. For each value of t, the coordinates of a point (x, y) were calculated. Because the position of the point (x, y) varies with t, the variable t is called the parameter. Both x and y are dependent variables and are functions of t.

Before we formally define parametric equations, experiment in the following Exploration.

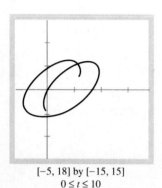

[−5, 18] by [−15, 15]
$0 \leq t \leq 10$

Figure 11.1
$X(T) = 5\cos T + \sin T + .5T$
and $Y(T) = 5\sin T + 2\cos T$.

🔍 EXPLORE WITH A GRAPHING UTILITY

Set a graphing calculator as follows:

- Rad mode,   Param mode
- Range: $T\text{min} = 0$, $T\text{max} = 10$, $T\text{step} = 0.1$
- Viewing rectangle: $[-5, 18]$ by $[-15, 15]$
- Define: $X_1(T) = 5\cos T + \sin T + 0.5T$ and $Y_1(T) = 5\sin T + 2\cos T$

Describe what happens when you press the graph key (see Fig. 11.1).

1. How is the curve different if $T\text{max}$ is changed to $T\text{max} = 15$? Or to $T\text{max} = 25$? Or to $T\text{max} = 30$?

2. As you move the trace cursor along the curve, how does the value of T relate to the values of X and Y on the grapher screen? How are these values related to the defining equations?

In this Exploration you experienced a curve that was defined by parametric equations. You saw that as t varies, the corresponding point (x, y) also varies. You saw that when $T\text{max}$ is increased, a longer curve is drawn. You have experienced the concepts defined in Definition 11.1.

Definition 11.1   Parametric Equations

Let f and g be two functions defined on an interval I. The relation of all ordered pairs $(f(t), g(t))$ for t in I is called a **curve C**. The equations

$$x = f(t) \qquad \text{and} \qquad y = g(t) \qquad \text{(for } t \text{ in } I)$$

are called **parametric equations** for C, and the variable t is the **parameter**.

If a curve C is defined by a pair of parametric equations, such as $x = f(t)$ and $y = g(t)$, with t in I, we say that the equations give a **parametrization of C** in terms of t.

Figure 11.2 shows several curves that could be defined by parametric equations.

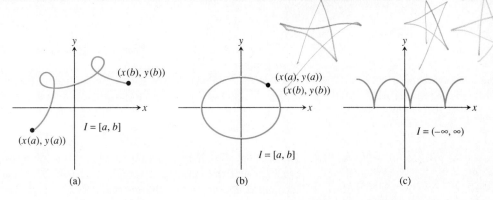

Figure 11.2 Several curves that can be defined by parametric equations.

The curves in Fig. 11.2(a, b) are defined for t in an interval $[a, b]$. The points $\big((x(a), y(a)\big)$ and $\big((x(b), y(b)\big)$ are called **endpoints** of the curve C. It is possible for a curve described parametrically to intersect itself, as shown in Fig. 11.2(a). This means that more than one value of t produces the same point in the coordinate plane.

EXAMPLE 1   Finding Endpoints of a Curve

Find the endpoints of the curve C defined by $x(t) = 1 - 2t$ and $y(t) = 2 - t$ for t in the interval $I = [0, 1]$. Then describe the nature of the curve as you move from one endpoint to the next.

Solution   To find the endpoints of the curve, evaluate the parametric equations at the endpoints of the interval I, that is, at $t = 0$ and $t = 1$: $x(0) = 1, y(0) = 2$, $x(1) = -1$, and $y(1) = 1$. Therefore, as t increases from 0 to 1, the curve goes from endpoint $(1, 2)$ to the endpoint $(-1, 1)$. See Fig. 11.3.

To describe the shape of the curve, consider that $x(t)$ and $y(t)$ are both linear functions. So x and y both decrease at a constant rate. That suggests that the curve is the line between the points $(1, 2)$ and $(-1, 1)$.

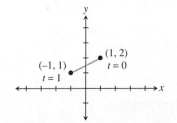

Figure 11.3   Curve C goes from $(1, 2)$ to $(-1, 1)$ as t goes from 0 to 1.

Eliminating the Parameter from a Parametric Representation

Sometimes a curve that is defined parametrically can also be described as the graph of a function. In that event it is often possible to describe the curve in terms of only the variables x and y. This process is called **eliminating the parameter**. Here is how to eliminate the parameter for the curve in Example 1.

$$x = 1 - 2t \quad \text{or} \quad t = 0.5(1 - x)$$

$$y = 2 - t \quad \text{or} \quad t = 2 - y$$

Since each equation has been solved for t, the two equations can be set equal to each other.

$$2 - y = 0.5(1 - x)$$

$$4 - 2y = 1 - x$$

$$2y - x = 3$$

The fact that this final equation is an equation of a straight line provides further evidence that the curve in Example 1 is part of a line. The extent of the line segment is determined by the interval I from which the parameter is chosen.

EXAMPLE 2 . Eliminating the Parameter

Eliminate the parameter from the curve C defined by $x(t) = t - 1$ and $y(t) = t^2$ for t in the interval $I = [0, 3]$. Describe this curve.

Solution Solve the first parametric equation for t and substitute in the second equation:

$$t = x + 1$$

$$y = t^2 = (x + 1)^2 = x^2 + 2x + 1 \quad \text{Square } t \text{ so that we can substitute for } t^2 = y.$$

Since $(x(0), y(0)) = (-1, 0)$ and $(x(3), y(3)) = (2, 9)$, we see that the curve C is that part of the parabola $y = x^2 + 2x + 1$ that lies between $(-1, 0)$ and $(2, 9)$ (see Fig. 11.4). ∎

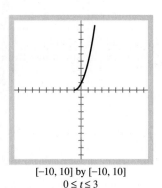

[−10, 10] by [−10, 10]
$0 \le t \le 3$

Figure 11.4 The curve C is the part of the parabola $y = x^2 + 2x + 1$ from $(-1, 0)$ to $(2, 9)$.

Describing Any Function $y = f(x)$ with Parametric Equations

It is not always possible to eliminate the parameter t as was done in Example 2. However, if you begin with a function $y = f(x)$, its graph can always be described parametrically using the parametric equations

$$x = t$$

$$y = f(t).$$

EXAMPLE 3 Describing a Function as Parametric Equations

Describe the graph of $y = 3x^4 + 7x^3 - 8x^2 - 3$ with parametric equations.

Solution The graph of this equation can be described by the parametric equations

$$x = t$$

$$y = 3t^4 + 7t^3 - 8t^2 - 3.$$ ∎

E X A M P L E   4   Finding Parametric Equations for a Circle

Find parametric equations for the circle with its center at the origin and a radius of 2.

Solution   Recall from Chapter 7 that if a point P on the unit circle determines an angle in standard position, then the coordinates of P are $(\cos\theta, \sin\theta)$ (see Fig. 11.5).

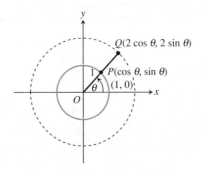

Figure 11.5   Coordinates of a point P on a unit circle and of a point Q on a circle with a radius of 2.

Parametric equations with parameter θ for a circle of radius 2 can be obtained by multiplying each coordinate function by 2 to obtain

$$x = 2\cos\theta$$

$$y = 2\sin\theta.$$

We obtain a complete circle if θ varies through any interval with a length of 2π, say $[0, 2\pi]$ (see Fig. 11.5). ≡

Recall that for a relation (x, y), the set of all x-values is the domain of the relation and the set of all y-values is the range of the relation. In Example 4 the domain of the relation is $-2 \leq x \leq 2$ and the range of the relation is $-2 \leq y \leq 2$. Notice that the domain and range of a curve are not the same set as the domain for the parameter. In Example 4 the domain for the parameter is $[0, 2\pi]$.

E X A M P L E   5   Graphing a Curve Defined Parametrically

Find the complete graph of the curve defined by $x = t\cos t$ and $y = t\sin t$ for $0 \leq t \leq 4\pi$.

Solution   The graph shown in Fig. 11.6 can be found with a graphing utility. ≡

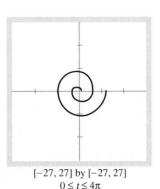

[−27, 27] by [−27, 27]
$0 \leq t \leq 4\pi$

Figure 11.6 $x = t\cos t$, $y = t\sin t$.

[−10, 10] by [−100, 100]
$0 \leq t \leq 20.5$

Figure 11.7 $x(t) = 5\sin t$ and $y(t) = 5t\cos t$. (See Example 6.)

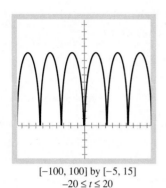

$[-100, 100]$ by $[-5, 15]$
$-20 \le t \le 20$

Figure 11.8 $x = 5t - 5\sin t$
and $y = 5 - 5\cos t$.

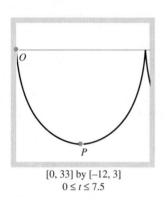

$[0, 33]$ by $[-12, 3]$
$0 \le t \le 7.5$

Figure 11.9 $x(t) = 5t - 5\sin t$
and $y(t) = -5 + 5\cos t$.

E X A M P L E   6   Graphing a Curve Defined Parametrically

Find the complete graph of the curve defined by $x(t) = 5\sin t$ and $y(t) = 5t\cos t$ for $0 \le t \le 20.5$.

Solution   Notice that $-5 \le x \le 5$. So use the viewing rectangle $[-10, 10]$ by $[-100, 100]$.

A graph of this curve appears in Fig. 11.7.   ≣

E X A M P L E   7   Graphing a Curve Defined Parametrically

Find a complete graph of the curve defined by the parametric equations $x = 5t - 5\sin t$ and $y = 5 - 5\cos t$.

Solution   Consider the range of values for x and y, and note that y is a periodic function of t. Since $-5\cos t$ varies from -5 to 5, observe that

$$0 \le y \le 10.$$

Likewise, $-5\sin t$ varies from -5 to 5. However, since $5t$ is an increasing function, x is not a periodic function. So

$$-\infty \le x \le \infty \quad \text{as } t \text{ varies from } -\infty \text{ to } \infty.$$

A complete graph of this curve for t in $[-20, 20]$ is seen in Fig. 11.8.   ≣

The graph of the parametric equations $x = a(t - \sin t)$ and $y = a(1 - \cos t)$ for any real number a and for all values of t is called a **cycloid**. So the graph in Fig. 11.8 is a cycloid.

Suppose one arc of a cycloid is reflected through the x-axis (see Fig. 11.9). Then, out of all possible curves connecting the origin to the point P (the first local minimum to the right of $x = 0$), a cycloid is the one that a ball will roll down, ignoring friction, in the *least* amount of time. Consequently, a physicist sometimes calls a cycloid a **curve of quickest descent**.

Exercises for Section 11.1

In Exercises 1 to 8, find the endpoints of the curve C defined by the given pair of parametric equations, and sketch a graph of the curve without using a graphing utility. Then support your work with a graphing utility.

1. $x(t) = 1 + t$ and $y(t) = t$ for t in $[0, 5]$

2. $x(t) = 1 + t$ and $y(t) = t$ for t in $[-3, 2]$

3. $x(t) = 2 - 3t$ and $y(t) = 5 + t$ for t in $[-1, 3]$

4. $x(t) = 2t - 3$ and $y(t) = 9 - 4t$ for t in $[3, 5]$

5. $x(t) = t$ and $y(t) = 2/t$ for t in $(0, 5]$

6. $x(t) = t + 2$ and $y(t) = 2/t$ for t in $[-3, 0) \cup (0, 3]$

7. $x(t) = 3\cos t$ and $y(t) = 3\sin t$ for t in $[0, 4\pi]$

8. $x(t) = 4\sin t$ and $y(t) = 4\cos t$ for t in $[-\pi/2, \pi/2]$

In Exercises 9 to 14, eliminate the parameter from the curve C defined by the given parametric equations. Then describe the curve.

9. $x(t) = 2 - 3t$ and $y(t) = 5 + t$ for t in $(-\infty, \infty)$

10. $x(t) = 5 - 3t$ and $y(t) = 2 + t$ for t in $[-2, 3]$

11. $x(t) = 2t$ and $y(t) = t^2$ for t in $[-3, 1]$

12. $x(t) = 3t - 1$ and $y(t) = t^2 + 2$ for t in $[-1, 4]$

13. $x(t) = 3\cos t$ and $y(t) = 3\sin t$ for t in $[0, \pi]$. (*Hint:* Use a trig identity.)

14. $x(t) = 2\sin t$ and $y(t) = 2\cos t$ for t in $[0, 3\pi/2]$.

In Exercises 15 to 18, use parametric equations to describe a curve that is the graph of the given functions.

15. $y = 3x^2 - 4x + 5$

16. $y = 9x^3 - 3x + 4$

17. $y = 7 + x^2 - 3x$

18. $y = \sin x + 4x^2$

19. Which of the curves in Exercises 1 to 8 are graphs of functions?

20. Which of the curves in Exercises 1 to 8 are graphs of one-to-one functions?

In Exercises 21 to 24, find the domain and range of each curve from the stated Exercise.

21. Exercise 2

22. Exercise 3

23. Exercise 5

24. Exercise 7

In Exercises 25 to 28, find parametric equations and sketch the graph of each circle with the given center and radius.

25. $(0,0)$, 5

26. $(10, 0)$, 4

27. $(0, 10)$, 6

28. (a, b), r

In Exercises 29 to 36, draw a complete graph of the curve defined by the given pair of parametric equations.

29. $x(t) = 4t - 2$ and $y = 8t^2$ for t in $(-\infty, \infty)$

30. $x(t) = 4\cos t$ and $y = 8\sin t$ for t in $(-2\pi, 2\pi)$

31. $x(t) = 1 + 1/t$ and $y = t - 1/t$ for t in $(0, 20]$

32. $x(t) = 2t - 2\sin t$ and $y(t) = 2 - 2\cos t$ for t in $[0, 40]$

33. $x(t) = 4t - 4\sin t$ and $y(t) = 4 - 4\cos t$ for t in $[0, 40]$

34. $x(t) = 6\cos t - 4\cos(\frac{3}{2}t)$ and $y(t) = 6\sin t - 4\sin(\frac{3}{2}t)$ for t in $[0, 2\pi]$. This is an *epicycloid*, the path of a point on a circle rolling on another circle.

35. $x(t) = 5\cos^3 t$ and $y(t) = 5\sin^3 t$ for t in $[0, 2\pi]$. This is a *hypocycloid* of four cusps.

36. $x(t) = 4(\cos t + t\sin t)$ and $y(t) = 4(\sin t - t\cos t)$ for t in $[0, 50]$. This is the *involute* of a circle. (*Hint:* Use a large viewing rectangle.)

37. Find the domain and range of the curve in Exercise 35.

38. Find the domain and range of the curve in Exercise 36.

39. Let $f(x) = 3 - x^2$. Show that the curve defined parametrically by $x(t) = at + b$ and $y(t) = f(t)$ for t in the interval $I = [c, d]$ is a *function* $y = g(x)$. Find a rule for $g(x)$. What is the domain of g?

40. Find the maximum value (if any) of $y(t)$ for the curve defined parametrically by $x(t) = 2t - 1$ and $y(t) = 4 - t^2$.

41. Find a complete graph of $x(t) = a(t - \sin t)$ and $y(t) = a(1 - \cos t)$ for $a = 1, 2, 3, 4$, and 5. Use zoom-in and determine the period of the curve and the maximum y-coordinate with the least positive x-coordinate.

42. Based on the results of Exercise 41, make a conjecture for the *period* and the maximum y-value with the least positive x-coordinate of the cycloid $x(t) = a(t - \sin t)$ and $y(t) = a(1 - \cos t)$ for an arbitrary value of a.

11.2 _____ Polar Coordinates and Graphs

Up to this point we have used a rectangular coordinate system. However, some curves cannot be described easily in a rectangular coordinate system. In this section we introduce a second coordinate system called the **polar coordinate system**.

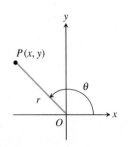

Figure 11.10 A point P with rectangular coordinates (x, y) and polar coordinates (r, θ).

Let $P(x, y)$ be a point in the rectangular coordinate system (Fig. 11.10). Point P lies on the terminal side of an angle θ in standard position and at a distance r from the origin O.

The pair of numbers (r, θ) are called **polar coordinates** of point P.

In the polar coordinate system the first coordinate describes the distance from the origin, and the second coordinate specifies an angle. Either degree measure or radian measure can be used to specify the second coordinate. Each number and angle pair determines a unique point. That is, no other point has these same polar coordinates.

E X A M P L E   1   Plotting Points with Polar Coordinates

Graph the points whose polar coordinates are: (a) $P(2, \pi/3)$, (b) $Q(1, 3\pi/4)$, (c) $R(3, -45°)$.

Solution   See Fig. 11.11.

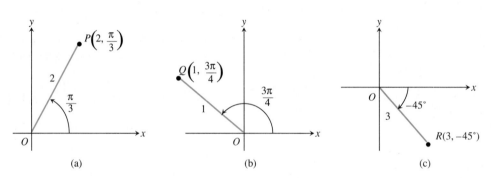

   (a)   (b)   (c)

Figure 11.11   Three points and their polar coordinates.

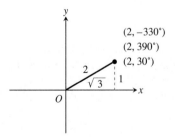

Figure 11.12   The point $P(\sqrt{3}, 1)$ with three different polar coordinates.

Example 1 illustrates that once a pair of polar coordinates is selected, a unique point has been determined. However, the converse is not true. The polar coordinates of a point $P(x, y)$ are *not unique*. For example, the polar coordinates $(2, 30°), (2, 390°)$, and $(2, -330°)$ all name the same point with rectangular coordinates $P(\sqrt{3}, 1)$ (see Fig. 11.12).

Fig. 11.11(c) shows a point with a negative second coordinate. The first coordinate can also be negative with the following interpretation. Suppose that $r > 0$. Figure 11.13 shows the relationship between the points whose polar coordinates are (r, θ) and $(-r, \theta)$. The distance of the point $P(-r, \theta)$ from the origin is r but in the direction opposite to the direction given by the terminal side of θ. So the polar coordinates $(-r, \theta)$ and $(r, \theta + \pi)$ name the same point.

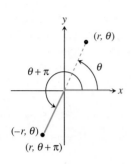

Figure 11.13 An interpretation for a negative value of r.

> **Theorem 11.1   Polar Coordinates of Points**
>
> Let (r, θ) be polar coordinates for a point P. Then, P also has the following for polar coordinates:
>
> $\quad (r, \theta + 2n\pi) \qquad$ (where n is any integer)
>
> $\quad (-r, \theta + \pi + 2n\pi) = (-r, \theta + (2n + 1)\pi) \qquad$ (where n is any integer)

The origin is assumed to have polar coordinates $(0, \theta)$ where θ can be any angle.

EXAMPLE 2   Finding Polar Coordinates of Points

Find three polar coordinates, using radian measure, for points whose rectangular coordinates are (a) $P(-\sqrt{3}, 1)$ and (b) $Q(-3, -3)$.

Solution   See Fig. 11.14.

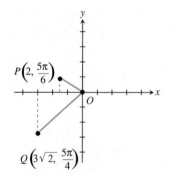

Figure 11.14   Reference triangles for the two points in Example 2.

a) The reference triangle for the point with rectangular coordinates $(-\sqrt{3}, 1)$ is a $30°$-$60°$ right triangle. Three of the many possible polar coordinates for point P are

$$\left(2, \frac{5\pi}{6}\right), \qquad \left(-2, \frac{-\pi}{6}\right), \qquad \text{and} \quad \left(-2, \frac{11\pi}{6}\right).$$

b) The reference triangle for the point with rectangular coordinates $(-3, -3)$ is a $45°$-$45°$ right triangle. Several polar coordinates for point Q are

$$\left(3\sqrt{2}, \frac{5\pi}{4}\right), \qquad \left(3\sqrt{2}, \frac{13\pi}{4}\right), \qquad \text{and} \quad \left(-3\sqrt{2}, \frac{\pi}{4}\right). \qquad \blacksquare$$

Conversion Equations

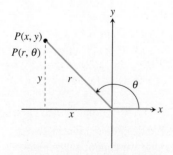

Figure 11.15   A point with polar coordinates (r, θ) and rectangular coordinates (x, y).

It is convenient for both computational and theoretical reasons to be able to convert between polar and rectangular coordinates. Figure 11.15 shows a point with rectangular coordinates $P(x, y)$ and polar coordinates $P(r, \theta)$ where r is positive. Using the reference triangle in this figure we obtain the following relationships:

$$x = r \cos \theta, \qquad\qquad r^2 = x^2 + y^2,$$

$$y = r \sin \theta, \qquad\qquad \tan \theta = \frac{y}{x} \; (x \neq 0).$$

It can be shown that these equations remain true when r is negative.

Theorem 11.2   Polar ↔ Cartesian Conversion Equations

Let a point P have rectangular coordinates (x, y) and polar coordinates (r, θ). Then

$$x = r \cos \theta, \qquad y = r \sin \theta, \qquad \textbf{(1)}$$

$$r^2 = x^2 + y^2, \qquad \tan \theta = \frac{y}{x} \ (x \neq 0). \qquad \textbf{(2)}$$

Example 3 gives the polar coordinates of points and asks you to find the rectangular coordinates.

E X A M P L E   3   Converting to Rectangular Coordinates

Find the rectangular coordinates of the points with the following polar coordinates: (a) $(3, 5\pi/6)$ and (b) $(2, -200°)$.

Solution

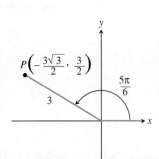

Figure 11.16   Converting $P(3, 5\pi/6)$ to rectangular coordinates.

a) Use Eq. (1) from Theorem 11.2 (see Fig. 11.16).

$$x = r \cos \theta \qquad\qquad y = r \sin \theta$$

$$= 3 \cos \frac{5\pi}{6} \qquad\qquad = 3 \sin \frac{5\pi}{6}$$

$$= -\frac{3\sqrt{3}}{2} \qquad\qquad = 3 \left(\frac{1}{2} \right) = \frac{3}{2}$$

The rectangular coordinates are $(-3\sqrt{3}/2, \frac{3}{2})$.

b) See Fig. 11.17.

$$x = r \cos \theta \qquad\qquad y = r \sin \theta$$

$$= 2 \cos(-200°) \qquad\qquad = 2 \sin(-200°)$$

$$= -1.88 \qquad\qquad = 0.68$$

The rectangular coordinates are $(-1.88, 0.68)$.   ▰

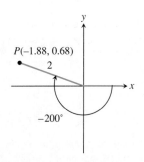

Figure 11.17   Converting $P(2, -200°)$ to rectangular coordinates.

In Example 4 the reverse situation occurs. The rectangular coordinates are given and some polar coordinates are found. (Notice that we cannot say *the* coordinates, because the polar coordinates are not unique.)

Suppose that we are given a point $P(x, y)$ in rectangular coordinates and want to find polar coordinates (r, θ) for P. For the first coordinate we can use the relation $r = \sqrt{x^2 + y^2}$ (Theorem 11.2). Finding the second coordinate θ is not always so straightforward. Recall that the inverse tangent on a calculator always returns values in radians between $-\pi/2$ and $\pi/2$. If P is in quadrants I or IV, the coordinates $(r, \tan^{-1}(y/x))$ are polar coordinates for P. However, if P is in quadrants II or III, the polar coordinates must be chosen more carefully, as illustrated in Example 4.

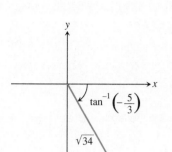

Figure 11.18 Converting $P(3, -5)$ to polar coordinates.

EXAMPLE 4   Converting to Polar Coordinates

Find polar coordinates for the points with the following rectangular coordinates: (a) $(3, -5)$, (b) $(-1, 1)$, and (c) $(-2, -3)$.

Solution

a) Point $P(3, -5)$ is in quadrant IV (see Fig. 11.18).

$$r = \sqrt{3^2 + (-5)^2} = \sqrt{34}$$

$$\tan\theta = -\frac{5}{3} \quad \text{or} \quad \theta = \tan^{-1}\left(-\frac{5}{3}\right) = -1.03$$

Polar coordinates of point P are $(\sqrt{34}, -1.03)$ or $(5.83, -1.03)$.

b) Point $P(-1, 1)$ is in quadrant II (see Fig. 11.19).

$$r = \sqrt{(-1)^2 + 1^2} = \sqrt{2}$$

$$\tan\theta = -1$$

Since $\tan^{-1}(-1) = -\pi/4$ is in the fourth quadrant, use the angle $\pi + \tan^{-1}(-1) = 3\pi/4$ in the second quadrant whose tangent is also -1.

Polar coordinates of P are $(\sqrt{2}, \dfrac{3\pi}{4})$.

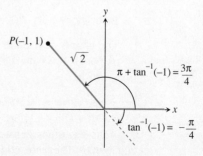

Figure 11.19 Converting $P(-1, 1)$ to polar coordinates.

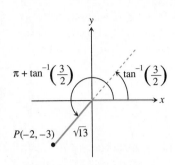

Figure 11.20 Converting $P(-2, -3)$ to polar coordinates.

c) The point $P(-2, -3)$ is in quadrant III (see Fig. 11.20).

$$r = \sqrt{(-2)^2 + (-3)^2} = \sqrt{13}$$

$$\tan \theta = \frac{-3}{-2}$$

Since $\tan^{-1}\left(\frac{3}{2}\right) = 0.98$ is in the first quadrant, use the angle $\pi + \tan^{-1}\left(\frac{3}{2}\right) = 4.12$ in the third quadrant whose tangent is also $\frac{3}{2}$.

So polar coordinates of $(-2, -3)$ are $(\sqrt{13}, 4.12)$.   ≡

The solution methods used in Example 4 can be generalized, as stated in Theorem 11.3.

Theorem 11.3   Polar Coordinates from Rectangular Coordinates

Let P have rectangular coordinates (x, y). Then, the following are polar coordinates for P where $r = \sqrt{x^2 + y^2}$:

a) $\left(r, \tan^{-1}\left(\frac{y}{x}\right)\right)$, if (x, y) is in the first or fourth quadrant.

b) $\left(r, \pi + \tan^{-1}\left(\frac{y}{x}\right)\right)$ if (x, y) is in the second or third quadrant.

Theorems 11.2 and 11.3 provide techniques for converting rectangular coordinates to polar coordinates and vice versa.

Polar Graphs

A function $r = f(\theta)$ where r and θ are polar coordinate variables can be graphed in the polar coordinate plane. The following definition applies to relations in addition to functions.

Definition 11.2   Graph of a Polar Equation

The **graph of a polar equation in the variables r and θ** is the set of all points (r, θ) in the polar coordinate plane where (r, θ) is a solution to the equation.

The equations considered in the next example are the simplest kind of polar equations. They are constant functions analogous to the rectangular coordinate equations of the form $x = a$ and $y = b$.

EXAMPLE 5 Drawing Graphs of Simple Polar Equations

Draw a complete graph of each polar equation: (a) $r = 2$ and (b) $\theta = 2$.

Solution

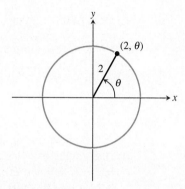

Figure 11.21   Polar coordinate graph of $r = 2$.

a) The graph of $r = 2$ consists of all points whose polar coordinates are $(2, \theta)$ where θ is any angle (see Fig. 11.21). The set of all such points is the circle with the center at the origin and a radius 2.

b) The graph of $\theta = 2$ consists of all points with polar coordinates $(r, 2)$ where r is any real number (see Fig. 11.22). The set of all such points is a straight line through the origin.

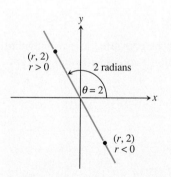

Figure 11.22   Polar coordinate graph of $\theta = 2$.

To draw the graph of a polar coordinate equation like $r = 3 + 3 \sin \theta$, consider all pairs (r, θ) as θ varies throughout an interval.

EXAMPLE 6 Graphing a Cardioid

Sketch a complete graph of the polar equation $r = 3 + 3 \sin \theta$ for $0 \le \theta \le 2\pi$.

Solution   If $0 \le \theta \le \pi/2$, then $0 \le \sin \theta \le 1$. Multiply all sides of this second inequality by 3 and add 3 to all sides to get

$$3 \le 3 + 3 \sin \theta \le 6.$$

Therefore, as θ increases from 0 to $\pi/2$, the variable r increases from 3 to 6. In like manner you can determine the behavior of r for $\pi/2 \le \theta \le 2\pi$. The results are summarized here.

θ	$\sin\theta$	$r = 3 + 3\sin\theta$
$0 \le \theta \le \dfrac{\pi}{2}$	Increases from 0 to 1	Increases from 3 to 6
$\dfrac{\pi}{2} \le \theta \le \pi$	Decreases from 1 to 0	Decreases from 6 to 3
$\pi \le \theta \le \dfrac{3\pi}{2}$	Decreases from 0 to -1	Decreases from 3 to 0
$\dfrac{3\pi}{2} \le \theta \le 2\pi$	Increases from -1 to 0	Increases from 0 to 3

Notice that the graph in Fig. 11.23 is traced in a counterclockwise fashion through the four quadrants beginning at $(3,0)$, moving to $(6,\pi/2)$, then to $(3,\pi)$, followed by $\left(0,\frac{3\pi}{2}\right)$, and ending with $(3,2\pi)$. ≡

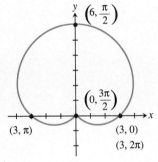

Figure 11.23 $y = 3 + 3\sin\theta$.

The graph in Fig. 11.23 is called a **cardioid** because of its heartlike shape. All the graphs of polar equations of the form $r = a \pm a\sin\theta$ or $r = a \pm a\cos\theta$ (where a is any nonzero constant real number) are cardioids.

Since the function $r = 3 + 3\sin\theta$ in Example 6 is a periodic function with a period of 2π, a complete graph was found restricting the domain to the interval $[0, 2\pi]$. If θ varies from 2π to 4π, the curve is completely retraced. In fact, the graph in Fig. 11.23 is also the graph of $r = 3 + 3\sin\theta$ for θ in $(-\infty, \infty)$. These facts can be supported using a parametric grapher, as illustrated in Example 7 later in this section.

Converting from Polar to Rectangular Form

The polar equation $r = 3 + 3\sin\theta$ in Example 6 can be converted to a rectangular equation in x and y by using the conversion equations from Theorem 11.2. For example,

$$r = 3 + 3\sin\theta$$

$$r = 3 + 3\frac{y}{r}$$

$$r^2 = 3r + 3y$$

$$x^2 + y^2 = 3\sqrt{x^2 + y^2} + 3y.$$

Notice that this equation in x and y is a relation that does not define a function $y = f(x)$. This confirms the observation that the vertical line test, a test that applies only to the rectangular coordinate system, is not satisfied for the graph in Fig. 11.23. This also demonstrates one of the reasons for using the polar coordinate system. Curves that cannot be described very easily in rectangular form often have simple polar equations. The cardioid is one such curve.

Graphing Polar Equations

Most modern graphing utilities can graph polar coordinate equations using the parametric graphing option illustrated in the next example.

Theorem 11.4   Polar Equations in Parametric Form

The graph of the polar equation $r = f(\theta)$ is the curve defined by the parametric equations

$$x(t) = f(t) \cos t$$

$$y(t) = f(t) \sin t.$$

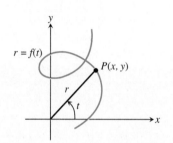

Figure 11.24   Consider a point $P(x, y)$ on a curve defined by a polar equation.

Proof   Let (x, y) be the rectangular coordinates of a point P on the polar graph $r = f(t)$ (see Fig. 11.24). By definition of the trig functions we have

$$\sin t = \frac{y}{r}, \qquad \cos t = \frac{x}{r}.$$

Thus $x = r \cos t = f(t) \cos t$, and $y = r \sin t = f(t) \sin t$. Notice that we have replaced θ with t in $r = f(\theta)$.   ≡

EXAMPLE 7   Finding the Parametric Form

Determine parametric equations for the curve $r = 7 \sin 2\theta$. Find a complete graph of the curve.

Solution   By Theorem 11.4 the parametric equations are

$$x(t) = 7 \sin 2t \cos t$$

$$y(t) = 7 \sin 2t \sin t.$$

A complete graph for $0 \le t \le 2\pi$ is shown in Fig. 11.25.   ≡

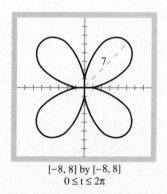

[−8, 8] by [−8, 8]
$0 \le t \le 2\pi$

Figure 11.25   The four-leafed rose $r = 7 \sin 2\theta$.

Notice that the length of each loop or petal of the graph in Fig. 11.25 is 7 units—a result of the fact that the maximum value of $r = 7 \sin 2\theta$ is 7. In general, the graph of equations in the form $r = a \sin 2\theta$ (where a is a constant real number) is a **four-petaled rose** whose petals have a length of $|a|$ units.

The graph in the next example is called a **spiral of Archimedes.**

EXAMPLE 8   Graphing the Spiral of Archimedes

Find the graph of $r = \theta$ as θ varies over the following intervals. Complete a separate graph for each interval.

a) $[0, 2\pi], [0, 4\pi], [0, 8\pi]$

b) $[-4\pi, 0], [-8\pi, 0], [-8\pi, 8\pi]$

Solution To find this graph use the parametric equations $x = t \cos t, y = t \sin t$.

a) Notice that the three curves in Fig. 11.26 are all counterclockwise spirals.

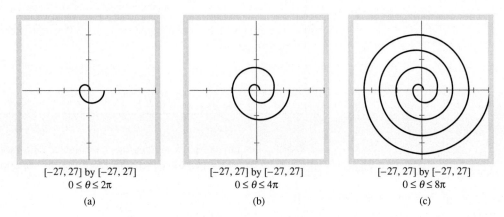

$[-27, 27]$ by $[-27, 27]$
$0 \le \theta \le 2\pi$

(a)

$[-27, 27]$ by $[-27, 27]$
$0 \le \theta \le 4\pi$

(b)

$[-27, 27]$ by $[-27, 27]$
$0 \le \theta \le 8\pi$

(c)

Figure 11.26 $r = \theta$ (spiral of Archimedes) for $\theta \ge 0$ over three intervals.

b) The two curves in Fig. 11.27(a,b) are clockwise spirals from the pole. Comparison of Figs. 11.26 and Fig. 11.27(a,b) shows that the spirals are counterclockwise as θ varies from zero to positive values and clockwise as θ varies from zero to negative values. The interval in Fig. 11.27(c) includes both positive and negative values, so both clockwise and counterclockwise spirals are present. ≡

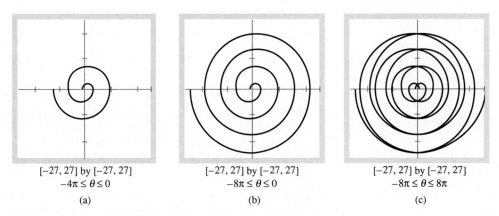

$[-27, 27]$ by $[-27, 27]$
$-4\pi \le \theta \le 0$

(a)

$[-27, 27]$ by $[-27, 27]$
$-8\pi \le \theta \le 0$

(b)

$[-27, 27]$ by $[-27, 27]$
$-8\pi \le \theta \le 8\pi$

(c)

Figure 11.27 $r = \theta$. (a, b) $\theta \le 0$ over two intervals, and (c) θ in an interval with positive and negative values.

Exercises for Section 11.2

In Exercises 1 to 4, compute the polar coordinates (r, θ) for $0 \leq \theta < 360°$ for each point with the given rectangular coordinates.

1. $(1, 1)$ **2.** $(-10, 0)$

3. $(-3, 4)$ **4.** $(-2, 5)$

In Exercises 5 to 10, compute the rectangular coordinates for each point with the given polar coordinates.

5. $(0, \pi)$ **6.** $(2, 30°)$ **7.** $(-3, 135°)$

8. $(-2, -120°)$ **9.** $\left(3, \dfrac{3\pi}{4}\right)$ **10.** $\left(2, \dfrac{\pi}{12}\right)$

In Exercises 11 to 18, find three polar coordinate pairs for the point with given rectangular coordinates. Include at least one pair with a negative first coordinate.

11. $(-2, 2)$ **12.** $(2\sqrt{3}, -2)$ **13.** $(-\sqrt{3}, 1)$

14. $(-4, -4)$ **15.** $(2, -3)$ **16.** $(1, 4)$

17. $(-3, -1)$ **18.** $(-2, 3)$

In Exercises 19 to 28, sketch a complete graph of each equation without using a graphing utility. If possible, support your answer with a polar graphing utility.

19. $r = 3$ **20.** $\theta = \dfrac{\pi}{4}$

21. $\theta = -\dfrac{\pi}{2}$ **22.** $r = -1$

23. $r = 3\cos\theta$ **24.** $r = 2\sin\theta$

25. $r = 2 + 2\cos\theta$ **26.** $r = 4 + 4\sin\theta$

27. $r = -1 + 2\cos\theta$ **28.** $r = \sin 2\theta$

In Exercises 29 to 32, write the polar equation in parametric form for θ in the given interval. Graph *both* the parametric and polar forms with an appropriate graphing utility.

29. $r = 3\theta, \ [0, 10\pi]$ **30.** $r = 5\sin\theta, \ [-\pi, \pi]$

31. $r = 5\sin 2\theta, \ [0, \pi]$ **32.** $r = 5\sin 3\theta, \ [0, 2\pi]$

In Exercises 33 to 36, use a graphing utility to find the polar graph for θ in each of the given intervals.

33. $r = 3\theta$
   a) $0 \leq \theta \leq \dfrac{\pi}{2}$
   b) $0 \leq \theta \leq \pi$
   c) $0 \leq \theta \leq 2\pi$
   d) $-\pi \leq \theta \leq \pi$
   e) $0 \leq \theta \leq 4\pi$

34. $r = 5\sin\theta$
   a) $0 \leq \theta \leq \dfrac{\pi}{2}$
   b) $0 \leq \theta \leq \pi$
   c) $0 \leq \theta \leq 2\pi$
   d) $-\pi \leq \theta \leq \pi$
   e) $0 \leq \theta \leq 4\pi$

35. $r = 5\cos 3\theta$
   a) $0 \leq \theta \leq \dfrac{\pi}{2}$
   b) $0 \leq \theta \leq \pi$

36. $r = 5\sin 2\theta$
   a) $0 \leq \theta \leq \dfrac{\pi}{2}$
   b) $0 \leq \theta \leq \pi$

   c) $0 \leq \theta \leq 2\pi$
   d) $-\pi \leq \theta \leq \pi$
   e) $0 \leq \theta \leq 4\pi$

   c) $0 \leq \theta \leq 2\pi$
   d) $-\pi \leq \theta \leq \pi$
   e) $0 \leq \theta \leq 4\pi$

In Exercises 37 to 42, use a polar graphing utility to find a complete graph of the polar equation. Specify an interval $a \leq \theta \leq b$ of smallest length that gives a complete graph.

37. $r = 2\theta$ **38.** $r = 0.275\theta$

39. $r = 2 - 3\cos\theta$ **40.** $r = 2\sin 3\theta$

41. $r = 3\sin^2\theta$ **42.** $r = 2 - 2\sin\theta$

43. Use a polar graphing utility to find a complete graph of $r = 5\sin n\theta$ for $n = 1, 2, 3, 4, 5$, and 6. Explain how the number of petals is related to n.

44. Use a polar graphing utility to find a complete graph of $r = 5\cos n\theta$ for $n = 1, 2, 3, 4, 5$, and 6. Explain how the number of petals is related to n.

For Exercises 45 and 46, use a polar graphing utility to find a complete graph of the given equation for $a = 1, 2, 3, 4, 5$, and 10. What is the effect of the parameter a on the graph?

45. $r = a\sin 2\theta$ **46.** $r = a\cos 3\theta$

In Exercises 47 to 50, determine the length of *one* petal.

47. $r = 5\sin 3\theta$ **48.** $r = 5\sin 2\theta$

49. $r = 8\sin 5\theta$ **50.** $r = 8\sin 4\theta$

For Exercises 51 to 54, draw the graph of $r = 5\sin 2\theta$ and $r = 5\sin 3\theta$ in the standard viewing rectangle.

51. Predict what the graph of $r = 5\sin 2.5\theta$ looks like. Then draw a complete graph of $r = 5\sin 2.5\theta$ with a polar graphing utility.

52. Give an algebraic argument for the appearance of the graph in Exercise 51.

53. Predict the graph of $r = 5\sin 3.5\theta$. Confirm your graph by using a polar graphing utility.

54. Predict the graph of

$$r = a\sin\left(\dfrac{m}{n}\theta\right)$$

where m and n are *relatively prime* positive integers (that is, m and n have no common factors).

55. Find polar coordinates of the vertices of a square with a side length of a whose center is at the origin. Assume that the square is positioned with two sides parallel to the x-axis.

56. Find polar coordinates of the vertices of a regular pentagon if the center is at the origin, one vertex is on the positive x-axis, and the distance from the center to a vertex is a.

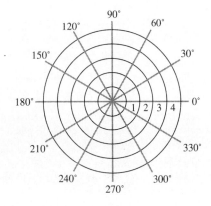

For Exercise 57

57. Before computers, polar graphs were often sketched using polar graph paper as shown in the figure. Use polar graph paper (you can make it yourself using a ruler, protractor, and compass) to sketch a complete graph of $r = 3 \sin 2\theta$ for $0 \le \theta \le 360°$. Plot points for $\theta = 0 + k \cdot 30°$, where $k = 0, 1, 2, \ldots, 12$.

In Exercises 58 to 61, use the parametric equation method of Example 7 to find the points of intersection of these graphs.

58. $\begin{cases} r = 5\sin\theta \\ r = 5\cos\theta \end{cases}$ **59.** $\begin{cases} r = 5\sin\theta \\ r = 5\sin 3\theta \end{cases}$

60. $\begin{cases} r = \theta/\pi \\ r = 3\sin\theta \end{cases}$ **61.** $\begin{cases} r = 2\cos\theta - 1 \\ r = 3\sin 2\theta \end{cases}$

62. Show that if P_1 and P_2 have polar coordinates (r_1, θ_1) and (r_2, θ_2) respectively, then the distance between P_1 and P_2 is $d(P_1, P_2) = \sqrt{r_1^2 + r_2^2 - 2r_1r_2\cos(\theta_2 - \theta_1)}$.

11.3 ———— Motion Problems and Parametric Equations

Motion Along a Line

In Section 2.6 we studied the projectile-motion problem situation in which a ball was thrown straight up in the air. The ball was imagined to be moving up and down along a vertical line (see Fig. 11.28).

In this section we consider other kinds of linear and nonlinear motion problem situations, and see how parametric equations can be used to represent them. Having briefly reviewed vertical motion, we now consider the case in which an object is moving along a horizontal line, say the x-axis.

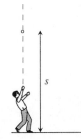

Figure 11.28 Height s of a ball thrown straight up in the air.

Motion-on-a-Line Problem Situation

The position (x-coordinate) of a particle moving on the x-axis is given by

$$x = s(t) = 2t^3 - 13t^2 + 22t - 5$$

where t is time in seconds. Describe the motion of the particle. When does it speed up? When does it slow down? When does it change direction?

See how many of these questions you can answer while completing the following Exploration.

🔍 EXPLORE WITH A GRAPHING UTILITY

Set a graphing calculator as follows:

- Rad mode,   Param mode
- Range: Tmin = 0, Tmax = 5, Tstep = 0.05
- Viewing rectangle: $[-10, 10]$ by $[-2, 6]$
- Define: $X_1(T) = 2T^3 - 13T^2 + 22T - 5$ and $Y_1(T) = 2$

1. Press the graph key. After the curve has been drawn, press the trace key. Use the left arrow key to move the trace cursor until the parameter has the value $T = 0$. You are now ready to do a simulation.

2. Hold down the right arrow key and watch the cursor move. Write a description of this motion.

3. For what values of t does the particle change directions? What is the x position where it changes direction?

4. For an alternate visualization, let $X_2(T) = 2T^3 - 13T^2 + 22T - 5$ and $Y_2(T) = T$. Set the calculator to Simul mode. Now press GRAPH. (Make sure that all four functions $X_1(T), Y_1(T), X_2(T),$ and $Y_2(T)$ are selected.)

This Exploration gave you experience with motion along a line. Next we use parametric equations to study motion in the plane.

Motion in the Plane

Recall the projectile-motion problem situation explored in Section 2.6. When an object is thrown straight up (that is, 90° from the horizontal) from a point s_0 feet above level ground with an initial velocity of v_0, then

$$s = -16t^2 + v_0 t + s_0, \tag{1}$$

where s is the distance of the object above ground level, t seconds after it is thrown.

Using parametric equations this problem situation can be extended to the case where the ball is thrown at an angle other than 90° from the horizontal.

Suppose that a ball is thrown with an initial velocity of 50 ft/sec at an angle of 60° with the x-axis, and assume that the only force acting on the object is due

Figure 11.29   Vector representing the velocity of a thrown ball.

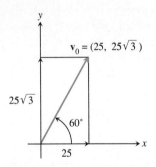

Figure 11.30   Vector components for the initial velocity of a ball thrown at an angle.

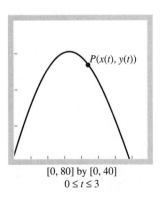

[0, 80] by [0, 40]
$0 \le t \le 3$

Figure 11.31   Complete graph of the problem situation in Example 1.

to gravity. Velocity is a vector quantity, so this throw can be represented by a vector as shown in Fig. 11.29.

If v_0 is the initial velocity vector, the horizontal component is $50 \cos 60°$ and the vertical component is $50 \sin 60°$. Thus $v_0 = (25, 25\sqrt{3})$. (See Fig. 11.30.) The horizontal direction of 25 ft/sec means that after t seconds the ball has traveled $x = 25t$ feet horizontally.

The vertical component of $25\sqrt{3}$ ft/sec represents the initial velocity in a $90°$ direction from the horizontal—precisely the projectile motion described generally by Eq. (1). So the y-coordinate after t seconds is $y = -16t^2 + 25\sqrt{3}t$. Therefore the position $P(x(t), y(t))$ of the ball t seconds after it is thrown is described by the parametric equations

$$x = 25t \tag{2a}$$

$$y = -16t^2 + 25\sqrt{3}t. \tag{2b}$$

Notice that, in using Eq. (1) to arrive at Eq. (2b), we let $s_0 = 0$, even though the ball leaves the thrower's hand a few feet above ground level. In the next example we will continue to make this assumption since it will not alter the results significantly, but it will simplify the calculations. Later examples will consider problem situations in which $s_0 \ne 0$.

EXAMPLE 1   APPLICATION: Projectile Motion at an Angle

A baseball is thrown with an initial velocity of 50 ft/sec at an angle of $60°$ with the positive x-axis. Assume that the only force acting on the baseball is due to gravity.

a) When will the ball hit the ground?

b) How far does the ball travel in the horizontal direction?

c) What is the maximum height attained by the ball?

Solution   The curve of the thrown ball is described by the parametric equations $x = 25t$ and $y = -16t^2 + 25\sqrt{3}t$. Find the complete graph shown in Fig. 11.31 and use TRACE to estimate that the ball hits the ground about 2.7 seconds after it is thrown and it lands about 67.5 feet away. Its maximum height is about 29.3 feet.

a) The ball will hit the ground when $y(t) = 0$.

$$y(t) = -16t^2 + 25\sqrt{3}t = 0$$

$$t(25\sqrt{3} - 16t) = 0$$

Now, $y(t) = 0$ when $t = 0$ or $t = 25\sqrt{3}/16$. Thus the object will hit the ground when $t = 25\sqrt{3}/16 = 2.7063294$, or approximately 2.71 seconds after launch.

b) The horizontal distance when it hits the ground is $x(t)$ when $t = 2.7063294$. That is,

$$x(2.7063294) = 25(2.7063294) = 67.658235.$$

The ball will travel 67.66 feet.

c) The path the ball travels is a parabola that opens down (see Fig. 11.31). Since its zeros occur when $t = 0$ or $t = 25\sqrt{3}/16$, the ball will reach its maximum height when t is halfway between $t = 25\sqrt{3}/32 = 1.3531647$. The maximum height will be

$$y\left(\frac{25\sqrt{3}}{32}\right) = 29.30 \text{ feet.}$$

In Example 1 the path of a thrown ball was described using parametric equations. With only a slight change in point of view, we can describe this path with vector notation.

The position of the ball at any time t of the object in vector form is

$$\mathbf{p} = (25t, 25\sqrt{3}t - 16t^2).$$

We can rewrite $\mathbf{p}$ as follows:

$$\begin{aligned}
\mathbf{p} &= (25t, 25\sqrt{3}t - 16t^2) \\
&= (25t, 25\sqrt{3}t) + (0, -16t^2) \\
&= t(25, 25\sqrt{3}) + (0, -16t^2)
\end{aligned}$$

So $\mathbf{p} = \mathbf{v}_1 + \mathbf{v}_2$ where $\mathbf{v}_1 = t\mathbf{v}_0 = t(25, 25\sqrt{3})$ and $\mathbf{v}_2 = (0, -16t^2)$. See Fig. 11.32.

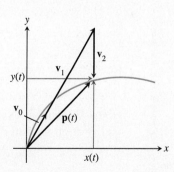

Figure 11.32   The path of an object is $\mathbf{p}(t) = \mathbf{v}_1 + \mathbf{v}_2$ where $\mathbf{v}_1 = t\mathbf{v}_0$.

The position of $\mathbf{p}$ at time t thus depends on the two vectors $\mathbf{v}_0$ and $\mathbf{v}_2$, where $\mathbf{v}_2$ depends only on gravity.

Using Vector and Parametric Equations to Solve Motion Problems

The next four examples illustrate application problems that can be solved using vector and parametric equations. Without the use of powerful graphing tools we could not easily solve these problems.

E X A M P L E   2   APPLICATION: Motion against the Wind

A baseball is hit when the ball is 3 feet above the ground and leaves the bat with initial velocity of 150 feet per second and at an angle of elevation of $20°$. A 6-mph wind is blowing in the horizontal direction against the batter. A 20-foot-high fence is 400 feet from home plate. Will the hit go over the fence to be a home run?

Solution   Find a vector equation that describes the position of the ball at any time t. The time t that the ball is 400 feet from home plate can be used to determine the height of the ball.

Set up a coordinate system with the origin at home plate. Assume that the batter hits the ball in the direction of the positive x-axis. Fig. 11.33 diagrams this problem situation.

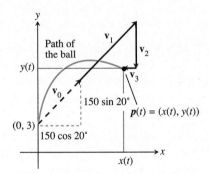

Figure 11.33   Vector diagram for Example 2. $\mathbf{p}(t)$ is the position of the ball at time t.

Initial Velocity $\mathbf{v_0}$ $\mathbf{v_0} = (150\cos 20°, 150\sin 20°)$. Ignoring gravity and the wind, the effect on the ball due to the hit at any time t is given by $\mathbf{v_1}$ where

$$\mathbf{v_1} = (150t\cos 20°, 150t\sin 20°).$$

Gravity Vector $\mathbf{v_2}$ We have seen when studying the projectile-motion problem situation that the vertical position at time t is given by $y(t) = -16t^2 + 150t\sin 20° + 3$. In other words,

$$\mathbf{v_2} = (0, 3 - 16t^2).$$
Notice that this vector takes into account that the ball was hit 3 feet off the ground.

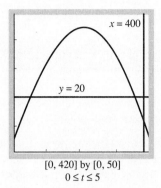

[0, 420] by [0, 50]
$0 \leq t \leq 5$

Figure 11.34 Curve described by the system of equations $x(t) = 150t \cos 20° - 8.8t$ and $y(t) = 150t \sin 20° + 3 - 16t^2$.

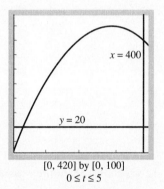

[0, 420] by [0, 100]
$0 \leq t \leq 5$

Figure 11.35 The ball clears the fence ($y = 20$) at 400 feet.

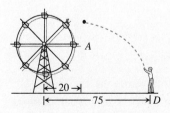

Figure 11.36 A person standing on the ground throws a ball to a person on a rotating ferris wheel.

Wind Vector v_3   60 mph is the same as 88 ft/sec so 6 mph is the same as 8.8 ft/sec. The wind vector is thus

$$\mathbf{v}_3 = (-8.8t, 0).$$

> The first coordinate is negative because the direction of the wind is opposite that of the hit ball, which is along the positive x-axis.

So the path of the ball is described by $\mathbf{p}(t)$ where

$$\mathbf{p}(t) = \mathbf{v}_1 + \mathbf{v}_2 + \mathbf{v}_3$$

$$= (150t \cos 20°, 150t \sin 20°) + (0, 3 - 16t^2) + (-8.8t, 0)$$

$$= (150t \cos 20° - 8.8t, 150t \sin 20° + 3 - 16t^2).$$

It now follows that

$$x(t) = 150t \cos 20° - 8.8t \qquad \text{and} \qquad y(t) = 150t \sin 20° + 3 - 16t^2 .$$

Figure 11.34 shows a graph of this pair of parametric equations. Clearly, when $x = 400$, $y < 20$, and the ball will *not* clear the fence. Therefore the hit will not be a home run. ≡

E X A M P L E   3   APPLICATION: Motion against the Wind

Suppose the ball of Example 2 leaves the bat at an angle of elevation of 30° but all other conditions of the example remain the same. Will this hit be a home run?

Solution   Only the angle value changes from the previous example. The parametric equations for the path of the ball in this case are

$$x(t) = 150t \cos 30° - 8.8t$$

$$y(t) = 150t \sin 30° + 3 - 16t^2 .$$

Fig. 11.35 shows the path of the ball. It is evident that at a distance of 400 feet the ball is high enough to clear a 20-foot fence. ≡

Now we use the information gained in previous examples to help solve the following problem posed by Neal Koblitz in the March 1988 issue of *The American Mathematical Monthly.*

E X A M P L E   4   APPLICATION: Throwing Ball at a Ferris Wheel

Eric is standing on the ground at point D, a distance of 75 feet from the bottom of a ferris wheel that is 20 feet in radius (see Fig. 11.36). His arm is at the same height as the bottom of the ferris wheel. Janice is on the ferris wheel, which makes one revolution counterclockwise every 12 seconds. At the instant she is at point A Eric throws a ball to her at 60 ft/sec at an angle of 60° above the horizontal.

Assume that $g = 32$ ft/sec^2 (force due to gravity), and neglect air resistance. Will the ball get to Janice?

Solution   To solve this problem, find parametric equations that describe the path of both the ferris wheel and the thrown ball. By graphing these two paths simultaneously, you will simulate the situation.

Place a coordinate system on the problem situation diagram so that the center of the ferris wheel is at point $(0, 20)$ and the ball is thrown from point $(75, 0)$.

Path of Ferris Wheel (Path A)   The parametric equations for the position of a point P on a circle with center $C(0, 20)$ and radius 20 is

$$x_A = 20\cos\theta$$

$$y_A = 20 + 20\sin\theta$$

where θ is the angle that radius CP makes with the positive x-axis (see Fig. 11.37).

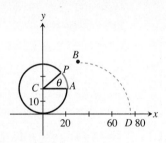

Figure 11.37   Diagram for Example 4.

The ferris wheel makes one revolution every 12 seconds. Therefore θ as a function of t in seconds is

$$\theta(t) = \frac{2\pi}{12}t = \frac{\pi}{6}t.$$

So the parametric equations that describe the position P of the friend on the ferris wheel are

$$x_A(t) = 20\cos\frac{\pi}{6}t$$

$$y_A(t) = 20 + 20\sin\frac{\pi}{6}t.$$

Path of Thrown Ball (Path B)   The ball is thrown towards the friend at a $60°$ angle with the ground, which makes an angle of $120°$ with respect to the positive x-axis. So the parametric equations that describe the path of the thrown ball are

$$x_B(t) = 75 + (60\cos 120°)t = 75 - 30t$$

$$y_B(t) = -16t^2 + (60\sin 120°)t = -16t^2 + 30\sqrt{3}\, t.$$

Graphing the two curves simultaneously shows that the ball comes close to Janice but does not reach her. Use the **trace** key to learn that the minimum distance between her and the ball occurs between 2.1 and 2.3 seconds.   ▤

We can use a graphing utility to investigate more closely what the minimum distance is between the ball and the person on the ferris wheel in Example 4.

E X A M P L E   5   APPLICATION: Minimum Distance

Find the minimum distance between the ball and the friend on the ferris wheel and the time at which the minimum occurs.

Solution   Earlier we saw that $x_A(t) = 20\cos(\pi t/6)$ and $y_A(t) = 20+20\sin(\pi t/6)$ are parametric equations for the path of the friend on the ferris wheel, and that $x_B(t) = 75 - 30t$ and $y_B(t) = 30\sqrt{3}\, t - 16t^2$ are parametric equations for the path of the ball.

The distance between the friend and the ball is given by

$$D(t) = \sqrt{[x_A(t) - x_B(t)]^2 + [y_A(t) - y_B(t)]^2}$$

$$= \sqrt{[20\cos(\tfrac{\pi}{6}t) - (75 - 30t)]^2 + [(20 + 20\sin(\tfrac{\pi}{6}t) - (30\sqrt{3}t - 16t^2)]^2}$$

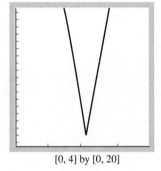

[0, 4] by [0, 20]

Figure 11.38   The distance between the friend and the ball is given by $D(t)$.

Fig. 11.38 shows the graph of $D(t)$ for t over the interval $[0, 4]$. Note that the ball hits the ground in a little over 3 seconds.

Using zoom-in, determine that the minimum distance is 1.59 feet with an error of at most 0.01, and that this minimum occurs when $t = 2.19$ seconds.   ▤

Exercises for Section 11.3

In Exercises 1 to 4, find a complete graph of the curve defined by the parametric equations.

1. $x(t) = 2t - 6\sin t$ and $y(t) = 2 - 6\cos t$

2. $x(t) = \cos^2 t$ and $y(t) = (1 - \cos t)\sin t$

3. $x(t) = 2 - 5\cos t$ and $y(t) = -2 + 4\cos t$

4. $x(t) = \dfrac{4}{1 + \sin t}\cos t$ and $y(t) = \dfrac{4}{1 + \sin t}\sin t$

5. An arrow is shot with an initial velocity of 205 ft/sec and at an angle of elevation of 48°. Find when and where the arrow will strike the ground.

6. With what initial velocity must a ball be thrown from the ground at an angle of 35° from the horizontal in order to travel a horizontal distance of 255 feet?

Exercises 7 to 12 refer to the following **problem situation**: A dart is thrown upward with an initial velocity of 58 ft/sec at an angle of elevation of 41°. Consider the position of the dart at any time t; $t = 0$ when the dart is thrown. Neglect air resistance.

7. Find parametric equations that model the problem situation.

8. Draw a complete graph of the model.

9. What portion of the graph represents the problem situation?

10. When will the dart hit the ground?

11. Find the maximum height of the dart. At what time will this occur?

12. How far does the dart travel in the horizontal direction? Neglect air resistance.

Exercises 13 and 14 refer to the following **problem situation**: A golfer hits a ball with an initial velocity of 133 ft/sec and at an angle of $36°$ from the horizontal.

13. Find when and where the ball will hit the ground.

14. Will the ball in Exercise 13 clear a fence 9 feet high that is at a distance of 275 feet from the golfer?

Exercises 15 to 20 refer to the following **problem situation**: Chris and Linda are standing 78 feet apart. At the same time they each throw a softball toward each other. Linda throws her ball with an initial velocity of 45 ft/sec with an angle of inclination of $44°$. Chris throws her ball with an initial velocity of 41 ft/sec with an angle of inclination of $39°$.

15. Find two sets of parametric equations that represent a model of the problem situation.

16. Find complete graphs of both sets of parametric equations in the same viewing rectangle.

17. What values of t make sense in this problem situation?

18. Find the maximum height of each ball. How far does each ball travel in the horizontal direction? When does each ball hit the ground? Whose ball hits first?

19. By choosing t_{max} carefully (guess and check), estimate how close the two balls get, and the time when they are closest (minimum distance). Be careful to use square windows.

20. Use the distance formula and zoom-in to find the minimum distance (and the time at which it occurs) with an error of less than 0.01.

Exercises 21 and 22 refer to the following **problem situation**: A river boat's paddle wheel has a diameter of 26 feet and makes one revolution clockwise in 2 seconds at full speed.

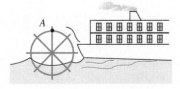

For Exercises 21 and 22

21. Write parametric equations describing the position of a point A on the paddle. Assume that, at $t = 0$, A is at the very top of the wheel.

22. How far has point A, which is fixed on the wheel, moved in 1 minute?

Exercises 23 to 26 refer to the ferris-wheel-and-ball **problem situation** described in Example 4.

23. Solve the problem if the radius of the ferris wheel is 26 feet and the ball is thrown with an initial velocity 76 ft/sec, at an angle of $52°$ with the horizontal, and from a distance of 62 feet from the bottom of the ferris wheel. Use parametric simulation and estimate your answer. (Assume that the ferris wheel revolves at a constant rate.)

24. Use the distance formula and zoom in to find the minimum distance between Janice and the ball.

25. Using the parametric simulation, vary the position of the ball thrower from 62 feet to see how close Eric can get the ball to Janice on the ferris wheel. Use a guess and check method. (Keep all other values the same.)

26. Using the parametric simulation, vary the angle of elevation from $52°$ to see how close you can get Janice and the ball. Use a guess and check method. (Keep all other values the same.)

Exercises 27 to 30 refer to the following **problem situation**: An NFL punter at the 15-yard line kicks a football downfield with an initial velocity of 85 ft/sec at an angle of elevation of $56°$.

27. Find a complete graph of the problem situation.

28. How far downfield will the football first hit the field?

29. Determine the maximum height of the ball above the field.

30. What is the "hang time" (the total time the football is in the air)?

Exercises 31 to 36 refer to the following **problem situation**: A major league baseball player hits a ball with an initial velocity of 103 ft/sec in the direction of a 10-foot fence that is 300 feet from home plate. For each exercise draw a complete graph of the problem situation and determine whether the hit is a home run (clears the fence). In Exercises 31 to 33, assume that gravity is the only force affecting the path of the ball; disregard air resistance in all the exercises in this group.

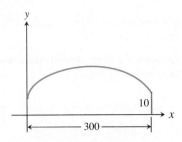

For Exercises 31 to 36

31. The hit is at an angle of elevation of $35°$.

32. The hit is at an angle of elevation of $43°$.

33. The hit is at an angle of elevation of $49°$.

34. The hit is at an angle of elevation of $41°$, and there is a wind blowing 22 ft/sec in the same direction as the horizontal path of the ball.

35. The hit is at an angle of elevation of $41°$, and there is a wind blowing 22 ft/sec in the direction opposite to the horizontal path of the ball.

36. The hit is at an angle of elevation of $41°$, and there is a wind blowing 22 ft/sec in the direction opposite to the horizontal path of the ball; and at an angle of depression of $12°$.

Exercises 37 to 40 refer to the following **problem situation** regarding projectile motion with air resistance: For many non-spinning projectiles the main effect on the path of the projectile, other than gravity, is a slowing-down influence due to air resistance. The effect is called the *drag force*, and it acts in a direction opposite to the velocity of the projectile. For projectiles moving through the air at low speeds, the drag can be assumed to be linear and directly proportional to the speed. Using this linear drag model it can be shown that the position of the particle at time t is given by

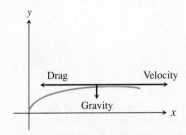

For Exercises 37 to 40

$$x(t) = \frac{v_0}{k} \cos \alpha (1 - e^{-kt})$$

$$y(t) = \frac{v_0}{k} \sin \alpha (1 - e^{-kt}) + \frac{32}{k^2}(1 - kt - e^{-kt})$$

where k is a constant representing the air density, v_0 is the initial velocity, and α is the initial angle of elevation. Suppose that $v_0 = 95$ ft/sec and $\alpha = 42°$.

37. Graph in the same viewing rectangle the motion of the particle assuming no air resistance and the motion of the particle assuming air resistance with $k = 0.3$.

38. Determine with and without drag the maximum height of the particle and the time when it occurs.

39. Determine with and without drag the range (horizontal distance) the particle travels and the time of impact.

40. Solve all parts of this problem for $k = 0.01$.

41. Show that the path of a fixed point P on a circle with radius a and center C that rolls on a straight line is the *cycloid* described by

$$x(\theta) = a(\theta - \sin \theta)$$

$$y(\theta) = a(1 - \cos \theta)$$

where θ represents the angle the radius CP has turned through. Assume the starting position is at the origin and that θ is a positive angle, even though the rotation is clockwise.

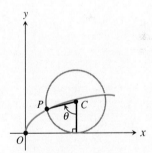

For Exercise 41

42. Design an experiment in physics to show the following remarkable property of cycloids. If Q is the lowest point of an arch of an inverted cycloid, then the time it takes for a frictionless bead to slide down the curve to point Q is independent of the starting point. That is, if A and B are dropped at the same time they will land at Q at the same time.

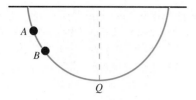

For Exercise 42

43. Writing to Learn   Write a paragraph that explains why Figs. 11.36 and 11.37 are actually distorted. How would

you change the viewing rectangle to see the shape of the actual path?

44. Writing to Learn   Explain how these parametric equations are related to Example 2.

$$x_1(t) = 400$$

$$y_1(t) = Y_{\max}(T/T_{\max})$$

$$x_2(t) = X_{\max}(T/T_{\max})$$

$$y_2(t) = 20$$

11.4   Conic Sections

Imagine two lines intersecting in three-dimensional space. When one line is fixed and the other rotates around the first, the resulting set of points is called a **cone**. The cone has two parts, called **nappes**, each of which looks like an ice cream cone. If the two lines maintain a constant angle between them during the rotation, then the result is a **double-napped right circular cone**.

A **conic section** (or simply a **conic**) is any curve obtained by intersecting a double-napped right circular cone with a plane. The three basic conic sections are the **parabola**, the **ellipse**, and the **hyperbola**. See Fig. 11.39. A circle is a special case of an ellipse. When a plane slices through only one nappe of the cone, either a parabola or an ellipse is formed, depending on the angle of the plane (see Fig. 11.39a,b). If the plane slices through both nappes of the cone, the result is a hyperbola (see Fig. 11.39c).

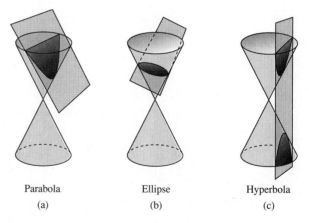

Parabola   Ellipse   Hyperbola
(a)   (b)   (c)

Figure 11.39   How the three basic conic sections are derived from the intersection of a right circular cone and a plane.

You were introduced informally to two of these conic sections—the parabola and the ellipse—in earlier chapters. In the material that follows we shall analyze all three conic sections from an algebraic point of view. We will give a formal definition and then develop standard forms for equations of each.

Parabolas

In Section 3.5 you learned that the graph of any quadratic function $y = ax^2 + bx + c$ can be obtained from the graph of $y = x^2$ by using vertical stretching or shrinking, reflection through the x-axis, vertical shifting, and horizontal shifting. The name *parabola* was used to refer to graphs of these functions. Here finally is a definition of a parabola.

Definition 11.3   Parabola

Let L be any line and $F(x_0, y_0)$ any point not on L. The set of all points $P(x, y)$ in the plane that are equidistant from L and F is called a **parabola** (see Fig. 11.40). The point F is the **focus of the parabola**, and the line L is the **directrix of the parabola**. The line perpendicular to L through the focus is the **line of symmetry of the parabola**, and the point common to the parabola and its line of symmetry is the **vertex of the parabola.**

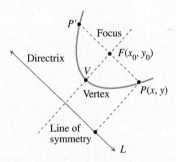

Figure 11.40 Terms used in defining a parabola.

Example 1 shows how you can find the equation of a parabola if the focus is on one axis and the directrix is parallel to the other axis.

E X A M P L E   1   Finding the Equation of a Parabola

Determine an equation for the parabola with focus $(0, a)$ and directrix $y = -a$ where $a > 0$ (see Fig. 11.41).

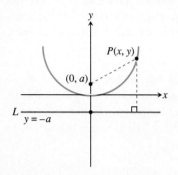

Figure 11.41 $x^2 = 4ay$, where $a > 0$. The distance from P to the focus $(0, a)$ is equal to the distance from P to L.

Solution In Fig. 11.41, the distance from $P(x, y)$ to the line $y = -a$ is $|y + a|$, and the distance from $P(x, y)$ to $(0, a)$ is $\sqrt{(x - 0)^2 + (y - a)^2}$. (Why?) Apply the definition of a parabola to obtain

$$\sqrt{x^2 + (y - a)^2} = |y + a|. \tag{1}$$

Next, square each side of Eq. (1) and simplify:

$$\left(\sqrt{x^2 + (y - a)^2}\right)^2 = |y + a|^2$$

$$x^2 + (y - a)^2 = (y + a)^2$$

$$x^2 + y^2 - 2ay + a^2 = y^2 + 2ay + a^2$$

$$x^2 = 4ay \tag{2}$$

Thus every point on the parabola is a solution to Eq. (2). Because the steps used to derive Eq. (2) from Eq. (1) are reversible, every solution to Eq. (2) corresponds to a point on the parabola. We can rewrite Eq. (2) in the form

$$y = \frac{1}{4a}x^2$$

to see that the graph can be obtained by starting with $y = x^2$ and applying a vertical stretch or shrink by the factor $1/4a$. The coordinates of the vertex are $(0, 0)$. Notice that a is half the distance from the focus to the directrix. ≡

Notice that the parabola developed in Example 1, whose equation is $x^2 = 4ay$, where $a > 0$, opens upward (see Fig. 11.41). If $a < 0$, the parabola $x^2 = 4ay$ opens downward (see Fig. 11.42a).

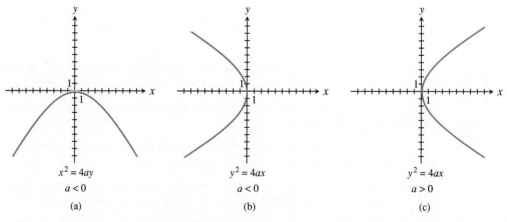

Figure 11.42 Parabolas whose equations are $x^2 = 4ay$ and $y^2 = 4ax$. The fourth case is shown in Fig. 11.41.

By repeating the algebra carried out in Example 1, we can establish that the parabola opens right or left in the case of $y^2 = 4ax$ (see Fig. 11.42b,c).

Consider a parabola with vertex (h, k) and focus $F(h, k+a)$ where $a > 0$ (see Fig. 11.43). Then the equation of the directrix would be $y = k - a$. The equation of the parabola can be obtained from $x^2 = 4ay$ by a horizontal and vertical shift, as the following development confirms.

$$\sqrt{(x-h)^2 + [y-(k+a)]^2} = |y - (k-a)|$$
$$(x-h)^2 + [(y-k)-a]^2 = [(y-k)+a]^2$$
$$(x-h)^2 + (y-k)^2 - 2a(y-k) + a^2 = (y-k)^2 + 2a(y-k) + a^2$$
$$(x-h)^2 = 4a(y-k)$$

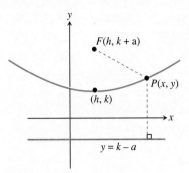

Figure 11.43 Vertex (h, k) and focus $F(h, k+a)$.

Theorem 11.5   Equations of Parabolas in Standard Form

The graph of each of the following equations is a parabola with vertex (h, k):

1. $(x-h)^2 = 4a(y-k)$: The focus is $(h, k+a)$, the directrix is $y = k - a$, and the line of symmetry is $x = h$.
2. $(y-k)^2 = 4a(x-h)$: The focus is $(h+a, k)$, the directrix is $x = h - a$, and the line of symmetry is $y = k$.

These equations are called **standard forms for the parabola**.

Once an equation for a parabola is in standard form, Theorem 11.5 can be used to find the important characteristics of the parabola.

E X A M P L E   2   Using the Standard Form of a Parabola

Find the vertex, line of symmetry, focus, and directrix of the parabola $(x+1)^2 = -12(y-3)$. Also find the x- and y-intercepts, and sketch a complete graph.

Solution   Since this equation is in standard form, use Theorem 11.5 to draw the following conclusions.

Vertex   Since an equation in standard form has vertex (h, k), the vertex of this parabola is the point $(-1, 3)$.

Line of Symmetry   Since the quadratic variable is x, the parabola opens upward or downward. So the line of symmetry is the line $x = -1$.

Focus   Since $4a = -12$, it follows that $a = -3$. Therefore the parabola opens downward, and the focus is the point $(-1, 3-3) = (-1, 0)$.

Directrix Since $a = -3$, the directrix is 3 units above the vertex. So it is the line $y = 6$.

To find the x- and y-intercepts substitute $(a, 0)$ and $(0, b)$ into the equation and solve for a and b.

$$(a + 1)^2 = -12(0 - 3)$$

$$(a + 1)^2 = 36$$

$$a + 1 = \pm 6$$

Therefore the points $(-7, 0)$ and $(5, 0)$ are x-intercepts. Similarly,

$$(0 + 1)^2 = -12(b - 3)$$

$$b - 3 = -\frac{1}{12}$$

$$b = -\frac{1}{12} + 3 = \frac{35}{12}.$$

The point $(0, 35/12)$ is the y-intercept.

With this information, sketch the graph shown in Fig. 11.44. Support your answer with a grapher.

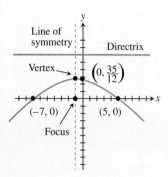

Figure 11.44
$(x + 1)^2 = -12(y - 3)$.

E X A M P L E   3   Finding the Standard Form of a Parabola

Find the standard form, vertex, focus, directrix, and line of symmetry of the parabola $y^2 - 6x + 2y + 13 = 0$.

Solution   Since this equation is quadratic in the variable y, complete the square on terms involving y.

$$y^2 - 6x + 2y + 13 = 0$$

$$y^2 + 2y = 6x - 13$$

$$y^2 + 2y + 1 = 6x - 13 + 1$$

$$(y + 1)^2 = 6x - 12$$

$$(y + 1)^2 = 6(x - 2).$$

This parabola opens to the right, has a vertex $(2, -1)$, and a line of symmetry $y = -1$. Since $4a = 6$, $a = 1.5$. The focus is $(3.5, -1)$, and the directrix is $x = 0.5$.

E X A M P L E   4   Finding a Complete Graph of a Parabola

Find a complete graph of the parabola $y^2 - 6x + 2y + 13 = 0$ with a graphing utility.

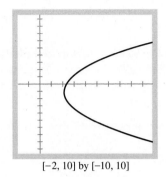

[−2, 10] by [−10, 10]

Figure 11.45
$y^2 - 6x + 2y + 13 = 0$.

Solution To sketch this parabola it is helpful first to change the equation to standard form as illustrated in Example 3. However, to find a complete graph on a graphing utility it is necessary to solve this original equation for y. Rewrite the original equation in the form $y^2 + 2y + (13 - 6x) = 0$, and use the quadratic formula to solve for y:

$$y^2 + 2y + (13 - 6x) = 0$$

$$y = \frac{-2 \pm \sqrt{4 - 4(13 - 6x)}}{2}$$

$$= -1 \pm \sqrt{1 - (13 - 6x)} \quad \text{(Why?)}$$

$$= -1 \pm \sqrt{6x - 12}.$$

To get a complete graph of the parabola (Fig. 11.45), it is necessary to graph both $y = -1 + \sqrt{6x - 12}$ and $y = -1 - \sqrt{6x - 12}$.

In the real world the reflective properties of objects with parabolic surfaces enable the parabola to be used in many applications. For example, if a source of light is placed at the focus of a parabolic surface, light will be reflected off the surface in lines parallel to its line of symmetry. This principle is used in the design of car headlights (see Fig. 11.46). Conversely, sound waves traveling *into* the opening of a parabola parallel to its line of symmetry will be reflected through the focus of the parabola. Parabolic microphones use this principle.

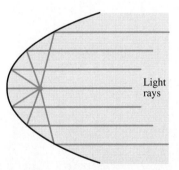

Light rays

Figure 11.46 Light rays from a source at the focus are reflected off a parabolic mirror in parallel directions.

EXAMPLE 5   APPLICATION: Parabolic Microphone

A parabolic microphone is formed by revolving the portion of the parabola $15y = x^2$ between $x = -9$ and $x = 9$ about its line of symmetry. Where should the sound receiver be placed?

Solution   The receiver should be placed at the focus of the parabola $15y = x^2$. Since $4a = 15$, $a = 3.75$. The focus is thus $(0, 3.75)$. The receiver should be placed 3.75 units from the vertex along its line of symmetry.

Ellipses

When a plane slices through just one nappe of a cone to form a closed curve, the resulting shape is called an ellipse. An algebraic description of an ellipse can also be given in a manner somewhat the same as for a parabola. One difference is that there are two focal points for the ellipse, rather than just one, as for the parabola.

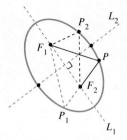

Figure 11.47 $|F_1 P| + |PF_2|$ is a constant for all points P on the ellipse.

Definition 11.4 Ellipse

Let F_1 and F_2 be any two points in the coordinate plane. An **ellipse** is the set of all points P in the plane such that the sum of the distances PF_1 and PF_2 is a constant (see Fig. 11.47). F_1 and F_2 are the **foci (focal points) of the ellipse**.

L_1, the line through the focal points, and L_2, the perpendicular bisector of line segment $F_1 F_2$, are both lines of symmetry for any ellipse determined by points F_1 and F_2.

For now we will consider only ellipses whose lines of symmetry are parallel to the coordinate axes; later in Section 11.4 we will examine ellipses not parallel to the coordinate axes.

E X A M P L E 6   Finding a Standard Equation of an Ellipse

Let $F_1 = (-c, 0)$ and $F_2 = (c, 0)$ be the two foci of the ellipse consisting of the points P where $d(P, F_1) + d(P, F_2) = 2a$ such that $a > c > 0$. Determine an equation for the ellipse, and the coordinates of the x-intercepts, the y-intercepts, and the center of the ellipse (see Fig. 11.48).

Solution Use the distance formula to obtain an equation for the ellipse:

$$d(P, F_1) + d(P, F_2) = 2a$$

$$\sqrt{(x + c)^2 + y^2} + \sqrt{(x - c)^2 + y^2} = 2a$$

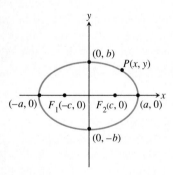

Figure 11.48 An ellipse with focal points F_1 and F_2 on the x-axis.

Next obtain an alternate form of this equation that does not involve radicals:

$$\sqrt{(x + c)^2 + y^2} + \sqrt{(x - c)^2 + y^2} = 2a$$

$$\sqrt{(x + c)^2 + y^2} = 2a - \sqrt{(x - c)^2 + y^2}$$

$$(x + c)^2 + y^2 = 4a^2 - 4a\sqrt{(x - c)^2 + y^2} + (x - c)^2 + y^2$$

$$x^2 + 2cx + c^2 + y^2 = 4a^2 - 4a\sqrt{(x - c)^2 + y^2} + x^2 - 2cx + c^2 + y^2$$

$$2cx = 4a^2 - 4a\sqrt{(x - c)^2 + y^2} - 2cx$$

$$4a\sqrt{(x - c)^2 + y^2} = 4a^2 - 4cx$$

$$a\sqrt{(x - c)^2 + y^2} = a^2 - cx \quad \text{Square each side and collect terms}$$

$$(a^2 - c^2)x^2 + a^2 y^2 = a^2(a^2 - c^2) \tag{3}$$

Divide each side of Eq. (3) by $a^2(a^2 - c^2)$ to obtain the following:

$$\frac{x^2}{a^2} + \frac{y^2}{a^2 - c^2} = 1 \qquad (4)$$

Because $a > c$ you can define a positive number b such that $b^2 = a^2 - c^2$ and rewrite Eq. (4) in the form

$$\frac{x^2}{a^2} + \frac{y^2}{b^2} = 1. \qquad (5)$$

Thus, every point on the ellipse is a solution to Eq. (5). It can also be shown that every solution of Eq. (5) corresponds to a point on the ellipse. This form is called the standard form for the equation of an ellipse. The x-intercepts are $\pm a$, and the y-intercepts are $\pm b$. (Why?) The center of the ellipse is $(0, 0)$. ≡

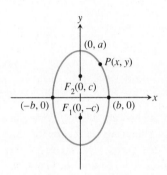

Figure 11.49 An ellipse with focal points F_1 and F_2 on the y-axis.

The **major axis** of the ellipse in Example 6 is the line segment from $(-a, 0)$ to $(a, 0)$, and the **minor axis** is the line segment from $(0, -b)$ to $(0, b)$. Note that, regardless of orientation, the focal points always lie on the major axis.

Now consider an ellipse with foci $F_1(0, -c)$ and $F_2(0, c)$ on the y-axis (see Fig. 11.49). It can be shown that the standard form for the equation of this ellipse, which satisfies $d(P, F_1) + d(P, F_2) = 2a$ such that $a > c > 0$, is

$$\frac{x^2}{b^2} + \frac{y^2}{a^2} = 1, \qquad (6)$$

where $b^2 = a^2 - c^2$. This equation is the same as Eq. (5) except that the number under x^2 is smaller than the number under y^2.

Equations (5) and (6) are the standard forms for an ellipse centered at the origin with axes parallel to the coordinate axes. If the center of an ellipse is the point (h, k), the standard forms of its equations are as stated in this theorem.

Theorem 11.6 Equations of Ellipses in Standard Form

Let $a > b$ and $c = \sqrt{a^2 - b^2}$. The graph of each of the following equations is an ellipse with center (h, k) and lines of symmetry $x = h$ and $y = k$ (see Fig. 11.50 on the following page).

1. $\dfrac{(x - h)^2}{a^2} + \dfrac{(y - k)^2}{b^2} = 1$ with foci $(h \pm c, k)$.

2. $\dfrac{(x - h)^2}{b^2} + \dfrac{(y - k)^2}{a^2} = 1$ with foci $(h, k \pm c)$.

These equations are the **standard forms for an ellipse.**

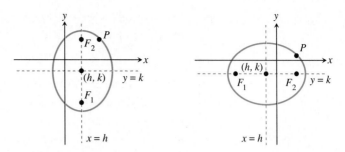

Figure 11.50 Ellipses with center (h, k) and axes parallel to the coordinate axes.

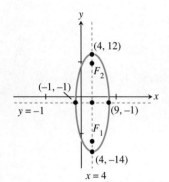

Figure 11.51
$$\frac{(x-4)^2}{25} + \frac{(y+1)^2}{169} = 1.$$

E X A M P L E   7   Using the Standard Form of an Ellipse

Find the center and the foci, the lines of symmetry, and the endpoints of the major and minor axes, and sketch a complete graph of

$$\frac{(x-4)^2}{25} + \frac{(y+1)^2}{169} = 1.$$

Solution Since the equation is in standard form, use Theorem 11.6 to conclude that the lines of symmetry are $x = 4$ and $y = -1$. Therefore the center of the ellipse is $(4, -1)$.

Now $a = 13$, $b = 5$, so that $c = 12$. The foci are $(4, -13)$ and $(4, 11)$. The endpoints of the major axis are $(4, -14)$ and $(4, 12)$, and the endpoints of the minor axis are $(-1, -1)$ and $(9, -1)$. Figure 11.51 shows a complete graph of the ellipse.

Ellipses, like parabolas, have reflective properties. Light or sound emitted at one focus of an ellipse is reflected by the ellipse through the other focus. One example of a real-world application is a lithotripter, a special device that produces ultra-high-frequency (UHF) shock waves moving through water to break up kidney stones. This device is in the shape of an **ellipsoid**. An ellipsoid is a three-dimensional solid that is formed by rotating an ellipse about its major axis. The foci of an ellipsoid are the same as for the ellipse used to generate it.

To use a lithotripter, doctors make careful measurements of the patient's kidney stones. The lithotripter is positioned so that the source producing the shock waves is at one focus of the ellipsoid and the kidney stones are at the other focus. The shock waves reflect off the inner surface of the ellipsoid and pass through the second focus to break up the kidney stones (see Fig. 11.52).

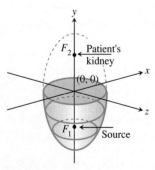

Figure 11.52 A lithotripter is an ellipsoidal device emitting UHF shock waves at one focus to break up kidney stones at the other focus.

E X A M P L E   8   APPLICATION: Lithotripter

Consider the following problem situation. Assume that the center of an ellipse rotated to form the ellipsoid of the lithotripter is $(0, 0)$. The two ends of the major axis are $(-6, 0)$ and $(6, 0)$, and one end of the minor axis is $(0, -2.5)$. Determine the coordinates of the lithotripter's foci.

Solution From the given information note that $a = 6$ and $b = 2.5$. Thus the equation for the ellipse that is rotated is $\dfrac{x^2}{6^2} + \dfrac{y^2}{2.5^2} = 1$. Now $c^2 = a^2 - b^2$, so $c^2 = 29.75$ and $c = 5.45$. Therefore the foci are $(-5.45, 0)$ and $(5.45, 0)$. The shock source (an underwater spark discharge) is placed at the negative focus and the patient's kidney at the positive focus. ≡

Hyperbolas

When a plane intersects two nappes of a cone, the resulting shape is a hyperbola.

Recall that an ellipse is defined algebraically in terms of the sum of two distances being constant. A hyperbola, on the other hand, is defined in terms of the difference of two distances being a constant.

Definition 11.5   Hyperbola

Let F_1 and F_2 be any two points in the coordinate plane. A **hyperbola** is the set of all points P in the plane such that the absolute value of the difference between the distances PF_1 and PF_2 is a constant. F_1 and F_2 are the **foci (focal points)**.

L_1, the line through the focal points, and line L_2, the perpendicular bisector of line segment F_1F_2, are both lines of symmetry for any hyperbola determined by points F_1 and F_2.

The line through the focal points, L_1, is called the **principal axis**, and line L_2 is called the **transverse axis**. The **center of the hyperbola** is the intersection of these two axes.

The calculation completed for an ellipse in Example 6 can be repeated with minor alterations for the hyperbola. In Fig. 11.53 the focal points are $F_1(-c, 0)$ and $F_2(c, 0)$. The hyperbola consists of all points P where $|d(P, F_1) - d(P, F_2)| = 2a$ such that $0 < a < c$.

Completing this calculation as we did in Example 6 leads to the following equation for a hyperbola:

$$\frac{x^2}{a^2} - \frac{y^2}{b^2} = 1 \tag{7}$$

where $b^2 = c^2 - a^2$. The x-intercepts $(-a, 0)$ and $(0, a)$ are called the **vertices of the hyperbola**.

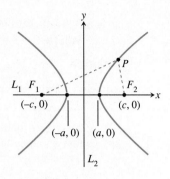

Figure 11.53 $\dfrac{x^2}{a^2} - \dfrac{y^2}{b^2} = 1.$

Notice from Fig. 11.53 that Eq. (7) describes a hyperbola whose principal axis is the x-axis. The next example considers the equation of a hyperbola whose principal axis is the y-axis.

EXAMPLE 9   Finding an Equation of a Hyperbola

Find the equation of the hyperbola with focal points $(0, 5)$ and $(0, -5)$ and vertices $(0, 4)$ and $(0, -4)$ (see Fig. 11.54).

Solution We see that $a = 4$, $c = 5$, and therefore $b = \sqrt{5^2 - 4^2} = 3$. Since the principal axis is the y-axis instead of the x-axis, the variables x and y must be reversed. Therefore the equation for this hyperbola is

$$\frac{y^2}{16} - \frac{x^2}{9} = 1.$$

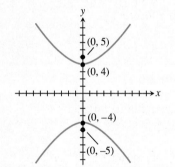

Figure 11.54 $\dfrac{y^2}{16} - \dfrac{x^2}{9} = 1.$
Note that the principal axis is the y-axis.

Asymptotes of a Hyperbola

Equation (7) can be rewritten as follows:

$$\frac{x^2}{a^2} - \frac{y^2}{b^2} = 1$$

$$\frac{x^2}{a^2} - 1 = \frac{y^2}{b^2}$$

$$y^2 = \frac{b^2 x^2}{a^2} - b^2$$

$$y^2 = \frac{b^2 x^2}{a^2}\left(1 - \frac{a^2}{x^2}\right) \tag{8}$$

From Eq. (8) it is apparent that, as the absolute value of x gets very large, a^2/x^2 approaches zero. Therefore

$$y^2 \qquad \text{is very close to} \qquad \frac{b^2 x^2}{a^2}.$$

So the two lines $y = bx/a$ and $y = -bx/a$ are the **asymptotes of the hyperbola**.

E X A M P L E   10   Finding the Graph of a Hyperbola

Find the asymptotes and sketch a complete graph of the hyperbola $\dfrac{x^2}{16} - \dfrac{y^2}{9} = 1$.

Solution   The given equation is in the form of Eq. (7). Its center is $(0,0)$, its principal axis is the x-axis, and $a = 4$ and $b = 3$. Therefore the asymptotes are

$$y = \frac{3}{4}x \qquad \text{and} \qquad y = -\frac{3}{4}x.$$

The foci are $(-5, 0)$ and $(5, 0)$ and the vertices are $(-4, 0)$ and $(4, 0)$. A complete graph is shown in Fig. 11.55. ≡

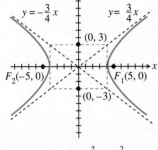

Figure 11.55 $\dfrac{x^2}{16} - \dfrac{y^2}{9} = 1.$

A horizontal and vertical shift moves a hyperbola centered at $(0, 0)$ to one centered at (h, k). The equations of the hyperbolas with axes parallel to the coordinate axes and centered at (h, k) are given in the following theorem.

Theorem 11.7   Equations of Hyperbolas in Standard Form

Let $c = \sqrt{a^2 + b^2}$. The graph of each of the following equations is a hyperbola with center (h, k) and lines of symmetry $x = h$ and $y = k$.

1. $\dfrac{(x - h)^2}{a^2} - \dfrac{(y - k)^2}{b^2} = 1$ with foci $(h \pm c, k)$ and vertices $(h \pm a, k)$; the asymptotes have a slope of $\pm b/a$.

2. $\dfrac{(y - k)^2}{a^2} - \dfrac{(x - h)^2}{b^2} = 1$ with foci $(h, k \pm c)$ and vertices $(h, k \pm a)$; the asymptotes have a slope of $\pm a/b$.

These equations are **standard forms for the hyperbola**.

E X A M P L E   11   Changing to Standard Form

Write $x^2 - 4y^2 + 2x - 24y = 39$ in standard form. Determine the center, foci, vertices, lines of symmetry, and asymptotes. Sketch a complete graph.

Solution   First group the terms involving x and the terms involving y, and then complete the square:

$$x^2 - 4y^2 + 2x - 24y = 39$$

$$(x^2 + 2x) - 4(y^2 + 6y) = 39$$

$$(x^2 + 2x + 1) - 4(y^2 + 6y + 9) = 39 + 1 - 4(9)$$

$$(x + 1)^2 - 4(y + 3)^2 = 4$$

$$\frac{(x + 1)^2}{4} - \frac{(y + 3)^2}{1} = 1$$

Use this standard form and refer to Theorem 11.7 to complete the example. The graph of this equation is a hyperbola whose center is $(-1, -3)$ and with lines of symmetry $x = -1$ and $y = -3$. Since $a = 2$ and $b = 1$, it follows that $c^2 = 5$. The vertices are $(-3, -3)$ and $(1, -3)$, and the foci are $(-1 - \sqrt{5}, -3) = (-3.24, -3)$ and $(-1 + \sqrt{5}, -3) = (1.24, -3)$. The asymptotes are $y + 3 = \pm\frac{1}{2}(x + 1)$ (see Fig. 11.56).

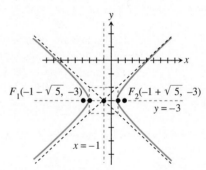

Figure 11.56   The asymptotes of $x^2 - 4y^2 + 2x - 24y = 39$ are $y + 3 = \pm\frac{1}{2}(x + 1)$.

EXAMPLE   12   *Using a Graphing Utility*

Use the quadratic formula and a graphing utility to find a complete graph of $x^2 - 4y^2 + 2x - 24y = 39$.

Solution   Solve this equation for y using the quadratic formula:

$$x^2 - 4y^2 + 2x - 24y = 39$$

$$-4y^2 - 24y + (x^2 + 2x - 39) = 0$$

$$4y^2 + 24y - (x^2 + 2x - 39) = 0$$

$$y = \frac{-24 \pm \sqrt{576 + 16(x^2 + 2x - 39)}}{8}$$

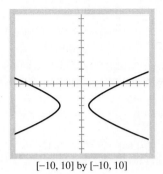

[-10, 10] by [-10, 10]

Figure 11.57
$x^2 - 4y^2 + 2x - 24y = 39.$

The graph of

$$y = \frac{-24 + \sqrt{576 + 16(x^2 + 2x - 39)}}{8}$$

produces the portion of the hyperbola in Fig. 11.56 that is above the line $y = -3$, and the graph of

$$y = \frac{-24 - \sqrt{576 + 16(x^2 + 2x - 39)}}{8}$$

produces the portion below the line $y = -3$. A complete graph is shown in Fig. 11.57. ≡

Reflective Properties of Hyperbolas

Hyperbolas have a reflective property that is important in the construction of lenses for cameras, glasses, and telescopes. A simple reflecting lens is created by coating one branch of a hyperbola with a substance that causes it to reflect light. A light ray aimed toward the focus F_1 behind that surface is reflected by the surface to the second focus F_2. See Fig. 11.58. A telescope is constructed by using both parabolic and hyperbolic lenses (see Fig. 11.59). The main lens is parabolic with focus F_1 and vertex F_2, and the secondary lens is hyperbolic with foci F_1 and F_2. Thus one focus of the hyperbola is also the focus of the parabola. The eye is positioned at the point F_2.

This application will be referred to in Exercises 73 to 75.

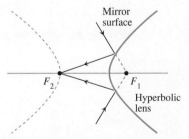

Figure 11.58 How a hyperbolic mirror works.

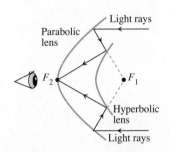

Figure 11.59 The reflective properties of the parabola and hyperbola combine in a telescope's lens system.

Graphing Equations in Quadratic Form

Next we use a function graphing utility to determine graphs of equations of the form

$$Ax^2 + Bxy + Cy^2 + Dx + Ey + F = 0 \qquad (9)$$

where $A, B,$ and C are not all zero. Recall from Section 10.4 that this is a general second-degree equation. It is also called a **quadratic form in variables x and y**. A complete graph of Eq. (9) is either one of the three ordinary conic sections (parabola, ellipse, or hyperbola), or it is a **degenerate conic**. Degenerate forms, formed when a plane passes through the vertex of a double-napped cone, include a pair of parallel lines, a pair of intersecting lines, one line, a single point, or no graph.

In Section 10.5 we saw that when $C \neq 0$, rewriting Eq. (9) as a quadratic in y^2 and using the quadratic formula results in the following two functions:

$$f(x) = \frac{-(Bx + E) + \sqrt{(Bx + E)^2 - 4C(Ax^2 + Dx + F)}}{2C} \tag{10a}$$

$$g(x) = \frac{-(Bx + E) - \sqrt{(Bx + E)^2 - 4C(Ax^2 + Dx + F)}}{2C} \tag{10b}$$

By graphing these two functions we obtain a complete graph of the conic of Eq. (9).

E X A M P L E 13   Finding a Complete Graph

Use the quadratic formula and a function graphing utility to obtain a complete graph of the ellipse $5x^2 + 3y^2 - 20x + 6y = -8$.

Solution   First rewrite the equation:

$$5x^2 + 3y^2 - 20x + 6y = -8$$

$$3y^2 + 6y + (5x^2 - 20x + 8) = 0$$

Next use the quadratic formula to solve for y:

$$y = \frac{-6 \pm \sqrt{36 - 12(5x^2 - 20x + 8)}}{6}$$

It is *not* necessary to simplify this equation before using a graphing utility. The graph of

$$y = \frac{-6 + \sqrt{36 - 12(5x^2 - 20x + 8)}}{6}$$

produces the upper half of the complete graph of the ellipse in Fig. 11.60, and the graph of

$$y = \frac{-6 - \sqrt{36 - 12(5x^2 - 20x + 8)}}{6}$$

produces the lower half.

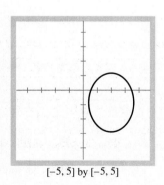

[−5, 5] by [−5, 5]

Figure 11.60
$5x^2 + 3y^2 - 20x + 6y = -8.$

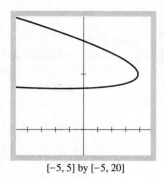

[−5, 5] by [−5, 20]

Figure 11.61 $x^2 + 4xy + 4y^2 - 30x - 90y + 450 = 0$.

EXAMPLE 14   Graphing a Conic in Quadratic Form

Use a graphing utility to determine a complete graph of the equation $x^2 + 4xy + 4y^2 - 30x - 90y + 450 = 0$.

Solution   Notice that in this equation $B = 4$. The functions of Eq. (10a,b) become

$$y = \frac{-(4x - 90) \pm \sqrt{(4x - 90)^2 - 16(x^2 - 30x + 450)}}{8}.$$

To make it easier to enter into a graphing utility, simplify this expression to obtain the functions:

$$f(x) = \frac{45 - 2x + \sqrt{225 - 60x}}{4} \quad \text{and} \quad g(x) = \frac{45 - 2x - \sqrt{225 - 60x}}{4}.$$

Figure 11.61 shows a complete graph of each of these functions in the same viewing rectangle. The result is a parabola. ≡

EXAMPLE 15   Graphing a Conic in Quadratic Form

Find a complete graph of $3x^2 + 4xy + 3y^2 - 12x + 2y + 7 = 0$.

Solution   Equations (10a,b) become

$$f(x) = \frac{-(4x + 2) + \sqrt{(4x + 2)^2 - 12(3x^2 - 12x + 7)}}{6}$$

$$g(x) = \frac{-(4x + 2) - \sqrt{(4x + 2)^2 - 12(3x^2 - 12x + 7)}}{6}.$$

Figure 11.62 shows a complete graph of these functions. The result is an ellipse. ≡

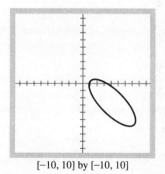

[−10, 10] by [−10, 10]

Figure 11.62 $3x^2 + 4xy + 3y^2 - 12x + 2y + 7 = 0$.

EXAMPLE 16   Graphing a Conic in Quadratic Form

Find a complete graph of $4x^2 - 6xy + 2y^2 - 3x + 10y - 6 = 0$.

Solution   Equation (10a,b) becomes

$$f(x) = \frac{(6x - 10) + \sqrt{(-6x + 10)^2 - 8(4x^2 - 3x - 6)}}{4}$$

$$g(x) = \frac{(6x - 10) - \sqrt{(-6x + 10)^2 - 8(4x^2 - 3x - 6)}}{4}.$$

Figure 11.63 shows a complete graph of these functions. The result is a hyperbola. ≡

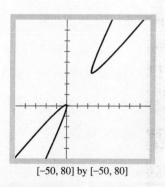

[−50, 80] by [−50, 80]

Figure 11.63
$4x^2 - 6xy + 2y^2 - 3x + 10y - 6 = 0$.

Examples 14 to 16 have shown that a graph of a quadratic form can be any one of the conics. Theorem 11.8 formalizes this observation.

> ### Theorem 11.8   Graphs of a Quadratic Form
>
> The graph of the equation $Ax^2 + Bxy + Cy^2 + Dx + Ey + F = 0$ is (possibly degenerate):
>
> 1. a parabola if $B^2 - 4AC = 0$;
> 2. an ellipse if $B^2 - 4AC < 0$;
> 3. a hyperbola if $B^2 - 4AC > 0$.

Exercises for Section 11.4

In Equations 1 to 8, find the vertex, line of symmetry, focus, and directrix of each parabola.

1. $24y = x^2$

2. $8x = y^2$

3. $12(y + 1) = (x - 3)^2$

4. $6(y - 3) = (x + 1)^2$

5. $(2 - y) = 16(x - 3)^2$

6. $22(x - 3) = (y + 5)^2$

7. $(x + 4)^2 = -6(y - 1)$

8. $(y - 7)^2 = 12x$

In Equations 9 to 12, list a sequence of transformations that when applied to the graph of $y^2 = x$ or $x^2 = y$ will result in the given parabola.

9. $12(x + 3) = (y + 4)^2$

10. $y = 18(x - 3)^2 + 7$

11. $(y - 2) = 6(x + 4)^2$

12. $x - 3 = 5(y + 6)^2 + 1$

In Exercises 13 to 15, determine an equation, the vertex, and the line of symmetry of the parabola, determined by the given focus and directrix. Also sketch a complete graph.

13. $(2, -1)$, $y = 3$

14. $(2, -1)$, $y = -3$

15. $(2, -1)$, $x = 3$

In Exercises 16 to 20, determine an equation, the focus, and the line of symmetry of the parabola, determined by the given vertex and directrix. Sketch a complete graph.

16. $(2, -1)$, $x = -3$

17. $(3, 2)$, $x = 5$

18. $(3, 2)$, $x = -5$

19. $(3, 2)$, $y = 5$

20. $(3, 2)$, $y = -5$

In Exercises 21 and 22, find the standard form, vertex, focus, directrix, and line of symmetry of each parabola, and sketch a complete graph without using a graphing utility. Then support your sketch with a graphing utility.

21. $x^2 + 2x - y + 3 = 0$

22. $3x^2 - 6x - 6y + 10 = 0$

23. Consider the graph of $y = 4x^2$. Explain how a horizontal shrink by a factor of $\frac{1}{2}$ applied to the graph of $y = x^2$ produces the same graph as applying a vertical stretch by a factor of 4 to $y = x^2$. [*Hint*: What happens to the point $(1, 1)$ on $y = x^2$?]

24. Consider the graph of $x = 4y^2$. Explain how a vertical shrink by a factor of $\frac{1}{2}$ applied to $x = y^2$ produces the same graph as applying a horizontal stretch by a factor of 4 to the graph of $x = y^2$.

In Exercises 25 to 28, for each ellipse give the endpoints of the major and minor axes, the coordinates of the center and foci, and the lines of symmetry. Sketch a complete graph without using a graphing utility.

25. $\dfrac{(x - 1)^2}{2} + \dfrac{(y + 3)^2}{4} = 1$

26. $(x + 3)^2 + 4(y - 1)^2 = 16$

27. $\dfrac{(x + 2)^2}{5} + 2(y - 1)^2 = 1$

28. $\dfrac{(x - 4)^2}{16} + 16(y + 4)^2 = 8$

In Exercises 29 to 32, draw a complete graph using only a graphing utility.

29. $2x^2 - 4x + y^2 - 6 = 0$

30. $3x^2 - 6x + 2y^2 + 8y + 5 = 0$

31. $2x^2 - y^2 + 4x + 6 = 0$

32. $3y^2 - 5x^2 + 2x - 6y - 9 = 0$

In Exercises 33 to 38, write the equation of the conic in standard form, and give the endpoints of the major and minor axes, the coordinates of the center and foci, the lines of symmetry, and the asymptotes (if any). Draw a complete graph, and support your sketch using a graphing utility.

33. $9x^2 + 4y^2 - 18x + 8y - 23 = 0$

34. $3x^2 + 5y^2 - 12x + 30y + 42 = 0$

35. $9x^2 - 4y^2 - 36x + 8y - 4 = 0$

36. $y^2 - 4y - 8x + 20 = 0$

37. $25y^2 - 9x^2 - 50y - 54x - 281 = 0$

38. $9x^2 + 16y^2 + 54x - 32y - 47 = 0$

In Exercises 39 and 40, determine the endpoints of the major and minor axes and standard form of the equation of the ellipse, and sketch a complete graph. Do not use a graphing utility.

39. Foci $(3, 0)$ and $(-3, 0)$; minor axis = 14

40. Foci $(0, 4)$ and $(0, -4)$; minor axis = 9

In Exercises 41 to 44, determine the endpoints of the major and minor axes and the standard form of the equation of the ellipse, and sketch a complete graph. Do not use a graphing utility.

41. The sum of the distances from the foci is 9; the foci are $(-4, 0)$ and $(4, 0)$.

42. The sum of the distances from the foci is 11; the foci are $(-0.5, 0)$ and $(0.5, 0)$.

43. The foci are $(1, 3)$ and $(1, 9)$; the major axis has a length of 12.

44. The center is $(1, -4)$, the foci are $(1, -2)$ and $(1, -6)$, and the minor axis has a length of 10.

In Exercises 45 to 48, determine the standard form of the equation, and sketch a complete graph of the hyperbola. Do not use a graphing utility.

45. The difference between the distances from any point on the hyperbola to the foci is 4; the foci are $(-3, 0)$ and $(3, 0)$.

46. The difference between the distances from any point on the hyperbola to the foci is 8; the foci are $(0, -8)$ and $(0, 8)$.

47. The difference between the distances from any point on the hyperbola to the foci is 3; the foci are $(-3, 2)$ and $(3, 2)$.

48. The difference between the distances from any point on the hyperbola to the foci is 6; the foci are $(1, -2)$ and $(9, -2)$.

In Exercises 49 to 52, determine the coordinates of the center, foci, and vertices of each hyperbola; find the lines of symmetry and the asymptotes; and sketch a complete graph. Do not use a graphing utility.

49. $\dfrac{x^2}{4} - \dfrac{(y-3)^2}{5} = 1$

50. $\dfrac{(y-3)^2}{9} - \dfrac{(x+2)^2}{4} = 1$

51. $4(y-1)^2 - 9(x-3)^2 = 36$

52. $4(x-2)^2 - 9(y+4)^2 = 1$

In Exercises 53 and 54, find the points of intersection (if any) between the line and the parabola.

53. $y = 2x^2 - 6x + 7$, $2x + 3y - 6 = 0$

54. $x = 3y^2 - 2y + 6$, $x - 4y - 10 = 0$

In Exercises 55 to 62, determine whether the graph of each of the equations is a parabola, ellipse, or hyperbola. Find the vertices, lines of symmetry, and foci of each.

55. $y^2 - 2y + 4x - 12 = 0$

56. $4y^2 - 9x^2 - 18x - 8y - 41 = 0$

57. $4x^2 + y^2 - 32x + 16y + 124 = 0$

58. $9y^2 - 9x - 6y - 5 = 0$

59. $16x^2 - y^2 - 32x - 6y - 57 = 0$

60. $2x^2 + 3y^2 + 12x - 24y + 60 = 0$

61. $2x^2 - 6x + 5y - 13 = 0$

62. $9x^2 + 4y^2 - 18x + 16y - 11 = 0$

In Exercises 63 to 66, the graph of each system of parametric equations is a conic. Substitute specific values for a, b, h, and k, and find a complete graph of the conic.

63. $\begin{cases} x = t + h \\ y = \dfrac{1}{4a}t^2 + k \end{cases}$ **64.** $\begin{cases} x = a\cos t + h \\ y = b\sin t + k \end{cases}$

65. $\begin{cases} x = \dfrac{a}{\cos t} + h \\ y = b\tan t + k \end{cases}$ **66.** $\begin{cases} x = \dfrac{1}{4a}t^2 + h \\ y = t + k \end{cases}$

67. A parabolic microphone is formed by revolving the portion of the parabola $10y = x^2$ between the lines $x = -7$ and $x = 7$ about its line of symmetry. Where should the sound receiver be placed for best reception?

68. A parabolic microphone is formed by revolving the portion of the parabola $18y = x^2$ between $x = -12$ and $x =$

12 about its line of symmetry. Where should the sound receiver be placed for best reception?

69. A parabolic headlight is formed by revolving the portion of the parabola $y^2 = 12x$ between the lines $y = -4$ and $y = 4$ about its line of symmetry. Where should the headlight bulb be placed for maximum illumination?

70. A parabolic headlight is formed by revolving the portion of the parabola $y^2 = 15x$ between the lines $y = -3$ and $y = 3$ about its line of symmetry. Where should the headlight bulb be placed for maximum illumination?

71. The form for a lithotripter derives from rotating the portion of an ellipse below its minor axis about its major axis. The *major diameter* (length of the major axis) is 26 inches, and the maximum depth from the major axis is 10 inches. Where should the shock-wave source and patient be placed for maximum effect? Give the appropriate measurements.

72. There are elliptical pool tables that have been constructed with a single pocket at one of the foci. Suppose such a table has a major diameter of 6 feet and minor diameter of 4 feet.

   a) Explain how a "pool shark" who knows conic geometry is at a great advantage over a "mark" who knows no conic geometry.

   b) How should the ball be hit so it bounces off the cushion directly into the pocket? Give specific measurements.

Exercises 73 to 75 refer to the parabolic-hyperbolic-lens **problem situation** represented here. Figure 11.59 in the text explains the arrangement of lenses.

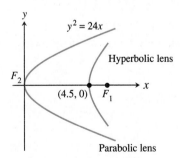

For Exercises 73 to 75

73. What are the coordinates of the foci of the hyperbola?

74. Determine the standard form of the equation of the generating hyperbola.

75. Find complete graphs of both conics in the same viewing rectangle. Explain how this lens arrangement works.

Exercises 76 to 78 refer to the parabolic-hyperbolic-lens **problem situation** shown here. See also Fig. 11.59.

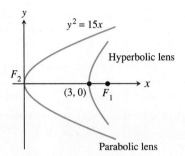

For Exercises 76 to 78

76. What are the coordinates of the foci of the hyperbola?

77. Determine the standard form of the equation of the generating hyperbola.

78. Find complete graphs of both conics in the same viewing rectangle. Explain how this lens arrangement works.

In Exercises 79 to 88, find a complete graph and identify the conic section.

79. $2x^2 - xy + 3y^2 - 3x + 4y - 6 = 0$

80. $-x^2 + 3xy + 4y^2 - 5x - 10y - 20 = 0$

81. $2x^2 - 4xy + 8y^2 - 10x + 4y - 13 = 0$

82. $2x^2 - 4xy + 2y^2 - 5x + 6y - 15 = 0$

83. $10x^2 - 8xy + 6y^2 + x - 5y + 20 = 0$

84. $10x^2 - 8xy + 6y^2 + x - 5y - 30 = 0$

85. $3x^2 - 2xy - 5x + 6y - 10 = 0$

86. $5xy - 6y^2 + 10x - 17y + 20 = 0$

87. $-3x^2 + 7xy - 2y^2 - x + 20y - 15 = 0$

88. $-3x^2 + 7xy - 2y^2 - 2x + 3y - 10 = 0$

89. Determine an equation for the ellipse with foci $(-1, 1)$ and $(1, 2)$ such that the sum of the distances of its points from the foci is 3.

90. Determine an equation for the hyperbola with foci $(-1, 1)$ and $(1, 2)$ such that the absolute value of the difference between the distances between its points from the foci is 1.

In Exercises 91 to 97, graph each degenerate conic.

91. $x^2 = -1$

92. $x^2 = 0$

93. $x^2 = 1$

94. $x^2 - xy = 0$

95. $x^2 + y^2 = 0$

96. $x^2 - y^2 = 0$

97. $x^2 + y^2 + 1 = 0$

11.5 _____ Polar Equations of Conics

In Section 11.4 we defined a parabola as the set of all points P such that the perpendicular distance from P to a fixed line (directrix) equals the distance from P to a fixed point (focus) not on the directrix. Ellipses and hyperbolas can also be described in terms of a focus and a directrix, when used with the concept of *eccentricity*—a concept also used in the polar form of the conics.

Eccentricity

> **Definition 11.6   Eccentricity**
>
> The **eccentricity** e of an ellipse or a hyperbola is defined by $e = c/a$, where $2c$ is the distance between foci F_1 and F_2 and $2a$ is the length of the major axis of an ellipse or the transverse axis of a hyperbola. The eccentricity of a parabola is defined to be 1. The eccentricity of a circle is defined to be 0.

Recall that for an ellipse $c = \sqrt{a^2 - b^2}$, so $0 < c < a$, and $e = \dfrac{c}{a} < 1$. For a hyperbola $c = \sqrt{a^2 + b^2}$. Thus, $c > a > 0$ so that $e = c/a > 1$.

Once the values for two of the constants a, b, and c of a conic are known, the eccentricity of that conic can be found.

E X A M P L E   1   Finding the Eccentricity

Find the eccentricity of each conic.

a) $\dfrac{x^2}{16} + \dfrac{y^2}{9} = 1$

b) $\dfrac{y^2}{16} - \dfrac{x^2}{9} = 1$

c) $4x^2 + 9y^2 - 24x + 36y + 36 = 0$

Solution

a) Because $a > b$, $a = 4$ and $b = 3$. Since $c = \sqrt{a^2 - b^2} = \sqrt{7}$, $e = c/a = \sqrt{7}/4$.

b) Here $a = 4$, $b = 3$, and $c = \sqrt{a^2 + b^2} = 5$. Thus $e = c/a = \frac{5}{4}$.

c) First complete the square for both variables x and y to find the standard form:

$$4x^2 + 9y^2 - 24x + 36y + 36 = 0$$
$$4x^2 - 24x + 9y^2 + 36y = -36$$
$$4(x^2 - 6x + 9) + 9(y^2 + 4y + 4) = 36$$
$$4(x - 3)^2 + 9(y + 2)^2 = 36$$
$$\frac{(x - 3)^2}{9} + \frac{(y + 2)^2}{4} = 36$$

From the standard form it is evident that $a = 3, b = 2$ and $c = \sqrt{a^2 - b^2} = \sqrt{5}$. Thus $e = c/a = \sqrt{5}/3$. ∎

It turns out that, if P is a point on either an ellipse or a hyperbola, the ratio $d(P, F)/d(P, Q)$ is equal to the eccentricity, where F is the closest focal point and $d(P, Q)$ is the perpendicular distance to the directrix. This fact is the subject of the next two theorems.

The next two theorems assume that the major axis (for an ellipse) or principal axis (for a hyperbola) is the x-axis. There are corresponding statements for the cases where the major axis or the principal axis lies on the y-axis.

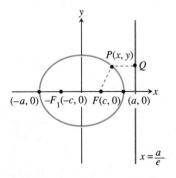

Figure 11.64   Directrix in an ellipse.

Theorem 11.9   An Ellipse and its Eccentricity

Suppose that $F(c, 0)$ (where $c > 0$) is a focus and that $e = c/a$ is the eccentricity of the ellipse

$$\frac{x^2}{a^2} + \frac{y^2}{b^2} = 1.$$

Let ℓ be the directrix defined as $x = a/e$ (see Fig. 11.64). If P is any point of the ellipse, and Q is a point on ℓ such that PQ is perpendicular to ℓ, then

$$\frac{d(P, F)}{d(P, Q)} = e.$$

Proof   Compute $d(P, F)$ where point $P(x, y)$ is on the ellipse.

$$d(P, F) = \sqrt{(x - c)^2 + y^2}$$

$$= \sqrt{(x - c)^2 + b^2 - \frac{b^2 x^2}{a^2}} \quad \text{Solve the given equation for } y^2 \text{ and substitute into the radical.}$$

$$= \sqrt{x^2 - 2cx + c^2 + b^2 - \frac{b^2 x^2}{a^2}}$$

$$= \sqrt{x^2 - 2cx + a^2 - b^2 + b^2 - \frac{b^2 x^2}{a^2}}$$

$$= \sqrt{x^2 \left(1 - \frac{b^2}{a^2}\right) - 2cx + a^2}$$

$$= \sqrt{x^2 \left(\frac{a^2 - b^2}{a^2}\right) - 2cx + a^2}$$

$$= \sqrt{\frac{c^2}{a^2} x^2 - 2cx + a^2}$$

$$= \sqrt{\frac{c^2}{a^2} \left(x^2 - \frac{2a^2}{c} x + \frac{a^4}{c^2}\right)}$$

$$= \sqrt{\frac{c^2}{a^2} \left(x - \frac{a^2}{c}\right)^2}$$

$$= \sqrt{\frac{c^2}{a^2} \left(x - \frac{a}{e}\right)^2}$$

$$= \frac{c}{a} \left|x - \frac{a}{e}\right|$$

$$= e \left|x - \frac{a}{e}\right|$$

$$= e \cdot d(P, Q)$$

Theorem 11.9 means that the vertical line $x = a/e$ is the directrix and the point $(c, 0)$ is the focus for an ellipse. In a similar way it can be shown that $x = -a/e$ can be taken as a directrix with respect to the focus $(-c, 0)$.

Theorem 11.10 establishes that a hyperbola can also be defined in terms of a focus and a directrix. Notice that for a hyperbola the directrix lies between the two foci.

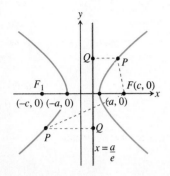

Figure 11.65 Directrix in a hyperbola.

Theorem 11.10 A Hyperbola and Its Eccentricity

Suppose that $F(c, 0)$ (where $c > 0$) is a focus and that $e = c/a$ is the eccentricity of the hyperbola

$$\frac{x^2}{a^2} - \frac{y^2}{b^2} = 1.$$

Let ℓ be the directrix defined as $x = a/e$ (see Fig. 11.65). If P is any point of the hyperbola, and Q be a point on ℓ such that PQ is perpendicular to ℓ, then

$$\frac{d(P, F)}{d(P, Q)} = e.$$

The conclusions of Theorems 11.9 and 11.10 are also true in the event that the centers of the conics are at point (h, k) instead of the origin $(0, 0)$.

We can now give the following alternative definition of a conic.

Definition 11.7 Conics in Terms of Focus and Directrix

Let F be a fixed point and ℓ be a line *not* containing F. A **conic** is the locus of all points P with $d(P, F)/d(P, Q) = e$ where e is a positive constant called the eccentricity and Q is the point on ℓ such that PQ is perpendicular to ℓ. F is a **focus** and ℓ is the **directrix of the conic**.

The conic in Definition 11.7 is an ellipse if $e < 1$, a parabola if $e = 1$, and a hyperbola if $e > 1$.

Polar Equations of Conics

In Section 11.4 the standard forms in a rectangular coordinate system were developed for equations of conic sections. In the case of the ellipse and the hyperbola, these standard forms are described in terms of the center of the conic. The simplest situation is when the center is the origin.

This section develops equations for the conics in a polar coordinate system. For a polar coordinate system it is most convenient to develop the equations assuming that a focus rather than the center of the conic is at the origin.

Consider a conic whose focus is the origin $(0, 0)$ and whose directrix is the line $x = -h$ (where $h > 0$). There are two cases to consider: whether a point P on the conic is on the same side of the directrix as the focus, or on the opposite side. Figure 11.66 shows the case where P is on the same side.

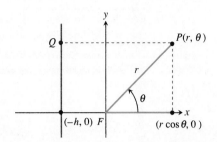

Figure 11.66   If $P(r, \theta)$ is a point on the conic, and P and the focus F are on the same side of the directrix, then $d(P, F) = e \cdot d(P, Q)$. (*Note*: Conic not shown.)

Using the polar coordinates to describe these distances we see that

$$d(P, F) = e \cdot d(P, Q)$$

$$r = e(h + r \cos \theta)$$

$$r - er \cos \theta = eh$$

$$r(1 - e \cos \theta) = eh$$

$$r = \frac{eh}{1 - e \cos \theta}.$$

Any point on the conic on the same side of the directrix as the focus has polar coordinates that satisfy Eq. (1).

On the other hand, suppose P is on the opposite side of the directrix from the focus (see Fig. 11.67). If (r, θ) is a polar coordinate of point P and $r < 0$, then $-r = d(P, F)$ and $d(P, Q) = -h - r \cos \theta$.

$$-r = e(-h - r \cos \theta)$$

$$r = eh + er \cos \theta$$

$$r = \frac{eh}{1 - e \cos \theta} \tag{1}$$

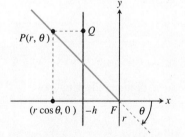

Figure 11.67   If P is a point on the conic and P and F are on opposite sides of the directrix, then $d(P, F) = ed(P, Q)$.

So if P is a point on a conic, then regardless of where the focus, directrix, and P are in relation to each other, its polar coordinates will satisfy an equation in the form of Eq. (1). It is important to observe that our development of Eq. (1) did not make any assertions about the eccentricity. If $0 < e < 1$, Eq. (1) is an ellipse, and if $1 < e$, Eq. (1) is a hyperbola.

A graphing utility can be used to find complete graphs of conics in polar form.

E X A M P L E   2   Finding a Complete Graph

Find complete graphs of

$$r = \frac{2e}{1 - e \cos \theta}$$

for e equal to 0.25, 0.5, 1.5, and 4.

Solution   For each of these equations the directrix is $x = -2$ and a focus is at the origin. See Fig. 11.68 for complete graphs.   ▤

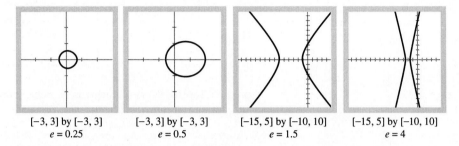

[−3, 3] by [−3, 3]	[−3, 3] by [−3, 3]	[−15, 5] by [−10, 10]	[−15, 5] by [−10, 10]
$e = 0.25$	$e = 0.5$	$e = 1.5$	$e = 4$

Figure 11.68 $r = 2e/(1 - e\cos\theta)$ for four values of e.

It is evident from Example 2 that when e is close to 0, the ellipse is close to being a circle, and that as $e > 1$ gets larger, the hyperbola becomes more and more like a pair of parallel lines.

Notice that Eq. (1) applies when the directrix is on the negative side of the y-axis. Using a development that parallels the one above, it can be shown that when the directrix is on the positive side of the y-axis, the polar equation is

$$r = \frac{eh}{1 + e\cos\theta}. \tag{2}$$

If $\cos\theta$ is replaced in Eqs. (1) and (2) by $\sin\theta$, a conic is again obtained.

Theorem 11.11 summarizes the equations for the polar coordinates of conics.

Theorem 11.11   **Polar Equations of Conics**

A nondegenerate conic with eccentricity e has one of the following polar equations:

1. $r = \dfrac{eh}{1 + e\cos\theta}$; directrix $x = +h$
2. $r = \dfrac{eh}{1 - e\cos\theta}$; directrix $x = -h$
3. $r = \dfrac{eh}{1 + e\sin\theta}$; directrix $y = +h$
4. $r = \dfrac{eh}{1 - e\sin\theta}$; directrix $y = -h$

Moreover, the graph of any such equation is a conic. The conic is an ellipse if and only if $0 < e < 1$, a parabola if and only if $e = 1$, and a hyperbola if and only if $1 < e$.

The next three examples explore conics in polar form.

EXAMPLE 3   Examining a Conic in Polar Form

Find a complete graph of

$$r = \frac{6}{4 - 3\cos\theta}.$$

Specify a directrix and a range for θ that produces a complete graph. Find the standard form for the equation of the conic.

Solution   Divide the numerator and denominator of this equation by 4 to put it into the form given in Theorem 11.11.

$$r = \frac{6}{4 - 3\cos\theta}$$

$$r = \frac{1.5}{1 - 0.75\cos\theta}$$

Then $eh = 1.5$ and $e = 0.75$ so $h = 2$. The conic is an ellipse whose directrix is $x = -2$. The range $0 \le \theta \le 2\pi$ produces a complete graph (Fig. 11.69).

When $\theta = 0, r = 6$, and when $\theta = \pi, r = -0.86$. The major axis vertices are thus $(-0.86, 0)$ and $(6, 0)$, and the center of the ellipse is $((-0.86 + 6)/2, 0)$, or $(2.57, 0)$.

Since c is the distance from the center to a focus and since one focus is $(0, 0)$, $c = 2.57$. The length of the major axis is $2a = 6 - (-0.86) = 6.86$, so $a = 3.43$.

$$b^2 = a^2 - c^2$$

$$b = \sqrt{(3.43)^2 - (2.57)^2} = 2.27$$

Therefore the standard form for the equation of this conic is

$$\frac{(x - 2.57)^2}{(3.43)^2} + \frac{y^2}{(2.27)^2} = 1.$$

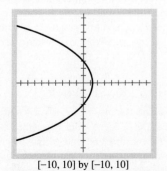

[-4, 8] by [-6, 6]

Figure 11.69 $r = \dfrac{6}{4 - 3\cos\theta}$ and $0 \le \theta \le 2\pi$.

EXAMPLE 4   Examining a Conic in Polar Form

Find a complete graph of

$$r = \frac{3}{1 + \cos\theta}.$$

Specify a directrix and a range for θ that produces a complete graph.

Solution   Notice from the form of the equation that $e = 1$ and $h = 3$. This conic is a parabola with directrix $x = 3$. A complete graph is obtained by letting $0 \le \theta \le 2\pi$ (Fig. 11.70).

[-10, 10] by [-10, 10]

Figure 11.70 $r = \dfrac{3}{1 + \cos\theta}$ and $0 \le \theta \le 2\pi$.

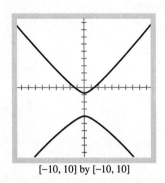

$$[-10, 10] \text{ by } [-10, 10]$$

Figure 11.71 $r = \dfrac{4}{3 - 4\sin\theta}$
and $0 \le \theta \le 2\pi$.

E X A M P L E   5   Examining a Conic in Polar Form

Find a complete graph of

$$r = \frac{4}{3 - 4\sin\theta}.$$

Specify a directrix and a range for θ that produces a complete graph.

Solution   Dividing numerator and denominator by 3 yields

$$r = \frac{\frac{4}{3}}{1 - \frac{4}{3}\sin\theta}.$$

Thus, $e = \frac{4}{3}$, so this conic is a hyperbola. Also $h = (4/3)(\frac{1}{e}) = 1$ so $y = -1$ is a directrix. A complete graph is obtained by allowing θ to vary from 0 to 2π (Fig. 11.71).   ∎

Exercises for Section 11.5

In Exercises 1 to 6, determine the eccentricity of the conic and sketch a complete graph. Support your sketch using a graphing utility.

1. $4x^2 + y^2 = 4$
2. $4x^2 + 25y^2 = 100$
3. $9x^2 - 16y^2 = 144$
4. $4x^2 - y^2 = 4$
5. $2x^2 - 3y^2 - 4x + 6y - 10 = 0$
6. $-6x^2 + 8y^2 - 6x + 9y + 10 = 0$

In Exercises 7 and 8, determine the center, length of the transverse axis, and the equations of the asymptotes.
7. the conic of Exercise 5
8. the conic of Exercise 6

In Exercises 9 and 10, estimate the eccentricity of the ellipse. (*Hint*: First estimate a and b. Then compute c and e.) Sketch a complete graph.

9. $2x^2 - 3xy + 6y^2 - 8x + 10y - 5 = 0$
10. $10x^2 + 52xy + 300y^2 - 100x + 250y - 500 = 0$

For Exercises 11 to 14, find complete graphs of the given conic for $e = 0.8, 1, 1.2$ in the same viewing rectangle.

11. $r = \dfrac{2e}{1 - e\cos\theta}$
12. $r = \dfrac{2e}{1 + e\cos\theta}$
13. $r = \dfrac{2e}{1 - e\sin\theta}$
14. $r = \dfrac{2e}{1 + e\sin\theta}$

In Exercises 15 to 20, identify and draw a complete graph of the conic in polar form. Specify a directrix and a range for θ that produces a complete graph.

15. $r = \dfrac{5}{1 - \cos\theta}$
16. $r = \dfrac{4}{2 - 4\sin\theta}$
17. $r = \dfrac{3}{4 - 2\cos\theta}$
18. $r = \dfrac{4}{3 + 4\sin\theta}$
19. $r = \dfrac{-8}{6 + 3\cos\theta}$
20. $r = \dfrac{-4}{4 - 2\sin\theta}$

In Exercises 21 and 22, draw a complete graph, identify the conic, and determine the standard form of the conic.

21. $r = \dfrac{16}{12 + 9\cos\theta}$
22. $r = \dfrac{-4}{2 + 6\sin\theta}$

23. Consider an ellipse in which the major axis has a length $2a = 8$ and the distance of a focus from the center is $c = 2$. Compute the eccentricity and find graphs of r_1 and r_2 in the same viewing rectangle. What conclusions can you draw?

$$r_1 = \frac{a - ce}{1 + e\cos\theta} \qquad r_2 = \frac{ce - a}{1 - e\cos\theta}$$

24. Consider an ellipse in which the major axis has a length $2a = 12$ and the distance of a focus from the center is $c = 3.5$. Compute the eccentricity and find graphs of r_1 and r_2 in the same viewing rectangle. What conclusions can you draw?

$$r_1 = \frac{a - ce}{1 + e\cos\theta}, \qquad r_2 = \frac{ce - a}{1 - e\cos\theta}$$

25. Consider the graph

$$r = \frac{eh}{-1 - e\cos\theta}$$

for $e = 7$ and $h = 2$. Is the graph a conic? What conic? Why?

26. Show that if an ellipse has major axis length of $2a$ and minor axis length of $2b$, then a polar equation of the ellipse is

$$r = \frac{b^2}{a + \sqrt{a^2 - b^2}\cos\theta}$$

where a focus is at the origin and the directrix is $x = h$ where $h > 0$.

In Exercises 27 to 30, compute the eccentricity and sketch the polar graphs of each ellipse. Assume that $a = 4$ and $b = \sqrt{12}$.

27. $r_1 = \dfrac{b^2}{a + \sqrt{a^2 - b^2}\cos\theta}$

28. $r_2 = \dfrac{-b^2}{a + \sqrt{a^2 - b^2}\cos\theta}$

29. $r_3 = \dfrac{-b^2}{a - \sqrt{a^2 - b^2}\cos\theta}$

30. $r_4 = \dfrac{b^2}{a - \sqrt{a^2 - b^2}\cos\theta}$

31. Find the graphs of the conics from Exercises 27 to 30 in the same viewing rectangle. What conclusions can you draw?

Chapter Review

KEY TERMS

asymptotes of a hyperbola	eccentricity e	hyperbola	spiral of Archimedes
cardioid	eliminating the parameter	line of symmetry of	standard form for
center of a hyperbola	ellipse	a parabola	an ellipse
cone	endpoints	major axis	standard form for
conic	focus of a conic	minor axis	hyperbola
conic section	focus of a parabola	parabola	standard form for
curve of quickest descent	foci (focal points) of	parametric equations	a parabola
cycloid	a hyperbola	parametrization of C	transverse axis
degenerate conic	foci (focal points) of	polar coordinates	vertex of a parabola
directrix of a conic	an ellipse	polar coordinate system	vertices of a hyperbola
directrix of a parabola	four-petaled rose	principal axis	
double-napped right	graph of a polar equation	quadratic form in variables	
circular cone	in variables r and θ	x and y	

REVIEW EXERCISES

In Exercises 1 to 3, describe each parametrically defined curve. Sketch the graph without using a graphing utility. Support your sketch using a parametric graphing utility.

1. $x(t) = 2 + 3t$, $y(t) = t$, t in $[0, 5]$

2. $x(t) = 2t$, $y(t) = 3/t$, t in $[1, 4]$

3. $x(t) = 4\cos t$, $y(t) = 4\sin t$, t in $[-2\pi, 2\pi]$

4. Which of the curves in Exercises 1 to 3 are functions?

5. What are the domains and ranges of the curves in Exercises 1 to 3?

In Exercises 6 to 10, find a complete graph.

6. $x(t) = 3t + 2$, $y = 6t^2$, t in $(-\infty, \infty)$

7. $x(t) = 2 - 1/t$ and $y = t + 1/t$, t in $(0, 20]$

8. $x(t) = \sin^2 t$, $y(t) = (1 - \sin t \cos t)$, t in $[0, 2\pi]$

9. $x(t) = t + \sin t$, $y(t) = 2 + \cos t$, t in $[-10, 10]$

10. $x(t) = 12 \cos t - 8 \cos \frac{3}{2}t$, $y(t) = 12 \sin t - 8 \sin \frac{3}{2}t$, t in $[0, 2\pi]$. (This is an *epicycloid*, the path of a point on a circle rolling on another circle.)

11. Find parametric equations and draw the graph of the circle centered at $(5, 0)$ with a radius of 4.

In Exercises 12 to 17, sketch a complete graph of each equation without using a graphing utility. Then support your answer with a graphing utility.

12. $r = 5$

13. $r = 2 \sin \theta$

14. $r = 3 + 3 \cos \theta$

15. $\theta = 78°$

16. $r = 1 - \sin \theta$

17. $r = \cos 3\theta$

In Exercises 18 and 19, use a graphing utility to draw the polar graph for θ over the given intervals.

18. $r = 4\theta$; $[0, \pi/2], [0, \pi], [0, 2\pi][-\pi, \pi], [0, 4\pi]$

19. $r = 5 \sin 3\theta$; $[0, \pi/2], [0, \pi], [0, 2\pi], [-\pi, \pi], [0, 4\pi]$

In Exercises 20 and 21, use a graphing utility to draw a complete graph of each polar equation. Specify an interval $a \le \theta \le b$ of smallest length that gives a complete graph.

20. $r = 2 \cos 4\theta$

21. $r = 3\theta$

22. Determine the length of one rose "petal" for $r = 6 \sin 2\theta$.

In Exercises 23 and 24, use the parametric equation method to find the points of intersection of the graph of each system.

23. $\begin{cases} r = 3 \cos \theta \\ r = 3 \sin \theta \end{cases}$

24. $\begin{cases} r = 2 + \sin \theta \\ r = 1 - \cos \theta \end{cases}$

In Exercises 25 and 26, determine an equation for the parabola from the given focus and directrix. Give the coordinates of the vertex and the line of symmetry, and draw a complete graph.

25. $(-2, 1)$, $y = -3$

26. $(-2, 1)$, $x = -3$

27. Determine an equation, the line of symmetry, and the focus of the parabola whose vertex is $(1, 4)$ and directrix is $x = 7$. Draw a complete graph.

28. Determine an equation, the line of symmetry, and the directrix of the parabola whose focus is $(0, 2)$ and vertex is $(0, -4)$. Draw a complete graph.

In Exercises 29 and 30, find the standard form, vertex, focus, directrix, and line of symmetry of each parabola. Find a complete graph without using a graphing utility, and then support your graph with a graphing utility.

29. $x^2 + 4x - y + 6 = 0$

30. $6y^2 - 12y - 12x + 20 = 0$

In Exercises 31 and 32, give the endpoints of the major and minor axes, the coordinates of the center and foci, and the lines of symmetry of each ellipse. Draw a complete graph of the ellipse without using a graphing utility.

31. $\dfrac{(x + 3)^2}{4} + \dfrac{(y - 1)^2}{6} = 1$

32. $(x - 1)^2 + 8(y + 2)^2 = 16$

In Exercises 33 to 35, determine the endpoints of the major and minor axes, and the standard form of the equation of each ellipse. Draw a complete graph without using a graphing utility.

33. The sum of the distances from the foci is 16; the foci are $(-5, 0)$ and $(5, 0)$.

34. The foci are $(2, 0)$ and $(-2, 0)$; the minor axis has a length of 10.

35. The foci are $(2, 3)$ and $(2, 9)$; the major axis has a length of 12.

In Exercises 36 and 37, write the equation of the ellipse in standard form. Give the endpoints of the major and minor axes, the coordinates of the center and foci, and the lines of symmetry. Draw a complete graph and support your answer using a graphing utility.

36. $4x^2 + 9y^2 + 8x - 36y + 4 = 0$

37. $4x^2 + 5y^2 - 24x + 10y + 21 = 0$

In Exercises 38 and 39, determine the coordinates of the center, foci, vertices, lines of symmetry, and asymptotes of each hyperbola. Draw a complete graph without using a graphing utility.

38. $\dfrac{x^2}{9} - \dfrac{(y + 2)^2}{6} = 1$

39. $3(y - 3)^2 - 5(x + 1)^2 = 15$

In Exercises 40 to 43, identify the conic, and write the equation in standard form. Give the foci, vertices, center, axes of symmetry, and asymptotes (if any). Draw a complete graph, and then support your answer using a graphing utility.

40. $25x^2 - 9y^2 - 50x - 36y - 236 = 0$

41. $y^2 - x + 6y + 9 = 0$

42. $5x^2 + 4y^2 + 30x - 8y + 29 = 0$

43. $4y^2 - 9x^2 + 24y + 35 = 0$

44. The parabola $y^2 - 4y + 2 = x$ does not define y as a function of x. How can it be graphed using only a function graphing utility?

45. Explain how a conic of the form $Ax^2 + Bxy + Cy^2 + Dx + Ey + F = 0$ can be graphed using a *function* graphing utility, not a special conic graphing utility.

In Exercises 46 to 49, find a complete graph, and identify the conic.

46. $4x^2 + 3xy - y^2 - 10x - 5y - 20 = 0$

47. $2x^2 - 4xy + 2y^2 + 6x - 5y - 15 = 0$

48. $6x^2 - 8xy + 10y^2 - 5x + y - 30 = 0$

49. $-2x^2 + 7xy - 3y^2 + 3x - 2y - 10 = 0$

50. Estimate the coordinates of the center and the equations of the asymptotes of the hyperbola $2x^2 - 3xy + y^2 + 2x - 3y - 2 = 0$.

51. Estimate the coordinates of the center, the endpoints of the major and minor axes, and lines of symmetry of the ellipse $3x^2 - xy + 2y^2 + 6x + 2y - 10 = 0$.

52. Determine a pair of equations that give an end behavior model of the hyperbola $4x^2 + 8xy - 3y^2 + 5x - 10y - 30 = 0$. Find graphs of the two equations and of the hyperbola in the same large viewing rectangle to support your answer.

In Exercises 53 and 54, list a sequence of transformations that when applied to the graph of $y = x^2$ will result in the graph of the given parabola.

53. $6(y - 1) = (x - 3)^2$ **54.** $x^2 - 2x - 6 = 2y$

55. Explain what transformations applied first to a circle in standard form will result in the ellipse $9x^2 + 16y^2 = 144$.

56. What transformations applied first to a conic in standard form will result in the conic $4x^2 + 9y^2 + 16x - 18y - 11 = 0$?

In Exercises 57 and 58, determine the standard form of the equation, and draw a complete graph of the hyperbola without using a graphing utility.

57. The absolute value of the difference of the distances from any point on the hyperbola to the foci is 2; the foci are $(-2, 0)$ and $(2, 0)$.

58. The absolute value of the difference of the distances from any point on the hyperbola to the foci is 10; the foci are $(0, -2)$ and $(0, 10)$.

59. Find the points of intersection of the line and the parabola (if any): $y = x^2 - 4x + 5$, $2x + y - 7 = 0$.

60. A parabola of the form $y = ax^2 + b$ passes through the points $(2, 4)$ and $(5, 8)$. Determine an equation of the parabola.

61. An ellipse has a major axis of length 10 along the x-axis and a minor axis along the y-axis of length 4. Determine the foci, standard form of the equation, and draw a complete graph without using a graphing utility

62. A golfer hits a ball with an initial velocity of 125 ft/sec and at an angle of $33°$ from the horizontal. Find when and where the ball will hit the ground.

63. A batter hits a ball with an initial velocity of 100 ft/sec and at an angle of $50°$ from the horizontal. Find the maximum height attained and the distance traveled by the ball.

Exercises 64 to 68 refer to the following **problem situation**: A dart is thrown upward with an initial velocity of 60 ft/sec at an angle of elevation $35°$. Consider the position of the dart at any time t ($t = 0$ when the dart is thrown). Neglect air resistance.

64. Find parametric equations that model the problem situation.

65. Draw a complete graph of the model.

66. What portion of the graph represents the problem situation?

67. When will the dart hit the ground?

68. Find the maximum height of the dart. At what time will it reach maximum height?

Exercises 69 to 72 refer to the following **problem situation**: An NFL punter at the 20-yard line kicks a football downfield with an initial velocity of 80 ft/sec at an angle of elevation of $55°$.

69. Draw a complete graph of the problem situation.

70. How far downfield will the football first hit the field?

71. Determine the maximum height above the field of the ball.

72. What is the "hang time" (the total time the football is in the air)?

CHAPTER 12

Sequences, Series, and Probability

12.1 Sequences

The word *sequence* as used in ordinary English means "one thing after another." A set of events occurs in sequence if first one occurs, then the next, then the next, and so on. A **sequence of numbers** is a set of numbers with a specific order. For example,

$$1, \frac{1}{2}, \frac{1}{3}, \frac{1}{4}, \ldots, b_n, \ldots$$

is an example of a sequence in mathematics. In order for a sequence to be uniquely determined, it is necessary that there be some rule that determines the nth term. The above sequence is uniquely defined by the rule

$$b_n = \frac{1}{n},$$

where it is understood that n has values $1, 2, 3, \ldots, n, \ldots$.

A second sequence,

$$2, 5, 8, 11, \ldots, a_n, \ldots$$

577

is defined by the rule $a_n = 3n - 1$.

Any function $f(x)$ whose domain includes all positive integers defines the sequence

$$f(1), f(2), f(3), \ldots, f(n), \ldots .$$

In fact, the function concept is key to understanding the concept of sequence.

Definition 12.1 Sequence

An **infinite sequence** is a function whose domain is the set of all positive integers $\{1, 2, 3, \ldots, n, \ldots\}$.

A **finite sequence** is a function whose domain is some initial subset of positive integers $\{1, 2, 3, \ldots, n\}$ for some fixed positive integer n.

A sequence is typically expressed in list form $a_1, a_2, a_3, \ldots, a_n, \ldots$, and the term a_n is called the nth term of the sequence. We often use the notation $\{a_n\}$ to denote a sequence whose nth term is a_n.

EXAMPLE 1 Finding Terms in Sequences

List the first three terms and the 15th term of the sequences (a) $a_n = (n^2 - 1)/n$ and (b) $b_n = (-1)^n 2^n$.

Solution

a)

$$a_1 = \frac{1^2 - 1}{1} = 0, \quad a_2 = \frac{2^2 - 1}{2} = \frac{3}{2}, \quad a_3 = \frac{3^2 - 1}{3} = \frac{8}{3},$$

and the 15th term is

$$a_{15} = \frac{15^2 - 1}{15} = \frac{224}{15}.$$

Therefore the sequence is

$$0, \frac{3}{2}, \frac{8}{3}, \ldots, \frac{224}{15}, \ldots, \frac{n^2 - 1}{n}, \ldots .$$

b) $b_1 = (-1) \cdot 2 = -2, \quad b_2 = (-1)^2 \cdot 2^2 = 4, \quad (-1)^3 \cdot 2^3 = -8$, and the 15th term is $a_{15} = (-1)^{15} \cdot 2^{15} = -32{,}768$. Therefore the sequence is

$$-2, 4, -8, \ldots, -32{,}768, \ldots, (-1)^n \cdot 2^n, \ldots .$$

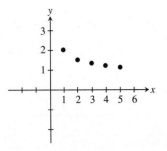

Figure 12.1   First five terms of $a_n = (n+1)/n$.

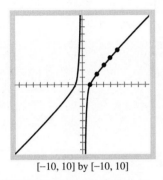

[−10, 10] by [−10, 10]

Figure 12.2   Graph of the sequence $a_n = (n^2 - 1)/n$.

Since a sequence is a function, the graph of the sequence is precisely its graph as a function. For example, to find the graph of the sequence $a_n = (n+1)/(n)$, simply plot the following set of points on the rectangular coordinate plane:

$$\{(1, 2), (2, 3/2), (3, 4/3), (4, 5/4), (5, 6/5), \ldots\}$$

See Fig. 12.1.

A second approach to finding the graph of a sequence involves finding a complete graph $y = f(x)$ where f is the function rule that defines the sequence. After finding the complete graph, place dots on the graph for the points that represent the graph of the sequence. This latter approach will be used in Example 2.

E X A M P L E   2   Graphing a Sequence

Find the graph of the sequence $a_n = (n^2 - 1)/n$.

Solution   First find the complete graph of $f(x) = (x^2 - 1)/x$. Then place dots on the graph for points

$$(1, f(1)), (2, f(2)), (3, f(3)), (4, f(4)), (5, f(5)), \ldots.$$

This graph is shown in Fig. 12.2.   ▤

The sequences in Example 1 were defined by stating an explicit formula that defined the nth term. A second method for specifying a sequence is to use a **recursive formula**. In a recursive formula the first few terms are given and the nth term a_n is defined in terms of previous terms of the sequence. Here is an example of a recursive formula:

$$a_n = 3 + a_{n-1}, \quad a_1 = 2.$$

The first few terms of this sequence are

$$a_1 = 2, \quad a_2 = 3 + a_1 = 3 + 2 = 5, \quad a_3 = 3 + a_2 = 3 + 5 = 8, \ldots.$$

E X A M P L E   3   Using a Recursive Formula

Determine the first four terms and the eighth term for the sequence $\{a_n\}$ defined by $a_n = 3 + a_{n-1}$ for $n \geq 2$, where $a_1 = 4$.

Solution   Use $a_n = 3 + a_{n-1}$ for $n = 2$ to find a_2. That is, $a_2 = 3 + a_1 = 3 + 4 = 7$. Also, $a_3 = 3 + a_2 = 3 + 7 = 10$, and $a_4 = 3 + a_3 = 3 + 10 = 13$.

Whenever a term of a recursively defined sequence is known, you can find the next term, or you can work backwards to find an earlier term in the sequence:

$$a_8 = 3 + a_7$$

$$= 3 + (3 + a_6)$$

$$= 6 + (3 + a_5)$$

$$= 9 + (3 + a_4)$$

$$= 12 + 13 = 25 \qquad \blacksquare$$

E X A M P L E   4   Finding the *n*th Term of a Recursive Formula

Discover a pattern and state a formula with variable n for the nth term of the sequence $\{a_n\}$ defined by $a_n = 3 + a_{n-1}$ for $n \geq 2$, where $a_1 = 4$.

Solution Compute terms of the sequence until a pattern is evident and you can conjecture a formula for the nth term.

$$a_2 = 3 + a_1$$

$$a_3 = 3 + a_2 = 2(3) + a_1$$

$$a_4 = 3 + a_3 = 3(3) + a_1$$

$$a_5 = 3 + a_4 = 4(3) + a_1$$

$$\vdots$$

The pattern seems to be clear. Conjecture that

$$a_n = 3(n - 1) + a_1 = 3(n - 1) + 4$$

and write $a_n = 3n + 1$. $\qquad \blacksquare$

In Section 12.5 we will introduce another method for verifying the nth term of a sequence, called mathematical induction. In the meantime use the "discover a pattern" method.

Example 4 illustrates that it is sometimes possible to express a_n as a formula with variable n. However, it is often difficult to determine such a formula. The next example introduces the **Fibonacci sequence**, a sequence that is easy to define recursively but difficult to express as a function of n.

Exercises 44 to 46 refer to a real-world occurrence of this sequence.

E X A M P L E   5   Finding Terms in the Fibonacci Sequence

Determine the first six terms of the sequence $\{a_n\}$ defined by $a_1 = a_2 = 1$, and $a_n = a_{n-1} + a_{n-2}$ for $n \geq 3$.

Solution Determine a_n for $n = 3, 4, 5$, and 6:

$$a_1 = 1$$

$$a_2 = 1$$

$$a_3 = a_2 + a_1 = 2$$
$$a_4 = a_3 + a_2 = 3$$
$$a_5 = a_4 + a_3 = 5$$
$$a_6 = a_5 + a_4 = 8$$

Arithmetic Progression

Certain groups of sequences are identified as being of the same type because they all have an identical pattern. Arithmetic sequences are one such group.

Definition 12.2   Arithmetic Sequences

A sequence $\{a_n\}$ is called an **arithmetic progression** or an **arithmetic sequence** if there is a real number d such that

$$a_n = a_{n-1} + d$$

for every positive integer n. The number d is called the **common difference** of the arithmetic sequence.

Suppose that $\{a_n\}$ is an arithmetic sequence with a common difference d. The sequence satisfies the pattern

$$a_2 = a_1 + d$$
$$a_3 = a_2 + d = (a_1 + d) + d = a_1 + 2d$$
$$a_4 = a_3 + d = (a_1 + 2d) + d = a_1 + 3d$$
$$\vdots$$
$$a_n = a_{n-1} + d = a_1 + (n-2)d + d = a_1 + (n-1)d.$$

This pattern suggests the following theorem.

Theorem 12.1   Arithmetic Sequences

If $\{a_n\}$ is an arithmetic sequence with a common difference d, then

$$a_n = a_1 + (n-1)d$$

for every positive integer n.

Notice that the a_n can be described as a function of n if the constant difference d and the first term a_1 are known. Examples 6 and 7 illustrate that in fact if any two terms of an arithmetic sequence are known, a_1 and d can be found.

EXAMPLE 6   Finding an Arithmetic Sequence

The first two terms of an arithmetic progression are -8 and -2. Find the 10th term and a formula for the nth term.

Solution $a_1 = -8, a_2 = -2$, and $a_2 = a_1 + d$. Therefore

$$a_2 = a_1 + d$$
$$-2 = -8 + d \quad \text{Substitute values for } a_1 \text{ and } a_2.$$
$$d = 6.$$

So, $a_{10} = a_1 + 9d = -8 + 9(6) = 46$. The nth term is thus

$$a_n = a_1 + (n-1)d = -8 + 6(n-1) = 6n - 14. \qquad \equiv$$

EXAMPLE 7   Finding an Arithmetic Sequence

The third and eighth terms of an arithmetic progression are 13 and 3, respectively. Determine the first term and a formula for the nth term.

Solution   Use $a_n = a_1 + (n-1)d$ to establish the following pair of equations:

$$a_3 = a_1 + 2d = 13$$
$$a_8 = a_1 + 7d = 3$$

Subtracting the first equation from the second yields $5d = -10$, so $d = -2$ and $a_1 = 17$. Therefore

$$a_n = a_1 + (n-1)d = 17 - 2(n-1) = 19 - 2n. \qquad \equiv$$

Geometric Progression

In an arithmetic sequence any term is obtained by adding a constant to the preceding term. The sequences known as geometric sequences satisfy the property that any given term is obtained from the preceding term by multiplying by a constant.

Definition 12.3   Geometric Sequences

A sequence $\{a_n\}$ is called a **geometric progression** or **geometric sequence** if there is a nonzero real number r such that

$$a_n = r \cdot a_{n-1}.$$

For every positive integer n, the number r is called the **common ratio** of the geometric sequence.

Suppose that $\{a_n\}$ is a geometric sequence with a common ratio r. Then the sequence satisfies the following pattern:

$$a_2 = a_1 r$$

$$a_3 = a_2 r = (a_1 r) \cdot r = a_1 r^2$$

$$a_4 = a_3 r = (a_1 r^2) \cdot r = a_1 r^3$$

$$\vdots$$

$$a_n = a_{n-1} r = (a_1 r^{n-2}) \cdot r = a_1 r^{n-1}$$

This pattern suggests the following theorem.

Theorem 12.2   Geometric Sequences

If $\{a_n\}$ is a geometric sequence with a common ratio r, then

$$a_n = a_1 r^{n-1}$$

for every positive integer n.

Notice that if a_k and a_{k+1} are successive terms of a geometric sequence, the ratio a_{k+1}/a_k simplifies as follows:

$$\frac{a_{k+1}}{a_k} = \frac{a_1 r^k}{a_1 r^{k-1}}$$

$$= r$$

This demonstrates why r is called the common ratio.

E X A M P L E   8   Finding a Geometric Sequence

The second and third terms of a geometric sequence are -6 and 12, respectively. Determine the first term and a formula for the nth term.

Solution   Since r is the ratio of successive terms,

$$r = \frac{a_3}{a_2} = \frac{12}{-6} = -2.$$

Since $a_n = a_1 r^{n-1}$ where $r = -2$, it follows that $a_2 = (-2)a_1 = -6$. Therefore $a_1 = 3$ and

$$a_n = 3 \cdot (-2)^{n-1}.$$ ≡

Example 9 revisits compound interest to illustrate that geometric sequences find application in the business world.

E X A M P L E   9   APPLICATION: Compound Interest

Two hundred dollars are deposited in an account that pays 9% annually, compounded monthly. Let P_n be the amount in the account at the end of the nth month. Show that $P_1, P_2, P_3, \ldots$ is a geometric sequence. Find the common ratio and the value of P_1.

Solution   To find the monthly interest rate, divide the annual rate by 12: $0.09/12 = 0.0075$. Using the formula for compound interest studied in Section 6.2, note that

$$P_n = 200(1 + 0.0075)^n.$$

Therefore

$$\frac{P_n}{P_{n-1}} = \frac{200(1.0075)^n}{200(1.0075)^{n-1}} = 1.0075.$$

Since the ratio of successive terms is 1.0075, this sequence is by definition a geometric sequence with a common ratio $r = 1.0075$. Therefore

$$P_n = P_1 \cdot r^{n-1} = 200(1.0075)^n = [200(1.0075)](1.0075)^{n-1}.$$

Consequently the first term $P_1 = 200(1.0075)$.   ≡

Exercises for Section 12.1

In Exercises 1 to 8, determine the first four terms and the tenth term of the sequence.

1. $a_n = (-1)^{n+1}$

2. $a_n = 2n - 1$

3. $a_n = \dfrac{n+1}{n}$

4. $a_n = (-1)^n 2n$

5. $a_n = \dfrac{n^3 - 1}{n+1}$

6. $a_n = \dfrac{4}{n+2}$

7. $a_n = (-1)^n \left(1 + \dfrac{1}{n}\right)$

8. $a_n = \dfrac{1}{8} \cdot 3^n$

In Exercises 9 to 12, determine the first four terms and the eighth term of the sequence and a rule for the nth term. That is, determine a_n as an explicit function of n.

9. $a_1 = 3; a_n = a_{n-1} + 1, n = 2, 3, \ldots$

10. $a_1 = -2; a_n = a_{n-1} + 2, n = 2, 3, \ldots$

11. $a_1 = 2; a_n = 2a_{n-1}, n = 2, 3, \ldots$

12. $a_1 = \dfrac{3}{2}; a_n = \dfrac{1}{2} a_{n-1}, n = 2, 3, \ldots$

In Exercises 13 to 16, discover a pattern and find a formula with variable n for the nth term of each sequence $\{a_n\}$.

13. $a_1 = 3; a_n = a_{n-1} + 2$ for $n \geq 2$.

14. $a_1 = -5; a_n = a_{n-1} + 7$ for $n \geq 2$.

15. $a_1 = 2; a_n = 3a_{n-1}$ for $n \geq 2$.

16. $a_1 = 3; a_n = (-2)a_{n-1}$ for $n \geq 2$.

In Exercises 17 to 20, determine the common difference, the 10th term, and a formula for the nth term of each arithmetic sequence.

17. $6, 10, 14, 18, \ldots$

18. $-4, 1, 6, 11, \ldots$

19. $-5, -2, 1, 4, \ldots$

20. $-7, 4, 15, 26, \ldots$

In Exercises 21 to 24, determine the common ratio, the eighth term, and a formula for the nth term of each geometric sequence.

21. $2, 6, 18, 54, \ldots$

22. $1, -2, 4, -8, 16 \ldots$

23. $3, 6, 12, 24, \ldots$

24. $-2, 2, -2, 2, \ldots$

25. The fourth and seventh terms of an arithmetic progression are -8 and 4, respectively. Determine the first term and a formula for the nth term.

26. The fifth and ninth terms of an arithmetic progression are -5 and -17, respectively. Determine the first term and a formula for the nth term.

Which sequences in Exercises 27 to 32 could be arithmetic or geometric? For arithmetic or geometric sequences, state the appropriate common difference or ratio, and determine a formula for the nth term.

27. $5, 10, 20, 40, \ldots$

28. $-0.25, 1, -4, 16, -64, \ldots$

29. $-16, -9, -2, 5, \ldots$

30. $10.1, 10.201, 10.30301, 10.4060401, \ldots$

31. $-2, 1, -\dfrac{1}{2}, \dfrac{1}{4}, \ldots$

32. $1, 5, 7, 11, 17, \ldots$

In Exercises 33 to 36, sketch a graph of each sequence.

33. $a_n = 2 - \dfrac{1}{n}$

34. $a_n = \sqrt{n} - 3$

35. $a_n = n^2 - 5$

36. $a_n = 3 + 2n$

37. Roberta had $1250 in a savings account 3 years ago. What will the value of her account be 2 years from now assuming no deposits or withdrawals are made and the account earns 6.5% interest compounded annually?

38. Ellen has $12,876 in a savings account today. She made no deposits or withdrawals during the past 6 years. What was the value of her account 6 years ago? Assume the account earned interest at 5.75% compounded monthly.

Exercises 39 to 41 refer to the following **problem situation**: The half-life of a certain unstable radioactive substance is 1 week. Suppose 1000 grams of the substance exist today. Let n represent the number of weeks the substance exists.

39. Determine an infinite geometric sequence that models the amount of the substance at week n, where $n = 1, 2, 3, \ldots$. List the first 10 terms of the sequence. What is the common ratio?

40. When will there be only 0.05 grams of the substance remaining?

41. Will the substance ever be reduced to nothing?

Exercises 42 and 43 refer to the following **problem situation**: The height of a certain fast-growing plant in a rain forest increases at the rate of 2.5% per month. Assume the plant is 15 inches in height today. Let n represent the number of months the plant grows, and assume the plant dies in 10 months.

42. Determine a finite geometric sequence that is a model for the height of the plant after n months. Write out all the terms of the sequence. What is the common ratio?

43. How long would the plant need to live in order to double in height?

Exercises 44 to 47 refer to the following rabbit population **problem situation**: Assume rabbits become fertile 1 month after birth and each male-female pair of fertile rabbits produces one new male-female pair of rabbits each month. Further assume the rabbit colony begins with one newborn male-female pair of rabbits and no rabbits die for 12 months. Let a_n represent the number of *pairs* of rabbits in the colony after $n - 1$ months.

44. Explain why $a_1 = 1$, $a_2 = 1$, and $a_3 = 2$.

45. Determine a_4, a_5, a_6, a_7, and a_8.

46. Explain why the sequence in Exercise 45 is a model for the size of the rabbit colony.

47. Compute the first seven terms of

$$a_n = \frac{1}{\sqrt{5}}\left(\frac{1 + \sqrt{5}}{2}\right)^n - \frac{1}{\sqrt{5}}\left(\frac{1 - \sqrt{5}}{2}\right)^n.$$

Do you recognize this sequence?

48. Investigate the value of $a_n = 10n \sin(\pi/n)$ for $n = 10{,}100$, and $10{,}000$. Compute the circumference of a circle with a radius of 5. What conclusions can you draw?

49. Sketch a graph of a_n for $1 \le n \le 100$ where a_n is defined as in Exercise 48. How does your graph relate to Exercise 48?

50. Consider the sequence $a_1 = 1$ and $a_n = na_{n-1}$. Compute the first six terms of the sequence, and determine a rule for a_n as an explicit function of n.

A sequence $\{a_n\}$ *converges to a real number K*, denoted by $a_n \to K$ as $n \to \infty$, if the line $y = K$ is a horizontal asymptote of the graph of a_n. For each sequence in Exercises 51 to 54, find a complete graph of a_n and a line $y = K$ in the same viewing rectangle to show that the sequence converges to a number K. Identify K.

51. $a_n = \dfrac{2n}{n + 1}$

52. $a_n = \left(1 + \dfrac{0.05}{n}\right)^n$

53. $a_n = 3 + \dfrac{(-1)^n}{n}$

54. $a_n = n \sin \dfrac{\pi}{2n}$

55. Let $f(x) = (\frac{1}{2})^x$, and define a sequence $a_n = f(a_{n-1})$ where $a_1 = f(1)$. Compute the first eight terms of this sequence. To what number does this sequence appear to converge?

56. Find complete graphs of $y = x$ and $f(x) = \left(\frac{1}{2}\right)^x$ in the same viewing rectangle. Zoom in to find a solution to the equation $f(x) = x$. How does this solution compare with the sequence in Exercise 55?

12.2   Finite and Infinite Series

Finite Series

In Section 12.1 we used the notation $\{a_n\}$ to denote a sequence. For example the terms of the sequence $\{a_n\}$ where $a_n = (2n - 1)^2$ are

$$1^2, 3^2, 5^2, 7^2, 9^2, \ldots, (2n - 1)^2, \ldots .$$

Consider the following sums:

$$S_1 = 1^2$$

$$S_2 = 1^2 + 3^2$$

$$S_3 = 1^2 + 3^2 + 5^2$$

$$S_4 = 1^2 + 3^2 + 5^2 + 7^2$$

$$\vdots$$

$$S_n = 1^2 + 3^2 + \cdots + (2n - 1)^2$$

Each sum S_n is called a **finite series** since there are a finite number of terms in each sum.

To illustrate the concept of *series* in general, consider the general sequence $\{a_n\}$. Then the **sequence of partial sums** of $\{a_n\}$ is the sequence $\{S_n\}$ shown here:

$$S_1 = a_1$$

$$S_2 = a_1 + a_2$$

$$S_3 = a_1 + a_2 + a_3$$

$$\vdots$$

$$S_n = a_1 + a_2 + \cdots + a_n$$

Again, each term S_k is an example of a finite series. The number S_n is called the **nth partial sum** of the sequence $\{a_n\}$.

The Greek capital letter Σ (sigma) is used as a symbol for sum.

Sigma Notation

The sum of n terms $a_1, a_2, \ldots, a_n$ is written as

$$S_n = \sum_{k=1}^{n} a_k = a_1 + a_2 + \cdots + a_n.$$

Read $\displaystyle\sum_{k=1}^{n} a_k$ as "the sum from $k = 1$ to n of a_k". a_k is called the **kth term of the sum**, and k is called the **index of summation.**

The sum $\displaystyle\sum_{k=1}^{n}$ is referred to as **sigma notation**, and the sum

$$a_1 + a_2 + \ldots + a_n$$

is referred to as **expanded notation.**

Example 1 illustrates how to convert from sigma notation to expanded form.

E X A M P L E   1   Expanding a Sum

Expand the sum $\displaystyle\sum_{k=1}^{n}(2k+3)^3$.

Solution

$$\sum_{k=1}^{n}(2k+3)^3 = 5^3 + 7^3 + 9^3 + \cdots + (2n+3)^3$$

≡

Sigma notation is often a notational convenience. When the form of expressions involving sigma notation needs to be changed, properties about the summation notation given by Theorem 12.3, stated here without proof, are useful.

Theorem 12.3   Summation Properties

Let $\{a_n\}$ and $\{b_n\}$ be two sequences, and let n be a positive integer. Then

1. $\displaystyle\sum_{k=1}^{n}(a_k + b_k) = \sum_{k=1}^{n}a_k + \sum_{k=1}^{n}b_k$

2. $\displaystyle\sum_{k=1}^{n}(a_k - b_k) = \sum_{k=1}^{n}a_k - \sum_{k=1}^{n}b_k$

3. $\displaystyle\sum_{k=1}^{n}ca_k = c\sum_{k=1}^{n}a_k$ for every real number c.

E X A M P L E   2   Using Summation Properties

Use Theorem 12.3 to combine the following expression into a single sum:

$$\sum_{k=1}^{n}(5k^2 - 4) + \sum_{k=1}^{n}(7 - 2k + k^2)$$

Solution

$$\sum_{k=1}^{n}(5k^2 - 4) + \sum_{k=1}^{n}(7 - 2k + k^2) = \sum_{k=1}^{n}[(5k^2 - 4) + (7 - 2k + k^2)]$$

$$= \sum_{k=1}^{n}(6k^2 - 2k + 3)$$

≡

Summation Formulas

The next theorem gives several summation formulas. These formulas can be proven using mathematical induction, a method that will be discussed in Section 12.5. Using these formulas, a sum can be replaced with an expression in the variable n.

Theorem 12.4   Summation Formulas

The following are true for all positive integers n:

1. $\displaystyle\sum_{k=1}^{n} c = cn$

2. $\displaystyle\sum_{k=1}^{n} k = \frac{n(n+1)}{2}$

3. $\displaystyle\sum_{k=1}^{n} k^2 = \frac{n(n+1)(2n+1)}{6}$

4. $\displaystyle\sum_{k=1}^{n} k^3 = \frac{n^2(n+1)^2}{4}$

E X A M P L E   3   Simplifying Sums

Use Theorems 12.3 and 12.4 to simplify $\displaystyle\sum_{k=1}^{n}(6k^2 - 2k + 3)$.

Solution

$$\sum_{k=1}^{n}(6k^2 - 2k + 3) = \sum_{k=1}^{n} 6k^2 - \sum_{k=1}^{n} 2k + \sum_{k=1}^{n} 3$$

$$= 6\sum_{k=1}^{n} k^2 - 2\sum_{k=1}^{n} k + 3n$$

$$= 6\frac{n(n+1)(2n+1)}{6} - 2\frac{n(n+1)}{2} + 3n$$

$$= n(2n^2 + 3n + 1) - (n^2 + n) + 3n$$

$$= 2n^3 + 2n^2 + 3n$$

$\blacksquare$

Finite Geometric Series

A **finite geometric series** is a finite series determined by a geometric sequence $a_1, a_1 r, a_1 r^2, \ldots, a_1 r^{n-1}, \ldots$. That is, this sum is a finite geometric series:

$$S_n = \sum_{k=1}^{n} a_1 r^{k-1} = a_1 + a_1 r + \cdots + a_1 r^{n-1}.$$

To develop a summation formula for a geometric series, start with expressions for S_n and rS_n.

$$S_n = \sum_{k=1}^{n} a_1 r^{k-1} = a_1 + a_1 r + \cdots a_1 r^{n-1} \qquad (1)$$

$$rS_n = \sum_{k=1}^{n} a_1 r^{k} = a_1 r + a_1 r^2 + \cdots a_1 r^{n} \qquad (2)$$

Subtracting Eq. (2) from Eq. (1) results in

$$S_n - rS_n = a_1 - a_1 r^n$$

$$(1 - r)S_n = a_1(1 - r^n)$$

$$S_n = a_1 \frac{1 - r^n}{1 - r}.$$

We have proved the following theorem.

Theorem 12.5   Finite Geometric Series

If S_n is equal to a finite geometric series

$$S_n = \sum_{k=1}^{n} a_1 r^{k-1} = a_1 + a_1 r + a_1 r^2 + \cdots + a_1 r^{n-1},$$

then

$$S_n = a_1 \frac{1 - r^n}{1 - r}.$$

E X A M P L E   4   Finding a Sum of a Finite Geometric Series

Determine the fourth partial sum of the geometric sequence $2, \frac{2}{3}, \frac{2}{9}, \ldots$.

Solution   To verify that these three terms are the beginning of a geometric sequence, check that the ratio of each pair of successive terms is the same.

$$r = \frac{\frac{2}{3}}{2} = \frac{\frac{2}{9}}{\frac{2}{3}} = \frac{1}{3}$$

Using Theorem 12.5 with $r = \dfrac{1}{3}, a_1 = 2$, and $n = 4$ we obtain

$$S_n = a_1 \frac{1 - r^n}{1 - r}$$

$$S_4 = 2\frac{1 - (\frac{1}{3})^4}{1 - (\frac{1}{3})}$$

$$= \frac{2(1 - 1/81)}{\frac{2}{3}}$$

$$= \frac{240}{81}$$

$$= 2.9629.$$

Infinite Series

So far in this section we have studied finite series, that is, the sums of the form

$$S_n = \sum_{k=1}^{n} a_k = a_1 + a_2 + \cdots + a_n.$$

If n is large, it may take a tremendous amount of computation time, but it is possible to actually add all the terms together.

We now introduce the concept of infinite series. An **infinite series** is denoted by the expression

$$\sum_{k=1}^{\infty} a_k = a_1 + a_2 + \cdots + a_n + \cdots. \tag{3}$$

Since an infinite number of terms cannot actually be added together, the sum of an infinite series cannot be found through direct addition.

In order to describe what the infinite sum of Eq. (3) means, consider the following sequence of partial sums:

$$S_1 = a_1$$

$$S_2 = a_1 + a_2$$

$$\vdots$$

$$S_n = a_1 + a_2 + \cdots + a_n$$

If there is a number S for which the line $y = S$ is a horizontal asymptote for the sequence $\{S_n\}$, then we say that "the sequence $\{S_n\}$ converges to S as n approaches infinity" and we call S the sum of the series. The notation for this is

$$S_n \to S \quad \text{as} \quad n \to \infty.$$

Definition 12.4   Sum of an Infinite Series

The **sum of an infinite series** $\displaystyle\sum_{k=1}^{\infty} a_k$, if it exists, is the number S where

$$\sum_{k=1}^{n} a_k \rightarrow S \quad \text{as} \quad n \rightarrow \infty.$$

The series is said to **converge** to S.

An infinite series of the form

$$\sum_{k=1}^{\infty} a_1 r^{k-1} = a_1 + a_1 r + a_1 r^2 + \cdots + a_1 r^{n-1} + \cdots$$

is called an **infinite geometric series**. Consider the following example.

E X A M P L E   5   Finding Sums of an Infinite Geometric Series

Find S_4, S_5, and S_6 for the infinite geometric series $\displaystyle\sum_{k=1}^{\infty} 2\left(\tfrac{1}{3}\right)^{k-1}$. Observe that $\{S_n\}$ appears to converge to 3.

Solution   Example 4 showed that $S_4 = 2.9629$. The other two sums are

$$S_5 = 2\frac{1 - \left(\tfrac{1}{3}\right)^5}{1 - \left(\tfrac{1}{3}\right)}$$

$$= \frac{2\left(1 - \tfrac{1}{243}\right)}{\tfrac{2}{3}}$$

$$= 2.9877,$$

$$S_6 = 2\frac{1 - \left(\tfrac{1}{3}\right)^6}{1 - \left(\tfrac{1}{3}\right)}$$

$$= \frac{2\left(1 - \tfrac{1}{729}\right)}{\tfrac{2}{3}}$$

$$= 2.9959.$$

The sequence of partial sums $\{S_n\} = \{2, 2.6667, 2.8889, 2.9629, 2.9877, 2.9959, \ldots\}$ appears to converge to 3.

Example 5 was based on direct computation. Now we develop a method for interpreting infinite geometric series graphically.

Theorem 12.5 states that the finite geometric series

$$\sum_{k=1}^{n} a_1 r^{k-1} \quad \text{is equal to} \quad a_1 \frac{1 - r^n}{1 - r}.$$

To obtain a visualization for the sum of the corresponding infinite series, consider the function

$$f(x) = a_1 \frac{1 - r^x}{1 - r}.$$

Then for each positive integer n, $f(n) = S_n$ is the nth partial sum of the infinite geometric series with the common ratio r. Consequently the graph of $\{S_n\}$ consists of some points on the graph of f, and we can investigate the convergence of

$$\sum_{k=1}^{\infty} a_n r^{k-1}$$

by considering the graph of $f(x)$.

Example 6 provides a graphical method for finding the sum of the infinite series found in Example 5.

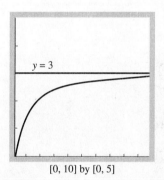

[0, 10] by [0, 5]

Figure 12.3 $y = 3$ and $f(x) = 3 - 3(\frac{1}{3})^x$.

E X A M P L E   6   Visualizing an Infinite Geometric Series

Use a graphical method to find the sum of the series

$$\sum_{k=1}^{\infty} 2\left(\frac{1}{3}\right)^{k-1} = 2 + \frac{2}{3} + \frac{2}{3^2} + \cdots.$$

Solution   In this geometric series $a_1 = 2$ and $r = \frac{1}{3}$. So consider the graph of

$$f(x) = 2 \cdot \frac{1 - r^x}{1 - r} = 2 \cdot \frac{1 - (\frac{1}{3})^x}{\frac{2}{3}} = 3 - 3\left(\frac{1}{3}\right)^x.$$

Figure 12.3 shows the graph of both $f(x)$ and $y = 3$. The line $y = 3$ is a horizontal asymptote for the graph of f. Since the graph of S_n consists of points on the graph of f, it follows that $S_n \to 3$ as $n \to \infty$.

Therefore the sum of this series is 3.   ▮

E X A M P L E   7   Visualizing an Infinite Geometric Series

Use a graphical method to find the sum of the series

$$\sum_{k=1}^{\infty} 4 \cdot 3^{k-1} = 4 + 4 \cdot 3 + 4 \cdot 3^2 + \cdots + 4 \cdot 3^{k-1} + \cdots.$$

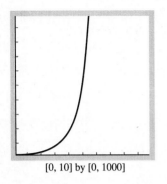

[0, 10] by [0, 1000]

Figure 12.4 $f(x) = -2 + 2 \cdot 3^x$.

Solution In this geometric series $a_1 = 4$ and $r = 3$. Consider the graph of

$$f(x) = 4 \cdot \frac{1 - 3^x}{1 - 3} = -2 + 2 \cdot 3^x.$$

Figure 12.4 shows a complete graph of f. It is evident that no horizontal asymptote exists. Therefore the sum of this infinite series does not exist. ■

When the sum of an infinite series does not exist, as illustrated in Example 7, the series is said to **diverge**.

Sum of an Infinite Geometric Series

We can see from Examples 6 and 7 that some infinite geometric series converge and some diverge. That raises the question, when does a geometric series converge and when does it diverge? The following Exploration addresses that question.

🔍 EXPLORE WITH A GRAPHING UTILITY

Find a complete graph of the function

$$f(x) = \frac{1 - r^x}{1 - r}$$

for each of the following values of r: (a) $r = 0.8$, (b) $r = 0.9$, (c) $r = 1.1$, and (d) $r = 1.2$.

For which of these values of r does the complete graph seem to have a horizontal asymptote?

Generalize For what values of r does this geometric series converge?

$$\sum_{k=1}^{\infty} a_1 r^{k-1} = a_1 + a_1 r + a_1 r^2 + \cdots + a_1 r^{k-1} + \cdots$$

It can be shown that a geometric series $\displaystyle\sum_{k=1}^{\infty} a_1 r^{k-1}$ converges if $|r| < 1$. It can also be shown that if $|r| < 1$, the sum is $a_1/(1 - r)$.

> ### Theorem 12.6   Convergence of an Infinite Geometric Series
>
> If $|r| < 1$, then the infinite geometric series
>
> $$\sum_{k=1}^{\infty} a_1 r^{k-1} = a_1 + a_1 r + a_1 r^2 + \cdots + a_1 r^{k-1} + \cdots$$
>
> has sum $a_1/(1 - r)$.

E X A M P L E   8   Finding the Sum of an Infinite Geometric Series

Find the sum of the infinite series

$$\sum_{k=1}^{\infty} 5\left(\frac{1}{2}\right)^{k-1} = 5 + \frac{5}{2} + \frac{5}{2^2} + \cdots + \frac{5}{2^{k-1}} + \cdots .$$

Solution   This series is a geometric series with $a_1 = 5$ and $r = 1/2$. Conclude from Theorem 12.6 that this series converges and has a sum of $\dfrac{5}{1 - (1/2)} = 10$.

∎

Annuities

Recall that an ordinary annuity is a sequence of equal periodic payments. Section 6.3 gave the following formula for the future value of an annuity.

> ### Future Value of an Ordinary Annuity
>
> The **future value S of an annuity** consisting of n equal payments of R dollars, each with interest rate i per period (payment interval), is given by
>
> $$S = R\frac{(1 + i)^n - 1}{i}.$$

We shall show that this formula is the sum of a finite geometric series.

Consider an annuity in which R dollars are deposited into an account at the end of each of n payment intervals. Suppose the account pays an interest rate i per period. The R dollars deposited at the end of the first payment interval earns interest for $n - 1$ intervals, so the value of the deposit at the end of the nth period is $R(1 + i)^{n-1}$ (see Fig. 12.5a on the next page).

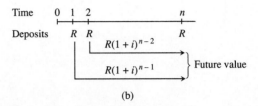

Figure 12.5 R is the amount deposited at the end of each payment interval, n is the number of payment intervals, and i is the interest per interval. a) How much the first payment earns by the end of the nth interval and b) how much the first and second payments earn by the end of the nth interval.

Similarly, the value of the R dollars deposited at the end of the second payment interval will have a value of $R(1 + i)^{n-2}$ at the end of the nth payment interval (see Fig. 12.5b).

Consequently the value of the n deposits at the end of the nth period is

$$S_n = R(1 + i)^{n-1} + R(1 + i)^{n-2} + \cdots + R(1 + i) + R. \qquad \textbf{(4)}$$

Equation (4) is a finite geometric series where $a_1 = R$ and $r = (1 + i)$. Theorem 12.5 states that this finite sum S_n is

$$S_n = a_1 \frac{1 - r^n}{1 - r} = R \frac{1 - (1 + i)^n}{1 - (1 + i)} = R \frac{(1 + i)^n - 1}{i}.$$

E X A M P L E 9   APPLICATION: Future Value of an Annuity

Bob deposits \$75 at the end of each month into an IRA (individual retirement account) that pays 9.5% APR compounded monthly. Find the value of Bob's account at the end of 20 years.

Solution This is an example of an annuity with a monthly interest rate $i = 0.095/12$. Find the future value of this account when $n = 240, i = 0.095/12$, and $R = 75$.

$$S = R \frac{(1 + i)^n - 1}{i}$$

$$= 75 \frac{(1 + 0.095/12)^{240} - 1}{0.095/12}$$

$$= 53,394.27$$

Pascal's Triangle

Consider the following array of numbers known as **Pascal's triangle**. What numbers should replace the dots in the next row of the array?

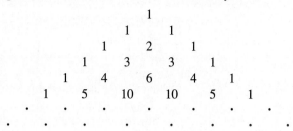

There are several important observations about the pattern in this array.

1. Each row begins and ends with a 1.

2. Each entry of a row is the sum of the two numbers directly above it in the preceding row.

3. The numbers of the nth row of this array are precisely the coefficients of the terms in the binomial expansion of $(a + b)^n$. Consider the 1 at the top of the triangle to be row zero.

Observe that row 6 of the array is

$$1 \quad 6 \quad 15 \quad 20 \quad 15 \quad 6 \quad 1.$$

E X A M P L E   1   Finding a Binomial Expansion

Expand $(a + b)^6$.

Solution   The sixth row of Pascal's triangle contains the coefficients of the terms in the expression.

$$(a + b)^6 = a^6 + \underline{\;?\;}\; a^5b + \underline{\;?\;}\; a^4b^2 + \underline{\;?\;}\, a^3b^3 + \underline{\;?\;}\, a^2b^4 + \underline{\;?\;}\, ab^5 + b^6$$

Therefore the correct expansion is

$$(a + b)^6 = a^6 + 6a^5b + 15a^4b^2 + 20a^3b^3 + 15a^2b^4 + 6ab^5 + b^6.$$ ≡

E X A M P L E   2   Finding a Binomial Expansion

Expand $(2x - 3y^2)^4$.

Solution   The binomial $2x - 3y^2$ can be rewritten as $[2x + (-3y^2)]$. Let $a = 2x$ and $b = -3y^2$, and substitute into the expression $(a + b)^4$.

$$(a + b)^4 = a^4 + 4a^3b + 6a^2b^2 + 4ab^3 + b^4$$

$$(2x - 3y^2)^4 = (2x)^4 + 4(2x)^3(-3y^2) + 6(2x)^2(-3y^2)^2 + 4(2x)(-3y^2)^3 + (-3y^2)^4$$

$$= 16x^4 + 4(-24)x^3y^2 + 6(36)x^2(y^2)^2 + 4(-54)x(y^2)^3 + 81(y^2)^4$$
$$= 16x^4 - 96x^3y^2 + 216x^2y^4 - 216xy^6 + 81y^8 \qquad \equiv$$

Binomial Coefficients $\binom{n}{r}$

While Pascal's triangle is handy to use if n is fairly small, it is not adequate for large values of n or in a situation when a formula is needed (for example, when writing a computer program) for the coefficient of the rth term in $(a + b)^n$.

Before introducing such a formula, we must introduce the concept of *factorial*. For any positive integer n we define **n factorial**, denoted $n!$, by

$$n! = 1 \cdot 2 \cdot \cdots \cdot n.$$

Notice that $n!$ is the product of all the positive integers starting with 1 and ending with n. For example,

$$3! = 1 \cdot 2 \cdot 3 = 6 \qquad \text{and} \qquad 5! = 1 \cdot 2 \cdot 3 \cdot 4 \cdot 5 = 120.$$

We also define $0! = 1$.

Definition 12.5   Binomial Coefficient $\binom{n}{r}$

If n and r are two nonnegative integers, the number called the **binomial coefficent n choose r**, denoted $\binom{n}{r}$, is defined by

$$\binom{n}{r} = \frac{n!}{r!(n-r)!}.$$

TRY THIS

Most graphing calculators have the capability to compute the calculation of binomial coefficients directly. Refer to your manual, and use your calculator to confirm the calculations in Examples 3 to 5.

Example 3 illustrates how to compute binomial coefficients.

EXAMPLE 3   Finding Binomial Coefficients

Find each of these constants: (a) $\binom{6}{4}$ and (b) $\binom{9}{5}$.

Solution

a) $\binom{6}{4} = \dfrac{6!}{4!(6-4)!} = \dfrac{6 \cdot 5}{2 \cdot 1} = 15$

b) $\binom{9}{5} = \dfrac{9!}{5!(9-5)!} = \dfrac{9 \cdot 8 \cdot 7 \cdot 6}{4 \cdot 3 \cdot 2 \cdot 1} = 126 \qquad \equiv$

Notice that $\binom{n}{r}$ is the rth entry in the nth row of Pascal's triangle, where the first entry is considered the zeroth entry. Evaluate each of these binomial coefficients and convince yourself that this array is really Pascal's triangle.

$$\binom{0}{0}$$

$$\binom{1}{0} \qquad \binom{1}{1}$$

$$\binom{2}{0} \qquad \binom{2}{1} \qquad \binom{2}{2}$$

$$\binom{3}{0} \qquad \binom{3}{1} \qquad \binom{3}{2} \qquad \binom{3}{3}$$

$$\binom{4}{0} \qquad \binom{4}{1} \qquad \binom{4}{2} \qquad \binom{4}{3} \qquad \binom{4}{4}$$

$$\binom{5}{0} \qquad \binom{5}{1} \qquad \binom{5}{2} \qquad \binom{5}{3} \qquad \binom{5}{4} \qquad \binom{5}{5}$$

We have seen earlier in this section that Pascal's triangle can be used to find the coefficients in a binomial expansion. This relationship is formalized in the **binomial theorem**.

Theorem 12.7   Binomial Theorem

$$(a+b)^n = \binom{n}{0}a^n + \binom{n}{1}a^{n-1}b + \binom{n}{2}a^{n-2}b^2 + \cdots + \binom{n}{n-1}ab^{n-1} + \binom{n}{n}b^n$$

where $\binom{n}{r} = \dfrac{n!}{r!(n-r)!}$.

E X A M P L E   4   Using the Binomial Theorem

Find the 12th term of $(2x+3y)^{15}$, where the leading term is considered the zeroth term.

Solution   From the binomial theorem note that the 12th term of $(2x+3y)^{15}$ is

$$\binom{15}{12}(2x)^{15-12}(3y)^{12} = \left(\frac{15!}{12!3!}\right)(2x)^3(3y)^{12}$$

$$= \frac{15 \cdot 14 \cdot 13}{3 \cdot 2 \cdot 1} \cdot 8x^3 \cdot 3^{12}y^{12}$$

$$= 5 \cdot 7 \cdot 13 \cdot 8x^3(531{,}441) \cdot y^{12}$$

$$= 1{,}934{,}445{,}240\, x^3 y^{12}.$$

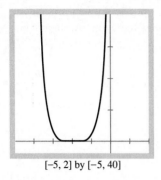

[−5, 2] by [−5, 40]

Figure 12.6 $f(x) = (x+2)^6$ overlaid with $y = x^6 + 12x^5 + 60x^4 + 160x^3 + 240x^2 + 192x + 64$.

E X A M P L E 5   Using the Binomial Theorem

Use the binomial theorem to represent $f(x) = (x+2)^6$ in the usual polynomial form.

Solution   See Fig. 12.6.

$$f(x) = (x+2)^6$$

$$= x^6 + \binom{6}{1}x^5(2) + \binom{6}{2}x^4(2^2) + \binom{6}{3}x^3(2^3) + \binom{6}{4}x^2(2^4) + \binom{6}{5}x(2^5) + 2^6$$

$$= x^6 + 6 \cdot 2x^5 + 15 \cdot 4x^4 + 20 \cdot 8x^3 + 15 \cdot 16x^2 + 6 \cdot 32x + 64$$

$$= x^6 + 12x^5 + 60x^4 + 160x^3 + 240x^2 + 192x + 64$$

      ■

Exercises for Section 12.3

1. Find the eighth row of Pascal's triangle.

2. Find the tenth row of Pascal's triangle.

In Exercises 3 to 10, expand each expression. Use Pascal's triangle to find the coefficients of each term.

3. $(a+b)^5$ **4.** $(a-b)^6$ **5.** $(x+2y)^4$

6. $(3x-y)^7$ **7.** $(x+y)^6$ **8.** $(a-2b^2)^4$

9. $(x-y)^6$ **10.** $(1+0.08)^5$

In Exercises 11 to 16, find each binomial coefficient.

11. $\binom{7}{3}$ **12.** $\binom{9}{4}$

13. $\binom{8}{4}$ **14.** $\binom{12}{3}$

15. $\binom{15}{11}$ **16.** $\binom{13}{7}$

In Exercises 17 to 20, find the coefficient of the given term in the binomial expansion.

17. x^5y^3 term, $(x+y)^8$ **18.** x^3y^5 term, $(x+y)^8$

19. x^4 term, $(x+4)^6$ **20.** x^6 term, $(x-3)^9$

In Exercises 21 to 26, use the binomial theorem to find a polynomial expansion for each function. Support your work with a graphing utility as for Figure 12.6.

21. $f(x) = (x-2)^5$ **22.** $g(x) = (x+3)^6$

23. $h(x) = (2x-1)^7$ **24.** $f(x) = (3x+4)^5$

25. $g(x) = (x+a)^4$ **26.** $h(x) = (3x-4)^8$

In Exercises 27 to 32, use the binomial theorem to find an expansion for each expression.

27. $(2x+y)^5$ **28.** $(\sqrt{x}+3)^4$

29. $(\sqrt{x}-\sqrt{y})^6$ **30.** $(2y-3x)^{12}$

31. $(x^{-2}+3)^5$ **32.** $(a-b)^{15}$

33. Show that $\binom{n}{r} = \binom{n}{n-r}$.

34. Show that $\binom{8}{3} + \binom{8}{4} = \binom{9}{4}$.

35. Show that, in general, $\binom{k}{r-1} + \binom{k}{r} = \binom{k+1}{r}$.

12.4

Polynomial Approximations to Functions

Polynomial functions are among the simplest functions discussed so far in this text. We are interested in exploring the extent to which a function can be approximated by a simpler function.

Consider the function $g(x) = (1 + x)^{10}$. Using the binomial theorem this function can be expanded to the form

$$g(x) = 1 + \binom{10}{1}x + \binom{10}{2}x^2 + \binom{10}{3}x^3 + \cdots + x^{10}.$$

Counting the 1 as the first term, the first six terms of this expansion form the fifth-degree polynomial

$$f(x) = 1 + 10x + 45x^2 + 120x^3 + 210x^4 + 252x^5.$$

For what values of x does $f(x)$ approximate

$$g(x) = (1 + x)^{10}?$$

We begin by considering these functions for the specific value $x = 0.06$.

E X A M P L E   1   Using a Binomial Expansion as Approximation

Compare the value of the sum of the first six terms of the binomial expansion of $(1 + 0.06)^{10}$ with the value of $(1.06)^{10}$.

Solution   Use a calculator to find that $(1.06)^{10} = 1.790847697$, which is accurate to 10 digits. To complete the comparison, use the binomial theorem to expand $(1 + 0.06)^{10}$.

$$(1 + 0.06)^{10} = 1 + \binom{10}{1}(0.06) + \binom{10}{2}(0.06)^2 + \binom{10}{3}(0.06)^3$$

$$+ \binom{10}{4}(0.06)^4 + \binom{10}{5}(0.06)^5 + \cdots + (0.06)^{10}$$

We are interested in how the value of the sum of the first 6 terms compares to the exact value of the sum of all 11 terms. So we use a calculator to find that

$$1 + \binom{10}{1}(0.06) + \binom{10}{2}(0.06)^2 + \binom{10}{3}(0.06)^3$$

$$+ \binom{10}{4}(0.06)^4 + \binom{10}{5}(0.06)^5$$

$$= 1 + 10(0.06) + 45(0.06)^2 + 120(0.06)^3 + 210(0.06)^4 + 252(0.06)^5$$

$$= 1.790837555.$$

The two values 1.790847697 and 1.790837555 agree through the fourth decimal place. ▤

From this example it is clear that the function $f(x)$ approximates $g(x)$ through the fourth decimal place when $x = 0.06$. We ask, for what other values of x is this approximation close?

Determine graphically an interval of values for x for which

$$f(x) = 1 + 10x + 45x^2 + 120x^3 + 210x^4 + 252x^5$$

is a good approximation to $g(x) = (1+x)^{10}$.

Solution   Figure 12.7(a) shows a graph of both f and g. It appears that f approximates g when $-0.2 \le x \le 0.2$.

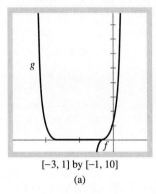

[−3, 1] by [−1, 10]

(a)

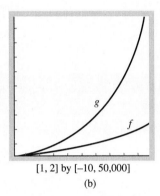

[1, 2] by [−10, 50,000]

(b)

Figure 12.7   Two views of $f(x) = 1 + 10x + 45x^2 + 120x^3 + 210x^4 + 252x^5$ and $g(x) = (1+x)^{10}$. (a) f is a good approximation to g over $[-0.2, 0.2]$. (b) f is not a good approximation over $[1, 2]$.

We say that f is a good approximation to g over the interval $[-0.2, 0.2]$.   ▤

Example 1 does not claim that the interval $[-0.2, 0.2]$ is the largest interval or the only interval on which the approximation is good. It is also of interest to observe in Fig. 12.7(b) that the approximation is not good on the interval $[1, 2]$. So an approximation may be good on some intervals and not on others.

Many functions can be approximated by polynomial functions. The intervals on which the approximation is good vary from one function to the next. The material that follows uses the two functions, $f(x) = \sin x$ and $g(x) = 1/(1-x)$, to illustrate that polynomial functions can be used as approximations to these functions on certain intervals.

Power Series Representation of sin x

This section investigates when the partial sum of a power series is a good approximation to the function $f(x) = \sin x$. We begin with a definition.

> ### Definition 12.6 Power Series
>
> A **power series** in x is any series of the form
>
> $$\sum_{k=0}^{\infty} a_k x^k = a_0 + a_1 x + a_2 x^2 + \cdots + a_n x^n + \cdots .$$

Notice that the partial sums of a power series are polynomials. Therefore a function that can be represented as a power series can be approximated by a polynomial function.

$$f_0(x) = a_0$$

$$f_1(x) = a_0 + a_1 x$$

$$f_2(x) = a_0 + a_1 x + a_2 x^2$$

$$\vdots$$

$$f_n(x) = a_0 + a_1 x + a_2 x^2 + \cdots + a_n x^n$$

Many of the functions studied earlier in this text can be represented by a power series. To do a complete study of all power series representations goes beyond the scope of this text. We simply illustrate power series representations for a few specific functions. For example, the function $f(x) = \sin x$ can be represented as a power series, which means that it can be approximated by polynomials.

> ### Power Series Representation of sin *x*
>
> It can be shown that for all real numbers x
>
> $$\sin x = x - \frac{x^3}{3!} + \frac{x^5}{5!} - \frac{x^7}{7!} + \cdots = \sum_{k=0}^{\infty} (-1)^k \frac{x^{2k+1}}{(2k+1)!}.$$

This power series representation of $f(x) = \sin x$ is valid for all real numbers. This means that for any real number a there is a positive integer n such that the nth partial sum of the power series is a good approximation to $\sin a$. Said another way, the power series converges to $\sin a$ for all values of a.

But the $(n+1)$th partial sum of this series is the degree-$(2n+1)$ polynomial

$$f_n(x) = \sum_{k=0}^{n} (-1)^k \frac{x^{2k+1}}{(2k+1)!} = x - \frac{x^3}{3!} + \frac{x^5}{5!} - \frac{x^7}{7!} + \cdots + (-1)^n \frac{x^{2n+1}}{(2n+1)!}.$$

Therefore $f(x) = \sin x$ can be approximated by polynomial functions.

Every power series converges for some interval of values of x. The interval can be a single point. We call this interval the **interval of convergence**.

Example 3 provides visual evidence that as n increases, the interval of convergence gets larger as well.

E X A M P L E   3   Finding Intervals of Convergence

Determine graphically intervals on which $f(x) = \sin x$ is approximated by

$$f_n(x) = \sum_{k=0}^{n}(-1)^k \frac{x^{2k+1}}{(2k+1)!}$$

for $n = 1, 2$, and 3.

Solution   We begin by finding a graph of $f(x) = \sin x$ in the same viewing rectangle with the graphs of

$$f_1(x) = x - \frac{1}{3!}x^3, \qquad f_2(x) = x - \frac{1}{3!}x^3 + \frac{1}{5!}x^5,$$

$$f_3(x) = x - \frac{1}{3!}x^3 + \frac{1}{5!}x^5 - \frac{1}{7!}x^7.$$

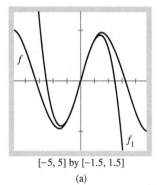

[−5, 5] by [−1.5, 1.5]

(a)

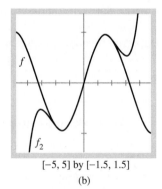

[−5, 5] by [−1.5, 1.5]

(b)

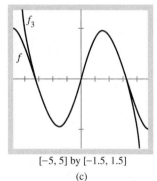

[−5, 5] by [−1.5, 1.5]

(c)

Figure 12.8 $f(x) = \sin x$ plotted with three partial sums. (a) $f_1(x) = x - \frac{1}{6}x^3$; (b) $f_2(x) = x - \frac{1}{6}x^3 + \frac{1}{120}x^5$; and (c) $f_3(x) = x - \frac{1}{6}x^3 + \frac{1}{120}x^5 - \frac{1}{5040}x^7$.

a) Fig. 12.8(a) shows that $f_1(x)$ gives a good approximation to $f(x) = \sin x$ over the interval $-1 \leq x \leq 1$.

b) Fig. 12.8(b) shows that $f_2(x)$ gives a good approximation to $f(x) = \sin x$ over the interval $-2 \leq x \leq 2$.

c) Fig. 12.8(c) shows that $f_3(x)$ gives a good approximation to $f(x) = \sin x$ over the interval $-3 \leq x \leq 3$.

It appears in Example 3 that the interval of values of x for which $f_n(x)$ is a good approximation to $f(x) = \sin x$ becomes larger as n increases. It can be shown that this is true for the power series representation for $f(x) = \sin x$. However, it is not true of power series representations of all functions.

Power Series Representation of $g(x) = 1/(1-x)$

Theorem 12.6 in Section 12.2 tells us that the infinite geometric series with the common ratio x,

$$\sum_{k=0}^{\infty} x^k,$$

converges to $1/(1-x)$ for all x in the interval $-1 < x < 1$. This gives a power series representation for $g(x) = 1/(1-x)$.

Power Series Representation for $g(x) = 1/(1-x)$

If x is a real number in the interval $(-1, 1)$, then

$$\frac{1}{1-x} = 1 + x + x^2 + x^3 + \cdots = \sum_{k=0}^{\infty} x^k.$$

The partial-sum polynomials

$$g_n(x) = 1 + x + x^2 + \cdots + x^n$$

are approximations to $g(x) = 1/(1-x)$. Although in this example x must satisfy the condition $-1 < x < 1$, it is true here, as it was in Example 3, that the interval of values for which the approximation is good becomes larger as n increases. However, Example 4 will show that for a particular value of n, say $n = 5$, the error in the approximation is not the same for all values of x.

E X A M P L E   4   Finding the Error of Approximation

Determine an interval of values for which $g_5(x) = 1 + x + x^2 + x^3 + x^4 + x^5$ is a good approximation to $g(x) = 1/(1-x)$. Then estimate the error in approximating $g(0.2)$ by $g_5(0.2)$ and $g(0.3)$ by $g_5(0.3)$.

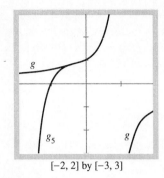

[−2, 2] by [−3, 3]

Figure 12.9 $g(x) = 1/(1-x)$ and $g_5(x)$.

Solution Figure 12.9 shows a graph of both $g(x) = 1/(1-x)$ and $g_5(x)$. This figure shows that $g_5(x)$ gives a good approximation to $g(x)$ over the interval $-0.7 \le x \le 0.7$.

In order to find an estimate on the error of approximation to $g(0.2)$ and $g(0.3)$, graph both g and g_5 in the viewing rectangles $[0.1999, 0.2001]$ by $[1.249, 1.251]$ and $[0.299, 0.301]$ by $[1.42, 1.43]$.

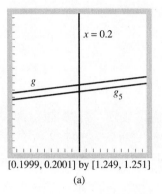

[0.1999, 0.2001] by [1.249, 1.251]

(a)

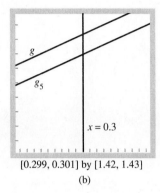

[0.299, 0.301] by [1.42, 1.43]

(b)

Figure 12.10 $g(x) = 1/(1-x)$ compared with a partial-sum approximation for two values of x. (a) $g(0.2)$ and $g_5(0.2)$; (b) $g(0.3)$ and $g_5(0.3)$.

Figure 12.10(a) shows that $g_5(0.2)$ underestimates $g(0.2)$ by about 0.0001. Similarly, $g_5(0.3)$ underestimates $g(0.3)$ by about 0.001. So we see that the approximation of g by g_5 is less accurate at the positive end of the interval of convergence. We would find the same pattern of decreasing accuracy if we tested smaller and smaller values of x at the negative end of this interval. ▤

Generalized Binomial Expansion

Using Theorem 12.7 of Section 12.3, we see that

$$f(x) = (1+x)^n = 1 + \binom{n}{1}x + \binom{n}{2}x^2 + \cdots + x^n. \qquad \textbf{(1)}$$

In the remainder of this section we will examine Eq. (1) for the case where $n = \frac{1}{2}$. This generalization results in a power series representation of an approximation for the function $f(x) = \sqrt{1+x}$.

Until now binomial coefficients $\binom{n}{r}$ have been defined only for nonnegative integers. To state this power series representation first requires finding an appropriate way to define $\binom{n}{r}$ in the case where n is a fraction. Using Definition 12.5 and dividing by $(n-r)!$, we obtain a new representation for $\binom{n}{r}$.

$$\binom{n}{r} = \frac{n!}{r!(n-r)!} = \frac{n(n-1)\cdots(n-r+1)}{r!} \qquad \textbf{(2)}$$

Using the right side of Eq. (2) where $n = \frac{1}{2}$, we obtain

$$\binom{0.5}{r} = \frac{0.5(0.5 - 1) \cdots (0.5 - r + 1)}{r!}.$$

For example,

$$\binom{0.5}{2} = \frac{0.5(0.5 - 1)}{2!} = -\frac{1}{8} \quad \text{and} \quad \binom{0.5}{3} = \frac{0.5(0.5 - 1)(0.5 - 2)}{3!} = \frac{1}{16}.$$

We can now state a power series representation for the function $f(x) = \sqrt{1 + x}$.

Power Series Representation for $f(x) = \sqrt{1 + x}$

It can be shown that for all real numbers x in the interval $[-1, 1]$,

$$\sqrt{1 + x} = 1 + \binom{0.5}{1}x + \binom{0.5}{2}x^2 + \binom{0.5}{3}x^3 + \cdots = \sum_{k=0}^{\infty} \binom{0.5}{k} x^k. \quad (3)$$

Equation (3) is sometimes called a **generalized binomial expansion.**

As Examples 3 and 4 have illustrated, the polynomials that are the partial sums of an infinite series approximate the function described by the power series. Example 4 compared the error in the approximation for two values in the interval of convergence.

In Example 5 we compare the error in the appoximation between the partial-sum polynomials $f_3(x)$ and $f_4(x)$ for the function $f(x) = \sqrt{1 + x}$.

E X A M P L E   5   Comparing Errors of Approximation

Let $f(x) = \sqrt{1 + x}$. Estimate graphically the error in approximating $\sqrt{1.5} = f(0.5)$ by $f_3(0.5)$ and by $f_4(0.5)$ where f_3 and f_4 are the following partial-sum approximations to the power series representation of $f(x)$.

$$f_3(x) = 1 + \frac{1}{2}x - \frac{1}{8}x^2 + \frac{1}{16}x^3, \qquad f_4(x) = 1 + \frac{1}{2}x - \frac{1}{8}x^2 + \frac{1}{16}x^3 - \frac{5}{128}x^4$$

Solution   Find the graphs of $f(x)$ and $f_3(x)$ in the viewing rectangle $[0.499, 0.501]$ by $[1.22, 1.23]$ and the graphs of $f(x)$ and $f_4(x)$ in the viewing rectangle $[0.4999, 0.5001]$ by $[1.224, 1.225]$.

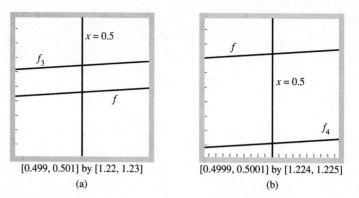

[0.499, 0.501] by [1.22, 1.23]   [0.4999, 0.5001] by [1.224, 1.225]

(a)   (b)

Figure 12.11 $f(x) = \sqrt{1+x}$ for $x = 0.5$ compared with two of its partial-sum approximations. (a) $f(0.5)$ and $f_3(0.5)$ and (b) $f(0.5)$ and $f_4(0.5)$.

Figure 12.11(a) shows that $f_3(0.5)$ is an overestimate of $f(0.5)$ by about 0.002. Similarly, Fig. 12.11(b) shows that $f_4(0.5)$ is an underestimate of $f(0.5)$ by about 0.0006.

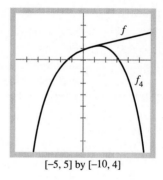

[−5, 5] by [−10, 4]

Figure 12.12 $f_4(x)$ and $f(x) = \sqrt{1+x}$. The approximation is good for x in $[-1, 1]$. ≡

Example 5 found the error in the approximation to $f(x) = \sqrt{1+x}$ by $f_4(x)$ where

$$f_4(x) = 1 + \frac{1}{2}x - \frac{1}{8}x^2 + \frac{1}{16}x^3 - \frac{5}{128}x^4$$

for $x = 0.5$. Figure 12.12 shows the graph of $f_4(x)$ overlaid onto the graph of f. From this global view it is clear that the approximation is good for x in the interval $[-1, 1]$.

This section ends with a summary of some of the conclusions that come from the examples in this section.

Summary

Suppose that $f(x)$ has a power series representation

$$\sum_{k=0}^{\infty} a_k x^k$$

over some interval (a, b).

1. As n increases, the interval of values for which the partial-sum polynomial $f_n(x)$ is a good approximation to f becomes larger.
2. The approximation to $f(x)$ by $f_n(x)$ may not be as good near the ends of the interval of convergence as toward the midpoint of the interval.
3. For a particular value $x = c$ the approximation $f_n(c)$ to $f(c)$ gets better as n increases.

Exercises for Section 12.4

Exercises 1 to 6 refer to the function $f(x) = (1 + x)^6$ whose partial-sum approximations are

$$f_1(x) = 1 + 6x$$

$$f_2(x) = 1 + 6x + 15x^2$$

$$f_3(x) = 1 + 6x + 15x^2 + 20x^3$$

$$f_4(x) = 1 + 6x + 15x^2 + 20x^3 + 15x^4$$

$$f_5(x) = 1 + 6x + 15x^2 + 20x^3 + 15x^4 + 6x^5$$

$$f_6(x) = 1 + 6x + 15x^2 + 20x^3 + 15x^4 + 6x^5 + x^6.$$

1. Verify that $f(x) = (1 + x)^6 = f_6(x)$.
2. Find complete graphs of $f_1, f_2, \ldots, f_6$ in the same viewing rectangle.
3. Use a graphing method to determine the error in using f_4 to approximate the value of $f(x) = (1 + x)^6$ when $x = 1$.
4. Compute $|f(1) - f_4(1)|$, and compare with the error estimate determined in Exercise 3.
5. Is $f_4(1)$ an underestimate or an overestimate of $f(1)$? Why?
6. Repeat Exercises 3 to 5 using f_5 to approximate $f(x) = (1 + x)^6$ when $x = 1$.

For Exercises 7 and 8 consider the infinite series

$$1 + \frac{1}{1!} + \frac{1}{2!} + \frac{1}{3!} + \cdots.$$

Assume the pattern continues as suggested.

7. Compute the first 10 partial sums of the series.
8. It can be shown the series converges to a number ℓ. Make a conjecture about the value of ℓ.

Exercises 9 to 12 refer to the following functions:

$$f_1(x) = 1 - x$$

$$f_2(x) = 1 - x + x^2$$

$$f_3(x) = 1 - x + x^2 - x^3$$

$$\vdots$$

$$f_n(x) = 1 - x + x^2 - x^3 + \cdots + (-1)^n x^n$$

9. Graph $f_1, f_2, f_3, f_4, f_5, f_6, f_7$, and f_8 together in the viewing rectangle $[-2, 2]$ by $[-5, 5]$.
10. Find a complete graph of $f(x) = 1/(x + 1)$. Compare this graph with the graphs in Exercise 9 to conclude that the power series $1 - x + x^2 - x^3 + \cdots + (-1)^n x^n + \cdots$ represents $f(x) = 1/(x + 1)$ for some values of x.
11. Based on Exercises 9 and 10, make a conjecture about the

interval of convergence of the power series expansion

$$\frac{1}{x+1} = 1 - x + x^2 - x^3 + \cdots + (-1)^n x^n + \cdots .$$

12. Relate the power series expansion of $1/(x+1)$ to a geometric series.

Exercises 13 to 18 refer to the following functions:

$$f_1(x) = 1 + x$$

$$f_2(x) = 1 + x + \frac{x^2}{2!}$$

$$f_3(x) = 1 + x + \frac{x^2}{2!} + \frac{x^3}{3!}$$

$$\vdots$$

$$f_n(x) = 1 + x + \frac{x^2}{2!} + \frac{x^3}{3!} + \cdots + \frac{x^n}{n!}$$

13. Find complete graphs of the six polynomial functions f_1, $f_2, \ldots, f_6$ in the viewing rectangle $[-2, 2]$ by $[-3, 8]$.

14. Find a complete graph of $f(x) = e^x$ and compare it with the graphs found in Exercise 13. Find complete graphs of $f(x) = e^x$ and f_6 in the same viewing rectangle.

15. Is $f_6(-8)$ a good estimate for e^{-8}? Why?

16. Is $f_6(3)$ a good estimate for e^3? Why?

17. On what interval is $f_6(x)$ a good approximation to e^x?

18. Use a graphing method to determine the error in using $f_3(3)$ to approximate e^3. Repeat using $f_4(3), f_5(3)$, and $f_6(3)$. Are they underestimates or overestimates?

Exercises 19 to 23 refer to the following functions:

$$f_1(x) = 1 - \frac{x^2}{2!}$$

$$f_2(x) = 1 - \frac{x^2}{2!} + \frac{x^4}{4!}$$

$$f_3(x) = 1 - \frac{x^2}{2!} + \frac{x^4}{4!} - \frac{x^6}{6!}$$

$$\vdots$$

$$f_n(x) = 1 - \frac{x^2}{2!} + \frac{x^4}{4!} - \frac{x^6}{6!} + \cdots + \frac{(-1)^n x^{2n}}{(2n)!}$$

19. Find complete graphs of the six polynomial functions f_1, $f_2, \ldots, f_6$ in the viewing rectangle $[-6, 6]$ by $[-3, 3]$.

20. Find a complete graph of $f(x) = \cos x$, and compare it with the graphs found in Exercise 19. Find complete graphs of $f(x) = \cos x$ and f_6 in the same viewing rectangle.

21. Is $f_6(-8)$ a good estimate for $\cos(-8)$? Why?

22. Is $f_6(3)$ a good estimate for $\cos 3$? Why?

23. Explain why $f_{10}(3)$ is a very good estimate for $\cos 3$. What is the error in the estimate? Is $f_{10}(3)$ an underestimate or an overestimate?

Exercises 24 to 28 refer to the family of functions $f_n(x)$ defined as follows:

$$f_n(x) = 1 + \frac{1}{3}x + \frac{\frac{1}{3}\left(-\frac{2}{3}\right)}{2!}x^2 + \frac{\frac{1}{3}\left(-\frac{2}{3}\right)\left(-\frac{5}{3}\right)}{3!}x^3$$

$$+ \cdots + \frac{\frac{1}{3}\left(-\frac{2}{3}\right)\left(-\frac{5}{3}\right)\cdots\left(\frac{1}{3}-n+1\right)}{n!}x^n$$

24. Determine f_1, f_2, f_3.

25. Find complete graphs of the polynomial functions f_1, f_2, f_3 in the same viewing rectangle, and compare them with the graph of $f(x) = \sqrt[3]{1+x}$.

26. On what interval do you think $f_n(x)$, for large values of n, closely approximates $f(x) = \sqrt[3]{1+x}$?

27. Use a graphing method to estimate the error in using $f_3(-0.25)$ as an estimate for $\sqrt[3]{0.75}$.

28. Use a graphing method to estimate the error in using $f_6(-0.25)$ as an estimate for $\sqrt[3]{0.75}$.

Exercises 29 to 31 give power series representations for several other functions. Use a graphing argument to complete each.

29. Give an argument that

$$\tan^{-1}(x) = x - \frac{x^3}{3} + \frac{x^5}{5} - \frac{x^7}{7} + \cdots + \frac{(-1)^n x^{2n+1}}{2n+1} + \cdots$$

for $-1 < x < 1$ by graphing $f(x) = \tan^{-1}(x)$ and the polynomial function consisting of the first eight terms of the power series $x - x^3/3 + x^5/5 - \cdots$ in the same viewing rectangle.

30. Give an argument that

$$\ln(1+x) = x - \frac{x^2}{2} + \frac{x^3}{3} + \cdots + (-1)^{n+1}\left(\frac{x^n}{n}\right) + \cdots$$

for $0 < x < 1$ by graphing $g(x) = \ln(1+x)$ and the polynomial function consisting of the first eight terms of the power series $x - x^2/2 + x^3/3 - x^4/4 + \cdots$ in the same viewing rectangle.

31. Give an argument that

$$\frac{e^x - e^{-x}}{2} = x + \frac{x^3}{3!} + \frac{x^5}{5!} + \cdots + \frac{x^{2n-1}}{(2n-1)!} + \cdots$$

for $-2 < x < 2$ by graphing $g(x) = (e^x - e^{-x})/2$ and the polynomial function equal to the first eight terms of the power series

$$x + \frac{x^3}{3!} + \frac{x^5}{5!} + \cdots + \frac{x^{2n-1}}{(2n-1)!} + \cdots$$

in the same viewing rectangle.

Exercises 32 and 33 refer to the *hyperbolic cosine* (cosh) function, which is defined as

$$\cosh x = \frac{e^x + e^{-x}}{2}.$$

32. Use the fact that $e^x = 1 + x + x^2/2! + x^3/3! + \cdots$ for all real number values of x (see Exercises 13 to 18) to show that

$$\cosh x = 1 + \frac{x^2}{2!} + \frac{x^4}{4!} + \frac{x^6}{6!} + \cdots$$

for all real x. Assume that an infinite series can be added term by term.

33. Graph $g(x) = \cosh x$ and the polynomial function f consisting of the first seven terms (up to the 6th power) of the power series $1 + x^2/2! + x^4/4! + \cdots$ in the same viewing rectangle. What conclusions can you draw? For what values of x is f a good approximation of $g(x) = \cosh x$?

Exercises 34 to 36 refer to the power series representation of $\sin x$,

$$\sin x = x - \frac{x^3}{3!} + \frac{x^5}{5!} - \frac{x^7}{7!} + \cdots.$$

34. How many terms of this power series must be used to obtain a good polynomial approximation to $f(x) = \sin x$ over $\left[-\pi/2, \pi/2\right]$? Use a graphing argument.

35. How many terms of this power series must be used to obtain a good polynomial approximation to $f(x) = \sin x$ over $[-\pi, \pi]$? Use a graphing argument.

36. How many terms of this power series must be used to obtain a good polynomial approximation to $f(x) = \sin x$ over $[-2\pi, 2\pi]$? Use a graphing argument.

It has been established in the previous exercises that

$$\sin x = x - \frac{x^3}{3!} + \frac{x^5}{5!} - \cdots$$

$$\cos x = 1 - \frac{x^2}{2!} + \frac{x^4}{4!} - \cdots$$

$$e^x = 1 + x + \frac{x^2}{2!} + \frac{x^3}{3!} + \cdots.$$

Use these power series to complete Exercises 37 and 38.

37. Show that $\cos x + i \sin x = e^{ix}$ (*Euler's formula*) by expanding e^u where $u = ix$. Assume infinite series can be added term by term.

38. The five most important constants in algebra are $0, 1, e, \pi$, and i. Use the results from Exercise 37 to link these five constants by showing that

$$e^{\pi i} + 1 = 0.$$

12.5 _____ Mathematical Induction

This section introduces a method of proof called the **principle of mathematical induction.** Let us consider the general sequence of partial sums:

$$S_1 = 1^2$$
$$S_2 = 1^2 + 2^2$$
$$S_3 = 1^2 + 2^2 + 3^2$$
$$S_4 = 1^2 + 2^2 + 3^2 + 4^2$$

$$\vdots$$

$$S_n = 1^2 + 2^2 + \cdots + n^2.$$

In Theorem 12.4 the following equality was stated without proof:

$$S_n = 1^2 + 2^2 + \cdots + n^2 = \frac{n(n+1)(2n+1)}{6}.$$

For what values of n is this equation true? The implication is that the equation is true for all positive integers n. How can this be proven?

We begin with an Exploration.

🔍 DISCUSS IN A SMALL GROUP

Let S be a set of numbers that have the following properties:

1. 1 is an element of S.

2. If k is in S, then $k + 1$ is also in S.

It is agreed that each element of S is obtained by applying these two properties.

What numbers are in the set S? Debate this question with members of your small group. Can the question be answered without additional information? Does your group agree?

Follow this reasoning. Since 1 is in S (by property 1), let $k = 1$ and conclude from property 2 that $1 + 1 = 2$ is also in S. Knowing that 2 is in S, apply property 2 again to conclude that $2 + 1 = 3$ is in S. Continuing this reasoning leads to the conclusion that all the positive integers are in S.

It is common for groups of students to conclude in this Exploration that S consists of the set of all integers $\{\ldots -3, -2, -1, 0, 1, 2, 3, \ldots\}$. This conclusion results from the following *false* reasoning:

1 is in S, so if $k + 1 = 1$ is in S, then $k = 0$ must also be in S.

Continuing this reasoning, you could conclude that -1 is in S, and so forth. What is false about this reasoning? It assumes that because you accept the statement

$$\text{if } k \text{ is in } S, \text{ then } k + 1 \text{ is also in } S, \qquad \textbf{(1)}$$

you can also accept the statement

$$\text{if } k + 1 \text{ is in } S, \text{ then } k \text{ is also in } S. \qquad \textbf{(2)}$$

Statement (2) is the **converse** of the first. It is not correct to accept the converse of a statement.

One way to remember that statement 1 and its converse are not both true is to visualize these falling dominoes.

Figure 12.13 Imagine a row of dominoes "sitting" on the real number line. Dominoes that have fallen or will eventually fall represent integers in the set S as a result of properties 1 and 2.

When the first domino, P_1, falls, it falls in only one direction. And then all the dominoes in that direction fall. The others remain standing.

This discussion leads us to the following axiom.

Axiom of Induction

Let S be a set of the positive integers with the following two properties:

1. S contains the integer 1.
2. S contains the integer $k + 1$ whenever S contains the integer k.

Then S is the entire set of positive integers.

E X A M P L E   1   Using the Axiom of Induction

Consider the sequence $\{a_n\}$ defined recursively by $a_1 = 4$ and $a_n = 3 + a_{n-1}$. Prove that for all positive integers n, $a_n = 3n + 1$.

Solution   Let S be the set of all positive integers for which the statement $a_n = 3n + 1$ is true. The goal is to show that this set S satisfies the two properties of the axiom of induction.

1. Demonstrating that 1 is in S: $a_1 = 4$ (given), and 4 is the value for $3n + 1$ when $n = 1$. Therefore the formula $a_n = 3n + 1$ is satisfied for $n = 1$. So 1 is in S.

2. Demonstrating that if k is in S, then $k+1$ is in S: If k is in S, then $a_k = 3k+1$.

$$a_{k+1} = 3 + a_k$$ This is true by the recursive definition of $a_n = 3 + a_{n-1}$.

$$= 3 + (3k + 1)$$ Replace a_k with its equivalent value $3k + 1$.

$$= (3k + 3) + 1$$

$$= 3(k + 1) + 1$$

Therefore $a_n = 3n + 1$ is true for $n = k + 1$. This shows that $k + 1$ is in S.

Since both properties of the axiom of induction are satisfied, conclude that S is the set of all positive integers. Since S is defined to be the set of all positive integers for which $a_n = 3n + 1$ is true, you can conclude that $a_n = 3n + 1$ is true for all positive integers n.   ≡

Example 1 illustrates how to use the principle stated in the next theorem.

Theorem 12.8   Principle of Mathematical Induction

Let P_n be a statement that is defined for each positive integer n. All the statements P_n are true provided the following two conditions are satisfied:

1. P_1 is true.
2. P_{k+1} is true whenever P_k is true.

Using the Principle of Mathematical Induction

Examples 2 to 4 show how to use Theorem 12.8 to prove that a statement P_n is true for all positive integers n.

E X A M P L E   2   Using Mathematical Induction

Use mathematical induction to prove that

$$1^2 + 3^2 + 5^2 + \cdots + (2n - 1)^2 = \frac{n(2n - 1)(2n + 1)}{3}$$

is true for every positive integer n.

Solution   Let P_n be the statement

$$1^2 + 3^2 + 5^2 + \cdots + (2n - 1)^2 = \frac{n(2n - 1)(2n + 1)}{3}. \tag{3}$$

For $n = 1$, the left-hand side of Eq. (3) is $1^2 = 1$, and the right-hand side is $1(2 - 1)(2 + 1)/3 = 1$. Thus P_1 is true.

Next show that if P_k is true, then P_{k+1} is true. If P_k is true, then

$$1^2 + 3^2 + 5^2 + \cdots + (2k - 1)^2 = \frac{k(2k - 1)(2k + 1)}{3}$$

is true. To show that P_{k+1} is true means showing that the following is true:

$$1^2 + 3^2 + 5^2 + \cdots + (2(k + 1) - 1)^2 = \frac{(k + 1)(2(k + 1) - 1)(2(k + 1) + 1)}{3},$$

$$1^2 + 3^2 + 5^2 + \cdots + (2k + 1)^2 = \frac{(k + 1)(2k + 1)(2k + 3)}{3}. \tag{4}$$

The second-to-last term on the left-hand side of Eq. (4) is $(2k - 1)^2$. (Why?) Use this fact to rewrite the left-hand side of Eq. (4):

$$1^2 + 3^2 + 5^2 + \cdots + (2k + 1)^2 = 1^2 + 3^2 + 5^2 + \cdots + (2k - 1)^2 + (2k + 1)^2$$

$$= \frac{k(2k - 1)(2k + 1)}{3} + (2k + 1)^2$$

$$= (2k + 1)\left[\frac{k(2k - 1)}{3} + 2k + 1\right]$$

$$= (2k + 1)\left(\frac{2k^2 - k + 6k + 3}{3}\right)$$

$$= \frac{(2k + 1)(2k^2 + 5k + 3)}{3}$$

$$= \frac{(2k + 1)(k + 1)(2k + 3)}{3}$$

$$= \frac{(k + 1)(2k + 1)(2k + 3)}{3}$$

Thus Eq. (4) is true, so P_{k+1} must be true. By Theorem 12.8,

$$1^2 + 3^2 + 5^2 + \cdots + (2n - 1)^2 = \frac{n(2n - 1)(2n + 1)}{3}$$

for all positive integers n.   ≡

Example 3 proves one of the summation formulas stated without proof in Theorem 12.4.

E X A M P L E   3   *Using Mathematical Induction*

Use mathematical induction to prove that

$$1^3 + 2^3 + \cdots + n^3 = \frac{n^2(n + 1)^2}{4}. \tag{5}$$

Solution Let P_n be the statement of Eq. (5). For $n = 1$ the left-hand side of Eq. (5) is $1^3 = 1$, and the right-hand side is $1^2(1+1)^2/4 = 1$. Thus P_1 is true.

Next show that if P_k is true, then P_{k+1} is true. That is, show that the following is true:

$$1^3 + 2^3 + \cdots + (k+1)^3 = \frac{(k+1)^2(k+1+1)^2}{4}$$

$$= \frac{(k+1)^2(k+2)^2}{4} \qquad (6)$$

The second-to-last term on the left-hand side of Eq. (6) is k^3. Therefore

$$1^3 + 2^3 + \cdots + k^3 + (k+1)^3 = \frac{k^2(k+1)^2}{4} + (k+1)^3$$

$$= (k+1)^2\left[\frac{k^2}{4} + (k+1)\right]$$

$$= (k+1)^2\left[\frac{k^2+4k+4}{4}\right]$$

$$= \frac{(k+1)^2(k+2)^2}{4}.$$

Thus

$$1^3 + 2^3 + \cdots + (k+1)^3 = \frac{(k+1)^2(k+2)^2}{4},$$

so P_{k+1} is true. By Theorem 12.8

$$1^3 + 2^3 + \cdots + n^3 = \frac{n^2(n+1)^2}{4}$$

is true for all positive integers n. ≡

Suppose that A dollars are invested in an account that compounds interest. If i is the interest rate paid per compounding period, then, as shown in Section 6.2, the amount in the account after n periods is $A(1+i)^n$. For example, if $200 is invested in an account that pays 9% annual interest compounded monthly, then $i = 0.09/12$ and the amount in the account after n months is

$$A(1+i)^n = 200\left(1 + \frac{0.09}{12}\right)^n.$$

EXAMPLE 4   APPLICATION: Compound Interest

Suppose A dollars are invested in a compound interest bearing account that pays interest rate i per compounding period. Use mathematical induction to prove that the amount in the account at the end of the nth period is $A(1+i)^n$.

Solution   Let P_n be the statement that the amount in the account at the end of the nth period is $A(1+i)^n$. First show that P_1 is true. At the end of the first period the amount in the account is the initial investment of A dollars plus the interest Ai earned during the first period. Thus

$$A + Ai = A(1+i).$$

Next show that if P_k is true, then P_{k+1} is true. Assuming that P_k is true means that the amount in the account at the end of the kth period is $A(1+i)^k$. You must show that the amount in the account at the end of the $(k+1)$st period is $A(1+i)^{k+1}$. The interest earned during the $(k+1)$st period on this investment is $A(1+i)^k i$. Thus the amount in the account at the end of the $(k+1)$st period is

$$A(1+i)^k + A(1+i)^k i = A(1+i)^k(1+i) = A(1+i)^{k+1}.$$

Therefore P_{k+1} is true and, by Theorem 12.8, P_n is true for all positive integers n. So the amount in the account at the end of n periods is $A(1+i)^n$ for every positive integer n. ▰

Exercises for Section 12.5

For each recursively defined sequence in Exercises 1 to 4, find a formula for a_n in terms of n, and prove that your formula is correct.

1. $a_n = a_{n-1} + 5, a_1 = 3$.   **2.** $a_n = a_{n-1} + 2, a_1 = 7$.

3. $a_n = 3a_{n-1}, a_1 = 2$.   **4.** $a_n = 5a_{n-1}, a_1 = 3$.

Each equation in Exercises 5 to 11 is a statement P_n. In each case write P_1, P_n, and P_{n+1}. (Do not prove these equations.)

5. $1 + 2 + \cdots + n = \dfrac{n(n+1)}{2}$

6. $S_n = 1^2 + 2^2 + \cdots + n^2 = \dfrac{n(n+1)(2n+1)}{6}$

7. $\dfrac{1}{1\cdot 2} + \dfrac{1}{2\cdot 3} + \cdots + \dfrac{1}{n\cdot(n+1)} = \dfrac{n}{n+1}$, for all integers $n \geq 1$.

8. $\displaystyle\sum_{k=1}^{n} k^4 = \dfrac{n(n+1)(2n+1)(3n^2+3n-1)}{30}$

9. $(a+b)^n = \displaystyle\sum_{i=0}^{n} a^i b^{n-i}$

10. $2^n < (n+2)!$ for all integers $n \geq 0$.

11. $\dbinom{n}{0} + \dbinom{n}{1} + \cdots + \dbinom{n}{n} = 2^n$

In Exercises 12 to 18 prove each statement by mathematical induction.

12. The nth term of an arithmetic progression is $a_n = a_1 + (n-1)d$ where a_1 is the first term and d is the common difference.

13. $1 + 2 + \cdots + n = \dfrac{n(n+1)}{2}$

14. $1^3 + 2^3 + \cdots + n^3 = \dfrac{n^2(n+1)^2}{4}$

15. $1 + 3 + 5 + \cdots + (2n-1) = n^2$

16. $1 + 5 + 9 + \cdots + (4n-3) = n(2n-1)$

17. $1 + 2 + 2^2 + \cdots + 2^{n-1} = 2^n - 1$

18. $\dfrac{1}{1\cdot 2} + \dfrac{1}{2\cdot 3} + \dfrac{1}{3\cdot 4} + \cdots + \dfrac{1}{n(n+1)} = \dfrac{n}{n+1}$

In Exercises 19 to 24, use any formula found in this chapter that applies to find each sum.

19. $1 + 2 + 3 + \cdots + 500$ **20.** $1^2 + 2^2 + \cdots + 250^2$

21. $4 + 5 + 6 + \cdots + n$

22. $1^3 + 2^3 + 3^3 + \cdots + 75^3$

23. $1 + 2 + 4 + 8 + \cdots + 2^{24}$

24. $1 + 8 + 27 + \cdots + 3375$

12.6 _____ Counting, Permutations, and Combinations

An area of mathematics that has achieved its own identity with the development of the computer is called discrete mathematics. A topic that is central to discrete mathematics is counting. A counting problem asks how many ways some event can occur.

Simple counting problems can be answered by listing all the possibilities. We begin with two examples of this type of counting problem.

E X A M P L E   1   Counting by Listing

How many three-letter codes are there using letters A, B, C, and D if no letter can be repeated.

Solution   Simply list all possibilities:

ABC	ABD	ACB	ACD	ADB	ADC
BAC	BAD	BCA	BCD	BDA	BCD
CAB	CAD	CBA	CBD	CDA	CDB
DAB	DAC	DBA	DBC	DCA	DCB

There are $4 \cdot 6 = 24$ possibilities. ▤

When completing a counting problem by listing all the possibilities, you should use a systematic method, that is, follow some pattern. As you read across the rows in the solution to Example 1, can you find a system?

If the number of possibilities is small enough, it is sometimes helpful to use a tree diagram to help structure the counting task.

E X A M P L E   2   Using a Tree Diagram

An experimental psychologist uses a sequence of two food rewards in an experiment regarding animal behavior. These two rewards are of three different varieties. How many different sequences of rewards are there if each variety can only be used once in each sequence?

Solution   Designate the three varieties of rewards as a, b, and c. The tree diagram in Fig. 12.14 shows all the possibilities.

There are six possible sequences. ▤

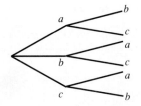

Figure 12.14   Each pathway along the tree from left to right represents a unique sequence of two rewards when there are three varieties of reward: a, b, and c.

Obviously a tree diagram is not practical if the number being counted is large. On the other hand, a method called the **fundamental counting principle**, which can be used for large numbers, is modeled after the tree-counting process.

Fundamental Counting Principle

Suppose that a certain procedure P can be broken into n successive ordered stages, $S_1, S_2, \ldots, S_n$, and suppose that

$$S_1 \text{ can occur in } r_1 \text{ ways,}$$
$$S_2 \text{ can occur in } r_2 \text{ ways,}$$
$$\vdots$$
$$S_n \text{ can occur in } r_n \text{ ways.}$$

Then the number of ways procedure P can occur is

$$r_1 \cdot r_2 \cdots r_n.$$

This fundamental counting principle is sometimes called the **multiplication principle.**

Using the Fundamental Counting Principle

When applying the fundamental counting principle, it is important to identify correctly the aspects of the particular counting problem under consideration that model the stages $S_1, S_2, \ldots, S_n$. Once these stages are correctly identified, the counting process proceeds according to the fundamental counting principle.

E X A M P L E   3   Using the Counting Principle

Suppose the license plates in a certain state begin with two letters followed by three digits. How many different license plates are possible? Assume that none of the characters (letters or numbers) repeats within each license plate.

Solution Let P be the procedure of writing down a license plate number, and let S_1 be the stage of selecting the first letter, S_2 the stage of selecting the second letter, and so forth.

Stages	S_1	S_2	S_3	S_4	S_5
Number of ways to complete each stage	26	25	10	9	8

Notice that S_2 can be completed in 25 ways since a letter cannot be repeated. The total number of license plates meeting the conditions of this problem is

$$26 \cdot 25 \cdot 10 \cdot 9 \cdot 8 = 468{,}000.$$

EXAMPLE 4   Using the Counting Principle

There are eight sprinters in a 100-meter final dash. How many different outcomes are possible to this race?

Solution   This problem is equivalent to the following one.

In how many different ways can eight different names be written down in order? This second problem can be thought of as the procedure of actually writing down the eight names of the eight contestants: S_1 is the act of writing the first name, S_2 is the act of writing the second name, and so on.

Stages	S_1	S_2	S_3	S_4	S_5	S_6	S_7	S_8
Number of ways to complete each stage	8	7	6	5	4	3	2	1

Using the fundamental counting principle, conclude that the total number of outcomes to the race is

$$8 \cdot 7 \cdot 6 \cdot 5 \cdot 4 \cdot 3 \cdot 2 \cdot 1 = 8! = 40{,}320. \qquad \equiv$$

TRY THIS

Most graphing calculators have the capability of calculating factorials. Refer to your manual, and use your calculator to confirm the results of Example 4.

Permutations

Examples 3 and 4 used the multiplication principle to find the number of different arrangements for letters, numbers, and names. We were in fact studying what is called a permutation.

Definition 12.7   Permutation

A **permutation** of n elements is an ordering of the n elements in a row.

Example 4 showed that the number of different permutations of eight objects is $8! = 40{,}320$. In general, the number of different permutations of n elements is $n!$.

Theorem 12.9   Number of Permutations of n Elements

There are $n!$ different permutations of n elements.

There are some situations dealing with permutations of elements in which only a subset of the elements are arranged in any one order. One such situation is considered in Example 5.

E X A M P L E   5   Finding the Number of Permutations

Suppose the 15 members of a club are to select three officers—president, vice president, and secretary-treasurer. In how many different ways can these offices be filled?

Solution   This problem is equivalent to asking how many ways three names, selected from the 15 persons, can be written in a specific order.

Using the multiplication principle we obtain the answer

$$15 \cdot 14 \cdot 13 = 2730.$$

Example 5 can be generalized to the situation of ordering r names selected from n names where $r < n$. We call this generalization an r-permutation.

Definition 12.8 r-Permutation

An **r-permutation** of a set of n elements is an ordered selection of r elements taken from the set of n elements. The number of r-permutations of a set of n elements is denoted $_nP_r$.

This next theorem states how $_nP_r$ can be calculated using the concept of *factorial*.

Theorem 12.10   A Formula for $_nP_r$

If n and r are integers and $0 \le r \le n$, then

$$_nP_r = \frac{n!}{(n-r)!}.$$

Proof   Apply the fundamental counting principle to conclude that

$$_nP_r = n \cdot (n-1) \cdots (n-r+1)$$

$$= n \cdot (n-1) \cdots (n-r+1)\frac{(n-r)\cdots 2 \cdot 1}{(n-r)\cdots 2 \cdot 1} \qquad \text{Multiply numerator and denominator by the same factors.}$$

$$= \frac{n!}{(n-r)!}.$$

E X A M P L E 6   Counting Permutations

How many different five-letter code words are there if no letter is repeated?

Solution   This problem asks us to count 5-permutations where $n = 26$.

$$_{26}P_5 = \frac{26!}{(26-5)!}$$

$$= \frac{26!}{21!}$$

$$= \frac{26(25)(24)(23)(22) \cdot 21!}{21!}$$

$$= 26 \cdot 25 \cdot 24 \cdot 23 \cdot 22$$

$$= 7,893,600 \qquad\qquad \equiv$$

TRY THIS

Most graphing calculators have the capability of calculating $_nP_r$. Refer to your manual and use your calculator to confirm the results of Example 6.

Combinations

The last counting situation that we will discuss is the problem of finding the number of subsets of r elements that can be selected from n elements. This is called counting the **combinations of n things taken r at a time.**

E X A M P L E 7   Counting Subsets

How many committees of three can be selected from four people?

Solution   To simplify the discussion of this problem, call the four people A, B, C, and D.

Example 1 gave a complete listing of all possible orderings of three of these four people. That list of 24 orderings is repeated here.

ABC	ABD	ACB	ACD	ADB	ADC
BAC	BAD	BCA	BCD	BDA	BCD
CAB	CAD	CBA	CBD	CDA	CDB
DAB	DAC	DBA	DBC	DCA	DCB

However, the committee consisting of persons A, B, and C, denoted $\{A, B, C\}$, is the same committee regardless of the order in which the three members are listed. For example, this committee can be listed in the following six ways:

ABC	ACB	BAC	BCA	CAB	CBA

The total number of different committees is thus equal to the number of different listings, $_4P_3$, divided by the 3! different orderings for each committee. Therefore the number of different committees is

$$_4P_3/3! = \frac{4!}{(4-3)!3!}$$

$$= \frac{4!}{1! \cdot 3!}. \qquad\qquad \equiv$$

Notice that when a counting problem is a combination problem, the order in which the elements are listed is not important.

The solution to Example 7 can be generalized to find the number of committees of r persons selected from a larger group of n persons.

1. First list all possible r-permutations. There are $n!/(n-r)!$ of them.

2. Each committee has been listed in all $r!$ of its different orderings.

3. The number of different committees is thus

$$\frac{n!}{r!(n-r)!}.$$

Notice that the number of combinations of n elements taken r at a time returns to the topic of binomial coefficients: The numbers $n!/[r!(n-r)!]$ are precisely the binomial coefficients studied in Section 12.3.

Theorem 12.11   Number of Combinations of n Elements Taken r at a Time

If n and r are nonnegative integers where $r \leq n$, then the number of combinations of n elements taken r at a time, denoted $_nC_r$, is

$$_nC_r = \frac{n!}{r!(n-r)!}.$$

Examples 8 and 9 show how Theorem 12.11 can be applied.

E X A M P L E   8   Finding the Number of Starting Teams

A certain basketball team has 12 players. How many different starting fives are possible?

Solution   This problem asks how many different five-person subsets can be selected from a set of 12 persons. That is, we must find $_nC_r$ when $n = 12$ and $r = 5$.

$$_{12}C_5 = \frac{12!}{5!(12-5)!}$$

$$= \frac{12 \cdot 11 \cdot 10 \cdot 9 \cdot 8}{5 \cdot 4 \cdot 3 \cdot 2 \cdot 1}$$

$$= 11 \cdot 9 \cdot 8 = 792$$

There are 792 different starting lineups.

TRY THIS

Most graphing calculators have the capability of calculating $_nC_r$. Refer to your manual and use your calculator to confirm the results of Examples 8 and 9.

The number of different subsets that can be chosen is often much greater than expected.

EXAMPLE 9   Counting Different Card Hands

In the game of bridge each player is dealt a 13-card hand selected from a deck of 52 cards. How many different bridge hands are there?

Solution   The order in which cards are held in a hand is not important. That is, you are interested in counting different subsets, not different orderings, so this is a combination problem, not a permutation problem. We must find $_nC_r$ when $n = 52$ and $r = 13$.

$$_{52}C_{13} = \frac{52!}{13!(52 - 13)!}$$

$$= 635,013,559,600$$

The number of different bridge hands is 635,013,559,600. Suppose a bridge hand can be dealt in 1 second. How many years would it take to deal all possible hands?

Exercises for Section 12.6

For Exercises 1 to 6 list all possibilities, or draw a tree diagram to count all the possibilities.

1. How many different three-letter code words are there, with no repeated letters, using the letters A, T, and X?

2. How many different three-letter code words are there, with no repeated letters, selecting from the letters R, S, T, and V?

3. There are three roads from town A to town B, and four roads from town B to town C. How many different routes are there from A to C?

4. Using the information in Exercise 3, how many different routes are there from A to C and back to A?

5. There are four candidates for homecoming queen and three candidates for king. How many king-and-queen pairs are possible?

6. When ordering an airline ticket you can request first class, business class, or coach. You can also choose a window, aisle, or middle seat. How many different ways can you order a ticket?

For Exercises 7 to 12 use the fundamental counting principle.

7. How many seven-digit telephone numbers are there? (A number may not begin with a 0 or a 1. Why?)

8. A social security number has the format XXX-XX-XXXX. How many different social security numbers are there?

9. How many different license plates are there that begin with two digits, two letters, and then three digits if no letter or digit repeats?

10. How many different license plates are there that consist of five symbols, either digit or letter? (Repetitions are allowed.)

11. A die is one of a pair of dice. Suppose that one red die and one green die are rolled. How many different outcomes are there?

12. How many different sequences of heads and tails are there if a coin is tossed 10 times?

In Exercises 13 to 20, calculate each value.

13. $_8P_5$ 14. $_{12}P_7$ 15. $_{18}P_6$ 16. $_{11}P_7$

17. $_{14}C_5$ 18. $_8C_6$ 19. $_{24}C_{15}$ 20. $_{18}C_8$

21. A 3-person committee is to be elected from an organization's membership of 25 persons. How many different committees can be elected?

22. How many different six-card hands can be dealt from a deck of 20 cards?

23. Jon has money to buy only three distinct titles from among the 48 discs available. How many different purchases can he make if he purchases no repeated titles?

24. A coin is tossed 20 times, and the heads and tails sequences are recorded. From among all possible sequences of heads and tails, how many have exactly seven heads?

25. How many different 13-card hands are there that include the ace and king of spades? (See Example 9.)

26. An employer interviews eight people for three openings. How many different groups of three can be employed?

27. Verify algebraically that $_nC_r + {_nC_{r+1}} = {_{n+1}C_{r+1}}$ where n and r are positive integers and $r + 1 \leq n$.

28. Writing to Learn Suppose a chain letter is sent to five people the first week of the year. Each of these five people sends a copy of the letter to five more people during the second week of the year, and this pattern is continued each week of the year. Explain how you know with certainty that you will receive a second copy of this letter later in the year. Why is it illegal to participate in "pyramid schemes" which involve money?

12.7 Probability

In today's complex society there are many situations with uncertain outcomes. We are concerned about the probability that outcomes will occur.

What are the chances that it will rain today? What are the chances that I will get the job I just applied for? A manufacturer wonders, what is the probability that a randomly selected item coming off the production line will be defective? An airline's booking agent asks, what is the probability that a passenger with a reservation will be a no-show? The scientists at the Center for Disease Control ask, what is the probability that someone exposed to a certain virus will contract the disease?

Each of these situations, and many more, can be thought of as an **experiment**. The various possible results of the experiment are called **outcomes** of the experiment, and the set of all possible outcomes is called the **sample space** of the experiment.

It is important to be able to identify the sample space of a probability experiment and to determine the number of elements in the sample space.

EXAMPLE 1 Finding the Sample Space

An experiment consists of tossing a red and a green die. List all the elements in sample space S.

Solution List all the pairs in sample space S. The first number of the pair represents the outcome of the red die, and the second number the outcome of the green die.

(1, 1)	(1, 2)	(1, 3)	(1, 4)	(1, 5)	(1, 6)
(2, 1)	(2, 2)	(2, 3)	(2, 4)	(2, 5)	(2, 6)
(3, 1)	(3, 2)	(3, 3)	(3, 4)	(3, 5)	(3, 6)
(4, 1)	(4, 2)	(4, 3)	(4, 4)	(4, 5)	(4, 6)
(5, 1)	(5, 2)	(5, 3)	(5, 4)	(5, 5)	(5, 6)
(6, 1)	(6, 2)	(6, 3)	(6, 4)	(6, 5)	(6, 6)

There are 36 elements in the sample space of this experiment.   ≡

A subset of a sample space is called an **event**. For example, in the experiment of Example 1, we can identify event D, "rolling doubles," or event N, "sum of 9," or event F, "sum less than 4." These events include the following outcomes:

D	(1, 1)	(3, 3)	(2, 2)	(4, 4)	(5, 5)	(6, 6)
N	(3, 6)	(5, 4)	(4, 5)	(6, 3)		
F	(1, 1)	(1, 2)	(2, 1)			

E X A M P L E   2   Finding the Sample Space

An experiment consists of flipping a coin three times in succession and recording the outcomes of heads (H) and tails (T). List all the elements of sample space S and all elements of the sample space in event E, "at least two heads."

Solution   The sample space is the set

$$S = \{HHH, HHT, HTH, THH, HTT, THT, TTH, TTT\},$$

and event E is the set

$$E = \{HHH, HHT, HTH, THH\}.$$ ≡

In the experiments considered so far it is assumed that the outcomes in the sample space are **equally likely**. This condition is described by saying the dice are "fair," or the coin is "fair."

The **theoretical probability** for an experiment of equally likely outcomes is the ratio of the number of elements in the event divided by the number of outcomes in the sample space.

We use the notation $n(S)$ to represent the number of outcomes in sample space S and $n(E)$ to represent the number of outcomes in event E.

> **Definition 12.9   Probability of an Event**
>
> In an experiment with a finite number of equally likely outcomes, the **probability** (or theoretical probability) of an event E, denoted $P(E)$, is
>
> $$P(E) = \frac{n(E)}{n(S)}.$$

Notice that, since $n(E)$ and $n(S)$ are positive integers where $n(E) \leq n(S)$, then $0 \leq P(E) \leq 1$ for any event E. An event A is impossible if and only if $P(A) = 0$, and an event B is certain if and only if $P(B) = 1$.

Finding the Probability of an Event

Finding the probability of an event requires calculating the quotient from Definition 12.9. Consequently, in any probability experiment it is important to identify the number of elements in the sample space and the number of elements in the event. Each of these tasks is a counting problem.

E X A M P L E   3   Finding the Probability of an Event

Find the probability of event E, "rolling a sum of 5," in the experiment of Example 1.

Solution   From Example 1, $n(S) = 36$. Since E consists of the set of outcomes $\{(1, 4), (2, 3), (3, 2), (4, 1)\}$, $n(E) = 4$. Therefore

$$P(E) = \frac{n(E)}{n(S)} = \frac{4}{36} = \frac{1}{9}.$$

E X A M P L E   4   Finding the Probability of an Event

What is the probability that a five-digit telephone number chosen at random has no repeated digits?

Solution   Let E be the event "no repeated digits," and let S represent the entire sample space. Use the fundamental counting principle to calculate

$$n(E) = 8 \cdot 9 \cdot 8 \cdot 7 \cdot 6 = 24{,}192.$$

(Recall that a telephone number cannot begin with a 0 or a 1.) Also,

$$n(S) = 8 \cdot 10 \cdot 10 \cdot 10 \cdot 10 = 80{,}000.$$

Therefore

$$P(E) = \frac{24{,}192}{80{,}000} = 0.3024.$$

Two events A and B from the same sample space are called **mutually exclusive events** if they have no outcomes in common. In the experiment of rolling a set of dice, discussed in Example 1, the events "rolling a sum of 5" and "rolling doubles" are mutually exclusive. By comparison, the events "rolling a sum of 5" and "red die is a 1" are not mutually exclusive events since the outcome $(1, 4)$ occurs in both events.

If two events are mutually exclusive, then the following probability formula applies.

Probability of Mutually Exclusive Events

If A and B are mutually exclusive events for the same experiment, then

$$P(A \text{ or } B) = P(A) + P(B). \qquad (1)$$

E X A M P L E   5   Probability of Mutually Exclusive Events

Suppose one card is drawn from a deck of the 20 cards consisting of one ace, king, queen, jack, and 10 in each of the four suits of spades, hearts, diamonds, and clubs. What is the probability of drawing a 10 or a face card (king, queen, or jack)?

Solution   Let A be the event "draw a 10," and let B be the event "draw a face card." Since a 10 is not a face card, events A and B are mutually exclusive. Then $P(A) = \frac{4}{20} = \frac{1}{5}$ and $P(B) = \frac{12}{20} = \frac{3}{5}$, and

$$P(A \text{ or } B) = P(A) + A(B) = \frac{1}{5} + \frac{3}{5} = \frac{4}{5}. \qquad \equiv$$

The **complement of an event** A, denoted A^c, is the set of all outcomes in the sample space that are not in event A. Notice that events A and A^c taken together consist of the entire sample space. Therefore, $P(A \text{ or } A^c) = 1$.

Events A and A^c are mutually exclusive by definition. Therefore

$$P(A \text{ or } A^c) = P(A) + P(A^c)$$

$$1 = P(A) + P(A^c)$$

$$P(A^c) = 1 - P(A).$$

To find the probability of an event it is often easier to think in terms of the complement.

E X A M P L E   6   Using the Complement of an Event

A 13-card hand is dealt from a standard 52-card deck. Find the probability that the hand has at least one heart.

Solution Let E be the event "at least one heart." That means one heart, two hearts, ... or 13 hearts. It will be much easier to determine the probability of E^c, the event "no hearts." Since the number of hands with no hearts is $_{39}C_{13}$,

$$P(E^c) = \frac{_{39}C_{13}}{_{52}C_{13}}$$

$$= \frac{39!39!}{26!52!}$$

$$= 0.01279.$$

Therefore

$$P(E) = 1 - P(E^c) = 1 - 0.01279 = 0.98721.$$

Independent Events

Two events are **independent events** if the occurrence of one has no effect on the occurrence of the other. For example, when tossing a fair coin, the event "head on the second toss" is independent of the event "tail on the first toss." The coin is not influenced by what happens on previous tosses.

When two events are known to be independent, we can find the probability of both occurring by using the following formula.

Probability of Independent Events

If A and B are independent events, then the probability that both will occur is

$$P(A \text{ and } B) = P(A) \cdot P(B). \tag{2}$$

Example 7 illustrates how to find the probability of an event that consists of a sequence of independent events.

E X A M P L E   7   Finding the Probability of Independent Events

Find the probability of the event "HHTTH" in the experiment of tossing a coin five times.

Solution Since each toss of the coin is an independent event, let the letters H and T refer to the events of rolling a head or a tail, respectively. So by Eq. (2)

$$P(\text{"HHTTH"}) = P(H) \cdot P(H) \cdot P(T) \cdot P(T) \cdot P(H)$$

$$= \left(\frac{1}{2}\right)^5 = \frac{1}{32}.$$

A coin that is tossed several times represents a set of independent events. Suppose that a coin is tossed four times. The binomial expansion provides a way to organize the probabilities of the events of obtaining exactly i tails on four tosses of a fair coin for $i = 0, 1, 2, 3, 4$. Consider the binomial expansion of $(H + T)^4$:

$$(H + T)^4 = \binom{4}{0} H^4 + \binom{4}{1} H^3 T + \binom{4}{2} H^2 T^2 + \binom{4}{3} H T^3 + \binom{4}{4} T^4. \quad \textbf{(3)}$$

Each coefficient $\binom{4}{i}$ gives the number of ways exactly i tails can occur when a coin is tossed four times; that is, $\binom{4}{i} = {}_4 C_i$.

If we let $H = T = \frac{1}{2}$, the probability of a head or a tail on one toss of a single coin, then we can rewrite the right-hand side of Eq. (3) in the following way:

$$1 = \left(\frac{1}{2} + \frac{1}{2} \right)^4 = \frac{{}_4 C_0}{16} + \frac{{}_4 C_1}{16} + \frac{{}_4 C_2}{16} + \frac{{}_4 C_3}{16} + \frac{{}_4 C_4}{16}$$

$$= \frac{1}{16} + \frac{4}{16} + \frac{6}{16} + \frac{4}{16} + \frac{1}{16}.$$

Each term ${}_4 C_i / 16$ represents the probability of the event consisting of exactly i tails occurring on a toss of four coins. This generalizes to tosses of any number of fair coins as illustrated in the next example. We note that a toss of n fair coins and n tosses of one fair coin are equivalent regarding events about the number of heads or tails that occur.

E X A M P L E   8   Finding the Probability of Independent Events

A fair coin is tossed seven times. Find the probability of obtaining exactly three tails on those seven tosses.

Solution   According to the discussion preceding this example, the desired probability is given by substituting $H = T = \frac{1}{2}$ in ${}_7 C_3 H^4 T^3$. Thus the probability of exactly three tails occurring on seven tosses of a fair coin is

$$_7 C_3 \left(\frac{1}{2} \right)^4 \left(\frac{1}{2} \right)^3 = \frac{7!}{4! 3!} \frac{1}{2^7} = \frac{35}{128}. \qquad \blacksquare$$

The analysis in Example 8 applies to any experiment that meets the two conditions: (a) There are two outcomes to the experiment, one called H and the other T; and (b) repetitions of the experiment are independent events. For example, a coin can be tossed n times with outcomes of "heads" (H) and "tails" (T). Or n light bulbs can be checked as they come off the assembly line with outcomes of "defective" (H) or "nondefective" (T). A basketball player can shoot n foul shots with outcomes of "made" (H) or "missed" (T). In each case, if $P(H) = k$ such that $0 \leq k \leq 1$, then $P(T) = 1 - k$.

Theorem 12.12   Independent Events with Two Outcomes

Suppose a certain experiment has only the two outcomes H and T, and suppose repetitions of the experiment are independent events. If $P(H) = k$, and E is the event "T occurs exactly r times in n repetitions," then

$$P(E) = {}_nC_r P(H)^{n-r} P(T)^r$$

$$= \frac{n!}{r!(n-r)!} k^{n-r}(1-k)^r.$$

E X A M P L E   9   APPLICATION: Defective Chips

Suppose it is known that one out of 1000 of a certain brand of computer chip is defective. Five computer chips are selected at random. What is the probability that a lot of five will contain one defective chip?

Solution   Let H represent the outcome that a selected computer chip is good, and T that it is defective. Then $P(H) = \frac{999}{1000} = 0.999$ and $P(T) = \frac{1}{1000} = 0.001$. Event E with exactly one defective computer chip can be represented by $\binom{5}{1} H^4 T$. The probability of this event is

$$P(E) = {}_5C_1 P(H)^4 P(T) = 5(0.999)^4(0.001)$$

$$= 0.00498003.$$

Thus the probability that one of the five selected computer chips is defective is about 0.00498. ≡

Experimental Probability

Throughout this section we have been calculating *theoretical* probability. For example, suppose a fair coin is tossed. The theoretical probability of obtaining a head on a single toss of a fair coin is $\frac{1}{2}$.

On the other hand, suppose this fair coin is physically tossed 100 times and that 48 heads occur. The **experimental probability** of heads is 0.48.

When a physical experiment is conducted, the experimental probability should be consistent with, though not identical to, the theoretical probability. In this sense the theoretical probability is a model of the real-world experiment.

Suppose a fair coin is tossed n times and H_n is the number of times a head occurs. Because the mathematical probability of obtaining a head on a given toss is $\frac{1}{2}$, we should expect that $H_n/n \to \frac{1}{2}$ as $n \to \infty$. In other words, the observed probability of a given event should be a good approximation to the mathematical probability if a large number of experiments are performed.

Exercises for Section 12.7 _____

In Experiments 1 to 5, list the elements of the sample space for each experiment.

1. A single die is rolled.

2. A single fair coin is tossed.

3. A penny, nickel, and dime are tossed at the same time.

4. Ten balls numbered 1 through 10 are in an urn. One ball is selected.

5. Five balls numbered 1 through 5 are in an urn. Two balls are selected from this urn; the second ball is drawn before the first has been replaced.

Exercises 6 to 17 refer to the following **problem situation**: A red and green die are rolled. List the outcomes in each of these events.

6. The sum is 9.   7. The sum is even.

8. The number on one die is one more than on the other die.

9. Both dice are even.

10. The sum is less than 10.

11. Both dice are odd.

12. Find the probability of the event in Exercise 6.

13. Find the probability of the event in Exercise 7.

14. Find the probability of the event in Exercise 8.

15. Find the probability of the event in Exercise 9.

16. Find the probability of the event in Exercise 10.

17. Find the probability of the event in Exercise 11.

Exercises 18 to 22 refer to the following **problem situation**: A deck of the 20 cards consists of five cards (ace, king, queen, jack and 10) in each of the four suits spades, hearts, diamonds, and clubs. An experiment consists of dealing a hand of five cards.

18. Find the probability that the hand consists of the five spades.

19. Find the probability that all five cards are from the same suit.

20. Find the probability that the hand includes all four aces.

21. Find the probability that the hand contains only aces and face cards (ace, king, queen, or jack).

22. Find the probability that the hand contains the king of clubs.

Exercises 23 to 27 refer to the experiment of tossing a fair coin 10 times.

23. Find the probability of "heads on the second toss."

24. Find the probability of "heads on the first and last toss."

25. Find the probability of "heads on all 10 tosses."

26. Find the probability of "exactly two heads."

27. Find the probability of "at least one head."

28. A factory's management knows that an item coming off an assembly line has a probability of 0.015 of being defective. If three items are selected at random during the course of a workday, find the probability that none of the items is defective.

29. A car agency has 25 cars available for rental, 12 compact cars, and 13 intermediate size cars. If two cars are selected at random, what is the probability that they are both compact?

30. In a game of *Yahtzee* five dice are tossed simultaneously. Find the probability of rolling five of a kind on a single roll.

31. Explain why the following statement cannot be true. The probabilities that a computer salesperson will sell no, one, two, or three computers in any one day are 0.12, 0.45, 0.38, and 0.15, respectively.

32. **Writing to Learn**   During July in a certain city, the probability of at least 1 hour a day of sunshine is 0.78, the probability of at least 30 minutes of rain is 0.44, and the probability that it will be cloudy all day is 0.22. Write a paragraph explaining whether this statement could be true.

Chapter Review

KEY TERMS

arithmetic progression
arithmetic sequence
axiom of induction
binomial
binomial coefficient
  n choose r
binomial theorem
combinations of n things
  selected r at a time
common difference
common ratio
complement of an event
convergence
converse
divergence

equally like events
event
expanded notation
experiment
experimental probability
Fibonacci sequence
finite geometric series
finite sequence
finite series
fundamental counting
  principle
future value S of
  an annuity
generalized binomial
  expansion

geometric progression
geometric sequence
independent events
index of summation
infinite sequence
infinite geometric series
infinite series
interval of convergence
kth term of the sum
multiplication principle
mutually exclusive events
n factorial
nth partial sum
outcomes
Pascal's triangle

permutation
power series
principle of mathematical
  induction
probability
recursive formula
r-permutation
sequence of numbers
sequence of partial sums
sigma notation
sum of an infinite series
sample space
theoretical probability

REVIEW EXERCISES

In Exercises 1 to 8, determine the first four terms and the 10th term of the sequence. Draw a graph of the sequence.

1. $a_n = (-1)^{n+1}(n-1)$

2. $a_n = 2n^2 - 1$

3. $a_n = 2^n - 1$

4. $a_n = \cos \pi n$

5. $a_n = a_{n-1} + 3, a_1 = 2$

6. $a_n = 5 - a_{n-1}, a_1 = 7$

7. $a_n = 3 \cdot a_{n-1}, a_1 = 5$

8. $a_n = (-2) \cdot a_{n-1}, a_1 = 1$

9. The fourth and seventh terms of an arithmetic progression are -8 and 16, respectively. Determine the first term and a formula for the nth term.

10. The fifth and ninth terms of an arithmetic progression are -5 and 13, respectively. Determine the first term and a formula for the nth term.

In Exercises 11 to 14, expand each summation for $n = 8$.

11. $\displaystyle\sum_{k=1}^{n}(3k+1)$

12. $\displaystyle\sum_{k=1}^{n} 3k^2$

13. $\displaystyle\sum_{k=1}^{n}(2^k - 1)$

14. $\displaystyle\sum_{k=1}^{n}(k^2 - 2k + 1)$

In Exercises 15 and 16, use summation notation to write the sum. Assume the patterns continue as suggested.

15. $-2 - 5 - 8 - 11 - \cdots - 29$

16. $4 + 16 + 64 + 256 + \cdots$

In Exercises 17 and 18, use summation notation to write the nth partial sum of the sequence. Assume the patterns continue as suggested.

17. $8, 6, 4, \ldots$

18. $-3, 6, -9, 12, \ldots$

In Exercises 19 to 22, use summation formulas to evaluate each expression.

19. $\displaystyle\sum_{k=1}^{25}(k^2 - 3k + 4)$

20. $\displaystyle\sum_{k=1}^{100}(k^3 - 2k)$

21. $\displaystyle\sum_{k=1}^{175}(3k^2 - 5k + 1)$

22. $\displaystyle\sum_{k=1}^{75}(k^3 - k^2 + 2)$

In Exercises 23 to 26 determine whether each infinite geometric series converges. If so, find its sum.

23. $\displaystyle\sum_{k=1}^{\infty} 3(0.5)^k$

24. $\displaystyle\sum_{k=1}^{\infty}(1.2)^k$

25. $\displaystyle\sum_{k=1}^{\infty} 2(0.01)^k$

26. $\displaystyle\sum_{k=1}^{\infty}\left(\frac{1}{1.05}\right)^k$

In Exercises 27 to 32, expand each expression.

27. $(2x + y)^5$

28. $(4a - 3b)^7$

29. $(3x^2 + y^3)^5$

30. $\left(1 + \dfrac{1}{x}\right)^6$

31. $(2a^3 - b^2)^9$

32. $(x^{-2} + y^{-1})^4$

Exercises 33 to 38 refer to the following sequence of polynomial functions:

$$f_1(x) = 1 - x$$

$$f_2(x) = 1 - x + \frac{x^2}{2!}$$

$$f_3(x) = 1 - x + \frac{x^2}{2!} - \frac{x^3}{3!}$$

$$\vdots$$

$$f_n(x) = 1 - x + \frac{x^2}{2!} - \frac{x^3}{3!} + \cdots + (-1)^n \frac{x^n}{n!}$$

33. Find complete graphs of the six polynomial functions $f_1, f_2, \ldots, f_6$ in the same viewing rectangle.

34. Find a complete graph of $f(x) = e^{-x}$, and compare it with the graphs in Exercise 33.

35. Is $f_6(-2)$ a good estimate for e^2? Why?

36. Is $f_6(4)$ a good estimate for e^{-4}? Why?

37. On what interval is $f_6(x)$ a good approximation for e^{-x}?

38. Use a graphing method to determine the error in using $f_3(-2)$ to approximate e^{-2}. Repeat using $f_4(-2)$, $f_5(-2)$, and $f_6(-2)$. Are they underestimates or overestimates?

In Exercises 39 to 43, use mathematical induction to prove that each of the following is true for all positive integer values of n.

39. $1 + 3 + 6 + \cdots + \dfrac{n(n + 1)}{2} = \dfrac{n(n + 1)(n + 2)}{6}$

40. $1 \cdot 2 + 2 \cdot 3 + 3 \cdot 4 + \cdots + n(n + 1) = \dfrac{n(n + 1)(n + 2)}{3}$

41. $\displaystyle\sum_{i=1}^{n} \left(\frac{1}{2}\right)^i = 1 - \frac{1}{2^n}$

42. $2^{n-1} \le n!$

43. $n^3 + 2n$ is divisible by 3.

44. Find $_{12}P_7$

45. Find $_{15}P_8$

46. Find $_{18}C_{12}$

47. Find $_{35}C_{28}$

48. How many license plates are there that begin with AT followed by one letter and four digits?

49. How many five-character code words are there if the first character is always a letter and the other characters are letters and/or digits?

50. A travel agent is trying to schedule a client's trip from city A to city B. There are three direct flights, three flights from A to a connecting city C, and four flights from this connecting city C to city B. How many trips are possible?

51. How many license plates are there that begin with two letters followed by four digits or that begin with three digits followed by three letters? Assume no letters or digits are repeated.

52. A club has 45 members, and the membership committee has three members. How many different membership committees are possible?

53. How many bridge hands are there that include the ace, king, and queen of spades?

54. How many bridge hands include all four aces and exactly one king?

55. Suppose a coin is tossed five times. How many different outcomes include at least two heads?

56. A certain small business has 35 employees, 21 women and 14 men. How many different employee representative committees are there if the committee must consist of two women and two men?

57. Show algebraically that

$$_nP_k \times {}_{n-k}P_j = {}_nP_{k+j}.$$

For Exercises 58 to 61 determine the theoretical probabilities of the following events. Assume all the coins are fair and have two distinct sides.

58. Obtaining exactly two heads in a toss of five coins.

59. Obtaining exactly three heads in a toss of five coins.

60. Obtaining exactly four tails in a toss of nine coins.

61. Obtaining exactly two heads in a toss of nine coins.

62. Suppose a fair coin with two distinct sides is tossed 50 times and *each* time it shows a head. What is the probability that the 51st toss will result in a head? How likely is obtaining no tails (all heads) on a toss of 50 coins? Be specific.

63. Suppose the probability of producing a defective bat is 0.02. Four bats are selected at random. What is the probability that the lot of four bats contains (a) no defective bats? (b) one defective bat?

64. Suppose the probability of producing a defective light bulb is 0.0004. Ten light bulbs are selected at random. What is the probability that the lot of 10 contains (a) no defective light bulbs? (b) two defective light bulbs?

Answers

CHAPTER 1

SECTION 1.1

1. Associative property of addition
3. Commutative property of addition
5.

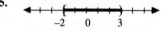

7.

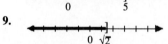

9.

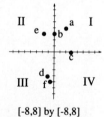

11. 8   **13.** $5 - \sqrt{3}$ **15.** 12
17. 4   **19.** $|x - 4|$ **21.**

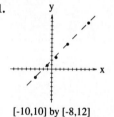

[-8,8] by [-8,8]

23. X scl $= 1$; Y scl $= 1$ **25.** X scl $= 5$; Y scl $= 1$
27. $\sqrt{10}$ **29.** $\sqrt{45}$ **31.** The length of each side is 5, therefore the quadrilateral is a rhombus.   **33.** $\sqrt{16 + y^2}$

35. $\sqrt{x^2 + 2x + 10}$ **37.** 8, -4
39. Answers depend on the grapher model.
41. If $a \geq 0$, then by definition, $|a| = a$, $a \geq 0$. If $a < 0$, then by definition, $|a| = -a$, $-a > 0$.

SECTION 1.2

1.

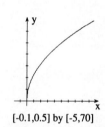

[-10,10] by [-8,12]

3.

[-0.1,0.5] by [-5,70]

x	0.01	0.04	0.09	0.16	0.25
y	10	20	30	40	50

5. The ordered pairs given satisfy the equation $y = x^2$.
7. **(a)** -10.75 **(b)** 8.00   **(c)** 26.75   **(d)** 70.50
9.

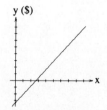

[0,500] by [-40,90]

11. No   **13.** No   **15.** Yes
17. **(a)** $[-10, 4]$ by $[7, 13]$ **(b)** $[-12, 21]$ by $[-4, 57]$
19. e

21.

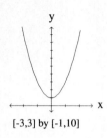

[-3,3] by [-1,10]

23.

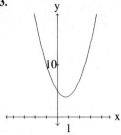

25.

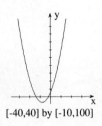

[-40,40] by [-10,100]

27.

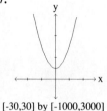

[-30,30] by [-1000,3000]

29.

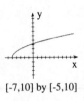

[-7,10] by [-5,10]

31.

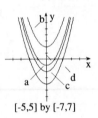

[-5,5] by [-7,7]

33.

x	0.25	0.5	1	1.5
y	-0.60	-0.30	0	0.18

x	2	3	4	5
y	0.30	0.48	0.60	0.70

35.

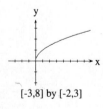

[-3,8] by [-2,3]

37.

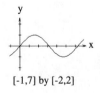

[-1,7] by [-2,2]

SECTION 1.3

1. 72   **3.** $\frac{1}{9}$ **5.** 343   **7.** 3   **9.** 4

11. $\frac{1}{4}$ **13.** 9   **15.** 1.47   **17.** 0.86   **19.** $3^{3/4}$

21. $12^{3/10}$, $3^{3/4}$, $4^{5/8}$

23. Yes   **25.** Yes

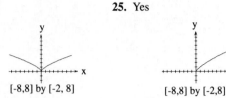

[-8,8] by [-2, 8]   [-8,8] by [-2,8]

27. For even positive values of n **29.** v^4

31. $\frac{16}{x^4}$ **33.** $\frac{1}{9x^4y^6}$ **35.** $\frac{x^3y^3}{8}$ **37.** $\frac{x-y}{x+y}$

39. $x^{1/3}$ **41.** $x^{3/2}y^{9/4}$ **43.** x^4y^4

45. 8% compounded monthly   **47.** d

49. $(a^3)^4 = (a \cdot a \cdot a)(a \cdot a \cdot a)(a \cdot a \cdot a)(a \cdot a \cdot a) = a^{12} = a^{3 \cdot 4}$

SECTION 1.4

1. Answers will vary.   **3.** Answers will vary.

5. $38.25

7. Degree = 4; leading coefficient = 3   **9.** $3x^2 + 5x + 2$

11. $-4x^2 - 7x - 17$ **13.** $6x^2 + 5x + 1$

15. $13x^2 - 3x - 1$ **17.** $-x^2 - 7x + 15$

19. $x^2 + 8x + 15$ **21.** $x^2 + 5x - 14$ **23.** $x^2 - 4x + 3$

25. $8x^2 + 14x + 3$ **27.** $-x^2 + 3x + 10$

29. $x^4 - 2x^2 - 3$ **31.** $x^5 + x^3 + 4x^2 + 4$

33. $x^{-3} + 3x^{-2} + x^{-1} + 3$ **35.** $x^3 + 6x^2 + 11x + 12$

37. False   **39.** False   **41.** False   **43.** False

45. b   **47.** $4(x - 16)$ **49.** $x(x^2 - 5x + 7)$

51. $(x - 3)(x + 2)(2x - 1)$ **53.** $(y + 2x)(y - 2x)$

55. $(x^2 + 9)(x + 3)(x - 3)$ **57.** $((x-1)^2 + 3)((x-1)^2 - 3)$

59. $(x + 3)^2$ **61.** $(x + 3)(x - 2)$ **63.** $(x + 6)(x + 2)$

65. $(x + 2y)(x + 3y)$ **67.** $2(2x + 1)(2x - 3)$

69. $2(2x + 3)(x - 2)$ **71.** $(x + 4)(x - 4)(x^2 + 2)$

SECTION 1.5

1. $4x$ **3.** x **5.** $x - 3$ **7.** $\frac{x}{3}$ **9.** $\frac{3x + 2}{x - 1}$

11. $\frac{x - 3}{x - 1}$ **13.** x^2 **15.** $\frac{x - y}{3}$ **17.** b   **19.** b

21. $\frac{x + 1}{3}$ **23.** $\frac{-1}{x - 3}$ **25.** $12y$ **27.** $\frac{3(x - 3)}{28}$

29. $\frac{x}{4(x - 3)}$ **31.** $\frac{(x + 1)^2}{(x - 1)^2}$ **33.** $\frac{(3x - 2)^3}{(2x - 1)^2}$

35. b   **37.** b   **39.** $\frac{5 + 2x}{5x}$ **41.** $\frac{7x - 11}{(x - 1)(x - 2)}$

43. $\frac{5x^2 + 7x - 15}{(x + 5)(x + 2)}$ **45.** $\frac{-3x + 2}{(x - 1)(x + 2)(x + 4)}$

47. $\frac{7x^2 + 3x}{(x + 1)(x - 1)(x + 2)}$ **49.** 6   **51.** $\frac{y + x}{xy}$

53. $2x$ **55.** $\dfrac{x^2 - 1}{x + 1} = \dfrac{(x+1)(x-1)}{x+1} = x - 1$ for all

$x \neq -1$. When $x = -1$, $\dfrac{x^2 - 1}{x + 1}$ is undefined because

$x + 1 = 0$.

67. $\dfrac{2x^3 + 13x^2 + 27x + 16}{(x+3)^2}$ **69.** $A = 125w$

[-2,2] by [-90,90]

Chapter 1 Review

1. Commutative property of addition, distributive property

3.   **5.**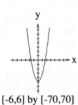

7.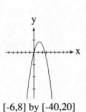

9. 2.5   **11.** 9   **13.** 3   **15.** 8

17. (a) $\sqrt{7} - 2.6$ (b) $\sqrt{7} - 2.6$ (c) $\pi - 3$ (d) $x - 5$

19. $(-2, -1)$ **21.** $\sqrt{13}$ **23.** $\sqrt{5}$ **25.** a

27. $\sqrt{y^2 - 6y + 13}$ **29.** d

31. $[-10, 4]$ by $[-9, 21]$

33.

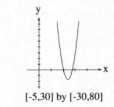

[-4,4] by [-7,9]

35.

[-6,6] by [-70,70]

37.

[-6,8] by [-40,20]

39.

[-5,30] by [-30,80]

41.

x	-3	-2	-1	0	1
y	0	1	1.414	1.732	2

x	2	3	4	5
y	2.236	2.449	2.646	2.828

43. $9x^5$ **45.** $\dfrac{8z^6 b^2}{a^5}$ **47.** $\dfrac{81v^8}{u}$

49. $x^3 - 4x^2 + 3x + 3$ **51.** $x^2 - 2x - 15$

53. $-6x^2 + 23x - 21$ **55.** $2x^2 - 19x + 45$

57. $9x^2 - 21x + 10$ **59.** $-6x^2 - xy + y^2$ **61.** $\dfrac{x+3}{x^2}$

63. $\dfrac{x^2 - 2x + 12}{(x-3)(x+2)}$ **65.** $\dfrac{x+3}{(x-1)(x^2 + 4x + 1)}$

71. $r = 6.91$ units

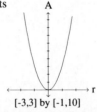

[-3,3] by [-1,10]

73. Problem situation: positive integer values of n

[-10,50] by [-20,15]

75. 37 tickets

77. The portion of the graph in quadrant I   **79.** Let
$x = $ length, $150 - x = $ width; then $A = l \cdot w$ yields
$A = x(150 - x)$.   **81.** $0 < x < 150$

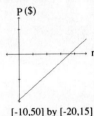

83. 553, 334 jars   **85.** $d = 48t$

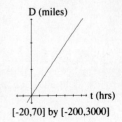

[-20,70] by [-200,3000]

87. $t \approx 25$ hours

CHAPTER 2

SECTION 2.1

1. Conditional equation   **3.** Identity
5. Conditional equation   **7.** 2 is a solution.
9. (a) -3 is a solution.   **(b)** -2 is not a solution.
(c) -1 is a solution.   **11.** 1   **13.** $-\dfrac{46}{9}$ **15.** $\dfrac{8}{19}$

17. $3, -5$ **19.** $\dfrac{5}{4}, \dfrac{7}{4}$ **21.** $-4, \dfrac{2}{3}$ **23.** $3, 2$

25. $1, 3$ **27.** $\dfrac{1}{2}, \dfrac{3}{2}$ **29.** $-5, 1$ **31.** $2 \pm \sqrt{2}$

33. $\dfrac{1}{2}, 1$ **35.** $-1, 4$ **37.** $\dfrac{\sqrt{3} \pm \sqrt{23}}{2}$ **39.** $y = 0$

41. ± 1 **43.** No real solutions
45. 2 real solutions   **47.** $C = \dfrac{5}{9}(F - 32)$

49. 3200 in^2 **51.** $y = \dfrac{5400}{30x} = \dfrac{180}{x}$ **53.** 15 cm
55. 0.75 liter   **57.** 25 years   **59.** 11.98 units
61. 440 units   **63.** 4 or 17 listings   **65.** As the
number increases to 10, profits increase. Beyond 10 listings,
profits decrease. More agents might be needed to handle
additional listings.

SECTION 2.2

1. $3, -2$ **3.** $1, 2$ **5.** $0, \pm 1$
7. 2 solutions; $[-4, 6]$ by $[-15, 5]$

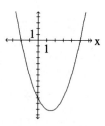

9. 2 solutions   **11.** 3 solutions

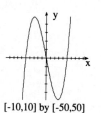

$[-50,50]$ by $[-500,1200]$ $[-10,10]$ by $[-50,50]$

13. 1 solution

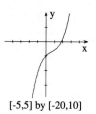

$[-5,5]$ by $[-20,10]$

15. The large range required for a complete graph makes it
difficult to estimate zeros between -1 and 1.

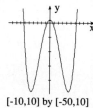

$[-10,10]$ by $[-50,10]$

17. 0.01   **19.** 0.5   **21.** 0.01   **23.** 0.326
25. Answers will vary. One sequence: $[1, 2]$ by $[-1, 1]$,
$[1.5, 1.6]$ by $[-0.1, 0.1]$, $[1.57, 1.58]$ by $[-0.01, 0.01]$,
and $[1.574, 1.575]$ by $[-0.001, 0.001]$.   **27.** 1.52
29. 10.19   **31.** 0.61, 4.39   **33.** 5.00, 15.00, 40.00
35. $-1.5, 4.5$ **37.** Answers will vary. Some
approximations: 2.15, 2.16, and 2.155. Exact solution: $\sqrt[3]{10}$.
39. 0.70, 3.39   **41.** 1.86, 5.00, 8.14 radians   **43.** 2858 cones
45. $A = \dfrac{x(320 - 2x)}{2} = x(160 - x)$ **47.** If $x = -40$,
$y = -40(160 - (-40)) = -8000$. $(-40, -8000)$ is a point on
the graph, but neither length nor width can be negative. The
coordinates have no meaning in the problem situation.
49. 0.003 cm   **51.** 1.28 inches   **53.** $p = \$78.40$;
$x = 256$ units (Problem situation requires an integer solution.)
55.

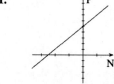   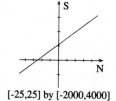

$[-10,10]$ by $[-20,10]$ $[0.5,1.5]$ by $[-0.5,0.5]$

SECTION 2.3

1.   **3.**

$[-40,20]$ by $[-50,100]$ $[-25,25]$ by $[-2000,4000]$

5. $A = 50L$ **7.**

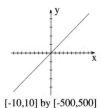

[-10,10] by [-500,500]

9. $P = 2L + 200$ **11.**

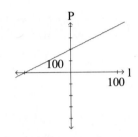

13. $A = 2W^2$ **15.** $P = 2(2W) + 2W = 6W$
17. 13.82 inches by 36.18 inches   **19.** If $x = -10$,
$y = -10(75 - (-10)) = -850$. $(-10, -850)$ is a point on the
graph, but neither length nor area can be negative. The
coordinates have no meaning in the problem situation.
21. $A = x(180 - x)$ **23.**

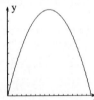

[0,180] by [0,8100]

25. $L \cdot W = 625$
27. The portion of the graph in quadrant I
29.

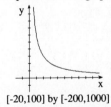

[-20,100] by [-200,1000]

31. $I = 0.085(12000 - x) + 0.07x$
33. The portion of the graph for $0 < x < 12,000$
35. $C = 30x + 100,000$ **37.** 8000 pairs   **39.** 5000 pairs
41. Answers will vary.   **43.** $8000 at 7%, $4000 at 8.5%

SECTION 2.4

1. Answers will vary. Choices include $x = -2, 0, 4$.
3. Answers will vary. Choices include $x = 0, 1, 2$.

5. Answers will vary. Choices include $x = 1, 2, 2.1$.
7. Answers will vary. Choices include $x = 4, 5, 6$.
9. $-3 \le x < 5$ **11.** $2 \le x \le 5$ **13.** $x < 4$
15. $x \le -2$ **17.** $(-1, 1)$ **19.** $[-1, 2)$
21. $(-\infty, 4]$ **23.**
                 -10
25.
   0   5   **27.**
       -2   0
29. $(3, 7)$; $3 < x < 7$ **31.** $(-\infty, -4]$; $x \le -4$
33. $x \le \dfrac{34}{7}$ **35.** $x < \dfrac{33}{13}$ **37.** $-4 \le x < 3$
39. $-\dfrac{1}{2} \le x \le \dfrac{17}{2}$ **41.** $x > 3.50$

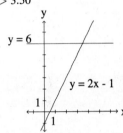

43. $(2, \infty)$ **45.** $(-33/13, \infty)$ **47.** $(-14/3, \infty)$
49. $x \le 4.23$ **51.** $r \ge 52.5$ mph
53. $0 < w < 34$ inches   **55.** $10 \le P \le 20$
57. $a < b$ if $b - a$ is a negative number.

SECTION 2.5

1.
   -4   0   2   **3.**
         0   3
5.
   0   2   5   **7.**
   -3   0   5
9.
   -3   0   3   **11.**
   -3   0   7
13.
   0   2   4
15. $|x| \le 4$ **17.** $|x - (-2)| < 1$ **19.** $|x - 4| \ge 3$
21. $(-\infty, 0] \cup (1, 3]$ **23.** $(-\infty, 0] \cup (2.5, \infty)$
25. $|x| \ge 1$ **27.** $|x - 1| \ge 1$ **29.** $(-\infty, \infty)$
31. $[-8, 2]$ **33.** $(-\infty, -2] \cup [8, \infty)$
35. $(-6, 14)$ **37.** $(-\infty, -4/3) \cup (4/3, \infty)$
39. $(-\infty, -2) \cup (-2, 3)$ **41.** $(-\infty, 3/2)$
43. $C \ge 100$ **45.** $0.42x - 20000 > 0$ **47.** $(4, \infty)$
49. $(-5/2, \infty)$ **51.**
   1.9   2.1
53. $0 < d < 0.003$

SECTION 2.6

1. 3 seconds, $1 \le t \le 4$
3. $-16t^2 + 80t > 10$; $-16t^2 + 80t \ge 10$
5. $s = -16t^2 + 32t + 120$
7. $(-\infty, -6), (-6, -5), (-5, \infty)$
9. $(-\infty, -5), (-5, -3), (-3, 2), (2, \infty)$
11. $(-\infty, 2), (2, 4), (4, \infty)$
13. $(-\infty, -2), (-2, -1), (-1, 1), (1, 2), (2, \infty)$
15. $(-\infty, -1 - \sqrt{2}), (-1 - \sqrt{2}, -1 + \sqrt{2}), (-1 + \sqrt{2}, 3),$
$(3, \infty)$ **17.** $y = 7x^3 - 2x^2 - 5x + 3$
19. $y = x^5 - 6x^2 - x - 3$ **21.** $[0, 3]$
23. $(-3, 7)$ **25.** $(0, 1)$ **27.** $[-2, 0] \cup [4, \infty)$
29. $(-\infty, -1.98) \cup (3.94, 7.04)$
31. $[0, 0.41) \cup (2.73, 6.69) \cup (9.01, 10]$, using radians
33. $(-\infty, -4) \cup (-1, 2)$ **35.** $(-3, 1)$
37. $[0.28, 2.39]$ **39.** $(-\infty, -3.66)$
41. The complete graph of the algebraic representation is shown. The graph of the problem situation is that portion in quadrant I.

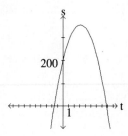

43. $t = 7.84$ sec

45. $A = (30 + 2x)(20 + 2x) - 600$

47. $1.86 < x < 3.19$ ft

49. $r \ge 0.28$

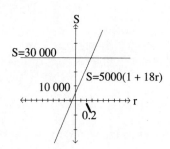

51. 10 years

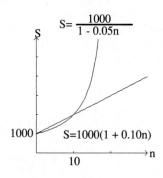

53. All values of x **55.** All values of x

Chapter 2 Review

1. $\dfrac{27}{40}$ **3.** $-3, 7$ **5.** $\pm\sqrt{3}$

7.
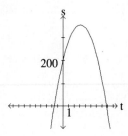
9.

11.   **13.**

15.   **17.**

19. $\pm\sqrt{6}$ **21.** $\dfrac{3 \pm \sqrt{65}}{4}$ **23.** $-0.44, 1.69$
25. 2.11 **27.** No real solutions   **29.** $-1.00, 0.50$
31. 2.23 **33.** ± 2.28 **35.** 0.85 **37.** $(-\infty, -9/2]$
39. $[1, 23/4)$ **41.** No real solutions
43. $(-\infty, -1] \cup [4, \infty)$ **45.** $(-\infty, -7] \cup [-3, \infty)$
47. $(-\infty, 2] \cup [3, \infty)$ **49.** $(-2, 0) \cup (3/2, \infty)$
51. $(-\infty, -2) \cup (5/2, \infty)$ **53.** $(-5, 2)$
55. $(-\infty, 0.23] \cup [1.43, \infty)$ **57.** $[-0.91, \infty)$
59. $[0, 1]$ by $[-1, 1]$; $[0.3, 0.4]$ by $[-0.1, 0.1]$; $[0.33, 0.34]$ by $[-0.01, 0.01]$; $[0.333, 0.334]$ by $[-0.001, 0.001]$
61. $y = \dfrac{420}{x}$; length $= 35$ cm
63. 6 pennies, 5 nickels, 12 dimes
65. $0 < w < 72.5$ in.
67. $P = 2x + 2w = 530$
    yields $w = 265 - x$.
    Then $A = l \cdot w = x(265 - x)$.

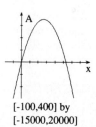

$[-100, 400]$ by
$[-15000, 20000]$

69. If $x = -100$, $y = (-100)[265 - (-100)] = -36500$. Thus $(-100, -36500)$ is a point on the graph, but neither length nor area can be negative. The coordinates have no meaning in the problem situation.
71. $0 < x < 8$ inches   **73.** $\frac{1}{2}(8.5)(x + 1) \le 36$
75. $P(x) = 15.25x - [(x - 100)^2 + 400]$

[-25,200] by [-1500,1500]

77. 74 or 142 books per week
79. $5.15x - (1.26x + 34000) \ge 42000$; $x \ge 19537.28$ lb.
81. $A = (230 + 2x)(125 + 2x) - 230 \cdot 125 = 4x^2 + 710x$
83. $3.99 < x < 5.33$ ft   **85.** The portion of the graph in quadrant I represents the problem situation.

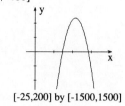

87. $x < 3$

CHAPTER 3

SECTION 3.1

1. $(3, 8)$ is in the relation because $2(3) - 8 = 6 - 8 = -2$. $(4, 2)$ is not because $2(4) - 2 = 8 - 2 \ne -2$.   **3.** $(-3, 6)$ is in the relation because $-3 + 6^2 = -3 + 36 = 33$. $(-2, 4)$ is not because $-2 + 4^2 = -2 + 16 \ne 33$.   **5.** No
7. No   **9.** No   **11.** Yes
13. x-intercepts: $(-2, 0)$, $(2, 0)$; y-intercepts: $(0, -1)$, $(0, 1)$
15. x-intercepts: $(-1, 0)$, $(1, 0)$; no y-intercepts
17. x-intercepts: $(-\sqrt{5}, 0)$, $(\sqrt{5}, 0)$; y-intercepts: $(0, -\sqrt{3})$, $(0, \sqrt{3})$ **19.** $(x - 1)^2 + (y - 2)^2 = 25$
21. $(x + 1)^2 + (y + 4)^2 = 9$ **23.** center $(3, 1)$; $r = 6$
25. **(a)** $(2, -3)$ **(b)** $(-2, 3)$ **(c)** $(-2, -3)$
27. **(a)** Symmetric with respect to y-axis   **(b)** Symmetric with respect to the origin

29.

31.

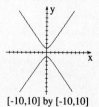

33. Symmetric with respect to y-axis
35. Symmetric with respect to the origin
37. Symmetric with respect to all three
39. Symmetric with respect to y-axis
41. Symmetric with respect to the origin

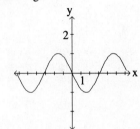

43. Line of symmetry: $x = 2$

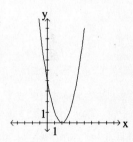

45. $x = -2$ **47.** $x = 3$
49. $y = \sqrt{2x^2 + 1}$; $y = -\sqrt{2x^2 + 1}$

51.

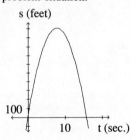

[-10,10] by [-10,10]   [-10,10] by [-10,10]

SECTION 3.2

1. $-1, 0$ **3.** $1, \dfrac{1}{2}$ **5.** $\dfrac{t}{2+t}$

7. $2, -3, 2$ **9.** $-\dfrac{1}{4}, 4.25$

11. (a) Function   (b) Not a function
13. (a) Not a function   (b) Not a function
15. $D = (-\infty, 3) \cup (3, \infty)$, $R = (-\infty, 0) \cup (0, \infty)$
17. $D = (-\infty, \infty)$, $R = [0, \infty)$
19. $D = (-\infty, 8]$, $R = [0, \infty)$
21. $D = (-1, \infty)$, $R = (0, \infty)$
23. $D = (-\infty, \infty)$, $R = [-16.25, \infty)$ **25.** d

27.

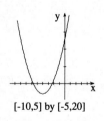

29.

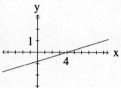

31.

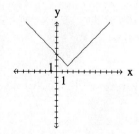

[-10,5] by [-5,20]

33.

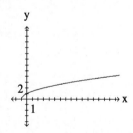

35.

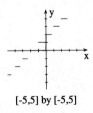

37.

[-5,5] by [-5,5]

39.

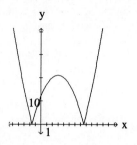

41.

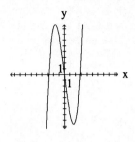

43.

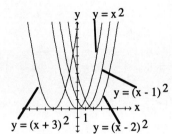

$y = x^2$
$y = (x - 1)^2$
$y = (x + 3)^2$ $y = (x - 2)^2$

45.

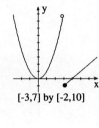

[-3,7] by [-2,10]

47.

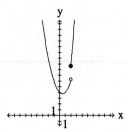

49. 6.30 hours   **51.** Only positive real values
53. $y = \left(\dfrac{x}{4}\right)^2 + \left(\dfrac{80 - x}{4}\right)^2$; $D = (0, 40)$ (in feet)
55. $y = C(t) = 0.48 + 0.28 \, INT(t)$ if $t > 0$, t not an integer.
$y = C(t) = 0.48 + 0.28(t - 1)$ if t is a positive integer.
$R = \{\, 0.48, 0.76, 1.04, \ldots \}$

[0,5] by [0,6]

57. Between 5 and 6 minutes
59. The portion of the graph in quadrant I

SECTION 3.3

1. $y = 3x$ and $y = \dfrac{1}{3}x$ rise.

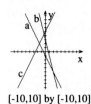

[-5,5] by [-5,5]

3. $y = 2x + 5$ rises.

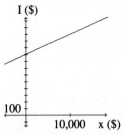

[-10,10] by [-10,10]

5. $-\dfrac{8}{3}$ **7.** $\dfrac{4}{5}$ **9.** $m = 2, b = -4$

11. $m = -\dfrac{2}{3}, b = \dfrac{2}{3}$ **13.** $m = -\dfrac{1}{2}, b = \dfrac{3}{2}$

15.

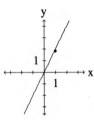

17.

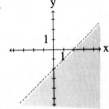

[-4,4] by [-3,5]

19. $y = \dfrac{3}{2}x + 3$ **21.** $y = \dfrac{13}{2}x + 300$

23. $[-4.8, 4.7]$ by $[-3.2, 3.1]$ with Xscl = Yscl = 1. Answers will vary for different calculators.

25. The slopes are the same but the first appears steeper.

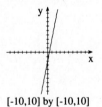

[-10,10] by [-10,10]

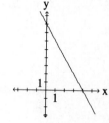

[-2,2] by [-10,10]

27. $[-2, 2]$ by $[-10, 10]$

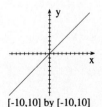

[-10,10] by [-10,10]

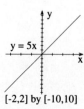

$y = 5x$

[-2,2] by [-10,10]

29. $m = \dfrac{y_2 - y_1}{x_2 - x_1} = \dfrac{-1(-y_2 + y_1)}{-1(-x_2 + x_1)} = \dfrac{y_1 - y_2}{x_1 - x_2}$

31. Not collinear **33.** $V = 3187.5t + 42000, t = 0$

35. 15.06 years after purchase

37.

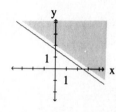

39. Year 2: 4%; Year 3: 3.85%; Year 4: 3.70%; Year 5: 3.57%

41.

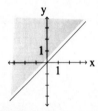

43.

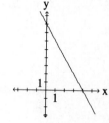

45.

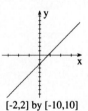

47.

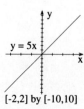

49. $2.50x + 3.75y > 1500$

SECTION 3.4

1. $y = \dfrac{3}{2}x + 2$ **3.** $y = \dfrac{1}{5}x - \dfrac{2}{3}$ **5.** $y = \dfrac{3}{2}x + \dfrac{3}{2}$

7. $y = 5$ **9.** $y = \dfrac{3}{2}x$ **11.** $y = \dfrac{1}{4}x + \dfrac{1}{4}$

13. $x = -2, y = 3$ **15.** $(2, 6)$ **17.** $\left(\dfrac{9}{2}, \dfrac{\sqrt{2}+2}{2}\right)$

19. $y = x - 2$ **21.** $y = \dfrac{1}{4}x + \dfrac{9}{2}$ **23.** $y = 2$

25. The slope (m_1) of the line segment from $(-1, 2)$ to $(-6, -2)$ is 4/5. The slope (m_2) of the line segment from $(-6, -2)$ to $(2, -12)$ is $-5/4$. $m_1 = -\dfrac{1}{m_2}$, thus the sides are perpendicular.

27. No

29. Length of side BC is $2\sqrt{10}$ but sides CA and AB have length $2\sqrt{5}$.

31. $y = \dfrac{6}{7}x, y = -12x + 30, y = -\dfrac{3}{4}x + \dfrac{15}{4}$

33. The four midpoints are $M_1 = \left(\dfrac{a}{2}, 0\right)$, $M_2 = \left(\dfrac{b+a}{2}, \dfrac{c}{2}\right)$,

$M_3 = \left(\dfrac{b+d}{2}, \dfrac{e+c}{2}\right)$, and $M_4 = \left(\dfrac{d}{2}, \dfrac{e}{2}\right)$. Show opposite

sides of $M_1 M_2 M_3 M_4$ are parallel by calculating slopes.
35. Label the vertices of the rectangle as: $(0,0)$, $(0,b)$, $(c,0)$, and (c,b). Then each diagonal has length $\sqrt{c^2 + b^2}$.
37. Consider the right triangle with vertices $(0,0)$, $(0,a)$, and $(b,0)$. The midpoint of the hypotenuse is $(\dfrac{b}{2}, \dfrac{a}{2})$ and its distance from each vertex is $\dfrac{1}{2}\sqrt{a^2 + b^2}$.
39. $(1.5, 3.75)$, $(4, 4.5)$ and $(6.5, 5.25)$
41. $y = -\dfrac{1}{11}x + \dfrac{35}{11}$ **43.** ℓ_1: $y = \left(\dfrac{c-a}{b}\right)x$; ℓ_2:

$x = a$; ℓ_3: $y = -\dfrac{a}{b}x + \dfrac{ac}{b}$. The point $\left(a, \dfrac{a(c-a)}{b}\right)$ is common to all three lines.

SECTION 3.5

1.

$y = 3(x+2)^2$ $y = 3(x-2)^2$

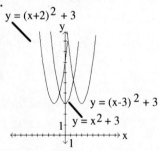

$y = 3x^2$

3.

$y = 2(x+1)^2$ $y = 2(x-1)^2$

$y = 2x^2$

5.

$y = (x+2)^2 + 3$

$y = (x-3)^2 + 3$
$y = x^2 + 3$

7. $y = 4x^2$ is above $y = 3x^2$.
9. $y = 3.21x^2$ is above $y = 3.021x^2$.   **11.** Horizontal shift right 1 unit   **13.** Horizontal shift right 3 units

15. Vertical stretch by a factor of 3 followed by a reflection in the x-axis

17. Horizontal shift left 1 unit

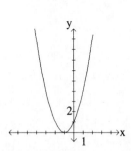

19. Vertical stretch by a factor of 3, reflection in the x-axis, followed by a vertical shift up 2 units

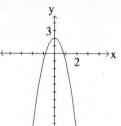

21. $(-2, -3)$, $x = -2$ **23.** $(\sqrt{3}, 4)$, $x = \sqrt{3}$
25. $(-4, 3)$, $x = -4$ **27.**

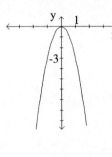

29.   **31.**

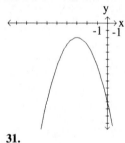

$[-5,10]$ by $[-5,10]$

33. $y = 3(x - 4)^2$ **35.** $y = 3x^2 + 4$
37. No. The equation for exercise 35 is $y = 3x^2 + 4$, but the equation for exercise 36 is

$y = 3(x^2 + 4) = 3x^2 + 12.$

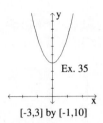

Ex. 35

[-3,3] by [-1,10]

Ex. 36

[-3,3] by [-1,20]

39. $y = -2(x - 4)^2 + 3$ **41.** $f(x) = (x - 3)^2 + 3$; horizontal shift right 3 units, vertical shift up 3 units, vertex: $(3, 3)$; line of symmetry: $x = 3$

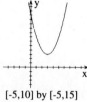

[-5,10] by [-5,15]

43. $f(x) = -(x + 8)^2 + 74$; horizontal shift left 8 units, reflection in the x-axis, vertical shift up 74 units; vertex: $(-8, 74)$; line of symmetry: $x = -8$ units

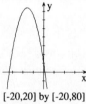

[-20,20] by [-20,80]

45. $b^2 - 4ac = 0$; one real zero

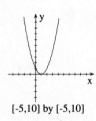

[-5,10] by [-5,10]

47. $b^2 - 4ac > 0$; two real zeros

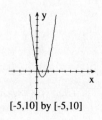

[-5,10] by [-5,10]

49. $b^2 - 4ac < 0$; no real zeros

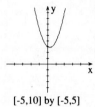

[-5,10] by [-5,5]

51. $(0.5, 0)$ **53.** $\left(\dfrac{a + b}{2}, \dfrac{-a^2 + 2ab - b^2}{4} \right)$

55. $f(x - 2) = |x - 2|$; horizontal shift right 2 units

57. $2f(x + 3) - 1 = 2|x + 3| - 1$; horizontal shift left 3 units, vertical stretch by a factor of 2, vertical shift down 1 unit

59. 3.5 ft   **61.** 11 ft and 9 ft   **63.** $31,250$ ft^2

SECTION 3.6

1. **(a)** $(f + g)(x) = x^2 + 2x - 1, D = (-\infty, \infty)$
(b) $(f - g)(x) = -x^2 + 2x - 1, D = (-\infty, \infty)$
(c) $(fg)(x) = 2x^3 - x^2, D = (-\infty, \infty)$
(d) $(f/g)(x) = \dfrac{2x - 1}{x^2}, D = (-\infty, 0) \cup (0, \infty)$

3. **(a)** $(f + g)(x) = x^2 + 2x, D = (-\infty, \infty)$
(b) $(f - g)(x) = x^2 - 2x, D = (-\infty, \infty)$
(c) $(fg)(x) = 2x^3, D = (-\infty, \infty)$
(d) $(f/g)(x) = \dfrac{x^2}{2x} = \dfrac{x}{2}, D = (-\infty, 0) \cup (0, \infty)$

5. **(a)** $(f + g)(x) = \dfrac{5x + 8}{3}, D = (-\infty, \infty)$
(b) $(f - g)(x) = \dfrac{x + 10}{3}, D = (-\infty, \infty)$
(c) $(fg)(x) = \dfrac{(x + 3)(2x - 1)}{3}, D = (-\infty, \infty)$
(d) $(f/g)(x) = \dfrac{3x + 9}{2x - 1}, D = (-\infty, 1/2) \cup (1/2, \infty)$

7. $D = (-\infty, -4) \cup (-4, \infty), R = \{1\}$

[-7,7,] by [-3,3]

9. $(f \circ g)(3) = 8, (g \circ f)(-2) = 3$
11. $(f \circ g)(3) = 9, (g \circ f)(-2) = 66$
13.   **(a)** $(f \circ g)(x) = \dfrac{1}{(x - 1)^2} - 1, D = (-\infty, 1) \cup$
$(1, \infty), R = (-1, \infty)$ **(b)** $(g \circ f)(x) = \dfrac{1}{x^2 - 2}$,
$D = (-\infty, -\sqrt{2}) \cup (-\sqrt{2}, \sqrt{2}) \cup (\sqrt{2}, \infty)$,
$R = (-\infty, 0) \cup (0, \infty)$

15. (a) $(f \circ g)(x) = x - 1$,
$D = [-1, \infty)$, $R = [-2, \infty)$ **(b)** $(g \circ f)(x) = \sqrt{x^2 - 1}$,
$D = (-\infty, -1] \cup [1, \infty)$, $R = [0, \infty)$
17. (a) $(f \circ g)(x) = x - 1$, $D = [-2, \infty)$, $R = [-3, \infty)$
(b) $(g \circ f)(x) = \sqrt{x^2 - 1}$, $D = (-\infty, -1] \cup [1, \infty)$,
$R = [0, \infty)$ **19.** Symmetry about $y = x$

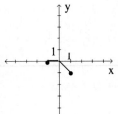

21. $g(x) = x - 3$ **23.** $g(x) = \dfrac{1}{x + 1}$, $h(x) = x^3$

25. $g(x) = (x - 3)^2$, $h(x) = \dfrac{2}{x}$

27. $g(x) = \sqrt{x}$, $h(x) = 3 - x$ **29.** $g(x) = x + 8$

31. $(h \circ g \circ f \circ k)(x)$ **33.**

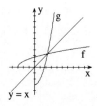

35.

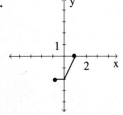

37.

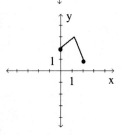

39.

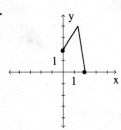

41.

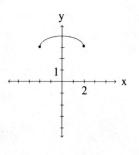

43.

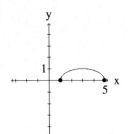

45.

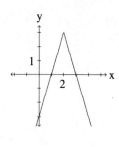

47.

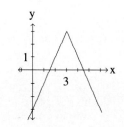

49.

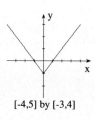

[-4,5] by [-3,4]

51. Horizontal shift right 3 units

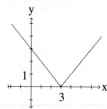

53. Horizontal shift right 4 units, vertical stretch by a factor of 3, followed by a vertical shift up 2 units

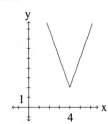

55. $(3, 8)$ **57.** $(3, 6)$ **59.** $b = 3$
61. $(4, 5)$, $(2, 3)$ **63.** $(4, -15)$, $(2, -9)$
65. $t = 6.68$ sec.   **67.** $t = 3.63$ sec.
69. $r = 3t$, $V = \dfrac{4}{3}\pi r^3 = 36\pi t^3$; $V = 3053.63$ in^3 when
$t = 3$ **71.** $S(r) = 4\pi r^2$, $g(r) = 1.6 - 0.0027t$,
$S(t) = 4\pi(1.6 - 0.0027t)^2$; $t = 592.59$ sec or 9.88 min
73. $C(x) = \begin{cases} 0.72[\![x + 1]\!], & 0 < x < 5 \\ 0.63[\![x - 4]\!] + 3.60, & 5 \le x < 15 \\ 0.51[\![x - 14]\!] + 9.90, & 15 \le x \end{cases}$

75.

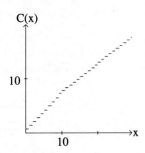

SECTION 3.7

1. If (a, b) is in the relation $y = x^3$, $b = a^3$. Thus, (b, a) satisfies the equation $x = y^3$. **3.** If (a, b) is in the relation $y = x^2 - 4$, $b = a^2 - 4$. Thus, (b, a) satisfies the equation $x = y^2 - 4$. **5.** $f(g(x)) = 3 \cdot \frac{1}{3}(x + 2) - 2 = x$; $g(f(x)) = \frac{1}{3}((3x - 2) + 2) = x$

7. $f(g(x)) = [(x - 1)^{1/3}]^3 + 1 = (x - 1) + 1 = x$; $g(f(x)) = ((x^3 + 1) - 1)^{1/3} = (x^3)^{1/3} = x$

9. Not one-to-one; fails horizontal test

[-10,10] by [-10,10]

11. Not one-to-one; fails horizontal test

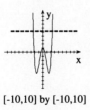

[-10,10] by [-10,10]

13. One-to-one; satisfies horizontal line test

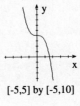

[-5,5] by [-5,10]

15. No   **17.** $(-4, -4)$
19.

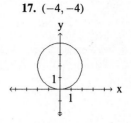

21. $f^{-1}(x) = x^2 + 2$ for $x \geq 0$. For f, $D = [2, \infty)$ and $R = [0, \infty)$; for f^{-1}, $D = [0, \infty)$ and $R = [2, \infty)$.
23. The graph satisfies the horizontal line test; one-to-one function; $f^{-1}(x) = \frac{1}{2}x - \frac{5}{2}$

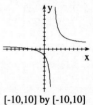

[-10,10] by [-10,10]

25. The graph satisfies the horizontal line test; one-to-one function $f^{-1}(x) = \frac{2x + 3}{x - 1}$

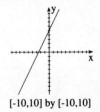

[-10,10] by [-10,10]

27. The graph satisfies the horizontal line test; one-to-one function $f^{-1}(x) = x^2 - 2$, with $x \geq 0$

[-6,10] by [-8,8]

29. f^{-1} is not a function.   **31.** f^{-1} is not a function.

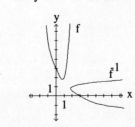

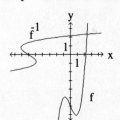

Chapter 3 Review

1.
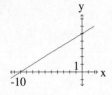

3.
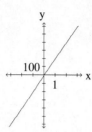

5. (a)
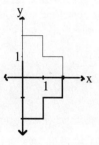

(b)
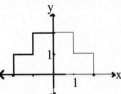

(c)
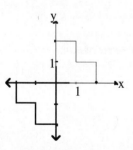

7. Symmetric with respect to the x-axis
9. Symmetric with respect to the origin
11. Symmetric with respect to the origin
13. $D = (-\infty, \infty)$; $R = [0, \infty)$; line of symmetry: $x = 3$; y is function of x

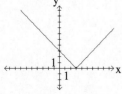

15. $D = [0, \infty)$; $R = (-\infty, \infty)$; line of symmetry: $y = 4$; Not a function

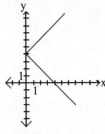

17. $D = (0, \infty)$; $R = (-\infty, 0) \cup (0, \infty)$; line of symmetry: $y = 0$; Not a function

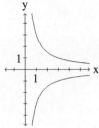

19. 2; 3; 11; 27; $t^2 + 2$; $t^2 + 2$; $\dfrac{1}{t^2} + 2$; $(a + h)^2 + 2$; $2a + h$ **21. (a)** 0; -2; 4 **(b)** 0, 3 **(c)** 0.25, 2.75

23.
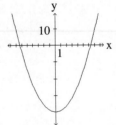

25.
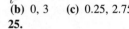
[-10,10] by [-10,10]

27.
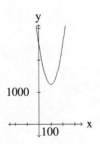

29. $D = [3, \infty)$; $R = [0, \infty)$
31. $D = [-3, \infty)$; $R = (-\infty, -2]$

33. $D = (-\infty, \infty)$; $R = (-\infty, \infty)$

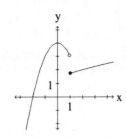

35. $D = (-\infty, \infty)$; $R = (0, \infty)$

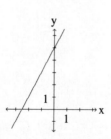

37. $D = (-\infty, \infty)$; $R = (-\infty, \infty)$

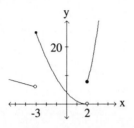

[-5,5] by [-40,40]

39.

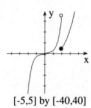

41. $m = -\dfrac{3}{2}$ **43.** $f(x) = -2x + 4$

45.

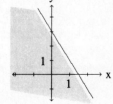

47.

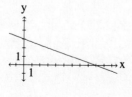

49. $y = -\dfrac{2}{3}x + 4$ **51.** $y = \dfrac{1}{5}x + \dfrac{23}{5}$ **53.** $(-1, 1.5)$

55. $y = -\dfrac{2}{3}x + 5$ **57. (a)** Only two sides are equal in length: $d(A, B) = \sqrt{74}$, $d(B, C) = \sqrt{74}$, $d(A, C) = 2\sqrt{2}$. **(b)** Midpoint is $D = (-3, 2)$. $m(AC) = 1$, $m(DB) = -1$. The slopes are negative reciprocals so $AC \perp DB$. **59.** Consider the square with vertices $A(0, 0)$, $B(0, a)$, $C(a, a)$, and $D(a, 0)$. $m(AC) = 1$, $m(BD) = -1$, so $AC \perp BD$. **61.** $y = -\dfrac{1}{7}x + \dfrac{6}{7}$

63. Reflection in the x-axis

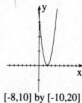

65. Reflection in the x-axis, vertical stretch by a factor of 2, horizontal shift left 3 units, vertical shift up 4 units

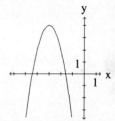

67. Vertical stretch by a factor of 4, horizontal shift right 2 units.

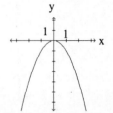

[-8,10] by [-10,20]

69. Reflection in the x-axis, vertical stretch by a factor of 2, horizontal shift left 3 units

[-8,5] by [-8,5]

71. Horizontal shift right 3 units, vertical stretch by a factor of 2

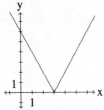

73. $b = 3$ **75. (a)** $y = 2x^2 + 1$

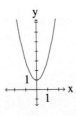

(b) $y = 2(x^2 + 1)$ **(c)** No, the second graph is shifted up 2 units instead of 1.

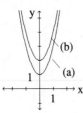

77. $f(x) = -(x + 3)^2 + 23$; reflection in the x-axis, horizontal shift left 3 units, vertical shift up 23 units
79. Reflection in the x-axis; vertical stretch by a factor of 2; horizontal shift right 3 units; vertical shift down 5 units

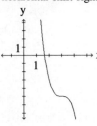

81.

83.

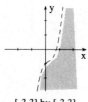

[-3,3] by [-3,3]

85. (a) $f(-2) > g(-2)$ **(b)** $f(2) < g(2)$
87. Horizontal shift left 3 units then vertical shift up 2 units

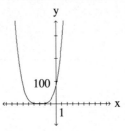

89. $f \circ g(-3) = -28$, $g \circ f(2) = 13$
91. $f \circ g(x) = \dfrac{x^2 + 6x + 17}{4}$, $g \circ f(x) = \dfrac{x^2 + 5}{2}$
93. (a) $g(x) = x - 5$ **(b)** $g(x) = x + 4$
95. $k \circ g \circ f \circ h(x)$ **97.** $g(x) = (x - 2)^2$, $h(x) = \dfrac{3}{x}$
99.

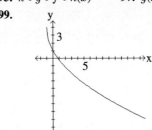

101. $x = y^2 - 2$; not a function

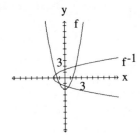

103. One-to-one; $f^{-1}(x) = \dfrac{x^2}{4} + 4$, with $x \geq 0$; func-

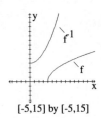

[-5,15] by [-5,15]

105. $0.75x + 1.10y \leq 0.999(x + y)$, $x \geq 0$, $y \geq 0$

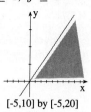

[-5,10] by [-5,20]

107. $s = -16t^2 + 70t + 200$
109. The portion of the graph in quadrant I
111. $0.39 < t < 3.98$ sec.

CHAPTER 4

SECTION 4.1

1.

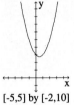

[-5,5] by [-2,10]

3.

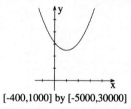

[-400,1000] by [-5000,30000]

5.

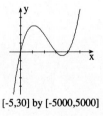

[-5,30] by [-5000,5000]

7.

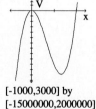

[-1000,3000] by
[-15000000,2000000]

9. Local min of 1 when $x = 2$ **11.** Local max of
2.25 when $x = 3.5$; local min of 0 when $x = 2$ or
$x = 5$ **13.** Zeros: $\pm\sqrt{10}$; local max of 10 when $x = 0$

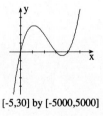

15. Zeros: 0, 10; local max of 0 when $x = 0$; local min of
-148.15 when $x = 6.67$

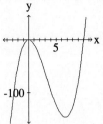

17. No real zeros; local max of 12.59 when $x = -0.41$; local
min of 11.91 when $x = -1.16$ and 3.51 when $x = 1.57$

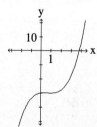

19. Zeros: 3.81; local max of -29.85 when $x = 0.33$; local
min of -30 when $x = 1$

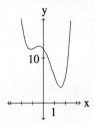

21. Zeros: -0.93; local max of 8.08 when $x = -0.44$;
local min of 2.59 when $x = 0.38$ and 0 when $x = -0.93$

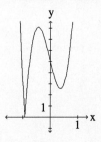

23. Zeros: 2.36; local max of 12.10 when $x = 0.79$; local
min of 11.90 when $x = 0.21$

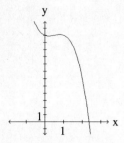

25. Increasing: $(1.5, \infty)$; decreasing: $(-\infty, 1.5)$
27. Increasing: $(-\infty, 0.67)$, $(2, \infty)$; decreasing: $(0.67, 2)$
29. Increasing: $(1.38, \infty)$; decreasing: $(-\infty, 1.38)$
31. Increasing: $(-\infty, 0.33)$, $(1, \infty)$; decreasing: $(0.33, 1)$
33. Reflection in the x-axis, vertical stretch by a factor of 2, horizontal shift left 3, then vertical shift up 1.
35. If $a > 0$, then increasing on $(-\infty, \infty)$; if $a < 0$, then decreasing on $(-\infty, \infty)$.   **37.** Dimensions: 262.5 by 525 ft; maximum area: $137{,}812.5 \text{ ft}^2$
39. Maximum height: 325 ft when $t = 1.25$ sec
41. Sides: 9.25 inches; maximum area: 171.13 in^2
43. $R(x) = (1900 + 20x)(450 - 15x), 0 \leq x \leq 30$, x an integer
45. $A(x) = \left(\frac{1}{4}x\right)^2 + \left(75 - \frac{1}{4}x\right)^2$
47. The portion of the graph for $0 \leq x \leq 300$
49. Let $x = 300$ or $x = 0$ and make only one frame.

51.

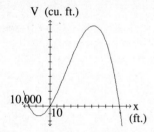

53. Dimensions: 30 by 70 ft; maximum volume: $63{,}000$ ft^3 **55.** The portion in quadrant I, $0 \leq x \leq 151$

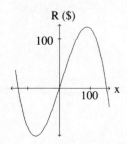

SECTION 4.2

1. Continuous   **3.** Continuous   **5.** Discontinuous; continuous on $[-4, 2)$, $(2, \infty)$; discontinous on $[-2, 3]$ or $(0, 5)$ (Answers vary.)   **7.** Discontinuous; continuous on $(-\infty, 2)$, $(2, 4)$, $(4, \infty)$; discontinous on $[0, 3]$ or $(3, 6)$ (Answers vary.)
9. Discontinuous at every integer value
11. No discontinuities
13. Discontinous at $x = 3$
15. $f(-10) = -42$ and $f(10) = 18$, thus $f(-10) \leq 5 \leq f(10)$. $c = 17/3$ **17.** $f(0) = -10$ and $f(10) = 230$, thus $f(0) \leq 50 \leq f(10)$. $c \approx 4.57$ **19.** $f(x) \to -\infty$ **21.** $f(x) \to 0$
23. $0 \leq x \leq 1019.62$ **25.** 676.52 lb; $1615.81
27. 0.87 ft^2 at $x = 1.73$ ft   **29.** $L(1.5) = 5$

SECTION 4.3

1. $q(x) = x - 1, r(x) = 2$
3. $q(x) = 2x^2 - 5x + 7/2, r(x) = -4.5$ **5.** $r = 3$
7. $r = 5$ **9.** Yes   **11.** Yes
13. $f(x) = (x - 3)(x - 2)$; real zeros: 2, 3
15. $f(x) = x(x - 3)(x + 3)$; real zeros: $\pm 3, 0$
17. $f(x) = (2x^2 - 5)(x^2 + 3)$; real zeros: $\pm\sqrt{5/2}$
19. $f(x) = (x + 3)(5x - 17)$; real zeros: $-3, 17/5$

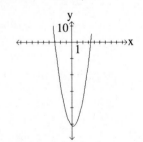

21. $f(x) = (x - 11)(x^2 + 1)$; real zeros: 11

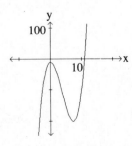

23. -4.97, -0.10, 2.07 **25.** -0.002
27. Maximum height: 36 ft when $t = 1.5$ sec
29. **(a)** 2   **(b)** 3   **(c)** 0.01, 0.91, 1.11

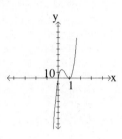

31. $f(x) = a(x - 2)^2$, $a \neq 0$ **33.** $f(x) = a(x + 1)^3$,
$a \neq 0$ or $f(x) = k(x + 1)(ax^2 + bx + c)$, $k \neq 0$, $b^2 < 4ac$
35. Equilibrium price: \$61.00; production level: 28,127
calculators   **37.** $x - 3$ or $x + 1$ **39.** **(a)** If
$50 = \frac{1}{2}xh$, then $h = \frac{100}{x}$ and $x^2 + (\frac{100}{x})^2 = (x + 2)^2$. Thus,
$10000 - 4x^3 - 4x^2 = 0$.   **(b)** 13.25

SECTION 4.4

1. ± 1, ± 2, ± 4 **3.** $\pm\frac{1}{2}$, ± 1, ± 2, $\pm\frac{5}{2}$, ± 5, ± 10
5. The only possible rational zeros are ± 1, but $f(-1) = -1$
and $f(1) = 3$.   **7.** The only possible rational zeros
are $\pm\frac{1}{2}$ and ± 1, but $f(-\frac{1}{2}) = \frac{5}{4}$, $f(\frac{1}{2}) = 1$, $f(-1) = 4$
and $f(1) = 2$.   **9.** Synthetic division by 2 leaves
a remainder of 0; $f(x) = (x - 2)(x + 4)(x - 1)$
11. Synthetic division by $-\frac{1}{2}$ leaves a remainder of 0;
$f(x) = (2x + 1)(x + \sqrt{3})(x - \sqrt{3})$
13. $q(x) = x^2 - 3$; $r(x) = 7$
15. $q(x) = x^3 - 3x^2 + 4x - 5$; $r(x) = 7$
17. No real zeros   **19.** 0
21. Rational: 1; irrational: $\dfrac{-5 \pm \sqrt{21}}{2}$;
$f(x) = (x - 1)(x^2 + 5x + 1)$

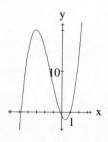

23. Rational: $7/3$; no irrational zeros;
$f(x) = (x - 7/3)(3x^2 + 6)$

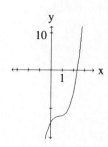

25. Rational: $-\frac{1}{2}$, 4; no irrational zeros
27. Rational: ± 3, $\frac{1}{2}$; no irrational zeros
29. Rational: ± 2; no irrational zeros
31. Upper bound: 4, lower bound: -2 (Answers vary.)
33. Upper bound: 2, lower bound: -3 (Answers vary.)
35. No rational zeros; irrational: 0.86, -1.11
37. $D = (-\infty, \infty)$; problem situation: $0 \leq d \leq 172$

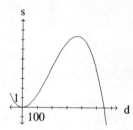

39. 3.35 ft deflection at 172 ft
41. 460 turkeys in 300 days   **43.** Answers will vary.
Example: Population increases until the food supply is
depleted.
45. Reflection in the x-axis

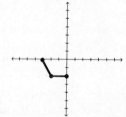

47. Vertical stretch by a factor of 2, reflection in the y-axis,
then vertical shift down 1 unit

49. Reflection in the x-axis, horizontal shift left 1 unit, then vertical shift up 2 units

51. Reflection in the x-axis

53. $-f(3 - x) = -f(-(x - 3))$; reflection in the x-axis, reflection in the y-axis, and horizontal shift right 3 units.

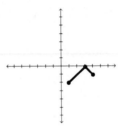

55. $-1 + 2f(1 - x) = -1 + 2f(-(x - 1))$; reflection in the y-axis, vertical stretch by a factor of 2, horizontal shift right 1 unit, then vertical shift down 1 unit

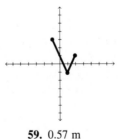

57. 0.653 m   **59.** 0.57 m

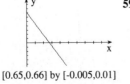

[0.65,0.66] by [-0.005,0.01]

SECTION 4.5

1. $8 - 3i$ **3.** $7 + 4i$ **5.** $1 + i$ **7.** $9 + 8i$
9. $2 + 3i$ **11.** $-3 - 4i$ **13.** $\frac{2}{5} - \frac{1}{5}i$ **15.** $\frac{3}{5} + \frac{4}{5}i$
17. $\frac{1}{2} - \frac{7}{2}i$
19. 2 nonreal complex zeros
21. 1 real zero, 2 nonreal complex zeros
23. 2 real zeros, 2 nonreal complex zeros
25. Integer: 1; nonreal complex: $\dfrac{-1 \pm \sqrt{19}i}{2}$
27. Integer: ± 1; nonreal complex: $\dfrac{-1 \pm \sqrt{23}i}{2}$
29. $f(1 + i) = 3(1 + i)^3 - 7(1 + i)^2 + 8(1 + i) - 2 = 0$;
zeros: $1 \pm i$, $1/3$ **31.** $f(x) = (x - 1)(x - i)(x + i)$
33. $f(x) = (x - 1)\left(x + \dfrac{1 + \sqrt{31}i}{4}\right)\left(x + \dfrac{1 - \sqrt{31}i}{4}\right)$
35. $a(x^2 - 4x + 13)$, $a \ne 0$
37. $a(x^3 - 5x^2 + 8x - 6)$, $a \ne 0$
39. $f(x) = k(x + 2)(x - (a + bi))(x - (a - bi))$, for k, a, $b \ne 0$.   **41.** $a(x^4 + 4x^3 - x^2 - 6x + 18)$, $a \ne 0$
43. 3.78 ft $(0 \le h \le 10)$ **45.** The ball will completely submerge since it is more dense than the liquid.   **47.** 2, $-1 \pm \sqrt{3}i$
49. $z \cdot \bar{z} = (a + bi)(a - bi) = a^2 - abi + abi - b^2i^2 = a^2 + b^2$

SECTION 4.6

1. $(-\sqrt{2}, 0) \cup (0, \sqrt{2})$ **3.** $(-1, 0) \cup (0, 1)$
5. $(-\infty, 0) \cup (0, 1)$ **7.** $(-1, 0) \cup (1, \infty)$ **9.** $(-2, \infty)$
11. $(-1, \infty)$ **13.** $(-\infty, 2)$ **15.** $(1, \infty)$
17. $(-1, 0) \cup (1, \infty)$ **19.** $[-1, 1] \cup [4, \infty)$
21.

[-5,10] by [-20,20]

23. $(0, 0.55] \cup [6.79, 7.50)$ **25.** $0 < x < 21.50$
27. $0 \le x \le 167.50$

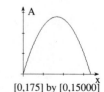

[0,175] by [0,15000]

29. From 30 to 586 customers **31.** (

(b)

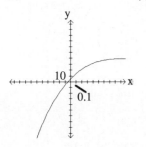

(c)

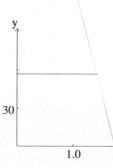

11. Real zeros: -1.26, 5; local max of -9.49 when $x = -0.35$ and -68.45 when $x = 3.71$; local min of -10.47 when $x = 0.39$;

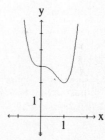

13. Answers vary: 6

33. No local extrema; real zero: 0.72; decreasing: $(-\infty, \infty)$

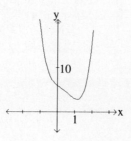

..s, local min of 2 when $x = 1$

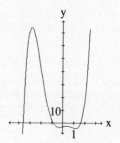

35. Local min of 2.84 when $x = 1.15$; no real zeros; decreasing: $(-\infty, 1.15)$; increasing: $(1, 15, \infty)$

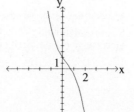

9. Real zeros: -3.60, -0.88, 1.63; local max of 74.12 when $x = -2.85$ and -2.52 when $x = 0.37$; local min of -3.43 when $x = -0.32$ and -4.33 when $x = 1.19$

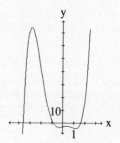

$c < 10$

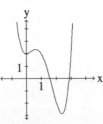

15. Answers vary: $-11.06 < c < -4.12$

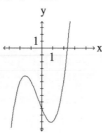

17. Answers vary: $2 < c < 2.35$

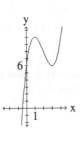

19. Real zeros: $-5.81, 1.04, 6.27$; local max of 211.00 when $x = -3.00$; local min of -132.00 when $x = 4.00$

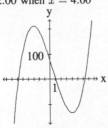

21. Real zeros: -3.63; local max of 80.12 when $x = -2.85$ and 3.48 when $x = 0.37$; local min of 2.57 when $x = -0.32$ and 1.67 when $x = 1.19$

$[-5,5]$ by $[-20,90]$

23. $D = (-\infty, \infty)$; $R = (-\infty, \infty)$; no points of discontinuity   **25.** $D = (-\infty, \infty)$; $R = $ the integers; discontinuous when x is an integer

27. $D = (-\infty, \infty)$; $R = (-1, \infty)$; discontinuous at $x = -2, 0$ **29.** $f(x) \to -\infty$ **31.** $f(x) \to 2$

33. $q(x) = 3x - 8$, $r(x) = 23$ **35.** $r(x) = 18$

37. $f(3) = 0$ so $x - 3$ is a factor.   **39.** $0, \pm\sqrt{8}$

41. $f(x) = (x - 2)(x^2 + 2x + 3)$; real zeros: 2

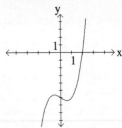

43. 5

45. No real zeros because the graph has no x-intercepts.

47. (a) For $m = -3$: 3 real zeros; 2 local extrema; increasing: $(-\infty, -0.5)$, $(0.5, \infty)$; decreasing: $(-0.5, 0.5)$

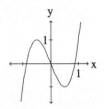

(b) For $m = -2$: 3 real zeros; 2 local extrema; increasing: $(-\infty, -0.41)$, $(0.41, \infty)$; decreasing: $(-0.41, 0.41)$

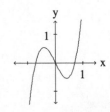

(c) For $m = 0$: 1 real zero; no local extrema; increasing: $(-\infty, \infty)$

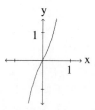

(d) For $m = 2$: 1 real zero; no local extrema; increasing: $(-\infty, \infty)$

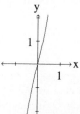

(e) For $m = 4$: 1 real zero; no local extrema; increasing: $(-\infty, \infty)$

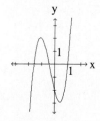

49. $k = -2$ **51.** Integer: ± 3 **53.** Possible: ± 1, $\pm\frac{1}{3}$, $\pm\frac{2}{3}$, ± 2; rational zero: 1; irrational zeros: $\dfrac{-3 \pm \sqrt{3}}{3}$

55. Rational zero: -2; irrational zeros: $\dfrac{-5 \pm \sqrt{41}}{2}$

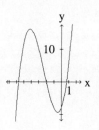

57. Upper bound: 1; lower bound: 0 (Answers will vary.)
59. $g(-3) = 0$ so $x + 3$ is a factor.   **61.** $2 + 11i$
63. $1 + 0i$ **65.** 1 real and 2 complex zeros
67. $a(x^2 - 2x + 5)$, $a \neq 0$
69. $a(x - 2)^2(x^2 - 6x + 10)$, $a \neq 0$
71. $D = (-\infty, \infty)$; problem situation: $0 \leq t \leq 24$
73. Approximately 6:46a.m. ($t = 0.76$) and 12:22a.m. ($t = 18.37$)   **75.** $29°$ at 5:01a.m ($t = 23.02$)
77.

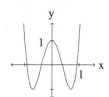

79. (a) Exer. 76: local min of -1 when $x = 0.5$; local max of 1 when $x = -0.5$ **(b)** Exer. 77: local min of -1 when $x = \pm 0.71$; local max of 1 when $x = 0$ **(c)** Exer. 78: local min of -1 when $x = -0.31$ and $x = 0.81$; local max of 1 when $x = -0.81$ and $x = 0.31$
81. (a)   **(b)**

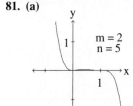 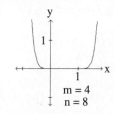

(c)

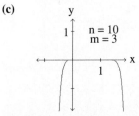

83. 82.61 or 233.40 ft from the west piling
85. The beam density is not uniform along its length.
87.

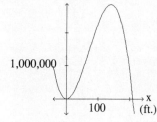

89. 70 ft   **91.**

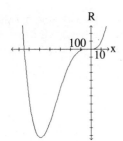

93. No maximum revenue
95. 182 pheasants in 111.65 days   **97.** Answers will vary. Example: Population increases until the food supply decreases.

CHAPTER 5

SECTION 5.1

1. $D = (-\infty, -1) \cup (-1, 2) \cup (2, \infty)$
3. $D = (-\infty, -3) \cup (-3, 1) \cup (1, \infty)$
5. $D = (-\infty, -1) \cup (-1, 1) \cup (1, \infty)$
7. $D = (-\infty, 2 - \sqrt{5}) \cup (2 - \sqrt{5}, 2 + \sqrt{5}) \cup (2 + \sqrt{5}, \infty)$
9. $D = (-\infty, -1) \cup (-1, 0) \cup (0, 1) \cup (1, \infty)$
11. HA: $y = 0$ **13.** HA: $y = -4$ **15.** HA: $y = -12$
17. HA: $y = 0$; VA: $x = -1$
19. HA: $y = 4$; VA: $x = -1$
21. HA: $y = 0$; VA: $x = 4$
23. Horizontal shift right 3 units; HA: $y = 0$; VA: $x = 3$

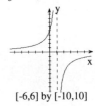

25. Vertical stretch by a factor of 2, reflection in the x-axis, horizontal shift left 5 units; HA: $y = 0$; VA: $x = -5$

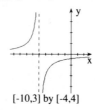

[-10,3] by [-4,4]

27. Horizontal shift left 1 unit, vertical shift down 3 units; HA: $y = -3$; VA: $x = -1$

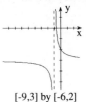

[-9,3] by [-6,2]

29. Vertical stretch by a factor of 5, reflection in the x-axis, horizontal shift right 1 unit; HA: $y = 0$; VA: $x = 1$

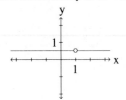

[-6,6] by [-10,10]

31. HA: $y = 3$; VA: $x = -2$
33. HA: $y = 2$; VA: $x = 3$
35. HA: $y = 1$; VA: $x = -4$ **37.** $f(x) \to 0$
39. $g(x) \to 4$ **41.** $D = (-\infty, 1) \cup (1, \infty)$; $R = \{\frac{1}{2}\}$;
HA: $y = \frac{1}{2}$; VA: none; removable discontinuity at $x = 1$

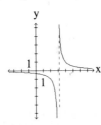

43. Vertical stretch by a factor of 2, horizontal shift right 1 unit, reflection in the x-axis, then a vertical shift up 3 units
45. Vertical stretch by a factor of $\frac{bc-ad}{c^2}$, horizontal shift of $-\frac{d}{c}$ units, followed by a vertical shift of $\frac{a}{c}$ units
47. $x \geq 80$ ounces
49. 60 ounces of 60% solution, 40 ounces of 10% solution
51. $D = (-\infty, -\frac{d}{c}) \cup (-\frac{d}{c}, \infty)$; $R = (-\infty, \frac{a}{c}) \cup (\frac{a}{c}, \infty)$, for $c \neq 0$

SECTION 5.2

1. $D = (-\infty, -1) \cup (-1, 1) \cup (1, \infty)$
3. $D = (-\infty, 0) \cup (0, \infty)$
5. $D = (-\infty, -1) \cup (-1, 1) \cup (1, \infty)$
7. $D = (-\infty, -1) \cup (-1, 3/2) \cup (3/2, \infty)$ **9.** $g(x) = \frac{1}{x}$
11. $g(x) = 3$ **13.** $g(x) = x$ **15.** VA: $x = 3$;

HA: $y = 0$; end behavior (EB) model: $g(x) = \frac{2}{x}$

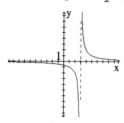

17. VA: none; HA: $y = 0$; EB model: $g(x) = \frac{1}{x}$

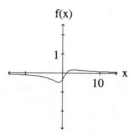

f(x)

19.

x	-1	-10	-100	-1000	-10,000
y	0.50	-0.11	-0.01	-0.001	-0.0001

21. $f(x) \to 0$　　**23.** $D = (-\infty, 0) \cup (0, \infty)$;
$R = [-0.25, \infty)$; VA: $x = 0$; HA: $y = 0$; EB model:
$g(x) = \frac{1}{x}$

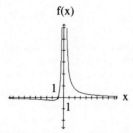

f(x)

25. $D = (-\infty, -1) \cup (-1, 1) \cup (0, \infty)$;
$R = (-\infty, -0.5) \cup (-0.5, 0) \cup (0, \infty)$; VA: $x = 1$; HA:
$y = 0$; removable discontinuity at $x = -1$; EB model:
$g(x) = \frac{1}{x}$

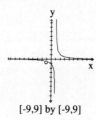

[-9,9] by [-9,9]

27. $D = (-\infty, -3.30) \cup (-3.30, 0.30) \cup (0.30, \infty)$;
$R = (-\infty, 0.12] \cup [0.65, \infty)$; VA: $x = -3.30$ and $x = 0.30$;
HA: $y = 0$; EB model: $g(x) = \frac{1}{x}$

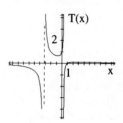

T(x)

29.

x	3	2.1	2.01	2.001	2.0001
$f(x)$	21	38.82	308.08	3008.01	30,008.00
$g(x)$	3	30	300	3000	30,000

31.

x	1	10	100	1000	10,000
$f(x)$	-1	200.38	20,000.03	2,000,000.00	200,000,000
$g(x)$	-3	0.38	0.03	0.003	0.0003

33. $f(x) \to \infty$　　**35.** $f(x) \to \infty$

37. End behavior asymptote (EBA): $y = x - 4$; VA: $x = -2$

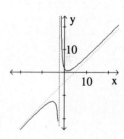

39. EBA: $y = x^2 + x + 1$; removable discontinuity at $x = 1$

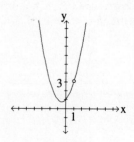

41. EBA: $y = x - 6$; VA: $x = -3$

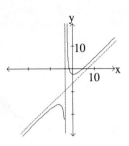

43. EBA: $y = x^3 + 2x^2 - 3x + 1$; removable discontinuity at $x = 5/2$.

[-5,5] by [-10,35]

45. $D = (-\infty, -1) \cup (-1, \infty)$;
$R = (-\infty, -9.66] \cup [1.66, \infty)$; VA: $x = -1$; EB model:
$g(x) = x$; EBA: $y = x - 3$

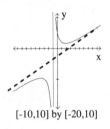

[-10,10] by [-20,10]

47. $D = (-\infty, -\sqrt[3]{3}) \cup (-\sqrt[3]{3}, \infty)$; $R = (-\infty, 2) \cup (2, \infty)$;
VA: $x = -\sqrt[3]{3}$; HA: $y = 2$; EB model: $g(x) = 2$

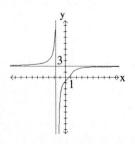

49. $D = (-\infty, \infty)$; $R = [0.18, \infty)$; EB model: $g(x) = x^2$;
EBA: $y = x^2 - 6$

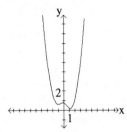

51. Increasing: $(-\infty, -1.00)$ $(1.00, \infty)$; decreasing:
$(-1.00, 0), (0, 1.00)$ **53.** Increasing: $(-2.27, -1.67)$
$(-1.67, -0.84)$, $(0.61, \infty)$; decreasing:
$(-\infty, -2.27)$, $(-0.84, 0.61)$ **55.** Local min of 0.92
when $x = -0.18$; increasing: $(-0.18, 0.5)$, $(0.5, \infty)$;
decreasing: $(-\infty, -0.18)$; zero: $x = 1.75$; EB model:
$g(x) = 0.5x^2$ **57.** Local min of 0.10 when
$x = -0.69$ and $x = 0$; local max of -5.28 when
$x = -3.42$ and 0.10 when $x = -0.40$; increasing:
$(-\infty, -3.42)$, $(-0.69, -0.40)$, $(0, \infty)$; decreasing:
$(-3.42, -2.42)$, $(-2.42, -0.69)$, $(-0.40, 0)$; no
zeros; EB model: $g(x) = 2x$ **59.** Local min of
3.32 when $x = -1.50$ and 180.28 when $x = 5.83$;
local max of -0.92 when $x = 0.75$; increasing:
$(-1.50, -1)$, $(-1, 0.75)$, $(5.83, \infty)$; decreasing:
$(-\infty, -1.50)$, $(0.75, 4)$, $(4, 5.83)$; no zeros; EB
model: $g(x) = 2x^2$ **61.** EB model: $g(x) = 3x^3$
EBA: $y = 3x^3 + 7x^2 + 3x - 30$

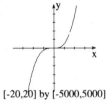

[-20,20] by [-5000,5000]

63. $P(x) = \dfrac{2x^2 + 750}{x}$; dimensions: 19.365 by 19.365 ft
perimeter: 77.46 ft

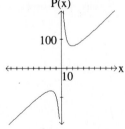

65. 102.16 ounces

SECTION 5.3

1. -3.5 **3.** $\dfrac{11 \pm \sqrt{73}}{8}$ **5.** 1

7. $-1, 0, 1$ **9.** $\dfrac{1 \pm \sqrt{13}}{6}$ **11.** $(-\infty, \frac{11}{4}) \cup (3, \infty)$

13. $(-\infty, \frac{7}{2}) \cup (\frac{38}{9}, \infty)$ **15.** $(-6.5, -4)$

17. $(-\infty, -1] \cup [1, \infty)$

19. $(-\infty, -2) \cup (-1, 5)$ **21.** $-2.04, 1.44$

23. $[-1.66, -1.00] \cup (3, \infty)$ **25.** Zeros: ± 1; y-int. at $(0, -1)$; VA: $x = -1.62$, $x = 0.62$; EBA: $g(x) = x^2 - x$

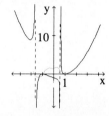

27. Zero: 1.46; y-int. at $(0, 5)$ VA: $x = -0.30$, $x = 3.30$; EBA: $g(x) = x^3 + 3x^2 + 9x + 30$. More than one view is needed for a complete graph.

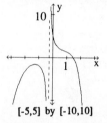

[-5,5] by [-10,10]

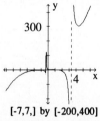

[-7,7,] by [-200,400]

29. VA; $x = 0$, $x = -43$; HA: $y = 0$; zero: -10.44

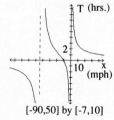

[-90,50] by [-7,10]

31. 20.45 mph   **33.**

[0,5] by [0,3]

35. $R(x) = \dfrac{2.3x}{2.3 + x}$ **37.** 6.52 ohms

39. $r > 0$

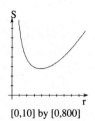

[0,10] by [0,800]

41. $P(L) = 2(L + \frac{900}{L})$ **43.** $L = 30.00$ ft; $P = 120.00$ ft

SECTION 5.4

1. $(1, \infty)$ **3.** $(0, 16)$ **5.** Vertical stretch by a factor of 2, reflection in the x-axis, horizontal shift left 3 units   **7.** Horizontal shift right 5 units, vertical shift down 3 units   **9.** Vertical stretch by a factor of 2, horizontal stretch by a factor of 3, horizontal shift right $5/3$ units   **11.**   **13.**

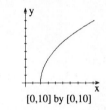

[0,10] by [0,10]

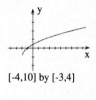

[-4,10] by [-3,4]

15.   **17.**

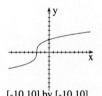

[-10,10] by [-10,10]

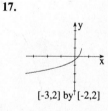

[-3,2] by [-2,2]

19. 38 **21.** 4.5 **23.** $\pm\sqrt{28}$ or ± 5.29

25. $\dfrac{3 + \sqrt{5}}{2}$ or 2.62 **27.** $\dfrac{161 \pm 33}{32}$ or $4.00, 6.06$

29. $(33, \infty)$ **31.** 2.84 **33.** $(-1.30, 1.30)$

35.   **37.**

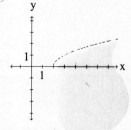

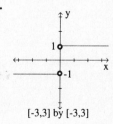

[-3,3] by [-3,3]

39. $f(x) \to \infty$ as $|x| \to \infty$ **41.** $4 - 2\sqrt{3}$ or 0.54
43. Minimum vertical distance of 21.00 when $x = 14.00$
45. $T(x) = \frac{\sqrt{x^2+400}}{30} + \frac{60-x}{50}$; $T(0) = 1.87$ hours to go to
B by boat then drive to C. $T(60) = 2.11$ hours to go to C
by boat.   **47.** Least amount of time is 1.73 hours if she
boats to a point 15 miles from B.   **49.** 2.34 ft
51. $r = 6.35$ ft, $h = 9.00$ ft

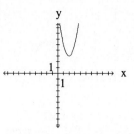

Chapter 5 Review

1. $D = (-\infty, -2) \cup (-2, 1) \cup (1, \infty)$
3. $D = (-\infty, -1) \cup (-1, 3) \cup (3, \infty)$
5. $D = (-\infty, \frac{3-\sqrt{5}}{2}) \cup (\frac{3-\sqrt{5}}{2}, \frac{3+\sqrt{5}}{2}) \cup (\frac{3+\sqrt{5}}{2}, \infty)$
7. VA: $x = -5$; HA: $y = 0$

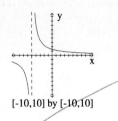

[-10,10] by [-10,10]

9. VA: $x = 3$; HA: $y = 5$

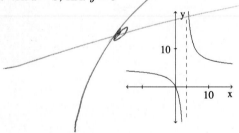

11. $D = (-\infty, 3) \cup (3, \infty)$; $R = (-\infty, 5) \cup (5, \infty)$
13. $f(x) \to 1$ **15.** Vertical stretch by a factor of 5,
horizontal shift right 2 units; HA: $y = 0$; VA: $x = 2$

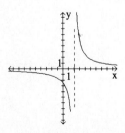

17. Vertical stretch by a factor of 2, horizontal shift right 2
units, vertical shift up 3 units;

19. $D = (-\infty, -4) \cup (-4, 5) \cup (5, \infty)$; $R = (-\infty, 0] \cup (3, \infty)$;
VA: $x = -4$, $x = 5$; EB asymptote: $g(x) = 3$; real zero: 0

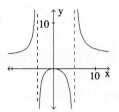

21. $D = (-\infty, -\sqrt[3]{2}) \cup (-\sqrt[3]{2}, \infty)$; $R = (-\infty, \infty)$ VA:
$x = -\sqrt[3]{2}$; EB asymptote: $g(x) = 2$; real zeros: -2.59,
-0.16, 1.24

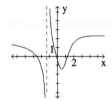

23. Increasing: $(-\infty, 0), (0, \infty)$
25. Local min of 3.47 when $x = -0.89$

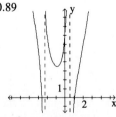

27. EB model: $g(x) = x$; VA: $x = -2$; no zeros;
local min of 2 when $x = 3$; local max of -18 when
$x = -7$; increasing: $(-\infty, -7)$, $(3, \infty)$; decreasing:
$(-7, -2)$, $(-2, 3)$

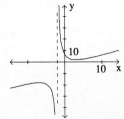

29. EB model: $g(x) = x^2$; EB asymptote: $g(x) = x^2 + 2x + 4$; removable discontinuity at $x = 2$ **31.** EB model: $g(x) = x^3$; EB asymptote: $g(x) = x^3 - 3x^2 - 5x + 7$ **33.** $f(x) \to \infty$

35. $f(x) \to -\infty$ **37.** $\dfrac{6 \pm \sqrt{6}}{2}$ or 1.78, 4.22

39. No real solutions **41.** $(-4, -2] \cup [2, \infty)$
43. $(-\infty, 2) \cup (3.25, \infty)$ **45.** No real solutions
47. $(-\sqrt[3]{7}, 2.39)$ **49.** 2 **51.** 3 **53.** The graph of $y_1 = \sqrt{x+5}$ is below the graph of $y_2 = 5 - \dfrac{x}{3}$ for $x < 5$. Solution: $(5.35, \infty)$

[-10,16] by [-5,10]

55. Reflection in the y-axis, vertical stretch by a factor of 2, horizontal shift right 5 units, then a vertical shift down 3 units

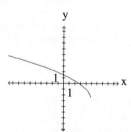

57. (a) $p(x) = 2x + \frac{1000}{x}$ (b) VA: $x = 0$; EB asymptote: $g(x) = 2x$

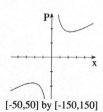

[-50,50] by [-150,150]

(c) Dimensions: 22.36 ft by 22.36 ft; minimum perimeter: 89.44 ft **59.** $\frac{22}{9}$ ft/sec **61.** 15.35 sec

63. $14{,}137.17$ in^3 **65.** $C(x) = \dfrac{75 + x}{150 + x}$

67. At least 190.91 ounces **69.** $T(x) = \frac{\sqrt{x^2+225}}{25} + \frac{55-x}{40}$; $T(0) = 1.975$ hours to go to B by boat then drive to C. $T(60) = 2.28$ hours to go to C by boat.
71. Toward a point 12 miles from B
73. $T(x) = \frac{11}{x} + \frac{45}{x+41}$ **75.** 34.40 mph

CHAPTER 6

SECTION 6.1

1. $3^0 = 5^0 = 10^0 = 1$

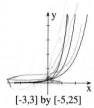

[-3,3] by [-5,25]

3. a and c **5.** Vertical shift down 4 units
7. Horizontal shift right 3 units **9.** Horizontal shift left 1 unit, vertical shift up 7 units
11. $x < 0$

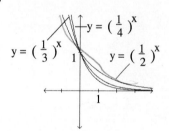

13. $x > 0$ (See graph for exercise 11.) **15.** a and c
17. b and c
19. **21.**

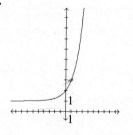
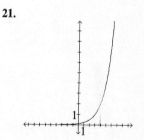

23.

25. $D = (-\infty, \infty)$; $R = (1, \infty)$ **27.** 4 **29.** -4

31. $D = (-\infty, \infty)$ **33.** $D = (-\infty, \infty)$

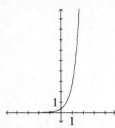   

35. Increasing: $(-\infty, \infty)$; no local extrema; $R = (0, \infty)$
37. Decreasing: $(-\infty, -0.91)$; increasing: $(-0.91, \infty)$; local min of -0.33 when $x = -0.91$; $R = [-0.33, \infty)$
39. Decreasing: $(-\infty, -0.85)$, $(0.85, \infty)$; increasing: $(-0.85, 0.85)$; local min of -0.52 when $x = -0.85$, local max of 0.52 when $x = 0.85$; $R = [-0.52, 0.52]$
41.

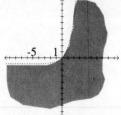

43. $(-0.77, 0.59)$, $(2, 4)$, $(4, 16)$ **45.** HA: $y = e^2$
(a)   **(b)**

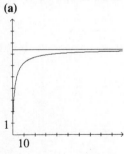

47. (a) 5000 bacteria   **(b)** 10,000 bacteria
(c) $2500(2)^{t/3}$ bacteria   **49.** 15.97 hours
51.

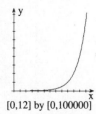

[0,12] by [0,100000]

53. Answers vary.   **55.** $15,689$ in 1915; $39,381$ in 1940
57. $P = 6.58(0.5)^{t/14}$; after 38.05 days   **59.** $\frac{1}{2}S$ grams; $\frac{1}{4}S$ grams; $\frac{1}{2^{t/1.5}}S$ grams   **61.** 2^{40} grams

SECTION 6.2

1. $I = \$200$; $S = \$1450$ **3.** \$641.13   **5.** \$981.79
7. \$33,492.13   **9.** \$36,374.39   **11.** \$10,382.24
13. 8% compounded annually   **15.** Ymax: 1600
(Answers will vary.)

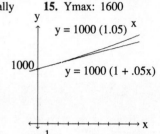

17. Simple interest: $y = 1000(1 + .05x)$; compound interest: $y = 1000(1.05)^x$; APR: 5%
19. $r = 0.125$ or 12.5%   **21.** \$1096.49   **23.** \$729.73
25. 13.54   **27.** \$669.11   **29.** \$674.43
31. \$674.93   **33.** \$7839.96   **35.** \$7877.60
37. 6.63 years
39. $r = 0.083$ or 8.3%   **41.** \$4161.39
43. $r = 0.043$ or 4.3%; Problem situation: A \$1500 investment earns interest compounded continuously. Determine the annual interest rate if the value of the investment is \$2300 after 10 years.   **45.** 17.62 years
47. \$0.46   **49.** \$94,260.33

SECTION 6.3

1. 6% compounded quarterly
3. 7.2% compounded daily   **5.** \$36,013.70
7. \$749.35
9. 9%; 4 payments per year   **11.** 12%; 12 payments per year (Alternate: 1%; 1 payment per year)
13.

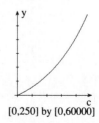

[0,250] by [0,60000]

15. $230.43   **17.** $884.61   **19.** $1028.61
21. 22 years 2 months   **23.** 11%; 4 payments per year
25. 9%; 12 payments per year (Alternate: 3%; 4 payments
per year)   **27.** The values of y in (a) and (b) represent
the present value of the loan based on x monthly payments at
8% APR and 12% APR, respectively.   **29.** $t = 69.66$, so
a $10,000$ loan at 12% annual rate with monthly payments of
$200 will be paid off in 70 months.   **31.** 35.71%
33. $0 \le t \le 6$ **35.**

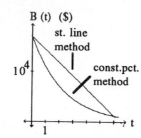

37.

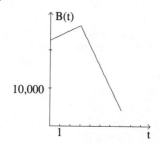

39. If $r < 0$, then $C(1 - r)^n = C(1 + |r|)^n$ where $|r| \ge 0$.
Then, for $r > 0$, $C(1 + |r|)^n = C(1 + r)^n = S$. Finally,
$1 + r > 1$ so $(1 + r)^n > 1^n = 1$ and $S = C(1 + r)^n > C$ for
all $n \ge 1$.

SECTION 6.4

1. 2   **3.** 3   **5.** -4 **7.** No solution
9.   **11.**

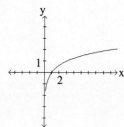 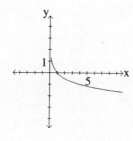

13. 81   **15.** 5   **17.** $\sqrt[9]{81}$ **19.** ± 3
21. $\log_7 y = x$ **23.** $\log_2(x + y) = 8$ **25.** $3^5 = x$
27. $3^{-2} = \dfrac{x}{y}$
29. $3 \log_2 x + 2 \log_2 y$, $y > 0$ and $x > 0$
31. $2 \log_a x - 3 \log_a y$, $x > 0$ and $y > 0$
33. $\log 5000 + \log x + 360 \log(1 + r)$, $r > -1$ and $x > 0$
35.   **37.**

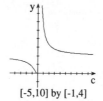

[-5,10] by [-1,4]   [-2,20] by [-0.5,2]

39. As $|x| \to \infty$, $f(x) \to 1$ **41.** As $x \to \infty$, $f(x) \to 1$
43. 20.22 years   **45.** 15,689 in 1915; 39,381 in 1940
47. After 117.48 days   **49.** The first set has a power rule
$y = ax^b$ with $a = 8.10$, $b = -0.115$ **51.** 5.45
53. The equations have the form $S = P(1 + r)^t$ where S is
the total in the account, P the principal, r the annual interest
rate. This is the formula for an investment with interest
compounded annually for t years.   **55.** 9.93 years
57. $m = 1.51$; $b = -21.80$

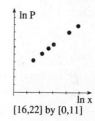

[16,22] by [0,11]

59. $P \approx 94,000$ days (Actual period is 90,520 days.)
61. $P(x) = 49.90 x^{0.25}$

SECTION 6.5

1. $[-2, 10]$ by $[-3, 3]$; $D = (0, \infty)$; $R = (-\infty, \infty)$

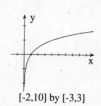

[-2,10] by [-3,3]

3. $[-2,5]$ by $[-1,5]$; $D = (0,\infty)$; $R = (-\infty,\infty)$

21.

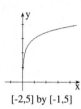

23.

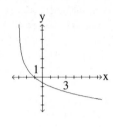

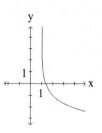

5. $[-1,5]$ by $[-1,10]$; $D = (0,\infty)$; $R = (-\infty,\infty)$

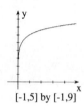

[-1,5] by [-1,9]

25.

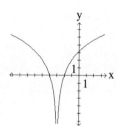

27.

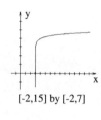

[-2,15] by [-2,7]

7.

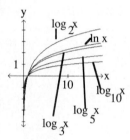

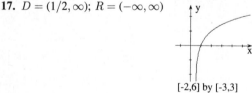

29. $(1,\infty)$ **31.** $(1,\infty)$
33. As $x \to \infty$, $f(x) \to \infty$; $f(x)$ not defined in $(-\infty,0]$
35. As $x \to \infty$, $f(x) \to 0$; $f(x)$ not defined in $(-\infty,0]$
37. Decreasing: $(0,0.61)$, increasing: $(0.61,\infty)$; local min of -0.18 when $x = 0.61$

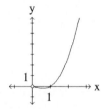

9. Horizontal shift left 5 units, vertical shift down 1 unit;
VA: $x = -5$ **11.** Reflection in the y-axis, horizontal
shift right 2 units; VA: $x = 2$ **13.** Horizontal shift left
$3/2$ units, vertical shift up $\ln 2 + 2$ units; VA: $x = -3/2$
15. Reflection in the y-axis, horizontal shift right 4 units,
reflection in the x-axis, vertical shift down 2 units; VA: $x = 4$
17. $D = (1/2,\infty)$; $R = (-\infty,\infty)$

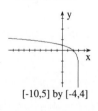

[-2,6] by [-3,3]

19. $D = (-\infty,3)$; $R = (-\infty,\infty)$

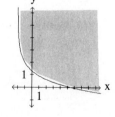

[-10,5] by [-4,4]

39. Decreasing: $(2.72,\infty)$, increasing: $(0,2.72)$; local max
of 0.37 when $x = 2.72$

41.

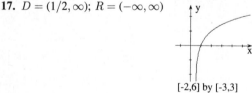

43. $(-2.02, 2.09)$, $(2.23, 2.98)$ **45.** $f(x) > g(x)$ in $(-\infty, 2.48) \cup (3, \infty)$; $f(x) = g(x)$ when $x = 2.48$ or 3; $f(x) < g(x)$ in $(2.48, 3)$ **47.** $f(x) > g(x)$ in $(0, 10)$; $f(x) = g(x)$ when $x = 10$; $f(x) < g(x)$ in $(10, \infty)$; $g(x) = x^x$ usually not defined for $x < 0$

49. $f(x) > g(x)$ in $(1, \infty)$; $g(x)$ not defined in $(-\infty, 1]$

51. Graph $y = \dfrac{\ln 4}{\ln x}$ or $y = \dfrac{\log 4}{\log x}$

53. $6 = \log\left(\dfrac{a_1}{T}\right) + B = \log a_1 - \log T + B$ and $4 = \log\left(\dfrac{a_2}{T}\right) + B = \log a_2 - \log T + B$. Subtraction yields $2 = \log a_1 - \log a_2 = \log\left(\dfrac{a_1}{a_2}\right)$. Then, $10^2 = \dfrac{a_1}{a_2}$ and $100 a_2 = a_1$.   **55.** $I(x) = 12(10)^{-0.00235x}$ **57.** 10.20 lumens   **59.** Line: $\log y = 0.48x + 0.54$

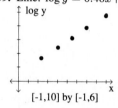
[-1,10] by [-1,6]

61. $\log(f(x)) = \log(ab^x) = \log a + x \log b = (\log b)x + \log a$. Thus, $m = \log b$ and $y_0 = \log a$.

63. (a)

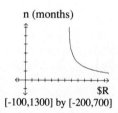
[-100,1300] by [-200,700]

(b) \$708.14   **(c)** 231 payments or 19 years 3 months

SECTION 6.6

1. 10,000   **3.** 5.25   **5.** 97   **7.** 16
9. 3   **11.** $\dfrac{e^3}{2}$ **13.** 1   **15.** $D_1 = (0, \infty)$, $R_1 = (-\infty, \infty)$; $D_2 = (-\infty, 0) \cup (0, \infty)$, $R_2 = (-\infty, \infty)$
17. $D_1 = D_2 = (0, \infty)$, $R_1 = R_2 = (-\infty, \infty)$
19. $\dfrac{\log 4.1}{\log 1.06}$ **21.** $\dfrac{\log 18.4}{\log 1.09}$ **23.** $\dfrac{\log(6 + \sqrt{37})}{\log 2}$
25. (a) 24.22   **(b)** -23.26 **(c)** 33.79   **(d)** 10.26
(e) 3.59   **(f)** ± 2.54 **27.** $D = (-\infty, \infty)$;

$R = [0, \infty)$; local min of 0 when $x = 0$; local max of 0.54 when $x = 2.00$; increasing: $(0, 2.00)$; decreasing: $(-\infty, 0)$, $(2.00, \infty)$

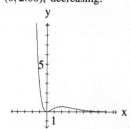

29. $D = (-\infty, \infty)$; $R = [0.67, \infty)$; local min of 0.67 when $x = 0$; increasing: $(0, \infty)$; decreasing: $(-\infty, 0)$

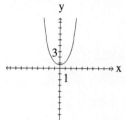

31. $D = (-\infty, -2) \cup (0, \infty)$; $R = (-\infty, 0) \cup (0, \infty)$; no local extrema; increasing: $(-\infty, -2)$, $(0, \infty)$

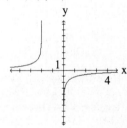

33. $(-1, 5)$ **35.** $(-\infty, -20.09]$ **37.** 0.41, 0.93
39. -0.94, 1.08, 58.77

41.

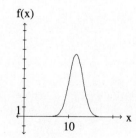

43.

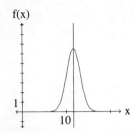

45. 9.69×10^{-4} lb/in^2 **47.** $r > 0$ **49.** 9.89%
51. $0 \le t \le 6$

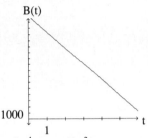

53. $f_{n-1}(x) = \dfrac{x^{n-1}}{(n-1)!} + \dfrac{x^{n-2}}{(n-2)!} + \ldots + x + 1$. Thus

$f_n(x) = \dfrac{x^n}{n!} + \dfrac{x^{n-1}}{(n-1)!} + \dfrac{x^{n-2}}{(n-2)!} + \ldots + x + 1 =$

$\dfrac{x^n}{n!} + f_{n-1}(x)$.   **55.** $(-1.32, 1.17)$

Chapter 6 Review

1.

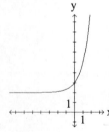

3.

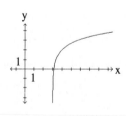

5.

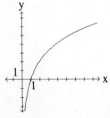

7. 5
9. $D = (-2, 2) \cup (2, \infty)$; $R = (-\infty, \infty)$; no local extrema

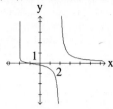

11. $D = (-\infty, 0) \cup (3, \infty)$; $R = (-\infty, 0) \cup (0, \infty)$; no local extrema

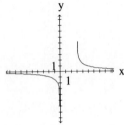

13. Decreasing: $(-\infty, \infty)$; no local extrema   **15.** 3
17. 3   **19.** $12\log(1 + r) - \log r$, $r > 0$
21. As $x \to \infty$, $f(x) \to \infty$
23. As $x \to 1^-$, $f(x) \to -\infty$
25. As $x \to \infty$, $f(x) \to \infty$, $f(x)$ not defined for
$x \le 0$ **27.** $3^{2/5}$ **29.** $D_1 = (0, \infty)$, $R_1 = (-\infty, 0)$;
$D_2 = (-\infty, -2) \cup (0, \infty)$, $R_2 = (-\infty, 0) \cup (0, \infty)$
31. -0.26 **33.** 2   **35.** 1.52   **37.** $(-\infty, 0.69]$
39. $(-0.77, 0.58)$, $(2, 4)$, $(4, 16)$; $2^x > x^2$ in
$(-0.77, 2) \cup (4, \infty)$; $x^2 > 2^x$ in $(-\infty, -0.77) \cup (2, 4)$
41. \$701.28   **43.** \$708.81   **45.** \$705.30
47. 6 years   **49.**

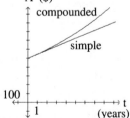

51. Negative and positive values near 0 (recent past and near future) make sense for the current growth rate.

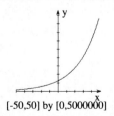

[-50,50] by [0,5000000]

53. The difference is less than 0.01 in $(0, 0.14)$

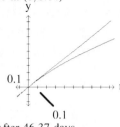

55. $A(t) = 4.62(\frac{1}{2})^{t/21}$ **57.** After 46.37 days
59. $a > 0$ **61.**

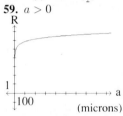

63. $i = 0.014$ or 1.4%
65. $\log f(x_1) = \log ab^{x_1} = \log a + x_1 \log b$
and $\log f(x_2) = \log ab^{x_2} = \log a + x_2 \log b$.
Then $\dfrac{\log f(x_2) - \log f(x_1)}{x_2 - x_1} =$
$\dfrac{(\log a + x_2 \log b) - (\log a + x_1 \log b)}{x_2 - x_1} = \dfrac{(x_2 - x_1)(\log b)}{x_2 - x_1} =$
$\log b$ **67. (a)** \$702.06 **(b)** 27.68 years

CHAPTER 7

SECTION 7.1

1. Quadrant III **3.** Quadrant II **5.** Quadrant I
7. $408°$ **9.** $345°$ **11.**

$415°, 775°, -305°,$ and $-665°$ are possible answers.
13.

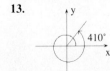

$50°, 770°, -310°,$ and $-670°$ are possible answers.

15.

$\frac{9\pi}{4}, \frac{17\pi}{4}, -\frac{7\pi}{4},$ and $-\frac{15\pi}{4}$ are possible answers.
17.

$\frac{13\pi}{6}, \frac{25\pi}{6}, -\frac{11\pi}{6},$ and $-\frac{23\pi}{6}$ are possible answers.
19.

$\frac{5\pi}{3}, \frac{11\pi}{3}, -\frac{7\pi}{3},$ and $-\frac{13\pi}{3}$ are possible answers.
21. Complement: $55°$; supplement: $145°$
23. Complement: $22°$; supplement: $112°$
25. Complement: $\frac{\pi}{6}$; supplement: $\frac{2\pi}{3}$
27. Complement: $\frac{3\pi}{26}$; supplement: $\frac{8\pi}{13}$ **29.** $180°$ or π
31. $45°$ or $\frac{\pi}{4}$ **33.** $315°$ or $\frac{7\pi}{4}$

35. $180°$ or π

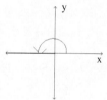

37. $480°$ or $\frac{8\pi}{3}$ **39.** $900°$ or 5π

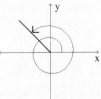 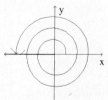

41. $\frac{\pi}{4}$ **43.** $\frac{3\pi}{4}$ **45.** $\frac{2\pi}{3}$ **47.** $\frac{23\pi}{180}$ or 0.40
49. $\frac{2\pi}{5}$ or 1.26 **51.** $75°$ **53.** $214.86°$ **55.** $\frac{\pi}{3}$
57. 15.58 **59.** 5.76 inches **61.** 6.125 cm

63.

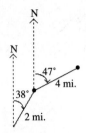

65. d: 10° south of current course

67.

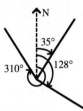

69. (a)

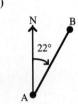

(b)

(c)

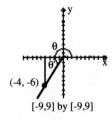

71. 37,699.11 ft/min

73. 10,555.75 ft/min

75. 50.27 inches

SECTION 7.2

1. $\sin A = \frac{8}{\sqrt{113}}$ **3.** $\tan A = \frac{8}{7}$ **5.** $\tan A = \frac{\sqrt{113}}{7}$

7. $\sin B = \frac{7}{\sqrt{113}}$, $\cos B = \frac{8}{\sqrt{113}}$, $\tan B = \frac{7}{8}$, $\cot B = \frac{8}{7}$, $\sec B = \frac{\sqrt{113}}{8}$, $\csc B = \frac{\sqrt{113}}{7}$ **9.** $\cos A = \frac{2\sqrt{26}}{15}$

11. $\cot A = \frac{2\sqrt{26}}{11}$ **13.** $\csc A = \frac{15}{11}$ **15.** $\sin 30° = \frac{1}{2}$, $\cos 30° = \frac{\sqrt{3}}{2}$, $\tan 30° = \frac{1}{\sqrt{3}}$, $\cot 30° = \sqrt{3}$, $\sec 30° = \frac{2}{\sqrt{3}}$, $\csc 30° = 2$ **17.** $\sin \frac{\pi}{3} = \frac{\sqrt{3}}{2}$, $\cos \frac{\pi}{3} = \frac{1}{2}$, $\tan \frac{\pi}{3} = \sqrt{3}$, $\cot \frac{\pi}{3} = \frac{1}{\sqrt{3}}$, $\sec \frac{\pi}{3} = 2$, $\csc \frac{\pi}{3} = \frac{2}{\sqrt{3}}$

19. See exercise 17 $\left(\frac{\pi}{3} = 60°\right)$ **21.** Note: For exercises 21 through 35, calculator values have been rounded to 4 decimal places.

$\sin 21° = 0.3584$, $\cos 21° = 0.9336$, $\tan 21° = 0.3839$

23. $\sin 1.23 = 0.9425$, $\cos 1.23 = 0.3342$, $\tan 1.23 = 2.8198$

25. $\sin 82° = 0.9903$, $\cos 82° = 0.1392$, $\tan 82° = 7.1154$

27. $\sin 0.27 = 0.2667$, $\cos 0.27 = 0.9638$, $\tan 0.27 = 0.2768$

29. $\cot 38° = 1.2799$, $\sec 38° = 1.2690$, $\csc 38° = 1.6243$

31. $\cot 0.83 = 0.9146$, $\sec 0.83 = 1.4818$, $\csc 0.83 = 1.3551$

33. $\cot 46° = 0.9657$, $\sec 46° = 1.4396$, $\csc 46° = 1.3902$

35. $\cot 1.35 = 0.2245$, $\sec 1.35 = 4.5661$, $\csc 1.35 = 1.0249$

37. $\sin \theta = \frac{3}{5}$, $\cos \theta = \frac{4}{5}$, $\tan \theta = \frac{3}{4}$, $\cot \theta = \frac{4}{3}$, $\sec \theta = \frac{5}{4}$, $\csc \theta = \frac{5}{3}$ **39.** $\sin \theta = \frac{1}{2}$, $\cos \theta = \frac{\sqrt{3}}{2}$, $\tan \theta = \frac{1}{\sqrt{3}}$, $\cot \theta = \sqrt{3}$, $\sec \theta = \frac{2}{\sqrt{3}}$, $\csc \theta = 2$

41. $\theta = 30° = 0.52$ **43.** $\theta = 36.87° = 0.64$

45. $\theta = 45° = 0.79$ **47.** $\theta = 22.93° = 0.40$

49. $\theta = 30° = 0.52$ **51.** $\theta = 59.04° = 1.03$

53. $\theta = 41.81° = 0.73$ **55.** $b = 33.79$, $c = 35.96$, $\angle B = 70°$ **57.** $a = 6.56$, $b = 7.55$, $\angle B = 49°$

59. $a = 4.90$, $\angle A = 44.42°$, $\angle B = 45.58°$

61. $c = 9.46$, $\angle A = 12.20°$, $\angle B = 77.80°$

63. $a = 12.58$, $b = 2.80$, $\angle A = 77.45°$ **65.** $\theta = 180°$; $\theta' = 0°$; $\sin \theta = 0$, $\cos \theta = -1$, $\tan \theta = 0$, $\cot \theta$ undefined, $\sec \theta = -1$, $\csc \theta$ undefined

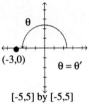

$(-3,0)$ $\theta = \theta'$

$[-5,5]$ by $[-5,5]$

67. $\theta = \theta' = 36.87°$; $\sin \theta = \frac{3}{5}$, $\cos \theta = \frac{4}{5}$, $\tan \theta = \frac{3}{4}$, $\cot \theta = \frac{4}{3}$, $\sec \theta = \frac{5}{4}$, $\csc \theta = \frac{5}{3}$

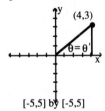

$(4,3)$ $\theta = \theta'$

$[-5,5]$ by $[-5,5]$

69. $\theta = 236.31°$; $\theta' = 56.31°$; $\sin \theta = -\frac{3}{\sqrt{13}}$, $\cos \theta = -\frac{2}{\sqrt{13}}$, $\tan \theta = \frac{3}{2}$, $\cot \theta = \frac{2}{3}$, $\sec \theta = -\frac{\sqrt{13}}{2}$, $\csc \theta = -\frac{\sqrt{13}}{3}$

$(-4, -6)$

$[-9,9]$ by $[-9,9]$

71. $\theta = 315°$; $\theta' = 45°$; $\sin \theta = -\frac{1}{\sqrt{2}}$, $\cos \theta = \frac{1}{\sqrt{2}}$, $\tan \theta = -1$, $\cot \theta = -1$, $\sec \theta = \sqrt{2}$, $\csc \theta = -\sqrt{2}$

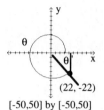

[-50,50] by [-50,50]

73. $\theta = 156°$; $\theta' = 24°$; $\sin \theta = \sin \theta' = 0.41$, $\cos \theta = -\cos \theta' = -0.91$, $\tan \theta = -\tan \theta' = -0.45$, $\cot \theta = -\cot \theta' = -2.25$, $\sec \theta = -\sec \theta' = -1.09$, $\csc \theta = \csc \theta' = 2.46$

[-10,10] by [-10,10]

75. $\theta = 614°$; $\theta' = 74°$; $\sin \theta = -\sin \theta' = -0.96$, $\cos \theta = -\cos \theta' = -0.28$, $\tan \theta = \tan \theta' = 3.49$, $\cot \theta = \cot \theta' = 0.29$, $\sec \theta = -\sec \theta' = -3.63$, $\csc \theta = -\csc \theta' = -1.04$

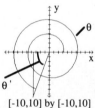

[-10,10] by [-10,10]

77. $h = 100$ ft

79. $s = 680.55$ ft

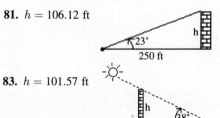

81. $h = 106.12$ ft

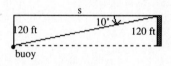

83. $h = 101.57$ ft

SECTION 7.3

1. $P(0, 1)$ **3.** $P\left(\frac{\sqrt{2}}{2}, -\frac{\sqrt{2}}{2}\right)$ **5.** $P(0, 1)$

7. $P\left(-\frac{\sqrt{2}}{2}, -\frac{\sqrt{2}}{2}\right)$ **9.** $P\left(\frac{\sqrt{3}}{2}, -\frac{1}{2}\right)$ **11.** $P\left(-\frac{1}{2}, \frac{\sqrt{3}}{2}\right)$

13. $\sin \frac{\pi}{6} = \frac{1}{2}$, $\cos \frac{\pi}{6} = \frac{\sqrt{3}}{2}$

15. $\sin \frac{\pi}{3} = \frac{\sqrt{3}}{2}$, $\cos \frac{\pi}{3} = \frac{1}{2}$

17. $\sin \frac{3\pi}{4} = \frac{\sqrt{2}}{2}$, $\cos \frac{3\pi}{4} = -\frac{\sqrt{2}}{2}$

19. $\sin -\frac{2\pi}{3} = -\frac{\sqrt{3}}{2}$, $\cos -\frac{2\pi}{3} = -\frac{1}{2}$

21. $\tan \frac{\pi}{6} = \frac{1}{\sqrt{3}}$, $\cot \frac{\pi}{6} = \sqrt{3}$, $\sec \frac{\pi}{6} = \frac{2}{\sqrt{3}}$, $\csc \frac{\pi}{6} = 2$

23. $\tan \frac{\pi}{3} = \sqrt{3}$, $\cot \frac{\pi}{3} = \frac{1}{\sqrt{3}}$, $\sec \frac{\pi}{3} = 2$, $\csc \frac{\pi}{3} = \frac{2}{\sqrt{3}}$

25. $\tan \frac{3\pi}{4} = -1$, $\cot \frac{3\pi}{4} = -1$, $\sec \frac{3\pi}{4} = -\frac{2}{\sqrt{2}}$, $\csc \frac{3\pi}{4} = \frac{2}{\sqrt{2}}$

27. $\tan \left(-\frac{2\pi}{3}\right) = \sqrt{3}$, $\cot \left(-\frac{2\pi}{3}\right) = \frac{1}{\sqrt{3}}$, $\sec \left(-\frac{2\pi}{3}\right) = -2$, $\csc \left(-\frac{2\pi}{3}\right) = -\frac{2}{\sqrt{3}}$ **29.** $\tan \frac{\pi}{2}$, $\sec \frac{\pi}{2}$ undefined

31. $\tan \frac{3\pi}{2}$, $\sec \frac{3\pi}{2}$ undefined   **33.** $\tan \frac{5\pi}{2}$, $\sec \frac{5\pi}{2}$ undefined   **35.** $\sin \frac{13\pi}{4} = -\frac{\sqrt{2}}{2}$, $\cos \frac{13\pi}{4} = -\frac{\sqrt{2}}{2}$ **37.** $\sin \frac{8\pi}{3} = \frac{\sqrt{3}}{2}$, $\cos \frac{8\pi}{3} = -\frac{1}{2}$ **39.** 0.34 (Quadrant I), -0.34 (Quadrant II)   **41.** 1.23 (Quadrant I), -1.23 (Quadrant IV)

43. $\frac{\sin^2 \theta}{\cos^2 \theta} + \frac{\cos^2 \theta}{\cos^2 \theta} = \frac{1}{\cos^2 \theta}$. Thus, $\tan^2 \theta + 1 = \sec^2 \theta$.

45. $\sin x$: +; $\cos x$: +; $\tan x$: +   **47.** $\sin x$: −; $\cos x$: −; $\tan x$: +   **49.** $\sin \frac{7\pi}{3} = \frac{\sqrt{3}}{2}$, $\cos \frac{7\pi}{3} = \frac{1}{2}$, $\tan \frac{7\pi}{3} = \sqrt{3}$

51. $\sin \frac{5\pi}{12} = 0.97$, $\cos \frac{5\pi}{12} = 0.26$, $\tan \frac{5\pi}{12} = 3.73$ **53.** $\sin \frac{11\pi}{24} = 0.99$, $\cos \frac{11\pi}{24} = 0.13$, $\tan \frac{11\pi}{24} = 7.60$

SECTION 7.4

1. Maximum: 4; amplitude: 4

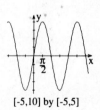

[-5,10] by [-5,5]

3. Maximum: 15; amplitude: 15

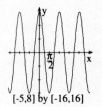

[-5,8] by [-16,16]

5. Maximum: 5; amplitude: 5

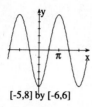

[-5,8] by [-6,6]

7. $D = (-\infty, \infty)$; $R = [-1, 1]$; period: $\frac{2\pi}{3}$

[-4,7] by [-1.5,2]

9. $D = (-\infty, \infty)$; $R = [-4, 4]$; period: $\frac{2\pi}{5}$

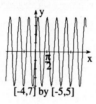

[-4,7] by [-5,5]

11. $D = (-\infty, \infty)$; $R = [-3, 3]$; period: π

[-4,7] by [-4,4]

13. $D = (-\infty, \infty)$; $R = [-1, 1]$; period: $\frac{2\pi}{3}$

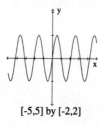

[-5,5] by [-2,2]

15. $D = (-\infty, \infty)$; $R = [1, 3]$; period: 2π

[-10,10] by [-4,4]

17. $D = (-\infty, \infty)$; $R = [-4, 2]$; period: 2π

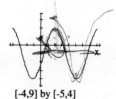

[-4,9] by [-5,4]

19. $D = (-\infty, \infty)$; $R = [-4, 2]$; period: 2π

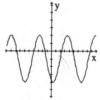

[-10,10] by [-6,6]

21. Answers will vary: $[0, \pi]$ by $[-2, 2]$
23. Answers will vary: $[0, 4\pi]$ by $[-3, 3]$
25. Answers will vary: $[0, 10\pi]$ by $[-4, 4]$ **27.** 0.52, 2.62
29. 0.93, 2.21   **31.** 0.93, 5.36   **33.** 0.60, 2.54
35. 0.79, 3.93   **37.** 1.70, 3.14, 4.60
39. $[0, 0.64) \cup (2.50, 2\pi)$ **41.** $[0, 2.28) \cup (4.00, 2\pi)$
43. Let $-\theta$ be the angle with $P(a, b)$ on its terminal side and θ be the angle in standard position. Then $\tan(-\theta) = b/a$ and $\tan(-\theta) = -\tan\theta$ **45.**

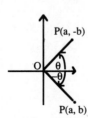

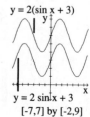

$y = 2(\sin x + 3)$

$y = 2 \sin x + 3$
[-7,7] by [-2,9]

47. 0.795 minutes or 47.7 seconds

SECTION 7.5

1. The graphs appear the same because each shows a complete graph of one period of the tangent function.

(a)

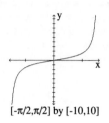

$[-\pi/2,\pi/2]$ by $[-10,10]$

(b)

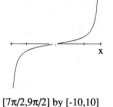

$[7\pi/2,9\pi/2]$ by $[-10,10]$

(c)

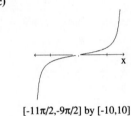

$[-11\pi/2,-9\pi/2]$ by $[-10,10]$

(d)

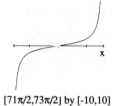

$[71\pi/2,73\pi/2]$ by $[-10,10]$

3.

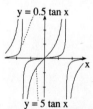

$y = 0.5 \tan x$

$y = 5 \tan x$

5. Answers will vary. The following windows show the graph of one complete period of $\sec x$: $[-\frac{\pi}{2}, \frac{3\pi}{2}]$ by $[-10, 10]$, $[\frac{7\pi}{2}, \frac{11\pi}{2}]$ by $[-10, 10]$, $[-\frac{11\pi}{2}, -\frac{7\pi}{2}]$ by $[-10, 10]$, $[\frac{51\pi}{2}, \frac{55\pi}{2}]$ by $[-10, 10]$ **7.** Period: $\frac{\pi}{2}$

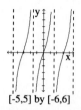

$[-\pi/4,5\pi/4]$ by $[-10,10]$

9. Period: π

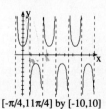

$[-\pi/4,11\pi/4]$ by $[-10,10]$

11. Period: $\frac{2\pi}{3}$

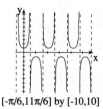

$[-\pi/6,11\pi/6]$ by $[-10,10]$

13. D: All reals except $x = \frac{\pi}{2} + k\pi$, k any integer; $R = (-\infty, \infty)$; period: π; VA: $x = \frac{\pi}{2} + k\pi$, k any integer

$[-5,5]$ by $[-6,6]$

15. D: All reals except $x = \frac{\pi}{2} + k\pi$, k any integer; $R = (-\infty, -\frac{1}{2}] \cup [\frac{1}{2}, \infty)$; period: 2π; VA: $x = \frac{\pi}{2} + k\pi$, k any integer

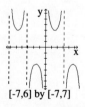

$[-5,8]$ by $[-4,4]$

17. D: All reals except $x = k\pi$, k any integer; $R = (-\infty, -3] \cup [3, \infty)$; period: 2π; VA: $x = k\pi$, k any integer

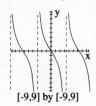

$[-7,6]$ by $[-7,7]$

19. D: All reals except $x = \pi + 2k\pi$, k any integer; $R = (-\infty, \infty)$; period: 2π; VA: $x = \pi + 2k\pi$, k any integer

$[-9,9]$ by $[-9,9]$

21. D: All reals except $x = k\pi$, k any integer; $R = (-\infty, -2] \cup [2, \infty)$; period: 2π; VA: $x = k\pi$, k any integer

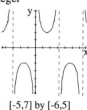

[-5,7] by [-6,5]

23. D: All reals except $x = \frac{\pi}{6} + \frac{k\pi}{3}$, k any integer; $R = (-\infty, \infty)$; period: $\frac{\pi}{3}$; VA: $x = \frac{\pi}{6} + \frac{k\pi}{3}$, k any integer

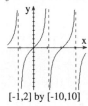

[-1,2] by [-10,10]

25. D: All reals except $x = 1 + 2k$, k any integer; $R = (-\infty, \infty)$; period: 2; VA: $x = 1 + 2k$, k any integer

[-4,4] by [-4,4]

27. D: All reals except $x = \frac{\pi}{4} + \frac{k\pi}{2}$, k any integer; $R = (-\infty, -3] \cup [3, \infty)$; period: π; VA: $x = \frac{\pi}{4} + \frac{k\pi}{2}$, k any integer

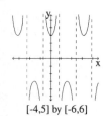

[-4,5] by [-6,6]

29. -5.01, -1.87, 1.27, 4.41 **31.** ± 0.59, ± 5.69
33. 0.67 **35.** ± 0.90 **37.** $(0.21, \frac{\pi}{2})$ **39.** $[0.67, \frac{\pi}{2})$
41.

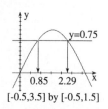

[-0.5,3.5] by [-0.5,1.5]

43.

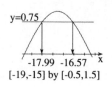

[-19,-15] by [-0.5,1.5]

45. $x + 2k\pi$, k any integer, where $x = 0.25$ or 2.89
47. $x + 2k\pi$, k any integer, where $x = 1.14$ or 5.15
49. $x + 2k\pi$, k any integer, where $-3.29 < x < 0.15$
51. $x + \frac{2k\pi}{3}$, k any integer, where $x = 0.19$ or 0.85
53. $x + 4k\pi$, k any integer, where $0.51 \le x \le 5.78$ or $2\pi < x < 4\pi$

SECTION 7.6

1. $\sin \theta = -\frac{1}{\sqrt{2}}$, $\cos \theta = -\frac{1}{\sqrt{2}}$, $\tan \theta = 1$, $\cot \theta = 1$, $\sec \theta = -\sqrt{2}$, $\csc \theta = -\sqrt{2}$ **3.** $\sin \theta = \frac{1}{\sqrt{2}}$, $\cos \theta = \frac{1}{\sqrt{2}}$, $\tan \theta = 1$, $\cot \theta = 1$, $\sec \theta = \sqrt{2}$, $\csc \theta = \sqrt{2}$ **5.** $\sin \theta = \frac{3}{5}$, $\cos \theta = \frac{4}{5}$, $\tan \theta = \frac{3}{4}$, $\cot \theta = \frac{4}{3}$, $\sec \theta = \frac{5}{4}$, $\csc \theta = \frac{5}{3}$
7. $\sin \theta = -\frac{2}{\sqrt{13}}$, $\cos \theta = -\frac{3}{\sqrt{13}}$, $\tan \theta = \frac{2}{3}$, $\cot \theta = \frac{3}{2}$, $\sec \theta = -\frac{\sqrt{13}}{3}$, $\csc \theta = -\frac{\sqrt{13}}{2}$ **9.** $63.43°$
11. $71.57°$ **13.** Quadrant III
15. Quadrant III
17. Height of pole: 30.09 ft; length of wire: 34.08 ft
19. 3290.53 ft   **21.** 167.82 ft
23. 84.85 miles; bearing of $140°$ **25.** $19.03°$
27. 637.85 ft   **29.** 9.78 ft   **31.** 2931.09 ft

Chapter 7 Review

1. Quadrant II; $\frac{3\pi}{4}$ or 2.36 **3.** Positive y-axis; $450°$
5. Quadrant I; $\frac{13\pi}{30}$ or 1.36 **7.** Quadrant I; $15°$
9. $270°$; $\frac{3\pi}{2}$

11. $63.43°$ or 1.11 **13.** $120°$ or 2.09
15. $296.57°$ or 5.18 **17.** $\frac{1}{2}$ **19.** -1 **21.** $\frac{2}{\sqrt{3}}$
23. $\frac{2}{\sqrt{3}}$ **25.** $-\frac{1}{2}$ **27.** -1 **29.** $\sin 0° = 0$, $\cos 0° = 1$, $\tan 0° = 0$, $\cot 0°$ undefined, $\sec 0° = 1$, $\csc 0°$ undefined   **31.** $\sin \frac{3\pi}{4} = \frac{1}{\sqrt{2}}$, $\cos \frac{3\pi}{4} = -\frac{1}{\sqrt{2}}$, $\tan \frac{3\pi}{4} =$

-1, $\cot \theta = -1$, $\sec \frac{3\pi}{4} = -\sqrt{2}$, $\csc \frac{3\pi}{4} = \sqrt{2}$ **33.** $\sin(-135°) = -\frac{1}{\sqrt{2}}$, $\cos(-135°) = -\frac{1}{\sqrt{2}}$, $\tan(-135°) = 1$, $\cot(-135°) = 1$, $\sec(-135°) = -\sqrt{2}$, $\csc(-135°) = -\sqrt{2}$
35. $\sin \angle A = \frac{12}{13}$, $\cos \angle A = \frac{5}{13}$, $\tan \angle A = \frac{12}{5}$, $\cot \angle A = \frac{5}{12}$, $\sec \angle A = \frac{13}{5}$, $\csc \angle A = \frac{13}{12}$ **37.** $\sin \theta = \frac{5}{13}$, $\cos \theta = \frac{12}{13}$, $\tan \theta = \frac{5}{12}$, $\cot \theta = \frac{12}{5}$, $\sec \theta = \frac{13}{12}$, $\csc \angle A = \frac{13}{5}$
39. $71.57°$ **41.** 0.22
43. $a = 6$, $\angle A = 36.87°$, $\angle B = 53.13°$
45. $a = 3.76$, $b = 7.06$, $\angle B = 62°$
47. $c = 7.72$, $\angle A = 18.90°$, $\angle B = 71.10°$
49. Quadrant II   **51.** Quadrant II
53. 0.71 in Quadrant I; -0.71 in Quadrant II   **55.** $\sin \theta = \frac{2}{\sqrt{5}}$, $\cos \theta = -\frac{1}{\sqrt{5}}$, $\tan \theta = -2$, $\cot \theta = -\frac{1}{2}$, $\sec \theta = -\sqrt{5}$, $\csc \theta = \frac{\sqrt{5}}{2}$ **57.** $\sin \theta = -\frac{3}{\sqrt{34}}$, $\cos \theta = -\frac{5}{\sqrt{34}}$, $\tan \theta = \frac{3}{5}$, $\cot \theta = \frac{5}{3}$, $\sec \theta = -\frac{\sqrt{34}}{5}$, $\csc \theta = -\frac{\sqrt{34}}{3}$
59.   **61.**

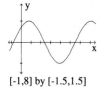
$[-1,8]$ by $[-1.5,1.5]$

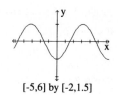
$[-5,6]$ by $[-2,1.5]$

63.   **65.**

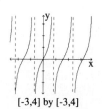
$[-3,4]$ by $[-3,4]$

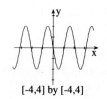
$[-4,4]$ by $[-4,4]$

67. $f(x)$ diverges as $x \to 0$ **69.** $50°$ or 0.87 **71.** $60°$ or 1.05 **73.** 0.25 **75.** Undefined
77. $(-3.99, -1.36) \cup (0.55, \infty)$ **79.** 23.78 ft
81. 1.62 miles   **83.** 4669.58 ft

CHAPTER 8

SECTION 8.1

1. Vertical stretch by a factor of 4, reflection in the x-axis, horizontal shrink by a factor of $1/2$, followed by horizontal shift right $\frac{\pi}{2}$ units and vertical shift up 3 units   **3.** Reflection in the x-axis, horizontal shift right π units, then vertical shift up 2 units

5.   **7.**

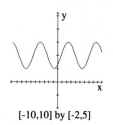
$[-10,10]$ by $[-2,5]$

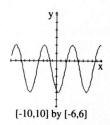
$[-10,10]$ by $[-6,6]$

9.   **11.**

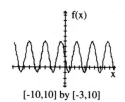
$[-10,10]$ by $[-3,10]$

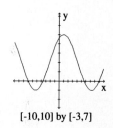
$[-10,10]$ by $[-3,7]$

13.

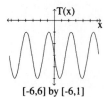
$[-6,6]$ by $[-6,1]$

15. D: all reals except $x = \frac{\pi}{2} + k\pi$, k any integer; $R = (-\infty, \infty)$; VA: $x = \frac{\pi}{2} + k\pi$, k any integer; period: π
17. $D = (-\infty, \infty)$; $R = [-2, 0]$; no asymptotes; period: 2π
19. Period: π; phase shift: $\frac{\pi}{2}$
21. Period: π; phase shift: $\frac{\pi}{4}$
23. Period: π; phase shift: $\frac{1}{4}$
25. $y = 3\sin(2x - \pi)$ **27.** $y = 2\sin\left(\frac{1}{2}x + \frac{\pi}{8}\right)$

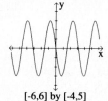
$[-6,6]$ by $[-4,5]$

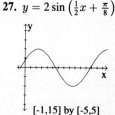
$[-1,15]$ by $[-5,5]$

29. $D = (-\infty, \infty)$; $R = [-3, 3]$; period: π; phase shift: 0

$[-2\pi, 2\pi]$ by $[-4,4]$

31. D: all reals except $x = k\pi$, k any integer; $R = (-\infty, \infty)$; period: π; phase shift: π

[-2π,2π] by [-4,4]

33. $D = (-\infty, \infty)$; $R = [-1, 5]$; period: $\frac{\pi}{2}$; phase shift: $\frac{\pi}{4}$

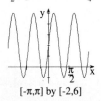

[-π,π] by [-2,6]

35. $\frac{\pi}{18} + \frac{2k\pi}{3}$, $\frac{5\pi}{18} + \frac{2k\pi}{3}$, for k any integer
37. $-2.66 + 4k\pi$, $2.66 + 4k\pi$ for k any integer
39. $0, \pi$ **41.** $(0.69, 3.83)$
43. $A = 3.61$, $b = 1$, $\alpha = 0.59$; $y = 3.61 \sin(x + 0.59)$

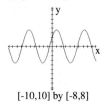

[-10,10] by [-8,8]

45. $A = 1.414$, $b = 1$, $\alpha = \frac{\pi}{4}$; $y = 1.414 \sin\left(x + \pi/4\right)$

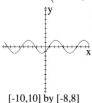

[-10,10] by [-8,8]

47. $D = (-\infty, \infty)$; $R = [-2, 1.13]$; period: 2π; absolute max of 1.13 when $x = 0.25$ or $x = 2.89$; local min of 0 when $x = 1.57$; absolute min of -2 when $x = 4.71$

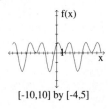

[-10,10] by [-4,5]

49. $D = (-\infty, \infty)$; $R = [-1.88, 1.88]$; period: 2π; absolute max of 1.88 when $x = 0.47$; local max of 0.15 when $x = 2.56$ and 1.06 when $x = 4.82$; local min of -1.06 when $x = 1.68$ and -0.15 when $x = 5.70$; absolute min of -1.88 when $x = 3.61$

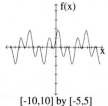

[-10,10] by [-5,5]

51. $D = (-\infty, \infty)$; $R = [-5.39, 5.39]$; period: 2π; absolute max of 5.39 when $x = 0.38$; absolute min of -5.39 when $x = 3.52$

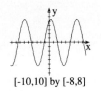

[-10,10] by [-8,8]

53. Period: $\frac{2\pi}{3}$; frequency: $\frac{3}{2\pi}$
55. Period: 4; frequency: $\frac{1}{4}$ **57.** 217.22 inches
59. 2.09 radians/sec   **61.** 11.42 mph
63. $\tan \theta = \dfrac{200t}{2055}$ or $\theta = \tan^{-1}\left(\dfrac{200t}{2055}\right)$; $\theta = 0.97$ or $55.59°$
65. Hottest: $86°$ on June 29 ($t = 90$); coldest: $30°$ on Dec. 26 ($t = 270$)   **67.** Problem situation: the portion of the graph to the right of y-axis ($t > 0$)

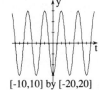

[-10,10] by [-20,20]

69. $y = -28 \cos(6\pi t)$; $t = 0.093 + \frac{k}{6}$ or $t = 0.24 + \frac{k}{6}$ for k any integer

SECTION 8.2

1. $D = [-\frac{1}{3}, \frac{1}{3}]$; $R = [-\frac{\pi}{2}, \frac{\pi}{2}]$

[-1,1] by [-2,2]

3. $D = [-2, 0]$; $R = [-\frac{\pi}{2}, \frac{\pi}{2}]$

[-3,1] by [-2,2]

5. $D = [\frac{3}{2}, \frac{5}{2}]$; $R = [0, 3\pi]$

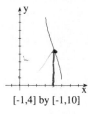

[-1,4] by [-1,10]

7. Reflection of arcsin x in the x-axis, vertical shift up 1 unit; $D = [-1, 1]$; $R = [-0.57, 2.57]$

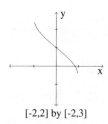

[-2,2] by [-2,3]

9. Vertical shrink of $\tan^{-1} x$ by a factor of 1/4, reflection in the x-axis, horizontal shift right π units; $D = (-\infty, \infty)$; $R = [-\frac{\pi}{8}, \frac{\pi}{8}]$

[-25,25] by [-0.7,0.7]

11. $D = [-1, 1]$; $R = [-1, 1]$

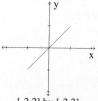

[-2,2] by [-2,2]

13. 21.22°   **15.** 7.13°   **17.** 0.48   **19.** 1.17
21. $\frac{\pi}{2}$ **23.** $\frac{\pi}{4}$ **25.** $-\frac{\pi}{3}$ **27.** 0.36   **29.** 0.42
31. Undefined   **33.** Undefined   **35.** 0.74   **37.** $\frac{\sqrt{3}}{2}$
39. $\frac{1}{2}$ **41.** 0.8   **43.** 1   **45.** 0.48   **47.** $\dfrac{x}{\sqrt{x^2 + 1}}$

49. $\dfrac{x}{\sqrt{1 - x^2}}$ **51.** $1.16 + k\pi$ for k any integer
53. $1.23 + 2k\pi$, $5.05 + 2k\pi$ for k any integer   **55.** $[-\pi, \pi]$
57. $\sin(-x) = -\sin x$ on $[-\frac{\pi}{2}, \frac{\pi}{2}]$. Let $y = \sin(-x)$. Then $y = -\sin x$ and $x = -\sin^{-1} y = \sin^{-1}(-y)$. Thus $-\sin^{-1} x = \sin^{-1}(-x)$.   **59.** Let $u = \arccos \theta$, $v = \arcsin \theta$. Then $\cos u = \sin v = \theta$. Since $\cos u = \sin(90 - u)$, $\sin(90 - u) = \sin v$ and $90 - u = v$, therefore $u + v = 90$.
61. $\theta = \tan^{-1} \frac{50}{L}$; problem situation: $L > 0$

[-200,200] by [-3,3]

63. $\sin \frac{\theta}{2} = \frac{c/2}{a} = \frac{c}{2a}$, so $c = 2a \sin \frac{\theta}{2}$. $\cos \frac{\theta}{2} = \frac{h}{a}$, so $h = a \cos \frac{\theta}{2}$. Then $A = \frac{1}{2}ch = \frac{1}{2}\left(2a \sin \frac{\theta}{2}\right)\left(a \cos \frac{\theta}{2}\right) = a^2 \sqrt{\frac{1 - \cos \theta}{2}} \sqrt{\frac{1 + \cos \theta}{2}} = \frac{1}{2}a^2 \sin^2 \theta$

SECTION 8.3

1. $4.71 + 2k\pi$ for k any integer

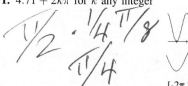

[-2π,2π] by [-3,3]

3. $1.02 + 2k\pi$, $2.13 + 2k\pi$ for k any integer

[-6,6] by [-4,4]

5. $0.78 + 2k\pi$, $2.37 + 2k\pi$ for k any integer   **7.** No solution
9. $\frac{\pi}{4}$, $\frac{5\pi}{4}$ **11.** $\frac{\pi}{6}$, $\frac{5\pi}{6}$ **13.** 0.62, 2.53, 3.76, 5.67
15. 0, π **17.** $\frac{\pi}{2}$, $\frac{3\pi}{2}$ **19.** $k\pi$ for k any integer
21. $0.52 + 2k\pi$, $2.62 + 2k\pi$ for k any integer
23. $\frac{\pi}{2} + 2k\pi$ for k any integer
25. $0.52 + 2k\pi$, $2.62 + 2k\pi$ for k any integer
27. $1.05 + 2k\pi$, $\pi + 2k\pi$, $5.24 + 2k\pi$ for k any integer
29. $[0, \frac{\pi}{6}) \cup (\frac{5\pi}{6}, 2\pi]$
31. $(1.96 + k\pi, 3.53 + k\pi)$ for k any integer   **33.** $\pm 2.28, 0$

35. $0, 1.28$ **37.** $(1.57+2k\pi, 2.84+2k\pi)\cup(4.71+2k\pi, 6.59+2k\pi)$ for k any integer   **39.** $r+2k\pi$ where $r = 1.18, 2.36, 2.75, 4.32, 5.50,$ or 5.89 (k any integer)

41. Local max of 5 when $x = 0$ or 12.57; local min of -1 when $x = 6.28$

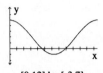

[0,12] by [-3,7]

43. Local max of 1 when $x = 0.64$ or 2.64; local min of -3 when $x = 1.64$

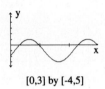

[0,3] by [-4,5]

45. The amplitude (x) increases with each x; thus the function values will not repeat in cycles.

[-20,20] by [-20,20]

47. Problem situation: $0 \le \theta \le \frac{\pi}{2}$

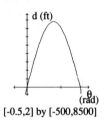

[-0.5,2] by [-500,8500]

49. 7812.5 ft   **51.** 0.63 or 0.94 radians ($36°$ or $54°$)
53. $f(x) \to 1$ as $|x| \to \infty$ (More than one view required for a complete graph.)

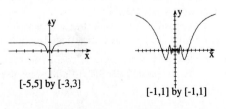

[-5,5] by [-3,3]   [-1,1] by [-1,1]

SECTION 8.4

1. $\sin\theta$ **3.** 1   **5.** $\tan^2 x$ **7.** 2   **9.** $\tan x$

11. $\dfrac{1}{\sin x \cos x}$ **13.** $\dfrac{1+2\sin t \cos t}{\sin^3 t \cos t}$ **15.** 1

17. Identity, the graphs coincide
19. Identity, the graphs coincide

21. $1 + \dfrac{\cos^2\theta}{\sin^2\theta} = \dfrac{\sin^2\theta + \cos^2\theta}{\sin^2\theta} = \dfrac{1}{\sin^2\theta} = \csc^2\theta$

23. $2\cos^2\theta + \sin^2\theta = \cos^2\theta + \cos^2\theta + \sin^2\theta = \cos^2\theta + 1$

25. $\dfrac{\sin x}{\tan x} = \dfrac{\sin x}{\frac{\sin x}{\cos x}} = \cos x$

27. $\cos^2 t - 2\sin t \cos t + \sin^2 t + \cos^2 t + 2\sin t \cos t + \sin^2 t = 2$

29. $\dfrac{1+\tan^2 x}{\sin^2 x + \cos^2 x} = 1 + \tan^2 x = \sec^2 x$

31. $\dfrac{(1+\cos\theta)}{(1+\cos\theta)} \cdot \dfrac{(1-\cos\theta)}{\sin\theta} = \dfrac{1-\cos^2\theta}{(1+\cos\theta)(\sin\theta)} =$

$\dfrac{\sin^2\theta}{(1+\cos\theta)(\sin\theta)} = \dfrac{\sin\theta}{1+\cos\theta}$ **33.** $\dfrac{2\sin^2 t - 1}{1+2\sin t \cos t} =$

$\dfrac{2\sin^2 t - (\sin^2 t + \cos^2 t)}{\sin^2 t + \cos^2 t + 2\sin t \cos t} = \dfrac{(\sin t + \cos t)(\sin t - \cos t)}{(\sin t + \cos t)^2} =$

$\dfrac{\sin t - \cos t}{\sin t + \cos t}$

35. $x^2\sin^2\alpha + 2xy \sin\alpha \cos\alpha + y^2\cos^2\alpha + x^2\cos^2\alpha - 2xy\cos\alpha\sin\alpha + y^2\sin^2\alpha = x^2(\sin^2\alpha + \cos^2\alpha) + y^2(\sin^2\alpha + \cos^2\alpha) = x^2 + y^2$

37. $\dfrac{\sin\theta}{1+\cos\theta} + \dfrac{1+\cos\theta}{\sin\theta} = \dfrac{\sin^2\theta + (1+\cos\theta)^2}{\sin\theta(1+\cos\theta)} =$

$\dfrac{\sin^2\theta + 1 + 2\cos\theta + \cos^2\theta}{\sin\theta(1+\cos\theta)} = \dfrac{2+2\cos\theta}{\sin\theta(1+\cos\theta)} = \dfrac{2}{\sin\theta} = $

$2\csc\theta$

SECTION 8.5

1. $\dfrac{\sqrt6 - \sqrt2}{4}$ **3.** $\dfrac{\sqrt6 + \sqrt2}{4}$ **5.** $\dfrac{\sqrt6 + \sqrt2}{4}$ **7.** $\dfrac{3+\sqrt3}{3-\sqrt3}$

9. $\cos x$ **11.** $-\sin x$
13. $\sin\left(\theta + \frac{\pi}{2}\right) = \sin\theta\cos\frac{\pi}{2} + \sin\frac{\pi}{2}\cos\theta = \cos\theta$

15. $\tan\left(\theta + \frac{\pi}{4}\right) = \dfrac{\tan\theta + \tan\frac{\pi}{4}}{1 - \tan\theta\tan\frac{\pi}{4}} = \dfrac{1+\tan\theta}{1-\tan\theta}$

17. $2\sin\theta\cos\theta + \cos\theta$
19. $2\sin\theta\cos\theta + \cos^3\theta - 3\sin^2\theta\cos\theta$
21. $2(2\sin\theta\cos\theta)(\cos^2\theta - \sin^2\theta) + \cos^3\theta - 3\sin^2\theta\cos\theta$

23. Period: $\frac{2\pi}{3}$; amplitude: 2.24; phase shift: 0.15 left

[-π,π] by [-3,3]

25. Period: 2π; amplitude: 4.64; phase shift: 1.37 left

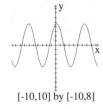

[-10,10] by [-10,8]

27. D: all reals except $x = \pm\sqrt{\frac{\pi}{2} + k\pi}$ for k nonnegative integer; $R = (-\infty, -1] \cup [1, \infty)$

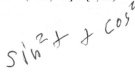

[-π,π] by [-5,5]

29. $D = (-\infty, \infty)$; $R = [0, 3]$

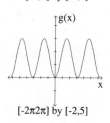

[-2π,2π] by [-2,5]

31. (a) $-\sqrt{5}/3$ **(b)** $3/2$ **33.** -2 **35.** $-\sqrt{3}$
37. $\frac{\pi}{6}, \frac{5\pi}{6}$ **39.** $\frac{\pi}{3}, \frac{2\pi}{3}$ **41.** $\frac{\pi}{2}, \frac{3\pi}{2}$ **43.** $0, \pi$
45. $\sin\left(\frac{\pi}{2} - \alpha\right) = \sin\frac{\pi}{2}\cos\alpha - \sin\alpha\cos\frac{\pi}{2} = \cos\alpha$
47. $\tan(\alpha + \beta) = \dfrac{\sin(\alpha + \beta)}{\cos(\alpha + \beta)} = \dfrac{\sin\alpha\cos\beta + \sin\beta\cos\alpha}{\cos\alpha\cos\beta - \sin\alpha\sin\beta} \cdot$
$\dfrac{1/(\cos\alpha\cos\beta)}{1/(\cos\alpha\cos\beta)} = \dfrac{\tan\alpha + \tan\beta}{1 - \tan\alpha\tan\beta}$
49. $\cos 2\theta = \cos\theta\cos\theta - \sin\theta\sin\theta = \cos^2\theta - \sin^2\theta$
51. $\tan 2\theta = \dfrac{\tan\theta + \tan\theta}{1 - \tan\theta\tan\theta} = \dfrac{2\tan\theta}{1 - \tan^2\theta}$ **53.** $\tan\left(\frac{\theta}{2}\right) =$

$\dfrac{\sin\frac{\theta}{2}}{\cos\frac{\theta}{2}} = \dfrac{\sqrt{\frac{1-\cos\theta}{2}}}{\sqrt{\frac{1+\cos\theta}{2}}} = \dfrac{\sqrt{1-\cos\theta}}{\sqrt{1+\cos\theta}} \cdot \dfrac{\sqrt{1+\cos\theta}}{\sqrt{1+\cos\theta}} = \dfrac{\sqrt{1-\cos^2\theta}}{1+\cos\theta} =$

$\dfrac{\sqrt{\sin^2\theta}}{1+\cos\theta} = \dfrac{\sin\theta}{1+\cos\theta}$ **55.** Answers will vary.
57. $\sin(\alpha - \beta) = \cos\left(\frac{\pi}{2} - (\alpha - \beta)\right) = \cos\left(\left(\frac{\pi}{2} - \alpha\right) + \beta\right) =$
$\cos\left(\frac{\pi}{2} - \alpha\right)\cos\beta - \sin\left(\frac{\pi}{2} - \alpha\right)\sin\beta = \sin\alpha\cos\beta - \cos\alpha\sin\beta$

SECTION 8.6

1. 0.30, 2.84 **3.** 0.98 **5.** $\frac{\pi}{6}, \frac{5\pi}{6}$
7. 0.52, 1.88, 2.62, 4.41 **9.** 1.05, 2.50, 3.79, 5.24
11. $0, \frac{\pi}{4}, \pi, \frac{5\pi}{4}$ **13.** $0, \frac{\pi}{2}, \frac{3\pi}{2}$
15. $\frac{\pi}{3}, \pi, \frac{5\pi}{3}$ **17.** 0 **19.** $\frac{2\pi}{3}, \frac{4\pi}{3}$ **21.** $\frac{\pi}{2}, \frac{7\pi}{6}$,
$\frac{11\pi}{6}$ **23.** $\frac{\pi}{3}, \pi, \frac{5\pi}{3}$ **25.** Let $x_1 = b\sin\theta_1$, $h = a\cos\theta_2$,
$x_2 = a\sin\theta_2$, $h = b\cos\theta_1$. Substitution in the expression in
Exercise 24 yields $A = \frac{1}{2}ab\sin\theta_1\cos\theta_2 + \frac{1}{2}ab\cos\theta_1\sin\theta_2$
27. $\dfrac{\sin\alpha}{\sin\beta} = 2.42$, then $\sin\beta = \dfrac{\sin\alpha}{2.42} = 0.413\sin\alpha$, and $\beta =$
$\sin^{-1}(0.413\sin\alpha)$; $D = [0, \frac{\pi}{2}]$

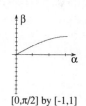

[0,π/2] by [-1,1]

29. 1.12 radians or 64.2° **31.** If $\tan x = \sec x$ then
$\frac{\sin x}{\cos x} = \frac{1}{\cos x}$ and $\sin x = 1$. Thus $x = \frac{\pi}{2} + 2k\pi$. But $\sec x$ is
undefined for these values of x so there is no solution, even
though the graph of $y = \tan x - \sec x$ appears to intersect the
x-axis.

Chapter 8 Review

1. Amplitude: 2; period: $\frac{2\pi}{3}$; phase shift: 0; $D = (-\infty, \infty)$;
$R = [-2, 2]$ **3.** Amplitude: 1.5; period: π; phase shift:
right $\frac{\pi}{8}$ units; $D = (-\infty, \infty)$; $R = [-1.5, 1.5]$

5. Amplitude: 4; period: π; phase shift: right 1/2 units; $D = (-\infty, \infty)$; $R = [-4, 4]$ **7.** Vertical stretch by a factor
of 3, horizontal shrink by a factor of 1/2, horizontal shift
right 1/2 unit, then vertical shift up 7 units **9.** Vertical
stretch by a factor of 5, horizontal shrink by a factor of 1/3,
horizontal shift left 0.5 unit, then vertical shift up 2.3 units

11. Vertical stretch by a factor of 2, horizontal shrink by a
factor of $\frac{1}{2\pi}$, horizontal shift left $\frac{3}{2\pi}$, then vertical shift down
2 units

13.

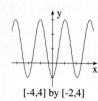

[-4,4] by [-2,4]

15.

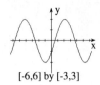

[-6,6] by [-3,3]

17. $A = 4.47$, $b = 1$, $\alpha = -1.11$; $y = 4.47(\sin x - 1.11)$

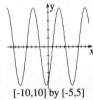

[-10,10] by [-5,5]

19. $A = 7.53$, $b = 2$, $\alpha = -1.44$ (phase shift: right 0.72 units); $y = 7.53(\sin 2x - 1.44)$ **21.** $A = 3.61$, $C = 0.59$

23. $A = 5.83$, $C = -0.54$

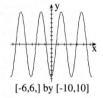

[-6,6,] by [-10,10]

25.

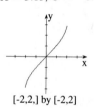

[-2,2,] by [-2,2]

27. Horizontal shrink of $y = \sin^{-1} x$ by a factor of 1/2

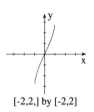

[-2,2,] by [-2,2]

29. Horizontal shrink of $y = \tan^{-1} x$ by a factor of 1/2

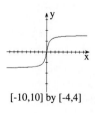

[-10,10] by [-4,4]

31. Horizontal shrink of $y = \sin^{-1} x$ by a factor of 1/3, horizontal shift right 1/3, vertical shift up 2 units

[-2,2] by [-2,5]

33. $\frac{\pi}{12} + k\pi$, $\frac{5\pi}{12} + k\pi$ for k any integer

35. $\frac{3\pi}{4} + k\pi$ for k any integer

37. $0.72 + k\pi$, $2.42 + k\pi$ for k any integer

39. $0.30 + 2k\pi$, $2.84 + 2k\pi$ for k any integer   **41.** 0.65

43. $D = (-\infty, \infty)$; $R = (-\infty, \infty)$

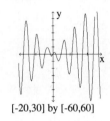

[-20,30] by [-60,60]

45. D: all reals except $x = k\pi$, k any integer; $R = (-\infty, \infty)$

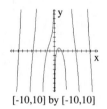

[-10,10] by [-10,10]

47. $D = (-\infty, \infty)$; $R = [0, 5]$

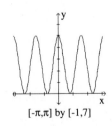

[-π,π] by [-1,7]

49. $D = [-1, 1]$; $R = [0, \pi^2/4]$

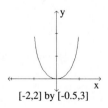

[-2,2] by [-0.5,3]

51. $\cos(3x) = \cos(2x + x) = \cos(2x)\cos x - \sin(2x)\sin x = (\cos^2 x - \sin^2 x)\cos x - 2\sin^2 x \cos x = \cos^3 x - 3\sin^2 x \cos x$

53. $\tan^2 x - \sin^2 x = \dfrac{\sin^2 x}{\cos^2 x} - \sin^2 x = \dfrac{\sin^2 x - \sin^2 x \cos^2 x}{\cos^2 x} = \dfrac{\sin^2 x (1 - \cos^2 x)}{\cos^2 x} = \dfrac{\sin^2 x \sin^2 x}{\cos^2 x} = \tan^2 x \sin^2 x$

55. $\csc x - \cos x \cot x = \dfrac{1}{\sin x} - \cos x \cdot \dfrac{\cos x}{\sin x} = \dfrac{1 - \cos^2 x}{\sin x} = \dfrac{\sin^2 x}{\sin x} = \sin x$ **57.** $\dfrac{1 + \frac{\sin\theta}{\cos\theta}}{1 - \frac{\sin\theta}{\cos\theta}} + \dfrac{1 + \frac{\cos\theta}{\sin\theta}}{1 - \frac{\cos\theta}{\sin\theta}} = \dfrac{\cos\theta + \sin\theta}{\cos\theta - \sin\theta} + \dfrac{\sin\theta + \cos\theta}{\sin\theta - \cos\theta} = \dfrac{\cos\theta + \sin\theta}{\cos\theta - \sin\theta} - \dfrac{\sin\theta + \cos\theta}{\cos\theta - \sin\theta} = 0$ **59.** True for all x except $\pi/2 + 2\pi k$ (where the left side of the equation is undefined).   **61.** $3\cos^2 x \sin x - \sin^3 x + 4\cos^3 x - 3\cos x$ **63.** $\cos^4 x - 2\cos^2 x \sin^2 x + \sin^4 x - 2\sin x \cos x$ **65.** $\sqrt{1 - x^2}$ **67.** $\sqrt{1 - x^2}$ **69.** $1.12 + 2k\pi, 5.16 + 2k\pi$ for k any integer   **71.** ± 1.15 **73.** $\frac{\pi}{12}, \frac{5\pi}{12}, \frac{13\pi}{12}, \frac{17\pi}{12}$ **75.** $0, \frac{\pi}{4}, \frac{3\pi}{4}, \pi, \frac{5\pi}{4}, \frac{7\pi}{4}$ **77.** $0, \frac{2\pi}{3}, \frac{4\pi}{3}$ **79.** $[0, \frac{\pi}{6}) \cup (\frac{5\pi}{6}, \frac{7\pi}{6}) \cup (\frac{11\pi}{6}, 2\pi)$ **81.** $(\frac{\pi}{3}, \frac{5\pi}{3})$ **83.** End behavior: $y \to 0$

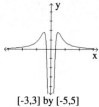

[-3,3] by [-5,5]

85.

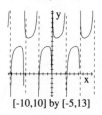

[-10,10] by [-5,13]

87. 0.96 or 54.72°

C H A P T E R   9

SECTION 9.1

Note: In sections 9.1 and 9.2, we assume a, b, and c represent positive lengths.
1. $a = 10$, $b = 18.23$, $c = 18.05$; $a = 50$, $b = 91.14$, $c = 90.23$ **3.** $\gamma = 110°$, $a = 12.86$, $c = 18.79$
5. $\alpha = 90°$, $\gamma = 60°$, $c = 10.39$
7. $\gamma = 68°$, $a = 3.88$, $c = 6.61$ **9.** $\beta = 73.25°$, $\gamma = 56.75°$, $c = 4.37$; $\beta = 106.75°$, $\gamma = 23.25°$, $c = 2.06$

11. $\alpha = 55.17°$, $\gamma = 86.83°$, $c = 19.46$; $\alpha = 124.83°$, $\gamma = 17.17°$, $c = 5.75$ **13.** No triangle possible
15. $\alpha = 22.06°$, $\gamma = 5.94°$, $c = 2.20$ **17. (a)** $6.69 < b < 10$ **(b)** $b \geq 10$ or $b = 6.69$ **(c)** $0 < b < 6.69$
19. From A: 19.70 miles; from B: 15.05 miiles; from the road: 11.86 miles   **21.** 0.72 miles
23. $\alpha = 128.89°$, $\gamma = 29.11°$, $c = 3.85$

SECTION 9.2

1. No solution   **3.** $\alpha = 24.56°$, $\beta = 99.22°$, $\gamma = 56.23°$
5. $a = 9.83$, $\beta = 89.32°$, $\gamma = 35.68°$
7. No solution   **9.** No solution   **11. (a)** $6.78 < b < 8$
(b) $b = 6.78$ or $b > 8$ **(c)** $0 < b < 6.78$
13. 17.55 square units   **15.** 110.35 square units
17. 5.56 square units   **19.** 841.22 ft   **21.** 93.27°
23. 42.50 ft   **25.** 41.56 ft
27. From A: 893.64 ft; height: 1123.56 ft   **29.** 61.73 ft
31. $A = \pi r^2 \cdot \dfrac{\theta}{2\pi} = \dfrac{r^2\theta}{2}$ **33.** $A = \dfrac{P\theta}{2(\theta + 2)^2}$ from exercise 32. Let $x = \theta$. For P constant, A is maximum when $f(x) = \dfrac{x}{2(x + 2)^2}$ is maximum.

SECTION 9.3

1. $2 + 7i$ **3.** $14 - 8i$ **5.** i
7. $a = 2$, $b = 2$, $|z_1| = 2\sqrt{2}$ **9.** $2\sqrt{2}(\cos\frac{\pi}{4} + i\sin\frac{\pi}{4})$
11. $3 + 0i$ **13.** $4 - 4i$

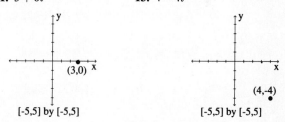

(3,0)   [-5,5] by [-5,5]

(4,-4)   [-5,5] by [-5,5]

15. $\sqrt{3} + i$

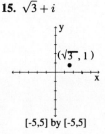

$(\sqrt{3}, 1)$

[-5,5] by [-5,5]

17. $\sqrt{2}(\cos\frac{\pi}{4} + i\sin\frac{\pi}{4})$ **19.** $4(\cos\frac{7\pi}{6} + i\sin\frac{7\pi}{6})$
21. $\sqrt{10}(\cos 1.25 + i\sin 1.25)$ **23.** $5(\cos 5.36 + i\sin 5.36)$
25. $\sqrt{13}(\cos 0.98 + i\sin 0.98)$
27. $\sqrt{66}(\cos 4.89 + i\sin 4.89)$ **29.** $1 + \sqrt{3}i$
31. $0.96 - 3.26i$ **33.** $6i$ **35.** $-0.36 + 2.42i$
37. Product: $0.26 + 0.97i$; quotient: $0.97 + 0.26i$
39. Product: $-2.20 + 8.20i$; quotient: $-2.05 + 0.55i$
41. $1 + 7i$ **43.** $11 + 6i$ **45.** $5\sqrt{13}$ **47.** $5 + 7i$

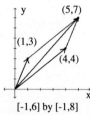

[-1,6] by [-1,8]

SECTION 9.4

1. $5(\cos 5.36 + i\sin 5.36)$ **3.** $\sqrt{34}(\cos 0.54 + i\sin 0.54)$
5. $2(\cos\frac{3\pi}{2} + i\sin\frac{3\pi}{2})$ **7.** $\cos\frac{3\pi}{4} + i\sin\frac{3\pi}{4}$ **9.** 2
11. $-4 - 4i$ **13.** -8 **15.** -1 **17.** (a) $(2+i)^2 =$
$[\sqrt{5}(\cos 0.4636 + i\sin 0.4636)]^2 = 5(\cos 0.9273 + i\sin 0.9273) =$
$3 + 4i$ (b) $(2+i)^2 = (2+i)(2+i) = 4 + 4i + i^2 = 3 + 4i$
19. $1, 0.31 \pm 0.95i, -0.81 \pm 0.59i$

[-2,2] by [-2,2]

21. (a) $(\frac{1}{\sqrt{2}} + \frac{1}{\sqrt{2}}i)^8 = (\cos\frac{\pi}{4} + i\sin\frac{\pi}{4})^8 = \cos 2\pi + i\sin 2\pi =$
1 (b) $(-\frac{1}{\sqrt{2}} + \frac{1}{\sqrt{2}}i)^8 = (\cos\frac{3\pi}{4} + i\sin\frac{3\pi}{4})^8 = \cos 6\pi +$
$i\sin 6\pi = 1$ (c) $(-\frac{1}{\sqrt{2}} - \frac{1}{\sqrt{2}}i)^8 = (\cos\frac{5\pi}{4} + i\sin\frac{5\pi}{4})^8 =$
$\cos 10\pi + i\sin 10\pi = 1$ (d) $(\frac{1}{\sqrt{2}} - \frac{1}{\sqrt{2}}i)^8 = (\cos\frac{7\pi}{4} +$
$i\sin\frac{7\pi}{4})^8 = \cos 14\pi + i\sin 14\pi = 1$
23. $\pm 1, \pm i, \frac{1}{\sqrt{2}} \pm \frac{1}{\sqrt{2}}i, -\frac{1}{\sqrt{2}} \pm \frac{1}{\sqrt{2}}i$

25. Roots: $\pm 1, \pm i$

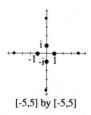

[-5,5] by [-5,5]

27. Roots: $\sqrt[8]{8}(\cos\theta + i\sin\theta)$ for $\theta = \frac{\pi}{16}, \frac{9\pi}{16}, \frac{17\pi}{16}, \frac{25\pi}{16}$

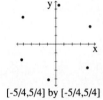

[-1.5,1.5] by [-1.5,1.5]

29. Roots: $\sqrt[12]{8}(\cos\theta + i\sin\theta)$ for $\theta = \frac{\pi}{8}, \frac{11\pi}{24}, \frac{19\pi}{24}, \frac{9\pi}{8}, \frac{35\pi}{24}, \frac{43\pi}{24}$

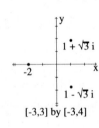

[-5/4,5/4] by [-5/4,5/4]

31. $z = -8$; roots: $-2, 1 \pm \sqrt{3}i$

[-3,3] by [-3,4]

33. Roots: $\sqrt[8]{50}(\cos\theta + i\sin\theta)$ for $\theta = 78.75°, 168.75°,$
$258.75°, 348.75°$

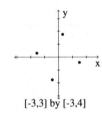

[-3,3] by [-3,4]

35. $(-1+i)^{12} = [\sqrt{2}(\cos\frac{3\pi}{4} + i\sin\frac{3\pi}{4})]^{12} = (\sqrt{2})^{12}(\cos 9\pi + i\sin 9\pi) = 64(-1 + 0i) = -64$

SECTION 9.5

1. $\sqrt{18}, 45°$ **3.** $\sqrt{10}, 341.47°$ **5.** $(1, 7)$
7. $(-3, 8)$ **9.** $(4, -9)$ **11.** $\sqrt{50}$

13. (a) $\mathbf{u} + \mathbf{v} = (4, 9)$ **(b)** $\mathbf{u} - \mathbf{v} = (-2, -3)$

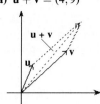 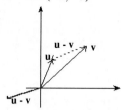

15. $(4, 2)$ **17.** $(12, 6)$ **19.** $(8, -11)$ **21.** $\sqrt{20}$
23. 0 **25.**

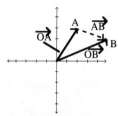

27. $-3\mathbf{i} + 6\mathbf{j}$ **29.** $-\mathbf{i} + 8\mathbf{j}$
31. For $\mathbf{u}$: $51.13°$; for $\mathbf{v}$: $0°$; angle between: $51.13°$
33. For $\mathbf{u}$: $116.57°$; for $\mathbf{v}$: $306.87°$; angle between: $167.70°$
35. $(5, 7) = \frac{19}{5}\mathbf{r} + \frac{3}{5}\mathbf{s}$; $\mathbf{v}$ is the diagonal vector of the parallelogram formed by vectors $\mathbf{r}$ and $\mathbf{s}$.   **37.** $(x, y) = t(a, b) + u(c, d)$ where $t = \dfrac{dx - cy}{ad - bc}$ and $u = \dfrac{ay - bx}{ad - bc}$ for any $a, b, c,$ and d, provided $ad - bc \neq 0$.   **39.** $(79.88, -453.01)$
41. Velocity: $(52.52, -528.19)$; speed: 530.79 mph; direction: $5.68°$ east of south   **43.** 433.49 mph; $2.72°$ north of west
45. Answers will vary with choice of graphing utility.
47. $(36t \cos 70°, 36t \sin 70°)$ **49.** This model ignores the effects of air resistance and gravity. According to this model, the ball will never return to the ground.
51. $t = 3.71$ sec   **53.** $t = 2.11$ sec   **55.** Law of cosines: $d^2 = |\mathbf{u}|^2 + |\mathbf{v}|^2 - 2|\mathbf{u}||\mathbf{v}| \cos \beta$ yields $\cos \beta = \dfrac{|\mathbf{u}|^2 + |\mathbf{v}|^2 - d^2}{2|\mathbf{u}||\mathbf{v}|}$. Then $\beta = \cos^{-1}\left(\dfrac{|\mathbf{u}|^2 + |\mathbf{v}|^2 - d^2}{2|\mathbf{u}||\mathbf{v}|} \right)$

Chapter 9 Review

Note: For Exercises 1 through 9, a, b, and c represent positive lengths.
1. $b = 3.88$, $\gamma = 68°$, $c = 6.61$
3. $\beta = 113.50°$, $b = 27.55$, $c = 18.16$
5. $\gamma = 72°$, $a = 2.94$, $b = 5.05$
7. $\alpha = 44.42°$, $b = 78.46°$, $\gamma = 57.12°$

9. (a) $5.63 < b < 12$
(b) $b = 5.63$ or $b \geq 12$ **(c)** $0 < b < 5.63$
11. 22.98 square units   **13.** 0.61 mi   **15.** $\alpha = 1.25$
17. $-2 - 5i$ **19.** $10 - 10i$ **21.** $-\frac{17}{58} - \frac{1}{58}i$
23.

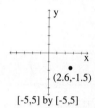

[-5,5] by [-5,5]
25. $3(\cos(-\frac{\pi}{6}) + \sin(\frac{\pi}{6})i \approx 2.6 - 1.5i$

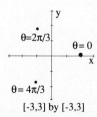

[-5,5] by [-5,5]
27. $5(\cos 126.87° + i \sin 126.87°)$ **29.** $23 + 14i$
31. $-16 + 30i$ **33.** $-2.60 + 1.5i$
35. $-3.20 + 2.39i$ **37.** $\sqrt{3}(\cos 2.19 + i \sin 2.19)$; $\sqrt{3}(\cos \theta + i \sin \theta)$ for $\theta = 2.19 + 2k\pi$, k any integer   **39.** $\sqrt{8}(\cos \frac{5\pi}{4} + i \sin \frac{5\pi}{4})$; $\sqrt{8}(\cos \theta + i \sin \theta)$ for $\theta = \frac{5\pi}{4} + 2k\pi$, k any integer
41. $5 + 5\sqrt{3}i$ **43.** $\frac{5\sqrt{2}}{4} + \frac{5\sqrt{2}}{4}i$
45. $\dfrac{3(\cos 30° + i \sin 30°)}{4(\cos 60° + i \sin 60°)} = \dfrac{\frac{3\sqrt{3}}{2} + \frac{3}{2}i}{2 + 2\sqrt{3}}$
$= \dfrac{\frac{3\sqrt{3}}{2} + \frac{3}{2}i}{2 + 2\sqrt{3}} \cdot \dfrac{2 + 2\sqrt{3}}{2 + 2\sqrt{3}} = \dfrac{6\sqrt{3} - 6i}{16} = \dfrac{3\sqrt{3}}{8} - \dfrac{3}{8}i$. Also
$\frac{3}{4}(\cos(-30°) + i \sin(-30°)) = \frac{3}{4}(\frac{\sqrt{3}}{2} + (-\frac{1}{2}i)) = \dfrac{3\sqrt{3}}{8} - \dfrac{3}{8}i$
47. $-128 + 221.70i$ **49.** $83190.41 + 83190.41i$

51. Roots: $2(\cos \theta + i \sin \theta)$ for $\theta = 0, \frac{2\pi}{3}, \frac{4\pi}{3}$

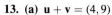

[-3,3] by [-3,3]

53. Roots: $\sqrt[8]{32}(\cos \theta + i \sin \theta)$ for $\theta = \frac{7\pi}{16}, \frac{15\pi}{16}, \frac{23\pi}{16}, \frac{31\pi}{16}$

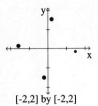

[-2,2] by [-2,2]

55. $(1,7)$ **57.** $\sqrt{10}$ **59.** $(3,6)$ **61.** $\sqrt{61}$
63. $-2\mathbf{i}+\mathbf{j}$
65. For $\mathbf{u}$: $36.87°$; for $\mathbf{v}$: $68.20°$; angle between: $31.33°$
67. $(x,y) = \frac{x+2y}{5}(1,2) + \frac{2x-y}{5}(2,-1)$
69. $\mathbf{v} = (90.14, -424.82)$; 434.28 mph; $11.98°$ east of south

C H A P T E R   10

SECTION 10.1

1. $(3,-17)$ **3.** $(50/7, -10/7)$
5. No solution, parallel lines   **7.** $(8,-2)$ **9.** $(4,2)$
11. No solution, parallel lines   **13. (a)** Substitution
(b)

[-150,150] by [-150,150]

(c) 2 solutions   **(d)** $(50+20\sqrt{5}, 50-20\sqrt{5})$, $(50-20\sqrt{5}, 50+20\sqrt{5})$ **15.** $(1/2, 6, 3)$ **17.** 50 yards by 60 yards
19. 380 student tickets, 72 nonstudent tickets
21. Small: \$0.57, medium: \$0.77, large: \$1
23. \$21,333.33 at 7.5%, \$16,666.67 at 6%
25. The algebraic solution is easier; the graphs are nearly identical in the standard VR. Solution: $(-5,1)$ **27.** \$23.15 when $x = 61.54$ units (62 units to nearest whole unit)
29. $(6.97, 43.03), (43.03, 6.97)$

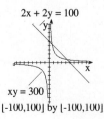

$2x + 2y = 100$

$xy = 300$

[-100,100] by [-100,100]

SECTION 10.2

1. Size: 3 by 4; 3 rows, 4 columns

3. $\begin{pmatrix} -1 & 2 & 3 & -1 \\ 3 & 2 & 4 & 3 \\ 2 & 6 & -2 & 3 \end{pmatrix}$ **5.** $\begin{pmatrix} -1 & 2 & 3 & -1 \\ 0 & 8 & 13 & 0 \\ 2 & 6 & -2 & 3 \end{pmatrix}$

7. $\begin{pmatrix} 1 & 0 & 0 & 50/49 \\ 0 & 1 & 0 & 13/98 \\ 0 & 0 & 1 & -4/49 \end{pmatrix}$

9. $a_{13} = -9$, $a_{32} = 0$, $a_{23} = -1$, $a_{25} = 3$, $a_{34} = -4$

11. $\begin{pmatrix} 3 & 0 & -9 & 2 & 1 \\ 1 & 1 & -1 & 0 & 3 \\ 0 & 0 & 0 & 0 & 0 \end{pmatrix}$

13. $\begin{pmatrix} 1 & 0 & -3 & 2/3 & 1/3 \\ 0 & 1 & 2 & -2/3 & 8/3 \\ 0 & 0 & 0 & 0 & 0 \end{pmatrix}$ **15.** $\begin{pmatrix} 1 & 0 & 0 & -1 \\ 0 & 1 & 0 & 1 \\ 0 & 0 & 1 & 2 \end{pmatrix}$

17. $\begin{pmatrix} 1 & -3 & 6 \\ 2 & 1 & 19 \end{pmatrix}$; solution: $(9,1)$ **19.** $\begin{pmatrix} 1 & -1 & 1 & 6 \\ 1 & 1 & 2 & -2 \end{pmatrix}$; solution:$(2 - 1.5z, -4 - 0.5z, z)$ for any real z

21. $\begin{pmatrix} 1 & -1 & 1 & 0 \\ 2 & 0 & -3 & -1 \\ -1 & -1 & 2 & -1 \end{pmatrix}$; solution: $(1,2,1)$

23. $\begin{pmatrix} 1 & 1 & -2 & 2 \\ 3 & -1 & 1 & 4 \\ -2 & -2 & 4 & 6 \end{pmatrix}$; no solution

25. $\begin{pmatrix} 1 & 1 & -2 & 2 \\ 3 & -1 & 1 & 1 \\ -2 & -2 & 4 & -4 \end{pmatrix}$; solution: $(0.75 + 0.25z, 1.25 + 1.75z, z)$ for any real z **27.** $\begin{pmatrix} 1 & 1 & -1 & 0 & 4 \\ 0 & 1 & 0 & 1 & 4 \\ 1 & -1 & 0 & 0 & 1 \\ 1 & 0 & 1 & 1 & 4 \end{pmatrix}$; solution: $(2, 1, -1, 3)$ **29.** $\begin{pmatrix} 2 & 1 & 1 & 2 & -3.5 \\ 1 & 1 & 1 & 1 & -1.5 \end{pmatrix}$; solution: $(-2 - w, 0.5 - z, z, w)$ for any real z and w
31. 724 children, 364 adults
33. \$7200 at 6%, \$3600 at 8%, \$9200 at 10%
35. $y = -x^2 + x + 10$ **37.** Answers may vary.

SECTION 10.3

1. $A \cdot B = \begin{pmatrix} -4 & -18 \\ -11 & -17 \end{pmatrix}$, $B \cdot A = \begin{pmatrix} 5 & -12 \\ 0 & -26 \end{pmatrix}$

3. $A \cdot B = \begin{pmatrix} 2 & 2 \\ -11 & 12 \end{pmatrix}$, $B \cdot A = \begin{pmatrix} 4 & 8 & -5 \\ -5 & 4 & -6 \\ -2 & -8 & 6 \end{pmatrix}$

5. $A \cdot B = \begin{pmatrix} 6 & -7 & -2 \\ 3 & 7 & 3 \\ 8 & -1 & -1 \end{pmatrix}$, $B \cdot A = \begin{pmatrix} 2 & 1 & 3 \\ 5 & 0 & 0 \\ -18 & -3 & 10 \end{pmatrix}$

7. $\begin{pmatrix} 2 & 5 \\ 1 & -2 \end{pmatrix} \begin{pmatrix} x \\ y \end{pmatrix} = \begin{pmatrix} -3 \\ 1 \end{pmatrix}$

9. $\begin{pmatrix} 5 & -7 & 1 \\ 2 & -3 & -1 \\ 1 & 1 & 1 \end{pmatrix} \begin{pmatrix} x \\ y \\ z \end{pmatrix} = \begin{pmatrix} 2 \\ 3 \\ -3 \end{pmatrix}$

11. $\begin{cases} 3x & - & y & = & -1 \\ 2x & + & 4y & = & 3 \end{cases}$

13. $\begin{cases} x & & - & 3z & = & 3 \\ 2x & - & y & + & 3z & = & -1 \\ -2x & + & 3y & - & 4z & = & 2 \end{cases}$

15. $\begin{pmatrix} -1/10 & 3/10 \\ -2/5 & 1/5 \end{pmatrix}$ **17.** No inverse; determinant is 0

19. $\begin{pmatrix} 2/3 & 0 & -1/6 \\ -2 & 1 & 0 \\ -1/3 & 0 & 1/3 \end{pmatrix}$ **21.** $(13/14, -12/7)$

23. $(2, 0)$ **25.** $(2.25, -0.75, -1.75)$

27. For A: $C(x) = x^2 - 8x + 13$; for B: $C(x) = x^2 - 4x - 1$

29. For A: 2.27 and 5.73; for B: -0.24 and 4.24

31. For A: $a_{11} + a_{22} = 8 = $ sum of eigenvalues of A; for B: $b_{11} + b_{22} = 4 = $ sum of eigenvalues of B. Conjecture: The sum of the main diagonal entries equals the sum of the eigenvalues of the matrix.   **33. (a)** $\begin{cases} 4a & + & 2b & + & c & = & 8 \\ 36a & + & 6b & + & c & = & 3 \\ 81a & + & 9b & + & c & = & 4 \end{cases}$

(b) $\begin{pmatrix} 4 & 2 & 1 \\ 36 & 6 & 1 \\ 81 & 9 & 1 \end{pmatrix} \begin{pmatrix} a \\ b \\ c \end{pmatrix} = \begin{pmatrix} 8 \\ 3 \\ 4 \end{pmatrix}$ **(c)** $\begin{pmatrix} 0.2261904762 \\ -3.05952381 \\ 13.2142857 \end{pmatrix}$;

$y = 0.23x^2 - 3.06x + 13.21$ **(d)** See graph in (e).

(e)

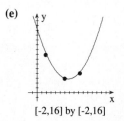

$[-2,16]$ by $[-2,16]$

35. (a) $\begin{cases} 8a & + & 4b & + & 2c & + & d & = & 8 \\ 64a & + & 16b & + & 4c & + & d & = & 5 \\ 216a & + & 36b & + & 6c & + & d & = & 3 \\ 729a & + & 81b & + & 9c & + & d & = & 4 \end{cases}$

(b) $\begin{pmatrix} 8 & 4 & 2 & 1 \\ 64 & 16 & 4 & 1 \\ 216 & 36 & 6 & 1 \\ 729 & 81 & 9 & 1 \end{pmatrix} \begin{pmatrix} a \\ b \\ c \\ d \end{pmatrix} = \begin{pmatrix} 8 \\ 5 \\ 3 \\ 4 \end{pmatrix}$

(c) $\begin{pmatrix} 0.202380952 \\ -0.1178571429 \\ -1.35952381 \\ 11.02857143 \end{pmatrix}$;

$y = 0.02x^3 - 0.12x^2 - 1.36x + 11.03$ **(d)** See graph in (e).

(e)

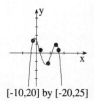

$[-10,20]$ by $[-20,40]$

37. (a) $\begin{cases} a & - & b & + & c & - & d & + & e & = & 8 \\ a & + & b & + & c & + & d & + & e & = & 2 \\ 256a & + & 64b & + & 16c & + & 4d & + & e & = & -6 \\ 2401a & + & 343b & + & 49c & + & 7d & + & e & = & 5 \\ 4096a & + & 512b & + & 64c & + & 8d & + & e & = & 2 \end{cases}$

(b) $\begin{pmatrix} 1 & -1 & 1 & -1 & 1 \\ 1 & 1 & 1 & 1 & 1 \\ 256 & 64 & 16 & 4 & 1 \\ 2401 & 343 & 49 & 7 & 1 \\ 4096 & 512 & 64 & 8 & 1 \end{pmatrix} \begin{pmatrix} a \\ b \\ c \\ d \\ e \end{pmatrix} = \begin{pmatrix} 8 \\ 2 \\ -6 \\ 5 \\ 2 \end{pmatrix}$

(c) $\begin{pmatrix} -0.0569444444 \\ 0.75 \\ -1.965277778 \\ -3.75 \\ 7.022222222 \end{pmatrix}$;

$y = -0.0569x^4 + 0.75x^3 - 1.9652x^2 - 3.75x + 7.0222$

(d) See graph in (e).   **(e)**

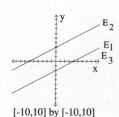

$[-10,20]$ by $[-20,25]$

SECTION 10.4

1. No solution; E_1 and E_2 are parallel.

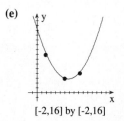

$[-10,10]$ by $[-10,10]$

3. $(6, 2)$ **5.** $(10, 10)$ **7.** Solution: $(3.14266, 15.713)$; max error of 0.001 in x; VR: $[3.142, 3.143]$ by $[15.71, 15.72]$; Xscl: 0.0001, Yscl: 0.001 (Answers may vary.)

9. $(2.236, 1.00), (-2.236, 1.00)$

11. $(-0.1034, -9.668)$, $(-1.5386, -0.650)$, $(3.1420, 0.318)$
13. $(-7.6426, -63.69)$, $(-0.5106, 8.718)$, $(1.1532, 10.977)$
15. $(1.1726, 1.612)$ **17.** There are an infinite number of solutions, all in Quadrant I. Solutions for $x < 5$ are:
$(0.5380, 1.859)$, $(2.1300, 0.469)$, $(3.8763, 0.258)$
19. $T(x) = \frac{11}{3}x^2 - \frac{32}{3}x + 5$
21. 5 nickels, 2 dimes, 10 quarters   **23.** 2 solutions

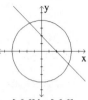

[-6,6] by [-6,6]

25. $(1+\sqrt{7}, 1-\sqrt{7})$, $(1-\sqrt{7}, 1+\sqrt{7})$ **27.** $(4.3060, 2.541)$, $(-4.3060, 2.541)$, $(3.5297, -3.541)$, $(-3.5297, -3.541)$

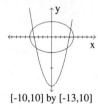

[-10,10] by [-13,10]

29. $V(x) = 4x^3 - 140x^2 + 1200x$
31. $x = 1.1490$ and 11.8890 (error in x at most 0.0001)
33. $23.25 when $x = 11.5091$ (12 units to the nearest whole unit)   **35.**

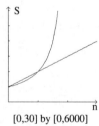

[0,30] by [0,6000]

37.

Years	19	19.5	19.9	19.99	20
Value	$20,000	$40,000	$200,000	$2,000,000	Undefined

SECTION 10.5

1. $(-1.4796, 1.7398)$, $(2.9196, -0.4598)$
3. $(-3.0981, 3.549)$, $(2.0981, 0.951)$ **5.** $(2.1965, 1.362)$, $(2.1965, -1.362)$, $(-2.1965, 1.362)$, $(-2.1965, -1.362)$
7. $(1.3657, 0.731)$, $(-1.3657, 0.731)$, $(1.0355, -0.856)$,

$(-1.0355, -0.856)$ **9.** $(-2.3166, 0.585)$, $(-2.3166, -0.585)$, $(4.3166, 1.913)$, $(4.3166, -1.913)$ **11.** $(0.2058, 1.8700)$, $(1.8700, 0.2058)$, $(-2.7459, -0.5299)$, $(-0.5299, -2.7459)$

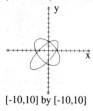

[-10,10] by [-10,10]

13. $(0.1518, 1.8436)$, $(1.6320, -0.238)$, $(-2.0784, 0.1890)$, $(-0.3675, -2.605)$

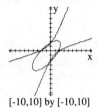

[-10,10] by [-10,10]

15.

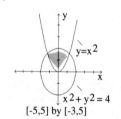

[-5,5] by [-3,5]

17.

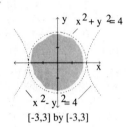

[-3,3] by [-3,3]

19. The solution is the shaded region inside the ellipse bounded by the right arm of the hyperbola.

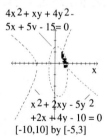

[-10,10] by [-5,3]

21. $\begin{cases} F(x) = \dfrac{0.58(84) + x}{84 + x} \\ g(x) \ge 0.7 \\ h(x) \le 0.8 \end{cases}$

$33.60 \le x \le 92.40$

23. $\begin{cases} x \ge 0 \\ y \ge 0.58 \end{cases}$ Solution:

25. $\begin{cases} A + B < 30,000 \\ A \ge 3000 \\ B \ge 8600 \\ 0.25A + 0.65B < 10,000 \end{cases}$

27.

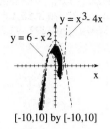

$y = 6 - x^2$

$y = x^3 - 4x$

x

[-10,10] by [-10,10]

Chapter 10 Review

1. $(5, 6)$ **3.** $(x, 2x - 3)$ for any real number x

5. $(4, 1, -5)$ **7.** $\begin{pmatrix} 1 & -1 & 1 & 6 \\ 1 & 1 & 2 & -4 \end{pmatrix}$; solution:

$(1 - 1.5z, -5 - 0.5z, z)$ for any real number z

9. $\begin{pmatrix} 4 & -2 & 0 & 0 \\ 1 & 3 & -1 & -3 \\ 0 & 6 & 2 & 16 \end{pmatrix}$; solution: $(5/13, 10/13, 74/13)$ (or,

in decimal form, $(0.3846, 0.7692, 5.6923))$

11. $\begin{pmatrix} 2 & -4 & 0 & 10 \\ 1 & 0 & -1 & -1 \\ 0 & 2 & -1 & -5 \end{pmatrix}$; no solution **13.** $\begin{pmatrix} 5 & -5 & -3 \\ 4 & -10 & 0 \end{pmatrix}$

15. $\begin{pmatrix} -1 & -1 & 6 \\ 4 & -18 & 20 \end{pmatrix}$

17. $(1.2143, 0.1429)$ (or, as fractions, $(17/14, 1/7))$

19. $(2.2128, 1.3844)$ **21.** $(1.0479, -1.0136, 0.4049)$

23. No solution **25.** $(-0.2944, 5.632), (6.7944, 14.493)$

27. $(-3.2623, 5.358)$ **29.** $(-6.3970, 49.676), (0.4018, 46.017),$

$(5.9730, 47.613)$ **31.** $(5.0804, -0.54), (-23.2622, 13.63)$

33. No solution **35.** 2 solutions

37. $(-1.2313, -1.342), (2.4807, 1.920)$ **39.** No solution

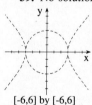

[-6,6] by [-6,6]

CHAPTER 11

SECTION 11.1

1. $(1, 0)$ and $(6, 5)$

[-2,7] by [-1,7]

3. $(5, 4)$ and $(-7, 8)$

[-8,6] by [-2,10]

5. $(5, 2/5)$, no left endpoint

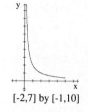

[-2,7] by [-1,10]

7. $(3, 0)$ and $(3, 0)$

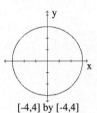

[-4,4] by [-4,4]

9. $x + 3y = 17$; line

11. $y = \dfrac{x^2}{4}$; parabola from $(-6, 9)$ to $(2, 1)$

13. $y = \sqrt{9 - x^2}$; semicircle with center $(0, 0)$, $r = 3$

15. $x(t) = t, y(t) = 3t^2 - 4t + 5$

17. $x(t) = t, y(t) = 7 + t^2 - 3t$

19. Functions: $1, 2, 3, 4, 5, 6$, and 8.

21. $D = [-2, 3], R = [-3, 2]$

23. $D = (0, 5], R = [0.4, \infty)$

25. $x(t) = 5 \cos t, y(t) = 5 \sin t$ for t in $[0, 2\pi]$

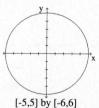

[-5,5] by [-6,6]

27. $x(t) = 6 \cos t, y(t) = 6 \sin t + 10$ for t in $[0, 2\pi]$

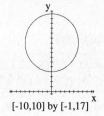

[-10,10] by [-1,17]

29.

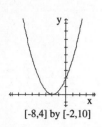

[-8,4] by [-2,10]

31.

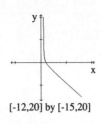

[-12,20] by [-15,20]

(e) $a = 5$; period: 10π; max: $y = 10$

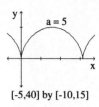

a = 5

[-5,40] by [-10,15]

33.

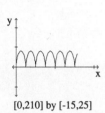

[0,210] by [-15,25]

35.

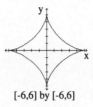

[-6,6] by [-6,6]

SECTION 11.2

1. $(\sqrt{2}, 45°)$ **3.** $(5, 126.87°)$ **5.** $(0, 0)$
7. $(2.12, -2.12)$ **9.** $(-2.12, 2.12)$
11. Answers will vary: $(\sqrt{8}, 135°), (\sqrt{8}, 11\pi/4), (-\sqrt{8}, -45°)$
13. Answers will vary: $(2, 150°), (2, 510°), (-2, -30°)$
15. Answers will vary: $(\sqrt{13}, -56.3°), (\sqrt{13}, 303.69°),$
$(-\sqrt{13}, 123.69°)$ **17.** Answers will vary: $(\sqrt{10}, -161.57°),$
$(\sqrt{10}, 198.43°), (-\sqrt{10}, 18.43°)$

37. $D = [-5, 5]$, $R = [-5, 5]$

39. $g(x) = 3 - \left(\dfrac{x - b}{a}\right)^2$; $D = [ac + b, ad + b]$ for $I = [c, d]$

41. (a) $a = 1$; period: 2π; max: $y = 2$

a = 1

[-5,12] by [-3,4]

(b) $a = 2$; period: 4π; max: $y = 4$

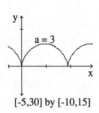

a = 2

[-5,20] by [-3,7]

(c) $a = 3$; period: 6π; max: $y = 6$

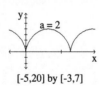

a = 3

[-5,30] by [-10,15]

(d) $a = 4$; period: 8π; max: $y = 8$

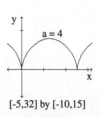

a = 4

[-5,32] by [-10,15]

19.

y

x

[-5,5] by [-3,5]

21. The graph is the y-axis.
23.

y

x

[-3,5] by [-3,5]

25.

y

x

[-3,6] by [-3,5]

27.

y

x

[-1,5] by [-3,3]

29. $x(t) = 3t\cos t$, $y(t) = 3t\sin t$ for t in $[0, 10\pi]$

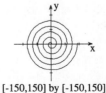

y

x

[-150,150] by [-150,150]

31. $x(t) = 5\sin 2t\cos t$, $y(t) = 5\sin 2t\sin t$ for t in $[0, \pi]$

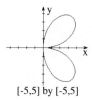

[-5,5] by [-5,5]

33. (a)

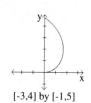

[-3,4] by [-1,5]

(b)

[-11,5] by [-3,8]

(c)

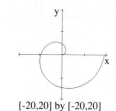

[-20,20] by [-20,20]

(d)

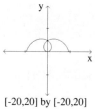

[-20,20] by [-20,20]

(e)

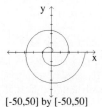

[-50,50] by [-50,50]

35. (a)

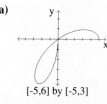

[-5,6] by [-5,3]

(b)

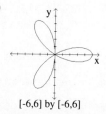

[-6,6] by [-6,6]

(c) See graph for part b   **(d)** See graph for part b   **(e)** See graph for part b   **37.** $-4\pi \leq \theta \leq 4\pi$

[-30,30] by [-30,30]

39. $0 \leq \theta \leq 2\pi$

[-6,2] by [-5,4]

41. $0 \leq \theta \leq 2\pi$

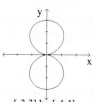

[-3,3] by [-4,4]

43. For n odd, there are n petals; for n even, $2n$ petals
45. All graphs are 4-petal roses; a determines the length of the petals.   **47.** 5 units   **49.** 8 units
51. 10 overlapping petals   **53.** 14 overlapping petals

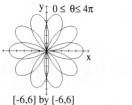

[-6,6] by [-6,6]

y $0 \leq \theta \leq 4\pi$

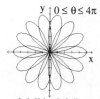

[-6,6] by [-6,6]

y $0 \leq \theta \leq 4\pi$

55. $(a/\sqrt{2}, \pi/4), (a/\sqrt{2}, 3\pi/4), (a/\sqrt{2}, 5\pi/4), (a/\sqrt{2}, 7\pi/4)$
57. 4-petal rose with petals of length 3

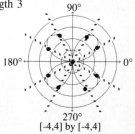

[-4,4] by [-4,4]

59. $(x, y) = (0,0), (2.5, 2.5), (-2.5, 2.5)$ (Note: Coordinates given in rectangular form for graphical solution.)
61. $(x, y) = (0,0), (0.96, 0.16), (0.96, -0.16), (2.29, 1.43), (2.29, -1.43), (0.41, 1.47), (0.41, -1.47)$ (Note: Coordinates given in rectangular form for graphical solution.)

SECTION 11.3

1.

[-25,25] by [-12,20]

3.

[-5,9] by [-6,4]

5. 1306.08 ft at 9.52 sec
7. $x(t) = 58t \cos 41°$, $y(t) = -16t^2 + 58t \sin 41°$
9. The portion in Quadrant I   **11.** 22.62 ft at 1.19 sec
13. 525.73 ft at 4.89 sec   **15.** Place Chris at the origin.
Chris: $x(t) = 41t \cos 39°$, $y(t) = -16t^2 + 41t \sin 39°$; Linda:
$x(t) = 78 - 45t \cos 44°$, $y(t) = -16t^2 + 45t \sin 44°$
17. $0 \le t \le 1.95$
19. Answers will vary. Example: 6.61 ft apart at $t = 1.2$ sec
21. $x(t) = 13 \cos(\pi/2 - \pi t)$, $y(t) = 13 + 13 \sin(\pi/2 - \pi t)$
23. Answers will vary. Example: 1.35 ft apart at 0.80 sec
25. A ball thrown from 59 ft away comes closest to Janice.
27.

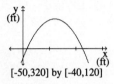

[-50,320] by [-40,120]

29. 77.59 ft   **31.** No home run; ball is 7.78 ft high when
300 ft from the plate.

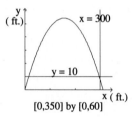

[0,350] by [0,60]

33. Home run; ball is 29.75 ft high when 300 ft from the plate.

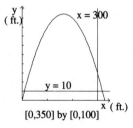

[0,350] by [0,100]

35. No home run; ball hits the ground 235.39 ft from the plate.

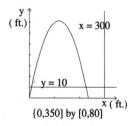

{0,350] by [0,80]

37.

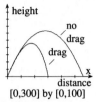

[0,300] by [0,100]

39. With resistance: $x = 150.55$ ft, $t = 3.41$ sec; without resistance: $x = 280$ ft, $t = 4$ sec,   **41.** Point P
has coordinates $(a\theta - a\sin\theta, a - a\cos\theta)$. The parametric
equations are $x(\theta) = a(\theta - \sin\theta)$ and $y(\theta) = a(1 - \cos\theta)$

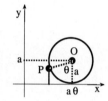

SECTION 11.4

1. Vertex: $(0,0)$; line of sym.: $x = 0$; focus: $(0,6)$; directrix: $y = -6$ **3.** Vertex: $(3,-1)$; line of sym.: $x = 3$;
focus: $(3,2)$; directrix: $y = -4$ **5.** Vertex: $(3,2)$; line of
sym.: $x = 3$; focus: $(3,127/64))$; directrix: $y = 129/64$
7. Vertex: $(-4,1)$; line of sym.: $x = -4$; focus: $(-4,-0.5)$;
directrix: $y = 2.5$ **9.** Horizontal shrink of $y^2 = x$ by a
factor of $1/12$, followed by horizontal shift left 3 units and
vertical shift down 4 units   **11.** Vertical stretch of $y = x^2$
by a factor of 6, then horizontal shift left 4 units and vertical
shift up 2 units
13. $-8(y - 1) = (x - 2)^2$; vertex: $(2,1)$; line of sym.: $x = 2$

[-7,10] by [-7,2]

15. $-2(x - 2.5) = (y + 1)^2$; vertex: $(2.5,-1)$; line of sym.:
$y = -1$

[-7,4] by [-6,5]

17. $-8(x-3) = (y-2)^2$; focus: $(1,2)$; line of sym.: $y = 2$

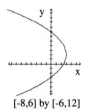

[-8,6] by [-6,12]

19. $-12(y-2) = (x-3)^2$; focus: $(3,-1)$; line of sym.: $x = 3$

[-7,15] by [-7,3]

21. $y-2 = (x+1)^2$; vertex: $(-1,2)$; focus: $(-1, 2.25)$; directrix: $y = 1.75$; line of sym.: $x = -1$

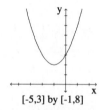

[-5,3] by [-1,8]

23. Vertical stretch of $y = x^2$ is $y = 4x^2$. A horizontal shrink by a factor of $1/2$ is given by $y = (2x)^2$. But $y = (2x)^2 = 4x^2$, so they are equivalent.   **25.** Major axis: $(1,-1)$, $(1,-5)$; minor axis: $(1-\sqrt{2}, -3)$, $(1+\sqrt{2}, -3)$; center: $(1,-3)$; foci: $(1,-3+\sqrt{2}, -3-\sqrt{2})$; lines of sym.: $x = 1$, $y = -3$

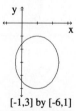

[-1,3] by [-6,1]

27. Major axis: $(-2+\sqrt{5}, 1)$, $(-2-\sqrt{5}, 1)$; minor axis: $\left(-2, 1+1/\sqrt{2}\right)$, $\left(-2, 1-1/\sqrt{2}\right)$; center: $(-2, 1)$; foci: $(-2+3/\sqrt{2}, 1)$, $(-2-3/\sqrt{2}, 1)$; lines of sym.: $x = -2$, $y = 1$

[-5,1] by [-1,3]

29.

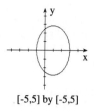

[-5,5] by [-5,5]

31.

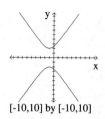

[-10,10] by [-10,10]

33. $\dfrac{(x-1)^2}{4} + \dfrac{(y+1)^2}{9} = 1$; major axis: $(1,2)$, $(1,-4)$; minor axis: $(-1,-1)$, $(3,-1)$; center: $(1,-1)$; foci: $(1, -1-\sqrt{5})$, $(1, -1+\sqrt{5})$; lines of sym.: $x = 1$, $y = -1$

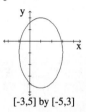

[-3,5] by [-5,3]

35. $\dfrac{(x-2)^2}{4} - \dfrac{(y-1)^2}{9} = 1$; center: $(2,1)$; foci: $(2+\sqrt{13}, 1)$, $(2-\sqrt{13}, 1)$; lines of sym.: $x = 2$, $y = 1$; asymptotes: $y-1 = \pm\frac{3}{2}(x-2)$; vertices: $(0,1)$, $(4,1)$

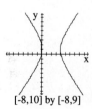

[-8,10] by [-8,9]

37. $\dfrac{(y-1)^2}{9} - \dfrac{(x+3)^2}{25} = 1$; center: $(-3,1)$; foci: $(-3, 1+\sqrt{34})$, $(-3, 1-\sqrt{34})$; lines of sym.: $x = -3$, $y = 1$; asymptotes: $y-1 = \pm\frac{3}{5}(x+3)$; vertices: $(-3,4)$, $(-3,-2)$

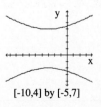

[-10,4] by [-5,7]

39. $\dfrac{x^2}{58} + \dfrac{y^2}{49} = 1$; major axis: $(\sqrt{58}, 0)$, $(-\sqrt{58}, 0)$; minor

axis: $(0, 7)$, $(0, -7)$

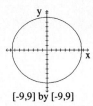

[-9,9] by [-9,9]

41. $\dfrac{x^2}{81/4} + \dfrac{y^2}{17/4} = 1$; major axis: $(9/2, 0)$, $(-9/2, 0)$; minor axis: $(0, \sqrt{17}/2)$, $(0, -\sqrt{17}/2)$

[-5,5] by [-3,3]

43. $\dfrac{(x-1)^2}{27} + \dfrac{(y-6)^2}{36} = 1$; major axis: $(1, 12)$, $(1, 0)$; minor axis: $(1 - 3\sqrt{3}, 6)$, $(1 + 3\sqrt{3}, 6)$

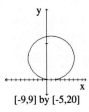

[-9,9] by [-5,20]

45. $\dfrac{x^2}{4} - \dfrac{y^2}{5} = 1$

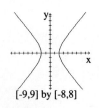

[-9,9] by [-8,8]

47. $\dfrac{x^2}{9/4} - \dfrac{(y-2)^2}{27/4} = 1$

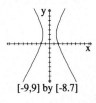

[-9,9] by [-8.7]

49. center: $(0, 3)$; foci: $(-3, 3)$, $(3, 3)$; vertices: $(-2, 3)$, $(2, 3)$; lines of sym.: $x = 0$, $y = 3$; asymptotes: $y - 3 = \pm\frac{\sqrt{5}}{2}x$

[-9,9] by [-6,10]

51. center: $(3, 1)$; foci: $(3, 1 + \sqrt{13})$, $(3, 1 - \sqrt{13})$; vertices: $(3, 4)$, $(3, -2)$; lines of sym.: $x = 3$, $y = 1$; asymptotes: $y - 1 = \pm\frac{3}{2}(x - 3)$

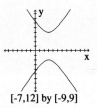

[-7,12] by [-9,9]

53. No points of intersection

55. Parabola; vertex: $(13/4, 1)$; focus: $(9/4, 1)$; line of sym.: $y = 1$ **57.** Ellipse; major axis: $(4, -10)$, $(4, -6)$; minor axis: $(3, -8)$, $(5, -8)$; foci: $(4, -8 + \sqrt{3})$, $(4, -8 - \sqrt{3})$; lines of sym.: $x = 4$, $y = -8$ **59.** Hyperbola; vertices: $(3, -3)$, $(-1, -3)$; foci: $(1 + \sqrt{68}, -3)$, $(1 - \sqrt{68}, -3)$; lines of sym.: $x = 1$, $y = -3$ **61.** Parabola; vertex: $(3/2, 7/2)$; focus: $(3/2, 23/8)$; line of sym.: $x = 3/2$

63. $h = 1$, $a = 1$, $k = 1$ (Answers may vary.)

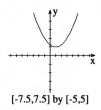

[-7.5,7.5] by [-5,5]

65. $h = 1$, $a = 2$, $b = 2$, $k = 1$ (Answers may vary.)

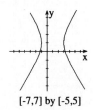

[-7,7] by [-5,5]

67. At the focus: $(0, 2.5)$ **69.** At the focus: $(3, 0)$
71. Place the patient at one focus and the sound source at the other. If the center of the machine is $(0, 0)$, the foci are at $(0, \sqrt{69})$ and $(0, -\sqrt{69})$, about 8.3 inches from the center.   **73.** $(0, 0), (6, 0)$ **75.** Light is reflected from the parabolic surface toward the focus. It is then reflected from the hyperbolic surface toward the second focus (the eyepiece).

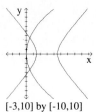

[-3,10] by [-10,10]

77. $\dfrac{(x - 15/8)^2}{81/64} - \dfrac{y^2}{9/4} = 1$
79. Ellipse

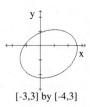

[-3,3] by [-4,3]

81. Ellipse

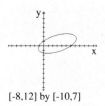

[-8,12] by [-10,7]

83. Degenerate conic, no graph

85. Hyperbola   **87.** Hyperbola

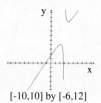

[-10,10] by [-6,12]

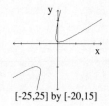

[-25,25] by [-20,15]

89. $20x^2 - 16xy + 32y^2 + 24x - 96y + 36 = 0$
91. No graph possible   **93.** Two lines: $x = \pm 1$
95. One point: $(0, 0)$ **97.** No graph possible

SECTION 11.5

1. $e = \sqrt{3}/2$

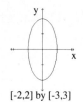

[-2,2] by [-3,3]

3. $e = 5/4$ **5.** $e = 1.29$

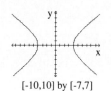

[-10,10] by [-7,7]

[-7,9] by [-6,6]

7. Center $(1, 1)$; length: $2\sqrt{3}$;
    Asymptotes: $y - 1 = \pm 0.816(x - 1)$
9. $e = 0.88$ (Answers will vary.)

[-3,6] by [-3,3]

11.

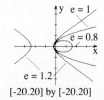

[-20,20] by [-20,20]

13.

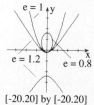

[-20,20] by [-20,20]

15. Parabola; $e = 1$; directrix: $x = -5$; $0 \le \theta \le 2\pi$

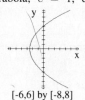

[-6,6] by [-8,8]

17. Ellipse; $e = 1/2$; directrix: $x = -3/2$; $0 \le \theta \le 2\pi$

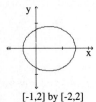

[-1,2] by [-2,2]

19. Ellipse; $e = 1/2$; directrix: $x = -8/3$; $0 \le \theta \le 2\pi$

[-4,4] by [-4,4]

21. Ellipse; $e = 3/4$; $\dfrac{(x + 2.29)^2}{(3.05)^2} + \dfrac{y^2}{(2.01)^2} = 1$

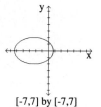

[-7,7] by [-7,7]

23. $e = 1/2$; $r_1 = r_2$ and the graphs coincide.

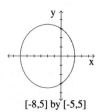

[-8,5] by [-5,5]

25. Hyperbola; $e > 1$

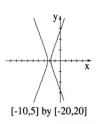

[-10,5] by [-20,20]

27. $e = 1/2$; see graph in exercise 31
29. $e = 1/2$; see graph in exercise 31   **31.** Graphs for exercises 27 and 29 are the same; graphs for exercises 28 and 30 are the same.

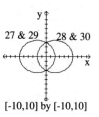

[-10,10] by [-10,10]

Chapter 11 Review

1. A straight line from $(2, 0)$ to $(17, 5)$

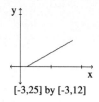

[-3,25] by [-3,12]

3. A circle with center $(0, 0)$ and radius 4

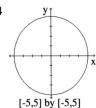

[-5,5] by [-5,5]

5. Exer. 1: $D = [2, 17]$, $R = [0, 5]$; Exer. 2: $D = [2, 8]$, $R = [3/4, 3]$; Exer. 3: $D = [-4, 4]$, $R = [-4, 4]$
7.   **9.**

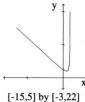

[-15,5] by [-3,22]

[-10,10] by [-3,7]

11. $x(t) = 5 + 4\cos t$ and $y(t) = 4\sin t$

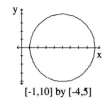

[-1,10] by [-4,5]

13.

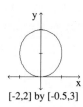

[-2,2] by [-0.5,3]

15.

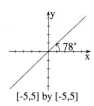

[-5,5] by [-5,5]

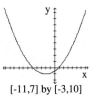

[-11,7] by [-3,10]

27. $x - 1 = -\frac{1}{24}(y-4)^2$; focus: $(-5, 4)$; line of sym.: $y = 4$

17.

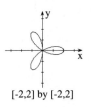

[-2,2] by [-2,2]

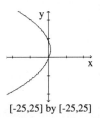

[-25,25] by [-25,25]

29. $y - 2 = (x+2)^2$; vertex: $(-2, 2)$; focus: $(-2, 9/4)$; directrix: $y = 7/4$; line of sym.: $x = -2$

19. (a)

(b)

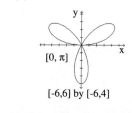

[0, π/2]

[-5,6] by [-6,4]

[0, π]

[-6,6] by [-6,4]

(c) For $0 \le \theta \le 2\pi$, see complete graph in (b)   **(d)** For $-\pi \le \theta \le \pi$, see complete graph in (b)   **(e)** For $0 \le \theta \le 4\pi$, see complete graph in (b)   **21.** $-20 \le \theta \le 20$ indicates the graph never repeats. There is no smallest interval for θ.

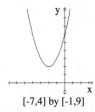

[-7,4] by [-1,9]

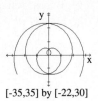

[-35,35] by [-22,30]

23. $(x, y) = (0, 0), (1.5, 1.5)$

31. Major axis: $(-3, 1 + \sqrt{6})$, $(-3, 1 - \sqrt{6})$; minor axis: $(-5, 1)$, $(-1, 1)$; center: $(-3, 1)$; foci: $(-3, 1 + \sqrt{2})$, $(-3, 1 - \sqrt{2})$; lines of sym.: $x = -3$, $y = 1$

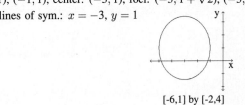

[-6,1] by [-2,4]

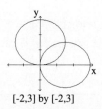

[-2,3] by [-2,3]

33. $\frac{x^2}{64} + \frac{y^2}{39} = 1$; major axis: $(8, 0)$, $(-8, 0)$; minor axis: $(0, \sqrt{39})$, $(0, -\sqrt{39})$

[-9,9] by [-7,8]

25. $y + 1 = \frac{1}{8}(x+2)^2$; vertex: $(-2, -1)$; line of sym.: $x = -2$

35. $\dfrac{(x-2)^2}{27} + \dfrac{(y-6)^2}{36} = 1$; major axis: $(2, 12)$, $(2, 0)$; minor axis: $(2 + 3\sqrt{3}, 6)$, $(2 - 3\sqrt{3}, 6)$

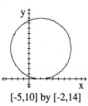

[-5,10] by [-2,14]

37. $\dfrac{(x-3)^2}{5} + \dfrac{(y+1)^2}{4} = 1$; major axis: $(3 + \sqrt{5}, -1)$, $(3 - \sqrt{5}, -1)$; minor axis: $(3, 1)$, $(3, -3)$; center: $(3, -1)$; foci: $(4, -1)$, $(2, -1)$; lines of sym.: $x = 3$, $y = -1$

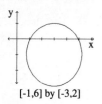

[-1,6] by [-3,2]

39. Center: $(-1, 3)$; foci: $(-1, 3+\sqrt{8})$, $(-1, 3-\sqrt{8})$; vertices: $(-1, 3 + \sqrt{5})$, $(-1, 3 - \sqrt{5})$; lines of sym.: $x = -1$, $y = 3$; asymptotes: $y - 3 = \pm\sqrt{5/3}\,(x + 1)$

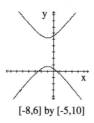

[-8,6] by [-5,10]

41. Parabola: $x = (y+3)^2$; focus: $(1/4, -3)$; vertex: $(0, -3)$; line of sym.: $y = -3$

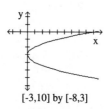

[-3,10] by [-8,3]

43. Hyperbola; $\dfrac{(y+3)^2}{1/4} - \dfrac{x^2}{1/9} = 1$; center: $(0, -3)$; foci: $(0, -3 + \sqrt{13}/6)$, $(0, -3 - \sqrt{13}/6)$; vertices: $(0, -5/2)$, $(0, -7/2)$; lines of sym.: $x = 0$, $y = -3$; asymptotes: $y + 3 = \pm\frac{3}{2}x$

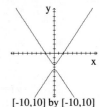

[-10,10] by [-10,10]

45. Use the quadratic formula to solve $Cy^2 + (Bx + E)y + (Ax^2 + Dx + F) = 0$ for y:
$$y = \dfrac{-(Bx+E) \pm \sqrt{(Bx+E)^2 - 4C(Ax^2 + Dx + F)}}{2C}.$$
Graph both equations in the same viewing rectangle.

47. Parabola

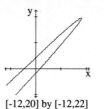

[-12,20] by [-12,22]

49. Hyperbola

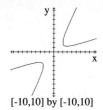

[-10,10] by [-10,10]

51. Center: $(-1.06, -0.86)$; major axis: $(0.03, 1.78)$, $(-2.12, -3.41)$; minor axis: $(-3.09, -0.02)$, $(0.79, -1.63)$; lines of sym.: $y = -0.43x - 1.32$, $y = 2.41x + 1.7$ (Answer may vary, especially if a non-square viewing rectangle is used.)
53. Vertical shrink of $y = x^2$ by a factor of $1/6$, horizontal shift right 3 units, vertical shift up 1 unit   **55.** Vertical stretch by a factor of 3 followed by horizontal stretch by a factor of 4   **57.** $\dfrac{x^2}{1} - \dfrac{y^2}{3} = 1$

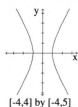

[-4,4] by [-4,5]

59. $(-0.73, 8.46)$, $(2.73, 1.54)$
61. $\dfrac{x^2}{25} + \dfrac{y^2}{4} = 1$; foci: $(\sqrt{21}, 0)$, $(-\sqrt{21}, 0)$

[-6,6] by [-4,4]

63. Max height: 91.69 ft; distance: 307.9 ft
65.

[-30,150] by [-50,35]

67. 2.15 sec   **69.**   **71.** 67.1 ft

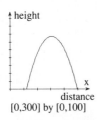

[0,300] by [0,100]

CHAPTER 12

SECTION 12.1

1. $a_1 = 1, a_2 = -1, a_3 = 1, a_4 = -1, a_{10} = -1$
3. $a_1 = 2, a_2 = 3/2, a_3 = 4/3, a_4 = 5/4, a_{10} = 11/10$
5. $a_1 = 0, a_2 = 7/3, a_3 = 13/2, a_4 = 63/5, a_{10} = 999/11$
7. $a_1 = -2, a_2 = 3/2, a_3 = -4/3, a_4 = 5/4, a_{10} = 11/10$
9. $a_1 = 3, a_2 = 4, a_3 = 5, a_4 = 6, a_8 = 10, a_n = n + 2$
11. $a_1 = 2, a_2 = 4, a_3 = 8, a_4 = 16, a_8 = 256, a_n = 2^n$
13. $a_n = 2n + 1$ **15.** $a_n = 2 \cdot 3^{n-1}$
17. $d = 4; a_{10} = 42; a_n = 2 + 4n$
19. $d = 3; a_{10} = 22; a_n = -8 + 3n$
21. $r = 3; a_8 = 4374; a_n = 2 \cdot 3^{n-1}$
23. $r = 2; a_8 = 384; a_n = 3 \cdot 2^{n-1}$
25. $a_1 = -20; d = 4; a_n = -24 + 4n$
27. Geometric: $a_1 = 5; r = 2; a_n = 5 \cdot 2^{n-1}$
29. Arithmetic: $a_1 = -16; d = 7; a_n = -23 + 7n$
31. Geometric: $a_1 = -2; r = -1/2; a_n = -2(-1/2)^{n-1}$
33.

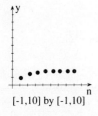

[-1,10] by [-1,10]

35.

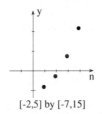

[-2,5] by [-7,15]

37. $1712.61   **39.** $a_n = 1000(1/2)^n$; $r = 1/2$; $a_1 = 500$, $a_2 = 250, a_3 = 125, a_4 = 62.5, a_5 = 31.25, a_6 = 15.625$, $a_7 = 7.8125, a_8 = 3.90625, a_9 = 1.953125, a_{10} = 0.9765625$
41. No   **43.** Just over 28 months ($n = 28.07$ months)
45. $a_4 = 3, a_5 = 5, a_6 = 8, a_7 = 13, a_8 = 21$ **47.** $a_1 = 1, a_2 = 1, a_3 = 2, a_4 = 3, a_5 = 5, a_6 = 8, a_7 = 13$; Fibonacci sequence
49. $a_n \to 31.42$ as $n \to \infty$

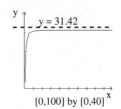

[0,100] by [0,40]

51. $K = 2$

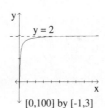

[0,100] by [-1,3]

53. $K = 3$

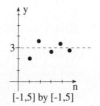

[-1,5] by [-1,5]

55. $a_1 = 0.5, a_2 = 0.7071, a_3 = 0.6125, a_4 = 0.6540, a_5 = 0.6355, a_6 = 0.6437, a_7 = 0.6401, a_8 = 0.6417$; sequence appears to converge to $K = 0.64$

SECTION 12.2

1. $4 + 16 + 36 + 64 + \cdots + 4n^2$

3. $2 + 5 + 8 + \cdots + (3n - 1)$ **5.** $\frac{3}{2} + \frac{3}{4} + \frac{3}{8} + \cdots + \frac{3}{2^n}$

7. $\dfrac{3n^2 + 7n}{2}$ **9.** $\dfrac{n^3 - 3n^2 + 8n}{3}$

11. $\dfrac{n^4 + 2n^3 + n^2 - 4n}{4}$ **13.** $S_n = 3(2^n - 1)$

15. $S_n = -4\left(1 - (\frac{1}{2})^n\right)$ **17.** $S_n = \frac{100}{11}\left(1 - (-\frac{1}{10})^n\right)$

19. $S_n = -2\left(\dfrac{1 - (-0.5)^n}{1.5}\right)$ **21.** $\displaystyle\sum_{k=1}^{10}(3k - 1)$

23. $\displaystyle\sum_{k=1}^{\infty}\left(\frac{1}{4}\right)^k$ **25.** $S_n = \displaystyle\sum_{k=1}^{n}(2k - 10)$

27. $S_n = \displaystyle\sum_{k=1}^{n}3k(-1)^{k+1}$

29. Geometric: $S_n = 2 - 2\left(\frac{1}{2}\right)^n$

31. Geometric: $S_n = -\frac{4}{3} + \frac{4}{3}\left(-\frac{1}{2}\right)^n$ **33.** $S_1 = 1/8$; $S_2 = 3/16$; $S_3 = 7/32$; $S_4 = 15/64$; $S_5 = 31/128$; $S_6 = 63/256$; series converges to $1/4$ **35.** $S_1 = \frac{3}{10}$; $S_2 = \frac{33}{100}$; $S_3 = \frac{333}{1000}$; $S_4 = \frac{3333}{10000}$; $S_5 = \frac{33333}{100000}$; $S_6 = \frac{333333}{1000000}$; converges to $\frac{1}{3}$ **37.** horizontal asymptote at $y = -40$ for $x \to -\infty$ but $f(x) \to \infty$ for $x \to \infty$; series diverges because $S_n = 2\left(\dfrac{1 - 1.05^n}{1 - 1.05}\right)$ diverges

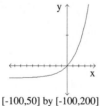

[-100,50] by [-100,200]

39. Converges to $S = 2.5$

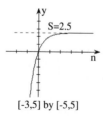

[-3,5] by [-5,5]

41. Converges to $S = 40$

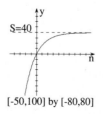

[-50,100] by [-80,80]

43. Converges to $S = 12/5$

45. Converges to $S = 1/9$ **47.** Converges to $S = 1$

49. $S_n = \displaystyle\sum_{k=1}^{n} 150\left(1 + \frac{0.07}{12}\right)^{n-k}$

51. $A_1 = \$1491.10$; $A_2 = \$1480.00$; $A_3 = \$1468.99$

53. $S_{240} = \$166{,}971.72$

SECTION 12.3

1. 1, 8, 28, 56, 70, 56, 28, 8, 1

3. $a^5 + 5a^4b + 10a^3b^2 + 10a^2b^3 + 5ab^4 + b^5$

5. $x^4 + 8x^3y + 24x^2y^2 + 32xy^3 + 16y^4$

7. $x^6 + 6x^5y + 15x^4y^2 + 20x^3y^3 + 15x^2y^4 + 6xy^5 + y^6$

9. $x^6 - 6x^5y + 15x^4y^2 - 20x^3y^3 + 15x^2y^4 - 6xy^5 + y^6$

11. 35   **13.** 70   **15.** 1365   **17.** 56   **19.** 240

21. $x^5 - 10x^4 + 40x^3 - 80x^2 + 80x - 32$

23. $128x^7 - 448x^6 + 672x^5 - 560x^4 + 280x^3 - 84x^2 + 14x - 1$

25. $x^4 + 4ax^3 + 6a^2x^2 + 4a^3x + a^4$

27. $32x^5 + 80x^4y + 80x^3y^2 + 40x^2y^3 + 10xy^4 + y^5$ **29.** $x^3 - 6x^{5/2}y^{1/2} + 15x^2y - 20x^{3/2}y^{3/2} + 15xy^2 - 6x^{1/2}y^{5/2} + y^3$

31. $x^{-10} + 15x^{-8} + 90x^{-6} + 270x^{-4} + 405x^{-2} + 243$

33. $\dbinom{n}{n-r} = \dfrac{n!}{(n-r)!\,(n-(n-r))!} =$

$\dfrac{n!}{(n-r)!\,(n-n+r)!} = \dfrac{n!}{(n-r)!\,r!} = \dfrac{n!}{r!\,(n-r)!} = \dbinom{n}{r}$

35. $\dbinom{k}{r-1} + \dbinom{k}{r} = \dfrac{k!}{(r-1)!\,(k-(r-1))!} + \dfrac{k!}{r!\,(k-r)!} =$

$\dfrac{r \cdot k! + k!\,(k-r+1)}{r!\,(k-r+1)!} = \dfrac{k!\,(k+1)}{r!\,(k+1-r)!} = \dfrac{(k+1)!}{r!\,((k+1)-r)!} =$

$\dbinom{k+1}{r}$

SECTION 12.4

1. From the binomial theorem and Pascal's triangle, $(1+x)^6 = 1 + 6x + 15x^2 + 20x^3 + 15x^4 + 6x^5 + x^6 = f_6(x)$.

3. Approximately 7 units

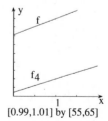

[0.99,1.01] by [55,65]

5. Underestimate; graph of f_4 is below graph of f at $x = 1$

7. 1, 2, 2.5, 2.67, 2.7083, 2.7167, 2.7181, 2.71825, 2.718279, 2.718282   **9.**

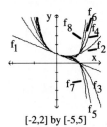

[-2,2] by [-5,5]

11. Approximately $(-0.5, 0.5)$ **13.**

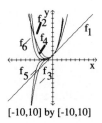

[-10,10] by [-10,10]

15. No, $|f_6(-8) - f(-8)| \approx 201.36$

17. Approximately $(-1.5, 1.5)$

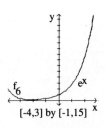

[-4,3] by [-1,15]

19.

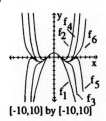

[-10,10] by [-10,10]

21. No, $|f_6(-8) - f(-8)| \approx 39.39$

23. Yes, $|f_{10}(3) - \cos(3)| < 2.74 \times 10^{-11}$; overestimate

25.

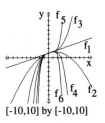

[-10,10] by [-10,10]

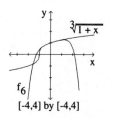

[-4,4] by [-4,4]

27. Approximately 0.00025 units

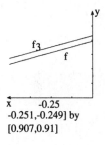

x   -0.25
-0.251,-0.249] by
[0.907,0.91]

29.

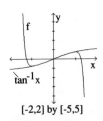

[-2,2] by [-5,5]

31.

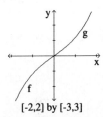

[-2,2] by [-3,3]

33. The polynomial f approximates g; $|f(x) - g(x)| < 0.01$ on $(-4, 4)$

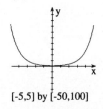

[-5,5] by [-50,100]

[4.99,5.01] by [74,75]

35. Polynomial with 5 terms approximates $f(x)$ within 0.01 units on $(-\pi/2, \pi/2)$

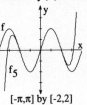

[-π,π] by [-2,2]

37. Let $u = ix$. Then, $e^u = e^{ix} = 1 + (ix) + \dfrac{(ix)^2}{2!} + \dfrac{(ix)^3}{3!} + \dfrac{(ix)^4}{4!} + \cdots = 1 + ix - \dfrac{x^2}{2!} - \dfrac{ix^3}{3!} + \dfrac{x^4}{4!} + \dfrac{ix^5}{5!} - \dfrac{x^6}{6!} - \cdots = \left(1 - \dfrac{x^2}{2!} + \dfrac{x^4}{4!} - \dfrac{x^6}{6!} + \cdots\right) + i \cdot \left(x - \dfrac{x^3}{3!} + \dfrac{x^5}{5!} - \dfrac{x^7}{7!} + \cdots\right)$
$= \cos x + i \sin x.$

SECTION 12.5

1. $a_n = 3 + (n-1)5 = 5n - 2$; by induction: $a_1 = 5(1) - 2 = 3$ is true. Assume $a_k = 5k - 2$, then $a_{k+1} = a_k + 5 = (5k - 2) + 5 = 5(k + 1) - 2$ so P_{k+1} is true. Thus $a_n = 5n - 2$ for all positive integers n. **3.** $a_n = 2(3)^{n-1}$; by induction: $a_1 = 2 \cdot 3^{1-1} = 2$ is true. Assume $a_k = 2 \cdot 3^{k-1}$. Then $a_{k+1} = 3a_k = 3 \cdot 2 \cdot 3^{k-1} = 2 \cdot 3 \cdot 3^{k-1} = 2 \cdot 3^k = 2 \cdot 3^{(k+1)-1}$ so P_{k+1} is true. Thus $a_n = 2 \cdot 3^{n-1}$ for all positive integers n. **5.** $P_1 = 1$; $P_k = 1 + 2 + \cdots + k = \dfrac{k(k+1)}{2}$; $P_{k+1} = 1 + 2 + \cdots + k + (k + 1) = \dfrac{(k+1)(k+2)}{2}$ **7.** $P_1 = 1/2$; $P_k = \dfrac{1}{1 \cdot 2} + \dfrac{1}{2 \cdot 3} + \cdots + \dfrac{1}{k \cdot (k+1)} = \dfrac{k}{k+1}$; $P_{k+1} = \dfrac{1}{1 \cdot 2} + \dfrac{1}{2 \cdot 3} + \cdots + \dfrac{1}{k \cdot (k+1)} + \dfrac{1}{(k+1) \cdot (k+2)} = \dfrac{k+1}{k+2}$. **9.** $P_1 = (a + b) = \displaystyle\sum_{i=0}^{1} a^i b^{1-i}$; $P_k = (a + b)^k = \displaystyle\sum_{i=0}^{k} a^i b^{k-i}$; $P_{k+1} = (a + b)^{k+1} = \displaystyle\sum_{i=0}^{k+1} a^i b^{(k+1)-i}$ **11.** $P_1 = \dbinom{1}{0} + \dbinom{1}{1} = 2$; $P_k = \dbinom{k}{0} + \dbinom{k}{1} + \cdots + \dbinom{k}{k} = 2^k$; $P_{k+1} = \dbinom{k+1}{0} + \dbinom{k+1}{1} + \cdots + \dbinom{k+1}{k} + \dbinom{k+1}{k+1} = 2^{k+1}$ **13.** $P_1 = \dfrac{1(1+1)}{2} = 1$ is true. Assume $P_k = 1 + 2 + \cdots + k = \dfrac{k(k+1)}{2}$ is true. Then $P_{k+1} = 1 + 2 + \cdots + k + (k+1) = \dfrac{k(k+1)}{2} + (k+1) = \dfrac{k(k+1) + 2(k+1)}{2} = \dfrac{(k+1)((k+1)+1)}{2}$ so P_{k+1} is true. Thus P_n is true for all positive integers n. **15.** $P_1 = 2(1) - 1 = 1 = 1^2$ is true. Assume $P_k = 1 + 3 + \cdots + (2k - 1) = k^2$ is true. Then $P_{k+1} = 1 + 3 + \cdots + (2k - 1) + 2(k + 1) - 1 = k^2 + 2k + 1 = (k + 1)^2$ so P_{k+1} is true. Thus P_n is true for all positive integers n. **17.** $P_1 = 1 = 2^1 - 1$ is true. Assume $P_k = 1 + 2 + 2^2 + \cdots + 2^{k-1} = 2^k - 1$ is true. Then $P_{k+1} = 1 + 2 + 2^2 + \cdots + 2^{k-1} + 2^k = 2^k - 1 + 2^k = 2 \cdot 2^k - 1 = 2^{k+1} - 1$ so P_{k+1} is true. Thus P_n is true for all positive integers n.

19. $125, 250$ **21.** $\dfrac{n(n+1)}{2} - 6$ or $\dfrac{(n+4)(n-3)}{2}$ **23.** $33,554,431$

SECTION 12.6

1. 6 **3.** 12 **5.** 12 **7.** 8,000,000
9. 19,656,000 **11.** 36 **13.** 6720 **15.** 13,366,080
17. 2002 **19.** 1,307,504 **21.** 2300 **23.** 17,296
25. $_{50}C_{11} = 37,353,738,800$ **27.** $_nC_r + _nC_{r+1} = \dfrac{n!}{r!(n-r)!} + \dfrac{n!}{(r+1)!(n-r-1)!} = \dfrac{(r+1)!n! + (n-r)n!}{(r+1)!(n-r)!} = \dfrac{n!(r+1+n-r)}{(r+1)!(n-r)!} = \dfrac{n!(n+1)}{(r+1)!(n-r)!} = \dfrac{(n+1)!}{(r+1)!((n+1)-(r+1))} = C_{n+1}C_{r+1}$

SECTION 12.7

1. $S = \{1, 2, 3, 4, 5, 6\}$ **3.** Order listed is penny, nickel, dime: $S = \{HHH, HHT, HTH, THH, TTH, THT, HTT, TTT\}$ **5.** $S = \{(1,2), (1,3), (1,4), (1,5), (2,1), (2,3), (2,4), (2,5), (3,1), (3,2), (3,4), (3,5), (4,1), (4,2), (4,3), (4,5), (5,1), (5,2), (5,3), (5,4)\}$ **7.** Order listed is (red, green): $S = \{(1,1), (1,3), (1,5), (2,2), (2,4), (2,6), (3,1), (3,3), (3,5), (4,2), (4,4), (4,6), (5,1), (5,3), (5,5), (6,2), (6,4), (6,6)\}$ **9.** Order listed is (red, green): $S = \{(2,2), (4,2), (6,2), (2,4), (4,4), (6,4), (2,6), (4,6), (6,6)\}$ **11.** Order listed is (red, green): $S = \{(1,1), (1,3), (1,5), (3,1), (3,3), (3,5), (5,1), (5,3), (5,5)\}$ **13.** 1/2 **15.** 1/4 **17.** 1/4 **19.** 4/15504 or 0.00026 **21.** 4368/15504 or 0.2817 **23.** 1/2 **25.** 1/1024 or 0.00098 **27.** 1023/1024 or 0.999 **29.** 132/625 or 0.21 **31.** The sum of the probabilities is greater than 1.

Chapter 12 Review

1. $a_1 = 0$, $a_2 = -1$, $a_3 = 2$, $a_4 = -3$, $a_{10} = -9$

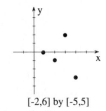

[-2,6] by [-5,5]

3. $a_1 = 1, a_2 = 3, a_3 = 7, a_4 = 15, a_{10} = 1023$

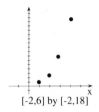

[-2,6] by [-2,18]

5. $a_1 = 2, a_2 = 5, a_3 = 8, a_4 = 11, a_{10} = 29$

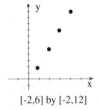

[-2,6] by [-2,12]

7. $a_1 = 5, a_2 = 15, a_3 = 45, a_4 = 135, a_{10} = 98,415$

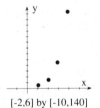

[-2,6] by [-10,140]

9. $a_1 = -32, a_n = 8n - 40$
11. $4 + 7 + 10 + 13 + 16 + 19 + 22 + 25$
13. $1 + 3 + 7 + 15 + 31 + 63 + 127 + 255$
15. $\displaystyle\sum_{k=1}^{10}(1 - 3k)$ **17.** $\displaystyle\sum_{k=1}^{n}(10 - 2k)$ **19.** 4650
21. $5,328,575$ **23.** Converges to 3
25. Converges to 2/99
27. $32x^5 + 80x^4y + 80x^3y^2 + 40x^2y^3 + 10xy^4 + y^5$
29. $243x^{10} + 405x^8y^3 + 270x^6y^6 + 90x^4y^9 + 15x^2y^{12} + y^{15}$
31. $512a^{27} - 2304a^{24}b^2 + 4608a^{21}b^4 - 5376a^{18}b^6 + 4032a^{15}b^8 - 2016a^{12}b^{10} + 672a^9b^{12} - 144a^6b^{14} + 18a^3b^{16} - b^{18}$
33.

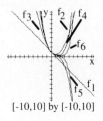

[-10,10] by [-10,10]

35. Yes, $|e^2 - f_6(-2)| = 0.0335$; approximation accurate to nearest 0.1
37. Approximation error less than 0.01 on $(-1.5, 1.5)$
39. $P_1 = \dfrac{1(1 + 1)(1 + 2)}{6} = 1$ is true. Assume $P_k = 1 + 3 + 6 + \cdots + \dfrac{k(k + 1)}{2} = \dfrac{k(k + 1)(k + 2)}{6}$ is true. Then $P_{k+1} = 1 + 3 + 6 + \cdots + \dfrac{k(k + 1)}{2}k + \dfrac{(k + 1)(k + 2)}{2} = \dfrac{k(k + 1)(k + 2)}{6} + \dfrac{(k + 1)(k + 2)}{2} = \dfrac{k(k + 1)(k + 2) + 3(k + 1)(k + 2)}{6} = \dfrac{(k + 1)(k + 2)(k + 3)}{6}$ so P_{k+1} is true. Thus the statement holds for all natural numbers.   **41.** $P_1 = \displaystyle\sum_{i=1}^{1}(\tfrac{1}{2})^i = \tfrac{1}{2} = 1 - \tfrac{1}{2}$ is true. Assume $P_k = \displaystyle\sum_{i=1}^{k}(\tfrac{1}{2})^i = 1 - \tfrac{1}{2^k}$ is true. Then $P_{k+1} = \displaystyle\sum_{i=1}^{k+1}(\tfrac{1}{2})^i = \displaystyle\sum_{i=1}^{k}(\tfrac{1}{2})^i + (\tfrac{1}{2})^{k+1} = 1 - \tfrac{1}{2^k} + (\tfrac{1}{2})^{k+1} = 1 - \dfrac{2}{2^{k+1}} + \dfrac{1}{2^{k+1}} = 1 - \dfrac{1}{2^{k+1}}$ so P_{k+1} is true. Thus the statement holds for all natural numbers.   **43.** $1^3 + 2 \cdot 1$ is divisible by 3 so P_1 is true. Assume $k^3 + 2k$ is divisible by 3 so $k^3 + 2k = 3t$ for some integer t. Then $(k + 1)^3 + 2(k + 1) = k^3 + 3k^2 + 3k + 1 + 2k + 2 = (k^3 + 2k) + 3(k^2 + k + 1) = 3t + 3(k^2 + k + 1)$, a number divisible by 3. So P_{k+1} is true and the statement holds for all natural numbers.   **45.** $259,459,200$
47. $6,724,520$ **49.** $43,670,016$ **51.** $14,508,000$
53. $8,217,822,536$ **55.** 26   **57.** $_nP_k \cdot _{n-k}P_j = \dfrac{n!}{(n - k)!} \cdot \dfrac{(n - k)!}{(n - k - j)!} = \dfrac{n!}{(n - k - j)!} = \dfrac{n!}{(n - (k + j)!} = _nP_{k+j}$ **59.** 5/16 or 0.3125   **61.** 36/512 or 0.0703
63. **(a)** 0.9224   **(b)** 0.0753

Index

Notes

Notes

Figure 15.15

"You go on home without me, Irene. I'm going to join this man's cult."

Drawing by Chas. Addams; © 1982
The New Yorker Magazine, Inc.

dented range of lifestyles and wants. As Martin Marty (1976) points out, many Americans use religion as a means toward self-fulfillment and the establishment of their identities. They are increasingly apt to pick and choose among religious organizations, rather like consumers looking for a particular product that best suits their own needs. Those who want mystical transcendence may join one group, those who want strict, unambiguous guidelines for behavior may choose another. Indeed, many of the new religions do not appeal, as older sects did, to the economically deprived: rather, they cater to the psychologically deprived, to people looking for meaning they cannot find elsewhere. Only time will tell whether some of the new religions, like others before them, will grow into the denominations of the future—or whether, like such bygone groups as the Diggers, the Shakers, and the Levellers, they totally disappear (Richardson, 1979; Robbins and Anthony, 1980; Levine, 1984; Hammond, 1985; Stark and Bainbridge, 1985).

Secularization: Fact or Myth?

In the preindustrial societies in which most human beings have lived throughout history, people accept without much question whatever religious beliefs their society offers. Their religion is simply another part of their reality, learned by everyone in the course of socialization. In these relatively simple societies, religion suffuses social life: everyday activities, such as eating, hunting, or caring for the sick, are surrounded with religious ritual. But as societies have industrialized, they have tended to undergo *secularization,* the process by which religion loses its social influence. In these highly diversified modern societies, traditional religion increasingly becomes a separate and distinct institution, its influence eroded by other institutions such as government, science, and education. Indeed, these societies typically include large numbers of people who have little real commitment to religion, or who are actually irreligious. How far has this trend toward secularization gone— and what future, if any, does religion have in the emerging postindustrial societies of the world?

One way to measure secularization is through public-opinion polls that periodically gather data on people's religious beliefs in various societies. Over the years, these polls have shown a general decline in religious commitment, and by 1975 the Gallup poll reported a "collapse" of religious belief in virtually all the industrialized nations it surveyed. The only significant exceptions to this pattern are the United States and, to a lesser extent, Canada. There has been some decline in religiosity in the United States over the past few decades, but most Americans remain very favorable toward religion. Opinion polls consistently find that around 95 percent of Americans believe in "God or a universal spirit," and Gallup polls in 1985 found that 55 percent feel religion is "very important" in their lives, 58 percent agree that "religion can answer all or most of today's problems," 66 percent have confidence in "the church or organized religion," and 91 percent express a preference for a specific faith. Canadians are somewhat less ardent in their religiosity, but their level of religious commitment is still remarkably high compared with other industrialized nations.

Also useful are data on the membership of religious organizations and on attendance at worship. These measures do have certain limitations, though. Membership figures are often unreliable because some groups count only those who have affirmed membership as an adult, while others count the entire group they feel ought to belong, including children. Attendance figures, too, may not be a good indication of how "religious" people actually are, especially in other aspects of their daily lives. One can attend worship for many reasons, ranging from habit to piety to desire for social status. The evidence from all industrialized socie-

PERCENTAGE ATTENDING CHURCH OR SYNAGOGUE
IN THE UNITED STATES DURING AVERAGE WEEK

1955	49	1971	40
1956	46	1972	40
1957	47	1973	40
1958	49	1974	40
1959	47	1975	40
1960	47	1976	42
1961	47	1977	41
1962	46	1978	41
1963	46	1979	40
1964	45	1980	40
1965	44	1981	41
1966	44	1982	41
1967	45	1983	40
1968	43	1984	40
1969	42	1985	42
1970	42	1986	40

SOURCE: Gallup polls.

Figure 15.16 *The percentage of Americans who attend church or synagogue during an average week seems to have leveled off after an earlier decline. American church attendance is still significantly higher than attendance in any other modern industrialized society.*

ties points to a decline, though an uneven one, in both membership of religious organizations and in attendance at worship. This trend appears in both the United States and Canada, but to a significantly lesser degree than in any other advanced industrialized society. In the United States in 1985, 71 percent of the population were members (rather than merely believers) in a particular faith, down from a high point of 76 percent in 1947. Average weekly church attendance in the United States declined somewhat in the early 1960s, but has since leveled off at around 40 percent (see Figure 15.16). Canadian attendance is lower—31 percent attended church in a typical week in 1986—but is still one of the highest rates in the world.

These findings raise an intriguing question. If advanced industrialization inevitably erodes traditional religious institutions, then why is it that the only exceptions to the trend are the United States, the first postindustrial society in the world, and Canada, a highly industrialized society with many cultural similarities to the United States? Clearly, we should expect the exact opposite to be the case. Peter Berger (1969) suggests a reason: the churches elsewhere have generally adhered to their traditional ways, and as a result have been pushed to the margins of their secular societies,

but the churches in North America have remained nearer the center of society by becoming secularized themselves. More concerned with self-preservation than with their original mission, the denominations have modified their doctrines and rituals in an attempt to become more "relevant" to the modern world. In effect, they participate in the secularized civil religion; only the sects, which uphold traditional doctrines, have become marginal to the society.

What, then, is the future of religion? We must distinguish carefully between secularization affecting traditional religion, and secularization affecting other orientations toward the sacred or supernatural. There is much evidence that traditional religion is being eroded; this in itself is hardly surprising, because social change alters all institutions over time. There is virtually no evidence, however, that public belief in some supernatural, transcendent reality is disappearing in North America or indeed anywhere else. Recent Gallup polls show that three-quarters of the American population know their astrological "sign," and 23 percent believe their lives are governed by the stars. In acknowledgment of widespread superstition, airlines have no row thirteen, and high-rise buildings have no thirteenth floor. Millions believe in one or more of such practices as fortune-telling, palmistry, numerology, hexing, tarot-card reading, and seances with the dead. One American in four believes in reincarnation. All these beliefs and practices run directly contrary to the teachings of the established churches, yet they thrive in North America and other advanced industrialized societies. Many people, too, adhere to an "invisible" or "silent" religion, acknowledging a supreme but unknowable force in the universe. And new sects and cults appear in unprecedented profusion, offering the prospect of further religious growth, in new directions, in the future (Greeley, 1975; Wuthnow, 1978; Westley, 1978; Campbell, 1978; Berger, 1979; Hammond, 1985; Stark and Bainbridge, 1985).

The fact that sociocultural evolution has generally meant secularization in the past does not mean that this must necessarily be so in the future. What is most likely is that there will be growing religious diversity in the postindustrial future, reflecting the increasing individualism and diversity of those societies. Particularly in times of uncertainty and rapid social change, people in the future may look, as they have in the past, to religious values to stabilize and revitalize their culture. It may well be the case, in fact, that the need for religion will eventually reassert itself most powerfully

Figure 15.17 *Traditional forms of religion still enjoy the allegiance of most of the people on earth. Even in modern societies, where some people switch from one faith to another and some even reject organized religion altogether, there is still ample evidence of a widespread belief in a higher power, in a sacred realm beyond everyday experience. This photograph was taken in a Tunisian synagogue.*

in precisely those societies that have become the most industrialized, rationalized, and materialistic.

For many years it was widely felt that as science progressively provided rational explanations for the mysteries of the universe, religion would have less and less of a role to play and would eventually disappear, unmasked as nothing more than superstition. But there are still gaps in our understanding that science can never fill. On the ultimately important questions—of the meaning and purpose of life and the nature of morality—science is utterly silent and, by its very nature, always will be. Few citizens of modern societies would utterly deny the possibility of some higher power in the universe, some supernatural, transcendental realm that lies beyond the boundaries of ordinary experience, and in this fundamental sense religion is probably here to stay.

Summary

1.   Religion is a system of communally held beliefs and rituals that are oriented toward some sacred, supernatural realm. According to Durkheim, all religions distinguish between the sacred and the profane.

2.   The sociological approach focuses on the social rather than the theological aspects of religion, and traces the interrelationships between religion and society.

3.   Religions can be conveniently classified into four main types: simple supernaturalism, animism, theism, and transcendent idealism. The major world religions have convincing theodicies that explain the human predicament.

4.   Durkheim concluded that the origins of religion are social rather than supernatural and that religious belief and ritual function to enhance social solidarity. The most important functions of religion are those of maintaining social solidarity; providing meaningful answers to ultimate questions; reinforcing social control; and offering psychological support to individuals in crisis. Some secular belief systems, such as communism, may serve as functional equivalents of religion in certain respects.

5.   Marx analyzed religion from a conflict perspective. He saw religious belief as a form of alienation and argued that the dominant religion tends to support the status quo in any unequal society. Religion does play this role in many societies and is often an element in social conflict between different groups.

6.   Religion can sometimes be a source of radical change. According to Weber's "Protestant ethic" thesis, modern capitalism arose partly as a result of the Puritan tendency to work hard and reinvest money rather than spend it. His theory allows a greater role for ideas in social change than·Marx's theory, in which ideas reflect rather than cause change. Another religious influence on social change is Islamic fundamentalism, which is a potent force in several Islamic societies that are undergoing rapid modernization.

7.   There are four main types of religious organization: the ecclesia, the denomination ("church"), the sect, and the cult. There is a dynamic relationship between denomination and sect, and this is a source of religious change.

8.   Distinctive features of American religion include the following: freedom of religion; breadth of religious commitment; religiosity as a value; religious pluralism; tolerance of diversity; religion as an ethnic characteristic; and the link between religion and social characteristics.

9.   Important trends in American religious life are the fundamentalist revival, which has challenged permissive trends through such means as the "electronic church"; the closer involvement of politics and religion, which has gone beyond the traditional "civil religion" into more controversial issues; and the rise of new sects and cults, such as the Hare Krishna movement, the Unification Church, and Scientology.

10.   Secularization can be measured in various ways; the general conclusion is that the influence of traditional religious forms is undermined by industrialization and the complex, heterogeneous societies that it creates. Various other beliefs in the sacred or supernatural abound, however, and new religions proliferate. A fully secularized society is unlikely: some forms of religion persist because they address vital issues that other belief systems ignore.

Important Terms

sacred (398)

profane (398)

ritual (398)

religion (398)

simple supernaturalism (399)

animism (399)

magic (400)

theism (400)

polytheism (400)

monotheism (400)

transcendent idealism (400)

theodicy (400)

functional equivalent (402)

alienation (403)

Protestant ethic (405)

fundamentalism (407)

ecclesia (409)

denomination (409)

sect (409)

cult (410)

secularization (419)

Suggested Readings

BERGER, PETER L. *A Rumor of Angels: Modern Society and the Rediscovery of the Supernatural.* New York: Doubleday, 1969.

Thoughtfully and elegantly written, this book argues that there is still a place for religion in the modern world and that a sociological approach to religion can be combined with religious faith.

CHALFANT, H. PAUL, ROBERT E. BECKLEY, and C. EDDIE PALMER. *Religion in Contemporary Society.* 2nd ed. Palo Alto, Calif.: Mayfield, 1986.

An excellent general introduction to the sociology of religion, recommended for a thorough overview of the field.

GREELEY, ANDREW M. *The American Catholic: A Social Portrait.* New York: Basic Books, 1977.

An important study of Catholics in the United States. Based on survey data, the study challenges many popular conceptions about Catholic attitudes and other social characteristics.

HADDEN, JEFFREY K., and CHARLES E. SWAN. *Prime Time Preachers: The Rising Power of Tele-Evangelism.* Reading, Mass.: Addison-Wesley, 1981.

An interesting study of the social bases and implications of the "electronic church."

LEVINE, SAUL P. *Radical Departures: Desperate Detours to Growing Up.* New York: Harcourt Brace Jovanovich, 1984.

An investigation into why people—particularly middle-class youths—join religious cults.

LIEBMAN, ROBERT C., and ROBERT WUTHNOW (eds.). *The New Christian Right: Mobilization and Legitimation.* Hawthorne, N.Y.: Aldine, 1983.

A collection of articles on a new phenomenon, the political activism of conservative fundamentalists.

ROBBINS, THOMAS, and DICK ANTHONY (eds.) *In Gods We Trust: New Patterns of Religious Pluralism in America.* New Brunswick, N.J.: Transaction Books, 1980.

A broad-ranging collection of articles dealing with the current religious ferment in America.

STARK, RODNEY, and WILLIAM SIMS BAINBRIDGE. *The Future of Religion: Secularization, Revival, and Cult Formation.* Berkeley, Calif.: University of California Press, 1985.

An informative survey of contemporary religious trends. The authors argue that religion, in various forms, is alive and well.

WILSON, JOHN N. *Religion in American Society: The Effective Presence.* Englewood Cliffs, N.J.: Prentice-Hall, 1978.

A detailed sociology of American religion. Wilson utilizes both conflict and functionalist perspectives and emphasizes religious changes.

CHAPTER 16

Medicine

Everybody gets sick. Disease and injury afflict us throughout our lives until, inevitably, some final assault on the body brings our existence to an end. Fortunately, most of us in modern industrialized societies can take relatively good health for granted most of the time. In fact, we tend to fully realize the importance of good health only when we or those close to us become seriously ill. At such times we keenly appreciate the ancient truism that health is our most precious asset, one for which we might readily sacrifice such worldly rewards as power, wealth, or fame.

Because ill health is a universal problem, affecting both the individual and society, the human response to sickness is always socially organized. No society leaves the responsibility for maintaining health and treating ill health entirely to the individual. Each society develops its own concepts of health and sickness and authorizes certain people to decide who is sick and how the sick should be treated. Around this focus there arises, over time, a stable cluster of norms, values, groups, statuses, and roles: in other words, an institution. To the sociologist, then, *medicine* is the institution concerned with the maintenance of health and the treatment of disease.

In the simplest preindustrial societies, medicine is usually an aspect of religion. The social arrangements for dealing with sickness are rudimentary, often involving only two roles: the sick person and the healer. The latter is typically also the priest, shaman, or witch doctor, who relies primarily on magical rituals both to identify and to treat disease: for example, bones may be thrown like dice to establish a cause (usually sorcery), and chants may be used to bring about a cure. In modern industrialized societies, on the other hand, the institution has become highly elaborate and specialized, including dozens of roles such as those of brain surgeon, anesthetist, druggist, and hospital administrator, linked with various organizations

Figure 16.1 *A socially recognized healing procedure exists in all human societies. In the most simple preindustrial communities, disease is commonly regarded as the result of sorcery or other malign spiritual influences. The tribal shaman or "witch doctor" serves as healer, combining magical rituals with herbal and other remedies—often with apparent success. The illustrations show historical shamanism among North American Indians and its modern counterpart in a South American tribe.*

such as nursing homes, insurance companies, medical schools, and pharmaceutical corporations. Medicine, in fact, has become the subject of intense sociological interest precisely because it is now one of the most pervasive, costly, and controversial institutions of modern society (Twaddle and Hessler, 1977; Freeman et al., 1979; Coe, 1978; Mechanic, 1978; Cockerham, 1986; Kurtz and Chalfant, 1984).

Sickness and Society

To a sick person, illness seems to be a highly individual issue, focused on the biological functioning of the body. Yet because every society has its own patterns of health, disease, and treatment, sickness can be fully understood only in its social context (Lyle, 1954; Moore et al., 1980).

Social Effects of Disease

Disease has many social effects, the most obvious being that it can disrupt a society by disabling its members. In this respect, disease can have an impact similar to that of other natural or social disasters, such as famine, earthquake, or war. Like these other phenomena, some diseases may confront a society continually, while others may occur infrequently. An **endemic disease** is one that is always present in a large part of a population. Dysentery, for example, is endemic in many parts of Africa and the Indian subcontinent, where it afflicts millions of people as a result of contaminated food and water supplies. On the other hand, an **epidemic disease** is one affecting a significant part of a population in which it is normally uncommon. Influenza, for example, always occurs as an epidemic, surging through a population and infecting an abnormally high number of people until it runs its course. Diseases of either kind can be acute or chronic. An **acute disease** is one of short duration; generally the victim either recovers from it or dies. Examples are measles and the common cold. A **chronic disease** is one of long duration; the victim may or may not die, but usually does not recover. Examples are diabetes and arthritis.

The direct impact of any disease, of course, falls on the individual, who may experience discomfort, pain, anxiety, confinement, or even death. But the effects can extend beyond the individual to the family, the community, and the whole society. The immediate family may have to deal emotionally and financially with the illness and the resulting incapacitation of its members. The community may be burdened, particularly in cases of widespread illness: sick people are typically unable to play their normal social roles, which must be either performed by others or abandoned. And disease may profoundly affect an entire society: in countries where malaria is endemic, for example, millions of people may have their energy sapped and their resistance to other diseases lowered, with devastating social and economic effects.

Epidemic diseases can have particularly striking consequences; in some cases they have destroyed entire societies. In the fourteenth century the terrible plague known as the Black Death swept through Europe, killing over a third of the population and shaking the economic, political, and religious foundations of the medieval world (Gottfried, 1983). In later centuries, European explorers brought to Africa and America diseases against which the indigenous peoples had no natural immunity. The entire Aztec civilization collapsed in the sixteenth century when smallpox was introduced into their society by a single Spanish soldier. Similar epidemics so ravaged other tribal peoples, such as the Hottentots of Africa, that they soon died out completely.

Despite all the advances that have been made in medicine, devastating epidemics still threaten modern industrialized societies. The influenza virus, for example, periodically shuffles its genes, producing deadly new forms of flu against which human populations have little immunity and existing vaccinations no effect. When this happened in

1918, some 20 million people died—more than had been killed in all the carnage of the preceding four years of World War I. A worldwide recurrence of such an influenza epidemic could well happen again (S. Hall, 1983). Indeed, as we shall see, disease—including new diseases—will always be with us. Our health exists only in relation to our environment—and that environment is constantly changing as new disease agents evolve, migrate, or are manufactured (Dubos, 1959, 1969).

Social Influences on Disease

Just as disease influences society, so social factors affect the manifestation of disease. Disease does not strike at random: there are always reasons why one person or group rather than another falls victim, even if those reasons are not immediately apparent. Genetic and constitutional factors play an important part in the genesis of disease, of course, but they do so in interaction with social and cultural factors. For example, until a few decades ago the Fore, a horticultural tribe of New Guinea, suffered from kuru, a fatal viral disease of the brain. At first, medical and social scientists could not understand why the Fore seemed so susceptible to this exceedingly rare disease, but they eventually found the reason. Kuru, it turned out, was transmitted by an unusual cultural practice of the tribe: as a mark of their deep respect for their dead kinsfolk, they ate them. In the course of cracking open skulls and preparing and eating the contents, they exposed themselves to the virus (Bingham, 1981).

Figure 16.2 An epidemic of bubonic plague, known as the "Black Death," killed about 75 million people in Europe between 1347 and 1351. The plague was widely perceived as divine punishment for sin. Many people joined a fundamentalist sect, the Brotherhood of the Flagellants, and publicly whipped themselves in the hope of appeasing an angry God. Some communities blamed the Jews instead, and burned their entire Jewish populations alive. Actually, the disease is spread through fleas carried by rats. There were several lesser plagues in Europe over succeeding centuries, but the disease is now rare—although isolated cases still occur all over the world, including the United States.

Fortunately, kuru has now virtually died out among the Fore, thanks to another cultural influence—interference in their cannibalism by disapproving Westerners.

Like the Fore, every society has typical patterns of health and disease closely linked to its cultural practices. The United States has one of the highest rates of heart disease in the world, a problem that arises in part from a general lack of exercise combined with a high consumption of animal fats in dairy products and red meat. Japan, in contrast, has a much lower rate of heart disease, in part because of a strong dietary preference for fish over fatty meats. In the same way, the rate of American deaths arising from lung cancer, traffic accidents, or drug overdoses is influenced by the extent of such cultural practices as smoking, private automobile use, and drug abuse.

A physician who takes a patient's case history is interested not only in "medical" facts but also in socially significant factors such as age, race, sex, marital status, religion, occupation, and social class. The reason is that, like cultural practices, these characteristics have a strong relationship to individual health. The young, for example, are more likely to suffer from acute diseases than the old, who are more prone to chronic ailments. Whites are generally more healthy than blacks. Women tend to live longer than men. Single people are more likely to suffer from depression than married people. Mormons, whose religion forbids drinking and smoking, enjoy better health than comparable non-Mormons. The higher one's social class, the better one's health is likely to be. In short, human health is shaped by interactions between the natural and social environments. This insight forms the basis of epidemiology.

Epidemiology

Patterns of health and disease constantly change as old ailments recur or new ones appear. To meet the challenge of any disease, we have to know what causes it, who is likely to get it, and how it is spread. These issues are the subject matter of *epidemiology,* the study of the origin, distribution, and means of transmission of disease in populations. Medical and sociological concerns often coincide in epidemiology, where researchers from both disciplines may work closely together.

The link between a disease and its source is often obscure, and the medical facts of a disease sometimes tell us surprisingly little about it. By looking at whatever social and cultural characteristics the victims have in common, we can often gain a great deal of further information about the disease: who gets it, under what conditions, and why. Epidemiological detective work can be an exciting and rewarding mission, particularly in cases where lives depend on a rapid solution to a medical mystery.

Tracing Disease Origins

The science of epidemiology emerged about the middle of the last century. A classic example of early epidemiological methods occurred in London in 1854, when a sudden epidemic of cholera broke out. Doctors had no idea what caused cholera, or how to prevent it. But one physician, Sir John Snow, decided on a novel approach: if the victims had anything in common other than cholera, he reasoned, then that might be the cause of the

Figure 16.3 *Urban cholera epidemics in the early nineteenth century were spread through contaminated water sources and unhygienic drinking vessels. Official carriers delivered water from house to house, unwittingly spreading contagion and death.*

disease. By noting such facts as where the victims lived, worked, ate, and the like, Snow soon found a common factor: they had all drunk water drawn from the Broad Street pump. Armed with this fact, Snow boldly removed the handle from the pump—and the cholera epidemic ended shortly afterward. His epidemiological analysis revealed both the source of the infection and a means of containing it, even though the germ responsible for cholera was not discovered until twenty-eight years later (Clendening, 1942).

The same methods are still used today to trace disease origins. In the summer of 1976 more than 200 Americans fell ill, and over 30 died, apparently from a pneumonia that did not respond to the usual treatments. Although the victims lived in various parts of the United States, they proved to have some characteristics in common: most were men of middle age or older who had recently at-tended a convention of the American Legion at a Philadelphia hotel. Painstaking research finally turned up a previously unknown bacterium in the hotel's air-conditioning system, and led to the re-cognition of legionnaires' disease. In 1979 and 1980, more than 1,500 young women fell ill and over 80 died from sudden, massive infections. Epi-demiological research showed that all the victims had menstruated shortly before becoming ill, and most had used a new form of tampon that encour-aged explosive bacterial growth. Again, a new dis-ease was recognized, toxic-shock syndrome.

AIDS

In early 1981 American physicians reported a mys-terious new disease that weakens the victims' immune systems, leaving them susceptible to rare forms of cancer, pneumonia, and other "opportun-istic" infections that do not affect people in normal health. The disease, AIDS (acquired immune defi-ciency syndrome), destroys certain blood cells that are essential to the body's fight against infection. For several reasons, public health officials realized that they might be facing "the disease of the cen-tury." AIDS seemed incurable and utterly lethal after the opportunistic infections set in: more than 80 percent of its victims were dead within two years of diagnosis. The disease spreads rapidly: the number of cases in the United States rose from 11 in early 1981 to over 30,000 six years later. If that rate of increase were to persist, there could be over 1 million American cases in the next decade—and AIDS is spreading all over the world. Moreover, the

incubation period (the time between infection and the onset of the first symptoms) ranges from a few months to seven or more years, meaning that cur-rent statistics reflect past infection patterns, not the invisible spread of the disease today.

Urgent questions arose as the implications of the epidemic became apparent. What was the cause of AIDS? How was it spread? Who was at risk? Where had it come from? Again, epidemiolo-gists found the necessary clues in the social char-acteristics of people with AIDS. Most of the early AIDS cases fell into three categories. The largest consisted of homosexual or bisexual men, many of whom had been quite sexually active. The second category included intravenous drug abusers, who are prone to share syringes and needles. The third

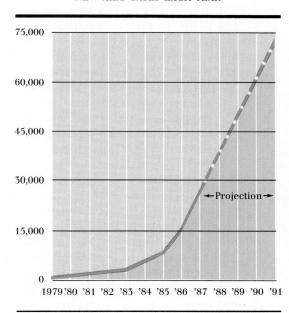

NEW AIDS CASES EACH YEAR

SOURCE: Centers for Disease Control and U.S. Public Health Service.

Figure 16.4 *As this graph shows, the number of new AIDS cases each year is increasing rapidly in the United States; it is expected that by 1991 there will be a cumulative total of over 270,000 cases. Additionally, there is a very much larger pool of people who have been infected, are currently without symptoms, but may be lifelong carriers of the disease. At the international level, the World Health Organization predicts that by 1991 there will be 10 million cases of AIDS, with a further 100 million people infected with the virus. Unless the disease can be checked, it will become a "pandemic"—a global epidemic.*

category contained hemophiliacs, who use a concentrate of donated blood to prevent their own uncontrolled bleeding. Most of the remaining victims were recipients of hospital blood transfusions, sexual partners (straight or gay) of people in high-risk groups, and infants born to high-risk mothers.

Diverse as these groups seemed to be, epidemiologists could conclude from the evidence that AIDS is an infectious disease spread through two methods: intimate sexual contact and contaminated blood. This information gave researchers a good idea of what to look for: a virus carried in blood and other bodily fluids. By 1984, less than three years after the discovery of AIDS, Luc Montagnier in France and then Robert Gallo in the United States isolated a previously unknown virus that is present in the bodily fluids—primarily blood and semen—of people with AIDS.

Where did AIDS come from? By 1985, international epidemiological studies pointed to Zaire and neighboring central African countries, where AIDS is rife, as the likely source. Traces of the disease are present in frozen blood samples taken in these countries in the early 1970s, and the local green-monkey population is infected with a closely related virus, leading researchers to believe that a mutant viral strain may have started to infect human beings in the region some years ago. The disease was probably carried to the Caribbean by Haitians who worked temporarily in Zaire; from there, migrants or vacationers brought it to the United States. Simultaneously, travelers from Africa spread the epidemic to Western Europe and on to other parts of the world.

Epidemiologists fear that the epidemic may be out of control. One cause of their alarm is the fact that sexually transmitted diseases are notoriously difficult to contain, for they involve private acts in which passion is liable to overwhelm discretion. A second reason is that actual AIDS cases represent only the tip of the iceberg. By 1986, about 300,000 Americans were suffering from AIDS-related complex (ARC), a milder form of the disease, and an estimated 1 to 3 million had been infected with the disease but showed no symptoms. It is not known how many of these people may eventually develop AIDS in the years or decades ahead (estimates range from 10 percent to almost 100 percent). It appears, however, that infected people may become permanent carriers of the disease, although they are usually unaware of it. The growing population of symptomless and unknowing carriers of the disease provides a huge potential for further dissemination of the epidemic. A crucial question is whether AIDS will spread significantly beyond the existing high-risk groups. Some 90 percent of the early American victims were male and 70 percent were homosexual or bisexual, a pattern similar to that in other industrialized societies. But in central Africa, where the disease has been established the longest, almost all people with AIDS are heterosexual, and the two sexes are equally affected. More time and research will be needed to explain these different patterns, but at the moment AIDS is spreading relatively slowly among American heterosexuals.

The AIDS epidemic shows clearly the influence of society on disease and of disease on society. Many social factors have helped spread the disease, ranging from global jet travel to changing sexual norms and drug-abuse patterns in the industrialized world. Social factors also delayed the medical response to AIDS, which was poorly funded until it became apparent in 1985 that the disease was spreading beyond the stigmatized high-risk groups; at that point, a wave of media coverage and public hysteria led to a sharp increase in budgets for research into and education about the disease, but valuable time, and perhaps lives, had been lost. The threat of AIDS has radically reduced promiscuous behavior among American gays, and is beginning to have a chastening effect on sexual mores in general. The full social impact of AIDS will depend, of course, on whether it remains relatively contained or becomes an endemic killer in the global population. In any event, it was the social characteristics of the early American victims that provided the epidemiological traces leading to the origin and cause of the disease—and which may lead, in time, to its prevention and cure (Fettner and Check, 1985; Slaff and Brubaker, 1985; Altman, 1986; Nichols, 1986; Gonda, 1986).

The Development of Medicine

Just as social factors affect disease, so they affect the way a medical system is organized to meet the challenge of disease. The historical development of modern medicine is essentially the story of how theories of disease and its treatment have evolved under changing social conditions, how various groups have successfully claimed the authority to practice medicine, and what effect these trends have had on the general health (Duffy, 1976; Twaddle and Hessler, 1977; Lyons and Petrucelli, 1978; Starr, 1982).

Figure 16.5 *The Hippocratic model held sway in the Western world for centuries, and traces of it still linger today. Under this model, good physical and mental health depended on a balance of body fluids, or "humors," such as blood and phlegm. Physicians' favored treatment was bleeding, which was supposed to correct fluid imbalances. Many doctors thought that if patients recovered after this treatment, the method was a success, but if they died, their fate proved only that they had not been bled enough. The practice of medicine was generally restricted to the clergy, but because religious scruples did not permit priests to cut human flesh, the job of surgery was relegated to the cutters of hair, the barbers. To this day, red and white stripes are used to signify a barber shop—a stylized reference to a time when they dried bloody bandages by hanging them on poles outside their premises. Also, we still speak of someone as being "hot blooded," "phlegmatic," or "ill-humored," and many graduating medical students still take a "Hippocratic oath" of allegiance to professional ethics.*

The Hippocratic Theory

Like much of the Western scientific tradition, the origins of modern medicine can be traced back to ancient Greece. The Greeks favored theory over practical investigations of the world, however, and many of their ideas lacked any grounding in fact. Thus, the greatest of the Greek philosophers, Aristotle, confidently but wrongly asserted that men had more teeth than women, without bothering to actually count the teeth in people's mouths. Such reliance on unsupported theories had a lasting effect on Western medicine. Around 2,500 years ago, the Greek physician Hippocrates developed a model according to which the health of the individual required a delicate balance of four "humors," or bodily fluids—blood, phlegm, yellow bile, and black bile. If the humors were in equilibrium, the individual was healthy, but any imbalance led to disorders of the body or the mind. Treatment of disease focused on the individual: for example, if the diagnosis of the patient's personality suggested an excess of "hot blood," the patient would be bled. Due attention was also paid to environmental factors that were believed to affect health, such as air temperature or wind direction. The heart, not the

head, was considered the seat of consciousness and emotion. With no knowledge of the pump, the Greeks could not understand the heart's function; but they did know the furnace, and so thought of the heart as a fire that warmed the body, with the lungs as the bellows and food as the fuel.

The Hippocratic model had a remarkable influence in Western history. The Church endorsed it, and for over a thousand years thereafter repressed any evidence that contradicted the official teachings; indeed, for the most part the Church resisted scientific inquiry of any kind, on the ground that mere mortals should not investigate the Creation. Medical practice, based on the Hippocratic model and combined with prayer and other religious rituals, was almost entirely restricted to the clergy.

The Hippocratic model was not much use in the treatment of illness. Indeed, throughout this long period physicians were, on the whole, a positive menace to the health and lives of their patients, and ordinary people with a modicum of common sense did their best to avoid them except as a last resort.

The Germ Theory

Around the fifteenth century the rebirth of learning and inquiry known as the Renaissance began in Europe. The Church's absolute authority over medicine and other forms of learning was slowly undermined, and the nonreligious roles of scientist and physician gradually emerged. Eventually, in the seventeenth and eighteenth centuries, new discoveries and inventions began to revolutionize medicine. The invention of the pump, for example, provided a model that finally enabled people to discover the function of the heart in the circulation of blood. The microscope paved the way for a more scientific investigation of disease by revealing, for the first time, the presence of microorganisms. The Hippocratic model was increasingly abandoned, although some of its methods persisted well into the nineteenth century.

By that time, some physicians began to wonder whether hospital conditions might not be causing rather than curing disease. The hospitals were filthy and overcrowded, and beds often contained two patients, each suffering from a different condition. All treatments were carried out in the public wards, whether they involved the delivery of an infant, an amputation, or the restraint of the mentally disordered. Patients and their linen were rarely washed, and both often crawled with vermin. The dead were sometimes left in bed with the living for hours, until someone could be bothered to remove them. To enter a hospital was to have one's chances of death substantially improved.

In 1847 a Hungarian physician working in Vienna, Ignaz Semmelweis, was dismayed to find that one of every five women who gave birth in his hospital died of "childbed," or puerperal, fever. In searching for the cause, he decided to focus not on the medical condition of the patients but rather on the social behavior of their doctors. He noticed that some physicians were dissecting corpses and then, without washing their hands, were proceeding to deliver babies. Semmelweis argued vehemently for the simple procedure of hand-washing, and actually showed, through careful statistics, that it saved lives. At first, his argument carried little weight with most of his colleagues. To them, washing their hands before surgery made as much sense as brushing their hair or buttoning their coats. The fundamental breakthrough came a few years later when Louis Pasteur found that diseases such as anthrax were linked to the presence of bacteria. The result was the new and revolutionary germ theory, which held that infectious organisms cause disease. This idea became easily the most

Figure 16.6 *Working in the middle of the last century, but using methods that would be familiar to contemporary scientists, Louis Pasteur launched the era of modern medicine when he discovered the role of germs in disease. His name gave rise to the word "pasteurization," which refers to the process of eliminating germs.*

powerful in the history of medicine. For the first time, medical practice could be reliable, for it was based on a scientific approach to disease. The germ theory offered the exciting prospect that all diseases might eventually be conquered, if science could only identify their specific causes and find ways to combat them.

The new theory helped to launch modern medicine as we know it. Armed with the germ theory, physicians and public health officials looked for disease-causing organisms and for ways to stop them from reaching their human hosts, or to kill them off once they got there. They achieved their greatest successes in the industrialized nations of the world, where most infectious diseases (such as polio, diphtheria, measles, tetanus, rubella, bubonic plague, mumps, and septicemia) are now controllable. In the less developed nations, progress has been much slower as a result of limited financial resources, overpopulation, unsanitary living conditions, and widespread poverty. Disease patterns there are consequently more similar to those that today's industrial societies experienced many decades ago.

Another important effect of the germ theory was a shift in the focus of medicine: doctors became absorbed in the study of disease rather than the care of the sick. As the body of medical knowledge grew, physicians used more sophisticated techniques and developed an arcane language, largely incomprehensible to outsiders, who could only marvel, like tribespeople in awe of the shaman, at "wonder drugs" and "miracle cures." A gulf developed in the communication between physician and patient (Twaddle, 1979; Thomas, 1983). Physicians enjoyed growing prestige, which they were quick to exploit. A powerful and highly trained profession emerged, insisting on the sole legal right to practice medicine. As we shall see, this did not happen by chance. Physicians (rather than patients or the community) seized control of the medical institution and largely directed its growth—unlike the parallel situation in, say, education, where the professionals, the teachers, are far more subject to community control in matters of training, salary, syllabus, rights in the classroom, and other working conditions (Starr, 1982; Shorter, 1986).

The Medical Profession

Whether their powers are real or imaginary, healers are generally believed to have access to knowledge that can mean the difference between sickness and health, even life and death. People who possess such rare and vital information are potentially able to enjoy high social status and the power, wealth, and prestige that come with it. These privileges are not automatic, however: the social status of physicians is shaped by social and historical forces unique to each society. In the Soviet Union, for example, standards of public health and medical care are generally lower than in most Western nations, so the job of physician is less prestigious (Kaser, 1976; Feshbach, 1984). Soviet doctors are employed by the state and earn only modest salaries, comparable to those of industrial workers. Nearly three-quarters of Soviet doctors are women, who in practice have much lower status than men in their society. In Western nations, in contrast, doctors have high social status, and they are mostly male; it is nursing, a job with less status, that is regarded primarily as women's work.

Figure 16.7 *When George Washington developed a severe cold and sore throat in 1799, his doctors bled him so profusely that he died. Other treatments in common use at the time were blistering (the creation of second-degree burns on the skin, supposedly to draw out infection through the formation of pus), and purging (the use of drugs that produced copious bowel movements or vomiting, in order to clean out the system). One of the most widely used medicines was calomel, which produced the devastating effects we now recognize as mercury poisoning. Physicians were doing the best they could with the limited knowledge they had, but, understandably, they were widely feared and had low prestige.*

The rising status of physicians over the past 150 years has resulted not just from improvements in medical knowledge and techniques but also from deliberate, organized attempts by doctors to advance their own interests. In the mid-nineteenth century the public regarded physicians with suspicion. Medical schools awarded credentials indiscriminately to almost any white male who applied. In fact, formal qualifications were not even needed, and many people simply declared themselves physicians and proceeded to practice medicine. Quacks and charlatans abounded, lending a bad reputation to even the most dedicated doctors. This chaotic situation changed in the United States when some physicians joined together and campaigned to have their occupation recognized not just as a job, but as a profession.

Professionalization

A *profession* is an occupation requiring extensive, systematic knowledge of, or training in, an art or science. Because their job requires knowledge that is unavailable to the general public, members of a profession are able to claim special privileges. Professionals in every field form associations to protect their interests, primarily by insisting on the sole legal right to perform the work. This right is based on a license to practice the profession. Because the licensing process is usually directly or indirectly controlled by existing members, they are able to restrict entry to their ranks. In comparison with other workers, professionals are able to command high fees and prestige, and they enjoy far more autonomy in their work (Moore, 1970; Larson, 1977; Freidson, 1970a, 1970b). (Professions are discussed in more detail in Chapter 17, "The Economic Order.")

In 1846, a group of doctors formed the American Medical Association (AMA). Under pressure from this professional association, state legislatures outlawed other forms of healing by requiring physicians to be suitably licensed and qualified. Additionally, most of the medical schools in the United States were closed down on the grounds that they did not meet satisfactory standards, leaving only a few schools that had high requirements for admission and graduation. By early in the twentieth century, the AMA had achieved a legal monopoly over the practice of medicine. Since then, physicians' prestige has risen spectacularly. When the American public is asked to rate dozens of occupations in order of their prestige, physicians rank the highest, above such eminent figures as judges and bankers (see Figure 10.6 in Chapter 10, "Social Stratification").

The exalted status of doctors distinguishes their job from most others and insulates them from normal workplace relationships. In their professional duties, doctors do not take orders from their clients (the patients) or their employers (such as hospital administrators). A physician's performance can supposedly be evaluated only by another physician, for outsiders are considered incompetent to make such judgments. Unlike most workers, doctors can generally insist on the right to set the fees for their own services, since people are reluctant to question doctors' opinions of what procedures are needed and what they should cost. As a result, American physicians enjoy higher average incomes than any other professionals (over $103,000 a year in 1986). No other profession enjoys quite this combination of prestige, autonomy,

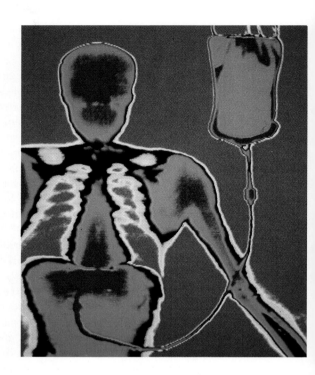

Figure 16.8 *Scientific and technological developments have helped to transform the medical profession and the public's attitude toward physicians. Doctors now have access to knowledge and techniques that are beyond the experience or understanding of most lay people, who are left in awe at the language, discoveries, methods, and even "miracles" of modern medicine.*

and income. It is hardly surprising that the professionalization of medicine has served as a model for dozens of other occupations, ranging from lawyers and architects to engineers and realtors.

Yet, as Paul Starr (1982) has pointed out, current social trends may bring the status of the medical profession more into line with that of other occupations. One important factor is that power in medicine is gradually passing from physicians to bureaucratic organizations, such as government departments and the large corporations that own more and more of the nation's laboratories, clinics, nursing homes, and hospitals. A second factor is that medicine is influenced by forces beyond the institution itself. Government, employers, unions, insurance companies, and similar interest groups all have a stake in changing the health care system, particularly in ways that will help contain costs or deliver services fairly. These social forces are likely to undermine doctors' unusual professional autonomy—if only because doctors are increasingly paid by large organizations.

Socialization for Medicine

Lengthy training is necessary to legally practice the profession of medicine. Sociological studies of this process in the United States have shown that medical students are disproportionately likely to be white, male, from high socioeconomic background, and to have a close relative (usually a parent) who is a doctor. This finding implies that preliminary socialization for medicine begins in the earlier years of life when tentative career choices are being made. Those who are poor, black, female, or lack physician role models are less likely to consider medicine as a career, or to have the financial resources to pursue it (Bloom, 1973; Haas and Shafir, 1977; Walsh, 1977; Jonas, 1978; Adler and Schuval, 1978; Coombs, 1978).

In a classic study of medical socialization, Howard Becker and his associates (1961) found that most students begin their training with considerable idealism about their chosen career, but find medical school a sobering experience. The students soon realize that they are required to absorb what seems to be an impossible amount of information. At first they try to memorize virtually everything, but, realizing that they cannot master more than a fraction of the material, they begin to learn only what they think will be in their exams. As the students progress through medical school, they also acquire a detachment in dealing with the human body, disease, and death. Lay people treat dead bodies with respect; medical students have to cut them to pieces, and often dispel the tension they experience by joking irreverently about cadavers—for example, by giving them nicknames. Similarly, the students learn to avoid emotional involvement with patients, for pain, dying, and death must be accepted as something a doctor will face repeatedly in the course of a career. As their socialization proceeds, the students come to realize that medical knowledge is full of gaps and uncertainties, and that physicians sometimes have to rely on guesswork and sometimes make mistakes. The students learn, too, some of the formal and informal norms that help maintain the status of their profession: to shun romantic or sexual relationships with patients; to try to hide their ignorance from the sick; to avoid criticizing another doctor in public. All these learning experiences bring a new realism about the possibilities and limits of modern medicine.

Of course, professional socialization does not end when physicians get their licenses; it continues throughout the medical career. Most American physicians become specialists, and must try to keep abreast of new developments in medical knowledge and technology. A great deal of informal socialization also takes place, particularly through continuing interaction with other medical personnel and with patients. Some observers have suggested that many physicians learn to relieve worries over life-and-death decisions by developing feelings of infallibility, which are reinforced because their judgment is so rarely questioned. This sense of infallibility is alleged to spill over into other aspects of physicians' lives: for example, doctors who fly private planes have much higher accident rates than other pilots, apparently because they fail to heed dangerous flying conditions (Sharaf and Levinson, 1974; Stein, 1979).

A fairly similar socialization process occurs among student nurses, who also enter their profession with high ideals about helping the sick. They, too, are apt to become somewhat cynical at first, when they discover that much of their work involves emptying bedpans, dealing with "difficult" patients, and handling arrogant superiors. In time, nurses also develop a more realistic understanding of their role and of how they can help patients. But although nurses have more opportunity for nurturant interaction with the sick than doctors, they also have much lower income and less workplace autonomy. This lack of a sense of being "professionals" doubtless contributes to the high "burnout" rate that drives most nurses from the job within six years (Davis, 1966; Psathas, 1968; Lorber, 1975).

The Medicalization of Society

The growth of a powerful and highly regarded medical profession has had a social impact far beyond the scientific battle against disease. Some sociologists suggest that we are witnessing a *medicalization of society,* a process in which the domain of medicine is extended over areas of life that were previously considered nonmedical (Freidson, 1970; Zola, 1972, 1975; Conrad and Schneider, 1980). There are four main indications of this trend in the United States.

1. *The growth of the medical institution.* The medical institution has grown steadily in size and social importance during this century, consuming an ever greater share of society's resources and thus diverting them from other goals. The number of doctors, nurses, and hospital beds has continued to climb, far outpacing increases in population size. The pharmaceutical industry has now become one of the largest in the economy. Health insurance has become a major personal or social

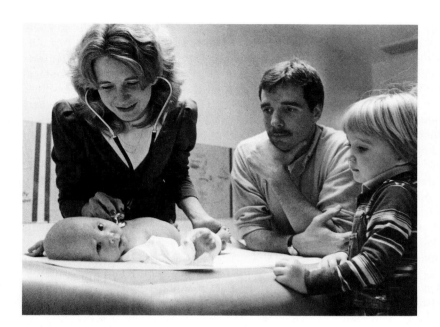

Figure 16.9 *More and more areas of society are becoming medicalized, or brought under the domain of the medical institution and its members. Pregnancy, childbirth, and infant care are cases in point. These have been regarded as "natural" rather than "medical" matters throughout history (and are still nonmedical for millions of people in less developed countries). In modern industrialized societies, however, it is automatically assumed that these processes warrant medical consultation and even intervention.*

cost. Medicine attracts a significant share of all funds available for scientific research. American health expenditures now account for over a tenth of the gross national product, and medicine, employing 7 percent of the work force, is the second largest industry. All these indicators suggest that the medical institution is of large and growing social and economic importance.

2. *Medicalization of life events.* Many events of life that were once considered natural and inevitable have now been redefined as medical and modifiable, even if they do not involve "disease" in any clinical sense. Less than a century ago, for example, most births in North America took place—as they still do in many parts of the world—without medical supervision, let alone hospitalization. Today, birth has become a major (and expensive) medical event. In fact, the claims of medicine now go much further—before birth, to such issues as fertility, conception, prenatal care, or abortion; after birth, to such matters as postnatal care, pediatrics, and child development generally. Throughout life, many common physical difficulties—such as getting too fat or being unable to sleep—are translated into medical diagnoses, such as obesity or insomnia, and treated accordingly. Medicine can even intervene in the physical appearances of age and sex: those who want to look younger can have plastic surgery or hair transplants, and individuals who would rather be of the opposite sex can have a "sex change" operation. Death, too, has become a medical event as well as a biological and social one: it usually takes place in a clinical set-

ting, where physicians sometimes make judgments about whether to keep people alive or let them die—or even to hasten their deaths. Some medical researchers are trying to discover how to stop the aging process, so that we can live indefinitely. (Some social and ethical implications of these trends are discussed in Chapter 22, "Technology and Environment.")

3. *The medicalization of deviance.* We noted in Chapter 8 ("Deviance") that many behaviors once considered sinful, criminal, or immoral are now regarded as medical problems instead. As a result, people who might formerly have been called "wicked" are now diagnosed as "sick"—which implies, for the most part, that they should be treated rather than punished. The deviant behaviors that have been largely medicalized include alcoholism, drug addiction, certain disciplinary problems of childhood and adolescence, exhibitionism and other forms of unconventional sexuality, attempted suicide, child abuse, spouse-beating, and compulsive stealing. Again, none of these behaviors is self-evidently "medical." They have become so only because physicians—and particularly psychiatrists—have successfully claimed authority over them. Society acquiesces, perhaps because it is more convenient or more humane to "treat" the offenders with therapy than to punish them with imprisonment. In certain cases of more serious deviance, psychiatrists venture opinions about whether an accused might be "bad" or "mad"—that is, sane and fit to stand trial, or insane and unfit to be tried.

4. *Public acceptance of medicalization.* The medicalization of society seems to have become part of our taken-for-granted reality. People implicitly accept a medical view of many personal, interpersonal, and social problems, forgetting that the labels "sick" and "healthy" are often metaphors, not clinical judgments. Someone whose behavior is outlandish is readily branded a "sicko"; someone else, whose approach is more conventional, is said to have a "healthy attitude." We have learned to view many ordinary difficulties of life as medical problems with medical solutions: there are pills to help us sleep and pills to keep us awake, pills to suppress our appetites and pills to make us hungry, pills to calm us down and pills to pep us up. There are psychiatrists to help us find out why we are too aggressive or too timid, too lazy or too active. Government and corporate bureaucracies accept physicians as a source of authority, relying on doctors to certify that people have been born, are fit for military service, are able to work, are entitled to disability benefits, or are definitely dead.

The medicalization of society is by no means complete or even unchallenged. Many critics have charged that medicine in general and psychiatry in particular have overextended themselves into fields that are not really medical (Szasz, 1970, 1986; Torrey, 1974; Clark, 1983). Physicians' claim to unquestioned professional authority is being challenged by patients, as evidenced by demands for patients' rights—ranging from the right to full information to the right to die in dignity (Fox, 1977; Strong, 1979). Nonetheless, medicine has achieved an impressive position, and remains one of the most dominant and highly regarded institutions of modern society.

Health-Seeking Behavior

When people feel ill, they try to return to health. They usually do so by seeking the attention of healers, a process that sociological research has shown to be surprisingly problematic.

Cultural Responses to Illness

We do not all respond the same way to the same illness. Instead, the assumptions of our particular culture or subculture influence the way we interpret our symptoms, as well as the kind of treatment (if any) we seek or receive. The same complaint might be interpreted in one group as the result of witchcraft, in another as a case of "tired blood," and in a third as a viral infection—with quite different consequences for treatment and possible cure. Even the question of whether we actually have a disease depends partly on social definitions. For example, infestation by parasites is not necessarily interpreted as a problem. A microscopic examination of your face at this moment would reveal a rich colony of revolting creatures foraging through your dead skin cells, but you would not regard this as disease. (You might learn to, though, if drug companies could persuade you that this population of parasites was a hygiene problem. Teenage acne, after all, was once simply accepted as a fact of life, but the medical profession and pharmaceutical industry have taught us to regard acne as a disease.) Similarly, in societies where intestinal amebic diseases are endemic, infected people do not currently consider themselves "sick" or seek treatment, for their symptoms are considered normal.

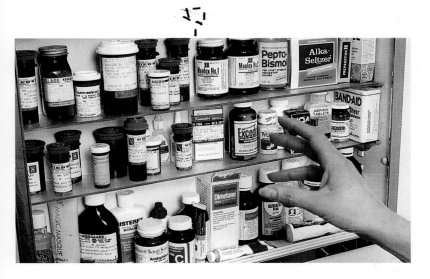

Figure 16.10 *In America, people who feel ill often resort first to self-medication. Typically, they turn to a bathroom medicine cabinet filled with pills—especially antibiotics—left over from previous episodes of disease. Actually, this behavior is potentially harmful for both the individual and society. Misuse of antibiotics can reduce the drugs' subsequent effectiveness for the persons concerned, and it also encourages the development of antibiotic-resistant strains of bacteria, which already kill thousands of people in the United States each year. An antibiotic should be taken only as directed—for a specific disease, in the doses and at the intervals prescribed, and until all the medication is used up.*

Even when people have decided that they are ill, their health-seeking behavior is influenced by cultural or subcultural assumptions. Members of some religious sects refuse medical treatment on the ground that Satan is the author of disease, and only God can cure it. Other people turn to faith healers, astrologers, and quacks of various kinds whose remedies (although they may occasionally appear successful) are scorned by licensed physicians. Thousands of American cancer patients, for example, have sought treatment with Laetrile, an apricot-pit extract, despite the fact that the medical establishment regards it as useless, even dangerous. In general, the various alternative healing systems attract patients who are suspicious of "conventional" medicine because it can do nothing for their complaints. One goes to a faith healer seeking a miraculous cure for blindness or lameness, not help for gonorrhea or pimples.

Mark Zborowski (1952, 1969) found that members of various American ethnic groups may have quite different responses to the experience of pain. Italians were very present-oriented about pain, and were primarily concerned with relieving it; Jews, on the other hand, were more future-oriented, and anxious about the long-term meaning of what they felt. Both groups freely expressed their emotions on the subject. Americans of white, Anglo-Saxon background, on the other hand, tended to complain less and to take a more detached, unemotional view of their symptoms.

Some ethnic Americans use their own unlicensed medical systems, either in preference to or in conjunction with the established system. Many Chinese-Americans, for example, subscribe to the ancient belief that health requires a balance of the "cold" and "hot" forces of *yin* and *yang,* which can be achieved by the use of specific herbs and foods. Traditional Chinese medicine also controls pain through the use of acupuncture, in which needles are inserted into specific parts of the body. Some acupuncture techniques do appear to "work," but they are generally ignored by mainstream medicine because they do not fit its current theories of human physiology (Hessler et al., 1975; Twaddle and Hessler, 1977).

American Indians, too, have a traditional system—one that, in the eighteenth and nineteenth centuries, was so much more effective than its European counterpart that many early settlers preferred the advice of Indian healers. This system is based on a view of the sacred relationship between humanity and nature, and relies on three techniques: the use of herbal and other drugs, religious or spiritual rituals, and physical manipula-

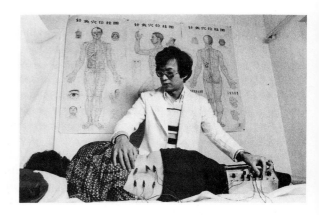

Figure 16.11 *People's health-seeking behavior does not depend only on their complaint or how ill they feel. Cultural or subcultural assumptions influence the kind of treatment people consider appropriate. In a heterogeneous society like the United States, health-seeking behavior can take many different forms, ranging from acupuncture to faith-healing.*

tions such as surgery, sweat baths, or poultices. The intent is to restore health, defined as a harmonious balance among all things in the universe, living and inanimate (Vogel, 1970; Kemnitzer, 1971; Weslager, 1973).

Similarly, many Mexican-Americans recognize certain illnesses that occur within their own group but not among "Anglos." These include *mal ojo, susto,* and *mal puesto,* which we can roughly translate as "evil eye," "shock," and "sorcery." "Anglo" doctors are considered unable to understand or treat such ailments; so patients go to *curanderos* or *curanderas,* healers who rely on Mexican folk medicine. This folk system, which includes ideas from medieval Spain, American Indian tribes, traditional Mexican healing, and even modern medicine, uses three main techniques of treatment—

foodstuffs and herbs, massages and manipulations of the body, and magical and religious symbols (Kiev, 1968; Clark, 1970; Willard, 1972; Roberts and Lee, 1980).

Most Americans, however, accept the medical profession's authority over disease and—perhaps after some delay, or an unsuccessful attempt at self-medication—they consult a doctor.

Illness, Disease, and Sickness

The patient goes to a physician with some worry or discomfort. The doctor's job is to make a diagnosis: that is, to apply a medical label to the patient's problem, converting a complaint into a disease. The doctor's professional status is largely based on this special skill. To know the name of the disease is, usually, to know how to treat it, and what its prognosis, or likely outcome, may be.

There are basic sociological distinctions made among the concepts of illness, disease, and sickness. *Illness* is the subjective sense that one is not well. *Disease* is an objective pathology of the body, such as an infection. *Sickness* is the condition of those who are socially recognized as unwell. In other words, illness is a psychological phenomenon—one "feels" ill. Disease is a biological phenomenon—one "has" a disease. Sickness is a social phenomenon—one "acts" sick, or behaves in a way typical of a sick person (Twaddle and Hessler, 1977).

We can readily see not only that illness, disease, and sickness are different, but that the presence of one does not necessarily imply the presence of the others. You can feel ill without having a disease (as in the case of psychosomatic illness). Or you can have a disease without feeling ill (as in the case of an undetected tumor). Or you can feel ill and be diseased, yet not be regarded as sick by other people (as in a case where others do not accept your claim to be unwell). The interaction between doctor and patient consists, in a sense, of the patient complaining of illness and the doctor looking for disease, which, if found, confirms the validity of the patient's sickness in the eyes of society.

There is also a difference between signs and symptoms—a distinction that is clear to the physician but probably not understood by the patient. "Signs" are objective features that the physician can detect by clinical testing or by examination of the patient, such as heart rate, skin blemishes, or blood-cholesterol level. "Symptoms," on the other hand, are subjective features that the physician knows only indirectly through the patient's re-

ports, such as nausea, stomach ache, or lack of energy. Patients may regard their symptoms as much more important than their signs, which they may not even be aware of. Doctors, however, are more inclined to pay attention to signs, which they regard as more reliable. Clearly, physician-patient interaction is fraught with opportunities for confusion and misunderstanding.

Physician-Patient Interaction

The encounter between physician and patient has long fascinated sociologists, for it is one of the most complex and subtle forms of social interaction. In fact, the medical and lay subcultures are so different that common understandings may be reached only with great difficulty, especially in cases where a wide gulf exists in the social, economic, and educational backgrounds of the participants (Jaco, 1979; Katz, 1984; Mischler et al., 1980).

In theory, the patient states a complaint on which the doctor bases a diagnosis and treatment, both of which the patient accepts. In practice, the interaction is rarely so simple. Most patients enter the medical world only occasionally, usually as strangers with a dim understanding of medical theory and practice. Physicians, on the other hand, are immersed daily in the medical subculture, and their approach is shaped by their professional training and clinical experience. Patients arrive feeling that their illness warrants the doctor's full time and attention, and their primary interest is the relief of their symptoms. But physicians are under pressure to deal with a large number of patients as quickly as possible, and they are interested mainly in the disease that underlies the symptoms. Patients and physicians think and talk differently about the body and its problems; not surprisingly, a good deal of information can get lost or corrupted in the process of translation. Patients may be confused about their symptoms, embarrassed about their body functions, and ignorant of medical terminology. Patients may want to know all about their diagnosis, but doctors are often reluctant to give them much information. Physicians' dominance of the interaction is threatened if the patients share their knowledge—particularly if the information reveals the doctor's own uncertainty or ignorance. Moreover, physicians may believe (often correctly) that some patients cannot understand or do not want to know the details of the diagnosis (Freidson, 1970; Waitzkin and Stoekle, 1976; Twaddle and Hessler, 1977; Tagliacazzo and Mauksh, 1979).

Figure 16.12 *This evocative painting by John Collier,* Sentence of Death, *captures the moment when a physician tells his patient that the disease will be fatal. Perhaps no other aspect of doctor-patient interaction is so fraught with emotion, tension, and potential misunderstanding. Many physicians are reluctant to tell patients they are dying, and many patients are unwilling to hear the truth. Extensive sociological research has shown, however, that denial of impending death usually leads to greater stress and confusion, for it inevitably creates a web of ever greater deception among patient, medical personnel, relatives, and friends. Death is more readily accepted if the dying person and intimate others confront the facts frankly and share mutual comfort with one another.*

Most physician-patient encounters do not involve serious disease, let alone the shrieking sirens and life-and-death decisions of TV melodrama. In emergencies we appreciate the skill and knowledge of physicians the most, but those situations are not typical. In the more routine interaction, patients visit a doctor because they are convinced they feel ill. But doctors can find nothing wrong with more than half the people who consult them: in other words, the patient claims symptoms of illness, but the doctor detects no clinical evidence of disease. To determine whether the patient is sick, therefore, both parties commonly enter a subtle negotiation in which each may make compromises in order to reach a mutually acceptable decision (Anderson and Helm, 1979). The physician who thinks there is nothing wrong, or who does not know what is wrong, may give a hint to that effect. Some patients appreciate the doctor's candor, but others are likely to see it as an admission of incompetence. In such cases, the physician implicitly negotiates a diagnosis with the patient by suggesting the likeliest label to fit the symptoms—"run down," "overstressed," "back strain," "looks like a fungus," "probably some virus," "could just be the heat." If the patient disagrees, the physician may restate the diagnosis more authoritatively, or may try another suggestion. If the patient refuses all diagnoses, the negotiation has broken down: the patient will probably seek other medical advice, and the doctor has lost a client.

Even when a diagnosis is accepted, it must usually be reinforced by a prescription, or patients are likely to feel that they have not received value for their time and money. In cases where no disease can be found or identified but the patients still insist that they are ill, physicians sometimes prescribe placebos—pharmacologically inactive substances disguised as real drugs, such as milk-sugar pills or salt-water injections. These are fully effective about 30 to 40 percent of the time, "curing" such problems as coughs, hayfever, seasickness, headaches, nausea, and even severe pain (Hennig, 1981; Shapiro, 1982).

Sore throats provide a notorious opportunity for this kind of implicit negotiation. In North America, people with sore throats often assume they have "strep throat," in the vague belief that the streptococcus bacterium is responsible. They go to the doctor expecting to be given antibiotics, which combat that germ very effectively. Unhappily, however, over 90 percent of sore throats are caused by viruses, against which antibiotics are useless. Knowing this, a responsible physician should tell the patient that there is probably nothing that can be done about the condition, except perhaps to gargle frequently. On the slight chance that a bacterium is responsible, the doctor should take a throat culture for laboratory analysis, and if a positive result is reported a few days later, should then prescribe the correct antibiotic. But patients are not inclined to pay a fat fee to a doctor, plus another fee for a lab test, just to be told to gargle and wait. They want "medicine," now, to stop their symptoms, immediately. So, just to keep the patients happy, many doctors implicitly accept the "strep throat" suggestion and irresponsibly prescribe antibiotics, knowing that the condition will probably improve soon in any case (Yedidia, 1980). This kind of negotiated outcome is arrived at with many other diseases, too. More than half the doctors in the United States admit to having prescribed antibiotics for another viral disease against which these drugs are utterly ineffective: the common cold (McKeown, 1978).

Medicine: A Functionalist View

Talcott Parsons, a leading functionalist theorist, was one of the first sociologists to show that sickness is a social as well as a biological phenomenon. He pointed out that a society can function smoothly only if most of its members are able to play their roles most of the time. When people are sick, their roles must be taken on by others or left unperformed, either of which situations places strains on the society as a whole. There is always a danger, however, that some people will feign illness in order to be excused from some of their duties. Society therefore has an interest not only in maintaining health and curing disease, but also in determining who is sick and who is not. According to Parsons, society makes this determination through an institutionalized sick role.

The Sick Role

Every society has a *sick role*—a pattern of behavior expected of someone who is ill. When you feel sufficiently ill, you do not behave normally. Instead, you change your social behavior: by announcing your symptoms, making your discomfort obvious, retiring to bed, seeking professional help, and so on. Like any other role, the sick role carries with it specific privileges and responsibilities. Parsons (1951, 1958, 1975) argues that the existence of this role, and the means for determining who can legitimately play it, are crucial for the normal functioning of society. In outline, Parsons's theory is as follows.

1. *Sickness is a form of deviance.* According to Parsons, the sick person is in a sense deviant, for he or she behaves in a socially undesirable way by violating norms of healthful behavior. But this deviance is of a special kind, for it is involuntary: the sick person does not choose to be sick and is not personally to blame for the condition.

2. *Sick people can claim exemption from social duties.* Society recognizes that the sick may be unable to play their roles, and allows them to abandon some of their responsibilities. It is well understood, for example, that a student who successfully claims sickness can avoid academic obligations such as term-paper deadlines.

3. *Sick people should want to get well.* It is not acceptable for people to enjoy the advantages of sickness, such as dependence on others. The sick person escapes the stigma of deviance only if he or she attempts to recover. Failure to make this attempt implies that the person is exploiting illness, or malingering, in order to escape social responsibilities.

4. *Sick people should seek technically competent help.* It is not enough to announce that one is sick and then expect sympathy and support from others. The sick role is legitimate only if one cooperates in the process of getting well by seeking technically competent help from a socially approved healer. Refusal to consult a doctor, refusal to follow the doctor's orders, or refusal to accept a doctor's view that one is not actually sick at all can lead to withdrawal of community support and the stigma of deviance.

Parsons's concept of the sick role has been an immensely influential one in sociology, although it has been much criticized (Segal, 1976; Twaddle, 1979; Arluke et al., 1979). One objection is that his theory focuses on acute diseases, such as influenza, and seems less appropriate for chronic ailments, such as incurable cancer. In such cases the sick person may have to adjust to the condition rather than work for recovery. A second criticism is that Parsons focuses too much on curative medicine and ignores society's interest in preventing people from getting sick in the first place. A third objection is that Parsons overlooks the variety of other ways in which people try to deal with illness, ranging from faith healing to simply gritting their teeth. And fourth, critics have pointed out that some conditions, such as mental disorders, leprosy, or venereal disease, do carry some stigma of deviance even if the patient cooperates in the process of getting well. Despite these criticisms, however, Parsons's work illuminates the way the sick role allows society to exercise some control over those who claim illness.

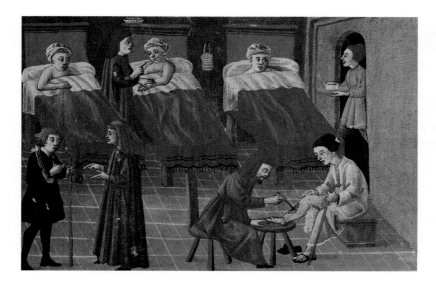 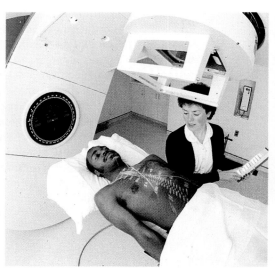

Figure 16.13 *All societies have some form of "sick role," the pattern of behavior expected of someone who is ill. In modern America, as in medieval Italy,* *the role usually involves the surrender of control over the treatment of disease to socially recognized experts in healing.*

Functions of Medicine

Bearing in mind the concept of the sick role and also our earlier discussion of the medicalization of society, we can now specify four major functions of the institution.

1. *The maintenance of health.* The medical institution has the obvious and important function of maintaining the health of society, for although individuals have ultimate responsibility for maintaining their own health, they often need to call on socially organized resources to do so. The health-maintenance function is fulfilled in a variety of ways, for example, through medical checkups, immunizations, health education, and various public health measures such as sanitation and water purification.

2. *The treatment of disease.* Everyone's health fails from time to time, and the medical institution is society's organized attempt to treat and if possible cure disease. A variety of personnel and organizations are involved—physicians, nurses, hospital administrators, pharmacies, drug companies, hospitals, nursing homes, and the like. Sick people are always, in some sense, a burden on society, and the disease-treatment function is vital in minimizing this problem.

3. *Research and innovation.* An important function of medicine involves research into the origins and spread of disease and innovation in technologies of treatment, such as surgery and drugs. Research takes many forms, ranging from fieldwork among diseased populations to laboratory research in the behavior of microorganisms. Research and innovation are performed primarily in university-affiliated teaching hospitals, government agencies, and corporate laboratories in such fields as pharmaceuticals and biotechnology. This function is essential if society is to conquer old diseases and confront new ones.

4. *Social control.* Medicine can serve as an agent of social control in several ways. First, medicine provides a means of approving the sick role for some but disallowing it for others; this ensures that ill people are relieved of some duties but controls malingering by those who feign illness. Second, physicians are now "gatekeepers" who control access to various social statuses and advantages: it is they who certify that people have been born, have been vaccinated, are too ill to work, are entitled to insurance payments, and so on. Third, psychiatrists are in some respects agents of social control, in that the threat of psychiatric labels and treatment serve to discourage various types of deviance. In all these respects, medicine helps to maintain conformity to the prevailing norms of the society.

Medicine: A Conflict View

The conflict view of medicine rests on two assumptions. The first is that good health is a highly valued resource. Like other valued resources, such as power, wealth, and prestige, good health tends to be unequally distributed in society. The second assumption is that competition over this resource shapes a society's health care system. The system may be organized so as to reduce, maintain, or increase the inequalities in health that already exist (Krause, 1977; Fuchs, 1986; Navarro, 1986; Waitzkin, 1986; Califano, 1985; Conrad and Kern, 1981). We shall look at each assumption in turn.

Inequalities in Health

Your chances of enjoying good health are improved if two conditions are met: first, that your living conditions tend not to induce disease; and second, that you have access to good health care. People with these advantages will tend to have consistently better health than those who lack them: in other words, there will be inequality of health in the society. Differences in health status, like other forms of social inequality, tend to be based on differences in socioeconomic status.

This principle is easily seen on a global scale, for there are striking health differences between the rich, industrialized societies and the poor, less developed ones. In impoverished countries such as Chad or the Central African Republic, life expectancy at birth is around 40 years. In contrast, it is over 70 years in such wealthy countries as Canada, Japan, or Switzerland. The main reason for this difference is that such a large proportion of infants and children die in the less developed nations. This high death rate is partly due to the indirect effects of poverty and overpopulation, such as malnourishment and poor sanitation. But another factor is a simple lack of basic medical facilities: every year children die by the millions from diseases that are easily preventable through immunizations or curable by antibiotics. These killer diseases could easily be wiped out if the resources were made available, as the case of smallpox shows. As recently as the 1960s, smallpox was present in 33 countries, where it infected 10 million people every year, killing a fifth of them. Through a concerted international campaign, the disease was eradicated by 1977 at a cost of $300 million—the equivalent of about five hours of international military expenditures at that time (Lown, 1982). It has been calculated that the world could wipe out ma-

laria, a disease affecting 300 million people in 66 countries, for less than half a single day's worth of global military spending (Chazof, 1982). International inequalities in health, then, parallel inequalities of power and wealth, with the lion's share of resources going to the wealthier nations.

Within a society, too, the distribution of good health tends to follow the lines of social stratification. In general, the higher one's social class, the more likely one is to enjoy good physical and mental health, to get superior medical treatment, and to live a long life. People in higher social classes are generally well educated, and have enough knowledge of their bodies and disease to recognize symptoms and to act on them immediately; poorer people may be inclined to endure symptoms, postponing medical intervention in the hope that the

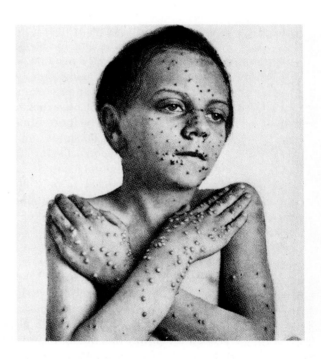

Figure 16.14 *Conflict theorists argue that many of the infectious diseases that kill millions of children in poor countries could be wiped out if the resources were made available. In fact, smallpox disease—illustrated here in a 1915 photograph— has been eliminated through an international campaign to exterminate the virus responsible. Today, the smallpox virus survives only in sealed laboratories in the United States and the Soviet Union—for each country is afraid the other might use it as a weapon in future biological warfare.*

problem will vanish—especially if a visit to the hospital may involve the loss of wages. Additionally, poor people are more likely than the nonpoor to live in crowded or unsanitary conditions, which makes them susceptible to infectious or parasitic diseases. Their standards of nutrition are likely to be lower, rendering them less resistant to most ailments. They are likely to have hazardous working conditions, which makes them liable to accidents and to job-related diseases such as asbestosis. They have less ready access to health care, especially the kind of personalized, quality care that money can buy. Rates of mental disorder, too, follow the lines of social class, probably because poorer people experience more social and economic stress, fail to seek treatment early, and are more likely to be hospitalized than to receive private therapy.

In the United States, patterns of health and disease are closely linked to race and class. Blacks have a poverty rate at least three times as high as whites. The life expectancy for whites is 75.3 years, but for blacks, at 69.3 years, it is some six years less. Infant mortality for whites is 10.5 deaths for each 1,000 live births, but for blacks it is nearly twice as high, at 20 deaths per 1,000 live births. (In fact, the United States ranks only twelfth among the nations of the world in preventing infant mortality, largely because of high death rates among poorer infants.) Similarly, there is a consistent relationship between social status and health status, with lower-income people having higher rates of most diseases and mental disorders, and therefore, shorter life expectancies. In the United States, as everywhere else, social and economic background literally affect one's life chances.

Health Care Systems

Nobody wants to be ill or dying, so those who control a cure are potentially in a position of advantage over the sick. The power to heal, then, can also be the power to exploit. According to conflict theorists, a society's health care system tends to be organized in a way that reflects the competing interests of the providers and the consumers. As in the case of any other institutional arrangements, health care systems reflect the power relationships within the society concerned (K. Davis, 1975; Roemer, 1977; Elling, 1980).

In most industrialized societies, health care is provided as a public service, either free of charge or at nominal cost. The British National Health Service, introduced soon after World War II, has

served as a model for many other countries. The British system allows for private physicians, profit-making hospitals, and fee-paying patients, but in practice almost all doctors, hospitals, and patients participate in the public system. The physicians are usually salaried employees of local communities, but they may also receive a fixed annual sum for each of their patients. Thus, doctors who attract patients have higher incomes than those who are less popular—but even so, they earn less than a third of what their American counterparts do. Medical care of any kind—physician consultations, diagnostic tests, hospitalization, major surgery, artificial limbs, and so on—is completely free. However, patients are expected to pay a flat fee of about a dollar for any prescription, regardless of what the drug or its actual cost may be. One major problem of the National Health Service is that the demand for free health care outstrips the supply, so the system is chronically short of cash (which comes, of course, from taxes), and there are sometimes long waiting lists for nonemergency treatment. Nevertheless, the system ensures great equality of health care and offers the British a longer life expectancy and lower infant mortality rate than Americans enjoy—and it does so at a much lower real cost, about 6 percent of the gross national product, compared with 11 percent in the United States. In the British view, health care should be distributed according to who needs it, not who can afford it.

The United States is the only modern industrialized nation in the world that does not have some form of national health insurance. Its health care system has evolved, over a few decades, from a virtual cottage industry dominated by family doctors and nonprofit hospitals into a huge "medical-industrial complex"—a vast, rambling system in which medical goods and services are sold for profit in much the same way as furniture or auto repairs (Relman, 1980; Wohl, 1984). With few exceptions, physicians set the charges for their work and collect payment—either from the patient or, more often, from a third party such as employers' health plans, government programs such as Medicaid, or private insurers such as Blue Cross and Blue Shield. Most older, city-center hospitals are still nonprofit (though not free), but newer facilities are increasingly located in suburbs and run for profit, often by large corporate chains. Some hospital corporations are larger than the entire medical systems of other countries: the Hospital Corporation of America, for example, has 367 facilities and employs 40,000 physicians. The main disadvantage of the American system is that it delivers health services unequally, for the best facilities are unavailable to many people, particularly the tens of millions who cannot afford adequate insurance coverage but are not poor enough to receive public assistance. The advantage of the system is that medical free enterprise has unquestionably enabled the United States to produce the most extensive and technologically advanced health care system in the entire world. It has also—and this is not an incidental matter—produced the world's richest doctors.

Opinion polls consistently show that most Americans would prefer a national health-insurance system. Yet, largely as a result of opposition from the AMA, all such proposals have been defeated in Congress for a period of more than forty years. Although the AMA represents less than half the nation's physicians, it is generally rated the single most powerful lobby in Washington, giving more money to senators and representatives (or their opponents) than any other interest group in the country. In brilliant campaigns to enlist public support, the AMA describes any health-insurance proposal as "socialized medicine," a phrase that suggests "socialism," which has a negative connotation for most Americans. The fact is, of course, that Americans already have socialized police forces, socialized elementary and secondary education, socialized fire fighting, and so on: you do not have to go out and hire a police officer if you are robbed, or a schoolteacher if your child needs

education, or a fire fighter if your house starts burning. Nor do you have to pay for any of these services according to your particular needs. The community regards them as social services and taxes everyone to make them freely available to all. The real question, for which there are strong arguments on both sides, is simply whether medicine, too, should be a social service, or whether it should remain primarily a commercial enterprise. The answer to that question, according to conflict theory, will depend on the power relations among the interests involved.

Health Costs in America

In 1985 health care in the United States cost almost $400 billion—more than a tenth of the gross national product. For years, medical costs have risen faster than the rate of inflation, and now they severely strain the budgets of government, employers, and families. The effects of prolonged or serious illness can be devastating to family finances, since most medical insurance provides coverage only for specific and limited dollar amounts or periods of illness. Indeed, more than half the personal bankruptcies in America each year are provoked by medical bills. Why is health care so expensive?

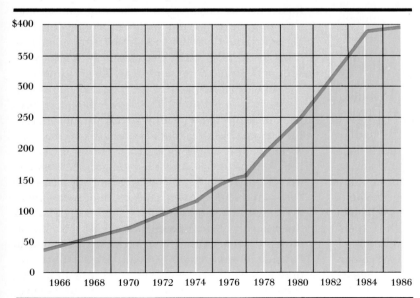

SPENDING ON HEALTH
Total public and private spending on health care for each year in billions of dollars

SOURCE: Department of Health and Human Services.

Figure 16.15 *A major problem of the American health care system is the extraordinary rise in medical costs. About one of every ten dollars spent in the United States goes on health-related items or services.*

1. *Pressure for profits.* There is strong pressure in the health care system to increase profits, but few incentives to control spending. Directly or indirectly, physicians determine most costs, for they make basic decisions about treatment and often set the fees. Patients rarely complain—partly because "doctor knows best," but also because, on average, they pay directly only about a third of physicians' fees and about a tenth of hospital bills. Most bills are paid by insurance companies, government programs, or employers. Ultimately, of course, the consumer pays the bill in insurance premiums, taxes, and higher product prices. General Motors, for example, adds an average of $340 to the price of a new car to pay its health care costs. But perception is more important than reality: consumers believe that someone else is paying the bills, so they have little incentive to question the pressure for profits.

2. *Medicaid and Medicare.* Another factor is the cost of the two federal assistance programs, Medicaid and Medicare, which in the past reimbursed doctors and hospitals for more or less whatever fees they charged. Medicaid pays part of the medical expenses of some poor people (although the program does not cover 60 percent of those below the poverty line). Many millions of dollars have been wasted through "medifraud" of the program by unscrupulous physicians. (In some cases, doctors set up a "Medicaid mill" in a slum area, where they perform phony tests, make false diagnoses, give useless treatments, and bill Medicaid for the costs.) Medicare, a much more expensive program, pays part of the medical bills of some 27 million aged and 3 million disabled people. The costs of Medicare are likely to rise astronomically in the decades ahead as the proportion of the population aged 65 or over grows larger—especially as older people require more medical care than the young. Attempts are now being made to contain costs by setting ceilings on the amount that these assistance programs will pay for specific procedures.

3. *Hospital costs.* Each morning about one million Americans wake up in the hospital, and by the end of the day have run up bills totaling more than $375 million. Hospitalization, in fact, accounts for nearly 70 percent of health care costs. Much of this bill represents overhead costs for the expensive, high-technology items, such as multimillion-dollar CAT scanners and magnetic resonance machines, that are now a standard feature of American hospitals. Sometimes these machines are needlessly duplicated in the same communities, particularly where for-profit hospitals try to attract patients away from nonprofit ones. Hospital costs have also been boosted by many new and expensive surgical procedures, such as open-heart surgery and organ transplants. Partly because these new machines and procedures require a large staff of technicians, the number of health care workers per hospital bed has tripled since 1960.

4. *Defensive medicine.* Physicians are requiring ever more extensive, and therefore more expensive, testing of their patients. The main reason seems to be a sharp rise in the number of malpractice lawsuits brought by patients who believe their doctor made a mistake. Some physicians in high-risk specialties, such as surgery or obstetrics, pay tens of thousands of dollars a year for insurance against these claims, a sum which is, of course, passed on to the consumer. To protect themselves further, many doctors practice "defensive medicine," ordering every conceivable test so that they cannot later be accused of negligently overlooking any. One recent study found that some American doctors ordered more than forty times as many tests for patients suffering from hypertension as their British counterparts did (Epstein and Hartley, 1984).

5. *Surplus doctors, redundant procedures.* The promise of high incomes has attracted a flood of entrants to the medical profession: in 1970, 334,000 doctors were licensed; in 1985, 500,000; and by 1990, there will be about 536,000. As a result, the United States has a surplus of doctors in general and of specialists in particular. This excess of doctors leads to an excess of doctoring, especially in fields such as surgery where, by common consensus, there are far too many practitioners. The United States has twice as many surgeons per capita as Britain and, not surprisingly, it has twice as much surgery per capita, too. Each year there are 150,000 heart-pacemaker and 170,000 coronary-bypass operations. These procedures can cost between $10,000 and $20,000 each, yet most medical scientists believe half of them are pointless. As the number of surgeons has risen, so has the number of births by Caesarean section, from less than 5 percent as recently as 1968 to over 20 percent in 1985—and about half these operations lead to further medical complications. Some hospitals use the procedure for 25 percent or even 30 percent of births. It seems either that American women are having unprecedented difficulty giving birth, or that American surgeons are boosting their incomes by performing unnecessary operations. Given that natural birth is, in fact, a thoroughly

tried and well proven means of entering the world, we may suspect that the fault lies with the surgeons rather than the mothers (Cohen and Estner, 1983).

Many steps are afoot to help contain medical costs. Insurance companies are encouraging and even requiring patients to get second opinions before major expenditures on surgery. Several state laws encourage physicians to prescribe generic drugs rather than identical, but more expensive, brand-name drugs. The federal government is setting limits on the amount it will reimburse hospitals for particular treatments under its aid programs. Many individuals and employers are joining health maintenance organizations (HMOs). An HMO is staffed by salaried physicians and provides a full range of treatment to consumers who pay a fixed annual fee for the service; if it is to be profitable, an HMO must minimize expenditures and so has an incentive to hold down costs. How much effect these piecemeal approaches will have remains to be seen.

Disease, Environment, and Lifestyle

In light of the high public regard for medicine, it may come as a surprise that modern medical techniques such as vaccinations and antibiotics have had no significant impact on the overall death rate in industrialized societies during the past century. Death rates in these societies have certainly declined sharply—but they did so *before* the introduction of vaccinations and antibiotics (McKinlay and McKinlay, 1977; McKeown, 1979). The drastic reduction in deaths was primarily the result of higher standards of nutrition (which increase resistance to disease) and innovations in public health, such as milk pasteurization, water purification, food inspection, and insect control (which reduce exposure to germs). In fact, despite a massive growth in medical knowledge, technology, and facilities, there is no sign whatever that the overall extent of disease is decreasing, even in the emerging postindustrial societies. Why is this?

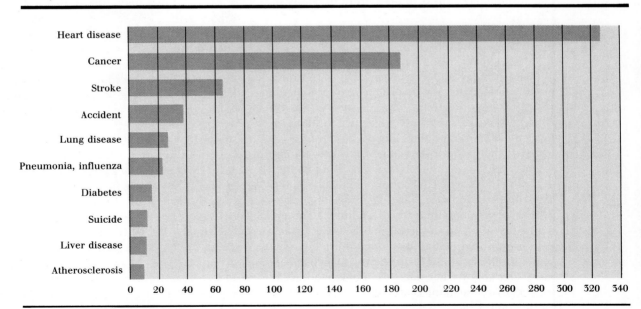

THE LEADING CAUSES OF DEATH IN THE UNITED STATES, 1985
Death rates per 100,000 people

SOURCE: Department of Health and Human Services.

Figure 16.16 *Most of the major killer diseases in the modern United States are degenerative conditions resulting from aging or environmental influences. Only influenza and pneumonia are caused by germs—and a high proportion of deaths from these diseases occur among elderly people whose immunity has been weakened by age or other disease.*

By the late twentieth century, it has become apparent that the germ theory is irrelevant to a great deal of disease: many of the most serious diseases in modern society are not caused by germs at all. Because people do not succumb to the acute, infectious diseases that once wrought havoc in childhood, they live longer—only to fall victim instead to chronic, incurable diseases of middle and old age, such as cancer, heart disease, emphysema, or strokes. In general, these ailments are becoming more prevalent in modern society, and consume an ever greater share of medical resources.

The causes of these diseases are many and complex, but fundamentally they arise from the relationship between individuals and their natural and social environment. In other words, the diseases involve interactions among such factors as genetic background, climate, diet, nutrition, weight, stress, occupation, physical activity, use of alcohol, tobacco, and other drugs, radiation, and chemical pollution of air, water, and food. Many diseases recognized today, in fact, seem to have a limited physical basis: migraine, gastric ulcers, hypertension, hysterical paralysis, asthma, and colitis are typically activated by episodes of stress. The same is true of mental disorders: most psychoses (such as schizophrenia) seem to be at least partly social in origin, and most neuroses (such as claustrophobia) appear to arise from previous social experience.

These chronic conditions are very resistant to medical intervention. They involve lengthier and more expensive treatment than acute diseases, and the prognosis for recovery is usually much poorer. Indeed, the ideal of their total elimination may prove to be a mirage, for new environmentally caused diseases are likely to appear as long as human technology and lifestyles continue to change. Many of our contemporary ailments are, in truth, the "diseases of civilization." But although they often cannot be cured, they can be prevented. Unfortunately, modern medical practice focuses primarily on the treatment rather than the prevention of disease—on surgery for failed hearts rather than preventing the habits that led those hearts to fail in the first place. We have grown accustomed to the idea that we become sick, and doctors make us well. In all too many cases, however, the truth is that we make ourselves sick, and the doctors can do little or nothing to make us better.

A prime example of this truth is tobacco use. The dangers of smoking are well known, yet some 50 million Americans still smoke—33 percent of adult men and 28 percent of adult women. Each year, Americans smoke over 620 billion cigarettes, and about 340,000 of them die of smoking-related causes. They spend over $23 billion on the drug, of which a third goes in taxes. Congress, which insists that health warnings be printed on cigarette packs and advertisements, has for many years subsidized the tobacco industry, which supports 500,000 farmers and supplies about 2 million other jobs. Every year, $1 billion worth of advertising urges Americans to take up or continue a medically unsound cultural habit.

Similarly, many Americans decline to use automobile seat belts, even though the practice drastically reduces the chance of death or serious injury in an accident. Many complain about and

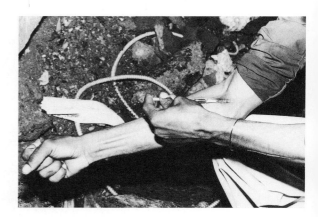

Figure 16.17 *Much of the ill health of modern society is created by individual and social practices. Good health is not something we can simply buy from doctors; to a great extent, we have to achieve and maintain it ourselves.*

The Epidemiology of Smoking and Disease

Does smoking contribute to disease? And why is the question controversial? It is sometimes difficult to establish a link between a particular disease and specific social or cultural factors. This is especially true when no infectious agent is involved, or when a long time passes between exposure to the cause and the final appearance of any symptoms. In such instances, years of research and statistical analysis may be needed before an unambiguous link can be shown. This is the case for the relationship between smoking, a practice deeply embedded in modern social, cultural, and economic life, and lung cancer, one of the major killer diseases of the twentieth century. The evidence for a causal connection rests on convincing statistical correlations, documented in a series of reports by the Surgeon General of the United States.

The statistical picture shows the following consistent links between cancer and smoking:

1. During this century, increased rates of smoking have been followed by increased rates of lung cancer.

2. The majority of lung-cancer victims—82 percent of them—have a history of smoking.

3. Men smoke more than women, and are more likely than women to get lung cancer.

4. As smoking has become more common among women, female lung-cancer rates have risen.

5. The longer people smoke, the higher their risk of lung cancer; and if they give up smoking, their risk is less than if they continue.

6. The more men smoke, the greater their chances of getting lung cancer: those who smoke less than one pack a day are ten times more likely to die of lung cancer than nonsmokers, but those who smoke more than one pack a day are thirty times more likely to die in this way.

Smoking has also been found to correlate strongly with other cancers: compared with nonsmokers, smokers are four times more likely to get cancer of the mouth and five times more likely to get cancer of the larynx. In addition, smoking appears to increase susceptibility to other diseases as well. Smokers are six times more likely to die of bronchitis or emphysema than nonsmokers. Asbestos workers who smoke have ninety times more risk of contracting lung cancer than people exposed neither to asbestos nor smoking. Smoking is associated with pregnancy problems, including lower birth weight, stillbirth, spontaneous abortion, and infant mortality. Smokers have shorter life expectancy than nonsmokers: for example, a 32-year-old smoker can expect to die seven years earlier than a comparable nonsmoker. Also, there is growing evidence that smoking causes disease in nonsmokers who inhale other people's smoke.

The tobacco industry has consistently refused to accept these statistical correlations as proof that smoking causes cancer and other health problems. Why? The fact that one variable correlates with another does not prove that one causes the other, or even that they are related at all. The link between them might be spurious—that is, it might be merely coincidental, and not imply any causal relationship. But no other plausible factor has been suggested to explain this particular correlation, or the fact that increases or decreases in one variable—smoking—lead to corresponding increases or decreases in the other—lung cancer and other diseases. The statistical correlations also have to be evaluated against a background of other facts. Most cancers are caused by environmental agents, and it seems reasonable to conclude that repeatedly inhaling the hundreds of chemicals that are present in cigarettes might eventually cause lung cancer. In any event, the evidence that smoking is dangerous to health, and often fatally so, has been sufficient to convince virtually everyone except the tobacco industry and some addicts of the drug.

SOURCE: From the Surgeon General's reports, 1983, 1984.

often exceed a 55 mph speed limit, although it saves 4,500 lives and prevents 90,000 severe head injuries each year. Millions eat themselves into cholesterol-induced heart disease, and still encourage their children to eat junk food. Millions become addicted to alcohol, barbiturates, cocaine, heroin, and other drugs whose dangers are common knowledge.

Having exposed themselves to the dangers of injury and disease, they then turn to the medical institution for help when the damage is done. The message of the sociological study of medicine is that it would be much cheaper, and far more effective, for individuals and society to make those changes that would prevent disease from occurring in the first place.

Recognition of this fact is gradually leading to another fundamental change in the direction of medicine. This change would involve devoting resources to prevention, as well as to cure; focusing on patients and their environment, as well as diseases and their diagnosis; and emphasizing individuals' responsibility for maintaining their own health instead of leaving it up to the doctors to cure them (Dubos, 1959; Illich, 1976; Carlson, 1976; Knowles, 1977; McKeown, 1979).

Summary

1. Medicine is the institution focused on disease and its social implications. Disease may be endemic or epidemic, acute or chronic. Sickness is a social as well as an individual matter, for disease has a social impact, and social factors influence disease.

2. Epidemiology is the science of the distribution of disease in populations. It emerged in the nineteenth century, and its methods are now applied to such problems as the cause and spread of AIDS.

3. The Hippocratic theory, based on a balance of four "humors," dominated Western medicine for centuries. It was followed by the germ theory, which revolutionized medicine by emphasizing infectious microorganisms.

4. Physicians have formed a profession, which helps ensure high earnings, prestige, and great autonomy in the workplace. This professional status requires a long period of socialization, primarily in medical school. The success of medicine has led to the medicalization of society, as shown by the growth of medicine, medicalization of life events, medicalization of deviance, and public acceptance of medicalization.

5. Health-seeking behavior is influenced by cultural factors, such as ethnic-group membership. Sociologists recognize a difference between illness (a personal, subjective condition), disease (a physical, objective condition), and sickness (a social, behavioral condition). Relationships between patients and physicians are complicated by their different backgrounds and assumptions. Diagnoses are sometimes "negotiated" by the participants, particularly in cases of minor ailments of uncertain cause, such as sore throats.

6. Talcott Parsons helped to develop the functionalist view of medicine through the concept of the sick role. He claimed that sickness is a form of deviance; sick people are exempted from social duties only if they want to get well and cooperate by seeking competent help. The functions of medicine are the maintenance of health, the treatment of disease, research and innovation, and (partly through the sick role) social control.

7. The conflict view of medicine emphasizes that patterns of health and of medical care reflect existing social inequalities. Inequalities of health follow the lines of stratification, as illustrated by international patterns of disease and death and by racial and class patterns within the United States. Similarly, health care systems reflect the power relations in society, as illustrated by the nonprofit British system and the American "medical-industrial complex."

8. Health costs in the United States are rising rapidly. The reasons include physicians' right to set their own fees; a lack of incentive by patients to contain costs paid by third parties; the high cost of Medicaid and particularly Medicare as the elderly population grows; costs of "high tech" equipment and procedures in hospitals; excessive testing, partly due to "defensive medicine" by physicians fearful of malpractice suits; and a surplus of surgeons and other specialists.

9. Despite the successes of medicine, serious disease is still widespread in modern societies. It is now recognized that many diseases are caused not by germs, but rather by environmental conditions and lifestyles.

Important Terms

medicine (425)   epidemiology (428)

endemic disease (426)   profession (434)

epidemic disease (426)   medicalization of society (435)

acute disease (426)   illness/disease/sickness (436)

chronic disease (426)   sick role (441)

Suggested Readings

BECKER, HOWARD S., et al. *Boys in White: Student Culture in Medical School.* Chicago: University of Chicago Press, 1961.
A classic study of socialization for medicine.

COCKERHAM, WILLIAM C. *Medical Sociology.* 3rd ed. Englewood Cliffs, N.J.: Prentice-Hall, 1986.
A good, up-to-date overview of the sociology of medicine.

CONRAD, PETER, and ROCHELLE KERN (eds.). *The Sociology of Health and Illness: Critical Perspectives.* New York: St. Martin's Press, 1981.
A useful selection of sociological articles on various aspects of medicine.

CONRAD, PETER, and JOSEPH W. SCHNEIDER. *Deviance and Medicalization: From Badness to Sickness.* St. Louis: Mosby, 1980.
An examination of the tendency for medicine to claim jurisdiction over various forms of deviance.

EPSTEIN, SAMUEL S. *The Politics of Cancer.* San Francisco: Sierra Club Books, 1978.
A controversial argument that modern industry has irresponsibly introduced a variety of cancer-causing substances into the environment.

FREIDSON, ELIOT. *Profession of Medicine.* New York: Dodd, Mead, 1970.
A classic sociological analysis of the medical profession.

GOTTFRIED, ROBERT S. *The Black Death: Natural and Human Disaster in Medieval Europe.* New York: Free Press, 1983.
An interesting historical account of the most disastrous epidemic of all time, with a consideration of its social consequences.

MECHANIC, DAVID (ed.). *Symptoms, Illness Behavior, and Health-Seeking.* New Brunswick, N.J.: Rutgers University Press, 1982.
A selection of articles on various aspects of patient-physician relationships.

STARR, PAUL. *The Social Transformation of American Medicine.* New York: Basic Books, 1982.
A detailed study of the origins, development, and current trends of the American medical system.

WAITZKIN, HOWARD. *The Second Sickness: Contradictions of Capitalist Health Care.* Chicago: University of Chicago Press, 1986.
An important critique of the American health care system, written from a conflict perspective.

CHAPTER 17

The Economic Order

The human animal needs food and shelter in order to survive: these are basic necessities. Beyond these requirements, people in all societies feel that they have "needs" for certain other goods and services as well—in one society, perhaps, for bows and arrows and the attention of a witch doctor; in another society, for a color TV set and the skills of an auto mechanic. Whether they are biological or social, human needs can usually be satisfied only by human effort. Most goods and services are scarce. People must work to produce them and must find some way of distributing them among the various members of the society. This activity, basic to our species, is the substance of economic life. The ***economic order*** is the institutionalized system for producing and distributing goods and services.

Economic activity is significant not only because it sustains life. Throughout this book we have noted the central importance of economic production for human culture and social structure as well. The principal means of production that a society uses—hunting and gathering, horticulture, pastoralism, agriculture, industrialism, or postindustrialism—strongly influences the size and complexity of the society and the character of its cultural and social life. Changes in the means of economic production are therefore inevitably accompanied by sweeping changes elsewhere in society. We have also noted the close link between economic inequality and other forms of social inequality—between different social classes, different racial and ethnic groups, different age groups, and even between men and women. Economic activity, too, is a vital part of our everyday existence, for our jobs usually provide our incomes and define our social status. Work is therefore a significant source of personal and social identity: in fact, one of the first questions we ask a person we have just met is "What do you do?" The answer to that

453

single question enables us to predict, with a good deal of accuracy, a person's social class, income, level of education, type of residential neighborhood, and various other social traits.

In this chapter we will be focusing on one of the most basic of all human activities, with implications that extend into many areas of individual and social life. We will not examine the actual mechanics of the economy in detail; that is primarily the task of economists. We will concentrate instead on the social basis and consequences of economic activity.

The Sociology of Occupations

The actual economic activity that people engage in depends largely on their society's basic subsistence strategy: in one society, perhaps, work means herding camels, while in another, it might mean serving hamburgers. Different economies offer people different kinds of jobs, and thus, indirectly, a variety of social and cultural styles. Sociologists who study economic life are therefore especially interested in the way the occupational structure of a society develops and changes, and the effects this structure has on human existence.

Primary, Secondary, and Tertiary Sectors

Any economy contains three basic sectors, with the proportion of the labor force in each sector depending on the society's basic subsistence strategy. The *primary sector* is the part of the economy that involves the gathering or extracting of undeveloped natural resources—for example, fishing, mining, forestry, or agriculture. The *secondary sector* is the part of the economy that involves turning the raw materials produced by the primary sector into manufactured goods—for example, houses, furniture, automobiles, canned foods. The *tertiary sector* is the part of the economy that involves providing services—for example, medicine, laundering, teaching, broadcasting. Over the course of sociocultural evolution, the economic emphasis shifts steadily from the primary to the secondary and then to the tertiary sector, with profound effects on the nature of work and, indeed, on society as a whole.

In *preindustrial* societies, virtually the entire population is engaged in the primary sector—hunting and gathering, tending herds or gardens, or plowing and harvesting fields. A few people may be occupied, often part-time, in the tiny secondary sector—making knives or clothing, for example. Even fewer work in the tertiary sector, providing such services as those of shaman or courtier. The overwhelming dominance of the primary sector has immediate implications for social and economic life. Communities are small, and people usually live and work in or around their tents or huts. The family is a unit of both production and consumption: its members grow their own food, catch their own game, and so on. Life is often hard and resources limited, but, within limits set primarily by natural factors such as the changing seasons, people have a fair amount of autonomy in their work—that is, personal control over working conditions, such as when and how the job should be done.

In *industrial* societies, most of the work force is engaged in "blue-collar" jobs in the secondary sector, producing manufactured goods in workshops and factories. The primary sector still exists, of course, to supply the raw materials for industry, and the tertiary sector begins to expand as new service occupations proliferate, like those of clerk, banker, manager, technician, and entertainer. The dominance of the secondary sector, however, shapes the general conditions of labor and life. People tend to live in cities rather than in small communities, for that is where the jobs are. They no longer work in or around their homes, but instead travel daily to and from the workplace. They rarely consume what they produce; rather, they produce for money, which they use to buy other people's products. And because they are wage laborers, paid by the hour or the week, they lose most of their job autonomy: they work for an employer, performing a specific job, in a specific place, for a specific period of time.

In *postindustrial* societies, most of the work force is engaged in the tertiary sector—providing services and processing information in locations like restaurants, hospitals, and offices. The primary sector, made highly productive through technological innovation, now employs only a tiny part of the work force, and the secondary sector steadily shrinks as jobs disappear through automation and through competition from cheaper labor in less developed foreign economies. The new dominance of the tertiary sector brings about fresh changes in the nature of economic and social life. Work becomes more diverse, often involving "business travel" away from the workplace as well

Figure 17.1 *There are three main sectors of work in an economy. Primary industry involves gathering or extracting raw materials; secondary industry involves manufacturing goods; and tertiary industry involves providing services. Over the course of economic development, the proportion of workers in secondary and, later, tertiary industry grows larger.*

as from the home; simultaneously, innovations in computer technology and telecommunications make it possible for many people to work at home once more. Rising standards of living lead to a growing emphasis on consumption rather than production, and a consumer ethic encourages a materialistic view of life. Many of the "white collar" workers in the tertiary sector enjoy a good deal of autonomy in their jobs, for much of their work requires individual judgments and skills in tasks involving people or information.

In the 1950s, the United States became the first country in the world to have more than half its labor force engaged in the tertiary sector, and this trend still continues. Today, American farm workers, who represented almost 40 percent of the work force at the turn of the century, comprise less than 3 percent of all workers; the industrial work force is shrinking rapidly, and now comprises less than 29 percent of all workers; and over 68 percent of workers are employed in providing services or handling information. Predictably, a shift of this magnitude does not take place without wrenching social changes, an issue we will discuss in more detail shortly.

The Division of Labor

Another important trend in the course of economic development is a refinement in the **division of labor,** the specialization by individuals or groups in particular economic activities. This specialization occurs in all societies because it is highly functional. By assigning particular people to do specific jobs, the division of labor helps ensure that they will become more expert at their work, and thus enhances the efficiency of economic life.

In *preindustrial* societies there is little division of labor. Hunting and gathering societies allocate some tasks according to age or sex, but there are very few full-time, specialized roles, and most people do much the same kinds of work. In pastoral, horticultural, and especially agricultural societies, there is rather more division of labor, for these societies produce some **surplus wealth**—more food and other goods than is necessary to meet their producers' basic needs. The surplus frees some people from basic subsistence activities and allows them to specialize in other roles—perhaps as traders, artists, or soldiers. The great bulk of the population, however, works in food production.

In *industrial* societies, the division of labor becomes very elaborate. One reason is that many new jobs are created by the diversity of industrial production and by the vast surplus that it creates. But another reason is that industrialism creates an entirely new form of the division of labor—the high degree of specialization found in factories where each individual contributes only a minute part to the final product. This specialization was hailed in the early days of industrialism by Adam Smith, the first advocate of modern capitalism. In the celebrated description of a pin factory that opens his book *The Wealth of Nations,* published in 1776, Smith reported that one worker could barely make 20 pins a day by himself, so ten workers would make about 200 pins. But if the job were broken down into simple operations, like drawing the wire or sharpening the point, ten workers doing specialized jobs could produce 48,000 pins a day. From such beginnings grew that symbol of specialization in industrial production, the modern assembly line.

In *postindustrial* societies, the division of labor reaches its highest degree of complexity. Economic development in these societies relies heavily on technological advances, which in turn require and create a series of new specialties and subspecialties, like computer designer, computer programmer, computer analyst, computer technician, computer operator. The contrast between the occupational structure of these societies and the simple societies of the past is striking.

In the simplest preindustrial society, the number of specialized occupational roles—if any exist at all—can probably be counted on the fingers of one hand. Even in the early stages of industrialism in the United States, the 1850 census recorded a grand total of 323 occupations. In the postindustrial United States today, in contrast, the Department of Labor records over 20,000 jobs. In 1977, the department's *Dictionary of Occupational Titles* listed such highly specialized occupations as blintz roller, alligator farmer, oxtail washer, cherry-bomb finisher, corset stringer, ear-muff assembler, gherkin pickler, and chicken sexer. But the number of job titles continued to increase so rapidly that a supplement to the dictionary was issued in 1982, this time including such specialties as bung driver, caponizer, singing messenger, tamale-machine feeder, braille proofreader, environmental epidemiologist, nuclear-criticality safety engineer, and laser-beam–color-scanner operator. These lists, of course, include only legitimate occupations. They leave out such jobs as dope pusher, pimp, pickpocket, counterfeiter, and con artist, all of which include many further subspecialties. But what does all this occupational diversity mean for modern society?

Specialization and Society

In his important work *The Division of Labor in Society* (1893), Emile Durkheim tried to identify the social consequences of the division of labor in the modern world. He concluded that increased specialization has two significant and related effects: it actually changes the very nature of the bonds that hold society together, and it encourages individualism at the expense of community—perhaps to a dangerous degree.

Traditional societies, Durkheim argued, are held together by *mechanical solidarity,* a form of social cohesion that is based on the similarity of the members. Because these societies are small and because everyone does much the same work, the members are all socialized in the same pattern, share the same experiences, and hold common values. These values, which are mainly religious in nature, form a "collective consciousness" for the community, a set of norms, beliefs, and assumptions shared by one and all. There is little individuality—for people think of themselves primarily in terms of their membership in, and loyalty to, the group. The society consists basically of a collection of kinship groups, all with similar characteristics.

Modern societies, on the other hand, are held together by *organic solidarity,* a form of social cohesion based on the differences among the members, which make them interdependent. People in modern societies play a variety of economic roles, have quite different experiences, hold different values, and socialize their children in many varying patterns. Consequently, they think of themselves as individuals first and as members of a kinship or wider social group second. The modern society thus consists of a series of interconnected individuals, each with different characteristics. Because they are now interdependent, however, they must rely on one another if their society is to function effectively. The basis for social solidarity is no longer the *similarity* of the members but rather their *differences.*

According to Durkheim, the end result of this division of labor, with its emphasis on differences and individuality, may be *anomie*—a condition of confusion that exists in both individual and society

Figure 17.2 *In a traditional, preindustrial society, there is hardly any division of labor except on the grounds of age and sex. People wear similar clothes, reside in similar dwellings, share similar ideas, and experience much the same lives. Such a society, Durkheim argued, is held together by "mechanical solidarity," or the basic similarity of its members. A diversified modern industrialized society, on the other hand, is held together by "organic solidarity," or the dissimilarity of people who have to depend on one another's specialized skills. These two pictures—one of a village on an island in the South Pacific, and one of a single street in Manhattan—give some idea of what this distinction can mean for the everyday life of the society.*

when social norms are weak, absent, or conflicting. As anomie spreads, people feel ever more detached from their fellows. Having little commitment to shared norms, they lack social guidelines for personal conduct and are inclined to pursue their private desires without regard for the interests of society as a whole. Social control of individual behavior becomes ineffective, and the society is threatened with extensive deviance, disorganization, or even disintegration as a result.

How valid do Durkheim's concerns seem today? He was probably correct in his view that the division of labor would lead to growing individualism and the breakdown of shared commitment to social norms. Indeed, we have touched on this issue at several points in this book. For example, we noted in Chapter 3 ("Culture") that self-fulfillment is becoming an important value in the postin-dustrial United States; in Chapter 8 ("Deviance"), that crime and other forms of deviant behavior seem much more widespread in modern societies than in traditionalist ones; in Chapter 14 ("The Family"), that people are increasingly inclined to judge family issues in terms of their own desires rather than their obligations to their kin; and, in Chapter 15 ("Religion"), that loyalty to traditional religion is being eroded in the most economically developed societies. In short, it seems plausible that there is widespread anomie in modern societies. Yet modern societies do retain enough consensus on norms and values to guide most individual behavior and to avert the social breakdown that Durkheim feared. Moreover, many people look favorably on the growth of individualism, with all it implies for personal freedom and the exercise of choice over one's own destiny.

Professions

One effect of specialization in modern economies is the appearance of professions. The word is often loosely used in everyday life—we hear of "professional" carpet layers or window cleaners—but the sociological use of the term is more rigorous. As we noted in our discussion of physicians in Chapter 16 ("Medicine"), a **profession** is an occupation requiring extensive, systematic knowledge of, or training in, an art or science. Professions are generally the most highly paid and prestigious of occupations, and professionals perform many of society's most important roles—such as those, for example, in teaching, scientific research, law, medicine, and technology (Parsons, 1954).

Professions are distinguished from other occupations by several characteristics. First, the skill of professionals is based on systematic, theoretical knowledge, not merely on training in particular techniques. This is a characteristic that distinguishes dentists, say, from dental assistants. Second, professionals have considerable autonomy over their work. Their clients are presumed to be incompetent to make judgments about the problems with which the profession is concerned: you can give instructions to a hairdresser or tailor, but cannot advise a doctor or lawyer on matters of medicine or law. Third, professionals form associations that regulate their profession's internal affairs and represent its interests to outside bodies. Psychiatrists or architects thus have a much greater sense of common identity than checkout clerks or janitors. Fourth, admission to a profession is carefully controlled by the existing members. Anyone can claim to be a salesperson or a carpenter, but someone who claims to be a surgeon or a professor without having the necessary credentials is an imposter. Becoming a professional involves taking an examination, receiving a license, and acquiring a title, and this process is usually regulated by the professional association concerned. Fifth, professions have a code of ethics that all their members are expected to adhere to; the penalty for a breach of this code may be expulsion from the profession. Most occupations have some of these characteristics to some degree, but only professions place such great emphasis on all of them (Greenwood, 1962; Etzioni, 1969).

The British playwright George Bernard Shaw once remarked that a profession is "a conspiracy against the layman." His implication was that professionals, by keeping their knowledge among themselves and by restricting access to the occupa-

Figure 17.3

INFRASTRUCTURALISTS AT WORK

Drawing by Ed Fisher; © 1982
The New Yorker Magazine, Inc.

tion, are merely protecting their own interests—even though they may claim that professionalization is for the benefit of the public. It is certainly common for nonprofessionals to try to "professionalize" their jobs in the hope of achieving greater prestige and income. This transformation generally follows a typical sequence. The first step is to create a professional association with specific qualifications for membership. The second step is to establish a code of ethics, which serves to raise the esteem in which the occupation is held and provides a means of keeping out "undesirable" members. The third step is to persuade political authorities to require all members of the occupation to have formal certification—and to ensure that training facilities fall, as far as possible, under the control of the professional association. The rationale for this crucial step is that certificates or other credentials are necessary to maintain sound professional standards, but requiring high qualifications serves an additional purpose: it restricts the number of new entrants to the field, thus ensuring a strong demand for the services of its existing members (Wilensky, 1964; W. Moore, 1970; Larson, 1977).

Attempts to professionalize jobs in the primary and secondary sectors of industry generally meet with only limited success. It is not enough, for example, to change the name of a job like "plumber" to "sanitary engineer." Blue-collar jobs usually do not involve sophisticated training, are often regarded by the public as "hard" or even "dirty" work, and continue to have relatively low prestige despite efforts at professionalization. In the white-collar jobs of the tertiary sector, however, professionalization tends to be more successful, and the number of jobs with "professional" or at least semi-professional status—such as realtor or travel agent—is expanding rapidly.

The Nature of Work

Work is a central part of our existence. Whether we see work as a source of fulfillment and satisfaction or as a cause of boredom and indignity, whether we view it as enjoyable in itself or simply as a means of earning a living, it is the activity that occupies most of our waking adult lives. Sociologists are therefore deeply interested in how people experience their work.

Work and Alienation

Industrialization transformed the nature of work. As early as 1776, Adam Smith became concerned about the effects of this change on the individual worker:

> The man whose whole life is spent in performing a few simple operations . . . has no occasion to exert his understanding or to exercise his invention. . . . He naturally loses, therefore, the habit of such exertion, and generally becomes as stupid and ignorant as it is possible for a human creature to become.

A more restrained comment was made by Alexis de Tocqueville, a French observer of early industrial development in the United States:

> What can be expected of a man who has spent twenty years of his life in making heads for pins? . . . When a workman has spent a considerable proportion of his existence in this manner, his thoughts are forever set upon the object of his daily toil. . . . The workman becomes more weak, more narrow-minded, and more dependent. [1954, orig. 1835]

Karl Marx took up this issue and made it a central part of his analysis of industrial societies. He believed that the capacity for labor is one of the most distinctive human characteristics. All other species, he argued, are merely objects in the world; human beings alone are subjects, because they consciously act on and create the world, shaping their lives, cultures, and personalities in the process. In modern societies, however, people have become estranged from their work, and thus from nature, from other human beings, and from themselves.

Marx referred to this sense of estrangement as *alienation*—the situation in which people lose their control over the social world they have created, with the result that they find themselves "alien" in a hostile environment. In his view, an important source of alienation in modern societies is the extreme division of labor. Each worker has a specific, restricted, and limiting role that makes it impossible to apply the full human capacities of the hands, the mind, and the emotions to work. The worker has diminished responsibility, does not own the tools with which the work is done, does not own the final product, does not have the right to make decisions—and is therefore reduced to a minute part of a process, a mere cog in a machine. Work becomes an enforced activity, not a creative and satisfying one. Marx claimed further that this situation is aggravated in capitalist economies, in which the profit produced by the labor of the worker goes to someone else.

Figure 17.4 *In this picture of a typical nineteenth-century factory, some workers are shown eating at their workbench while others continue at their jobs. Many employers viewed their workers as little more than adjuncts to the machinery, and would have regarded the modern idea of a "lunch hour" as absurd.*

Worker Satisfaction

Is there alienation in a modern economy like that of the United States—and if so, how much? That many people dislike their jobs is no secret. A 1973 report by the U.S. Department of Health, Education, and Welfare, *Work in America,* focused on the issue of alienation. The report told of extensive "blue-collar blues" and "white-collar woes," caused by "dull, repetitive, seemingly meaningless tasks, offering little challenge or autonomy." But although these and similar findings seem to indicate widespread alienation, sociologists have found the concept too vague to measure with real precision. Instead, they have focused on the degree of worker satisfaction, which may give a broad indication of the level of alienation.

How satisfied are American workers? To some extent, the answer depends on how the question is put to them. When people are asked if, given the opportunity, they would do the same job over again, only 43 percent of white-collar workers and 24 percent of blue-collar workers say they would. And if people are asked whether they enjoy their work so much that they would find it hard to give up, only one-third say they enjoy it that much (Glenn and Weaver, 1984). These findings seem to indicate a general lack of enthusiasm for the job. But the answers could be muddied by the actual questions, which may be tapping people's vague feelings of disquiet about what else they could be doing with their lives.

If we ask Americans more directly whether they are "satisfied with their jobs," the answer is a convincing "yes." In 1985, for example, the Gallup poll found that 70 percent of workers were satisfied, 20 percent were dissatisfied, and 10 percent had no opinion. Moreover, when people are asked whether they would carry on working if they won enough money to live as comfortably as they wished for the rest of their lives, an overwhelming majority—around 70 percent—assert that they would continue to work. And, in fact, one recent study of people who became millionaires through lottery wins found that over 60 percent of them were still working the following year (Kaplan, 1985). All in all, such data seem to indicate a high level of job satisfaction.

What factors are important in overall job satisfaction? In surveys on the subject, one factor is cited by about three-quarters of all workers: good pay. But money alone does not make workers satisfied; they look for much more, including the meaningfulness of the job and the opportunity to develop individual potentials. A large majority of workers wish for recognition of their efforts, for interesting tasks, for chances to learn new skills, for good prospects of advancement, and for respectful treatment. Different categories of workers have different emphases—blue-collar workers, for example, cite job security as an important consideration, while professional women regard the chance for advancement as even more important than good pay. But on the whole, the greater a worker's sense of autonomy and discretion in the workplace, the less the alienation, at least as this is measured by worker satisfaction or dissatisfaction. This finding is hardly surprising in a postindustrial society where self-fulfillment has become an important value for the individual (Mortimer, 1979; Lacy, Bokemeier, and Shepard, 1983; Kagan, 1983).

Workplace Trends

Before industrialization, most Americans had a good deal of autonomy in their work. In 1800, close to 80 percent of all workers were self-employed, mainly as farmers or craft workers. But as the secondary sector grew during the nineteenth century, farm workers migrated to the cities, where they were transformed into industrial laborers. These workers had little autonomy in the new world of manufacturing, because employers tried to maximize productivity by minimizing their employees' freedom and discretion. This trend continued until, by the beginning of the twentieth century, the industrial laborer was regarded as little more than another machine. A new profession of "efficiency experts" completely ignored the workers' social and psychological needs, and concentrated instead on the physical aspects of the job to be done. The chief advocate of this approach was Frederick Winslow Taylor, an engineer who fathered "time-and-motion" studies of work and recommended "scientific management." Taylor believed that workers should be strictly disciplined and that all physical movements involved in the job should be carefully planned in advance, right down to the tiniest detail. This was his recipe for success:

> Let me give one simple piece of advice beyond all others. Every day, year in and year out, each man should ask himself, over and over again, two questions. First, "What is the name of the man I am now working for?", and having answered this definitely, then, "What does this man want me to do, right now?"

There was no assumption that laborers should be satisfied with their work, and no idea that their satisfaction, or lack of it, could affect their productivity. All that was thought important was that they show up on time and do exactly what they were told—which, increasingly, meant keeping pace with the machinery.

This approach was shattered by sociological research conducted during the 1930s by Elton Mayo and his associates at the Hawthorne plant of the Western Electric company. In their most famous experiment, the researchers systematically altered the working conditions of a group of employees to find out how the changes would influence productivity. First, they changed the method of payment from hourly wages to group piecework. Production went up. Then they introduced brief rest periods. Production rose again. Next they served refreshments twice a day. Production rose once more. The researchers tried new experiments, introducing additional breaks in the working day, or letting workers go home early. With each change, production rose. Finally, the researchers returned the group to their original working conditions—and production rose to even greater heights! What was happening? The answer was that the experiment had been contaminated by the subjects' assumptions about what the researchers were trying to prove—the now-notorious "Hawthorne Effect." Flattered by the attention that they were receiving and the variety that was introduced into their working lives, the workers had formed a close-knit primary group. They had established their own norms for productivity and were trying to please the researchers by working harder (Roethlisberger and Dickson, 1939; Mayo, 1966). Sociologists are now fully aware of the influence of peer-group norms on worker productivity. It is not so much wages or even working conditions that seem to directly affect output; it is the consensus of the workers regarding what a reasonable output should be.

Mayo's findings led to a new "human relations" approach to the workplace—one that drew heavily on the insights gained from sociological research into industrial relations. Gradually, managers began to give more attention to the human needs of their employees: for example, they used incentives, rather than mere discipline, to motivate them. Simultaneously, the growth of labor unions strengthened workers' collective bargaining powers, and they used this resource to negotiate improved wages, shorter hours, better workplace conditions, and fringe benefits. Then, as the tertiary sector began to expand, the nature of many jobs changed. The new occupations required interaction with people rather than labor with machines, and demanded a higher proportion of skilled, better-educated workers. Inevitably, these workers demanded greater responsibility and autonomy, and a series of workplace innovations has resulted. Sometimes, for example, jobs are rotated to make work more varied; profits are shared to encourage the workers' identification with their company's fortunes; or, to eliminate the frustrations that come from a minute division of labor, teams are given joint responsibility for a finished product. Increasingly, too, workers are encouraged to participate in actual workplace decisions. As a result of such trends, the environment of the contemporary office or even the factory is infinitely more congenial than it was only a few decades ago.

Is worker alienation, as measured by satisfaction or dissatisfaction, likely to increase or decrease? On the one hand, we live in an age where self-fulfillment is increasingly seen as an important personal goal. Yet today only 8 percent of American workers are self-employed, and the rest work in government or corporate bureacracies—

Figure 17.5 *In general, people who have a good deal of workplace autonomy appear more satisfied with their jobs than people who work under close supervision with little opportunity to exercise personal judgment. Many of the new jobs in the postindustrial economy do offer a high degree of autonomy, for they require specialized knowledge and skills.*

relatively anonymous environments where the individual has little sense of contribution to the final product. On the other hand, the shift from an industrial to a postindustrial economy is making most work easier, cleaner, and in some respects more satisfying than before. But there are many exceptions to this trend, for the tertiary sector contains two main groups of employees—information workers (such as managers and lawyers) and service workers (such as waiters and cleaners). Unlike the more skilled information workers, service workers are often trapped in jobs that may offer low pay, few rewards, and little job satisfaction—and there is little prospect that this situation will change.

Capitalism and Socialism

There are now two basic economic systems in the world. One is **capitalism,** an economic system in which the means of production and distribution are privately owned. The other is **socialism,** an economic system in which the means of production and distribution are publicly owned.

There are strong ideological differences between countries adopting either strategy, and as a result, the differences between these systems are often overemphasized. In fact, however, there is little basis for the common view that capitalism and socialism represent "either/or" alternatives, since neither system exists in a pure form. In practice there is great variety in these two kinds of economy, ranging from the most capitalist societies, such as the United States and Canada, through intermediate societies, such as Britain, Sweden, and Yugoslavia, to the most socialist societies, such as China and Albania. There is, moreover, great variety in the political systems that are associated with both capitalism and socialism, for democratic and authoritarian forms of government are found in each type of economy. For example, Sweden is socialist but democratic, while Cuba is socialist but authoritarian; Switzerland is capitalist and democratic, but Chile is capitalist and authoritarian.

The concepts of "capitalism" and "socialism" each represent merely an **ideal type,** an abstract description constructed from a number of real cases in order to reveal their essential features. Before we consider actual examples of these types, we must examine the concept of property, for the ownership of property is the chief bone of contention between the advocates of each system.

The Concept of Property

In everyday speech we think of "property" as objects. Strictly speaking, however, **property** is the set of rights that the owner of something has in relation to others who do not own it. Property is established in a society through social norms, often expressed in law, that define the conditions under which people may own objects.

Property exists because resources are scarce; if they were all as unlimited and inexhaustible as the air, nobody would think to claim ownership. Ownership of property may take one of three forms:

1. *Communal ownership* exists when property belongs to the community as a whole and may be used by any member of the community. Communal ownership of land is frequently found in small preindustrial societies—it was the traditional form, for example, among most American Indian tribes.

2. *Private ownership* exists when property belongs to specific persons. Private property is recognized in all societies. In some it may be restricted to a few household possessions; in others it may include assets worth millions of dollars. (Corporations are regarded as "persons" for legal purposes, so corporate ownership is a form of private ownership.)

3. *Public ownership* exists when property belongs to the state or some other political authority that claims the property on behalf of the people as a whole. A good deal of property in all modern societies (such as highways and schools) is publicly owned.

The main reason the ownership of property is such a controversial matter is that those who own the means of producing and distributing goods and services—means such as land, factories, and capital funds—are potentially in a position of power over those who do not. The debate between the advocates of capitalism and socialism hinges on this issue. Advocates of capitalism contend that the interests of all are served best if there is a minimum of public ownership of the means of production and distribution. Advocates of socialism argue that private ownership leads to exploitation and inequality, which can be avoided if the means of production and distribution are publicly owned. The issue is so important that it has divided the major industrialized societies of the modern world into two opposing, armed camps.

Capitalism

In its ideal form, capitalism contains two essential ingredients. The first is the deliberate pursuit of *personal profit* as the goal of economic activity. As Max Weber remarked, the outstanding characteristic of capitalism is production "for the pursuit of profit, and ever renewed profit." There is nothing unusual about people seeking their own self-interest, but the distinguishing feature of capitalism is that it defines this activity as normal, morally acceptable, and socially desirable. The second essential ingredient is *market competition* as the mechanism for determining what is produced, at what price, and for which consumers.

Why is the pursuit of profit and an atmosphere of unrestricted competition so necessary for capitalism? The reason, Adam Smith argued in 1776, is that under these conditions the market forces of supply and demand will ensure the production of the best possible products at the lowest possible price. The profit motive will provide the incentive for individual capitalists to produce the goods and services the public wants. Competition among capitalists will give the public the opportunity to compare the quality and prices of goods, so that any producers who are inefficient or who charge excessive prices will be put out of business. The "invisible hand" of market forces thus ensures the greatest good for the entire society. Efficient producers are rewarded with profits, and consumers get quality products at competitive prices. For the system to work, however, there should ideally be a minimum of government interference in economic life. If the government attempts to regulate the supply of, or demand for, goods, the forces of the market will be upset, producers will lose their incentive to produce, and prices will be artificially distorted. The government should therefore adopt a policy of *laissez faire,* meaning "leave it alone."

The United States conforms most closely to the ideal model of capitalism. In practice, though, pure capitalism has never existed, although it was perhaps approximated in the early phases of industrial development. But since the Great Depression, when the capitalist system seemed in danger of total collapse, it has been generally accepted that the federal government must supervise many details of economic activity. For example, the government sets minimum prices for some commodities and puts ceilings on the prices of others. It intervenes in international trade and concerns itself with the balance of payments with other countries. It protects some natural resources and encourages

Figure 17.6 *John D. Rockefeller was one of the most successful capitalists of all time, and, not too surprisingly, was an enthusiastic advocate of the system, which he saw as "a working out of a law of nature and a law of God." Rockefeller was disturbed, however, by his public image as a hard and greedy man, so every year, on his birthday, he would encourage some young boy to become a capitalist by giving him a nickel. In his later years, Rockefeller increased his annual largess to a dime.*

the exploitation of others. It lays down minimum wage standards, provides for unemployment benefits, and sometimes supervises labor-management relations. It tries to ensure the safety of the workplace and of manufactured goods. It regulates the level of production and consumption through its fiscal policies. It also has the authority to safeguard competition in the marketplace by preventing the growth of a **monopoly,** a single firm that dominates an industry, or of an **oligopoly,** a group of a few firms that dominates an industry.

Modern American capitalism is thus unlike the classical model in many respects. It has certain drawbacks, too, that are common to all capitalist systems: marked social inequality, a large and impoverished lower class, and repeated cycles of prosperity and recession, employment and unemployment. No capitalist society has yet found a way out of these dilemmas. Nevertheless, Americans remain convinced that their social and economic interests are best served if the means of production and distribution are privately owned, and both political parties strongly endorse free competition and the pursuit of private profit. These features make the United States the most capitalistic society on earth, and, for those who can afford them, this economic system has certainly delivered the goods. With just over 5 percent of the world's population, the United States accounts for over 20 percent of its output.

Socialism

In its ideal form, socialism also contains two essential ingredients: the fulfillment of *social needs* as the goal of economic activity, and reliance on *centralized planning* as the mechanism for determining what is produced, at what price, and for which consumers. Socialism thus rests on entirely different assumptions from those of capitalism. The pursuit of private profit is regarded as fundamentally immoral, because one person's profit is another person's loss. Under capitalism, it is argued, workers are paid less than the value of what they produce, and the surplus wealth is seized as profit by the owners. In addition, competition among different firms producing similar products is a waste of resources. Thus, the ultimate result of capitalism is social inequality and social conflict.

Socialism, on the other hand, proposes that production should be designed to serve social needs, and whether it is profitable or not is of secondary importance. Since private owners exploit both workers and consumers and will not produce unprofitable goods or services, whatever the social need for them, it is necessary for the means of production to be taken into public ownership and run in the best interests of society as a whole. Similarly, the means of distribution of wealth must be publicly owned to ensure that goods and services flow to those who need them rather than only to those who can afford them. The aims of a socialist economy, then, are the efficient production of needed goods and services and the achievement of social equality by preventing the accumulation of private wealth. To this end, the government must regulate the economy in accordance with long-term national plans, and it must not hesitate to establish artificial price levels or to run important industries at a loss if necessary.

In actuality, there are two very divergent forms of socialism in the modern world—one practiced in authoritarian, communist-ruled societies, mostly in Eastern Europe and Asia, and one practiced in democratic, pluralist societies, mostly in Western Europe. These versions differ markedly in their degree of centralized control of the economy, and in the liberties their citizens enjoy.

Soviet-Style Socialism

Soviet-style socialism exists in the Soviet Union and other countries that are ruled by communist parties, such as Bulgaria or Vietnam. In every case, the governments of these societies seized power through revolution or other use of force. These countries are often called "communist" in the United States, but they never describe themselves that way. Although they are ruled by communist parties, they consider themselves to be in a stage of socialism, a preparatory step toward their true goal. That goal is **communism,** a hypothetical egalitarian political and economic system in which the means of production and distribution would be communally owned.

Since no communist society has ever existed, and since the writings of Marx and other advocates of communism are somewhat vague in their vision of one, it is not entirely clear what a communist society would look like. In general, however, it would have some of the characteristics implied in the previously described communal-ownership pattern that is currently found only in primitive societies. The role of the state would shrink; there would be an abundance of goods and services; people would no longer regard property as "private"; and wealth and power would be shared in harmony by the community as a whole. Under socialism, people are paid according to their work, but under communism, individuals would contribute according to their abilities and receive according to their needs. The history of human alienation and strife would be over, and each person would be able to fulfill his or her human potential to the full. The major problem with such a society is that nobody seems to know quite how to arrive there. The Soviet Communist Party predicted in 1961 that a communist society would essentially be in place in the Soviet Union by 1980. Obviously, this did not happen, and in 1985, the party revised its program. The party still declares that "the advance of humanity toward communism is inexorable," but it no longer offers a target date for the process (Schmemann, 1985). It is now clear that the Soviet Union and other communist-ruled societies are "stuck" in the socialist stage and have virtually no idea of how to get beyond it.

The economy of the Soviet Union conforms in some respects, however, to the ideal socialist model. The means of production and distribution—land, machines, factories, capital funds, banks, retail outlets, and so on—are publicly owned. Speculative investment and the pursuit of private profit are not only considered undesirable; they are crimes of theft punishable in certain instances with the death penalty. Citizens are permitted private ownership of personal items, such as household goods and automobiles, but generally may not own wealth-producing property. (However, there is a tiny private sector in agriculture, which consists of less than 2 percent of the farmland but which produces a third of the total meat and vegetable output.) The economy is closely regulated in accordance with national economic plans that are designed to meet specified national goals—even if this means depriving people of inessentials, such as the latest in fashionable clothing, in favor of investment in heavy industry that might generate more wealth in the long run. The degree of this centralized regulation is astonishing to outsiders: for example, a 1983 report of the proceedings of the Politburo, the highest political authority in the Soviet Union, showed that one of the topics the members discussed was the price of fur collars for winter coats. Critics allege that overly centralized planning leads to inefficiency; plant managers, for example, are simply ordered by distant authorities to produce quotas of products, without any regard for local conditions of supply and demand.

Every Soviet citizen is guaranteed health care, a job, and a home, so people have no real fear of medical costs, unemployment, or destitution. In all Soviet-style societies, however, there are significant differences in income between ordinary workers and those in managerial or other executive positions. The Soviet Union and most of these countries are now experimenting with "incentive payments" to encourage higher productivity—a practice not very different from offering them greater "profit" for working harder. Actually, productivity is relatively poor, giving the Soviet Union one of the lowest standards of living of all industrialized societies. In America, for example, there are 79 telephones per 100 residents; in the Soviet Union, there are 8. Overall, American per capita consumption is about three times that of the Soviet Union.

It is important to recognize that when Marx advocated communism, it was the concept of communism already outlined that he had in mind, not the Soviet version of socialism. Much of the antagonism to Marxist thought in the United States stems from a confusion between Marx's ideas and contemporary Soviet practice. On the basis of his writings, however, it seems highly unlikely that Marx would have regarded modern Soviet society with much enthusiasm.

Figure 17.7 *These Russian women are relaxing after the ordeal of a day spent shopping. Because of fundamental inefficiencies in the country's economy, there are chronic shortages of consumer items of every kind. The women—who like many Russians, take string bags with them when they leave home so that they can carry back any suitable consumer items that suddenly become available—may have to wait for hours in line to make a single purchase. Some communist-ruled countries, such as Hungary and Rumania, have more efficient economies because they rely far less on bureaucratic central planning.*

Democratic Socialism

Many of the countries of Western Europe, such as Denmark or Austria, practice one form or another of *democratic socialism,* a political and economic system that aims to preserve individual freedom in the context of social equality achieved through a centrally planned economy.

Under democratic socialism—also known as the "welfare state"—the state takes ownership of only strategic industries and services, such as railways, airlines, mines, banks, radio, TV, telephone systems, medical services, colleges, and important manufacturing enterprises such as chemicals and steel. Private ownership of other means of production is permitted, even encouraged, but the economy is closely regulated in accordance with national priorities. High tax rates are used to prevent excessive profits or an undue concentration of wealth. A measure of social equality is ensured through extensive welfare services. In Great Britain, for example, college education and medical services are available free of charge, and about a quarter of the population lives in heavily subsidized public housing.

None of these democratic socialist societies aspires to communism, and they zealously guard their democratic traditions. Most are politically allied to the United States, although sometimes they are critical of American foreign policy—particularly of American support for authoritarian governments that face socialist-inspired unrest and even revolution in impoverished third-world countries.

Most of the countries of Western Europe have had periods of both socialist and nonsocialist rule since World War II, as their electorates have periodically switched allegiance from one political party to another. Currently, most of these countries have been moving in a more capitalistic direction—for example, by selling off nationalized industries (such as British Airways and British Telecom) to private owners once more. Several less developed countries elsewhere in the world, like India, Nigeria, and Argentina, are also shifting away from a centrally planned economy and toward one driven by free enterprise. The reason seems to be that, while socialist societies may distribute wealth more evenly than capitalist ones, they are less efficient at creating wealth in the first place. The twentieth century has provided overwhelming evidence that socialist economies are more bureaucratized and less productive than capitalist ones (Berger, 1986).

Convergence Theory

The example of democratic socialism, with its blend of capitalist and socialist elements, has led some observers to postulate *convergence theory,* the hypothesis that the similar problems faced by capitalist and socialist societies may influence their evolution toward a common ultimate form (Hollander, 1978; Form, 1979).

There are many similarities between the advanced capitalist and socialist societies. Both are heavily industrialized, urbanized, and bureaucratized. Both face the need for constant growth to satisfy the demands of their respective consumer cultures and to avoid economic stagnation. Both face problems of resource depletion and environmental pollution. Both must find incentives for their workers to produce, and means to distribute the production among the population in a way that is perceived as fair. But do these similarities necessarily mean convergence?

Actually, a good deal of convergence has already taken place. The United States, as we have seen, is by no means a pure capitalist society. Many services have to be provided, for example, even if they profit nobody—so schools, sewers, police forces, and the like are socialized and publicly owned. Government intervenes repeatedly in the "free" market, in ways more reminiscent of a socialist country—saving mammoth corporations like Lockheed, Chrysler, Penn Central, and Continental Illinois Bank from bankruptcy, supporting agricultural prices, giving direct and indirect subsidies to industries, regulating the money supply, shifting income from workers to Social Security recipients, and so on. Similar trends are evident in all other advanced capitalist societies.

Conversely, there are indisputable signs that the communist-ruled societies are embracing aspects of capitalism, especially through their use of financial incentives. The Soviet Union and its allies are finally confronting the fact that their system is inherently inefficient. Any comparison of roughly similar capitalist and Soviet-style socialist societies yields the same impression about the relative living standards of the populace. The United States is more prosperous than the Soviet Union; West Germany is more prosperous than East Germany; South Korea, more so than North Korea; Taiwan, more so than China. Even within the Soviet bloc, the most productive and prosperous societies are those, like Hungary and Rumania, that have the least centralized economies and the most "capitalistic" incentives. The trend in all these societies,

Figure 17.8 *The Soviet Union built the Berlin wall to prevent East Germans from fleeing to the West to escape communist rule. In doing so, they gave the West a considerable propaganda advantage. As Western leaders are fond of pointing out, their countries have never had to build a wall to keep their people in.*

therefore, is now toward greater rewards for individual effort.

Economic convergence does appear to be taking place—but will political convergence also follow? All democratic socialist societies and all advanced capitalist societies are democracies, with a free press, an independent judiciary, and regular free elections. There is no prospect that this situation will change. On the other hand, no communist-ruled country is a democracy: a communist party has never been elected to national office in a free election anywhere in the world, and, once in office, communists have never permitted free elections thereafter. Ultimately, "convergence" may depend on whether more liberal economic policies will lead to democratization in the Soviet-style economies.

Whither China?

Over two centuries ago, Napoleon commented that China was "a sleeping giant, and when she wakes, she will shake the world." Much the same could be said today. China is an impoverished, predominantly agricultural society. More than 80 percent of the population are peasants, most of them living in harsh conditions. But, with over 1 billion inhabitants—over a fifth of all humanity—China is the most populous society on earth.

Since the revolution of 1949, China has been a communist-ruled socialist society. For much of

that time its former leader, Mao Tse Tung, kept China in almost total isolation from the rest of the world. Highly critical of the Soviet Union, which he believed had abandoned Marx's vision, Mao tried to guide the society toward complete equality and true communism. Mao attempted, for example, to obliterate all distinctions of rank. During a "cultural revolution" that he instigated, professional work was downgraded, professors were stripped of their titles, students received no degrees, and the insignia of military rank were abolished. Virtually the entire population wore the same drab, loose-fitting garments—especially the "Mao tunic." Private ownership of land was abolished, and peasants were grouped into communes under the slogan "Let everyone eat from the same pot." Each commune had a production quota, and food was to be cooked and eaten communally, not by the individual family. Creativity in art or literature was despised as the output of "stinking intellectuals." All authority was concentrated in the party, which provided the only avenue for the limited social mobility that was available.

Mao died in 1976, and his successors were faced with a society in stagnation. Gradually, the new Chinese leadership under Deng Xiaoping abandoned many of Mao's policies, and cautiously introduced reforms that may yet take China down the "capitalist road." The new regime is pragmatic, lavishly praising communist ideals but much more interested in immediate results; as Deng commented, "It doesn't matter what color a cat is, so long as it catches mice." The regime has introduced a "responsibility system," under which hundreds of millions of Chinese peasants are allowed to work individual farm plots in addition to communal land. The result has been an explosion of productivity that has produced a series of record-breaking harvests. (In their own slogan, the peasants are "energetic as a dragon on the private plot, sluggish as worms on the public fields.") Between 1978 and 1983, average peasant income doubled to reach about $117 per year—making peasants more prosperous, for the most part, than city dwellers. In 1984, a successful chicken farmer became the first person in thirty-five years to buy a private car in China.

Inevitably, reform is spreading to the cities. Planning is being decentralized, and limited pri-

Figure 17.9 *China is not yet going down the "capitalist road"—but the current Chinese government, while professing unflagging loyalty to communist principles, has perceptibly moved the economy in that direction.*

vate enterprise is permitted. Some 11 million Chinese—still a minuscule fraction of the population—now work in privately owned street stalls, restaurants, repair shops, and factories. Consumer goods are plentiful in urban areas, as consumers develop appetites for wristwatches, radios, and televisions. Higher incomes are implicitly recognized as a means of providing incentives and rewarding achievements—a suspiciously capitalistic notion. Within the state bureaucracy there are now twenty-four grades, from clerks at the bottom to the party chairman at the top, and each has a corresponding level of pay. Similarly, there are twelve ranks of professors, sixteen of actors, eight of industrial laborers, and four of cooks.

Old-line Chinese communists are resentful of these changes, arguing that the use of incentives will revive class differences. Successful farmers, for example, might come to act like prerevolutionary landlords, hiring others to do their work for them. The leadership's reply to this criticism is "Some will prosper early, some will prosper later"—a slogan that captures the dominant view that China is now irrevocably embarked on the path to industrialization and modernization. Yet China has a long way to go; for example, in rural areas where electricity is available, peasant families, even now, are often permitted only one 25-watt bulb a year to light their homes. China is still determinedly socialist and authoritarian. It will be interesting to see how far the country will stray from the socialist path and whether economic liberalization will in turn lead to political democratization. Given China's size and potential, its economic future will be of world-historical significance (White, 1983; Mosher, 1983; Wren, 1984a, 1984b; Tsou, 1985).

Corporate Capitalism

The modern American economy, as we have seen, is no longer based on the competitive efforts of innumerable private capitalists. Although there are hundreds of thousands of businesses, a mere 500 of them account for three-quarters of the gross national product. The economy is now dominated not by the individual entrepreneur but rather by the ***corporation,*** a legally recognized organization whose existence, powers, and liabilities are separate and distinct from those of its owners or employees. The largest commercial and industrial corporations exert enormous political and economic power.

Corporations and the American Economy

The corporation is a relatively new social invention that first achieved prominence in the late nineteenth century. Corporations have no single owner. They are owned by thousands or even hundreds of thousands of stockholders, and some of these stockholders are other corporations. In fact, most corporate stock in the United States is actually owned by corporate investors. In theory, the stockholders control the corporation by electing a board of directors and by voting on company policies at annual stockholders' meetings. In practice, the widely dispersed stockholders cannot effectively control corporate activities, and they merely rubber-stamp decisions that have already been made for them. The boards of directors are essentially self-perpetuating bodies whose recommendations, including nominations for new board members, are approved by stockholders as a matter of course. The day-to-day running of the corporation is in the hands of the management, which not only supervises company operations but also makes most of the major policy decisions, which in turn are usually approved by the board. The most important effect of this situation is that it tends to separate *ownership* of the firm from *control* of the firm. Those who control the corporation—the managers and to a lesser extent the directors—are for most purposes responsible to nobody but themselves. As long as they continue to maximize profits, the stockholders generally remain content.

The size and economic power of the major corporations are immense. The largest 100 corporations own 49 percent of all the manufacturing assets in the United States, and the largest 200 corporations own 61 percent of these assets (Bureau of the Census, 1986a). Some of the largest corporations, such as Exxon and General Motors, have budgets that are larger than those of every country in the world other than the United States and the Soviet Union.

The largest corporations are linked together through **interlocking directorates,** social networks consisting of individuals who are members of several different corporate boards. The directors of the board of General Motors, for example, sit on 29 other corporate boards. The members of those boards, in turn, sit on the boards of an additional 650 corporations. The total directorate of the leading corporations resembles a tightly spun web, making the influence of these organizations all the

more concentrated (Mintz and Schwartz, 1981, 1984; Dye, 1983; Useem, 1980, 1984). The domination of the American economy by large corporations has several important consequences. One of them, more fully explored in Chapter 18 ("The Political Order"), is that these corporations are able to apply political leverage on national policy, winning favors for themselves, influencing the country's tax structure, and successfully blocking efforts to prevent the growth of oligopolies in particular industries. In fact, about 60 percent of manufacturing in the United States is oligopolistic, with a handful of firms controlling most of the output of such products as automobiles, cigarettes, and steel.

One feature of American capitalism is that many corporations compete not through the quality or price of their products but rather through their advertising. The automobile, banking, and airline industries, for example, devote resources to the production of basically similar goods and services and to extensive advertising designed to make them appear different. In fact, the United States accounts for more advertising expenditures than the rest of the world put together. Americans are literally bombarded with ads, receiving many hundreds of commercial messages each day from such sources as TV, radio, newspapers, and billboards. This advertising represents a diversion of more than $87 billion each year from other potential uses (U.S. Bureau of the Census, 1986a; *World Advertising Expenditures,* 1985).

Americans tend to take this deluge of advertising for granted, but sociologists are keenly interested in its social effects. The manifest function of advertising, of course, is to encourage sales. But advertising has other, latent functions. For example, it creates markets where there were no markets before, by arousing consumer desires for items or services that were previously nonexistent. The implication is that the economy is not merely satisfying human "needs," but is endlessly creating more of them. The further implication is that modern consumers are learning always to want "more"—and that each increment of "more" may leave them just as unsatisfied as before, yet seeking still "more" in the hope of achieving greater satisfaction. This was, in fact, Durkheim's vision of a society entering a state of *anomie*—a vision of individuals endlessly seeking a gratification which, because there was no clear, socially defined horizon to their desires, was always retreating into the distance.

Another striking feature of modern corporate

Figure 17.10 *Thanks largely to the way that corporate capitalism creates both products and the public demand for them, Americans have become the world's greatest consumers. Indeed, these two figures could only be American, and would be instantly recognized as such almost anywhere in the world. Actually, the pair—entitled* Couple with Shopping Bags—*were created, in vinyl, by the contemporary American artist Duane Hanson.*

capitalism is "paper entrepreneurialism"—the pursuit of profits, not by producing goods or services, but by using clever accounting procedures, manipulating the tax laws, and buying, selling, or dismembering other corporations. Some leading corporations have become conglomerates, whose primary business is taking over other corporations. The International Telephone and Telegraph Corporation (ITT), for example, has at one time or another engulfed some 275 other corporations in fields ranging from hotels to insurance. Each year, more than 2,000 American corporations are taken over or merged with others. These moves often make economic sense, but sometimes they seem to represent little more than piracy. One practice, for example, is "greenmail," in which a hostile investor buys a large block of stock in a corporation and threatens to take it over and perhaps fire its executives and sell off its assets; the corporation then buys back the stock at a premium price to persuade the investor to go away. Billions of dollars have been "earned" in this way. A whole vocabulary has arisen around corporate takeovers: the "white knight," a friendly investor who buys control of a threatened corporation to rescue it from a hostile investor; the "poison pill," any provision—such as huge debts—that makes a corporation less attractive as a takeover candidate; and the "golden parachute," a guarantee by a target corporation to give huge severance payments (often of many millions of dollars) to its senior executives in the event of a takeover. The various activities of "paper entrepreneurialism" bring us a long way from the original impulse of capitalism: to supply the consumer with the best possible product at the lowest possible price.

One further feature of corporate capitalism in the United States merits consideration: what Galbraith (1966, 1979) has termed the contrast between "private affluence" and "public squalor." The American public has learned to prefer to spend its money on the consumption of goods and services provided by private enterprise rather than on taxes for goods and services provided by public authorities. Despite perennial grumbling about their tax rates, Americans actually pay substantially less of their income for taxes—and thus for social services and amenities—than the inhabitants of virtually all other industrialized societies. The United States therefore has a generally affluent private life in the midst of generally squalid public facilities such as mass-transit systems and urban schools. This ordering of priorities would seem peculiar to many other societies, but it is taken for granted in the United States, where people have learned to value the wants of the individual more highly than those of the community.

Multinational Corporations

In the past, corporations concentrated their efforts in one country. Today, many have also established an international presence, often diversifying into various industries in the process. A **multinational corporation** is a corporate enterprise which, although headquartered in one country, conducts its operations through subsidiaries that it owns or controls around the world. ITT, for example, employs over 400,000 workers in sixty-eight countries. Exxon operates in nearly a hundred countries, and its fleet of oil tankers constitutes a navy as large as Great Britain's. General Motors is active in thirty-nine countries, where it sells over $80 bil-

THE WORLD'S 50 LARGEST CORPORATIONS

Company Name	Headquarters	Value (In billions)
IBM	Armonk, N.Y.	$87.6
Exxon	New York	44.0
General Electric	Fairfield, Conn.	36.8
Tokyo Electric	Tokyo	32.4
AT&T	New York	27.1
Sumitomo Bank	Osaka, Japan	25.9
Toyota Motor	Toyota City, Japan	25.1
General Motors	Detroit	24.7
Dai-Ichi Kangyo Bank	Tokyo	23.7
Nomura Securities	Tokyo	23.1
Royal Dutch Petroleum	The Hague, Netherlands	21.5
Mitsubishi Bank	Tokyo	21.4
Fuji Bank	Tokyo	21.4
Daimler-Benz	Stuttgart, W. Germany	20.8
British Telecom	London	20.4
Du Pont	Wilmington, Del.	20.0
BellSouth	Atlanta	19.2
Industrial Bank of Japan	Tokyo	19.0
Sanwa Bank	Osaka, Japan	18.3
Philip Morris	New York	17.8
Sears Roebuck	Chicago	17.6
British Petroleum	London	16.6
Matsushita Electric Industrial	Osaka, Japan	16.2
Coca-Cola	Atlanta	16.1
Amoco	Chicago	15.5
Mitsubishi Estate	Tokyo	15.1
Hitachi	Tokyo	14.9
Merck	Rahway, N.J.	14.6
Wal-Mart Stores	Bentonville, Ark.	14.5
Ford Motor	Dearborn, Mich.	14.3
Kansai Electric Power	Osaka, Japan	14.2
Bell Atlantic	Philadelphia	13.8
American Express	New York	13.8
Nynex	New York	13.6
American Home Products	New York	13.6
Shell Transport & Trading	London	13.4
Siemens	Munich, W. Germany	13.4
Seibu Railway	Toshimaku, Japan	13.4
Procter & Gamble	Cincinnati, Ohio	13.4
Johnson & Johnson	New Brunswick, N.J.	13.2
Eastman Kodak	Rochester, N.Y.	13.2
RJR Nabisco	Winston-Salem, N.C.	13.2
Ameritech	Chicago	13.1
Sumitomo Trust & Banking	Osaka, Japan	13.1
Chevron	San Francisco	13.0
3M	St. Paul, Minn.	13.0
Mobil	New York	12.9
Allianz	Munich, W. Germany	12.8
Abbott Laboratories	Chicago	12.8
NEC	Tokyo	12.7

SOURCE: *Wall Street Journal*, 1986.

Figure 17.11 *The economies of the Western nations, and of much of the rest of the world, are dominated by a handful of giant corporations, many of them American.*

lion worth of products every year. In fact, some of these corporations are substantially wealthier than many of their host countries. The multinationals are already responsible for more than a quarter of total world economic production, and they are expected to account for over half by the end of the century—one of the most remarkable trends in the modern world (Barnet and Muller, 1974; Said and Simmons, 1975; Modelski, 1979; Heilbroner, 1982).

About 300 of the largest 500 multinationals are headquartered in one country, the United States. The international influence of these organizations, therefore, is primarily an American one. Decisions made by a small group of people in the United States can mean prosperity or unemployment in nations thousands of miles away. Multinational corporations dominate the economies of many less developed countries, influencing the level of wages, the kind of crops that are grown, or how national resources are allocated. Even developed nations are subject to this influence: more than half of Canada's industry is owned by American and British multinationals, making it difficult for the Canadians to control their own economy. In fact, American corporate industry abroad is now the third largest economy in the world, after that of the United States and the Soviet Union. Such a situation raises the prospect of *neocolonialism,* the informal political and economic domination of one society over another, such that the former is able to exploit the labor and resources of the latter for its own purposes (Wallerstein, 1979; Masden, 1980; Kumar, 1980).

American-based multinationals have an impressive record of interference in the affairs of the host countries, with activities ranging from bribery of local officials to attempts to overthrow foreign governments. As long ago as 1953, international oil companies helped to overturn the populist Iranian prime minister Mohammed Mussadegh and to consolidate the dictatorial rule of the shah—thereby incurring the enduring wrath of the Iranian people toward the United States. In 1954, a dispute between the United Fruit Company and the elected president of Guatemala led to the president's ouster and a period of dictatorship. In 1970, ITT, fearing for the safety of its investments, plotted to overthrow the elected president of Chile; the corporation not only spent millions of dollars within Chile for that purpose, but even secretly asked the U.S. government for help and offered to contribute a further $1 million toward any federal expenses involved. When these and similar facts became public in the mid-1970s, Congress demanded extensive investigations of illicit corpo-

Figure 17.12 *The world is rapidly becoming a single marketplace, in which the same products appear in countries all over the globe. In the process, many multinational corporations have become important actors on the world political and economic scene. In some instances, these corporations have greater financial resources than the countries in which they operate, and decisions by corporate executives in the developed world can have a profound impact on nations thousands of miles away.*

rate activity. Exxon, it was soon discovered, had paid nearly $60 million to government officials in fifteen nations, including $27 million to several Italian political parties. Lockheed had distributed nearly $200 million in bribes and payoffs in several countries, and the resulting scandals implicated the prince of the Netherlands, the prime minister of Japan, military leaders in Colombia, and cabinet members in Italy. Overwhelmed by the size of their task, federal investigators offered corporations immunity in return for full confessions. In all, more than 500 major American corporations, most of them multinational, admitted giving bribes or other questionable payments to government officials in order to obtain benefits for themselves (Sampson, 1973; Hougan, 1976; Hirsh, 1982).

The multinationals do offer many useful resources to the less developed countries. They encourage economic growth by importing the necessary capital and technology, and they create new industries and markets all over the world. But their motives are purely selfish—to exploit cheap labor and resources on an international scale for the benefit of a handful of stockholders in wealthy

countries. Their activities have had a significant impact within the United States, too, for the multinationals export not only capital, but also jobs: if an item can be manufactured more cheaply in Hong Kong than Detroit, the multinationals may close down their American plant, open one in Asia, and import the finished item back to the United States. They are also able to shift assets and operations around the world—recording losses in high-tax nations and profits in low-tax nations, or evading safety regulations or labor laws in one country by moving to another that lacks them. The multinationals are joining nation-states as the major actors on the international stage, for they inevitably develop worldwide interests and the "foreign policies" that go with them. These huge organizations have developed much more quickly than have the means of applying social control over them. Dedicated to the pursuit of profit and subject to the authority of no one nation, run by a tiny elite of managers and directors who have a largely fictional responsibility to their far-flung shareholders, they represent a disturbing and growing concentration of global power and influence (Ball, 1975; Vernon, 1977; Evans, 1981; Bornschier and Hoby, 1981).

Unemployment

Although some groups in the United States have always faced high rates of unemployment, the period since the Great Depression has been, until relatively recently, one of almost continuous economic expansion. Since the mid-1970s, however, a series of recessions has created a serious problem of unemployment. In 1983 the unemployment rate soared to a postwar record of nearly 11 percent, and over 11 million American workers found themselves without a job. More recently, the unemployment rate has fluctuated around 7 percent.

No society ever has completely full employment, in the sense that everybody able to work actually has a job. There is always a certain amount of unemployment, because even under the most favorable conditions, there are potential workers who are ill for long periods, who are changing jobs, or who are looking for work after graduating from school. For this reason, most countries consider that they have full employment if the unemployment rate is about 2 percent or less. In the United States a somewhat higher unemployment rate—around 4 percent of the work force—is regarded as tolerable, and there is real alarm only if the rate goes much above that level. In practice, official statistics probably underestimate the extent of unemployment, for the Bureau of Labor Statistics classifies people as unemployed only if they have actively looked for a job during the previous four weeks but have not worked at all in the previous week. The people who have simply given up looking for a job and the people who have worked only a few hours at a temporary job in the previous week are therefore not counted as unemployed. And since the bureau bases its information on random telephone surveys, it also excludes migrant workers, drifters, and others who do not have a permanent home with a listed telephone number.

The loss of a job can have a devastating impact on the individual. The immediate effect, of course, is a sharp drop in income. Unemployment benefits typically offer less than half the individual's previous earnings, and many people are not even entitled to these benefits—for example, the self-employed, recent graduates who have not held a steady job in the previous year, and people who have been unemployed for a long period. (Most unemployment benefits last for only nine months, and none are payable after more than a year of unemployment.) The economic strain on the jobless is severe, particularly for those who have young children or long-term commitments for expenses such as mortgages or college tuitions.

But the effects of unemployment are not merely financial; they are also social and psychological. In American society, the holder of a respected, well-paid job is honored, whereas the person who is poorly paid is likely to be looked down on, and someone who is habitually out of work is apt to be dismissed as "worthless." As one out-of-work teacher put it:

> It's difficult when you strip away all the things that supposedly hold you together in terms of an identity. Your work, your money, whatever is power to you, whatever is responsibility, whatever means freedom and choice. I had to ask myself, "Who am I now? What will I do now?" [Maurer, 1979]

Prolonged unemployment may thrust the individual into boredom, despair, ill-temper, apathy, and, perhaps, conflict with other family members or alcoholism. Even those who keep their jobs are affected by high rates of unemployment, for they begin to fear for their own future.

Why has unemployment become a problem in the United States in recent years? The answers are complex, but some of the causes are fairly clear.

First, however, we should distinguish between the *general* rate of unemployment in the society as a whole and the *specific* rate of unemployment among categories of the population, for they do not necessarily have the same origins.

The general rate of unemployment depends on factors influencing the entire economy. In recent years, for example, unemployment in the United States has been aggravated by changes in the price of oil, which caused economic disruption; by cycles of recession and recovery, which are common to all capitalist societies; and by the flooding of the labor market with unprecedented numbers of women and young workers of the "baby boom" generation. Societal factors like these tend to translate into increases in unemployment, unless deliberate countermeasures are taken. In Soviet-style socialist societies, for example, unemployment is avoided at all costs, even if it means hiring people at low wages in unproductive government jobs. In Japan, the major corporations are willing to temporarily lose money rather than lay off their employees.

Specific rates of unemployment depend on factors that influence only certain categories of the population. As we might expect, these are the same categories that bear the brunt of discrimination in virtually every other aspect of social life: hence, the rate is higher for women than for men, higher

Figure 17.13 *In recent years, depressed economic conditions have led to widespread unemployment. Millions of Americans have been thrown out of work, including many who had taken their job security for granted.*

for nonwhites than for whites, and higher for blue-collar (working-class) workers than for white-collar (middle- and upper-class) workers. Several other categories also face high rates of unemployment—people approaching the usual retirement age of sixty-five, migrant and seasonal workers, and people living in places (particularly decaying inner cities and depressed rural regions) that have persistent pockets of unemployment because the residents lack work skills and the communities lack industries.

High unemployment exists and is likely to persist among blue-collar workers in industries where jobs are being eroded by foreign competition and by automation. Several of these industries—shoes, textiles, toys, plastics, and even backbone industries like steel—are in danger of extinction. The main reason is that the United States and a handful of other industrialized societies have lost their near monopoly on global manufacturing. Americans now compete not just with each other, but with the world—and in international terms, many Americans earn too much for the skills they bring to the job. For example, a garment worker earns over $5 an hour in the United States, compared with 16¢ an hour in China. An American auto

UNEMPLOYMENT RATES IN
SELECTED CATEGORIES

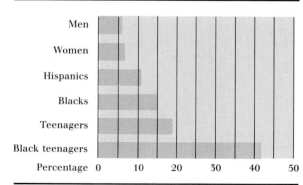

SOURCE: Bureau of Labor Statistics, 1986.

Figure 17.14 *As this chart shows, unemployment is not randomly distributed among the population in general: it is likely to affect some categories of workers more than others. In general, the categories that suffer high rates of unemployment are those that are relatively disadvantaged, or even discriminated against, in other areas of life.*

worker makes over $20 an hour, but a South Korean auto worker earns about $2 an hour. Inevitably, millions of jobs that were captive in the industrialized world are now being performed elsewhere, raising the hopes and living standards of other people just as they once did for an earlier generation of Americans. Simultaneously, American corporations are improving productivity through automation, replacing workers with industrial robots and other machines. The prospects for these displaced laborers seem bleak: to return to the work force, they may have to either upgrade their skills or take lower-paying service jobs (Bluestone and Harrison, 1982; Reich, 1983).

A popular response to foreign competition is to demand quotas, tariffs, subsidies, or anything that will help protect the threatened industries. American economists generally oppose protectionism, on the grounds that it would force higher prices on the American consumer, make it difficult for American goods to compete abroad, encourage multinationals to export even more jobs and capital, and encourage retaliation by other countries. A better strategy, most argue, is the one which Japan has long followed: to abandon older industries as they become uncompetitive, and to shift resources to emerging ones—such as genetic engineering, microelectronics, fiber optics, and aerospace technology. This may be good advice for the society, but it is of little immediate help to the individual—say, to a middle-aged worker who earned $25,000 a year at a blast furnace that has closed forever, and who has no other marketable skills.

One category of the population that has suffered more from underemployment than unemployment is that of recent college graduates, who have sometimes found themselves working below their level of skill as cab drivers or tour guides, rather than in the high-paying jobs they expected to occupy. The reason for this phenomenon is that, from about 1973 to 1984, the colleges turned out more graduates than there were graduate-level jobs. Economic expansion is changing this situation, but there is still so much slack to be taken up that there may be a small but persistent surplus of graduates for some time. In the longer term, however, the prospects for new graduates look quite promising. Now that the baby-boom generation has completed its education, the present generation of college students has the advantage of being at the leading edge of a steady decline in the number of college graduates, which means you will face less competition for jobs and, later, for promotions (Williams, 1985).

Postindustrial America

The United States is pioneering the transition from an industrial to a postindustrial society. There will still be farms and smokestacks in the new economy, of course, but most people will be employed elsewhere. Jobs in the secondary sector, which comprised 24 percent of the total in 1980, will drop to around 11 percent by the end of the century, while jobs in the tertiary sector will rise from 62 percent of the total in 1980 to 86 percent.

The postindustrial economy calls for a new kind of worker. The American labor force is becoming much better educated: twenty years ago one worker in ten had a college degree, compared with one in five today. Women are also going to work in unprecedented numbers: 38 percent were in the labor force in 1960; more than half are at work today, and over 60 percent are expected to be employed by 1995. On the other hand, labor unions, which had a proud history in the early industrial era, seem to be losing membership and influence in the postindustrial economy. Union membership represented 25 percent of the labor force in 1970, 23 percent in 1980, and less than 19 percent in 1985. Long associated with blue-collar occupations, the unions have had particular difficulty attracting white-collar workers in new, high-technology industries.

Technology may change many aspects of the workplace. The central office, for example, may become something of an anachronism in certain respects. Working from 9 to 5 in such a location is designed for maximum control, not maximum productivity, and advances in computer and telecommunications technology have already made it feasible for many of these jobs to be done at home, with substantial savings in transport costs, travel time, office space, cafeteria expenses, real estate taxes, and other hidden expenses. But, although high technology is the soul of the new economy, it will not create vast numbers of new, high-paying jobs. True, highly skilled jobs in technology are rapidly increasing in number, but they are a small part of the total work force. Between 1973 and 1983, for example, the number of computer-systems analysts increased by 171 percent—a greater increase than in any other job—but the actual number of new positions was only 127,000, less than a third of the increase in the number of cooks. Most high-technology jobs are very routine and do not demand high qualifications or offer high pay. Most new jobs in the expanding tertiary sector, in fact, will be low-paying service positions, such as secretaries, nurses' aides, sales clerks, cashiers, and janitors.

The shift to a postindustrial future occurs at a time when the United States has become part of a world market—a market, in fact, that American multinational corporations have helped to create. Before the 1960s, foreign trade was not a significant part of the American economy. In 1970, America exported about 9 percent of its products and also imported about 9 percent of its needs; by 1980, it exported 19 percent and imported 22 percent. More important, 70 percent of all goods in the United States are in active competition with goods from elsewhere in the world. In short, the world is becoming a single marketplace, where capital, jobs, and products may move with little regard for national boundaries. A computer designed and marketed in Texas may have its casing built in Mexico, its microchip in Japan, its circuit boards in Singapore, its keyboard in Taiwan, its disks in Germany. The combined effects of international competition and technological development may lead to a wave of what the economist Joseph Schumpeter has called "creative destruction"—the reallocation of resources from old industries to the enterprises of the future, in ways that may change the face of economy and society. The ubiquitous microchip, after all, was not even invented in 1970; who knows what the innovation of the day, or its implications, will be in 2000?

Summary

1.   The economic order is the institutionalized system for distributing goods and services. Economic activity is important because it sustains life, because a society's main means of economic production influences culture and social structure, because economic and other inequalities are very closely linked, and because an individual's work is a major source of personal identity and social status.

2.   Any economy contains three sectors, the primary (extracting raw materials), the secondary (producing manufactured goods), and the tertiary (providing services or information). In preindustrial societies, the predominating sector is the primary sector; in industrial societies, the secondary sector; in postindustrial societies, the tertiary sector.

3.   Every society establishes a division of labor among its members. There has been a general trend toward increased specialization, which has gone furthest in postindustrial societies because of their large surplus wealth. Durkheim distinguished between societies integrated by mechanical solidarity (similarity of members) and organic solidarity (differences of members); the latter are more prone to anomie, or normlessness. One trend in modern economies is the appearance of professions and of attempts by nonprofessionals to gain professional status.

4.   Alienation refers to the sense of powerlessness and meaninglessness experienced by people when they lose control over, and are estranged from, their environment. Marx linked alienation to the extreme division of labor, which reduces workers' autonomy. Worker alienation may be roughly measured in terms of worker satisfaction or dissatisfaction. Many workers are now gaining more autonomy over their work: the nature of many jobs is changing, and employers recognize that involved and satisfied workers are more productive.

5.   Two basic economic systems are capitalism and socialism. Both represent ideal types that are only approximated by specific countries. The two systems differ primarily over the extent to which property and other economic resources should be privately or publicly owned. Socialism includes two varieties, one under communist rule and one under democratic rule. Convergence theory suggests that socialist and capitalist societies will evolve toward similar forms as a result of common problems. China is one socialist society that is adopting some "capitalistic" elements.

6.   The American economy is dominated by large corporations whose power and influence have important implications for the economy and society. Many corporations have now become multinational in scope and influence, and they represent a disturbing concentration of economic—and therefore political—power.

7.   The general rate of unemployment results from structural factors in the economy as a whole; specific rates result from factors that affect only certain categories of the population, such as minorities, women, or blue-collar workers in decaying industries.

8.   The United States is moving to a postindustrial future in the context of a global economy; this shift is likely to involve the abandonment of older, noncompetitive industries in favor of newer ones, and may have profound effects on economic and social life.

Important Terms

economic order (453)

primary sector (454)

secondary sector (454)

tertiary sector (454)

division of labor (455)

surplus wealth (455)

mechanical solidarity (456)

organic solidarity (456)

anomie (456)

profession (458)

alienation (459)   communism (464)

capitalism (462)   democratic socialism (466)

socialism (462)   convergence theory (466)

ideal type (462)   corporation (468)

property (462)   interlocking directorates (469)

monopoly (463)   multinational corporation (470)

oligopoly (463)   neocolonialism (471)

Suggested Readings

BERGER, PETER. *The Capitalist Revolution.* New York: Basic Books, 1986.

An important sociological analysis of modern capitalism. Berger argues that capitalism is more productive than socialism and is also more likely to nourish democracy.

FUCHS, VICTOR S. *How We Live: An Economic Perspective on Americans from Birth to Death.* Cambridge, Mass.: Harvard University Press, 1983.

An interesting account of how economic forces affect almost every aspect of Americans' lives.

KANTER, ROSABETH M. *Men and Women of the Corporation.* New York: Basic Books, 1977.

An influential study of the inner workings of an American corporation, with a special focus on the position of women in the organization.

MARX, KARL. *Selected Writings in Sociology and Social Philosophy.* Tom Bottomore and Maximilian Rubel (eds.). Baltimore, Md.: Penguin, 1964.

A selection of excerpts from Marx's major works. The selections include Marx's writings on the concept of alienation and his impassioned denunciations of alienated labor.

NADER, RALPH, et al. *Taming the Giant Corporation.* New York: W. W. Norton, 1976.

A critical study of large modern corporations. Nader and his associates suggest some ways to make these organizations more socially responsible.

RITZER, GEORGE, and DAVID WALCZAK. *Working: Conflict and Change.* 3rd ed. Englewood Cliffs, N.J.: Prentice-Hall, 1986.

A good sociological overview of work in modern America.

TERKEL, STUDS. *Working.* New York: Random House, 1974.

A fascinating collection of tape-recorded interviews with workers across the United States. The book, which became a best seller, has great human interest as well as sociological significance.

TOFFLER, ALVIN. *The Third Wave.* New York: Morrow, 1980.

A best-selling popular account of some potential implications of the transition to a postindustrial economy.

VERNON, RAYMOND. *Storm over the Multinationals: The Real Issues.* Cambridge, Mass.: Harvard University Press, 1977.

A useful discussion of multinational corporations, with a full analysis of their advantages and disadvantages for other nations.

CHAPTER 18

The Political Order

Over 2,000 years ago the philosopher Aristotle observed that we are political animals. We are indeed, and necessarily so, for politics is an inevitable consequence of social living. In every society some valued resources are scarce, and politics is essentially the process of deciding "who gets what, when, and how" (Lasswell, 1936). The character of political institutions and behavior varies a great deal from one society or group to another, but the political process itself is universal.

The *political order* is the institutionalized system through which some individuals or groups acquire and exercise power over others. In this chapter we will focus primarily on these processes as they occur at the level of the *state,* the supreme political authority in society. Max Weber (1946), who laid the foundations of modern political sociology, pointed out that the state is the only authority that can successfully claim a monopoly on the right to use force within a given territory. Of course, the state may choose to delegate some of its powers to other agencies, such as local authorities, the police, or the military. In the final analysis, however, the state can override all other agencies and is thus the central and most vital component of the political order. The "state," incidentally, is not quite the same thing as the "government." The state is an impersonal social authority, whereas the government is the collection of individuals who happen to be directing the power of the state at any given moment.

Power

Politics is about power—about who gets it, how it is obtained, how it is applied, and to what purposes it is put. As Weber defined it, *power* is the ability to control the behavior of others, even in the absence of their consent. Put another way, power is the capacity to participate effectively in a decision-making process. Those who for one reason or another cannot affect the process are therefore powerless. Power may be exercised blatantly or subtly, legally or illegally, justly or unjustly. It may derive from any of a number of resources, such as wealth, prestige, numbers, or organizational efficiency. Its ultimate basis, however, is the ability to compel obedience, if necessary through the threat or use of force.

The exercise of power may be either legitimate or illegitimate. As we noted in Chapter 10 ("Social Stratification"), *legitimacy* is the generally held belief that a political system is valid and justified. Power, therefore, is considered legitimate only if people generally recognize that those who apply it have the right to do so—perhaps because they are elected government officials, perhaps because they are an aristocracy whose commands are never questioned, perhaps because they are believed to be inspired by God. According to Weber, *authority* is the form of power whose legitimacy is recognized by those to whom it is applied. Power is considered illegitimate, on the other hand, if people believe that those who apply it do not have the right to do so—perhaps because they are acting illegally, perhaps because they hold no public office, perhaps because they are newly successful revolutionaries who have not yet entrenched their regime. To Weber, *coercion* is the form of power whose legitimacy is denied by those to whom it is applied.

A simple example will illustrate this distinc-

tion more fully. If a judge rules that you must pay a fine, you will probably obey: if you do not, the judge has the power to make you suffer other negative consequences. If an armed mugger in the street demands your money, you will likewise probably hand it over: the mugger also has the power to make you suffer negative consequences if you refuse. But you regard the judge's demand as legitimate. It rests on judicial authority, and you recognize that the judge has the *right* to fine you even if you disagree with and resent the decision. You do not accept, however, that the mugger has any *right* whatever to take your money. You pay up simply because you are being coerced.

Power based on authority is usually unquestioningly accepted by those to whom it is applied, for obedience to it has become a social norm. Power based on coercion, on the other hand, tends to be unstable, because people obey only out of fear and will disobey at the first opportunity. For this reason every political system must be regarded as legitimate by its participants if it is to survive. Most people must consider it desirable, workable, and better than any alternatives. If the bulk of the citizens in any society no longer consider their political system legitimate, it is doomed, for its power can then rest only on coercion, which will fail in the long run. The French, Russian, American, and Iranian revolutions, for example, were preceded by an erosion of the legitimacy of the existing systems. The authority of the respective monarchies was questioned and their power, based increasingly on coercion rather than on unquestioning loyalty, inevitably crumbled.

Figure 18.1 *If it is to survive, a political system must be regarded as legitimate by the people subject to it. When the rulers have to rely on the almost continuous use of violence to maintain their position—as is the case in South Africa—their actions are a sign of weakness, not of strength, for their regime has lost its legitimacy.*

Types of Authority

Max Weber distinguished three basic types of legitimate authority: traditional authority, legal-rational authority, and charismatic authority. Each type is legitimate because it rests on the implicit or explicit consent of the governed. A person who can successfully claim one of these types of authority is regarded as having the right to compel obedience, at least within socially specified limits.

Traditional Authority

Traditional authority is a type of authority in which power is legitimated by ancient custom. Chieftainships and monarchies, for example, have always relied on traditional authority, and historically it has been the most common source of legitimation of power. Traditional authority is generally founded on unwritten laws and has an almost sacred quality. The competence or policies of a particular ruler are not really at issue in such a system, so long as he or she has a legitimate claim to the throne or other traditional ruling status.

People obey traditional authority because "it has always been that way": the right of the king to rule is not open to question. Claim to traditional authority is usually based on birthright, with the status of ruler generally passing to the eldest son of the incumbent. In some cases the power of the ruler over the subjects seems virtually unlimited, but in practice there are always informal social norms setting the boundaries within which power

Figure 18.2 *There are three different sources of legitimate political authority. The power of hereditary rulers, such as Queen Elizabeth I of England, is legitimated by traditional authority: people tend to obey simply because that is the historical practice. In contrast, the power of most modern leaders—such as Mikhail Gorbachev, general secretary of the Soviet Communist Party—is legitimated by legal-rational authority: people obey because the leader has achieved a legally recognized public office by socially prescribed means. Finally, the power of certain leaders is legitimated by charismatic authority. A leader like Iran's Ayatollah Khomeini gained obedience, not because of any public position he inherited or achieved, but because of the exceptional and almost supernatural qualities that his followers saw in him.*

can be exercised. If a ruler exceeds these limits, as many Roman emperors did, people may regard such use of power as illegitimate and coercive, and may even try to depose the ruler. However, they are likely to remain loyal to the system of traditional authority, often recognizing the close kin of the overthrown ruler as having the strongest claim to the succession. But when a society begins to modernize, support for systems based on traditional authority wanes, and some people look for a more rational alternative.

Legal-Rational Authority

Legal-rational authority is a type of authority in which power is legitimated by explicit rules and procedures that define the rights and obligations of the rulers. The rules and procedures are typically found in a written constitution and set of laws that, at least in theory, have been socially agreed upon. This form of authority is characteristic of the political systems of most modern societies.

Legal-rational authority stresses a government of laws, not of specific rulers. The power of an official in a country such as the United States, Canada, or the Soviet Union derives from the office the person holds, not from personal characteristics such as birthright. Officials can exercise power only within legally defined limits that have been formally set in advance. Americans thus acknowledge the right of a president or even of a minor bureaucrat to exercise power, provided that person does not exceed the specific boundaries of authority that attach to his or her respective office. When President Nixon did overstep these boundaries by using his office to persecute his opponents and to obstruct criminal investigations of his aides' activities, his actions were considered illegitimate—an abuse of power—and he was forced to resign. A similar or worse fate would doubtless await a modern Soviet leader who used power in ways considered illegitimate in that country.

Charismatic Authority

Charismatic authority is a type of authority in which power is legitimated by the unique and remarkable qualities that people attribute to a specific leader. Weber called this extraordinary quality "charisma," from a Greek word meaning "gift of grace." Typical charismatic leaders include such figures as Jesus, Joan of Arc, Hitler, Gandhi, Napoleon, Mao, Castro, Julius Caesar, Alexander the Great, Churchill, and the Ayatollah Khomeini. The charismatic leader is seen as a person of destiny who is inspired by unusual vision, by lofty principles, or even by God. The charisma of these leaders is itself sufficient to make their authority seem legitimate to their followers. Whether they can also lay claim to traditional or legal-rational authority is of little relevance to their popular appeal.

Charisma is a spontaneous, irrational phenomenon that often poses a threat to systems based on traditional or legal-rational authority. Revolutions are commonly led by charismatic figures who win personal allegiance and are regarded as the symbol of radical changes to come. Yet charismatic authority is inherently unstable. It has no traditions or rules to guide conduct, and because it rests on the unique characteristics of a particular individual, it is undermined if the leader fails or dies. Successful revolutions led by charismatic figures such as Mao, Castro, or Khomeini almost always face a problem of succession, for those who take over are unlikely to have the qualities of their predecessor. For this reason, systems based on charismatic authority are usually short-lived. Many of them collapse. Others gradually evolve into legal-rational systems based on bureaucratic rules and procedures, or—more commonly in the past than today—into traditional systems in which power passes to the descendants of the original leader.

Each of these forms of authority represents an **ideal type,** an abstract description constructed from a number of real cases in order to reveal their essential features. In practice, political systems and political leaders may derive their authority from more than one source. The power of the American presidency, for example, is legitimated primarily by legal-rational authority, but the office has existed for so long that it now seems to have traditional authority as well. Sometimes, too, the occupant may have charismatic appeal. John F. Kennedy, who had considerable charisma, may be said to have enjoyed legitimacy from all three sources of authority—charismatic, legal-rational, and traditional.

The Rise of the State

In most parts of the world, the state is a relatively recent historical development. As the anthropologist George Murdock (1949) observed, people lived in small groups without formal government for perhaps 99 percent of the time our species has existed. Even when chieftainships and kingdoms emerged, their political authority was often shaky and unpredictable. Rulers certainly laid claim to authority over large areas, but there was little sense of nationhood and few means of asserting power over long distances. Often, in fact, the rulers' authority was confined to an urban area and its hinterland, in a combined territory called a city-state. Even the early empires, such as those of Rome and Persia, were, in effect, alliances between city-states, each of which claimed authority over its own citizens and only grudgingly recognized the center of power. Until as recently as two centuries ago, most of the peoples of the world lived under the often informal authority of local rulers. But since then, the state has emerged as the main source of social authority, successfully claiming a monopoly of the legitimate use of force within a given territory. That territory comprises a nation—a geographically distinct collectivity of people under the authority of a single state. The city-state has virtually disappeared, to be replaced by the modern nation-state.

The emergence of the state as a separate institution is closely linked to a society's level of cultural evolution, and in particular to its means of subsistence (Fried, 1967; Service, 1971, 1975; Lenski and Lenski, 1978). As we noted in Chapter 4 ("Society"), formal political institutions are absent in *hunting and gathering* societies. Each community is independent, and decisions are made by group consensus. In *pastoral* and *horticultural* societies, where populations are larger and there may be a food surplus, some individuals become more wealthy and powerful than others. They pass their status on to their descendants, and patterns of chieftainship emerge. In *agricultural* societies a very large food surplus is possible, and this can be converted into wealth and power. Entire categories of the population become wealthier than others, and social classes appear for the first time. In these societies, the state emerges as a distinct social institution, with power typically concentrated in the hands of a monarch or emperor. The power of the ruler is legitimated by traditional authority, and an elaborate court bureaucracy and full-time military organization are established.

In *industrial* and *postindustrial* societies the nature of the state changes radically. The unprecedented wealth produced by industrialism creates a large, politically sophisticated middle class that will no longer accept arbitrary rule. Regimes based on traditional authority crumble or are overthrown, and legal-rational authority becomes the new basis for the state's legitimacy. In all these societies, the responsibilities of the state steadily expand as it comes to regulate more and more areas of social life, such as welfare, education, medicine, public transport, scientific research, and economic planning.

One measure of this growth is the extraordinary rise in government expenditures. Just under two centuries ago, George Washington's administration spent an average of $20,000 a day. In 1934,

Figure 18.3 *The state does not exist in the simplest of preindustrial societies. Among these Middle Eastern pastoralists, for example, all decisions are made through consensus among the males in the group, and the power of the headman is very limited. The state is present only in societies that are stratified into castes or classes.*

Franklin Roosevelt became known as a "big spender" when his administration spent $18 million a day. By 1986, Ronald Reagan's administration was spending well over $2.7 billion a day—enough, in $1 bills, to blanket a 21-foot road from New York to San Franciso. Reagan, in fact, was the first president to have an annual budget over $1 trillion. The size of the government bureaucracy has shown a corresponding increase. A century and a half ago, the federal government employed 5,000 people. Today it employs 2.9 million civilians, and the total of all federal, state, and local government employees exceeds 16 million people (Bureau of the Census, 1986a). Why has the state become such a central social institution?

The State: A Functionalist View

From the functionalist perspective, the emergence of the state and its dominant position in modern societies can be explained in terms of the functions that it serves in the maintenance of the social system as a whole (Parsons, 1969). Four major functions of the state can be identified.

1. *Enforcement of norms.* In small, traditional communities, norms are usually unwritten and are generally enforced by spontaneous community action. In a highly complex and rapidly changing modern society such a system would be unworkable. The state accordingly takes the responsibility for codifying important norms in the form of laws.

It also tries to ensure that these norms are obeyed by applying formal negative sanctions to offenders. Laws are used to define and suppress certain forms of deviance; these are the criminal laws. Laws are also used to define and protect the rights of individuals and groups; these are the civil laws.

2. *Arbitration of conflict.* The state provides an institutionalized process for deciding "who gets what, when, and how." Conflict over the allocation of scarce resources and over national goals must be kept within manageable limits, or society might become a jungle in which different groups pursue their own interests without restraint. The state acts as arbitrator, or umpire, between conflicting interests, establishing means for resolving disputes and determining policies.

3. *Planning and direction.* A complex modern society requires coordinated and systematic planning and direction. The economy must be closely monitored and attempts made to prevent unemployment, inflation, or recession. The output of trained workers must be geared to the demands of industry and commerce. Research funds must be allocated in accordance with national priorities. Highways must be put where people need them. Welfare must be distributed to the poor, and pensions to the aged. The decisions involved in these and countless other actions must be based on knowledge derived from reliable data, which have to be systematically collected and analyzed. To a greater or lesser degree, policy making must be centralized if coherent policies are to emerge.

4. *Relations with other societies.* The state is responsible for political, economic, and military

Figure 18.4 *Although the modern state has many functions, its underlying theme is the preservation of law and order.*

relations with other societies. It joins alliances with friendly states and participates in international organizations. It forms trading agreements with other societies and attempts to protect its country's foreign investments. It engages in acts of diplomacy and sometimes of defense or aggression against other states. None of these functions could be met without a high degree of centralized control and authority. If the state is to be effective in its relations with other states, it must have the capacity to be taken seriously.

A single theme underlies all four functions: the preservation of social order. More than 300 years ago, the English philosopher Thomas Hobbes (1588–1697) speculated that without a strong political authority, life would be "solitary, poor, nasty, brutish, and short." To Hobbes, people created the state by an implicit social contract, in which they surrendered much of their own liberty to a higher authority in order to prevent chaos. This basic notion is still widely accepted in the United States and elsewhere—that is, that the main duty of the state is to maintain law and order.

The State: A Conflict View

An early conflict view of the state held that it exists largely to safeguard the interests of the privileged. In other words, the state protects the "haves" in their conflict with the "have nots." This idea was forcefully expressed over 200 years ago by the French philosopher Jean Jacques Rousseau (1712–1778). He argued that the emergence of the state was the cause of people's problems, not the solution: "Man is born free, yet everywhere he is in chains." The state, claimed Rousseau, does not apply impartial justice; it merely protects the interests of the wealthy.

The most influential conflict theory of the state is, of course, that of Karl Marx, as put forward in the *Communist Manifesto* (1848) and elsewhere. Marx claimed that all except the most primitive societies are divided into two or more classes, one of which dominates and exploits the others. The ruling class always uses social institutions to maintain its privileged position. For this reason, institutions like the state always serve to maintain the status quo, not to change it. The state itself is simply the "executive committee of the ruling class," protecting that class's interests and allowing it to enjoy the surplus wealth produced by the workers.

Figure 18.5

"When my distinguished colleague refers to the will of the 'people,' does he mean his 'people' or my 'people'?"

Drawing by Richter; © 1976
The New Yorker Magazine, Inc.

Marx declared that "the history of all hitherto existing societies is the history of class struggle." He traced this history through a series of stages. The first is *primitive communism,* in which there is no private property and therefore there are no classes. The second is *slavery,* in which one class owns and exploits the members of another. The third is *feudalism,* in which a class of aristocratic landowners exploits the mass of peasants. The fourth is *capitalism,* in which the owners of wealth exploit the mass of industrial workers. The fifth stage, *socialism,* occurs when the industrial workers have finally revolted. They establish a temporary "dictatorship of the proletariat" to prevent attempts by reactionaries to return to the old system and to guide social change toward the final stage. This is the stage of *communism,* in which property is communally owned and in which, Marx believed, people would enjoy true freedom and the fulfillment of their human potential for the first time in history. But if the state exists primarily to safeguard the interests of the ruling class, then what happens to the state in the classless communist society? Marx's collaborator, Friedrich Engels, declared optimistically that it would just "wither away."

Most modern conflict theorists have serious reservations about Marx's theory. He was no doubt correct that a *major* function of the state is to protect the interests of the ruling class. As we have seen, the state comes into existence only when classes emerge in society; and in all societies the ruling class is the economically dominant class as well. Institutions and other cultural arrangements do, indeed, generally support the status quo, and therefore the interests of the class that benefits from it. But Marx failed to recognize that the state has many functions that are not necessarily related to class conflict—functions that would have to be fulfilled in any modern society, with or without classes. Certainly there seems to be no chance that the state could wither away. A socialist or communist society, in fact, must regulate the lives of its citizens even more closely than a capitalist society has to, because it supervises not only the production but also the distribution of wealth. In countries that are currently at the stage of socialism, like the Soviet Union and Cuba, the state is exceptionally powerful—and their governments obviously have no idea of how to abolish the state, nor any wish to do it.

Modern conflict theorists have broadened Marx's focus from class conflict to social conflict in general. They point out that the state is the main arena of conflict among a variety of competing groups—for example, among racial and ethnic groups, officials and citizens, inner-city residents and suburbanites, consumers and producers, conservatives and liberals, social movements for and against the right to abortion, and so on. Even in communist-ruled societies, which claim to have abolished classes, social conflict persists: in Poland, for example, there is immense hostility between the country's workers and its bureaucratic elite. In any state, then, a variety of different groups use the political process to advance their own interests. Usually, the outcome of any conflict favors the wealthier group, but ongoing conflict can lead to shifts in the distribution of power, and thus can bring about social change (Tilly, 1978; Zald and McCarthy, 1979; Collins, 1974, 1979).

Forms of Government

Forms of government may be classified according to the relationships between the rulers and the ruled: Is the government answerable to the public, or is the public answerable to the government? In the modern world there are three basic forms of government—the authoritarian, the totalitarian, and the democratic. Again, each of these is an ideal type, which actual governments approximate to a greater or lesser degree.

Authoritarianism

Authoritarianism is a form of government in which the rulers tolerate little or no public opposition, and generally cannot be removed from office by legal means. Authoritarian regimes are of several different kinds. A few are *monarchies,* in which power is held by a hereditary claimant to a throne, although such rule is now rare. One of the last examples was the late shah of Iran—"King of Kings, Shadow of the Almighty, God's Vicar, and Center of the Universe"—who inherited his throne from his father and ruled his country with notable greed and arrogance until his people deposed him in 1979. Some are *dictatorships,* in which power is gained and held by a single individual. In the Caribbean country of Haiti, for example, "Baby Doc" Duvalier enjoyed the official position of President-for-Life, until popular unrest forced him to flee the country in 1986. Some authoritarian governments are *juntas,* in which power is seized by military officers in a coup against the existing government. An example is the Chilean junta, headed by General Pinochet, which has ruled the country with an iron fist since the elected president was deposed and murdered in a 1973 coup. Authoritarian rule by the military used to be the norm in Latin America, and is now quite common in Africa. About half of the fifty African countries that gained independence as democracies during the 1960s are now ruled by authoritarian military regimes, sometimes involving one coup after another. Democratic transition from one government to another is almost unknown in Africa, where more than seventy leaders have been deposed through coups in the past quarter century.

Authoritarian governments permit no direct challenge to their own authority, but their concerns are often limited to the immediate political sphere. They may permit public debate, for example, on economic policy, and they frequently acknowledge and deal with other centers of influence, such as business, religious, or labor interests. In the modern world, specific authoritarian governments tend to be relatively short-lived, usually surviving only a few decades at most. One reason is that dictators (such as Franco in Spain) eventually die. Another is that some of them (such as Somoza in Nicaragua) become the target of successful revolutions. And some of them (such as the military junta of Argentina) tire of running the country, declare that the people are "ready" for civilian government, and resign. Authoritarian regimes, therefore, may sometimes be the precursors to more democratic governments.

Figure 18.6 *A characteristic feature of virtually all totalitarian societies is their formal military "body language." Typically, soldiers in totalitarian societies such as Nazi Germany and the Soviet Union use the "goose step" when on parade—a march in which the foot, encased in a jackboot, is held high* *and then stamped on the ground. This action provides a powerful image, and implicitly reminds onlookers of the authority of the state and of its capacity to use force. In democratic societies, the goose step is not used; indeed, it is regarded as rather ridiculous.*

Totalitarianism

Totalitarianism is an authoritarian form of government in which the rulers recognize no limits to their authority and are willing to regulate virtually any aspect of social life. The term "totalitarian" derives from the "totality" of the rulers' ambitions: they tolerate no opposition in any sphere and aim for complete control of the society and its future. Totalitarianism is a twentieth-century phenomenon, in part because it relies on such modern techniques as mass indoctrination of the populace and sophisticated surveillance of potential dissidents. The outstanding examples of totalitarian government are the three that were responsible for perhaps the most grotesque acts of genocide in history: Nazi Germany, Stalinist Russia, and, more recently, Cambodia under the Khmer Rouge regime. In each case, terror was used as an instrument of policy, and millions of people were slaughtered at the whim of a regime that was utterly convinced of its own righteousness.

Totalitarian governments are marked by several characteristics (Friedrich and Brzezinski, 1979). These are an elaborate ideology that covers every phase of the individual's life; a single political party that is identical with the government; widespread use of intimidation; complete control of mass media; monopoly control of weaponry and armed forces; and direction of the economy by the state bureaucracy. Iran shows signs of totalitarian tendencies under its Islamic fundamentalist regime, but the principal examples of totalitarianism in the modern world are the various communist-ruled societies, such as the Soviet Union, North Korea, and Albania. Like authoritarian regimes, totalitarian governments cannot be legally removed from office—but unlike authoritarian regimes, they seem highly resistant to revolution or to evolution toward more democratic forms. No communist government, for example, has ever been overthrown, and none has ever permitted a free election. To an individual who is brutalized by a government, it matters little whether that government is totalitarian or merely authoritarian, but in the long run it may make a considerable difference to the society in question.

Democracy

Democracy is a form of government in which it is recognized that ultimate authority belongs to the people, who have the right to participate in the decision-making process and to appoint and dismiss their rulers. "Democracy" actually comes from a Greek word meaning "rule of the people," and this is no doubt what Lincoln had in mind when he defined democracy as "government of the people, by the people, and for the people." In practice, no such system has ever existed. Pure democracy would mean that every citizen would have the

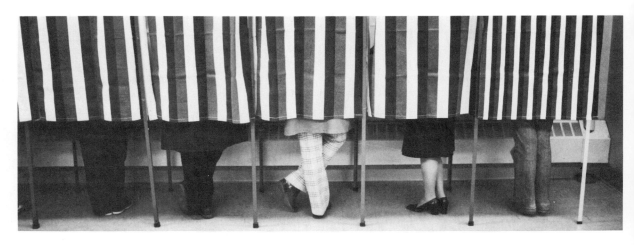

Figure 18.7 *In true representative democracy, voters can choose among genuine alternatives by secret ballot at regular intervals. Such democracy is very rare in the modern world.*

right to participate in every decision, a situation that would lead to complete chaos and would leave little time for all kinds of other activities. This ideal form of democracy has been approximated only in very small communities, such as the ancient Greek city-states and early New England towns. Even in these cases, however, the right of participation was denied to certain people—specifically, both slaves and women in Greece, and non-property-holders and women in New England.

In practice, the societies we consider democratic are those that have institutionalized procedures for periodically choosing among contenders for public office. They have a *representative democracy;* that is, the voters elect representatives who are responsible for making political decisions. In all democracies the right of the individual to choose among alternatives is held in high regard, and this right presupposes such basic civil liberties as freedom of speech and assembly.

Representative democracy is historically recent, rare, and fragile. It is found almost exclusively in a handful of Western European countries and in a few areas that these countries colonized and successfully implanted with their democratic traditions, such as North America, Australia, and India. Some countries, particularly in Africa and communist-ruled Eastern Europe, do have the trappings of representative democracy in that they hold periodic elections—but since there is only one party to choose from, the outcome is a foregone conclusion. The practice of one-party "democracy" is defended on the grounds that the party already "knows" what the people want, or that party strife would be socially divisive. In the ab-

sence of free elections, there is obviously no way of finding out whether these assumptions are correct. The suspicion must linger that a party that is reluctant to face a free election is afraid it might lose the contest.

Prerequisites for Democracy

Why is democratic government so rare? It seems that democracy can thrive only when most of several basic conditions have been met.

1. *Advanced economic development.* In a classic study, Seymour Martin Lipset (1959a) surveyed data from forty-eight societies and found that, although advanced economic development does not necessarily lead to democracy, it is rare to find stable democracy in societies that are not economically advanced. Gerhard Lenski (1966) also found that advanced industrialization is often associated with political democratization. One reason for this relationship is that an advanced economy always contains an urbanized, literate, and sophisticated population that expects some participation in the political process. A second reason is that these societies tend to be politically stable, because their large middle class has a stake in the system and is reluctant to support political upheavals of any kind. These countries can afford to offer citizens political alternatives without fearing that the society would be torn apart in any resulting conflict. In societies with a large, impoverished lower class—such as most of the nations of Africa, Asia, and Latin America—there is likely to be strong opposition from the ruling class to any meaningful exten-

sion of democratic rights. There are some exceptions, however, to the general link between economic development and democracy. In particular, the totalitarian nature of all communist-ruled societies has made them highly resistant to democratization, no matter how economically advanced they are (Berger, 1986).

2. *Restraints on government power.* Democracy is best served if there are institutional checks on the power of the state. These restraints can be of many different kinds. The most obvious are formal restraints such as laws limiting the exercise of power, constitutional arrangements for the impeachment of officials, or guarantees of free criticism by the press and other media. Yet written and legal restraints alone do not assure democracy—the Soviet constitution contains many guarantees that are not worth the paper they are written on, while Britain, one of the most democratic societies in the world, does not even have a written constitution or bill of rights. What is ultimately more important than formal restrictions on the abuse of government power are informal restraints. These restraints, expressed in widely shared norms and values, set limits that public officials dare not violate. These underlying assumptions about the "rules of the game" are an invisible but vital part of any democratic system.

3. *Absence of major cleavages.* Democracy is most likely to survive in a society in which there is a general consensus on basic values and a widespread commitment to the existing political order. Minor competition among several cross-cutting interests is generally healthy for democracy, but a sharp political cleavage, or split, tends to divide society into militant camps that are unwilling to make the compromises necessary for democracy to work. Potential or actual conflict of this kind may put pressure on the government to become "strong" in order to contain it. In societies marked by extreme disunity—such as Lebanon with its religious divisions, South Africa with its racial divisions, or Bolivia with its economic divisions—democratic institutions are generally either unstable or absent. Bolivia, for example, has stumbled between democratic and authoritarian governments so often that it has had over 190 governments since its independence in 1825—an average of more than one per year.

4. *Tolerance of dissent.* A tolerance of criticism and of dissenting opinions is fundamental to democracy. Governing parties must resist the temptation to equate their own policies with the national good, or they will tend to regard opposition as disloyal or even treasonable. Similarly, democ-

racies must avoid the danger of the "tyranny of the majority." In some cases the democratic process may work in such a way that a small minority—Sikhs in India, for example—is rendered permanently powerless. For groups in this position, democracy might as well not exist, and it is important that government should recognize the grievances of minorities that have little political clout. If the losers in the political process do not accept the legitimacy of the process under which they have lost, they may resort to more radical tactics outside the institutional framework.

5. *Access to information.* A democracy requires its citizens to make informed choices. If citizens or their representatives are denied access to the information they need to make these choices, or if they are given false or misleading information, the democratic process may become a sham. It is therefore important that the media not be censored, that citizens have the right of free speech, and that public officials tell the truth. When some presidents concealed information from, or lied to, Congress and the public, their actions were contrary to democratic values and damaged public faith in American political institutions. President Johnson, for example, campaigned against an air war in Vietnam when he was running for reelection, even though he had already given orders to launch such a war. President Nixon had Cambodia bombed for over a year while denying that he was doing so, and he secretly invaded Laos in violation of specific prohibitions voted by Congress and signed by himself. President Reagan publicly urged an international arms embargo of Iran but approved secret arms sales to that country—and the profits were illicitly used to support revolutionary guerrillas in Nicaragua. Under such circumstances, the people cannot use their rights in a meaningful way.

6. *Diffusion of power.* If power is diffuse and no one group can obtain a monopoly over it, the prospects for democracy are enhanced. One way of diffusing power is to distribute it among various branches of government. The U.S. Constitution separates the powers of the executive, legislative, and judicial branches, and they often provide an effective check on one another. Another way of diffusing power is to distribute it to regional and local governments. Power may also be spread beyond government into other institutions and organizations. The existence of separate centers of power in labor unions, corporations, churches, and elsewhere provides a system of checks and balances and ensures that each group must take account of the others.

A Note on Liberty and Equality

The Soviet-style socialist societies of Eastern Europe and Asia claim to be democratic and dedicated to human freedom, although their political systems have few of the features that we have identified as prerequisites for democracy. Yet the leaders of these societies are not necessarily being cynical. They, and no doubt many of their citizens, believe that they live in democracies and that their people are free. Conversely, they also believe that our societies are undemocratic and unfree. How can this be?

The source of the difficulty lies in the way "freedom" is defined. In our society we are primarily concerned with freedom "of": freedom of speech, freedom of assembly, freedom of the press, freedom of the individual to make a fortune. In their societies they are primarily concerned with freedom "from": freedom from want, freedom from hunger, freedom from unemployment, freedom from exploitation by people who want to make a fortune. Put another way, we interpret freedom as meaning "liberty"; they interpret it as meaning "equality."

Liberty and equality are uneasy bedfellows. In general, the more you have of one, the less you will have of the other. Your liberty to be richer than anyone else violates other people's right to be your equal; other people's right to be your equal violates your liberty to earn more than anyone else. The United States has chosen to emphasize personal liberty, an emphasis that can lead only to social inequality. Socialist societies like the Soviet Union have stressed equality, an emphasis that can lead only to infringements of personal liberty. Most Western European countries have chosen a middle way, that of "democratic socialism"; they attempt to balance the demands of liberty and equality more evenly. There is no way to *prove* that any one of these solutions is more desirable, moral, or "right" than any other. The question is a matter of philosophic preference.

Most people, of course, do not rationally consider the various alternatives. No matter what country they inhabit, they tend simply to accept the system they have been socialized to believe in. So Soviet citizens learn, on the whole, to overlook their lack of liberty, and Americans learn, on the whole, to overlook their lack of equality. Extensive research on political socialization has shown that people take the legitimacy of their particular political system for granted very early in life, and usually adopt the political views of their parents. By the time they are in elementary school, children all over the world take an overwhelmingly favorable view of their own country's system and of its national leaders (Greenstein, 1965; Hyman, 1969; Jaros, 1974; Jennings and Niemi, 1974; Renshon, 1977).

Figure 18.8 *People in every society are readily socialized into an acceptance of its particular political system. These photographs show two Nicaraguan children—one, a supporter of the country's revolutionary Sandinista government; the other, a soldier of the Contra counterrevolutionaries. It is not difficult to see how, under different circumstances, each child might hold the opposite allegiance.*

Figure 18.9 *The American political process differs from that of most other democracies in that the parties are essentially loose coalitions with no specific programs. In other democracies, legislators almost always vote according to the "party line," but American representatives can vote more independently—and so are more subject to informal outside influence.*

The American Political Process

The American political process involves an interplay of both explicit, formal elements and informal, sometimes hidden, ones. You are no doubt already familiar with the formal elements of the American political system, such as the electoral process, the role of the presidency, and the way legislation is passed. In this chapter, therefore, we shall focus on the more informal but no less vital processes of party politics and interest-group lobbying. These processes are "unofficial"—that is, they are not included in any formal diagram of how the system "works." But they are very important, nonetheless.

Political Parties

A **political party** is an organization whose purpose is to gain legitimate control of government. Parties are a vital element in a democracy. They link the voter to government; they define policy alternatives; they transmit public opinion from the level of the citizen to the level of the leadership; and they mobilize grass-roots political participation; and they recruit and offer candidates for public office.

Most democracies have several major political parties. These parties are usually narrowly based, partisan movements with very definite policies and very specific programs. The United States, how-

ever, has only two major parties, the Republican and the Democratic. These parties are broad, umbrellalike coalitions of various interests that offer only general statements of policy and vaguely delineated programs. Why are American parties so different from most others?

Maurice Duverger (1954) suggested that the answer lies in the nature of a country's voting system. Many democracies, such as Italy and several other Western European countries, have a voting system based on *proportional representation:* if a party gets, say, 15 percent of the vote nationally, it is allocated 15 percent of the seats in the national legislature. This voting system ensures that minority parties are represented; in fact, there are sometimes so many parties in the legislature that none has a majority, and several parties may have to join together to form a coalition government. Proportional representation encourages the development of minority parties with firm, clear policies that can win enough support to assure at least a few seats—and thereby, perhaps, a chance at participation in a coalition government after the elections.

In contrast, the United States (and a few other countries like Canada) have a voting system based on *simple plurality:* the candidates who win the most votes in each district win the seats. Under this system, a party that consistently gets only 15 percent of the votes will have no congressional representation at all. People are therefore inclined to regard a vote for minority parties as a "waste," and do not seriously consider supporting them. The American voting system thus discourages parties with very strong views and narrow electoral bases. Instead, it produces parties that aim to win elections by forming coalitions before the elections and then appealing to the majority of the people with middle-of-the-road programs.

These basic differences are linked to a number of other distinctive features. In other democracies, parties are usually closely tied to either the working class or to the middle and upper classes. They have very specific programs, which are contained in policy documents issued before elections, and their differences over policy are usually clear-cut and significant. Every member of a party is expected to support every aspect of the party's program in public, and failure to do so can lead to expulsion from the party. Each party applies strict discipline over its legislators, requiring them to be present for voting and instructing them on how to vote. People may become candidates for a party nomination only if they are approved by the party organization. There are no primary elections, and candidates are selected behind closed doors by a small group of party activists. The electorate generally votes for the party, not the individual, because voters are oriented toward policies, not personalities. A politician who is expelled from a party therefore has little chance of being re-elected. Being an incumbent is of little help if the party nominates someone else.

Figure 18.10

"Good God! He's giving the white-collar voters' speech to the blue collars."

Drawing by Joseph Farris; © 1984
The New Yorker Magazine, Inc.

American parties are different in several respects. Although there is a tendency for the lower and working classes to vote Democratic and the upper middle and upper classes to vote Republican, both parties have a wide base of support and try to avoid any mention of "class" in their campaigns. Each party has a liberal and a conservative wing, and it is possible for voters to be faced with a choice between a liberal Republican and a conservative Democrat. The parties usually try to avoid very specific or controversial policy proposals, and their platforms most often take the form of bland generalizations intended to appeal to the political center. There is no expectation that candidates will support every detail of the party platform and no means of disciplining them if they do not. Both parties have weak national organizations: in effect, they are federations of state and local parties that meet together only once every four years to select a presidential candidate. Any member of a party can seek its nomination for any local, state, or national office, and in states where there are primary elections, a person can win the nominations even in the face of opposition from party officials. Americans are willing to vote for the individual, not the party; so an incumbent who is well known has a strong advantage in an election.

A Political Realignment?

Although both parties aim at the middle ground in politics, this does not mean that they are merely a Tweedledum and a Tweedledee, espousing almost identical programs. People have long regarded the Democrats as the party more likely to favor the underdog, and the Republicans as the party more closely tied to business interests. And for most of the past half century, since Franklin D. Roosevelt promised in 1932 that his party would help the nation out of the Great Depression, a majority of the American people have preferred the Democrats.

Roosevelt's election constituted a major event in American politics. He put together a new coalition that consisted, with some overlaps, of high proportions of white Southerners, blacks, white ethnics, Catholics, Jews, young people, Easterners, liberals, union members, and the big-city working class generally. This formidable grouping gave the Democrats a built-in majority: although the party lost the White House in some presidential elections, it controlled the Senate for all but eight years from 1932 until 1984, and the House of Representatives for all but four years in that period.

Ronald Reagan's election in 1980 and his massive, forty-nine–state sweep in 1984 raised the question of whether a new Republican majority might be emerging. Like Roosevelt, Reagan put together a coalition that revitalized his party. This grouping contains high proportions of white Southerners, Christian fundamentalists, young people, Westerners, conservatives, small-town and suburban residents, business people, and upwardly mobile urban professionals. Is this the beginning of a major realignment that will change the face of American politics for years, perhaps decades, to come?

It is too early to know the answer, but some current trends may well work in favor of the Republicans. White Southerners—traditionally hostile to the Republicans, the party of Lincoln—are now reliably Republican in presidential elections and are increasingly so in state contests. Population shifts have greatly enhanced the importance of the Southern and Western states: in fact, these twenty-nine states now have enough votes to decide a presidential election. Young voters' support of the Republicans bodes well for the party's future, because people tend to keep their early party identification for most of their lives. The Republicans, too, have finally shaken off their reputation as the party of hard times, which had dogged them since the Hoover administration ushered in the Great Depression. In fact, the Republicans are now widely viewed as the party of prosperity, while the Democrats have become associated with such economic woes as recession, inflation, and high interest rates. Labor unions, long a bastion of Democratic support, are in decline, while workers in new high-technology industries are more likely to be Republican. Finally, there has recently been a shift in Americans' declared party allegiance: the proportion who declare themselves Democrats has shrunk, while the proportion of Republicans and independents has risen.

It may be the case, however, that the Republican coalition simply reflected Ronald Reagan's personal popularity rather than an underlying switch in party allegiance—and that the Republicans may have trouble holding together such disparate interests as small-town fundamentalists and well-educated urban professionals. It could be that we are witnessing not so much a realignment as a dealignment—a breakdown of traditional loyalties in favor of a more fluid party system, in which people pick and choose among personalities and positions with little regard for party labels. Americans are quite happy to split their tickets—to vote for candidates of each party for different offices. Indeed, a 1986 Roper poll found that only 23 percent of the public considers it important what party a presidential candidate belongs to, and in the elections of that year, the Democrats regained control of the Senate. Certainly, a trend toward a dealignment of party loyalties would not be unexpected in a postindustrial society whose hallmarks are individualism and choice.

Interest Groups

Another effect of the distinctive American party system is that it encourages people to try to influence the way individual legislators vote on specific issues. In other democracies, there is little doubt about the outcome of a vote in the legislature, because most legislators "toe the party line" and are not subject to much external influence. Thus, if the Australian Labor Party has, say, a 20-seat majority in Parliament, it can rely on a 20-vote majority—minus any legislators who are unable to attend—on virtually any vote. In contrast, the loose nature of American parties and their lack of internal discipline means that it is most unusual for all Republican or all Democratic legislators to vote the same way. Instead, a new and different coalition of congressional votes has to be assembled on every issue. This feature gives outsiders a genuine opportunity to affect the law-making process—and many of them seize that chance. An *interest group* is a group or organization that attempts to influence political decisions that might have an impact on its members or their goals. These groups may be large or small, temporary or permanent, secretive or open, but they all try to gain access to, and sway, those who have power.

Interest groups may use a variety of tactics. They may collect petitions, take court action, advertise in the media, organize floods of letters to legislators on particular issues, pledge their members' votes to certain candidates, donate money to election campaigns, or even resort to outright bribery. Frequently, they use *lobbying,* the tactic of directly persuading decision makers. (The word derives from the British Parliament earlier in this century: members did not have any office space, so constituents waited to meet their representatives in the lobby of the Parliament building.) Many large interest groups—including over 500 corporations—maintain highly paid, full-time professional staffs of lobbyists who meet regularly with legislators and government officials. Other groups hire the services of free-lance lobbying firms, which are often staffed by former members of Congress

Figure 18.11 *Competition between organized interest groups is a vital part of the American democratic system. By the use of lobbying and other tactics, these groups try to influence the lawmaking process—sometimes in public, sometimes behind the scenes.*

and government officials. The professional lobbyists usually charge handsomely for their services: it is not uncommon for an interest group to pay $7,000 for getting a bill introduced, $10,000 for getting it through a committee, and $25,000 for its passage on the House or Senate floor. By 1986, there were 8,200 registered lobbyists—more than twice as many as in 1976—but the total number, including those who do not register because of loopholes in the relevant regulations, is believed to be around 20,000, or more than 30 for each member of Congress (E. Thomas, 1986).

Many interest groups make generous donations to help politicians get elected. It can be very costly to run for election to Congress: in 1984, the winner of a House seat spent an average of $325,000—and the bigger-spending candidate was the victor in twenty-eight of the thirty closest contests. Senate campaigns are even more costly: the average winner in 1984 spent nearly $3 million. (The record was set in the 1984 North Carolina senatorial contest, in which the loser spent $9.5 million, and the winner, $16.5 million. The cost of

that single election, in fact, was more than twice the total amount spent by all candidates of all parties to contest all 630 parliamentary seats in the last British national election.) Who pays for all this? A large part of the money—about a third of the cost of House campaigns and about a fifth of those for the Senate—comes from political action committees (PACs), which are organizations established by interest groups for the purpose of raising and distributing campaign funds. We may well suspect that these interest groups expect and obtain some payoff in return for their generosity; one does not shower lawmakers with money, year after year, for no reason (Green and Newfield, 1980; Jacobson, 1980).

Some PACs act on behalf of broad constituencies, such as conservatives or environmentalists, but most represent very narrow interests, and some of them are established for the purpose of promoting or opposing a single piece of legislation. The number of these organizations is increasing rapidly, which suggests that interest groups consider them useful and effective. In 1974 there were about 600 PACs in operation, and they contributed about $12 million to candidates; by 1984 there were more than 4,000 PACs, and their contributions had swelled to over $104 million. About two-thirds of the contributions go to incumbents; about one-sixth goes to challengers of incumbents; and about one-sixth goes to candidates in "open" contests in which no incumbent is running. Incumbents are usually reelected; on average, about 90 percent of House members and a slightly lesser proportion of senators are returned to office (Drew, 1983; Sabato, 1984).

Legislators' dependence on campaign donations raises serious questions about the behind-the-scenes influence of private groups in the political process. For example, when Congress recently considered a proposal that warranties be required for used automobiles, used-car dealers formed a PAC that distributed around $1 million in campaign funds, and the proposal was defeated. The American Medical Association (AMA), which has always opposed the introduction of a national health-insurance program, has spent more than $10 million over the years in supporting candidates who favor its views and trying to unseat those who do not. More than two-thirds of the members of Congress have received funds from this organization. Another highly effective interest group is the National Rifle Association (NRA), whose lobbying

efforts and campaign donations have helped to kill fourteen different gun-control bills since the 1960s, despite opinion polls that consistently show a large majority of the people in favor of such legislation. The NRA has donated money to about a quarter of Congress.

Political sociologists are divided over whether the activities of interest groups are beneficial or harmful to democracy. On the one hand, these groups, frequently operating in secrecy, are often able to win favors that might not be in the public interest. The ordinary voter's influence is thus reduced. Also, how can someone who is not rich and who refuses to accept PAC money run for Congress on an equal basis against those who accept such donations? On the other hand, the existence of a number of interest groups, many of them with conflicting goals, may prevent the development of a monopoly of power and influence. Furthermore, the interest group provides an effective means for otherwise powerless citizens to gain political influence. A mass of unorganized citizens concerned about environmental pollution or child abuse, for example, has little means of exerting influence. If they form an interest group, they have a potentially far greater access to the decision-making process.

American political culture thus encourages an informal, behind-the-scenes interaction among parties, elected officials, and private interest groups. An understanding of this process gives a much fuller picture of the political order than an analysis of formal processes alone. But where does power really lie? Who makes the decisions?

Who Rules?

In a democracy, power is theoretically vested in the people, who periodically delegate it to their representatives. The difficulty is, of course, that power may become vested in the representatives themselves and in those individuals and interests who have privileged access to the decision-making process. The growth of mass political parties in the late nineteenth and early twentieth centuries appeared at first to promise an end to the ancient pattern of rule by a small elite. Yet disillusion set in early when it seemed that even in these new, theoretically democratic parties, power was concentrated in the hands of the leadership.

Three important social scientists of this period addressed the problem, and they all came to similar conclusions. Robert Michels (1911) argued that

Figure 18.12

"According to our estimates, a campaign budget around six point two million is needed to successfully sing your praises."

Drawing by Bernard Schoenbaum; © 1984
The New Yorker Magazine, Inc.

in any organization, concentration of power was essential to efficiency and would thus lead to oligarchy, or rule by the few (see Chapter 7, "Social Groups"). Vilfredo Pareto (1935) pointed out that elites are present in all societies, communities, and organizations. Some people have greater skill, determination, ambition, intelligence, or manipulative ability than others, and they tend to dominate the group. Pareto saw no reason why political life should be any different. He believed it is important, however, that political systems be "open," permitting new rulers to replace old ones in a continual "circulation of elites." Gaetano Mosca (1939) insisted that every society contains a class that rules and a class that is ruled; the ruling class is always a minority. This situation, he argued, will always be found in any society.

Do these principles apply to the United States? Is there a "ruling class," and do the ordinary voters have much influence over the political decisions that affect their lives? We will look first at two important theories on the subject, and then at some empirical evidence.

The Power-Elite Model

The **power-elite model** is a view of the political process that sees power as being held by, and exercised primarily in the interest of, a privileged few (Mills, 1956; Dye, 1983; Useem, 1980, 1984). In his classic book *The Power Elite,* C. Wright Mills (1956) argued that the United States is dominated by a small, informal group of powerful and influential individuals. This "power elite" is not a conspiracy; the members have usually not even sought the extraordinary power that they enjoy. Rather, they exercise this power because they happen to hold important positions in the three sets of great organizations that, over the course of this century, have come to dominate American society: government bureaucracy, large corporations, and the military.

America's advanced capitalist system, Mills argues, requires highly coordinated, long-range decision making among government, corporations, and the military, which is by far the biggest single spender and consumer in the United States. The leading officials of these organizations are therefore in constant contact with one another, and they often make informal decisions of great social and political importance. The power elite is composed of men of very similar social background. They are mostly born in America of American parents; they are from urban areas; they are

predominantly Protestant; and a great number of them have attended Ivy League colleges. Except for the politicians, most of them are from the East. The members of the power elite know one another personally and share very similar attitudes, values, and interests. They sit together on corporation boards and government commissions, where they coordinate their activities and policies.

Mills argues that there are three distinct levels of power and influence in the United States. At the highest level is the power elite, which operates informally and invisibly and makes all the most important decisions in domestic and especially foreign policy. The middle level consists of the legislative branch of government, the various interest groups, and local opinion leaders. Decisions at this level, made mostly through lobbying and the legislative process, are usually of secondary importance. At the third and lowest level is the mass of powerless, unorganized citizens, who have little direct influence on decisions that may affect their lives and, in fact, are often unaware that the decisions are even being made.

The Pluralist Model

The **pluralist model** is a view of the political process that sees many competing interest groups as having access to government and shaping its decisions. This view is held by some sociologists who reject Mills's argument, mainly on the grounds that they do not believe power is as concentrated as Mills suggests (Riesman, 1961; Dahl, 1981, 1982). Instead, these sociologists emphasize the diversity rather than the similarity of the many organizations and groups that exercise power and influence.

In an influential statement of this position, David Riesman (1961) acknowledges that power is unequally shared in American society, but denies that the decision makers are a unified group. Rather, there are so many competing groups at the upper levels of power that no one group is able to maintain a monopoly of the decision-making process. Riesman claims that there are two basic levels of power in the United States. The upper level consists of what he calls "veto groups," strong interest groups that use the formal and informal political process to protect themselves by blocking any of the other groups' proposals that might encroach on their own interests. Power is not highly centralized; instead, shifting coalitions emerge depending on the issue at stake, and in the long run no one

Figure 18.13 *When Americans have been asked over the years whether their government is run "for the benefit of all" or "by a few big interests looking out for themselves," a fluctuating but significant proportion answer that big interests run the government.*

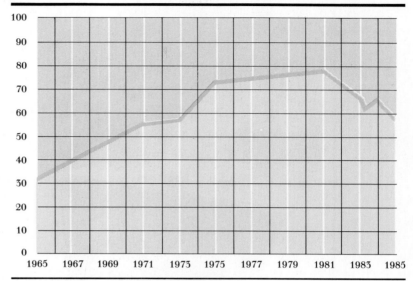

OPINIONS ON WHO RUNS GOVERNMENT
Percentage believing that "government is run by a few big interests looking out for themselves"

SOURCE: *Public Opinion*, August/September 1985.

group is favored over the others. At the lower level of power is the unorganized public, which Riesman believes is not so much dominated by the veto groups as it is sought by them as an ally in their campaigns.

Robert Dahl (1981, 1982) generally supports this view. He argues that power in the United States is dispersed among various groups, each of which is interested only in defending its own interests—not in dominating the society as a whole. Major corporations, for example, may lobby intensively on issues like tax reform, but they are unlikely to become involved in debates over school prayer or crime prevention. On any particular issue, too, various interests dilute power by competing with one another—corporate interests with labor interests, taxpayers' interests with those of Social Security recipients, and so on. Moreover, the government itself is divided into separate legislative, executive, and judicial branches, thus further dispersing the centers of power and influence. In Dahl's view, there is no coordinated elite that dominates society in its own interests—although, like Riesman, Dahl concedes that the general public has little direct influence on the decision-making process.

Empirical Studies

It is difficult to evaluate these models, because they deal with a largely invisible and informal process that cannot easily be studied. Nevertheless, research in some areas can throw light on the issue. Sociologists have done important studies of the backgrounds of the country's political, industrial, and military elite; of the extent of popular participation in the political process; of local community politics; and of the "military-industrial complex."

The "Governing Class"

In a systematic attempt to discover whether the United States has a "governing class" of the kind described by Mills, G. William Domhoff (1967, 1971, 1983) tried to find out who the members of the American upper class were. His criteria for membership in this class included being listed in the exclusive *Social Register*, having gone to a select private school, having millionaire status, and belonging to prestigious men's clubs in large cities.

Domhoff found that this uppermost social

Figure 18.14

"Let's not split hairs, Senator. We both know that big government and private enterprise worship at the same church."

Drawing by Stan Hunt; © 1978
The New Yorker Magazine, Inc.

class consisted of not more than 0.5 percent of the population. The members were not only extremely wealthy. A disproportionate number of them held high-level positions in important social organizations. These included corporations, banks, insurance companies, the diplomatic service, the CIA, charitable foundations, the military, the mass media, the National Security Council, the Council on Foreign Relations, government departments, and the boards of trustees of universities and colleges. Moreover, these people were closely knit through intermarriage, attendance at the same schools and universities, membership in the same clubs, and service on boards of important governmental and economic organizations. Other studies of the nation's economic and political elite have generally confirmed this picture. As noted in Chapter 17 ("The Economic Order"), the boards of the largest and most powerful corporations form an "interlocking directorate," in which the same individuals are directors of numerous firms. Additionally, there is a "revolving door" through which high-status individuals move back and forth be-

tween positions of political and economic influence, a further indication of a tight social network at this level (Allen, 1974; G. Moore, 1979; Useem, 1979, 1980, 1984; Dye, 1983; Mintz and Schwartz, 1985).

This group clearly bears many similarities to the "power elite" described by Mills, and seems to constitute the governing class of the United States. The evidence seems convincing, but the case is not proved. The members of this elite may not necessarily work for their own advantage; there may be severe disagreements among them; and there may be many restraints on the power that they exercise. The fact that the elite exists seems beyond dispute, but how much power it has and how it uses it remains debatable.

Political Participation

To what extent are people at the other end of the power structure—the ordinary voters—actively involved in the political process? Most people, it seems, take little active part in politics. Polls show that only about 8 percent of the population belong to a political organization, and less than 20 percent have ever contacted a local, state, or national official on any political issue.

The turnout of voters in American elections is strikingly low compared with that in most other democracies (see Figure 18.15). About a quarter of Americans who are eligible to vote do not bother to register—and even then, only a little over half of the registered electorate votes in national elections. Moreover, the percentage of registered voters who actually take the trouble to vote has declined for most of the past quarter century, even for widely publicized and hotly contested presidential elections. The trend is clear: 62.8 percent of registered voters cast a ballot in 1960; 61.9 percent in 1964; 60.9 percent in 1968; 55.5 percent in 1972; 54.4 percent in 1976; 52.3 percent in 1980; and 52.9 percent in 1984. In that year, Ronald Reagan swept the election—but since so many voting-age Americans either did not register or did not vote, his "landslide" victory was based on the support of less than a third of the potential electorate. Voter turnout in years when there is no presidential contest is even lower, and it is common for around 100 million Americans of voting age to stay away from the polls on election day. In the 1986 elections, only 37.7 percent of those eligible to vote actually cast a ballot.

Who are these nonvoters? Research has shown clearly that political participation is correlated with social class. The lower a person's social class,

TURNOUT IN MOST RECENT NATIONAL ELECTION

Vote as a Percentage of Voting-Age Population	
1. Italy	94.0
2. Austria	89.3
3. Belgium	88.7
4. Sweden	86.8
5. Portugal	85.9
6. Greece	84.9
7. Netherlands	84.7
8. Australia	83.1
9. Denmark	82.1
10. Norway	81.8
11. Germany	81.1
12. New Zealand	78.5
13. France	78.0
14. United Kingdom	76.0
15. Japan	74.4
16. Spain	73.0
17. Canada	67.4
18. Finland	63.0
19. Ireland	62.3
20. United States	52.6
21. Switzerland	39.4

SOURCE: *Public Opinion*, December/January 1984.

Figure 18.15 *As this table shows, Americans have a remarkably low rate of turnout in national elections compared to the citizens of other democracies. (The table compares voting in the most recent elections as of 1983; but in the 1986 elections, American turnout was even lower, 37.7.) Americans' lack of interest in voting is a paradox, for the United States prides itself on its dedication to the democratic way of life.*

the less likely that person is to register as a voter, to vote, to belong to a political organization, or to attempt to influence the views of others. For example, the great majority of those earning under $5,000 per year fail to vote, while the great majority of those earning over $25,000 do so. Blacks are also less likely to vote than whites, although this seems to be a matter of class rather than race; middle- and upper-class blacks are as likely to vote as are their white counterparts. The failure of low-income people to vote is a distinctive feature of American politics; in most other democracies, there is relatively little difference in class voting patterns.

Why do poorer Americans fail to participate in the electoral process? One reason may be that the United States, unlike other democracies, lacks a major political party that directly addresses the interests of the working and lower classes. Many

low-income people may not bother to vote because they perceive no real relationship between voting and political influence. Surveys of nonvoters tend to support this view: a high proportion cite feelings of political alienation as a reason for their apathy. From the point of view of the middle and upper classes, on the other hand, voting is a way of protecting their investment in the society. Their participation helps sustain the vitality of a system in which both parties are committed to the preservation of the existing social order (Ladd, 1978; Hadley, 1978; Wolfinger and Rosenstone, 1980). The low participation of the poor in voting finds its counterpart in the high participation of the wealthy in elected office. In 1986, nearly 10 percent of the members of Congress (including one-third of the senators) had a net worth of over $1 million.

Community Politics

The relatively small scale of towns and cities makes it comparatively easy to analyze their political processes. A number of studies have done this, sometimes in the hope that patterns of power and influence in communities will provide insights into those of the wider society.

The general finding of these studies has been that power is exercised by small elites, although the nature of the elites varies from one community to another. In the late nineteenth and early twentieth centuries, for example, large cities such as New York, Philadelphia, Boston, and San Francisco were ruled by the party "machine," the local organization of the dominant party. These machines, headed by a party "boss," effectively traded votes for jobs and other benefits. The base of the machine's power was the working class, in most cases containing large numbers of new immigrants. This system survived in Chicago into the 1970s, but is now largely a thing of the past.

Studies made over the past few decades have reported different patterns. In his study of Atlanta, Georgia, Floyd Hunter (1953) found that most decisions were made by an economic elite consisting mainly of corporation executives and bankers. These men communicated informally, shared a similar point of view on major community issues, and determined local policies. Ordinary members of the community were not aware that this elite existed, and they regarded their elected public officials as their real leaders. Hunter found, however, that the elected leaders were not the actual decision makers; they carried out decisions made by others who had the ability to influence them. And when Hunter (1980) restudied Atlanta a quarter century later, he found the situation essentially unchanged.

In a study of New Haven, Connecticut, Robert Dahl (1961) found that the community power structure was much less centralized than in Atlanta, with a far wider participation in decision making. The upper class, Dahl found, had withdrawn from the community political arena by moving to the suburbs. The working class was also excluded from decision making, since it had no effective means of asserting influence. The actual power structure was a shifting coalition of public officials and private individuals, with different people participating in decisions on different issues. Men and women from the middle and upper middle class appeared to have the greatest influence but took part only in decisions affecting their own particular interests. Other community studies reveal no consistent pattern other than that decisions are made by small elites in every case. Who these elites are, how much influence they have, and to what extent they are unified are questions that seem to depend on the characteristics of the community itself.

The Military-Industrial Complex

The **military-industrial complex** is an informal system of mutual influence between the Pentagon, which buys armaments, and the major U.S. corporations that sell them. The phrase was first used by President Dwight Eisenhower in his farewell address to the American people. Eisenhower warned that

> the conjunction of an immense military establishment and a large arms industry is new to the American experience. The total influence . . . economic, political, even spiritual . . . is felt in every statehouse, every office of the Federal government. . . . We must not fail to recognize its grave implications. Our toil, resources, and livelihood are all involved; so is the very structure of our society. In the councils of government we must guard against the unwarranted influence, whether sought or unsought, by the military-industrial complex. The potential for a disastrous rise of misplaced power exists and will persist. [Quoted in Melman, 1970]

Despite Eisenhower's warning, the military-industrial complex has become a dominant feature of American economic and political life. The Pentagon has immense importance in the U.S. economy. It consumes one-quarter of the federal budget. It is the largest single formal organization in world history. It is the world's largest home builder. It finances half of all federal government research. It owns more property than any one single organization in the world, and controls an area of land equal to the size of New York State. One in every nine jobs in the United States is dependent on the military establishment, and over a third of federal civilian employees work for the Pentagon. Defense money flows into more than three-fourths of the nation's congressional districts, and some 350 American communities have at least one defense plant or factory.

The Pentagon relies heavily on the small number of giant corporations that have the technological expertise to supply sophisticated weaponry. The corporations, in turn, are dependent on the Pentagon, because manufacturing goods for the military is much more profitable than competitive commercial production. Less than 10 percent of Pentagon contracts are open for competitive bidding, and the Pentagon has allowed corporations to make very large profits and to incur vast "cost overruns" on the original estimated prices of products. Such arrangements naturally appeal to corporations, and they have flocked to gain a piece of the action: the Pentagon signs agreements with over 20,000 prime contractors and more than 100,000 smaller contractors. About two dozen major corporations, however, hold more than 50 percent of the prime contracts.

Inefficiency, waste, and even outright fraud in the manufacture and testing of American military equipment are now legendary. Relatively minor examples of price gouging are regularly reported. In recent years, for example, the Pentagon has paid $7,622 each for coffee brewers, $659 for ashtrays, and $640 for toilet seats; it bought plastic caps (valued at 25¢) for $1,118 apiece, and light bulbs (valued at 17¢) for $44 each. In such cases, the lay person can grasp how public money is being squandered, for the sums are comprehensible and the items are familiar. When it comes to sophisticated arms or total weapons systems, however, it is much harder for the ordinary person—or even members of Congress—to exercise informed judgment. A Trident submarine costs $1.2 billion; who knows whether that is a great buy or an outrageous ripoff?

One thing is clear: colossal amounts of tax money have been wasted on equipment—like the unreliable Sergeant York Air Defense Gun or the defective Bradley Infantry Fighting Vehicle—which is so inadequate that, if used in wartime, it could jeopardize the safety and lives of the Ameri-

FEDERAL BUDGET OUTLAYS FOR NATIONAL DEFENSE: 1975 TO 1985
In billions of dollars

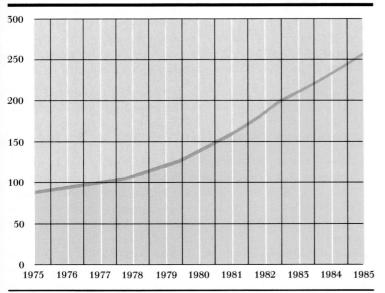

SOURCE: U.S. Bureau of the Census, *Statistical Abstract of the United States, 1986*
(Washington, D.C.: U.S. Government Printing Office, 1986).

Figure 18.16 *As this graph shows, U.S. military expenditures have increased sharply in recent years. Much of this rise is due to inflation and is roughly proportional to the overall increase in federal spending; however, military expenditure consumes roughly a quarter of the total federal budget each year.*

can fighting personnel who relied on it. Why does the Pentagon tolerate this situation? Because it is a captive of the major corporations: if they should collapse into bankruptcy through loss of Pentagon contracts and handouts, the United States would be left without a weapons supply. In 1986, almost half of the top 100 corporate defense contractors were under investigation for fraud. But, if the past is any guide, those corporations found guilty of plundering the Pentagon's purse will receive only a slap on the wrist, such as a temporary suspension of their right to bid on new weapons (Stubbing and Mendel, 1986; Biddle, 1986; Cushman, 1986). (The military-industrial complex and problems with modern weaponry are discussed in more detail in Chapter 23, "War and Peace.")

Because large corporations such as Lockheed and General Dynamics derive most of their income from defense contracts, they constantly lobby the Pentagon and Congress to spend ever larger sums on defense. Most of the corporations have permanent lobbyists in Washington, and many try to maintain their links with the Pentagon by hiring ex-military officers: it is estimated that at least 5,000 ex-officers are in the defense industry. Many of these men presumably retained influence with their former colleagues. Military officials who are responsible for negotiating contracts and who may hope for a corporate appointment when they retire are also, to say the least, put in a compromising situation. The Pentagon itself employs the largest professional lobby in Washington—one lobbyist for every two members of Congress. These lobbyists urge Congress to increase defense expenditures and to take care of the interests of prime contractors.

Mills argued that "military capitalism" is at the heart of the power elite, a view that seems highly plausible. The soaring level of defense expenditure, at a time when the United States has long had the capacity to destroy life on the planet several times over, is partly, of course, a response to the perceived threat of Soviet military and political ambitions. But the size of the defense budget can be fully explained only in terms of continuing corporate pressure for the profits to be gained from weapons production—whether or not these weapons provide sufficient "bang for the buck."

What, then, is the nature of the American power structure: a "power elite" or a series of competing "veto groups"? We still lack the detailed information we need to give a definitive answer to this question, but on the basis of the available evidence it seems that both views are too simplistic. It is likely that decision making in foreign policy is controlled by a very small elite, but that domestic issues are determined by shifting coalitions of elites. There are probably a number of power elites in American society that are united on some issues but in disagreement on others. What does seem clear, however, is that most important political decisions are made behind the scenes by a very small and privileged part of the population. This group consists primarily, though not exclusively, of officials in the executive branch of the federal government and at the head of the great industrial and financial corporations. And because these people influence the policies of the world's most powerful nation, they help shape the course of social change around the world.

Summary

1.   The political order is the institutionalized system through which some people acquire and exercise power over others. The highest level of power is that of the state, the institution that claims a monopoly on the legitimate use of force within a given territory.

2.   Power is the ability to compel obedience, even in the absence of consent by those who obey. Power may be regarded as legitimate (authority) or illegitimate (coercion). There are three basic types of authority: traditional, legal-rational, and charismatic.

3.   The emergence of the state is linked to the level of evolution of a society; it appears first in agricultural societies and becomes a dominant institution in industrial societies. The functionalist perspective emphasizes the functions of the state in maintaining social order: enforcing norms; arbitrating conflict; planning and giving direction; and regulating relationships with other societies. The conflict perspective derives from the Marxist view that the state protects the interests of the dominant class, but modern conflict theorists emphasize that a variety of groups and interests compete for access to the state's resources. The functionalist and conflict approaches are not necessarily incompatible.

4.   Three principal forms of government, at least in ideal type, are authoritarianism, totalitarianism, and democracy. Democracy is rare and exists only as representative democracy. The prerequisites for democracy are advanced economic development; restraints on government power; absence of major cleavage; tolerance of dissent; free access to information; and diffusion of power. Liberty and equality are to some extent incompatible: capitalist societies emphasize liberty; socialist societies, equality.

5.   Largely because of the American simple-plurality voting system, American parties are loose coalitions. The Democrats have been the majority party for five decades, but a party realignment—or dealignment—may be emerging. Because legislators' votes are to some extent unpredictable, powerful interest groups may lobby for their own advantage, sometimes through the use of PACs, which help finance election campaigns.

6.   Mills argued that the United States is ruled by a power elite. Riesman argued that important decisions are made through the interplay of groups in a more pluralistic process. Studies of the governing class, of political participation, of community politics, and of the military-industrial complex all indicate that important decisions are made by powerful interests.

Important Terms

political order (479)	authority (480)
state (479)	coercion (480)
power (479)	traditional authority (481)
legitimacy (480)	legal-rational authority (482)

charismatic authority (482)

ideal type (482)

authoritarianism (486)

totalitarianism (487)

democracy (487)

political party (491)

interest group (493)

lobbying (493)

power-elite model (496)

pluralist model (496)

military-industrial
complex (500)

Suggested Readings

EBENSTEIN, WILLIAM. *Today's Isms*. Englewood Cliffs, N.J.: Prentice-Hall, 1980.

A short and readable explanation of some of the major ideologies that operate in the contemporary political world.

EPSTEIN, LEON B. *Political Parties in Western Democracies*. 2nd ed. New Brunswick, N.J.: Transaction Books, 1979.

An excellent comparative study of political parties, focusing mainly on those of the United States and Great Britain.

DAHL, ROBERT A. *Dilemmas of Pluralist Democracy*. New Haven, Conn.: Yale University Press, 1982.

A discussion of the American political system and its future by an author who favors the pluralist model of the distribution of power.

DYE, THOMAS R. *Who's Running America?* 3rd ed. Englewood Cliffs, N.J.: Prentice-Hall, 1983.

A useful overview of research on America's elite and the networks through which they exercise their influence.

MILLS, C. WRIGHT. *The Power Elite*. New York: Oxford University Press, 1956.

This is the book that first raised the issue of "who rules" in the United States. Mills argues forcefully that American political life is dominated by a "power elite" drawn from the executive branch of government, the military, and major corporations.

MOORE, BARRINGTON. *Social Origins of Dictatorship and Democracy*. Boston: Beacon Press, 1966.

An important and interesting analysis of the way societies achieve either democratic or dictatorial governments.

ORUM, ANTHONY M. *Introduction to Political Sociology*. 2nd ed. Englewood Cliffs, N.J.: Prentice-Hall, 1983.

An excellent overview of theory and research in political sociology. The book is recommended for a general introduction to the field.

SABATO, LARRY J. *PAC Power: Inside the World of Political Action Committees*. New York: Norton, 1984.

A survey of the power, influence, and activities of political action committees, a relatively new but important influence on American political life.

Social Change in the Modern World

Everything changes, and human societies are no exception. Yet throughout the greater part of the history of our species, social change has been relatively slow. Most people lived much the same lives as their parents and grandparents before them, and they expected that their children and grandchildren would lead similar lives as well. Today this is no longer true. The modern world is in a state of constant and rapid social change, and we take it for granted that social and technological innovations will continue to transform our lives in the years that lie ahead.

The chapters in this unit deal with some of the issues involved in the process of change. The first chapter attempts to explain social change in general, and to analyze some specific factors that can cause it. The second chapter discusses collective behavior and social movements—those concerted acts through which people break out of their ordinary routines and alter their social surroundings. The third chapter deals with two striking features of the contemporary world, explosive population growth and the rapid urbanization that accompanies it. The fourth chapter in the unit focuses on modern technology and its effects upon both the social and the natural environments. Finally, we turn to a phenomenon that may threaten the very survival of human society in our own time—war, and especially nuclear war.

The illustration opposite, which ironically captures both the challenges and the perils of rapid innovation in the late twentieth century, is Columbia at Booster Separation, *painted for the NASA archives by the contemporary American artist Bob McCall.*

CHAPTER 19

Social Change

"Everything changes," observed the ancient Greek philosopher Heraclitus. It was he who pointed out that a man cannot step twice into the same river—for he is not quite the same man, nor is it quite the same river. This principle applies to every phenomenon known to us, from the dance of subatomic particles to the expansion of the universe, from the growth and decay of living organisms to the development of individual personality. Societies, as we are only too well aware in the modern world, also change. We have pointed to these changes throughout this book, placing particular emphasis on the transformation that accompanies the shift from traditional, preindustrial society to modern, industrialized society. Yet, although social change is a central concern of sociology, the question of how, why, and in what specific ways societies change remains one of the most intriguing and difficult problems in the discipline.

Social change is the alteration in patterns of culture, social structure, and social behavior over time. No society can successfully prevent change, not even those that try to do so, although some societies are more resistant to change than others. But the rate, nature, and direction of change differ greatly from one society to another. Over the past 200 years, the United States has changed from a predominantly agricultural society into an industrial and then a postindustrial one. In the same period, the society of the BaMbuti Pygmies of the Central African forests has changed hardly at all. Why? What caused the great civilizations of the past to flourish, and what led to their ruin? Why did civilization arise in India long before it appeared in Europe? Why did industrialism emerge in Europe rather than in India? Does social change take place in a haphazard manner, or are recurrent patterns to be found in all societies? Are all human societies moving toward similar social forms and a common destiny, or will they differ in the future as much as they have in the past?

Figure 19.1 *The tempo of social change in any society is reflected in its art. In ancient Egypt, an unusually static society, all painting followed an almost identical style for several centuries—people and animals were always portrayed in profile, with no attempt at depth or perspective. In modern industrialized societies, on the other hand, artistic styles change rapidly and a variety of styles exist simultaneously—trends that reflect the rapidly changing and diverse nature of these countries.*

These are important questions, and they are as old as sociology itself. The man who first coined the term "sociology," Auguste Comte, believed that the new science could lay bare the processes of social change and thus make it possible to plan the human future in a rational way. Almost without exception, the most distinguished sociologists of the nineteenth and twentieth centuries have grappled with the problem of social change. As yet, however, sociology has failed to fully meet the challenge. Many theories have been offered, but none has been able to win general acceptance. As Wilbert Moore (1960) comments: "The mention of 'theory of social change' will make most social scientists appear defensive, furtive, guiltridden, or frightened."

Why does the study of social change present such problems? One reason is that social change involves not only the past and present, but also the future—and the future, of course, cannot be known with certainty. A second reason for the difficulty is that social change usually involves a complex of interacting factors—environmental, technological, personal, cultural, political, religious, economic, and so on. To discover the cause or causes of change is therefore very difficult indeed—especially since we cannot "rerun" history or conduct laboratory experiments in large-scale social change to test our theories. And because each society is unique, we must be hesitant about using the experiences of one society as the basis for confident predictions about changes in another. Nevertheless, these problems are not impossible to overcome, and sociologists already have a good, though partial and tentative, understanding of the processes that social change involves (Etzioni-Halevy, 1981; Lauer, 1982).

In this chapter we will consider three major aspects of social change: first, some specific factors that can cause social change; second, some general theories of social change; and third, the foremost example of sweeping social change in the modern world, global development toward industrialization. We will then examine revolutions as an example of radical social change. Finally, we will assess the prospects for predicting social change in the future.

Some Sources of Social Change

Sociologists have identified a number of specific factors that, in their interaction with other factors, may generate changes in all societies. The precise nature and direction of the changes, however, depend to a great extent on the unique conditions of the social and historical context in which they occur.

The Physical Environment

As we saw in Chapter 3 ("Culture"), the physical environment has a strong influence on the culture and social structure of a society. Thus, people living in the arctic tundra must obviously evolve social forms different from those of people living in arid deserts or on tropical islands. Australia had no indigenous animals suitable for domestication and virtually no indigenous plants suitable for systematic cultivation, so it is hardly surprising that the aboriginal inhabitants remained hunters and gatherers and did not become a pastoral, horticultural, or agricultural society. Another example of interaction between social and environmental forces is the way societies that have been located at geographic crossroads—such as those at the land bridge between Europe, Asia, and Africa—have always been centers of social change. In contrast, societies that have been geographically less accessible have tended to change less. It is no accident that the least developed societies of the world have been cut off from other societies by oceans, deserts, mountain ranges, or jungle.

The physical environment, then, may influence the character of a society and its culture, and it may set limits on some forms of social change. Additionally, environmental factors may actually provoke local or even societal changes. Around 1500 B.C., for example, a volcanic eruption in the Aegean Sea created a massive tidal wave that destroyed the highly developed Minoan civilization on the island of Crete—a catastrophe, incidentally, that probably gave rise to the legend of Atlantis, a civilization that allegedly sank beneath the sea. Other environmental phenomena such as severe earthquakes, floods, or droughts may cause changes in population structure or may even provoke migrations. In the United States, for example, the continued development and even survival of many urban areas in the Southwest will depend on the availability of new water sources for their growing populations. If these cities cannot meet their water needs, they will face the doom that has ultimately overtaken all desert civilizations of the past.

The relationship between environmental factors and social change is actually more complicated than it might seem. We are not completely at the mercy of a capricious environment; on the contrary, we often alter the environment to suit our own purposes, sometimes with results we did not anticipate. Much of the desert in drought-stricken North Africa, for example, was created by over-

Figure 19.2 *Although environmental changes are usually too slow to cause noticeable social change, there are certain exceptions. For example, an earthquake devastated San Francisco in 1906, and the "dustbowl" conditions in Oklahoma in the 1930s caused a large-scale migration of impoverished farmers toward California.*

grazing and other human interference with the ecology of the region, as was land erosion that has destroyed farmland around the world. Currently, the worldwide burning of fossil fuels and the destruction of tropical rain forests are increasing the amount of carbon dioxide in the atmosphere. The result may be a rise in global temperature which, by early in the next century, could begin to melt polar ice caps, raise sea levels, and inundate existing coastal areas. And the future growth of highly industrialized societies may eventually be restricted by the finite capacity of the environment to tolerate increasing pollution and resource depletion. (Some of these pressing issues are considered in more detail in Chapter 22, "Technology and Environment.")

Cultural Innovation

Changes in a society's culture tend to involve social changes as well. As we have already noted in Chapter 3 ("Culture"), there are three distinct sources of cultural innovation: discovery, invention, and diffusion.

Discovery

A *discovery* is a new perception of an aspect of reality that already exists: the principle of the lever, a new continent, the composition of the atmosphere, or the moons of Saturn. A discovery, if shared within the society, becomes an addition to the society's culture and store of knowledge. It becomes a source of social change, however, only when it is put to use. The highly conservative rulers of ancient Tibet knew of the wheel, but, fearing its potential for social change, they banned it from their mountain kingdom for almost a thousand years. The ancient Greeks discovered the principle of steam power; in fact, a steam engine was built as a toy in Alexandria around 100 A.D. But the principle was not put to serious use, and thus did not generate social change, for nearly 1,700 years after it was discovered. In the same way, Europeans knew of other continents for centuries, but it was only when they colonized parts of these territories that social change resulted, in both the colonies and the countries that colonized them.

Invention

An *invention* is the combination or new use of existing knowledge to produce something that did not exist before. Inventions may be either material (cigarettes, can openers, microchips) or social (slavery, democratic institutions, corporations). All inventions are based on previous knowledge, discoveries, and inventions. For this reason, the nature and rate of inventions in a particular society depend on its existing store of knowledge. The cave dweller had little knowledge to work with, and merely to produce a bow and arrow was a considerable intellectual achievement. We are no cleverer than our "primitive" ancestors; we simply have more knowledge to build on. As Ralph Linton (1936) remarked, "If Einstein had been born into a primitive tribe which was unable to count beyond three, lifelong application to mathematics probably would not have carried him beyond the development of a decimal system based on fingers and toes." Inventions occur exponentially: the more inventions that exist in a culture, the more rapidly

SIMULTANEOUS DISCOVERIES AND INVENTIONS

Discovery of the planet Neptune	Adams (1845) Leverrier (1845)
Discovery of oxygen	Scheele (1774) Priestly (1774)
Logarithms	Napier-Briggs (1614) Burgi (1620)
Photography	Daguerre-Niepce (1839) Talbot (1839)
Kinetic theory of gases	Clausius (1850) Rankine (1850)
Discovery of sunspots	Galileo (1611) Fabricius (1611) Scheiner (1611) Harriott (1611)
Laws of heredity	Mendel (1865) DeVries (1900) Correns (1900) Tschermak (1900)

SOURCE: William F. Ogburn, *Social Change* (New York: Viking, 1922), pp. 90–122.

Figure 19.3 *These are some of the 150 discoveries and inventions that William Ogburn found had been made almost simultaneously. In most cases the investigators were unaware of one another's work. They all lived in similar cultures, however, and so had access to the same store of cultural knowledge. Once sufficient knowledge has been accumulated in a particular field, new inventions become almost inevitable.*

further inventions can be made. Given a sufficient cultural store of knowledge, new inventions become almost inevitable. William Ogburn (1950) listed 150 inventions that were made almost simultaneously by different scientists living in the same or similar cultures (see Figure 19.3).

Diffusion

Diffusion is the spread of cultural elements from one society to another. Diffusion may result from many factors, such as travel, trade, conquest, migration, or telecommunications. George Murdock (1934) estimated that about 90 percent of the contents of every culture has been acquired from other societies, and some social scientists have argued that diffusion is the main source of cultural and social change. One of the most outstanding contemporary social changes is the diffusion of industrialism from the advanced to the less developed societies.

Diffusion may involve not only material artifacts like knives or computers, but also aspects of nonmaterial culture, like norms and values. Ideas, for example, may arise in one cultural context, become "detached" from that context, then have an independent effect in another time or place. For instance, the ban on artificial birth control by the Catholic Church and some other Christian groups stems ultimately from the stern morality of the ancient Israelites. The Israelites were a small tribe, subject to a high infant death rate and surrounded by enemies, so they placed great value on large families. This value was transmitted to early Christianity, and, many centuries later, the "immorality" of artificial birth control became part of the official doctrine of several churches in modern countries where quite different conditions prevail. And this diffusion from the past carries still further potential for social change in the future. For example, in those Catholic countries where condoms are hard to obtain, a vital barrier to the spread of AIDS is lacking. Similarly, religious opposition to birth control is encouraging rapid population growth in impoverished nations in Latin America and elsewhere—thus worsening a problem of overpopulation and poverty that may, in time, lead to other political and economic changes.

As a general rule, however, material artifacts are apt to diffuse more readily from one culture to another than new norms, values, or beliefs. For these reasons, white settlers in America accepted the Indians' tobacco—but not their religion.

Population

Any significant decrease or increase in population size or growth rates may affect or even disrupt social life. A population that grows too slowly or even declines in numbers faces the danger of extinction. A population that grows too large puts impossible demands on resources. The result, as it has so often been in history, may be mass migration, usually resulting in cultural diffusion and sometimes in wars as the migrants invade other territories. Or the result may be upheaval and conflict over scarce resources within the society itself. The problem of population decrease is not one that most societies have to face today, but overpopulation is one of the most pressing social problems in the contemporary world. If global population con-

tinues to increase at anything like its current rate, demands for food, living space, and other natural resources may become insupportable. Excessive social changes would follow, including an abrupt population decline as the death rate soars due to malnutrition, disease, and, quite probably, even wars.

Changes in the demographic structure of a population also cause social changes. The post-World War II "baby boom" gave the United States a disproportionate number of young people, which, among other things, made a massive expansion of educational facilities necessary in the 1950s and 1960s. The subsequent "birth dearth" resulted in a reduced population of young people, so many colleges are now finding themselves short of students. As the "baby boom" generation ages, the United States will become "top heavy" with old people, resulting in still further social changes. Medical science will focus increasingly on the problems of the aged, and geriatrics will become a growth area in medicine. New provision will have to be made for the elderly, probably through an extension of old-age homes and similar facilities. Younger workers may find that an increasing part of what they earn goes in taxes to support the growing ranks of the retired, and funeral homes will enjoy an unprecedented boom. (The social impact of population changes is discussed in more detail in Chapter 21, "Population and Urbanization.")

Technology

A major source of social change is **technology**, the practical applications of scientific or other knowledge. We have only to look around us to see how our way of life and social behavior are influenced by various technologies, ranging from kitchen gadgets to automobiles.

Most technological innovations are based on existing scientific knowledge and technology. The more advanced a society is in this respect, therefore, the faster the pace of technological change is likely to be. And the more rapid the technological change, the more rapid is the social change that it generates.

A mere sixty-six years elapsed between the first faltering flight of the Wright brothers and the landing of the first astronauts on the moon. The rate of technological change in modern industrialized societies has no historical precedent. Throughout most of history, people lived in a world little different from that of their parents, and they expected their children and grandchildren to

Figure 19.4 *The rate of technological change in modern societies is without precedent. This glider, piloted by Orville Wright, was considered something of a marvel in 1908; the space craft that brought this astronaut to the moon is already obsolete. One reason for the rapid pace of technological innovation is that each advance builds on previous ones. The greater the accumulation of technology, therefore, the faster the rate of innovation is likely to be.*

live much the same lives as they did. In the modern world, however, we accept change as the norm. We look for novelty, we are oriented to the future rather than the past, and we expect constant improvements in our material environment.

The pace of technological change has implications for every area of society. Medical advances have helped to lengthen life expectancy and to slash the death rate, radically altering population structure. Innovations in industrial technology displace thousands of workers and render recently manufactured machinery obsolete within a few years. Cultural activities are transformed through such innovations as computers and video cassettes. The socialization process, which in simple societies consists almost entirely of passing the culture of one generation on to the next, becomes both more complex and more inadequate, for the knowledge of one generation grows obsolete in some respects even before it can be transmitted to the young; and the young, for their part, cannot be fully socialized for a future that cannot be anticipated with any certainty.

The influence of technology on society seems so powerful that some sociologists have supported the theory of ***technological determinism***—the view that the technology available to a society is an important determinant of its culture, social structure, and even of its history. For example, William Ogburn (1922) argued that the invention of the cotton gin in 1793 encouraged the use of slavery in the United States. The cotton gin greatly increased the productivity and thus the profits of the textile industry, and many more slaves were needed to work on the new cotton plantations that sprang into being. Ogburn also emphasized the division of culture into material and nonmaterial elements, and claimed that changes usually occur in the material culture first. But although people accept new tools much more readily than they accept new ideas, values, or norms, technological innovations inevitably lead to other cultural changes. The result is often ***culture lag,*** a delay between a change in material culture and the adjustment of nonmaterial culture to the change. Ogburn argued that this "catching up" process is a continuing feature of modern life. For example, there has been a substantial delay between the invention of the computer and its general use in routine office work, in part because many people were perplexed by, and resisted, such a novel machine.

The argument for technological determinism seems persuasive, as you will appreciate if you consider the social impact of such innovations as gunpowder, the compass, the printing press, the automobile, the elevator (which makes skyscrapers practical), the jet engine, or nuclear weapons. But the theory has its limitations. Technological change, such as the introduction of the cotton gin, always occurs in the context of other influences. It is very difficult, if not impossible, to prove that the technological factor was the main cause of social change. Moreover, the precise effect of technological innovation depends on the culture into which it is introduced. Technology and other elements in society are best seen as parts of an interacting system. (These issues are discussed in more detail in Chapter 22, "Technology and Environment.")

Human Action

One obvious source of social change is human action, which may bring about social changes whether they are intended and foreseen or not. Two types of human action are particularly important: the acts of powerful leaders and other crucially placed individuals; and the collective action of large numbers of people.

Individual Action

The precise influence of individuals on the course of history and social change is very difficult to judge. Take the case of the Roman general Julius Caesar. Some 2,000 years ago, he made a historic decision to overthrow Rome's republican form of government and to replace it with a dictatorship. His act led directly to an imperial form of government, and the great Roman empire passed from him, through his adopted son Augustus, to tyrants and madmen such as Nero and Caligula. If Caesar had not seized power, the Roman republic might have survived; Augustus, Nero, Caligula, and the rest would not have become emperors, and the history of the Western world over the next twenty centuries, right up to our own time, would have taken a different course. Or would it have? We cannot know. We cannot conduct an experiment in which we remove Caesar from the scene and wait to see what happens.

Historians and biographers often adopt what is sometimes called the "great man" theory of history and social change. Sociologists have generally rejected this approach, taking the view that history makes individuals rather than that individuals make history. Sociologists see the personality and ambitions of leaders, like those of anyone else, as being strongly influenced by the culture in which the particular figures were born and socialized.

From the sociological perspective, the social changes that individuals appear to have created are better seen as the product of deeper social forces. Caesar could destroy the Roman republic only because it was already on its last legs; fifty years earlier his seizure of power would have been impossible and even unthinkable. If he had not acted when he did, others might have done so instead, and later events might have followed a broadly similar course. Similarly, we cannot attribute World War II solely to the personality and ambitions of Adolf Hitler. The German dictator certainly influenced the course of events, but if there had not been severe social, ethnic, and economic strains in Germany at the time, he might never have come to power or have had the opportunity to put his policies into effect. If a person of the same personality and ideas were to appear in a different society or a different period—say, in modern-day Canada—his impact on history would extend no further than the local prison or mental hospital.

Additionally, it is not only "great" individuals who may influence the course of social change: some quite obscure people may have significant effect, if they are crucially placed. A warehouse clerk with a mail-order rifle ended John F. Kennedy's presidency in 1963, bringing about the presidency of Lyndon Johnson, which, in turn, led to policies that included war in Vietnam. One evening in 1972, an alert watchman at the Watergate building in Washington noticed that a burglary was in progress, and called the police—thus setting in motion a series of investigations that led to the disgrace and downfall of Richard Nixon and to the presidency of Gerald Ford. Events of this kind may seem to lie beyond the scope of scientific analysis, but as Robert Nisbet (1969, 1970) points out, the actual event need not always be the decisive factor in social change. The system as a whole may sometimes be "ripe" for change, and the event may merely "trigger" it. Corruption and deceit in American politics is a problem of long standing. Sooner or later someone was likely to get caught, and that someone happened to be Richard Nixon. The United States has its share of psychopaths and lacks a responsible system of gun control; sooner or later someone was likely to assassinate a president. Attempts were made in the past half century, in fact, on the lives of presidents Roosevelt, Truman, Kennedy, Ford, and Reagan; the president who became a fatal victim was John Kennedy. To at least some extent, then, the historic actions of individuals can be explained in terms of existing social conditions.

Collective Action

Collective social action by large numbers of people is easier to analyze sociologically than the acts of individuals. Sometimes such action takes the form that sociologists refer to as **collective behavior**—relatively spontaneous action that occurs when people try to work out common responses to ambiguous situations. This behavior, which includes fads, fashions, rumors, and even riots and lynch mobs, represents an attempt by people to change aspects of their social environment (Smelser, 1962). Often these behaviors have little lasting effect, but sometimes they can bring about significant social change. For example, rioting mobs provoked the French and Russian revolutions, and in 1986 the Marcos regime in the Philippines fell when crowds of demonstrators refused to disperse and the military refused to act against them.

Other social action takes the more structured form of a **social movement**—a large number of people who have joined together to bring about or resist some social or cultural change. Social movements—such as those for national independence, civil rights, and gay liberation, or against abortion, slavery, and nuclear weapons—arise when people mobilize their resources to influence the course of events (Zald and McCarthy, 1979). The campaigns of social movements also illustrate the importance of ideas (often expressed as slogans) in furthering change. The cry for "liberty, equality, fraternity" in the French Revolution influenced social and political history around the world. The concept of "the brotherhood of man" was used by those who wished to abolish slavery in the United States and elsewhere. Appeals by crusading movements for

Figure 19.5 *Ideas and beliefs are created by human beings, but can then act on other people in later years, influencing their behavior. The persecution of Jews, for example, has a long history, extending from the time when they suffered suspicion and prejudice as a religious minority in medieval Europe. The first picture shows Jews being burned in the fifteenth century, when they were blamed for epidemics of the plague. The second picture shows an annual custom in some European towns of the eighteenth century, the stoning of Jews in Lent. The final picture was taken in 1945 in a German concentration camp, one of several centers where the Nazis murdered millions of Jews.*

"democracy" or "justice" helped swing American public opinion in favor of extending the vote to women and to blacks. Yet none of these ideas or movements existed in a vacuum; they were influential only in the context of other social and historical forces that lent them particular weight. (These forms of collective action are discussed in more detail in Chapter 20, "Collective Behavior and Social Movements.")

Theories of Social Change

A full grasp of social change needs more than an understanding of some specific factors that can provoke change. We need a broader theory of change—one that explains how, why, and in what direction social change in general takes place. Several such theories have been proposed, not only by sociologists but also by historians and anthropologists, for their respective disciplines all have a common interest in the subject. The study of these theories, incidentally, gives us an interesting insight into the sociology of knowledge and belief: each type of theory won acceptance because it fitted so well with popular assumptions that prevailed at the time.

Some theories, now abandoned, were based on the vague impression that social change occurs in cycles, or repetitive patterns. For example, Ibn Khaldun, a fourteenth-century Arab scholar, believed that societies alternate between a nomadic and a sedentary way of life—a view that was influenced, no doubt, by the collapse of his own settled society under attacks of nomadic tribes. Soon after the senseless carnage of World War I, a German writer, Oswald Spengler (1926), claimed that all civilizations go through a cycle of birth, maturity, old age, and death. Western civilization, he asserted, was in its last throes—as proved, supposedly, by the dreadful war that had just occurred. Another cyclical theory came from a British historian, Arnold Toynbee (1945). He argued that all civilizations go through a cycle of growth and decay, but that each civilization learns from its predecessors—so the cycles build on each other toward a higher point, rather like a circular staircase.

Cyclical theories of social change may at first seem attractive because they deal with an observed historical fact: all civilizations of the past have risen and fallen. But this does not mean that historical and social change is necessarily cyclical. The fact that the sun has risen and set every day in

Figure 19.6 *Cyclical theories of social change focus on the rise and fall of civilizations, attempting to explain these patterns of growth and decay. This picture shows some of the giant stone statues that have stood for centuries on the remote Easter Island, off the Pacific coast of South America. Little is known about who created these massive figures, or why they did so.*

recorded history gives us good reason to suppose that it will do so again tomorrow. Changes in human societies, however, are not subject to such inexorable "laws"—or if they are, the cyclical theorists have failed to discover them. To say that cyclical changes are caused by a tendency for change to occur in cycles explains nothing: it is like explaining the movement of an automobile in terms of its "automotive tendency." These theories also place too much emphasis on mysterious forces such as "destiny" and too little emphasis on social forces. Although no sociologist would be so foolish as to reject the possibility that Western civilization and the societies that share it might ultimately be doomed, cyclical theories are simply not convincing.

A successful theory of social change must do more than describe events: it must *explain* how and why change takes the forms that it does. There are three explanations of social change which go some way toward meeting that requirement, and we have encountered them repeatedly in this book. They are sociocultural-evolution theory, functionalist theory, and conflict theory. How do they account for change?

Sociocultural-Evolution Theory

The evolutionary approach to social change is based on the assumption that societies gradually develop from simple beginnings into ever more complex forms. This assumption rests on both anthropological and historical evidence. We know from the cross-cultural data that there have been and still are many small-scale, simple societies, such as those of hunters and gatherers, horticulturalists, and pastoralists. We know from the historical data that many small, simple societies have grown steadily larger, and some of them have been transformed into the industrial and even postindustrial societies of the modern world. But what does this evidence mean?

Early Evolutionary Theory

Actually, the evolutionary theory of social change had an unpromising start. Nineteenth-century theorists believed that human societies evolve in a *unilinear* way—that is, in "one line" of development from the simple to the complex that recurs in every society. They were convinced, too, that "change" meant "progress" toward something better. This unilinear view arose in an era of colonial expansion, in which European soldiers, missionaries, merchants, and adventurers brought back tales of strange and exotic peoples in distant, "backward" lands. Working with this kind of second-hand, ethnocentric information, early anthropologists came to the conclusion that all societies passed through the same stages, beginning in primitive origins and climaxing, of course, in Western civilization.

This view drew much of its impetus from Charles Darwin's contention that all life forms evolved from different origins, and that the general direction of biological evolution was toward greater complexity. Other writers immediately used this theory to explain social change. Herbert Spencer, for example, applied Darwin's principle of "the survival of the fittest" to human societies. He claimed that Western "races," classes, or societies had survived and evolved to "higher" levels than non-Western ones because they were better adapted to face the conditions of life. This view, known as "social Darwinism," won extraordinarily wide acceptance in the late nineteenth century. It survived in both Europe and the United States until World War I, and was used to justify the dominance of whites over nonwhites, of the rich over the poor, and of the powerful over the weak.

It is easy to see why this early evolutionary

Figure 19.7 *The early evolutionary theories of the nineteenth century assumed that all societies evolved in the same unilinear manner through a series of "stages," culminating in Western civilization. Actually, this approach was little more than an ideology that justified the interests of the colonial powers, for it enabled them to proclaim their natural superiority over the peoples whose lands they seized. This portrait of Queen Victoria and one of her subject chiefs conveys the tenor of those times.*

doctrine was accepted. It provided an ideology that legitimized the political and economic ambitions of the European colonial powers. The enforced spread of Western culture was conveniently pictured as "the white man's burden"—the thankless but noble task of bringing "higher" forms of civilization to "inferior" peoples. But unilinear evolutionary theory was fatally flawed. One problem was that it described but did not explain social change: it offered no account of how or why societies should evolve toward the Western pattern. The second problem was that the theory was based on faulty data. As first-hand ethnographic evidence became available, social scientists realized that the diverse societies of the world did not follow the orderly sequences that armchair theorists had dreamed up. By the 1920s, unilinear evolutionary theory was as dead as the dodo.

Modern Evolutionary Theory

Yet an evolutionary theory of society is still alive and well, this time in a form that is grounded in fact and is more respectful of cultural diversity. As we noted in Chapter 4 ("Society"), *sociocultural evolution* is the tendency for societies' social structures and cultures to grow more complex over time. Modern social scientists see this process as a *tendency*, not a universal "law," and they do not press the analogy between societies and living organisms. They point out, however, that societies generally tend to move from small-scale, simple forms of social structure and culture to large-scale, complex forms. They agree that this process is *multilinear:* change occurs in many different ways, and does not necessarily follow exactly the same course, direction, or speed in every society. Additionally, social scientists no longer believe that "change" necessarily means "progress," or that greater social complexity will inevitably produce greater human happiness. This view, much more tentative than that of the early evolutionists, has found its way into the mainstream of anthropological and sociological thought (for example, Steward, 1956; Fried, 1967; Parsons, 1966; Service, 1971; Lenski and Lenski, 1982).

An advantage of sociocultural-evolution theory is that it shows *how* changes take place. The main source of change is a shift in a society's basic means of subsistence—say, from agricultural to industrial, or from industrial to postindustrial. Because each succeeding subsistence strategy is more productive than its predecessor, it yields a greater economic surplus—which, in turn, makes possible larger populations, a more affluent mate-

rial life, greater cultural diversity, a variety of new statuses and roles, and a broader base for further and faster development. As a theory of social change, this one is useful as far as it goes. However, the concept of sociocultural evolution does not offer a fully satisfactory theory, for it deals with only one aspect of change—the evolution of societies from the simple to the complex. Sociocultural evolution tells us little, for example, about wars, migrations, revolutions, or other important forms of change.

Functionalist Theory

Ever since Emile Durkheim laid the basis for functionalism around the turn of the century, functionalist theory has emphasized social order rather than social change. As we have seen, Durkheim's method was to ask what function social phenomena like education and religion had in maintaining—but not changing—the social system as a whole. In later decades, the American sociologist Talcott Parsons built on Durkheim's work to produce not only a functionalist theory of social order but also one of social change.

Parsons's Theory of Social Order

Parsons's writings are wordy, abstract, and make singularly difficult reading. The basic idea of his early work, however, is not very complex. In brief, Parsons (1937, 1951) argued that a society consists of interdependent parts, each of which helps to maintain the stability of the entire social system. The system as a whole has a tendency to constantly seek equilibrium, or balance—in much the same way as the human body (by sweating, shivering, or metabolizing food) tries to maintain a constant internal temperature. According to Parsons, society is able to minimize disruptive forces because conservative cultural patterns, particularly shared norms and values, serve to resist radical changes. In this conception of society, Parsons gave little attention to social change. Indeed, he seemed to regard changes as unwelcome irritants that disturbed the smooth functioning of the social system.

Throughout the 1940s and 1950s, Parsons's work dominated American sociology. The United States was enjoying a period of relative cohesion and stability, and Parsons's view of society as a balanced system that integrated small yet necessary changes was in tune with the times. But the major social conflict in the United States in the late 1950s and throughout the 1960s raised many doubts about Parsons's assumptions. Critics questioned whether a theory of equilibrium and stability is relevant to societies that are in a state of constant change and social conflict (Lockwood, 1956; Dahrendorf, 1958; Mills, 1959). In his later writings, Parsons confronted this problem and attempted to include social change in his functionalist model.

Parsons's Theory of Social Change

Parsons (1961, 1966) came to see change not as something that disturbs the social equilibrium, but as something that alters it—so as to produce a new, and qualitatively different, equilibrium. In other words, social change occurs when internal or external strains (such as unemployment or war) throw the system out of balance. This imbalance provokes adjustments that help bring the system back into equilibrium once more—but the new equilibrium contains different social arrangements and cultural components than the previous one did. In short, social change is simply a means of getting from one form of social stability to another. A rough analogy might be the changes that take place over time in the human body. Internal and external factors (such as hormones or injuries) may throw the body out of its previous harmony, so it makes adjustments that lead to change. In due course, the body becomes different, yet balanced once more.

Parsons was particularly interested in the evolutionary changes that occur in a society as it grows more complex. This process, he argued, involves two related processes: *differentiation* and *integration*. In simple societies there are few institutions, and any one of them may have several functions—the family, for example, is responsible for reproduction, education, and economic production. When such a society grows more complex, differentiation takes place: different institutions, such as schools or the corporate economy, emerge to take over the functions that were previously undifferentiated. But the new institutions must be linked together, this time through integration. For example, new norms might evolve to help smooth the relationship between school and family, or law courts might emerge to resolve conflicts between government and corporations. In this way, society changes in the direction of greater complexity, but maintains its equilibrium because the new components are integrated with one another.

Parsons's work is an ambitious attempt to explain both social order and social change, although his focus is still overwhelmingly on the former. His theory remains limited, however, in that it deals only with the institutional changes that take place as a society grows more complex. Other functionalists have nevertheless accepted that tensions may cause social changes of many types, even in the most harmonious social system. Robert Merton (1968), for example, writes of the "strain, tension, contradiction, and discrepancy between the component parts of social structure" that may provoke social change. In so doing, however, he is borrowing concepts from conflict theories of change. As we shall see, a blend of conflict and functionalist ideas can prove fruitful.

Figure 19.8 *In a small-scale, preindustrial society, such as that of the Senufo tribespeople of West Africa, social institutions are undifferentiated: for example, the family is responsible for education, economic production, and many aspects of religious ceremony, political decision making, and so on. According to functionalist theory, social change consists largely of the process by which such functions are differentiated into several new, interrelated institutions as a society becomes more complex.*

Figure 19.9 *Although Karl Marx focused on class as the primary source of social change, modern conflict theorists emphasize a wide variety of tensions and competition as potential causes of change. In the 1960s, for example, conflict arose in the United States over the country's involvement in* *the Vietnam war, and eventually led to American withdrawal. In the 1980s, there has been considerable conflict in Poland between the nation's workers and its pro-Soviet bureaucratic elite—conflict that may bring about significant changes in that country's policies.*

Conflict Theory

The conflict theory of social change holds that many changes are caused by tensions between competing interests in society. Conflict theorists regard conflict as a normal, not an abnormal, process. They see change as a constant and inevitable feature of society, for they believe that the existing social conditions always contain the seeds of a different future. The conflict theory of change derives from the work of Karl Marx, but has been much modified by later sociologists.

Marx: Class Conflict

"All history," Marx and Engels wrote in *The Communist Manifesto* (1848), "is the history of class conflict." As we have noted earlier, Marx believed that the character of social and cultural forms is influenced by the economic base of society—specifically, by its mode of production and by the relationships that exist between those who own the means of production and those who work for them. History is the story of conflict between the exploiting and the exploited classes. In Marx's vision, this conflict would repeat itself again and again until capitalism was overthrown by the oppressed class. The victorious workers would then

create socialism, a new system in which the means of production would be owned by the public. Socialism would eventually be replaced by communism, in which all inequalities would be abolished and people would finally achieve true fulfillment of their human potential. In Marx's view, the most dramatic social changes occur through outright violence. Reviewing the evidence of the past, Marx declared that "violence is the midwife of history"; and, in a similar vein, the Chinese communist leader Mao wrote that "change comes from the barrel of a gun."

Modern Theorists: Social Conflict

Ralf Dahrendorf (1958) regards the view that "all history is the history of class conflict" as an "unjustifiable oversimplification." He is one of many modern conflict theorists who focus not just on *class* conflict but on *social* conflict in general. Most American conflict theorists are not Marxists, and although they acknowledge the importance of class, they point to other conflicts—perhaps between different nations, racial groups, political parties, religions, or regions. Tensions between such interests as management and workers, teachers and students, the old and the young, males and females, bureaucrats and the public, conservatives and liberals, "prolife" and "prochoice" advocates, and so on, are an enduring feature of modern social life. These and other conflicts are not necessarily class-based, yet they generate change when dissatisfied groups mobilize their resources in order to get what they want. New social and cultural arrangements continually emerge out of this competition, with the outcome generally favoring whichever group has the greatest power in the interaction (Tilly, 1978; Zald and McCarthy, 1979; Collins, 1974, 1979).

Conflict theory does not explain all forms of social change, but it does give us a means of analyzing some of the most significant events in history and contemporary society. It can be applied, for example, to the overthrow of feudalism and its replacement by capitalist industrialism, or to the civil rights and women's movements in the United States and continuing changes in patterns of race relations and gender roles. Yet it is not a comprehensive theory of social change. Conflict theory cannot, for example, tell us why technology is having such a dramatic effect on the rate of social change in the United States. It cannot tell us why forms of family organization are changing. Above all, it cannot tell us much about the future direction of social change. Even hard-line Marxists have been unable to predict successfully the countries, or the periods, in which socialist revolutions will occur, although they are able to provide plausible explanations of similar changes in the past. But a fully satisfactory theory must do more than explain history. It must also give us sufficient understanding of social dynamics for us to be able to predict, at least in broad outline, the future implications of present trends.

A Synthesis

No single contemporary theory seems able to account for all social change. Where, then, does our survey leave us?

The theory of sociocultural evolution seems promising. It fits the facts: societies generally tend to evolve from the small and simple to the larger and more complex, from the traditional to the modern. They do so in different ways, but a change in the mode of production is usually involved. The theory also explains why this evolution takes place. People will always seek the most efficient subsistence strategy—that is, the one that will give them the greatest return for their effort. In finding and exploiting more efficient strategies—such as industrialism rather than agriculture—people will produce a greater economic surplus. That surplus serves, in turn, as the foundation for further social and cultural diversification and development. The theory, then, gives us a general context for understanding social change.

What of functionalist and conflict theories? As usual, they seem at first sight to be at odds with one another. Functionalism emphasizes stability, integration, and shared values; conflict theory emphasizes change, tension, and coercion. But as we have seen on a number of occasions, the two approaches can often complement each other in the final analysis. The reason for this apparent paradox lies in the contradictory nature of society itself. Societies *are* stable, enduring systems, but they *do* experience conflict and continuous change. The functionalist and conflict approaches are merely focusing on different aspects of social reality: one mainly on stability, one mainly on change. There seems to be no logical reason, then, why the two theories cannot be integrated to a considerable extent. As we have noted, Merton has introduced the concepts of "strain" and "tension" from conflict theory into functionalist theory. In a similar vein, Lewis Coser (1956) has written about the "functions" of conflict in society. Conflict, Coser points out, can be functional for the social system because it prevents stagnation and generates necessary changes.

Evolutionary theory, in its multilinear form, is compatible with either functionalist or conflict theory. If we take the perspective of sociocultural evolution and combine it with functionalist or conflict theory—or, where appropriate, with both—we have the best general theory of social change. Each approach contributes to our overall understanding. Sociocultural evolution provides the broad framework in which society and culture undergo change toward greater complexity. Functionalist theory helps explain how, even in the midst of change, societies generally retain their order and stability. Conflict theory shows how competition over values and resources can generate social change as various groups try to further their interests. Throughout this book, in fact, we have located social phenomena (such as stratification, the family, or the political system) in a preindustrial, industrial, or postindustrial sociocultural context, and have then applied functionalist and conflict approaches to them. As a general theory of social change, this combination admittedly remains imperfect, but it does enhance our understanding of how and why societies change in the way that they do. We can apply this understanding to the phenomenon of social and economic development.

Figure 19.10 *As a result of social forces over which they have no control whatever, children born into different societies have quite different life chances. Most of the people living in the poorer societies of the "third world" will remain in poverty all their lives. The painting* Echo of a Scream, *by the Mexican artist David Alfaro Siqueiros, conveys the despair of this situation.*

Global Development and Underdevelopment

As we have seen throughout this book, one of the most significant of all social changes is the transition from a preindustrial to an industrial type of society. Yet only a handful of countries have achieved that transition. Accordingly, the various societies of the world can be roughly grouped into two categories. The ***developed countries*** are highly industrialized and comparatively affluent societies. Most of them are in Europe and North America, although there are a few, such as Japan and Australia, elsewhere in the world. The ***less developed countries*** are comparatively poor nations that have not achieved a predominantly industrial mode of production. These societies are mostly located in the "third world"—Africa, Asia, and Latin America.

In the developed countries, most people enjoy high standards of nutrition, housing, education, health care, workplace conditions, transport, social services, and other amenities. In contrast, the bulk of the people in the less developed countries are ill-housed, poorly nourished, chronically diseased, and impoverished. A few key facts convey some idea of the gap in living standards. In the developed nations, average life expectancy is seventy-three years; gross national product is over $9,500 per capita; 72 percent of the population live in cities; and nearly all adults can read and write. In the less developed countries, average life expectancy is fifty-eight years; gross national product is $700 per capita; 66 percent of the population live in rural areas; and a large part of the adult population cannot read or write.

In some societies, conditions are even more bleak: in Zaire, for example, the per capita gross national product is $170; in Sierra Leone, average life expectancy is thirty-four years; in Nepal, 82 percent of adults are illiterate. Most poignant of all, perhaps, is the contrast in infant death rates. In Norway, a highly industrialized country, 8 of every 1,000 babies die in the first year of life; in Gambia, a desperately poor country, the rate is nearly twenty-two times higher, 174 deaths per 1,000 births. To make matters worse, the less developed countries are experiencing a population explosion which is literally eating into their already meager resources. Three-quarters of the world's people live in the less developed countries, and at present growth rates, their population will actually double in a little more than thirty years (Population Reference Bureau, 1986).

As we noted earlier in this book, the "sociological imagination" enables us to see the link between private lives and social forces. An outstanding example of such a link is the contrast in life chances between people in developed and in less developed countries. A child born in, say, the United States or Switzerland is not an intrinsically better or more deserving person than one born in Ethiopia or Brazil. Yet because of social forces beyond individual control, each child faces the prospect of living out a lifetime under utterly different material conditions. Why should this be?

What can account for the fact that some societies have become heavily industrialized and economically advanced, while others are changing so much more slowly? Social scientists have offered two rather different explanations. One emphasizes a universal but uneven process of modernization and economic growth; the other focuses on a worldwide system of political and economic inequality.

The Modernization Model

Some social scientists view development in terms of *modernization,* a process of economic, social, and cultural change that facilitates the transition from preindustrial to industrial society. Modernization theorists claim that the various countries of the world are converging on a basically similar societal type, the modern industrialized society. Some 250 years ago, the developed countries of today also had rudimentary, preindustrial economies, but because they modernized relatively quickly, they now have productive economies that offer high living standards. During the same period, however, the poor countries have been slow to modernize. Differences in development, therefore, are largely the result of uneven modernization; but, as "modern" features diffuse from the developed to the less developed countries, they too will follow the path to industrialization and affluence (Rostow, 1960, 1962; Moore, 1979).

What kinds of change does modernization entail? Some modernization theorists emphasize a change in individual psychology. They claim that people in the developed societies are more likely to have a work ethic, a desire for achievement, a willingness to defer gratification, a sense of control over their destiny, a strong sense of individualism. In contrast, a lack of ambition, an orientation toward the present, a fatalistic outlook, and a weak sense of individualism are said to be typical of people in more traditional societies. Other modernization theorists emphasize sweeping structural changes in society. Developed countries, for example, invariably have a nuclear family system, which facilitates social and geographical mobility. Traditional societies are more likely to have an extended family system, in which kinship obligations encourage people to remain, physically and socially, where they started from. Similarly, modernization involves such features as heavy urbanization, extensive schooling, advanced technology, low population growth, a legal-rational political

Figure 19.11 *According to modernization theory, the less developed societies will achieve higher standards of living once they modernize and "catch up" with the more developed societies. This picture shows both sides of the border between a developed and a less developed society—the United States and Mexico.*

system, and a range of sophisticated services such as efficient transport, banking, and communications. On the whole, these features are lacking or inadequate in less developed countries, where government is usually authoritarian, the population is predominantly rural and ill-educated, and the necessary services are not in place (Lerner, 1958; McClelland, 1961; Haagen, 1962; Berman, 1982; Inkeles, 1983).

The modernization model implies that the less developed countries need only look to the developed ones to see the image of their own futures. They should even be able to hasten the modernization process—by internal political, educational, and other reforms, and by external infusions of capital, technology, and foreign aid. This approach seems to offer a fairly optimistic view of the world's future, but it runs into some difficulties. One problem is that the whole argument seems rather circular, for it is not clear whether modernization causes, helps, or results from development— or even whether development and modernization might be much the same process. A more practical problem is that the less developed countries, on the whole, are not catching up with the developed ones; indeed, in the 1970s and 1980s the gap in overall living standards has actually widened. It is beginning to look, in fact, as though the poorer countries may well be "stuck" in their present state for the foreseeable future. Why is this so?

Unhappily, the less developed countries face conditions very unlike those in which the developed countries first began to industrialize. The United States, for example, started out with abundant land and resources, a small, manageable population, and a domestic economy that was largely isolated from the rest of the world. In contrast, the less developed countries have large populations that put great strain on land and other resources, and they are junior partners in a world of intense economic competition. In fact, virtually all the less developed countries were brought into the global network after invasion and colonization by a few European powers—England, France, Spain, Portugal, Belgium, Germany, and the Netherlands. These European countries were not interested in building independent economies in their colonies. They simply used the colonies as a source of raw materials for their own developing economies, and as a captive market for their manufactured goods. Modernization in the third world may still be impeded by the legacy of that colonial dependency.

The World-System Model

Other social scientists, notably Immanuel Wallerstein (1979), view development in the context of the *world system,* a network of unequal economic and political relationships among the developed and the less developed countries. This international system consists of a "core" of highly industrialized countries, and a "periphery" of less developed countries that are dependent on and exploited by those at the core. World-system theorists point out that the peoples of the third world were quite capable of providing for themselves before "modern" ideas and technologies began to "diffuse" from the colonial powers. In fact, they claim, development and underdevelopment proceeded simultaneously over a period of more than two centuries as the richer countries financed their own industrial expansion by draining the surplus resources of the poorer ones. The colonial system finally broke down when the last of the colonies won their formal independence around the middle of the twentieth century. But by then a new international relationship had been established: *neocolonialism,* the informal political and economic domination of some societies by others, such that the former are able to exploit the labor and resources of the latter for their own purposes. In essence, the world system is a form of international stratification, with a wealthy minority enjoying a disproportionate share of the planet's resources and using various means—political, economic, and sometimes military—to maintain their position (Cockroft et al., 1972; Amin, 1976; Chirot, 1977; Chirot and Hall, 1982).

According to world-system theorists, the less developed countries are kept in a situation of permanent dependence primarily by the following three factors.

1. *Export dependency.* Before the colonial era, the third-world economies were diversified and self-sufficient. The European colonial powers totally reorganized these economies to produce a handful of products, like copper or coffee, for their own markets. A large part of the local population was forced to abandon traditional economic activities and to become wage laborers, producing goods not for their own use but for export. This situation has persisted, leaving the third-world countries dependent on world commodity prices— which they cannot control—for their exports and their livelihood. (One exception is oil. Until the 1970s, oil prices were set by the consumer nations of the developed world, but since then, OPEC, a cartel of mostly third-world oil producers, has had considerable influence over the price of this commodity. The effect has been a significant transfer of wealth from the developed countries to a few of the less developed ones—to the outrage of many people in the developed world.)

2. *The debt trap.* Many of the less developed countries are deep in debt, and some are getting in

deeper still. In 1986, for example, Mexico and Brazil both owed around $100 billion to foreign creditors, with little foreseeable prospect of being able to repay it. Why do less developed countries get into this situation? The reason is that their own economies do not provide enough capital for investment—but without that investment, they face further stagnation. Meanwhile, their restless and growing populations demand an escape from poverty through economic growth. So the governments borrow money from abroad, hoping to use it for economic expansion, which, in turn, should provide the means to repay the loan. But if the expansion does not take place, or if world commodity prices slump, or if interest rates rise, or if their currencies lose value, then the borrowers fall into the debt trap—a situation in which they have to borrow more money merely to pay the interest on what they already owe. The main creditors are American and West European banks and two international bodies dominated by the United States, the World Bank and the International Monetary Fund. The effect of the debt trap is thus to further reduce the less developed countries' control of their own destinies and to increase their dependence on the "core" countries of the world system (Dalmaide, 1984; Kaletsky, 1985).

3. *Multinational corporations.* As we noted earlier in Chapter 17 ("The Economic Order"), a ***multinational corporation*** is a corporate enterprise which, though headquartered in one country, conducts its operations through subsidiaries that it owns or controls around the world. The organizations, mostly based in the United States, Western Europe, and Japan, have become major actors on the international stage, for some of them are wealthier than many of the countries they operate in. The less developed countries often welcome the multinationals because they are a source of investment and jobs. Yet their presence has its drawbacks, for these organizations soon develop immense political and economic influence in the host countries. Development becomes concentrated in a few industries that are oriented to the needs of outsiders; profits are frequently exported rather than reinvested; and local benefits go mainly to a small ruling elite whose interests are tied to those of the foreigners rather than to those of their own people. The effect is to further increase export dependency and to limit the less developed countries' control of their own economies (Masden, 1980; Kumar, 1980; Bornschier and Hoby, 1981; Stack and Zimmerman, 1982).

In the world-system model, both development and underdevelopment result from competition for scarce global resources and the resulting domination of some societies over others. This approach implies that international inequalities can be resolved only if the less developed countries are able to achieve liberation and real autonomy over their destinies. But the world-system model also has

Figure 19.12 *According to world-system theorists, the countries of the world are divided into two main groups, with the developed countries exploiting the cheap labor and natural resources of the less developed ones. Extensive poverty in the third world results from a global imbalance in the distribution of wealth, and this situation is unlikely to change. The scene in this photograph is a typical slum in the Philippines.*

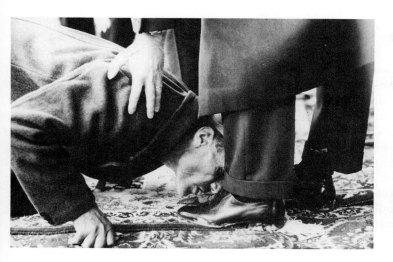

Figure 19.14 *The shoe in the first picture is that of the late shah of Iran, an absolute ruler who was installed in 1953 by the United States Central Intelligence Agency and who enjoyed American support until a successful revolution in 1979. The head in the second picture represents that of Ferdinand Marcos, who had firm U.S. backing as the virtual dictator of the Philippines until his people drove him from office in 1986. Notable for their arrogance, and greedy beyond the dreams of avarice, both rulers looted hundreds of millions of dollars from their respective public treasuries. The United States has often found itself supporting third-world juntas, dictators, and other authoritarian rulers, so long as they are anticommunist. In the Philippines, the United States withdrew support from Marcos in time to be able to retain friendly relations with the new government of that country; but in Iran, the United States supported the shah for too long. The revolutionary regime is hostile to the United States, which Iranians continue to regard as "the Great Satan."*

example of this trend, but it conforms to a widespread pattern. The final victors are usually the most disciplined and even ruthless of the revolutionaries. A revolution tends to be followed by the creation of a nondemocratic government, largely because the new regime fears challenges to its legitimacy, but authoritarian controls may be gradually lessened if the society becomes more stable.

One of the paradoxes of the modern age is that the United States—a country born in revolution and explicitly committed to the right of people everywhere to revolt against tyranny—has become the greatest antirevolutionary power on earth. Only in isolated situations like Afghanistan, where guerrillas are fighting a communist government, is the United States supportive of revolutionaries. For most of this century, the United States has directly or indirectly opposed revolutions in third-world countries, even when the targets have been authoritarian regimes or brutal dictatorships. And in several cases—such as Iran under the shah, Nicaragua under the Somoza family, or Zaire under General Mobuto—the original dictators were actually installed through direct or indirect American intervention.

The basic reason for this antirevolutionary policy is the fear that revolutions will result in socialist or communist governments. Such a situation could place local American economic interests in jeopardy, while yielding strategic or diplomatic benefits to the Soviet Union. Revolutionary movements are, indeed, often influenced or controlled by communists. The United States has therefore found it preferable to tolerate or actively support a variety of dictatorships, military juntas, and other authoritarian regimes that are reliably anticommunist. This policy is often futile, for many of the revolutions are successful anyway—for example, undemocratic governments that had enjoyed U.S. support have been overthrown in such countries as Cuba, Nicaragua, Angola, Zimbabwe, Mozambique, and Iran.

The ordinary people in impoverished and undemocratic countries of the third world probably know little of, and care even less about, the international rivalry between the United States and the Soviet Union. But they do know who seems to be on their side and who seems to be against them in their own struggle against tyranny. It is a sad irony that the United States, one of the world's greatest democracies, has become allied with authoritarian regimes, while the Soviet Union, one of the most totalitarian states on earth, has become a champion of the oppressed. As Jonathan Kwitny (1984) observes, this situation has created "endless enemies" for the United States, and much anti-American sentiment all over the world. He argues that American support for undemocratic regimes merely plays into the communists' hands, and suggests that a more appropriate role for the United States would be to encourage democratization in repressed third-world societies before a revolutionary situation develops. There are now some signs that such a policy is developing: in 1986, the United States helped to depose two dictators it had previously supported—Jean-Claude Duvalier in Haiti and Ferdinand Marcos in the Philippines—just at the point where successful revolutions seemed inevitable.

Predicting the Future

The Mexican writer Octavio Paz (1985) comments that the future "has no face and is sheer possibility." But to what extent does our present understanding of social change permit us to predict the future? We are able to do so within limits, particularly for societies that are less developed: we have a good idea, for example, of what industrialization will mean to an agricultural society. But when we look to our own future, we have no example to guide us. We can, however, make fairly confident predictions about specific areas of society. We can anticipate the likely effect of population growth and can project future trends in urbanization, for example. But when it comes to predicting the overall form of our society in the future, we are somewhat in the dark.

Nevertheless, there is no shortage of attempts to predict the future. Donella Meadows and her associates (1972) warn that modern societies will be "self-extinguishing" because they will collapse under the burdens of overpopulation, resource depletion, and pollution. Christopher Evans (1979) writes about the "micro millennium," a society in which life is transformed for the better by computers. Fred Hirsch (1976) declares that a future society will have to recognize limits to development, and will have to create a "steady state," no-growth economy. Alvin Toffler (1980) explains that humanity, after undergoing two waves of change as a result of the agricultural and industrial revolutions, is now witnessing a "third wave" of postindustrial change that will bring unprecedented opportunities. John Diebold (1985) prophesies the "information age," in which the very nature of jobs and work is transformed. William Ophuls (1977) describes a "scarcity society" in which depletion of resources leads to a lower standard of living and a strong, authoritarian state that regulates conflict among groups struggling for their piece of the pie. Julian Simon (1981) assures us that by using our "ultimate resource"—the ingenuity of our minds—we will enjoy ever more abundance. Jonathan

Schell (1982) surveys the evidence and concludes that the "fate of the earth" could be total destruction in a nuclear holocaust.

We cannot yet know whether there will be an ecological collapse, a micro millennium, a third wave, a scarcity society, a nuclear war, or any of the other future scenarios that are envisaged for us. All these are very different predictions, for the reason that each writer focuses on one or a few aspects of change in the modern world and projects this trend, largely through guesswork, into the future. Precise predictions about the long-term future will ever elude us: change always depends on the unique events that have gone before, and always has unique effects on the events that are still to come. In any case, accurate prediction of the course of history involves an insuperable logical flaw. If we knew what was to happen, we would be able to prevent it from happening—in which case the prediction would be false. The future may not be for us to know, but it is surely ours to make.

Figure 19.15 *Predicting the future is no easy task, for prophets are always bound by the assumptions of their own time and place, even though they may be unaware of the fact. The drawing on the opposite page, nearly a hundred years old, shows one Frenchman's view of what the twentieth century would be like. He extended his own assumptions—about fashions of dress, the use of cast iron in manufacturing, and architecture, for example—into the future, but with results that are wildly inaccurate. The painting,* Moonport, *was made in 1956 by the American artist Jim Powers, and attempts to portray life in the next century. Yet this vision, too, is beginning to seem dated (notice the tail fins on the automobile!). How might our contemporary views of the future look a hundred years from now?*

Summary

1.   Social change is the alteration in patterns of culture, social structure, and social behavior over time. The process is universal but occurs at different rates and in different ways. Social change is difficult to analyze because it involves so many factors, including future unknowns.

2.   Some specific sources of change are the influences of the physical environment; cultural innovation, which takes the forms of discovery, invention, and diffusion; population dynamics, such as population growth; technology, which generates changes in culture and society, sometimes causing a culture lag; and human action, including both individual actions and collective behavior and social movements.

3.   The most useful general theories of change are sociocultural-evolution theory, functionalist theory, and conflict theory. Early evolutionary theory was faulty, but modern sociocultural-evolution theory helps explain the evolution of societies from simple to more complex forms. Functionalist theory focuses mainly on social order, but Parsons saw change as a process by which the social equilibrium is altered so that a new equilibrium results. Conflict theorists see competition and tension as intrinsic to society and as the main source of social change. Marx emphasized class conflict, but later theorists have focused on social conflict in general. Taken together, the theories can help explain various aspects of change.

4.   The societies of the world may be roughly divided into developed countries and less developed countries, according to their degree of industrialization and economic growth. The modernization model explains development as a process of diffusion of certain characteristics from the developed to the less developed societies. The world-system model explains differences in development as a result of global patterns of inequality and exploitation.

7.   Revolutions are rare events, generally requiring several preconditions: widespread grievance, rising expectations, blockage of change, loss of legitimacy, and military breakdown. During this century the United States, fearing communist influence, has generally opposed revolutions.

8.   Although the future may be predicted in broad outline and sometimes in its specifics, there are practical and logical obstacles to knowing the future with much certainty.

Important Terms

social change (507)

discovery (510)

invention (510)

diffusion (510)

technology (511)

technological determinism (512)

culture lag (512)

collective behavior (514)

social movement (514)

sociocultural evolution (517)

developed country (521)   neocolonialism (523)

less developed country (521)   multinational corporation (524)

modernization (522)   revolution (525)

world system (523)   coup d'état (525)

Suggested Readings

BARNEY, GERALD O. *The Global 2000 Report to the President.* New York: Pergamon, 1982.

A summary of rather pessimistic projections about future economic and population trends in the world.

CHIROT, DANIEL. *Social Change in the Twentieth Century.* New York: Harcourt Brace Jovanovich, 1977.

A good survey of global social change, with a strong emphasis on the world-system model.

LAUER, ROBERT H. (ed.). *Perspectives on Social Change.* 3rd ed. Boston: Allyn and Bacon, 1982.

A useful survey of theory and research on the phenomenon of social and cultural change.

MOORE, WILBERT E. *World Modernization: The Limits of Convergence.* New York: Elsevier, 1979.

A careful analysis of global development in terms of a reevaluated modernization model.

NISBET, ROBERT T. *History of the Idea of Progress.* New York: Basic Books, 1979.

An elegantly written account of the Western idea that change implies progress toward something better.

OGBURN, WILLIAM F. *Social Change.* New York: Viking, 1950.

A classic work in the field. Ogburn presents his concept of "culture lag" and discusses the social disorganization that technological changes can create.

PASCARELLA, PERRY. *Technology: Fire in a Dark World.* New York: Van Nostrand Reinhold, 1979.

An interesting defense of the virtues of technology and technological advance in the modern world.

SKOCPOL, THEDA. *States and Social Revolutions.* New York: Cambridge University Press, 1979.

An important analysis of the preconditions for revolution, illustrated by actual cases.

TOFFLER, ALVIN. *The Third Wave.* New York: Morrow, 1980.

An account for the lay person of the implications of the transition to postindustrial society—the "third wave" after the agricultural and industrial revolutions.

CHAPTER 20

Collective Behavior and Social Movements

Most social behavior follows a regular and patterned course, for people generally conduct themselves according to the norms that define the behavior expected in various situations. Consider social behavior in your own sociology lecture class. People arrive more or less on time, they seat themselves in an orderly way, they listen and take notes, they ask questions at appropriate points, and they leave when the lecture is over. There are an infinite number of other things that a group of students could do in a room, but in practice everyone behaves in a fairly predictable fashion.

But suppose that a fire suddenly breaks out in the room. Immediately, the norms that prevailed a few moments before are suspended, and social behavior becomes unstructured and unpredictable. It is even possible, although certainly not inevitable, that a panic will result. If this happens, cooperative behavior will break down. There will be a disorderly rush to the exits, even though this response will actually reduce everyone's chance of escape. It is also possible that there will be little panic, especially if leaders emerge to direct an orderly exit. But whether the crowd panics or not, its behavior is no longer guided by everyday norms.

Certain social behavior, then, occurs in contexts in which social norms are unclear or absent. Often, in fact, it seems that the people concerned are collectively improvising new conduct on the spot. Sociologists call this phenomenon *collective behavior*—relatively spontaneous social action that occurs when people try to work out common responses to ambiguous situations. The concept includes a wide range of social behavior, much of it unusual or even bizarre: a crowd in panic, a lynch mob, a craze, fad, or fashion, rumors, riots, mass hysteria, and the ebb and flow of public opinion. We need only consider social action in a much more structured setting—say, in a formal organization such as a government bureaucracy—to ap-

Figure 20.1 *Collective behavior involves relatively unstructured and spontaneous social action: the usual norms that govern conduct become ambiguous or actually break down, so that people are unsure of how to behave. This photograph shows some of these features: notice, for example, how the "body language" of people in the crowd reveals their uncertainty. Not all collective behavior is quite so dramatic, but the same basic principles apply.*

preciate the contrast between the more routine activities of human groups and these episodes of collective behavior.

There is another form of social behavior that can also disturb the established patterns of social life—sometimes in more profound and lasting ways. This is the behavior of a ***social movement***—a large number of people who have joined together to bring about or resist some social or cultural change. Examples include the civil rights movement, the antinuclear movement, the gay rights movement, the women's movement, the environmental movement, and various revolutionary movements that aim at overthrowing entire governments.

Formerly, many sociologists regarded social movements as yet another example of collective behavior. Hostile to the efforts of social movements to change society, they dismissed these campaigns as examples of irrational collective behavior: they implied that there was nothing much wrong with society, so there must be something wrong with the people who challenged it. Today, however, most sociologists see social movements as an essentially separate phenomenon. Although collective behavior and social movements both represent a social response to problematic conditions,

social movements are relatively more structured and long-lasting. The members of these movements are more likely to formulate long-term goals and to actually *organize* their activities in pursuit of these objectives. Admittedly, some social movements—such as the "hippie" counterculture of the 1960s—seem to have many characteristics of collective behavior. Such movements have little organization, their norms are flexible, and their goals are vague. Many social movements, however, are highly structured, may endure for years, do hold clearly defined goals, and have well-established statuses, roles, and norms. For the analytic purposes of this chapter we will regard collective behavior and social movements as distinct forms of social action, while still recognizing that there are sometimes similarities between them.

Collective Behavior

Collective behavior is difficult for sociologists to study. To begin with, the behavior is so unstructured that it may be hard to find underlying regularities or to generalize from one specific incident to others. In addition, collective behavior often occurs as a spontaneous outburst, and cannot be easily created or reproduced for the convenience of the researcher. A third problem is that the concept of "collective behavior" is something of a grab bag, for it includes an extraordinary range of phenomena that seem to have unique features. Despite these difficulties, it is possible to draw up a checklist of the kinds of conditions that lead to these episodes.

Conditions for Collective Behavior

According to Neil Smelser (1962), collective behavior is essentially an attempt by people to alter their environment when they are under conditions of uncertainty, threat, or strain. For example, fads and crazes can be interpreted as a response to a situation of boredom; panics, as a response to a situation of threat; or riots, to a situation of strain and resentment. If people have a limited understanding of the problem that faces them, they are likely to respond in a relatively unstructured way—say, through a rumor that seems to explain the problem, or through mass hysteria. The more elaborate their understanding, the more structured their reaction will be, perhaps even taking the form of an organized social movement.

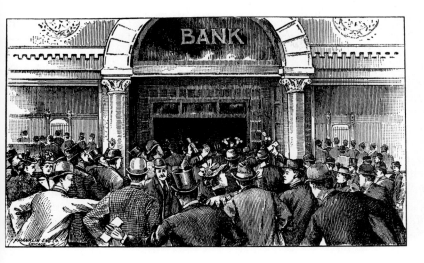

Figure 20.2 *Collective behavior will not occur unless certain preconditions are met, starting with the structural conditions that make the particular outburst possible in the first place. A typical episode of collective behavior was the financial panic that occurred at the beginning of the Great Depression of 1929. Banks did not have enough cash available to repay their depositors, so when rumors spread that the banks were in trouble, a self-fulfilling prophecy resulted—people rushed to withdraw their money, causing the banks to fail. Similarly, panicked investors tried to sell their stocks as quickly as possible, thus ensuring that stock prices would collapse. In trying to protect their individual interests, people worsened the situation for themselves and everyone else.*

Smelser argues that collective behavior involves six basic conditions, and will occur only if *all* six are met:

1. *Structural conduciveness.* This term refers to the surrounding conditions that make a particular form of collective behavior possible in the first place. For example, the financial panic that began the Great Depression was possible only because the United States had a stock market on which stock could be bought and sold in a short space of time, and a banking system in which banks never had enough ready cash to be able to repay all their depositors.

2. *Structural strains.* Any social condition that places a strain on people—poverty, conflict, discrimination, uncertainty about their future—encourages them to make a collective effort to relieve the problem. Prison riots, for instance, are examples of collective behavior that arises in response to a structural strain imposed by the confining and often tense nature of prison life.

3. *Generalized belief.* Structural conduciveness and structural strains are not in themselves sufficient to provoke collective behavior. People must also develop some general belief about their situation—by identifying the problem, forming their opinions about it, and defining appropriate responses. The members of racist lynch mobs in the United States, for example, had developed a generalized belief about the need to repress blacks and about methods for doing so. This belief was used to justify the collective action of lynching.

4. *Precipitating factors.* Even if the preceding conditions are present, collective behavior does not "just happen." Some event is necessary to trigger a response. In all the ghetto riots that have been studied, for example, a specific incident—usually one involving a conflict between local residents and the police—precipitated the outbreak of violence.

5. *Mobilization for action.* Even when the precipitating incident has taken place, collective behavior will not occur unless people join in the action. If leaders emerge and encourage the others to act, collective behavior will probably follow. When police raided a gay bar in Greenwich Village in New York in 1969, some of the patrons strenuously resisted arrest. Their example mobilized other patrons and sympathetic onlookers, and a serious riot followed. (In turn, the national publicity from this event helped launch a new social movement for gay liberation.)

6. *Failure of social control.* Even if the preceding conditions have been met, social control may prevent an outburst of collective behavior. For example, a crowd may obey a police order to disperse. Sometimes, however, social-control mechanisms may be too weak to prevent the behavior; or they may be counterproductive and may actually magnify the behavior. At this point, collective behavior is inevitable.

An Illustration: The Peoples Temple Mass Suicide

The Peoples Temple was an American religious sect founded in 1956 by Jim Jones, a preacher and community activist. Most of the members were poor and most were black, and it seems they were attracted by the sect's combination of fundamentalist Christianity and an activist philosophy that offered a refuge from, and a challenge to, hypocrisy, racism, and evil. In 1974 Jones cleared a 900-acre jungle site in the South American country of Guyana in order to set up a utopian community, far from the pressures of the secular world. In due course, over a thousand members of the sect emigrated to the new community, which their leader egotistically named Jonestown. What later happened in the jungle was one of the most extraordinary and tragic episodes of collective behavior in American history (J. Hall, 1979; Reston, 1981; Naipaul, 1981; Feinsod, 1981).

In this isolated environment, the members increasingly came to rely on and even to adulate their leader. At the same time, Jones's personality, apparently already unstable, began to deteriorate; in particular, he was subject to bouts of paranoid suspicion and delusions of grandeur. Rumors began to circulate in the United States that Jones sexually abused the members; that sadistic beatings were used to maintain discipline; that armed guards prevented people from leaving of their own free will. In 1978, California congressman Leo Ryan visited the community to investigate these rumors. Peoples Temple members shot and killed Ryan, three accompanying news reporters, and one defector from the sect. Jones, convinced by now that American or Guyanese authorities would destroy his community, decided that death would

be preferable—not just for himself, but for the entire sect. He summoned his followers and—taking care to tape-record the proceedings for posterity—he told them that life was no longer worth living, that they should "die with dignity" in a "revolutionary suicide protesting the conditions of an inhumane world." A large vat of Kool-Aid spiked with cyanide was prepared. The children in the community were the first to die; mothers watched as nurses squirted the poison into the mouths of infants. The adults followed; a few struggled and were forced to swallow the mixture, but most drank it voluntarily. At the end more than 900 Americans, including Jones, lay dead, their bodies piled two and even three deep around the main compound.

This bizarre episode cannot be satisfactorily explained in the simplistic terms of pop psychology (for example, that Jones had a magnetic personality and had brainwashed his followers); we need to examine the entire social context of the events in order to comprehend them. Smelser's theory provides a useful framework to achieve such an understanding, for each of his six preconditions was met at Jonestown.

1. *Structural conduciveness.* If someone like Jim Jones appeared in your sociology class and suggested that everyone immediately commit revolutionary suicide, he would probably be ignored, laughed at, or thrown out; the structural conduciveness that might make his appeal effective would be absent. In Jonestown, however, things were different: a close-knit group of highly disciplined people were isolated from the outside world and almost idolized their leader, a man who had brought meaning and hope to their lives. These conditions made an episode of collective behavior possible in the first place.

2. *Structural strain.* The members of the community were under great strain. They had come to Jonestown because it offered an escape from the secular world; now investigators from the United States government had arrived in the community, and, according to Jones, they intended to destroy it. Jonestown, in fact, had become a "total institution" like a prison or mental hospital, in which the inhabitants had lost the power to make meaningful decisions over their lives.

3. *Generalized belief.* Jones's own paranoid suspicions about the motives of outsiders had come to be shared by virtually all the members of the community: they felt that they were threatened by the Guyanese and American governments, by defectors, even by self-doubt. Jones, in fact, had made a habit of playing on the guilt feelings of the

Figure 20.3 *The 1978 mass suicide of American members of the Peoples Temple sect was one of the most remarkable episodes of collective behavior in the nation's history. The actions of the people concerned can be fully understood only in terms of their social context at the time.*

members by making them write letters of confession if they seemed to deviate from the beliefs of the group.

4. *Precipitating factors.* The precipitating factor in this case was the murder of a congressman and of representatives of the mass media. It is not clear whether these acts were committed on Jones's specific instructions, but they made it certain that full-scale investigations and prosecutions would follow and that the community's days would be numbered.

5. *Mobilization for action.* The mobilization of the members for action came when Jones summoned them to a meeting and, using all the sources of authority at his command, urged them to kill themselves. There had even been some preparatory mobilization for this event: on previous occasions, Jones had called the members together and ordered them to prove their faith by drinking from a poisoned vat—telling them only afterward that the drink was harmless.

6. *Failure of social control.* The social control that might have existed if the event had occurred elsewhere—in an American city, say—was entirely absent: there were no officials or even neighbors who might apply pressure on the group or on individuals within it to behave differently. Within the community, the leader demanded mass suicide, peer-group pressure supported it, and armed guards enforced it.

Crowds

In studying the contexts in which collective behavior takes place, some sociologists distinguish between a crowd and a mass. A **crowd** is a temporary collection of people who are in close enough proximity to interact with one another. Crowds are inherently unstable, for they have little structure, lack elaborate goals or plans, and cannot sustain themselves for long periods. The crowd provides an environment for certain kinds of collective behavior, such as riots or panics. On the other hand, a **mass** is a collection of people who are concerned with the same phenomenon without being in one another's presence. The members of a mass may not even know of one another's existence, yet they respond to the same events or issues. In a mass, kinds of collective behavior may occur that do not require close physical proximity, such as changes in fashions or in public opinion.

Many sociologists do not find this distinction between a crowd and a mass useful, however, particularly since certain kinds of collective behavior, such as rumor, can occur in both a crowd and a mass. Indeed, some sociologists believe there is really no such thing as a mass: they claim that a mass is simply a very diffuse crowd, in which members do interact with one another, if only through the media or through their everyday contacts with other people. Consider a classic case of mass behavior: the worldwide sense of shock and dismay at the assassination of President Kennedy on November 23, 1963. The emotional impact of Kennedy's murder was so great, and so universally felt, that virtually everyone who was old enough to be aware of the event still remembers exactly what they were doing when they first heard the news. Yet people did not learn of the event in total isolation—they heard of it from others, in person or through the media. They took emotional cues from their informants, passed on the news to those who had not heard it, and shared their feelings with friends, relatives, neighbors, coworkers, and even complete strangers. So in a sense, some sociologists argue, even the global mass of people can be considered a loose kind of crowd.

In any event, the most striking episodes of collective behavior—including destructive and apparently irrational outbursts—occur in the context of collections of people in close proximity. How can such behavior be explained? There are two main theories, contagion theory and emergent-norms theory.

Contagion Theory

Almost a century ago, the French social psychologist Gustave Le Bon (1960, orig. 1895) wrote a highly influential book on crowd behavior, *The Mind of the Crowd.* In this work, he advanced the **contagion theory,** which explains crowd behavior as a loss of individuality resulting from the infectious spread of emotion and action through the group. Le Bon argued that a "collective mind" emerges in crowd situations, with the conscious personality of the individual members almost disappearing.

According to Le Bon, the members of a crowd are dominated by a single impulse and act almost identically. People are less capable of rational thought once they are caught up in the frenzy of the crowd, and the "collective mind" is, in effect, merely the lowest common denominator of the emotions of the members. Le Bon was an aristocrat, and like most members of upper classes everywhere, he thoroughly disliked crowds of ordinary citizens, particularly dissatisfied ones. The reason, of course, was that a frustrated crowd

Figure 20.4 *Sociologists are particularly interested in why people in crowds seem to behave in a similar manner, particularly when their behavior is out of the ordinary. This picture shows the start of a riot at the 1985 European Soccer Cup final in Belgium—a riot that left forty people killed and hundreds more injured.*

readily becomes a militant mob, which is why governments facing popular unrest often go to great lengths to ban all public gatherings, even of as few as three people. Le Bon was firmly convinced that a person in a crowd "descends several rungs in the ladder of civilization. Isolated, he may be a cultivated individual; in a crowd, he is a barbarian; that is, a creature acting by instinct."

Today, Le Bon's idea of a "collective mind" is regarded as a quaint fallacy. The behavior of a crowd is the sum of the behavior of its individual members, and there is no crowd "mind" with an independent existence, any more than there is a crowd brain. Yet other parts of Le Bon's theory remain influential, and many social scientists have attempted to analyze the way individual personality seems to become merged into and influenced by the crowd.

For example, Herbert Blumer (1951) claims that people in crowds tend to respond to one another in an emotional, unreflecting way, creating a sort of ripple effect that he calls a "circular reaction." Blumer compares this circular reaction to the behavior of a herd of animals. One beast becomes agitated, and the others, noticing this behavior, begin to act in the same way. The excitement circles back to the first animal, which becomes still more aroused. The process is repeated and further intensified—and eventually a

stampede results. In the same way, a precipitating incident may arouse some members of a crowd. People start to mill around, perhaps talking, arguing, jostling. The mood of the crowd, which may range from anger to fear, is steadily amplified, until people become focused on some common objective and act without thinking rationally. Furthermore, people feel anonymous in the crowd context, and so are inclined to act less responsibly than they might otherwise do.

How valid is contagion theory? It does seem true that people in crowds tend to narrow their emotional and intellectual focus and allow themselves to be influenced by others. This is particularly true if the crowd is closely packed. For this reason, religious and political speakers whose audience is scattered about a room often ask those present to move to the front and fill any vacant seats. It is sometimes possible to manipulate crowds by "planting" supporters in the room with instructions to applaud at prearranged points: once a few people start clapping (or laughing or even coughing), others usually do so as well. However, these situations merely prove that people in crowds take cues from one another—not that their specific behaviors are in some way due to contagion. In fact, the concept of "contagion" is little more than a metaphor—it describes an apparently infectious process, but does not really explain it. Also, contagion theory tends to regard crowd behavior as a unique phenomenon, lying beyond the normal boundaries of social scientific investigation. Many sociologists argue strongly that crowd behavior can be analyzed in terms of the ordinary social and psychological processes that shape other human behavior.

Emergent-Norms Theory

Rejecting the idea that crowd behavior is unique, Ralph Turner and Lewis Killian (1972) propose the *emergent-norms theory,* which explains crowd behavior as the result of norms that arise in the course of social interaction among crowd members. They point out that in most social situations, people rely on existing definitions and norms to tell them "what's going on." In the case of some crowds, however, the situation is unclear, and people look to one another for cues. Because they are anxious and uncertain, they tend to be suggestible, and quickly accept whatever norms seem to be prevailing.

Turner (1964) challenges the assumption that crowd members behave in the same way as a result of "contagion." In fact, he argues, there are considerable differences in the motives, attitudes, and actions of crowd members. Some of those present may be impulsive participants, others passive supporters, others dissidents, others passersby who have become onlookers, others opportunistic individuals who are joining in "for the hell of it." The unanimity of crowds is often an illusion. Even in the midst of a riot, people may have varying motives, intentions, and behaviors. Subsequent research has generally confirmed that crowd members often act and think very differently from one another (McPhail and Wohlstein, 1982).

According to emergent-norms theory, seemingly unified crowd behavior is simply another example of a common social phenomenon, conformity to the group. Group norms define appropriate behavior in the crowd situation and arise from the visible actions of a few people. In the ambiguous crowd situation, these few activists are able to define the norms—whether they are norms regarding applause, violence, or anything else—for most of the other members. Many of the others do not agree with the direction that is being taken, but out of fear of ridicule, coercion, or even personal injury, they refrain from offering opposition. As a result, casual observers may believe that the crowd is unanimous. Crowd behavior can thus be explained in the same terms as other social behavior: that is, it is influenced by the prevailing social norms. The only difference is that the crowd itself improvises the norms on the spot and then starts to enforce them, informally, on its members. In fact, we have already seen examples of such conduct in Chapter 7 ("Social Groups"), in our discussion of bystander apathy. This phenomenon occurs when people look to others for cues on how to react to an apparent emergency—and if others appear unconcerned, the individual bystander is unlikely to react any differently.

Mobs

As Herbert Blumer (1951) points out, there are four basic types of crowd. A *casual* crowd consists of a loose collection of individuals who have little or no purpose in common, such as people who gather at the scene of a street accident. A *conventional* crowd is one that follows well-established norms, such as an audience at a graduation ceremony. An *expressive* crowd consists of people who are looking for some personal gratification in groups like a religious revival meeting or a rock concert. And an

acting crowd, as the name implies, is a crowd in action—perhaps rioting or fleeing. Of course, a precipitating event like a fire or explosion can easily turn one of the other types into an acting crowd.

Although the acting crowd is the least common type, it is sometimes the most socially significant—particularly when it takes the form of a **mob,** an emotionally aroused crowd intent on violent or destructive action. Although mobs usually have leaders and impose strong conformity on their members, they have limited objectives and are a particularly unstable form of collective behavior. But their hostile outbursts pose a direct challenge to social order and to political authority. At times, mobs have even helped change the course of history: the French Revolution, for example, was precipitated by a mob assault on the notorious Paris prison, the Bastille.

One example of mob behavior, common in American history but extremely rare elsewhere, is the lynch mob. Lynching is part of an American vigilante tradition, in which self-appointed groups of citizens, in order to serve their own version of law and order, kill people whom they define as criminal or undesirable. Lynching is thus a curious combination of moral self-righteousness and brutal sadism. The practice has historically taken place primarily in the West and the South. Until the

Figure 20.5 *This picture shows a lynching in the 1930s—one of more than 3,000 that occurred in the United States during the first half of this century.*

turn of the century the victims were both white and nonwhite, but during this century they were increasingly and overwhelmingly black. During the Reconstruction period after the Civil War, "nigger hunts" were organized in which whole groups of freed slaves were rounded up and murdered: in the decade 1889–1899, some 1,875 lynchings were reported, and many more doubtless went unrecorded (Cantril, 1963). Between 1900 and 1950, well over 3,000 people were lynched in the United States, fewer than 200 of them white. Contrary to popular belief, lynching of blacks was not usually associated with charges of sexual offenses against white women. Rape or attempted rape was allegedly involved in only one-fourth of the cases. Other blacks were hanged, shot, mutilated, and burned to death for such offenses as "trying to act like a white man," "making boastful remarks," "insisting on voting," "giving poor entertainment," "being too prosperous," and "riding in a train with white passengers" (Raper, 1933).

Virtually all the lynchings recorded in this century were the result of mob action, often by the Ku Klux Klan and almost always with little or no opposition from social-control agencies. Local social norms, in fact, appeared to allow police and prison officials to give mere token resistance to lynching attempts, and even this resistance was tolerated only because it would safeguard the officials in the event of a subsequent inquiry. Participants in lynch mobs were typically whites of very low social status, and their acts may be interpreted as a venting of their frustrations onto a defenseless scapegoat group. The lynch mob now seems to have faded from the American scene, to be replaced by less spontaneous forms of violence, such as the firebombing of homes.

An important form of mob behavior is the riot, a hostile outburst aimed at the creation of disorder through attacks on property, people, or both. Rioters are typically people who lack significant access to power, and so resort instead to destructive action in order to vent their feelings. The riot has a long history in the United States, and many previous outbreaks were much more bloody than those of recent decades. Extensive antidraft riots took place in New York in 1863 when working-class whites protested attempts to draft them into the Civil War. Labor history in the United States was marked by bitter conflict and riots until the 1930s. Serious race riots took place in many cities earlier in this century, notably in Chicago in 1919 and Detroit in 1943. These riots were initiated by white mobs who engaged mainly in acts of violence against individual blacks.

Figure 20.6 *Urban riots have been a recurrent feature of the American scene. The first picture shows striking workers rioting in New York in 1889; the second shows a racially motivated riot in Miami in 1983. Riot participants are generally disaffected citizens who have minimal access to power and influence.*

Blacks initiated extensive ghetto riots in the 1960s. In contrast to those of the 1940s and 1980, these riots were directed primarily against property rather than people. Although the police and national guard who attempted to suppress the riots were mostly white, these disturbances were not "race" riots as such; there was little interracial conflict between ordinary citizens. The worst of the riots took place in over twenty cities in 1967 and caused so much concern that a National Commission on Civil Disorders was appointed to investigate them. The commission reported that in every instance there had been a reservoir of growing discontent, and that a single precipitating factor, usually involving white police, had sparked the riot. Efforts at social control had often aggravated the situation, leading to fresh and more extensive outbursts, and exaggerated rumors had often heightened tension on the part of both rioters and police. The underlying cause of the riots, the commission found, was frustration and resentment at a society that promised equality but did not deliver it. More recent riots with racial and ethnic overtones occurred in Miami in 1980 and again in 1983.

Panics

A *panic* is a form of collective behavior in which people faced with an immediate threat react in a fearful, spontaneous, and uncoordinated way. This behavior causes cooperative social relationships to break down, often with the result that the people's fear and danger are actually increased.

The progress of a panic follows a fairly typical course. A sudden crisis occurs; people experience intense fear; normal social expectations are disrupted; each individual tries desperately to escape from the source of danger; mutual cooperation breaks down; and the situation becomes even more threatening as a result. Panics are especially likely to occur in unusual conditions in which everyday norms have little relevance, such as fires, floods, shipwrecks, earthquakes, or military invasions. Some kind of response is necessary in these situations, but there are few, if any, social norms that specify an appropriate reaction. Thus, when a passenger aircraft makes a crash landing, people may attempt to flee before fire breaks out and causes an explosion, but they only succeed in hampering themselves and others by creating bottlenecks at the exits. Awareness of the bottlenecks may lead to increased panic, with people fighting and trampling one another in the effort to escape. Despite intensive training of airline personnel in emergency evacuation procedures, a high proportion of passenger fatalities are caused by a panic that prevents people from escaping in time.

The most dramatic panics are those that occur in situations of extreme emergency. In 1903, for example, a fire broke out in Chicago's Iroquois Theater. The fire was soon extinguished and did little damage to the building—but over 600 people died, smothered or trampled to death in a panic-stricken rush to the exits. Bodies were piled eight deep in the bottlenecks, many with heel marks on their faces and some with clothes and even flesh torn from their bodies. A similar panic occurred when a fire broke out in the Beverly Hills Supper Club in 1977: some 164 people died because the exits were blocked by the rush to escape.

We might expect that people would panic in the aftermath of major natural or technological disasters such as earthquakes or poison-gas spills, but in fact they rarely do so. Panics tend to occur immediately before or in the first moments of a threatening event, not afterward. Panic is such an extreme emotional state that it cannot be sustained for long; if the threat persists, the result is more likely to be shock than continued panic. Major disasters actually produce not less but *more* structure and cohesion in the communities affected. Once the initial stress of an event like a hurricane or a bombing has worn off, people tend to take on new roles and extra communal duties, going out of their way to help neighbors and even strangers (Raphael, 1985; Turner, Nigg, and Paz, 1986).

Figure 20.7 *Natural or technological disasters usually do not lead to panic and social disintegration. Rather, they tend to produce increased social cohesion, with people abandoning their normal roles in order to help one another. The picture shows a rescue after a volcanic eruption led to a mudslide that buried a Colombian town in 1986.*

Rumors

A *rumor* is information that is transmitted informally from anonymous sources. A rumor may be false, true, or a combination of truth and falsehood. Its origin is usually difficult to check, for it is passed along outside the formal communications system of press, TV, government statements, and the like. The spreading of a rumor is itself a form of collective behavior, and rumors may in turn be an important element in virtually all other kinds of collective behavior. For example, in a strained situation such as an excitable, milling crowd, provocative rumors can easily stimulate mob action.

Rumors are especially likely to arise in situations where people are deprived of information or where they do not trust the official information they are given. A rumor is thus a substitute for hard news: people want information in doubtful or ambiguous situations, and rumor fills their need if reliable information is lacking (Rosnow and Fine, 1976). One insight into the importance of rumor in a tense, strained situation came in the aftermath of serious riots that took place in Detroit in 1967, when a newspaper strike eliminated an important source of "official" information. A rumor-control center was established in the city, and within less than a month it had received some 10,000 calls from people wanting confirmation of rumors they had heard, including reports of concentration camps for blacks and incidents of interracial violence and even castration (Rosenthal, 1971).

The way rumors are passed on has been quite thoroughly studied through the use of controlled experiments and analyses of actual cases. Experiments have usually been sophisticated versions of the children's game of "pass it on." People are given a story and asked to spread it to others, and then various versions of the rumor are compared. Gordon Allport and Leo Postman (1947) showed that what happens to the rumor depends on its content, on the number of people involved in the chain of transmission, and on their attitudes toward the rumor. Some rumors change little, but others, especially those that excite emotions, may be severely distorted. In general, part of the content drops out and the remainder is organized around some dominant theme. The ultimate form of the rumor is often influenced by the special interests of the people involved, because they tend to reshape and pass on those parts of the rumor that fit their preconceptions about the subject matter.

Tamotsu Shibutani (1966) points out that the transmission of a rumor is a "collective" effort, in that many people contribute to the spread of a rumor, and they can play many different roles in doing so. Some take the role of "messenger" by relaying the rumor. Some take the role of "interpreter" by placing it in context and speculating on its implications. Others may be "skeptics" who urge caution and express doubt. Some become "protagonists," forcefully arguing in favor of one interpretation rather than another. Others play the role of "decision makers" and try to initiate action on the basis of the rumor. Most people become an "audience" and are mere spectators in the process. A rumor can thus be seen as a form of communication in which people pool their resources to construct a meaningful interpretation of an ambiguous situation. In doing so they may sometimes improve the accuracy of the rumor rather than distort the truth.

The Death of Paul McCartney

A classic example of rumor as a form of collective behavior occurred in 1969 when a story about the death of a Beatle, Paul McCartney, spread to at least three continents within a few days. According to the rumor, McCartney had died in an auto accident some years previously, but his record company had replaced him with a look-alike and persuaded the remaining Beatles to hush up the event in the interests of future album sales.

In the weeks following, thousands of people ransacked Beatles albums in search of clues to "prove" the rumor. After playing records in the normal way and discovering many lyrics supposedly referring to the death, ingenious investigators began to play them backward, and found even more startling evidence. On one track, "Revolution No. 9," for example, a ghostly voice was heard intoning "Turn me on, dead man." On the front cover of the *Sergeant Pepper* album, a hand was spotted above McCartney's head—a symbol of death, it was alleged, in ancient Greek or perhaps Indian mythology—while McCartney himself wore an armband reading "OPD," presumably short for "Officially Pronounced Dead." On the back cover of the album, moreover, all the Beatles were facing outward—except McCartney, who had his back turned to the camera. And in the *Magical Mystery Tour* album photograph, McCartney was found to be wearing, significantly, a black carnation. Eventually, investigators noted that the word "Beatles" on the reversed cover of *Magical Mystery Tour,* if viewed with an appropriate squint, yielded a London telephone number, whereupon the owner

Figure 20.8 *In their search for evidence to confirm the rumors of Paul McCartney's death, Beatles fans looked for and found hidden meanings on album covers. On the* Abbey Road *cover, the Beatles appeared to be walking in funeral procession. John Lennon was in white (the priest), Ringo Starr was in a black suit (the undertaker), McCartney was barefooted, out of step, and had his eyes closed (the corpse), and George Harrison was in working clothes (the gravedigger). To clinch matters, a car in the background had the registration number 28IF, meaning—what else?—that McCartney would have been twenty-eight if he were still alive. By such imaginative theorizing, distraught fans found dozens of similar "clues" on album covers and in song lyrics, and the rumors multiplied accordingly.*

of the number, a British journalist, received hundreds of calls—most of them from the United States and most of them collect—from determined Beatles fans. When repeated denials by record-company officials failed to have much impact on the rumor, Paul McCartney finally squashed it himself, while admitting, "If I were dead, I'd be the last to know about it."

To understand the spread of this irrational rumor we must consider the relationship of the Beatles to the youth culture of the time. The Beatles were by far the most popular and influential rock group. They had pioneered or spread a number of innovative trends, not only in music but also in fashions (notably long hair for males) and in fads (such as dabbling in Eastern religion and using psychedelic drugs as a route to new consciousness). For this reason, *any* rumor about the Beatles was likely to spread; there was an eager audience for news about all their doings, however trivial. But why should this particular rumor have been so widely believed? Part of the reason was that there was already a shortage of hard news about the group, for they were secretly in the process of breaking up. In fact, the Beatles had not appeared together in public for several years, so it would have been at least possible for a fake McCartney to have been substituted in records and photographs. Also, the rock audience was accustomed to analyzing rock lyrics for hidden significance, and the surrealistic images of many Beatles songs lent themselves to whatever interpretation people chose to put on them. Moreover, several leading rock stars had died in the eighteen months preceding the McCartney rumor, providing an atmosphere in which the story seemed more credible. Finally, there was growing disillusion in the "counterculture," which appeared to be disintegrating from within. It is not surprising that this anxiety and disillusion were projected through rumor onto the youth movement's most prominent symbol, the Beatles.

The Satanic Logo

In 1982, rumors spread among some Christian fundamentalist groups in the American South and Southwest that Procter & Gamble, one of the major household-products corporations, was engaged in devil worship. According to the rumor, a vice president of the company had admitted on television, on the "Phil Donahue Show," that a percentage of the corporation's profits was "given to Satan." Further proof, according to the rumor, was a satanic device that appeared on all the company's packages, a logo in the form of a man's face surrounded by stars.

Procter & Gamble quickly tried to stop the rumor. Company officials announced publicly that the symbol, which had been on its products since 1882, merely represented the man in the moon—a popular graphic at the time—with stars representing the thirteen colonies. Additionally, the company filed lawsuits against individuals who were believed to be spreading the rumor. Representatives of the Donahue show also denied that the

Figure 20.9 *This logo, used on Procter & Gamble household products for more than a century, came under attack in 1982 when some fundamentalist groups became convinced that it was a satanic device.*

purported interview had ever taken place. At first the rumor seemed to die down, but it resurfaced again in 1985, this time spreading to the Northeast and even to some Catholic groups. Again Procter & Gamble resisted the rumor, by calling press conferences, distributing statements to churches and schools, and even establishing a toll-free hotline, which drew thousands of inquiries. But these efforts have been to no avail, and the company, perhaps deciding the logo was more of a headache than it was worth, removed the century-old symbol from many of its packages.

What are we to make of this rumor? It appears to have been a response by some fundamentalists to a situation of ambiguity and uncertainty—the problem of identifying who their enemies are. Some fundamentalist preachers, including certain television evangelists, regularly blame social and moral decay on "secular humanists," apparently a conspiratorial group of liberals and atheists who promote everything the fundamentalists abhor, from sexual permissiveness to the theory of evolution. However, there is no organization of secular humanists, no leadership that claims to speak for them, and no direct evidence that such people even exist. Some fundamentalists, it seems, therefore looked for the enemy in certain sources of

power and influence—large corporations and the media. Procter & Gamble was a likely target at the time, for a fundamentalist group, Coalition for Better Television, was urging a consumer boycott of companies that sponsored shows it considered morally offensive. Procter & Gamble, which has a $500 million annual advertising budget, was inevitably in the line of fire, and its name had been circulated on lists of potential boycott candidates. Phil Donahue, too, was an obvious ingredient for the rumor, since his show has the reputation of viewing social problems from a liberal viewpoint. It seems that somebody, somewhere, noticed an occult-seeming logo on the packages of a suspect company—and, in speculating about it, started a grass-roots rumor that a mighty corporation could do nothing to stop.

Urban Legends

Ancient peoples, such as the Greeks and the Romans, had a rich tradition of folklore. Many of these oral tales recounted the exploits of legendary heroes whose deeds set an implicit example for others to follow: when listeners heard about Jason's search for the golden fleece, Hercules's many labors, or Ulysses's quest for adventure, they learned moral lessons about human behavior. We no longer tell quite this kind of tale in the modern world, but we do have a form of contemporary folklore known as ***urban legends***—realistic but untrue stories with an ironic twist concerning recent alleged events. Like rumors, these "legends" are a collective reaction to situations of ambiguity.

According to Jan Brunvand (1981), who has collected many of these stories in hundreds of different versions, urban legends have three necessary ingredients: they have a strong story appeal, they seem believable, and they teach a lesson. The legends are an integral part of the culture, passed along by people who believe the truth lies one or two informants back down the line of transmission of the tale. The legends gain credibility from specific references to time and place, or to authorities who supposedly served as the source of the information. The physical settings of the events are usually close by, and the event in question typically happened to a "friend of a friend" or someone equally close.

A fairly typical urban legend, known to folklorists as "The Boyfriend's Death," goes as follows:

This happened just a few years ago out on the road that turns off 59 highway by the Holiday Inn. This couple were parked under a tree out on this road. Well, it got to be time for the girl to be back at the dorm, so she told her boyfriend that they should start back. But the car wouldn't start, so he told her to lock herself in the car and he would go down to the Holiday Inn and call for help. Well, he didn't come back and he didn't come back, and pretty soon she started hearing a scratching noise on the roof of the car. "Scratch, scratch . . . scratch, scratch." She got scareder and scareder, but he didn't come back. Finally, when it was almost daylight, some people came along and stopped and helped her out of the car, and she looked up and there was her boyfriend hanging from the tree, and his feet were scraping against the roof of the car. This is why the road is called "Hangman's Road."

Various other versions of the tale have the boyfriend skinned, decapitated, or hanging upside down, so that his fingernails scrape the roof of the car. The moral, of course, is that young people should not be "making out" in cars in secluded places, and the tale reflects the ambiguity felt by parents over the way their offspring can isolate themselves by means of the automobile. A similar tale, "The Hook," which has appeared in communities all over the United States, found its way into the popular "Dear Abby" newspaper column:

Figure 20.10 *Many urban legends concern automobiles, and particularly the dangers that might face teenage boys and girls who drive off alone. These legends express public concern about the way automobiles have made it possible for young people to gain immediate privacy away from parental control.*

DEAR ABBY: If you are interested in teenagers, you will print this story. I don't know whether it's true or not, but it doesn't matter because it served its purpose for me:

A fellow and his date pulled into their favorite "lovers' lane" to listen to the radio and do a little necking. The music was interrupted by an announcer who said there was an escaped convict in the area who had served time for rape and robbery. He was described as having a hook instead of a right hand. The couple became frightened and drove away. When the boy took his girl home, he went around to open the car door for her. Then he saw—a hook on the door handle! I don't think I will ever park to make out as long as I live. I hope this does the same for other kids.

JEANETTE

Legends about putting a living creature in an oven have circulated for decades. In one of them, "Hot Dog," an old lady (or a young child) puts a pet in a microwave in order to dry it off—an implicit warning about the unknown dangers of microwaves. A related version, widely circulated in the 1960s and still reappearing periodically, is "The Hippie Babysitter." In this one, a teenage babysitter, high on drugs, puts an infant into an oven thinking the baby is a turkey. This legend has two morals: first, don't trust strangers with your children; and second, drugs make you crazy.

One common contemporary legend is "Snake in the Blanket" (or blouse, sweater, carpet, or other fabric):

A woman was looking through the blouses at K-Mart and stuck herself with a pin. At least that's what she thought. It hurt so she went on home. Later her hand started swelling so she called the doctor. He examined it and said she hadn't stuck it with a pin, but that it had been bitten by a snake. An investigation was held at the K-Mart and two snakes were found in with the blouses. They discovered that the blouses had come over here from Hong Kong and that the snakes had apparently been in with the blouses.

The common feature of all these snake tales is that the fabric was imported from a foreign country. Moral: don't buy imported goods.

Perhaps the commonest legends of all concern the contents of food in foreign or fast-food restaurants—worms or kangeroo meat in the local McDonald's hamburgers, for example. A classic version of this legend is "Kentucky Fried Rat":

Two couples stopped one night at a notable carry-out for a fried chicken snack. The husband returned to the car with the chicken. While sitting there in the car eating their chicken, his wife said, "My chicken tastes funny." She continued to eat and continued to complain.

After a while the husband said, "Let me see it." The driver of the car decided to put the light on and then it was discovered that the woman was eating a rodent, nicely floured and fried crisp. The woman went into shock and was rushed to the hospital. It was reported that the husband was approached by lawyers representing the carry-out and offered the sum of $35,000. The woman remained on the critical list for several days. Spokesmen from the hospital would not divulge the facts about the case and nurses were instructed to keep their mouths shut. And it is also reported that a second offer was made for $75,000, and was refused. The woman died and presumably the case will come to court.

This legend has two obvious morals: first, don't trust fast foods; and second, if you have a problem, sue somebody. However, the legend also contains another more subtle lesson. In an analysis of some 115 different versions of "Kentucky Fried Rat," Gary Fine (1980) found that the victim is always a woman—one who is neglecting her traditional role as food preparer and who, as one version states, resorted to fast food because "she didn't have anything ready for supper." The fried rat is her reward.

Urban legends, then, are a collective if indirect response to ambiguities of life, such as teenage independence and sexuality, drug use, foreign influences, and changing gender roles.

Mass Hysteria

Mass hysteria is a form of collective behavior involving widespread anxiety, caused by some unfounded belief. The hysteria may be fairly localized within a specific community, or it may be quite extensive in the society as a whole. As a result of their anxiety, people behave in irrational ways in order to protect themselves. Episodes of mass hysteria are self-limiting, for the absurdity of the situation eventually becomes so apparent that the anxiety dissipates. We can illustrate this process through three specific examples.

The Martian Invasion of Earth

In 1938 a radio dramatization of H. G. Wells's novel about an invasion from Mars, *The War of the Worlds,* was broadcast in the New York area. The program took the form of a music concert that was suddenly interrupted by news bulletins and eyewitness accounts of an alien attack in progress. The result was mass hysteria and even outright panic, involving perhaps as many as 1 million of the 6 million people who heard the broadcast.

Although an announcer had made the fictional nature of the program clear at the outset, people who tuned in late heard "on the spot" descriptions of the havoc wreaked by horrible-looking creatures from outer space. Many of them accepted this broadcast as fact, not fiction. Some of them hid in cellars. Others bundled their children into their cars and drove as fast as they could from the scene of the supposed invasion. Others telephoned their relatives to give them the terrible news and to say farewell. Others simply prayed and waited for the inevitable end. Crowds gathered excitedly in public places, and fresh rumors about the invasion were generated.

Why did such an improbable tale of invasion from outer space have such a devastating effect? One reason was undoubtedly that the "bulletin" format, with comments from supposed scientific experts and public officials, gave a certain credibility to the events. Equally important was the fact that in this pretelevision age people relied heavily on the radio for up-to-the-minute news, much of which at this time dealt with the growing tensions in Europe, which stood on the brink of World War II. Listeners were glued to their radio sets as never before, had learned to expect interruptions of their scheduled programs, and anticipated that these interruptions might deal with conflict and warfare. In addition, knowledge of other planets was far less extensive than it is today. Observations of Mars had led some astronomers to the mistaken conclusion that its surface was criss-crossed by "canals," presumably constructed by highly intelligent Martians. Belief in the possibility of advanced life forms on Mars was quite widespread among the public (Cantril, 1940; Koch, 1970).

The Seattle Windshield-Pitting Epidemic

In late March 1954, Seattle newspapers carried occasional reports of damage to automobile windshields in a city eighty miles to the north—damage that the police suspected was caused by vandals. On the morning of April 14, newspapers reported windshield damage in a town only sixty-five miles away, and later that day similar cases were reported only forty-five miles from the city limits. On the same evening, the mysterious windshield-pitting agent struck Seattle itself: between April 14 and April 15, more than 15,000 people called the Seattle police department complaining about windshield damage, which usually consisted of small pitting marks. On the evening of April 15, the mayor of Seattle dramatically announced that the pitting was "no longer a police matter" and called on the state governor and the president of the United States for help. Yet on April 16 police received only forty-six complaints; on April 17, only ten; and thereafter, none at all. The epidemic was over almost as soon as it had begun.

Careful scientific analysis of the pitted windshields revealed that the amount of pitting increased with the age and mileage of the car in question, and that there was no evidence of pitting that could not be explained by ordinary road damage. What had happened was that the residents of Seattle, for the first time, had started to look *at* their windshields instead of *through* them. In a study of the epidemic, Nahum Medalia and Otto Larsen (1958) found that for two months before the episode, Seattle newspapers had been printing reports about recent H-bomb tests in the Pacific and the resulting radioactive fallout, "hinting darkly at doom and disaster." The epidemic, they suggest, may have served to relieve the tensions that had been built up, if only by focusing these vague anxieties on a very narrow area of experience, automobile windshields.

AIDS Hysteria

A more diffuse form of mass hysteria is the recent public concern over the contagiousness of AIDS. Although the disease was first reported in 1981, it was largely ignored by the media until 1985, when it suddenly became headline news. Responding to public concern, scientists and health officials gave assurances that AIDS is not casually transmitted. In particular, they repeatedly pointed out that none of the medical attendants or family members of the 13,000 people diagnosed with AIDS up to that time had become infected through their own casual contact with the patients. A large part of the population, however, was unconvinced. A 1985 *New York Times*/CBS News poll found that 80 percent of the public claimed to "know a lot about AIDS"— but 47 percent thought the disease could be spread through drinking glasses; 32 percent, through kissing; 28 percent, from a toilet seat; and 12 percent, from the touch or presence of an infected person. Many people acted on these beliefs. In some parts of the country, for example, police and other officials who might have to deal with AIDS patients were issued protective gear, such as gloves and masks. Some people refused to work with an AIDS victim, threatening to leave their jobs unless the person was fired. Camera crews walked off the set of TV programs in which people with AIDS were to be interviewed. In some places, notably New York City, many parents kept their children home from school rather than risk having them come into contact with others infected with the disease— although, since well over 1 million Americans were unknowingly carrying the AIDS virus at that time, the chance of such contact was at least as great in the street or department store.

Why this irrational fear of casual infection with AIDS? The precipitating incident in 1985 was the death from the disease of the movie actor Rock Hudson—a person who was well "known" to virtually all Americans, though his homosexuality was not. Publicity over this event gave the disease familiarity, and touched off deeper concerns. AIDS arouses ambiguous feelings in many people: in fact, a 1985 Gallup poll found that one American in five believes AIDS is "a judgment from God." AIDS hysteria was particularly noticeable, too, in communities where the media had emphasized the emotive aspects of the disease: the sensationalist *New York Post*, for example, had been running stories along the lines of gay-bug-kills-granny.

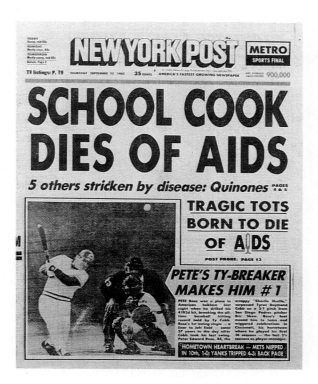

Figure 20.11 *Outbreaks of AIDS hysteria were particularly common and intense in areas where the local media treated the disease in a sensationalist way. In New York, where the* New York Post *repeatedly played on people's fears, many parents kept their children home from school for fear that they might somehow "catch" the disease.*

Additionally, in an age of "wonder drugs" and "miracle cures," the appearance of a new, lethal, and incurable disease was unexpected and threatening. The problem of uncertainty was compounded by the fact that, in principle, scientists cannot prove that something will never happen—only that it is very unlikely to happen if, over thousands of cases, it has never happened yet. So when public health officials declared that, on the evidence thus far, AIDS is not transmitted through casual contact, part of the public detected a hint of ambiguity. Accustomed, perhaps, to being somewhat skeptical of "experts," many people remained doubtful—and acted on their fears (Altman, 1986).

Fashions

Fashions are the currently valued styles of appearance and behavior. The fact that some style is called a "fashion" implies a social recognition that it is temporary and will eventually be replaced by a new style. In small-scale, traditional societies,

fashions are virtually unknown. In these communities everyone of similar age and sex wears much the same clothing, and there is little change in styles from year to year or even from generation to generation. In modern societies, however, fashions may change very rapidly indeed: automobile bodies assume new contours every year, and women's hemlines rise and fall with the passage of the seasons.

One reason for the emphasis on fashion in modern societies is that these societies are oriented toward the future rather than the past; novelty is considered desirable rather than threatening. A second reason, closely related, is that powerful commercial interests encourage changes in fashions because they profit from the demand for new styles. A further reason is that in a competitive, status-conscious society, fashion is used to indicate one's social characteristics to others. People may wish to appear attractive, distinctive, or affluent, and a new fashion enables them to show off—for a while at least (Brooks, 1981).

Not all fashions are deliberately imposed on the population, however, and people may resist new fashions, even in the face of massive advertis-

Figure 20.12 *Clothing fashions are related to broader social trends. There is a distinct relationship, for example, between women's clothing and society's attitude toward sexuality. During the highly restrictive Victorian era, women's bodies* *were almost completely concealed; during the permissive 1960s, the miniskirt was the rage; and in the more conservative sexual climate of today, longer and less revealing skirts have come into fashion.*

ing campaigns designed to influence public taste. One of the greatest flops in auto-industry history was the Ford Edsel, lavishly promoted in the 1950s but almost unanimously scorned by American consumers, who considered it monstrously ugly. In the past, fashions were set by the social elite. Today, however, fashions can arise at any level of society and can then spread outward from their point of origin. Blue jeans, for example, are the traditional clothes of the working class, but they can now be desirable "designer" items for members of the middle and upper classes. A new fashion is generally more likely to be accepted if it does not differ too much from existing fashions. If you consider consecutive changes in automobile styles, for example, you will find few, if any, abrupt changes in appearance. Each new fashion is essentially a modification of its predecessor.

Fads

A *fad* is a temporary form of conduct that is followed enthusiastically by large numbers of people. Fads differ from fashions not only in that they are typically even more temporary but also in that they are usually mildly scorned by the majority of the population. Those who participate in a fad are labeled as faddists; they are believed to follow a fad simply because it has "caught on," not because it has any intrinsic value. Those who are "in fashion," on the other hand, are more positively regarded, for their behavior is appropriate for as long as the fashion lasts.

Some notable fads in recent decades have involved the hula hoop, "streaking," roller-disco, pet rocks, Rubik's Cube, Pac Man, Cabbage Patch dolls, and Trivial Pursuit. A fad often provides a means of asserting personal identity. It is a way of showing that one is worth noticing, that one is a little different from everyone else (Klapp, 1969). For this reason, fads tend to appeal primarily to young people, who often have less stable identities than their elders. When a fad becomes so widespread that it no longer offers a distinctive identity to its adherents, it tends to be regarded as something of a bore and is usually abandoned.

Some fads win popularity because they offer the promise—frequently illusory—of personal advantage to their adherents. Typical of such fads is the financial craze, which involves widespread and reckless investment in dubious ventures, ranging from a gold rush to speculation in marginal real estate. One of the most extraordinary of

Figure 20.13 *A short-lived but popular fad of the 1950s, much practiced by college students, was telephone-booth cramming. Fads tend to appeal mostly to young people, who are often anxious to assert their identity by being a little "different" and doing something "new." Once the fad becomes too commonplace, of course, it quickly loses its appeal.*

these crazes was the tulip mania that occurred in Holland in 1634. The Dutch suddenly developed a passion for tulips, which rose rapidly in value. People at every level of society invested in the flowers and their bulbs, and many speculators made vast fortunes. Hoping to get rich quick, many people sold their homes and land to invest even more money in tulips, which at the height of the craze were worth their weight in gold. But suddenly, a rumor spread that the price of tulips was about to fall. Tulip owners desperately tried to sell their bulbs and blooms, but there were no buyers. The price of the flowers fell to well below its normal level, and thousands of speculators were ruined. But even today, the Dutch are internationally famous for the quality of their tulips—an indication of how a brief episode of collective behavior can leave lingering social effects.

Public Opinion

Many forms of collective behavior involve a certain amount of direct contact among the participants. The study of public opinion presents a somewhat different picture, however, because the participants are much more dispersed, although there is still some interaction among them.

A *public* is a substantial number of people with a shared interest in some issue on which there are differing opinions. We sometimes speak loosely of the whole population as "the public," but this conception is really a fiction. In practice, there are as many publics as there are issues, and there is no issue for which the entire population is a public, simply because many people are ignorant of, or uninterested in, any specific issue. The Gallup poll, for example, has found that it is very rare for more than 80 percent of the American population to be aware of a particular issue, and the percentage is often very much lower. The public for a single issue—such as abortion, a political scandal, fluoridation of water, or protection of the environment—expands or contracts as more people gain or lose interest in the topic.

The activities of a public may be more rational than those of a crowd. Some members of a public may think and feel alike, but they are individuals making personal decisions over time, and so are less vulnerable to group pressure. Some of the interaction within a public takes place on a face-to-face basis among friends, associates, and family members, but much of it occurs indirectly through the mass media. A public does not act together (although some of its members may join in collective behavior or social movements), but it does form views on the issue around which it is focused.

Public opinion is the sum of the decisions of the members of a public on a particular issue. Because people may constantly change their views, opinion on many issues is often in a state of flux. An assessment of public opinion is therefore valid only for the time and place in which it was made. People may be quite willing, however, to express opinions on subjects they know nothing about. In 1983 a *New York Times*/CBS News poll asked Americans about a major foreign-policy issue, the U.S. government's involvement in Central America. The administration was supporting an attempt by the government of El Salvador to suppress a revolution, and at the same time supporting a revolution against the government of Nicaragua. The poll found that 68 percent of the public felt that Central America is "very important" to American defense interests—but only 25 percent knew which side the United States was supporting in El Salvador, and only 13 percent knew which side it was supporting in Nicaragua. Even so, one-third of the respondents favored sending American combat troops to El Salvador, and one-quarter favored armed intervention in Nicaragua.

Despite such anomalies, considerable importance is placed on public opinion in the United States. The society is a democratic one in which elected officials must pay some attention to the views of their electorates, and it is a capitalist society in which commercial interests must take account of consumer attitudes toward various goods and services. A great deal of effort consequently goes into finding out what the public thinks about particular issues—and into influencing or changing these opinions. Billions of dollars are spent annually on public-opinion polls and market surveys and on media campaigns to build favorable public images of candidates, policies, corporations, and products. These campaigns are actually forms of *propaganda*—information or viewpoints that are presented with the deliberate intention of persuading the audience to adopt a particular opinion. Propaganda may be true or false, but its objective is always the same: to influence public opinion toward a specific conclusion.

Public opinion arises in an informal way, making it difficult to study. We do know, however, that people are not the passive victims of advertisers and other media persuaders. Opinions are not formed in a vacuum; they are made in the context of existing cultural and personal preconceptions. Moreover, people do not necessarily get their opinions directly from media sources. Information and viewpoints are sifted through other people, particularly family, friends, and workmates. For example, we are more likely to be influenced to see a movie by a friend who recommends it to us than by a newspaper advertisement. A public is also influenced by opinion leaders, usually people who spend greater time studying the controversy, form definite opinions about it, and interpret the issue for others. Labor union officials, for example, are likely to have a strong influence over union members' opinions on various economic and labor issues, and this influence may extend to other areas as well.

Awareness of others' views may also play a role in the formation of public opinion through what is known as the "bandwagon" effect. If it appears that opinion is swinging in one direction, some people—particularly those who were previ-

Propaganda Techniques

Propagandists can use several very simple methods to persuade their audiences. All these techniques have one element in common: they make an appeal to the values and attitudes of the audience. The next time you watch advertisements on television, you might try to identify the particular techniques being used.

1. *Glittering generalities* is a technique of surrounding a product, candidate, or policy with rather empty phrases that evoke a favorable response. Politicians, for example, become lyrical about "freedom," "democracy," "the individual," or "a better future," and have successfully campaigned on such slogans as "New Frontier," "Great Society," or even "Law and Order."

2. *Name calling* is a method used in negative propaganda: it attempts to attach an unfavorable label to something that the propagandist opposes. Opponents of plans for a national health insurance program, for example, have successfully branded these plans as "socialized medicine." This phrase conjures up images of socialism, a concept to which the American public generally reacts very unfavorably.

3. *Transfer* is a method of winning approval for something by associating it with something else that is known to be viewed favorably. The most obvious example is the practice of associating commercial products with attractive models, however irrelevant the link between the two may be.

4. *Testimonial* is the technique of using people—often "celebrities"—to make public statements favoring or opposing something. Commercial advertisers, for example, commonly use sports heroes, movie stars, or even retired astronauts to recommend their products on television and in magazines.

5. *Plain folks* is the method of identifying the propagandist's ideas, product, or person with "ordinary" people. Political candidates, for example, try to create a down-to-earth, common-sense image by being filmed driving tractors, wearing hard hats, or mingling in street crowds.

6. *Card stacking* is an argument in which the facts (or falsehoods) are arranged in such a way that only one conclusion seems to be logically possible. This method is commonly used in commercial advertisements that compare one brand to another.

7. *Bandwagon* is a method that tries to build support for a particular viewpoint or product by creating the impression that "everyone is doing it." The implication is that the audience is being "left out" of a popular trend and should "get with it."

SOURCE: Adapted from Alfred McClung Lee and Elizabeth Bryant Lee, *The Fine Art of Propaganda* (New York: Octagon, 1971).

---

ously undecided or who had no very strong commitment to the other side—tend to change their viewpoints. This is why commercial advertisers often stress an "everybody is doing it" theme and why candidates in presidential primaries are so eager to do well in the early stages of their campaigns—to build that vital "momentum."

The expressed opinions of the public can now be measured by opinion polls with a high degree of accuracy. But as we noted in Chapter 2 ("Doing Sociology: The Methods of Research"), there are significant problems in constructing, using, and interpreting measures of public opinion. A notorious misreading of opinion occurred in 1985, when the Coca-Cola company announced that it would change the formula of its popular soft drink. The company reached this decision after spending over $4 million on an extensive survey of consumer preferences. The findings seemed convincing: in over 200,000 taste tests, the new, sweeter formula seemed rather more popular than the old one. Yet the change provoked a strongly negative reaction. Some people formed a group called Old Cola Drinkers of America to demand a return to the old formula. Tens of thousands more called the company to protest. American distributors reported that many consumers thought the new formula was an insipid brew, lacking the zing of the original. Foreign distributors did not even want to handle the new product. After three months, the Coca-Cola company announced that the original formula would be reintroduced and marketed alongside the new beverage. By the end of 1985, the "classic" version was outselling the new version by 2 to 1, and by 1986, by 4 to 1.

What went wrong? One problem is that people will often prefer the sweeter of two tastes in a single test—but not repeatedly over a long period.

Figure 20.14 *In a remarkable misreading of public opinion, the Coca-Cola company tried in 1985 to abandon its old soft-drink formula. Coke loyalists quickly—and successfully—demanded their old drink back.*

More important, the researchers had not realized the emotional attachment that many people have to Coca-Cola as an American cultural symbol. In sampling public opinion, the researchers had not told people that their preference for the sweeter taste would mean saying goodbye to the Coca-Cola they had known since childhood. The new beverage flopped not just because of its taste (in blind tests, even the founder of Old Cola Drinkers of America could not tell the two formulas apart), but because it represented unwelcome change (Hollie, 1986).

Social Movements

Compared to most episodes of collective behavior, social movements are a much more deliberate and organized form of action. Social movements are found only in certain societies. They are uncommon in simple preindustrial societies, largely because the inhabitants tend to be suspicious of change, and to take their social system for granted. Such social movements as do arise in these societies frequently take the form of religious cults or sects, for preindustrial peoples often interpret their misfortunes in religious rather than social, political, or economic terms.

Movements of this kind seem to fall at the borderline between an outburst of collective behavior and a full-fledged social movement. Frequently, they take the form of a *millenarian movement*—one that prophesies a cataclysmic upheaval within

the immediate future. The word comes from "millennium," the prophesied thousand-year reign of Christ; but the cataclysm may involve a radical change in the conditions of life, a return to some golden age of the past, or even the end of the world. Although millenarian movements have been recorded on every continent, they all have one theme in common: a reversal of the social order, in which those who accept the prophecy will be triumphant over their enemies (who are usually their rulers). In fourteenth-century Europe, for example, hordes of peasants flogged themselves on long marches from one town to the next, hoping thereby to bring about the earthly rule of a messiah king and a relief from such woes as poverty and the plague. The participants were typically uprooted, homeless, and unemployed laborers, who hoped for divine intervention to better their own lives and to torment their persecutors (Cohn, 1962).

Most millenarian movements have been recorded in preindustrial societies that have been colonized by Europeans. In these cases, the millenarian prophecy often contains a modified version of Judeo-Christian beliefs: the colonized people equate themselves with the Israelites in search of the promised land, and the colonizers with the doomed Egyptian oppressors. One such millenarian movement arose among the Xhosa, a tribe of nomadic pastoralists in southern Africa. In the middle of the past century they came into competition with Dutch settlers, themselves nomadic pastoralists, who were penetrating the continent from the south. The two groups fought several bloody

Figure 20.15 *A millenarian movement, the Ghost Dance cult, arose among the Plains Indians of the United States during the 1870s and 1890s, at the time of the Indians' desperate defense of their lands and cultures against the invading settlers. Various prophets foretold that if the appropriate dances and rituals were performed, dead ancestors would arise from the grave, the tribes would be immune to the invaders' bullets, the whites would be driven back to the ocean, the vanishing buffalo would return in vast numbers, and the old way of life would be restored. Belief in the Ghost Dance cult was destroyed by the slaughter of the Indians at the Battle of Wounded Knee.*

wars, which the Dutch settlers won as a result of their superior military technology. A prophet arose among the Xhosa, claiming that if the people slaughtered all their cattle and destroyed all their stores of food, the sun would rise blood-red the following day. Cattle, grain, and guns would emerge from the ground, the dead ancestors would return, and the whites would be driven back to the ocean from which they had come. The Xhosa accepted the prophecy, destroyed their cattle and food, and

waited on the hilltops for the blood-red dawn. At least twenty thousand starved to death.

During this century, a series of millenarian movements called "cargo cults" arose in the Melanesian islands of the South Pacific. When the native peoples were colonized by Europeans, they were deeply impressed by the quantity and variety of strange goods that arrived as cargo into their country—yet the cargo went only to the colonists, never to them. Prophets began to declare that the cargo was being manufactured for the islanders by their own ancestors, but was being intercepted by the colonists. Millenarian movements arose, typically prophesying that if all crops and food were destroyed and if makeshift harbors (and later, airstrips) were built, the cargo would miraculously appear. In a few cases the prophecies were actually fulfilled: when the Melanesians had destroyed their food stocks, the colonial administration was obliged to ship in fresh supplies to prevent mass starvation—an event that gave added impetus to the movements (Worsely, 1968).

Millenarian social movements are, in effect, "religions of the oppressed." Before adopting the new religion, the members have felt a sense of injustice or deprivation. The religion offers compensation—not as "pie-in-the-sky" in the hereafter, but here on earth, and soon. The recruits are people whose traditional norms and values are no longer relevant to their new plight. In their confusion or desperation they will grasp at any hope, and they turn to a new religious vision because supernatural resources, for better or worse, are the only resources they believe they have. An important feature of these movements is that they often serve as the forerunner to militant, politically motivated social movements, for they help to identify the source of the problem, to lay the basis for group organization, and to advance the concept of social change through collective action. Around the middle of this century, for example, a nationalist movement in Kenya, the Mau Mau, hastened the end of British colonial rule in that country. This movement gained members among the indigenous people by combining some religious elements, such as ritual oaths, with a military and political strategy for overthrowing and transforming the social system (Cohn, 1962; Lanternari, 1963; Worsely, 1968; B. Wilson, 1973; Tilly, 1978).

Although a few millenarian movements (such as the Jehovah's Witnesses) do exist in modern industrialized societies, they generally have little impact on the course of events. But social movements with a more secular, political orientation are very much a part of the modern world. Indeed, many of today's nation-states came into being as a result of the efforts of nationalist or revolutionary movements. However, social movements are rare in undemocratic societies, for the simple reason that authoritarian or totalitarian governments do not tolerate them. Thus there is no independent peace movement or women's movement in the Soviet Union, and Polish authorities try their utmost to restrict the activities of the Polish workers' movement, Solidarity (Ash, 1984). On the whole, social movements are found primarily in societies that have democratic systems and so permit dissent. In these heterogeneous and generally tolerant societies, there are always groups or interests anxious to influence the course of events, and their activities are an essential part of an ongoing political process through which decisions about the future are made.

Social movements are important precisely because they deliberately intervene in history. Their members are not content to be the passive playthings of social forces: instead, they try to affect the social order through direct action. Many of these movements, of course, have little or no impact, but others have brought about lasting and profound social and cultural changes. Our lives today would be utterly different had it not been for the efforts of the diverse social movements that were responsible for, say, the American Revolution, the abolition of slavery, the introduction of compulsory schooling, the extension of the vote to women, or the legalization of birth-control devices.

Explaining Social Movements

A major concern of sociologists has been to find out what causes social movements to arise in the first place. Three general explanations have been offered: psychological theories, strain theories, and resource-mobilization theory.

Psychological Theories

Early writers on the subject, notably Gustave Le Bon (1895), tended to focus on the psychological characteristics of those who took part in social movements. As we have already seen, these theorists were typically hostile to social movements, which they regarded as simply one more form of

Figure 20.16 *Social movements play a vital role in the formation of public opinion. The movements draw attention to controversial social issues and provoke debates about these subjects. Social change often emerges from the ensuing clash of interests and opinions.*

irrational collective behavior. From this viewpoint, those who challenge the existing order are, almost by definition, unbalanced, and social movements are little more than long-lasting mobs. This analysis persisted until the 1960s, although the psychological explanations became much more subtle. Essentially, the various writers who took this approach suggested that social movements attract people who have a personality defect of some kind, and that membership in the movements meets their psychological needs by making them feel important or useful (Cantril, 1942; Hoffer, 1951; Toch, 1965; Feuer, 1969). But there are obvious problems with this approach. First, if social movements exist purely to express psychological discontent, why should people join one movement rather than another—say, the Ku Klux Klan rather than the civil rights movement? Second, why should some movements (such as that for women's liberation) be largely successful, while others (such as the movement to make Sunday sport illegal) make little or no headway? Third, might it not be possible that the sources of social movements lie not in psychological conditions, but, rather, in social ones; that is, is it not possible that there is sometimes something "wrong" with society, not with the people who try to change it?

Strain Theories

Largely in response to these criticisms, several sociologists began to develop a new approach. According to this view, which became popular in the 1960s, the main factor behind the emergence of social movements is some form of social "strain." Smelser's theory of collective behavior is one such strain theory, and, in fact, Smelser originally intended that it should be applicable to social movements as well as to such phenomena as riots and panics. As applied to the ecology movement, for example, this theory would hold that the strain caused by the existence of pollution in a society supposedly committed to the preservation of health and of the environment led to a new social movement aimed at resolving that strain. Other sociologists offer a somewhat different but related argument: they propose that people's feelings of *deprivation* are the source of social movements. This deprivation can be absolute (when people totally lack some social reward or rewards) or relative (when people have a lesser share of these rewards than other groups to whom they compare themselves). According to these sociologists, griev-

ances that are caused by deprivation encourage people to launch a social movement that would improve their situation (Davies, 1962, 1971; Klapp, 1969; Gurr, 1971).

This approach has the virtue of locating the source of social movements more firmly in social rather than in presumed psychological conditions. But it also runs into a serious problem. There is, surely, a certain amount of strain in all societies at some time or another, and virtually everyone feels deprived (either absolutely, or relative to other people) in some respects. Yet these conditions of strain or deprivation do not automatically lead to social movements. American blacks, for example, were subject to strain and deprivation long before the civil rights movement, as were women before the women's movement, gays before the gay liberation movement, and so on. Why did these movements arise when they did, rather than earlier—or later? Theories of strain do not really answer this question, still less make it possible to predict when a social movement will arise. Indeed, some social movements have occurred at times when virtually nobody, including sociologists, foresaw that they would. The student movement of the 1960s, for example, suddenly disrupted campuses across the nation at a time when scholars and editorial writers were deploring student apathy; the women's movement was so unexpected that its main problem, in its early years, was to convince most women (let alone men) that women were, in fact, subject to any strain or deprivation at all. There is a dangerous circularity in strain theories: How do we know there was strain? Because a social movement arose. Why did the social movement arise? Because there was strain. Clearly, theories focusing on strain or deprivation are inadequate in several important respects (Guerney and Tierney, 1982).

Resource-Mobilization Theory

A more recent approach, associated particularly with the work of John McCarthy and Mayer Zald, overcomes many of these difficulties. This theory emphasizes *resource mobilization,* the ability to organize and use available resources, such as time, money, people, and skills. Dissatisfaction may well exist in society—whether because of psychological frustration, social strain, feelings of deprivation, or for any other reason—but a social movement will not emerge until people organize and take action by using the resources at their command. These resources may include access to a duplicating machine, the services of professional organizers, contacts with the media, links with other social movements, the presence of sympathizers, or even the ability to tap millions of dollars of campaign funds from individuals and groups that favor the movement's goals. The focus of sociological attention, therefore, should be on how and why people actually do mobilize their resources and launch a movement (McCarthy and Zald, 1977; Zald and McCarthy, 1979; Oberschall, 1973; Gamson, 1975; Tilly, 1978).

McCarthy and Zald place particular emphasis on the role of outsiders in getting a social movement launched. These outsiders may be amateurs who sympathize with the group concerned, or they may even be professionals whose job it is to organize people into movements of one sort or another. In either case, the outsiders help to mobilize the group's resources and thus to bring the social movement into being—or, if it already exists, to inject new dynamism into it. For example, white liberal Northerners, often college students, played an active part in the early days of the civil rights movement, which they encouraged by such means as organizing sit-ins at segregated facilities and helping with voter registration. A similar process can be seen at the international level. In nearly all the less developed nations of the world, the bulk of the population lives in poverty under the rule of antidemocratic regimes. Yet this situation of strain and deprivation is generally insufficient to provoke a major social movement for revolution. The Soviet Union is well aware of this fact, and has consistently attempted, often through the use of Cuban or East German "advisers," to mobilize popular resentment into revolutionary movements and to ensure the subsequent success of those movements. The United States, too, has helped provide and mobilize resources for revolutionary movements in countries like Afghanistan, Cuba, and Nicaragua.

Resource-mobilization theory helps explain why movements might get off the ground and become successful, but it has been criticized for downplaying whatever conditions of strain or dissatisfaction already exist. It seems logical to assume that if people are already "ripe" for mobilization, then the emergence of a social movement seems more likely, but if they have no particular interest in the issue, mobilization of resources, particularly by outsiders, may have little impact (Wood and Jackson, 1982; McAdam, 1982; Jenkins, 1983; Klandermans, 1984).

Social-Movement Characteristics

Although there is extraordinary diversity in the goals, tactics, membership, size, and fate of social movements, they do tend to display certain recurrent features.

Types of Social Movements

All social movements have an *ideology,* a set of beliefs that explains and justifies some actual or potential social arrangements. The ideology of every movement provides a diagnosis of the problem the movement wishes to rectify, an explanation of how the problem came about and why it persists, a prescription for how to correct the situation, and a scenario of how matters would get worse if the movement were to fail. Although the leaders of social movements may have very specific ideas about the nature of the ideology, ordinary members or sympathizers often have only a vague conception of its content.

Social movements can be classified into different types, largely according to the kind of ideology they hold and the implications that it has for their activities.

1. *Regressive movements.* These are social movements that aim to "set back the clock." Their members view certain social changes with suspicion and distaste, and try to reverse the current trends. The "Moral Majority" was an example of just such a regressive movement, in this case one that resisted the trends toward permissiveness and secularization that have taken place in the course of this century.

2. *Reform movements.* The members of some movements are basically satisfied with the existing social order but believe certain reforms are necessary, usually in specific areas of society. The antinuclear movement, the ecology movement, and the consumer movement are all examples of this type of social movement.

3. *Revolutionary movements.* These movements are deeply dissatisfied with the existing social order and work to reorganize the entire society in accordance with their own ideological blueprint. A successful revolutionary movement, such as those that gave birth to the United States, the Soviet Union, and the People's Republic of China, can launch sweeping social and historical change.

Figure 20.17 *Of all types of social movements, the ones that can have the greatest social impact are revolutionary movements. The revolutionaries in America and in Iran (shown here toppling equestrian statues of, respectively, George III and the shah) radically altered the history and culture of their societies. Many other revolutionary movements, of course, are unsuccessful.*

4. *Utopian movements.* The members of these movements envision a radically changed and blissful life, either on a large scale at some time in the future or on a smaller scale in the present. The utopian ideal and the means of achieving it are often vague. The "counterculture" of the 1960s and several contemporary religious cults are examples of utopian movements.

Social-Movement Organizations

A social movement—particularly a large and successful one—often contains a number of smaller groups, which sociologists call social-movement organizations. These are formal organizations with constitutions, officials, rules and regulations, and the like. For example, the ecology movement includes the Sierra Club and Friends of the Earth; the social movement of the aged includes the Gray Panthers and the American Association of Retired Persons. Some social-movement organizations, such as Ralph Nader's consumer-rights crusades, may have no members as such, and may collect their resources from idealistic supporters—who may be a different group from the potential beneficiaries of the movement's program.

The general trend in modern societies, in keeping with their overall tendency toward bureaucratization, is for social movements to become highly organized and professionalized at an early stage of their existence (McCarthy and Zald, 1973). In fact, a movement may become so highly structured that it really ceases to be a social movement any longer, and simply becomes a formal organization representing the interests of its particular constituents—a far cry from the millenarian movements of preindustrial societies.

Tactics of Social Movements

All social movements must use tactics of some sort to further their goals. One purpose of these tactics is to retain and enhance the loyalty of the members and to increase their number. A social movement usually contains a small, central "core" of leaders and other devotees; beyond that, there is a wider circle of members and participants who play a greater or lesser part in the movement's activities; and further beyond that, there is a general constituency of potential supporters who are vaguely sympathetic to the movement's objectives. The tactics of the movement should therefore aim at mobilizing this entire reservoir of support. A second purpose of the tactics is to persuade those who are not sympathetic to the movement's goals (and this probably includes the political authorities) to change their attitudes. If those with political power do not respond to the movement's demands, then the movement may adopt disruptive tactics aimed at forcing change.

The actual tactics that are adopted depend in some measure on what type of movement is involved: a reform movement is far less likely than a revolutionary one to use violence, for it is concerned to retain the good will of those in positions of power, and its leaders and members are likely to have strong moral objections to the use of violence. A second important influence on tactics is the degree to which the movement has become institutionalized. A movement that already has access to the power structure, such as the National Association for the Advancement of Colored People, is more likely to work through private lobbying than through spectacular public demonstrations. Movements that have little access to power, however, are more likely to create "news events," for they soon learn that they will otherwise be ignored. For that reason, some members of the early anti-Vietnam-war movement publicly burned their draft cards; some members of the early antinuclear movement occupied the construction site of a new reactor in Seabrook, New Hampshire; some members of the antibusing movement tried to physically prevent the passage of school buses; some members of the antiabortion movement have firebombed abortion clinics. Such events are quickly seized on by the press and television, which, in effect, give free publicity to the movement involved and increase public awareness of its beliefs and goals.

Sometimes, too, social movements turn to outright violence as a means of achieving their objectives. In general, they do so only when other channels are blocked or ineffective, or when those in positions of power use violence to repress the movements. Unhappily, it seems that violence can often be a successful tactic and therefore, from the point of view of those who espouse it, a rational one. William Gamson (1975) studied fifty-three groups that had challenged the American power structure between 1800 and 1945. These movements, which ranged from the American Birth Control League to the Communist Labor Party, used a wide variety of tactics, but the 25 percent or so that were involved in violent confrontations were, on the whole, more successful than the majority that were not.

Terrorism

A few social movements may resort to the tactic of **terrorism**—the use of violence against civilian targets for the purpose of intimidation to achieve political ends. In America, the stereotyped image of terrorism probably involves Middle Easterners hijacking an airplane or planting a bomb in a crowded street. Although terrorism takes much more diverse forms than that, most terrorist acts are one of two basic kinds.

1. *State terrorism.* All over the world, authoritarian and totalitarian governments use terror against their own populations as an instrument of political and social control. Tens of millions of innocent people have died during the course of this century as a result of these acts of repression, most notably in the Soviet Union during the 1930s, in Nazi Germany in the 1940s, and in Cambodia in the 1970s. Amnesty International, a human-rights organization, reports that even in the 1980s, the governments of no fewer than ninety-eight countries practice torture on suspected dissidents. These acts include flogging people, pulling out their fingernails, giving them electric shocks, hanging them upside down, holding them under water, burning them with cigarettes, and in some cases blinding or otherwise mutilating them. In some countries, such as Syria and Uganda, tens of thousands of civilians have died in massacres by their own country's military forces (Grantham, 1984).

2. *Revolutionary terrorism.* Some radical social movements (and some small groups that hope to become a social movement) resort to violence to achieve their goals. Their tactics typically include such acts as bombings, assassinations, hijackings, kidnappings, and holding people for ransom. Revolutionary groups that have used such tactics in recent years include the Palestine Liberation Organization in the Middle East, the Mujahedeen in Iran, the Red Brigade in Italy, the Red Army in Japan, the Bader-Meinhof group in West Germany, the Contras in Nicaragua, the Shining Path in Peru, the Irish Republican Army in Northern Ireland, and the Basque separatists in Spain. Altogether, these and hundreds of similar groups commit thousands of terrorist acts in the world every year, frequently maiming and killing innocent people in the process (Lodge, 1981).

There is often a close link between state terrorism and revolutionary terrorism, for one of them may call forth the other. By blocking legitimate channels of change, repressive governments may encourage attempts at violent revolution.

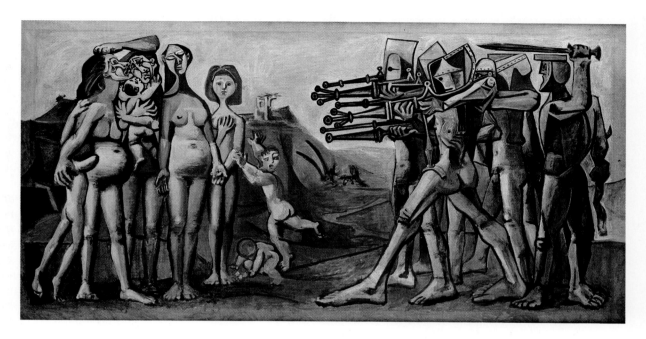

Figure 20.18 *The vast majority of the terrorist acts during this century have been perpetrated by government forces on their own people. Pablo Picasso's painting* The Korean Massacres *(1951), with its*   *image of machinelike executioners, captures the impersonal but devastating nature of the state terrorism that has claimed so many millions of lives during the course of this century.*

Conversely, revolutionary terrorism may provoke repressive governments into acts of widespread and even random violence against suspected dissidents or their supporters. In fact, a vicious cycle often develops in which revolutionaries and regimes perpetrate fresh atrocities on one another in retaliation for the previous acts of the other side. Within the past two decades, for example, hundreds of thousands of people have been murdered by police or military "death squads" in countries that were embroiled in guerrilla warfare, such as Argentina, El Salvador, Ethiopia, Sri Lanka, Guatemala, and Chile. Actually, state terrorism may benefit revolutionaries in the long run, for it polarizes the society by forcing people to take sides. As the moderate center collapses, the battle lines are clarified—with the revolutionaries appearing as the only alternative to the existing rulers.

Revolutionary terrorism attracts much more publicity in the United States than does state terrorism. One reason is that revolutionary terrorists sometimes target American citizens, airliners, and embassy facilities, for they perceive the United States as the principal supporter of the governments they oppose. The main reason, however, is that revolutionary terrorists thrive on publicity.

Whereas the perpetrators of state terrorism try to hide their behavior from international scrutiny, the revolutionary terrorists want to draw worldwide attention to their cause. Their brutal acts are often merely the start of a sustained public performance that includes communiqués, demands, threats, deadlines, negotiations, and a final climax or anticlimax—a drama that is conducted, via instantaneous telecommunication, for the benefit of a vast global audience (Rubin and Friedland, 1986).

This manipulation of the media is often highly successful, for it gives terrorists publicity—and thus the power to instill fear—that is out of proportion to their real numbers or strength. In 1986, as a result of publicity surrounding two terrorist attacks in Europe and a subsequent American reprisal raid on Libya, millions of Americans cancelled their European vacation plans. Yet the actual chance of an American abroad being involved in a terrorist attack is negligible. True, several hundred American civilians have lost their lives in foreign terrorist attacks over the past twenty years. But staying at home could be a lot more dangerous—among many other hazards, about 18,000 people are murdered in the United

Figure 20.19 *Revolutionary terrorists are generally people who lack any resources other than violence, or the threat of violence, to achieve their ends. They thrive on publicity, for it brings their claims to the attention of a vast audience that would otherwise completely ignore them.*

States each year, and over 40,000 are killed in traffic accidents. The irrational response to the perceived threat of terrorism merely proves how effective it can be as a tool of intimidation.

Why do some groups turn to revolutionary terrorism instead of more peaceful means? Two factors seem to be relevant. First, terrorists are fanatics. They always perceive themselves as "freedom fighters," and are so utterly convinced of the righteousness of their cause that they consider almost any act justified, as long as it will serve their ends. Second, terrorists are people who lack the means or the patience to achieve their goals by less violent methods. Without resort to terrorism, they would be too weak to make an effective challenge to their enemies—so they use terrorism as a resource to equalize the terms of the struggle.

Terrorism can pose a serious problem to democratic societies. The acts of terrorist movements and groups create danger to people and property, cause appalling moral dilemmas in situations where hostages are involved, and necessitate a variety of cumbersome and costly precautions at airports and elsewhere. There is no easy answer to this problem, although there is now a consensus among Western governments that, if at all possible, terrorist demands should not be granted for fear of encouraging still further terrorism.

Life Course of Social Movements

Social movements—particularly reform movements—play a vital part in the process by which a social problem is brought to public attention. Some undesirable conditions can exist for years or even centuries before they are recognized as social problems. Slavery, poverty, and pollution were all generally regarded as either unimportant or inevitable until social movements drew these conditions to public attention, mobilized public opinion, and campaigned for change.

The degree of success of a social movement determines not only to what extent a social problem is resolved but also what happens to the movement itself. The interplay of social problems and social movements produces a "life course," or "natural history," which Malcolm Spector and John Kitsuse (1977) suggest may involve four stages.

1. *Agitation.* In the early stage of the life course, members of the new movement try to stir up public opinion in favor of their viewpoint. In most cases, these efforts are unsuccessful, and the would-be movement simply withers away. The reasons for this early failure can be many. The claims the members make on behalf of their cause may be false or outrageously exaggerated—or may seem so to most people. Or the movement may be composed of people too powerless and lacking in resources to have much public impact. Or the members may use counterproductive tactics that merely antagonize rather than persuade the public. Or the movement may collide with other movements that have far greater resources and be overwhelmed in the resulting competition for public support. This is frequently the fate of social movements of the poor or other less privileged groups (Useem, 1975; Piven and Cloward, 1979).

2. *Legitimation.* If it survives at all, a movement may enter a stage in which its objectives gain widespread support and the movement itself becomes respectable. At this point, government or other authorities recognize that the movement's claims are valid. Leaders who were once dismissed as cranks may now find that the increasing success of the movement has made them celebrities; they are sought after by the media and consulted by government agencies. Once the civil rights movement became a national force, for example, federal and state authorities that had earlier ignored or even tried to suppress the movement began, instead, to invite civil rights leaders to participate in the commissions and agencies responsible for future policy in the area. Similarly, corporations that once had all-male boards of di-

rectors as a matter of course are now appointing women directors, if only in token numbers. One effect of this success, however, is that the social movement loses much of its initiative to established governmental or other organizations.

3. *Bureaucratization.* In the third stage the social-movement organizations grow steadily more bureaucratized, and so tend to become more engrossed in day-to-day administrative tasks than in the long-term challenge of confronting the problems they were originally set up to solve. Failure to deal effectively with these problems rarely leads to the abolition of the organization responsible, however: indeed, it is likely to demand a larger budget and still more officials on the grounds that its existing resources are inadequate to achieve solutions. Inevitably, a public reaction sets in, and the organization focuses more on the growing complaints about its failure to solve the problems than on actually solving them. This has been the fate, for example, of some organizations within the American labor movement. In the late nineteenth century, American workers were deeply resentful of their low pay, poor working conditions, and lack of the right to form unions. Labor unions emerged, and after many years of tension and violence, they won official recognition from Congress and employers. Many unions grew and prospered, became vast formal organizations, and are in some cases now part of the very establishment that the early labor movement set out to attack. The Teamsters' Union, to cite one of the more notorious examples, has a president who enjoys an annual salary of over $500,000. The union has strayed so far from its original purpose, in fact, that it has been accused, among many other charges, of betraying its members' interests, of diverting their pension funds to organized crime, and of using illegal and even violent methods to enforce conformity among its members.

Figure 20.20

"Would a study shut them up?"

Copyright Wm. Hamilton

4. *Reemergence of the movement.* Eventually, discontent may accumulate to such an extent that the movement reemerges, although this time it campaigns not only against the social conditions in question but also against the relevant policies, programs, and organizations that have become institutionalized in the name of changing those conditions. Sometimes members of the original movement may regroup and renew their campaigns, but often new movements emerge, led and supported by people who were previously uninvolved but who now see themselves as victims of bureaucratic incompetence and insensitivity. Thus the cycle begins again. But the process has not been entirely unfruitful; although dissatisfaction may persist, it is likely that some progress will have been made. Social problems are rarely, if ever, solved through single, dramatic strokes of policy. Rather, they are ameliorated, or made better, through a series of piecemeal approaches that gradually eliminate most of the conditions that gave rise to the problem.

Summary

1.   Collective behavior refers to relatively spontaneous action that occurs when people try to work out common responses to ambiguous situations. Social movements are more structured, and consist of a large number of people who have joined together to bring about or resist some social or cultural change.

2.   Smelser argues that collective behavior will occur only if six conditions are met: structural conduciveness, structural strains, generalized belief, precipitating factors, mobilization for action, and failure of social control. The Peoples Temple mass suicide is a clear example of this sequence.

3. Much collective behavior occurs in the context of crowds. The contagion theory holds that crowd members lose their personal identity in crowd situations and are easily influenced by others; the emergent-norms theory holds that crowd behavior involves a collective improvisation of new norms.

4. Mobs are acting crowds bent on violence or destruction; their members typically have little access to power. Examples are lynch mobs and riots. Panics involve fearful, spontaneous, and uncoordinated behavior. Some occur in situations of immediate threat (such as fires), others in more diffuse situations of threat (such as stock-market collapses). Disasters are generally not followed by panics.

5. A rumor is information transmitted informally from anonymous sources, generally when "hard" information is lacking. Examples are the "death" of Paul McCartney and the "satanic" logo. Urban legends are realistic but untrue stories concerning recent alleged events. Their content involves ambiguous situations and has an implicit lesson or moral.

6. Mass hysteria is an outbreak of widespread anxiety caused by some unfounded belief. Examples of this phenomenon are the Martian invasion of earth, the Seattle windshield-pitting epidemic, and AIDS hysteria.

7. Fashions are currently valued styles. They are found primarily in industrialized societies, where they are used to signal individual status. Fads are more temporary forms of conduct that people follow with great enthusiasm; they are often a means of asserting personal identity.

8. Public opinion is the sum of the views of members of the public on a particular issue. There is a different and constantly changing public for every issue. Despite the difficulties involved in measurement and interpretation, public opinion can usually be quite reliably measured by polls.

9. Social movements may achieve changes of great historical importance. In preindustrial societies, they often take the religious form of millenarian movements, but in modern democracies, they are more oriented toward social, economic, and political goals. Their emergence has been explained as the result of their members' psychological needs; as the result of social strain or deprivation; and as the result of people's mobilization of resources such as skills and money.

10. Social movements frequently contain several social-movement organizations within them. Depending on their ideology, social movements may be of four basic types: regressive movements, reform movements, revolutionary movements, and utopian movements.

11. Social movements vary in their tactics; the less successful they are, the more likely they are to resort to publicity-seeking gimmicks or even violence. Terrorism may be used by the state or by revolutionary movements. Social movements often go through a four-stage "life cycle": agitation, legitimation, bureaucratization, and reemergence, in which a new movement arises.

Important Terms

collective behavior (533)
social movement (534)
crowd (537)
mass (537)
contagion theory (537)
emergent-norms theory (538)
mob (539)
panic (541)
rumor (542)
urban legend (544)

mass hysteria (546)
fashion (548)
fad (549)
public opinion (550)
propaganda (550)
millenarian movement (552)
resource mobilization (555)
ideology (556)
terrorism (558)

Suggested Readings

FREEMAN, JO (ed.). *Social Movements of the Sixties and Seventies.* New York: Longman, 1983.

A useful collection of articles covering the rise and sometimes the decline of some of the social movements that have helped shape many aspects of modern life.

PIVEN, FRANCES FOX, and RICHARD A. CLOWARD. *Poor People's Movements: Why They Succeed, How They Fail.* New York: Vintage, 1979.

An important analysis of the success or failure of four social movements—of the unemployed, of industrial workers, and for civil rights and welfare rights.

ROSE, JERRY D. *Outbreaks: The Sociology of Collective Behavior.* New York: Free Press, 1982.

A good, up-to-date overview of current sociological understanding of various forms of collective behavior.

ROSNOW, RALPH L., and GARY ALAN FINE. *Rumor and Gossip.* New York: Elsevier, 1976.

A readable study of rumor and its relationship to some other forms of collective behavior.

SMELSER, NEIL J. *Theory of Collective Behavior.* New York: Free Press, 1962.

A highly influential analysis of various forms of collective behavior. Smelser interprets collective behavior as an attempt by people to alter some aspect of their social environment.

TILLY, CHARLES. *From Mobilization to Revolution.* Reading, Mass.: Addison-Wesley, 1978.

An excellent and well-written analysis of various social movements over the past five centuries.

WORSLEY, PETER. *The Trumpet Shall Sound.* London: MacGibbon & Kee, 1957.

An interesting descriptive and analytical account of the various "cargo-cult" movements in the South Pacific. Worsley's account throws light on other, less exotic social movements nearer home.

ZALD, MAYER N., and JOHN D. MCCARTHY (eds.). *The Dynamics of Social Movements.* Cambridge, Mass.: Winthrop, 1979.

An important collection of articles representative of the resource-mobilization approach to social movements.

CHAPTER 21

Population and Urbanization

By this time tomorrow, about a quarter of a million more human beings will have been born. Some 50,000 years ago, when our ancestors lived in small bands of hunters and gatherers, there was 1 person for every 200 square miles of the earth's surface—but if current rates of population growth persist, within less than a thousand years there will be 100 people for each square yard! Of course, such an absurdity will not occur, if only because, one way or another, population growth is going to stop long before that point is reached. But already, the world has a population of around 5 billion people, a number that will rise beyond 6 billion by the end of this century and will probably exceed 8 billion well within the lifetime of most of today's students.

This population growth represents one of the most critical social problems in the modern world, with potential consequences in terms of sheer human misery that are almost unimaginable. At least 10 million people die every year from the effects of starvation, at least 500 million more are undernourished or malnourished, and most of the remaining human population lives in conditions of poverty or hardship—yet 90 percent of the billion or so births that will occur before the end of the century will take place in the world's poorest countries. Even for the richer nations, population growth presents problems. No natural environment can withstand an infinite increase in the animal or plant populations that it supports. It is questionable whether the planet can continue to provide the food and other raw materials that huge increases in the human population will require, or whether it can tolerate the pollution caused by ever expanding industrial production (Brown, 1978, 1981; Crittenden, 1981; Birdsall, 1982; Gupte, 1984).

The tremendous impact of population growth is felt most keenly in cities. In fact, the growth of cities is one of the most significant trends in the modern world. The human animal has been around for well over 3 million years, yet our ancestors lived in small primary groups for all but about the past 6,000 years. The growth of cities that contain most of a society's members is a very recent development: until 1850 not more than 5 percent of the global population was urban, and only one city, London, had more than 1 million inhabitants. Yet most people in all the industrialized societies are now urban residents, and there are over 150 cities with a population exceeding 1 million. If present trends continue, there will be more than 500 cities with 1 million inhabitants by the end of the century—60 of them containing over 5 million people, and 6 of them with populations of over 20 million. By then, more than half the people in the world will live in cities (Salas, 1980). This new, highly urbanized environment offers challenges and opportunities that are without precedent in the history of the species.

In this chapter we will examine two related areas of sociological inquiry. The first area is *demography,* the study of the size, composition, distribution, and changes in human populations. The second is *urbanism,* the nature and meaning of city life. These two subfields of the discipline are linked not only by some common sources of information—both demographers and urban sociologists rely heavily on population census data—but also by the close connection between the processes of population growth and distribution.

The Study of Population

No human population is ever completely stable. Some populations grow and others decline. The size of some populations changes rapidly, while that of others changes much more slowly. Some populations have a high proportion of young people, others, of old people. Most populations contain more females than males, particularly in the oldest generation, but the exact ratio of the sexes varies over time and from place to place. These and other population characteristics are the result of processes that can be scientifically analyzed.

The Science of Demography

The science of demography is a subdiscipline of sociology for the reason that population dynamics strongly affect, and are affected by, social factors. If

a society places restrictions on abortion or the use of contraceptives, the number of births will tend to be high. If a society places taboos on premarital sex or on sex for some time after childbirth, the number of births will tend to be low. Social values that encourage large families exert pressure for population increase; values that encourage women to pursue independent careers tend to depress population growth. Standards of nutrition and public health obviously affect the length of the average life in any given society.

Demography thus consists of much more than simply extending lines on graphs. The science must take full account of all factors, social, cultural, and environmental, that may affect population trends. Since such factors cannot always be accurately forecast, demographic projections into the distant future are necessarily inexact. Nor is unpredictability the only problem that demographers have to face. Many of the statistics that they have to work with are merely estimates, which in many cases are unreliable. A number of less developed nations do not have an efficient and regular population census, and demographic statistics from many of these countries are based to some extent on guesswork. The United States has an elaborate population census every ten years, but the Bureau of the Census believes that about 7 million people—vagrants, illegal immigrants, illiterates, and others—were omitted from its last census in 1980. Despite these limitations, however, demographers can use current data to give reasonably accurate projections for the relatively short term—say, the next quarter century or so. They can also offer long-range projections, but these will hold good only under specified hypothetical conditions.

Population Dynamics

Population growth or decline in a given society is affected by three factors: the birth rate, the death rate, and the rate of migration into or out of the society.

Birth Rate

The *birth rate* is the annual number of births per thousand members of a population. In the impoverished Asian country of Bangladesh, for example, the birth rate is high, 47 per thousand; in Canada it is low, 15 per thousand. In addition to these societal birth rates, demographers can also determine more specific birth rates for particular subgroups

Figure 21.1 *The fertility of women (the actual number of children they bear) rarely approaches their fecundity (the number they are theoretically capable of bearing). Although some women, like the mother of this Wisconsin family of a century ago, may approach the fecundity level of twenty or more children, in practice very few women do so.*

in a population, such as Hindus in Bangladesh or French speakers in Canada.

The birth rate allows us to determine a society's *fertility,* the actual number of children the average woman is bearing. Fertility must be distinguished from *fecundity,* the potential number of children that could be born to a woman of childbearing age. The fecundity of a physically normal woman during this period is about twenty to twenty-five children. In practice the actual fertility of women in any society does not even approach this level of fecundity, because a variety of cultural, social, economic, and health factors prevent such prolific breeding.

Death Rate

The *death rate* is the annual number of deaths per thousand members of a population. In Bangladesh the death rate is high, 17 per thousand, while in Canada it is comparatively low, 7 per thousand. Again, it is possible to construct specific death rates for particular categories in the population. The infant death rate for American blacks, for example, is 20 per thousand, while that for whites is 10.5 per thousand.

The death rate is related to *life expectancy,* the number of years that the average newborn in a particular population can be expected to live. In the United States, life expectancy has increased from about forty-seven years at the turn of the century to about seventy-five years today, largely as a result of a decline in the infant mortality rate. Life expectancy must be distinguished from *life span,* the maximum length of life possible in a particular species. Although human life expectancy in most societies has increased markedly during this century, the life span has increased little, if at all, and very few people live beyond a hundred. We have been unable to extend the life span because we have been unable to combat the diseases of old age—cancer and degenerative conditions of the heart, lungs, kidneys, and other organs—as easily as the infectious diseases of childhood.

Migration Rate

The *migration rate* is the annual difference between the number of immigrants (people entering) or emigrants (people leaving) per thousand members of the population. Again, specific rates can be constructed for particular categories of immigrants and emigrants.

Migration rates obviously do not affect the increase or decrease in global population, but they may be an important factor in specific societies. The United States is a case in point: in recent years, immigration has accounted for more than half of the society's annual growth rate. Immigration to North America in the late nineteenth and early twentieth centuries was part of the most massive migration in history, in which some 75 million Europeans left their continent and settled in North and South America, parts of Africa, and Australasia. Migration is the product of two interacting factors. The first is "push," which refers to the conditions that encourage people to emigrate from an area (such as the potato famine in Ireland). The second factor is "pull," which refers to the conditions that encourage them to immigrate into a particular place (such as the promise of a new and better life in the United States).

Growth Rate

Changes in population size are measured by the **growth rate,** the difference between the number of people added to, and the number of people subtracted from, a population, expressed as an annual percentage. The average world growth rate at the moment is about 1.7 percent per year. The United States now has a relatively low annual growth rate of 0.7 percent, and a few areas in Europe, such as Hungary and West Germany, actually have negative growth rates, meaning that their populations are shrinking. The industrialized countries of the world generally have growth rates under 1 percent, but the less developed countries typically have rates that are well above 2 percent. Some, such as Syria and Guatemala, have rates above 3 percent.

Expressed in percentage terms, these differences seem small. But their long-term impact is staggering. The reason is that population growth is *exponential:* the increase each year is based not on the original figure but on the accumulated total up to that time. A population of 10,000 with a growth rate of 3 percent will thus increase in ten years not by 30 percent, to 13,000, but by about 34 percent, to 13,439. A very useful concept in analyzing the effects of exponential growth is **doubling time,** the period it takes for a population to double its numbers. A population growing at 1 percent will double itself in 70 years; a population growing at 2 percent will double itself in 35 years; and a population growing at 3 percent will double itself in 23 years. Thus the population of Belgium, currently growing at around 0.1 percent each year, would take about 1,155 years to double if present rates were maintained, but the population of Mexico, growing at 2.6 percent each year, would double within 27 years.

The history of world population growth gives some idea of the dizzying speed and numbers exponential growth can produce. In 8000 B.C. the total human population was probably about 5 million people. By A.D. 1 it had risen to about 250 million. A thousand years later it had increased to around 300 million, and by 1650, to half a billion. By the end of the next two centuries, it had doubled to a billion; eighty years later, in 1930, it had doubled again, to 2 billion. The most recent doubling to 4 billion was completed in fifty years, by 1980; and if the present growth rate continues, the next doubling to 8 billion will take around forty years. About one out of every twenty persons who have ever inhabited this planet is alive today, and by the year 2000 the world will contain well over twice as many people as when most readers of this book were born.

Obviously, population cannot continue to increase at this rate. The process can be halted only by a sharp decrease in the birth rate, by a sharp increase in the death rate, or by some combination of the two. If each set of parents reproduced only enough children to replace themselves (about 2.1 children per family, taking into account those who died young or who for other reasons did not reproduce themselves), we would ultimately have **zero population growth** (ZPG), a situation in which population size would remain stable.

WORLD POPULATION GROWTH FROM 8000 B.C. TO THE PRESENT
Population in billions

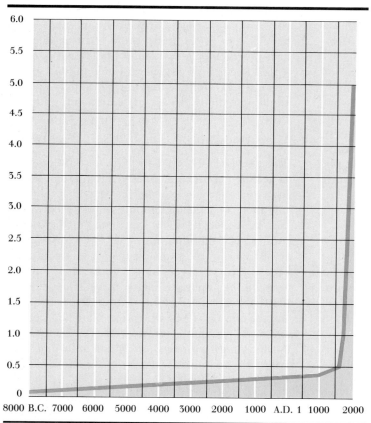

SOURCE: Population Reference Bureau.

Figure 21.2 *This graph gives some idea of the implications of exponential population growth. Clearly, growth at this rate will have to come to a drastic halt, either through a decline in the birth rate, an increase in the death rate, or both.*

Age Structure

A stable world population is a long way off, however. Even if every set of parents in the world had only 2.1 children from this moment on, world population would continue to increase for many years. The reason is that the children who have already been born would still grow up and reproduce themselves. A society's *age structure*—the relative proportions of different age categories in a population—is therefore an important element in predicting demographic trends. The younger a population is, the more "momentum" it has for further growth.

In most developed societies roughly one-fourth of the population are under the age of fifteen. In Denmark, for example, the figure is 18 percent; in East Germany, 19 percent; in Canada, 22 percent; and in the United States, 22 percent. But in the developing nations the proportion of people under fifteen is very much larger. In Brazil, it is 38 percent; in Algeria, 46 percent; in Kenya, 53 percent. These countries consequently have a vast potential for future population growth, regardless of whether their birth rates decline in the next few years. Indeed, even if parents the world over reproduced only enough children to replace themselves from now on, population would still soar to around 7 billion before it stabilized. But although the birth rate is stabilizing in many countries, there appears to be little prospect of any drastic decline in global birth rates—a fact that makes the alternative "solution," a sharp increase in the death rate through famine, disease, and war, all the more probable.

Let us look at the population problem in more detail, first in the world as a whole, and then in the United States.

The World Population Problem

Birth rates were always very high in preindustrial societies. In most of these societies large families were greatly valued, for each new member was an economic asset in groups that had to hunt or tend animals or wrest their living from the soil. Additionally, high infant death rates encouraged people to raise large numbers of children in the hope that at least some of them would survive into adulthood. It was only in the early stages of the Industrial Revolution in England that the value of large families was seriously questioned for the first time.

AGE STRUCTURES OF SWEDEN AND PAKISTAN

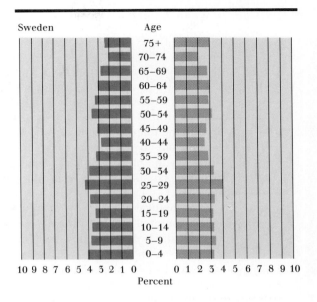

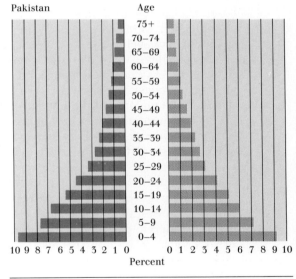

SOURCE: Adapted from Robert H. Weller and Leon F. Bouvier, *Population: Demography and Policy* (New York: St. Martin's Press, 1981), p. 44.

Figure 21.3 *The age structure of a population tells us a great deal about its demographic future. The proportion of young people is very much smaller in Sweden, a developed country, than in Pakistan, a less developed country. Pakistan therefore has a far greater potential for population increase as the younger members grow up and reproduce themselves. You can visualize what might happen to the age structures of each country if the same pattern repeats itself for another generation or more.*

The Malthusian Trap

In 1798, an English parson, Thomas Malthus, published his *Essay on the Principles of Population,* a work that outraged many of his contemporaries. Malthus lived in an age of great optimism, dominated by the idea of the "perfectibility of man." According to this notion, a new golden age of abundance and bliss would be achieved in the future through the marvels of industrial technology. Malthus set out to shatter this idea through a very simple argument, based on his observation that the European population was growing rapidly at the time.

The natural tendency of population growth, Malthus pointed out, is to increase exponentially. But food supply depends on a fixed amount of land, so increases in agricultural production can be made only in a simple, additive fashion by bringing new land under cultivation. Inevitably, therefore, population tends to outrun the means of subsistence. At this point certain factors intervene to keep population within the limits set by food supply—those factors being "war, pestilence, and famine." Human beings, Malthus argued, were destined forever to press against the limits of the food supply. Misery, hunger, and poverty were the inevitable fate of the majority of the human species.

This argument was not a popular one, and Malthus became known as the "gloomy parson." His analysis certainly seemed to offer little hope. The only suggestions he made were the abolition of poor relief—in order to cut the growth rate of the lower classes—and "moral restraint" on the part of the rest of the population. (He himself had three children, only one of whom lived to maturity.) Yet for a while it seemed that Malthus was wrong. He did not anticipate subsequent technical improvements in agriculture, which made possible a vastly increased yield from a fixed amount of land; nor did he foresee the decline in birth rates, combined with growing affluence, that took place in the industrialized nations in the nineteenth and twentieth centuries. Since then, however, an unprecedented population explosion has occurred in the poorer nations of the world, and we have come to recognize that the high living standards of the developed countries have depended in part on their exploitation of the limited resources of the less developed countries. The underlying logic of Malthus's argument is difficult to refute: although we may be able to put off the day of reckoning, population cannot increase indefinitely in a world that has finite resources. We may find ourselves in the Malthusian trap once more.

In demographic terms, the countries of the world fall into two main categories: the developed nations, such as Japan and Canada, which have relatively low birth and growth rates, and the less developed nations, such as Nigeria and Haiti, with relatively high birth and growth rates. Between these two lies a third group of countries with intermediate birth and growth rates; these are mostly the smaller and more industrialized of the developing nations, such as South Korea and Singapore. Rapid population growth is therefore primarily a problem of the poorest nations of the world: in Asia, life expectancy is fifty-nine years and the per capita gross national product is $940; in Africa, life expectancy is fifty years and the per capita gross national product is $740. In Europe and North America, by contrast, life expectancy is around seventy-five years, while the per capita gross national product is over $8,200 in Europe and nearly $14,000 in North America.

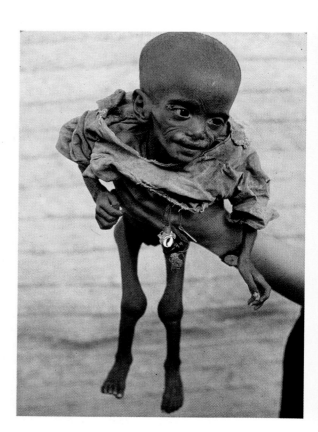

Figure 21.4 *A scene such as this is likely to become more, rather than less, common in the decades ahead. Much of the world's population is undernourished, and famines are now frequent, especially in Africa.*

Much of the poverty in the less developed countries results from an unequal distribution of global resources. If all the world's food were equally distributed, there would be enough to maintain the present population above subsistence level. But in fact, half the world's grain is fed not to people but to livestock, so that a small part of the global population may enjoy a diet high in animal meat and fats. In years when millions of children in other countries literally starve, the United States government pays farmers millions of dollars to keep land idle, in order to avoid local surpluses and maintain prices. And even if the various political and distribution problems could be overcome, the world's food would feed only a third of the present population at the dietary level that North Americans take for granted.

Moreover, the gap between the rich and the poor nations is steadily widening and is likely to continue to do so. If we project future demographic trends in some of the less developed countries, the picture becomes bleaker still. Kenya, growing at a rate of 4.2 percent a year, with a per capita gross national product of $340, will double its population in 17 years. Mexico, with a population of 82 million people, and a per capita gross national product of $2,180, would have about 2 billion people in 100 years if present growth rates were to continue—a population equal to about 40 percent of all the people in the world today.

The Causes of Rapid Population Growth

Why is population increasing at such a speed in the less developed nations? The main reason is a change and resulting imbalance in the ratio of births to deaths. The death rate in these societies has been sharply reduced by the introduction, however haphazard, of modern standards of sanitation, nutrition, and medicine—but the birth rate has remained extremely high. In the industrialized societies, similar innovations in public health occurred over many decades, and there was time for cultural values about family size to adjust to the changed material conditions. In the newly developing nations, however, vaccinations, sewage systems, pesticides, and new dietary practices have been introduced with dramatic suddenness, causing a sharp drop in death rates while the birth rates remain at or near their previous levels. (Nepal, for example, has a birth rate of 42 and a death rate of 18; Mexico, a birth rate of 32 and a death rate of 6.) A complicating factor is that the less developed

countries, unlike the early industrial societies, are facing rapid population growth at a time when they already have very large populations—so even a small annual growth rate produces huge numbers of babies.

Given this sharp decline in death rates and an already existing population strain, why have birth rates remained high in the less developed nations? The reason is that people everywhere are reluctant to accept changes in cultural values, particularly those related to the family. In many traditional societies a man's virility is gauged by the number of children he fathers, and most traditional societies emphasize the domestic role of the wife as mother and child-rearer. Poorly educated people in a tradition-bound society may have difficulty appreciating that the value of a large family has changed within the course of a generation or so. Even today, in fact, a large family may serve important functions for parents in developing societies. In countries that lack a system of social security, children provide the only guarantee that one will be looked after in old age.

A Demographic Transition?

There is a glimmer of hope in this otherwise bleak picture. We have noted that the early industrial societies faced a rapid population increase as their living standards rose and their death rates fell. We noted also that their growth rates tended to level off afterward as a result of a fall in the birth rates. This historical sequence has led some demographers to ask whether the same process might occur in other countries as they also industrialize.

Demographers refer to this process as the *demographic transition*—the tendency for birth rates to drop and population to stabilize once a society has achieved a certain level of economic development. According to demographic-transition theory, people generally have as many children as they believe they can support—and parents in urban, industrialized societies, where children are an economic burden rather than a benefit, prefer small families. The problem in the less developed societies, then, is that although they are beginning to urbanize and industrialize, there is a culture lag between parents' values and their rapidly changing material circumstances.

The demographic transition appears to proceed through three basic stages:

1. *High birth rate, high death rate: stable population.* This is the situation in all traditional socie-

ties. People have a large number of children, but there is a very high death rate, especially among infants. Births and deaths more or less cancel each other out, so population numbers remain fairly stable.

2. *High birth rate, low death rate: population increase.* This is the situation found in all developing societies as they shift from preindustrial to industrial modes of production. The birth rate remains very high but the death rate drops sharply because of improved living standards and medical care. As a result, population grows rapidly.

3. *Low birth rate, low death rate: stable population.* This is the situation found in the advanced industrial and the emerging postindustrial societies. The birth rate drops as large families come to be seen as a liability, and the death rate remains low. As a result, births and deaths tend to become balanced once more, and the population growth rate declines toward zero.

The demographic transition is now almost complete in Europe, North America, and Japan. Encouragingly, several of the less developed nations—such as Tunisia and China—are showing a steady decline in birth rates, suggesting that they are in transition between stages two and three.

THE DEMOGRAPHIC TRANSITION

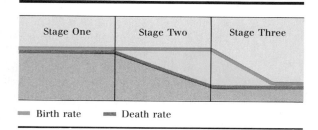

Figure 21.5 *According to demographic-transition theory, the high population growth rate in the less developed countries should be only a temporary phenomenon—if they follow the same "demographic transition" that occurred historically in the developed societies. According to this theory, a preindustrial society usually has similar birth and death rates (stage one). As the society industrializes, the death rate drops, but the birth rate remains constant, leading to population increase (stage two). But with further industrialization, the birth rate declines to much the same level as the death rate (stage three). It is uncertain, however, whether some of the less developed societies will achieve such a transition.*

Other less developed nations, however, such as Uganda and Ecuador, are in stage two. But in time—if the demographic-transition theory is correct—their birth rate should also decline.

How valid is this theory? First, we must recognize that it is merely a hypothesis. The fact that some societies have followed a pattern of demographic transition does not mean that every society will do so. It is possible that specific factors operating in a particular society could speed the transition—or delay it, or even "freeze" it at a particular point. A second problem is that demographic-transition theory assumes that an economic "threshold" of urbanization and industrialization must be reached before the transition will take place. Yet the poorest and most populous nations are precisely those that find economic advancement most difficult. The reasons lie in the vicious cycle of poverty and overpopulation.

A country with a rapidly growing population has a disproportionate number of children—perhaps 40 to 50 percent of the inhabitants. As a result, the work force must put much or most of its efforts into feeding relatively unproductive members of society. Per capita income is therefore very low, and living standards and educational levels are consequently depressed. Moreover, capital cannot be accumulated in the quantities necessary to spur economic development. As a result, whatever economic advances these countries make may be literally eaten up by their increasing populations and used to accommodate more people rather than improve the health and welfare of the existing population. A country whose population doubles in twenty or thirty years has to double its national income in that period—a staggering task—merely to maintain the same level of subsistence.

What, then, are the prospects for a global demographic transition? Some writers venture predictions of impending doom, but many similar past prophecies of mass starvation and other dire consequences have not been fulfilled (Sax, 1960; Osborn, 1962; Erlich, 1968). In fact, the world population growth rate has declined from around 2.0 percent in 1970 to 1.7 percent today, largely because birth rates have dropped significantly in the two most populous nations on earth, China and India. During this period, too, food production has kept ahead of population growth on every continent except Africa, where famines are now commonplace (Enzer, 1978; Scrimshaw and Taylor, 1980; Selim, 1980). In the light of these general trends, other writers have taken a more optimistic view. Julian Simon (1981), for example, claims that human beings will always be able to use the "ulti-

Figure 21.6

"*Excuse me, sir. I am prepared to make you a rather attractive offer for your square.*"

Drawing by Weber; © 1971
The New Yorker Magazine, Inc.

mate resource" of their ingenuity to find new technologies to exploit the environment, and that the world will therefore be able to support many more people, just as it always has in the past.

This is a comfortable assumption, particularly for those who do not have to eke out an existence on a daily basis in an impoverished, overpopulated country, but it may prove as ill-founded as the alarmism of the extreme pessimists. After all, the difference between a global growth rate of 2.0 and one of 1.7 is the difference between a doubling time of 36 years and one of 41 years, which in a world of around 5 billion people is hardly cause for celebration. It may prove to be the case that the planet lacks the resources to support many billions of people at anything remotely resembling the standard of living of the developed countries. Nor is it easy to see how the environment could tolerate the amount of pollution involved in a world consisting entirely of heavily populated and fully industrialized societies. It is possible that some of the less developed societies will never reach the level of socioeconomic development that has historically been necessary before a demographic transition occurred (Barnes, 1982). The best that can be said is that, at present, the demographic fate of the world and its peoples hangs in precarious balance.

Population in the United States

The United States is the world's wealthiest nation, fully capable of supporting its population at a very high standard of consumption. Does the society have a population problem? To answer this question, we must first look at the society's demographic characteristics.

American Demographic Characteristics

The current population of the United States exceeds 240 million. The birth rate is low and reflects a consistent trend of declining fertility over the past 150 years. In 1820, the birth rate was 55 per thousand, but this level dropped steadily until it hit a low of 17 per thousand during the Great Depression of the 1930s. The years after World War II saw a "baby boom," resulting from a backlog of delayed marriages and a greatly improved economic climate, and the birth rate rose again to around 25 per thousand in the late 1950s. Then it declined once more to a record low of just under 15 in 1970, before rising to almost 16 in 1980, where it now seems to have stabilized. The baby boom was not anticipated by demographers, and neither was the "birth dearth" of the 1970s. The baby-boom generation is now of marriageable age, and there should be an "echo effect" as this large generation reproduces itself, although there are few signs that this is taking place as yet. The reasons include women's desire to have a career outside the home, the tendency of many young adults to postpone marriage, a growing unwillingness to raise large families, improved birth-control techniques, and easier access to abortions.

The death rate in the United States is also low, at 9 per thousand, and life expectancy is extremely high at 75 years of age. Average life expectancy varies according to race and sex: 78.5 years for white females, 73 years for black females, 71.1 years for white males, and only 64.4 for black males. The median age of the population, about 31 years, is relatively high, both in comparison with most other countries and with the nation's past. About 12 percent of the population is sixty-five and over, and this proportion will increase markedly as the baby-boom generation grows older in the years ahead. The death rate will therefore increase noticeably as this generation reaches its seventieth decade.

An American Population Problem?

An affluent society with a low birth and growth rate may not at first sight appear to have a population problem. But the national Commission on Population Growth and the American Future (1972) reported that population growth threatens severe problems for American society—and for the rest of the world—and recommended a national policy of zero population growth.

Zero population growth is still some way off, however. At present, the average American woman is bearing 1.8 children, somewhat less than the 2.1 figure required for zero population growth. Demographers expect the rate to increase slightly, however, as the economic climate improves and as young adults who have delayed marriage begin to raise families. Consequently, zero population growth may not be achieved until well into the next century, probably at a level exceeding 300 million people. The results would be more crowded cities, more demands for energy, and more pollution of the environment—especially if we expect this larger population to enjoy a higher standard of living than it does at present. Immense sums would have to be spent on duplicating existing facilities, such as schools and hospitals; and fresh sources of food, lumber, minerals, and other raw materials—including water, which is already in short supply in many parts of the United States— would have to be found. The commission looked for economic advantages in population increase but found none. Instead, it reported, the quality of life would suffer.

Moreover, American population growth has a global impact. In international terms, a new American child is something of a disaster, for he or she presents a greater threat to the ecology of the planet than fifty Asian babies. With less than 6 percent of the world's population, Americans use more than a third of the earth's energy and material resources and generate almost half of its pollution. The United States already uses, for example, a third of the world's tin, half of its newsprint and rubber, a fourth of its steel, and a fifth of its cotton. Adding another 30 million Americans to the population—which we shall probably do by the year 2000—would be the equivalent, in ecological terms, of adding another 1.5 billion or so Asians to the world. American population growth cannot be considered in isolation from the rest of the world, for the various nations are increasingly interdependent. The American economy relies on the minerals and other raw materials of other nations; if those materials are exhausted, or if other peo-

ples need to use them to support their own growing populations, the American way of life will suffer.

What Can Be Done?

In an effort to avoid a dismal and overcrowded future, many nations, including most of the less developed countries, have adopted policies aimed at reducing birth rates.

Population-Control Strategies

In general, the nations of the world are trying to control their population growth through one or more of three strategies: family planning; antinatalism (that is, antibirth policies); and economic improvements.

1. *Family planning.* This strategy involves parents' use of contraception to limit the number of their offspring. Nearly all the nations of Asia and many countries in other parts of the world are already committed to population limitation through family planning. But no society has yet managed to achieve a significant drop in its birth rate through this means alone. The main reason is that family planning, by definition, permits parents to determine how large their family is to be, and the parents' notion of the ideal family size may not accord with the needs of society. Westerners are often guilty of the "technological fallacy," the belief that merely applying technology to a problem will solve it. But people have to be persuaded to make use of contraceptive technology, and they will not do so if the technology runs counter to their values. Although hundreds of millions of people in the world have been sterilized or have accepted contraceptives, it seems that many of them, perhaps the majority, have done so only *after* they have produced what they believe is a sufficiently large family. Family planning is an essential element in population limitation, but the strategy is not sufficient in itself.

2. *Antinatalism.* This strategy involves public policies intended to discourage births. These policies always include educational programs aimed at changing social values and attitudes about family size, and sometimes offer incentives, such as a cash payment or a gift of a radio or other item, to people who accept contraception or sterilization. Sometimes antinatalism goes even further, involving what most Americans would regard as authori-

YOU SHENG OU YU ZHEN XING ZHONG HUA

Figure 21.7 *China—a country whose population represents a fifth of humanity—has achieved a significant decline in the birth rate through a vigorous antinatalist policy. This policy includes penalties for having more than two children, easy access to contraception and abortion, and continuing publicity for the ideal of a one-child family.*

tarian intrusion into private life. The Japanese government followed a particularly dramatic antinatalist policy after World War II: by encouraging widespread abortions, it achieved the sharpest drop in birth rates ever recorded—from 34 to 14 per thousand in the space of a decade. The outstanding contemporary example of antinatalism is China's: there is an official limit of two children per family, but parents are strongly urged to have only one. Contraception, sterilization, and abortions are freely available, and local officials check on families to make sure they do not exceed their limit. Couples who have only one child receive financial benefits and preferential treatment in jobs and housing; those who have more than two are regarded as antisocial deviants, no small penalty in a highly conformist society (Tien, 1983).

3. *Economic improvements.* As we have seen, the demographic transition is closely linked to economic development, but many of the less developed nations may not have the means to achieve the rapid economic growth necessary to raise living standards to the appropriate level. There is evidence, however, that a different kind of economic reform might bring about a lower birth rate: a fairer distribution of the society's resources. In other words, if people are allowed to enjoy such basics of life as food, shelter, clothing, health care, education (especially for women), and a sense that things will get better in the future, then they tend to voluntarily limit the size of their families. The family-planning efforts of many less developed nations fail, it seems, because the resources of these societies are unfairly shared: typically, a tiny elite enjoys a disproportionate share (and its birth

rate drops), but the mass of the people remain in hopeless poverty (and maintain high birth rates). If this analysis is correct, then policies that focus on a sharing of resources, rather than exclusively on economic development that may benefit only a minority, may be a promising way to reduce global population growth (Hernandez, 1974; Ehrlich and Ehrlich, 1979; Alba, 1980).

Ideological Influences

Political, religious, and other ideological influences affect social attitudes concerning population limitation. Many religions emphasize some version of the Judeo-Christian injunction to "be fruitful and multiply." An old Arab proverb declares that "to have many children is to be blessed by Allah," and Islamic religion in several countries is opposed to birth control. The Catholic Church, which is particularly influential in South America—where very high birth rates and grinding poverty are prevalent almost everywhere—has always opposed the use of contraceptives. To complicate matters further, some governments regard high birth rates as essential for their nations' economic or political strength. Argentina banned the use of contraceptives in 1974 as part of a planned campaign to double its population as soon as possible, in the supposed interests of economic development. In 1980 Chile launched a campaign for "a significant increase in population," in order to ensure "national security." Orthodox Marxists, too, have long held that there is no population problem: there is merely a problem of exploitation of poor people and poor countries by rich people and rich countries. China, in fact, adopted a strongly pronatalist policy for two decades after the communist revolution of 1949—and ended up with more than 1 billion mouths to feed and the strongest antinatalist policy in the world.

Ideological shifts on population control can make strange bedfellows. At the first International Conference on Population in Belgrade in 1964, the United States was a lonely voice strongly urging population control in the interests of the planetary environment and the future of humanity. Arrayed on the other side were the communist countries, Catholic countries, and most of the less developed nations—all of them arguing that economic development would solve population problems. At the most recent conference, in Mexico City in 1984, the United States was again in isolation—this time arguing, against virtually the rest of the world, that "population growth is a neutral phenomenon" whose problems can be solved by capitalism. The reason for the American change of position lay in domestic politics rather than demography: the Reagan administration wanted to appease the powerful right-to-life movement, which is hostile to population control because in some countries it may involve abortion. Only Chile, Costa Rica, and the Vatican shared the administration's position— a position that profoundly embarrassed most American demographers.

Urbanization

Urbanization is the process by which population is concentrated in cities. Urbanization has become a master trend of the modern age, transforming, in the course of a generation or two, the way most people in the world live their lives. But why did it take so long for cities to develop at all, how did urbanization come about, and why has urbanization spread so rapidly in the course of this century?

A hint of the answer lies in the sociological definition of a *city:* a permanent concentration of relatively large numbers of people who do not produce their own food. The emergence of cities depended initially on the development of a food surplus. Only when farmers could produce more food than they needed to sustain themselves was it possible for large numbers of people to abandon agriculture and to engage instead in other specialized and often more rewarding roles, such as those of merchant or craft worker. These roles, unlike that of the farmer, require minimal land area and are more conveniently performed in a concentrated human population. Thus the city was born. But the subsequent growth and spread of cities was hampered for centuries by inadequate means of transporting and storing food. The larger the concentration of people in a city, the more food they require and the greater the distance it must be transported. Large-scale urbanization had to await the Industrial Revolution, which led to highly developed facilities for road, rail, sea, and air transport and advanced technologies for storage by such means as canning, refrigeration, and the use of chemical preservatives (Childe, 1950; Sjoberg, 1960; Mumford, 1961; Berry, 1981; Light, 1983).

The Historical City

The first urban settlements appeared around 6,000 years ago in the Middle East and in Asia, on the fertile banks of the Nile, Tigris, Euphrates, Indus, and Yellow rivers. In later centuries, techniques for domesticating animals and plants were either invented in, or diffused to, other parts of the world, and urban settlements began to appear elsewhere in Asia and the Middle East, in Europe, in Central and South America, and in North and West Africa.

By modern standards, the earliest of these preindustrial settlements were so small that we would hardly consider them cities at all. The biblical city of Ur occupied only about 220 acres, while Babylon covered a mere 3.2 square miles. Even ancient Rome, largest of all the ancient cities and seat of a mighty empire that ruled the Mediterranean world for centuries, never had a population of more than about 350,000 people—about the current size of Omaha, Nebraska. The small scale of these historical cities resulted from several factors. The rudimentary agricultural techniques of the time could not produce a very large surplus; on average, it took about seventy-five farmers to support one city inhabitant. Facilities for communication and transport were primitive. Roads hardly existed (the wheel was unknown in many early settlements) and food usually had to be laboriously carried by human beings or animals from farming areas to the cities.

The major urban centers that developed in Europe after the collapse of the Roman empire were also relatively small, for their populations rarely exceeded 50,000 people. Nor, by contemporary standards, were they very attractive places to live. Their outstanding characteristic was stench. There was an almost total lack of sanitation, so human and domestic wastes were simply dumped

Figure 21.8 *The historical city, such as this one pictured by the fourteenth-century Italian artist Ambrogio Lorenzetti, differed radically from the city in modern industrialized societies. It was very much smaller—we would call it a town, not a city—and its social organization was based on kinship networks. There was no "downtown," because commercial operations were spread throughout the city, with particular crafts and trades concentrated in their own areas.*

through windows or doors into puddles and open sewers that ran along the winding streets, which were often so narrow as to be mere pathways. Largely as a result of these crowded and unsanitary conditions, death rates in the cities were higher than in the rural areas; occasionally, in fact, an epidemic might wipe out half a city's population in a matter of weeks. The most notorious epidemic, the "Black Death," killed about a third of the population of Europe as it spread across the continent between the years 1347 and 1351. Nor did these cities offer the "bright lights" and after-hours entertainment that we take for granted today. There was no illumination of public areas at night, and usually no public police or guards, so few people ventured from their homes after dark. Why, then, did anybody bother to migrate from the countryside to this fetid, dangerous environment? They did so for the same reasons that people have always moved to the city: the prospects of new possibilities, including perhaps social mobility and excitement. In agricultural areas, most people spend their lifetimes working in a routine manner in another person's fields; but the migrant to the city may live an utterly transformed life.

The migrant to the historical city found an environment that differed from the modern industrial city in features other than size and amenities. Kinship networks were the basis of social organization within these cities. With rare exceptions, such as some of the democratic city-states of ancient Greece, the governments were monarchies or oligarchies. There was usually no separate commercial district; the equivalent of "downtown" was the political and religious center of the community. Because most people traveled by foot, traders and artisans worked at home, using their houses as shops, and people following particular trades or crafts often lived and worked in distinct parts of the city. The city itself was commonly divided into "quarters" for various occupational, religious, or other social groups. In many cases the quarters were walled off from one another and their inhabitants locked into their own districts at night. In medieval Europe, for example, Jews were confined to specific areas of the city, called ghettos. Traces of ancient quarters can still be found in many North African towns today.

Small as all these preindustrial cities were, they revolutionized human social organization. Economic and political institutions became more complex. The city-state, in which an urban settlement dominated its hinterland, became the typical political unit and the source of legal and military authority. The relatively large market offered by the urban population encouraged occupational specialization and an increasingly refined division of labor. The cities became—and have always remained—a crossroads for trade, communication, and ideas, and the center of learning and innovation.

The Contemporary City

As we have seen, it is no accident that the rapid growth and spread of cities coincided with the advance of the Industrial Revolution. The huge modern city must rest, at least to some extent, on an industrial base that includes mechanized agriculture, sophisticated communications, transport, and storage facilities, and the variety of specialized, nonagricultural jobs that industrialism provides. However, there are notable differences between the typical cities of the less developed countries that are still attempting to industrialize, and those of the highly industrialized developed countries.

Figure 21.9 *In today's less developed societies, cities often contain a small but fairly affluent center. Immediately beyond this center, however, there are usually poor neighborhoods, frequently including shantytowns and squatter settlements. People from rural areas flock to these urban areas in search of work, but the overpopulated cities have few jobs to offer. This photograph shows contrasting neighborhoods in Rio de Janeiro.*

Cities in Less Developed Societies

Most of the cities in the less developed countries display two characteristic features: rapid growth and extensive poverty. A flood of rural migrants is overwhelming these cities at a time when industrial development has not created enough jobs to support a huge, nonagricultural population. Urban unemployment rates are therefore extremely high, while wages are low and basic facilities such as transport, housing, utilities, medical services, and social security are inadequate or lacking. The Egyptian capital of Cairo, for example, is a thousand-year-old city whose population has soared from half a million to 12 million in the course of this century. One-third of the city's residents have

homes that are not connected to any sewage system, and population density is so great that hundreds of thousands of people live in and among tombs in old graveyards. In the Indian city of Calcutta, many people live on what they can beg from others, and more than 70 percent of the population of 10 million exists on $8 or less per month. Half of all Calcutta homes have no indoor toilets. Most families live in a single room, and over half a million people live, raise children, and die, on the city streets.

Urban areas in less developed societies have a typical layout that reflects the social makeup of their populations. There is usually a city center, often quite smart and affluent in appearance, that contains the political and commercial hub of the area together with the homes of a very wealthy minority. Immediately surrounding this area are established neighborhoods of poor people, and beyond them are the slums and shantytowns of squatters and other recent arrivals from the rural areas.

Cities in Developed Societies

The cities of the industrialized nations grew in a much slower and more orderly fashion than those in the developing world; and for the most part they can quite easily absorb the trickle of migrants who still come from the rural areas. By international standards, these cities offer a superior environment for the bulk of their inhabitants—although they typically do include some poor neighborhoods and tawdry facilities.

The larger cities in the developed societies generally have a fairly similar form. The urban area contains a central city, often inhabited by a small number of the very wealthy and a large number of the very poor. The central city is typically surrounded by suburbs, primarily residential areas that have grown up around the city as the urban population has expanded. A *metropolis* is an urban area containing a city and its surrounding suburbs, and it forms an economic and geographic unity. In several modern societies, metropolitan areas have expanded to such an extent that they have merged with adjacent metropolises. The result is a *megalopolis,* a virtually unbroken urban tract consisting of two or more central cities and their surrounding suburbs. If current trends persist, most inhabitants of modern industrialized societies will eventually live in sprawling megalopolises containing many millions of people and stretching in some instances for hundreds of miles.

At present, great cities are primarily a phenomenon of the developed world: of the ten largest cities in the world, seven are in industrialized societies. But by the year 2020, only one of them—Tokyo—will still be on the list. The nine other largest cities of the time will be located in the developing nations. If any place on earth is the city of the future, it is the one that will be largest of them all, Mexico City. Three decades ago, the Mexican capital was home to 5 million people; today it contains 17 million, by the year 2000 it is expected to hold 26 million, and by 2025, 37 million. Despite the elegance and sophistication of its center, much of Mexico City seems scarcely livable today. Half of all Mexican industry is located in and around the city; it spews forth over 10,000 tons of chemical pollution every day, contributing to tens of thousands of deaths a year. More than 2 million residents have no running water. Some 3 million have no sewage facilities. About 40 percent of the work force is unemployed. Half the population has no access to medical treatment. City facilities are becoming ever more inadequate under the pressure of population numbers—yet rural migrants continue to stream in at the rate of about a thousand every day, seeking the elusive fortune that only urban life can offer. For most of the human population, this is what urbanization has come to mean—a way of life that is unprecedented in the human experience, and a far cry from our ancestral communities of a handful of cave dwellers.

Figure 21.10 *Seattle, like most other cities in the developed societies of the modern world, contains a thriving central commercial and administrative district. Beyond this center are a variety of areas of different land use, such as manufacturing districts and upper-, middle-, and lower-income residential neighborhoods.*

Urban Ecology

Like other social trends, urbanization follows certain patterns. Cities do not dot the earth randomly, nor do they grow in a completely unpredictable fashion. They are cultural artifacts that develop as a result of a complex interplay of environmental and social factors. As we noted in Chapter 3 ("Culture"), the *ecological approach* is one that analyzes cultural elements in the context of the total environment. Urban sociologists have found this approach useful in analyzing urban land use and growth.

Several factors in the natural environment determine the location of cities. Large cities, for example, are generally not found in inhospitable zones—jungles, deserts, polar regions, or at very high altitudes. Most major cities developed from villages and towns that grew up along shorelines or navigable rivers or, more recently, railroads. These settlements became centers of trade and communication and thus had the potential to develop into cities. Various factors in the surrounding natural environment also influence the growth pattern of an urban settlement. For example, mountains must be skirted, lakes and marshes must be drained or avoided, and housing and industry must be placed conveniently near water and raw materials.

Social factors also influence the appearance and development of cities. For instance, a city may be established as a result of a political decision: Brazil created the new capital of Brasilia in the remote interior in order to stimulate the economic development of the surrounding area; and Great Britain has built several entirely new towns to relieve population pressure on existing cities. Prevailing ideas about town planning, such as the grid-pattern concept applied to Manhattan and some American cities, also influence urban layout. The actual use to which land is put often depends on economic factors, because owners tend to

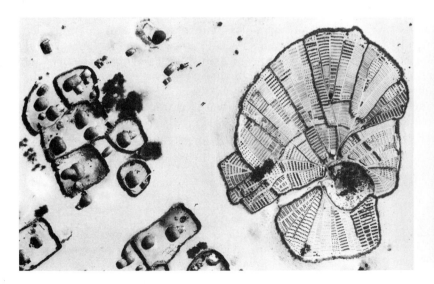

Figure 21.11 *The ecological approach to urban analysis focuses on the natural, social, and other environmental factors that influence the physical arrangements of human settlements. In the first picture, which shows a small community in the Sahara desert, you will notice that the houses (left) are set some distance away from the oasis (right). The reason for this arrangement is that the gardens on which these people depend for food must be situated as closely as possible to the water* source, *so that the labor of carrying water to the plants is minimized. In the second picture, which shows a housing development in Florida, the dwellings are located close to the water, which the residents use for recreation rather than horticulture. The waterfront is so valued in Florida, in fact, that much of this housing development is on artificial islands. The factors that determine the layout of an entire urban area are not always so easily determined, but the same basic principles apply.*

devote their land to whatever use gives them the greatest gain. Land on a hillside, with a commanding view of a valley below, is of more value for upper-class residential property than for factories, which are more conveniently situated on flat land near major transport arteries.

The location of the neighborhoods of different groups is related to such factors as their relative incomes, which determine where they can afford to live, and to their feelings of group solidarity or prejudice against outsiders. The arrival of a group considered "undesirable" by existing residents frequently results in their mass departure, although their exodus may not be immediate. The first intrusions may pass unnoticed, but at a certain stage, the "tipping point," older residents seem to agree that the character of the neighborhood is irreversibly changed for the worse, and that they should leave if possible.

Technological inventions such as the automobile and mass transit systems also influence urban patterns. If workers have to walk to their factories every day, their homes must be near the workplace, but if they can drive to work, they can easily live fifteen miles away. If large numbers of the urban labor force move away from the city center, services and facilities will tend to follow them, perhaps leaving a vacuum that is filled by deterioration. If people can work at home with computer terminals, they can live far from their employers in the city center.

Urban sociologists have offered three specific models of the distribution of people and facilities in the space of a modern city.

1. *The concentric-zone model.* Using Chicago data, Robert Park, Ernest Burgess, and R. D. McKenzie (1925) concluded that a city consists of zones of different land use that radiate out in circles from a central business and administrative district. The first circle beyond this center is a formerly prosperous zone that has now become shabby, and includes marginal businesses and minority-group ghettos. The successive zones thereafter are primarily residential, with homes of working people in the next circle and then the homes of the more affluent at progressively greater distances from the center.

2. *The sector model.* Homer Hoyt (1939) modified this model through this "sector" theory. Hoyt claimed that cities grow in wedge-shaped sectors of different land use that extend out from the center to the periphery, rather like pieces cut from a pie. The reason for this pattern is that a newly developed area takes on the same character as the existing adjacent area: for example, wealthy suburbs develop beyond existing suburbs rather than next to existing ghettos. Industrial areas, too, may take a wedge-shaped form because they tend to follow watercourses and railroad lines.

3. *The multiple-nuclei model.* C. D. Harris and Edward Ullman (1945) reformulated these models further. With more awareness of the impact of automobiles and highways on the development of such cities as Los Angeles, they emphasized that urban areas have several "nuclei," or specialized areas centered on such uses as entertainment, light manufacturing, or retailing. Each of these nuclei, they claimed, influences the character and development of the area around it.

These models are intended to be just that, and not exact descriptions of particular cities. Taken together, they seem to be valid, at least for many North American cities. These urban areas do tend to grow more or less concentrically from the center, but there are "wedges" of similar land use within this pattern, and several "minicenters" are usually present as well. Modern sociologists point out, too, that the development of cities is not just a matter of thousands of individuals (or their elected representatives) making choices over land use. The big players of the urban real estate game are such powerful interests as developers, utilities, highway lobbies, mortgage lenders, and commercial and industrial enterprises. Decisions about where to put shopping malls, highways, and skyscrapers, or about which neighborhoods to demolish in urban-renewal plans, have vast implications for ordinary urban residents but are rarely in their hands (Castells, 1977; Feagin, 1983).

The Nature of Urban Life

Urbanization has radically changed traditional patterns of social life and the nature of human communities. A *community* is a social group with a common territorial base and a sense of shared interests and "belonging." The differences between a community of a few hundred people and one of several millions are so great that some sociologists doubt whether a large city can be usefully described as a "community" at all. What are the defining characteristics of urban life, and in what ways does the urban community differ from the small rural community?

Figure 21.12 *These contrasting pictures suggest the differences between small-scale, traditional communities and the large-scale urban environment of today. The first picture,* Dance of the Peasants, *by Pieter Bruegel the Elder, was painted about 1567. The work captures the features of what Tönnies called the* Gemeinschaft—*its intimacy of interpersonal relationships and sense of community solidarity. The second picture,* The Subway, *was painted in 1950 by the American artist George Tooker. This work reflects some features of the* Gesellschaft—*its anonymity and lack of shared commitment. But while there is some truth in both of these portraits, the features of each are exaggerated. It is unlikely that the peasant community was always so sociable, and the modern city is hardly so impersonal.*

Classical Views

Classical sociological views of the city, published in the late nineteenth and early twentieth century, tended to take a rather pessimistic view: urban life was seen as imposing severe strains on human relationships.

Tönnies: *Gemeinschaft* and *Gesellschaft*

Ferdinand Tönnies (1855–1936) was one of the first sociologists to examine the differences between urban and rural communities. His analysis, first published in Germany in 1887, distinguished between the **Gemeinschaft,** a "community" in which most people know one another, and the **Gesellschaft,** an "association" in which most people are strangers to one another.

In the *Gemeinschaft,* interpersonal relationships are close, people are oriented toward the interests and values of the community as a whole, and they have a strong feeling of shared group membership. Kinship ties are strong, and social life centers on the family. In the *Gesellschaft,* on the other hand, relationships are impersonal and are often based on the practical need that people have for one another, rather than on any emotional commitment. People do not necessarily hold the same values, and they are oriented toward individual rather than group goals. Tradition and custom no longer have a strong influence on individual behavior, and kinship ceases to be the most important basis of social organization. In short, urbanization implies that the community with strong interpersonal bonds is replaced by an association of individuals, most of whose relationships are temporary and impersonal.

Wirth: Urbanism as a Way of Life

Tönnies's work influenced sociologists at the University of Chicago in the 1920s and 1930s, who were especially interested in the problems of the city. The classic statement of the Chicago School's position is contained in Louis Wirth's 1938 essay "Urbanism as a Way of Life."

Wirth argued that three distinctive features of the city—its size, population density, and social diversity—combine to create a style of life that is very different from that of small communities. The *size* of the city produces an anonymous existence, for the individual becomes almost insignificant in a mass environment and cannot know more than a tiny fraction of the other inhabitants. The *density* of the city forces people into contact with one another, but only in terms of highly specific roles—like mail carrier or merchant—and not as whole people. Relationships therefore become rational

and calculated rather than warm and affectionate. The *social diversity* of the city produces an awareness of many different viewpoints and lifestyles, and so tends to break down the individual's unquestioning allegiance to traditional values. In short, the close-knit rural community cannot be reproduced in the impersonal city, where in Wirth's words, "the clock and the traffic signal are symbolic of the basis of our social order."

Modern Views

Modern sociologists are inclined to take a more benign view of the city, emphasizing the opportunities it offers. The Chicago theorists, they suggest, may have suffered from unconscious biases: most of them had small-town origins, and did most of their research in Chicago at a time of economic recession, racial tension, and high crime rates.

Gans: The Urban Mosaic

Herbert Gans (1962a, 1962b, 1968) rejects the view that the city is essentially impersonal. He argues that the city, despite its size, is really a mosaic of different groups and neighborhoods. The individual resident, he claims, experiences city life within

these much smaller and more manageable environments, not in the anonymous city as a whole.

The diversity of the city, according to Gans, results, not from its size, but rather from the fact that it contains people who differ widely in their cultural, ethnic, economic, and other characteristics. The result is a heterogeneous population composed of groups ranging from young adventurers and upwardly mobile professionals, who may avidly enjoy urban life, to ghetto residents and impoverished people, who may feel trapped in the city. Gans insists that there are real communities within the city, which he calls "urban villages." Some of these communities are ethnic neighborhoods in which kinship ties remain strong and there is a genuine sense of community loyalty and shared values. Other communities consist of scattered individuals whose shared interests and pursuits give them a sense of common identity that transcends their physical distance. Urban artists, writers, or intellectuals, for example, may form a community without actually living in the same area of the city. Other research has supported Gans's view. For example, Gerald Suttles (1970) has shown that strong feelings of community solidarity exist in slum neighborhoods, where residents are often acutely aware of the identity, membership, and boundaries of their communities.

Figure 21.13 *Many modern sociologists take a more optimistic view of urban life than their predecessors. They argue that people do not necessarily experience the city as an impersonal environment. The city is actually a mosaic of different communities and subcultures, in which the individual can find a variety of opportunities that would be unavailable in a small-town or rural environment.*

Fischer: Urban Subcultures

Claude Fischer (1975, 1982, 1984) offers a more recent view of urbanism that combines elements of previous theories. His basic idea is that the city actually gives people a sense of belonging because it contains a variety of subcultures that support and cater to interests that cannot be satisfied anywhere else.

In nonurban areas, according to Fischer, people with unusual or even deviant interests are too few in number to form a subculture or community. But in the city, the necessary "critical mass" of potential members exists. In other words, there are enough people devoted to particular kinds of politics, music, art, recreation, drugs, sexual practices, or religious cults for groups to emerge that support these interests and values. So, although the size, density, and social diversity of the city may facilitate unconventional and even deviant behavior, urban life does not necessarily destroy the sense of community. On the contrary, it may help create and develop subcultural communities—private worlds that give people a sense of intimacy and belonging despite the impersonality of the wider city environment.

It seems, then, that a fair reassessment of urban life must take account of both its drawbacks and its advantages. There is little doubt that urban life can be more impersonal and isolating than life in a traditional rural community. The city cuts people off from the beauty of the natural environment and exposes them to too many people, too much noise, and too much pollution. It immerses them in social problems such as poverty, racial conflict, drug addiction, and crime.

But rural life is not all wine and roses. The traditional community lacks many of the comforts and amenities of the city. Large urban populations can support a cultural life of a richness and diversity never found in a small community. The city allows occupational specialization and therefore greater opportunities for fulfilling talents. Its anonymity is something for which many people are grateful. The close relationships of the small community can too often mean that everyone pries into everyone else's affairs. Nonconformists thrive in the more tolerant atmosphere of the city, where behavior that might scandalize a traditional community is ignored or may even be accepted. The city provides a more cosmopolitan outlook, in contrast to the relatively narrow, conservative, and provincial outlook of the small community. Urban living thus offers a much greater opportunity for intellectual and personal freedom.

The American City and Its Problems

The United States is one of the most urbanized societies in the world. You probably live in an urban area: most Americans do. Yet the first U.S. census in 1790 recorded only twenty-four urban places, of which only two had populations of more than

25,000. In 1820 nearly 80 percent of the American people still lived on farms. But by 1920 half the population lived in urban areas; by 1950, 65 percent; and by 1985 the proportion had risen to 76 percent. Two out of every three Americans now reside in urban areas of at least 1 million people, more than 50 percent of the population lives on 1 percent of the nation's land mass, and less than 3 percent live or work on farms.

Population has not only been shifting toward the cities; it has also shifted from the older cities of the Northeast and Midwest to the "sunbelt" cities of the South and Southwest. States such as Arizona, Texas, Nevada, and Florida exert a dual appeal to "snowbelt" residents: they have a more favorable climate and may offer better economic opportunities. The long-term consequences of this migration may be immense, for it signifies the slow demise of the old Northeastern center of economic power and influence and the emergence of a new one centered in the South and West and based on new, high-technology industries such as aerospace development or electronics production. Political power will inevitably follow this demographic and economic shift (Perry and Watkins, 1978; Butler and Chinetz, 1982).

The Metropolis

The fact that most Americans live in urban areas does not mean that they necessarily live in the central cities. In fact, slightly more Americans reside in the suburbs of metropolitan areas than the central cities themselves, and many others live in urban areas with relatively small populations. The Bureau of the Census regards any locality with more than 2,500 inhabitants as an urban area, and it deliberately ignores the boundaries of cities and suburbs in its analysis of urban data. The bureau recognizes that the political boundaries are less important than the social, economic, and communications network that integrates various urban communities into one unit, and it analyzes large-scale urban settlements through the concept of a *metropolitan statistical area* (MSA)—basically, any area that contains a city (or a combination of a city and its surrounding suburbs) that has a total population of 50,000 or more. At present the bureau recognizes over 280 MSAs, containing three-quarters of the American population.

The bureau also recognizes eighteen megalopolises, containing adjacent metropolises that have developed or will shortly develop into continuous urban sprawls. The outstanding megalopolis at present is the chain of hundreds of cities and suburbs on the eastern seaboard from Massachusetts to Virginia—a tract that runs through ten states and contains some 45 million people. Other important megalopolises are currently developing in California (San Francisco–Los Angeles–San Diego), Florida (Jacksonville–Tampa–Miami), Texas (Dallas–San Antonio–Houston), and the Great Lakes area (Chicago–Pittsburgh).

The Suburbs

The growth of suburbs is one of the outstanding features of urbanization in the United States. In 1940, only 20 percent of the American population lived in suburbs; but by 1980 nearly 40 percent were suburbanites. Almost within a single generation, more Americans had come to live in the suburbs than in either the central cities or the rural areas. The rush to the suburbs was facilitated by federally subsidized highways, by the shortage of central-city housing, by economic growth in the 1950s and 1960s, and, perhaps most important, by the sense that suburban living offered the ideal compromise between urban and rural life: one could be close enough to the city to enjoy its amenities, but far away enough to avoid its inconveniences. The single-family detached home, in a development with a countrified name like Park Forest, Oak Glen, or Hillside Acres, became an almost essential part of the American dream.

Life in the suburbs has been the object of a great deal of scorn and satire. It is often thought that the suburbs are dull, homogeneous middle-class bastions, in which the residents are obsessed with the neatness of their lawns and "keeping up with the Joneses." There may be some truth in this picture, but it is probably exaggerated. Suburban residents in general are doubtless more politically conservative, more morally conventional, and more oriented toward family life and the local community than city residents. But the suburbs—many of which are now predominantly working-class or include a high proportion of residents from diverse racial and ethnic backgrounds—appear to be much more heterogeneous and less unlike some central-city neighborhoods than popular beliefs allow. The character of many suburbs, in fact, is changing swiftly. A large and rapidly growing proportion of suburbanites now work in their own suburbs, or in other suburbs nearby. Factories, superhighways, and office complexes are mushrooming, and many of the symptoms generally associated with urban decay are appearing.

Figure 21.14 *Suburban living has often been scorned and satirized, yet it has a very strong* *appeal for many Americans—including the millions who have fled the central cities in recent decades.*

Moreover, the ideal of the single-family detached home may prove a mirage for most Americans. The United States is one of the very few countries in which a majority of families do own their homes, but inflation has now brought the average price of a new single-family home to over $86,000, a figure beyond the means of most American families. For many Americans, then, home ownership is likely to take the form of a condominium, a multiple-unit structure of which each tenant owns only a part. This form of home ownership represented about 5 percent of the housing stock by the end of the 1970s and is becoming the norm so rapidly that by the turn of the century most American families are expected to live in condominiums of one kind or another.

The Central Cities

The Greek philosopher Aristotle once described the city as "a common life to a noble end." That is hardly the kind of description we would apply to central cities in America today, especially those of the older metropolises. The word "city" is more likely to bring to mind images of decaying housing, rundown schools, high rates of crime and drug addiction, racial segregation and tension, overburdened welfare rolls, and deteriorating public services. Why are so many social problems concen-

trated in the central cities of metropolitan areas?

An underlying factor is the growth of the suburbs, which has largely removed the middle class and its local tax money from the central cities. These cities have therefore had to rely for their income on a population that consists disproportionately of poor people, making it generally impossible to compensate for the shrinkage of revenue by raising taxes. The poorer city residents simply cannot afford to pay higher taxes. In addition, higher taxes are likely to act as a further incentive to wealthier residents and businesses to move to the suburbs, where property taxes are frequently lower. To make matters worse, the central city has comparatively more ancient buildings, a far higher crime rate, older public facilities and schools, and a greater proportion of unemployed residents. As a result, it must spend much more money per capita on fire and police protection, building maintenance, transport systems, schools, and welfare if it is to offer services comparable to those of the suburbs. Central-city residents not only pay more than many suburban residents in local taxes; they also get less for their money.

Under these circumstances it is hardly surprising that the urban environment has generally continued to deteriorate and that the suburbs have continued to expand. And because racial and class divisions tend to overlap, the suburbs have been and remain primarily white, while the cities are becoming steadily more black. Almost three-fourths of black Americans now live in metropolitan areas, and of these, 80 percent live in the central cities, mostly in ghettos. Metropolitan residential patterns have thus created a state of segregation almost as effective as that once imposed in the South by law.

One major obstacle to effective metropolitan planning is the fragmentation of metropolitan governments. The problems of the metropolis—highways, mass transit, pollution, school segregation, police protection, public utilities—are regional. The city and the suburbs are politically separate but interdependent in all other respects. The suburbs are viable only because a large number of their residents are able to work in the central cities. Moreover, suburban residents rely on many city services that they do not support through their taxes. Yet some metropolitan regions have dozens of different local authorities, each jealously guarding its own domain in the name of the American tradition of "community control." Los Angeles, for example, has a small central city, a county of nine other cities, and sixty-seven smaller self-governing communities. A rational solution to many problems would be to recognize that the political boundaries between cities and suburbs are outdated. There is little sign, however, that any proposal to integrate urban and suburban communities will be widely adopted in the United States. The suburbanites, who have more political muscle than the central-city residents, usually believe that they have everything to gain by preserving their distance from the troubled central cities.

Various efforts have been made to revitalize the central cities, but the results have been mixed. During the 1950s and 1960s, massive "urban renewal" projects razed many city neighborhoods—including, in some cases, "ethnic villages"—and replaced them with high-rise office buildings and luxury apartments. Most of these "renewed" urban areas are arid, uninteresting places to live or even to walk about in. With buildings that lack any architectural diversity or human scale, they seem cold and colorless. Yet a lesson has been learned from these disasters, and many cities are now beginning to "recycle" older buildings by putting them to new uses. One form of recycling is "gentrification," in which middle-class people ("gentry") buy and renovate older buildings in central-city neighborhoods, turning rooming houses, warehouses, abandoned firehouses, and the like into single-family homes. Gentrification has radically altered formerly decaying neighborhoods such as Park Slope in Brooklyn, SoHo in Manhattan, Queen's Village in Philadelphia, and Adams-Morgan in Washington, D.C. In some cases, however, the process has displaced poorer residents who cannot afford to live in the upgraded neighborhoods. A second form of recycling is the renovation, through public funds, of deteriorating or abandoned central-city facilities, such as old markets or docklands. Twenty years ago these areas would have been targeted for "urban renewal," to be demolished and replaced by featureless high-rise buildings. Instead, careful recycling has produced such immensely successful projects as Ghirardelli Square in San Francisco, the rehabilitated Skid Row in Sacramento, Harborside in Baltimore, South Street Seaport in Manhattan, and Quincy Market in Boston—lively and colorful market areas that attract millions of visitors every year. Unlike so many other urban-planning episodes, these renovations have not neglected the human element that is essential to bringing a great city to life.

Figure 21.15 *The South Bronx in New York has come to symbolize urban decay in America. The scene shows a vandalized statue of George Washington, surrounded by blocks of abandoned houses and apartment buildings.*

Summary

1.   Rapid population growth in a context of limited resources is one of the most serious social problems in the modern world. Much of this population growth has taken place in urban areas.

2.   Demography is the study of population composition and change. The principal factors involved in demographic change are the birth rate, the death rate, and the migration rate. Population growth rate, which is exponential, is also influenced by the age structure of the population concerned.

3.   Malthus pointed out that population tends to grow faster than the food supply. This problem has been averted in advanced industrial societies, but now threatens less developed societies, where population has exploded because death rates have declined while birth rates have remained high. In these societies cultural values concerning large families have been slow to change.

4.   The theory of demographic transition holds that birth rates will decline once developing societies become more industrialized, but the poorest nations may have great difficulty in reaching an adequate level of industrialization.

5.   Despite low birth, death, and growth rates, U.S. population increases will tax natural resources and will place a disproportionate burden on other societies.

6.   There are three possible strategies for reducing birth rates: family planning, antinatalism, and economic improvements.

7.   A city is a permanent concentration of fairly large numbers of people who do not produce their own food. Urbanization is one of the most significant trends in the modern world. Historical cities remained small, but industrialization has encouraged the growth of large cities. In the less developed countries, cities contain an affluent center surrounded by slums. In fully industrialized societies, cities contain a central city and suburbs, which together form a metropolis. When metropolises merge, they form a megalopolis.

8.   The ecological approach attempts to explain the appearance and growth of cities in terms of influences from both the social and natural environment. Three main models of urban growth have been proposed: the concentric-zone model, the sector model, and the multiple-nuclei model.

9.   Classical theories of urban life focused on the drawbacks of city life. Tönnies saw the city as an association rather than a community, and Wirth stressed the impersonality of urban life. Modern theories focus more on the opportunities of city life. Gans sees the city as a mosaic of communities, and Fischer stresses the city's subcultural diversity.

10. The United States is a highly urbanized society, with most people living in metropolitan areas. Suburbs have expanded rapidly and now contain more people than central cities do. The central cities face continuing problems, largely as a result of the flight of middle-class residents and their local tax money to the suburbs.

Important Terms

demography (566)

urbanism (566)

birth rate (566)

fertility (567)

fecundity (567)

death rate (567)

life expectancy (567)

life span (567)

migration rate (567)

growth rate (568)

doubling time (568)

zero population growth (568)

age structure (569)

demographic transition (571)

urbanization (576)

city (576)

metropolis (579)

megalopolis (579)

ecological approach (580)

community (580)

Gemeinschaft (582)

Gesellschaft (582)

metropolitan statistical area (MSA) (585)

Suggested Readings

BARNEY, GERALD O. *The Global 2000 Report to the President of the U.S.* New York: Pergamon Press, 1980.

The report of a presidential commission on the long-term consequences of population growth and resource depletion; the conclusions are generally pessimistic.

FISCHER, CLAUDE S. *The Urban Experience.* 2nd ed. New York: Harcourt Brace Jovanovich, 1984.

A short and very readable introduction to urban sociology, recommended for an overview of the field.

GUPTE, PRANAY. *The Crowded Earth: People and the Politics of Population.* New York: Norton, 1984.

A good overview of the social and environmental effects of population growth, and of the political ramifications of population control.

JONES, LANDON. *Great Expectations: America and the Baby Boom Generation.* New York: Ballantine, 1981.

An interesting account of the past, present, and potential future effects of the baby-boom generation on American society.

MUMFORD, LEWIS. *The City in History.* New York: Harcourt Brace Jovanovich, 1961.

A rich and fascinating account of the rise and role of cities in history by one of the foremost experts in the field.

SALE, KIRKPATRICK. *Human Scale.* New York: Coward, McCann, and Geohegan, 1980.

An interesting discussion of urban planning by a writer who advocates small-scale developments as a means of countering urban impersonality.

SIMON, JULIAN L. *The Ultimate Resource.* Princeton: Princeton University Press, 1981.

Simon presents the controversial argument that resources are essentially inexhaustible because human technology will always find substitutes or new ways of exploiting existing resources.

U.S. BUREAU OF THE CENSUS. *Statistical Abstract of the United States.* Washington, D.C.: U.S. Government Printing Office.

An annual Census Bureau publication, containing up-to-date information on the American population and a remarkable variety of aspects of American life.

CHAPTER 22

Technology and Environment

One of the most distinctive of all human characteristics is that we are tool-using animals. True, a few other animals have learned to employ implements in a rudimentary way: for example, sea otters sometimes use rocks to smash mollusk shells, and chimpanzees occasionally use twigs to extract termites from their nests. But the tool use of other species has little if any permanent effect on their social or natural environments. People, in contrast, have used increasingly sophisticated techniques to act on the social and the natural world for thousands of years—and they have done so in ways that have transformed, and continue to transform, the very conditions of life on the planet.

Over the generations, such cultural artifacts as the knife, the wheel, the plow, gunpowder, irrigation, screws, windmills, dams, the compass, clocks, the printing press, steam engines, vaccinations, pesticides, television, rockets, lasers, and nuclear reactors have dramatically influenced our social and sometimes our natural surroundings. These and countless similar items are all examples of **technology,** the practical applications of scientific or other knowledge. Modern civilization depends on our ability to translate knowledge of nature into a multitude of gadgets, contraptions, processes, implements, and techniques: aircraft and antibiotics, computers and plastics, assembly lines and telecommunications, synthetic fabrics and skyscrapers.

A recent U.S. Air Force recruitment slogan declares "Technology is taking over the world. Keep up with it or you're going to be left behind." As the slogan correctly implies, technological and social change are intimately connected, particularly in the modern world, where rapid technological and social change tend to go hand in hand. The slogan also implies that technological advancement is desirable. Many people in modern societies, in fact, seem to implicitly assume that techno-

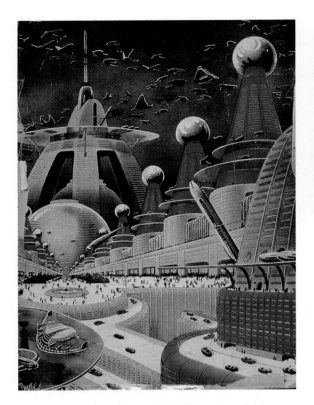

Figure 22.1 *Throughout history, many peoples have had little concept of "progress" toward a better life; and others have seen "progress" as a matter of spiritual development toward a society better attuned to moral, religious, or spiritual values. Since the Industrial Revolution, however, people in the Western world have tended to think of progress in terms of technological advances toward greater material conveniences. Our visions of the future portray, not more happiness, but rather more things—whether in Frank Paul's* City of the Future (1942), *or Syd Mead's* Megastructure (1969).

logical development and human progress are much the same thing. But although some observers see advanced technology as the key to a brighter future, others wonder if it may sometimes be more of a curse than a blessing. Modern technology has certainly offered admirable achievements, but it has also created dismaying problems. We will examine some of those achievements and problems shortly, but first we must consider the relationship of technology to science.

Science and Society

The words "science" and "technology" are often used as synonyms in ordinary speech. But although the two happen to be closely linked in industrialized societies, they are actually quite distinct phenomena. **Science** refers to the logical, systematic methods by which knowledge is obtained, and to the actual body of knowledge produced by these methods. Science, therefore, is concerned with the pursuit of certain kinds of knowledge, while technology is concerned with putting any knowledge—scientific or otherwise—to practical use.

Technology, in fact, is much older than science. Even the most simple societies have some body of knowledge on which their technology is based, even if it extends only to making fire, canoes, or bows and arrows. But that kind of knowledge is not science, for it is based only on trial-and-error experience, not on any understanding of the abstract principles involved. The cave dweller may know how to light a fire—but does not know why it burns, or why some substances burn whereas others do not.

Science, unlike technology, has appeared only rarely in human societies in the past. Scientific knowledge requires a logical, systematic understanding of the principles that underlie natural events, but throughout history the inhabitants of most societies have explained the phenomena of the natural world in mythical, magical, or religious terms. A scientific understanding of the world is necessary, however, for an advanced technology:

automobiles or intercontinental ballistic missiles cannot be invented without a precise knowledge of the relevant scientific principles. The close linkage between science and technology that we take for granted today is a comparatively recent development, yet it is altering our social and natural environments in radical ways.

Science has now emerged as a major social institution in all industrialized societies, where it has become the foundation for technological innovation. How and why did this development take place?

The Historical Background

A few ancient peoples, such as the Arabs, the Greeks, and the Mayans, accumulated a considerable amount of scientific knowledge, particularly in the fields of mathematics and astronomy. These societies recognized very few specialized scientific roles, however, and made little effort to link science with technology. The Greeks possessed a particularly elaborate science, which, had they applied it to technology, might have speeded up the modernization process by many centuries. Why did they fail to do so? The reason seems to lie in the values and social structure of ancient Greek society. The Greeks rigidly differentiated between slaves, who were responsible for work, and citizens, who ideally refrained from such lowly activity and instead pursued intellectual pleasures. The Greeks regarded science as simply an aspect of philosophy, and they sought knowledge of the world for its own sake—not for its relevance to the practical concerns of craft workers such as tanners, silversmiths, coopers, or millers (Farrington, 1949). The ancient Romans were less interested than the Greeks in abstract ideas, and although Greek scientific knowledge was available to them, they based most of their own technology on rule-of-thumb methods rather than scientific principles. With the fall of the Roman empire, scientific advance in the Western world came to a nearly complete halt for almost a thousand years, largely because systematic inquiry into nature was discouraged by the medieval Church.

The rebirth of learning in Europe in the sixteenth and seventeenth centuries marked the beginning of modern science and the first real awareness of technology's potential for influencing social change. However, there were no specialized scientific roles; even in England, where the

most significant scientific innovations of the era took place, science was practiced, almost as a hobby, by gentlemen of leisure. The handful of scientists in this period can still be counted and named, and nearly all of them made notable scientific discoveries. The issues they dealt with, however, were increasingly relevant to the technological problems that faced their society and economy: the bulk of their research was in fields related to warfare, navigation, or industry (Merton, 1970). Eventually, by the end of the nineteenth century, inventors such as Alexander Graham Bell and Thomas Edison used existing scientific research to create such important new technologies as the telephone and the electric light. Even so, science at the turn of the twentieth century was still widely regarded as little more than a respectable leisure activity.

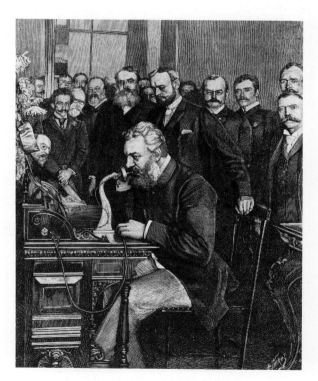

Figure 22.2 *Science and technology became systematically linked only a century or so ago, when scientific knowledge was used to create such technological artifacts as the telegraph and the telephone. This illustration shows Alexander Graham Bell testing the first telephone in 1876.*

The Modern Institution

In the course of this century, the relationship between science and technology has become fully recognized and exploited. The "little science" of the previous centuries has now become "big science," deeply involved in big organizations, big money, and big politics. In all industrialized societies, and particularly in the emerging postindustrial societies such as the United States, science has become a central and highly respected social institution. The number of scientific roles in the United States has expanded enormously; there are now more than 3 million scientists and engineers in the country, more than a quarter of whom are engaged in full-time research. Unlike the scientists of previous centuries, these research scientists rarely work independently in their own private laboratories. Nearly all of them are employed by large formal organizations: private industry employs a majority of scientists, and most of the rest work in the educational institution or for government agencies. The scientists who work in a university or college still have considerable freedom to choose the area of their research, provided some organization or interest can be persuaded to fund the investigation. But in industry or government, the scientist's specific tasks are usually set by the organization in accordance with its own goals and priorities. This is an important consideration, for it explains why American scientific resources are overwhelmingly devoted to such areas as commercial or military research (Dickson, 1984; Noble, 1984).

A highly technological society such as the United States supports science and scientists because it expects some sort of payoff. The federal government provides slightly more than half of the funds that are used for scientific research, and most of the rest is supplied by industry. These sponsors are mainly interested in useful technologies; consequently, they tend to allocate most funds to **applied research,** systematic inquiry that tries to find practical uses for existing knowledge, rather than to **basic research,** systematic inquiry that is concerned with establishing new knowledge. Thus, the determination of how research money should be allocated, be it for AIDS research or "star wars" technology, is the outcome of a political process and has little to do with what scientists themselves consider the most pressing social or scientific problems.

NUMBER OF NOBEL PRIZES FOR SCIENCE, BY NATIONALITY, 1901–1984

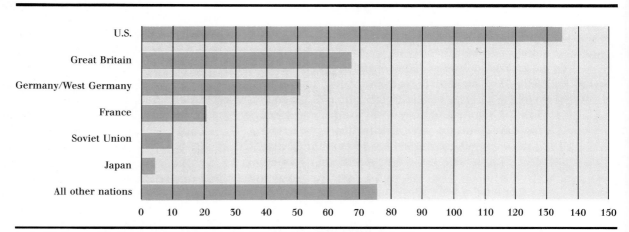

SOURCE: U.S. Bureau of the Census, *Statistical Abstract of the United States, 1986* (Washington, D.C.: U.S. Government Printing Office, 1986).

Figure 22.3 *The United States has won a remarkably high proportion of Nobel prizes in science. The main reasons for this performance appear to be an atmosphere that encourages scientific initiative, and the extensive support that government, industry, and educational institutions give to research. For such a large and powerful country, the Soviet Union does poorly in this respect— probably because state bureaucracies are the only source of research funds, and the atmosphere of academic freedom that is so vital to research is lacking.*

Scientific Innovation

Like football, courtship, or war, scientific research is itself a form of social behavior, and as such is a topic of sociological interest in its own right. Over the past four decades, sociologists have carefully studied the social process of scientific innovation—that is, the way new scientific knowledge is discovered, disseminated, and received.

Science is not just the creation of curious individuals performing whatever experiments happen to capture their fancy. Scientific research is merely one aspect of the *social construction of reality,* the process by which people create their understanding of their environment. As we noted in our discussion of this process in Chapter 6 ("Social Interaction in Everyday Life"), our understandings of even such basic concepts as time and space are constantly modified under changing social conditions. Inevitably, the topics that scientists study, the questions they ask, and the reactions of the scientific community to an individual's research are all influenced by social forces, both within and beyond the scientific community. Actually, what scientists see in the world depends not just on what they look at. It also depends on what their training and unconscious assumptions have predisposed them to find (Kuhn, 1962; Boorstin, 1984; Brannigan, 1981).

Not too surprisingly, discoveries that challenge important existing assumptions or values may provoke intense controversy and even resistance. It is quite common, in fact, for a major new theory or discovery to cause an intellectual scandal in the scientific community and in the society beyond. Galileo's colleagues refused to look through his telescope to see the moons of Jupiter. Giordano Bruno was burned at the stake for proclaiming that the earth revolved around the sun. Pasteur's germ theory was ignored by the surgeons of his time, who could have saved countless lives simply by washing their hands and instruments before operating on patients. Harvey's theory of the circulation of the blood was greeted with howls of laughter when he delivered a paper on the subject to other physicians. Darwin was reviled for his theory of evolution (on one occasion a bishop asked him in public whether he was related to an ape on his father's or his mother's side). Freud was shouted down by his outraged colleagues when he outlined his theory of sexual and other unconscious motivations for behavior. The discoveries of modern physics, such as gravitation, relativity, wave theory, and quantum theory, were vigorously resisted by many scientists for years after they were first announced. Yet, in time, these ideas have come to be taken for granted by the scientific community, and in some cases have led to significant new technologies. What means does the scientific community have for ensuring that valid new knowledge is developed, disseminated, evaluated, and eventually accepted?

The Norms of Science

Writing from a functionalist perspective, Robert Merton (1942) asserts that the scientific community has developed a set of four shared norms that help to ensure the orderly advance of scientific research. Essentially, the norms are as follows:

1. *Universalism.* This norm emphasizes the universal nature of science and its findings: the enterprise must be open to any scientist who has a contribution to make. Particular characteristics of individual scientists—such as their race, class, religion, or national origin—are irrelevant. Research findings must be evaluated purely in terms of their scientific merit.

2. *Communalism.* Scientific knowledge should be made available to the entire scientific community. All science rests on a shared heritage of past discoveries, and no individual can claim property rights over research results. A few scientists may have their discoveries named after them (Boyle's law, Halley's comet, Einstein's theory of relativity), but the discoveries are common property. (Technology, in contrast, can become private or corporate property through the use of patents.)

3. *Altruism.* Scientists are expected to be "disinterested"—that is, free from self-interest in their professional work. Of course, scientists may legitimately hope that their work will be recognized and praised by the scientific community, but their main aim should be to advance scientific knowledge. In other careers—in business, say, or in politics—it is almost expected that people will distort the facts to serve their own ends, but in the scientific community the dishonest manipulation of data or any other fraudulent practice is intolerable.

4. *Organized skepticism.* Scientists are expected to be skeptical, and to suspend judgment until all the facts are at hand. No theory, however ancient and respected or new and revolutionary, can be accepted uncritically. There are no areas in science so sacred that they may not be investi-

gated, even if political or religious dogma forbids it. This skepticism is "organized" in the sense that it is built into the scientific method itself and is binding on all members of the community.

Merton (1973) recognizes that these norms, like any others, are sometimes violated, and there is growing evidence that scientists are by no means as universalist, unselfish, altruistic, or open-minded as the norms may seem to imply (Edge and Mulkay, 1976; Broad and Wade, 1983; A. Kohn, 1986). For example, scientists often violate the norm of universalism, preferring to evaluate research results on the basis of such personal criteria as a researcher's reputation. As Merton himself has noted, there is a "Matthew effect" in science (the term derives from the biblical promise that "To everyone that hath, more shall be given"). Prominent scientists tend to enjoy more credibility and a wider audience than unknown scientists, regardless of the quality of the current work of each. Similarly, scientists often violate the norm of communalism by keeping their ongoing research secret, for fear that other scientists will "steal" their work and thus get credit for it. For example, in the mid-1980s two of the leading French and American AIDS researchers, Luc Montagnier and Robert Gallo, systematically denied each other access to their own work, and even went to court to settle the question of who discovered the AIDS virus first. (They eventually settled privately, agreeing to share the credit.)

Scientists may also violate the norm of altruism, for they may be as greedy or as ambitious as anyone else. There is actually some outright fraud in science—deliberate bias, plagiarism, suppression of inconvenient facts, bogus claims, and even forgery of research results. In the late 1970s, for example, a prominent Harvard medical researcher was found to have faked his results in more than 100 research publications over a period of some fourteen years; he was caught when a junior assistant rummaged through the contents of his trash can and found forged "data" for experiments that had never been conducted (McKean, 1981; Silberner, 1982). And the norm of organized skepticism is perhaps the most frequently violated of all. Like the rest of us, scientists have their private values and prejudices, and they may be passionately committed to particular viewpoints or theories. In a study of forty-two leading scientists who took part in the Apollo moon research project, Ian Mitroff (1974b) found that every one of them "thought the notion of the objective, emotionally disinterested scientist naive."

Even if the norms are sometimes violated, however, they are still the norms—and thus provide a moral framework for the scientific enterprise, helping to ensure that the production of new knowledge, and perhaps its eventual application to technology, is not arbitrarily hindered.

Competition in Science

Many sociologists, particularly those writing from a conflict perspective, point out that another important factor in scientific innovation is competition among scientists (Mulkay, 1974; Mitroff, 1974a). Fame and honor go to the scientist who arrives first at a discovery. The scientist who gets there second by independent work is ignored, no matter how meritorious his or her work. (In fact, one reason that scientific fraud may go undetected is that so few research findings are ever replicated, or independently verified. Researchers get no acclaim for following in the footsteps of others, and so prefer to break new ground instead.)

Professional recognition is of great importance to the scientist. Particularly in the United States, this recognition is essential for a successful career in higher education. The university or college scientist must "publish or perish" because tenure and promotion usually depend on a continuing output of journal articles and scholarly books. The more original work a scientist publishes, the more honors—in the form of prizes, awards, honorary degrees, promotions, or citation by others in their own publications—he or she receives. For this reason, the course of research on a particular topic sometimes involves a *priority dispute,* an argument about who made a particular discovery first. One study found that more than 60 percent of scientists had been "scooped," or anticipated by others at least once in their careers, 17 percent had been anticipated more than twice, and about a third were worried about being anticipated in their present research (Hagstrom, 1974).

The desire for recognition may hamper scientific innovation in that it encourages secrecy, but it has several useful effects as well. First, it encourages scientists to make their findings known as soon as possible. For example, Darwin tinkered with his theory of evolution for seventeen years before he published it; he was finally spurred to write his book, in the space of a few months, only by the realization that he was about to be "scooped" by someone who had independently reached the same conclusion, Alfred Russel Wallace. Second, competition reduces a wasteful du-

Figure 22.4

Drawing by D. Reilly; © 1985
The New Yorker Magazine, Inc.

plication of effort, for scientists are motivated to tackle only those problems that others are not working on. Scientific effort is thus efficiently allocated among the various problems that exist. Third, competition encourages scientists to explore new specialties or even to found new disciplines in existing areas of ignorance, where their chances of making significant contributions are greatest. In fact, some new disciplines were created by applying knowledge from one field to an entirely new field. Sociology, for example, was originally conceived by Auguste Comte as "social physics," in the novel belief that "laws" analogous to those of the natural sciences could be applied to human society. Similarly, molecular biology was created primarily by nuclear physicists who deserted their own field in order to apply its concepts to the science of living organisms. Competition among scientists thus provides impetus and direction to the research process (Hagstrom, 1965, 1974; Polanyi, 1951).

Paradigms in Science

In an influential analysis of scientific innovation, Thomas Kuhn (1962) points out that there are two rather different kinds of scientific innovation: the cumulative increase of knowledge during the "normal" or routine process of research, and the radical change in knowledge that results from a scientific "revolution," in which scientists come to look at their subject matter in an entirely different way. Most scientific innovation is of the normal kind, but occasionally—as when Darwin's theory of evolution transformed the study of biology—a scientific revolution takes place.

Kuhn argues that science does not develop merely through a series of individual discoveries. What often happens is that scientists in a particular field develop what Kuhn calls a *paradigm*—a shared set of concepts, methods, and assumptions about a scientific discipline. A paradigm determines what scientists regard as a problem, a solution, an appropriate research method, or a discovery. Physicists committed to the Newtonian paradigm, for example, interpreted phenomena in one way; physicists committed to the Einsteinian paradigm interpret them in another way. The work of the scientist is, in effect, an attempt to fit nature into the conceptual box provided by the paradigm.

A paradigm, however, is necessary for "normal" scientific innovation. Nature is too vast and complex for haphazard, random investigations to be very successful. A paradigm defines the problems that must be solved and the means that should be used to solve them, and thus focuses the attention of a scientific community upon them. If a science has no paradigm, little progress will be made. Such was the case, for example, with the investigation of electricity until Benjamin Franklin supplied a set of assumptions that were generally fruitful. Research guided by a paradigm therefore helps in the accumulation of scientific knowledge.

Why, then, do scientific "revolutions" occasionally come about? The reason is that research under a particular paradigm will continue to generate new questions—some of which cannot be answered in terms of the paradigm's assumptions. At first these anomalies may be shelved or ignored, or the paradigm may be modified to take account of them. In the end, however, so many anomalies may emerge that the paradigm becomes a mere patchwork, incapable of containing or explaining the mounting inconsistencies. At this point, scientists begin to cast around for some entirely new paradigm that will yield better results. If a fresh paradigm is proposed that makes more sense of reality, it will eventually triumph over the old paradigm. In this way, the Copernican view of the universe finally replaced the centuries-old Ptolemaic system, in which the earth was supposed to be the center of the universe. In similar fashion Einstein's view of the universe provided answers to anomalies that Newton's view could not explain, resulting in a major scientific revolution in physics.

The response to a paradigm, incidentally, can be strongly influenced by nonscientific considera-

Figure 22.5 *Until Benjamin Franklin's experiments with electricity, researchers on the subject were making little progress, for they did not really understand the phenomenon or how to investigate* *it. Franklin's work provided them with a useful "paradigm," or set of assumptions that made sense of electricity and pointed the way for future research.*

tions. Despite its extraordinary technological implications, Einstein's theory was scorned by Nazi Germany in the 1930s simply because Einstein was Jewish. And between the mid-1940s and the mid-1960s, agriculture in the Soviet Union suffered serious setbacks because the Communist Party endorsed the eccentric biological paradigm of the geneticist Trofim Lysenko. This scientific charlatan claimed, incorrectly, that organisms could pass on to their descendants any characteristics they had acquired from the environment in their lifetimes, and much of Soviet agriculture was organized to take advantage of this "fact." The state imprisoned and persecuted many of Lysenko's critics—with the result that Soviet biologists are now so far behind their Western counterparts that they have become mere onlookers in the new scientific revolution that is occurring in modern biotechnology (Reichlin, 1984).

Technology and Change

For most of the period since the Industrial Revolution, people have tended to see scientific and technological innovation as the route to human happiness. Faith in the direction of technological change began to falter, however, when the first atomic bomb was dropped on Hiroshima at the end of World War II, for the explosion brought the realization that modern science could now be applied in ways that could destroy life on earth. Since then, the prestige of technology has been further eroded by mounting evidence of its potentially disruptive effects on the social and natural environments. Recent opinion polls show that people still acknowledge the extraordinary benefits to be derived from technology, but that many are becoming less enthusiastic about the unknown consequences of headlong technological advance.

In a 1986 U.S. News/CNN poll, for example, a quarter of the public felt that technology would cause more harm than good over the next twenty years.

Problems of Technology

Modern technology is problematic because it has become such an important factor in social change. Major technological changes are introduced in the belief that they will help to solve problems, and they often do so quite successfully. But in solving problems of one kind, technological changes sometimes generate new and different problems, including some that were not foreseen. The response to this situation is usually what Alvin Weinberg (1966) called the **technological fix**—the use of technology to solve problems, including those that prior technology has created. The result may be a complex cycle in which one new technology after another is applied to an ever more complicated situation, with the whole process taking us further and further from the original problem and its solution.

For example, the birth-control pill was introduced as a convenient technology for family planning. It soon had the effect, however, of stimulating a "sexual revolution" in which permissiveness became more socially acceptable than before. Many single women became sexually active without using the pill, with the result that greater numbers of unwanted children were conceived than ever before. One result of this trend was a sharp increase in the number of abortions and the number of single mothers. Now a new technological fix is in the offing: an "abortion" pill that will induce an early miscarriage—and which will be as easy to take after conception as the birth-control pill is to take before the act. Thus an old problem leads to a new technology, which in turn leads to a new problem, which in turn generates a new technological fix, which still leaves other complications unaddressed.

Significant technological innovation also causes economic dislocation, for it makes existing products, processes, and sometimes workers obsolete. Modern industry is becoming increasingly dependent on **automation,** the replacement of workers by nonhuman means of production. To be replaced in one's job by a machine can be a humiliating experience, but to employers, automated labor often makes economic sense: machines can work almost continuously, without breaks for food and sleep, and they require no pension plans or

Figure 22.6 *Technological innovations can have far-reaching and complex social effects, many of which were unintended and unanticipated. For example, automobiles were first used by a small leisure class for the ostentatious display of wealth, but once mass-production techniques were applied to car manufacture, pervasive social changes followed. The assembly line, first developed in the car industry, has been duplicated in countless other manufacturing processes. Huge multinational corporations have emerged to produce millions of cars a year. Gasoline has become a critical factor in international trade and politics. A national system of roads and highways has been created, linking communities in ways that the horse or railroad never could have done. Elaborate traffic laws have been introduced. Tens of thousands of Americans are killed every year in auto accidents. Cities have become congested with traffic, and residential patterns have been changed by the development of commuter suburbs. Air pollution from auto exhausts has become a major problem. Leisure and dating patterns have changed. Few of these changes were expected or desired, but all can be traced directly or indirectly to a single technological innovation. Moreover, new innovations have been added to help solve the problems that the auto has created—traffic lights to control vehicle flow, emission devices to cut air pollution, seat belts to protect passengers, weight reductions to conserve fuel, and so on.*

medical benefits. It is hardly surprising, therefore, that human bank tellers are being replaced by automated tellers, or that assembly-line welders are yielding their jobs to robots. As we noted in Chapter 17 ("The Economic Order"), the transition from an industrial to a postindustrial society is causing a wave of "creative destruction" in which old industries and technologies are replaced by new ones. Despite the dislocation it causes, technological innovation creates many new occupations and opportunities—although this is small consolation to millions of workers whose jobs and sometimes careers have been destroyed.

Faith in technology is also shaken periodically by technological disasters, particularly highly publicized failures of artifacts of advanced technology. Such disasters include the sinking of the *Titanic,* the burning of the *Hindenburg,* the crashes of the flawed DC 10 aircraft, the poison gas leak at Bhopal, India, that claimed thousands of lives, the nuclear accidents at Three Mile Island in the United States and at Chernobyl in the Soviet Union, and the explosion of the space shuttle *Challenger.* In each case, a combination of seemingly minor and unrelated failures—in design, engineering, and human organization—combined to create a system breakdown (Allman, 1985). Perhaps, as Charles Perrow (1984) suggests, many technological disasters are simply "normal accidents," an inevitable feature in a world of advanced and rapidly changing technology where we learn from our mistakes as well as our successes.

Another nagging question concerns the purpose of all our technological innovations. We are surrounded by marvelous mechanical and electronic creations, ranging from supersonic passenger jets to cars that talk to us about our unfastened seatbelts. But does all this technological progress make us any *happier?* Do you gain any more satisfaction from a modern automobile than your grandparents might have gained from a Model T Ford? If your children have more sophisticated automobiles than you do today, will they be happier with their lives and more fulfilled as human beings? Do we have a rational reason for climbing ever higher technological peaks, or do we do it simply because they are there? Critics of modern technology such as Philip Slater (1970) wonder whether we are becoming intoxicated with our own technological cleverness—which now ranges from the capacity to conceive babies in a dish to the capacity to wipe out much of the life on the planet within a matter of minutes. The ancient Greeks had a word for the pride of heroes who overreached themselves: *hubris,* an arrogance that defies the gods—and that invariably comes before a fall.

The rapid pace of technological innovation can be a disconcerting problem in itself. At a relatively trivial level, rapid innovation continually

Figure 22.7 *Public faith in the latest technologies is sometimes shaken by technological disasters, such as the destruction of the "unsinkable" passenger liner* Titanic *in 1912, the airship* Hindenburg *in 1937, and the space shuttle* Challenger *in 1986.*

Such disasters capture public attention because of their dramatic nature, while more serious but less visible disasters—such as the pollution of the environment with pesticides and other noxious chemicals—tend to be overlooked.

renders current products (such as computers, video recorders, audio equipment) obsolete soon after they are marketed, so consumers are eternally chasing a material fulfillment that they can never achieve. Perhaps more important, people find that the world alters so rapidly that they barely have time to assimilate the transformations before new changes arrive. But why does technological change occur so quickly in modern industrial and postindustrial societies? As we noted in Chapter 3 ("Culture"), all inventions are based on previous discoveries and inventions. Technological innovations therefore tend to occur exponentially: the more inventions that exist in a culture, the more rapidly further inventions can be made. Consequently, there is a quickening reduction in the lead time between one major technological development and the next—it took centuries, for example, for military technology to proceed from the arrow to the musket, but only a few years to go from the propeller bomber to the jet bomber to the nuclear missile.

Social Control of Technology

Perhaps understandably, some people have come to see technology as an autonomous force—a sort of Frankenstein's monster that is out of control (Winner, 1977; Barrett, 1978). The idea is not new. The nineteenth-century writer Ralph Waldo Emerson declared ominously that "things are in the saddle, and ride mankind"; and in his 1932 novel, *Brave New World*, Aldous Huxley described a utopia in which an impersonal technology kept humanity in comfort, free of want and pain—but without any real experience of choice, creativity, freedom, or the natural world. The French sociologist Jacques Ellul (1964) claims that we have forgotten that technological innovation is a means, not an end, and so have allowed techniques to become a goal in themselves. We have adapted ourselves to technology, rather than the other way around, and now live in a technological rather than a natural environment. As Philip Slater (1970) writes:

> We poke our noses out the door each day and wonder breathlessly what new disruptions technology has in store for us. We talk of technology as the servant of man, but it is a servant that now dominates the household, too powerful to fire, upon whom everyone is helplessly dependent. We tiptoe about and speculate upon his mood. What will be the effects of such-and-such an invention? How will it change our daily lives? We never ask, do we *want* this, is it worth it? . . . We simply say "You can't stop progress" and shuffle back inside.

As we noted in Chapter 20 ("Social Change"), a few sociologists have adopted the position of *technological determinism*—the view that the technology available to a society is an important determinant of its culture, social structure, and even of its history. Most sociologists, however, speak of technology as *influencing* rather than determining change. They point out that technological innovation always occurs in the context of other forces—historical, social, political, economic—which themselves help shape the technology and its uses. It is easy to blame technology for auto accidents, pollution, the bomb, or human alienation, but technology is actually only one of several interacting elements in a cultural system. Technology acquires its meaning only in a social context: a technological innovation takes root only when there is some perceived need for it, some resources to devote to it, and some social acceptance of whatever conveniences (or inconveniences) it offers. For example, the United States leads the world in weapons research and production not because some voracious technological monster demands it, but because Congress perceives the need for a huge defense industry, allocates public money to sustain it, and generally enjoys electoral support for this policy. Technology itself is neutral; it is human beings who decide whether or how to use it (Rybczynski, 1983).

Science and technology are not somehow independent of society, although they may sometimes appear that way. Like any other cultural products, they are created and controlled by countless individual men and women. The difficulty is that this control is often haphazard. In a classic example of *culture lag*—the delay between a change in material culture and the adjustment of nonmaterial culture to the change—we have created a complex technology, but have established few social means of monitoring and controlling the consequences.

The lack of systematic social control over scientific and technological innovation presents three main problems. The first, of course, is that haphazard innovations may have many unforeseen and even calamitous effects on social life and on our natural surroundings. The second is that unless innovations take place in accordance with defined social goals, priorities may become distorted—say, toward such trivia as self-heating shaving cream rather than toward more socially desirable ends, such as medical research or energy conservation. The third problem is that a highly technological society poses a possible threat to democracy. Public participation in the decision-making process may become difficult if the relevant facts about important issues—such as the wisdom of building breeder reactors—are beyond the comprehension of both voters and their representatives. Such a situation could ultimately lead to a behind-the-scenes *technocracy,* or rule by technical experts whose specialized knowledge and recommendations are relied upon by those who are officially responsible for decisions (Galbraith, 1979; Lakoff, 1977).

Currently, it is not clear who has—or who should have—the moral responsibility for decisions about research that may have far-reaching consequences. At present, scientists usually cannot and do not control the uses to which their work is put. Ought the responsibility for decisions about new research and technology to rest with scientists themselves, or with industrial and commercial interests, or with government, or with some new control agency such as a "science court" with full legal powers to restrict certain research or applications? So far in the United States, one small step has been taken: Congress has established an Office of Technology Assessment to determine which innovations are likely to have important long-range effects and which innovations should be encouraged or discouraged. It remains to be seen whether this agency, with its vast task and limited resources, will have much influence on the future course of technological change.

With these considerations in mind, we can examine some specific issues concerning the impact of technology on the social and natural environments.

Technology and the Social Environment

The United States is today the most scientifically and technologically advanced society in history. It is also a society in which, perhaps more than in any other, technological development is equated with human progress. The prospect of further technological innovation can certainly be a thrilling one, offering us the prospect of unprecedented material conveniences and ventures into all the realms that are technically possible—even, literally, reaching for the stars. Invariably, however, technological innovations have unanticipated social consequences, and we may consider some of them here.

Mass Media

The mass media are the various forms of communication that reach a large audience without any personal contact between the senders and the receivers. These media are of two basic kinds: the print media, such as books, magazines, and newspapers; and the electronic media, such as sound recordings, radio, and television. All these forms of communication are called "mass" media because, unlike a private conversation or a personal letter, they are directed at a general category of people rather than toward anyone in particular. Over the centuries, the mass media have increasingly broadened the cultural horizons of ordinary people—and, in doing so, have made them aware of new possibilities for themselves and their societies. In this way, media technologies have helped to generate a variety of profound changes in the social world.

We take the mass media so much for granted today that it is difficult even to imagine what intellectual life must have been like before the invention of the printing press. Until that event, almost everyone in the Western world was illiterate, except for the members of a tiny religious and political elite. Consequently, the bulk of the population lived in gross ignorance, knowing little of history or even of the way of life of others in communities more than a few miles away. If they were to gain any knowledge of the world beyond the immediate orbit of family and village, people had to rely on the spoken words of religious figures, elders, storytellers, minstrels, and occasional visitors from distant places. Even the privileged few who were able to read had access to only a relatively small number of manuscripts, since the reproduction of books was a laborious process in which manuscripts had to be copied by hand from the originals, one at a time. By the fourteenth century, however, some books were actually printed through a rather primitive process: the type for each page was carved in mirror image on the face of a block of wood, which was then inked and applied to paper (McMurtie, 1976).

This situation was transformed in the middle of the fifteenth century when a German printer, Johann Gutenberg, developed a revolutionary printing press. This press used moveable type—a stock of wooden or metal letters and numbers that could be freely arranged to create and print an infinite number of pages of text. This printing press became one of the most influential technological innovations in history. Versions of the press

Figure 22.8 *The birth of the mass media dates to the invention of the printing press in the fifteenth century—one of the most significant technological innovations in human history.*

quickly spread throughout Europe, and by the end of the fifteenth century more than 40,000 books were in circulation. The result was an explosive dissemination of philosophical, political, and religious ideas, which reached into almost every aspect of life at the time and served as a catalyst for the upheaval of the Protestant Reformation. As literacy gradually became more widespread, a growing part of the population of Europe was freed from the confines of ancient ignorance, and the ground was eventually cleared for the collapse of an old social order and the beginnings of the Industrial Revolution. Once that revolution began some 250 years ago, mass literacy became inevitable; and today, of course, it is an essential founda-

tion for the emerging postindustrial societies of the world.

Twentieth-century innovations in the mass media have also had a profound effect on the social environment. Unlike the print media, modern electronic media such as radio and TV provide telecommunication, or instant transmittal of information over distance. As a result, people can now be aware of an event virtually at the moment that it happens, even if it takes place hundreds or thousands of miles away. When President Lincoln was shot in 1865, it took weeks for dispatch riders to carry the news to certain parts of the country. But when President Kennedy was shot in 1963, two-thirds of all American adults heard the news within 30 minutes, and 92 percent within two hours. It is interesting to note, incidentally, that when a serious nuclear accident occurred at Three Mile Island, Pennsylvania, in 1979, most Americans and even Europeans heard about the incident in a matter of hours—but some people living within a few miles of the stricken reactor did not learn of it until several days later. The reason is that they belonged to the Old Order Amish, a religious sect whose members refuse to use electricity and so have no telephones, radio, or television (Wright, 1986).

Telecommunications technology has helped to internationalize, and even homogenize, much of the culture of the modern world. Particularly now that extensive satellite networks are in place, it is possible for radio or television programming from one source to be relayed to a public virtually anywhere else on earth, provided equipment is available to receive it. In this sense, therefore, much of the planetary population belongs to a "global village" in which news, information, entertainment, and propaganda can be disseminated and shared with little regard for geographic boundaries. The United States, with its immense media resources and unparalleled motion picture industry, has become the dominant force in this process, often to the discomfort of other governments. News and entertainment broadcasts from the United States and its allies, particularly Great Britain, are regularly listened to by people in foreign lands who do not trust their own media to tell the truth. Additionally, listeners and viewers all over the world are exposed to a steady stream of American rock music, soap operas, sitcoms, movies, fashions, and, by implication, values—a deluge which some foreigners regard as a form of "cultural pollution" that encourages their young people to lose touch with their own traditions. (To understand this concern, you might wonder how Americans would feel if, year in and year out, most of their movies, books, TV dramas, films, top-forty recordings, and the like came from, say, Turkey or Russia, and consistently portrayed that society's view of the world.)

Like any other kind of technology, the mass media are not independent forces in society; they are organized according to the resources and priorities of the countries in which they exist. For economic and sometimes political reasons, the media in other societies are often limited in their variety and scope. Most countries have far fewer newspapers than the United States, and in many societies there are severe restrictions on the freedom of the press to report the facts, make criticisms, or offer comments. Also, most countries have only one or two television channels and a mere handful of radio stations, and these media are typically under direct or indirect government control. Sometimes, as in Great Britain, this control is used to enhance program quality, by insisting on a high ratio of "high culture" to "popular culture" in media fare. In other situations, the control can have deeper implications. Both the Soviet Union and China, for example, have made extensive use of wired radios rather than regular receivers. These sets, which are essentially loudspeakers that simply relay whatever program is fed into them, are located in public places such as factories and recreation areas. Wired receivers provide an economic solution to the problem of bringing radio to large countries with relatively poor populations, while at the same time ensuring that the public hears only what it is supposed to hear. As totalitarian controls in the Soviet Union have eased in recent years, ordinary receivers (which can pick up Western broadcasts) have become much more common, but in China the wired receiver is still the norm.

No other country is as permeated by the mass media as the United States. There are over 9,000 American newspapers, and more than 63 million copies are circulated every day. There are some 8,470 radio stations, and 99 percent of all households have radios, with the average household owning more than five sets. Additionally, there are 2,023 television stations; 98 percent of all households have TV, and there are nearly two sets for every household (Bureau of the Census, 1986a). As befits a heterogeneous postindustrial society, these media cater to an astonishing variety of highly specialized interests. Most of the American media are privately owned as profit-making businesses, and their success depends on attracting advertisers and audiences. As a result, program content is strongly influenced by commercial rather than political considerations. Indeed, media advertising has become a fundamental part of the American capitalist system and consumer culture (Ewen and Ewen, 1982; Schudson, 1985).

Television, with its extraordinary visual immediacy, is generally considered to be the most influential of the media. A television set is switched on for more than seven hours a day in the average American home, and, as we noted in Chapter 5 ("Socialization"), its influence is much debated. There does seem to be some evidence that fictional violence on television may encourage actual violence in some viewers, and it seems that heavy television viewers think of the world as a more dangerous, violent, and threatening place than light viewers (Gerbner et al., 1981, 1982). It does not seem justified, however, to blame "television" for such things as high crime rates, sexual permissiveness, poor school performance, and so on, for television is simply a neutral technology. It is people who decide how to use it.

We use television and other media not only for entertainment, information, advertising, and the socialization of the young, but also for setting society's "agenda" of the important topics that command public attention. This agenda is largely shaped by news coverage, for events are considered important only if they are reported and emphasized by the media. Conversely, the multitude of events that are not "news" are unimportant, or even nonexistent, to the public. News is never just a factual report of events as they happen. Rather, the news is socially constructed, for what "gets into the news" is often the outcome of intense negotiation and bargaining for "space" among reporters, editors, station managers, and sometimes advertisers or other influential outsiders, all of whom have their own values, biases, and interests to advance or protect (Gans, 1975; Tuchman, 1978; Fishman, 1980). In any event, modern telecommunication technologies enhance the agenda-setting function of the media, and thus amplify the influence of the media on society. During the 1960s, for example, television brought the Vietnam war into American homes by showing almost daily footage of scenes from that conflict. This coverage undoubtedly encouraged the growing domestic opposition to the war. In the early 1970s, the mass media contributed significantly to the downfall of Richard Nixon, first by uncovering details of the Watergate scandal and then by publicizing the subsequent con-

Figure 22.9

"*Good evening. Here is this evening's news, according to television.*"

Drawing by Modell; © 1986
The New Yorker Magazine, Inc.

Computers

During the past three decades, computers have become an integral part of modern life. Although the inner workings of the machines are a mystery to most people, computers and the information they manipulate now pervade everyday social activities, particularly in the emerging postindustrial societies of the world. National and international banking and telecommunications, for example, are now utterly dependent on the computer. As David Burnham (1983) observes, computers today are as essential to the life of our planet as the central nervous system is to the human body.

The first electronic computer was built in 1946. It occupied the space of a two-car garage, cost half a million dollars, and contained some 18,000 vacuum tubes, 6,000 switches, 10,000 capacitors, and 70,000 resistors. It was a technological marvel at the time—yet it would be easily outperformed by a modern desk-top computer costing a few hundred dollars. Rapid innovations in computer technology, notably the integrated circuit and the microprocessor, have dramatically reduced the size and cost of the machines while vastly increasing their power and speed. The computers of the future are expected to employ advanced technologies that will bring us closer to the creation of an "artificial intelligence" in computers that can understand information conveyed by sight, speech, and movement, and that can "think" and reason somewhat like human beings.

Predictably, the rapid introduction of this extraordinary new technology created a culture lag. For example, it took several years for the computer's usefulness to be widely accepted, in part because many adults feared they would not "understand" the machines. Male business executives, too, often had a strong resistance to computers, for they associated keyboards with the work of female secretaries. Another culture lag arose in the legal field, for some laws had to be enacted, and others amended, to cover computer crimes. These crimes typically involved acts of theft and embezzlement that used electronic techniques previously unknown to law enforcement agencies or the courts. Even today, perplexing legal questions still remain about whether certain electronic information is a form of property that can be stolen, or whether the usual libel laws apply to statements disseminated through computer "bulletin boards."

The computerization of society may also threaten the individual's privacy—something that

gressional investigations. More recently, television coverage of the Iran-Contra scandal brought the controversy to public attention in a way that traditional print media could not have done.

Interestingly, innovations in telecommunications technology now make it theoretically possible for the United States to have a mass, participatory democracy. Television viewers, by pressing a button attached to specially adapted "interactive" TV sets, can record a "yes" or "no" response to a televised question, and the results of the ballot can be almost instantaneously tallied and then relayed back to the public. Such a system has already been used, on a local basis, to measure public opinion on specific issues. It is technically possible, therefore, for the general public to vote, on a national basis, and as often as desired, on virtually any political issue, including taxation and other legislative proposals. The voters could do so, in fact, after extensive televised presentation of the issues. This would be true participatory democracy, a modern version of the kind pioneered in the tiny Greek city-states of thousands of years ago. Yet there is little pressure for such a democratic system from elected representatives, who (perhaps imagining the public voting to reduce taxes) seem inclined to dismiss any proposals for such a participatory democracy as dangerous or impractical.

is hardly considered a right at all in many countries, but which Americans take very seriously indeed. It is estimated that the government has about fifteen files for the average citizen, running the gamut from medical data to tax, employment, and other business records. Most of this information is accurate, but much of it contains clerical and other errors. Before the advent of the computer, the task of physically collating the various data on any individual would have been immensely time-consuming and cumbersome, but today computers can link numerous data banks together and produce a welter of material on a specific person in seconds. Although there are some legal protections of privacy, they do not extend very far: even the IRS, the most confidential of all government agencies, is required by law to share its data with some thirty-eight other government offices. Already, in fact, several government agencies run computer matching programs, in which one office checks its records against others in search of tax cheats, welfare frauds, students who have failed to register with the Selective Service System, and the like. Other commercial interests, such as department stores or credit-card companies, also have extensive computer records of people's consumer patterns, travel habits, and the like. We leave a semipublic electronic trail throughout our lives in postindustrial society, and our privacy may be in jeopardy as a result (Samuels, 1983).

Industrial sociologists are especially interested in how the computer is affecting the experience of work. An immediate result of computerization is that many jobs become redundant as assembly-line workers are replaced by robots, or as accounting departments find they need fewer staff members. Another effect is that many workers—such as word processors and stockbrokers—are now able to work at home, connected to their central office through a personal computer and a telephone line. It appears, however, that most people who could work at home prefer to go to their office, primarily to experience face-to-face contact and fellowship with their co-workers. Depending on their jobs, some workers find that the computer gives them a greater sense of autonomy, while others find themselves under closer supervision than ever before. The computer itself can monitor and record the performance of the operator, perhaps counting errors or comparing productivity with the norms for the work group as a whole.

As we noted in Chapter 5 ("Socialization"), learning to think is an important part of the sociali-

Figure 22.10

"Roger, it won't kill you to help your father with his computer."

Drawing by Modell; © 1984
The New Yorker Magazine, Inc.

zation process. For thousands of years the tools of thought changed little: they were essentially ink, paper, and a means of applying the former to the latter. The computer has the potential to give intellectual activity a new shape, but thus far there is disagreement on the precise impact of the machine. For example, Theodore Roszak (1986) claims that computers have a vulgarizing effect—that information takes the place of ideas, that video graphics are equated with art, that the manipulation of data passes for thinking. (Roszak admits, though, that he writes on a word processor, and that he uses electronic data bases for his research.) Sherry Turkle (1984) finds that regular users of computers tend to compare their thinking or "programming" with that of machines and, in becoming more aware of their own thought processes, they implicitly reconsider what it means to be human and to think. Incidentally, computers have spread with such rapidity that the young often know more about them than their elders do—a situation that creates an unusual opportunity for "reverse socialization," in which the young pass on knowledge to their elders.

Unlike the United States, the Soviet Union is not a highly computerized society. In fact, computers are quite scarce in the Soviet Union—and most of those that do exist are outdated copies of American machines. During the 1950s, the Soviet leader Josef Stalin denounced cybernetics, the science on which modern computers are based, and this attitude has lingered in various forms in the Soviet Union for many years afterward. The country has long feared that an explosion in information would allow ordinary citizens to become privy to state secrets, and that widespread access to computers could lead to a tidal wave of illicit publications. For that reason, the Soviet Union bans the private ownership of copying machines, printing presses, and computers. Today there are only a few thousand microcomputers and personal computers in the Soviet Union (compared to about 25 million in the United States); modems to link one computer telephonically to another scarcely exist; and even such simple devices as pocket calculators are generally unavailable. A revolution in computer science and technology will be necessary if the Soviet Union is ever to become a postindustrial society—but that development, if it takes place, will inevitably help to undermine the society's secretive, centralized government bureaucracy. If that happens, the ultimate global ramifications of the new technology could be profound.

Genetic Engineering

For millions of years, life on earth has evolved in response to the changing pressures and opportunities of the natural environment. The result is the profusion of distinct species that currently live on the planet. As we approach the twenty-first century, however, scientists are developing the ability to break down the boundaries between the various species. Emerging technologies may make it possible to reorganize existing animal and plant forms into an infinite number of other biological combinations. We stand, therefore, on the brink of a biological revolution whose potential social, economic, and ecological consequences could transform the world as we know it.

The new technology of genetic engineering is based on knowledge derived from the discipline of molecular biology. This science has shown that all life forms utilize the same basic genetic material, DNA, although the molecules are arranged in different sequences in each animal or plant species. It is now possible for scientists, using "recombinant DNA" techniques, to chemically "snip" genes from one organism and "splice" them into another. The result may be a new or altered organism, one that will transmit to its descendants whatever genetic traits the scientists have introduced into it (Cherfas, 1983; Yoxen, 1984; Zimmerman, 1984).

What benefits might genetic engineering offer to humanity? The technology is still in its infancy, but experts in the field foresee an immense range of applications. For example, some genetic engineers predict the creation of specialized bacteria that could scavenge metal from ores, break down water pollutants, or clean up oil spills. Others visualize food crops that can resist the ravages of frost and insects, or that can draw their nitrogen directly from the atmosphere rather than from expensive fertilizers applied to the ground. Some scientists hope to produce cattle that would be genetically altered to reach maturity in a fraction of the usual time; others envision all-female herds of cows the size of elephants; others plan to replace cows altogether with vats of blue-green algae that would be given a gene to synthesize casein, the milk protein. Clearly, innovations of this kind would have multiple and often unanticipated effects in industry, agriculture, and the society beyond (Baskin, 1984; Judson, 1985).

Already, in fact, the new biology is becoming an industry in itself. So far, genetic engineers have focused primarily on one of the lowest life forms, bacteria. Certain bacteria, they have found, can be genetically altered to produce substances, such as medically useful drugs, that have vast profit-making potential. Such bacteria can produce bil-

Figure 22.11 *This mouse, a product of genetic engineering, is programmed to lose all its hair within a couple of weeks of birth, and then to develop heavily wrinkled skin. The possibilities for altering life forms through genetic engineering are theoretically limitless.*

lions of genetically identical versions of themselves within a few days, and these can then be harvested for the useful products that have been bred into them. Already, genetically engineered substances such as insulin and human growth hormone are being produced by this method; and genetically engineered vaccines against malaria, rabies, and hepatitis are being tested. Recognizing the potential for lucrative new products, businesses are employing the most knowledgeable experts in the field—many of whom are research scientists in universities. Consequently, many researchers now have private contracts with biotechnology corporations, which pay them in various ways in return for exclusive access to research findings. These scientists are therefore unwilling or legally unable to share their information with others in the scientific community, in violation of the traditional scientific norm of communalism (Rensberger, 1981; Bouton, 1983).

Every significant technology has its consequences, and an extraordinary technology may well have extraordinary consequences. For this reason, the new technology has stirred a good deal of public unease. The main concern is that genetic engineers, reckless with their own enthusiasm and unmindful of their own ignorance, may release potentially harmful new organisms into the environment. Thus far, little is known about the ability of genetically altered organisms to thrive outside the laboratory, and important questions will have to be answered in the case of each altered life form. Can a specific organism survive in the environment? Can it grow and multiply? Can it transfer harmful material to other organisms? Can it damage the environment? Does it pose risks of communicable diseases or other threats to health? What happens if it is found to be potentially harmful, but is released by accident?

Experts in genetic engineering have assured the public that, provided there is appropriate regulation, such fears are groundless. That may well be the case. But technological "experts" have been wrong so often in the past that the lay person may be reluctant to share the experts' optimism this time. Consider the case of pesticides. In 1947, the Department of Agriculture was given full authority to regulate the introduction and marketing of these chemicals. Over the next two decades, experts gave approval for the manufacture and use of what later proved to be some of the most hazardous substances ever introduced to the environment—DDT, heptachlor, EDB, aldrin, kepone, and toxaphene. The result was an appalling threat to human and animal welfare in the form of widespread chemical pollution of land, water, and food sources. Most of the offending chemicals have now been banned or severely restricted because of their carcinogenic (cancer-causing) or other toxic effects—but a great deal of permanent damage has already been done. In much the same way, representatives of the early nuclear-power industry exuded confidence in the safety of nuclear reactors, yet today the disposal of radioactive waste has become a serious problem, and the very safety of the reactors is in question.

But concerns about genetic engineering go beyond the engineering of new genes for bacteria. Some genetic engineers are interested in redesigning the genetic core of higher organisms, including human beings. It is for this reason that the President's Commission for the Study of Ethical Problems (1983) called genetic engineering one of the greatest technological revolutions in history. As the commission pointed out, it may become possible for us to change the makeup of human cells in such a way as to alter the behavior, intellect, and physical appearance of our species. And the prospects go even further: it might be possible, for example, to hybridize subhuman creatures, by splicing the genes of humans with those of other primates.

Genetic engineering—although conceived as a useful technology for the betterment of social and economic life—may eventually prove to be a practical and ethical minefield. In a controversial argument, Jeremy Rifkin (1983) sees this technology as a classic case of human *hubris,* in which the boundaries between creatures and the sacredness of life seem no longer to warrant our respect. He claims that the more we learn about the chemistry of life, the more we are inclined to reduce living organisms to mere packages of information—collections of data, to be assembled and reassembled at our will. In "playing God" in this way, Rifkin argues, we are really playing a kind of ecological roulette in which our mistakes may prove irretrievable. Many religious thinkers have also come to the conclusion that the genetic modification of human life threatens to produce a theologically unacceptable notion of what human life is. In 1984, a group of sixty-four prominent American religious leaders called for a ban on any experiments that could alter the genetic traits of our species. Genetic engineering seems to offer the prospects of both hope and peril, depending on the directions in which society allows the new technology to develop.

Biomedicine

The science and technology of medicine are transforming the treatment of the diseased and the injured, and millions of people owe their health and lives to the dramatic medical innovations of the past few decades. Some of the new technologies, however, are creating new problems even as they solve old ones. In particular, the new technologies have given doctors and patients a range of difficult life-or-death choices that they did not have even a few years ago. For example, terminally ill patients can now be kept alive through artificial respiration, intravenous feeding, electronic heart stimulation, mechanical organ substitutes, or even transplants of body parts from other people or animals. Consequently, medical dilemmas frequently become moral and legal ones as well.

Until the 1940s, most Americans were born and died at home. Births and deaths happened when they happened, often without medical intervention. If a baby was too premature or defective, or if a seriously ill person was dying, there was little the family doctor could do about it other than

to offer comfort. Today, most Americans are born and die in hospitals under the supervision of medical personnel who sometimes decide to keep them alive long beyond the point at which they would normally have died. Patients can be hooked up for days, months, or years to machines that sustain their lives, and this step may be taken even if they are in constant pain or even if they are permanently comatose. Thus, technologies that were intended to save people from unnecessary death may actually have the effect of depriving them of a dignified death.

Physicians are expected to do all they can to sustain life, even in the case of grossly deformed newborn infants who, in the natural order of things, would have no chance of survival for more than a few hours. Frequently, these babies are destined for short lives of extreme pain, suffering, and mental retardation. In practice, some physicians try to keep these infants alive, but others do not; some parents insist that the attempt be made, while others hope that the child will die. Parents and doctors thus become involved in a process that Jeff Lyon (1985) calls "playing God in the nursery."

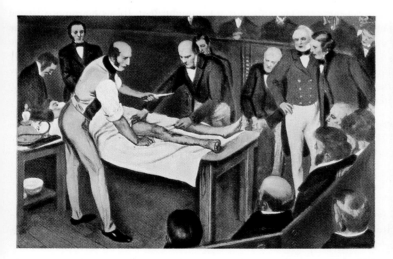

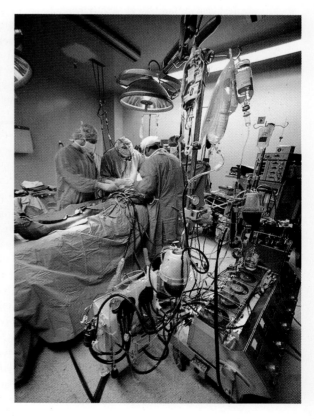

Figure 22.12 *Particularly during the course of this century, the medical profession has come to rely ever more heavily on scientific and technological innovations. The physicians of a century ago would have very little understanding of the techniques used by their counterparts today—but they were also spared the kinds of moral dilemmas and life-or-death decisions that modern physicians sometimes face.*

A Right to Die?

The following account by a close observer highlights one of the most profound and wrenching questions to arise from modern biological technology.

Her chief complaint is that she wants to die and that the doctors will not let her.

She is 96 years old. She has attended the burial of her husband, two daughters-in-law, and all the people who were close friends throughout her lifetime. A woman of fierce and independent spirit, she never wanted to live with her children, to be supported by them or to be what she calls "a burden." After being widowed 24 years ago, she achieved those goals for a long time because she was in good health and her modest fiscal needs were met by the interest of the trust fund left by her husband.

Until 11 years ago, she lived alone and maintained her own apartment. She spent her time walking, talking with neighbors, reading, watching television, playing card games, attending religious services and traveling to visit children, grandchildren, and great-grandchildren in different cities. At age 85, however, she began to dislike shopping and cooking for herself; and she began to worry about living 60 miles away from her nearest relative. She moved, in a city where a son and grandchildren lived, into an apartment residence building that was the "congregate setting" of a geriatric center. The setting provided her with lunch, dinner, a social life and her own small apartment, in which she prepared her own breakfast.

On her 90th birthday, although in excellent mental and physical health, she began complaining that she had become too old. Her stated desire was to die in her sleep, preferably not on a night before she was scheduled to visit her great-grandchildren. When hospitalized with an episode of pneumonia that winter, she said, "My time has come." She bid a loving goodbye to each child, grandchild and great-grandchild who came to see her, and gave them a farewell blessing. When she recovered—thanks to intravenous fluids and antibiotics—she was surprised and somewhat dismayed, but she resumed her former life, remaining independent and perky.

During the next few years, she grew progressively more frail. She began having episodes of faintness, due to paroxysms of atrial fibrillation, but the episodes were brief, and the symptoms would vanish when she lay down briefly. She began walking with the aid of a cane. Although she would no longer travel long distances alone, her mind remained clear and her life independent. With each winter, however, she was rehospitalized with another bout of pneumonia. Each time she was sicker than before; each time she was prepared and wanted to die; and each time she received vigorous therapy and recovered.

During an episode three years ago, however, she had a spell of faintness while in the bathroom of her hospital room. Uncertain that she could successfully get back to her bed, she treated the symptom in her usual manner. She lay down calmly on the floor, closed her eyes and waited. In that position, and with a rapid irregular pulse, she was found by a nurse who promptly issued an emergency "Code" alarm. By the time the doctors and equipment arrived, she actually felt much better; but the excitement of the aggregated "team" convinced her she must be moribund. When she failed to die, she became angry and depressed. "I want to die, and I am ready to die," she said, "but the doctors won't let me."

He records the case of a pair of twins who were born prematurely and would not have lived without modern medical technology. One of the children is today developing normally; the other is blind, has no measurable intelligence, and must be fed entirely through tubes. The mother poignantly sums up the dilemma: "I feel like saying, 'Thank you, modern medicine, and damn you, modern medicine.'" Thus far, there is no social or legal consensus on the ethical issues involved, for they are without precedent in medical history.

Biomedical technology is also affecting the process of human conception and pregnancy. Artificial insemination of a woman, usually by sperm introduced from an anonymous donor, has been available for over two decades, and a quarter of a million Americans have been conceived and born through this technique. But today new technologies are creating a variety of ways for childless couples to have children. An egg from the mother, for example, can be implanted in another woman, there to be artificially inseminated by the husband of the first woman or by a donor. Eggs have been fertilized in a dish and the developing embryo subsequently reinserted in the uterus of the mother or of a surrogate mother who agrees to bear the child. Variations on these techniques are likely to become more common—and in the process, they

After she returned to her small apartment, she became less depressed as she became persuaded that she needed to live at least another year to attend the religious confirmation of her youngest granddaughter. During that year, she became more frail, but her mind stayed clear and her spirits high. She traveled four hours in each direction by private car to go to the confirmation ceremony, and she took special pleasure in participating in it. During the trip, she laughed, sang, and joked, exchanging stories of the old days with a brother-in-law whom she seldom sees and who had come a long distance to ride with her to the ceremony.

Several days after her return home, she had a stroke. She became confused and disoriented. Although physically able to function, she could no longer take care of herself. She could not cook or successfully make her way alone to and from the dining room. When lucidity transiently drifted in, she would complain unhappily and bitterly about having a "companion," who had been hired to be with her during waking hours, and about having become "a burden."

About a week later, she re-entered the hospital with another, more severe stroke. She was conscious, seemed aware of her surroundings, and could state the names of her family visitors, but she made no other conversation. Moving her eyes toward the sky, she seemed to be pleading with God to take her at long last. When she developed anorexia, fever and pneumonia, her children asked the house staff to let her alone, but they and the attending physicians insisted that they could not "do nothing." Before one of her sons—a physician at a medical school in a distant city—could arrive to dispute the doctors' plan, she was given intravenous antibiotics, fluids and other vigorous support.

She recovered, left the hospital and now resides in a nursing home. She can still recognize her family visitors, say their names, and engage in trivial conversation, but her mind is substantially destroyed. She does not know where she is or how long she has been there. She cannot read, watch television, walk alone, use a telephone or play card games. She retains bladder and bowel continence, but she cannot dress herself, feed herself or transfer from bed to chair to bathroom.

She is no longer aware of her plight, and expresses no suggestion of despair, but everything she wanted to avoid has happened. In a semivegetating state, she has lost her functional and mental independence; and she is about to become a financial as well as a physical burden. Because she has the trust fund, the government will not pay for the costs of the nursing home; but the trust fund interest is not large enough to cover the charge of $80 a day. She had hoped to leave the trust-fund principal to her grandchildren, but now it will be gradually transferred to the nursing home.

As her visitors deal with the agony of her vegetation, they wonder why this problem has been created. Since the preservation of her life helps no one, and is desired neither by her nor by those who love her most dearly, why could her doctors not be content to let her die in peace and serenity? Why did they pursue a vigorous therapy that would benefit no one except their own satisfaction in thwarting death, regardless of the consequences?

I do not know the answers to these questions. But I, the physician son of this woman, weep for my mother and for what has happened to my profession.

SOURCE: Dr. Alvan R. Feinstein, "The State of the Art," *Journal of the American Medical Associaton,* 255, March 21, 1986, p. 1488.

will raise unprecedented practical, ethical, legal, and familial dilemmas (Singer and Wells, 1985).

Indeed, biomedical science is changing concepts of pregnancy and birth faster than the English language can create words for them. We have no real name, for example, for a woman who bears a child conceived from another woman's egg, or for a man who becomes an anonymous father by donating his sperm to a woman he will never know. Lacking even the words, we have no clear idea of what kind of relationships are being created by these developments. Take the relatively simple issue of artificial insemination: if a married woman bears the child of an anonymous donor, is the child legitimate? Courts in half the states have held that the child is legitimate, provided the woman's husband consents; in other states, the situation is uncertain. Other issues have still to be settled. For example, should a child conceived through artificial insemination have the right to try to find out the identity of the biological father, in the way that adopted children may do under certain circumstances in some states? Is frozen sperm an inheritable form of property—for example, could a dying man leave his sperm to his wife or girlfriend, so that she could later bear his children? If, by accident or design, a child is conceived through artificial insemination by closely related partners, has incest been committed—even though no incestuous sex act has occurred?

Pregnancy through surrogate mothers raises even more unsettling questions. In most of these cases, a couple pays another woman to bear and then to hand over a child conceived with the egg of the female partner. But half the states forbid payment to a woman who bears a child for adoption—selling children is, after all, a serious offense—and the other states seem confused over the issue. Consequently, these private "surrogate" contracts are not legally binding—and situations have already arisen where the couple, disliking the appearance of their child, have refused to take it, or where the surrogate mother, growing attached to the baby, has refused to hand it over. Who is legally the owner, or parent, of the child in such circumstances? And does a surrogate mother have the right to abort another woman's child, or can she be sued or even prosecuted for doing so? Should the child have the right to know the identity of the surrogate mother, and should the surrogate mother have visiting or other rights for the child she bore? Who owns an embryo in a dish—the donor of the egg, the donor of the sperm, the hospital where the dish is located, the intending parents, or the mother who has contracted to be the incubator? These are not idle questions; an Australian government committee was recently confronted with the issue of whether a frozen embryo has the right to life and the right to inherit property: the biological parents had been killed in a plane crash, leaving a million dollars and no other heirs. (The Australians decided, amid wide protests, that frozen embryos do not have a right to life.) And what might be the precise relationships among children in the same family who, although they are not the products of adultery, adoption, or previous marriage, have different biological parents from each other? These issues may well seem exotic at the moment, but in time more and more parents will have to take them into account, and, through trial and error, new family norms, values, and laws will be needed to deal with these social and cultural by-products of the new technology.

Other technologies that may affect parents and their families are also in the offing. Already there are successful experimental techniques that could enable parents to select the sex of their children. A marketable product is likely to emerge, with commercial interests encouraging widespread sex selection. This may sound like a socially useful technology—until we consider one factor. Opinion polls in the United States and a number of other countries have indicated that a large majority of parents would prefer to have boys rather than girls (Williamson, 1976). The result of sex selection might be a society in which males significantly outnumber females, with important effects on population structure, family patterns, and sexual norms. Does society want this kind of situation, and should the decision be left to the marketplace?

Similarly, new technologies may make it possible for parents to artificially influence some of the genetic characteristics of their offspring. Biomedical scientists are interested in using "gene therapy" to cure some of the 3,000 or so hereditary disorders, such as hemophilia and sickle-cell anemia, that affect about 2 percent of all infants. Such a technology would involve modifying the genetic makeup of the infant before birth by introducing the correct genes to the fetus. Again, this sounds like a socially useful technology—but where might "gene therapy" end? What is the legitimate boundary, if any, between correcting genetic "defects" and making genetic "improvements" in, say, an infant's potential height, skin color, or other genetically influenced characteristics? What might be the long-range consequences of the genetic manipulation of the unborn?

Additionally, researchers in the field of biomedicine are currently working on the fulfillment of one of humanity's most ancient dreams: the postponement of death by prolonging the length of life itself. As we noted in Chapter 21 ("Population and Urbanization"), our life span—the maximum length of life possible in our species—is fairly inflexible. Few people live beyond 100, and the upper limit seems to be approximately 115 years, about what it was many centuries ago. Human aging appears to be based on processes within individual cells: when cultured in the laboratory, most cells divide about fifty times, and then stop and die. Some scientists believe that we are genetically programmed to age, and liken the process to the inexorable ticking of a biological clock; others hold that aging is the result of cumulative cellular damage that occurs during a lifetime. Either way, scientists now hope to intervene in the aging process in such a way as to delay or even halt it. It is not impossible that they might succeed. But what would be the personal and social effects, in an already overcrowded world, of people's living much longer, if not indefinitely? Such a technology would have an unprecedented impact, for it could eventually create a situation in which there was no room for succeeding generations (Walford, 1983; Eckholm, 1986; Maranto, 1984).

Technology and the Natural Environment

Other animals can sustain themselves directly from the environment—for example, by grazing on vegetation or preying on other species. Human beings, however, rely on tools for their subsistence, whether these are as simple as a hunting knife or as complex as a modern agricultural enterprise backed by fertilizers, combine harvesters, irrigation networks, storage and transportation facilities, and electric power. But this difference between ourselves and other creatures can be a deceptive one. In the modern industrialized world, we often feel insulated from nature and confident that our technology can give us mastery over the natural environment. We forget all too easily that we too are animals, ultimately as dependent on the environment for our survival as any other species.

The Science of Ecology

Ecology is the science of the relationship between living organisms and their environments. The discipline emerged as a natural science in the late nineteenth century and is still primarily the domain of biologists. Recently, however, an awareness of an "ecological crisis" has led social and natural scientists from several disciplines to focus on the complex interrelationship among industrialization, technology, population growth, and the global environment.

If all societies still relied on hunting and gathering for their subsistence, world population would have leveled off at around 10 million people. But the industrial and postindustrial modes of pro-

Figure 22.13 *Over the centuries, our technological innovations have had ever greater potential for environmental damage. Preindustrial societies drew their energy directly from such natural resources as wind and water. Early industrial societies utilized indirect energy—for example, burning coal to produce heat to make steam to drive an engine. In the modern world we rely extensively on electricity derived from even more sophisticated sources, such as nuclear reactors. Each advance yields greater resources of energy, but it does so at greater risk. Incidentally, the twin reactors shown here are at Diablo Canyon, California. They are built almost directly on top of an earthquake fracture line, and, due to a mixup in the blueprints, their structural supports were inadvertently installed back to front.*

duction, which are always linked to advanced medical and other technologies, permit a small part of the population to feed the rest and thus make high population growth rates possible. However, the technology of large-scale industrialization poses two major problems. First, it generates pollution of the natural environment, threatening or destroying life in a chain reaction that can run from the tiniest microorganism to human beings. Second, it depletes natural resources such as wood, oil, and minerals, many of which are in short supply and cannot be replaced. The question that arises is whether a world population that will double in forty years, and thus produce twice as many people to consume and pollute—perhaps more profligately than they do at present—can be supported by the environment.

Life on earth exists only in the biosphere, a thin film of soil, air, and water at or near the surface of the planet. Within this biosphere all living organisms exist in a delicate balance with one another and with the environmental resources that support them. A fundamental ecological concept is the *ecosystem,* a self-sustaining community of organisms within its natural environment. An ecosystem may be as small as a drop of pond water or as large as the biosphere itself, but the same principle of mutual interdependence always applies. Energy and inorganic (nonliving) matter are both essential for life. The energy is derived directly or indirectly from the sun, and the inorganic matter from the soil and the air. Green plants convert the sun's energy and the inorganic nutrients into organic, living matter. The plants are eaten by animals, many of which are consumed in turn by other animals in highly complex food chains. Finally, insects, bacteria, fungi, and other decomposers break down the dead bodies of plants and animals, releasing the nutrients back into the ecosystem and completing the cycle.

We may think nothing of the bacteria in the soil, but if we destroy them, we destroy ourselves, for all life depends on these lowly creatures. We poison insects at our peril, for insects are an element in a food chain that may ultimately concentrate the poison in the bodies of animals, including ourselves, for whom it was never intended. In preindustrial societies people traditionally treated nature with respect, considering themselves a part of, rather than set apart from, the natural world; this attitude was typical, for example, among the Indian tribes of North America in pre-Colonial times. In industrialized societies our attitude is different. We consider ourselves the lords of creation and see nature primarily as a resource for exploi-

tation. As our "needs" increase, our capacity for exploitation expands. We do not see our ravaging of the environment as "ravaging" at all; it is "progress" or "development." We are so used to exploiting natural resources and dumping our waste products into the environment that we frequently forget that resources are limited and exhaustible and that pollution can disrupt the ecological balance on which our survival depends.

Pollution

Over the past quarter century, pollution of the environment has begun to threaten the ecological balance of the planet and the health of many of its species, including ourselves. The pollution problem is an exceedingly difficult one to solve, for several reasons. First, some people and governments see pollution as a regrettable but inevitable by-product of desired economic development—"where there's smoke, there's jobs." Second, control of pollution sometimes requires international coordination, for one country's emissions or pesticides can end up in other countries' air or food. Third, the effects of pollution may not show up for many years, so severe environmental damage can occur with little public awareness that it is taking place. Fourth, preventing or correcting pollution can be costly, technically complex, and sometimes—when the damage is irreversible—impossible. In general, the most industrialized nations are now actively trying to limit the effects of pollution, but the populous less developed societies are more concerned with economic growth, and tend to see pollution as part of the price they have to pay for it.

Living with Chemicals

One important source of environmental pollution is the widespread agricultural use of hundreds of chemical poisons in the form of herbicides and insecticides, which, as we have noted, can be transmitted and concentrated through the food chain until they turn up, sometimes years later, in the bodies of other organisms. These chemicals are now found in every part of the world—even in antarctic penguins and arctic polar bears, thousands of miles from the original source of the pollution. Most of the food we eat is tainted in some degree with traces of pesticides—some of them applied recently in the United States or elsewhere, some of them residues that have remained in the environment after being banned many years ago.

Figure 22.14 *A major contributor to the chemical pollution of the environment is the agricultural use of pesticides. But despite extensive application of these substances, the proportion of crops lost to pests is now the same as it was before the chemicals came into common use forty years ago. One reason is that a great many insects have now developed resistance to most pesticides; another is that the poisons have killed off other creatures that were predators of the pests.*

Serious though the spread of pesticides may be, it is only a minor aspect of the problem of chemical pollution. Over 60,000 synthetic chemicals are now on the market, where they are used—often to our great benefit—in such areas as medicine, food processing, and manufacturing. However, more than half of these chemicals are classified by the Environmental Protection Agency as either potentially or definitely harmful to human health. Additionally, new chemicals are constantly being synthesized and manufactured; in the United States alone, scientists create at least 1,000 new compounds every year. The great majority of these substances do not exist in nature, so we have evolved no natural defenses against any harmful effects they might have. Even the components of common household products include thousands of suspect substances (such as the formaldehyde in particle board or the fiber glass in wall insulation) whose long-term effects are not known. But environmental factors are responsible for many diseases, including the great majority of cancers. Vinyl chloride, for example, has been linked to liver cancer; asbestos, to lung cancer; and benzene, to leukemia. In many cases, these and other diseases do not show up for many years after exposure to the substances that cause them. It is highly likely that people all over the world are being exposed right now to supposedly safe substances that will prove, in time, to have dangerous and even lethal consequences (S. Epstein, 1978; M. Brown, 1980).

As many American communities are discovering, the disposal of industrial wastes has created one of the most serious of all pollution problems. Manufacturing processes produce millions of tons of unwanted and hazardous chemical by-products each year. Most of this material is dumped, legally or illegally, into landfills, fields, swamps, and sometimes lakes and rivers. There are tens of thousands of toxic waste dumps all over the United States, many of them long abandoned and most of them lacking an efficient lining that might prevent their poisons from leaching into the ground water and thence, years later, into the drinking supply of distant communities. The Office of Technology Assessment estimates that at least 10,000 of these sites require a "priority" cleanup, and that it could easily cost over $100 billion to render the others safe—an extraordinarily expensive technological fix to a problem that arose from technological innovations in the first place. Unfortunately, the problem is one that cannot be easily buried. Already, many homes and even two entire communities—Love Canal, New York, and Times Beach, Missouri—have had to be abandoned because of toxic pollution seeping up from the ground (Levine, 1982).

Water Pollution

Federal clean-water legislation has led to significant improvements in the quality of American surface water, and although many rivers and lakes remain severely polluted, almost all are in better condition than they were a decade or two ago. Although millions of gallons of raw sewage are still pumped into the lower reaches of the Hudson, parts of the upper river are now swimmable. The Cuyahoga River, which was so polluted that on one occasion it burst into flames, now supports fish. So does lake Erie, which a few years ago had become almost devoid of aquatic animal life. But ground water—which more than half the American population relies on for domestic use—is a different matter. This vast reservoir, lying in aquifers anywhere from a few feet to half a mile below the earth's surface, accumulates and moves very slowly as water percolates down from the land above. Ground water is being increasingly contaminated by thousands of different chemicals, ranging from agricultural pesticides and household cleaners to industrial wastes; indeed, the Environmental Protection Agency calculates that three-quarters of the known toxic-waste disposal sites may be leaking their contents into aquifers. Once polluted, ground water is virtually impossible to clean, so the contamination of this huge and vital water supply may be irreversible. We are conducting a massive but unwitting experiment on human exposure to low levels of water-borne toxic chemicals, and the result may be disastrous health consequences in the form of widespread poisonings, cancers, and birth defects (Maranto, 1985).

Air Pollution

After decades of carelessly dumping noxious gases and particulates into the atmosphere, most of the industrialized societies are now enforcing clean-air standards, and air quality in these societies is generally much better than at any time in the past fifteen years. In the United States, for example, auto-emission controls have reduced the amount of carbon monoxide in the air by 40 percent since 1970. But clean air is a relative matter, and vast amounts of pollution from American manufacturing, power generation, waste incineration, and transport still reach the skies each year, including more than 3 billion pounds of some thirty-six

Figure 22.15

"The sky is certainly a beautiful blue today, isn't it, Miss Simkins? Check with production and see if something's wrong."

chemicals suspected of causing cancer and other chronic ailments. In the less developed countries there are few controls on air pollution, and as these nations industrialize, they are steadily increasing the sum total of planetary pollution.

The chemistry of atmospheric pollution is extremely complex, for rain and sunlight blend various compounds into a constantly changing photochemical brew. Scientists are particularly worried about the effect of air pollution on the planet's ozone layer. Ozone is a rare form of oxygen that is concentrated at very high altitudes, where it absorbs about 99 percent of the ultraviolet radiation from space. Ultraviolet radiation is highly dangerous to living things, for it can induce cancer, burn skin, cause blindness, and destroy the vegetation and plankton on which terrestrial and aquatic life ultimately depend. Unfortunately, some atmospheric pollutants—particularly nitrogen dioxide and chlorofluorocarbons from solvents and refrigerants—destroy ozone. It seems that increasing pollution is gradually depleting the ozone layer, allowing more radiation to reach the earth's surface. If this trend continues, the loss of ozone could irreversibly alter the earth's ability to support life (National Research Council, 1984).

Another significant problem is acid rain. This phenomenon is found primarily in heavily industrialized areas of Western Europe and the eastern United States, although it is spreading to adjacent regions, such as parts of southern Europe and Canada. Acid rain is believed to result primarily from the burning of fossil fuels such as coal and gasoline. This combustion pours oxides of sulfur and nitrogen into the atmosphere, where they mix with moisture, form acids, and are brought to the earth in rain and snow. The effects on many tree species are catastrophic, and vast forest areas in the affected regions have been damaged or even destroyed, particularly at higher altitudes. Additionally, thousands of lakes in these areas are becoming sterile, for they are now too acidic for most fish and other aquatic life. Ironically, the acid-rain problem may have been aggravated by new technologies that "scrub" ash, which is mostly alkaline, from factory emissions, thereby increasing the overall acidity of industrial pollutants (Sitwell, 1984; Postel, 1985).

The most far-reaching effect of air pollution, however, is a change in the global climate. As a result of the burning of fuels and wastes and the razing of forests, the amount of carbon dioxide in the atmosphere is steadily increasing. This gas creates a "greenhouse effect" on the planet, for it allows solar rays to reach the earth's surface but prevents heat from radiating back into space. The consequence will be a global warming, which will eventually cause the melting of the polar ice caps, a rise in sea levels, and changes in weather patterns. This warming effect is already under way, and average global temperature is expected to rise by 3 to 8 degrees Fahrenheit by 2030. This seems like a small change, but minor fluctuations in global temperature can have drastic consequences: during the last ice age, when much of North America was covered with sheets of ice more than a mile thick, average temperature was only about 5 degrees cooler than today.

What will the warmer climate expected in the next century mean? Among other things, it will bring about changes in the global circulation patterns that drive the weather; more powerful storms and more numerous hurricanes; a three-foot rise in sea levels; flooding of river delta cities such as Cairo and New Orleans; inundation of low-lying areas like the Netherlands and the Sacramento Valley; seepage of salt water into many fresh-water sources; and aridity in previously fertile areas such as America's Midwestern "breadbasket." By the end of the twenty-first century, global temperature may have increased by as much as 9 degrees, raising sea levels by ten to twelve feet, turning tropical areas into deserts, and creating a climate far warmer than anything humanity has ever experienced. Most of the climatic, agricultural, and ecological patterns we are familiar with today would be completely disrupted, and there is no knowing what the ultimate consequences would be for life on the planet and for human society (Yulsman, 1984; MacCracken and Luther, 1985; Eckholm, 1986).

Two countries generate more than 40 percent of the world's carbon-dioxide emissions—the United States (about 23 percent) and the Soviet Union (about 18 percent). This and other atmospheric pollution is not an inevitable outcome of industrial technology; it derives also from political decisions to tolerate pollution rather than bear the costs—probably including slower economic growth—of limiting it. The United States has some of the world's most stringent antipollution laws, but these are clearly insufficient to prevent potentially grave damage to the atmosphere. Further control of pollution is politically difficult, however, for the economic interests behind "smokestack" industries are a powerful political lobby that is reluctant to commit the necessary resources to the task.

Incidentally, modern technology is even polluting space beyond the upper atmosphere. At present, there are over 15,000 detectable artificial objects orbiting the earth, of which only about 235 are operational satellites. The rest are space junk—nonfunctioning satellites, spent rockets, exploded boosters, oxygen cylinders, and the like. Additionally, there are several million other objects that are too small to track, most of them bits and pieces resulting from collisions of space junk and from intentional detonations by experimental "killer" satellites. Further collisions among these various objects create a constant rain of new fragments. Because of its high impact velocity, this orbiting garbage now represents a serious threat to spacecraft and working satellites. A piece of metal as small as a walnut traveling at six miles a second has the explosive impact of a hand grenade, and could easily penetrate a space shuttle, killing its occupants. Some multimillion-dollar satellites are already believed to have stopped functioning because of such damage, and any future space station will have to be protected against space-junk impacts. In fact, the possibility of collisions would be a continuing threat to any space-based missile defense system, for its "star wars" components could be accidentally disabled by chance encounters with space debris. Again, scientists are looking for a technological fix in the form of a scavenger satellite—a sort of orbiting trash can that would monitor and collect the junk (Murphy, 1981; Oberg, 1984).

Resources

In preindustrial societies, human technology made comparatively little demand on the resources of the environment. Populations were relatively small, and for the most part people's material needs were fairly limited and easily satisfied. Industrialization, however, has brought about rapid population increases—and also an apparently endless expansion in people's material desires. The most technologically advanced societies are now digging ever deeper into the planetary environment for the raw materials and energy they need to fuel their economic development. The United States, as the most industrialized society on earth, is also the greatest consumer of resources. This single society uses a third of the world's energy, more than 60 percent of its natural gas, more than 40 percent of its aluminum and coal, a third of its petroleum, platinum, and copper, and about a quarter of its gold, iron, silver, lead, and zinc. A child born in the United States at the start of the 1980s is expected to consume, in his or her lifetime, some 226 tons of coal, 1,782 barrels of petroleum, and 5.7 million cubic feet of natural gas. Yet contemporary Americans, more affluent than any people in history, seem less than satisfied by this unprecedented consumption, and demand even more. If the same voracious pattern persists in the future in other industrializing societies, an expanding demand may well exceed the planet's finite resources.

Indeed, if current patterns of extraction are continued, most of the known reserves of such minerals as iron, chromium, nickel, aluminum, copper, lead, tin, and zinc will be exhausted fairly soon, in many cases within a century. New resources will no doubt be found, but the rate of discovery of new deposits is dropping off rapidly. In some cases, shortages can be met by resorting to lower-grade deposits that were considered too expensive to exploit in the past. In other cases, a technological fix comes to the rescue in the form of synthetic substitutes, such as plastic for wood or carbon fiber for steel. As demand grows in the future, however, some shortages and resulting price increases are inevitable. In the case of vital commodities, the results could be economic dislocation. For example, rises in the price of oil in the early 1970s—when gasoline was 38 cents a gallon at American pumps—shocked the world economy. In the inflation and slump that followed, some 45 million workers in the industrialized countries lost their jobs. Thanks largely to energy conservation, there has been an oil glut during most of the 1980s, and prices, though higher, are stable for the time being; but oil is a nonrenewable resource which will inevitably be exhausted one day.

Some resources, of course, are plentiful: the United States, for example, has coal deposits that will last for centuries and can be burned to generate energy as other resources fail. But the use of a resource cannot be considered in isolation from its potentially complex environmental impacts. As we have seen, the burning of coal produces sulfur and carbon dioxide, and the more coal we burn, the more we pollute the atmosphere. The sulfur helps form acid rain, which has a drastic effect on another resource, forests. Most of the trees that are to be cut for housing in the year 2030 are already growing, and in many cases already dying. We will have to rely for the foreseeable future on whatever timberland can survive increasing acid rain over the next few decades, but studies in the affected regions already show losses of 20 to 30 percent in the growth and biomass of forests. And the carbon dioxide from increased coal burning would contribute to the "greenhouse effect" that would scorch the Great Plains and shift the world's "breadbasket" northward—to the vast tracts of currently empty land in Canada and the Soviet Union. A simple solution to society's energy needs thus turns out not to be so "simple" after all. Other apparently simple solutions—such as the use of winds, tides, or sunlight—still appear, after years of intensive research, to be too inefficient or uneconomic for large-scale use at present.

In the years immediately after World War II, nuclear power was seen as the energy resource of the future—one that would provide electricity "too cheap to meter." Today, nuclear reactors seem monuments to a god that failed. There are over 200 nuclear plants in some twenty-five countries, but many of them are managerial, financial, or engineering disasters. About 80 plants are operational in the United States, producing about 13 percent of the electricity consumed, but their high costs and perceived dangers have given them such a bad reputation that no new plant has been ordered since 1978. The principal public fear is that a "meltdown" at a nuclear reactor could release a plume of deadly radiation into the atmosphere, perhaps before people in surrounding communities could be warned and evacuated. Despite consistent assurances from the industry that nuclear reactors are safe, opinion polls show that the public is unconvinced—especially since the seri-

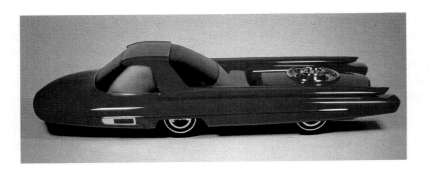

Figure 22.16 *During the early days of nuclear power, experts and public alike foresaw the "Uranium Age," an era of unlimited energy and abundance. This prototype automobile of the 1950s is the "uranium powered" Ford Nucleon, which was to supposed to draw its energy from a little reactor at the rear of the vehicle.*

ous nuclear accidents at Three Mile Island and Chernobyl. (Actually, a nuclear accident of much greater magnitude seems to have occurred near Kyshtym in Russia in 1957, spreading radioactive debris over a wide area which is now believed to be uninhabitable for centuries. The full story of the disaster has never been told, but the names of about 30 small towns in the region have disappeared from Soviet maps, and an elaborate system of canals has been built, presumably to carry rivers and other water systems around the contaminated area.)

Nuclear reactors produce notoriously hazardous wastes. So far, the American plants have disgorged over 15,000 tons of radioactive garbage, to which a further 1,400 tons is added each year. Most of it is "temporarily" stored on site or in Hanford, Washington, in aging containers, some of which have already leaked. What is needed is a place that will safely contain the waste for at least 10,000 years, which is long enough for most of it to decay. The location of such a site is a ticklish political problem, for the obvious reason that people are generally unenthused about the prospect of having a radioactive dump in their own neighborhood. Congress has opted for the solution of eventually creating two securely buried superdumps—one soon in the West, where there is the most empty space; and one later in the East, where most nuclear plants are. When the sites are finally chosen, the target states may decline the selection, unless both houses of Congress override the refusal. The disposal problem seems to be one that has no acceptable technological fix, so in this case a political solution may have to suffice (Bartlett and Steel, 1985).

One resource that is very much in short supply, in the United States and elsewhere, is fresh water. Although ours is a watery planet, most of the water is in the oceans. The bulk of the fresh water is frozen in icecaps or hidden in underground aquifers, so less than 1 percent of all the earth's water is available at the surface for human use— and much of this is in the "wrong" place. Yet modern industrial societies require huge amounts of water for domestic, agricultural, and industrial purposes: it takes 120 gallons of water to put an egg on the breakfast table, 15,000 gallons to grow a bushel of wheat, and 60,000 gallons to produce a ton of steel. American society consumes enormous quantities of water—more than 2,000 gallons a day per person, which is more than three times as much as the Japanese use.

Most American rainfall is in the East and the Pacific Northwest. This presents a problem for other parts of the country, such as the great agricultural plains that run from Nebraska to Texas and provide the "breadbasket" for the nation and for much of the rest of the world. Lacking an adequate rainfall, farmers in this huge region rely heavily on water pumped from the Ogallala aquifer, the greatest reserve of ground water in the world. Unhappily, water is being taken from the aquifer at six times the rate at which natural runoff is replenishing it. The water table in the region has fallen drastically during this century, and at current rates of use the immense reservoir will run dry in thirty years. Without a dependable water supply, this vital region would be largely useless for agricultural purposes—a situation that could cause extensive food shortages and make the economic plight of today's farmers pale by comparison.

Similarly, the growing desert cities of the American Southwest, such as Phoenix and Los Angeles, have a totally inadequate surface-water supply. A temporary solution to the problem has been to pump ground water, but this source is fast disappearing. Already, in fact, there is extensive ground subsidence in the region, and cracks several feet wide and deep now run for miles across the desert floor. The favored technological fix, of course, is to pipe water in from other sources, sometimes hundreds of miles away. Thus the mighty Colorado River, which has carved out the Grand Canyon over 200 million years, is now dammed and controlled through a computer, which regulates its flow according to the needs of the expanding Southwestern cities. Water shortages in the Southwest are already sparking social conflict—not only among the various cities and states in the region, but also between consumers and the owners of water rights, who frequently include the local Indian tribes that have owned the rights since a time when water was almost valueless (Worster, 1985).

Given the interrelationship among technology, ecology, and resources, can global industrialization continue indefinitely? Some writers, such as William Ophuls (1977), glumly foresee a new era of scarcity, in which economic growth would be replaced, at best, by economic stability—and at worst, by economic shrinkage. Others, such as Julian Simon (1981), are highly optimistic that we can continue on our present path, relying on technological innovations to solve problems in the future as they have in the past. But predicting the future is a risky matter at the best of times, and to project highly complex trends for many decades into the future, when one cannot be aware of subsequent technological and other factors that might affect them, is not a very reliable way of making forecasts. If data on agricultural production a century ago had been used to project trends into the 1980s, they would have pointed to global mass starvation at this moment. But the "green revolution" (the introduction of new hybrid species of high-yield grain) and highly mechanized agricultural techniques have greatly increased food production in a way that could not have been anticipated. In 1850, New York City was faced with a "horse crisis." The number of horses was increasing exponentially and the streets were piled with horse dung. A simple projection would have indicated that the streets of New York would eventually be impassible and the city uninhabitable, but this prediction could not take account of several intervening factors, most notably the replacement of horses by automobiles.

Yet nobody denies that the planet has a finite amount of resources or that it can tolerate only a limited amount of pollution. If world population continues to grow rapidly, if industrialism spreads around the world, and if pollution and resource depletion continue at an increasing rate—and all these things are happening—where is human society headed? The most optimistic answer to these questions would be that, one way or another, sweeping social changes await us.

Species Extinction

The march of industrial civilization, which we generally equate with progress toward a better future, is having a devastating effect on the other life forms of the planet. In fact, in the latter part of the twentieth century we are witnessing a catastrophic extinction of other species: not by the dozens, or the hundreds, or even the thousands—but by the millions. This quiet apocalypse probably represents the greatest ecological disaster in the long history of life on earth. Indeed, if some different creature were to have the calamitous effects on other plants and animals that we ourselves do, we would undoubtedly consider it the most noxious and virulent pest ever to crawl upon on the face of the earth.

Because they have the most developed technologies for altering the natural environment, the highly advanced industrialized societies have caused the greatest destruction of planetary ecosystems in the past. Today they are taking the lead—however hesitantly—in efforts to protect the threatened and endangered species. In fact, the United States was the first country with the vision to establish a system of national parks, wilderness areas, and wildlife refuges, and these areas are admired the world over for their awesome grandeur and the flora and fauna they protect. Even so, less than 2 percent of the land in the continental United States has been designated as wilderness areas, to be kept forever wild, and each day there is less and less other "undeveloped" land that might still be protected. Moreover, there is constant pressure on these lands by economic interests that claim the federal government is "locking up" land needed for oil exploration, logging, mining, or housing and recreation facilities.

All over the world, and especially in the less developed societies, the pressure of the human population and its technologies is devastating natural ecosystems. This pressure takes many forms—urbanization and highway construction; transformation of virgin land into farmland; chemical pollution of fresh water; dredging and landfill in coastal areas; uncontrolled hunting and poaching, especially of African wildlife; deliberate and accidental poisoning of wildlife with pesticides; disruption of natural predator-prey relationships; strangulation of millions of birds and fish with discarded styrofoam pellets, plastic bags, and other synthetic flotsam; dam construction and irrigation; and massive deforestation.

Biologists estimate that there are anywhere between 5 million and 30 million species on earth. Of these, only about 1.6 million have been classified. The rest—plants, insects, fish, reptiles, birds, and even some mammals—are still almost complete mysteries to us. They have never been named, cataloged, or studied, yet many are becoming extinct even before we know of their existence. This wholesale extinction of life forms occurs primarily in the tropical rain forests, a primordial green girdle stretching around parts of Central and South America, the Congo Basin in Africa, and Indonesian islands in the Pacific. These forests cover less than 6 percent of the planet, yet they contain most of its species. Under pressure from ranchers and peasants, the rain forest is being cut down and burned. More than 40 percent of the original rain forest has disappeared since World War II, and at present 100 acres fall to axes and bulldozers every minute. If this process continues, more than a million species will be extinct by the end of the century, by which time most of the remaining rain forest will be degraded or destroyed (Ehrlich and Ehrlich, 1981; Forsythe and Miyata, 1984; Myers,

Figure 22.17 *These two photographs show the early steps in the permanent destruction of the tropical rain forest—an ecosystem that contains the most abundant life on the planet, with as many as 200 different species in a single acre. First, a road is bulldozed through the virgin forest. Soon thereafter, farmers or ranchers move in and burn the jungle to the ground, destroying all animal habitats and plant life. The newcomers then try to convert the land to agricultural purposes—but within a few years, it becomes barren wasteland,* *and the farmers move on to repeat the process elsewhere. Despite the luxuriant appearance of the jungle, the soil in these areas is very poor. The rain forest has evolved over 60 million years in such a way that decaying materials are immediately broken down by humidity and fungi and returned to the plants, so virtually all the nutrients are held in the vegetation itself. Once the forest cover is gone, rainfall soon leaches the remaining nutrients from the soil, leaving a moonscape in place of abundant life.*

1984; Caufield, 1985). To some observers, the disappearance of other species as a result of human activity is a matter of no particular consequence. To others, it represents the height of human *hubris,* in that we are making ourselves the ultimate arbiters of which species may survive and which may be obliterated.

Actually, there are many practical reasons why human society should protect other life forms. Tropical forests are a stabilizing factor in the global climate, for they absorb vast amounts of atmospheric carbon dioxide. Many plants are medically valuable: most anticancer compounds, for example, come from plants of the rain forest, and this pharmaceutical cornucopia is still mostly untapped. Wild species are a "storehouse" for agricultural scientists who interbreed them with domestic species in order to create more fruitful or resistant strains. The rain forest is itself a vast and irreplaceable "library" from which genetic engineers of the future may draw their raw material. Many species among the millions of uncataloged

plants will surely prove to be edible, and could become major crops in the future. And the trees and the flowers, the beasts of the field and the fowls of the air, are an aesthetic treasure, capable of delighting our senses and giving us some vision of what we are so carelessly destroying.

There is another argument for protecting other life forms, however, and it has nothing to do with any social benefit to ourselves. The breathtaking diversity of species has evolved in delicate and precarious balance over many millions of years. Most of the plants and animals with which we share the earth have been here a great deal longer than we have. For a fleeting moment in planetary history, our technology has given us domain over them. In awe, respect, and humility, we might just let them be.

There is one technology, however, that threatens not only other species with extinction, but humanity as well. That is the technology of thermonuclear warfare, to which we turn in the final chapter.

Summary

1.   Technology refers to the practical applications of scientific and other knowledge. Many simple technologies are not based on science, but the advanced technologies of the modern world rely on sophisticated scientific knowledge. Science has therefore become a major institution in the industrialized world.

2.   Scientific innovation is a social process, for it is influenced by factors within the scientific community and in the wider society. Merton claims that there are four important norms that guide the scientific enterprise: universalism, communalism, altruism, and organized skepticism. The norms are sometimes violated, however. Competition among scientists may also spur them to make original contributions. Scientists generally work under a paradigm, or set of general assumptions about a particular discipline. A scientific revolution takes place when one paradigm is replaced by another that explains the evidence more convincingly.

3.   Technology is problematic because it is a factor in social change— particularly in the modern world, where complex technological fixes are applied to existing social and technological problems, only to produce still more problems. Society has not yet evolved an effective means of controlling the direction and content of technological change.

4.   The influence of technology on the social environment is illustrated by the mass media, which have revolutionized human communication; the computer, which is an essential element in post-industrialized society; genetic engineering, which is altering the nature of living things; and biomedicine, which now influences life, death, and pregnancy in ways that were not generally foreseen.

5.   Advanced industrial technology can have dramatic ecological effects. It is leading to extensive pollution of air, water, and land, with disruptive effects on the health of organisms and the climate of the planet. It is also leading to the rapid depletion of resources, such as minerals and fresh water. Additionally, the combined effects of pollution and habitat destruction are causing a mass extinction of other species.

Important Terms

technology (591)

science (592)

applied research (594)

basic research (594)

social construction of reality (595)

priority dispute (596)

paradigm (597)

technological fix (599)

automation (599)

technological determinism (601)

culture lag (601)

technocracy (602)

ecology (613)

ecosystem (614)

Suggested Readings

CAUFIELD, CATHERINE. *In the Rainforest.* New York: Knopf, 1985.

An important and informative discussion of rain-forest ecology, which is now under such grave threat.

CRONON, WILLIAM. *Changes in the Land: Indians, Colonists, and the Ecology of New England.* New York: Hill and Wang, 1984.

A superb work of historical ecology, in which Cronon uses trends in early New England to illustrate fundamental relationships between people and nature.

HILGARTNER, STEPHEN, RICHARD C. BELL, and RORY O'CONNOR. *Nukespeak: The Selling of Nuclear Technology in America.* New York: Penguin, 1984.

A highly critical view of the American nuclear power industry.

KNORR-CETINA, KARIN D., and MICHAEL MULKAY (eds.). *Science Observed: Perspectives on the Social Study of Science, 1983.*

A good introductory collection of articles on the sociology of science.

KOHN, ALEXANDER. *False Prophets.* New York: Basil Blackwell, 1986.

The author details several fascinating studies of fraudulent practices in science.

KUHN, THOMAS S. *The Structure of Scientific Revolutions.* Chicago: University of Chicago Press, 1962.

A highly influential book. Kuhn outlines his concept of the scientific paradigm and shows the role of paradigms in both "normal" and "revolutionary" scientific innovation.

MERTON, ROBERT K. *Sociology of Science: Theoretical and Empirical Investigations.* Chicago: University of Chicago Press, 1973.

An important collection of articles on the sociology of science by Robert Merton, the leading sociologist in the field.

PERROW, CHARLES. *Normal Accidents: Living with High-Risk Technologies.* New York: Basic Books, 1984.

A careful analysis of risky and even disastrous technologies, which the author suggests will inevitably yield regular accidents.

TURKLE, SHERRY. *The Second Self: Computers and the Human Spirit.* New York: Simon and Schuster, 1984.

An interesting study of the impact of computers on their users, and particularly the user's thinking processes.

TOCH, ALBERT H. (ed.). *Technology and the Future.* 4th ed. New York: St. Martins, 1986.

A useful collection of articles that cover various issues of technological and social concern.

WRIGHT, CHARLES R. *Mass Communication: A Sociological Perspective.* New York: Random House, 1986.

A brief and up-to-date introduction to the sociology of the mass media.

CHAPTER 23

War and Peace

In the darkness before the dawn of July 16, 1945, a small group of American scientists waited to test an experimental bomb in the New Mexico desert. They were not quite sure what would happen: some expected an explosion of one kind or another, while others thought the weapon would not work at all. But when the countdown ended, the onlookers gazed upon a burst of light such as had never been seen on the planet before. A violent blast-wave raced across the desert floor, and a ball of fire of dazzling luminosity lighted the sky, changing shape and color as it soared to the heavens. The elemental force of atoms, freed from bonds of billions of years, had been broken by human technology in a spectacle of terrible beauty. Awestruck by the unearthly force he had helped create, the principal designer of the bomb, Robert Oppenheimer, recalled a phrase from ancient Hindu mythology: "Now I am become death, destroyer of worlds." The nuclear age had begun, and all humanity has lived in the shadow of the bomb ever since.

Nuclear warfare started shortly after that first test in the desert. On August 6, 1945, an American aircraft dropped a nuclear bomb on a civilian target, the Japanese city of Hiroshima, killing at least 75,000 people outright. Two days later, a second nuclear bomb was exploded on the city of Nagasaki. Aware that further bombings were being planned, the Japanese government surrendered to the United States two days thereafter. In the four decades since then, the world's nuclear stockpile has increased from a single bomb to more than 50,000 weapons. The potential energy of these devices is equal to about four tons of the explosive TNT for every man, woman, and child on the planet, enough to kill all of humanity dozens of times over. War—which has long been one of the nastiest of all human endeavors—now threatens the survival of civilization as we know it, and perhaps even the existence of our species.

"War," General William Tecumseh Sherman declared, "is hell." A more sociological definition would be that **war** is sustained military conflict between politically organized groups. Usually, the organized groups in question are societies, but sometimes war can occur within a society in the form of revolutionary war or civil war. Conversely, **peace** is sustained amicable relationships between politically organized groups. It is important to note that peace is a positive and constructive state of affairs, and not just the absence of war. For example, the United States is today at peace with Great Britain, for the two countries have an enduring and amicable relationship, and there is no prospect whatever that either would attack the other. However, the United States cannot be said to be at peace with the Soviet Union, because each society has the plans and the means to reduce the other to smoldering rubble within thirty minutes. Rather, these two societies are in a state of hostility, a sort of limbo between peace and war. In fact, the Soviet Union and the United States, which together have less than 11 percent of the world's population, account for 23 percent of its armed forces, 60 percent of its military expenditures, 80 percent of its weapons research, and 97 percent of its nuclear warheads and bombs (Sivard, 1986). Whether their mutual hostility turns to war or peace is perhaps the most vital question affecting the future of humanity, and we shall concentrate on that issue in this chapter.

Perhaps surprisingly, the sociological study of war and peace is still in its infancy, for the subject has traditionally fallen within the disciplines of political science and, to a lesser extent, anthropology. In recent years, however, sociologists have begun to apply their own perspective to these ancient phenomena.

War and Society

Over the centuries, warfare has shaped and disrupted societies, altered the course of history, and led to the slaughter of hundreds of millions of people, combatants and noncombatants alike. Why do people go to war, and how have we reached our present state of military preparedness?

Why War?

Since warfare is highly unpleasant for the combatants, why is warfare such a common phenomenon? An answer frequently offered, it seems, is that we humans are naturally warlike. As we noted in Chapter 3 ("Culture"), many people assume that "human nature" includes some kind of an aggressive "instinct," and popular writers have advanced this view widely. Thus Konrad Lorenz (1966), an expert in animal behavior, claimed that humanity

Figure 23.1 *Whether or not a society is "warlike" depends on social factors that vary from one time and place to another. The Iranian government uses a variety of highly emotional methods to encourage enmity toward Iraq among its own people. The photograph shows a "fountain of blood" that serves as a memorial to the Iranian "martyrs" who have fallen in battle in Iraq. Actually, the liquid in the fountain is colored water.*

shares an aggressive drive with lower animals, and Robert Ardrey (1970), a playwright, argued that we are descended from "killer apes" and so are destined to do battle with one another. An obvious problem with this approach is that one could just as easily make the reverse argument. Most people and societies are *not* at war most of the time—so on this evidence we could say that human nature includes a "peaceful instinct," and that we are destined to cooperate with one another! In fact, we are all capable of both aggression and friendship, war and peace—but we are not biologically driven to them. Some people seem willing to fight, some people do not. Some societies, like the Jalé of New Guinea or the Yanamamö of South America, seem warlike. Other societies seem peaceful: Sweden and Switzerland, for example, have chosen to be neutral and have stayed out of all wars for a century and a half. Human society has survived thus far, not because we are a fundamentally aggressive species, but because we are a fundamentally sociable and cooperative one (Otterbein, 1970, 1973; Montagu, 1973, 1978; Fried, Harris, and Murphy, 1986).

Then why war? The answer is that war occurs as a result of a political decision—usually a decision by older men that younger men should fight for what the older men believe to be worth fighting for. There can be no war unless the leaders of at least two societies with conflicting interests decide that they prefer war to any alternative means of settling their differences. The soldiers themselves go to war—frequently not knowing what they are fighting for, and usually terrified of meeting the enemy in battle—because a legitimate political authority is determined on that course of action. War is actually a highly structured social activity. It cannot be sustained without a strong political authority that can persuade people to risk their lives for a purpose beyond themselves (Barnet, 1970; Falk and Kim, 1980).

Many factors may influence the decision to go to war—the personalities of the leaders; the influence of nationalist, religious, or other ideologies; the extent of popular support for war; the anticipated economic gains or losses; the ambitions or advice of the military; perceptions or misperceptions of the other side's motives and intentions; the expected reaction of the international community; and, of course, expectations about the likely outcome of the conflict. But one factor that seems particularly likely to encourage war is preparations for it. A military build-up by country X may make country Y feel threatened, leading Y to begin a de-fensive build-up. Country X perceives the new build-up as a hostile move and increases its armaments, proving to Y that its suspicions about X were right all along and that more arms are needed—and so on. In general, militarized nations tend to fight with other militarized nations, and countries that prepare for war tend to become engaged in war (Naroll, 1966; Blainey, 1973; Wallace, 1979). At times, however, even countries that are totally unprepared for war find themselves in one.

Development of War

The history of war is largely the story of the development of ever more technologically advanced weapons and the means of delivering them. The first weapons were rocks, clubs, spears, and swords, wielded or thrown by human beings. Gradually, ways were found to strike further, more accurately, and with greater force—with slings, catapults, bows and arrows, crossbows. The invention of gunpowder and similar explosives led to the musket, the rifle, the cannon, the grenade, the bomb. These weapons were mounted on land vehicles, ships, and eventually aircraft. Today, missiles can travel thousands of miles from one continent to another and deliver their warheads with an accuracy that can be measured in feet and seconds. Ever since weapons first appeared on the scene, defenses have also evolved in such forms as shields, armor, fortresses, antiaircraft guns, electronic jamming devices, antimissile missiles, and so on. One effect of innovations in military technology is to make killing—even mass killing—impersonal. A few centuries ago, war meant soldiers physically attacking one another. Today, a handful of people can obliterate a city thousands of miles away by deciding to push a button.

Over the centuries, the number of people involved in, and killed by, warfare has also increased dramatically. Alexander the Great set out to conquer the world as he knew it with an army of less than 40,000 men. William the Conqueror invaded England with 50,000 men. The Napoleonic Wars involved hundreds of thousands of soldiers. In the American Civil War, nearly 2 million men were under arms. During World War I, some 65 million troops were mobilized, and 19 million people were killed. The carnage of that pointless and dreadful conflict so stunned the world that people called it "the war to end all wars," for they knew humanity would never commit such folly again. World War II followed a mere twenty-one years later—and this

Figure 23.2 *The history of warfare is marked by constant technological developments that have greatly extended the range and destructive force of weaponry. This illustration shows an assault on a* *fifteenth-century city in France. The weapons seem primitive to us, in an age when it is possible for dozens of cities to be destroyed within minutes at the touch of a button.*

time, almost 100 million people took up arms, and an estimated 38 million soldiers and civilians were killed. All told in this century, there have been over forty wars that resulted in 100,000 deaths or more, with a total loss of life of about 83 million people. Today, the major powers maintain huge standing armies, even though they are not at war. The United States has 2.2 million people in its armed forces, the Soviet Union has 3.8 million, and China has over 4 million. Of course, in nuclear war, the size of armies would be irrelevant, for the entire civilian populations of the countries concerned would be brought into the arena of battle—along with much of the rest of the world's population.

To a visitor from another planet, it would seem that the modern world is obsessed with preparations for "defense" (it is never called "offense"). Many countries spend more of their budgets for military purposes than they do for education or medical care. Altogether, the international military establishment employs an estimated 100 million people. World military expenditures in 1986—the "International Year of Peace"—were a record $900 billion. Over the past quarter century, global spending for military purposes has consumed an estimated $14 trillion (that is, $14,000,000,000,000). This represents a colossal diversion of funds from socially useful goals: for example, a single hour's

TWENTIETH-CENTURY WARS WITH DEATHS OF 100,000 OR MORE

Location	Date	Identification of Conflict	Deaths
Latin America			
Bolivia	1932–35	Paraguay vs Bolivia	200,000
Columbia	1949–62	"La Violencia"; civil war	300,000
Mexico	1910–20	Liberals & Radicals vs Govt.	250,000
Europe			
Greece	1945–49	Civil war; UK intervening	160,000
Poland	1919–20	USSR vs Poland	100,000
Spain	1936–39	Civil war; Italy, Portugal & Germany intervening	1,200,000
Turkey	1915	Armenians deported	1,000,000
USSR	1904–05	Japan vs Russia	130,000
	1918–20	Civil war; Allied intervention	1,300,000
Europe and Other			
	1914–18	World War I	19,617,000
	1939–45	World War II	38,351,000
Middle East			
Iraq	1961–70	Civil war; massacres	105,000
	1982–86	Iran attack following Iraq invasion	600,000
Lebanon	1975–76	Civil war; Syria intervening	100,000
Yemen, AR	1962–69	Coup; civil war; Egypt intervening	101,000
South Asia			
Afghanistan	1978–86	Civil war; USSR intervening	500,000
Bangladesh	1971	Bengalis vs Pak; India invad.; famine & massacres	1,500,000
India	1946–48	Muslims vs Hindus; UK intervening; massacres	800,000
Far East			
Cambodia	1970–75	Civil war; NV, US intervening	156,000
	1975–78	Pol Pot Govt. vs people; famine and massacres	2,000,000
China	1928	Muslim rebellion vs Govt.	200,000
	1930–35	Civil war	500,000
	1937–41	Japan vs China	1,800,000
	1946–50	Civil war	1,000,000
	1950–51	Govt. executes landlords	1,000,000
	1956–59	Tibetan revolt	100,000
Indonesia	1965–66	Abortive coup; massacres	500,000
	1975–80	Annexation of East Timor; famine & massacres	100,000
Korea	1950–53	Korean War; UN intervening	2,889,000
Vietnam	1945–54	War of independence from France	600,000
	1960–65	Civil war; US intervening	300,000
	1965–75	Peak of Indo-China War; US bombing	2,058,000
Africa			
Algeria	1954–62	Civil war; France intervening	320,000
Burundi	1972	Hutu vs Govt.; massacres	100,000
Ethiopia	1974–86	Eritrean revolt and famine	545,000
Mozambique	1981–86	Famine worsened by civil war	100,000
Nigeria	1967–70	Civil war; famine & massacres	2,000,000
Rwanda	1956–65	Tutsis vs Govt.; massacres	108,000
Sudan	1963–72	Christians vs Arab Govt.; massacres	300,000
Tanzania	1905–07	Revolt against Germany; massacres	150,000
Uganda	1971–78	Civil war, Idi Amin coup; massacres	300,000
	1981–85	Army vs people; massacres	102,000
Zaire	1960–65	Katanga secession; UK, Belgium intervening	100,000
			83,642,000

SOURCE: Ruth Leger Sivard, *World Military and Social Expenditures, 1986* (Washington, D.C.: World Priorities, 1986), p. 26.

Figure 23.3 *This table gives some idea of the appalling loss of life that has occurred through war in the twentieth century. The table lists only major conflicts; if the death toll in minor wars were also included, the total number of fatalities would probably be about 100 million—and the century is by no means over yet.*

worth of these expenditures would suffice to save, through immunization, the 120,000 children around the world who die each day from preventable infectious diseases (Sivard, 1986).

Superpower Hostility

The United States and the Soviet Union—the two greatest powers the world has ever known—confront one another with suspicion and hostility. This fact is not particularly surprising. Powerful nations are often rivals, for the simple reason that they frequently have conflicting goals within a common sphere of influence. The hostility between the two contemporary superpowers is greatly increased, however, by the fact that they also represent quite different ways of life. Although both societies claim to offer the best hope for the human future, the Soviet Union is a totalitarian society that advocates communism, while the United States is a democratic society that advocates capitalism.

Whenever two societies are in a state of hostility, each tends to "demonize" the other—that is, to attribute all manner of wickedness to the opposing side. For example, Iranians tend to demonize Iraqis, and Iraqis tend to demonize Iranians; Israelis tend to demonize Syrians, and Syrians tend to demonize Israelis. What is often striking to outside observers is the similarity of each side's images of the other. Thus, the United States and the Soviet Union both view their own country as peace-loving and the other country as warmongering. Each nation believes the other is liable to start a major war, and each claims to build up its own military defenses to forestall the other's aggression. Each society claims that the other seeks world domination, in the form of either communist "enslavement" or capitalist "exploitation." Each country charges the other with trying to enforce its political will on its immediate neighbors: the United States sees the Soviet Union as bullying Poland or Afghanistan, while the Soviet Union sees the United States as bullying Nicaragua or Grenada. Both societies accuse one another of unjustified meddling in distant lands: the United States claims that the Soviet Union foments revolution around the world, while the Soviet Union claims that the United States props up unjust and unpopular dictatorships. Each sees the other side as unreasonable, untrustworthy, and fundamentally treacherous. Yet, for all their strong opinions, the citizens of each country are remarkably uninformed about even the most basic facts regarding the other country. Relying on fragments of limited information from their schools and mass media, the peoples of both countries think of each other largely in terms of negative stereotypes (Shipler, 1985).

Winston Churchill once described the Soviet Union as a "riddle wrapped in a mystery inside an enigma," a remark that still seems valid in some respects. The Soviet Union is dominated by its principal constituent republic, Russia. The Russian people have never known democracy; their society went straight from the rule of a hereditary monarchy to that of an unelected communist elite in the Revolution of 1917. Observers often comment that Russia seems a paranoid nation, obsessed with secrecy and fear of outsiders. It is also a highly militarized society in which the armed forces (whose uniformed members are a constant public presence) are held in great esteem. To many, this concern with secrecy and military power seems to reflect the regime's feelings of pervasive insecurity, not of strength.

Such insecurity has deep historical roots, for in the course of this century, the West has invaded Russia three times. German forces marched into Russia during World War I. Shortly thereafter, in 1920, several Western nations, including the United States, sent troops in an unsuccessful attempt to crush the Russian Revolution. Then, in World War II, the German army launched a massive invasion that was finally turned back within sight of Moscow. The people of the Soviet Union see World War II in a very different way from Americans—they call the conflict the "Great Patriotic War." If you examine American history textbooks, you will learn that World War II was primarily a conflict between the United States and both Germany and Japan, a two-theater war in which American forces liberated Europe from Nazi Germany and then drove Japan to defeat in the Pacific. If you examine British textbooks, you will discover that World War II was primarily a conflict between Britain and Nazi Germany, in which Britain saved the world for democracy while waiting for a reluctant United States to enter the war. But if you consult Soviet textbooks, you will find that World War II was a titanic struggle between communist Russia and fascist Germany, and that all other conflicts were a mere sideshow. In terms of wartime casualties, the Soviet interpretation is best supported by the facts. Fewer than 300,000 Ameri-

Figure 23.4 *Although the United States and the Soviet Union are both highly militarized societies, the military is a more obvious public presence in the Soviet Union. The high prestige of the Soviet military derives from its exploits in the "Great Patriotic War" against Nazi Germany.*

cans, almost all of them combatants, were killed in the war. The Soviet Union, in contrast, lost some 20 million people, including 7 million civilians. No other country in history has suffered such a catastrophic loss of life in war, and Soviet policy is obsessively focused on ensuring that nothing like it ever happens again.

Few Americans understand this aspect of Soviet culture, for their schools teach next to nothing about the history or society of their country's principal rival. A 1985 *New York Times* poll found that a large majority of Americans do not know that the United States once invaded the Soviet Union to put down its revolution, do not know that the Soviets suffered greater casualties in World War II than the United States did, and do not even know that the two countries were allies during that war. Yet in the same opinion poll, some 46 percent of the respondents expressed the view that Americans care more about their children than the Russians do.

How did the two great powers become such overt antagonists? At the conclusion of World War II, Soviet forces drove the German army from Eastern Europe but—partly to spread communism and partly to create a series of buffer states between itself and the West—the Soviet Union proceeded to install puppet communist regimes wherever it could. Fearing the spread of communism and further Russian encroachment, the United States, Canada, and several Western European countries formed the North Atlantic Treaty Organization, whose members are pledged to support one another in the event of a Soviet invasion. The Soviet Union and its new East European allies responded by creating the Warsaw Pact, which similarly pledges its members to mutual military aid. The United States went further and promised to use nuclear weapons to defend Western Europe against a conventional Soviet attack. Both countries began to look for supporters elsewhere in the postwar world, and the two sides have been frozen into this hostile stance ever since.

The Arms Race

The most menacing expression of superpower rivalry is the *arms race,* a process in which each side continuously attempts to gain or maintain superiority in weaponry. The arms race has given the world an astonishing variety of new conventional weapons, as well as a growing arsenal of nuclear weapons and the means of delivering

them from bombers, submarines, and land-based missiles. The United States held a clear lead in this "race" for several years after World War II, and took advantage of its superiority during the Cuban missile crisis of 1961—an event that probably marked the closest the superpowers have ever come to war. In that year the Soviet Union tried to install its missiles in Cuba in response to the basing of American missiles in Turkey. President Kennedy demanded that the Soviet missiles be withdrawn, and made clear his willingness to use force to achieve that end. The Soviet Union eventually withdrew the missiles in return for an American pledge to remove missiles from Turkey and never to invade Cuba. The Soviet leadership had little choice but to comply with Kennedy's demand, for at that time the country had only a few hundred missiles, while the United States had several thousand. Determined never to negotiate from a position of weakness again, the Soviet Union began a systematic military build-up, and achieved rough parity with the United States in deterrence sometime in the late 1970s. Despite extensive efforts by both sides since then, neither now seems able to get the edge over the other.

The arms race is propelled not only by the rivalry between the superpowers, but also by entrenched interests within both countries. An important feature of American society is the *military-industrial complex,* an informal system of mutual influence between the Pentagon, which buys armaments, and the major U.S. corporations that sell them. As we noted in Chapter 19 ("The Political Order"), the Pentagon has become dependent on the handful of corporations that have the resources to produce sophisticated weapons systems; and these corporations have in turn become dependent on the Pentagon for the bulk of their business and profits. As a result, the Pentagon has a strong incentive to protect its weapons manufacturers by insulating them from the rigors of free competition, while the manufacturers eagerly encourage the Pentagon to spend ever more money on developing and buying weaponry.

Decisions about which corporation is to build what weapon tend to become political as well as military issues. One reason is that corporations frequently build components of a weapons system in as many states as possible, in order to encourage members of Congress to vote the necessary funds. For example, parts of the B1 intercontinental bomber are being built in 47 states and 400 congressional districts. Congress has voted funds for the manufacture of 100 of these airplanes, even though they will be obsolete by the mid-1990s and even though the first few planes to be built are so defective in electronics and maneuverability that they would be useless in wartime. Each of these bombers costs over $200 million—which is more, incidentally, than the total federal spending on AIDS education and research in 1986—and modifications to the planes will cost hundreds of millions of dollars more. Yet it would be politically difficult for the Pentagon or Congress to cancel this latest entry into the arms race, for much of the support for the project is now based on local economic considerations, rather than on international strategic ones.

The Pentagon spends more than any other organization in the United States—about $500 million a day. Much of this money, no doubt, is spent well, in ways that enhance the nation's security. But much of it is simply wasted. Indeed, the military-industrial complex is notorious for producing overpriced and ineffective weapons systems. One reason, regrettably, is outright fraud. In the mid-1980s, nine of the Pentagon's largest ten contractors, and forty-five of the largest hundred, were under criminal investigation, mostly for various kinds of fraud and theft. A second reason is the lack of competition in the bidding and production process: because corporate manufacturers are almost guaranteed a substantial profit, they have little in-

centive to impose stringent quality controls or to hold down costs. A third reason for high costs and unreliability is that American weapons rely on ever more complicated technology. Typically, new weapons are "gold plated"—that is, loaded with every conceivable electronic or other "high-tech" device—even though the final product is often less useful in combat than the simpler, cheaper, and more numerous items that it replaces.

Consider the recent case of the Sergeant York air-defense gun, an expensive and complicated weapon that was originally designed for use against low-flying airplanes. It soon became apparent that the gun could not hit airplanes, so the Pentagon determined that its real function should be to attack helicopters. Almost anything can shoot down a helicopter—the army lost 4,643 in Vietnam, mostly to infantry fire—but not the Sergeant York. Eventually, after spending more than $2 billion in an effort to make the gun work, the Pentagon canceled the entire project. Yet, for the price of one of these guns, the army could have bought thirty highly reliable conventional antiaircraft weapons. A similar case is the Bradley Infantry Fighting Vehicle, which is supposed to carry troops into battle against Soviet forces in Europe. Thanks to "gold-plating," the vehicle now contains so much ammunition and other gear that it stands ten feet tall, making it an unusually inviting target for enemy fire—especially since it has to come to a complete halt to use its own antitank missile. To complicate matters, cheap and accurate hand-held rockets, which are standard equipment among Soviet infantry, can easily penetrate the carrier's armor and cause a fireball inside. And although the vehicle is supposed to cross rivers with ease, it is apt to sink at the first opportunity. If troops can be persuaded to ride in it at all, this hapless contraption will carry a crew and a grand total of six soldiers into battle, at a cost of nearly $2 million per vehicle, which is 64 percent more than its estimated cost. Further modifications are likely to add more than $70,000 to the price of each unit—a sum which alone could have bought a more efficient, commodious, and safer standard troop carrier.

Unfortunately, such "high-tech" mishaps have become almost normal in the American armaments industry. The B-70 aircraft, developed at a cost of over $1.5 billion, was such a disaster that only two of the planes were ever built, and one of these promptly crashed. The Sheridan tank cost $1 billion to develop, but was unfit for battle. A nuclear submarine launched in California immediately sank to the bottom of the ocean (the salvage

Figure 23.5

"No, no. When I say this new secret weapon can slip past their defenses undetected, I'm not referring to the Russians, I'm referring to Congress."

Drawing by Stevenson; © 1986
The New Yorker Magazine, Inc.

THE ARMS RACE: ACTION/REACTION

Action		Reaction
U.S. 1945	Atomic bomb	1949 U.S.S.R.
U.S. 1948	Intercontinental bomber	1955 U.S.S.R.
U.S. 1951	Jet bomber	1954 U.S.S.R.
U.S. 1952	Thermonuclear bomb	1953 U.S.S.R.
U.S.S.R. 1957	Intercontinental ballistic missile (ICBM)	1958 U.S.
U.S.S.R. 1957	Man-made satellite	1958 U.S.
U.S. 1960	Photo reconnaissance from satellite	1962 U.S.S.R.
U.S. 1960	Submarine-launched ballistic missile (SLBM)	1968 U.S.S.R.
U.S. 1962	Solid-fueled ICBM	1966 U.S.S.R.
U.S. 1966	Multiple warhead (MRV)	1968 U.S.S.R.
U.S.S.R. 1968	Antiballistic missile (ABM)	1972 U.S.
U.S. 1970	Multiple independently targeted warhead (MIRV)	1975 U.S.S.R.
U.S. 1982	Long-range cruise missile	1984 U.S.S.R.
U.S. 1983	Neutron bomb	198? U.S.S.R.
U.S. 198?	Antisatellite weapon	198? U.S.S.R.

SOURCE: Ruth Leger Sivard, *World Military and Social Expenditures, 1985* (Washington, D.C.: World Priorities, 1985), p. 16.

Figure 23.6 *As this table suggests, the arms race is essentially an action-reaction phenomenon, in which each contender tries to catch up with or get ahead of the other.*

costs alone were estimated at $35 million). The Safeguard missile defense system was built at a cost of $5.7 billion, only to be taken out of operation as useless some ten months later. The Viper antitank weapon ended up costing ten times its original estimate—but it cannot pierce the front of Soviet tanks, and so cannot be used by troops facing the enemy. The F/A-18 Hornet aircraft costs $30 million apiece, triple its original estimate, and uses so much fuel that it has only half the range of the A-7 it replaces. The cost of an AH-64 Apache helicopter rose from $9 million to over $17 million— and it has to hover motionless for up to 30 seconds in battle to fire its laser-guided missile, making it much easier to shoot down than its cheaper predecessor. The Stinger, intended to be a light, shoulder-held portable missile especially suited for use in rough terrain, turned out to be so heavy that it now requires a truck and trailer to transport

it. The M-1 tank costs $2.7 million each—45 percent more than originally projected, and three times as much as the tank it replaces. But because it breaks down five times as often and must refuel 40 percent more often (it uses about 2 gallons per mile), it is available for combat only half as often— meaning that the army can now field only one-sixth as many battle tanks for the same price as before.

It is often considered "patriotic" to favor increased military spending. But quantity of money does not equal quality of product, and the missile that does not fire, the radio that fails, the helicopter that stalls, the gun that jams, offer no benefit to Americans risking their lives in battle. Yet the Pentagon tolerates such inefficiencies, partly because it is a virtual captive of the defense contractors, and partly because of its own nature as a huge formal organization. As we noted in Chapter 7 ("Social Groups"), bureaucracies tend to develop a number of internal problems that are unrelated to their original goals. In many respects, the Pentagon, by far the biggest single bureaucracy in the world, has lost sight of its original job—to win wars—and has become overly concerned with moving paper, maintaining budgets, and advancing careers (Hadley, 1986; Gabriel, 1986). The military is now bloated with officers: for example, there are four times as many majors and colonels for every 100 enlisted soldiers as there were during wartime in 1945. The effects of this bureaucracy were tellingly revealed in a poorly planned and executed operation against the tiny Caribbean island of Grenada in 1983, when it took 7,000 U.S. troops three days to overcome 200 Cuban soldiers and a Grenadan army that would not fight. After the operation, the army gave out more medals than there were soldiers involved—8,612 in all, including many to officers who got no nearer to the action than their desks in Washington.

Little is known about the internal forces that propel the Soviet Union on its course in the arms race, but that country must have a military-industrial complex of its own. There is no private armaments industry, of course, so weapons manufacturing is in the hands of large state bureaucracies that are also closely tied to the military. The military itself has a great deal of overt power, prestige, and influence in the Soviet Union, where national days are often celebrated with displays of weaponry and military, might. Moreover, the Soviet arms industry does not have to face the kind of public scrutiny that its American counterpart must face, for its plans and budgets—and failures—are kept secret.

The good news, from the American point of view, is that the Soviet Union is also stumbling toward ever more expensive and technologically complicated equipment, much of it a poor copy of outdated American originals. Soviet weaponry has repeatedly proved itself inferior when used in battle by countries such as Syria and Libya (Cockburn, 1982; Gervasi, 1986).

If the arms race continues in the future, we can expect efforts to create a host of new destructive devices, such as neutron bombs, X-ray lasers, microwave weapons, particle-beam weapons, gamma-ray lasers, rail guns, and germ or chemical warfare. For the present, however, there are two major elements in the arms race: innovations in the deployment of nuclear weapons, and early steps toward the creation of a "star wars" missile defense system. We will look at each in turn.

Nuclear Strategy

The most feared weapon on the planet is the nuclear bomb. This weapon is based on Albert Einstein's insight that matter is merely a form of "frozen" energy, which can be released through nuclear fission or fusion to yield immense force. The bomb that destroyed Hiroshima was the equivalent of 13 kilotons, a kiloton being the equivalent of 1,000 tons of TNT. Today's nuclear bombs are more commonly measured in terms of the megaton—1 million tons of TNT (which, if it were to be transported by rail, would require a train more than 400 miles long). Some contemporary bombs have the force of 20 megatons or more; the largest ever tested, by the Soviet Union in 1961, was equal to 50 million tons of conventional explosive (Riordan, 1982; Sivard, 1986).

From the point of view of military strategy, nuclear weapons are the most paradoxical of devices. The superpowers seem as reluctant to use them as they are eager to build them. In fact, nuclear strategy generally assumes that the weapons will be used, not as weapons, but rather as threats to deter the other side from using its weapons. The awful risk, of course, is that the weapons may one day be used as just that—weapons.

Many people seem to regard nuclear strategy as a highly complicated matter that is better left to the experts, who alone might understand the complexities involved. Actually, the strategy of nuclear warfare is fairly simple; it is much easier to grasp, certainly, than the strategy of a board game such as chess. And in the matter of nuclear strategy, blind faith in the judgment of experts is tantamount to surrendering one's democratic right to help shape one's own and one's society's future. In any war, after all, the "experts" of at least one side must have chosen the wrong strategy or miscalculated the outcome, for in warfare there is invariably at least one loser!

Actually, nuclear strategy has evolved considerably since the dawn of the atomic age. When the United States was the only nation in the world with nuclear weapons, nuclear strategy was simple indeed. The United States threatened to use the bomb on the Soviet Union if that country engaged in unacceptable military action. Since there was no defense of any kind against nuclear weapons, this system of unilateral deterrence worked very well—from the American point of view. The Soviet Union, naturally enough, did not like this form of deterrence too well, and in 1949 it developed its own nuclear bomb.

Once the superpowers both had nuclear weapons, each nation was able to hold the other's population as hostage, for an attack by one side could be met with a devastating counterattack by the other. To ensure that such an attack and a counterattack would be possible, both superpowers developed a strategic "triad" consisting of bombers, land-based missiles, and submarine-based missiles. The three elements in the triad have different advantages and disadvantages that complement one another. Bombers require several hours to reach their targets, but they can take to the air when under attack and can be recalled in the event of error or change of policy. Land-based intercontinental missiles are sited in fixed locations and so can become targets themselves, but they can deliver powerful warheads quickly and accurately, striking the enemy within half an hour of launch. Submarines are almost undetectable, so their missiles can deter an enemy even if the other two elements in the triad are destroyed or somehow fail. A single Trident submarine, for example, carries enough nuclear weapons to destroy the Soviet Union by obliterating its 240 largest cities. That is more firepower than was used in all of World War II—and the United States already has six Tridents and plans fourteen more. This system of mutual deterrence has long been known as MAD, for "mutually assured destruction."

Gradually, however, the superpowers are attempting to abandon their reliance on MAD. The

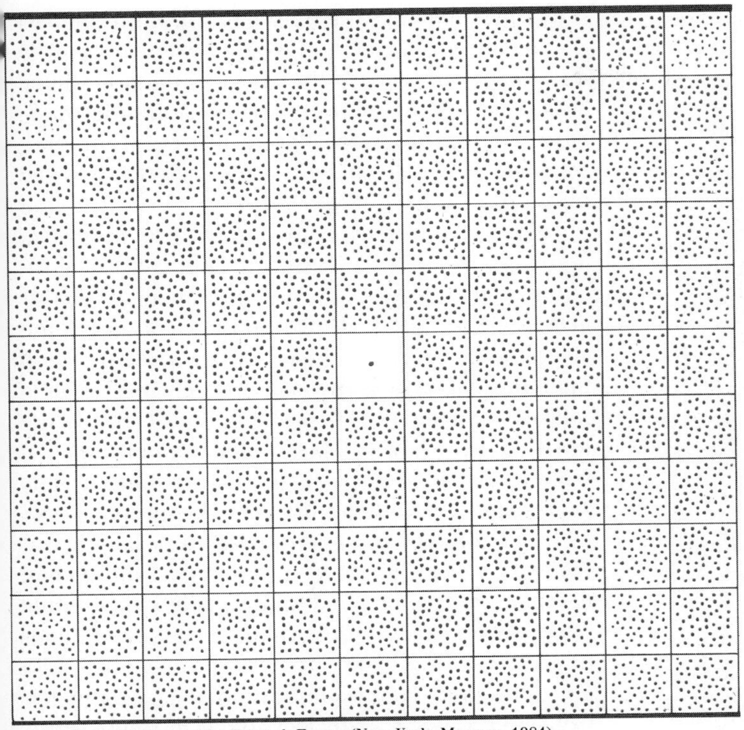

SOURCE: Harold Willens, *The Trimtab Factor* (New York: Morrow, 1984).

Figure 23.7 *This chart compares the world's fire-power in the mid-1980s to that of World War II. The dot in the center square represents all the fire-power in World War II. The other dots represent the firepower of the world's current nuclear weaponry. Three dots represent the firepower of a single Poseidon submarine, which would be sufficient to destroy the 200 largest cities in the Soviet Union. The United States has thirty of these submarines. Eight dots—equal to the firepower of eight World War IIs—represents the firepower of a new Trident submarine, which would be enough to destroy 240 major cities in the Northern Hemisphere. The United States has six of these submarines, and plans a fleet of twenty. Any two squares on this chart represent enough firepower to destroy every large and medium-size city on earth.*

main reason seems to be that the system produces a kind of nuclear stalemate in which neither side has any real edge. This is an unsatisfactory situation for rivals in an arms race, and Soviet and American strategists have turned to new nuclear devices in the hope of securing some advantages. The newly emerging strategy is one of "flexible response," which offers a variety of different op-

tions for deterrence—or even for offense. One of these options is based on a recent innovation, the "battlefield" or "theater" nuclear bomb—a relatively small device that is designed for deployment in conventional warfare, on the risky assumption that its use will not provoke a massive nuclear retaliation. Another innovation is the cruise missile, which can carry a nuclear warhead and is small enough to be launched from a boat or truck. These missiles could be used for a "surgical strike" against a limited target. Some strategists now speak of a shift from MAD to NUTS, for "nuclear-use theories."

The most crucial new strategy, however, is the development of nuclear missiles, such as the American MX, which are so accurate that in theory they could destroy the other side's missiles by exploding virtually on top of them. This innovation raises the theoretical possibility of a "first strike" by one superpower on the land-based missiles of the other, in the hope of inducing the weakened victim to surrender rather than face a second barrage aimed at its cities. Of course, the victim might still choose to respond in kind, striking at the aggressor with any remaining land-based missiles and with its bombers and submarine missiles. Moreover, one country's suspicion or fear that its own land-based missiles might soon be under attack could prompt it to a preemptive strike of its own—"use it or lose it." So, despite all these innovations, MAD is not likely to disappear until nuclear weapons do.

"Star Wars"

If one country's missiles can hit another country's missiles while they are on the ground, then a logical next step in the arms race would be a weapons system that could hit incoming missiles in their flight before they hit their targets. The idea of an antiballistic missile system—one that could destroy incoming missiles—is not new. In fact, the superpowers agreed to strictly limit the use of such systems when they signed the Antiballistic Missile Treaty in 1972. At that time, both sides regarded such a system as potentially dangerous, because it would upset the cautious balance provided by mutually assured destruction. However, the concept was revived by President Reagan in 1983, and it is likely to remain controversial, whether his specific proposals are put into practice in the future or not (Ball, 1985).

Figure 23.8 *This recent air-force recruitment poster captures the "star wars" imagery that has come to symbolize American plans to deploy a space-based missile defense system.*

President Reagan's Strategic Defense Initiative—universally dubbed "star wars"—calls for a ground- and space-based defense against intercontinental ballistic missiles. The defense would use various weapons—including exotic new devices such as X-ray lasers—to intercept and destroy incoming Soviet missiles and warheads at successive stages in their flight. As visualized by Reagan, the system would protect the American people from Soviet or other missiles so effectively that these nuclear weapons would become obsolete. This is an imaginative and morally appealing idea, for it seems to substitute defense and safety for offense and danger in nuclear strategy. Unhap-

pily, there is general agreement among scientists that no antimissile system would be able to provide an effective shield for the population as a whole. Most strategic planners therefore see "star wars" as providing only indirect protection to the public—by protecting American missiles against a Soviet first strike (Carter, 1984).

Even as a missile protector, the proposed strategic defense system would run into serious difficulties. The cost would be astronomical—probably around $1 trillion, making it by far the most expensive single project in history. The system would have to track and respond to tens of thousands of missiles and decoys, all arriving almost simultaneously at speeds of 10,000 miles an hour, and it would have to work perfectly the first time. If only 1 percent of the incoming missile shower penetrated the defenses, the United States could be effectively destroyed. The wretched performance of defense contractors in building relatively simple weapons on earth in the past does not inspire confidence that they could create an efficient or workable antiballistic missile system in space in the future—let alone a perfect one. One apparently insuperable problem is that the software for the necessary computer programs would require millions of lines of code, with little tolerance for the usual "bugs" or errors that occur in even a simple program. Since "star wars" could never be tested in practice, it would be impossible to discover and remove the many thousands of bugs that it would inevitably contain. Additionally, the problems of constructing and installing hundreds of sensors, rocket battle stations, and other devices in space would be an unprecedented technological challenge. Materials would have to be launched into space at more than fifty times the annual rate achieved by the already troubled space-shuttle program, and a new space "truck" would have to be built, at a cost of at least $60 billion, to do the job (Parnas, 1985; H. Brown, 1986).

Even if the system were eventually in place and in working order, the Soviet Union could take numerous steps to foil it. For example, the system could be "blinded" by such means as high-altitude nuclear explosions. Or, since warheads and especially decoys are much cheaper to build than the weapons to defend against them, thousands of additional warheads and decoys could be used to overwhelm the system. The Soviet Union could also attack the defense system itself, with existing missiles or by using killer satellites or even by placing "space mines" in orbit near the "star wars" components, where they would await instructions to explode on command. And the Soviet Union could completely circumvent the system (which is designed to stop only missiles that pass through space) by delivering nuclear weapons from offshore submarines, on low-flying cruise missiles, or even in suitcases smuggled into the United States and left in city apartments for later detonation. Or the Soviet Union could escalate the arms race beyond nuclear warfare—to some new strategy involving chemical or biological weaponry (Hecht, 1984; Stares, 1986).

Unfortunately, a "star wars" system could make the world even more insecure by increasing superpower tension and encouraging a new arms race in space. The Soviet Union, for example, might build its own system. Then each side would be tempted to create means of attacking the other's system as well as defending its own. In fact, "star wars" itself could be used for attack as well as defense, for its weaponry, should it ever become effective at all, could be turned on satellites and other objects in space besides missiles, and also on "soft" military, industrial, and urban targets on the ground (Boffey, 1985).

The greatest danger, however, is the instability that would develop if the United States actually did combine its existing potential to attack the Soviet Union with a new potential to defend itself from Soviet counterattack. Such a pairing of offense and defense would be extraordinarily provocative to the Soviet Union, for it would leave that society highly vulnerable. We can understand the intense Soviet anxiety about the "star wars" system if we imagine the system in reverse—the Soviet Union having the ability to attack the United States while having a potential defense against an American response. No American leader would allow such a situation to develop, and it is prudent to assume that no Soviet leader would allow his country to be so jeopardized either.

Throughout the history of warfare, people have grasped for some ultimate weapon or defense—one that would finally provide permanent security. For example, Hiram Maxim, the inventor of the machine gun, thought he had invented a weapon to end war: "Only a general who was a barbarian would send his men to certain death against the concentrated power of my new gun." But sent they were; in World War I, tens of thousands were mowed down in a single day. Orville Wright believed that his flying machine would make further wars impossible, for the old ways of conducting battle would be obsolete. Instead, the airplane increased military capacity to an unprecedented degree (Hellman, 1985). After World War I, France built the Maginot Line, a string of border fortifications designed to prevent Germany from ever invading France again. But in World War II, German forces simply detoured around the line: they invaded Belgium and swept into France by a different, undefended route, a tactic the Maginot planners had not seriously considered.

"Star wars" may be yet another of these supposedly "ultimate" security devices. After all, if the Soviet Union built a defense system that made it immune to American missile attack, what would the United States do? Surely, it would either find some way to outwit the system, or else it would develop some new weapon entirely. There is no reason whatever to suppose that the Soviet Union would not take similar steps against any American missile defense. Once that happened, the "star wars" system would become a mere irrelevance, a high-tech Maginot Line in the sky. Abandoned and forgotten, the trillion-dollar space junk would orbit the planet in eerie silence for many thousands of years after the superpowers of today had fought their war, or made their peace, and disappeared into the dust of history.

Figure 23.9 *This photograph shows a test firing of a gun in France's Maginot Line, a supposedly impregnable border defense that was built during the 1930s to prevent any future German invasion. The line was never put to the test, for in 1939 Germany simply circumvented the line by invading France from a different direction. The Maginot Line is remembered today as a classic "ultimate defense" that proved to be irrelevant in actual warfare.*

Nuclear War

If full-scale nuclear war ever occurred, it would be, to put it mildly, an event of the greatest social significance. Such a war would shatter many contemporary societies, destroy the existing world order, and reshape whatever human history might be left.

Can It Happen?

When considering the possibility of nuclear war, we are apt to regard it as unthinkable. But "unthinkable" merely means that we choose not to think about it—and in turning to the illusion that all will surely be well, we may ignore the reality of our danger and so increase the chances of war. Naturally, people have great resistance to the idea that they may one day destroy themselves. They therefore tend to think of reasons why nuclear war cannot happen ("Nobody would be crazy enough to start one"), rather than to acknowledge the circumstances in which it could happen. We already know, from more than four decades of experience with the bomb, that nuclear war can be avoided; but there are factors that have made and continue to make such a war a distinct possibility. The mere fact that several nations are arming for such a conflict is in itself evidence of that (Calder, 1980; Beres, 1982; Kennan, 1982).

How might a nuclear war break out? A calculated surprise attack by one superpower on the other is the least likely possibility, because each side has so many weapons that the victim nation would probably still be able to mount a catastrophic retaliation. Even so, nuclear strategists are deeply concerned about the possibility of such a first strike and about ways to defend against it, such as the "star wars" system.

There is a much greater possibility of a deliberate attack occurring during a time of extreme tension between the superpowers. Obviously, one side would resort to such a step only if it believed that the consequences of not striking would be worse than the consequences of striking. However, if country X believes that country Y is likely to use nuclear weapons, then it could be a military advantage for country X to use its weapons first, in a preemptive strike designed to destroy most of the other side's weapons before they can be used. Unhappily, nuclear deterrence has a built-in trap. Neither side wants to use the weapons, but each must bluff the other side that it is willing to do so. After all, if we are *certain* that they will not use their weapons, or if they are *certain* that we will

not use ours, then the weapons have no deterrent value at all. But what if the bluff is too convincing? If we become *certain* (rightly or wrongly) that they intend to use theirs, or if they become *certain* (rightly or wrongly) that we intend to use ours, then a first strike is the logical response—and nuclear war is under way. In practice, extreme international tension is likely to be marked by *uncertainty*—a situation in which each side is *almost* convinced that the other side will (or will not) use the weapons. In this situation, the slightest miscalculation or mistake—a misinterpretation of the other side's troop mobilization, a skirmish between two naval vessels, a computer error in a missile warning system—could precipitate war.

Another source of danger is superpower involvement in such "hot spots" as Central America, the Middle East, or southern Africa. The growing interdependence of nations has produced a network of vital interests all over the world that the superpowers are pledged to defend. The United States, for example, has made it clear that it will use any necessary force to protect its oil interests in the Middle East. The danger exists that a local conflict—say, between Israel and Syria—could quickly involve the superpowers in conventional and then nuclear war. The Cuban missile crisis, for example, started out as a local issue but eventually brought the superpowers eyeball to eyeball—until both made concessions.

The proliferation of nuclear weapons adds to the danger. Clearly, the more weapons there are and the more countries that have them, the greater is the peril that they will eventually be used. Presently, only the United States, the Soviet Union, Great Britain, France, and China admit to having nuclear weapons. It is widely believed that Israel and South Africa—both "hot spot" countries in strategically important locations—have also produced the bomb. India and Pakistan, which have a long tradition of hostility, also have the capability to make nuclear weapons. Over the next two decades, a sizable number of other countries will have the ability to make nuclear bombs, including such nations as Libya, Iran, and North Korea—three nations whose current leaders are often viewed in the West as lunatics. Once there are enough nuclear powers in the world, it may become possible for one of them to use a warhead on another country anonymously. For example, a fanatical leader of a minor nation could launch a nuclear cruise missile from a fishing vessel at the capital city of a major power. Additionally, the proliferation of nuclear weapons greatly increases the probability that terrorists will eventually capture a bomb and

THE SPREAD OF NUCLEAR WEAPONS

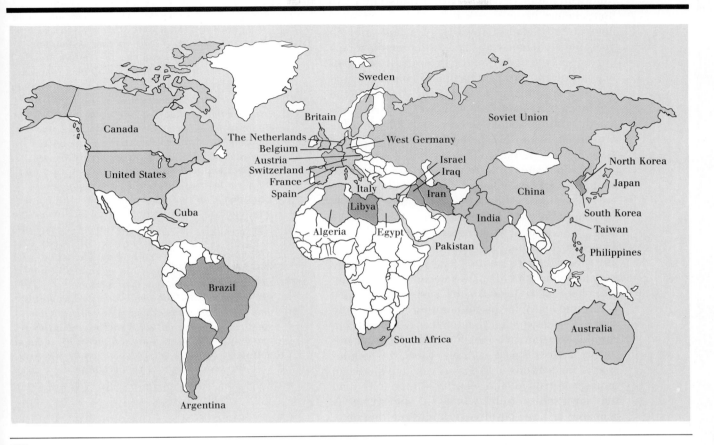

Have nuclear weapons.

Are believed to have nuclear weapons or weapon components in various stages of development and deployment.

Have made efforts to develop or acquire nuclear weapons.

Are believed able, but unlikely, to build or develop nuclear weapons.

SOURCE: Nuclear Control Institute.

Figure 23.10 *As this map suggests, there is considerable danger of a quite widespread proliferation of nuclear weapons in the future. Any further spread of these weapons must increase the danger of nuclear war—partly because the mathematical probability of nuclear war will automatically be increased, and partly because some of the future nuclear powers already have recent records of political instability and even aggression against other societies.*

use it to threaten a major power in pursuit of their goals (Meyer, 1984).

Nuclear war could also begin by accident— say, by the misfiring of a missile, particularly in a time of crisis. Actually, there have been at least thirty-two serious nuclear-weapon accidents involving American planes, missiles, or vessels, including some in which nuclear bombs crashed to the ground unexploded or were lost at sea. The Soviet Union has doubtless had accidents of its own, but few details are known (Cox, 1977). More worrisome is the possibility that war may break out as a result of false alarms, of which there have been many American (and no doubt Soviet) instances over the years. During the 1950s, a flock of Canadian geese picked up by radar led Americans to believe that a Soviet bomber attack was under way. In 1960, a meteor shower was interpreted as an assault by enemy missiles. In 1961, an early-warning station misinterpreted a moon echo as a launch against the United States, and in response American bombers flew off toward Russia for two hours before being recalled. In 1978, a technician inadvertently loaded a war-games tape into an operational system, causing a Soviet missile attack to be displayed at the American Strategic Air Command. In 1980, a 46-cent computer chip failed, and led to a warning of a submarine strike on the American mainland. In each case, the error was caught in time, thanks to cross-checking and the human element that is built into the warning system (Wicker, 1982).

In some situations, however, there is little or no time for human judgments. New short-range missiles allow less and less warning time between launch and arrival. Intercontinental missiles take about half an hour to complete their journey, but American Pershing missiles in Europe can hit Moscow within six minutes. This gives virtually no time for Soviet personnel to determine whether an alarm is real or false, so the Soviet Union must ignore the alarm, or permit a junior officer on the spot to decide whether to launch Soviet missiles in response, or it must leave the decision up to a computer. In this respect, as in all others, the technological innovations of the arms race have created more problems for the security of humanity than they have solved. Nobody knows if nuclear war is probable or not—but it is certainly very possible.

Figure 23.11 *The illustration on the facing page shows the hypothetical sequence of events that might follow a 1-megaton nuclear explosion above New York City. The skyline of the city, viewed from the west, is drawn to scale, and the detonation point is some 6,500 feet above the Empire State Building. (1) In the first moment of the explosion, there is a brilliant flash of light, a wave of radiant heat, an electromagnetic pulse, and a burst of lethal radiation—all traveling at the speed of light. Additionally, a blast wave begins to travel faster than the speed of sound from the center of the explosion. (2) The blast spreads across the city, crushing and flattening most structures. Dust and other radioactive particles are swept up by the explosion's updraft. Combustible materials burst into flame. (3) Fires begin to merge into major conflagrations. (4) The conflagrations coalesce into a massive fire covering what is left of the city. (5) A firestorm ensues, driven by in-rushing winds of over 100 miles per hour. Huge quantities of smoke and dust are carried into the atmosphere. (6) The fire burns out, and the smoke and dust from this and other explosions extend over a large region, effectively blocking out sunlight and drastically reducing surface temperature. In actuality, a major industrial, military, and economic center like New York City would be hit with more than 1 megaton—certainly with 20, and perhaps as many as 100, megatons.*

Immediate Effects

In an all-out war, the nuclear powers would strike at targets of military, economic, and industrial significance. Because so many of these targets are in or near urban areas, many or most of the large cities in both societies would be hit by nuclear warheads. The immediate effects on these populated areas would depend in part on the number and power of the striking warheads. For simplicity's sake, we can consider the effects primarily in terms of a single (and relatively small) 1-megaton explosion. Such an explosion would have four principal types of immediate effect on populated areas (Glastone and Dolan, 1977; Lewis, 1979; Riordan, 1982; Tsipis, 1982).

1. *Electromagnetic pulse.* A nuclear explosion creates an electromagnetic pulse, a burst of energy that can produce thousands of volts in a fraction of a second. The pulse is harmless to people, but induces destructive surges of current in electrical and electronic systems, burning out circuits in a random fashion. The higher the nuclear weapon is

exploded, the more widespread the pulse; a large nuclear weapon exploded high above the earth could blanket an area half the size of the United States, knocking out many radio and television stations, telephones, computer networks, and other electrical equipment—including much of the military command and control system. In war, some nuclear weapons would certainly be used in this way in order to cripple the enemy's ability to respond militarily.

2. *Blast.* Most of the immediate damage from a bomb exploded at or near the earth's surface comes from an explosive blast. At ground zero, the point on the earth where the explosion is centered, the blast digs out a large crater; a 1-megaton bomb, for example, could create a hole about 1,000 feet wide and 200 feet deep. The cratering causes earthquakelike tremors that will collapse buildings miles away. The blast also spreads out laterally from ground zero, traveling faster than the speed of sound. There are actually two components in the blast—"overpressure," a compression

of air that crushes objects in its path, and "dynamic pressure," a rushing shock wave that hits surfaces like a powerful wind. Most structures within about five miles of ground zero would be destroyed or flattened, and the rubble would be carried along by the winds. At some distance from ground zero, the steel framework of some buildings would be left standing, but the windows and contents, including the occupants, might be blown out. Billions of pieces of shattered glass would slice through the air at speeds of over 100 miles an hour, maiming or killing anyone in their path.

3. *Heat.* A nuclear bomb produces radiant energy in the form of heat and light, with temperatures in the hottest regions of the explosion reaching millions of degrees Centigrade. The heat and light travel at the speed of light—much faster than the sound of the blast—so there is no warning to take cover. The heat from a 1-megaton bomb would cause first-degree burns (similar to bad sunburn) at about seven miles from ground zero; second-degree burns (leading to blisters and infection) at six miles, and third-degree burns (destroying skin tissue) at up to five miles. Without medical treatment, a third-degree burn over a quarter of the body, or a second-degree burn over a third of the body, would be fatal. The radiant heat would ignite most flammable material, including oil- and gas-storage facilities, within five miles of ground zero. The light from the bomb could cause temporary flash blindness to observers as much as fifty miles away.

4. *Radiation.* A nuclear weapon creates two forms of potentially lethal radiation. The first is "direct radiation," a single invisible burst of energy that travels in straight lines in all directions at the speed of light, with its intensity diminishing with distance from ground zero. The second is "fallout radiation," consisting of particles of debris that have been carried up in the mushroom cloud and made radioactive by the explosion. This material is a poison that can be eaten, breathed, or absorbed through the skin. Some of the fallout returns to earth within minutes and lands close to ground zero, but much of it is carried away in a plume downwind of the explosion—a long thin plume if the wind is strong, a shorter and wider one if the wind is slow. This fallout may remain in the atmosphere for days, weeks, months, or even years until it settles to earth or is brought down by rain. The various radioactive materials produced by the bomb decay at different rates, but the area near ground zero would become safe by normal standards within about ten years, and outlying areas within two or three years.

In short, the immediate effects of a single 1-megaton nuclear bomb would be the social and physical destruction of the affected area and the pulverizing, broiling, and irradiating of many or most of the inhabitants. In practice, major cities might be hit by 20 or more megatons in the course of a full-scale nuclear war. What would be the aftermath for any who survived?

Long-Term Effects

Moments after an all-out attack, somewhere in the region of 80 million Americans would be dead, and about 50 million more would die during the next few weeks, primarily as a result of injuries, burns, radiation sickness, disease, starvation, and exposure to the elements. The Soviet Union, which is a less urbanized society with a more dispersed population, would probably suffer a somewhat lower number of deaths. In all likelihood, many tens of millions more would be dead in the countries of Eastern and Western Europe. In addition to the loss of life, the attack would profoundly damage both the physical and the social structure of the target societies (Schell, 1982; Katz, 1982; Tucker and Gleisner, 1982).

The first psychological response to nuclear attack, if the experience of Hiroshima is anything to go by, would be profound shock. The familiar world would be gone—relatives and friends dead or missing, homes destroyed, city centers vaporized, services and power sources lacking, nearly all social values stripped of their meaning. In a study of the aftermath of the Hiroshima bombing, Robert Lifton (1967) found that the survivors did not panic. Rather, they seemed emotionless: they simply moved, slowly and dully, away from the center of the destruction, many of them seeming to be walking in a dream, as though they were not really alive. Lifton suggests that this reaction was simply a closing of the mind to prevent the surrounding horror from penetrating it. The normal human response to such a grotesque scene of death and destruction is not rage, panic, depression, fear, or mourning, but merely mental paralysis. In other disasters, such as a flood or a volcanic explosion, there is at least a hopeful sense that the rest of the world is intact and that help is on the way, but in the case of nuclear holocaust, these fundamental certainties do not apply (Barnaby, 1977; Finch, 1979; Lifton and Erikson, 1982).

After the initial shock wore off, the survivors would begin to attend to their immediate problems. These would include taking care of their own and others' injuries as best they could without the benefit of professional help or medications; and trying to find uncontaminated food, water, and shelter. Shelter would be essential for the survivors to limit their exposure to radioactive fallout. The radioactivity would probably dissipate within two or three weeks. In some areas, however, incoming warheads might have damaged nuclear power reactors and released their contents into the atmosphere; these areas could be uninhabitable for many years, even centuries.

Conditions in the shelters would generally be appalling, for hungry people, many of them sick or dying from the effects of radiation, would be living in close proximity in a highly unsanitary environment. This situation would be made worse by the fact that radiation weakens the immune system, causing people to die of burns and other medical problems that would not usually be fatal. Even relatively small doses of radiation cause severe effects that become apparent slowly in the days and weeks after exposure, including nausea, vomiting, diarrhea, fever, bleeding, ulcerations, and hair loss. All the survivors, no matter how well protected, would be exposed to unsafe levels of radiation. Consequently, many babies would be born deformed in the months after the war, and millions of survivors would eventually develop cancers as a result of their exposure.

The survivors would also be exposed, in time, to such long-forgotten infections as cholera and typhoid—but without most of civilization's usual barriers against disease, such as medication, clean water, sanitary waste disposal, good nutrition, refrigeration, uncontaminated food, and insecticides. One disease that could well become rampant is the plague. This disease is endemic among rats and other rodents in the westernmost part of the United States, and nuclear war would create the ideal conditions for its transmission to humans—crowded and unsanitary living conditions, an absence of antibiotics, and a multiplication of rats gorging themselves on corpses (Adams, 1982; Adams and Cullen, 1982; Chivian, 1982).

Social organization in the postattack period would have to be built again almost from scratch. The old division of labor would be irrelevant, since the vast majority of jobs—particularly the information-processing ones of the destroyed postindustrial society—would no longer exist. Government functions would have collapsed; the national political and bureaucratic leadership would probably have been largely "decapitated" by a massive and early strike on Washington. Central government might survive, but it is possible that localities and regions would become the new political units. Basic services, such as education, sanitation, and policing, would have to be reassembled at the local level. Most of the computer records that track and give identity to modern Americans would be lost. Major banks would have disappeared along with prominent corporations that were headquartered

Figure 23.12 *This photograph of the city of Hiroshima after the atomic bomb gives some idea of the world that would be left after full-scale nuclear war.*

in target cities. Currency would be useless, and goods and services would be exchanged through barter. Security would be a serious problem, for armed bandits would prey on the resources of the other survivors. Millenarian and other religious movements would probably flourish, each of them offering its own interpretation of the events that had occurred and its own prophecies for the future.

The survivors would soon have to get down to the difficult and complex job of restoring production—primarily production of food. This would be an urgent task, for if existing supplies ran out before new food could be produced, a downward spiral would begin, leading to almost medieval conditions. The greatest danger would be that starving people would seize and eat the grain to be planted for the following year's crop. Even with adequate seed supplies, however, survivors might find that oil and gasoline resources were inadequate to permit mechanized agriculture. It is quite conceivable that, for the first time, Americans would experience the kind of existence they once saw on TV reports from famine-ridden countries like Ethiopia—except that in this case, there would be no airlifted supplies from the outside world to aid the desperate and the hungry. Of course, the collapse of the American, Soviet, and European economies would plunge most of the other countries of the world into an unprecedented economic depression, followed by social and political chaos. To those who remained alive after the nuclear apocalypse, the world of today would seem like a paradise lost. With the haunting realization that civilization had squandered its heritage, they might well ask: How did it happen? Could nobody see it coming? Why didn't anybody stop it?

There is some question, however, of whether very many people—or even any people—would survive an all-out nuclear war. This uncertainty stems primarily from our general ignorance about the environmental and climatic effects of a full-scale nuclear war. Scientists have only recently come to realize that if the United States and the Soviet Union used even half of their weapons in a nuclear barrage directed at major military, industrial, and urban targets, the result would be vast conflagrations of burning cities, forests, factories, and fuels. Hundreds of millions of tons of smoke and toxic fumes would be dumped into the atmosphere, forming a thick veil of soot over much of the Northern Hemisphere and blocking out much of the sunlight for days if not weeks. The result would be a dramatic fall in temperature, although nobody can be sure of how much, since the height, extent, composition, and distribution of the pollutants are largely a matter of guesswork. Early estimates were that temperatures would fall about 45 degrees centigrade for weeks or months on end; more recent estimates are that they would dip about half that much. In any event, much or most of the world's agricultural production would surely be lost, and freezing weather would be added to the hunger and misery of the survivors. But if global temperatures fell far enough for a long enough period, then the superpowers might have truly found a doomsday weapon that could push our species toward extinction.

Prospects for Peace

Global preparations for "defense" consume an immense and growing proportion of human financial, material, and personal resources, in a world that is already overburdened with social and economic problems. As we approach the twenty-first century, there is one physician for every 1,030 people on the planet, but one soldier for every 43 people. All over the world, hundreds of thousands of scientists and engineers devote their skills to planning new and more efficient ways for humans to kill one another; millions of workers labor to manufacture instruments of death; and tens of millions of soldiers train for combat—and some of them actually go to war. From a moral and even an economic point of view, this vast investment of human ingenuity and energy seems a tragic waste. Unlike other economic goods, such as cars or computers, the weapons of war are rarely put to any use—and if they are used at all, it is to destroy economies, not to build them. And looming over all these military preparations and counterpreparations is humanity's ultimate threat, the unleashing of full-scale nuclear war.

For millennia, people have hoped for peace in their time. Today, as usual, there is no shortage of grand proposals for peace—such as new defensive devices, or the acceptance of one religion or another, or the establishment of a world government, or even the reform of so-called human nature. Yet arms races and wars continue as before, sometimes creating the discouraging idea that hopes for peace are too "idealistic." And indeed, we are likely to be disappointed if we expect dramatic results in the form of an immediate end to war and militarism. The prospects for peace look much more encouraging, however, once we recognize that war and peace are really opposite ends of a continuum, and that movement along this continuum, in either direction, is the result of social processes that develop and change over time under the influence of government policies and popular pressures.

We can see this process in the hostile, intricate dance of the superpowers as they waver along the continuum between war and peace—sometimes tending one way, sometimes another. As we have noted, the policies of both the Soviet Union and the United States are constrained by the knowledge that if one side pushes the other too far, nuclear war could result. Consequently, both countries test one another—but only within the perceived limits of their mutual tolerance. The Soviet Union and the United States are generally careful to avoid direct confrontation, and instead participate openly or covertly in wars in other countries, often through the use of foreign "proxy" forces, such as the Cubans in Angola or the Contras in Nicaragua. Both countries, it seems, share an unwritten understanding—essentially, that if a country is already communist-ruled, the Soviet Union will be permitted to intervene to keep it that way, and if it is already noncommunist, the United States will be permitted to intervene to maintain the status quo.

Thus, when the United States sent troops to prevent the communist side from winning a civil war in Vietnam, the Soviet Union objected mightily, but did no more than send covert assistance to its own sympathizers. Similarly, when the Soviet Union invaded Afghanistan to prevent a communist regime from being overthrown, the United States protested vehemently, but took no direct action other than to send covert aid to the rebels. Both countries also grant each other the implicit "right" to dominate and even invade bordering countries: over the years, for example, the United States has intervened with impunity in such countries as Grenada, Nicaragua, and the Dominican Republic, while the Soviet Union has readily used force or the threat of force in such countries as Hungary, Czechoslovakia, and Poland. War and peace, therefore, are not either/or alternatives, for the various actions or inactions of the superpowers tend to move the world one way or another along the continuum between military holocaust and peaceful harmony. Seen in this light, steps designed to enhance the prospects for peace rather than war are matters of practical reality, not impractical ideals. In what ways, then, can nuclear war between the superpowers be avoided, and peace be achieved?

Nuclear Deterrence

Many people hold the view that nuclear weapons have helped to prevent war. Throughout the more than four decades since these destructive devices appeared on the scene, the United States and the Soviet Union have avoided outright military conflict. Obviously, we cannot know for certain whether the two nations would have fought one another had there not been a nuclear threat. There can be little doubt, however, that the prospect of mutually assured destruction has deterred war by making its potential consequences utterly intolerable. This record has encouraged the widespread view that the best way to avoid war is for each side to hold the other's population as hostage under nuclear threat. The drawback to this approach, of course, is that the threat of mutually assured destruction is an "all-or-nothing" gamble with the highest stakes imaginable. As long as the threat "works," war is avoided; but if the strategy fails—through design, miscalculation, or error—then the result is the obliteration of the societies that depended on it.

Moreover, a strategy of mutually assured destruction is most likely to work if there is a balance of power between the two main nations or blocs. If the contending parties are evenly balanced, neither will be likely to strike first, for there can be no certainty of victory. On the other hand, if one of the

Figure 23.13

"Well, that takes care of that—unless, of course, somebody can suggest an even harder line."

Drawing by Stevenson; © 1984
The New Yorker Magazine, Inc.

parties gains (or appears to be gaining) superiority, war becomes more likely—either because the superior power is tempted to take advantage of its position, or because the inferior one is tempted to strike before its own position deteriorates further. As a matter of historical fact, that is precisely the situation that precipitated many wars of this century, most notably World War I (Diehl, 1985).

Unfortunately, however, the arms race introduces recurrent instability into the balance of power, for each new weapon or defense seems to offer one side or the other a chance to gain or maintain some temporary advantage. In practice, therefore, reliance on nuclear deterrence means a continuation of the arms race and the constant threat of annihilation. Nuclear weapons do not guarantee that war cannot happen—only that it will be calamitous if it does. They do not so much defend as threaten, and in threatening, they elicit still more threats in return—as the world's growing stockpile of bombs and missiles attests. The obsessive focus on the threat of weapons as the way to avoid war also blinds us to the central question: Is *anything* that the Soviet Union or the United States values so important that it justifies risking the destruction of both societies, the murder of hundreds of millions of people, and the jeopardizing of our very species?

Arms Control

An alternative to deterrence based on a continuing arms race, therefore, is **arms control**—mutually agreed limitations on the nature, numbers, and uses of weapons and defenses. But for arms control to be successful, certain conditions must be met. First, both sides have to be willing to give up the possibility of gaining further advantages over the other in their military technology. Second, both sides must trust one another sufficiently to enter the agreement at all—and trust is in short supply between any contending powers, as a result of their tendency to demonize the other side as villainous, evil, and treacherous. So a third condition is needed, in the form of some means of verifying that the other side is indeed keeping its word, and not illicitly hoarding old weapons or developing new ones. Unfortunately, the proliferation of nuclear weapons is rapidly making verification more and more difficult. Various spying techniques, notably satellite reconnaisance, made it easy in the past for both superpowers to count submarines as they were built or land-based missiles as they were

installed in their silos. But the construction of thousands of small, mobile, and easily hidden cruise missiles will soon make accurate inspection and verification exceedingly difficult—providing yet another example of how military technologies may create more problems than they solve.

Despite the difficulties, a number of significant arms-control treaties have already been achieved. Many countries, including the United States and the Soviet Union, have signed multilateral agreements restricting the testing, spread, and potential use of nuclear weapons. The Antarctic Treaty of 1959, for example, signed by 30 nations, bans nuclear testing in Antarctica; the Partial Test Ban Treaty of 1963, signed by 112 countries, bans nuclear tests in the atmosphere, in outer space, and under water; and the Non-Proliferation Treaty of 1968, signed by 132 countries, bans the transfer of nuclear weapons and technology beyond the five states that already have them. In addition, the two superpowers have signed several important bilateral agreements. The Hot-Line Agreements of 1963 establish direct links between heads of the two governments to ensure instant communication in times of crisis. The Anti-Ballistic Missile Treaty of 1972 limits the use of these defensive systems by both sides. The Strategic Arms Limitation Treaty (SALT) Interim Agreement of 1972 sets a ceiling on the number of ballistic-missile launchers for both countries. The Prevention of Nuclear War Agreement of 1973 requires consultation between the two countries if there is a danger of nuclear war. The Threshold Test Ban Treaty of 1974 places limits on the size of underground tests. The SALT II Treaty of 1979, long observed by the United States but not ratified by the Senate, limits the number of strategic missiles and bombers each side may have.

Of course, a treaty is only as good as the willingness of each party to abide by it, in letter and in spirit. That willingness is influenced by the prevailing attitudes in Washington and Moscow, and both countries have adopted a "hard line" at different times. The Reagan administration accelerated the arms race in the hopes of gaining superiority over the Soviet Union. Generally hostile to arms control, President Reagan decided to abandon the SALT II limits on nuclear warheads and to "reinterpret" the Antiballistic Missile Treaty in order to proceed with the "star wars" defensive system. During the same period, the Soviet Union under Mikhail Gorbachev was unusually conciliatory: it offered a moratorium on all nuclear testing and a suspension of antisatellite weapons tests, but the

Figure 23.14 *For more than four decades, the leaders of the United States and the Soviet Union have met at summit conferences to discuss the precarious balance of peace in the world. The photographs show Franklin D. Roosevelt with Josef Stalin; Dwight D. Eisenhower with Nikita Khru-* *shchev; Richard Nixon with Leonid I. Brezhnev; and Ronald Reagan with Mikhail Gorbachev. Although several arms-control agreements have been achieved, the total nuclear arsenals of both of the superpowers have greatly increased during this period.*

United States rejected both proposals. A particularly significant opportunity was lost at a summit meeting between the Soviet and American leaders in Reykjavik, Iceland, in 1986. At that meeting, the Soviet leader made an unexpected proposal: to immediately dismantle intermediate-range weapons in Europe; to reduce strategic nuclear weapons by half by 1990; to eliminate all remaining nuclear weapons by the end of the century; and to ban them from the planet forever afterward. This startling offer was conditional upon the United States keeping its "star wars" technology at the testing stage for a period of ten years. President Reagan declined the proposal, on the grounds that he might want to deploy the "star wars" system sooner. The outcome was a major propaganda victory for the Soviet Union, for it left the United States in the awkward position of refusing to eliminate nuclear weapons, merely so that it could build a system that would be pointless if the weapons were eliminated—for what is the function of an antimissile defense if there are no missiles?

Disarmament

Ideally, successful experience of arms control would eventually lead toward *disarmament,* or the steady reduction in the nature, numbers, and uses of weapons and defenses. In effect, disarmament means putting the arms race into reverse. If the process were to occur, it would almost certainly be a gradual one—partly because so much money is currently spent on military purposes that rapid disarmament would jolt the economies of the superpowers and indeed of the world, and partly because disarmament requires increasing trust between the parties involved. In all probability, therefore, the process would begin with a freeze on the manufacture and deployment of nuclear weapons; then, if tension eased and a climate of trust developed, existing bombs, warheads, and delivering systems would be scrapped in a series of carefully verified stages.

The prospect of the United States and the Soviet Union getting rid of all or most of their nuclear weapons may seem remote. But it is not impossible, for neither country has much to gain from the alternative—continued diversion of economic and human resources into an ever more costly and indefinitely prolonged arms race. Again, a major stumbling block to disarmament is the issue of trust, for each country finds it difficult to believe that the other would really abandon its supposed ambitions for "world domination." Americans, for example, are generally unaware of just how threatened the Soviet government and people feel, not only as a result of their past history but also because of a number of present circumstances. After all, the Soviet Union is a much less affluent and technologically advanced society than the United States, and so is worse equipped to prepare for war. Worldwide, the Soviet Union has far fewer allies—and far fewer military bases—than the United States. Several Soviet allies, in fact, are highly unreliable: it is quite possible, for example, that Polish forces would mutiny rather than obey Soviet orders to fight American troops. Moreover, the Soviet Union suffers the particular disadvantage of having to maintain a huge army to protect its long border with its unfriendly neighbor, China. And whereas the United States has only one nuclear enemy, the Soviet Union faces missiles pointed at it by every other nuclear power in the world—the United States, Great Britain, France, and China. And the Soviet Union's sense of menace is further increased by the fact that its principal enemy is the only nation in the world that has ever used nuclear weapons.

International Peace-Making

An important element in any peace process is the international community and its mechanisms for restraining conflict among its members. Trade, travel, and telecommunications have made the nations of the modern world more interdependent than ever before. Yet today's societies entered the nuclear age with political institutions inherited from a previous era. The human population is spread among a series of sovereign independent states—most of them with their own armed forces—and so there is a built-in potential for warfare whenever two nations have conflicting interests. Karl von Clausewitz, a nineteenth-century military strategist, shrewdly expressed this potential in his famous definition: "War is simply the continuation of state policy by other means." In fact, before the twentieth century, there were few institutionalized ways for hostile nations to achieve peaceful settlements. When negotiations took place, they often occurred only after a war—for the purpose of agreeing to a peace treaty that would specify the spoils of the victor. Although the structure of international peace-making is still rudimentary, it now offers infinitely better prospects for helping nations to avoid war.

Particularly in a world where all nations face a common threat of direct or indirect involvement in nuclear warfare, some reliable method is needed to limit conflicts among sovereign states. If we anticipate that some benign and fair "world government" will take on the task, we are likely to be disappointed; but if we look for progress along that continuum that runs from war to peace, the prospects are much more encouraging. Already, two vital elements for international peace-making are in place. The first is the United Nations, which provides a forum for world opinion and a mechanism for conflict resolution. The second is a growing body of international law that specifies the rights and obligations that nations have toward one another—particularly with respect to aggression. Over the years, the United Nations has intervened successfully in a number of wars (for example, in Korea and in the Middle East) and in several situations that might have led to war (for example, in the superpower crises involving Cuba and Berlin).

A major difficulty with international peace-making, of course, is that compliance with the resolutions of the United Nations and the rulings of its World Court are voluntary, for no country is willing to surrender its sovereignty to an international body. The United Nations is most effective, in fact, when both superpowers are able to agree on a course of action and mobilize their blocs to support it. Even so, the organization provides an influential forum for world opinion, and, while it does not always prevent war, it surely helps make it less likely.

Collective Action

Ultimately, the prospects for peace depend on the collective action of ordinary people. This may seem paradoxical at first, for individuals often feel powerless in the face of distant governments and mighty arsenals. Yet if sociology has a central lesson, it is that societies, together with all the social institutions and social behavior they contain, are continuously created and re-created by the acts of countless individuals, whether these individuals realize their role in the grand sweep of history or not. If a modern society goes to war, it is not just because the leaders have opted for war, but because the people have implicitly or explicitly done so also—or at least, they have not opted for peace. In the United States the public actually places informal, unspoken restraints on the ability of the leaders to wage war. For example, although the United States has tactical nuclear weapons that it could have used in local conflicts such as the Korean and Vietnam wars, it has not employed these devices—primarily because such a resort to nuclear weapons would be unacceptable and im-

moral to the American people. Similar restraints operate in other countries, although they are felt most strongly in democracies.

As we noted in Chapter 20 ("Collective Behavior and Social Movements"), historically significant change is often brought about by the organized efforts of a *social movement*—a large number of people who have come together to bring about or resist some social or cultural change. National and international social movements that demand the elimination of nuclear weaponry are now a persistent feature of the Western world. In 1982, for example, more than 2 million Americans signed a petition calling for a nuclear freeze, and resolutions endorsing the proposal were passed by hundreds of town meetings and at least one legislature in each of twenty-three American states. Often, significant pressure for peace comes from the acts of a handful of individuals. In 1981, an American doctor and a Russian doctor founded International Physicians for the Prevention of War, a group that focuses on the medical consequences of nuclear warfare. Within five years, the organization had over 150,000 members in forty-nine countries, and it had won a Nobel prize for peace. Similarly, a small group of Japanese activists conceived the idea of "nuclear free zones"—places that formally refuse to allow nuclear weapons inside their boundaries. Within a few years, nineteen countries had explicitly prohibited the presence of nuclear weapons on their

Figure 23.15 *Two decades ago, the United States underwent the highly traumatic experience of an ugly and apparently pointless war in Vietnam. The end of the war was greatly hastened by an antiwar movement that included large numbers of young people, particularly college students.*

soil, and more than 3,400 communities—cities, counties, and provinces—in twenty-four countries had declared themselves "nuclear free" (Bentley, 1984).

None of these movements, however, has achieved any lasting success. One reason is that they are restricted to the Western world. There is no independent antiwar or antinuclear movement in the Soviet Union, so Westerners are discouraged by the lack of visible evidence that the Soviet people also want peace, or can pressure their government into searching for it. But in this respect, the unfolding of sociocultural evolution offers good grounds for hope. As we noted in Chapter 4 ("Society"), the Soviet Union is still an industrial society, not a postindustrial one. If the society remains primarily industrial, it will tend to stagnate relative to the more technologically and economically advanced United States, a situation that will be unacceptable to the Soviet leadership. But if the Soviet Union attempts to achieve a transition to a postindustrial economy, the leadership will increasingly have to tolerate the free flow of ideas and information—particularly through computers and telecommunications—that is the lifeblood of a postindustrial economy. Already there are signs that this is happening under the new Soviet leadership, which is eliminating many controls over dissidents and the media, in an effort to create greater *glasnost,* or "openness." This trend does not mean that the Soviet Union will soon become democratized in the Western sense—but once the faucet of liberty is opened, it could prove exceedingly difficult to shut off, and the Soviet Union could be irrevocably embarked on a course that would give its people a greater say in their own destiny.

A striking example of collective action to stop war occurred during the 1960s, when the United States became embroiled in the longest and most humiliating military conflict in its history. Vietnam was involved in civil war between the north, ruled by communists, and the south, ruled by an undemocratic regime that called for American help. Determined to "fight communism," the United States stumbled into an obscure but vicious conflict on behalf of peasants who seemed largely indifferent to the outcome of the fighting and to America's ideology. At first, American public opinion gave patriotic support to the war. But as the nation became more deeply involved, the Vietnam war became a quagmire that drained its energy, strength, credibility, treasure, and blood. As casualties mounted and troops became more demoralized, the war began to tear American society apart, dividing neighbor from neighbor, friend from friend, family

members from one another. Some sons volunteered for war, some were drafted, some became conscientious objectors, some evaded the draft by going into hiding or fleeing their country. Those who fought and those who refused to fight branded each other with such names as traitor, brute, coward, dupe. Altogether, more than 2 million young Americans went to this unfamiliar place to fight an unwanted war for uncertain ends. Some 57,000 of them were killed, and about 300,000 wounded. To some extent, the war divides Americans still, but there is now a general consensus that, somehow, a terrible mistake was made. The memory of that mistake places an informal social restraint on American leaders, for there is intense public resistance to any prospect of "another Vietnam" in the jungles of Central America or anywhere else.

The Vietnam war came to an end largely as a result of the antiwar movement, a social movement that consisted disproportionately of young people, including many college students. When the antiwar movement first challenged the war, it received little support from politicians or the press, and its goals seemed almost hopeless. But the tide of public opinion gradually began to shift. In the 1968 presidential primaries, an antiwar candidate backed by student volunteers did unexpectedly well and President Johnson decided not to run for reelection. From that point on, political debate on the war focused not on how to stay in it, but on how to get out of it. Through collective action, ordinary people with few resources other than their own determination had changed a national consensus for war to a national consensus for peace.

A fundamental insight of sociology is that once people no longer take their world for granted, but instead understand the social authorship of their lives and futures, they can become an irresistible force in history. Whether we choose to destroy our civilization or save it is a collective decision—and it is one that may well be made within the lifetimes of most readers of this book. If more and more nuclear weapons are built, and if more sophisticated means of delivering them are devised, and if more and more nations get control of these vile devices, then we surely risk our own destruction. If ways are found to reverse that process, then we can divert unprecedented energy and resources to the real problems that face us, including poverty, disease, overpopulation, injustice, oppression, and the devastation of our natural environment. We may hope and trust that our ultimate choice will be to enhance the life on the bright and lovely planet on which all five billion of us share our adventure.

Summary

1.   War and peace are both common features of human society. In the nuclear age, the threat of war has become perhaps the most important issue facing humanity.

2.   War is a social phenomenon that has social causes; it occurs when leaders choose war over other alternatives to resolving a dispute. The development of war has been marked by increasingly sophisticated weapons that involve an ever larger population in the arena of conflict.

3.   The United States and the Soviet Union are hostile superpowers that tend to demonize one another. They are embarked on an arms race in which each side tries to gain temporary superiority. The arms race is driven by both international factors and by a domestic linkage between industry and the military.

4.   Nuclear strategy has long been based on the concept of mutually assured destruction. New weapons, however, may encourage either side to contemplate limited use of nuclear weapons, or even a major strike at the opponent's missiles. The proposed "star wars" defensive system might offer some protection to American missiles, but it is questionable whether the system would be practicable or reliable.

5.   Nuclear war is possible: through deliberate calculation, through miscalculation, through superpower involvement in local conflicts, through proliferation or even terrorism, and through error or accident.

6.   A nuclear explosion causes immediate effects of electromagnetic pulse, blast, heat, and radiation, with highly destructive effects. Long-term effects would place the survival of the affected societies in jeopardy, and perhaps endanger the species itself.

7.   There are various prospects for peace: continued reliance on nuclear deterrence; arms control; disarmament; international peace-making; and collective action by concerned citizens.

Important Terms

war   (626)

peace   (626)

arms race   (631)

military-industrial complex   (631)

arms control   (646)

disarmament   (648)

social movement   (649)

Suggested Readings

ARBATOV, GEORGI. *The Soviet Viewpoint.* New York: Dodd, Mead, 1981.

A good introduction to the Soviet Union's view of the world.

HADLEY, ARTHUR T. *The Straw Giant.* New York: Random House, 1986.

A critical analysis of the American military, including its weaponry and performance in the field.

KATZ, ARTHUR M. *Life After Nuclear War.* Cambridge, Mass.: Ballinger, 1982.

The author summarizes what is known about the likely effects of nuclear war on human society in the postattack environment.

LIFTON, ROBERT J. *Death in Life: Survivors of Hiroshima.* New York: Random House, 1967.

A classic study of the psychological effects of nuclear warfare.

MCNEILL, WILLIAM H. *Technology, Armed Force, and Society Since A.D. 1000.* Chicago: University of Chicago Press, 1982.

A detailed and interesting historical overview of the relationships among the military, technology, and society.

RIORDAN, MICHAEL (ed.) *The Day After Midnight.* Palo Alto, Calif.: Cheshire Books, 1982.

A shocking summary of the immediate effects of nuclear war on an urban society.

SCHELL, JONATHAN. *The Fate of the Earth.* New York: Knopf, 1982.

An important book that traces the potential effects and meanings of nuclear war.

APPENDIX

Techniques of Library Research

Among its many resources, the library has a wealth of information that is useful in sociological research. Every library is systematically organized so that this knowledge can be easily located and retrieved, and the purpose of this appendix is to acquaint you with some of the ways you can "plug into" the sociological information that the library contains.

Your method of tracking down information will depend very much on the exact kind of information you are looking for. The following categories cover most situations.

If you are looking for general information on a particular subject:

A useful place to start might be a general encyclopedia such as the *Britannica* or the *Americana;* or you can try the seventeen-volume *International Encyclopaedia of the Social Sciences,* which contains general reviews written by experts in various fields. These sources can provide broad background information on the topic you are interested in and can also help you to narrow the focus of your search to specific areas of the topic. Every encyclopedia contains instructions on how to use it, and at the end of each article you will find additional references that you can use for follow-up.

If you want current information on a specific subject:

A good place to begin your search for current information is the computer reference files. Most libraries have one or more data-base computer files that provide indexed references to a vast range of current periodicals and books. Basically, what you do is ask the computer to "search" such a file for your topic—say, unemployment or drug abuse— and the computer will display listings of books and articles that deal with that topic. The computer first displays the subtopics under which the file's listings are arranged. For example, listings for unemployment will fall under such categories as "Unemployment Among Ghetto Youth," "Unemployment Benefits," "Unemployment in the U.S.," etc.; similarly, drug abuse will be listed under such categories as "Drug Abuse Among Adolescents," "Drug Abuse in the Workplace," "Drug Abuse, Social Costs," etc. After scanning the subtopics available, call up the ones that seem most closely related to your area of research, and the computer will show you all the references the file has listed under the specified subtopics.

Some data-base reference files list both scholarly and popular publications; others list only scholarly publications. (Ask a librarian about the type of reference files that are available in your library.) The nonscholarly sources, such as *Time, Newsweek,* and the *New Republic,* often provide a useful introduction to some issue, but they usually lack the objectivity and precision of good sociology. For specifically sociological information you may be more interested in articles found in the major journals covering various aspects of the discipline. Four highly regarded journals that print articles of general sociological interest are the *American Journal of Sociology,* the *American Sociological Review, Social Forces,* and the *British Journal of Sociology.* There are also a number of journals on specific areas, such as *Sociology of Education, Journal of Health and Social Behavior, Social Problems, Public Opinion Quarterly, Issues in Criminology, Journal of Marriage and the Family,* and *Journal of Abnormal and Social Psychology.* You may also be interested in scholarly articles that appear in professional psychology journals, criminology journals, economics journals, etc. All of these are listed in data-base computer files.

If you are looking for information about specific events or people, the sources that will be particularly helpful to you may be newspaper articles.

Certain newspapers are known as "journals of record"—in other words, they not only cover "newsworthy" events but also try to preserve a record of significant social events, and print lengthy extracts from government reports and similar material. The two outstanding journals of record in the English-speaking world are the *New York Times* and the London *Times*. The computer file will direct you to relevant articles published in these newspapers.

Once you have located the sources that seem most pertinent to your research, print out the titles and then consult the library catalogue to see which ones are available in your library.

If you are looking for general information that is not current:

Most computer reference files go back only five to ten years in their listings, and their listings may be incomplete. For this reason it is important that you be familiar with the standard bound reference sources, which are organized chronologically, span decades of publication, and collectively provide the most complete listing of sources. If you are looking for older material, or additional material (or if a computer reference file is not available to you), you can consult the *Reader's Guide to Periodical Literature,* which lists nonscholarly sources, and the *Social Sciences Index,* which will direct you to more reliable sources in sociology and related fields. For specifically sociological information, you can start with *Sociological Abstracts,* which arranges all sociological books, articles, and papers presented to professional meetings, according to subject area. The publication includes a brief summary of the content of each item, together with the names of the authors and the source of the material. Similar abstracts are available in related areas, such as *Psychological Abstracts, Crime and Delinquency Abstracts, Education Abstracts,* and *Poverty and Human Resources Abstracts.* There is also a *Dissertation Abstracts,* covering unpublished doctoral dissertations. The *New York Times* and the London *Times* maintain an index of all names and events that have appeared in their columns, and this index will direct you to any article they have published on subjects you are interested in.

If you want information about particular people:

One obvious source is the newspaper files just mentioned (obituaries in newspapers are a particularly useful source of information about people who are dead). Information can also be obtained from such volumes as *Who's Who, Who Was Who, Current Biography,* or *American Men and Women of Science.* The latter is in two volumes, one covering the physical and biological sciences and the other covering the behavioral sciences and humanities.

If you want statistical information:

The best place to start is usually *Statistical Abstracts,* an annual publication that contains information about virtually every aspect of American life on which statistics are kept. The *Census Report,* published every ten years, gives many details about the characteristics of the American population. You might also consult *Statistical Sources: A Subject Guide to Data on Industrial Business, Social, Educational, Financial, and Other Topics for the U.S. and Internationally.* This useful volume will direct you to other sources of information that you may not know about: if you are looking for information on crime trends, for example, it will direct you to such sources as the annual *Uniform Crime Reports* of the FBI.

You will always find that sources generate more sources, because each reference will lead you to several more. Unless you want a broad overview of a topic, then, it is best to have very specific information in mind, or you might be overwhelmed by the richness of the data waiting for you. Above all, remember that when you are in any difficulty, you should not hesitate to *ask the librarian.* Some people are reluctant to "bother" the librarian, or feel that he or she may not know about the specific information that is sought. But the librarian is a professional trained in library science, and has an intimate knowledge of the general methods for locating information and of the specific resources of your library. The librarian will be glad to help, so if you are unable to find what you are looking for, just ask.

GLOSSARY

Absolute deprivation The inability to afford minimal standards of food, clothing, shelter, and health care.

Achieved status One that depends to some extent on characteristics over which the individual has some control.

Acute disease One of short duration; generally the victim either recovers or dies.

Adultery Sexual relations involving partners at least one of whom is married to someone else.

Age structure The relative proportions of different age categories in a population.

Ageism The belief that one age category is in some respects inferior to other age categories and that unequal treatment of them is therefore justified.

Agents of socialization Significant individuals, groups, or institutions that provide structured situations in which socialization takes place.

Aggregate A collection of people who happen to be in the same place at the same time, such as the passengers in a bus or a crowd in a street.

Agricultural society A society relying for its subsistence primarily on the cultivation of crops through the use of plows and draft animals.

Alienation The situation in which people lose their control over the social world they have created, with the result that they find themselves "alien" in a hostile social environment.

Animism A type of religion that recognizes active, animate spirits operating in the world.

Anomie A condition of confusion that exists in both individual and society when social norms are weak, absent, or conflicting.

Applied research Systematic inquiry that tries to find practical uses for existing knowledge.

Arms control Mutually agreed limitations on the nature, numbers, and uses of weapons and defenses.

Arms race A process in which each side continually attempts to gain or maintain superiority in weaponry.

Art Unique, skilled, and creative cultural products intended to inspire or entertain.

Ascribed status One that is attached to people on grounds over which they have no control.

Authoritarianism A form of government in which the rulers tolerate little or no public opposition, and generally cannot be removed from office by legal means.

Authoritarian personality A distinctive set of traits, including conformity, intolerance, and insecurity, that seem typical of many prejudiced people.

Authority The form of power whose legitimacy is recognized by those to whom it is applied.

Automation The replacement of workers by nonhuman means of production.

Basic research Systematic inquiry that is concerned with establishing new knowledge.

Bias The tendency, often unconscious, to interpret facts according to one's own values.

Bilateral system One in which descent and inheritance are traced through both sides of the family.

Birth rate The annual number of births per thousand members of a population.

Bisexuality Sexual orientation toward both sexes.

Bureaucracy A hierarchical authority structure that operates under explicit rules and procedures.

Bystander apathy The reluctance of people to "get involved" in an apparent emergency affecting a stranger in public.

Capitalism An economic system in which the means of production and distribution are privately owned.

Case study A complete and detailed record of an event, group, or social process.

Caste system A closed form of social stratification in which status is determined by birth and is lifelong.

Category A number of people who may never have met each other but who share similar characteristics, such as age, race, or sex.

Charismatic authority A type of authority in which power is legitimated by the unique and remarkable qualities that people attribute to a specific leader.

Chronic disease One of long duration; the victim may not die, but usually does not recover.

City A permanent concentration of relatively large numbers of people who do not produce their own food.

Class consciousness An objective awareness of the lower stratum's common plight and interests as an oppressed group.

Classless society One with no economically based strata.

Class system An open form of stratification based primarily on economic statuses, which may be subject to change.

Coercion The form of power whose legitimacy is denied by those to whom it is applied.

Cohort A category of people who are born during the same period, such as a period of one, five, or ten years.

Collective behavior Relatively spontaneous social action that occurs when people try to work out common responses to ambiguous situations.

Colonialism The formal political and economic domination of one nation by a more powerful nation: in effect, the subordinate country is "owned" by the dominant one.

Communism A hypothetical egalitarian political and economic system in which the means of production and distribution would be communally owned.

Community A social group with a common territorial base and a sense of shared interests and "belonging."

Conflict perspective A view of society that focuses on social processes of tension, competition, and change.

Contagion theory An explanation of crowd behavior as a loss of individuality resulting from the infectious spread of emotion and action through the group.

Control group The subjects in an experiment who are exposed to all the experimental conditions except the independent variable.

Controls Ways of excluding the possibility that some other factors might be influencing the relationship between two variables.

Control theory An approach that explains deviance as the outcome of a failure of social control.

Convergence theory The hypothesis that the similar problems faced by capitalist and socialist societies may influence their evolution toward a common ultimate form.

Corporation A legally recognized organization whose existence, powers, and liabilities are separate and distinct from those of its owners or employees.

Corrections The sanctions and other measures that society applies to convicted criminals—in the United States, primarily imprisonment, probation, and parole.

Correlation A relationship between two variables that occurs regularly.

Counterculture A subculture whose values, norms, and lifestyle are fundamentally at odds with the dominant culture.

Coup d'état The restricted use of force to replace one set of leaders with another, usually consisting of military officers.

Crime An act that contravenes a law.

Crowd A temporary collection of people who are in close enough proximity to interact with one another.

Cult A loosely organized religious movement that is independent of the religious tradition of the surrounding society.

Cultural anthropology The study of the ways of life of other peoples.

Cultural deprivation Deficiencies in home, family, and neighborhood background that hinder the ability to compete in the larger culture.

Cultural integration A tendency for norms, values, beliefs, practices, and other characteristics to complement one another.

Cultural relativism The recognition that one culture cannot be arbitrarily judged by the standards of another.

Cultural-transmission theory An approach that explains deviance as behavior that is learned in the same way as conformity—through interaction with other people.

Cultural universals Practices that are found in every society.

Culture All the shared products of human society.

Culture lag A delay between a change in material culture and the adjustment of nonmaterial culture to the change.

Death rate The annual number of deaths per thousand members of a population.

Democracy A form of government in which it is recognized that ultimate authority belongs to the people, who have the right to participate in the decision-making process and to appoint and dismiss their rulers.

Democratic socialism A political and economic system that aims to preserve individual freedom in the context of social equality achieved through a centrally planned economy.

Demographic transition The tendency for birth rates to drop and population to stabilize once a society has achieved a certain level of economic development.

Demography The study of the size, composition, distribution, and changes in human population.

Denomination One of two or more well-established, relatively tolerant religious organizations that claim the allegiance of a substantial part of the population.

Dependent variable A variable that is influenced by another variable—in other words, it is affected.

Detached observation A method in which the researcher remains as aloof as possible, and the subjects may not even know they are being studied.

Developed country A highly industrialized and comparatively affluent society.

Deviance Behavior that violates significant social norms and is disapproved by large numbers of people as a result.

Differential association Social relationships oriented toward particular types of people, such as criminals, through which deviant behavior is learned.

Diffusion The spread of cultural elements from one culture to another.

Disarmament The steady reduction in the nature, numbers, and uses of weapons and defenses.

Discovery A new perception of an aspect of reality that already exists.

Discrimination Unequal treatment of people on the grounds of their group membership.

Disease An objective pathology of the body, such as an infection.

Division of labor The specialization by individuals or groups in particular economic activities.

Double standard An unspoken expectation that restrictive rules of sexual conduct should be applied strictly to women, but leniently to men.

Doubling time The period it takes for a population to double its numbers.

Dramaturgy A method of analyzing social interaction as though the participants were actors on a stage.

Dyad A group containing two people.

Dysfunction A negative consequence that may disrupt the social system.

Ecclesia A religious organization that claims the membership of everyone in a society or even in several societies.

Ecological approach One that analyzes social and cultural elements in the context of the total environment in which a society exists.

Ecology The science of the relationship between living organisms and their environments.

Economic order The institutionalized system for producing and distributing goods and services.

Ecosystem A self-sustaining community of organisms within its natural environment.

Education The systematic, formalized transmission of knowledge, skills, and values.

Egalitarian marriage A system in which the husband and wife have a more or less equal say in family matters.

Emergent-norms theory An explanation of crowd behavior as the result of norms that arise in the course of social interaction among crowd members.

Endemic disease One that is always present in a large part of a population.

Endogamy Marriage within the same social category.

Epidemic disease One affecting a significant part of a population in which it is normally uncommon.

Epidemiology The study of the origin, distribution, and means of transmission of disease in populations.

Ethnic group A category of people who, as a result of their shared cultural heritage, are regarded as socially distinct.

Ethnocentrism The tendency to judge other cultures by the standards of one's own.

Ethnography An anthropological report about some aspects of a people's way of life.

Ethnomethodology The study of how people construct and share their definitions of reality in their everyday interactions.

Exchange mobility Changes in people's social statuses as they exchange places with one another at different levels of the hierarchy.

Exogamy Marriage outside a particular social category.

Experiment A method for studying the relationship between two variables under carefully controlled conditions.

Experimental group The subjects in an experiment who are exposed to the independent variable.

Expressive leadership The kind of leadership necessary to create harmony and solidarity among group members.

Extended family One in which more than two generations of the same kinship line live together.

Fad A temporary form of conduct that is followed enthusiastically by large numbers of people.

False consciousness A subjective understanding of one's situation that does not accord with the objective facts.

Family A relatively permanent group of people related by ancestry, marriage, or adoption, who live together, form an economic unit, and take care of their young.

Family of orientation The family into which we are born.

Family of procreation The family that we create ourselves.

Fashion A currently valued style of appearance and behavior.

Fecundity The potential number of children that could be born to a woman of childbearing age.

Fertility The actual number of children the average woman is bearing.

Folkways The ordinary usages and conventions of everyday life.

Formal organization Large secondary groups that are deliberately and rationally designed to achieve specific objectives.

Function A positive consequence for a whole social system.

Functional equivalent A social or cultural feature that has the same effect as another, and may in that sense serve as a substitute for it.

Functionalist perspective A view of society that focuses on the way various parts of society have functions, or positive effects, that maintain the stability of the whole.

Fundamentalism A commitment to, and reliance on, the traditional basics of religious doctrine.

Gemeinschaft A "community" in which most people know one another.

Gender The culturally learned differences between men and women.

Gender roles The behavior patterns, obligations, and privileges that are considered appropriate for each sex.

Generalizations Statements that apply not just to a specific case but to most cases of the same type.

Generalized other The attitudes and viewpoint of society as a whole.

Genocide The extermination of entire populations.

Gesellschaft An "association" in which most people are strangers to one another.

Group A collection of people interacting together in an orderly way on the basis of shared expectations about each other's behavior.

Growth rate The difference between the number of people added to, and the number of people subtracted from, a population, expressed as an annual percentage.

Hawthorne effect The contamination of an experiment by the subjects' assumptions about what the experimenter is trying to discover.

Heterosexuality Sexual orientation toward the opposite sex.

High culture Creations of a relatively profound and serious nature that appeal to, and are supported by, a fairly small and elite group.

Homogamy Marriage between partners who share similar social characteristics.

Homosexuality Sexual orientation toward the same sex.

Horticultural society A society relying for its subsistence primarily on the hoe cultivation of domesticated plants.

Hunting and gathering society A society relying for its subsistence on such wild animals and vegetation as its members can hunt or gather.

Hypothesis A tentative statement that predicts a relationship between variables.

Ideal culture The norms and values a society adheres to in principle.

Ideal type An abstract description constructed from a number of real cases in order to reveal their essential features.

Ideology A set of beliefs that explains and justifies some actual or potential social arrangements.

Illegitimate birth Birth to a mother who is not married to the father.

Illness The subjective sense that one is not well.

Incest taboo A powerful moral prohibition against sexual contact between certain categories of relatives.

Independent variable A variable that influences another variable—in other words, it acts as a cause.

Industrial society A society relying for its subsistence primarily on mechanized production.

Ingroup Any group one belongs to and identifies with.

Institution A stable cluster of values, norms, statuses, roles, and groups that develops around a basic social need.

Institutionalized discrimination Unequal treatment, on the grounds of group membership, that is entrenched in social customs.

Instrumental leadership The kind of leadership necessary to organize a group in pursuit of its goal.

Interactionist perspective A view of society that focuses on the way in which people act toward, respond to, and influence one another.

Interest group A group or organization that attempts to influence political decisions that might have an impact on its members or their goals.

Intergenerational mobility Movement up and down the hierarchy by family members from one generation to the next.

Interlocking directorates Social networks consisting of individuals who are members of several different corporate boards.

Internalization of norms The unconscious process of making conformity to the norms of one's culture a part of one's personality, so that one usually follows social expectations automatically, without question.

Invention The combination or new use of existing knowledge to produce something that did not exist before.

Kinship A social network of people related by common ancestry, adoption, or marriage.

Labeling theory A theory that explains deviance as a process by which some people successfully define others as deviant.

Latent function An unrecognized and unintended consequence of some element in a social system.

Law A rule that has been formally enacted by a political authority and is backed by the power of the state.

Leader Someone who, largely by virtue of certain personality characteristics, is consistently able to influence the behavior of others.

Legal discrimination Unequal treatment, on the grounds of group membership, that is upheld by law.

Legal-rational authority A type of authority in which power is legitimated by explicit rules and procedures that define the rights and obligations of the rulers.

Legitimacy The generally held belief that a given political system is valid and justified.

Legitimate birth Birth to a mother and father who are married to each other.

Less developed country A comparatively poor nation that has not achieved a predominantly industrial mode of production.

Life chances Probabilities of benefiting or suffering from the opportunities or disadvantages one's society offers.

Life course The biological and social sequence of birth, childhood, maturity, old age, and death.

Life expectancy The number of years that the average newborn in a particular population can be expected to live.

Life span The maximum length of life possible in a particular species.

Linguistic-relativity hypothesis Holds that speakers of a particular language must necessarily interpret the world through the unique vocabulary and grammar their language supplies.

Lobbying The tactic of directly persuading decision makers.

Looking-glass self A self-concept derived from a social "mirror" in which we can observe how others react to us.

Magic Rituals intended to harness supernatural power for human ends.

Manifest function An obvious and intended consequence of some element in a social system.

Marriage A socially approved mating arrangement between two or more people.

Mass A collection of people who are concerned with the same phenomenon without being in one another's presence.

Mass hysteria A form of collective behavior involving widespread anxiety, caused by some unfounded belief.

Mass media The various forms of communication that reach a large audience without any personal contact between the senders and the receivers: newspapers, magazines, books, television, radio, movies, videos, and records.

Master status The position most important in establishing an individual's social identity.

Material culture All the artifacts, or physical objects, human beings create and give meaning to—such as wheels, clothing, schools, factories, cities, books, spacecraft, totem poles.

Matriarchy A system in which the wife has the greater authority in family matters.

Matrilineal system One in which descent and inheritance pass through the female side of the family.

Matrilocal residence The custom in which married partners settle in or near the household of the wife's father.

Mechanical solidarity A form of social cohesion based on the similarity of the members.

Medicalization of society A process in which the domain of medicine is extended over areas of life that were previously considered nonmedical.

Medicine The institution concerned with the maintenance of health and the treatment of disease.

Megalopolis A virtually unbroken urban tract consisting of two or more central cities and their surrounding suburbs.

Mental disorder The psychological inability to cope realistically and effectively with the ordinary challenges of life.

Methodology A system of rules, principles, and procedures that guides scientific investigation.

Metropolis An urban area containing a city and its surrounding suburbs, and forming an economic and geographic unity.

Metropolitan Statistical Area (MSA) Basically, any area that contains a city (or a combination of a city and its surrounding suburbs) that has a total population of 50,000 or more.

Migration rate The annual difference between the number of immigrants (people entering) or emigrants (people leaving) per thousand members of the population.

Military-industrial complex An informal system of mutual influence between the Pentagon, which buys armaments, and the major U.S. corporations that sell them.

Millenarian movement One that prophesies a cataclysmic upheaval within the immediate future.

Minority group People whose physical appearance or cultural practices are unlike those of the dominant group, making them susceptible to different and unequal treatment.

Mob An emotionally aroused crowd intent on violent or destructive action.

Modernization A process of economic, social, and cultural change that facilitates the transition from preindustrial to industrial society.

Monogamy Marriage involving one spouse of each sex.

Monopoly A single firm that dominates an industry.

Monotheism The belief in a single supreme being.

Mores Strong norms that are regarded as morally significant, and violations of which are considered a serious matter.

Multinational corporation A corporate enterprise which, though headquartered in one country, conducts its operations through subsidiaries that it owns or controls around the world.

Natural sciences Disciplines that study physical and biological phenomena.

Negotiated reality An organization that derives its existence and character from the social interaction through which the members continuously create and recreate it.

Neocolonialism The informal political and economic domination of some societies by others, such that the former are able to exploit the labor resources of the latter for their own purposes.

Neolocal residence The custom in which marriage partners establish a new residence separate from the kin of either spouse.

Nonmaterial culture Abstract human creations—languages, ideas, beliefs, rules, customs, myths, skills, family patterns, political systems.

Nonverbal communication The exchange of information through nonlinguistic symbols such as signs, gestures, and facial expressions.

Norms Shared values or guidelines that describe the behavior appropriate in a given situation.

Nuclear family One in which the family group consists only of the parents and their dependent children, living apart from other relatives.

Objectivity An interpretation that eliminates the influence of personal values and experience.

Oligarchy Rule by the few.

Oligopoly A group of a few firms that dominates an industry.

Operational definition A definition that states a concept, for the purposes of research, in terms that can be measured.

Organic solidarity A form of social cohesion based on the differences among the members, which make them interdependent.

Outgroup Any alternative group that one does not belong to or identify with.

Panic A form of collective behavior in which people faced with an immediate threat react in a fearful, spontaneous, and uncoordinated way.

Paradigm A shared set of concepts, methods, and assumptions about a scientific discipline.

Participant observation A method in which the researcher becomes directly involved in the social behavior under study.

Particular other Specific other people such as parents.

Pastoral society A society relying for its subsistence primarily on domesticated herd animals.

Patriarchy A system in which the husband has the greater authority in family matters.

Patrilineal system One in which descent and inheritance pass through the male side of the family.

Patrilocal residence The custom in which marriage partners settle in or near the household of the husband's father.

Peace Sustained amicable relations between politically organized groups.

Peers People of roughly equivalent age and other social characteristics.

Permissiveness Acceptance of some latitude in sexual norms and conduct.

Personality The fairly stable patterns of thought, feeling, and action that are typical of an individual.

Pluralist model A view of the political process that sees many competing interest groups as having access to government and shaping its decisions.

Political order The institutionalized system through which some individuals or groups acquire and exercise power over others.

Political party An organization whose purpose is to gain legitimate control of government.

Polyandry Marriage between one wife and more than one husband.

Polygamy Marriage involving a spouse of one sex and two or more spouses of the opposite sex.

Polygyny Marriage between one husband and more than one wife.

Polytheism A belief in a number of gods.

Popular culture Creations of a relatively less serious and less intellectually demanding nature that appeal primarily to, and are supported by, a large audience of typical members of the society.

Pornography Pictorial and written material intended to arouse sexual excitement.

Postindustrial society A society relying for its subsistence primarily on the production of services and information.

Power The ability to control the behavior of others, even in the absence of their consent.

Power-elite model A view of the political process that sees power as being held by, and exercised primarily in the interest of, a privileged few.

Prejudice An irrational, inflexible attitude toward an entire category of people.

Primary deviance Nonconformity that is temporary, exploratory, trivial, or easily concealed.

Primary group A small number of people who interact over a relatively long period on a direct, intimate basis.

Primary sector The part of the economy that involves the gathering or extracting of undeveloped natural resources—for example, fishing, mining, forestry, or agriculture.

Priority dispute An argument about who made a particular discovery first.

Profane Anything that is regarded as part of the ordinary rather than the supernatural world; as such it may be considered familiar, mundane, even corrupting.

Profession An occupation requiring extensive, systematic knowledge of, or training in, an art or science.

Propaganda Information or viewpoints that are presented with the deliberate intention of persuading the audience to adopt a particular opinion.

Property The set of rights that the owner of something has in relation to others who do not own it.

Prostitution The relatively indiscriminate exchange of sexual favors for economic gain.

Protestant ethic A disciplined, moral commitment to regular, conscientious work and deferred gratification.

Psychosis A profound mental disturbance involving such a severe break with reality that the affected person cannot function in society.

Public opinion The sum of the decisions of the members of a public on a particular issue.

Race A category of people who are regarded as socially distinct because they share genetically transmitted physical characteristics.

Racism The belief that one racial or ethnic group is inferior to another and that unequal treatment is therefore justified.

Random sample A sample chosen in such a way that every member of the population in question has the same chance of being selected.

Rape Forcible sexual intercourse against the will of the victim.

Rationalization The way in which traditional, spontaneous, rule-of-thumb methods of social organization are replaced by abstract, explicit, carefully calculated rules and procedures.

Real culture The norms and values a society adheres to in practice.

Recidivism Repeated crime by those who have been convicted before.

Reference group A group to which people refer when making evaluations of themselves and their behavior.

Relative deprivation The inability to maintain the living standards customary in the society.

Religion A system of communally shared beliefs and rituals that are oriented toward some sacred, supernatural realm.

Research design The actual plan for the collection and analysis of data.

Resocialization Learning that involves a sharp break with the past and socialization into radically different norms and values.

Resource mobilization The ability to organize and use available resources, such as time, money, people, and skills.

Respondents The actual subjects of a survey.

Restrictiveness Insistence on adherence to narrowly defined sexual norms.

Revolution The violent overthrow of an existing political or social system.

Rites of passage Formal ceremonies that mark an individual's transition from one age status to another.

Ritual A formal, stylized procedure, such as prayer, incantation, or ceremonial cleansing.

Ritual pollution Types of contact or proximity between members of different castes that are considered unclean for the superior caste.

Role A set of expected behavior patterns, obligations, and privileges attached to a particular social status.

Role conflict A situation in which two or more of a person's roles have contradictory requirements.

Role expectation The generally expected social norms that prescribe how a role ought to be played.

Role performance The actual behavior of a person playing a role.

Role strain A situation in which contradictory expectations are built into a single role.

Role-taking Pretending to take or actually taking the roles of other people, so that one can see the world and one's self from their viewpoints.

Rumor Information that is transmitted informally from anonymous sources.

Sacred Anything that is regarded as part of the supernatural rather than the ordinary world; as such it inspires awe, reverence, and deep respect.

Sample A small number of individuals drawn from a larger population.

Sanctions Rewards for conformity and punishments for nonconformity.

Scapegoating Placing the blame for one's troubles on some relatively powerless individual or group.

Science The logical, systematic methods by which knowledge is obtained, and the actual body of knowledge produced by those methods.

Secondary deviance Persistent nonconformity by a person who accepts the label of deviant.

Secondary group A number of people who interact on a relatively temporary, anonymous and impersonal basis.

Secondary sector The part of the economy that involves turning the raw materials produced by the primary sector into manufactured goods—for example, houses, furniture, automobiles, canned foods.

Sect An exclusive and uncompromising religious organization, usually one that has split off from a denomination for doctrinal reasons.

Secularization The process by which religion loses its social influence.

Self The individual's conscious experience of a distinct personal identity that is separate from all other people and things.

Self-fulfilling prophecy A prediction that leads to behavior that makes the prediction come true.

Self-fulfillment The commitment to achieving the development of one's individual personality, talents, and potential.

Sex The biological distinction between male and female.

Sexism The belief that one sex is inferior to another and that unequal treatment is therefore justified.

Sick role A pattern of behavior expected of someone who is ill.

Sickness The condition of those who are socially recognized as unwell.

Simple supernaturalism A type of religion that does not recognize specific gods or spirits, but does assume that supernatural forces influence human events for better or worse.

Small group A group that contains few enough members for the participants to relate to one another as individuals.

Social change The alteration in patterns of culture, social structure, and social behavior over time.

Social class A category of people of roughly equivalent status in an unequal society.

Social construction of reality The process by which people create their understanding of the nature of their environment.

Social control A set of means of ensuring that people generally behave in expected and approved ways.

Social gerontology The study of the social aspects of aging.

Social inequality The unequal sharing of such social rewards as wealth, power, and prestige.

Social interaction The process by which people act toward or respond to other people.

Social mobility Movement from one social status to another.

Social movement A large number of people who have joined together to bring about or resist some social or cultural change.

Social networks Webs of relationships that link the individual directly to other people, and through these others, indirectly to even more people.

Social psychology The study of how personality and behavior are influenced by the social context.

Social sciences Disciplines that study various aspects of human behavior.

Social stratification The structured inequality of entire categories of people, who have different access to social rewards as a result of their status in a social hierarchy.

Social structure The pattern of relationships among the basic components in a social system.

Socialism An economic system in which the means of production and distribution are publicly owned.

Socialization The process of social interaction through which people acquire personality and learn the way of life of their society.

Society A population that occupies the same territory, is subject to the same political authority, and participates in a common culture.

Sociocultural evolution The tendency for societies' social structures and cultures to grow more complex over time.

Socioeconomic status (SES) A complex of factors such as income, type of occupation, years of education, and sometimes place of residence.

Sociology The scientific study of human society and social behavior.

Sport Competitive physical activity guided by established rules.

Spurious correlation A correlation that is merely coincidental and does not imply any causal relationship whatsoever.

State The supreme political authority in society.

Status A position in society.

Status inconsistency A situation in which an individual's status or statuses appear contradictory.

Stereotype A rigid mental image that summarizes whatever is believed to be typical about a group.

Stigma The mark of social disgrace that sets the deviant apart from those who consider themselves "normal."

Structural mobility Changes in people's social statuses as a result of changes in the structure of the economy.

Structural-strain theory An approach that explains deviance as the outcome of social strains that put pressure on some people to deviate.

Structure A set of interrelated components such as head, limbs, a heart, and so on.

Subculture A group that shares in the overall culture of the society but also has its own distinctive values, norms, and lifestyle.

Subjectivity An interpretation based on personal values and experiences.

Surplus wealth More goods and services than are necessary to meet their producers' basic needs.

Survey A method for systematically obtaining standardized information about the attitudes, behavior, and other characteristics of a population.

Symbol Anything that can meaningfully represent something else.

Symbolic interaction The interaction between people that takes place through such symbols as signs, gestures, and language.

Taboo A powerful social belief that some specific act is utterly loathsome.

Technocracy Rule by technical experts whose specialized knowledge and recommendations are relied upon by those who are officially responsible for decisions.

Technological determinism The view that the technology available to a society is an important determinant of its culture, social structure, and even of its history.

Technological fix The use of technology to solve problems, including those that prior technology has created.

Technology The practical applications of scientific or other knowledge.

Terrorism The use of violence against civilian targets for the purpose of intimidation to achieve political ends.

Tertiary sector The part of the economy that involves producing services—for example, medicine, laundering, teaching, broadcasting.

Theism A type of religion that centers on a belief in gods.

Theodicy An emotionally satisfying explanation for such great problems of earthly existence as human origins, suffering, and death.

Theoretical perspective A broad assumption about society and social behavior that provides a point of view for the study of specific problems.

Theory A statement that organizes a set of concepts in a meaningful way by explaining the relationship among them.

Thomas theorem "If people define situations as real, they are real in their consequences."

Total institution A place of residence where the inmates are confined for a set period of their lives, where they are cut off from the rest of society, and where they surrender personal control of their lives, submitting instead to the almost absolute rule of a hierarchy of officials.

Totalitarianism An authoritarian form of government in which the rulers recognize no limits to their authority and are willing to regulate virtually any aspect of social life.

Traditional authority A type of authority in which power is legitimated by ancient custom.

Transcendent idealism A type of religion that centers not on the worship of a god but rather on sacred principles of thought and conduct.

Triad A group containing three people.

Urban legend A realistic but untrue story with an ironic twist concerning a recent alleged event.

Urbanism The nature and meaning of city life.

Urbanization The process by which population is concentrated in the cities.

Value-freedom The absence of personal values or biases.

Value judgment An opinion based on personal values or biases.

Values Socially shared ideas about what is good, right, and desirable.

Variable Any characteristic that can change or differ—for example, from time to time, from place to place, or from one individual to another.

Verstehen Subjective interpretation of a social actor's behavior and intentions.

War Sustained military conflict between politically organized groups.

World system A network of unequal economic and political relationships among the developed and the less developed countries.

Zero population growth (ZPG) A situation in which population size would remain stable.

REFERENCES

AARON, HENRY, and WILLIAM B. SCHWARTZ. 1984. *The Painful Prescription: Rationing Hospital Care.* Washington, D.C.: Brookings Institution.

ACUÑA, RODOLFO. 1980. *Occupied America: A History of Chicanos.* New York: Harper & Row.

ADAM, BARRY B. 1978. *The Survival of Domination: Inferiorization and Everyday Life.* New York: Elsevier.

ADAM, HERIBERT. 1972. *Modernizing Racial Domination: The Dynamics of South African Politics.* Berkeley: University of California Press.

ADAMS, BERT N. 1986. *The Family: A Sociological Introduction.* 4th ed. San Diego, Calif.: Harcourt Brace Jovanovich.

ADAMS, HERBERT L. 1982. "Survivors of Nuclear War: Infection and the Spread of Disease," in Eric Chivian et al. (eds.). *Last Aid: The Medical Dimensions of Nuclear War.* San Francisco: Freeman.

ADAMS, ROBERT L., and ROBERT J. FOX. 1972. "Mainlining Jesus: The new trip." *Society,* 9:4, 50–56.

ADAMS, RUTH, and SUSAN CULLEN. *The Final Epidemic: Physicians and Scientists on Nuclear War.* Chicago: University of Chicago Press, 1982.

ADAMSON, MADELEINE, and SETH BORGOS. 1984. *This Mighty Dream: Social Protest Movements in the United States.* Boston: Routledge and Kegan Paul.

ADLER, ISRAEL, and JUDITH T. SCHUVAL. 1978. "Cross pressures during socialization for medicine." *American Sociological Review,* 43, pp. 693–704.

ADORNO, THEODORE W., et al. 1950. *The Authoritarian Personality.* New York: Norton.

AKERS, RONALD L. 1985. *Deviant Behavior: A Social Learning Approach.* 3rd ed. Belmont, Calif.: Wadsworth.

ALBA, FRANCISCO. 1980. *The Population of Mexico.* New Brunswick, N.J.: Transaction Books.

ALBA, RICHARD D., and GWEN MOORE. 1982. "Ethnicity in the American elite." *American Sociological Review,* 47, pp. 373–383.

ALBERT, ETHEL M. 1963. "Women of Burundi: A study of social values," in Denise Paulme (ed.), *Women of Tropical Africa.* Berkeley, Calif.: University of California Press.

ALCORN, PAUL A. 1986. *Social Issues in Technology.* Englewood Cliffs., N.J.: Prentice-Hall.

ALFORD, ROBERT R. 1975. *Health Care Politics.* Chicago: University of Chicago Press.

———, and ROGER FRIEDLAND. 1975. "Political participation," in Alex Inkeles et al. (eds.), *Annual Review of Sociology.* Palo Alto, Calif.: Annual Reviews.

ALLEN, I. L. 1983. *The Language of Ethnic Conflict.* New York: Columbia University Press.

ALLEN, MICHAEL PATRICK. 1974. "The structure of interorganizational elite cooptation: Interlocking corporate directors." *American Sociological Review,* 39, pp. 393–406.

ALLMAN, WILLIAM F. 1985. "Staying alive in the 20th century." *Science '85,* October, pp. 31–41.

ALLPORT, GORDON W., and LEO J. POSTMAN. 1947. *The Psychology of Rumor.* New York: Holt, Rinehart and Winston.

ALTMAN, DENNIS. 1986. AIDS *in the Mind of America.* Garden City, N.Y.: Doubleday/Anchor.

ALTMAN, LAWRENCE K. 1984. "Mysterious form of hepatitis seen as widespread threat." *New York Times,* August 28, Section C, pp. 1, 9.

ALTORKI, SORAYA. 1986. *Women in Saudi Arabia.* 1986. New York: Columbia University Press.

AMERICAN SOCIOLOGICAL ASSOCIATION. 1982. "Revised A.S.A. code of professional ethics: Reactions solicited." *ASA Footnotes,* 10 (March), pp. 9-10.

AMIN, SAMIR. 1976. *Unequal Development: An Essay on Social Formations of Peripheral Capitalism.* New York: Monthly Review Press.

AMIR, MENACHEM. 1971. *Patterns of Forcible Rape.* Chicago: University of Chicago Press.

ANDERSON, JERVIS. 1985. *Guns in American Life.* New York: Random House.

ANDERSON, W. TIMOTHY, and DAVID T. HELM. 1979. "The physician-patient encounter: A process of reality negotiation." in E. Gartly Jago (ed.), *Patients, Physicians, and Illness.* New York: Free Press.

ANTHONY, DICK, et al. 1980. "Legitimating repression." *Society,* 17:3, 39–42.

APA MONITOR. 1974. "Homosexuality dropped as mental disorder," 5 (February), pp. 1, 9.

APPLE, MICHAEL W. 1982. *Education and Power: Reproduction and Contradiction in Education.* London: Routledge & Kegan Paul.

ARDREY, ROBERT. 1970. *The Social Contract.* New York: Dell.

ARENDT, HANNAH. 1958. *The Origins of Totalitarianism.* Cleveland: World.

ARGYLE, MICHAEL. 1969. *Social Interaction.* London: Methuen.

ARIÈS, PHILIPPE. 1962. *Centuries of Childhood: A Social History of Family Life.* New York: Knopf.

ARLUKE, ARNOLD, LOUANNE KENNEDY, and RONALD C. KESSLER. 1979. "Reexamining the sick role concept: An empirical assessment." *Journal of Health and Social Behavior,* 20, pp. 432–439.

ARNEY, WILLIAM RAY, and BERNARD J. BERGEN. 1984. *Medicine and the Management of Living.* Chicago: University of Chicago Press.

ASCH, SOLOMON. 1955. "Opinions and social pressure." *Scientific American,* 193, pp. 31–35.

ASH, T. G. 1984. *The Polish Revolution: Solidarity.* New York: Scribner's.

ASHMORE, HARRY S. 1982. *Hearts and Minds: The Anatomy of Racism from Roosevelt to Reagan.* New York: McGraw-Hill.

ASTIN, ALEXANDER W. 1977. *Four Critical Years.* San Francisco: Jossey-Bass.

———. 1985. *Achieving Educational Excellence.* San Francisco: Jossey-Bass.

———, and KENNETH C. GREEN. 1986. *The American Freshman: Twenty-Year Trends, 1966–1985.* Los Angeles: American Council on Education.

ATTORNEY-GENERAL'S COMMISSION ON PORNOGRAPHY. 1986. *Report to the Attorney General.* Washington, D.C.: Government Printing office.

AULETTA, KEN. 1982. *The Underclass.* New York: McGraw-Hill.

AVERITT, ROBERT T. 1968. *The Dual Economy: The Dynamics of American Industry Structure*. New York: Norton.

AXTHELM, PETE. 1970. *The City Game: Basketball in New York*. New York: Harper & Row.

BABBIE, EARL. 1985. *The Practice of Social Research*. 4th ed. Belmont, Calif.: Wadsworth.

BAIL, DONALD W. and JOHN W. LOY. 1975. *Sport and Social Order*. Reading, Mass.: Addison-Wesley.

BALDASSARE, MARK. 1986. *Trouble in Paradise: The Suburban Transformation in America*. New York: Columbia University Press.

BALES, ROBERT F. 1950. *Interaction Process Analysis: A Method for the Study of Small Groups*. Reading, Mass.: Addison-Wesley.

——————. 1953. "The equilibrium problem in small groups," in Talcott Parsons et al. (eds.), *Working Papers in the Theory of Action*. Glencoe, Ill.: Free Press.

——————. 1970. *Personality and Interpersonal Behavior*. New York: Holt, Rinehart and Winston.

——————, and FRED L. STRODTBECK. 1951. "Phases in group problem solving." *Journal of Abnormal and Social Psychology*, 46, pp. 485–494.

BALL, GEORGE W. (ed.). 1975. *Global Companies: The Political Economy of World Business*. Englewood Cliffs, N.J.: Prentice-Hall.

——————. 1985. "The war for star wars." *New York Review of Books*, April 11, pp. 38–44.

BALL, JOHN C., LAWRENCE BALL, JOHN A. FLICK, and DAVID NURCO. 1981. "The criminality of heroin addicts when addicted and when off opiates," in James A. Inciardy (ed.), *The Drugs-Crime Connection*. Beverly Hills, Calif.: Sage.

BALLANTINE, JEANNE H. 1983. *The Sociology of Education*. Englewood Cliffs, N.J.: Prentice-Hall.

——————. (ed.). 1985. *Schools and Society: A Reader in Education and Sociology*. Palo Alto, Calif.: Mayfield.

BANDURA, ALBERT. 1977. *Social Learning Theory*. Englewood Cliffs, N.J.: Prentice-Hall.

——————, and RICHARD H. WALTERS. 1963. *Social Learning and Personality Development*. New York: Holt, Rinehart and Winston.

BANE, MARY JO. 1976. *Here to Stay: American Families in the Twentieth Century*. New York: Basic Books.

BARAN, PAUL. 1957. *The Political Economy of Growth*. New York: Monthly Review Press.

BARASH, DAVID P. 1977. *Sociobiology and Behavior*. New York: Elsevier.

——————. 1983. *Aging: An Exploration*. Seattle: University of Washington Press.

BARBER, THEODORE, et al. 1969. "Five attempts to replicate the experimenter bias effect." *Journal of Consulting and Clinical Psychology*, 3, pp. 1–6.

BARBOUR, IAN G. 1980. *Technology, Environment, and Human Values*. New York: Praeger.

BARKER, EILEEN. 1984. *The Making of a Moonie: Brainwashing or Choice?* Oxford: Basil Blackwell.

BARNABY, FRANK C. 1977. "Hiroshima and Nagasaki: The Survivors." *New Scientists*, 75, pp. 472–475.

BARNET, RICHARD. 1970. *Roots of War*. New York: Penguin.

——————, and RONALD MULLER. 1974. *Global Reach: Power and the Multinational Corporations*. New York: Simon and Schuster.

BARNEY, GERALD O. 1980. *The Global 2000 Report to the President of the U.S.* New York: Pergamon Press.

BARR, REBECCA, and ROBERT DREEBEN. 1983. *How Schools Work*. Chicago: University of Chicago Press.

BARRET, WILLIAM. 1978. *The Illusion of Technique*. Garden City, N.Y.: Doubleday.

BARRY, HERBERT, et al. 1957. "A cross-cultural survey of some sex differences in socialization." *Journal of Abnormal and Social Psychology*, 55, pp. 327–332.

BARTLETT, DAVID L., and JAMES B. STEEL. 1985. *Forevermore: Nuclear Wastes in America*. New York: Norton.

BARTON, JOHN H. 1981. *The Politics of Peace: An Evaluation of Arms Control*. Stanford, Calif.: Stanford University Press.

BASKIN, YVONNE. 1984. "Doctoring the genes." *Science '84*, December, pp. 52–60.

BAYER, RONALD. 1981. *Homosexuality and American Psychiatry: The Politics of Diagnosis*. New York: Basic Books.

BEACH, FRANK A. (ed.). 1965. *Sex and Behavior*. New York: Wiley.

——————. (ed.). 1977. *Human Sexuality in Four Perspectives*. Baltimore: Johns Hopkins University Press.

BEAUCHAMP, TOM L., et al. (eds.). 1982. *Ethical Issues in Social Science Research*. Baltimore: Johns Hopkins University Press.

BECKER, HOWARD S. 1953. "Becoming a marijuana user." *American Journal of Sociology*, 50 (November), pp. 235–242.

——————. (ed.). 1963a. *The Other Side*. New York: Free Press.

——————. 1963b. *Outsiders: Studies in the Sociology of Deviance*. New York: Free Press.

——————. 1982. *Art Worlds*. Berkeley, Calif.: University of California Press.

——————, et al. 1961. *Boys in White: Student Culture in Medical School*. Chicago: University of Chicago Press.

——————, et al. 1968. *Making the Grade: The Academic Side of College Life*. New York: Wiley.

——————, and BLANCHE GREER. 1958. "The fate of idealism in medical school." *American Sociological Review*, 23, pp. 50–56.

BEIER, RUTH. 1984. *Science and Gender: A Critique of Biology and Its Theories on Women*. New York: Pergamon Press.

BELL, ALAN P., and MARTIN S. WEINBERG. 1978. *Homosexualities: A Study of Diversity Among Men and Women*. New York: Simon and Schuster.

——————, MARTIN S. WEINBERG, and SUE KIEFER HAMMERSMITH. 1981. *Sexual Preference: Its Development in Men and Women*. Indianapolis: Indiana University Press.

BELL, DANIEL. 1973. *The Coming of Postindustrial Society*. New York: Basic Books.

——————. 1976. *The Cultural Contradiction of Capitalism*. New York: Basic Books.

BELL, LELAND V. 1980. *Treating the Mentally Ill: From Colonial Times to the Present*. New York: Praeger.

BELLAH, ROBERT N. 1970. *Beyond Belief*. New York: Harper & Row.

——————, and RICHARD MADSEN, WILLIAM M. SULLIVAN, ANN SWIDLER, and STEVEN M. TIPTON. 1985. *Habits of the Heart*. Berkeley, Calif: University of California Press.

BEM, SANDRA, and DARYL BEM. 1970. "We're all nonconscious sexists." *Psychology Today*, 4, p. 22.

BEN-DAVID, JOSEPH. 1971. *The Scientist's Role in Society*. Englewood Cliffs, N.J.: Prentice-Hall.

——————. 1984. *The Scientist's Role in Society: A Comparative Study*. Chicago: University of Chicago Press.

BENDERLY, BERYL LIEFF. 1982. "Rape free or rape prone," *Science*, 82, pp. 40–43.

BENEDICT, RUTH. 1961. *Patterns of Culture*. Boston: Houghton Mifflin.

BENINGER, JAMES R. 1986. *The Control Revolution: Technological and Economic Origins of the Information Society*. Cambridge, Mass.: Harvard University Press.

BENNETT, JOHN W. 1976. *The Ecological Transition: Cultural Anthropology and Human Adaptation*. New York: Pergamon.

BENTLEY, JUDITH. 1984. *The Nuclear Freeze Movement*. New York: Franklin Watts.

BERES, LOUIS RENÉ. 1982. *Apocalypse: Nuclear Catastrophe in World Politics*. Chicago: University of Chicago Press, 1982.

BERG, IVAR. 1970. *Education and Jobs: The Great Training Robbery*. New York: Praeger.

—————, et al. 1978. *Managers and Work Reform: A Limited Engagement.* New York: Free Press.

BERGER, KATHLEEN STASSEN. 1986. *The Developing Person.* 3rd ed. New York: Worth.

BERGER, PETER L. 1963. *Invitation to Sociology: A Humanistic Perspective.* New York: Doubleday.

—————. 1964. "Some general observations on the problem of work," in Peter L. Berger (ed.), *The Human Shape of Work.* New York: Macmillan.

—————. 1967. *The Sacred Canopy: Elements of a Sociological Theory of Religion.* New York: Doubleday.

—————. 1969. *A Rumor of Angels: Modern Society and the Rediscovery of the Supernatural.* New York: Doubleday.

—————. 1979. *The Heretical Imperative: Contemporary Possibilities of Religious Affirmation.* New York: Doubleday.

—————. 1986. *The Capitalist Revolution.* New York: Basic Books.

—————, and THOMAS LUCKMANN. 1963. *The Social Construction of Reality.* New York: Doubleday.

BERGMAN, BARBARA. 1986. *The Economic Emergence of Women.* New York: Basic Books.

BERK, RICHARD A., et al. 1980. "Poverty and crime: Some experimental evidence from ex-offenders." *American Sociological Review,* 45:5, 766–786.

BERK, SARAH FENSTERMAKER. 1985. *The Gender Factory: The Apportionment of Work in American Households.* New York: Plenum.

BERKUN, M., et al. 1962. "Experimental studies of psychological stress in man." *Psychological Monographs: General and Applied,* 76:15, 1–39.

BERLE, A. A., and G. C. MEANS. 1933. *The Modern Corporation and Private Property.* New York: Macmillan.

BERLIN, BRENT, and PAUL KAY. 1969. *Basic Color Terms: Their Universality and Evolution.* Berkeley, Calif.: University of California Press.

BERMAN, MARSHALL. 1982. *All That Is Solid Melts into Thin Air: The Experience of Modernity.* New York: Simon and Schuster.

BERNARD, JESSIE. 1956. *Remarriage: A Study of Marriage.* New York: Dryden.

—————. 1981. *The Female World.* New York: Free Press.

—————. 1982. *The Future of Marriage.* 2nd ed. New Haven: Yale University Press.

BERNARD, L. L. 1924. *Instinct.* New York: Holt, Rinehart and Winston.

BERNSTEIN, BASIL, 1971. *Class, Codes, and Control.* London: Routledge & Kegan Paul.

BERREMAN, GERALD D. 1973. *Caste in the Modern World.* Morristown, N.J.: General Learning Press.

BERRY, BRIAN J. C. 1981. *Comparative Urbanization.* New York: St. Martin's Press.

BEST, RAPHAELA. 1983. *We've All Got Scars: What Boys and Girls Learn in Elementary School.* Bloomington: Indiana University Press.

BETTELHEIM, BRUNO. 1959. "Feral children and autistic children." *American Journal of Sociology,* 64, pp. 455–467.

BETTS, JOHN R. 1974. *America's Sporting Heritage 1850–1950.* Reading, Mass.: Addison-Wesley.

BIDDLE, WAYNE. 1986. "How much bang for the buck?" *Discover* (September), pp. 50–63.

BIEBER, IRVING, et al. 1962. *Homosexuality: A Psychoanalytic Study.* New York: Basic Books.

BIELBY, WILLIAM T., and JAMES N. BARON. 1986 "Men and women at work: Sex segregation and statistical discrimination." *American Journal of Sociology,* 91:4, 759–799.

BINGHAM, ROGER. 1981. "Outrageous ardor." *Science,* 81, pp. 56–61.

BIRD, CAROLINE. 1975. *The Case Against College.* New York: McKay.

—————. 1979. *The Two-Paycheck Marriage.* New York. Rawson Wade.

BIRDSALL, NANCY. 1982. "Population growth and poverty in the developing world." *Population Bulletin,* 35:5.

BIRDWHISTELL, RAY L. 1970. *Kinesics and Context.* Philadelphia: Pennsylvania University Press.

BLACK, CYRIL, et al. 1975. *The Modernization of Japan and Russia.* New York: Free Press.

BLACKWELL, JAMES E. 1985. *The Black Community: Diversity and Unity.* 2nd ed. New York: Harper & Row.

—————, and PHILIP HART. 1982. *Cities, Suburbs, and Blacks.* New York: General Hall.

BLAINEY, GEOFFREY. 1973. *The Causes of War.* New York: Free Press.

BLANKENSHIP, RALPH (ed.). 1977. *Colleagues in Organization: The Social Construction of Professional Work.* New York: Wiley.

BLAU, FRANCINE D., and MARIANE A. FERBER. 1986. *Economics of Women, Men, and Work.* Englewood Cliffs., N.J.: Prentice-Hall.

BLAU, PETER M. 1964. *Exchange and Power in Social Life.* New York: Wiley.

—————, and W. RICHARD SCOTT. 1962. *Formal Organizations.* San Francisco: Chandler.

—————, and OTIS DUDLEY DUNCAN. 1967. *The American Occupational Structure.* New York: Wiley.

—————, and MARSHALL W. MEYER. 1973. *Bureaucracy in Modern Society.* 3rd ed. New York: Random House.

BLEDSTEIN, BURTON J. 1976. *The Culture of Professionalism: The Middle Class and the Development of Higher Education in America.* New York: Norton.

BLISHEN, BERNARD R., and H. A. MCROBERTS. 1976. "A revised socioeconomic index for occupations in Canada." *Canadian Review of Sociology and Anthropology,* 13, pp. 71–79.

BLOOM, SAMUEL W. 1973. *Power and Dissent in the Medical School.* New York: Free Press.

BLUESTONE, BARRY, and BENNET HARRISON. 1982. *The Deindustrialization of America.* New York: Basic Books.

BLUMER, HERBERT. 1951. "Collective behavior," in Alfred McLung Lee (ed.), *New Outline of the Principles of Sociology.* New York: Barnes & Noble.

—————. 1962. "Society as symbolic interaction," in Arnold Rose (ed.), *Human Behavior and Social Processes: An Interactionist Approach.* Boston: Houghton Mifflin.

—————. 1969. *Symbolic Interactionism: Perspective and Method.* Englewood Cliffs, N.J.: Prentice-Hall.

—————. 1974. "Social movements," in R. Serge Denisoff (ed.), *The Sociology of Dissent.* New York: Harcourt Brace Jovanovich.

BLUMSTEIN, PHILIP, and PEPPER SCHWARTZ. 1974. "The acquisition of sexual identity: The bisexual case." Paper presented at the Annual Meetings of the American Sociological Association, August 25–29, Montreal, Canada.

—————, and PEPPER SCHWARTZ. 1983. *American Couples.* New York: Morrow.

BOCK, KENNETH. 1981. *Human Nature and History: A Response to Sociobiology.* New York: Columbia University Press.

BOFFEY, PHILIP M. 1985. "Dark side of 'star wars': System could also attack." March 7, *New York Times,* pp. 1, 22.

BOGGS, CARL. 1986. *Social Movements and Political Power.* Philadelphia: Temple University Press.

BOLTER, DAVID. 1984. *Turing's Man: Western Culture in the Computer Age.* Chapel Hill: University of North Carolina Press.

BONACICH, EDNA. 1972. "A theory of ethnic antagonism: The split-labor market." *American Sociological Review,* 37, pp. 547–559.

BOOCOCK, SARANE SPENCE. 1980. *Sociology of Education.* Boston: Houghton Mifflin.

BOORSTIN, DANIEL J. 1984. *The Discoverers.* New York: Random House.

BORNSCHIER, VOLKER, and JEAN-PIERRE HOBY. 1981. "Economic policy and multinational corporations in development: The measurable impact in cross-national perspective." *Social Problems,* 28, pp. 363–377.

BOSE, CHRISTINE E. 1985. *Jobs and Gender: A Study of Occupational Prestige.* New York: Praeger.

—————, and PETER H. ROSSI. 1983. "Gender and jobs: Prestige

standings of occupations as affected by gender." *American Sociological Review,* 48, pp. 316–330.

BOSWELL, JAMES. 1980. *Christianity, Homosexuality, and Social Tolerance.* Chicago: University of Chicago Press.

BOSWELL, THOMAS D., and JAMES R. CURTIS. 1984. *The Cuban-American Experience.* Totowa, N.J.: Rowman and Allanheld.

BOTT, ELIZABETH. 1971. *Family and Social Network.* New York: Free Press.

BOUDON, RAYMOND. 1974. *Education, Opportunity, and Social Inequality.* New York: Wiley.

BOULDING, KENNETH. 1959. "Foreword" to Thomas Malthus, *Population: The First Essay.* Ann Arbor, Mich.: University of Michigan Press.

_____. 1964. *The Meaning of the Twentieth Century: The Great Transition.* New York: Harper & Row.

_____. 1978. *Ecodynamics: A New Theory of Societal Evolution.* Beverly Hills, Calif.: Sage.

_____. 1985. *The World as a Total System.* Beverly Hills, Calif: Sage.

BOURDIEU, PIERRE. 1977. *Reproduction in Education, Society, and Culture.* Beverly Hills, Calif.: Sage.

BOURNE, RICHARD, and ELI H. NEWBERGER (eds.). 1979. *Critical Perspectives on Child Abuse.* Lexington, Mass.: D. C. Heath.

BOUTON, KATHERINE. 1983. "Academic research and big business: A delicate balance." *New York Times Magazine,* September 11, pp. 62–63, 118–126, 151.

BOWEN, HOWARD R. 1977. *Investment in Learning: The Individual and the Social Value of American Higher Education.* San Francisco: Jossey-Bass.

BOWLBY, JOHN. 1969. *Attachment and Loss.* Vol. 1. New York: Basic Books.

BOWLES, SAMUEL, and HERBERT GINTIS. 1976. *Schooling in Capitalist America.* New York: Basic Books.

BOYER, ERNEST L. 1983. *High School.* New York: Harper & Row.

BRANNIGAN, AUGUSTINE. 1981. *The Social Basis of Scientific Discoveries.* New York: Cambridge University Press.

BRIERE, JOHN, NEIL MALAMUTH, and JOE CENITI. 1981. "Self-assessed rape proclivity: Attitudinal and sexual correlates." Paper presented at the American Psychological Association Meetings, Los Angeles, August.

BRINTON, CRANE. 1960. *The Anatomy of Revolution.* New York: Random House.

BROAD, WILLIAM, and NICHOLAS WADE. 1983. *Betrayers of the Truth.* New York: Simon and Schuster.

BROD, CRAIG, and WES ST. JOHN. 1984. *Technostress: The Human Cost of the Computer Revolution.* Reading, Mass.: Addison-Wesley.

BROMLEY, DAVID G., and ANSON D. SHUPE. 1979. *"Moonies" in America: Cult, Church, and Crusade.* Beverly Hills, Calif.: Sage.

_____, and JAMES T. RICHARDSON (eds.). 1983. *The Brainwashing/Deprogramming Controversy.* Lewiston, N.Y.: Edwin Mellen Press.

BRONFENBRENNER, URIE. 1970. *Two Worlds of Childhood.* New York: Russell Sage Foundation.

BROOKS, CHARLES H. 1980. "Social, economic, and biologic correlates of infant mortality in city neighborhoods." *Journal of Health and Social Behavior,* 21, pp. 2–11.

BROPHY, J. E., and T. L. GOOD. 1970. "Teachers' communication of differential expectations for children's classroom performance: Some behavioral data." *Journal of Educational Psychology,* 61, p. 356.

BROWN, HAROLD. 1986. "Is SDI technically feasible?" *Foreign Affairs,* 64, pp. 435–445.

BROWN, LESTER R. 1978. *The Twenty-ninth Day.* New York: Norton.

_____. 1981. "World food resources and population: The narrowing margin." *Population Bulletin,* 56:3.

_____, and EDWARD C. WOLF. 1987. "Charting a sustainable course," in Lester R. Brown (ed.), *State of the World: 1987.* Washington, D.C.: Worldwatch Institute.

BROWN, MICHAEL. 1980. *Laying Waste.* New York: Pantheon.

BROWN, RAY (ed.). *Children and Television.* Beverly Hills, Calif: Sage, 1976.

BROWN, ROGER. 1965. *Social Psychology.* New York: Free Press.

BROWNMILLER, SUSAN. 1975. *Against Our Will: Men, Women, and Rape.* New York: Simon and Schuster.

_____. 1984. *Feminity.* New York: Linden Press/Simon and Schuster.

BROWNSTEIN, RONALD, and NINA EASTON. 1983. *Reagan's Ruling Class: Portraits of the President's Top One Hundred Officials.* New York: Pantheon.

BRUCE-BIGGS, B. (ed.). 1979. *The New Class?* New Brunswick, N.J.: Transaction Books.

BRUNVAND, JAN H. 1981. *The Vanishing Hitchhiker: American Urban Legends and Their Meanings.* New York: Norton.

BRYANT, JAMES H. 1965. "Apprenticeships in prostitution." *Social Problems,* 12, pp. 278–297.

BUCKLEY, W. 1958. "Social stratification and the functional theory of social differentiation." *American Sociological Review,* 23, pp. 369–375.

BULLOUGH, VERN L. 1976. *Sexual Variance in Society and History.* New York: Wiley.

_____, and BONNIE BULLOUGH. 1979. *Prostitution: An Illustrated Social History.* New York: Crown.

BULMER, MARTIN (ed.). 1982. *Social Research Ethics.* New York: Holmes and Meier, 1982.

BUNDY, WILLIAM P. (ed.). *The Nuclear Controversy.* New York: Meridian.

BUREAU OF JUSTICE STATISTICS. 1984. "Criminal victimization in the United States, 1982." Washington, D.C.: U.S. Government Printing Office.

BUREAU OF THE CENSUS, 1986a. *Statistical Abstract of the United States: 1986.* Washington, D.C.: U.S. Government Printing Office.

BUREAU OF THE CENSUS, 1986b. "Household wealth and asset ownership: 1984." *Current Population Reports,* Series P-70, no. 7. Washington, D.C.: U.S. Government Printing Office.

BUREAU OF THE CENSUS, 1986c. "Money income of households, families, and persons in the United States: 1984." *Current Population Reports,* Series P-60, no. 151.

BURGOON, JUDEE K., and STEPHEN B. JONES. 1976. "Toward a theory of personal space expectations and their violations." *Human Communication Research,* 2, pp. 131–146.

BURNHAM, DAVID. 1983. *The Rise of the Computer State.* New York: Random House.

BURNHAM, JAMES. 1941. *The Managerial Revolution.* New York: John Day.

BURRIDGE, KENELM O. L. 1957. "Disputing in Tangu." *American Anthropologist,* 59, pp. 763–780.

BUTLER, KATHLEEN, and BEN CHINETZ. 1982. "Urban growth in the sunbelt," in Gary Gappert and Richard V. Knight (eds.), *Cities in the Twenty-First Century.* Beverly Hills, Calif.: Sage

BUTLER, SANDRA. 1979. *Conspiracy of Silence: The Trauma of Incest.* New York: Bantam.

BUTTERFIELD, FOX. 1985. "Chinese organized crime said to rise in U.S." *New York Times,* January 13, pp. 1, 42.

_____. 1985. "Violent incidents against Asian-Americans seen as part of racist pattern." *New York Times,* August 31, p. 8.

CAFFERTY, PASTORA, et al. 1983. *The Dilemma of American Immigration: Beyond the Golden Door.* New Brunswick, N.J.: Transaction Books.

CAHILL, SPENCER E. 1980. "Directions for an interactionist study of gender development." *Symbolic Interaction,* 13, pp. 123–138.

_____. 1983. "Reexamining the acquisition of sex roles: A social interactionist approach." *Sex Roles,* 12, pp. 1–5.

CALDER, NIGEL. 1980. *Nuclear Nightmares: An Investigation in Possible Wars.* New York: Viking.

CALIFANO, JOSEPH A. 1985. *America's Health Care Revolution.* New York: Random House.

CAMPBELL, BERNARD. 1985. *Human Ecology.* Hawthorne, N.Y.: Aldine.

CAMPBELL, COLIN. 1978. "The secret religion of the educated classes." *Sociological Analysis,* 59:2, 146–156.

CANTRIL, HADLEY. 1940. *The Invasion from Mars.* Princeton, N.J.: Princeton University Press.

—————. 1941. *The Psychology of Social Movements.* New York: Wiley.

—————. 1963. *The Psychology of Social Movements.* New York: Wiley.

CAPLAN, ARTHUR L. (ed.). 1978. *The Sociobiology Debate.* New York: Harper & Row.

CARGAN, LEONARD. 1982. *Singles: Myths and Realities.* Beverly Hills, Calif.: Sage.

CARLSON, RICK. 1976. *The End of Medicine.* New York: Wiley.

CARMEN, ARLENE, and HOWARD MOODY. 1985. *Working Women: The Subterranean World of Street Prostitution.* New York: Harper & Row.

CARMODY, DENISE. 1979. *Women and World Religions.* Nashville: Abingdon.

CARR, RAYMOND. 1984. *Puerto Rico: A Colonial Experiment.* New York: New York University Press/Vintage.

CARROLL, JACKSON, BARBARA HARGROVE, and ADAIR LUMMIS. 1982. *Women of the Cloth.* New York: Harper & Row.

CARTER, ASHTON B. 1984. *Directed Energy Missile Defense in Space.* Washington, D.C.: U.S. Government Printing Office.

CARTER, DOUGLAS, and STEPHEN STRICKLAND. 1975. *TV Violence and the Child: The Evolution and Fate of the Surgeon General's Report.* New York: Russell Sage Foundation.

CARTER, HUGH, and PAUL C. GLICK. 1976. *Marriage and Divorce: A Social and Economic Study.* Cambridge, Mass.: Harvard University Press.

CASTELLS, MANUEL. 1977. *The Urban Question.* Cambridge, Mass.: MIT Press.

CAUFIELD, CATHERINE. 1985. *In the Rainforest.* New York: Knopf.

CAUGHEY, JOHN L. 1984. *Imaginary Social Worlds: A Cultural Approach.* Lincoln: University of Nebraska Press.

CHAFETZ, JANET SALTZMAN. 1984. *Sex and Advantage: A Comparative, Macro-Structural Theory of Sex Stratification.* Totowa, N.J.: Rowmann and Allanheld.

CHAGNON, NAPOLEON A. 1967. "Yanamamö social organization and warfare," in Morton Fried et al. (eds.), *War: The Anthropology of Armed Conflict and Aggression.* New York: Doubleday.

—————. 1977. *Yanamamö: The Fierce People.* 2nd ed. New York: Holt, Rinehart and Winston.

CHALFANT, H. PAUL, ROBERT E. BECKLEY, and C. EDDIE PALMER. 1986. *Religion in Contemporary Society.* 2nd ed. Palo Alto, Calif.: Mayfield.

CHAMBLISS, WILLIAM J. 1973. "The Saints and the Roughnecks." *Society,* 11, pp. 24–31.

—————, and MILTON MANKOFF (eds.). 1976. *Whose Law? What Order?* New York: Wiley.

—————, and ROBERT SEIDMAN. 1982. *Law, Order, and Power.* 2nd ed. Reading, Mass.: Addison-Wesley.

CHANG, PAO-MIN. 1983. *Continuity and Change: A Profile of Chinese Americans.* New York: Vantage.

CHAPMAN, JANE ROBERTS, and MARGARET GATES (eds.). 1978. *The Victimization of Women.* Beverly Hills, Calif.: Sage.

CHAPPELL, DUNCAN, et al. (eds.). 1977. *Rape: The Victim and the Offender.* New York: Columbia University Press.

CHARMAZ, KATHY. 1980. *The Social Reality of Death.* Reading, Mass.: Addison-Wesley.

CHAZOV, EVGENII I. 1982. "Physicians for Nuclear Disarmament," in Eric Chivian et al. (eds.). *Last Aid: The Medical Dimensions of Nuclear War.* San Francisco: Freeman.

CHEEK, WILLIAM F. 1970. *Black Resistance Before the Civil War.* Beverly Hills, Calif.: Glencoe Press.

CHERFAS, JEREMY. 1983. *Man-Made Life: An Overview of the Science, Technology and Commerce of Genetic Engineering.* New York: Pantheon.

CHERLIN, ANDREW. 1978. "Remarriage as an incomplete institution." *American Journal of Sociology,* 84, pp. 634–650.

—————. 1983. *Marriage, Divorce, and Remarriage.* Cambridge, Mass.: Harvard University Press.

CHESLER, PHYLLIS. 1972. *Women and Madness.* New York: Avon.

CHILDE, V. GORDON. 1950. "The urban revolution." *Town Planning Review,* 21, pp. 3-17.

CHIRICOS, THEODORE G., and GORDON P. WALDO. 1975. "Socioeconomic status and criminal sentencing: An empirical assessment of a conflict proposition." *American Sociological Review,* 40, pp. 753–772.

CHIROT, DANIEL. 1977. *Social Change in the Twentieth Century.* New York: Harcourt Brace Jovanovich.

—————. 1986. *Social Change in the Modern Era.* 2nd ed. San Diego, Calif.: Harcourt Brace Jovanovich.

—————, and THOMAS H. HALL. 1982. "World-system theory," in RALPH H. TURNER and JAMES F. SHORT (eds.), *Annual Review of Sociology,* 8. Palo Alto, Calif.: Annual Reviews.

CHIVIAN, ERIC, et al. (eds.). 1982. *Last Aid: The Medical Dimensions of Nuclear War.* San Francisco: Freeman.

CHOROVER, STEPHAN. 1979. *From Genesis to Genocide.* Cambridge, Mass.: MIT Press.

CHURCH, JOSEPH. 1978. "Two flew over the cuckoo's nest." *New York Times Book Review,* March 26, p. 11.

CICOUREL, AARON. 1974. *Cognitive Sociology.* New York: Free Press.

CLARK, BURTON R. 1960. "The 'cooling-out' function in higher education." *American Journal of Sociology,* 65, pp. 569–576.

CLARK, CANDACE. 1983. "Sickness and social control," in Howard Robboy and Candace Clark (eds.), *Social Interaction: Readings in Sociology.* 2nd ed. New York: St. Martin's Press.

CLARK, MARGARET. 1970. *Health in the Mexican-American Culture: a Community Study.* 2nd ed. Berkeley: University of California Press.

CLARK, REGINALD M. 1983. *Family Life and School Achievement.* Chicago: University of Chicago Press.

CLAUSEN, JOHN. 1986. *The Life Course: A Sociological Perspective.* Englewood Cliffs, N.J.: Prentice-Hall.

CLAYTON, RICHARD R., and HARWIN L. VOSS. 1977. "Shacking up: Cohabitation in the 1970s." *Journal of Marriage and the Family,* 39:2, 273–283.

CLEMENT, WALLACE. 1975. *The Canadian Corporate Elite: An Analysis of Economic Power.* Toronto: McClelland and Stewart.

CLENDENING, LOGAN (ed.). 1942. *Sourcebook of Medical History.* New York: Dover Publications.

CLEVELAND, DIANE. 1985. *Incest.* Lexington, Mass.: Lexington Books.

CLINARD, MARSHALL B., and PETER C. YEAGER. 1980. *Corporate Crime.* New York: Free Press.

CLOWARD, RICHARD A., and LLOYD E. OHLIN. 1960. *Delinquency and Opportunity: A Theory of Delinquent Gangs.* New York: Free Press.

COAKLEY, JAY J. 1982. *Sport in Society: Issues and Controversies.* 2nd ed. St. Louis: Mosby.

COCKBURN, ANDREW. 1982. *Inside the Soviet Military Machine.* New York: Random House.

COCKERHAM, WILLIAM C. 1981. *Sociology of Mental Disorder.* Englewood Cliffs, N.J.: Prentice-Hall.

—————. 1986. *Medical Sociology.* 3rd ed. Englewood Cliffs, N.J.: Prentice-Hall.

COCKROFT, JAMES D., et al. (eds.). 1972. *Dependence and Underdevelopment.* Garden City, N.Y.: Anchor.

COE, RODNEY M. 1978. *Sociology of Medicine.* 2nd ed. New York: McGraw-Hill.

COHEN, ALBERT K. 1955. *Delinquent Boys: The Culture of the Gang.* New York: Free Press.

COHEN, BERNARD. 1980. *Deviant Street Networks: Prostitution in New York City.* Lexington, Mass.: D. C. Heath.

COHEN, YEHUDI A. (ed.). 1974. *Man in Adaptation: The Cultural Present,* 2nd ed. Chicago: Aldine.

COHN, NORMAN. 1962. *The Pursuit of the Millennium.* New York: Oxford University Press.

COLE, STEPHEN, and JONATHAN COLE. 1977. *Social Stratification in Science.* Chicago: University of Chicago Press.

COLEMAN, JAMES C. 1976. *Abnormal Psychology and Modern Life.* 5th ed. Glenview, Ill.: Scott, Foresman.

COLEMAN, JAMES S., THOMAS HOFFER, and SALLY KILGORE. 1982. *High School Achievement: Public, Catholic, and Private Schools Compared.* New York: Basic Books.

——————, et al. 1966. *Equality of Educational Opportunity.* Washington, D.C.: U.S. Government Printing Office.

——————, et al. 1975. *Trends in School Desegregation, 1968–1973.* Washington, D.C.: Urban Institute.

——————, and THOMAS HOFFER. 1986. *Public and Private High Schools: The Impact of Communities.* New York: Basic Books.

COLEMAN, JAMES W. 1985. *Criminal Elite: The Sociology of White-Collar Crime.* New York: St. Martin's Press.

COLLINS, RANDALL. 1971a. "A conflict theory of sexual stratification." *Social Problems,* 19, pp. 3–12.

——————. 1971b. "Functional and conflict theories of educational stratification." *American Sociological Review,* 36:6, 1002–1019.

——————. 1974. *Conflict Sociology: Toward an Explanatory Science.* New York: Academic Press.

——————. 1979. *The Credential Society.* New York: Academic Press.

——————. 1985. *Sociology of Marriage and the Family: Gender, Love, and Property.* Chicago: Nelson Hall.

COMMISSION ON POPULATION GROWTH AND THE AMERICAN FUTURE. 1972. *Population and the American Future: The Report of the Commission on Population Growth and the American Future.* Washington, D.C.: U.S. Government Printing Office.

COMSTOCK, GEORGE, et al. 1978. *Television and Human Behavior.* New York: Columbia University Press.

——————. 1980. *Television in America.* Beverly Hills, Calif.: Sage.

CONDRY, JOHN, and SANDRA CONDRY. 1976. "Sex differences: A study of the eye of the beholder." *Child Development,* 47, pp. 812–819.

CONKLIN, JOHN E. 1986. *Criminology.* 2nd ed. New York: Macmillan.

CONNOR, WALTER D. 1979. *Socialism, Politics, and Equality.* New York: Columbia University Press.

——————. 1980. *Hierarchy and Change in Eastern Europe and the U.S.S.R.* New York: Columbia University Press.

CONRAD, JOHN P. 1983. "Deterrence, the death penalty, and the data." In Ernest van den Haag and John P. Conrad (eds.), *The Death Penalty: A Debate.* New York: Plenum.

CONRAD, PETER. 1975. "The discovery of hyperkinesis: Notes on the medicalization of deviant behavior." *Social Problems,* 23, pp. 12–21.

——————, and ROCHELLE KERN (eds.). 1985. *Sociology of Health and Illness: Critical Perspectives.* 2nd ed. New York: St. Martin's Press.

——————, and JOSEPH W. SCHNEIDER, 1980. *Deviance and Medicalization: From Badness to Sickness.* St. Louis: Mosby.

CONSTANTINE, LARRY L. 1978. "Multilateral relations revisited: Group marriage in extended perspective," in Bernard I. Murstein (ed.), *Exploring Intimate Life Styles.* New York: Springer.

——————, and JOAN M. CONSTANTINE. 1974. *Group Marriage.* New York: Macmillan.

COOLEY, CHARLES HORTON. 1902. *Human Nature and the Social Order.* New York: Scribner's.

COOMBS, ROBERT H. 1978. *Mastering Medicine: Professional Socialization in Medical School.* New York: Free Press.

COSER, LEWIS A. 1956. *The Functions of Social Conflict.* Glencoe, Ill.: Free Press.

COURTWRIGHT, DAVID T. 1982. *Dark Paradise: Opiate Addiction in America before 1940.* Cambridge, Mass.: Harvard University Press.

COWGILL, DONALD O. 1974. "Aging and modernization: A revision of the theory," in Jon Hendricks and C. Davis Hendricks (eds.), *Dimensions of Aging.* Cambridge, Mass.: Winthrop.

COX, HARVEY. 1977. *Turning East: The Promise and Peril of the New Orientalism.* New York: Simon and Schuster.

COX, JOHN. 1977. *Overkill.* New York: Thomas Crowell.

COX, OLIVER C. 1976. *Race Relations: Elements and Social Dynamics.* Detroit: Wayne State University Press.

CRAPANZANO, VINCENT. 1985. *Waiting: The Whites of South Africa.* New York: Random House.

CRITTENDEN, ANN. 1981. "Demand outpaces world food supply." *New York Times,* August 16, pp. 1, 12.

CROLL, ELIZABETH, et al. (eds.). 1985. *China's One-Child Family Policy.* New York: St. Martin's Press.

CROSBIE, PAUL V. (ed.). 1975. *Interaction in Small Groups.* New York: Macmillan.

CROSSMAN, RICHARD (ed.). 1952. *The God That Failed.* New York: Bantam.

CUMMING, ELAINE, and WILLIAM E. HENRY. 1961. *Growing Old: The Process of Disengagement.* New York: Basic Books.

CUMMINGS, JUDITH. 1983. "Breakup of black families imperils gains of decades. *New York Times,* November 20, pp. 1, 56.

CURLE, ADAM. 1971. *Making Peace.* London: Tavistock.

CURRIE, ELLIOTT. 1986. *Confronting Crime: An American Challenge.* New York: Pantheon.

CURTISS, SUSAN. 1977. *Genie: A Psycholinguistic Study of a Modern-Day "Wild Child."* New York: Academic Press.

CUSHMAN, JOHN H. 1986. "Experts see risk in troop carrier." *New York Times,* September 21, pp. 1, 36.

DAALDER, HANS, and PETER MAIR (eds.). 1983. *Western European Party Systems.* Beverly Hills, Calif: Sage.

DAHL, ROBERT. 1961. *Who Governs?* New Haven: Yale University Press.

——————. 1981. *Democracy in the United States.* 4th ed. Boston: Houghton Mifflin.

DAHRENDORF, RALF. 1958. "Toward a theory of social conflict." *The Journal of Conflict Resolution,* 11, pp. 170–183.

——————. 1959. *Class and Class Conflict in Industrial Society.* Berkeley, Calif.: Stanford University Press.

DALMAIDE, DARRELL. 1984. *Debt Shock.* New York: Doubleday.

DALPHIN, JOHN. 1981. *The persistence of social inequality in America.* Cambridge, Mass.: Schenkman.

DALY, MARY. 1973. *Beyond God the Father.* Boston: Beacon Press.

D'ANDRADE, ROY G. 1966. "Sex differences and cultural institutions," in Eleanor E. Maccoby (ed.), *The Development of Sex Differences.* Palo Alto, Calif.: Stanford University Press.

DANER, FRANCINE. 1976. *The American Children of Krsna: A Study of the Hare Krsna Movement.* New York: Holt, Rinehart & Winston.

DANK, BARRY M. 1971. "Coming out in the gay world." *Psychiatry,* 34, pp. 180–197.

DANZIGER, SHELDON H., and DANIEL H. WEINBERG. 1986. *Fighting Poverty: What Works and What Doesn't.* Cambridge, Mass.: Harvard University Press.

DARLEY, JOHN M., and BIBB LATANÉ. 1968. "Bystander intervention in emergencies: Diffusion of responsibility." *Journal of Personality and Social Psychology,* 8, pp. 377–383.

DAVIES, JAMES C. 1962. "Toward a theory of revolution." *American Sociological Review,* 27, pp. 5–18.

——————(ed.). 1971. *When Men Revolt—and Why.* New York: Free Press.

DAVIES, MARK, and DENISE B. KANDEL. 1981. "Parental and peer influences on adolescents' educational plans: Some further evidence." *American Journal of Sociology,* 87, pp. 363–387.

DAVIES, NIGEL. 1981. *Human Sacrifice.* New York: Morrow.

DAVIES, PAUL. 1984. *Superforce: The Search for a Grand Theory of Nature.* New York: Simon and Schuster.

DAVIS, ALAN J. 1968. "Sexual assaults in the Philadelphia prison system." *Transaction,* 6, pp. 28–35.

DAVIS, CARY, CARL HAUB, and JOANNE WILLETTE. 1983. *U.S. Hispanics: Changing the Face of America.* Washington, D.C.: Population Reference Bureau.

DAVIS, FRED (ed.). 1966. *The Nursing Profession.* New York: Wiley.

DAVIS, GEORGE, and GLEGG WATSON. 1982. *Black Life in Corporate America.* New York: Doubleday/Anchor.

DAVIS, KAREN. 1975. *National Health Insurance.* Washington, D.C.: Brookings Institution.

DAVIS, KINGSLEY. 1932. "The sociology of prostitution." *American Sociological Review,* 2, pp. 744–755.

——————. 1940. "Extreme social isolation of a child." *American Journal of Sociology,* 45, pp. 554–564.

——————. 1945. *The World Demographic Transition.* Annals of the American Academy of Political and Social Sciences, 237, pp. 1–11.

——————. 1947. "Final note on a case of extreme isolation." *American Journal of Sociology,* 50, pp. 432–437.

——————. 1948. *Human Society.* New York: Macmillan.

——————, and WILBERT E. MOORE. 1945. "Some principles of stratification." *American Sociological Review,* 10, pp. 242–249.

——————. 1976. "Sexual behavior," in Robert K. Merton and Robert Nisbet (eds.), *Contemporary Social Problems.* 3rd ed. New York: Harcourt Brace Jovanovich.

DAVIS, NANETTE J. 1971. "The prostitute: Developing a deviant identity," in James M. Henslin (ed.), *Studies in the Sociology of Sex.* New York: Appleton-Century-Crofts.

DAY, ROBERT A., and JOANNE V. DAY. 1977. "A review of the current state of negotiated order theory: An appreciation and a critique." *Sociological Quarterly,* Winter, p. 18.

DE MAUSE, LLOYD (ed.). 1974. *The History of Childhood.* New York: Psychohistory Press.

DE TOCQUEVILLE, ALEXIS. 1954, originally published 1835. *Democracy in America II.* Phillips Bradley (ed.). New York: Random House.

DEGLER, CARL N. 1980. *At Odds: Women and Family in America from the Revolution to the Present.* New York: Oxford University Press.

DEKMEJIAN, R. HRAIR. 1985. *Islam in Revolution: Fundamentalism in the Arab World.* Syracuse: Syracuse University Press.

DELUTZ, THOMAS JR. 1985. *A Bowling Career.* Unpublished manuscript: William Paterson College, Wayne, N.J.

DEMERATH, N. J., and RHYS H. WILLIAMS. 1984. "A mythical past and uncertain future." *Society,* 21, pp. 3–10.

DENNIS, WAYNE. 1960. "Causes of retardation among institutionalized children: Iran." *Journal of Genetic Psychology,* 96, pp. 47–59.

——————. 1973. *Children of the Creche.* New York: Appleton-Century-Crofts.

DEPARTMENT OF LABOR. 1977. *Dictionary of Occupational Titles.* Washington, D.C.: U.S. Government Printing Office.

DESPELDER, LYNNE ANNE, and ALBERT LEE STRICKLAND. 1983. *The Last Dance: Encountering Death and Dying.* Palo Alto, Calif.: Mayfield.

DEUTSCHER, IRWIN. 1973. *What We Say, What We Do: Sentiments and Acts.* Glenview, Ill.: Scott, Foresman.

DIAMOND, MILTON. 1977. "Human sexual development: Biological foundations for social development," in Frank A. Beach (ed.), *Human Sexuality in Four Perspectives.* Baltimore: Johns Hopkins University Press.

DICKSON, DAVID. 1984. *The New Politics of Science.* New York: Pantheon.

DIEBOLD, JOHN. 1985. *Making the Future Work.* New York: Simon and Schuster.

DIEHL, PAUL F. 1985. "Arms races to war: What are the empirical linkages?" *Sociological Quarterly,* 26, pp. 331–349.

DIENER, EDWARD, and RICK CRANDALL. 1978. *Ethics in Social and Behavioral Research.* Chicago: University of Chicago Press.

DOBSON, RICHARD B. 1977. "Mobility and stratification in the Soviet Union." *Annual Review of Sociology.* Palo Alto, Calif.: Annual Reviews.

DOHRENWEND, BRUCE P. 1975. "Sociocultural and social-psychological factors in the genesis of mental disorders." *Journal of Health and Social Behavior,* 16, pp. 365–392.

DOLESCHAL, EUGENE, and NORAH KLAPMUTS. 1973. *Toward a New Criminology.* Hackensack, N.J.: National Council on Crime and Delinquency.

DOMHOFF, G. WILLIAM. 1967. *Who Rules America?* Englewood Cliffs, N.J.: Prentice-Hall.

——————. 1970. *The Higher Circles.* New York: Random House.

——————. 1978. *Who Really Rules?* New Brunswick, N.J.: Transaction Books.

——————. (ed.). 1980. *Power Structure Research.* Beverly Hills, Calif.: Sage.

——————. 1983. *Who Rules America Now?* Englewood Cliffs, N.J.: Prentice-Hall.

DOOB, LEONARD W. 1981. *The Pursuit of Peace.* Westport, Conn.: Greenwood Press.

DORE, RONALD. 1976. *The Diploma Disease: Education, Qualification, and Development.* London: Allen and Unwin.

DOUNTON, JAMES V. 1979. *Sacred Journeys: The Conversion of Young Americans to Divine Light Mission.* New York: Columbia University Press.

DOYLE, JAMES A. 1983. *The Male Experience.* Dubuque, Iowa: Wm. C. Brown.

——————. 1985. *Sex and Gender: The Human Experience.* Dubuque, Iowa: Wm. C. Brown.

DREITZEL, HANS P. 1970. *Recent Sociology No. 2: Patterns of Communicative Behavior.* New York: Macmillan.

DREW, DAVID E. (ed.). 1978. *Competency, Careers, and College: New Directions for Education and Work.* San Francisco: Jossey-Bass.

DREW, ELIZABETH. 1983. *Politics and Money: The New Road to Corruption.* New York: Macmillan.

DUBERMAN, LUCILLE. 1975. *The Reconstructed Family.* Chicago: Nelson-Hall.

DUBOS, RENÉ. 1959. *Health as Mirage.* New York: Doubleday.

——————. 1969. *Man, Medicine, and Environment.* New York: Mentor.

DUERR, HANS PETER. 1985. *Dreamtime: Concerning the Boundary Between Wilderness and Civilization.* Oxford: Basil Blackwell.

DUFFY, JOHN. 1976. *The Healers: The Rise of the Medical Establishment.* New York: McGraw-Hill.

DUNBAR, L. W. (ed.). 1984. *Minority Report.* New York: Pantheon.

DUNCAN, GREG J. 1982. "Who gets ahead? And who gets left behind?" *American Demographics,* 4, pp. 38–41.

DUNCAN, OTIS DUDLEY, DAVID L. FEATHERMAN, and BEVERLY DUNCAN. 1972. *Socioeconomic background and achievement.* New York: Academic Press.

DUNN, JOHN, and CAROL KENDRICK. 1983. *Siblings: Love, Envy, and Understanding.* Cambridge, Mass.: Harvard University Press.

DURKHEIM, EMILE. 1954, originally published 1912. *The Elementary Forms of Religious Life.* Joseph W. Swain (trans.). Glencoe, Ill.: Free Press.

——————. 1964a, originally published 1893. *The Division of Labor in Society.* George Simpson (trans.). Glencoe, Ill.: Free Press.

——————. 1964b, originally published 1897. *Suicide.* Glencoe, Ill.: Free Press.

DUTTON, DIANA B. 1978. "Explaining the low use of health services by the poor: Costs, attitudes, or delivery systems?" *American Sociological Review,* 43, pp. 348–368.

DUVERGER, MAURICE. 1954. *Political Parties.* New York: Wiley.

DWORKIN, ANDREA. 1981. *Pornography: Men Possessing Women*. New York: Putnam.

DYE, THOMAS R. 1983. *Who's Running America?* 3rd ed. Englewood Cliffs, N.J.: Prentice-Hall.

EATON, WILLIAM W. 1980. *The Sociology of Mental Disorders*. New York: Praeger.

ECKHOLM, ERIC. 1986. "Significant rise in sea level now seems certain." *New York Times*, February 18.

—————. 1986. "Aging: Studies point toward ways to slow it," *New York Times*, June 10, Section C, pp. 1, 3.

EDGE, D. O., and MICHAEL MULKAY. 1976. *Astronomy Transformed*. New York: Wiley Interscience.

EDWARDS, CHRISTOPHER. 1979. *Crazy for God*. Englewood Cliffs, N.J.: Prentice-Hall.

EDWARDS, HARRY. 1969. *The Revolt of the Black Athlete*. New York: Free Press.

—————. 1973. *Sociology of Sport*. Homewood, Ill.: Dorsey.

—————. 1982. "Race in contemporary American sports," *National Forum*, 62, pp. 19–22.

EHRBAR, A. F. 1983. "Grasping the new unemployment," *Fortune*, May 16, pp. 107–112.

EHRLICH, ISAAC. 1975. "The deterrent effect of capital punishment: A question of life and death." *American Economic Review*, 65, pp. 397–417.

EHRLICH, PAUL R. 1968. *The Population Bomb*. New York: Macmillan.

—————, et al. 1977. *Ecoscience: Population, Resources, Environment*. San Francisco: Freeman.

—————, and ANNE EHRLICH. 1981. *Extinction*. New York: Random House.

EITZEN, D. STANLEY (ed.). 1982. *Sport in Contemporary Society: An Anthology*. New York: St. Martin's Press.

—————, (ed.). 1984. *Sport in American Society*. 2nd ed. New York: St. Martin's Press.

EKMAN, PAUL. 1985. *Telling Lies*. New York: Norton.

—————, et al. 1972. *Emotion in the Human Face*. New York: Pergamon Press.

ELDER, GLEN. 1974. *Children of the Great Depression*. Chicago: University of Chicago Press.

ELDREDGE, NILES. 1985. *Time Frames*. New York: Simon and Schuster.

ELIAS, NORBERT. 1978. *What Is Sociology?* New York: Columbia University Press.

ELKIND, DAVID. 1984. *All Grown Up and No Place to Go: Teenagers in Crisis*. Reading, Mass.: Addison-Wesley.

ELKINS, STANLEY M. 1963. *Slavery: A Problem in American Institutional and Intellectual Life*. New York: Grosset & Dunlap.

ELLING, RAY H. 1980. *Cross-National Study of Health Systems*. New Brunswick, N.J.: Transaction Books.

ELLIOTT, DELBERT S., DAVID HUIZINGA, and SUSANNE S. AGETON. 1985. *Explaining Delinquency and Drug Use*. Beverly Hills, Calif.: Sage.

ELLIS, ALBERT. 1970. "Group marriage: A possible alternative?" in Herbert A. Otto (ed.), *The Family in Search of a Future*. New York: Appleton-Century-Crofts.

ELLIS, LEE. 1979. "Toward neurologically-specific theories of criminal behavior." *Contemporary Sociology*, 8, pp. 372–376.

ELLUL, JACQUES. 1964. *The Technological Society*. New York: Knopf.

EMERY, ROBERT E., et al. 1984. "Divorce, children, and social policy," in Harold W. Stevenson and Alberta E. Siegal (eds.), *Child Development Research and Social Policy*. Chicago. University of Chicago Press.

ENGELS, FRIEDRICH. 1942. *The Origin of the Family, Private Property, and the State*. New York: International Publishing.

ENROTH, RONALD E. 1977. *Youth, Brainwashing, and Extremist Cults*. Grand Rapids, Mich.: Zondervan.

EPSTEIN, CYNTHIA FUCHS, and ROSE LAUD COSER (eds.). 1981. *Access to Power: Cross-National Studies of Women and Elites*. Boston: Allen and Unwin.

EPSTEIN, SAMUEL S. 1978. *The Politics of Cancer*. San Francisco: Sierra Club Books.

—————, LESTER BROWN, and CARL POPE. 1983. *Hazardous Waste in America*. San Francisco: Sierra Club Books.

ERMANN, DAVID M. and RICHARD J. LUNDMAN. 1982. *Corporate Deviance*. New York: Holt, Rinehart and Winston.

ETTMORE, E. M. 1980. *Lesbians, Women, and Society*. London: Routledge and Kegan Paul.

ETZIONI, AMITAI (ed.). 1969. *The Semi-Professions and Their Organization*. New York: Free Press.

—————. 1975. *A Comparative Analysis of Complex Organizations*. Revised and enlarged ed. Glencoe, Ill.: Free Press.

—————. 1982. *An Immodest Agenda: Rebuilding America before the Twenty-First Century*. New York: McGraw-Hill.

ETZIONI-HALEVY, EVA. 1981. *Social Change*. London: Routledge & Kegan Paul.

EVANS, CHRISTOPHER. 1979. *The Mico Millennium*. New York: Viking.

EVANS, LAURA J. 1978. "Sexual harassment: Women's hidden occupational hazard," in Jane R. Chapman and Margaret Gates (eds.), *The Victimization of Women*. Beverly Hills, Calif.: Sage.

EWEN, STUART, and ELIZABETH EWEN. 1982. *Channels of Desire: Mass Images and the Shaping of American Consciousness*. New York: McGraw-Hill.

FADERMAN, L. 1981. *Surpassing the Love of Men*. New York: Morrow.

FALK, RICHARD A., and SAMUEL S. KIM (eds.). 1980. *The War System: An Interdisciplinary Approach*. Boulder, Col.: Westview Press.

FALLOWS, JAMES. 1985. "The Case Against Credentialism." *Atlantic Monthly* (December), pp. 49–67.

FARBER, SUSAN I. 1981. *Identical Twins Reared Apart*. New York: Basic Books.

FARLEY, REYNOLDS. 1984. *Blacks and Whites: Narrowing the Gap?* Cambridge, Mass.: Harvard University Press.

FARRINGTON, BENJAMIN. 1949. *Greek Science, II*. London: Penguin.

FAST, JULIUS. 1970. *Body Language*. New York: Evans.

FAUST, BEATRICE. 1980. *Women, Sex, and Pornography*. New York: Macmillan.

FAUSTO-STERLING, ANNE. 1985. *Myths of Gender: Biological Theories about Women and Men*. New York: Basic Books.

FEAGIN, JOE R. 1975. *Subordinating the Poor: Welfare and American Beliefs*. Englewood Cliffs, N.J.: Prentice-Hall.

FEATHERMAN, DAVID. 1981. "Stratification and social mobility," in James Short (ed.), *The State of Sociology*. Beverly Hills, Calif.: Sage.

—————, and ROBERT M. HAUSER. 1978. *Opportunity and Change*. New York: Academic Press.

FEINSOD, ETHAN. 1981. *Awake in a Nightmare*. New York: Norton.

FELDMAN, KENNETH A., and THEODORE NEWCOMB. 1969. *The Impact of College upon Students*. San Francisco: Jossey-Bass.

FELIPE, N., and R. SOMMER. 1966. "Invasions of personal space." *Social Problems*, 14, pp. 206–214.

FESHBACH, MURRAY. 1984. "Soviet health problems," *Society*, March/April, 80–89.

FESTINGER, LEON, et al. 1956. *When Prophecy Fails*. New York: Harper & Row.

FETTNER, ANN GIUDICI and WILLIAM A. CHECK. 1984. *The Truth about AIDS: Evolution of an epidemic*. New York: Holt, Rinehart and Winston.

FEYERABEND, PAUL. 1982. *Science in a Free Society*. London: Verso.

FINCH, STUART C. 1979. "The study of atomic bomb survivors in Japan." *American Journal of Medicine*, 66, pp. 899–901.

FINE, GARY ALAN. 1984. "Negotiated orders and organizational cultures," in Ralph H. Turner (ed.), *Annual Review of Sociology*, 12. Palo Alto, Calif.: Annual Reviews.

FINKELHOR, DAVID. 1984. *Child Sexual Abuse: New Theory and Research*. New York: Free Press.

—————, et al. (eds.). 1983. *The Dark Side of Families*. Beverly Hills, Calif.: Sage.

FISCHER, CLAUDE S. 1975. "Toward a subcultural theory of urbanism." *American Journal of Sociology*, 80:6, 1319–1341.

—————. 1984. *The Urban Experience*. 2nd ed. New York: Harcourt Brace Jovanovich.

FISHMAN, PAMELA M. 1978. "Interaction: The work women do" *Social Problems*, 25, pp. 397–406.

—————. 1980. "Conversational insecurity," in Howard Giles, W. Peter Robinson and Philip M. Smith (eds.), *Language: Social and Psychological Perspectives*. New York: Pergamon Press.

FLAKE, CAROL. 1984. *Redemptorama: Culture, Politics, and the New Evangelicalism*. Garden City, N.Y.: Anchor.

FONER, ANNE. 1980. "The sociology of age stratification: A review of some recent publications." *Contemporary Sociology*, 9:6, 771–779.

—————. 1986. *Aging and Old Age: New Perspectives*. Englewood Cliffs, N.J.: Prentice-Hall.

FONER, NANCY. 1984. *Ages in Conflict*. New York: Columbia University Press.

FORD, CLELLAN S., and FRANK A. BEACH. 1951. *Patterns of Sexual Behavior*. New York: Harper & Row.

FORER, LUCILLE K. 1976. *The Birth Order Factor*. New York: David McKay.

FORM, WILLIAM. 1979. "Comparative industrial sociology and the convergence hypothesis," in Alex Inkeles, James Coleman, and Ralph H. Turner (eds.), *Annual Review of Sociology*, 5. Palo Alto, Calif: Annual Reviews.

FORSYTHE, ADRIAN, and KENNETH MIYATA. 1984. *Tropical Nature*. New York: Scribner's.

FOX, RENEE. 1957. "Training for uncertainty," in Robert K. Merton, George C. Reader and Patricia Kendall (eds.), *The Student Physician*. Cambridge, Mass: Harvard University Press.

—————. 1977. "The medicalization and demedicalization of American society." *Daedalus*, Winter.

FOX, THOMAS G., and S. M. MILLER. 1965. "Inter-country variations: Occupational stratification and mobility." *Studies in Comparative International Development*, 1, pp. 3–10.

—————, and S. M. MILLER. 1966. "Economic, political, and social determinants of mobility: An international cross-sectional analysis." *Acta Sociologica*, 9:1–2, 76–93.

FRAKER, SUSAN. 1984. "Why women aren't getting to the top." *Fortune*, April 16, pp. 40–45.

FRANK, JEROME D. 1982. *Sanity or Survival in the Nuclear Age*. 2nd ed. New York: Random House.

FRANKLIN, CLYDE W. 1984. *The Changing Definition of Masculinity*. New York: Plenum Press.

FRAZIER, E. FRANKLIN. 1963. *The Negro Church in America*. New York: Schocken.

FREDERICKSON, GEORGE M. 1981. *White Supremacy: A Comparative Study in American and South African History*. New York: Oxford University Press.

FREEDMAN, MARCIA, and IVAR BERG. 1978. "Investments in education: Public policies and private risks," in David E. Drew (ed.), *Competency, Careers, and College*. San Francisco: Jossey-Bass.

FREEMAN, HOWARD E., SOL LEVINE, and LEO G. REEDER (eds.). 1972. *Handbook of Medical Sociology*. 2nd ed. Englewood Cliffs, N.J.: Prentice-Hall.

FREEMAN, JO. 1975. *The Politics of Women's Liberation*. New York: David McKay.

————— (ed.). 1984. *Women: A Feminist Perspective*. 3rd ed. Palo Alto, Calif.: Mayfield.

FREEMAN, RICHARD. 1976. *The Overeducated American*. New York: Academic Press.

FREIDSON, ELIOT. 1970. *Profession of Medicine*. New York: Dodd, Mead.

—————. 1970b. *Professional Dominance*. Chicago: Aldine.

—————. 1975. *Doctoring Together*. New York: Elsevier.

—————. 1980. *Doctoring Together: A Study of Professional Social Control*. Chicago: University of Chicago Press.

FRIED, MORTON. 1967. *The Evolution of Political Society*. New York: Random House.

—————, MARVIN HARRIS, and ROBERT MURPHY. 1986 *War: The Anthropology of Armed Conflict and Aggression*. Garden City, N.Y.: Doubleday.

FRIEDL, ERNESTINE. 1975. *Women and Men: An Anthropologist's View*. New York: Holt, Rinehart and Winston.

FRIEDRICH, CARL J., and ZBIGNIEW K. BRZEZINSKI. 1965. *Totalitarian Dictatorship and Autocracy*. Cambridge, Mass.: Harvard University Press.

FRIEDRICHS, GUENTER, and ADAM SCHAFF (eds.). 1983. *Microelectronics and Society: A Report to the Club of Rome*. New York: Mentor.

FRITH, SIMON. 1982. *Sound Effects: Youth, Leisure, and the Politics of Rock and Roll*. New York: Pantheon.

FUCHS, VICTOR R. 1983. *How We Live: An Economic Perspective on Americans from Birth to Death*. Cambridge, Mass.: Harvard University Press.

—————. 1986. *The Health Economy*. Cambridge, Mass.: Harvard University Press.

GABRIEL, RICHARD A. 1986. *Military Incompetence: Why the American Military Doesn't Win*. New York: Hill and Wang/Farrar, Straus & Giroux.

GAENSBAUER, THEODORE, and SUSAN HIATT. 1984. *The Psychobiology of Affective Development*. Hillsdale, N.J.: Erlbaum.

GAGER, NANCY, and KATHLEEN SCHURR. 1976. *Sexual Assault*. New York: Grosset and Dunlap.

GAGNON, JOHN, and WILLIAM SIMON (eds.). 1967. *Sexual Deviance*. Chicago: Aldine.

—————, and WILLIAM SIMON. 1973. *Sexual Conduct: The Social Sources of Human Sexuality*. Chicago: Aldine.

GALBRAITH, JOHN KENNETH. 1966. *The Affluent Society*. Boston: Beacon.

—————. 1979. *The New Industrial State*. 3rd rev. ed. New York: New American Library.

GALTUNG, JOHN. 1971. "A structural theory of imperialism." *Journal of Peace Research*, 8:2, 81–117.

GAMSON, WILLIAM. 1968. *Power and Discontent*. Homewood, Ill.: Dorsey.

—————. 1975. *The Strategy of Social Protest*. Homewood, Ill.: Dorsey.

GANS, HERBERT J. 1962a. "Urbanism and suburbanism as ways of life," in Arnold M. Rose (ed.), *Human Behavior and Social Processes*. Boston: Houghton Mifflin.

—————. 1962b. *The Urban Villagers*. New York: Free Press.

————— (ed.). 1968. *People and Plans: Essays on Urban Problems and Solutions*. New York: Basic Books.

—————. 1973. *More Equality*. New York: Pantheon.

—————. 1979. *Deciding What's News*. New York: Pantheon.

GARDNER, HOWARD. 1981. *The Quest for Mind*. 2nd ed. Chicago: University of Chicago Press.

—————. 1983. *Frames of Mind: The Theory of Multiple Intelligences*. New York: Basic Books.

GARDNER, ROBERT W., BRYANT ROBEY, and PETER C. SMITH. 1985. *Asian Americans: Growth, Change, and Diversity*. Washington, D.C.: Population Reference Bureau.

GARFINKEL, HAROLD. 1956. "Conditions of successful degradation ceremonies." *American Journal of Sociology*, 61, pp. 420–424.

_____. 1967. *Studies in Ethnomethodology.* Englewood Cliffs, N.J.: Prentice-Hall.

_____. 1970. "The ethnomethodological paradigm," in Hans Peter Dreitzel (ed.), *Recent Sociology No. 2: Patterns of Communicative Behavior.* New York: Macmillan.

GARTNER, ALAN, COLIN CREER, and FRANK REISSMAN. 1982. *What Reagan Is Doing to Us.* New York: Harper & Row.

GASTON, JERRY. 1978. *The Reward System in British and American Science.* New York: Wiley.

GATHORNE-HARDY, JONATHAN. 1978. *The Old School Tie: The Phenomenon of the English Public School.* New York: Viking.

GEERTZ, CLIFFORD. 1968. "The impact of the concept of culture on the concept of man," in Yehudi A. Cohen (ed.), *Man and Adaptation: The Cultural Present.* Chicago: Aldine.

GELANTER, MARK, et al. 1979. "The Moonies: A psychological study of conversion membership in a contemporary religious sect." *American Journal of Psychiatry,* 136, pp. 165–170.

GELLES, RICHARD J. 1979. *Family Violence.* Beverly Hills, Calif.: Sage.

_____, and CLAIRE PEDRICK CORNELL (eds.). 1983. *International Perspectives on Family Violence.* Lexington, Mass.: Lexington Books.

_____, and CLAIRE PEDRICK CORNELL. 1985. *Intimate Violence in Families.* Beverly Hills, Calif.: Sage.

GERSHMAN, CARL. 1984. "Psychiatric abuse in the Soviet Union." *Society,* 21:5, 55–59.

GERVASI, TOM. 1986. *The Myth of Soviet Military Supremacy.* New York: Harper & Row.

GERZON, MARK. 1982. *A Choice of Heroes: The Changing Faces of American Manhood.* Boston: Houghton Mifflin.

GIBBS, JACK P. 1975. *Crime, Punishment, and Deterrence.* New York: Elsevier.

_____. 1981. *Norms, Deviance, and Social Control.* New York: Elsevier.

GILBERT, DENNIS, and JOSEPH A. KAHL. 1982. *The American Class Structure: A New Synthesis.* Homewood, Ill.: Dorsey.

GILDER, GEORGE. 1981. *Wealth and Poverty.* New York: Basic Books.

GINTIS, HERBERT. 1971. "Education and the characteristics of worker productivity." *American Economic Review,* 61, pp. 266–279.

GIROUARD, MARK. 1985. *Cities and People: An Architectural History.* New Haven: Yale University Press.

GLASER, BARNEY G., and ANSELM L. STRAUSS. 1965. *Awareness of Dying.* Chicago: Aldine.

_____. 1968. *Time for Dying.* Chicago: Aldine.

GLASGOW, DOUGLAS G. 1980. *The Black Underclass.* San Francisco: Jossey-Bass.

GLASSTONE, SAMUEL, and PHILIP J. DOLAN (eds.). 1977. *The Effects of Nuclear Weapons.* 3rd ed. Washington, D.C.: U.S. Department of Defense.

GLENN, NORVAL D., and CHARLES N. WEAVER. 1982. "Enjoyment of work by full-time workers in the U.S., 1955 and 1980." *Public Opinion Quarterly,* 46, pp. 459–470.

GLICK, PAUL C. 1979. "The Future of the American Family." *Current Population Reports, Bureau of the Census,* Special Studies, Series P-23, No. 78. Washington, D.C.: U.S. Government Printing Office.

GLOCK, CHARLES Y., and ROBERT N. BELLAH (eds.). 1976. *The New Religious Consciousness.* Berkeley, Calif.: University of California Press.

GLUECK, SHELDON, and ELEANOR GLUECK. 1956. *Physique and Delinquency.* New York: Harper & Row.

GOFFMAN, ERVING. 1959. *The Presentation of the Self in Everyday Life.* New York: Doubleday.

_____. 1961. *Asylums: Essays on the Social Situation of Mental Patients and Other Inmates.* Chicago: Aldine.

_____. 1963a. *Behavior in Public Places.* New York: Free Press.

_____. 1963b. *Stigma: Notes on the Management of Spoiled Identity.* Englewood-Cliffs, N.J.: Prentice-Hall.

_____. 1966. *Encounters.* Indianapolis: Bobbs-Merrill.

_____. 1967. *Interaction Ritual: Essays on Face-to-Face Behavior.* New York: Doubleday.

_____. 1969. *Strategic Interaction.* Philadelphia: University of Pennsylvania Press.

_____. 1971. *Relations in Public.* New York: Basic Books.

_____. 1974. *Frame Analysis: An Essay on the Organization of Experience.* New York: Harper & Row.

_____. 1976. *Gender Advertisements.* New York: Harper & Row.

GOLDENBERG, NAOMI. 1979. *Changing of the Gods.* Boston: Beacon Press.

GOLDFARB, WILLIAM. 1945. "Psychological privation in infancy and subsequent adjustment." *American Journal of Orthopsychiatry,* 15, pp. 247–253.

GOLDSTONE, JACK A. 1986. *Revolutions: Theoretical, Comparative, and Historical Studies.* San Diego, Calif.: Harcourt Brace Jovanovich.

GOLDTHORPE, JOHN H. 1980. *Social Mobility and Class Structure in Modern Britain.* London: Routledge & Kegan Paul.

GOLEMAN, DANIEL. 1984. "Order found in development of emotions." *New York Times,* June 19, Section C, pp. 1, 8.

GONDA, MATTHEW ALLEN. 1986. "The natural history of AIDS." *Natural History,* May, pp. 78–81.

GOODE, WILLIAM J. 1963. *World Revolution and Family Patterns.* New York: Free Press.

_____. 1982. *The Family.* 2nd ed. Englewood Cliffs, N.J.: Prentice-Hall.

GOODLAD, JOHN I. 1983. *A Place Called School.* New York: McGraw-Hill.

GORDON, MICHAEL. 1978. *The American Family: Past, Present, and Future.* New York: Random House.

_____. 1983. *The American Family in Social-Historical Perspective.* 3rd ed. New York: St. Martin's Press.

GORDON, MILTON M. 1961. "Assimilation in America: Theory and reality." *Daedalus,* 90, pp. 363–365.

_____. 1978. *Human Nature, Class, and Ethnicity.* New York: Oxford University Press.

GORDON, THEODORE J., HERBERT GERJUOY, and MARK ANDERSON. 1980. *Life-Extending Technologies: A Technology Assessment.* Elmsford, N.Y.: Pergamon Press.

GOTTFRIED, ROBERT S. 1983. *The Black Death: Natural and Human Disaster in Medieval Europe.* New York: Free Press.

GOUGH, KATHLEEN E. 1959. "The Nayars and the definition of marriage." *Journal of the Royal Anthropological Institute,* 89, pp. 23–24.

GOULD, ROGER L. 1978. *Transformations.* New York: Simon and Schuster.

GOULDNER, ALVIN W. 1970. *The Coming Crisis of Western Sociology.* New York: Avon.

_____. 1979. *The Future of Intellectuals and the Rise of the New Class.* New York: Seabury Press.

GOVE, WALTER R. (ed.). 1980. *The Labeling of Deviance: Evaluating a Perspective.* Beverly Hills, Calif.: Sage.

GRANOVETTER, MARK. 1973. *Getting a Job: A Study of Contacts and Careers.* Cambridge, Mass.: Harvard University Press.

GRANTHAM, P. 1984. *Torture in the Eighties.* London: Amnesty International Publications.

GREELEY, ANDREW M. 1976. *Ethnicity, Domination, and Inequality.* Beverly Hills, Calif.: Sage.

_____. 1977. *The American Catholic: A Social Portrait.* New York: Basic Books.

GREEN, MARK, and JACK NEWFIELD. 1980. "Who owns Congress?" *The Village Voice,* April 21, pp. 1, 16–22.

GREEN, PHILIP. 1981. *Pursuit of Inequality.* New York: Pantheon.

GREEN, RICHARD, and JOHN MONEY. 1969. *Transsexualism and Sex Reassignment.* Baltimore: Johns Hopkins University Press.

GREENSTEIN, FRED I. 1965. *Children and Politics.* New Haven: Yale University Press.

GREENWOOD, E. 1962. "Attributes of a profession," in S. Nosow and W. H. Form (eds.), *Man, Work and Society*. New York: Basic Books.

GREGERSEN, EDGAR. 1982. *Sexual Practices: The Story of Human Sexuality*. London: Mitchell Beazley.

GRIBBIN, JOHN. 1982. "The 1% advantage: Human vs. gorilla." *Science Digest,* August, pp. 73–77.

GRIFFIN, L. J., and K. A. ALEXANDER. 1978. "Schooling and socioeconomic attainments: High school and college influences." *American Journal of Sociology,* 84, pp. 319–347.

GROSS, MARTIN. 1978. *The Psychological Society*. New York: Random House.

GRUNEAU, RICHARD S. "Sport, social differentiation, and social inequality," in Donald W. Ball and John W. Loy (eds.), *Sport and Social Order*. Reading, Mass.: Addison-Wesley.

GRUSKY, DAVID B., and ROBERT M. HAUSER. 1984. "Comparative social mobility revisited: Models of convergence and divergence in 16 countries." *American Sociological Review,* 49, pp. 19–38.

GUERNEY, JOAN NEFF, and KATHLEEN J. TIERNEY. 1982. "Relative deprivation and social movements: A critical look at twenty years of theory and research." *Sociological Quarterly,* 23, pp. 33–47.

GUILBAUT, SERGE. 1983. *How New York Stole the Idea of Modern Art*. Chicago: University of Chicago Press.

GUINZBERG, SUZANNE. 1983. "Education's Earning Power." *Psychology Today,* 17 (October), pp. 20–21.

GUPTE, PRANAY. 1984. *The Crowded Earth: People and the Politics of Population*. New York: Norton.

GURR, TED. 1970. *Why Men Rebel*. Princeton, N.J.: Princeton University Press.

HAAS, AARON. 1979. *Teenage Sexuality*. New York: Macmillan.

HAAS, JACK, and WILLIAM SHAFIR. 1977. "The professionalization of medical students: Developing competence and a cloak of competence." *Symbolic Interaction,* 1, pp. 71–88.

HADDEN, JEFFREY K. 1969. *The Gathering Storm in the Churches*. Garden City, N.Y.: Doubleday.

—————, and CHARLES E. SWAN. 1981. *Prime Time Preachers: The Rising Power of Tele-Evangelism*. Reading, Mass.: Addison-Wesley.

HADLEY, ARTHUR T. 1986. *The Straw Giant*. New York: Random House.

HAGEN, EVERETT E. 1962. *On the Theory of Social Change: How Economic Growth Begins*. Homewood, Ill.: Dorsey.

HAGSTROM, WILLIAM O. 1965. *The Scientific Community*. New York: Basic Books.

—————. 1974. "Competition in science." *American Sociological Review,* 39, pp. 1–18.

HALBERSTAM, DAVID. 1979. *The Powers That Be*. New York: Dell.

HALL, EDWARD T. 1959. *The Silent Language*. New York: Doubleday.

—————. 1966. *The Hidden Dimension*. New York: Doubleday.

—————, and MILDRED R. HALL. 1976. "The sounds of silence," in Jeffrey E. Nash and James P. Spradley (eds.), *Sociology: A Descriptive Approach*. Chicago: Rand McNally.

—————. 1981. *Beyond Culture*. Garden City, N.Y.: Doubleday.

—————. 1983. *The Dance of Life: The Other Dimension of Time*. Garden City, N.Y.: Anchor.

HALL, FRANCINE S., and DOUGLAS T. HALL. 1979. *The Two-Career Couple*. Reading, Mass.: Addison-Wesley.

HALL, RICHARD H. 1982. *Organizations*. 3rd ed. Englewood Cliffs., N.J.: Prentice-Hall.

HALL, STEPHEN S. 1983. "The Flu," *Science '83,* 4:9, 56–64.

HAMMOND, PHILLIP E. (ed.). 1985. *The Sacred in a Secular Age: Toward Revision in the Scientific Study of Religion*. Berkeley, Calif.: University of California Press.

HANDEL, WARREN. 1982. *Ethnomethodology: How People Make Sense*. Englewood Cliffs, N.J.: Prentice-Hall.

HANSEN, MARCUS L. 1952. "The third generation in America" *Commentary,* 14:5, 492–500.

HARDESTY, DONALD L. 1977. *Ecological Anthropology*. New York: Wiley.

HARDESTY, SARAH, and NEHEMA JACOBS. 1986. *Success and Betrayal: The Crisis of Women in Corporate America*. New York: Franklin Watts.

HARE, A. PAUL. 1976 *Handbook of Small Group Research*. 2nd ed. New York: Free Press.

—————, et al. (eds.). 1965. *Small Groups: Studies in Social Interaction*. New York: Knopf.

—————, et al. (eds.). 1979. *South Africa: Sociological Analysis*. Cape Town: Oxford University Press.

HARLOW, HARRY F. 1958. "The nature of love." *American Psychologist,* 13, pp. 673–685.

—————. 1965. "The affectional systems," in Allan Schrier et al. (eds.), *Behavior of Nonhuman Primates: Modern Research Trends*. New York: Academic Press.

—————, and MARGARET K. HARLOW. 1962. "Social deprivation in monkeys." *Scientific American,* 207, pp. 137–147.

—————, and R. R. ZIMMERMAN. 1959. "Affectional responses in the infant monkey." *Science,* 130, pp. 421–423.

HARRINGTON, MICHAEL. 1984. *The New American Poverty*. New York: Holt, Rinehart and Winston.

HARRIS, C. D., and EDWARD L. ULLMAN. 1945. "The nature of cities." *The Annals of the American Academy of Political and Social Science,* 242, pp. 7–17.

HARRIS, MARVIN. 1974. *Cows, Pigs, Wars, and Witches: The Riddles of Culture*. New York: Random House.

—————. 1977. *Cannibals and Kings: The Origins of Cultures*. New York: Random House.

—————. 1980. *Cultural Materialism: The Struggle for a Science of Culture*. New York: Vintage.

—————. 1982. *America Now*. New York: Simon and Schuster.

—————. 1986. *Good to Eat: Riddles of Food and Culture*. New York: Simon and Schuster.

HARRON, FRANK, JOHN BURNSIDE, and TOM BEAUCHAMP. 1983. *Health and Human Values*. New Haven: Yale University Press.

HARTLEY, EUGENE. 1946. *Problems in Prejudice*. New York: King's Crown Press.

HARTMANN, HEIDI I. 1985. *Comparable Worth*. Washington, D.C.: National Academy of Sciences.

HAUSER, ROBERT M., and DAVID L. FEATHERMAN. 1977. *The Process of Stratification: Trends and Analysis*. New York: Academic Press.

—————, and DAVID L. FEATHERMAN. 1978. *Opportunity and Change*. New York: Academic Press.

HECHT, JEFF. 1984. *Beam Weapons: The Next Arms Race*. New York: Plenum.

HELLMAN, MARTIN (ed.). 1985. *Beyond War: A New Way of Thinking*. Palo Alto, Calif.: Beyond War.

HENDRICKS, JON, and C. DAVIS HENDRICKS. 1986. *Aging in Mass Society: Myths and Realities*. 3rd ed. Boston: Little, Brown.

HENLEY, NANCY M. 1977. *Body Politics: Power, Sex, and Nonverbal Communication*. Englewood Cliffs, N.J.: Prentice-Hall.

HENNIG, ROBIN MARANTZ. 1981. "The placebo effect: It's not all in your mind." *SciQuest,* 54, pp. 16–20.

HENRY, JULES. 1963. *Culture Against Man*. New York: Random House.

HENSLIN, JAMES M. 1975. *Introducing Sociology*. New York: Free Press.

—————, and MAE A. BRIGGS. 1971. "Dramaturgical desexualization: The sociology of the vaginal examination," in James M. Heslin (ed.), *Studies in the Sociology of Sex*. New York: Appleton-Century-Crofts.

—————— (ed.). 1985. *Marriage and Family in a Changing Society*. 2nd ed. New York: Free Press.

HERBERS, JOHN. 1984. "Political and religious shifts rekindle church-state issue." *New York Times,* September 2, pp. 1, 20.

HERDT, GILBERT. 1981. *Guardians of the Flutes: Idioms of Masculinity*. New York: McGraw-Hill.

_____ (ed.). 1982. *Rituals of Manhood.* Berkeley, Calif.: University of California Press.

_____. 1985. *Ritual Homosexuality in Melanesia.* Berkeley, Calif.: University of California Press.

HERITAGE, JOHN. 1984. *Garfinkel and Ethnomethodology.* New York: Basil Blackwell.

HERMAN, EDWARD S. 1981. *Corporate Control, Corporate Power.* New York: Cambridge University Press.

HERNANDEZ, CARROL A., et al. (eds.). 1976. *Chicanos: Social and Psychological Perspectives.* 2nd ed. St. Louis: Mosby.

HERNANDEZ, JOSE. 1974. *People, Power, and Policy: A New View on Population.* Palo Alto, Calif.: National Press Books.

HERSH, SEYMOUR M. 1970. *My Lai 4: A Report on the Massacre and Its Aftermath.* New York: Vintage.

_____. 1982. "The price of power: Kissinger, Nixon, and Chile." *Atlantic Monthly,* December, pp. 31–58.

HERTZ, ROSANNA. 1986. *More Equal than Others: Women and Men in Dual Career Marriages.* Berkeley, Calif.: University of California Press.

HERZBERG, FREDERICK. 1966. *Work and the Nature of Man.* Cleveland: World.

HESS, BETH B., and ELIZABETH MARKSON (eds.). 1984. *Growing Old in America.* 3rd ed. New Brunswick, N.J.: Transaction Books.

HESSLER, RICHARD M., et al. 1975. "Intraethnic diversity: Health care of the Chinese Americans." *Human Organization,* 34, pp. 253–262.

HEYL, BARBARA S. 1977. *The Madame as Entrepreneur: The Political Economy of a House of Prostitution.* New Brunswick, N.J.: Transaction Books.

HILBERMAN, ELAINE. 1976. *The Rape Victim.* New York: Basic Books.

HILGARTNER, STEPHEN, RICHARD C. BELL, and RORY O'CONNOR. 1982. *Nukespeak: The Selling of Nuclear Technology in America.* New York: Penguin.

HILL, JANE H. 1978. "Apes and language." *Annual Review of Anthropology.* Palo Alto, Calif.: Annual Reviews.

HINDELANG, MICHAEL J., et al. 1979. "Correlates of delinquency: The illusion of discrepancy between self-report and official measures." *American Sociological Review,* 44, pp. 995–1014.

_____, TRAVIS HIRSCHI, and JOSEPH G. WEIS. 1981. *Measuring Delinquency.* Beverly Hills, Calif.: Sage.

HIRSCHI, TRAVIS. 1969. *Causes of Delinquency.* Berkeley, Calif.: University of California Press.

HOBBES, THOMAS. 1958, originally published 1598. *Leviathan.* New York: Liberal Arts Press.

HOCHSCHILD, ARLIE RUSSELL. 1975. "The sociology of feeling and emotion," in Marcia Millman and Rosabeth Moss Kanter, *Another Voice.* Garden City, N.Y.: Doubleday/Anchor.

_____. 1979. "Emotion work, feeling rules, and social structure." *American Journal of Sociology,* 85:3, 55–575.

HODGE, ROBERT W., et al. 1964. "Occupational prestige in the United States, 1925–1963." *American Journal of Sociology,* 70, pp. 286–302.

_____, and DONALD J. TREIMAN. 1968. "Class identification in the United States." *American Journal of Sociology,* 73, pp. 535–547.

HOEPNER, B. J. (ed.). 1974. *Women's Athletics: Coping with Controversy.* Washington, D.C.: American Association for Health, Physical Education, and Recreation.

HOFFER, ERIC. 1951. *The True Believer.* New York: Holt, Rinehart and Winston.

HOFFMAN, ERIK P., and ROBBIN F. LAIRD (eds.). 1984. *The Soviet Polity in the Modern Era.* Hawthorne, N.Y.: Aldine.

HOLDEN, CONSTANCE. 1980. "Twins reunited." *Science,* 80:1, 55–59.

_____. 1983. "Simon and Kahn versus Global 2000." *Science,* 221, pp. 341–343.

HOLLANDER, PAUL. 1978. *Soviet and American Society: A Comparison.* New York: Oxford University Press.

HOLLIE, PAMELA G. "Keeping New Coke alive." *New York Times,* July 20, Section F, p. 6

HOLLINGSHEAD, AUGUST B. 1949. *Elmstown's Youth.* New York: Wiley.

_____, and FREDERICK REDLICH. 1958. *Social Class and Mental Disorder.* New York: Wiley.

HOLLOWAY, DAVID. 1983. *The Soviet Union and the Arms Race.* New Haven, Conn.: Yale University Press.

HOLMAN, M. CARL. 1985. "How to stop the miseducation of black children." *Ebony,* 40:12, 43–50.

HOLMSTROM, LINDA LYTLE, and ANN WOLBERT BURGESS. 1976. *The Victim of Rape: Institutional Reactions.* New York: Wiley.

HOMANS, GEORGE C. 1950. *The Human Group.* New York: Harcourt Brace Jovanovich.

_____. 1974. *Social Behavior: Its Elementary Forms.* Rev. ed. New York: Harcourt Brace Jovanovich.

HOOKER, EVELYN. 1965. "An empirical study of some relations between sexual patterns and gender identity in male homosexuals," in John Money (ed.), *Sex Research—New Developments.* New York: Holt, Rinehart and Winston.

_____. 1969. "Parental relations and male homosexuality in patient and nonpatient samples." *Journal of Consulting and Clinical Psychology,* 33, pp. 140–142.

HOPE, KEITH. 1982. "Vertical and nonvertical class mobility in three countries." *American Sociological Review,* 47, pp. 99–113.

HORN, MARJORIE C., and CHRISTINE A. BACHRACH. 1985. "Marriage and first intercourse, marital dissolution, and remarriage: United States, 1982. Washington, D.C.: National Center for Health Statistics.

HOROWITZ, IRVING LOUIS. 1967. *The Rise and Fall of Project Camelot.* Cambridge, Mass.: MIT Press.

HOSKIN, FRAN. 1980. "Women and Health: Genital and Sexual Mutilation." *International Journal of Women's Studies,* 3 (May-June), pp. 300–316.

HOUGAN, JIM. 1976. "The business of buying friends." *Harper's* (December), pp. 43–62.

HOYT, HOMER. 1939. *The Structure and Growth of Residential Neighborhoods in American Cities.* Washington, D.C.: Federal Housing Authority.

HUGHES, ROBERT. 1981. *The Shock of the New: Art in the Century of Change.* New York: Knopf.

HUMPHREY, CRAIG R. and FREDERICK R. BUTTEL. 1982. *Environment, Energy, and Society.* Belmont, Calif.: Wadsworth.

HUMPHREYS, LAUD. 1970. *Tearoom Trade: Impersonal Sex in Public Places.* Chicago: Aldine.

_____. 1972. *Out of the Closets: The Sociology of Homosexual Liberation.* Englewood Cliffs, N.J.: Prentice-Hall.

HUNT, MORTON. 1959. *The Natural History of Love.* New York: Knopf.

_____. 1974. *Sexual Behavior in the 1970's.* New York: Dell.

HUNTER, FLOYD. 1953. *Community Power Structure.* Chapel Hill: University of North Carolina Press.

_____. 1980. *Community Power Succession: Atlanta's Policy-Makers Revisited.* Chapel Hill: University of North Carolina Press.

HURN, CHRISTOPHER. 1985. *The Limits and Possibilities of Schooling: An Introduction to the Sociology of Education.* 2nd ed. Boston: Allyn and Bacon.

HUTNER, FRANCES E. 1986. *Equal Pay for Comparable Worth.* New York: Praeger.

HUTTON, J. H. 1963. *Caste in India: Its Nature, Functions, and Origins.* 4th ed. London: Oxford University Press.

HYDE, JANET S. 1981. "How large are cognitive gender differences?" *American Psychologist,* 36, pp 892–901.

_____. 1985. *Half the Human Experience: The Psychology of Women.* 3rd ed. Lexington, Mass.: Lexington Books.

HYMAN, HERBERT H. 1969. *Political Socialization: A Study in the Psychology of Political Behavior.* New York: Free Press.

_____, and CHARLES R. WRIGHT. 1979. *Education's Lasting Influence on Values.* Chicago: University of Chicago Press.

_____, et al. 1975. *The Enduring Effects of Education.* Chicago: University of Chicago Press.

ILCHMAN, ALICE S., et al. 1985. *Women's Work, Men's Work: Sex Segregation on the Job.* Washington, D.C.: National Academy Press.

ILLICH, IVAN. 1976. *Medical Nemesis: The Expropriation of Health.* New York: Pantheon.

IMPERATO, PASCAL J. 1985. *Acceptable Risks.* New York: Viking.

INCIARDY, JAMES A. (ed.). 1981. *The Drugs-Crime Connection.* Beverly Hills, Calif.: Sage.

INKELES, ALEX. 1968. *Social Change in Soviet Russia.* Cambridge, Mass.: Harvard University Press.

——————. 1983. *Exploring Individual Modernity.* New York: Columbia University Press.

——————, and PETER H. ROSSI. 1956. "National comparisons of occupational prestige." *American Journal of Sociology,* 66, pp. 329–339.

——————, and DAVID H. SMITH. 1974. *Becoming Modern: Individual Change in Six Developing Countries.* Cambridge, Mass.: Harvard University Press.

INSEL, PAUL, and RUDOLF MOOS (eds.). 1974. *Health and the Social Environment.* Lexington, Mass.: D. C. Heath.

IRONS, PETER. 1983. *Justice at War.* New York: Oxford University Press.

JACKSON, DONALD. 1974. "Justice for none." *New Times,* 2, January 11, pp. 48–57.

JACO, E. GARTLEY (ed.). 1979. *Patients, Physicians, and Illness.* 3rd ed. New York: Free Press.

JACOBS, JANE. 1961. *The Death and Life of Great American Cities.* New York: Random House.

JACOBSON, GARY C. 1980. *Money in Congressional Elections.* New Haven: Yale University Press.

JAMES, DAVIS. 1982. "Up and down opportunity's ladder." *Public Opinion,* 5:3, pp. 11–15, 48–51.

JANIS, IRVING L. 1972. *Victims of Groupthink.* Boston: Houghton Mifflin.

——————, and LEON MANN. 1977. *Decision Making: A Psychological Analysis of Conflict, Choice, and Commitment.* New York: Free Press.

JAROS, DEAN. 1974. *Socialization to Politics.* New York: Praeger.

JENCKS, CHRISTOPHER. 1980. "Heredity, environment, and public policy reconsidered," *American Sociological Review,* 45, pp. 723–736.

——————. 1985. "How poor are the poor?" *New York Review of Books,* 32:9, 41–49.

——————, et al. 1972. *Inequality: A Reassessment of the Effect of Family and Schooling in America.* New York: Basic Books.

——————, et al. 1979. *Who Gets Ahead? The Determinants of Economic Success in America.* New York: Basic Books.

JENKINS, J. CRAIG. 1983. "Resource mobilization theory and the study of social movements." *Annual Review of Sociology,* 9. Palo Alto, Calif.: Annual Reviews.

JENNINGS, HUMPHREY. 1985. *Pandemonium: The Coming of the Machine as Seen by Contemporary Observers, 1660–1886.* Chicago: University of Chicago Press.

JENNINGS, M. KENT, and RICHARD G. NIEMI. 1974. *The Political Character of Adolescence.* Princeton, N.J.: Princeton University Press.

JENSEN, ARTHUR. 1969. "How much can be we boost IQ and scholastic achievement?" *Howard Educational Review,* 39, pp. 273–274.

——————. 1979. *Bias in Mental Testing.* New York: Free Press.

JERVIS, ROBERT. 1984. *The Illogic of American Nuclear Strategy.* Ithaca, N.Y.: Cornell University Press.

JOHNSON, GREGORY. 1976. "The Hare Krishna movement in San Francisco," in Charles Y. Glock and Robert N. Bellah (eds.), *The New Religious Consciousness.* Berkeley, Calif.: University of California Press.

JOHNSON, NORRIS, JAMES C. STEMLER, and DEBORAH HUNTER. 1977. "Crowd behavior as 'risky shift': A laboratory experiment." *Sociometry,* 40, pp. 183–187.

JOHNSTONE, RONALD L. 1983. *Religion and Society in Interaction: The Sociology of Religion.* 2nd ed. Englewood Cliffs, N.J.: Prentice-Hall.

JONAS, STEPHEN. 1978. *Medical Mystery: The Training of Doctors in the United States.* New York: Norton.

JONES, ELSIE F., et al. 1985. "Teenage pregnancy in developed countries: Determinants and policy implications." *Family Planning Perspectives,* 17:2, 53–63.

JONES, LANDON. 1981. *Great Expectations: America and the Baby Boom Generation.* New York: Ballantine.

JORGENSEN, JAMES. 1980. *The Graying of America.* New York: Dial Press.

JOSEPHY, ALVIN M. 1982. *Now that the Buffalo's Gone: A Study of Today's American Indians.* New York: Knopf.

JUDAH, J. STILLSON. 1974. *Hare Krishna and the Counterculture.* New York: Wiley.

JUDSON, HORACE FREELAND. 1985. "Who shall play God?" *Science Digest,* May, pp. 52–54, 82–83.

JUSTICE, BLAIR, and RITA JUSTICE. 1979. *The Broken Taboo: Sex in the Family.* New York: Human Sciences Press.

KAGAN, JEROME. 1984. *Emotions, Cognition, and Behavior.* New York: Cambridge University Press.

KAHN, HERMAN. 1979. *World Economic Development.* New York: Morrow.

KALETSKY, ANATOLE. 1985. *The Costs of Default.* New York: Priority Press.

KAMIN, LEON J. 1975. *The Science and Politics of I.Q.* Hillsdale, N.J.: Erlbaum.

——————. 1986. "Is crime in the genes? The answer may depend on who chooses what evidence." *Scientific American,* February, pp. 22–27.

KANTER, ROSABETH MOSS. 1973. *Communes: Creating and Managing the Collective Life.* New York: Harper & Row.

——————. 1977. *Work and Family in the United States.* New York: Russell Sage Foundation.

——————, and BARRY STEIN (eds.). 1979. *Life in Organizations: Workplaces as People Experience Them.* New York: Basic Books, 1979.

KAPLAN, H. ROY. 1985. "Lottery winners and work commitment." *Journal of the Institute for Socioeconomic Studies,* 10:2, 82–94.

KARNOW, STANLEY. 1984. *Vietnam: A History.* New York: Penguin.

KARP, DAVID, and WILLIAM YOELS. 1986. *Sociology and Everyday Life.* Itasca, Ill.: F. E. Peacock.

——————, and WILLIAM C. YORK. 1982. *Experiencing the Life Cycle: A Social Psychology of Aging.* Springfield, Ill.: Charles C. Thomas.

KART, GARY S. 1985. *The Social Realities of Aging.* 2nd ed. Boston: Allyn and Bacon.

KASER, MICHAEL. 1976. *Health Care in the Soviet Union and Eastern Europe.* Boulder, Col.: Westview Press.

KATZ, ARTHUR M. 1982. *Life After Nuclear War.* Cambridge, Mass.: Ballinger.

KATZ, JAY. 1984. *The Silent World of Doctor and Patient.* New York: Free Press.

——————. 1986. *The Silent World of Doctor and Patient.* Chicago: University of Chicago Press.

KAYE, KENNETH. 1983. *The Mental and Social Life of Babies: How Parents Create Persons.* Chicago: University of Chicago Press.

KEELEY, CHARLES B. 1982. "Illegal migration." *Scientific American,* 246 (March), pp. 41–47.

KELLERMANN, ARTHUR L., and DONALD T. REAY. 1986. "Protection or peril? An analysis of firearm-related deaths in the home." *New England Journal of Medicine,* 314:24, pp. 1557–1560.

KELLY, DEAN M. 1972. *Why the Conservative Churches Are Growing: A Study in the Sociology of Religion.* New York: Harper & Row.

KELLY, RAYMOND C. 1977. *Etoro Social Structure: A Study in Cultural Contradiction.* Ann Arbor: University of Michigan Press.

KEMNITZER, L. 1971. "Yuwipi medicine: Healing and the Indian response to the white man's culture." Paper presented at the meeting of the Society for Applied Anthropology, Miami, Fla., April.

KEMPE, C. HENRY, and RAY E. HELFER (eds.). 1980. *The Battered Child.* 3rd ed. Chicago: University of Chicago Press.

KEMPER, THEODORE D. 1976. "Marxist and functionalist theories of the study of stratification." *Social Forces*, 54:3, 559–578.

———. 1978. "Toward a sociology of emotions." *American Sociologist*, 13, pp. 30–41.

KENNAN, GEORGE. 1982. *The Nuclear Delusion.* New York: Pantheon.

KEPHART, WILLIAM M. 1983. *Extraordinary Groups: The Sociology of Unconventional Life-Styles.* 2nd ed. New York: St. Martin's Press.

KERBO, HAROLD R. 1983. *Social Stratification and Inequality: Class Conflict in the United States.* New York: McGraw-Hill.

KESSLER, RONALD C., and PAUL D. CLEARY. 1980. "Social class and psychological distress." *American Sociological Review*, 45, pp. 463–478.

KESSLER-HARRIS, ALICE. 1983. *Out to Work: A History of Wage-Earning Women in the United States.* New York: Oxford University Press.

KETT, JOSEPH F. 1979. *Rites of Passage.* New York: Basic Books.

KIEV, ARI. 1968. *Curanderismo: Mexican American Folk Psychiatry.* New York: Free Press.

KINSEY, ALFRED C., et al. 1948. *Sexual Behavior in the Human Male.* Philadelphia: W. B. Saunders.

———, et al. 1953. *Sexual Behavior in the Human Female.* Philadelphia: W. B. Saunders.

KIRKHAM, GEORGE L. 1971. "Homosexuality in prison," in James M. Henslin (ed.), *Studies in the Sociology of Sex.* New York: Appleton-Century-Crofts.

KITANO, HARRY L. 1976. *Japanese Americans: The Evolution of a Subculture.* 2nd ed. Englewood Cliffs, N.J.: Prentice-Hall.

KITTRIE, NICHOLAS N. 1974. *The Right to Be Different: Deviance and Enforced Therapy.* Baltimore: Penguin.

KLANDERMANS, BERT. 1984. "Mobilization and participation: Social psychological explanations of resource mobilization theory." *American Sociological Review*, 49, pp. 583–600.

KLAPP, ORIN. 1969. *Collective Search for Identity.* New York: Holt, Rinehart and Winston.

KLEIN, VIOLA. 1975. *The Feminine Character: History of an Ideology.* Urbana, Ill.: University of Illinois Press.

KLEINMAN, ARTHUR. 1979. Patients and Healers in the Context of Culture. Berkeley, Calif.: University of California Press.

———, and BYRON GOOD (eds.). 1985. *Culture and Depression: Studies in the Anthropology and Cross-Cultural Psychiatry of Affect and Disorder.* Berkeley, Calif.: University of California Press.

KLEMESRUD, JUDY. 1981. "Voice of authority: Still male." *New York Times*, February 2, p. 16.

KLUCKHOHN, CLYDE. 1948. "As an anthropologist views it," in Albert Deutch (ed.), *Sex Habits of American Men.* New York: Prentice-Hall.

———. 1962. "Universal categories of culture," in Sol Tax (ed.), *Anthropology Today: Selections.* Chicago: University of Chicago Press.

KLUEGEL, JAMES R., and ELIOT R. SMITH. 1986. *Beliefs about Inequality: Americans' Views of What Is and What Ought to Be.* Hawthorne, N.Y.: Aldine.

KNAPP, JACQUELYN J., and ROBERT N. WHITEHURST. 1978. "Sexually open marriages and relationships: Issues and prospects," in Bernard I. Murstein (ed.), *Exploring Intimate Life Styles.* New York: Springer.

KNOWLES, JOHN H. 1977. "The responsibility of the individual." *Daedalus*, 106 (Winter), pp. 57–80.

KOCHEN, MANFRED, and KARL W. DEUTCH. 1980. *Decentralization.* Cambridge, Mass.: Oelgeschlager, Gunn, and Haine.

KOESTLER, ARTHUR. 1959. *The Sleepwalkers: A History of Man's Changing View of the Universe.* London: Hutchinson.

KOGAN, N., and WALLACH, M. A. 1964. *Risk Taking: A Study in Cognition and Personality.* New York: Holt, Rinehart and Winston.

KOHLBERG, LAWRENCE. 1966. "A cognitive-developmental analysis of children's sex-role concepts and attitudes," in Eleanor E. Maccoby (ed.), *The Development of Sex Differences.* Palo Alto, Calif.: Stanford University Press.

———. 1969. "Stage and sequence: The cognitive-development approach to socialization," in David A. Goslin (ed.), *Handbook of Socialization Theory and Research.* Chicago: Rand McNally.

KOHN, ALEXANDER. 1986. *False Prophets.* New York: Basil Blackwell.

KOHN, MELVIN L. 1963. "Social class and parent-child relationships: An interpretation." *American Journal of Sociology*, 68, pp. 471–480.

———. 1971. "Bureaucratic man: A portrait and an interpretation." *American Sociological Review*, 36, pp. 461–474.

———. 1973. "Social class and schizophrenia: A critical review and reformulation," *Schizophrenia Bulletin*, 7 (Winter), pp. 60–79.

———. 1976. "Occupational structure and alienation," *American Journal of Sociology*, 82, pp. 111–130.

———. 1977. *Class and Conformity.* 2nd ed. Homewood, Ill.: Dorsey.

———. 1978. "The benefits of bureaucracy." *Human Nature*, August.

KOISTINEN, PAUL. 1980. *The Military Industrial Complex.* New York: Praeger.

KOLLOCK, PETER, PHILIP BLUMSTEIN, and PEPPER SCHWARTZ. 1985. "Sex and power in interaction: Conversational privileges and duties." *American Sociological Review*, 50:1, 34–46.

KOMAROVSKY, MIRRA. 1962. *Blue-Collar Marriage.* New York: Random House.

———. 1973. "Cultural contradictions and sex roles: The masculine case." *American Journal of Sociology*, 78, pp. 873–884.

KORNHAUSER, RUTH ROSNER. 1978. *Social Sources of Delinquency.* Chicago: University of Chicago Press.

KORNHAUSER, WILLIAM. 1966. "'Power elite' or 'veto groups'?" in Reinhard Bendix and Seymour Martin Lipset (eds.), *Class, Status, and Power.* 2nd ed. New York: Free Press.

KRAMARAE, CHERIS. 1980. *The Voices and Words of Men and Women.* Oxford: Pergamon Press.

KRAUSE, ELLIOT A. 1977. *Power and Illness: The Political Sociology of Health and Medical Care.* New York: Elsevier.

KRICUS, RICHARD. 1976. *Pursuing the American Dream: White Ethnics and the New Populism.* Bloomington, Ind.: Indiana University Press.

KROHN, MARVIN D., and MASSEY, JAMES L. "Social control and delinquent behavior: An examination of the social bond." *The Sociological Quarterly*, 21, pp. 529–543.

KÜBLER-ROSS, ELISABETH. 1969. *On Death and Dying.* New York: Macmillan.

———. 1972. "Facing up to death." *Today's Education*, 16, pp. 30–32.

———. 1975. *Death: The Final Stage of Growth.* Englewood Cliffs, N.J.: Prentice-Hall.

KUHN, MANFORD, and THOMAS S. MCPARTLAND. 1954. "An empirical investigation of self-attitudes." *American Sociological Review*, 19, pp. 68–76.

KUHN, THOMAS S. 1962. *The Structure of Scientific Revolutions.* Chicago: University of Chicago Press.

KUMAR, KRISHNA (ed.). 1980. *Transnational Enterprises: Their Impact on Third World Societies and Cultures.* Boulder, Colo: Westview Press.

KUPER, LEO. (ed.). 1975. *Race, Science, and Society.* New York: Columbia University Press.

KURTZ, RICHARD A., and H. PAUL CHALFANT. 1984. *Sociology of Medicine and Illness.* Boston: Allyn and Bacon.

KWITNY, JONATHAN. 1984. *Endless Enemies: The Making of an Unfriendly World.* New York: Congdon and Weed.

LA BARRE, WESTON. 1954. *The Human Animal.* Chicago: University of Chicago Press.

LACY, W. B., J. L. BOKEMEIER, and J. M. SHEPHARD. 1983. "Job attribute preference and work commitment in the United States." *Personnel Psychology*, 36, pp. 315–319.

LAKOFF, SANFORD A. 1977. "Scientists, technologists, and political power," in Ina Spiegel-Rösing and Derek de Solla Price (eds.), *Science, Technology, and Society.* Beverly Hills, Calif.: Sage.

LANDES, DAVID S. 1983. *Revolution in Time: Clocks and the Making of the Modern World.* Cambridge, Mass.: Harvard University Press.

LANE, DAVID. 1976. *The Socialist Industrial State.* London: Allen and Unwin.

_____. 1978. *Politics and Society in the U.S.S.R.* New York: New York University Press.

LANE, HARLAN. 1976. *The Wild Boy of Aveyron.* Cambridge, Mass.: Harvard University Press.

LANER, MARY RIEGE. 1974. "Prostitution as an illegal vocation: A sociological overview," in Clifton D. Bryant (ed.), *Deviant Behavior.* Chicago: Rand McNally.

LANTERNARI, VITTORIO. 1963. *Religions of the Oppressed: A Study of Modern Messianic Cults.* New York: Knopf.

LAPHAM, LEWIS H., et al. 1984. "On the place of pornography," *Harper's,* November, pp. 32–45.

LAPIDUS, GAIL WARSHOFSKY. 1978. *Women in Soviet Society.* Berkeley, Calif.: University of California Press.

LAPIERE, RICHARD T. 1934. "Attitudes versus action." *Social Forces,* 13, pp. 230–237.

LARSON, DONALD E., and IRVING ROOTMAN. 1976. "Physician role performance and patient satisfaction." *Social Science and Medicine,* 10, pp. 29–32.

LARSON, MARGALI SARFATTI. 1977. *The Rise of Professionalism: A Sociological Analysis.* Berkeley: University of California Press.

LARWOOD, LAURIE, ANN H. STROMBERG, and BARBARA A. GUTEK (eds.). 1985. *Women and Work.* Beverly Hills, Calif.: Sage.

LASCH, CHRISTOPHER. 1977. *Haven in a Heartless World: The Family Besieged.* New York: Basic Books.

_____. 1979. *The Culture of Narcissism.* New York: Norton.

LASLETT, PETER. 1971. *The World We Have Lost.* 2nd ed. New York: Scribner's.

_____. 1977. "Characteristics of the Western family considered over time." *Journal of Family History,* 2:2, 89–115.

_____, and RICHARD WALL (eds.). 1972. *Household and Family in Past Time.* Cambridge, Eng.: Cambridge University Press.

LASSWELL, HAROLD D. 1936. *Politics: Who Gets What, When, and How.* New York: McGraw-Hill.

LATANÉ, BIBB, and JOHN M. DARLEY. 1968. "Group inhibition of bystander intervention." *Journal of Personality and Social Psychology,* 8, pp. 377–383.

_____, and JOHN M. DARLEY. 1969. "Bystander apathy." *American Scientist,* 57, pp. 244–268.

_____, and JEAN A. RODIN. 1969. "A lady in distress: Inhibiting effects of friends and strangers on bystander intervention." *Journal of Experimental Social Psychology,* 5, pp. 189–202.

LAUER, ROBERT H. 1982. *Perspectives on Social Change.* 3rd ed. Boston: Allyn and Bacon.

LE BON, GUSTAVE. 1960, originally published 1895. *The Mind of the Crowd.* New York: Viking.

LEDERER, LAURA (ed.). 1980. *Take Back the Night: Women on Pornography.* New York: Morrow.

LEE, RICHARD B. 1968. "What hunters do for a living, or how to make out on scarce resources," in Richard B. Lee and Irvin DeVore (eds.), *Man the Hunter.* Chicago: Aldine.

_____. 1979. *The !Kung San: Men, Women, and Work in a Foraging Society.* New York: Cambridge University Press.

LEHMAN, EDWARD W., and AMITAI ETZIONI (eds.). 1980. *Sociology of Complex Organizations.* 3rd ed. New York: Holt, Rinehart and Winston.

LEITER, KENNETH. 1980. *A Primer on Ethnomethodology.* New York: Oxford University Press.

LEMERT, EDWIN M. 1951. *Social Pathology.* New York: McGraw-Hill.

_____. 1967. *Human Deviance, Social Problems, and Social Control.* Englewood Cliffs, N.J.: Prentice-Hall.

_____. 1974. "Beyond Mead: The societal reaction to deviance." *Social Problems,* 21, pp. 457–468.

LENGERMAN, PATRICIA M., and RUTH A. WALLACE. 1985. *Gender in America.* Englewood Cliffs, N.J.: Prentice-Hall.

LENSKI, GERHARD. 1966. *Power and Privilege: A Theory of Social Stratification.* New York: McGraw-Hill.

_____, and JEAN LENSKI. 1982. *Human Societies.* 4th ed. New York: McGraw-Hill.

LEO, JOHN. 1984. "The revolution is over." *Time,* April 9, pp. 74–83.

LEONARD, KAREN ISAKSEN. 1978. *Social History of an Indian Caste.* Berkeley, Calif.: University of California Press.

LEONARD, WILBERT M. 1980. *A Sociological Perspective of Sport.* Minneapolis: Burgess.

LEONTIEF, WASSILY, and FAYE DUCHIN. 1983. *Military Spending.* New York: Oxford University Press.

LERNER, DANIEL. 1958. *The Passing of Traditional Society.* New York: Free Press.

LERNER, M. J., and C. H. SIMMONS. 1966. "Observer's reaction to the 'innocent victim': Compassion or rejection?" *Journal of Personality and Social Psychology,* 4, pp. 203–210.

LEVIN, JACK, and WILLIAM C. LEVIN. 1980. *Prejudice and Discrimination against the Elderly.* Belmont, Calif.: Wadsworth.

_____. 1982. *The Functions of Prejudice.* 2nd ed. New York: Harper & Row.

LEVIN, SAUL V. 1984. *Radical Departures: Desperate Detours to Growing Up.* New York: Harcourt Brace Jovanovich.

LEVINE, ADELINE GORDON. 1982. *Love Canal: Science, Politics, and People.* Lexington, Mass.: Lexington Books.

LEVINSON, DANIEL. 1978. *Seasons of a Man's Life.* New York: Knopf.

LÉVI-STRAUSS, CLAUDE. 1966. *The Savage Mind.* Chicago: University of Chicago Press.

LEVITAN, SAR A., and RICHARD S. BELOUS. 1981. *What's Happening to the American Family?* Baltimore: Johns Hopkins University Press.

LEWIS, KEVIN N. 1979. "The Prompt and Delayed Effects of Nuclear War." *Scientific American,* 241 (July), pp. 35–47.

LEWIS, MICHAEL. 1978. *The Culture of Inequality.* New York: New American Library.

LI, WEN LANG. 1982. "Chinese Americans: Exclusion from the Melting Pot," in Anthony G. Dworkin and Rosalind J. Dworkin (eds.), *The Minority Report* (2nd ed.). New York: Holt, Rinehart and Winston.

LIAZOS, ALEXANDER. 1972. "The poverty of the sociology of deviance: Nuts, sluts, and preverts." *Social Problems,* 20, pp. 103–120.

LIBBY, ROGER W. 1978. "Creative singlehood as a life style: Beyond marriage as a rite of passage," in Bernard I. Murstein (ed.), *Exploring Intimate Life Styles.* New York: Springer.

LIEBERSON, STANLEY. 1980. *A Piece of the Pie.* Berkeley: University of California Press.

_____. 1982. "Stereotypes: Their Consequences for Race and Ethnic Relations," in Robert M. Hauser et al. (eds.), *Social Structure and Behavior: Essays in Honor of William Hamilton Sewell.* New York: Academic Press.

LIEBMAN, ROBERT C., and ROBERT WUTHNOW (eds.). 1983. *The New Christian Right: Mobilization and Legitimation.* Hawthorne, N.Y.: Aldine.

LIEBMAN-SMITH, RICHARD. 1986. *The Question of AIDS.* New York: New York Academy of Sciences.

LIEBOW, ELLIOT. 1967. *Tally's Corner: A Study of Negro Streetcorner Men.* Boston: Little, Brown.

LIENHARDT, GODFREY. 1966. *Social Anthropology.* London: Oxford University Press.

LIFTON, ROBERT J. 1967. *Death in Life: Survivors of Hiroshima.* New York: Random House.

_____, and KAI ERIKSON. 1982. "Survivors of Nuclear War: Psychological and Communal Breakdown," in Eric Chivian et al. (eds), *Last Aid: The Medical Dimensions of Nuclear War.* San Francisco: Freeman.

LIGHT, IVAN. 1983. *Cities in World Perspective.* New York: Macmillan.

LIGHTFOOT, SARAH LAWRENCE. 1983. *The Good High School.* New York: Basic Books.

LIN, NAM, WALTER M. ENSLER, and JOHN C. VAUGHN. 1981. "Social resources and strength of ties: Structural factors in occupational status attainment." *American Sociological Review,* 46, pp. 393–405.

LINCOLN, ERIC C. 1974. *The Black Church since Frazier.* New York: Schocken.

LINDSEY, ROBERT. 1984. "Scientology chief got millions, ex-aides say." *New York Times,* July 11, pp. 1, 21.

LINTON, RALPH. 1936. *The Study of Man.* New York: Appleton-Century-Crofts.

—————. 1943. "Nativistic movements." *American Anthropologist,* 45, pp. 230–240.

—————. 1945. *The Cultural Background of Personality.* New York: Free Press.

LIPKOWITZ, MARTIN H., and SUDHARAM IDUPUGANTI. 1983. "Diagnosing schizophrenia in 1980: A survey of U.S. psychiatrists." *American Journal of Psychiatry,* 140, pp. 52–55.

LIPSET, SEYMOUR MARTIN. 1959a. "Democracy and working-class authoritarianism." *American Sociological Review,* 24, pp. 482–501.

—————. 1959b. *Political Man.* New York: Doubleday.

—————. 1959c. "Some social prerequisites for democracy: Economic development and political legitimacy." *American Political Science Review,* 53, pp. 74–86.

—————. 1973. "Commentary: Social stratification research and Soviet scholarship," in Murray Yanovitch and Westley A. Fischer (trans. and eds.), *Social Stratification and Mobility in the USSR.* White Plains, N.Y.: International Arts and Sciences Press.

—————, et al. 1956. *Union Democracy: The Inside Politics of the International Typographical Union.* Glencoe, Ill.: Free Press.

—————. 1972. "Social mobility and equal opportunity." *Public Interest,* 29 (Fall), pp. 90–108.

—————— (ed.). 1979. *The Third Century: America as a Postindustrial Society.* Chicago: University of Chicago Press.

—————, and REINHARD BENDIX. 1959. *Social Mobility in Industrial Society.* Berkeley, Calif.: University of California Press.

LITWACK, LEON F. 1979. *Been in the Storm So Long: The Aftermath of Slavery.* New York: Knopf.

LLANES, JOSE. 1982. *Cuban Americans.* Cambridge, Mass.: Abt Books.

LOCKWOOD, DANIEL. 1979. *Prison Sexual Violence.* New York: Elsevier.

LOCKWOOD, DAVID. 1956. "Some notes on 'The Social System'." *British Journal of Sociology,* 7, p. 2.

LODGE, JULIET. 1981. *Terrorism: A Challenge to the State.* New York: St. Martin's Press.

LOFLAND, JOHN. 1966. *Doomsday Cult.* Englewood Cliffs, N.J.: Prentice-Hall.

—————. 1969. *Deviance and Identity.* Englewood Cliffs, N.J.: Prentice-Hall.

—————. 1977. *Doomsday Cult.* Enlarged ed. New York: Irvington.

LOFLAND, LYNN H. 1979. *The Craft of Dying.* Beverly Hills, Calif.: Sage.

LOMBROSO, CESARE. 1911. *Crime: Its Causes and Remedies.* Boston: Little, Brown.

LONDON, HOWARD B. 1978. *The Culture of a Community College.* New York: Praeger.

LONG, FRANKLIN A., DONALD HAFFNER, and JERRY BOUTWELL (eds.). 1986. *Weapons in Space.* New York: Norton.

LOOMIS, CAROL J. 1982. "The madness of executive compensation." *Fortune,* July 12, pp. 41–51.

LOPEZ, ADALBERTO (ed.). 1980. *The Puerto Ricans.* Cambridge, Mass.: Schenkman.

LORBER, JUDITH. 1975. "Good patients and problem patients: Conformity and deviance in a general hospital." *Journal of Health and Social Behavior,* 16, pp. 213–225.

LORENZ, KONRAD. 1966. *On Aggression.* New York: Harcourt Brace Jovanovich.

LORTIE, DAN C. 1975. *School Teacher: A Sociological Study.* Chicago: University of Chicago Press.

LOWE, MARIAN, and RUTH HUBBARD (eds.). 1983. *Woman's Nature: Rationalizations of Inequality.* New York: Pergamon Press.

LOWIE, ROBERT H. 1940. *Introduction to Cultural Anthropology.* New York: Holt, Rinehart and Winston.

LOWN, BERNARD. 1982. "Physicians and nuclear war," in Eric Chivian et al. (eds.), *Last Aid: The Medical Dimensions of Nuclear War.* San Francisco: Freeman.

LOY, JOHN W. 1969. "The study of sport and social mobility," in Gerald S. Kenyon (ed.), *Aspects of Contemporary Sport Sociology.* Chicago: Athletic Institute.

—————, et al. 1978. *Sport and Social Systems.* Reading, Mass.: Addison-Wesley.

LUFT, JOSEPH. 1984. *Group Processes: An Introduction to Group Dynamics.* 3rd ed. Palo Alto, Calif.: Mayfield.

LUKER, KRISTIN. 1985. *Abortion and the Politics of Motherhood.* Berkeley, Calif.: University of California Press.

LUMSDEN, CHARLES J., and EDWARD O. WILSON. 1983. *Promethean Fire: Reflections on the Origin of Mind.* Cambridge, Mass.: Harvard University Press.

LURIE, ALISON. 1981. *The Language of Clothes.* New York: Random House.

LUSCHEN, GUNTHER. 1969. "Social stratification and social mobility among young sportsmen," in John W. Loy and Gerald S. Kenyon (eds.), *Sport, Culture, and Society.* New York: Macmillan.

—————, and GEORGE H. SAGE (eds.). 1981. *Handbook of Social Science of Sport.* Champaign, Ill.: Stipes.

LYME, S. LEONARD, and LISA F. BERKMAN. 1976. "Social class, susceptibility, and sickness." *American Journal of Epidemiology,* 104, pp. 1–8.

LYND, ROBERT S., and HELEN M. LYND. 1929. *Middletown: A Study in American Culture.* New York: Harcourt Brace.

LYON, JEFF. 1985. *Playing God in the Nursery.* New York: Norton.

LYONS, ALBERT S., and R. JOSEPH PETRUCELLI. 1978. *Medicine: An Illustrated History.* St. Louis: Mosby/Times Mirror.

MACCOBY, ELEANOR. (1980). *Social Development.* New York: Harcourt Brace Jovanovich.

—————, and CAROL N. JACKLIN. 1974. *The Psychology of Sex Differences.* Palo Alto, Calif.: Stanford University Press.

—————, and CAROL N. JACKLIN. 1980. "Sex differences in aggression: A rejoinder and reprise." *Child Development,* 51, pp. 964–980.

MACCRACKEN, MICHAEL C., and FREDERICK M. LUTHER (eds.). 1985. *The Potential Climatic Effects of Increasing Carbon Dioxide.* Washington, D.C.: U.S. Department of Energy.

MACK, RAYMOND W. 1956. "Do we really believe in the bill of rights?" *Social Problems,* 3, pp. 264–269.

MADSEN, AXEL. 1980. *Private Power: Multinational Corporations for the Survival of our Planet.* New York: Morrow.

MAIN, JEREMY. 1983. "The bull market's biggest winners." *Fortune,* August 8, pp. 36–43.

MALAMUTH, NEIL M. 1981. "Rape proclivity among men." *Journal of Social Issues,* 37, p. 4.

—————, and EDWARD DONNERSTEIN. 1984. *Pornography and Sexual Aggression.* Orlando: Academic Press.

MALCOLM, ANDREW H. 1985. "New generation of poor youths emerges in U.S." *New York Times,* October 20, pp. 1, 56.

MALINOWSKI, BRONISLAW. 1922. *The Argonauts of the Western Pacific.* New York: Dutton.

—————. 1926. *Crime and Custom in Savage Society.* New York: Harcourt, Brace.

—————. 1948. *Magic, Science and Religion and Other Essays.* Glencoe, Ill.: Free Press.

MALSON, LUCIEN. 1972. *Wolf Children and the Problem of Human Nature.* New York: Monthly Review Press.

MANKOFF, MILTON. 1971. "Societal reaction and career deviance: A critical analysis." *Sociological Quarterly,* 12, pp. 204–218.

MARANTO, GINA. 1984. "Aging: Can we slow the inevitable?" *Discover,* December, pp. 17–21.

_____. 1985. "The creeping poison underground." *Discover,* February, pp. 74–78.

MARKHAM, WILLIAM T., et al. 1983. "A note on sex, geographic mobility, and career advancement." *Social Forces,* 61, pp. 1138–1146.

MARMOR, JUDD. 1980. *Homosexual Behavior: A Modern Reappraisal.* New York: Basic Books.

MARSHALL, VICTOR W. 1975. "Socialization for impending death in a retirement village." *American Journal of Sociology,* 80, pp. 1124–1144.

MARTIN, M. KAY, and **BARBARA VOORHIES.** 1975. *Female of the Species.* New York: Columbia University Press.

MARTY, MARTIN E. 1976. *A Nation of Behavers.* Chicago: University of Chicago Press.

MARX, KARL. 1964a. *Economic and Political Manuscripts of 1844.* New York: International Publishers.

_____. 1964b, originally published in 1848. *Selected Writings in Sociology and Social Philosophy.* T. B. Bottomore and Maximillian Rubel (eds.). Baltimore, Md.: Penguin.

_____. 1967, originally published 1843. *Critique of Hegel's Philosophy of Right,* in Lloyd D. Easton and Kurt Guddat (trans. and eds.), *Writings of the Young Marx on Philosophy and Society.* New York: Doubleday.

_____. 1967, originally published 1867–1895. *Das Capital.* New York: International Publishers.

_____. 1969, originally published 1852. "The eighteenth brumaire of Louis Napoleon," in *Karl Marx: Selected Works.* Vol. 1. Moscow: Progress Publishers.

_____, and **FRIEDRICH ENGELS.** 1970. *Selected Works.* Vol. 3. Moscow: Progress Publishers.

MASNICK, GEORGE, and **MARY JO BANE.** 1980. *The Nation's Families.* Cambridge, Mass.: Harvard University Press.

MASSEY, DOUGLAS S. 1981. "Social class and ethnic segregation: A reconsideration of methods and conclusions. *American Sociological Review,* 46, pp. 641–650.

MASTERS, WILLIAM H., and **VIRGINIA E. JOHNSON.** 1979. *Homosexuality in Perspective.* Boston: Little, Brown.

MATTHEWS, JAY, and **LINDA MATTHEWS.** 1983. *One Billion: A China Chronicle.* New York: Random House.

MAURER, HARRY. 1979. *Not Working: An Oral History of the Unemployed.* New York: Holt, Rinehart and Winston.

MAYER, J. P. 1943. *Max Weber and German Politics.* London: Faber & Faber.

MAYO, ELTON. 1966. *Human Problems of an Industrial Civilization.* New York: Viking.

MCADAM, D. 1982. *Political Process and the Development of Black Insurgency, 1930–1970.* Chicago: University of Chicago Press.

MCCANN, H. GILMAN. 1978. *Chemistry Transformed.* Norwood, N.J.: Ablex.

MCCARTHY, JOHN D., and **MAYER N. ZALD.** 1973. *The Trend of Social Movements in America: Professionalization and Resource Mobilization.* Morristown, N.J.: General Learning Press.

_____, and **MAYER N. ZALD.** 1977. "Resource mobilization and social movements: A partial theory." *American Journal of Sociology,* 82:6, 1212–1241.

MCCLELLAND, DAVID C. 1961. *The Achieving Society.* New York: Van Nostrand.

MCCLENDON, MCKEE J. 1980. "Structural and exchange components of occupational mobility: A cross-national analysis." *Sociological Quarterly,* 21, pp. 493–509.

MCCLOSKY, HERBERT, and **ALIDA BRILL.** *Dimensions of Tolerance: What Americans Believe about Civil Liberties.* New York: Russell Sage Foundation, 1983.

MCCREADY, WILLIAM C., and **ANDREW M. GREELEY.** 1976. *The Ultimate Values of the American Population.* Beverly Hills, Calif.: Sage.

MCGAHEY, RICHARD M. 1980. "Dr. Ehrlich's magic bullet: Econometric theory, econometrics, and the death penalty." *Crime and Delinquency,* 26, pp. 485–502.

MCGEE, REECE. 1975. *Points of Departure.* Hinsdale, Ill.: Dryden Press.

MCGRATH, JOSEPH E. 1978. "Small group research." *American Behavioral Scientist,* 21:5, 651–671.

MCGUIRE, MEREDITH B. 1981. *Control of Charisma.* Philadelphia: Temple University Press.

_____. 1981. *Religion: The Social Context.* Belmont, Calif.: Wadsworth.

MCKEAN, KEVIN. 1981. "A scandal in the laboratory." *Discover,* November, pp. 18–23.

MCKEOWN, THOMAS. 1978. "Determinants of health." *Human Nature,* 1, pp. 64–71.

_____. 1979. *The Role of Medicine.* Princeton, N.J.: Princeton University Press.

MCKINLAY, JOHN B. 1975. "Who is really ignorant—patient or physician?" *Journal of Health and Social Behavior,* 16, pp. 3–11.

MCKINLAY, JOHN B., and **SONIA M. MCKINLAY.** 1977. "The questionable contribution of medical measures to the decline of mortality in the United States in the twentieth century." *Health and Society,* 55:3.

MCKINNON, CATHERINE A. 1979. *Sexual Harassment of Working Women: A Case of Sex Discrimination.* New Haven: Yale University Press.

MCLEAN, CHARLES. 1978. *The Wolf Children.* New York: Hill and Wang.

MCLEMORE, S. DALE. 1983. *Racial and Ethnic Relations in America.* 2nd ed. Boston: Allyn and Bacon.

MCMURTIE, DOUGLAS C. 1976. *The Story of Printing and Bookmaking.* 3rd ed. New York: Oxford University Press.

MCNEILL, WILLIAM H. 1982. *Technology, Armed Force, and Society Since A.D. 1000.* Chicago: University of Chicago Press.

MCPHAIL, CLARK, and **RONALD T. WALSTEIN.** 1983. "Individual and collective behaviors within gatherings, demonstrations, and riots." *Annual Review of Sociology,* 9. Palo Alto, Calif.: Annual Reviews.

MCPHERSON, J. MILLER, and **LYNN SMITH-LOVIN.** 1982. "Women and weak ties: Differences by sex in the size of voluntary organizations." *American Journal of Sociology,* 87, pp. 883–904.

MCROBERTS, HUGH A., and **KEVIN SELBEE.** 1981. "Trends in occupational mobility in Canada and the United States: A comparison." *American Sociological Review,* 46, pp. 406–421.

MEAD, GEORGE HERBERT. 1934. *Mind, Self, and Society: From the Standpoint of a Social Behaviorist.* Charles W. Morris (ed.). Chicago: University of Chicago Press.

MEAD, MARGARET. 1935. *Sex and Temperament in Three Primitive Societies.* New York: Dell.

_____. 1970. *Culture and Commitment.* New York: Doubleday.

MEADOWS, DONNELLA H., et al. 1972. *The Limits to Growth.* New York: New American Library.

MEANS, GARDINER S. 1970. "Economic concentration," in Maurice Zeitlin (ed.), *American Society Inc.* Chicago: Markham.

MEARS, WALTER R. 1977. "Ending the welfare myths." *New York Post,* May 27, p. 36.

MECHANIC, DAVID. 1976. *The Growth of Bureaucratic Medicine.* New York: Wiley.

_____. 1978. *Medical Sociology.* 2nd ed. New York: Free Press.

_____. 1980a. *Mental Health and Social Policy.* 2nd ed. Englewood Cliffs, N.J.: Prentice-Hall.

_____ (ed.). 1980b. *Readings in Medical Sociology.* New York: Free Press.

_____ (ed.). 1982. *Symptoms, Illness Behavior, and Help-seeking.* New Brunswick, N.J.: Rutgers University Press.

_____. 1986. *From Advocacy to Allocation: The Evolving American Health Care System.* Chicago: University of Chicago Press.

MEDALIA, NAHUM Z., and OTTO N. LARSEN. 1958. "Diffusion and belief in a collective delusion: The Seattle windshield pitting epidemic." *American Sociological Review,* 23, pp. 221–232.

MEDNICK, SARNOFF A., and KARL O. CHRISTIANSEN (eds.). 1977. *Biosocial Bases of Criminal Behavior.* New York: Gardner Press.

MEDVEDEV, ROY, A. and ZHORES MEDVEDEV. 1979. *A Question of Madness.* New York: Norton.

MEIER, ROBERT F. 1982. "Perspectives on the concept of social control," in Ralph H. Turner (ed.), *Annual Review of Sociology.* Palo Alto, Calif.: Annual Reviews.

MELMAN, SEYMOUR. 1970. *Pentagon Capitalism: The Political Economy of War.* New York: McGraw-Hill.

MELTON, J. GORDON. 1979. *Encyclopaedia of American Religions.* Gaithersburg, Md.: Consortium Books.

MELVILLE, KEITH. 1972. *Communes and the Counter Culture.* New York: Morrow.

MEREDITH, NIKI. 1984. "The gay dilemma." *Psychology Today,* January, pp. 56–62.

MERTON, ROBERT K. 1938. "Social structure and anomie." *American Sociological Review,* 3, pp. 672–682.

_____. 1942. "Science and technology in a democratic order." *Journal of Legal and Political Science,* 1, pp. 115–126.

_____. 1949. "Discrimination and the American creed," in Robert M. McIver (ed.), *Discrimination and National Welfare.* New York: Harper.

_____. 1968. *Social Theory and Social Structure.* 2nd ed. New York: Free Press.

_____. 1970, originally published 1938. *Science, Technology, and Society in Seventeenth Century England.* New York: Howard Fertig.

_____. 1971. "Social problems and sociological theory," in Robert K. Merton and Robert Nisbet (eds.), *Contemporary Social Problems.* 3rd ed. New York: Harcourt Brace Jovanovich.

_____. 1973. *Sociology of Science: Theoretical and Empirical Investigations.* Norman W. Storer (ed.). Chicago: University of Chicago Press.

_____, GEORGE C. READER, and PATRICIA KENDALL (eds.). 1957. *The Student Physician.* Cambridge, Mass: Harvard University Press.

METHENY, E. 1977. *Vital Issues.* Washington, D.C.: American Association for Health, Physical Education, and Recreation.

MEYER, MARSHALL W., WILLIAM STEVENSON, and STEPHEN WEBSTER. 1984. *Limits to Bureaucratic Growth.* Hawthorne, N.Y.: Aldine.

MEYER, MARY COELI, et al. 1981. *Sexual Harassment.* New York: Petrocelli Books.

MEYER, STEPHEN M. 1984. *The Dynamics of Nuclear Proliferation.* Chicago: University of Chicago Press.

MICHELS, ROBERT. 1967, originally published 1911. *Political Parties.* New York: Free Press.

MICHIE, DONALD, and RORY JOHNSON. 1985. *The Knowledge Machine.* New York: Morrow.

MIDDLETON, RUSSELL. 1962. "Brother-sister and father-daughter marriage in ancient Egypt." *American Sociological Review,* 27, pp. 103–111.

MILGRAM, STANLEY. 1967. "The small world problem." *Psychology Today,* 1, pp. 61–67.

_____. 1973. *Obedience to Authority: An Experimental View.* New York: Harper & Row.

_____, and R. LANCE SHOTLAND. 1973. *Television and antisocial behavior: Field experiments.* New York: Academic Press.

MILLAR, RONALD. 1974. *The Piltdown Man.* New York: St. Martin's Press.

MILLER, DAVID. 1985. *Introduction to Collective Behavior.* Belmont, Calif.: Wadsworth.

MILLER, JUDITH. 1983. "Moslem world is unsettled by surge in fundamentalism." *New York Times,* December 18, pp. 1, 20.

MILLER, WALTER. 1958. "Lower class culture as a generating milieu of gang delinquency." *Journal of Sociological Issues,* 14, pp. 5–19.

MILLMAN, MARCIA. 1977. *The Unkindest Cut.* New York: Morrow.

MILLS, C. WRIGHT. 1956. *The Power Elite.* New York: Oxford University Press.

_____. 1959. *The Sociological Imagination.* New York: Oxford University Press.

MILLS, THEODORE. 1967. *The Sociology of Small Groups.* Englewood Cliffs, N.J.: Prentice-Hall.

MINDEL, CHARLES, and ROBERT W. HABENSTEIN. 1982. *Ethnic Families in America: Patterns and Variations.* New York: Elsevier.

MINTZ, BETH A., and MICHAEL SCHWARTZ. 1981. "Interlocking directorates and interest group formation." *American Sociological Review,* 46, pp. 857–869.

_____. 1985. *The Power Structure of American Business.* Chicago: University of Chicago Press.

MIRANDE, ALFREDO. 1985. *The Chicano Experience.* South Bend, Ind.: Notre Dame Press.

MISCHLER, ELIOT G., et al. 1981. *Social Contexts of Health, Illness, and Patient Care.* Cambridge, Eng.: Cambridge University Press.

MITCHELL, JACK N. 1978. *Social Exchange, Dramaturgy, and Ethnomethodology.* New York: Elsevier.

MITROFF, IAN I. 1974a. *The Subjective Side of Science.* Amsterdam: Elsevier.

_____. 1974b. "Norms and counter-norms in a select group of the Apollo moon scientists: A case study in the ambivalence of scientists." *American Sociological Review,* 39, pp. 579–595.

MODELSKI, GEORGE (ed.). 1979. *Transnational Corporations and the World Order.* San Francisco: Freeman.

MONEY, JOHN, and ANKE A. EHRHARDT. 1972. *Man and Woman, Boy and Girl.* Baltimore, Md.: Johns Hopkins University Press.

_____, and PATRICIA TUCKER. 1975. *Sexual Signatures: On Being a Man or a Woman.* Boston: Little, Brown.

MONTAGU, ASHLEY (ed.). 1973. *Man and Aggression.* 2nd ed. New York: Oxford University Press.

_____ (ed.). 1975. *Race and IQ.* New York: Oxford University Press.

_____ (ed.). 1978. *Learning Non-Aggression: The Experience of Non-Literate Societies.* New York: Oxford University Press.

_____ (ed.). 1980. *Sociobiology Examined.* New York: Oxford University Press.

MOODY, PETER R. 1985. *Chinese Politics After Mao.* New York: Praeger.

MOONEY, JAMES. 1965. *The Ghost-Dance Religion and Sioux Outbreak of 1890.* Chicago: University of Chicago Press.

MOORE, BARRINGTON. 1966. *Social Origins of Dictatorship and Democracy.* Boston: Beacon.

_____. 1979. *Injustice: The Social Bases of Obedience and Revolt.* New York: Pantheon.

MOORE, GWEN. 1979. "The structure of a national elite network." *American Sociological Review,* 44, pp. 673–692.

MOORE, LORNA G., et al. 1980. *The Biocultural Basis of Health: Expanding Views of Medical Anthropology.* St. Louis: Mosby.

MOORE, MARK H., et al. 1985. *Dangerous Offenders.* Cambridge, Mass.: Harvard University Press.

MOORE, WILBERT E. 1960. "A reconsideration of theories of social change." *American Sociological Review,* 25, pp. 810–818.

_____. 1970. *The Professions.* Beverly Hills, Calif.: Sage.

_____. 1974. *Social Change.* 2nd ed. Englewood Cliffs, N.J.: Prentice-Hall.

_____. 1979. *World Modernization: The Limits of Convergence.* New York: Elsevier.

MORRIS, DESMOND. 1977. *Manwatching: A Field Guide to Human Behavior.* New York: Abrams.

_____, et al. 1979. *Gestures.* New York: Stein and Day.

MORRISON, ANN M. 1982. "Those executive bailout deals." *Fortune,* December 13, pp. 82–87.

MORTIMER, JEYLAND T. 1979. *Changing Attitudes Toward Work.* Scarsdale, N.Y.: Work in America Institute.

MORTIMER, KENNETH P., et al. 1984. *Involvement In Learning.* Washington, D.C.: National Institute of Education.

MOSCA, GAETANO. 1939. *The Ruling Class.* New York: McGraw-Hill.

MOSHER, STEVEN W. 1983. *Broken Earth: The Rural Chinese.* New York: Free Press.

MOSSE, GEORGE L. 1978. *Toward the Final Solution: A History of European Racism.* New York: Howard Fertig.

MOTTAHEDEH, ROY. 1985. *The Mantle of the Prophet: Religion and Politics in Iran.* New York: Simon and Schuster.

MOUNIN, GEORGES. 1976. "Chimpanzees, language, and communication." *Current Anthropology,* 17, pp. 1–22.

MOUSTAFA, TAHER, and GERTRUD WEISS. 1968. *Health Status and Practices of Mexican Americans.* Los Angeles: University of California Press.

MOYNIHAN, DANIEL PATRICK. 1965. *The Negro Family: The Case for National Action.* Washington, D.C.: Office of Policy Planning and Research, U.S. Department of Labor.

MULKAY, MICHAEL J. 1972. *The Social Process of Innovation: A Study in the Sociology of Science.* New York: Macmillan.

——————. 1976. "Norms and ideology in science." *Social Science Information,* 15, pp. 637–656.

MULLINS, LYNN S., and RICHARD E. KOPELMAN. 1984. "The best seller as an indicator of societal narcissism: Is there a trend?" *Public Opinion Quarterly,* 48, pp. 720–730.

MUMFORD, LEWIS. 1961. *The City in History.* New York: Harcourt Brace Jovanovich.

MUNCY, RAYMOND LEE. 1974. *Sex and Marriage in Utopian Communities.* Baltimore: Penguin.

MURDOCK, GEORGE P. 1934. *Our Primitive Contemporaries.* New York: Macmillan.

——————. 1935. "Comparative data on the division of labor by sex." *Social Forces,* 15, pp. 551–553.

——————. 1945. "The common denominator of cultures," in Ralph Linton (ed.), *The Science of Man and the World Crisis.* New York: Columbia University Press.

——————. 1949. *Social Structure.* New York: Macmillan.

——————. 1957. "World ethnographic sample." *American Anthropologist,* 54, pp. 664–687.

MURPHY, JAMIE. 1981. "Dodging celestial garbage." *Time,* May 21, p. 92.

MURRAY, CHARLES. 1984. *Losing Ground: American Social Policy 1950–1980.* New York: Basic Books.

MYERS, DAVID G., and HELMUT LAMM. 1976. "The group polarization phenomenon." *Psychology Bulletin,* 83, pp. 602–627.

MYERS, NORMAN. 1984. *The Primary Source: Tropical Forests and Our Future.* New York: Norton.

MYRDAL, GUNNAR. 1944. *An American Dilemma.* New York: Harper & Row.

NAKELL, BARRY, and KENNETH A. HARDY. 1987. *The Arbitrariness of the Death Penalty.* Philadelphia: Temple University Press.

NANCE, JOHN. 1975. *The Gentle Tasaday: A Stone Age People in the Philippine Rain Forest.* New York: Harcourt Brace Jovanovich.

NAROLL, RAOUL. 1966. "Does military deterrence deter?" *Transaction,* 3, pp. 4–20.

NASH, MANNING. 1962. "Race and the ideology of race." *Current Anthropology,* 3, pp. 285–288.

NATIONAL ADVISORY COMMISSION ON CIVIL DISORDERS (KERNER COMMISSION). 1968. *Report of National Advisory Commission on Civil Disorders.* New York: Bantam.

NATIONAL COMMISSION ON EXCELLENCE IN EDUCATION. 1983. *A Nation at Risk.* Washington, D.C.: U.S. Government Printing Office.

NATIONAL EDUCATION ASSOCIATION. 1968. *Ability Grouping: Research Summary 1968–se.* Washington, D.C.: NEA Research Division.

NATIONAL INSTITUTE OF MENTAL HEALTH. 1982. *Television and Behavior: Ten Years of Scientific Progress and Implications for the Eighties.* Washington, D.C.: U.S. Government Printing Office.

NATIONAL RESEARCH COUNCIL. 1984. *Causes and Effects of Changes in Stratospheric Ozone.* Washington, D.C.: National Academy Press.

NAVARRO, VICENTE. 1976. *Medicine under Capitalism.* New York: Prodist.

——————. 1986. *Crisis, Health, and Medicine.* New York: Tavistock.

NAVASKY, VICTOR S. 1980. *Naming Names.* New York: Viking.

NICHOLS, EVE K. 1986. *Mobilizing Against AIDS.* Cambridge, Mass.: Harvard University Press.

NIEBUHR, RICHARD H. 1929. *The Social Sources of Denominationalism.* New York: Holt.

NIELSEN, JOYCE MCCARL. 1978. *Sex in Society: Perspectives on Stratification.* Belmont, Calif.: Wadsworth.

NISBET, ROBERT A. 1953. *The Quest for Community.* New York: Oxford University Press.

——————. 1969. *Social Change and History.* New York: Oxford University Press.

——————. 1970. *The Social Bond.* New York: Knopf.

NIXON, HOWARD L. 1979. *The Small Group.* Englewood Cliffs, N.J.: Prentice-Hall.

NOBLE, DAVID F. 1984. *Forces of Production: A Social History of Industrial Automation.* New York: Knopf.

NOEL, DON. 1968. "The theory of the origin of ethnic stratification." *Social Problems,* 16, pp. 157–172.

——————. (ed.). 1972. *The Origins of American Slavery and Racism.* Columbus, Ohio: Merrill.

NORTH, JAMES. 1985. *Freedom Rising.* New York: Macmillan.

NORTON, ELEANOR HOLMES. 1985. "Restoring the black family." *New York Times Magazine,* June 2, pp. 43–96.

NORUM, G. A., et al. 1967. "Seating patterns and group tasks." *Psychology in the Schools,* 4, p. 3.

NOVAK, M. A. 1979. "Social recovery of monkeys isolated for the first year of life: II. Long term assessment." *Developmental Psychology,* 11, pp. 453–461.

NOVAK, MICHAEL. 1971. "White ethnic." *Harper's,* 243, pp. 44–50.

NUNN, CLYDE Z., et al. 1978. *Tolerance for Nonconformity: A National Survey of Americans' Changing Commitment to Civil Liberties.* San Francisco: Jossey-Bass.

NYE, IVAN F. 1958. *Family Relationships and Delinquent Behavior.* New York: Wiley.

OAKES, JEANNIE. 1985. *Keeping Track: How Schools Structure Inequality.* New Haven: Yale University Press.

OBERG, ALECESTIS. 1984. "Trashing the orbital frontier." *Science Digest,* October, pp. 41–44, 83.

OBERSCHALL, ANTHONY. 1973. *Social Conflict and Social Movements.* Englewood Cliffs, N.J.: Prentice-Hall.

OGBURN, WILLIAM F. 1950. *Social Change.* New York: Viking.

O'KELLY, CHARLOTTE G., and LARRY S. CARNEY (eds.). 1985. *Women and Men in Society: Cross-Cultural Perspectives on Gender Stratification.* Belmont, Calif.: Wadsworth.

OLSBERG, LARS. 1983. *Economic Inequality in the United States.* Armonk, N.Y.: M. E. Sharpe.

O'NEIL, NENA, and GEORGE O'NEIL. 1973. *Open Marriage.* New York: Avon.

OPHULS, WILLIAM. 1974. "The scarcity society." *Harper's,* 246, pp. 47–52.

——————. 1977. *Ecology and the Politics of Scarcity.* San Francisco: W. H. Freeman.

ORFIELD, GARY. 1983. *Public School Desegregation in the United States, 1968–1980.* Washington, D.C.: Joint Center for Political Studies.

ORUM, ANTHONY. 1983. *Introduction to Political Sociology.* 2nd ed. New York: Prentice-Hall.

ORWELL, G. 1949. *1984*. New York: New American Library.

OSTLING, RICHARD N. 1985. "Jerry Falwell's Crusade." *Time*, September 2, pp. 48–57.

OTTERBEIN, KEITH. 1970. *The Evolution of War*. New Haven, Conn.: Human Relations Area Files.

————. 1973. "The anthropology of war," in John J. Honnigman (ed.), *Handbook of Social and Cultural Anthropology*. Chicago: Rand McNally.

OUCHI, WILLIAM. 1981. *Theory Z: How American Business Can Meet the Japanese Challenge*. Reading, Mass.: Addison-Wesley.

PACEY, ARNOLD. 1984. *The Culture of Technology*. Cambridge, Mass.: MIT Press.

PAGE, BENJAMIN I. 1983. *Who Gets What from Government*. Berkeley, Calif.: University of California Press.

PALMORE, ERDMAN, and K. MANTON. 1974. "Modernization and the status of the aged: International correlations." *Journal of Gerontology*, 29, pp. 205–210.

PARETO, VILFREDO. 1935. *Mind and Society*. New York: Harcourt Brace Jovanovich.

PARK, ROBERT E., et al. 1925. *The City*. Chicago: University of Chicago Press.

PARKE, ROSS D. 1979. "The father of the child." *The Sciences*, 19, pp. 12–15.

PARKIN, DAVID (ed.). 1985. *The Anthropology of Evil*. Oxford: Basil Blackwell.

PARNAS, DAVID LORGE. 1985. "Software aspects of strategic defense systems." *American Scientist*, 73:5, pp. 432–440.

PARRILLO, VINCENT. 1985. *Strangers to These Shores*. 2nd ed. New York: Macmillan.

PARSONS, TALCOTT. 1937. *The Structure of Social Action*. New York: McGraw-Hill.

————. 1940. "An analytic approach to the theory of social stratification." *American Journal of Sociology*, 45, pp. 841–862.

————. 1951. *The Social System*. Glencoe, Ill.: Free Press.

————. 1954. "The professions and social structure," in Talcott Parsons (ed.), *Essays in Sociological Theory*. New York: Free Press.

————. 1958. "Definitions of health and illness in the light of American values and social structure," in E. Gartly Jaco, *Patients, Physicians, and Illness*. New York: Free Press.

————. 1959. *Politics and Social Structure*. New York: Free Press.

————. 1961. "Some considerations on the theory of social change." *Rural Sociology*, 26, pp. 219–239.

————. 1966. *Societies: Evolutionary and Comparative Perspectives*. Englewood Cliffs, N.J.: Prentice-Hall.

————. 1975. "The sick role and the role of the physician reconsidered." *Health and Society*, Summer, pp. 257–278.

————, et al. 1955. *Family, Socialization, and Interaction Process*. Glencoe, Ill.: Free Press.

PASCALE, RICHARD TANNER, and ANTHONY G. ATHOS. 1981. *The Art of Japanese Management*. New York: Warner Books.

PATRICK, TED. 1976. *Let Our Children Go*. New York: Ballantine.

PATTERSON, JAMES T. 1982. *America's Struggle Against Poverty, 1900–1980*. Cambridge, Mass.: Harvard University Press.

PATTERSON, M. L., et al. 1971. "Compensatory reactions to spatial intrusion." *Sociometry*, 34, pp. 114–121.

PATTERSON, ORLANDO. 1977. *Ethnic Chauvinism: The Reactionary Impulse*. New York: Stein and Day.

PATTISON, E. MANSELL (ed.). 1979. *The Experience of Dying*. Englewood Cliffs, N.J.: Prentice-Hall.

PEAR, ROBERT. 1986. "Poverty rate down slightly in 1985, to level of '81." *New York Times*, August 27, p. 17.

PEARCE, DIANA. 1979. "Gatekeepers and homeseekers: Institutional factors in racial steering." *Social Problems*, 26: 3, 325–342.

PEARLIN, LEONARD. 1980. "Life strains and psychological distress among adults," in Neil Smelser and Erik Erikson (eds.), *Of Love and Work and Adulthood*. Cambridge, Mass.: Harvard University Press.

PEBLEY, ANN R., and CHARLES F. WESTOFF. 1982. "Women's sex preferences in the United States: 1970 to 1975." *Demography*, 19:2, 177–190.

PEDERSON, D. M. 1973. "Developmental trends in personal space." *Journal of Psychology*, 83, pp. 3–9.

PEPITONE-ROCKWELL, FRAN (ed.). 1980. *Dual Career Couples*. Beverly Hills, Calif.: Sage.

PERROW, CHARLES. 1986. *Normal Accidents: Living with High-Risk Technologies*. New York: Basic Books.

————. 1986. *Complex Organizations: A Critical Essay*. 3rd ed. New York: Random House.

PERRY, DAVID C., and ALFRED J. WATKINS (eds.). 1978. *The Rise of the Sunbelt Cities*. Beverly Hills, Calif.: Sage.

PETER, LAURENCE J. 1986. *The Peter Pyramid*. New York: Morrow.

PETTIGREW, THOMAS. 1958. "Personality and socio-cultural factors in intergroup attitudes: A cross-national comparison." *Journal of Conflict Resolution*, 2, pp. 29–42.

————. 1959. "Regional differences in anti-negro prejudice." *Journal of Abnormal and Social Psychology*, 59, pp. 28–36.

————. 1971. *Racially Separate or Together?* New York: McGraw-Hill.

————. 1982. "Prejudice," in Thomas F. Pettigrew et al. (eds.), *Prejudice: Dimensions of Ethnicity*. Cambridge, Mass.: Harvard University Press.

————, and ROBERT GREEN. 1976. "School desegregation in large cities: A critique of the Coleman 'white flight' thesis." *Harvard Educational Review*, 46, pp. 1–53.

————, et al. (eds.). 1982. *Prejudice*. Cambridge, Mass.: Harvard University Press.

PHILLIPS, JOHN C. 1976. "Toward an explanation of racial variations in top level sports participation." *International Review of Sport Sociology*, November, pp. 39–55.

PIAGET, JEAN. 1950. *The Psychology of Intelligence*. London: Routledge & Kegan Paul.

————. 1954. *The Construction of Reality in the Child*. New York: Basic Books.

————, and BARBEL INHELDER. 1969. *The Psychology of the Child*. New York: Basic Books.

PICKERING, ANDREW. 1986. *Constructing Quarks: A Sociological History of Particle Physics*. Chicago: University of Chicago Press.

PIFER, ALAN, and LYDIA BRONTE (eds.). 1986. *Our Aging Society: Paradox and Promise*. New York: Norton.

PILIAVAN, IRVIN, and SCOTT BRIAR. 1964. "Police encounters with juveniles." *American Journal of Sociology*, 70, pp. 206–214.

PINEO, PETER C., and JOHN PORTER. 1967. "Occupational prestige in Canada." *Canadian Review of Sociology and Anthropology*, 4, pp. 24–40.

PINES, MAYA. 1981. "The civilizing of Genie." *Psychology Today*, September, pp. 28–34.

————. 1982. "Behavior and heredity: Links for specific traits are growing stronger." *New York Times*, June 29, pp. 19, 22.

PIVEN, FRANCES FOX, and RICHARD A. CLOWARD. 1977. *Poor Peoples' Movements: Why They Succeed, How They Fail*. New York: Pantheon.

PLECK, JOSEPH. 1981. *The Myth of Masculinity*. Cambridge, Mass.: MIT Press.

POLANYI, MICHAEL. 1951. *The Logic of Liberty*. London: Routledge & Kegan Paul.

POLSKY, NED. 1964. *Hustlers, Beats, and Others*. Chicago: Aldine.

PONSE, BARBARA. 1978. *Identities in the Lesbian World: The Social Construction of Self*. Westport, Conn.: Greenwood Press.

POPE, DANIEL. 1983. *The Making of Modern Advertising.* New York: Basic Books.

POPPER, KARL R. 1959. *The Logic of Scientific Discovery.* New York: Basic Books.

POPULATION REFERENCE BUREAU. 1986. *1986 World Population Data Sheet.* Washington, D.C.: Population Reference Bureau, Inc.

PORTER, BLAINE R. 1979. "Single-parent families," in Nick Stinnet, (ed.), *Building Family Strengths: Blueprints for Action.* Omaha: University of Nebraska Press.

PORTER, BRUCE, and MARVIN DUNN. 1984. *The Miami Riot of 1980.* Lexington, Mass.: Lexington Books.

PORTER, JOHN. 1965. *The Vertical Mosaic: An Analysis of Social Class and Power in Canada.* Toronto: University of Toronto Press.

POSTEL, SANDRA. 1985. *Air Pollution, Acid Rain, and the Future of Forests.* Washington, D.C.: Worldwatch Institute.

POSTMAN, NEIL. 1979. *Teaching as a Conserving Activity.* New York: Delacorte Press.

——————. 1981. *The Disappearance of Childhood.* New York: Dell.

POULANTZAS, NICOS. 1973. *Political Power and Social Classes.* New York: New Left Books.

POWES, JOHN. 1974. "On the limitations of modern medicine," in Robert L. Kane (ed.), *The Challenges of Community Medicine.* New York: Springer.

PREMACK, DAVID, and ANN J. PREMACK. 1983. *The Mind of an Ape.* New York: Norton.

PRESIDENT'S COMMISSION FOR THE STUDY OF ETHICAL PROBLEMS IN MEDICINE AND BIOMEDICAL AND BEHAVIORAL RESEARCH. 1983. *Splicing Life.* Washington, D.C.: U.S. Government Printing Office.

PRESIDENT'S COMMISSION ON OBSCENITY AND PORNOGRAPHY. 1970. *Report of the President's Commission on Obscenity and Pornography.* New York: Bantam.

PRICE, DEREK J. DE SOLLA. 1963. *Big Science, Little Science.* New York: Columbia University Press.

PROVENCE, S., and LIPTON, R. C. 1962. *Infants in Institutions.* New York: International Universities Press.

PRUCHA, FRANCIS PAUL. 1985. *The Indians in American Society: From the Revolutionary War to the Present.* Berkeley, Calif.: University of California Press.

PSATHAS, GEORGE (ed.). 1979. *Everyday Language: Studies in Ethnomethodology.* New York: Lovington.

——————. 1968. *The Student Nurse and the Diploma School of Nursing.* New York: Springer.

PUGH, M. D., and RALPH WAHRMAN. 1983. "Neutralizing sexism in mixed sex groups: Do women have to do better than men?" *American Journal of Sociology,* 89, pp. 746–761.

QUEEN, STUART A., ROBERT HABENSTEIN, and JILL QUADAGNO. 1985. *The Family in Various Cultures.* 5th ed. New York: Harper & Row.

QUINNEY, RICHARD. 1979. *Criminology.* Boston: Little, Brown.

——————. 1980. *Class, State, and Crime.* 2nd ed. New York: Longman.

RADCLIFFE-BROWN, A. R. 1935. "On the concept of functionalism in the social sciences." *American Anthropologist,* 37, pp. 394–402.

——————. 1952. *Structure and Function in Primitive Society.* Glencoe, Ill.: Free Press.

RAINES, HOWELL. 1979. "American Indians: Struggling for power and identity." New York Times Magazine, February 11, pp. 21–54.

RAINWATER, LEE, and RICHARD COLEMAN. 1978. *Social Standing in America: New Dimensions of Class.* New York: Basic Books.

RAPER, ARTHUR. 1933. *The Tragedy of Lynching.* Chapel Hill, N.C.: University of North Carolina Press.

RAPHAEL, BEVERLEY. 1985. *When Disaster Strikes: How Communities and Individuals Cope with Disasters.* New York: Basic Books.

RAPPOPORT, RHONA, and ROBERT RAPPOPORT. 1976. *Dual Career Families Re-examined.* New York: Harper & Row.

RATHJE, W. L., and W. W. HUGHES. 1976. "The garbage project as a non-reactive approach: Garbage in—garbage out," in H. W. Sinaiko and L. A. Broedling (eds.), *Perspectives on Attitude Assessment: Surveys and Their Alternatives.* Champaign, Ill.: Pendleton Publications.

RAVITCH, DIANNE. 1978. *The Revisionists Revised: A Critique of the Radical Attack on the Schools.* New York: Basic Books.

——————. 1983. *The Troubled Crusade: American Education 1945–1980.* New York: Basic Books.

READ, KENNETH. 1965. *The High Valley.* New York: Scribner's.

RECKLESS, WALTER. 1973. *The Crime Problem.* 4th ed. New York: Appleton-Century-Crofts.

REDDAWAY, PETER, and SIDNEY BLOCH. 1977. *Psychiatric Terror.* New York: Basic Books.

REEDER, LEO G. 1972. "The patient-client as consumer: Some observations on the changing professional-client relationship." *Journal of Health and Social Behavior,* 13, pp. 406–412.

REICH, MICHAEL. 1981. *Racial Inequality: A Political Economic Analysis.* Princeton, N.J.: Princeton University Press.

REICH, ROBERT B. 1983. *The Next American Frontier.* New York: Times Books.

REICHLIN, IGOR. 1984. "How dogma cripples Soviet science." *Science Digest,* March, pp. 66–69, 101–103.

REID, JOHN. 1980. *Black America.* Washington, D.C.: Population Reference Bureau.

——————. 1982. *Black America in the 1980's.* Washington, D.C.: Population Reference Bureau.

REIMAN, JEFFREY H. 1984. *The Rich Get Richer and the Poor Get Prison.* 2nd ed. New York: Wiley.

REISCHAUER, EDWIN O. 1981. *The Japanese.* Cambridge, Mass.: Harvard University Press.

REISS, ALBERT J. 1961. "The social integration of peers and queers." *Social Problems,* 9, pp. 102–120.

——————. 1968. "Police brutality: Answers to key questions." *Transaction,* 5, pp. 10–19.

——————. 1971. *The Police and the Public.* New Haven: Yale University Press.

RELMAN, ARNOLD S. 1980. "The new medical industrial complex." *New England Journal of Medicine,* 303, pp. 963–970.

RENSBERGER, BOYCE. 1981. "Tinkering with life." *Science '81,* November, pp. 45–49.

RENSHON, STANLEY ALLEN (ed.). 1977. *Handbook of Political Socialization: Theory and Research.* New York: Free Press.

RESKIN, BARBARA F. 1985. *Sex Segregation in the Workplace.* New York: National Academy Press.

REYNOLDS, PAUL D. 1979. *Ethical Dilemmas and Social Science Research.* San Francisco: Jossey-Bass.

——————. 1982. *Ethics and Social Science Research.* Englewood Cliffs, N.J.: Prentice-Hall.

RICHARDSON, JAMES T., et al. 1979. *Organized Miracles.* New Brunswick, N.J.: Transaction Books.

—————— (ed.). 1979. *Conversion Careers: In and Out of the New Religions.* Garden City, N.Y.: Doubleday.

RICHMOND-ABBOTT, MARIE. 1979. *The Contemporary American Woman: Her Past, Her Present, Her Future Prospects.* New York: Holt, Rinehart, and Winston.

RIESMAN, DAVID. 1961. *The Lonely Crowd.* New Haven: Yale University Press.

RIFKIN, JEREMY. 1983. *Algeny.* New York: Viking.

RILEY, MATILDA W. 1971. "Social gerontology and the age stratification of society." *Gerontologist,* 11, pp. 79–87.

——————, et al. 1972. *Aging and Society. Volume 3. A Sociology of Age Stratification.* New York: Russell Sage Foundation.

RIORDAN, MICHAEL (ed.). 1982. *The Day After Midnight*. Palo Alto, Calif.: Cheshire Books.

RIST, RAY C. 1970. "Student social class and teacher expectations: The self-fulfilling prophecy in ghetto education." *Harvard Educational Review*, 40, pp. 411–451.

—————. (ed.). 1979. *Desegregated Schools: Appraisals of an American Experiment*. New York: Academic Press.

RITCHIE, JOHN W. 1977. "The magic feather: Education and the power of positive thinking." *Teachers College Record*, 78:4, 477–486.

RITZER, GEORGE, and DAVID WALCZAK. 1986. *Working: Conflict and Change*. 3rd ed. Englewood Cliffs., N.J.: Prentice-Hall.

ROBBINS, THOMAS, and DICK ANTHONY (eds.). 1979. *In Gods We Trust: New Patterns of Religious Pluralism in America*. New Brunswick, N.J.: Transaction Books.

ROBERTS, KEITH A. 1984. *Religion in Sociological Perspective*. Homewood, Ill.: Dorsey.

ROBERTS, ROBERT F., and EUN SUL LEE. 1980. "Medical care use by Mexican Americans: Evidence from the human population laboratory studies." *Medical Care*, 43, pp. 166–281.

ROBERTSON, IAN. 1976. "Social stratification," in David E. Hunter and Phillip Whitten (eds.), *The Study of Anthropology*. New York: Harper & Row.

—————. 1978. "Education in South Africa," in Ian Robertson and Phillip Whitten (eds.), *Race and Politics in South Africa*. New Brunswick, N.J.: Transaction Books.

—————. 1980. *Social Problems*. 2nd ed. New York: Random House.

ROBINS, CORRINE. 1984. *The Pluralist Era: American Art 1968–1981*. New York, Harper & Row.

ROBINSON, I. E., and D. JEDLICKA. 1980. "Changes in sexual attitudes and behavior of college students from 1956 to 1980: A research note." *Journal of Marriage and the Family*, 44, pp. 237–240.

ROCKFORD, E. BURKE. 1985. *Hare Krishna in America*. New Brunswick, N.J.: Rutgers University Press.

RODGERS, HARRELL R. 1986. *Poor Women, Poor Families*. Armonk, N.Y.: M. E. Sharpe.

RODRIGUEZ, RICHARD. 1983. *Hunger of Memory*. New York: Bantam.

ROEMER, MILTON I. 1977. *Comparative National Policies on Health Care*. New York: Marcel Dekker.

ROETHLISBERGER, FRITZ J., and WILLIAM J. DICKSON. 1939. *Management and the Worker*. Cambridge: Harvard University Press.

ROHLEN, THOMAS P. 1979. *For Harmony and Strength: Japanese White Collar Organization in Anthropological Perspective*. Berkeley, Calif.: University of California Press.

ROLLINS, JOAN H. 1982. *Hidden Minorities: The Persistence of Ethnicity in American Life*. Washington, D.C.: University Press of America.

ROSA, EUGENE, and ALLAN MAZUR. 1979. "Incipient status in small groups." *Social Forces*, 58:1, 18–37.

ROSALDO, MICHELLE ZIMBALIST. 1974. "Woman, culture, and society: A theoretical overview," in Michelle Zimbalist Rosaldo and Louise Lamphere (eds.), *Women, Culture, and Society*. Stanford, Calif.: Stanford University Press.

ROSALDO, RENATO, and R. A. CALVERT (eds.). 1981. *Chicanos: The Evolution of a People*. Huntingdon, N.Y.: Krieger.

ROSE, PETER I. 1980. *They and We: Racial and Ethnic Relations in the United States*. 3rd ed. New York: Random House.

ROSE, STEVEN. 1986. "Stalking the criminal chromosome." *The Nation*, 242:20, 732–736.

ROSEN, R. D. 1977. *Psychobabble: Fast Talk and Quick Cure in the Era of Feeling*. New York: Atheneum.

ROSENFELD, JEFFREY P. 1978. *The Legacy of Aging: A Sociology of Inheritance and Disinheritance*. Norwood, N.J.: Ablex.

ROSENGRANT, T. 1973. "The relationship of race and sex on proxemic behavior and source credibility." Paper, International Communication Association, Montreal, April.

ROSENTHAL, M. 1971. "Where rumor raged." *Transaction*, 8, pp. 34–43.

ROSENTHAL, ROBERT. 1966. *Experimenter Effects in Behavioral Research*, New York: Appleton-Century-Crofts.

—————, and LENORE JACOBSON. 1968. *Pygmalion in the Classroom: Teacher Expectation and Pupils' Intellectual Development*. New York: Holt, Rinehart and Winston.

ROSNOW, RALPH L., and GARY ALAN FINE. 1976. *Rumor and Gossip*. New York: Elsevier.

ROSS, JAMES B., and MARY M. MCLAUGHLIN (eds.). 1949. *The Portable Medieval Reader*. New York: Viking.

ROSSELL, CHRISTINE. 1976. "School desegregation and white flight." *Political Science Quarterly*, 90, pp. 675–698.

—————, and WILLIS D. HAWLEY (eds.) 1983. *The Consequences of School Desegregation*. Philadelphia: Temple University Press.

ROSSIDES, DANIEL W. 1976. *The American Class System*. Boston: Houghton Mifflin.

ROSTOW, WALT W. 1960. *The Stages of Economic Growth*. New York: Cambridge University Press.

—————. 1962. *The Process of Economic Growth*. New York: Norton.

ROSZAK, THEODORE. 1969. *The Making of a Counter-Culture: Reflections on the Technocratic Society and Its Youthful Opposition*. New York: Doubleday.

—————. 1986. *The Cult of Information*. New York: Pantheon.

ROTHMAN, ROBERT A. 1978. *Inequality and Stratification in the United States*. Englewood Cliffs, N.J.: Prentice-Hall.

ROTHMAN, SHEILA M. 1978. *Woman's Proper Place: A History of Changing Ideals and Practices, 1870 to the Present*. New York: Basic Books.

ROTHSCHILD-WHITT, JOYCE. 1979. "The collectivist organization: An alternative to rational-bureaucratic models." *American Sociological Review*, 44, pp. 509–527.

ROUSSEAU, JEAN JACQUES. 1950, originally published 1762. *The Social Contract*. New York: Dutton.

ROZMAN, GILBERT. 1981. *The Modernization of China*. New York: Free Press.

RUBIN, BARRY. 1983. "Iran's year of turmoil." *Current History*, January, pp. 28–31.

RUBIN, LILLIAN. 1976. *Worlds of Pain: Life in the Working Class Family*. New York: Basic Books.

—————. 1979. *Women of a Certain Age*. New York: Harper & Row.

RUBOVITS, P. C., and A. L. MAEHR. 1971. "Pygmalion analyzed: Toward an explanation of the Rosenthal-Jacobson findings." *Journal of Personality and Social Psychology*, 19, pp. 197–203.

—————, and A. L. MAEHR. 1973. "Pygmalion black and white." *Journal of Personality and Social Psychology*, 25, pp. 210–218.

RUDE, GEORGE. 1980. *Ideology and Popular Protest*. New York: Pantheon.

RUSSELL, DIANA E. H. 1975. *The Politics of Rape: The Victim's Perspective*. New York: Stein and Day.

—————. 1984. *Sexual Exploitation: Rape, Child Sexual Abuse, and Workplace Harassment*. Beverly Hills, Calif.: Sage.

—————. 1986. *The Secret Trauma: Incest in the Lives of Girls and Women*. New York: Basic Books.

RUTTER, MICHAEL. 1974. *The Qualities of Mothering: Maternal Deprivation Reassessed*. New York: Aronson.

—————, et al. 1979. *Fifteen Thousand Hours*. Cambridge, Mass.: Harvard University Press.

—————. 1983. "School effects on pupil progress: Research findings and policy implications." *Child Development*, 54, pp. 1–29.

RYAN, WILLIAM. 1976. *Blaming the Victim*. Rev. ed. New York: Vintage.

—————. 1982. *Equality*. New York: Vintage.

RYBCZYNSKI, WITOLD. 1983. *Taming the Tiger: The Struggle to Control Technology*. New York: Viking.

SABATO, LARRY J. 1984. *PAC Power: Inside the World of Political Action Committees*. New York: Norton.

SABIN, THEODORE R., and JAMES C. MANCUSO. 1980. *Schizophrenia: Medical Diagnosis or Moral Verdict.* New York: Pergamon Press.

SAFILIOS-ROTHSCHILD, CONSTANTINE. 1974. *Woman and Social Policy.* Englewood Cliffs, N.J.: Prentice-Hall.

SAGARIN, EDWARD. 1973. "The good guys, the bad guys, and the gay guys." *Contemporary Sociology,* 2, pp. 3–13.

——————. 1975. *Deviants and Deviance.* New York: Praeger.

SAHLINS, MARSHALL D. 1972. *Stone Age Economics.* Chicago: Aldine.

——————. 1976. *The Use and Abuse of Biology.* Ann Arbor: University of Michigan Press.

——————, and ELMAN R. SERVICE. 1960. *Evolution and Culture.* Ann Arbor: University of Michigan Press.

SAID, ABDUL A., and LUIZ R. SIMMONS. 1975. *The New Sovereigns: Multinational Corporations as World Powers.* Englewood Cliffs, N.J.: Prentice-Hall.

SAID, EDWARD. 1979. *Orientalism.* New York: Pantheon.

SALAS, RAFAEL M. 1980. *Annual Report of the Executive Director, United Nations Fund for Population Activities.* New York: United Nations.

SAMORA, J. L. SAUNDERS, and R. LARSON. 1961. "Medical vocabulary knowledge among hospital patients." *Journal of Health and Social Behavior,* 2, pp. 83–92.

SAMPSON, ANTHONY. 1973. *The Sovereign State of ITT.* Greenwich, Conn.: Fawcett.

——————. 1983. *The Changing Anatomy of Britain.* New York: Random House.

SAMUELS, DOROTHY J. 1983. "Privacy vs. computers." *New York Times,* September 12.

SAMUELSON, ROBERT J. 1985. "The myths of comparable worth." *Newsweek,* April 22, p. 57.

SANDAY, PEGGY REEVES. 1981a. "The sociocultural context of rape: A cross-cultural study." *Journal of Social Issues,* 17:4.

——————. 1981b. *Female Power and Male Dominance: On the Origins of Sexual Inequality.* New York: Cambridge University Press.

SANDEEN, ERNEST R. 1970. *The Roots of Fundamentalism.* Chicago: University of Chicago Press.

SANDIFER, MYRON G., CHARLES PETTUS, and DANA QUADE. 1964. "A study of psychiatric diagnosis." *Journal of Nervous Mental Disease,* 139, pp. 350–356.

SAPIR, EDWARD. 1929. "The status of linguistics as a science." *Language,* 5, pp. 207–214.

SAPIRO, VIRGINIA. 1986. *Women in American Society.* Palo Alto, Calif.: Mayfield.

SARAN, PARMATMA, and EDWIN EAMES. 1980. *The New Ethnics: Asian Indians in the United States.* New York: Praeger.

SAUNDERS, LYLE. 1954. *Cultural Differences and Medical Care.* New York: Russell Sage Foundation.

SAWHILL, ISABEL, and JOHN PALMER. 1984. *The Reagan Record.* Washington, D.C.: Urban Institute.

SAX, KARL. 1960. *Standing Room Only.* Boston: Beacon Press.

SAXON, LLOYD. 1985. *The Individual, Marriage, and the Family.* 6th ed. Belmont, Calif.: Wadsworth.

SCARR, SANDRA. 1981. *Race, Social Class, and Individual Differences in I.Q.* Hillsdale, N.J.: Erlbaum.

SCHACHTER, STANLEY, and JEROME E. SINGER. 1962. "Cognitive, social, and physiological determinants of emotional state." *Psychological Review,* 69, pp. 379–399.

SCHAEFER, RICHARD T. 1984. *Racial and Ethnic Groups.* 2nd ed. Boston: Little, Brown.

SCHANK, ROGER C., and PETER G. CHILDERS. 1985. *The Cognitive Computer.* Reading, Mass.: Addison-Wesley.

SCHARAF, MYRON R., and DANIEL LEVINSON. 1974. "The quest for omnipotence in professional training—the case of the psychiatric resident." *Psychiatry,* 27, pp. 135–149.

SCHEFF, THOMAS. 1984. *Being Mentally Ill: A Sociological Theory. 2nd ed.* Hawthorne, N.Y.: Aldine.

SCHELL, JONATHAN. 1982. *The Fate of the Earth.* New York: Knopf.

SCHLEGEL, ALICE. 1972. *Male Dominance and Female Autonomy.* New Haven: Human Relations Area Files Press.

——————(ed.). 1977. *Sexual Stratification: A Cross-Cultural View.* New York: Columbia University Press.

SCHMEMANN, SERGE. 1985. "Moscow offers a more modest plan for achieving true communism." New York Times, October 26, pp. 1, 6.

SCHNEIDER, CARL E., and MARIS A. VINOVSKIS (eds.). 1980. *The Law and Politics of Abortion.* Lexington, Mass.: Lexington Books.

SCHNEIDER, STEPHEN H., and RANDI LONDER. 1984. *The Coevolution of Climate and Life.* San Francisco: Sierra Club Books.

SCHNEIDER, WILLIAM, and I. A. LEWIS. 1984. "The straight story on homosexual rights." *Public Opinion,* 7:1, 16–20, 59–60.

SCHNEIDMAN, EDWIN (ed.). 1984. *Death: Current Perspectives.* Palo Alto, Calif.: Mayfield.

SCHOSTAK, ARTHUR, GARY MCLOUTH, and LYNN SENG. 1983. *Men and Abortion.* New York: Praeger.

SCHRAM, DONNA D. 1978. "Rape," in James R. Chapman and Margaret Gates (eds.), *The Victimization of Women.* Beverly Hills, Calif.: Sage.

SCHUCKIT, MARK A., et al. 1979. *The Genetic Aspects of Psychiatric Syndrome Relating to Antisocial Problems in Youth.* Seattle: Center for Law and Justice.

SCHUDSON, MICHAEL. 1985. *Advertising, the Uneasy Persuasion: Its Dubious Impact on American Society.* New York: Basic Books.

SCHUMAN, HOWARD, CHARLETTE STEEN, and LAWRENCE BOBO. 1985. *Racial Attitudes in America: Trends and Interpretations.* Cambridge, Mass.: Harvard University Press.

SCHUR, EDWIN M. 1965. *Crimes Without Victims—Deviant Behavior and Public Policy.* Englewood Cliffs, N.J.: Prentice-Hall.

——————. 1976. *The Awareness Trap: Self Absorption Instead of Social Change.* New York: Quandrangle.

——————. 1980. *The Politics of Deviance.* Englewood Cliffs, N.J.: Prentice-Hall.

SCHWARTZ, HOWARD and C. S. KART (eds.). 1978. *Dominant Issues in Medical Sociology.* Reading, Mass.: Addison-Wesley.

SCRIMSHAW, NEVIN S., and LANCE TAYLOR. 1980. "Food." *Scientific American,* 243, pp. 78–88.

SCULL, ANDREW T. 1977. *Decarceration: Community Treatment and the Deviant—A Radical View.* Englewood Cliffs, N.J.: Prentice-Hall.

——————. 1979. *Museums of Madness: The Social Organization of Insanity in Nineteenth-Century England.* New York: St. Martin's Press.

SCULLY, DIANA, and JOSEPH MAROLLA. 1983. "Incarcerated rapists: Exploring a sociological model." *Final Report for the Department of Health and Human Services.* Washington, D.C.: National Institutes of Mental Health.

SEGAL, ALEXANDER. 1976. "The sick role concept: Understanding illness behavior." *Journal of Health and Social Behavior,* 17, pp. 162–169.

SELIGMAN, DANIEL. 1984. "Why are people poor?" *Fortune,* October 1, pp. 189–191.

SELIGMAN, JEAN, et al. 1984. "The date who rapes." *Newsweek,* April 9, p. 91.

SELIM, ROBERT. 1980. "The 1980's: A decade of hunger?" *The Futurist,* 14, pp. 29–38.

SELLIN, THORSTEN. 1938. *Culture Conflict and Crime.* New York: Social Science Research Council.

——————. 1980. *The Penalty of Death.* Beverly Hills, Calif.: Sage.

SERVICE, ELMAN R. 1971. *Primitive Social Organization: An Evolutionary Perspective.* New York: Random House.

——————. 1975. *Origins of the State and Civilization: The Process of Cultural Evolution.* New York: Norton.

SEWELL, WILLIAM H. 1971. "Inequality of opportunity for higher education." *American Sociological Review,* 36, pp. 793–808.

——————, and ROBERT M. HAUSER. 1975. *Education, Occupation, and Earnings.* New York: Academic Press.

_____, and **ROBERT M. HAUSER** (eds.). 1976. *Schooling and Achievement in American Society.* New York: Academic Press.

_____, **ROBERT M. HAUSER**, and **WENDY C. WOLF**. 1980. "Sex, schooling, and occupational status." *American Journal of Sociology,* 86, pp. 551–583.

SHAFFER, KAY T. 1981. *Sex Roles and Human Behavior.* Cambridge, Mass.: Winthrop.

SHAPIRO, ARTHUR K. 1982. "The placebo effect," in W. G. Clark and J. del Guidice, *Principles of Pharmacology.* 2nd ed. New York: Academic Press.

SHATTUCK, ROGER. 1980. *The Forbidden Experiment.* New York: Farrar, Straus and Giroux.

SHAW, MARVIN E. 1981. *Group Dynamics: The Psychology of Small Group Behavior.* 3rd ed. New York: McGraw-Hill.

SHELER, JEFFREY L., et al. 1985. "Lobbyists go for it." *U.S. News and World Report.* June 17, pp. 30–54.

SHELP, EARL E. 1986. *Born to Die? Deciding the Fate of Critically Ill Newborns.* Chicago: University of Chicago Press.

SHERIF, MUZAFER. 1956. "Experiments in group conflict." *Scientific American,* 195, pp. 54–58.

SHERMAN, JULIA. 1978. *Sex-Related Cognitive Differences.* Springfield, Ill.: Charles C Thomas.

SHIBUTANI, TAMOTSU. 1966. *Improvised News: A Sociological Study of Rumor.* Indianapolis: Bobbs-Merrill.

SHIELDS, PETE. 1981. *Guns Don't Die—People Do.* New York: Arbor House.

SHIPLER, DAVID K. 1982. *Russia: Broken Idols, Solemn Dreams.* New York: Times Books.

_____. 1985. "The view from America." *New York Times Magazine,* November 10, pp. 33–48, 72–89.

SHORTER, EDWARD. 1975. *The Making of the Modern Family.* New York: Basic Books.

_____. 1986. *Bedside Manners: The Troubled History of Doctors and Patients.* New York: Simon and Schuster.

SHOSTAK, ARTHUR B., and **GARY MCLOUTH**. 1984. *Men and Abortion: Losses, Lessons, and Love.* New York: Human Sciences Press.

SHOTT, SUSAN. 1979. "Emotion and social life: A symbolic interactionist analysis." *American Journal of Sociology,* 84:6, 1317–1334.

SHRAG, PETER. 1978. *Mind Control.* New York: Random House.

SHUPE, ANSON D., and **DAVID G. BROMLEY**. 1980. *The New Vigilantes: Deprogrammers, Anti-cultists and the New Religions.* Beverly Hills, Calif.: Sage.

SIDEL, RUTH. 1986. *Women and Children Last: The Plight of Poor Women in Affluent America.* New York: Viking.

SILBERMAN, CHARLES E. 1971. *Crisis in the Classroom: The Remaking of American Education.* New York: Random House.

_____. 1978. *Criminal Violence, Criminal Justice.* New York: Random House.

SILBERNER, JOANNE. 1982. "Cheating in the labs." *Science Digest,* August, pp. 38–41.

SIMENAUER, JACQUELINE, and **DAVID CARROLL**. 1982. *Singles: The New Americans.* New York: Simon and Schuster.

SIMKUS, ALBERT A. 1981. "Comparative stratification and mobility." *International Journal of Comparative Sociology,* 22, pp. 213–216.

SIMMEL, GEORG. 1904. "The sociology of conflict," Albion Small (transl.). *American Journal of Sociology,* 9, p. 490 ff.

_____. 1955. *Conflict and the Web of Group Affiliations.* Kurt Wolff (transl.). Glencoe, Ill.: Free Press.

_____. 1964. "The metropolis and mental life," in Kurt Wolff (ed.), *The Sociology of Georg Simmel.* New York: Free Press.

SIMON, DAVID R., and **STANLEY D. EITZEN**. 1982. *Elite Deviance.* Boston: Allyn and Bacon.

SIMON, JULIAN L. 1981. *The Ultimate Resource.* Princeton: Princeton University Press.

SIMONS, GEOFF. 1985. *Silicon Shock: The Menace of Computer Invasion.*

Oxford: Basil Blackwell.

SIMPSON, GEORGE E., and **J. MILTON YINGER**. 1985. *Racial and Cultural Minorities: An Analysis of Prejudice and Discrimination.* 5th ed. New York: Plenum.

SINGER, PETER, and **DEANE WELLS**. 1985. *Making Babies: The New Science and Ethics of Conception.* New York: Scribner's.

SINGH, J. A. L., and **ROBERT M. ZINGG**. 1942. *Wolf Children and Feral Man.* New York: Harper & Row.

SITKOFF, HARVARD. 1982. *The Struggle for Black Equality, 1954–1980.* New York: Hill and Wang.

SITWELL, NIGEL. 1984. "Our trees are dying." *Science Digest,* September, pp. 39–48, 96.

SIVARD, RUTH LEGER. 1986. *World Military and Social Expenditures, 1986.* Washington, D.C.: World Priorities.

SIZER, THEODORE R. 1984. *Horace's Compromise: The Dilemma of the American High School.* Boston: Houghton Mifflin.

SJOBERG, GIDEON. 1960. *The Preindustrial City.* New York: Free Press.

SKINNER, B. F. 1971. *Beyond Freedom and Dignity.* New York: Knopf.

SKJEI, ERIC, and **RICHARD RABKIN**. 1981. *The Male Ordeal: Role Crisis in a Changing World.* New York: Putnam.

SKLARE, MARSHALL. 1971. *America's Jews.* New York: Random House.

_____ (ed.). 1974. *The Jew in American Society.* New York: Behrman House.

SKOCPOL, THEDA. 1979. *States and Social Revolutions.* New York: Cambridge University Press.

SKOLNICK, ARLENE S., and **JEROME H. SKOLNICK**. (eds.). 1986. *Family in Transition: Rethinking Marriage, Sexuality, Childrearing, and Family Organization.* 5th ed. Boston: Little, Brown.

SKULLY, GERALD W. 1974. "Discrimination: The case of baseball," in Roger G. Noll (ed.), *Government and the Sports Business.* Washington, D.C.: Brookings Institution.

SLAFF, JAMES, and **JOHN K. BRUBAKER**. 1985. *The AIDS Epidemic.* New York: Warner.

SLATER, PHILIP E. 1955. "Role differentiation in small groups," in A. Paul Hare et al. (eds.), *Small Groups: Studies in Social Interaction.* New York: Knopf.

_____. 1970. *The Pursuit of Loneliness: American Culture at the Breaking Point.* Boston: Beacon.

SMART, CAROL. 1984. *The Ties that Bind: Law, Marriage, and the Reproduction of Patriarchal Relations.* London: Routledge & Kegan Paul.

SMELSER, NEIL J. 1962. *Theory of Collective Behavior.* New York: Free Press.

SMITH, ADAM. 1910. *The Wealth of Nations.* London: Dent.

SMITH, JAMES R., and **LYNN G. SMITH** (eds.). 1974. *Beyond Monogamy: Recent Studies of Sexual Alternatives in Marriage.* Baltimore: Johns Hopkins University Press.

SMITH, LILLIAN. 1949. *Killers of the Dream.* New York: Norton.

SMITH, TERRENCE. 1984. "Iran: Five years of fanaticism." *New York Times Magazine,* February 12, pp. 21–32.

SNIDER, WILLIAM D. 1985. *Helms and Hunt: The North Carolina Senate Race, 1984.* Chapel Hill: University of North Carolina Press.

SNOW, DAVID A., and **CYNTHIA L. PHILLIPS**. 1982. "The changing self-orientations of college students: From institutions to impulse." *Social Science Quarterly,* 63, pp. 462–476.

SNYDER, ELDON E., and **ELMER A. SPREITZER**. 1983. *Social Aspects of Sport.* 2nd ed. Englewood Cliffs, N.J.: Prentice-Hall.

SOKOLOFF, NATALIE J. 1981. *Between Money and Love: The Dialectics of Women's Home and Market Work.* New York: Praeger.

SOLOMON, LEWIS C., et al. 1977. *College as a Training Ground for Jobs.* New York: Praeger.

SOMMER, ROBERT. 1979. *Personal Space.* Englewood Cliffs, N.J.: Prentice-Hall.

SOROKIN, PITIRIM A. 1937. *Social and Cultural Dynamics.* New York: American Books.

_____. 1941. *The Crisis of Our Age.* New York: E. P. Dutton.

SOWELL, THOMAS. 1977. "New light on the black IQ controversy." *New York Times Magazine,* March 27, pp. 56–63.

_____. 1981. *Ethnic America: A History.* New York: Basic Books.

_____. 1983. *The Economics and Politics of Race.* New York: Morrow.

SPATES, JAMES L. 1983. "The sociology of values." *Annual Review of Sociology,* 9, Palo Alto: Calif: Annual Reviews.

SPECTOR, MALCOLM. 1977. "Legitimizing homosexuality." *Society,* 41, pp. 52–56.

_____, and JOHN I. KITSUSE. 1973. "Social problems: A re-formulation." *Social Problems,* 21, pp. 145–159.

_____, and JOHN I. KITSUSE. 1977. *Constructing Social Problems.* Menlo Park, Calif.: Cummings.

SPENGLER, OSWALD. 1962, originally published 1918, 1922. *The Decline of the West.* New York: Knopf.

SPICER, EDWARD H. 1980. "American Indians," in Stephan Thernstrom, *Harvard Encyclopedia of American Ethnic Groups.* Cambridge, Mass.: Harvard University Press.

SPITZ, RENÉ A. 1945. "Hospitalism: An inquiry into the genesis of psychiatric conditions in early childhood," in Anna Freud et al. (eds.), *The Psychoanalytic Study of the Child.* New York: International Universities Press.

SPRADLEY, JAMES P., and DAVID W. MCCURDY (eds.). 1980. *Conformity and Conflict: Readings in Cultural Anthropology.* Boston: Little, Brown.

SQUIRES, GREGORY D. 1979. *Education, Jobs, and the U.S. Class Structure.* New Brunswick, N.J.: Transaction Books.

SRINIVAS, M. N. 1966. *Social Change in Modern India.* Berkeley, Calif.: University of California Press.

SROLE, LEO, et al. 1962. *Mental Health in the Metropolis.* New York: McGraw-Hill.

_____, et al. 1977. *Mental Health in the Metropolis.* Rev. ed. New York: Harper & Row.

ST. JOHN, NANCY H. 1975. *School Desegregation: Outcomes for Children.* New York: Wiley.

_____. 1981. "The effects of school desegregation on children: A new look at the evidence," in Adam Yarmolinsky et al., (eds.), *Race and Schooling in the City.* Cambridge, Mass.: Harvard University Press.

STACK, STEVEN, and DELORE ZIMMERMAN. 1982. "The effect of world economy on income inequality: A reassessment." *The Sociological Quarterly,* 23, pp. 345–358.

STAMPP, KENNETH. 1956. *The Peculiar Institution.* New York: Knopf.

STANLEY, STEVEN M. 1982. *Fossils, Genes, and the Origin of Species.* New York: Basic Books.

STAPLES, ROBERT. 1986. *The Urban Plantation: Racism and Colonialism in the Post Civil Rights Era.* San Francisco: Black Scholar Press.

STARES, PAUL B. 1986. *The Militarization of Space.* Ithaca, N.Y.: Cornell University Press.

STARK, RODNEY, and WILLIAM SIMS BAINBRIDGE. 1985. *The Future of Religion: Secularization, Revival, and Cult Formation.* Berkeley, Calif.: University of California Press.

STARR, PAUL. 1982. *The Social Transformation of American Medicine.* New York: Basic Books.

STEIN, HOWARD F., and ROBERT F. HILL. 1977. *The Ethnic Imperative.* University Park, Pa.: Penn State University Press.

STEIN, LEONARD I. 1967. "The doctor-nurse game." *Archives of General Psychiatry,* 16, pp. 699–703.

STEIN, PETER J. 1976. *Single.* Englewood Cliffs, N.J.: Prentice-Hall.

_____, (ed.). 1981. *Single Life: Unmarried Adults in Social Context.* New York: St Martin's Press.

STEINBERG, STEPHEN. 1981. *The Ethnic Myth: Race, Ethnicity, and Class in America.* New York: Atheneum.

STEINER, STAN. 1974. *The Islands: The Worlds of the Puerto Ricans.* New York: Harper & Row.

STEWARD, JULIAN H. 1955. *Theory of Culture Change.* Urbana, Ill.: University of Illinois Press.

STINNET, NICK, and CRAIG WAYNE BIRDSONG. 1978. *The Family and Alternate Life Styles.* Chicago: Nelson Hall.

STOCKARD, JEAN, and MIRIAM M. JOHNSON. 1980. *Sex Roles: Sex Inequality and Sex Role Development.* Englewood Cliffs, N.J.: Prentice-Hall.

STOCKTON, WILLIAM. 1978. "Going home: The Puerto Ricans' new migration." *New York Times,* May 12, pp. 20–22, 88–93.

STOGDILL, RALPH M. 1974. *Handbook of Leadership: A Survey of Theory and Research.* New York: Free Press.

STOLTE, JOHN F. 1983. "The legitimation of structural inequality." *American Sociological Review,* 48, pp. 331–342.

STONE, JOHN. 1986. *Racial Conflict in Contemporary Society.* Cambridge, Mass.: Harvard University Press.

STONE, LAWRENCE. 1977. *The Family, Sex, and Marriage in England, 1500–1800.* New York: Harper & Row.

STONER, J. A. F. 1961. "A comparison of individual and group decisions involving risk." Unpublished master's thesis, Massachusetts Institute of Technology.

STORER, NORMAN W. (ed.). 1973. *Sociology of Science: Theoretical and Empirical Investigations.* Chicago: University of Chicago Press.

STRAUS, MURRAY A., et al. 1979. *Behind Closed Doors: A Study of Family Violence in America.* Garden City, N.Y.: Doubleday.

_____, and GERALD T. HOTALING. 1980. *The Social Causes of Husband-Wife Violence.* Minneapolis: University of Minneapolis Press.

STRAUSS, ANSELM. 1978. *Negotiations: Varieties, Contexts, Processes, and Social Order.* San Francisco: Jossey-Bass.

STRONG, P. M. 1979. "Sociological imperialism and the profession of medicine: A critical examination of the thesis of medical imperialism." *Social Science and Medicine,* 13A: 2, pp. 199–215.

STRYKER, SHELDON. 1980. *Symbolic Interaction.* Menlo Park, Calif.: Cummings.

STUBBING, RICHARD A., and RICHARD A. MENDEL. 1986. *The Defense Game.* New York: Harper & Row.

SUDMAN, SEYMOUR and NORMAN M. BRADBURN. 1982. *Asking Questions: A Practical Guide to Questionnaire Design.* San Francisco: Jossey-Bass.

SUDNOW, DAVID. 1972. *Studies in Social Interaction.* New York: Free Press.

SUMNER, WILLIAM GRAHAM. 1906. *Folkways.* Boston: Ginn

SURANSKY, VALERIE P. 1982. *The Erosion of Childhood.* Chicago: University of Chicago Press.

SUTHERLAND, EDWIN H. 1939. *Principles of Criminology.* Philadelphia: Lippincott.

_____. 1940. "White collar criminality." *American Sociological Review,* 5, pp. 1–12.

SUTTIES, GERALD. 1970. *The Social Order of the Slum.* Chicago: University of Chicago Press.

SWANSON, GUY E. 1960. *The Birth of the Gods.* Ann Arbor: University of Michigan Press.

SWEET, ELLEN. 1985. "Date rape." *Ms.,* October, pp. 56–59.

SYMANSKI, RICHARD. 1981. *The Immoral Landscape: Female Prostitution in the Western World.* Toronto: Butterworth.

SZASZ, THOMAS. 1961. *The Myth of Mental Illness.* New York: Harper & Row.

_____. 1970. *The Manufacture of Madness.* New York: Dell.

_____. 1970. *Ideology and Insanity.* New York: Anchor.

_____. 1974. *The Myth of Mental Illness.* Rev. ed. New York: Harper & Row.

SZYMANSKI, ALBERT. 1983. *Class Structure: A Critical Perspective.* New York: Praeger.

TAGLIACOZZO, DAISY L., and HANS O. MAUKSCH. 1979. "The patient's view of the patient's role," in E. Gartley Jaco (ed.), *Patient's Physicians, and Illness.* New York: Free Press.

TAKOOSHIAN, HAROLD, and HERZEL BODINGER. 1979. "Street crime in 18 American cities: A national field experiment." Paper presented at the annual meeting of the American Sociological Association, Boston, August.

TANNER, DONNA M. 1978. *The Lesbian Couple*. Lexington, Mass.: Heath.

TAVRIS, CAROL, and CAROLE WADE. 1984. *The Longest War: Sex Differences in Perspective*. 2nd ed. New York: Harcourt Brace Jovanovich.

TAYLOR, GORDON RATTRAY. 1970. *Sex in History*. New York: Vanguard.

TAYLOR, HOWARD F. 1980. *The I.Q. Game*. New Brunswick, N.J.: Rutgers University Press.

TAYLOR, IAN, et al. 1973. *The New Criminology*. London: Routledge & Kegan Paul.

TEICH, ALBERT H. (ed.) 1986. *Technology and the Future*. 4th ed. New York: St. Martin's Press.

THERNSTROM, STEPHAN. 1980. *Harvard Encyclopedia of American Ethnic Groups*. Cambridge, Mass.: Harvard University Press.

THOMAS, EVAN. 1986. "Peddling influence." *Time*, March 3, pp. 26–36.

THOMAS, LEWIS. 1983. *The Youngest Science: Notes of a Medicine Watcher*. New York: Viking.

THOMPSON, ANTHONY P. 1983. "Extramarital sex: A review of the literature." *The Journal of Sex Research*. February, pp. 1–21.

THOMPSON, SPENCER K. 1975. "Gender labels and early sex-role development." *Child Development*, 46, pp. 339–347.

THORNE, BARRIE, and NANCY HENLEY. 1975. *Language and Sex: Difference and Dominance*. Rowley, Mass.: Newbury House.

THUROW, LESTER C. 1984. "The leverage of our wealthiest 400." *New York Times*, Oct. 11, p. 27.

TIEN, H. YUAN. 1983. "China: Demographic billionaire." *Population Bulletin*, 38:2, pp. 1–42.

TILLY, CHARLES. 1978. *From Mobilization to Revolution*. Reading, Mass.: Addison-Wesley.

TITTLE, CHARLES R., et al. 1978. "The myth of social class and criminality: An empirical assessment of the empirical evidence." *American Sociological Review*, 43, pp. 643–656.

TOBEY, JACKSON. 1980. "Crime in the American Public Schools." *The Public Interest*, 58 (Winter), pp. 18–42.

TOBIAS, SHEILA, and CAROL WEISSBROD. 1980. "Anxiety and Mathematics: An Update." *Harvard Educational Review*, 50, pp. 63–70.

TOCH, ALBERT H. (ed.). 1986. *Technology and the Future*. 4th ed. New York: St. Martin's Press.

TOCH, HANS. 1965. *The Social Psychology of Social Movements*. Indianapolis: Bobbs-Merrill.

TOFFLER, ALVIN. 1980. *The New Wave*. New York: Morrow.

TÖNNIES, FERDINAND. 1957, originally published in 1887. *Community and Society*. East Lansing, Mich.: Michigan State University Press.

TORREY, E. F. 1974. *The Death of Psychiatry*. New York: Penguin.

TOURAINE, ALAN. 1971. *The Post-Industrial Society*. New York: Random House.

TOYNBEE, ARNOLD. 1946. *A Study of History*. New York: Oxford University Press.

TRACY, PAUL E., MARVIN E. WOLFGANG, and ROBERT M. FIGLIO. 1985. *Delinquency in Two Birth Cohorts*. Washington, D.C.: U.S. Department of Justice.

TRAVERS, ANDREW. 1982. "Ritual power in interaction." *Symbolic Interaction*, 5:2, 277–286.

TREIMAN, DONALD J. 1977. *Occupational Prestige in Comparative Perspective*. New York: Academic Press.

_____, and HEIDI I. HARTMANN. 1981. *Women, Work, and Wages*. Washington, D.C.: National Academy of Sciences.

_____, and PATRICIA A. ROOS. 1983. "Sex and earnings in industrial society: A nine-nation comparison." *American Journal of Sociology*, 89:3, pp. 612–650.

TROELTSCH, ERNST. 1931. *The Social Teachings of the Christian Churches*. New York: Macmillan.

TSIPIS, KOSTA. 1982. "The physical effects of a nuclear explosion," in Eric Chivian, et al. (eds.). *Last Aid: The Medical Dimensions of Nuclear War*. San Francisco: W. H. Freeman.

_____. 1983. *Arsenal: Understanding Weapons in the Nuclear Age*. New York: Simon and Schuster.

TSOU, TANG. 1985. *The Cultural Revolution and Post-Mao Reforms*. Chicago: University of Chicago Press.

TUCHMAN, GAYE. 1978. *Making News: A Study in the Construction of Reality*. New York: Free Press.

_____, ARLENE KAPLAN DANIELS, and JAMES BENET (eds.). 1978. *Hearth and Home: Images of Women in the Mass Media*. New York: Oxford University Press.

TUCKER, ANTHONY, and JOHN GLEISNER. 1982. *Crucible of Despair: The Effects of Nuclear War*. London: Menard Press.

TUMIN, MELVIN M. 1953. "Some principles of stratification: A critical analysis." *American Sociological Review*, 18, pp. 378–394.

_____. 1955. "Rewards and task orientations." *American Sociological Review*, 20, pp. 419–423.

_____. 1963. "On inequality." *American Sociological Review*, 28, pp. 19–26.

TURK, AUSTIN T. 1982. *Political Crime: The Defiance and Defense of Authority*. Beverley Hills, Calif.: Sage.

TURKLE, SHERRY. 1984. *The Second Self: Computers and the Human Spirit*. New York: Simon and Schuster.

TURNER, JEFFREY S., and DONALD B. HELMS. 1979. *Life Span Development*. Philadelphia: Saunders.

TURNER, RALPH H. 1964. "Collective behavior," in Robert E. L. Fatis (ed.), *Handbook of Modern Sociology*. Chicago: Rand McNally.

_____, and LEWIS M. KILLIAN. 1972. *Collective Behavior*. 2nd ed. Englewood Cliffs, N.J.: Prentice-Hall.

_____, JOANNE M. NIGG, and DENISE HELLER PAZ. 1986. *Waiting for Disaster: Earthquake Watch in California*. Berkeley: University of California Press.

TWADDLE, ANDREW. 1973. "Illness and deviance." *Social Science and Medicine*, 7, pp. 751–762.

_____. 1979. *Sickness Behavior and the Sick Role*. Cambridge, Mass.: Schenkman.

_____, and RICHARD HESSLER. 1986. *A Sociology of Health*. 2nd ed. New York: Macmillan.

TYREE, ANDREA, MOSHE SEMYONOV, and ROBERT W. HODGE. 1979. "Gaps and glissandos: Inequality, economic development, and social mobility in 24 countries." *American Sociological Review*, 44, pp. 410–424.

UNGER, RHODA K. 1980. *Female and Male: Sex and Gender*. Harper & Row.

USEEM, MICHAEL. 1978. "The inner group of the American capitalist class." *Social Problems*, 25, pp. 225–240.

_____. 1979. "The social organization of the American business elite and participation of corporation directors in the governance of American institutions." *American Sociological Review*, 44, pp. 553–572.

_____. 1984. *The Inner Circle: Large Corporations and the Rise of the Business Political Activity in the U.S. and U.K.*. New York: Oxford University Press.

_____. 1980. "Corporations and the corporate elite." *Annual Review of Sociology*, 6. Palo Alto, Calif.: Annual Reviews.

VAN BAAL, J. 1966. *Dema: Description and Analysis of Manind-anim Culture (South New Guinea)*. The Hague: M. Nijhoff.

VAN DEN BERGHE, PIERRE. 1978. *Race and Racism: A Comparative Perspective*. 2nd ed. New York: Wiley.

VANDER ZANDEN, JAMES W. 1983. *American Minority Relations*. 4th ed. New York: Knopf.

VANFOSSEN, BETH E. 1979. *The Structure of Social Inequality*. Boston: Little, Brown.

VAYDA, ANDREW P. (ed.). 1969. *Environment and Cultural Behavior.* Garden City, N.Y.: Natural History Press.

VEBLEN, THORSTEIN. 1922. *The Instinct of Workmanship.* New York: Huebsch.

VERBA, SIDNEY, and NORMAN H. NIE. 1972. *Participation in America.* New York: Harper & Row.

VERNON, BRIAN. 1985. *Objectively Correct Inspections.* London: World Books.

VERNON, RAYMOND. 1977. *Storm over the Multinationals.* Cambridge, Mass.: Harvard University Press.

VIDAL, FEDERICO S. 1976. "Mutayr: A tribe of Saudi Arabian pastoral nomads," in David E. Hunter and Phillip Whitten (eds.), *The Study of Anthropology.* New York: Harper & Row.

VOGEL, EZRA F. 1980. *Japan as Number One: Lessons for America.* New York: Harper Colophon.

VOGEL, VIRGIL. 1970. *American Indian Medicine Man.* New York: Ballantine.

VOSLENSKY, MICHAEL. 1984. *Nomenklatura: The Soviet Ruling Class.* New York: Doubleday.

WAGLEY, CHARLES, and MARVIN HARRIS. 1964. *Minorities in the New World.* New York: Columbia University Press.

WAITZKIN, HOWARD. 1986. *The Second Sickness: Contradictions of Capitalist Health Care.* Chicago: University of Chicago Press.

——————, and BARBARA WATERMAN. 1974. *The Exploitation of Illness in Capitalist Society.* Indianapolis: Bobbs-Merrill.

——————, and JOHN D. STOECKLE. 1976. "Information and control and the micro-politics of health care." *Social Science and Medicine,* 6, pp. 263–276.

WALFORD, ROY. 1983. *Maximum Life Span.* New York: Norton.

WALKER, MARCIA, and STANLEY BRODKSY. 1976. *Sexual Assault: The Victim and the Rapist.* Lexington, Mass.: Lexington Books.

WALKER, PAT. 1979. *Between Labor and Capital.* Boston, Mass.: South End Press.

WALLACE, ANTHONY F. C. 1956. "Revitalization movements." *American Anthropologist,* 58, pp. 264–281.

WALLACE, MICHAEL D. 1979. "The role of arms races in the escalation of disputes into war: Some new evidence." *Journal of Conflict Resolution,* 32:1, pp. 3–16.

WALLERSTEIN, IMMANUEL. 1974. *The Modern World System.* New York: Academic Press.

——————. 1979. *The Capitalist World-Economy.* New York: Cambridge University Press.

WALLIS, ROY. 1977. *The Road to Total Freedom: A Sociological Analysis of Scientology.* New York: Columbia University Press.

WALSH, MARY ROTH. 1977. *Doctors Wanted: Women Need Not Apply.* New Haven: Yale University Press.

WALUM, LAUREL RICHARDSON. "The changing door ceremony: Notes on the operation of sex roles." *Urban Life and Culture* 2 (January, 1974), pp. 506–515.

WARHEIT, GEORGE J., CHARLES E. HOLZER, and SANDRA A. AREY. 1975. "Race and mental illness: An epidemiological update." *Journal of Health and Social Behavior,* 16, pp. 243–356.

WARNER, W. LLOYD, and PAUL S. LUNT. 1941. *The Social Life of a Modern Community.* New Haven: Yale University Press.

——————. and PAUL S. LUNT, et al. 1949. *Social Class in America.* New York: Harper.

WATERS, HARRY P. 1977. "What TV does to kids." *Newsweek,* February 21, pp. 62–70.

WATSON, J. B. 1924. *Behavior.* New York: Norton.

WAX, ROSALIE. 1978. *Doing Fieldwork.* Chicago: University of Chicago Press.

WEBER, MAX. 1922. *Economy and Society.* Ephraim Fischoff et al. (transl.), 1968. New York: Bedminster Press.

——————. 1946. *From Max Weber: Essays in Sociology.* H. H. Gerth and C. Wright Mills (trans./eds.). New York: Oxford University Press.

——————. 1951. *The Religion of China.* New York: Free Press.

——————. 1952. *Ancient Judaism.* New York: Free Press.

——————. 1958a. *The Protestant Ethic and the Spirit of Capitalism.* New York: Scribner's.

——————. 1958b. *The Religion of India.* New York: Free Press.

——————. 1963. *The Sociology of Religion.* Boston: Beacon Press.

WEINBERG, ALVIN M. 1966. "Can technology replace social engineering?" *University of Chicago Magazine,* 59 (October), pp. 6–10.

WEINBERG, MARTIN S., and COLIN J. WILLIAMS. 1974. *Male Homosexuals: Their Problems and Adjustments.* New York: Oxford University Press.

WEISBERG, D. KELLY. 1985. *Children of the Night.* Lexington, Mass.: Lexington Books.

WEISS, CAROL H., and ALLEN H. BARTON. 1979. *Making Bureaucracies Work.* Beverly Hills, Calif.: Sage.

WEISS, ROBERT S. 1975. *Marital Separation.* New York: Basic Books.

——————. 1979. *Going It Alone: The Family Life and Social Situation of the Single Parent.* New York: Basic Books.

WEITZ, SHIRLEY. 1977. *Sex Roles: Biological, Psychological, and Social Foundations.* New York: Oxford University Press.

——————. (ed.). 1979. *Nonverbal Communication.* New York: Oxford University Press.

WEITZMAN, LENORE. 1979. *Sex Role Socialization.* Palo Alto, Calif.: Mayfield.

——————. 1985. *Divorce Revolution: The Unexpected Social and Economic Consequences for Women and Children in America.* New York: Free Press.

WELCH, SUSAN, JOHN COMER, and MICHAEL STEINMAN. 1973. "Some social and behavioral correlates of health care among Mexican Americans." *Journal of Health and Social Behavior,* 14, pp. 205–213.

WENNBERG, ROBERT N. 1985. *Life in the Balance: Exploring the Abortion Controversy.* Grand Rapids, Mich.: Eerdmans.

WESLAGER, C. A. 1973. *Magic Medicine of the Indians.* Somerset, N.J.: Middle Atlantic Press.

WEST, CANDACE, and DON H. ZIMMERMAN. 1977. "Women's place in everyday talk: Reflections on parent-child interactions." *Social Problems,* 24, pp. 521–528.

WESTHUES, KENNETH. 1972. *Society's Shadow: Studies in the Sociology of Countercultures.* Toronto: McGraw-Hill Ryerson.

WESTIE, FRANK R. 1965. "The American dilemma: An empirical test." *American Sociological Review,* 30, pp. 527–538.

WESTLEY, FRANCES. 1978. "'The cult of man': Durkheim's predictions and the new religious movements." *Sociological Analysis,* 39:2, pp. 135–145.

WEYLER, REX. 1982. *Blood on the Land: The Government and Corporate War against the American Indian Movement.* New York: Everest House.

WHITE, LESLIE A. 1959. *The Evolution of Culture.* New York: McGraw-Hill.

——————. 1969. *The Science of Culture.* New York: Farrar, Straus & Giroux.

WHITE, RALPH K., and RONALD O. LIPPITT. 1960. *Autocracy and Democracy.* New York: Harper & Row.

WHITE, THEODORE H. 1983. "China: Burnout of a revolution." *Time,* September 26, pp. 30–49.

WHITEHEAD, HARRIET. 1974. "Reasonably fantastic: Some perspectives on scientology, science fiction, and occultism," in Irving I. Zaretsky and Mark P. Leone (eds.), *Religious Movements in Contemporary American.* Princeton, N.J.: Princeton University Press.

WHYTE, WILLIAM F. 1943. *Street-Corner Society: The Social Structure of an Italian Slum.* Chicago: University of Chicago Press.

WHYTE, WILLIAM H. 1956. *The Organization Man.* New York: Simon and Schuster.

WICKER, TOM. 1982. "War by accident." *New York Times*, November 21, p. 32.

WILENSKY. H. L. 1964. "The professionalization of everyone?" *American Journal of Sociology*, 70, pp. 137–158.

WILL, GEORGE F. 1985. "Battling the racial spoils system." *Newsweek*, June 10, p. 96.

WILLARD, W. 1972. *Curanderismo and Health Care.* Tucson, Ariz.: College of Medicine, University of Arizona.

WILLIAMS, FREDERICK, et al. 1981. *Children, Television, and Sex-Role Stereotyping.* New York: Praeger.

WILLIAMS, LENA. 1985. "To blacks, the surburbs prove both pleasant and troubling." *New York Times*, May 20, pp. A1, B4.

WILLIAMS, MONCI JO. 1985. "The baby bust hits the job market." *Fortune*, May 27,

WILLIAMS, ROBIN M., JR. 1970. *American Society: A Sociological Interpretation.* 3rd ed. New York: Knopf.

WILLIAMSON, NANCY E. 1976. *Sons or Daughters: A Cross-Cultural Survey of Parental Preference.* Beverly Hills, Calif.: Sage.

WILLIE, CHARLES V. 1976. *A New Look at Black Families.* Bayside, N.Y.: General Hall.

_____. 1980. *The Caste and Class Controversy.* Bayside, N.Y.: General Hall.

WILSON, EDWARD O. 1975. *Sociobiology: The New Synthesis.* Cambridge, Mass.: Harvard University Press.

_____. 1978. *On Human Nature.* Cambridge, Mass.: Harvard University Press.

WILSON, JAMES Q. 1983. *Thinking about Crime.* Rev. ed. New York: Basic Books.

_____ (ed.). 1983. *Crime and Public Policy.* New York: ICS Press.

_____, and RICHARD J. HERNSTEIN. 1985. *Crime and Human Nature.* New York: Simon and Schuster.

WILSON, JOHN. 1973. *Introduction to Social Movements.* New York: Basic Books.

_____. 1982. *Religion in American Society: The Effective Presence.* 2nd ed. Englewood Cliffs, N.J.: Prentice-Hall.

WILSON, ROBERT A., and BILL HOSOKAWA. 1980. *East to America: A History of the Japanese in the United States.* New York: Morrow.

WILSON, WILLIAM J. 1973. *Power, Racism, and Privilege.* New York: Free Press.

_____. 1980. *The Declining Significance of Race: Blacks and Changing American Institutions.* 2nd ed. Chicago: University of Chicago Press.

WINERIP, MICHAEL. 1985. "Asian Americans question Ivy League's entry policies." *New York Times*, May 30, pp. 1, 4.

WINN, MARIE. 1983. *Children without Childhood.* New York: Pantheon.

WINNER, LANGDON. 1977. *Autonomous Technology.* Cambridge, Mass.: MIT Press.

WINNICK, MARIANN P., and CHARLES WINNICK. 1979. *The Television Experience: What Children See.* Beverly Hills, Calif.: Sage.

WIRTH, LOUIS. 1931. "Culture conflict and misconduct." *Social Forces*, 9, pp. 484–492.

_____. 1938. "Urbanism as a way of life." *American Journal of Sociology*, 44, pp. 8–20.

_____. 1945. "The problem of minority groups," in Ralph Linton (ed.), *The Science of Man in the World Crisis.* New York: Columbia University Press.

WOHL, STANLEY. 1984. *The Medical Industrial Complex.* New York: Harmony Books.

WOLF, DEBORAH GOLEMAN. 1979. *The Lesbian Community.* Berkeley, Calif.: University of California Press.

WOLF, WENDY, and FLIGSTEIN, NEIL. 1979. "Sex and authority in the workplace: The causes of sexual inequality." *American Sociological Review*, 44, pp. 235–252.

WOLFE, TOM. 1975. *The Painted Word.* New York: Farrar, Strauss, & Giroux.

_____, 1976. "The 'me' decade and the third great awakening." *New York*, August 23, pp. 26–40.

WOLFF, JANET. 1981. *The Social Production of Art.* New York: St. Martin's Press.

WOLFINGER, RAYMOND E., and STEVEN J. ROSENSTONE. 1980. *Who Votes?* New Haven: Yale University Press.

WOLINSKY, FREDRIC D. 1980. *The Sociology of Health: Principles, Professions, and Issues.* Boston: Little, Brown.

WONG, BERNARD P. 1982. *Chinatown: Economic Adaptation and Ethnic Identity of the Chinese.* New York: Holt, Rinehart, and Winston.

WOODRUM, ERIC. 1981. "An assessment of Japanese-American assimilation, pluralism, and subordination." *American Journal of Sociology*, 87, pp. 157–169.

WORSLEY, PETER. 1957. *The Trumpet Shall Sound.* London: MacGibbon & Kee.

WORSTER, DONALD. 1985. *Rivers of Empire: Water, Aridity, and the Growth of the American West.* New York: Pantheon.

WREN, CHRISTOPHER. 1984. "Despite rural China's gains, poverty grips some regions." *New York Times*, December 18, pp. 1, 10.

_____. 1984. "Improving quality of life is first priority in Peking." *New York Times*, December 16, pp. 1, 14.

WRIGHT, CHARLES. 1986. *Mass Communication: A Sociological Perspective.* 3rd ed. New York: Random House.

WRIGHT, ERIK OLIN. 1979. *Class Structure and Income Determination.* New York: Academic Press.

_____, DAVID HACHEN, CYNTHIA COSTELLO, and JOEY SPRAGUE. 1982. "The American class structure." *American Sociological Review*, 47, pp. 709–726.

WRIGHT, JAMES D., PETER H. ROSSI, and KATHLEEN DALY. 1983. *Under the Gun: Weapons, Crime, and Violence in America.* Hawthorne, N.Y.: Aldine.

WRONG, DENNIS H. 1959. "The functional theory of stratification: Some neglected considerations." *American Sociological Review*, 24, pp. 772–782.

_____. 1961. "The oversocialized conception of man in modern sociology." *American Sociological Review*, 26, pp. 183–193.

WUTHNOW, ROBERT. 1976. *The Consciousness Revolution.* Berkeley, Calif.: University of California Press.

_____. 1978. *Experimentation in American Religion: The New Mysticisms and Their Implications for the Churches.* Berkeley: University of California Press.

WYNNE, EDWARD A. 1986. "Will the Young Support the Old?" in Alan Pifer and Lydia Bronte (eds.). *Our Aging Society: Paradox and Promise.* New York: Norton.

YANKELOVICH, DANIEL. 1981. *New Rules: Searching for Self-Fulfillment in a World Turned Upside Down.* New York: Random House.

YANOWITCH, MURRAY. 1977. *Social and Economic Inequality in the Soviet Union.* White Plains, N.Y.: M. E. Sharpe.

_____ (ed.). 1986. *The Social Structure of the USSR.* Armonk, N.Y.: M. E. Sharpe.

YARROW, L. J. 1963. "Research in dimensions of early maternal care." *Merrill-Palmer Quarterly*, 9, pp. 101–114.

YEDIDIA, MICHAEL. 1980. "The lay-professional division of knowledge in health care delivery," in Julius A. Roth (ed.), *Research in the Sociology of Health Care.* Greenwich, Conn.: JAI Press.

YETMAN, NORMAN R., and D. STANLEY EITZEN. 1982. "Racial dynamics in American sport: Continuity and change," in Norman R. Yetman (ed.), *Majority and Minority: The Dynamics of Race and Ethnicity in American Life.* 3rd ed. Boston: Allyn and Bacon.

_____ (ed.). 1986. *Majority and Minority: The Dynamics of Race and Ethnic Relations.* 4th ed. Rockleigh, N.J.: Allyn and Bacon.

YINGER, MILTON J. 1982. *Countercultures: The Promise and Peril of a World Turned Upside Down.* New York: Free Press.

YORBURG, BETTY. 1974. *Sexual Identity: Sex Roles and Social Change.* New York: Wiley.

YOUNG, JOCK. 1971. *The Drugtakers.* London: Paladin.

YOXEN, EDWARD. 1984. *The Gene Business: Who Should Control Biotechnology?* New York: Harper & Row.

YULSMAN, TOM. 1984. "Greenhouse earth." *Science Digest,* February, pp. 41–45, 98–101.

YUNKER, JAMES A. 1982. "The relevance of the identification problem to statistical research on capital punishment." *Crime and Delinquency,* 28, pp. 96–124.

ZALD, MAYER N., and JOHN D. MCCARTHY (eds.). 1979. *The Dynamics of Social Movements.* Cambridge, Mass.: Winthrop.

—————, and MICHAEL A. BERGER. 1978. "Social movements in organizations: Coups d'etat, insurgency, and mass movements." *American Journal of Sociology,* 83, pp. 823–861.

ZANDER, ALVIN. 1979. "The psychology of group processes." *Annual Review of Psychology.* Palo Alto, Calif.: Annual Reviews, Inc.

ZANGWILL, ISRAEL. 1933. *The Melting Pot.* New York: Macmillan.

ZBOROWSKI, MARK. 1969. *People in Pain.* San Francisco: Jossey-Bass.

ZELIZER, VIVIANA A. 1985. *Pricing the Priceless Child.* New York: Basic Books.

ZELNICK, MELVIN, and JOHN F. KANTER. 1980. "Sexual activity, contraceptive use and pregnancy among metropolitan area teenagers: 1971–1979." *Family Planning Perspectives,* 12, pp. 230–231, 233–237.

ZERUBAVEL, EVIATAR. 1981. *Hidden Rhythms: Schedules and Calendars in Social Life.* Chicago: University of Chicago Press.

—————. 1982. "The standardization of time: A sociohistorical perspective." *American Journal of Sociology,* 88:1, 1–23.

—————. 1985. *The Seven Day Circle: The History and Meaning of the Week.* New York: Free Press.

ZILBERGELD, BERNIE. 1983. *The Shrinking of America: Myths of Psychological Change.* Boston: Little, Brown.

ZIMBARDO, PHILIP G. 1969. "The human choice: Individuation, reason, and order vs. deindividuation, impulse, and chaos." *Nebraska Symposium on Motivation,* 17, pp. 237–307.

ZIMMERMAN, BURKE K. 1984. *Biofuture: Confronting the Genetic Era.* New York: Plenum.

ZIMMERMAN, DON H., and CANDACE WEST. 1975. "Sex roles, interruptions, and silences in conversation," in Barrie Thorne and Nancy Henley, *Language and Sex.* Rowley, Mass.: Newbury House.

ZINSSER, HANS. 1971. *Rats, Lice, and History.* New York: Bantam Books.

ZOLA, IRVING K. 1966. "Culture and symptoms—An analysis of patient's presenting complaints." *American Sociological Review,* 33, pp. 615–630.

—————. 1972. "Medicine as an institution of social control." *Sociological Review,* 20, pp. 480–504.

—————. 1975. "In the name of health and illness: on the socio-political consequences of medical influence." *Social Science and Medicine,* 9, pp. 83–87.

ZURCHER, LOUIS A. 1977. *The Mutable Self: A Self-Concept for Change.* Beverly Hills, Calif.: Sage.

ZWEIGENHAFT, RICHARD L. 1982. "Recent patterns of Jewish representation in the corporate and social elite." *Contemporary Jewry,* 6, pp. 36–46.

ZWERDLING, DANIEL. 1980. *Workplace Democracy.* New York: Harper & Row.

ACKNOWLEDGMENTS

TEXT PERMISSIONS

Page 27   From *Invitation to Sociology* by Peter L. Berger. Copyright © 1963 by Peter L. Berger. Reprinted by permission of Doubleday & Company, Inc.

Page 113   From "Pathology of Imprisonment" by Philip G. Zimbardo. Copyright (1972) by Transaction, Inc. Reprinted by permission of Transaction, Inc.

Page 133   From "Our Forebears Made Childhood a Nightmare" by Lloyd DeMause. Copyright © 1975 American Psychological Association. Reprinted with permission of *Psychology Today* magazine.

Page 140   From *Genie* by Susan Curtiss, Academic Press, 1977. Reprinted by permission of Academic Press.

Page 156   From *Obedience to Authority: An Experimental View* by Stanley Milgram, Harper & Row, 1973. Copyright © 1973 by Stanley Milgram. Reprinted by permission of the author.

Page 219   From "The Saints and the Roughnecks" by William Chambliss. Copyright (1973) by Transaction, Inc. Reprinted by permission of Transaction, Inc.

Page 372   From "Mating Power Among the Tiwi" by Cherry Lindholm and Charles Lindholm, *Science Digest*, Sept./Oct. 1980. Reprinted by permission of the authors.

UNIT OPENERS

1. *Sunday Afternoon on the Island of La Grande Jatte* (detail), Georges Seurat, 1884–1886. Oil on canvas, 81″ × 120⅜″. Helen Birch Bartlett Collection. © The Art Institute of Chicago. All Rights Reserved.

2. *Portrait of Nicholas Wilder 1966*, David Hockney. Acrylic on canvas, 183 cm × 183 cm. © David Hockney 1966.

3. *Target with Four Faces*, Jasper Johns, 1955. Encaustic on newspaper over canvas, 26″ × 26″ (66 × 66 cm), surmounted by four tinted plaster faces in wood box with hinged front. Box closed, 3¾″ × 26″ × 3½″ (9.5 × 66 × 8.9 cm). Overall dimensions with box open, 33⅝″ × 26″ × 3″ (85.3 × 66 × 7.6 cm). Collection, The Museum of Modern Art, New York. Gift of Mr. and Mrs. Robert C. Scull.

4. *The Presidential Family*, Fernando Botero, 1967. Oil on canvas, 6′8⅛″ × 6′5¼″. Collection, The Museum of Modern Art, New York. Gift of Warren D. Benedek.

5. *Columbia at Booster Separation*, Bob McCall, 1981. Oil, 54″ × 38″. Courtesy NASA Art Program.

CHAPTER 1

1.0   © Geoffrey Gove
1.1   © Michael McCoy/Photo Researchers
1.2   from top to bottom, © Leonard Freed/Magnum Photos; © John Moss/Photo Researchers; © Loren McIntyre 1973/Woodfin Camp & Associates
1.3   The Bettmann Archive
1.5   © M. Serraillier/Photo Researchers

1.6–1.8   The Bettmann Archive
1.9   The Granger Collection
1.10   The Bettmann Archive
1.11 and 1.12   The Granger Collection
1.13   American Sociological Association
1.14   Ben Martin, *Time* magazine © Time, Inc.
1.15   Courtesy Columbia University, Office of Public Information
1.16   © Lowell Georgia/Photo Researchers
1.17   © Dennis Brack/Black Star
1.18   © Donald Smetzer/Click/Chicago Ltd.
1.19   left, © Brian Seed/Click/Chicago Ltd.; right, © Thomas Hopker/Woodfin Camp & Associates

CHAPTER 2

1.0   © Howard Sochurek 1983/Woodfin Camp & Associates
2.1   The Bettmann Archive
2.2   © Charles Gupton/Stock, Boston
2.3   © Syndication International
2.4   The Granger Collection
2.5   © Owen Franken/Stock, Boston
2.6   UPI/Bettmann Newsphotos
2.8   © Ellis Herwig/Stock, Boston
2.9   © Andy Levin 1985/Black Star
2.10   left, The Bettmann Archive; right, AP/Wide World Photos
2.12   Museo Nacional de Arte Moderna, Mexico City, photograph © Bradley Smith/Gemini Smith, Inc., La Jolla

CHAPTER 3

3.0   © Victor Englebert/Photo Researchers
3.1   © J. G. Ross/Photo Researchers
3.2   from left to right, © Ylla/Photo Researchers; © Russ Kinne/Photo Researchers; © Toni Angermayer/Photo Researchers
3.3   © Jack Drake 1980/Black Star
3.4   left, Massachusetts Historical Society; right, © Spooner 1984/Gamma-Liaison
3.5   Courtesy of the Norman Rockwell Museum at the Old Corner House, Stockbridge, Mass.
3.6   top, The Bettmann Archive; bottom, © Photri 1986
3.7   top, © C. Bonington 1982/Woodfin Camp & Associates; bottom, © Malcolm S. Kirk/Peter Arnold, Inc.
3.8   © Ira Kirschenbaum/Stock, Boston
3.9   © Black Star 1985
3.11   left, © Claus Meyer/Black Star; right, © Eve Arnold/Magnum Photos
3.12   Haseler/Art Resource
3.14   © Bonnie Freer 1978/Photo Researchers
3.15   top, © Bill Gallery/Stock, Boston; bottom, © Leslie E. Spatt/Dance Theatre of Harlem
3.16   © Tim Carson/Stock, Boston

3.17 top, The Granger Collection; bottom, Collection of Marcia S. Weisman, photograph Sotheby's

3.18 © Marc & Evelyne Bernheim/Woodfin Camp & Associates

CHAPTER 4

4.0 © Frank Cezus/Click/Chicago Ltd.

4.1 © P. Frillet/SIPA/Special Features

4.4 © Tom McHugh/Photo Researchers

4.7 © Phyllis Greenberg/Photo Researchers

4.8 © Brian Seed 1981/Click/Chicago Ltd.

4.9 © Peter Menzel 1985/Stock, Boston

4.10 © Loren McIntyre/Woodfin Camp & Associates

4.11 © Mathias Oppersdorff/Photo Researchers

4.12 © Michael Mauney/Click/Chicago Ltd.

4.13 © C. Lee/Click/Chicago Ltd.

CHAPTER 5

5.0 © Brian Seed/Click/Chicago Ltd.

5.1 left, © Erika Stone 1979; right, © John Launois/Black Star

5.2 The Bettmann Archive

5.3 © Harry F. Harlow, University of Wisconsin Primate Laboratory

5.4 © Erika Stone 1985

5.5 © Jan Lukas/Photo Researchers

5.6 © Sybil Shelton/Peter Arnold, Inc.

5.7 © Kenneth Karp/Omni-Photo Communications

5.8 left, © Don Steffan/Photo Researchers; right, © Deborah Kahn 1985/Stock, Boston

5.9 © Paul Conklin/Monkmeyer Press Photo Service

5.10 © Leif Skoogfors 1982/Woodfin Camp & Associates

5.12 Colonial Williamsburg Foundation

5.13 Fritz Goro, *Life* magazine © 1955 Time, Inc.

5.15 © B. D. Vidibar/Photo Researchers

CHAPTER 6

6.0 © Stephane Pfriender/The Stock Market

6.2 top, © Melissa Hayes English/Photo Researchers; bottom, © Paul Conklin

6.5 © Jan Lukas/Photo Researchers

6.7 © Charles Gatewood

6.8 © Michael Abramson/Gamma-Liaison

6.9 From P. Ekman and W. V. Friesen, *Pictures of Facial Affect.* Palo Alto, California: Consulting Psychologists Press, 1976

6.10 © Sybil Shelton/Peter Arnold, Inc.

6.11 © Thomas Hopker/Woodfin Camp & Associates

6.13 The Bettmann Archive

6.14 © Richard Pasley/Stock, Boston

6.15 Musée Condé, Chantilly, photograph Giraudon/Art Resource

6.16 © Joel Gordon 1982

CHAPTER 7

7.0 © Jasmin/Gamma-Liaison

7.1 © Victor Engelbert/Photo Researchers

7.2 © Chuck Fishman 1984/Woodfin Camp & Associates

7.3 © Thomas Hopker/Woodfin Camp & Associates

7.7 The Metropolitan Museum of Art, George A. Hearn Fund, 1956

7.8 *Newsweek*-Bernard Gotfryd

7.9 © Hazel Hankin/Stock, Boston

7.11 AP/Wide World Photos

7.13 © Bruno J. Zehnder/Peter Arnold, Inc.

CHAPTER 8

8.0 © Wesley Bocxe/Photo Researchers

8.1 left, Courtesy of Tattoo Art Museum, San Francisco, photograph © Charles Gatewood; right, © Alan Carey/The Image Works

8.2 left, Culver Pictures; right NYT Pictures

8.3 © Bob Combs/Photo Researchers

8.5 © Christopher Morris 1982/Black Star

8.7 © Peter Garfield, Washington, D.C.

8.8 © Tim Chapman 1982, Miami Herald/Black Star

8.13 AP/Wide World Photos

8.14 The Bettman Archive

8.15 © Christopher Morris 1982/Black Star

8.17 left, Culver Pictures; right, UPI/Bettmann Newsphotos

CHAPTER 9

9.0 © Jan Lukas/Photo Researchers

9.1 © Richard Steedman/The Stock Market

9.2 from top left to bottom right, © Jacques Jangoux/Peter Arnold, Inc.; © Malcolm S. Kirk/Peter Arnold, Inc.; © Chuck Fishman/Woodfin Camp & Associates; © Richard Lee Rue III/Monkmeyer Press Photo Service; © George Holton/Photo Researchers; © Malcolm S. Kirk/Peter Arnold, Inc.

9.3 © Robert Frerck 1982/Woodfin Camp & Associates

9.5 Carmine Church, Florence, photograph Scala/Art Resource

9.6 Jeu de Paume, Paris, photograph Scala/Art Resource

9.7 The Bettmann Archive

9.9 © Joel Gordon 1980

9.10 © Andrew Lawson

9.12 © Jan Lukas 1979/Photo Researchers

9.14 © Jean-Marie Simon/Taurus Photos

9.15 Museo Correr, Venice, photograph Scala/Art Resource

9.16 © Jim Anderson 1981/Woodfin Camp & Associates

CHAPTER 10

10.0 © Richard Hutchings/Photo Researchers

10.1 © Paolo Koch/Photo Researchers

10.2 © Charles Kennard/Stock, Boston

10.3 © Daniel Zirinsky/Photo Researchers

10.4 Culver Pictures

10.5 The Bettmann Archive

10.8 © Ian Berry/Magnum Photos

10.9 Musée Condé, Chantilly, photograph Giraudon/Art Resource

10.11 The Bettmann Archive

10.14 © Yvonne Freund 1975/Photo Researchers

10.15 left, © David Campbell/Click/Chicago Ltd.; right, © Gabe Palmer/The Stock Market

10.17 left, The Bettmann Archive; right, © Diana Walker/Gamma-Liaison

10.19 © Tim Kelly 1983/Black Star

CHAPTER 11

11.0 © Mark Antman/The Image Works

11.1 from bottom left to bottom right, © Tom Pix 1984/Peter Arnold, Inc.; © Paul Conklin; © Eric Kroll 1979/Taurus Photos; (both) © Paul Conklin; © Yoram Kahana/Peter Arnold, Inc.; © Beryl Goldberg; © Paolo Koch/Photo Researchers; © Topham/The Image Works

11.2 © Richard Tomkins 1982/Gamma-Liaison

11.3 Woolarac Museum, Bartlesville, Oklahoma

11.4 UPI/Bettmann Newsphotos

11.5 © Michael Grecco/Stock, Boston

11.6 The Bettmann Archive

11.7 left, Culver Pictures; right, AP/Wide World Photos

11.8 The Bettmann Archive

11.9 top left to bottom right, The Bettmann Archive; AP/Wide World Photos; *Ebony* magazine, Johnson Publishing Company; © Paul Meredith/Click/Chicago Ltd.

11.10 The Phillips Collection, Washington, D.C.

11.11 © Lester Sloan/Woodfin Camp & Associates

11.12 © Cynthia Johnson/Gamma-Liaison

11.13 © Paul Conklin

11.14 Hansel Mieth, *Life* magazine © Time, Inc.

11.15 Culver Pictures

CHAPTER 12

12.0 © Jim Olive 1982/Peter Arnold, Inc.

12.1 left, © Victor Englebert 1976/Photo Researchers; right, © David Wells 1980/Gamma-Liaison

12.3 Oil on masonite, 19½″ × 97½″ (sight), 1934. The Fine Arts Museums of San Francisco, Gift of Mr. and Mrs. John D. Rockefeller 3rd

12.6 bottom and top left, The Granger Collection; top right, The Bettmann Archive

12.7 *Popular Mechanics,* 1950, courtesy of Library of Congress

12.8 both, © June Lundborg Whitworth 1986

12.9 Museum Ludwig, Cologne

12.12 © Ann Hagen Griffiths/Omni-Photo Communications

12.13 © Beryl Goldberg

12.14 The Bettmann Archive

12.16 © Paul Conklin

12.18 © B. D. Vidibar/Photo Researchers

12.19 © Paul Conklin

CHAPTER 13

13.0 © Tom Martin/The Stock Market

13.1 left, © Rick Smolan/Woodfin Camp & Associates; right, © Brent Bear/Click/Chicago Ltd.

13.2 © Mimi Forsyth/Monkmeyer Press Photo Service

13.4 © Marta Sentis/Photo Researchers

13.5 © Hazel Hankin 1983

13.6 left, The Metropolitan Museum of Art, Gift of Frederic H. Hatch, 1926; right, originally published by *New England Monthly*

13.7 left, The Bettmann Archive; right, Culver Pictures

13.8 The Metropolitan Museum of Art, Bequest of Catherine Lorillard Wolfe, 1887. Catherine Lorillard Wolfe Collection

13.11 © Karen Rosenthal/Stock, Boston

13.12 left, © P. Davidson 1986/The Image Works; right, © Anna Clopet/SIPA/Special Features

CHAPTER 14

14.0 © David Burnett 1986/Woodfin Camp & Associates

14.1 © Michael S. Yamashita 1981/Woodfin Camp & Associates

14.3 top, Nat & Yanna Brandt 1985/Photo Researchers; bottom, © Susan Johns/Photo Researchers

14.5 Oil on canvas, 63⅞″ × 45″, 1932. Collection, The Museum of Modern Art, New York. Gift of Philip Johnson

14.6 © Barbara Kirk/The Stock Market

14.8 © Gabe Palmer/The Stock Market

14.9 © Alex Webb/Magnum Photos

14.11 *Time* magazine © Time, Inc.

14.12 Yale University Art Gallery. The Mabel Brady Garvan Collection

14.13 © Ellis Herwig/Stock, Boston

CHAPTER 15

15.0 © Richard J. Quataert/Taurus Photos

15.1 left, © Thomas Hopker 1984/Woodfin Camp & Associates; right, © Jehangir Gazdar/Woodfin Camp & Associates

15.2 Oil on canvas, 54¾″ × 147½″ (139.1 × 374.6 cm). Tomkins Collection, courtesy Museum of Fine Arts, Boston.

15.3 © John Troha 1979/Black Star

15.5 left, *Torture Chamber,* Alessandro Magnasco. Reproduced by courtesy of the Board of Directors of the Budapest Museum of Fine Arts; right, The Bettmann Archive

15.6 Oil on beaver board, 29⅞″ × 25″, 1930. Friends of American Art Collection. © The Art Institute of Chicago. All rights reserved.

15.7 © Mehmet Biber/Photo Researchers

15.9 © Roger Werth 1983/Woodfin Camp & Associates

15.11 left, © Eddie Adams/Gamma-Liaison; right, © Sepp Seitz 1977/Woodfin Camp & Associates

15.12 © Dennis Brack 1986/Black Star

15.13 © Lawrence Manning 1980/Click/Chicago Ltd.

15.14 © Bettina Cirone/Photo Researchers

15.17 © Edna Douthat 1981/Photo Researchers

CHAPTER 16

16.0 © William Stroke 1984/Black Star

16.1 top, *Medicine Man Curing a Patient,* color lithograph by Christian Schuessele (after Seth Eastman), 1851. Philadelphia Museum of Art, Smith Kline Beckman Corporation Fund; bottom, © Martin Rogers 1985/Woodfin Camp & Associates

16.2 and 16.3 The Bettmann Archive

16.5 left, The Bettmann Archive; right, © Beryl Goldberg 1986

16.6 Chateau Versailles, photograph Giraudon/Art Resource

16.7 Courtesy of The New York Historical Society, New York

16.8 © Howard Sochurek 1982/Woodfin Camp & Associates

16.9 © Joel Gordon 1983

16.10 © Ray Ellis 1986/Photo Researchers

16.11 top, © Bonnie Freer 1978/Photo Researchers; bottom, © Charles Kennard/Stock, Boston

16.12 The Mansell Collection

16.13 left, Laurentian Library, Florence, photograph Scala/Art Resource; right, © Charles Steiner/Picture Group

16.14 The Bettmann Archive

16.17 top, © Yvonne Hemsey/Gamma Liaison; bottom, © Joel Gordon 1978

CHAPTER 17

17.0 © Dick Durrance II 1984/Woodfin Camp & Associates

17.1 from left to right, EPA-Documerica; © Will McIntyre 1983/Photo Researchers; © Clyde H. Smith/Peter Arnold, Inc.

17.2 left, © Malcolm Kirk/Peter Arnold, Inc.; right, © Raimondo Borea

17.4 The Bettmann Archive

17.5 © John Blaustein/Woodfin Camp & Associates

17.6 *New York Daily News* photo

17.7 © Lebeck, *Stern*/Black Star

17.8 © Flip Schulke 1980/Black Star

17.9 © John Lei/Omni-Photo Communications

17.10 Cast vinyl polychromed in oil, lifesize, 1976. Courtesy O. K. Harris Gallery, New York

17.12 © J. P. Laffont/Sygma

17.13 © Andrew Sacks 1982/Black Star

CHAPTER 18

18.0 © Shelly Katz 1984/Black Star

18.1 © David Turnley 1985/Black Star

18.2 top left, The Granger Collection; top right, © Jasmin/Gamma-Liaison; bottom © Gamma-Liaison 1984

18.3 © Anthony Howarth 1982/Woodfin Camp & Associates

18.4 © Mark Reinstein/Click/Chicago Ltd.

18.6 left, The Bettmann Archive; right, © Ilkka Ranta/Woodfin Camp & Associates

18.7 © Jim Anderson 1978/Woodfin Camp & Associates

18.8 left, © Chris Brown/Stock, Boston; right, © James Nachtwey 1983/Black Star

18.9 © Mark Reinstein/Click/Chicago Ltd.

18.11 left, reprinted by permission of National Rifle Association of America; right, reprinted by permission of Handgun Control, Inc.

CHAPTER 19

19.0 © Frank Siteman 1979/Taurus Photos

19.1 © Brian Brake/Photo Researchers

19.2   both, The Bettmann Archive

19.4   top, The Bettmann Archive; bottom, © NASA/Photo Researchers

19.5   top, both, The Bettmann Archive; bottom, Culver Pictures

19.6   © George Holton/Photo Researchers

19.7   The Granger Collection

19.8   © Marc & Evelyne Bernheim/Woodfin Camp & Associates

19.9   left, © Daniel Brody/Stock, Boston; right, © C. Niedenthal 1982/ Black Star

19.10   Ducco on wood, 48″ × 36″, 1937. Collection, The Museum of Modern Art, New York. Gift of Edward M. M. Warburg

19.11   *Newsweek*-Lester Sloan

19.12   © Christopher Morris 1985/Black Star

19.13   The Bettmann Archive

19.14   left, © Thomas Hopker 1981/Woodfin Camp & Associates; right, © Charlyn Zlotnik/Woodfin Camp & Associates

19.15   left, The Bettmann Archive; right; photo courtesy Smithsonian Institution Traveling Exhibition Service. From SITES exhibition *Yesterday's Tomorrows: Past Visions of the American Future*

CHAPTER 20

20.0   © Don Smetzer/Click/Chicago Ltd.

20.1   © Klaus D. Francke/Peter Arnold, Inc.

20.2   Culver Pictures

20.3   © Tim Chapman/Black Star

20.4   © Mark Deville/Gamma-Liaison

20.5   © Danny Lyon/Magnum Photos

20.6   top, The Bettmann Archive; bottom, © *Miami Herald* 1983/Black Star

20.7   © B. Diederich 1985/Woodfin Camp & Associates

20.8   E.M.I. Recording, Capitol Records, Inc.

20.10   © Barbara Kirk 1985/The Stock Market

20.11   © Bernard Gotfryd 1985/Woodfin Camp & Associates

20.12   from left to right, The Granger Collection; Vernon Merritt, *Life* magazine © Time, Inc. 1969; © George Zimbel/Monkmeyer Press Photo Service

20.13   © Joe Munroe/Photo Researchers

20.14   © Mark Kauffman 1985

20.15   The Bettmann Archive

20.16   from left to right, © John Ficara 1985/Woodfin Camp & Associates; © Jim Anderson 1980/Woodfin Camp & Associates; © Lawrence Migdale 1986/Photo Researchers

20.17   left, The Bettmann Archive; right, © P. Chauvel/Sygma

20.18   Musée Picasso, Paris. © S.P.A.D.E.M., Paris/V.A.G.A., New York 1986

20.19   Courtesy ABC News

CHAPTER 21

21.0   © Stephanie Maze/Woodfin Camp & Associates

21.1   Brown Brothers

21.4   © Arnaud Borrel/Gamma-Liaison

21.8   The Granger Collection

21.9   © Charles Trainor/Photo Researchers

21.10   © Summer Productions/Taurus Photos

21.11   left, © Georg Gerster/Photo Researchers; right, © Russ Kinne 1975/ Photo Researchers

21.12   left, Uffizi, Florence, photograph Scala/Art Resource; right, Egg tempera on composition board, 18″ × 36″, 1950. Collection of Whitney Museum of American Art. Juliana Force Purchase. Acq. #50.23

21.13   © June Lundborg Whitworth 1981

21.14   © Van Bucher 1972/Photo Researchers

21.15   © Rafael Marcia 1984/Photo Researchers

CHAPTER 22

22.0   © Jeffrey D. Smith/Woodfin Camp & Associates

22.1   both photos courtesy Smithsonian Institution Traveling Exhibition Service. From SITES exhibition *Yesterday's Tomorrows: Past Visions of the American Future*, photographer Joe A. Goulait

22.2   The Bettmann Archive

22.5   The Granger Collection

22.6   © Tom McHugh/Photo Researchers

22.7   left, UPI/Bettmann Newsphotos; right, The Bettmann Archive

22.8   The Granger Collection

22.11   © Richard Howard 1983

22.12   left, The Bettmann Archive; right, © Ronald Seymour/Click/ Chicago Ltd.

22.13   top left, The Bettmann Archive; top right, The Granger Collection; bottom, © Rick Browne 1981/Black Star

22.14   © Jack Fields/Photo Researchers

22.16   photo courtesy Smithsonian Institution Traveling Exhibition Service. From SITES exhibition *Yesterday's Tomorrows: Past Visions of the American Future*, photographer Joe A. Goulait

22.17   left, © H. W. Silvester/Photo Researchers; right, © Jacques Jangoux/Peter Arnold, Inc.

CHAPTER 23

23.0   © Fred Ward 1983/Black Star

23.1   © H. Nagakura/Gamma-Liaison

23.2   The Granger Collection

23.4   © A.P.N./Gamma-Liaison

23.8   © Photri 1986

23.9   AP/Wide World Photos

23.12   Brown Brothers

23.14   from top left to bottom left, UPI/Bettmann Newsphotos; bottom right, AP/Wide World Photos

23.15   Larry Burrows, LIFE magazine © 1971 Time, Inc.

23   End   © John Giannicchi/Science Source/Photo Researchers

INDEX